OFFICIAL
SCRABBLE
BRAND Crossword Game
LISTS

by Darryl Francis and Allan Simmons

Collins

HarperCollins Publishers
Westerhill Road
Bishopbriggs
Glasgow
G64 2QT
Great Britain

Second Edition 2008

Reprint 10 9 8 7 6 5 4 3 2 1 0

© HarperCollins Publishers 2005,
2006, 2008

ISBN 978-0-00-727848-0

Collins® is a registered trademark
of HarperCollins Publishers Limited

SCRABBLE® is a registered
trademark of J. W. Spear & Son Ltd a
subsidiary of Mattel, Inc.
© 2008 Mattel, Inc.

www.collinslanguage.com

A catalogue record for this book is
available from the British Library

Typeset by Interactive Sciences Ltd,
Gloucester

Printed in Italy by
LEGO Spa, Lavis (Trento), Italy

FOR THE PUBLISHER
Ian Brookes
Robert Groves
Elaine Higgleton
Helen Hucker

COMPUTING SUPPORT
Thomas Callan

Contents

WESPA – the World English-language Scrabble® Players Association

Scrabble is played in numerous English-speaking countries around the World (including African countries, India, Singapore, and Malaysia, as well as Great Britain, Ireland, USA, Canada, Australia, and New Zealand). English-language Scrabble is also played where English is not the first-language (eg in Thailand, Japan, Netherlands, and Sweden). Over 30 nations were represented at the 2007 World Scrabble Championship, and there are estimated to be more than 25,000 tournament players world-wide.

WESPA is a relatively new regulatory body for Scrabble, established and run by competitive players to coordinate international tournaments, to provide an international rating system, to make decisions on policy (such as a standard word-list), and to represent the interests of players globally, especially in matters that involve the owners of the Scrabble trademark. WESPA is also committed to development of organized Scrabble and runs an annual World Youth Scrabble Championship as part of this objective.

Most national organizations (such as the Association of British Scrabble Players) are members of WESPA, although WESPA also offers individual membership where a national association does not exist or has not joined.

WESPA is formally approved by Mattel, the owners of the Scrabble trademark outside of North America.

Visit the websites at www.wespa.org and www.absp.org.uk

Foreword – My Top 100 Words

Philip Nelkon, Scrabble Clubs Manager, Mattel Inc.

Picking 100 words from the many thousands that feature in *Collins Scrabble Lists* is rather like being shown the wonders of the whole world and then being asked to live on a rock in the Pacific. I've tried, however, even with this small sample, to give a flavour of all of the words in the book.

My main principle in selecting such words has been usefulness for playing Scrabble. If you learn just a few of them, I'm sure they'll increase the scores you get. I've included a lot of words that will not be in most people's general vocabulary, although, having said that, it's amazing how often a word that you have learnt for Scrabble crops up in 'real life'. I well remember watching a play about an unsuccessful expedition to Africa in the nineteenth century, where one of the characters staggered about the stage shouting 'Atebrin, atebrin!' and thinking, somewhat smugly, to myself that I must have been one of the few people in the audience who knew that ATEBRIN was a medicine used against malaria – a fact I had learnt when adding the word to my Scrabble vocabulary.

I did indulge myself slightly by picking ten words that just sounded good, the reason why you'll find BORSCHT and SQUAMAE in the list and surely one of the most unbelievable – KGOTLAS.

Whether you're looking to become the next World Scrabble Champion or just to learn a few words to enable you to turn the tables on that friend or relation who always seems to beat you. I'm sure you'll find that *Collins Scrabble Lists* is an invaluable addition to your armoury.

ACOEMETI:	Byzantine monks
AEGIRINE:	green mineral
AIA:	maidservant or nursemaid
AINEE:	elder
AL:	Chaucerian spelling of all
ALA:	wing or winglike structure
ALEURONE:	protein found in the outer layer of cereal grains
ANESTRA:	periods of sexual inactivity in nonhuman mammals
ATEBRIN:	drug formerly used to treat malaria
AZO:	consisting of, or containing, the divalent group -N:N-
BAGH:	garden
BOHO:	bohemian
BORSCHT:	Russian and Polish soup based on beetroot

CH:	dialect word for I
CHOG:	core of a piece of fruit
DEBE:	tin
DEF:	very good
EAU:	water
EGOITIES:	personalities
ENTERATE:	possessing an alimentary canal
EQUID:	equine
ERIONITE:	white crystalline mineral
ET:	and
ETAERIO:	aggregate fruit such as the raspberry
ETESIAN:	recurring annually in the summer
ETOURDIE:	foolish
EUOI:	cry of Dionysian frenzy
EUOUAE:	Gregorian cadence
FAQIR:	Muslim ascetic
FY:	fie
GAUJE:	Scots word for a fellow
GNOW:	ground-dwelling bird
GREX:	group of plants from the same hybrid parent group
IDEE:	idea or concept
INDUCIAE:	time by which a defendant must appear in court
ISATINE:	yellowish-red crystalline compound
ITA:	type of palm tree
IZARD:	sure-footed goat antelope
JAFA:	offensive name for a person from Auckland
JIAO:	unit of Chinese currency
JINN:	demon in Muslim belief
JIZ:	wig

JO:	Scots word for sweetheart
KEX:	hollow-stemmed plant
KGOTLAS:	assemblies of Botswanan elders
KOMITAJI:	Balkan guerilla
KY:	cattle
LAIRISE:	dress flashily
METANOIA:	repentance
MYXO:	myxomatosis
NABK:	edible berries of the Zizyphys Lotus tree
NARQUOIS:	malicious
NIDI:	nests of small animals
NODI:	problematic situation
ODEA:	buildings for musical performances
OESTRAL:	of the period of sexual receptivity in female mammals
OXO:	containing oxygen
PHIZ:	face or facial expression
QADI:	Muslim judge
QAID:	Muslim leader
QANAT:	ancient water-supply system
QAT:	evergreen shrub
QI:	vital energy in Chinese medicine
QIBLA:	direction of the Kaaba in Mecca
QOPH:	letter of the Hebrew alphabet
QUAT:	evergreen shrub
QUENA:	Andean flute
REORIENT:	adjust or align in a new or different way
RESIDUA:	residues
SAOUARI:	butternut tree
SEROTINE:	insectivorous bat

SHEQEL:	currency of Israel
SIPE:	ooze
SOHO:	exclamation announcing the sighting of a hare
SQUAMAE:	scales or scalelike structures
SQUEG:	oscillate irregularly
SWARAJ:	self-government
TAENIAE:	headbands
TAI:	member of the Tai-speaking tribes of Southeast Asia
TALA:	standard monetary unit of Samoa
TALAQ:	Muslim divorce
TANH:	hyperbolic tangent
TRANQ:	tranquilizer
TWAL:	Scots variant of twelve
UINTAITE:	natural bitumen
URINOSE:	of urine
VATU:	standard monetary unit of Vanuatu
VEGO:	vegetarian
WAQF:	charitable donation of land
WILI:	ghost of a betrothed girl who died before her wedding
WUD:	Scots word for wood
WUDU:	Islamic practice of ritual washing before daily prayer
WULL:	will
WUS:	casual term of address
XI:	fourteenth letter of the Greek alphabet
XU:	Vietnamese unit of currency
ZED:	the letter Z
ZERDA:	fennec fox
ZITI:	pasta tubes
ZO:	Tibetan animal bred from cows and yaks

Introduction

Collins Scrabble Lists is the companion volume to *Collins Scrabble Tournament and Club Word List*, the official wordlist for Scrabble. While the *Word List* contains the complete list of words that are valid in Scrabble, this *Lists* book provides strategies for memorizing the most useful of these words. With over 260,000 words eligible for play in Scrabble, it is virtually impossible for anyone to learn them all. What this book does is to provide the best of the words – those that are most useful in the game – in a manner in which they can be easily learned and remembered for Scrabble situations. Essentially, *Collins Scrabble Lists* is a collection of lists, each of which groups together words for exploiting a particular tactic. The lists allow for learning different groups of words and spotting opportunities to play them during a game

In various parts of the book, you will come across specific terminology – power tiles, benjamins, stems, hooks, blockers, awkward combinations, multiplets, alphagrams, and the like. If you're not familiar with these terms, each is explained in the appropriate text prior to associated lists of words.

Here is just a flavour of some of the lists presented in this book. You will find straightforward lists of all the two-, three- and four-letter words. There are lists of words using the power tiles, JQXZ, sorted by the individual letter and word length. There are lists of words beginning with particular prefixes, and ending with particular suffixes, encouraging the player to consider these prefixes and suffixes when searching for bonus plays. There are lists of words which will be helpful in offloading excessive vowels from your rack and offloading awkward combinations of consonants. There are extensive lists of hook words, whereby you can add a single letter at the front or end of a word, allowing you to play another word perpendicularly. And then there are blockers, the opposite of hooks, words which cannot have a letter added at the front or end.

There are extensive lists of six-letter stems, groups of six letters which are particularly productive in combining with a seventh letter to form valid seven-letter words. And beyond that, there are the seven-letter stems which are most productive when combining with an eighth letter.

There are lists of variant spellings – which should help you with recalling whether, for example, a particular word is spelled COSEY, COSIE, COSY, COZEY, COZIE or COZY (All six are valid!). And what about those -ISE and -IZE endings? Are they always interchangeable? And, occupying about 400 pages, you can check to see whether any particular set of seven- or eight-letters forms one or more valid words.

You'll be introduced to word families, words from varieties of English around the world, words which are placenames, and many more.

The lists in this book bring to the fore a great many words that will be unfamiliar to most people, and even to most Scrabble players. By adding these words to their vocabulary, players are equipping themselves with a powerful arsenal that they can deploy on the Scrabble board. These words, and the varied approaches to word-learning in this book, should enable any player to improve his or her game, no matter at what level the game is played.

Chapter 1: Short Words

While long words may yield spectacular scores in Scrabble – and words of up to 15 letters in length can be formed – the chances to achieve such coups are few and far between. A Scrabble player's best chance of consistently high scores comes not from long words but from remembering the short, useful words that can ensure a good play in even the most difficult situations. Short words are easy to squeeze onto the board when there is little or no room for longer words and can still score well if they contain one of the higher-scoring letters. They can also serve to open up the board easily if that is required. The short words containing only or mostly vowels also serve to help resolve a vowel-heavy rack (eg AI, OU, EAU, AIA, ILIA, UNAU).

Two-letter words

Two-letter words are vital to the serious Scrabble player. While very few two-letter words afford big scores in their own right, they are crucial linking elements in the game. Essentially, two-letter words are the nuts and bolts of the game, allowing longer words to be played parallel to each other or for slotting in a high-scoring letter on a premium square to form words in two directions. There are 124 valid two-letter words in Scrabble, all of which are listed in this section.

AA	DO	IF	NY	SO
AB	EA	IN	OB	ST
AD	ED	IO	OD	TA
AE	EE	IS	OE	TE
AG	EF	IT	OF	TI
AH	EH	JA	OH	TO
AI	EL	JO	OI	UG
AL	EM	KA	OM	UH
AM	EN	KI	ON	UM
AN	ER	KO	OO	UN
AR	ES	KY	OP	UP
AS	ET	LA	OR	UR
AT	EX	LI	OS	US
AW	FA	LO	OU	UT
AX	FE	MA	OW	WE
AY	FY	ME	OX	WO
BA	GI	MI	OY	XI
BE	GO	MM	PA	XU
BI	GU	MO	PE	YA
BO	HA	MU	PI	YE
BY	HE	MY	PO	YO
CH	HI	NA	QI	YU
DA	HM	NE	RE	ZA
DE	HO	NO	SH	ZO
DI	ID	NU	SI	

Three-letter words

Three-letter words aren't quite as important as two-letter words, but they are still an essential weapon in every Scrabble player's armoury. It's especially worth noting those three-letter words that are one-letter extensions (hooks) of two-letter words (before or after). You should at least be familiar with those that are -S plurals of two-letter words.

There are 1,292 valid three-letter words in Scrabble, all of which are listed in this section. Not all are valuable in Scrabble but are all listed here for completeness.

AAH	ANY	BEG	CAP	DAS
AAL	APE	BEL	CAR	DAW
AAS	APO	BEN	CAT	DAY
ABA	APP	BES	CAW	DEB
ABB	APT	BET	CAY	DEE
ABO	ARB	BEY	CAZ	DEF
ABS	ARC	BEZ	CEE	DEG
ABY	ARD	BIB	CEL	DEI
ACE	ARE	BID	CEP	DEL
ACH	ARF	BIG	CHA	DEN
ACT	ARK	BIN	CHE	DEV
ADD	ARM	BIO	CHI	DEW
ADO	ARS	BIS	CID	DEX
ADS	ART	BIT	CIG	DEY
ADZ	ARY	BIZ	CIS	DIB
AFF	ASH	BOA	CIT	DID
AFT	ASK	BOB	CLY	DIE
AGA	ASP	BOD	COB	DIF
AGE	ASS	BOG	COD	DIG
AGO	ATE	BOH	COG	DIM
AGS	ATT	BOI	COL	DIN
AHA	AUA	BOK	CON	DIP
AHI	AUE	BON	COO	DIS
AHS	AUF	BOO	COP	DIT
AIA	AUK	BOP	COR	DIV
AID	AVA	BOR	COS	DOB
AIL	AVE	BOS	COT	DOC
AIM	AVO	BOT	COW	DOD
AIN	AWA	BOW	COX	DOE
AIR	AWE	BOX	COY	DOF
AIS	AWL	BOY	COZ	DOG
AIT	AWN	BRA	CRU	DOH
AKA	AXE	BRO	CRY	DOL
AKE	AYE	BRR	CUB	DOM
ALA	AYS	BRU	CUD	DON
ALB	AYU	BUB	CUE	DOO
ALE	AZO	BUD	CUM	DOP
ALF	BAA	BUG	CUP	DOR
ALL	BAC	BUM	CUR	DOS
ALP	BAD	BUN	CUT	DOT
ALS	BAG	BUR	CUZ	DOW
ALT	BAH	BUS	CWM	DOY
AMA	BAL	BUT	DAB	DRY
AMI	BAM	BUY	DAD	DSO
AMP	BAN	BYE	DAE	DUB
AMU	BAP	BYS	DAG	DUD
ANA	BAR	CAA	DAH	DUE
AND	BAS	CAB	DAK	DUG
ANE	BAT	CAD	DAL	DUH
ANI	BAY	CAG	DAM	DUI
ANN	BED	CAM	DAN	DUN
ANT	BEE	CAN	DAP	DUO

Three-letter words

DUP	EXO	GAB	HAE	ICH
DUX	EYE	GAD	HAG	ICK
DYE	FAA	GAE	HAH	ICY
DZO	FAB	GAG	HAJ	IDE
EAN	FAD	GAL	HAM	IDS
EAR	FAE	GAM	HAN	IFF
EAS	FAG	GAN	HAO	IFS
EAT	FAH	GAP	HAP	IGG
EAU	FAN	GAR	HAS	ILK
EBB	FAP	GAS	HAT	ILL
ECH	FAR	GAT	HAW	IMP
ECO	FAS	GAU	HAY	INK
ECU	FAT	GAY	HEH	INN
EDH	FAW	GED	HEM	INS
EDS	FAX	GEE	HEN	ION
EEK	FAY	GEL	HEP	IOS
EEL	FED	GEM	HER	IRE
EEN	FEE	GEN	HES	IRK
EFF	FEG	GEO	HET	ISH
EFS	FEH	GET	HEW	ISM
EFT	FEM	GEY	HEX	ISO
EGG	FEN	GHI	HEY	ITA
EGO	FER	GIB	HIC	ITS
EHS	FES	GID	HID	IVY
EIK	FET	GIE	HIE	IWI
EKE	FEU	GIF	HIM	JAB
ELD	FEW	GIG	HIN	JAG
ELF	FEY	GIN	HIP	JAI
ELK	FEZ	GIO	HIS	JAK
ELL	FIB	GIP	HIT	JAM
ELM	FID	GIS	HMM	JAP
ELS	FIE	GIT	HOA	JAR
ELT	FIG	GJU	HOB	JAW
EME	FIL	GNU	HOC	JAY
EMO	FIN	GOA	HOD	JEE
EMS	FIR	GOB	HOE	JET
EMU	FIT	GOD	HOG	JEU
END	FIX	GOE	HOH	JEW
ENE	FIZ	GON	HOI	JIB
ENG	FLU	GOO	HOM	JIG
ENS	FLY	GOR	HON	JIN
EON	FOB	GOS	HOO	JIZ
ERA	FOE	GOT	HOP	JOB
ERE	FOG	GOV	HOS	JOE
ERF	FOH	GOX	HOT	JOG
ERG	FON	GOY	HOW	JOL
ERK	FOP	GUB	HOX	JOR
ERN	FOR	GUE	HOY	JOT
ERR	FOU	GUL	HUB	JOW
ERS	FOX	GUM	HUE	JOY
ESS	FOY	GUN	HUG	JUD
EST	FRA	GUP	HUH	JUG
ETA	FRO	GUR	HUI	JUN
ETH	FRY	GUS	HUM	JUS
EUK	FUB	GUT	HUN	JUT
EVE	FUD	GUV	HUP	KAB
EVO	FUG	GUY	HUT	KAE
EWE	FUM	GYM	HYE	KAF
EWK	FUN	GYP	HYP	KAI
EWT	FUR	HAD	ICE	KAK

KAM	LEX	MIC	NIL	OOF
KAS	LEY	MID	NIM	OOH
KAT	LEZ	MIG	NIP	OOM
KAW	LIB	MIL	NIS	OON
KAY	LID	MIM	NIT	OOP
KEA	LIE	MIR	NIX	OOR
KEB	LIG	MIS	NOB	OOS
KED	LIN	MIX	NOD	OOT
KEF	LIP	MIZ	NOG	OPE
KEG	LIS	MNA	NOH	OPS
KEN	LIT	MOA	NOM	OPT
KEP	LOB	MOB	NON	ORA
KET	LOD	MOC	NOO	ORB
KEX	LOG	MOD	NOR	ORC
KEY	LOO	MOE	NOS	ORD
KHI	LOP	MOG	NOT	ORE
KID	LOR	MOI	NOW	ORF
KIF	LOS	MOL	NOX	ORS
KIN	LOT	MOM	NOY	ORT
KIP	LOU	MON	NTH	OSE
KIR	LOW	MOO	NUB	OUD
KIS	LOX	MOP	NUN	OUK
KIT	LOY	MOR	NUR	OUP
KOA	LUD	MOS	NUS	OUR
KOB	LUG	MOT	NUT	OUS
KOI	LUM	MOU	NYE	OUT
KON	LUR	MOW	NYS	OVA
KOP	LUV	MOY	OAF	OWE
KOR	LUX	MOZ	OAK	OWL
KOS	LUZ	MUD	OAR	OWN
KOW	LYE	MUG	OAT	OWT
KUE	LYM	MUM	OBA	OXO
KYE	MAA	MUN	OBE	OXY
KYU	MAC	MUS	OBI	OYE
LAB	MAD	MUT	OBO	OYS
LAC	MAE	MUX	OBS	PAC
LAD	MAG	MYC	OCA	PAD
LAG	MAK	NAB	OCH	PAH
LAH	MAL	NAE	ODA	PAL
LAM	MAM	NAG	ODD	PAM
LAP	MAN	NAH	ODE	PAN
LAR	MAP	NAM	ODS	PAP
LAS	MAR	NAN	OES	PAR
LAT	MAS	NAP	OFF	PAS
LAV	MAT	NAS	OFT	PAT
LAW	MAW	NAT	OHM	PAV
LAX	MAX	NAW	OHO	PAW
LAY	MAY	NAY	OHS	PAX
LEA	MED	NEB	OIK	PAY
LED	MEE	NED	OIL	PEA
LEE	MEG	NEE	OKA	PEC
LEG	MEL	NEF	OKE	PED
LEI	MEM	NEG	OLD	PEE
LEK	MEN	NEK	OLE	PEG
LEP	MES	NEP	OLM	PEH
LES	MET	NET	OMS	PEN
LET	MEU	NEW	ONE	PEP
LEU	MEW	NIB	ONO	PER
LEV	MHO	NID	ONS	PES
LEW	MIB	NIE	ONY	PET

Three-letter words

PEW	RAS	SAL	SOW	TIN
PHI	RAT	SAM	SOX	TIP
PHO	RAW	SAN	SOY	TIS
PHT	RAX	SAP	SPA	TIT
PIA	RAY	SAR	SPY	TIX
PIC	REB	SAT	SRI	TOC
PIE	REC	SAU	STY	TOD
PIG	RED	SAV	SUB	TOE
PIN	REE	SAW	SUD	TOG
PIP	REF	SAX	SUE	TOM
PIR	REG	SAY	SUI	TON
PIS	REH	SAZ	SUK	TOO
PIT	REI	SEA	SUM	TOP
PIU	REM	SEC	SUN	TOR
PIX	REN	SED	SUP	TOT
PLU	REO	SEE	SUQ	TOW
PLY	REP	SEG	SUR	TOY
POA	RES	SEI	SUS	TRY
POD	RET	SEL	SWY	TSK
POH	REV	SEN	SYE	TUB
POI	REW	SER	SYN	TUG
POL	REX	SET	TAB	TUI
POM	REZ	SEW	TAD	TUM
POO	RHO	SEX	TAE	TUN
POP	RHY	SEY	TAG	TUP
POS	RIA	SEZ	TAI	TUT
POT	RIB	SHA	TAJ	TUX
POW	RID	SHE	TAK	TWA
POX	RIF	SHH	TAM	TWO
POZ	RIG	SHY	TAN	TWP
PRE	RIM	SIB	TAO	TYE
PRO	RIN	SIC	TAP	TYG
PRY	RIP	SIF	TAR	UDO
PSI	RIT	SIK	TAS	UDS
PST	RIZ	SIM	TAT	UEY
PUB	ROB	SIN	TAU	UFO
PUD	ROC	SIP	TAV	UGH
PUG	ROD	SIR	TAW	UGS
PUH	ROE	SIS	TAX	UKE
PUL	ROK	SIT	TAY	ULE
PUN	ROM	SIX	TEA	ULU
PUP	ROO	SKA	TEC	UMM
PUR	ROT	SKI	TED	UMP
PUS	ROW	SKY	TEE	UMU
PUT	RUB	SLY	TEF	UNI
PUY	RUC	SMA	TEG	UNS
PYA	RUD	SNY	TEL	UPO
PYE	RUE	SOB	TEN	UPS
PYX	RUG	SOC	TES	URB
QAT	RUM	SOD	TET	URD
QIS	RUN	SOG	TEW	URE
QUA	RUT	SOH	TEX	URN
RAD	RYA	SOL	THE	URP
RAG	RYE	SOM	THO	USE
RAH	SAB	SON	THY	UTA
RAI	SAC	SOP	TIC	UTE
RAJ	SAD	SOS	TID	UTS
RAM	SAE	SOT	TIE	UTU
RAN	SAG	SOU	TIG	UVA
RAP	SAI	SOV	TIL	VAC

VAE	VUM	WIS	YAR	YUS
VAG	WAB	WIT	YAW	ZAG
VAN	WAD	WIZ	YAY	ZAP
VAR	WAE	WOE	YEA	ZAS
VAS	WAG	WOF	YEH	ZAX
VAT	WAI	WOG	YEN	ZEA
VAU	WAN	WOK	YEP	ZED
VAV	WAP	WON	YES	ZEE
VAW	WAR	WOO	YET	ZEK
VEE	WAS	WOP	YEW	ZEL
VEG	WAT	WOS	YEX	ZEP
VET	WAW	WOT	YGO	ZEX
VEX	WAX	WOW	YID	ZHO
VIA	WAY	WOX	YIN	ZIG
VID	WEB	WRY	YIP	ZIN
VIE	WED	WUD	YOB	ZIP
VIG	WEE	WUS	YOD	ZIT
VIM	WEM	WYE	YOK	ZIZ
VIN	WEN	WYN	YOM	ZOA
VIS	WET	XIS	YON	ZOL
VLY	WEX	YAD	YOS	ZOO
VOE	WEY	YAE	YOU	ZOS
VOL	WHA	YAG	YOW	ZUZ
VOR	WHO	YAH	YUG	ZZZ
VOW	WHY	YAK	YUK	
VOX	WIG	YAM	YUM	
VUG	WIN	YAP	YUP	

Four-letter words

Four-letter words are generally even less valuable than three-letter words. The ones that are most useful during play tend to be those that can be formed by hooking three-letter words before or after (eg ALOW, LOWE), those that contain awkward combinations of letters (eg VEHM) or three vowels (eg HIOI) that help to resolve problems, or those that contain a power tile (eg ROJI). All the 5,454 four-letter words are listed here for completeness.

AAHS	ACES	AFAR	AHIS	AKIN
AALS	ACHE	AFFY	AHOY	ALAE
ABAC	ACHY	AFRO	AIAS	ALAN
ABAS	ACID	AGAR	AIDE	ALAP
ABBA	ACME	AGAS	AIDS	ALAR
ABBE	ACNE	AGED	AIGA	ALAS
ABBS	ACRE	AGEE	AILS	ALAY
ABED	ACTA	AGEN	AIMS	ALBA
ABET	ACTS	AGER	AINE	ALBE
ABID	ACYL	AGES	AINS	ALBS
ABLE	ADAW	AGHA	AIRN	ALCO
ABLY	ADDS	AGIN	AIRS	ALEC
ABOS	ADDY	AGIO	AIRT	ALEE
ABRI	ADIT	AGLU	AIRY	ALEF
ABUT	ADOS	AGLY	AITS	ALES
ABYE	ADRY	AGMA	AITU	ALEW
ABYS	ADZE	AGOG	AJAR	ALFA
ACAI	AEON	AGON	AJEE	ALFS
ACCA	AERO	AGUE	AKED	ALGA
ACED	AERY	AHED	AKEE	ALIF
ACER	AESC	AHEM	AKES	ALIT

Three-letter words

ALKO	APOS	AURA	BALL	BEGO
ALKY	APPS	AUTO	BALM	BEGS
ALLS	APSE	AVAL	BALS	BEIN
ALLY	APSO	AVAS	BALU	BELL
ALMA	APTS	AVEL	BAMS	BELS
ALME	AQUA	AVER	BANC	BELT
ALMS	ARAK	AVES	BAND	BEMA
ALOD	ARAR	AVID	BANE	BEND
ALOE	ARBA	AVOS	BANG	BENE
ALOW	ARBS	AVOW	BANI	BENI
ALPS	ARCH	AWAY	BANK	BENJ
ALSO	ARCO	AWDL	BANS	BENS
ALTO	ARCS	AWED	BANT	BENT
ALTS	ARDS	AWEE	BAPS	BERE
ALUM	AREA	AWES	BAPU	BERG
AMAH	ARED	AWLS	BARB	BERK
AMAS	AREG	AWNS	BARD	BERM
AMBO	ARES	AWNY	BARE	BEST
AMEN	ARET	AWOL	BARF	BETA
AMIA	AREW	AWRY	BARK	BETE
AMID	ARFS	AXAL	BARM	BETH
AMIE	ARIA	AXED	BARN	BETS
AMIN	ARID	AXEL	BARP	BEVY
AMIR	ARIL	AXES	BARS	BEYS
AMIS	ARIS	AXIL	BASE	BHAT
AMLA	ARKS	AXIS	BASH	BHEL
AMMO	ARLE	AXLE	BASK	BHUT
AMOK	ARMS	AXON	BASS	BIAS
AMPS	ARMY	AYAH	BAST	BIBB
AMUS	ARNA	AYES	BATE	BIBS
AMYL	AROW	AYIN	BATH	BICE
ANAL	ARPA	AYRE	BATS	BIDE
ANAN	ARSE	AYUS	BATT	BIDI
ANAS	ARSY	AZAN	BAUD	BIDS
ANCE	ARTI	AZON	BAUK	BIEN
ANDS	ARTS	AZYM	BAUR	BIER
ANES	ARTY	BAAL	BAWD	BIFF
ANEW	ARUM	BAAS	BAWL	BIGA
ANGA	ARVO	BABA	BAWN	BIGG
ANIL	ARYL	BABE	BAWR	BIGS
ANIS	ASAR	BABU	BAYE	BIKE
ANKH	ASCI	BABY	BAYS	BILE
ANNA	ASEA	BACH	BAYT	BILK
ANNO	ASHY	BACK	BEAD	BILL
ANNS	ASKS	BACS	BEAK	BIMA
ANOA	ASPS	BADE	BEAM	BIND
ANON	ATAP	BADS	BEAN	BINE
ANOW	ATES	BAEL	BEAR	BING
ANSA	ATMA	BAFF	BEAT	BINK
ANTA	ATOC	BAFT	BEAU	BINS
ANTE	ATOK	BAGH	BECK	BINT
ANTI	ATOM	BAGS	BEDE	BIOG
ANTS	ATOP	BAHT	BEDS	BIOS
ANUS	ATUA	BAIL	BEDU	BIRD
APAY	AUFS	BAIT	BEEF	BIRK
APED	AUKS	BAJU	BEEN	BIRL
APER	AULA	BAKE	BEEP	BIRO
APES	AULD	BALD	BEER	BIRR
APEX	AUNE	BALE	BEES	BISE
APOD	AUNT	BALK	BEET	BISH

BISK	BOLT	BREW	BURY	CARK
BIST	BOMA	BREY	BUSH	CARL
BITE	BOMB	BRIE	BUSK	CARN
BITO	BONA	BRIG	BUSS	CARP
BITS	BOND	BRIK	BUST	CARR
BITT	BONE	BRIM	BUSY	CARS
BIZE	BONG	BRIN	BUTE	CART
BLAB	BONK	BRIO	BUTS	CASA
BLAD	BONY	BRIS	BUTT	CASE
BLAE	BOOB	BRIT	BUYS	CASH
BLAG	BOOH	BROD	BUZZ	CASK
BLAH	BOOK	BROG	BYDE	CAST
BLAM	BOOL	BROO	BYES	CATE
BLAT	BOOM	BROS	BYKE	CATS
BLAW	BOON	BROW	BYRE	CAUF
BLAY	BOOR	BRRR	BYRL	CAUK
BLEB	BOOS	BRUS	BYTE	CAUL
BLED	BOOT	BRUT	CAAS	CAUM
BLEE	BOPS	BRUX	CABA	CAUP
BLET	BORA	BUAT	CABS	CAVA
BLEW	BORD	BUBA	CACA	CAVE
BLEY	BORE	BUBO	CADE	CAVY
BLIN	BORK	BUBS	CADI	CAWK
BLIP	BORM	BUBU	CADS	CAWS
BLOB	BORN	BUCK	CAFE	CAYS
BLOC	BORS	BUDA	CAFF	CEAS
BLOG	BORT	BUDI	CAGE	CECA
BLOT	BOSH	BUDO	CAGS	CEDE
BLOW	BOSK	BUDS	CAGY	CEDI
BLUB	BOSS	BUFF	CAID	CEES
BLUE	BOTA	BUFO	CAIN	CEIL
BLUR	BOTH	BUGS	CAKE	CELL
BOAB	BOTS	BUHL	CAKY	CELS
BOAK	BOTT	BUHR	CALF	CELT
BOAR	BOUK	BUIK	CALK	CENS
BOAS	BOUN	BUKE	CALL	CENT
BOAT	BOUT	BULB	CALM	CEPE
BOBA	BOWL	BULK	CALO	CEPS
BOBS	BOWR	BULL	CALP	CERE
BOCK	BOWS	BUMF	CALX	CERO
BODE	BOXY	BUMP	CAMA	CERT
BODS	BOYF	BUMS	CAME	CESS
BODY	BOYG	BUNA	CAMO	CETE
BOEP	BOYO	BUND	CAMP	CHAD
BOET	BOYS	BUNG	CAMS	CHAI
BOFF	BOZO	BUNK	CANE	CHAL
BOGS	BRAD	BUNN	CANG	CHAM
BOGY	BRAE	BUNS	CANN	CHAO
BOHO	BRAG	BUNT	CANS	CHAP
BOHS	BRAK	BUOY	CANT	CHAR
BOIL	BRAN	BURA	CANY	CHAS
BOIS	BRAS	BURB	CAPA	CHAT
BOKE	BRAT	BURD	CAPE	CHAV
BOKO	BRAW	BURG	CAPH	CHAW
BOKS	BRAY	BURK	CAPI	CHAY
BOLA	BRED	BURL	CAPO	CHEF
BOLD	BREE	BURN	CAPS	CHER
BOLE	BREI	BURP	CARB	CHEW
BOLL	BREN	BURR	CARD	CHEZ
BOLO	BRER	BURS	CARE	CHIA

Four-letter words

CHIB	COAT	CORN	CUNT	DATA
CHIC	COAX	CORS	CUPS	DATE
CHID	COBB	CORY	CURB	DATO
CHIK	COBS	COSE	CURD	DAUB
CHIN	COCA	COSH	CURE	DAUD
CHIP	COCH	COSS	CURF	DAUR
CHIS	COCK	COST	CURL	DAUT
CHIT	COCO	COSY	CURN	DAVY
CHIV	CODA	COTE	CURR	DAWD
CHIZ	CODE	COTH	CURS	DAWK
CHOC	CODS	COTS	CURT	DAWN
CHOG	COED	COTT	CUSH	DAWS
CHON	COFF	COUP	CUSK	DAWT
CHOP	COFT	COUR	CUSP	DAYS
CHOU	COGS	COVE	CUSS	DAZE
CHOW	COHO	COWK	CUTE	DEAD
CHUB	COIF	COWL	CUTS	DEAF
CHUG	COIL	COWP	CWMS	DEAL
CHUM	COIN	COWS	CYAN	DEAN
CHUT	COIR	COWY	CYMA	DEAR
CIAO	COIT	COXA	CYME	DEAW
CIDE	COKE	COXY	CYST	DEBE
CIDS	COKY	COYS	CYTE	DEBS
CIEL	COLA	COZE	CZAR	DEBT
CIGS	COLD	COZY	DABS	DECK
CILL	COLE	CRAB	DACE	DECO
CINE	COLL	CRAG	DACK	DEED
CION	COLS	CRAM	DADA	DEEK
CIRE	COLT	CRAN	DADO	DEEM
CIRL	COLY	CRAP	DADS	DEEN
CIST	COMA	CRAW	DAES	DEEP
CITE	COMB	CRAY	DAFF	DEER
CITO	COME	CRED	DAFT	DEES
CITS	COMM	CREE	DAGO	DEET
CITY	COMP	CREM	DAGS	DEEV
CIVE	COMS	CREW	DAHL	DEFI
CLAD	COND	CRIB	DAHS	DEFT
CLAG	CONE	CRIM	DAIS	DEFY
CLAM	CONF	CRIS	DAKS	DEGS
CLAN	CONI	CRIT	DALE	DEID
CLAP	CONK	CROC	DALI	DEIF
CLAT	CONN	CROG	DALS	DEIL
CLAW	CONS	CROP	DALT	DEKE
CLAY	CONY	CROW	DAME	DELE
CLEF	COOF	CRUD	DAMN	DELF
CLEG	COOK	CRUE	DAMP	DELI
CLEM	COOL	CRUS	DAMS	DELL
CLEW	COOM	CRUX	DANG	DELO
CLIP	COON	CUBE	DANK	DELS
CLOD	COOP	CUBS	DANS	DELT
CLOG	COOS	CUDS	DANT	DEME
CLON	COOT	CUED	DAPS	DEMO
CLOP	COPE	CUES	DARB	DEMY
CLOT	COPS	CUFF	DARE	DENE
CLOU	COPY	CUIF	DARG	DENI
CLOW	CORD	CUIT	DARI	DENS
CLOY	CORE	CUKE	DARK	DENT
CLUB	CORF	CULL	DARN	DENY
CLUE	CORK	CULM	DART	DERE
COAL	CORM	CULT	DASH	DERM

DERN	DITZ	DOSH	DUDS	ECCE
DERO	DIVA	DOSS	DUED	ECCO
DERV	DIVE	DOST	DUEL	ECHE
DESI	DIVI	DOTE	DUES	ECHO
DESK	DIVS	DOTH	DUET	ECHT
DEUS	DIXI	DOTS	DUFF	ECOD
DEVA	DIXY	DOTY	DUGS	ECOS
DEVS	DJIN	DOUC	DUIT	ECRU
DEWS	DOAB	DOUK	DUKA	ECUS
DEWY	DOAT	DOUM	DUKE	EDDO
DEXY	DOBS	DOUN	DULE	EDDY
DEYS	DOBY	DOUP	DULL	EDGE
DHAK	DOCK	DOUR	DULY	EDGY
DHAL	DOCO	DOUT	DUMA	EDHS
DHOL	DOCS	DOUX	DUMB	EDIT
DHOW	DODO	DOVE	DUMP	EECH
DIAL	DODS	DOWD	DUNE	EELS
DIBS	DOEK	DOWF	DUNG	EELY
DICE	DOEN	DOWL	DUNK	EERY
DICH	DOER	DOWN	DUNS	EEVN
DICK	DOES	DOWP	DUNT	EFFS
DICT	DOFF	DOWS	DUOS	EFTS
DIDO	DOGE	DOWT	DUPE	EGAD
DIDY	DOGS	DOXY	DUPS	EGAL
DIEB	DOGY	DOYS	DURA	EGER
DIED	DOHS	DOZE	DURE	EGGS
DIEL	DOIT	DOZY	DURN	EGGY
DIES	DOJO	DRAB	DURO	EGIS
DIET	DOLE	DRAC	DURR	EGMA
DIFF	DOLL	DRAD	DUSH	EGOS
DIFS	DOLS	DRAG	DUSK	EHED
DIGS	DOLT	DRAM	DUST	EIDE
DIKA	DOME	DRAP	DUTY	EIKS
DIKE	DOMS	DRAT	DWAM	EILD
DILL	DOMY	DRAW	DYAD	EINA
DIME	DONA	DRAY	DYED	EINE
DIMP	DONE	DREE	DYER	EISH
DIMS	DONG	DREG	DYES	EKED
DINE	DONS	DREK	DYKE	EKES
DING	DOOB	DREW	DYNE	EKKA
DINK	DOOK	DREY	DZHO	ELAN
DINO	DOOL	DRIB	DZOS	ELDS
DINS	DOOM	DRIP	EACH	ELFS
DINT	DOON	DROP	EALE	ELHI
DIOL	DOOR	DROW	EANS	ELKS
DIPS	DOOS	DRUB	EARD	ELLS
DIPT	DOPA	DRUG	EARL	ELMS
DIRE	DOPE	DRUM	EARN	ELMY
DIRK	DOPS	DRYS	EARS	ELSE
DIRL	DOPY	DSOS	EASE	ELTS
DIRT	DORB	DUAD	EAST	EMES
DISA	DORE	DUAL	EASY	EMEU
DISC	DORK	DUAN	EATH	EMIC
DISH	DORM	DUAR	EATS	EMIR
DISK	DORP	DUBS	EAUS	EMIT
DISS	DORR	DUCE	EAUX	EMMA
DITA	DORS	DUCI	EAVE	EMMY
DITE	DORT	DUCK	EBBS	EMOS
DITS	DORY	DUCT	EBON	EMPT
DITT	DOSE	DUDE	ECAD	EMUS

EMYD	EWKS	FAUT	FILA	FOAM	
EMYS	EWTS	FAUX	FILE	FOBS	
ENDS	EXAM	FAVA	FILL	FOCI	
ENES	EXEC	FAVE	FILM	FOEN	
ENEW	EXED	FAWN	FILO	FOES	
ENGS	EXES	FAWS	FILS	FOGS	
ENOL	EXIT	FAYS	FIND	FOGY	
ENOW	EXON	FAZE	FINE	FOHN	
ENUF	EXPO	FEAL	FINI	FOHS	
ENVY	EXUL	FEAR	FINK	FOID	
EOAN	EYAS	FEAT	FINO	FOIL	
EONS	EYED	FECK	FINS	FOIN	
EORL	EYEN	FEDS	FIRE	FOLD	
EPEE	EYER	FEEB	FIRK	FOLK	
EPHA	EYES	FEED	FIRM	FOND	
EPIC	EYNE	FEEL	FIRN	FONE	
EPOS	EYOT	FEEN	FIRS	FONS	
ERAS	EYRA	FEER	FISC	FONT	
ERED	EYRE	FEES	FISH	FOOD	
ERES	EYRY	FEET	FISK	FOOL	
EREV	FAAN	FEGS	FIST	FOOT	
ERGO	FAAS	FEHM	FITS	FOPS	
ERGS	FABS	FEHS	FITT	FORA	
ERIC	FACE	FEIS	FIVE	FORB	
ERKS	FACT	FELL	FIXT	FORD	
ERNE	FADE	FELT	FIZZ	FORE	
ERNS	FADO	FEME	FLAB	FORK	
EROS	FADS	FEMS	FLAG	FORM	
ERRS	FADY	FEND	FLAK	FORT	
ERST	FAFF	FENI	FLAM	FOSS	
ERUV	FAGS	FENS	FLAN	FOUD	
ESES	FAHS	FENT	FLAP	FOUL	
ESKY	FAIK	FEOD	FLAT	FOUR	
ESNE	FAIL	FERE	FLAW	FOUS	
ESPY	FAIN	FERM	FLAX	FOWL	
ESSE	FAIR	FERN	FLAY	FOXY	
ESTS	FAIX	FESS	FLEA	FOYS	
ETAS	FAKE	FEST	FLED	FOZY	
ETAT	FALL	FETA	FLEE	FRAB	
ETCH	FALX	FETE	FLEG	FRAE	
ETEN	FAME	FETS	FLEW	FRAG	
ETHE	FAND	FETT	FLEX	FRAP	
ETHS	FANE	FEUD	FLEY	FRAS	
ETIC	FANG	FEUS	FLIC	FRAT	
ETNA	FANK	FEYS	FLIM	FRAU	
ETUI	FANO	FIAR	FLIP	FRAY	
EUGE	FANS	FIAT	FLIR	FREE	
EUGH	FARD	FIBS	FLIT	FRET	
EUKS	FARE	FICE	FLIX	FRIB	
EUOI	FARL	FICO	FLOC	FRIG	
EURO	FARM	FIDO	FLOE	FRIS	
EVEN	FARO	FIDS	FLOG	FRIT	
EVER	FARS	FIEF	FLOP	FRIZ	
EVES	FART	FIER	FLOR	FROE	
EVET	FASH	FIFE	FLOW	FROG	
EVIL	FAST	FIFI	FLUB	FROM	
EVOE	FATE	FIGO	FLUE	FROS	
EVOS	FATS	FIGS	FLUS	FROW	
EWER	FAUN	FIKE	FLUX	FRUG	
EWES	FAUR	FIKY	FOAL	FUBS	

FUCI	GANS	GHAT	GNOW	GREN
FUCK	GANT	GHEE	GNUS	GREW
FUDS	GAOL	GHIS	GOAD	GREX
FUEL	GAPE	GIBE	GOAF	GREY
FUFF	GAPO	GIBS	GOAL	GRID
FUGS	GAPS	GIDS	GOAS	GRIG
FUGU	GAPY	GIED	GOAT	GRIM
FUJI	GARB	GIEN	GOBO	GRIN
FULL	GARE	GIES	GOBS	GRIP
FUME	GARI	GIFT	GOBY	GRIS
FUMS	GARS	GIGA	GODS	GRIT
FUMY	GART	GIGS	GOEL	GROG
FUND	GASH	GILA	GOER	GROK
FUNG	GASP	GILD	GOES	GROT
FUNK	GAST	GILL	GOEY	GROW
FUNS	GATE	GILT	GOFF	GRUB
FURL	GATH	GIMP	GOGO	GRUE
FURR	GATS	GING	GOLD	GRUM
FURS	GAUD	GINK	GOLE	GUAN
FURY	GAUM	GINN	GOLF	GUAR
FUSC	GAUN	GINS	GOLP	GUBS
FUSE	GAUP	GIOS	GONE	GUCK
FUSS	GAUR	GIPS	GONG	GUDE
FUST	GAUS	GIRD	GONK	GUES
FUTZ	GAVE	GIRL	GONS	GUFF
FUZE	GAWD	GIRN	GOOD	GUGA
FUZZ	GAWK	GIRO	GOOF	GUID
FYCE	GAWP	GIRR	GOOG	GULA
FYKE	GAYS	GIRT	GOOK	GULE
FYLE	GAZE	GISM	GOOL	GULF
FYRD	GAZY	GIST	GOON	GULL
GABS	GEAL	GITE	GOOP	GULP
GABY	GEAN	GITS	GOOR	GULS
GADE	GEAR	GIVE	GOOS	GULY
GADI	GEAT	GIZZ	GORA	GUMP
GADS	GECK	GJUS	GORE	GUMS
GAED	GEDS	GLAD	GORI	GUNG
GAEN	GEED	GLAM	GORM	GUNK
GAES	GEEK	GLED	GORP	GUNS
GAFF	GEEP	GLEE	GORY	GUPS
GAGA	GEES	GLEG	GOSH	GURL
GAGE	GEEZ	GLEI	GOSS	GURN
GAGS	GEIT	GLEN	GOTH	GURS
GAID	GELD	GLEY	GOUK	GURU
GAIN	GELS	GLIA	GOUT	GUSH
GAIR	GELT	GLIB	GOVS	GUST
GAIT	GEMS	GLID	GOWD	GUTS
GAJO	GENA	GLIM	GOWF	GUVS
GALA	GENE	GLIT	GOWK	GUYS
GALE	GENS	GLOB	GOWL	GYAL
GALL	GENT	GLOM	GOWN	GYBE
GALS	GENU	GLOP	GOYS	GYMP
GAMA	GEOS	GLOW	GRAB	GYMS
GAMB	GERE	GLUE	GRAD	GYNY
GAME	GERM	GLUG	GRAM	GYPS
GAMP	GERT	GLUM	GRAN	GYRE
GAMS	GEST	GLUT	GRAT	GYRI
GAMY	GETA	GNAR	GRAV	GYRO
GANE	GETS	GNAT	GRAY	GYTE
GANG	GEUM	GNAW	GREE	GYVE

Four-letter words

HAAF	HAUT	HILA	HOOF	HUSS
HAAR	HAVE	HILD	HOOK	HUTS
HABU	HAWK	HILI	HOON	HWAN
HACK	HAWM	HILL	HOOP	HWYL
HADE	HAWS	HILT	HOOT	HYED
HADJ	HAYS	HIMS	HOPE	HYEN
HADS	HAZE	HIND	HOPS	HYES
HAED	HAZY	HING	HORA	HYKE
HAEM	HEAD	HINS	HORE	HYLA
HAEN	HEAL	HINT	HORI	HYLE
HAES	HEAP	HIOI	HORN	HYMN
HAET	HEAR	HIPS	HORS	HYPE
HAFF	HEAT	HIPT	HOSE	HYPO
HAFT	HEBE	HIRE	HOSS	HYPS
HAGG	HECH	HISH	HOST	HYTE
HAGS	HECK	HISN	HOTE	IAMB
HAHA	HEED	HISS	HOTS	IBEX
HAHS	HEEL	HIST	HOUF	IBIS
HAIK	HEFT	HITS	HOUR	ICED
HAIL	HEHS	HIVE	HOUT	ICER
HAIN	HEID	HIYA	HOVE	ICES
HAIR	HEIL	HIZZ	HOWE	ICHS
HAJI	HEIR	HOAR	HOWF	ICKY
HAJJ	HELD	HOAS	HOWK	ICON
HAKA	HELE	HOAX	HOWL	IDEA
HAKE	HELL	HOBO	HOWS	IDEE
HAKU	HELM	HOBS	HOYA	IDEM
HALE	HELO	HOCK	HOYS	IDES
HALF	HELP	HODS	HUBS	IDLE
HALL	HEME	HOED	HUCK	IDLY
HALM	HEMP	HOER	HUED	IDOL
HALO	HEMS	HOES	HUER	IDYL
HALT	HEND	HOGG	HUES	IFFY
HAME	HENS	HOGH	HUFF	IGAD
HAMS	HENT	HOGS	HUGE	IGGS
HAND	HEPS	HOHA	HUGS	IGLU
HANG	HEPT	HOHS	HUGY	IKAN
HANK	HERB	HOIK	HUHU	IKAT
HANT	HERD	HOKA	HUIA	IKON
HAPS	HERE	HOKE	HUIC	ILEA
HAPU	HERL	HOKI	HUIS	ILEX
HARD	HERM	HOLD	HULA	ILIA
HARE	HERN	HOLE	HULE	ILKA
HARK	HERO	HOLK	HULK	ILKS
HARL	HERS	HOLM	HULL	ILLS
HARM	HERY	HOLP	HUMA	ILLY
HARN	HESP	HOLS	HUMF	IMAM
HARO	HEST	HOLT	HUMP	IMID
HARP	HETE	HOLY	HUMS	IMMY
HART	HETH	HOMA	HUNG	IMPI
HASH	HETS	HOME	HUNH	IMPS
HASK	HEWN	HOMO	HUNK	INBY
HASP	HEWS	HOMS	HUNS	INCH
HAST	HEYS	HOMY	HUNT	INFO
HATE	HICK	HOND	HUPS	INGO
HATH	HIDE	HONE	HURL	INIA
HATS	HIED	HONG	HURT	INKS
HAUD	HIES	HONK	HUSH	INKY
HAUF	HIGH	HONS	HUSK	INLY
HAUL	HIKE	HOOD	HUSO	INNS

INRO	JEED	JOUR	KARA	KICK
INTI	JEEL	JOWL	KARK	KIDS
INTO	JEEP	JOWS	KARN	KIEF
IONS	JEER	JOYS	KARO	KIER
IOTA	JEES	JUBA	KART	KIFF
IRED	JEEZ	JUBE	KATA	KIFS
IRES	JEFE	JUCO	KATI	KIKE
IRID	JEFF	JUDO	KATS	KILD
IRIS	JEHU	JUDS	KAVA	KILL
IRKS	JELL	JUDY	KAWA	KILN
IRON	JEON	JUGA	KAWS	KILO
ISBA	JERK	JUGS	KAYO	KILP
ISIT	JESS	JUJU	KAYS	KILT
ISLE	JEST	JUKE	KAZI	KINA
ISMS	JETE	JUKU	KBAR	KIND
ISNA	JETS	JUMP	KEAS	KINE
ISOS	JEUX	JUNK	KEBS	KING
ITAS	JEWS	JUPE	KECK	KINK
ITCH	JIAO	JURA	KEDS	KINO
ITEM	JIBB	JURE	KEEF	KINS
IURE	JIBE	JURY	KEEK	KIPE
IWIS	JIBS	JUST	KEEL	KIPP
IXIA	JIFF	JUTE	KEEN	KIPS
IZAR	JIGS	JUTS	KEEP	KIRK
JAAP	JILL	JUVE	KEET	KIRN
JABS	JILT	JYNX	KEFS	KIRS
JACK	JIMP	KAAL	KEGS	KISH
JADE	JINK	KAAS	KEIR	KISS
JAFA	JINN	KABS	KEKS	KIST
JAGA	JINS	KADE	KELL	KITE
JAGG	JINX	KADI	KELP	KITH
JAGS	JIRD	KAED	KELT	KITS
JAIL	JISM	KAES	KEMB	KIVA
JAKE	JIVE	KAFS	KEMP	KIWI
JAKS	JIVY	KAGO	KENO	KLAP
JAMB	JIZZ	KAGU	KENS	KLIK
JAMS	JOBE	KAID	KENT	KNAG
JANE	JOBS	KAIE	KEPI	KNAP
JANN	JOCK	KAIF	KEPS	KNAR
JAPE	JOCO	KAIK	KEPT	KNEE
JAPS	JOES	KAIL	KERB	KNEW
JARK	JOEY	KAIM	KERF	KNIT
JARL	JOGS	KAIN	KERN	KNOB
JARP	JOHN	KAIS	KERO	KNOP
JARS	JOIN	KAKA	KESH	KNOT
JASP	JOKE	KAKI	KEST	KNOW
JASS	JOKY	KAKS	KETA	KNUB
JASY	JOLE	KALE	KETE	KNUR
JATO	JOLL	KALI	KETO	KNUT
JAUK	JOLS	KAMA	KETS	KOAN
JAUP	JOLT	KAME	KEWL	KOAP
JAVA	JOMO	KAMI	KEYS	KOAS
JAWS	JONG	KANA	KHAF	KOBO
JAXY	JOOK	KANE	KHAN	KOBS
JAYS	JORS	KANG	KHAT	KOEL
JAZY	JOSH	KANS	KHET	KOFF
JAZZ	JOSS	KANT	KHIS	KOHA
JEAN	JOTA	KAON	KHOR	KOHL
JEAT	JOTS	KAPA	KHUD	KOIS
JEDI	JOUK	KAPH	KIBE	KOJI

Four-letter words

KOLA	LAIK	LEEP	LIMP	LOON
KOLO	LAIN	LEER	LIMY	LOOP
KOND	LAIR	LEES	LIND	LOOR
KONK	LAKE	LEET	LINE	LOOS
KONS	LAKH	LEFT	LING	LOOT
KOOK	LAKY	LEGS	LINK	LOPE
KOPH	LALL	LEHR	LINN	LOPS
KOPS	LAMA	LEIR	LINO	LORD
KORA	LAMB	LEIS	LINS	LORE
KORE	LAME	LEKE	LINT	LORN
KORO	LAMP	LEKS	LINY	LORY
KORS	LAMS	LEKU	LION	LOSE
KORU	LANA	LEME	LIPA	LOSH
KOSS	LAND	LEND	LIPE	LOSS
KOTO	LANE	LENG	LIPO	LOST
KOWS	LANG	LENO	LIPS	LOTA
KRAB	LANK	LENS	LIRA	LOTE
KRIS	LANT	LENT	LIRE	LOTH
KSAR	LANX	LEPS	LIRI	LOTI
KUDO	LAPS	LEPT	LIRK	LOTO
KUDU	LARD	LERE	LISK	LOTS
KUEH	LARE	LERP	LISP	LOUD
KUES	LARI	LESS	LIST	LOUN
KUFI	LARK	LEST	LITE	LOUP
KUIA	LARN	LETS	LITH	LOUR
KUKU	LARS	LEUD	LITS	LOUS
KULA	LASE	LEVA	LITU	LOUT
KUNA	LASH	LEVE	LIVE	LOVE
KUNE	LASS	LEVO	LOAD	LOWE
KURI	LAST	LEVY	LOAF	LOWN
KURU	LATE	LEWD	LOAM	LOWP
KUTA	LATH	LEYS	LOAN	LOWS
KUTI	LATI	LEZZ	LOBE	LOWT
KUTU	LATS	LIAR	LOBI	LOYS
KUZU	LATU	LIAS	LOBO	LUAU
KVAS	LAUD	LIBS	LOBS	LUBE
KYAK	LAUF	LICE	LOCA	LUCE
KYAR	LAVA	LICH	LOCH	LUCK
KYAT	LAVE	LICK	LOCI	LUDE
KYBO	LAVS	LIDO	LOCK	LUDO
KYES	LAWK	LIDS	LOCO	LUDS
KYLE	LAWN	LIED	LODE	LUES
KYND	LAWS	LIEF	LODS	LUFF
KYNE	LAYS	LIEN	LOFT	LUGE
KYPE	LAZE	LIER	LOGE	LUGS
KYTE	LAZO	LIES	LOGO	LUIT
KYUS	LAZY	LIEU	LOGS	LUKE
LABS	LEAD	LIFE	LOGY	LULL
LACE	LEAF	LIFT	LOID	LULU
LACK	LEAK	LIGS	LOIN	LUMA
LACS	LEAL	LIKE	LOIR	LUMP
LACY	LEAM	LILL	LOKE	LUMS
LADE	LEAN	LILO	LOLL	LUNA
LADS	LEAP	LILT	LOMA	LUNE
LADY	LEAR	LILY	LOME	LUNG
LAER	LEAS	LIMA	LONE	LUNK
LAGS	LEAT	LIMB	LONG	LUNT
LAHS	LECH	LIME	LOOF	LUNY
LAIC	LEED	LIMN	LOOK	LURE
LAID	LEEK	LIMO	LOOM	LURK

LURS	MANY	MEMO	MINO	MONO
LUSH	MAPS	MEMS	MINT	MONS
LUSK	MARA	MEND	MINX	MONY
LUST	MARC	MENE	MINY	MOOD
LUTE	MARD	MENG	MIPS	MOOI
LUTZ	MARE	MENO	MIRE	MOOK
LUVS	MARG	MENT	MIRI	MOOL
LUXE	MARK	MENU	MIRK	MOON
LWEI	MARL	MEOU	MIRO	MOOP
LYAM	MARM	MEOW	MIRS	MOOR
LYCH	MARS	MERC	MIRV	MOOS
LYES	MART	MERE	MIRY	MOOT
LYME	MARY	MERI	MISE	MOPE
LYMS	MASA	MERK	MISO	MOPS
LYNE	MASE	MERL	MISS	MOPY
LYNX	MASH	MESA	MIST	MORA
LYRA	MASK	MESE	MITE	MORE
LYRE	MASS	MESH	MITT	MORN
LYSE	MAST	MESS	MITY	MORS
LYTE	MASU	META	MIXT	MORT
MAAR	MATE	METE	MIXY	MOSE
MAAS	MATH	METH	MIZZ	MOSH
MABE	MATS	METS	MNAS	MOSK
MACE	MATT	MEUS	MOAI	MOSS
MACH	MATY	MEVE	MOAN	MOST
MACK	MAUD	MEWL	MOAS	MOTE
MACS	MAUL	MEWS	MOAT	MOTH
MADE	MAUN	MEZE	MOBE	MOTI
MADS	MAUT	MEZZ	MOBS	MOTS
MAES	MAWK	MHOS	MOBY	MOTT
MAGE	MAWN	MIBS	MOCH	MOTU
MAGG	MAWR	MICA	MOCK	MOUE
MAGI	MAWS	MICE	MOCS	MOUP
MAGS	MAXI	MICH	MODE	MOUS
MAID	MAYA	MICK	MODI	MOVE
MAIK	MAYO	MICO	MODS	MOWA
MAIL	MAYS	MICS	MOER	MOWN
MAIM	MAZE	MIDI	MOES	MOWS
MAIN	MAZY	MIDS	MOFO	MOXA
MAIR	MEAD	MIEN	MOGS	MOYA
MAKE	MEAL	MIFF	MOHR	MOYL
MAKI	MEAN	MIGG	MOIL	MOYS
MAKO	MEAT	MIGS	MOIT	MOZE
MAKS	MECK	MIHA	MOJO	MOZO
MALA	MEDS	MIHI	MOKE	MOZZ
MALE	MEED	MIKE	MOKI	MUCH
MALI	MEEK	MILD	MOKO	MUCK
MALL	MEER	MILE	MOLA	MUDS
MALM	MEES	MILK	MOLD	MUFF
MALS	MEET	MILL	MOLE	MUGG
MALT	MEFF	MILO	MOLL	MUGS
MAMA	MEGA	MILS	MOLS	MUID
MAMS	MEGS	MILT	MOLT	MUIL
MANA	MEIN	MIME	MOLY	MUIR
MAND	MELA	MINA	MOME	MULE
MANE	MELD	MIND	MOMI	MULL
MANG	MELL	MINE	MOMS	MUMM
MANI	MELS	MING	MONA	MUMP
MANO	MELT	MINI	MONG	MUMS
MANS	MEME	MINK	MONK	MUMU

Four-letter words

MUNG	NAVE	NISI	NURL	OLDY
MUNI	NAVY	NITE	NURR	OLEA
MUNS	NAYS	NITS	NURS	OLEO
MUNT	NAZE	NIXE	NUTS	OLES
MUON	NAZI	NIXY	NYAS	OLID
MURA	NEAL	NOAH	NYED	OLIO
MURE	NEAP	NOBS	NYES	OLLA
MURK	NEAR	NOCK	OAFS	OLMS
MURL	NEAT	NODE	OAKS	OLPE
MURR	NEBS	NODI	OAKY	OMBU
MUSE	NECK	NODS	OARS	OMEN
MUSH	NEDS	NOEL	OARY	OMER
MUSK	NEED	NOES	OAST	OMIT
MUSO	NEEM	NOGG	OATH	OMOV
MUSS	NEEP	NOGS	OATS	ONCE
MUST	NEFS	NOIL	OBAS	ONER
MUTE	NEGS	NOIR	OBES	ONES
MUTI	NEIF	NOLE	OBEY	ONIE
MUTS	NEKS	NOLL	OBIA	ONLY
MUTT	NEMA	NOLO	OBIS	ONOS
MUZZ	NEMN	NOMA	OBIT	ONST
MYAL	NENE	NOME	OBOE	ONTO
MYCS	NEON	NOMS	OBOL	ONUS
MYNA	NEPS	NONA	OBOS	ONYX
MYTH	NERD	NONE	OCAS	OOFS
MYXO	NERK	NONG	OCCY	OOFY
MZEE	NESH	NONI	OCHE	OOHS
NAAM	NESS	NOOK	OCTA	OOMS
NAAN	NEST	NOON	ODAH	OONS
NABE	NETE	NOOP	ODAL	OONT
NABK	NETS	NOPE	ODAS	OOPS
NABS	NETT	NORI	ODDS	OOSE
NACH	NEUK	NORK	ODEA	OOSY
NADA	NEUM	NORM	ODES	OOTS
NADS	NEVE	NOSE	ODIC	OOZE
NAFF	NEVI	NOSH	ODOR	OOZY
NAGA	NEWS	NOSY	ODSO	OPAH
NAGS	NEWT	NOTA	ODYL	OPAL
NAIF	NEXT	NOTE	OFAY	OPED
NAIK	NIBS	NOTT	OFFS	OPEN
NAIL	NICE	NOUL	OGAM	OPES
NAIN	NICK	NOUN	OGEE	OPPO
NALA	NIDE	NOUP	OGLE	OPTS
NAME	NIDI	NOUS	OGRE	OPUS
NAMS	NIDS	NOUT	OHED	ORAD
NAMU	NIED	NOVA	OHIA	ORAL
NANA	NIEF	NOWL	OHMS	ORBS
NANE	NIES	NOWN	OHOS	ORBY
NANS	NIFE	NOWS	OIKS	ORCA
NAOI	NIFF	NOWT	OILS	ORCS
NAOS	NIGH	NOWY	OILY	ORDO
NAPA	NILL	NOYS	OINK	ORDS
NAPE	NILS	NUBS	OINT	ORES
NAPS	NIMB	NUDE	OKAS	ORFE
NARC	NIMS	NUFF	OKAY	ORFS
NARD	NINE	NUKE	OKEH	ORGY
NARE	NIPA	NULL	OKES	ORLE
NARK	NIPS	NUMB	OKRA	ORRA
NARY	NIRL	NUNS	OKTA	ORTS
NATS	NISH	NURD	OLDS	ORYX

ORZO	PALE	PEES	PILI	POGO
OSAR	PALL	PEGH	PILL	POGY
OSES	PALM	PEGS	PILY	POIS
OSSA	PALP	PEHS	PIMA	POKE
OTIC	PALS	PEIN	PIMP	POKY
OTTO	PALY	PEKE	PINA	POLE
OUCH	PAMS	PELA	PINE	POLK
OUDS	PAND	PELE	PING	POLL
OUKS	PANE	PELF	PINK	POLO
OULD	PANG	PELL	PINS	POLS
OULK	PANS	PELT	PINT	POLT
OUMA	PANT	PEND	PINY	POLY
OUPA	PAPA	PENE	PION	POME
OUPH	PAPE	PENI	PIOY	POMO
OUPS	PAPS	PENK	PIPA	POMP
OURN	PARA	PENS	PIPE	POMS
OURS	PARD	PENT	PIPI	POND
OUST	PARE	PEON	PIPS	PONE
OUTS	PARK	PEPO	PIPY	PONG
OUZO	PARP	PEPS	PIRL	PONK
OVAL	PARR	PERE	PIRN	PONS
OVEL	PARS	PERI	PIRS	PONT
OVEN	PART	PERK	PISE	PONY
OVER	PASE	PERM	PISH	POOD
OVUM	PASH	PERN	PISO	POOF
OWED	PASS	PERP	PISS	POOH
OWER	PAST	PERT	PITA	POOK
OWES	PATE	PERV	PITH	POOL
OWLS	PATH	PESO	PITS	POON
OWLY	PATS	PEST	PITY	POOP
OWNS	PATU	PETS	PIUM	POOR
OWRE	PATY	PEWS	PIXY	POOS
OWSE	PAUA	PFFT	PIZE	POOT
OWTS	PAUL	PFUI	PLAN	POPE
OXEN	PAVE	PHAT	PLAP	POPS
OXER	PAVS	PHEW	PLAT	PORE
OXES	PAWA	PHIS	PLAY	PORK
OXID	PAWK	PHIZ	PLEA	PORN
OXIM	PAWL	PHOH	PLEB	PORT
OYER	PAWN	PHON	PLED	PORY
OYES	PAWS	PHOS	PLEW	POSE
OYEZ	PAYS	PHOT	PLEX	POSH
PAAL	PEAG	PHUT	PLIE	POSS
PACA	PEAK	PIAL	PLIM	POST
PACE	PEAL	PIAN	PLOD	POSY
PACK	PEAN	PIAS	PLOP	POTE
PACO	PEAR	PICA	PLOT	POTS
PACS	PEAS	PICE	PLOW	POTT
PACT	PEAT	PICK	PLOY	POUF
PACY	PEBA	PICS	PLUE	POUK
PADI	PECH	PIED	PLUG	POUR
PADS	PECK	PIER	PLUM	POUT
PAGE	PECS	PIES	PLUS	POWN
PAHS	PEDS	PIET	POAS	POWS
PAID	PEED	PIGS	POCK	POXY
PAIK	PEEK	PIKA	POCO	POZZ
PAIL	PEEL	PIKE	PODS	PRAD
PAIN	PEEN	PIKI	POEM	PRAM
PAIR	PEEP	PILA	POEP	PRAO
PAIS	PEER	PILE	POET	PRAT

Four-letter words

PRAU	PUPS	RAIK	REEN	RINK
PRAY	PUPU	RAIL	REES	RINS
PREE	PURE	RAIN	REFS	RIOT
PREM	PURI	RAIS	REFT	RIPE
PREP	PURL	RAIT	REGO	RIPP
PREX	PURR	RAJA	REGS	RIPS
PREY	PURS	RAKE	REHS	RIPT
PREZ	PUSH	RAKI	REIF	RISE
PRIG	PUSS	RAKU	REIK	RISK
PRIM	PUTS	RALE	REIN	RISP
PROA	PUTT	RAMI	REIS	RITE
PROB	PUTZ	RAMP	REKE	RITS
PROD	PUYS	RAMS	RELY	RITT
PROF	PYAS	RANA	REMS	RITZ
PROG	PYAT	RAND	REND	RIVA
PROM	PYES	RANG	RENK	RIVE
PROO	PYET	RANI	RENS	RIVO
PROP	PYIC	RANK	RENT	RIZA
PROS	PYIN	RANT	RENY	ROAD
PROW	PYNE	RAPE	REOS	ROAM
PRUH	PYOT	RAPS	REPO	ROAN
PRYS	PYRE	RAPT	REPP	ROAR
PSIS	PYRO	RARE	REPS	ROBE
PSST	QADI	RARK	RESH	ROBS
PTUI	QAID	RASE	REST	ROCH
PUBE	QATS	RASH	RETE	ROCK
PUBS	QOPH	RASP	RETS	ROCS
PUCE	QUAD	RAST	REVS	RODE
PUCK	QUAG	RATA	REWS	RODS
PUDS	QUAI	RATE	RHEA	ROED
PUDU	QUAT	RATH	RHOS	ROES
PUER	QUAY	RATO	RHUS	ROIL
PUFF	QUEP	RATS	RIAL	ROIN
PUGH	QUEY	RATU	RIAS	ROJI
PUGS	QUID	RAUN	RIBA	ROKE
PUHA	QUIM	RAVE	RIBS	ROKS
PUIR	QUIN	RAWN	RICE	ROKY
PUJA	QUIP	RAWS	RICH	ROLE
PUKA	QUIT	RAYA	RICK	ROLF
PUKE	QUIZ	RAYS	RICY	ROLL
PUKU	QUOD	RAZE	RIDE	ROMA
PULA	QUOP	RAZZ	RIDS	ROMP
PULE	RABI	READ	RIEL	ROMS
PULI	RACA	REAK	RIEM	RONE
PULK	RACE	REAL	RIFE	RONG
PULL	RACH	REAM	RIFF	RONT
PULP	RACK	REAN	RIFS	ROOD
PULS	RACY	REAP	RIFT	ROOF
PULU	RADE	REAR	RIGG	ROOK
PULY	RADS	REBS	RIGS	ROOM
PUMA	RAFF	RECK	RILE	ROON
PUMP	RAFT	RECS	RILL	ROOP
PUMY	RAGA	REDD	RIMA	ROOS
PUNA	RAGE	REDE	RIME	ROOT
PUNG	RAGG	REDO	RIMS	ROPE
PUNK	RAGI	REDS	RIMU	ROPY
PUNS	RAGS	REED	RIMY	RORE
PUNT	RAHS	REEF	RIND	RORT
PUNY	RAIA	REEK	RINE	RORY
PUPA	RAID	REEL	RING	ROSE

ROST	SABE	SCAN	SERK	SIGN
ROSY	SABS	SCAR	SERR	SIJO
ROTA	SACK	SCAT	SERS	SIKA
ROTE	SACS	SCAW	SESE	SIKE
ROTI	SADE	SCOG	SESH	SILD
ROTL	SADI	SCOP	SESS	SILE
ROTO	SADO	SCOT	SETA	SILK
ROTS	SADS	SCOW	SETS	SILL
ROUE	SAFE	SCRY	SETT	SILO
ROUL	SAFT	SCUD	SEWN	SILT
ROUM	SAGA	SCUG	SEWS	SIMA
ROUP	SAGE	SCUL	SEXT	SIMI
ROUT	SAGO	SCUM	SEXY	SIMP
ROUX	SAGS	SCUP	SEYS	SIMS
ROVE	SAGY	SCUR	SHAD	SIND
ROWS	SAIC	SCUT	SHAG	SINE
ROWT	SAID	SCYE	SHAH	SING
RUBE	SAIL	SEAL	SHAM	SINH
RUBS	SAIM	SEAM	SHAN	SINK
RUBY	SAIN	SEAN	SHAT	SINS
RUCK	SAIR	SEAR	SHAW	SIPE
RUCS	SAIS	SEAS	SHAY	SIPS
RUDD	SAKE	SEAT	SHEA	SIRE
RUDE	SAKI	SECH	SHED	SIRI
RUDS	SALE	SECO	SHES	SIRS
RUED	SALL	SECS	SHET	SISS
RUER	SALP	SECT	SHEW	SIST
RUES	SALS	SEED	SHIM	SITE
RUFF	SALT	SEEK	SHIN	SITH
RUGA	SAMA	SEEL	SHIP	SITS
RUGS	SAME	SEEM	SHIR	SITZ
RUIN	SAMP	SEEN	SHIT	SIZE
RUKH	SAMS	SEEP	SHIV	SIZY
RULE	SAND	SEER	SHMO	SJOE
RULY	SANE	SEES	SHOD	SKAG
RUME	SANG	SEGO	SHOE	SKAS
RUMP	SANK	SEGS	SHOG	SKAT
RUMS	SANS	SEIF	SHOO	SKAW
RUND	SANT	SEIK	SHOP	SKEE
RUNE	SAPS	SEIL	SHOT	SKEG
RUNG	SARD	SEIR	SHOW	SKEN
RUNS	SARI	SEIS	SHRI	SKEO
RUNT	SARK	SEKT	SHUL	SKEP
RURP	SARS	SELD	SHUN	SKER
RURU	SASH	SELE	SHUT	SKET
RUSA	SASS	SELF	SHWA	SKEW
RUSE	SATE	SELL	SIAL	SKID
RUSH	SATI	SELS	SIBB	SKIM
RUSK	SAUL	SEME	SIBS	SKIN
RUST	SAUT	SEMI	SICE	SKIO
RUTH	SAVE	SENA	SICH	SKIP
RUTS	SAVS	SEND	SICK	SKIS
RYAL	SAWN	SENE	SICS	SKIT
RYAS	SAWS	SENS	SIDA	SKOL
RYES	SAXE	SENT	SIDE	SKRY
RYFE	SAYS	SEPS	SIDH	SKUA
RYKE	SCAB	SEPT	SIEN	SKUG
RYND	SCAD	SERA	SIES	SKYF
RYOT	SCAG	SERE	SIFT	SKYR
RYPE	SCAM	SERF	SIGH	SLAB

Four-letter words

SLAE	SOCA	SPAE	SUBS	SYPE
SLAG	SOCK	SPAG	SUCH	SYPH
SLAM	SOCS	SPAM	SUCK	TAAL
SLAP	SODA	SPAN	SUDD	TABI
SLAT	SODS	SPAR	SUDS	TABS
SLAW	SOFA	SPAS	SUED	TABU
SLAY	SOFT	SPAT	SUER	TACE
SLED	SOGS	SPAW	SUES	TACH
SLEE	SOHO	SPAY	SUET	TACK
SLEW	SOHS	SPAZ	SUGH	TACO
SLEY	SOIL	SPEC	SUID	TACT
SLID	SOJA	SPED	SUIT	TADS
SLIM	SOKE	SPEK	SUKH	TAED
SLIP	SOLA	SPET	SUKS	TAEL
SLIT	SOLD	SPEW	SULK	TAES
SLOB	SOLE	SPIC	SULU	TAGS
SLOE	SOLI	SPIE	SUMO	TAHA
SLOG	SOLO	SPIF	SUMP	TAHR
SLOP	SOLS	SPIK	SUMS	TAIG
SLOT	SOMA	SPIM	SUMY	TAIL
SLOW	SOME	SPIN	SUNG	TAIN
SLUB	SOMS	SPIT	SUNK	TAIS
SLUE	SOMY	SPIV	SUNN	TAIT
SLUG	SONE	SPOD	SUNS	TAKA
SLUM	SONG	SPOT	SUPE	TAKE
SLUR	SONS	SPRY	SUPS	TAKI
SLUT	SOOK	SPUD	SUQS	TAKS
SMEE	SOOL	SPUE	SURA	TAKY
SMEW	SOOM	SPUG	SURD	TALA
SMIR	SOON	SPUN	SURE	TALC
SMIT	SOOP	SPUR	SURF	TALE
SMOG	SOOT	SRIS	SUSS	TALI
SMUG	SOPH	STAB	SUSU	TALK
SMUR	SOPS	STAG	SWAB	TALL
SMUT	SORA	STAP	SWAD	TAME
SNAB	SORB	STAR	SWAG	TAMP
SNAG	SORD	STAT	SWAM	TAMS
SNAP	SORE	STAW	SWAN	TANA
SNAR	SORI	STAY	SWAP	TANE
SNAW	SORN	STED	SWAT	TANG
SNEB	SORT	STEM	SWAY	TANH
SNED	SOSS	STEN	SWEE	TANK
SNEE	SOTH	STEP	SWEY	TANS
SNIB	SOTS	STET	SWIG	TAOS
SNIG	SOUK	STEW	SWIM	TAPA
SNIP	SOUL	STEY	SWIZ	TAPE
SNIT	SOUM	STIE	SWOB	TAPS
SNOB	SOUP	STIM	SWOP	TAPU
SNOD	SOUR	STIR	SWOT	TARA
SNOG	SOUS	STOA	SWUM	TARE
SNOT	SOUT	STOB	SYBO	TARN
SNOW	SOVS	STOP	SYCE	TARO
SNUB	SOWF	STOT	SYED	TARP
SNUG	SOWL	STOW	SYEN	TARS
SNYE	SOWM	STUB	SYES	TART
SOAK	SOWN	STUD	SYKE	TASH
SOAP	SOWP	STUM	SYLI	TASK
SOAR	SOWS	STUN	SYNC	TASS
SOBA	SOYA	STYE	SYND	TATE
SOBS	SOYS	SUBA	SYNE	TATH

TATS	TEXT	TITE	TORT	TUGS
TATT	THAE	TITI	TORY	TUIS
TATU	THAN	TITS	TOSA	TULE
TAUS	THAR	TIVY	TOSE	TUMP
TAUT	THAT	TIZZ	TOSH	TUMS
TAVA	THAW	TOAD	TOSS	TUNA
TAVS	THEE	TOBY	TOST	TUND
TAWA	THEM	TOCK	TOTE	TUNE
TAWS	THEN	TOCO	TOTS	TUNG
TAWT	THEW	TOCS	TOUK	TUNS
TAXA	THEY	TODS	TOUN	TUNY
TAXI	THIG	TODY	TOUR	TUPS
TAYS	THIN	TOEA	TOUT	TURD
TEAD	THIO	TOED	TOWN	TURF
TEAK	THIR	TOES	TOWS	TURK
TEAL	THIS	TOEY	TOWT	TURM
TEAM	THON	TOFF	TOWY	TURN
TEAR	THOU	TOFT	TOYO	TUSH
TEAS	THRO	TOFU	TOYS	TUSK
TEAT	THRU	TOGA	TOZE	TUTS
TECH	THUD	TOGE	TRAD	TUTU
TECS	THUG	TOGS	TRAM	TUZZ
TEDS	THUS	TOHO	TRAP	TWAE
TEDY	TIAR	TOIL	TRAT	TWAL
TEED	TICE	TOIT	TRAY	TWAS
TEEK	TICH	TOKE	TREE	TWAT
TEEL	TICK	TOKO	TREF	TWAY
TEEM	TICS	TOLA	TREK	TWEE
TEEN	TIDE	TOLD	TRES	TWIG
TEER	TIDS	TOLE	TRET	TWIN
TEES	TIDY	TOLL	TREW	TWIT
TEFF	TIED	TOLT	TREY	TWOS
TEFS	TIER	TOLU	TREZ	TYDE
TEGG	TIES	TOMB	TRIE	TYED
TEGS	TIFF	TOME	TRIG	TYEE
TEGU	TIFT	TOMO	TRIM	TYER
TEHR	TIGE	TOMS	TRIN	TYES
TEIL	TIGS	TONE	TRIO	TYGS
TELA	TIKA	TONG	TRIP	TYIN
TELD	TIKE	TONK	TROD	TYKE
TELE	TIKI	TONS	TROG	TYMP
TELL	TILE	TONY	TRON	TYND
TELS	TILL	TOOK	TROP	TYNE
TELT	TILS	TOOL	TROT	TYPE
TEME	TILT	TOOM	TROW	TYPO
TEMP	TIME	TOON	TROY	TYPP
TEMS	TIND	TOOT	TRUE	TYPY
TEND	TINE	TOPE	TRUG	TYRE
TENE	TING	TOPH	TRYE	TYRO
TENS	TINK	TOPI	TRYP	TYTE
TENT	TINS	TOPO	TSAR	TZAR
TEPA	TINT	TOPS	TSKS	UDAL
TERF	TINY	TORA	TUAN	UDON
TERM	TIPI	TORC	TUBA	UDOS
TERN	TIPS	TORE	TUBE	UEYS
TEST	TIPT	TORI	TUBS	UFOS
TETE	TIRE	TORN	TUCK	UGHS
TETH	TIRL	TORO	TUFA	UGLY
TETS	TIRO	TORR	TUFF	UKES
TEWS	TIRR	TORS	TUFT	ULAN

Four-letter words

ULES	VALE	VILD	WAIR	WEEM
ULEX	VALI	VILE	WAIS	WEEN
ULNA	VAMP	VILL	WAIT	WEEP
ULUS	VANE	VIMS	WAKA	WEER
ULVA	VANG	VINA	WAKE	WEES
UMBO	VANS	VINE	WAKF	WEET
UMPH	VANT	VINO	WALD	WEFT
UMPS	VARA	VINS	WALE	WEID
UMPY	VARE	VINT	WALI	WEIL
UNAI	VARS	VINY	WALK	WEIR
UNAU	VARY	VIOL	WALL	WEKA
UNBE	VASA	VIRE	WALY	WELD
UNCE	VASE	VIRL	WAME	WELK
UNCI	VAST	VISA	WAND	WELL
UNCO	VATS	VISE	WANE	WELT
UNDE	VATU	VITA	WANG	WEMB
UNDO	VAUS	VITE	WANK	WEMS
UNDY	VAUT	VIVA	WANS	WENA
UNIS	VAVS	VIVE	WANT	WEND
UNIT	VAWS	VIVO	WANY	WENS
UNTO	VEAL	VIZY	WAPS	WENT
UPAS	VEEP	VLEI	WAQF	WEPT
UPBY	VEER	VOAR	WARB	WERE
UPDO	VEES	VOES	WARD	WERO
UPGO	VEGA	VOID	WARE	WERT
UPON	VEGO	VOLA	WARK	WEST
UPSY	VEHM	VOLE	WARM	WETA
UPTA	VEIL	VOLK	WARN	WETS
URAO	VEIN	VOLS	WARP	WEXE
URBS	VELA	VOLT	WARS	WEYS
URDE	VELD	VORS	WART	WHAE
URDS	VELE	VOTE	WARY	WHAM
URDY	VELL	VOWS	WASE	WHAP
UREA	VENA	VRIL	WASH	WHAT
URES	VEND	VROT	WASM	WHEE
URGE	VENT	VROU	WASP	WHEN
URIC	VERA	VROW	WAST	WHET
URNS	VERB	VUGG	WATE	WHEW
URPS	VERD	VUGH	WATS	WHEY
URSA	VERS	VUGS	WATT	WHID
URUS	VERT	VULN	WAUK	WHIG
URVA	VERY	VUMS	WAUL	WHIM
USED	VEST	WAAC	WAUR	WHIN
USER	VETO	WABS	WAVE	WHIO
USES	VETS	WACK	WAVY	WHIP
UTAS	VEXT	WADD	WAWA	WHIR
UTES	VIAE	WADE	WAWE	WHIT
UTIS	VIAL	WADI	WAWL	WHIZ
UTUS	VIAS	WADS	WAWS	WHOA
UVAE	VIBE	WADT	WAXY	WHOM
UVAS	VIBS	WADY	WAYS	WHOP
UVEA	VICE	WAES	WEAK	WHOT
VACS	VIDE	WAFF	WEAL	WHOW
VADE	VIDS	WAFT	WEAN	WHUP
VAES	VIED	WAGE	WEAR	WHYS
VAGI	VIER	WAGS	WEBS	WICE
VAGS	VIES	WAID	WEDS	WICH
VAIL	VIEW	WAIF	WEED	WICK
VAIN	VIGA	WAIL	WEEK	WIDE
VAIR	VIGS	WAIN	WEEL	WIEL

WIFE	WORE	YAWN	YODE	ZEAL
WIGS	WORK	YAWP	YODH	ZEAS
WILD	WORM	YAWS	YODS	ZEBU
WILE	WORN	YAWY	YOGA	ZEDS
WILI	WORT	YAYS	YOGH	ZEES
WILL	WOST	YBET	YOGI	ZEIN
WILT	WOTS	YEAD	YOKE	ZEKS
WILY	WOVE	YEAH	YOKS	ZELS
WIMP	WOWF	YEAN	YOLD	ZEPS
WIND	WOWS	YEAR	YOLK	ZERK
WINE	WRAP	YEAS	YOMP	ZERO
WING	WREN	YEBO	YOND	ZEST
WINK	WRIT	YECH	YONI	ZETA
WINN	WUDS	YEDE	YONT	ZEZE
WINO	WUDU	YEED	YOOF	ZHOS
WINS	WULL	YEGG	YOOP	ZIFF
WINY	WUSS	YELD	YORE	ZIGS
WIPE	WYCH	YELK	YORK	ZILA
WIRE	WYES	YELL	YORP	ZILL
WIRY	WYLE	YELM	YOUK	ZIMB
WISE	WYND	YELP	YOUR	ZINC
WISH	WYNN	YELT	YOUS	ZINE
WISP	WYNS	YENS	YOWE	ZING
WISS	WYTE	YEPS	YOWL	ZINS
WIST	XYST	YERD	YOWS	ZIPS
WITE	YAAR	YERK	YUAN	ZITE
WITH	YABA	YESK	YUCA	ZITI
WITS	YACK	YEST	YUCH	ZITS
WIVE	YADS	YETI	YUCK	ZIZZ
WOAD	YAFF	YETT	YUFT	ZOBO
WOCK	YAGI	YEUK	YUGA	ZOBU
WOES	YAGS	YEVE	YUGS	ZOEA
WOFS	YAHS	YEWS	YUKE	ZOIC
WOGS	YAKS	YGOE	YUKO	ZOLS
WOKE	YALD	YIDS	YUKS	ZONA
WOKS	YALE	YIKE	YUKY	ZONE
WOLD	YAMS	YILL	YULE	ZONK
WOLF	YANG	YINS	YUMP	ZOOM
WOMB	YANK	YIPE	YUNX	ZOON
WONK	YAPP	YIPS	YUPS	ZOOS
WONS	YAPS	YIRD	YURT	ZOOT
WONT	YARD	YIRK	YUTZ	ZORI
WOOD	YARE	YIRR	YUZU	ZOUK
WOOF	YARK	YITE	YWIS	ZULU
WOOL	YARN	YLEM	ZACK	ZUPA
WOON	YARR	YLKE	ZAGS	ZURF
WOOS	YATE	YMPE	ZANY	ZYGA
WOOT	YAUD	YMPT	ZAPS	ZYME
WOPS	YAUP	YOBS	ZARF	ZZZS
WORD	YAWL	YOCK	ZATI	

Chapter 2: Power Tiles

The highest-scoring tiles in the game are J, Q, X, and Z, with J and X scoring eight points each, while Q and Z are worth ten. These 'power tiles' are the most potent weapons in the Scrabble player's arsenal, but need to be carefully deployed. This isn't always a matter of using them in a long word – a carefully positioned short word can be just as good a move. You should also remember that, on average, in a two-player game you are only likely to get each one every other game so it isn't worth concentrating just on these words at the expense of learning new short words or bonus-scoring words.

This section lists all of the power-tile words of two and three letters, with a brief definition for each. It's worth learning all of these words as they can be tremendously useful, combining the assets of all short words with the high scores afforded by the power tiles. Knowing the definitions of these words will help you commit them to memory.

The subsequent lists include all of the power-tile words from four to eight letters. While there may be too many of these to remember, studying the list will provide you with a range of useful options for game situations where you have one of these valuable tiles on your rack. You should initially focus on four or five letter words that begin or end in a power tile because that is a standard length between a double or triple letter square and a double or triple word square.

Using J

There is only one J tile in Scrabble, so for any word with two Js (eg HAJJ or JUJU) a blank is required. When you are trying to use a word with J for parallel play, remember that there are only two two-letter words with J – JA and JO. The J can be as awkward as the Q and is not as flexible as the X and Z so it is wise to try and use it as soon as it arrives on your rack rather than hold onto it hoping for a better score later. Don't forget unusual combinations like the FJ in FJELD and FJORD, or the DJ in DJIN, DJINN and their plurals. An examination of the following lists will also reveal a number of words that contain a JR combination, including BAJRA, BAJRI, and HIJRA. Learning some of these more unusual words will give you greater ammunition to make the best use of the J if more common words are unplayable. If there is a Z on the board or on your rack when you have a J, there are several words that could impress your opponent (eg JIZ, JAZY).

Two-letter words

JA	yes
JO	Scots word for sweetheart

Three-letter words

GJU	type of violin used in Shetland
HAJ	pilgrimage a Muslim makes to Mecca
JAB	poke sharply
JAG	period of uncontrolled indulgence in an activity
JAI	victory (to)
JAK	device for raising a motor vehicle or other heavy object
JAM	pack tightly into a place
JAP	splash
JAR	wide-mouthed container, usu round and made of glass
JAW	one of the bones in which the teeth are set
JAY	bird with a pinkish body and blue-and-black wings
JEE	mild exclamation of surprise, admiration, etc
JET	aircraft driven by jet propulsion
JEU	game
JEW	obsolete offensive word for haggle
JIB	taunt or jeer
JIG	type of lively dance
JIN	Chinese unit of weight
JIZ	wig
JOB	occupation or paid employment
JOE	Scots word for sweetheart
JOG	run at a gentle pace, esp for exercise
JOL	party
JOR	movement in Indian music
JOT	write briefly
JOW	ring (a bell)
JOY	feeling of great delight or pleasure
JUD	large block of coal
JUG	container for liquids, with a handle and small spout
JUN	North and South Korean monetary unit worth one hundredth of a won
JUS	right, power, or authority
JUT	project or stick out
RAJ	(in India) government
TAJ	tall conical cap worn as a mark of distinction by Muslims

Four-letter words

AJAR	JAGS	JAUP	JELL	JINN
AJEE	JAIL	JAVA	JEON	JINS
BAJU	JAKE	JAWS	JERK	JINX
BENJ	JAKS	JAXY	JESS	JIRD
DJIN	JAMB	JAYS	JEST	JISM
DOJO	JAMS	JAZY	JETE	JIVE
FUJI	JANE	JAZZ	JETS	JIVY
GAJO	JANN	JEAN	JEUX	JIZZ
GJUS	JAPE	JEAT	JEWS	JOBE
HADJ	JAPS	JEDI	JIAO	JOBS
HAJI	JARK	JEED	JIBB	JOCK
HAJJ	JARL	JEEL	JIBE	JOCO
JAAP	JARP	JEEP	JIBS	JOES
JABS	JARS	JEER	JIFF	JOEY
JACK	JASP	JEES	JIGS	JOGS
JADE	JASS	JEEZ	JILL	JOHN
JAFA	JASY	JEFE	JILT	JOIN
JAGA	JATO	JEFF	JIMP	JOKE
JAGG	JAUK	JEHU	JINK	JOKY

JOLE	JOTA	JUDO	JUPE	MOJO
JOLL	JOTS	JUDS	JURA	PUJA
JOLS	JOUK	JUDY	JURE	RAJA
JOLT	JOUR	JUGA	JURY	ROJI
JOMO	JOWL	JUGS	JUST	SIJO
JONG	JOWS	JUJU	JUTE	SJOE
JOOK	JOYS	JUKE	JUTS	SOJA
JORS	JUBA	JUKU	JUVE	
JOSH	JUBE	JUMP	JYNX	
JOSS	JUCO	JUNK	KOJI	

Five-letter words

AFLAJ	JAFAS	JEBEL	JINGO	JOUAL
AJIVA	JAGAS	JEDIS	JINKS	JOUGS
AJUGA	JAGER	JEELS	JINNE	JOUKS
AJWAN	JAGGS	JEELY	JINNI	JOULE
BAJAN	JAGGY	JEEPS	JINNS	JOURS
BAJRA	JAGIR	JEERS	JIRDS	JOUST
BAJRI	JAGRA	JEFES	JIRGA	JOWAR
BAJUS	JAILS	JEFFS	JIRRE	JOWED
BANJO	JAKES	JEHAD	JISMS	JOWLS
BHAJI	JAKEY	JEHUS	JIVED	JOWLY
BIJOU	JALAP	JELAB	JIVER	JOYED
BUNJE	JALOP	JELLO	JIVES	JUBAS
BUNJY	JAMBE	JELLS	JIVEY	JUBES
CAJON	JAMBO	JELLY	JNANA	JUCOS
CAJUN	JAMBS	JEMBE	JOBED	JUDAS
DJINN	JAMBU	JEMMY	JOBES	JUDGE
DJINS	JAMES	JENNY	JOCKO	JUDOS
DOJOS	JAMMY	JERID	JOCKS	JUGAL
EEJIT	JANES	JERKS	JODEL	JUGUM
EJECT	JANNS	JERKY	JOEYS	JUICE
ENJOY	JANNY	JERRY	JOHNS	JUICY
FALAJ	JANTY	JESSE	JOINS	JUJUS
FJELD	JAPAN	JESTS	JOINT	JUKED
FJORD	JAPED	JESUS	JOIST	JUKES
FUJIS	JAPER	JETES	JOKED	JUKUS
GADJE	JAPES	JETON	JOKER	JULEP
GADJO	JARKS	JETTY	JOKES	JUMAR
GAJOS	JARLS	JEUNE	JOKEY	JUMBO
GANJA	JARPS	JEWED	JOKOL	JUMBY
GAUJE	JARTA	JEWEL	JOLED	JUMPS
HADJI	JARUL	JEWIE	JOLES	JUMPY
HAJES	JASEY	JHALA	JOLLS	JUNCO
HAJIS	JASPE	JIAOS	JOLLY	JUNKS
HAJJI	JASPS	JIBBS	JOLTS	JUNKY
HEJAB	JATOS	JIBED	JOLTY	JUNTA
HEJRA	JAUKS	JIBER	JOMON	JUNTO
HIJAB	JAUNT	JIBES	JOMOS	JUPES
HIJRA	JAUPS	JIFFS	JONES	JUPON
HODJA	JAVAS	JIFFY	JONGS	JURAL
JAAPS	JAVEL	JIGGY	JONTY	JURAT
JABOT	JAWAN	JIGOT	JOOKS	JUREL
JACAL	JAWED	JIHAD	JORAM	JUROR
JACKS	JAXIE	JILLS	JORUM	JUSTS
JACKY	JAZZY	JILTS	JOTAS	JUTES
JADED	JEANS	JIMMY	JOTTY	JUTTY
JADES	JEATS	JIMPY	JOTUN	JUVES

KANJI	NINJA	PUNJI	ROJIS	THUJA
KHOJA	OBJET	RAJAH	SAJOU	UNJAM
KOJIS	OJIME	RAJAS	SHOJI	UPJET
KOPJE	OUIJA	RAJES	SIJOS	WILJA
LAPJE	POLJE	REJIG	SLOJD	YOJAN
MAJOR	POOJA	REJON	SOJAS	ZANJA
MOJOS	PUJAH	RIOJA	SUJEE	
MUJIK	PUJAS	ROJAK	TAJES	

Six-letter words

ABJECT	EVEJAR	JACARE	JAPING	JEERER
ABJURE	FAJITA	JACENT	JAPPED	JEFFED
ACAJOU	FANJET	JACKAL	JARFUL	JEHADI
ADJIGO	FEIJOA	JACKED	JARGON	JEHADS
ADJOIN	FIGJAM	JACKER	JARINA	JEJUNA
ADJURE	FINJAN	JACKET	JAROOL	JEJUNE
ADJUST	FJELDS	JACKSY	JARPED	JELABS
AJIVAS	FJORDS	JADERY	JARRAH	JELLED
AJOWAN	FRIJOL	JADING	JARRED	JELLOS
AJUGAS	GADJES	JADISH	JARTAS	JEMBES
AJWANS	GAIJIN	JAEGER	JARULS	JEMIMA
BAJADA	GANJAH	JAGAED	JARVEY	JENNET
BAJANS	GANJAS	JAGERS	JARVIE	JERBIL
BAJRAS	GARJAN	JAGGED	JASEYS	JERBOA
BAJREE	GAUJES	JAGGER	JASIES	JEREED
BAJRIS	GIDJEE	JAGHIR	JASMIN	JERIDS
BANJAX	GOUJON	JAGIRS	JASPER	JERKED
BANJOS	GURJUN	JAGRAS	JASPES	JERKER
BEJADE	GYTTJA	JAGUAR	JASPIS	JERKIN
BEJANT	HADJEE	JAILED	JASSES	JERQUE
BENJES	HADJES	JAILER	JASSID	JERRID
BHAJAN	HADJIS	JAILOR	JATAKA	JERSEY
BHAJEE	HAJJAH	JAKEYS	JAUKED	JESSED
BHAJIS	HAJJES	JALAPS	JAUNCE	JESSES
BIJOUS	HAJJIS	JALOPS	JAUNSE	JESSIE
BIJOUX	HANJAR	JALOPY	JAUNTS	JESTED
BOOJUM	HEJABS	JAMBED	JAUNTY	JESTEE
BUNJEE	HEJIRA	JAMBEE	JAUPED	JESTER
BUNJES	HEJRAS	JAMBER	JAVELS	JESUIT
BUNJIE	HIJABS	JAMBES	JAWANS	JETLAG
CAJOLE	HIJACK	JAMBOK	JAWARI	JETONS
COJOIN	HIJRAH	JAMBOS	JAWBOX	JETSAM
CONJEE	HIJRAS	JAMBUL	JAWING	JETSOM
CROJIK	HOBJOB	JAMBUS	JAXIES	JETSON
DEEJAY	HODJAS	JAMJAR	JAYGEE	JETTED
DEJECT	INJECT	JAMMED	JAYVEE	JETTON
DJEBEL	INJERA	JAMMER	JAZIES	JETWAY
DJEMBE	INJURE	JAMPAN	JAZZBO	JEWELS
DJINNI	INJURY	JAMPOT	JAZZED	JEWIES
DJINNS	INKJET	JANDAL	JAZZER	JEWING
DJINNY	JABBED	JANGLE	JAZZES	JEZAIL
DONJON	JABBER	JANGLY	JEANED	JHALAS
EEJITS	JABBLE	JANKER	JEBELS	JHATKA
EJECTA	JABERS	JANSKY	JEEING	JIBBAH
EJECTS	JABIRU	JANTEE	JEELED	JIBBED
ENJAMB	JABOTS	JAPANS	JEELIE	JIBBER
ENJOIN	JACALS	JAPERS	JEEPED	JIBERS
ENJOYS	JACANA	JAPERY	JEERED	JIBING

JICAMA	JOCKOS	JOVIAL	JUNGLI	OUTJET
JIGGED	JOCOSE	JOWARI	JUNGLY	OUTJUT
JIGGER	JOCUND	JOWARS	JUNIOR	PAJAMA
JIGGLE	JODELS	JOWING	JUNKED	PAJOCK
JIGGLY	JOGGED	JOWLED	JUNKER	POLJES
JIGJIG	JOGGER	JOWLER	JUNKET	POOJAH
JIGOTS	JOGGLE	JOYFUL	JUNKIE	POOJAS
JIGSAW	JOHNNY	JOYING	JUNTAS	POPJOY
JIHADI	JOINED	JOYOUS	JUNTOS	PRAJNA
JIHADS	JOINER	JOYPOP	JUPATI	PROJET
JILBAB	JOINTS	JUBATE	JUPONS	PUJAHS
JILGIE	JOISTS	JUBBAH	JURANT	PUNJIS
JILLET	JOJOBA	JUBHAH	JURATS	PYJAMA
JILTED	JOKERS	JUBILE	JURELS	RAJAHS
JILTER	JOKIER	JUDDER	JURIED	RAMJET
JIMINY	JOKILY	JUDGED	JURIES	REJECT
JIMJAM	JOKING	JUDGER	JURIST	REJIGS
JIMMIE	JOLING	JUDGES	JURORS	REJOIN
JIMPER	JOLLED	JUDIES	JUSTED	RHANJA
JIMPLY	JOLLEY	JUDOGI	JUSTER	RIOJAS
JIMSON	JOLLOP	JUDOKA	JUSTLE	ROJAKS
JINGAL	JOLTED	JUGALS	JUSTLY	ROMAJI
JINGKO	JOLTER	JUGATE	JUTTED	SAJOUS
JINGLE	JOOKED	JUGFUL	JYMOLD	SANJAK
JINGLY	JORAMS	JUGGED	JYNXES	SEJANT
JINKED	JORDAN	JUGGLE	KANJIS	SHINJU
JINKER	JORUMS	JUGLET	KHODJA	SHOJIS
JINNEE	JOSEPH	JUGULA	KHOJAS	SLOJDS
JINNIS	JOSHED	JUGUMS	KOPJES	SOOJEY
JINXED	JOSHER	JUICED	LAPJES	SUJEES
JINXES	JOSHES	JUICER	LOGJAM	SVARAJ
JIRBLE	JOSKIN	JUICES	MAJLIS	SWARAJ
JIRGAS	JOSSER	JUJUBE	MAJORS	TAJINE
JISSOM	JOSSES	JUKING	MASJID	THUJAS
JITNEY	JOSTLE	JULEPS	MATJES	TINAJA
JITTER	JOTTED	JUMARS	MEJLIS	TRIJET
JIVERS	JOTTER	JUMART	MOJOES	UJAMAA
JIVIER	JOTUNN	JUMBAL	MOUJIK	UNJAMS
JIVING	JOTUNS	JUMBIE	MUJIKS	UNJUST
JIZZES	JOUALS	JUMBLE	MUSJID	UPJETS
JNANAS	JOUKED	JUMBLY	MUZJIK	VEEJAY
JOANNA	JOULED	JUMBOS	NINJAS	WILJAS
JOBBED	JOULES	JUMPED	OBJECT	WILTJA
JOBBER	JOUNCE	JUMPER	OBJETS	YOJANA
JOBBIE	JOUNCY	JUNCOS	OBJURE	YOJANS
JOBING	JOURNO	JUNCUS	OJIMES	ZANJAS
JOCKEY	JOUSTS	JUNGLE	OUIJAS	

Seven-letter words

ABJECTS	ADJOURN	AJUTAGE	BEJADED	BONJOUR
ABJOINT	ADJUDGE	ALFORJA	BEJADES	BOOJUMS
ABJURED	ADJUNCT	ANTIJAM	BEJANTS	BRINJAL
ABJURER	ADJURED	APAREJO	BEJESUS	BUNJEES
ABJURES	ADJURER	AZULEJO	BEJEWEL	BUNJIES
ACAJOUS	ADJURES	BAJADAS	BHAJANS	CAJAPUT
ADJIGOS	ADJUROR	BAJREES	BHAJEES	CAJEPUT
ADJOINS	ADJUSTS	BANJOES	BLOWJOB	CAJOLED
ADJOINT	AJOWANS	BASENJI	BLUEJAY	CAJOLER

CAJOLES	INJOINT	JAMBERS	JAUNSES	JERKING
CAJONES	INJUNCT	JAMBEUX	JAUNTED	JERKINS
CAJUPUT	INJURED	JAMBIER	JAUNTEE	JERQUED
CARJACK	INJURER	JAMBING	JAUNTIE	JERQUER
CATJANG	INJURES	JAMBIYA	JAUPING	JERQUES
COJOINS	JABBERS	JAMBOKS	JAVELIN	JERREED
COJONES	JABBING	JAMBONE	JAWARIS	JERRIDS
CONJECT	JABBLED	JAMBOOL	JAWBONE	JERRIES
CONJEED	JABBLES	JAMBULS	JAWFALL	JERSEYS
CONJEES	JABIRUS	JAMDANI	JAWHOLE	JESSAMY
CONJOIN	JACALES	JAMESES	JAWINGS	JESSANT
CONJURE	JACAMAR	JAMJARS	JAWLESS	JESSIES
CONJURY	JACANAS	JAMLIKE	JAWLIKE	JESSING
CROJIKS	JACARES	JAMMERS	JAWLINE	JESTEES
DEEJAYS	JACCHUS	JAMMIER	JAYBIRD	JESTERS
DEJECTA	JACINTH	JAMMIES	JAYGEES	JESTFUL
DEJECTS	JACKALS	JAMMING	JAYVEES	JESTING
DEJEUNE	JACKASS	JAMPANI	JAYWALK	JESUITS
DISJECT	JACKDAW	JAMPANS	JAZZBOS	JETBEAD
DISJOIN	JACKEEN	JAMPOTS	JAZZERS	JETFOIL
DISJUNE	JACKERS	JANDALS	JAZZIER	JETLAGS
DJEBELS	JACKETS	JANGLED	JAZZILY	JETLIKE
DJEMBES	JACKIES	JANGLER	JAZZING	JETPORT
DJIBBAH	JACKING	JANGLES	JAZZMAN	JETSAMS
DONJONS	JACKLEG	JANITOR	JAZZMEN	JETSOMS
EJECTED	JACKMAN	JANIZAR	JEALOUS	JETSONS
EJECTOR	JACKMEN	JANKERS	JEELIED	JETTIED
ENJAMBS	JACKPOT	JANNIES	JEELIES	JETTIER
ENJOINS	JACKSIE	JANNOCK	JEELING	JETTIES
ENJOYED	JACOBIN	JANSKYS	JEEPERS	JETTING
ENJOYER	JACOBUS	JANTIER	JEEPING	JETTONS
EVEJARS	JACONET	JANTIES	JEEPNEY	JETWAYS
FAJITAS	JACUZZI	JAPINGS	JEERERS	JEWELED
FANJETS	JADEDLY	JAPPING	JEERING	JEWELER
FEIJOAS	JADEITE	JARFULS	JEFFING	JEWELRY
FIGJAMS	JADITIC	JARGONS	JEHADIS	JEWFISH
FINJANS	JAEGERS	JARGONY	JEJUNAL	JEZAILS
FJORDIC	JAGAING	JARGOON	JEJUNUM	JEZEBEL
FRIJOLE	JAGGARY	JARHEAD	JELLABA	JHATKAS
GANJAHS	JAGGERS	JARINAS	JELLIED	JIBBAHS
GARJANS	JAGGERY	JARKMAN	JELLIES	JIBBERS
GIDJEES	JAGGIER	JARKMEN	JELLIFY	JIBBING
GJETOST	JAGGIES	JARLDOM	JELLING	JIBBONS
GOUJONS	JAGGING	JAROOLS	JEMADAR	JIBBOOM
GURJUNS	JAGHIRE	JARPING	JEMIDAR	JICAMAS
GYTTJAS	JAGHIRS	JARRAHS	JEMIMAS	JIFFIES
HADJEES	JAGLESS	JARRING	JEMMIED	JIGABOO
HAJJAHS	JAGUARS	JARSFUL	JEMMIER	JIGAJIG
HANDJAR	JAILERS	JARVEYS	JEMMIES	JIGAJOG
HANJARS	JAILING	JARVIES	JENNETS	JIGGERS
HARIJAN	JAILORS	JASMINE	JENNIES	JIGGIER
HEJIRAS	JAKESES	JASMINS	JEOFAIL	JIGGING
HIJACKS	JALAPIC	JASPERS	JEOPARD	JIGGISH
HIJINKS	JALAPIN	JASPERY	JERBILS	JIGGLED
HIJRAHS	JALOPPY	JASSIDS	JERBOAS	JIGGLES
HOBJOBS	JALOUSE	JATAKAS	JEREEDS	JIGJIGS
IJTIHAD	JAMADAR	JAUKING	JERKERS	JIGLIKE
INJECTS	JAMBART	JAUNCED	JERKIER	JIGSAWN
INJELLY	JAMBEAU	JAUNCES	JERKIES	JIGSAWS
INJERAS	JAMBEES	JAUNSED	JERKILY	JIHADIS

JILBABS	JOINTER	JUBBAHS	JUNKIES	OUTJINX
JILGIES	JOINTLY	JUBHAHS	JUNKING	OUTJUMP
JILLETS	JOISTED	JUBILEE	JUNKMAN	OUTJUTS
JILLION	JOJOBAS	JUBILES	JUNKMEN	OVERJOY
JILTERS	JOKIEST	JUDASES	JUPATIS	PAJAMAS
JILTING	JOLLEYS	JUDDERS	JURALLY	PAJOCKE
JIMJAMS	JOLLIED	JUDGERS	JURANTS	PAJOCKS
JIMMIED	JOLLIER	JUDGING	JURIDIC	PERJINK
JIMMIES	JOLLIES	JUDOGIS	JURISTS	PERJURE
JIMMINY	JOLLIFY	JUDOIST	JURYING	PERJURY
JIMPEST	JOLLILY	JUDOKAS	JURYMAN	PIROJKI
JIMPIER	JOLLING	JUGFULS	JURYMEN	POOJAHS
JINGALL	JOLLITY	JUGGING	JUSSIVE	POPJOYS
JINGALS	JOLLOPS	JUGGINS	JUSTERS	PRAJNAS
JINGLED	JOLLYER	JUGGLED	JUSTEST	PREJINK
JINGLER	JOLTERS	JUGGLER	JUSTICE	PROJECT
JINGLES	JOLTIER	JUGGLES	JUSTIFY	PROJETS
JINGLET	JOLTILY	JUGHEAD	JUSTING	PROPJET
JINGOES	JOLTING	JUGLETS	JUSTLED	PYJAMAS
JINJILI	JONESED	JUGSFUL	JUSTLES	RAMJETS
JINKERS	JONESES	JUGULAR	JUTTIED	REEJECT
JINKING	JONNOCK	JUGULUM	JUTTIES	REENJOY
JINXING	JONQUIL	JUICERS	JUTTING	REJECTS
JIPYAPA	JONTIES	JUICIER	JUVENAL	REJOICE
JIRBLED	JOOKERY	JUICILY	KAJAWAH	REJOINS
JIRBLES	JOOKING	JUICING	KAJEPUT	REJONEO
JISSOMS	JORDANS	JUJITSU	KHANJAR	REJONES
JITNEYS	JOSEPHS	JUJUBES	KHODJAS	REJOURN
JITTERS	JOSHERS	JUJUISM	KILLJOY	REJUDGE
JITTERY	JOSHING	JUJUIST	KUNJOOS	RESOJET
JIVEASS	JOSKINS	JUJUTSU	LOCKJAW	RHANJAS
JIVIEST	JOSSERS	JUKEBOX	LOGJAMS	ROMAJIS
JOANNAS	JOSTLED	JUKSKEI	MAATJES	SANJAKS
JOANNES	JOSTLER	JUMARED	MAHJONG	SAPAJOU
JOBBERS	JOSTLES	JUMARTS	MAJAGUA	SEJEANT
JOBBERY	JOTTERS	JUMBALS	MAJESTY	SHINJUS
JOBBIES	JOTTING	JUMBIES	MAJORAT	SJAMBOK
JOBBING	JOTUNNS	JUMBLED	MAJORED	SKYJACK
JOBLESS	JOUKERY	JUMBLER	MAJORLY	SOJOURN
JOBNAME	JOUKING	JUMBLES	MANJACK	SOOJEYS
JOCKEYS	JOULING	JUMBUCK	MASJIDS	SUBJECT
JOCKNEY	JOUNCED	JUMELLE	MISJOIN	SUBJOIN
JOCULAR	JOUNCES	JUMPERS	MOJARRA	TAJINES
JODHPUR	JOURNAL	JUMPIER	MOUJIKS	TINAJAS
JOGGERS	JOURNEY	JUMPILY	MUDEJAR	TOLARJI
JOGGING	JOURNOS	JUMPING	MUNTJAC	TRAJECT
JOGGLED	JOUSTED	JUMPOFF	MUNTJAK	TRIJETS
JOGGLER	JOUSTER	JUNCATE	MUSJIDS	TWINJET
JOGGLES	JOWARIS	JUNCOES	MUZJIKS	UJAMAAS
JOGTROT	JOWLERS	JUNGLED	NAARTJE	UNJADED
JOHNNIE	JOWLIER	JUNGLES	NARTJIE	UNJOINT
JOHNSON	JOWLING	JUNGLIS	NONJURY	VEEJAYS
JOINDER	JOYANCE	JUNIORS	OBJECTS	WILTJAS
JOINERS	JOYLESS	JUNIPER	OBJURED	WUDJULA
JOINERY	JOYPOPS	JUNKERS	OBJURES	YOJANAS
JOINING	JOYRIDE	JUNKETS	OUTJEST	ZANJERO
JOINTED	JOYRODE	JUNKIER	OUTJETS	

Eight-letter words

ABJECTED	CONJOINT	JACKBOOT	JANITORS	JELLABAS
ABJECTLY	CONJUGAL	JACKDAWS	JANITRIX	JELLYING
ABJOINTS	CONJUNCT	JACKEENS	JANIZARS	JELUTONG
ABJURERS	CONJUNTO	JACKEROO	JANIZARY	JEMADARS
ABJURING	CONJURED	JACKETED	JANNOCKS	JEMIDARS
ADJACENT	CONJURER	JACKFISH	JANTIEST	JEMMIEST
ADJOINED	CONJURES	JACKINGS	JAPANISE	JEMMYING
ADJOINTS	CONJUROR	JACKLEGS	JAPANIZE	JEOFAILS
ADJOURNS	CRACKJAW	JACKPOTS	JAPANNED	JEOPARDS
ADJUDGED	CUNJEVOI	JACKROLL	JAPANNER	JEOPARDY
ADJUDGES	DEEJAYED	JACKSIES	JAPERIES	JEREMIAD
ADJUNCTS	DEJECTED	JACKSTAY	JAPINGLY	JEREPIGO
ADJURERS	DEJEUNER	JACOBINS	JAPONICA	JERKIEST
ADJURING	DEJEUNES	JACONETS	JARARACA	JERKINGS
ADJURORS	DEMIJOHN	JACQUARD	JARARAKA	JEROBOAM
ADJUSTED	DISJECTS	JACULATE	JARGONED	JERQUERS
ADJUSTER	DISJOINS	JACUZZIS	JARGONEL	JERQUING
ADJUSTOR	DISJOINT	JADEITES	JARGOONS	JERREEDS
ADJUTAGE	DISJUNCT	JADELIKE	JARHEADS	JERRICAN
ADJUTANT	DISJUNES	JADERIES	JARLDOMS	JERRYCAN
ADJUVANT	DJELLABA	JADISHLY	JAROSITE	JERSEYED
AJUTAGES	DJIBBAHS	JAGGEDER	JAROVISE	JESTBOOK
ALFORJAS	DOORJAMB	JAGGEDLY	JAROVIZE	JESTINGS
APAREJOS	EJECTING	JAGGHERY	JARRINGS	JESUITIC
AZULEJOS	EJECTION	JAGGIEST	JASMINES	JESUITRY
BANJAXED	EJECTIVE	JAGHIRES	JASPISES	JETBEADS
BANJAXES	EJECTORS	JAILABLE	JAUNCING	JETFOILS
BANJOIST	ENJAMBED	JAILBAIT	JAUNDICE	JETLINER
BASENJIS	ENJOINED	JAILBIRD	JAUNSING	JETPLANE
BEJABERS	ENJOINER	JAILLESS	JAUNTIER	JETPORTS
BEJADING	ENJOYERS	JAKFRUIT	JAUNTIES	JETTIEST
BEJEEZUS	ENJOYING	JALAPENO	JAUNTILY	JETTISON
BEJESUIT	FLAPJACK	JALAPINS	JAUNTING	JETTYING
BEJEWELS	FORJUDGE	JALOPIES	JAVELINA	JEWELERS
BEJUMBLE	FRABJOUS	JALOUSED	JAVELINS	JEWELING
BENJAMIN	FRIJOLES	JALOUSES	JAWBONED	JEWELLED
BIJUGATE	GJETOSTS	JALOUSIE	JAWBONER	JEWELLER
BIJUGOUS	GOUJEERS	JAMADARS	JAWBONES	JEZEBELS
BIJWONER	HANDJARS	JAMBARTS	JAWBOXES	JIBBERED
BLOWJOBS	HARIJANS	JAMBEAUX	JAWFALLS	JIBBINGS
BLUEJACK	HIGHJACK	JAMBIERS	JAWHOLES	JIBBOOMS
BLUEJAYS	HIJACKED	JAMBIYAH	JAWLINES	JIBINGLY
BOERTJIE	HIJACKER	JAMBIYAS	JAYBIRDS	JICKAJOG
BOOTJACK	IJTIHADS	JAMBOLAN	JAYWALKS	JIGABOOS
BRINJALS	INJECTED	JAMBONES	JAZERANT	JIGAJIGS
CAJAPUTS	INJECTOR	JAMBOOLS	JAZZIEST	JIGAJOGS
CAJEPUTS	INJOINTS	JAMBOREE	JAZZLIKE	JIGGERED
CAJOLERS	INJUNCTS	JAMDANIS	JEALOUSE	JIGGIEST
CAJOLERY	INJURERS	JAMMABLE	JEALOUSY	JIGGINGS
CAJOLING	INJURIES	JAMMIEST	JEANETTE	JIGGLIER
CAJUPUTS	INJURING	JAMMINGS	JEELYING	JIGGLING
CARCAJOU	JABBERED	JAMPANEE	JEEPNEYS	JIGSAWED
CARJACKS	JABBERER	JAMPANIS	JEERINGS	JIHADISM
CARJACOU	JABBLING	JANGLERS	JEHADISM	JIHADIST
CATJANGS	JACAMARS	JANGLIER	JEHADIST	JILLAROO
COJOINED	JACINTHE	JANGLING	JEJUNELY	JILLIONS
CONJECTS	JACINTHS	JANIFORM	JEJUNITY	JIMCRACK
CONJOINS	JACKAROO	JANISARY	JELLABAH	JIMMYING

JIMPIEST	JONESING	JUNCUSES	NINJITSU	SOJOURNS
JIMPNESS	JONGLEUR	JUNGLIER	NINJUTSU	STICKJAW
JINGALLS	JONQUILS	JUNGLIST	NONJUROR	SUBJECTS
JINGBANG	JORDELOO	JUNIPERS	NONMAJOR	SUBJOINS
JINGKOES	JOSTLERS	JUNKANOO	OBJECTED	SUCURUJU
JINGLERS	JOSTLING	JUNKETED	OBJECTOR	SUPERJET
JINGLETS	JOTTINGS	JUNKETER	OBJURING	SVARAJES
JINGLIER	JOUNCIER	JUNKIEST	OUTJESTS	SWARAJES
JINGLING	JOUNCING	JUNKYARD	OUTJUMPS	TJANTING
JINGOISH	JOURNALS	JURASSIC	OVERJOYS	TOLARJEV
JINGOISM	JOURNEYS	JURATORY	OVERJUMP	TRAJECTS
JINGOIST	JOUSTERS	JURISTIC	OVERJUST	TURBOJET
JINJILIS	JOUSTING	JURYLESS	PAJAMAED	TWINJETS
JIPIJAPA	JOVIALLY	JURYMAST	PAJOCKES	UNDERJAW
JIPYAPAS	JOVIALTY	JUSSIVES	PEJORATE	UNJAMMED
JIRBLING	JOWLIEST	JUSTICER	PERJURED	UNJOINED
JIRKINET	JOYANCES	JUSTICES	PERJURER	UNJOINTS
JITTERED	JOYFULLY	JUSTLING	PERJURES	UNJOYFUL
JIUJITSU	JOYOUSLY	JUSTNESS	POPINJAY	UNJOYOUS
JIUJUTSU	JOYRIDER	JUTELIKE	POPJOYED	UNJUDGED
JOBATION	JOYRIDES	JUTTYING	PREJUDGE	UNJUSTER
JOBBINGS	JOYSTICK	JUVENALS	PROJECTS	UNJUSTLY
JOBNAMES	JUBILANT	JUVENILE	PROPJETS	UPJETTED
JOBSHARE	JUBILATE	KABELJOU	PULSEJET	VERJUICE
JOCKETTE	JUBILEES	KAJAWAHS	PULSOJET	WATERJET
JOCKEYED	JUDDERED	KAJEPUTS	PYJAMAED	WHIPJACK
JOCKNEYS	JUDGMENT	KHANJARS	QUILLAJA	WUDJULAS
JOCOSELY	JUDICIAL	KILLJOYS	RAJASHIP	ZABAJONE
JOCOSITY	JUDOISTS	KINKAJOU	READJUST	ZANJEROS
JOCUNDLY	JUGGINGS	KNEEJERK	REEJECTS	
JODELLED	JUGGLERS	KOMITAJI	REENJOYS	
JODHPURS	JUGGLERY	LOCKJAWS	REINJECT	
JOGGINGS	JUGGLING	LOGJUICE	REINJURE	
JOGGLERS	JUGHEADS	LONGJUMP	REINJURY	
JOGGLING	JUGULARS	MAHARAJA	REJACKET	
JOGPANTS	JUGULATE	MAHJONGG	REJECTED	
JOGTROTS	JUICIEST	MAHJONGS	REJECTEE	
JOHANNES	JUJITSUS	MAJAGUAS	REJECTER	
JOHNBOAT	JUJUISMS	MAJESTIC	REJECTOR	
JOHNNIES	JUJUISTS	MAJLISES	REJIGGED	
JOHNSONS	JUJUTSUS	MAJOLICA	REJIGGER	
JOINABLE	JUKSKEIS	MAJORATS	REJOICED	
JOINDERS	JULIENNE	MAJORING	REJOICER	
JOININGS	JUMARING	MAJORITY	REJOICES	
JOINTERS	JUMARRED	MANJACKS	REJOINED	
JOINTING	JUMBLERS	MARJORAM	REJONEOS	
JOINTURE	JUMBLIER	MARYJANE	REJOURNS	
JOISTING	JUMBLING	MEJLISES	REJUDGED	
JOKESOME	JUMBOISE	MICROJET	REJUDGES	
JOKESTER	JUMBOIZE	MIJNHEER	REJUGGLE	
JOKINESS	JUMBUCKS	MISJOINS	REOBJECT	
JOKINGLY	JUMELLES	MISJUDGE	RESOJETS	
JOLLEYER	JUMPABLE	MOJARRAS	SAPAJOUS	
JOLLIERS	JUMPIEST	MULTIJET	SCRAMJET	
JOLLIEST	JUMPINGS	MUNTJACS	SERJEANT	
JOLLYERS	JUMPOFFS	MUNTJAKS	SJAMBOKS	
JOLLYING	JUMPSUIT	NAARTJES	SKIJORER	
JOLTHEAD	JUNCATES	NAARTJIE	SKIPJACK	
JOLTIEST	JUNCTION	NARTJIES	SKYJACKS	
JONCANOE	JUNCTURE	NIGHTJAR	SLAPJACK	

Using Q

Along with Z, Q is the highest-scoring letter in Scrabble. Unlike Z, Q can be tricky to use because the majority of words that contain Q also require a U. You shouldn't unnecessarily hold onto the Q and hope for a U to go with it. It is better being played as soon as possible and there are a number of words that contain Q but no U which can help. A complete list of these follows in this section. It's easy enough to learn all of these, especially the more likely shorter ones. There's only one two-letter word with Q, QI, which is very useful as you are either likely to have an I on your rack or one available on the board. It's also worth committing the few three-letter Q words to memory. If you are lucky enough to have a Q and U on your rack, or a U is available on the board then the four or five-letter Q words are more likely to get you the best scores. It can help to remember some of them in sets such as (QUAD, QUID, QUOD) and (QUINA, QUINE, QUINO).

Two-letter words

QI	22nd letter of the Greek alphabet, a consonant, transliterated as CH or rarely KH

Three-letter words

QAT	white-flowered evergreen shrub of Africa and Arabia whose leaves have narcotic properties
QIS	plural of qi
QUA	in the capacity of
SUQ	suck (to)

Four-letter words

AQUA	QUAD	QUEP	QUIP	SUQS
QADI	QUAG	QUEY	QUIT	WAQF
QAID	QUAI	QUID	QUIZ	
QATS	QUAT	QUIM	QUOD	
QOPH	QUAY	QUIN	QUOP	

Five-letter words

AQUAE	QANAT	QUALE	QUBIT	QUICH
AQUAS	QIBLA	QUALM	QUEAN	QUICK
BURQA	QOPHS	QUANT	QUEEN	QUIDS
EQUAL	QORMA	QUARE	QUEER	QUIET
EQUID	QUACK	QUARK	QUELL	QUIFF
EQUIP	QUADS	QUART	QUEME	QUILL
FAQIR	QUAFF	QUASH	QUENA	QUILT
FIQUE	QUAGS	QUASI	QUERN	QUIMS
MAQUI	QUAIL	QUASS	QUERY	QUINA
NIQAB	QUAIR	QUATE	QUEST	QUINE
PIQUE	QUAIS	QUATS	QUEUE	QUINO
QADIS	QUAKE	QUAYD	QUEYN	QUINS
QAIDS	QUAKY	QUAYS	QUEYS	QUINT

QUIPO	QUITS	QUOPS	SQUAD	TALAQ
QUIPS	QUOAD	QUOTA	SQUAT	TOQUE
QUIPU	QUODS	QUOTE	SQUAW	TRANQ
QUIRE	QUOIF	QUOTH	SQUEG	TUQUE
QUIRK	QUOIN	QURSH	SQUIB	UMIAQ
QUIRT	QUOIT	QUYTE	SQUID	USQUE
QUIST	QUOLL	ROQUE	SQUIT	WAQFS
QUITE	QUONK	SQUAB	SQUIZ	

Six-letter words

ACQUIT	OPAQUE	QUATRE	QUINOS	SAIQUE
ASQUAT	PIQUED	QUAVER	QUINSY	SEQUEL
BARQUE	PIQUES	QUAZZY	QUINTA	SEQUIN
BASQUE	PIQUET	QUBITS	QUINTE	SHEQEL
BISQUE	PLAQUE	QUBYTE	QUINTS	SQUABS
BOSQUE	PULQUE	QUEACH	QUINZE	SQUADS
BUQSHA	QABALA	QUEANS	QUIPOS	SQUAIL
BURQAS	QANATS	QUEASY	QUIPPU	SQUALL
CAIQUE	QASIDA	QUEAZY	QUIPPY	SQUAMA
CALQUE	QAWWAL	QUEENS	QUIPUS	SQUAME
CASQUE	QIBLAS	QUEENY	QUIRED	SQUARE
CHEQUE	QIGONG	QUEERS	QUIRES	SQUARK
CHEQUY	QINDAR	QUEEST	QUIRKS	SQUASH
CINQUE	QINTAR	QUEINT	QUIRKY	SQUATS
CIRQUE	QIVIUT	QUELCH	QUIRTS	SQUAWK
CLAQUE	QORMAS	QUELEA	QUISTS	SQUAWS
CLIQUE	QUACKS	QUELLS	QUITCH	SQUEAK
CLIQUY	QUACKY	QUEMED	QUITED	SQUEAL
CLOQUE	QUAERE	QUEMES	QUITES	SQUEGS
COQUET	QUAFFS	QUENAS	QUIVER	SQUIBS
DIQUAT	QUAGGA	QUENCH	QUOHOG	SQUIDS
EQUALI	QUAGGY	QUERNS	QUOIFS	SQUIER
EQUALS	QUAHOG	QUESTS	QUOINS	SQUIFF
EQUANT	QUAICH	QUETCH	QUOIST	SQUILL
EQUATE	QUAIGH	QUETHE	QUOITS	SQUINT
EQUIDS	QUAILS	QUEUED	QUOKKA	SQUINY
EQUINE	QUAINT	QUEUER	QUOLLS	SQUIRE
EQUIPE	QUAIRS	QUEUES	QUONKS	SQUIRM
EQUIPS	QUAKED	QUEYNS	QUOOKE	SQUIRR
EQUITY	QUAKER	QUEZAL	QUORUM	SQUIRT
EXEQUY	QUAKES	QUICHE	QUOTAS	SQUISH
FAQIRS	QUALIA	QUICKS	QUOTED	SQUITS
FAQUIR	QUALMS	QUIDAM	QUOTER	SQUUSH
FIQUES	QUALMY	QUIETS	QUOTES	TALAQS
HAIQUE	QUANGO	QUIFFS	QUOTHA	TOQUES
JERQUE	QUANTA	QUIGHT	QUOTUM	TOQUET
LASQUE	QUANTS	QUILLS	QURUSH	TORQUE
LIQUID	QUARER	QUILTS	QUYTED	TRANQS
LIQUOR	QUARKS	QUINAS	QUYTES	TUQUES
LOQUAT	QUARRY	QUINCE	QWERTY	UBIQUE
MANQUE	QUARTE	QUINES	REQUIN	UMIAQS
MAQUIS	QUARTO	QUINIC	REQUIT	UNIQUE
MARQUE	QUARTS	QUINIE	RISQUE	USQUES
MASQUE	QUARTZ	QUININ	ROQUES	YANQUI
MOSQUE	QUASAR	QUINOA	ROQUET	YAQONA
NIQABS	QUATCH	QUINOL	SACQUE	

Seven-letter words

ACEQUIA	CUMQUAT	MESQUIT	QUANTUM	QUICKIE
ACQUEST	DAQUIRI	MEZQUIT	QUAREST	QUICKLY
ACQUIRE	DIQUARK	MOSQUES	QUARREL	QUIDAMS
ACQUIST	DIQUATS	OBLIQUE	QUARTAN	QUIDDIT
ACQUITE	DOCQUET	OBLOQUY	QUARTER	QUIDDLE
ACQUITS	ENQUIRE	OBSEQUY	QUARTES	QUIESCE
ALFAQUI	ENQUIRY	OPAQUED	QUARTET	QUIETED
ALIQUOT	EQUABLE	OPAQUER	QUARTIC	QUIETEN
ANTIQUE	EQUABLY	OPAQUES	QUARTOS	QUIETER
AQUAFER	EQUALED	OQUASSA	QUARTZY	QUIETLY
AQUARIA	EQUALLY	PARQUET	QUASARS	QUIETUS
AQUATIC	EQUANTS	PASQUIL	QUASHED	QUIGHTS
AQUAVIT	EQUATED	PERIQUE	QUASHEE	QUILLAI
AQUEOUS	EQUATES	PICQUET	QUASHER	QUILLED
AQUIFER	EQUATOR	PIQUANT	QUASHES	QUILLET
AQUILON	EQUERRY	PIQUETS	QUASHIE	QUILLON
AQUIVER	EQUINAL	PIQUING	QUASSES	QUILTED
ASQUINT	EQUINES	PIROQUE	QUASSIA	QUILTER
BANQUET	EQUINIA	PLAQUES	QUASSIN	QUINARY
BAROQUE	EQUINOX	PREQUEL	QUATRES	QUINATE
BARQUES	EQUIPES	PULQUES	QUAVERS	QUINCES
BASQUED	EQUITES	QABALAH	QUAVERY	QUINCHE
BASQUES	ESQUIRE	QABALAS	QUAYAGE	QUINELA
BEQUEST	FAQUIRS	QASIDAS	QUBYTES	QUINIES
BEZIQUE	GRECQUE	QAWWALI	QUEACHY	QUININA
BISQUES	HAIQUES	QAWWALS	QUEECHY	QUININE
BOSQUES	INQILAB	QIGONGS	QUEENED	QUININS
BOSQUET	INQUERE	QINDARS	QUEENIE	QUINNAT
BOUQUET	INQUEST	QINTARS	QUEENLY	QUINOAS
BRIQUET	INQUIET	QIVIUTS	QUEERED	QUINOID
BRUSQUE	INQUIRE	QUACKED	QUEERER	QUINOLS
BUQSHAS	INQUIRY	QUACKER	QUEERLY	QUINONE
CACIQUE	JERQUED	QUACKLE	QUEESTS	QUINTAL
CAIQUES	JERQUER	QUADDED	QUELEAS	QUINTAN
CALQUED	JERQUES	QUADRAT	QUELLED	QUINTAR
CALQUES	JONQUIL	QUADRIC	QUELLER	QUINTAS
CASQUED	KUMQUAT	QUAERED	QUEMING	QUINTES
CASQUES	LACQUER	QUAERES	QUERIDA	QUINTET
CAZIQUE	LACQUEY	QUAFFED	QUERIED	QUINTIC
CHARQUI	LALIQUE	QUAFFER	QUERIER	QUINTIN
CHEQUER	LASQUES	QUAGGAS	QUERIES	QUINZES
CHEQUES	LEQUEAR	QUAHAUG	QUERIST	QUIPPED
CINQUES	LIQUATE	QUAHOGS	QUESTED	QUIPPER
CIRQUES	LIQUEFY	QUAICHS	QUESTER	QUIPPUS
CLAQUER	LIQUEUR	QUAIGHS	QUESTOR	QUIRING
CLAQUES	LIQUIDS	QUAILED	QUETHES	QUIRKED
CLIQUED	LIQUIFY	QUAKERS	QUETSCH	QUIRTED
CLIQUES	LIQUORS	QUAKIER	QUETZAL	QUITING
CLIQUEY	LOQUATS	QUAKILY	QUEUERS	QUITTAL
CLOQUES	MACAQUE	QUAKING	QUEUING	QUITTED
COEQUAL	MADOQUA	QUALIFY	QUEYNIE	QUITTER
COMIQUE	MAQUILA	QUALITY	QUEZALS	QUITTOR
CONQUER	MARQUEE	QUAMASH	QUIBBLE	QUIVERS
COQUETS	MARQUES	QUANGOS	QUIBLIN	QUIVERY
COQUINA	MARQUIS	QUANNET	QUICHED	QUIXOTE
COQUITO	MASQUER	QUANTAL	QUICHES	QUIZZED
CROQUET	MASQUES	QUANTED	QUICKEN	QUIZZER
CROQUIS	MESQUIN	QUANTIC	QUICKER	QUIZZES

QUODDED	REEQUIP	SHEQELS	SQUEAKS	SQUISHY
QUODLIN	RELIQUE	SILIQUA	SQUEAKY	SQUITCH
QUOHOGS	REPIQUE	SILIQUE	SQUEALS	SQUOOSH
QUOIFED	REQUERE	SQUABBY	SQUEEZE	SUBAQUA
QUOINED	REQUEST	SQUACCO	SQUEEZY	TEQUILA
QUOISTS	REQUIEM	SQUADDY	SQUELCH	TOQUETS
QUOITED	REQUINS	SQUAILS	SQUIDGE	TORQUED
QUOITER	REQUIRE	SQUALID	SQUIDGY	TORQUER
QUOKKAS	REQUITE	SQUALLS	SQUIERS	TORQUES
QUOMODO	REQUITS	SQUALLY	SQUIFFY	TSADDIQ
QUONDAM	REQUOTE	SQUALOR	SQUILLA	TZADDIQ
QUONKED	RISQUES	SQUAMAE	SQUILLS	UNEQUAL
QUOPPED	ROCQUET	SQUAMES	SQUINCH	UNIQUER
QUORATE	ROQUETS	SQUARED	SQUINNY	UNIQUES
QUORUMS	RORQUAL	SQUARER	SQUINTS	UNQUEEN
QUOTERS	SACQUES	SQUARES	SQUINTY	UNQUIET
QUOTING	SAIQUES	SQUARKS	SQUIRED	UNQUOTE
QUOTUMS	SEQUELA	SQUASHY	SQUIRES	VAQUERO
QURSHES	SEQUELS	SQUATLY	SQUIRMS	YANQUIS
QUYTING	SEQUENT	SQUATTY	SQUIRMY	YAQONAS
QWERTYS	SEQUINS	SQUAWKS	SQUIRRS	
RACQUET	SEQUOIA	SQUAWKY	SQUIRTS	

Eight-letter words

ACEQUIAS	AQUATINT	CLAQUERS	ENQUIRER	HUAQUERO
ACQUAINT	AQUATONE	CLAQUEUR	ENQUIRES	ILLIQUID
ACQUESTS	AQUAVITS	CLINIQUE	EQUALING	INEQUITY
ACQUIGHT	AQUEDUCT	CLIQUIER	EQUALISE	INIQUITY
ACQUIRAL	AQUIFERS	CLIQUING	EQUALITY	INQILABS
ACQUIRED	AQUILINE	CLIQUISH	EQUALIZE	INQUERED
ACQUIREE	AQUILONS	CLIQUISM	EQUALLED	INQUERES
ACQUIRER	ARQUEBUS	COEQUALS	EQUATING	INQUESTS
ACQUIRES	BANQUETS	COEQUATE	EQUATION	INQUIETS
ACQUISTS	BARBEQUE	COLLOQUE	EQUATORS	INQUIRED
ACQUITES	BAROQUES	COLLOQUY	EQUINELY	INQUIRER
ADEQUACY	BASQUINE	COMIQUES	EQUINIAS	INQUIRES
ADEQUATE	BEDQUILT	CONQUERS	EQUINITY	JACQUARD
AEQUORIN	BELIQUOR	CONQUEST	EQUIPAGE	JERQUERS
ALFAQUIN	BEQUEATH	CONQUIAN	EQUIPPED	JERQUING
ALFAQUIS	BEQUESTS	COQUETRY	EQUIPPER	JONQUILS
ALIQUANT	BEZIQUES	COQUETTE	EQUISETA	KUMQUATS
ALIQUOTS	BIUNIQUE	COQUILLA	EQUITANT	LACQUERS
ANTIQUED	BLANQUET	COQUILLE	EQUITIES	LACQUEYS
ANTIQUER	BOSQUETS	COQUINAS	EQUIVOKE	LALIQUES
ANTIQUES	BOUQUETS	COQUITOS	ESQUIRED	LEQUEARS
ANTIQUEY	BOUTIQUE	COTQUEAN	ESQUIRES	LIQUABLE
APPLIQUE	BRELOQUE	CRITIQUE	ESQUISSE	LIQUATED
AQUACADE	BRIQUETS	CROQUETS	EXEQUIAL	LIQUATES
AQUAFARM	BRUSQUER	CUMQUATS	EXEQUIES	LIQUESCE
AQUAFERS	CACIQUES	DAIQUIRI	FILIOQUE	LIQUEURS
AQUALUNG	CALQUING	DAQUIRIS	FREQUENT	LIQUIDLY
AQUANAUT	CAZIQUES	DETRAQUE	GODSQUAD	LIQUIDUS
AQUARIAL	CHAQUETA	DIQUARKS	GRECQUES	LIQUORED
AQUARIAN	CHARQUID	DISQUIET	HAQUETON	LOQUITUR
AQUARIST	CHARQUIS	DOCQUETS	HENEQUEN	LUSTIQUE
AQUARIUM	CHEQUERS	ELOQUENT	HENEQUIN	MACAQUES
AQUASHOW	CHEQUING	EMBUSQUE	HENIQUEN	MADOQUAS
AQUATICS	CINQUAIN	ENQUIRED	HENIQUIN	MAQUETTE

MAQUILAS	QINDARKA	QUARTILE	QUIBBLER	QUIPPIER
MAROQUIN	QUAALUDE	QUARTZES	QUIBBLES	QUIPPING
MARQUEES	QUACKERS	QUASHEES	QUIBLINS	QUIPPISH
MARQUESS	QUACKERY	QUASHERS	QUICHING	QUIPSTER
MARQUISE	QUACKIER	QUASHIES	QUICKENS	QUIRKIER
MASQUERS	QUACKING	QUASHING	QUICKEST	QUIRKILY
MBAQANGA	QUACKISH	QUASSIAS	QUICKIES	QUIRKING
MESQUINE	QUACKISM	QUASSINS	QUICKSET	QUIRKISH
MESQUITE	QUACKLED	QUATCHED	QUIDDANY	QUIRTING
MESQUITS	QUACKLES	QUATCHES	QUIDDITS	QUISLING
MEZQUITE	QUADDING	QUATORZE	QUIDDITY	QUITCHED
MEZQUITS	QUADPLEX	QUATRAIN	QUIDDLED	QUITCHES
MIQUELET	QUADRANS	QUAVERED	QUIDDLER	QUITRENT
MISQUOTE	QUADRANT	QUAVERER	QUIDDLES	QUITTALS
MOQUETTE	QUADRATE	QUAYAGES	QUIDNUNC	QUITTERS
MORESQUE	QUADRATS	QUAYLIKE	QUIESCED	QUITTING
MOSQUITO	QUADRICS	QUAYSIDE	QUIESCES	QUITTORS
MUQADDAM	QUADRIGA	QUAZZIER	QUIETENS	QUIVERED
MUSQUASH	QUADROON	QUEACHES	QUIETERS	QUIVERER
MYSTIQUE	QUAESTOR	QUEASIER	QUIETEST	QUIXOTES
NARQUOIS	QUAFFERS	QUEASILY	QUIETING	QUIXOTIC
NONEQUAL	QUAFFING	QUEAZIER	QUIETISM	QUIXOTRY
NONQUOTA	QUAGGIER	QUEENDOM	QUIETIST	QUIZZERS
OBLIQUED	QUAGMIRE	QUEENIER	QUIETIVE	QUIZZERY
OBLIQUER	QUAGMIRY	QUEENIES	QUIETUDE	QUIZZIFY
OBLIQUES	QUAHAUGS	QUEENING	QUIGHTED	QUIZZING
OBLIQUID	QUAICHES	QUEENITE	QUILLAIA	QUODDING
OBSEQUIE	QUAILING	QUEENLET	QUILLAIS	QUODLINS
ODALIQUE	QUAINTER	QUEERDOM	QUILLAJA	QUOIFING
OLDSQUAW	QUAINTLY	QUEEREST	QUILLETS	QUOINING
OPAQUELY	QUAKIEST	QUEERING	QUILLING	QUOITERS
OPAQUEST	QUAKINGS	QUEERISH	QUILLMAN	QUOITING
OPAQUING	QUALMIER	QUEERITY	QUILLMEN	QUOMODOS
OQUASSAS	QUALMING	QUELCHED	QUILLONS	QUONKING
OUTQUOTE	QUALMISH	QUELCHES	QUILTERS	QUOPPING
PARAQUAT	QUANDANG	QUELLERS	QUILTING	QUOTABLE
PARAQUET	QUANDARY	QUELLING	QUINCHED	QUOTABLY
PAROQUET	QUANDONG	QUENCHED	QUINCHES	QUOTIENT
PARQUETS	QUANNETS	QUENCHER	QUINCUNX	QURUSHES
PASQUILS	QUANTICS	QUENCHES	QUINELAS	QWERTIES
PEQUISTE	QUANTIFY	QUENELLE	QUINELLA	RACQUETS
PERIQUES	QUANTILE	QUERCINE	QUINIELA	RAMEQUIN
PERRUQUE	QUANTING	QUERIDAS	QUININAS	REEQUIPS
PETANQUE	QUANTISE	QUERIERS	QUININES	RELIQUES
PHYSIQUE	QUANTITY	QUERISTS	QUINNATS	REMARQUE
PICQUETS	QUANTIZE	QUERYING	QUINOIDS	REPIQUED
PIQUANCE	QUANTONG	QUESTANT	QUINOLIN	REPIQUES
PIQUANCY	QUARRELS	QUESTERS	QUINONES	REQUERED
PIQUETED	QUARRIAN	QUESTING	QUINSIED	REQUERES
PIQUILLO	QUARRIED	QUESTION	QUINSIES	REQUESTS
PIROQUES	QUARRIER	QUESTORS	QUINTAIN	REQUIEMS
POSTIQUE	QUARRIES	QUETCHED	QUINTALS	REQUIGHT
PRATIQUE	QUARRION	QUETCHES	QUINTANS	REQUIRED
PREQUELS	QUARTANS	QUETHING	QUINTARS	REQUIRER
QABALAHS	QUARTERN	QUETZALS	QUINTETS	REQUIRES
QABALISM	QUARTERS	QUEUEING	QUINTETT	REQUITAL
QABALIST	QUARTETS	QUEUINGS	QUINTICS	REQUIGHT
QAIMAQAM	QUARTETT	QUEYNIES	QUINTILE	REQUITED
QALAMDAN	QUARTICS	QUEZALES	QUINTINS	REQUITER
QAWWALIS	QUARTIER	QUIBBLED	QUIPPERS	REQUOTED

REQUOTES	SQUADRON	SQUAWKED	SQUINIES	TORQUATE
REQUOYLE	SQUAILED	SQUAWKER	SQUINTED	TORQUERS
ROCQUETS	SQUAILER	SQUAWMAN	SQUINTER	TORQUING
ROQUETED	SQUALENE	SQUAWMEN	SQUIRAGE	TRANQUIL
ROQUETTE	SQUALLED	SQUEAKED	SQUIREEN	TRUQUAGE
RORQUALS	SQUALLER	SQUEAKER	SQUIRELY	TRUQUEUR
SEAQUAKE	SQUALOID	SQUEALED	SQUIRESS	TSADDIQS
SEQUELAE	SQUALORS	SQUEALER	SQUIRING	TURQUOIS
SEQUENCE	SQUAMATE	SQUEEGEE	SQUIRISH	TZADDIQS
SEQUENCY	SQUAMOSE	SQUEEZED	SQUIRMED	UBIQUITY
SEQUENTS	SQUAMOUS	SQUEEZER	SQUIRMER	UMQUHILE
SEQUINED	SQUAMULA	SQUEEZES	SQUIRRED	UNEQUALS
SEQUITUR	SQUAMULE	SQUEGGED	SQUIRREL	UNIQUELY
SEQUOIAS	SQUANDER	SQUEGGER	SQUIRTED	UNIQUEST
SERVQUAL	SQUARELY	SQUELCHY	SQUIRTER	UNQUEENS
SHEQALIM	SQUARERS	SQUIBBED	SQUISHED	UNQUIETS
SILIQUAE	SQUAREST	SQUIDDED	SQUISHES	UNQUOTED
SILIQUAS	SQUARIAL	SQUIDGED	SQUIZZES	UNQUOTES
SILIQUES	SQUARING	SQUIDGES	SQUOOSHY	USQUABAE
SOLIQUID	SQUARISH	SQUIFFED	SQUUSHED	USQUEBAE
SQUABASH	SQUARSON	SQUIFFER	SQUUSHES	VANQUISH
SQUABBED	SQUASHED	SQUIGGLE	SUBEQUAL	VAQUEROS
SQUABBER	SQUASHER	SQUIGGLY	SURQUEDY	VEHMIQUE
SQUABBLE	SQUASHES	SQUILGEE	TAQUERIA	VERQUERE
SQUACCOS	SQUATTED	SQUILLAE	TEQUILAS	VERQUIRE
SQUADDED	SQUATTER	SQUILLAS	TEQUILLA	
SQUADDIE	SQUATTLE	SQUINIED	TOQUILLA	

Q but not U

There are few things more infuriating in Scrabble than having a Q on your rack but no U with which to play it! But this situation needn't be disastrous: there are a surprisingly high number of words that have a Q but not U. A complete list of these words is included here. These have short definitions to help you remember them; it is well worth learning them all, as they can be extremely useful. Note that the A is a key vowel in quite a few of these words.

FAQIR	FAQIRS	
INQILAB	INQILABS	
MBAQANGA	MBAQANGAS	
NIQAB	NIQABS	
QABALA		
QABALAH	QABALAHS	QABALAS
QABALISM	QABALISMS	
QABALIST	QABALISTIC	QABALISTS
QADI	QADIS	
QAID	QAIDS	
QAIMAQAM	QAIMAQAMS	
QALAMDAN	QALAMDANS	
QANAT	QANATS	
QASIDA	QASIDAS	
QAT	QATS	
QAWWAL	QAWWALI	
QAWWALIS	QAWWALS	
QI		
QIBLA	QIBLAS	
QIGONG	QIGONGS	
QINDAR	QINDARKA	QINDARS

QINTAR	QINTARS	
QIS		
QOPH	QOPHS	
QORMA	QORMAS	
QWERTIES	QWERTY	QWERTYS
SHEQALIM	SHEQEL	SHEQELS
TALAQ	TALAQS	
TRANQ	TRANQS	
TSADDIQ	TSADDIQIM	TSADDIQS
TZADDIQ	TZADDIQIM	TZADDIQS
WAQF	WAQFS	
YAQONA	YAQONAS	

Q and K

Looking at the words that contain Q but not U, you may well notice that many are of Arabic or Hebrew origin. Of course, these languages aren't written using the Roman alphabet, so these words are transliterations from a different script. It's an interesting – and helpful – fact that the Arabic consonant that is represented as a Q in Roman script can also be transliterated as a K, which means that many of the Q-but-no-U words can also be spelt with a K. This is useful for two reasons. Firstly, looking at the list of K alternatives will help you remember the Q-only words. Secondly, K is a sort of 'semi-power' tile, scoring five points and being the most valuable letter after the power tiles. Thus it's quite useful to know these unusual words using K for their own sake.

FAQIR	FAKIR	QAIMAQAMS	KAIMAKAMS	SHEQEL	SHEKEL
FAQIRS	FAKIRS	QALAMDAN	KALAMDAN	SHEQELS	SHEKELS
QABALA	KABALA	QALAMDANS	KALAMDANS	TALAQ	TALAK
QABALAS	KABALAS	QAT	KAT	TALAQS	TALAKS
QABALISM	KABALISM	QATS	KATS	TRANQ	TRANK
QABALISMS	KABALISMS	QI	KI	TRANQS	TRANKS
QABALIST	KABALIST	QIBLA	KIBLA	TSADDIQ	TSADDIK
QABALISTIC	KABALISTIC	QIBLAS	KIBLAS	TSADDIQIM	TSADDIKIM
QABALISTS	KABALISTS	QIS	KIS	TSADDIQS	TSADDIKS
QADI	KADI	QOPH	KOPH	TZADDIQ	TZADDIK
QADIS	KADIS	QOPHS	KOPHS	TZADDIQIM	TZADDIKIM
QAID	KAID	QORMA	KORMA	TZADDIQS	TZADDIKS
QAIDS	KAIDS	QORMAS	KORMAS	WAQF	WAKF
QAIMAQAM	KAIMAKAM	SHEQALIM	SHEKALIM	WAQFS	WAKFS

Using X

X is perhaps the most versatile of the power tiles, simply because of the extensive number of two- and three-letter words that contain it. It can reap many points through parallel play, especially if the X falls on a premium square, because there is a two-letter word for every vowel. It is fairly easy to spot words that end in X so it's worth learning a few words that begin with X when a board may not favour X-ending words (eg XENIA, XYST). Of all the power tiles, the X is the only one that it can be worthwhile holding back in the hope of a better score later, providing you can score reasonably well with your other tiles meanwhile.

Q but not U

Two-letter words

AX	tool with a sharp blade for felling trees or chopping wood
EX	not including
OX	castrated bull
XI	14th letter in the Greek alphabet
XU	Vietnamese currency unit

Three-letter words

AXE	tool with a sharp blade for felling trees or chopping wood
BOX	container with a firm flat base and sides
COX	coxswain
DEX	dextroamphetamine
DUX	(in Scottish and certain other schools) the top pupil ina class or school
EXO	excellent
FAX	electronic system for sending facsimiles of documents by telephone
FIX	make or become firm, stable, or secure
FOX	reddish-brown bushy-tailed animal of the dog family
GOX	gaseous oxygen
HEX	of or relating to hexadecimal notation
HOX	hamstring
KEX	any of several large hollow-stemmed umbelliferous plants, such as cow parsnip and chervil
LAX	not strict
LEX	system or body of laws
LOX	load fuel tanks of spacecraft with liquid oxygen
LUX	unit of illumination
MAX	reach the full extent
MIX	combine or blend into one mass
MUX	spoil
NIX	be careful! watch out!
NOX	nitrogen oxide
OXO	acid that contains oxygen
OXY	castrated bull
PAX	kiss of peace
PIX	any receptacle for the Eucharistic Host
POX	disease in which skin pustules form
PYX	any receptacle for the Eucharistic Host
RAX	stretch or extend
REX	king
SAX	saxophone
SEX	state of being male or female
SIX	one more than five
SOX	informal spelling of 'socks'
TAX	compulsory payment levied by a government on income, property, etc to raise revenue
TEX	unit of weight used to measure yarn density
TIX	tickets
TUX	short for tuxedo
VEX	frustrate, annoy
VOX	voice or sound
WAX	solid shiny fatty or oily substance used for sealing, making candles, etc
WEX	wax
WOX	wax
XIS	plural, 14th letter in the Greek alphabet

YEX	hiccup			
ZAX	saxophone			
ZEX	tool for cutting roofing slate			

Four-letter words

APEX	DIXI	FLAX	MAXI	PLEX
AXAL	DIXY	FLEX	MINX	POXY
AXED	DOUX	FLIX	MIXT	PREX
AXEL	DOXY	FLUX	MIXY	ROUX
AXES	EAUX	FOXY	MOXA	SAXE
AXIL	EXAM	GREX	MYXO	SEXT
AXIS	EXEC	HOAX	NEXT	SEXY
AXLE	EXED	IBEX	NIXE	TAXA
AXON	EXES	ILEX	NIXY	TAXI
BOXY	EXIT	IXIA	ONYX	TEXT
BRUX	EXON	JAXY	ORYX	ULEX
CALX	EXPO	JEUX	OXEN	VEXT
COAX	EXUL	JINX	OXER	WAXY
COXA	FAIX	JYNX	OXES	WEXE
COXY	FALX	LANX	OXID	XYST
CRUX	FAUX	LUXE	OXIM	YUNX
DEXY	FIXT	LYNX	PIXY	

Five-letter words

ADDAX	CALYX	EXECS	FOXES	LOXES
ADMIX	CAREX	EXEEM	FOXIE	LUREX
AFFIX	CAXON	EXEME	GALAX	LUXES
ANNEX	CHOUX	EXERT	GOXES	MALAX
ATAXY	CIMEX	EXIES	HAPAX	MAXED
AUXIN	CODEX	EXILE	HELIX	MAXES
AXELS	COMIX	EXINE	HEXAD	MAXIM
AXIAL	COXAE	EXING	HEXED	MAXIS
AXILE	COXAL	EXIST	HEXER	MIREX
AXILS	COXED	EXITS	HEXES	MIXED
AXING	COXES	EXODE	HEXYL	MIXEN
AXIOM	CULEX	EXONS	HOXED	MIXER
AXION	CYLIX	EXPAT	HOXES	MIXES
AXITE	DEOXY	EXPEL	HYRAX	MIXTE
AXLED	DESEX	EXPOS	IMMIX	MIXUP
AXLES	DETOX	EXTOL	INDEX	MOXAS
AXMAN	DEWAX	EXTRA	INFIX	MOXIE
AXMEN	DEXES	EXUDE	IXIAS	MUREX
AXOID	DEXIE	EXULS	IXORA	MUXED
AXONE	DIXIE	EXULT	IXTLE	MUXES
AXONS	DIXIT	EXURB	JAXIE	MYXOS
BEAUX	DOXIE	FAXED	KEXES	NEXTS
BEMIX	DRUXY	FAXES	KYLIX	NEXUS
BOLIX	DUXES	FEDEX	LATEX	NIXED
BORAX	EMBOX	FIXED	LAXER	NIXER
BOXED	ENFIX	FIXER	LAXES	NIXES
BOXEN	EPOXY	FIXES	LAXLY	NIXIE
BOXER	EXACT	FIXIT	LEXES	NOXAL
BOXES	EXALT	FLAXY	LEXIS	NOXES
BRAXY	EXAMS	FLEXO	LIMAX	ORIXA
BUXOM	EXCEL	FOREX	LINUX	OXBOW
CALIX	EXEAT	FOXED	LOXED	OXERS

OXEYE	PYXIS	SIXES	UNBOX	XEBEC
OXIDE	RADIX	SIXMO	UNFIX	XENIA
OXIDS	RAXED	SIXTE	UNMIX	XENIC
OXIME	RAXES	SIXTH	UNSEX	XENON
OXIMS	REDOX	SIXTY	UNTAX	XERIC
OXLIP	REDUX	SOREX	VARIX	XEROX
OXTER	REFIX	TAXED	VEXED	XERUS
PANAX	RELAX	TAXER	VEXER	XOANA
PAXES	REMEX	TAXES	VEXES	XYLAN
PHLOX	REMIX	TAXIS	VEXIL	XYLEM
PIXEL	RETAX	TAXOL	VIBEX	XYLIC
PIXES	REWAX	TAXON	VITEX	XYLOL
PIXIE	REXES	TAXOR	VIXEN	XYLYL
PODEX	SALIX	TAXUS	VOXEL	XYSTI
POXED	SAXES	TELEX	WAXED	XYSTS
POXES	SEXED	TEXAS	WAXEN	YEXED
PREXY	SEXER	TEXES	WAXER	YEXES
PROXY	SEXES	TEXTS	WAXES	ZAXES
PYREX	SEXTO	TOXIC	WEXED	ZEXES
PYXED	SEXTS	TOXIN	WEXES	
PYXES	SILEX	TUXES	WOXEN	
PYXIE	SIXER	TWIXT	WUXIA	

Six-letter words

ADIEUX	BEMBEX	COMMIX	EXACUM	EXODOI
ADMIXT	BEMBIX	CONFIX	EXALTS	EXODOS
ADNEXA	BEMIXT	CONVEX	EXAMEN	EXODUS
AFFLUX	BIAXAL	CORTEX	EXARCH	EXOGEN
ALEXIA	BIFLEX	COWPOX	EXCAMB	EXOMIS
ALEXIC	BIJOUX	COXIER	EXCEED	EXONIC
ALEXIN	BOLLIX	COXING	EXCELS	EXONYM
ALKOXY	BOLLOX	CRUXES	EXCEPT	EXOPOD
ANNEXE	BOMBAX	DEFLEX	EXCESS	EXOTIC
ANOXIA	BOMBYX	DEIXES	EXCIDE	EXPAND
ANOXIC	BONXIE	DEIXIS	EXCISE	EXPATS
APEXES	BOXCAR	DELUXE	EXCITE	EXPECT
ATAXIA	BOXERS	DENTEX	EXCUSE	EXPELS
ATAXIC	BOXFUL	DESOXY	EXEATS	EXPEND
ATWIXT	BOXIER	DEXIES	EXEDRA	EXPERT
AUSPEX	BOXILY	DEXTER	EXEEMS	EXPIRE
AUXINS	BOXING	DEXTRO	EXEMED	EXPIRY
AXEMAN	BOYAUX	DIAXON	EXEMES	EXPORT
AXEMEN	BRUXED	DIOXAN	EXEMPT	EXPOSE
AXENIC	BRUXES	DIOXID	EXEQUY	EXPUGN
AXILLA	CALXES	DIOXIN	EXERTS	EXSECT
AXIOMS	CARFAX	DIPLEX	EXEUNT	EXSERT
AXIONS	CARFOX	DIXIES	EXHALE	EXTANT
AXISED	CAUDEX	DIXITS	EXHORT	EXTASY
AXISES	CAXONS	DOGFOX	EXHUME	EXTEND
AXITES	CERVIX	DOXIES	EXILED	EXTENT
AXLIKE	CHENIX	DUPLEX	EXILER	EXTERN
AXOIDS	CLAXON	EARWAX	EXILES	EXTINE
AXONAL	CLIMAX	EFFLUX	EXILIC	EXTIRP
AXONES	COAXAL	ELIXIR	EXINES	EXTOLD
AXONIC	COAXED	ETHOXY	EXISTS	EXTOLL
AXSEED	COAXER	EUTAXY	EXITED	EXTOLS
BANJAX	COAXES	EXACTA	EXODES	EXTORT
BAXTER	COCCYX	EXACTS	EXODIC	EXTRAS

EXUDED	IMBREX	ORYXES	REFLUX	TEXTER
EXUDES	IMPLEX	OUTBOX	REMIXT	THORAX
EXULTS	INFLUX	OUTFOX	REXINE	TOXICS
EXURBS	ISOLEX	OXALIC	RHEXES	TOXINE
EXUVIA	IXODID	OXALIS	RHEXIS	TOXINS
FAXING	IXORAS	OXBOWS	SAXAUL	TOXOID
FIXATE	IXTLES	OXCART	SAXONY	TUTRIX
FIXERS	JAWBOX	OXEYES	SCOLEX	TUXEDO
FIXING	JAXIES	OXFORD	SEXERS	ULEXES
FIXITY	JINXED	OXGANG	SEXFID	UNAXED
FIXIVE	JINXES	OXGATE	SEXIER	UNFIXT
FIXURE	JYNXES	OXHEAD	SEXILY	UNISEX
FLAXEN	KLAXON	OXHIDE	SEXING	UNMIXT
FLAXES	LARNAX	OXIDES	SEXISM	UNSEXY
FLEXED	LARYNX	OXIDIC	SEXIST	UNVEXT
FLEXES	LAXEST	OXIMES	SEXPOT	URTEXT
FLEXOR	LAXISM	OXLAND	SEXTAN	VERNIX
FLEXOS	LAXIST	OXLIKE	SEXTET	VERTEX
FLIXED	LAXITY	OXLIPS	SEXTON	VEXERS
FLIXES	LEXEME	OXSLIP	SEXTOS	VEXILS
FLUXED	LEXICA	OXTAIL	SEXUAL	VEXING
FLUXES	LOXING	OXTERS	SILVEX	VIXENS
FORFEX	LUMMOX	OXYGEN	SIXAIN	VOLVOX
FORNIX	LUXATE	OXYMEL	SIXERS	VORTEX
FOXIER	LUXURY	PAXWAX	SIXMOS	VOXELS
FOXIES	LYNXES	PEGBOX	SIXTES	WAXERS
FOXILY	MAGNOX	PEROXO	SIXTHS	WAXEYE
FOXING	MASTIX	PEROXY	SKYBOX	WAXIER
FRUTEX	MATRIX	PHENIX	SMILAX	WAXILY
GALAXY	MAXIMA	PICKAX	SPADIX	WAXING
GREXES	MAXIMS	PINXIT	SPHINX	WEXING
GUANXI	MAXING	PIXELS	SPHYNX	WRAXLE
HALLUX	MAXIXE	PIXIES	STORAX	WUXIAS
HANDAX	MENINX	PLEXAL	STYRAX	XEBECS
HATBOX	MINXES	PLEXES	SUBFIX	XENIAL
HAYBOX	MIXENS	PLEXOR	SUFFIX	XENIAS
HEXACT	MIXERS	PLEXUS	SUPLEX	XENIUM
HEXADE	MIXIER	POLEAX	SURTAX	XENONS
HEXADS	MIXING	POLLEX	SYNTAX	XEROMA
HEXANE	MIXUPS	POXIER	SYRINX	XOANON
HEXENE	MOXIES	POXING	TAXEME	XYLANS
HEXERS	MUSKOX	PRAXES	TAXERS	XYLEMS
HEXING	MUXING	PRAXIS	TAXIED	XYLENE
HEXONE	MYXOID	PREFIX	TAXIES	XYLOID
HEXOSE	MYXOMA	PREMIX	TAXING	XYLOLS
HEXYLS	NEXTLY	PRETAX	TAXITE	XYLOMA
HOAXED	NIXERS	PREXES	TAXMAN	XYLOSE
HOAXER	NIXIES	PROLIX	TAXMEN	XYLYLS
HOAXES	NIXING	PTYXES	TAXOLS	XYSTER
HOTBOX	NONTAX	PTYXIS	TAXONS	XYSTOI
HOXING	ONYXES	PYXIES	TAXORS	XYSTOS
IBEXES	OREXIS	PYXING	TEABOX	XYSTUS
ICEBOX	ORIFEX	RAXING	TETTIX	YEXING
ILEXES	ORIXAS	REFLEX	TEXTED	YUNXES

Seven-letter words

ABAXIAL	ABRASAX	ADAXIAL	ADMIXED	ADNEXAL
ABAXILE	ABRAXAS	ADDAXES	ADMIXES	AFFIXAL

AFFIXED	BOXCARS	DIOXIDE	EXCUSAL	EXPOSED
AFFIXER	BOXFISH	DIOXIDS	EXCUSED	EXPOSER
AFFIXES	BOXFULS	DIOXINS	EXCUSER	EXPOSES
ALEXIAS	BOXHAUL	DISTRIX	EXCUSES	EXPOSIT
ALEXINE	BOXIEST	DRUXIER	EXECUTE	EXPOUND
ALEXINS	BOXINGS	EDITRIX	EXEDRAE	EXPRESS
ALLOXAN	BOXLIKE	ELIXIRS	EXEEMED	EXPUGNS
ANAXIAL	BOXROOM	EMBOXED	EXEGETE	EXPULSE
ANNEXED	BOXWOOD	EMBOXES	EXEMING	EXPUNCT
ANNEXES	BRAXIES	ENFIXED	EXEMPLA	EXPUNGE
ANOREXY	BROADAX	ENFIXES	EXEMPLE	EXPURGE
ANOXIAS	BRUXING	EPAXIAL	EXEMPTS	EXSCIND
ANTEFIX	BRUXISM	EPITAXY	EXERGUE	EXSECTS
ANTHRAX	BUREAUX	EPOXIDE	EXERTED	EXSERTS
ANTISEX	BUXOMER	EPOXIED	EXHALED	EXTATIC
ANTITAX	BUXOMLY	EPOXIES	EXHALES	EXTENDS
ANXIETY	CACHEXY	EPOXYED	EXHAUST	EXTENSE
ANXIOUS	CADEAUX	EQUINOX	EXHEDRA	EXTENTS
APOPLEX	CALYXES	ETHOXYL	EXHIBIT	EXTERNE
APRAXIA	CARAPAX	EUTAXIA	EXHORTS	EXTERNS
APRAXIC	CASHBOX	EUTEXIA	EXHUMED	EXTINCT
APTERYX	CELOTEX	EXABYTE	EXHUMER	EXTINES
ARUSPEX	CHAMOIX	EXACTAS	EXHUMES	EXTIRPS
ASEXUAL	CHOENIX	EXACTED	EXIGENT	EXTOLLS
ASPHYXY	CLAXONS	EXACTER	EXILERS	EXTORTS
ATARAXY	COALBOX	EXACTLY	EXILIAN	EXTRACT
ATAXIAS	COANNEX	EXACTOR	EXILING	EXTRAIT
ATAXICS	COAXERS	EXACUMS	EXILITY	EXTREAT
ATAXIES	COAXIAL	EXALTED	EXISTED	EXTREMA
AUXESES	COAXING	EXALTER	EXITING	EXTREME
AUXESIS	COEXERT	EXAMENS	EXOCARP	EXTRUDE
AUXETIC	COEXIST	EXAMINE	EXODERM	EXUDATE
AUXINIC	COMMIXT	EXAMPLE	EXODIST	EXUDING
AXEBIRD	COMPLEX	EXAPTED	EXOGAMY	EXULTED
AXIALLY	CONFLUX	EXARATE	EXOGENS	EXURBAN
AXILLAE	CONTEXT	EXARCHS	EXOMION	EXURBIA
AXILLAR	CORIXID	EXARCHY	EXONYMS	EXUVIAE
AXILLAS	COTEAUX	EXCAMBS	EXOPODS	EXUVIAL
AXINITE	COXALGY	EXCEEDS	EXORDIA	EXUVIUM
AXOLOTL	COXCOMB	EXCEPTS	EXOSMIC	FAREBOX
AXONEME	COXIEST	EXCERPT	EXOTICA	FEDEXED
AXSEEDS	COXITIS	EXCHEAT	EXOTICS	FEDEXES
BANDBOX	COXLESS	EXCIDED	EXOTISM	FEEDBOX
BATEAUX	CULEXES	EXCIDES	EXPANDS	FIREBOX
BAUXITE	CURTAXE	EXCIMER	EXPANSE	FIXABLE
BAXTERS	DEINDEX	EXCIPLE	EXPECTS	FIXATED
BEATBOX	DESEXED	EXCISED	EXPENDS	FIXATES
BEESWAX	DESEXES	EXCISES	EXPENSE	FIXATIF
BEMIXED	DETOXED	EXCITED	EXPERTS	FIXEDLY
BEMIXES	DETOXES	EXCITER	EXPIATE	FIXINGS
BETAXED	DEWAXED	EXCITES	EXPIRED	FIXTURE
BETWIXT	DEWAXES	EXCITON	EXPIRER	FIXURES
BIAXIAL	DEXTERS	EXCITOR	EXPIRES	FLAXIER
BOLIXED	DEXTRAL	EXCLAIM	EXPLAIN	FLEXILE
BOLIXES	DEXTRAN	EXCLAVE	EXPLANT	FLEXING
BONXIES	DEXTRIN	EXCLUDE	EXPLODE	FLEXION
BOOMBOX	DIAXONS	EXCRETA	EXPLOIT	FLEXORS
BORAXES	DIGOXIN	EXCRETE	EXPLORE	FLEXURE
BOSTRYX	DIOXANE	EXCUDIT	EXPORTS	FLIXING
BOXBALL	DIOXANS	EXCURSE	EXPOSAL	FLUMMOX

FLUXING	JAMBEUX	OXBLOOD	PYREXIA	SONOVOX
FLUXION	JINXING	OXCARTS	PYREXIC	SOREXES
FLUXIVE	JUKEBOX	OXFORDS	PYXIDES	SPANDEX
FOREXES	KICKBOX	OXGANGS	PYXIDIA	SUBTAXA
FOWLPOX	KLAXONS	OXGATES	QUIXOTE	SUBTEXT
FOXFIRE	KLEENEX	OXHEADS	RADIXES	SYNAXES
FOXFISH	LATEXES	OXHEART	REAFFIX	SYNAXIS
FOXHOLE	LAXATOR	OXHIDES	REANNEX	TALKBOX
FOXHUNT	LAXISMS	OXIDANT	RECTRIX	TAXABLE
FOXIEST	LAXISTS	OXIDASE	REDOXES	TAXABLY
FOXINGS	LAXNESS	OXIDATE	REEXPEL	TAXEMES
FOXLIKE	LEXEMES	OXIDISE	REFIXED	TAXEMIC
FOXSHIP	LEXEMIC	OXIDIZE	REFIXES	TAXICAB
FOXSKIN	LEXICAL	OXLANDS	REINDEX	TAXIING
FOXTAIL	LEXICON	OXONIUM	RELAXED	TAXIMAN
FOXTROT	LEXISES	OXSLIPS	RELAXER	TAXIMEN
FUNPLEX	LINUXES	OXTAILS	RELAXES	TAXINGS
GALAXES	LIXIVIA	OXTERED	RELAXIN	TAXITES
GATEAUX	LOCKBOX	OXYACID	REMIXED	TAXITIC
GEARBOX	LOXYGEN	OXYGENS	REMIXES	TAXIWAY
GRAVLAX	LUREXES	OXYMELS	RESEAUX	TAXLESS
GUANXIS	LUXATED	OXYMORA	RETAXED	TAXPAID
HAPAXES	LUXATES	OXYNTIC	RETAXES	TAXWISE
HELIXES	MAILBOX	OXYPHIL	REWAXED	TAXYING
HELLBOX	MALAXED	OXYSALT	REWAXES	TECTRIX
HEXACTS	MALAXES	OXYSOME	REXINES	TELEFAX
HEXADES	MARTEXT	OXYTONE	SALPINX	TELETEX
HEXADIC	MAXILLA	PACKWAX	SALTBOX	TELEXED
HEXAGON	MAXIMAL	PANAXES	SANDBOX	TELEXES
HEXANES	MAXIMIN	PANCHAX	SAXAULS	TEXASES
HEXAPLA	MAXIMUM	PARADOX	SAXHORN	TEXTERS
HEXAPOD	MAXIMUS	PAXIUBA	SAXTUBA	TEXTILE
HEXARCH	MAXIXES	PEMPHIX	SEALWAX	TEXTING
HEXENES	MAXWELL	PERPLEX	SEEDBOX	TEXTUAL
HEXEREI	MEATAXE	PERSPEX	SEXFOIL	TEXTURE
HEXINGS	METHOXY	PHALANX	SEXIEST	TOOLBOX
HEXONES	MILIEUX	PHARYNX	SEXISMS	TORTRIX
HEXOSAN	MINIMAX	PHENOXY	SEXISTS	TOXEMIA
HEXOSES	MINXISH	PHLOXES	SEXLESS	TOXEMIC
HEXYLIC	MIREXES	PHOENIX	SEXPERT	TOXICAL
HOAXERS	MIXABLE	PICKAXE	SEXPOTS	TOXINES
HOAXING	MIXDOWN	PILLBOX	SEXTAIN	TOXOIDS
HOMOSEX	MIXEDLY	PIXYISH	SEXTANS	TREEWAX
HUMIDEX	MIXIBLE	PLANXTY	SEXTANT	TRIAXON
HYDROXY	MIXIEST	PLEXORS	SEXTETS	TRIOXID
HYPOXIA	MIXTION	PLEXURE	SEXTETT	TRIPLEX
HYPOXIC	MIXTURE	PODEAXE	SEXTILE	TUBIFEX
HYRAXES	MONAXON	POLEAXE	SEXTONS	TUXEDOS
IMMIXED	MUREXES	POSTBOX	SEXTUOR	ULEXITE
IMMIXES	MYXOMAS	POSTFIX	SHOEBOX	UNBOXED
INDEXAL	NARTHEX	POSTTAX	SHOWBOX	UNBOXES
INDEXED	NEXUSES	POXIEST	SILEXES	UNFIXED
INDEXER	NOXIOUS	PREMIXT	SIMPLEX	UNFIXES
INDEXES	ORATRIX	PRETEXT	SIXAINE	UNMIXED
INDOXYL	OUTJINX	PREXIES	SIXAINS	UNMIXES
INEXACT	OVERLAX	PRINCOX	SIXFOLD	UNSEXED
INFIXED	OVERMIX	PROXIES	SIXTEEN	UNSEXES
INFIXES	OVERTAX	PROXIMO	SIXTHLY	UNTAXED
INVEXED	OXALATE	PYREXES	SIXTIES	UNTAXES
IXODIDS	OXAZINE		SOAPBOX	UNVEXED

Using X

UNWAXED	WAXABLE	WOODBOX	XERARCH	XYLENES
URTEXTS	WAXBILL	WOODWAX	XERASIA	XYLENOL
UXORIAL	WAXEYES	WORKBOX	XEROMAS	XYLIDIN
VAUDOUX	WAXIEST	WRAXLED	XEROSES	XYLITOL
VEXEDLY	WAXINGS	WRAXLES	XEROSIS	XYLOGEN
VEXILLA	WAXLIKE	XANTHAM	XEROTES	XYLOMAS
VEXINGS	WAXWEED	XANTHAN	XEROTIC	XYLONIC
VICTRIX	WAXWING	XANTHIC	XEROXED	XYLOSES
VITEXES	WAXWORK	XANTHIN	XEROXES	XYSTERS
VITRAUX	WAXWORM	XENOPUS	XERUSES	ZEUXITE
VIXENLY	WOADWAX	XERAFIN	XIPHOID	ZOOTAXY

Eight-letter words

ACETOXYL	AXOLEMMA	CACOMIXL	CURTALAX	EPITAXIC
ADMIXING	AXOLOTLS	CAMAIEUX	CURTAXES	EPITAXIS
AFFIXERS	AXONEMAL	CARBOXYL	CYBERSEX	EPOXIDES
AFFIXIAL	AXONEMES	CARFAXES	DEFLEXED	EPOXYING
AFFIXING	AXOPLASM	CARFOXES	DEFLEXES	ETHOXIDE
AFFLUXES	BANDEAUX	CARNIFEX	DEIXISES	ETHOXIES
AFTERTAX	BANJAXED	CATHEXES	DENTEXES	ETHOXYLS
ALDOXIME	BANJAXES	CATHEXIS	DESEXING	EUTAXIAS
ALEXINES	BANXRING	CAUDEXES	DETOXIFY	EUTAXIES
ALEXINIC	BATTEAUX	CERVIXES	DETOXING	EUTAXITE
ALKOXIDE	BAUXITES	CHAPEAUX	DEWAXING	EUTEXIAS
ALLOXANS	BAUXITIC	CHATEAUX	DEXTRANS	EUXENITE
AMPHIOXI	BEAUXITE	CHENIXES	DEXTRINE	EXABYTES
AMPLEXUS	BEMBEXES	CHRONAXY	DEXTRINS	EXACTERS
ANATOXIN	BEMBIXES	CICATRIX	DEXTROSE	EXACTEST
ANNEXING	BEMIXING	CINEPLEX	DEXTROUS	EXACTING
ANNEXION	BERCEAUX	CLACKBOX	DIGOXINS	EXACTION
ANNEXURE	BICONVEX	CLANGBOX	DIOXANES	EXACTORS
ANOREXIA	BIOTOXIN	CLIMAXED	DIOXIDES	EXAHERTZ
ANOREXIC	BISEXUAL	CLIMAXES	DIPLEXER	EXALTERS
ANOXEMIA	BOBBYSOX	COCCYXES	DISANNEX	EXALTING
ANOXEMIC	BOLIXING	COEXERTS	DOGFOXES	EXAMINED
ANTEFIXA	BOLLIXED	COEXISTS	DOXASTIC	EXAMINEE
ANTHELIX	BOLLIXES	COEXTEND	DOXOLOGY	EXAMINER
APOMIXES	BOLLOXED	COMMIXED	DRUXIEST	EXAMINES
APOMIXIS	BOLLOXES	COMMIXES	DUPLEXED	EXAMPLAR
APOPLEXY	BOMBAXES	CONFIXED	DUPLEXER	EXAMPLED
APPENDIX	BOMBYXES	CONFIXES	DUPLEXES	EXAMPLES
APRAXIAS	BORDEAUX	CONTEXTS	DUXELLES	EXANTHEM
APYREXIA	BOXBALLS	CONVEXED	DYSLEXIA	EXAPTIVE
ASPHYXIA	BOXBERRY	CONVEXES	DYSLEXIC	EXARCHAL
ATARAXIA	BOXBOARD	CONVEXLY	DYSTAXIA	EXCAMBED
ATARAXIC	BOXHAULS	CORIXIDS	EARTHWAX	EXCAVATE
AUXETICS	BOXINESS	CORTEXES	EARWAXES	EXCEEDED
AUXILIAR	BOXROOMS	COTURNIX	ECONOBOX	EXCEEDER
AUXOCYTE	BOXTHORN	COUTEAUX	ECOTOXIC	EXCELLED
AVIATRIX	BOXWOODS	COWPOXES	EFFLUXES	EXCEPTED
AXEBIRDS	BRAINBOX	COXALGIA	EKTEXINE	EXCEPTOR
AXIALITY	BREADBOX	COXALGIC	EMBOXING	EXCERPTA
AXILEMMA	BROADAXE	COXCOMBS	ENDEIXES	EXCERPTS
AXILLARS	BRUXISMS	COXINESS	ENDEIXIS	EXCESSED
AXILLARY	BUXOMEST	COXSWAIN	ENDEXINE	EXCESSES
AXINITES	CACHEXIA	CREATRIX	ENFIXING	EXCHANGE
AXIOLOGY	CACHEXIC	CRUCIFIX	EPICALYX	EXCHEATS
AXLETREE	CACODOXY	CURATRIX	EPITAXES	EXCIDING

EXCIMERS	EXHUMING	EXPIRANT	EXTRORSE	HEXAGLOT
EXCIPLES	EXIGEANT	EXPIRERS	EXTRUDED	HEXAGONS
EXCISING	EXIGENCE	EXPIRIES	EXTRUDER	HEXAGRAM
EXCISION	EXIGENCY	EXPIRING	EXTRUDES	HEXAMINE
EXCITANT	EXIGENTS	EXPLAINS	EXTUBATE	HEXANOIC
EXCITERS	EXIGIBLE	EXPLANTS	EXUDATES	HEXAPLAR
EXCITING	EXIGUITY	EXPLICIT	EXULTANT	HEXAPLAS
EXCITONS	EXIGUOUS	EXPLODED	EXULTING	HEXAPODS
EXCITORS	EXILABLE	EXPLODER	EXURBIAS	HEXAPODY
EXCLAIMS	EXIMIOUS	EXPLODES	EXUVIATE	HEXARCHY
EXCLAVES	EXISTENT	EXPLOITS	FABLIAUX	HEXEREIS
EXCLUDED	EXISTING	EXPLORED	FEDEXING	HEXOSANS
EXCLUDEE	EXITANCE	EXPLORER	FIXATIFS	HEXYLENE
EXCLUDER	EXITLESS	EXPLORES	FIXATING	HOMEOBOX
EXCLUDES	EXOCARPS	EXPONENT	FIXATION	HORSEBOX
EXCRETAL	EXOCRINE	EXPORTED	FIXATIVE	HORSEPOX
EXCRETED	EXOCYTIC	EXPORTER	FIXATURE	HOTBOXES
EXCRETER	EXODERMS	EXPOSALS	FIXITIES	HYDROXYL
EXCRETES	EXODISTS	EXPOSERS	FIXTURES	HYPOXIAS
EXCUBANT	EXODUSES	EXPOSING	FLAXIEST	ICEBOXES
EXCURSED	EXOERGIC	EXPOSITS	FLAXSEED	IMMIXING
EXCURSES	EXOGAMIC	EXPOSURE	FLEXAGON	IMPLEXES
EXCURSUS	EXOMIONS	EXPOUNDS	FLEXIBLE	INDEXERS
EXCUSALS	EXOMISES	EXPRESSO	FLEXIBLY	INDEXING
EXCUSERS	EXONUMIA	EXPUGNED	FLEXIONS	INDOXYLS
EXCUSING	EXOPHAGY	EXPULSED	FLEXTIME	INEXPERT
EXCUSIVE	EXOPLASM	EXPULSES	FLEXUOSE	INFIXING
EXECRATE	EXORABLE	EXPUNCTS	FLEXUOUS	INFIXION
EXECUTED	EXORCISE	EXPUNGED	FLEXURAL	INFLEXED
EXECUTER	EXORCISM	EXPUNGER	FLEXURES	INFLUXES
EXECUTES	EXORCIST	EXPUNGES	FLUXGATE	INTERMIX
EXECUTOR	EXORCIZE	EXPURGED	FLUXIONS	INTERREX
EXECUTRY	EXORDIAL	EXPURGES	FORFEXES	INTERSEX
EXEEMING	EXORDIUM	EXSCINDS	FOURPLEX	ISOLEXES
EXEGESES	EXOSMOSE	EXSECANT	FOXBERRY	JAMBEAUX
EXEGESIS	EXOSPORE	EXSECTED	FOXFIRES	JANITRIX
EXEGETES	EXOTERIC	EXSERTED	FOXGLOVE	JAWBOXES
EXEGETIC	EXOTISMS	EXTASIES	FOXHOLES	KETOXIME
EXEMPLAR	EXOTOXIC	EXTENDED	FOXHOUND	KLAXONED
EXEMPLES	EXOTOXIN	EXTENDER	FOXHUNTS	LARYNXES
EXEMPLUM	EXPANDED	EXTENSOR	FOXINESS	LAXATION
EXEMPTED	EXPANDER	EXTERIOR	FOXSHARK	LAXATIVE
EXEQUIAL	EXPANDOR	EXTERNAL	FOXSHIPS	LAXATORS
EXEQUIES	EXPANSES	EXTERNAT	FOXSKINS	LAXITIES
EXERCISE	EXPECTED	EXTERNES	FOXTAILS	LEXICONS
EXERGUAL	EXPECTER	EXTINCTS	FOXTROTS	LEXIGRAM
EXERGUES	EXPEDITE	EXTIRPED	GALAXIES	LIXIVIAL
EXERTING	EXPELLED	EXTOLLED	GENETRIX	LIXIVIUM
EXERTION	EXPELLEE	EXTOLLER	GENITRIX	LOOSEBOX
EXERTIVE	EXPELLER	EXTORTED	GEOTAXES	LOXYGENS
EXHALANT	EXPENDED	EXTORTER	GEOTAXIS	LUMMOXES
EXHALENT	EXPENDER	EXTRACTS	GIAMBEUX	LUNCHBOX
EXHALING	EXPENSED	EXTRADOS	GLOXINIA	LUXATING
EXHAUSTS	EXPENSES	EXTRAITS	HANDAXES	LUXATION
EXHEDRAE	EXPERTED	EXTRANET	HARUSPEX	LUXMETER
EXHIBITS	EXPERTLY	EXTREATS	HATBOXES	LUXURIES
EXHORTED	EXPIABLE	EXTREMAL	HAYBOXES	LUXURIST
EXHORTER	EXPIATED	EXTREMER	HERETRIX	LYNXLIKE
EXHUMATE	EXPIATES	EXTREMES	HERITRIX	MAGNOXES
EXHUMERS	EXPIATOR	EXTREMUM	HEXAFOIL	MALAXAGE

MALAXATE	OXALISES	PONTIFEX	SEXTANTS	TAXIWAYS
MALAXING	OXAZEPAM	POXVIRUS	SEXTARII	TAXONOMY
MANTEAUX	OXAZINES	PRAXISES	SEXTETTE	TAXPAYER
MARTEXTS	OXBLOODS	PREAXIAL	SEXTETTS	TEABOXES
MASTIXES	OXHEARTS	PRECIEUX	SEXTILES	TEGUEXIN
MATCHBOX	OXIDABLE	PREEXIST	SEXTOLET	TELETEXT
MATRIXES	OXIDANTS	PREFIXAL	SEXTUORS	TELEXING
MAXICOAT	OXIDASES	PREFIXED	SEXTUPLE	TETRAXON
MAXILLAE	OXIDASIC	PREFIXES	SEXTUPLY	TETROXID
MAXILLAR	OXIDATED	PREMIXED	SEXUALLY	TETTIXES
MAXILLAS	OXIDATES	PREMIXES	SILOXANE	TEXTBOOK
MAXIMALS	OXIDISED	PRETEXTS	SILVEXES	TEXTILES
MAXIMINS	OXIDISER	PROLIXLY	SIXAINES	TEXTLESS
MAXIMISE	OXIDISES	PROTOXID	SIXPENCE	TEXTUARY
MAXIMIST	OXIDIZED	PROXEMIC	SIXPENNY	TEXTURAL
MAXIMITE	OXIDIZER	PROXIMAL	SIXSCORE	TEXTURED
MAXIMIZE	OXIDIZES	PTYXISES	SIXTEENS	TEXTURES
MAXIMUMS	OXIMETER	PYREXIAL	SIXTIETH	THORAXES
MAXWELLS	OXIMETRY	PYREXIAS	SIXTYISH	THYROXIN
MEATAXES	OXONIUMS	PYROXENE	SKYBOXES	TOADFLAX
MEGAPLEX	OXPECKER	PYROXYLE	SMALLPOX	TONNEAUX
METHOXYL	OXTERING	PYXIDIUM	SMILAXES	TOXAEMIA
MICROLUX	OXTONGUE	QUADPLEX	SNUFFBOX	TOXAEMIC
MILLILUX	OXYACIDS	QUINCUNX	SOUNDBOX	TOXEMIAS
MIREPOIX	OXYGENIC	QUIXOTES	SPADIXES	TOXICANT
MIXDOWNS	OXYMORON	QUIXOTIC	SPARAXIS	TOXICITY
MIXOLOGY	OXYPHILE	QUIXOTRY	SPHINXES	TOXOCARA
MIXTIONS	OXYPHILS	REEXPELS	SPHYNXES	TRACTRIX
MIXTURES	OXYSALTS	REEXPORT	SPINIFEX	TRANSFIX
MONAXIAL	OXYSOMES	REEXPOSE	SPINTEXT	TRIAXIAL
MONAXONS	OXYTOCIC	REFIXING	STORAXES	TRIAXONS
MONOXIDE	OXYTOCIN	REFLEXED	STYRAXES	TRIOXIDE
MORCEAUX	OXYTONES	REFLEXES	SUBAXIAL	TRIOXIDS
MUSKOXEN	PAINTBOX	REFLEXLY	SUBFIXES	TRUMEAUX
MYXAMEBA	PANMIXES	REFLUXED	SUBINDEX	TUTRIXES
MYXEDEMA	PANMIXIA	REFLUXES	SUBOXIDE	TUXEDOED
MYXOCYTE	PANMIXIS	RELAXANT	SUBTAXON	TUXEDOES
MYXOMATA	PARADOXY	RELAXERS	SUBTEXTS	ULEXITES
NALOXONE	PARALLAX	RELAXING	SUFFIXAL	UNBOXING
NAPROXEN	PARAXIAL	RELAXINS	SUFFIXED	UNDERTAX
NEOTOXIN	PAROXYSM	REMIXING	SUFFIXES	UNEXOTIC
NEURAXON	PAXIUBAS	RETAXING	SUPERFIX	UNEXPERT
NEXTDOOR	PAXWAXES	REWAXING	SUPERMAX	UNFIXING
NEXTNESS	PEGBOXES	RHEXISES	SUPERSEX	UNFIXITY
NITROXYL	PEROXIDE	RONDEAUX	SUPERTAX	UNFLEXED
NONTAXES	PEROXIDS	ROULEAUX	SUPLEXES	UNIAXIAL
NONTOXIC	PHENIXES	SARDONYX	SURTAXED	UNISEXES
NOUVEAUX	PHORMINX	SAUCEBOX	SURTAXES	UNMIXING
OCTUPLEX	PHYLAXIS	SAXATILE	SWEATBOX	UNSEXING
OPOPANAX	PICKAXED	SAXHORNS	SWINEPOX	UNSEXIST
OREXISES	PICKAXES	SAXICOLE	SYNTAXES	UNSEXUAL
ORIFEXES	PIXIEISH	SAXONIES	SYNTEXIS	UNTAXING
ORTHODOX	PIXINESS	SAXONITE	SYRINXES	UXORIOUS
OTOTOXIC	PLATEAUX	SAXTUBAS	TABLEAUX	VERNIXES
OUTBOXED	PLEXURES	SCRUMPOX	TAXABLES	VERTEXES
OUTBOXES	PLEXUSES	SEXFOILS	TAXATION	VEXATION
OUTFOXED	POLEAXED	SEXINESS	TAXATIVE	VEXATORY
OUTFOXES	POLEAXES	SEXOLOGY	TAXIARCH	VEXILLAR
OXALATED	POLYAXON	SEXPERTS	TAXICABS	VEXILLUM
OXALATES	PONCEAUX	SEXTAINS	TAXINGLY	VEXINGLY

VIDEOTEX	WAXWINGS	XANTHOMA	XERANTIC	XYLOGENS
VIXENISH	WAXWORKS	XANTHONE	XERAPHIM	XYLOIDIN
VOLVOXES	WAXWORMS	XANTHOUS	XERASIAS	XYLOLOGY
VORTEXES	WRAXLING	XENOGAMY	XEROMATA	XYLOMATA
WATCHBOX	XANTHAMS	XENOGENY	XEROSERE	XYLONITE
WATERPOX	XANTHANS	XENOLITH	XEROXING	XYLOTOMY
WAXBERRY	XANTHATE	XENOPHYA	XIPHOIDS	ZELATRIX
WAXBILLS	XANTHEIN	XENOTIME	XYLENOLS	ZEUXITES
WAXCLOTH	XANTHENE	XENURINE	XYLIDINE	ZOOTOXIC
WAXINESS	XANTHINE	XERAFINS	XYLIDINS	ZOOTOXIN
WAXPLANT	XANTHINS	XERANSES	XYLITOLS	
WAXWEEDS	XANTHISM	XERANSIS	XYLOCARP	

Using Z

Z scores the same as Q: ten points. But is an easier letter to use primarily because of the two two-letter words (ZA, ZO). Occasionally it may be worth considering holding the Z back if no great scores are immediately available but generally you should look to play it sooner rather than later. It is worth familiarizing yourself with some unusual three-, four- and five-letter words with the Z, especially those with low-scoring other letters (eg ZEA, ZOA, ZEIN, ZILA, ZONAE, ZANTE). There are a few Z words that also contain another power tile (JIZ, JAZY, ZAX, ZEX, QUIZ). Although these appear to very useful, in practice if you have two power tiles on your rack, it can be wiser to play them separately over two turns. There are also quite a few words with a double Z (eg BUZZ and FUZZ).

Two-letter words

ZA	pizza
ZO	Tibetan breed of cattle, developed by crossing the yak with common cattle

Three-letter words

ADZ	tool with an arched blade at right angles to the handle
AZO	of, consisting of, or containing the divalent group -N-
BEZ	part of deer's horn
BIZ	business
CAZ	casual
COZ	cousin
CUZ	cousin
DZO	Tibetan breed of cattle, developed by crossing the yak with common cattle
FEZ	brimless tasselled cap, orig. from Turkey
FIZ	make a hissing or bubbling noise
JIZ	wig
LEZ	lesbian (offensive)
LUZ	supposedly indestructible bone of the human body
MIZ	misery
MOZ	hex
POZ	positive
REZ	informal word for an instance of reserving; reservation
RIZ	(in some dialects) past form of rise
SAZ	Middle Eastern stringed instrument

Using X

SEZ	informal spelling of 'says'
WIZ	wizard
ZAG	change direction sharply
ZAP	kill (by shooting)
ZAS	pizzas
ZAX	saxophone
ZEA	corn silk
ZED	British and New Zealand spoken form of the letter Z
ZEE	zed
ZEK	Soviet prisoner
ZEL	Turkish cymbal
ZEP	type of long sandwich
ZEX	tool for cutting roofing slate
ZHO	Tibetan breed of cattle, developed by crossing the yak with common cattle
ZIG	change direction sharply
ZIN	zinfandel
ZIP	zipper
ZIT	spot or pimple
ZIZ	short sleep
ZOA	plural of zoon
ZOL	South African slang for a cannabis cigarette
ZOO	place where live animals are kept for show
ZOS	plural of zo
ZUZ	ancient Hebrew silver coin
ZZZ	informal word for sleep

Four-letter words

ADZE	GIZZ	OOZE	YUZU	ZINE
AZAN	HAZE	OOZY	ZACK	ZING
AZON	HAZY	ORZO	ZAGS	ZINS
AZYM	HIZZ	OUZO	ZANY	ZIPS
BIZE	IZAR	OYEZ	ZAPS	ZITE
BOZO	JAZY	PHIZ	ZARF	ZITI
BUZZ	JAZZ	PIZE	ZATI	ZITS
CHEZ	JEEZ	POZZ	ZEAL	ZIZZ
CHIZ	JIZZ	PREZ	ZEAS	ZOBO
COZE	KAZI	PUTZ	ZEBU	ZOBU
COZY	KUZU	QUIZ	ZEDS	ZOEA
CZAR	LAZE	RAZE	ZEES	ZOIC
DAZE	LAZO	RAZZ	ZEIN	ZOLS
DITZ	LAZY	RITZ	ZEKS	ZONA
DOZE	LEZZ	RIZA	ZELS	ZONE
DOZY	LUTZ	SITZ	ZEPS	ZONK
DZHO	MAZE	SIZE	ZERK	ZOOM
DZOS	MAZY	SIZY	ZERO	ZOON
FAZE	MEZE	SPAZ	ZEST	ZOOS
FIZZ	MEZZ	SWIZ	ZETA	ZOOT
FOZY	MIZZ	TIZZ	ZEZE	ZORI
FRIZ	MOZE	TOZE	ZHOS	ZOUK
FUTZ	MOZO	TREZ	ZIFF	ZULU
FUZE	MOZZ	TUZZ	ZIGS	ZUPA
FUZZ	MUZZ	TZAR	ZILA	ZURF
GAZE	MZEE	VIZY	ZILL	ZYGA
GAZY	NAZE	WHIZ	ZIMB	ZYME
GEEZ	NAZI	YUTZ	ZINC	ZZZS

Five-letter words

ABUZZ	COZED	GLAZY	MIZEN	SOYUZ
ADOZE	COZEN	GLITZ	MIZZY	SOZIN
ADZED	COZES	GLOZE	MOTZA	SPAZA
ADZES	COZEY	GONZO	MOZED	SPAZZ
AGAZE	COZIE	GRAZE	MOZES	SPITZ
AIZLE	CRAZE	GRENZ	MOZOS	SQUIZ
AMAZE	CRAZY	GRIZE	MUZZY	SWIZZ
ASSEZ	CROZE	GROSZ	MZEES	TAZZA
AVIZE	CZARS	GYOZA	NAZES	TAZZE
AVYZE	DARZI	HAFIZ	NAZIR	TEAZE
AZANS	DAZED	HAMZA	NAZIS	TIZZY
AZIDE	DAZER	HAZAN	NEEZE	TOAZE
AZIDO	DAZES	HAZED	NERTZ	TOPAZ
AZINE	DIAZO	HAZEL	NIZAM	TOUZE
AZLON	DITZY	HAZER	NUDZH	TOUZY
AZOIC	DIZEN	HAZES	OOZED	TOWZE
AZOLE	DIZZY	HEEZE	OOZES	TOWZY
AZONS	DOOZY	HERTZ	ORZOS	TOZED
AZOTE	DOZED	HIZEN	OUZEL	TOZES
AZOTH	DOZEN	HUZZA	OUZOS	TOZIE
AZUKI	DOZER	HUZZY	OZEKI	TROOZ
AZURE	DOZES	IZARD	OZONE	TZARS
AZURN	DURZI	IZARS	OZZIE	ULZIE
AZURY	DZHOS	IZZAT	PEAZE	UNZIP
AZYGY	ENZYM	JAZZY	PEIZE	VEZIR
AZYME	FAZED	KANZU	PIEZO	VIZIR
AZYMS	FAZES	KARZY	PIZED	VIZOR
BAIZA	FEAZE	KAZIS	PIZES	VOZHD
BAIZE	FEEZE	KAZOO	PIZZA	WALTZ
BAZAR	FEZES	KHAZI	PLAZA	WANZE
BAZOO	FEZZY	KLUTZ	PLOTZ	WAREZ
BEZEL	FIZZY	KRANZ	PONZU	WAZIR
BEZES	FORZA	KUDZU	POZZY	WAZOO
BEZIL	FORZE	KUZUS	PRIZE	WEIZE
BIZES	FRITZ	LAZAR	PUZEL	WHIZZ
BIZZO	FRIZE	LAZED	PZAZZ	WINZE
BIZZY	FRIZZ	LAZES	RAZED	WIZEN
BLAZE	FROZE	LAZOS	RAZEE	WIZES
BLITZ	FURZE	LAZZI	RAZER	WOOTZ
BONZA	FURZY	LAZZO	RAZES	WOOZY
BONZE	FUZED	LEAZE	RAZOO	YUZUS
BOOZE	FUZEE	LEZES	RAZOR	ZABRA
BOOZY	FUZES	LEZZA	RITZY	ZACKS
BORTZ	FUZIL	LEZZY	RIZAS	ZAIRE
BOZOS	FUZZY	LOZEN	ROZET	ZAKAT
BRAZA	GAUZE	MAIZE	ROZIT	ZAMAN
BRAZE	GAUZY	MATZA	SADZA	ZAMBO
BRIZE	GAZAL	MATZO	SAZES	ZAMIA
BUAZE	GAZAR	MAZED	SCUZZ	ZANJA
BUZZY	GAZED	MAZER	SEAZE	ZANTE
BWAZI	GAZER	MAZES	SEIZE	ZANZA
CAPIZ	GAZES	MAZEY	SENZA	ZANZE
CEAZE	GAZON	MAZUT	SIZAR	ZAPPY
CHIZZ	GAZOO	MEZES	SIZED	ZARFS
CLOZE	GHAZI	MEZZE	SIZEL	ZATIS
COBZA	GINZO	MEZZO	SIZER	ZAXES
COLZA	GIZMO	MILTZ	SIZES	ZAYIN
COOZE	GLAZE	MIRZA	SMAZE	ZAZEN

ZEALS	ZIGAN	ZIPPY	ZONAE	ZORIS
ZEBEC	ZILAS	ZIRAM	ZONAL	ZORRO
ZEBRA	ZILCH	ZITIS	ZONDA	ZOUKS
ZEBUB	ZILLA	ZIZEL	ZONED	ZOWIE
ZEBUS	ZILLS	ZIZIT	ZONER	ZULUS
ZEINS	ZIMBI	ZLOTE	ZONES	ZUPAN
ZERDA	ZIMBS	ZLOTY	ZONKS	ZUPAS
ZERKS	ZINCO	ZOAEA	ZOOEA	ZURFS
ZEROS	ZINCS	ZOBOS	ZOOEY	ZUZIM
ZESTS	ZINCY	ZOBUS	ZOOID	ZYGAL
ZESTY	ZINEB	ZOCCO	ZOOKS	ZYGON
ZETAS	ZINES	ZOEAE	ZOOMS	ZYMES
ZEXES	ZINGS	ZOEAL	ZOONS	ZYMIC
ZEZES	ZINGY	ZOEAS	ZOOTY	
ZHOMO	ZINKE	ZOISM	ZOPPA	
ZIBET	ZINKY	ZOIST	ZOPPO	
ZIFFS	ZIPPO	ZOMBI	ZORIL	

Six-letter words

ABLAZE	BAIZED	BOOZEY	COZILY	EPIZOA
ABRAZO	BAIZES	BORZOI	COZING	ERSATZ
ADZING	BANZAI	BRAIZE	COZZES	EVZONE
ADZUKI	BARAZA	BRAZAS	CRAZED	FAZING
AGAZED	BAZAAR	BRAZED	CRAZES	FEAZED
AGNIZE	BAZARS	BRAZEN	CROZER	FEAZES
AGRIZE	BAZAZZ	BRAZER	CROZES	FEEZED
AGRYZE	BAZOOS	BRAZES	CRUZIE	FEEZES
AGUIZE	BEDAZE	BRAZIL	CUZZES	FEZZED
AIZLES	BEEZER	BREEZE	CZAPKA	FEZZES
ALTEZA	BEGAZE	BREEZY	DARZIS	FIZGIG
AMAZED	BENZAL	BRIZES	DAZERS	FIZZED
AMAZES	BENZIL	BRONZE	DAZING	FIZZEN
AMAZON	BENZIN	BRONZY	DAZZLE	FIZZER
APOZEM	BENZOL	BROUZE	DEFUZE	FIZZES
ASSIZE	BENZYL	BUAZES	DEZINC	FIZZLE
AVIZED	BEZANT	BUZUKI	DIAZIN	FLOOZY
AVIZES	BEZAZZ	BUZZED	DIAZOS	FOOZLE
AVYZED	BEZELS	BUZZER	DITZES	FOZIER
AVYZES	BEZILS	BUZZES	DIZAIN	FRANZY
AZALEA	BEZOAR	BWAZIS	DIZENS	FRAZIL
AZERTY	BEZZLE	BYZANT	DONZEL	FREEZE
AZIDES	BIZAZZ	CEAZED	DOOZER	FRENZY
AZINES	BIZONE	CEAZES	DOOZIE	FRIEZE
AZIONE	BIZZES	CHAZAN	DORIZE	FRIZED
AZLONS	BIZZOS	CHINTZ	DOZENS	FRIZER
AZOLES	BLAIZE	CIZERS	DOZERS	FRIZES
AZOLLA	BLAZED	CLOZES	DOZIER	FRIZZY
AZONAL	BLAZER	COBZAS	DOZILY	FROUZY
AZONIC	BLAZES	COLZAS	DOZING	FROWZY
AZOTED	BLAZON	COOZES	DRAZEL	FROZEN
AZOTES	BLINTZ	COROZO	DURZIS	FURZES
AZOTHS	BLOWZE	CORYZA	DZEREN	FUTZED
AZOTIC	BLOWZY	COUZIN	ECZEMA	FUTZES
AZUKIS	BONZER	COZENS	ENTREZ	FUZEES
AZURES	BONZES	COZEYS	ENZIAN	FUZILS
AZYGOS	BOOZED	COZIED	ENZONE	FUZING
AZYMES	BOOZER	COZIER	ENZYME	FUZZED
BAIZAS	BOOZES	COZIES	ENZYMS	FUZZES

FUZZLE	HUZOOR	MAZHBI	PEIZES	SAZZES
GAUZES	HUZZAH	MAZIER	PEZANT	SCAZON
GAZABO	HUZZAS	MAZILY	PHEEZE	SCHIZO
GAZALS	IMBIZO	MAZING	PHIZES	SCHIZY
GAZARS	IODIZE	MAZOUT	PHIZOG	SCHNOZ
GAZEBO	IONIZE	MAZUMA	PIAZZA	SCOZZA
GAZERS	IZARDS	MAZUTS	PIAZZE	SCRUZE
GAZIER	IZZARD	MEAZEL	PIZAZZ	SCUZZY
GAZING	IZZATS	MEZAIL	PIZING	SEAZED
GAZONS	JAZIES	MEZCAL	PIZZAS	SEAZES
GAZOON	JAZZBO	MEZUZA	PIZZAZ	SEIZED
GAZOOS	JAZZED	MEZZES	PIZZLE	SEIZER
GAZUMP	JAZZER	MEZZOS	PLAZAS	SEIZES
GEEZAH	JAZZES	MIRZAS	PODZOL	SEIZIN
GEEZER	JEZAIL	MIZENS	PONZUS	SEIZOR
GHAZAL	JIZZES	MIZUNA	POTZER	SHAZAM
GHAZEL	KAIZEN	MIZZEN	POZOLE	SIZARS
GHAZIS	KAMEEZ	MIZZES	PREZES	SIZELS
GIZMOS	KANZUS	MIZZLE	PRIZED	SIZERS
GIZZEN	KAZOOS	MIZZLY	PRIZER	SIZIER
GIZZES	KHAZEN	MOMZER	PRIZES	SIZING
GLAZED	KHAZIS	MOTZAS	PUTZED	SIZISM
GLAZEN	KIBITZ	MOZING	PUTZES	SIZIST
GLAZER	KLUTZY	MOZZES	PUZELS	SIZZLE
GLAZES	KOLHOZ	MOZZIE	PUZZEL	SLEAZE
GLITZY	KOLKOZ	MOZZLE	PUZZLE	SLEAZO
GLOZED	KRANTZ	MUZAKY	QUARTZ	SLEAZY
GLOZES	KUDZUS	MUZHIK	QUAZZY	SLEEZY
GOZZAN	KUVASZ	MUZJIK	QUEAZY	SMAZES
GRAZED	KWANZA	MUZZED	QUEZAL	SNAZZY
GRAZER	LAZARS	MUZZES	QUINZE	SNEEZE
GRAZES	LAZIED	MUZZLE	RANZEL	SNEEZY
GRIZES	LAZIER	MZUNGU	RAZEED	SNOOZE
GROSZE	LAZIES	NAZIFY	RAZEES	SNOOZY
GROSZY	LAZILY	NAZIRS	RAZERS	SOZINE
GUIZER	LAZING	NEEZED	RAZING	SOZINS
GUTZER	LAZOED	NEEZES	RAZOOS	SOZZLE
GUZZLE	LAZOES	NIZAMS	RAZORS	SOZZLY
GYOZAS	LAZULI	NOZZER	RAZURE	SPELTZ
HALUTZ	LEAZES	NOZZLE	RAZZED	SPRITZ
HAMZAH	LEZZAS	NUZZER	RAZZES	STANZA
HAMZAS	LEZZES	NUZZLE	RAZZIA	STANZE
HAZANS	LEZZIE	NYANZA	RAZZLE	STANZO
HAZARD	LIZARD	OOZIER	REBOZO	SUIVEZ
HAZELS	LIZZIE	OOZILY	RESIZE	SYZYGY
HAZERS	LOZELL	OOZING	REZERO	TARZAN
HAZIER	LOZENS	OUZELS	REZONE	TAZZAS
HAZILY	LUTZES	OYEZES	REZZES	TEAZED
HAZING	LUZERN	OZAENA	RHIZIC	TEAZEL
HAZMAT	LUZZES	OZALID	RITZES	TEAZES
HAZZAN	MAHZOR	OZEKIS	RIZARD	TEAZLE
HEEZED	MAIZES	OZONES	RIZZAR	TENZON
HEEZES	MAMZER	OZONIC	RIZZER	TIZWAS
HEEZIE	MATZAH	OZZIES	RIZZOR	TIZZES
HIZENS	MATZAS	PANZER	RONZER	TOAZED
HIZZED	MATZOH	PATZER	ROZETS	TOAZES
HIZZES	MATZOS	PAZAZZ	ROZITS	TOLZEY
HOWZAT	MATZOT	PEAZED	ROZZER	TOUZED
HOWZIT	MAZARD	PEAZES	SADZAS	TOUZES
HUTZPA	MAZERS	PEIZED	SAZHEN	TOUZLE

TOWZED	WIZIER	ZARIBA	ZINCOS	ZONKED
TOWZES	WIZZEN	ZARNEC	ZINEBS	ZONOID
TOZIES	WIZZES	ZAYINS	ZINGED	ZONULA
TOZING	WURZEL	ZAZENS	ZINGEL	ZONULE
TREZES	WUZZLE	ZEALOT	ZINGER	ZONURE
TUZZES	YAKUZA	ZEATIN	ZINKED	ZOOEAE
TWEEZE	YUTZES	ZEBECK	ZINKES	ZOOEAL
TZETSE	ZABETA	ZEBECS	ZINNIA	ZOOEAS
TZETZE	ZABRAS	ZEBRAS	ZIPPED	ZOOIDS
TZURIS	ZADDIK	ZEBUBS	ZIPPER	ZOOIER
ULZIES	ZAFFAR	ZECHIN	ZIPPOS	ZOOMED
UMFAZI	ZAFFER	ZELANT	ZIPTOP	ZOONAL
UNZIPS	ZAFFIR	ZELOSO	ZIRAMS	ZOONED
UPGAZE	ZAFFRE	ZENANA	ZIRCON	ZOONIC
UPSIZE	ZAFTIG	ZENDIK	ZITHER	ZOOZOO
VEZIRS	ZAGGED	ZENITH	ZIZELS	ZORILS
VIZARD	ZAIKAI	ZEPHYR	ZIZITH	ZORINO
VIZIED	ZAIRES	ZERDAS	ZIZZED	ZORROS
VIZIER	ZAKATS	ZEREBA	ZIZZES	ZOSTER
VIZIES	ZAMANG	ZERIBA	ZIZZLE	ZOUAVE
VIZIRS	ZAMANS	ZEROED	ZLOTYS	ZOUNDS
VIZORS	ZAMBOS	ZEROES	ZOAEAE	ZOYSIA
VIZSLA	ZAMBUK	ZEROTH	ZOAEAS	ZUFOLI
VIZZIE	ZAMIAS	ZESTED	ZOARIA	ZUFOLO
VOZHDS	ZANANA	ZESTER	ZOCALO	ZUPANS
WANZED	ZANDER	ZEUGMA	ZOCCOS	ZYDECO
WANZES	ZANIED	ZHOMOS	ZODIAC	ZYGOID
WAZIRS	ZANIER	ZIBETH	ZOECIA	ZYGOMA
WAZOOS	ZANIES	ZIBETS	ZOETIC	ZYGOSE
WEAZEN	ZANILY	ZIGANS	ZOFTIG	ZYGOTE
WEIZED	ZANJAS	ZIGGED	ZOISMS	ZYMASE
WEIZES	ZANTES	ZIGZAG	ZOISTS	ZYMITE
WEZAND	ZANZAS	ZILLAH	ZOMBIE	ZYMOID
WHEEZE	ZANZES	ZILLAS	ZOMBIS	ZYMOME
WHEEZY	ZAPATA	ZIMBIS	ZONARY	ZYTHUM
WHIZZY	ZAPPED	ZIMMER	ZONATE	
WINZES	ZAPPER	ZINCED	ZONDAS	
WIZARD	ZARAPE	ZINCIC	ZONERS	
WIZENS	ZAREBA	ZINCKY	ZONING	

Seven-letter words

ABRAZOS	ALFEREZ	AVIZING	BAIZING	BENZILS
ADONIZE	ALIZARI	AVYZING	BANZAIS	BENZINE
ADZUKIS	ALTEZAS	AZALEAS	BAPTIZE	BENZINS
AGATIZE	ALTEZZA	AZIMUTH	BARAZAS	BENZOIC
AGENIZE	AMAZING	AZIONES	BAZAARS	BENZOIN
AGNIZED	AMAZONS	AZOLLAS	BAZOOKA	BENZOLE
AGNIZES	ANALYZE	AZOTISE	BAZOOMS	BENZOLS
AGONIZE	ANODIZE	AZOTIZE	BAZOUKI	BENZOYL
AGRIZED	ANZIANI	AZOTOUS	BEDAZED	BENZYLS
AGRIZES	APOZEMS	AZULEJO	BEDAZES	BEZANTS
AGRYZED	APPRIZE	AZUREAN	BEDIZEN	BEZIQUE
AGRYZES	ARABIZE	AZURINE	BEEZERS	BEZOARS
AGUIZED	ASSIZED	AZURITE	BEGAZED	BEZZANT
AGUIZES	ASSIZER	AZYGIES	BEGAZES	BEZZAZZ
ALBIZIA	ASSIZES	AZYGOUS	BEMAZED	BEZZLED
ALCAZAR	ATHEIZE	AZYMITE	BENZALS	BEZZLES
ALCORZA	ATOMIZE	AZYMOUS	BENZENE	BIZARRE

BIZARRO	CHALAZA	DITZIER	FLOOZIE	GOZZANS
BIZNAGA	CHALUTZ	DIZAINS	FOOZLED	GRAZERS
BIZONAL	CHAMETZ	DIZENED	FOOZLER	GRAZIER
BIZONES	CHAZANS	DIZZARD	FOOZLES	GRAZING
BIZZIES	CHAZZAN	DIZZIED	FORZATI	GRECIZE
BLAZERS	CHAZZEN	DIZZIER	FORZATO	GRIZZLE
BLAZING	CHINTZY	DIZZIES	FOZIEST	GRIZZLY
BLAZONS	CHIZZED	DIZZILY	FRAWZEY	GROZING
BLINTZE	CHIZZES	DOCKIZE	FRAZILS	GUEREZA
BLITZED	CHOMETZ	DONZELS	FRAZZLE	GUIZERS
BLITZER	CHORIZO	DOOZERS	FREEZER	GUTZERS
BLITZES	CHUTZPA	DOOZIES	FREEZES	GUZZLED
BLOWZED	CITIZEN	DOPIAZA	FRIEZED	GUZZLER
BLOWZES	COALIZE	DORIZED	FRIEZES	GUZZLES
BONANZA	COGNIZE	DORIZES	FRITZES	HAFIZES
BOOZERS	COROZOS	DOZENED	FRIZERS	HAMZAHS
BOOZIER	CORYZAL	DOZENTH	FRIZING	HAZANIM
BOOZILY	CORYZAS	DOZIEST	FRIZZED	HAZARDS
BOOZING	COUZINS	DOZINGS	FRIZZER	HAZELLY
BORAZON	COZENED	DRAZELS	FRIZZES	HAZIEST
BORTZES	COZENER	DRIZZLE	FRIZZLE	HAZINGS
BORZOIS	COZIERS	DRIZZLY	FRIZZLY	HAZMATS
BRAIZES	COZIEST	DUALIZE	FURZIER	HAZZANS
BRAZENS	COZYING	DZERENS	FUTZING	HEEZIES
BRAZERS	CRAZIER	EBONIZE	FUZZIER	HEEZING
BRAZIER	CRAZIES	ECHOIZE	FUZZILY	HEROIZE
BRAZILS	CRAZILY	ECTOZOA	FUZZING	HERTZES
BRAZING	CRAZING	ECZEMAS	FUZZLED	HIZZING
BREEZED	CROZERS	EGOTIZE	FUZZLES	HOATZIN
BREEZES	CROZIER	ELEGIZE	GALLIZE	HORIZON
BRITZKA	CRUIZIE	EMBLAZE	GAUZIER	HUMBUZZ
BROMIZE	CRUZADO	EMPRIZE	GAUZILY	HUTZPAH
BRONZED	CRUZIES	ENDOZOA	GAZABOS	HUTZPAS
BRONZEN	CYANIZE	ENFROZE	GAZANIA	HUZOORS
BRONZER	CYCLIZE	ENTOZOA	GAZEBOS	HUZZAED
BRONZES	CZAPKAS	ENZIANS	GAZEFUL	HUZZAHS
BROUZES	CZARDAS	ENZONED	GAZELLE	HUZZIES
BRULZIE	CZARDOM	ENZONES	GAZETTE	ICONIZE
BUMBAZE	CZARINA	ENZYMES	GAZIEST	IDOLIZE
BUZUKIA	CZARISM	ENZYMIC	GAZINGS	IMBIZOS
BUZUKIS	CZARIST	EPAZOTE	GAZOOKA	IMBLAZE
BUZZARD	DAMOZEL	EPIZOAN	GAZOONS	IODIZED
BUZZCUT	DANAZOL	EPIZOIC	GAZUMPS	IODIZER
BUZZERS	DAZEDLY	EPIZOON	GEEZAHS	IODIZES
BUZZIER	DAZZLED	EROTIZE	GEEZERS	IONIZED
BUZZING	DAZZLER	EVZONES	GENIZAH	IONIZER
BUZZWIG	DAZZLES	FAHLERZ	GENIZOT	IONIZES
BYZANTS	DEFROZE	FANZINE	GHAZALS	IRIDIZE
CABEZON	DEFUZED	FAZENDA	GHAZELS	IRONIZE
CADENZA	DEFUZES	FEAZING	GHAZIES	ISOZYME
CALZONE	DEGLAZE	FEEZING	GINZOES	ITEMIZE
CALZONI	DENIZEN	FILAZER	GIZZARD	IZZARDS
CANZONA	DEUTZIA	FIZGIGS	GIZZENS	JACUZZI
CANZONE	DEZINCS	FIZZENS	GLAZERS	JANIZAR
CANZONI	DIALYZE	FIZZERS	GLAZIER	JAZZBOS
CAPIZES	DIARIZE	FIZZGIG	GLAZILY	JAZZERS
CAPSIZE	DIAZINE	FIZZIER	GLAZING	JAZZIER
CAZIQUE	DIAZINS	FIZZING	GLITZED	JAZZILY
CEAZING	DIAZOES	FIZZLED	GLITZES	JAZZING
CERVEZA	DIAZOLE	FIZZLES	GLOZING	JAZZMAN

JAZZMEN	MEZUZAH	PAZZAZZ	RHIZOMA	SNEEZES
JEZAILS	MEZUZAS	PEAZING	RHIZOME	SNOOZED
JEZEBEL	MEZUZOT	PECTIZE	RHIZOPI	SNOOZER
KAIZENS	MIDSIZE	PEIZING	RIOTIZE	SNOOZES
KARZIES	MILTZES	PEPTIZE	RITZIER	SNOOZLE
KHAZENS	MITZVAH	PEZANTS	RITZILY	SNUZZLE
KIBBITZ	MIZMAZE	PHEAZAR	RIZARDS	SOVKHOZ
KIBBUTZ	MIZUNAS	PHEEZED	RIZZARS	SOYUZES
KLEZMER	MIZZENS	PHEEZES	RIZZART	SOZINES
KLUTZES	MIZZLED	PHIZOGS	RIZZERS	SOZZLED
KOLHOZY	MIZZLES	PHIZZES	RIZZORS	SOZZLES
KOLKHOZ	MOMZERS	PIAZZAS	ROMANZA	SPATZLE
KOLKOZY	MOZETTA	PIZAZZY	RONZERS	SPAZZED
KRANZES	MOZETTE	PIZZAZZ	ROZELLE	SPAZZES
KREUZER	MOZZIES	PIZZLES	ROZETED	SPITZES
KUNZITE	MOZZLES	PLOTZED	ROZITED	SPREAZE
KWANZAS	MUEZZIN	PLOTZES	ROZZERS	SPREEZE
KYANIZE	MUZHIKS	PODZOLS	SAZERAC	SPULZIE
LAICIZE	MUZJIKS	POETIZE	SAZHENS	SQUEEZE
LAIRIZE	MUZZIER	POLYZOA	SCAZONS	SQUEEZY
LAYDEEZ	MUZZILY	POTZERS	SCHANZE	STANZAS
LAZARET	MUZZING	POZOLES	SCHERZI	STANZES
LAZIEST	MUZZLED	POZZIES	SCHERZO	STANZOS
LAZOING	MUZZLER	PRENZIE	SCHIZOS	STARETZ
LAZULIS	MUZZLES	PRETZEL	SCHIZZY	STYLIZE
LAZYING	MYTHIZE	PREZZIE	SCHMALZ	SUBZERO
LAZYISH	MZUNGUS	PRIZERS	SCHMELZ	SUBZONE
LEZZIES	NEEZING	PRIZING	SCHMOOZ	SWAZZLE
LIONIZE	NETIZEN	PUTZING	SCHNOZZ	SWIZZED
LIZARDS	NONZERO	PUZZELS	SCOZZAS	SWIZZES
LIZZIES	NOZZERS	PUZZLED	SCRUZED	SWIZZLE
LOZELLS	NOZZLES	PUZZLER	SCRUZES	SWOZZLE
LOZENGE	NUDZHED	PUZZLES	SCUZZES	SYZYGAL
LOZENGY	NUDZHES	PZAZZES	SEAZING	TAILZIE
LUZERNS	NUZZERS	QUARTZY	SEIZERS	TARZANS
MACHZOR	NUZZLED	QUETZAL	SEIZING	TEAZELS
MADZOON	NUZZLER	QUEZALS	SEIZINS	TEAZING
MAHZORS	NUZZLES	QUINZES	SEIZORS	TEAZLED
MAMZERS	NYANZAS	QUIZZED	SEIZURE	TEAZLES
MATZAHS	OBELIZE	QUIZZER	SELTZER	TENDENZ
MATZOHS	ODORIZE	QUIZZES	SHEGETZ	TENZONS
MATZOON	ODZOOKS	RANZELS	SHIATZU	THIAZIN
MATZOTH	OOZIEST	RAZORED	SHMALTZ	THIAZOL
MAZARDS	ORGANZA	RAZURES	SHMOOZE	TIZZIES
MAZEDLY	OUTGAZE	RAZZIAS	SHOWBIZ	TOAZING
MAZEFUL	OUTSIZE	RAZZING	SIAMEZE	TOLZEYS
MAZHBIS	OXAZINE	RAZZLES	SIZABLE	TOPAZES
MAZIEST	OXIDIZE	REALIZE	SIZABLY	TOUZIER
MAZOUTS	OZAENAS	REBOZOS	SIZEISM	TOUZING
MAZUMAS	OZALIDS	REFROZE	SIZEIST	TOUZLED
MAZURKA	OZONATE	REGLAZE	SIZIEST	TOUZLES
MAZZARD	OZONIDE	REPRIZE	SIZINGS	TOWZIER
MEAZELS	OZONISE	RESEIZE	SIZISMS	TOWZING
MENAZON	OZONIZE	RESIZED	SIZISTS	TRAPEZE
MESTIZA	OZONOUS	RESIZES	SIZZLED	TRIAZIN
MESTIZO	PALAZZI	REZEROS	SIZZLER	TRIZONE
METAZOA	PALAZZO	REZONED	SIZZLES	TUILZIE
MEZAILS	PANZERS	REZONES	SLEAZES	TWEEZED
MEZCALS	PARAZOA	RHIZINE	SNEEZED	TWEEZER
MEZQUIT	PATZERS	RHIZOID	SNEEZER	TWEEZES

TWIZZLE	WIZARDS	ZEALANT	ZINCIER	ZONULES
TZADDIK	WIZENED	ZEALFUL	ZINCIFY	ZONULET
TZADDIQ	WIZIERS	ZEALOTS	ZINCING	ZONURES
TZARDOM	WIZZENS	ZEALOUS	ZINCITE	ZOOECIA
TZARINA	WOOTZES	ZEATINS	ZINCKED	ZOOGAMY
TZARISM	WOOZIER	ZEBECKS	ZINCODE	ZOOGENY
TZARIST	WOOZILY	ZEBRAIC	ZINCOID	ZOOGLEA
TZETSES	WRIZLED	ZEBRANO	ZINCOUS	ZOOGONY
TZETZES	WURZELS	ZEBRASS	ZINGANI	ZOOIDAL
TZIGANE	WUZZLED	ZEBRINA	ZINGANO	ZOOIEST
TZIGANY	WUZZLES	ZEBRINE	ZINGARA	ZOOLITE
TZIMMES	ZABETAS	ZEBROID	ZINGARE	ZOOLITH
TZITZIS	ZABTIEH	ZEBRULA	ZINGARI	ZOOLOGY
TZITZIT	ZACATON	ZEBRULE	ZINGARO	ZOOMING
UMFAZIS	ZADDICK	ZECCHIN	ZINGELS	ZOONING
UNCRAZY	ZADDIKS	ZECHINS	ZINGERS	ZOONITE
UNFAZED	ZAFFARS	ZEDOARY	ZINGIER	ZOONOMY
UNFROZE	ZAFFERS	ZELANTS	ZINGING	ZOOPERY
UNISIZE	ZAFFIRS	ZELATOR	ZINKIER	ZOOTAXY
UNITIZE	ZAFFRES	ZELKOVA	ZINKIFY	ZOOTIER
UNRAZED	ZAGGING	ZEMSTVA	ZINKING	ZOOTOMY
UNSIZED	ZAIKAIS	ZEMSTVO	ZINNIAS	ZOOTYPE
UNZONED	ZAITECH	ZENAIDA	ZIPLESS	ZOOZOOS
UPGAZED	ZAKUSKA	ZENANAS	ZIPLOCK	ZORBING
UPGAZES	ZAKUSKI	ZENDIKS	ZIPPERS	ZORGITE
UPSIZED	ZAMANGS	ZENITHS	ZIPPIER	ZORILLA
UPSIZES	ZAMARRA	ZEOLITE	ZIPPING	ZORILLE
UTILIZE	ZAMARRO	ZEPHYRS	ZIRCONS	ZORILLO
VIZARDS	ZAMBUCK	ZEPPOLE	ZITHERN	ZORINOS
VIZIERS	ZAMBUKS	ZEPPOLI	ZITHERS	ZOSTERS
VIZORED	ZAMOUSE	ZEREBAS	ZIZANIA	ZOUAVES
VIZSLAS	ZAMPONE	ZERIBAS	ZIZZING	ZOYSIAS
VIZYING	ZAMPONI	ZEROING	ZIZZLED	ZUFFOLI
VIZZIED	ZANANAS	ZESTERS	ZIZZLES	ZUFFOLO
VIZZIES	ZANDERS	ZESTFUL	ZLOTIES	ZYDECOS
WALTZED	ZANELLA	ZESTIER	ZLOTYCH	ZYGOMAS
WALTZER	ZANIEST	ZESTILY	ZOARIAL	ZYGOSES
WALTZES	ZANJERO	ZESTING	ZOARIUM	ZYGOSIS
WANZING	ZANYING	ZETETIC	ZOCALOS	ZYGOTES
WARZONE	ZANYISH	ZEUGMAS	ZOCCOLO	ZYGOTIC
WAZZOCK	ZANYISM	ZEUXITE	ZODIACS	ZYMASES
WEAZAND	ZAPATEO	ZIBETHS	ZOECIUM	ZYMITES
WEAZENS	ZAPPERS	ZIFFIUS	ZOEFORM	ZYMOGEN
WEIZING	ZAPPIER	ZIGANKA	ZOISITE	ZYMOMES
WEZANDS	ZAPPING	ZIGGING	ZOMBIES	ZYMOSAN
WHAIZLE	ZAPTIAH	ZIGZAGS	ZOMBIFY	ZYMOSES
WHEEZED	ZAPTIEH	ZIKURAT	ZONALLY	ZYMOSIS
WHEEZER	ZARAPES	ZILCHES	ZONATED	ZYMOTIC
WHEEZES	ZAREBAS	ZILLAHS	ZONINGS	ZYMURGY
WHEEZLE	ZAREEBA	ZILLION	ZONKING	ZYTHUMS
WHIZZED	ZARIBAS	ZIMMERS	ZONULAE	ZYZZYVA
WHIZZER	ZARNECS	ZIMOCCA	ZONULAR	
WHIZZES	ZARNICH	ZINCATE	ZONULAS	

Eight-letter words

ACTIVIZE	AGATIZED	AGENIZES	AGONIZES	AGUIZING
ADONIZED	AGATIZES	AGNIZING	AGRIZING	ALBITIZE
ADONIZES	AGENIZED	AGONIZED	AGRYZING	ALBIZIAS

ALBIZZIA	BAPTIZES	BROMIZED	COGNIZER	DISPRIZE
ALCAZARS	BAROMETZ	BROMIZES	COGNIZES	DISSEIZE
ALCORZAS	BARTIZAN	BRONZERS	COLONIZE	DITZIEST
ALGUAZIL	BAZAZZES	BRONZIER	COLORIZE	DIVINIZE
ALIZARIN	BAZOOKAS	BRONZIFY	COMPRIZE	DIZENING
ALIZARIS	BAZOUKIS	BRONZING	COZENAGE	DIZYGOUS
ALKALIZE	BEDAZING	BRONZITE	COZENERS	DIZZARDS
ALLOZYME	BEDAZZLE	BRUILZIE	COZENING	DIZZIEST
ALTEZZAS	BEDIZENS	BRULZIES	COZINESS	DIZZYING
AMAZEDLY	BEGAZING	BRUNIZEM	CRAZIEST	DOCKIZED
AMORTIZE	BEJEEZUS	BRYOZOAN	CREDENZA	DOCKIZES
ANALYZED	BEMUZZLE	BULLDOZE	CREOLIZE	DOPIAZAS
ANALYZER	BENZENES	BUMBAZED	CREUTZER	DORIZING
ANALYZES	BENZIDIN	BUMBAZES	CROZIERS	DOUZEPER
ANNALIZE	BENZINES	BURDIZZO	CROZZLED	DOWNSIZE
ANODIZED	BENZOATE	BUZKASHI	CRUIZIES	DOWNZONE
ANODIZES	BENZOINS	BUZZARDS	CRUZADOS	DOZENING
ANTICIZE	BENZOLES	BUZZCUTS	CRUZEIRO	DOZENTHS
APHETIZE	BENZOYLS	BUZZIEST	CURARIZE	DOZINESS
APHORIZE	BENZYLIC	BUZZINGS	CUTINIZE	DRIZZLED
APPETIZE	BENZYLIC	BUZZWIGS	CYANIZED	DRIZZLES
APPRIZED	BEZAZZES	BUZZWORD	CYANIZES	DUALIZED
APPRIZER	BEZIQUES	CABEZONE	CYCLIZED	DUALIZES
APPRIZES	BEZONIAN	CABEZONS	CYCLIZES	DYNAMIZE
ARABIZED	BEZZANTS	CADENZAS	CZARDOMS	EBENEZER
ARABIZES	BEZZLING	CALABAZA	CZAREVNA	EBIONIZE
ARBORIZE	BITESIZE	CALORIZE	CZARINAS	EBONIZED
ARCHAIZE	BIZARRES	CALZONES	CZARISMS	EBONIZES
ARMOZEEN	BIZARROS	CANALIZE	CZARISTS	ECHOIZED
ARMOZINE	BIZAZZES	CANONIZE	CZARITSA	ECHOIZES
ARRHIZAL	BIZCACHA	CANZONAS	CZARITZA	ECTOZOAN
ASSIZERS	BIZNAGAS	CANZONES	DAIDZEIN	ECTOZOIC
ASSIZING	BLAZERED	CANZONET	DAMOZELS	ECTOZOON
ATHEIZED	BLAZONED	CAPONIZE	DANAZOLS	EGOTIZED
ATHEIZES	BLAZONER	CAPSIZAL	DAZZLERS	EGOTIZES
ATHETIZE	BLAZONRY	CAPSIZED	DAZZLING	ELEGIZED
ATMOLYZE	BLINTZES	CAPSIZES	DEFREEZE	ELEGIZES
ATOMIZED	BLITZERS	CATALYZE	DEFROZEN	EMBEZZLE
ATOMIZER	BLITZING	CAZIQUES	DEFUZING	EMBLAZED
ATOMIZES	BLIZZARD	CENOZOIC	DEGLAZED	EMBLAZER
ATRAZINE	BLOWZIER	CERVEZAS	DEGLAZES	EMBLAZES
ATTICIZE	BLOWZILY	CHALAZAE	DEIONIZE	EMBLAZON
AUTOLYZE	BONANZAS	CHALAZAL	DEMONIZE	EMBOLIZE
AVIANIZE	BOOZIEST	CHALAZAS	DENAZIFY	EMPERIZE
AZIMUTHS	BOOZINGS	CHALAZIA	DENIZENS	EMPRIZES
AZOTEMIA	BORAZONS	CHAZANIM	DEPUTIZE	ENDOZOIC
AZOTEMIC	BOTANIZE	CHAZZANS	DEUTZIAS	ENDOZOON
AZOTISED	BOUZOUKI	CHAZZENS	DEZINCED	ENERGIZE
AZOTISES	BOZZETTI	CHINTZES	DIALYZED	ENFREEZE
AZOTIZED	BOZZETTO	CHIZZING	DIALYZER	ENFROZEN
AZOTIZES	BRAZENED	CHORIZOS	DIALYZES	ENTOZOAL
AZOTURIA	BRAZENLY	CHROMIZE	DIARIZED	ENTOZOAN
AZULEJOS	BRAZENRY	CHUTZPAH	DIARIZES	ENTOZOIC
AZURINES	BRAZIERS	CHUTZPAS	DIAZEPAM	ENTOZOON
AZURITES	BRAZIERY	CITIZENS	DIAZINES	ENZONING
AZYGOSES	BRAZILIN	CIVILIZE	DIAZINON	ENZOOTIC
AZYMITES	BREEZIER	COALIZED	DIAZOLES	EPAZOTES
BANALIZE	BREEZILY	COALIZES	DIGITIZE	EPIZOANS
BAPTIZED	BREEZING	COENZYME	DIMERIZE	EPIZOISM
BAPTIZER	BRITZKAS	COGNIZED	DIPLOZOA	EPIZOITE

EPIZOOTY	FUZZIEST	HEROIZED	KLEZMERS	MESTIZAS
EQUALIZE	FUZZLING	HEROIZES	KLUTZIER	MESTIZOS
ERGOTIZE	FUZZTONE	HIZZONER	KOLHOZES	METALIZE
EROTIZED	GADZOOKS	HOACTZIN	KOLKHOZY	METAZOAL
EROTIZES	GALLIZED	HOATZINS	KOLKOZES	METAZOAN
ERSATZES	GALLIZES	HOLOZOIC	KRANTZES	METAZOIC
ETERNIZE	GARBANZO	HOMINIZE	KREUTZER	METAZOON
ETHERIZE	GAUZIEST	HORIZONS	KREUZERS	METRAZOL
ETHICIZE	GAZABOES	HOWITZER	KUNZITES	MEZEREON
EULOGIZE	GAZANIAS	HUMANIZE	KUVASZOK	MEZEREUM
EUPHUIZE	GAZEBOES	HUTZPAHS	KYANIZED	MEZQUITE
EXAHERTZ	GAZELLES	HUZZAHED	KYANIZES	MEZQUITS
EXORCIZE	GAZEMENT	HUZZAING	LAICIZED	MEZUZAHS
FABULIZE	GAZETTED	HYDROZOA	LAICIZES	MEZUZOTH
FANZINES	GAZETTES	HYLOZOIC	LAIRIZED	MIDSIZED
FARADIZE	GAZOGENE	ICONIZED	LAIRIZES	MINIMIZE
FAZENDAS	GAZOOKAS	ICONIZES	LATERIZE	MISPRIZE
FEMINAZI	GAZPACHO	IDEALIZE	LATINIZE	MITZVAHS
FEMINIZE	GAZUMPED	IDOLIZED	LAZARETS	MITZVOTH
FIBERIZE	GAZUMPER	IDOLIZER	LAZINESS	MIZMAZES
FILAZERS	GAZUNDER	IDOLIZES	LAZULITE	MIZZLIER
FINALIZE	GENIZAHS	IMBLAZED	LAZURITE	MIZZLING
FIZZGIGS	GENIZOTH	IMBLAZES	LEGALIZE	MOBILIZE
FIZZIEST	GIZZARDS	IMMUNIZE	LIONIZED	MOMZERIM
FIZZINGS	GIZZENED	INFAMIZE	LIONIZER	MONAZITE
FIZZLING	GLAZIERS	IODIZERS	LIONIZES	MONETIZE
FLOOZIES	GLAZIERY	IODIZING	LOCALIZE	MORALIZE
FLUIDIZE	GLAZIEST	IONIZERS	LOGICIZE	MOTORIZE
FOCALIZE	GLAZINGS	IONIZING	LOZENGED	MOZETTAS
FOOZLERS	GLITZIER	IRIDIZED	LOZENGES	MOZZETTA
FOOZLING	GLITZILY	IRIDIZES	LYRICIZE	MOZZETTE
FORZANDI	GLITZING	IRONIZED	LYSOZYME	MUEZZINS
FORZANDO	GLOZINGS	IRONIZES	MACARIZE	MUZZIEST
FORZATOS	GOHONZON	ISOZYMES	MACHZORS	MUZZLERS
FOZINESS	GOLDSIZE	ISOZYMIC	MADERIZE	MUZZLING
FRANCIZE	GRAECIZE	ITEMIZED	MADZOONS	MYTHIZED
FRANZIER	GRAZABLE	ITEMIZER	MAGAZINE	MYTHIZES
FRAWZEYS	GRAZIERS	ITEMIZES	MAHZORIM	NASALIZE
FRAZZLED	GRAZINGS	IZVESTIA	MAMZERIM	NAZIFIED
FRAZZLES	GRAZIOSO	JACUZZIS	MANZELLO	NAZIFIES
FREEZERS	GRECIZED	JANIZARS	MARZIPAN	NEBULIZE
FREEZING	GRECIZES	JANIZARY	MATZOONS	NETIZENS
FRENZIED	GRIZZLED	JAPANIZE	MAXIMIZE	NIZAMATE
FRENZIES	GRIZZLER	JAROVIZE	MAZAEDIA	NODALIZE
FRENZILY	GRIZZLES	JAZERANT	MAZARINE	NOMADIZE
FRIEZING	GUEREZAS	JAZZIEST	MAZELIKE	NOTARIZE
FRIZETTE	GUZZLERS	JAZZLIKE	MAZELTOV	NOVELIZE
FRIZZERS	GUZZLING	JEZEBELS	MAZEMENT	NUDZHING
FRIZZIER	HALAZONE	JUMBOIZE	MAZINESS	NUZZLERS
FRIZZIES	HALUTZIM	KAMEEZES	MAZOURKA	NUZZLING
FRIZZILY	HAZARDED	KAMIKAZE	MAZURKAS	OBELIZED
FRIZZING	HAZARDER	KAZACHKI	MAZZARDS	OBELIZES
FRIZZLED	HAZARDRY	KAZACHOK	MECHITZA	ODORIZED
FRIZZLER	HAZELHEN	KAZATSKI	MELANIZE	ODORIZES
FRIZZLES	HAZELNUT	KAZATSKY	MELODIZE	OOZINESS
FROUZIER	HAZINESS	KAZATZKA	MEMORIZE	OPALIZED
FROWZIER	HAZZANIM	KHAZENIM	MENAZONS	OPSONIZE
FROWZILY	HEBRAIZE	KIBITZED	MESOZOAN	OPTIMIZE
FROZENLY	HEMOLYZE	KIBITZER	MESOZOIC	ORGANIZE
FURZIEST	HEPATIZE	KIBITZES	MESPRIZE	ORGANZAS

OUTBLAZE	POLYZOIC	RITZIEST	SIZINESS	SUBITIZE
OUTGAZED	POLYZOON	RIVALIZE	SIZZLERS	SUBSIZAR
OUTGAZES	POZZOLAN	RIZZARED	SIZZLING	SUBZONAL
OUTPRIZE	PREFROZE	RIZZARTS	SLEAZIER	SUBZONES
OUTSIZED	PRETZELS	RIZZERED	SLEAZILY	SURPRIZE
OUTSIZES	PREZZIES	RIZZORED	SLEAZOID	SUZERAIN
OVERSIZE	PRIZABLE	ROBOTIZE	SLEEZIER	SWAZZIES
OVERZEAL	PRIZEMAN	ROMANIZE	SMORZATO	SWIZZING
OXAZEPAM	PRIZEMEN	ROMANZAS	SNAZZIER	SWIZZLED
OXAZINES	PROTOZOA	ROYALIZE	SNAZZILY	SWIZZLER
OXIDIZED	PTYALIZE	ROZELLES	SNEEZERS	SWIZZLES
OXIDIZER	PUZZLERS	ROZETING	SNEEZIER	SWOZZLES
OXIDIZES	PUZZLING	ROZITING	SNEEZING	SYZYGIAL
OZONATED	PYRAZOLE	RURALIZE	SNOOZERS	SYZYGIES
OZONATES	PYRITIZE	SALINIZE	SNOOZIER	TAILZIES
OZONIDES	PYROLIZE	SAMIZDAT	SNOOZING	TEAZELED
OZONISED	PYROLYZE	SANITIZE	SNOOZLED	TEAZLING
OZONISER	QUANTIZE	SARRAZIN	SNOOZLES	TERRAZZO
OZONISES	QUARTZES	SATIRIZE	SNUZZLED	TERZETTA
OZONIZED	QUATORZE	SAZERACS	SNUZZLES	TERZETTI
OZONIZER	QUAZZIER	SCHANTZE	SOBERIZE	TERZETTO
OZONIZES	QUEAZIER	SCHANZES	SODOMIZE	TETANIZE
PAGANIZE	QUETZALS	SCHERZOS	SOLARIZE	THEORIZE
PALAZZOS	QUEZALES	SCHIZIER	SOLECIZE	THIAZIDE
PAPALIZE	QUIZZERS	SCHIZOID	SOLONETZ	THIAZINE
PARALYZE	QUIZZERY	SCHIZONT	SORORIZE	THIAZINS
PARAZOAN	QUIZZIFY	SCHMALTZ	SOVKHOZY	THIAZOLE
PARAZOON	QUIZZING	SCHMALZY	SOZZLIER	THIAZOLS
PARTIZAN	RACEMIZE	SCHMELZE	SOZZLING	TIZWASES
PATINIZE	RAZEEING	SCHMOOZE	SPAETZLE	TOPAZINE
PAZAZZES	RAZMATAZ	SCHMOOZY	SPATZLES	TOTALIZE
PECTIZED	RAZORING	SCHNOZES	SPAZZING	TOUZIEST
PECTIZES	REALIZED	SCRUZING	SPELTZES	TOUZLING
PENALIZE	REALIZER	SCUZZIER	SPETSNAZ	TOWZIEST
PEPTIZED	REALIZES	SEIZABLE	SPETZNAZ	TRAPEZED
PEPTIZER	REFREEZE	SEIZINGS	SPOROZOA	TRAPEZES
PEPTIZES	REFROZEN	SEIZURES	SPREAZED	TRAPEZIA
PETUNTZE	REGLAZED	SELTZERS	SPREAZES	TRAPEZII
PEZIZOID	REGLAZES	SFORZATI	SPREEZED	TRIAZINE
PHEAZARS	REGULIZE	SFORZATO	SPREEZES	TRIAZINS
PHEEZING	RENDZINA	SHIATZUS	SPRITZED	TRIAZOLE
PHENAZIN	REPRIZED	SHKOTZIM	SPRITZER	TRISTEZA
PIAZZIAN	REPRIZES	SHMALTZY	SPRITZES	TRIZONAL
PINTSIZE	RESEIZED	SHMOOZED	SPRITZIG	TRIZONES
PIROZHKI	RESEIZES	SHMOOZES	SPUILZIE	TSARITZA
PIROZHOK	RESINIZE	SHVARTZE	SPULZIED	TUILZIED
PIZAZZES	RESIZING	SIAMEZED	SPULZIES	TUILZIES
PIZZAZES	REZEROED	SIAMEZES	SQUEEZED	TUTORIZE
PIZZAZZY	REZEROES	SIEROZEM	SQUEEZER	TWEEZERS
PIZZELLE	REZONING	SIMAZINE	SQUEEZES	TWEEZING
PIZZERIA	RHIZINES	SIMILIZE	SQUIZZES	TWIZZLED
PLOTZING	RHIZOBIA	SIMONIZE	STANZAED	TWIZZLES
PODZOLIC	RHIZOIDS	SINICIZE	STANZAIC	TZADDIKS
POETIZED	RHIZOMES	SIRENIZE	STANZOES	TZADDIQS
POETIZER	RHIZOMIC	SIRONIZE	STARGAZE	TZARDOMS
POETIZES	RHIZOPOD	SITZMARK	STRELITZ	TZAREVNA
POLARIZE	RHIZOPUS	SIZEABLE	STYLIZED	TZARINAS
POLEMIZE	RIBOZYME	SIZEABLY	STYLIZER	TZARISMS
POLONIZE	RIGIDIZE	SIZEISMS	STYLIZES	TZARISTS
POLYZOAN	RIOTIZES	SIZEISTS	SUBERIZE	TZARITZA

TZATZIKI	WHAIZLES	ZARZUELA	ZINGIBER	ZOONOSES
TZIGANES	WHEEZERS	ZASTRUGA	ZINGIEST	ZOONOSIS
TZITZITH	WHEEZIER	ZASTRUGI	ZINKIEST	ZOONOTIC
UNAMAZED	WHEEZILY	ZEALANTS	ZIPPERED	ZOOPATHY
UNDAZZLE	WHEEZING	ZEALLESS	ZIPPIEST	ZOOPERAL
UNFREEZE	WHEEZLED	ZEALOTRY	ZIRCALOY	ZOOPHAGY
UNFROZEN	WHEEZLES	ZEBRANOS	ZIRCONIA	ZOOPHILE
UNGAZING	WHIZBANG	ZEBRINAS	ZIRCONIC	ZOOPHILY
UNGLAZED	WHIZZERS	ZEBRINES	ZITHERNS	ZOOPHOBE
UNGRAZED	WHIZZIER	ZEBRINNY	ZIZANIAS	ZOOPHORI
UNIONIZE	WHIZZING	ZEBRULAS	ZIZYPHUS	ZOOPHYTE
UNITIZED	WIZARDLY	ZEBRULES	ZIZZLING	ZOOSCOPY
UNITIZER	WIZARDRY	ZECCHINE	ZOCCOLOS	ZOOSPERM
UNITIZES	WIZENING	ZECCHINI	ZODIACAL	ZOOSPORE
UNMUZZLE	WOMANIZE	ZECCHINO	ZOETROPE	ZOOTHOME
UNPRIZED	WOOZIEST	ZECCHINS	ZOIATRIA	ZOOTIEST
UNPUZZLE	WURTZITE	ZELATORS	ZOISITES	ZOOTOMIC
UNSEIZED	WUZZLING	ZELATRIX	ZOMBIISM	ZOOTOXIC
UNVIZARD	YAHRZEIT	ZELKOVAS	ZOMBORUK	ZOOTOXIN
UNZIPPED	YOKOZUNA	ZEMINDAR	ZONATION	ZOOTROPE
UPGAZING	ZABAIONE	ZEMSTVOS	ZONELESS	ZOOTYPES
UPSIZING	ZABAJONE	ZENAIDAS	ZONETIME	ZOOTYPIC
URBANIZE	ZABTIEHS	ZENITHAL	ZONULETS	ZOPILOTE
UTILIZED	ZACATONS	ZEOLITES	ZOOBLAST	ZORBINGS
UTILIZER	ZADDIKIM	ZEOLITIC	ZOOCHORE	ZORGITES
UTILIZES	ZAIBATSU	ZEPPELIN	ZOOCHORY	ZORILLAS
VALORIZE	ZAITECHS	ZEPPOLES	ZOOCYTIA	ZORILLES
VAPORIZE	ZAKOUSKA	ZERUMBET	ZOOECIUM	ZORILLOS
VELARIZE	ZAKOUSKI	ZESTIEST	ZOOGENIC	ZUCCHINI
VIRILIZE	ZAMARRAS	ZESTLESS	ZOOGLEAE	ZUCHETTA
VITALIZE	ZAMARROS	ZETETICS	ZOOGLEAL	ZUCHETTO
VIZAMENT	ZAMBOMBA	ZEUXITES	ZOOGLEAS	ZUGZWANG
VIZARDED	ZAMBUCKS	ZIBELINE	ZOOGLOEA	ZWIEBACK
VIZCACHA	ZAMINDAR	ZIGANKAS	ZOOGRAFT	ZYGAENID
VIZIRATE	ZAMOUSES	ZIGGURAT	ZOOLATER	ZYGANTRA
VIZIRIAL	ZAMPOGNA	ZIGZAGGY	ZOOLATRY	ZYGODONT
VIZORING	ZAMZAWED	ZIKKURAT	ZOOLITES	ZYGOMATA
VOCALIZE	ZANELLAS	ZIKURATS	ZOOLITHS	ZYGOSITY
VOLUMIZE	ZANINESS	ZILLIONS	ZOOLITIC	ZYGOTENE
VOWELIZE	ZANJEROS	ZIMOCCAS	ZOOLOGIC	ZYLONITE
VUVUZELA	ZANYISMS	ZINCATES	ZOOMANCY	ZYMOGENE
WALTZERS	ZAPATEOS	ZINCIEST	ZOOMANIA	ZYMOGENS
WALTZING	ZAPPIEST	ZINCITES	ZOOMETRY	ZYMOGRAM
WARZONES	ZAPTIAHS	ZINCKIER	ZOOMORPH	ZYMOLOGY
WAZZOCKS	ZAPTIEHS	ZINCKIFY	ZOONITES	ZYMOSANS
WEAZANDS	ZARATITE	ZINCKING	ZOONITIC	ZYMOTICS
WEAZENED	ZAREEBAS	ZINCODES	ZOONOMIA	ZYZZYVAS
WHAIZLED	ZARNICHS	ZINDABAD	ZOONOMIC	

Chapter 3: Word Families

by Allan Simmons

You wouldn't be reading this book if you weren't interested in learning some useful word for Scrabble! But not everyone finds it easy nor has the patience to learn tedious lists of words. I have always found it ideal to learn words in small manageable sets that are going to have a high yield on the Scrabble board. To be manageable a list has to be fairly short and restricted to a single page. To have a high yield the list has to focus on words that are likely to crop up during play.

It was with these criteria in mind that I first created the concept of word families – a sort of mind-map of words centred around a short root word. Two- and three-letter words regularly appear on the board so showing how those words can be developed is very relevant. And because all the words in the 'family' contain the embedded root word, clumps of words with similar patterns naturally occur and these can be grouped together for convenient learning. Through careful arrangement of family members with shorter words near the centre and longer words further away, it is also possible to reflect the natural extension of the shorter words into longer words (hooks). Generally, I try to show the words that start with the root word flowing to the right of each diagram and those that contain the root word flowing to the left, but this will always depend on the number of words in the family that start or end with the root word. The overall aim is to provide an aesthetically pleasing and useful arrangement of words of relevance to the game.

In selecting the best words to use as root words I have analysed the two letter words to ascertain those that produce the more useful and pleasing families. For example, there is little point in using the two-letter word IT because it will generate far too many words, and the 'IT' within longer words will not be a significant component of most of those words. Whereas a root word with a higher-scoring tile or an unusual combination of two-letters (eg KO, ZO, IO) generate shorter lists where the two-letter sequence for the most part remains a key component of the family members.

The maximum length of words selected for each family is mostly five, or sometimes six depending on the volume of words generated in each case. In order to keep the families uncluttered all -S plurals of words have been excluded. However, so that the reader can easily identify those that do and do not take an -S extension, an asterisk (*) follows every word that can NOT be extended by -S. That does not mean that such words cannot be pluralized because in some cases the plural may be something other than an -S. Inflected forms ending in -ES have been included, providing they are within the length criteria.

I trust you find the word families of great use and interest to improve your Scrabble vocabulary. They've also been fun to compile and I'm sure I've learned one or two new words in the process as well. You might like to try and create further families yourself, making use of the extensive lists in this book to find the appropriate words. Happy Families!

AARTI
AALII

AARGH*
AARRGH*

FAAN*
BAAL KAAL* PAAL TAAL

AAHED*

MAAED* CAAED* BAAED*

AAL

AAH

MAA CAA BAA FAA

JAAP WAAC

BAAS* KAAS* MAAS*

HAAF HAAR MAAR

NAAM NAAN

ALAAP PRAAM PLAAS*

DWAAL CRAAL GRAAL KRAAL

BRAAI KIAAT

LAARI MAARE*

TAATA KAAMA

* = word does not take an -s extension

PSOAE *
STOAE *

CAESE *

CAECA *
FAENA

ANSAE *
ANTAE *

RIMAE *
MINAE *
VITAE *

LAEVO *

PAEAN
PAEON

AEON

AESIR *

AERO
AERY *

FAERY *

AECIA *
AERIE

AEDES *
AEGIS *

TUBAE *
PUPAE *

ISNAE *
ULNAE *
URSAE *

AQUAE *
ZOEAE *

VIAE *
UVAE *

FAE *

SAE *

ALAE *

AESC *

CLAES *

BLAER *
SPAER *
SPAED *

SCRAE
STRAE
THRAE *

SETAE *
TELAE *
VENAE *

NAEVE
NAEVI

VAE

NAE *
MAE

* A₁ E₁ *

SPAE
SLAE
BLAE
BRAE
FRAE *
THAE *
TWAE *
WHAE *

AREAE *
AURAE *

KANAE *

ZOAEA

URAEI *

CYMAE *
GYNAE *

ZONAE
COMAE
COXAE
NOVAE
VOLAE

ALGAE *
BIGAE *
NUGAE *
RUGAE *
TOGAE *

KAED *
TAED *

KAE
TAE
DAE
GAE
HAE

WAE *
YAE *

BAAED *
CAAED *
MAAED *

HOAED *
TEAED *

LAER

GAED *
HAED *

GAEN *
HAEN *
HAEM
HAET

BAEL
TAEL

OLPAE *

POTAE *
PORAE *
PARAE *
MORAE *
MARAE

* = word does not take an -s extension

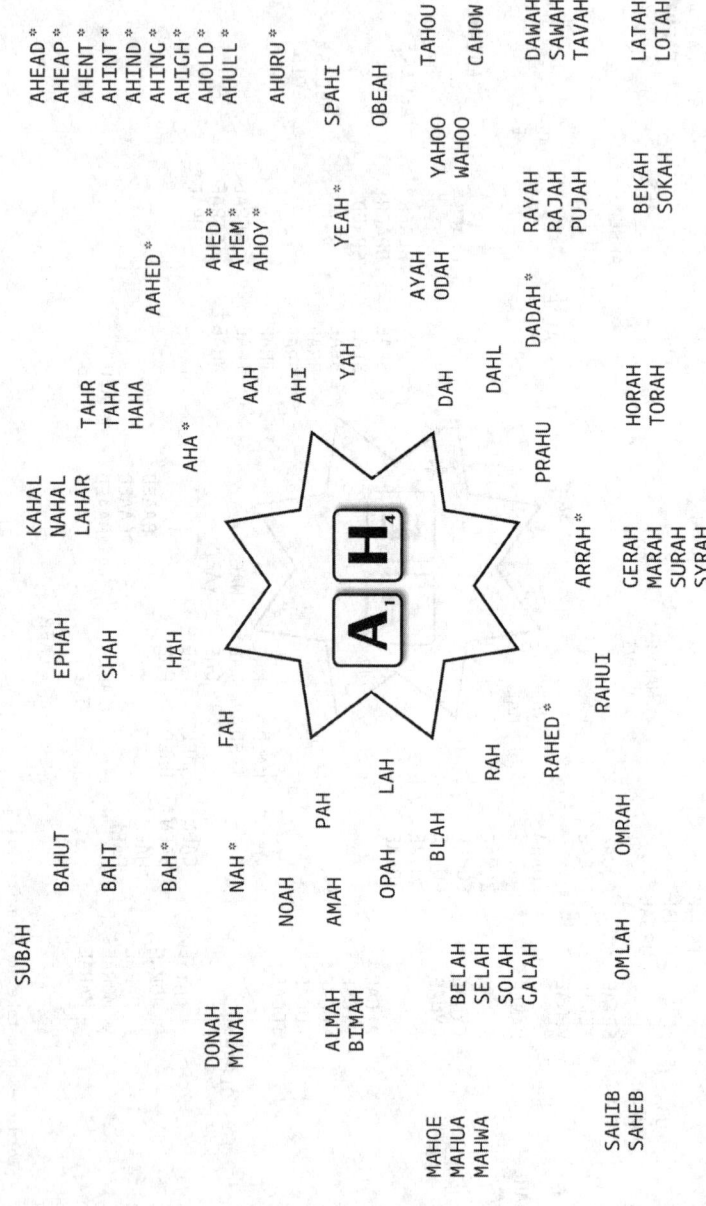

AHEAD*
AHEAP*
AHENT*
AHINT*
AHIND*
AHING*
AHIGH*
AHOLD*
AHULL*

AHURU*

SPAHI
OBEAH

TAHOU
CAHOW

DAWAH
SAWAH
TAVAH

LATAH
LOTAH

AAHED*

AHED*
AHEM*
AHOY*

YAHOO
WAHOO

RAYAH
RAJAH
PUJAH

BEKAH
SOKAH

TAHR
TAHA
HAHA

AHA*

YEAH*

AYAH
ODAH

AAH
AHI

YAH

DAH
DAHL

DADAH*

HORAH
TORAH

KAHAL
NAHAL
LAHAR

PRAHU

ARRAH*

GERAH
MARAH
SURAH
SYRAH

EPHAH
SHAH
HAH

RAHUI

A₁ H₄

SUBAH

BAHUT
BAHT
BAH*

NAH*
FAH

RAHED*
RAH

OMRAH

DONAH
MYNAH

NOAH

ALMAH
BIMAH

AMAH
OPAH

PAH
LAH
BLAH

BELAH
SELAH
SOLAH
GALAH

OMLAH

MAHOE
MAHUA
MAHWA

SAHIB
SAHEB

* = word does not take an -s extension

ADDAX *

ATAXY *

GALAX *
MALAX *
HAPAX *
PANAX *
LIMAX *
BORAX *
HYRAX *

AXIAL *
AXILE *
AXITE

BRAXY *
FLAXY *

AXING

AXLED *

AXOID
AXONE

AXIOM
AXION

AXED

AXAL *
AXEL
AXIL
AXLE
AXIS *
AXON

AXMAN *
AXMEN *

AXE

FLAX *

AXE

SAXE

FAX *
MAX *
RAX *
TAX *
WAX *

COAX *
HOAX *

LAX *
PAX *
SAX *
ZAX *

A₁ X₈

FAXES *
MAXES *
RAXES *
TAXES *
WAXES *

LAXES *
PAXES *
SAXES *
ZAXES *

TAXER
WAXER
LAXER *

FAXED *
MAXED *
RAXED *
TAXED *
WAXED *

WAXY *
JAXY *

MAXIM

WAXEN *

JAXIE

CAXON
TAXON

TAXOL
TAXOR

TAXA
TAXI
MAXI

TAXUS *

RETAX *
REWAX *
RELAX *

LAXLY *

DEWAX *
UNTAX *

* = word does not take an -s extension

DRACHM

RHYTHM

MEGOHM

ASHMAN *
ASHMEN *

MAHMAL

PASHM

ABOHM

OHMAGE

OHMIC *

OHM

HMM *

SHMEK

SHMEAR

ASTHMA
BRAHMA

FEHM *
VEHM *

FEHME *
VEHME *

FEHMIC *
VEHMIC *

H₄ M₃

ISTHMI *
MISHMI

SHMO *
SCHMO
SCHMOE

SHMOCK
SHMUCK

* = word does not take an -s extension

FIORD
KIOSK
RIOJA

KIORE

AIOLI

PIONY*
PIOYE

ADDIO
AMNIO

ARIOT*
GRIOT

DANIO

BIOME
BIONT

RADIO
RATIO
PATIO

AGIO
OLIO

NGAIO

FUGIO
CURIO
AUDIO

FOLIO
POLIO
HELIO

HIOI

BIO
GIO

BRIO
SKIO
TRIO
THIO*
WHIO*

I O

DIODE

CION
LION

DIOL
VIOL

PION
PIOY

VIOLA
VIOLD*

PIOUS*

RIOT

BIOG

BIOTA
DIOTA

IOTA

IODIC*
IODID
IODIN
IONIC

ADIOS*
APIOL
AVION
AXIOM
AXION

ION

CRIOS*
SCION
PSION
PRION
PRIOR
TRIOR
TRIOL
THIOL

ANION
INION
ONION
UNION

IDIOM
IDIOT

* = word does not take an -s extension

JODEL
JOCKO
JOKOL *
JOKER
JOKEY *

JONTY *
JOTTY *

JOLTY *
JOLLY *
JOWLY *

JOCK
JOCO *
JOKE
JOKY *

JOULE
JOUAL
JOUGS *
JONES *

JOMON *

JOEY

JOOK
JOUK

JOUR

JOSH *
JOSS *

JOBE
JOLE
JOLT
JOLL
JOWL

JOE

SJOE *

JOMO
JOIN
JOHN
JONG

JOY

JOB
JOG

JOL
JOW

JORAM
JORUM

JOR

JOT

JOTA

JOTUN

JOWAR

ENJOY

JOYED *
JOBED *
JOKED *
JOLED *
JOWED *

BANJO
GADJO *

BIJOU
SAJOU

DOJO
GAJO
SIJO
MOJO

FJORD

MAJOR

CAJON *
REJON *

JOINT
JOIST
JOUST

* = word does not take an -s extension

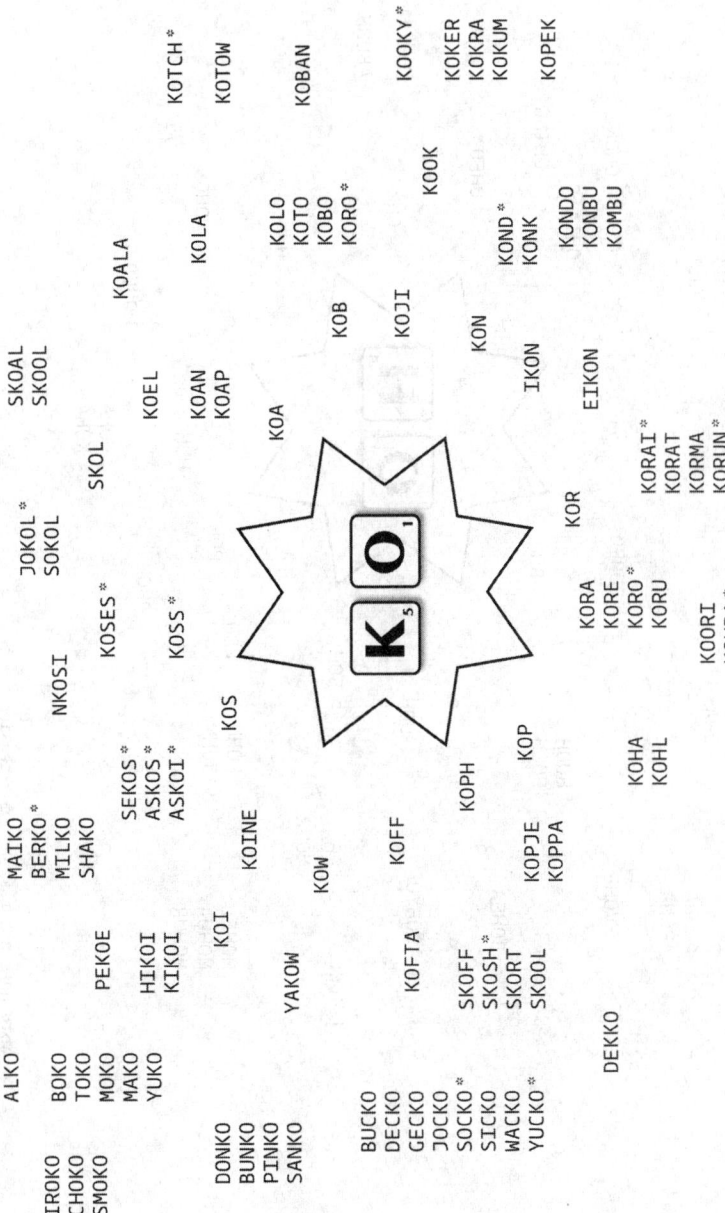

KOTCH *
KOTOW

KOBAN

KOOKY *
KOKER
KOKRA
KOKUM
KOPEK

KOOK

KOALA

KOLA

KOLO
KOTO
KOBO
KORO *

KOND *
KONK

KONDO
KONBU
KOMBU

KOB

KOJI

KON

IKON

EIKON

KORAI *
KORAT
KORMA
KORUN *

KOA

KOR

KOORI
KOURA *

KORA
KORE
KORO *
KORU

KOHA
KOHL

KOP

KOPH

KOPJE
KOPPA

KOFF

KOW

KOINE

KOI

YAKOW

KOFTA

SKOFF
SKOSH *
SKORT
SKOOL

DEKKO

BUCKO
DECKO
GECKO
JOCKO
SOCKO *
SICKO
WACKO
YUCKO *

DONKO
BUNKO
PINKO
SANKO

PEKOE

HIKOI
KIKOI

SEKOS *
ASKOS *
ASKOI *

KOS

NKOSI

KOSES *

KOSS *

SKOL

SKOAL
SKOOL

KOEL

KOAN
KOAP

SOKOL

JOKOL *

MAIKO
BERKO *
MILKO
SHAKO

ALKO

BOKO
TOKO
MOKO
MAKO
YUKO

IROKO
CHOKO
SMOKO

* = word does not take an -s extension

BOHO
COHO
SOHO*
TOHO

OHONE*

OHIA

OHO

OOH

OHING*

OHED*

OHM

OHMIC*

ABOHM

NOH*

NOHOW*

HOHED*

O_1 H_4

HOH

HOHA*
KOHA

POH*

OOHED*

BOH

SOH

FOH

DOH

PHOH

COHOE
COHOG

COHAB

BOOH
POOH

FOHN
JOHN

EVOHE*

BOHEA

DOHYO

KOHL
MOHR

ALOHA
AROHA

LOHAN

MOHEL
MOHUA*
MOHUR

* = word does not take an -s extension

WOXEN *
BOXEN *

BOXER

COXAE *
COXAL *
DOXIE
MOXIE
FOXIE

COXA *
MOXA

BOXY *
COXY *
DOXY *
FOXY *
POXY *

WOX *
BOX *
COX *
LOX *
FOX *
HOX *
POX *

BOXES *
COXES *
LOXES *
FOXES *
HOXES *
POXES *

BOXED *
COXED *
LOXED *
FOXED *
HOXED *
POXED *

OXIDE
OXIME

OXBOW
OXEYE
OXLIP
OXTER

NOXES *
GOXES *

NOXAL *

OXID
OXIM
OXEN *
OXER
OXES *

NOX *
GOX *

EPOXY *
PROXY *

*

O_1 X_8

VOXEL

SOX *
VOX *

EMBOX *
UNBOX *

PHLOX *

DETOX *
REDOX *
XEROX *

OXO *

OXY *

DEOXY *

TOXIC
TOXIN

* = word does not take an -s extension

Central tiles: Q₁₀ U₁ A₁ *

QUATRE

EQUANT
EQUATE

EQUALI *

SQUARE

SQUAIL
SQUALL

SQUAMA *
SQUAME

ASQUAT *

DIQUAT
LOQUAT

SQUASH *
SQUAWK
SQUARK

SQUAB
SQUAD
SQUAT
SQUAW

AQUA

AQUAE *

EQUAL

QUARE *
QUATE *
QUALE *

QUANT
QUART
QUAIL
QUAIR
QUALM

QUANTA *
QUARRY *
QUAERE *
QUARER *

QUALIA *
QUALMY *

QUARTE
QUARTO
QUARTZ *

QUAKED *
QUAKER
QUAVER

QUASH *
QUASI *
QUASS *

QUAFF

QUARK
QUAKE
QUAKY *
QUACK

QUASAR

QUAINT *
QUATCH *
QUAICH
QUAIGH

QUAZZY *
QUAGGY *

QUAGGA
QUAHOG

QUANGO

QUAYD *

QUAT
QUAD
QUAG

QUAI
QUAY

* = word does not take an -s extension

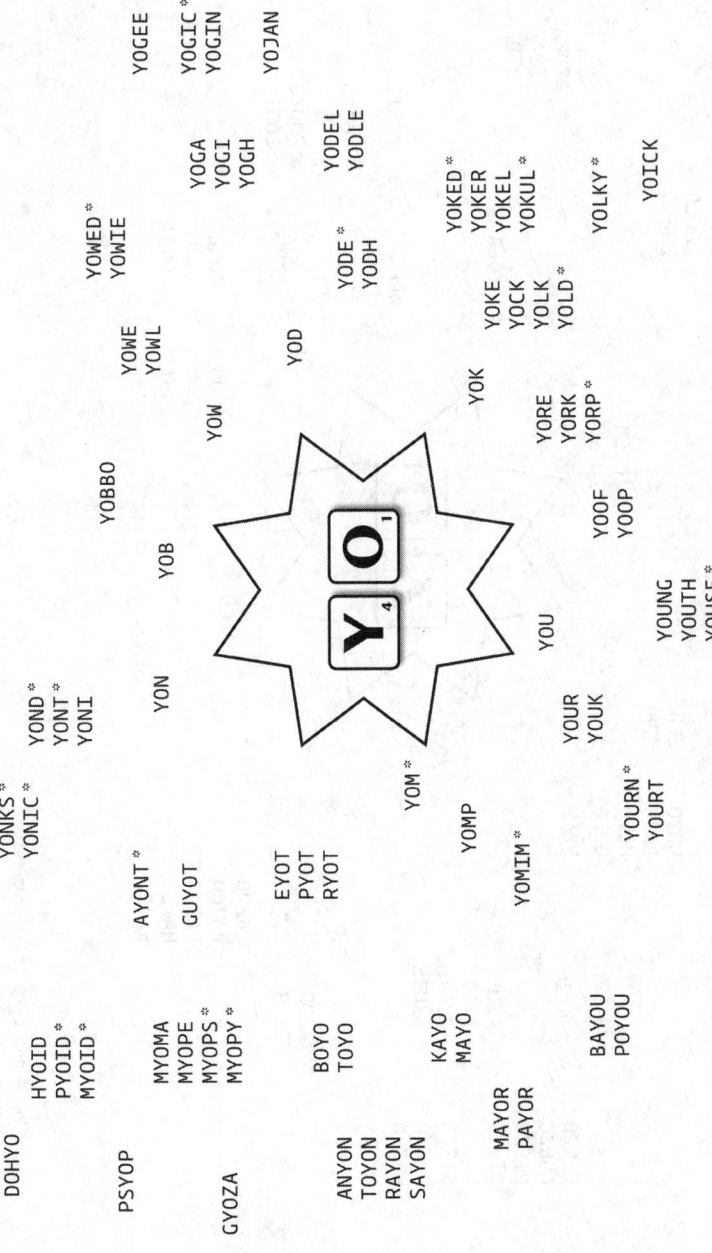

YOGEE
YOGIC* YOGIN
YOJAN

YOGA
YOGI
YOGH

YODEL
YODLE

YOWED* YOWIE

YOKED* YOKER YOKEL YOKUL*

YODE* YODH

YOWE YOWL

YOKE YOCK YOLK YOLD*

YOLKY*

YOICK

YOD

YOW

YORE YORK YORP*

YOBBO

YOB

YOK

YOOF YOOP

YOU

YOUNG YOUTH YOUSE*

YON

YOUR YOUK

YOM*

YOMP

YOURN* YOURT

YONKS* YONIC*

YOND* YONT* YONI

AYONT*
GUYOT

EYOT PYOT RYOT

YOMIM*

DOHYO

HYOID PYOID* MYOID*

PSYOP

MYOMA MYOPE MYOPS* MYOPY*

GYOZA

BOYO TOYO

KAYO MAYO

ANYON TOYON RAYON SAYON

MAYOR PAYOR

BAYOU POYOU

* = word does not take an -s extension

ZOMBI
ZOWIE *

ZOEAL *
ZOEAE *
ZOAEA
ZOOEA

ZOPPA *
ZOPPO *
ZOCCO
ZORRO

ZORIL
ZOOID

ZOOKS *
ZOOTY *

ZOEA

ZOOEY *

ZORI

ZONAE *
ZONAL *

ZONED *
ZONER
ZONDA

ZOISM
ZOIST

ZOIC *

ZOL

ZOOM
ZOON
ZOOT *

ZOUK

Z₁₀ O₁

ZONA *

ZONE

ZONK

ZOBO
ZOBU

ZOA *

ZOO

OZONE

DZO

AZO *

AZON

BOZO
LAZO
MOZO
OUZO
ORZO

GAZON

GAZOO
BAZOO
KAZOO
RAZOO
WAZOO

MATZO

AZOLE
AZOIC *
AZOTH
AZOTE

RAZOR
VIZOR

GINZO *
GONZO *
PIEZO *
DIAZO

BIZZO *
LAZZO *
MEZZO

* = word does not take an -s extension

Chapter 4: Beginnings and Endings

Prefixes

It's very useful to be aware of the common prefixes in English, as these provide a wealth of opportunities for building on words that are already on the board. Moreover, they can help players find bonus words on their rack by forming prefixes and seeing if the remaining letters, maybe using a letter on the board, fit with it to make a valid seven- or eight-letter word. The following lists show the most common prefixes in English, along with the valid words of seven and eight letters that they form from other existing words. Only those words which can be formed from a word already on the board are shown. In some cases, the words shown are not strictly examples of the prefix in question: ABALONE (AB-ALONE), for instance. These are still included, however, because they work in the same way on the Scrabble board, and are useful in encouraging a little lateral thinking when trying to build on words already in play.

Also included is a list of three-letter extensions to five-letter words – these are the so-called 'benjamins'. The value of these words for Scrabble comes from the fact that the first play on a board is often a five-letter play in order to use a double-letter square in conjunction with the central double-word square. If such a word is played to the left then it may be possible to later reap the benefits of the triple word square by adding three-letters before it. Some are straightforward prefixes (eg MOUNT becoming DISMOUNT) but others are more interesting because the form of the word changes (eg CHANT becoming PENCHANT or GLAND becoming GANGLAND). To be most relevant to the game only those five letter words that begin with a letter worth two or more points have been included because a player is more likely to play that letter on the double-letter square. The equivalent suffix extensions to extend a word to the right triple word square have not been listed because they are more straightforward to spot with many of them being simple -ING extensions.

Words that begin with AB-

Seven-letter words

ABACTOR	ABFARAD	ABOUGHT	ABROADS	ABUSAGE
ABALONE	ABHENRY	ABRAIDS	ABSEILS	ABUSERS
ABASHED	ABJOINT	ABRAYED	ABSENTS	ABUSING
ABASHES	ABLATED	ABREACT	ABSOLVE	ABUTTER
ABAXIAL	ABLINGS	ABREAST	ABSORBS	ABVOLTS
ABAXILE	ABLUTED	ABREGES	ABSTAIN	ABWATTS
ABDUCES	ABOLLAS	ABRIDGE	ABSURDS	
ABDUCTS	ABOMASA	ABROACH	ABTHANE	

Eight-letter words

ABACTORS	ABASHING	ABEGGING	ABFARADS	ABLEGATE
ABAMPERE	ABDUCTED	ABERRANT	ABHENRYS	ABNEGATE
ABAPICAL	ABEARING	ABESSIVE	ABJOINTS	ABNORMAL

ABOMASAL	ABRAYING	ABROOKED	ABSOLVER	ABSTRICT
ABOMASUM	ABREACTS	ABSEILED	ABSOLVES	ABTHANES
ABORALLY	ABRIDGED	ABSENTED	ABSONANT	ABUSABLE
ABORIGIN	ABRIDGER	ABSOLUTE	ABSORBED	ABUSAGES
ABRAIDED	ABRIDGES	ABSOLVED	ABSTAINS	ABUTTERS

Words that begin with AD-

Seven-letter words

ADAGIOS	ADDREST	ADLANDS	ADREADS	ADVISES
ADAPTED	ADDUCES	ADMIRED	ADRENAL	ADVISOR
ADAPTER	ADDUCTS	ADMIRES	ADSORBS	ADWARDS
ADAWING	ADHERES	ADMIXED	ADVENTS	ADWARES
ADAXIAL	ADJOINS	ADMIXES	ADVERBS	ADWOMAN
ADDEEMS	ADJOINT	ADNOUNS	ADVERSE	ADWOMEN
ADDICTS	ADJUDGE	ADOPTED	ADVERTS	
ADDOOMS	ADJUROR	ADOPTER	ADVICES	
ADDRESS	ADJUSTS	ADPRESS	ADVISED	

Eight-letter words

ADAPTING	ADENOSIS	ADJUDGES	ADMONISH	ADUMBRAL
ADDEBTED	ADEQUATE	ADJURORS	ADNATION	ADUNCATE
ADDEEMED	ADESSIVE	ADJUSTED	ADOPTERS	ADVERSER
ADDICTED	ADJACENT	ADJUSTER	ADOPTING	ADVERTED
ADDOOMED	ADJOINED	ADMASSES	ADOPTION	ADVISING
ADDUCTED	ADJOINTS	ADMIRING	ADSCRIPT	ADVISORS
ADENOSES	ADJUDGED	ADMIXING	ADSORBED	ADWARDED

Words that begin with AIR-

Seven-letter words

AIRBAGS	AIRFOIL	AIRLINE	AIRSHIP	AIRWARD
AIRBASE	AIRGAPS	AIRLOCK	AIRSHOT	AIRWAVE
AIRBOAT	AIRGLOW	AIRMAIL	AIRSHOW	AIRWAYS
AIRCREW	AIRHEAD	AIRPARK	AIRSICK	AIRWISE
AIRDATE	AIRHOLE	AIRPLAY	AIRSIDE	
AIRDROP	AIRLESS	AIRPORT	AIRSTOP	
AIRFARE	AIRLIFT	AIRPOST	AIRTIME	
AIRFLOW	AIRLIKE	AIRSHED	AIRTING	

Eight-letter words

AIRBASES	AIRDATES	AIRHOLES	AIRPROOF	AIRSTRIP
AIRBOATS	AIRDRAWN	AIRLIFTS	AIRSCAPE	AIRTHING
AIRBORNE	AIRDROME	AIRLINER	AIRSCREW	AIRTIGHT
AIRBOUND	AIRDROPS	AIRLINES	AIRSHAFT	AIRTIMES
AIRBRICK	AIRFARES	AIRLOCKS	AIRSHEDS	AIRWARDS
AIRBRUSH	AIRFIELD	AIRMAILS	AIRSHIPS	AIRWAVES
AIRBURST	AIRFLOWS	AIRPARKS	AIRSHOTS	AIRWOMAN
AIRBUSES	AIRFOILS	AIRPLANE	AIRSHOWS	AIRWOMEN
AIRCHECK	AIRFRAME	AIRPLAYS	AIRSIDES	
AIRCOACH	AIRGLOWS	AIRPORTS	AIRSPACE	
AIRCRAFT	AIRGRAPH	AIRPOSTS	AIRSPEED	
AIRCREWS	AIRHEADS	AIRPOWER	AIRSTOPS	

Words that begin with AB-

Words that begin with BE-

Seven-letter words

BEACHED	BEDUNGS	BEKNOTS	BEPUFFS	BESTING
BEACHES	BEDUSTS	BEKNOWN	BEQUEST	BESTIRS
BEADMAN	BEDWARF	BELABOR	BERAKED	BESTORM
BEADMEN	BEECHES	BELACED	BERAKES	BESTOWS
BEARISH	BEFALLS	BELACES	BERATED	BESTREW
BEAVERS	BEFLAGS	BELATED	BERATES	BESTROW
BEBLOOD	BEFLEAS	BELAUDS	BERAYED	BESTUCK
BEBUNGS	BEFLECK	BELAYED	BEREAVE	BESTUDS
BECALLS	BEFOAMS	BELAYER	BERHYME	BESWARM
BECALMS	BEFOOLS	BELEAPS	BERIMED	BETAKEN
BECAUSE	BEFOULS	BELEAPT	BERIMES	BETAKES
BECHALK	BEFRETS	BELIEFS	BEROBED	BETAXED
BECHARM	BEGALLS	BELIERS	BESAINT	BETEEMS
BECLASP	BEGAZED	BELIEVE	BESCOUR	BETHANK
BECLOAK	BEGAZES	BELONGS	BESEEMS	BETHINK
BECLOGS	BEGIFTS	BELOVED	BESHAME	BETHORN
BECLOUD	BEGILDS	BELOVES	BESHINE	BETHUMB
BECLOWN	BEGIRDS	BELYING	BESHONE	BETHUMP
BECOMES	BEGLADS	BEMADAM	BESHOUT	BETIDED
BECRAWL	BEGLOOM	BEMAULS	BESHREW	BETIDES
BECRIME	BEGNAWS	BEMAZED	BESIDES	BETIGHT
BECROWD	BEGOING	BEMEANS	BESIEGE	BETIMED
BECRUST	BEGONIA	BEMEANT	BESIGHS	BETIMES
BECURLS	BEGORED	BEMEDAL	BESINGS	BETITLE
BECURSE	BEGRIME	BEMETED	BESLAVE	BETOILS
BECURST	BEGROAN	BEMETES	BESLIME	BETOKEN
BEDAMNS	BEGUILE	BEMIRED	BESMEAR	BETRAYS
BEDAUBS	BEGULFS	BEMIRES	BESMILE	BETREAD
BEDAZED	BEGUNKS	BEMISTS	BESMOKE	BETRIMS
BEDAZES	BEHAVER	BEMIXED	BESMUTS	BETROTH
BEDECKS	BEHAVES	BEMIXES	BESNOWS	BETWEEN
BEDELLS	BEHEADS	BEMOANS	BESORTS	BETWIXT
BEDEMAN	BEHESTS	BEMOCKS	BESPAKE	BEVOMIT
BEDEVIL	BEHIGHT	BEMOILS	BESPATE	BEWAILS
BEDEWED	BEHINDS	BEMOUTH	BESPEAK	BEWARED
BEDIGHT	BEHOLDS	BEMUSED	BESPEED	BEWARES
BEDIRTY	BEHOOFS	BEMUSES	BESPICE	BEWEARY
BEDIZEN	BEHOOVE	BENAMED	BESPITS	BEWEEPS
BEDRAIL	BEHOVED	BENAMES	BESPOKE	BEWHORE
BEDRAPE	BEHOVES	BENEATH	BESPORT	BEWITCH
BEDROLL	BEHOWLS	BENEMPT	BESPOTS	BEWORMS
BEDROPS	BEINKED	BENIGHT	BESPOUT	BEWORRY
BEDROPT	BEJADED	BENUMBS	BESTAIN	BEWRAPS
BEDRUGS	BEJADES	BEPAINT	BESTARS	BEWRAPT
BEDUCKS	BEJESUS	BEPEARL	BESTEAD	
BEDUMBS	BEJEWEL	BEPELTS	BESTICK	
BEDUNCE	BEKNAVE	BEPROSE	BESTILL	

Eight-letter words

BEACHIER	BEBOPPER	BECHALKS	BECLOAKS	BECOWARD
BEACHING	BECALLED	BECHANCE	BECLOTHE	BECRAWLS
BEARABLE	BECALMED	BECHARMS	BECLOUDS	BECRIMED
BEBLOODS	BECAPPED	BECLAMOR	BECLOWNS	BECRIMES
BEBOPPED	BECARPET	BECLASPS	BECOMING	BECROWDS

BECRUSTS	BEGEMMED	BELITTLE	BERHYMED	BESPOUTS
BECUDGEL	BEGETTER	BELONGED	BERHYMES	BESPREAD
BECURLED	BEGIFTED	BELONGER	BERIMING	BESPRENT
BECURSED	BEGILDED	BELOVING	BERINGED	BESTAINS
BECURSES	BEGINNER	BEMADAMS	BEROBBED	BESTEADS
BEDABBLE	BEGIRDED	BEMADDED	BEROUGED	BESTICKS
BEDAGGLE	BEGIRDLE	BEMADDEN	BESAINTS	BESTILLS
BEDAMNED	BEGLAMOR	BEMAULED	BESCORCH	BESTORMS
BEDARKEN	BEGLOOMS	BEMEANED	BESCOURS	BESTOWED
BEDASHED	BEGNAWED	BEMEDALS	BESCRAWL	BESTOWER
BEDASHES	BEGOTTEN	BEMETING	BESCREEN	BESTREAK
BEDAUBED	BEGRIMED	BEMINGLE	BESEEING	BESTREWN
BEDAZING	BEGRIMES	BEMIRING	BESEEMED	BESTREWS
BEDAZZLE	BEGROANS	BEMISTED	BESEEMLY	BESTRIDE
BEDEAFEN	BEGRUDGE	BEMIXING	BESETTER	BESTRODE
BEDECKED	BEGUILER	BEMOANED	BESHADOW	BESTROWN
BEDESMAN	BEGUILES	BEMOANER	BESHAMED	BESTROWS
BEDEVILS	BEGULFED	BEMOCKED	BESHAMES	BESUITED
BEDEWING	BEHALVES	BEMOILED	BESHINES	BESWARMS
BEDIAPER	BEHAPPEN	BEMOUTHS	BESHIVER	BETAKING
BEDIGHTS	BEHATTED	BEMUDDED	BESHOUTS	BETATTER
BEDIMMED	BEHAVERS	BEMUDDLE	BESHREWS	BETEEMED
BEDIMPLE	BEHAVING	BEMUFFLE	BESHROUD	BETHANKS
BEDIZENS	BEHAVIOR	BEMURMUR	BESIEGED	BETHINKS
BEDOTTED	BEHEADED	BEMUSING	BESIEGER	BETHORNS
BEDRAILS	BEHEADER	BEMUZZLE	BESIEGES	BETHRALL
BEDRAPED	BEHIGHTS	BENAMING	BESIGHED	BETHUMBS
BEDRAPES	BEHOLDEN	BENETTED	BESLAVED	BETHUMPS
BEDRENCH	BEHOLDER	BENIGHTS	BESLAVER	BETHWACK
BEDRIVEL	BEHOOVED	BENUMBED	BESLAVES	BETIDING
BEDROLLS	BEHOOVES	BEPAINTS	BESLIMED	BETIMING
BEDUCKED	BEHOVING	BEPATTED	BESLIMES	BETITLED
BEDUMBED	BEHOWLED	BEPEARLS	BESMEARS	BETITLES
BEDUNCES	BEJABERS	BEPELTED	BESMILED	BETOILED
BEDUNGED	BEJADING	BEPEPPER	BESMILES	BETOKENS
BEDUSTED	BEJESUIT	BEPESTER	BESMIRCH	BETONIES
BEDWARFS	BEJEWELS	BEPIMPLE	BESMOKED	BETOSSED
BEDYEING	BEJUMBLE	BEPITIED	BESMOKES	BETOSSES
BEFALLEN	BEKISSED	BEPITIES	BESMOOTH	BETREADS
BEFINGER	BEKISSES	BEPLUMED	BESMUDGE	BETROTHS
BEFINNED	BEKNAVES	BEPOMMEL	BESMUTCH	BETWEENS
BEFITTED	BEKNIGHT	BEPOWDER	BESNOWED	BEUNCLED
BEFLECKS	BELABORS	BEPRAISE	BESOOTHE	BEVOMITS
BEFLOWER	BELABOUR	BEPROSED	BESORTED	BEWAILED
BEFOAMED	BELACING	BEPROSES	BESOTTED	BEWAILER
BEFOGGED	BELADIES	BEPUFFED	BESOUGHT	BEWARING
BEFOOLED	BELAUDED	BEQUESTS	BESOULED	BEWETTED
BEFOULED	BELAYERS	BERAKING	BESPEAKS	BEWHORED
BEFOULER	BELAYING	BERASCAL	BESPEEDS	BEWHORES
BEFRIEND	BELEAPED	BERATING	BESPICED	BEWIGGED
BEFRINGE	BELEEING	BERAYING	BESPICES	BEWILDER
BEFUDDLE	BELIEVER	BEREAVED	BESPOKEN	BEWINGED
BEGALLED	BELIQUOR	BEREAVER	BESPORTS	BEWORMED
BEGAZING		BEREAVES	BESPOUSE	

Words that begin with BE-

Words that begin with BI-

Seven-letter words

BIASSES	BICYCLE	BILIMBI	BIPACKS	BITABLE
BIAXIAL	BIDENTS	BILOBAR	BIPARTY	BITINGS
BIBASIC	BIDINGS	BILOBED	BIPEDAL	BITONAL
BIBLESS	BIFACES	BIMETAL	BIPLANE	BIVALVE
BIBLIST	BIFILAR	BIMODAL	BIPOLAR	BIVINYL
BICARBS	BIFOCAL	BIMORPH	BIPRISM	BIZONAL
BICHORD	BIKINGS	BIOLOGY	BISECTS	BIZONES
BICOLOR	BILAYER	BIONTIC	BISHOPS	
BICORNS	BILEVEL	BIOPTIC	BISTATE	

Eight-letter words

BIACETYL	BIDENTAL	BILINEAR	BIPARTED	BISTABLE
BIANNUAL	BIELDING	BILOBATE	BIPHASIC	BISTOURY
BICAUDAL	BIFACIAL	BIMANUAL	BIPHENYL	BITEWING
BICHROME	BIFORKED	BIMENSAL	BIPLANES	BITINGLY
BICOLORS	BIFORMED	BIMESTER	BIPRISMS	BIUNIQUE
BICOLOUR	BIGEMINY	BIMETALS	BIRACIAL	BIVALVED
BICONVEX	BIHOURLY	BIMETHYL	BIRADIAL	BIVALVES
BICUSPID	BIJUGATE	BIMORPHS	BIRAMOSE	BIVINYLS
BICYCLED	BILABIAL	BIOBLAST	BIRAMOUS	BIWEEKLY
BICYCLER	BILANDER	BIOTITIC	BISECTOR	BIYEARLY
BICYCLES	BILAYERS	BIOVULAR	BISERIAL	
BICYCLIC	BILEVELS	BIPAROUS	BISEXUAL	

Words that begin with COM-

Seven-letter words

COMAKES	COMFIER	COMMONS	COMPASS	COMPONE
COMARBS	COMFITS	COMMOTE	COMPAST	COMPONY
COMARTS	COMFORT	COMMOTS	COMPEAR	COMPORT
COMATES	COMICES	COMMOVE	COMPEER	COMPOSE
COMBATS	COMMAND	COMMUTE	COMPEND	COMPOST
COMBIER	COMMEND	COMPACT	COMPERE	COMPOTE
COMBINE	COMMENT	COMPAGE	COMPILE	COMPOTS
COMBING	COMMERE	COMPAND	COMPING	COMRADE
COMBUST	COMMIXT	COMPARE	COMPLEX	COMUSES
COMETIC	COMMODE	COMPART	COMPLOT	

Eight-letter words

COMAKING	COMFORTS	COMMOTES	COMPARED	COMPILES
COMBATED	COMINGLE	COMMOVED	COMPARER	COMPINGS
COMBINER	COMMENDS	COMMOVES	COMPARES	COMPLAIN
COMBINES	COMMERES	COMMUTED	COMPARTS	COMPLEAT
COMBINGS	COMMERGE	COMMUTER	COMPEARS	COMPLIED
COMBLESS	COMMIXED	COMMUTES	COMPEERS	COMPLIER
COMBUSTS	COMMIXES	COMPACTS	COMPENDS	COMPLIES
COMEMBER	COMMODES	COMPADRE	COMPERES	COMPLOTS
COMETHER	COMMONER	COMPAGES	COMPILED	COMPORTS
COMFIEST	COMMONEY	COMPANDS	COMPILER	COMPOSED

| COMPOSER | COMPOSTS | COMPOUND | COMPRINT | COMPRIZE |
| COMPOSES | COMPOTES | COMPRESS | COMPRISE | COMPULSE |

Words that begin with CON-

Seven-letter words

CONACRE	CONDOLE	CONFORM	CONJURY	CONTENT
CONARIA	CONDOMS	CONFUSE	CONKIER	CONTEST
CONCAVE	CONDONE	CONGAED	CONKING	CONTEXT
CONCEDE	CONDORS	CONGEAL	CONNOTE	CONTORT
CONCENT	CONDUCE	CONGEED	CONSEIL	CONTOUR
CONCERT	CONDUCT	CONGEES	CONSENT	CONTRAT
CONCHAL	CONDUIT	CONGEST	CONSIGN	CONTUND
CONCHAS	CONFABS	CONGOES	CONSIST	CONURES
CONCORD	CONFESS	CONGREE	CONSOLE	CONVENT
CONCREW	CONFEST	CONGRUE	CONSOLS	CONVERT
CONCURS	CONFINE	CONJEED	CONSORT	CONVIVE
CONCUSS	CONFIRM	CONJEES	CONTACT	
CONDIES	CONFITS	CONJOIN	CONTAIN	
CONDOES	CONFLUX	CONJURE	CONTEND	

Eight-letter words

CONACRED	CONDUCES	CONGLOBE	CONSISTS	CONTRAIL
CONACRES	CONDUCTS	CONGREED	CONSOLED	CONTRATS
CONCAUSE	CONDUITS	CONGREES	CONSOLER	CONTRIST
CONCAVED	CONFINED	CONGREET	CONSOLES	CONTRITE
CONCAVES	CONFINER	CONGRUED	CONSORTS	CONTUNDS
CONCEDED	CONFINES	CONGRUES	CONSPIRE	CONURBAN
CONCEDER	CONFIRMS	CONJOINS	CONSTATE	CONURBIA
CONCEDES	CONFIXED	CONJOINT	CONTACTS	CONVENTS
CONCENTS	CONFIXES	CONJUGAL	CONTAINS	CONVERGE
CONCERTS	CONFOCAL	CONJUNTO	CONTANGO	CONVERSE
CONCLAVE	CONFORMS	CONJUROR	CONTEMPO	CONVERSO
CONCOLOR	CONFOUND	CONNOTED	CONTEMPT	CONVERTS
CONCORDS	CONFRERE	CONNOTES	CONTENDS	CONVEXED
CONCOURS	CONFRONT	CONQUEST	CONTENTS	CONVEXES
CONCREWS	CONFUSED	CONSEILS	CONTESTS	CONVIVES
CONDENSE	CONFUSES	CONSENTS	CONTEXTS	CONVOLVE
CONDOLED	CONGEALS	CONSERVE	CONTORTS	
CONDOLES	CONGENIC	CONSIDER	CONTOURS	
CONDONER	CONGESTS	CONSIGNS	CONTRACT	

Words that begin with DE-

Seven-letter words

DEADMAN	DEBASES	DEBRIEF	DECANES	DECLASS
DEADMEN	DEBATED	DEBUNKS	DECANTS	DECLAWS
DEAIRED	DEBATES	DEBURRS	DECARBS	DECLINE
DEALATE	DEBEAKS	DEBUSED	DECARES	DECODED
DEASHED	DEBEARD	DEBUSES	DECEASE	DECODER
DEASHES	DEBONED	DECADES	DECIDED	DECODES
DEBARKS	DEBONER	DECAFFS	DECIDER	DECOKED
DEBASED	DEBONES	DECAMPS	DECIDES	DECOKES
DEBASER	DEBRIDE	DECANAL	DECLAIM	DECOLOR

Words that begin with COM-

DECOYED
DECOYER
DECREED
DECREES
DECREWS
DECRIED
DECRIER
DECRIES
DECROWN
DECRYPT
DECURIA
DECURVE
DEDUCES
DEDUCTS
DEFACED
DEFACER
DEFACES
DEFAMED
DEFAMES
DEFANGS
DEFAULT
DEFEATS
DEFENCE
DEFENDS
DEFIERS
DEFILED
DEFILER
DEFILES
DEFINED
DEFINER
DEFINES
DEFLEAS
DEFOAMS
DEFOCUS
DEFORCE
DEFORMS
DEFOULS
DEFRAGS

DEFRAUD
DEFRAYS
DEFROCK
DEFROST
DEFROZE
DEFUELS
DEFUNDS
DEFUSED
DEFUSES
DEFUZED
DEFUZES
DEGAMES
DEGASES
DEGAUSS
DEGERMS
DEGLAZE
DEGOUTS
DEGRADE
DEGREED
DEGREES
DEGUSTS
DEHORNS
DEICERS
DEICING
DEICTIC
DEINDEX
DEJEUNE
DELAPSE
DELATED
DELAYED
DELAYER
DELEADS
DELEAVE
DELIGHT
DELIMED
DELIMES
DELIMIT
DELISTS

DELIVER
DELOPED
DELOPES
DELOUSE
DELUDES
DELUGED
DELUGES
DEMAINS
DEMARKS
DEMASTS
DEMEANE
DEMEANS
DEMERGE
DEMERIT
DEMERSE
DEMESNE
DEMISES
DEMISTS
DEMOSES
DEMOTED
DEMOTES
DEMOUNT
DEMURED
DEMURES
DENOTED
DENOTES
DENUDER
DENUDES
DENYING
DEONTIC
DEORBIT
DEPAINT
DEPARTS
DEPENDS
DEPERMS
DEPLANE
DEPLOYS
DEPLUME

DEPONES
DEPORTS
DEPOSED
DEPOSER
DEPOSES
DEPOSIT
DEPRESS
DERAILS
DERANGE
DERATED
DERATES
DERAYED
DERIDER
DERIDES
DERIVED
DERIVER
DERIVES
DESALTS
DESANDS
DESCALE
DESCANT
DESCEND
DESCENT
DESERVE
DESEXED
DESEXES
DESIGNS
DESINED
DESINES
DESIRED
DESIRES
DESISTS
DESKILL
DESNOOD
DESORBS
DESPITE
DESPOIL
DESPOTS

DESTAIN
DESTOCK
DESTROY
DESUGAR
DESYNED
DESYNES
DETAILS
DETAINS
DETENTS
DETENUE
DETESTS
DETICKS
DETORTS
DETOURS
DETRACT
DETRAIN
DETUNED
DETUNES
DEVALUE
DEVEINS
DEVESTS
DEVICES
DEVISED
DEVISES
DEVISOR
DEVOICE
DEVOLVE
DEVOTED
DEVOTES
DEWATER
DEWAXED
DEWAXES
DEWOOLS
DEWORMS
DEZINCS

Eight-letter words

DEAERATE
DEAIRING
DEALATED
DEALATES
DEARLING
DEASHING
DEBAGGED
DEBARKED
DEBARKER
DEBARRED
DEBASING
DEBATING
DEBEAKED
DEBEARDS
DEBELLED
DEBITING
DEBONERS
DEBONING

DEBOSHES
DEBOSSED
DEBOSSES
DEBOUCHE
DEBRIDED
DEBRIDES
DEBRIEFS
DEBRUISE
DEBUDDED
DEBUGGED
DEBUGGER
DEBUNKED
DEBUNKER
DEBURRED
DEBUSING
DEBUSSED
DEBUSSES
DECADENT

DECALLED
DECAMPED
DECANTED
DECANTER
DECEASED
DECEASES
DECENTER
DECENTRE
DECERNED
DECIDERS
DECIDING
DECIPHER
DECLAIMS
DECLAWED
DECLINAL
DECLINES
DECLUTCH
DECODERS

DECODING
DECOKING
DECOLORS
DECOLOUR
DECOMMIT
DECOUPLE
DECOYING
DECREASE
DECREWED
DECRIERS
DECROWNS
DECRYING
DECRYPTS
DECUBITI
DECURIAS
DECURIES
DECURVED
DECURVES

DEDUCTED
DEFACERS
DEFACING
DEFAMING
DEFANGED
DEFATTED
DEFAULTS
DEFEATED
DEFEATER
DEFENCED
DEFENCES
DEFENDED
DEFENDER
DEFIANCE
DEFILERS
DEFILING
DEFINERS
DEFINING

DEFINITE	DEHORNER	DEMONISM	DERIDERS	DESTOCKS
DEFLEXED	DEIONISE	DEMONIST	DERIDING	DESTROYS
DEFLEXES	DEIONIZE	DEMOTION	DERIGGED	DESUGARS
DEFLOWER	DELAPSED	DEMOUNTS	DERINGER	DESULFUR
DEFLUENT	DELAPSES	DEMURING	DERIVERS	DESYNING
DEFOAMED	DELAYERS	DENATURE	DERIVING	DETACHES
DEFOAMER	DELAYING	DENAZIFY	DESALTED	DETAILED
DEFOGGED	DELEADED	DENETTED	DESALTER	DETAILER
DEFOGGER	DELEAVED	DENOTATE	DESANDED	DETASSEL
DEFORCED	DELEAVES	DENOTING	DESCALED	DETENUES
DEFORCER	DELEGACY	DEORBITS	DESCALES	DETESTED
DEFORCES	DELEGATE	DEPAINTS	DESCANTS	DETESTER
DEFOREST	DELIBATE	DEPARTED	DESCENDS	DETHATCH
DEFORMED	DELIGHTS	DEPARTER	DESCENTS	DETHRONE
DEFORMER	DELIMING	DEPEINCT	DESCHOOL	DETICKED
DEFOULED	DELIMITS	DEPENDED	DESCRIBE	DETICKER
DEFRAUDS	DELISTED	DEPEOPLE	DESCRIED	DETOURED
DEFRAYED	DELIVERS	DEPERMED	DESCRIES	DETRACTS
DEFREEZE	DELIVERY	DEPLANED	DESCRIVE	DETRAINS
DEFROCKS	DELOPING	DEPLANES	DESELECT	DETUNING
DEFROSTS	DELOUSED	DEPLOYED	DESERVED	DEVALUED
DEFROZEN	DELOUSER	DEPLUMED	DESERVER	DEVALUES
DEFUELED	DELOUSES	DEPLUMES	DESERVES	DEVEINED
DEFUNDED	DELUGING	DEPOLISH	DESEXING	DEVERBAL
DEFUSING	DELUSTER	DEPONENT	DESIGNED	DEVESTED
DEFUZING	DEMANNED	DEPORTED	DESIGNEE	DEVIATOR
DEGASSED	DEMARKED	DEPORTER	DESIGNER	DEVISING
DEGASSER	DEMARKET	DEPOSERS	DESILVER	DEVISORS
DEGASSES	DEMASTED	DEPOSING	DESINING	DEVOICED
DEGENDER	DEMEANED	DEPOSITS	DESIRING	DEVOICES
DEGERMED	DEMEANES	DERAILED	DESISTED	DEVOLVED
DEGLAZED	DEMERGED	DERAILER	DESKILLS	DEVOLVES
DEGLAZES	DEMERGER	DERANGED	DESNOODS	DEVOTING
DEGRADED	DEMERGES	DERANGER	DESOLATE	DEWATERS
DEGRADER	DEMERITS	DERANGES	DESORBED	DEWAXING
DEGRADES	DEMERSES	DERATING	DESPIGHT	DEWITTED
DEGREASE	DEMESNES	DERATION	DESPITED	DEWOOLED
DEGUMMED	DEMISTED	DERATTED	DESPITES	DEWORMED
DEGUSTED	DEMISTER	DERAYING	DESPOILS	DEWORMER
DEHORNED	DEMOBBED	DERELICT	DESTAINS	DEZINCED

Words that begin with DIS-

Seven-letter words

DISABLE	DISCORD	DISJOIN	DISMISS	DISPRAD
DISALLY	DISCURE	DISKING	DISNEST	DISRANK
DISARMS	DISCUSS	DISLEAF	DISOBEY	DISRATE
DISAVOW	DISEASE	DISLEAL	DISOWNS	DISROBE
DISBAND	DISEDGE	DISLIKE	DISPACE	DISROOT
DISBARK	DISFAME	DISLIMB	DISPARK	DISSAVE
DISBARS	DISFORM	DISLIMN	DISPART	DISSEAT
DISBUDS	DISGEST	DISLINK	DISPEND	DISSECT
DISCAGE	DISGOWN	DISLOAD	DISPLAY	DISSENT
DISCANT	DISGUST	DISMALS	DISPLED	DISSING
DISCARD	DISHELM	DISMANS	DISPONE	DISTAIN
DISCASE	DISHING	DISMASK	DISPORT	DISTEND
DISCIDE	DISHOME	DISMAST	DISPOSE	DISTENT
DISCOED	DISHORN	DISMAYS	DISPOST	DISTICH

Words that begin with DE-

DISTILL	**DIS**TOME	**DIS**TUNE	**DIS**USES
DISTILS	**DIS**TORT	**DIS**USED	**DIS**YOKE

Eight-letter words

DISABLED	**DIS**CLOSE	**DIS**HOMES	**DIS**PACES	**DIS**SECTS
DISABLER	**DIS**COLOR	**DIS**HONOR	**DIS**PARKS	**DIS**SEISE
DISABLES	**DIS**CORDS	**DIS**HORNS	**DIS**PARTS	**DIS**SEIZE
DISABUSE	**DIS**COUNT	**DIS**HORSE	**DIS**PATCH	**DIS**SENTS
DISADORN	**DIS**COURE	**DIS**HOUSE	**DIS**PEACE	**DIS**SERVE
DISAGREE	**DIS**COVER	**DIS**INTER	**DIS**PENCE	**DIS**SEVER
DISALLOW	**DIS**CROWN	**DIS**INURE	**DIS**PENDS	**DIS**SIGHT
DISANNEX	**DIS**CURED	**DIS**JOINS	**DIS**PERSE	**DIS**SOLVE
DISANNUL	**DIS**CURES	**DIS**JOINT	**DIS**PLACE	**DIS**TAINS
DISAPPLY	**DIS**EASED	**DIS**LEAFS	**DIS**PLANT	**DIS**TALLY
DISARMED	**DIS**EASES	**DIS**LEAVE	**DIS**PLAYS	**DIS**TASTE
DISARMER	**DIS**EDGED	**DIS**LIKED	**DIS**PLING	**DIS**TENDS
DISARRAY	**DIS**EDGES	**DIS**LIKEN	**DIS**PLUME	**DIS**TILLS
DISASTER	**DIS**ENDOW	**DIS**LIKER	**DIS**PONES	**DIS**TINCT
DISAVOWS	**DIS**ENROL	**DIS**LIKES	**DIS**POSED	**DIS**TOMES
DISBANDS	**DIS**FAMES	**DIS**LIMBS	**DIS**POSER	**DIS**TORTS
DISBARKS	**DIS**FAVOR	**DIS**LIMNS	**DIS**POSES	**DIS**TRACT
DISBENCH	**DIS**FLESH	**DIS**LINKS	**DIS**POSTS	**DIS**TRAIL
DISBOSOM	**DIS**FORMS	**DIS**LOADS	**DIS**PRIZE	**DIS**TRAIN
DISBOUND	**DIS**FROCK	**DIS**LODGE	**DIS**PROOF	**DIS**TRAIT
DISBOWEL	**DIS**GAVEL	**DIS**LOYAL	**DIS**PROVE	**DIS**TRESS
DISBURSE	**DIS**GESTS	**DIS**MASKS	**DIS**PURSE	**DIS**TRUST
DISCAGED	**DIS**GORGE	**DIS**MASTS	**DIS**QUIET	**DIS**TUNED
DISCAGES	**DIS**GOWNS	**DIS**MAYED	**DIS**RANKS	**DIS**TUNES
DISCANDY	**DIS**GRACE	**DIS**MOUNT	**DIS**RATED	**DIS**UNION
DISCANTS	**DIS**GRADE	**DIS**NESTS	**DIS**RATES	**DIS**UNITE
DISCARDS	**DIS**GUISE	**DIS**OBEYS	**DIS**ROBED	**DIS**UNITY
DISCASED	**DIS**GUSTS	**DIS**ODIUM	**DIS**ROBES	**DIS**USAGE
DISCASES	**DIS**HABIT	**DIS**ORBED	**DIS**ROOTS	**DIS**USING
DISCIDED	**DIS**HABLE	**DIS**ORDER	**DIS**SAVED	**DIS**VALUE
DISCIDES	**DIS**HELMS	**DIS**OWNED	**DIS**SAVES	**DIS**VOUCH
DISCINCT	**DIS**HINGS	**DIS**OWNER	**DIS**SEATS	**DIS**YOKED
DISCLAIM	**DIS**HOMED	**DIS**PACED	**DIS**SEATS	**DIS**YOKES

Words that begin with EM-

Seven-letter words

EMAILED	**EM**BAYED	**EM**BRACE	**EM**MOVED	**EM**PLACE
EMBAILS	**EM**BLAZE	**EM**BRAID	**EM**MOVES	**EM**PLANE
EMBALED	**EM**BLOOM	**EM**BRAVE	**EM**PAIRE	**EM**PLOYS
EMBALES	**EM**BOILS	**EM**BREAD	**EM**PALED	**EM**PLUME
EMBALLS	**EM**BOLUS	**EM**BROIL	**EM**PALER	**EM**POWER
EMBALMS	**EM**BOSKS	**EM**BROWN	**EM**PALES	**EM**PRESS
EMBANKS	**EM**BOSOM	**EM**BRUTE	**EM**PANEL	**EM**PRISE
EMBARKS	**EM**BOUND	**EM**BUSED	**EM**PARED	**EM**PRIZE
EMBASED	**EM**BOWED	**EM**BUSES	**EM**PARES	**EM**PUSES
EMBASES	**EM**BOWEL	**EM**ENDED	**EM**PARTS	
EMBASSY	**EM**BOWER	**EM**ENDER	**EM**PEACH	
EMBASTE	**EM**BOXED	**EM**IRATE	**EM**PERCE	
EMBATHE	**EM**BOXES	**EM**MEWED	**EM**PIGHT	

Eight-letter words

EMAILING	EMBLAZON	EMBRAIDS	EMMOVING	EMPLACED
EMBAILED	EMBLOOMS	EMBRAVED	EMPACKET	EMPLACES
EMBALING	EMBODIED	EMBRAVES	EMPAIRED	EMPLANED
EMBALLED	EMBODIES	EMBREADS	EMPAIRES	EMPLANES
EMBALMED	EMBOGGED	EMBROILS	EMPALING	EMPLEACH
EMBANKED	EMBOILED	EMBROWNS	EMPANADA	EMPLONGE
EMBANKER	EMBOLDEN	EMBRUTED	EMPANELS	EMPLOYED
EMBARKED	EMBORDER	EMBRUTES	EMPARING	EMPLUMED
EMBARRED	EMBOSOMS	EMBUSIED	EMPARLED	EMPLUMES
EMBASING	EMBOSSED	EMBUSIES	EMPARTED	EMPOISON
EMBATHED	EMBOSSER	EMBUSING	EMPATHIC	EMPOLDER
EMBATHES	EMBOSSES	EMBUSSED	EMPATRON	EMPOWERS
EMBATTLE	EMBOUNDS	EMBUSSES	EMPEOPLE	EMPRISES
EMBAYING	EMBOWELS	EMDASHES	EMPERCED	EMPRIZES
EMBEDDED	EMBOWERS	EMENDERS	EMPERCES	EMPURPLE
EMBEZZLE	EMBOWING	EMENDING	EMPERISH	EMPYEMIC
EMBITTER	EMBOXING	EMMARBLE	EMPHASES	
EMBLAZED	EMBRACED	EMMESHED	EMPHASIS	
EMBLAZER	EMBRACER	EMMESHES	EMPHATIC	
EMBLAZES	EMBRACES	EMMEWING	EMPIERCE	

Words that begin with EN-

Seven-letter words

ENABLED	ENCRYPT	ENFRAME	ENJAMBS	ENROLLS
ENABLER	ENCYSTS	ENFREED	ENJOINS	ENROOTS
ENABLES	ENDARTS	ENFREES	ENJOYED	ENROUGH
ENACTED	ENDEARS	ENFROZE	ENLACED	ENROUND
ENACTOR	ENDEMIC	ENGAGED	ENLACES	ENSEALS
ENAMINE	ENDEWED	ENGAGER	ENLARDS	ENSEAMS
ENAMOUR	ENDINGS	ENGAGES	ENLARGE	ENSEARS
ENARMED	ENDITED	ENGAOLS	ENLIGHT	ENSERFS
ENCAGED	ENDITES	ENGILDS	ENLINKS	ENSEWED
ENCAGES	ENDIVES	ENGIRDS	ENLISTS	ENSHELL
ENCALMS	ENDORSE	ENGLOBE	ENLIVEN	ENSIGNS
ENCAMPS	ENDOWED	ENGLOOM	ENLOCKS	ENSILED
ENCASED	ENDOWER	ENGLUTS	ENMEWED	ENSILES
ENCASES	ENDUING	ENGORED	ENMOVED	ENSKIED
ENCAVED	ENDURED	ENGORES	ENMOVES	ENSKIES
ENCAVES	ENDURES	ENGORGE	ENNOBLE	ENSKYED
ENCHAFE	ENDUROS	ENGRACE	ENOLOGY	ENSLAVE
ENCHAIN	ENFACED	ENGRAFF	ENOUNCE	ENSNARE
ENCHANT	ENFACES	ENGRAFT	ENPLANE	ENSNARL
ENCHARM	ENFELON	ENGRAIL	ENPRINT	ENSOULS
ENCHASE	ENFEOFF	ENGRAIN	ENQUIRE	ENSTAMP
ENCHEER	ENFEVER	ENGRAMS	ENRACED	ENSTEEP
ENCLASP	ENFILED	ENGRASP	ENRACES	ENSTYLE
ENCLAVE	ENFIRED	ENGRAVE	ENRAGED	ENSUING
ENCLOSE	ENFIRES	ENGROSS	ENRAGES	ENSURED
ENCLOUD	ENFIXED	ENGUARD	ENRANGE	ENSURER
ENCODED	ENFIXES	ENGULFS	ENRANKS	ENSURES
ENCODER	ENFLAME	ENGULPH	ENRHEUM	ENSWEEP
ENCODES	ENFLESH	ENHALOS	ENRINGS	ENSWEPT
ENCORED	ENFOLDS	ENHANCE	ENRIVEN	ENTAILS
ENCORES	ENFORCE	ENISLED	ENROBED	ENTAMED
ENCRUST	ENFORMS	ENISLES	ENROBES	ENTAMES

ENTICED	ENTRAIL	ENTRIST	ENVYING	ENZONED
ENTICES	ENTRAIN	ENTRUST	ENWALLS	ENZONES
ENTIRES	ENTRANT	ENTWINE	ENWHEEL	ENZYMES
ENTITLE	ENTRAPS	ENTWIST	ENWINDS	ENZYMIC
ENTOILS	ENTREAT	ENVAULT	ENWOMBS	
ENTOMBS	ENTREES	ENVENOM	ENWOUND	
ENTOPIC	ENTRIES	ENVIERS	ENWRAPS	

Eight-letter words

ENABLING	ENCRUSTS	ENGIRDED	ENLIVENS	ENSILAGE
ENACTING	ENCRYPTS	ENGIRDLE	ENLOCKED	ENSILING
ENACTION	ENCUMBER	ENGLOBED	ENLUMINE	ENSKYING
ENACTIVE	ENCYCLIC	ENGLOBES	ENMESHED	ENSLAVED
ENACTORS	ENDAMAGE	ENGLOOMS	ENMESHES	ENSLAVER
ENACTURE	ENDANGER	ENGORGED	ENMEWING	ENSLAVES
ENAMINES	ENDARTED	ENGORGES	ENMOSSED	ENSNARED
ENAMOURS	ENDASHES	ENGORING	ENMOVING	ENSNARER
ENARCHED	ENDEARED	ENGRACED	ENNOBLER	ENSNARES
ENARCHES	ENDEIXES	ENGRACES	ENNOBLES	ENSNARLS
ENARMING	ENDEIXIS	ENGRAFFS	ENOUNCES	ENSOULED
ENAUNTER	ENDERMIC	ENGRAFTS	ENPLANED	ENSPHERE
ENCAGING	ENDEWING	ENGRAILS	ENPLANES	ENSTAMPS
ENCALMED	ENDITING	ENGRAINS	ENPRINTS	ENSTEEPS
ENCAMPED	ENDORSER	ENGRAMMA	ENQUIRED	ENSTYLED
ENCARPUS	ENDORSES	ENGRAMME	ENQUIRES	ENSTYLES
ENCASHED	ENDOSSED	ENGRASPS	ENRACING	ENSURING
ENCASHES	ENDOSSES	ENGRAVED	ENRAGING	ENSWATHE
ENCASING	ENDOWERS	ENGRAVEN	ENRANGED	ENSWEEPS
ENCAVING	ENDOWING	ENGRAVER	ENRANGES	ENTAILED
ENCHAFED	ENDURING	ENGRAVES	ENRANKED	ENTAILER
ENCHAFES	ENFACING	ENGRIEVE	ENRAUNGE	ENTAMING
ENCHAINS	ENFEEBLE	ENGROOVE	ENRAVISH	ENTANGLE
ENCHANTS	ENFELONS	ENGUARDS	ENRHEUMS	ENTELLUS
ENCHARGE	ENFEOFFS	ENGULFED	ENRICHED	ENTENDER
ENCHARMS	ENFETTER	ENGULPHS	ENRICHER	ENTHETIC
ENCHASED	ENFEVERS	ENHALOED	ENRICHES	ENTHRALL
ENCHASER	ENFIERCE	ENHALOES	ENRIDGED	ENTHRONE
ENCHASES	ENFIRING	ENHANCES	ENRINGED	ENTHUSES
ENCHEERS	ENFIXING	ENHEARSE	ENROBING	ENTICING
ENCHORIC	ENFLAMED	ENHUNGER	ENROLLED	ENTITLED
ENCIPHER	ENFLAMES	ENHYDROS	ENROLLER	ENTITLES
ENCIRCLE	ENFLOWER	ENISLING	ENROOTED	ENTOILED
ENCLASPS	ENFOLDED	ENJAMBED	ENROUGHS	ENTOMBED
ENCLAVES	ENFOLDER	ENJOINED	ENROUNDS	ENTRAILS
ENCLITIC	ENFORCED	ENJOINER	ENSAMPLE	ENTRAINS
ENCLOSED	ENFORCER	ENJOYING	ENSCONCE	ENTRANCE
ENCLOSER	ENFORCES	ENKERNEL	ENSCROLL	ENTRANTS
ENCLOSES	ENFOREST	ENKINDLE	ENSEALED	ENTREATS
ENCLOTHE	ENFORMED	ENLACING	ENSEAMED	ENTREATY
ENCLOUDS	ENFRAMED	ENLARDED	ENSEARED	ENTRENCH
ENCODERS	ENFRAMES	ENLARGEN	ENSEMBLE	ENTROPIC
ENCODING	ENFREEZE	ENLARGER	ENSEWING	ENTRUSTS
ENCOLOUR	ENFROZEN	ENLARGES	ENSHEATH	ENTWINED
ENCOLURE	ENGAGERS	ENLIGHTS	ENSHELLS	ENTWINES
ENCORING	ENGAGING	ENLINKED	ENSHIELD	ENTWISTS
ENCRADLE	ENGAOLED	ENLISTED	ENSHRINE	ENURESES
ENCREASE	ENGENDER	ENLISTEE	ENSHROUD	ENURESIS
ENCRINAL	ENGILDED	ENLISTER	ENSIGNED	ENURETIC

ENVASSAL	ENVIABLE	ENVISION	ENWALLOW	ENWREATH
ENVAULTS	ENVIABLY	ENVYINGS	ENWHEELS	ENZONING
ENVENOMS	ENVISAGE	ENWALLED	ENWOMBED	

Words that begin with EX-

Seven-letter words

EXACTED	EXCITER	EXPENDS	EXPULSE	EXTORTS
EXACTOR	EXCITES	EXPERTS	EXPURGE	EXTRACT
EXALTER	EXCLAIM	EXPLAIN	EXSECTS	EXTRAIT
EXAMENS	EXCLAVE	EXPLANT	EXTENDS	EXTREAT
EXAMINE	EXCURSE	EXPORTS	EXTENSE	EXTREMA
EXAMPLE	EXEMPTS	EXPOSED	EXTENTS	EXURBAN
EXAPTED	EXHALED	EXPOSER	EXTERNE	EXURBIA
EXCHEAT	EXHALES	EXPOSES	EXTERNS	
EXCIDED	EXODIST	EXPOSIT	EXTINCT	
EXCIDES	EXOSMIC	EXPOUND	EXTINES	
EXCITED	EXPANDS	EXPRESS	EXTOLLS	

Eight-letter words

EXACTING	EXCIDING	EXODISTS	EXPOSERS	EXTENSOR
EXACTION	EXCITERS	EXOGAMIC	EXPOSING	EXTERNAL
EXACTORS	EXCITING	EXOSMOSE	EXPOSITS	EXTERNES
EXALTERS	EXCLAIMS	EXPANDER	EXPOUNDS	EXTINCTS
EXAMINES	EXCLAVES	EXPENDED	EXPULSED	EXTOLLED
EXANTHEM	EXCURSED	EXPERTLY	EXPULSES	EXTOLLER
EXCELLED	EXCURSES	EXPLAINS	EXPURGED	EXTRACTS
EXCESSED	EXCURSUS	EXPLANTS	EXPURGES	EXTRAITS
EXCESSES	EXEMPTED	EXPONENT	EXSECANT	EXTREATS
EXCHANGE	EXHALING	EXPORTED	EXTENDED	EXTUBATE
EXCHEATS	EXHUMATE	EXPORTER	EXTENDER	EXURBIAS

Words that begin with FOOT-

Seven-letter words

FOOTAGE	FOOTBOY	FOOTLES	FOOTPAD	FOOTWAY
FOOTBAG	FOOTERS	FOOTMAN	FOOTRAS	
FOOTBAR	FOOTLED	FOOTMEN	FOOTROT	

Eight-letter words

FOOTAGES	FOOTGEAR	FOOTNOTE	FOOTROPE	FOOTWAYS
FOOTBAGS	FOOTHILL	FOOTPACE	FOOTROTS	FOOTWEAR
FOOTBALL	FOOTHOLD	FOOTPADS	FOOTRULE	FOOTWELL
FOOTBARS	FOOTLESS	FOOTPAGE	FOOTSIES	FOOTWORK
FOOTBATH	FOOTLIKE	FOOTPATH	FOOTSLOG	FOOTWORN
FOOTBOYS	FOOTLING	FOOTPOST	FOOTSORE	
FOOTERED	FOOTMARK	FOOTRACE	FOOTSTEP	
FOOTFALL	FOOTMUFF	FOOTREST	FOOTWALL	

Words that begin with EN-

Words that begin with FOR-

Seven-letter words

FORAGED	FORDING	FORGOER	FORMALS	FORSAYS
FORAGER	FORDOES	FORGOES	FORMATE	FORSLOE
FORAGES	FORDONE	FORGONE	FORMATS	FORSLOW
FORAMEN	FORESTS	FORHENT	FORMICA	FORSOOK
FORBADE	FOREVER	FORHOWS	FORMING	FORTIES
FORBARE	FOREXES	FORKIER	FORMOLS	FORTING
FORBEAR	FORFAIR	FORKING	FORPETS	FORTUNE
FORBIDS	FORFEND	FORLANA	FORPINE	FORWARD
FORBODE	FORGAVE	FORLEND	FORPITS	FORWARN
FORBORE	FORGETS	FORLENT	FORRAYS	FORWENT
FORCATS	FORGING	FORLORE	FORSAID	FORWORN
FORCEPS	FORGIVE	FORLORN	FORSAKE	FORZATI

Eight-letter words

FORAGERS	FORESTER	FORJUDGE	FORSAKER	FORSWINK
FORAGING	FORFAIRS	FORLANAS	FORSAKES	FORSWORE
FORAMENS	FORFAULT	FORLENDS	FORSLACK	FORSWORN
FORBEARS	FORFENDS	FORLESES	FORSLOES	FORTHINK
FORBODED	FORGINGS	FORMATED	FORSLOWS	FORTRESS
FORBODES	FORGIVEN	FORMATES	FORSOOTH	FORTUNED
FORBORNE	FORGIVER	FORMICAS	FORSPEAK	FORTUNES
FORDOING	FORGIVES	FORMINGS	FORSPEND	FORWARDS
FOREKING	FORGOERS	FORPINED	FORSPENT	FORWARNS
FORELAIN	FORGOING	FORPINES	FORSPOKE	FORWASTE
FORELAND	FORHENTS	FORRAYED	FORSWEAR	FORWEARY

Words that begin with IM-

Seven-letter words

IMAGERS	IMBRAST	IMPAINT	IMPEACH	IMPOSED
IMAGING	IMBROWN	IMPAIRS	IMPEARL	IMPOSER
IMAGISM	IMBRUTE	IMPALAS	IMPEDES	IMPOSES
IMAGIST	IMBURSE	IMPALED	IMPENDS	IMPOSTS
IMAMATE	IMMASKS	IMPALER	IMPERIL	IMPOUND
IMARETS	IMMENSE	IMPALES	IMPIETY	IMPOWER
IMBALMS	IMMERGE	IMPANEL	IMPINGS	IMPRESA
IMBARKS	IMMERSE	IMPARKS	IMPIOUS	IMPRESE
IMBASED	IMMEWED	IMPARTS	IMPLANT	IMPRESS
IMBASES	IMMIXED	IMPASSE	IMPLATE	IMPREST
IMBATHE	IMMIXES	IMPASTE	IMPLEAD	IMPRINT
IMBLAZE	IMMORAL	IMPAVED	IMPLIED	IMPROVE
IMBOSKS	IMMURED	IMPAVES	IMPLIES	IMPULSE
IMBOSOM	IMMURES	IMPAVID	IMPONES	IMPURER
IMBOWER	IMPACTS	IMPAWNS	IMPORTS	

Eight-letter words

IMAGINGS	IMAMATES	IMBARRED	IMBATHES	IMBLAZED
IMAGISMS	IMBALMED	IMBASING	IMBEDDED	IMBLAZES
IMAGISTS	IMBARKED	IMBATHED	IMBITTER	IMBODIED

IMBODIES	IMMESHED	IMPARKED	IMPLEADS	IMPOUNDS
IMBOLDEN	IMMESHES	IMPARLED	IMPLEDGE	IMPOWERS
IMBORDER	IMMEWING	IMPARTED	IMPLEXES	IMPRESES
IMBOSOMS	IMMINGLE	IMPARTER	IMPLUNGE	IMPRESTS
IMBOSSED	IMMINUTE	IMPASSES	IMPLYING	IMPRINTS
IMBOSSES	IMMIXING	IMPASTED	IMPOCKET	IMPRISON
IMBOWERS	IMMOBILE	IMPASTES	IMPOLDER	IMPROPER
IMBROWNS	IMMODEST	IMPAVING	IMPOLICY	IMPROVED
IMBRUTED	IMMOMENT	IMPAWNED	IMPOLITE	IMPROVER
IMBRUTES	IMMORTAL	IMPEARLS	IMPONENT	IMPROVES
IMBURSES	IMMOTILE	IMPENDED	IMPOROUS	IMPUDENT
IMMANENT	IMMURING	IMPERILS	IMPORTED	IMPULSED
IMMANTLE	IMPAINTS	IMPINGED	IMPORTER	IMPULSES
IMMASKED	IMPAIRED	IMPINGER	IMPOSERS	IMPURELY
IMMATURE	IMPAIRER	IMPLANTS	IMPOSING	IMPUREST
IMMERGED	IMPALING	IMPLATED	IMPOSTED	IMPURITY
IMMERGES	IMPANELS	IMPLATES	IMPOSTER	IMPURPLE
IMMERSES	IMPARITY	IMPLEACH	IMPOTENT	

Words that begin with IN-

Seven-letter words

INANGAS	INCURVE	INFIXES	INLANDS	INSTALL
INAPTLY	INDARTS	INFLAME	INLAYER	INSTARS
INARMED	INDENES	INFLOWS	INLIERS	INSTATE
INBEING	INDENTS	INFOLDS	INLOCKS	INSTEAD
INBOARD	INDEWED	INFORCE	INLYING	INSTEPS
INBOUND	INDEXES	INFORMS	INMATES	INSTILL
INBREAK	INDICES	INFRACT	INNARDS	INSURED
INBREDS	INDICTS	INFUSED	INNERVE	INSURER
INBREED	INDITED	INFUSES	INORBED	INSURES
INBRING	INDITES	INGATES	INPHASE	INSWEPT
INBUILT	INDOLES	INGENUS	INPOURS	INSWING
INBURST	INDOORS	INGESTS	INQUEST	INTAKES
INCAGED	INDORSE	INGLOBE	INQUIET	INTENDS
INCAGES	INDOWED	INGOING	INQUIRE	INTENSE
INCANTS	INDRAFT	INGRAFT	INROADS	INTENTS
INCASED	INDRAWN	INGRAIN	INSANER	INTERNE
INCASES	INDUCES	INGRATE	INSCAPE	INTERNS
INCAVED	INDUCTS	INGROSS	INSCULP	INTINES
INCAVES	INDUING	INGROUP	INSEAMS	INTITLE
INCEDED	INDWELL	INGROWN	INSECTS	INTOMBS
INCEDES	INDWELT	INGULFS	INSEEMS	INTONED
INCENSE	INEARTH	INGULPH	INSHELL	INTONER
INCENTS	INEXACT	INHABIT	INSHIPS	INTONES
INCHASE	INFALLS	INHALED	INSHORE	INTORTS
INCITED	INFAMED	INHALER	INSIDER	INTRANT
INCITER	INFAMES	INHALES	INSIDES	INTREAT
INCITES	INFANCY	INHAULS	INSIGHT	INTRONS
INCIVIL	INFARES	INHERES	INSINEW	INTRUST
INCLASP	INFAUNA	INHOOPS	INSISTS	INTURNS
INCLINE	INFEOFF	INHUMAN	INSNARE	INTWINE
INCLIPS	INFESTS	INISLED	INSOFAR	INTWIST
INCLOSE	INFIELD	INISLES	INSOLES	INURNED
INCOMER	INFIGHT	INJELLY	INSOOTH	INUTILE
INCOMES	INFILLS	INJOINT	INSOULS	INVADED
INCROSS	INFIRMS	INLACED	INSPANS	INVADES
INCRUST	INFIXED	INLACES	INSPIRE	INVALID

Words that begin with IM-

INVENTS	INVEXED	INWALLS	INWINDS	INWRAPS
INVERSE	INVITAL	INWARDS	INWORKS	
INVERTS	INVOICE	INWEAVE	INWOUND	
INVESTS	INVOLVE	INWICKS	INWOVEN	

Eight-letter words

INACTION	INDICTED	INFORMER	INQUIRES	INTERNED
INACTIVE	INDIGEST	INFOUGHT	INRUSHES	INTERNES
INARABLE	INDIRECT	INFRACTS	INSANELY	INTHRALL
INARCHED	INDITING	INFRINGE	INSANEST	INTHRONE
INARCHES	INDOCILE	INFRUGAL	INSANIES	INTIMIST
INARMING	INDOLENT	INFUSING	INSANITY	INTITLED
INAURATE	INDORSER	INFUSION	INSCAPES	INTITLES
INBEINGS	INDORSES	INGATHER	INSCIENT	INTITULE
INBOARDS	INDOWING	INGLOBED	INSCONCE	INTOMBED
INBOUNDS	INDRAFTS	INGLOBES	INSCRIBE	INTONERS
INBREAKS	INDRENCH	INGOINGS	INSCROLL	INTONING
INBREEDS	INDUCTED	INGRAFTS	INSCULPS	INTRANTS
INBRINGS	INDWELLS	INGRAINS	INSCULPT	INTREATS
INBURSTS	INEARTHS	INGRATES	INSEAMED	INTRENCH
INCAGING	INEDIBLE	INGROOVE	INSECURE	INTREPID
INCANTED	INEDITED	INGROUND	INSEEMED	INTRUSTS
INCASING	INEQUITY	INGROUPS	INSETTER	INTUBATE
INCAVING	INERRANT	INGROWTH	INSHEATH	INTURNED
INCEDING	INESSIVE	INGULFED	INSHELLS	INTWINED
INCENSED	INEXPERT	INGULPHS	INSHRINE	INTWINES
INCENSER	INFAMING	INHABITS	INSIDERS	INTWISTS
INCENSES	INFAMOUS	INHALERS	INSIGHTS	INUNDATE
INCENSOR	INFAUNAE	INHALING	INSINEWS	INURBANE
INCENTER	INFAUNAL	INHAULER	INSISTED	INURNING
INCENTRE	INFAUNAS	INHEARSE	INSISTER	INUSTION
INCHASED	INFECUND	INHOLDER	INSNARED	INVADING
INCHASES	INFEOFFS	INHOOPED	INSNARER	INVENTED
INCITERS	INFERIAE	INHUMANE	INSNARES	INVENTER
INCITING	INFESTER	INHUMATE	INSOLATE	INVERITY
INCIVISM	INFIELDS	INISLING	INSOULED	INVERSED
INCLASPS	INFIGHTS	INJOINTS	INSPHERE	INVERSES
INCLINES	INFILLED	INJURIES	INSPIRED	INVERTED
INCLOSED	INFINITE	INLACING	INSPIRES	INVESTED
INCLOSER	INFIRMED	INLANDER	INSPIRIT	INVIABLE
INCLOSES	INFIRMER	INLAYERS	INSTABLE	INVIABLY
INCOMERS	INFIRMLY	INLAYING	INSTALLS	INVIRILE
INCOMING	INFIXING	INLOCKED	INSTANCE	INVISCID
INCORPSE	INFLAMED	INMESHED	INSTATED	INVOICED
INCREASE	INFLAMER	INMESHES	INSTATES	INVOICES
INCREATE	INFLAMES	INNATIVE	INSTILLS	INVOLUTE
INCRUSTS	INFLATUS	INNERVED	INSTRESS	INVOLVED
INCUMBER	INFLEXED	INNERVES	INSTROKE	INVOLVES
INCURRED	INFLIGHT	INNOCENT	INSUCKEN	INWALLED
INCURVED	INFLUENT	INORBING	INSURING	INWEAVED
INCURVES	INFLUXES	INORNATE	INSWATHE	INWEAVES
INDARTED	INFOLDED	INPOURED	INSWINGS	INWICKED
INDEBTED	INFOLDER	INPUTTED	INTARSIA	INWORKED
INDECENT	INFORCED	INPUTTER	INTENDED	
INDENTED	INFORCES	INQUESTS	INTENDER	
INDEVOUT	INFORMAL	INQUIETS	INTENSER	
INDEWING	INFORMED	INQUIRED	INTERNAL	

Words that begin with ISO-

Seven-letter words

ISOAMYL	ISODOSE	ISOGRAM	ISOMERE	ISOTONE
ISOBARE	ISOFORM	ISOLATE	ISONOME	ISOTOPE
ISOBARS	ISOGAMY	ISOLEAD	ISOPODS	ISOTRON
ISOBASE	ISOGONE	ISOLINE	ISOSPIN	ISOTYPE
ISOBATH	ISOGONS	ISOLOGS	ISOTACH	ISOZYME

Eight-letter words

ISOAMYLS	ISOCHORE	ISOGRAMS	ISONOMES	ISOTONIC
ISOBARES	ISOCLINE	ISOGRAPH	ISONOMIC	ISOTOPES
ISOBARIC	ISODOSES	ISOLATED	ISOPHONE	ISOTOPIC
ISOBASES	ISOFORMS	ISOLEADS	ISOSPINS	ISOTRONS
ISOBATHS	ISOGAMIC	ISOLEXES	ISOTACHS	ISOTYPES
ISOBUTYL	ISOGENIC	ISOLINES	ISOTHERE	ISOTYPIC
ISOCHASM	ISOGLOSS	ISOMERES	ISOTHERM	ISOZYMES
ISOCHIME	ISOGRAFT	ISOMORPH	ISOTONES	ISOZYMIC

Words that begin with MAN-

Seven-letter words

MANAGED	MANGELS	MANKIER	MANNITE	MANTIDS
MANAGER	MANGING	MANKIND	MANNOSE	MANTIES
MANAGES	MANGLED	MANLESS	MANPACK	MANTOES
MANAKIN	MANGOES	MANLIER	MANREDS	MANTRAM
MANANAS	MANGOLD	MANLIKE	MANRENT	MANTRAP
MANDATE	MANHOLE	MANLILY	MANROPE	MANURES
MANDOMS	MANHOOD	MANMADE	MANSARD	MANWARD
MANGABY	MANHUNT	MANNANS	MANTEEL	MANWISE
MANGALS	MANJACK	MANNISH	MANTELS	

Eight-letter words

MANAGERS	MANFULLY	MANJACKS	MANRENTS	MANTEELS
MANAGING	MANGOLDS	MANKINDS	MANRIDER	MANTRAMS
MANDATED	MANGROVE	MANNITES	MANROPES	MANTRAPS
MANDATES	MANHOLES	MANNOSES	MANSARDS	MANURIAL
MANDRAKE	MANHOODS	MANPACKS	MANSHIFT	MANWARDS
MANDRILL	MANHUNTS	MANPOWER	MANSWORN	

Words that begin with MIS-

Seven-letter words

MISACTS	MISBIND	MISCOOK	MISDEED	MISDRAW
MISADDS	MISBORN	MISCOPY	MISDEEM	MISDREW
MISAIMS	MISCALL	MISCUED	MISDIAL	MISEASE
MISALLY	MISCAST	MISCUES	MISDIET	MISEATS
MISAVER	MISCITE	MISCUTS	MISDOER	MISEDIT
MISBIAS	MISCODE	MISDATE	MISDOES	MISERES
MISBILL	MISCOIN	MISDEAL	MISDONE	MISFALL

MISFARE	MISKENS	MISMATE	MISSEEM	MISTEND
MISFEED	MISKENT	MISMEET	MISSEEN	MISTERM
MISFELL	MISKEPT	MISMOVE	MISSEES	MISTIER
MISFILE	MISKEYS	MISNAME	MISSELS	MISTIME
MISFIRE	MISKICK	MISPAGE	MISSEND	MISTING
MISFITS	MISKNEW	MISPART	MISSENT	MISTOLD
MISFORM	MISKNOW	MISPENS	MISSETS	MISTOOK
MISGAVE	MISLAID	MISPLAN	MISSHOD	MISTUNE
MISGIVE	MISLAIN	MISPLAY	MISSIES	MISTYPE
MISGOES	MISLAYS	MISPLED	MISSILE	MISUSED
MISGONE	MISLEAD	MISRATE	MISSING	MISUSER
MISGREW	MISLIES	MISREAD	MISSORT	MISUSES
MISGROW	MISLIKE	MISRELY	MISSOUT	MISWEEN
MISHAPS	MISLIVE	MISRULE	MISSTEP	MISWEND
MISHEAR	MISLUCK	MISSAID	MISSTOP	MISWENT
MISHITS	MISMADE	MISSALS	MISSUIT	MISWORD
MISJOIN	MISMAKE	MISSAYS	MISTAKE	MISWRIT
MISKEEP	MISMARK	MISSEAT	MISTELL	MISYOKE

Eight-letter words

MISACTED	MISCOOKS	MISFILES	MISLIVES	MISRATED
MISADAPT	MISCOUNT	MISFIRED	MISLODGE	MISRATES
MISADDED	MISCREED	MISFIRES	MISLUCKS	MISREADS
MISAGENT	MISCUING	MISFOCUS	MISLYING	MISREFER
MISAIMED	MISDATED	MISFORMS	MISMAKES	MISROUTE
MISALIGN	MISDATES	MISFRAME	MISMARKS	MISRULED
MISALLOT	MISDEALS	MISGAUGE	MISMARRY	MISRULES
MISALTER	MISDEALT	MISGIVEN	MISMATCH	MISSABLE
MISAPPLY	MISDEEDS	MISGIVES	MISMATED	MISSEATS
MISARRAY	MISDEEMS	MISGOING	MISMATES	MISSEEMS
MISASSAY	MISDEMPT	MISGRADE	MISMEETS	MISSENDS
MISATONE	MISDIALS	MISGRAFF	MISMETRE	MISSENSE
MISAVERS	MISDIETS	MISGRAFT	MISMOVED	MISSHAPE
MISAWARD	MISDIGHT	MISGROWN	MISMOVES	MISSILES
MISBEGAN	MISDOERS	MISGROWS	MISNAMED	MISSISES
MISBEGIN	MISDOING	MISGUESS	MISNAMES	MISSORTS
MISBEGOT	MISDONNE	MISGUIDE	MISOLOGY	MISSOUND
MISBEGUN	MISDOUBT	MISHEARD	MISORDER	MISSOUTS
MISBILLS	MISDRAWN	MISHEARS	MISPAGED	MISSPACE
MISBINDS	MISDRAWS	MISINFER	MISPAGES	MISSPEAK
MISBIRTH	MISDREAD	MISINTER	MISPAINT	MISSPELL
MISBOUND	MISDRIVE	MISJOINS	MISPARSE	MISSPELT
MISBRAND	MISDROVE	MISJUDGE	MISPARTS	MISSPEND
MISBUILD	MISEASES	MISKEEPS	MISPATCH	MISSPENT
MISBUILT	MISEATEN	MISKEYED	MISPLACE	MISSPOKE
MISCALLS	MISEDITS	MISKICKS	MISPLANS	MISSTAMP
MISCARRY	MISENROL	MISKNOWN	MISPLANT	MISSTART
MISCASTS	MISENTER	MISKNOWS	MISPLAYS	MISSTATE
MISCHIEF	MISENTRY	MISLABEL	MISPLEAD	MISSTEER
MISCHOSE	MISEVENT	MISLABOR	MISPOINT	MISSTEPS
MISCITED	MISFAITH	MISLAYER	MISPOISE	MISSTOPS
MISCITES	MISFALLS	MISLEADS	MISPRICE	MISSTYLE
MISCLAIM	MISFARED	MISLEARN	MISPRINT	MISSUITS
MISCLASS	MISFARES	MISLIGHT	MISPRISE	MISSUSES
MISCODED	MISFEEDS	MISLIKED	MISPRIZE	MISTAKEN
MISCODES	MISFEIGN	MISLIKER	MISPROUD	MISTAKER
MISCOINS	MISFIELD	MISLIKES	MISQUOTE	MISTAKES
MISCOLOR	MISFILED	MISLIVED	MISRAISE	MISTEACH

MISTELLS	MISTINGS	MISTRUST	MISUNION	MISWRITE
MISTENDS	MISTITLE	MISTRUTH	MISUSAGE	MISWROTE
MISTERMS	MISTOUCH	MISTRYST	MISUSERS	MISYOKED
MISTHINK	MISTRACE	MISTUNED	MISUSING	MISYOKES
MISTHREW	MISTRAIN	MISTUNES	MISVALUE	
MISTHROW	MISTREAT	MISTUTOR	MISWEENS	
MISTIMED	MISTRESS	MISTYPED	MISWENDS	
MISTIMES	MISTRIAL	MISTYPES	MISWORDS	

Words that begin with NON-

Seven-letter words

NONACID	NONCOMS	NONGAYS	NONORAL	NONSTOP
NONAGED	NONCORE	NONHEME	NONPAID	NONSUCH
NONAGES	NONDRIP	NONHERO	NONPAST	NONSUIT
NONAGON	NONDRUG	NONHOME	NONPEAK	NONUSER
NONANES	NONEGOS	NONIRON	NONPLAY	NONUSES
NONARTS	NONFACT	NONJURY	NONPLUS	NONWAGE
NONBANK	NONFANS	NONLIFE	NONPOOR	NONWARS
NONBODY	NONFARM	NONMEAT	NONPROS	NONWOOL
NONBOOK	NONFOOD	NONNEWS	NONSELF	NONWORD
NONCASH	NONFUEL	NONNIES	NONSKID	NONWORK
NONCOLA	NONGAME	NONOILY	NONSLIP	NONZERO

Eight-letter words

NONACIDS	NONEVENT	NONLEVEL	NONPASTS	NONTIDAL
NONACTOR	NONFACTS	NONLIVES	NONPLAYS	NONTITLE
NONADULT	NONFATAL	NONLOCAL	NONPOINT	NONTONAL
NONAGONS	NONFATTY	NONLOYAL	NONPOLAR	NONTONIC
NONBANKS	NONFINAL	NONLYRIC	NONPRINT	NONTOXIC
NONBASIC	NONFLUID	NONMAJOR	NONQUOTA	NONTRUMP
NONBEING	NONFOCAL	NONMETAL	NONRATED	NONTRUTH
NONBLACK	NONGLARE	NONMETRO	NONRIGID	NONUNION
NONBOOKS	NONGREEN	NONMODAL	NONRIVAL	NONURBAN
NONBRAND	NONGUEST	NONMONEY	NONROYAL	NONUSERS
NONCLASS	NONGUILT	NONMORAL	NONRURAL	NONUSING
NONCLING	NONHARDY	NONMUSIC	NONSENSE	NONVALID
NONCOLAS	NONHUMAN	NONNASAL	NONSKIER	NONVIRAL
NONCOLOR	NONIDEAL	NONNAVAL	NONSOLAR	NONVITAL
NONCRIME	NONIMAGE	NONNOBLE	NONSOLID	NONVOCAL
NONDAIRY	NONINERT	NONNOVEL	NONSTICK	NONVOTER
NONDANCE	NONIONIC	NONOBESE	NONSTOPS	NONWHITE
NONELECT	NONISSUE	NONOHMIC	NONSTORY	NONWOODY
NONELITE	NONJUROR	NONOWNER	NONSTYLE	NONWORDS
NONEMPTY	NONLABOR	NONPAGAN	NONSUGAR	NONWOVEN
NONENTRY	NONLEAFY	NONPAPAL	NONSUITS	
NONEQUAL	NONLEGAL	NONPARTY	NONTAXES	

Words that begin with OUT-

Seven-letter words

OUTACTS	OUTASKS	OUTBARK	OUTBEAM	OUTBRAG
OUTADDS	OUTBACK	OUTBARS	OUTBEGS	OUTBRED
OUTAGES	OUTBAKE	OUTBAWL	OUTBIDS	OUTBULK

Words that begin with MIS-

OUTBURN	**OUT**GAIN	**OUT**LETS	**OUT**RIDE	**OUT**SWUM
OUTBUYS	**OUT**GATE	**OUT**LIED	**OUT**RIGS	**OUT**TAKE
OUTCALL	**OUT**GAVE	**OUT**LIER	**OUT**RING	**OUT**TALK
OUTCAST	**OUT**GAZE	**OUT**LIES	**OUT**ROAR	**OUT**TASK
OUTCHID	**OUT**GIVE	**OUT**LINE	**OUT**ROCK	**OUT**TELL
OUTCITY	**OUT**GLOW	**OUT**LIVE	**OUT**RODE	**OUT**TOLD
OUTCOME	**OUT**GNAW	**OUT**LOOK	**OUT**ROLL	**OUT**TOOK
OUTCOOK	**OUT**GOER	**OUT**LOVE	**OUT**ROOP	**OUT**TOPS
OUTCROP	**OUT**GOES	**OUT**MANS	**OUT**ROOT	**OUT**TROT
OUTCROW	**OUT**GONE	**OUT**MODE	**OUT**ROPE	**OUT**TURN
OUTDARE	**OUT**GREW	**OUT**MOST	**OUT**ROWS	**OUT**VIED
OUTDATE	**OUT**GRIN	**OUT**MOVE	**OUT**RUNG	**OUT**VIES
OUTDOER	**OUT**GROW	**OUT**NAME	**OUT**RUNS	**OUT**VOTE
OUTDOES	**OUT**GUNS	**OUT**NESS	**OUT**RUSH	**OUT**WAIT
OUTDONE	**OUT**GUSH	**OUT**PACE	**OUT**SAID	**OUT**WALK
OUTDOOR	**OUT**HAUL	**OUT**PART	**OUT**SAIL	**OUT**WARD
OUTDRAG	**OUT**HEAR	**OUT**PASS	**OUT**SANG	**OUT**WARS
OUTDRAW	**OUT**HIRE	**OUT**PEEP	**OUT**SAYS	**OUT**WASH
OUTDREW	**OUT**HITS	**OUT**PEER	**OUT**SEEN	**OUT**WEAR
OUTDROP	**OUT**HOWL	**OUT**PITY	**OUT**SEES	**OUT**WEED
OUTDUEL	**OUT**HUNT	**OUT**PLAN	**OUT**SELL	**OUT**WEEP
OUTDURE	**OUT**JEST	**OUT**PLAY	**OUT**SETS	**OUT**WELL
OUTEARN	**OUT**JETS	**OUT**PLOD	**OUT**SHOT	**OUT**WENT
OUTEATS	**OUT**JINX	**OUT**PLOT	**OUT**SIDE	**OUT**WEPT
OUTECHO	**OUT**JUMP	**OUT**POLL	**OUT**SING	**OUT**WICK
OUTEDGE	**OUT**JUTS	**OUT**PORT	**OUT**SINS	**OUT**WILE
OUTFACE	**OUT**KEEP	**OUT**POST	**OUT**SITS	**OUT**WILL
OUTFALL	**OUT**KEPT	**OUT**POUR	**OUT**SIZE	**OUT**WIND
OUTFAST	**OUT**KICK	**OUT**PRAY	**OUT**SOAR	**OUT**WING
OUTFAWN	**OUT**KILL	**OUT**PULL	**OUT**SOLD	**OUT**WINS
OUTFEEL	**OUT**KISS	**OUT**PUSH	**OUT**SOLE	**OUT**WISH
OUTFELT	**OUT**LAID	**OUT**PUTS	**OUT**SPAN	**OUT**WITH
OUTFIND	**OUT**LAIN	**OUT**RACE	**OUT**SPED	**OUT**WITS
OUTFIRE	**OUT**LAND	**OUT**RAGE	**OUT**STAY	**OUT**WORE
OUTFISH	**OUT**LASH	**OUT**RANG	**OUT**STEP	**OUT**WORK
OUTFITS	**OUT**LAST	**OUT**RANK	**OUT**SULK	**OUT**WORN
OUTFLEW	**OUT**LAWS	**OUT**RATE	**OUT**SUMS	**OUT**WRIT
OUTFLOW	**OUT**LAYS	**OUT**RAVE	**OUT**SUNG	**OUT**YELL
OUTFOOL	**OUT**LEAD	**OUT**READ	**OUT**SWAM	**OUT**YELP
OUTFOOT	**OUT**LEAP	**OUT**REDS	**OUT**SWIM	

Eight-letter words

OUTACTED	**OUT**BLUSH	**OUT**BULKS	**OUT**CLOMB	**OUT**DARES
OUTADDED	**OUT**BOARD	**OUT**BULLY	**OUT**COACH	**OUT**DATED
OUTARGUE	**OUT**BOAST	**OUT**BURNS	**OUT**COMES	**OUT**DATES
OUTASKED	**OUT**BOUND	**OUT**BURNT	**OUT**COOKS	**OUT**DODGE
OUTBACKS	**OUT**BOXED	**OUT**BURST	**OUT**COUNT	**OUT**DOERS
OUTBAKED	**OUT**BOXES	**OUT**CALLS	**OUT**CRAWL	**OUT**DOING
OUTBAKES	**OUT**BRAGS	**OUT**CAPER	**OUT**CRIED	**OUT**DOORS
OUTBARKS	**OUT**BRAVE	**OUT**CASTE	**OUT**CRIES	**OUT**DRAGS
OUTBAWLS	**OUT**BRAWL	**OUT**CASTS	**OUT**CROPS	**OUT**DRANK
OUTBEAMS	**OUT**BREAK	**OUT**CATCH	**OUT**CROSS	**OUT**DRAWN
OUTBITCH	**OUT**BREED	**OUT**CAVIL	**OUT**CROWD	**OUT**DRAWS
OUTBLAZE	**OUT**BRIBE	**OUT**CHARM	**OUT**CROWS	**OUT**DREAM
OUTBLEAT	**OUT**BROKE	**OUT**CHEAT	**OUT**CURSE	**OUT**DRESS
OUTBLESS	**OUT**BUILD	**OUT**CHIDE	**OUT**CURVE	**OUT**DRINK
OUTBLOOM	**OUT**BUILT	**OUT**CLASS	**OUT**DANCE	**OUT**DRIVE
OUTBLUFF	**OUT**BULGE	**OUT**CLIMB	**OUT**DARED	**OUT**DROPS

OUTDROVE	**OUT**GROWN	**OUT**PLANS	**OUT**SHAME	**OUT**SWUNG
OUTDRUNK	**OUT**GROWS	**OUT**PLAYS	**OUT**SHINE	**OUT**TAKEN
OUTDUELS	**OUT**GUARD	**OUT**PLODS	**OUT**SHONE	**OUT**TAKES
OUTDURED	**OUT**GUESS	**OUT**PLOTS	**OUT**SHOOT	**OUT**TALKS
OUTDURES	**OUT**GUIDE	**OUT**POINT	**OUT**SHOTS	**OUT**TASKS
OUTDWELL	**OUT**HAULS	**OUT**POLLS	**OUT**SHOUT	**OUT**TELLS
OUTDWELT	**OUT**HEARD	**OUT**PORTS	**OUT**SIDER	**OUT**THANK
OUTEARNS	**OUT**HEARS	**OUT**POSTS	**OUT**SIDES	**OUT**THINK
OUTEATEN	**OUT**HIRED	**OUT**POURS	**OUT**SIGHT	**OUT**THREW
OUTEDGES	**OUT**HIRES	**OUT**POWER	**OUT**SINGS	**OUT**THROB
OUTFABLE	**OUT**HOMER	**OUT**PRAYS	**OUT**SIZED	**OUT**THROW
OUTFACED	**OUT**HOUSE	**OUT**PREEN	**OUT**SIZES	**OUT**TOWER
OUTFACES	**OUT**HOWLS	**OUT**PRESS	**OUT**SKATE	**OUT**TRADE
OUTFALLS	**OUT**HUMOR	**OUT**PRICE	**OUT**SKIRT	**OUT**TRICK
OUTFASTS	**OUT**HUNTS	**OUT**PRIZE	**OUT**SLEEP	**OUT**TROTS
OUTFAWNS	**OUT**JESTS	**OUT**PULLS	**OUT**SLEPT	**OUT**TRUMP
OUTFEAST	**OUT**JUMPS	**OUT**PUNCH	**OUT**SLICK	**OUT**TURNS
OUTFEELS	**OUT**KEEPS	**OUT**PUPIL	**OUT**SMART	**OUT**VALUE
OUTFENCE	**OUT**KICKS	**OUT**QUOTE	**OUT**SMELL	**OUT**VAUNT
OUTFIELD	**OUT**KILLS	**OUT**RACED	**OUT**SMELT	**OUT**VENOM
OUTFIGHT	**OUT**LANDS	**OUT**RACES	**OUT**SMILE	**OUT**VOICE
OUTFINDS	**OUT**LASTS	**OUT**RAGED	**OUT**SMOKE	**OUT**VOTED
OUTFIRED	**OUT**LAUGH	**OUT**RAGES	**OUT**SNORE	**OUT**VOTER
OUTFIRES	**OUT**LAWED	**OUT**RAISE	**OUT**SOARS	**OUT**VOTES
OUTFLANK	**OUT**LEADS	**OUT**RANCE	**OUT**SOLES	**OUT**VYING
OUTFLASH	**OUT**LEAPS	**OUT**RANGE	**OUT**SPANS	**OUT**WAITS
OUTFLIES	**OUT**LEAPT	**OUT**RANKS	**OUT**SPEAK	**OUT**WALKS
OUTFLING	**OUT**LEARN	**OUT**RATED	**OUT**SPEED	**OUT**WARDS
OUTFLOAT	**OUT**LIERS	**OUT**RATES	**OUT**SPELL	**OUT**WASTE
OUTFLOWN	**OUT**LINED	**OUT**RAVED	**OUT**SPELT	**OUT**WATCH
OUTFLOWS	**OUT**LINER	**OUT**RAVES	**OUT**SPEND	**OUT**WEARS
OUTFLUSH	**OUT**LINES	**OUT**REACH	**OUT**SPENT	**OUT**WEARY
OUTFOOLS	**OUT**LIVED	**OUT**READS	**OUT**SPOKE	**OUT**WEEDS
OUTFOOTS	**OUT**LIVER	**OUT**REIGN	**OUT**SPORT	**OUT**WEEPS
OUTFOUND	**OUT**LIVES	**OUT**RIDER	**OUT**STAND	**OUT**WEIGH
OUTFOXED	**OUT**LOOKS	**OUT**RIDES	**OUT**STARE	**OUT**WELLS
OUTFOXES	**OUT**LOVED	**OUT**RIGHT	**OUT**START	**OUT**WHIRL
OUTFROWN	**OUT**LOVES	**OUT**RINGS	**OUT**STATE	**OUT**WICKS
OUTGAINS	**OUT**LYING	**OUT**RIVAL	**OUT**STAYS	**OUT**WILED
OUTGASES	**OUT**MARCH	**OUT**ROARS	**OUT**STEER	**OUT**WILES
OUTGATES	**OUT**MATCH	**OUT**ROCKS	**OUT**STEPS	**OUT**WILLS
OUTGAZED	**OUT**MODES	**OUT**ROLLS	**OUT**STOOD	**OUT**WINDS
OUTGAZES	**OUT**MOVED	**OUT**ROOPS	**OUT**STRIP	**OUT**WINGS
OUTGIVEN	**OUT**MOVES	**OUT**ROOTS	**OUT**STUDY	**OUT**WORKS
OUTGIVES	**OUT**NAMED	**OUT**ROPER	**OUT**STUNT	**OUT**WORTH
OUTGLARE	**OUT**NAMES	**OUT**ROPES	**OUT**SULKS	**OUT**WOUND
OUTGLEAM	**OUT**NIGHT	**OUT**ROWED	**OUT**SWARE	**OUT**WREST
OUTGLOWS	**OUT**PACED	**OUT**SAILS	**OUT**SWEAR	**OUT**WRITE
OUTGNAWN	**OUT**PACES	**OUT**SAVOR	**OUT**SWEEP	**OUT**WROTE
OUTGNAWS	**OUT**PAINT	**OUT**SCOLD	**OUT**SWELL	**OUT**YELLS
OUTGOERS	**OUT**PARTS	**OUT**SCOOP	**OUT**SWEPT	**OUT**YELPS
OUTGOING	**OUT**PEEPS	**OUT**SCORE	**OUT**SWIMS	**OUT**YIELD
OUTGRINS	**OUT**PEERS	**OUT**SCORN	**OUT**SWING	
OUTGROSS	**OUT**PITCH	**OUT**SELLS	**OUT**SWORE	
OUTGROUP	**OUT**PLACE	**OUT**SERVE	**OUT**SWORN	

Words that begin with OUT-

Words that begin with OVER-

Seven-letter words

OVERACT	OVERCUT	OVERFIT	OVERMAN	OVERSEA
OVERAGE	OVERDID	OVERFLY	OVERMEN	OVERSEE
OVERALL	OVERDOG	OVERGET	OVERMIX	OVERSET
OVERAPT	OVERDRY	OVERGOT	OVERNET	OVERSEW
OVERARM	OVERDUB	OVERHIT	OVERNEW	OVERSOW
OVERATE	OVERDUE	OVERHOT	OVERPAY	OVERSUP
OVERAWE	OVERDYE	OVERJOY	OVERPLY	OVERTAX
OVERBED	OVEREAT	OVERLAP	OVERRAN	OVERTIP
OVERBET	OVEREGG	OVERLAX	OVERRED	OVERTOP
OVERBID	OVEREYE	OVERLAY	OVERREN	OVERUSE
OVERBIG	OVERFAR	OVERLET	OVERRUN	OVERWET
OVERBUY	OVERFAT	OVERLIE	OVERSAD	
OVERCOY	OVERFED	OVERLIT	OVERSAW	

Eight-letter words

OVERABLE	OVERCOOK	OVERFOLD	OVERHOPE	OVERLOVE
OVERACTS	OVERCOOL	OVERFOND	OVERHUNG	OVERLUSH
OVERAGED	OVERCRAM	OVERFOUL	OVERHUNT	OVERMANS
OVERAGES	OVERCRAW	OVERFREE	OVERHYPE	OVERMANY
OVERALLS	OVERCROP	OVERFULL	OVERIDLE	OVERMAST
OVERARCH	OVERCROW	OVERFUND	OVERJOYS	OVERMEEK
OVERARMS	OVERCURE	OVERGALL	OVERJUMP	OVERMELT
OVERAWED	OVERCUTS	OVERGANG	OVERJUST	OVERMILD
OVERAWES	OVERDARE	OVERGAVE	OVERKEEN	OVERMILK
OVERBAKE	OVERDEAR	OVERGEAR	OVERKEEP	OVERMINE
OVERBEAR	OVERDECK	OVERGETS	OVERKEPT	OVERMUCH
OVERBEAT	OVERDOER	OVERGILD	OVERKEST	OVERNAME
OVERBETS	OVERDOES	OVERGILT	OVERKILL	OVERNEAR
OVERBIDS	OVERDOGS	OVERGIRD	OVERKIND	OVERNEAT
OVERBILL	OVERDONE	OVERGIRT	OVERKING	OVERNETS
OVERBITE	OVERDOSE	OVERGIVE	OVERKNEE	OVERNICE
OVERBLEW	OVERDRAW	OVERGLAD	OVERLADE	OVERPACK
OVERBLOW	OVERDREW	OVERGOAD	OVERLAID	OVERPAGE
OVERBOIL	OVERDUBS	OVERGOES	OVERLAIN	OVERPAID
OVERBOLD	OVERDUST	OVERGONE	OVERLAND	OVERPART
OVERBOOK	OVERDYED	OVERGREW	OVERLAPS	OVERPASS
OVERBOOT	OVERDYER	OVERGROW	OVERLARD	OVERPAST
OVERBORE	OVERDYES	OVERHAIR	OVERLATE	OVERPAYS
OVERBORN	OVEREASY	OVERHALE	OVERLAYS	OVERPEER
OVERBRED	OVEREATS	OVERHAND	OVERLEAF	OVERPERT
OVERBRIM	OVEREDIT	OVERHANG	OVERLEAP	OVERPLAN
OVERBROW	OVEREGGS	OVERHARD	OVERLEND	OVERPLAY
OVERBULK	OVEREYED	OVERHATE	OVERLENT	OVERPLOT
OVERBURN	OVEREYES	OVERHAUL	OVERLETS	OVERPLUS
OVERBUSY	OVERFALL	OVERHEAD	OVERLEWD	OVERPOST
OVERBUYS	OVERFAST	OVERHEAP	OVERLIER	OVERPUMP
OVERCALL	OVERFEAR	OVERHEAR	OVERLIES	OVERRACK
OVERCAME	OVERFEED	OVERHEAT	OVERLIVE	OVERRAKE
OVERCAST	OVERFELL	OVERHELD	OVERLOAD	OVERRANK
OVERCLAD	OVERFILL	OVERHENT	OVERLOCK	OVERRASH
OVERCLOY	OVERFINE	OVERHIGH	OVERLONG	OVERRATE
OVERCOAT	OVERFISH	OVERHITS	OVERLOOK	OVERREAD
OVERCOLD	OVERFLEW	OVERHOLD	OVERLORD	OVERREDS
OVERCOME	OVERFLOW	OVERHOLY	OVERLOUD	OVERRENS

OVERRICH	**OVER**SETS	**OVER**STAY	**OVER**TIRE	**OVER**WEAR
OVERRIDE	**OVER**SEWN	**OVER**STEP	**OVER**TOIL	**OVER**WEEN
OVERRIFE	**OVER**SEWS	**OVER**STIR	**OVER**TONE	**OVER**WENT
OVERRIPE	**OVER**SHOE	**OVER**SUDS	**OVER**TOOK	**OVER**WETS
OVERRODE	**OVER**SHOT	**OVER**SUPS	**OVER**TOPS	**OVER**WIDE
OVERRUDE	**OVER**SICK	**OVER**SURE	**OVER**TRIM	**OVER**WILY
OVERRUFF	**OVER**SIDE	**OVER**SWAM	**OVER**TRIP	**OVER**WIND
OVERRULE	**OVER**SIZE	**OVER**SWAY	**OVER**TURN	**OVER**WING
OVERRUNS	**OVER**SKIP	**OVER**SWIM	**OVER**TYPE	**OVER**WISE
OVERSAIL	**OVER**SLIP	**OVER**SWUM	**OVER**URGE	**OVER**WORD
OVERSALE	**OVER**SLOW	**OVER**TAKE	**OVER**USED	**OVER**WORE
OVERSALT	**OVER**SOAK	**OVER**TALK	**OVER**USES	**OVER**WORK
OVERSAVE	**OVER**SOFT	**OVER**TAME	**OVER**VEIL	**OVER**WORN
OVERSEAS	**OVER**SOLD	**OVER**TART	**OVER**VIEW	**OVER**YEAR
OVERSEED	**OVER**SOON	**OVER**TASK	**OVER**VOTE	**OVER**ZEAL
OVERSEEN	**OVER**SOUL	**OVER**TEEM	**OVER**WARM	
OVERSEER	**OVER**SOWN	**OVER**THIN	**OVER**WARY	
OVERSEES	**OVER**SOWS	**OVER**TIME	**OVER**WASH	
OVERSELL	**OVER**SPIN	**OVER**TIPS	**OVER**WEAK	

Words that begin with PER-

Seven-letter words

PERACID	**PER**FINS	**PER**KING	**PER**PEND	**PER**TAKE
PERAEON	**PER**FORM	**PER**KINS	**PER**PENT	**PER**TEST
PERCASE	**PER**FUME	**PER**KISH	**PER**PLEX	**PER**TOOK
PERCENT	**PER**FUMY	**PER**LITE	**PER**SALT	**PER**UKES
PERCHER	**PER**FUSE	**PER**LOUS	**PER**SANT	**PER**USED
PERCINE	**PER**HAPS	**PER**MING	**PER**SING	**PER**USER
PERCUSS	**PER**ICON	**PER**MUTE	**PER**SIST	**PER**USES
PERDUES	**PER**JINK	**PER**NODS	**PER**SONS	**PER**VADE
PERDURE	**PER**JURE	**PER**ONES	**PER**SUED	**PER**VERT
PEREGAL	**PER**JURY	**PER**ORAL	**PER**SUES	
PEREONS	**PER**KIER	**PER**OXID	**PER**TAIN	

Eight-letter words

PERACIDS	**PER**FUMED	**PER**MEANT	**PER**PENTS	**PER**TAINS
PERACUTE	**PER**FUMER	**PER**MEASE	**PER**RADII	**PER**TAKEN
PERAEONS	**PER**FUMES	**PER**MUTED	**PER**SALTS	**PER**TAKES
PERCENTS	**PER**FUSED	**PER**MUTES	**PER**SAUNT	**PER**USERS
PERCOLIN	**PER**FUSES	**PER**NANCY	**PER**SEITY	**PER**USING
PERDURED	**PER**IODIC	**PER**ORATE	**PER**SISTS	**PER**VADED
PERDURES	**PER**IODID	**PER**OXIDE	**PER**SPIRE	**PER**VADES
PERFORCE	**PER**ISHES	**PER**OXIDS	**PER**SPIRY	**PER**VERSE
PERFORMS	**PER**LITES	**PER**PENDS	**PER**SUING	**PER**VERTS

Words that begin with PRE-

Seven-letter words

PREACED	**PRE**AMPS	**PRE**BAKE	**PRE**BOIL	**PRE**CAST
PREACES	**PRE**ANAL	**PRE**BEND	**PRE**BOOK	**PRE**CAVA
PREACHY	**PRE**ARMS	**PRE**BIDS	**PRE**BOOM	**PRE**CEDE
PREACTS	**PRE**AVER	**PRE**BILL	**PRE**BORN	**PRE**CENT
PREAGED	**PRE**BADE	**PRE**BIND	**PRE**BUYS	**PRE**CESS

Words that begin with OVER-

PRECODE	**PREFADE**	**PREMISS**	**PRERIOT**	**PRETERM**
PRECOOK	**PREFARD**	**PREMIXT**	**PREROCK**	**PRETEST**
PRECOOL	**PREFILE**	**PREMOLD**	**PRESAGE**	**PRETEXT**
PRECOUP	**PREFIRE**	**PREMOLT**	**PRESALE**	**PRETOLD**
PRECURE	**PREFORM**	**PREMOVE**	**PRESELL**	**PRETORS**
PRECUTS	**PREFUND**	**PRENAME**	**PRESENT**	**PRETRIM**
PREDATE	**PREGAME**	**PRENOON**	**PRESETS**	**PRETYPE**
PREDAWN	**PREHEAT**	**PREORAL**	**PRESHIP**	**PREVAIL**
PREDIAL	**PREHEND**	**PREPACK**	**PRESHOW**	**PREVENT**
PREDICT	**PREJINK**	**PREPAID**	**PRESIDE**	**PREVERB**
PREDIED	**PRELACY**	**PREPARE**	**PRESIFT**	**PREVIEW**
PREDIES	**PRELATE**	**PREPAVE**	**PRESOAK**	**PREVISE**
PREDIVE	**PRELIFE**	**PREPAYS**	**PRESOLD**	**PREWARM**
PREDOOM	**PRELOAD**	**PREPILL**	**PRESONG**	**PREWARN**
PREDUSK	**PRELUDE**	**PREPLAN**	**PRESORT**	**PREWASH**
PREEDIT	**PREMADE**	**PREPONE**	**PRESTED**	**PREWIRE**
PREEMPT	**PREMEAL**	**PREPOSE**	**PRETAPE**	**PREWORK**
PREEVES	**PREMEDS**	**PREPUCE**	**PRETEEN**	**PREWORN**
PREFABS	**PREMEET**	**PREPUPA**	**PRETELL**	**PREWRAP**
PREFACE	**PREMISE**	**PRERACE**	**PRETEND**	**PREWYNS**

Eight-letter words

PREACHED	**PRECHILL**	**PREFADED**	**PREMOVED**	**PRESALES**
PREACHES	**PRECHOSE**	**PREFADES**	**PREMOVES**	**PRESCORE**
PREACING	**PRECINCT**	**PREFIGHT**	**PRENAMES**	**PRESCUTA**
PREACTED	**PRECITED**	**PREFILED**	**PRENASAL**	**PRESELLS**
PREADAPT	**PRECLEAN**	**PREFILES**	**PRENATAL**	**PRESENTS**
PREADMIT	**PRECLEAR**	**PREFIRED**	**PRENOMEN**	**PRESERVE**
PREADOPT	**PRECODED**	**PREFIRES**	**PREORDER**	**PRESHAPE**
PREADULT	**PRECODES**	**PREFIXED**	**PREOWNED**	**PRESHIPS**
PREALLOT	**PRECOOKS**	**PREFIXES**	**PREPACKS**	**PRESHOWN**
PREALTER	**PRECOOLS**	**PREFLAME**	**PREPARED**	**PRESHOWS**
PREAMBLE	**PRECRASH**	**PREFOCUS**	**PREPARER**	**PRESIDED**
PREAPPLY	**PRECURED**	**PREFORMS**	**PREPARES**	**PRESIDER**
PREARMED	**PRECURES**	**PREFRANK**	**PREPASTE**	**PRESIDES**
PREASSES	**PRECURSE**	**PREFROZE**	**PREPAVED**	**PRESIFTS**
PREAUDIT	**PREDATED**	**PREFUNDS**	**PREPAVES**	**PRESLEEP**
PREAVERS	**PREDATES**	**PREGAMES**	**PREPLACE**	**PRESLICE**
PREAXIAL	**PREDAWNS**	**PREGUIDE**	**PREPLANS**	**PRESOAKS**
PREBAKED	**PREDEATH**	**PREHEATS**	**PREPLANT**	**PRESOLVE**
PREBAKES	**PREDIALS**	**PREHENDS**	**PREPONES**	**PRESORTS**
PREBASAL	**PREDICTS**	**PREHUMAN**	**PREPOSED**	**PRESPLIT**
PREBENDS	**PREDOOMS**	**PREJUDGE**	**PREPOSES**	**PRESTAMP**
PREBILLS	**PREDRAFT**	**PRELEGAL**	**PREPRESS**	**PRESTING**
PREBINDS	**PREDRIED**	**PRELIMIT**	**PREPRICE**	**PRESTORE**
PREBIRTH	**PREDRIES**	**PRELIVES**	**PREPRINT**	**PRETAPED**
PREBLESS	**PREDRILL**	**PRELOADS**	**PREPUBES**	**PRETAPES**
PREBOARD	**PREDUSKS**	**PRELOVED**	**PREPUBIS**	**PRETASTE**
PREBOILS	**PREDYING**	**PRELUDES**	**PREPUCES**	**PRETEENS**
PREBOOKS	**PREEDITS**	**PRELUNCH**	**PREPUNCH**	**PRETELLS**
PREBOUND	**PREELECT**	**PREMEDIC**	**PREPUPAE**	**PRETENDS**
PREBUILD	**PREEMPTS**	**PREMISES**	**PREPUPAL**	**PRETENSE**
PREBUILT	**PREENACT**	**PREMIXED**	**PREPUPAS**	**PRETERMS**
PRECASTS	**PREERECT**	**PREMIXES**	**PRERADIO**	**PRETESTS**
PRECEDED	**PREEXIST**	**PREMOLAR**	**PRERENAL**	**PRETEXTS**
PRECEDES	**PREFACED**	**PREMOLDS**	**PRERINSE**	**PRETONIC**
PRECENTS	**PREFACER**	**PREMORAL**	**PRESAGER**	**PRETRAIN**
PRECHECK	**PREFACES**	**PREMORSE**	**PRESAGES**	**PRETREAT**

PRETRIAL	PREUNITE	PREVIEWS	PREWARMS	PREWORKS
PRETRIMS	PREVAILS	PREVISED	PREWARNS	PREWRAPS
PRETYPED	PREVALUE	PREVISES	PREWEIGH	
PRETYPES	PREVENTS	PREVISIT	PREWIRED	
PREUNION	PREVERBS	PREVISOR	PREWIRES	

Words that begin with PRO-

Seven-letter words

PROBALL	PROFANE	PROLONG	PROPEND	PROTEND
PROBAND	PROFESS	PROMINE	PROPENE	PROTEST
PROBANG	PROFILE	PROMISE	PROPINE	PROTONS
PROBATE	PROFITS	PROMOTE	PROPONE	PROTORE
PROBING	PROFUSE	PRONAOI	PROPOSE	PROVANT
PROBITS	PROGRAM	PRONAOS	PRORATE	PROVEND
PROCARP	PROJETS	PRONEST	PROSAIC	PROVERB
PROCESS	PROKING	PRONOTA	PROSECT	PROVERS
PROCURE	PROLATE	PRONOUN	PROSERS	PROVIDE
PRODRUG	PROLEGS	PROOTIC	PROSING	PROVINE
PRODUCE	PROLINE	PROPAGE	PROSOMA	PROWEST
PRODUCT	PROLING	PROPALE	PROSTIE	
PROFACE	PROLOGS	PROPANE	PROTEAS	

Eight-letter words

PROBANDS	PROFILES	PRONOTAL	PROPOSES	PROTENSE
PROBANGS	PROFOUND	PRONOTUM	PROPOUND	PROTESTS
PROBATED	PROGRADE	PRONOUNS	PROPYLON	PROTONIC
PROBATES	PROGRAMS	PROPAGED	PRORATED	PROTORES
PROCARPS	PROLABOR	PROPAGES	PRORATES	PROTRACT
PROCHAIN	PROLAPSE	PROPALED	PROROGUE	PROTRADE
PROCINCT	PROLATED	PROPALES	PROSAIST	PROUNION
PROCLAIM	PROLINES	PROPANES	PROSECTS	PROVENDS
PROCURED	PROLONGE	PROPENDS	PROSEMEN	PROVERBS
PROCURER	PROLONGS	PROPENES	PROSINGS	PROVINED
PROCURES	PROMETAL	PROPHAGE	PROSODIC	PROVINES
PRODROME	PROMINES	PROPHASE	PROSOMAS	PROVIRAL
PRODRUGS	PROMISER	PROPINED	PROSTATE	PROVIRUS
PRODUCES	PROMISES	PROPINES	PROSTIES	PROVISOR
PRODUCTS	PROMOTED	PROPOLIS	PROSTYLE	
PROFANES	PROMOTES	PROPONES	PROTAMIN	
PROFILED	PROMOTOR	PROPOSED	PROTEASE	
PROFILER	PRONATES	PROPOSER	PROTENDS	

Words that begin with RE-

Seven-letter words

REACHED	READORN	REAMEND	REAROSE	REBAITS
REACHES	REAFFIX	REANNEX	REAVAIL	REBATED
REACTED	REAGENT	REAPERS	REAVERS	REBATES
REACTOR	REAKING	REAPING	REAVOWS	REBECKS
READAPT	REALIGN	REAPPLY	REAWAKE	REBEGAN
READDED	REALIST	REARGUE	REAWOKE	REBEGIN
READMIT	REALLOT	REARISE	REBACKS	REBEGUN
READOPT	REALTER	REARMED	REBADGE	REBILLS

REBINDS	RECORKS	REFEELS	REGRIND	REMANET
REBIRTH	RECOUNT	REFENCE	REGROOM	REMARKS
REBITES	RECOUPE	REFIGHT	REGROUP	REMARRY
REBLEND	RECOUPS	REFILED	REGROWN	REMATCH
REBLENT	RECOURE	REFILES	REGROWS	REMATED
REBLOOM	RECOVER	REFILLS	REGULAR	REMATES
REBOARD	RECOWER	REFILMS	REHANGS	REMEADS
REBOILS	RECRATE	REFINDS	REHEARD	REMEETS
REBOOKS	RECROSS	REFINED	REHEARS	REMELTS
REBOOTS	RECROWN	REFINER	REHEATS	REMENDS
REBORED	RECURED	REFINES	REHEELS	REMERCY
REBORES	RECURES	REFIRED	REHINGE	REMERGE
REBOUND	RECURVE	REFIRES	REHIRED	REMINDS
REBOZOS	RECYCLE	REFIXED	REHIRES	REMINTS
REBRACE	REDATED	REFIXES	REHOUSE	REMISES
REBRAND	REDATES	REFLAGS	REIMAGE	REMIXED
REBREED	REDEALS	REFLIES	REINCUR	REMIXES
REBUFFS	REDEALT	REFLOAT	REINDEX	REMODEL
REBUILD	REDEARS	REFLOOD	REINKED	REMOLDS
REBUILT	REDEEMS	REFLOWN	REINTER	REMORAS
REBUKES	REDIALS	REFLOWS	REISSUE	REMORSE
REBUSES	REDOCKS	REFOCUS	REJOINS	REMOTES
RECALLS	REDOING	REFOLDS	REJONES	REMOULD
RECANED	REDOUBT	REFOOTS	REJUDGE	REMOUNT
RECANES	REDOUTS	REFORGE	REKEYED	REMOVED
RECANTS	REDRAFT	REFORMS	REKNITS	REMOVER
RECARRY	REDRAWN	REFOUND	REKNOTS	REMOVES
RECASTS	REDRAWS	REFRACT	RELABEL	RENAILS
RECATCH	REDREAM	REFRAME	RELACED	RENAMED
RECEDED	REDRESS	REFRESH	RELACES	RENAMES
RECEDES	REDRIED	REFRIED	RELANDS	RENESTS
RECENSE	REDRIES	REFRIES	RELAPSE	RENEWED
RECHART	REDRILL	REFRONT	RELATED	RENEWER
RECHEAT	REDRIVE	REFROZE	RELATER	RENYING
RECHECK	REDROVE	REFUELS	RELAXER	REOCCUR
RECHEWS	REDUCES	REFUNDS	RELAXES	REOFFER
RECHOSE	REDUITS	REFUSED	RELAYED	REOILED
RECITAL	REEARNS	REFUSES	RELEARN	REOPENS
RECITED	REECHED	REGAINS	RELEASE	REORDER
RECITER	REECHES	REGALES	RELENDS	REPACKS
RECITES	REEDIFY	REGALLY	RELIEFS	REPAINT
RECLADS	REEDITS	REGAUGE	RELIERS	REPAIRS
RECLAIM	REEJECT	REGEARS	RELIEVE	REPANEL
RECLAME	REEKING	REGENTS	RELIGHT	REPAPER
RECLASP	REELECT	REGESTS	RELINED	REPARKS
RECLEAN	REELMEN	REGILDS	RELINES	REPASTS
RECLIMB	REEMITS	REGIVEN	RELINKS	REPATCH
RECLINE	REENACT	REGIVES	RELISTS	REPAVED
RECLOSE	REENDOW	REGLAZE	RELIVED	REPAVES
RECOALS	REENJOY	REGLOSS	RELIVER	REPEALS
RECOATS	REENTER	REGLOWS	RELIVES	REPEATS
RECOCKS	REENTRY	REGLUED	RELOADS	REPENTS
RECODED	REEQUIP	REGLUES	RELOANS	REPERKS
RECODES	REERECT	REGORGE	RELOCKS	REPINED
RECOILS	REEVOKE	REGRADE	RELOOKS	REPINES
RECOINS	REEXPEL	REGRAFT	RELYING	REPIQUE
RECOLOR	REFACED	REGRANT	REMAILS	REPLACE
RECOMBS	REFACES	REGRATE	REMAINS	REPLANS
RECOOKS	REFALLS	REGREEN	REMAKER	REPLANT
RECORDS	REFEEDS	REGREET	REMAKES	REPLATE

REPLAYS	REROUTE	RESORTS	RETENES	REVERBS
REPLEAD	RESAILS	RESOUND	RETESTS	REVERSE
REPLICA	RESALES	RESOWED	RETHINK	REVERSO
REPLIED	RESAWED	RESPACE	RETILED	REVERTS
REPLIER	RESCALE	RESPADE	RETILES	REVESTS
REPLIES	RESCORE	RESPEAK	RETIMED	REVIEWS
REPLOTS	RESEALS	RESPELL	RETIMES	REVILER
REPLOWS	RESEATS	RESPELT	RETINES	REVISED
REPLUMB	RESECTS	RESPIRE	RETINTS	REVISES
REPOINT	RESEEDS	RESPITE	RETIRED	REVISIT
REPOLLS	RESEEKS	RESPLIT	RETIRES	REVISOR
REPONES	RESEIZE	RESPOKE	RETITLE	REVIVER
REPORTS	RESELLS	RESPOOL	RETOOLS	REVIVES
REPOSED	RESENDS	RESPOTS	RETORTS	REVOICE
REPOSER	RESENTS	RESPRAY	RETOTAL	REVOLTS
REPOSES	RESERVE	RESTACK	RETOUCH	REVOLVE
REPOSIT	RESEWED	RESTAFF	RETOURS	REVOTED
REPOSTS	RESHAPE	RESTAGE	RETRACE	REVOTES
REPOURS	RESHAVE	RESTAMP	RETRACK	REVYING
REPOWER	RESHINE	RESTART	RETRACT	REWAKED
REPRESS	RESHIPS	RESTATE	RETRAIN	REWAKEN
REPRICE	RESHOED	RESTEMS	RETRAIT	REWAKES
REPRIME	RESHOES	RESTIFF	RETREAD	REWARDS
REPRINT	RESHONE	RESTING	RETREAT	REWARMS
REPRISE	RESHOOT	RESTIVE	RETREES	REWAXED
REPRIZE	RESHOWN	RESTOCK	RETRIAL	REWAXES
REPROBE	RESHOWS	RESTOKE	RETRIED	REWEARS
REPROOF	RESIDED	RESTORE	RETRIES	REWEAVE
REPROVE	RESIDER	RESTUDY	RETRIMS	REWEIGH
REPULPS	RESIDES	RESTUFF	RETUNDS	REWELDS
REPULSE	RESIFTS	RESTUMP	RETUNED	REWIDEN
REPUMPS	RESIGHT	RESTYLE	RETUNES	REWINDS
REPURED	RESIGNS	RESURGE	RETURFS	REWIRED
REPURES	RESILED	RETABLE	RETURNS	REWIRES
REQUEST	RESILES	RETACKS	RETWIST	REWOKEN
REQUINS	RESINED	RETAILS	RETYING	REWORDS
REQUIRE	RESISTS	RETAINS	RETYPED	REWORKS
REQUITE	RESITED	RETAKEN	RETYPES	REWOUND
REQUITS	RESITES	RETAKER	REUNIFY	REWOVEN
REQUOTE	RESIZED	RETAKES	REUNION	REWRAPS
RERACKS	RESIZES	RETALLY	REUNITE	REWRAPT
RERAILS	RESKEWS	RETAPED	REURGED	REWRITE
RERAISE	RESKILL	RETAPES	REURGES	REWROTE
REREADS	RESLATE	RETASTE	REUSING	REZEROS
REREDOS	RESMELT	RETAXED	REUTTER	REZONED
RERENTS	RESOAKS	RETAXES	REVALUE	REZONES
RERISEN	RESOLED	RETEACH	REVAMPS	
RERISES	RESOLES	RETEAMS	REVEALS	
REROLLS	RESOLVE	RETEARS	REVENGE	
REROOFS	RESORBS	RETELLS	REVENUE	

Eight-letter words

REABSORB	REACTANT	READDICT	READVISE	REALLIES
REACCEDE	REACTING	READDING	REAFFIRM	REALLOTS
REACCENT	REACTION	READJUST	REAGENCY	REALTERS
REACCEPT	REACTIVE	READMITS	REAGENTS	REAMENDS
REACCUSE	REACTORS	READOPTS	REALIGNS	REANOINT
REACHING	READAPTS	READORNS	REALLIED	REANSWER

Words that begin with RE-

REAPPEAR	REBURIED	RECOOKED	REDYEING	REFORMAT
REARGUED	REBURIES	RECOPIED	REEARNED	REFORMED
REARGUES	REBUTTED	RECOPIES	REECHING	REFORMER
REARISEN	REBUTTER	RECORDED	REECHOED	REFOUGHT
REARISES	REBUTTON	RECORDER	REECHOES	REFOUNDS
REARMING	REBUYING	RECORKED	REEDITED	REFRACTS
REAROUSE	RECALLED	RECOUNTS	REEJECTS	REFRAMED
REARREST	RECALLER	RECOUPED	REELECTS	REFRAMES
REASCEND	RECANING	RECOUPLE	REEMBARK	REFREEZE
REASCENT	RECANTED	RECOURED	REEMBODY	REFRINGE
REASSAIL	RECANTER	RECOURES	REEMERGE	REFRONTS
REASSERT	RECAPPED	RECOURSE	REEMPLOY	REFROZEN
REASSESS	RECAPTOR	RECOVERS	REENACTS	REFRYING
REASSIGN	RECARPET	RECOWERS	REENDOWS	REFUELED
REASSORT	RECAUGHT	RECRATED	REENGAGE	REFUNDED
REASSUME	RECEDING	RECRATES	REENJOYS	REFUNDER
REASSURE	RECEMENT	RECREANT	REENLIST	REFUSING
REATTACH	RECENSED	RECREATE	REENROLL	REFUSION
REATTACK	RECENSES	RECROWNS	REENTERS	REGAINED
REATTAIN	RECENSOR	RECURING	REEQUIPS	REGAINER
REAVAILS	RECENTER	RECURRED	REERECTS	REGATHER
REAVOWED	RECENTRE	RECURVED	REEVOKED	REGAUGED
REAWAKED	RECESSED	RECURVES	REEVOKES	REGAUGES
REAWAKEN	RECESSES	RECYCLED	REEXPELS	REGEARED
REAWAKES	RECHANGE	RECYCLER	REEXPORT	REGELATE
REAWOKEN	RECHARGE	RECYCLES	REEXPOSE	REGILDED
REBACKED	RECHARTS	REDAMAGE	REFACING	REGIVING
REBADGED	RECHEATS	REDATING	REFALLEN	REGLAZED
REBADGES	RECHECKS	REDECIDE	REFASTEN	REGLAZES
REBAITED	RECHEWED	REDEEMED	REFELLED	REGLOWED
REBATING	RECHOOSE	REDEFEAT	REFENCED	REGLUING
REBEGINS	RECHOSEN	REDEFECT	REFENCES	REGORGED
REBELLED	RECIRCLE	REDEFIED	REFIGHTS	REGORGES
REBELLOW	RECITALS	REDEFIES	REFIGURE	REGRADED
REBIDDEN	RECITERS	REDEFINE	REFILING	REGRADES
REBILLED	RECITING	REDEMAND	REFILLED	REGRAFTS
REBIRTHS	RECLAIMS	REDENIED	REFILMED	REGRANTS
REBITING	RECLAMES	REDENIES	REFILTER	REGRATED
REBITTEN	RECLASPS	REDEPLOY	REFINERS	REGRATER
REBLENDS	RECLEANS	REDESIGN	REFINERY	REGRATES
REBLOOMS	RECLIMBS	REDIALED	REFINING	REGREENS
REBOARDS	RECLINES	REDIGEST	REFINISH	REGREETS
REBODIED	RECLOSED	REDIPPED	REFIRING	REGRINDS
REBODIES	RECLOSES	REDIRECT	REFITTED	REGROOMS
REBOILED	RECLOTHE	REDISTIL	REFIXING	REGROOVE
REBOOKED	RECOALED	REDIVIDE	REFLEXED	REGROUND
REBOOTED	RECOATED	REDOCKED	REFLEXES	REGROUPS
REBORING	RECOCKED	REDOLENT	REFLOATS	REGROWTH
REBORROW	RECODIFY	REDONNED	REFLOODS	REHAMMER
REBOTTLE	RECODING	REDOUBLE	REFLOWED	REHANDLE
REBOUGHT	RECOILED	REDOUBTS	REFLOWER	REHANGED
REBOUNDS	RECOILER	REDRAFTS	REFLUENT	REHARDEN
REBRACED	RECOINED	REDRAWER	REFLUXED	REHASHED
REBRACES	RECOLLET	REDREAMS	REFLUXES	REHASHES
REBRANCH	RECOLORS	REDREAMT	REFLYING	REHEARSE
REBRANDS	RECOMBED	REDRILLS	REFOLDED	REHEATED
REBREEDS	RECOMMIT	REDRIVEN	REFOOTED	REHEATER
REBUFFED	RECONFER	REDRIVES	REFOREST	REHEELED
REBUILDS	RECONNED	REDRYING	REFORGED	REHEMMED
REBURIAL	RECONVEY	REDUBBED	REFORGES	REHINGED

REHINGES	RELIABLE	REOCCUPY	REPOUSSE	RESAYING
REHIRING	RELIEVER	REOCCURS	REPOWERS	RESCALED
REHOUSED	RELIGHTS	REOFFEND	REPREEVE	RESCALES
REHOUSES	RELINING	REOFFERS	REPRICED	RESCHOOL
REIGNITE	RELINKED	REOILING	REPRICES	RESCORED
REILLUME	RELISTED	REOPENED	REPRIEFE	RESCORES
REIMAGED	RELIVERS	REOPENER	REPRIEVE	RESCREEN
REIMAGES	RELIVING	REOPPOSE	REPRIMED	RESCRIPT
REIMPORT	RELOADED	REORDAIN	REPRIMES	RESCULPT
REIMPOSE	RELOADER	REORDERS	REPRINTS	RESEALED
REINCITE	RELOANED	REORIENT	REPRISED	RESEARCH
REINCURS	RELOCATE	REOUTFIT	REPRISES	RESEASON
REINDICT	RELOCKED	REPACIFY	REPRIZED	RESEATED
REINDUCE	RELOOKED	REPACKED	REPRIZES	RESECURE
REINDUCT	RELUCENT	REPAINTS	REPROBED	RESEEDED
REINFECT	RELUMINE	REPAIRED	REPROBES	RESEEING
REINFORM	REMAILED	REPAIRER	REPROOFS	RESEIZED
REINFUSE	REMAINED	REPANELS	REPROVED	RESEIZES
REINJECT	REMAKERS	REPAPERS	REPROVER	RESELECT
REINJURE	REMAKING	REPARKED	REPROVES	RESELLER
REINJURY	REMANENT	REPASSED	REPUBLIC	RESEMBLE
REINKING	REMANIES	REPASSES	REPULPED	RESENTED
REINSERT	REMANNED	REPASTED	REPULSED	RESERVED
REINSTAL	REMAPPED	REPAVING	REPULSER	RESERVER
REINSURE	REMARKED	REPAYING	REPULSES	RESERVES
REINTERS	REMARKER	REPEALED	REPUMPED	RESETTER
REINVADE	REMARKET	REPEGGED	REPURIFY	RESETTLE
REINVENT	REMARQUE	REPEOPLE	REPURING	RESEWING
REINVEST	REMASTER	REPERKED	REPURSUE	RESHAPED
REINVITE	REMATING	REPERUSE	REQUESTS	RESHAPER
REINVOKE	REMEDIAL	REPHRASE	REQUIGHT	RESHAPES
REISSUED	REMELTED	REPINING	REQUIRED	RESHAVED
REISSUER	REMEMBER	REPINNED	REQUIRES	RESHAVEN
REISSUES	REMENDED	REPIQUED	REQUITED	RESHAVES
REJACKET	REMERGED	REPIQUES	REQUITES	RESHINED
REJIGGED	REMERGES	REPLACED	REQUOTED	RESHINES
REJIGGER	REMINDED	REPLACER	REQUOTES	RESHOOTS
REJOINED	REMINDER	REPLACES	RERACKED	RESHOWED
REJUDGED	REMINTED	REPLANTS	RERAILED	RESHOWER
REJUDGES	REMIXING	REPLATED	RERAISED	RESIDERS
REJUGGLE	REMODELS	REPLATES	RERAISES	RESIDING
REKEYING	REMODIFY	REPLAYED	RERECORD	RESIFTED
REKINDLE	REMOLDED	REPLEADS	REREMIND	RESIGHTS
RELABELS	REMORSES	REPLEDGE	RERENTED	RESIGNED
RELACHES	REMOTION	REPLIERS	REREPEAT	RESIGNER
RELACING	REMOULDS	REPLOWED	REREVIEW	RESILING
RELANDED	REMOUNTS	REPLUMBS	REREVISE	RESILVER
RELAPSED	REMOVERS	REPLUNGE	REREWARD	RESINING
RELAPSER	REMOVING	REPLYING	RERIGGED	RESISTED
RELAPSES	REMURMUR	REPOINTS	RERISING	RESISTER
RELAUNCH	RENAILED	REPOLISH	REROLLED	RESITING
RELAYING	RENAMING	REPOLLED	REROLLER	RESIZING
RELEARNS	RENATURE	REPORTED	REROOFED	RESKETCH
RELEARNT	RENEGATE	REPORTER	REROUTED	RESKEWED
RELEASED	RENESTED	REPOSERS	REROUTES	RESKILLS
RELEASER	RENEWING	REPOSING	RESADDLE	RESLATED
RELEASES	RENOTIFY	REPOSITS	RESAILED	RESLATES
RELEGATE	RENUMBER	REPOSTED	RESALUTE	RESMELTS
RELETTER	REOBJECT	REPOTTED	RESAMPLE	RESMOOTH
RELEVANT	REOBTAIN	REPOURED	RESAWING	RESOAKED

Words that begin with RE-

RESODDED	**RE**STAGED	**RE**TAILER	**RE**TUNING	**RE**VISITS
RESOFTEN	**RE**STAGES	**RE**TAILOR	**RE**TURFED	**RE**VISORS
RESOLDER	**RE**STAMPS	**RE**TAKERS	**RE**TURNED	**RE**VIVERS
RESOLING	**RE**STARTS	**RE**TAKING	**RE**TURNER	**RE**VIVIFY
RESOLUTE	**RE**STATED	**RE**TAPING	**RE**TWISTS	**RE**VOICED
RESOLVED	**RE**STATES	**RE**TARGET	**RE**TYPING	**RE**VOICES
RESOLVER	**RE**STINGS	**RE**TASTED	**RE**UNIONS	**RE**VOLUTE
RESOLVES	**RE**STITCH	**RE**TASTES	**RE**UNITED	**RE**VOLVED
RESONANT	**RE**STOCKS	**RE**TAUGHT	**RE**UNITER	**RE**VOLVES
RESORBED	**RE**STOKED	**RE**TAXING	**RE**UNITES	**RE**VOTING
RESORTED	**RE**STOKES	**RE**TEAMED	**RE**UPTAKE	**RE**WAKENS
RESORTER	**RE**STORED	**RE**TELLER	**RE**URGING	**RE**WAKING
RESOUGHT	**RE**STORER	**RE**TEMPER	**RE**USABLE	**RE**WARDED
RESOUNDS	**RE**STORES	**RE**TESTED	**RE**UTTERS	**RE**WARDER
RESOURCE	**RE**STRAIN	**RE**THINKS	**RE**VALUED	**RE**WARMED
RESOWING	**RE**STRESS	**RE**THREAD	**RE**VALUES	**RE**WASHED
RESPACED	**RE**STRICT	**RE**TIEING	**RE**VAMPED	**RE**WASHES
RESPACES	**RE**STRIKE	**RE**TILING	**RE**VAMPER	**RE**WAXING
RESPADED	**RE**STRING	**RE**TIMING	**RE**VEALED	**RE**WEAVED
RESPADES	**RE**STRIVE	**RE**TINTED	**RE**VEALER	**RE**WEAVES
RESPEAKS	**RE**STROVE	**RE**TIRING	**RE**VENGED	**RE**WEDDED
RESPELLS	**RE**STRUCK	**RE**TITLED	**RE**VENGER	**RE**WEIGHS
RESPIRED	**RE**STRUNG	**RE**TITLES	**RE**VENGES	**RE**WELDED
RESPIRES	**RE**STUFFS	**RE**TOOLED	**RE**VENUES	**RE**WETTED
RESPITED	**RE**STUMPS	**RE**TOTALS	**RE**VERIFY	**RE**WIDENS
RESPITES	**RE**STYLED	**RE**TOURED	**RE**VERIST	**RE**WINDED
RESPLICE	**RE**STYLES	**RE**TRACED	**RE**VERSAL	**RE**WINDER
RESPLITS	**RE**SUBMIT	**RE**TRACER	**RE**VERSED	**RE**WIRING
RESPOKEN	**RE**SUMMON	**RE**TRACES	**RE**VERSER	**RE**WORDED
RESPOOLS	**RE**SUPINE	**RE**TRACKS	**RE**VERSES	**RE**WORKED
RESPRANG	**RE**SUPPLY	**RE**TRACTS	**RE**VERSOS	**RE**WRITER
RESPRAYS	**RE**SURGED	**RE**TRAINS	**RE**VERTED	**RE**WRITES
RESPREAD	**RE**SURGES	**RE**TRAITS	**RE**VESTED	**RE**ZEROED
RESPRING	**RE**SURVEY	**RE**TREADS	**RE**VESTRY	**RE**ZEROES
RESPROUT	**RE**TABLES	**RE**TREATS	**RE**VETTED	**RE**ZONING
RESPRUNG	**RE**TACKED	**RE**TRENCH	**RE**VIEWED	
RESTABLE	**RE**TACKLE	**RE**TRIALS	**RE**VIEWER	
RESTACKS	**RE**TAGGED	**RE**TRYING	**RE**VISING	
RESTAFFS	**RE**TAILED	**RE**TUNDED	**RE**VISION	

Words that begin with RED-

Seven-letter words

REDACTS	**RED**CAPS	**RED**FOOT	**RED**RAFT	**RED**SKIN
REDATES	**RED**COAT	**RED**HEAD	**RED**RAWN	**RED**TAIL
REDBACK	**RED**DENS	**RED**LEGS	**RED**RAWS	**RED**TOPS
REDBAIT	**RED**DING	**RED**LINE	**RED**REAM	**RED**WARE
REDBAYS	**RED**DISH	**RED**NECK	**RED**RILL	**RED**WING
REDBIRD	**RED**EARS	**RED**NESS	**RED**RIVE	**RED**WOOD
REDBONE	**RED**EYES	**RED**OUTS	**RED**ROOT	
REDBUDS	**RED**FINS	**RED**OXES	**RED**ROVE	
REDBUGS	**RED**FISH	**RED**POLL	**RED**SEAR	

Eight-letter words

REDACTED	**RED**BACKS	**RED**BIRDS	**RED**COATS	**RED**HEADS
REDACTOR	**RED**BAITS	**RED**BONES	**RED**DINGS	**RED**HORSE
REDARGUE	**RED**BELLY	**RED**BRICK	**RED**FOOTS	**RED**LINED

REDLINER	REDRAFTS	REDROOTS	REDSHORT	REDWINGS
REDLINES	REDRAWER	REDSHANK	REDSKINS	REDWOODS
REDNECKS	REDREAMS	REDSHARE	REDSTART	
REDOLENT	REDRILLS	REDSHIFT	REDTAILS	
REDONNED	REDRIVEN	REDSHIRE	REDWARES	
REDPOLLS	REDRIVES	REDSHIRT	REDWATER	

Words that begin with SEA-

Seven-letter words

SEABAGS	SEAFOWL	SEALING	SEASIDE	SEAWARE
SEABANK	SEAGIRT	SEAMAID	SEASING	SEAWAYS
SEABEDS	SEAGULL	SEAMARK	SEASONS	SEAWEED
SEABIRD	SEAHAWK	SEAMING	SEASURE	SEAWIFE
SEABOOT	SEAHOGS	SEAPORT	SEATING	SEAWORM
SEACOCK	SEAKALE	SEARATS	SEAWALL	SEAZING
SEADOGS	SEALANT	SEAREST	SEAWANS	
SEAFOLK	SEALIFT	SEARING	SEAWANT	
SEAFOOD	SEALINE	SEASICK	SEAWARD	

Eight-letter words

SEABANKS	SEAFLOOR	SEALIFTS	SEAROBIN	SEAWANTS
SEABEACH	SEAFOLKS	SEALINES	SEASCAPE	SEAWARDS
SEABIRDS	SEAFOODS	SEALINGS	SEASCOUT	SEAWARES
SEABLITE	SEAFOWLS	SEAMAIDS	SEASHELL	SEAWATER
SEABOARD	SEAFRONT	SEAMANLY	SEASHORE	SEAWEEDS
SEABOOTS	SEAGOING	SEAMARKS	SEASIDES	SEAWIVES
SEABORNE	SEAGULLS	SEAMOUNT	SEASPEAK	SEAWOMAN
SEACOAST	SEAHAWKS	SEAPIECE	SEASURES	SEAWOMEN
SEACOCKS	SEAHORSE	SEAPLANE	SEATINGS	SEAWORMS
SEACRAFT	SEAHOUND	SEAPORTS	SEATRAIN	
SEADROME	SEAKALES	SEAQUAKE	SEATROUT	
SEAFARER	SEALANTS	SEARINGS	SEAWALLS	

Words that begin with SUB-

Seven-letter words

SUBACID	SUBDEBS	SUBIDEA	SUBRENT	SUBTEND
SUBACTS	SUBDEWS	SUBITEM	SUBRING	SUBTEST
SUBALAR	SUBDUAL	SUBJOIN	SUBRULE	SUBTEXT
SUBAQUA	SUBDUCE	SUBLATE	SUBSALE	SUBTILE
SUBAREA	SUBDUCT	SUBLETS	SUBSECT	SUBTONE
SUBARID	SUBDUED	SUBLIME	SUBSERE	SUBTYPE
SUBATOM	SUBDUES	SUBLINE	SUBSETS	SUBUNIT
SUBBASE	SUBECHO	SUBLOTS	SUBSIDE	SUBURBS
SUBBASS	SUBEDIT	SUBMENU	SUBSIST	SUBVERT
SUBBING	SUBERIC	SUBMISS	SUBSITE	SUBWAYS
SUBCELL	SUBFEUS	SUBNETS	SUBSOIL	SUBZERO
SUBCLAN	SUBFILE	SUBORAL	SUBSONG	SUBZONE
SUBCODE	SUBFUSC	SUBOVAL	SUBTACK	
SUBCOOL	SUBGOAL	SUBPART	SUBTASK	
SUBCULT	SUBGUMS	SUBPLOT	SUBTAXA	
SUBDEAN	SUBHEAD	SUBRACE	SUBTEEN	

Words that begin with RED-

Eight-letter words

SUBABBOT	**SUB**DEANS	**SUB**IMAGO	**SUB**RENTS	**SUB**TESTS
SUBACRID	**SUB**DEPOT	**SUB**INDEX	**SUB**RINGS	**SUB**TEXTS
SUBACTED	**SUB**DEWED	**SUB**ITEMS	**SUB**RULES	**SUB**THEME
SUBACUTE	**SUB**DUALS	**SUB**JOINS	**SUB**SALES	**SUB**TIDAL
SUBADULT	**SUB**DUCES	**SUB**LATED	**SUB**SCALE	**SUB**TILER
SUBAGENT	**SUB**DUCTS	**SUB**LEASE	**SUB**SECTS	**SUB**TITLE
SUBAREAS	**SUB**DUING	**SUB**LEVEL	**SUB**SENSE	**SUB**TONES
SUBATOMS	**SUB**DUPLE	**SUB**LIMED	**SUB**SERES	**SUB**TONIC
SUBAUDIO	**SUB**DURAL	**SUB**LIMES	**SUB**SERVE	**SUB**TOPIC
SUBAURAL	**SUB**DWARF	**SUB**LIMIT	**SUB**SHAFT	**SUB**TOTAL
SUBAXIAL	**SUB**EDITS	**SUB**LINES	**SUB**SHELL	**SUB**TRACT
SUBBASAL	**SUB**ENTRY	**SUB**LUNAR	**SUB**SHRUB	**SUB**TREND
SUBBASES	**SUB**EPOCH	**SUB**MENTA	**SUB**SIDED	**SUB**TRIBE
SUBBASIN	**SUB**EQUAL	**SUB**MENUS	**SUB**SIDER	**SUB**TRIST
SUBBINGS	**SUB**ERECT	**SUB**MERGE	**SUB**SIDES	**SUB**TUNIC
SUBBLOCK	**SUB**EROSE	**SUB**MERSE	**SUB**SISTS	**SUB**TYPES
SUBBREED	**SUB**FEUED	**SUB**NASAL	**SUB**SITES	**SUB**UNITS
SUBCASTE	**SUB**FIELD	**SUB**NICHE	**SUB**SIZAR	**SUB**URBAN
SUBCAUSE	**SUB**FILES	**SUB**NODAL	**SUB**SKILL	**SUB**URBIA
SUBCELLS	**SUB**FIXES	**SUB**OCEAN	**SUB**SOILS	**SUB**VERSE
SUBCHIEF	**SUB**FLOOR	**SUB**OPTIC	**SUB**SOLAR	**SUB**VERST
SUBCHORD	**SUB**FLUID	**SUB**ORDER	**SUB**SONGS	**SUB**VERTS
SUBCLAIM	**SUB**FRAME	**SUB**OVATE	**SUB**SONIC	**SUB**VICAR
SUBCLANS	**SUB**GENRE	**SUB**OXIDE	**SUB**SPACE	**SUB**VIRAL
SUBCLASS	**SUB**GENUS	**SUB**PANEL	**SUB**STAGE	**SUB**VIRUS
SUBCLERK	**SUB**GOALS	**SUB**PARTS	**SUB**STATE	**SUB**VOCAL
SUBCODES	**SUB**GRADE	**SUB**PHASE	**SUB**STYLE	**SUB**WAYED
SUBCOOLS	**SUB**GRAPH	**SUB**PHYLA	**SUB**TACKS	**SUB**WORLD
SUBCOSTA	**SUB**GROUP	**SUB**PLOTS	**SUB**TASKS	**SUB**ZONAL
SUBCRUST	**SUB**HEADS	**SUB**POLAR	**SUB**TAXON	**SUB**ZONES
SUBCULTS	**SUB**HUMAN	**SUB**PRIOR	**SUB**TEENS	
SUBCUTES	**SUB**HUMID	**SUB**PUBIC	**SUB**TENDS	
SUBCUTIS	**SUB**IDEAS	**SUB**RACES	**SUB**TENSE	

Words that begin with SUN-

Seven-letter words

SUNBACK	**SUN**BOWS	**SUN**DOWN	**SUN**LAND	**SUN**SETS
SUNBAKE	**SUN**BURN	**SUN**FAST	**SUN**LESS	**SUN**SPOT
SUNBATH	**SUN**DAES	**SUN**FISH	**SUN**LIKE	**SUN**STAR
SUNBEAM	**SUN**DARI	**SUN**GARS	**SUN**NIES	**SUN**SUIT
SUNBEAT	**SUN**DECK	**SUN**GLOW	**SUN**RAYS	**SUN**TANS
SUNBEDS	**SUN**DEWS	**SUN**HATS	**SUN**RISE	**SUN**TRAP
SUNBELT	**SUN**DIAL	**SUN**KETS	**SUN**ROOF	**SUN**WARD
SUNBIRD	**SUN**DOGS	**SUN**LAMP	**SUN**ROOM	**SUN**WISE

Eight-letter words

SUNBAKED	**SUN**BELTS	**SUN**BURNT	**SUN**DIALS	**SUN**GLASS
SUNBAKES	**SUN**BERRY	**SUN**BURST	**SUN**DOWNS	**SUN**GLOWS
SUNBATHE	**SUN**BIRDS	**SUN**CHOKE	**SUN**DRESS	**SUN**GREBE
SUNBATHS	**SUN**BLIND	**SUN**DARIS	**SUN**DRIES	**SUN**LAMPS
SUNBEAMS	**SUN**BLOCK	**SUN**DECKS	**SUN**DRILY	**SUN**LANDS
SUNBEAMY	**SUN**BURNS	**SUN**DERED	**SUN**DROPS	**SUN**LIGHT

SUNPORCH	SUNROOFS	SUNSHADE	SUNSPOTS	SUNSUITS
SUNPROOF	SUNROOMS	SUNSHINE	SUNSTARS	SUNTRAPS
SUNRISES	SUNSCALD	SUNSHINY	SUNSTONE	SUNWARDS

Words that begin with TRI-

Seven-letter words

TRIABLE	TRICEPS	TRIGAMY	TRIOXID	TRISOME
TRIACID	TRICLAD	TRIGONS	TRIPACK	TRISOMY
TRIAGED	TRICORN	TRIGRAM	TRIPART	TRITEST
TRIAGES	TRICOTS	TRIJETS	TRIPIER	TRITIDE
TRIARCH	TRIDARN	TRILITH	TRIPLED	TRITONE
TRIAXON	TRIDENT	TRILOBE	TRIPLEX	TRITONS
TRIBADE	TRIDUAN	TRILOGY	TRIPODS	TRIUMPH
TRIBALS	TRIENES	TRINARY	TRIPSIS	TRIVETS
TRIBLET	TRIFLED	TRIODES	TRISECT	TRIVIAL
TRIBUTE	TRIFOLD	TRIONES	TRISEME	TRIZONE
TRICARS	TRIFORM	TRIOSES	TRISHAW	

Eight-letter words

TRIACIDS	TRICHINA	TRIGRAPH	TRIPEDAL	TRISTATE
TRIAGING	TRICHORD	TRILEMMA	TRIPHASE	TRISTICH
TRIALIST	TRICLADS	TRILITHS	TRIPHONE	TRITHING
TRIANGLE	TRICOLOR	TRILOBED	TRIPLANE	TRITICAL
TRIAXIAL	TRICORNS	TRILOBES	TRIPLIED	TRITIDES
TRIAXONS	TRICYCLE	TRIMETER	TRIPLIES	TRITONES
TRIAZINE	TRIDARNS	TRIMORPH	TRIPLING	TRIUNITY
TRIAZOLE	TRIDENTS	TRIMOTOR	TRIPODAL	TRIVALVE
TRIBALLY	TRIETHYL	TRINODAL	TRIPOLIS	TRIZONAL
TRIBASIC	TRIFLING	TRIOLEIN	TRIPOSES	TRIZONES
TRIBLETS	TRIFOCAL	TRIOXIDE	TRISECTS	
TRIBRACH	TRIGLYPH	TRIOXIDS	TRISEMES	
TRIBUTES	TRIGRAMS	TRIPACKS	TRISHAWS	

Words that begin with UN-

Seven-letter words

UNACTED	UNAWARE	UNBITTS	UNBRACE	UNCASES
UNADDED	UNBAKED	UNBLENT	UNBRAID	UNCEDED
UNADEPT	UNBALED	UNBLESS	UNBRAKE	UNCHAIN
UNADULT	UNBALES	UNBLEST	UNBROKE	UNCHAIR
UNAGILE	UNBARED	UNBLIND	UNBUILD	UNCHARM
UNAGING	UNBARES	UNBLOCK	UNBUILT	UNCHARY
UNAIDED	UNBARKS	UNBLOWN	UNBULKY	UNCHECK
UNAIMED	UNBASED	UNBOLTS	UNBURNT	UNCHILD
UNAIRED	UNBATED	UNBONED	UNCAGED	UNCHOKE
UNAKING	UNBEARS	UNBONES	UNCAGES	UNCITED
UNALIKE	UNBEGET	UNBOOTS	UNCAKED	UNCIVIL
UNALIST	UNBEGOT	UNBORNE	UNCAKES	UNCLAMP
UNALIVE	UNBEGUN	UNBOSOM	UNCANNY	UNCLASP
UNAPTLY	UNBEING	UNBOUND	UNCAPED	UNCLEAN
UNARMED	UNBELTS	UNBOWED	UNCAPES	UNCLEAR
UNASKED	UNBENDS	UNBOXED	UNCARTS	UNCLEFT
UNAWAKE	UNBINDS	UNBOXES	UNCASED	UNCLEWS

UNCLING	UNFAMED	UNHITCH	UNMINED	UNRIGHT
UNCLIPS	UNFANCY	UNHIVED	UNMITER	UNRIMED
UNCLIPT	UNFAZED	UNHIVES	UNMITRE	UNRIPER
UNCLOAK	UNFENCE	UNHOARD	UNMIXED	UNRISEN
UNCLOGS	UNFEUED	UNHOODS	UNMIXES	UNRIVEN
UNCLOSE	UNFILED	UNHOOKS	UNMOLDS	UNRIVET
UNCLOUD	UNFIRED	UNHOOPS	UNMOORS	UNROBED
UNCOCKS	UNFITLY	UNHOPED	UNMORAL	UNROBES
UNCODED	UNFIXED	UNHORSE	UNMOULD	UNROLLS
UNCOILS	UNFIXES	UNHOUSE	UNMOUNT	UNROOFS
UNCOLTS	UNFLESH	UNHUMAN	UNMOVED	UNROOST
UNCOMIC	UNFLUSH	UNHUSKS	UNNAILS	UNROOTS
UNCOPED	UNFOLDS	UNIDEAL	UNNAMED	UNROPED
UNCOPES	UNFOOLS	UNJADED	UNNEATH	UNROPES
UNCORDS	UNFORMS	UNJOINT	UNNERVE	UNROUGH
UNCORKS	UNFOUND	UNKEMPT	UNNESTS	UNROUND
UNCOUTH	UNFREED	UNKINGS	UNNOBLE	UNROVEN
UNCOVER	UNFREES	UNKINKS	UNNOISY	UNROYAL
UNCOWLS	UNFROCK	UNKNITS	UNNOTED	UNRUFFE
UNCRATE	UNFROZE	UNKNOTS	UNOFTEN	UNRULED
UNCRAZY	UNFUMED	UNKNOWN	UNOILED	UNRULES
UNCROSS	UNFUNNY	UNLACED	UNORDER	UNSAFER
UNCROWN	UNFURLS	UNLACES	UNOWNED	UNSAINT
UNCUFFS	UNFUSED	UNLADED	UNPACED	UNSATED
UNCURBS	UNFUSSY	UNLADEN	UNPACKS	UNSAVED
UNCURED	UNGATED	UNLADES	UNPAGED	UNSAWED
UNCURLS	UNGEARS	UNLATCH	UNPAINT	UNSCALE
UNCURSE	UNGILDS	UNLAWED	UNPANEL	UNSCARY
UNDATED	UNGIRDS	UNLEADS	UNPAPER	UNSCREW
UNDEALT	UNGIRTH	UNLEARN	UNPARED	UNSEALS
UNDECKS	UNGLOVE	UNLEASH	UNPAVED	UNSEAMS
UNDEIFY	UNGLUED	UNLEVEL	UNPERCH	UNSEATS
UNDERNS	UNGLUES	UNLIKED	UNPICKS	UNSEELS
UNDIGHT	UNGODLY	UNLIKES	UNPILED	UNSELFS
UNDINES	UNGORED	UNLIMED	UNPILES	UNSELLS
UNDOCKS	UNGOWNS	UNLIMES	UNPLACE	UNSENSE
UNDOERS	UNGROWN	UNLINED	UNPLAIT	UNSEWED
UNDOING	UNGUARD	UNLINES	UNPLUGS	UNSEXED
UNDRAPE	UNGULAR	UNLINKS	UNPLUMB	UNSEXES
UNDRAWN	UNGYVED	UNLIVED	UNPLUME	UNSHALE
UNDRAWS	UNGYVES	UNLIVES	UNPOPES	UNSHAPE
UNDRESS	UNHABLE	UNLOADS	UNPOSED	UNSHARP
UNDREST	UNHAIRS	UNLOBED	UNPRAYS	UNSHELL
UNDRIED	UNHANDS	UNLOCKS	UNPROPS	UNSHENT
UNDRUNK	UNHANDY	UNLOOSE	UNPURSE	UNSHEWN
UNDYING	UNHANGS	UNLORDS	UNQUEEN	UNSHIFT
UNEAGER	UNHAPPY	UNLOVED	UNQUIET	UNSHIPS
UNEARED	UNHARDY	UNLOVES	UNQUOTE	UNSHOED
UNEARTH	UNHASPS	UNLUCKY	UNRACED	UNSHOES
UNEASES	UNHASTY	UNMACHO	UNRAKED	UNSHOOT
UNEATEN	UNHEADS	UNMAKER	UNRAKES	UNSHORN
UNEDGED	UNHEALS	UNMAKES	UNRATED	UNSHOUT
UNEDGES	UNHEARD	UNMANLY	UNRAVEL	UNSHOWN
UNENDED	UNHEART	UNMARRY	UNRAZED	UNSHOWY
UNEQUAL	UNHEEDY	UNMASKS	UNREADY	UNSHUTS
UNFACTS	UNHELED	UNMATED	UNREAVE	UNSIGHT
UNFADED	UNHELES	UNMEANT	UNREELS	UNSINEW
UNFAIRS	UNHELMS	UNMERRY	UNREEVE	UNSIZED
UNFAITH	UNHINGE	UNMETED	UNREINS	UNSLAIN
UNFAKED	UNHIRED	UNMEWED	UNRESTS	UNSLICK

UNSLING	UNSTAID	UNTAXES	UNTUNES	UNWILLS
UNSLUNG	UNSTATE	UNTEACH	UNTURFS	UNWINDS
UNSMART	UNSTEEL	UNTEAMS	UNTURNS	UNWIPED
UNSMOTE	UNSTEPS	UNTENTS	UNTWINE	UNWIRED
UNSNAGS	UNSTICK	UNTENTY	UNTWIST	UNWIRES
UNSNAPS	UNSTOCK	UNTHAWS	UNTYING	UNWISER
UNSNARL	UNSTOPS	UNTHINK	UNURGED	UNWITCH
UNSNECK	UNSTOWS	UNTILED	UNUSUAL	UNWITTY
UNSOBER	UNSTRAP	UNTILES	UNVAILS	UNWIVED
UNSOLID	UNSTRIP	UNTIMED	UNVEILS	UNWIVES
UNSONSY	UNSTUCK	UNTIRED	UNVEXED	UNWOMAN
UNSOOTE	UNSTUNG	UNTOMBS	UNVISOR	UNWOOED
UNSOULS	UNSUITS	UNTONED	UNVITAL	UNWORKS
UNSOUND	UNSUNNY	UNTRACE	UNVOCAL	UNWORTH
UNSOWED	UNSURED	UNTRACK	UNVOICE	UNWOUND
UNSPARS	UNSURER	UNTREAD	UNWAGED	UNWOVEN
UNSPEAK	UNSWEAR	UNTRIDE	UNWAKED	UNWRAPS
UNSPELL	UNSWEET	UNTRIED	UNWARES	UNWRITE
UNSPENT	UNSWEPT	UNTRIMS	UNWATER	UNWROTE
UNSPIDE	UNSWORE	UNTRUER	UNWAXED	UNWRUNG
UNSPIED	UNSWORN	UNTRULY	UNWAYED	UNYOKED
UNSPILT	UNTACKS	UNTRUSS	UNWEALS	UNYOKES
UNSPLIT	UNTAKEN	UNTRUST	UNWEARY	UNYOUNG
UNSPOKE	UNTAMED	UNTRUTH	UNWEAVE	UNZONED
UNSPOOL	UNTAMES	UNTUCKS	UNWHIPT	
UNSTACK	UNTAXED	UNTUNED	UNWHITE	

Eight-letter words

UNABATED	UNBARING	UNBOBBED	UNBURIED	UNCHEWED
UNABUSED	UNBARKED	UNBODIED	UNBURIES	UNCHICLY
UNACHING	UNBARRED	UNBODING	UNBURNED	UNCHILDS
UNACIDIC	UNBASTED	UNBOILED	UNBURROW	UNCHOKED
UNACTIVE	UNBATHED	UNBOLTED	UNBUSTED	UNCHOKES
UNADORED	UNBEARED	UNBONDED	UNBUTTON	UNCHOSEN
UNAFRAID	UNBEATEN	UNBONING	UNCAGING	UNCHURCH
UNAGEING	UNBEDDED	UNBONNET	UNCAKING	UNCIPHER
UNAGREED	UNBEGETS	UNBOOKED	UNCALLED	UNCLAMPS
UNALLIED	UNBEGGED	UNBOOTED	UNCANDID	UNCLASPS
UNAMAZED	UNBEINGS	UNBOSOMS	UNCANNED	UNCLASSY
UNAMUSED	UNBELIEF	UNBOTTLE	UNCAPING	UNCLAWED
UNANCHOR	UNBELTED	UNBOUGHT	UNCAPPED	UNCLENCH
UNANELED	UNBENDED	UNBOUNCY	UNCARDED	UNCLEWED
UNARCHED	UNBENIGN	UNBOWING	UNCARING	UNCLINCH
UNARGUED	UNBEREFT	UNBOXING	UNCARTED	UNCLOAKS
UNARISEN	UNBESEEM	UNBRACED	UNCARVED	UNCLOSED
UNARMING	UNBIASED	UNBRACES	UNCASHED	UNCLOSES
UNARTFUL	UNBIASES	UNBRAIDS	UNCASING	UNCLOTHE
UNATONED	UNBIDDEN	UNBRAKED	UNCASKED	UNCLOUDS
UNAVOWED	UNBILLED	UNBRAKES	UNCATCHY	UNCLOUDY
UNAWAKED	UNBISHOP	UNBREECH	UNCAUGHT	UNCLOVEN
UNBACKED	UNBITTED	UNBRIDLE	UNCAUSED	UNCLOYED
UNBAGGED	UNBITTEN	UNBRIGHT	UNCHAINS	UNCLUTCH
UNBAITED	UNBITTER	UNBROKEN	UNCHAIRS	UNCOATED
UNBALING	UNBLAMED	UNBUCKLE	UNCHANCY	UNCOCKED
UNBANDED	UNBLINDS	UNBUDDED	UNCHARGE	UNCOFFIN
UNBANKED	UNBLOCKS	UNBUILDS	UNCHARMS	UNCOILED
UNBANNED	UNBLOODY	UNBUNDLE	UNCHASTE	UNCOINED
UNBARBED	UNBLOWED	UNBURDEN	UNCHECKS	UNCOLTED

Words that begin with UN-

UNCOMBED	UNEASIER	UNFOUGHT	UNHEDGED	UNLAWING
UNCOMELY	UNEASILY	UNFRAMED	UNHEEDED	UNLAYING
UNCOMMON	UNEDGING	UNFREEZE	UNHELING	UNLEADED
UNCOOKED	UNEDIBLE	UNFRIEND	UNHELMED	UNLEARNS
UNCOOLED	UNEDITED	UNFROCKS	UNHELPED	UNLEARNT
UNCOPING	UNELATED	UNFROZEN	UNHEROIC	UNLEASED
UNCORDED	UNENDING	UNFUNDED	UNHIDDEN	UNLETHAL
UNCORKED	UNENVIED	UNFURLED	UNHINGED	UNLETTED
UNCOSTLY	UNEQUALS	UNFURRED	UNHINGES	UNLEVELS
UNCOUPLE	UNERASED	UNGAGGED	UNHIPPER	UNLEVIED
UNCOVERS	UNEROTIC	UNGAINLY	UNHIVING	UNLICKED
UNCOWLED	UNERRING	UNGALLED	UNHOARDS	UNLIDDED
UNCRATED	UNESPIED	UNGARBED	UNHOLIER	UNLIKELY
UNCRATES	UNEVADED	UNGAUGED	UNHOLILY	UNLIMBER
UNCREATE	UNEVENER	UNGAZING	UNHOLPEN	UNLIMING
UNCREWED	UNEVENLY	UNGEARED	UNHOMELY	UNLINEAL
UNCROWNS	UNEXOTIC	UNGELDED	UNHONEST	UNLINING
UNCUFFED	UNEXPERT	UNGENIAL	UNHOODED	UNLINKED
UNCULLED	UNFABLED	UNGENTLE	UNHOOKED	UNLISTED
UNCURBED	UNFADING	UNGENTLY	UNHOOPED	UNLIVELY
UNCURLED	UNFAIRED	UNGIFTED	UNHORSED	UNLIVING
UNCURSED	UNFAIRER	UNGILDED	UNHORSES	UNLOADED
UNCURSES	UNFAIRLY	UNGIRDED	UNHOUSED	UNLOADER
UNCURVED	UNFAITHS	UNGIRTHS	UNHOUSES	UNLOCKED
UNDAMMED	UNFALLEN	UNGIVING	UNHUNTED	UNLOOKED
UNDAMNED	UNFAMOUS	UNGLAZED	UNHUSKED	UNLOOSED
UNDAMPED	UNFANNED	UNGLOVED	UNIDEAED	UNLOOSEN
UNDARING	UNFASTEN	UNGLOVES	UNIMBUED	UNLOOSES
UNDASHED	UNFAULTY	UNGLUING	UNINURED	UNLOPPED
UNDAZZLE	UNFEARED	UNGODDED	UNIONISE	UNLORDED
UNDECENT	UNFELLED	UNGORGED	UNIONIZE	UNLORDLY
UNDECKED	UNFELTED	UNGOTTEN	UNIRONED	UNLOVELY
UNDEEDED	UNFENCED	UNGOWNED	UNIRONIC	UNLOVING
UNDEFIED	UNFENCES	UNGRACED	UNISSUED	UNMAILED
UNDENIED	UNFETTER	UNGRADED	UNJAMMED	UNMAIMED
UNDENTED	UNFEUDAL	UNGRAZED	UNJOINED	UNMAKERS
UNDERATE	UNFILIAL	UNGREEDY	UNJOINTS	UNMAKING
UNDESERT	UNFILLED	UNGROUND	UNJOYFUL	UNMANFUL
UNDEVOUT	UNFILMED	UNGUARDS	UNJOYOUS	UNMANNED
UNDIGHTS	UNFISHED	UNGUIDED	UNJUDGED	UNMANTLE
UNDIMMED	UNFITTED	UNGUILTY	UNJUSTER	UNMAPPED
UNDINTED	UNFITTER	UNGUMMED	UNJUSTLY	UNMARKED
UNDIPPED	UNFIXING	UNGYVING	UNKEELED	UNMARRED
UNDIVINE	UNFIXITY	UNHACKED	UNKENNED	UNMASKED
UNDOABLE	UNFLASHY	UNHAILED	UNKENNEL	UNMASKER
UNDOCILE	UNFLAWED	UNHAIRED	UNKINDER	UNMATTED
UNDOCKED	UNFLEXED	UNHALLOW	UNKINDLY	UNMEETLY
UNDOINGS	UNFLUTED	UNHALSED	UNKINGED	UNMELLOW
UNDOOMED	UNFOILED	UNHALVED	UNKINGLY	UNMELTED
UNDOTTED	UNFOLDED	UNHANDED	UNKINKED	UNMENDED
UNDOUBLE	UNFOLDER	UNHANGED	UNKISSED	UNMESHED
UNDRAPED	UNFOOLED	UNHARMED	UNKISSES	UNMESHES
UNDRAPES	UNFOOTED	UNHASPED	UNKNIGHT	UNMEWING
UNDREAMT	UNFORBID	UNHATTED	UNKNOWNS	UNMILKED
UNDRIVEN	UNFORCED	UNHEADED	UNKOSHER	UNMILLED
UNDROSSY	UNFORGED	UNHEALED	UNLACING	UNMINDED
UNDUBBED	UNFORGOT	UNHEALTH	UNLADING	UNMINGLE
UNDULLED	UNFORKED	UNHEARSE	UNLASHED	UNMISSED
UNEARNED	UNFORMAL	UNHEARTS	UNLASHES	UNMITERS
UNEARTHS	UNFORMED	UNHEATED	UNLAWFUL	UNMITRED

UNMITRES	UNPOISON	UNRINSED	UNSHADED	UNSTARRY
UNMIXING	UNPOLISH	UNRIPELY	UNSHADOW	UNSTATED
UNMOANED	UNPOLITE	UNRIPEST	UNSHAKED	UNSTATES
UNMODISH	UNPOLLED	UNRIPPED	UNSHAKEN	UNSTAYED
UNMOLDED	UNPOSTED	UNRIVETS	UNSHALED	UNSTEADY
UNMOLTEN	UNPOTTED	UNROBING	UNSHALES	UNSTEELS
UNMONIED	UNPRAISE	UNROLLED	UNSHAMED	UNSTICKS
UNMOORED	UNPRAYED	UNROOFED	UNSHAPED	UNSTITCH
UNMOULDS	UNPREACH	UNROOSTS	UNSHAPEN	UNSTOCKS
UNMOUNTS	UNPRETTY	UNROOTED	UNSHAPES	UNSTONED
UNMOVING	UNPRICED	UNROPING	UNSHARED	UNSTOWED
UNMUFFLE	UNPRIEST	UNROTTED	UNSHAVED	UNSTRAPS
UNMUZZLE	UNPRIMED	UNROTTEN	UNSHAVEN	UNSTRESS
UNNAILED	UNPRISON	UNROUGED	UNSHELLS	UNSTRING
UNNATIVE	UNPRIZED	UNROUNDS	UNSHIFTS	UNSTRIPS
UNNEEDED	UNPROBED	UNROUSED	UNSHOOTS	UNSTRUCK
UNNERVED	UNPROPER	UNRUBBED	UNSHOUTS	UNSTRUNG
UNNERVES	UNPROVED	UNRUFFLE	UNSHROUD	UNSTUFFY
UNNESTED	UNPROVEN	UNRULIER	UNSHRUNK	UNSUBTLE
UNNETTED	UNPRUNED	UNRUSHED	UNSICKER	UNSUBTLY
UNNOBLES	UNPUCKER	UNRUSTED	UNSIFTED	UNSUCKED
UNOBEYED	UNPULLED	UNSADDLE	UNSIGHTS	UNSUITED
UNOPENED	UNPURELY	UNSAFELY	UNSIGNED	UNSUMMED
UNORDERS	UNPURGED	UNSAFEST	UNSILENT	UNSUNNED
UNORNATE	UNPURSED	UNSAFETY	UNSINEWS	UNSUPPLE
UNPACKED	UNPURSES	UNSAILED	UNSINFUL	UNSURELY
UNPACKER	UNPUZZLE	UNSAINED	UNSLAKED	UNSUREST
UNPADDED	UNQUEENS	UNSAINTS	UNSLICED	UNSWATHE
UNPAINED	UNQUIETS	UNSALTED	UNSLINGS	UNSWAYED
UNPAINTS	UNQUOTED	UNSAPPED	UNSLUICE	UNSWEARS
UNPAIRED	UNQUOTES	UNSASHED	UNSMOKED	UNTACKED
UNPANELS	UNRACKED	UNSATING	UNSMOOTH	UNTACKLE
UNPANGED	UNRAISED	UNSAVORY	UNSNARLS	UNTAGGED
UNPAPERS	UNRAKING	UNSAYING	UNSNECKS	UNTAILED
UNPARTED	UNRANKED	UNSCALED	UNSOAKED	UNTAMING
UNPATHED	UNRAVELS	UNSCALES	UNSOAPED	UNTANGLE
UNPAYING	UNREALLY	UNSCREWS	UNSOCIAL	UNTANNED
UNPEELED	UNREAPED	UNSEALED	UNSOCKET	UNTAPPED
UNPEERED	UNREASON	UNSEAMED	UNSODDEN	UNTARRED
UNPEGGED	UNREAVED	UNSEARED	UNSOILED	UNTASTED
UNPENNED	UNREAVES	UNSEASON	UNSOLDER	UNTAUGHT
UNPEOPLE	UNRECKED	UNSEATED	UNSOLEMN	UNTAXING
UNPERSON	UNREELED	UNSECRET	UNSOLVED	UNTEAMED
UNPICKED	UNREELER	UNSEEDED	UNSONSIE	UNTEMPER
UNPILING	UNREEVED	UNSEEING	UNSORTED	UNTENANT
UNPINKED	UNREEVES	UNSEELED	UNSOUGHT	UNTENDED
UNPINNED	UNREINED	UNSEELIE	UNSOULED	UNTENDER
UNPITIED	UNRENTED	UNSEEMLY	UNSOURED	UNTENTED
UNPITTED	UNREPAID	UNSEIZED	UNSPARED	UNTESTED
UNPLACED	UNREPAIR	UNSELDOM	UNSPEAKS	UNTETHER
UNPLACES	UNRESTED	UNSELFED	UNSPELLS	UNTHATCH
UNPLAITS	UNRETIRE	UNSELVES	UNSPHERE	UNTHAWED
UNPLAYED	UNRHYMED	UNSENSED	UNSPOILT	UNTHINKS
UNPLIANT	UNRIBBED	UNSENSES	UNSPOKEN	UNTHREAD
UNPLOWED	UNRIDDEN	UNSERVED	UNSPOOLS	UNTHRIFT
UNPLUMBS	UNRIDDLE	UNSETTLE	UNSPRUNG	UNTHRONE
UNPLUMED	UNRIFLED	UNSEWING	UNSTABLE	UNTIDIED
UNPLUMES	UNRIGGED	UNSEXING	UNSTABLY	UNTIDIER
UNPOETIC	UNRIGHTS	UNSEXIST	UNSTACKS	UNTIDIES
UNPOISED	UNRINGED	UNSEXUAL	UNSTARCH	UNTIDILY

Words that begin with UN-

UNTIEING	UNTRUSTY	UNVENTED	UNWASHED	UNWINGED
UNTILING	UNTRUTHS	UNVERSED	UNWASHEN	UNWIRING
UNTILLED	UNTUCKED	UNVESTED	UNWASTED	UNWISDOM
UNTILTED	UNTUFTED	UNVETTED	UNWATERS	UNWISELY
UNTIMELY	UNTUNING	UNVIABLE	UNWATERY	UNWISEST
UNTINGED	UNTURBID	UNVIEWED	UNWEANED	UNWISHED
UNTINNED	UNTURFED	UNVIRTUE	UNWEAPON	UNWISHES
UNTIPPED	UNTURNED	UNVISORS	UNWEAVES	UNWITTED
UNTIRING	UNTWINED	UNVIZARD	UNWEBBED	UNWIVING
UNTITLED	UNTWINES	UNVOICED	UNWEDDED	UNWOMANS
UNTOMBED	UNTWISTS	UNVOICES	UNWEEDED	UNWONTED
UNTOWARD	UNUNITED	UNVULGAR	UNWEENED	UNWOODED
UNTRACED	UNUSABLE	UNWALLED	UNWEIGHT	UNWORDED
UNTRACES	UNUSABLY	UNWANING	UNWELDED	UNWORKED
UNTRACKS	UNUSEFUL	UNWANTED	UNWETTED	UNWORMED
UNTRADED	UNVAILED	UNWARDED	UNWIELDY	UNWORTHS
UNTREADS	UNVALUED	UNWARIER	UNWIFELY	UNWORTHY
UNTRENDY	UNVARIED	UNWARILY	UNWIGGED	UNWRITES
UNTRUEST	UNVEILED	UNWARMED	UNWILFUL	UNYEANED
UNTRUISM	UNVEILER	UNWARNED	UNWILLED	UNYOKING
UNTRUSTS	UNVEINED	UNWARPED	UNWINDER	UNZIPPED

Words that begin with UP-

Seven-letter words

UPBEARS	UPDIVED	UPHOORD	UPRIVER	UPSWEEP
UPBEATS	UPDIVES	UPHURLS	UPROARS	UPSWELL
UPBINDS	UPDRAFT	UPKEEPS	UPROLLS	UPSWEPT
UPBLOWN	UPDRAGS	UPKNITS	UPROOTS	UPSWING
UPBLOWS	UPDRAWN	UPLANDS	UPROUSE	UPSWUNG
UPBOILS	UPDRAWS	UPLEADS	UPSCALE	UPTAKEN
UPBORNE	UPDRIED	UPLEANS	UPSENDS	UPTAKES
UPBOUND	UPDRIES	UPLEANT	UPSHIFT	UPTALKS
UPBRAID	UPENDED	UPLEAPS	UPSHOOT	UPTEARS
UPBRAST	UPFIELD	UPLEAPT	UPSHOTS	UPTEMPO
UPBRAYS	UPFILLS	UPLIFTS	UPSIDES	UPTHREW
UPBREAK	UPFLING	UPLIGHT	UPSIZED	UPTHROW
UPBRING	UPFLOWS	UPLINKS	UPSIZES	UPTICKS
UPBROKE	UPFLUNG	UPLOADS	UPSKILL	UPTIGHT
UPBUILD	UPFOLDS	UPLOCKS	UPSLOPE	UPTILTS
UPBUILT	UPFRONT	UPLOOKS	UPSOARS	UPTIMES
UPBURST	UPFURLS	UPLYING	UPSPAKE	UPTOWNS
UPCASTS	UPGANGS	UPMAKER	UPSPEAK	UPTRAIN
UPCATCH	UPGAZED	UPMAKES	UPSPEAR	UPTREND
UPCHEER	UPGAZES	UPPILED	UPSPOKE	UPTURNS
UPCHUCK	UPGIRDS	UPPILES	UPSTAGE	UPTYING
UPCLIMB	UPGOING	UPPINGS	UPSTAIR	UPVALUE
UPCLOSE	UPGRADE	UPPROPS	UPSTAND	UPWAFTS
UPCOAST	UPGROWN	UPRAISE	UPSTARE	UPWARDS
UPCOILS	UPGROWS	UPRATED	UPSTART	UPWELLS
UPCOMES	UPHANGS	UPRATES	UPSTATE	UPWHIRL
UPCOURT	UPHAUDS	UPREACH	UPSTAYS	UPWINDS
UPCURLS	UPHEAPS	UPREARS	UPSTEPS	UPWOUND
UPCURVE	UPHEAVE	UPRESTS	UPSTIRS	UPWRAPS
UPDARTS	UPHILLS	UPRIGHT	UPSTOOD	
UPDATED	UPHOARD	UPRISEN	UPSURGE	
UPDATER	UPHOIST	UPRISER	UPSWARM	
UPDATES	UPHOLDS	UPRISES	UPSWAYS	

Eight-letter words

UPBEARER	UPFLINGS	UPLEANED	UPRUSHED	UPSTROKE
UPBOILED	UPFLOWED	UPLEAPED	UPRUSHES	UPSURGED
UPBRAIDS	UPFOLDED	UPLIFTED	UPSCALED	UPSURGES
UPBRAYED	UPFOLLOW	UPLIFTER	UPSCALES	UPSWARMS
UPBREAKS	UPFURLED	UPLIGHTS	UPSETTER	UPSWAYED
UPBRINGS	UPGATHER	UPLINKED	UPSHIFTS	UPSWEEPS
UPBROKEN	UPGAZING	UPLOADED	UPSHOOTS	UPSWELLS
UPBUILDS	UPGIRDED	UPLOCKED	UPSIZING	UPSWINGS
UPBURSTS	UPGOINGS	UPLOOKED	UPSKILLS	UPTAKING
UPCAUGHT	UPGRADED	UPMAKERS	UPSOARED	UPTALKED
UPCHEERS	UPGRADER	UPMAKING	UPSPEAKS	UPTEMPOS
UPCHUCKS	UPGRADES	UPMARKET	UPSPEARS	UPTHROWN
UPCLIMBS	UPGROWTH	UPPILING	UPSPOKEN	UPTHROWS
UPCLOSED	UPGUSHED	UPRAISED	UPSPRANG	UPTHRUST
UPCLOSES	UPGUSHES	UPRAISER	UPSPRING	UPTILTED
UPCOILED	UPHEAPED	UPRAISES	UPSPRUNG	UPTOSSED
UPCOMING	UPHEAVED	UPRATING	UPSTAGED	UPTOSSES
UPCURLED	UPHEAVER	UPREARED	UPSTAGER	UPTRAINS
UPCURVED	UPHEAVES	UPRIGHTS	UPSTAGES	UPTRENDS
UPCURVES	UPHOARDS	UPRISERS	UPSTAIRS	UPTURNED
UPDARTED	UPHOISTS	UPRISING	UPSTANDS	UPVALUED
UPDATERS	UPHOLDER	UPRIVERS	UPSTARED	UPVALUES
UPDATING	UPHOORDS	UPROARED	UPSTARES	UPWAFTED
UPDIVING	UPHUDDEN	UPROLLED	UPSTARTS	UPWELLED
UPDRAFTS	UPHURLED	UPROOTED	UPSTATER	UPWHIRLS
UPDRYING	UPJETTED	UPROOTER	UPSTATES	
UPENDING	UPLANDER	UPROUSED	UPSTAYED	
UPFILLED	UPLAYING	UPROUSES	UPSTREAM	

Words that begin with WAR-

Seven-letter words

WARBIER	WARHEAD	WARMING	WARRENS	WARWOLF
WARBLED	WARKING	WARPAGE	WARRING	WARWORK
WARDENS	WARLESS	WARPATH	WARSAWS	WARWORN
WARDING	WARLIKE	WARPING	WARSHIP	WARZONE
WARDOGS	WARLING	WARRAND	WARSLED	
WARDROP	WARLOCK	WARRANT	WARTIER	
WARFARE	WARLORD	WARRAYS	WARTIME	

Eight-letter words

WARBLING	WARFARER	WARLORDS	WARPLANE	WARTIMES
WARCRAFT	WARFARES	WARMAKER	WARPOWER	WARTWEED
WARDERED	WARHABLE	WARMINGS	WARRANDS	WARWORKS
WARDINGS	WARHEADS	WARMOUTH	WARRANTS	WARZONES
WARDRESS	WARHORSE	WARPAGES	WARRAYED	
WARDROPS	WARLINGS	WARPATHS	WARSHIPS	
WARFARED	WARLOCKS	WARPINGS	WARSLING	

Benjamins

ABAPICAL	ABIDINGS	ACADEMES	ACIDOSES	ADEQUATE
ABIDANCE	ABOMASUS	ACADEMIC	ACUPOINT	ADIPOSES

Words that begin with UP-

AGAMETES	ANABASIS	ATOMISER	BASQUINE	BETHORNS
AGEMATES	ANAGLYPH	ATOMISES	BATFOWLS	BETHUMPS
AIMFULLY	ANAGRAMS	ATOMISTS	BATGIRLS	BETWEENS
AIRBASES	ANAPESTS	ATYPICAL	BATHORSE	BEVVYING
AIRBOATS	ANAPHASE	AUMBRIES	BATHOSES	BIACETYL
AIRBORNE	ANEMOSES	AUSFORMS	BATWOMAN	BIBCOCKS
AIRBOUND	ANICONIC	AVIFAUNA	BATWOMEN	BICYCLED
AIRBRICK	ANIMALIC	AVIGATOR	BAUBLING	BIDDINGS
AIRBRUSH	ANIMATED	AVOWRIES	BAWCOCKS	BIGFOOTS
AIRBURST	ANIMATER	AWAKINGS	BAWDRIES	BIGGINGS
AIRBUSES	ANIMATES	AWLBIRDS	BAYBERRY	BIGHEADS
AIRCHECK	ANIMISTS	AWLWORTS	BAYWOODS	BIGHORNS
AIRCOACH	ANIMUSES	AXEBIRDS	BEACONED	BIGMOUTH
AIRCRAFT	ANODALLY	AXOPLASM	BEADINGS	BILBERRY
AIRCREWS	ANODYNES	AZYMITES	BEADROLL	BINDINGS
AIRDATES	ANTBEARS	BABBITTS	BEAMINGS	BIOBLAST
AIRDRAWN	ANTBIRDS	BABBLING	BECHANCE	BIOCHIPS
AIRDROME	ANTHELIX	BACCARAT	BECHARMS	BIOCIDES
AIRDROPS	ANTHEMIC	BACCHANT	BEDBOARD	BIOCLEAN
AIRFARES	ANTHILLS	BACKINGS	BEDCHAIR	BIOCYCLE
AIRFIELD	ANYPLACE	BADMOUTH	BEDCOVER	BIOFACTS
AIRFLOWS	ANYWHERE	BAFFLING	BEDDINGS	BIOFILMS
AIRFOILS	APEHOODS	BAGGAGES	BEDFRAME	BIOFUELS
AIRFRAME	APIMANIA	BAGGINGS	BEDGOWNS	BIOGASES
AIRGLOWS	APOCARPS	BAGHOUSE	BEDMAKER	BIOGENIC
AIRGRAPH	APOCOPES	BAGPIPED	BEDMATES	BIOGRAPH
AIRHEADS	APOCRINE	BAGPIPER	BEDPLATE	BIOHERMS
AIRHOLES	APODOSES	BAGPIPES	BEDPOSTS	BIOMETER
AIRMAILS	APOGAMIC	BAGWORMS	BEDQUILT	BIOMORPH
AIRPARKS	APOGRAPH	BALKINGS	BEDWARDS	BIOPLASM
AIRPLANE	APOMIXES	BALMORAL	BEEBREAD	BIOPLAST
AIRPLAYS	APOPHONY	BANDARIS	BEEFIEST	BIRDINGS
AIRPORTS	APOPLAST	BANDINGS	BEEHIVES	BISCUITS
AIRPOSTS	ARABISES	BANDOOKS	BEEYARDS	BISHOPED
AIRPOWER	ARABIZES	BANDURAS	BEGGINGS	BIVVYING
AIRPROOF	ARAPONGA	BANDYING	BEGHARDS	BLADINGS
AIRWARDS	ARAPUNGA	BANGINGS	BELDAMES	BLAWORTS
AIRWAVES	ARCCOSES	BANJOIST	BELFRIED	BLAZONED
AIRWOMAN	ARCHINGS	BANKINGS	BELFRIES	BLAZONER
AIRWOMEN	ARCHIVED	BARBARIC	BENDINGS	BLEWARTS
ALAMODES	ARCHIVES	BARBATED	BENZINES	BLOWHOLE
ALCHEMIC	ARCKINGS	BARBELLS	BERBERES	BOBBITTS
ALEBENCH	ARMBANDS	BARBERRY	BERGAMAS	BOBBLING
ALECOSTS	ARMCHAIR	BARBLESS	BERGERES	BOBFLOAT
ALEHOUSE	ARMGAUNT	BARBOLAS	BESCOURS	BOBWHEEL
ALEPINES	ARMHOLES	BARFLIES	BESCRAWL	BOBWHITE
ALEWIVES	ARTFULLY	BARGAINS	BESHAMED	BOGBEANS
ALICANTS	ARTWORKS	BARGEESE	BESHAMES	BOGWOODS
ALIQUANT	ARUGULAS	BARGESTS	BESHIVER	BOMBARDE
ALLHEALS	ASHCAKES	BARGHEST	BESHOUTS	BOMBARDS
ALPHORNS	ASHFALLS	BARGOONS	BESMILES	BOMBASTS
ALTHORNS	ASHPLANT	BARGOOSE	BESMOKES	BOMBINGS
ALTHOUGH	ASPHALTS	BARGUEST	BESMUDGE	BOMBLETS
ALUMINAS	ASSHOLES	BARKEEPS	BESMUTCH	BOMBORAS
ALUMINES	ASSWAGED	BARKHANS	BESPEAKS	BONDINGS
AMICABLE	ASSWAGES	BARMAIDS	BESPORTS	BONFIRES
AMIDINES	ATABRINE	BARWARES	BESPOUTS	BONGRACE
AMPHORAL	ATABRINS	BARWOODS	BESPRENT	BONHOMIE
AMPHORAS	ATEBRINS	BARYONIC	BESWARMS	BONKINGS
ANABASES	ATEMOYAS	BASHINGS	BETHANKS	BOOBIRDS

BOOBOOKS	**BUF**FIEST	**CAN**DOCKS	**CHA**CONNE	**COF**FLING	
BOODYING	**BUG**BANES	**CAN**DYING	**CHA**GRINS	**COF**FRETS	
BOOFIEST	**BUG**BEARS	**CAN**FIELD	**CHA**MISES	**COG**GINGS	
BOOKINGS	**BUG**GINGS	**CAN**VASES	**CHA**MISOS	**COG**WHEEL	
BOOMINGS	**BUG**HOUSE	**CAN**ZONES	**CHA**PLAIN	**COL**CHICA	
BOOZINGS	**BUG**WORTS	**CAP**MAKER	**CHE**CHIAS	**COM**BATED	
BORDERED	**BUL**BLETS	**CAP**PINGS	**CHE**DITES	**COM**BINER	
BORDURES	**BUL**WADDY	**CAR**BARNS	**CHE**KISTS	**COM**BINES	
BOSCAGES	**BUL**WARKS	**CAR**BENES	**CHE**MISES	**COM**BINGS	
BOTFLIES	**BUM**BLING	**CAR**BIDES	**CHE**MISTS	**COM**BLESS	
BOTHOLES	**BUM**BOATS	**CAR**BINES	**CHE**VALET	**COM**BUSTS	
BOTHYMEN	**BUM**FLUFF	**CAR**BORAS	**CHE**VYING	**COM**FIEST	
BOUVIERS	**BUM**MOCKS	**CAR**BOYED	**CHE**WINKS	**COM**FORTS	
BOWFRONT	**BUM**PINGS	**CAR**BURET	**CHI**BOUKS	**COM**MENDS	
BOWHEADS	**BUN**COMBE	**CAR**CAKES	**CHI**CANED	**COM**MERES	
BOWKNOTS	**BUN**DOOKS	**CAR**CASED	**CHI**CANER	**COM**MERGE	
BOWWOWED	**BUN**DYING	**CAR**CASES	**CHI**CANES	**COM**MIXED	
BOWYANGS	**BUR**BLING	**CAR**DINGS	**CHI**DINGS	**COM**MIXES	
BOXBALLS	**BUR**DOCKS	**CAR**FARES	**CHI**KARAS	**COM**MODES	
BOXBERRY	**BUR**GAGES	**CAR**FAXES	**CHI**KHORS	**COM**MONER	
BOXBOARD	**BUR**GLARY	**CAR**FOXES	**CHI**MERES	**COM**MONEY	
BOXHAULS	**BUR**GOUTS	**CAR**GEESE	**CHI**VVYING	**COM**MOTES	
BOXWOODS	**BUR**GRAVE	**CAR**GOING	**CHO**PINES	**COM**MOVED	
BOYCHICK	**BUR**GUNDY	**CAR**GOOSE	**CHO**WRIES	**COM**MOVES	
BOYCHIKS	**BUR**KITES	**CAR**JACKS	**CHU**PATTY	**COM**MUTED	
BOYCOTTS	**BUR**WEEDS	**CAR**MAKER	**CHY**MISTS	**COM**MUTER	
BOYHOODS	**BUS**GIRLS	**CAR**MINES	**CIA**BATTA	**COM**MUTES	
BRACEROS	**BUS**HELED	**CAR**PALES	**CIN**DERED	**COM**PACTS	
BRECHAMS	**BUS**HINGS	**CAR**PARKS	**CIN**GULAR	**COM**PADRE	
BREVIERS	**BUS**KINGS	**CAR**PINGS	**CIR**CITER	**COM**PAGES	
BREVISES	**BUT**CHEST	**CAR**POOLS	**CIR**CLING	**COM**PANDS	
BREWAGES	**BUY**BACKS	**CAR**PORTS	**CIR**CLIPS	**COM**PARED	
BREWINGS	**BUZ**ZINGS	**CAS**CABLE	**CIR**CUITS	**COM**PARER	
BREWISES	**CAB**BALAS	**CAS**CADES	**CIT**HERNS	**COM**PARES	
BRICOLES	**CAD**DICES	**CAS**HABLE	**CLA**VIERS	**COM**PARTS	
BRIDALLY	**CAD**DYING	**CAT**BIRDS	**CLA**YLIKE	**COM**PEARS	
BRIDEMAN	**CAL**CINES	**CAT**BOATS	**CLE**VISES	**COM**PEERS	
BRIGADES	**CAL**CITES	**CAT**BRIER	**CLI**MATED	**COM**PENDS	
BRIMINGS	**CAL**FLICK	**CAT**CALLS	**CLI**MATES	**COM**PERES	
BROCADES	**CAL**KINGS	**CAT**CLAWS	**CLI**MAXED	**COM**PILED	
BROCAGES	**CAL**MINGS	**CAT**FACES	**CLI**MAXES	**COM**PILER	
BROCARDS	**CAL**PACKS	**CAT**FALLS	**CLI**PARTS	**COM**PILES	
BROKINGS	**CAL**PAINS	**CAT**FIGHT	**CLO**CHARD	**COM**PINGS	
BROMATED	**CAL**VARIA	**CAT**HEADS	**CLU**BLAND	**COM**PLAIN	
BROMATES	**CAL**YCLED	**CAT**HEXES	**CLU**BROOM	**COM**PLEAT	
BROMINES	**CAL**ZONES	**CAT**HOLES	**CLU**BRUSH	**COM**PLIED	
BROMISES	**CAM**BOOSE	**CAT**HOODS	**COA**GENTS	**COM**PLIER	
BRUCELLA	**CAM**PHENE	**CAT**HOUSE	**COA**MINGS	**COM**PLIES	
BRUCINES	**CAM**PINGS	**CAT**MINTS	**COB**BLING	**COM**PLOTS	
BRUCITES	**CAM**PIONS	**CAT**WALKS	**COB**WEBBY	**COM**PORTS	
BRUHAHAS	**CAM**PLING	**CAT**WORKS	**COC**HAIRS	**COM**POSED	
BUBBLING	**CAM**PONGS	**CAT**WORMS	**COC**KADES	**COM**POSER	
BUCKAROO	**CAM**POUTS	**CAU**DALLY	**COC**KEREL	**COM**POSES	
BUCKEENS	**CAM**PUSES	**CAU**DATED	**COC**KEYED	**COM**POSTS	
BUCKINGS	**CAM**WOODS	**CAU**DATES	**COD**PIECE	**COM**POTES	
BUDDINGS	**CAN**BANKS	**CAU**DEXES	**COE**DITED	**COM**POUND	
BUDDYING	**CAN**CELLI	**CAU**DICES	**COE**HORNS	**COM**PRESS	
BUDWORMS	**CAN**CERED	**CEP**HEIDS	**COE**QUATE	**COM**PRINT	
BUFFABLE	**CAN**CRINE	**CER**VICES	**COE**VOLVE	**COM**PRISE	
BUFFETED		**CHA**BOUKS	**COF**FINED	**COM**PRIZE	

COMPULSE	**CORBEAUS**	**CUB**HOODS	**DEN**DROID	**DIS**CAGED
CONCAUSE	**CORDIALS**	**CUD**BEARS	**DEODATES**	**DIS**CAGES
CONCAVED	**CORDINER**	**CUD**WEEDS	**DERMISES**	**DIS**CANDY
CONCAVES	**CORDINGS**	**CUFFLING**	**DESCANTS**	**DIS**CANTS
CONCEDED	**CORDITES**	**CULVERTS**	**DESCENTS**	**DIS**CARDS
CONCEDER	**CORDUROY**	**CUMQUATS**	**DESCRIED**	**DIS**CASED
CONCEDES	**CORMUSES**	**CUP**BOARD	**DESCRIER**	**DIS**CASES
CONCENTS	**CORPORAL**	**CUP**CAKES	**DESCRIES**	**DIS**CIDED
CONCERTS	**CORPUSES**	**CUP**GALLS	**DESKILLS**	**DIS**CIDES
CONCLAVE	**CORVINAS**	**CUP**HEADS	**DESMINES**	**DIS**CINCT
CONCOLOR	**COSMESES**	**CUP**PINGS	**DESPAIRS**	**DIS**CLAIM
CONCORDS	**COSMETIC**	**CURB**INGS	**DESPATCH**	**DIS**CLOSE
CONCOURS	**COSMINES**	**CURB**LESS	**DESPIGHT**	**DIS**COLOR
CONCREWS	**COSMISTS**	**CUR**CHEFS	**DESPISES**	**DIS**CORDS
CONDENSE	**COSMOSES**	**CUR**CUMIN	**DESPONDS**	**DIS**COUNT
CONDOLED	**COTQUEAN**	**CURVITAL**	**DETHATCH**	**DIS**COURE
CONDOLES	**COUCHANT**	**CUSPATED**	**DEWBERRY**	**DIS**COVER
CONDONER	**COUGUARS**	**CUT**BACKS	**DEWCLAWS**	**DIS**CROWN
CONDUCES	**COUPLING**	**CUT**BANKS	**DEWDROPS**	**DIS**CURED
CONDUCTS	**COUPURES**	**CUT**DOWNS	**DEWFALLS**	**DIS**CURES
CONDUITS	**COUVADES**	**CUT**GLASS	**DEWPOINT**	**DIS**FAMES
CONFINED	**COUVERTS**	**CUT**GRASS	**DIABASES**	**DIS**FAVOR
CONFINER	**COWBANES**	**CUT**PURSE	**DIABASIC**	**DIS**FLESH
CONFINES	**COWBELLS**	**CUT**WATER	**DIABETES**	**DIS**FORMS
CONFIRMS	**COWBERRY**	**CUT**WORKS	**DIABOLOS**	**DIS**FROCK
CONFIXED	**COWBINDS**	**CUT**WORMS	**DIACETYL**	**DIS**GAVEL
CONFIXES	**COWBIRDS**	**CYMBALER**	**DIAGLYPH**	**DIS**GESTS
CONFOCAL	**COWBOYED**	**CYMBLING**	**DIAGRAMS**	**DIS**GORGE
CONFORMS	**COWFLAPS**	**DABBLING**	**DIAGRAPH**	**DIS**GOWNS
CONFOUND	**COWFLOPS**	**DAB**CHICK	**DIAGRIDS**	**DIS**GRACE
CONFRERE	**COWGIRLS**	**DADDOCKS**	**DIAMETER**	**DIS**GRADE
CONFRONT	**COWGRASS**	**DAFFIEST**	**DIAMINES**	**DIS**GUISE
CONFUSED	**COWHANDS**	**DAGGINGS**	**DIAPASES**	**DIS**GUSTS
CONFUSES	**COWHEARD**	**DAGWOODS**	**DIAPAUSE**	**DIS**HABIT
CONGEALS	**COWHEELS**	**DALGYTES**	**DIAPHONE**	**DIS**HABLE
CONGENIC	**COWHERBS**	**DAMBOARD**	**DIAPHONY**	**DIS**HELMS
CONGESTS	**COWHERDS**	**DAMBRODS**	**DIAZINES**	**DIS**HINGS
CONGLOBE	**COWHIDED**	**DAMPENED**	**DIBBLING**	**DIS**HOMED
CONGREED	**COWHIDES**	**DAMPINGS**	**DIDDERED**	**DIS**HOMES
CONGREES	**COWHOUSE**	**DANDERED**	**DIEBACKS**	**DIS**HONOR
CONGREET	**COWPLOPS**	**DAPPLING**	**DIEHARDS**	**DIS**HORNS
CONGRUED	**COWPOKES**	**DAUBINGS**	**DIEMAKER**	**DIS**HORSE
CONGRUES	**COWPOXES**	**DAUBRIES**	**DIFFRACT**	**DIS**HOUSE
CONJOINS	**COXCOMBS**	**DAWBAKES**	**DIFFUSED**	**DIS**JOINS
CONJOINT	**CREDITED**	**DAWBRIES**	**DIFFUSES**	**DIS**JOINT
CONJUGAL	**CREMAINS**	**DAWCOCKS**	**DIGGABLE**	**DIS**MASKS
CONJUNTO	**CREMATED**	**DAY**BOOKS	**DIGGINGS**	**DIS**MASTS
CONJUROR	**CREMATES**	**DAY**BREAK	**DIMPLIER**	**DIS**MAYED
CONQUEST	**CREMINIS**	**DAY**CARES	**DIMPLING**	**DIS**MOUNT
CONVENTS	**CREMONAS**	**DAY**DREAM	**DINGOING**	**DIS**PACED
CONVERGE	**CREMORNE**	**DAY**FLIES	**DIP**CHICK	**DIS**PACES
CONVERSE	**CREPANCE**	**DAY**GLOWS	**DIPHONES**	**DIS**PARKS
CONVERSO	**CREVICED**	**DAY**MARES	**DIPPINGS**	**DIS**PARTS
CONVERTS	**CREVICES**	**DAY**MARKS	**DISBANDS**	**DIS**PATCH
CONVEXED	**CRIBROSE**	**DAY**WORKS	**DISBARKS**	**DIS**PEACE
CONVEXES	**CRIMINIS**	**DEACONED**	**DISBENCH**	**DIS**PENCE
CONVIVES	**CROMACKS**	**DECKINGS**	**DISBOSOM**	**DIS**PENDS
CONVOLVE	**CROMORNE**	**DEEPENED**	**DISBOUND**	**DIS**PERSE
COOKINGS	**CRUDITES**	**DEICIDES**	**DISBOWEL**	**DIS**PLACE
COOKOFFS	**CUBBINGS**	**DEIFIERS**	**DISBURSE**	**DIS**PLANT

DISPLAYS	DRYWALLS	ENCHAINS	EXECRATE	FINDINGS
DISPLING	DRYWELLS	ENCHANTS	EXECUTER	FINDRAMS
DISPLUME	DUBBINGS	ENCHARMS	EXECUTES	FINFOOTS
DISPONES	DUCKINGS	ENDBRAIN	EXIGENTS	FINMARKS
DISPORTS	DUECENTO	ENDGAMES	EXOCARPS	FIPPENCE
DISPOSED	DULCITES	ENDPAPER	EXOCRINE	FISHABLE
DISPOSER	DULCOSES	ENDPLATE	EXODERMS	FISHINGS
DISPOSES	DUMFOUND	ENDPLAYS	EXOGAMIC	FITCHEWS
DISPOSTS	DUMMERER	ENDPOINT	EXOMISES	FITFULLY
DISPRIZE	DUMPINGS	ENSHEATH	EXOPLASM	FIZZINGS
DISPROOF	DUMPLING	ENSHELLS	EXUDATES	FLAGRANT
DISPROVE	DURMASTS	ENSWEEPS	EYEBALLS	FLAMINES
DISPURSE	DYEWEEDS	ENTWINED	EYEBANKS	FLAVINES
DISQUIET	DYEWOODS	ENTWINES	EYEBATHS	FLOKATIS
DISVALUE	DYSGENIC	ENTWISTS	EYEBEAMS	FLOWAGES
DISVOUCH	DYSMELIC	ENWHEELS	EYEBLACK	FLYBACKS
DISYOKED	EARBALLS	EPIBLAST	EYEBLINK	FLYBANES
DISYOKES	EARDROPS	EPICALYX	EYEBOLTS	FLYBELTS
DITHEIST	EARDRUMS	EPICARPS	EYEBROWS	FLYBLOWN
DIVVYING	EARFLAPS	EPICEDES	EYEDROPS	FLYBLOWS
DOBCHICK	EARMARKS	EPICISTS	EYEFOLDS	FLYBOATS
DOCKINGS	EARMUFFS	EPICURES	EYEGLASS	FLYBOOKS
DODDERED	EARPHONE	EPICYCLE	EYEHOLES	FLYHANDS
DODGINGS	EARPICKS	EPIDEMIC	EYEHOOKS	FLYMAKER
DOGBANES	EARPIECE	EPIDERMS	EYEPIECE	FLYPAPER
DOGBERRY	EARPLUGS	EPIDOTES	EYEPOINT	FLYPASTS
DOGBOLTS	EARWAXES	EPIDURAL	EYEWATER	FLYPITCH
DOGCARTS	EARWIGGY	EPIFAUNA	EYEWINKS	FLYWHEEL
DOGFACES	EARWORMS	EPIFOCAL	FAGGINGS	FOAMINGS
DOGFIGHT	ECOCIDES	EPIGAMIC	FALBALAS	FODDERED
DOGFOXES	ECOFREAK	EPIGENIC	FALCADES	FOGBOUND
DOGGINGS	EDIFICES	EPIGRAMS	FANBASES	FOGFRUIT
DOGGONER	EDIFIERS	EPIGRAPH	FANFARED	FOGGAGES
DOGHOLES	EDUCABLE	EPIMERES	FANFARES	FOGHORNS
DOGHOUSE	EDUCATES	EPIZOISM	FANFOLDS	FOLDINGS
DOGVANES	EELFARES	EPIZOOTY	FANGLIKE	FOLDOUTS
DOGWATCH	EELGRASS	EREMITES	FANWORTS	FONDANTS
DOGWOODS	EELPOUTS	EREWHILE	FANZINES	FONDUING
DOLDRUMS	EELWORMS	ERLKINGS	FARDINGS	FORBEARS
DONDERED	EELWRACK	ERODENTS	FARMINGS	FORBODED
DOOFUSES	EGGFRUIT	EROGENIC	FASCINES	FORBODES
DOPPINGS	EGGHEADS	ERUDITES	FASCISTS	FORBORNE
DORHAWKS	EGGPLANT	ESCHEATS	FATBACKS	FORDOING
DORMERED	EGGWHISK	ESCHEWED	FATBIRDS	FORFAIRS
DORMOUSE	EGOMANIA	ESCHEWER	FATHEADS	FORFAULT
DOUBLETS	EILDINGS	ESTHETES	FATHOMED	FORFENDS
DOUBLING	ELEGISTS	ETAGERES	FATHOMER	FORGINGS
DOUCINES	ELFHOODS	ETAMINES	FATWOODS	FORGIVEN
DRACONES	ELICITED	ETCHANTS	FAUBOURG	FORGIVER
DRACONIC	ELKHOUND	ETCHINGS	FAUCHONS	FORGIVES
DRAGOONS	ELLWANDS	ETYPICAL	FEEBLEST	FORGOERS
DRAGROPE	ELMWOODS	EVIDENTS	FEEBLING	FORGOING
DRAPIERS	ELOCUTES	EVOCABLE	FEEDHOLE	FORHENTS
DRAWINGS	ELOGISTS	EVOCATES	FEEDINGS	FORJUDGE
DREVILLS	EMICATES	EXABYTES	FELWORTS	FORMATED
DRIBLETS	EMIGRANT	EXAHERTZ	FENDERED	FORMATES
DROPOUTS	EMIGRATE	EXAMINED	FEUDALLY	FORMICAS
DRYBEATS	EMPYESES	EXAMINER	FEUDINGS	FORMINGS
DRYMOUTH	ENABLING	EXAMINES	FIGWORTS	FORPINED
DRYPOINT	ENAMINES	EXCHEATS	FINBACKS	FORPINES

FORWARDS	GANGLIAL	GODCHILD	GUNWALES	HENBANES
FORWARNS	GARBLESS	GODDAMNS	GWEDUCKS	HENCOOPS
FORWASTE	GARBLING	GODHEADS	HACKINGS	HENHOUSE
FORWEARY	GARBOARD	GODHOODS	HADDOCKS	HENPECKS
FOUDRIES	GARBOILS	GODWARDS	HAEMATIN	HERBLESS
FOUGADES	GARDANTS	GOLDARNS	HAGBERRY	HERBLETS
FOUMARTS	GARPIKES	GOLDURNS	HAGBOLTS	HERMETIC
FOXBERRY	GASFIELD	GONDELAY	HAGDOWNS	HEYDUCKS
FOXFIRES	GASHOUSE	GONFANON	HALFLING	HICCOUGH
FOXGLOVE	GASKINGS	GONGLIKE	HALYARDS	HILDINGS
FOXHOLES	GASPINGS	GOOFIEST	HAMBLING	HINDERED
FOXHOUND	GASWORKS	GORBELLY	HAMBONED	HIPBONES
FOXHUNTS	GAUCHEST	GORBLIMY	HAMBONES	HIPPARCH
FOYBOATS	GAUGINGS	GORCOCKS	HAMBURGS	HIPPINGS
FRACASES	GAUPUSES	GORCROWS	HAMMERED	HIPPUSES
FRAGRANT	GAWPUSES	GORDITAS	HAMMERER	HIRPLING
FRAMINGS	GAYWINGS	GOSHAWKS	HAMMOCKS	HIZZONER
FREDAINE	GEEBUNGS	GOSPORTS	HANDOFFS	HOBBLING
FRIGATES	GEEPOUND	GOUGERES	HANDOUTS	HOECAKES
FRIJOLES	GELDINGS	GOUJEERS	HANDOVER	HOEDOWNS
FRIVOLED	GEMCLIPS	GRADATED	HANDRAIL	HOGBACKS
FROGLIKE	GEMMATED	GRADATES	HANDROLL	HOGGINGS
FROMAGES	GEMMATES	GRADINES	HANGABLE	HOGHOODS
FROWARDS	GEMMEOUS	GRADUALS	HANGINGS	HOGMANES
FRUGALLY	GEMMULES	GRAMERCY	HANGOUTS	HOGWARDS
FRYBREAD	GENDERED	GRAVITAS	HAPPENED	HOGWEEDS
FUCKINGS	GEODUCKS	GRAZINGS	HARBORED	HOLDINGS
FUCKOFFS	GEOFACTS	GREGALES	HARBORER	HOLDOUTS
FUFFIEST	GEOMETER	GRIMACED	HARMALAS	HOLDOVER
FULCRATE	GEOMYOID	GRIMACER	HARMINES	HOMBURGS
FULFILLS	GEOPHONE	GRIMACES	HARMOSTS	HOMMOCKS
FULMINED	GEOPROBE	GRIMOIRE	HARPINGS	HOMMOSES
FULMINES	GERMAINS	GROGRAMS	HARPOONS	HOPBINDS
FUMBLING	GERMANIC	GROWINGS	HARVESTS	HOPBINES
FUNBOARD	GIBBETED	GRYPHONS	HATBANDS	HOPHEADS
FUNDINGS	GIDDYING	GUAYULES	HATBOXES	HOPPINGS
FUNFAIRS	GILDINGS	GUIDANCE	HATBRUSH	HOPPLING
FUNFESTS	GIMBALED	GUIDINGS	HATCHECK	HORDOCKS
FUNHOUSE	GIMCRACK	GUIPURES	HATGUARD	HORMONAL
FURBELOW	GIMMICKS	GULFIEST	HATMAKER	HOTBLOOD
FURCATES	GIMMICKY	GUMBALLS	HAUBERKS	HOTBOXES
FURFAIRS	GINGALLS	GUMBOILS	HAWBUCKS	HOTCAKES
FURFURAL	GINGELLY	GUMBOOTS	HAWFINCH	HOTFOOTS
FURFURAN	GINHOUSE	GUMDROPS	HAWKEYED	HOTHEADS
FURFUROL	GIRDINGS	GUMMINGS	HAWKINGS	HOTHOUSE
FUTHARKS	GLAZINGS	GUMMITES	HAYBANDS	HOTPLATE
GABBARDS	GLIDINGS	GUMMOSES	HAYBOXES	HOTPRESS
GABBLING	GLOBALLY	GUMWEEDS	HAYCOCKS	HOUMUSES
GABFESTS	GLOBATED	GUMWOODS	HAYFIELD	HOWDYING
GADFLIES	GLOZINGS	GUNBOATS	HAYFORKS	HUFFIEST
GADWALLS	GLUCOSES	GUNFIGHT	HAYMAKER	HUGGABLE
GADZOOKS	GLYCERIA	GUNFIRES	HAYWARDS	HUIPILES
GAMBETTA	GLYCERIC	GUNFLINT	HAYWIRES	HUMBLEST
GAMBIERS	GLYCINES	GUNHOUSE	HEADINGS	HUMBLING
GAMBLING	GLYCOLIC	GUNMAKER	HEADRAIL	HUMDRUMS
GAMMOCKS	GLYCONIC	GUNMETAL	HEADREST	HUMMINGS
GAMMONER	GLYCOSES	GUNPAPER	HEDGINGS	HUMMOCKS
GANDERED	GNAWINGS	GUNPLAYS	HEEHAWED	HUMMUSES
GANGINGS	GNOMISTS	GUNPOINT	HELMETED	HUSBANDS
GANGLAND	GOBBLING	GUNPORTS	HELPINGS	HUSKINGS

HUSWIFES	**ITA**CONIC	**KEB**BOCKS	**LAN**GLEYS	**LOG**BOARD
HUSWIVES	**ITCH**INGS	**KEB**BUCKS	**LAN**YARDS	**LOG**BOOKS
HYACINES	**ITE**MISER	**KEE**PINGS	**LAP**BOARD	**LOG**GINGS
HYLDINGS	**ITE**MISES	**KEM**BOING	**LAP**PINGS	**LOG**JUICE
IAMBUSES	**JAB**BLING	**KEM**PINGS	**LAP**WINGS	**LOG**WOODS
ICEBALLS	**JACK**AROO	**KER**BINGS	**LAP**WORKS	**LON**GINGS
ICEBERGS	**JACK**EENS	**KER**CHIEF	**LAR**BOARD	**LOO**KISTS
ICEBLINK	**JACK**INGS	**KER**MISES	**LAR**GESSE	**LOO**PINGS
ICEBOATS	**JAG**HIRES	**KER**PLUNK	**LAS**HINGS	**LOP**GRASS
ICEBOUND	**JAK**FRUIT	**KEY**BOARD	**LAT**HINGS	**LOP**PINGS
ICEBOXES	**JAM**BEAUX	**KEY**BUGLE	**LAU**WINES	**LOR**DINGS
ICEFALLS	**JAM**BIERS	**KEY**CARDS	**LAW**BOOKS	**LOR**DOSES
ICEFIELD	**JAM**BONES	**KEY**HOLES	**LAW**FULLY	**LOW**BALLS
ICEHOUSE	**JAM**BOOLS	**KEY**PUNCH	**LAW**GIVER	**LOW**BROWS
ICEMAKER	**JAM**BOREE	**KEY**WORDS	**LAW**MAKER	**LOW**DOWNS
ICEPACKS	**JAM**MINGS	**KHE**DIVAS	**LAY**BACKS	**LOW**VELDS
ICEWINES	**JAR**GOONS	**KHE**DIVES	**LAY**WOMAN	**LUB**BARDS
IMAGINGS	**JAR**HEADS	**KIB**BLING	**LAY**WOMEN	**LUG**GABLE
IMAGISMS	**JAS**MINES	**KICK**OFFS	**LEA**DINGS	**LUG**GAGES
IMAGISTS	**JAS**PISES	**KID**DYING	**LEAD**OFFS	**LUG**HOLES
IMAMATES	**JAW**BONED	**KID**GLOVE	**LEA**FIEST	**LUG**WORMS
INDWELLS	**JAW**BONER	**KIM**BOING	**LEE**BOARD	**LUM**BANGS
INEDITED	**JAW**BONES	**KIN**CHINS	**LEE**WARDS	**LUR**KINGS
INKBERRY	**JAW**BOXES	**KIN**FOLKS	**LEG**GINGS	**LUT**FISKS
INKBLOTS	**JAW**FALLS	**KIN**GLIKE	**LEG**GISMS	**LUT**HERNS
INKHORNS	**JAW**HOLES	**KIP**PAGES	**LEG**HORNS	**LUX**METER
INKWELLS	**JAY**BIRDS	**KIR**KINGS	**LEG**WEARS	**LYD**DITES
INKWOODS	**JAY**WALKS	**KIS**METIC	**LEG**WORKS	**MAC**HAIRS
INNYARDS	**JEO**FAILS	**KLA**VIERS	**LEK**KINGS	**MAC**HETES
INSCAPES	**JEO**PARDS	**KNE**VELLS	**LEM**MINGS	**MAC**KEREL
INSHEATH	**JEO**PARDY	**KNO**WINGS	**LEN**DINGS	**MAD**BRAIN
INSHELLS	**JER**KINGS	**KOL**BASIS	**LEO**PARDS	**MAD**DOCKS
INSWINGS	**JET**BEADS	**KOL**BASSI	**LET**DOWNS	**MAD**HOUSE
INTWINED	**JET**FOILS	**KOS**MOSES	**LEU**CINES	**MAD**WOMAN
INTWINES	**JET**PLANE	**KOU**MISES	**LEU**CITES	**MAD**WOMEN
INTWISTS	**JET**PORTS	**KOU**PREYS	**LEU**COMAS	**MAD**WORTS
IREFULLY	**JIB**BINGS	**KUM**QUATS	**LEU**KOSES	**MAD**ZOONS
ISCHEMIC	**JIB**BOOMS	**KYP**HOSES	**LIB**BARDS	**MAF**FLING
ISOBARES	**JIG**GINGS	**LACK**EYED	**LIC**KINGS	**MAH**JONGS
ISOBARIC	**JIM**CRACK	**LAC**MUSES	**LIG**GINGS	**MAI**MINGS
ISOBASES	**JIN**GALLS	**LAC**QUEYS	**LIL**YLIKE	**MAL**POSED
ISOBATHS	**JIR**BLING	**LAD**DERED	**LIM**BECKS	**MAL**WARES
ISOBUTYL	**JOB**BINGS	**LAD**HOODS	**LIM**BLESS	**MAM**BOING
ISOCHASM	**JOCK**EYED	**LAD**YLIKE	**LIM**BUSES	**MAM**MERED
ISOCHIME	**JOG**GINGS	**LAG**GINGS	**LIM**PINGS	**MAM**MITIS
ISOCHORE	**JOG**PANTS	**LAI**GHEST	**LIN**GULAR	**MAM**MOCKS
ISOCLINE	**JON**CANOE	**LAM**BASTE	**LIN**GULAS	**MAM**MOTHS
ISODOSES	**JOY**FULLY	**LAM**BASTS	**LIP**PENED	**MAM**PARAS
ISOFORMS	**JUD**DERED	**LAM**BINGS	**LIP**PINGS	**MAN**DATED
ISOGAMIC	**JUG**GINGS	**LAM**BLING	**LIS**PINGS	**MAN**DATES
ISOGENIC	**JUG**HEADS	**LAM**MINGS	**LIS**POUND	**MAN**DRAKE
ISOGLOSS	**JUM**BLING	**LAM**PASES	**LIT**HATES	**MAN**DRILL
ISOGRAFT	**JUM**BUCKS	**LAM**PASSE	**LIT**HEMIC	**MAN**FULLY
ISOGRAMS	**JUM**PINGS	**LAM**PERNS	**LIT**HOING	**MAN**GOLDS
ISOGRAPH	**JUN**CATES	**LAM**PINGS	**LIT**MUSES	**MAN**GROVE
ISOMERES	**KAB**BALAS	**LAM**PIONS	**LOA**DINGS	**MAN**HOLES
ISOMORPH	**KAL**PISES	**LAM**POONS	**LOB**WORMS	**MAN**HOODS
ISOPHONE	**KAM**PONGS	**LAM**PREYS	**LOC**KINGS	**MAN**HUNTS
ISOZYMES	**KAT**CHINA	**LAN**DINGS	**LOC**KNUTS	**MAN**JACKS
ISOZYMIC	**KAU**PAPAS	**LAND**RAIL	**LOD**GINGS	**MAN**KINDS

MANPACKS	MIDWEEKS	MISFAITH	MISPRIZE	MUSCADET
MANPOWER	MIDWIFED	MISFALLS	MISPROUD	MUSCLING
MANWARDS	MIDWIFES	MISFARED	MISQUOTE	MUSCONES
MAPMAKER	MIDWIVED	MISFARES	MISVALUE	MUSPIKES
MAPPINGS	MIDWIVES	MISFEEDS	MISWEENS	MUSQUASH
MARBLING	MIDYEARS	MISFEIGN	MISWENDS	MYOBLAST
MARCELLA	MIFFIEST	MISFIELD	MISWORDS	MYOGENIC
MARDYING	MILDEWED	MISFILED	MISWRITE	MYOGRAMS
MARGENTS	MILFOILS	MISFILES	MISWROTE	MYOGRAPH
MARGRAVE	MILKINGS	MISFIRED	MISYOKED	MYRBANES
MARJORAM	MIMMICKS	MISFIRES	MISYOKES	MYTHISTS
MARKHORS	MINDINGS	MISFOCUS	MIXDOWNS	NANDINES
MARKINGS	MIRBANES	MISFORMS	MIZMAZES	NANKEENS
MARMITES	MISBEGAN	MISFRAME	MOBBINGS	NARCISTS
MARMOSES	MISBEGIN	MISGAUGE	MOBBLING	NARCOMAS
MARPLOTS	MISBEGOT	MISGIVEN	MOCHELLS	NARCOSES
MASHINGS	MISBEGUN	MISGIVES	MOCKINGS	NARWHALE
MASKINGS	MISBILLS	MISGOING	MOIDERED	NAVVYING
MATFELON	MISBINDS	MISGRADE	MOLDERED	NAYWARDS
MATGRASS	MISBIRTH	MISGRAFF	MOLDINGS	NAYWORDS
MATWEEDS	MISBOUND	MISGRAFT	MONDAINE	NECKINGS
MATZOONS	MISBRAND	MISGROWN	MONGEESE	NEOBLAST
MAUVEINS	MISBUILD	MISGROWS	MONGOOSE	NEOMORPH
MAUVINES	MISBUILT	MISGUESS	MONKEYED	NEOPAGAN
MAWBOUND	MISCALLS	MISGUIDE	MOODYING	NEOPLASM
MAWPUSES	MISCARRY	MISHEARD	MOPBOARD	NERVINES
MAXWELLS	MISCASTS	MISHEARS	MOPHEADS	NETBALLS
MAYBIRDS	MISCHIEF	MISJOINS	MORBIDER	NETHEADS
MAYFLIES	MISCHOSE	MISJUDGE	MORBUSES	NETWORKS
MAYPOLES	MISCITED	MISKEEPS	MORDANTS	NEWCOMER
MAYWEEDS	MISCITES	MISKEYED	MORDENTS	NEWFOUND
MEACOCKS	MISCLAIM	MISKICKS	MOSHINGS	NEWWAVER
MEDFLIES	MISCLASS	MISKNOWN	MOUCHARD	NIBBLING
MENDINGS	MISCODED	MISKNOWS	MOUCHOIR	NICKNACK
MENFOLKS	MISCODES	MISMAKES	MOWBURNS	NIDDICKS
MERCHANT	MISCOINS	MISMARKS	MOWBURNT	NIFFIEST
MERCHILD	MISCOLOR	MISMARRY	MRIDANGS	NIMBLEST
MERFOLKS	MISCOOKS	MISMATCH	MUCHELLS	NIMBUSED
MERGINGS	MISCOUNT	MISMATED	MUDBATHS	NIMBUSES
MERMAIDS	MISCREED	MISMATES	MUDDYING	NIOBATES
MESDAMES	MISCUING	MISMEETS	MUDFLAPS	NIOBITES
MESHINGS	MISDATED	MISMETRE	MUDFLATS	NIPPLING
MESPRISE	MISDATES	MISMOVED	MUDFLOWS	NISBERRY
MESPRIZE	MISDEALS	MISMOVES	MUDGUARD	NITHINGS
MESQUINE	MISDEALT	MISPAGED	MUDHOLES	NITPICKS
MESQUITE	MISDEEDS	MISPAGES	MUDHOOKS	NITPICKY
MESQUITS	MISDEEMS	MISPAINT	MUDPACKS	NOBBLING
METCASTS	MISDEMPT	MISPARSE	MUDPUPPY	NODDINGS
METHYLIC	MISDIALS	MISPARTS	MUDWORTS	NOGGINGS
MEZQUITE	MISDIETS	MISPATCH	MUFFLING	NONBANKS
MEZQUITS	MISDIGHT	MISPLACE	MUGGINGS	NONBASIC
MICHINGS	MISDOERS	MISPLANS	MUGWORTS	NONBEING
MICKEYED	MISDOING	MISPLANT	MULBERRY	NONBLACK
MIDBRAIN	MISDONNE	MISPLAYS	MULMULLS	NONBOOKS
MIDCULTS	MISDOUBT	MISPLEAD	MUMBLING	NONBRAND
MIDFIELD	MISDRAWN	MISPOINT	MUMMINGS	NONCLASS
MIDMONTH	MISDRAWS	MISPOISE	MUMMOCKS	NONCLING
MIDMOSTS	MISDREAD	MISPRICE	MUNGOOSE	NONCOLAS
MIDPOINT	MISDRIVE	MISPRINT	MURDERED	NONCOLOR
MIDWATCH	MISDROVE	MISPRISE	MURMURED	NONCRIME

NONDAIRY	OATHABLE	OUTBLUSH	OUTDRESS	OUTGUIDE
NONDANCE	OATMEALS	OUTBOARD	OUTDRINK	OUTHAULS
NONFACTS	OBSCURED	OUTBOAST	OUTDRIVE	OUTHEARD
NONFATAL	OBSCURER	OUTBOUND	OUTDROPS	OUTHEARS
NONFATTY	OBSCURES	OUTBOXED	OUTDROVE	OUTHIRED
NONFINAL	ODDBALLS	OUTBOXES	OUTDRUNK	OUTHIRES
NONFLUID	ODOGRAPH	OUTBRAGS	OUTDUELS	OUTHOMER
NONFOCAL	ODOMETER	OUTBRAVE	OUTDURED	OUTHOUSE
NONGLARE	OFFBEATS	OUTBRAWL	OUTDURES	OUTHOWLS
NONGREEN	OFFCASTS	OUTBREAK	OUTDWELL	OUTHUMOR
NONGUEST	OFFPRINT	OUTBREED	OUTDWELT	OUTHUNTS
NONGUILT	OHMMETER	OUTBRIBE	OUTFABLE	OUTJESTS
NONHARDY	OILBIRDS	OUTBROKE	OUTFACED	OUTJUMPS
NONHUMAN	OILCAMPS	OUTBUILD	OUTFACES	OUTKEEPS
NONJUROR	OILCLOTH	OUTBUILT	OUTFALLS	OUTKICKS
NONMAJOR	OILFIELD	OUTBULGE	OUTFASTS	OUTKILLS
NONMETAL	OILFIRED	OUTBULKS	OUTFAWNS	OUTMARCH
NONMETRO	OILGASES	OUTBULLY	OUTFEAST	OUTMATCH
NONMODAL	OILHOLES	OUTBURNS	OUTFEELS	OUTMODES
NONMONEY	OILPAPER	OUTBURNT	OUTFENCE	OUTMOVED
NONMORAL	OILPROOF	OUTBURST	OUTFIELD	OUTMOVES
NONMUSIC	OKIMONOS	OUTCALLS	OUTFIGHT	OUTPACED
NONPAGAN	OLDWIVES	OUTCAPER	OUTFINDS	OUTPACES
NONPAPAL	OLEFINES	OUTCASTE	OUTFIRED	OUTPAINT
NONPARTY	OLICOOKS	OUTCASTS	OUTFIRES	OUTPARTS
NONPASTS	OLIGISTS	OUTCATCH	OUTFLANK	OUTPEEPS
NONPLAYS	OLIGOMER	OUTCAVIL	OUTFLASH	OUTPEERS
NONPOINT	OLIVINES	OUTCHARM	OUTFLIES	OUTPITCH
NONPOLAR	OLIVINIC	OUTCHEAT	OUTFLING	OUTPLACE
NONPRINT	OLOGISTS	OUTCHIDE	OUTFLOAT	OUTPLANS
NONQUOTA	OLYCOOKS	OUTCLASS	OUTFLOWN	OUTPLAYS
NONVALID	OMOHYOID	OUTCLIMB	OUTFLOWS	OUTPLODS
NONVIRAL	OMOPLATE	OUTCLOMB	OUTFLUSH	OUTPLOTS
NONVITAL	OMPHALOS	OUTCOACH	OUTFOOLS	OUTPOINT
NONVOCAL	ONYCHIAS	OUTCOMES	OUTFOOTS	OUTPOLLS
NONVOTER	OOSPERMS	OUTCOOKS	OUTFOUND	OUTPORTS
NONWHITE	OOSPORES	OUTCOUNT	OUTFOXED	OUTPOSTS
NONWOODY	OPAQUEST	OUTCRAWL	OUTFOXES	OUTPOURS
NONWORDS	OPOPANAX	OUTCRIED	OUTFROWN	OUTPOWER
NONWOVEN	ORACLING	OUTCRIES	OUTGAINS	OUTPRAYS
NORWARDS	ORCHARDS	OUTCROPS	OUTGASES	OUTPREEN
NOTHINGS	OREWEEDS	OUTCROSS	OUTGATES	OUTPRESS
NOWHENCE	ORIFICES	OUTCROWD	OUTGAZED	OUTPRICE
NOWHERES	OROGENIC	OUTCROWS	OUTGAZES	OUTPRIZE
NUBBLING	OROMETER	OUTCURSE	OUTGIVEN	OUTPULLS
NUMCHUCK	ORTHOSES	OUTCURVE	OUTGIVES	OUTPUNCH
NUNDINES	OSTMARKS	OUTDANCE	OUTGLARE	OUTPUPIL
NUNHOODS	OTOCYSTS	OUTDARED	OUTGLEAM	OUTQUOTE
NUTBROWN	OUTBACKS	OUTDARES	OUTGLOWS	OUTVALUE
NUTCASES	OUTBAKED	OUTDATED	OUTGNAWN	OUTVAUNT
NUTGALLS	OUTBAKES	OUTDATES	OUTGNAWS	OUTVENOM
NUTGRASS	OUTBARKS	OUTDODGE	OUTGOERS	OUTVOICE
NUTHATCH	OUTBAWLS	OUTDOERS	OUTGOING	OUTVOTED
NUTHOUSE	OUTBEAMS	OUTDOING	OUTGRINS	OUTVOTER
NUTMEALS	OUTBITCH	OUTDOORS	OUTGROSS	OUTVOTES
NUTMEATS	OUTBLAZE	OUTDRAGS	OUTGROUP	OUTVYING
NUTPICKS	OUTBLEAT	OUTDRANK	OUTGROWN	OUTWAITS
NUTWOODS	OUTBLESS	OUTDRAWN	OUTGROWS	OUTWALKS
OARWEEDS	OUTBLOOM	OUTDRAWS	OUTGUARD	OUTWARDS
OATCAKES	OUTBLUFF	OUTDREAM	OUTGUESS	OUTWASTE

OUTWATCH	**PAN**PIPES	**PER**FORMS	**PIS**CINES	**PRE**BUILT
OUTWEARS	**PAP**PUSES	**PER**FUMED	**PIS**MIRES	**PRE**CASTS
OUTWEARY	**PAR**BAKED	**PER**FUMER	**PIT**CHOUT	**PRE**CEDED
OUTWEEDS	**PAR**BAKES	**PER**FUMES	**PIT**FALLS	**PRE**CEDES
OUTWEEPS	**PAR**BOILS	**PER**FUSED	**PIT**HEADS	**PRE**CENTS
OUTWEIGH	**PAR**BREAK	**PER**FUSES	**PIT**PROPS	**PRE**CHECK
OUTWELLS	**PAR**CLOSE	**PER**MEANT	**PLAC**ABLE	**PRE**CHILL
OUTWHIRL	**PAR**DALES	**PER**MEASE	**PLA**CARDS	**PRE**CHOSE
OUTWICKS	**PAR**DALIS	**PER**MUTED	**PLA**CATER	**PRE**CINCT
OUTWILED	**PAR**DONER	**PER**MUTES	**PLA**CATES	**PRE**CITED
OUTWILES	**PAR**FLESH	**PER**PENDS	**PLA**CIDER	**PRE**CLEAN
OUTWILLS	**PAR**FOCAL	**PER**PENTS	**PLA**FONDS	**PRE**CLEAR
OUTWINDS	**PAR**GINGS	**PER**VADED	**PLAY**LIKE	**PRE**CODED
OUTWINGS	**PAR**KADES	**PER**VADES	**PLI**CATES	**PRE**CODES
OUTWORKS	**PAR**KINGS	**PER**VERSE	**PLUM**AGES	**PRE**COOKS
OUTWORTH	**PAR**PANES	**PER**VERTS	**PLUM**ISTS	**PRE**COOLS
OUTWOUND	**PAR**PENDS	**PET**CHARY	**PLUM**ULES	**PRE**CRASH
OUTWREST	**PAR**PENTS	**PET**COCKS	**PLU**VIALS	**PRE**CURED
OUTWRITE	**PAR**POINT	**PHIM**OSES	**PLY**WOODS	**PRE**CURES
OUTWROTE	**PAR**VENUE	**PICK**EREL	**POCH**ARDS	**PRE**CURSE
OUTYELLS	**PAR**VENUS	**PICK**INGS	**POD**CASTS	**PRE**DATED
OUTYELPS	**PAR**VISES	**PICK**OFFS	**POE**CHORE	**PRE**DATES
OUTYIELD	**PAS**CHALS	**PID**DOCKS	**POL**DERED	**PRE**DAWNS
OVICIDES	**PAT**BALLS	**PIE**BALDS	**POLK**AING	**PRE**DEATH
OVIDUCAL	**PATH**OGEN	**PIE**CRUST	**POM**FRETS	**PRE**DIALS
OVIDUCTS	**PATH**OSES	**PIE**FORTS	**POM**PIONS	**PRE**DICTS
OVIPOSIT	**PAX**WAXES	**PIE**HOLES	**POM**POONS	**PRE**DOOMS
OXAZINES	**PAY**BACKS	**PIE**PLANT	**POM**WATER	**PRE**DRAFT
OXIDANTS	**PAY**CHECK	**PIF**FLING	**PON**DERED	**PRE**DRIED
OXIDATED	**PAY**GRADE	**PIG**BOATS	**POO**FIEST	**PRE**DRIES
OXIDATES	**PAY**PHONE	**PIG**FACES	**POP**CORNS	**PRE**DRILL
OXIMETER	**PEA**BERRY	**PIG**FEEDS	**POP**JOYED	**PRE**DUSKS
OXYGENIC	**PEA**COATS	**PIG**GINGS	**POP**PLIER	**PRE**DYING
OXYMORON	**PEA**COCKS	**PIG**MEATS	**POP**PLING	**PRE**FACED
PACKINGS	**PEA**COCKY	**PIG**WEEDS	**POR**POISE	**PRE**FACER
PADDINGS	**PEA**FOWLS	**PIL**CHARD	**POT**BELLY	**PRE**FACES
PADDOCKS	**PEB**BLING	**PIL**CORNS	**POT**BOILS	**PRE**FADED
PALMATED	**PEC**CABLE	**PIL**CROWS	**POT**BOUND	**PRE**FADES
PALMISTS	**PECK**INGS	**PIL**FERER	**POT**HEADS	**PRE**FIGHT
PALPATED	**PEG**BOARD	**PIMP**LIER	**POT**HERBS	**PRE**FILED
PALPATES	**PEG**BOXES	**PIN**BALLS	**POT**HOLED	**PRE**FILES
PAMPASES	**PEG**GINGS	**PIN**BONES	**POT**HOLES	**PRE**FIRED
PAMPEANS	**PEL**VISES	**PIN**CASES	**POT**HOOKS	**PRE**FIRES
PANBROIL	**PEM**BROKE	**PIN**CERED	**POT**HOUSE	**PRE**FIXED
PANCAKED	**PEN**CHANT	**PIN**CHECK	**POW**DERED	**PRE**FIXES
PANCAKES	**PEN**CRAFT	**PIND**ARIS	**POW**WOWED	**PRE**FLAME
PANDARED	**PEN**DANTS	**PIN**DOWNS	**POX**VIRUS	**PRE**FOCUS
PANDEMIC	**PEN**DENTS	**PIN**FALLS	**PRE**BAKED	**PRE**FORMS
PANDERED	**PEN**DULES	**PIN**FOLDS	**PRE**BAKES	**PRE**FRANK
PANDOORS	**PEN**FOLDS	**PIN**GRASS	**PRE**BASAL	**PRE**FROZE
PANDOWDY	**PEN**KNIFE	**PIN**HEADS	**PRE**BENDS	**PRE**FUNDS
PANDURAS	**PEN**POINT	**PIN**HOLES	**PRE**BILLS	**PRE**GAMES
PANDYING	**PEN**WOMAN	**PIN**KINGS	**PRE**BINDS	**PRE**GUIDE
PANFRIED	**PEN**WOMEN	**PIN**POINT	**PRE**BIRTH	**PRE**HEATS
PANFRIES	**PEO**PLING	**PIN**PRICK	**PRE**BLESS	**PRE**HENDS
PANGAMIC	**PER**CENTS	**PIN**WALES	**PRE**BOARD	**PRE**HUMAN
PANGENES	**PER**COLIN	**PIN**WEEDS	**PRE**BOILS	**PRE**JUDGE
PANGRAMS	**PER**DURED	**PIN**WHEEL	**PRE**BOOKS	**PRE**MEDIC
PANHUMAN	**PER**DURES	**PIN**WORKS	**PRE**BOUND	**PRE**MISES
PANMIXES	**PER**FORCE	**PIN**WORMS	**PRE**BUILD	**PRE**MIXED

PREMIXES	PROCURER	PUMPIONS	RAPHIDES	RENDERED
PREMOLAR	PROCURES	PUNDONOR	RAPPINGS	RENFORCE
PREMOLDS	PRODROME	PURBLIND	RAPPORTS	RENVERSE
PREMORAL	PRODRUGS	PURCHASE	RASBORAS	RENVERST
PREMORSE	PRODUCES	PURFLING	RASPINGS	REOPENED
PREMOVED	PRODUCTS	PURGINGS	RATFINKS	REOVIRUS
PREMOVES	PROFANES	PURPLIER	RATHOLES	REPPINGS
PREPACKS	PROFILED	PURPLING	RATHOUSE	RESCORED
PREPARED	PROFILER	PURPORTS	RATPACKS	RESCORES
PREPARER	PROFILES	PURPOSED	RATPROOF	RESCUING
PREPARES	PROFOUND	PURPOSES	RAUPATUS	RESHAVEN
PREPASTE	PROGRADE	PURPURES	RAWBONED	RESHAVES
PREPAVED	PROGRAMS	PURPURIN	RAWHEADS	RESHOOTS
PREPAVES	PROMETAL	PURVIEWS	RAWHIDED	RESKETCH
PREPLACE	PROMINES	PUSHOVER	RAWHIDES	RESKILLS
PREPLANS	PROMISER	PUTCHOCK	RAYGRASS	RESMELTS
PREPLANT	PROMISES	PUTDOWNS	READINGS	RESPACED
PREPONES	PROMOTED	PYEBALDS	READOUTS	RESPACES
PREPOSED	PROMOTES	PYODERMA	READYING	RESPEAKS
PREPOSES	PROMOTOR	PYOGENIC	REAGENTS	RESPELLS
PREPRESS	PROPAGED	QAWWALIS	REAMENDS	RESPONDS
PREPRICE	PROPAGES	QUADRANT	REAVAILS	RESPOOLS
PREPRINT	PROPALED	QUADRATS	REAVOWED	RESPRANG
PREPUBES	PROPALES	QUAKINGS	REAWAKED	RESPRAYS
PREPUBIS	PROPANES	QUAYLIKE	REAWAKEN	RETWISTS
PREPUCES	PROPENDS	QUIBLINS	REAWAKES	RHAGADES
PREPUNCH	PROPENES	RABBETED	REAWOKEN	RHIZINES
PREPUPAE	PROPHAGE	RABBITER	RECHARTS	RHUBARBS
PREPUPAL	PROPHASE	RABBITOS	RECHATES	RHUBARBY
PREPUPAS	PROPINED	RABBLING	RECHEATS	RHYMISTS
PREVAILS	PROPINES	RACCOONS	RECHECKS	RIBBANDS
PREVALUE	PROPOLIS	RACHIDES	RECHEWED	RIBBINGS
PREVENTS	PROPONES	RACKINGS	RECHOSEN	RIBBONED
PREVERBS	PROPOSED	RADWASTE	RECYCLED	RIBCAGES
PREVIEWS	PROPOSER	RAFFLING	REDBACKS	RIBGRASS
PREVISED	PROPOSES	RAGBOLTS	REDBAITS	RIBWORKS
PREVISES	PROPOUND	RAGGINGS	REDBELLY	RIBWORTS
PREVISIT	PROPYLON	RAGHEADS	REDBIRDS	RIDDANCE
PREVISOR	PROVENDS	RAGWEEDS	REDBONES	RIDGINGS
PREWARMS	PROVERBS	RAGWHEEL	REDBRICK	RIFFLING
PREWARNS	PROVINED	RAGWORKS	REDCOATS	RIGGINGS
PREWEIGH	PROVINES	RAGWORMS	REDDINGS	RIMFIRES
PREWIRED	PROVIRAL	RAGWORTS	REDFOOTS	RIMMINGS
PREWIRES	PROVIRUS	RAIDINGS	REDHEADS	RIMPLING
PREWORKS	PROVISOR	RAMBLING	REDHORSE	RINGINGS
PREWRAPS	PSCHENTS	RAMPAGED	REDPOLLS	RINGLIKE
PRIMAGES	PSYCHICS	RAMPAGER	REDWARES	RIPCORDS
PRIMATES	PTOMAINS	RAMPAGES	REDWATER	RIPPIERS
PRIMINES	PUCCOONS	RAMPARTS	REDWINGS	RIPPLIER
PRIMINGS	PUDDERED	RAMPICKS	REDWOODS	RIPPLING
PRIMUSES	PUDDINGS	RAMPIKES	REEDINGS	RISPETTI
PROBANDS	PUDDINGY	RAMPINGS	REEDITED	RISPETTO
PROBANGS	PUDDOCKS	RAMPIONS	REEFABLE	RISPINGS
PROBATED	PUFFIEST	RAMPOLES	REEFIEST	ROADINGS
PROBATES	PUGGINGS	RANCIDER	REEMERGE	ROAMINGS
PROCARPS	PUGGREES	RANCORED	REEQUIPS	ROCKIERS
PROCHAIN	PUGMARKS	RANCOURS	REGMAKER	ROCKINGS
PROCINCT	PULMOTOR	RANGINGS	REIFIERS	RODDINGS
PROCLAIM	PULPALLY	RANKINGS	REIMAGES	ROEBUCKS
PROCURED	PULVILLI	RANPIKES	REMBLING	RONDINOS

RONDURES	SARKINGS	SEAQUAKE	SIGMATES	SORBUSES
ROOFIEST	SARMENTA	SEAWALLS	SILVATIC	SORDINES
ROTGRASS	SASHAYED	SEAWANTS	SILVEXES	SOUBISES
ROUGHEST	SAVVYING	SEAWARDS	SIMMERED	SOUMINGS
ROUMINGS	SAWBILLS	SEAWARES	SIMPLING	SOUPLING
ROWBOATS	SAWBLADE	SEAWATER	SINDINGS	SOWBACKS
RUBBABOO	SAWBONES	SEAWEEDS	SINFULLY	SOWBELLY
RUBBINGS	SAWBUCKS	SEAWIVES	SINGABLE	SOWBREAD
RUBBLING	SAWDERED	SEAWOMAN	SINGINGS	SOYBEANS
RUBBOARD	SAWDUSTS	SEAWOMEN	SINGULAR	SOYMILKS
RUBDOWNS	SAWDUSTY	SEAWORMS	SINKINGS	SPADEMAN
RUBYLIKE	SAWFLIES	SEECATCH	SIPHONED	SPADICES
RUCHINGS	SAWHORSE	SEEDINGS	SIPPLING	SPAVINED
RUDDOCKS	SAWMILLS	SEEMINGS	SIRGANGS	SPYGLASS
RUDDYING	SAXHORNS	SEEPAGES	SITFASTS	SPYHOLES
RUEFULLY	SCABLAND	SEICENTO	SITHENCE	SPYPLANE
RUFFLIER	SCAGLIAS	SEIZINGS	SIXPENCE	SPYWARES
RUFFLING	SCAPULAS	SELCOUTH	SIXPENNY	STABILES
RUGGINGS	SCAVENGE	SELFISTS	SKIPLANE	STABLEST
RUMBELOW	SCEDULES	SEMBLING	SKYBOARD	STABLING
RUMBLING	SCHMATTE	SENDINGS	SKYBORNE	STADIALS
RUMMAGES	SCHMECKS	SENDOFFS	SKYBOXES	STAGINGS
RUMPLIER	SCHMEERS	SENGREEN	SKYDIVED	STAMENED
RUMPLING	SCHMOCKS	SENHORAS	SKYDIVER	STAMINAS
RUMPUSES	SCHMOOSE	SEPPUKUS	SKYDIVES	STAPEDES
RUNBACKS	SCHMUCKS	SERGINGS	SKYHOMES	STAPLING
RUNDALES	SCIMITER	SERKALIS	SKYHOOKS	STEWARDS
RUNDOWNS	SCOPULAS	SERMONER	SKYJACKS	STEWINGS
RUSHINGS	SCOWRIES	SERPENTS	SKYWALKS	STIBINES
RYEBREAD	SCUCHINS	SERVANTS	SKYWARDS	STIFLING
RYEFLOUR	SEABANKS	SERVICED	SKYWRITE	STIPENDS
RYEGRASS	SEABEACH	SERVICES	SKYWROTE	STIPULED
RYEPECKS	SEABIRDS	SETBACKS	SLADANGS	STIPULES
SABBATHS	SEABLITE	SETWALLS	SLIDINGS	STOMACHS
SABKHATS	SEABOARD	SEXFOILS	SLIPOUTS	STOMACKS
SACCADES	SEABOOTS	SEXPERTS	SLOBLAND	STOMATES
SACCOSES	SEABORNE	SHABRACK	SLOWINGS	STOPINGS
SACHEMIC	SEACOAST	SHADINGS	SLYBOOTS	STOWAGES
SACKINGS	SEACOCKS	SHADOWED	SMOKINGS	STOWINGS
SAFFRONS	SEACRAFT	SHADOWER	SNAGLIKE	STUDENTS
SAGGINGS	SEADROME	SHAGREEN	SNAPLINK	STUDYING
SAIBLING	SEAFARER	SHAKINGS	SNIPINGS	STUPRATE
SAKKOSES	SEAFLOOR	SHAKUDOS	SNOBLING	SUBBASAL
SALBANDS	SEAFOLKS	SHAMANIC	SOAKINGS	SUBBASES
SALCHOWS	SEAFOODS	SHAMINAS	SOBBINGS	SUBBASIN
SALFERNS	SEAFOWLS	SHAMUSES	SOCCAGES	SUBBINGS
SALPIANS	SEAFRONT	SHAPINGS	SOGGINGS	SUBBLOCK
SAMBUKES	SEAGOING	SHEBANGS	SOLDADOS	SUBBREED
SAMPLING	SEAGULLS	SHEBEANS	SOLDERED	SUBCASTE
SANDALED	SEAHAWKS	SHEKELIM	SOLVENTS	SUBCAUSE
SANDINGS	SEAHORSE	SHIPLAPS	SOMBRING	SUBCELLS
SANDIVER	SEAHOUND	SHOFROTH	SONDELIS	SUBCHIEF
SANGHATS	SEAKALES	SHOWINGS	SONGLIKE	SUBCHORD
SAPHEADS	SEAMAIDS	SHOWRING	SONHOODS	SUBCLAIM
SAPPLING	SEAMANLY	SIAMANGS	SOOPINGS	SUBCLANS
SAPWOODS	SEAMARKS	SIAMESES	SOPHISTS	SUBCLASS
SARCODES	SEAMOUNT	SIAMEZES	SOPPINGS	SUBCLERK
SARCOMAS	SEAPIECE	SIEVERTS	SORBATES	SUBCODES
SARDINED	SEAPLANE	SIFFLING	SORBENTS	SUBCOOLS
SARDINES	SEAPORTS	SIGMATED	SORBITES	SUBCOSTA

SUBCRUST	SUFFERER	SUPPOSES	TAMPINGS	TIECLASP
SUBCULTS	SUFFETES	SUPPRESS	TAMPIONS	TIFFINED
SUBCUTES	SUFFICES	SURBASED	TAMWORTH	TIMBALES
SUBCUTIS	SUFFIXED	SURBASES	TANBARKS	TINFOILS
SUBDEANS	SUFFIXES	SURBATED	TANDOORS	TINHORNS
SUBDEPOT	SUFFUSED	SURBATES	TANGENTS	TINPLATE
SUBDEWED	SUFFUSES	SURCEASE	TANGOING	TINWARES
SUBDUALS	SUGGESTS	SURCOATS	TANGRAMS	TINWORKS
SUBDUCES	SUGGINGS	SURFABLE	TANKINGS	TIPCARTS
SUBDUCTS	SUICIDED	SURFACED	TANYARDS	TIPPINGS
SUBDUING	SUICIDES	SURFACER	TAPHOLES	TIPPLING
SUBDUPLE	SUIPLAPS	SURFACES	TAPHOUSE	TISWASES
SUBDURAL	SULFATED	SURFIEST	TAPPINGS	TITHABLE
SUBDWARF	SULFATES	SURGINGS	TARDYING	TITHINGS
SUBFEUED	SULPHONE	SURMISER	TARPAPER	TITMOUSE
SUBFIELD	SUMMATED	SURMISES	TARWEEDS	TIZWASES
SUBFILES	SUMMATES	SURMOUNT	TARWHINE	TOADYING
SUBFIXES	SUMMERED	SURPRINT	TASKBARS	TOECLIPS
SUBFLOOR	SUMMINGS	SURPRISE	TASKINGS	TOEHOLDS
SUBFLUID	SUMMISTS	SURPRIZE	TAWDRIER	TOEPIECE
SUBFRAME	SUMMONER	SURVEILS	TAWDRIES	TOEPLATE
SUBGENRE	SUNBAKED	SURVIEWS	TAWDRILY	TOFFIEST
SUBGENUS	SUNBAKES	SURVIVER	TAXPAYER	TOLBOOTH
SUBGOALS	SUNBATHE	SURVIVES	TAYBERRY	TOMBACKS
SUBGRADE	SUNBATHS	SUSPENCE	TEABERRY	TOMBLESS
SUBGRAPH	SUNBEAMS	SUSPENDS	TEABOARD	TOMBOLAS
SUBGROUP	SUNBEAMY	SYLVATIC	TEABOWLS	TOMBOLOS
SUBHEADS	SUNBELTS	SYLVINES	TEABOXES	TOMFOOLS
SUBHUMAN	SUNBERRY	SYMBIONT	TEABREAD	TOMPIONS
SUBHUMID	SUNBIRDS	SYMBOLES	TEACAKES	TONDINOS
SUBJOINS	SUNBLIND	SYMPHONY	TEACARTS	TOPCOATS
SUBMENTA	SUNBLOCK	SYMPLAST	TEAHOUSE	TOPCROSS
SUBMENUS	SUNBURNS	SYMPODIA	TEAMAKER	TOPKICKS
SUBMERGE	SUNBURNT	SYNCARPS	TEAMINGS	TOPKNOTS
SUBMERSE	SUNBURST	SYNCLINE	TEAWARES	TOPMAKER
SUBPANEL	SUNCHOKE	SYNCOPAL	TEDDERED	TOPMASTS
SUBPARTS	SUNDARIS	SYNCOPES	TEGMENTA	TOPPINGS
SUBPHASE	SUNDECKS	SYNDINGS	TELFORDS	TOPPLING
SUBPHYLA	SUNDERED	SYNDROME	TEMPESTS	TOPWORKS
SUBPLOTS	SUNDIALS	SYNFUELS	TEMPLATE	TORCHERE
SUBPOLAR	SUNDOWNS	SYNGAMIC	TEMPORAL	TORCHONS
SUBPRIOR	SUNDRESS	SYNGASES	TENDANCE	TORMENTA
SUBPUBIC	SUNDRIES	SYNGENIC	TENDERED	TORQUATE
SUBVERSE	SUNDRILY	SYNGRAPH	TENFOLDS	TOUGHEST
SUBVERST	SUNDROPS	SYPHONED	TENPENCE	TOWBOATS
SUBVERTS	SUNGLASS	TABBISES	TENPENNY	TOWHEADS
SUBVICAR	SUNGLOWS	TACHISTS	TERGITES	TOWPATHS
SUBVIRAL	SUNGREBE	TACKINGS	TERMINER	TOWPLANE
SUBVIRUS	SUNPORCH	TADPOLES	TERMINUS	TOYWOMAN
SUBVOCAL	SUNPROOF	TAFFETAS	TERMITES	TOYWOMEN
SUBWAYED	SUNWARDS	TAFFRAIL	TERPENES	TRADINGS
SUBWORLD	SUPPAWNS	TAGBOARD	TEUCHATS	TRADUCES
SUBZONAL	SUPPLANT	TAGGANTS	TEUCHEST	TRAGULES
SUBZONES	SUPPLIED	TAGGINGS	TEUGHEST	TRAMELLS
SUCCADES	SUPPLIER	TAGMEMES	THAWINGS	TRAPUNTO
SUCCINCT	SUPPLIES	TALKINGS	THYMINES	TRAVAILS
SUCCORED	SUPPLING	TAMBALAS	THYMUSES	TRAVERSE
SUCCORER	SUPPORTS	TAMBURAS	TICKINGS	TRAVISES
SUCCOURS	SUPPOSED	TAMBURIN	TIEBACKS	TREBLING
SUCKINGS	SUPPOSER	TAMPALAS	TIEBREAK	TRECENTO

TREFOILS	TURFIEST	UNSPELLS	VIRGULES	WAYBREAD
TREPANGS	TURGITES	UNSPOOLS	VISCOSES	WAYFARED
TREVISES	TURMOILS	UNSWAYED	VISCOUNT	WAYFARER
TRIBALLY	TUSKINGS	UNSWEARS	VOIDANCE	WAYFARES
TRIBASIC	TUTWORKS	UNTHATCH	VOIDINGS	WAYGOING
TRIBLETS	TWIBILLS	UNTHAWED	VOLPLANE	WAYGOOSE
TRIBRACH	TWICHILD	UNTWINED	VULGATES	WAYMARKS
TRIBUTES	TWIGLIKE	UNTWINES	WABBLING	WAYPOINT
TRICHINA	TWOFOLDS	UNTWISTS	WADDINGS	WAYPOSTS
TRICHORD	TWOPENCE	UPADAISY	WADDYING	WAYWISER
TRICLADS	TWOPENNY	UPCHUCKS	WADMOLLS	WEBBINGS
TRICOLOR	TYMPANIC	UPSHOOTS	WAFFLIER	WEBCASTS
TRICORNS	TYPHOONS	UPSKILLS	WAFFLING	WEBMAILS
TRICYCLE	UDOMETER	UPSPEAKS	WAGGONER	WEBPAGES
TRIDARNS	UNABATED	UPSPEARS	WAGMOIRE	WEBWHEEL
TRIDENTS	UNABUSED	UPSPRANG	WALKINGS	WEBWORKS
TRIFLING	UNAGREED	UPSWARMS	WALKYRIE	WEBWORMS
TRIFOCAL	UNAKITES	UPSWAYED	WAMBLING	WEDDERED
TRIGLYPH	UNAMAZED	UPSWEEPS	WAMMUSES	WEDDINGS
TRIGRAMS	UNAMUSED	UPSWELLS	WAMPUSES	WEDGINGS
TRIGRAPH	UNAVOWED	UPSWINGS	WANDERED	WEEDINGS
TRIMETER	UNAWAKED	UREDINES	WANHOPES	WEEKLONG
TRIMORPH	UNAWARES	URICASES	WANWORDY	WEEPINGS
TRIMOTOR	UNCHAINS	URIDINES	WANWORTH	WELCOMER
TRIPACKS	UNCHAIRS	URNFIELD	WARBLING	WELCOMES
TRIPEDAL	UNCHARMS	UROCHORD	WARCRAFT	WELDINGS
TRIPHASE	UNCHASTE	URODELES	WARDERED	WELFARES
TRIPHONE	UNCHECKS	UROMERES	WARDINGS	WERGELDS
TRIPLANE	UNCHEWED	UROPODAL	WARDRESS	WERGELTS
TRIPLIED	UNCHOKED	USEFULLY	WARDROPS	WERGILDS
TRIPLIES	UNCHOKES	UTOPIANS	WARFARED	WETBACKS
TRIPLING	UNCHOSEN	VACCINES	WARFARER	WETPROOF
TRIPODAL	UNEDITED	VALKYRIE	WARFARES	WETWARES
TRIPOLIS	UNEVADED	VAMBRACE	WARHABLE	WHEYLIKE
TRIPOSES	UNIBROWS	VAMPINGS	WARHEADS	WHIPLASH
TRIVALVE	UNICOLOR	VAMPLATE	WARHORSE	WHIPRAYS
TRIZONAL	UNICORNS	VANDYKED	WARMAKER	WIBBLING
TRIZONES	UNICYCLE	VANDYKES	WARMINGS	WICKINGS
TROCHARS	UNIFACES	VANGUARD	WARMOUTH	WIGGINGS
TROCHILI	UNIFIERS	VANPOOLS	WARPAGES	WIGMAKER
TROMINOS	UNIFILAR	VARMINTS	WARPATHS	WILDERED
TROPICAL	UNIFORMS	VENDACES	WARPINGS	WILDINGS
TROPINES	UNIPOLAR	VENDINGS	WARPLANE	WILFULLY
TRUCAGES	UNIQUEST	VERBALLY	WARPOWER	WIMBLING
TRYWORKS	UNIVALVE	VERBILES	WARWORKS	WIMPLING
TUBBINGS	UNIVERSE	VERBINGS	WARZONES	WINDINGS
TUBFASTS	UNIVOCAL	VERBLESS	WASHABLE	WINDOCKS
TUGBOATS	UNOPENED	VERDICTS	WASHINGS	WINDOWED
TUGGINGS	UNSCREWS	VERDITES	WASHOUTS	WINDROWS
TUMBLING	UNSHADED	VERDURED	WATCHOUT	WINGLIKE
TUNBELLY	UNSHALED	VERDURES	WAXBERRY	WINKINGS
TUPPENCE	UNSHALES	VERJUICE	WAXBILLS	WISHINGS
TUPPENNY	UNSHAMED	VERMELLS	WAXCLOTH	WITHOUTS
TURBANDS	UNSHARED	VERMINED	WAXPLANT	WITWALLS
TURBANED	UNSHAVEN	VERMOUTH	WAXWEEDS	WOBBLING
TURBANTS	UNSHELLS	VERQUIRE	WAXWINGS	WOEFULLY
TURBETHS	UNSHOOTS	VIADUCTS	WAXWORKS	WOLFLING
TURBINAL	UNSHOUTS	VIAMETER	WAXWORMS	WONDERED
TURBINES	UNSPARED	VIEWINGS	WAYBILLS	WOODHOLE
TURBONDS	UNSPEAKS	VIRGATES	WAYBOARD	WOODWALE

WOOFIEST	YARDANGS	ZAMBUCKS	ZINCODES	ZOOGENIC
WORDINGS	YARDINGS	ZECCHINE	ZINGIBER	ZOOGRAFT
WORKINGS	YAWMETER	ZECCHINO	ZIRCONIA	ZOOMANIA
WOSBIRDS	YAWPINGS	ZECCHINS	ZIRCONIC	ZOOMORPH
WRYBILLS	YELPINGS	ZEPPOLES	ZITHERNS	ZORBINGS
YAMMERED	YEOMANLY	ZINCATES	ZOOBLAST	ZORGITES
YAMMERER	YOGHURTS	ZINCITES	ZOOCHORE	

Suffixes

Suffixes are just as useful as prefixes for the same reasons, but it can be less easy to spot opportunities to employ them. Therefore, it's a good idea to study the lists of the most commonly available suffixes to help you find those elusive bonus words. This list is also useful for remembering which adjective stems also form adverbs, as a glance at the -LY list demonstrates. As with the prefixes list, words which end in the suffix letters by coincidence rather than etymology are included, as they are useful in exactly the same way, and may be less obvious. Unlike prefixes though, the root part of the word may not always be a stand-alone word because often the root is modified when the suffix is added (eg DUTIFUL, EQUABLE).

Words that end with -ABLE

Seven-letter words

ACCABLE	DYEABLE	LIKABLE	POKABLE	TAMABLE
ACTABLE	EATABLE	LINABLE	POSABLE	TAXABLE
ADDABLE	EFFABLE	LIVABLE	POTABLE	TENABLE
AFFABLE	EQUABLE	LOSABLE	RATABLE	TOTABLE
AMIABLE	ERRABLE	LOVABLE	RETABLE	TOWABLE
ASTABLE	EYEABLE	MAKABLE	RIDABLE	TRIABLE
BATABLE	FADABLE	MINABLE	ROPABLE	TUNABLE
BITABLE	FINABLE	MIRABLE	ROWABLE	TYPABLE
BUYABLE	FIXABLE	MIXABLE	RULABLE	UNHABLE
CAPABLE	FLYABLE	MOVABLE	SALABLE	USEABLE
CITABLE	FRIABLE	MUTABLE	SAVABLE	VATABLE
CODABLE	FRYABLE	NAMABLE	SAYABLE	VOCABLE
CURABLE	GELABLE	NOTABLE	SEEABLE	VOLABLE
DATABLE	GETABLE	OWNABLE	SEWABLE	VOTABLE
DISABLE	GIVABLE	PACABLE	SIZABLE	WADABLE
DOWABLE	HATABLE	PAPABLE	SKIABLE	WAXABLE
DRYABLE	HEWABLE	PARABLE	SOWABLE	WIRABLE
DUPABLE	HIDABLE	PAYABLE	SUEABLE	
DURABLE	HIRABLE	PLIABLE	TAKABLE	

Eight-letter words

ABATABLE	AMUSABLE	BARRABLE	BINDABLE	BONDABLE
ABUSABLE	ARGUABLE	BEARABLE	BISTABLE	BOOKABLE
ADORABLE	ATONABLE	BEATABLE	BITEABLE	BOOTABLE
AGITABLE	AVOWABLE	BEDDABLE	BLAMABLE	BRIBABLE
ALLIABLE	BAILABLE	BENDABLE	BOATABLE	BUFFABLE
AMENABLE	BANKABLE	BIDDABLE	BOILABLE	BURNABLE
AMICABLE	BANNABLE	BILLABLE	BOMBABLE	CALLABLE

CARTABLE	FURLABLE	LOCKABLE	REAPABLE	SUMMABLE
CASCABLE	GAGEABLE	LOVEABLE	REEFABLE	SURFABLE
CASHABLE	GAINABLE	LUGGABLE	REELABLE	SWAYABLE
CASTABLE	GETTABLE	MAILABLE	RELIABLE	SYLLABLE
CAUSABLE	GIFTABLE	MAKEABLE	RENTABLE	TAKEABLE
CHEWABLE	GIVEABLE	MAPPABLE	RESTABLE	TALKABLE
CITEABLE	GNAWABLE	MASKABLE	REUSABLE	TAMEABLE
CLOSABLE	GRADABLE	MELTABLE	RIDEABLE	TANNABLE
CLUBABLE	GRAZABLE	MENDABLE	RINSABLE	TAPEABLE
COINABLE	GROWABLE	MILLABLE	RIPPABLE	TAPPABLE
COOKABLE	GUIDABLE	MINEABLE	ROCKABLE	TASTABLE
COPYABLE	GULLABLE	MISSABLE	ROLLABLE	TEARABLE
CULPABLE	GUSTABLE	MOCKABLE	ROPEABLE	TEASABLE
CURBABLE	HACKABLE	MOLDABLE	RUINABLE	TELLABLE
CUTTABLE	HANGABLE	MOOTABLE	RUNNABLE	TESTABLE
DAMNABLE	HATEABLE	MOVEABLE	RUSTABLE	TILLABLE
DATEABLE	HEALABLE	NAMEABLE	SACKABLE	TILTABLE
DENIABLE	HEARABLE	NESTABLE	SAILABLE	TIPPABLE
DIGGABLE	HEATABLE	NETTABLE	SALEABLE	TITHABLE
DIMMABLE	HELPABLE	OATHABLE	SALVABLE	TITRABLE
DIPPABLE	HIREABLE	OBEYABLE	SANDABLE	TOLLABLE
DISHABLE	HITTABLE	OBVIABLE	SATIABLE	TOTEABLE
DRAPABLE	HOLDABLE	OPENABLE	SAVEABLE	TRADABLE
DRAWABLE	HUGGABLE	OPERABLE	SCALABLE	TUBBABLE
DRIVABLE	HUMMABLE	OPINABLE	SEALABLE	TUNEABLE
DUTIABLE	HUNTABLE	OUTFABLE	SEISABLE	TURNABLE
EDITABLE	IMITABLE	OVENABLE	SEIZABLE	TYPEABLE
EDUCABLE	INARABLE	OVERABLE	SELLABLE	UNDOABLE
ENVIABLE	INSTABLE	OXIDABLE	SENDABLE	UNSTABLE
ERASABLE	INVIABLE	PACKABLE	SERVABLE	UNUSABLE
ERODABLE	ISOLABLE	PALPABLE	SHAKABLE	UNVIABLE
EVADABLE	ISSUABLE	PANTABLE	SHAMABLE	VALUABLE
EVITABLE	JAILABLE	PARSABLE	SHAPABLE	VARIABLE
EVOCABLE	JAMMABLE	PASSABLE	SHARABLE	VENDABLE
EXILABLE	JOINABLE	PAWNABLE	SHAVABLE	VIEWABLE
EXORABLE	JUMPABLE	PECCABLE	SHEDABLE	VIOLABLE
EXPIABLE	KEEPABLE	PEELABLE	SHOWABLE	VITIABLE
FACEABLE	KICKABLE	PETTABLE	SIGNABLE	VOIDABLE
FARMABLE	KILLABLE	PICKABLE	SINGABLE	VOTEABLE
FEEDABLE	KISSABLE	PINTABLE	SINKABLE	WADEABLE
FELLABLE	KNOWABLE	PITIABLE	SIZEABLE	WALKABLE
FILEABLE	LAPSABLE	PLACABLE	SLAKABLE	WARHABLE
FILLABLE	LAUDABLE	PLAYABLE	SLAYABLE	WASHABLE
FILMABLE	LEASABLE	PLOWABLE	SLIDABLE	WASTABLE
FINDABLE	LENDABLE	PORTABLE	SMOKABLE	WEARABLE
FINEABLE	LETTABLE	POSEABLE	SOCIABLE	WELDABLE
FIREABLE	LEVIABLE	POURABLE	SOLVABLE	WETTABLE
FISHABLE	LIENABLE	PRIZABLE	SORBABLE	WILLABLE
FITTABLE	LIFTABLE	PROBABLE	SORTABLE	WINDABLE
FOAMABLE	LIKEABLE	PROVABLE	SPARABLE	WINNABLE
FOILABLE	LINEABLE	PRUNABLE	STATABLE	WORKABLE
FOLDABLE	LINKABLE	QUOTABLE	STEWABLE	WRITABLE
FORDABLE	LIQUABLE	RADIABLE	STONABLE	
FORMABLE	LISTABLE	RAISABLE	STORABLE	
FRAMABLE	LIVEABLE	RATEABLE	STOWABLE	
FUNDABLE	LOANABLE	READABLE	SUITABLE	

Words that end with -AGE

Seven-letter words

ABUSAGE	COWHAGE	LINKAGE	PRESAGE	TEENAGE
ACREAGE	CRANAGE	LOCKAGE	PRIMAGE	TENTAGE
AJUTAGE	CUTTAGE	LUGGAGE	PRISAGE	THANAGE
AMENAGE	DISCAGE	MASSAGE	PROPAGE	THENAGE
APANAGE	DOCKAGE	MELTAGE	QUAYAGE	TILLAGE
ARRIAGE	DRAYAGE	MESSAGE	RAMPAGE	TOLLAGE
ASSUAGE	DUNNAGE	MILEAGE	REIMAGE	TONNAGE
ASSWAGE	ECOTAGE	MILLAGE	REMUAGE	TRUCAGE
AULNAGE	ESCUAGE	MINTAGE	RESTAGE	TUNNAGE
AVERAGE	ETALAGE	MISPAGE	RIBCAGE	UMBRAGE
BAGGAGE	FALDAGE	MOCKAGE	RIFFAGE	UNITAGE
BANDAGE	FARDAGE	MONTAGE	ROOTAGE	UPSTAGE
BARRAGE	FLOTAGE	MOORAGE	RUMMAGE	VANTAGE
BEERAGE	FLOWAGE	MOULAGE	SACKAGE	VENDAGE
BONDAGE	FOGGAGE	NONWAGE	SALVAGE	VENTAGE
BOSCAGE	FOLIAGE	ONSTAGE	SAUSAGE	VIDUAGE
BOSKAGE	FOOTAGE	OUTRAGE	SCALAGE	VILLAGE
BREWAGE	FROMAGE	OUVRAGE	SCAVAGE	VINTAGE
BROCAGE	FULLAGE	OVERAGE	SCUTAGE	VITRAGE
BROKAGE	GARBAGE	PACKAGE	SEEPAGE	VOLTAGE
BULKAGE	GUIDAGE	PANNAGE	SELVAGE	VORLAGE
BUOYAGE	GUNNAGE	PASSAGE	SEPTAGE	WAFTAGE
BURGAGE	HAULAGE	PAWNAGE	SERFAGE	WAINAGE
CABBAGE	HAYLAGE	PAYSAGE	SIGNAGE	WANTAGE
CARNAGE	HEADAGE	PEERAGE	SINKAGE	WARPAGE
CARTAGE	HERBAGE	PEONAGE	SOAKAGE	WASTAGE
CENTAGE	HIREAGE	PIERAGE	SOCCAGE	WATTAGE
COINAGE	HOSTAGE	PILLAGE	SOILAGE	WEBPAGE
COLLAGE	KEELAGE	PIPEAGE	SONDAGE	WEFTAGE
COMPAGE	KIPPAGE	PLUMAGE	SPINAGE	WINDAGE
CORDAGE	LAIRAGE	PLUSAGE	STORAGE	WORDAGE
CORKAGE	LASTAGE	PONDAGE	STOWAGE	YARDAGE
CORNAGE	LEAFAGE	PONTAGE	SULLAGE	
CORSAGE	LEAKAGE	PORTAGE	TALLAGE	
COTTAGE	LIGNAGE	POSTAGE	TANKAGE	
COURAGE	LINEAGE	POTTAGE	TANNAGE	

Eight-letter words

ACCORAGE	BRASSAGE	DIALLAGE	FRONTAGE	LAYERAGE
ACIERAGE	BREAKAGE	DISUSAGE	FROTTAGE	LEVERAGE
ADJUTAGE	BROCKAGE	DRAINAGE	FRUITAGE	MALAXAGE
AGIOTAGE	CABOTAGE	DRESSAGE	FUSELAGE	MARITAGE
ALIENAGE	CARRIAGE	DRIFTAGE	GRAFTAGE	MARRIAGE
ALTARAGE	CARUCAGE	ENALLAGE	GRAINAGE	MESSUAGE
AMPERAGE	CHANTAGE	ENDAMAGE	GRAMMAGE	METAYAGE
APPANAGE	CHUMMAGE	ENSILAGE	GRILLAGE	METERAGE
BADINAGE	CLEARAGE	ENVISAGE	GROUPAGE	MISUSAGE
BARONAGE	CLEAVAGE	EQUIPAGE	GUARDAGE	MORTGAGE
BERTHAGE	CLOUDAGE	FERRIAGE	HELOTAGE	MUCILAGE
BEVERAGE	COMANAGE	FLOATAGE	HERITAGE	MULTIAGE
BIRDCAGE	COVERAGE	FLOORAGE	HOMEPAGE	NONIMAGE
BLINDAGE	COZENAGE	FOOTPAGE	INTERAGE	OFFSTAGE
BLOCKAGE	CREEPAGE	FRAUTAGE	LANGRAGE	OVERPAGE
BRAKEAGE	CRIBBAGE	FRONDAGE	LANGUAGE	PILOTAGE

PLANT**AGE**	SEWER**AGE**	STEAR**AGE**	TASSW**AGE**	VERBI**AGE**
PLOTT**AGE**	SHORT**AGE**	STEER**AGE**	THIRL**AGE**	VICAR**AGE**
PLUSS**AGE**	SLIPP**AGE**	STERN**AGE**	TRACK**AGE**	VICIN**AGE**
POUND**AGE**	SMALL**AGE**	STILL**AGE**	TRUCK**AGE**	WAGON**AGE**
PROPH**AGE**	SPILL**AGE**	STOCK**AGE**	TRUQU**AGE**	WATER**AGE**
PUCEL**AGE**	SPOIL**AGE**	STOPP**AGE**	TUTEL**AGE**	WEIGH**AGE**
PUPIL**AGE**	SPOUS**AGE**	STRAV**AGE**	TUTOR**AGE**	WHARF**AGE**
REDAM**AGE**	SQUIR**AGE**	STREW**AGE**	UMPIR**AGE**	WRAPP**AGE**
REENG**AGE**	STAFF**AGE**	STUMP**AGE**	UNDER**AGE**	WRECK**AGE**
ROUGH**AGE**	STALL**AGE**	SUBST**AGE**	VAULT**AGE**	
SABOT**AGE**	STEAL**AGE**	SUFFR**AGE**	VAUNT**AGE**	

Words that end with -ANCE

Seven-letter words

ADV**ANCE**	CRE**ANCE**	JOY**ANCE**	SON**ANCE**
AID**ANCE**	DUR**ANCE**	NOY**ANCE**	SUR**ANCE**
ASK**ANCE**	ENH**ANCE**	PEN**ANCE**	VAC**ANCE**
BAL**ANCE**	FIN**ANCE**	ROM**ANCE**	VAL**ANCE**

Eight-letter words

ABEY**ANCE**	BRIS**ANCE**	FEAS**ANCE**	OUTD**ANCE**	RESI**ANCE**
ABID**ANCE**	BUOY**ANCE**	GUID**ANCE**	OUTR**ANCE**	RIDD**ANCE**
ACUT**ANCE**	CREP**ANCE**	INST**ANCE**	PARL**ANCE**	SORT**ANCE**
ADAM**ANCE**	DEFI**ANCE**	ISSU**ANCE**	PAST**ANCE**	TADV**ANCE**
AFFI**ANCE**	DEVI**ANCE**	ITER**ANCE**	PIQU**ANCE**	TEND**ANCE**
ALLI**ANCE**	DIST**ANCE**	LAIT**ANCE**	PITT**ANCE**	VALI**ANCE**
AMBI**ANCE**	ELEG**ANCE**	NOND**ANCE**	PORT**ANCE**	VARI**ANCE**
AMOR**ANCE**	ENTR**ANCE**	NUIS**ANCE**	RADI**ANCE**	VIBR**ANCE**
BECH**ANCE**	EXIT**ANCE**	ORDN**ANCE**	RELI**ANCE**	VOID**ANCE**

Words that end with -ANCY

Seven-letter words

ERR**ANCY**	PLI**ANCY**	TEN**ANCY**	UNF**ANCY**
INF**ANCY**	SON**ANCY**	TRU**ANCY**	VAC**ANCY**

Eight-letter words

ABEY**ANCY**	DEVI**ANCY**	INST**ANCY**	PIQU**ANCY**	VAGR**ANCY**
ADAM**ANCY**	DORM**ANCY**	MORD**ANCY**	RADI**ANCY**	VALI**ANCY**
BLAT**ANCY**	ELEG**ANCY**	MYOM**ANCY**	RAMP**ANCY**	VERD**ANCY**
BUOY**ANCY**	GEOM**ANCY**	PECC**ANCY**	REGN**ANCY**	VIBR**ANCY**
CLAM**ANCY**	IMIT**ANCY**	PERN**ANCY**	UNCH**ANCY**	ZOOM**ANCY**

Words that end with -ARCH

Seven-letter words

AUT**ARCH**	HEX**ARCH**	MON**ARCH**	NOM**ARCH**	TRI**ARCH**
END**ARCH**	MES**ARCH**	NAV**ARCH**	TOP**ARCH**	XER**ARCH**

Eight-letter words

ETHNARCH	HIPPARCH	OUTMARCH	PHYLARCH	TAXIARCH
HEPTARCH	OLIGARCH	OVERARCH	POLYARCH	TETRARCH
HIERARCH	OMNIARCH	PENTARCH	RESEARCH	UNSTARCH

Words that end with -BACK

Seven-letter words

BUYBACK	FINBACK	OUTBACK	SETBACK	TOMBACK
CUTBACK	FLYBACK	PAYBACK	SOWBACK	WETBACK
DIEBACK	HOGBACK	REDBACK	SUNBACK	
FATBACK	LAYBACK	RUNBACK	TIEBACK	

Eight-letter words

BAREBACK	FEEDBACK	HOLDBACK	PULLBACK	SWAYBACK
BLOWBACK	FIREBACK	HOWLBACK	ROLLBACK	TAILBACK
BLUEBACK	FLATBACK	HUMPBACK	ROORBACK	TALKBACK
CALLBACK	FOLDBACK	KICKBACK	SCATBACK	TURNBACK
CASHBACK	FULLBACK	LIFTBACK	SEATBACK	WINGBACK
CLAWBACK	GIVEBACK	LOANBACK	SKEWBACK	ZWIEBACK
COMEBACK	GRAYBACK	MOSSBACK	SLOTBACK	
DRAWBACK	GREYBACK	PICKBACK	SLOWBACK	
FALLBACK	HALFBACK	PLAYBACK	SNAPBACK	
FASTBACK	HARDBACK	PLOWBACK	SOFTBACK	

Words that end with -BALL

Seven-letter words

BOXBALL	GUMBALL	NETBALL	PINBALL
EARBALL	ICEBALL	ODDBALL	PROBALL
EYEBALL	LOWBALL	PATBALL	

Eight-letter words

BASEBALL	FIREBALL	GOOFBALL	KORFBALL	SOFTBALL
BEANBALL	FISHBALL	HAIRBALL	MEATBALL	SOURBALL
BLOWBALL	FOOSBALL	HANDBALL	MOTHBALL	SPITBALL
BLUEBALL	FOOTBALL	HARDBALL	PITHBALL	TRAPBALL
COALBALL	FORKBALL	HEELBALL	PUFFBALL	WASHBALL
CORNBALL	FOURBALL	HIGHBALL	PUSHBALL	
FASTBALL	GOALBALL	KICKBALL	SNOWBALL	

Words that end with -BAND

Seven-letter words

ARMBAND	HATBAND	HUSBAND	RIBBAND	TURBAND
DISBAND	HAYBAND	PROBAND	SALBAND	

Words that end with -ARCH

Eight-letter words

BACK**BAND**	FAHL**BAND**	NECK**BAND**	PLAT**BAND**	SIDE**BAND**
BASE**BAND**	HAIR**BAND**	NOSE**BAND**	RAIN**BAND**	WAVE**BAND**
BROW**BAND**	HEAD**BAND**	PASS**BAND**	SARA**BAND**	WIDE**BAND**

Words that end with -BIRD

Seven-letter words

ANT**BIRD**	BOO**BIRD**	FAT**BIRD**	OIL**BIRD**	SUN**BIRD**
AWL**BIRD**	CAT**BIRD**	JAY**BIRD**	RED**BIRD**	WOS**BIRD**
AXE**BIRD**	COW**BIRD**	MAY**BIRD**	SEA**BIRD**	

Eight-letter words

BELL**BIRD**	FIRE**BIRD**	LADY**BIRD**	RAIL**BIRD**	SONG**BIRD**
BLUE**BIRD**	GAOL**BIRD**	LOVE**BIRD**	RAIN**BIRD**	SURF**BIRD**
CAGE**BIRD**	HANG**BIRD**	LYRE**BIRD**	REED**BIRD**	WHIP**BIRD**
COCK**BIRD**	JAIL**BIRD**	OVEN**BIRD**	RICE**BIRD**	YARD**BIRD**
FERN**BIRD**	KING**BIRD**	PUFF**BIRD**	SNOW**BIRD**	

Words that end with -DOM

Seven-letter words

BABU**DOM**	DOLL**DOM**	FREE**DOM**	JARL**DOM**	SERF**DOM**
BORE**DOM**	DUKE**DOM**	GEEK**DOM**	KING**DOM**	SHAH**DOM**
BOSS**DOM**	EARL**DOM**	GURU**DOM**	PAPA**DOM**	STAR**DOM**
CHEF**DOM**	FIEF**DOM**	HALI**DOM**	POPE**DOM**	TSAR**DOM**
CZAR**DOM**	FILM**DOM**	HEIR**DOM**	RHAB**DOM**	TZAR**DOM**
DOGE**DOM**	FOGY**DOM**	HOBO**DOM**	SELF**DOM**	WIFE**DOM**

Eight-letter words

BABEL**DOM**	FOGEY**DOM**	MOVIE**DOM**	QUEEN**DOM**	UNSEL**DOM**
BIRTH**DOM**	GIPSY**DOM**	NOVEL**DOM**	QUEER**DOM**	UNWIS**DOM**
BLOKE**DOM**	GYPSY**DOM**	PACHA**DOM**	REBEL**DOM**	VILLA**DOM**
CHIEF**DOM**	HIPPY**DOM**	PAGAN**DOM**	SAINT**DOM**	WHORE**DOM**
CLERK**DOM**	HOTEL**DOM**	PAPPA**DOM**	SHEIK**DOM**	
DEVIL**DOM**	LEECH**DOM**	PASHA**DOM**	SWELL**DOM**	
DUNCE**DOM**	LIEGE**DOM**	POPPA**DOM**	THANE**DOM**	
FAIRY**DOM**	MOTOR**DOM**	PUPPY**DOM**	THRAL**DOM**	

Words that end with -EAUX

Seven-letter words

BAT**EAUX**	CAD**EAUX**	GAT**EAUX**	RES**EAUX**
BUR**EAUX**	COT**EAUX**		

Eight-letter words

BANDEAUX	CHAPEAUX	MANTEAUX	PONCEAUX	TONNEAUX
BATTEAUX	CHATEAUX	MORCEAUX	RONDEAUX	TRUMEAUX
BERCEAUX	COUTEAUX	NOUVEAUX	ROULEAUX	
BORDEAUX	JAMBEAUX	PLATEAUX	TABLEAUX	

Words that end with -ENCE

Seven-letter words

ABSENCE	ESSENCE	LATENCE	POTENCE	SILENCE
CADENCE	FAIENCE	LICENCE	REFENCE	UNFENCE
COGENCE	FAYENCE	LUCENCE	REGENCE	URGENCE
DEFENCE	FLUENCE	OFFENCE	SCIENCE	VALENCE

Eight-letter words

AMBIENCE	EXIGENCE	OUTFENCE	SENTENCE	TUPPENCE
AUDIENCE	FIPPENCE	PATIENCE	SEQUENCE	TWOPENCE
CLARENCE	FLORENCE	PRESENCE	SITHENCE	VERGENCE
COMMENCE	LENIENCE	PRETENCE	SIXPENCE	VIOLENCE
CREDENCE	MERGENCE	PRUDENCE	SUSPENCE	
DISPENCE	NASCENCE	PUNGENCE	TANGENCE	
EMINENCE	NOWHENCE	SALIENCE	TENDENCE	
EVIDENCE	OPULENCE	SAPIENCE	TENPENCE	

Words that end with -ENCY

Seven-letter words

ARDENCY	FLUENCY	PATENCY	REGENCY
CADENCY	LATENCY	POTENCY	URGENCY
COGENCY	LUCENCY	PUDENCY	VALENCY
DECENCY	ORIENCY	RECENCY	VIVENCY

Eight-letter words

CLEMENCY	FERVENCY	OPULENCY	SAPIENCY	TURGENCY
COAGENCY	FULGENCY	PENDENCY	SEQUENCY	VERGENCY
CURRENCY	LAMBENCY	PUNGENCY	SOLVENCY	
EMINENCY	LENIENCY	REAGENCY	TANGENCY	
EXIGENCY	NASCENCY	SALIENCY	TENDENCY	

Words that end with -EST

Seven-letter words

ACHIEST	AIRIEST	ARTIEST	BADDEST	BLUIEST
ACIDEST	AMPLEST	ASHIEST	BALDEST	BOLDEST
ACQUEST	ANAPEST	AULDEST	BARGEST	BONIEST
ACUTEST	ARCHEST	AVIDEST	BASSEST	BOSSEST
ADDREST	ARIDEST	AWAREST	BEQUEST	BOXIEST
AERIEST	ARMREST	AWNIEST	BIGGEST	BRAVEST
AGILEST	ARSIEST	BABIEST	BLATEST	BRAWEST

Words that end with -EAUX

BUFFEST	EASIEST	INKIEST	NEATEST	RORIEST
BUMMEST	EDGIEST	INQUEST	NESHEST	ROSIEST
BUSIEST	EELIEST	IRATEST	NIGHEST	RUBIEST
CAGIEST	EERIEST	JIMPEST	NOBLEST	RULIEST
CAKIEST	EGGIEST	JIVIEST	NOSIEST	RUMMEST
CALMEST	ELMIEST	JOKIEST	NUMBEST	SADDEST
CAMPEST	EVENEST	JUSTEST	OAKIEST	SAFTEST
CANIEST	EVILEST	KEENEST	OARIEST	SAGIEST
CANTEST	FABBEST	KEWLEST	OBESEST	SAIDEST
CHICEST	FADIEST	KINDEST	OILIEST	SAIREST
CLOSEST	FAINEST	LACIEST	ONLIEST	SALTEST
COKIEST	FAIREST	LAKIEST	OOFIEST	SAMIEST
COLDEST	FALSEST	LANGEST	OORIEST	SEAREST
CONFEST	FASTEST	LANKEST	OOSIEST	SEIKEST
CONGEST	FATTEST	LARGEST	OOZIEST	SEXIEST
CONTEST	FAUREST	LAZIEST	OPENEST	SICKEST
COOLEST	FEATEST	LEALEST	ORBIEST	SIZIEST
COSIEST	FELLEST	LEANEST	OULDEST	SKEWEST
COWIEST	FIKIEST	LEFTEST	OURIEST	SKYIEST
COXIEST	FIRMEST	LENGEST	OUTJEST	SLOWEST
COZIEST	FITTEST	LEWDEST	OWLIEST	SNIDEST
CRUDEST	FLUIEST	LIEFEST	OWRIEST	SOFTEST
CURTEST	FONDEST	LIEVEST	PACIEST	SOONEST
DAFTEST	FOULEST	LIMIEST	PAIREST	SOUREST
DAMPEST	FOXIEST	LIMPEST	PALIEST	SPAREST
DANKEST	FOZIEST	LINIEST	PERTEST	SPRIEST
DARKEST	FULLEST	LITHEST	PINIEST	SPRYEST
DEADEST	FUMIEST	LOGIEST	PINKEST	STALEST
DEAFEST	FUNFEST	LONGEST	PIPIEST	STEYEST
DEAREST	FUNNEST	LOOSEST	POKIEST	SUAVEST
DEEDEST	GABFEST	LOTHEST	POOREST	SUBTEST
DEEPEST	GAINEST	LOUDEST	PORIEST	SUGGEST
DEFFEST	GAMIEST	LOWSEST	POSHEST	TAKIEST
DEFTEST	GAPIEST	LUNIEST	POSIEST	TALLEST
DEIDEST	GASHEST	LUSHEST	POXIEST	TANNEST
DEIFEST	GAZIEST	MADDEST	PRETEST	TARTEST
DENSEST	GLUIEST	MAINEST	PRONEST	TAUTEST
DEWIEST	GOLDEST	MATIEST	PROTEST	TAWIEST
DICIEST	GOOIEST	MAUVEST	PROWEST	TEDIEST
DIKIEST	GORIEST	MAZIEST	PUIREST	TEMPEST
DIMMEST	GOWDEST	MEANEST	PULIEST	TENSEST
DINKEST	GRAVEST	MEEKEST	PUNIEST	TERSEST
DISGEST	GRAYEST	MEETEST	PUNKEST	TIDIEST
DISNEST	GREYEST	MIDDEST	QUAREST	TINIEST
DOMIEST	HADDEST	MILDEST	RACIEST	TOEIEST
DOPIEST	HARDEST	MIMMEST	RADDEST	TONIEST
DOTIEST	HARVEST	MINIEST	RADGEST	TOOMEST
DOUCEST	HAZIEST	MIRIEST	RANKEST	TOWIEST
DOUREST	HEPPEST	MIRKEST	RASHEST	TRITEST
DOVIEST	HIGHEST	MITIEST	RATHEST	TUNIEST
DOWIEST	HIPPEST	MIXIEST	REALEST	TYPIEST
DOZIEST	HOKIEST	MOOTEST	REDDEST	UGLIEST
DROLEST	HOLIEST	MOPIEST	RENKEST	UNBLEST
DUFFEST	HOMIEST	MOSTEST	REQUEST	UNCOEST
DULLEST	HOTTEST	MOTIEST	RICHEST	UNDREST
DUMBEST	ICKIEST	MURKEST	RICIEST	VAGUEST
DUNNEST	ICKLEST	NAFFEST	RILIEST	VAINEST
DUSKEST	IFFIEST	NAIFEST	RIMIEST	VASTEST
DYKIEST	IMPREST	NAIVEST	ROKIEST	VERIEST
EARNEST	INANEST	NEAREST	ROPIEST	VIBIEST

VINIEST	WANNEST	WAXIEST	WILDEST	WOTTEST
VOGIEST	WARIEST	WEAKEST	WILIEST	WOWFEST
WACKEST	WARMEST	WEETEST	WILLEST	YUKIEST
WALIEST	WATTEST	WETTEST	WINIEST	ZANIEST
WANIEST	WAVIEST	WHITEST	WIRIEST	ZOOIEST

Eight-letter words

ACERBEST	BLINDEST	CADGIEST	CURLIEST	DRUXIEST
ACIDIEST	BLINGEST	CALMIEST	CURNIEST	DUCKIEST
ACRIDEST	BLITHEST	CAMPIEST	CURVIEST	DUDDIEST
ADEPTEST	BLOKIEST	CANNIEST	CUSHIEST	DULLIEST
AFFOREST	BLONDEST	CANTIEST	CUTTIEST	DUMMIEST
ALCAHEST	BLOWIEST	CARNIEST	DAFFIEST	DUMPIEST
ALERTEST	BLUDIEST	CATTIEST	DAGGIEST	DUNGIEST
ALKAHEST	BLUFFEST	CAULDEST	DAMNDEST	DUNNIEST
ALMAGEST	BLUNTEST	CHARIEST	DAMPIEST	DURGIEST
ANAPAEST	BODGIEST	CHASTEST	DANCIEST	DURNDEST
ANGRIEST	BOGGIEST	CHEAPEST	DANDIEST	DUSKIEST
ANTSIEST	BONEYEST	CHEWIEST	DARNDEST	DUSTIEST
ARBALEST	BONNIEST	CHIEFEST	DASHIEST	DWARFEST
ARBELEST	BOOFIEST	CHILLEST	DAUBIEST	EAGEREST
ARTSIEST	BOOKIEST	CHIRKEST	DEBBIEST	EARLIEST
ASTUTEST	BOOKREST	CHOICEST	DEEDIEST	EMONGEST
BACKREST	BOOMIEST	CHOKIEST	DEFOREST	EMPTIEST
BAGGIEST	BOOZIEST	CHUFFEST	DEMUREST	ENFOREST
BALDIEST	BORTIEST	CISSIEST	DICKIEST	EVILLEST
BALKIEST	BOSKIEST	CLAYIEST	DICTIEST	EXACTEST
BALMIEST	BOSSIEST	CLEANEST	DIDDIEST	FADDIEST
BANALEST	BOUSIEST	CLEAREST	DILLIEST	FAGGIEST
BANDIEST	BOYSIEST	COALIEST	DINGIEST	FAINTEST
BARDIEST	BRAGGEST	COARSEST	DINKIEST	FANCIEST
BARGHEST	BRAIDEST	COATTEST	DIPPIEST	FARTHEST
BARGUEST	BRAKIEST	COBBIEST	DIRTIEST	FATTIEST
BARKIEST	BRASHEST	COCKIEST	DISHIEST	FAWNIEST
BARMIEST	BRENTEST	COMBIEST	DITSIEST	FEEBLEST
BARNIEST	BRIEFEST	COMFIEST	DITZIEST	FEINTEST
BARRIEST	BRILLEST	CONKIEST	DIVINEST	FELTIEST
BASSIEST	BRINIEST	CONQUEST	DIZZIEST	FEMMIEST
BATTIEST	BRISKEST	COOMIEST	DOCILEST	FENDIEST
BAWDIEST	BROADEST	COPSIEST	DODDIEST	FENNIEST
BEADIEST	BROWNEST	CORKIEST	DODGIEST	FERLIEST
BEAKIEST	BRUSKEST	CORNIEST	DOGGIEST	FERNIEST
BEAMIEST	BUDDIEST	COULDEST	DOILTEST	FESTIEST
BEATIEST	BUFFIEST	COUTHEST	DONSIEST	FETIDEST
BEEFIEST	BUGGIEST	CRANKEST	DOOMIEST	FICKLEST
BEERIEST	BULGIEST	CRAPIEST	DORKIEST	FIERCEST
BENDIEST	BULKIEST	CRASSEST	DORTIEST	FIERIEST
BENTIEST	BULLIEST	CRAZIEST	DOTTIEST	FILMIEST
BILGIEST	BUMPIEST	CREPIEST	DOTTLEST	FINNIEST
BIRKIEST	BUNTIEST	CRISPEST	DOWDIEST	FIRRIEST
BIRSIEST	BURLIEST	CRONKEST	DOWLIEST	FISHIEST
BITSIEST	BURRIEST	CROOKEST	DOWNIEST	FISTIEST
BITTIEST	BUSHIEST	CROSSEST	DRABBEST	FITLIEST
BLACKEST	BUSTIEST	CRUELEST	DREAREST	FIZZIEST
BLANDEST	BUTCHEST	CRUMPEST	DROLLEST	FLAKIEST
BLANKEST	BUXOMEST	CULTIEST	DRONIEST	FLAMIEST
BLEAKEST	BUZZIEST	CUPPIEST	DRUNKEST	FLARIEST
BLEAREST	CACKIEST	CURDIEST	DRUSIEST	FLASHEST

Words that end with -EST

FLATTEST	GLARIEST	HERBIEST	LAIRIEST	MEALIEST
FLAWIEST	GLAZIEST	HILLIEST	LAMBIEST	MEATIEST
FLAXIEST	GLEGGEST	HINKIEST	LANKIEST	MELTIEST
FLEETEST	GLIBBEST	HIPPIEST	LARDIEST	MERRIEST
FLIPPEST	GLIDDEST	HISSIEST	LARKIEST	MESHIEST
FLORIEST	GLUMMEST	HOARIEST	LARNIEST	MESSIEST
FLUKIEST	GOATIEST	HOARSEST	LATHIEST	MICKLEST
FLUSHEST	GOBBIEST	HOLEYEST	LAWNIEST	MIDGIEST
FLUTIEST	GODLIEST	HOODIEST	LEADIEST	MIFFIEST
FOAMIEST	GOLDIEST	HOOKIEST	LEAFIEST	MIGHTEST
FOGGIEST	GOODIEST	HOOLIEST	LEAKIEST	MILKIEST
FOLKIEST	GOOFIEST	HOOTIEST	LEARIEST	MILTIEST
FOOTIEST	GOONIEST	HOPPIEST	LEAVIEST	MIMSIEST
FOOTREST	GOOPIEST	HORNIEST	LEDGIEST	MINCIEST
FORKIEST	GOOSIEST	HORSIEST	LEERIEST	MINGIEST
FRAILEST	GORMIEST	HOUSIEST	LEGGIEST	MINTIEST
FRANKEST	GORSIEST	HUFFIEST	LEISHEST	MINUTEST
FRESHEST	GOUTIEST	HUGGIEST	LICHTEST	MIRKIEST
FROWIEST	GRANDEST	HULKIEST	LIGHTEST	MIRLIEST
FUBBIEST	GRAPIEST	HULLIEST	LIMBIEST	MISSIEST
FUBSIEST	GREATEST	HUMANEST	LINGIEST	MISTIEST
FUFFIEST	GREENEST	HUMBLEST	LINTIEST	MOCHIEST
FUGGIEST	GRIMIEST	HUMIDEST	LIPPIEST	MOISTEST
FUGLIEST	GRIMMEST	HUMPIEST	LITTLEST	MOLDIEST
FUNKIEST	GRIPIEST	HUNKIEST	LIVIDEST	MOODIEST
FUNNIEST	GRITTEST	HUSHIEST	LOAMIEST	MOONIEST
FURRIEST	GRODIEST	HUSKIEST	LOATHEST	MOORIEST
FURTHEST	GROSSEST	IMMODEST	LOFTIEST	MOPPIEST
FURZIEST	GROUSEST	IMPUREST	LOGGIEST	MOROSEST
FUSSIEST	GRUFFEST	INDIGEST	LOOBIEST	MOSSIEST
FUSTIEST	GRUMMEST	INEPTEST	LOONIEST	MOTHIEST
FUTILEST	GUCKIEST	INERTEST	LOOPIEST	MOTLIEST
FUZZIEST	GULFIEST	INSANEST	LOPPIEST	MOTTIEST
GABBIEST	GULPIEST	INTEREST	LOSSIEST	MOUSIEST
GAMMIEST	GUMMIEST	IRONIEST	LOURIEST	MUCKIEST
GAPPIEST	GUNGIEST	ITCHIEST	LOUSIEST	MUDDIEST
GASPIEST	GUNKIEST	JAGGIEST	LOVEFEST	MUGGIEST
GASSIEST	GURLIEST	JAMMIEST	LOWLIEST	MUMSIEST
GAUCHEST	GUSHIEST	JANTIEST	LOYALEST	MURKIEST
GAUCIEST	GUSTIEST	JAZZIEST	LUCIDEST	MURLIEST
GAUDIEST	GUTSIEST	JEMMIEST	LUCKIEST	MUSHIEST
GAUMIEST	GUTTIEST	JERKIEST	LUMMIEST	MUSKIEST
GAUNTEST	HAILIEST	JETTIEST	LUMPIEST	MUSSIEST
GAUZIEST	HAIRIEST	JIGGIEST	LURIDEST	MUSTIEST
GAWCIEST	HAMMIEST	JIMPIEST	LUSHIEST	MUZZIEST
GAWKIEST	HANDIEST	JOLLIEST	LUSTIEST	MYTHIEST
GAWSIEST	HANGNEST	JOLTIEST	MALMIEST	NAGGIEST
GEEKIEST	HAPPIEST	JOWLIEST	MALTIEST	NAKEDEST
GELIDEST	HARDIEST	JUICIEST	MANGIEST	NAPPIEST
GEMMIEST	HARSHEST	JUMPIEST	MANIFEST	NARKIEST
GENTIEST	HASHIEST	JUNKIEST	MANKIEST	NASTIEST
GENTLEST	HASTIEST	KEDGIEST	MANLIEST	NATTIEST
GERMIEST	HEADIEST	KEMPIEST	MARDIEST	NEDDIEST
GIDDIEST	HEADREST	KERKIEST	MARLIEST	NEEDIEST
GIMPIEST	HEAPIEST	KICKIEST	MASHIEST	NERDIEST
GINNIEST	HEAVIEST	KIDGIEST	MASSIEST	NERVIEST
GIRLIEST	HEDGIEST	KINKIEST	MASTIEST	NETTIEST
GIRNIEST	HEFTIEST	KITTLEST	MATUREST	NEWSIEST
GLADDEST	HEMPIEST	KOOKIEST	MAWKIEST	NIFFIEST
GLADIEST	HENNIEST	LAIGHEST	MEAGREST	NIFTIEST

NIMBLEST	POOVIEST	ROARIEST	SKIEYEST	STIVIEST
NIPPIEST	POPPIEST	ROCKIEST	SKINTEST	STONIEST
NIRLIEST	PORKIEST	ROILIEST	SKIVIEST	STOUTEST
NITTIEST	PORNIEST	ROOFIEST	SLACKEST	STYLIEST
NOBBIEST	PORTIEST	ROOKIEST	SLATIEST	SUBTLEST
NODDIEST	POSTTEST	ROOMIEST	SLEEKEST	SUCKIEST
NOISIEST	POTTIEST	ROOPIEST	SLICKEST	SUDSIEST
NONGUEST	POUTIEST	ROOTIEST	SLIMIEST	SUETIEST
NOOKIEST	PRICIEST	RORTIEST	SLIMMEST	SULKIEST
NOUNIEST	PRIMMEST	ROUGHEST	SLOPIEST	SUNNIEST
NOWTIEST	PRIVIEST	ROUNDEST	SLUGFEST	SUPPLEST
NUBBIEST	PROSIEST	ROUPIEST	SMALLEST	SURFIEST
NURDIEST	PROUDEST	ROWDIEST	SMARTEST	SURGIEST
NUTSIEST	PUDGIEST	RUDDIEST	SMOKIEST	SURLIEST
NUTTIEST	PUDSIEST	RUGGIEST	SMUGGEST	SVELTEST
OBTUSEST	PUFFIEST	RUMMIEST	SNAKIEST	SWALIEST
OFTENEST	PUGGIEST	RUNNIEST	SNARIEST	SWANKEST
ONERIEST	PULPIEST	RUNTIEST	SNELLEST	SWEETEST
OPAQUEST	PUNKIEST	RUSHIEST	SNIDIEST	SWEIREST
ORANGEST	PUNNIEST	RUSTIEST	SNIPIEST	SWELLEST
ORNATEST	PURPLEST	RUTTIEST	SNODDEST	SWIFTEST
OUTWREST	PURSIEST	SAGGIEST	SNOWIEST	SWIPIEST
OVERKEST	PURTIEST	SALTIEST	SNUGGEST	SWISHEST
PALLIEST	PUSHIEST	SANDIEST	SOAPIEST	TACKIEST
PALMIEST	PUSSIEST	SAPPIEST	SOBEREST	TAGGIEST
PALSIEST	QUAKIEST	SARKIEST	SODDIEST	TALCIEST
PAPPIEST	QUEEREST	SASSIEST	SOGGIEST	TALKFEST
PARKIEST	QUICKEST	SAUCIEST	SOILIEST	TALKIEST
PASTIEST	QUIETEST	SAVAGEST	SOLIDEST	TANGIEST
PAWKIEST	RABIDEST	SAVVIEST	SOMBREST	TARDIEST
PEAKIEST	RAGGIEST	SCALIEST	SONGFEST	TARRIEST
PEARTEST	RAINIEST	SCANTEST	SONSIEST	TARTIEST
PEATIEST	RAMMIEST	SCARCEST	SOOTHEST	TASTIEST
PECKIEST	RANDIEST	SCARIEST	SOOTIEST	TATTIEST
PEERIEST	RANGIEST	SCODIEST	SOPPIEST	TAWNIEST
PEPPIEST	RAPIDEST	SEAMIEST	SORRIEST	TAWTIEST
PERKIEST	RASPIEST	SECUREST	SOUNDEST	TEARIEST
PESKIEST	RATTIEST	SEDATEST	SOUPIEST	TECHIEST
PESTIEST	RAUCLEST	SEDGIEST	SPACIEST	TEENIEST
PETTIEST	READIEST	SEEDIEST	SPARSEST	TENTIEST
PHATTEST	REAMIEST	SEELIEST	SPEWIEST	TEPIDEST
PHONIEST	REARREST	SEEPIEST	SPICIEST	TESTIEST
PICKIEST	REDDIEST	SEMPLEST	SPICKEST	TEUCHEST
PIGGIEST	REDIGEST	SERENEST	SPIKIEST	TEUGHEST
PINKIEST	REEDIEST	SEVEREST	SPINIEST	THAWIEST
PIPPIEST	REEFIEST	SHADIEST	SPIRIEST	THEWIEST
PITHIEST	REEKIEST	SHAKIEST	SPRUCEST	THICKEST
PLAINEST	REFOREST	SHALIEST	SPUMIEST	THINNEST
PLATIEST	REINVEST	SHARPEST	SQUAREST	THYMIEST
PLUMIEST	REMOTEST	SHEEREST	STABLEST	TICHIEST
PLUMMEST	RESTIEST	SHINIEST	STAGIEST	TIDDIEST
PLUMPEST	RIBBIEST	SHOALEST	STAIDEST	TIGHTEST
PLUSHEST	RICHTEST	SHORTEST	STARKEST	TILLIEST
POCKIEST	RIDGIEST	SHOWIEST	STEEPEST	TIMIDEST
PODDIEST	RIFTIEST	SILKIEST	STEEVEST	TINNIEST
PODGIEST	RIGHTEST	SILLIEST	STERNEST	TINTIEST
POLITEST	RIGIDEST	SILTIEST	STEWIEST	TIPPIEST
PONCIEST	RINDIEST	SIMPLEST	STIEVEST	TIPSIEST
PONGIEST	RISKIEST	SINKIEST	STIFFEST	TIREDEST
POOFIEST	RITZIEST	SISSIEST	STILLEST	TOCKIEST

Words that end with -EST

TOFFIEST	TUSKIEST	VIEWIEST	WEEPIEST	WOOZIEST
TOSHIEST	TWINIEST	VIVIDEST	WEIRDEST	WORDIEST
TOSSIEST	UNHONEST	VOGUIEST	WENNIEST	WORMIEST
TOTTIEST	UNIQUEST	VUGGIEST	WERSHEST	WOULDEST
TOUGHEST	UNPRIEST	VUGHIEST	WHEYIEST	WRONGEST
TOUSIEST	UNRIPEST	VUTTIEST	WHINIEST	WUSSIEST
TOUTIEST	UNSAFEST	WACKIEST	WHITIEST	YAPPIEST
TOUZIEST	UNSUREST	WALLIEST	WIFTIEST	YAWNIEST
TOWNIEST	UNTRUEST	WALTIEST	WIGGIEST	YOLKIEST
TOWSIEST	UNWISEST	WANKIEST	WIMPIEST	YOUNGEST
TOWZIEST	URBANEST	WARBIEST	WINDIEST	YUCKIEST
TRAPNEST	UTTEREST	WARTIEST	WINGIEST	YUKKIEST
TRIFFEST	VAIRIEST	WASHIEST	WISPIEST	YUMMIEST
TRIGGEST	VALIDEST	WASPIEST	WITHIEST	ZAPPIEST
TRIMMEST	VAMPIEST	WASPNEST	WITTIEST	ZESTIEST
TRIPIEST	VAPIDEST	WEARIEST	WOMBIEST	ZINCIEST
TUBBIEST	VASTIEST	WEBBIEST	WONKIEST	ZINGIEST
TUFTIEST	VEALIEST	WEDGIEST	WOODIEST	ZINKIEST
TUMPIEST	VEILIEST	WEEDIEST	WOOFIEST	ZIPPIEST
TURFIEST	VEINIEST	WEENIEST	WOOLIEST	ZOOTIEST

Words that end with -ETTE

Seven-letter words

AILETTE	CURETTE	LADETTE	NAVETTE	ROSETTE
ARIETTE	CUVETTE	LAYETTE	NEDETTE	STRETTE
AVIETTE	DINETTE	LORETTE	NONETTE	SYRETTE
BLUETTE	FOUETTE	LUNETTE	OCTETTE	TONETTE
BURETTE	FUMETTE	MINETTE	PALETTE	VEDETTE
BUVETTE	GALETTE	MOFETTE	PIPETTE	VIDETTE
CASETTE	GAZETTE	MOZETTE	POPETTE	
CUNETTE	GENETTE	MUSETTE	PROETTE	

Eight-letter words

AIGRETTE	COQUETTE	GRISETTE	PALMETTE	SEXTETTE
AMUSETTE	CORVETTE	HACKETTE	PARKETTE	SOCKETTE
ANISETTE	CREVETTE	JEANETTE	PIANETTE	SPINETTE
BAGNETTE	DANCETTE	JOCKETTE	POCHETTE	SUEDETTE
BAGUETTE	DISKETTE	MAQUETTE	RACLETTE	TOILETTE
BARBETTE	DRABETTE	MOFFETTE	REINETTE	UMBRETTE
BARRETTE	FAUVETTE	MOQUETTE	ROOMETTE	VIGNETTE
BIMBETTE	FLATETTE	MOZZETTE	ROQUETTE	
BRUNETTE	FOSSETTE	NOISETTE	ROULETTE	
CASSETTE	FRISETTE	OMELETTE	SEPTETTE	
CHAVETTE	FRIZETTE	PALLETTE	SESTETTE	

Words that end with -EUR

Seven-letter words

AMATEUR	FLANEUR	MASSEUR	REMUEUR
DANSEUR	FRISEUR	MINCEUR	SABREUR
DOUCEUR	HAUTEUR	PRIMEUR	SIGNEUR
FARCEUR	LIQUEUR	PRONEUR	TRACEUR

Eight-letter words

BATELEUR	COIFFEUR	GRANDEUR	SECATEUR	TROUVEUR
BLAGUEUR	ECRASEUR	JONGLEUR	SEIGNEUR	TRUQUEUR
CHASSEUR	FROIDEUR	LONGUEUR	SIFFLEUR	VOYAGEUR
CISELEUR	FRONDEUR	MONSIEUR	SIGNIEUR	
CLAQUEUR	FROTTEUR	SABOTEUR	TAILLEUR	

Words that end with -FISH

Seven-letter words

BATFISH	FINFISH	JEWFISH	PIGFISH	SELFISH
BOXFISH	FOXFISH	LUBFISH	PINFISH	SERFISH
CATFISH	GARFISH	MUDFISH	PUPFISH	SUNFISH
CODFISH	GEMFISH	MUFFISH	RAFFISH	TOFFISH
COWFISH	HAGFISH	OARFISH	RATFISH	TUBFISH
DEAFISH	HOGFISH	OUTFISH	REDFISH	WAIFISH
DOGFISH	HUFFISH	PANFISH	SAWFISH	WOLFISH

Eight-letter words

BAITFISH	DRUMFISH	JACKFISH	ROCKFISH	STUDFISH
BILLFISH	DWARFISH	KINGFISH	ROSEFISH	SUCKFISH
BLOWFISH	FALLFISH	LADYFISH	SAILFISH	SURFFISH
BLUEFISH	FILEFISH	LIONFISH	SALTFISH	TILEFISH
BOARFISH	FLATFISH	LUMPFISH	SANDFISH	TOADFISH
BONEFISH	FOOLFISH	LUNGFISH	SCARFISH	WALLFISH
CAVEFISH	FROGFISH	MILKFISH	SCOMFISH	WEAKFISH
COALFISH	GOATFISH	MONKFISH	SCUMFISH	WOLFFISH
CRAWFISH	GOLDFISH	MOONFISH	SNIFFISH	
CRAYFISH	GRAYFISH	NUMBFISH	SPOFFISH	
DEALFISH	GRUFFISH	OVERFISH	STARFISH	
DRAFFISH	HEADFISH	PIPEFISH	STIFFISH	

Words that end with -FORM

Seven-letter words

ACIFORM	CONFORM	ISOFORM	PREFORM
ALIFORM	DEIFORM	MISFORM	TRIFORM
AUSFORM	DIFFORM	OVIFORM	UNIFORM
AVIFORM	DISFORM	PERFORM	ZOEFORM

Eight-letter words

AERIFORM	FUSIFORM	NAPIFORM	PISIFORM	ROTIFORM
ARCIFORM	GASIFORM	NATIFORM	PLANFORM	SETIFORM
AURIFORM	GRUIFORM	NUBIFORM	PLATFORM	SLIPFORM
COLIFORM	IODOFORM	OMNIFORM	POSTFORM	TUBIFORM
CONIFORM	JANIFORM	PALIFORM	PYRIFORM	UNCIFORM
CUBIFORM	LANDFORM	PARAFORM	RAMIFORM	URSIFORM
CUNIFORM	LAVAFORM	PEDIFORM	RANIFORM	VARIFORM
ENSIFORM	LYRIFORM	PICIFORM	REINFORM	VASIFORM
FILIFORM	MANIFORM	PILIFORM	RENIFORM	WAVEFORM
FREEFORM	MURIFORM	PIRIFORM	RETIFORM	

Words that end with -EUR

Words that end with -FUL

Seven-letter words

ARMSFUL	EASEFUL	HORNFUL	PALMFUL	SONGFUL
BAGSFUL	FACTFUL	HURTFUL	PESTFUL	SOULFUL
BALEFUL	FATEFUL	HUSHFUL	PIPEFUL	SWAYFUL
BANEFUL	FEARFUL	JARSFUL	PITHFUL	TACTFUL
BASHFUL	FISHFUL	JESTFUL	PITIFUL	TALEFUL
BOATFUL	FISTFUL	JUGSFUL	PLAYFUL	TANKFUL
BODEFUL	FOODFUL	KISTFUL	PLOTFUL	TEARFUL
BOOKFUL	FORKFUL	LIFEFUL	POKEFUL	TEEMFUL
BOWLFUL	FORMFUL	LISTFUL	POUTFUL	TEENFUL
BRIMFUL	FRETFUL	LOCKFUL	PREYFUL	TENTFUL
CAGEFUL	GAINFUL	LOOFFUL	PUSHFUL	TOILFUL
CANSFUL	GASHFUL	LUNGFUL	RACKFUL	TRAYFUL
CAREFUL	GAZEFUL	LUSTFUL	RAGEFUL	TUBEFUL
CARTFUL	GLADFUL	MASTFUL	RESTFUL	TUNEFUL
CROPFUL	GLEEFUL	MAZEFUL	RISKFUL	VIALFUL
CUPSFUL	GUSTFUL	MINDFUL	ROOMFUL	WAILFUL
DAREFUL	GUTSFUL	MISTFUL	RUTHFUL	WAKEFUL
DEEDFUL	HANDFUL	MOANFUL	SACKFUL	WAMEFUL
DERNFUL	HARMFUL	MUSEFUL	SHEDFUL	WILEFUL
DIREFUL	HATEFUL	NEEDFUL	SHIPFUL	WILLFUL
DISHFUL	HATSFUL	NESTFUL	SHOPFUL	WISHFUL
DOLEFUL	HEADFUL	ODORFUL	SIGHFUL	WISTFUL
DOOMFUL	HEEDFUL	PAGEFUL	SKEPFUL	WORKFUL
DUREFUL	HELPFUL	PAILFUL	SKILFUL	ZEALFUL
DUTIFUL	HOPEFUL	PAINFUL	SKINFUL	ZESTFUL

Eight-letter words

APRONFUL	FORKSFUL	MOURNFUL	SLOTHFUL	TRUSTFUL
AVAILFUL	FOUNTFUL	MOUTHFUL	SMILEFUL	TRUTHFUL
BASINFUL	FRAUDFUL	NIEVEFUL	SNEERFUL	UDDERFUL
BELLYFUL	FREAKFUL	NOISEFUL	SNOOTFUL	UNARTFUL
BLAMEFUL	FRISKFUL	ODOURFUL	SOOTHFUL	UNJOYFUL
BLISSFUL	FRUITFUL	PAILSFUL	SPADEFUL	UNLAWFUL
BLUSHFUL	GHASTFUL	PAUSEFUL	SPEEDFUL	UNMANFUL
BOASTFUL	GLASSFUL	PEACEFUL	SPELLFUL	UNSINFUL
CHARMFUL	GLOOMFUL	PLAINFUL	SPITEFUL	UNUSEFUL
CHEEKFUL	GRACEFUL	PLATEFUL	SPOILFUL	UNWILFUL
CHEERFUL	GRATEFUL	POUCHFUL	SPOONFUL	VAUNTFUL
CHESTFUL	GRIEFFUL	POWERFUL	SPORTFUL	VENGEFUL
CHOCKFUL	GROANFUL	PRANKFUL	STAGEFUL	VOICEFUL
COLORFUL	GUILEFUL	PRESSFUL	STARTFUL	WAGONFUL
CRATEFUL	HANDSFUL	PRIDEFUL	STICKFUL	WASTEFUL
CRIMEFUL	HASTEFUL	PROUDFUL	STORMFUL	WATCHFUL
DEARNFUL	HONEYFUL	PURSEFUL	SURGEFUL	WEARIFUL
DEATHFUL	HOUSEFUL	RIGHTFUL	TABLEFUL	WORTHFUL
DIRGEFUL	HUMORFUL	SACKSFUL	TASTEFUL	WRACKFUL
DOUBTFUL	LADLEFUL	SCENTFUL	THANKFUL	WRATHFUL
DREADFUL	LAUGHFUL	SCOOPFUL	TOOTHFUL	WREAKFUL
DREAMFUL	LIGHTFUL	SCORNFUL	TRADEFUL	WRECKFUL
EVENTFUL	LOATHFUL	SENSEFUL	TRAINFUL	WRONGFUL
FAITHFUL	MENSEFUL	SHAMEFUL	TRISTFUL	WROTHFUL
FANCIFUL	MERCIFUL	SHEENFUL	TROTHFUL	YOUTHFUL
FAULTFUL	MIGHTFUL	SHELFFUL	TROUTFUL	
FEASTFUL	MIRTHFUL	SHELLFUL	TRUCKFUL	
FORCEFUL	MOISTFUL	SKILLFUL	TRUNKFUL	

Words that end with -GEN

Seven-letter words

ACROGEN	HALOGEN	LOXYGEN	MUTAGEN	SMIDGEN
ANLAGEN	HUMOGEN	LUCIGEN	ONCOGEN	TRUDGEN
ANTIGEN	INDIGEN	LYSOGEN	PIROGEN	TWIGGEN
CRYOGEN	IONOGEN	MITOGEN	PYROGEN	XYLOGEN
ENDOGEN	KEROGEN	MUCIGEN	RONTGEN	ZYMOGEN

Eight-letter words

ABORIGEN	COLLAGEN	ESTROGEN	HYDROGEN	PHOTOGEN
ALLERGEN	CULTIGEN	FLORIGEN	MISCEGEN	ROENTGEN
AMIDOGEN	CYANOGEN	GLYCOGEN	NITROGEN	STARAGEN
AMYLOGEN	DIPLOGEN	HISTOGEN	OSTEOGEN	
ANDROGEN	ENLARGEN	HYALOGEN	PATHOGEN	

Words that end with -GRAM

Seven-letter words

ANAGRAM	EPIGRAM	ISOGRAM	PANGRAM	TANGRAM
DIAGRAM	GROGRAM	MYOGRAM	PROGRAM	TRIGRAM

Eight-letter words

AEROGRAM	ETHOGRAM	KYMOGRAM	NANOGRAM	SONOGRAM
BAROGRAM	GENOGRAM	LEXIGRAM	NOMOGRAM	TELEGRAM
DECAGRAM	HEXAGRAM	LIPOGRAM	ONDOGRAM	TOMOGRAM
DECIGRAM	HOLOGRAM	LOGOGRAM	PARAGRAM	VENOGRAM
DEKAGRAM	IDEOGRAM	MAILGRAM	PICOGRAM	ZYMOGRAM
ECHOGRAM	IDIOGRAM	MARIGRAM	RENOGRAM	
ERGOGRAM	KILOGRAM	MONOGRAM	SKIAGRAM	

Words that end with -HOLE

Seven-letter words

AIRHOLE	CATHOLE	JAWHOLE	MUDHOLE	POTHOLE
ARMHOLE	DOGHOLE	KEYHOLE	OILHOLE	RATHOLE
ASSHOLE	EYEHOLE	LUGHOLE	PIEHOLE	SPYHOLE
BOTHOLE	FOXHOLE	MANHOLE	PINHOLE	TAPHOLE

Eight-letter words

ANETHOLE	COALHOLE	KNEEHOLE	PLUGHOLE	WEEPHOLE
ARSEHOLE	DOWNHOLE	KNOTHOLE	PORTHOLE	WELLHOLE
BLOWHOLE	FEEDHOLE	LAMPHOLE	POSTHOLE	WOODHOLE
BOLTHOLE	FUNKHOLE	LOOPHOLE	SHITHOLE	WORMHOLE
BOREHOLE	GUNKHOLE	PEEPHOLE	SHOTHOLE	
BUNGHOLE	HELLHOLE	PESTHOLE	SINKHOLE	

Words that end with -HOOD

Seven-letter words

APE**HOOD**	CUB**HOOD**	HOG**HOOD**	NUN**HOOD**	
BOY**HOOD**	ELF**HOOD**	LAD**HOOD**	SON**HOOD**	
CAT**HOOD**	GOD**HOOD**	MAN**HOOD**		

Eight-letter words

AUNT**HOOD**	IDLE**HOOD**	MISS**HOOD**	PUMP**HOOD**	WIVE**HOOD**
BABY**HOOD**	KING**HOOD**	MONK**HOOD**	SELF**HOOD**	
DOLL**HOOD**	LADY**HOOD**	PAGE**HOOD**	SERF**HOOD**	
GIRL**HOOD**	MAID**HOOD**	POPE**HOOD**	WIFE**HOOD**	

Words that end with -HORN

Seven-letter words

ALP**HORN**	BIG**HORN**	FOG**HORN**	SAX**HORN**
ALT**HORN**	COE**HORN**	INK**HORN**	TIN**HORN**
BET**HORN**	DIS**HORN**	LEG**HORN**	UNS**HORN**

Eight-letter words

BOX**THORN**	CRUM**HORN**	HAW**THORN**	LONG**HORN**	SLUG**HORN**
BUCK**HORN**	DEER**HORN**	KRUM**HORN**	RAMS**HORN**	STAG**HORN**
BULL**HORN**	GEMS**HORN**	LAN**THORN**	SHOE**HORN**	WALD**HORN**

Words that end with -IBLE

Seven-letter words

ADD**IBLE**	DOC**IBLE**	MIX**IBLE**	RIS**IBLE**
AUD**IBLE**	FUS**IBLE**	PAT**IBLE**	VIS**IBLE**
DEL**IBLE**	LEG**IBLE**	RIB**IBLE**	

Eight-letter words

CRED**IBLE**	EVAD**IBLE**	FUNG**IBLE**	PASS**IBLE**	TENS**IBLE**
CRUC**IBLE**	EVAS**IBLE**	GULL**IBLE**	POSS**IBLE**	TERR**IBLE**
EDUC**IBLE**	EXIG**IBLE**	HORR**IBLE**	REND**IBLE**	THUR**IBLE**
ELID**IBLE**	FALL**IBLE**	INED**IBLE**	RINS**IBLE**	UNED**IBLE**
ELIG**IBLE**	FEAS**IBLE**	LAPS**IBLE**	RUNC**IBLE**	VEND**IBLE**
ELUD**IBLE**	FENC**IBLE**	MAND**IBLE**	SENS**IBLE**	VINC**IBLE**
EROD**IBLE**	FLEX**IBLE**	MISC**IBLE**	SUAS**IBLE**	
EROS**IBLE**	FORC**IBLE**	PART**IBLE**	TANG**IBLE**	

Words that end with -IFY

Seven-letter words

ACET**IFY**	ANGL**IFY**	CALC**IFY**	CERT**IFY**	CLAR**IFY**
ACID**IFY**	BEAT**IFY**	CAPR**IFY**	CHYL**IFY**	COAL**IFY**
AMPL**IFY**	BRUT**IFY**	CARN**IFY**	CHYM**IFY**	CORN**IFY**

CRUCIFY	HORRIFY	MORTIFY	RECTIFY	TIPSIFY
DAMNIFY	ICONIFY	MUMMIFY	REEDIFY	TORRIFY
DANDIFY	JELLIFY	MUNDIFY	REUNIFY	UNDEIFY
DENSIFY	JOLLIFY	MYSTIFY	RUSSIFY	VERBIFY
DIGNIFY	JUSTIFY	NIGRIFY	SACRIFY	VERSIFY
DULCIFY	LIGNIFY	NITRIFY	SALSIFY	VITRIFY
FALSIFY	LIQUIFY	NULLIFY	SCARIFY	YUPPIFY
FANCIFY	LITHIFY	OPACIFY	SCORIFY	ZINCIFY
FARCIFY	MAGNIFY	PETRIFY	SIGNIFY	ZINKIFY
FISHIFY	MATTIFY	PLEBIFY	SPECIFY	ZOMBIFY
FORTIFY	MERCIFY	PONTIFY	TACKIFY	
FRUTIFY	METRIFY	PROSIFY	TERRIFY	
GLORIFY	MICRIFY	PULPIFY	TESTIFY	
GRATIFY	MOLLIFY	QUALIFY	THURIFY	

Eight-letter words

ALKALIFY	EMULSIFY	KARSTIFY	RENOTIFY	SILICIFY
AMMONIFY	ESTERIFY	LAPIDIFY	REPACIFY	SIMPLIFY
BEAUTIFY	ETHERIFY	MOISTIFY	REPURIFY	SOLIDIFY
BRONZIFY	FLINTIFY	OPSONIFY	RESINIFY	STELLIFY
CLASSIFY	FLUIDIFY	PRETTIFY	REVERIFY	STRATIFY
COCKNIFY	FRUCTIFY	QUANTIFY	REVIVIFY	STULTIFY
COPURIFY	GENTRIFY	QUIZZIFY	RIGIDIFY	TRENDIFY
DENAZIFY	GLASSIFY	READEDIFY	SANCTIFY	ZINCKIFY
DETOXIFY	HUMIDIFY	RECODIFY	SANGUIFY	
DIVINIFY	IDENTIFY	REMODIFY	SAPONIFY	

Words that end with -INGS

Seven-letter words

ABLINGS	CASINGS	ERRINGS	HYPINGS	MAYINGS
ACHINGS	CAVINGS	FACINGS	IMPINGS	MERINGS
ACTINGS	CAWINGS	FADINGS	INNINGS	MININGS
AGEINGS	CODINGS	FILINGS	JAPINGS	MOWINGS
AIRINGS	COMINGS	FININGS	JAWINGS	MUSINGS
ANTINGS	COOINGS	FIRINGS	KEYINGS	NAMINGS
ARCINGS	COPINGS	FIXINGS	KITINGS	NIDINGS
ARMINGS	COVINGS	FLYINGS	LACINGS	NOSINGS
ASKINGS	CRYINGS	FOXINGS	LADINGS	OFFINGS
AUDINGS	DARINGS	FROINGS	LAKINGS	OGLINGS
AWNINGS	DATINGS	FRYINGS	LASINGS	ONDINGS
BAAINGS	DICINGS	GAMINGS	LAWINGS	OUTINGS
BAKINGS	DIVINGS	GAPINGS	LAYINGS	PAGINGS
BESINGS	DONINGS	GATINGS	LIKINGS	PALINGS
BIDINGS	DOPINGS	GAZINGS	LIMINGS	PARINGS
BIKINGS	DOTINGS	GIVINGS	LININGS	PAVINGS
BITINGS	DOZINGS	GORINGS	LIVINGS	PAYINGS
BLUINGS	DRYINGS	HAVINGS	LOBINGS	PIKINGS
BODINGS	DYEINGS	HAYINGS	LORINGS	PILINGS
BONINGS	EARINGS	HAZINGS	LOSINGS	PIPINGS
BORINGS	EATINGS	HEWINGS	LOVINGS	POLINGS
BOWINGS	EDGINGS	HEXINGS	LOWINGS	POSINGS
BOXINGS	EFFINGS	HIDINGS	LUGINGS	PRYINGS
BUSINGS	ELDINGS	HIRINGS	LUTINGS	PULINGS
CAKINGS	ENDINGS	HOLINGS	MAKINGS	RACINGS
CANINGS	ENRINGS	HOMINGS	MATINGS	RAGINGS

Words that end with -IFY

RAKINGS	SAVINGS	STRINGS	TOYINGS	WADINGS
RATINGS	SAWINGS	TAKINGS	TRYINGS	WAKINGS
RAVINGS	SAYINGS	TAMINGS	TUBINGS	WANINGS
RAWINGS	SEEINGS	TARINGS	TUNINGS	WAVINGS
RIDINGS	SEWINGS	TAWINGS	TYPINGS	WAXINGS
RISINGS	SIDINGS	TAXINGS	ULLINGS	WIPINGS
ROBINGS	SIZINGS	TIDINGS	UNKINGS	WIRINGS
RODINGS	SKIINGS	TILINGS	UPPINGS	WONINGS
ROPINGS	SORINGS	TIMINGS	URGINGS	WOOINGS
ROVINGS	SOWINGS	TIRINGS	URNINGS	YOKINGS
ROWINGS	SPAINGS	TOLINGS	VEXINGS	ZONINGS
RUEINGS	SPRINGS	TONINGS	VIKINGS	
RULINGS	SPYINGS	TOWINGS	VOTINGS	

Eight-letter words

ABIDINGS	BOLTINGS	CHIDINGS	DIPPINGS	FEELINGS
AISLINGS	BOMBINGS	CIELINGS	DISHINGS	FEERINGS
AMBLINGS	BONDINGS	CISSINGS	DOATINGS	FELTINGS
ANGLINGS	BONKINGS	CLONINGS	DOCKINGS	FENCINGS
ARCHINGS	BOOKINGS	CLOSINGS	DODGINGS	FERNINGS
ARCKINGS	BOOMINGS	COAMINGS	DOGGINGS	FEUDINGS
AWAKINGS	BOOZINGS	COATINGS	DOPPINGS	FILLINGS
BACKINGS	BOWLINGS	CODLINGS	DRAWINGS	FINDINGS
BAGGINGS	BRACINGS	COGGINGS	DRIVINGS	FIRRINGS
BAITINGS	BREWINGS	COININGS	DROVINGS	FISHINGS
BALKINGS	BRIMINGS	COLLINGS	DUBBINGS	FITTINGS
BALLINGS	BROKINGS	COMBINGS	DUCKINGS	FIZZINGS
BANDINGS	BRUTINGS	COMPINGS	DUCTINGS	FLUTINGS
BANGINGS	BUCKINGS	CONNINGS	DUFFINGS	FLYTINGS
BANKINGS	BUDDINGS	COOKINGS	DUMPINGS	FOAMINGS
BANTINGS	BUFFINGS	CORDINGS	DUNNINGS	FOILINGS
BARRINGS	BUGGINGS	COWLINGS	DUSTINGS	FOLDINGS
BASHINGS	BULLINGS	CRAVINGS	EANLINGS	FOOLINGS
BASTINGS	BUMPINGS	CUBBINGS	EARNINGS	FOOTINGS
BATTINGS	BUNTINGS	CULLINGS	EARRINGS	FOPLINGS
BAWLINGS	BURNINGS	CUNNINGS	EASTINGS	FORGINGS
BEADINGS	BUSHINGS	CUPPINGS	EBAYINGS	FORMINGS
BEAMINGS	BUSKINGS	CURBINGS	EDITINGS	FOULINGS
BEARINGS	BUSSINGS	CURLINGS	EEVNINGS	FOWLINGS
BEATINGS	BUSTINGS	CURSINGS	EILDINGS	FRAMINGS
BEDDINGS	BUZZINGS	CUTTINGS	EMPTINGS	FRAYINGS
BEGGINGS	CABLINGS	CYCLINGS	ENVYINGS	FUCKINGS
BELLINGS	CALKINGS	CYMLINGS	ERLKINGS	FUNDINGS
BELTINGS	CALLINGS	DAFFINGS	ETCHINGS	FURRINGS
BENDINGS	CALMINGS	DAGGINGS	EVENINGS	GADLINGS
BETTINGS	CAMPINGS	DAMPINGS	FABLINGS	GAFFINGS
BIASINGS	CANNINGS	DANCINGS	FAGGINGS	GAININGS
BIDDINGS	CANTINGS	DARLINGS	FAILINGS	GANGINGS
BIGGINGS	CAPPINGS	DARNINGS	FAIRINGS	GASKINGS
BILLINGS	CARDINGS	DAUBINGS	FALLINGS	GASPINGS
BINDINGS	CARLINGS	DAWNINGS	FANNINGS	GASSINGS
BIRDINGS	CARPINGS	DEALINGS	FARCINGS	GAUGINGS
BIRLINGS	CARVINGS	DECKINGS	FARDINGS	GAYWINGS
BITTINGS	CASTINGS	DEVLINGS	FARMINGS	GEARINGS
BLADINGS	CATLINGS	DIALINGS	FASTINGS	GELDINGS
BLUEINGS	CEASINGS	DIETINGS	FATLINGS	GETTINGS
BOATINGS	CEILINGS	DIGGINGS	FAWNINGS	GILDINGS
BOILINGS	CHASINGS	DILLINGS	FEEDINGS	GINNINGS

GIRDINGS	HUSKINGS	LEKKINGS	MOUSINGS	PRIMINGS
GLAZINGS	HUSTINGS	LEMMINGS	MUGGINGS	PROSINGS
GLEYINGS	HUTTINGS	LENDINGS	MUMMINGS	PROVINGS
GLIDINGS	HYLDINGS	LETTINGS	MUNTINGS	PRUNINGS
GLOVINGS	IMAGINGS	LICKINGS	NAILINGS	PUDDINGS
GLOZINGS	INBEINGS	LIGGINGS	NECKINGS	PUFFINGS
GNAWINGS	INBRINGS	LIMPINGS	NERVINGS	PUGGINGS
GODLINGS	INGOINGS	LIPPINGS	NESTINGS	PUNNINGS
GOLFINGS	INKLINGS	LISPINGS	NETTINGS	PURGINGS
GOSLINGS	INSWINGS	LISTINGS	NITHINGS	PURLINGS
GRATINGS	IRONINGS	LOADINGS	NODDINGS	PURRINGS
GRAVINGS	ITCHINGS	LOAFINGS	NOGGINGS	PUTTINGS
GRAZINGS	JACKINGS	LOANINGS	NOONINGS	PYONINGS
GREYINGS	JAMMINGS	LOCKINGS	NOTHINGS	QUAKINGS
GRICINGS	JARRINGS	LODGINGS	NULLINGS	QUEUINGS
GROWINGS	JEERINGS	LOGGINGS	NURSINGS	RACKINGS
GUIDINGS	JERKINGS	LONGINGS	NUTTINGS	RAFTINGS
GUISINGS	JESTINGS	LOONINGS	OAKLINGS	RAGGINGS
GUMMINGS	JIBBINGS	LOOPINGS	ONGOINGS	RAIDINGS
GUNNINGS	JIGGINGS	LOOSINGS	OPENINGS	RAILINGS
HACKINGS	JOBBINGS	LOOTINGS	OUTRINGS	RAISINGS
HAININGS	JOGGINGS	LOPPINGS	OUTSINGS	RAMPINGS
HALLINGS	JOININGS	LORDINGS	OUTWINGS	RANGINGS
HALTINGS	JOTTINGS	LOURINGS	PACKINGS	RANKINGS
HANGINGS	JUGGINGS	LUGEINGS	PADDINGS	RANTINGS
HARLINGS	JUMPINGS	LURKINGS	PAIRINGS	RAPPINGS
HARPINGS	KARTINGS	MADLINGS	PANNINGS	RASPINGS
HASTINGS	KAYOINGS	MAILINGS	PANTINGS	RATLINGS
HATTINGS	KEELINGS	MAIMINGS	PARGINGS	RATTINGS
HAWKINGS	KEENINGS	MALLINGS	PARKINGS	READINGS
HEADINGS	KEEPINGS	MALTINGS	PARSINGS	REDDINGS
HEALINGS	KEGLINGS	MAPPINGS	PARTINGS	REDWINGS
HEARINGS	KEMPINGS	MARKINGS	PASSINGS	REEDINGS
HEATINGS	KENNINGS	MARLINGS	PASTINGS	REEFINGS
HEAVINGS	KERBINGS	MASHINGS	PAUSINGS	REELINGS
HEDGINGS	KERNINGS	MASKINGS	PECKINGS	RENNINGS
HEELINGS	KIDLINGS	MATTINGS	PEELINGS	RENTINGS
HELPINGS	KILLINGS	MEANINGS	PEGGINGS	REPPINGS
HERLINGS	KILTINGS	MEETINGS	PELTINGS	RESTINGS
HERRINGS	KIRKINGS	MELTINGS	PERFINGS	RIBBINGS
HIDLINGS	KITLINGS	MENDINGS	PETTINGS	RIDGINGS
HILDINGS	KNIFINGS	MERGINGS	PHASINGS	RIFLINGS
HINTINGS	KNOWINGS	MERLINGS	PICKINGS	RIGGINGS
HIPPINGS	LAGGINGS	MESHINGS	PIECINGS	RIGLINGS
HIRLINGS	LALLINGS	MICHINGS	PIGGINGS	RIMMINGS
HISSINGS	LAMBINGS	MILKINGS	PIGLINGS	RINGINGS
HOGGINGS	LAMMINGS	MILLINGS	PILLINGS	RINSINGS
HOLDINGS	LAMPINGS	MINCINGS	PINKINGS	RIOTINGS
HOPPINGS	LANDINGS	MINDINGS	PINNINGS	RISPINGS
HORNINGS	LAPPINGS	MISTINGS	PIONINGS	ROADINGS
HORSINGS	LAPWINGS	MOANINGS	PITTINGS	ROAMINGS
HOSTINGS	LASHINGS	MOBBINGS	PLACINGS	ROARINGS
HOTTINGS	LASTINGS	MOCKINGS	PLATINGS	ROCKINGS
HOUSINGS	LATHINGS	MOLDINGS	POLLINGS	RODDINGS
HOUTINGS	LEADINGS	MOORINGS	POSTINGS	ROLFINGS
HOWLINGS	LEANINGS	MOOTINGS	POURINGS	ROLLINGS
HUFFINGS	LEASINGS	MORLINGS	POUTINGS	ROOFINGS
HUMMINGS	LEAVINGS	MORNINGS	PRATINGS	ROOTINGS
HUNTINGS	LEERINGS	MOSHINGS	PRAYINGS	ROUMINGS
HURLINGS	LEGGINGS	MOSLINGS	PRICINGS	ROUTINGS

Words that end with -INGS

RUBBINGS	SIGNINGS	SUMMINGS	TUFTINGS	WAULINGS
RUCHINGS	SINDINGS	SURFINGS	TUGGINGS	WAWLINGS
RUGGINGS	SINGINGS	SURGINGS	TUNNINGS	WAXWINGS
RUININGS	SINKINGS	SWALINGS	TURFINGS	WEANINGS
RUNNINGS	SITTINGS	SWAYINGS	TURNINGS	WEARINGS
RUSHINGS	SKATINGS	SYNDINGS	TUSKINGS	WEAVINGS
RUSTINGS	SKIVINGS	TABLINGS	TUTTINGS	WEBBINGS
RUTTINGS	SLATINGS	TACKINGS	TWININGS	WEDDINGS
SACKINGS	SLICINGS	TAGGINGS	UNBEINGS	WEDGINGS
SACRINGS	SLIDINGS	TAILINGS	UNDOINGS	WEEDINGS
SAGGINGS	SLOWINGS	TALKINGS	UNITINGS	WEEPINGS
SAILINGS	SMILINGS	TAMPINGS	UNSLINGS	WELDINGS
SALTINGS	SMOKINGS	TANKINGS	UNTYINGS	WELLINGS
SALVINGS	SNARINGS	TANLINGS	UPBRINGS	WELTINGS
SANDINGS	SNIPINGS	TANNINGS	UPFLINGS	WESTINGS
SAPLINGS	SNORINGS	TAPPINGS	UPGOINGS	WETTINGS
SARKINGS	SOAKINGS	TARRINGS	UPSWINGS	WHALINGS
SCALINGS	SOARINGS	TASKINGS	VAMPINGS	WHININGS
SCORINGS	SOBBINGS	TASTINGS	VANNINGS	WHITINGS
SCRYINGS	SOGGINGS	TATTINGS	VARYINGS	WICKINGS
SEALINGS	SOILINGS	TEAMINGS	VEERINGS	WIGGINGS
SEARINGS	SOOPINGS	TEASINGS	VEILINGS	WILDINGS
SEATINGS	SOPPINGS	TELLINGS	VEININGS	WINCINGS
SEEDINGS	SORNINGS	TENTINGS	VENDINGS	WINDINGS
SEELINGS	SORTINGS	TESTINGS	VENTINGS	WINKINGS
SEEMINGS	SOSSINGS	THAWINGS	VERBINGS	WINNINGS
SEININGS	SOTTINGS	TICKINGS	VERSINGS	WISHINGS
SEISINGS	SOUMINGS	TIFFINGS	VESTINGS	WITLINGS
SEIZINGS	SOURINGS	TILLINGS	VIEWINGS	WITTINGS
SELFINGS	SOUSINGS	TILTINGS	VOGUINGS	WOLFINGS
SENDINGS	SPACINGS	TINNINGS	VOICINGS	WOLVINGS
SENSINGS	SPAEINGS	TINTINGS	VOIDINGS	WONNINGS
SERGINGS	SPILINGS	TIPPINGS	WADDINGS	WORDINGS
SERVINGS	STAGINGS	TITHINGS	WAFTINGS	WORKINGS
SETTINGS	STARINGS	TITLINGS	WAILINGS	WRITINGS
SHADINGS	STEWINGS	TOILINGS	WAITINGS	YARDINGS
SHAKINGS	STONINGS	TOLLINGS	WALKINGS	YAWNINGS
SHAPINGS	STOPINGS	TOOLINGS	WALLINGS	YAWPINGS
SHARINGS	STOVINGS	TOPPINGS	WANTINGS	YEALINGS
SHAVINGS	STOWINGS	TOSSINGS	WARDINGS	YELLINGS
SHOEINGS	STYLINGS	TOTTINGS	WARLINGS	YELPINGS
SHORINGS	SUBBINGS	TOURINGS	WARMINGS	YOWLINGS
SHOVINGS	SUBRINGS	TOUSINGS	WARNINGS	ZORBINGS
SHOWINGS	SUCKINGS	TRACINGS	WARPINGS	
SIBLINGS	SUGGINGS	TRADINGS	WASHINGS	
SIFTINGS	SUITINGS	TUBBINGS	WASTINGS	

Words that end with -ISE

Seven-letter words

ABSCISE	APPRISE	CHEMISE	DIARISE	ENDWISE
ADONISE	ARABISE	COALISE	DOCKISE	EROTISE
AGATISE	ATHEISE	COGNISE	DUALISE	FADAISE
AGENISE	ATOMISE	CONCISE	EBONISE	FANWISE
AGONISE	AZOTISE	COTTISE	ECHOISE	GALLISE
AIRWISE	BAPTISE	CYANISE	EGOTISE	GENOISE
ANODISE	BROMISE	CYCLISE	ELEGISE	GRECISE
ANYWISE	CHAMISE	DESPISE	EMPRISE	HEROISE

ICONISE	MALAISE	OZONISE	PROMISE	SUNRISE
IDOLISE	MANNISE	PARVISE	REALISE	SUNWISE
IRIDISE	MAPWISE	PECTISE	REARISE	SURMISE
IRONISE	MORTISE	PENTISE	REPRISE	TAXWISE
ITEMISE	MYTHISE	PEPTISE	RERAISE	TRENISE
KYANISE	NICOISE	POETISE	RIOTISE	UNITISE
LAICISE	OBELISE	PRECISE	SOUBISE	UPRAISE
LAIRISE	ODORISE	PREMISE	STYLISE	UTILISE
LIONISE	OXIDISE	PREVISE	SUCCISE	

Eight-letter words

ACTIVISE	DEPUTISE	IDEALISE	OPTIMISE	SIRENISE
ALBITISE	DIGITISE	IMMUNISE	ORGANISE	SIRONISE
ALKALISE	DIMERISE	INFAMISE	OUTRAISE	SOBERISE
AMORTISE	DISGUISE	JAPANISE	OVERWISE	SODOMISE
ANNALISE	DISSEISE	JAROVISE	PAGANISE	SOLARISE
ANTICISE	DIVINISE	JUMBOISE	PAIRWISE	SOLECISE
APHETISE	DROPWISE	LATERISE	PALEWISE	SOMEWISE
APHORISE	DYNAMISE	LATINISE	PAPALISE	SORORISE
APPETISE	EBIONISE	LEGALISE	PARADISE	STEPWISE
APPRAISE	EDGEWISE	LIKEWISE	PATINISE	SUBERISE
ARBORISE	EGLOMISE	LOCALISE	PENALISE	SUBITISE
ARCHAISE	ELSEWISE	LOGICISE	POLARISE	SUCHWISE
ARCHWISE	EMBOLISE	LONGWISE	POLEMISE	SURPRISE
ATHETISE	EMPERISE	LYRICISE	POLONISE	TEAMWISE
ATTICISE	ENERGISE	MACARISE	PORPOISE	TELEVISE
AVIANISE	EQUALISE	MADERISE	PORTOISE	TENTWISE
BANALISE	ERGOTISE	MARQUISE	PRACTISE	TETANISE
BENDWISE	ETERNISE	MAUVAISE	PTYALISE	THEORISE
BEPRAISE	ETHERISE	MAXIMISE	PYRITISE	THUSWISE
BOTANISE	ETHICISE	MELANISE	PYROLISE	TORTOISE
BRANDISE	EULOGISE	MELODISE	QUANTISE	TOTALISE
CALORISE	EUPHUISE	MEMORISE	RACEMISE	TRAVOISE
CANALISE	EXERCISE	MESPRISE	READVISE	TREATISE
CANONISE	EXORCISE	METALISE	REGULISE	TUTORISE
CAPONISE	FABULISE	MINIMISE	REREVISE	UNIONISE
CHASTISE	FARADISE	MISPOISE	RESINISE	UNPRAISE
CHROMISE	FEMINISE	MISPRISE	RIGIDISE	URBANISE
CIVILISE	FESSWISE	MISRAISE	RINGWISE	VALORISE
COLONISE	FIBERISE	MOBILISE	RIVALISE	VAPORISE
COLORISE	FINALISE	MONETISE	ROBOTISE	VELARISE
COMBWISE	FLATWISE	MOONRISE	ROMANISE	VIRILISE
COMPRISE	FLUIDISE	MORALISE	ROYALISE	VITALISE
COVETISE	FOCALISE	MOTORISE	RURALISE	VOCALISE
CRABWISE	FRANCISE	NASALISE	SALINISE	VOLUMISE
CREOLISE	GRAECISE	NEBULISE	SANITISE	VOWELISE
CURARISE	HEBRAISE	NODALISE	SATIRISE	WARPWISE
CUTINISE	HEPATISE	NOMADISE	SIDEWISE	WEFTWISE
DEBRUISE	HIGHRISE	NOTARISE	SIMILISE	WOMANISE
DEIONISE	HOMINISE	NOVELISE	SIMONISE	
DEMONISE	HUMANISE	OPSONISE	SINICISE	

Words that end with -ISH

Seven-letter words

ABOLISH	ANGUISH	BADDISH	BATFISH	BEARISH
ALUMISH	BABYISH	BALDISH	BEAMISH	BEAUISH

Words that end with -ISE

BIGGISH	ENGLISH	HUFFISH	PANFISH	SNOWISH
BLEMISH	EVANISH	HUNNISH	PARKISH	SOFTISH
BLOKISH	FADDISH	JEWFISH	PEAKISH	SOTTISH
BLUEISH	FAIRISH	JIGGISH	PECKISH	SOURISH
BOARISH	FALSISH	KADDISH	PERKISH	STONISH
BOBBISH	FASTISH	KERNISH	PERKISH	STYLISH
BOGGISH	FATTISH	KIDDISH	PETTISH	SUNFISH
BOOBISH	FENNISH	KNAVISH	PIEDISH	SWINISH
BOOKISH	FILMISH	LADDISH	PIGFISH	TALLISH
BOORISH	FINEISH	LADYISH	PIGGISH	TANNISH
BOXFISH	FINFISH	LARGISH	PINFISH	TARNISH
BRINISH	FLEMISH	LARKISH	PINKISH	TARTISH
BRUTISH	FOGYISH	LAZYISH	PIXYISH	TIGRISH
BUCKISH	FOLKISH	LEFTISH	PLANISH	TITTISH
BULLISH	FOOLISH	LOGGISH	PLENISH	TOADISH
BURNISH	FOPPISH	LOMPISH	POORISH	TOFFISH
CADDISH	FOXFISH	LONGISH	POPPISH	TONNISH
CARLISH	FULLISH	LOUDISH	PRUDISH	TOWNISH
CATFISH	FURBISH	LOUTISH	PUBLISH	TUBBISH
CATTISH	FURNISH	LUBFISH	PUCKISH	TUBFISH
CHAVISH	GAMPISH	LUMPISH	PUGGISH	TUNDISH
CHERISH	GARFISH	LUSKISH	PUNKISH	VAMPISH
CLAYISH	GARNISH	MADDISH	PUPFISH	VARNISH
COCKISH	GAWKISH	MAIDISH	RAFFISH	VOGUISH
CODFISH	GEMFISH	MANNISH	RAMMISH	WAGGISH
COLDISH	GIRLISH	MAWKISH	RANKISH	WAIFISH
COLTISH	GNOMISH	MINXISH	RASPISH	WAMPISH
COOLISH	GOATISH	MISSISH	RATFISH	WANNISH
COWFISH	GOLDISH	MOBBISH	RATTISH	WARMISH
CRONISH	GOODISH	MONKISH	REDDISH	WASPISH
CUBBISH	GRAYISH	MOONISH	REDFISH	WEAKISH
CULTISH	GREYISH	MOORISH	RELLISH	WEARISH
CURRISH	GUARISH	MOREISH	RIGGISH	WEBLISH
DAMPISH	GULLISH	MUDFISH	ROGUISH	WENNISH
DANKISH	HAGFISH	MUFFISH	ROINISH	WETTISH
DARKISH	HAGGISH	MUGGISH	ROMPISH	WHEYISH
DEAFISH	HAIMISH	MUMPISH	ROOKISH	WHITISH
DERVISH	HARDISH	MURKISH	ROYNISH	WHORISH
DIMMISH	HASHISH	NEBBISH	RUBBISH	WILDISH
DOGFISH	HAWKISH	NEDDISH	RUMMISH	WIMPISH
DOGGISH	HEIMISH	NERDISH	RUNTISH	WISPISH
DOLLISH	HELLISH	NICEISH	RUTTISH	WOGGISH
DOLTISH	HENNISH	NOIRISH	SADDISH	WOLFISH
DONNISH	HICKISH	NOURISH	SALTISH	WOLVISH
DOVEISH	HIGHISH	NUNNISH	SAWFISH	WORDISH
DRONISH	HIPPISH	NURDISH	SELFISH	WORMISH
DULLISH	HOBBISH	OARFISH	SERFISH	YOBBISH
DUMPISH	HOGFISH	OGREISH	SICKISH	ZANYISH
DUNCISH	HOGGISH	OOFTISH	SLAVISH	
DUNNISH	HORNISH	OUTFISH	SLOWISH	
DUSKISH	HOTTISH	OUTWISH	SNAKISH	

Eight-letter words

ACTORISH	BAITFISH	BLEAKISH	BLOWFISH	BOOBYISH
ADMONISH	BAKSHISH	BLIMPISH	BLUEFISH	BRACKISH
ASTONISH	BILLFISH	BLOCKISH	BLUNTISH	BRAINISH
BABELISH	BLACKISH	BLOKEISH	BOARFISH	BRANDISH
BAIRNISH	BLANDISH	BLONDISH	BONEFISH	BRASSISH

BRATTISH	ESSAYISH	LUMPFISH	SAINTISH	STUDFISH
BRISKISH	ETHERISH	LUNGFISH	SALTFISH	SUCKFISH
BROADISH	FAINTISH	MILKFISH	SANDFISH	SUMPHISH
BROGUISH	FALLFISH	MINIDISH	SCAMPISH	SURFFISH
BROWNISH	FEEBLISH	MONKFISH	SCARFISH	SWAINISH
CAMELISH	FEVERISH	MOONFISH	SCOMFISH	SWAMPISH
CAVEFISH	FIENDISH	NABOBISH	SCUMFISH	SWEETISH
CEORLISH	FIFTYISH	NANNYISH	SHARPISH	SWELLISH
CHEAPISH	FILEFISH	NINNYISH	SHEEPISH	SYLPHISH
CHILDISH	FLATFISH	NOHOWISH	SHORTISH	THICKISH
CHURLISH	FLATTISH	NOVELISH	SHREWISH	THIEVISH
CLANNISH	FLIRTISH	NUMBFISH	SISSYISH	THINNISH
CLAPDISH	FLOURISH	NYMPHISH	SIXTYISH	THUGGISH
CLERKISH	FOGEYISH	ORANGISH	SKIRMISH	TICKLISH
CLIQUISH	FOOLFISH	OVERFISH	SKITTISH	TIGERISH
CLODDISH	FORTYISH	PAGANISH	SLANGISH	TIGHTISH
CLOTTISH	FRAILISH	PIPEFISH	SLIMMISH	TILEFISH
CLOWNISH	FREAKISH	PIXIEISH	SLOBBISH	TINGLISH
CLUBBISH	FRESHISH	PLAINISH	SLUGGISH	TOADFISH
CLUMPISH	FROGFISH	PLUMPISH	SLUTTISH	TOADYISH
COALFISH	FRUMPISH	POKERISH	SMALLISH	TOLLDISH
COARSISH	GHOULISH	POSERISH	SMARTISH	TOUGHISH
COMPLISH	GIPSYISH	PRANKISH	SNAPPISH	TOVARISH
CRANKISH	GLUMPISH	PRIGGISH	SNEAKISH	TRAMPISH
CRAWFISH	GOATFISH	PROUDISH	SNIFFISH	TRICKISH
CRAYFISH	GOLDFISH	PSEUDISH	SNOBBISH	UNMODISH
CROSSISH	GRAYFISH	PUPPYISH	SNOUTISH	UNPOLISH
DANDYISH	GREENISH	PURPLISH	SNUBBISH	VAGARISH
DEALFISH	GRUFFISH	PYGMYISH	SOLIDISH	VANQUISH
DEMOLISH	GRUMPISH	QUACKISH	SORRYISH	VAPORISH
DEPOLISH	GYPSYISH	QUALMISH	SPARKISH	VIGORISH
DEVILISH	HEADFISH	QUEERISH	SPOFFISH	VIPERISH
DIMINISH	IDIOTISH	QUIPPISH	SPOOKISH	VIXENISH
DOWDYISH	JACKFISH	QUIRKISH	SQUARISH	WALLFISH
DRABBISH	JINGOISH	RAWMAISH	SQUIRISH	WATERISH
DRAFFISH	KINGFISH	REFINISH	STABLISH	WEAKFISH
DREGGISH	KNACKISH	REPOLISH	STANDISH	WOLFFISH
DROLLISH	LADYFISH	RIGHTISH	STARFISH	WOMANISH
DROOGISH	LANGUISH	ROCKFISH	STARTISH	YOKELISH
DRUMFISH	LEMONISH	ROSEFISH	STEEPISH	YOUNGISH
DWARFISH	LIGHTISH	ROUGHISH	STIFFISH	
DWEEBISH	LIONFISH	ROUNDISH	STILTISH	
EMPERISH	LITTLISH	ROWDYISH	STOCKISH	
ENRAVISH	LIVERISH	SAILFISH	STOUTISH	

Words that end with -ISM

Seven-letter words

ABLEISM	BARDISM	CHORISM	DODOISM	ETATISM
AMORISM	BIPRISM	CLADISM	DONNISM	EXOTISM
ANIMISM	BOGYISM	CLONISM	DUALISM	FADDISM
ASTEISM	BOSSISM	COPYISM	ECHOISM	FALSISM
ATAVISM	BROMISM	COSMISM	EGOTISM	FASCISM
ATHEISM	BRUTISM	CRETISM	ELITISM	FATTISM
ATOMISM	BRUXISM	CULTISM	ENTRISM	FAUVISM
BAALISM	CAMBISM	CZARISM	EPICISM	FIDEISM
BABUISM	CHARISM	DADAISM	EROTISM	FOGYISM
BAPTISM	CHEMISM	DIORISM	ETACISM	FOODISM

Words that end with -ISH

GURUISM	LEFTISM	ODYLISM	RANKISM	TSARISM
HANDISM	LEGGISM	OGREISM	REALISM	TYCHISM
HEROISM	LIONISM	ONANISM	SELFISM	TZARISM
HEURISM	LOCOISM	ORALISM	SENSISM	URANISM
HOBOISM	LOOKISM	ORPHISM	SIZEISM	UTOPISM
IDOLISM	MAIDISM	PEONISM	SLUMISM	WHOLISM
IMAGISM	MOBBISM	PHAEISM	SOPHISM	YOBBISM
ITACISM	MYALISM	PHOBISM	STATISM	ZANYISM
JUJUISM	MYTHISM	PHOTISM	TACHISM	
KARAISM	NARCISM	PIANISM	TACTISM	
LADYISM	NEURISM	PIETISM	TOURISM	
LAICISM	OBELISM	PLENISM	TROPISM	

Eight-letter words

ACOSMISM	DEVILISM	IDIOTISM	OPTIMISM	SCRIBISM
ACROTISM	DIMERISM	INCIVISM	ORGANISM	SEISMISM
ACTINISM	DIOECISM	INTIMISM	PACIFISM	SIMPLISM
ACTIVISM	DIRIGISM	IOTACISM	PAEANISM	SINAPISM
ALARMISM	DITHEISM	JEHADISM	PAGANISM	SNOBBISM
ALBINISM	DONATISM	JIHADISM	PALUDISM	SOLARISM
ALGORISM	DOWDYISM	JINGOISM	PAPALISM	SOLECISM
ALIENISM	DRUDGISM	KABALISM	PARECISM	SOLIDISM
ALLELISM	DRUIDISM	LABORISM	PARTYISM	SOMATISM
ALPINISM	DWARFISM	LACONISM	PELORISM	STOICISM
ALTRUISM	DYNAMISM	LEGALISM	PETALISM	STRABISM
ANEURISM	EBIONISM	LOBBYISM	PEYOTISM	SWINGISM
APHORISM	EMBOLISM	LOCALISM	PHALLISM	SYBOTISM
APTERISM	ENDEMISM	LOGICISM	PHRENISM	TANTRISM
ARCHAISM	ENTRYISM	LOOKSISM	PLUMBISM	TERATISM
ASTERISM	EPIZOISM	LOYALISM	POLONISM	THUGGISM
ATROPISM	ERETHISM	LUMINISM	POPULISM	TIGERISM
ATTICISM	ERGOTISM	LYRICISM	PRIAPISM	TITANISM
AUTECISM	ESCAPISM	MACARISM	PRIGGISM	TOADYISM
BABELISM	ETHERISM	MACHOISM	PROSAISM	TOKENISM
BATHMISM	ETHICISM	MELANISM	PSELLISM	TOTALISM
BETACISM	EUGENISM	MERYCISM	PSEPHISM	TOTEMISM
BINARISM	EUMERISM	METOPISM	PSYCHISM	TRIADISM
BOGEYISM	EUPHUISM	MINIMISM	PTYALISM	TRIALISM
BOOBYISM	EXORCISM	MODALISM	PUGILISM	TROILISM
BOTULISM	FAIRYISM	MONADISM	PUPPYISM	TUTORISM
BOYARISM	FAKIRISM	MORALISM	PYGMYISM	ULTRAISM
BULLYISM	FAMILISM	MORONISM	QABALISM	UNDINISM
CABALISM	FARADISM	NABOBISM	QUACKISM	UNIONISM
CAFFEISM	FATALISM	NASALISM	QUIETISM	UNTRUISM
CASTEISM	FEMINISM	NATIVISM	RACEMISM	URBANISM
CENTRISM	FINALISM	NATURISM	REGALISM	VEGANISM
CHARTISM	FINITISM	NAVALISM	RIGHTISM	VIRILISM
CIVICISM	FOGEYISM	NEGROISM	RIGORISM	VITALISM
CLASSISM	FUTURISM	NEPHRISM	ROBOTISM	VOCALISM
CLIQUISM	GIANTISM	NEPOTISM	ROWDYISM	VOLTAISM
CLUBBISM	GYPSYISM	NIHILISM	ROYALISM	WOMANISM
COLORISM	HEDONISM	NIMBYISM	RURALISM	XANTHISM
CRONYISM	HELOTISM	NOMADISM	SAINTISM	YAHOOISM
CULLYISM	HOBBYISM	NOVELISM	SAPPHISM	ZOMBIISM
CYNICISM	HUMANISM	OBEAHISM	SATANISM	
DANDYISM	HYLICISM	OCKERISM	SAVAGISM	
DEMONISM	IDEALISM	OPIUMISM	SCIOLISM	

Words that end with -IST

Seven-letter words

ABLEIST	CORNIST	FATTIST	MAPPIST	RHYMIST
ACQUIST	COSMIST	FAUNIST	METRIST	SACRIST
AGONIST	CULTIST	FAUVIST	MIDLIST	SELFIST
ALTOIST	CYCLIST	FEUDIST	MYALIST	SENSIST
AMORIST	CZARIST	FIDEIST	MYTHIST	SIZEIST
ANGLIST	DADAIST	FLORIST	NAIVIST	SOLOIST
ANIMIST	DENTIST	FLUTIST	NARCIST	SOPHIST
ATAVIST	DIALIST	FUGUIST	OCULIST	STATIST
ATHEIST	DIARIST	GAMBIST	OLIGIST	STYLIST
ATOMIST	DIETIST	GNOMIST	OLOGIST	SUBSIST
ATTRIST	DUALIST	HARPIST	ONANIST	SUMMIST
BAPTIST	DUELIST	HERBIST	ORALIST	SUMOIST
BASSIST	DUMAIST	HORNIST	PALMIST	TACHIST
BIBLIST	EBONIST	HYGEIST	PERSIST	TENNIST
BUNDIST	ECHOIST	HYLOIST	PHOBIST	TITLIST
CAMBIST	EGOTIST	HYMNIST	PIANIST	TOURIST
CASUIST	ELEGIST	IAMBIST	PIARIST	TROPIST
CELLIST	ELITIST	IDOLIST	PIETIST	TSARIST
CHEKIST	ELOGIST	IDYLIST	PLENIST	TUBAIST
CHEMIST	ENTRIST	IMAGIST	PLUMIST	TZARIST
CHORIST	ENTWIST	INTWIST	POLLIST	UNALIST
CHUTIST	EPEEIST	IRONIST	POLOIST	UNTWIST
CHYMIST	EPICIST	IVORIST	PROTIST	UPHOIST
CLADIST	ETATIST	JUDOIST	QUERIST	UTOPIST
COEXIST	EXODIST	JUJUIST	REALIST	VACUIST
CONSIST	FADDIST	LEFTIST	RETWIST	VIOLIST
COPYIST	FASCIST	LOOKIST	REVUIST	WHOLIST

Eight-letter words

ACOSMIST	BURINIST	DYNAMIST	HEDONIST	LUMINIST
ACTIVIST	CABALIST	ENTRYIST	HOBBYIST	LUNARIST
ALARMIST	CALORIST	ERRORIST	HOMILIST	LUTANIST
ALIENIST	CANOEIST	ESCAPIST	HUMANIST	LUTENIST
ALPINIST	CANONIST	ESSAYIST	HUMORIST	LUXURIST
ALTRUIST	CENTOIST	ETHERIST	HYGIEIST	LYRICIST
ANNALIST	CENTRIST	ETHICIST	HYLICIST	MAXIMIST
APHORIST	CERAMIST	EUGENIST	HYPOCIST	MEDALIST
APIARIST	CHARTIST	EULOGIST	IDEALIST	MELANIST
AQUARIST	CIVILIST	EUPHUIST	IDYLLIST	MELODIST
ARBALIST	CLASSIST	EXORCIST	INTIMIST	METALIST
ARBORIST	CLUBBIST	FABULIST	JEHADIST	MINIMIST
ARCANIST	COASSIST	FATALIST	JIHADIST	MODALIST
ARCHAIST	COLONIST	FEMINIST	JINGOIST	MODELIST
ARMORIST	COLORIST	FIGURIST	JUNGLIST	MONODIST
ARSONIST	CONTRIST	FINALIST	KABALIST	MORALIST
ATTICIST	CREOLIST	FLAUTIST	LABORIST	MOTORIST
AVANTIST	DEMONIST	FUTURIST	LAPIDIST	MURALIST
AVIARIST	DEMOTIST	GARAGIST	LEGALIST	NATIVIST
BACKLIST	DIALLIST	GLOSSIST	LIBELIST	NATURIST
BANJOIST	DIGAMIST	GREYLIST	LINGUIST	NEPOTIST
BIGAMIST	DITHEIST	GROUPIST	LOBBYIST	NIELLIST
BLURBIST	DRUGGIST	HAGADIST	LOCALIST	NIHILIST
BONGOIST	DUELLIST	HALAKIST	LOGICIST	NOVELIST
BOTANIST	DUETTIST	HANDLIST	LOYALIST	ODONTIST

OGHAMIST	PREEXIST	RURALIST	SODOMIST	ULTRAIST
OOLOGIST	PROSAIST	SAFARIST	SOLARIST	UNIONIST
OPTICIST	PSALMIST	SAPPHIST	SOLECIST	UNSEXIST
OPTIMIST	PSYCHIST	SARODIST	SOLIDIST	URBANIST
ORGANIST	PUCKFIST	SATANIST	SOMATIST	VEGETIST
PACIFIST	PUGILIST	SATIRIST	STOCKIST	VISAGIST
PAGANIST	QABALIST	SCIOLIST	SUBTRIST	VITALIST
PANELIST	QUIETIST	SEMITIST	TANGOIST	VOCALIST
PAPALIST	RALLYIST	SHITLIST	TENORIST	VOLUMIST
PARODIST	REENLIST	SHOOTIST	THEORIST	VOTARIST
PEYOTIST	REGALIST	SILURIST	TOTALIST	WAITLIST
PHALLIST	REVERIST	SIMONIST	TOTEMIST	WOMANIST
PLAYLIST	RIGHTIST	SIMPLIST	TRIADIST	
POLEMIST	RIGORIST	SITARIST	TRIALIST	
POPULIST	ROYALIST	SODALIST	TROILIST	

Words that end with -ITY

Seven-letter words

ABILITY	CLARITY	FURMITY	PANEITY	SURDITY
ACIDITY	CRUDITY	GASEITY	PAUCITY	TENSITY
AGILITY	CURVITY	GRAVITY	PIOSITY	TENUITY
AMENITY	DABBITY	INANITY	PRAVITY	TRINITY
AMINITY	DACOITY	JOLLITY	PRIVITY	UNICITY
ANALITY	DAKOITY	LAICITY	PROBITY	UTILITY
ANILITY	DENSITY	NULLITY	QUALITY	VACUITY
ANNUITY	DIGNITY	OBESITY	RABBITY	VARSITY
ARIDITY	DUALITY	OMNEITY	RAUCITY	VASTITY
AUREITY	EDACITY	OPACITY	REALITY	VIDUITY
AVIDITY	EGALITY	ORALITY	RUBBITY	
BIGGITY	EXILITY	OUTCITY	SICCITY	
BREVITY	FALSITY	OUTPITY	SPIRITY	
CHARITY	FATUITY	OVALITY	SUAVITY	

Eight-letter words

ACERBITY	CALAMITY	ETERNITY	GRATUITY	INVERITY
ACRIDITY	CALIDITY	EXIGUITY	GULOSITY	IONICITY
ACTIVITY	CANINITY	FACILITY	HELICITY	JEJUNITY
ADUNCITY	CAPACITY	FATALITY	HEREDITY	JOCOSITY
AFFINITY	CELERITY	FELICITY	HILARITY	LABILITY
ALACRITY	CHASTITY	FELINITY	HUMANITY	LANOSITY
ALGIDITY	CIRCUITY	FEMALITY	HUMIDITY	LATINITY
ALTERITY	CIVILITY	FEMINITY	HUMILITY	LEGALITY
ANTICITY	CONCEITY	FERACITY	IDEALITY	LEGERITY
ASPERITY	CONICITY	FEROCITY	IDENTITY	LIVIDITY
ASTUCITY	CUBICITY	FETIDITY	IDONEITY	LOCALITY
ATROCITY	CUPIDITY	FIDELITY	IMMANITY	LUCIDITY
AUDACITY	DEBILITY	FINALITY	IMMUNITY	MAJORITY
AURALITY	DICACITY	FLUIDITY	IMPARITY	MATURITY
AXIALITY	DISUNITY	FORTUITY	IMPUNITY	MEGACITY
BANALITY	DIVINITY	FUGACITY	IMPURITY	MINACITY
BASICITY	DOCILITY	FUMOSITY	INEQUITY	MINORITY
BIFIDITY	DUMOSITY	FURACITY	INFINITY	MOBILITY
BISCUITY	ENORMITY	FUTILITY	INIQUITY	MODALITY
BOVINITY	EQUALITY	FUTURITY	INSANITY	MOLALITY
CADUCITY	EQUINITY	GELIDITY	INTIMITY	MOLARITY

MORALITY	PENALITY	RURALITY	SONORITY	VALIDITY
MORONITY	PERSEITY	SAGACITY	SORORITY	VAPIDITY
MOROSITY	PILOSITY	SALACITY	SPARSITY	VELLEITY
MOTILITY	POLARITY	SALINITY	TEMERITY	VELOCITY
MOTIVITY	POROSITY	SANCTITY	TENACITY	VENALITY
MUCIDITY	PRIORITY	SAPIDITY	TEPIDITY	VENOSITY
MUCOSITY	PUDICITY	SATANITY	TIMIDITY	VERACITY
MULTEITY	QUANTITY	SCANTITY	TONALITY	VICINITY
NASALITY	QUEERITY	SCARCITY	TONICITY	VINOSITY
NATALITY	QUIDDITY	SECURITY	TOROSITY	VIRIDITY
NATIVITY	RABIDITY	SEDULITY	TOTALITY	VIRILITY
NIHILITY	RAMOSITY	SENILITY	TOXICITY	VITALITY
NOBILITY	RAPACITY	SERENITY	TRIALITY	VIVACITY
NODALITY	RAPIDITY	SEROSITY	TRIUNITY	VIVIDITY
NODOSITY	REGALITY	SEVERITY	TUMIDITY	VOCALITY
NUBILITY	RIGIDITY	SODALITY	UBIQUITY	VORACITY
OBTUSITY	RIMOSITY	SODICITY	UNFIXITY	ZYGOSITY
ORGANITY	RIVALITY	SOLICITY	URBANITY	
OTIOSITY	RUGOSITY	SOLIDITY	VAGILITY	

Words that end with -IUM

Seven-letter words

ALODIUM	ELUVIUM	LITHIUM	RHENIUM	TRITIUM
ALUMIUM	ERODIUM	MUONIUM	RHODIUM	TRIVIUM
BALLIUM	EXUVIUM	NATRIUM	SPODIUM	URANIUM
BOHRIUM	FERMIUM	NIOBIUM	STADIUM	UREDIUM
CADMIUM	GALLIUM	ORARIUM	STIBIUM	YTTRIUM
CAESIUM	HAFNIUM	OXONIUM	STOMIUM	ZOARIUM
CALCIUM	HAHNIUM	PALLIUM	TAEDIUM	ZOECIUM
CAMBIUM	HASSIUM	PLAGIUM	TERBIUM	
CRANIUM	HOLMIUM	PREMIUM	TERTIUM	
DUBNIUM	IRIDIUM	PROTIUM	THORIUM	
ELOGIUM	ISCHIUM	PYTHIUM	THULIUM	

Eight-letter words

ACHENIUM	COREMIUM	GYNECIUM	OPSONIUM	SEDILIUM
ACTINIUM	CORONIUM	HELENIUM	ORDALIUM	SELENIUM
AECIDIUM	CYATHIUM	HYMENIUM	OSSARIUM	SILICIUM
AEROBIUM	CYMATIUM	ILLINIUM	PATAGIUM	SILPHIUM
ALLODIUM	DELIRIUM	ILLUVIUM	PECULIUM	SIMULIUM
ALLUVIUM	DIDYMIUM	IMPERIUM	PEPONIUM	SOLARIUM
AMMONIUM	DILUVIUM	INDICIUM	PERIDIUM	SOLATIUM
APTERIUM	DISODIUM	INDUSIUM	PHORMIUM	SOREDIUM
AQUARIUM	DOMATIUM	INGENIUM	POLONIUM	SPLENIUM
ASCIDIUM	DOMINIUM	LIXIVIUM	PROPRIUM	SUDARIUM
ASPIDIUM	EMPORIUM	LUTECIUM	PSYLLIUM	SYCONIUM
BASIDIUM	ENCOMIUM	LUTETIUM	PUPARIUM	THALLIUM
BDELLIUM	ERYNGIUM	MASURIUM	PYGIDIUM	TITANIUM
BIENNIUM	EULOGIUM	MECONIUM	PYXIDIUM	TRILLIUM
BOTHRIUM	EUROPIUM	MOTORIUM	RANARIUM	UNUNBIUM
BRACHIUM	EXORDIUM	MYCELIUM	REFUGIUM	VANADIUM
CALADIUM	FRANCIUM	NEBULIUM	ROSARIUM	VELARIUM
CHROMIUM	FUSARIUM	NOBELIUM	RUBIDIUM	VENIDIUM
CIBORIUM	GERANIUM	ONCIDIUM	SAMARIUM	VIVARIUM
CONARIUM	GONIDIUM	ONYCHIUM	SCANDIUM	ZOOECIUM
CONIDIUM	GRAPHIUM	OOGONIUM	SCHOLIUM	

Words that end with -ITY

Words that end with -KIN

Seven-letter words

BARMKIN	CATSKIN	GHERKIN	LORDKIN	RAMAKIN
BAWDKIN	COWSKIN	GRISKIN	LUMPKIN	RAMEKIN
BODIKIN	CUTIKIN	HUFFKIN	MANAKIN	REDSKIN
BOOMKIN	DOESKIN	KIDSKIN	MANIKIN	SHINKIN
BRODKIN	DOGSKIN	KIPSKIN	MINIKIN	SIMPKIN
BUMPKIN	DOITKIN	LADYKIN	OILSKIN	WOLFKIN
CANAKIN	FINIKIN	LAMBKIN	PIGSKIN	
CANIKIN	FOXSKIN	LIMPKIN	PUMPKIN	

Eight-letter words

BAUDEKIN	CAPESKIN	DUNNAKIN	MOLESKIN	SWANSKIN
BEARSKIN	CIDERKIN	FINICKIN	MOUSEKIN	THUMBKIN
BOOTIKIN	COONSKIN	FISHSKIN	MUNCHKIN	TURNSKIN
BRODEKIN	COOTIKIN	FORESKIN	MUTCHKIN	WINESKIN
BUCKSKIN	CUITIKIN	GOATSKIN	PANNIKIN	WOLFSKIN
BYRLAKIN	DAMASKIN	LAMBSKIN	PONYSKIN	WOODSKIN
CALFSKIN	DEERSKIN	LARRIKIN	SEALSKIN	WOOLSKIN
CANNIKIN	DEVILKIN	MANNIKIN	SPILIKIN	

Words that end with -LAND

Seven-letter words

BADLAND	FENLAND	HOLLAND	NORLAND	WETLAND
BOGLAND	GARLAND	LALLAND	OUTLAND	
COTLAND	GOLLAND	LAWLAND	RIMLAND	
DRYLAND	GOWLAND	LOWLAND	SUNLAND	
ELFLAND	HIELAND	MIDLAND	TROLAND	

Eight-letter words

BACKLAND	EASTLAND	HOMELAND	PINELAND	TIDELAND
BOOKLAND	FARMLAND	LACKLAND	PLAYLAND	TOWNLAND
BUSHLAND	FILMLAND	LAKELAND	PLOWLAND	WASHLAND
CLUBLAND	FLATLAND	MAINLAND	PORTLAND	WILDLAND
CORNLAND	FOLKLAND	MOORLAND	SCABLAND	WOODLAND
CROPLAND	FORELAND	MOSSLAND	SHETLAND	YARDLAND
DOCKLAND	GANGLAND	OVERLAND	SLOBLAND	
DOWNLAND	HEADLAND	PARKLAND	SNOWLAND	
DUNELAND	HIGHLAND	PEATLAND	SOAPLAND	

Words that end with -LESS

Seven-letter words

AGELESS	ARTLESS	BARLESS	BRALESS	CUBLESS
AIDLESS	ASHLESS	BEDLESS	BUDLESS	DEWLESS
AIMLESS	AWELESS	BIBLESS	CAPLESS	EARLESS
AIRLESS	AWNLESS	BITLESS	CARLESS	EBBLESS
ARMLESS	BAGLESS	BOWLESS	COXLESS	EGGLESS

EGOLESS	HAPLESS	LAWLESS	RIMLESS	TOYLESS
ENDLESS	HATLESS	LEGLESS	RODLESS	TUGLESS
EYELESS	HIPLESS	LIDLESS	RUNLESS	UNBLESS
FATLESS	HITLESS	LIPLESS	SACLESS	USELESS
FEELESS	HUELESS	MANLESS	SAPLESS	VOWLESS
FINLESS	ICELESS	MAPLESS	SEXLESS	WARLESS
FLYLESS	INKLESS	MATLESS	SINLESS	WAYLESS
FOGLESS	INNLESS	NAPLESS	SONLESS	WEBLESS
FURLESS	IRELESS	NETLESS	SUMLESS	WIGLESS
GAPLESS	JAGLESS	OARLESS	SUNLESS	WINLESS
GASLESS	JAWLESS	ORBLESS	TAXLESS	WITLESS
GODLESS	JOBLESS	PEGLESS	TIELESS	ZIPLESS
GUMLESS	JOYLESS	PIPLESS	TIPLESS	
GUNLESS	KEYLESS	RAYLESS	TOELESS	
GUTLESS	KINLESS	RIBLESS	TOPLESS	

Eight-letter words

BACKLESS	CROPLESS	FRETLESS	HURTLESS	MOONLESS
BARBLESS	CUFFLESS	FUMELESS	HYMNLESS	MOVELESS
BARKLESS	CURBLESS	FUNDLESS	IDEALESS	NAILLESS
BASELESS	CURELESS	FUSELESS	IRONLESS	NAMELESS
BASHLESS	DATELESS	GAINLESS	ISLELESS	NATHLESS
BATELESS	DEBTLESS	GAOLLESS	JAILLESS	NECKLESS
BATHLESS	DEEDLESS	GARBLESS	JURYLESS	NEEDLESS
BEAKLESS	DEVILESS	GATELESS	KEELLESS	NEWSLESS
BEAMLESS	DINTLESS	GAUMLESS	KINDLESS	NORMLESS
BEATLESS	DISKLESS	GEARLESS	KINGLESS	NOSELESS
BEEFLESS	DOORLESS	GIFTLESS	KNOTLESS	NOTELESS
BELTLESS	DOWNLESS	GOALLESS	LACELESS	NOUNLESS
BLOTLESS	DRIPLESS	GOLDLESS	LANDLESS	ODORLESS
BODILESS	DUCTLESS	GORMLESS	LEADLESS	OUTBLESS
BOLTLESS	DUSTLESS	GRITLESS	LEAFLESS	PAINLESS
BONDLESS	EASELESS	GUSTLESS	LEAKLESS	PANELESS
BONELESS	ECHOLESS	HAIRLESS	LENSLESS	PANGLESS
BOOKLESS	EDGELESS	HALTLESS	LIFELESS	PASSLESS
BOONLESS	EXITLESS	HANDLESS	LIMBLESS	PASTLESS
BOOTLESS	FACELESS	HARMLESS	LIMELESS	PATHLESS
BRIMLESS	FADELESS	HATELESS	LINELESS	PEAKLESS
BROWLESS	FAMELESS	HEADLESS	LINTLESS	PEERLESS
BUSHLESS	FANGLESS	HEATLESS	LISTLESS	PELTLESS
CALFLESS	FEARLESS	HEEDLESS	LOAMLESS	PILELESS
CARELESS	FECKLESS	HEELLESS	LOFTLESS	PIPELESS
CASHLESS	FEETLESS	HEIRLESS	LORDLESS	PITHLESS
CHADLESS	FERNLESS	HELMLESS	LOSSLESS	PITILESS
CHAPLESS	FILMLESS	HELPLESS	LOVELESS	PLANLESS
CHINLESS	FINELESS	HERBLESS	LUCKLESS	PLAYLESS
CLAWLESS	FIRELESS	HIDELESS	LUSTLESS	PLOTLESS
CLOYLESS	FIRMLESS	HILTLESS	MAIDLESS	PLUGLESS
CLUELESS	FISHLESS	HIVELESS	MAILLESS	POETLESS
COALLESS	FLAGLESS	HOLELESS	MAKELESS	POLELESS
COATLESS	FLAPLESS	HOMELESS	MANELESS	POPELESS
CODELESS	FLAWLESS	HOODLESS	MASSLESS	PORTLESS
COMBLESS	FOAMLESS	HOOFLESS	MASTLESS	PREBLESS
COOKLESS	FOODLESS	HOOKLESS	MATELESS	PULPLESS
CORDLESS	FOOTLESS	HOOPLESS	MEALLESS	PUMPLESS
CORELESS	FORDLESS	HOPELESS	MEATLESS	RAILLESS
COSTLESS	FORKLESS	HORNLESS	MILKLESS	RAINLESS
CREWLESS	FORMLESS	HUMPLESS	MINDLESS	RANKLESS

Words that end with -LESS

RECKLESS	SCARLESS	SOUPLESS	TIMELESS	WAGELESS
REDELESS	SCUMLESS	SPANLESS	TINTLESS	WAKELESS
REINLESS	SEAMLESS	SPINLESS	TIRELESS	WARDLESS
RESTLESS	SEATLESS	SPOTLESS	TOADLESS	WARELESS
RIFTLESS	SEEDLESS	SPURLESS	TOILLESS	WARTLESS
RIMELESS	SEEMLESS	STARLESS	TOMBLESS	WATTLESS
RINDLESS	SELFLESS	STAYLESS	TONELESS	WAVELESS
RINGLESS	SHIPLESS	STEMLESS	TOOLLESS	WEEDLESS
RISKLESS	SHITLESS	STIRLESS	TOWNLESS	WEETLESS
RITELESS	SHOELESS	STOPLESS	TRAMLESS	WELDLESS
RIVALESS	SHUNLESS	SUCKLESS	TREELESS	WICKLESS
ROADLESS	SIGHLESS	SUDSLESS	TUBELESS	WIFELESS
ROCKLESS	SIGNLESS	TACKLESS	TUNELESS	WINDLESS
ROOFLESS	SKILLESS	TACTLESS	TURFLESS	WINELESS
ROOTLESS	SKINLESS	TAILLESS	TUSKLESS	WINGLESS
ROSELESS	SLIPLESS	TAMELESS	TWIGLESS	WIRELESS
RULELESS	SLITLESS	TANKLESS	TYRELESS	WISHLESS
RUMPLESS	SMOGLESS	TAPELESS	VANELESS	WITELESS
RUNGLESS	SNAPLESS	TASKLESS	VEILLESS	WONTLESS
RUSTLESS	SNOWLESS	TEARLESS	VEINLESS	WOODLESS
RUTHLESS	SOAPLESS	TEEMLESS	VENTLESS	WORDLESS
SACKLESS	SOCKLESS	TENTLESS	VERBLESS	WORKLESS
SAIKLESS	SODALESS	TERMLESS	VESTLESS	YOKELESS
SAILLESS	SOILLESS	TEXTLESS	VETOLESS	YOLKLESS
SALTLESS	SOLELESS	THAWLESS	VICELESS	ZEALLESS
SANDLESS	SONGLESS	THEWLESS	VIEWLESS	ZESTLESS
SASHLESS	SOOTLESS	THOWLESS	VINELESS	ZONELESS
SATELESS	SOULLESS	TIDELESS	VOTELESS	

Words that end with -LET

Seven-letter words

ANNULET	COVELET	HARSLET	OVERLET	STARLET
ARCHLET	CUMULET	HERBLET	PARTLET	STEMLET
BEAMLET	DEERLET	HOOKLET	PIKELET	STERLET
BENDLET	DEVILET	HORNLET	PLAYLET	SWALLET
BOMBLET	DOUBLET	JINGLET	QUILLET	TARTLET
BOOKLET	DOVELET	KINGLET	RINGLET	TEMPLET
BOOMLET	DRIBLET	LAKELET	RIPPLET	TOWNLET
BULBLET	DROPLET	LEAFLET	RIVULET	TRIBLET
CACOLET	EPAULET	LOBELET	ROOTLET	TRIOLET
CANTLET	FLATLET	MANTLET	ROYALET	TRIPLET
CAPELET	FONTLET	MARTLET	RUNDLET	VEINLET
CHAMLET	FORTLET	MEDALET	SCARLET	WAVELET
CHAPLET	FROGLET	MOONLET	SERVLET	WINGLET
CIRCLET	GANTLET	NECKLET	SINGLET	ZONULET
CORSLET	GURGLET	NOTELET	SKILLET	
COUPLET	HACKLET	OSSELET	SNIGLET	

Eight-letter words

BANDELET	CHAINLET	CROSSLET	FRONTLET	HEARTLET
BARRULET	CHEVALET	CROWNLET	FRUITLET	HERBELET
BRACELET	CLOUDLET	DRIBBLET	GAUNTLET	LANCELET
BRACTLET	CORSELET	DRUPELET	GLOBULET	MANTELET
BROOKLET	COURTLET	FLAMELET	GREENLET	MIQUELET
CAPELLET	COVERLET	FOVEOLET	GROUPLET	MURRELET

NERVE**LET**	PLANT**LET**	ROUND**LET**	STATE**LET**	UNDER**LET**
NONUP**LET**	PLATE**LET**	SEXTO**LET**	SWIFT**LET**	VALVE**LET**
OCTUP**LET**	PLUME**LET**	SPANG**LET**	TERCE**LET**	VEINU**LET**
PAMPH**LET**	QUEEN**LET**	SPARK**LET**	TRICK**LET**	VERSE**LET**
PANTA**LET**	RECOL**LET**	SPIKE**LET**	TROUT**LET**	WRIST**LET**
PISTO**LET**	RONDE**LET**	SPIRE**LET**	UMBEL**LET**	

Words that end with -LIKE

Seven-letter words

AIR**LIKE**	EEL**LIKE**	HOG**LIKE**	NUN**LIKE**	SAW**LIKE**
ANT**LIKE**	ELF**LIKE**	HUT**LIKE**	NUT**LIKE**	SIC**LIKE**
APE**LIKE**	EYE**LIKE**	ICE**LIKE**	OAK**LIKE**	SKY**LIKE**
ARM**LIKE**	FAD**LIKE**	INK**LIKE**	OAR**LIKE**	SON**LIKE**
ASS**LIKE**	FAN**LIKE**	IVY**LIKE**	OAT**LIKE**	SUN**LIKE**
BAG**LIKE**	FAT**LIKE**	JAM**LIKE**	OWL**LIKE**	TAG**LIKE**
BAT**LIKE**	FIN**LIKE**	JAW**LIKE**	PEA**LIKE**	TEA**LIKE**
BED**LIKE**	FOX**LIKE**	JET**LIKE**	PEG**LIKE**	TIN**LIKE**
BEE**LIKE**	GEM**LIKE**	JIG**LIKE**	PIG**LIKE**	TOE**LIKE**
BIB**LIKE**	GOD**LIKE**	KID**LIKE**	POD**LIKE**	TOY**LIKE**
BOW**LIKE**	GUM**LIKE**	LAW**LIKE**	POT**LIKE**	TUB**LIKE**
BOX**LIKE**	GUT**LIKE**	LEG**LIKE**	PUS**LIKE**	UNA**LIKE**
BUD**LIKE**	HAG**LIKE**	LIP**LIKE**	RAT**LIKE**	URN**LIKE**
CAT**LIKE**	HAT**LIKE**	MAN**LIKE**	RAY**LIKE**	WAR**LIKE**
CUP**LIKE**	HEN**LIKE**	MAP**LIKE**	RIB**LIKE**	WAX**LIKE**
DIS**LIKE**	HIP**LIKE**	MIS**LIKE**	ROD**LIKE**	WEB**LIKE**
DOG**LIKE**	HOB**LIKE**	NET**LIKE**	RUG**LIKE**	WIG**LIKE**
EAR**LIKE**	HOE**LIKE**	NIB**LIKE**	SAC**LIKE**	

Eight-letter words

AGUE**LIKE**	CRAB**LIKE**	FUME**LIKE**	HOOP**LIKE**	LION**LIKE**
AUNT**LIKE**	CULT**LIKE**	FUSE**LIKE**	HORN**LIKE**	LOFT**LIKE**
BALM**LIKE**	DAWN**LIKE**	GAME**LIKE**	HOSE**LIKE**	LORD**LIKE**
BARN**LIKE**	DEER**LIKE**	GATE**LIKE**	HUMP**LIKE**	LYNX**LIKE**
BEAD**LIKE**	DISC**LIKE**	GERM**LIKE**	HUSK**LIKE**	MASK**LIKE**
BEAK**LIKE**	DISH**LIKE**	GLEN**LIKE**	HYMN**LIKE**	MAST**LIKE**
BEAM**LIKE**	DISK**LIKE**	GLUE**LIKE**	IRON**LIKE**	MAZE**LIKE**
BEAN**LIKE**	DOME**LIKE**	GNAT**LIKE**	JADE**LIKE**	MILK**LIKE**
BEAR**LIKE**	DOVE**LIKE**	GOAD**LIKE**	JAZZ**LIKE**	MOAT**LIKE**
BIRD**LIKE**	DOWN**LIKE**	GOAT**LIKE**	JUTE**LIKE**	MOON**LIKE**
BOAT**LIKE**	DRUM**LIKE**	GONG**LIKE**	KILT**LIKE**	MOSS**LIKE**
BOLT**LIKE**	DUNE**LIKE**	GULF**LIKE**	KING**LIKE**	MOTH**LIKE**
BOWL**LIKE**	DUST**LIKE**	HAIR**LIKE**	KITE**LIKE**	NECK**LIKE**
BUSH**LIKE**	EPIC**LIKE**	HALO**LIKE**	KNOB**LIKE**	NEST**LIKE**
CAGE**LIKE**	FANG**LIKE**	HAND**LIKE**	KNOT**LIKE**	NOOK**LIKE**
CALF**LIKE**	FAUN**LIKE**	HARE**LIKE**	LACE**LIKE**	NOSE**LIKE**
CAVE**LIKE**	FAWN**LIKE**	HAWK**LIKE**	LADY**LIKE**	NOVA**LIKE**
CLAM**LIKE**	FELT**LIKE**	HEAD**LIKE**	LAKE**LIKE**	OVEN**LIKE**
CLAW**LIKE**	FERN**LIKE**	HEMP**LIKE**	LAMB**LIKE**	PALM**LIKE**
CLAY**LIKE**	FILM**LIKE**	HERB**LIKE**	LARD**LIKE**	PARK**LIKE**
COCK**LIKE**	FISH**LIKE**	HERD**LIKE**	LATH**LIKE**	PEAK**LIKE**
COKE**LIKE**	FOAM**LIKE**	HIVE**LIKE**	LAVA**LIKE**	PINE**LIKE**
COMB**LIKE**	FOLK**LIKE**	HOME**LIKE**	LEAF**LIKE**	PIPE**LIKE**
CORD**LIKE**	FOOT**LIKE**	HOOD**LIKE**	LIFE**LIKE**	PITH**LIKE**
CORK**LIKE**	FORK**LIKE**	HOOF**LIKE**	LILY**LIKE**	PLAY**LIKE**
CORM**LIKE**	FROG**LIKE**	HOOK**LIKE**	LINE**LIKE**	PLUM**LIKE**

POET**LIKE**	SACK**LIKE**	SOAP**LIKE**	TILE**LIKE**	WAND**LIKE**
POPE**LIKE**	SALT**LIKE**	SONG**LIKE**	TOAD**LIKE**	WART**LIKE**
PUMP**LIKE**	SAND**LIKE**	SOUL**LIKE**	TOMB**LIKE**	WASP**LIKE**
PUSS**LIKE**	SCAB**LIKE**	SOUP**LIKE**	TRAP**LIKE**	WAVE**LIKE**
QUAY**LIKE**	SCUM**LIKE**	SPAR**LIKE**	TREE**LIKE**	WEED**LIKE**
RASH**LIKE**	SEAL**LIKE**	STAR**LIKE**	TUBE**LIKE**	WHEY**LIKE**
REED**LIKE**	SEAM**LIKE**	STEM**LIKE**	TURF**LIKE**	WHIP**LIKE**
RING**LIKE**	SEED**LIKE**	STEP**LIKE**	TUSK**LIKE**	WIFE**LIKE**
ROCK**LIKE**	SERF**LIKE**	SUCH**LIKE**	TWIG**LIKE**	WING**LIKE**
ROOF**LIKE**	SHED**LIKE**	SUIT**LIKE**	VASE**LIKE**	WIRE**LIKE**
ROOT**LIKE**	SIGH**LIKE**	SURF**LIKE**	VEIL**LIKE**	WISP**LIKE**
ROPE**LIKE**	SILK**LIKE**	SWAN**LIKE**	VEIN**LIKE**	WOLF**LIKE**
ROSE**LIKE**	SKIN**LIKE**	TAIL**LIKE**	VEST**LIKE**	WOMB**LIKE**
RUBY**LIKE**	SLAB**LIKE**	TANK**LIKE**	VICE**LIKE**	WOOL**LIKE**
RUFF**LIKE**	SLIT**LIKE**	TAPE**LIKE**	VINE**LIKE**	WORM**LIKE**
RUNE**LIKE**	SNAG**LIKE**	TENT**LIKE**	VISE**LIKE**	
RUSH**LIKE**	SNOW**LIKE**	TIDE**LIKE**	WAIF**LIKE**	

Words that end with -LOGY

Seven-letter words

ANA**LOGY**	ECO**LOGY**	NEO**LOGY**	TRI**LOGY**
APO**LOGY**	ENO**LOGY**	NOO**LOGY**	UFO**LOGY**
BIO**LOGY**	GEO**LOGY**	ORO**LOGY**	URO**LOGY**
DYS**LOGY**	MYO**LOGY**	OTO**LOGY**	ZOO**LOGY**

Eight-letter words

AERO**LOGY**	CHAO**LOGY**	IDEO**LOGY**	OPTO**LOGY**	SINO**LOGY**
AGRO**LOGY**	CODO**LOGY**	KIDO**LOGY**	OREO**LOGY**	SITO**LOGY**
ALGO**LOGY**	CYTO**LOGY**	MENO**LOGY**	OURO**LOGY**	THEO**LOGY**
ANTI**LOGY**	DEKA**LOGY**	MISO**LOGY**	PARA**LOGY**	TOCO**LOGY**
APIO**LOGY**	DEMO**LOGY**	MIXO**LOGY**	PEDO**LOGY**	TOKO**LOGY**
ARCO**LOGY**	DOSO**LOGY**	MONO**LOGY**	PELO**LOGY**	TOPO**LOGY**
AREO**LOGY**	DOXO**LOGY**	MYCO**LOGY**	PENO**LOGY**	TYPO**LOGY**
ATMO**LOGY**	ETHO**LOGY**	NOMO**LOGY**	PODO**LOGY**	VENO**LOGY**
AUTO**LOGY**	ETIO**LOGY**	NOSO**LOGY**	POMO**LOGY**	VINO**LOGY**
AXIO**LOGY**	FETO**LOGY**	OECO**LOGY**	POSO**LOGY**	VIRO**LOGY**
BATO**LOGY**	GEMO**LOGY**	OENO**LOGY**	PYRO**LOGY**	XYLO**LOGY**
BRYO**LOGY**	HOMO**LOGY**	OINO**LOGY**	RHEO**LOGY**	ZYMO**LOGY**
CACO**LOGY**	HORO**LOGY**	ONCO**LOGY**	SERO**LOGY**	
CETO**LOGY**	IDEA**LOGY**	ONTO**LOGY**	SEXO**LOGY**	

Words that end with -LY

Seven-letter words

ACRID**LY**	ALIEN**LY**	APHYL**LY**	BALKI**LY**	BEERI**LY**
ACTOR**LY**	ALONE**LY**	APISH**LY**	BALMI**LY**	BEETF**LY**
ACUTE**LY**	ALOOF**LY**	AREAL**LY**	BANAL**LY**	BIFID**LY**
ADDED**LY**	AMIAB**LY**	AUDIB**LY**	BASAL**LY**	BLACK**LY**
ADEPT**LY**	ANGER**LY**	AURAL**LY**	BAWDI**LY**	BLAND**LY**
ADULT**LY**	ANGRI**LY**	AWFUL**LY**	BEADI**LY**	BLANK**LY**
AFFAB**LY**	ANOMA**LY**	AXIAL**LY**	BEAMI**LY**	BLEAK**LY**
AGILE**LY**	ANTIC**LY**	BAGGI**LY**	BEAST**LY**	BLIND**LY**
ALERT**LY**	APETA**LY**	BAIRN**LY**	BEEFI**LY**	BLOWF**LY**

BLUFF**LY**	CUSHI**LY**	FLUID**LY**	GYRAL**LY**	LOFTI**LY**
BLUNT**LY**	DAFFI**LY**	FLUKI**LY**	HAMMI**LY**	LOOBI**LY**
BOGUS**LY**	DANDI**LY**	FOAMI**LY**	HANDI**LY**	LOONI**LY**
BONNI**LY**	DATED**LY**	FOCAL**LY**	HAPPI**LY**	LOOPI**LY**
BOOZI**LY**	DAYLI**LY**	FOGGI**LY**	HARDI**LY**	LOOSE**LY**
BOSSI**LY**	DAZED**LY**	FRAIL**LY**	HARSH**LY**	LOUSI**LY**
BRAMB**LY**	DEARN**LY**	FRANK**LY**	HARTE**LY**	LOVAB**LY**
BRASH**LY**	DEATH**LY**	FRECK**LY**	HASTI**LY**	LOVER**LY**
BRAVE**LY**	DEEDI**LY**	FRESH**LY**	HAZEL**LY**	LOWLI**LY**
BRIEF**LY**	DEERF**LY**	FRIAR**LY**	HEADI**LY**	LOYAL**LY**
BRISK**LY**	DENSE**LY**	FRITF**LY**	HEART**LY**	LUCID**LY**
BRIST**LY**	DICYC**LY**	FRIZZ**LY**	HEAVI**LY**	LUCKI**LY**
BRITT**LY**	DINGI**LY**	FUGAL**LY**	HEFTI**LY**	LUMPI**LY**
BROAD**LY**	DIRTI**LY**	FUGGI**LY**	HOARI**LY**	LURID**LY**
BRUTE**LY**	DISAL**LY**	FUNKI**LY**	HORNI**LY**	LUSTI**LY**
BUIRD**LY**	DIZZI**LY**	FUNNI**LY**	HORSI**LY**	LYING**LY**
BULKI**LY**	DOOMI**LY**	FURRI**LY**	HUFFI**LY**	MAJOR**LY**
BUMPI**LY**	DOTTI**LY**	FUSIB**LY**	HUMAN**LY**	MANGI**LY**
BURLI**LY**	DOUCE**LY**	FUSSI**LY**	HUMID**LY**	MANLI**LY**
BUSHF**LY**	DOWDI**LY**	FUSTI**LY**	HUSKI**LY**	MASCU**LY**
BUSHI**LY**	DREAD**LY**	FUZZI**LY**	IDEAL**LY**	MAZED**LY**
BUXOM**LY**	DRIBB**LY**	GALLF**LY**	IGNOB**LY**	MEATI**LY**
CAMPI**LY**	DRIZZ**LY**	GASSI**LY**	INANE**LY**	MERRI**LY**
CANNI**LY**	DROPF**LY**	GAUDI**LY**	INAPT**LY**	MESAL**LY**
CANTI**LY**	DUCAL**LY**	GAUNT**LY**	INEPT**LY**	MESSI**LY**
CAPAB**LY**	DUMPI**LY**	GAUZI**LY**	INERT**LY**	METAL**LY**
CATTI**LY**	DUOPO**LY**	GAWKI**LY**	INJEL**LY**	MIFFI**LY**
CAVAL**LY**	DURAB**LY**	GELID**LY**	INNER**LY**	MILKI**LY**
CECAL**LY**	DUSKI**LY**	GEMMI**LY**	IRATE**LY**	MIRKI**LY**
CHARI**LY**	DUSTI**LY**	GHAST**LY**	ITCHI**LY**	MISAL**LY**
CHEAP**LY**	DYING**LY**	GHOST**LY**	JADED**LY**	MISER**LY**
CHEER**LY**	EAGER**LY**	GIANT**LY**	JAZZI**LY**	MISRE**LY**
CHIEF**LY**	EARTH**LY**	GIDDI**LY**	JERKI**LY**	MISTI**LY**
CHILD**LY**	ELDER**LY**	GINGE**LY**	JOINT**LY**	MIXED**LY**
CHIMB**LY**	EMPTI**LY**	GLAZI**LY**	JOLLI**LY**	MODAL**LY**
CIVIL**LY**	EPIBO**LY**	GLOWF**LY**	JOLTI**LY**	MOIST**LY**
CLEAN**LY**	EQUAB**LY**	GODLI**LY**	JUICI**LY**	MONTH**LY**
CLEAR**LY**	EQUAL**LY**	GOOFI**LY**	JUMPI**LY**	MOODI**LY**
CLERK**LY**	ERECT**LY**	GOUTF**LY**	JURAL**LY**	MOONI**LY**
CLOSE**LY**	EROSE**LY**	GOUTI**LY**	KINKI**LY**	MORAL**LY**
COCKI**LY**	EXACT**LY**	GRADE**LY**	KNOBB**LY**	MOUSI**LY**
CORNF**LY**	FADED**LY**	GRAND**LY**	KNUBB**LY**	MOVAB**LY**
CORNI**LY**	FAINT**LY**	GRAVE**LY**	KNUCK**LY**	MUCKI**LY**
COURT**LY**	FAIRI**LY**	GRAYF**LY**	LADYF**LY**	MUDDI**LY**
COWED**LY**	FALSE**LY**	GREAT**LY**	LAIRD**LY**	MUGGI**LY**
CRACK**LY**	FANCI**LY**	GREEN**LY**	LAITH**LY**	MURKI**LY**
CRANK**LY**	FATAL**LY**	GREIS**LY**	LANKI**LY**	MUSHI**LY**
CRASS**LY**	FATTI**LY**	GRIES**LY**	LARGE**LY**	MUSKI**LY**
CRAZI**LY**	FETID**LY**	GRIMI**LY**	LEAKI**LY**	MUSSI**LY**
CRINK**LY**	FIERI**LY**	GRISE**LY**	LEERI**LY**	MUSTI**LY**
CRISP**LY**	FIFTH**LY**	GRIST**LY**	LEGAL**LY**	MUTAB**LY**
CROSS**LY**	FILMI**LY**	GRIZZ**LY**	LEGIB**LY**	MUTED**LY**
CRUDE**LY**	FINAL**LY**	GROSS**LY**	LEVEL**LY**	MUZZI**LY**
CRUEL**LY**	FIREF**LY**	GRUFF**LY**	LICHT**LY**	NAIVE**LY**
CRUMB**LY**	FIRST**LY**	GRUMB**LY**	LICIT**LY**	NAKED**LY**
CRUMP**LY**	FISHI**LY**	GRYSE**LY**	LIGHT**LY**	NARGI**LY**
CRUSI**LY**	FIXED**LY**	GUMMI**LY**	LITHE**LY**	NASAL**LY**
CUBIC**LY**	FLAKI**LY**	GUSHI**LY**	LIVID**LY**	NASTI**LY**
CURAB**LY**	FLEET**LY**	GUSTI**LY**	LOATH**LY**	NATTI**LY**
CURLI**LY**	FLESH**LY**	GUTSI**LY**	LOCAL**LY**	NAVAL**LY**

Words that end with -LY

NEEDILY	PUSHILY	SHEERLY	STONILY	TWINKLY
NERVILY	QUAKILY	SHINGLY	STOUTLY	UNAPTLY
NIFTILY	QUEENLY	SHINILY	STUBBLY	UNFITLY
NIGHTLY	QUEERLY	SHOGGLY	STUMBLY	UNGODLY
NINTHLY	QUICKLY	SHOOFLY	SUAVELY	UNMANLY
NIPPILY	QUIETLY	SHOOGLY	SULKILY	UNTRULY
NOBBILY	RABIDLY	SHORTLY	SUNNILY	USEABLY
NODALLY	RAINILY	SHOWILY	SURLILY	USUALLY
NOISILY	RANDILY	SHRILLY	SWEETLY	UTTERLY
NONOILY	RANGILY	SIGHTLY	SWIFTLY	VAGALLY
NOTABLY	RAPIDLY	SILKILY	SWITHLY	VAGUELY
NOTEDLY	RATABLY	SILLILY	TACITLY	VALIDLY
NOVELLY	RATTILY	SIXTHLY	TACKILY	VAPIDLY
NUTTILY	RAVELLY	SIZABLY	TAILFLY	VENALLY
NYMPHLY	READILY	SLACKLY	TARDILY	VERMILY
OBESELY	REAPPLY	SLANTLY	TARTILY	VEXEDLY
OCTUPLY	REEDILY	SLEEKLY	TASTILY	VICARLY
ORDERLY	REGALLY	SLICKLY	TATTILY	VIRALLY
OVATELY	RETALLY	SLIMILY	TAWNILY	VISIBLY
OVERFLY	RIANTLY	SMARTLY	TAXABLY	VITALLY
OVERPLY	RIGHTLY	SMICKLY	TEARILY	VIVIDLY
OVERTLY	RIGIDLY	SMOKILY	TECHILY	VIXENLY
PANOPLY	RISIBLY	SNAKILY	TENABLY	VOCABLY
PAPALLY	RISKILY	SNIDELY	TENSELY	VOCALLY
PASTILY	RITZILY	SNIFFLY	TENTHLY	VOLUBLY
PAWKILY	ROCKILY	SNOWILY	TEPIDLY	VOWELLY
PAYABLY	ROOMILY	SNUFFLY	TERSELY	VYINGLY
PEARTLY	ROUGHLY	SOAPILY	TESTILY	WACKILY
PENALLY	ROUNDLY	SOBERLY	TEUGHLY	WASHILY
PEPPILY	ROUPILY	SOGGILY	THEGNLY	WASPILY
PERKILY	ROWDILY	SOLIDLY	THICKLY	WEARILY
PESKILY	ROYALLY	SOLUBLY	THIRDLY	WEASELY
PETTILY	RUDDILY	SOOTHLY	THISTLY	WEEDILY
PHONILY	RUMMILY	SOOTILY	THRILLY	WEEPILY
PICKILY	RURALLY	SOPPILY	TIDALLY	WEEVILY
PIOUSLY	RUSTILY	SORRILY	TIGERLY	WEIRDLY
PITHILY	RUTTILY	SOUNDLY	TIGHTLY	WHITELY
PLAINLY	SAINTLY	SPANGLY	TIMIDLY	WIGHTLY
PLIABLY	SALABLY	SPARELY	TINNILY	WINDILY
PLUMPLY	SALTILY	SPARKLY	TIPSILY	WISPILY
PLUSHLY	SANDFLY	SPICILY	TIREDLY	WITTILY
POCKILY	SAPPILY	SPIKILY	TONALLY	WOFULLY
PODGILY	SASSILY	SPINDLY	TOSSILY	WOMANLY
PRICILY	SAUCILY	SPRAWLY	TOTALLY	WOOZILY
PRICKLY	SAVVILY	SQUALLY	TOUGHLY	WORDILY
PRIMELY	SCANTLY	SQUATLY	TREACLY	WORLDLY
PRIORLY	SCARILY	STAGILY	TREMBLY	WORMFLY
PRIVILY	SCRAWLY	STAIDLY	TRICKLY	WRIGGLY
PRONELY	SEEDILY	STALELY	TRIFOLY	WRINKLY
PROSILY	SHADFLY	STARKLY	TRITELY	WRONGLY
PROUDLY	SHADILY	STARTLY	TUFTILY	YOUNGLY
PUDGILY	SHAKILY	STATELY	TUMIDLY	YOUTHLY
PUFFILY	SHAMBLY	STEEPLY	TUNABLY	ZESTILY
PULPILY	SHAPELY	STERNLY	TWADDLY	ZONALLY
PURSILY	SHARPLY	STIFFLY	TWIDDLY	

Eight-letter words

ABASEDLY	BIYEARLY	CLOUDILY	DOGGEDLY	FLOPPILY
ABJECTLY	BLACKFLY	CLUBBILY	DOOLALLY	FLORALLY
ABORALLY	BLAMABLY	CLUMSILY	DORSALLY	FLORIDLY
ABRUPTLY	BLEARILY	COARSELY	DOTARDLY	FLOSSILY
ABSENTLY	BLITHELY	COEVALLY	DOTINGLY	FLUENTLY
ABSURDLY	BLOODILY	COGENTLY	DRAFTILY	FLUFFILY
ACHINGLY	BLOUSILY	COITALLY	DREAMILY	FOETIDLY
ACTIVELY	BLOWSILY	COMELILY	DREARILY	FOLKSILY
ACTUALLY	BLOWZILY	COMMONLY	DRESSILY	FORCEDLY
ADORABLY	BLURRILY	CONVEXLY	DRIPPILY	FORCIBLY
ADROITLY	BODINGLY	COOINGLY	DROOPILY	FORKEDLY
AERIALLY	BORINGLY	COSTALLY	DROWSILY	FORMABLY
AFFINELY	BOTCHILY	COUSINLY	DUDISHLY	FORMALLY
AGUISHLY	BOUNCILY	COVERTLY	DULCETLY	FORMERLY
AIMFULLY	BOVINELY	COWARDLY	EARTHILY	FOURTHLY
ALDERFLY	BOWINGLY	COYISHLY	EASTERLY	FREAKILY
ALPINELY	BOYISHLY	CRABBILY	EFFETELY	FRENZILY
AMAZEDLY	BRAINILY	CRAFTILY	EIGHTHLY	FRIENDLY
AMENABLY	BRASSILY	CRAGGILY	ELATEDLY	FRIGIDLY
AMICABLY	BRAWNILY	CRANEFLY	ELFISHLY	FRISKILY
AMORALLY	BRAZENLY	CRANKILY	ELIGIBLY	FRIZZILY
AMUSEDLY	BREEZILY	CRAVENLY	ELVISHLY	FROSTILY
ANIMALLY	BRIDALLY	CREAKILY	ENTIRELY	FROTHILY
ANNUALLY	BRIGHTLY	CREAMILY	ENVIABLY	FROWZILY
ANODALLY	BROKENLY	CREDIBLY	EPICALLY	FROZENLY
APICALLY	BROODILY	CREEPILY	EQUINELY	FRUGALLY
ARCANELY	BRUTALLY	CRISPILY	ERRANTLY	FRUITILY
ARDENTLY	BUCCALLY	CROAKILY	ERRINGLY	FRUMPILY
ARGUABLY	BUNCHILY	CROUPILY	EVANGELY	FUMINGLY
ARGUTELY	CAECALLY	CROUSELY	EXPERTLY	FUTILELY
ARRANTLY	CANDIDLY	CRUSTILY	FACETELY	GAGEABLY
ARTFULLY	CARNALLY	CRYINGLY	FACIALLY	GAPINGLY
ASSEMBLY	CASUALLY	CULPABLY	FACILELY	GARISHLY
ASTRALLY	CATCHFLY	CURSEDLY	FALLIBLY	GAUCHELY
ASTUTELY	CAUDALLY	CURVEDLY	FAMOUSLY	GENIALLY
ATONALLY	CAUSALLY	CUSSEDLY	FATHERLY	GIBINGLY
AUGUSTLY	CHANCILY	CYCLICLY	FAULTILY	GIFTEDLY
AVERSELY	CHASTELY	CYMOSELY	FAUNALLY	GINGELLY
AVOWABLY	CHATTILY	DAINTILY	FEASIBLY	GINGERLY
AVOWEDLY	CHEEKILY	DAMNABLY	FEISTILY	GLASSILY
BADGERLY	CHEERILY	DAPPERLY	FELINELY	GLITZILY
BANKERLY	CHEESILY	DARINGLY	FELLOWLY	GLOBALLY
BARRENLY	CHESTILY	DATIVELY	FERVIDLY	GLOOMILY
BAULKILY	CHILLILY	DECENTLY	FESTALLY	GLOSSILY
BEARABLY	CHIRPILY	DEMISSLY	FEUDALLY	GLUMPILY
BEASTILY	CHOICELY	DEMURELY	FIERCELY	GOLDENLY
BEGGARLY	CHOPPILY	DENIABLY	FILIALLY	GORBELLY
BEHOVELY	CHORALLY	DENTALLY	FILTHILY	GORGEDLY
BENIGNLY	CHUBBILY	DEUCEDLY	FINITELY	GOSPELLY
BESEEMLY	CHUMMILY	DEVOUTLY	FISCALLY	GRAITHLY
BIASEDLY	CHUNKILY	DIRECTLY	FITFULLY	GRASSILY
BIDDABLY	CHURCHLY	DISAPPLY	FLABBILY	GRAVELLY
BIHOURLY	CLAMMILY	DISMALLY	FLASHILY	GRAVIDLY
BINATELY	CLASSILY	DISTALLY	FLEECILY	GREASILY
BITCHILY	CLEVERLY	DIVERSLY	FLESHILY	GREEDILY
BITINGLY	CLINALLY	DIVINELY	FLEXIBLY	GREENFLY
BITTERLY	CLOGGILY	DOCILELY	FLIMSILY	GRITTILY
BIWEEKLY	CLONALLY	DOCTORLY	FLINTILY	GROGGILY

Words that end with -LY

GRUBBILY	KNOTTILY	MODESTLY	PIPINGLY	RECTALLY
GRUFFILY	LABIALLY	MODISHLY	PITCHILY	REDBELLY
GRUMPILY	LAICALLY	MOLTENLY	PITIABLY	REFLEXLY
GUILTILY	LATENTLY	MOMENTLY	PLACABLY	RELIABLY
GULLABLY	LATTERLY	MONOPOLY	PLACIDLY	REMISSLY
GULLIBLY	LAUDABLY	MOPINGLY	PLAGUILY	REMOTELY
HEARTILY	LAVISHLY	MOPISHLY	PLIANTLY	REPANDLY
HEATEDLY	LAWFULLY	MORBIDLY	PLUCKILY	RESUPPLY
HEAVENLY	LAWYERLY	MOROSELY	PLUGUGLY	RETRALLY
HECTICLY	LEADENLY	MORTALLY	PLURALLY	RIBALDLY
HECTORLY	LETHALLY	MOTHERLY	PLUSHILY	RIMOSELY
HEROICLY	LIMBERLY	MOUTHILY	PLYINGLY	RITUALLY
HIDDENLY	LIMPIDLY	MOVEABLY	POLITELY	ROBUSTLY
HITCHILY	LINEALLY	MOVINGLY	POPISHLY	ROOTEDLY
HOARSELY	LINEARLY	MULISHLY	POROUSLY	ROTTENLY
HOLLOWLY	LIQUIDLY	MULTIPLY	PORTABLY	ROTUNDLY
HOMELILY	LISSOMLY	MUSINGLY	PORTERLY	ROVINGLY
HONESTLY	LITHERLY	MUTUALLY	POSINGLY	RUEFULLY
HONIEDLY	LIVELILY	MYOPHILY	POSSIBLY	RUGGEDLY
HOPINGLY	LIVINGLY	MYSTICLY	POSTALLY	RUGOSELY
HORRIBLY	LOBATELY	NARGHILY	POTBELLY	RUSTICLY
HORRIDLY	LOBLOLLY	NARROWLY	POTENTLY	SACREDLY
HORSEFLY	LONELILY	NATANTLY	PREAPPLY	SAILORLY
HOUSEFLY	LOSINGLY	NATIVELY	PREPPILY	SALEABLY
HOVERFLY	LOUCHELY	NEURALLY	PRETTILY	SALLOWLY
HUMANELY	LOVEABLY	NEWISHLY	PRIESTLY	SALVABLY
HUNGERLY	LOVELILY	NOCENTLY	PRIMALLY	SATIABLY
HUNGRILY	LOVINGLY	NORMALLY	PRINCELY	SAVAGELY
HUNTEDLY	LUBBERLY	NOUNALLY	PRISSILY	SAVINGLY
HUSHEDLY	LUCENTLY	OAFISHLY	PROBABLY	SAVORILY
IMMANELY	LUMBERLY	OBLATELY	PROLIXLY	SAVOURLY
IMPISHLY	LUMPENLY	OBLONGLY	PROMPTLY	SCABBILY
IMPURELY	LUNATELY	OBTUSELY	PROPERLY	SCALABLY
INDIGNLY	LURINGLY	OCCULTLY	PROVABLY	SCANTILY
INEDIBLY	LYRATELY	OCULARLY	PROVENLY	SCARCELY
INFIRMLY	MAIDENLY	ODIOUSLY	PRYINGLY	SCATTILY
INNATELY	MALIGNLY	OFFISHLY	PUBLICLY	SCRABBLY
INSANELY	MANFULLY	OGRISHLY	PULINGLY	SCRAGGLY
INTACTLY	MANNERLY	ONWARDLY	PULPALLY	SCRIBBLY
INTENTLY	MANUALLY	OPAQUELY	PUNCHILY	SCRIGGLY
INVIABLY	MARKEDLY	OPERABLY	PUTRIDLY	SCRIMPLY
INWARDLY	MARTYRLY	ORNATELY	QUAINTLY	SCUMMILY
IREFULLY	MASSEDLY	OTIOSELY	QUEASILY	SCURVILY
ISSUABLY	MASTERLY	OUTBULLY	QUIRKILY	SEAMANLY
JADISHLY	MATRONLY	OVERHOLY	QUOTABLY	SECANTLY
JAGGEDLY	MATTEDLY	OVERWILY	RACIALLY	SECONDLY
JAPINGLY	MATURELY	OWLISHLY	RADIALLY	SECRETLY
JAUNTILY	MEAGERLY	PALLIDLY	RAGGEDLY	SECUNDLY
JEJUNELY	MEAGRELY	PALPABLY	RAGINGLY	SECURELY
JIBINGLY	MEDIALLY	PALTRILY	RAKISHLY	SEDATELY
JOCOSELY	MEDIANLY	PANDERLY	RAMOSELY	SELDOMLY
JOCUNDLY	MELLOWLY	PASSABLY	RAMOUSLY	SELECTLY
JOKINGLY	MENIALLY	PASSIBLY	RANCIDLY	SENILELY
JOVIALLY	MENTALLY	PASTORLY	RANDOMLY	SENSIBLY
JOYFULLY	MESIALLY	PATCHILY	RASCALLY	SERENELY
JOYOUSLY	METABOLY	PATENTLY	RATEABLY	SERIALLY
KERNELLY	MIGHTILY	PATRONLY	RAVINGLY	SEVERELY
KINDLILY	MINUTELY	PEACHILY	READABLY	SEXTUPLY
KISSABLY	MISAPPLY	PEDATELY	READERLY	SEXUALLY
KNIGHTLY	MODERNLY	PETTEDLY	RECENTLY	SHABBILY

SHAGGILY	SOMBERLY	SUDDENLY	UNCHICLY	VENIALLY
SHAMABLY	SOMBRELY	SUITABLY	UNCIALLY	VENOUSLY
SHAUCHLY	SORDIDLY	SULLENLY	UNCOMELY	VERBALLY
SHIFTILY	SORTABLY	SULTRILY	UNCOSTLY	VERNALLY
SHIRTILY	SOTTEDLY	SUMMERLY	UNEASILY	VESTALLY
SHITTILY	SOUTERLY	SUNDRILY	UNEVENLY	VEXINGLY
SHODDILY	SOVRANLY	SUPERBLY	UNFAIRLY	VINCIBLY
SHREWDLY	SOWBELLY	SUPINELY	UNGAINLY	VINOUSLY
SICKERLY	SPARKILY	SUPPLELY	UNGENTLY	VIOLABLY
SICKLILY	SPARSELY	SVELTELY	UNHOLILY	VIRGINLY
SIGNALLY	SPEEDILY	SWANKILY	UNHOMELY	VIRILELY
SILENTLY	SPIFFILY	SWEATILY	UNIQUELY	VISCIDLY
SILVERLY	SPINALLY	SWIMMILY	UNITEDLY	VISUALLY
SINFULLY	SPIRALLY	SYMPHILY	UNJUSTLY	VOTIVELY
SISTERLY	SPONGILY	TAKINGLY	UNKINDLY	VULGARLY
SIZEABLY	SPOOKILY	TANGIBLY	UNKINGLY	WANTONLY
SKIMPILY	SPOONILY	TARNALLY	UNLIKELY	WATERILY
SLANGILY	SPORTILY	TARTARLY	UNLIVELY	WEASELLY
SLEAZILY	SPOTTILY	TASSELLY	UNLORDLY	WEEVILLY
SLEEPILY	SPRITELY	TAWDRILY	UNLOVELY	WESTERLY
SLIGHTLY	SPRUCELY	TAXINGLY	UNMEETLY	WHEEZILY
SLINKILY	SPUNKILY	TENDERLY	UNPURELY	WHIMSILY
SLIPPILY	SQUARELY	TENSIBLY	UNREALLY	WHITEFLY
SLOPPILY	SQUIGGLY	TERRIBLY	UNRIPELY	WICKEDLY
SLOVENLY	SQUIRELY	TETCHILY	UNSAFELY	WILFULLY
SLUSHILY	STALKILY	THORNILY	UNSEEMLY	WINGEDLY
SMALMILY	STANCHLY	THRAWNLY	UNSTABLY	WINTERLY
SMARMILY	STARRILY	THWARTLY	UNSUBTLY	WINTRILY
SMEARILY	STATEDLY	TIMOUSLY	UNSURELY	WITTOLLY
SMIRKILY	STEADILY	TINSELLY	UNTIDILY	WIZARDLY
SMOOTHLY	STEAMILY	TONISHLY	UNTIMELY	WOEFULLY
SMUDGILY	STEEVELY	TOOTHILY	UNUSABLY	WONTEDLY
SMUTTILY	STICKILY	TORPIDLY	UNWARELY	WOODENLY
SNAPPILY	STIEVELY	TORRIDLY	UNWARILY	WOOINGLY
SNARKILY	STINGILY	TOUCHILY	UNWIFELY	WOOLLILY
SNAZZILY	STOCKILY	TOWARDLY	UNWISELY	WORKABLY
SNEAKILY	STODGILY	TOYISHLY	UPPISHLY	WORTHILY
SNIFFILY	STOLIDLY	TRASHILY	UPWARDLY	WOUNDILY
SNIPPILY	STONEFLY	TRENDILY	URBANELY	WRATHILY
SNIVELLY	STORMILY	TREVALLY	URGENTLY	WRITERLY
SNOBBILY	STRAGGLY	TRIBALLY	URGINGLY	YEASTILY
SNOOPILY	STRAITLY	TRICKILY	USEFULLY	YELLOWLY
SNOOTILY	STRICTLY	TRUANTLY	UVULARLY	YEOMANLY
SNOTTILY	STRONGLY	TRUSTILY	VACANTLY	YONDERLY
SNUFFILY	STUBBILY	TRYINGLY	VALUABLY	ZOOPHILY
SOCIABLY	STUFFILY	TUNBELLY	VARIABLY	
SOCIALLY	STUMPILY	TUNEABLY	VARIEDLY	
SODDENLY	STUPIDLY	TURBIDLY	VEILEDLY	
SOLEMNLY	STURDILY	TURGIDLY	VENDIBLY	

Words that end with -MAN

Seven-letter words

ADWOMAN	AUTOMAN	BELLMAN	BOGYMAN	BYREMAN
ALMSMAN	BASEMAN	BELTMAN	BONDMAN	CASEMAN
ANATMAN	BATSMAN	BILLMAN	BOOKMAN	CAVEMAN
ANTIMAN	BEADMAN	BIRDMAN	BRAHMAN	CHAPMAN
ARTSMAN	BEDEMAN	BOATMAN	BUSHMAN	CLUBMAN

Words that end with -LY

COALMAN	HANUMAN	LOCKMAN	PORTMAN	SURFMAN
CREWMAN	HARDMAN	LOCOMAN	POSTMAN	SWAGMAN
DAYSMAN	HEADMAN	MAGSMAN	PROPMAN	TAPSMAN
DEADMAN	HELIMAN	MAILMAN	PULLMAN	TAXIMAN
DECUMAN	HERDMAN	MALTMAN	RAFTMAN	TELEMAN
DESKMAN	HIGHMAN	MARKMAN	RAILMAN	TOLLMAN
DOORMAN	HOODMAN	MASHMAN	REEDMAN	TONGMAN
DRAYMAN	HOSEMAN	MEATMAN	REELMAN	TOOLMAN
DUSTMAN	INHUMAN	MESSMAN	REPOMAN	TOPSMAN
FACEMAN	IRONMAN	MILKMAN	RINGMAN	TRUEMAN
FIREMAN	ISLEMAN	MOBSMAN	ROADMAN	TURFMAN
FLAGMAN	JACKMAN	MOORMAN	RODSMAN	UNHUMAN
FOOTMAN	JARKMAN	MOOTMAN	RUCKMAN	UNWOMAN
FOREMAN	JAZZMAN	NEWSMAN	SAGAMAN	WAKEMAN
FREEMAN	JUNKMAN	OARSMAN	SANDMAN	WINGMAN
FROGMAN	JURYMAN	ODDSMAN	SEEDMAN	WIREMAN
GADSMAN	KEELMAN	ORRAMAN	SHIPMAN	WOODMAN
GATEMAN	KINSMAN	OTTOMAN	SHOPMAN	WOOLMAN
GLEEMAN	KIRKMAN	OVERMAN	SHOWMAN	WORKMAN
GOODMAN	LANDMAN	PACKMAN	SIDEMAN	YARDMAN
GOWNMAN	LEADMAN	PASSMAN	SNOWMAN	YEGGMAN
GRIPMAN	LENSMAN	PEATMAN	SOCKMAN	
GUDEMAN	LIFTMAN	PIKEMAN	SOKEMAN	
HACKMAN	LINEMAN	PLOWMAN	SONGMAN	
HANGMAN	LINKMAN	POLLMAN	SPAEMAN	

Eight-letter words

AIRWOMAN	CORPSMAN	HIELAMAN	PILOTMAN	SIDESMAN
ALDERMAN	CRAGSMAN	HOASTMAN	PITCHMAN	SONARMAN
BAILSMAN	DAIRYMAN	HOISTMAN	PIVOTMAN	SOUNDMAN
BANDSMAN	DALESMAN	HORSEMAN	PLACEMAN	SPACEMAN
BANDYMAN	DOOMSMAN	HOTELMAN	PLAIDMAN	SPADEMAN
BANKSMAN	DOORSMAN	HOUSEMAN	PLATEMAN	SPEARMAN
BARGEMAN	DRAGOMAN	HUNTSMAN	POINTMAN	SQUAWMAN
BATWOMAN	DRAGSMAN	ISLESMAN	PREHUMAN	STAFFMAN
BEADSMAN	DUTCHMAN	KNIFEMAN	PRESSMAN	STALLMAN
BEDESMAN	EARTHMAN	LANDSMAN	PRIZEMAN	STEELMAN
BLUESMAN	EVERYMAN	LAYWOMAN	PROSEMAN	STICKMAN
BOARDMAN	FERRYMAN	LEADSMAN	PUNTSMAN	STILLMAN
BOATSMAN	FOILSMAN	LIEGEMAN	QUILLMAN	STOCKMAN
BOGEYMAN	FORGEMAN	LINESMAN	RADIOMAN	STOREMAN
BONDSMAN	FREEDMAN	LINKSMAN	RAFTSMAN	STUNTMAN
BOOGYMAN	FRESHMAN	LOCKSMAN	RAMPSMAN	SUBHUMAN
BOTHYMAN	FRONTMAN	LODESMAN	RANCHMAN	SUPERMAN
BRAKEMAN	FUGLEMAN	LOFTSMAN	REINSMAN	SWAGSMAN
BRIDEMAN	FUNNYMAN	MADWOMAN	RIFLEMAN	SWEETMAN
BRINKMAN	GAMESMAN	MARCHMAN	RIVERMAN	SWINGMAN
BUTTYMAN	GANGSMAN	MARKSMAN	ROADSMAN	SWORDMAN
CHAINMAN	GAVELMAN	MERESMAN	ROUTEMAN	TACKSMAN
CHAIRMAN	GILDSMAN	MERRYMAN	SALESMAN	TALESMAN
CHESSMAN	GLASSMAN	MONEYMAN	SCENEMAN	TALISMAN
CHINAMAN	GOADSMAN	MOTORMAN	SEAWOMAN	TALLYMAN
CHOIRMAN	GOWNSMAN	NOBLEMAN	SEEDSMAN	TIDESMAN
CHOREMAN	HANDYMAN	NONHUMAN	SHAREMAN	TOWNSMAN
CLANSMAN	HEADSMAN	OVERSMAN	SHEARMAN	TOYWOMAN
CLASSMAN	HELMSMAN	PANHUMAN	SHEEPMAN	TRACKMAN
COACHMAN	HENCHMAN	PENWOMAN	SHIREMAN	TRAINMAN
COLORMAN	HERDSMAN	PETERMAN	SHOREMAN	TRASHMAN

TREWSMAN	VERSEMAN	WEIGHMAN	WINCHMAN
TRUCHMAN	WATCHMAN	WHALEMAN	WOODSMAN
TRUCKMAN	WATERMAN	WHEELMAN	YACHTMAN
UNDERMAN	WEALSMAN	WIDOWMAN	YARRAMAN

Words that end with -MEN

Seven-letter words

ABDOMEN	DEADMEN	HOODMEN	MOOTMEN	SHOWMEN
ADWOMEN	DESKMEN	HOSEMEN	NEWSMEN	SIDEMEN
AGNOMEN	DOORMEN	IRONMEN	OARSMEN	SNOWMEN
ALBUMEN	DRAYMEN	ISLEMEN	ODDSMEN	SOCKMEN
ALMSMEN	DURAMEN	JACKMEN	ORRAMEN	SOKEMEN
ARTSMEN	DUSTMEN	JARKMEN	OVERMEN	SONGMEN
AUTOMEN	FACEMEN	JAZZMEN	PACKMEN	SPAEMEN
BASEMEN	FIREMEN	JUNKMEN	PASSMEN	SUDAMEN
BATSMEN	FLAGMEN	JURYMEN	PEATMEN	SURFMEN
BEADMEN	FLEHMEN	KEELMEN	PIKEMEN	SWAGMEN
BEDEMEN	FOOTMEN	KINSMEN	PLOWMEN	TAPSMEN
BELLMEN	FORAMEN	KIRKMEN	POLLMEN	TAXIMEN
BELTMEN	FOREMEN	LANDMEN	PORTMEN	TEGUMEN
BILLMEN	FREEMEN	LEADMEN	POSTMEN	TELEMEN
BIRDMEN	FROGMEN	LENSMEN	PROPMEN	TOLLMEN
BITUMEN	GADSMEN	LIFTMEN	PUTAMEN	TONGMEN
BOATMEN	GATEMEN	LINEMEN	RAFTMEN	TOOLMEN
BOGYMEN	GLEEMEN	LINKMEN	RAILMEN	TOPSMEN
BONDMEN	GOODMEN	LOCKMEN	REEDMEN	TRUEMEN
BOOKMEN	GOWNMEN	LOCOMEN	REELMEN	TURFMEN
BUSHMEN	GRIPMEN	MAGSMEN	REGIMEN	VELAMEN
BYREMEN	GUDEMEN	MAILMEN	REPOMEN	WAKEMEN
CACUMEN	HACKMEN	MALTMEN	RINGMEN	WINGMEN
CASEMEN	HANGMEN	MARKMEN	ROADMEN	WIREMEN
CAVEMEN	HARDMEN	MASHMEN	RODSMEN	WOODMEN
CERUMEN	HEADMEN	MEATMEN	RUCKMEN	WOOLMEN
CHAPMEN	HEGUMEN	MESSMEN	SAGAMEN	WORKMEN
CLUBMEN	HELIMEN	MILKMEN	SANDMEN	YARDMEN
COALMEN	HERDMEN	MOBSMEN	SEEDMEN	YEGGMEN
CREWMEN	HIGHMEN	MOLIMEN	SHIPMEN	
DAYSMEN	HILLMEN	MOORMEN	SHOPMEN	

Eight-letter words

AIRWOMEN	BOTHYMEN	COLORMEN	FREEDMEN	HENCHMEN
ALDERMEN	BRAKEMEN	CORPSMEN	FRESHMEN	HERDSMEN
BAILSMEN	BRIDEMEN	CRAGSMEN	FRONTMEN	HOASTMEN
BANDSMEN	BRINKMEN	CYCLAMEN	FUGLEMEN	HOISTMEN
BANDYMEN	BUTTYMEN	DAIRYMEN	FUNNYMEN	HORSEMEN
BANKSMEN	CHAINMEN	DALESMEN	GAMESMEN	HOTELMEN
BARGEMEN	CHAIRMEN	DOOMSMEN	GANGSMEN	HOUSEMEN
BATWOMEN	CHESSMEN	DOORSMEN	GAVELMEN	HUNTSMEN
BEADSMEN	CHINAMEN	DRAGOMEN	GILDSMEN	ISLESMEN
BEDESMEN	CHOIRMEN	DRAGSMEN	GLASSMEN	KNIFEMEN
BLUESMEN	CHOREMEN	DUTCHMEN	GOADSMEN	LANDSMEN
BOARDMEN	CLANSMEN	EARTHMEN	GOWNSMEN	LAYWOMEN
BOATSMEN	CLASSMEN	EVERYMEN	GRAVAMEN	LEADSMEN
BOGEYMEN	CLINAMEN	FERRYMEN	HANDYMEN	LIEGEMEN
BONDSMEN	COACHMEN	FOILSMEN	HEADSMEN	LINESMEN
BOOGYMEN	COGNOMEN	FORGEMEN	HELMSMEN	LINKSMEN

LOCKSMEN	PLATEMEN	SEAWOMEN	STILLMEN	TRUCHMEN
LODESMEN	POINTMEN	SEEDSMEN	STOCKMEN	TRUCKMEN
LOFTSMEN	PRENOMEN	SHAREMEN	STOREMEN	UNDERMEN
MADWOMEN	PRESSMEN	SHEARMEN	STUNTMEN	VERSEMEN
MARCHMEN	PRIZEMEN	SHEEPMEN	SUPERMEN	WATCHMEN
MARKSMEN	PROSEMEN	SHIREMEN	SWAGSMEN	WATERMEN
MERESMEN	PUNTSMEN	SHOREMEN	SWEETMEN	WEALSMEN
MERRYMEN	QUILLMEN	SIDESMEN	SWINGMEN	WEIGHMEN
MONEYMEN	RADIOMEN	SONARMEN	SWORDMEN	WHALEMEN
MOTORMEN	RAFTSMEN	SOUNDMEN	TACKSMEN	WHEELMEN
NOBLEMEN	RAMPSMEN	SPACEMEN	TALESMEN	WIDOWMEN
OVERSMEN	RANCHMEN	SPADEMEN	TALLYMEN	WINCHMEN
PENWOMEN	REINSMEN	SPEARMEN	TIDESMEN	WOODSMEN
PETERMEN	RIFLEMEN	SPECIMEN	TOWNSMEN	YACHTMEN
PILOTMEN	RIVERMEN	SQUAWMEN	TOYWOMEN	YARRAMEN
PITCHMEN	ROADSMEN	STAFFMEN	TRACKMEN	
PIVOTMEN	ROUTEMEN	STALLMEN	TRAINMEN	
PLACEMEN	SALESMEN	STEELMEN	TRASHMEN	
PLAIDMEN	SCENEMEN	STICKMEN	TREWSMEN	

Words that end with -NESS

Seven-letter words

ALLNESS	FARNESS	ICINESS	ONENESS	SLYNESS
APTNESS	FATNESS	ILLNESS	OUTNESS	TWONESS
BADNESS	FEWNESS	LAXNESS	PATNESS	WAENESS
BIGNESS	FEYNESS	LIONESS	RAWNESS	WANNESS
COYNESS	FITNESS	LOWNESS	REDNESS	WETNESS
DIMNESS	FULNESS	MADNESS	RUMNESS	WITNESS
DRYNESS	GAYNESS	NEWNESS	SADNESS	WOENESS
DUENESS	HARNESS	NOWNESS	SETNESS	WRYNESS
DULNESS	HIPNESS	ODDNESS	SHINESS	
DUNNESS	HOTNESS	OLDNESS	SHYNESS	

Eight-letter words

ACHINESS	BUSINESS	DEARNESS	FAIRNESS	GOODNESS
ACIDNESS	BUSYNESS	DEEPNESS	FASTNESS	GORINESS
AGEDNESS	CAGINESS	DEFTNESS	FELLNESS	GRAYNESS
AIRINESS	CAGYNESS	DEMONESS	FINENESS	GREYNESS
ALBINESS	CAKINESS	DEWINESS	FIRMNESS	GRIMNESS
ARCHNESS	CALMNESS	DIRENESS	FLATNESS	GRUMNESS
ARIDNESS	CAMPNESS	DONENESS	FONDNESS	HALENESS
ARTINESS	CANONESS	DOPINESS	FOULNESS	HALFNESS
ASHINESS	CHICNESS	DOURNESS	FOXINESS	HARDNESS
AVIDNESS	COLDNESS	DOWFNESS	FOZINESS	HAZINESS
AWAYNESS	COOLNESS	DOZINESS	FREENESS	HERENESS
BALDNESS	COSINESS	DRABNESS	FULLNESS	HIGHNESS
BARENESS	COXINESS	DULLNESS	GAMENESS	HOKINESS
BARONESS	COZINESS	DUMBNESS	GAMINESS	HOLINESS
BASENESS	CURTNESS	DUSKNESS	GAMYNESS	HOMINESS
BASSNESS	CUTENESS	EASINESS	GASTNESS	HUGENESS
BEINNESS	DAFTNESS	EDGINESS	GLADNESS	ICKINESS
BIASNESS	DAMPNESS	EERINESS	GLEGNESS	IDLENESS
BLUENESS	DANKNESS	EVENNESS	GLIBNESS	IFFINESS
BOLDNESS	DARKNESS	EVILNESS	GLUINESS	INKINESS
BONINESS	DEADNESS	EYEDNESS	GLUMNESS	IRONNESS
BOXINESS	DEAFNESS	FAINNESS	GONENESS	JIMPNESS

JOKINESS	MEEKNESS	PIEDNESS	SEARNESS	TITANESS
JUSTNESS	MEETNESS	PINKNESS	SEEDNESS	TRIGNESS
KEENNESS	MILDNESS	PIPINESS	SELFNESS	TRIMNESS
KINDNESS	MIRINESS	PIXINESS	SEXINESS	TRUENESS
LACINESS	MOOTNESS	POKINESS	SICKNESS	TWEENESS
LAMENESS	MOPINESS	POORNESS	SIZINESS	UGLINESS
LANKNESS	MORENESS	PORINESS	SKEWNESS	VAINNESS
LATENESS	MUCHNESS	POSHNESS	SLIMNESS	VASTNESS
LAZINESS	MUTENESS	PRIMNESS	SLOWNESS	VILDNESS
LEANNESS	NAFFNESS	PUNINESS	SMUGNESS	VILENESS
LEWDNESS	NAIFNESS	PURENESS	SNUBNESS	VOIDNESS
LIKENESS	NEARNESS	RACINESS	SNUGNESS	WARINESS
LIMINESS	NEATNESS	RANKNESS	SOFTNESS	WARMNESS
LIMPNESS	NESHNESS	RAPTNESS	SOLENESS	WASTNESS
LITENESS	NEXTNESS	RARENESS	SORENESS	WAVINESS
LIVENESS	NICENESS	RASHNESS	SOURNESS	WAXINESS
LOGINESS	NIGHNESS	REALNESS	SPRYNESS	WEAKNESS
LONENESS	NOSINESS	RICHNESS	SUCHNESS	WELLNESS
LONGNESS	NUDENESS	RIFENESS	SURENESS	WHATNESS
LORNNESS	NULLNESS	RIMINESS	TALLNESS	WIDENESS
LOSTNESS	NUMBNESS	RIPENESS	TAMENESS	WILDNESS
LOTHNESS	OILINESS	ROPINESS	TARTNESS	WILINESS
LOUDNESS	OOZINESS	ROSINESS	TAUTNESS	WIRINESS
LUNINESS	OPENNESS	RUDENESS	THATNESS	WISENESS
LUSHNESS	OVALNESS	SAFENESS	THINNESS	WOODNESS
MALENESS	PACKNESS	SAGENESS	THISNESS	WORNNESS
MATINESS	PALENESS	SALTNESS	THUSNESS	ZANINESS
MAZINESS	PASTNESS	SAMENESS	TIDINESS	
MEANNESS	PERTNESS	SANENESS	TININESS	

Words that end with -OID

Seven-letter words

ACAROID	COLLOID	FIBROID	MYELOID	SIGMOID
ADENOID	CORMOID	FUNGOID	NAEVOID	SIMIOID
AGAMOID	COSMOID	GLENOID	NEGROID	SPAROID
AGATOID	COTTOID	GLOBOID	NEUROID	SPIROID
AMBROID	CRICOID	GOBIOID	OBOVOID	SPOROID
AMEBOID	CRINOID	HAEMOID	OCELOID	STEROID
AMYLOID	CTENOID	HAPLOID	OCHROID	STYLOID
ANDROID	CYCLOID	HELCOID	OIDIOID	TABLOID
ANEROID	CYSTOID	HISTOID	OSTEOID	TENIOID
ANTHOID	DELTOID	HYALOID	PERCOID	THEROID
ARCTOID	DENTOID	HYDROID	PHACOID	THYROID
ASTROID	DERMOID	HYENOID	PHYTOID	TIGROID
BYSSOID	DESMOID	HYPNOID	PIGMOID	TURDOID
CACTOID	DIPLOID	LABROID	PLACOID	TYPHOID
CESTOID	DISCOID	LENTOID	PYGMOID	VALGOID
CHELOID	EMEROID	LIANOID	QUINOID	VESPOID
CHOROID	ERICOID	LITHOID	RHIZOID	VISCOID
CIRSOID	ETHMOID	MASTOID	SARCOID	XIPHOID
CISSOID	EUPLOID	MATTOID	SAUROID	ZEBROID
COCCOID	FACTOID	MUSCOID	SIALOID	ZINCOID

Eight-letter words

ACTINOID	AMBEROID	AMOEBOID	ARILLOID	ATHETOID
ALKALOID	AMMONOID	ANCONOID	ASTEROID	AUTACOID

Words that end with -NESS

AUTOCOID	ERGATOID	MELANOID	PSYCHOID	SQUALOID
BLASTOID	GABBROID	MUCINOID	PYRANOID	STURNOID
BOTRYOID	GALENOID	MYCELOID	PYRENOID	TAENIOID
CALYCOID	GEOMYOID	MYTILOID	RACEMOID	TAPIROID
CAMELOID	GROUPOID	NEMATOID	RESINOID	TARSIOID
CANCROID	GYNECOID	NEPHROID	RETINOID	TERATOID
CARDIOID	HELICOID	NOCTUOID	RHABDOID	TETANOID
CATENOID	HEMATOID	NUCLEOID	RHOMBOID	THALLOID
CENTROID	HISTIOID	ODONTOID	SCAPHOID	THYREOID
CERATOID	HOMALOID	OMOHYOID	SCHIZOID	THYRSOID
CHOREOID	HOMINOID	ONISCOID	SCINCOID	TRENDOID
CHORIOID	HUMANOID	PARANOID	SCIUROID	TRICHOID
CICHLOID	HYDATOID	PAROTOID	SCLEROID	TRIPLOID
CLUPEOID	HYRACOID	PETALOID	SEPALOID	TROCHOID
CONCHOID	INDIGOID	PEZIZOID	SESAMOID	TUBEROID
CORACOID	ISTHMOID	PHALLOID	SILUROID	VARICOID
CORONOID	KERATOID	PHELLOID	SINUSOID	VIBRIOID
COTYLOID	LAMBDOID	PHYLLOID	SISTROID	VIRUSOID
DENDROID	LEMUROID	PINACOID	SLEAZOID	VOLUTOID
DORIDOID	LIGULOID	PINAKOID	SOLENOID	YPSILOID
ECHINOID	LIMULOID	PITYROID	SORICOID	
ELYTROID	LYMPHOID	PLASMOID	SPHENOID	
EMBRYOID	MANATOID	POLYPOID	SPHEROID	
EMULSOID	MEDUSOID	PRISMOID	SPONGOID	

Words that end with -OR

Seven-letter words

ABACTOR	COACTOR	FUNCTOR	NEGATOR	SCISSOR
ABETTOR	CREATOR	GENITOR	NONPOOR	SENATOR
ABLATOR	CURATOR	GRANTOR	OBLIGOR	SEPTUOR
ADAPTOR	DEBITOR	GYRATOR	OFFEROR	SETTLOR
ADJUROR	DECOLOR	HERITOR	OUTDOOR	SEXTUOR
ADVISOR	DELATOR	HUMIDOR	PANDOOR	SIGNIOR
AERATOR	DEVISOR	IGNITOR	PARADOR	SIMILOR
AGISTOR	DILATOR	IMPEDOR	PARITOR	SPONSOR
ALASTOR	DILUTOR	INCISOR	PICADOR	SQUALOR
ALIENOR	DIVISOR	ISOCHOR	PLEDGOR	STENTOR
ANAPHOR	DONATOR	JANITOR	PLESSOR	STERTOR
ASSUROR	EDUCTOR	LANGUOR	PRAETOR	STRIDOR
ATHANOR	EJECTOR	LAXATOR	PRESSOR	TANDOOR
AUDITOR	ELECTOR	LEGATOR	PROCTOR	TEMBLOR
AVIATOR	EMPEROR	LEVATOR	QUESTOR	TRACTOR
BELABOR	EMULSOR	LOCATOR	QUITTOR	TRAITOR
BICOLOR	ENACTOR	MACHZOR	REACTOR	TRUSTOR
BIOPHOR	EQUATOR	MALODOR	REALTOR	TWISTOR
CAMPHOR	ERECTOR	MAORMOR	RECOLOR	UNVISOR
CHADDOR	EVERTOR	MARKHOR	RELATOR	VAVASOR
CHANTOR	EVICTOR	MATADOR	REVISOR	VENATOR
CHIKHOR	EXACTOR	MIRADOR	REVIVOR	VISITOR
CITATOR	EXCITOR	MONITOR	ROTATOR	WARRIOR
CLANGOR	FEOFFOR	MORMAOR	SANTOOR	ZELATOR

Eight-letter words

ABDUCTOR	ACCEPTOR	ADDUCTOR	ADULATOR	ALACHLOR
ACCENTOR	ACTUATOR	ADJUSTOR	AGITATOR	ANCESTOR

ANIMATOR	CURSITOR	IMPELLOR	NONMAJOR	RETAILOR
ANTERIOR	CUSPIDOR	IMPOSTOR	OBJECTOR	RONCADOR
APPELLOR	DEFECTOR	INCENSOR	OBSESSOR	SCULPTOR
ARRESTOR	DEFLATOR	INCEPTOR	OBVIATOR	SEAFLOOR
ASPERSOR	DEMEANOR	INDENTOR	OCCLUSOR	SECRETOR
ASSENTOR	DEPICTOR	INDICTOR	OPERATOR	SECTATOR
ASSERTOR	DETECTOR	INDORSOR	OUTHUMOR	SEDUCTOR
ASSESSOR	DEVIATOR	INDUCTOR	OUTSAVOR	SEIGNIOR
ASSIGNOR	DICTATOR	INFECTOR	PALPATOR	SELECTOR
ASSISTOR	DIFFUSOR	INFERIOR	PARACHOR	SERVITOR
ATTESTOR	DIGESTOR	INFLATOR	PATENTOR	SPLENDOR
AVIGATOR	DIRECTOR	INJECTOR	PHOSPHOR	STRESSOR
BACHELOR	DISCOLOR	INTERIOR	PISCATOR	SUBFLOOR
BACKDOOR	DISFAVOR	INVENTOR	PLEDGEOR	SUBPRIOR
BARRATOR	DISHONOR	INVERTOR	PREDATOR	SUPERIOR
BARRETOR	EDUCATOR	INVESTOR	PREVISOR	SURVEYOR
BECLAMOR	EFFECTOR	IODOPHOR	PRODITOR	SURVIVOR
BEGLAMOR	ELEVATOR	ISOLATOR	PROLABOR	TESTATOR
BEHAVIOR	ELICITOR	KOMONDOR	PROMISOR	THEREFOR
BELIQUOR	EMANATOR	KURVEYOR	PROMOTOR	THRUSTOR
BISECTOR	EMBRASOR	LABRADOR	PRONATOR	TITRATOR
CANEPHOR	EMULATOR	LAUDATOR	PROVEDOR	TOREADOR
CAVEATOR	ENDEAVOR	LICENSOR	PROVIDOR	TRADITOR
CHELATOR	ENDORSOR	MAINDOOR	PROVISOR	TRAPDOOR
COANCHOR	EPILATOR	MANDATOR	PULMOTOR	TRICOLOR
COAUTHOR	EVOCATOR	MARKHOOR	PULSATOR	TRIMOTOR
CODEBTOR	EXCEPTOR	MEDIATOR	PUNDONOR	ULTERIOR
COEDITOR	EXECUTOR	METAPHOR	PURVEYOR	UNANCHOR
COENAMOR	EXPANDOR	MIGRATOR	QUAESTOR	UNICOLOR
COFACTOR	EXPIATOR	MISCOLOR	RADIATOR	URINATOR
COLESSOR	EXTENSOR	MISLABOR	RECAPTOR	UTILIDOR
COLLATOR	EXTERIOR	MISTUTOR	RECENSOR	VALUATOR
CONCOLOR	FELLATOR	NARRATOR	RECEPTOR	VARACTOR
CONJUROR	GILLYVOR	NEIGHBOR	REDACTOR	VARISTOR
CONVENOR	GOVERNOR	NEXTDOOR	REDUCTOR	VAVASSOR
CONVEYOR	HELIODOR	NITRATOR	REGRATOR	VERDEROR
COPASTOR	HYDRATOR	NONACTOR	REJECTOR	VIBRATOR
CORRIDOR	IDOLATOR	NONCOLOR	RELEASOR	VIOLATOR
CREDITOR	IMITATOR	NONJUROR	REMITTOR	VITIATOR
CREMATOR	IMPACTOR	NONLABOR	RESISTOR	WHEREFOR

Words that end with -OUS

Seven-letter words

ACAJOUS	ARENOUS	BURNOUS	CORIOUS	FIBROUS
ACEROUS	ATHEOUS	CACHOUS	CORMOUS	FOLIOUS
ACETOUS	ATOKOUS	CALLOUS	COYPOUS	FULVOUS
ACINOUS	AZOTOUS	CARIOUS	CUPROUS	FUNGOUS
ADIPOUS	AZYGOUS	CASEOUS	CURIOUS	FURIOUS
AENEOUS	AZYMOUS	CEREOUS	DEVIOUS	FUSCOUS
AGAMOUS	BADIOUS	CESIOUS	DUBIOUS	GALLOUS
AMADOUS	BILIOUS	CHYLOUS	DUTEOUS	GASEOUS
AMOROUS	BINIOUS	CHYMOUS	EMULOUS	GEALOUS
ANUROUS	BIVIOUS	CIRROUS	ENVIOUS	GIBBOUS
ANXIOUS	BOUBOUS	CITROUS	ESTROUS	GLEBOUS
APODOUS	BRUMOUS	COCCOUS	FATUOUS	GLOBOUS
AQUEOUS	BULBOUS	CONGOUS	FEATOUS	GRUMOUS
ARDUOUS	BULLOUS	COPIOUS	FERROUS	GUMMOUS

Words that end with -OR

HEINOUS	NIMIOUS	PARLOUS	RUBIOUS	UMBROUS
HERBOUS	NIOBOUS	PERLOUS	RUINOUS	URANOUS
HIDEOUS	NITROUS	PETROUS	SANIOUS	URINOUS
HOUMOUS	NIVEOUS	PICEOUS	SARCOUS	USUROUS
HUGEOUS	NOCUOUS	PILEOUS	SERIOUS	VACUOUS
HYDROUS	NOXIOUS	PISTOUS	SIMIOUS	VALGOUS
IGNEOUS	OBVIOUS	PITEOUS	SINUOUS	VARIOUS
IMPIOUS	OCHROUS	PLUMOUS	SOUKOUS	VEINOUS
INVIOUS	ODOROUS	POMPOUS	SPINOUS	VICIOUS
JEALOUS	OMINOUS	PORTOUS	SPUMOUS	VIDUOUS
LENTOUS	ONEROUS	PULPOUS	SUCCOUS	VILLOUS
LEPROUS	ONYMOUS	RAMEOUS	TALCOUS	VISCOUS
LIMBOUS	OPACOUS	RAUCOUS	TEDIOUS	VOUDOUS
LUTEOUS	OSMIOUS	RHODOUS	TENUOUS	ZEALOUS
MEVROUS	OSSEOUS	RIOTOUS	TIMEOUS	ZINCOUS
NACROUS	OZONOUS	ROUCOUS	TYPHOUS	
NERVOUS	PAPPOUS	ROUTOUS	UBEROUS	

Eight-letter words

ACARPOUS	COUSCOUS	FEVEROUS	MIASMOUS	RAVENOUS
ACAULOUS	COVETOUS	FIDDIOUS	MUCINOUS	RESINOUS
ACOELOUS	COVINOUS	FLATUOUS	MUTICOUS	RIGOROUS
ADUNCOUS	CRANKOUS	FLEXUOUS	MUTINOUS	ROSINOUS
AMBEROUS	CRIBROUS	FRABJOUS	NACREOUS	RUCTIOUS
ANGINOUS	CROCEOUS	FRONDOUS	NAUSEOUS	RUMOROUS
ANGULOUS	CROUPOUS	GEMINOUS	NEBULOUS	SABULOUS
ANOUROUS	CUMBROUS	GEMMEOUS	NEMOROUS	SAPAJOUS
ANSEROUS	CUMULOUS	GENEROUS	NIDOROUS	SAPOROUS
ANTICOUS	CUPREOUS	GLABROUS	NODULOUS	SAVOROUS
APHONOUS	DARTROUS	GLAREOUS	NUBILOUS	SCABIOUS
APHTHOUS	DECOROUS	GLAUCOUS	NUMEROUS	SCABROUS
APTEROUS	DESIROUS	GLORIOUS	NUMINOUS	SCARIOUS
ARACEOUS	DEXTROUS	GOITROUS	OCHEROUS	SCIOLOUS
ARANEOUS	DIDYMOUS	GORGEOUS	OCHREOUS	SCLEROUS
ARBOROUS	DIECIOUS	GRACIOUS	OESTROUS	SCORIOUS
ARSENOUS	DIGAMOUS	GRIEVOUS	OOGAMOUS	SEDULOUS
ARSONOUS	DIGYNOUS	GRISEOUS	ORAGIOUS	SELENOUS
ASPEROUS	DIMEROUS	GYPSEOUS	ORDUROUS	SENSUOUS
ASTOMOUS	DIOICOUS	HALITOUS	ORGULOUS	SEPALOUS
ATROPOUS	DIPNOOUS	HAMULOUS	OVARIOUS	SETULOUS
BIBULOUS	DITOKOUS	HUMOROUS	PABULOUS	SIBILOUS
BIGAMOUS	DIZYGOUS	ICHOROUS	PALUDOUS	SOMBROUS
BIJUGOUS	DOLOROUS	IDONEOUS	PAPULOUS	SONOROUS
BIMANOUS	EDACIOUS	IMPOROUS	PATULOUS	SOPOROUS
BIPAROUS	ELYTROUS	INCUBOUS	PERILOUS	SPACIOUS
BIRAMOUS	ENGINOUS	INERMOUS	PERVIOUS	SPECIOUS
BUTYROUS	ENORMOUS	INFAMOUS	PETALOUS	SPERMOUS
CADUCOUS	EPIGEOUS	KOUSKOUS	PLUMBOUS	SPURIOUS
CAESIOUS	EUROKOUS	LACTEOUS	PLUVIOUS	SQUAMOUS
CANOROUS	EXIGUOUS	LAMINOUS	POACEOUS	STANNOUS
CAPTIOUS	EXIMIOUS	LEAPROUS	POLYPOUS	STOCIOUS
CARIBOUS	FABULOUS	LIBELOUS	POPULOUS	STOTIOUS
CARNEOUS	FACTIOUS	LIGNEOUS	PORTEOUS	STRATOUS
CAUTIOUS	FASHIOUS	LUMINOUS	PRECIOUS	STRUMOUS
CERNUOUS	FASTUOUS	LUSCIOUS	PREVIOUS	STUDIOUS
CHLOROUS	FEATEOUS	LUSTROUS	PYRITOUS	SUBEROUS
CHROMOUS	FEATUOUS	MANITOUS	PYRRHOUS	SUDOROUS
CITREOUS	FELONOUS	MARABOUS	RACEMOUS	TEMEROUS
CORNEOUS	FERREOUS	MELANOUS	RAMULOUS	TENUIOUS

THALLOUS	TUBULOUS	UNJOYOUS	VENULOUS	WAVEROUS
TIMOROUS	TUMOROUS	USURIOUS	VERTUOUS	WONDROUS
TINAMOUS	TUMULOUS	UXORIOUS	VIGOROUS	WRONGOUS
TITANOUS	TURACOUS	VALOROUS	VIPEROUS	XANTHOUS
TORTIOUS	ULCEROUS	VANADOUS	VIRTUOUS	YTTRIOUS
TORTUOUS	UNCTUOUS	VAPOROUS	VITREOUS	
TRAPPOUS	UNDULOUS	VENOMOUS	VOMITOUS	
TUBEROUS	UNFAMOUS	VENTROUS	WAMEFOUS	

Words that end with -OUT

Seven-letter words

ASPROUT	COOKOUT	HIDEOUT	ROLLOUT	TURNOUT
BACKOUT	DROPOUT	HOLDOUT	SELLOUT	UNSHOUT
BAILOUT	EELPOUT	LOCKOUT	SHUTOUT	WALKOUT
BESHOUT	FADEOUT	LOOKOUT	SICKOUT	WASHOUT
BESPOUT	FALLOUT	MISSOUT	SLIPOUT	WIDEOUT
BLOWOUT	FOLDOUT	PASSOUT	SPINOUT	WIPEOUT
BURGOUT	GRAYOUT	PULLOUT	SURTOUT	WITHOUT
BURNOUT	HANDOUT	RAINOUT	TAKEOUT	WORKOUT
CAMPOUT	HANGOUT	READOUT	TIMEOUT	

Eight-letter words

BLACKOUT	FREAKOUT	PHASEOUT	SHAKEOUT	THEREOUT
BREAKOUT	GADABOUT	PITCHOUT	SHOOTOUT	UNDEVOUT
BROWNOUT	HORNPOUT	PRINTOUT	SLEEPOUT	WATCHOUT
BULLPOUT	INDEVOUT	RACAHOUT	SPEAKOUT	WHEREOUT
CARRYOUT	KNOCKOUT	RESPROUT	STAKEOUT	WHITEOUT
CHECKOUT	LAYABOUT	RUNABOUT	STANDOUT	
CLOSEOUT	MARABOUT	SEASCOUT	STICKOUT	
FLAMEOUT	OUTSHOUT	SEATROUT	TACAHOUT	

Words that end with -SET

Seven-letter words

BACKSET	FILMSET	KNESSET	OVERSET	TYPESET
BONESET	HANDSET	LOCKSET	SEAMSET	
BRASSET	HARDSET	MINDSET	SIROSET	
CHIPSET	HAROSET	MOONSET	TOOLSET	
CRESSET	HEADSET	NAILSET	TWINSET	

Eight-letter words

CHAROSET	HEAVYSET	PHOTOSET	SOMERSET	THORNSET
EARTHSET	MARMOSET	QUICKSET	THICKSET	UNDERSET

Words that end with -SHIP

Seven-letter words

AIRSHIP	FOXSHIP	KINSHIP	PALSHIP	WARSHIP
DOGSHIP	GODSHIP	LUDSHIP	PRESHIP	WORSHIP
DONSHIP	GUNSHIP	MIDSHIP	SIBSHIP	
ENDSHIP	HERSHIP	NUNSHIP	SONSHIP	

Words that end with -OUS

Eight-letter words

AMID**SHIP**	DUKE**SHIP**	HEIR**SHIP**	PEAT**SHIP**	TRAN**SHIP**
ANTI**SHIP**	EARL**SHIP**	HERO**SHIP**	POET**SHIP**	TREE**SHIP**
BARD**SHIP**	FIRE**SHIP**	KING**SHIP**	POPE**SHIP**	TWIN**SHIP**
CHUM**SHIP**	FLAG**SHIP**	LADY**SHIP**	RAJA**SHIP**	WARD**SHIP**
CLAN**SHIP**	FORE**SHIP**	LONG**SHIP**	SERF**SHIP**	WIND**SHIP**
DEAN**SHIP**	GURU**SHIP**	LORD**SHIP**	STAR**SHIP**	
DEMY**SHIP**	HARD**SHIP**	MAGE**SHIP**	TANK**SHIP**	
DOGE**SHIP**	HEAD**SHIP**	MATE**SHIP**	TOWN**SHIP**	

Words that end with -SKIN

Seven-letter words

CAT**SKIN**	DOG**SKIN**	KID**SKIN**	PIG**SKIN**
COW**SKIN**	FOX**SKIN**	KIP**SKIN**	RED**SKIN**
DOE**SKIN**	GRI**SKIN**	OIL**SKIN**	

Eight-letter words

BEAR**SKIN**	COON**SKIN**	FORE**SKIN**	PONY**SKIN**	WINE**SKIN**
BUCK**SKIN**	DAMA**SKIN**	GOAT**SKIN**	SEAL**SKIN**	WOLF**SKIN**
CALF**SKIN**	DEER**SKIN**	LAMB**SKIN**	SWAN**SKIN**	WOOD**SKIN**
CAPE**SKIN**	FISH**SKIN**	MOLE**SKIN**	TURN**SKIN**	WOOL**SKIN**

Words that end with -SMAN

Seven-letter words

ALM**SMAN**	GAD**SMAN**	MES**SMAN**	ODD**SMAN**	TOP**SMAN**
ART**SMAN**	KIN**SMAN**	MOB**SMAN**	PAS**SMAN**	
BAT**SMAN**	LEN**SMAN**	NEW**SMAN**	ROD**SMAN**	
DAY**SMAN**	MAG**SMAN**	OAR**SMAN**	TAP**SMAN**	

Eight-letter words

BAIL**SMAN**	CRAG**SMAN**	HEAD**SMAN**	MARK**SMAN**	SWAG**SMAN**
BAND**SMAN**	DALE**SMAN**	HELM**SMAN**	MERE**SMAN**	TACK**SMAN**
BANK**SMAN**	DOOM**SMAN**	HERD**SMAN**	OVER**SMAN**	TALE**SMAN**
BEAD**SMAN**	DOOR**SMAN**	HUNT**SMAN**	PRESS**MAN**	TALI**SMAN**
BEDE**SMAN**	DRAG**SMAN**	ISLE**SMAN**	PUNT**SMAN**	TIDE**SMAN**
BLUE**SMAN**	FOIL**SMAN**	LAND**SMAN**	RAFT**SMAN**	TOWN**SMAN**
BOAT**SMAN**	GAME**SMAN**	LEAD**SMAN**	RAMP**SMAN**	TREW**SMAN**
BOND**SMAN**	GANG**SMAN**	LINE**SMAN**	REIN**SMAN**	WEAL**SMAN**
CHESS**MAN**	GILD**SMAN**	LINK**SMAN**	ROAD**SMAN**	WOOD**SMAN**
CLAN**SMAN**	GLAS**SMAN**	LOCK**SMAN**	SALE**SMAN**	
CLAS**SMAN**	GOAD**SMAN**	LODE**SMAN**	SEED**SMAN**	
CORP**SMAN**	GOWN**SMAN**	LOFT**SMAN**	SIDE**SMAN**	

Words that end with -SMEN

Seven-letter words

ALM**SMEN**	BAT**SMEN**	GAD**SMEN**	LEN**SMEN**	MES**SMEN**
ART**SMEN**	DAY**SMEN**	KIN**SMEN**	MAG**SMEN**	MOB**SMEN**

NEWSMEN	ODDSMEN	RODSMEN	TOPSMEN
OARSMEN	PASSMEN	TAPSMEN	

Eight-letter words

BAILSMEN	CRAGSMEN	HEADSMEN	MARKSMEN	SWAGSMEN
BANDSMEN	DALESMEN	HELMSMEN	MERESMEN	TACKSMEN
BANKSMEN	DOOMSMEN	HERDSMEN	OVERSMEN	TALESMEN
BEADSMEN	DOORSMEN	HUNTSMEN	PRESSMEN	TIDESMEN
BEDESMEN	DRAGSMEN	ISLESMEN	PUNTSMEN	TOWNSMEN
BLUESMEN	FOILSMEN	LANDSMEN	RAFTSMEN	TREWSMEN
BOATSMEN	GAMESMEN	LEADSMEN	RAMPSMEN	WEALSMEN
BONDSMEN	GANGSMEN	LINESMEN	REINSMEN	WOODSMEN
CHESSMEN	GILDSMEN	LINKSMEN	ROADSMEN	
CLANSMEN	GLASSMEN	LOCKSMEN	SALESMEN	
CLASSMEN	GOADSMEN	LODESMEN	SEEDSMEN	
CORPSMEN	GOWNSMEN	LOFTSMEN	SIDESMEN	

Words that end with -SOME

Seven-letter words

AWESOME	FULSOME	NOISOME	TRISOME	WAESOME
BEESOME	GAYSOME	NOYSOME	TWASOME	WAGSOME
EPISOME	IRKSOME	OXYSOME	TWOSOME	WINSOME
EYESOME	LISSOME	TOYSOME	UROSOME	WOESOME

Eight-letter words

ACROSOME	FLAYSOME	HANDSOME	LOVESOME	ROOMSOME
AUTOSOME	FLEASOME	HEALSOME	LYSOSOME	TEDISOME
BORESOME	FOURSOME	HOLESOME	MEROSOME	TIRESOME
CLOYSOME	FRETSOME	JOKESOME	MESOSOME	TOILSOME
CYTOSOME	GAMESOME	LARKSOME	MONOSOME	TWIGSOME
DARKSOME	GLADSOME	LIFESOME	MURKSOME	WAILSOME
DOLESOME	GLEESOME	LIPOSOME	PLAYSOME	WORKSOME
DUELSOME	GONOSOME	LONESOME	POLYSOME	
ENDOSOME	GREWSOME	LONGSOME	PYROSOME	
FEARSOME	GRUESOME	LOTHSOME	RIBOSOME	

Words that end with -TIME

Seven-letter words

AIRTIME	BIGTIME	LAYTIME	PASTIME	TEATIME
ANYTIME	CENTIME	MISTIME	RAGTIME	WARTIME
BEDTIME	DAYTIME	ONETIME	SEPTIME	

Eight-letter words

CHOWTIME	HALFTIME	MEANTIME	SEEDTIME	XENOTIME
DOWNTIME	LIFETIME	NOONTIME	SHOWTIME	ZONETIME
FLEXTIME	LONGTIME	OVERTIME	SOMETIME	
FORETIME	MARITIME	PLAYTIME	TERMTIME	
GOODTIME	MEALTIME	REALTIME		

Words that end with -SMEN

Words that end with -TION

Seven-letter words

ALATION	COCTION	ENATION	OVATION	TACTION
AMATION	COITION	FACTION	PACTION	TUITION
AMOTION	DICTION	FICTION	PORTION	UNCTION
AUCTION	EDITION	LECTION	RECTION	UNITION
BASTION	ELATION	MENTION	RUCTION	
CANTION	ELUTION	MICTION	SECTION	
CAPTION	EMOTION	MIXTION	STATION	
CAUTION	EMPTION	ORATION	SUCTION	

Eight-letter words

ABLATION	DILATION	FUNCTION	LUNATION	RELATION
ABLUTION	DILUTION	GELATION	LUXATION	REMOTION
ABORTION	DONATION	GUMPTION	MONITION	ROGATION
ADAPTION	DOTATION	GYRATION	MUNITION	ROTATION
ADDITION	DURATION	HALATION	MUTATION	SANCTION
ADNATION	EDUCTION	HIMATION	NATATION	SCONTION
ADOPTION	EGESTION	IDEATION	NEGATION	SEDATION
AERATION	EJECTION	IGNITION	NIDATION	SEDITION
AGNATION	ELECTION	ILLATION	NIVATION	SOLATION
AMBITION	EMICTION	INACTION	NODATION	SOLUTION
AUDITION	ENACTION	INUSTION	NOLITION	SORPTION
AVIATION	EQUATION	IODATION	NOTATION	STICTION
BIBATION	ERECTION	JOBATION	NOVATION	SUDATION
CIBATION	ERUPTION	JUNCTION	NUDATION	SWAPTION
CITATION	EVECTION	LAVATION	NUTATION	TAXATION
COACTION	EVICTION	LAXATION	OBLATION	TRACTION
CONATION	EXACTION	LEGATION	PACATION	VACATION
COOPTION	EXERTION	LENITION	PETITION	VENATION
CREATION	FETATION	LIBATION	POSITION	VEXATION
DELATION	FIXATION	LIGATION	POTATION	VOCATION
DELETION	FLECTION	LIMATION	PUNITION	VOLITION
DEMOTION	FRACTION	LOBATION	PUPATION	VOLUTION
DERATION	FRICTION	LOCATION	QUESTION	ZONATION
DEVOTION	FRUITION	LOCUTION	REACTION	

Words that end with -URE

Seven-letter words

ABATURE	DISCURE	GYPLURE	PASTURE	SEISURE
BORDURE	EPICURE	HACHURE	PERDURE	SEIZURE
BRAVURE	ERASURE	LEASURE	PERJURE	SEYSURE
BRISURE	FACTURE	LECTURE	PICTURE	SOILURE
CAPTURE	FAILURE	LEISURE	PLEXURE	STATURE
CENSURE	FEATURE	MEASURE	POSTURE	TEXTURE
CLOSURE	FISSURE	MIXTURE	PRECURE	TONSURE
CLOTURE	FIXTURE	MONTURE	PROCURE	TORTURE
COENURE	FLEXURE	MORSURE	PULTURE	VENTURE
CONJURE	FRISURE	MULTURE	PURPURE	VERDURE
COUPURE	FRITURE	NERVURE	RAPTURE	VESTURE
COUTURE	GARBURE	NURTURE	RECOURE	VOITURE
CULTURE	GESTURE	OBSCURE	RONDURE	VULTURE
DASYURE	GRAVURE	OUTDURE	RUPTURE	WAFTURE
DENTURE	GUIPURE	PARTURE	SEASURE	

Eight-letter words

ANNEXURE	CREATURE	GENITURE	OVERSURE	RESECURE
APERTURE	CUBATURE	HUMITURE	OVERTURE	ROUNDURE
ARCATURE	CYNOSURE	IMMATURE	PAINTURE	SCISSURE
ARMATURE	DENATURE	INCISURE	PEDICURE	SCRIMURE
AVENTURE	DISCOURE	INSECURE	PLEASURE	SINECURE
BROCHURE	DISINURE	JOINTURE	PRESSURE	TAINTURE
CEINTURE	DOUBLURE	JUNCTURE	PUNCTURE	TINCTURE
CINCTURE	ENACTURE	LIGATURE	REASSURE	TOURNURE
CISELURE	ENCOLURE	LINCTURE	REFIGURE	TREASURE
COCKSURE	EXPOSURE	MANICURE	REINJURE	TRESSURE
COENDURE	FILATURE	MOISTURE	REINSURE	TUBULURE
COIFFURE	FIXATURE	OSSATURE	RENATURE	
COINSURE	FRACTURE	OVERCURE	REPOSURE	

Words that end with -WARD

Seven-letter words

AIRWARD	FROWARD	LEEWARD	OUTWARD	SUNWARD
AWKWARD	GODWARD	MANWARD	SEAWARD	VANWARD
BEDWARD	HAYWARD	NAYWARD	SKYWARD	WAYWARD
FORWARD	HOGWARD	NORWARD	STEWARD	WEYWARD

Eight-letter words

BACKWARD	FOREWARD	HOMEWARD	PARKWARD	THRAWARD
BEARWARD	GOALWARD	KIRKWARD	POLEWARD	UNTOWARD
BECOWARD	HEADWARD	LANDWARD	REARWARD	WESTWARD
CITYWARD	HELLWARD	LEFTWARD	REREWARD	WINDWARD
DOWNWARD	HINDWARD	MISAWARD	SELFWARD	WOODWARD
EASTWARD	HIVEWARD	MOONWARD	SIDEWARD	WOOLWARD

Words that end with -WARDS

Seven-letter words

ADWARDS	INWARDS	REWARDS	UPWARDS	VAWARDS
COWARDS	ONWARDS	TOWARDS	USWARDS	

Eight-letter words

AIRWARDS	GODWARDS	MANWARDS	SEAWARDS
BEDWARDS	HAYWARDS	NAYWARDS	SKYWARDS
FORWARDS	HOGWARDS	NORWARDS	STEWARDS
FROWARDS	LEEWARDS	OUTWARDS	SUNWARDS

Words that end with -WAY

Seven-letter words

ARCHWAY	BIKEWAY	CUTAWAY	FARAWAY	FOLKWAY
AREAWAY	CARAWAY	DOORWAY	FISHWAY	FOOTWAY
BELTWAY	CARTWAY	FAIRWAY	FLYAWAY	FREEWAY

Words that end with -URE

GANGWAY	LAYAWAY	RAILWAY	SKIDWAY	TRAMWAY
GATEWAY	LICHWAY	RINGWAY	SLIPWAY	WALKWAY
GETAWAY	LIFEWAY	ROADWAY	SOMEWAY	WELAWAY
HADAWAY	PACEWAY	RODEWAY	SPURWAY	WINDWAY
HALFWAY	PACKWAY	ROLLWAY	TAXIWAY	WIREWAY
HALLWAY	PARKWAY	ROPEWAY	THRUWAY	
HEADWAY	PARTWAY	RUNAWAY	TIDEWAY	
HIGHWAY	PATHWAY	SHIPWAY	TOLLWAY	
LANEWAY	RACEWAY	SIDEWAY	TOWAWAY	

Eight-letter words

AISLEWAY	DRANGWAY	HEREAWAY	ROLLAWAY	TEARAWAY
ALLEYWAY	DRIVEWAY	HIDEAWAY	ROUTEWAY	THATAWAY
BROADWAY	ENTRYWAY	HOISTWAY	SLIDEWAY	THISAWAY
CABLEWAY	EVERYWAY	HORSEWAY	SOAKAWAY	TRACKWAY
CARRAWAY	FADEAWAY	HUNTAWAY	SOARAWAY	TRAINWAY
CASTAWAY	FALLAWAY	LOCKAWAY	SPEEDWAY	UNDERWAY
CAUSEWAY	FLOODWAY	MOTORWAY	SPILLWAY	WALKAWAY
CLEARWAY	FOLDAWAY	MULLOWAY	STAIRWAY	WASHAWAY
COLORWAY	GIVEAWAY	OVERSWAY	STAYAWAY	WASTEWAY
CRAWLWAY	GREENWAY	RIDGEWAY	STERNWAY	WATERWAY
CROSSWAY	GUIDEWAY	RIVERWAY	STOWAWAY	WELLAWAY
CYCLEWAY	HATCHWAY	ROCKAWAY	TAKEAWAY	WIDTHWAY

Words that end with -WISE

Seven-letter words

AIRWISE	ENDWISE	MANWISE	SUNWISE
ANYWISE	FANWISE	MAPWISE	TAXWISE

Eight-letter words

ARCHWISE	EDGEWISE	LONGWISE	SIDEWISE	TENTWISE
BENDWISE	ELSEWISE	OVERWISE	SOMEWISE	THUSWISE
COMBWISE	FESSWISE	PAIRWISE	STEPWISE	WARPWISE
CRABWISE	FLATWISE	PALEWISE	SUCHWISE	WEFTWISE
DROPWISE	LIKEWISE	RINGWISE	TEAMWISE	

Words that end with -WOOD

Seven-letter words

BARWOOD	CAMWOOD	ELMWOOD	LOGWOOD	SAPWOOD
BAYWOOD	DAGWOOD	FATWOOD	NUTWOOD	
BOGWOOD	DOGWOOD	GUMWOOD	PLYWOOD	
BOXWOOD	DYEWOOD	INKWOOD	REDWOOD	

Eight-letter words

AGALWOOD	BEEFWOOD	CORDWOOD	FIREWOOD	HAREWOOD
BACKWOOD	BENTWOOD	CORKWOOD	FUELWOOD	IRONWOOD
BASSWOOD	BLUEWOOD	CRABWOOD	GILTWOOD	KINGWOOD
BEARWOOD	COLTWOOD	DEADWOOD	HARDWOOD	LACEWOOD

LATEWOOD	PEARWOOD	PULPWOOD	SOFTWOOD	WILDWOOD
MILKWOOD	PINEWOOD	ROSEWOOD	SOURWOOD	WORMWOOD
OVENWOOD	PORKWOOD	SASSWOOD	TEAKWOOD	

Words that end with -WORK

Seven-letter words

ARTWORK	LEGWORK	PINWORK	TINWORK	WAXWORK
CUTWORK	NETWORK	PREWORK	TOPWORK	WEBWORK
DAYWORK	NONWORK	RAGWORK	TUTWORK	
LAPWORK	OUTWORK	RIBWORK	WARWORK	

Eight-letter words

BACKWORK	FIREWORK	IRONWORK	PARTWORK	STUDWORK
BEADWORK	FLATWORK	KNOTWORK	PILEWORK	TASKWORK
BODYWORK	FLUEWORK	KOFTWORK	PIPEWORK	TEAMWORK
BOOKWORK	FOOTWORK	LACEWORK	RACKWORK	TIMEWORK
BUHLWORK	FORMWORK	LATHWORK	RINGWORK	TUBEWORK
BUSYWORK	FRETWORK	LEADWORK	ROADWORK	WIREWORK
CAGEWORK	HACKWORK	LIFEWORK	ROCKWORK	WOODWORK
CAPEWORK	HAIRWORK	LINKWORK	ROPEWORK	WOOLWORK
CASEWORK	HANDWORK	MESHWORK	SALTWORK	YARDWORK
CRIBWORK	HEADWORK	MILLWORK	SCUTWORK	
DUCTWORK	HOMEWORK	OPENWORK	SEATWORK	
FARMWORK	HORNWORK	OVERWORK	SLOPWORK	

Words that end with -WORM

Seven-letter words

BAGWORM	CUTWORM	LOBWORM	RAGWORM	WEBWORM
BUDWORM	EARWORM	LUGWORM	SEAWORM	
CATWORM	EELWORM	PINWORM	WAXWORM	

Eight-letter words

ARMYWORM	FISHWORM	HORNWORM	MUCKWORM	SLOWWORM
BOLLWORM	FLATWORM	INCHWORM	PILLWORM	SPANWORM
BOOKWORM	GAPEWORM	LEAFWORM	RINGWORM	TAPEWORM
CASEWORM	GLOWWORM	LINDWORM	ROOTWORM	TUBEWORM
CLAMWORM	GRUBWORM	LUNGWORM	SANDWORM	WHIPWORM
CORNWORM	HAIRWORM	MALTWORM	SHIPWORM	WIREWORM
FIREWORM	HOOKWORM	MEALWORM	SILKWORM	WOODWORM

Words that end with -WORT

Seven-letter words

AWLWORT	FANWORT	MADWORT	RAGWORT
BLAWORT	FELWORT	MUDWORT	RIBWORT
BUGWORT	FIGWORT	MUGWORT	

Words that end with -WOOD

Eight-letter words

BELL**WORT**	FLEA**WORT**	LUNG**WORT**	PILE**WORT**	SOAP**WORT**
COLE**WORT**	GOUT**WORT**	MILK**WORT**	PILL**WORT**	STAR**WORT**
DAME**WORT**	HONE**WORT**	MODI**WORT**	PIPE**WORT**	WALL**WORT**
DANE**WORT**	HORN**WORT**	MOON**WORT**	SALT**WORT**	WART**WORT**
DROP**WORT**	LEAD**WORT**	MOOR**WORT**	SAND**WORT**	

Words that end with -YARD

Seven-letter words

BEE**YARD**	INN**YARD**	LAN**YARD**	TAN**YARD**
HAL**YARD**			

Eight-letter words

BACK**YARD**	DEER**YARD**	HAUL**YARD**	METE**YARD**	TILT**YARD**
BALL**YARD**	DOCK**YARD**	JUNK**YARD**	RICK**YARD**	VINE**YARD**
BARN**YARD**	DOOR**YARD**	KAIL**YARD**	SALE**YARD**	WHIN**YARD**
BOAT**YARD**	FARM**YARD**	KALE**YARD**	SAVO**YARD**	WILL**YARD**
BONE**YARD**	FEED**YARD**	KIRK**YARD**	SHIP**YARD**	WOOD**YARD**
COAL**YARD**	FORE**YARD**	MAIN**YARD**	SHOW**YARD**	

Vowel endings

E aside, it can be difficult to think of words that end in the vowels. But these words can be very useful. A, I, O and U represent almost a third of the tiles in the game, and there are a great many two-letter words that begin or end with vowels other than E. Words that end in vowels give you great opportunities for tagging your main word onto an existing word making a two-letter word with the vowel in the process. Or it may be that the vowel you need to end with for a double- or triple-word score is already on the board. The lists in this section detail all words from two letters to eight in length, ending in A, I, O or U. Definitions are provided for the two-letter and three-letter words.

Words that end with -A

Two-letter words

AA	volcanic rock
BA	symbol for the soul in Ancient Egyptian religion
DA	Burmese knife
EA	river
FA	musical note
HA	exclamation expressing triumph, surprise, or scorn
JA	yes
KA	in ancient Egypt, one's spirit or soul
LA	musical note
MA	mother
NA	not
PA	father
TA	a thank you
YA	you
ZA	pizza

Three-letter words

ABA	type of cloth from Syria
AGA	Turkish commander or chief officer
AHA	(to utter an) exclamation expressing triumph, surprise
AIA	female servant in East
AKA	vine found in New Zealand
ALA	wing or winglike part
AMA	Oriental nurse
ANA	collection of gossip
AUA	yellow-eye mullet
AVA	aromatic plant of pepper family
AWA	away
BAA	make the bleating sound of a sheep
BOA	large nonvenomous snake
BRA	brassiere
CAA	to call
CHA	tea
ERA	period of time
ETA	seventh letter in the Greek alphabet
FAA	to fall
FRA	brother: a title given to an Italian monk or friar
GOA	type of gazelle
HOA	to cause to stop
ITA	type of palm
KEA	large brownish-green parrot
KOA	Hawaiian leguminous tree
LEA	meadow
MAA	(of goats) bleat
MNA	Greek weight
MOA	large extinct flightless New Zealand bird
OBA	a Yoruba chief or ruler
OCA	any of various South American herbaceous plants
ODA	room in a harem
OKA	unit of weight used in Turkey
ORA	plural of os, bone
OVA	plural of ovum, egg
PEA	plant with seeds growing in pods
PIA	membrane that covers the brain and spinal cord
POA	type of grass
PYA	monetary unit of Myanmar
QUA	in the capacity of
RIA	drowned valley
RYA	handwoven rug from Scandinavia
SEA	mass of salt water covering much of the earth's surface
SHA	be quiet
SKA	type of West Indian pop music of the 1960s
SMA	small
SPA	resort with a mineral-water spring
TEA	drink made from infusing the dried leaves of an Asian bush in boiling water
TWA	two
UTA	side-blotched lizard
UVA	grape or fruit resembling this
VIA	a roadway
WHA	who
YEA	yes
ZEA	a maize extract
ZOA	plural of zoon, creature

Words that end with -A

Four-letter words

ABBA	DATA	JAVA	NAGA	ROMA
ACCA	DEVA	JOTA	NALA	ROTA
ACTA	DIKA	JUBA	NANA	RUGA
AGHA	DISA	JUGA	NAPA	RUSA
AGMA	DITA	JURA	NEMA	SAGA
AIGA	DIVA	KAKA	NIPA	SAMA
ALBA	DONA	KAMA	NOMA	SENA
ALFA	DOPA	KANA	NONA	SERA
ALGA	DUKA	KAPA	NOTA	SETA
ALMA	DUMA	KARA	NOVA	SHEA
AMIA	DURA	KATA	OBIA	SHWA
AMLA	EGMA	KAVA	OCTA	SIDA
ANGA	EINA	KAWA	ODEA	SIKA
ANNA	EKKA	KETA	OHIA	SIMA
ANOA	EMMA	KINA	OKRA	SKUA
ANSA	EPHA	KIVA	OKTA	SOBA
ANTA	ETNA	KOHA	OLEA	SOCA
AQUA	EYRA	KOLA	OLLA	SODA
ARBA	FAVA	KORA	ORCA	SOFA
AREA	FETA	KUIA	ORRA	SOJA
ARIA	FILA	KULA	OSSA	SOLA
ARNA	FLEA	KUNA	OUMA	SOMA
ARPA	FORA	KUTA	OUPA	SORA
ASEA	GAGA	LAMA	PACA	SOYA
ATMA	GALA	LANA	PAPA	STOA
ATUA	GAMA	LAVA	PARA	SUBA
AULA	GENA	LEVA	PAUA	SURA
AURA	GETA	LIMA	PAWA	TAHA
BABA	GIGA	LIPA	PEBA	TAKA
BEMA	GILA	LIRA	PELA	TALA
BETA	GLIA	LOCA	PICA	TANA
BIGA	GORA	LOMA	PIKA	TAPA
BIMA	GUGA	LOTA	PILA	TARA
BOBA	GULA	LUMA	PIMA	TAVA
BOLA	HAHA	LUNA	PINA	TAWA
BOMA	HAKA	LYRA	PIPA	TAXA
BONA	HILA	MALA	PITA	TELA
BORA	HIYA	MAMA	PLEA	TEPA
BOTA	HOHA	MANA	PROA	TIKA
BUBA	HOKA	MARA	PUHA	TOEA
BUDA	HOMA	MASA	PUJA	TOGA
BUNA	HORA	MAYA	PUKA	TOLA
BURA	HOYA	MEGA	PULA	TORA
CABA	HUIA	MELA	PUMA	TOSA
CACA	HULA	MESA	PUNA	TUBA
CAMA	HUMA	META	PUPA	TUFA
CAPA	HYLA	MICA	RACA	TUNA
CASA	IDEA	MIHA	RAGA	ULNA
CAVA	ILEA	MINA	RAIA	ULVA
CECA	ILIA	MOLA	RAJA	UPTA
CHIA	ILKA	MONA	RANA	UREA
COCA	INIA	MORA	RATA	URSA
CODA	IOTA	MOWA	RAYA	URVA
COLA	ISBA	MOXA	RHEA	UVEA
COMA	ISNA	MOYA	RIBA	VARA
COXA	IXIA	MURA	RIMA	VASA
CYMA	JAFA	MYNA	RIVA	VEGA
DADA	JAGA	NADA	RIZA	VELA

VENA	VITA	WEKA	YOGA	ZOEA
VERA	VIVA	WENA	YUCA	ZONA
VIGA	VOLA	WETA	YUGA	ZUPA
VINA	WAKA	WHOA	ZETA	ZYGA
VISA	WAWA	YABA	ZILA	

Five-letter words

ABACA	BANDA	COALA	ETYMA	HALVA
ABAKA	BANIA	COBIA	EXTRA	HAMBA
ABAYA	BARCA	COBRA	FACIA	HAMZA
ABOMA	BARRA	COBZA	FAENA	HANSA
ABUNA	BASTA	COCOA	FANGA	HAOMA
ACETA	BATTA	COLZA	FATWA	HASTA
ADYTA	BELGA	COMMA	FAUNA	HATHA
AECIA	BETTA	CONGA	FELLA	HEJRA
AFARA	BHUNA	CONIA	FERIA	HENNA
AGAMA	BIGHA	COPRA	FESTA	HERMA
AGILA	BIOTA	CORIA	FETTA	HEVEA
AGITA	BIVIA	COSTA	FETWA	HIJRA
AGORA	BOCCA	COTTA	FINCA	HODJA
AGRIA	BOHEA	CRENA	FITNA	HOLLA
AINGA	BONZA	CRURA	FLORA	HONDA
AJIVA	BORNA	CULPA	FLOTA	HOOKA
AJUGA	BOYLA	CUPPA	FOLIA	HOSTA
AKELA	BRAVA	CURIA	FONDA	HOVEA
AKITA	BRAZA	DABBA	FORZA	HUDNA
ALAPA	BUBBA	DACHA	FOSSA	HURRA
ALDEA	BUFFA	DAGGA	FOVEA	HUTIA
ALIYA	BULLA	DARGA	FRENA	HUZZA
ALOHA	BUNIA	DELTA	FURCA	HYDRA
ALPHA	BUNYA	DERMA	GALEA	HYENA
ALULA	BURKA	DICTA	GAMBA	HYPHA
AMEBA	BURQA	DINNA	GAMMA	IDOLA
AMIGA	BURSA	DIOTA	GANJA	INFRA
AMNIA	BWANA	DOBLA	GARDA	INTRA
ANANA	CAECA	DOBRA	GEMMA	INULA
ANATA	CALLA	DOGMA	GENOA	IXORA
ANIMA	CALPA	DOLIA	GENUA	JAGRA
ANTRA	CANNA	DOLMA	GLEBA	JARTA
AORTA	CARTA	DONGA	GOGGA	JHALA
APNEA	CAUDA	DONNA	GOMPA	JIRGA
ARABA	CAUSA	DOONA	GONIA	JNANA
ARECA	CEIBA	DORBA	GONNA	JUNTA
ARENA	CELLA	DORSA	GOTTA	KAAMA
AREPA	CERIA	DOULA	GOURA	KACHA
AROBA	CESTA	DOUMA	GRAMA	KAIKA
AROHA	CHARA	DOURA	GRANA	KALPA
AROMA	CHAYA	DOWNA	GROMA	KANGA
ASANA	CHEKA	DRAMA	GUANA	KAPPA
ASYLA	CHELA	DUKKA	GUAVA	KARMA
ATRIA	CHICA	DULIA	GUMMA	KASHA
BABKA	CHINA	DUMKA	GUSLA	KEHUA
BACCA	CHOLA	DURRA	GUTTA	KERMA
BACHA	CHOTA	EDEMA	GYOZA	KHAYA
BAIZA	CHUFA	ENEMA	HAIKA	KHEDA
BAJRA	CILIA	ENTIA	HAKEA	KHOJA
BAKRA	CIRCA	ERBIA	HALFA	KIBLA
BALSA	CNIDA	ERICA	HALMA	KINDA

Words that end with -A

KIPPA	MEDIA	PACHA	REATA	SORDA
KOALA	MEKKA	PACTA	RECTA	SORRA
KOFTA	MENSA	PADMA	REDIA	SORTA
KOKRA	MENTA	PAISA	REGMA	SPAZA
KOPPA	MICRA	PAKKA	REGNA	SPICA
KORMA	MIKRA	PALEA	RENGA	SPINA
KOURA	MILIA	PALLA	REPLA	SPUTA
KRONA	MILPA	PAMPA	RETIA	STELA
KURTA	MIRZA	PANDA	RHYTA	STIPA
KWELA	MISSA	PANGA	RIATA	STOMA
LABDA	MOCHA	PARKA	RIOJA	STRIA
LABIA	MOHUA	PARRA	ROOSA	STUPA
LABRA	MOIRA	PASHA	RUANA	SUBHA
LAIKA	MOLLA	PASTA	RUMBA	SULFA
LAKSA	MOMMA	PELMA	RUPIA	SUMMA
LAMIA	MOOLA	PELTA	RUSMA	SUNNA
LARVA	MORIA	PENNA	SABRA	SUPRA
LAURA	MORRA	PEPLA	SACRA	SURRA
LAVRA	MOTZA	PEREA	SADZA	SUTRA
LEHUA	MOWRA	PHOCA	SAIGA	SUTTA
LEMMA	MUDRA	PHYLA	SAKIA	SYLVA
LEPRA	MUGGA	PICRA	SALPA	TAATA
LEPTA	MULGA	PIETA	SALSA	TABLA
LEZZA	MULLA	PILEA	SAMBA	TAFIA
LIANA	MUNGA	PINNA	SANGA	TAGMA
LIBRA	MURRA	PINTA	SANSA	TAIGA
LIMBA	MURVA	PITTA	SAUBA	TAIRA
LIMMA	MUSCA	PIZZA	SAUNA	TALEA
LIMPA	MUSHA	PLAYA	SCALA	TALMA
LINGA	MUTHA	PLAZA	SCAPA	TALPA
LLAMA	MYOMA	PLENA	SCENA	TANGA
LOGIA	NABLA	PLICA	SCHWA	TANKA
LONGA	NAIRA	POAKA	SCOPA	TANNA
LOOFA	NAKFA	PODIA	SCUBA	TAPPA
LOUMA	NALLA	POLKA	SCUTA	TAYRA
LUBRA	NAMMA	PONGA	SELLA	TAZZA
LUFFA	NANNA	POOJA	SELVA	TECTA
LUTEA	NANUA	POOKA	SENNA	TEGUA
LYCEA	NAPPA	POPPA	SENSA	TELIA
LYCRA	NERKA	PORTA	SENZA	TENIA
LYSSA	NGANA	PRANA	SEPIA	TERGA
LYTTA	NGOMA	PRESA	SEPTA	TERRA
MAFIA	NINJA	PRIMA	SERRA	TESLA
MAGMA	NORIA	PRUTA	SESSA	TESTA
MAHUA	NORMA	PSORA	SHAMA	TETRA
MAHWA	NUBIA	PUCKA	SHAYA	THANA
MALVA	NUCHA	PUKKA	SHEVA	THECA
MALWA	NULLA	PULKA	SHIVA	THEMA
MAMBA	NYALA	PUNGA	SHOLA	THETA
MAMMA	NYSSA	PUNKA	SHURA	THUJA
MANGA	OCREA	PURDA	SIDHA	THUYA
MANIA	OIDIA	QIBLA	SIGLA	TIARA
MANNA	OMASA	QORMA	SIGMA	TIBIA
MANTA	OMEGA	QUENA	SIGNA	TICCA
MARIA	OPERA	QUINA	SILVA	TIKKA
MARKA	ORGIA	QUOTA	SIMBA	TINEA
MASSA	ORIXA	RAGGA	SIRRA	TOMIA
MATZA	OSSIA	RAITA	SITKA	TONGA
MBIRA	OSTIA	RASTA	SOFTA	TONKA
MECCA	OUIJA	RATHA	SOPRA	TORTA

TREFA	UVULA	VITTA	WINNA	YUCCA
TREMA	VACUA	VIVDA	WIRRA	YURTA
TRONA	VANDA	VODKA	WISHA	ZABRA
TRYMA	VARIA	VOEMA	WOKKA	ZAMIA
TSUBA	VARNA	VOILA	WONGA	ZANJA
TUGRA	VEENA	VOLTA	WUXIA	ZANZA
TUINA	VERRA	VOLVA	XENIA	ZEBRA
TULPA	VESPA	VULVA	XOANA	ZERDA
ULAMA	VESTA	WAGGA	YABBA	ZILLA
ULEMA	VIFDA	WALLA	YACCA	ZOAEA
ULTRA	VIGIA	WANNA	YACKA	ZONDA
UMBRA	VILLA	WHATA	YAKKA	ZOOEA
UNCIA	VINCA	WICCA	YARFA	ZOPPA
URBIA	VIOLA	WIGGA	YARTA	
URENA	VIRGA	WILGA	YENTA	
USNEA	VISTA	WILJA	YERBA	

Six-letter words

ABASIA	ANOPIA	BATATA	CANULA	CLOACA
ABELIA	ANOXIA	BAUERA	CAPITA	CLUSIA
ABOLLA	ANTARA	BEFANA	CARDIA	COAITA
ABULIA	ANTLIA	BEFLEA	CARINA	COBAEA
ACACIA	ANURIA	BELUGA	CASABA	CODEIA
ACEDIA	APHTHA	BEMATA	CASAVA	CONCHA
ADNEXA	APNOEA	BERTHA	CASITA	CONIMA
AFTOSA	APORIA	BHAKTA	CASSIA	CONTRA
AGENDA	ARAARA	BILBOA	CATENA	COPITA
AGGADA	ARALIA	BOCCIA	CEDULA	COPPRA
AGOUTA	ARCANA	BODEGA	CEMBRA	COPULA
AHIMSA	AREOLA	BONITA	CENTRA	CORNEA
AIKONA	ARGALA	BOONGA	CESURA	CORNUA
AKATEA	ARISTA	BOORKA	CHACMA	CORONA
AKHARA	ARMADA	BOSHTA	CHAETA	CORREA
ALALIA	ARNICA	BRAATA	CHAKRA	CORYZA
ALASKA	AROLLA	BRAHMA	CHALLA	COSMEA
ALBATA	ARRIBA	BREGMA	CHANGA	COWPEA
ALEXIA	ARROBA	BROLGA	CHAPKA	CRACKA
ALISMA	ASRAMA	BUCKRA	CHARKA	CRANIA
ALODIA	ASTHMA	BUDDHA	CHARTA	CRESTA
ALOGIA	ATAATA	BUGSHA	CHATTA	CRISSA
ALPACA	ATAXIA	BUNNIA	CHICHA	CRISTA
ALTEZA	ATOCIA	BUQSHA	CHIGGA	CROWEA
ALTHEA	ATONIA	BUSERA	CHIMLA	CRUSTA
ALUMNA	AUCUBA	BUSHWA	CHOANA	CUBICA
AMARNA	AURORA	CABALA	CHOKRA	CUESTA
AMELIA	AVRUGA	CABANA	CHOLLA	CUMBIA
AMENTA	AXILLA	CADAGA	CHORDA	CUPOLA
AMOEBA	AZALEA	CAEOMA	CHOREA	CUPULA
AMRITA	AZOLLA	CAFILA	CHORIA	CURARA
AMUSIA	BACKRA	CALESA	CHROMA	CUTCHA
ANATTA	BACULA	CALIMA	CHUKKA	CZAPKA
ANCORA	BAHADA	CALTHA	CHUPPA	DAGABA
ANEMIA	BAJADA	CAMBIA	CICADA	DAGOBA
ANGINA	BALATA	CAMERA	CICALA	DAHLIA
ANGOLA	BALBOA	CAMISA	CICUTA	DATCHA
ANGORA	BANANA	CANADA	CINEMA	DATURA
ANICCA	BARAZA	CANCHA	CITOLA	DEFLEA
ANNONA	BARYTA	CANOLA	CLIVIA	DHAMMA

Words that end with -A

DHARMA	GEISHA	JEJUNA	LINGUA	MURENA
DHARNA	GELADA	JEMIMA	LIPOMA	MURRHA
DHOORA	GENERA	JERBOA	LITHIA	MUTUCA
DHURNA	GENEVA	JHATKA	LOBOLA	MYOPIA
DHURRA	GITANA	JICAMA	LOCHIA	MYRICA
DOLINA	GLIOMA	JOANNA	LOGGIA	MYXOMA
DOOSRA	GLORIA	JOJOBA	LOMATA	NAGANA
DUENNA	GLOSSA	JUDOKA	LORCHA	NATURA
DUHKHA	GNAMMA	JUGULA	LORICA	NAUSEA
DUKKHA	GOANNA	KABAKA	LUCUMA	NEBULA
DUMELA	GOONDA	KABALA	LUMINA	NEPETA
ECZEMA	GOPURA	KABAYA	LUNULA	NOCTUA
EGESTA	GORGIA	KACCHA	LUSTRA	NOMINA
EIDOLA	GOTCHA	KAFILA	MABELA	NOVENA
EJECTA	GRAMMA	KAHUNA	MACOYA	NUMINA
ELODEA	GRAMPA	KAINGA	MACULA	NUTRIA
ELUVIA	GRAPPA	KALMIA	MAFFIA	NYANZA
ELYTRA	GRINGA	KAMALA	MAKUTA	NYMPHA
EMPUSA	GUINEA	KAMELA	MALTHA	OBELIA
ENCINA	GYTTJA	KAMILA	MANAIA	OCHREA
ENIGMA	HALALA	KANAKA	MANANA	OEDEMA
ENTERA	HALLOA	KANGHA	MANAWA	OMENTA
EPEIRA	HAMADA	KANTHA	MANILA	OMERTA
EPIZOA	HANIWA	KANUKA	MANTRA	ONYCHA
EPOCHA	HAPUKA	KAPUKA	MANTUA	OPTIMA
ERRATA	HARIRA	KARAKA	MANUKA	ORARIA
ESPADA	HAWALA	KATANA	MARACA	ORBITA
EUPNEA	HEBONA	KEMBLA	MARINA	ORGANA
EUREKA	HEDERA	KENTIA	MARKKA	ORISHA
EXACTA	HEGIRA	KERRIA	MASALA	OSCULA
EXEDRA	HEJIRA	KETMIA	MASHUA	OSETRA
EXUVIA	HEMINA	KGOTLA	MASULA	OTTAVA
FACULA	HERNIA	KHANDA	MATATA	OZAENA
FAJITA	HILLOA	KHANGA	MAUNNA	PAELLA
FANEGA	HOLLOA	KHODJA	MAXIMA	PAGODA
FARINA	HOLMIA	KHURTA	MAZUMA	PAJAMA
FASCIA	HOODIA	KINARA	MEDAKA	PAKEHA
FATSIA	HOOPLA	KINEMA	MEDINA	PAKORA
FAVELA	HRYVNA	KISHKA	MEDUSA	PALAMA
FECULA	HULLOA	KOCHIA	MEGARA	PALAPA
FEDORA	HUTZPA	KORORA	MELENA	PALLIA
FEIJOA	HYAENA	KORUNA	MESETA	PANADA
FEMORA	HYDRIA	KUMARA	METEPA	PANAMA
FERULA	IDEATA	KUMERA	MEZUZA	PAPAYA
FIBULA	IGUANA	KUTCHA	MGANGA	PAPULA
FIESTA	IMPALA	KWACHA	MIASMA	PARERA
FLAUTA	INANGA	KWANZA	MIMOSA	PARURA
FOOTRA	INDABA	LABARA	MINIMA	PASELA
FOUSSA	INDUNA	LACUNA	MIZUNA	PASHKA
FOUTRA	INFIMA	LAGENA	MODENA	PATACA
FRAENA	INFULA	LAGUNA	MODICA	PATAKA
FRISKA	INJERA	LAMBDA	MOKSHA	PATERA
FRUSTA	INSULA	LAMINA	MONERA	PATINA
FULCRA	INTIMA	LATINA	MOORVA	PAYOLA
FUNKIA	INYALA	LATRIA	MORCHA	PELOTA
FUSUMA	ISCHIA	LEIPOA	MORULA	PENNIA
GALENA	ISTANA	LEXICA	MOTUCA	PERAEA
GAMBIA	JACANA	LIGULA	MUCOSA	PEREIA
GARRYA	JARINA	LIKUTA	MULETA	PESETA
GARUDA	JATAKA	LIMINA	MUMMIA	PESEWA

PESHWA	RAMONA	SENECA	SYNURA	UTOPIA
PETARA	RANULA	SENEGA	TABULA	VAGINA
PHARMA	RAPHIA	SENORA	TAENIA	VAHANA
PHOBIA	RAZZIA	SEROSA	TAFFIA	VALETA
PIAZZA	REALIA	SHAMBA	TAHINA	VALUTA
PICARA	REDOWA	SHARIA	TAIAHA	VARROA
PILULA	REGINA	SHEILA	TAIHOA	VEDUTA
PINATA	REGULA	SHELTA	TALUKA	VELETA
PINETA	RELATA	SHERIA	TAMARA	VESICA
PIRANA	REMORA	SHERPA	TANKIA	VICUNA
PIRAYA	REMUDA	SHIKSA	TANTRA	VIHARA
PITARA	RESEDA	SHIRRA	TAONGA	VIMANA
PITAYA	RETAMA	SHISHA	TAPETA	VIMINA
PLANTA	RETINA	SHOORA	TARAMA	VIZSLA
PLASMA	RHANJA	SIDDHA	TARSIA	VOMICA
PLEURA	RHUMBA	SIENNA	TEGULA	WAIATA
PNEUMA	RISTRA	SIERRA	TELEGA	WAIRUA
POISHA	ROSTRA	SIESTA	TEPHRA	WHATNA
POPERA	ROSULA	SIFAKA	TERATA	WHENUA
PORINA	ROTULA	SILICA	TERBIA	WILTJA
POSADA	RUCOLA	SISTRA	TEREFA	WOMERA
PRAJNA	RUGOLA	SITULA	TERTIA	XEROMA
PREMIA	RUGOSA	SKOLIA	THANNA	XYLOMA
PROTEA	RUMINA	SMEGMA	THORIA	YAKUZA
PRUINA	RUSSIA	SOLERA	THULIA	YANTRA
PSYLLA	SABKHA	SOMATA	TINAJA	YAQONA
PTERIA	SAHIBA	SONATA	TIPULA	YARPHA
PULKHA	SALINA	SPIREA	TIPUNA	YAUTIA
PUNCTA	SALIVA	SQUAMA	TORANA	YOJANA
PURANA	SALVIA	SRADHA	TORULA	YTTRIA
PYEMIA	SAMARA	STADDA	TOTARA	YUKATA
PYJAMA	SAMOSA	STADIA	TRAUMA	ZABETA
PYROLA	SANCTA	STANZA	TREIFA	ZANANA
PYURIA	SAPOTA	STATUA	TRIVIA	ZAPATA
QABALA	SASTRA	STELLA	TROIKA	ZAREBA
QASIDA	SATARA	STEMMA	TSAMBA	ZARIBA
QUAGGA	SATYRA	STERNA	TUATUA	ZENANA
QUALIA	SCARPA	STIGMA	TUGHRA	ZEREBA
QUANTA	SCHEMA	STIRRA	TUNDRA	ZERIBA
QUELEA	SCILLA	STOMIA	TUNICA	ZEUGMA
QUINOA	SCLERA	STRATA	TUPUNA	ZINNIA
QUINTA	SCOLIA	STRIGA	UJAMAA	ZOARIA
QUOKKA	SCORIA	STROMA	ULTIMA	ZOECIA
QUOTHA	SCOTIA	STRUMA	UNGULA	ZONULA
RADULA	SCOZZA	SUBSEA	URANIA	ZOYSIA
RAFFIA	SCROTA	SULPHA	UREDIA	ZYGOMA
RAMADA	SEMEIA	SUNDRA	UREMIA	
RAMBLA	SEMINA	SYLVIA	URTICA	

Seven-letter words

ABOMASA	ACHARYA	ADDENDA	AGRAPHA	ALGEBRA
ABOULIA	ACHENIA	ADENOMA	AKRASIA	ALGESIA
ABROSIA	ACHOLIA	ADHARMA	ALAMEDA	ALLODIA
ACANTHA	ACICULA	ADIPSIA	ALBIZIA	ALLUVIA
ACAPNIA	ACRASIA	AECIDIA	ALCHERA	ALPACCA
ACCIDIA	ACROMIA	AEROBIA	ALCORZA	ALTEZZA
ACEQUIA	ACTINIA	AGEUSIA	ALFALFA	ALTHAEA
ACEROLA	ACUSHLA	AGNOSIA	ALFORJA	ALUMINA

Words that end with -A

AMADODA	AUREOLA	CABOMBA	CITHARA	DOGMATA
AMANDLA	BABESIA	CADENZA	CLARKIA	DOMATIA
AMANITA	BACCARA	CAESURA	COAGULA	DONGOLA
AMBOINA	BACHCHA	CAFFILA	COCHLEA	DOPATTA
AMBOYNA	BACLAVA	CALDERA	CODEINA	DOPIAZA
AMENTIA	BAKLAVA	CALLUNA	CODETTA	DOULEIA
AMMONIA	BAKLAWA	CALUMBA	CODILLA	DRACENA
AMNESIA	BALISTA	CAMELIA	COMITIA	DRACHMA
AMOKURA	BANDANA	CAMISIA	COMMATA	DROSERA
AMOROSA	BANDORA	CAMORRA	CONARIA	DUODENA
AMPHORA	BANDURA	CAMPANA	CONIDIA	DUPATTA
AMPULLA	BANKSIA	CANASTA	COPAIBA	DVANDVA
AMREETA	BANSELA	CANDELA	COPAIVA	DYSPNEA
ANAEMIA	BARBOLA	CANDIDA	COQUINA	DYSURIA
ANALGIA	BARILLA	CANELLA	CORALLA	ECHIDNA
ANALOGA	BARISTA	CANNULA	CORBINA	ECTASIA
ANCHUSA	BARTSIA	CANTALA	CORDOBA	ECTHYMA
ANCILIA	BASIDIA	CANTATA	CORELLA	ECTOPIA
ANCILLA	BATAVIA	CANTINA	COREMIA	ECTOZOA
ANERGIA	BATTUTA	CANZONA	COROLLA	EDEMATA
ANESTRA	BAZOOKA	CAPUERA	CORPORA	EMBLEMA
ANGARIA	BEFFANA	CARAMBA	CORRIDA	EMERITA
ANGIOMA	BEGONIA	CARANNA	CORTINA	EMPORIA
ANHINGA	BEGORRA	CARAUNA	CORVINA	EMPYEMA
ANNATTA	BERETTA	CARBORA	COTINGA	ENCOMIA
ANONYMA	BERGAMA	CARIAMA	CRAPOLA	ENDOZOA
ANOPSIA	BHANGRA	CARIOCA	CREMONA	ENEMATA
ANOSMIA	BIDARKA	CASCARA	CRIMINA	ENTASIA
ANTENNA	BIENNIA	CASSABA	CROTALA	ENTOZOA
APADANA	BIODATA	CASSATA	CURACOA	EPHEDRA
APEPSIA	BIRETTA	CASSAVA	CURCUMA	EPISCIA
APHAGIA	BISNAGA	CASSENA	CURIOSA	EPYLLIA
APHAKIA	BIZNAGA	CASSINA	CURTANA	EQUINIA
APHASIA	BOFFOLA	CATALPA	CYATHIA	EROTEMA
APHELIA	BOHEMIA	CATASTA	CYMATIA	EROTICA
APHONIA	BOLIVIA	CATAWBA	CYPSELA	EUGENIA
APLASIA	BOLOGNA	CAVALLA	CZARINA	EUGLENA
APRAXIA	BOMBORA	CEDILLA	DAMIANA	EULOGIA
APTERIA	BONAMIA	CELESTA	DAPHNIA	EUPNOEA
AQUARIA	BONANZA	CELOSIA	DAROGHA	EUTAXIA
ARABICA	BONSELA	CEMENTA	DATARIA	EUTEXIA
ARAROBA	BORONIA	CEREBRA	DAVIDIA	EXCRETA
ARCADIA	BOTHRIA	CERVEZA	DECIDUA	EXEMPLA
ARCHAEA	BOTTEGA	CHACHKA	DECURIA	EXHEDRA
ARGYRIA	BOURKHA	CHALAZA	DEJECTA	EXORDIA
ARIETTA	BRACCIA	CHALUPA	DELENDA	EXOTICA
ARMILLA	BRACHIA	CHAMISA	DELIRIA	EXTREMA
ARUGOLA	BRAVURA	CHARKHA	DEODARA	EXURBIA
ARUGULA	BRECCIA	CHECHIA	DEUTZIA	FALBALA
ASCIDIA	BRITSKA	CHIASMA	DHOURRA	FALCULA
ASHRAMA	BRITZKA	CHICANA	DIANOIA	FARINHA
ASPIDIA	BRUHAHA	CHIKARA	DICAMBA	FARRUCA
ASTASIA	BUBINGA	CHIMERA	DIGAMMA	FAUNULA
ASTERIA	BUCCINA	CHOLERA	DIHEDRA	FAVELLA
ATALAYA	BULIMIA	CHRISMA	DILEMMA	FAZENDA
ATEMOYA	BULLOSA	CHUTZPA	DILUVIA	FELICIA
ATHLETA	BUMELIA	CIBORIA	DIORAMA	FELUCCA
ATRESIA	BURSERA	CIMELIA	DIPLOMA	FERMATA
ATROPIA	BUZUKIA	CINEREA	DIPTERA	FIBROMA
AURELIA	CABBALA	CINGULA	DIPTYCA	FILARIA

FIMBRIA	HARISSA	KOPIYKA	MARKKAA	OCTAPLA
FISTULA	HARMALA	KUCHCHA	MARSALA	OLEARIA
FLORULA	HELLOVA	LABELLA	MASCARA	OLESTRA
FLUTINA	HELLUVA	LACINIA	MASTABA	OMMATEA
FONTINA	HEMIOLA	LAMBADA	MATILDA	OMNIANA
FORLANA	HETAERA	LAMELLA	MAXILLA	ONDATRA
FORMICA	HETAIRA	LAMPUKA	MAZURKA	ONYCHIA
FORMULA	HEUREKA	LANGAHA	MEDACCA	OOGONIA
FOSSULA	HEXAPLA	LANTANA	MEDULLA	OOTHECA
FOVEOLA	HIDALGA	LASAGNA	MEGILLA	OPHIURA
FREESIA	HIMATIA	LATAKIA	MELISMA	OPUNTIA
FRENULA	HOROEKA	LATILLA	MELODIA	OQUASSA
FUCHSIA	HOSANNA	LAVOLTA	MEROPIA	ORGANZA
FURCULA	HRYVNIA	LEMMATA	MESHUGA	OROPESA
FURLANA	HRYVNYA	LEMPIRA	MESTIZA	OSMUNDA
FUSARIA	HYDROMA	LEUCOMA	METAZOA	OSSETRA
GALABEA	HYGROMA	LEUKOMA	MICELLA	OSTEOMA
GALABIA	HYMENIA	LEWISIA	MILITIA	OSTRACA
GALANGA	HYPOGEA	LINGULA	MINEOLA	OSTRAKA
GALATEA	HYPONEA	LIPEMIA	MINORCA	OTALGIA
GALLETA	HYPOXIA	LIPURIA	MINUTIA	OUGUIYA
GALLICA	IGNATIA	LIXIVIA	MITUMBA	OVERSEA
GANGLIA	IKEBANA	LOBELIA	MOCHILA	OVIPARA
GANGSTA	ILLUVIA	LOCUSTA	MOJARRA	OXYMORA
GAROUPA	IMPERIA	LOGANIA	MOMENTA	PADELLA
GASTREA	IMPRESA	LOMENTA	MONARDA	PAENULA
GAZANIA	INDICIA	LORDOMA	MONILIA	PAISANA
GAZOOKA	INDUSIA	MACCHIA	MORPHIA	PALABRA
GENISTA	INEDITA	MACUMBA	MORRHUA	PALINKA
GERBERA	INERTIA	MADEIRA	MOUSAKA	PALMYRA
GERMINA	INFANTA	MADONNA	MOVIOLA	PALOOKA
GERTCHA	INFAUNA	MADOQUA	MOZETTA	PANACEA
GIARDIA	INGESTA	MADRASA	MUDIRIA	PANDORA
GINGIVA	INOCULA	MADRONA	MULATTA	PANDURA
GLOMERA	INTRADA	MAGENTA	MURAENA	PANOCHA
GLUCINA	IPOMOEA	MAGMATA	MUTANDA	PAPAUMA
GOBURRA	ISODICA	MAHATMA	MYALGIA	PAPILLA
GODETIA	ISODOMA	MAHONIA	MYCELIA	PAPRICA
GONDOLA	JAMBIYA	MAJAGUA	MYCELLA	PAPRIKA
GONIDIA	JELLABA	MALACCA	MYELOMA	PARATHA
GORDITA	JIPYAPA	MALACIA	MYOMATA	PARAZOA
GORILLA	KABBALA	MALANGA	MYRINGA	PAREIRA
GOSPODA	KACHCHA	MALARIA	NANDINA	PARELLA
GRANDMA	KACHINA	MAMILLA	NAPHTHA	PARERGA
GRANDPA	KALIMBA	MAMPARA	NARCOMA	PARGANA
GRANITA	KANTELA	MANCALA	NEMESIA	PARTITA
GRANOLA	KARAKIA	MANDALA	NEUROMA	PASSATA
GRAVIDA	KARANGA	MANDIRA	NEURULA	PASTINA
GUARANA	KATCINA	MANDOLA	NGARARA	PATAGIA
GUEREZA	KATORGA	MANDORA	NIGELLA	PATELLA
GUMMATA	KATSURA	MANILLA	NIHONGA	PAVLOVA
GUNNERA	KAUPAPA	MANIOCA	NIRVANA	PAXIUBA
GYNECIA	KEITLOA	MANUMEA	NONCOLA	PECULIA
HAFTARA	KERBAYA	MANYATA	NORTENA	PEISHWA
HAGGADA	KERYGMA	MAQUILA	NOTANDA	PELORIA
HALACHA	KHALIFA	MARANTA	NOTITIA	PEMBINA
HALAKHA	KHEDIVA	MARASCA	NOUMENA	PENTHIA
HAMMADA	KIBITKA	MAREMMA	NOVALIA	PEREIRA
HARAMDA	KITHARA	MARGOSA	NOVELLA	PERGOLA
HARIANA	KOEKOEA	MARIMBA	OCARINA	PERIDIA

Words that end with -A

PERILLA	RASBORA	SCOTOMA	SYRINGA	VALONEA
PERINEA	RATAFIA	SCYBALA	TACHINA	VALONIA
PERSONA	REFUGIA	SECRETA	TAFFETA	VALVULA
PESSIMA	REGALIA	SEDILIA	TAGMATA	VANESSA
PETUNIA	REGATTA	SELECTA	TALARIA	VANILLA
PHILTRA	REGMATA	SENHORA	TALOOKA	VARIOLA
PIASABA	REPLICA	SENOPIA	TAMASHA	VASCULA
PIASAVA	RESIDUA	SEQUELA	TAMBALA	VEDALIA
PICCATA	RETSINA	SEQUOIA	TAMBURA	VELARIA
PIGNORA	RHIZOMA	SERIEMA	TAMPALA	VENTANA
PINNULA	RHODORA	SERINGA	TANAGRA	VERANDA
PINTADA	RHYTINA	SERPULA	TANIWHA	VERBENA
PIRAGUA	RICKSHA	SESTINA	TANTARA	VERRUCA
PIRANHA	RICOTTA	SEVRUGA	TAPIOCA	VERRUGA
PISCINA	RIFFOLA	SHAHADA	TARAMEA	VETTURA
PITUITA	RIKISHA	SHAMINA	TARTANA	VEXILLA
PLACITA	RIVIERA	SHASTRA	TAUPATA	VIATICA
PLANULA	ROBINIA	SHEHITA	TAVERNA	VICUGNA
PLATINA	ROBUSTA	SHEIKHA	TEDESCA	VIDENDA
PLECTRA	ROMAIKA	SHICKSA	TEGMINA	VIHUELA
PLEROMA	ROMANZA	SHORTIA	TEMPERA	VINCULA
PLUGOLA	ROMNEYA	SIGNORA	TEMPURA	VIRANDA
PLUMULA	ROSACEA	SILESIA	TEQUILA	VIREMIA
PODAGRA	ROSALIA	SILIQUA	TEREBRA	VISCERA
PODESTA	ROSARIA	SILPHIA	TESSERA	VIVARIA
POGONIA	ROSELLA	SINOPIA	THANGKA	VIVERRA
POLACCA	ROSEOLA	SITELLA	THEMATA	VOLUSPA
POLENTA	ROTUNDA	SKIMMIA	THRIMSA	WAKANDA
POLYNIA	RUBELLA	SOKAIYA	THRYMSA	WALLABA
POLYNYA	RUBEOLA	SOLARIA	TIKANGA	WANKSTA
POLYOMA	RUELLIA	SOLATIA	TILAPIA	WEIGELA
POLYZOA	RUFIYAA	SOREDIA	TIMPANA	WHOOPLA
POTASSA	RUNANGA	SPATULA	TITANIA	WIRILDA
PRECAVA	RUSALKA	SPECTRA	TOCCATA	WOMMERA
PREPUPA	RUSSULA	SPECULA	TOHEROA	WOODSIA
PRIMULA	SABELLA	SPICULA	TOHUNGA	WOOMERA
PRONOTA	SABURRA	SPINULA	TOMBOLA	WOORARA
PROPRIA	SACELLA	SPIRAEA	TOMENTA	WUDJULA
PROPYLA	SADHANA	SPIRULA	TORMINA	XERASIA
PROSOMA	SAGITTA	SPLENIA	TOSTADA	YAMALKA
PTERYLA	SAGRADA	SQUILLA	TOXEMIA	YAMULKA
PUDENDA	SAMBUCA	SRADDHA	TRACHEA	YESHIVA
PUKATEA	SAMSARA	STAMINA	TREHALA	ZAKUSKA
PUNALUA	SANGOMA	STASIMA	TRIELLA	ZAMARRA
PUPARIA	SANGRIA	STHENIA	TRISULA	ZANELLA
PUPUNHA	SANTERA	STOMATA	TRITOMA	ZAREEBA
PURPURA	SAPHENA	STRETTA	TRYMATA	ZEBRINA
PYAEMIA	SARCINA	STRIATA	TSANTSA	ZEBRULA
PYGIDIA	SARCOMA	SUBAQUA	TSARINA	ZELKOVA
PYREXIA	SARDANA	SUBAREA	TUATARA	ZEMSTVA
PYXIDIA	SATSUMA	SUBIDEA	TUATERA	ZENAIDA
QUASSIA	SAVANNA	SUBPENA	TURISTA	ZIGANKA
QUERIDA	SAXTUBA	SUBTAXA	TUTANIA	ZIMOCCA
QUINELA	SCAGLIA	SUCCUBA	TYMPANA	ZINGARA
QUININA	SCANDIA	SUDARIA	TZARINA	ZIZANIA
RABANNA	SCAPULA	SULTANA	ULNARIA	ZOOECIA
RADIATA	SCHISMA	SUMATRA	URAEMIA	ZOOGLEA
RAMENTA	SCHOLIA	SYCONIA	URETHRA	ZORILLA
RAOULIA	SCOPULA	SYNOVIA	VACCINA	ZYZZYVA

Eight-letter words

ABDOMINA	ASPERMIA	BUDDLEIA	CLAUSULA	DYSLEXIA
ABRACHIA	ASPHYXIA	BURLETTA	CLITELLA	DYSMELIA
ABSCISSA	ASPIRATA	CAATINGA	COCCIDIA	DYSPNOEA
ACADEMIA	ASTHENIA	CABRESTA	COCINERA	DYSTAXIA
ACELDAMA	ASTIGMIA	CABRETTA	COCOBOLA	DYSTOCIA
ACHAENIA	ASYNDETA	CABRILLA	COENOBIA	DYSTONIA
ACHILLEA	ATARAXIA	CACHEXIA	COLCHICA	DYSTOPIA
ACIDEMIA	ATHEROMA	CACHUCHA	COLLEGIA	EARTHPEA
ACIDURIA	ATROPHIA	CACUMINA	COLLUVIA	ECCLESIA
ADESPOTA	AUBRETIA	CALABAZA	COLLYRIA	EFFLUVIA
ADULARIA	AUBRIETA	CALAMATA	COLOBOMA	EGOMANIA
ADYNAMIA	AURICULA	CALATHEA	COLUMNEA	EMPANADA
AGENESIA	AUTOMATA	CALCANEA	COMATULA	ENCAENIA
AGLOSSIA	AUTOPSIA	CALCARIA	CONFERVA	ENDAMEBA
AGNOMINA	AVIFAUNA	CALCTUFA	CONSULTA	ENDOSTEA
AGRAPHIA	AXILEMMA	CALDARIA	CONTAGIA	ENGRAMMA
AGRYPNIA	AXOLEMMA	CALISAYA	CONTESSA	ENIGMATA
AKINESIA	AYURVEDA	CALVARIA	CONTINUA	ENTAMEBA
ALBIZZIA	AZOTEMIA	CALYPTRA	CONURBIA	EPENDYMA
ALGAROBA	AZOTURIA	CAMBOGIA	COPREMIA	EPHEMERA
ALIGARTA	BABIRUSA	CAMELLIA	COPROSMA	EPICEDIA
ALLELUIA	BABUSHKA	CAMPAGNA	COQUILLA	EPIFAUNA
ALOCASIA	BACTERIA	CAPITULA	CORMIDIA	EPIMYSIA
ALOPECIA	BAIDARKA	CAPOEIRA	COXALGIA	EPITHECA
AMBERINA	BALLISTA	CAPONATA	CREDENDA	EPITHEMA
AMBROSIA	BANDANNA	CAPYBARA	CREDENZA	EPOPOEIA
AMPHIBIA	BAPTISIA	CARACARA	CRIBELLA	EQUISETA
AMYGDALA	BARATHEA	CARAGANA	CRITERIA	ERYTHEMA
ANABAENA	BARRANCA	CARNAUBA	CROMORNA	ESTANCIA
ANACONDA	BASILICA	CARPALIA	CTENIDIA	ESTHESIA
ANALECTA	BATTALIA	CASTELLA	CUBICULA	ETCETERA
ANALEMMA	BAUHINIA	CATHEDRA	CUNABULA	EUPEPSIA
ANAPHORA	BEDSONIA	CATHISMA	CUTICULA	EUPHOBIA
ANASARCA	BERGENIA	CATTLEYA	CYMBIDIA	EUPHONIA
ANATHEMA	BERRETTA	CAVATINA	CZAREVNA	EUPHORIA
ANECDOTA	BERYLLIA	CECROPIA	CZARITSA	EUTHYMIA
ANGELICA	BETHESDA	CELOMATA	CZARITZA	EXCERPTA
ANOESTRA	BIGNONIA	CERCARIA	DAHABIYA	EXONUMIA
ANOOPSIA	BIRRETTA	CHALAZIA	DECENNIA	FALDETTA
ANOREXIA	BISCACHA	CHAMPACA	DEMENTIA	FANEGADA
ANOXEMIA	BIZCACHA	CHAQUETA	DEMERARA	FANTASIA
ANTEFIXA	BLASTEMA	CHARANGA	DENTALIA	FASCIOLA
ANTHELIA	BLASTOMA	CHARISMA	DENTARIA	FASCISTA
ANTHEMIA	BLASTULA	CHATCHKA	DIARRHEA	FENESTRA
ANTHODIA	BOLTONIA	CHICKPEA	DIASPORA	FETERITA
ANTIDORA	BONSELLA	CHILLADA	DIASTEMA	FIBRILLA
ANTISERA	BORRELIA	CHIMAERA	DICENTRA	FISTIANA
APIMANIA	BOTANICA	CHINAMPA	DICHASIA	FLABELLA
APOLOGIA	BRACIOLA	CHINKARA	DIELYTRA	FLAGELLA
APOSITIA	BRANCHIA	CHIRAGRA	DIPLEGIA	FLOTILLA
APYREXIA	BRASSICA	CHLOASMA	DIPLOPIA	FOCACCIA
ARAPAIMA	BREGMATA	CHOLEMIA	DIPLOZOA	FORAMINA
ARAPONGA	BRITZSKA	CHURINGA	DJELLABA	FRITTATA
ARAPUNGA	BROMELIA	CHYLURIA	DRACAENA	FUGHETTA
ARBORETA	BRONCHIA	CIABATTA	DULCIANA	FURCRAEA
ARETHUSA	BROUGHTA	CINCHONA	DULCINEA	GALABIYA
ARMONICA	BROUHAHA	CISTERNA	DYSCHROA	GALLABEA
ARYTHMIA	BRUCELLA	CLAUSTRA	DYSLALIA	GALLABIA

Words that end with -A

GALLERIA	HYPHEMIA	MALAROMA	OLIGURIA	PRESIDIA
GALTONIA	HYPOGAEA	MALVASIA	OMBRELLA	PROFORMA
GAMBETTA	HYPONOIA	MAMALIGA	OMNIVORA	PROGERIA
GAMBUSIA	HYPOPNEA	MAMMILLA	ONGAONGA	PROTOZOA
GAMMADIA	HYSTERIA	MANDIOCA	OPERCULA	PRUNELLA
GAMMATIA	ICEKHANA	MANDORLA	OPERETTA	PRYTANEA
GARCINIA	IMPLUVIA	MANTILLA	OPUSCULA	PSORALEA
GARDENIA	INSIGNIA	MANTISSA	ORCHELLA	PTERYGIA
GASTRAEA	INSOMNIA	MANUBRIA	ORCHILLA	PUERPERA
GASTRULA	INTARSIA	MANYATTA	PAHAUTEA	PUTAMINA
GELSEMIA	INTIFADA	MARCELLA	PALESTRA	PYCNIDIA
GEMATRIA	ISABELLA	MARCHESA	PALLADIA	PYODERMA
GERARDIA	ISCHEMIA	MARINARA	PALPEBRA	PYORRHEA
GEROPIGA	ISCHURIA	MARINERA	PANATELA	QINDARKA
GESNERIA	IZVESTIA	MARIPOSA	PANCETTA	QUADRIGA
GLABELLA	JAPONICA	MARSUPIA	PANDEMIA	QUILLAIA
GLADIOLA	JARARACA	MARTYRIA	PANETELA	QUILLAJA
GLAUCOMA	JARARAKA	MASSOOLA	PANMIXIA	QUINELLA
GLIOMATA	JAVELINA	MATADORA	PANORAMA	QUINIELA
GLORIOSA	JIPIJAPA	MATAMATA	PARABEMA	RACHILLA
GLOSSINA	KALAMATA	MAUSOLEA	PARABOLA	RADIALIA
GLOXINIA	KALYPTRA	MAZAEDIA	PARANOEA	RAKSHASA
GLUMELLA	KAMAAINA	MAZOURKA	PARANOIA	RAMTILLA
GLYCEMIA	KARATEKA	MBAQANGA	PARAPARA	RANGIORA
GLYCERIA	KAREAREA	MECHITZA	PARHELIA	RAPHANIA
GOLCONDA	KATAKANA	MELANOMA	PAROEMIA	REDDENDA
GOLFIANA	KATCHINA	MELODICA	PAROSMIA	RENDZINA
GOLGOTHA	KAUMATUA	MENSTRUA	PAROUSIA	REPTILIA
GUERILLA	KAVAKAVA	MESHUGGA	PASHMINA	RESINATA
GURDWARA	KAWAKAWA	MESOGLEA	PELLAGRA	RESPONSA
GYMKHANA	KAZATZKA	METANOIA	PENUMBRA	RETICULA
GYMNASIA	KERATOMA	METASOMA	PEPONIDA	RETINULA
GYNAECEA	KHANSAMA	MIASMATA	PERFECTA	REWAREWA
GYNAECIA	KIELBASA	MILIARIA	PERIAGUA	RHIZOBIA
GYNOECIA	KINAKINA	MILTONIA	PETECHIA	ROSTELLA
HABANERA	KRAMERIA	MINNEOLA	PHACELIA	RUTABAGA
HACIENDA	LABRUSCA	MOKOPUNA	PHELONIA	SACRARIA
HAMARTIA	LAVALAVA	MOLLUSCA	PHOTINIA	SALICETA
HAPHTARA	LAVATERA	MONSTERA	PHOTOPIA	SALSILLA
HAPLOPIA	LECANORA	MONTARIA	PHRYGANA	SANTERIA
HATTERIA	LEKGOTLA	MOUSSAKA	PHYSALIA	SAPREMIA
HEARTPEA	LEUCEMIA	MOVIEOLA	PIASSABA	SAPUCAIA
HEKETARA	LEUKEMIA	MOZZETTA	PIASSAVA	SARMENTA
HEMATOMA	LEVODOPA	MRIDANGA	PIGNOLIA	SASARARA
HEMIOLIA	LINGUICA	MYCETOMA	PITAHAYA	SASTRUGA
HEMIOPIA	LINGUISA	MYOTONIA	PIZZERIA	SAYONARA
HEPATICA	LIPAEMIA	MYXAMEBA	PLACENTA	SCABIOSA
HEPATOMA	LIPOMATA	MYXEDEMA	PLANARIA	SCHAPSKA
HERBARIA	LISTERIA	MYXOMATA	PLANURIA	SCHEMATA
HETAIRIA	LITHEMIA	NASSELLA	PLATANNA	SCIATICA
HEUCHERA	LODICULA	NAVICULA	PLATYSMA	SCLEREMA
HINAHINA	LONICERA	NOCTURIA	PLETHORA	SCLEROMA
HIRAGANA	LYMPHOMA	NONQUOTA	PLUMERIA	SCOLIOMA
HORDEOLA	MACAHUBA	NUBECULA	POLLINIA	SCOTOMIA
HOROKAKA	MADRASSA	NYMPHAEA	POLYGALA	SCOTOPIA
HOSPITIA	MAGNESIA	OCCIPITA	POLYPNEA	SCROFULA
HYDREMIA	MAGNOLIA	ODONTOMA	POLYURIA	SCUTELLA
HYDRILLA	MAHARAJA	OEDEMATA	POSTCAVA	SEMANTRA
HYDROZOA	MAIOLICA	OITICICA	PREDELLA	SEMICOMA
HYPALGIA	MAJOLICA	OLIGEMIA	PRESCUTA	SEMIGALA

SEMINOMA	STOCCATA	TEGMENTA	TRIPUDIA	VIRTUOSA
SEMOLINA	STOKESIA	TEGUMINA	TRISTEZA	VISCACHA
SEMUNCIA	STOMODEA	TENACULA	TRITONIA	VISCARIA
SENORITA	STOTINKA	TENTORIA	TROCHLEA	VITICETA
SENSILLA	STROBILA	TEQUILLA	TROPARIA	VIVIPARA
SENSORIA	STROMATA	TERATOMA	TSAREVNA	VIZCACHA
SEPARATA	STRONTIA	TERRARIA	TSARITSA	VULSELLA
SEPTARIA	SUBCOSTA	TERRELLA	TSARITZA	VUVUZELA
SEPTLEVA	SUBMENTA	TERZETTA	TZAREVNA	WAHCONDA
SERENATA	SUBPHYLA	TESSELLA	TZARITZA	WEIGELIA
SHAMIANA	SUBPOENA	TETRAPLA	ULTIMATA	WISTARIA
SHECHITA	SUBTOPIA	THERIACA	UMBRELLA	WISTERIA
SHIGELLA	SUBUCULA	THIOTEPA	UNDERSEA	XANTHOMA
SHILLALA	SUBURBIA	THIOUREA	UNGUENTA	XENOPHYA
SHRADDHA	SUDAMINA	TIGRIDIA	UREDINIA	XEROMATA
SIDALCEA	SVASTIKA	TITHONIA	URINEMIA	XYLOMATA
SIGNORIA	SWASTICA	TOKONOMA	UROPYGIA	YARMULKA
SILICULA	SWASTIKA	TOPALGIA	VACCINIA	YERSINIA
SIMARUBA	SWEETPEA	TOQUILLA	VAGINULA	YOKOZUNA
SINFONIA	SYMPODIA	TORMENTA	VALENCIA	YTTERBIA
SITTELLA	SYMPOSIA	TORTILLA	VALLONIA	ZAKOUSKA
SONATINA	SYNANGIA	TOURISTA	VELAMINA	ZAMBOMBA
SORBARIA	SYNAPHEA	TOXAEMIA	VELATURA	ZAMPOGNA
SPARTINA	SYNCYTIA	TOXOCARA	VENDETTA	ZARZUELA
SPIRILLA	SYNECHIA	TRACHOMA	VERATRIA	ZASTRUGA
SPORIDIA	SYNEDRIA	TRAPEZIA	VERONICA	ZIRCONIA
SPOROZOA	SYNERGIA	TRAUMATA	VERTEBRA	ZOIATRIA
SQUAMULA	SYNKARYA	TRICHINA	VESICULA	ZOOCYTIA
STAPELIA	SYNTAGMA	TRIDACNA	VESTIGIA	ZOOGLOEA
STAROSTA	SYSSITIA	TRIENNIA	VIBRISSA	ZOOMANIA
STEATOMA	TAKAMAKA	TRIFECTA	VICTORIA	ZOONOMIA
STEMMATA	TAMANDUA	TRIFORIA	VIEWDATA	ZUCHETTA
STERIGMA	TAMBOURA	TRIHEDRA	VINIFERA	ZYGANTRA
STICHERA	TAPADERA	TRILEMMA	VIRAEMIA	ZYGOMATA
STIGMATA	TAQUERIA	TRIPTYCA	VIRGINIA	

Words that end with -I

Two-letter words

AI	three-toed sloth of South America
BI	bisexual person
DI	a plural of deus, god
GI	loose-fitting white martial-art suit
HI	hello
KI	(Chinese medicine) life force, same as qi
LI	Chinese measurement of distance
MI	musical note
OI	interjection
PI	sixteenth letter in the Greek alphabet
QI	(Chinese medicine) life force
SI	musical note
TI	musical note
XI	14th letter in the Greek alphabet

Words that end with -A

Three-letter words

AHI	yellowfin tuna
AMI	male friend
ANI	tropical American bird
BOI	lesbian who dresses like a boy
CHI	22nd letter of the Greek alphabet
DEI	a plural of deus, god
DUI	a plural of duo, duet
GHI	clarified butter
HOI	interjection
HUI	meeting of Maori people
IWI	any Maori tribe
JAI	victory (to)
KAI	food
KHI	same as CHI, letter of the Greek alphabet
KOI	any of various ornamental forms of the common carp
LEI	garland of flowers
MOI	me, used in mock affectation
OBI	broad sash tied in a large flat bow at the back, worn by Japanese women and children
PHI	21st letter in the Greek alphabet
POI	Hawaiian dish made from taro root
PSI	23rd letter of the Greek alphabet
RAI	type of Algerian popular music
REI	former Portuguese coin
SAI	South American monkey
SEI	type of whale
SKI	to glide over snow or water
SRI	title of respect used when addressing a Hindu
SUI	of itself
TAI	Japanese sea-bream
TUI	New Zealand bird
UNI	university
WAI	in New Zealand, water

Four-letter words

ABRI	DIVI	HORI	LOTI	NAZI
ACAI	DIXI	IMPI	LWEI	NEVI
ANTI	DUCI	INTI	MAGI	NIDI
ARTI	ELHI	JEDI	MAKI	NISI
ASCI	ETUI	KADI	MALI	NODI
BANI	EUOI	KAKI	MANI	NONI
BENI	FENI	KALI	MAXI	NORI
BIDI	FIFI	KAMI	MERI	PADI
BREI	FINI	KATI	MIDI	PENI
BUDI	FOCI	KAZI	MIHI	PERI
CADI	FUCI	KEPI	MINI	PFUI
CAPI	FUJI	KIWI	MIRI	PIKI
CEDI	GADI	KOJI	MOAI	PILI
CHAI	GARI	KUFI	MODI	PIPI
CONI	GLEI	KURI	MOKI	PTUI
DALI	GORI	KUTI	MOMI	PULI
DARI	GYRI	LARI	MOOI	PURI
DEFI	HAJI	LATI	MOTI	QADI
DELI	HILI	LIRI	MUNI	QUAI
DENI	HIOI	LOBI	MUTI	RABI
DESI	HOKI	LOCI	NAOI	RAGI

RAKI	SATI	TABI	TORI	WILI
RAMI	SEMI	TAKI	UNAI	YAGI
RANI	SHRI	TALI	UNCI	YETI
ROJI	SIMI	TAXI	VAGI	YOGI
ROTI	SIRI	TIKI	VALI	YONI
SADI	SOLI	TIPI	VLEI	ZATI
SAKI	SORI	TITI	WADI	ZITI
SARI	SYLI	TOPI	WALI	ZORI

Five-letter words

AALII	CESTI	HAJJI	MUFTI	SAKAI
AARTI	CHILI	HANGI	MURRI	SALMI
ABACI	CHOLI	HIKOI	MURTI	SAMPI
ACARI	CIPPI	HONGI	MYTHI	SATAI
ACINI	CIRRI	HOURI	NAEVI	SCAPI
ADUKI	CLAVI	IAMBI	NASHI	SCUDI
AGAMI	COATI	IMARI	NGATI	SEGNI
AGGRI	COCCI	IMSHI	NIMBI	SENGI
AGUTI	COMBI	INDRI	NISEI	SENSI
AIDOI	CORGI	ISSEI	NKOSI	SENTI
AIOLI	CORNI	JINNI	NOMOI	SERAI
ALIBI	CROCI	KANJI	OBELI	SHCHI
AMICI	CULTI	KARRI	OBOLI	SHIAI
ANIMI	CUNEI	KATTI	OCULI	SHOGI
APPUI	CURLI	KAURI	OKAPI	SHOJI
ARDRI	CURSI	KHADI	ORIBI	SOLDI
ARIKI	DARZI	KHAKI	OVOLI	SOLEI
ASKOI	DASHI	KHAZI	OZEKI	SPAHI
ASSAI	DESHI	KIBBI	PADRI	STOAI
ATIGI	DHOBI	KIBEI	PAGRI	STYLI
AULOI	DHOTI	KIKOI	PALKI	SUCCI
AUREI	DHUTI	KIRRI	PALPI	SULCI
AZUKI	DILLI	KOORI	PAOLI	SUSHI
BAJRI	DISCI	KORAI	PAPPI	SWAMI
BALTI	DOLCI	KRUBI	PARDI	TAKHI
BAMBI	DUOMI	KUKRI	PARKI	TANGI
BASSI	DURZI	KULFI	PARTI	TANTI
BASTI	ELCHI	LAARI	PENNI	TARSI
BEEDI	ELEMI	LANAI	PERAI	TAWAI
BENNI	ENNUI	LASSI	PETTI	TELOI
BESTI	ENOKI	LATHI	PILEI	TEMPI
BHAJI	ENVOI	LAZZI	PIRAI	TERAI
BIALI	FARCI	LENTI	POORI	TETRI
BINDI	FASCI	LIBRI	PRIMI	THAGI
BLINI	FASTI	LICHI	PSOAI	THALI
BOCCI	FERMI	LIMBI	PULLI	THOLI
BRAAI	FILMI	LITAI	PUNJI	THYMI
BRAVI	FRATI	LOGOI	PUTTI	TONDI
BUFFI	FUNDI	LUNGI	QUASI	TOPHI
BUSTI	FUNGI	LURGI	RABBI	TOPOI
BWAZI	GADDI	MACHI	RADII	TORII
BYSSI	GARNI	MANDI	RAHUI	TORSI
CACTI	GENII	MAQUI	RANGI	TRAGI
CAMPI	GHAZI	MARRI	RECTI	TSADI
CARDI	GIBLI	MATAI	REIKI	TUTTI
CARPI	GLOBI	MAURI	RISHI	UGALI
CEILI	GOBBI	MEDII	ROSHI	UMAMI
CELLI	GUSLI	MODII	ROSTI	URAEI
CERCI	HADJI	MOOLI	RUBAI	URALI

Words that end with -I

URARI	VILLI	WONGI	ZIMBI	
UTERI	VOLTI	XYSTI	ZOMBI	

Six-letter words

ACULEI	CURARI	KABIKI	OORALI	SIDDHI
ADSUKI	CYATHI	KABUKI	OURALI	SIFREI
ADZUKI	CYTISI	KAIKAI	OURARI	SIGLOI
AGAPAI	DALASI	KAMAHI	OUREBI	SILENI
AGOUTI	DECANI	KIMCHI	PAKAHI	SIMPAI
ALFAKI	DEGAMI	KOKIRI	PAKIHI	SMALTI
ALKALI	DENARI	KONAKI	PALAGI	SMRITI
ALUMNI	DEWANI	KONINI	PANINI	SOLIDI
AMBARI	DHOOTI	KORARI	PAPYRI	SOMONI
ANNULI	DJINNI	KOUROI	PATIKI	SONERI
ARCHEI	DROMOI	KOWHAI	PERITI	SOUARI
ARGALI	DUELLI	KROONI	PETSAI	STELAI
ARGULI	DUETTI	KULAKI	PHALLI	STRATI
ARILLI	ECHINI	KUMARI	PIROGI	SUNDRI
ARIOSI	ELTCHI	LAOGAI	PITHOI	SURIMI
ASKARI	EMBOLI	LAZULI	PITURI	TABULI
AVANTI	EPHEBI	LIMULI	PLUTEI	TAHINI
BAILLI	EPHORI	LITCHI	POHIRI	TAMARI
BANZAI	EQUALI	LOBULI	POLYPI	TANUKI
BHAKTI	EURIPI	LOCULI	PRIAPI	TAPETI
BHINDI	EXODOI	LUNGYI	PROTEI	TATAMI
BHISTI	FAMULI	MALLEI	PURIRI	TATSOI
BIKINI	FLOCCI	MALOTI	PUTELI	TAUIWI
BINDHI	FRACTI	MANATI	PYLORI	TAWHAI
BINGHI	FUMULI	MARABI	RAGINI	TENUTI
BOLETI	GARDAI	MARARI	RAMULI	THALLI
BONACI	GELATI	MAULVI	RAPINI	THOLOI
BONSAI	GEMINI	MAZHBI	REGULI	THYRSI
BOOHAI	GHARRI	MEHNDI	RENVOI	TIFOSI
BORZOI	GHIBLI	MEISHI	RHOMBI	TIRITI
BUIBUI	GILGAI	MILADI	ROMAJI	TITOKI
BUKSHI	GLUTEI	MIRCHI	RUBATI	TITULI
BURITI	GOMUTI	MIRITI	RUMAKI	TOITOI
BUZUKI	GRIGRI	MISHMI	SACCOI	TORULI
CADAGI	GUANXI	MODULI	SAFARI	TROCHI
CALAMI	GURAMI	MOIRAI	SAIKEI	TROPHI
CANTHI	HAIKAI	MOKIHI	SAKKOI	TSOTSI
CAROLI	HAKARI	MOOLVI	SALAMI	TUFOLI
CASINI	HAMULI	MOPANI	SALUKI	TULADI
CENTAI	HEGARI	MUESLI	SAMITI	TUMULI
CESTOI	HEISHI	MUNSHI	SANCAI	UAKARI
CESTUI	HERMAI	MYTHOI	SANDHI	UMFAZI
CHADRI	HUMERI	NAGARI	SANSEI	UNCINI
CHATTI	ILLUPI	NEINEI	SATORI	URACHI
CHICHI	INCAVI	NEROLI	SBIRRI	WAKIKI
CHILLI	INCUBI	NIELLI	SCAMPI	WAPITI
CHOKRI	ISTHMI	NIGIRI	SCYPHI	WARAGI
CHOWRI	JAWARI	NILGAI	SENITI	WASABI
CLYPEI	JEHADI	NOSTOI	SENSEI	XYSTOI
COLOBI	JIHADI	NUCLEI	SESELI	YANQUI
COLONI	JOWARI	OCELLI	SHALLI	YIDAKI
CONGII	JUDOGI	OCTOPI	SHANTI	YOGINI
CUBITI	JUNGLI	OCTROI	SHTCHI	ZAIKAI
CUMULI	JUPATI	ONAGRI	SHUFTI	ZUFOLI

Seven-letter words

ABOMASI	CHOREGI	INTAGLI	PALAZZI	SERKALI
ACANTHI	CHUPATI	JACUZZI	PANDANI	SERRATI
ACOUCHI	CLARINI	JAMDANI	PARODOI	SHIKARI
AFGHANI	COENURI	JAMPANI	PECCAVI	SHIVITI
ALFAQUI	COLIBRI	JINJILI	PENTITI	SIGNORI
ALIZARI	COLOSSI	JUKSKEI	PENUCHI	SKYPHOI
ALVEOLI	CORTILI	KABADDI	PIEROGI	SONDELI
AMORINI	CREMINI	KACHERI	PIGNOLI	SOPRANI
ANESTRI	CRIMINI	KAHAWAI	PINDARI	SORDINI
ANZIANI	DACTYLI	KAMICHI	PIROGHI	SPINONI
APICULI	DAKOITI	KAROSHI	PIROJKI	SPLENII
APPALTI	DAQUIRI	KOKOWAI	PLATYPI	SPUMONI
ARCHAEI	DASHEKI	KOLBASI	POLYNYI	STAMNOI
ASSAGAI	DASHIKI	KONGONI	PORANGI	STICHOI
ASSEGAI	DEMENTI	KOROWAI	PORCINI	STIMULI
ASTATKI	DENARII	LAMPUKI	POWHIRI	STRETTI
BACCHII	DIDAKAI	LAPILLI	PRELUDI	SUCCUBI
BACILLI	DIDAKEI	LECYTHI	PRONAOI	SUFFARI
BAMBINI	DIDICOI	LEKYTHI	PULVINI	SUNDARI
BANDARI	DOCHMII	MACRAMI	QAWWALI	SURCULI
BANOFFI	EFFENDI	MAESTRI	QUILLAI	SYLLABI
BASENJI	ELENCHI	MAFIOSI	RABBONI	TABOULI
BASMATI	EMERITI	MAMMATI	RANGOLI	TANKINI
BAZOUKI	EPHEBOI	MARCONI	RAPPINI	TAWHIRI
BHISHTI	EPIGONI	MARTINI	RAURIKI	TERMINI
BILIMBI	EPINAOI	MATSURI	RAVIOLI	THALAMI
BIRIANI	EREMURI	MELTEMI	REMBLAI	THROMBI
BIRYANI	ETOURDI	MENISCI	REREMAI	TIMPANI
BOUILLI	FAGOTTI	MERANTI	REVERSI	TOFUTTI
BREWSKI	FIASCHI	MINISKI	RHIZOPI	TOLARJI
BROCOLI	FLOKATI	MODELLI	RHOMBOI	TONDINI
BRONCHI	FORZATI	MODIOLI	RHONCHI	TORTONI
BUSUUTI	FUMETTI	MOLOSSI	RHYTHMI	TRIPOLI
CADUCEI	FUSILLI	MONOSKI	RIKISHI	TSUNAMI
CALATHI	GHILGAI	NAUPLII	RILIEVI	TURFSKI
CALCULI	GINGELI	NAUTILI	RIPIENI	TYMPANI
CALZONI	GINGILI	NEGRONI	SACCULI	URCEOLI
CAMOODI	GLUTAEI	NILGHAI	SAIMIRI	VENTURI
CANNOLI	GNOCCHI	NONETTI	SAMADHI	VIRELAI
CANZONI	GOURAMI	NUCELLI	SAMITHI	VITELLI
CAVETTI	GRADINI	NURAGHI	SAMURAI	VOLVULI
CEMBALI	GUARANI	NYLGHAI	SANTIMI	WISTITI
CHAPATI	HALLALI	OBLASTI	SANYASI	WOORALI
CHARPAI	HALOUMI	OMPHALI	SAOUARI	WOORARI
CHARQUI	HARAMDI	ORIGAMI	SARANGI	WOURALI
CHIANTI	HAVARTI	OUAKARI	SASHIMI	ZAKUSKI
CHIASMI	HEITIKI	OUSTITI	SCALENI	ZAMPONI
CHILIOI	HELLERI	PACHISI	SCHERZI	ZEPPOLI
CHIVARI	HEXEREI	PADRONI	SCIRRHI	ZINGANI
CHONDRI	HIBACHI	PAESANI	SECONDI	ZINGARI
CHORAGI	HOKONUI	PAHLAVI	SENARII	ZUFFOLI

Eight-letter words

ACERVULI	AMARETTI	ANOESTRI	BANDITTI	BIRIYANI
ACOEMETI	AMORETTI	ANTENATI	BERIBERI	BISCOTTI
ALBERGHI	AMPHIOXI	ASSEGAAI	BIMBASHI	BONAMANI

Words that end with -I

BORLOTTI	DAISHIKI	KIRIGAMI	PACHOULI	SIGISBEI
BOSTANGI	DECUBITI	KOFTGARI	PARCHESI	SIGNIORI
BOUSOUKI	DIADOCHI	KOHLRABI	PARCHISI	SOFFIONI
BOUZOUKI	DIGERATI	KOLBASSI	PASTICCI	SOLFEGGI
BOZZETTI	DIPTEROI	KOLINSKI	PASTRAMI	SOUVLAKI
BRAHMANI	DIVIDIVI	KOMITAJI	PASTROMI	STACCATI
BRINDISI	DOUPIONI	KUMBALOI	PATUTUKI	STAPEDII
BROCCOLI	DRACHMAI	KUMIKUMI	PECORINI	STOTINKI
BUMALOTI	DUPONDII	LEKYTHOI	PEDICULI	STROBILI
BUZKASHI	DURUKULI	LEMNISCI	PEPERONI	SUKIYAKI
CALAMARI	DUUMVIRI	LEYLANDI	PERFECTI	SUMOTORI
CALCANEI	ESOPHAGI	LIBRETTI	PERIBOLI	TABBOULI
CALYCULI	FASCISMI	LINGUINI	PERRADII	TAGLIONI
CANCELLI	FASCISTI	LITERATI	PIHOIHOI	TANDOORI
CANTHARI	FEDELINI	LUMBRICI	PIROSHKI	TARAKIHI
CAPITANI	FEMINAZI	MACARONI	PIROZHKI	TEDESCHI
CAPRICCI	FLOCCULI	MAHARANI	POPLITEI	TEOCALLI
CASTRATI	FORZANDI	MAHIMAHI	POSTNATI	TERAKIHI
CHAPATTI	FRASCATI	MALIHINI	PRINCIPI	TERIYAKI
CHAPPATI	FUNICULI	MALLEOLI	PRODROMI	TERZETTI
CHIGETAI	GINGELLI	MANUHIRI	PULVILLI	THESAURI
CHUPATTI	GINGILLI	MARAVEDI	RASMALAI	TRAPEZII
CICERONI	GINGLYMI	MARCHESI	RENMINBI	TROCHILI
CICISBEI	GLADIOLI	MARIACHI	RETIARII	TZATZIKI
CLAFOUTI	GRAFFITI	MENOMINI	RIGATONI	UMBILICI
CONCEPTI	GRISSINI	MONOKINI	RISPETTI	URANISCI
CONCERTI	HAEREMAI	MORBILLI	RYOTWARI	UTRICULI
CONCETTI	HALLOUMI	NANNYGAI	SANNYASI	VIRTUOSI
CONDUCTI	HETAIRAI	NARCISSI	SARTORII	WATERSKI
CONFETTI	HYDROSKI	NENNIGAI	SASTRUGI	WHARENUI
CORNETTI	IGNORAMI	NIRAMIAI	SCALDINI	YAKITORI
COTHURNI	KACHAHRI	NOTTURNI	SEXTARII	ZAKOUSKI
CROSTINI	KAKARIKI	NUCLEOLI	SFORZATI	ZASTRUGI
CUMBUNGI	KAZACHKI	OBLIGATI	SHANGHAI	ZECCHINI
CUNJEVOI	KAZATSKI	OSTINATI	SHERWANI	ZOOPHORI
DAIQUIRI	KIELBASI	OUISTITI	SHILINGI	ZUCCHINI

Words that end with -O

Two-letter words

BO	familiar term of address for a man
DO	to perform or complete (a deed or action)
GO	to move to or from a place
HO	cessation
IO	interjection
JO	Scots word for sweetheart
KO	Maori digging stick
LO	look!
MO	moment
NO	denial, disagreement, or refusal
OO	(Scots) wool
PO	chamber pot
SO	such an extent
TO	indicating movement towards
WO	archaic spelling of woe, grief
YO	expression used as a greeting or to attract someone's attention
ZO	Tibetan breed of cattle

Three-letter words

ABO	aborigine
ADO	fuss, trouble
AGO	in the past
APO	type of protein
AVO	Macao currency unit
AZO	of, consisting of, or containing the divalent nitrogen group -N-
BIO	biography
BOO	to shout disapproval
BRO	place for which one feels great affinity
COO	(of a dove or pigeon) to make a soft murmuring sound
DOO	dove
DSO	Tibetan breed of cattle
DUO	duet
DZO	Tibetan breed of cattle
ECO	short for ecology
EGO	conscious mind of an individual
EMO	type of music combining hard rock with emotional lyrics
EVO	informal Australian word for evening
EXO	informal Australian word for excellent
FRO	away
GEO	gully, creek
GIO	gully, creek
GOO	sticky substance
HAO	monetary unit of Vietnam
HOO	interjection
ISO	short segment of film that can be replayed easily
LOO	lavatory
MHO	unit of electrical conductance
MOO	(of a cow) to make a long deep cry
NOO	now
OBO	ship carrying oil and ore
OHO	exclamation expressing surprise, exultation, or derision
ONO	Hawaiian fish
OXO	containing oxygen
PHO	interjection of contempt
POO	to defecate
PRO	professional person
REO	language in general (Maori)
RHO	17th letter in the Greek alphabet
ROO	kangaroo
TAO	(in Confucian philosophy) path of virtuous conduct
THO	though
TOO	also, as well
TWO	one more than one
UDO	stout perennial plant of Japan and China
UFO	flying saucer
UPO	upon
WHO	which person
WOO	to seek the love or affection of
YGO	obsolete past tense of go
ZHO	Tibetan breed of cattle
ZOO	place where live animals are kept for show

Four-letter words

AERO	DERO	JOCO	MOJO	SKIO
AFRO	DIDO	JOMO	MOKO	SOHO
AGIO	DINO	JUCO	MONO	SOLO
ALCO	DOCO	JUDO	MOZO	SUMO
ALKO	DODO	KAGO	MUSO	SYBO
ALSO	DOJO	KARO	MYXO	TACO
ALTO	DURO	KAYO	NOLO	TARO
AMBO	DZHO	KENO	ODSO	THIO
AMMO	ECCO	KERO	OLEO	THRO
ANNO	ECHO	KETO	OLIO	TIRO
APSO	EDDO	KILO	ONTO	TOCO
ARCO	ERGO	KINO	OPPO	TOHO
ARVO	EURO	KOBO	ORDO	TOKO
AUTO	EXPO	KOLO	ORZO	TOMO
BEGO	FADO	KORO	OTTO	TOPO
BIRO	FANO	KOTO	OUZO	TORO
BITO	FARO	KUDO	PACO	TOYO
BOHO	FICO	KYBO	PEPO	TRIO
BOKO	FIDO	LAZO	PESO	TYPO
BOLO	FIGO	LENO	PISO	TYRO
BOYO	FILO	LEVO	POCO	UMBO
BOZO	FINO	LIDO	POGO	UNCO
BRIO	GAJO	LILO	POLO	UNDO
BROO	GAPO	LIMO	POMO	UNTO
BUBO	GIRO	LINO	PRAO	UPDO
BUDO	GOBO	LIPO	PROO	UPGO
BUFO	GOGO	LOBO	PYRO	URAO
CALO	GYRO	LOCO	RATO	VEGO
CAMO	HALO	LOGO	REDO	VETO
CAPO	HARO	LOTO	REGO	VINO
CERO	HELO	LUDO	REPO	VIVO
CHAO	HERO	MAKO	RIVO	WERO
CIAO	HOBO	MANO	ROTO	WHIO
CITO	HOMO	MAYO	SADO	WINO
COCO	HUSO	MEMO	SAGO	YEBO
COHO	HYPO	MENO	SECO	YUKO
DADO	INFO	MICO	SEGO	ZERO
DAGO	INGO	MILO	SHMO	ZOBO
DATO	INRO	MINO	SHOO	
DECO	INTO	MIRO	SIJO	
DELO	JATO	MISO	SILO	
DEMO	JIAO	MOFO	SKEO	

Five-letter words

ABMHO	ANDRO	BANJO	BINGO	BUROO
ACHOO	ANGLO	BARDO	BIZZO	BURRO
ADDIO	APPRO	BARRO	BOFFO	BUTEO
ADOBO	ASPRO	BASHO	BOMBO	CACAO
AGGRO	AUDIO	BASSO	BONGO	CAMEO
AGLOO	AVISO	BASTO	BORGO	CAMPO
ALAMO	AWATO	BAZOO	BRAVO	CANSO
ALTHO	AWETO	BEANO	BROMO	CANTO
AMIDO	AZIDO	BENTO	BUCKO	CARBO
AMIGO	BABOO	BERKO	BUFFO	CARGO
AMINO	BACCO	BIFFO	BUMBO	CASCO
AMNIO	BALOO	BILBO	BUNCO	CELLO
ANCHO	BANCO	BIMBO	BUNKO	CENTO

CHACO	FOLIO	KIMBO	PATIO	SEGNO
CHADO	FORDO	KONDO	PEDRO	SERVO
CHEMO	FORGO	KUSSO	PENGO	SEXTO
CHIAO	FUERO	LAEVO	PESTO	SHAKO
CHICO	FUGIO	LARGO	PETTO	SHISO
CHIMO	FUNGO	LASSO	PHONO	SICKO
CHINO	GADJO	LAZZO	PHOTO	SIXMO
CHIRO	GADSO	LENTO	PIANO	SKIMO
CHOCO	GALVO	LESBO	PIEZO	SMOKO
CHOKO	GAMBO	LEUCO	PILAO	SOCKO
CHOLO	GARBO	LIMBO	PINGO	SOLDO
CISCO	GAZOO	LINGO	PINKO	SORBO
CLARO	GECKO	LITHO	PINTO	SORDO
COCCO	GENRO	LLANO	PISCO	SORGO
COMBO	GESSO	LOTTO	POLIO	SPADO
COMMO	GINZO	MACHO	PONGO	STENO
COMPO	GIPPO	MACRO	PORNO	STYLO
CONDO	GISMO	MAIKO	POSHO	SULFO
CONGO	GIZMO	MAMBO	POTOO	TABOO
CONTO	GOBBO	MANGO	POTTO	TACHO
CONVO	GODSO	MANTO	PRIMO	TANGO
CORNO	GOMBO	MATLO	PROMO	TANTO
CORSO	GONZO	MATZO	PROSO	TARDO
CREDO	GREGO	MENTO	PULAO	TELCO
CUFFO	GUACO	MESTO	PULMO	TEMPO
CURIO	GUANO	METHO	PUNTO	TENNO
CUSSO	GUIRO	METRO	PUTTO	THORO
CUTTO	GUMBO	MEZZO	QUINO	TIMBO
CYANO	GUSTO	MICRO	QUIPO	TONDO
CYCLO	GYPPO	MILKO	RADIO	TORSO
DANIO	HALLO	MIMEO	RATIO	TRIGO
DATTO	HELIO	MISDO	RATOO	TRUGO
DECKO	HELLO	MISGO	RAUPO	TURBO
DEFFO	HILLO	MOLTO	RAZOO	TYPTO
DEKKO	HIMBO	MONDO	REALO	UREDO
DERRO	HIPPO	MONGO	RECCO	VERSO
DIAZO	HOLLO	MORRO	RECTO	VIDEO
DILDO	HOWSO	MOSSO	REFFO	VIREO
DINGO	HULLO	MOTTO	REGGO	VISTO
DIPSO	HYDRO	MUCHO	REPRO	VULGO
DISCO	IGAPO	MUCRO	RESTO	WACKO
DITTO	IGLOO	MUNGO	RETRO	WAHOO
DOBRO	IMAGO	NACHO	RHINO	WALDO
DOGGO	IMIDO	NAPOO	RODEO	WAZOO
DOHYO	IMINO	NARCO	ROMEO	WHAMO
DONKO	INTRO	NEGRO	RONDO	WHOSO
DRACO	IROKO	NGAIO	RONEO	WILCO
DSOBO	JAMBO	NITRO	RUMBO	YAHOO
DSOMO	JELLO	NUTSO	RUMPO	YARCO
DUBBO	JINGO	ORTHO	SADDO	YARTO
DUMBO	JOCKO	OUTDO	SALTO	YOBBO
DUNNO	JUMBO	OUTGO	SALVO	YUCKO
DUOMO	JUNCO	OUTRO	SAMBO	YUMMO
ERUGO	JUNTO	OVOLO	SANGO	ZAMBO
ESTRO	KAROO	PANTO	SANKO	ZHOMO
FANGO	KAZOO	PAOLO	SANTO	ZINCO
FATSO	KEENO	PAREO	SARGO	ZIPPO
FIBRO	KEMBO	PARGO	SCHMO	ZOCCO
FILLO	KENDO	PARVO	SCUDO	ZOPPO
FLEXO	KIDDO	PASEO	SECCO	ZORRO

Words that end with -O

Six-letter words

ABRAZO	CATALO	GHERAO	MACACO	RABATO
ADAGIO	CHARRO	GHETTO	MADURO	RANCHO
ADJIGO	CHEAPO	GIGOLO	MAMAKO	REBATO
AERUGO	CHEERO	GINGKO	MANITO	REBOZO
AHCHOO	CHOCHO	GINKGO	MANOAO	REECHO
AIKIDO	CHOCKO	GITANO	MAOMAO	REGULO
AKIMBO	CHROMO	GIUSTO	MATICO	REZERO
ALBEDO	CHURRO	GOMBRO	MATIPO	RIALTO
ALBINO	CICERO	GOMUTO	MEDICO	RIGHTO
ALBUGO	COGITO	GONGYO	MELANO	ROADEO
ALNICO	COLUGO	GOOROO	MENUDO	ROBALO
AMMINO	COMEDO	GORGIO	MERINO	ROCOCO
AMMONO	COMODO	GREEBO	MIKADO	ROMANO
ANATTO	CONCHO	GRINGO	MIOMBO	ROTOLO
ANGICO	COOCOO	GROTTO	MODULO	RUBATO
APOLLO	COROZO	GUANGO	MOKORO	RUBIGO
ARIOSO	CRAMBO	HAIRDO	MONOAO	SAMFOO
ARISTO	CRYPTO	HALLOO	MOOLOO	SANCHO
ARROYO	CUATRO	HERETO	MORPHO	SANPRO
ARSENO	CUCKOO	HETERO	NANDOO	SAPEGO
ARSINO	DAIMIO	HOLLOO	NARDOO	SBIRRO
ASIAGO	DAIMYO	HONCHO	NIELLO	SCAMTO
AUSUBO	DAYGLO	HOODOO	NONEGO	SCHIZO
AWHATO	DEXTRO	HOOPOO	NOSTRO	SCRUTO
AWHETO	DINERO	HOOROO	NUNCIO	SHACKO
BABACO	DOMINO	HULLOO	NYMPHO	SHEEPO
BAGNIO	DOODOO	HUPIRO	OBENTO	SHIPPO
BAGUIO	DOPPIO	IGNARO	OCTAVO	SHIVOO
BAMBOO	DORADO	IMBIZO	OLINGO	SHYPOO
BAROLO	DRONGO	INCAVO	OVERDO	SISSOO
BARRIO	DUELLO	INDIGO	OVERGO	SKIDOO
BASUCO	DUETTO	JAZZBO	PAKOKO	SLEAZO
BAYAMO	DYNAMO	JINGKO	PALOLO	SMALTO
BEENTO	EMBRYO	JOURNO	PANINO	SOLANO
BILLYO	ENDURO	KAKAPO	PARAMO	SOLITO
BISTRO	ENHALO	KARORO	PEDALO	SORGHO
BLANCO	ENVIRO	KARROO	PEPINO	SPEEDO
BLOTTO	ERINGO	KATIPO	PERNIO	SPINTO
BOLERO	ERYNGO	KEKENO	PEROXO	STALKO
BONITO	ESCUDO	KIMONO	PHYLLO	STANZO
BONOBO	FASCIO	KLEPTO	PHYSIO	STEREO
BOOBOO	FIASCO	KOKAKO	PICARO	STINGO
BOOCOO	FINITO	KOODOO	PIOPIO	STINKO
BOOHOO	FINSKO	KORERO	PLONKO	STUCCO
BOOKOO	FOREDO	KOUSSO	POMATO	STUDIO
BRASCO	FOREGO	KWAITO	POMELO	SUBITO
BRILLO	FORHOO	LADINO	PONCHO	TAPALO
BROCHO	FRANCO	LANUGO	POTATO	TATTOO
BRONCO	FRESCO	LATIGO	PRESTO	TECHNO
BUMALO	FUGATO	LATINO	PRONTO	TENUTO
BURGOO	FUMADO	LAVABO	PSEUDO	TERCIO
CABRIO	GABBRO	LEGATO	PSYCHO	TEREDO
CALICO	GALAGO	LIBERO	PUEBLO	THICKO
CALIGO	GAUCHO	LIBIDO	PUKEKO	THUGGO
CAMSHO	GAZABO	LIVEDO	PUMELO	TIFOSO
CARDIO	GAZEBO	LOBOLO	PUNCTO	TOLEDO
CASHOO	GELATO	LOLIGO	QUANGO	TOMATO
CASINO	GENTOO	LUCUMO	QUARTO	TORERO

TRILLO	ULTIMO	VIRINO	WEIRDO	ZOCALO
TROPPO	VAUDOO	VOMITO	WHACKO	ZOOZOO
TUKTOO	VELCRO	VOODOO	WHAMMO	ZORINO
TUPELO	VIBRIO	VORAGO	WHATSO	ZUFOLO
TURACO	VIGORO	VOSTRO	WHOMSO	ZYDECO
TUXEDO	VIRAGO	WANDOO	ZELOSO	

Seven-letter words

AGITATO	CEMBALO	LUMBAGO	PERSICO	SENTIMO
AILANTO	CENTAVO	MADRONO	PIANINO	SERPIGO
AKIRAHO	CENTIMO	MAESTRO	PICACHO	SERRANO
ALBERGO	CHAMISO	MAFIOSO	PICCOLO	SFUMATO
ALFREDO	CHANOYO	MAGNETO	PIFFERO	SHAKUDO
ALLEGRO	CHEERIO	MALICHO	PIMENTO	SHAMPOO
AMORINO	CHICANO	MANGEAO	PINTADO	SIROCCO
AMOROSO	CHORIZO	MARCATO	PINTANO	SKIDDOO
ANIMATO	CLARINO	MARENGO	PLACEBO	SMOKEHO
ANNATTO	COMMODO	MARRANO	PLENIPO	SOLDADO
APAREJO	CONCEDO	MEMENTO	POBLANO	SOPRANO
APPALTO	COQUITO	MENDIGO	POINADO	SORDINO
ARBORIO	CORANTO	MESTESO	POMPANO	SQUACCO
ARNATTO	CORNUTO	MESTINO	POMPELO	STRETTO
ARNOTTO	CRIOLLO	MESTIZO	PORCINO	SUBECHO
ARRIERO	CRUSADO	MISTICO	PORRIGO	SUBZERO
ASINICO	CRUZADO	MOCKADO	PORTICO	SUPREMO
ATISHOO	CURACAO	MODELLO	POTOROO	SYNCHRO
AVOCADO	CYMBALO	MOMENTO	PRIMERO	TALLYHO
AZULEJO	DIABOLO	MONTERO	PRIVADO	TAMARAO
BACALAO	DINITRO	MORELLO	PROVISO	TANGELO
BAMBINO	EIGHTVO	MORENDO	PROXIMO	TEDESCO
BANDITO	ELECTRO	MORISCO	PRURIGO	TENTIGO
BAROCCO	EMBARGO	MOROCCO	PUMMELO	TESTUDO
BARRICO	ESPARTO	MULATTO	QUOMODO	THEORBO
BATTERO	ETAERIO	NATHEMO	RABBITO	THERETO
BEEFALO	FAGOTTO	NAVARHO	REJONEO	TIMPANO
BIZARRO	FARRAGO	NELUMBO	RELIEVO	TOBACCO
BONIATO	FERRUGO	NITROSO	RELLENO	TOMBOLO
BOTARGO	FINNSKO	NONETTO	REVERSO	TONDINO
BRACCIO	FORZATO	NONHERO	RIDOTTO	TORNADO
BRACERO	FUMETTO	NONZERO	RILIEVO	TORPEDO
BRASERO	FURIOSO	NORTENO	RIPIENO	TOSTADO
BRAVADO	GAMBADO	OKIMONO	RISOTTO	TOURACO
BRONCHO	GESTAPO	OLOROSO	ROGALLO	TREMOLO
BUDGERO	GIOCOSO	OREGANO	RONDINO	TROMINO
BUFFALO	GRADINO	OUTECHO	ROSOLIO	TWIGLOO
BUGABOO	GUANACO	PACHUCO	RUBABOO	TYMPANO
BUMMALO	HAPKIDO	PAESANO	SAGUARO	UNDERDO
BURRITO	HIDALGO	PAISANO	SAHUARO	UNDERGO
BUSHIDO	HISTRIO	PAKAPOO	SALTATO	UNMACHO
CABILDO	HORNITO	PALAZZO	SAMSHOO	UPTEMPO
CALALOO	HUANACO	PAMPERO	SANTERO	VAQUERO
CALANDO	IMPASTO	PAPILIO	SAPSAGO	VERISMO
CALYPSO	INFERNO	PASSADO	SCALADO	VERTIGO
CANTICO	JIGABOO	PATRICO	SCHERZO	VIBRATO
CARABAO	KARENGO	PEDRERO	SCIOLTO	VILIACO
CASSINO	KERCHOO	PEEKABO	SECONDO	VILIAGO
CATTALO	LENTIGO	PEKEPOO	SEMIPRO	VIRANDO
CAVETTO	LLANERO	PENTITO	SENECIO	VOLCANO

Words that end with -O

VOLPINO	WHERETO	ZANJERO	ZEMSTVO	ZOCCOLO
WENDIGO	WINDIGO	ZAPATEO	ZINGANO	ZORILLO
WHERESO	ZAMARRO	ZEBRANO	ZINGARO	ZUFFOLO

Eight-letter words

ALFRESCO	CONTANGO	HUBBUBOO	OCOTILLO	SMORZATO
AMARETTO	CONTEMPO	IMPETIGO	ORATORIO	SOLIDAGO
AMORETTO	CONTINUO	INNUENDO	OSTINATO	SOMBRERO
ANTIHERO	CONTORNO	INTAGLIO	OTTAVINO	SPADILLO
ARMIGERO	CONVERSO	INTONACO	PACHINKO	SPICCATO
ARPEGGIO	CORAGGIO	JACKAROO	PADERERO	STACCATO
ASSIENTO	CORNETTO	JACKEROO	PALAMINO	STAMPEDO
ATAMASCO	COROCORO	JALAPENO	PALISADO	STICCADO
AUTOGIRO	COURANTO	JEREPIGO	PALMETTO	STICCATO
AUTOGYRO	CROSTINO	JILLAROO	PALOMINO	STILETTO
BALLYHOO	CRUZEIRO	JORDELOO	PARLANDO	STOCCADO
BARBASCO	CURCULIO	JUNKANOO	PASTITSO	SUBAUDIO
BARGELLO	DOLCETTO	KAKEMONO	PATERERO	SUBIMAGO
BARRANCO	DOLOROSO	KAMOKAMO	PECORINO	SUPEREGO
BESOGNIO	DUECENTO	KANGAROO	PEDERERO	SUPERLOO
BISCOTTO	DUETTINO	KORIMAKO	PEEKABOO	SUPERPRO
BOCACCIO	ELDORADO	KOROMIKO	PEEKAPOO	SUPPEAGO
BONAMANO	ENCIERRO	LARGANDO	PEPERINO	TALEGGIO
BORACHIO	ESCALADO	LEGGIERO	PERDENDO	TAPACOLO
BORDELLO	ESCAPADO	LENTANDO	PERFECTO	TAPACULO
BOZZETTO	ESPRESSO	LIBECCIO	PIMIENTO	TAPADERO
BUCKAROO	ESPUMOSO	LIBRETTO	PIQUILLO	TENEBRIO
BUCKAYRO	EXPRESSO	LITERATO	PLUMBAGO	TERRAZZO
BUCKEROO	FALSETTO	LOCOFOCO	POIGNADO	TERZETTO
BURDIZZO	FANDANGO	LOTHARIO	POLITICO	TOKOTOKO
CABESTRO	FAROLITO	MACHISMO	PRELUDIO	TORNILLO
CABRESTO	FASCISMO	MAESTOSO	PRERADIO	TRAPUNTO
CACAFOGO	FELLATIO	MAKIMONO	PRESIDIO	TRECENTO
CALLALOO	FINNESKO	MALGRADO	PRUNELLO	TUCOTUCO
CAMISADO	FINOCHIO	MALLECHO	PULVILIO	TUCUTUCO
CAPITANO	FLAMENCO	MAMELUCO	PYINKADO	TWELVEMO
CAPUCCIO	FLAMINGO	MANCANDO	RANCHERO	UMBRELLO
CASTRATO	FORZANDO	MANZELLO	REDDENDO	VARGUENO
CAUDILLO	FRICANDO	MARTELLO	RENEGADO	VARLETTO
CAVALERO	GALAPAGO	MERCAPTO	RIRORIRO	VERDELHO
CHARANGO	GARBANZO	MICROMHO	RISOLUTO	VIGOROSO
CHARNECO	GARDYLOO	MILESIMO	RISPETTO	VILLAGIO
CHECHAKO	GAZPACHO	MILLIMHO	RITENUTO	VILLIAGO
CHUBASCO	GERONIMO	MINIMOTO	ROSOGLIO	VINDALOO
CICISBEO	GILLAROO	MIROMIRO	RUBBABOO	VIRTUOSO
CILANTRO	GRACIOSO	MODERATO	SALTANDO	VITILIGO
CIOPPINO	GRAFFITO	MOKOMOKO	SARGASSO	WALLAROO
CLASSICO	GRAZIANO	MONTANTO	SCALDINO	WANDEROO
COCKAPOO	GUACHARO	MOSQUITO	SCENARIO	WATERLOO
COCKATOO	HABANERO	MUCHACHO	SCIROCCO	WAYLEGGO
COCOBOLO	HALLALOO	MUNDUNGO	SCORDATO	WHAKAIRO
COLORADO	HEREINTO	NEUTRINO	SEICENTO	YAKIMONO
COMMANDO	HEREUNTO	NOCTILIO	SEMIHOBO	ZECCHINO
CONCERTO	HITHERTO	NONMETRO	SERAGLIO	ZUCHETTO
CONCETTO	HOROPITO	NOPALITO	SESTETTO	
CONFETTO	HUAQUERO	NOTTURNO	SFORZATO	
CONJUNTO	HUARACHO	OBLIGATO	SIGISBEO	

Words that end with -U

Two-letter words

GU	
MU	12th letter in the Greek alphabet, a consonant, transliterated as M
NU	13th letter in the Greek alphabet
OU	man, bloke, or chap
XU	Vietnamese currency unit
YU	jade

Three-letter words

AMU	unit of mass
AYU	small Japanese fish
BRU	(South African) informal word for a friend
CRU	(in France) a vineyard
EAU	river
ECU	any of various former French gold or silver coins
EMU	Australian flightless bird
FEU	to grant use of land with a particular type of tenure
FLU	any of various viral infections
FOU	bushel
GAU	district set up by the Nazi Party during the Third Reich
GJU	type of violin used in Shetland
GNU	South African antelope
JEU	a game (as if French)
KYU	(in judo) one of the five student grades for inexperienced competitors
LEU	standard monetary unit of Romania and Moldova
LOU	(Scots) to love
MEU	European plant
MOU	Scots form of mouth
PIU	more (quickly, softly, etc)
PLU	beaver skin used as a unit of value in the fur trade
SAU	Vietnamese currency unit
SOU	former French coin
TAU	19th letter in the Greek alphabet
ULU	type of knife
UMU	type of oven
UTU	reward
VAU	obsolete letter of Greek alphabet
YOU	person or people addressed

Four-letter words

AGLU	EMEU	JUKU	LUAU	PUKU
AITU	FRAU	KAGU	LULU	PULU
BABU	FUGU	KORU	MASU	PUPU
BAJU	GENU	KUDU	MENU	RAKU
BALU	GURU	KUKU	MEOU	RATU
BAPU	HABU	KURU	MOTU	RIMU
BEAU	HAKU	KUTU	MUMU	RURU
BEDU	HAPU	KUZU	NAMU	SULU
BUBU	HUHU	LATU	OMBU	SUSU
CHOU	IGLU	LEKU	PATU	TABU
CLOU	JEHU	LIEU	PRAU	TAPU
ECRU	JUJU	LITU	PUDU	TATU

Words that end with -U

TEGU	TOFU	UNAU	WUDU	ZOBU
THOU	TOLU	VATU	YUZU	ZULU
THRU	TUTU	VROU	ZEBU	

Five-letter words

ADIEU	CHIRU	KONBU	PERDU	TAHOU
AHURU	CORNU	KUDZU	PIKAU	TATOU
BANTU	COYPU	LASSU	PILAU	TENDU
BATTU	FICHU	MAPAU	POILU	TUKTU
BAYOU	FONDU	MIAOU	PONZU	UHURU
BIJOU	HAIKU	MUNTU	POYOU	URUBU
BITOU	HINAU	NAIRU	PRAHU	VERTU
BOYAU	HOKKU	NANDU	QUIPU	VIRTU
BUCHU	JAMBU	NIKAU	SADHU	VODOU
BUCKU	KANZU	NOYAU	SAJOU	VOULU
BUNDU	KAURU	OTAKU	SAMFU	WUSHU
BUSSU	KAWAU	PAREU	SHOYU	
CENTU	KOMBU	PENDU	SNAFU	

Six-letter words

ABATTU	COTEAU	KIKUYU	MZUNGU	SAMSHU
ACAJOU	COYPOU	KOKOPU	NHANDU	SENRYU
ALLYOU	DETENU	KOTUKU	NILGAU	SHINJU
AMADOU	EPERDU	LANDAU	NOGAKU	SUBFEU
APERCU	GAGAKU	MADAFU	ORIHOU	TAMANU
BATEAU	GATEAU	MAHEWU	ORMOLU	TAUHOU
BHIKHU	GOMOKU	MAKUTU	PILLAU	TELEDU
BINIOU	GRUGRU	MALIBU	PISTOU	VOUDOU
BOUBOU	HALERU	MAMAKU	PIUPIU	WHANAU
BUREAU	HAPUKU	MANATU	QUIPPU	YNAMBU
CACHOU	INGENU	MANITU	RAWARU	
CADEAU	JABIRU	MEVROU	RESEAU	
CALALU	KARAMU	MILIEU	ROUCOU	
CONGOU	KERERU	MUUMUU	SADDHU	

Seven-letter words

ANTIFLU	CHANOYU	MANITOU	PURLIEU	TAMANDU
BABASSU	CHAPEAU	MANTEAU	RAUPATU	TAMARAU
BANDEAU	CHATEAU	MARABOU	ROKKAKU	TAUHINU
BATTEAU	CORBEAU	MOINEAU	RONDEAU	TIMARAU
BEBEERU	COUTEAU	MORCEAU	ROULEAU	TINAMOU
BERCEAU	DAIMOKU	MWALIMU	SANTIMU	TONNEAU
BUNRAKU	FABLIAU	NILGHAU	SAPAJOU	TRUMEAU
CAMAIEU	INCONNU	NOUVEAU	SEPPUKU	TURACOU
CARDECU	JAMBEAU	NYLGHAU	SHIATSU	UMLUNGU
CARIBOU	JUJITSU	PARVENU	SHIATZU	WAMEFOU
CATECHU	JUJUTSU	PLATEAU	SUBMENU	WAREHOU
CATTABU	MAMAKAU	PONCEAU	TABLEAU	

Eight-letter words

ABOIDEAU	FELDGRAU	KEIRETSU	PIRARUCU	TIRAMISU
ABOITEAU	FLAMBEAU	KINKAJOU	PRIEDIEU	TSUTSUMU
BERIMBAU	FROUFROU	MAIREHAU	PYENGADU	TUCUTUCU
CARCAJOU	HAUSFRAU	MINSHUKU	ROUSSEAU	VERMOULU
CARIACOU	JIUJITSU	NINJITSU	SUCURUJU	WILLIWAU
CARJACOU	JIUJUTSU	NINJUTSU	SURUCUCU	ZAIBATSU
COUMAROU	KABELJOU	NUNCHAKU	THANKYOU	

Chapter 5: Vowel and Consonant Themes

Awkward vowel combinations

A problem every Scrabble player faces is an unpromising combination of letters. With the exception of E, drawing duplicates of any vowel can be awkward. In this respect duplicate As and Os are bad enough, but duplicate Is and Us are even worse. If you find yourself with three or more of a particular vowel on your rack, it's a good idea to try and offload the excess ones. With three Is on your rack, you should try to play a word with two of them. And because I is one of the most common letters in the game, if you don't get rid of both Is in a single turn, you are highly likely to end up with the same problem in the next round. It's a very good idea, therefore, to have a cache of words that uses duplicate vowels so that you can deal with the problem as soon as it arises, allowing you to clear out the excess vowels on your rack without falling behind on the score. The lists in this section provide three- and four-letter words with two of each vowel (except E), and five and six-letter words with three or more Os or Us.

Using As

Three-letter words with two As

AAH	AGA	ALA	AVA	FAA
AAL	AHA	AMA	AWA	MAA
AAS	AIA	ANA	BAA	
ABA	AKA	AUA	CAA	

Four-letter words with two As

AAHS	ALFA	ASAR	DATA	KAWA
AALS	ALGA	ASEA	FAAN	LAMA
ABAC	ALMA	ATAP	FAAS	LANA
ABAS	AMAH	ATMA	FAVA	LAVA
ABBA	AMAS	ATUA	GAGA	MAAR
ACAI	AMIA	AULA	GALA	MAAS
ACCA	AMLA	AURA	GAMA	MALA
ACTA	ANAL	AVAL	HAAF	MAMA
ADAW	ANAN	AVAS	HAAR	MANA
AFAR	ANAS	AWAY	HAHA	MARA
AGAR	ANGA	AXAL	HAKA	MASA
AGAS	ANNA	AYAH	JAAP	MAYA
AGHA	ANOA	AZAN	JAFA	NAAM
AGMA	ANSA	BAAL	JAGA	NAAN
AIAS	ANTA	BAAS	JAVA	NADA
AIGA	APAY	BABA	KAAL	NAGA
AJAR	AQUA	CAAS	KAAS	NALA
ALAE	ARAK	CABA	KAKA	NANA
ALAN	ARAR	CACA	KAMA	NAPA
ALAP	ARBA	CAMA	KANA	PAAL
ALAR	AREA	CAPA	KAPA	PACA
ALAS	ARIA	CASA	KARA	PAPA
ALAY	ARNA	CAVA	KATA	PARA
ALBA	ARPA	DADA	KAVA	PAUA

PAWA	RATA	TAKA	TAWA	WAWA
RACA	RAYA	TALA	TAXA	YAAR
RAGA	SAGA	TANA	VARA	YABA
RAIA	SAMA	TAPA	VASA	
RAJA	TAAL	TARA	WAAC	
RANA	TAHA	TAVA	WAKA	

Five-letter words with three As

ABACA	AFARA	ALAPA	ARABA	TAATA
ABAKA	AGAMA	ANANA	ASANA	
ABAYA	ALAAP	ANATA	KAAMA	

Six-letter words with three As

ABACAS	ANABAS	BALATA	KABAKA	PANAMA
ABAKAS	ANANAS	BANANA	KABALA	PAPAYA
ABASIA	ANATAS	BARAZA	KABAYA	PATACA
ABAYAS	ANATTA	BATATA	KAMALA	PATAKA
ACACIA	ANTARA	BAZAAR	KANAKA	QABALA
AFARAS	ARABAS	BRAATA	KARAKA	RAMADA
AGAMAS	ARALIA	CABALA	KATANA	SALAAM
AGAPAE	ARCANA	CABANA	LABARA	SAMAAN
AGAPAI	ARGALA	CADAGA	MANAIA	SAMARA
AGGADA	ARMADA	CANADA	MANANA	SATARA
AKATEA	ASANAS	CASABA	MANAWA	TAATAS
AKHARA	ASRAMA	CASAVA	MARACA	TAIAHA
ALAAPS	ATABAL	DAGABA	MASALA	TAMARA
ALALIA	ATAMAN	HALALA	MATATA	TARAMA
ALAPAS	ATAXIA	HAMADA	NAGANA	UJAMAA
ALASKA	AVATAR	HAWALA	PAJAMA	VAHANA
ALBATA	AZALEA	JACANA	PALAMA	WAIATA
ALPACA	BAHADA	JATAKA	PALAPA	ZANANA
AMARNA	BAJADA	KAAMAS	PANADA	ZAPATA

Using Es

Four-letter words with three Es

EPEE

Five-letter words with three Es

BELEE	EMEER	GELEE	NEEZE	SEMEE
BESEE	EPEES	HEEZE	PEECE	TEENE
DEERE	ETWEE	KEEVE	PEEPE	TEPEE
DEEVE	EXEEM	LEESE	PEEVE	WEEKE
EERIE	EXEME	LEVEE	PEWEE	WEETE
EEVEN	FEESE	MELEE	REEDE	
ELPEE	FEEZE	NEELE	REEVE	
EMCEE	GEESE	NEESE	RESEE	

Six-letter words with four Es

BEEBEE	TEEPEE	VEEPEE	WEEWEE
PEEWEE			

Using As

Using Is

Four-letter words with two Is

BIDI	ILIA	IWIS	NIDI	TIPI
DIVI	IMID	IXIA	NISI	TITI
DIXI	IMPI	KIWI	PIKI	WILI
FIFI	INIA	LIRI	PILI	ZITI
FINI	INTI	MIDI	PIPI	
HILI	IRID	MIHI	SIMI	
HIOI	IRIS	MINI	SIRI	
IBIS	ISIT	MIRI	TIKI	

Five-letter words with two Is

AALII	DIXIT	INDRI	LIPIN	RICIN
ACINI	FICIN	INFIX	LITAI	RIGID
AIDOI	FILMI	INION	LIVID	RISHI
AIOLI	FINIS	INTIL	MEDII	SHIAI
ALIBI	FIRIE	INTIS	MIDIS	SIGIL
AMICI	FIXIT	INWIT	MIHIS	SIMIS
ANIMI	GENII	IODIC	MILIA	SIRIH
ARIKI	GIBLI	IODID	MIMIC	SIRIS
ATIGI	HIKOI	IODIN	MINIM	TEIID
BIALI	HIOIS	IONIC	MINIS	TIBIA
BIDIS	IAMBI	IRIDS	MIRIN	TIKIS
BIFID	ICIER	IRING	MITIS	TIMID
BIKIE	ICILY	ISSEI	MODII	TIPIS
BINDI	ICING	IVIED	NHIL	TITIS
BINIT	ICTIC	IVIES	NIMBI	TORII
BIVIA	IDIOM	IXIAS	NISEI	VIGIA
BLINI	IDIOT	JINNI	NITID	VIGIL
CEILI	ILIAC	KIBBI	NIXIE	VILLI
CHILI	ILIAD	KIBEI	OBIIT	VINIC
CILIA	ILIAL	KIKOI	OIDIA	VIRID
CIPPI	ILIUM	KILIM	ORIBI	VISIE
CIRRI	IMARI	KININ	PIING	VISIT
CIVIC	IMIDE	KIRRI	PIKIS	VIVID
CIVIE	IMIDO	KIWIS	PILEI	VIZIR
CIVIL	IMIDS	LIBRI	PILIS	WIFIE
DIDIE	IMINE	LICHI	PIPIS	WILIS
DIGIT	IMINO	LICIT	PIPIT	YITIE
DILLI	IMMIT	LIKIN	PIRAI	ZIMBI
DINIC	IMMIX	LIMBI	PIXIE	ZITIS
DISCI	IMPIS	LIMIT	PRIMI	ZIZIT
DIVIS	IMSHI	LININ	RADII	
DIXIE	INDIE	LIPID	REIKI	

Six-letter words with three Is

BIKINI	IRIDIC	IRITIS	NIGIRI
IMIDIC	IRITIC	MIRITI	TIRITI

Using Os

Five-letter words with three Os

OVOLO
POTOO

Six-letter words with three Os

BONOBO	COOCOO	GOOROO	LOBOLO	POTOOS
BGOBOO	COROZO	HOLLOO	MOKORO	ROCOCO
BOOCOO	DOOCOT	HOODOO	MONOAO	ROTOLO
BOOHOO	DOODOO	HOOPOE	MOOLOO	VOODOO
BOOKOO	DOOWOP	HOOPOO	OOLOGY	ZOOZOO
COCOON	FORHOO	HOOROO	OOLONG	
COMODO	GOOGOL	KOODOO	OVOLOS	

Using Us

Three-letter words with two Us

ULU   UTU
UMU

Four-letter words with two Us

BUBU	KUDU	LULU	RURU	URUS
FUGU	KUKU	MUMU	SULU	UTUS
GURU	KURU	PUDU	SUSU	WUDU
HUHU	KUTU	PUKU	TUTU	YUZU
JUJU	KUZU	PULU	ULUS	ZULU
JUKU	LUAU	PUPU	UNAU	

Five-letter words with two Us

AHURU	FUGUS	KUZUS	RUBUS	UNGUM
AUGUR	GURUS	LUAUS	RURUS	UPRUN
AURUM	HUDUD	LULUS	SULUS	URUBU
BUBUS	HUHUS	LUPUS	SUNUP	USQUE
BUCHU	HUMUS	LUSUS	SUSUS	USUAL
BUCKU	JUGUM	MUCUS	TUKTU	USURE
BUNDU	JUJUS	MUMUS	TUQUE	USURP
BUSSU	JUKUS	MUNTU	TUTUS	USURY
BUTUT	KAURU	PUDUS	UHURU	UVULA
CUTUP	KUDUS	PUKUS	UNAUS	VOULU
DUFUS	KUDZU	PULUS	UNCUS	WUDUS
DURUM	KUKUS	PUPUS	UNCUT	WUSHU
FUCUS	KURUS	QUEUE	UNDUE	YUZUS
FUGUE	KUTUS	QUIPU	UNDUG	ZULUS

Six-letter words with three Us

MUTUUM
UHURUS
URUBUS

Light words

While duplicate vowels on your rack can be a real pain, having too many vowels in general can be frustrating. For this reason, it's helpful to have a number of 'light' words up your sleeve – words that contain a high proportion of vowels. The lists of light words include words from two to eight letters, of which more than half are vowels. Words of four or more letters are listed alphabetically according to the vowels they contain.

Two-letter words (two vowels)

AA	AI	EE	OE	OO
AE	EA	IO	OI	OU

Three-letter words (three vowels)

AIA	AUE	EAU
AUA		

Four-letter words (three vowels or more)

AAE	ALAE		AWEE		ZOEA		OHIA		EUGE
	AREA		EALE	**AEU**	AGUE	**AIU**	AITU	**EIO**	ONIE
	ASEA		EASE		AUNE		HUIA	**EIOU**	EUOI
AAI	ACAI		EAVE		BEAU		KUIA	**EIU**	ETUI
	AIAS	**AEI**	AIDE		EAUS		QUAI		IURE
	AIGA		AINE		EAUX		UNAI		LIEU
	AMIA		AMIE		UREA	**AOU**	AUTO	**EOO**	OBOE
	ARIA		EINA		UVAE		OUMA		OLEO
	RAIA		IDEA		UVEA		OUPA		OOSE
AAO	ANOA		ILEA	**AII**	ILIA		URAO		OOZE
AAU	AQUA		KAIE		INIA	**AUU**	LUAU	**EOU**	EURO
	ATUA		VIAE		IXIA		UNAU		MEOU
	AULA	**AEO**	AEON	**AIO**	AGIO	**EEE**	EPEE		MOUE
	AURA		AERO		CIAO	**EEI**	EIDE		ROUE
	PAUA		ALOE		IOTA		EINE	**IIO**	HIOI
AEE	AGEE		EOAN		JIAO		IDEE	**IOO**	MOOI
	AJEE		ODEA		MOAI	**EEO**	EVOE		OLIO
	AKEE		OLEA		NAOI		OGEE	**OOU**	OUZO
	ALEE		TOEA		OBIA	**EEU**	EMEU		

Five-letter words (four vowels)

AAEE	AREAE	**AEEI**	AERIE	**AEOO**	ZOOEA		MIAOU		OORIE
AAEI	AECIA		AINEE	**AIIO**	AIDOI		OUIJA	**EIOU**	LOUIE
AAEO	ZOAEA	**AEEO**	ZOEAE		AIOLI	**EEEI**	EERIE		OURIE
AAEU	AQUAE	**AEIU**	ADIEU		OIDIA	**EEOO**	COOEE		
	AURAE		AUREI	**AIOU**	AUDIO	**EEUU**	QUEUE		
AAII	AALII		URAEI		AULOI	**EIOO**	LOOIE		

Six-letter words (four vowels or more)

AAAA	ARAARA		GATEAU		FAERIE		FEIJOA	**AIIO**	AIKIDO
	ATAATA		LAURAE		FERIAE		GOALIE		AIOLIS
AAAE	AGAPAE		NAUSEA		HEARIE		HOAGIE		ARIOSI
	AKATEA	**AAII**	AALIIS		IDEAED		IODATE		DAIMIO
	AZALEA		HAIKAI		IDEATE		LEIPOA		MOIRAI
AAAI	ABASIA		KAIKAI		KEAVIE		OAKIER	**AIIU**	TAUIWI
	ACACIA		ZAIKAI		LAESIE		OAKIES	**AIOO**	ARIOSO
	AGAPAI	**AAIO**	ADAGIO		MEALIE		OARIER		BOOHAI
	ALALIA		AIKONA		MEANIE		OBELIA		HOODIA
	ARALIA		ALODIA		MEDIAE		OPIATE		OOIDAL
	ATAXIA		ALOGIA		PEREIA		ROADIE		OOMIAC
	MANAIA		ANOPIA		REDIAE		ROARIE		OOMIAK
	TAIAHA		ANOXIA		SEMEIA		SOAPIE		OORALI
	WAIATA		APORIA		TENIAE		ZOECIA		OORIAL
AAAU	UJAMAA		ASIAGO	**AEEO**	AEROBE	**AEIU**	ACULEI	**AIOU**	AGOUTI
AAEE	AERATE		ATOCIA		APOGEE		ADIEUS		AUDIOS
	AKEAKE		ATONIA		AREOLE		ADIEUX		BAGUIO
	AMEBAE		COAITA		COATEE		AECIUM		GIAOUR
	EATAGE		LAOGAI		ELODEA		AGUISE		MIAOUS
	GALEAE		ORARIA		EVOVAE		AGUIZE		OUIJAS
	PALEAE		TAIHOA		FOVEAE		AUDILE		OURALI
	PERAEA		ZOARIA		GOATEE		AUGITE		OURARI
	TALEAE	**AAIU**	ABULIA		OCREAE		AUNTIE		QUINOA
AAEEO	ZOAEAE		AMUSIA		OEDEMA		CAIQUE		SOUARI
AAEI	ABELIA		ANURIA		OLEATE		CURIAE		UTOPIA
	ACEDIA		AUDIAL	**AEEOO**	ZOOEAE		DAUTIE	**AOOO**	MONOAO
	AECIAL		AUMAIL	**AEEOUU**	EUOUAE		ELUVIA	**AOOU**	VAUDOO
	AERIAL		GUAIAC	**AEEU**	AEMULE		EQUALI	**AOUU**	AUROUS
	ALEXIA		IGUANA		AENEUS		EUCAIN		AUSUBO
	AMELIA		QUALIA		AVENUE		EXUVIA		TAUHOU
	ANEMIA		UAKARI		BAUBEE		GAUCIE	**EEEE**	BEEBEE
	ARAISE		URANIA		ELUATE		GUINEA		PEEWEE
	AVAILE		WAIRUA		EPAULE		HAIQUE		TEEPEE
	AVIATE		YAUTIA		EQUATE		SAIQUE		VEEPEE
	FACIAE	**AAOO**	MANOAO		EUPNEA		SAULIE		WEEWEE
	IDEATA		MAOMAO		EUREKA		TAUPIE	**EEEI**	DEEPIE
	LAMIAE	**AAOU**	ACAJOU		FEAGUE		UNCIAE		EELIER
	REALIA		AGOUTA		HEAUME		UREDIA		EERIER
	TAENIA		AMADOU		LEAGUE		UREMIA		FEERIE
AAEO	AGORAE		AOUDAD		QUAERE	**AEOO**	AMOOVE		HEEZIE
	AMOEBA		AURORA		QUELEA		ROADEO		JEELIE
	AORTAE		OUBAAS		RESEAU		ZOOEAL		KEELIE
	APNOEA	**AAUU**	AUCUBA		UNEASE		ZOOEAS		MEEMIE
	AREOLA		TUATUA		UREASE	**AEOU**	AERUGO		PEERIE
	CAEOMA	**AEEE**	HEALEE	**AEII**	AIRIER		AROUSE		REEKIE
	COBAEA	**AEEI**	AEDILE		BAILIE		AUTOED		SEELIE
	OARAGE		AEDINE		LIAISE		AVOURE		WEENIE
	OZAENA		AERIED		SAIKEI		COTEAU		WEEPIE
	ZOAEAS		AERIER		TIBIAE		DOUANE	**EEEO**	EOCENE
AAEU	ACUATE		AERIES	**AEIO**	AEONIC		OPAQUE	**EEPOPEE**	
	ALULAE		APIECE		ANOMIE		OUTAGE	**EEEU**	EKUELE
	AUBADE		BAILEE		ARIOSE		OUTATE		EMEUTE
	AURATE		BEANIE		AZIONE		OUTEAT	**EEII**	FEIRIE
	BATEAU		DEARIE		BOATIE		ZOUAVE		HEINIE
	BAUERA		DEAWIE		CODEIA	**AEUU**	AUREUS		KIEKIE
	CADEAU		EASIED		EIDOLA		AUTEUR		KIERIE
	CAUDAE		EASIER		EOLIAN		BUREAU		MEINIE
	CAUSAE		EASIES		EONIAN		URAEUS		MIELIE
	FAUNAE		EPEIRA		EPIZOA		UVULAE		NEINEI

WIENIE	QUEUER	FOOTIE	WOODIE	OIDIUM
EEIO EOSINE	QUEUES	GOODIE	WOOLIE	**IIUU** BUIBUI
ETOILE	**EIIO** IODIDE	GOOIER	WOOPIE	PIUPIU
LOERIE	IODINE	GOOLIE	ZOOIER	**I00U** IODOUS
OLEINE	IODISE	GOONIE	**EIOU** BOUGIE	KOUROI
OREIDE	IODIZE	GOORIE	COURIE	ODIOUS
SOIREE	IOLITE	HOODIE	FOULIE	ORIHOU
TOEBIE	IONISE	HOOLIE	LOUIES	**0000** BOOBOO
TOEIER	IONIZE	IONONE	LOURIE	BOOCOO
VOIDEE	OILIER	KOOKIE	MOUSIE	BOOHOO
EEIU ECURIE	**EIIU** EURIPI	LOOIES	OUGLIE	BOOKOO
EPUISE	MILIEU	LOONIE	OUREBI	COOCOO
EQUINE	QUINIE	LOOSIE	OURIER	DOODOO
EQUIPE	**EIOO** BLOOIE	NOOGIE	OUTLIE	GOOROO
UREIDE	BOOBIE	NOOKIE	OUTVIE	HOODOO
EE00 BOOTEE	BOODIE	OOFIER	POURIE	HOOPOO
COOEED	BOOGIE	OOLITE	SOUTIE	HOOROO
COOEES	BOOKIE	OORIER	TOURIE	KOODOO
DOOLEE	BOOTIE	OOSIER	TOUTIE	MOOLOO
SOOGEE	COOKIE	OOZIER	**EIUU** UBIQUE	VOODOO
TOETOE	COOLIE	ORIOLE	UNIQUE	ZOOZOO
EEOU COULEE	COORIE	OROIDE	**E000** HOOPOE	**00UU** BOUBOU
COUPEE	COOTIE	OTIOSE	**E00U** QUOOKE	ROUCOU
EVOLUE	DOOBIE	ROOFIE	**EOUU** UVEOUS	VOUDOU
MEOUED	DOOLIE	ROOKIE	**II00** OPIOID	**UUUU** MUUMUU
OEUVRE	DOOZIE	ROOMIE	PIOPIO	
OUTSEE	EXODOI	SOOGIE	TOITOI	
TOUPEE	FLOOIE	TOONIE	**IIOU** BINIOU	
EEUU QUEUED	FOODIE	TOORIE	IONIUM	

Seven-letter words (five vowels or more)

AAAEI ANAEMIA	AGEUSIA	SAOUARI	**AEEOO** KOEKOEA	MOINEAU
AAAIU AQUARIA	AURELIA	**AEEEI** ALIENEE	**AEEOU** AENEOUS	SEQUOIA
AAEEI TAENIAE	CAMAIEU	EATERIE	AUREOLE	**AEOUU** AQUEOUS
AAEEO AMOEBAE	EUTAXIA	**AEEEU** EVACUEE	EUPNOEA	AUTOCUE
AREOLAE	URAEMIA	**AEEII** AIERIES	**AEEOUU** EUOUAES	COUTEAU
AAEEU AUREATE	**AAEOU** AUREOLA	**AEEIO** ETAERIO	**AEIIO** EPINAOI	NOUVEAU
AAEII AECIDIA	AURORAE	**AEEIU** AUDITEE	**AEIIU** EQUINIA	ROULEAU
AAEIO AEOLIAN	**AAIIO** DIANOIA	EUCAINE	**AEIOO** IPOMOEA	**AIOOO** OOGONIA
AEONIAN	**AAIOU** ABOULIA	EUGARIE	ZOOECIA	**AIOUU** OUGUIYA
AEROBIA	OUABAIN	EUGENIA	**AEIOU** DOULEIA	**EEEIU** EPUISEE
OLEARIA	OUAKARI	EUTEXIA	EULOGIA	QUEENIE
AAEIU ACEQUIA	RAOULIA	EXUVIAE	MIAOUED	**IIIOO** OIDIOID

Eight-letter words (five vowels or more)

AAAAE ANABAENA	**AAAEU** ACAUDATE	AQUARIAN	**AAEEI** ACIERAGE	ERADIATE
AAAAI ARAPAIMA	AGUACATE	AULARIAN	ACIERATE	FACETIAE
ATARAXIA	AQUACADE	AVIFAUNA	AGACERIE	HAEREMAI
KAMAAINA	PAHAUTEA	MAIASAUR	AGENESIA	TAENIATE
AAAEE KAREAREA	**AAAII** APIARIAN	SAPUCAIA	ALIENAGE	**AAEEO** AMOEBEAN
AAAEI ACADEMIA	APIMANIA	**AAAOU** AUTOMATA	ALIENATE	ANAEROBE
ACHAENIA	RADIALIA	**AAAUU** AQUANAUT	AWEARIED	AREOLATE
ANAEMIAS	**AAAIO** ALOCASIA	KAUMATUA	EMACIATE	OEDEMATA
ASSEGAAI	PARANOIA	**AAEEE** AMEERATE	ENCAENIA	**AAEEOU** AUREOLAE
MAZAEDIA	**AAAIU** ADULARIA	DEAERATE	EPIGAEAL	**AAEEU** ACULEATE
AAAEO PARANOEA	AQUARIAL	HETAERAE	EPIGAEAN	ADEQUATE

CAESURAE	**AAEOU** ACAULOSE	**AEEII** AEGIRINE	OOTHECAE	CAESIOUS
ECAUDATE	AERONAUT	AEGIRITE	PAHOEHOE	DIALOGUE
EVACUATE	ANALOGUE	AERIFIED	PEEKABOO	DOUANIER
EVALUATE	AQUATONE	AERIFIES	PEEKAPOO	DOULEIAS
LAUREATE	ARACEOUS	ASEITIES	ZOOGLEAE	EDACIOUS
NAUSEATE	ARANEOUS	EPICEDIA	**AEEOU** AEGLOGUE	EQUATION
PAENULAE	AUREOLAS	GAIETIES	ALEHOUSE	EUDAIMON
SEAQUAKE	AUROREAN	IDEALISE	ALEURONE	EULOGIAS
AAEII ACIDEMIA	AUTOCADE	IDEALIZE	AUREOLED	EUPHOBIA
ACTINIAE	AUTOMATE	IDEATIVE	AUREOLES	EUPHONIA
AECIDIAL	MAUSOLEA	INERTIAE	COEQUATE	EUPHORIA
AKINESIA	OCEANAUT	INFERIAE	EUDAEMON	EUSOCIAL
APIARIES	OUBAASES	METAIRIE	EUPNOEAS	EXONUMIA
AVIANISE	**AAEUU** FAUNULAE	WEIGELIA	FEATEOUS	JALOUSIE
AVIANIZE	QUAALUDE	**AEEIO** ACOEMETI	JEALOUSE	MOINEAUS
AVIARIES	USQUABAE	AEROLITE	OUTEATEN	ODALIQUE
CAVIARIE	**AAIII** MILIARIA	AMEIOSES	REAROUSE	OUTRAISE
FILARIAE	NIRAMIAI	ETAERIOS	TEAHOUSE	POULAINE
HETAIRAI	**AAIIO** APOSITIA	ETIOLATE	**AEEUU** NEURULAE	SAUTOIRE
HETAIRIA	AVIATION	FOEDARIE	URAEUSES	SEQUOIAS
LACINIAE	DIANOIAS	OEDIPEAN	USQUEBAE	THIOUREA
LIPAEMIA	MAIOLICA	OEILLADE	**AEIII** INITIATE	**AEIUU** AUGURIES
VIRAEMIA	ZOIATRIA	PAEONIES	RETIARII	AUTUNITE
AAEIO AERATION	**AAIIU** ACIDURIA	**AEEIOO** EPOPOEIA	**AEIIO** AMEIOSIS	FAUTEUIL
AGIOTAGE	AUXILIAR	**AEEIOU** EULOGIAE	HEMIOLIA	**AEOOO** ZOOGLOEA
ALOPECIA	BAUHINIA	**AEEIU** ACQUIREE	HEMIOPIA	**AEOOU** ACOELOUS
ANOREXIA	IGUANIAN	AEDICULE	IBOGAINE	APOLOGUE
ANOXEMIA	QUILLAIA	AGUELIKE	IDEATION	AUTOSOME
APOGAEIC	UNIAXIAL	AUDIENCE	IODINATE	POACEOUS
AZOTEMIA	**AAIOO** ANOOPSIA	AUDITEES	NOTITIAE	**AEOUU** AUTOCUES
CAPOEIRA	APOLOGIA	BANLIEUE	OLIGEMIA	AUTOTUNE
EGOMANIA	ZOOMANIA	BEAUTIED	TAENIOID	BEAUCOUP
METANOIA	**AAIOU** ABOULIAS	BEAUTIES	**AEIIU** ACUITIES	COUTEAUX
OLEARIAS	AUTACOID	BEAUXITE	AECIDIUM	FEATUOUS
PAROEMIA	AUTOPSIA	CAUSERIE	AIGUILLE	HUAQUERO
TOXAEMIA	AZOTURIA	DECIDUAE	AQUILINE	NAUSEOUS
ZABAIONE	CARIACOU	ELUVIATE	AUDITIVE	NOUVEAUX
AAEIOU ABOIDEAU	GUAIACOL	EQUALISE	AURIFIED	OUTARGUE
ABOITEAU	OUABAINS	EQUALIZE	AURIFIES	OUTVALUE
AAEIU ACAULINE	OUAKARIS	EQUIPAGE	EQUINIAS	ROULEAUS
ACEQUIAS	PAROUSIA	EQUISETA	INDUCIAE	ROULEAUX
ACICULAE	RAOULIAS	EUCAINES	INDUVIAE	ROUSSEAU
AGEUSIAS	SAOUARIS	EUGARIES	MAIEUTIC	**AIIIO** OITICICA
ALLELUIA	**AAIUU** AQUARIUM	EUGENIAS	MINUTIAE	**AIIIU** DAIQUIRI
AUBRETIA	AURICULA	EUPEPSIA	QUINIELA	**AIIOO** AVOISION
AUBRIETA	GUAIACUM	EUTAXIES	SILIQUAE	IODATION
AUMAILED	**AAOUU** ACAULOUS	EUTAXITE	UINTAITE	**AIIOU** AUDITION
AURELIAN	**AEEEE** EMEERATE	EUTEXIAS	UREDINIA	MIAOUING
AURELIAS	RELEASEE	EXEQUIAL	URINEMIA	OLIGURIA
CAMAIEUX	**AEEEI** ALIENEES	EXUVIATE	**AEIOO** AEROFOIL	**AIOOO** OOGONIAL
DIAPAUSE	DETAINEE	LEUCEMIA	AMOEBOID	ORATORIO
EPIFAUNA	EARPIECE	LEUKEMIA	COENOBIA	ZOONOMIA
EUTAXIAS	EATERIES	MAUVEINE	IPOMOEAS	**AIOOU** AUTOCOID
INAURATE	EMERITAE	QUEASIER	MOVIEOLA	AUTOGIRO
INFAUNAE	EXAMINEE	QUEAZIER	OOGAMIES	ORAGIOUS
MAIREHAU	SEAPIECE	UNEASIER	OVARIOLE	OVARIOUS
MAUVAISE	**AEEEU** AGUEWEED	UNIDEAED	PATOOTIE	**AIOUU** CAUTIOUS
PERIAGUA	EMERAUDE	**AEEOO** AEROTONE	**AEIOU** AEQUORIN	GUAIOCUM
TAQUERIA	EVACUEES	FOVEOLAE	AEROBIUM	OUGUIYAS
URAEMIAS	SEQUELAE	OOGAMETE	AGOUTIES	SUBAUDIO

Light words

AOOOU	OOGAMOUS		EBIONISE	**EEIOU**	BOUDERIE	**EIIOO**	ONIONIER	**EOOOO**	BOOHOOED
AOOUU	ANOUROUS		EBIONIZE		EPIGEOUS	**EIIOU**	DIECIOUS		HOODOOED
	COUMAROU		EGOITIES		EPILOGUE		EXIMIOUS		VOODOOED
EEEEI	EYEPIECE		EOLIPILE		EQUIVOKE		FILIOQUE	**EOOUU**	DUOLOGUE
EEEEU	SQUEEGEE		EPIZOITE		ETOURDIE		UNIONISE		EUROKOUS
EEEIO	EOLIENNE		ERIONITE		EULOGIES		UNIONIZE		OUTHOUSE
	TOEPIECE		MEIONITE		EULOGISE	**EIIUU**	BIUNIQUE		OUTQUOTE
EEEIU	EUXENITE		MOIETIES		EULOGIZE	**EIOOO**	FORHOOIE		VOUDOUED
	EXEQUIES		OILERIES		EUPNOEIC		OOLOGIES	**IIIOO**	PIHOIHOI
	MEUNIERE		OSIERIES		EUROKIES	**EIOOU**	IDONEOUS	**IIIOU**	OUISTITI
	QUEENIER	**EEIIU**	EQUITIES		ICEHOUSE		ISOLOGUE	**IIOOU**	DIOICOUS
	QUEENIES		PRIEDIEU		OBSEQUIE		OUTVOICE		DOUPIONI
	QUEENITE		QUIETIVE		OUVRIERE		ZOOECIUM	**IOOOU**	OOGONIUM
	UNSEELIE		UBIETIES	**EEIUU**	EUPHUISE	**EIOUU**	BOUTIQUE	**IOOUU**	BOUSOUKI
EEEOU	ETOUFFEE	**EEIOO**	COOEEING		EUPHUIZE		EULOGIUM		BOUZOUKI
EEIIO	BOISERIE		EOLOPILE		QUEUEING		EUROPIUM		UXORIOUS
	DEIONISE		MOVIEOKE		QUIETUDE		EXIGUOUS	**IOUUU**	USURIOUS
	DEIONIZE		OOGENIES	**EEOOU**	EURONOTE		OUTGUIDE		
	DIOECIES		OPTIONEE	**EIIIO**	IDIOCIES		TENUIOUS		

Awkward consonant combinations

Certain consonants can be just as awkward as vowels when they show up more than one at a time on your rack. The following lists provide words of three to five letters with doubles of B, C, F, H, V, W and Y (where such words exist; but note that there are no three-letter words with two Cs).

Using Bs

Three-letter words with two Bs

ABB	BOB	EBB
BIB	BUB	

Four-letter words with two Bs

ABBA	BABY	BLUB	BUBA	COBB
ABBE	BARB	BOAB	BUBO	EBBS
ABBS	BIBS	BOBA	BUBS	JIBB
BABA	BLAB	BOBS	BUBU	SIBB
BABE	BLEB	BOMB	BULB	
BABU	BLOB	BOOB	BURB	

Five-letter words with two or more Bs

ABBAS	BABUL	BILBO	BOBAK	BUBAL
ABBED	BABUS	BILBY	BOBAS	BUBAS
ABBES	BAMBI	BIMBO	BOBBY	BUBBA
ABBEY	BARBE	BLABS	BOBOL	BUBBY
ABBOT	BARBS	BLEBS	BOMBE	BUBUS
BABAS	BARBY	BLOBS	BOMBO	BULBS
BABEL	BEBOP	BLUBS	BOMBS	BUMBO
BABES	BEROB	BLURB	BOOBS	BURBS
BABKA	BIBBS	BOABS	BOOBY	BUSBY
BABOO	BIBLE	BOBAC	BRIBE	CABBY

CABOB	EBBED	KABAB	NUBBY	TUBBY
COBBS	EBBET	KABOB	RABBI	WEBBY
COBBY	FUBBY	KEBAB	REBBE	YABBA
CUBBY	GABBY	KEBOB	RIBBY	YABBY
CUBEB	GOBBI	KIBBE	RUBBY	YOBBO
DABBA	GOBBO	KIBBI	SIBBS	ZEBUB
DEBBY	GOBBY	LOBBY	SLUBB	
DIBBS	HOBBY	MOBBY	SUBBY	
DOBBY	HUBBY	NABOB	SYBBE	
DUBBO	JIBBS	NOBBY	TABBY	

Using Cs

Four-letter words with two Cs

ACCA	CHIC	COCH	CROC	OCCY
CACA	CHOC	COCK	ECCE	
CECA	COCA	COCO	ECCO	

Five-letter words with two or more Cs

ACCAS	CECUM	CIVIC	COOCH	CYNIC
ACCOY	CERCI	CLACH	COSEC	ICTIC
ACMIC	CERIC	CLACK	COUCH	LECCY
ACOCK	CHACE	CLECK	CRACK	MECCA
BACCA	CHACK	CLICK	CRAIC	MUCIC
BACCO	CHACO	CLOCK	CRICK	OCCAM
BACCY	CHECK	CLUCK	CROCI	OCCUR
BICCY	CHICA	COACH	CROCK	PICCY
BOCCA	CHICH	COACT	CROCS	RECCE
BOCCE	CHICK	COCAS	CRUCK	RECCO
BOCCI	CHICO	COCCI	CUBIC	RECCY
CABOC	CHICS	COCCO	CULCH	SECCO
CACAO	CHOCK	COCKS	CUMEC	SUCCI
CACAS	CHOCO	COCKY	CURCH	TICCA
CACHE	CHOCS	COCOA	CUSEC	WICCA
CACKY	CHUCK	COCOS	CUTCH	YACCA
CACTI	CINCH	CODEC	CWTCH	YECCH
CAECA	CINCT	COLIC	CYCAD	YUCCA
CASCO	CIRCA	COMIC	CYCAS	YUCCH
CATCH	CIRCS	CONCH	CYCLE	ZOCCO
CECAL	CISCO	CONIC	CYCLO	

Using Fs

Three-letter words with two Fs

AFF	IFF
EFF	OFF

Four-letter words with two or more Fs

AFFY	BUFF	DAFF	EFFS	FIFI
BAFF	CAFF	DIFF	FAFF	FUFF
BIFF	COFF	DOFF	FIEF	GAFF
BOFF	CUFF	DUFF	FIFE	GOFF

Using Bs

GUFF	KIFF	NAFF	RAFF	TUFF
HAFF	KOFF	NIFF	RIFF	WAFF
HUFF	LUFF	NUFF	RUFF	YAFF
IFFY	MEFF	OFFS	TEFF	ZIFF
JEFF	MIFF	PFFT	TIFF	
JIFF	MUFF	PUFF	TOFF	

Five-letter words with two or more Fs

AFFIX	CUFFS	GLIFF	NIFFY	SNIFF
BAFFS	DAFFS	GOFFS	NUFFS	SNUFF
BAFFY	DAFFY	GRAFF	NYAFF	SOWFF
BIFFO	DEFFO	GRIFF	OFFAL	SPIFF
BIFFS	DIFFS	GRUFF	OFFED	STAFF
BIFFY	DOFFS	GUFFS	OFFER	STIFF
BLAFF	DRAFF	HAFFS	PLUFF	STUFF
BLUFF	DUFFS	HOUFF	POUFF	TAFFY
BOFFO	EFFED	HOWFF	PUFFS	TEFFS
BOFFS	FAFFS	HUFFS	PUFFY	TIFFS
BUFFA	FEOFF	HUFFY	QUAFF	TOFFS
BUFFE	FIEFS	JEFFS	QUIFF	TOFFY
BUFFI	FIFED	JIFFS	RAFFS	TRIFF
BUFFO	FIFER	JIFFY	REFFO	TUFFE
BUFFS	FIFES	KOFFS	RIFFS	TUFFS
BUFFY	FIFTH	LUFFA	RUFFE	WAFFS
CAFFS	FIFTY	LUFFS	RUFFS	WAUFF
CHAFF	FLAFF	MEFFS	SCAFF	WHIFF
CHUFF	FLUFF	MIFFS	SCOFF	YAFFS
CLIFF	FUFFS	MIFFY	SCUFF	ZIFFS
CLOFF	FUFFY	MUFFS	SKIFF	
COFFS	GAFFE	NAFFS	SKOFF	
CUFFO	GAFFS	NIFFS	SLUFF	

Using Hs

Three-letter words with two Hs

HAH	HOH	SHH
HEH	HUH	

Four-letter words with two Hs

HAHA	HECH	HISH	HUHU	SHAH
HAHS	HEHS	HOGH	HUNH	
HASH	HETH	HOHA	HUSH	
HATH	HIGH	HOHS	PHOH	

Five-letter words with two Hs

AHIGH	HARSH	HEIGH	HILCH	HORAH
CHETH	HASHY	HETHS	HITCH	HOTCH
CHICH	HATCH	HEUCH	HITHE	HOUGH
EPHAH	HATHA	HEUGH	HOGHS	HUHUS
HAHAS	HAUGH	HEWGH	HOHED	HUMPH
HAITH	HEATH	HIGHS	HOOCH	HUNCH
HANCH	HECHT	HIGHT	HOOSH	HUSHY

HUTCH	KHAPH	PHPHT	SHCHI	THIGH
HYPHA	KHETH	SHAHS	SHISH	WHICH
HYTHE	PHOHS	SHASH	SHUSH	WHISH

Using Vs

Four-letter words with two Vs

VAVS	VIVE
VIVA	VIVO

Five-letter words with two Vs

BEVVY	LUVVY	VARVE	VIVDA	VOLVA
BIVVY	NAVVY	VERVE	VIVER	VOLVE
CIVVY	SAVVY	VIVAS	VIVES	VULVA
DIVVY	VALVE	VIVAT	VIVID	

Using Ws

Three-letter words with two Ws

WAW
WOW

Four-letter words with two Ws

WAWA	WAWL	WHEW	WOWF
WAWE	WAWS	WHOW	WOWS

Five-letter words with two Ws

EWHOW	WAWAS	WAWLS	WIDOW	WOWEE
PAWAW	WAWES	WHEWS	WOWED	WRAWL

Using Ys

Four-letter words with two Ys

EYRY	TYPY	YAYS	YUKY
GYNY	YAWY		

Five-letter words with two Ys

AZYGY	FLYBY	PYGMY	WRYLY	YESTY
BOYSY	GAYLY	SHYLY	XYLYL	YEUKY
BYWAY	GYNNY	SKYEY	YABBY	YIPPY
COYLY	GYPPY	SLYLY	YAMPY	YOLKY
DOYLY	GYPSY	STYMY	YAPPY	YUCKY
DRYLY	HAYEY	THYMY	YAWEY	YUKKY
DYKEY	MYOPY	TYIYN	YAWNY	YUMMY
FEYLY	MYTHY	TYPEY	YECHY	YUPPY

Using Hs

Heavy words

In contrast to light words, 'heavy' words have a high proportion of consonants. (Y is used as a vowel in many words, but counts as a consonant here for our purposes.) These lists contain words with no vowels (apart from Y), of two to five letters, and words of six letters that contain either no vowels or only one. Noun plurals ending in S have not been included in these lists.

Two-letter words (no vowels except Y)

BY	FY	KY	MY	SH
CH	HM	MM	NY	ST

Three-letter words (no vowels except Y)

BRR	GYP	PRY	SNY	TWP
CLY	HMM	PST	SPY	TYG
CRY	HYP	PYX	STY	VLY
CWM	LYM	RHY	SWY	WHY
DRY	MYC	SHH	SYN	WRY
FLY	NTH	SHY	THY	WYN
FRY	PHT	SKY	TRY	ZZZ
GYM	PLY	SLY	TSK	

Four-letter words (no vowels except Y)

BRRR	HYMN	PSST	SYNC	TYPY
BYRL	JYNX	RYND	SYND	WYCH
CYST	KYND	SCRY	SYPH	WYND
FYRD	LYCH	SKRY	TRYP	WYNN
GYMP	LYNX	SKYF	TYMP	XYST
GYNY	MYTH	SKYR	TYND	YMPT
HWYL	PFFT	SPRY	TYPP	

Five-letter words (no vowels except Y)

CHYND	GLYPH	LYNCH	SHYLY	TRYST
CRWTH	GRYPT	MYRRH	SLYLY	WRYLY
CRYPT	GYNNY	MYTHY	STYMY	XYLYL
CWTCH	GYPPY	NYMPH	SYLPH	
DRYLY	GYPSY	PHPHT	SYNCH	
FLYBY	KYDST	PSYCH	SYNTH	
GHYLL	LYMPH	PYGMY	THYMY	

Six-letter words (one vowel)

BLANCH	BORSHT	CATCHT	CLASPT	CRANCH
BLENCH	BRANCH	CHINCH	CLATCH	CRANTS
BLIGHT	BRICHT	CHINTS	CLENCH	CRATCH
BLINTZ	BRIGHT	CHINTZ	CLINCH	CROTCH
BLOTCH	BROWST	CHRISM	CLUNCH	CRUNCH
BORSCH	BRUNCH	CHURCH	CLUTCH	CRUTCH

CULTCH	PLONGD	SHLUMP	SPLASH	STRUCK
DIRNDL	PRANCK	SHMOCK	SPLENT	STRUNG
DRACHM	PROMPT	SHMUCK	SPLIFF	STRUNT
DRENCH	PUTSCH	SHNAPS	SPLINT	SWARTH
DROWND	RHYTHM	SHRANK	SPLOSH	SWATCH
FLANCH	SCARPH	SHREWD	SPRACK	SWITCH
FLENCH	SCARTH	SHRIFT	SPRANG	SWOWND
FLETCH	SCATCH	SHRILL	SPRAWL	TCHICK
FLIGHT	SCHELM	SHRIMP	SPREDD	THATCH
FLINCH	SCHISM	SHRINK	SPRENT	THETCH
FLITCH	SCHIST	SHROFF	SPRING	THIRST
FLYSCH	SCHLEP	SHROWD	SPRINT	THRALL
FRATCH	SCHLUB	SHRUNK	SPRITZ	THRANG
FRENCH	SCHNOZ	SHTCHI	SPRONG	THRASH
FRICHT	SCHORL	SHTETL	SPRUNG	THRAWN
FRIGHT	SCHRIK	SHTICK	SPRUSH	THRESH
FROWST	SCHROD	SHTUCK	STANCH	THRIFT
GLITCH	SCHTIK	SHTUMM	STANCK	THRILL
GLUMPS	SCHULN	SKARTH	STARCH	THRIST
GLUNCH	SCHUSS	SKETCH	STENCH	THRONG
GRINCH	SCLAFF	SKITCH	STITCH	THROWN
GROWTH	SCLIFF	SKLENT	STOWND	THRUSH
GRUMPH	SCORCH	SKLIFF	STRAFF	THRUST
GRUTCH	SCOTCH	SKRIMP	STRAMP	THWACK
HIGHTH	SCOWTH	SKRUMP	STRAND	THWART
KIRSCH	SCRAMB	SLATCH	STRANG	TRENCH
KITSCH	SCRAWL	SLIGHT	STRASS	TROGGS
KLATCH	SCRAWM	SLUTCH	STRATH	TROWTH
KLEPHT	SCRAWP	SMATCH	STRAWN	TSKING
KNICKS	SCRIMP	SMIGHT	STRESS	TSKTSK
KNIGHT	SCRIPT	SMIRCH	STREWN	TWIGHT
KNITCH	SCROLL	SMUTCH	STRICH	TWITCH
KRANTZ	SCRORP	SNATCH	STRICK	WARMTH
KVETCH	SCROWL	SNITCH	STRICT	WHILST
LENGTH	SCRUFF	SPARTH	STRIFT	WHISHT
MENSCH	SCRUMP	SPELTZ	STRING	WRENCH
MONGST	SCRUNT	SPERST	STRIPT	WRETCH
PHLEGM	SCULCH	SPETCH	STROLL	WRIGHT
PLANCH	SCULPT	SPHINX	STROMB	
PLENCH	SCUTCH	SPHYNX	STROND	
PLIGHT	SHLEPP	SPIGHT	STRONG	
PLINTH	SHLOCK	SPILTH	STROWN	

Chapter 6: Bonus Words

No matter what letters you have on your rack, using all of them in a single turn is usually the best way to score points. The 50-point bonus that you get for using all the letters on your rack is likely to exceed any other score except that from an exceptionally high-scoring word that lands on a triple-word square. For this reason, any serious Scrabble player should devote serious effort to mastering 'bonus words' – words of seven or eight letters that will allow you to empty your rack in one go. This section contains a number of different methods of memorizing words that will help you to scoop up those 50-point bonuses.

Stems and mnemonics

Knowing whether the letters on your rack can be used to form a word that will use up all your tiles gives you a great advantage in a game. If you know that there is a seven- or eight-letter word that fits your letters, then it's simply a matter of finding the right word from the letters. If, on the other hand, you know that there isn't a valid word that you can fit on the board, you won't need to waste time looking for one. One invaluable way of knowing whether your rack can furnish you with a bonus word is to be aware of 'stems'. Stems are groups of six and seven letters which combine with one more letter to form a valid word. This can be a daunting task, but it's made much easier if you concentrate only on the stems that are both likely and rewarding (ie those that are most common, and which will combine with many letters). In the following lists, the best stems have been determined for you, based on an algorithm of likelihood applied to the words in **Collins Tournament and Club Word List**

Another way to help remember which letters combine with which stems is through the use of 'mnemonics'. To create a mnemonic, identify the letters that combine with a given stem, and arrange those letters into a short phrase or sentence. It doesn't matter if you have to repeat some of the letters. Then find a common or easy-to-spot word that can be made from the letters of the stem that could possibly be connected to the phrase or sentence. In other words, establish a link between the stem and the phrase. For example, the six-letter stem **AEINRT** goes with B C D E F G H I J K L M N O P R S T U W. So for the sentence, you might come up with: Keep light brown ducks from Jim. A common word that can be made from the letters of the AEINRT stem is RETAIN. So you would then up with:

RETAIN - Keep light brown ducks from Jim

Similarly:

EINORST goes with A B C D E G H I J K L N O P R S T U V Y Z

ORIENTS: Eastern helpers buy good jazzy stock every time

Alternatively, form a mnemonic from the stem letters and the letters that don't work with it.

For example:

AEINST goes with A B C D E F G H I J K L M N O P R S T U V W X Z

So, with reference to James Bond, you could ask:

Y Q is neat

This is easy to remember, and it's obvious that Y and Q are the letters in question, and that **IS NEAT** is the stem.

Many veteran Scrabble players will have their own mnemonics, but if you are new to the game, try devising some for yourself from the stems and combining sets listed here. The key is getting a memorable phrase with a strong association with the stem word. This is a great test of your skill with anagrams, and your creativity generally; if you can come up with some good mnemonics, you will be honing your Scrabble skills in the process!

Six-letter stems

The 250 stems given here are derived from an algorithm which was developed by Mike Barron to assess the usefulness of each stem for Scrabble play. The first list here shows the rankings of usefulness: the most useful stem is AEINRT, followed by AEINST, then AEIRST, and so on. Against each stem is shown the most common word that can be made from the letters of the stem. The subsequent lists show each of the six-letter stems in alphabetical order, along with their ranking of usefulness, a common word which can be made from the stem's letters, the letters which can be added to the stem, and the seven-letter words which can be formed.

Six-letter stems in order of usefulness

1: AEINRT - RETINA	25: EINRST - INSERT	49: AEIRTT - ATTIRE
2: AEINST - TISANE	26: EILORT - TOILER	50: AENRTU - NATURE
3: AEIRST - SATIRE	27: AINORT - RATION	51: ADENOT - DONATE
4: EIORST - SORTIE	28: ADEINS - DAINES	52: AEGNRT - GARNET
5: ADEINR - RAINED	29: EEIRST - RETIES	53: AELNRT - ANTLER
6: AEILNR - LINEAR	30: AEERST - TEASER	54: AEENRT - NEATER
7: EINORS - SENIOR	31: EILOST - TOILES	55: ADEORT - ORATED
8: AENORT - ORNATE	32: AEILNS - ALIENS	56: DEINST - IDENTS
9: AEORST - ORATES	33: EILNOS - LESION	57: EIINRT - TINIER
10: AEINRS - SARNIE	34: EILNOT - LIONET	58: AEIRRT - IRATER
11: EINORT - ORIENT	35: EILNOR - NEROLI	59: AEIMNT - INMATE
12: EEINRT - ENTIRE	36: DEIORS - ROSIED	60: EEINST - SEITEN
13: EINOST - TONIES	37: AEILST - SALTIE	61: DEEINR - DENIER
14: AENRST - ASTERN	38: AENOST - ATONES	62: ADEILS - SAILED
15: AEILRT - RETAIL	39: EILORS - OILERS	63: AEGORT - TOERAG
16: AEGINR - REGINA	40: AELORT - LORATE	64: AELNRS - LEARNS
17: AEILNT - ENTAIL	41: EINRTU - UNITER	65: AELOST - SOLATE
18: ADEIRS - AIDERS	42: AEILNO - EOLIAN	66: AELNST - LATENS
19: ADEIRT - TIRADE	43: ADEORS - SOARED	67: EGINOR - REGION
20: ENORST - STONER	44: AEEINT - TENIAE	68: AIORST - RATIOS
21: DEINOR - IRONED	45: ADEINT - DETAIN	69: EENRST - ENTERS
22: AENORS - REASON	46: AELORS - SOLERA	70: DEIOST - TODIES
23: AEILRS - SERIAL	47: DEIORT - EDITOR	71: EILRST - TILERS
24: ADEILR - DERAIL	48: AELRST - SLATER	72: ADENST - STANED

73: EEINRS - SERINE	133: ACENOT - OCTANE	193: AERSTT - TREATS
74: AEGINS - EASING	134: CEIORT - EROTIC	194: GINORT - TRIGON
75: DEINOS - ONSIDE	135: EGILNT - TINGLE	195: ABEIRT - BAITER
76: AELNOS - LANOSE	136: ADEERS - SEARED	196: AEIRTV - TAIVER
77: EGINRT - ENGIRT	137: DEEINT - ENDITE	197: DEENRS - SENDER
78: ADERST - TREADS	138: EEILRT - RETILE	198: CEINOT - NOTICE
79: DEINRU - RUINED	139: AEGRST - GREATS	199: AEOPRT - PROTEA
80: EILNST - TINSEL	140: AENRTT - NATTER	200: AEGNST - AGENTS
81: AEEIRS - EASIER	141: EINOPR - PROINE	201: AEIMNS - AMINES
82: EIORTU - TOURIE	142: ADELOR - RELOAD	202: ACEORS - COARSE
83: ADINOR - ORDAIN	143: AEIPRS - PRAISE	203: DELORT - RETOLD
84: AEIORS - ARIOSE	144: ADEILN - NAILED	204: AAENST - ANSATE
85: DEINRS - DINERS	145: EEIORT - TOEIER	205: DEIINT - INDITE
86: AINRST - TRAINS	146: EEIORS - SOIREE	206: EGIORT - GOITRE
87: DEEIRS - RESIDE	147: DEENOR - REDONE	207: EEILNS - SENILE
88: ELORST - OSTLER	148: ADELNR - DARNEL	208: AEIMST - MATIES
89: DEORST - STRODE	149: EINRTT - TINTER	209: ADEGOT - DOTAGE
90: AEGNOR - ORANGE	150: DENORS - DRONES	210: DEEINS - DENIES
91: AEIMRT - MATIER	151: AEGIRT - TRIAGE	211: EIOPST - POSTIE
92: EEORST - STEREO	152: AEINPT - PANTIE	212: AAELOR - AREOLA
93: AELNOT - TOLANE	153: EINSTU - UNTIES	213: DEILNO - INDOLE
94: EIINST - TINIES	154: EILNRS - LINERS	214: AILNST - INSTAL
95: EEILRS - RELIES	155: ADINRT - INDART	215: AERRST - ARREST
96: AEINTU - AUNTIE	156: ADEEIR - DEARIE	216: ELNOST - STOLEN
97: ACEINR - CARNIE	157: EEILNT - LENITE	217: ADELNT - DENTAL
98: ADENRT - RANTED	158: ENORSU - ROUENS	218: DEINTU - UNTIED
99: AEIMNR - REMAIN	159: AILOST - OSTIAL	219: EINOPS - PONIES
100: AEGILN - GENIAL	160: AEINPR - RAPINE	220: CEINOR - COINER
101: AEENRS - RANEES	161: ACEINT - ENATIC	221: ADELST - SALTED
102: AEELRT - RELATE	162: AINORS - NORIAS	222: EINRSU - INSURE
103: INORST - INTROS	163: AEISTT - TATIES	223: EINNRT - INTERN
104: DEIRST - STRIDE	164: EEILST - ELITES	224: AEILMR - MAILER
105: DEILOR - ROILED	165: ENRSTU - UNREST	225: EGINST - TINGES
106: AEENST - SENATE	166: DEGINR - RINGED	226: ACDEIR - CARDIE
107: AGINRT - RATING	167: AEGIST - AGEIST	227: ABDEIR - ABIDER
108: EIRSTU - URITES	168: AAEINT - TAENIA	228: AEIMRS - ARMIES
109: ANORST - TRONAS	169: ADELRS - ALDERS	229: EORSTU - ROUTES
110: AEMNOR - MOANER	170: ABEORT - BOATER	230: ELNORS - ENROLS
111: AAERST - SEARAT	171: AEELNT - LATEEN	231: CEIOST - OECIST
112: ADENRS - SNARED	172: AEGNRS - RANGES	232: ADENOS - ANODES
113: DEINOT - OINTED	173: EIOOST - OTIOSE	233: AILNOS - ALISON
114: AEELNR - LEANER	174: AERSTU - URATES	234: AGINOT - GITANO
115: ADEERT - TEARED	175: EINORR - IRONER	235: AEMNOT - OMENTA
116: AEIPRT - PIRATE	176: ACEORT - RECOAT	236: ADINRS - DRAINS
117: ADENRU - UNREAD	177: ADELOS - ALDOSE	237: EIRSTT - SITTER
118: AEELRS - RESALE	178: DENORU - UNDOER	238: AEGORS - SORAGE
119: EGINOS - SOIGNE	179: AEGLNR - REGNAL	239: AEIMNO - ANOMIE
120: AELNOR - RELOAN	180: ADEEST - TEASED	240: AEELST - TEASEL
121: ADEIOR - ROADIE	181: EEILNR - RELINE	241: DEEILR - RELIED
122: EGINRS - SINGER	182: AINRTU - NUTRIA	242: ADEELT - ELATED
123: DEILOS - SOILED	183: AEEGNR - ENRAGE	243: AEELNS - ENSEAL
124: DENORT - RODENT	184: AGINOR - OARING	244: EORRST - STORER
125: EILNRT - LINTER	185: ENORTU - TENOUR	245: EINNST - TENNIS
126: DEINRT - TINDER	186: AEINNT - INNATE	246: AEEGNT - NEGATE
127: ABEINT - BINATE	187: AENSTU - UNSEAT	247: AEILMN - MENIAL
128: DENOST - STONED	188: ADENTU - UNDATE	248: AILNRST - TRIALS
129: AEGINT - EATING	189: DEORTU - TOURED	249: ENNORT - TONNER
130: DEILRT - TIRLED	190: AEILRR - RERAIL	250: AEIRRS - SIERRA
131: AILNOT - LATINO	191: AENRRT - RANTER	
132: ADELRT - DARTLE	192: ACENRT - TRANCE	

aaeint 168 - taenia

E TAENIAE	M AMENTIA	P PATINAE	TAENIAS
L ANTLIAE	ANIMATE	S ENTASIA	

aaelor 212 - areola

C ACEROLA	I OLEARIA	S AREOLAS	U AUREOLA
E AREOLAE	R AREOLAR		

aaenst 204 - ansate

A ANATASE	G AGNATES	L SEALANT	P ANAPEST	SANTERA
C CATENAS	I ENTASIA	M NAMASTE	PEASANT	V SAVANTE
D ANSATED	TAENIAS	N ANNATES	R ANESTRA	W SEAWANT

aaerst 111 - searat

B ABATERS	G AGRASTE	ATRESIA	N ANESTRA	S SEARATS
ABREAST	GASTREA	K KARATES	SANTERA	U AURATES
C ACATERS	TEARGAS	L TARSEAL	O AEROSAT	W AWAREST
CARATES	I ARISTAE	M AMEARST	P PETARAS	
E AERATES	ASTERIA	RETAMAS	R ERRATAS	

abdeir 227 - abider

A BRAAIED	BRIGADE	M EMBRAID	RABIDER	SIDEBAR
C CARBIDE	L BALDIER	N BANDIER	S ABIDERS	T REDBAIT
D BRAIDED	BEDRAIL	BRAINED	BARDIES	TRIBADE
E BEADIER	BRAILED	R BARDIER	BRAISED	U DAUBIER
BEARDIE	RAILBED	BRAIDER	DARBIES	W BAWDIER
G ABRIDGE	RIDABLE	BRIARED	SEABIRD	X AXEBIRD

abeint 127 - binate

C CABINET	I BAINITE	O NIOBATE	S BANTIES	BESTAIN
E BETAINE	K BEATNIK	P BEPAINT	BASINET	T TABINET
G BEATING	M AMBIENT	R ATEBRIN	BESAINT	

abeirt 195 - baiter

D REDBAIT	F BAREFIT	N ATEBRIN	BARITES	BIRETTA
TRIBADE	L LIBRATE	R ARBITER	REBAITS	RATBITE
E BEATIER	TABLIER	RAREBIT	TERBIAS	V VIBRATE
EBRIATE	TRIABLE	S BAITERS	T BATTIER	

abeort 170 - boater

A AEROBAT	L BLOATER	R ABORTER	BORATES	TABORET
D ABORTED	M BROMATE	ARBORET	REBATOS	
BORATED	N BARONET	TABORER	SORBATE	
TABORED	REBOANT	S BOASTER	T ABETTOR	
E ABORTEE	P PROBATE	BOATERS	BATTERO	

Six-letter stems

acdeir 226 - cardie

A CARDIAE	H CHAIRED	N CAIRNED	R ACRIDER	SIDECAR
B CARBIDE	I ACIDIER	CARNIED	CARRIED	U DECURIA
E DECIARE	L DECRIAL	DANCIER	S CARDIES	
F FARCIED	RADICEL	P EPACRID	DARCIES	
G CADGIER	RADICLE	PERACID	RADICES	

aceinr 97 - carnie

A ACARINE	E CINEREA	M CARMINE	ARSENIC	CREATIN
CARINAE	F FANCIER	N CANNIER	CARNIES	CRINATE
B CARBINE	G ANERGIC	NARCEIN	CERASIN	NACRITE
D CAIRNED	GRECIAN	P CAPRINE	T CANTIER	TACRINE
CARNIED	H ARCHINE	R CARNIER	CERATIN	
DANCIER	L CARLINE	S ARCSINE	CERTAIN	

aceint 161 - enatic

B CABINET	O ACONITE	CREATIN	CINEAST	Y CYANITE
H CHANTIE	ANOETIC	CRINATE	T NICTATE	Z ZINCATE
K ANTICKE	P PICANTE	NACRITE	TETANIC	
M EMICANT	R CANTIER	TACRINE	U TUNICAE	
NEMATIC	CERATIN	S ACETINS	V VENATIC	
N ANCIENT	CERTAIN	CANIEST	X INEXACT	

acenot 133 - octane

C COENACT	COGNATE	L LACTONE	S COSTEAN
D TACNODE	I ACONITE	N CONNATE	OCTANES
E ACETONE	ANOETIC	P PATONCE	T ATTONCE
G COAGENT	J JACONET	R ENACTOR	V CENTAVO

acenrt 192 - trance

A CATERAN	H CHANTER	NACRITE	NECTARS	UNCRATE
D CANTRED	TRANCHE	TACRINE	RECANTS	UNTRACE
TRANCED	I CANTIER	L CENTRAL	SCANTER	Y ENCRATY
E CENTARE	CERATIN	M CREMANT	TANECS	NECTARY
CRENATE	CERTAIN	O ENACTOR	TRANCES	
REENACT	CREATIN	S CANTERS	T TRANECT	
F CANTREF	CRINATE	CARNETS	U CENTAUR	

aceors 202 - coarse

A ROSACEA	ORACHES	ORACLES	EARCONS	U ACEROUS
B BORACES	ROACHES	RECOALS	NARCOSE	CAROUSE
D SARCODE	I CARIOSE	SOLACER	R COARSER	W CROWEAS
E ACEROSE	ORACIES	M AMORCES	CORREAS	X COAXERS
G CARGOES	SCORIAE	N CANOERS	S ROSACES	
CORSAGE	L CLAROES	CARNOSE	T COASTER	
SOCAGER	COALERS	COARSEN	COATERS	
H CHOREAS	ESCOLAR	CORNEAS	RECOATS	

aceort 176 - recoat

D CORDATE	I EROTICA	R ACROTER	S COASTER	U OUTRACE
REDCOAT	L LOCATER	CREATOR	COATERS	V OVERACT
E OCREATE	N ENACTOR	REACTOR	RECOATS	X EXACTOR

adeeir 156 - dearie

B BEADIER	D DEAIRED	FEDARIE	R READIER	W WEARIED
BEARDIE	READIED	H HEADIER	S DEARIES	
C DECIARE	F AREFIED	L LEADIER	READIES	

adeelt 242 - elated

A DEALATE	G GELATED	LATENED	RELATED	VELATED
B BELATED	LEGATED	P PETALED	TREADLE	X EXALTED
BLEATED	TEAGLED	PLEATED	S DELATES	Z TEAZLED
C CLEATED	M MEDALET	R ALERTED	STEALED	
D DELATED	METALED	ALTERED	T LADETTE	
F DEFLATE	N EDENTAL	REDEALT	V VALETED	

adeers 136 - seared

B BEADERS	HEADERS	REDEALS	R DREARES	REDATES
DEBASER	HEARSED	M REMADES	READERS	SEDATER
SABERED	HEDERAS	REMEADS	REDEARS	STEARED
C CREASED	SHEARED	SMEARED	REDSEAR	TASERED
DECARES	I DEARIES	N DEANERS	REREADS	V ADVERSE
SEARCED	READIES	ENDEARS	S RESEDAS	EVADERS
D DEADERS	K DEKARES	O OREADES	T DEAREST	W DRAWEES
G DRAGEES	SKEARED	P PREASED	DERATES	RESAWED
GREASED	L DEALERS	RESPADE	ESTRADE	
H ADHERES	LEADERS	SPEARED	REASTED	

adeert 115 - teared

A AERATED	CREATED	ALTERED	R RETREAD	TASERED
B BERATED	REACTED	REDEALT	TREADER	T ARETTED
BETREAD	D DERATED	RELATED	S DEAREST	TREATED
DEBATER	REDATED	TREADLE	DERATES	V AVERTED
REBATED	TREADED	M REMATED	ESTRADE	TAVERED
TABERED	F DRAFTEE	P ADEPTER	REASTED	W DEWATER
C CATERED	H EARTHED	PREDATE	REDATES	TARWEED
CEDRATE	HEARTED	RETAPED	SEDATER	WATERED
CERATED	L ALERTED	TAPERED	STEARED	X RETAXED

adeest 180 - teased

B BESTEAD	F DEAFEST	L DELATES	DERATES	TASERED
DEBATES	DEFASTE	STEALED	ESTRADE	S SEDATES
C TEDESCA	DEFEATS	M STEAMED	REASTED	T ESTATED
D DEADEST	FEASTED	N STANDEE	REDATES	U SAUTEED
SEDATED	H HEADSET	STEANED	SEDATER	W SWEATED
STEADED	I IDEATES	R DEAREST	STEARED	Y YEASTED

adegot 209 - dotage

E DOGEATE	F FAGOTED	L GLOATED	R GAROTED	DOTAGES
GOATEED	I GODETIA	N TANGOED	S DOGATES	T TOGATED

adeiln 144 - nailed

C INLACED	DEALING	K KNAIDEL	S DENIALS	V ANDVILE
E ALIENED	LEADING	N ANNELID	SNAILED	ANVILED
DELAINE	H HIELAND	LINDANE	U ALIUNDE	X INDEXAL
G ALIGNED	INHALED	P PLAINED	UNIDEAL	

adeilr 24 - derail

A RADIALE	RADICEL	I DELIRIA	PEDRAIL	T DILATER
B BALDIER	RADICLE	IRIDEAL	PREDIAL	REDTAIL
BEDRAIL	D DIEDRAL	L DALLIER	R LARDIER	TRAILED
BRAILED	DRAILED	DIALLER	S DERAILS	U UREDIAL
RAILBED	E LEADIER	RALLIED	DIALERS	V RIVALED
RIDABLE	G GLADIER	O DARIOLE	REDIALS	VALIDER
C DECRIAL	GLAIRED	P LIPREAD	SIDERAL	Y READILY

adeils 62 - sailed

B BALDIES	H HALIDES	MEDIALS	LAPIDES	T DETAILS
DIABLES	I DAILIES	MISDEAL	PAIDLES	DILATES
DISABLE	LIAISED	MISLEAD	PALSIED	U AUDILES
C SCAILED	SEDILIA	N DENIALS	PLEIADS	DEASIUL
D DAIDLES	K SKAILED	SNAILED	R DERAILS	DUALISE
LADDIES	L DALLIES	O DEASOIL	DIALERS	V DEVISAL
E AEDILES	DISLEAL	ISOLEAD	REDIALS	Y DIALYSE
DEISEAL	LALDIES	P ALIPEDS	SIDERAL	EYLIADS
F DISLEAF	SALLIED	ELAPIDS	S AIDLESS	
G SILAGED	M MAELIDS	LAIPSED	DEASILS	

adeinr 5 - rained

A ARANEID	DRAINED	GRAINED	O ANEROID	T ANTIRED
B BANDIER	F FRIANDE	READING	P PARDINE	DETRAIN
BRAINED	G AREDING	H HANDIER	R DRAINER	TRAINED
C CAIRNED	DEARING	I DENARII	RANDIER	U UNAIRED
CARNIED	DERAIGN	M ADERMIN	S RANDIES	URANIDE
DANCIER	EARDING	INARMED	SANDIER	V INVADER
D DANDIER	GRADINE	N NARDINE	SARDINE	RAVINED

adeins 28 - daines

A NAIADES	F FADEINS	MEDINAS	SPAINED	NIDATES
B BANDIES	G AGNISED	SIDEMAN	R RANDIES	SAINTED
BASINED	K KANDIES	N DANNIES	SANDIER	SATINED
C CANDIES	L DENIALS	O ADONISE	SARDINE	STAINED
INCASED	SNAILED	ANODISE	S SDAINES	V INVADES
D DANDIES	M DEMAINS	SODAINE	T DESTAIN	W DEWANIS
SDAINED	MAIDENS	P PANDIES	DETAINS	
E ANISEED	MEDIANS	PANSIED	INSTEAD	

adeint 45 - detain

D NIDATED	P DEPAINT	TRAINED	SAINTED	V DEVIANT
F DEFIANT	PAINTED	S DESTAIN	SATINED	
FAINTED	PATINED	DETAINS	STAINED	
I INEDITA	R ANTIRED	INSTEAD	T TAINTED	
M MEDIANT	DETRAIN	NIDATES	U AUDIENT	

adeior 121 - roadie

D RADIOED	N ANEROID	SOREDIA	AVOIDER
L DARIOLE	S ROADIES	V AVODIRE	X EXORDIA

adeirs 18 - aiders

A ARAISED	READIES	K DAIKERS	SANDIER	ASTRIDE
B ABIDERS	F FARSIDE	DARKIES	SARDINE	DIASTER
BARDIES	FRAISED	L DERAILS	O ROADIES	DISRATE
BRAISED	G AGRISED	DIALERS	SOREDIA	STAIDER
DARBIES	H AIRSHED	REDIALS	P ASPIRED	STAIRED
SEABIRD	DASHIER	SIDERAL	DESPAIR	TARDIES
SIDEBAR	HARDIES	M ADMIRES	DIAPERS	TIRADES
C CARDIES	SHADIER	MARDIES	PRAISED	U RESIDUA
DARCIES	I AIRSIDE	MISREAD	R ARRIDES	V ADVISER
RADICES	DAIRIES	SEDARIM	RAIDERS	VARDIES
SIDECAR	DIARIES	SIDEARM	T ARIDEST	X RADIXES
E DEARIES	DIARISE	N RANDIES	ASTERID	

adeirt 19 - tirade

A AIRDATE	H AIRTHED	DETRAIN	S ARIDEST	TARDIES
RADIATE	K TRAIKED	TRAINED	ASTERID	TIRADES
TIARAED	L DILATER	P DIPTERA	ASTRIDE	T ATTIRED
B REDBAIT	REDTAIL	PARTIED	DIASTER	V TARDIVE
TRIBADE	TRAILED	PIRATED	DISRATE	Y DIETARY
D TARDIED	M READMIT	R TARDIER	STAIDER	
G TRIAGED	N ANTIRED	TARRIED	STAIRED	

adelnr 148 - darnel

A ADRENAL	G DANGLER	M MANDREL	RELANDS	RUNDALE
B BLANDER	GNARLED	O LADRONE	SLANDER	Y DEARNLY
C CANDLER	H HANDLER	S DARNELS	SNARLED	
D DANDLER	K RANKLED	ENLARDS	U LAUNDER	
E LEARNED	L LANDLER	LANDERS	LURDANE	

adelnt 217 - dental

A LANATED	LATENED	O TALONED	SLANTED	W WETLAND
C CANTLED	G TANGLED	P PLANTED	U LUNATED	
E EDENTAL	M MANTLED	S DENTALS	UNDEALT	

adelor 142 - reload

B LABORED	ORACLED	I DARIOLE	M EARLDOM	P LEOPARD
C CAROLED	F ALFREDO	L ODALLER	N LADRONE	PAROLED

Six-letter stems

	PRELOAD	ORDEALS	T	DELATOR	U	ROULADE
S	LOADERS	RELOADS		LEOTARD		

adelos 177 - aldose

B	ALBEDOS	I	DEASOIL	P	DEPOSAL	S	ALDOSES	W	WALDOES
C	COLEADS		ISOLEAD		PEDALOS		LASSOED		
	SOLACED	K	SKOALED	R	LOADERS	T	SALTOED		
E	ELODEAS	M	DAMOSEL		ORDEALS		SOLATED		
H	SHOALED	N	LOADENS		RELOADS	V	SALVOED		

adelrs 169 - alders

B	BEDRALS	E	DEALERS		DIALERS		LANDERS	R	LARDERS
	BLADERS		LEADERS		REDIALS		RELANDS	S	RASSLED
C	CRADLES		REDEALS		SIDERAL		SLANDER		SARDELS
	RECLADS	F	FARDELS	K	DARKLES		SNARLED	T	DARTLES
	SCALDER	G	DARGLES	L	LADLERS	O	LOADERS		SLARTED
D	LADDERS	H	HARELDS	M	MEDLARS		ORDEALS	U	LAUDERS
	RADDLES		HERALDS	N	DARNELS		RELOADS	W	WARSLED
	SADDLER	I	DERAILS		ENLARDS	P	PEDLARS	Z	DRAZELS

adelrt 132 - dartle

A	LATERAD	E	ALERTED		TREADLE	O	DELATOR	T	RATTLED
B	BLARTED		ALTERED	I	DILATER		LEOTARD	W	TRAWLED
C	CLARTED		REDEALT		REDTAIL	S	DARTLES	X	DEXTRAL
D	DARTLED		RELATED		TRAILED		SLARTED	Y	LYRATED

adelst 221 - salted

B	BALDEST	E	DELATES		STALKED		SOLATED	T	SLATTED
	BLASTED		STEALED	L	STALLED	P	SPALTED	U	AULDEST
	STABLED	H	DALETHS	M	MALTEDS		STAPLED		SALUTED
C	CASTLED	I	DETAILS	N	DENTALS	R	DARTLES		
	SCLATED		DILATES		SLANTED		SLARTED		
D	STADDLE	K	SKLATED	O	SALTOED	S	DESALTS		

adenos 232 - anodes

C	ACNODES		ANODISE		MASONED	P	DAPSONE	U	DOUANES
	DEACONS		SODAINE		MODENAS	T	ASTONED	Y	NOYADES
G	SONDAGE	L	LOADENS		MONADES		DONATES		
I	ADONISE	M	DAEMONS		NOMADES		ONSTEAD		

adenot 51 - donate

B	BATONED	G	TANGOED		TONEPAD		ONSTEAD
C	TACNODE	L	TALONED	R	TORNADE	T	NOTATED
D	DONATED	O	ODONATE	S	ASTONED	V	NOVATED
	NODATED	P	NOTEPAD		DONATES	Z	ZONATED

adenrs 112 - snared

B BANDERS	GARDENS	LANDERS	R DARNERS	DANSEUR
C DANCERS	H HANDERS	RELANDS	ERRANDS	DAUNERS
D DANDERS	HARDENS	SLANDER	SNARRED	W DAWNERS
E DEANERS	I RANDIES	SNARLED	S SANDERS	WANDERS
ENDEARS	SANDIER	M DAMNERS	SARSDEN	WARDENS
F FARDENS	SARDINE	MANREDS	T ENDARTS	Z ZANDERS
SNARFED	K DARKENS	RANDEMS	STANDER	
G DANGERS	L DARNELS	REMANDS	STARNED	
GANDERS	ENLARDS	P PANDERS	U ASUNDER	

adenrt 98 - ranted

B BARTEND	GRANTED	S ENDARTS	NATURED	Y DENTARY
C CANTRED	I ANTIRED	STANDER	UNRATED	TRAYNED
TRANCED	DETRAIN	STARNED	UNTREAD	TYRANED
D DRANTED	TRAINED	T TRANTED	V VERDANT	
G DRAGNET	O TORNADE	U DAUNTER	X DEXTRAN	

adenru 117 - unread

B UNBARED	RAUNGED	LURDANE	O RONDEAU	T DAUNTER
C DURANCE	H UNHEARD	RUNDALE	P UNDRAPE	NATURED
UNRACED	I UNAIRED	M DURAMEN	UNPARED	UNRATED
D DAUNDER	URANIDE	MANURED	S ASUNDER	UNTREAD
E UNEARED	K UNRAKED	MAUNDER	DANSEUR	Y UNREADY
G ENGUARD	L LAUNDER	UNARMED	DAUNERS	Z UNRAZED

adenst 72 - staned

A ANSATED	H HANDSET	STAINED	O ASTONED	STARNED
C DECANTS	I DESTAIN	K DANKEST	DONATES	T ATTENDS
DESCANT	DETAINS	STANKED	ONSTEAD	U SAUNTED
SCANTED	INSTEAD	L DENTALS	P PEDANTS	UNSATED
E STANDEE	NIDATES	SLANTED	PENTADS	V ADVENTS
STEANED	SAINTED	M TANDEMS	R ENDARTS	Y STAYNED
G STANGED	SATINED	N STANDEN	STANDER	

adentu 188 - undate

B UNBATED	H HAUNTED	UNTAMED	UNTREAD	V VAUNTED
C UNACTED	I AUDIENT	P UNADEPT	S SAUNTED	X UNTAXED
D DAUNTED	J JAUNTED	Q QUANTED	UNSATED	
UNDATED	L LUNATED	R DAUNTER	T ATTUNED	
G GAUNTED	UNDEALT	NATURED	NUTATED	
UNGATED	M UNMATED	UNRATED	TAUNTED	

adeors 43 - soared

C SARCODE	I ROADIES	M RADOMES	T DOATERS	V OVERSAD
D DEODARS	SOREDIA	O ROADEOS	ROASTED	SAVORED
E OREADES	L LOADERS	R ADORERS	TORSADE	W REDOWAS
F FEDORAS	ORDEALS	DROSERA	TROADES	
G DOGEARS	RELOADS	S SARODES	U AROUSED	

Six-letter stems

adeort 55 - orated

B ABORTED	G GAROTED	O ODORATE	TORSADE	OUTREAD
BORATED	K TROAKED	P ADOPTER	TROADES	READOUT
TABORED	L DELATOR	READOPT	T ROTATED	
C CORDATE	LEOTARD	S DOATERS	TROATED	
REDCOAT	N TORNADE	ROASTED	U OUTDARE	

aderst 78 - treads

B DABSTER	STEARED	ASTRIDE	M SMARTED	DARTRES
TABERDS	TASERED	DIASTER	N ENDARTS	RETARDS
C REDACTS	F STRAFED	DISRATE	STANDER	STARRED
SCARTED	G RADGEST	STAIDER	STARNED	TRADERS
D ADDREST	H DEARTHS	STAIRED	O DOATERS	T STARTED
RADDEST	HARDEST	TARDIES	ROASTED	TETRADS
E DEAREST	HARDSET	TIRADES	TORSADE	V ADVERTS
DERATES	HATREDS	K DARKEST	TROADES	STARVED
ESTRADE	THREADS	STARKED	P DEPARTS	W STEWARD
REASTED	TRASHED	STRAKED	DRAPETS	STRAWED
REDATES	I ARIDEST	L DARTLES	PETARDS	WRASTED
SEDATER	ASTERID	SLARTED	R DARTERS	Y STRAYED

adinor 83 - ordain

B INBOARD	GRADINO	P PADRONI	ORDAINS
D ANDROID	ROADING	PONIARD	SADIRON
E ANEROID	L ORDINAL	R ORDINAR	T DIATRON
G ADORING	N ANDIRON	S INROADS	V VIRANDO

adinrs 236 - drains

A RADIANS	SARDINE	K DISRANK	O INROADS	T INDARTS
B RIBANDS	F FRIANDS	L ALDRINS	ORDAINS	U DURIANS
E RANDIES	G DARINGS	M MANDIRS	SADIRON	SUNDARI
SANDIER	GRADINS	N INNARDS	Q QINDARS	W INWARDS

adinrt 155 - indart

A INTRADA	E ANTIRED	F INDRAFT	O DIATRON	U TRIDUAN
RADIANT	DETRAIN	G DARTING	R TRIDARN	UNITARD
B ANTBIRD	TRAINED	TRADING	S INDARTS	

aeegnr 183 - enrage

B REBEGAN	GRANDEE	L ENLARGE	S ENRAGES	U RENAGUE
C ENGRACE	GRENADE	GENERAL	T GRANTEE	UNEAGER
D ANGERED	F FREEGAN	GLEANER	GREATEN	V AVENGER
DERANGE	G ENGAGER	M GERMANE	NEGATER	ENGRAVE
ENRAGED	I REGINAE	N ENRANGE	REAGENT	

aeegnt 246 - negate

C CENTAGE	E TEENAGE	L ELEGANT	GREATEN	S NEGATES
D AGENTED	F FANTEEG	M GATEMEN	NEGATER	T TENTAGE
NEGATED	H THENAGE	R GRANTEE	REAGENT	V VENTAGE

aeeint 44 - teniae

A TAENIAE	L LINEATE	MATINEE	RETINAE	S ETESIAN
B BETAINE	M ETAMINE	R ARENITE	TRAINEE	V NAIVETE

aeeirs 81 - easier

D DEARIES	FREESIA	M SEAMIER	R REARISE	W WEARIES
READIES	I AIERIES	SERIEMA	RERAISE	
F AREFIES	L EARLIES	P APERIES	T AERIEST	
FAERIES	REALISE	EPEIRAS	SERIATE	

aeelnr 114 - leaner

B ENABLER	G ENLARGE	M REELMAN	RELEARN	ETERNAL
C CLEANER	GENERAL	N LERNEAN	S LEANERS	TELERAN
RECLEAN	GLEANER	P REPANEL	T ALTERNE	W RENEWAL
D LEARNED	I ALIENER	R LEARNER	ENTERAL	

aeelns 243 - enseal

B BALEENS	SCALENE	MELENAS	S ENSEALS	LEAVENS
ENABLES	D LEADENS	O ENOLASE	T ELANETS	W WEANELS
C CLEANSE	I SEALINE	P ALPEENS	LATEENS	
ELANCES	K ALKENES	SPELEAN	LEANEST	
ENLACES	M ENAMELS	R LEANERS	V ENSLAVE	

aeelnt 171 - lateen

B TENABLE	G ELEGANT	M MANTEEL	ETERNAL	LEANEST
C LATENCE	H LETHEAN	TELEMAN	TELERAN	Y ENTAYLE
D EDENTAL	I LINEATE	R ALTERNE	S ELANETS	
LATENED	K KANTELE	ENTERAL	LATEENS	

aeelrs 118 - resale

C ALERCES	G GALERES	P LEAPERS	SEALERS	REVEALS
CEREALS	REGALES	PLEASER	T ELATERS	SEVERAL
RELACES	H HEALERS	PRESALE	REALEST	VEALERS
RESCALE	I EARLIES	RELAPSE	RELATES	X RELAXES
SCLERAE	REALISE	REPEALS	RESLATE	Y SEALERY
D DEALERS	K LEAKERS	S EARLESS	STEALER	
LEADERS	M MEALERS	LEASERS	U LEASURE	
REDEALS	N LEANERS	RESALES	V LAVEERS	
E RELEASE	O AREOLES	RESEALS	LEAVERS	

aeelrt 102 - relate

A LAETARE	RELATED	M LAMETER	PRELATE	REALEST
B BLEATER	TREADLE	N ALTERNE	REPLATE	RELATES
RETABLE	F REFLATE	ENTERAL	R ALERTER	RESLATE
C TREACLE	H HALTERE	ETERNAL	ALTERER	STEALER
D ALERTED	LEATHER	TELERAN	REALTER	X EXALTER
ALTERED	I ATELIER	P PETRALE	RELATER	
REDEALT	REALTIE	PLEATER	S ELATERS	

aeelst 240 - teasel

B BELATES	LEGATES	LATEENS	STEALER	VALETES
C CELESTA	SEGETAL	LEANEST	S ALTESSE	VELETAS
SELECTA	TEAGLES	O OLEATES	STEALES	X LATEXES
D DELATES	TELEGAS	R ELATERS	TEASELS	Y EYALETS
STEALED	H LATHEES	REALEST	U ELUATES	Z TEAZELS
G EAGLETS	L LEALEST	RELATES	SETUALE	TEAZLES
GELATES	N ELANETS	RESLATE	V SALVETE	

aeenrs 101 - ranees

C CAREENS	ENDEARS	M MEANERS	P PANEERS	EASTERN
CASERNE	G ENRAGES	RENAMES	R EARNERS	NEAREST
ENRACES	H ARSHEEN	N ENSNARE	REEARNS	RATEENS
RECANES	K SNEAKER	RENNASE	S ENSEARS	W WEANERS
D DEANERS	L LEANERS	O ARENOSE	T EARNEST	

aeenrt 54 - neater

C CENTARE	REAGENT	K RETAKEN	R TERRANE	RATTEEN
CRENATE	H EARTHEN	L ALTERNE	S EARNEST	TERNATE
REENACT	HEARTEN	ENTERAL	EASTERN	V AVENTRE
G GRANTEE	I ARENITE	ETERNAL	NEAREST	NERVATE
GREATEN	RETINAE	TELERAN	RATEENS	VETERAN
NEGATER	TRAINEE	M REMANET	T ENTREAT	

aeenst 106 - senate

C CETANES	I ETESIAN	MEANEST	EASTERN	SENSATE
TENACES	J SEJEANT	N NEATENS	NEAREST	STEANES
D STANDEE	L ELANETS	P NEPETAS	RATEENS	T NEATEST
STEANED	LATEENS	PENATES	S ENTASES	
G NEGATES	LEANEST	PESANTE	SATEENS	
H ETHANES	M ENTAMES	R EARNEST	SENATES	

aeerst 30 - teaser

A AERATES	REDATES	SERIATE	N EARNEST	SAETERS
B BEATERS	SEDATER	K RETAKES	EASTERN	SEAREST
BERATES	STEARED	SAKERET	NEAREST	SEATERS
REBATES	TASERED	L ELATERS	RATEENS	STEARES
C CERATES	F AFREETS	REALEST	O ROSEATE	TEASERS
CREATES	FEASTER	RELATES	P REPEATS	TESSERA
ECARTES	G ERGATES	RESLATE	RETAPES	T ESTREAT
SECRETA	RESTAGE	STEALER	R RETEARS	RESTATE
D DEAREST	H AETHERS	M REMATES	SERRATE	RETASTE
DERATES	HEATERS	RETEAMS	TEARERS	U AUSTERE
ESTRADE	REHEATS	STEAMER	S EASTERS	W SWEATER
REASTED	I AERIEST	TEAMERS	RESEATS	X RETAXES

aegiln 100 - genial

C ANGELIC	GALENIC	DEALING	E LINEAGE	FINAGLE
ANGLICE	D ALIGNED	LEADING	F FEALING	LEAFING

G EAGLING	M GEMINAL	PEALING	REGINAL	TAGLINE
GEALING	LEAMING	PLEAING	S LEASING	U LINGUAE
LIGNAGE	MEALING	R ALIGNER	LINAGES	UNAGILE
H HEALING	N ANELING	ENGRAIL	SEALING	V LEAVING
K LEAKING	EANLING	LAERING	T ATINGLE	VEALING
LINKAGE	LEANING	LEARING	ELATING	Y ALEYING
L GALLEIN	NEALING	NARGILE	GELATIN	YEALING
NIGELLA	P LEAPING	REALIGN	GENITAL	

aeginr 16 - regina

A ANERGIA	F FEARING	M GERMAIN	R ANGRIER	REGINAS
B BEARING	G GEARING	GERMINA	EARRING	SEARING
C ANERGIC	NAGGIER	MANGIER	GRAINER	SERINGA
GRECIAN	H HEARING	MEARING	RANGIER	T GRANITE
D AREDING	K REAKING	REAMING	REARING	GRATINE
DEARING	L ALIGNER	N AGINNER	S ANGRIES	INGRATE
DERAIGN	ENGRAIL	EARNING	EARINGS	TANGIER
EARDING	LAERING	ENGRAIN	ERASING	TEARING
GRADINE	LEARING	GRANNIE	GAINERS	V REAVING
GRAINED	NARGILE	NEARING	GRAINES	VINEGAR
READING	REALIGN	O ORIGANE	REAGINS	W WEARING
E REGINAE	REGINAL	P REAPING	REGAINS	Z ZINGARE

aegins 74 - easing

B SABEING	LINAGES	P PEASING	REGINAS	INGESTA
C CEASING	SEALING	SPAEING	SEARING	SEATING
INCAGES	M ENIGMAS	SPINAGE	SERINGA	TAGINES
D AGNISED	GAMINES	R ANGRIES	S AGNISES	TANGIES
E AGENISE	MEASING	EARINGS	SEASING	TEASING
F FEASING	SEAMING	ERASING	T EASTING	TSIGANE
G AGEINGS	N INNAGES	GAINERS	EATINGS	U GUINEAS
SIGNAGE	SEANING	GRAINES	GAINEST	Y EASYING
K SINKAGE	O AGONIES	REAGINS	GENISTA	Z AGNIZES
L LEASING	AGONISE	REGAINS	INGATES	SEAZING

aegint 129 - eating

B BEATING	GENITAL	GENTIAN	EATINGS	TANGIES
F FEATING	TAGLINE	R GRANITE	GAINEST	TEASING
H GAHNITE	M MINTAGE	GRATINE	GENISTA	TSIGANE
HEATING	TEAMING	INGRATE	INGATES	U UNITAGE
L ATINGLE	TEGMINA	TANGIER	INGESTA	V VINTAGE
ELATING	N ANTEING	TEARING	SEATING	Z TEAZING
GELATIN	ANTIGEN	S EASTING	TAGINES	TZIGANE

aegirt 151 - triage

C CIGARET	RAGTIME	TEARING	SEAGIRT	V VIRGATE
D TRIAGED	N GRANITE	O GOATIER	STAGIER	VITRAGE
F FRIGATE	GRATINE	S AGISTER	STRIGAE	
G TAGGIER	INGRATE	AIGRETS	TIRAGES	
M MIGRATE	TANGIER	GAITERS	TRIAGES	

aegist 167 - ageist

A AGATISE	TAIGLES	INGESTA	AIGRETS	SAGIEST
C CAGIEST	M GAMIEST	SEATING	GAITERS	U AUGITES
D AGISTED	SIGMATE	TAGINES	SEAGIRT	Y GASEITY
G STAGGIE	N EASTING	TANGIES	STAGIER	Z GAZIEST
L AGILEST	EATINGS	TEASING	STRIGAE	
AIGLETS	GAINEST	TSIGANE	TIRAGES	
GELATIS	GENISTA	P GAPIEST	TRIAGES	
LIGATES	INGATES	R AGISTER	S AGEISTS	

aeglnr 179 - regnal

A ALNAGER	GENERAL	LEARING	P GRAPNEL	TRANGLE
B BRANGLE	GLEANER	NARGILE	S ANGLERS	U GRANULE
C CLANGER	F FLANGER	REALIGN	ERLANGS	W WANGLER
GLANCER	G GANGREL	REGINAL	LANGERS	WRANGLE
D DANGLER	I ALIGNER	J JANGLER	LARGENS	Y ANGERLY
GNARLED	ENGRAIL	L LANGREL	SLANGER	
E ENLARGE	LAERING	M MANGLER	T TANGLER	

aegnor 90 - orange

B BEGROAN	I ORIGANE	O OREGANO	ORANGES	
C ACROGEN	K KARENGO	R GROANER	T NEGATOR	
CORNAGE	M MARENGO	ORANGER	W WAGONER	
D GROANED	MEGARON	S ONAGERS	Y ORANGEY	

aegnrs 172 - ranges

B BANGERS	H GNASHER	REAGINS	LARGENS	RANGERS
GRABENS	HANGERS	REGAINS	SLANGER	S SANGERS
D DANGERS	REHANGS	REGINAS	M ENGRAMS	SERANGS
GANDERS	SHERANG	SEARING	GERMANS	T ARGENTS
GARDENS	I ANGRIES	SERINGA	MANGERS	GARNETS
E ENRAGES	EARINGS	K SKANGER	O ONAGERS	STRANGE
G GANGERS	ERASING	L ANGLERS	ORANGES	U RAUNGES
GRANGES	GAINERS	ERLANGS	P ENGRASP	UNGEARS
NAGGERS	GRAINES	LANGERS	R GARNERS	W GNAWERS

aegnrt 52 - garnet

A TANAGER	REAGENT	TEARING	N REGNANT	GARNETS
D DRAGNET	F ENGRAFT	L TANGLER	O NEGATOR	STRANGE
GRANTED	I GRANITE	TRANGLE	P TREPANG	U GAUNTER
E GRANTEE	GRATINE	M GARMENT	R GRANTER	W TWANGER
GREATEN	INGRATE	MARGENT	REGRANT	Y AGENTRY
NEGATER	TANGIER	RAGMENT	S ARGENTS	

aegnst 200 - agents

A AGNATES	EATINGS	SEATING	L GELANTS	O ONSTAGE
D STANGED	GAINEST	TAGINES	LANGEST	R ARGENTS
E NEGATES	GENISTA	TANGIES	TANGLES	GARNETS
H STENGAH	INGATES	TEASING	M MAGNETS	STRANGE
I EASTING	INGESTA	TSIGANE	N GANNETS	T GESTANT

aegors 238 - sorage

A	AGAROSE		CORSAGE	H	GHERAOS	N	ONAGERS		ORGEATS
	OARAGES		SOCAGER	L	GALORES		ORANGES		STORAGE
B	BORAGES	D	DOGEARS		GAOLERS	S	SORAGES		TOERAGS
C	CARGOES	F	FORAGES	M	ROMAGES	T	GAROTES	U	AERUGOS

aegort 63 - toerag

D	GAROTED		LEGATOR		POTAGER		STORAGE
F	FAGOTER	N	NEGATOR	R	GARROTE		TOERAGS
I	GOATIER	O	ROOTAGE	S	GAROTES	T	GAROTTE
L	GLOATER	P	PORTAGE		ORGEATS	U	OUTRAGE

aegrst 139 - greats

A	AGRASTE		GARGETS		STAGIER	O	GAROTES	S	GASTERS
	GASTREA		STAGGER		STRIGAE		ORGEATS		STAGERS
	TEARGAS		TAGGERS		TIRAGES		STORAGE	T	TARGETS
B	BARGEST	H	GATHERS		TRIAGES		TOERAGS	V	GRAVEST
D	RADGEST	I	AGISTER	L	LARGEST	P	PARGETS	Y	GRAYEST
E	ERGATES		AIGRETS	N	ARGENTS	R	GARRETS		GYRATES
	RESTAGE		GAITERS		GARNETS		GARTERS		STAGERY
G	GAGSTER		SEAGIRT		STRANGE		GRATERS		

aeilmn 247 - menial

A	LAMINAE	G	GEMINAL	M	MAILMEN	R	MANLIER		MENIALS
B	MINABLE		LEAMING	N	LINEMAN		MARLINE		SEMINAL
C	CNEMIAL		MEALING		MELANIN		MINERAL	T	AILMENT
	MELANIC	H	HELIMAN	O	MINEOLA		RAILMEN		ALIMENT
F	FEMINAL	K	MANLIKE	P	IMPANEL	S	ISLEMAN	U	ALUMINE
	INFLAME	L	MANILLE		MANIPLE		MALINES		

aeilmr 224 - mailer

B	BALMIER		RECLAIM	M	MALMIER		IMPEARL		REMAILS
	LAMBIER	E	MEALIER	N	MANLIER		LEMPIRA	T	LAMITER
	MIRABLE	F	FLAMIER		MARLINE		PALMIER		MALTIER
	REMBLAI	G	GREMIAL		MINERAL	R	LARMIER		MARLITE
C	CALMIER		LAMIGER		RAILMEN		MARLIER		
	CLAIMER	I	RAMILIE	O	LOAMIER	S	MAILERS		
	MIRACLE	K	ARMLIKE	P	IMPALER		REALISM		

aeilno 42 - eolian

A	AEOLIAN	M	MINEOLA	R	AILERON		ALIENOR	T	ELATION
K	KAOLINE	P	OPALINE		ALERION	S	ANISOLE		TOENAIL

aeilnr 6 - linear

C	CARLINE		ENGRAIL		NARGILE	H	HERNIAL	K	LANKIER
E	ALIENER		LAERING		REALIGN		INHALER	L	RALLINE
G	ALIGNER		LEARING		REGINAL	I	AIRLINE	M	MANLIER

MARLINE	ALIENOR	S ALINERS	RATLINE	W LAWNIER
MINERAL	P PEARLIN	NAILERS	RELIANT	X RELAXIN
RAILMEN	PLAINER	RENAILS	RETINAL	Y INLAYER
O AILERON	PRALINE	T ENTRAIL	TRENAIL	NAILERY
ALERION	R LARNIER	LATRINE	V RAVELIN	

aeilns 32 - aliens

B LESBIAN	LINAGES	O ANISOLE	SILANES	TENAILS
C INLACES	SEALING	P ALPINES	T EASTLIN	U INSULAE
SANICLE	H INHALES	PINEALS	ELASTIN	INULASE
SCALENI	K ALKINES	SPANIEL	ENTAILS	V ALEVINS
D DENIALS	L AINSELL	SPLENIA	NAILSET	VALINES
SNAILED	M ISLEMAN	R ALINERS	SALIENT	W LAWINES
E SEALINE	MALINES	NAILERS	SALTINE	X ALEXINS
F FINALES	MENIALS	RENAILS	SLAINTE	Y ELYSIAN
G LEASING	SEMINAL	S SALINES	STANIEL	

aeilnt 17 - entail

A ANTLIAE	TAGLINE	R ENTRAIL	ELASTIN	TENAILS
E LINEATE	K ANTLIKE	LATRINE	ENTAILS	U ALUNITE
F INFLATE	M AILMENT	RATLINE	NAILSET	V VENTAIL
G ATINGLE	ALIMENT	RELIANT	SALIENT	
ELATING	O ELATION	RETINAL	SALTINE	
GELATIN	TOENAIL	TRENAIL	SLAINTE	
GENITAL	P PANTILE	S EASTLIN	STANIEL	

aeilrr 190 - rerail

C CERRIAL	F FLARIER	K LARKIER	N LARNIER	RETRIAL
D LARDIER	FRAILER	L RALLIER	S RAILERS	TRAILER
E EARLIER	G GLARIER	M LARMIER	RERAILS	
LEARIER	I LAIRIER	MARLIER	T RETIRAL	

aeilrs 23 - serial

A AERIALS	E EARLIES	SERKALI	P PALSIER	T REALIST
B BAILERS	REALISE	L RALLIES	PARLIES	RETAILS
C CLARIES	G GLAIRES	SALLIER	R RAILERS	SALTIER
ECLAIRS	GRAILES	M MAILERS	RERAILS	SALTIRE
SCALIER	H HAILERS	REALISM	S AIRLESS	SLATIER
D DERAILS	SHALIER	REMAILS	RESAILS	TAILERS
DIALERS	I LAIRISE	N ALINERS	SAILERS	V REVISAL
REDIALS	J JAILERS	NAILERS	SERIALS	W SWALIER
SIDERAL	K LAIKERS	RENAILS	SERIALS	WAILERS

aeilrt 15 - retail

B LIBRATE	D DILATER	K RATLIKE	MALTIER	RETINAL
TABLIER	REDTAIL	TALKIER	MARLITE	TRENAIL
TRIABLE	TRAILED	L LITERAL	N ENTRAIL	P PLAITER
C ARTICLE	E ATELIER	TALLIER	LATRINE	PLATIER
RECITAL	REALTIE	TRIELLA	RATLINE	R RETIRAL
TALCIER	H LATHIER	M LAMITER	RELIANT	RETRIAL

```
  TRAILER      SALTIER        TAILERS      W WALTIER        TEARILY
S REALIST      SALTIRE      T TERTIAL      Y IRATELY
  RETAILS      SLATIER      U URALITE        REALITY
```

aeilst 37 - saltie

```
B ABLEIST      SALICET      I LAITIES        SLAINTE        SLATIER
  ALBITES    D DETAILS      K LAKIEST        STANIEL        TAILERS
  ASTILBE      DILATES        TALKIES        TENAILS      S SALTIES
  BASTILE    F FETIALS      L SITELLA      O ISOLATE      U SITULAE
  BESTIAL      SEALIFT        TAILLES      P APLITES      V ESTIVAL
  BLASTIE    G AGILEST        TALLIES        PALIEST      W WALIEST
  LIBATES      AIGLETS      N EASTLIN        PLATIES      Y TAILYES
  STABILE      GELATIS        ELASTIN        TALIPES      Z LAZIEST
C ASTELIC      LIGATES        ENTAILS      R REALIST
  ELASTIC      TAIGLES        NAILSET        RETAILS
  LACIEST    H HALITES        SALIENT        SALTIER
  LATICES      HELIAST        SALTINE        SALTIRE
```

aeimno 239 - anomie

```
C ENCOMIA      DOMAINE      R MORAINE      S ANOMIES      U MOINEAU
D AMIDONE    L MINEOLA        ROMAINE      T AMNIOTE
```

aeimnr 99 - remain

```
B MIRBANE      GERMINA      L MANLIER      R MARINER        RAIMENT
C CARMINE      MANGIER        MARLINE      S MARINES      V VERMIAN
D ADERMIN      MEARING        MINERAL        REMAINS      W WIREMAN
  INARMED      REAMING        RAILMEN        SEMINAR
E REMANIE    H HARMINE      O MORAINE        SIRNAME
F FIREMAN      MANKIER        ROMAINE      T MERANTI
G GERMAIN      RAMEKIN      P PERMIAN        MINARET
```

aeimns 201 - amines

```
A AMNESIA    E MEANIES        HEMINAS      O ANOMIES        MAINEST
  ANEMIAS      NEMESIA      J JASMINE      R MARINES        MANTIES
C AMNESIC    F FAMINES      K KINEMAS        REMAINS        TAMEINS
  CINEMAS      INFAMES      L ISLEMAN        SEMINAR        TAMINES
D DEMAINS    G ENIGMAS        MALINES        SIRNAME      W MANWISE
  MAIDENS      GAMINES        MENIALS      S INSEAMS
  MEDIANS      MEASING        SEMINAL        SAMISEN
  MEDINAS      SEAMING      M AMMINES      T ETAMINS
  SIDEMAN    H HAEMINS        MISNAME        INMATES
```

aeimnt 59 - inmate

```
A AMENTIA    E ETAMINE      I INTIMAE      R MERANTI        MANTIES
  ANIMATE      MATINEE        MINIATE        MINARET        TAMEINS
B AMBIENT    G MINTAGE      L AILMENT        RAIMENT        TAMINES
C EMICANT      TEAMING        ALIMENT      S ETAMINS      X TAXIMEN
  NEMATIC      TEGMINA      N MANNITE        INMATES      Y AMENITY
D MEDIANT    H HEMATIN      O AMNIOTE        MAINEST        ANYTIME
```

aeimrs 228 - armies

B	AMBRIES	G	GISARME	M MAIMERS
D	ADMIRES		IMAGERS	RAMMIES
	MARDIES		MAIGRES	N MARINES
	MISREAD		MIRAGES	REMAINS
	SEDARIM	H MASHIER		SEMINAR
	SIDEARM		MISHEAR	SIRNAME
E	SEAMIER	L MAILERS		P IMPRESA
	SERIEMA		REALISM	SAMPIRE
F	MISFARE		REMAILS	R MARRIES

B AMBRIES	G GISARME	M MAIMERS	SIMARRE	SMARTIE
D ADMIRES	IMAGERS	RAMMIES	S MASSIER	U UREMIAS
MARDIES	MAIGRES	N MARINES	SARMIES	V MISAVER
MISREAD	MIRAGES	REMAINS	T IMARETS	W AWMRIES
SEDARIM	H MASHIER	SEMINAR	MAESTRI	SEMIRAW
SIDEARM	MISHEAR	SIRNAME	MAISTER	Y RIMAYES
E SEAMIER	L MAILERS	P IMPRESA	MASTIER	
SERIEMA	REALISM	SAMPIRE	MISRATE	
F MISFARE	REMAILS	R MARRIES	SEMITAR	

aeimrt 91 - matier

A AMIRATE	G MIGRATE	M MARMITE	S IMARETS	SMARTIE
C MATRICE	RAGTIME	TRAMMIE	MAESTRI	U MURIATE
D READMIT	I AIRTIME	N MERANTI	MAISTER	V VITAMER
E EMERITA	L LAMITER	MINARET	MASTIER	W WARTIME
EMIRATE	MALTIER	RAIMENT	MISRATE	
MEATIER	MARLITE	P PRIMATE	SEMITAR	

aeimst 208 - maties

C ACMITES	I AMITIES	MANTIES	MAESTRI	SAMITES
ETACISM	ATIMIES	TAMEINS	MAISTER	TAMISES
MICATES	K KETMIAS	TAMINES	MASTIER	T ETATISM
SEMATIC	MISTAKE	O AMOSITE	MISRATE	MATIEST
D DIASTEM	M MISMATE	ATOMIES	SEMITAR	MATTIES
MISDATE	SEMIMAT	ATOMISE	SMARTIE	Z MAZIEST
E STEAMIE	TAMMIES	OSMIATE	S ASTEISM	MESTIZA
G GAMIEST	N ETAMINS	P IMPASTE	MISEATS	
SIGMATE	INMATES	PASTIME	MISSEAT	
H ATHEISM	MAINEST	R IMARETS	SAMIEST	

aeinnt 186 - innate

C ANCIENT	GENTIAN	P PANTINE	S INANEST
F INFANTE	K NEATNIK	PINNATE	STANINE
G ANTEING	M MANNITE	R ENTRAIN	TANNIES
ANTIGEN	O ENATION	TRANNIE	T ANTIENT

aeinpr 160 - rapine

C CAPRINE	G REAPING	PLAINER	P NAPPIER	PERTAIN
D PARDINE	H HEPARIN	PRALINE	S PANIERS	REPAINT
E PERINEA	K RANPIKE	M PERMIAN	RAPINES	
F FIREPAN	L PEARLIN	N PANNIER	T PAINTER	

aeinpt 152 - pantie

A PATINAE	PAINTED	N PANTINE	REPAINT	SPINATE
B BEPAINT	PAINTED	PINNATE	S PANTIES	T PATIENT
C PICANTE	H PENTHIA	R PAINTER	PATINES	U PETUNIA
D DEPAINT	L PANTILE	PERTAIN	SAPIENT	Y PANEITY

aeinrs 10 - sarnie

C ARCSINE	ERASING	J INJERAS	O ERASION	RESIANT
ARSENIC	GAINERS	K SNAKIER	P PANIERS	RETAINS
CARNIES	GRAINES	L ALINERS	RAPINES	RETINAS
CERASIN	REAGINS	NAILERS	R SIERRAN	RETSINA
D RANDIES	REGAINS	RENAILS	SNARIER	STAINER
SANDIER	REGINAS	M MARINES	S ARSINES	STARNIE
SARDINE	SEARING	REMAINS	SARNIES	STEARIN
F INFARES	SERINGA	SEMINAR	T ANESTRI	V AVENIRS
SERAFIN	H ARSHINE	SIRNAME	ANTSIER	RAVINES
G ANGRIES	HERNIAS	N INSANER	NASTIER	
EARINGS	I SENARII	INSNARE	RATINES	

aeinrt 1 - retina

B ATEBRIN	F FAINTER	L ENTRAIL	REPAINT	STEARIN
C CANTIER	FENITAR	LATRINE	R RETRAIN	T INTREAT
CERATIN	G GRANITE	RATLINE	TERRAIN	ITERANT
CERTAIN	GRATINE	RELIANT	TRAINER	NATTIER
CREATIN	INGRATE	RETINAL	S ANESTRI	NITRATE
CRINATE	TANGIER	TRENAIL	ANTSIER	TARTINE
NACRITE	TEARING	M MERANTI	NASTIER	TERTIAN
TACRINE	H HAIRNET	MINARET	RATINES	U RUINATE
D ANTIRED	INEARTH	RAIMENT	RESIANT	TAURINE
DETRAIN	THERIAN	N ENTRAIN	RETAINS	URANITE
TRAINED	I INERTIA	TRANNIE	RETINAS	URINATE
E ARENITE	J JANTIER	O OTARINE	RETSINA	W TAWNIER
RETINAE	NARTJIE	P PAINTER	STAINER	TINWARE
TRAINEE	K KERATIN	PERTAIN	STARNIE	

aeinst 2 - tisane

A ENTASIA	G EASTING	L EASTLIN	P PANTIES	TANSIES
TAENIAS	EATINGS	ELASTIN	PATINES	TISANES
B BANTIES	GAINEST	ENTAILS	SAPIENT	T INSTATE
BASINET	GENISTA	NAILSET	SPINATE	SATINET
BESAINT	INGATES	SALIENT	R ANESTRI	U AUNTIES
BESTAIN	INGESTA	SALTINE	ANTSIER	SINUATE
C ACETINS	SEATING	SLAINTE	NASTIER	V NAIVEST
CANIEST	TAGINES	STANIEL	RATINES	NATIVES
CINEAST	TANGIES	TENAILS	RESIANT	VAINEST
D DESTAIN	TEASING	M ETAMINS	RETAINS	W AWNIEST
DETAINS	TSIGANE	INMATES	RETINAS	TAWNIES
INSTEAD	H SHEITAN	MAINEST	RETSINA	WANIEST
NIDATES	STHENIA	MANTIES	STAINER	WANTIES
SAINTED	I ISATINE	TAMEINS	STARNIE	X ANTISEX
SATINED	J JANTIES	TAMINES	STEARIN	SEXTAIN
STAINED	TAJINES	N INANEST	S ENTASIS	Z ZANIEST
E ETESIAN	K INTAKES	STANINE	NASTIES	ZEATINS
F FAINEST	KENTIAS	TANNIES	SEITANS	
NAIFEST	TANKIES	O ATONIES	SESTINA	

aeintu 96 - auntie

C TUNICAE	K UNAKITE	QUINATE	URINATE
D AUDIENT	L ALUNITE	R RUINATE	S AUNTIES
G UNITAGE	P PETUNIA	TAURINE	SINUATE
J JAUNTIE	Q ANTIQUE	URANITE	V VAUNTIE

Six-letter stems

aeiors 84 - ariose

B ISOBARE	SCORIAE	N ERASION	OTARIES
C CARIOSE	D ROADIES	P SOAPIER	V OVARIES
ORACIES	SOREDIA	T OARIEST	

aeiprs 143 - praise

A SPIRAEA	G GASPIER	SAMPIRE	RASPIER	PIASTER
C EPACRIS	PRISAGE	N PANIERS	REPAIRS	PIASTRE
SCRAPIE	SPAIRGE	RAPINES	S ASPIRES	PIRATES
SPACIER	H HARPIES	O SOAPIER	PARESIS	PRATIES
D ASPIRED	SHARPIE	P APPRISE	PARISES	TRAIPSE
DESPAIR	K PARKIES	SAPPIER	PRAISES	U SPURIAE
DIAPERS	SPARKIE	R ASPIRER	PRAISES	UPRAISE
PRAISED	L PALSIER	PARRIES	T PAIREST	V PARVISE
E APERIES	PARLIES	PRAISER	PARTIES	PAVISER
EPEIRAS	M IMPRESA	RAPIERS	PASTIER	W WASPIER

aeiprt 116 - pirate

A APTERIA	E PEATIER	REPAINT	PIASTER	V PRIVATE
C PARETIC	L PLAITER	P PERIAPT	PIASTRE	W WIRETAP
PICRATE	PLATIER	R PARTIER	PIRATES	
D DIPTERA	M PRIMATE	S PAIREST	PRATIES	
PARTIED	N PAINTER	PARTIES	TRAIPSE	
PIRATED	PERTAIN	PASTIER	T PARTITE	

aeirrs 250 - sierra

B BARRIES	RERAISE	SIMARRE	RASPIER	TARRIES
BRASIER	H HARRIES	N SIERRAN	REPAIRS	TARSIER
C CARRIES	K KERRIAS	SNARIER	S ARRISES	V ARRIVES
SCARIER	SARKIER	P ASPIRER	RAISERS	VARIERS
D ARRIDES	L RAILERS	PARRIES	SIERRAS	
RAIDERS	RERAILS	PRAISER	T ARTSIER	
E REARISE	M MARRIES	RAPIERS	SERRATI	

aeirrt 58 - irater

A TARAIRE	D TARDIER	TRAILER	R TARRIER	T RATTIER
B ARBITER	TARRIED	N RETRAIN	S ARTSIER	RETRAIT
RAREBIT	E TEARIER	TERRAIN	SERRATI	TARTIER
C CIRRATE	L RETIRAL	TRAINER	TARRIES	W WARTIER
ERRATIC	RETRIAL	P PARTIER	TARSIER	Y RETIARY

aeirst 3 - satire

A ARISTAE	RACIEST	TARDIES	STAGIER	KARITES
ASTERIA	STEARIC	TIRADES	STRIGAE	L REALIST
ATRESIA	D ARIDEST	E AERIEST	TIRAGES	RETAILS
B BAITERS	ASTERID	SERIATE	TRIAGES	SALTIER
BARITES	ASTRIDE	F FAIREST	H HASTIER	SALTIRE
REBAITS	DIASTER	G AGISTER	SHERIAT	SLATIER
TERBIAS	DISRATE	AIGRETS	I AIRIEST	TAILERS
C ATRESIC	STAIDER	GAITERS	IRISATE	M IMARETS
CRISTAE	STAIRED	SEAGIRT	K ARKITES	MAESTRI

	MAISTER		RETAINS	PASTIER	S	ARSIEST		STRIATE
	MASTIER		RETINAS	PIASTER		ARTSIES		TASTIER
	MISRATE		RETSINA	PIASTRE		SAIREST		TERTIAS
	SEMITAR		STAINER	PIRATES		SATIRES	V	TAIVERS
	SMARTIE		STARNIE	PRATIES		TIRASSE		VASTIER
N	ANESTRI		STEARIN	TRAIPSE	T	ARTIEST		VERITAS
	ANTSIER	O	OARIEST	R	ARTSIER	ARTISTE	W	WAISTER
	NASTIER		OTARIES	SERRATI		ATTIRES		WAITERS
	RATINES	P	PAIREST	TARRIES		IRATEST		WARIEST
	RESIANT		PARTIES	TARSIER		RATITES		WASTRIE

aeirtt 49 - attire

A	ARIETTA	E	ARIETTE	TARTINE	ATTIRES		TITRATE
B	BATTIER		ITERATE	TERTIAN	IRATEST	V	TAIVERT
	BIRETTA	F	FATTIER	P	PARTITE	RATITES	W	TAWTIER
	RATBITE	L	TERTIAL	R	RATTIER	STRIATE	X	EXTRAIT
C	ATRETIC	N	INTREAT	RETRAIT	TASTIER		
	CATTIER		ITERANT	TARTIER	TERTIAS		
	CITRATE		NATTIER	S	ARTIEST	T	ATTRITE
D	ATTIRED		NITRATE	ARTISTE	TATTIER		

aeirtv 196 - taiver

A	VARIATE	E	EVIRATE	M	VITAMER	VASTIER	Y	VARIETY
B	VIBRATE	G	VIRGATE	P	PRIVATE	VERITAS		
D	TARDIVE		VITRAGE	S	TAIVERS	T	TAIVERT

aeistt 163 - taties

A	SATIATE	H	ATHEIST	SATINET	ATTIRES		TATTIES
B	BATISTE		STAITHE	O	OSTIATE	IRATEST	U	SITUATE
	BISTATE	K	TAKIEST	TOASTIE	RATITES	V	STATIVE
C	CATTIES	M	ETATISM	P	PATTIES	STRIATE	W	TAWIEST
	STATICE		MATIEST	TAPETIS	TASTIER		TWAITES
	TIETACS		MATTIES	R	ARTIEST	TERTIAS	X	TAXITES
F	FATTIES	N	INSTATE	ARTISTE	T	ETATIST	Y	SATIETY

aelnor 120 - reloan

C	CORNEAL		ALERION	M	ALMONER	ORLEANS	V	VERONAL
D	LADRONE		ALIENOR	NEMORAL	RELOANS		
I	AILERON	L	LLANERO	S	LOANERS	U	ALEURON

aelnos 76 - lanose

B	BONSELA	G	ENGAOLS	O	ALSOONE	ORLEANS
C	SECONAL	H	ENHALOS	P	ESPANOL	RELOANS
D	LOADENS	I	ANISOLE	NOPALES	T	ETALONS
E	ENOLASE	M	MELANOS	R	LOANERS	TOLANES

aelnot 93 - tolane

B	NOTABLE	H	ANETHOL	M	LOMENTA	S	ETALONS
C	LACTONE		ETHANOL	OMENTAL	TOLANES
D	TALONED	I	ELATION	TELAMON	V	VOLANTE
G	TANGELO		TOENAIL	P	POLENTA	Y	ANOLYTE

Six-letter stems

aelnrs 64 - learns

A ARSENAL	RELANDS	LARGENS	LANNERS	T ANTLERS
B BRANLES	SLANDER	SLANGER	O LOANERS	RENTALS
BRANSLE	SNARLED	I ALINERS	ORLEANS	SALTERN
C LANCERS	E LEANERS	NAILERS	RELOANS	SLANTER
RANCELS	F SALFERN	RENAILS	P PLANERS	STERNAL
D DARNELS	G ANGLERS	K RANKLES	REPLANS	V VERLANS
ENLARDS	ERLANGS	M ALMNERS	R SNARLER	Y LARNEYS
LANDERS	LANGERS	N ENSNARL	S RANSELS	Z RANZELS

aelnrt 53 - antler

B BRANTLE	G TANGLER	RELIANT	PLANTER	STERNAL
C CENTRAL	TRANGLE	RETINAL	REPLANT	T TRENTAL
E ALTERNE	H ENTHRAL	TRENAIL	S ANTLERS	U NEUTRAL
ENTERAL	I ENTRAIL	L ENTRALL	RENTALS	V VENTRAL
ETERNAL	LATRINE	N LANTERN	SALTERN	
TELERAN	RATLINE	P PANTLER	SLANTER	

aelnst 66 - latens

A SEALANT	G GELANTS	SLAINTE	O ETALONS	LATTENS
C CANTLES	LANGEST	STANIEL	TOLANES	TALENTS
CENTALS	TANGLES	TENAILS	P PLANETS	U ELUANTS
LANCETS	H HANTLES	K ANKLETS	PLATENS	LUNATES
SCANTLE	I EASTLIN	ASKLENT	R ANTLERS	UNLASTE
D DENTALS	ELASTIN	LANKEST	RENTALS	V LEVANTS
SLANTED	ENTAILS	M LAMENTS	SALTERN	Y STANYEL
E ELANETS	NAILSET	MANTELS	SLANTER	Z ZELANTS
LATEENS	SALIENT	MANTLES	STERNAL	
LEANEST	SALTINE	N STANNEL	T LATENTS	

aelors 46 - solera

A AREOLAS	SOLACER	G GALORES	RELOANS	SEROSAL
B LABROSE	D LOADERS	GAOLERS	O AEROSOL	SOLERAS
C CLAROES	ORDEALS	H SHOALER	ROSEOLA	T OESTRAL
COALERS	RELOADS	L ROSELLA	P PAROLES	OLESTRA
ESCOLAR	E AREOLES	M MORALES	REPOSAL	
ORACLES	F LOAFERS	N LOANERS	S LASSOER	
RECOALS	SAFROLE	ORLEANS	OARLESS	

aelort 40 - lorate

B BLOATER	FLOREAT	RATHOLE	RELATOR	TORULAE
C LOCATER	REFLOAT	L REALLOT	S OESTRAL	V LEVATOR
D DELATOR	G GLOATER	M MOLERAT	OLESTRA	Y ROYALET
LEOTARD	LEGATOR	P PROLATE	T RETOTAL	Z ZELATOR
F FLOATER	H LOATHER	R REALTOR	U ROTULAE	

aelost 65 - solate

B BOATELS	C ALECOST	LOCATES	TALCOSE	SOLATED
OBLATES	LACTOSE	SCATOLE	D SALTOED	E OLEATES

F FOLATES	I ISOLATE	TOLANES	OLESTRA
G GELATOS	K SKATOLE	P APOSTLE	S SOLATES
LEGATOS	M MALTOSE	PELOTAS	V SOLVATE
H LOATHES	N ETALONS	R OESTRAL	Z ZEALOTS

aelrst 48 - slater

A TARSEAL	RELATES	TAILERS	OLESTRA	STARTLE
B ALBERTS	RESLATE	K STALKER	P PALTERS	TATLERS
BATLERS	STEALER	TALKERS	PERSALT	U ESTRUAL
BLASTER	F FALTERS	L STELLAR	PLASTER	SALUTER
LABRETS	G LARGEST	TELLARS	PLATERS	V TRAVELS
STABLER	H HALTERS	M ARMLETS	PSALTER	VARLETS
C CARTELS	HARSLET	LAMSTER	STAPLER	VESTRAL
CLARETS	LATHERS	MARTELS	S ARTLESS	W WARSTLE
CRESTAL	SLATHER	TRAMELS	LASTERS	WASTREL
SCARLET	THALERS	N ANTLERS	SALTERS	WRASTLE
TARCELS	I REALIST	RENTALS	SLATERS	Y RAYLETS
D DARTLES	RETAILS	SALTERN	TARSELS	
SLARTED	SALTIER	SLANTER	T RATTLES	
E ELATERS	SALTIRE	STERNAL	SLATTER	
REALEST	SLATIER	O OESTRAL	STARLET	

aemnor 110 - moaner

A AMARONE	FOREMAN	L ALMONER	S ENAMORS	V OVERMAN
C CREMONA	G MARENGO	NEMORAL	MOANERS	Y ANYMORE
ROMANCE	MEGARON	N MONERAN	OARSMEN	ROMNEYA
D MADRONE	H MENORAH	P MANROPE	T TONEARM	
ROADMEN	I MORAINE	REPOMAN	U ENAMOUR	
F FORAMEN	ROMAINE	R ORRAMEN	NEUROMA	

aemnot 235 - omenta

B BOATMEN	MONTAGE	OMENTAL	NONMEAT	U AUTOMEN
G GEOMANT	H NATHEMO	TELAMON	R TONEARM	NOTAEUM
MAGNETO	I AMNIOTE	M MOMENTA	S MANTOES	OUTNAME
MEGATON	L LOMENTA	N MONTANE	T TOMENTA	

aenors 22 - reason

B BORANES	NARCOSE	I ERASION	OARSMEN	SANTERO
C CANOERS	E ARENOSE	L LOANERS	P PERSONA	SENATOR
CARNOSE	G ONAGERS	ORLEANS	R SERRANO	TREASON
COARSEN	ORANGES	RELOANS	S REASONS	U ARENOUS
CORNEAS	H HOARSEN	M ENAMORS	SENORAS	
EARCONS	SENHORA	MOANERS	T ATONERS	

aenort 8 - ornate

B BARONET	G NEGATOR	N NORTENA	R ORNATER	TREASON
REBOANT	H ANOTHER	P OPERANT	S ATONERS	U OUTEARN
C ENACTOR	I OTARINE	PRONATE	SANTERO	V VENATOR
D TORNADE	M TONEARM	PROTEAN	SENATOR	

aenost 38 - atones

B ONBEATS	DONATES	L ETALONS	R ATONERS	S ASTONES
C COSTEAN	ONSTEAD	TOLANES	SANTERO	T ATTONES
OCTANES	G ONSTAGE	M MANTOES	SENATOR	NOTATES
D ASTONED	I ATONIES	P TEOPANS	TREASON	U SOUTANE

aenrrt 191 - ranter

A NARRATE	REGRANT	TRAINER	S ERRANTS	Y TERNARY
E TERRANE	I RETRAIN	O ORNATER	RANTERS	
G GRANTER	TERRAIN	P PARTNER	T TRANTER	

aenrst 14 - astern

A ANESTRA	EASTERN	RETINAS	SARMENT	RANTERS
SANTERA	NEAREST	RETSINA	SMARTEN	S SARSNET
B BANTERS	RATEENS	STAINER	N TANNERS	TRANSES
BARNETS	G ARGENTS	STARNIE	O ATONERS	T NATTERS
C CANTERS	GARNETS	STEARIN	SANTERO	RATTENS
CARNETS	STRANGE	K RANKEST	SENATOR	U AUNTERS
NECTARS	H ANTHERS	STARKEN	TREASON	NATURES
RECANTS	HARTENS	TANKERS	P ARPENTS	SAUNTER
SCANTER	THENARS	L ANTLERS	ENTRAPS	V SERVANT
TANRECS	I ANESTRI	RENTALS	PANTERS	TAVERNS
TRANCES	ANTSIER	SALTERN	PARENTS	VERSANT
D ENDARTS	NASTIER	SLANTER	PASTERN	W STRAWEN
STANDER	RATINES	STERNAL	PERSANT	WANTERS
STARNED	RESIANT	M ARTSMEN	TREPANS	Y TRAYNES
E EARNEST	RETAINS	MARTENS	R ERRANTS	

aenrtt 140 - natter

A TARTANE	TERNATE	TARTINE	REPTANT	Y NATTERY
C TRANECT	I INTREAT	TERTIAN	R TRANTER	
D TRANTED	ITERANT	L TRENTAL	S NATTERS	
E ENTREAT	NATTIER	N ENTRANT	RATTENS	
RATTEEN	NITRATE	P PATTERN	U TAUNTER	

aenrtu 50 - nature

A NATURAE	NATURED	UNHEART	L NEUTRAL	T TAUNTER
TAUREAN	UNRATED	URETHAN	M TRUEMAN	V VAUNTER
C CENTAUR	UNTREAD	I RUINATE	O OUTEARN	W UNWATER
UNCRATE	G GAUNTER	TAURINE	S AUNTERS	
UNTRACE	H HAUNTER	URANITE	NATURES	
D DAUNTER	UNEARTH	URINATE	SAUNTER	

aenstu 187 - unseat

B BUTANES	SINUATE	O SOUTANE	SAUNTER	TETANUS
SUNBEAT	L ELUANTS	P PEANUTS	S NASUTES	UNSTATE
C NUTCASE	LUNATES	PESAUNT	UNSEATS	X UNTAXES
D SAUNTED	UNLASTE	Q EQUANTS	T ATTUNES	
UNSATED	M UNTAMES	R AUNTERS	NUTATES	
I AUNTIES	UNTEAMS	NATURES	TAUTENS	

aeoprt 199 - protea

B PROBATE	G PORTAGE	N OPERANT	PRORATE	T PORTATE
D ADOPTER	POTAGER	PRONATE	S ESPARTO	V OVERAPT
READOPT	H PHORATE	PROTEAN	PROTEAS	
E OPERATE	L PROLATE	R PRAETOR	PROTEAS	
			SEAPORT	

aeorst 9 - orates

A AEROSAT	RECOATS	STORAGE	OLESTRA	P ESPARTO
B BOASTER	D DOATERS	TOERAGS	M AMORETS	PROTEAS
BOATERS	ROASTED	H ASTHORE	MAESTRO	SEAPORT
BORATES	TORSADE	EARSHOT	OMERTAS	R ROASTER
REBATOS	TROADES	HAROSET	N ATONERS	S OSETRAS
SORBATE	E ROSEATE	I OARIEST	SANTERO	OSSETRA
C COASTER	G GAROTES	OTARIES	SENATOR	T ROTATES
COATERS	ORGEATS	L OESTRAL	TREASON	TOASTER

aerrst 215 - arrest

A ERRATAS	STARRED	GARTERS	STARKER	RASTERS
B BARRETS	TRADERS	GRATERS	M ARMREST	STARERS
BARTERS	E RETEARS	H TRASHER	SMARTER	T RATTERS
C CARTERS	SERRATE	I ARTSIER	N ERRANTS	RESTART
CRATERS	TEARERS	SERRATI	RANTERS	STARTER
TRACERS	F FRATERS	TARRIES	O ROASTER	V STARVER
D DARTERS	RAFTERS	TARSIER	P PARTERS	Y STRAYER
DARTRES	STRAFER	K KARTERS	PRATERS	
RETARDS	G GARRETS	KRATERS	S ARRESTS	

aerstt 193 - treats

B BATTERS	SHATTER	SLATTER	SPATTER	TATTERS
TABRETS	THREATS	STARLET	TAPSTER	U ASTUTER
C SCATTER	I ARTIEST	STARTLE	R RATTERS	STATURE
D STARTED	ARTISTE	TATLERS	RESTART	V VATTERS
TETRADS	ATTIRES	M MATTERS	STARTER	W SWATTER
E ESTREAT	IRATEST	SMATTER	S ASTERTS	TEWARTS
RESTATE	RATITES	N NATTERS	STARETS	Y YATTERS
RETASTE	STRIATE	RATTENS	STATERS	Z STARETZ
G TARGETS	TASTIER	O ROTATES	TASTERS	
H HATTERS	TERTIAS	TOASTER	T STRETTA	
RATHEST	L RATTLES	P PATTERS	TARTEST	

aerstu 174 - urates

A AURATES	CRUSTAE	M MATURES	UPRATES	T ASTUTER
B ARBUTES	CURATES	STRUMAE	UPSTARE	STATURE
BURSATE	E AUSTERE	N AUNTERS	UPTEARS	U AUTEURS
SURBATE	F FAUREST	NATURES	Q QUAREST	Y ESTUARY
C ACTURES	L ESTRUAL	SAUNTER	QUARTES	
CAUTERS	SALUTER	P PASTURE	QUATRES	

aginor 184 - oaring

C ORGANIC	GRADINO	E ORIGANE	L RANGOLI	P PIGNORA
D ADORING	ROADING	H HOARING	M ROAMING	PORANGI

R ROARING	ORIGANS	SOARING	ROATING
S IGNAROS	SIGNORA	T ORATING	Z ZINGARO

aginot 234 - gitano

B BOATING	F ANTIFOG	N ATONING	GITANOS	Z TOAZING
C COATING	G GIGATON	R ORATING	U AUTOING	
COTINGA	L ANTILOG	ROATING	OUTGAIN	
D DOATING	M MOATING	S AGONIST	V OVATING	

aginrt 107 - rating

A GRANITA	INGRATE	I AIRTING	ROATING	STARING
C CARTING	TANGIER	RAITING	P PARTING	TARINGS
CRATING	TEARING	K KARTING	PRATING	T RATTING
TRACING	F FARTING	L RATLING	TRAPING	TARTING
D DARTING	INGRAFT	M MARTING	R TARRING	W RINGTAW
TRADING	RAFTING	MIGRANT	S GASTRIN	Y GIANTRY
E GRANITE	G GRATING	N RANTING	GRATINS	
GRATINE	TARGING	O ORATING	RATINGS	

ailnos 233 - alison

B ALBINOS	LADINOS	M MALISON	S ALISONS
C ALNICOS	E ANISOLE	MONIALS	SIALONS
OILCANS	I LIAISON	SOMNIAL	T LATINOS
D DOLINAS	K KAOLINS	N SOLANIN	TALIONS

ailnot 131 - latino

A AILANTO	B BITONAL	TOENAIL	N ANTLION	TALIONS
ALATION	E ELATION	G ANTILOG	S LATINOS	U OUTLAIN

ailnst 214 - instal

A LATINAS	ENTAILS	TENAILS	L INSTALL	T LATTINS
C CATLINS	NAILSET	G ANGLIST	O LATINOS	U UNALIST
TINCALS	SALIENT	LASTING	TALIONS	Y NASTILY
D TINDALS	SALTINE	SALTING	P PLAINTS	SAINTLY
E EASTLIN	SLAINTE	SLATING	R RATLINS	
ELASTIN	STANIEL	STALING	S INSTALS	

ailost 159 - ostial

A SOLATIA	E ISOLATE	M SOMITAL	TOPSAIL	TAILORS
B OBLASTI	G GALIOTS	N LATINOS	R ORALIST	T ALTOIST
C CITOLAS	LATIGOS	TALIONS	RIALTOS	U OUTSAIL
STOICAL	SALIGOT	P APOSTIL	SLIOTAR	X OXTAILS

ailrst 248 - trials

A LARIATS	B TRIBALS	E REALIST	SALTIER	SLATIER
LATRIAS	C CITRALS	RETAILS	SALTIRE	TAILERS

I LIATRIS	N RATLINS	SLIOTAR	U RITUALS	
M MISTRAL	O ORALIST	TAILORS	TRISULA	
RAMTILS	RIALTOS	T STARLIT	Y TRYSAIL	

ainors 162 - norias

C SARONIC	E ERASION	SIGNORA	PORINAS	W WARISON
D INROADS	F INSOFAR	SOARING	SOPRANI	
ORDAINS	G IGNAROS	M MAINORS	T AROINTS	
SADIRON	ORIGANS	P PARISON	RATIONS	

ainort 27 - ration

B TABORIN	E OTARINE	J JANITOR	S AROINTS	X TRIAXON
C CAROTIN	G ORATING	M TORMINA	RATIONS	
CORTINA	ROATING	O ORATION	U RAINOUT	
D DIATRON	H ORTHIAN	P ATROPIN	W WAITRON	

ainrst 86 - trains

A ANTIARS	NASTIER	STEARIN	L RATLINS	SANTIRS
ARTISAN	RATINES	G GASTRIN	M MARTINS	STRAINS
TSARINA	RESIANT	GRATINS	O AROINTS	T STRAINT
B BRISANT	RETAINS	RATINGS	RATIONS	TRANSIT
C NARCIST	RETINAS	STARING	P SPIRANT	U NUTRIAS
D INDARTS	RETSINA	TARINGS	SPRAINT	
E ANESTRI	STAINER	H TARNISH	Q QINTARS	
ANTSIER	STARNIE	K KIRTANS	S INSTARS	

ainrtu 182 - nutria

C CURTAIN	E RUINATE	F ANTIFUR	P PURITAN	Y UNITARY
TURACIN	TAURINE	M NATRIUM	UPTRAIN	
D TRIDUAN	URANITE	N URINANT	Q QUINTAR	
UNITARD	URINATE	O RAINOUT	S NUTRIAS	

aiorst 68 - ratios

B ORBITAS	ORGIAST	RIALTOS	P AIRPOST	U SAUTOIR
D ASTROID	H AIRSHOT	SLIOTAR	AIRSTOP	V TRAVOIS
E OARIEST	SHORTIA	TAILORS	PAROTIS	VIATORS
OTARIES	THORIAS	M AMORIST	S AORISTS	Y OSTIARY
F FAITORS	K TROIKAS	N AROINTS	ARISTOS	
G AGISTOR	L ORALIST	RATIONS	SATORIS	

anorst 109 - tronas

A TORANAS	E ATONERS	L LATRONS	SANTOOR	ROTTANS
B BARTONS	SANTERO	M MATRONS	P PARTONS	U ROUSANT
C CANTORS	SENATOR	TRANSOM	PATRONS	SANTOUR
CARTONS	TREASON	N NATRONS	TARPONS	Y AROYNTS
CONTRAS	I AROINTS	NONARTS	T ATTORNS	
CRATONS	RATIONS	O RATOONS	RATTONS	

Six-letter stems

ceinor 220 - coiner

B BICORNE	INFORCE	P PERICON	CRONIES	NOTICER
C CORNICE	G COREIGN	PONCIER	ORCEINS	RECTION
CROCEIN	H CHORINE	PORCINE	ORCINES	U COENURI
CROCINE	I ONEIRIC	R CORNIER	RECOINS	NOURICE
F COINFER	K CONKIER	S COINERS	SERICON	V CORVINE
CONIFER	M INCOMER	CRINOSE	T COINTER	Y ORIENCY

ceinot 198 - notice

A ACONITE	NOTICED	M CENTIMO	NEPOTIC	SECTION
ANOETIC	H HENOTIC	ENTOMIC	R COINTER	T ENTOTIC
C CONCEIT	K KENOTIC	TONEMIC	NOTICER	TONETIC
D CTENOID	KETONIC	O COONTIE	RECTION	X EXCITON
DEONTIC	L LECTION	P ENTOPIC	S NOTICES	

ceiort 134 - erotic

A EROTICA	G ERGOTIC	M MORTICE	TERCIOS	XEROTIC
C CEROTIC	H ROTCHIE	N COINTER	T COTTIER	
ORECTIC	THEORIC	NOTICER	V EVICTOR	
D CORDITE	K TOCKIER	RECTION	W COWRITE	
E COTERIE	L CORTILE	S EROTICS	X EXCITOR	

ceiost 231 - oecist

A SOCIATE	TOISECH	P POETICS	T COTTISE	EXOTICS
D CESTOID	K COKIEST	R EROTICS	SCOTTIE	Y SOCIETY
COEDITS	L CITOLES	TERCIOS	V COSTIVE	Z COZIEST
COTISED	N NOTICES	S COSIEST	W COWIEST	
E COESITE	SECTION	COTISES	X COEXIST	
H ECHOIST	O COOTIES	OECISTS	COXIEST	

deeilr 241 - relied

A LEADIER	REFILED	RELINED	T RETILED	W WIELDER
D DREIDEL	G GELIDER	O REOILED	V DELIVER	Y REEDILY
F DEFILER	LEDGIER	P PERILED	LIVERED	YIELDER
FERLIED	LEIDGER	REPLIED	RELIVED	
FIELDER	N REDLINE	S RESILED	REVILED	

deeinr 61 - denier

B BENDIER	FENDIER	H INHERED	RIPENED	W REWIDEN
INBREED	REFINED	K REINKED	R DERNIER	WIDENER
C CEDRINE	G DREEING	L REDLINE	NERDIER	X INDEXER
D NEDDIER	ENERGID	RELINED	S DENIERS	REINDEX
E NEEDIER	GREINED	M ERMINED	NEREIDS	
F DEFINER	REEDING	O ORDINEE	RESINED	
ENFIRED	REIGNED	P REPINED	U UREDINE	

deeins 210 - denies

A ANISEED	D DESINED	SDEINED	G SDEIGNE	K ENSKIED
C INCEDES	NEDDIES	F DEFINES	SEEDING	SKEINED

L ENISLED	SIDEMEN	RESINED	STEINED	SINEWED
ENSILED	N INDENES	S DESINES	V DEVEINS	X INDEXES
LINSEED	R DENIERS	T DESTINE	ENDIVES	
M DESMINE	NEREIDS	ENDITES	W ENDWISE	

deeint 137 - endite

C ENTICED	F FEINTED	M DEMENTI	ENDITES	U DETINUE
D ENDITED	I DIETINE	N DENTINE	STEINED	V EVIDENT
TEINDED	L LENITED	S DESTINE	T DINETTE	

deeirs 87 - reside

A DEARIES	E SEEDIER	O OREIDES	SERRIED	V DERIVES
READIES	F DEFIERS	OSIERED	S DESIRES	DEVISER
B BREDIES	SERIFED	P PREDIES	RESIDES	DIVERSE
DERBIES	G SEDGIER	PRESIDE	T DIESTER	REVISED
C DECRIES	L RESILED	SPEIRED	DIETERS	W SWEIRED
DEICERS	M REMEIDS	SPIERED	REEDITS	Z RESIZED
D DERIDES	REMISED	R DERRIES	REISTED	
DESIRED	N DENIERS	DESIRER	RESITED	
DIEDRES	NEREIDS	REDRIES	U RESIDUE	
RESIDED	RESINED	RESIDER	UREIDES	

deenor 147 - redone

B DEBONER	ENCORED	N ENDERON	T ERODENT
ENROBED	G ENGORED	O RONEOED	W ENDOWER
REDBONE	I ORDINEE	P REPONED	REENDOW
C ENCODER	M MODERNE	S ENDORSE	Z REZONED

deenrs 197 - sender

A DEANERS	SERENED	RESINED	P SPENDER	TENDRES
ENDEARS	SNEERED	L LENDERS	R RENDERS	U ENDURES
B BENDERS	F FENDERS	RELENDS	S REDNESS	ENSURED
C DECERNS	G GENDERS	SLENDER	RESENDS	V VENDERS
SCERNED	H HERDENS	M MENDERS	SENDERS	Z DZERENS
D REDDENS	I DENIERS	REMENDS	T STERNED	
E NEEDERS	NEREIDS	O ENDORSE	TENDERS	

deginr 166 - ringed

A AREDING	B BREDING	REEDING	O ERODING	S DINGERS
DEARING	C CRINGED	REIGNED	GROINED	ENGIRDS
DERAIGN	D GRINDED	IGNORED	U DUNGIER	
EARDING	REDDING	F FRINGED	NEGROID	W REDWING
GRADINE	E DREEING	H HERDING	REDOING	WRINGED
GRAINED	ENERGID	I DINGIER	R GRINDER	Y YERDING
READING	GREINED	N GRINNED	REGRIND	
		RENDING		

deiint 205 - indite

A INEDITA	D INDITED	EDITING	TENIOID	S INDITES
C IDENTIC	E DIETINE	IGNITED	R INDITER	TINEIDS
INCITED	G DIETING	O EDITION	NITRIDE	V INVITED

deilno 213 - indole

E ELOINED	O EIDOLON	INDOLES	T LENTOID
G GLENOID	S DOLINES	SONDELI	U UNOILED

deilor 105 - roiled

A DARIOLE	E REOILED	K RODLIKE	S SOLDIER
B BROILED	G GLORIED	L DOLLIER	SOLIDER
C DOCILER	GODLIER	M MOLDIER	T DOILTER
D DROILED	GOLDIER	P LEPORID	W DOWLIER

deilos 123 - soiled

A DEASOIL	I DOILIES	SMOILED	DIPLOES	SOLIDER
ISOLEAD	IDOLISE	N DOLINES	DIPOLES	V LIVEDOS
B BOLIDES	K KELOIDS	INDOLES	PELOIDS	Y DOYLIES
C COLDIES	L DOLLIES	SONDELI	SOLIPED	
D DILDOES	M MELOIDS	O DOOLIES	SPOILED	
E OILSEED	MIDSOLE	P DESPOIL	R SOLDIER	

deilrt 130 - tirled

A DILATER	D TIDDLER	H THIRLED	TRINDLE	W TWIRLED
REDTAIL	E RETILED	K KIRTLED	O DOILTER	Y TIREDLY
TRAILED	F FLIRTED	L TRILLED	P TRIPLED	
B DRIBLET	TRIFLED	N TENDRIL	U DILUTER	

deinor 21 - ironed

A ANEROID	IGNORED	N ENDIRON	INDORSE	W DOWNIER
B INORBED	NEGROID	P POINDER	ORDINES	WINDORE
D NODDIER	REDOING	PROINED	ROSINED	
E ORDINEE	H HORDEIN	R DRONIER	SORDINE	
G ERODING	J JOINDER	S DINEROS	U DOURINE	
GROINED	M MINORED	DONSIER	NEUROID	

deinos 75 - onside

A ADONISE	G DINGOES	SONDELI	SPINODE	S ONSIDES
ANODISE	H HOIDENS	M DOMINES	R DINEROS	T DITONES
SODAINE	I IODINES	EMODINS	DONSIER	STONIED
C CODEINS	IONISED	MISDONE	INDORSE	
CONDIES	K DOESKIN	N DONNIES	ORDINES	
SECONDI	L DOLINES	ONDINES	ROSINED	
D NODDIES	INDOLES	P DISPONE	SORDINE	

deinot 113 - ointed

C CTENOID	D DENTOID	TENIOID	N INTONED	S DITONES
DEONTIC	G INGOTED	J JOINTED	NOINTED	STONIED
NOTICED	I EDITION	L LENTOID	P POINTED	

deinrs 85 - diners

A RANDIES	E DENIERS	H HINDERS	REMINDS	P PINDERS
SANDIER	NEREIDS	NERDISH	N DINNERS	T TINDERS
SARDINE	RESINED	SHRINED	ENDRINS	U INSURED
B BINDERS	F FINDERS	I INSIDER	O DINEROS	V VERDINS
INBREDS	FRIENDS	SNIDIER	DONSIER	W REWINDS
REBINDS	REDFINS	K KINDERS	INDORSE	WINDERS
C CINDERS	REFINDS	KINREDS	ORDINES	
DISCERN	G DINGERS	REDSKIN	ROSINED	
RESCIND	ENGIRDS	M MINDERS	SORDINE	

deinrt 126 - tinder

A ANTIRED	NITRIDE	S TINDERS	UNTIRED	Y TINDERY
DETRAIN	L TENDRIL	T TRIDENT	UNTIRDE	
TRAINED	TRINDLE	U INTRUDE	UNTRIED	
I INDITER	P PRINTED	TURDINE	X DEXTRIN	

deinru 79 - ruined

A UNAIRED	F UNFIRED	M UNRIMED	R NURDIER	UNTRIDE
URANIDE	G DUNGIER	N DUNNIER	S INSURED	UNTRIED
C INDUCER	H UNHIRED	INURNED	T INTRUDE	W UNWIRED
D UNDRIED	I URIDINE	O DOURINE	TURDINE	
E UREDINE	J INJURED	NEUROID	UNTIRED	

deinst 56 - idents

A DESTAIN	E DESTINE	K DINKEST	STONIED	STINTED
DETAINS	ENDITES	KINDEST	P DIPNETS	U DISTUNE
INSTEAD	STEINED	L DENTILS	STIPEND	DUNITES
NIDATES	F SNIFTED	M MINDSET	R TINDERS	Y DENSITY
SAINTED	G NIDGETS	MISTEND	S DISNEST	DESTINY
SATINED	STEDING	N DENTINS	DISSENT	
STAINED	STINGED	INDENTS	SNIDEST	
B BIDENTS	I INDITES	INTENDS	T DENTIST	
D DISTEND	TINEIDS	O DITONES	DISTENT	

deintu 218 - untied

A AUDIENT	L DILUENT	MUTINED	TURDINE	S DISTUNE
C UNCITED	UNTILED	UNTIMED	UNTIRED	DUNITES
E DETINUE	M MINUTED	N DUNNITE	UNTRIDE	
G DUETING	MUNITED	R INTRUDE	UNTRIED	

deiors 36 - rosied

A ROADIES	SODDIER	M MISDOER	SORDINE	ROISTED
SOREDIA	E OREIDES	MOIDERS	O ODORISE	ROSITED
B BORIDES	OSIERED	N DINEROS	OROIDES	SORTIED
DISROBE	H RHODIES	DONSIER	P PERIODS	STEROID
C DISCOER	I IODISER	INDORSE	S DORISES	STORIED
SCODIER	L SOLDIER	ORDINES	DOSSIER	TIERODS
D DORISED	SOLIDER	ROSINED	T EDITORS	TRIODES

Six-letter stems

| V DEVISOR | VISORED | W DOWRIES | WEIRDOS |
| DEVOIRS | VOIDERS | ROWDIES | Z DORIZES |

deiort 47 - editor

B DEBITOR	I DIORITE	R DORTIER	STORIED	OUTRIDE
DEORBIT	L DOILTER	S EDITORS	TIERODS	Z ROZITED
ORBITED	P DIOPTER	ROISTED	TRIODES	
C CORDITE	DIOPTRE	ROSITED	T DOTTIER	
G GOITRED	PERIDOT	SORTIED	U ETOURDI	
H THEROID	PROTEID	STEROID	IODURET	

deiost 70 - todies

A IODATES	J JOISTED	P DEPOSIT	ROSITED	U OUTSIDE
TOADIES	M DISTOME	DOPIEST	SORTIED	TEDIOUS
C CESTOID	DOMIEST	PODITES	STEROID	V DOVIEST
COEDITS	MODISTE	POSITED	STORIED	W DOWIEST
COTISED	MOISTED	SOPITED	TIERODS	X EXODIST
D TODDIES	N DITONES	TOPSIDE	TRIODES	Z DOZIEST
F FOISTED	STONIED	R EDITORS	T DOTIEST	
H HOISTED	O OSTEOID	ROISTED	STOITED	

deirst 104 - stride

A ARIDEST	BISTRED	SHIRTED	STEROID	U DUSTIER
ASTERID	C CREDITS	I DIRTIES	STORIED	REDUITS
ASTRIDE	DIRECTS	DITSIER	TIERODS	STUDIER
DIASTER	E DIESTER	TIDIERS	TRIODES	V DIVERTS
DISRATE	DIETERS	K SKIRTED	P SPIRTED	STRIVED
STAIDER	REEDITS	N TINDERS	STRIPED	VERDITS
STAIRED	REISTED	O EDITORS	R STIRRED	
TARDIES	RESITED	ROISTED	STRIDER	
TIRADES	F FRISTED	ROSITED	S DISSERT	
B BESTRID	H DITHERS	SORTIED	STRIDES	

delort 203 - retold

A DELATOR	I DOILTER	P DROPLET	STRODLE	
LEOTARD	L TROLLED	PRETOLD	T DOTTLER	
D TODDLER	N ENTROLD	S DROLEST	DOTTREL	
F TELFORD	O ROOTLED	OLDSTER	U TROULED	

denors 150 - drones

B BONDERS	E ENDORSE	SORDINE	R DRONERS	UNDOERS
C CONDERS	H DEHORNS	L RONDELS	S SONDERS	V VENDORS
CORSNED	I DINEROS	M MODERNS	T RODENTS	W DOWNERS
SCORNED	DONSIER	RODSMEN	SNORTED	WONDERS
D DONDERS	INDORSE	P PERNODS	U ENDUROS	Y YONDERS
NODDERS	ORDINES	PONDERS	RESOUND	
SNODDER	ROSINED	RESPOND	SOUNDER	

denort 124 - rodent

| A TORNADE | E ERODENT | H NORTHED | THORNED | L ENTROLD |
| D TRODDEN | F FRONTED | THONDER | THRONED | M MORDENT |

| N DONNERT | P PORTEND | S RODENTS | SNORTED |
| TENDRON | PROTEND | | |

denoru 178 - undoer

A RONDEAU		UNDERDO	I DOURINE	P POUNDER		SOUNDER
B BOUNDER	F FOUNDER		NEUROID		UNROPED	UNDOERS
REBOUND		REFOUND	L LOUNDER	R RONDURE		W REWOUND
UNROBED	G GUERDON		ROUNDEL		ROUNDER	WOUNDER
C CRUNODE		UNDERGO	ROUNDLE		UNORDER	
D REDOUND		UNGORED	M MOURNED	S ENDUROS		
ROUNDED	H HOUNDER		N ENROUND		RESOUND	

denost 128 - stoned

A ASTONED	C DOCENTS		STONIED		TENDONS	SNORTED
DONATES	E DENOTES	K STONKED		O SNOOTED		T SNOTTED
ONSTEAD	F FONDEST	M ENDMOST			STOODEN	U DEUTONS
B OBTENDS	I DITONES	N STONNED		R RODENTS		SNOUTED

deorst 89 - strode

A DOATERS		FROSTED		TIERODS	P DEPORTS		OUTREDS
ROASTED	G STODGER		TRIODES		REDTOPS	REDOUTS
TORSADE	H DEHORTS	K STROKED			SPORTED	ROUSTED
TROADES		SHORTED	L DROLEST	R DORTERS		W STROWED
B DEBTORS	I EDITORS		OLDSTER		RODSTER	WORSTED
STROBED		ROISTED		STRODLE	T DETORTS	Y DESTROY
E OERSTED		ROSITED	M STORMED		DOTTERS	ROYSTED
ROSETED		SORTIED	N RODENTS	U DETOURS		STROYED
TEREDOS		STEROID		SNORTED		DOUREST	
F DEFROST		STORIED	O ROOSTED		DOUTERS	

deortu 189 - toured

A OUTDARE		REDOUBT	I ETOURDI	P TROUPED		REDOUTS
OUTREAD	C COURTED		IODURET	Q TORQUED		ROUSTED
READOUT		EDUCTOR		OUTRIDE	S DETOURS		T TUTORED
B DOUBTER	F FOUTRED	L TROULED			DOUREST	U OUTDURE
OBTRUDE	G DROGUET	O OUTDOER			DOUTERS	W OUTDREW
OUTBRED		GROUTED		OUTRODE		OUTREDS	

eeilnr 181 - reline

A ALIENER	D REDLINE		REELING	S LIERNES
B BERLINE		RELINED	M ERMELIN		RELINES
C RECLINE	G LEERING	O ELOINER	V LIVENER

eeilns 207 - senile

A SEALINE		LINSEED	O OLEINES		SENILES		TENSILE
C LICENSE	F FELINES	P PENSILE		SENSILE	Y YEELINS
SELENIC	G LEESING	R LIERNES		SILENES
SILENCE		SEELING		RELINES	T LENITES
D ENISLED	L NELLIES	S ENISLES		LISENTE
ENSILED	M ISLEMEN		ENSILES		SETLINE

Six-letter stems

eeilnt 157 - lenite

A LINEATE	D LENITED	K NETLIKE	S LENITES	TENSILE
C CENTILE	G GENTILE	N LENIENT	LISENTE	T ENTITLE
LICENTE	H THEELIN	P PENLITE	SETLINE	V VEINLET

eeilrs 95 - relies

A EARLIES	REFILES	RELLIES	S IRELESS	RELIVES
REALISE	REFLIES	N LIERNES	RESILES	REVILES
B BELIERS	RELIEFS	RELINES	T LEISTER	SERVILE
C CEILERS	G LEIGERS	O LOERIES	RETILES	VEILERS
D RESILED	LIEGERS	P REPLIES	STERILE	X EXILERS
E SEELIER	H LEISHER	SPIELER	U LEISURE	
F FERLIES	L LEISLER	R RELIERS	V LEVIERS	

eeilrt 138 - retile

A ATELIER	D RETILED	M MELTIER	S LEISTER	
REALTIE	F FELTIER	O TROELIE	RETILES	
C RETICLE	FERTILE	P PERLITE	STERILE	
TIERCEL	L TREILLE	REPTILE	T RETITLE	

eeilst 164 - elites

C SECTILE	G ELEGIST	N LENITES	PELITES	V EVILEST
D ISLETED	ELEGITS	LISENTE	R LEISTER	LEVITES
E EELIEST	H SHELTIE	SETLINE	RETILES	LIEVEST
STEELIE	K KELTIES	TENSILE	STERILE	VELITES
F FELSITE	SLEEKIT	O ESTOILE	S LISTEES	X SEXTILE
LEFTIES	L TELLIES	ETOILES	TELESIS	
LIEFEST	M ELMIEST	P EPISTLE	TIELESS	

eeinrs 73 - serine

C CERESIN	FINEERS	N NERINES	ENTRIES	VERSINE
SCRIENE	REFINES	P EREPSIN	NERITES	W NEWSIER
SINCERE	G GREISEN	REPINES	RETINES	WEINERS
D DENIERS	H HENRIES	R RERISEN	TRENISE	WIENERS
NEREIDS	INHERES	RESINER	TRIENES	X REXINES
RESINED	RESHINE	S SEINERS	V ENVIERS	
E ESERINE	L LIERNES	SEREINS	INVERSE	
F ENFIRES	RELINES	SERINES	VEINERS	
FEERINS	M ERMINES	T ENTIRES	VENIRES	

eeinrt 12 - entire

A ARENITE	F FEINTER	I ERINITE	RENTIER	TRIENES
RETINAE	G GENTIER	NITERIE	TERRINE	T NETTIER
TRAINEE	INTEGER	K KERNITE	S ENTIRES	TENTIER
B BENTIER	TEERING	N INTERNE	ENTRIES	U NEURITE
C ENTERIC	TREEING	P INEPTER	NERITES	RETINUE
ENTICER	H NEITHER	R INERTER	RETINES	REUNITE
E TEENIER	THEREIN	REINTER	TRENISE	UTERINE

eeinst 60 - seiten

A ETESIAN	I SIENITE	N INTENSE	RETINES	V TENSIVE
C ENTICES	L LENITES	TENNIES	TRENISE	VENITES
D DESTINE	LISENTE	P PENTISE	TRIENES	X EXTINES
ENDITES	SETLINE	R ENTIRES	S SEITENS	SIXTEEN
STEINED	TENSILE	ENTRIES	SESTINE	Y SYENITE
H THEINES	M EMETINS	NERITES	T NETTIES	

eeiors 146 - soiree

B EBRIOSE	OSIERED	L LOERIES	R ROSIERE	T EROTISE
D OREIDES	H HEROISE	M ISOMERE	S SOIREES	V EROSIVE

eeiort 145 - toeier

A ETAERIO	L TROELIE	S EROTISE	Z EROTIZE
C COTERIE			

eeirst 29 - reties

A AERIEST	RESITED	METIERS	TRIENES	S RESITES
SERIATE	E EERIEST	REEMITS	O EROTISE	T TESTIER
B REBITES	F FESTIER	RETIMES	P PESTIER	U SUETIER
C CERITES	H HEISTER	TREMIES	RESPITE	V RESTIVE
RECITES	K KEISTER	TRISEME	R ETRIERS	SIEVERT
TIERCES	KIESTER	N ENTIRES	REITERS	STIEVER
D DIESTER	L LEISTER	ENTRIES	RESTIER	VERIEST
DIETERS	RETILES	NERITES	RETIRES	VERITES
REEDITS	STERILE	RETINES	RETRIES	W STEWIER
REISTED	M MEISTER	TRENISE	TERRIES	Z ZESTIER

eenrst 69 - enters

A EARNEST	RETENES	K RENKEST	R RENTERS	RETUNES
EASTERN	TEENERS	L NESTLER	RERENTS	TENURES
NEAREST	G GERENTS	RELENTS	STERNER	TUREENS
RATEENS	REGENTS	SLENTER	S NESTERS	V VENTERS
C CENTERS	H THRENES	N RENNETS	RENESTS	VENTRES
CENTRES	I ENTIRES	TENNERS	RESENTS	W WESTERN
TENRECS	ENTRIES	O ESTRONE	STRENES	X EXTERNS
D STERNED	NERITES	P PENSTER	T NETTERS	Y STYRENE
TENDERS	RETINES	PRESENT	TENTERS	YESTERN
TENDRES	TRENISE	REPENTS	TESTERN	
E ENTREES	TRIENES	SERPENT	U NEUTERS	

eeorst 92 - stereo

A ROSEATE	I EROTISE	METEORS	STEREOS	VETOERS
D OERSTED	J RESOJET	REMOTES	T ROSETTE	X XEROTES
ROSETED	K RESTOKE	N ESTRONE	V ESTOVER	Y ESOTERY
TEREDOS	L SOLERET	R RESTORE	OVERSET	
H HETEROS	M EMOTERS	S OSSETER	REVOTES	

egilnt 135 - tingle

A ATINGLE	TINGLED	K KINGLET	TINGLER	T ETTLING
ELATING	E GENTILE	L GILLNET	TRINGLE	LETTING
GELATIN	F FELTING	TELLING	S GLISTEN	U ELUTING
GENITAL	H ENLIGHT	M MELTING	LESTING	W WELTING
TAGLINE	LIGHTEN	O LENTIGO	SINGLET	WINGLET
B BELTING	I LIGNITE	P PELTING	SNIGLET	
D GLINTED	J JINGLET	R RINGLET	TINGLES	

eginor 67 - region

A ORIGANE	NEGROID	O GOONIER	S ERINGOS	V OVERING
C COREIGN	REDOING	P PERIGON	IGNORES	Z ZEROING
D ERODING	F FOREIGN	PIROGEN	REGIONS	
GROINED	M MOERING	PONGIER	SIGNORE	
IGNORED	N NEGRONI	R IGNORER	T GENITOR	

eginos 119 - soigne

A AGONIES	E GENOISE	LIGNOSE	P EPIGONS	U IGNEOUS
AGONISE	SOIGNEE	LINGOES	PIGEONS	W WIGEONS
B BINGOES	H HONGIES	LONGIES	PINGOES	Y ISOGENY
BIOGENS	SHOEING	M MISGONE	R ERINGOS	Z GINZOES
C COGNISE	J JINGOES	O GOONIES	IGNORES	
COIGNES	L ELOIGNS	ISOGONE	REGIONS	
D DINGOES	LEGIONS	NOOGIES	SIGNORE	

eginrs 122 - singer

A ANGRIES	D DINGERS	SLINGER	SPRINGE	RUEINGS
EARINGS	ENGIRDS	M GERMINS	R ERRINGS	SIGNEUR
ERASING	E GREISEN	MERINGS	GIRNERS	V SERVING
GAINERS	F FINGERS	MINGERS	RINGERS	VERSING
GRAINES	FRINGES	N ENRINGS	SERRING	W SWINGER
REAGINS	G GINGERS	GINNERS	S INGRESS	WINGERS
REGAINS	NIGGERS	O ERINGOS	RESIGNS	Y SYRINGE
REGINAS	SERGING	IGNORES	SIGNERS	Z ZINGERS
SEARING	SNIGGER	REGIONS	SINGERS	
SERINGA	H HINGERS	SIGNORE	T RESTING	
B BINGERS	L GIRNELS	P PERSING	STINGER	
C CRINGES	LINGERS	PINGERS	U REUSING	

eginrt 77 - engirt

A GRANITE	INTEGER	TIGRINE	N RENTING	T GITTERN
GRATINE	TEERING	L RINGLET	RINGENT	RETTING
INGRATE	TREEING	TINGLER	TERNING	U TRUEING
TANGIER	H RIGHTEN	TRINGLE	O GENITOR	V VERTING
TEARING	I IGNITER	M METRING	S RESTING	Y RETYING
E GENTIER	TIERING	TERMING	STINGER	

eginst 225 - tinges

A EASTING	GENISTA	SEATING	TEASING	D NIDGETS
EATINGS	INGATES	TAGINES	TSIGANE	STEDING
GAINEST	INGESTA	TANGIES	B BESTING	STINGED

H NIGHEST	SINGLET	SENTING	T SETTING	WESTING
I IGNITES	SNIGLET	TENSING	TESTING	Z ZESTING
J JESTING	TINGLES	R RESTING	U GUNITES	
K KESTING	M STEMING	STINGER	V VESTING	
L GLISTEN	TEMSING	S INGESTS	W STEWING	
LESTING	N NESTING	SIGNETS	TWINGES	

egiort 206 - goitre

A GOATIER	D GOITRED	S GOITERS	GORIEST	V VERTIGO
C ERGOTIC	N GENITOR	GOITRES	U GOUTIER	Z ZORGITE

eiinrt 57 - tinier

A INERTIA		NITRIDE	TIGRINE	TERMINI	VITRINE
C CITRINE	E ERINITE	H INHERIT	N TINNIER	W TWINIER
CRINITE	NITERIE	L LINTIER	T NITRITE	
INCITER	F NIFTIER	NITRILE	NITTIER	
NERITIC	G IGNITER	M INTERIM	TINTIER	
D INDITER	TIERING	MINTIER	V INVITER	

eiinst 94 - tinies

A ISATINE	F FINITES	M MINIEST	TIEPINS	VINIEST
B STIBINE	NIFTIES	N INTINES	T SITTINE	W WINIEST
C INCITES	G IGNITES	TINNIES	TINIEST	
D INDITES	K INKIEST	O INOSITE	U UNITIES	
TINEIDS	L LINIEST	P PINIEST	UNITISE	
E SIENITE	LINTIES	PINITES	V INVITES	

eilnor 35 - neroli

A AILERON	E ELOINER	P PLERION	S NEROLIS	
ALERION	N ONLINER	PROLINE	T RETINOL	
ALIENOR	O LOONIER	R LORINER		

eilnos 33 - lesion

A ANISOLE		SONDELI	LONGIES	M LOMEINS	INSOLES
B BOLINES	E OLEINES	I ELISION	MOLINES	LESIONS
C CINEOLS	F OLEFINS	ISOLINE	O LOONIES	LIONESS
CONSEIL	G ELOIGNS	LIONISE	P EPSILON	T ENTOILS
INCLOSE	LEGIONS	K SONLIKE	PINOLES	LIONETS
D DOLINES	LIGNOSE	L LIONELS	R NEROLIS	ONLIEST
INDOLES	LINGOES	NIELLOS	S ESLOINS	U ELUSION

eilnot 34 - lionet

A ELATION	H HOTLINE	PONTILE	LIONETS	W TOWLINE
TOENAIL	NEOLITH	POTLINE	ONLIEST	
C LECTION	I ETIOLIN	TOPLINE	U ELUTION	
D LENTOID	M MOLINET	R RETINOL	OUTLINE	
G LENTIGO	P POINTEL	S ENTOILS	V VIOLENT	

eilnrs 154 - liners

A ALINERS	RELINES	RESILIN	MERLINS	SNIRTLE
NAILERS	G GIRNELS	K LINKERS	O NEROLIS	V SILVERN
RENAILS	LINGERS	RELINKS	P PILSNER	
B BERLINS	SLINGER	SLINKER	T LINTERS	
E LIERNES	I INLIERS	M LIMNERS	SLINTER	

eilnrt 125 - linter

A ENTRAIL	RETINAL	G RINGLET	NITRILE	SLINTER
LATRINE	TRENAIL	TINGLER	K TINKLER	SNIRTLE
RATLINE	D TENDRIL	TRINGLE	O RETINOL	Y INERTLY
RELIANT	TRINDLE	I LINTIER	S LINTERS	

eilnst 80 - tinsel

A EASTLIN	LECTINS	SNIGLET	O ENTOILS	LISTENS
ELASTIN	STENCIL	TINGLES	LIONETS	SILENTS
ENTAILS	D DENTILS	I LINIEST	ONLIEST	TINSELS
NAILSET	E LENITES	LINTIES	P LEPTINS	U LUNIEST
SALIENT	LISENTE	K LENTISK	PINTLES	LUTEINS
SALTINE	SETLINE	TINKLES	PLENIST	UNTILES
SLAINTE	TENSILE	L LENTILS	R LINTERS	UTENSIL
STANIEL	G GLISTEN	LINTELS	SLINTER	V VENTILS
TENAILS	LESTING	TELLINS	SNIRTLE	W WESTLIN
C CLIENTS	SINGLET	N LINNETS	S ENLISTS	WINTLES

eilors 39 - oilers

B BOILERS	SOLIDER	N NEROLIS	LOSSIER	LOUSIER
LIBEROS	E LOERIES	O ORIOLES	RISSOLE	SOILURE
REBOILS	G GLOIRES	P SLOPIER	T ESTRIOL	V OLIVERS
C COILERS	GLORIES	SPOILER	LOITERS	VIOLERS
RECOILS	I SOILIER	R LORRIES	TOILERS	W LOWRIES
D SOLDIER	M MOILERS	S LORISES	U LOURIES	

eilort 26 - toiler

B TRILOBE	F LOFTIER	N RETINOL	S ESTRIOL	TRIOLET
C CORTILE	TREFOIL	O TROOLIE	LOITERS	U OUTLIER
D DOILTER	J JOLTIER	P POITREL	TOILERS	V OVERLIT
E TROELIE	M MOTLIER	POLITER	T TORTILE	

eilost 31 - toiles

A ISOLATE	H EOLITHS	M MOTILES	P PIOLETS	U OUTLIES
B BETOILS	HOLIEST	N ENTOILS	PISTOLE	V OLIVETS
C CITOLES	HOSTILE	LIONETS	R ESTRIOL	VIOLETS
E ESTOILE	I IOLITES	ONLIEST	LOITERS	W OWLIEST
ETOILES	OILIEST	O OOLITES	TOILERS	Z ZLOTIES
G ELOGIST	L OILLETS	OSTIOLE	T LITOTES	
LOGIEST	TOLLIES	STOOLIE	TOILETS	

eilrst 71 - tilers

A REALIST	RETILES	J JILTERS	SNIRTLE	STILTER
RETAILS	STERILE	K KILTERS	O ESTRIOL	TESTRIL
SALTIER	F FILTERS	KIRTLES	LOITERS	TILTERS
SALTIRE	LIFTERS	KLISTER	TOILERS	TITLERS
SLATIER	STIFLER	L RILLETS	P RESPLIT	U LUSTIER
TAILERS	TRIFLES	STILLER	SPIRTLE	RULIEST
B BLISTER	G GLISTER	TILLERS	TRIPLES	RUTILES
BRISTLE	GRISTLE	TRELLIS	S LISTERS	Y STYLIER
RIBLETS	H SLITHER	M MILTERS	RELISTS	
C RELICTS	I RILIEST	N LINTERS	T LITTERS	
E LEISTER	SILTIER	SLINTER	SLITTER	

einnrt 223 - intern

A ENTRAIN	G RENTING	H THINNER	NOINTER	S INTERNS
TRANNIE	RINGENT	I TINNIER	TERNION	TINNERS
E INTERNE	TERNING	O INTONER	P ENPRINT	V VINTNER

einnst 245 - tennis

A INANEST	INTENDS	I INTINES	SPINNET	T INTENTS
STANINE	E INTENSE	TINNIES	TENPINS	TENNIST
TANNIES	TENNIES	L LINNETS	R INTERNS	U TUNNIES
C INCENTS	G NESTING	O INTONES	TINNERS	V INVENTS
D DENTINS	SENTING	TENSION	S SENNITS	
INDENTS	TENSING	P PINNETS	SINNETS	

einopr 141 - proine

C PERICON	PIONEER	I RIPIENO	R PORNIER	PTERION
PONCIER	F FORPINE	L PLERION	S ORPINES	REPOINT
PORCINE	G PERIGON	PROLINE	PIONERS	TROPINE
D POINDER	PIROGEN	M PROMINE	PROINES	V PROVINE
PROINED	PONGIER	P POPERIN	T POINTER	
E PEREION	H PHONIER	PROPINE	PROTEIN	

einops 219 - ponies

A EPINAOS	PIGEONS	L EPSILON	SPINONE	T PINTOES
SENOPIA	PINGOES	PINOLES	P PEPINOS	POINTES
D DISPONE	H PHONIES	M IMPONES	R ORPINES	PONTIES
SPINODE	I PIONIES	PEONISM	PIONERS	W POWNIES
E PEONIES	SINOPIE	N PENSION	PROINES	WINESOP
G EPIGONS	K PINKOES	PINONES	S SPINOSE	Y PIONEYS

einorr 175 - ironer

C CORNIER	E ONERIER	H HORNIER	L LORINER	S IRONERS
D DRONIER	G IGNORER	I IRONIER	P PORNIER	ROSINER

einors 7 - senior

A ERASION	CRONIES	RECOINS	DONSIER	ROSINED
C COINERS	ORCEINS	SERICON	INDORSE	SORDINE
CRINOSE	ORCINES	D DINEROS	ORDINES	G ERINGOS

Six-letter stems

IGNORES	NOISIER	P ORPINES	SONSIER	V ENVIROS
REGIONS	J JOINERS	PIONERS	T NORITES	RENVOIS
SIGNORE	REJOINS	PROINES	OESTRIN	VERSION
H HEROINS	L NEROLIS	R IRONERS	ORIENTS	W SNOWIER
INSHORE	M MERINOS	ROSINER	STONIER	
I IONISER	MERSION	S ORNISES	TERSION	
IRONIES	N RONNIES	SENIORS	TRIONES	
IRONISE	O EROSION	SONERIS	U URINOSE	

einort 11 - orient

A OTARINE	J JOINTER	PROTEIN	ORIENTS	W NOWTIER
B BORNITE	L RETINOL	PTERION	STONIER	TOWNIER
C COINTER	N INTONER	REPOINT	TERSION	Z TRIZONE
NOTICER	NOINTER	TROPINE	TRIONES	
RECTION	TERNION	S NORITES	T TRITONE	
G GENITOR	P POINTER	OESTRIN	U ROUTINE	

einost 13 - tonies

A ATONIES	HISTONE	MONTIES	PONTIES	SONTIES
B BONIEST	I INOSITE	SENTIMO	R NORITES	STONIES
EBONIST	J JONTIES	N INTONES	OESTRIN	T SNOTTIE
C NOTICES	L ENTOILS	TENSION	ORIENTS	TONIEST
SECTION	LIONETS	O ISOTONE	STONIER	TONITES
D DITONES	ONLIEST	TOONIES	TERSION	W TOWNIES
STONIED	M MESTINO	P PINTOES	TRIONES	TWONIES
H ETHIONS	MOISTEN	POINTES	S NOSIEST	X TOXINES

einrst 25 - insert

A ANESTRI	D TINDERS	SKINTER	OESTRIN	TINTERS
ANTSIER	E ENTIRES	STINKER	ORIENTS	U NUTSIER
NASTIER	ENTRIES	TINKERS	STONIER	TRIUNES
RATINES	NERITES	L LINTERS	TERSION	UNITERS
RESIANT	RETINES	SLINTER	TRIONES	V INVERTS
RETAINS	TRENISE	SNIRTLE	P NIPTERS	STRIVEN
RETINAS	TRIENES	M ENTRISM	PTERINS	W TWINERS
RETSINA	F SNIFTER	MINSTER	S ESTRINS	WINTERS
STAINER	G RESTING	MINTERS	INSERTS	Y SINTERY
STARNIE	STINGER	REMINTS	SINTERS	
STEARIN	H HINTERS	N INTERNS	T ENTRIST	
C CISTERN	NITHERS	TINNERS	RETINTS	
CRETINS	K REKNITS	O NORITES	STINTER	

einrsu 222 - insure

B BURNIES	RUEINGS	N SUNNIER	UPRISEN	T NUTSIER
RUBINES	SIGNEUR	UNREINS	Q REQUINS	TRIUNES
SUBERIN	J INJURES	UNRISEN	R INSURER	UNITERS
D INSURED	M MUREINS	O URINOSE	RUINERS	W UNWIRES
F INFUSER	MURINES	P PRUINES	S INSURES	UNWISER
G REUSING	NEURISM	PURINES	SUNRISE	

einrtt 149 - tinter

A INTREAT	B BITTERN	RETTING	O TRITONE	W TWINTER
ITERANT	C CITTERN	I NITRITE	S ENTRIST	WRITTEN
NATTIER	D TRIDENT	NITTIER	RETINTS	
NITRATE	E NETTIER	TINTIER	STINTER	
TARTINE	TENTIER	K KNITTER	TINTERS	
TERTIAN	G GITTERN	TRINKET	U NUTTIER	

einrtu 41 - uniter

A RUINATE	D INTRUDE	REUNITE	O ROUTINE	V UNRIVET
TAURINE	TURDINE	UTERINE	P REPUNIT	VENTURI
URANITE	UNTIRED	G TRUEING	R RUNTIER	W UNWRITE
URINATE	UNTRIDE	M MINUTER	S NUTSIER	
B BUNTIER	UNTRIED	MUNTRIE	TRIUNES	
TRIBUNE	E NEURITE	UNMITER	UNITERS	
TURBINE	RETINUE	UNMITRE	T NUTTIER	

einstu 153 - unties

A AUNTIES	I UNITIES	M MINUETS	P PUNIEST	UNITERS
SINUATE	UNITISE	MINUTES	PUNTIES	S INTUSES
C NEUSTIC	L LUNIEST	MISTUNE	Q INQUEST	T TUNIEST
D DISTUNE	LUTEINS	MUNITES	QUINTES	
DUNITES	UNTILES	MUTINES	R NUTSIER	
G GUNITES	UTENSIL	N TUNNIES	TRIUNES	

eioost 173 - otiose

B BOOTIES	OOFIEST	OSTIOLE	R OORIEST	T TOOTSIE
C COOTIES	G GOOIEST	STOOLIE	ROOTIES	Z OOZIEST
D OSTEOID	H TOOSHIE	N ISOTONE	SOOTIER	ZOOIEST
F FOOTIES	K STOOKIE	TOONIES	TOORIES	
FOOTSIE	L OOLITES	P ISOTOPE	S OOSIEST	

eiopst 211 - postie

A ATOPIES	E POETISE	N PINTOES	RIPOSTE	TIPTOES
OPIATES	H ETHIOPS	POINTES	ROPIEST	U PITEOUS
C POETICS	OPHITES	PONTIES	S POSIEST	X EXPOSIT
D DEPOSIT	K POKIEST	O ISOTOPE	POSTIES	POXIEST
DOPIEST	L PIOLETS	P POTPIES	POTSIES	Y ISOTYPE
PODITES	PISTOLE	R PERIOST	SEPIOST	
POSITED	M MOPIEST	PORIEST	SOPITES	
SOPITED	OPTIMES	PROSTIE	T POTTIES	
TOPSIDE	STOMPIE	REPOSIT	SPOTTIE	

eiorst 4 - sortie

A OARIEST	TERCIOS	STEROID	F FOISTER	H HERIOTS
OTARIES	D EDITORS	STORIED	FORTIES	HOISTER
B ORBIEST	ROISTED	TIERODS	G GOITERS	SHORTIE
SORBITE	ROSITED	TRIODES	GOITRES	TOSHIER
C EROTICS	SORTIED	E EROTISE	GORIEST	I RIOTISE

Six-letter stems

K	ROKIEST		OESTRIN	P	PERIOST	S	ROSIEST		STOURIE
L	ESTRIOL		ORIENTS		PORIEST		SIROSET		TOURIES
	LOITERS		STONIER		PROSTIE		SORITES		TOUSIER
	TOILERS		TERSION		REPOSIT		SORTIES	V	TORSIVE
M	EROTISM		TRIONES		RIPOSTE		STORIES	W	OWRIEST
	MOISTER	O	OORIEST		ROPIEST		TOSSIER		TOWSIER
	MORTISE		ROOTIES	R	RIOTERS		TRIOSES		
	TRISOME		SOOTIER		ROISTER	T	STOITER		
N	NORITES		TOORIES		RORIEST	U	OURIEST		

eiortu 82 - tourie

D	ETOURDI	G	GOUTIER	N	ROUTINE		STOURIE	V	VOITURE
	IODURET	H	OUTHIRE	P	POUTIER		TOURIES	Z	TOUZIER
	OUTRIDE		ROUTHIE	Q	QUOITER		TOUSIER		
F	OUTFIRE	L	OUTLIER	S	OURIEST	T	TOUTIER		

eirstt 237 - sitter

A	ARTIEST	C	TRISECT	L	LITTERS		STINTER	T	STRETTI
	ARTISTE	E	TESTIER		SLITTER		TINTERS		TITTERS
	ATTIRES	F	FITTERS		STILTER	O	STOITER		TRITEST
	IRATEST		TITFERS		TESTRIL	P	PITTERS	U	TERTIUS
	RATITES	H	HITTERS		TILTERS		SPITTER	V	TRIVETS
	STRIATE		TITHERS		TITLERS		TIPSTER	W	RETWIST
	TASTIER	J	JITTERS	M	METRIST	R	RITTERS		TWISTER
	TERTIAS		TRIJETS	N	ENTRIST		TERRITS		WITTERS
B	BITTERS	K	SKITTER		RETINTS	S	SITTERS		

eirstu 108 - urites

B	BUSTIER		STUDIER		TUSKIER	O	OURIEST	R	RUSTIER
	RUBIEST	E	SUETIER	L	LUSTIER		STOURIE	S	SUITERS
C	CUITERS	F	FUSTIER		RULIEST		TOURIES	T	TERTIUS
	CURIETS		SURFEIT		RUTILES		TOUSIER	V	REVUIST
	CURITES	G	GUSTIER	M	MUSTIER	P	PERITUS		STUIVER
	ICTERUS		GUTSIER	N	NUTSIER		PUIREST		VIRTUES
D	DUSTIER	H	HIRSUTE		TRIUNES	Q	QUERIST		
	REDUITS	K	TURKIES		UNITERS		REQUITS		

elnors 230 - enrols

A	LOANERS	C	CLONERS	G	LONGERS	L	ENROLLS	S	NORSELS
	ORLEANS		CORNELS	I	NEROLIS	M	MERLONS	T	LENTORS
	RELOANS	D	RONDELS	K	SNORKEL	N	RONNELS	U	NOURSLE

elnost 216 - stolen

A	ETALONS	G	LONGEST	L	STOLLEN	R	LENTORS	V	SOLVENT
	TOLANES	I	ENTOILS	M	LOMENTS	S	TELSONS		
B	NOBLEST		LIONETS		MELTONS	T	TONLETS		
F	TEFLONS		ONLIEST	P	LEPTONS	U	LENTOUS		

elorst 88 - ostler

A	OESTRAL	B	BOLSTER		LOBSTER		CORSLET		LECTORS
	OLESTRA		BOLTERS	C	COLTERS		COSTREL	D	DROLEST

	OLDSTER	I	ESTRIOL		MOLTERS		REPLOTS		TOLTERS
	STRODLE		LOITERS	N	LENTORS	S	OSTLERS	U	ELUTORS
E	SOLERET		TOILERS	O	LOOTERS		STEROLS		OUTLERS
F	FLORETS	J	JOLTERS		RETOOLS		TORSELS		TROULES
	LOFTERS		JOSTLER		ROOTLES	T	LOTTERS	V	REVOLTS
H	HOLSTER	L	TOLLERS		TOOLERS		SETTLOR	W	TROWELS
	HOSTLER	M	MERLOTS	P	PETROLS		SLOTTER		WORTLES

ennort 249 - tonner

A	NORTENA	E	ENTERON	G	RONTGEN		TERNION		TONNERS
D	DONNERT		TENONER	I	INTONER	O	NORTENO	U	NEUTRON
	TENDRON	F	FORNENT		NOINTER	S	STONERN		

enorst 20 - stoner

A	ATONERS	D	RODENTS		OESTRIN	M	MENTORS		STONERS
	SANTERO		SNORTED		ORIENTS		MONSTER		TENSORS
	SENATOR	E	ESTRONE		STONIER		MONTRES	T	ROTTENS
	TREASON	F	FRONTES		TERSION	N	STONERN		SNOTTER
B	BRETONS	G	TONGERS		TRIONES		TONNERS		STENTOR
	SORBENT	H	HORNETS	K	REKNOTS	O	ENROOTS	U	TENOURS
C	CONSTER		SHORTEN		STONKER	P	POSTERN		TONSURE
	CORNETS		THRENOS		STROKEN		PRONEST	Y	TYRONES
	CRESTON		THRONES		TONKERS	R	SNORTER		
	CRONETS	I	NORITES	L	LENTORS	S	NESTORS		

enorsu 158 - rouens

A	ARENOUS		ROUNCES	G	SURGEON		NONUSER	V	NERVOUS
B	BOURNES	D	ENDUROS	H	UNHORSE	O	ONEROUS	W	UNSWORE
	UNROBES		RESOUND	I	URINOSE	P	UNROPES	Z	ZONURES
	UNSOBER		SOUNDER	L	NOURSLE	T	TENOURS		
C	CONURES		UNDOERS	N	NEURONS		TONSURE		

enortu 185 - tenour

A	OUTEARN		RECOUNT	I	ROUTINE		REMOUNT		TONSURE
C	CORNUTE		TROUNCE	M	MONTURE	N	NEUTRON	W	UNWROTE
	COUNTER	F	FORTUNE		MOUNTER	S	TENOURS	Y	TOURNEY

enrstu 165 - unrest

A	AUNTERS	C	ENCRUST	G	GUNTERS		UNITERS		TONSURE
	NATURES	D	RETUNDS		GURNETS	L	RUNLETS	P	PUNSTER
	SAUNTER		UNDREST		SURGENT	M	MUNSTER		PUNTERS
B	BRUNETS	E	NEUTERS	H	HUNTERS		MUNTERS	R	RETURNS
	BUNTERS		RETUNES		SHUNTER		STERNUM		TURNERS
	BURNETS		TENURES		UNHERST	N	RUNNETS	S	UNRESTS
	BURSTEN		TUREENS	I	NUTSIER		STUNNER	T	ENTRUST
	SUBRENT	F	FUNSTER		TRIUNES	O	TENOURS		NUTTERS

eorrst 244 - storer

A	ROASTER		RODSTER	H	RHETORS	I	RIOTERS	K	STROKER
C	RECTORS	E	RESTORE		ROTHERS		ROISTER	M	STORMER
D	DORTERS	G	GROSERT		SHORTER		RORIEST		TERMORS

Six-letter stems

TREMORS	PRESORT	S RESORTS	STERTOR	TROUSER
N SNORTER	PRETORS	ROSTERS	TORRETS	V TROVERS
O ROOSTER	REPORTS	SORTERS	U RETOURS	W STROWER
ROOTERS	SPORTER	STORERS	ROUSTER	Y ROYSTER
TOREROS	R RORTERS	T RETORTS	ROUTERS	STROYER
P PORTERS	TERRORS	ROTTERS	TOURERS	

eorstu 229 - routes

B OBTUSER	FOUTRES	M MOUTERS	Q QUESTOR	OUSTERS
C COUTERS	H SHOUTER	OESTRUM	QUOTERS	SOUREST
CROUTES	SOUTHER	N TENOURS	ROQUETS	SOUTERS
SCOUTER	I OURIEST	TONSURE	TORQUES	STOURES
D DETOURS	STOURIE	P PETROUS	R RETOURS	TOUSERS
DOUREST	TOURIES	POSTURE	ROUSTER	TROUSES
DOUTERS	TOUSIER	POUTERS	ROUTERS	TUSSORE
OUTREDS	J JOUSTER	PROTEUS	TOURERS	T OUTSERT
REDOUTS	L ELUTORS	SEPTUOR	TROUSER	STOUTER
ROUSTED	OUTLERS	SPOUTER	S ESTROUS	TOUTERS
F FOUTERS	TROULES	TROUPES	OESTRUS	X SEXTUOR

ginort 194 - trigon

A ORATING	I IGNITOR	TROPING	TRIGONS	TOURING
ROATING	RIOTING	R RORTING	T ROTTING	W ROWTING
D DORTING	K TROKING	S ROSTING	U OUTGRIN	TROWING
E GENITOR	O ROOTING	SORTING	OUTRING	
F FORTING	P PORTING	STORING	ROUTING	

inorst 103 - intros

A AROINTS	CORTINS	TRIONES	H HORNIST	TORSION
RATIONS	E NORITES	F FORINTS	I IRONIST	P TROPINS
B RIBSTON	OESTRIN	G ROSTING	L NOSTRIL	T INTORTS
C CISTRON	ORIENTS	SORTING	N INTRONS	TRITONS
CITRONS	R STONIER	STORING	O ISOTRON	U NITROUS
CORNIST	TERSION	TRIGONS	NITROSO	TURIONS

Seven-letter stems

Seven-letter stems in order of usefulness

As with the six-letter stems, the top 250 seven-letter stems are listed here in order of usefulness. The most useful combination of tiles is AEINORT, followed by AEINRST, then EINORST, and so on. Underneath the list, the individual stems are shown in alphabetical order together with the words that can be formed by combining them with another letter.

1: AEINORT - OTARINE	9: AEEIRST - SERIATE	17: AEEILRT - ATELIER
2: AEINRST - NASTIER	10: AEEINRT - TRAINEE	18: AEENRST - EASTERN
3: EINORST - ORIENTS	11: EEINRST - ENTRIES	19: ADEINST - STAINED
4: AEIORST - OTARIES	12: AEILRST - REALIST	20: DEINORS - ROSINED
5: AENORST - TREASON	13: AEINORS - ERASION	21: AEGILNR - REALIGN
6: AEILNRT - RELIANT	14: ADEIRST - TIRADES	22: EILNOST - ONLIEST
7: ADEINRT - TRAINED	15: AEILNRS - RENAILS	23: EILORST - TOILERS
8: ADEINRS - SARDINE	16: AEINOST - ATONIES	24: AEINRTU - URINATE

25: AEGINRT - TEARING	85: ENORSTU - TONSURE	145: AEORSTT - TOASTER
26: ADEINOR - ANEROID	86: AAEILNT - ANTLIAE	146: ADEILNS - DENIALS
27: AELORST - OLESTRA	87: AEINSTT - INSTATE	147: AEGINOR - ORIGANE
28: DEIORST - STEROID	88: AEILRTT - TERTIAL	148: DEEORST - TEREDOS
29: AEILNOT - TOENAIL	89: AEEORST - ROSEATE	149: ABEORST - BOASTER
30: AINORST - RATIONS	90: AEINRRT - TRAINER	150: AILORST - TAILORS
31: AEGINRS - SEARING	91: ADEIORS - ROADIES	151: EEILORS - LOERIES
32: ADENORT - TORNADE	92: EGINRST - STINGER	152: EEINRTT - TENTIER
33: EILNORS - NEROLIS	93: AEIMNRT - RAIMENT	153: AEINSTV - VAINEST
34: ADEGINR - READING	94: AEIIRST - AIRIEST	154: AAEINST - TAENIAS
35: AEIINRT - INERTIA	95: ADEINRU - UNAIRED	155: AEGINOS - AGONIES
36: EILNORT - RETINOL	96: EEGINRS - GREISEN	156: AEILRTU - URALITE
37: DEEIRST - DIETERS	97: ADENOST - DONATES	157: AEIINRS - SENARII
38: AEILOST - ISOLATE	98: ADINORS - INROADS	158: CEINOST - SECTION
39: AEGINST - SEATING	99: AEEGNRT - REAGENT	159: EIMORST - MORTISE
40: AEINPRT - REPAINT	100: AEINNOT - ENATION	160: AEILRRT - TRAILER
41: EENORST - ESTRONE	101: DEILNOS - SONDELI	161: AEHINRT - HAIRNET
42: DEEINST - DESTINE	102: EINORTU - ROUTINE	162: AGILNOT - ANTILOG
43: ACEINRT - CERTAIN	103: ADENRTU - UNRATED	163: EINOPRS - PROINES
44: AEILNOR - AILERON	104: ADEGORT - GAROTED	164: AGINRST - STARING
45: AEINRTT - NITRATE	105: ABEINST - BESTAIN	165: EGINORT - GENITOR
46: AEGILNT - GELATIN	106: AEIMNST - INMATES	166: ADEILOR - DARIOLE
47: AEELRST - STEALER	107: ADEERST - DEAREST	167: AEILNPT - PANTILE
48: ADEILRT - TRAILED	108: AEIPRST - TRAIPSE	168: ADEIMNR - INARMED
49: AEILNST - SALIENT	109: ACENORT - ENACTOR	169: ACINORT - CORTINA
50: AEELNRT - ETERNAL	110: AEGNRST - STRANGE	170: AAEIRST - ATRESIA
51: ADEINOS - SODAINE	111: ADEEIST - IDEATES	171: DEENORT - ERODENT
52: ADEILRS - DERAILS	112: ADEEIRS - READIES	172: CEINORS - CRONIES
53: EEIORST - EROTISE	113: AEORRST - ROASTER	173: DEILORT - DOILTER
54: DEINOST - STONIED	114: AEINNRT - TRANNIE	174: EILRSTU - LUSTIER
55: ADINORT - DIATRON	115: AEHIRST - HASTIER	175: AEINPST - PANTIES
56: EGINORS - REGIONS	116: ADEIOST - TOADIES	176: EEINSTT - NETTIES
57: EINRSTU - UNITERS	117: EEILORT - TROELIE	177: AEGILRS - GRAILES
58: AEILNOS - ANISOLE	118: ADIORST - ASTROID	178: AEEGINS - AGENISE
59: EIORSTU - TOUSIER	119: AEGILNS - SEALING	179: EIILRST - SILTIER
60: AENRSTU - SAUNTER	120: ACEINRS - ARSENIC	180: AGINORS - SOARING
61: AEEILRS - REALISE	121: EEGINRT - INTEGER	181: ADEIINT - INEDITA
62: AEIRSTT - TASTIER	122: EIORRST - RIOTERS	182: AEIMNOT - AMNIOTE
63: AEEILNT - LINEATE	123: EEIINRT - NITERIE	183: AEINSTU - AUNTIES
64: AEEGINR - REGINAE	124: AEIINST - ISATINE	184: AEENORS - ARENOSE
65: DEEINRS - RESINED	125: ACEINOT - ACONITE	185: ADEGNOR - GROANED
66: AEEINST - ETESIAN	126: ADEILST - DILATES	186: DEIORTU - OUTRIDE
67: EEILRST - STERILE	127: AADEIRT - RADIATE	187: BEINOST - BONIEST
68: AEIMRST - SMARTIE	128: DEENORS - ENDORSE	188: DEILORS - SOLDIER
69: DEINRTU - UNTRIED	129: AGINORT - ORATING	189: AEMNORS - OARSMEN
70: EINORTT - TRITONE	130: ADEEILR - LEADIER	190: ADENRST - STANDER
71: DEINRST - TINDERS	131: ADEENRS - ENDEARS	191: AELNORU - ALEURON
72: AELNRST - ANTLERS	132: ADEEGNR - GRENADE	192: EIOPRST - ROPIEST
73: AEEILNR - ALIENER	133: EIORSTT - STOITER	193: DEINSTU - DUNITES
74: AEEILNS - SEALINE	134: ADEILOS - ISOLEAD	194: ADEEINS - ANISEED
75: EEILNST - TENSILE	135: AEIMNRS - SEMINAR	195: ADINRST - INDARTS
76: DEILNOT - LENTOID	136: EELORST - SOLERET	196: ACEILRT - ARTICLE
77: ADEORST - ROASTED	137: AEEIMRT - MEATIER	197: AEINPRS - RAPINES
78: AEIRRST - TARRIES	138: EINNORT - TERNION	198: DEEILNR - RELINED
79: AAENRST - SANTERA	139: AILNOST - LATINOS	199: EEILNRS - RELINES
80: CEINORT - RECTION	140: AEGORST - TOERAGS	200: DENORST - SNORTED
81: EILNRST - SNIRTLE	141: AEIRSTW - WAITERS	201: EINORSS - SENIORS
82: AEINNRS - INSNARE	142: AEILPRT - PLATIER	202: AEGNORT - NEGATOR
83: ACEINST - CINEAST	143: AENORSU - ARENOUS	203: EINOPRT - POINTER
84: AENORTU - OUTEARN	144: AEINSST - TISANES	204: AEIRSST - SATIRES

Seven-letter stems

205: AEMORST - MAESTRO	221: DEEILNS - LINSEED	237: AEIRSTV - VERITAS
206: EIINORS - NOISIER	222: AENNORT - NORTENA	238: ADEELST - STEALED
207: ADELNOR - LADRONE	223: AEINRRS - SNARIER	239: EGNORST - TONGERS
208: ADEELRT - RELATED	224: EHIORST - HOISTER	240: AEENRTT - ENTREAT
209: EEGILNR - REELING	225: AEOPRST - SEAPORT	241: DEENRTU - TENURED
210: ADEEILS - AEDILES	226: DEIRSTU - STUDIER	242: AEINRSS - SARNIES
211: ADEIRTT - ATTIRED	227: BEIORST - SORBITE	243: ACDEINR - DANCIER
212: AEERRST - TEARERS	228: AELNORS - RELOANS	244: AEIILNR - AIRLINE
213: ADEGILN - LEADING	229: EINORSU - URINOSE	245: AEGNORS - ORANGES
214: AENRSTT - NATTERS	230: ADEEILN - DELAINE	246: ADEINTU - AUDIENT
215: DEINRSU - INSURED	231: AEMNORT - TONEARM	247: ADEINPT - PAINTED
216: AEIORSV - OVARIES	232: EGIORST - GORIEST	248: DEIINOT - EDITION
217: ADEIPRS - PRAISED	233: DEGINOR - REDOING	249: EINOSTT - TONITES
218: AIORSTU - SAUTOIR	234: ADEIMNO - DOMAINE	250: ADEELNT - LATENED
219: ACEORST - COASTER	235: DEIINRT - NITRIDE	
220: AELRSTU - SALUTER	236: EINRSTT - TINTERS	

aadeirt 127 - radiate

C RADICATE	E ERADIATE	N DENTARIA	S AIRDATES	RADIATES
D RADIATED	L LARIATED	RAINDATE	DATARIES	V VARIATED

aaeilnt 86 - antliae

C ANALCITE	E ALIENATE	H ANTHELIA	M ALAIMENT	P PALATINE
LAITANCE	G AGENTIAL	K ANTILEAK	ANTIMALE	T ANTLIATE
D DENTALIA	ALGINATE	L ALLANITE	LAMINATE	V AVENTAIL

aaeinst 154 - taenias

B BASANITE	H ASTHENIA	ARTESIAN	SEATRAIN	TANAISTE
C ESTANCIA	M AMENTIAS	RATANIES	S ENTASIAS	V SANATIVE
F FANTASIE	ANIMATES	RESINATA	T ASTATINE	
G SAGINATE	R ANTISERA	SANTERIA	SANITATE	

aaeirst 170 - atresia

D AIRDATES	M AMIRATES	RESINATA	PARASITE	T ARIETTAS
DATARIES	N ANTISERA	SANTERIA	SEPTARIA	ARISTATE
RADIATES	ARTESIAN	SEATRAIN	S ASTERIAS	V VARIATES
H HETAIRAS	RATANIES	P ASPIRATE	ATRESIAS	W AWAITERS

aaenrst 79 - santera

B ANTBEARS	SERENATA	RATANIES	L ASTERNAL	S SANTERAS
RATSBANE	G STARAGEN	RESINATA	M SARMENTA	T TARTANES
C CANASTER	TANAGERS	SANTERIA	SEMANTRA	V TAVERNAS
CATERANS	I ANTISERA	SEATRAIN	O ANOESTRA	TSAREVNA
E ARSENATE	ARTESIAN	J NAARTJES	R NARRATES	

abeinst 105 - bestain

A BASANITE	G BEATINGS	L INSTABLE	OBEISANT	S BASINETS
C BASCINET	H ABSINTHE	M AMBIENTS	P BEPAINTS	BASSINET
CABINETS	I BAINITES	O BOTANIES	R ATEBRINS	BESAINTS
D BANDIEST	K BEATNIKS	BOTANISE	BANISTER	BESTAINS
E BETAINES	SNAKEBIT	NIOBATES	BARNIEST	T TABINETS

abeorst 149 - boaster

A AEROBATS	E ABORTEES	SORTABLE	R ABORTERS	T ABETTORS
RABATOES	REBATOES	STORABLE	ARBORETS	BATTEROS
C CABESTRO	H BATHORSE	M BROMATES	TABORERS	TABORETS
CABRESTO	I SABOTIER	N BARONETS	S BOASTERS	U SABOTEUR
D BROADEST	L BLOATERS	P PROBATES	SORBATES	

acdeinr 243 - dancier

A CANARIED	RIDDANCE	I ACRIDINE	T CRINATED
RADIANCE	E DERACINE	N CRANNIED	DICENTRA
D CANDIDER	H INARCHED	R RANCIDER	

aceilrt 196 - article

A TAILRACE	M METRICAL	P PARTICLE	ARTICLES	T TRACTILE
D ARTICLED	N CLARINET	PRELATIC	RECITALS	U RETICULA
LACERTID	O EROTICAL	R CLARTIER	SELICTAR	V VERTICAL
K TALCKIER	LORICATE	S ALTRICES	STERICAL	Y LITERACY

aceinot 125 - aconite

C ACETONIC	INCHOATE	ANORETIC	CANOEIST	INVOCATE
D ACTIONED	M COINMATE	CREATION	SONICATE	X EXACTION
CATENOID	N ENACTION	REACTION	T TACONITE	
H ETHANOIC	R ACTIONER	S ACONITES	V CONATIVE	

aceinrs 120 - arsenic

A ACARINES	RESIANCE	I RIANCIES	O SCENARIO	CISTERNA
CANARIES	F FANCIERS	K SKINCARE	S ARCSINES	CREATINS
CESARIAN	FRANCISE	L CARLINES	ARSENICS	NACRITES
SARCINAE	G CREASING	LANCIERS	CERASINS	SCANTIER
B BRISANCE	GRECIANS	M CARMINES	RACINESS	TACRINES
CARBINES	SEARCING	CREMAINS	T CANISTER	
E CINEREAS	H ARCHINES	N CRANNIES	CARNIEST	
INCREASE	INARCHES	NARCEINS	CERATINS	

aceinrt 43 - certain

A CARINATE	CREATINE	REACTING	S CANISTER	TACRINES
CRANIATE	INCREATE	I ARENITIC	CARNIEST	T INTERACT
B BACTERIN	ITERANCE	L CLARINET	CERATINS	U ANURETIC
C ACENTRIC	G ARGENTIC	O ACTIONER	CISTERNA	V NAVICERT
D CRINATED	CATERING	ANORETIC	CREATINS	X XERANTIC
DICENTRA	CITRANGE	CREATION	NACRITES	
E CENTIARE	CREATING	REACTION	SCANTIER	

aceinst 83 - cineast

A ESTANCIA	F FANCIEST	M AMNESTIC	O ACONITES	CISTERNA
B BASCINET	H ASTHENIC	SEMANTIC	CANOEIST	CREATINS
CABINETS	CHANTIES	N ANCIENTS	SONICATE	NACRITES
D DANCIEST	I ANTICISE	CANNIEST	R CANISTER	SCANTIER
DISTANCE	CANITIES	INSECTAN	CARNIEST	TACRINES
E CINEASTE	L CANISTEL	INSTANCE	CERATINS	S CINEASTS

Seven-letter stems

SCANTIES	ENTASTIC	TETANICS	VESICANT	Z ZINCATES
T CANTIEST	NICTATES	V CISTVAEN	Y CYANITES	

acenort 109 - enactor

C ACCENTOR	H ANCHORET	REACTION	S ANCESTOR	T CONTRATE
D CARTONED	I ACTIONER	O CORONATE	ENACTORS	U COURANTE
NOTECARD	ANORETIC	P COPARENT	SARCONET	OUTRANCE
E CAROTENE	CREATION	PORTANCE	SORTANCE	Y ENACTORY

aceorst 219 - coaster

B CABESTRO	G ESCARGOT	ENACTORS	REACTORS	OVERCAST
CABRESTO	H CHAROSET	SARCONET	S COARSEST	X EXACTORS
C ECTOSARC	THORACES	SORTANCE	COASTERS	
D REDCOATS	L LOCATERS	P POSTRACE	T SECTATOR	
E CREASOTE	SECTORAL	R ACROTERS	U OUTRACES	
F FORECAST	N ANCESTOR	CREATORS	V OVERACTS	

acinort 169 - cortina

A RAINCOAT	ANORETIC	K ANTIROCK	CONTRAIR	U NOCTURIA
C CRATONIC	CREATION	L CILANTRO	S CANTORIS	Y CARYOTIN
NARCOTIC	REACTION	CONTRAIL	CAROTINS	
D TORNADIC	F FRACTION	M ROMANTIC	CORTINAS	
E ACTIONER	H ANORTHIC	R CARROTIN	T TRACTION	

adeegnr 132 - grenade

A GADARENE	E RENEGADE	M GENDARME	GARNERED	UNAGREED
C ENGRACED	H REHANGED	N ENDANGER	S DERANGES	UNDERAGE
D DANGERED	I REGAINED	ENRANGED	GRANDEES	UNGEARED
DERANGED	L ENLARGED	O RENEGADO	GRENADES	V ENGRAVED
GANDERED	LANGERED	R DERANGER	U DUNGAREE	
GARDENED	LARGENED	GARDENER	RENAGUED	

adeeiln 230 - delaine

B DENIABLE	F ENFILADE	M ENDEMIAL	S DELAINES	ENTAILED
D DEADLINE	H HEADLINE	R RENAILED	T DATELINE	LINEATED

adeeilr 130 - leadier

B RIDEABLE	L REALLIED	P PEDALIER	RESAILED	RETAILED
D DEADLIER	M REMAILED	R DERAILER	SIDEREAL	Z REALIZED
DERAILED	REMEDIAL	RERAILED	T DETAILER	
REDIALED	N RENAILED	S REALISED	ELATERID	

adeeils 210 - aediles

B ABSEILED	K LAKESIDE	R REALISED	IDEALESS	
BELADIES	M LIMEADES	RESAILED	T LEADIEST	
H DEISHEAL	N DELAINES	SIDEREAL	V DISLEAVE	
I IDEALISE	P PLEIADES	S DEISEALS	Y EYELIADS	

adeeins 194 - aniseed

G AGENISED	INSEAMED	R ARSENIDE	NEARSIDE
L DELAINES	N ADENINES	DENARIES	S ANISEEDS
M DEMAINES	ANDESINE	DRAISENE	T ANDESITE

adeeirs 112 - readies

B BEARDIES	L REALISED	DENARIES	RERAISED	V READVISE
C DECIARES	RESAILED	DRAISENE	T READIEST	
F FEDARIES	SIDEREAL	NEARSIDE	SERIATED	
G DISAGREE	M MADERISE	P AIRSPEED	SIDERATE	
J JADERIES	N ARSENIDE	R DREARIES	STEADIER	

adeeist 111 - ideates

B BEADIEST	H ATHEISED	M MEDIATES	SIDERATE	V DEVIATES
DIABETES	HEADIEST	N ANDESITE	STEADIER	SEDATIVE
D STEADIED	J JADEITES	R READIEST	S STEADIES	
F SAFETIED	L LEADIEST	SERIATED	U AUDITEES	

adeelnt 250 - latened

B BANDELET	I DATELINE	M LAMENTED	T TALENTED	Y ENTAYLED
C LANCETED	ENTAILED	P ENDPLATE	U UNELATED	
G DANEGELT	LINEATED	R ANTLERED	V LEVANTED	

adeelrt 208 - related

C CLARETED	FALTERED	ELATERID	P PALTERED	TREADLES
DECRETAL	REFLATED	RETAILED	REPLATED	V TRAVELED
TREACLED	H HALTERED	L TELLARED	R TREADLER	
D TREADLED	LATHERED	M TRAMELED	S DESALTER	
F DEFLATER	I DETAILER	N ANTLERED	RESLATED	

adeelst 238 - stealed

A DEALATES	I LEADIEST	R DESALTER	DETASSEL	
D DESALTED	M MEDALETS	RESLATED	TASSELED	
E TEASELED	O DESOLATE	TREADLES	T LADETTES	
F DEFLATES	P PEDESTAL	S DATELESS	Y SEDATELY	

adeenrs 131 - endears

C ASCENDER	GRANDEES	NEARSIDE	N ENSNARED	UNSEARED
REASCEND	GRENADES	K KNEADERS	O REASONED	W ANSWERED
E ENSEARED	I ARSENIDE	M AMENDERS	S DEARNESS	Y YEARENDS
SERENADE	DENARIES	MEANDERS	U UNDERSEA	
G DERANGES	DRAISENE	REAMENDS	UNERASED	

adeerst 107 - dearest

B BETREADS	E RESEATED	I READIEST	K STREAKED	M MASTERED
BREASTED	F DRAFTEES	SERIATED	L DESALTER	STREAMED
DEBATERS	G RESTAGED	SIDERATE	RESLATED	P PEDERAST
C CEDRATES	H HEADREST	STEADIER	TREADLES	PREDATES

Seven-letter stems

	REPASTED	RASTERED	S ASSERTED	RETASTED	Y ESTRAYED
	TRAPESED	RETREADS	ESTRADES	W DEWATERS	
R	ARRESTED	SERRATED	T ASTERTED	TARWEEDS	
	DREAREST	TREADERS	RESTATED	WASTERED	

adegiln 213 - leading

B	BLINDAGE	I GLIADINE	O GALENOID	DEARLING	SIGNALED
C	DECALING	M MALIGNED	P PEDALING	DRAGLINE	T DELATING
F	FINAGLED	MEDALING	PLEADING	S DEALINGS	Y DELAYING
H	HEALDING	N LADENING	R DANGLIER	LEADINGS	

adeginr 34 - reading

A	AREADING	E REGAINED	DRAGLINE	S DERAIGNS	Y DERAYING
	DRAINAGE	H ADHERING	M DREAMING	GRADINES	READYING
	GARDENIA	HEADRING	MARGINED	READINGS	YEARDING
B	BEARDING	I DEAIRING	MIDRANGE	T DERATING	
	BREADING	K DAKERING	N GRANNIED	GRADIENT	
D	DREADING	L DANGLIER	O ORGANDIE	REDATING	
	READDING	DEARLING	R DREARING	TREADING	

adegnor 185 - groaned

B	BONDAGER	F FRONDAGE	J JARGONED	N ANDROGEN	P DOGNAPER
E	RENEGADO	I ORGANDIE	M DRAGOMEN	DRAGONNE	T DRAGONET

adegort 104 - garoted

B	BOGARTED	I ERGATOID	R GARROTED	U OUTRAGED
E	DEROGATE	N DRAGONET	S GOADSTER	RAGOUTED
H	GOATHERD	P PORTAGED	T GAROTTED	W WATERDOG

adeiiint 181 - inedita

C	ACTINIDE	INDICATE	O IDEATION	R DAINTIER	V VANITIED
	CTENIDIA	G IDEATING	IODINATE	S ADENITIS	
	DIACTINE	M MINIATED	TAENIOID	DAINTIES	

adeilns 146 - denials

D	ISLANDED	G DEALINGS	K SANDLIKE	O NODALISE	U UNSAILED
	LANDSIDE	LEADINGS	N ANNELIDS	P SANDPILE	V ANDVILES
E	DELAINES	SIGNALED	LINDANES	R ISLANDER	

adeilor 166 - dariole

F	FORELAID	L ARILLODE	SOLIDARE	T IDOLATER	V OVERLAID
G	DIALOGER	S DARIOLES	SOREDIAL	TAILORED	X EXORDIAL

adeilos 134 - isolead

C	COALISED	MELODIAS	OPALISED	SOLIDARE	DEASOILS
G	GOLIASED	N NODALISE	SEPALOID	SOREDIAL	ISOLEADS
M	DAMOISEL	P EPISODAL	R DARIOLES	S ASSOILED	T DIASTOLE

| ISOLATED | SOLIDATE | Z DIAZOLES |
| SODALITE | U DOULEIAS | SLEAZOID |

adeilrs 52 - derails

A SALARIED	RADICLES	I LAIRISED	SOLIDARE	SPIRALED
B BEDRAILS	D DIEDRALS	L DALLIERS	SOREDIAL	T DILATERS
DISABLER	E REALISED	DIALLERS	P LIPREADS	LARDIEST
RAILBEDS	RESAILED	M DISMALER	PARSLIED	REDTAILS
C DECRIALS	SIDEREAL	N ISLANDER	PEDRAILS	U RESIDUAL
RADICELS	G SLAIRGED	O DARIOLES	PREDIALS	Y DIALYSER

adeilrt 48 - trailed

A LARIATED	E DETAILER	O IDOLATER	S DILATERS	Y DIELYTRA
B LIBRATED	ELATERID	TAILORED	LARDIEST
C ARTICLED	RETAILED	P DIPTERAL	REDTAILS
LACERTID	L TRIALLED	TRIPEDAL	T DETRITAL

adeilst 126 - dilates

B BALDIEST	G GLADIEST	O DIASTOLE	P TALIPEDS	V VALIDEST
C CITADELS	I IDEALIST	ISOLATED	R DILATERS	Y DIASTYLE
DIALECTS	M MEDALIST	SODALITE	LARDIEST	STEADILY
E LEADIEST	MISDEALT	SOLIDATE	REDTAILS

adeimno 234 - domaine

C COMEDIAN	L MELANOID	R RADIOMEN	NOMADIES	U EUDAIMON
DAEMONIC	N DEMONIAN	S AMIDONES	NOMADISE	Z NOMADIZE
DEMONIAC	MONDAINE	DAIMONES	T DOMINATE
G AMIDOGEN	P DOPAMINE	DOMAINES	NEMATOID

adeimnr 168 - inarmed

A MARINADE	G DREAMING	I MERIDIAN	S ADERMINS	Y DAIRYMEN
B BRIDEMAN	MARGINED	O RADIOMEN	SIRNAMED	Z ZEMINDAR
E REMAINED	MIDRANGE	R MANRIDER	U MURAENID

adeinor 26 - aneroid

B DEBONAIR	M RADIOMEN	S ANEROIDS	DERATION	U DOUANIER
D ORDAINED	R ORDAINER	DONARIES	ORDINATE
G ORGANDIE	REORDAIN	T AROINTED	RATIONED

adeinos 51 - sodaine

B BEDSONIA	ANODISED	DAIMONES	S ADENOSIS	Z ADONIZES
C CODEINAS	G AGONISED	DOMAINES	ADONISES	ANODIZES
DIOCESAN	DIAGNOSE	NOMADIES	ANODISES
OCEANIDS	H ADHESION	NOMADISE	T ASTONIED
D ADENOIDS	L NODALISE	R ANEROIDS	SEDATION
ADONISED	M AMIDONES	DONARIES	X DIOXANES

Seven-letter stems

adeinpt 247 - painted

A PATINAED	PENTADIC	L PANTILED	O ANTIPODE	S DEPAINTS
C PEDANTIC	E DIAPENTE	N PINNATED	R DIPTERAN	

adeinrs 8 - sardine

A ARANEIDS	NEARSIDE	M ADERMINS	SERRANID	UNRAISED
B BRANDIES	F FRIANDES	SIRNAMED	S ARIDNESS	URANIDES
BRANDISE	G DERAIGNS	N INSNARED	SARDINES	V INVADERS
D SARDINED	GRADINES	O ANEROIDS	T DETRAINS	SANDIVER
E ARSENIDE	READINGS	DONARIES	RANDIEST	Y SYNEDRIA
DENARIES	I DRAISINE	P SPRAINED	STRAINED	
DRAISENE	L ISLANDER	R DRAINERS	U DENARIUS	

adeinrt 7 - trained

A DENTARIA	RETAINED	I DAINTIER	S DETRAINS	RUINATED
RAINDATE	G DERATING	O AROINTED	RANDIEST	URINATED
C CRINATED	GRADIENT	DERATION	STRAINED	
DICENTRA	REDATING	ORDINATE	T NITRATED	
D INDARTED	TREADING	RATIONED	U DATURINE	
E DETAINER	H ANTHERID	P DIPTERAN	INDURATE	

adeinru 95 - unaired

F UNFAIRED	M MURAENID	UNREPAID	URANIDES	RUINATED
H UNHAIRED	O DOUANIER	S DENARIUS	T DATURINE	URINATED
I UREDINIA	P UNPAIRED	UNRAISED	INDURATE	V UNVARIED

adeinst 19 - stained

B BANDIEST	G SEDATING	M MEDIANTS	R DETRAINS	T INSTATED
C DANCIEST	STEADING	TIDESMAN	RANDIEST	U AUDIENTS
DISTANCE	H HANDIEST	O ASTONIED	STRAINED	SINUATED
D DANDIEST	I ADENITIS	SEDATION	S DESTAINS	V DEVIANTS
E ANDESITE	DAINTIES	P DEPAINTS	SANDIEST	Y DESYATIN

adeintu 246 - audient

B UNBAITED	N ANTIDUNE	R DATURINE	URINATED	
C INCUDATE	INUNDATE	INDURATE	S AUDIENTS	
L UNTAILED	Q ANTIQUED	RUINATED	SINUATED	

adeiors 91 - roadies

C IDOCRASE	F FORESAID	SOREDIAL	P DIASPORE	V AVODIRES
D ROADSIDE	L DARIOLES	N ANEROIDS	PARODIES	AVOIDERS
SIDEROAD	SOLIDARE	DONARIES	T ASTEROID	

adeiost 116 - toadies

G GODETIAS	SODALITE	N ASTONIED	R ASTEROID	
L DIASTOLE	SOLIDATE	SEDATION	X OXIDATES	
ISOLATED	M ATOMISED	P DIOPTASE	Z AZOTISED	

adeiprs 217 - praised

A PARADISE	H RAPHIDES	SPIRALED	R DRAPIERS	TRAIPSED
C EPACRIDS	I PRESIDIA	N SPRAINED	S DESPAIRS	U UPRAISED
PERACRIDS	L LIPREADS	O DIASPORE	T DIPTERAS	W RIPSAWED
D DISPREAD	PARSLIED	PARODIES	RAPIDEST	
E AIRSPEED	PEDRAILS	P APPRISED	SPIRATED	
G SPAIRGED	PREDIALS	DRAPPIES	TARSIPED	

adeirst 14 - tirades

A AIRDATES	D DISRATED	L DILATERS	O ASTEROID	DISRATES
DATARIES	E READIEST	LARDIEST	P DIPTERAS	T STRAITED
RADIATES	SERIATED	REDTAILS	RAPIDEST	STRIATED
B BARDIEST	SIDERATE	M MARDIEST	SPIRATED	TARDIEST
BRAIDEST	STEADIER	MISRATED	TARSIPED	W TAWDRIES
RABIDEST	H HAIRSTED	READMITS	TRAIPSED	
REDBAITS	HARDIEST	N DETRAINS	S ASTERIDS	
TRIBADES	I IRISATED	RANDIEST	DIASTERS	
C ACRIDEST	K STRAIKED	STRAINED	DISASTER	

adeirtt 211 - attired

C CITRATED	E ITERATED	N NITRATED	STRIATED	TITRATED
TETRACID	L DETRITAL	O TERATOID	TARDIEST	
TETRADIC	M ADMITTER	S STRAITED	T ATTRITED	

adelnor 207 - ladrone

B BANDEROL	E OLEANDER	P PONDERAL	U UNLOADER	RONDAVEL
C COLANDER	RELOANED	S LADRONES	URODELAN	
CONELRAD	F FORELAND	SOLANDER	V OVERLAND	

adenort 32 - tornade

C CARTONED	I AROINTED	RATIONED	P PRONATED	W DANEWORT
NOTECARD	DERATION	N NONRATED	S TORNADES	TEARDOWN
G DRAGONET	ORDINATE	O RATOONED	T ATTORNED	Y AROYNTED

adenost 97 - donates

C ENDOCAST	E ENDOSTEA	SEDATION	P NOTEPADS	R TORNADES
TACNODES	I ASTONIED	O ODONATES	TONEPADS	S ONSTEADS

adenrst 190 - stander

B BANDSTER	STRANDED	RANDIEST	S STANDERS	X DEXTRANS
BARTENDS	G DRAGNETS	STRAINED	U DAUNTERS	
C CANTREDS	GRANDEST	O TORNADES	TRANSUDE	
D DARNDEST	I DETRAINS	R STRANDER	UNTREADS	

adenrtu 103 - unrated

B BREADNUT	UNCRATED	D DRAUNTED	UNDERATE	I DATURINE
TURBANED	UNDERACT	UNTRADED	UNDEREAT	INDURATE
C UNCARTED	UNTRACED	E DENATURE	H UNTHREAD	RUINATED

Seven-letter stems

URINATED	P DEPURANT	S DAUNTERS	T TRUANTED	
L DENTURAL	UNPARTED	TRANSUDE	X UNDERTAX	
M UNDREAMT	R UNTARRED	UNTREADS		

adeorst 77 - roasted

B BROADEST	L DELATORS	N TORNADES	READOPTS	U OUTDARES
C REDCOATS	LEOTARDS	P ADOPTERS	R ROADSTER	OUTREADS
G GOADSTER	LODESTAR	ASPORTED	S ASSORTED	READOUTS
I ASTEROID	M STROAMED	PASTORED	TORSADES	X EXTRADOS

adinors 98 - inroads

B INBOARDS	E ANEROIDS	N ANDIRONS	T DIATRONS
C SARDONIC	DONARIES	P PONIARDS	INTRADOS
D ANDROIDS	G ROADINGS	R ORDINARS	U DINOSAUR
DISADORN	L ORDINALS	S SADIRONS	V VIRANDOS

adinort 55 - diatron

A ANTIDORA	DERATION	L TRINODAL	S DIATRONS
C TORNADIC	ORDINATE	N ORDINANT	INTRADOS
E AROINTED	RATIONED	O TANDOORI	U DURATION

adinrst 195 - indarts

A INTRADAS	E DETRAINS	F INDRAFTS	K STINKARD	R TRIDARNS
RADIANTS	RANDIEST	G TRADINGS	O DIATRONS	U UNITARDS
B ANTBIRDS	STRAINED	I DISTRAIN	INTRADOS	

adiorst 118 - astroid

C CAROTIDS	I TARSIOID	INTRADOS	S ASTROIDS	U AUDITORS
E ASTEROID	L DILATORS	P PARODIST	SARODIST	
G GORDITAS	N DIATRONS	PAROTIDS	T STRADIOT	

aeeginr 64 - reginae

B BAREGINE	G AGREEING	M GERMAINE	S ANERGIES	INTERAGE
BERGENIA	I AEGIRINE	P PERIGEAN	GESNERIA	Z RAZEEING
D REGAINED	L ALGERINE	R REGAINER	T GRATINEE	

aeegins 178 - agenise

A AGENESIA	L ENSILAGE	GESNERIA	ASSIGNEE	V ENVISAGE
C AGENCIES	LINEAGES	S AGENESIS	T SAGENITE	Z AGENIZES
D AGENISED	R ANERGIES	AGENISES	U EUGENIAS	

aeegnrt 99 - reagent

A TAGAREEN	RENEGATE	I GRATINEE	L REGENTAL	N GENERANT
E GENERATE	TEENAGER	INTERAGE	M AGREMENT	R ETRANGER

S ESTRANGE	GREATENS	REAGENTS	SERGEANT	U GAUNTREE
GRANTEES	NEGATERS	SEGREANT	STERNAGE	

aeeilnr 73 - aliener

C CARELINE	D RENAILED	P PERINEAL	T ELATERIN
CINEREAL	F FLANERIE	R NEARLIER	ENTAILER
RELIANCE	G ALGERINE	S ALIENERS	TREENAIL

aeeilns 74 - sealine

B BASELINE	E ALIENEES	M MELANISE	PENALISE	S SEALINES
C SALIENCE	G ENSILAGE	N SELENIAN	SEPALINE	V VASELINE
D DELAINES	LINEAGES	P ALEPINES	R ALIENERS	X ALEXINES

aeeilnt 63 - lineate

A ALIENATE	G GALENITE	M MELANITE	ENTAILER	
D DATELINE	GELATINE	P PETALINE	TREENAIL	
ENTAILED	LEGATINE	TAPELINE	V ELVANITE	
LINEATED	L TENAILLE	R ELATERIN	VENTAILE	

aeeilrs 61 - realise

C ESCALIER	SERAFILE	MEASLIER	S REALISES	REALTIES
D REALISED	G GASELIER	N ALIENERS	T ATELIERS	V VELARISE
RESAILED	H SHIRALEE	P ESPALIER	EARLIEST	Y YEARLIES
SIDEREAL	L REALLIES	PEARLIES	LATERISE	Z REALIZES
F FILAREES	M ALMERIES	R REALISER	LEARIEST	SLEAZIER

aeeilrt 17 - atelier

B LIBERATE	H ETHERIAL	ENTAILER	EARLIEST	V LEVIRATE
D DETAILER	L LAETRILE	TREENAIL	LATERISE	RELATIVE
ELATERID	M EREMITAL	O AEROLITE	LEARIEST	Z LATERIZE
RETAILED	MATERIEL	P PEARLITE	REALTIES	
F FEATLIER	REALTIME	R RETAILER	T LATERITE	
FRAILTEE	N ELATERIN	S ATELIERS	LITERATE	

aeeimrt 137 - meatier

B AMBERITE	E EMERITAE	L EREMITAL	S EMERITAS	V VIAMETER
C CEMITARE	G EMIGRATE	MATERIEL	EMIRATES	
D DIAMETER	REMIGATE	REALTIME	REAMIEST	
REMEDIAT	I METAIRIE	N ANTIMERE	STEAMIER	

aeeinrt 10 - trainee

C CENTIARE	RETAINED	I INERTIAE	TREENAIL	ARSENITE
CREATINE	G GRATINEE	K ANKERITE	M ANTIMERE	RESINATE
INCREATE	INTERAGE	KREATINE	P APERIENT	STEARINE
ITERANCE	H ATHERINE	L ELATERIN	R RETAINER	TRAINEES
D DETAINER	HERNIATE	ENTAILER	S ARENITES	

Seven-letter stems

aeeinst 66 - etesian

B BETAINES	M ETAMINES	R ARENITES	TRAINEES	TETANIES
C CINEASTE	MATINEES	ARSENITE	S ETESIANS	TETANISE
D ANDESITE	MISEATEN	RESINATE	TENIASES	V NAIVETES
G SAGENITE	SEMINATE	STEARINE	T ANISETTE	

aeeirst 9 - seriate

D READIEST	LATERISE	ARSENITE	REASTIER	W SWEATIER
SERIATED	LEARIEST	RESINATE	S SERIATES	TAWERIES
SIDERATE	REALTIES	STEARINE	T ARIETTES	WASTERIE
STEADIER	M EMERITAS	TRAINEES	ITERATES	WEARIEST
E EATERIES	EMIRATES	O ETAERIOS	TEARIEST	Y YEASTIER
H HEARTIES	REAMIEST	P PARIETES	TREATIES	
L ATELIERS	STEAMIER	PETARIES	TREATISE	
EARLIEST	N ARENITES	R ARTERIES	V EVIRATES	

aeelnrt 50 - eternal

B RENTABLE	H LEATHERN	M LAMENTER	ETERNALS	W TREELAWN
D ANTLERED	I ELATERIN	N LANNERET	TELERANS	X EXTERNAL
E LATEENER	ENTAILER	R RELEARNT	V LEVANTER	
G REGENTAL	TREENAIL	S ALTERNES	RELEVANT	

aeelrst 47 - stealer

A LAETARES	D DESALTER	LATERISE	PLEATERS	TESSERAL
B ARBELEST	RESLATED	LEARIEST	PRELATES	T ALERTEST
BLEAREST	TREADLES	REALTIES	REPLATES	U RESALUTE
BLEATERS	E TEASELER	M LAMETERS	R ALTERERS	X EXALTERS
RESTABLE	F REFLATES	N ALTERNES	REALTERS	Y EASTERLY
RETABLES	H HALTERES	ETERNALS	RELATERS	
C CLEAREST	LEATHERS	TELERANS	S RESLATES	
SCELERAT	I ATELIERS	O OLEASTER	STEALERS	
TREACLES	EARLIEST	P PETRALES	TEARLESS	

aeenors 184 - arenose

B SEABORNE	P PERAEONS	R REASONER	SEASONER	RESONATE
D REASONED	PERSONAE	S RESEASON	T EARSTONE	

aeenrst 18 - eastern

A ARSENATE	F FASTENER	SERGEANT	J SERJEANT	EARNESTS
SERENATA	FENESTRA	STERNAGE	L ALTERNES	SARSENET
B ABSENTER	REFASTEN	H HASTENER	ETERNALS	T ENTREATS
C CENTARES	G ESTRANGE	HEARTENS	TELERANS	RATTEENS
ENCASTRE	GRANTEES	I ARENITES	M REMANETS	U SAUTERNE
REASCENT	GREATENS	ARSENITE	O EARSTONE	V AVENTRES
REENACTS	NEGATERS	RESINATE	RESONATE	VETERANS
SARCENET	REAGENTS	STEARINE	R TERRANES	
E SERENATE	SEGREANT	TRAINEES	S ASSENTER	

aeenrtt 240 - entreat

A ANTEATER	RATTENED	THREATEN	RATTEENS	Y ENTREATY
B BATTENER	E ENTERATE	R NATTERER	V ANTEVERT	
D ATTENDER	F FATTENER	RATTENER	X EXTERNAT	
NATTERED	H HATERENT	S ENTREATS	EXTRANET	

aeeorst 89 - roseate

B ABORTEES	I ETAERIOS	L OLEASTER	RESONATE	V OVEREATS
REBATOES	K KERATOSE	M EROTEMAS	P OPERATES	
C CREASOTE	KREASOTE	N EARSTONE	PROTEASE	

aeerrst 212 - tearers

B REBATERS	RASTERED	K RETAKERS	R ARRESTER	U AUSTERER
TABRERES	RETREADS	STREAKER	REARREST	TREASURE
TEREBRAS	SERRATED	L ALTERERS	S ASSERTER	V AVERTERS
C CATERERS	TREADERS	REALTERS	REASSERT	TRAVERSE
RECRATES	E ARRESTEE	RELATERS	SERRATES	W WATERERS
RETRACES	F FERRATES	M REMASTER	TERRASES	
TERRACES	G REGRATES	STREAMER	T RETRATES	
D ARRESTED	I ARTERIES	N TERRANES	RETREATS	
DREAREST	REASTIER	P TAPERERS	TREATERS	

aegilnr 21 - realign

A GERANIAL	G GANGLIER	MALINGER	REALIGNS	TERAGLIN
REGALIAN	LAGERING	N LEARNING	SALERING	TRIANGLE
B BLEARING	REGALING	O GERANIOL	SANGLIER	V RAVELING
C CLEARING	H NARGHILE	REGIONAL	SIGNALER	X RELAXING
RELACING	NARGILEH	P GRAPLINE	SLANGIER	Y LAYERING
D DANGLIER	I GAINLIER	PEARLING	T ALERTING	RELAYING
DEARLING	J JANGLIER	R GNARLIER	ALTERING	YEARLING
DRAGLINE	L ALLERGIN	S ALIGNERS	INTEGRAL	
E ALGERINE	M GERMINAL	ENGRAILS	RELATING	
F FINAGLER	MALIGNER	NARGILES	TANGLIER	

aegilns 119 - sealing

B SIGNABLE	H HEALINGS	LEANINGS	SANGLIER	GENITALS
SINGABLE	LEASHING	O GASOLINE	SIGNALER	STEALING
D DEALINGS	SHEALING	P ELAPSING	SLANGIER	TAGLINES
LEADINGS	K LINKAGES	PLEASING	S GAINLESS	V LEAVINGS
SIGNALED	SNAGLIKE	R ALIGNERS	GLASSINE	SLEAVING
E ENSILAGE	L GALLEINS	ENGRAILS	LEASINGS	W SWEALING
LINEAGES	NIGELLAS	NARGILES	SEALINGS	Y YEALINGS
F FINAGLES	M MEASLING	REALIGNS	T EASTLING	
G LIGNAGES	N EANLINGS	SALERING	GELATINS	

aegilnt 46 - gelatin

A AGENTIAL	BLEATING	D DELATING	LEGATINE	TEAGLING
ALGINATE	TANGIBLE	E GALENITE	G GELATING	H ATHELING
B BELATING	C CLEATING	GELATINE	LEGATING	K GNATLIKE

M LIGAMENT	O GELATION	INTEGRAL	S EASTLING	V VALETING
METALING	LEGATION	RELATING	GELATINS	X EXALTING
TEGMINAL	P PLEATING	TANGLIER	GENITALS	Z TEAZLING
N GANTLINE	R ALERTING	TERAGLIN	STEALING	
LATENING	ALTERING	TRIANGLE	TAGLINES	

aegilrs 177 - grailes

A GASALIER	E GASELIER	ENGRAILS	SLANGIER	REGALIST
LAIRAGES	G SLAGGIER	NARGILES	O GASOLIER	Y GREASILY
REGALIAS	M GREMIALS	REALIGNS	GIRASOLE	Z GLAZIERS
C GLACIERS	LAMIGERS	SALERING	SERAGLIO	
GRACILES	REGALISM	SANGLIER	S GLASSIER	
D SLAIRGED	N ALIGNERS	SIGNALER	T GLARIEST	

aeginor 147 - origane

| B ABORIGEN | L GERANIOL | R ORANGIER | ORGANISE | Z ORGANIZE |
| D ORGANDIE | REGIONAL | S IGNAROES | ORIGANES | |

aeginos 155 - agonies

B BEGONIAS	DIAGNOSE	N ANGINOSE	ORGANISE	Z AGONIZES
C COINAGES	G SEAGOING	GANOINES	ORIGANES	
D AGONISED	L GASOLINE	R IGNAROES	S AGONISES	

aeginrs 31 - searing

A ANERGIAS	G GEARINGS	SIGNALER	R EARRINGS	RANGIEST
ANGARIES	GREASING	SLANGIER	GRAINERS	REASTING
ARGINASE	SNAGGIER	M GERMAINS	S ASSIGNER	STEARING
B BEARINGS	H HEARINGS	SMEARING	REASSIGN	TASERING
SABERING	HEARSING	N AGINNERS	SEARINGS	V VINEGARS
C CREASING	SHEARING	EARNINGS	SERINGAS	W RESAWING
GRECIANS	K SKEARING	ENGRAINS	T ANGRIEST	SWEARING
SEARCING	L ALIGNERS	GRANNIES	ANGSTIER	WEARINGS
D DERAIGNS	ENGRAILS	O IGNAROES	ASTRINGE	Y RESAYING
GRADINES	NARGILES	ORGANISE	GANISTER	SYNERGIA
READINGS	REALIGNS	ORIGANES	GANTRIES	
E ANERGIES	SALERING	P PREASING	GRANITES	
GESNERIA	SANGLIER	SPEARING	INGRATES	

aeginrt 25 - tearing

A AERATING	REDATING	RELATING	GANISTER	V AVERTING
B BERATING	TREADING	TANGLIER	GANTRIES	GRIEVANT
REBATING	E GRATINEE	TERAGLIN	GRANITES	TAVERING
TABERING	INTERAGE	TRIANGLE	INGRATES	VINTAGER
C ARGENTIC	H EARTHING	M EMIGRANT	RANGIEST	W TWANGIER
CATERING	HEARTING	REMATING	REASTING	WATERING
CITRANGE	INGATHER	P RETAPING	STEARING	X RETAXING
CREATING	K RETAKING	TAPERING	TASERING	
REACTING	L ALERTING	S ANGRIEST	T ARETTING	
D DERATING	ALTERING	ANGSTIER	GNATTIER	
GRADIENT	INTEGRAL	ASTRINGE	TREATING	

aeginst 39 - seating

A SAGINATE	GELATINS	GENTIANS	REASTING	TANGIEST
B BEATINGS	GENITALS	STEANING	STEARING	U SAUTEING
D SEDATING	STEALING	R ANGRIEST	TASERING	UNITAGES
STEADING	TAGLINES	ANGSTIER	S EASTINGS	V VINTAGES
E SAGENITE	M MANGIEST	ASTRINGE	GENISTAS	W SWEATING
F FEASTING	MINTAGES	GANISTER	GIANTESS	Y YEASTING
G NAGGIEST	MISAGENT	GANTRIES	SEATINGS	Z TZIGANES
H GAHNITES	STEAMING	GRANITES	TEASINGS	
HEATINGS	TEAMINGS	INGRATES	TSIGANES	
L EASTLING	N ANTIGENS	RANGIEST	T ESTATING	

aegnors 245 - oranges

B BEGROANS	ORGANISE	O OREGANOS	ORANGEST
C ACROGENS	ORIGANES	R GROANERS	RAGSTONE
CORNAGES	K KARENGOS	T ESTRAGON	STONERAG
I IGNAROES	M MEGARONS	NEGATORS	W WAGONERS

aegnort 202 - negator

D DRAGONET	S ESTRAGON	RAGSTONE	U OUTRANGE
F FRONTAGE	NEGATORS	STONERAG	Y NEGATORY
N NEGATRON	ORANGEST	T TETRAGON	

aegnrst 110 - strange

A STARAGEN	REAGENTS	GANISTER	TANGLERS	STONERAG
TANAGERS	SEGREANT	GANTRIES	TRANGLES	P TREPANGS
B BANGSTER	SERGEANT	GRANITES	M GARMENTS	R GRANTERS
D DRAGNETS	STERNAGE	INGRATES	MARGENTS	REGRANTS
GRANDEST	F ENGRAFTS	RANGIEST	RAGMENTS	STRANGER
E ESTRANGE	G GANGSTER	REASTING	O ESTRAGON	S STRANGES
GRANTEES	I ANGRIEST	STEARING	NEGATORS	U STRAUNGE
GREATENS	ANGSTIER	TASERING	ORANGEST	W TWANGERS
NEGATERS	ASTRINGE	L STRANGLE	RAGSTONE	

aegorst 140 - toerags

C ESCARGOT	L GLOATERS	ORANGEST	P PORTAGES	T GAROTTES
D GOADSTER	LEGATORS	RAGSTONE	POTAGERS	U OUTRAGES
F FAGOTERS	N ESTRAGON	STONERAG	R GARROTES	
H SHORTAGE	NEGATORS	O ROOTAGES	S STORAGES	

aehinrt 161 - hairnet

D ANTHERID	G EARTHING	O ANTIHERO	INEARTHS	W TARWHINE
E ATHERINE	HEARTING	P PERIANTH	THERIANS	
HERNIATE	INGATHER	S HAIRNETS	U HAURIENT	

aehirst 115 - hastier

A HETAIRAS	D HAIRSTED	I HAIRIEST	O HOARIEST	U THESAURI
C CHARIEST	HARDIEST	N HAIRNETS	P TRIPHASE	W SWATHIER
STICHERA	E HEARTIES	INEARTHS	R TRASHIER	WATERISH
THERIACS	F FAITHERS	THERIANS	S SHERIATS	Y HYSTERIA

Seven-letter stems

aeiilnr 244 - airline

B BILINEAR	G GAINLIER	R AIRLINER	SNAILIER
C IRENICAL	H HAIRLINE	S AIRLINES	T INERTIAL

aeiinrs 157 - senarii

B BINARIES	K KAISERIN	N SIRENIAN	RAINIEST
C RIANCIES	L AIRLINES	S AIRINESS	Y YERSINIA
D DRAISINE	SNAILIER	T INERTIAS	

aeiinrt 35 - inertia

C ARENITIC	E INERTIAE	L INERTIAL	P PAINTIER	RAINIEST
D DAINTIER	F FAINTIER	N TRIENNIA	S INERTIAS	Z TRIAZINE

aeiinst 124 - isatine

B BAINITES	F FAINITES	M MINIATES	S ISATINES	X AXINITES
C ANTICISE	K KAINITES	P PATINISE	SANITIES	Z SANITIZE
CANITIES	L ALIENIST	PIANISTE	SANITISE	
D ADENITIS	LATINISE	R INERTIAS	TENIASIS	
DAINTIES	LITANIES	RAINIEST	V VANITIES	

aeiirst 94 - airiest

D IRISATED	LISTERIA	RAINIEST	SATIRISE	Z SATIRIZE
F RATIFIES	M AIRTIMES	P PARITIES	V VAIRIEST	
H HAIRIEST	SERIATIM	R RARITIES	W WISTERIA	
L LAIRIEST	N INERTIAS	S IRISATES	X SEXTARII	

aeilnor 44 - aileron

C ACROLEIN	F FORELAIN	P PELORIAN	T ORIENTAL
COLINEAR	G GERANIOL	S AILERONS	RELATION
CREOLIAN	REGIONAL	ALERIONS	TAILERON
LONICERA	L ALLERION	ALIENORS	V OVERLAIN

aeilnos 58 - anisole

D NODALISE	MINEOLAS	R AILERONS	T ELATIONS
G GASOLINE	SEMOLINA	ALERIONS	INSOLATE
K KAOLINES	N SOLANINE	ALIENORS	TOENAILS
M LAMINOSE	P OPALINES	S ANISOLES	X SILOXANE

aeilnot 29 - toenail

B TAILBONE	G GELATION	R ORIENTAL	S ELATIONS	T TONALITE
D DELATION	LEGATION	RELATION	INSOLATE	
F OLEFIANT	P ANTIPOLE	TAILERON	TOENAILS	

aeilnpt 167 - pantile

A PALATINE	C PECTINAL	D PANTILED	TAPELINE	O ANTIPOLE
B PINTABLE	PLANETIC	E PETALINE	G PLEATING	P PIEPLANT

R INTERLAP	TRIPLANE	PANTILES	T TINPLATE	
TRAPLINE	S PANELIST	PLAINEST	Y PENALITY	

aeilnrs 15 - renails

B RINSABLE	REALIGNS	M MARLINES	R SNARLIER	TRENAILS
C CARLINES	SALERING	MINERALS	S RAINLESS	U LUNARIES
LANCIERS	SANGLIER	MISLEARN	T ENTRAILS	V RAVELINS
D ISLANDER	SIGNALER	O AILERONS	LARNIEST	X RELAXINS
E ALIENERS	SLANGIER	ALERIONS	LATRINES	Y INLAYERS
G ALIGNERS	H INHALERS	ALIENORS	RATLINES	SNAILERY
ENGRAILS	I AIRLINES	P PEARLINS	REINSTAL	
NARGILES	SNAILIER	PRALINES	RETINALS	

aeilnrt 6 - reliant

C CLARINET	INTEGRAL	TRAMLINE	TRIPLANE	TRENAILS
E ELATERIN	RELATING	N INTERNAL	S ENTRAILS	T RATTLINE
ENTAILER	TANGLIER	O ORIENTAL	LARNIEST	U AUNTLIER
TREENAIL	TERAGLIN	RELATION	LATRINES	RETINULA
F INFLATER	TRIANGLE	TAILERON	RATLINES	TENURIAL
G ALERTING	I INERTIAL	P INTERLAP	REINSTAL	V INTERVAL
ALTERING	M TERMINAL	TRAPLINE	RETINALS	Y INTERLAY

aeilnst 49 - salient

B INSTABLE	I ALIENIST	SMALTINE	LARNIEST	NAILSETS
C CANISTEL	LATINISE	O ELATIONS	LATRINES	SALIENTS
F INFLATES	LITANIES	INSOLATE	RATLINES	SALTINES
G EASTLING	K LANKIEST	TOENAILS	REINSTAL	STANIELS
GELATINS	M AILMENTS	P PANELIST	RETINALS	U ALUNITES
GENITALS	ALIMENTS	PANTILES	TRENAILS	INSULATE
STEALING	MANLIEST	PLAINEST	S EASTLINS	V VENTAILS
TAGLINES	MELANIST	R ENTRAILS	ELASTINS	W LAWNIEST

aeilost 38 - isolate

C ALOETICS	ISOLATED	G LATIGOES	N ELATIONS	R SOTERIAL
COALIEST	SODALITE	OTALGIES	INSOLATE	S ISOLATES
SOCIETAL	SOLIDATE	K KEITLOAS	TOENAILS	T TOTALISE
D DIASTOLE	F FOLIATES	M LOAMIEST	P SPOLIATE	V VIOLATES

aeilprt 142 - platier

A PARIETAL	TRIPEDAL	N INTERLAP	R PALTRIER	V LIVETRAP
B PARTIBLE	E PEARLITE	TRAPLINE	PRETRIAL	
C PARTICLE	I LIPARITE	TRIPLANE	S PILASTER	
PRELATIC	REPTILIA	O EPILATOR	PLAISTER	
D DIPTERAL	K TRAPLIKE	PETIOLAR	PLAITERS	

aeilrrt 160 - trailer

A ARTERIAL	O RETAILOR	S RETIRALS	T RATTLIER
C CLARTIER	P PALTRIER	RETRIALS	U RURALITE
E RETAILER	PRETRIAL	TRAILERS	Y LITERARY

Seven-letter stems

aeilrst 12 - realist

B BLASTIER	E ATELIERS	K LARKIEST	N ENTRAILS	R RETIRALS
LIBRATES	EARLIEST	STALKIER	LARNIEST	RETRIALS
TABLIERS	LATERISE	STARLIKE	LATRINES	TRAILERS
C ALTRICES	LEARIEST	L LITERALS	RATLINES	S REALISTS
ARTICLES	REALTIES	TALLIERS	REINSTAL	SALTIERS
RECITALS	F FLARIEST	TRIELLAS	RETINALS	SALTIRES
SELICTAR	FRAILEST	M LAMISTER	TRENAILS	SLAISTER
STERICAL	G GLARIEST	LAMITERS	O SOTERIAL	T TERTIALS
D DILATERS	REGALIST	MARLIEST	P PILASTER	U URALITES
LARDIEST	I LAIRIEST	MARLITES	PLAISTER	
REDTAILS	LISTERIA	MISALTER	PLAITERS	

aeilrtt 88 - tertial

B TITRABLE	E LATERITE	G AGLITTER	N RATTLINE	S TERTIALS
C TRACTILE	LITERATE	I LITERATI	O LITERATO	Y ALTERITY
D DETRITAL	F FILTRATE	M REMITTAL	R RATTLIER	

aeilrtu 156 - uralite

C RETICULA	G LIGATURE	RETINULA	REQUITAL	V VAULTIER
F FAULTIER	L TAILLEUR	TENURIAL	R RURALITE	Z LAZURITE
FILATURE	N AUNTLIER	Q QUARTILE	S URALITES	

aeimnot 182 - amniote

A METANOIA	NEMATOID	NOMINATE	MASONITE	Z MONAZITE
C COINMATE	M AMMONITE	P PTOMAINE	MISATONE	
D DOMINATE	N ANTINOME	S AMNIOTES	SOMNIATE	

aeimnrs 135 - seminar

B MIRBANES	G GERMAINS	MINERALS	R MARINERS	U ANEURISM
C CARMINES	SMEARING	MISLEARN	S SEMINARS	Y SEMINARY
CREMAINS	H HARMINES	N REINSMAN	SIRNAMES	
D ADERMINS	SHIREMAN	O MORAINES	T MERANTIS	
SIRNAMED	K RAMEKINS	ROMAINES	MINARETS	
E REMANIES	L MARLINES	ROMANISE	RAIMENTS	

aeimnrt 93 - raiment

A ANIMATER	REMATING	S MERANTIS	MARTINET	
MARINATE	L TERMINAL	MINARETS	U RUMINATE	
E ANTIMERE	TRAMLINE	RAIMENTS	W WARIMENT	
G EMIGRANT	N TRAINMEN	T INTERMAT	Y TYRAMINE	

aeimnst 106 - inmates

A AMENTIAS	SEMANTIC	MATINEES	G MANGIEST	TEAMINGS
ANIMATES	D MEDIANTS	MISEATEN	MINTAGES	H HEMATINS
B AMBIENTS	TIDESMAN	SEMINATE	MISAGENT	I MINIATES
C AMNESTIC	E ETAMINES	F MANIFEST	STEAMING	K MANKIEST

	MISTAKEN		MELANIST		MASONITE		MINARETS
L	AILMENTS		SMALTINE		MISATONE		RAIMENTS
	ALIMENTS	N	MANNITES		SOMNIATE	S	MANTISES
	MANLIEST	O	AMNIOTES	R	MERANTIS		MATINESS

aeimrst 68 - smartie

A	AMIRATES		EMIRATES		SITKAMER		MINARETS		SMARTIES
B	BARMIEST		REAMIEST	L	LAMISTER		RAIMENTS	T	MISTREAT
C	CERAMIST		STEAMIER		LAMITERS	O	AMORTISE		TERATISM
	MATRICES	G	MAGISTER		MARLIEST		ATOMISER	U	MURIATES
	MISTRACE		MIGRATES		MARLITES	P	APTERISM		SEMITAUR
	SCIMETAR		RAGTIMES		MISALTER		PRIMATES	V	VITAMERS
D	MARDIEST		STERIGMA	M	MARMITES	S	ASTERISM	W	WARTIMES
	MISRATED	I	AIRTIMES		RAMMIEST		MAISTERS	X	MATRIXES
	READMITS		SERIATIM		TRAMMIES		MISRATES	Y	SYMITARE
E	EMERITAS	K	MISTAKER	N	MERANTIS		SEMITARS		

aeinnot 100 - enation

C	ENACTION	G	NEGATION	R	ANOINTER	S	ENATIONS	V	INNOVATE
D	ANOINTED	M	ANTINOME		INORNATE		SONATINE		VENATION
	ANTINODE		NOMINATE		REANOINT	T	INTONATE		

aeinnrs 82 - insnare

C	CRANNIES	G	AGINNERS	I	SIRENIAN	R	INSNARER	U	ANEURINS
	NARCEINS		EARNINGS	M	REINSMAN	S	INSNARES		UNARISEN
D	INSNARED		ENGRAINS	O	RAISONNE	T	ENTRAINS	W	SWANNIER
E	ANSERINE		GRANNIES	P	PANNIERS		TRANNIES		

aeinnrt 114 - trannie

I	TRIENNIA	M	TRAINMEN		INORNATE	R	INERRANT		TRANNIES
L	INTERNAL	O	ANOINTER		REANOINT	S	ENTRAINS	T	INTRANET

aeinors 13 - erasion

B	BARONIES	F	FARINOSE		ALERIONS	N	RAISONNE		NOTARIES
	SEAROBIN	G	IGNAROES		ALIENORS	S	ERASIONS		NOTARISE
C	SCENARIO		ORGANISE	M	MORAINES		SENSORIA		ROSINATE
D	ANEROIDS		ORIGANES		ROMAINES	T	ANOESTRI		SENORITA
	DONARIES	L	AILERONS		ROMANISE		ARSONITE	V	AVERSION

aeinort 1 - otarine

A	AERATION		ANORETIC		RATIONED		INORNATE		NOTARIES
B	BARITONE		CREATION	H	ANTIHERO		REANOINT		NOTARISE
	OBTAINER		REACTION	L	ORIENTAL	P	ATROPINE		ROSINATE
	REOBTAIN	D	AROINTED		RELATION	R	ANTERIOR		SENORITA
	TABORINE		DERATION		TAILERON	S	ANOESTRI	T	TENTORIA
C	ACTIONER		ORDINATE	N	ANOINTER		ARSONITE	Z	NOTARIZE

aeinost 16 - atonies

B BOTANIES	SONICATE	M AMNIOTES	P SAPONITE	SENORITA
BOTANISE	D ASTONIED	MASONITE	R ANOESTRI	S ASSIENTO
NIOBATES	SEDATION	MISATONE	ARSONITE	ASTONIES
OBEISANT	L ELATIONS	SOMNIATE	NOTARIES	V STOVAINE
C ACONITES	INSOLATE	N ENATIONS	NOTARISE	X SAXONITE
CANOEIST	TOENAILS	SONATINE	ROSINATE	

aeinprs 197 - rapines

A PANARIES	G PREASING	K RANPIKES	T PAINTERS	REPAINTS
D SPRAINED	SPEARING	L PEARLINS	PANTRIES	U UNPRAISE
E NAPERIES	H HEPARINS	PRALINES	PERTAINS	W SPAWNIER
F FIREPANS	PARISHEN	N PANNIERS	PINASTER	
PANFRIES	SERAPHIN	P SNAPPIER	PRISTANE	

aeinprt 40 - repaint

A ANTIRAPE	H PERIANTH	O ATROPINE	PERTAINS	U PAINTURE
D DIPTERAN	I PAINTIER	R PRETRAIN	PINASTER	X EXPIRANT
E APERIENT	L INTERLAP	TERRAPIN	PRISTANE	
G RETAPING	TRAPLINE	S PAINTERS	REPAINTS	
TAPERING	TRIPLANE	PANTRIES	T TRIPTANE	

aeinpst 175 - panties

B BEPAINTS	PIANISTE	N PANTINES	PERTAINS	STEAPSIN
D DEPAINTS	K SNAKEPIT	O SAPONITE	PINASTER	T PATIENTS
H PENTHIAS	L PANELIST	P NAPPIEST	PRISTANE	U PETUNIAS
THESPIAN	PANTILES	R PAINTERS	REPAINTS	SUPINATE
I PATINISE	PLAINEST	PANTRIES	S SAPIENTS	Y EPINASTY

aeinrrs 223 - snarier

D DRAINERS	G EARRINGS	L SNARLIER	RETRAINS	TRANSIRE
SERRANID	GRAINERS	M MARINERS	STRAINER	
E REARISEN	H SHARNIER	N INSNARER	TERRAINS	
F REFRAINS	K SNARKIER	T RESTRAIN	TRAINERS	

aeinrrt 90 - trainer

E RETAINER	P PRETRAIN	RETRAINS	TRAINERS	V VERATRIN
N INERRANT	TERRAPIN	STRAINER	TRANSIRE	W INTERWAR
O ANTERIOR	S RESTRAIN	TERRAINS	T RETIRANT	

aeinrss 242 - sarnies

C ARCSINES	F FAIRNESS	H ARSHINES	SENSORIA	STEARINS
ARSENICS	SANSERIF	I AIRINESS	T ARTINESS	U ANURESIS
CERASINS	SERAFINS	L RAINLESS	RESIANTS	SENARIUS
RACINESS	G ASSIGNER	M SEMINARS	RETSINAS	W WARINESS
D ARIDNESS	REASSIGN	SIRNAMES	SNARIEST	X XERANSIS
SARDINES	SEARINGS	N INSNARES	STAINERS	
E SENARIES	SERINGAS	O ERASIONS	STARNIES	

aeinrst 2 - nastier

A	ANTISERA		STRAINED	H	HAIRNETS		TRANNIES	S	ARTINESS
	ARTESIAN	E	ARENITES		INEARTHS	O	ANOESTRI		RESIANTS
	RATANIES		ARSENITE		THERIANS		ARSONITE		RETSINAS
	RESINATA		RESINATE	I	INERTIAS		NOTARIES		SNARIEST
	SANTERIA		STEARINE		RAINIEST		NOTARISE		STAINERS
	SEATRAIN		TRAINEES	J	NARTJIES		ROSINATE		STARNIES
B	ATEBRINS	F	FAINTERS	K	KERATINS		SENORITA		STEARINS
	BANISTER		FENITARS		NARKIEST	P	PAINTERS	T	INTREATS
	BARNIEST	G	ANGRIEST	L	ENTRAILS		PANTRIES		NITRATES
C	CANISTER		ANGSTIER		LARNIEST		PERTAINS		STRAITEN
	CARNIEST		ASTRINGE		LATRINES		PINASTER		TARTINES
	CERATINS		GANISTER		RATLINES		PRISTANE		TERTIANS
	CISTERNA		GANTRIES		REINSTAL		REPAINTS	U	RUINATES
	CREATINS		GRANITES		RETINALS	R	RESTRAIN		TAURINES
	NACRITES		INGRATES		TRENAILS		RETRAINS		URANITES
	SCANTIER		RANGIEST	M	MERANTIS		STRAINER		URINATES
	TACRINES		REASTING		MINARETS		TERRAINS	W	TINWARES
D	DETRAINS		STEARING		RAIMENTS		TRAINERS		
	RANDIEST		TASERING	N	ENTRAINS		TRANSIRE		

aeinrtt 45 - nitrate

A	ATTAINER	G	ARETTING	M	INTERMAT	P	TRIPTANE		STRAITEN
	REATTAIN		GNATTIER		MARTINET	R	RETIRANT		TARTINES
C	INTERACT		TREATING	N	INTRANET	S	INTREATS		TERTIANS
D	NITRATED	L	RATTLINE	O	TENTORIA		NITRATES	U	TAINTURE

aeinrtu 24 - urinate

A	INAURATE		INDURATE	L	AUNTLIER	Q	ANTIQUER		URINATES
B	BRAUNITE		RUINATED		RETINULA		QUAINTER	T	TAINTURE
	URBANITE		URINATED		TENURIAL	S	RUINATES	V	VAUNTIER
C	ANURETIC	H	HAURIENT	M	RUMINATE		TAURINES		
D	DATURINE	J	JAUNTIER	P	PAINTURE		URANITES		

aeinsst 144 - tisanes

A	ENTASIAS		GENISTAS		TENIASIS	O	ASSIENTO		SESTINAS
B	BASINETS		GIANTESS	K	SNAKIEST		ASTONIES	T	ANTSIEST
	BASSINET		SEATINGS	L	EASTLINS	P	SAPIENTS		INSTATES
	BESAINTS		TEASINGS		ELASTINS		STEAPSIN		NASTIEST
	BESTAINS		TSIGANES		NAILSETS	R	ARTINESS		SATINETS
C	CINEASTS	H	ANTHESIS		SALIENTS		RESIANTS		TITANESS
	SCANTIES		SHANTIES		SALTINES		RETSINAS	U	SINUATES
D	DESTAINS		SHEITANS		STANIELS		SNARIEST	X	SEXTAINS
	SANDIEST		STHENIAS	M	MANTISES		STAINERS		
E	ETESIANS	I	ISATINES		MATINESS		STARNIES		
	TENIASES		SANITIES	N	INSANEST		STEARINS		
G	EASTINGS		SANITISE		STANINES	S	SAINTESS		

aeinstt 87 - instate

A	ASTATINE		TANAISTE	C	CANTIEST		NICTATES	D	INSTATED
	SANITATE	B	TABINETS		ENTASTIC		TETANICS	E	ANISETTE

TETANIES	H HESITANT	R INTREATS	S ANTSIEST	T NATTIEST
TETANISE	J JANTIEST	NITRATES	INSTATES	V TASTEVIN
F FAINTEST	N ANTIENTS	STRAITEN	NASTIEST	W TAWNIEST
G ESTATING	STANNITE	TARTINES	SATINETS	
TANGIEST	P PATIENTS	TERTIANS	TITANESS	

aeinstu 183 - aunties

D AUDIENTS	J JAUNTIES	P PETUNIAS	R RUINATES	S SINUATES
SINUATED	K UNAKITES	SUPINATE	TAURINES	V SUIVANTE
G SAUTEING	L ALUNITES	Q ANTIQUES	URANITES	
UNITAGES	INSULATE	QUANTISE	URINATES	

aeinstv 153 - vainest

A SANATIVE	D DEVIANTS	I VANITIES	O STOVAINE
C CISTVAEN	E NAIVETES	K KISTVAEN	T TASTEVIN
VESICANT	G VINTAGES	L VENTAILS	U SUIVANTE

aeiorst 4 - otaries

B SABOTIER	L SOTERIAL	NOTARIES	ROTARIES	VIATORES
D ASTEROID	M AMORTISE	NOTARISE	T TOASTIER	VOTARIES
E ETAERIOS	ATOMISER	ROSINATE	U OUTRAISE	
H HOARIEST	N ANOESTRI	SENORITA	SAUTOIRE	
J JAROSITE	ARSONITE	R ROARIEST	V TRAVOISE	

aeiorsv 216 - ovaries

C COVARIES	G VIRAGOES	VARIOLES	R SAVORIER	VOTARIES
VARICOSE	J JAROVISE	VOLARIES	S SAVORIES	W AVOWRIES
D AVODIRES	L OVERSAIL	N AVERSION	T TRAVOISE	
AVOIDERS	VALORISE	P VAPORISE	VIATORES	

aeiprst 108 - traipse

A ASPIRATE	D DIPTERAS	I PARITIES	PERTAINS	RASPIEST
PARASITE	RAPIDEST	K PARKIEST	PINASTER	TRAIPSES
SEPTARIA	SPIRATED	L PILASTER	PRISTANE	V PRIVATES
B BAPTISER	TARSIPED	PLAISTER	REPAINTS	W WIRETAPS
C CRAPIEST	TRAIPSED	PLAITERS	P PERIAPTS	Y ASPERITY
CRISPATE	E PARIETES	M APTERISM	R PARTIERS	
PARETICS	PETARIES	PRIMATES	S PASTRIES	
PICRATES	G GRAPIEST	N PAINTERS	PIASTERS	
PRACTISE	H TRIPHASE	PANTRIES	PIASTRES	

aeirrst 78 - tarries

B ARBITERS	F FRATRIES	N RESTRAIN	O ROARIEST	T RETRAITS
BARRIEST	H TRASHIER	RETRAINS	ROTARIES	STRAITER
RAREBITS	I RARITIES	STRAINER	P PARTIERS	TARRIEST
C ERRATICS	L RETIRALS	TERRAINS	R STARRIER	W STRAWIER
E ARTERIES	RETRIALS	TRAINERS	TARRIERS	
REASTIER	TRAILERS	TRANSIRE	S TARSIERS	

aeirsst 204 - satires

A	ASTERIAS	H	SHERIATS	M	ASTERISM		STAINERS	S	ASSISTER
	ATRESIAS	I	IRISATES		MAISTERS		STARNIES		TIRASSES
C	SCARIEST		SATIRISE		MISRATES		STEARINS	T	ARTISTES
D	ASTERIDS	K	ASTERISK		SEMITARS	P	PASTRIES		ARTSIEST
	DIASTERS		SARKIEST		SMARTIES		PIASTERS		STRIATES
	DISASTER	L	REALISTS	N	ARTINESS		PIASTRES	V	TRAVISES
	DISRATES		SALTIERS		RESIANTS		RASPIEST	W	WAISTERS
E	SERIATES		SALTIRES		RETSINAS		TRAIPSES		WAITRESS
G	AGISTERS		SLAISTER		SNARIEST	R	TARSIERS		WASTRIES

aeirstt 62 - tastier

A	ARIETTAS		TARDIEST	M	MISTREAT	R	RETRAITS		TARTIEST
	ARISTATE	E	ARIETTES		TERATISM		STRAITER		TITRATES
B	BIRETTAS		ITERATES	N	INTREATS		TARRIEST		TRISTATE
C	CITRATES		TEARIEST		NITRATES	S	ARTISTES	W	WARTIEST
	CRISTATE		TREATIES		STRAITEN		ARTSIEST	X	EXTRAITS
	SCATTIER		TREATISE		TARTINES		STRIATES	Z	TRISTEZA
D	STRAITED	G	STRIGATE		TERTIANS	T	ATTRITES		
	STRIATED	L	TERTIALS	O	TOASTIER		RATTIEST		

aeirstv 237 - veritas

A	VARIATES	G	VIRGATES	M	VITAMERS		VOTARIES	Y	VESTIARY
B	VIBRATES		VITRAGES	O	TRAVOISE	P	PRIVATES		
E	EVIRATES	I	VAIRIEST		VIATORES	S	TRAVISES		

aeirstw 141 - waiters

A	AWAITERS		TAWERIES	H	SWATHIER	M	WARTIMES	S	WAISTERS
B	WARBIEST		WASTERIE		WATERISH	N	TINWARES		WAITRESS
D	TAWDRIES		WEARIEST	I	WISTERIA	P	WIRETAPS		WASTRIES
E	SWEATIER	F	WASTRIFE	K	WATERSKI	R	STRAWIER	T	WARTIEST

aelnors 228 - reloans

D	LADRONES	I	AILERONS	L	LLANEROS		PSORALEN	V	VERONALS
	SOLANDER		ALERIONS	M	ALMONERS	U	ALEURONS		
F	FARNESOL		ALIENORS	P	PERSONAL		NEUROSAL		

aelnoru 191 - aleuron

D	UNLOADER	E	ALEURONE	S	ALEURONS	T	OUTLEARN
	URODELAN	N	NEURONAL		NEUROSAL		

aelnrst 72 - antlers

A	ASTERNAL	G	STRANGLE		LATRINES	P	PANTLERS		TRENTALS
B	BRANTLES		TANGLERS		RATLINES		PLANTERS	U	NEUTRALS
C	CENTRALS		TRANGLES		REINSTAL		REPLANTS	V	VENTRALS
E	ALTERNES	H	ENTHRALS		RETINALS	S	SALTERNS		
	ETERNALS	I	ENTRAILS		TRENAILS		SLANTERS		
	TELERANS		LARNIEST	N	LANTERNS	T	SLATTERN		

aelorst 27 - olestra

B	BLOATERS		LODESTAR	H	LOATHERS		POLESTAR	U	ROSULATE
	SORTABLE	E	OLEASTER		RATHOLES		PROLATES	V	LEVATORS
	STORABLE	F	FLOATERS	I	SOTERIAL	R	REALTORS		OVERSALT
C	LOCATERS		FORESTAL	L	REALLOTS		RELATORS	Y	ROYALETS
	SECTORAL		REFLOATS		ROSTELLA		RESTORAL	Z	ZELATORS
D	DELATORS	G	GLOATERS	M	MOLERATS	S	OLESTRAS		
	LEOTARDS		LEGATORS	P	PETROSAL	T	RETOTALS		

aelrstu 220 - saluter

B	BALUSTER	F	REFUTALS	I	URALITES	P	APLUSTRE	V	VAULTERS
	RUSTABLE	G	GAULTERS	M	STAUMREL	S	SALUTERS		VESTURAL
C	RAUCLEST		GESTURAL	N	NEUTRALS	T	LUSTRATE		
E	RESALUTE		TRAGULES	O	ROSULATE		TUTELARS		

aemnors 189 - oarsmen

A	AMARONES	F	FORAMENS	I	MORAINES	P	MANROPES		TONEARMS
C	CREMONAS	G	MEGARONS		ROMAINES		PROSEMAN	U	ENAMOURS
	ROMANCES	H	HORSEMAN		ROMANISE	R	RANSOMER		NEUROMAS
D	MADRONES		MENORAHS	L	ALMONERS	T	MONSTERA	V	OVERMANS
	RANSOMED		RHAMNOSE	N	MONERANS		ONSTREAM		OVERSMAN
	ROADSMEN		SHOREMAN		SONARMEN		STOREMAN	Y	ROMNEYAS

aemnort 231 - tonearm

A	EMANATOR	P	EMPATRON		STOREMAN	U	ROUTEMAN
N	ORNAMENT	S	MONSTERA		TONEARMS	Y	MONETARY
O	ANTEROOM		ONSTREAM	T	TORMENTA		

aemorst 205 - maestro

B	BROMATES		FORMATES		ATOMISER		ONSTREAM	R	REARMOST
D	STROAMED		MORTSAFE	L	MOLERATS		STOREMAN	S	MAESTROS
E	EROTEMAS	H	TERAOHMS	M	MARMOSET		TONEARMS	V	OVERMAST
F	FOREMAST	I	AMORTISE	N	MONSTERA	O	TEAROOMS		

aennort 222 - nortena

D	NONRATED		INORNATE	P	PATRONNE	U	UNORNATE
G	NEGATRON		REANOINT	S	NORTENAS	W	WANTONER
I	ANOINTER	M	ORNAMENT		RESONANT		

aenorst 5 - treason

A	ANOESTRA		RESONATE		ARSONITE		TONEARMS		SANTEROS
B	BARONETS	F	SEAFRONT		NOTARIES	N	NORTENAS		SENATORS
C	ANCESTOR	G	ESTRAGON		NOTARISE		RESONANT		STARNOSE
	ENACTORS		NEGATORS		ROSINATE	P	OPERANTS		TREASONS
	SARCONET		ORANGEST		SENORITA		PRONATES	T	ORNATEST
	SORTANCE		RAGSTONE	M	MONSTERA		PROTEANS	U	OUTEARNS
D	TORNADES		STONERAG		ONSTREAM	R	ANTRORSE	V	VENATORS
E	EARSTONE	I	ANOESTRI		STOREMAN	S	ASSENTOR	W	STONERAW

aenorsu 143 - arenous

A ARANEOUS	F FURANOSE	M ENAMOURS	S ANSEROUS	V RAVENOUS
C CARNEOUS	L ALEURONS	NEUROMAS	ARSENOUS	
NACREOUS	NEUROSAL	N UNREASON	T OUTEARNS	

aenortu 84 - outearn

A AERONAUT	OUTRANCE	L OUTLEARN	N UNORNATE
C COURANTE	G OUTRANGE	M ROUTEMAN	S OUTEARNS

aenrstt 214 - natters

A TARTANES	RATTEENS	TARTINES	N ENTRANTS	TRAPNEST
C TRANECTS	I INTREATS	TERTIANS	O ORNATEST	R TRANTERS
TRANSECT	NITRATES	L SLATTERN	P PATTERNS	S TARTNESS
E ENTREATS	STRAITEN	TRENTALS	TRANSEPT	U TAUNTERS

aenrstu 60 - saunter

B UNBRASTE	TRANSUDE	UNHEARTS	M ANESTRUM	T TAUNTERS
URBANEST	UNTREADS	URETHANS	MENSTRUA	V VAUNTERS
C CENTAURS	E SAUTERNE	I RUINATES	TRANSUME	W UNWATERS
RECUSANT	F AFTERSUN	TAURINES	O OUTEARNS	
UNCRATES	G STRAUNGE	URANITES	P PERSAUNT	
UNTRACES	H HAUNTERS	URINATES	S ANESTRUS	
D DAUNTERS	UNEARTHS	L NEUTRALS	SAUNTERS	

aeoprst 225 - seaport

B PROBATES	E OPERATES	POTSHARE	PROTEANS	PROTASES
C POSTRACE	PROTEASE	L PETROSAL	P TRAPPOSE	SEAPORTS
D ADOPTERS	F FOREPAST	POLESTAR	R PRAETORS	T PROSTATE
ASPORTED	G PORTAGES	PROLATES	PRORATES	U APTEROUS
PASTORED	POTAGERS	N OPERANTS	S ESPARTOS	V OVERPAST
READOPTS	H PHORATES	PRONATES	PORTASES	

aeorrst 113 - roaster

A AERATORS	REACTORS	RELATORS	PRORATES	ROASTERS
B ABORTERS	D ROADSTER	RESTORAL	R ARRESTOR	T ROSTRATE
ARBORETS	G GARROTES	M REARMOST	S ASSERTOR	
TABORERS	I ROARIEST	N ANTRORSE	ASSORTER	
C ACROTERS	ROTARIES	O SORORATE	ORATRESS	
CREATORS	L REALTORS	P PRAETORS	REASSORT	

aeorstt 145 - toaster

A AEROSTAT	C SECTATOR	L RETOTALS	S STRATOSE	U OUTRATES
B ABETTORS	G GAROTTES	N ORNATEST	TOASTERS	OUTSTARE
BATTEROS	H RHEOSTAT	P PROSTATE	T ATTESTOR	SEATROUT
TABORETS	I TOASTIER	R ROSTRATE	TESTATOR	

agilnot 162 - antilog

A GALTONIA	E GELATION	GOATLING	TAGLIONI	SALTOING
B BLOATING	LEGATION	H LOATHING	P PLOATING	SOLATING
OBLIGANT	F FLOATING	I INTAGLIO	R TRIGONAL	T TOTALING
C LOCATING	G GLOATING	LIGATION	S ANTILOGS	Y ANTILOGY

aginors 180 - soaring

C ORGANICS	ORIGANES	M ORGANISM	S ASSIGNOR	ROASTING
D ROADINGS	H ORANGISH	ROAMINGS	SIGNORAS	U AROUSING
E IGNAROES	I SIGNORIA	R GARRISON	SOARINGS	V SAVORING
ORGANISE	L RANGOLIS	ROARINGS	T ORGANIST	

aginort 129 - orating

B ABORTING	I RIGATONI	O ROGATION	TROATING	
BORATING	K TROAKING	S ORGANIST	V GRAVITON	
TABORING	L TRIGONAL	ROASTING	Y GYRATION	
G GAROTING	N IGNORANT	T ROTATING	ORGANITY	

aginrst 164 - staring

A GRANITAS	GRANITES	H TRASHING	O ORGANIST	V STARVING
B BRASTING	INGRATES	K KARTINGS	ROASTING	W RINGTAWS
C SCARTING	RANGIEST	STARKING	P PARTINGS	STRAWING
TRACINGS	REASTING	L RATLINGS	PRATINGS	WRASTING
D TRADINGS	STEARING	SLARTING	R STARRING	Y STINGRAY
E ANGRIEST	TASERING	STARLING	TARRINGS	STRAYING
ANGSTIER	F INGRAFTS	M MIGRANTS	S GASTRINS	
ASTRINGE	RAFTINGS	SMARTING	STARINGS	
GANISTER	STRAFING	N RANTINGS	T RATTINGS	
GANTRIES	G GRATINGS	STARNING	STARTING	

ailnost 139 - latinos

A AILANTOS	INSOLATE	SALTOING	N ANTLIONS	Y LANOSITY
ALATIONS	TOENAILS	SOLATING	O SOLATION	
E ELATIONS	G ANTILOGS	L STALLION	R TONSILAR	

ailorst 150 - tailors

B LABORIST	D DILATORS	O ISOLATOR	SOLARIST	
ORBITALS	E SOTERIAL	OSTIOLAR	U SUTORIAL	
STROBILA	M MORALIST	S ORALISTS	Y ROYALIST	
C CALORIST	N TONSILAR	SLIOTARS	SOLITARY	

ainorst 30 - rations

B TABORINS	E ANOESTRI	G ORGANIST	O ORATIONS	W WAITRONS
C CANTORIS	ARSONITE	ROASTING	P ATROPINS	X TRIAXONS
CAROTINS	NOTARIES	H TRAHISON	S ARSONIST	
CORTINAS	NOTARISE	J JANITORS	T STRONTIA	
D DIATRONS	ROSINATE	K SKIATRON	U RAINOUTS	
INTRADOS	SENORITA	L TONSILAR	SUTORIAN	

aiorstu 218 - sautoir

D AUDITORS	SAUTOIRE	L SUTORIAL	SUTORIAN	T TOURISTA
E OUTRAISE	F FAITOURS	N RAINOUTS	S SAUTOIRS	V VIRTUOSA

beinost 187 - boniest

A BOTANIES	B NOBBIEST	K STEINBOK	R BORNITES	U BOUNTIES
BOTANISE	E BETONIES	N BONNIEST	RIBSTONE	
NIOBATES	EBONITES	O BONITOES	S EBONISTS	
OBEISANT	I NIOBITES	EOBIONTS	T BOTTINES	

beiorst 227 - sorbite

A SABOTIER	DEORBITS	L STROBILE	RIBSTONE	S SORBITES
C BISECTOR	I ORBITIES	TRILOBES	O ROBOTISE	T BORTIEST
D DEBITORS	K REITBOKS	N BORNITES	R ORBITERS	Y SOBRIETY

ceinors 172 - cronies

A SCENARIO	FORENSIC	I RECISION	P CONSPIRE	RECTIONS
B BICORNES	FORINSEC	SORICINE	INCORPSE	U COINSURE
C CONCISER	FORNICES	L INCLOSER	R RESORCIN	NOURICES
CORNICES	INFORCES	LICENSOR	S NECROSIS	ROUNCIES
CROCEINS	G COGNISER	M CREMOSIN	SERICONS	
D CONSIDER	COREIGNS	INCOMERS	T COINTERS	
F COINFERS	COSIGNER	SERMONIC	CORNIEST	
CONIFERS	H CHORINES	N INCENSOR	NOTICERS	

ceinort 80 - rection

A ACTIONER	D CENTROID	H NOTCHIER	R TRICORNE	CORNETTI
ANORETIC	DOCTRINE	J INJECTOR	S COINTERS	U NEUROTIC
CREATION	E ERECTION	M INTERCOM	CORNIEST	UNEROTIC
REACTION	NEOTERIC	P ENTROPIC	NOTICERS	V CONTRIVE
C CONCERTI	F INFECTOR	INCEPTOR	RECTIONS	
NECROTIC	G GERONTIC	PRETONIC	T CONTRITE	

ceinost 158 - section

A ACONITES	SEICENTO	M CENTIMOS	RECTIONS	X EXCITONS
CANOEIST	G ESCOTING	O COONTIES	S SECTIONS	Y CYTOSINE
SONICATE	K CONKIEST	P PONCIEST	T CENTOIST	
C CONCEITS	KENOTICS	R COINTERS	STENOTIC	
D DEONTICS	L LECTIONS	CORNIEST	TONETICS	
E ICESTONE	TELSONIC	NOTICERS	U COUNTIES	

deeilnr 198 - relined

A RENAILED	C DECLINER	E NEEDLIER	REEDLING	R REDLINER
B LINEBRED	RECLINED	G ENGIRDLE	K REKINDLE	S REDLINES
RENDIBLE	D REDLINED	LINGERED	RELINKED	U UNDERLIE

deeilns 221 - linseed

A DELAINES	E SELENIDE	K SILKENED	S IDLENESS	LISTENED
C DECLINES	G SEEDLING	O ESLOINED	LINSEEDS	TINSELED
LICENSED	H ENSHIELD	LESIONED	T ENLISTED	V SNIVELED
SILENCED	I SIDELINE	R REDLINES	LINTSEED	Y DYELINES

deeinrs 65 - resined

A ARSENIDE	F DEFINERS	RESHINED	S DIRENESS	V INVERSED
DENARIES	G DESIGNER	K DEERSKIN	T INSERTED	W REWIDENS
DRAISENE	ENERGIDS	L REDLINES	NERDIEST	WIDENERS
NEARSIDE	REDESIGN	N SINNERED	RESIDENT	X INDEXERS
B INBREEDS	READINGS	O INDORSEE	SINTERED	
E NEREIDES	RESIGNED	ORDINEES	TRENDIES	
REDENIES	H DRISHEEN	P SPENDIER	U UREDINES	

deeinst 42 - destine

A ANDESITE	G INGESTED	LISTENED	O SIDENOTE	S DESTINES
B BENDIEST	SIGNETED	TINSELED	P PENTISED	T DINETTES
D DESTINED	STEEDING	M DEMENTIS	R INSERTED	INSETTED
NEDDIEST	H DISTHENE	SEDIMENT	NERDIEST	U DETINUES
E NEEDIEST	I DIETINES	TIDESMEN	RESIDENT	V EVIDENTS
F FENDIEST	L ENLISTED	N DENTINES	SINTERED	INVESTED
INFESTED	LINTSEED	DESINENT	TRENDIES	

deeirst 37 - dieters

A READIEST	D REDDIEST	M DEMERITS	O EROTISED	T TIREDEST
SERIATED	E REEDIEST	DEMISTER	P PREEDITS	U ERUDITES
SIDERATE	F RESIFTED	DIMETERS	PRIESTED	SURETIED
STEADIER	G DIGESTER	MISTERED	RESPITED	V VERDITES
B BESTRIDE	ESTRIDGE	N INSERTED	R DESTRIER	W WEIRDEST
BISTERED	REDIGEST	NERDIEST	S DIESTERS	
C DESERTIC	H DIETHERS	RESIDENT	EDITRESS	
DISCREET	I SIDERITE	SINTERED	RESISTED	
DISCRETE	L RELISTED	TRENDIES	SISTERED	

deenors 128 - endorse

A REASONED	ENCODERS	E ENDORSEE	SERMONED	T ERODENTS
B DEBONERS	NECROSED	I INDORSEE	N ENDERONS	W ENDOWERS
REDBONES	SECONDER	ORDINEES	R ENDORSER	REENDOWS
C CENSORED	D ENDORSED	M MODERNES	S ENDORSES	WORSENED

deenort 171 - erodent

C CENTRODE	I ORIENTED	M ENTODERM	S ERODENTS
H DETHRONE	L REDOLENT	MENTORED	U DEUTERON
THRENODE	RONDELET	O ENROOTED	

deenrtu 241 - tenured

A DENATURE	UNDEREAT	E NEUTERED	REUNITED	N UNRENTED
UNDERATE	D RETUNDED	I RETINUED	L UNDERLET	UNTENDER

	O DEUTERON	S DENTURES	UNDERSET	UNRESTED	
	R RETURNED	SEDERUNT	UNDESERT	V VENTURED	

deeorst 148 - teredos

B BESORTED	F DEFOREST	M MODESTER	R RESORTED	TETRODES
BESTRODE	FORESTED	N ERODENTS	RESTORED	X DEXTROSE
C CORSETED	FOSTERED	P DOPESTER	ROSTERED	Y OYSTERED
ESCORTED	G GOSTERED	POSTERED	S DOSSERET	STOREYED
SECTORED	I EROTISED	REEDSTOP	OERSTEDS	
E STEREOED	K RESTOKED	REPOSTED	T ROSETTED	

deginor 233 - redoing

A ORGANDIE	O RODEOING	R ORDERING	U GUERIDON	RINGDOVE
C RECODING	P PROIGNED	S NEGROIDS	V DOVERING	W DOWERING

deiinot 248 - edition

A IDEATION	TAENIOID	L TOLIDINE	S EDITIONS	Y IDONEITY
IODINATE	F NOTIFIED	R RETINOID	SEDITION	

deiinrt 235 - nitride

A DAINTIER	REINDICT	M DIRIMENT	S DISINTER	RINDIEST
C INDICTER	D NITRIDED	O RETINOID	INDITERS	U UNTIDIER
INDIRECT	G DIRIGENT	P INTREPID	NITRIDES	

deilnos 101 - sondeli

A NODALISE	LESIONED	I LIONISED	R DISENROL	U DELUSION
C INCLOSED	G GLENOIDS	O EIDOLONS	S SONDELIS	INSOULED
E ESLOINED	SIDELONG	SOLENOID	T LENTOIDS	UNSOILED

deilnot 76 - lentoid

A DELATION	ENTOILED	N INDOLENT	S LENTOIDS
E DELETION	I TOLIDINE	P TOPLINED	U OUTLINED

deilors 188 - soldier

A DARIOLES	C SCLEROID	N DISENROL	T STOLIDER
SOLIDARE	I IDOLISER	P LEPORIDS	U SOULDIER
SOREDIAL	L DOLLIERS	S SOLDIERS	Y SOLDIERY

deilort 173 - doilter

A IDOLATER	B TRILOBED	LOITERED	S STOLIDER
TAILORED	E DOLERITE	L TROLLIED	Y ELYTROID

deinors 20 - rosined

A ANEROIDS	D INDORSED	G NEGROIDS	IRONISED	J JOINDERS
DONARIES	E INDORSEE	H HORDEINS	IRONSIDE	L DISENROL
C CONSIDER	ORDINEES	I DERISION	RESINOID	N ENDIRONS

Seven-letter stems

P DISPONER	R INDORSER	T DRONIEST	W DISOWNER
POINDERS	S INDORSES	U DOURINES	WINDORES
PRISONED	SORDINES	SOURDINE	WINDROSE

deinost 54 - stonied

A ASTONIED	D NODDIEST	I EDITIONS	M DEMONIST	W DOWNIEST
SEDATION	E SIDENOTE	SEDITION	R DRONIEST	
C DEONTICS	H HEDONIST	L LENTOIDS	S DONSIEST	

deinrst 71 - tinders

A DETRAINS	NERDIEST	I DISINTER	TENDRILS	TRIDENTS
RANDIEST	RESIDENT	INDITERS	TRINDLES	U INTRUDES
STRAINED	SINTERED	NITRIDES	O DRONIEST	NURDIEST
D STRIDDEN	TRENDIES	RINDIEST	P SPRINTED	X DEXTRINS
E INSERTED	G STRINGED	L SNIRTLED	T STRIDENT	

deinrsu 215 - insured

A DENARIUS	C INDUCERS	URIDINES	S INSUREDS
UNRAISED	E UREDINES	N UNRINSED	SUNDRIES
URANIDES	G GRUNDIES	O DOURINES	T INTRUDES
B BURNSIDE	I DISINURE	SOURDINE	NURDIEST

deinrtu 69 - untried

A DATURINE	B TURBINED	E RETINUED	M RUDIMENT	R INTRUDER
INDURATE	UNDERBIT	REUNITED	UNMITRED	S INTRUDES
RUINATED	C REINDUCT	I UNTIDIER	N INTURNED	NURDIEST
URINATED	D INTRUDED	L UNDERLIT	P TURNIPED	W UNDERWIT

deinstu 193 - dunites

A AUDIENTS	G DUNGIEST	L DILUENTS	DUNNITES	U UNSUITED
SINUATED	I DISUNITE	INSULTED	Q SQUINTED	
D DISTUNED	NUDITIES	UNLISTED	R INTRUDES	
E DETINUES	UNITISED	M MISTUNED	NURDIEST	
F UNSIFTED	UNTIDIES	N DUNNIEST	S DISTUNES	

deiorst 28 - steroid

A ASTEROID	GRODIEST	N DRONIEST	PROTEIDS	OUTRIDES
B DEBITORS	STODGIER	P DIOPTERS	RIPOSTED	OUTSIDER
DEORBITS	I DIORITES	DIOPTRES	TOPSIDER	SUITORED
C CORDITES	K DORKIEST	DIPTEROS	S STEROIDS	W ROWDIEST
E EROTISED	L STOLIDER	PERIDOTS	T DORTIEST	WORDIEST
G DIGESTOR	M MORTISED	PORTSIDE	U IODURETS	

deiortu 186 - outride

B TUBEROID	F OUTFIRED	S IODURETS	SUITORED
C OUTCRIED	H OUTHIRED	OUTRIDES	V OUTDRIVE
E ETOURDIE	R OUTRIDER	OUTSIDER	

deirstu 226 - studier

C CRUDITES	SURETIED	N INTRUDES	P DISPUTER	STUDIERS
CURDIEST	G DURGIEST	NURDIEST	STUPIDER	STURDIES
CURTSIED	L DILUTERS	O IODURETS	Q SQUIRTED	T DETRITUS
D RUDDIEST	LURIDEST	OUTRIDES	R STURDIER	X DRUXIEST
STURDIED	STUDLIER	OUTSIDER	S DIESTRUS	
E ERUDITES	M DIESTRUM	SUITORED	DRUSIEST	

denorst 200 - snorted

A TORNADES	M MORDENTS	PROTENDS	UNSORTED
E ERODENTS	N TENDRONS	U ROUNDEST	Y DRYSTONE
I DRONIEST	P PORTENDS	TONSURED	

eegilnr 209 - reeling

A ALGERINE	REEDLING	O ELOIGNER	T GREENLIT
C CREELING	F FLEERING	R LINGERER	U REGULINE
D ENGIRDLE	G LEGERING	S LEERINGS	V LEVERING
LINGERED	I LINGERIE	REELINGS	REVELING

eeginrs 96 - greisen

A ANERGIES	REEDINGS	H GREENISH	INGENERS	REESTING
GESNERIA	RESIGNED	REHINGES	SERENING	STEERING
B BIGENERS	E ENERGIES	SHEERING	SNEERING	STREIGNE
BREINGES	ENERGISE	J JEERINGS	O ERINGOES	U SEIGNEUR
REBEGINS	GREENIES	K KREESING	P SPEERING	V SEVERING
C CREESING	RESEEING	SKEERING	SPREEING	VEERINGS
GENERICS	F FEERINGS	L LEERINGS	R RESIGNER	W RESEWING
D DESIGNER	FEIGNERS	REELINGS	S GREISENS	SEWERING
ENERGIDS	REEFINGS	M REGIMENS	T GENTRIES	SWEERING
REDESIGN	G GREESING	N ENGINERS	INTEGERS	

eeginrt 121 - integer

A GRATINEE	I REIGNITE	N ENTERING	STEERING	X EXERTING
INTERAGE	RETIEING	P PETERING	STREIGNE	GENETRIX
C ERECTING	L GREENLIT	S GENTRIES	U GENITURE	
GENTRICE	M METERING	INTEGERS	V EVERTING	
G GREETING	REGIMENT	REESTING	W TWEERING	

eeiinrt 123 - niterie

A INERTIAE	REINCITE	O ERIONITE	T INTERTIE
B BENITIER	G REIGNITE	S ERINITES	RETINITE
C ICTERINE	RETIEING	NITERIES	V REINVITE

eeilnrs 199 - relines

A ALIENERS	SILENCER	M ERMELINS	T ENLISTER	V LIVENERS
B BERLINES	D REDLINES	O ELOINERS	LISTENER	SNIVELER
C LICENSER	G LEERINGS	P PILSENER	REENLIST	
RECLINES	REELINGS	S REINLESS	SILENTER	

Seven-letter stems

eeilnst 75 - tensile

B STILBENE	TINSELED	H THEELINS	P PENLITES	S LITENESS
TENSIBLE	E ENLISTEE	I LENITIES	PLENTIES	SETLINES
C CENTILES	SELENITE	K NESTLIKE	R ENLISTER	T ENTITLES
D ENLISTED	G GENTILES	N LENIENTS	LISTENER	V VEINLETS
LINTSEED	SLEETING	SENTINEL	REENLIST	
LISTENED	STEELING	O NOSELITE	SILENTER	

eeilors 151 - loeries

B EROSIBLE	I OILERIES	N ELOINERS	TROELIES	VOLERIES
C CREOLISE	K ROSELIKE	P PELORIES	V OVERLIES	W OWLERIES
F FORELIES	L ORSEILLE	T LITEROSE	RELIEVOS	

eeilort 117 - troelie

A AEROLITE	LOITERED	K LORIKEET	R LOITERER	TROELIES
D DOLERITE	H HOTELIER	M MOTELIER	S LITEROSE	

eeilrst 67 - sterile

A ATELIERS	TIERCELS	I TILERIES	SILENTER	SPIRELET
EARLIEST	TRISCELE	K TRISKELE	O LITEROSE	S LEISTERS
LATERISE	D RELISTED	L TREILLES	TROELIES	RITELESS
LEARIEST	E LEERIEST	M TERMLIES	P EPISTLER	TIRELESS
REALTIES	SLEETIER	N ENLISTER	PELTRIES	T RETITLES
C RETICLES	STEELIER	LISTENER	PERLITES	
SCLERITE	F FERLIEST	REENLIST	REPTILES	

eeinrst 11 - entries

A ARENITES	RESIDENT	I ERINITES	R INSERTER	TRIENTES
ARSENITE	SINTERED	NITERIES	REINSERT	U ESURIENT
RESINATE	TRENDIES	K KERNITES	REINTERS	NEURITES
STEARINE	E ETERNISE	L ENLISTER	RENTIERS	RETINUES
TRAINEES	TEENSIER	LISTENER	TERRINES	REUNITES
C CENTRIES	F FERNIEST	REENLIST	S INTERESS	V NERVIEST
ENTERICS	INFESTER	SILENTER	SENTRIES	REINVEST
ENTICERS	G GENTRIES	M MISENTER	TRENISES	SERVIENT
SCIENTER	INTEGERS	N INTENSER	T INERTEST	SIRVENTE
SECRETIN	REESTING	INTERNES	INSETTER	X INTERSEX
D INSERTED	STEERING	O ONERIEST	INTEREST	Y SERENITY
NERDIEST	STREIGNE	SEROTINE	STERNITE	

eeinrtt 152 - tentier

B REBITTEN	TEENTIER	L NETTLIER	S INERTEST	TRIENTES
C RETICENT	H THIRTEEN	N INTERNET	INSETTER	Y ENTIRETY
D RETINTED	I INTERTIE	RENITENT	INTEREST	ETERNITY
E REINETTE	RETINITE	O TENORITE	STERNITE	

eeinstt 176 - netties

A ANISETTE	B BENTIEST	E TEENIEST	I ENTITIES	N SENTIENT
TETANIES	D DINETTES	F FEINTEST	L ENTITLES	O NOISETTE
TETANISE	INSETTED	G GENTIEST	M MINETTES	TEOSINTE

P INEPTEST	INSETTER	TRIENTES	W TENTWISE
SPINETTE	INTEREST	T NETTIEST	TWENTIES
R INERTEST	STERNITE	TENTIEST	X EXISTENT

eeiorst 53 - erotise

A ETAERIOS	G ERGOTISE	L LITEROSE	SEROTINE	EROTISES
C COTERIES	H ISOTHERE	TROELIES	P POETISER	Z EROTIZES
ESOTERIC	THEORIES	M TIRESOME	POETRIES	
D EROTISED	THEORISE	N ONERIEST	S EROTESIS	

eelorst 136 - soleret

A OLEASTER	SELECTOR	TROELIES	S SOLERETS
C CORSELET	E SLOETREE	L SOLLERET	T LORETTES
ELECTORS	H HOSTELER	M MOLESTER	U RESOLUTE
ELECTROS	I LITEROSE	N ENTRESOL	V OVERLETS

eenorst 41 - estrone

A EARSTONE	SOFTENER	L ENTRESOL	O OESTRONE	V OVERNETS
RESONATE	G ESTROGEN	M SERMONET	ROESTONE	X EXTENSOR
D ERODENTS	H HONESTER	STOREMEN	P PROTENSE	
F ENFOREST	I ONERIEST	N ENTERONS	S ESTRONES	
RESOFTEN	SEROTINE	TENONERS	T ONSETTER	

eginors 56 - regions

A IGNAROES	COREIGNS	L RESOLING	SPONGIER	ROSETING
ORGANISE	COSIGNER	M NEGROISM	R IGNORERS	W RESOWING
ORIGANES	D NEGROIDS	N NEGRONIS	S GORINESS	Y SEIGNORY
B SOBERING	E ERINGOES	P PERIGONS	SIGNORES	
C COGNISER	I SEIGNIOR	REPOSING	T GENITORS	

eginort 165 - genitor

C GERONTIC	RINGTONE	T OTTERING	V REVOTING	Z ROZETING
H THROEING	S GENITORS	U OUTREIGN	W TOWERING	
N NITROGEN	ROSETING	ROUTEING	X OXTERING	

eginrst 92 - stinger

A ANGRIEST	TASERING	IGNITERS	N RENTINGS	TRESSING
ANGSTIER	C CRESTING	REISTING	STERNING	TRIGNESS
ASTRINGE	D STRINGED	RESITING	O GENITORS	T GITTERNS
GANISTER	E GENTRIES	STINGIER	ROSETING	V STERVING
GANTRIES	INTEGERS	STRIGINE	P PRESTING	W STREWING
GRANITES	REESTING	L LINGSTER	R RESTRING	WRESTING
INGRATES	STEERING	RINGLETS	RINGSTER	
RANGIEST	STREIGNE	STERLING	STRINGER	
REASTING	H RIGHTENS	TINGLERS	S RESTINGS	
STEARING	I GIRNIEST	TRINGLES	STINGERS	

egiorst 232 - goriest

D DIGESTOR	E ERGOTISE	GORMIEST	S GORSIEST	V VERTIGOS
GRODIEST	H GHOSTIER	N GENITORS	STRIGOSE	Y OYSTRIGE
STODGIER	M ERGOTISM	ROSETING	U GOUSTIER	Z ZORGITES

egnorst 239 - tongers

A ESTRAGON	RAGSTONE	G GONGSTER	N RONTGENS	T TONGSTER
NEGATORS	STONERAG	I GENITORS	R STRONGER	U STURGEON
ORANGEST	E ESTROGEN	ROSETING	S SONGSTER	W WRONGEST

ehiorst 224 - hoister

A HOARIEST	THEORISE	ORNITHES	HOSTRIES	SHOUTIER
C ROTCHIES	G GHOSTIER	P TROPHIES	SHORTIES	V OVERHITS
THEORICS	M ISOTHERM	R HERITORS	T THEORIST	W WORTHIES
E ISOTHERE	MOITHERS	S HOISTERS	THORITES	
THEORIES	N HORNIEST	HORSIEST	U OUTHIRES	

eiilrst 179 - siltier

A LAIRIEST	E TILERIES	M LIMITERS	O ROILIEST	U UTILISER
LISTERIA	F FILISTER	MIRLIEST	P TRIPLIES	
B TRILBIES	G GIRLIEST	N NIRLIEST	T SLITTIER	
D REDISTIL	L STILLIER	NITRILES	STILTIER	

eiinors 206 - noisier

B BRIONIES	IRONISED	L LIONISER	SIRONISE	Z IONIZERS
C RECISION	IRONSIDE	P RIPIENOS	T IRONIEST	IRONIZES
SORICINE	RESINOID	S IONISERS	V REVISION	SIRONIZE
D DERISION	G SEIGNIOR	IRONISES	VISIONER	

eilnors 33 - nerolis

A AILERONS	LICENSOR	I LIONISER	PROLINES	
ALERIONS	D DISENROL	M MISENROL	R LORINERS	
ALIENORS	E ELOINERS	N ONLINERS	S IRONLESS	
C INCLOSER	G RESOLING	P PLERIONS	T RETINOLS	

eilnort 36 - retinol

A ORIENTAL	I TRIOLEIN	R RITORNEL	U OUTLINER	
RELATION	P TERPINOL	S RETINOLS	W TOWNLIER	
TAILERON	TOPLINER	T TROTLINE		

eilnost 22 - onliest

A ELATIONS	TELSONIC	HOTLINES	M MOLINETS	P POINTELS
INSOLATE	D LENTOIDS	NEOLITHS	N INSOLENT	PONTILES
TOENAILS	E NOSELITE	I ETIOLINS	O LOONIEST	POTLINES
C LECTIONS	H HOLSTEIN	L STELLION	OILSTONE	TOPLINES

| R RETINOLS | OUTLINES | VIOLENTS | W TOWLINES |
| U ELUTIONS | V NOVELIST | | |

eilnrst 81 - snirtle

A ENTRAILS	D SNIRTLED	G LINGSTER	K LINKSTER	SNIRTLES
LARNIEST	TENDRILS	RINGLETS	STRINKLE	U INSULTER
LATRINES	TRINDLES	STERLING	TINKLERS	LUSTRINE
RATLINES	E ENLISTER	TINGLERS	M MINSTREL	Y TINSELRY
REINSTAL	LISTENER	TRINGLES	O RETINOLS	
RETINALS	REENLIST	I NIRLIEST	P SPLINTER	
TRENAILS	SILENTER	NITRILES	S SLINTERS	

eilorst 23 - toilers

A SOTERIAL	COSTLIER	F FLORIEST	N RETINOLS	T TRIOLETS
B STROBILE	CREOLIST	TREFOILS	O OESTRIOL	U LOURIEST
TRILOBES	D STOLIDER	I ROILIEST	TROOLIES	OUTLIERS
C CLOISTER	E LITEROSE	L TRILLOES	P POITRELS	
COISTREL	TROELIES	TROLLIES	S ESTRIOLS	

eilrstu 174 - lustier

A URALITES	D DILUTERS	I UTILISER	OUTLIERS	SURTITLE
B BURLIEST	LURIDEST	M MURLIEST	Q QUILTERS	V RIVULETS
SUBTILER	STUDLIER	N INSULTER	R SULTRIER	
C CURLIEST	G GURLIEST	LUSTRINE	S SURLIEST	
UTRICLES	H LUTHIERS	O LOURIEST	T SLUTTIER	

eimorst 159 - mortise

A AMORTISE	G ERGOTISM	ROOMIEST	TRISOMES	WORMIEST
ATOMISER	GORMIEST	P IMPOSTER	T OMITTERS	Y ISOMETRY
C MORTICES	H ISOTHERM	R MORTISER	U MISROUTE	
D MORTISED	MOITHERS	STORMIER	MOISTURE	
E TIRESOME	O MOORIEST	S EROTISMS	V VOMITERS	
F SETIFORM	MOTORISE	MORTISES	W MISWROTE	

einnort 138 - ternion

A ANOINTER	D INDENTOR	H INTHRONE	NOINTERS	U NEUTRINO
INORNATE	G NITROGEN	N NONINERT	TERNIONS	V INVENTOR
REANOINT	RINGTONE	S INTONERS	T TONTINER	NOVERINT

einoprs 163 - proines

C CONSPIRE	PIONEERS	PROLINES	R PRISONER	REPOINTS
INCORPSE	F FORPINES	M PROMINES	S PORINESS	TROPINES
D DISPONER	G PERIGONS	O POISONER	PRESSION	U PRUINOSE
POINDERS	REPOSING	SNOOPIER	ROPINESS	V OVERSPIN
PRISONED	SPONGIER	SPOONIER	T POINTERS	PROVINES
E ISOPRENE	I RIPIENOS	P POPERINS	PORNIEST	
PEREIONS	L PLERIONS	PROPINES	PROTEINS	

einoprt 203 - pointer

A	ATROPINE	D	DIPTERON	L	TERPINOL		PORNIEST	U	ERUPTION
C	ENTROPIC	H	TRIPHONE		TOPLINER		PROTEINS		
	INCEPTOR	I	POINTIER	M	ORPIMENT		REPOINTS		
	PRETONIC		POITRINE	S	POINTERS		TROPINES		

einorss 201 - seniors

A	ERASIONS	E	ESSOINER		SIRONISE		PRESSION	U	NEUROSIS
	SENSORIA	G	GORINESS	L	IRONLESS		ROPINESS		RESINOUS
C	NECROSIS		SIGNORES	M	MERSIONS	R	ROSINERS	V	VERSIONS
	SERICONS	H	HERISSON	N	IRONNESS	S	ROSINESS		
D	INDORSES	I	IONISERS	O	EROSIONS	T	OESTRINS		
	SORDINES		IRONISES	P	PORINESS		TERSIONS		

einorst 3 - orients

A	ANOESTRI		CORNIEST		ORNITHES	P	POINTERS	T	SNOTTIER
	ARSONITE		NOTICERS	I	IRONIEST		PORNIEST		TENORIST
	NOTARIES		RECTIONS	J	JOINTERS		PROTEINS		TRITONES
	NOTARISE	D	DRONIEST	K	INSTROKE		REPOINTS	U	ROUTINES
	ROSINATE	E	ONERIEST	L	RETINOLS		TROPINES		SNOUTIER
	SENORITA		SEROTINE	N	INTONERS	R	INTRORSE	V	INVESTOR
B	BORNITES	G	GENITORS		NOINTERS		SNORTIER	Y	SEROTINY
	RIBSTONE		ROSETING		TERNIONS	S	OESTRINS		TYROSINE
C	COINTERS	H	HORNIEST	O	SNOOTIER		TERSIONS	Z	TRIZONES

einorsu 229 - urinose

C	COINSURE	D	DOURINES	M	INERMOUS	P	PRUINOSE	T	ROUTINES
	NOURICES		SOURDINE		MONSIEUR	S	NEUROSIS		SNOUTIER
	ROUNCIES	F	REFUSION	N	REUNIONS		RESINOUS	V	SOUVENIR

einortt 70 - tritone

A	TENTORIA	D	INTORTED	K	KNOTTIER	S	SNOTTIER	U	RITENUTO
C	CONTRITE	E	TENORITE	L	TROTLINE		TENORIST		
	CORNETTI	G	OTTERING	N	TONTINER		TRITONES		

einortu 102 - routine

C	NEUROTIC		ROUTEING	N	NEUTRINO		SNOUTIER
	UNEROTIC	J	JOINTURE	P	ERUPTION	T	RITENUTO
G	OUTREIGN	L	OUTLINER	S	ROUTINES		

einostt 249 - tonites

B	BOTTINES	E	NOISETTE	J	JETTISON	R	SNOTTIER		STONIEST
C	CENTOIST		TEOSINTE	N	TINSTONE		TENORIST	T	TOTIENTS
	STENOTIC	F	FISTNOTE		TONTINES		TRITONES	W	NOWTIEST
	TONETICS	G	TENTIGOS	P	NEPOTIST	S	SNOTTIES		TOWNIEST

einrstt 236 - tinters

A INTREATS	C CENTRIST	INTEREST	K KNITTERS	STINTERS
NITRATES	CITTERNS	STERNITE	TRINKETS	U RUNTIEST
STRAITEN	D STRIDENT	TRIENTES	O SNOTTIER	W TWINTERS
TARTINES	TRIDENTS	G GITTERNS	TENORIST	Y ENTRYIST
TERTIANS	E INERTEST	I NITRITES	TRITONES	
B BITTERNS	INSETTER	STINTIER	S ENTRISTS	

einrstu 57 - uniters

A RUINATES	D INTRUDES	UNITISER	N RUNNIEST	Q SQUINTER
TAURINES	NURDIEST	L INSULTER	STURNINE	T RUNTIEST
URANITES	E ESURIENT	LUSTRINE	O ROUTINES	V UNRIVETS
URINATES	NEURITES	M MUNTRIES	SNOUTIER	VENTURIS
B TRIBUNES	RETINUES	TERMINUS	P REPUNITS	W UNWRITES
TURBINES	REUNITES	UNMITERS	UNPRIEST	
C CURNIEST	I NEURITIS	UNMITRES	UNRIPEST	

eioprst 192 - ropiest

C PERSICOT	E POETISER	N POINTERS	S PERIOSTS	SPOTTIER
D DIOPTERS	POETRIES	PORNIEST	PROSIEST	U ROUPIEST
DIOPTRES	F FIREPOTS	PROTEINS	PROSTIES	SPOUTIER
DIPTEROS	PIEFORTS	REPOINTS	REPOSITS	V OVERTIPS
PERIDOTS	POSTFIRE	TROPINES	RIPOSTES	PIVOTERS
PORTSIDE	H TROPHIES	O PORTOISE	SPORTIES	SORPTIVE
PROTEIDS	K PORKIEST	ROOPIEST	TRIPOSES	SPORTIVE
RIPOSTED	L POITRELS	R PIERROTS	T PORTIEST	
TOPSIDER	M IMPOSTER	SPORTIER	RISPETTO	

eiorrst 122 - rioters

A ROARIEST	H HERITORS	SNORTIER	TERROIRS	U STOURIER
ROTARIES	I RIOTRIES	O ROOTSIER	S RESISTOR	V OVERSTIR
B ORBITERS	M MORTISER	P PIERROTS	ROISTERS	SERVITOR
F FROSTIER	STORMIER	SPORTIER	SORRIEST	
ROTIFERS	N INTRORSE	R ERRORIST	T RORTIEST	

eiorstt 133 - stoiter

A TOASTIER	THORITES	TRITONES	SPOTTIER	V VIRETOTS
B BORTIEST	L TRIOLETS	O ROOTIEST	R RORTIEST	W SWOTTIER
C COTTIERS	M OMITTERS	TORTOISE	S STOITERS	
D DORTIEST	N SNOTTIER	P PORTIEST	U TOUSTIER	
H THEORIST	TENORIST	RISPETTO	TUTORISE	

eiorstu 59 - tousier

A OUTRAISE	OUTSIDER	SHOUTIER	SNOUTIER	TUTORISE
SAUTOIRE	SUITORED	L LOURIEST	P ROUPIEST	V VIRTUOSE
C CITREOUS	F FOUSTIER	OUTLIERS	SPOUTIER	VITREOUS
OUTCRIES	OUTFIRES	M MISROUTE	Q QUOITERS	VOITURES
D IODURETS	G GOUSTIER	MOISTURE	R STOURIER	
OUTRIDES	H OUTHIRES	N ROUTINES	T TOUSTIER	

Seven-letter stems

enorstu 85 - tonsure

A OUTEARNS	RECOUNTS	G STURGEON	MOUNTERS	V VENTROUS
B BURSTONE	TROUNCES	H SOUTHERN	REMOUNTS	Y TOURNEYS
RUBSTONE	D ROUNDEST	I ROUTINES	N NEUTRONS	
C CONSTRUE	TONSURED	SNOUTIER	O OUTSNORE	
CORNUTES	UNSORTED	L TURNSOLE	S TONSURES	
COUNTERS	F FORTUNES	M MONTURES	T STENTOUR	

AEIOU bonus words

These two short lists contain the very few seven- and eight-letter words to contain one each of all five vowels. It's worth learning these words for occasions when you find yourself with a vowel-heavy rack. Definitions are provided for these words as an aide-memoire.

Seven-letter words

DOULEIA	inferior veneration accorded to saints and angels
EULOGIA	blessing
MIAOUED	made the crying sound of a cat
MOINEAU	small fortification
SEQUOIA	giant Californian tree

Eight-letter words

AEQUORIN	type of protein
AEROBIUM	organism that requires oxygen to live
AGOUTIES	small South American rodents
CAESIOUS	having a waxy bluish-grey coating
DIALOGUE	conversation between two people
DOUANIER	customs officer
DOULEIAS	inferior venerations accorded to saints and angels
EDACIOUS	devoted to eating
EQUATION	mathematical statement that two expressions are equal
EUDAIMON	good spirit
EULOGIAS	blessings
EUPHOBIA	fear of good news
EUPHONIA	agreeable sound
EUPHORIA	sense of elation
EUSOCIAL	using division of labour
EXONUMIA	numismatic objects that are not coins, such as medals and tokens
JALOUSIE	outside shutter with slats
MOINEAUS	small fortifications
ODALIQUE	female slave in a harem
OUTRAISE	to raise more money than
POULAINE	tapering toe of shoe
SAUTOIRE	heraldic design
SEQUOIAS	giant Californian trees
THIOUREA	white water-soluble crystalline substance with a bitter taste

Non-words

Six-letter words that do not combine with another letter

In addition to remembering some of the bonus-word sets listed in this chapter, it's a good idea to remember that sometimes you will draw a rack which cannot form a seven-letter bonus word. If you can recognize such combinations early on, it will save you valuable time, and allow you to look for other options. The first list of 'non-words' contains valid six-letter words which cannot be changed into any valid word with the addition of another letter. If you can form one of the six-letter words with the letters on your rack, you can tell straight away that there is no valid seven-letter word to be formed from them; the only possibility of making a bonus play is to find an eight-letter word utilizing a letter already on the board. The six-letter word list contains just over 200 words. Words with any of JKQXZ have been removed, words with more than three of the same letter have been removed (eg no words with three Es), words with more than two repeated letters have been removed (eg no words with 2 Es and 2 Ns). The 200-plus words are presented in alphabetic order. The first word on the six-letter list is ABUNAS - and just to reiterate, there is no seven-letter word which can be made containing these letters.

ABUNAS	DRIFTY	FRONDS	LOUCHE	PIBALS
ADAPTS	DRILLS	FUGIOS	MAFTED	PIVOTS
ADIPIC	DROOLY	FUNNED	MAUVER	POLITY
ADOBOS	DUVETS	FUTONS	MAVENS	POOVES
AERIFY	EGOITY	GAVOTS	MAWGER	PRUTAH
AFLAME	ETYMIC	GAWPED	MEETLY	PUNCTA
AFLOAT	EULOGY	GLAURY	MERELY	PUNNED
AIMFUL	EURIPI	GLOVED	MIAOUS	PURITY
ANBURY	EVENLY	GOOFED	MIAOWS	RAGULY
ARIOSI	FAMULI	GRAFTS	MIEVES	RARELY
ASTOOP	FANALS	GREEDY	MIHIED	REMEDY
AUDIAL	FAUNAE	GRYDES	MIRVED	RIVERY
AVIARY	FAUNAS	GUIDED	MOATED	ROOTSY
AWEIGH	FAVEST	GYLDEN	MONACT	RUBATI
AWHATO	FAVOSE	HALFEN	MOULTS	SAFETY
AWHIRL	FAWNED	HALVED	MOUPED	SANIFY
BAVINS	FAYEST	HENGES	MUTINY	SAYONS
BEAUTY	FAYNES	HENNAS	NINETY	SNIFTY
BEGETS	FEALTY	HERYED	NOUNAL	SNOTTY
BEWIGS	FENMAN	HOBOED	NOVITY	SNOUTY
BIGOTS	FERVID	HOLONS	NOWAYS	STROWN
BINMEN	FEVERS	HOOVED	NULLED	SUETTY
BITTED	FEYEST	HOOVEN	OBTECT	SUGARY
BOLLEN	FOEHNS	HORRID	ODDITY	SWIPED
BOOHED	FOGIES	HOUSEY	ODIOUS	SWIVED
BRANDY	FOLEYS	HOVEAS	OIDIUM	TAIHOA
BRAWNS	FONNED	HUGEST	ORIHOU	TAWDRY
BUOYED	FORGOT	INBENT	OTALGY	THEMED
CABMEN	FOUNTS	INFIMA	OUBAAS	THRAWN
CLONAL	FOYNED	LARVAS	OVOIDS	TIGLIC
CLOVEN	FOYNES	LAWMEN	OWELTY	TINCTS
DAWNED	FRANCO	LEGACY	PANTRY	TODAYS
DEFOGS	FRIARS	LOOKED	PARODY	TOMBED
DRAFTY	FRIGID	LOOVES	PENURY	TOWERY

TRIPLY	UNSOFT	VATTED	VOGUED	WILIER
TRYPAN	UNTIDY	VAUNTY	VORAGO	WISPED
TUFTED	UNWONT	VAWTED	WAIFED	WOADED
TURGID	UPDOVE	VEDUTE	WAIFTS	WRISTY
TWEEDY	UPGOES	VELDTS	WAILED	YBRENT
TWEENY	UPGONE	VENERY	WANNEL	YIRRED
TWIRLS	VACANT	VIBIER	WANNER	YITIES
TWIRLY	VAGROM	VIFDAS	WAURED	YOWIES
TWIRPS	VANMEN	VINTRY	WAVERY	
UNCUTE	VANNED	VIOLAS	WEFTED	
UNMIRY	VATMAN	VISTAS	WHINEY	

Seven-letter words that do not combine with another letter

The seven-letter word list is slightly different in concept. These are valid seven-letter words, and potentially playable on a board. However, if you find that the seven-letter word isn't playable, you may begin to consider whether an eight-letter can be played through a letter already on the board. None of these seven-letter words combines with an eighth letter, so you can avoid wasting time by searching for any. The criteria for inclusion in the seven-letter are the same as for the six-letter list. The seven-letter word list contains over 200 words. Words with any of JKQXZ have been removed, words with more than three of the same letter have been removed (eg no words with three Es), words with more than two repeated letters have been removed (eg no words with 2 Es and 2 Ns). The 200-plus words are presented in alphabetic order. The first word on the seven-letter list is ABEYANT - and just to be clear, although this is a valid seven-letter word, there is no valid eight-letter word which can be made containing these letters.

ABEYANT	AVOIDED	DAWTING	FOODIES	HOODIAS
ABUSIVE	BEDIRTY	DEFANGS	FOREDID	HOSIERY
ACAROID	BESPATE	DEVIOUS	FORGAVE	HURTLED
ADIPOUS	BILGIER	DILUTED	FOSSATE	IMAGERY
ADOPTED	BINDERY	DITHIOL	FUNGOES	INNERLY
AEFAULD	BIODATA	DITTANY	GAUCIER	INSWEPT
AEOLIAN	BIRDIES	DOCIBLE	GAUDERY	INVADED
AEROBIA	BODGIER	DODGIER	GAWCIER	INVIOUS
AGATOID	BOILERY	DOTARDS	GHASTED	IRACUND
AGELONG	BONEYER	DOVEISH	GHOSTED	IRONMAN
AGOUTAS	BOOFIER	DOWDIER	GIFTEES	IVORIED
ALIBIED	BOOGIED	EBRIETY	GLADIUS	LAWNIER
ALIYOTH	BOOSTED	ENTROPY	GLOUTED	LEAFERY
ALONELY	BOUGIES	EPINAOI	GONADIC	LEAGUED
ALSOONE	BOVINES	EVINCES	GOOFIER	LETHIED
ALUMNAE	BRACTED	FADDIER	GOVERNS	LITHOID
AMATIVE	BRAVOED	FAGOTTI	GOWDEST	MEADOWS
AMOEBAS	BRIGUED	FAITHED	GREYEST	MIAOWED
AMOEBIC	CAEOMAS	FANEGAS	GRITTED	MIDGIER
ANNUITY	CANOLAS	FANNERS	GROUPED	MILORDS
ANTIGAY	COOMIER	FEAGUED	HARILY	MIOCENE
ARRIVED	DADOING	FERVENT	HOARILY	MISWENT
AUDITED	DAIKONS	FESTIVE	HOGTIED	NAUPLII
AUREITY	DAIMIOS	FOISTED	HONDLES	NAYSAID
AUTOMAN	DATURIC	FOLIOED	HONGIED	NERVILY

NOISILY	OVERBIG	SIALOID	TIPTOED	VESPINE
NONWAGE	OVERGOT	SNAFUED	TOWNEES	VOMICAE
NOTCHED	OVIPARA	SNOTTED	TRIFOLD	VUTTIER
NOVELTY	PAVONES	SOVIETS	TURDOID	WAFERED
NOVENAS	PEAVIES	STALLED	TURTLED	WAIRING
OBELION	PENSIVE	STIFLED	TUYERES	WAIRUAS
OBOVATE	PERENTY	SUDARIA	TWINGED	WANIONS
OLDWIFE	PLONGES	SUDATES	UNNEATH	WANNEST
OLITORY	POOFIER	SWINERY	UNOFTEN	WAREHOU
ORGANDY	POOVIER	TAGUANS	UNROYAL	WAURING
ORIENCY	POYNTED	TAUIWIS	UNSWEET	WAVIEST
OUTGAVE	RESTUDY	TEAPOYS	UNWAGED	WAYGONE
OUTGREW	REUNIFY	TENUITY	URINARY	WIFTIER
OUTLAID	RILIEVO	TEUGHER	UVEITIS	WIREMEN
OUTWENT	RORTING	THIEVED	VALGOID	WURLIES
OVARIAN	RUINOUS	THINNED	VANNERS	YAUTIAS
OVATELY	SATIETY	THRIVED	VAWNTIE	YONNIES

Special eights

If you are landed with a 'non-word' rack, you needn't abandon all hope of playing a bonus word. Some racks that don't form seven-letter words will form eight-letter words with letters on the board. This is where 'special eights' come in handy. Special eights are eight-letter words that have no other eight-letter anagrams, and contain no seven-letter words. These are great words to know, as each of them is a solution to eight different problem racks. The top 200 special eights are listed below, in alphabetical order.

ABNEGATE	ATHETOID	DILATATE	FUSIONAL	IRONLIKE
ABOIDEAU	AUDITION	DILATIVE	GAIETIES	IRONWARE
ABOITEAU	AUDITIVE	DOLOMITE	GEODETIC	IRRIGATE
ABSENTEE	AURIFIED	DOTATION	GLEETIER	JETLINER
ACUITIES	AUTACOID	DROOLIER	GOLDTONE	LATEWOOD
ADDITION	AUTODYNE	DUETTINO	GROOLIER	LIGATIVE
ADULATOR	AUTOGENY	DYSTONIA	GUILTIER	LITIGATE
AEDICULE	AUTOGIRO	EBENISTE	HABANERO	LOOSENER
AEGIRITE	AUTUNITE	ECLOGITE	HAEREMAI	LOTHARIO
AEQUORIN	AVIANISE	EGOISTIC	HANDOVER	LOWERIER
AEROBIUM	AVIARIES	ELOINING	HAURIANT	LOWERING
AEROFOIL	AVIATION	ENCAENIA	HELOTAGE	MEUNIERE
AEROTONE	AVOIDANT	ENVIABLE	HORDEOLA	MIRLITON
AGIOTAGE	BANNERET	EUCARYON	IANTHINE	MOTORAIL
ALEHOUSE	BARONIAL	EUPHONIA	IDEALITY	MOUTERED
ALOPECIA	BEMOANER	EURONOTE	IDEOGRAM	NAUSEATE
AMARETTO	BETOILED	EVECTION	IDONEOUS	NEATENED
ANAEROBE	BIENNALE	EXERTION	ILLATION	NEONATAL
ANNEALED	BIOMETER	EXPIATOR	ILMENITE	NEOTENIC
ANNULOSE	BOUDERIE	EYELINER	INDAGATE	NODALITY
ANOREXIA	BOUNTREE	EYESTONE	INDUCIAE	NONGLARE
ANOREXIC	CAPOEIRA	FACETIAE	INDUVIAE	NOTATION
ANTIWEED	COENOBIA	FAROLITO	INFERIAE	NUTATION
AORTITIS	COOEEING	FETATION	INFERNAL	OCEANAUT
APERITIF	COROTATE	FLEABITE	INITIATE	OEDIPEAN
APOSITIA	DETAINEE	FONTANEL	INTOMBED	OEILLADE
AQUATONE	DEVOTION	FOREHAND	INTUITED	OILFIRED
ARTIFICE	DIGITATE	FOREREAD	INVERTOR	OLIGEMIA
ATENOLOL	DIGITULE	FRUITION	IODATION	ONIONIER

Seven-letter words that do not combine with another letter

OOGAMETE	RADIATOR	SARTORII	TOILETED	VENEREAL
OPIATING	RAILROAD	SEMIOVAL	TOLEWARE	VENOSITY
OPTIONEE	RAINWEAR	SIALIDAN	TRIBUNAL	VESTIGIA
OREODONT	REBOOTED	SOLIDARY	TRIZONAL	VINIFERA
ORONASAL	RECOILER	TABEFIED	TROOPIAL	VIOLATOR
OUTEATEN	RELOADED	TALEGGIO	UINTAITE	VOIDABLE
OVERFINE	RELOADER	TAPENADE	UNEASIER	WAGMOIRE
OVERLOAD	RETIARII	TAQUERIA	UNHAIRER	WAILSOME
PARANOEA	ROTAVATE	TENEBRAE	UNPITIED	WANDEROO
PATOOTIE	ROTOVATE	TERATOMA	UNSEELIE	WANTONED
PELERINE	ROYALISE	THIONATE	VANITORY	WATERLOO

Multiplets

Multiplets, a word borrowed from physics, are groups of letters with a given number of anagrams. So, a couplet is a set of two anagrams; a triplet is a set of three anagrams; a quadruplet is a set of four anagrams; and so on. The lists here contain seven-letter words. You'll see that the largest group in any of these lists contains 11 anagrams.

The benefit of studying these words is that if you get the requisite letters on your rack, you don't need to waste any time on looking for bonus words that aren't there. Also, multiplets can serve as memory-joggers for other anagrams in the same group. For example, remembering that there are 11 anagrams of RETAINS should enable you to recall the others. If you are interested in multiplet eight-letter anagrams, you could compile your own lists using the eight-letter anagrams section of this book.

Couplets

ABACTOR	ABLINGS	ACARINE	ACCUSED	ACHIRAL
ACROBAT	SABLING	CARINAE	SUCCADE	RACHIAL
ABATERS	ABLUENT	ACATERS	ACERBIC	ACIDEST
ABREAST	TUNABLE	CARATES	BRECCIA	DACITES
ABATORS	ABOUNDS	ACATOUR	ACEROUS	ACIFORM
RABATOS	BAUSOND	AUTOCAR	CAROUSE	FORMICA
ABDUCES	ABRASAX	ACCITES	ACETALS	ACNODAL
SCUBAED	ABRAXAS	ASCETIC	LACTASE	CALANDO
ABETTER	ABRIDGE	ACCOILS	ACETOSE	ACNODES
BERETTA	BRIGADE	CALICOS	COATEES	DEACONS
ABIDDEN	ABSENTS	ACCOMPT	ACETYLS	ACOLYTE
BANDIED	BASNETS	COMPACT	SCYTALE	COTYLAE
ABIOSES	ABYEING	ACCOYLD	ACHARNE	ACONITE
ISOBASE	EBAYING	CACODYL	ARCHEAN	ANOETIC
ABLATED	ABYSMAL	ACCRUAL	ACHENES	ACORNED
DATABLE	BALSAMY	CARACUL	ENCHASE	DRACONE
ABLATES	ACANTHI	ACCRUED	ACHIEST	ACQUIST
ASTABLE	TACHINA	CARDECU	AITCHES	ACQUITS

ACRIDER	ADVENED	AGENDUM	AIRPORT	ALKANET
CARRIED	DAVENED	GUDEMAN	PARITOR	KANTELA
ACROGEN	ADVERSE	AGENTED	AIRTING	ALLAYER
CORNAGE	EVADERS	NEGATED	RAITING	AREALLY
ACTINGS	ADVERTS	AGGADAH	ALANYLS	ALLEDGE
CASTING	STARVED	HAGGADA	NASALLY	ALLEGED
ACUTEST	ADVISER	AGGRADE	ALBUGOS	ALLICES
SCUTATE	VARDIES	GARAGED	SUBGOAL	CAILLES
ADAPTER	ADVISES	AGISTOR	ALCADES	ALLISES
READAPT	DISSAVE	ORGIAST	SCALADE	SALLIES
ADDICTS	ADWARES	AGNAMED	ALCAICS	ALLODIA
DIDACTS	SEAWARD	MANAGED	CICALAS	ALODIAL
ADDREST	ADWOMEN	AGNISES	ALCOVES	ALLONGE
RADDEST	WOMANED	SEASING	COEVALS	GALLEON
ADDUCES	AEDILES	AGNIZES	ALDOSES	ALLOVER
SCAUDED	DEISEAL	SEAZING	LASSOED	OVERALL
ADERMIN	AEGISES	AGNOMEN	ALEGARS	ALLUDED
INARMED	ASSIEGE	NONGAME	LAAGERS	DUALLED
ADHARMA	AERIEST	AGNOSIC	ALEMBIC	ALLUDES
HARAMDA	SERIATE	ANGICOS	CEMBALI	ALUDELS
ADHERED	AEROSOL	AGONIES	ALEPINE	ALLURED
REDHEAD	ROSEOLA	AGONISE	ELAPINE	UDALLER
ADHERER	AFFAIRS	AGONIST	ALETHIC	ALLURES
REHEARD	RAFFIAS	GITANOS	ETHICAL	LAURELS
ADIPSIA	AFFIXER	AGRISES	ALEVINS	ALMANAC
ASPIDIA	REAFFIX	GASSIER	VALINES	MANCALA
ADMIRAL	AFFYING	AGUISED	ALEYING	ALMONDS
AMILDAR	YAFFING	GAUDIES	YEALING	DOLMANS
ADMIRED	AFREETS	AIBLINS	ALFAKIS	ALMONER
MARDIED	FEASTER	BILIANS	KAFILAS	NEMORAL
ADONIZE	AGAMETE	AIDLESS	ALIENED	ALMUCES
ANODIZE	AGEMATE	DEASILS	DELAINE	MACULES
ADOPTER	AGAROSE	AILANTO	ALINING	ALMUDES
READOPT	OARAGES	ALATION	NAILING	MEDUSAL
ADORERS	AGEINGS	AILMENT	ALISMAS	ALNICOS
DROSERA	SIGNAGE	ALIMENT	SALAMIS	OILCANS
ADORNER	AGEISTS	AIRBASE	ALISONS	ALOGIAS
READORN	SAGIEST	ARABISE	SIALONS	LAOGAIS
ADUSTED	AGELESS	AIRIEST	ALIUNDE	ALPEENS
SUDATED	ALGESES	IRISATE	UNIDEAL	SPELEAN

Couplets

ALSIKES	AMISSES	ANGLIFY	APERCUS	APTOTES
ASSLIKE	MESSIAS	FLAYING	SCAUPER	TEAPOTS
ALYSSUM	AMITIES	ANGUINE	APERIES	ARAYSED
ASYLUMS	ATIMIES	GUANINE	EPEIRAS	DARESAY
AMABILE	AMMETER	ANGUISH	APHESES	ARAYSES
AMIABLE	METAMER	HAUSING	SPAHEES	ASSAYER
AMANDLA	AMMINES	ANICUTS	APHETIC	ARBITER
MANDALA	MISNAME	NAUTICS	HEPATIC	RAREBIT
AMARANT	AMNESIA	ANKLING	APHIDES	ARBORES
MARANTA	ANEMIAS	LANKING	DIPHASE	BRASERO
AMATION	AMNESIC	ANNELID	APICALS	ARCADES
ANIMATO	CINEMAS	LINDANE	SPACIAL	ASCARED
AMBARIS	AMOOVES	ANNOYED	APLENTY	ARCHERS
MARABIS	VAMOOSE	ANODYNE	PENALTY	CRASHER
AMBOINA	AMPERES	ANSWERS	APNOEAS	ARCHILS
BONAMIA	EMPARES	RAWNESS	PAESANO	CARLISH
AMBONES	AMRITAS	ANTHEMS	APNOEIC	ARCHLET
BEMOANS	TAMARIS	HETMANS	PAEONIC	TRACHLE
AMEARST	AMULETS	ANTIBUG	APOLLOS	ARCMINS
RETAMAS	MULETAS	TABUING	PALOLOS	NARCISM
AMELIAS	ANADEMS	ANTICLY	APOMICT	ARCTANS
MALAISE	MAENADS	CANTILY	POTAMIC	CANTARS
AMENDED	ANAPEST	ANTIFLU	APOSTIL	ARCTOID
DEADMEN	PEASANT	FLUTINA	TOPSAIL	CAROTID
AMENING	ANCILIA	ANTINGS	APOSTLE	AREFIED
MEANING	LACINIA	STANING	PELOTAS	FEDARIE
AMENITY	ANCONES	ANTIQUE	APPENDS	ARETTED
ANYTIME	SONANCE	QUINATE	SNAPPED	TREATED
AMENTIA	ANCRESS	ANTISEX	APPLIES	ARGALIS
ANIMATE	CASERNS	SEXTAIN	LAPPIES	GARIALS
AMERCER	ANDVILE	ANTRUMS	APPOSED	ARGHANS
CREAMER	ANVILED	UNSMART	PEAPODS	HANGARS
AMIDASE	ANERGIC	ANUROUS	APPOSER	ARGLING
SEAMAID	GRECIAN	URANOUS	POPERAS	GLARING
AMIDINE	ANESTRA	ANYMORE	APPRESS	ARGONON
DIAMINE	SANTERA	ROMNEYA	SAPPERS	ORGANON
AMIDINS	ANETHOL	APEDOMS	APPRISE	ARGUERS
DIAMINS	ETHANOL	POMADES	SAPPIER	SUGARER
AMIDONE	ANGINAS	APELIKE	APPRIZE	ARGYLES
DOMAINE	INANGAS	PEALIKE	ZAPPIER	GRAYLES

ARIETTE	ASININE	ASTUTER	AVALING	BACCIES
ITERATE	INSANIE	STATURE	VAGINAL	SEBACIC
ARISTAS	ASKINGS	ASTYLAR	AVARICE	BACKERS
TARSIAS	GASKINS	SATYRAL	CAVIARE	REBACKS
ARKITES	ASPERGE	ATELIER	AVENGED	BACKOUT
KARITES	PRESAGE	REALTIE	VENDAGE	OUTBACK
ARMINGS	ASPORTS	ATHAMES	AVENGER	BACKPAY
MARGINS	PASTORS	HAMATES	ENGRAVE	PAYBACK
ARMLOCK	ASPREAD	ATHEIST	AVENGES	BAETYLS
LOCKRAM	PARADES	STAITHE	GENEVAS	BEASTLY
ARMREST	ASQUINT	ATLATLS	AVENIRS	BAGARRE
SMARTER	QUINTAS	TALLATS	RAVINES	BARRAGE
ARNOTTO	ASSARTS	ATOCIAS	AVERTED	BAGASSE
RATTOON	SASTRAS	COAITAS	TAVERED	SEABAGS
AROINTS	ASSENTS	ATOPIES	AVGASES	BAGFULS
RATIONS	SNASTES	OPIATES	SAVAGES	BAGSFUL
ARRIDES	ASSERTS	ATRIUMS	AVIATIC	BAGGERS
RAIDERS	TRASSES	MATSURI	VIATICA	BEGGARS
ARRIERO	ASSIGNS	ATTONES	AVIETTE	BAGNIOS
ROARIER	SASSING	NOTATES	EVITATE	GABIONS
ARRIVES	ASSUAGE	ATTRIST	AVISING	BAGUETS
VARIERS	SAUSAGE	ATTRITS	VISAING	TUBAGES
ARROBAS	ASSUMED	AUCTION	AVOCETS	BAKINGS
RASBORA	MEDUSAS	CAUTION	OCTAVES	BASKING
ARSHINE	ASSURED	AUGMENT	AVODIRE	BALDING
HERNIAS	RUDASES	MUTAGEN	AVOIDER	BLADING
ARSHINS	ASSURER	AULDEST	AWAKENS	BALEENS
SHAIRNS	RASURES	SALUTED	WAKANES	ENABLES
ARSINES	ASSURES	AULNAGE	AWELESS	BALLAST
SARNIES	SARUSES	LEGUAAN	WEASELS	BALLATS
ARTSMAN	ASTARTS	AUNTIES	AWESOME	BALLUTE
MANTRAS	STRATAS	SINUATE	WAESOME	BULLATE
ARUGULA	ASTHENY	AUTOCUE	AWMRIES	BALSAMS
AUGURAL	SHANTEY	COUTEAU	SEMIRAW	SAMBALS
ASCITES	ASTHMAS	AUTOING	BABBLED	BAMPOTS
ECTASIS	MATSAHS	OUTGAIN	BLABBED	SPAMBOT
ASCITIC	ASTRALS	AUTOPSY	BABIEST	BANDARS
SCIATIC	TARSALS	PAYOUTS	TABBIES	SANDBAR
ASEPSIS	ASTRAND	AVAILED	BABOOSH	BANDIER
ASPISES	TARANDS	VEDALIA	HABOOBS	BRAINED

Couplets

BANDIES	BARRIES	BEADIER	BEENTOS	BENISON
BASINED	BRASIER	BEARDIE	BONESET	BONNIES
BANDORE	BARYTES	BEAKERS	BEETING	BENTHIC
BROADEN	BETRAYS	BERAKES	BEIGNET	BITCHEN
BANGERS	BASALLY	BEARERS	BEEYARD	BERDASH
GRABENS	SALABLY	BREARES	BERAYED	BRASHED
BANKERS	BASHERS	BEATIER	BEEZERS	BERGAMA
BARKENS	BRASHES	EBRIATE	BREEZES	MEGABAR
BANTAMS	BASHLIK	BECALMS	BEFANAS	BERRIED
BATSMAN	KIBLAHS	SCAMBLE	FANBASE	BRIERED
BANTERS	BASIONS	BECRUST	BEFLUMS	BERTHES
BARNETS	BONSAIS	BECURST	FUMBLES	SHERBET
BAPTISM	BASSEST	BEDERAL	BEGIRDS	BESCOUR
BITMAPS	BASSETS	BLEARED	BRIDGES	OBSCURE
BARAZAS	BASTARD	BEDIGHT	BEGUINS	BESINGS
BAZAARS	TABARDS	BIGHTED	BUNGIES	BIGNESS
BARBIES	BASTLES	BEDLAMS	BELACED	BESLIME
RABBIES	STABLES	BELDAMS	DEBACLE	BESMILE
BARDING	BATBOYS	BEDLESS	BELATED	BESPAKE
BRIGAND	BOBSTAY	BLESSED	BLEATED	BESPEAK
BARGING	BATCHER	BEDRALS	BELAYED	BESTEAD
GARBING	BRACHET	BLADERS	DYEABLE	DEBATES
BARISTA	BATISTE	BEDRAPE	BELGARD	BESTILL
BARTSIA	BISTATE	PREBADE	GARBLED	BILLETS
BARKEEP	BATTERS	BEDROCK	BELTERS	BESTORM
PREBAKE	TABRETS	BROCKED	TREBLES	MOBSTER
BARKIER	BATTLED	BEDSORE	BELTMAN	BESTREW
BRAKIER	BLATTED	SOBERED	LAMBENT	WEBSTER
BARKING	BAUBLES	BEDTIME	BELUGAS	BESTRID
BRAKING	BUBALES	BETIMED	BLAGUES	BISTRED
BARLESS	BAUERAS	BEDUINS	BEMETES	BESTUCK
BRALESS	SUBAREA	BUNDIES	BETEEMS	BUCKETS
BAROLOS	BAWBLES	BEDUSTS	BEMIRED	BETIDED
ROBALOS	WABBLES	BESTUDS	BERIMED	DEBITED
BARONET	BAWLERS	BEECHES	BEMUSED	BHAKTAS
REBOANT	WARBLES	BESEECH	EMBUSED	SABKHAT
BARONGS	BAWLEYS	BEEFIER	BEMUSES	BHINDIS
BROGANS	BYELAWS	FREEBIE	EMBUSES	BINDHIS
BARRETS	BAWLING	BEEGAHS	BENDIER	BICOLOR
BARTERS	BLAWING	BHAGEES	INBREED	BROCOLI

BICORNS	BLATHER	BLOWUPS	BOODIES	BOUCHES
BICRONS	HALBERT	UPBLOWS	DOOBIES	SUBECHO
BIFTERS	BLEARER	BLUBBED	BOOGERS	BOUGETS
FIBSTER	ERRABLE	BUBBLED	GOOBERS	OUTBEGS
BILBOES	BLEATER	BLUBBER	BOOGIES	BOULDER
LOBBIES	RETABLE	BUBBLER	GOOBIES	DOUBLER
BILLERS	BLENDER	BLUDGER	BOOHING	BOULTED
REBILLS	REBLEND	BURGLED	HOBOING	DOUBLET
BILOBED	BLETHER	BLUEING	BOOKERS	BOULTER
LOBBIED	HERBLET	BULGINE	REBOOKS	TROUBLE
BILTONG	BLINDER	BLUEISH	BOOKIER	BOUNCED
BOLTING	BRINDLE	HELIBUS	BROOKIE	BUNCOED
BIMBOES	BLOATED	BLUIEST	BOOKIES	BOUNDEN
MOBBIES	LOBATED	SUBTILE	BOOKSIE	UNBONED
BINGOES	BLOBBED	BLUNDER	BOONGAS	BOUSIER
BIOGENS	BOBBLED	BUNDLER	GABOONS	OUREBIS
BIOGENY	BLOGGER	BLUNGED	BOOSTER	BOUTONS
OBEYING	BOGGLER	BUNGLED	REBOOTS	UNBOOTS
BIOPICS	BLONDES	BLUNGER	BOOZERS	BOWELED
BIOPSIC	BOLDENS	BUNGLER	REBOZOS	ELBOWED
BIPEDAL	BLOODED	BLUNGES	BORACIC	BOWINGS
PIEBALD	BOODLED	BUNGLES	BRACCIO	BOWSING
BIPOLAR	BLOOMER	BLUSHER	BORDURE	BOWLDER
PARBOIL	REBLOOM	BURHELS	BOURDER	LOWBRED
BIRDIES	BLOTTED	BLUSHES	BOREENS	BOWLEGS
BRIDIES	BOTTLED	BUSHELS	ENROBES	WEBLOGS
BIRDING	BLOTTER	BOATELS	BORIDES	BOWSERS
BRIDING	BOTTLER	OBLATES	DISROBE	BROWSES
BIRSIER	BLOUSED	BOCAGES	BORKING	BOXWOOD
RIBIERS	DOUBLES	BOSCAGE	BROKING	WOODBOX
BIRSLED	BLOUSES	BODICES	BORSCHT	BOYARDS
BRIDLES	BOLUSES	CEBOIDS	BORTSCH	BYROADS
BIRSLES	BLOWERS	BOMBERS	BORTIER	BRADOON
RIBLESS	BOWLERS	MOBBERS	ORBITER	ONBOARD
BISTORT	BLOWFLY	BOMBING	BOSHTER	BRAHMAS
BITTORS	FLYBLOW	MOBBING	BOTHERS	SAMBHAR
BITTURS	BLOWING	BONDAGE	BOSSEST	BRAILLE
TURBITS	BOWLING	DOGBANE	BOSSETS	LIBERAL
BIZARRE	BLOWSES	BONIEST	BOSSIER	BRAIRDS
BRAZIER	BOWLESS	EBONIST	RIBOSES	BRIARDS

BRAIZES	BROMINS	BUMMLED	BYREMAN	CALLOPS
ZERIBAS	MISBORN	MUMBLED	MYRBANE	SCALLOP
BRANDER	BROOSES	BUNDIST	CACHETS	CALLOSE
REBRAND	SORBOSE	DUSTBIN	CATCHES	LOCALES
BRANLES	BROUZES	BUNTALS	CACHING	CALLUNA
BRANSLE	SUBZERO	TULBANS	CHACING	LACUNAL
BRASHER	BRUCKLE	BURDASH	CACKLED	CALMANT
HERBARS	BUCKLER	RHABDUS	CLACKED	CLAMANT
BRASSED	BRUISED	BURIALS	CACTOID	CALMEST
SERDABS	BURDIES	RAILBUS	OCTADIC	CAMLETS
BRAWEST	BRUMOUS	BURLERS	CADRANS	CALQUES
WABSTER	UMBROUS	BURRELS	CANARDS	CLAQUES
BRAWLED	BRUSHES	BURNOUT	CAESTUS	CALTROP
WARBLED	BUSHERS	OUTBURN	CUESTAS	PROCTAL
BRAWLER	BRUSKER	BURPING	CAIMANS	CALVARY
WARBLER	BURKERS	UPBRING	MANIACS	CAVALRY
BRAWLIE	BRUTELY	BURSERA	CAITIVE	CALYCES
WIRABLE	BUTLERY	SABREUR	VICIATE	CYCLASE
BREAKUP	BRUTERS	BURYING	CAKIEST	CALYCLE
UPBREAK	BURSTER	RUBYING	TACKIES	CECALLY
BREDIES	BUCKSAW	BUSBIES	CALALUS	CAMARON
DERBIES	SAWBUCK	SUBBIES	CLAUSAL	NARCOMA
BRETONS	BUDDERS	BUSIEST	CALAMUS	CAMBREL
SORBENT	REDBUDS	SUBSITE	MACULAS	CLAMBER
BRIBERS	BUFFERS	BUSINGS	CALDERA	CAMOTES
RIBBERS	REBUFFS	BUSSING	CRAALED	COMATES
BRIBING	BUFFEST	BUSTICS	CALENDS	CAMPERS
RIBBING	BUFFETS	CUBISTS	CANDLES	SCAMPER
BRICOLE	BUGLING	BUSTIER	CALIBER	CAMPLED
CORBEIL	BULGING	RUBIEST	CALIBRE	CLAMPED
BRIGUES	BUILDUP	BUSTING	CALICES	CANDIES
RUGBIES	UPBUILD	TUBINGS	CELIACS	INCASED
BRINING	BUISTED	BUSTLES	CALICHE	CANDOUR
INBRING	SUBEDIT	SUBLETS	CHALICE	CAUDRON
BRISTLY	BULGHUR	BUTANES	CALIMAS	CANFULS
TRILBYS	BURGHUL	SUNBEAT	CAMAILS	CANSFUL
BRISTOL	BULKERS	BUTENES	CALIPER	CANGLES
STROBIL	BURLESK	SUBTEEN	REPLICA	GLANCES
BRITTLE	BULLOUS	BUYOUTS	CALKING	CANGUES
TRIBLET	LOBULUS	OUTBUYS	LACKING	UNCAGES

CANKERS	CARBONS	CASCADE	CAUSTIC	CETANES
SNACKER	CORBANS	SACCADE	CICUTAS	TENACES
CANNERS	CARDERS	CASQUES	CAUTELS	CHACHKA
SCANNER	SCARRED	SACQUES	SULCATE	KACHCHA
CANNIER	CAREERS	CASSOCK	CAVEATS	CHACOES
NARCEIN	CREASER	COSSACK	VACATES	COACHES
CANTRED	CARGOED	CASTLED	CAVERNS	CHAINED
TRANCED	CORDAGE	SCLATED	CRAVENS	ECHIDNA
CANULAE	CARHOPS	CASTLES	CAWKERS	CHAINES
LACUNAE	COPRAHS	SCLATES	WACKERS	INCHASE
CANULAR	CARIOUS	CASTOFF	CEASING	CHAKRAS
LACUNAR	CURIOSA	OFFCAST	INCAGES	CHARKAS
CANULAS	CARNEYS	CASTORS	CEILING	CHALKED
LACUNAS	SCENARY	COSTARS	CIELING	HACKLED
CANYONS	CAROCHE	CASUALS	CELESTA	CHALLIE
SONANCY	COACHER	CAUSALS	SELECTA	HELICAL
CAPABLE	CAROLED	CATALOS	CELOSIA	CHAMISA
PACABLE	ORACLED	COASTAL	COALISE	CHIASMA
CAPERER	CAROMED	CATCHER	CENSING	CHAMISO
PRERACE	COMRADE	RECATCH	SCENING	CHAMOIS
CAPITAL	CAROTIN	CATCHUP	CENTILE	CHANCER
PLACITA	CORTINA	UPCATCH	LICENTE	CHANCRE
CAPITAN	CARPING	CATHOLE	CENTRED	CHANGED
CAPTAIN	CRAPING	CHOLATE	CREDENT	GANCHED
CAPIZES	CARRIES	CATLING	CERAMIC	CHANGES
CAPSIZE	SCARIER	TALCING	RACEMIC	GANCHES
CAPLETS	CARROTS	CATLINS	CERIUMS	CHANSON
PLACETS	TROCARS	TINCALS	MURICES	NONCASH
CAPLINS	CARSEYS	CATSUPS	CEROTIC	CHANTER
INCLASP	SCRAYES	UPCASTS	ORECTIC	TRANCHE
CAPORAL	CARTOON	CATTILY	CERTIFY	CHAPKAS
CRAPOLA	CORANTO	TACITLY	RECTIFY	PACHAKS
CAPOUCH	CARVERS	CAUDLES	CERVIDS	CHARGES
PACHUCO	CRAVERS	CEDULAS	SCRIVED	CREAGHS
CAPTION	CARVING	CAULOME	CESIUMS	CHARIOT
PACTION	CRAVING	LEUCOMA	MISCUES	HARICOT
CARACKS	CASABAS	CAUSEYS	CESSERS	CHARMED
CRACKAS	CASSABA	CAYUSES	CRESSES	MARCHED
CARBEEN	CASAVAS	CAUSING	CESSPIT	CHARMER
CARBENE	CASSAVA	SAUCING	SEPTICS	MARCHER

CHARNEL	CHERISH	CHOKING	CHYMIST	CLASPED
LARCHEN	SHRIECH	HOCKING	TYCHISM	SCALPED
CHARPAI	CHESILS	CHOLENT	CHYPRES	CLASSED
HAIRCAP	CHISELS	NOTCHEL	CYPHERS	DECLASS
CHARTED	CHETAHS	CHOLERS	CIDARIS	CLASSES
RATCHED	HATCHES	ORCHELS	SCIARID	SACLESS
CHARTER	CHEVETS	CHOLINE	CILICES	CLAVIES
RECHART	VETCHES	HELICON	ICICLES	VESICAL
CHASTEN	CHEVIES	CHOOSER	CINGULA	CLEANER
NATCHES	SEVICHE	SOROCHE	GLUCINA	RECLEAN
CHATTEL	CHEWERS	CHOPINE	CINQUES	CLEANUP
LATCHET	RECHEWS	PHOCINE	QUINCES	UNPLACE
CHATTER	CHIASMS	CHOPINS	CIPOLIN	CLEFTED
RATCHET	SCHISMA	PHONICS	PICOLIN	DEFLECT
CHAWING	CHICEST	CHORDAE	CIRCARS	CLEUCHS
CHINWAG	HECTICS	ROACHED	RICRACS	CULCHES
CHEAPED	CHICLES	CHORDAL	CIRCLES	CLEUGHS
PEACHED	CLICHES	DORLACH	CLERICS	GULCHES
CHEAPER	CHICONS	CHORING	CIRRATE	CLIMATE
PEACHER	COCHINS	OCHRING	ERRATIC	METICAL
CHECKER	CHIDERS	CHORISM	CISTERN	CLIMBER
RECHECK	HERDICS	CHRISOM	CRETINS	RECLIMB
CHEEPED	CHIELDS	CHORIST	CITATOR	CLINGER
DEPECHE	CHILDES	OSTRICH	RICOTTA	CRINGLE
CHEERED	CHIGRES	CHOROID	CITHERN	CLINKED
REECHED	SCREIGH	OCHROID	CITHREN	NICKLED
CHEERLY	CHIKORS	CHORTEN	CITIZEN	CLINKER
LECHERY	CHOKRIS	NOTCHER	ZINCITE	CRINKLE
CHELOID	CHIMERS	CHOUSES	CITOLAS	CLIPPER
HELCOID	MICHERS	HOCUSES	STOICAL	CRIPPLE
CHELONE	CHIMING	CHOWDER	CLADDER	CLOBBER
ECHELON	MICHING	COWHERD	CRADLED	COBBLER
CHEMISE	CHIPSET	CHOWSED	CLANGER	CLOCKED
SCHEMIE	PITCHES	COWSHED	GLANCER	COCKLED
CHEMIST	CHIVIES	CHROMAS	CLAQUER	CLOCKER
MITCHES	VICHIES	MORCHAS	LACQUER	COCKLER
CHENARS	CHOICER	CHUNDER	CLARINO	CLODDED
RANCHES	CHOREIC	CHURNED	CLARION	CODDLED
CHENETS	CHOKEYS	CHYLOUS	CLASHES	CLOGGED
TENCHES	HOCKEYS	SLOUCHY	SEALCHS	COGGLED

CLOISON	CODEINA	COMBERS	CONSIST	CORDATE
SCOLION	OCEANID	RECOMBS	TOCSINS	REDCOAT
CLOKING	CODLING	COMBIER	CONSORT	CORDERS
LOCKING	LINGCOD	MICROBE	CROTONS	RECORDS
CLONERS	CODRIVE	COMICES	CONSULT	CORELLA
CORNELS	DIVORCE	MOCCIES	UNCOLTS	OCELLAR
CLOSEST	CODROVE	COMPARE	CONSUME	CORKIER
CLOSETS	VOCODER	COMPEAR	MUSCONE	ROCKIER
CLOSURE	COENURI	COMPEER	CONURES	CORKING
COLURES	NOURICE	COMPERE	ROUNCES	ROCKING
CLOTTER	COFFERS	COMPILE	CONVEYS	CORNERS
CROTTLE	SCOFFER	POLEMIC	COVYNES	SCORNER
CLOVERS	COGENER	COMPOST	COOKERS	CORNILY
VELCROS	CONGREE	COMPOTS	RECOOKS	LYRICON
CLUEING	COGNISE	COMUSES	COOKOUT	CORNUAL
LUCIGEN	COIGNES	MUSCOSE	OUTCOOK	COURLAN
CLUMBER	COHEIRS	CONARIA	COOLANT	CORONAS
CRUMBLE	HEROICS	OCARINA	OCTANOL	RACOONS
CLUMPER	COIFFES	CONCENT	COOLERS	CORONER
CRUMPLE	OFFICES	CONNECT	CREOSOL	CROONER
CLUNKER	COILERS	CONDOES	COOLEST	CORPSES
CRUNKLE	RECOILS	SECONDO	OCELOTS	PROCESS
CNEMIAL	COLEADS	CONDORS	COOLING	CORSIVE
MELANIC	SOLACED	CORDONS	LOCOING	VOICERS
COAGENT	COLITIS	CONDUIT	COOPERS	COSIERS
COGNATE	SOLICIT	NOCTUID	SCOOPER	CRIOSES
COALTAR	COLLOPS	CONGAED	COOSERS	COSMIST
CROTALA	SCOLLOP	DECAGON	ROSCOES	SITCOMS
COARSER	COLLUDE	CONGIUS	COOTERS	COSTEAN
CORREAS	LOCULED	SOUCING	SCOOTER	OCTANES
COATING	COLOBUS	CONICAL	COPITAS	COSTING
COTINGA	SUBCOOL	LACONIC	PSOATIC	GNOSTIC
COCAINE	COLONES	CONIINE	COPOUTS	COTTISE
OCEANIC	CONSOLE	INCONIE	OCTOPUS	SCOTTIE
COCKERS	COLORER	CONKERS	COPTERS	COUNSEL
RECOCKS	RECOLOR	RECKONS	PROSECT	UNCLOSE
COCKILY	COMARBS	CONKING	COPULAR	COUPLET
COLICKY	CRAMBOS	NOCKING	CUPOLAR	OCTUPLE
CODDLES	COMBATS	CONSENT	CORCASS	COUPONS
SCOLDED	TOMBACS	NOCENTS	CORSACS	SOUPCON

COURIES	CREMSIN	CRUSADE	CURNIER	DAMAGER
SCOURIE	MINCERS	SCAURED	REINCUR	MEGARAD
COURTED	CREOLES	CRUSTAL	CURPELS	DAMMERS
EDUCTOR	RECLOSE	CURTALS	SCRUPLE	SMARMED
COUTILS	CREPING	CRYINGS	CURTAIL	DAMPEST
OCULIST	PERCING	SCRYING	TRUCIAL	STAMPED
COUZINS	CRETISM	CUDDLES	CURTAIN	DAMPISH
ZINCOUS	METRICS	SCUDDLE	TURACIN	PHASMID
COVERER	CRIMINA	CUFFLES	CURTESY	DANDIER
RECOVER	MINICAR	SCUFFLE	CURTSEY	DRAINED
COWRIES	CRIMSON	CUISHES	CUSPATE	DANDIES
SCOWRIE	MICRONS	CUSHIES	TEACUPS	SDAINED
COYOTES	CRISPED	CULMENS	CUSSING	DANGLED
OOCYTES	DISCERP	MESCLUN	SCUSING	GLADDEN
CRAFTED	CRISPER	CULTIER	CUTOFFS	DANGLER
FRACTED	PRICERS	UTRICLE	OFFCUTS	GNARLED
CRAFTER	CROQUET	CUMBERS	CYCLISE	DANKEST
REFRACT	ROCQUET	SCUMBER	CYLICES	STANKED
CRAMPIT	CROSSED	CUMMERS	CYSTEIN	DANTONS
PTARMIC	SCORSED	SCUMMER	CYSTINE	DONNATS
CRANING	CROSSES	CUNNERS	CYTASES	DARINGS
RANCING	SCORSES	SCUNNER	ECSTASY	GRADINS
CRANIUM	CROUPED	CUPELED	DABBLES	DARLING
CUMARIN	PRODUCE	DECUPLE	SLABBED	LARDING
CRAPPIE	CROUPER	CUPFULS	DABSTER	DARSHAN
EPICARP	PROCURE	CUPSFUL	TABERDS	DHARNAS
CRASHED	CROWERS	CUPPERS	DADDLES	DARTING
ECHARDS	SCOWRER	SCUPPER	SADDLED	TRADING
CREASES	CROWNED	CUPRITE	DAFTIES	DARTLES
SEARCES	DECROWN	PICTURE	FADIEST	SLARTED
CRECHES	CROWNER	CURACAO	DAGGLES	DASHERS
SCREECH	RECROWN	CURACOA	SLAGGED	SHADERS
CREDITS	CRUDEST	CURAGHS	DAIDLES	DASHING
DIRECTS	CRUSTED	SCRAUGH	LADDIES	SHADING
CREEPED	CRUELTY	CURATED	DAIKERS	DATARIA
PRECEDE	CUTLERY	TRADUCE	DARKIES	RADIATA
CREMATE	CRUISED	CURDIER	DALLIED	DAUNTED
MEERCAT	DISCURE	CURRIED	DIALLED	UNDATED
CREMONA	CRUIVES	CURDLES	DALTONS	DAWDING
ROMANCE	CURSIVE	SCUDLER	SANDLOT	WADDING

DAWDLED	DECREWS	DEHORTS	DEMURES	DERNIER
WADDLED	SCREWED	SHORTED	RESUMED	NERDIER
DAWTIES	DECRIES	DEIDEST	DENDRON	DERVISH
WAISTED	DEICERS	TEDDIES	DONNERD	SHRIVED
DAYWORK	DECTETS	DEIFIED	DENGUES	DESANDS
WORKDAY	DETECTS	EDIFIED	UNEDGES	SADDENS
DEAIRED	DEDIMUS	DEIFIES	DENIALS	DESCEND
READIED	MUDDIES	EDIFIES	SNAILED	SCENDED
DEANERS	DEDUCES	DEINDEX	DENNETS	DESCENT
ENDEARS	SEDUCED	INDEXED	STENNED	SCENTED
DEARIES	DEEDEST	DEISTIC	DENSITY	DESERVE
READIES	STEEDED	DICIEST	DESTINY	SEVERED
DEASOIL	DEEDILY	DEKARES	DENTALS	DESIGNS
ISOLEAD	YIELDED	SKEARED	SLANTED	SDEIGNS
DEAVING	DEEDING	DELATES	DENTELS	DESIRES
EVADING	DEIGNED	STEALED	NESTLED	RESIDES
DEBASES	DEEPEST	DELATOR	DENTING	DESKILL
SEABEDS	STEEPED	LEOTARD	TENDING	SKILLED
DEBTORS	DEFACER	DELENDA	DENUDER	DESMANS
STROBED	REFACED	LADENED	ENDURED	MADNESS
DECAMPS	DEFAULT	DELIGHT	DEPERMS	DESMINE
SCAMPED	FAULTED	LIGHTED	PREMEDS	SIDEMEN
DECANES	DEFIANT	DELIMIT	DEPICTS	DESNOOD
ENCASED	FAINTED	LIMITED	DISCEPT	SNOODED
DECERNS	DEFIERS	DELIRIA	DEPLANE	DESPISE
SCERNED	SERIFED	IRIDEAL	PANELED	PEDESIS
DECIDER	DEFILED	DELVING	DEPLOYS	DESUGAR
DECRIED	FIELDED	DEVLING	PODLEYS	SUGARED
DECILES	DEFOCUS	DEMANDS	DEPONES	DESYNES
DELICES	FOCUSED	MADDENS	SPONDEE	ENDYSES
DECKELS	DEFORMS	DEMERGE	DEPOSAL	DETAILS
DECKLES	SERFDOM	EMERGED	PEDALOS	DILATES
DECKOED	DEFOULS	DEMESNE	DEPOSED	DETENTE
DECOKED	FLOUSED	SEEDMEN	SEEDPOD	NEDETTE
DECODER	DEFROCK	DEMISED	DEPOSER	DETENTS
RECODED	FROCKED	MISDEED	REPOSED	STENTED
DECREED	DEFROST	DEMOING	DEPOSES	DETENUS
RECEDED	FROSTED	MENDIGO	SPEEDOS	DETUNES
DECREET	DEFUSER	DEMOUNT	DERAYED	DETERGE
ERECTED	REFUSED	MOUNTED	YEARDED	GREETED

DETICKS	DICKERS	DINNLES	DISSERT	DOLINAS
STICKED	SCRIKED	LINDENS	STRIDES	LADINOS
DETORTS	DICTIER	DINTING	DISSING	DONATED
DOTTERS	ICTERID	TINDING	SIDINGS	NODATED
DETRACT	DIDDLER	DIOXIDS	DISTUNE	DONGLES
TRACTED	RIDDLED	IXODIDS	DUNITES	GOLDENS
DEUCING	DIEDRAL	DIPHONE	DITCHES	DONGOLA
EDUCING	DRAILED	PHONIED	SICHTED	GONDOLA
DEUTONS	DIEHARD	DIPNETS	DITHERS	DONINGS
SNOUTED	DIHEDRA	STIPEND	SHIRTED	ONDINGS
DEVEINS	DIEOFFS	DIPNOAN	DITHIOL	DONNERT
ENDIVES	OFFSIDE	NONPAID	LITHOID	TENDRON
DEVOLVE	DIGESTS	DIRHAMS	DITONES	DONNIES
EVOLVED	DISGEST	MIDRASH	STONIED	ONDINES
DEWITTS	DIGNITY	DIRTIED	DIURONS	DOODLER
TWISTED	TIDYING	TIDDIER	DURIONS	DROOLED
DEWLAPS	DIGONAL	DISCOER	DIVERGE	DOOFERS
SPAWLED	LOADING	SCODIER	GRIEVED	FORDOES
DHANSAK	DILUENT	DISEASE	DIVISOR	DOOKETS
KHANDAS	UNTILED	SEASIDE	VIROIDS	STOOKED
DHURRIE	DILUTES	DISEURS	DOCKERS	DOOLANS
HURRIED	DUELIST	SUDSIER	REDOCKS	ONLOADS
DIALYSE	DIMNESS	DISGOWN	DODGERS	DOOMILY
EYLIADS	MISSEND	DOWSING	GORSEDD	MOODILY
DIASTEM	DINDLES	DISHORN	DODGING	DOORMAN
MISDATE	SLIDDEN	DRONISH	GODDING	MADRONO
DIATOMS	DINGERS	DISMAYD	DODMANS	DOORMEN
MASTOID	ENGIRDS	MIDDAYS	ODDSMAN	MORENDO
DIAXONS	DINGEYS	DISMAYL	DOGATES	DOPINGS
DIOXANS	DYEINGS	LADYISM	DOTAGES	PONGIDS
DIAZINS	DINKEST	DISPELS	DOGEATE	DORISED
DIZAINS	KINDEST	DISPLES	GOATEED	SODDIER
DIBBLER	DINKEYS	DISPLED	DOGLEGS	DORISES
DRIBBLE	KIDNEYS	PIDDLES	SLOGGED	DOSSIER
DICHTED	DINKIES	DISPONE	DOGLIKE	DORMANT
DITCHED	KINDIES	SPINODE	GODLIKE	MORDANT
DICINGS	DINKING	DISROOT	DOGSHIP	DORMINS
DISCING	KINDING	TOROIDS	GODSHIP	NIMRODS
DICKENS	DINNERS	DISSEAT	DOILIES	DORTERS
SNICKED	ENDRINS	SAIDEST	IDOLISE	RODSTER

DOSAGES	DRAYAGE	DUALIST	DUNNIES	EARWIGS
SEADOGS	YARDAGE	TULADIS	UNDINES	GAWSIER
DOSSERS	DRAYING	DUCTILE	DUNSHES	EBAYERS
DROSSES	YARDING	DULCITE	SNUSHED	EYEBARS
DOTCOMS	DRAYMAN	DUDDIER	DUNTING	EBONIES
TOMCODS	YARDMAN	RUDDIED	TUNDING	EBONISE
DOTIEST	DRAYMEN	DUELERS	DUOTONE	ECHOIST
STOITED	YARDMEN	ELUDERS	OUTDONE	TOISECH
DOTTLER	DREADED	DUETTOS	DUPIONS	ECONOMY
DOTTREL	READDED	TESTUDO	UNIPODS	MONOECY
DOURINE	DREADLY	DUFFEST	DURANCE	EDENTAL
NEUROID	LADDERY	STUFFED	UNRACED	LATENED
DOUSING	DRESSER	DUGITES	DURIANS	EDGINGS
GUIDONS	REDRESS	GIUSTED	SUNDARI	SNIGGED
DOWAGER	DRILLER	DUGONGS	DURMAST	EDITION
WORDAGE	REDRILL	GUNDOGS	MUSTARD	TENIOID
DOWNERS	DROGUET	DUIKERS	DUSTERS	EELIEST
WONDERS	GROUTED	DUSKIER	TRUSSED	STEELIE
DOWNIER	DROICHS	DUKKAHS	DWARVES	EEVNING
WINDORE	ORCHIDS	DUKKHAS	SWARVED	EVENING
DOWSERS	DROOMES	DULCIAN	DWINDLE	EFTSOON
DROWSES	SMOORED	INCUDAL	WINDLED	FESTOON
DRAFTER	DROPLET	DULOSIS	DWINING	EGGLERS
REDRAFT	PRETOLD	SOLIDUS	WINDING	LEGGERS
DRAGEES	DROPOUT	DUMAIST	DYELINE	EGOISMS
GREASED	OUTDROP	STADIUM	NEEDILY	MISGOES
DRAGNET	DROWSED	DUMMIER	EARFLAP	EGOISTS
GRANTED	SWORDED	IMMURED	PARAFLE	STOGIES
DRAGOON	DRUGGED	DUMMIES	EARLIER	EGOTISE
GADROON	GRUDGED	MEDIUMS	LEARIER	GOETIES
DRAINER	DRUGGER	DUMPIER	EARLIES	EILDING
RANDIER	GRUDGER	UMPIRED	REALISE	ELIDING
DRAPERS	DRUMBLE	DUMPLES	EARLIKE	EISWEIN
SPARRED	RUMBLED	SLUMPED	LEAKIER	WIENIES
DRAPPIE	DRUPELS	DUNGING	EARNERS	ELATION
PREPAID	SLURPED	NUDGING	REEARNS	TOENAIL
DRAWEES	DRUSIER	DUNNEST	EARTHED	ELCHEES
RESAWED	DURRIES	STUNNED	HEARTED	LEECHES
DRAWING	DUALINS	DUNNIER	EARTHEN	ELECTOR
WARDING	SUNDIAL	INURNED	HEARTEN	ELECTRO

ELEGIES	EMPORIA	ENDOWER	ENROUGH	ENTWIST
ELEGISE	MEROPIA	REENDOW	ROUGHEN	TWINSET
ELEGIST	EMPTIES	ENDURES	ENSIGNS	ENWOUND
ELEGITS	SEPTIME	ENSURED	SENSING	UNOWNED
ELEMENT	EMPTINS	ENDWISE	ENSKIED	EPACRID
TELEMEN	PIMENTS	SINEWED	SKEINED	PERACID
ELOGIST	EMPTION	ENEWING	ENSKIES	EPARCHS
LOGIEST	PIMENTO	WEENING	KINESES	PARCHES
ELOPERS	EMULGES	ENFOLDS	ENSLAVE	EPARCHY
LEPROSE	LEGUMES	FONDLES	LEAVENS	PREACHY
ELUATES	EMUNGED	ENFRAME	ENSNARE	EPEIRIC
SETUALE	GUDEMEN	FREEMAN	RENNASE	EPICIER
ELUENTS	ENAMELS	ENGINED	ENSNARL	EPHEBOS
UNSTEEL	MELENAS	NEEDING	LANNERS	PHOEBES
ELUTION	ENAMOUR	ENGINER	ENSOULS	EPIGRAM
OUTLINE	NEUROMA	INGENER	NOUSLES	PRIMAGE
EMAILED	ENCAVED	ENGLISH	ENSTAMP	EPILATE
LIMEADE	VENDACE	SHINGLE	TAPSMEN	PILEATE
EMBLICS	ENCHARM	ENGLUTS	ENSTEEP	EPIMERE
LIMBECS	MARCHEN	GLUTENS	STEEPEN	PREEMIE
EMBRUED	ENCLASP	ENGORES	ENSTYLE	EPINAOS
UMBERED	SPANCEL	NEGROES	TENSELY	SENOPIA
EMENDER	ENCLAVE	ENGUARD	ENTAMES	EPISODE
REEDMEN	VALENCE	RAUNGED	MEANEST	POESIED
EMERGES	ENCODER	ENJOYER	ENTASIA	EPISTLE
MERGEES	ENCORED	REENJOY	TAENIAS	PELITES
EMICANT	ENCODES	ENLIGHT	ENTERIC	EPOXIDE
NEMATIC	SECONDE	LIGHTEN	ENTICER	EPOXIED
EMITTER	ENCORES	ENLOCKS	ENTERON	EPSILON
TERMITE	NECROSE	SLOCKEN	TENONER	PINOLES
EMONGES	ENCRATY	ENMOVED	ENTOPIC	EQUATOR
GENOMES	NECTARY	VENOMED	NEPOTIC	QUORATE
EMOTING	ENDARCH	ENOLOGY	ENTOTIC	EQUINAL
MITOGEN	RANCHED	NEOLOGY	TONETIC	QUINELA
EMPALER	ENDINGS	ENQUIRE	ENTOZOA	ERATHEM
PREMEAL	SENDING	INQUERE	OZONATE	THERMAE
EMPANEL	ENDITED	ENRACED	ENTRAIN	ERECTER
EMPLANE	TEINDED	RECANED	TRANNIE	REERECT
EMPARED	ENDNOTE	ENRINGS	ENTRUST	EREPSIN
PREMADE	TENONED	GINNERS	NUTTERS	REPINES

ERGATES	ETALAGE	EXCURSE	FALSERS	FAUTORS
RESTAGE	GALEATE	EXCUSER	FLASERS	FOUTRAS
ERINITE	ETALONS	EXPANDS	FALSIES	FAVORER
NITERIE	TOLANES	SPANDEX	FILASSE	OVERFAR
ERISTIC	ETAMINE	EXPERTS	FAMINES	FEATHER
RICIEST	MATINEE	SEXPERT	INFAMES	TEREFAH
EROTICS	ETATIST	EXPIRES	FANGLED	FECHTER
TERCIOS	TATTIES	PREXIES	FLANGED	FETCHER
ERRANTS	ETCHERS	EXPOSED	FANGLES	FEEDERS
RANTERS	RETCHES	PODEXES	FLANGES	REFEEDS
ERRATUM	ETHIONS	EXPOSIT	FANKLED	FEEDING
MATURER	HISTONE	POXIEST	FLANKED	FEIGNED
ERUPTED	ETHIOPS	EXTINES	FANNELL	FEELERS
REPUTED	OPHITES	SIXTEEN	FLANNEL	REFEELS
ERYNGOS	ETHNICS	EYELIDS	FANTAIL	FEELING
GROYNES	STHENIC	SEEDILY	TAILFAN	FLEEING
ESCROCS	ETTLING	EYESPOT	FARCERS	FELLATE
SOCCERS	LETTING	PEYOTES	SCARFER	LEAFLET
ESPADAS	EUMONGS	FACIEND	FARCIES	FELTIER
PASSADE	MUNGOES	FANCIED	FIACRES	FERTILE
ESPANOL	EVANISH	FACTORS	FARDENS	FEMINAL
NOPALES	VAHINES	FORCATS	SNARFED	INFLAME
ESPIERS	EVENTER	FACTURE	FARFELS	FEODARY
PRESSIE	EVERNET	FURCATE	RAFFLES	FORAYED
ESPOUSE	EVOKERS	FAIENCE	FARMERS	FERNIER
POSEUSE	REVOKES	FIANCEE	FRAMERS	REFINER
ESQUIRE	EVOLUTE	FAINEST	FARMING	FERROUS
QUERIES	VELOUTE	NAIFEST	FRAMING	FURORES
ESSOYNE	EVOLVER	FAINNES	FARMOST	FETIALS
NOYESES	REVOLVE	FANNIES	FORMATS	SEALIFT
ESTEEMS	EXACTER	FAINTER	FARSIDE	FETICHE
MESTEES	EXCRETA	FENITAR	FRAISED	FITCHEE
ESTHETE	EXAMPLE	FAIRISH	FASTENS	FETTLES
TEETHES	EXEMPLA	HAIRIFS	FATNESS	LEFTEST
ESTOILE	EXCEPTS	FALCONS	FASTERS	FEUTRED
ETOILES	EXPECTS	FLACONS	STRAFES	REFUTED
ESTREPE	EXCIDES	FALLERS	FASTEST	FEUTRES
STEEPER	EXCISED	REFALLS	SAFTEST	REFUTES
ESTRUAL	EXCITOR	FALLOUT	FATSOES	FICKLED
SALUTER	XEROTIC	OUTFALL	FOSSATE	FLICKED

Couplets

FICKLER	FLATCAR	FLYOVER	FRENUMS	GADGETS
FLICKER	FRACTAL	OVERFLY	SURFMEN	STAGGED
FIERIER	FLECKER	FOALING	FRESHER	GAHNITE
REIFIER	FRECKLE	LOAFING	REFRESH	HEATING
FILAREE	FLEMISH	FOCUSER	FRESHET	GALERES
LEAFIER	HIMSELF	REFOCUS	HEFTERS	REGALES
FILLERS	FLENSER	FOCUSES	FRESHIE	GALLEIN
REFILLS	FRESNEL	FUCOSES	HEIFERS	NIGELLA
FILMERS	FLESHED	FOISTER	FRETFUL	GALLICA
REFILMS	SHELFED	FORTIES	TRUFFLE	GLACIAL
FILMSET	FLESHER	FOLDERS	FRETSAW	GALLIES
LEFTISM	HERSELF	REFOLDS	WAFTERS	GALLISE
FINALIS	FLETTON	FOLDUPS	FRONTER	GALLING
FINIALS	FONTLET	UPFOLDS	REFRONT	GINGALL
FINGERS	FLIRTED	FONDLER	FUGLIER	GALLNUT
FRINGES	TRIFLED	FORLEND	GULFIER	NUTGALL
FINITES	FLIRTER	FONDUED	FUGLING	GALLONS
NIFTIES	TRIFLER	FOUNDED	GULFING	GOLLANS
FINKING	FLITING	FORAMEN	FULNESS	GALORES
KNIFING	LIFTING	FOREMAN	UNSELFS	GAOLERS
FIRELIT	FLOORER	FORBARE	FUNDERS	GAMBIST
FITLIER	FORLORE	FORBEAR	REFUNDS	GAMBITS
FIREPOT	FLOOSIE	FORESTS	FUNDIES	GAMBLER
PIEFORT	FOLIOSE	FOSTERS	INFUSED	GAMBREL
FIRLOTS	FLORETS	FORETOP	FUNFAIR	GAMETES
FLORIST	LOFTERS	POOFTER	RUFFIAN	METAGES
FIRMEST	FLOURED	FORFEIT	FURANES	GAMIEST
FREMITS	FOULDER	TOFFIER	UNSAFER	SIGMATE
FISTING	FLUATES	FORMERS	FUROLES	GAMMERS
SIFTING	SULFATE	REFORMS	OURSELF	GRAMMES
FITNESS	FLUERIC	FORRAYS	FUSIBLE	GAMONES
INFESTS	LUCIFER	ORFRAYS	SUBFILE	MANGOES
FITTERS	FLUIEST	FORWARD	FUSTIER	GANGING
TITFERS	SULFITE	FROWARD	SURFEIT	NAGGING
FITTING	FLUSHED	FOUNDER	GABBLER	GANSEYS
TIFTING	SHEDFUL	REFOUND	GRABBLE	GAYNESS
FIZZERS	FLUTIER	FOUTERS	GABELLE	GANTING
FRIZZES	FUTILER	FOUTRES	GELABLE	TANGING
FLARIER	FLUVIAL	FRANGER	GABNASH	GAOLING
FRAILER	VIALFUL	GRANFER	NASHGAB	GOALING

GARNERS	GERMING	GIRONNY	GLOSSED	GOOSIES
RANGERS	MERGING	ROYNING	GODLESS	SOOGIES
GASLESS	GESTATE	GIRSHES	GLOSSER	GORGETS
GLASSES	TAGETES	SIGHERS	REGLOSS	TOGGERS
GASPERS	GIBBONS	GIRTHED	GLOVERS	GORINGS
SPARGES	SOBBING	RIGHTED	GROVELS	GRINGOS
GASSERS	GILDING	GIRTING	GLOWERS	GOSLING
GRASSES	GLIDING	RINGGIT	REGLOWS	OGLINGS
GASTERS	GILLERS	GITTERN	GLOWING	GOWANED
STAGERS	GRILLES	RETTING	GOWLING	WAGONED
GASTRIC	GILLNET	GLACIER	GLUEING	GRADDAN
TRAGICS	TELLING	GRACILE	LUGEING	GRANDAD
GATEWAY	GIMMERS	GLADIER	GLUGGED	GRADERS
GETAWAY	MEGRIMS	GLAIRED	GUGGLED	REGARDS
GAUDGIE	GINGALS	GLAIKET	GLUIEST	GRADING
GUIDAGE	LAGGINS	TAGLIKE	UGLIEST	NIGGARD
GAUFERS	GINGELY	GLAIRES	GLUTTED	GRADINI
GAUFRES	GLEYING	GRAILES	GUTTLED	RAIDING
GAUNTED	GINGKOS	GLEAVES	GNARRED	GRAFTER
UNGATED	GINKGOS	SELVAGE	GRANDER	REGRAFT
GEARING	GINNELS	GLEEING	GNASHED	GRAHAMS
NAGGIER	LENSING	NEGLIGE	HAGDENS	GRAMASH
GELATOS	GINNERY	GLEEMAN	GOALIES	GRANDAM
LEGATOS	RENYING	MELANGE	SOILAGE	GRANDMA
GELDING	GINNIER	GLIBBER	GODDENS	GRANTER
NIGGLED	REINING	GRIBBLE	GODSEND	REGRANT
GEMMATE	GINSHOP	GLIMPSE	GODLING	GRAPING
TAGMEME	POSHING	MEGILPS	LODGING	PARGING
GENOISE	GIPPERS	GLINTED	GOLOSHE	GRAPLIN
SOIGNEE	GRIPPES	TINGLED	SHOOGLE	PARLING
GENTLED	GIRAFFE	GLISTER	GONGING	GRASPER
GLENTED	RIFFAGE	GRISTLE	NOGGING	SPARGER
GENTLES	GIRASOL	GLOATER	GONIFFS	GRATING
LENGEST	GLORIAS	LEGATOR	OFFINGS	TARGING
GENUINE	GIRDERS	GLOIRES	GOODIES	GRAVELS
INGENUE	RIDGERS	GLORIES	SOOGIED	VERGLAS
GENUSES	GIRLOND	GLOMERA	GOOLIES	GRAVURE
NEGUSES	LORDING	GOMERAL	OLOGIES	VERRUGA
GERENTS	GIRNING	GLONOIN	GOORIES	GREASER
REGENTS	RINGING	LOONING	GOOSIER	REGEARS

GREATER	GRUELED	GUTLESS	HALLANS	HARDMEN
REGRATE	REGLUED	TUGLESS	NALLAHS	HERDMAN
GREENED	GRUMOSE	GUTROTS	HALLOED	HAREEMS
RENEGED	MORGUES	ROTGUTS	HOLLAED	MAHSEER
GREETER	GRUNGES	GUTTIER	HALLOOS	HARELDS
REGREET	SNUGGER	TURGITE	HOLLOAS	HERALDS
GREMIAL	GRUNTED	GUYLING	HALLOWS	HARISSA
LAMIGER	TRUDGEN	UGLYING	SHALLOW	SHARIAS
GRIEVES	GRUSHIE	GYMNAST	HALTERE	HARPIES
REGIVES	GUSHIER	SYNTAGM	LEATHER	SHARPIE
GRIFFIN	GRUTTEN	GYMPIES	HALTING	HARVEST
RIFFING	TURGENT	PYGMIES	LATHING	THRAVES
GRINDED	GUBBINS	GYRATED	HAMBLES	HASSLED
REDDING	SUBBING	TRAGEDY	SHAMBLE	SLASHED
GRINDER	GUDDLES	HACKLES	HAMMERS	HASSOCK
REGRIND	SLUDGED	SHACKLE	SHAMMER	SHACKOS
GRINNED	GULLIES	HACKSAW	HANDERS	HASTIER
RENDING	LIGULES	KWACHAS	HARDENS	SHERIAT
GRIPMAN	GULPERS	HADARIM	HANDLES	HASTING
RAMPING	SPLURGE	HARAMDI	HANDSEL	TASHING
GROANER	GUNDIES	HAEMINS	HANDOFF	HATFULS
ORANGER	SUEDING	HEMINAS	OFFHAND	HATSFUL
GROOMER	GUNLESS	HAGBORN	HANGOUT	HATTING
REGROOM	GUNSELS	HORNBAG	TOHUNGA	TATHING
GROOVED	GUNSHIP	HAGDONS	HANGUPS	HAULING
OVERDOG	PUSHING	SANDHOG	UPHANGS	NILGHAU
GROSERS	GURGING	HAGRIDE	HANJARS	HAVINGS
GROSSER	RUGGING	HEADRIG	RHANJAS	SHAVING
GROSSED	GURRIES	HAILERS	HANKERS	HAWKIES
SODGERS	SURGIER	SHALIER	HARKENS	WEAKISH
GROUPER	GURSHES	HAILING	HANTING	HAYRIDE
REGROUP	GUSHERS	NILGHAI	TANGHIN	HYDRIAE
GROUPIE	GUSHING	HAIQUES	HAPLESS	HAZMATS
PIROGUE	SUGHING	QUASHIE	PLASHES	MATZAHS
GROWERS	GUSTIER	HALAKAH	HAPLONT	HEADPIN
REGROWS	GUTSIER	HALAKHA	NAPHTOL	PINHEAD
GROWNUP	GUSTILY	HALITES	HARDASS	HEAVERS
UPGROWN	GUTSILY	HELIAST	SRADHAS	RESHAVE
GRUEING	GUSTING	HALITUS	HARDIER	HEEDING
GUNGIER	GUTSING	THULIAS	HARRIED	NEIGHED

HEELERS	HILLERS	HOLSTER	HUMITES	ILLICIT
REHEELS	RELLISH	HOSTLER	TUMSHIE	ILLITIC
HEIRESS	HILLOES	HOMAGES	HUNGANS	ILLIPES
HERISSE	HOLLIES	OHMAGES	UNHANGS	PILLIES
HELIMEN	HILTING	HONGIES	HURLIES	ILLUDES
HEMLINE	LITHING	SHOEING	LUSHIER	SULLIED
HELLERI	HINDGUT	HOODMAN	HURRIES	IMBOSOM
HELLIER	UNDIGHT	MANHOOD	RUSHIER	MIOMBOS
HELLERS	HINGING	HOOPING	HURTFUL	IMBOWER
SHELLER	NIGHING	POOHING	RUTHFUL	WOMBIER
HEMPIES	HINTERS	HOPPERS	HURTLES	IMBRUTE
IMPHEES	NITHERS	SHOPPER	HUSTLER	TERBIUM
HEPCATS	HINTING	HORMONE	HUSHERS	IMPAINT
PATCHES	NITHING	MOORHEN	SHUSHER	TIMPANI
HEPTADS	HIPBONE	HORRENT	HYACINE	IMPALED
SPATHED	HOPBINE	NORTHER	HYAENIC	IMPLEAD
HERMITS	HIPPENS	HORSING	HYALINS	IMPALES
MITHERS	SHIPPEN	SHORING	LINHAYS	PALMIES
HERNIAL	HIPPIES	HORSTES	HYDRATE	IMPANEL
INHALER	SHIPPIE	TOSHERS	THREADY	MANIPLE
HEROINS	HIRINGS	HOSTING	HYDROUS	IMPASSE
INSHORE	SHIRING	TOSHING	SHROUDY	PESSIMA
HEROISM	HIRSELS	HOTCHES	HYLISTS	IMPASTE
MOREISH	HIRSLES	SHOCHET	STYLISH	PASTIME
HERRIED	HISSELF	HOTLINE	ICECAPS	IMPASTO
REHIRED	SELFISH	NEOLITH	IPECACS	MATIPOS
HERRIES	HITTERS	HOTTING	ICELESS	IMPEDES
REHIRES	TITHERS	TONIGHT	SIECLES	SEMIPED
HESPING	HITTING	HOUTING	ICHNITE	IMPLATE
PHESING	TITHING	THOUING	NITCHIE	PALMIET
HEURISM	HOARSEN	HOWEVER	ICINESS	IMPONES
MUSHIER	SENHORA	WHOEVER	INCISES	PEONISM
HICATEE	HODDENS	HOWLETS	IDEATUM	IMPORTS
TEACHIE	SHODDEN	THOWELS	TAEDIUM	TROPISM
HIDLING	HOEDOWN	HUDDLER	IDENTIC	IMPOSES
HILDING	WOODHEN	HURDLED	INCITED	MOPSIES
HIELAND	HOLDUPS	HUMECTS	IGNITOR	IMPOSTS
INHALED	UPHOLDS	MUTCHES	RIOTING	MISSTOP
HIGHTED	HOLINGS	HUMIDOR	IGNOBLE	IMPRESA
THIGHED	LONGISH	RHODIUM	INGLOBE	SAMPIRE

IMPREST	INGESTS	INSURES	IODIDES	JACKMAN
PERMITS	SIGNETS	SUNRISE	IODISED	MANJACK
IMPUGNS	INHUMER	INTAGLI	IODINES	JALOUSE
SPUMING	RHENIUM	TAILING	IONISED	JEALOUS
IMPURER	INISLED	INTENSE	IOLITES	JAMBOKS
PRIMEUR	LINDIES	TENNIES	OILIEST	SJAMBOK
IMPUTER	INKPOTS	INTENTS	IONIUMS	JAMBONE
TUMPIER	INKSPOT	TENNIST	NIMIOUS	JOBNAME
INAPTLY	INLAYER	INTERNS	IONIZER	JAMBULS
PTYALIN	NAILERY	TINNERS	IRONIZE	JUMBALS
INCANTS	INLIERS	INTIMAE	IONOMER	JAMMIES
STANNIC	RESILIN	MINIATE	MOONIER	JEMIMAS
INCESTS	INNAGES	INTINES	IRELESS	JANTIER
INSECTS	SEANING	TINNIES	RESILES	NARTJIE
INCISED	INNINGS	INTONED	IRISING	JANTIES
INDICES	SINNING	NOINTED	NIGIRIS	TAJINES
INCLUDE	INQUEST	INTONES	IRKSOME	JARFULS
NUCLIDE	QUINTES	TENSION	SMOKIER	JARSFUL
INDEWED	INSANER	INTORTS	IRONERS	JAWINGS
WIDENED	INSNARE	TRITONS	ROSINER	JIGSAWN
INDEXER	INSCAPE	INTRADA	IRONING	JAYVEES
REINDEX	PINCASE	RADIANT	ROINING	VEEJAYS
INDITER	INSEAMS	INTWIST	IRRUPTS	JERBILS
NITRIDE	SAMISEN	NITWITS	STIRRUP	JIRBLES
INDITES	INSIDER	INVADED	ISOSPIN	JERKINS
TINEIDS	SNIDIER	VIDENDA	SINOPIS	JINKERS
INDOORS	INSTATE	INVADER	ISOTONE	JITTERS
SORDINO	SATINET	RAVINED	TOONIES	TRIJETS
INDRAWN	INSTEPS	INVERTS	ISSUANT	JOINERS
WINNARD	SPINETS	STRIVEN	SUSTAIN	REJOINS
INDUSIA	INSULAE	INVITER	ISSUERS	JOLLITY
SUIDIAN	INULASE	VITRINE	RISUSES	JOLTILY
INDWELT	INSULAR	INVITES	ITCHIER	JOLTERS
WINTLED	URINALS	VINIEST	TICHIER	JOSTLER
INFARES	INSULIN	INWRAPS	IVORIST	JOUNCES
SERAFIN	INULINS	RIPSAWN	VISITOR	JUNCOES
INFEFTS	INSULSE	IODATED	IVRESSE	JOURNOS
STIFFEN	SILENUS	TOADIED	REVISES	SOJOURN
INFIDEL	INSURER	IODATES	JACKIES	JOYPOPS
INFIELD	RUINERS	TOADIES	JACKSIE	POPJOYS

JUGFULS	KELLIES	KIRNING	LACINGS	LARMIER
JUGSFUL	SKELLIE	RINKING	SCALING	MARLIER
JUJITSU	KELSONS	KIRPANS	LADINGS	LASINGS
JUJUIST	SLOKENS	PARKINS	LIGANDS	SIGNALS
JUMARED	KELTIES	KISSING	LADRONS	LASKETS
MUDEJAR	SLEEKIT	SKIINGS	LARDONS	SKLATES
KAISERS	KENOTIC	KISTFUL	LADYISH	LASQUES
KARSIES	KETONIC	LUTFISK	SHADILY	SQUEALS
KALMIAS	KEPHIRS	KITSCHY	LAGERED	LATINOS
KAMILAS	PERKISH	SHTICKY	REGALED	TALIONS
KANGHAS	KERRIAS	KNEADER	LAIKERS	LATTICE
KHANGAS	SARKIER	NAKEDER	SERKALI	TACTILE
KANTING	KETMIAS	KNEIDEL	LAIRAGE	LAUNCED
TANKING	MISTAKE	LIKENED	REGALIA	UNLACED
KARAMUS	KEYINGS	KNITTER	LAISSES	LAVAGES
KUMARAS	YESKING	TRINKET	LASSIES	SALVAGE
KARYONS	KEYRING	KNURLED	LAKIEST	LAWINGS
RYOKANS	YERKING	RUNKLED	TALKIES	SWALING
KASBAHS	KIDDERS	KOORIES	LAKINGS	LAYINGS
SABKHAS	SKIDDER	ROOKIES	SLAKING	SLAYING
KASHERS	KIDNAPS	KRAKENS	LAMINAL	LAYOUTS
SHAKERS	SKIDPAN	SKANKER	MANILLA	OUTLAYS
KAYOING	KILLERS	KREESED	LAMINAR	LAYOVER
OKAYING	RESKILL	SKEERED	RAILMAN	OVERLAY
KEELERS	KILTING	KUMARIS	LAMMIES	LAYTIME
SLEEKER	KITLING	RUMAKIS	MELISMA	MEATILY
KEENEST	KIMMERS	KUMITES	LAMPING	LEACHER
KETENES	SKIMMER	MISTEUK	PALMING	RELACHE
KEENING	KIMONOS	KURSAAL	LANCERS	LEAGUER
KNEEING	MONOSKI	RUSALKA	RANCELS	REGULAE
KEEPING	KINDLES	KYANISE	LANGARS	LEAKING
PEEKING	SLINKED	YANKIES	RAGLANS	LINKAGE
KEESTER	KINGCUP	KYLIKES	LANGUID	LEARNER
SKEETER	PUCKING	SKYLIKE	LAUDING	RELEARN
KEGGERS	KINGPIN	LABELER	LANIARD	LEASHED
SKEGGER	PINKING	RELABEL	NADIRAL	SHEALED
KEISTER	KINSHIP	LABOURS	LAPPING	LEAVIER
KIESTER	PINKISH	SUBORAL	PALPING	VEALIER
KEITLOA	KIPPERS	LABRUMS	LARIATS	LEAVING
OATLIKE	SKIPPER	LUMBARS	LATRIAS	VEALING

Couplets

LECHWES	LIGATED	LINIEST	LOCOMEN	LOUVARS
WELCHES	TAIGLED	LINTIES	MONOCLE	VALOURS
LEEPING	LIGHTER	LINSEYS	LOCULES	LOVABLE
PEELING	RELIGHT	LYSINES	OCELLUS	VOLABLE
LEERING	LIGNANS	LINTIER	LOCUSTA	LOVINGS
REELING	LINSANG	NITRILE	TALCOUS	SOLVING
LEESING	LIGNINS	LIONELS	LOFTIER	LOWERED
SEELING	LININGS	NIELLOS	TREFOIL	ROWELED
LEEWAYS	LIGROIN	LIPPENS	LOGGERS	LOWPING
WEASELY	ROILING	NIPPLES	SLOGGER	PLOWING
LEGGISM	LIGULAS	LIQUATE	LOMEINS	LOWSEST
MIGGLES	LUGSAIL	TEQUILA	MOLINES	SLOWEST
LEIGERS	LIKINGS	LISTERS	LOMENTS	LOXYGEN
LIEGERS	SILKING	RELISTS	MELTONS	XYLOGEN
LEIRING	LILTING	LITOTES	LOMPISH	LUCITES
LINGIER	TILLING	TOILETS	PHLOMIS	LUETICS
LEISLER	LIMACEL	LITTERY	LOOKERS	LUCUMOS
RELLIES	MICELLA	TRITELY	RELOOKS	OSCULUM
LEMURES	LIMACES	LITTLIE	LOOKOUT	LUDSHIP
RELUMES	MALICES	TILLITE	OUTLOOK	SULPHID
LENGTHY	LIMACON	LIVINGS	LOOKUPS	LUMINED
THEGNLY	MALONIC	SLIVING	UPLOOKS	UNLIMED
LENTISK	LIMITER	LIVYERS	LOOMING	LUMPENS
TINKLES	MILTIER	SILVERY	MOOLING	PLENUMS
LESSONS	LIMMERS	LOACHES	LOOPING	LUMPERS
SONLESS	SLIMMER	OSCHEAL	POOLING	RUMPLES
LETTERN	LIMNERS	LOAFERS	LOOSEST	LUMPIER
NETTLER	MERLINS	SAFROLE	LOTOSES	PLUMIER
LEVERED	LIMPEST	LOATHER	LOOTING	LUMPING
REVELED	LIMPETS	RATHOLE	TOOLING	PLUMING
LEWDEST	LINCHET	LOATHLY	LOPPERS	LUNATED
SWELTED	TINCHEL	TALLYHO	PROPELS	UNDEALT
LEXISES	LINEMAN	LOBBERS	LORDOMA	LUNGIES
SILEXES	MELANIN	SLOBBER	MALODOR	SLUEING
LIAISES	LINGAMS	LOCKERS	LOTHEST	LUNKERS
SILESIA	MALIGNS	RELOCKS	SHOTTLE	RUNKLES
LICHENS	LINGUAE	LOCKETS	LOTIONS	LURRIES
LINCHES	UNAGILE	LOCKSET	SOLITON	SURLIER
LIERNES	LINGUAL	LOCKUPS	LOUNDED	LUSHING
RELINES	LINGULA	UPLOCKS	NODULED	SHULING

LUSKING	MANIHOC	MARQUES	MATRONS	MEINEYS
SULKING	MOHICAN	MASQUER	TRANSOM	MENYIES
LUTITES	MANITOS	MARRANO	MATROSS	MELICKS
TITULES	STAMNOI	ORRAMAN	STROAMS	MICKLES
LYCHEES	MANITOU	MARRIES	MATTERS	MELLAYS
SLEECHY	TINAMOU	SIMARRE	SMATTER	MESALLY
LYDDITE	MANKIER	MARRUMS	MATURES	MENDERS
TIDDLEY	RAMEKIN	MURRAMS	STRUMAE	REMENDS
MACABER	MANPACK	MARTIAN	MAUGRES	MERCERY
MACABRE	PACKMAN	TAMARIN	MURAGES	REMERCY
MADRONE	MANRENT	MARTING	MAULERS	MERELLS
ROADMEN	REMNANT	MIGRANT	SERUMAL	SMELLER
MAGIANS	MANROPE	MASALAS	MAUMETS	MERINOS
SIAMANG	REPOMAN	SALAAMS	SUMMATE	MERSION
MAGNONS	MANTEEL	MASCOTS	MAUVEIN	MERISIS
SONGMAN	TELEMAN	SCAMTOS	MAUVINE	MISSIER
MAGPIES	MANTRAP	MASHIER	MAXIMIN	MERISMS
MISPAGE	RAMPANT	MISHEAR	MINIMAX	SIMMERS
MAIMERS	MANTUAS	MASHIES	MAZIEST	MERLOTS
RAMMIES	TAMANUS	MESSIAH	MESTIZA	MOLTERS
MAISTRY	MAORMOR	MASHING	MEANERS	MESEEMS
SYMITAR	MORMAOR	SHAMING	RENAMES	SEMEMES
MAKEUPS	MAPLESS	MASHUPS	MEANIES	MESETAS
UPMAKES	SAMPLES	SMASHUP	NEMESIA	SEAMSET
MAKINGS	MARBLED	MASONRY	MEDAKAS	MESTERS
MASKING	RAMBLED	MORNAYS	SMAAKED	RESTEMS
MALANGA	MARBLER	MASQUES	MEDALET	METRING
NAGMAAL	RAMBLER	SQUAMES	METALED	TERMING
MALICHO	MARCONI	MASSIER	MEDICOS	METTLES
MOCHILA	MINORCA	SARMIES	MISCODE	STEMLET
MANATIS	MARENGO	MASSIVE	MEDUSAN	MIDTERM
STAMINA	MEGARON	MAVISES	SUDAMEN	TRIMMED
MANDOLA	MARITAL	MASTERS	MEERING	MIGRATE
MONADAL	MARTIAL	STREAMS	REGIMEN	RAGTIME
MANDRIL	MARKERS	MASTICH	MEETING	MIKRONS
RIMLAND	REMARKS	TACHISM	TEEMING	MORKINS
MANEGES	MARMITE	MATCHER	MEGASSE	MILDEST
MENAGES	TRAMMIE	REMATCH	MESSAGE	MISTLED
MANGELS	MAROONS	MATLESS	MEGILLA	MILLETS
MANGLES	ROMANOS	SAMLETS	MILLAGE	MISTELL

Couplets

MILREIS	MITISES	MOORIER	MUCOIDS	NAPPIES
SLIMIER	STIMIES	ROOMIER	MUSCOID	PINESAP
MIMESES	MITOSES	MOORING	MUDGERS	NARKING
MISSEEM	SOMITES	ROOMING	SMUDGER	RANKING
MINCEUR	MITTENS	MOORVAS	MUGGERS	NASTILY
NUMERIC	SMITTEN	VAROOMS	SMUGGER	SAINTLY
MINDERS	MODELER	MOOTING	MUISTED	NASUTES
REMINDS	REMODEL	TOOMING	TEDIUMS	UNSEATS
MINDSET	MODERNS	MOPPIER	MUNDANE	NATRONS
MISTEND	RODSMEN	POMPIER	UNNAMED	NONARTS
MINIMUS	MODULES	MORAINE	MURDERS	NATTERS
MINIUMS	MOUSLED	ROMAINE	SMURRED	RATTENS
MINUEND	MOITHER	MORONIC	MURLAIN	NATURAE
UNMINED	MOTHIER	OMICRON	RUMINAL	TAUREAN
MIREXES	MOLLAHS	MOROSER	MURREES	NAVARIN
REMIXES	OLLAMHS	ROOMERS	RESUMER	NIRVANA
MISDOER	MOMENTO	MORTALS	MUSIMON	NEAPING
MOIDERS	MOOTMEN	STROMAL	OMNIUMS	PEANING
MISEASE	MOMENTS	MOTIVED	MUSINGS	NEBULAS
SIAMESE	MONTEMS	VOMITED	MUSSING	UNBALES
MISERLY	MOMUSES	MOTTIER	MUSKLES	NEGATON
MISRELY	MOUSMES	OMITTER	SKELUMS	TONNAGE
MISHAPS	MONARCH	MOULDER	MUSMONS	NEITHER
PASHIMS	NOMARCH	REMOULD	SUMMONS	THEREIN
MISPLAN	MONAULS	MOUSERS	MUSSELS	NERVIER
PLASMIN	SOLANUM	SMOUSER	SUMLESS	VERNIER
MISSEES	MONGERS	MOUSING	MUTANDA	NESTLES
SEMISES	MORGENS	SOUMING	TAMANDU	NETLESS
MISSOUT	MONISMS	MOUSSED	MUTUALS	NETTIER
SUMOIST	NOMISMS	SMOUSED	UMLAUTS	TENTIER
MISTERS	MONITOR	MOUSSES	MUTUELS	NETTING
SMITERS	TROMINO	SMOUSES	MUTULES	TENTING
MISTERY	MONOMER	MOUSTED	MUTULAR	NETTLES
SMYTRIE	MOORMEN	SMOUTED	TUMULAR	TELNETS
MISTLES	MONOSIS	MOUTERS	MYOSOTE	NEURONS
SMILETS	SIMOONS	OESTRUM	TOYSOME	NONUSER
MISTRAL	MONTANE	MOWINGS	MYTHIER	NEXUSES
RAMTILS	NONMEAT	SOWMING	THYMIER	UNSEXES
MITERER	MOONLET	MUCHELS	NANDINE	NHANDUS
TRIREME	TOOLMEN	MULCHES	NANNIED	UNHANDS

NICKERS	NOVALIA	OFFTAKE	OPUNTIA	OUTJEST
SNICKER	VALONIA	TAKEOFF	UTOPIAN	OUTJETS
NICTATE	NOWHERE	OGRISMS	ORATING	OUTLIED
TETANIC	WHEREON	SIMORGS	ROATING	TOLUIDE
NIFFERS	NOWTIER	OILCUPS	ORBIEST	OUTNESS
SNIFFER	TOWNIER	UPCOILS	SORBITE	TONUSES
NIPPERS	NUCLEUS	OILLETS	ORDERER	OUTPASS
SNIPPER	NUCULES	TOLLIES	REORDER	PASSOUT
NIPTERS	NURDLED	OILNUTS	OREIDES	OUTPOST
PTERINS	RUNDLED	ULTIONS	OSIERED	OUTTOPS
NITROUS	NURSING	OLIVERS	ORGONES	OUTPULL
TURIONS	URNINGS	VIOLERS	OROGENS	PULLOUT
NOIRISH	NURSLES	OLIVETS	ORPHISM	OUTPUTS
ROINISH	RUNLESS	VIOLETS	ROMPISH	PUTOUTS
NONETTI	NURTURE	OMELETS	ORRISES	OUTRIGS
TONTINE	UNTRUER	TELOMES	ROSIERS	RIGOUTS
NONPAST	NUZZLES	OMNEITY	OSETRAS	OUTROLL
PANTONS	SNUZZLE	OMNIETY	OSSETRA	ROLLOUT
NONSTOP	OARIEST	ONAGERS	OSPREYS	OUTRUNS
PONTONS	OTARIES	ORANGES	PYROSES	RUNOUTS
NOODLES	OARSMAN	ONEYERS	OSSETER	OUTSELL
SNOOLED	RAMONAS	ONEYRES	STEREOS	SELLOUT
NOOKIER	OBDURES	OOMPAHS	OSSUARY	OUTSETS
ROOINEK	ROSEBUD	SHAMPOO	SUASORY	SETOUTS
NORITIC	ODDNESS	OORALIS	OSTIATE	OUTSIDE
TIRONIC	SODDENS	OORIALS	TOASTIE	TEDIOUS
NOSHERS	ODORISE	OOZIEST	OTTERED	OUTSINS
SENHORS	OROIDES	ZOOIEST	TETRODE	USTIONS
NOSTOCS	OESTRAL	OPCODES	OUGHTED	OUTSPED
ONCOSTS	OLESTRA	SCOOPED	TOUGHED	SPOUTED
NOTCHES	OEUVRES	OPERONS	OUTACTS	OUTSTEP
TECHNOS	OVERUSE	SNOOPER	OUTCAST	TOUPETS
NOTEPAD	OFFENDS	OPINING	OUTDOER	OUTTAKE
TONEPAD	SENDOFF	PIONING	OUTRODE	TAKEOUT
NOTICES	OFFERER	OPPRESS	OUTDRAW	OUTTURN
SECTION	REOFFER	PORPESS	OUTWARD	TURNOUT
NOUGATS	OFFPUTS	OPPUGNS	OUTGUNS	OUTWALK
OUTSANG	PUTOFFS	POPGUNS	OUTSUNG	WALKOUT
NOUNIER	OFFSETS	OPSONIC	OUTHIRE	OUTWASH
REUNION	SETOFFS	POCOSIN	ROUTHIE	WASHOUT

OUTWITH	PALLONE	PARTIAL	PAULINS	PENCILS
WITHOUT	PLEONAL	PATRIAL	SPINULA	SPLENIC
OUTWORK	PALMARY	PARTURE	PAUNCES	PENNATE
WORKOUT	PALMYRA	RAPTURE	UNCAPES	PENTANE
OVARIAL	PALSHIP	PARTYER	PAUPERS	PENNIES
VARIOLA	SHIPLAP	PETRARY	UPSPEAR	PINENES
OVERATE	PALSIER	PARURES	PAYINGS	PENSELS
OVEREAT	PARLIES	UPREARS	SPAYING	SPLEENS
OVERLIE	PANDITS	PARVISE	PAYSLIP	PENSIVE
RELIEVO	SANDPIT	PAVISER	SAPPILY	VESPINE
OVERMEN	PANGENS	PASEARS	PEACODS	PEPPIER
VENOMER	PENANGS	SARAPES	PEASCOD	PREPPIE
OVERNEW	PANIERS	PASSADO	PEANUTS	PEPTISE
REWOVEN	RAPINES	POSADAS	PESAUNT	TIPPEES
OVERPLY	PANNERS	PASSELS	PEARTER	PERCALE
PLOVERY	SPANNER	SAPLESS	TAPERER	REPLACE
OVERRED	PANTINE	PASSING	PECKIER	PERCENT
REDROVE	PINNATE	SPAINGS	PICKEER	PRECENT
OVERRUN	PARETIC	PASSMAN	PEDALED	PERCEPT
RUNOVER	PICRATE	SAMPANS	PLEADED	PRECEPT
OVERSAD	PARIAHS	PASTELS	PEDANTS	PERCUSS
SAVORED	RAPHIAS	STAPLES	PENTADS	SPRUCES
OVERTIP	PARIANS	PASTEUP	PEDDERS	PERDURE
PIVOTER	PIRANAS	PUPATES	SPREDDE	REPURED
OWRIEST	PARKIES	PASTILS	PEDDLES	PEREION
TOWSIER	SPARKIE	SPITALS	SPELDED	PIONEER
OYSTERS	PARODIC	PATENTS	PEDICEL	PERFECT
STOREYS	PICADOR	PATTENS	PEDICLE	PREFECT
PACKERS	PAROLES	PATRICK	PEDLERS	PERFORM
REPACKS	REPOSAL	TRIPACK	SPELDER	PREFORM
PADANGS	PARPING	PATROLS	PEERIES	PERILED
PADNAGS	RAPPING	PORTALS	SEEPIER	REPLIED
PADRONI	PARROTS	PATROON	PEERING	PERITUS
PONIARD	RAPTORS	PRONOTA	PREEING	PUIREST
PAINIMS	PARROTY	PATTERN	PEEVERS	PERJINK
PIANISM	PORTRAY	REPTANT	PREEVES	PREJINK
PALETTE	PARSONS	PATTIES	PEISING	PERKINS
PELTATE	SANPROS	TAPETIS	PIGSNIE	PINKERS
PALLIER	PARTERS	PATTLES	PELORIC	PERLITE
PERILLA	PRATERS	PELTAST	POLICER	REPTILE

PERORAL	PIGNORA	PITSAWS	PLOWERS	POLOIST
PREORAL	PORANGI	SAWPITS	REPLOWS	TOPSOIL
PERSUES	PIGNUTS	PLACITS	PLUGGED	POODLES
PERUSES	STUPING	PLASTIC	PUGGLED	SPOOLED
PERTUSE	PILEUPS	PLACOID	PLUMBER	POPERIN
REPUTES	UPPILES	PODALIC	REPLUMB	PROPINE
PERUSER	PILLAUS	PLAGUES	PLUMBIC	PORGIES
REPURES	PILULAS	PLUSAGE	UPCLIMB	SERPIGO
PERVING	PINANGS	PLAICES	PLUMOSE	PORKERS
PREVING	SPANING	SPECIAL	PUMELOS	PROKERS
PESTERS	PINCHES	PLAITED	PLUNGED	PORKING
PRESETS	SPHENIC	TALIPED	PUNGLED	PROKING
PESTIER	PINDARI	PLAITER	PLUNGES	PORTAGE
RESPITE	PRIDIAN	PLATIER	PUNGLES	POTAGER
PETALED	PINGLES	PLANERS	PLUSSES	PORTEND
PLEATED	SPIGNEL	REPLANS	PUSSELS	PROTEND
PETASOS	PINIONS	PLANETS	PLUTEUS	PORTICO
SAPOTES	SPINONI	PLATENS	PUSTULE	PROOTIC
PETITES	PINNERS	PLASHER	PLUTONS	PORTING
PETTIES	SPINNER	SPHERAL	PULTONS	TROPING
PETROLS	PINOCLE	PLASMIC	POCOSEN	PORTOUS
REPLOTS	PLEONIC	PSALMIC	POONCES	UPROOTS
PHAETON	PIOLETS	PLECTRE	PODIUMS	POSINGS
PHONATE	PISTOLE	PRELECT	SPODIUM	POSSING
PHENOMS	PIONIES	PLERION	POGONIP	POSNETS
SHOPMEN	SINOPIE	PROLINE	POOPING	STEPSON
PHILTER	PIPINGS	PLEROMA	POINDER	POSSERS
PHILTRE	SIPPING	RAMPOLE	PROINED	PROSSES
PHRASED	PIPLESS	PLOATED	POISERS	POSTBOY
SHARPED	SIPPLES	TADPOLE	PROSSIE	POTBOYS
PHYTOID	PISMIRE	PLODDED	POISONS	POSTERN
TYPHOID	PRIMSIE	PODDLED	POISSON	PRONEST
PICAROS	PISSANT	PLODGES	POITREL	POSTING
PROSAIC	PTISANS	SPLODGE	POLITER	STOPING
PICENES	PISSERS	PLOPPED	POLDERS	POSTMEN
PIECENS	PRISSES	POPPLED	PRESOLD	TOPSMEN
PICKETS	PISTOLS	PLOTFUL	POLINGS	POTASSA
SKEPTIC	POSTILS	TOPFULL	SLOPING	SAPOTAS
PICKLER	PITIERS	PLOUTER	POLLERS	POTLUCK
PRICKLE	TIPSIER	POULTER	REPOLLS	PUTLOCK

Couplets

POUDERS	PREMIER	PROPERS	PURSIER	RAGGIES
POUDRES	REPRIME	PROSPER	UPRISER	SAGGIER
POULPES	PRENTED	PROTIST	PURSUED	RAGTAGS
UPSLOPE	PRETEND	TROPIST	USURPED	TAGRAGS
POUNCED	PREPAYS	PROTORE	PURSUER	RAGWEED
UNCOPED	YAPPERS	TROOPER	USURPER	WAGERED
POUNCES	PREPONE	PRUNERS	PUTTERS	RAILERS
UNCOPES	PROPENE	SPURNER	SPUTTER	RERAILS
POUNDER	PRESHIP	PRUSIKS	PUTTIED	RAKINGS
UNROPED	SHIPPER	SPRUIKS	TITUPED	SARKING
POURERS	PRESONG	PSALMED	PUZZELS	RALLIES
REPOURS	SPONGER	SAMPLED	PUZZLES	SALLIER
POURIES	PRESSES	PSEUDOS	PYEMIAS	RAMSONS
SOUPIER	SPERSES	SPOUSED	YAMPIES	RANSOMS
POURSUE	PRESSOR	PUDDERS	PYRALID	RAMSTAM
UPROUSE	PROSERS	SPUDDER	RAPIDLY	TAMMARS
POUSSES	PRESUME	PUDDLES	PYRITES	RANDOMS
SPOUSES	SUPREME	SPUDDLE	STRIPEY	RODSMAN
POUSSIN	PRETEEN	PUISNES	PYROPES	RASHERS
SPINOUS	TERPENE	SUPINES	YOPPERS	SHARERS
POWNIES	PREVISE	PULSANT	QUEERER	RASSLED
WINESOP	PRIEVES	PULTANS	REQUERE	SARDELS
POWTERS	PREWRAP	PULSION	QUELEAS	RATLIKE
PROWEST	WRAPPER	UPSILON	SEQUELA	TALKIER
PRAETOR	PRINTER	PUMPERS	QUERIER	RATOONS
PRORATE	REPRINT	REPUMPS	REQUIRE	SANTOOR
PRAWNED	PRISONS	PUNCHER	QUERIST	RATTILY
PREDAWN	SPINORS	UNPERCH	REQUITS	TARTILY
PRAWNER	PRISSED	PUNIEST	QUESTER	RATTING
PREWARN	SPIDERS	PUNTIES	REQUEST	TARTING
PREARMS	PROETTE	PUNKIES	QUIETER	RAUNCHY
RAMPERS	TREETOP	SPUNKIE	REQUITE	UNCHARY
PREDOOM	PROGENY	PUNNETS	QUINNAT	RAUNGES
PROMOED	PYROGEN	UNSPENT	QUINTAN	UNGEARS
PREEDIT	PROLLED	PUNSTER	RABATTE	RAVAGES
TEPIDER	REDPOLL	PUNTERS	TABARET	SAVAGER
PREFILE	PRONAOS	PURITAN	RACISTS	RAWHEAD
PRELIFE	SOPRANO	UPTRAIN	SACRIST	WARHEAD
PREIFES	PROOFER	PURLERS	RACKERS	RAYLESS
PRIEFES	REPROOF	SLURPER	RERACKS	SLAYERS

REALTOR	REEDILY	REROLLS	RETREAD	REWRAPS
RELATOR	YIELDER	ROLLERS	TREADER	WARPERS
REAMERS	REESTED	REROOFS	RETREES	RHUMBAS
SMEARER	STEERED	ROOFERS	STEERER	SAMBHUR
REAMIER	REFUTAL	RESEEDS	RETRIMS	RIBAUDS
REREMAI	TEARFUL	SEEDERS	TRIMERS	SUBARID
REAPERS	REGRESS	RESELLS	RETUNDS	RIBBONS
SPEARER	SERGERS	SELLERS	UNDREST	ROBBINS
REARISE	REGROWN	RESHOWS	RETURNS	RICKEYS
RERAISE	WRONGER	SHOWERS	TURNERS	YICKERS
REASONS	REISSUE	RESIDUE	REUTTER	RIDGIER
SENORAS	SEISURE	UREIDES	UTTERER	RIGIDER
REAVAIL	REIVING	RESIGHT	REVAMPS	RIKISHA
VELARIA	RIEVING	SIGHTER	VAMPERS	SHIKARI
REAVING	RELEVES	RESISTS	REVENUE	RILIEST
VINEGAR	SLEEVER	SISTERS	UNREEVE	SILTIER
REBORES	RELIVER	RESIZES	REVIEWS	RIMLESS
SOBERER	REVILER	SEIZERS	VIEWERS	SMILERS
REBUSES	REMEIDS	RESKEWS	REWAKED	RIPTIDE
SUBSERE	REMISED	SKEWERS	WREAKED	TIDERIP
RECITED	REMORAS	RESTIFF	REWAKEN	RISTRAS
TIERCED	ROAMERS	STIFFER	WAKENER	STIRRAS
RECLUSE	REMORSE	RESTING	REWEIGH	RITTERS
RECULES	ROEMERS	STINGER	WEIGHER	TERRITS
RECULED	RENAGUE	RESTYLE	REWELDS	RITUALS
ULCERED	UNEAGER	TERSELY	WELDERS	TRISULA
RECURED	RENNETS	RESURGE	REWIDEN	RIVALED
REDUCER	TENNERS	REURGES	WIDENER	VALIDER
REDACTS	RENOWNS	RETAKES	REWINDS	RIVERET
SCARTED	WONNERS	SAKERET	WINDERS	RIVETER
REDBAIT	REPEATS	RETELLS	REWIRED	RIVETED
TRIBADE	RETAPES	TELLERS	WEIRDER	VERDITE
REDDEST	REPINED	RETHINK	REWIRES	RIVIERA
TEDDERS	RIPENED	THINKER	SWEIRER	VAIRIER
REDDLES	REPINER	RETICLE	REWORDS	ROADIES
SLEDDER	RIPENER	TIERCEL	SWORDER	SOREDIA
REDLINE	REPLIES	RETIRER	REWORKS	RODENTS
RELINED	SPIELER	TERRIER	WORKERS	SNORTED
REDWING	RERISEN	RETRACK	REWOUND	ROGUING
WRINGED	RESINER	TRACKER	WOUNDER	ROUGING

Couplets

ROLLTOP	RUNDLET	SANDERS	SAXTUBA	SEETHER
TROLLOP	TRUNDLE	SARSDEN	SUBTAXA	SHEETER
ROOTLET	RUNNETS	SANGERS	SCAMPIS	SEEWING
TOOTLER	STUNNER	SERANGS	SPASMIC	SWEEING
RORTERS	RUSTRES	SANIOUS	SCAPING	SEITENS
TERRORS	TRUSSER	SUASION	SPACING	SESTINE
RORTIER	SABELLA	SANNIES	SCEDULE	SELFIST
TERROIR	SALABLE	SIENNAS	SECLUDE	STIFLES
ROSALIA	SACBUTS	SANNUPS	SCHOUTS	SELSYNS
SOLARIA	SUBACTS	UNSNAPS	SCOUTHS	SLYNESS
ROSYING	SACHETS	SANSEIS	SCHTICK	SEMMITS
SIGNORY	SCATHES	SASINES	TCHICKS	TSIMMES
ROTATED	SACKBUT	SANTOLS	SCHTIKS	SENNITS
TROATED	SUBTACK	STANOLS	SHTICKS	SINNETS
ROTATES	SACKERS	SANTONS	SCOURGE	SENSUAL
TOASTER	SCREAKS	SONANTS	SCROUGE	UNSEALS
ROTCHIE	SACRIFY	SANTURS	SCOWING	SEPHENS
THEORIC	SCARIFY	SUNSTAR	SOWCING	SPHENES
ROTULAE	SADDISH	SAPOURS	SCOWLER	SEPTATE
TORULAE	SIDDHAS	UPSOARS	SCROWLE	SPATTEE
ROTULAS	SAGENES	SARCOUS	SCREAKY	SERENER
TORULAS	SENEGAS	SOUCARS	YACKERS	SNEERER
ROUSANT	SAIMINS	SAROSES	SCREICH	SERRANS
SANTOUR	SIMIANS	SEROSAS	SCRIECH	SNARERS
ROUSING	SALADES	SARSNET	SCRIEVE	SERVERS
SOURING	SALSAED	TRANSES	SERVICE	VERSERS
ROWDILY	SALINES	SAUCIER	SCULKED	SERVEWE
WORDILY	SILANES	URICASE	SUCKLED	WEEVERS
ROWINGS	SALOONS	SAUNTED	SDEIGNE	SERVING
WORSING	SOLANOS	UNSATED	SEEDING	VERSING
ROWTING	SALTANT	SAVINES	SEAMIER	SERVLET
TROWING	TALANTS	VINASSE	SERIEMA	SVELTER
ROYSTER	SALTISH	SAVIOUR	SEAWORM	SESELIS
STROYER	TAHSILS	VARIOUS	WOMERAS	SESSILE
RUBACES	SALTOED	SAVORER	SECKELS	SESTETS
SUBRACE	SOLATED	SEROVAR	SECKLES	TSETSES
RUBELLA	SALUTES	SAWDERS	SEEKING	SETTEES
RULABLE	TALUSES	SWEARDS	SKEEING	TESTEES
RUINOUS	SAMOYED	SAWYERS	SEETHED	SETTING
URINOUS	SOMEDAY	SWAYERS	SHEETED	TESTING

SEWINGS	SIDLERS	SLEWING	SOVIETS	STATING
SWINGES	SLIDERS	SWINGLE	STOVIES	TASTING
SHAITAN	SIDLING	SLIPWAY	SOWARRY	STATINS
TAHINAS	SLIDING	WASPILY	YARROWS	TANISTS
SHAPEUP	SIERRAN	SLITTED	SOWINGS	STATUTE
UPHEAPS	SNARIER	STILTED	SOWSING	TAUTEST
SHAWLIE	SIESTAS	SLOPIER	SPALTED	STAYING
WHAISLE	TASSIES	SPOILER	STAPLED	STYGIAN
SHEIKHS	SIEVING	SMOKILY	SPEEDER	STEEVES
SHIKSEH	VISEING	SOYMILK	SPEERED	VESTEES
SHEITAN	SIGNARY	SMOODGE	SPINARS	STELLAR
STHENIA	SYRINGA	SMOOGED	SPRAINS	TELLARS
SHEWELS	SIGNING	SNAFUED	SPIRANT	STEMING
WELSHES	SINGING	UNDEAFS	SPRAINT	TEMSING
SHIATSU	SILOING	SNEAPED	SPIRITS	STERVED
THIASUS	SOILING	SPEANED	TRIPSIS	VERDETS
SHICKER	SILVERS	SNICKET	SPIRTED	STEWERS
SKRIECH	SLIVERS	TICKENS	STRIPED	WESTERS
SHINERS	SIPHONS	SNOOPED	SPURIAE	STICKUP
SHRINES	SONSHIP	SPOONED	UPRAISE	UPTICKS
SHIRKED	SIPPLED	SNOOTED	SPUTNIK	STIDDIE
SHRIKED	SLIPPED	STOODEN	UPKNITS	TIDDIES
SHIRRAS	SITTINE	SNORERS	SPYWARE	STINGOS
SIRRAHS	TINIEST	SORNERS	YAWPERS	TOSSING
SHIVERS	SITUSES	SNORING	STABBED	STIPELS
SHRIVES	TISSUES	SORNING	TEBBADS	TIPLESS
SHLOCKY	SIZEIST	SNOWING	STACKET	STIPPLE
SHYLOCK	SIZIEST	WONINGS	TACKETS	TIPPLES
SHOUTED	SKIVING	SOLANDS	STALKER	STIRING
SOUTHED	VIKINGS	SOLDANS	TALKERS	TIRINGS
SHOUTER	SKLATED	SOLDIER	STANDEE	STIRRED
SOUTHER	STALKED	SOLIDER	STEANED	STRIDER
SHOVERS	SKREIGH	SOLLERS	STARDOM	STOKERS
SHROVES	SKRIEGH	SORELLS	TSARDOM	STROKES
SHYSTER	SKRYING	SOMBERS	STARTED	STOMPER
THYRSES	SKYRING	SOMBRES	TETRADS	TROMPES
SICKLED	SLAMMED	SOREXES	STARTUP	STONERN
SLICKED	SMALMED	XEROSES	UPSTART	TONNERS
SIDEWAY	SLEEPRY	SOULDAN	STATELY	STONILY
WAYSIDE	YELPERS	UNLOADS	STYLATE	TYLOSIN

Couplets

STONING	STUDIES	SUNSUIT	SWINGER	TANNAHS
TONINGS	TISSUED	UNSUITS	WINGERS	THANNAS
STONNED	STUMBLE	SUNTRAP	SWINKER	TANNERY
TENDONS	TUMBLES	UNSTRAP	WINKERS	TYRANNE
STOOKER	STURNUS	SUNWARD	SWIPIER	TANNEST
STROOKE	UNTRUSS	UNDRAWS	WISPIER	TENANTS
STOOLED	STURTED	SUPPING	SWIRLED	TANTARA
TOLEDOS	TRUSTED	UPPINGS	WILDERS	TARTANA
STOPPLE	STUSHIE	SURAMIN	SWISHED	TARDIER
TOPPLES	TUSHIES	URANISM	WHISSED	TARRIED
STOTTIE	STYLITE	SURGING	SWISHER	TARTLET
TOTTIES	TESTILY	URGINGS	WISHERS	TATTLER
STOUTEN	STYLIZE	SWADDIE	SWISHES	TATUING
TENUTOS	ZESTILY	WADDIES	WHISSES	TAUTING
STOVERS	STYRENE	SWAGGER	SWOONED	TAWIEST
VOTRESS	YESTERN	WAGGERS	WOODENS	TWAITES
STOVING	SUBDEAN	SWALIER	SWOOPED	TAWNIER
VOTINGS	UNBASED	WAILERS	WOOPSED	TINWARE
STOWAGE	SUEABLE	SWALLOW	SWOUNED	TAXWISE
TOWAGES	USEABLE	WALLOWS	UNSOWED	WAXIEST
STRAINT	SUITORS	SWANKER	TABLEAU	TEABOWL
TRANSIT	TSOURIS	WANKERS	TABULAE	TOWABLE
STRAWEN	SULLENS	SWAPPER	TACKLED	TEAZELS
WANTERS	UNSELLS	WAPPERS	TALCKED	TEAZLES
STREELS	SULPHUR	SWARDED	TACTICS	TEAZING
TRESSEL	UPHURLS	WADDERS	TICTACS	TZIGANE
STREETY	SUMATRA	SWATTED	TAKEUPS	TEETERS
SYRETTE	TRAUMAS	WADSETT	UPTAKES	TERETES
STRETTE	SUNDECK	SWATTER	TALLEST	TEMENOS
TETTERS	UNDECKS	TEWARTS	TALLETS	TONEMES
STREWED	SUNDERS	SWEEPER	TALLOWY	TEMPLAR
WRESTED	UNDRESS	WEEPERS	TOLLWAY	TRAMPLE
STREWER	SUNLIKE	SWIGGER	TAMARAS	TENDRIL
WRESTER	UNLIKES	WIGGERS	TARAMAS	TRINDLE
STROWED	SUNROOF	SWILLER	TAMPANS	TENOURS
WORSTED	UNROOFS	WILLERS	TAPSMAN	TONSURE
STUDDIE	SUNROOM	SWINDGE	TANGLER	TENSIVE
STUDIED	UNMOORS	SWINGED	TRANGLE	VENITES
STUDENT	SUNSPOT	SWINDLE	TANGRAM	THIRSTS
STUNTED	UNSTOPS	WINDLES	TRANGAM	THRISTS

THIRSTY	TUBULIN	UNFURLS	UPSPAKE	WELTING
THRISTY	UNBUILT	URNFULS	UPSPEAK	WINGLET
THRAWED	TUFTIER	UNGLUED	UPSWARM	WENCHES
WRATHED	TURFITE	UNGULED	WARMUPS	WHENCES
TICKLER	TUILZIE	UNITIES	UPSWELL	WESANDS
TRICKLE	UTILIZE	UNITISE	UPWELLS	WESSAND
TILTING	TULCHAN	UNLADES	UPWINDS	WESKITS
TITLING	UNLATCH	UNLEADS	WINDUPS	WISKETS
TITANIS	TUMBLER	UNLIVES	VAILING	WESTLIN
TITIANS	TUMBREL	UNVEILS	VIALING	WINTLES
TOOLSET	TURKIES	UNMATED	VALETED	WETHERS
TOOTLES	TUSKIER	UNTAMED	VELATED	WRETHES
TOPWORK	TURNIPS	UNNAILS	VALISES	WHEEDLE
WORKTOP	UNSTRIP	UNSLAIN	VESSAIL	WHEELED
TORPEDO	TURNUPS	UNNOTED	VAMPIER	WHITIER
TROOPED	UPTURNS	UNTONED	VAMPIRE	WITHIER
TORTILE	TWEEDLE	UNRAVEL	VENTERS	WHITIES
TRIOLET	TWEELED	VENULAR	VENTRES	WITHIES
TORTIVE	TWINERS	UNRIVET	VENTOSE	WHITING
VIRETOT	WINTERS	VENTURI	VOTEENS	WITHING
TORTURE	TWINTER	UNROOST	VIRGATE	WHITRET
TROUTER	WRITTEN	UNROOTS	VITRAGE	WHITTER
TOSSILY	TWIRING	UNSEENS	VIRINOS	WIGGLER
TYLOSIS	WRITING	UNSENSE	VIRIONS	WRIGGLE
TOWNIES	ULICONS	UNSPILT	VIRTUAL	WILLEST
TWONIES	UNCOILS	UNSPLIT	VITULAR	WILLETS
TOWTING	UNAIRED	UNSTACK	VODOUNS	WILTING
WOTTING	URANIDE	UNTACKS	VOUDONS	WITLING
TRAVOIS	UNALIVE	UNSTUCK	VOLATIC	WINKLER
VIATORS	UNVAILE	UNTUCKS	VOLTAIC	WRINKLE
TREVETS	UNBARES	UNSWEAR	WANGLER	WISENTS
VETTERS	UNBEARS	UNWARES	WRANGLE	WITNESS
TRIDUAN	UNCAPED	UNTAMES	WARNERS	ZAFFERS
UNITARD	UNPACED	UNTEAMS	WARRENS	ZAFFRES
TRISHAW	UNCASES	UNWIRES	WASHIER	ZANIEST
WRAITHS	USANCES	UNWISER	WEARISH	ZEATINS
TRIVIAL	UNDRAPE	UPDATER	WEIRING	
VITRAIL	UNPARED	UPRATED	WINGIER	
TROWELS	UNFILDE	UPDRAWS	WELKINS	
WORTLES	UNFILED	UPWARDS	WINKLES	

Couplets

Triplets

ABASING	ACHINGS	AGRASTE	AMBERED	ANOINTS
BAAINGS	CASHING	GASTREA	BREAMED	NATIONS
BISNAGA	CHASING	TEARGAS	EMBREAD	ONANIST
ABETTOR	ACROTER	AGREGES	AMENDES	ANOPIAS
BATTERO	CREATOR	RAGGEES	DEMEANS	ANOPSIA
TABORET	REACTOR	REGGAES	SEEDMAN	PAISANO
ABLEISM	ACTINAL	AILERON	AMERCED	ANTEING
EMBAILS	ALICANT	ALERION	CREAMED	ANTIGEN
LAMBIES	ANTICAL	ALIENOR	RACEMED	GENTIAN
ABORDED	ACTINON	AIRDATE	AMERCES	ANTHERS
BOARDED	CANTION	RADIATE	CAREMES	HARTENS
ROADBED	CONTAIN	TIARAED	RACEMES	THENARS
ABORTED	ACTIONS	AIRNING	AMNIONS	ANTIARS
BORATED	ATONICS	INGRAIN	MANSION	ARTISAN
TABORED	CATIONS	RAINING	ONANISM	TSARINA
ABORTER	ACTRESS	AIRPOST	AMORETS	ANTICKS
ARBORET	CASTERS	AIRSTOP	MAESTRO	CATKINS
TABORER	RECASTS	PAROTIS	OMERTAS	CATSKIN
ABREACT	ADMIRER	AIRSHOT	AMOUNTS	ANTIRED
BEARCAT	MARDIER	SHORTIA	MOUTANS	DETRAIN
CABARET	MARRIED	THORIAS	OUTMANS	TRAINED
ABREGES	ADONISE	AISLING	AMTRACS	ANURIAS
BAREGES	ANODISE	NILGAIS	RAMCATS	SAURIAN
BARGEES	SODAINE	SAILING	TARMACS	URANIAS
ABRUPTS	ADORING	ALBATAS	AMUSERS	AORISTS
SUBPART	GRADINO	ATABALS	ASSUMER	ARISTOS
UPBRAST	ROADING	BALATAS	MASSEUR	SATORIS
ABSCISE	ADPRESS	ALERTLY	ANCHORS	APPERIL
SCABIES	SPADERS	ELYTRAL	ARCHONS	APPLIER
SEBASIC	SPREADS	RETALLY	RANCHOS	ARIPPLE
ABSEILS	AETHERS	ALIBIES	ANGELED	APPLETS
ISABELS	HEATERS	BAILIES	GELANDE	LAPPETS
LABISES	REHEATS	BIALIES	GLEANED	STAPPLE
ACARIDS	AFFRETS	ALIGNED	ANGELIC	APPULSE
ASCARID	RESTAFF	DEALING	ANGLICE	PAPULES
CARDIAS	STAFFER	LEADING	GALENIC	UPLEAPS
ACCRUES	AGELAST	ALINERS	ANGELUS	APTNESS
ACCURSE	ALGATES	NAILERS	LAGUNES	PATNESS
ACCUSER	LASTAGE	RENAILS	LANGUES	PESANTS
ACERBER	AGGRESS	ALTESSE	ANIMIST	ARBUTES
CEREBRA	SAGGERS	STEALES	INTIMAS	BURSATE
REBRACE	SEGGARS	TEASELS	SANTIMI	SURBATE
ACETINS	AGNAMES	AMBEERS	ANKLETS	ARCHING
CANIEST	MANAGES	BEAMERS	ASKLENT	CHAGRIN
CINEAST	SAGAMEN	BESMEAR	LANKEST	CHARING

ARCTIID	ASCIANS	AUTOMEN	BASTION	BIGENER
TRIACID	CASSINA	NOTAEUM	BONITAS	BREINGE
TRIADIC	SANCAIS	OUTNAME	OBTAINS	REBEGIN
AREFIES	ASEPTIC	AVENTRE	BATHERS	BIMETAL
FAERIES	PACIEST	NERVATE	BERTHAS	LIMBATE
FREESIA	SPICATE	VETERAN	BREATHS	TIMBALE
ARENITE	ASPHALT	AVIDEST	BATTIER	BINDERS
RETINAE	SPATHAL	DATIVES	BIRETTA	INBREDS
TRAINEE	TAPLASH	VISTAED	RATBITE	REBINDS
ARGENTS	ASPINES	AVOWERS	BATTLER	BLISTER
GARNETS	PANSIES	OVERSAW	BLATTER	BRISTLE
STRANGE	SAPIENS	REAVOWS	BRATTLE	RIBLETS
ARGUSES	ASRAMAS	AWNINGS	BEADERS	BLUDIER
SAUGERS	SAMARAS	SNAWING	DEBASER	BUILDER
USAGERS	SAMSARA	WANINGS	SABERED	REBUILD
ARISHES	ASTHORE	BABBLER	BEADMEN	BLURBED
RASHIES	EARSHOT	BLABBER	BEDEMAN	BURBLED
SHERIAS	HAROSET	BRABBLE	BENAMED	RUBBLED
ARISTAE	ASTONED	BACKETS	BEARDED	BOILERS
ASTERIA	DONATES	BACKSET	BREADED	LIBEROS
ATRESIA	ONSTEAD	SETBACK	DEBEARD	REBOILS
ARKOSES	ASUNDER	BAILOUT	BEATERS	BOLSTER
RESOAKS	DANSEUR	OBITUAL	BERATES	BOLTERS
SOAKERS	DAUNERS	TABOULI	REBATES	LOBSTER
ARMADAS	ATHIRST	BALDEST	BEDROOM	BORINGS
MADRASA	RATTISH	BLASTED	BOREDOM	ROBINGS
RAMADAS	TARTISH	STABLED	BROOMED	SORBING
ARMFULS	ATRETIC	BALDIES	BEDRUGS	BOSSING
ARMSFUL	CATTIER	DIABLES	BUDGERS	GIBSONS
FULMARS	CITRATE	DISABLE	REDBUGS	OBSIGNS
ARMPITS	ATTORNS	BANSHEE	BELDAME	BOULLES
IMPARTS	RATTONS	BEENAHS	BEMEDAL	LOBULES
MISPART	ROTTANS	SHEBEAN	EMBALED	SOLUBLE
ARRESTS	ATTRITE	BARBELS	BELLIED	BOUNDER
RASTERS	TATTIER	RABBLES	DELIBLE	REBOUND
STARERS	TITRATE	SLABBER	LIBELED	UNROBED
ARRISES	ATTUNED	BARBETS	BEMIRES	BOURNES
RAISERS	NUTATED	RABBETS	BERIMES	UNROBES
SIERRAS	TAUNTED	STABBER	BIREMES	UNSOBER
ARTICLE	AUDILES	BASEMEN	BESORTS	BREEDER
RECITAL	DEASIUL	BEMEANS	SORBETS	BREERED
TALCIER	DUALISE	BENAMES	STROBES	REBREED
ASCENTS	AUNTERS	BASSIER	BETRIMS	BRIDALS
SECANTS	NATURES	BRAISES	TIMBERS	LABRIDS
STANCES	SAUNTER	BRASSIE	TIMBRES	RIBALDS

Triplets

BRIEFED	CAMBERS	CARTERS	CESTOID	CHOREUS
DEBRIEF	CEMBRAS	CRATERS	COEDITS	CHOUSER
FIBERED	CRAMBES	TRACERS	COTISED	ROUCHES
BRISURE	CANALED	CARTING	CESURAL	CHOUSED
BRUISER	CANDELA	CRATING	RECUSAL	DOUCHES
BURIERS	DECANAL	TRACING	SECULAR	HOCUSED
BUGLERS	CANDORS	CASEINS	CHALETS	CIERGES
BULGERS	CARDONS	CASSINE	LATCHES	GRECISE
BURGLES	DACRONS	INCASES	SATCHEL	GRIECES
BUMMELS	CANGLED	CASEMEN	CHAPTER	CINDERS
BUMMLES	CLANGED	EMACSEN	PATCHER	DISCERN
MUMBLES	GLANCED	MENACES	REPATCH	RESCIND
BUNTIER	CANINES	CATTIES	CHARISM	CINEOLS
TRIBUNE	ENCINAS	STATICE	CHIMARS	CONSEIL
TURBINE	NANCIES	TIETACS	CHRISMA	INCLOSE
BURNIES	CANTHUS	CATTISH	CHASERS	CITHERS
RUBINES	CHAUNTS	CHATTIS	CRASHES	ESTRICH
SUBERIN	STAUNCH	TACHIST	ESCHARS	RICHEST
CACKLER	CAPELIN	CENTARE	CHETNIK	CLARIES
CLACKER	PANICLE	CRENATE	KITCHEN	ECLAIRS
CRACKLE	PELICAN	REENACT	THICKEN	SCALIER
CAFILAS	CAPERED	CENTAUR	CHILDER	CLASHER
FACIALS	PEARCED	UNCRATE	CHIRLED	LARCHES
FASCIAL	PREACED	UNTRACE	ELDRICH	RASCHEL
CAGANER	CAPOTES	CENTERS	CHINING	CLEANED
CARNAGE	SCOPATE	CENTRES	INCHING	ELANCED
CRANAGE	TOECAPS	TENRECS	NICHING	ENLACED
CAHIERS	CAPSTAN	CENTIMO	CHIRTED	CLIENTS
CASHIER	CAPTANS	ENTOMIC	DITCHER	LECTINS
ERIACHS	CATNAPS	TONEMIC	RICHTED	STENCIL
CAIRNED	CARGOES	CERESIN	CHOKERS	CLOSERS
CARNIED	CORSAGE	SCRIENE	HOCKERS	CRESOLS
DANCIER	SOCAGER	SINCERE	SHOCKER	ESCROLS
CAISSON	CARINAL	CERIPHS	CHOLERA	CLOTURE
CASINOS	CLARAIN	CIPHERS	CHORALE	CLOUTER
CASSINO	CRANIAL	SPHERIC	CHOREAL	COULTER
CAKINGS	CARIOSE	CERITES	CHORALS	COASTER
CASKING	ORACIES	RECITES	LORCHAS	COATERS
SACKING	SCORIAE	TIERCES	SCHOLAR	RECOATS
CALKERS	CARLOTS	CESSION	CHORDEE	CODEINS
LACKERS	CROTALS	COSINES	COHERED	CONDIES
SLACKER	SCROTAL	OSCINES	OCHERED	SECONDI
CALVERS	CARPERS	CESTODE	CHOREAS	CODILLE
CARVELS	SCARPER	ESCOTED	ORACHES	COLLIDE
CLAVERS	SCRAPER	TEDESCO	ROACHES	COLLIED

COEXIST	COSMINE	CRUELLS	DARNERS	DEMIREP
COXIEST	INCOMES	CULLERS	ERRANDS	EPIDERM
EXOTICS	MESONIC	SCULLER	SNARRED	IMPEDER
COINFER	COUPERS	CRUISER	DARNING	DENIERS
CONIFER	CROUPES	CURRIES	NARDING	NEREIDS
INFORCE	RECOUPS	SUCRIER	RANDING	RESINED
COINTER	COURSED	CRUISES	DAUBERS	DENTARY
NOTICER	SCOURED	CRUSIES	EARBUDS	TRAYNED
RECTION	SOURCED	CUISSER	SUBEDAR	TYRANED
CONATUS	COURSER	CTENOID	DAWDLER	DENTINS
NOCTUAS	CRUORES	DEONTIC	DRAWLED	INDENTS
TOUCANS	SCOURER	NOTICED	WADDLER	INTENDS
CONDERS	COUTERS	CUATROS	DAWDLES	DENTIST
CORSNED	CROUTES	SURCOAT	SWADDLE	DISTENT
SCORNED	SCOUTER	TURACOS	WADDLES	STINTED
CONTOUR	COUTHER	CURTEST	DAWNERS	DENTURE
CORNUTO	RETOUCH	CUTTERS	WANDERS	RETUNED
CROUTON	TOUCHER	SCUTTER	WARDENS	TENURED
CONTUSE	COUVERT	CUTLETS	DEADEST	DENUDES
ECONUTS	CUTOVER	CUTTLES	SEDATED	DUDEENS
UNCOEST	OVERCUT	SCUTTLE	STEADED	DUENDES
COPERED	CRADLES	CUTLINE	DEALERS	DEPAINT
PRECODE	RECLADS	LINECUT	LEADERS	PAINTED
PROCEED	SCALDER	TUNICLE	REDEALS	PATINED
COPIERS	CRASSER	DABBLER	DEBITOR	DEPARTS
COPSIER	SCARERS	DRABBLE	DEORBIT	DRAPETS
PERSICO	SCARRES	RABBLED	ORBITED	PETARDS
COPULAS	CREASED	DAILIES	DEBONER	DEPORTS
CUPOLAS	DECARES	LIAISED	ENROBED	REDTOPS
SCOPULA	SEARCED	SEDILIA	REDBONE	SPORTED
COPYISM	CREEING	DAIMONS	DECANTS	DEPRAVE
MISCOPY	ENERGIC	DOMAINS	DESCANT	PERVADE
MYOPICS	GENERIC	MADISON	SCANTED	REPAVED
CORKERS	CREMINI	DALLIER	DECRIAL	DEPRESS
RECORKS	CRIMINE	DIALLER	RADICEL	PRESSED
ROCKERS	MINCIER	RALLIED	RADICLE	SPERSED
CORNICE	CREPIER	DANGERS	DEIFIER	DEPRIVE
CROCEIN	PIERCER	GANDERS	EDIFIER	PREDIVE
CROCINE	REPRICE	GARDENS	REIFIED	PRIEVED
CORVETS	CRISPEN	DAPPLES	DELAYER	DERATED
COVERTS	PINCERS	SAPPLED	LAYERED	REDATED
VECTORS	PRINCES	SLAPPED	RELAYED	TREADED
COSIEST	CRUDDLE	DARKEST	DELETES	DERIVER
COTISES	CUDDLER	STARKED	SLEETED	REDRIVE
OECISTS	CURDLED	STRAKED	STEELED	RIVERED

Triplets

DESERTS	DISNEST	DROGUES	ELAPSES	ENDGAME
DESSERT	DISSENT	GOURDES	PLEASES	MANEGED
TRESSED	SNIDEST	GROUSED	SAPELES	MENAGED
DESINED	DISPORT	DROLEST	ELICHES	ENERVES
NEDDIES	TORPIDS	OLDSTER	HELICES	EVENERS
SDEINED	TRIPODS	STRODLE	LICHEES	VENEERS
DESTINE	DIVERTS	DROWNED	ELISION	ENGRAMS
ENDITES	STRIVED	ROWNDED	ISOLINE	GERMANS
STEINED	VERDITS	WONDRED	LIONISE	MANGERS
DESTOCK	DOLINES	DUELING	ELITISM	ENISLED
DOCKETS	INDOLES	ELUDING	LIMIEST	ENSILED
STOCKED	SONDELI	INDULGE	LIMITES	LINSEED
DESTROY	DOMINES	DUFFELS	ELUANTS	ENLARGE
ROYSTED	EMODINS	DUFFLES	LUNATES	GENERAL
STROYED	MISDONE	SLUFFED	UNLASTE	GLEANER
DEWATER	DONDERS	DUNGERS	ELUTORS	ENRIVEN
TARWEED	NODDERS	GERUNDS	OUTLERS	INNERVE
WATERED	SNODDER	NUDGERS	TROULES	NERVINE
DIALING	DOOMIER	DUSTIER	EMANATE	ENSUING
GLIADIN	MOIDORE	REDUITS	ENEMATA	GUNNIES
LAIDING	MOODIER	STUDIER	MANATEE	INGENUS
DIESELS	DORSELS	DUSTPAN	EMERITA	ENTOILS
IDLESSE	RODLESS	STANDUP	EMIRATE	LIONETS
SEIDELS	SOLDERS	UPSTAND	MEATIER	ONLIEST
DIETING	DOTTELS	EAGLING	EMIGRES	ENTREAT
EDITING	DOTTLES	GEALING	REGIMES	RATTEEN
IGNITED	SLOTTED	LIGNAGE	REMIGES	TERNATE
DIETIST	DOWRIES	EARFULS	EMOTERS	ENTREES
DITTIES	ROWDIES	FERULAS	METEORS	RETENES
TIDIEST	WEIRDOS	REFUSAL	REMOTES	TEENERS
DILATER	DRAGGLE	EARPLUG	EMPTING	ENVIOUS
REDTAIL	GARGLED	GRAUPEL	PIGMENT	NIVEOUS
TRAILED	RAGGLED	PLAGUER	TEMPING	VEINOUS
DIMPLES	DRAPIER	EATCHES	EMULING	ENVIROS
MISPLED	PARRIED	ESCHEAT	GUMLINE	RENVOIS
SIMPLED	RAPIDER	TEACHES	LEGUMIN	VERSION
DIPTERA	DRAUNTS	EIGHTHS	EMULSIN	ENWRAPS
PARTIED	DURANTS	HEIGHTS	LUMINES	PAWNERS
PIRATED	TUNDRAS	HIGHEST	UNLIMES	SPAWNER
DIRTIES	DREAMER	EKISTIC	ENAMORS	EOLITHS
DITSIER	REARMED	ICKIEST	MOANERS	HOLIEST
TIDIERS	REDREAM	TICKIES	OARSMEN	HOSTILE
DISHING	DREIDLS	ELANETS	ENDARTS	EOSINIC
HIDINGS	RIDDLES	LATEENS	STANDER	ICONISE
SHINDIG	SLIDDER	LEANEST	STARNED	NICOISE

EPACRIS	FANCIES	FLOATER	GARGLES	GESTAPO
SCRAPIE	FASCINE	FLOREAT	LAGGERS	POSTAGE
SPACIER	FIANCES	REFLOAT	RAGGLES	POTAGES
EPIGONS	FARTING	FLOODER	GARMENT	GINGERY
PIGEONS	INGRAFT	FLOORED	MARGENT	GREYING
PINGOES	RAFTING	REFLOOD	RAGMENT	NIGGERY
ERBIUMS	FASTIES	FLOWING	GARNISH	GIRDING
IMBRUES	FIESTAS	FOWLING	RASHING	GRIDING
IMBURSE	FISSATE	WOLFING	SHARING	RIDGING
ESPARTO	FATHERS	FLUENTS	GARRETS	GIRDLED
PROTEAS	HAFTERS	NESTFUL	GARTERS	GLIDDER
SEAPORT	SHAFTER	NETFULS	GRATERS	GRIDDLE
ESPYING	FEALING	FLUSTER	GARVIES	GIRNELS
PEYSING	FINAGLE	FLUTERS	GRAVIES	LINGERS
PIGSNEY	LEAFING	RESTFUL	RIVAGES	SLINGER
ESSOINS	FELSITE	FOETORS	GASPIER	GLAIRIN
OSSEINS	LEFTIES	FOOTERS	PRISAGE	LAIRING
SESSION	LIEFEST	REFOOTS	SPAIRGE	RAILING
ESTRAYS	FELTERS	FOOTIES	GASTING	GLOBINS
STAYERS	REFLETS	FOOTSIE	GATINGS	GOBLINS
STAYRES	TELFERS	OOFIEST	STAGING	LOBINGS
ESTREAT	FERRIED	FORPITS	GAULTER	GLORIED
RESTATE	REFIRED	PROFITS	TEGULAR	GODLIER
RETASTE	REFRIED	SPORTIF	TRAGULE	GOLDIER
ESTRINS	FERRIES	FRANTIC	GELANTS	GNOMISH
INSERTS	REFIRES	INFARCT	LANGEST	HOMINGS
SINTERS	REFRIES	INFRACT	TANGLES	MOSHING
ESTRIOL	FERULES	FRATERS	GELATED	GOGLETS
LOITERS	FUELERS	RAFTERS	LEGATED	LOGGETS
TOILERS	REFUELS	STRAFER	TEAGLED	TOGGLES
ESTRUMS	FIFTIES	FRITURE	GELIDER	GOITERS
MUSTERS	IFFIEST	FRUITER	LEDGIER	GOITRES
STUMERS	STIFFIE	TURFIER	LEIDGER	GORIEST
ETATISM	FIGHTER	GALIOTS	GEMINAL	GOONIES
MATIEST	FREIGHT	LATIGOS	LEAMING	ISOGONE
MATTIES	REFIGHT	SALIGOT	MEALING	NOOGIES
ETHYLIC	FISHERS	GALLATE	GEMMIER	GORPING
LECYTHI	SERFISH	GALLETA	GREMMIE	GROPING
TECHILY	SHERIFS	TALLAGE	IMMERGE	PORGING
ETOURDI	FISSURE	GANGERS	GENESIS	GOSTERS
IODURET	FUSSIER	GRANGES	SEEINGS	GROSETS
OUTRIDE	SURFIES	NAGGERS	SIGNEES	STORGES
FALSEST	FLANEUR	GAPINGS	GERMINS	GRASPED
FATLESS	FRENULA	GASPING	MERINGS	SPADGER
FESTALS	FUNERAL	PAGINGS	MINGERS	SPARGED

Triplets

GRAYEST	HARPERS	HOMERIC	INKLESS	ISOTRON
GYRATES	PHRASER	MOCHIER	KINLESS	NITROSO
STAGERY	SHARPER	MORICHE	SILKENS	TORSION
GREENER	HASLETS	HOTPOTS	INKLING	KAROROS
REGREEN	HATLESS	HOTSPOT	KILNING	KARROOS
RENEGER	SHELTAS	POTSHOT	LINKING	KORORAS
GREISLY	HASTENS	HUNTERS	INLACES	KARTERS
GRIESLY	SNATHES	SHUNTER	SANICLE	KRATERS
GRISELY	SNEATHS	UNHERST	SCALENI	STARKER
GREMLIN	HAWSERS	HURTING	INROADS	KASHRUT
MERLING	SWASHER	UNGIRTH	ORDAINS	KHURTAS
MINGLER	WASHERS	UNRIGHT	SADIRON	TUSHKAR
GRINGAS	HAWSING	HUSTLES	INSCULP	KELTERS
RAGINGS	SHAWING	LUSHEST	SCULPIN	KESTREL
SIRGANG	WASHING	SLEUTHS	UNCLIPS	SKELTER
GRIPMEN	HEARERS	ICKLEST	INSTARS	KILTERS
IMPREGN	REHEARS	STICKLE	SANTIRS	KIRTLES
PERMING	SHEARER	TICKLES	STRAINS	KLISTER
GUERDON	HEEDERS	IGNITER	INTAKES	KINDERS
UNDERGO	HEREDES	TIERING	KENTIAS	KINREDS
UNGORED	SHEERED	TIGRINE	TANKIES	REDSKIN
GUILERS	HEGARIS	IMMURES	INTERIM	KISTING
LIGURES	HEGIRAS	MUMSIER	MINTIER	KITINGS
LURGIES	HIRAGES	RUMMIES	TERMINI	SKITING
GUNTERS	HELIUMS	IMPETUS	INTONER	KITTELS
GURNETS	HUMLIES	IMPUTES	NOINTER	KITTLES
SURGENT	MUHLIES	UPTIMES	TERNION	SKITTLE
GUSTFUL	HENRIES	IMPOSER	INURING	KREESES
GUTFULS	INHERES	PROMISE	RUINING	RESEEKS
GUTSFUL	RESHINE	SEMIPRO	URINING	SEEKERS
HAIRNET	HEROONS	INANEST	IRATELY	LADDERS
INEARTH	ONSHORE	STANINE	REALITY	RADDLES
THERIAN	SOREHON	TANNIES	TEARILY	SADDLER
HALSING	HEWINGS	INCHERS	IRENICS	LAMENTS
LASHING	SHEWING	NICHERS	SERICIN	MANTELS
SHALING	WHINGES	RICHENS	SIRENIC	MANTLES
HAMMALS	HIDDERS	INCISAL	ISMATIC	LAMITER
MAHMALS	REDDISH	SALICIN	ITACISM	MALTIER
MASHLAM	SHIDDER	SINICAL	SIMATIC	MARLITE
HAPTENE	HINDERS	INGINES	ISOMERS	LAPPERS
HEPTANE	NERDISH	INSIGNE	MOISERS	RAPPELS
PHENATE	SHRINED	SEINING	MOSSIER	SLAPPER
HAPTICS	HOLIDAY	INGROUP	ISONOME	LAPSING
PATHICS	HYALOID	POURING	MOONIES	PALINGS
SPATHIC	HYOIDAL	ROUPING	NOISOME	SAPLING

LATENTS	LINGUAS	LOUDEST	MASCLES	MISDIET
LATTENS	NILGAUS	OULDEST	MESCALS	MISEDIT
TALENTS	SALUING	TOUSLED	SCAMELS	STIMIED
LAUNDER	LINKERS	LOUNDER	MASTERY	MISLIES
LURDANE	RELINKS	ROUNDEL	MAYSTER	MISSILE
RUNDALE	SLINKER	ROUNDLE	STREAMY	SIMILES
LEAPING	LINKUPS	LOURIES	MASTICS	MISMATE
PEALING	SKULPIN	LOUSIER	MISACTS	SEMIMAT
PLEAING	UPLINKS	SOILURE	MISCAST	TAMMIES
LEASING	LINTERS	LOUVERS	MASTING	MISUSER
LINAGES	SLINTER	LOUVRES	MATINGS	MUSSIER
SEALING	SNIRTLE	VELOURS	TAMINGS	SURMISE
LEISTER	LIPPERS	LUCARNE	MEDLING	MONTURE
RETILES	RIPPLES	NUCLEAR	MELDING	MOUNTER
STERILE	SLIPPER	UNCLEAR	MINGLED	REMOUNT
LENDERS	LIPREAD	LUSTIER	MEETERS	MOOTEST
RELENDS	PEDRAIL	RULIEST	REMEETS	MOTTOES
SLENDER	PREDIAL	RUTILES	TEEMERS	TOOMEST
LENTILS	LISTEES	LUSTING	MELOIDS	MOPIEST
LINTELS	TELESIS	LUTINGS	MIDSOLE	OPTIMES
TELLINS	TIELESS	SINGULT	SMOILED	STOMPIE
LEOPARD	LISTETH	LUSTRED	MENTORS	MOTHERS
PAROLED	LITHEST	RUSTLED	MONSTER	SMOTHER
PRELOAD	THISTLE	STRUDEL	MONTRES	THERMOS
LEPTINS	LITERAL	MAILERS	MERANTI	MOTIEST
PINTLES	TALLIER	REALISM	MINARET	MOTTIES
PLENIST	TRIELLA	REMAILS	RAIMENT	TITMOSE
LIBRATE	LOADERS	MALATES	MERCHES	MUNSTER
TABLIER	ORDEALS	MALTASE	SCHEMER	MUNTERS
TRIABLE	RELOADS	TAMALES	SCHMEER	STERNUM
LICENSE	LOANERS	MALISON	MESSILY	MUREINS
SELENIC	ORLEANS	MONIALS	MILSEYS	MURINES
SILENCE	RELOANS	SOMNIAL	SMILEYS	NEURISM
LICKERS	LOMENTA	MANITUS	MILADIS	MUTISMS
RICKLES	OMENTAL	SANTIMU	MISDIAL	SUMMIST
SLICKER	TELAMON	TSUNAMI	MISLAID	SUMMITS
LIMINGS	LORISES	MANURES	MINTAGE	NAGARIS
SLIMING	LOSSIER	MURENAS	TEAMING	SANGRIA
SMILING	RISSOLE	SURNAME	TEGMINA	SARANGI
LIMOSES	LOTUSES	MAPPERS	MIOTICS	NAIVEST
LISSOME	SOLUTES	PAMPERS	MISTICO	NATIVES
SMOILES	TOUSLES	PREAMPS	SOMITIC	VAINEST
LINGOTS	LOUDENS	MARACAS	MIRIEST	NEEDERS
TIGLONS	NODULES	MARASCA	MISTIER	SERENED
TOLINGS	NOUSLED	MASCARA	RIMIEST	SNEERED

Triplets

NEPETAS	OBSERVE	PANDIES	PEELERS	PINNETS
PENATES	OBVERSE	PANSIED	SLEEPER	SPINNET
PESANTE	VERBOSE	SPAINED	SPEELER	TENPINS
NEPHRIC	OERSTED	PANTLER	PENSILS	PINTOES
PHRENIC	ROSETED	PLANTER	SPINELS	POINTES
PINCHER	TEREDOS	REPLANT	SPLINES	PONTIES
NESTING	OOLITES	PAPERER	PENSION	PISHERS
SENTING	OSTIOLE	PREPARE	PINONES	RESHIPS
TENSING	STOOLIE	REPAPER	SPINONE	SERIPHS
NESTLER	OPERANT	PARISON	PERICON	PISTONS
RELENTS	PRONATE	PORINAS	PONCIER	POSTINS
SLENTER	PROTEAN	SOPRANI	PORCINE	SPINTOS
NESTORS	OPPOSER	PARKEES	PERIGON	PITTERS
STONERS	POOPERS	RESPEAK	PIROGEN	SPITTER
TENSORS	PROPOSE	SPEAKER	PONGIER	TIPSTER
NETTERS	OPTIONS	PARKERS	PERIQUE	PLANATE
TENTERS	POSITON	REPARKS	REEQUIP	PLANTAE
TESTERN	POTIONS	SPARKER	REPIQUE	PLATANE
NEWSIER	ORIGINS	PARTING	PERNODS	PLANTAS
WEINERS	SIGNIOR	PRATING	PONDERS	PLATANS
WIENERS	SIGNORI	TRAPING	RESPOND	SALTPAN
NICKELS	ORPINES	PARTLET	PERSING	PLESSOR
NICKLES	PIONERS	PLATTER	PINGERS	SLOPERS
SLICKEN	PROINES	PRATTLE	SPRINGE	SPLORES
NIDGETS	OSSELET	PARTONS	PERTEST	POOREST
STEDING	TELOSES	PATRONS	PETTERS	POOTERS
STINGED	TOELESS	TARPONS	PRETEST	STOOPER
NIDINGS	OSTENTS	PARULIS	PERUSAL	POPSTER
SINDING	STETSON	SPIRULA	PLEURAS	STOPPER
SNIDING	TESTONS	UPRISAL	SERPULA	TOPPERS
NITRITE	OSTLERS	PASCUAL	PHYTONS	POSEURS
NITTIER	STEROLS	PAUCALS	PYTHONS	SEROPUS
TINTIER	TORSELS	SCAPULA	TYPHONS	SOUPERS
NOOSERS	OUTDARE	PASTERS	PICKERS	POSTMAN
SEROONS	OUTREAD	REPASTS	RIPECKS	TAMPONS
SOONERS	READOUT	SPAREST	SPICKER	TOPSMAN
NOSIEST	OUTSERT	PATTERS	PIERROT	POTHERS
SONTIES	STOUTER	SPATTER	PORTIER	STROPHE
STONIES	TOUTERS	TAPSTER	PRERIOT	THORPES
NUPTIAL	PAINTER	PEARLIN	PIGSKIN	POTTERS
PATULIN	PERTAIN	PLAINER	PIKINGS	PROTEST
UNPLAIT	REPAINT	PRALINE	SPIKING	SPOTTER
NUTSIER	PALASES	PEASING	PINIEST	POTTIES
TRIUNES	PASELAS	SPAEING	PINITES	SPOTTIE
UNITERS	PLAASES	SPINAGE	TIEPINS	TIPTOES

POULDER	QUAREST	RENTING	REVISIT	RUMPIES
POULDRE	QUARTES	RINGENT	STIVIER	SPUMIER
PROULED	QUATRES	TERNING	VISITER	UMPIRES
PRAYERS	RANDIES	RERISES	REVUIST	RUSSETS
RESPRAY	SANDIER	SERRIES	STUIVER	TRUSSES
SPRAYER	SARDINE	SIRREES	VIRTUES	TUSSERS
PREASED	RANKEST	RESEAUS	REWARMS	RUTTERS
RESPADE	STARKEN	SEASURE	SWARMER	TRUSTER
SPEARED	TANKERS	UREASES	WARMERS	TURRETS
PRESELL	RASHEST	RESIFTS	REWEARS	SACHEMS
RESPELL	SHASTER	SIFTERS	SWEARER	SAMECHS
SPELLER	TRASHES	STRIFES	WEARERS	SCHEMAS
PRESSER	RATTANS	RESPLIT	RHETORS	SALIVAS
REPRESS	TANTRAS	SPIRTLE	ROTHERS	SALVIAS
SPERRES	TARTANS	TRIPLES	SHORTER	VASSAIL
PRISING	RATTERS	RESTOCK	RICKETS	SALLETS
RISPING	RESTART	ROCKETS	STICKER	STELLAS
SPIRING	STARTER	STOCKER	TICKERS	TASSELL
PROYNES	RATTIER	RESTUFF	RINGLET	SALVETE
PYONERS	RETRAIT	STUFFER	TINGLER	VALETES
PYRONES	TARTIER	TRUFFES	TRINGLE	VELETAS
PRUDENT	REBATER	RESTUMP	RIOTERS	SALVING
PRUNTED	TABRERE	STUMPER	ROISTER	SLAVING
UPTREND	TEREBRA	SUMPTER	RORIEST	VALSING
PRUINES	RECURES	RETEARS	RIPPLET	SEAGULL
PURINES	RESCUER	SERRATE	TIPPLER	SULLAGE
UPRISEN	SECURER	TEARERS	TRIPPLE	ULLAGES
PRYINGS	REDCAPS	RETIRAL	RISQUES	SEEDLIP
PRYSING	SCARPED	RETRIAL	SQUIERS	SPEILED
SPRINGY	SCRAPED	TRAILER	SQUIRES	SPIELED
PUDSIER	REDNESS	RETIRED	RONDURE	SEINERS
SIRUPED	RESENDS	RETRIED	ROUNDER	SEREINS
UPDRIES	SENDERS	TIREDER	UNORDER	SERINES
PULIEST	REDOUND	RETRAIN	ROOSTER	SENDUPS
PUTELIS	ROUNDED	TERRAIN	ROOTERS	SUSPEND
STIPULE	UNDERDO	TRAINER	TOREROS	UPSENDS
PULSATE	REEVING	RETRATE	ROTTENS	SERVANT
PUTEALS	REGIVEN	RETREAT	SNOTTER	TAVERNS
SPATULE	VEERING	TREATER	STENTOR	VERSANT
PUSLEYS	REMADES	RETWIST	ROWDIER	SETWALL
PUSSLEY	REMEADS	TWISTER	WORDIER	SWALLET
SPULYES	SMEARED	WITTERS	WORRIED	WALLETS
PUSSIER	RENTERS	REUSING	RUCKLES	SHREIKS
SUSPIRE	RERENTS	RUEINGS	SCULKER	SHRIEKS
UPRISES	STERNER	SIGNEUR	SUCKLER	SHRIKES

Triplets

SHUTING	SPROUTS	STRETTI	TAIVERS	WARLESS
TUSHING	STROUPS	TITTERS	VASTIER	WARSLES
UNSIGHT	STUPORS	TRITEST	VERITAS	WRASSLE
SISTRUM	STERNED	STRINGY	TEWHITS	WARSTLE
TRISMUS	TENDERS	STYRING	WETTISH	WASTREL
TRUISMS	TENDRES	TRYINGS	WHITEST	WRASTLE
SITELLA	STEWARD	SUNBELT	THAIRMS	WEATHER
TAILLES	STRAWED	UNBELTS	THIRAMS	WHEREAT
TALLIES	WRASTED	UNBLEST	THRIMSA	WREATHE
SKIRRET	STEWING	SUNNIER	THEATER	WENDIGO
SKIRTER	TWINGES	UNREINS	THEATRE	WIDGEON
STRIKER	WESTING	UNRISEN	THEREAT	WONGIED
SNOTTIE	STORMER	SWATHER	TRAVELS	WHERRIT
TONIEST	TERMORS	THAWERS	VARLETS	WHIRRET
TONITES	TREMORS	WREATHS	VESTRAL	WRITHER
SONNETS	STOTTER	SWELTER	UNHEALS	
STONNES	STRETTO	WELTERS	UNLEASH	
TENSONS	TOTTERS	WRESTLE	UNSHALE	
SPARTHE	STOWING	SWIPING	UNIPEDS	
TEPHRAS	TOWINGS	WIPINGS	UNSPIDE	
THREAPS	TOWSING	WISPING	UNSPIED	
SPELDIN	STRETTA	SWITHER	VERSUTE	
SPINDLE	TARTEST	WITHERS	VERTUES	
SPLINED	TATTERS	WRITHES	VESTURE	

Quadruplets

ABUSERS	AGAINST	ALGESIS	AMBLING	APRICOT
BUSERAS	AGITANS	GLASSIE	BALMING	APROTIC
RUBASSE	ANTISAG	LIGASES	BLAMING	PAROTIC
SURBASE	GITANAS	SILAGES	LAMBING	PATRICO
ACMITES	AIMLESS	ALLERGY	AMOSITE	APRONED
ETACISM	MESAILS	GALLERY	ATOMIES	OPERAND
MICATES	SAMIELS	LARGELY	ATOMISE	PADRONE
SEMATIC	SEISMAL	REGALLY	OSMIATE	PANDORE
ACRASIN	AIRSHED	ALMAINS	ANELING	ARBORED
ARNICAS	DASHIER	ANIMALS	EANLING	BOARDER
CARINAS	HARDIES	LAMINAS	LEANING	BROADER
SARCINA	SHADIER	MANILAS	NEALING	REBOARD
ACTURES	AIRSIDE	ALPINES	ANGRILY	ARCINGS
CAUTERS	DAIRIES	PINEALS	NARGILY	RACINGS
CRUSTAE	DIARIES	SPANIEL	RANGILY	SACRING
CURATES	DIARISE	SPLENIA	RAYLING	SCARING
ADEPTER	ALERTER	ALTERNE	APLITES	ARCKING
PREDATE	ALTERER	ENTERAL	PALIEST	CARKING
RETAPED	REALTER	ETERNAL	PLATIES	CRAKING
TAPERED	RELATER	TELERAN	TALIPES	RACKING

ARCSINE	ATONERS	CALLERS	CARPETS	CLEANSE
ARSENIC	SANTERO	CELLARS	PREACTS	ELANCES
CARNIES	SENATOR	RECALLS	PRECAST	ENLACES
CERASIN	TREASON	SCLERAL	SPECTRA	SCALENE
ARMLETS	ATRESIC	CALMIER	CARVIES	CLEARED
LAMSTER	CRISTAE	CLAIMER	CAVIERS	CREEDAL
MARTELS	RACIEST	MIRACLE	VARICES	DECLARE
TRAMELS	STEARIC	RECLAIM	VISCERA	RELACED
ARTISTS	AWNIEST	CALORIE	CASSENE	CLOSEUP
SITTARS	TAWNIES	CARIOLE	ENCASES	COUPLES
STRAITS	WANIEST	COALIER	SEANCES	OPUSCLE
TSARIST	WANTIES	LORICAE	SENECAS	UPCLOSE
ARTSIER	BAITERS	CAMERAL	CATERER	COLORED
SERRATI	BARITES	CARAMEL	RECRATE	CROODLE
TARRIES	REBAITS	CERAMAL	RETRACE	CROOLED
TARSIER	TERBIAS	MACERAL	TERRACE	DECOLOR
ARTSMEN	BALMIER	CANTLES	CENSERS	COLTERS
MARTENS	LAMBIER	CENTALS	SCERNES	CORSLET
SARMENT	MIRABLE	LANCETS	SCREENS	COSTREL
SMARTEN	REMBLAI	SCANTLE	SECERNS	LECTORS
ASCRIBE	BANTIES	CANTORS	CERATES	CONSTER
CABRIES	BASINET	CARTONS	CREATES	CORNETS
CARBIES	BESAINT	CONTRAS	ECARTES	CRESTON
CARIBES	BESTAIN	CRATONS	SECRETA	CRONETS
ASHIEST	BARDIER	CAPITOL	CESTUIS	COPINGS
SAITHES	BRAIDER	COALPIT	CUEISTS	COPSING
STASHIE	BRIARED	OPTICAL	CUTISES	PICONGS
TAISHES	RABIDER	TOPICAL	ICTUSES	SCOPING
ASHLERS	BASTERS	CAPSULE	CHEAPOS	CORNUTE
HALSERS	BESTARS	SCALEUP	EPOCHAS	COUNTER
LASHERS	BRASSET	SPECULA	POACHES	RECOUNT
SLASHER	BREASTS	UPSCALE	SHOEPAC	TROUNCE
ASHLESS	BECHARM	CARDIES	CIRROSE	CREESED
HASSELS	BRECHAM	DARCIES	CORRIES	DECREES
HASSLES	CHAMBER	RADICES	CROSIER	RECEDES
SLASHES	CHAMBRE	SIDECAR	ORRICES	SECEDER
ASPIRED	BEMOILS	CAREENS	CISTRON	CRESSET
DESPAIR	EMBOILS	CASERNE	CITRONS	RESECTS
DIAPERS	MOBILES	ENRACES	CORNIST	SCREETS
PRAISED	OBELISM	RECANES	CORTINS	SECRETS
ASTERTS	BLUSTER	CARLESS	CITADEL	CROSSER
STARETS	BUSTLER	CLASSER	DELTAIC	RECROSS
STATERS	BUTLERS	SCALERS	DIALECT	SCORERS
TASTERS	SUBTLER	SCLERAS	EDICTAL	SCORSER
ATOMICS	BURBLES	CAROLUS	CITRINE	CUITERS
MATICOS	LUBBERS	OCULARS	CRINITE	CURIETS
OSMATIC	RUBBLES	OSCULAR	INCITER	CURITES
SOMATIC	SLUBBER	RUCOLAS	NERITIC	ICTERUS

Quadruplets

CUNDIES	DERAILS	DURAMEN	ENTRIST	FINDERS
INCUDES	DIALERS	MANURED	RETINTS	FRIENDS
INCUSED	REDIALS	MAUNDER	STINTER	REDFINS
INDUCES	SIDERAL	UNARMED	TINTERS	REFINDS
CUSTODE	DERIDER	EARNEST	ERETHIC	FLOWERS
DOUCEST	REDDIER	EASTERN	ETHERIC	FOWLERS
DOUCETS	REDRIED	NEAREST	HERETIC	REFLOWS
SCOUTED	RIDERED	RATEENS	TECHIER	WOLFERS
DALLIES	DERIDES	EARTHLY	ERINGOS	FRISEUR
DISLEAL	DESIRED	HARTELY	IGNORES	FRISURE
LALDIES	DIEDRES	HEARTLY	REGIONS	FURRIES
SALLIED	RESIDED	LATHERY	SIGNORE	SURFIER
DAMNERS	DERIVES	EMPARLS	EROTISM	GAGSTER
MANREDS	DEVISER	LAMPERS	MOISTER	GARGETS
RANDEMS	DIVERSE	PALMERS	MORTISE	STAGGER
REMANDS	REVISED	SAMPLER	TRISOME	TAGGERS
DANGLES	DEVISOR	EMPARTS	ERRINGS	GAROTES
GLANDES	DEVOIRS	RESTAMP	GIRNERS	ORGEATS
LAGENDS	VISORED	STAMPER	RINGERS	STORAGE
SLANGED	VOIDERS	TAMPERS	SERRING	TOERAGS
DAUNTER	DINGLES	ENDUROS	ESLOINS	GATEMAN
NATURED	ELDINGS	RESOUND	INSOLES	MAGENTA
UNRATED	ENGILDS	SOUNDER	LESIONS	MAGNATE
UNTREAD	SINGLED	UNDOERS	LIONESS	NAMETAG
DEAFEST	DIOPTER	ENFIRES	ESTOVER	GELDERS
DEFASTE	DIOPTRE	FEERINS	OVERSET	LEDGERS
DEFEATS	PERIDOT	FINEERS	REVOTES	REDLEGS
FEASTED	PROTEID	REFINES	VETOERS	SLEDGER
DEANERY	DISTOME	ENGINES	EVILEST	GENTIER
RENAYED	DOMIEST	GENNIES	LEVITES	INTEGER
YEAREND	MODISTE	NEESING	LIEVEST	TEERING
YEARNED	MOISTED	SNEEING	VELITES	TREEING
DEFILER	DOATERS	ENIGMAS	FAUNIST	GEOMANT
FERLIED	ROASTED	GAMINES	FIAUNTS	MAGNETO
FIELDER	TORSADE	MEASING	FUSTIAN	MEGATON
REFILED	TROADES	SEAMING	INFAUST	MONTAGE
DEFINER	DONATOR	ENLISTS	FEERING	GINGERS
ENFIRED	ODORANT	LISTENS	FEIGNER	NIGGERS
FENDIER	TANDOOR	SILENTS	FREEING	SERGING
REFINED	TORNADO	TINSELS	REEFING	SNIGGER
DELAPSE	DOUBTER	ENTERER	FERLIES	GINGLES
ELAPSED	OBTRUDE	REENTER	REFILES	LEGGINS
PLEASED	OUTBRED	TERREEN	REFLIES	NIGGLES
SEPALED	REDOUBT	TERRENE	RELIEFS	SNIGGLE
DELIVER	DRAWERS	ENTRISM	FILTERS	GIRKINS
LIVERED	REDRAWS	MINSTER	LIFTERS	GRISKIN
RELIVED	REWARDS	MINTERS	STIFLER	KRISING
REVILED	WARDERS	REMINTS	TRIFLES	RISKING

GISARME	HISTING	LAMMERS	LOOTERS	MARINES
IMAGERS	INSIGHT	RAMMELS	RETOOLS	REMAINS
MAIGRES	SHITING	RAMMLES	ROOTLES	SEMINAR
MIRAGES	SITHING	SLAMMER	TOOLERS	SIRNAME
GLURGES	HORNETS	LASCARS	LOTTERS	MELTERS
GURGLES	SHORTEN	RASCALS	SETTLOR	REMELTS
LUGGERS	THRENOS	SACRALS	SLOTTER	RESMELT
SLUGGER	THRONES	SCALARS	TOLTERS	SMELTER
GNASHER	IGNAROS	LASSOER	LOWINGS	MERISES
HANGERS	ORIGANS	OARLESS	LOWSING	MESSIER
REHANGS	SIGNORA	SEROSAL	SLOWING	MISERES
SHERANG	SOARING	SOLERAS	SOWLING	REMISES
GRANTEE	IMPALER	LATESTS	LUMBERS	MESTINO
GREATEN	IMPEARL	SALTEST	RUMBLES	MOISTEN
NEGATER	LEMPIRA	STALEST	SLUMBER	MONTIES
REAGENT	PALMIER	TASLETS	UMBRELS	SENTIMO
GRISONS	IMPRESS	LEGLINS	LUNIEST	MINUTED
INGROSS	PREMISS	LINGELS	LUTEINS	MUNITED
SIGNORS	SIMPERS	LINGLES	UNTILES	MUTINED
SORINGS	SPIREMS	SELLING	UTENSIL	UNTIMED
GUNSHOT	INCEPTS	LENITES	LURDENS	MINUTER
HOGNUTS	INSPECT	LISENTE	NURDLES	MUNTRIE
NOUGHTS	PECTINS	SETLINE	NURSLED	UNMITER
SHOTGUN	PEINCTS	TENSILE	RUNDLES	UNMITRE
HASPING	INERTER	LEPROUS	MACHERS	MISTING
PASHING	REINTER	PELORUS	MARCHES	SMITING
PHASING	RENTIER	PERLOUS	MESARCH	STIMING
SHAPING	TERRINE	SPORULE	SCHMEAR	TIMINGS
HATTERS	INGRESS	LIMPERS	MADRONA	MOLDERS
RATHEST	RESIGNS	PRELIMS	MANDORA	REMOLDS
SHATTER	SIGNERS	RIMPLES	MONARDA	SLORMED
THREATS	SINGERS	SIMPLER	ROADMAN	SMOLDER
HAUNTER	INSEEMS	LINEUPS	MAELIDS	NAPPERS
UNEARTH	MISSEEN	LUPINES	MEDIALS	PARPENS
UNHEART	NEMESIS	SPINULE	MISDEAL	PARSNEP
URETHAN	SIEMENS	UNPILES	MISLEAD	SNAPPER
HEAPERS	INSPIRE	LISPING	MAINTOP	NESTERS
RESHAPE	PIRNIES	PILINGS	PTOMAIN	RENESTS
SPHAERE	SNIPIER	SLIPING	TAMPION	RESENTS
SPHEARE	SPINIER	SPILING	TIMPANO	STRENES
HEPSTER	IONISER	LISTING	MANDIOC	NEURITE
PETHERS	IRONIES	SILTING	MONACID	RETINUE
SPERTHE	IRONISE	STILING	MONADIC	REUNITE
THREEPS	NOISIER	TILINGS	NOMADIC	UTERINE
HERIOTS	ISLEMAN	LOOPERS	MANLIER	NEUTERS
HOISTER	MALINES	POOLERS	MARLINE	RETUNES
SHORTIE	MENIALS	RESPOOL	MINERAL	TENURES
TOSHIER	SEMINAL	SPOOLER	RAILMEN	TUREENS

Quadruplets

NORTHED	PARTANS	PERDUES	QUESTOR	RILLETS
THONDER	SPARTAN	PERSUED	QUOTERS	STILLER
THORNED	TARPANS	PERUSED	ROQUETS	TILLERS
THRONED	TRAPANS	SUPERED	TORQUES	TRELLIS
OORIEST	PASSIVE	PERRIES	REIVERS	ROSTING
ROOTIES	PAVISES	PRISERE	REVERSI	SORTING
SOOTIER	PAVISSE	REPRISE	REVISER	STORING
TOORIES	SPAVIES	RESPIRE	RIEVERS	TRIGONS
OPENEST	PASTIES	PETRALE	REKNITS	RUINATE
PENTOSE	PATSIES	PLEATER	SKINTER	TAURINE
POSTEEN	PETSAIS	PRELATE	STINKER	URANITE
POTEENS	TAPISES	REPLATE	TINKERS	URINATE
ORALIST	PASTINA	PIECERS	REKNOTS	SALVERS
RIALTOS	PATINAS	PIERCES	STONKER	SERVALS
SLIOTAR	PINATAS	PRECISE	STROKEN	SLAVERS
TAILORS	TAIPANS	RECIPES	TONKERS	VERSALS
ORNISES	PASTURE	PLUSING	REMATES	SKATERS
SENIORS	UPRATES	PULINGS	RETEAMS	STRAKES
SONERIS	UPSTARE	PULSING	STEAMER	STREAKS
SONSIER	UPTEARS	PUSLING	TEAMERS	TASKERS
OURIEST	PEARLED	POINTEL	RESERVE	SKATING
STOURIE	PEDALER	PONTILE	REVERES	STAKING
TOURIES	PLEADER	POTLINE	REVERSE	TAKINGS
TOUSIER	REPLEAD	TOPLINE	SEVERER	TASKING
OUSTING	PEARTLY	PREDIES	RESEWED	STAWING
OUTINGS	PEYTRAL	PRESIDE	SEWERED	TAWINGS
OUTSING	PRELATY	SPEIRED	SWEERED	TAWSING
TOUSING	PTERYLA	SPIERED	WEEDERS	WASTING
OUTGRIN	PELMETS	PROIGNS	RESORTS	STIVERS
OUTRING	STEMPEL	PROSING	ROSTERS	STRIVES
ROUTING	STEMPLE	ROPINGS	SORTERS	TREVISS
TOURING	TEMPLES	SPORING	STORERS	VERISTS
PANTIES	PELTERS	PULPERS	RETORTS	SYSTOLE
PATINES	PETRELS	PURPLES	ROTTERS	TOLSEYS
SAPIENT	RESPELT	REPULPS	STERTOR	TOYLESS
SPINATE	SPELTER	SUPPLER	TORRETS	TYLOSES
PARINGS	PENSTER	PURISTS	REVESTS	WAISTER
PARSING	PRESENT	SPRUITS	STERVES	WAITERS
RASPING	REPENTS	UPRISTS	VERSETS	WARIEST
SPARING	SERPENT	UPSTIRS	VERSTES	WASTRIE

Quintuplets

ABORTUS	ADHERES	ADMIRES	AGILEST	AGINNER
OUTBARS	HEADERS	MARDIES	AIGLETS	EARNING
ROBUSTA	HEARSED	MISREAD	GELATIS	ENGRAIN
RUBATOS	HEDERAS	SEDARIM	LIGATES	GRANNIE
TABOURS	SHEARED	SIDEARM	TAIGLES	NEARING

AIRINGS	ANGLIST	ATINGLE	CATERED	DEMERSE
ARISING	LASTING	ELATING	CEDRATE	EMERSED
RAGINIS	SALTING	GELATIN	CERATED	MEDRESE
RAISING	SLATING	GENITAL	CREATED	REDEEMS
SAIRING	STALING	TAGLINE	REACTED	REMEDES

AIRLESS	ANGRIER	ATTUNES	CENSUAL	DERRIES
RESAILS	EARRING	NUTATES	LACUNES	DESIRER
SAILERS	GRAINER	TAUTENS	LAUNCES	REDRIES
SERAILS	RANGIER	TETANUS	UNLACES	RESIDER
SERIALS	REARING	UNSTATE	UNSCALE	SERRIED

ALBERTS	ANOSMIC	BALDIER	CERUSES	DIESTER
BATLERS	CAMIONS	BEDRAIL	CESURES	DIETERS
BLASTER	CONIMAS	BRAILED	RECUSES	REEDITS
LABRETS	MANIOCS	RAILBED	RESCUES	REISTED
STABLER	MASONIC	RIDABLE	SECURES	RESITED

ALECOST	ANTLERS	BATLETS	CHEEROS	DREARES
LACTOSE	RENTALS	BATTELS	CHOREES	READERS
LOCATES	SALTERN	BATTLES	COHERES	REDEARS
SCATOLE	SLANTER	BLATEST	ECHOERS	REDSEAR
TALCOSE	STERNAL	TABLETS	RECHOSE	REREADS

ALERCES	ARCHEST	BERATED	CLUSTER	DREEING
CEREALS	CHARETS	BETREAD	CULTERS	ENERGID
RELACES	CHASTER	DEBATER	CUSTREL	GREINED
RESCALE	RACHETS	REBATED	CUTLERS	REEDING
SCLERAE	RATCHES	TABERED	RELUCTS	REIGNED

ALERTED	ARCUSES	BESTIRS	COURSES	EARLESS
ALTERED	CAUSERS	BISTERS	SCOURSE	LEASERS
REDEALT	CESURAS	BISTRES	SCOUSER	RESALES
RELATED	SAUCERS	BITSERS	SOURCES	RESEALS
TREADLE	SUCRASE	BREISTS	SUCROSE	SEALERS

ALNAGES	ARSIEST	BOASTER	DAEMONS	ELATERS
ANLAGES	ARTSIES	BOATERS	MASONED	REALEST
GALENAS	SAIREST	BORATES	MODENAS	RELATES
LAGENAS	SATIRES	REBATOS	MONADES	RESLATE
LASAGNE	TIRASSE	SORBATE	NOMADES	STEALER

AMBLERS	ARTLESS	BRUNETS	DARTERS	ELOIGNS
BLAMERS	LASTERS	BUNTERS	DARTRES	LEGIONS
LAMBERS	SALTERS	BURNETS	RETARDS	LIGNOSE
MARBLES	SLATERS	BURSTEN	STARRED	LINGOES
RAMBLES	TARSELS	SUBRENT	TRADERS	LONGIES

ANGERED	ASPIRES	CALIVER	DEMAINS	ENISLES
DERANGE	PARESIS	CAVILER	MAIDENS	ENSILES
ENRAGED	PARISES	CLAVIER	MEDIANS	SENILES
GRANDEE	PRAISES	VALERIC	MEDINAS	SENSILE
GRENADE	SPIREAS	VELARIC	SIDEMAN	SILENES

ANGLERS	ASTELIC	CARTELS	DEMERIT	ENTASES
ERLANGS	ELASTIC	CLARETS	DIMETER	SATEENS
LANGERS	LACIEST	CRESTAL	MERITED	SENATES
LARGENS	LATICES	SCARLET	MITERED	SENSATE
SLANGER	SALICET	TARCELS	RETIMED	STEANES

Quintuplets

ENVIERS	GLISTEN	LETTERS	PARSERS	RESTIVE
INVERSE	LESTING	LETTRES	RASPERS	SIEVERT
VEINERS	SINGLET	SETTLER	SPARERS	STIEVER
VENIRES	SNIGLET	STERLET	SPARRES	VERIEST
VERSINE	TINGLES	TRESTLE	SPARSER	VERITES
ERODING	GRANITE	LEVIERS	POINTER	RETESTS
GROINED	GRATINE	RELIVES	PROTEIN	SETTERS
IGNORED	INGRATE	REVILES	PTERION	STREETS
NEGROID	TANGIER	SERVILE	REPOINT	TERSEST
REDOING	TEARING	VEILERS	TROPINE	TESTERS
ESCAPER	HALTERS	LOGIONS	PORTERS	RETOURS
PEARCES	HARSLET	LOOSING	PRESORT	ROUSTER
PERCASE	LATHERS	OLINGOS	PRETORS	ROUTERS
PREACES	SLATHER	SOLOING	REPORTS	TOURERS
RESPACE	THALERS	SOOLING	SPORTER	TROUSER
ESCARPS	HOOTERS	MARSHES	POSIEST	SOWTERS
PARSECS	RESHOOT	MASHERS	POSTIES	STOWERS
SCRAPES	SHEROOT	SHAMERS	POTSIES	STOWRES
SECPARS	SHOOTER	SHMEARS	SEPIOST	TOWSERS
SPACERS	SOOTHER	SMASHER	SOPITES	WORSETS
ESPIALS	INTRUDE	MINUETS	RACKETS	
LAIPSES	TURDINE	MINUTES	RESTACK	
LAPISES	UNTIRED	MISTUNE	RETACKS	
LIPASES	UNTRIDE	MUNITES	STACKER	
PALSIES	UNTRIED	MUTINES	TACKERS	
GASTRIN	LAVEERS	OPENERS	RATTLES	
GRATINS	LEAVERS	PEREONS	SLATTER	
RATINGS	REVEALS	PERONES	STARLET	
STARING	SEVERAL	REOPENS	STARTLE	
TARINGS	VEALERS	REPONES	TATLERS	
GERMAIN	LEAPERS	PARLEYS	RECUSED	
GERMINA	PLEASER	PARSLEY	REDUCES	
MANGIER	PRESALE	PLAYERS	RESCUED	
MEARING	RELAPSE	REPLAYS	SECURED	
REAMING	REPEALS	SPARELY	SEDUCER	

Sextuplets

ABIDERS	ASPERSE	ASTEISM	CANOERS	CLAROES
BARDIES	PARESES	MISEATS	CARNOSE	COALERS
BRAISED	PRAESES	MISSEAT	COARSEN	ESCOLAR
DARBIES	PREASES	SAMIEST	CORNEAS	ORACLES
SEABIRD	PREASSE	SAMITES	EARCONS	RECOALS
SIDEBAR	SERAPES	TAMISES	NARCOSE	SOLACER
AMENDER	ASPIRER	CAMELID	CHEATER	CORSETS
ENARMED	PARRIES	CLAIMED	HECTARE	COSTERS
MEANDER	PRAISER	DECIMAL	RECHATE	ESCORTS
REAMEND	RAPIERS	DECLAIM	RECHEAT	SCOTERS
REEDMAN	RASPIER	MALICED	RETEACH	SCROTES
RENAMED	REPAIRS	MEDICAL	TEACHER	SECTORS

DARNELS	DINEROS	ETAMINS	LUSTERS	PHRASES
ENLARDS	DONSIER	INMATES	LUSTRES	SERAPHS
LANDERS	INDORSE	MAINEST	RESULTS	SHAPERS
RELANDS	ORDINES	MANTIES	RUSTLES	SHERPAS
SLANDER	ROSINED	TAMEINS	SUTLERS	SPHAERS
SNARLED	SORDINE	TAMINES	ULSTERS	SPHEARS

DEARTHS	EAGLETS	ETRIERS	MEISTER	PORTESS
HARDEST	GELATES	REITERS	METIERS	POSTERS
HARDSET	LEGATES	RESTIER	REEMITS	PRESTOS
HATREDS	SEGETAL	RETIRES	RETIMES	REPOSTS
THREADS	TEAGLES	RETRIES	TREMIES	RESPOTS
TRASHED	TELEGAS	TERRIES	TRISEME	STOPERS

DEPOSIT	ENTASIS	HECTORS	NORITES	REALIST
DOPIEST	NASTIES	ROCHETS	OESTRIN	RETAILS
PODITES	SEITANS	ROTCHES	ORIENTS	SALTIER
POSITED	SESTINA	TOCHERS	STONIER	SALTIRE
SOPITED	TANSIES	TORCHES	TERSION	SLATIER
TOPSIDE	TISANES	TROCHES	TRIONES	TAILERS

DESPOIL	ENTIRES	INTREAT	PALTERS	RECEPTS
DIPLOES	ENTRIES	ITERANT	PERSALT	RESPECT
DIPOLES	NERITES	NATTIER	PLASTER	SCEPTER
PELOIDS	RETINES	NITRATE	PLATERS	SCEPTRE
SOLIPED	TRENISE	TARTINE	PSALTER	SPECTER
SPOILED	TRIENES	TERTIAN	STAPLER	SPECTRE

DETOURS	ENTRAIL	LITTERS	PERIOST	
DOUREST	LATRINE	SLITTER	PORIEST	
DOUTERS	RATLINE	STILTER	PROSTIE	
OUTREDS	RELIANT	TESTRIL	REPOSIT	
REDOUTS	RETINAL	TILTERS	RIPOSTE	
ROUSTED	TRENAIL	TITLERS	ROPIEST	

Septuplets

ALIGNER	AREDING	CANTERS	CARPELS	DESTAIN
ENGRAIL	DEARING	CARNETS	CLASPER	DETAINS
LAERING	DERAIGN	NECTARS	CRAPLES	INSTEAD
LEARING	EARDING	RECANTS	PARCELS	NIDATES
NARGILE	GRADINE	SCANTER	PLACERS	SAINTED
REALIGN	GRAINED	TANRECS	RECLASP	SATINED
REGINAL	READING	TRANCES	SCALPER	STAINED

ALIPEDS	ARPENTS	CANTIER	COINERS	GILDERS
ELAPIDS	ENTRAPS	CERATIN	CRINOSE	GIRDLES
LAIPSED	PANTERS	CERTAIN	CRONIES	GLIDERS
LAPIDES	PARENTS	CREATIN	ORCEINS	GRISLED
PAIDLES	PASTERN	CRINATE	ORCINES	LIDGERS
PALSIED	PERSANT	NACRITE	RECOINS	REGILDS
PLEIADS	TREPANS	TACRINE	SERICON	RIDGELS

Sextuplets

IMARETS	PETROUS	ROSIEST
MAESTRI	POSTURE	SIROSET
MAISTER	POUTERS	SORITES
MASTIER	PROTEUS	SORTIES
MISRATE	SEPTUOR	STORIES
SEMITAR	SPOUTER	TOSSIER
SMARTIE	TROUPES	TRIOSES

Octuplets

ABLEIST	ARTIEST	EASTERS	EMPIRES
ALBITES	ARTISTE	RESEATS	EMPRISE
ASTILBE	ATTIRES	SAETERS	EPIMERS
BASTILE	IRATEST	SEAREST	IMPRESE
BESTIAL	RATITES	SEATERS	PERMIES
BLASTIE	STRIATE	STEARES	PREMIES
LIBATES	TASTIER	TEASERS	PREMISE
STABILE	TERTIAS	TESSERA	SPIREME

AGISTER	DEAREST	EDITORS	PAIREST
AIGRETS	DERATES	ROISTED	PARTIES
GAITERS	ESTRADE	ROSITED	PASTIER
SEAGIRT	REASTED	SORTIED	PIASTER
STAGIER	REDATES	STEROID	PIASTRE
STRIGAE	SEDATER	STORIED	PIRATES
TIRAGES	STEARED	TIERODS	PRATIES
TRIAGES	TASERED	TRIODES	TRAIPSE

Nontuplets

ARIDEST	EASTLIN	ESPRITS	ESTROUS
ASTERID	ELASTIN	PERSIST	OESTRUS
ASTRIDE	ENTAILS	PRIESTS	OUSTERS
DIASTER	NAILSET	SITREPS	SOUREST
DISRATE	SALIENT	SPRIEST	SOUTERS
STAIDER	SALTINE	SPRITES	STOURES
STAIRED	SLAINTE	STIRPES	TOUSERS
TARDIES	STANIEL	STRIPES	TROUSES
TIRADES	TENAILS	TRIPSES	TUSSORE

Decuplets

ANGRIES
EARINGS
ERASING
GAINERS
GRAINES
REAGINS
REGAINS
REGINAS
SEARING
SERINGA

Undecuplets

ANESTRI	EASTING
ANTSIER	EATINGS
NASTIER	GAINEST
RATINES	GENISTA
RESIANT	INGATES
RETAINS	INGESTA
RETINAS	SEATING
RETSINA	TAGINES
STAINER	TANGIES
STARNIE	TEASING
STEARIN	TSIGANE

Chapter 7: Variants

One of the confusing things about the English language is the number of variant spellings that exist. But to a Scrabble player, variant spellings can be a great opportunity. If you know that a word can end in -EY as well as -Y, for example, then you have an extra possibility for playing it, maybe using up a surplus E.

American spellings are one great source of variants – think of all the -RE words that are spelt -ER in the US, for example. But there are also many other variations, which you will find in the lists below. These lists contain most of the common variant spellings in English; the words are listed in alphabetical order. Excluded from this section are the most obvious set of variants – verbs that end in -IZE or -ISE. There are simply far too many of these to include; instead, you will find a list of all the verbs ending in -ISE that **don't** have a variant ending in -IZE where you might expect them to, and vice versa.

-ABLE/-IBLE

ADDABLE – ADDIBLE
EDUCABLE – EDUCIBLE
ERODABLE – ERODIBLE
EVADABLE – EVADIBLE
GULLABLE – GULLIBLE

LAPSABLE – LAPSIBLE
MIXABLE – MIXIBLE
PASSABLE – PASSIBLE
RINSABLE – RINSIBLE
VENDABLE – VENDIBLE

-AE/-E

ACHAENIA – ACHENIA
AEDILE – EDILE
AEDILES – EDILES
AEGIS – EGIS
AEGISES – EGISES
AEMULE – EMULE
AEMULED – EMULED
AEMULES – EMULES
AEMULING – EMULING
AEOLIAN – EOLIAN
AEON – EON
AEONIAN – EONIAN
AEONS – EONS
AERUGO – ERUGO
AERUGOS – ERUGOS
AESTHETE – ESTHETE
AESTIVAL – ESTIVAL
AETHER – ETHER
AETHERIC – ETHERIC
AETHERS – ETHERS
AGAPAE – AGAPE
ALTHAEA – ALTHEA
ALTHAEAS – ALTHEAS
ANAEMIA – ANEMIA
ANAEMIAS – ANEMIAS
ANAEMIC – ANEMIC
ANAPAEST – ANAPEST
APOGAEIC – APOGEIC
ARCHAEAN – ARCHEAN

ARCHAEI – ARCHEI
ARCHAEUS – ARCHEUS
AREOLAE – AREOLE
CAECA – CECA
CAECAL – CECAL
CAECALLY – CECALLY
CAECITIS – CECITIS
CAECUM – CECUM
CAERULE – CERULE
CAESIOUS – CESIOUS
CAESIUM – CESIUM
CAESIUMS – CESIUMS
CAESTUS – CESTUS
CAESURA – CESURA
CAESURAE – CESURAE
CAESURAL – CESURAL
CAESURAS – CESURAS
CESURAE – CESURE
CHIMAERA – CHIMERA
COAEVAL – COEVAL
COAEVALS – COEVALS
DAEDAL – DEDAL
DAEMON – DEMON
DAEMONIC – DEMONIC
DAEMONS – DEMONS
DRACAENA – DRACENA
EPIGAEAL – EPIGEAL
EPIGAEAN – EPIGEAN
EUDAEMON – EUDEMON

FAECAL – FECAL
FAECES – FECES
FRAENA – FRENA
FRAENUM – FRENUM
FRAENUMS – FRENUMS
GASTRAEA – GASTREA
GLUTAEAL – GLUTEAL
GLUTAEI – GLUTEI
GLUTAEUS – GLUTEUS
GRAECISE – GRECISE
GRAECIZE – GRECIZE
GYNAECIA – GYNECIA
HAEMAL – HEMAL
HAEMATAL – HEMATAL
HAEMATIC – HEMATIC
HAEMATIN – HEMATIN
HAEMIC – HEMIC
HAEMIN – HEMIN
HAEMINS – HEMINS
HAEMOID – HEMOID
HAEREDES – HEREDES
HAERES – HERES
HYAENA – HYENA
HYAENAS – HYENAS
HYAENIC – HYENIC
HYPOGAEA – HYPOGEA
LAERED – LERED
LAERING – LERING
LAEVO – LEVO
LAEVULIN – LEVULIN
LERNAEAN – LERNEAN
LIPAEMIA – LIPEMIA
MAENAD – MENAD
MAENADS – MENADS
MURAENA – MURENA
MURAENAS – MURENAS
NAEVE – NEVE
NAEVES – NEVES
NAEVI – NEVI
NAEVOID – NEVOID
NAEVUS – NEVUS
OLPAE – OLPE
PAEON – PEON
PAEONIES – PEONIES
PAEONS – PEONS

PAEONY – PEONY
PERAEA – PEREA
PERAEON – PEREON
PERAEONS – PEREONS
PIGMAEAN – PIGMEAN
PINNULAE – PINNULE
PRAECIPE – PRECIPE
PRAEDIAL – PREDIAL
PRAEFECT – PREFECT
PRAELECT – PRELECT
PRAESES – PRESES
PRAETOR – PRETOR
PRAETORS – PRETORS
PYAEMIA – PYEMIA
PYAEMIAS – PYEMIAS
PYAEMIC – PYEMIC
PYGMAEAN – PYGMEAN
QUAESTOR – QUESTOR
RAPHAE – RAPHE
REAEDIFY – REEDIFY
RHAPHAE – RHAPHE
SAECULUM – SECULUM
SPELAEAN – SPELEAN
SPHAERE – SPHERE
SPHAERES – SPHERES
SPIRAEA – SPIREA
SPIRAEAS – SPIREAS
TAEDIUM – TEDIUM
TAEDIUMS – TEDIUMS
TAENIA – TENIA
TAENIAE – TENIAE
TAENIAS – TENIAS
TAENIOID – TENIOID
TOXAEMIA – TOXEMIA
TOXAEMIC – TOXEMIC
URAEMIA – UREMIA
URAEMIAS – UREMIAS
URAEMIC – UREMIC
VALVULAE – VALVULE
VIRAEMIA – VIREMIA
VIRAEMIC – VIREMIC
ZOAEA – ZOEA
ZOAEAE – ZOEAE
ZOAEAS – ZOEAS

-EI/-IE

BEIN – BIEN
BREI – BRIE
BREIS – BRIES
CEIL – CIEL
CEILED – CIELED
CEILING – CIELING
CEILINGS – CIELINGS
CEILS – CIELS
DEIL – DIEL
DREIGH – DRIEGH
FEINT – FIENT
FEINTS – FIENTS

FEIST – FIEST
GREISLY – GRIESLY
HEID – HIED
KEIR – KIER
KEIRS – KIERS
KEISTER – KIESTER
KEISTERS – KIESTERS
LEIGER – LIEGER
LEIGERS – LIEGERS
LEIR – LIER
LEIRS – LIERS
MEIN – MIEN

-AE/-E

MEINS – MIENS
NEIF – NIEF
NEIFS – NIEFS
NEIVE – NIEVE
NEIVES – NIEVES
OMNEITY – OMNIETY
POLEIS – POLIES
PREIF – PRIEF
PREIFE – PRIEFE
PREIFES – PRIEFES
PREIFS – PRIEFS
REIVE – RIEVE
REIVER – RIEVER
REIVERS – RIEVERS
REIVES – RIEVES
REIVING – RIEVING
SCREICH – SCRIECH
SCREICHS – SCRIECHS
SHEILING – SHIELING

SHREIK – SHRIEK
SHREIKED – SHRIEKED
SHREIKS – SHRIEKS
SKREIGH – SKRIEGH
SKREIGHS – SKRIEGHS
SPEIL – SPIEL
SPEILED – SPIELED
SPEILING – SPIELING
SPEILS – SPIELS
SPEIR – SPIER
SPEIRED – SPIERED
SPEIRING – SPIERING
SPEIRS – SPIERS
VLEIS – VLIES
WEIL – WIEL
WEILS – WIELS
WEINER – WIENER
WEINERS – WIENERS

EN-/IN-

ENACTION – INACTION
ENACTIVE – INACTIVE
ENARCH – INARCH
ENARCHED – INARCHED
ENARCHES – INARCHES
ENARM – INARM
ENARMED – INARMED
ENARMING – INARMING
ENARMS – INARMS
ENCAGE – INCAGE
ENCAGED – INCAGED
ENCAGES – INCAGES
ENCAGING – INCAGING
ENCASE – INCASE
ENCASED – INCASED
ENCASES – INCASES
ENCASING – INCASING
ENCAVE – INCAVE
ENCAVED – INCAVED
ENCAVES – INCAVES
ENCAVING – INCAVING
ENCHASE – INCHASE
ENCHASED – INCHASED
ENCHASES – INCHASES
ENCLASP – INCLASP
ENCLASPS – INCLASPS
ENCLOSE – INCLOSE
ENCLOSED – INCLOSED
ENCLOSER – INCLOSER
ENCLOSES – INCLOSES
ENCREASE – INCREASE
ENCRUST – INCRUST
ENCRUSTS – INCRUSTS
ENCUMBER – INCUMBER
ENDART – INDART
ENDARTED – INDARTED
ENDARTS – INDARTS
ENDEW – INDEW

ENDEWED – INDEWED
ENDEWING – INDEWING
ENDEWS – INDEWS
ENDITE – INDITE
ENDITED – INDITED
ENDITES – INDITES
ENDITING – INDITING
ENDORSE – INDORSE
ENDORSED – INDORSED
ENDORSEE – INDORSEE
ENDORSER – INDORSER
ENDORSES – INDORSES
ENDORSOR – INDORSOR
ENDOW – INDOW
ENDOWED – INDOWED
ENDOWING – INDOWING
ENDOWS – INDOWS
ENDUE – INDUE
ENDUED – INDUED
ENDUES – INDUES
ENDUING – INDUING
ENFANT – INFANT
ENFANTS – INFANTS
ENFEOFF – INFEOFF
ENFEOFFS – INFEOFFS
ENFESTED – INFESTED
ENFIX – INFIX
ENFIXED – INFIXED
ENFIXES – INFIXES
ENFIXING – INFIXING
ENFLAME – INFLAME
ENFLAMED – INFLAMED
ENFLAMES – INFLAMES
ENFOLD – INFOLD
ENFOLDED – INFOLDED
ENFOLDER – INFOLDER
ENFOLDS – INFOLDS
ENFORCE – INFORCE

ENFORCED – INFORCED
ENFORCES – INFORCES
ENFORM – INFORM
ENFORMED – INFORMED
ENFORMS – INFORMS
ENGINE – INGINE
ENGINES – INGINES
ENGLOBE – INGLOBE
ENGLOBED – INGLOBED
ENGLOBES – INGLOBES
ENGRAFT – INGRAFT
ENGRAFTS – INGRAFTS
ENGRAIN – INGRAIN
ENGRAINS – INGRAINS
ENGRAM – INGRAM
ENGROOVE – INGROOVE
ENGROSS – INGROSS
ENGULF – INGULF
ENGULFED – INGULFED
ENGULFS – INGULFS
ENGULPH – INGULPH
ENGULPHS – INGULPHS
ENHEARSE – INHEARSE
ENISLE – INISLE
ENISLED – INISLED
ENISLES – INISLES
ENISLING – INISLING
ENLACE – INLACE
ENLACED – INLACED
ENLACES – INLACES
ENLACING – INLACING
ENLOCK – INLOCK
ENLOCKED – INLOCKED
ENLOCKS – INLOCKS
ENMESH – INMESH
ENMESHED – INMESHED
ENMESHES – INMESHES
ENNAGE – INNAGE
ENNAGES – INNAGES
ENQUIRE – INQUIRE
ENQUIRED – INQUIRED
ENQUIRER – INQUIRER
ENQUIRES – INQUIRES
ENQUIRY – INQUIRY
ENSCONCE – INSCONCE
ENSCROLL – INSCROLL
ENSEAM – INSEAM
ENSEAMED – INSEAMED
ENSEAMS – INSEAMS
ENSHEATH – INSHEATH
ENSHELL – INSHELL
ENSHELLS – INSHELLS
ENSHRINE – INSHRINE
ENSNARE – INSNARE
ENSNARED – INSNARED
ENSNARER – INSNARER

ENSNARES – INSNARES
ENSOUL – INSOUL
ENSOULED – INSOULED
ENSOULS – INSOULS
ENSPHERE – INSPHERE
ENSURE – INSURE
ENSURED – INSURED
ENSURER – INSURER
ENSURERS – INSURERS
ENSURES – INSURES
ENSURING – INSURING
ENSWATHE – INSWATHE
ENSWEPT – INSWEPT
ENTENDER – INTENDER
ENTERS – INTERS
ENTHRAL – INTHRAL
ENTHRALL – INTHRALL
ENTHRALS – INTHRALS
ENTHRONE – INTHRONE
ENTIRE – INTIRE
ENTITLE – INTITLE
ENTITLED – INTITLED
ENTITLES – INTITLES
ENTOMB – INTOMB
ENTOMBED – INTOMBED
ENTOMBS – INTOMBS
ENTRANT – INTRANT
ENTRANTS – INTRANTS
ENTREAT – INTREAT
ENTREATS – INTREATS
ENTRENCH – INTRENCH
ENTROLD – INTROLD
ENTRUST – INTRUST
ENTRUSTS – INTRUSTS
ENTWINE – INTWINE
ENTWINED – INTWINED
ENTWINES – INTWINES
ENTWIST – INTWIST
ENTWISTS – INTWISTS
ENURE – INURE
ENURED – INURED
ENURES – INURES
ENURING – INURING
ENVEIGLE – INVEIGLE
ENVIABLE – INVIABLE
ENVIABLY – INVIABLY
ENVIOUS – INVIOUS
ENWALL – INWALL
ENWALLED – INWALLED
ENWALLS – INWALLS
ENWIND – INWIND
ENWINDS – INWINDS
ENWOUND – INWOUND
ENWRAP – INWRAP
ENWRAPS – INWRAPS

-ER/-OR

ABATER – ABATOR	IMPOSTER – IMPOSTOR
ABETTER – ABETTOR	INCENSER – INCENSOR
ACCEPTER – ACCEPTOR	INDENTER – INDENTOR
ADAPTER – ADAPTOR	INDICTER – INDICTOR
ADJURER – ADJUROR	INDORSER – INDORSOR
ADJUSTER – ADJUSTOR	INFECTER – INFECTOR
ADVISER – ADVISOR	INFLATER – INFLATOR
AGISTER – AGISTOR	INVENTER – INVENTOR
ALIENER – ALIENOR	INVERTER – INVERTOR
ANIMATER – ANIMATOR	JAILER – JAILOR
ARMER – ARMOR	KRONER – KRONOR
ARRESTER – ARRESTOR	LESSER – LESSOR
ASPERSER – ASPERSOR	LICENSER – LICENSOR
ASSENTER – ASSENTOR	LOCATER – LOCATOR
ASSERTER – ASSERTOR	NARRATER – NARRATOR
ASSIGNER – ASSIGNOR	NEGATER – NEGATOR
ASSISTER – ASSISTOR	NESTER – NESTOR
ASSURER – ASSUROR	OBLIGER – OBLIGOR
ATTESTER – ATTESTOR	OFFERER – OFFEROR
BAILER – BAILOR	OUTDOER – OUTDOOR
BARRATER – BARRATOR	PARADER – PARADOR
BETTER – BETTOR	PAWNER – PAWNOR
BEVER – BEVOR	PAYER – PAYOR
BITTER – BITTOR	PLEDGER – PLEDGEOR – PLEDGOR
CANTER – CANTOR	PRESSER – PRESSOR
CASTER – CASTOR	PROMISER – PROMISOR
CENSER – CENSOR	PROMOTER – PROMOTOR
CHANTER – CHANTOR	PROVIDER – PROVIDOR
CLANGER – CLANGOR	QUESTER – QUESTOR
CONDER – CONDOR	QUITTER – QUITTOR
CONJURER – CONJUROR	RAZER – RAZOR
CONVENER – CONVENOR	REALTER – REALTOR
CONVEYER – CONVEYOR	REGRATER – REGRATOR
CURSER – CURSOR	REJECTER – REJECTOR
DEFLATER – DEFLATOR	RELATER – RELATOR
DEPICTER – DEPICTOR	RELEASER – RELEASOR
DETECTER – DETECTOR	REMITTER – REMITTOR
DEVISER – DEVISOR	RESISTER – RESISTOR
DIFFUSER – DIFFUSOR	RETAILER – RETAILOR
DIGESTER – DIGESTOR	REVISER – REVISOR
DILATER – DILATOR	REVIVER – REVIVOR
DILUTER – DILUTOR	RIZZER – RIZZOR
DIRECTER – DIRECTOR	SAILER – SAILOR
EFFECTER – EFFECTOR	SALVER – SALVOR
ENDORSER – ENDORSOR	SECRETER – SECRETOR
ERECTER – ERECTOR	SEISER – SEISOR
EXACTER – EXACTOR	SEIZER – SEIZOR
EXCITER – EXCITOR	SETTLER – SETTLOR
EXECUTER – EXECUTOR	STATER – STATOR
EXPANDER – EXPANDOR	STRIDER – STRIDOR
FEOFFER – FEOFFOR	SUITER – SUITOR
GIMMER – GIMMOR	SURVIVER – SURVIVOR
GRANTER – GRANTOR	TABER – TABOR
HUMIDER – HUMIDOR	TAILER – TAILOR
IDOLATER – IDOLATOR	TAXER – TAXOR
IGNITER – IGNITOR	TENSER – TENSOR
IMPACTER – IMPACTOR	TERMER – TERMOR
IMPEDER – IMPEDOR	THRUSTER – THRUSTOR
IMPELLER – IMPELLOR	TRIER – TRIOR

TRUSTER – TRUSTOR	VERDERER – VERDEROR
TUSSER – TUSSOR	VIOLATER – VIOLATOR
TWISTER – TWISTOR	VISITER – VISITOR
VENDER – VENDOR	WELDER – WELDOR

-EY/-IE/-Y

AERIE – AERY	CABBAGY – CABBAGEY
AGLY – AGLEY	CABBIE – CABBY
ALKIE – ALKY	CADDIE – CADDY
ALLY – ALLEY	CAGY – CAGEY
ANOMIE – ANOMY	CAKY – CAKEY
APPLY – APPLEY	CALORIE – CALORY
ARSY – ARSEY	CANDIE – CANDY
AUNTIE – AUNTY	CANNIE – CANNY
AWMRIE – AWMRY	CARDIE – CARDY
BADDIE – BADDY	CARNEY – CARNIE – CARNY
BAGGIE – BAGGY	CATTIE – CATTY
BAILEY – BAILIE	CAVIE – CAVY
BARBIE – BARBY	CHALLIE – CHALLY
BARDIE – BARDY	CHANCY – CHANCEY
BARMIE – BARMY	CHANTEY – CHANTIE – CHANTY
BARNY – BARNEY	CHAPPIE – CHAPPY
BARRIE – BARRY	CHARLEY – CHARLIE
BATTERIE – BATTERY	CHEAPIE – CHEAPY
BAWTIE – BAWTY	CHEWIE – CHEWY
BEANIE – BEANY	CHIMBLY – CHIMBLEY
BEARDIE – BEARDY	CHINKIE – CHINKY
BHEESTIE – BHEESTY	CHIPPIE – CHIPPY
BIGGIE – BIGGY	CHOKY – CHOKEY
BILLIE – BILLY	CHOOSY – CHOOSEY
BITTIE – BITTY	CHRISTIE – CHRISTY
BLASTIE – BLASTY	CHUCKIE – CHUCKY
BLIMY – BLIMEY	CIGGIE – CIGGY
BLOCKIE – BLOCKY	CLIQUY – CLIQUEY
BLOOEY – BLOOIE	COLLIE – COLLY
BLOWIE – BLOWY	COLY – COLEY
BLUDIE – BLUDY	COMMIE – COMMY
BOGEY – BOGIE – BOGY	CONCHIE – CONCHY
BOLSHIE – BOLSHY	CONY – CONEY
BONEY – BONIE – BONY	COOKEY – COOKIE – COOKY
BONNIE – BONNY	COOLIE – COOLY
BOOBIE – BOOBY	COONTIE – COONTY
BOODIE – BOODY	CORBIE – CORBY
BOOGEY – BOOGIE – BOOGY	CORY – COREY
BOOKIE – BOOKY	COSEY – COSIE – COSY
BOOKSIE – BOOKSY	COUTHIE – COUTHY
BOOTIE – BOOTY	COWRIE – COWRY
BOOZY – BOOZEY	COZEY – COZIE – COZY
BOTHIE – BOTHY	CRAPPIE – CRAPPY
BOWSEY – BOWSIE	CREEPIE – CREEPY
BRASSIE – BRASSY	CREPY – CREPEY
BRAWLIE – BRAWLY	CRICKY – CRICKEY
BRICKIE – BRICKY	CROPPIE – CROPPY
BROWNIE – BROWNY	CROWDIE – CROWDY
BUNGEY – BUNGIE – BUNGY	CRUMMIE – CRUMMY
BUNJIE – BUNJY	CRUNCHIE – CRUNCHY
BUPPIE – BUPPY	CRUSIE – CRUSY
BURLY – BURLEY	CUDDIE – CUDDY
BUSHIE – BUSHY	CURNY – CURNEY

-ER/-OR

CURRIE – CURRY
CURTSY – CURTSEY
CURVY – CURVEY
CUSHIE – CUSHY
CUTESIE – CUTESY
CUTEY – CUTIE
DARKEY – DARKIE – DARKY
DEARIE – DEARY
DEAWIE – DEAWY
DEXIE – DEXY
DICKEY – DICKIE – DICKY
DIDDLY – DIDDLEY
DIDIE – DIDY
DINGY – DINGEY
DINKEY – DINKIE – DINKY
DIXIE – DIXY
DOBBIE – DOBBY
DOBIE – DOBY
DOGEY – DOGIE – DOGY
DOGGIE – DOGGY
DONSIE – DONSY
DOOLIE – DOOLY
DOOZIE – DOOZY
DOPY – DOPEY
DORMIE – DORMY
DOVEKEY – DOVEKIE
DOXIE – DOXY
DOYLY – DOYLEY
DRAPPIE – DRAPPY
DRUGGIE – DRUGGY
DUCKIE – DUCKY
DUDDIE – DUDDY
DURRIE – DURRY
EATERIE – EATERY
EERIE – EERY
EYRIE – EYRY
FAERIE – FAERY
FANTASIE – FANTASY
FARCIE – FARCY
FERLIE – FERLY
FIDDLY – FIDDLEY
FLAKY – FLAKEY
FLATTIE – FLATTY
FLEECIE – FLEECY
FLOOEY – FLOOIE
FLOOSIE – FLOOSY
FLOOZIE – FLOOZY
FLOSSIE – FLOSSY
FLUKY – FLUKEY
FLUNKEY – FLUNKIE – FLUNKY
FLUTY – FLUTEY
FOGEY – FOGIE – FOGY
FOLEY – FOLIE
FOLKIE – FOLKY
FOODIE – FOODY
FOOTIE – FOOTY
FOOTSIE – FOOTSY
FOXIE – FOXY
FROWIE – FROWY
FUNDIE – FUNDY

GALLY – GALLEY
GAMY – GAMEY
GARBAGY – GARBAGEY
GARVEY – GARVIE
GAUCIE – GAUCY
GAWSIE – GAWSY
GILLIE – GILLY
GILPY – GILPEY
GINGELY – GINGELEY
GIRLIE – GIRLY
GLASSIE – GLASSY
GOODIE – GOODY
GOOLEY – GOOLIE – GOOLY
GOONEY – GOONIE – GOONY
GOORIE – GOORY
GOOSY – GOOSEY
GRANNIE – GRANNY
GRAPY – GRAPEY
GREENIE – GREENY
GREMMIE – GREMMY
GRIESIE – GRIESY
GRIPY – GRIPEY
GROUPIE – GROUPY
GRUMPHIE – GRUMPHY
GULLY – GULLEY
GUSSIE – GUSSY
GUSTIE – GUSTY
GYNIE – GYNY
GYNNY – GYNNEY
GYPPIE – GYPPY
HANKIE – HANKY
HAWKEY – HAWKIE
HEMPIE – HEMPY
HICKEY – HICKIE
HIPPIE – HIPPY
HOAGIE – HOAGY
HOLY – HOLEY
HOMEY – HOMIE – HOMY
HONKEY – HONKIE – HONKY
HOODIE – HOODY
HOOKY – HOOKEY
HOOLEY – HOOLIE – HOOLY
HORSY – HORSEY
HOTTIE – HOTTY
HOWDIE – HOWDY
HUNKEY – HUNKIE – HUNKY
HURLY – HURLEY
INCONIE – INCONY
JACKSIE – JACKSY
JARVEY – JARVIE
JASY – JASEY
JAUNTIE – JAUNTY
JAXIE – JAXY
JEELIE – JEELY
JIMMIE – JIMMY
JIVY – JIVEY
JOHNNIE – JOHNNY
JOKY – JOKEY
JOLLY – JOLLEY
JUMBIE – JUMBY

JUNKIE – JUNKY
KARSY – KARSEY
KELPIE – KELPY
KELTIE – KELTY
KIDDIE – KIDDY
KILTIE – KILTY
KINDIE – KINDY
KLUDGY – KLUDGEY
KOOKIE – KOOKY
LACY – LACEY
LALDIE – LALDY
LAMBIE – LAMBY
LAMMIE – LAMMY
LEFTIE – LEFTY
LEZZIE – LEZZY
LIMPSY – LIMPSEY
LIMY – LIMEY
LINNY – LINNEY
LINTIE – LINTY
LINY – LINEY
LIPPIE – LIPPY
LOGGIE – LOGGY
LOGIE – LOGY
LOOEY – LOOIE
LOONEY – LOONIE – LOONY
LOURIE – LOURY
LOWRIE – LOWRY
LUCKIE – LUCKY
LUVVIE – LUVVY
MALARKY – MALARKEY
MAMEY – MAMIE
MAMMEY – MAMMIE – MAMMY
MANGABY – MANGABEY
MANGY – MANGEY
MASHIE – MASHY
MATY – MATEY
MAZY – MAZEY
MEALIE – MEALY
MEANIE – MEANY
MEINEY – MEINIE – MEINY
MICKY – MICKEY
MIDDIE – MIDDY
MIDGIE – MIDGY
MIMSY – MIMSEY
MINNIE – MINNY
MOBBIE – MOBBY
MOBIE – MOBY
MOCHIE – MOCHY
MOGGIE – MOGGY
MOLLIE – MOLLY
MONEY – MONIE – MONY
MOOLY – MOOLEY
MOPY – MOPEY
MOSSIE – MOSSY
MOUSEY – MOUSIE – MOUSY
MURRY – MURREY
MUSKIE – MUSKY
NANNIE – NANNY
NAPPIE – NAPPY
NELLIE – NELLY

NETTIE – NETTY
NEWSIE – NEWSY
NIGHTIE – NIGHTY
NIRLIE – NIRLY
NITERIE – NITERY
NIXIE – NIXY
NOOKIE – NOOKY
NOSHERIE – NOSHERY
NOSY – NOSEY
OBSEQUIE – OBSEQUY
OCHRY – OCHREY
OLDIE – OLDY
ONIE – ONY
ORANGY – ORANGEY
ORGANDIE – ORGANDY
OVERLIE – OVERLY
PACY – PACEY
PALMIE – PALMY
PANTIE – PANTY
PARDIE – PARDY
PARKIE – PARKY
PARLY – PARLEY
PASTIE – PASTY
PATTIE – PATTY
PEAVY – PEAVEY
PEERIE – PEERY
PERDIE – PERDY
PERENTIE – PERENTY
PHONY – PHONEY
PIGGIE – PIGGY
PIGSNEY – PIGSNIE – PIGSNY
PINKEY – PINKIE – PINKY
PINNIE – PINNY
PINY – PINEY
PIONY – PIONEY
PIXIE – PIXY
PLAGUY – PLAGUEY
PLISKIE – PLISKY
PLOOKIE – PLOOKY
PLOTTIE – PLOTTY
PLOUKIE – PLOUKY
PLUMPIE – PLUMPY
PODDIE – PODDY
POGY – POGEY
POKEY – POKIE – POKY
POLLICIE – POLLICY
POLONIE – POLONY
POLY – POLEY
POMMIE – POMMY
PONCY – PONCEY
PONTIE – PONTY
PONY – PONEY
POPSIE – POPSY
PORGIE – PORGY
POSY – POSEY
POTSIE – POTSY
POWNEY – POWNIE – POWNY
PRATIE – PRATY
PREMIE – PREMY
PREPPIE – PREPPY

PRICY – PRICEY
PUDSY – PUDSEY
PUGGIE – PUGGY
PUMIE – PUMY
PUNKEY – PUNKIE – PUNKY
PURPIE – PURPY
PUSSLY – PUSSLEY
PUTTIE – PUTTY
QUEENIE – QUEENY
RANDIE – RANDY
REALLIE – REALLY
REALTIE – REALTY
REECHIE – REECHY
REEKIE – REEKY
RELIE – RELY
RENY – RENEY
REVERIE – REVERY
RHODIE – RHODY
RICY – RICEY
ROARIE – ROARY
ROOFIE – ROOFY
ROOKIE – ROOKY
ROOMIE – ROOMY
ROPY – ROPEY
RORIE – RORY
ROUGHIE – ROUGHY
SALTIE – SALTY
SARNEY – SARNIE
SAVVY – SAVVEY
SCARY – SCAREY
SCROGGIE – SCROGGY
SCRUMMIE – SCRUMMY
SEELIE – SEELY
SHALY – SHALEY
SHANTY – SHANTEY
SHARPIE – SHARPY
SHAWLEY – SHAWLIE
SHEENEY – SHEENIE – SHEENY
SHELTIE – SHELTY
SHIMMY – SHIMMEY
SHINNY – SHINNEY
SHORTIE – SHORTY
SILKIE – SILKY
SKELLIE – SKELLY
SKIVIE – SKIVY
SKOLLIE – SKOLLY
SLATY – SLATEY
SMARTIE – SMARTY
SMOKY – SMOKEY
SMOOTHIE – SMOOTHY
SNAKY – SNAKEY
SNOTTIE – SNOTTY
SOAPIE – SOAPY
SOFTIE – SOFTY
SONSIE – SONSY
SPACY – SPACEY
SPAMMIE – SPAMMY
SPARKIE – SPARKY
SPICY – SPICEY
SPIE – SPY

SPIKY – SPIKEY
SPINNY – SPINNEY
SPOONY – SPOONEY
SPOTTIE – SPOTTY
SPUNKIE – SPUNKY
SPURRY – SPURREY
SQUADDIE – SQUADDY
STAGGIE – STAGGY
STAGY – STAGEY
STEAMIE – STEAMY
STEELIE – STEELY
STEY – STIE – STY
STIE – STY – STEY
STIFFIE – STIFFY
STIMIE – STIMY
STOGEY – STOGIE – STOGY
STONY – STONEY
STORY – STOREY
STOURIE – STOURY
STRIPY – STRIPEY
STUBBIE – STUBBY
STY – STEY – STIE
STYMIE – STYMY
SUBBIE – SUBBY
SURFIE – SURFY
SWABBIE – SWABBY
SWADDIE – SWADDY
SWANKEY – SWANKIE – SWANKY
SWANNIE – SWANNY
SWEENY – SWEENEY
SWEETIE – SWEETY
SWIFTIE – SWIFTY
TACKY – TACKEY
TALKIE – TALKY
TAMMIE – TAMMY
TANGIE – TANGY
TATTIE – TATTY
TAWNY – TAWNEY
TECHIE – TECHY
TEDDIE – TEDDY
TENTIE – TENTY
THICKIE – THICKY
THY – THEY
THYMY – THYMEY
TICKY – TICKEY
TIDDLY – TIDDLEY
TINNIE – TINNY
TITTIE – TITTY
TOASTIE – TOASTY
TOLLIE – TOLLY
TONY – TONEY
TOOTSIE – TOOTSY
TOTTIE – TOTTY
TOUGHIE – TOUGHY
TOWIE – TOWY
TOWNIE – TOWNY
TRANNIE – TRANNY
TREY – TRIE – TRY
TRICKIE – TRICKY
TRIPY – TRIPEY

TROELIE – TROELY
TROLLY – TROLLEY
TUSHIE – TUSHY
TWEENIE – TWEENY
TYPY – TYPEY
UMPIE – UMPY
UNSONSIE – UNSONSY
UNWARIE – UNWARY
UPSY – UPSEY
VAUNTIE – VAUNTY
VERRY – VERREY
VISNOMIE – VISNOMY
WADDIE – WADDY
WALLIE – WALLY
WANY – WANEY
WASPIE – WASPY
WASTERIE – WASTERY
WASTRIE – WASTRY
WAVY – WAVEY
WEBBIE – WEBBY
WEDGIE – WEDGY

WEENIE – WEENY
WEEPIE – WEEPY
WEIRDIE – WEIRDY
WELLIE – WELLY
WHEELIE – WHEELY
WHIMSY – WHIMSEY
WHINY – WHINEY
WHISKY – WHISKEY
WHITY – WHITEY
WIDDIE – WIDDY
WIFEY – WIFIE
WILLEY – WILLIE – WILLY
WINY – WINEY
WOODIE – WOODY
WOOLIE – WOOLY
WURLEY – WURLIE
YABBIE – YABBY
YAPPIE – YAPPY
YAWY – YAWEY
YIPPIE – YIPPY
YUPPIE – YUPPY

-LL/-L

ALLAY – ALAY
ALLAYED – ALAYED
ALLAYING – ALAYING
ALLAYS – ALAYS
ALLEE – ALEE
ALLEGGE – ALEGGE
ALLEGGED – ALEGGED
ALLEGGES – ALEGGES
ALLERION – ALERION
ALLEYED – ALEYED
ALLOD – ALOD
ALLODIA – ALODIA
ALLODIAL – ALODIAL
ALLODIUM – ALODIUM
ALLODS – ALODS
ALLOW – ALOW
ALLURE – ALURE
ALLURES – ALURES
ANVILLED – ANVILED
APPALL – APPAL
APPALLS – APPALS
APPERILL – APPERIL
BAILLIE – BAILIE
BAILLIES – BAILIES
BALLADIN – BALADIN
BALLISTA – BALISTA
BARBELL – BARBEL
BARBELLS – BARBELS
BASTILLE – BASTILE
BEDELL – BEDEL
BEDELLS – BEDELS
BELLYING – BELYING
BEVELLED – BEVELED
BEVELLER – BEVELER
BOLLIX – BOLIX
BOLLIXED – BOLIXED

BOLLIXES – BOLIXES
BONSELLA – BONSELA
BORRELL – BORREL
BORSTALL – BORSTAL
BOULLE – BOULE
BOULLES – BOULES
BOWELLED – BOWELED
BRAILLED – BRAILED
BRIMFULL – BRIMFUL
BULLBAR – BULBAR
BULLGINE – BULGINE
BULLRUSH – BULRUSH
BURRELL – BURREL
BURRELLS – BURRELS
CALLALOO – CALALOO
CALLID – CALID
CALLIPEE – CALIPEE
CALLIPER – CALIPER
CAMELLIA – CAMELIA
CANALLED – CANALED
CAPELLET – CAPELET
CAROLLED – CAROLED
CAROLLER – CAROLER
CARRELL – CARREL
CARRELLS – CARRELS
CAVILLED – CAVILED
CAVILLER – CAVILER
CHALLAH – CHALAH
CHALLAHS – CHALAHS
CHALLAN – CHALAN
CHALLANS – CHALANS
CHALLOT – CHALOT
CHALLOTH – CHALOTH
CHILLI – CHILI
CHILLIES – CHILIES
CHILLIS – CHILIS

-EY/-IE/-Y

CHOLLA – CHOLA
CHOLLAS – CHOLAS
CHOLLERS – CHOLERS
COLL – COL
COLLED – COLED
COLLIES – COLIES
COLLINS – COLINS
COLLS – COLS
COLLY – COLY
COOLLY – COOLY
CROPFULL – CROPFUL
CRUELLER – CRUELER
CRUELLS – CRUELS
CULLET – CULET
CULLETS – CULETS
CUPELLED – CUPELED
CUPELLER – CUPELER
DECALLED – DECALED
DEVELLED – DEVELED
DEVILLED – DEVILED
DHOLL – DHOL
DHOLLS – DHOLS
DIALLED – DIALED
DIALLER – DIALER
DIALLERS – DIALERS
DIALLING – DIALING
DIALLIST – DIALIST
DISTILL – DISTIL
DISTILLS – DISTILS
DOWELLED – DOWELED
DROLLER – DROLER
DROLLEST – DROLEST
DUELLED – DUELED
DUELLER – DUELER
DUELLERS – DUELERS
DUELLING – DUELING
DUELLIST – DUELIST
DULLNESS – DULNESS
DULLY – DULY
EISELL – EISEL
EISELLS – EISELS
ELLOPS – ELOPS
ELLOPSES – ELOPSES
EMBALLED – EMBALED
ENROLL – ENROL
ENROLLS – ENROLS
ENTHRALL – ENTHRAL
EQUALLED – EQUALED
ESCALLOP – ESCALOP
ESCROLL – ESCROL
ESCROLLS – ESCROLS
EVILLER – EVILER
EVILLEST – EVILEST
EXTOLL – EXTOL
EXTOLLS – EXTOLS
FANNELL – FANNEL
FANNELLS – FANNELS
FAVELL – FAVEL
FAVELLA – FAVELA
FAVELLAS – FAVELAS

FILLE – FILE
FILLES – FILES
FILLET – FILET
FILLETED – FILETED
FILLETS – FILETS
FILLIBEG – FILIBEG
FILLING – FILING
FILLINGS – FILINGS
FILLO – FILO
FILLOS – FILOS
FUELLED – FUELED
FUELLER – FUELER
FUELLERS – FUELERS
FUELLING – FUELING
FULFILL – FULFIL
FULFILLS – FULFILS
FULLNESS – FULNESS
GALLABEA – GALABEA
GALLABIA – GALABIA
GALLANT – GALANT
GALLIOT – GALIOT
GALLIOTS – GALIOTS
GALLIPOT – GALIPOT
GALLOOT – GALOOT
GALLOOTS – GALOOTS
GALLOP – GALOP
GALLOPED – GALOPED
GALLOPS – GALOPS
GALLUMPH – GALUMPH
GAVELLED – GAVELED
GELLANT – GELANT
GELLANTS – GELANTS
GILLET – GILET
GILLETS – GILETS
GINGALL – GINGAL
GINGALLS – GINGALS
GINGELLI – GINGELI
GINGELLY – GINGELY
GINGILLI – GINGILI
GRAVELLY – GRAVELY
GRUELLED – GRUELED
GRUELLER – GRUELER
HALLAL – HALAL
HALLALS – HALALS
HALLING – HALING
HALLOUMI – HALOUMI
HOVELLED – HOVELED
IDYLL – IDYL
IDYLLIST – IDYLIST
IDYLLS – IDYLS
ILLIAD – ILIAD
ILLIADS – ILIADS
INSTALL – INSTAL
INSTALLS – INSTALS
INSTILL – INSTIL
INSTILLS – INSTILS
INTHRALL – INTHRAL
JEWELLED – JEWELED
JEWELLER – JEWELER
JINGALL – JINGAL

JINGALLS – JINGALS
JOLL – JOL
JOLLED – JOLED
JOLLING – JOLING
JOLLS – JOLS
LABELLED – LABELED
LABELLER – LABELER
LAPELLED – LAPELED
LEVELLED – LEVELED
LEVELLER – LEVELER
LIBELLED – LIBELED
LIBELLEE – LIBELEE
LIBELLER – LIBELER
LOYALLER – LOYALER
MALLAM – MALAM
MALLAMS – MALAMS
MALLEATE – MALEATE
MANDRILL – MANDRIL
MANILLA – MANILA
MANILLAS – MANILAS
MARSHALL – MARSHAL
MEDALLED – MEDALED
MELL – MEL
MELLS – MELS
MERELL – MEREL
MERELLS – MERELS
METALLED – METALED
MILLIARY – MILIARY
MODELLED – MODELED
MODELLER – MODELER
MOLLA – MOLA
MOLLAS – MOLAS
MORALL – MORAL
MORALLS – MORALS
MUCHELL – MUCHEL
MUCHELLS – MUCHELS
MULLED – MULED
MULLEY – MULEY
MULLEYS – MULEYS
MULLING – MULING
MULMULL – MULMUL
MULMULLS – MULMULS
MURALLED – MURALED
MYALL – MYAL
NALLA – NALA
NALLAS – NALAS
NELLIES – NELIES
NEWELL – NEWEL
NEWELLS – NEWELS
NILL – NIL
NILLS – NILS
PALLET – PALET
PALLETS – PALETS
PALLETTE – PALETTE
PANELLED – PANELED
PEDALLED – PEDALED
PEDALLER – PEDALER
PERILLED – PERILED
PETALLED – PETALED
PILLAR – PILAR

PILLAU – PILAU
PILLAUS – PILAUS
PLIMSOLL – PLIMSOL
POLLICES – POLICES
POLLICY – POLICY
POLLIES – POLIES
POLLING – POLING
POLLINGS – POLINGS
PROLLED – PROLED
PROLLER – PROLER
PROLLERS – PROLERS
PROLLING – PROLING
PULLI – PULI
PULLUS – PULUS
PUPILLAR – PUPILAR
QUINELLA – QUINELA
RAMILLIE – RAMILIE
RAVELLED – RAVELED
RAVELLER – RAVELER
RECALL – RECAL
RECALLS – RECALS
REFELL – REFEL
REFILLED – REFILED
RELLIES – RELIES
RELLISH – RELISH
REPOSALL – REPOSAL
REVELLED – REVELED
REVELLER – REVELER
RIGOLL – RIGOL
RIGOLLS – RIGOLS
RIVALLED – RIVALED
ROWELLED – ROWELED
SALL – SAL
SALLAD – SALAD
SALLADS – SALADS
SALLAL – SALAL
SALLALS – SALALS
SALLET – SALET
SALLETS – SALETS
SCULL – SCUL
SCULLS – SCULS
SELLE – SELE
SELLES – SELES
SEPALLED – SEPALED
SHALLOT – SHALOT
SHALLOTS – SHALOTS
SIBYLLIC – SIBYLIC
SILLER – SILER
SILLERS – SILERS
SKELLUM – SKELUM
SKELLUMS – SKELUMS
SKILLFUL – SKILFUL
SOLLAR – SOLAR
SOLLARS – SOLARS
SOLLER – SOLER
SOLLERET – SOLERET
SOLLERS – SOLERS
SORELL – SOREL
SORELLS – SORELS
SPALLE – SPALE

SPALLES – SPALES
SPILLED – SPILED
SPILLING – SPILING
STELLA – STELA
STELLAR – STELAR
SWILLER – SWILER
SWILLERS – SWILERS
TALLENT – TALENT
TALLENTS – TALENTS
TASSELL – TASSEL
TASSELLS – TASSELS
TEQUILLA – TEQUILA
TESTRILL – TESTRIL
THALLI – THALI
TOPFULL – TOPFUL
TOTALLED – TOTALED
TOWELLED – TOWELED
TRAMELL – TRAMEL
TRAMELLS – TRAMELS
TULLE – TULE
TULLES – TULES
TWIBILL – TWIBIL
TWIBILLS – TWIBILS
UMBELLED – UMBELED
VALLONIA – VALONIA
VELLUM – VELUM

VIALLED – VIALED
VIALLING – VIALING
VILLIAGO – VILIAGO
WADMOLL – WADMOL
WADMOLLS – WADMOLS
WALLIER – WALIER
WALLIES – WALIES
WALLIEST – WALIEST
WALLING – WALING
WALLY – WALY
WEASELLY – WEASELY
WEEVILLY – WEEVILY
WELLAWAY – WELAWAY
WILLFUL – WILFUL
WOOLLED – WOOLED
WOOLLEN – WOOLEN
WOOLLENS – WOOLENS
WOOLLIER – WOOLIER
WOOLLIES – WOOLIES
WOOLLY – WOOLY
WOOSELL – WOOSEL
WOOSELLS – WOOSELS
YODELLED – YODELED
YODELLER – YODELER
ZILLA – ZILA
ZILLAS – ZILAS

-OE/-E

AMOEBA – AMEBA
AMOEBAE – AMEBAE
AMOEBAN – AMEBAN
AMOEBAS – AMEBAS
AMOEBEAN – AMEBEAN
AMOEBIC – AMEBIC
AMOEBOID – AMEBOID
ANOESTRA – ANESTRA
ANOESTRI – ANESTRI
ANOETIC – ANETIC
APNOEA – APNEA
APNOEAL – APNEAL
APNOEAS – APNEAS
APNOEIC – APNEIC
CHOENIX – CHENIX
COELIAC – CELIAC
COELIACS – CELIACS
COELOM – CELOM
COELOMIC – CELOMIC
COELOMS – CELOMS
COENACLE – CENACLE
DYSPNOEA – DYSPNEA
EUPNOEA – EUPNEA
EUPNOEAS – EUPNEAS
EUPNOEIC – EUPNEIC
FOEDARIE – FEDARIE
FOETAL – FETAL
FOETID – FETID
FOETIDER – FETIDER

FOETIDLY – FETIDLY
FOETOR – FETOR
FOETORS – FETORS
FOETUS – FETUS
FOETUSES – FETUSES
GYNOECIA – GYNECIA
OECOLOGY – ECOLOGY
OEDEMA – EDEMA
OEDEMAS – EDEMAS
OEDEMATA – EDEMATA
OENOLOGY – ENOLOGY
OESTRAL – ESTRAL
OESTRIN – ESTRIN
OESTRINS – ESTRINS
OESTRIOL – ESTRIOL
OESTRONE – ESTRONE
OESTROUS – ESTROUS
OESTRUM – ESTRUM
OESTRUMS – ESTRUMS
OESTRUS – ESTRUS
PHOENIX – PHENIX
SUBPOENA – SUBPENA
ZOOEA – ZOEA
ZOOEAE – ZOEAE
ZOOEAL – ZOEAL
ZOOEAS – ZOEAS
ZOOECIA – ZOECIA
ZOOECIUM – ZOECIUM
ZOOGLOEA – ZOOGLEA

-OUR/-OR

ARBOUR – ARBOR
ARDOUR – ARDOR
ARMOUR – ARMOR
BELABOUR – BELABOR
BICOLOUR – BICOLOR
BITTOUR – BITTOR
CANDOUR – CANDOR
CLAMOUR – CLAMOR
CLANGOUR – CLANGOR
COLOUR – COLOR
DECOLOUR – DECOLOR
DOLOUR – DOLOR
ENAMOUR – ENAMOR
FAITOUR – FAITOR
FAVOUR – FAVOR
FERVOUR – FERVOR
FLAVOUR – FLAVOR
FULGOUR – FULGOR
GLAMOUR – GLAMOR
HARBOUR – HARBOR
HAVIOUR – HAVIOR
HONOUR – HONOR

HUMOUR – HUMOR
LABOUR – LABOR
MAINOUR – MAINOR
MALODOUR – MALODOR
ODOUR – ODOR
PARLOUR – PARLOR
PAVIOUR – PAVIOR
RANCOUR – RANCOR
RIGOUR – RIGOR
RUMOUR – RUMOR
SAPOUR – SAPOR
SAVIOUR – SAVIOR
SAVOUR – SAVOR
STENTOUR – STENTOR
SUCCOUR – SUCCOR
TABOUR – TABOR
TENOUR – TENOR
TUMOUR – TUMOR
VALOUR – VALOR
VAPOUR – VAPOR
VAVASOUR – VAVASOR
VIGOUR – VIGOR

-RE/-ER

BAYADERE – BAYADEER
BISTRE – BISTER
BRERE – BREER
CABRE – CABER
CADASTRE – CADASTER
CALIBRE – CALIBER
CENTRE – CENTER
CHAMBRE – CHAMBER
CHANCRE – CHANCER
COMPERE – COMPEER
DARTRE – DARTER
DECENTRE – DECENTER
DIOPTRE – DIOPTER
EAGRE – EAGER
FERE – FEER
FIBRE – FIBER
FOUTRE – FOUTER
GAUFRE – GAUFER
GOITRE – GOITER
INCENTRE – INCENTER
LARE – LAER
LERE – LEER
LETTRE – LETTER
LITRE – LITER
LOUVRE – LOUVER
LUSTRE – LUSTER
MACABRE – MACABER
MAUGRE – MAUGER
MEAGRE – MEAGER

METRE – METER
MITRE – MITER
NITRE – NITER
OCHRE – OCHER
OMBRE – OMBER
ONEYRE – ONEYER
OUTRE – OUTER
PHILTRE – PHILTER
PIASTRE – PIASTER
POUDRE – POUDER
POULDRE – POULDER
RECENTRE – RECENTER
SABRE – SABER
SALTIRE – SALTIER
SCEPTRE – SCEPTER
SEMPRE – SEMPER
SOMBRE – SOMBER
SPARRE – SPARER
SPECTRE – SPECTER
TENDRE – TENDER
THEATRE – THEATER
TIMBRE – TIMBER
TITRE – TITER
TWIRE – TWIER
UMBRE – UMBER
UNMITRE – UNMITER
VENTRE – VENTER
ZAFFRE – ZAFFER

-SMAN/-MAN

BATSMAN – BATMAN	LINESMAN – LINEMAN
BEADSMAN – BEADMAN	LINKSMAN – LINKMAN
BEDESMAN – BEDEMAN	LOCKSMAN – LOCKMAN
BOATSMAN – BOATMAN	MARKSMAN – MARKMAN
BONDSMAN – BONDMAN	OVERSMAN – OVERMAN
DESMAN – DEMAN	RAFTSMAN – RAFTMAN
DOORSMAN – DOORMAN	ROADSMAN – ROADMAN
GOWNSMAN – GOWNMAN	RODSMAN – RODMAN
HEADSMAN – HEADMAN	SEEDSMAN – SEEDMAN
HERDSMAN – HERDMAN	SIDESMAN – SIDEMAN
ISLESMAN – ISLEMAN	SWAGSMAN – SWAGMAN
LANDSMAN – LANDMAN	TOPSMAN – TOPMAN
LEADSMAN – LEADMAN	WOODSMAN – WOODMAN

-ISE not -IZE

ABSCISE	DISFRANCHISE	IMPARADISE	PRESURMISE	TREATISE
ADVISE	DISGUISE	IMPROVISE	PREVISE	TRENISE
AFFRANCHISE	DISPRAISE	INCISE	READVERTISE	UNMORTISE
BRANDISE	EGLOMISE	MISADVISE	READVISE	UNPARADISE
CHASTISE	EMPARADISE	MORTISE	SEXERCISE	VALISE
CIRCUMCISE	ENFRANCHISE	OVERADVERTISE	SUBINCISE	VICHYSSOISE
COTISE	EXCISE	OVEREXERCISE	SUCCISE	WALISE
COTTISE	EXERCISE	PARVISE	SUPERVISE	WARRANTISE
COVETISE	FAINEANTISE	PENTISE	SURMISE	
DISCOURTEISE	FRANCHISE	POSTEXERCISE	TELEVISE	
DISENFRANCHISE	GALLIARDISE	PRACTISE	TRAVOISE	

-IZE not -ISE

ASSIZE	DISPRIZE	PREJUDIZE
CAPSIZE	HAZARDIZE	

Chapter 8: Hooks and Blockers

Hooks are words that can be transformed into other valid words by the addition of a single letter at the beginning or the end. Such words are called hooks because they allow other words to be attached to them: if you wish to play a word which has a letter that will go with a hook already on the board, you can attach the new word on the hook by playing the new word perpendicular to it, forming a longer word in the process. Hooks that form valid words with a letter added to their beginning are known as front-hooks; those that take a letter at the end are, naturally enough, end-hooks. Many words are both front-hooks and end-hooks. As an example, the word HOOK itself is both a front-hook and an end-hook, as it can form SHOOK (or CHOOK) and HOOKS (or HOOKA or HOOKY). It may well be that the word RETAINS on your rack can only played on the board by utilizing the front hook of HOOK, make SHOOK and RETAINS at the same time.

Hooks arranged by hook word

The lists in this section contain short words (two, three and four letters) that act as hooks for longer words (three, four and five letters). These are listed alphabetically, with the hook word itself in **bold** and the words formed by hooking shown after each hook word. The lists here contain all the two-letter hook words, then the three-letter hook words, and then the four-letter words.

Two-letter root words

AA	BAD	SAE	AGS	AIN
BAA	CAD	TAE	**AH**	AIR
CAA	DAD	VAE	AAH	AIS
FAA	FAD	WAE	BAH	AIT
MAA	GAD	YAE	DAH	**AL**
AAH	HAD	**AG**	FAH	AAL
AAL	LAD	BAG	HAH	BAL
AAS	MAD	CAG	LAH	DAL
AB	PAD	DAG	NAH	GAL
CAB	RAD	FAG	PAH	MAL
DAB	SAD	GAG	RAH	PAL
FAB	TAD	HAG	YAH	SAL
GAB	WAD	JAG	AHA	ALA
JAB	YAD	LAG	AHI	ALB
KAB	ADD	MAG	AHS	ALE
LAB	ADO	NAG	**AI**	ALF
NAB	ADS	RAG	JAI	ALL
SAB	ADZ	SAG	KAI	ALP
TAB	**AE**	TAG	RAI	ALS
WAB	DAE	VAG	SAI	ALT
ABA	FAE	WAG	TAI	**AM**
ABB	GAE	YAG	WAI	BAM
ABO	HAE	ZAG	AIA	CAM
ABS	KAE	AGA	AID	DAM
ABY	MAE	AGE	AIL	GAM
AD	NAE	AGO	AIM	HAM

JAM	ARS	VAW	BEL	DAW
KAM	ART	WAW	BEN	DAY
LAM	ARY	YAW	BES	**DE**
MAM	**AS**	AWA	BET	IDE
NAM	AAS	AWE	BEY	ODE
PAM	BAS	AWL	BEZ	DEB
RAM	DAS	AWN	**BI**	DEE
SAM	EAS	**AX**	OBI	DEF
TAM	FAS	FAX	BIB	DEG
YAM	GAS	LAX	BID	DEI
AMA	HAS	MAX	BIG	DEL
AMI	KAS	PAX	BIN	DEN
AMP	LAS	RAX	BIO	DEV
AMU	MAS	SAX	BIS	DEW
AN	NAS	TAX	BIT	DEX
BAN	PAS	WAX	BIZ	DEY
CAN	RAS	ZAX	**BO**	**DI**
DAN	TAS	AXE	ABO	DIB
EAN	VAS	**AY**	OBO	DID
FAN	WAS	BAY	BOA	DIE
GAN	ZAS	CAY	BOB	DIF
HAN	ASH	DAY	BOD	DIG
MAN	ASK	FAY	BOG	DIM
NAN	ASP	GAY	BOH	DIN
PAN	ASS	HAY	BOI	DIP
RAN	**AT**	JAY	BOK	DIS
SAN	BAT	KAY	BON	DIT
TAN	CAT	LAY	BOO	DIV
VAN	EAT	MAY	BOP	**DO**
WAN	FAT	NAY	BOR	ADO
ANA	GAT	PAY	BOS	UDO
AND	HAT	RAY	BOT	DOB
ANE	KAT	SAY	BOW	DOC
ANI	LAT	TAY	BOX	DOD
ANN	MAT	WAY	BOY	DOE
ANT	NAT	YAY	**BY**	DOF
ANY	OAT	AYE	ABY	DOG
AR	PAT	AYS	BYE	DOH
BAR	QAT	AYU	BYS	DOL
CAR	RAT	**BA**	**CH**	DOM
EAR	SAT	ABA	ACH	DON
FAR	TAT	OBA	ECH	DOO
GAR	VAT	BAA	ICH	DOP
JAR	WAT	BAC	OCH	DOR
LAR	ATE	BAD	CHA	DOS
MAR	ATT	BAG	CHE	DOT
OAR	**AW**	BAH	CHI	DOW
PAR	CAW	BAL	**DA**	DOY
SAR	DAW	BAM	ODA	**EA**
TAR	FAW	BAN	DAB	KEA
VAR	HAW	BAP	DAD	LEA
WAR	JAW	BAR	DAE	PEA
YAR	KAW	BAS	DAG	SEA
ARB	LAW	BAT	DAH	TEA
ARC	MAW	BAY	DAK	YEA
ARD	NAW	**BE**	DAL	ZEA
ARE	PAW	OBE	DAM	EAN
ARF	RAW	BED	DAN	EAR
ARK	SAW	BEE	DAP	EAS
ARM	TAW	BEG	DAS	EAT

EAU	SEL	PES	FER	HAS
ED	TEL	RES	FES	HAT
BED	ZEL	TES	FET	HAW
FED	ELD	YES	FEU	HAY
GED	ELF	ESS	FEW	**HE**
KED	ELK	EST	FEY	CHE
LED	ELL	**ET**	FEZ	SHE
MED	ELM	BET	**GI**	THE
NED	ELS	FET	GIB	HEH
PED	ELT	GET	GID	HEM
RED	**EM**	HET	GIE	HEN
SED	FEM	JET	GIF	HEP
TED	GEM	KET	GIG	HER
WED	HEM	LET	GIN	HES
ZED	MEM	MET	GIO	HET
EDH	REM	NET	GIP	HEW
EDS	WEM	PET	GIS	HEX
EE	EME	RET	GIT	HEY
BEE	EMO	SET	**GO**	**HI**
CEE	EMS	TET	AGO	AHI
DEE	EMU	VET	EGO	CHI
FEE	**EN**	WET	YGO	GHI
GEE	BEN	YET	GOA	KHI
JEE	DEN	ETA	GOB	PHI
LEE	EEN	ETH	GOD	HIC
MEE	FEN	**EX**	GOE	HID
NEE	GEN	DEX	GON	HIE
PEE	HEN	HEX	GOO	HIM
REE	KEN	KEX	GOR	HIN
SEE	MEN	LEX	GOS	HIP
TEE	PEN	REX	GOT	HIS
VEE	REN	SEX	GOV	HIT
WEE	SEN	TEX	GOX	**HM**
ZEE	TEN	VEX	GOY	OHM
EEK	WEN	WEX	**GU**	HMM
EEL	YEN	YEX	GUB	**HO**
EEN	END	ZEX	GUE	MHO
EF	ENE	EXO	GUL	OHO
DEF	ENG	**FA**	GUM	PHO
KEF	ENS	FAA	GUN	RHO
NEF	**ER**	FAB	GUP	THO
REF	FER	FAD	GUR	WHO
TEF	HER	FAE	GUS	ZHO
EFF	PER	FAG	GUT	HOA
EFS	SER	FAH	GUV	HOB
EFT	ERA	FAN	GUY	HOC
EH	ERE	FAP	**HA**	HOD
FEH	ERF	FAR	AHA	HOE
HEH	ERG	FAS	CHA	HOG
PEH	ERK	FAT	SHA	HOH
REH	ERN	FAW	WHA	HOI
YEH	ERR	FAX	HAD	HOM
EHS	ERS	FAY	HAE	HON
EL	**ES**	**FE**	HAG	HOO
BEL	BES	FED	HAH	HOP
CEL	FES	FEE	HAJ	HOS
DEL	HES	FEG	HAM	HOT
EEL	LES	FEH	HAN	HOW
GEL	MES	FEM	HAO	HOX
MEL	OES	FEN	HAP	HOY

ID	LIS	KAM	LOT	MOL
AID	MIS	KAS	LOU	MOM
BID	NIS	KAT	LOW	MON
CID	PIS	KAW	LOX	MOO
DID	QIS	KAY	LOY	MOP
FID	SIS	**KI**	**MA**	MOR
GID	TIS	SKI	AMA	MOS
HID	VIS	KID	SMA	MOT
KID	WIS	KIF	MAA	MOU
LID	XIS	KIN	MAC	MOW
MID	ISH	KIP	MAD	MOY
NID	ISM	KIR	MAE	MOZ
RID	ISO	KIS	MAG	**MU**
TID	**IT**	KIT	MAK	AMU
VID	AIT	**KO**	MAL	EMU
YID	BIT	KOA	MAM	UMU
IDE	CIT	KOB	MAN	MUD
IDS	DIT	KOI	MAP	MUG
IF	FIT	KON	MAR	MUM
DIF	GIT	KOP	MAS	MUN
GIF	HIT	KOR	MAT	MUS
KIF	KIT	KOS	MAW	MUT
RÏF	LIT	KOW	MAX	MUX
SIF	NIT	**KY**	MAY	**MY**
IFF	PIT	SKY	**ME**	MYC
IFS	RIT	KYE	EME	**NA**
IN	SIT	KYU	MED	ANA
AIN	TIT	**LA**	MEE	MNA
BIN	WIT	ALA	MEG	NAB
DIN	ZIT	LAB	MEL	NAE
FIN	ITA	LAC	MEM	NAG
GIN	ITS	LAD	MEN	NAH
HIN	**JA**	LAG	MES	NAM
JIN	JAB	LAH	MET	NAN
KIN	JAG	LAM	MEU	NAP
LIN	JAI	LAP	MEW	NAS
PIN	JAK	LAR	**MI**	NAT
RIN	JAM	LAS	AMI	NAW
SIN	JAP	LAT	MIB	NAY
TIN	JAR	LAV	MIC	**NE**
VIN	JAW	LAW	MID	ANE
WIN	JAY	LAX	MIG	ENE
YIN	**JO**	LAY	MIL	ONE
ZIN	JOB	**LI**	MIM	NEB
INK	JOE	LIB	MIR	NED
INN	JOG	LID	MIS	NEE
INS	JOL	LIE	MIX	NEF
IO	JOR	LIG	MIZ	NEG
BIO	JOT	LIN	**MM**	NEK
GIO	JOW	LIP	HMM	NEP
ION	JOY	LIS	UMM	NET
IOS	**KA**	LIT	**MO**	NEW
IS	AKA	**LO**	EMO	**NO**
AIS	OKA	LOB	MOA	ONO
BIS	SKA	LOD	MOB	NOB
CIS	KAB	LOG	MOC	NOD
DIS	KAE	LOO	MOD	NOG
GIS	KAF	LOP	MOE	NOH
HIS	KAI	LOR	MOG	NOM
KIS	KAK	LOS	MOI	NON

NOO	FOE	OON	TOR	OWT
NOR	GOE	SON	VOR	**OX**
NOS	HOE	TON	ORA	BOX
NOT	JOE	WON	ORB	COX
NOW	MOE	YON	ORC	FOX
NOX	ROE	ONE	ORD	GOX
NOY	TOE	ONO	ORE	HOX
NU	VOE	ONS	ORF	LOX
GNU	WOE	ONY	ORS	NOX
NUB	OES	**OO**	ORT	POX
NUN	**OF**	BOO	**OS**	SOX
NUR	DOF	COO	BOS	VOX
NUS	OOF	DOO	COS	WOX
NUT	WOF	GOO	DOS	OXO
NY	OFF	HOO	GOS	OXY
ANY	OFT	LOO	HOS	**OY**
ONY	**OH**	MOO	IOS	BOY
SNY	BOH	NOO	KOS	COY
NYE	DOH	POO	LOS	DOY
NYS	FOH	ROO	MOS	FOY
OB	HOH	TOO	NOS	GOY
BOB	NOH	WOO	OOS	HOY
COB	OOH	ZOO	POS	JOY
DOB	POH	OOF	SOS	LOY
FOB	SOH	OOH	WOS	MOY
GOB	OHM	OOM	YOS	NOY
HOB	OHO	OON	ZOS	SOY
JOB	OHS	OOP	OSE	TOY
KOB	**OI**	OOR	**OU**	OYE
LOB	BOI	OOS	FOU	OYS
MOB	HOI	OOT	LOU	**PA**
NOB	KOI	**OP**	MOU	SPA
ROB	MOI	BOP	SOU	PAC
SOB	POI	COP	YOU	PAD
YOB	OIK	DOP	OUD	PAH
OBA	OIL	FOP	OUK	PAL
OBE	**OM**	HOP	OUP	PAM
OBI	DOM	KOP	OUR	PAN
OBO	HOM	LOP	OUS	PAP
OBS	MOM	MOP	OUT	PAR
OD	NOM	OOP	**OW**	PAS
BOD	OOM	POP	BOW	PAT
COD	POM	SOP	COW	PAV
DOD	ROM	TOP	DOW	PAW
GOD	SOM	WOP	HOW	PAX
HOD	TOM	OPE	JOW	PAY
LOD	YOM	OPS	KOW	**PE**
MOD	OMS	OPT	LOW	APE
NOD	**ON**	**OR**	MOW	OPE
POD	BON	BOR	NOW	PEA
ROD	CON	COR	POW	PEC
SOD	DON	DOR	ROW	PED
TOD	EON	FOR	SOW	PEE
YOD	FON	GOR	TOW	PEG
ODA	GON	JOR	VOW	PEH
ODD	HON	KOR	WOW	PEN
ODE	ION	LOR	YOW	PEP
ODS	KON	MOR	OWE	PER
OE	MON	NOR	OWL	PES
DOE	NON	OOR	OWN	PET

Hooks arranged by hook word

PEW	SHE	TAX	**UM**	GUS
PI	SHH	TAY	BUM	JUS
PIA	SHY	**TE**	CUM	MUS
PIC	**SI**	ATE	FUM	NUS
PIE	PSI	UTE	GUM	OUS
PIG	SIB	TEA	HUM	PUS
PIN	SIC	TEC	LUM	SUS
PIP	SIF	TED	MUM	WUS
PIR	SIK	TEE	RUM	YUS
PIS	SIM	TEF	SUM	USE
PIT	SIN	TEG	TUM	**UT**
PIU	SIP	TEL	VUM	BUT
PIX	SIR	TEN	YUM	CUT
PO	SIS	TES	UMM	GUT
APO	SIT	TET	UMP	HUT
UPO	SIX	TEW	UMU	JUT
POA	**SO**	TEX	**UN**	MUT
POD	DSO	**TI**	BUN	NUT
POH	ISO	TIC	DUN	OUT
POI	SOB	TID	FUN	PUT
POL	SOC	TIE	GUN	RUT
POM	SOD	TIG	HUN	TUT
POO	SOG	TIL	JUN	UTA
POP	SOH	TIN	MUN	UTE
POS	SOL	TIP	NUN	UTS
POT	SOM	TIS	PUN	UTU
POW	SON	TIT	RUN	**WE**
POX	SOP	TIX	SUN	AWE
POZ	SOS	**TO**	TUN	EWE
QI	SOT	TOC	UNI	OWE
QIS	SOU	TOD	UNS	WEB
RE	SOV	TOE	**UP**	WED
ARE	SOW	TOG	CUP	WEE
ERE	SOX	TOM	DUP	WEM
IRE	SOY	TON	GUP	WEN
ORE	**ST**	TOO	HUP	WET
PRE	EST	TOP	OUP	WEX
URE	PST	TOR	PUP	WEY
REB	STY	TOT	SUP	**WO**
REC	**TA**	TOW	TUP	TWO
RED	ETA	TOY	YUP	WOE
REE	ITA	**UG**	UPO	WOF
REF	UTA	BUG	UPS	WOG
REG	TAB	DUG	**UR**	WOK
REH	TAD	FUG	BUR	WON
REI	TAE	HUG	CUR	WOO
REM	TAG	JUG	FUR	WOP
REN	TAI	LUG	GUR	WOS
REO	TAJ	MUG	LUR	WOT
REP	TAK	PUG	NUR	WOW
RES	TAM	RUG	OUR	WOX
RET	TAN	TUG	PUR	**XI**
REV	TAO	VUG	SUR	XIS
REW	TAP	YUG	URB	**YA**
REX	TAR	UGH	URD	PYA
REZ	TAS	UGS	URE	RYA
SH	TAT	**UH**	URN	YAD
ASH	TAU	DUH	URP	YAE
ISH	TAV	HUH	**US**	YAG
SHA	TAW	PUH	BUS	YAH

YAK	KYE	YEP	YOU	ZAP
YAM	LYE	YES	YOW	ZAS
YAP	NYE	YET	**YU**	ZAX
YAR	OYE	YEW	AYU	**ZO**
YAW	PYE	YEX	KYU	AZO
YAY	RYE	**YO**	YUG	DZO
YE	SYE	YOB	YUK	ZOA
AYE	TYE	YOD	YUM	ZOL
BYE	WYE	YOK	YUP	ZOO
DYE	YEA	YOM	YUS	ZOS
EYE	YEH	YON	**ZA**	
HYE	YEN	YOS	ZAG	

Three-letter root words

AAH	DACE	PADS	AGEE	AIAS	
AAHS	FACE	RADS	AGEN	**AID**	
AAL	LACE	SADS	AGER	CAID	
BAAL	MACE	TADS	AGES	GAID	
KAAL	PACE	WADS	**AGO**	KAID	
PAAL	RACE	YADS	DAGO	LAID	
TAAL	TACE	**ADZ**	KAGO	MAID	
AALS	ACED	ADZE	SAGO	PAID	
AAS	ACER	**AFF**	AGOG	QAID	
BAAS	ACES	BAFF	AGON	RAID	
CAAS	**ACH**	CAFF	**AGS**	SAID	
FAAS	BACH	DAFF	BAGS	WAID	
KAAS	EACH	FAFF	CAGS	AIDE	
MAAS	MACH	GAFF	DAGS	AIDS	
ABA	NACH	HAFF	FAGS	**AIL**	
BABA	RACH	NAFF	GAGS	BAIL	
CABA	TACH	RAFF	HAGS	FAIL	
YABA	ACHE	WAFF	JAGS	HAIL	
ABAC	ACHY	YAFF	LAGS	JAIL	
ABAS	**ACT**	AFFY	MAGS	KAIL	
ABB	FACT	**AFT**	NAGS	MAIL	
ABBA	PACT	BAFT	RAGS	NAIL	
ABBE	TACT	DAFT	SAGS	PAIL	
ABBS	ACTA	HAFT	TAGS	RAIL	
ABO	ACTS	RAFT	VAGS	SAIL	
ABOS	**ADD**	SAFT	WAGS	TAIL	
ABS	WADD	WAFT	YAGS	VAIL	
CABS	ADDS	**AGA**	ZAGS	WAIL	
DABS	ADDY	GAGA	**AHA**	AILS	
FABS	**ADO**	JAGA	HAHA	**AIM**	
GABS	DADO	NAGA	TAHA	KAIM	
JABS	FADO	RAGA	**AHI**	MAIM	
KABS	SADO	SAGA	AHIS	SAIM	
LABS	ADOS	AGAR	**AHS**	AIMS	
NABS	**ADS**	AGAS	AAHS	**AIN**	
SABS	BADS	**AGE**	DAHS	CAIN	
TABS	CADS	CAGE	FAHS	FAIN	
WABS	DADS	GAGE	HAHS	GAIN	
ABY	FADS	MAGE	LAHS	HAIN	
BABY	GADS	PAGE	PAHS	KAIN	
GABY	HADS	RAGE	RAHS	LAIN	
ABYE	LADS	SAGE	YAHS	MAIN	
ABYS	MADS	WAGE	**AIA**	NAIN	
ACE	NADS	AGED	RAIA	PAIN	

RAIN	NALA	GALS	RAND	PAPE
SAIN	TALA	MALS	SAND	RAPE
TAIN	ALAE	PALS	WAND	TAPE
VAIN	ALAN	SALS	ANDS	APED
WAIN	ALAP	ALSO	**ANE**	APER
AINE	ALAR	**ALT**	BANE	APES
AINS	ALAS	DALT	CANE	APEX
AIR	ALAY	HALT	FANE	**APO**
FAIR	**ALB**	MALT	GANE	CAPO
GAIR	ALBA	SALT	JANE	GAPO
HAIR	ALBE	ALTO	KANE	APOD
LAIR	ALBS	ALTS	LANE	APOS
MAIR	**ALE**	**AMA**	MANE	**APP**
PAIR	BALE	CAMA	NANE	YAPP
SAIR	DALE	GAMA	PANE	APPS
VAIR	EALE	KAMA	SANE	**APT**
WAIR	GALE	LAMA	TANE	RAPT
AIRN	HALE	MAMA	VANE	APTS
AIRS	KALE	SAMA	WANE	**ARB**
AIRT	MALE	AMAH	ANES	BARB
AIRY	PALE	AMAS	ANEW	CARB
AIS	RALE	**AMI**	**ANI**	DARB
DAIS	SALE	KAMI	BANI	GARB
KAIS	TALE	RAMI	MANI	WARB
PAIS	VALE	AMIA	RANI	ARBA
RAIS	WALE	AMID	ANIL	ARBS
SAIS	YALE	AMIE	ANIS	**ARC**
TAIS	ALEC	AMIN	**ANN**	MARC
WAIS	ALEE	AMIR	CANN	NARC
AIT	ALEF	AMIS	JANN	ARCH
BAIT	ALES	**AMP**	ANNA	ARCO
GAIT	ALEW	CAMP	ANNO	ARCS
RAIT	**ALF**	DAMP	ANNS	**ARD**
TAIT	CALF	GAMP	**ANT**	BARD
WAIT	HALF	LAMP	BANT	CARD
AITS	ALFA	RAMP	CANT	EARD
AITU	ALFS	SAMP	DANT	FARD
AKA	**ALL**	TAMP	GANT	HARD
HAKA	BALL	VAMP	HANT	LARD
KAKA	CALL	AMPS	KANT	MARD
TAKA	FALL	**AMU**	LANT	NARD
WAKA	GALL	NAMU	PANT	PARD
AKE	HALL	AMUS	RANT	SARD
BAKE	LALL	**ANA**	SANT	WARD
CAKE	MALL	KANA	VANT	YARD
FAKE	PALL	LANA	WANT	ARDS
HAKE	SALL	MANA	ANTA	**ARE**
JAKE	TALL	NANA	ANTE	BARE
LAKE	WALL	RANA	ANTI	CARE
MAKE	ALLS	TANA	ANTS	DARE
RAKE	ALLY	ANAL	**ANY**	FARE
SAKE	**ALP**	ANAN	CANY	GARE
TAKE	CALP	ANAS	MANY	HARE
WAKE	SALP	**AND**	WANY	LARE
AKED	ALPS	BAND	ZANY	MARE
AKEE	**ALS**	FAND	**APE**	NARE
AKES	AALS	HAND	CAPE	PARE
ALA	BALS	LAND	GAPE	RARE
GALA	BALS	MAND	JAPE	TARE
MALA	DALS	PAND	NAPE	VARE

WARE	MART	PATE	AWED	**BAD**
YARE	PART	RATE	AWEE	BADE
AREA	TART	SATE	AWES	BADS
ARED	WART	TATE	**AWL**	**BAG**
AREG	ARTI	WATE	BAWL	BAGH
ARES	ARTS	YATE	PAWL	BAGS
ARET	ARTY	ATES	WAWL	**BAH**
AREW	**ARY**	**ATT**	YAWL	BAHT
ARF	MARY	BATT	AWLS	**BAL**
BARF	NARY	MATT	**AWN**	BALD
ZARF	OARY	TATT	BAWN	BALE
ARFS	VARY	WATT	DAWN	BALK
ARK	WARY	**AUA**	FAWN	BALL
BARK	ARYL	PAUA	LAWN	BALM
CARK	**ASH**	**AUF**	MAWN	BALS
DARK	BASH	CAUF	PAWN	BALU
HARK	CASH	HAUF	RAWN	**BAM**
JARK	DASH	LAUF	SAWN	BAMS
KARK	FASH	AUFS	YAWN	**BAN**
LARK	GASH	**AUK**	AWNS	BANC
MARK	HASH	BAUK	AWNY	BAND
NARK	LASH	CAUK	**AXE**	BANE
PARK	MASH	JAUK	SAXE	BANG
RARK	PASH	WAUK	AXED	BANI
SARK	RASH	AUKS	AXEL	BANK
WARK	SASH	**AVA**	AXES	BANS
YARK	TASH	CAVA	**AYE**	BANT
ARKS	WASH	FAVA	BAYE	**BAP**
ARM	ASHY	JAVA	AYES	BAPS
BARM	**ASK**	KAVA	**AYS**	BAPU
FARM	BASK	LAVA	BAYS	**BAR**
HARM	CASK	TAVA	CAYS	KBAR
MARM	HASK	AVAL	DAYS	BARB
WARM	MASK	AVAS	FAYS	BARD
ARMS	TASK	**AVE**	GAYS	BARE
ARMY	ASKS	CAVE	HAYS	BARF
ARS	**ASP**	EAVE	JAYS	BARK
BARS	GASP	FAVE	KAYS	BARM
CARS	HASP	GAVE	LAYS	BARN
EARS	JASP	HAVE	MAYS	BARP
FARS	RASP	LAVE	NAYS	BARS
GARS	WASP	NAVE	PAYS	**BAS**
JARS	ASPS	PAVE	RAYS	ABAS
LARS	**ASS**	RAVE	SAYS	OBAS
MARS	BASS	SAVE	TAYS	BASE
OARS	JASS	WAVE	WAYS	BASH
PARS	LASS	AVEL	YAYS	BASK
SARS	MASS	AVER	**AYU**	BASS
TARS	PASS	AVES	AYUS	BAST
VARS	SASS	**AVO**	**AZO**	**BAT**
WARS	TASS	AVOS	LAZO	BATE
ARSE	**ATE**	AVOW	AZON	BATH
ARSY	BATE	**AWA**	**BAA**	BATS
ART	CATE	KAWA	BAAL	BATT
CART	DATE	PAWA	BAAS	**BAY**
DART	FATE	TAWA	**BAC**	BAYE
FART	GATE	WAWA	ABAC	BAYS
GART	HATE	AWAY	BACH	BAYT
HART	LATE	**AWE**	BACK	**BED**
KART	MATE	WAWE	BACS	ABED

Hooks arranged by hook word

BEDE	IBIS	**BOR**	BUDI	SCAG
BEDS	OBIS	BORA	BUDO	CAGE
BEDU	BISE	BORD	BUDS	CAGS
BEE	BISH	BORE	**BUG**	CAGY
BEEF	BISK	BORK	BUGS	**CAM**
BEEN	BIST	BORM	**BUM**	SCAM
BEEP	**BIT**	BORN	BUMF	CAMA
BEER	OBIT	BORS	BUMP	CAME
BEES	BITE	BORT	BUMS	CAMO
BEET	BITO	**BOS**	**BUN**	CAMP
BEG	BITS	ABOS	BUNA	CAMS
BEGO	BITT	OBOS	BUND	**CAN**
BEGS	**BIZ**	BOSH	BUNG	SCAN
BEL	BIZE	BOSK	BUNK	CANE
BELL	**BOA**	BOSS	BUNN	CANG
BELS	BOAB	**BOT**	BUNS	CANN
BELT	BOAK	BOTA	BUNT	CANS
BEN	BOAR	BOTH	**BUR**	CANT
BEND	BOAS	BOTS	BURA	CANY
BENE	BOAT	BOTT	BURB	**CAP**
BENI	**BOB**	**BOW**	BURD	CAPA
BENJ	BOBA	BOWL	BURG	CAPE
BENS	BOBS	BOWR	BURK	CAPH
BENT	**BOD**	BOWS	BURL	CAPI
BES	BODE	**BOX**	BURN	CAPO
OBES	BODS	BOXY	BURP	CAPS
BEST	BODY	**BOY**	BURR	**CAR**
BET	**BOG**	BOYF	BURS	SCAR
ABET	BOGS	BOYG	BURY	CARB
YBET	BOGY	BOYO	**BUS**	CARD
BETA	**BOH**	BOYS	BUSH	CARE
BETE	BOHO	**BRA**	BUSK	CARK
BETH	BOHS	BRAD	BUSS	CARL
BETS	**BOI**	BRAE	BUST	CARN
BEV	BOIL	BRAG	BUSY	CARP
OBEY	BOIS	BRAK	**BUT**	CARR
BEYS	**BOK**	BRAN	ABUT	CARS
BIB	BOKE	BRAS	BUTE	CART
BIBB	BOKO	BRAT	BUTS	**CAT**
BIBS	BOKS	BRAW	BUTT	SCAT
BID	**BON**	BRAY	**BUY**	CATE
ABID	EBON	**BRO**	BUYS	CATS
BIDE	BONA	BROD	**BYE**	**CAW**
BIDI	BOND	BROG	ABYE	SCAW
BIDS	BONE	BROO	BYES	CAWK
BIG	BONG	BROS	**BYS**	CAWS
BIGA	BONK	BROW	ABYS	**CAY**
BIGG	BONY	**BRR**	**CAA**	CAYS
BIGS	**BOO**	BRRR	CAAS	**CEE**
BIN	BOOB	**BRU**	**CAB**	CEES
BIND	BOOH	BRUS	SCAB	**CEL**
BINE	BOOK	BRUT	CABA	CELL
BING	BOOL	BRUX	CABS	CELS
BINK	BOOM	**BUB**	**CAD**	CELT
BINS	BOON	BUBA	ECAD	**CEP**
BINT	BOOR	BUBO	SCAD	CEPE
BIO	BOOS	BUBS	CADE	CEPS
BIOG	BOOT	BUBU	CADI	**CHA**
BIOS	**BOP**	**BUD**	CADS	CHAD
BIS	BOPS	BUDA	**CAG**	CHAI

CHAL	COLT	**COZ**	ODAL	DELO
CHAM	COLY	COZE	UDAL	DELS
CHAO	**CON**	COZY	DALE	DELT
CHAP	ICON	**CRU**	DALI	**DEN**
CHAR	COND	ECRU	DALS	DENE
CHAS	CONE	CRUD	DALT	DENI
CHAT	CONF	CRUE	**DAM**	DENS
CHAV	CONI	CRUS	DAME	DENT
CHAW	CONK	CRUX	DAMN	DENY
CHAY	CONN	**CRY**	DAMP	**DEV**
CHE	CONS	SCRY	DAMS	DEVA
ACHE	CONY	**CUB**	**DAN**	DEVS
ECHE	**COO**	CUBE	DANG	**DEW**
OCHE	COOF	CUBS	DANK	DEWS
CHEF	COOK	**CUD**	DANS	DEWY
CHER	COOL	SCUD	DANT	**DEX**
CHEW	COOM	CUDS	**DAP**	DEXY
CHEZ	COON	**CUE**	DAPS	**DEY**
CHI	COOP	CUED	**DAS**	DEYS
CHIA	COOS	CUES	ODAS	**DIB**
CHIB	COOT	**CUM**	DASH	DIBS
CHIC	**COP**	SCUM	**DAW**	**DID**
CHID	SCOP	**CUP**	ADAW	DIDO
CHIK	COPE	SCUP	DAWD	DIDY
CHIN	COPS	CUPS	DAWK	**DIE**
CHIP	COPY	**CUR**	DAWN	DIEB
CHIS	**COR**	SCUR	DAWS	DIED
CHIT	CORD	CURB	DAWT	DIEL
CHIV	CORE	CURD	**DAY**	DIES
CHIZ	CORF	CURE	DAYS	DIET
CID	CORK	CURF	**DEB**	**DIF**
ACID	CORM	CURL	DEBE	DIFF
CIDE	CORN	CURN	DEBS	DIFS
CIDS	CORS	CURR	DEBT	**DIG**
CIG	CORY	CURS	**DEE**	DIGS
CIGS	**COS**	CURT	IDEE	**DIM**
CIS	ECOS	**CUT**	DEED	DIME
CIST	COSE	SCUT	DEEK	DIMP
CIT	COSH	CUTE	DEEM	DIMS
CITE	COSS	CUTS	DEEN	**DIN**
CITO	COST	**CWM**	DEEP	DINE
CITS	COSY	CWMS	DEER	DING
CITY	**COT**	**DAB**	DEES	DINK
COB	SCOT	DABS	DEET	DINO
COBB	COTE	**DAD**	DEEV	DINS
COBS	COTH	DADA	**DEF**	DINT
COD	COTS	DADO	DEFI	**DIP**
ECOD	COTT	DADS	DEFT	DIPS
CODA	**COW**	**DAE**	DEFY	DIPT
CODE	SCOW	DAES	**DEG**	**DIS**
CODS	COWK	**DAG**	DEGS	DISA
COG	COWL	DAGO	**DEI**	DISC
SCOG	COWP	DAGS	DEID	DISH
COGS	COWS	**DAH**	DEIF	DISK
COL	COWY	ODAH	DEIL	DISS
COLA	**COX**	DAHL	**DEL**	**DIT**
COLD	COXA	DAHS	DELE	ADIT
COLE	COXY	**DAK**	DELF	EDIT
COLL	**COY**	DAKS	DELI	DITA
COLS	COYS	**DAL**	DELL	DITE

DITS	**DOR**	DUOS	MEAT	KEEL
DITT	ODOR	**DUP**	NEAT	PEEL
DITZ	DORB	DUPE	PEAT	REEL
DIV	DORE	DUPS	SEAT	SEEL
DIVA	DORK	**DYE**	TEAT	TEEL
DIVE	DORM	DYED	EATH	WEEL
DIVI	DORP	DYER	EATS	EELS
DIVS	DORR	DYES	**EAU**	EELY
DOB	DORS	**DZO**	BEAU	**EEN**
DOBS	DORT	DZOS	EAUS	BEEN
DOBY	DORY	**EAN**	EAUX	DEEN
DOC	**DOS**	BEAN	**EBB**	FEEN
DOCK	ADOS	DEAN	EBBS	KEEN
DOCO	UDOS	GEAN	**ECH**	PEEN
DOCS	DOSE	JEAN	EECH	REEN
DOD	DOSH	LEAN	HECH	SEEN
DODO	DOSS	MEAN	LECH	TEEN
DODS	DOST	PEAN	PECH	WEEN
DOE	**DOT**	REAN	SECH	**EFF**
DOEK	DOTE	SEAN	TECH	JEFF
DOEN	DOTH	WEAN	YECH	MEFF
DOER	DOTS	YEAN	ECHE	TEFF
DOES	DOTY	EANS	ECHO	EFFS
DOF	**DOW**	**EAR**	ECHT	**EFS**
DOFF	DOWD	BEAR	**ECO**	KEFS
DOG	DOWF	DEAR	DECO	NEFS
DOGE	DOWL	FEAR	SECO	REFS
DOGS	DOWN	GEAR	ECOD	TEFS
DOGY	DOWP	HEAR	ECOS	**EFT**
DOH	DOWS	LEAR	**ECU**	DEFT
DOHS	DOWT	NEAR	ECUS	HEFT
DOL	**DOY**	PEAR	**EDH**	LEFT
IDOL	DOYS	REAR	EDHS	REFT
DOLE	**DRY**	SEAR	**EDS**	WEFT
DOLL	ADRY	TEAR	BEDS	EFTS
DOLS	DRYS	WEAR	FEDS	**EGG**
DOLT	**DSO**	YEAR	GEDS	TEGG
DOM	ODSO	EARD	KEDS	YEGG
DOME	DSOS	EARL	MEDS	EGGS
DOMS	**DUB**	EARN	NEDS	EGGY
DOMY	DUBS	EARS	PEDS	**EGO**
DON	**DUD**	**EAS**	REDS	BEGO
UDON	DUDE	CEAS	TEDS	REGO
DONA	DUDS	KEAS	WEDS	SEGO
DONE	**DUE**	LEAS	ZEDS	VEGO
DONG	DUED	PEAS	**EEK**	EGOS
DONS	DUEL	SEAS	DEEK	**EHS**
DOO	DUET	TEAS	GEEK	FEHS
DOOB	**DUG**	YEAS	KEEK	HEHS
DOOK	DUGS	ZEAS	LEEK	PEHS
DOOL	**DUI**	EASE	MEEK	REHS
DOOM	DUIT	EAST	PEEK	**EIK**
DOON	**DUN**	EASY	REEK	REIK
DOOR	DUNE	**EAT**	SEEK	SEIK
DOOS	DUNG	BEAT	TEEK	EIKS
DOP	DUNK	FEAT	WEEK	**EKE**
DOPA	DUNS	GEAT	**EEL**	DEKE
DOPE	DUNT	HEAT	FEEL	LEKE
DOPS	**DUO**	JEAT	HEEL	PEKE
DOPY		LEAT	JEEL	REKE

EKED	MELT	CENS	KERN	EUKS	
EKES	PELT	DENS	PERN	**EVE**	
ELD	TELT	FENS	TERN	LEVE	
GELD	WELT	GENS	ERNE	MEVE	
HELD	YELT	HENS	ERNS	NEVE	
MELD	ELTS	KENS	**ERR**	YEVE	
SELD	**EME**	LENS	SERR	EVEN	
TELD	DEME	PENS	ERRS	EVER	
VELD	FEME	RENS	**ERS**	EVES	
WELD	HEME	SENS	HERS	EVET	
YELD	LEME	TENS	SERS	**EVO**	
ELDS	MEME	WENS	VERS	LEVO	
ELF	SEME	YENS	ERST	EVOE	
DELF	TEME	**EON**	**ESS**	EVOS	
PELF	EMES	AEON	CESS	**EWE**	
SELF	EMEU	JEON	FESS	EWER	
ELFS	**EMO**	NEON	JESS	EWES	
ELK	DEMO	PEON	LESS	**EWK**	
WELK	MEMO	EONS	MESS	EWKS	
YELK	EMOS	**ERA**	NESS	**EWT**	
ELKS	**EMS**	SERA	SESS	NEWT	
ELL	FEMS	VERA	ESSE	EWTS	
BELL	GEMS	ERAS	**EST**	**EXO**	
CELL	HEMS	**ERE**	BEST	EXON	
DELL	MEMS	BERE	FEST	**EYE**	
FELL	REMS	CERE	GEST	EYED	
HELL	TEMS	DERE	HEST	EYEN	
JELL	WEMS	FERE	JEST	EYER	
KELL	**EMU**	GERE	KEST	EYES	
MELL	EMUS	HERE	LEST	**FAA**	
PELL	**END**	LERE	NEST	FAAN	
SELL	BEND	MERE	PEST	FAAS	
TELL	FEND	PERE	REST	**FAB**	
VELL	HEND	SERE	TEST	FABS	
WELL	LEND	WERE	VEST	**FAD**	
YELL	MEND	ERED	WEST	FADE	
ELLS	PEND	ERES	YEST	FADO	
ELM	REND	EREV	ZEST	FADS	
HELM	SEND	**ERF**	ESTS	FADY	
YELM	TEND	KERF	**ETA**	**FAG**	
ELMS	VEND	SERF	BETA	FAGS	
ELMY	WEND	TERF	FETA	**FAH**	
ELS	ENDS	**ERG**	GETA	FAHS	
BELS	**ENE**	BERG	KETA	**FAN**	
CELS	BENE	ERGO	META	FAND	
DELS	DENE	ERGS	SETA	FANE	
EELS	GENE	**ERK**	WETA	FANG	
GELS	MENE	BERK	ZETA	FANK	
MELS	NENE	JERK	ETAS	FANO	
SELS	PENE	MERK	ETAT	FANS	
TELS	SENE	NERK	**ETH**	**FAR**	
ZELS	TENE	PERK	BETH	AFAR	
ELSE	ENES	SERK	HETH	FARD	
ELT	ENEW	YERK	METH	FARE	
BELT	**ENG**	ZERK	TETH	FARL	
CELT	LENG	ERKS	ETHE	FARM	
DELT	MENG	**ERN**	ETHS	FARO	
FELT	ENGS	DERN	**EUK**	FARS	
GELT	**ENS**	FERN	NEUK	FART	
KELT	BENS	HERN	YEUK	**FAS**	

FASH	FIGO	**FOU**	GAGA	GEEP
FAST	FIGS	FOUD	GAGE	GEES
FAT	**FIL**	FOUL	GAGS	GEEZ
FATE	FILA	FOUR	**GAL**	**GEL**
FATS	FILE	FOUS	EGAL	GELD
FAW	FILL	**FOX**	GALA	GELS
FAWN	FILM	FOXY	GALE	GELT
FAWS	FILO	**FOY**	GALL	**GEM**
FAY	FILS	FOYS	GALS	GEMS
OFAY	**FIN**	**FRA**	**GAM**	**GEN**
FAYS	FIND	FRAB	OGAM	AGEN
FED	FINE	FRAE	GAMA	GENA
FEDS	FINI	FRAG	GAMB	GENE
FEE	FINK	FRAP	GAME	GENS
FEEB	FINO	FRAS	GAMP	GENT
FEED	FINS	FRAT	GAMS	GENU
FEEL	**FIR**	FRAU	GAMY	**GEO**
FEEN	FIRE	FRAY	**GAN**	GEOS
FEER	FIRK	**FRO**	GANE	**GET**
FEES	FIRM	AFRO	GANG	GETA
FEET	FIRN	FROE	GANS	GETS
FEG	FIRS	FROG	GANT	**GHI**
FEGS	**FIT**	FROM	**GAP**	GHIS
FEH	FITS	FROS	GAPE	**GIB**
FEHM	FITT	FROW	GAPO	GIBE
FEHS	**FIX**	**FUB**	GAPS	GIBS
FEM	FIXT	FUBS	GAPY	**GID**
FEME	**FIZ**	**FUD**	**GAR**	GIDS
FEMS	FIZZ	FUDS	AGAR	**GIE**
FEN	**FLU**	**FUG**	GARB	GIED
FEND	FLUB	FUGS	GARE	GIEN
FENI	FLUE	FUGU	GARI	GIES
FENS	FLUS	**FUM**	GARS	**GIF**
FENT	FLUX	FUME	GART	GIFT
FER	**FOB**	FUMS	**GAS**	**GIG**
FERE	FOBS	FUMY	AGAS	GIGA
FERM	**FOE**	**FUN**	GASH	GIGS
FERN	FOEN	FUND	GASP	**GIN**
FES	FOES	FUNG	GAST	AGIN
FESS	**FOG**	FUNK	**GAT**	GING
FEST	FOGS	FUNS	GATE	GINK
FET	FOGY	**FUR**	GATH	GINN
FETA	**FOH**	FURL	GATS	GINS
FETE	FOHN	FURR	**GAU**	**GIO**
FETS	FOHS	FURS	GAUD	AGIO
FETT	**FON**	FURY	GAUM	GIOS
FEU	FOND	**GAB**	GAUN	**GIP**
FEUD	FONE	GABS	GAUP	GIPS
FEUS	FONS	GABY	GAUR	**GIS**
FEY	FONT	**GAD**	GAUS	EGIS
FEYS	**FOP**	EGAD	**GAY**	GISM
FIB	FOPS	IGAD	GAYS	GIST
FIBS	**FOR**	GADE	**GED**	**GIT**
FID	FORA	GADI	AGED	GITE
FIDO	FORB	GADS	GEDS	GITS
FIDS	FORD	**GAE**	**GEE**	**GJU**
FIE	FORE	GAED	AGEE	GJUS
FIEF	FORK	GAEN	OGEE	**GNU**
FIER	FORM	GAES	GEED	GNUS
FIG	FORT	**GAG**	GEEK	**GOA**

GOAD	GULP	HAME	**HEP**	**HIP**
GOAF	GULS	HAMS	HEPS	CHIP
GOAL	GULY	**HAN**	HEPT	SHIP
GOAS	**GUM**	KHAN	**HER**	WHIP
GOAT	GUMP	SHAN	CHER	HIPS
GOB	GUMS	THAN	HERB	HIPT
GOBO	**GUN**	HAND	HERD	**HIS**
GOBS	GUNG	HANG	HERE	AHIS
GOBY	GUNK	HANK	HERL	CHIS
GOD	GUNS	HANT	HERM	GHIS
GODS	**GUP**	**HAO**	HERN	KHIS
GOE	GUPS	CHAO	HERO	PHIS
YGOE	**GUR**	**HAP**	HERS	THIS
GOEL	GURL	CHAP	HERY	HISH
GOER	GURN	WHAP	**HES**	HISN
GOES	GURS	HAPS	SHES	HISS
GOEY	GURU	HAPU	HESP	HIST
GON	**GUS**	**HAS**	HEST	**HIT**
AGON	GUSH	CHAS	HET	CHIT
GONE	GUST	HASH	**HET**	SHIT
GONG	**GUV**	HASK	KHET	WHIT
GONK	GUVS	HASP	SHET	HITS
GONS	**GUV**	HAST	WHET	**HOA**
GOO	GUVS	**HAT**	HETE	WHOA
GOOD	**GUY**	BHAT	HETH	HOAR
GOOF	GUYS	CHAT	HETS	HOAS
GOOG	**GYM**	GHAT	**HEW**	HOAX
GOOK	GYMP	KHAT	CHEW	**HOB**
GOOL	GYMS	PHAT	PHEW	HOBO
GOON	**GYP**	SHAT	SHEW	HOBS
GOOP	GYPS	THAT	THEW	**HOC**
GOOR	**HAD**	WHAT	WHEW	CHOC
GOOS	CHAD	HATE	HEWN	HOCK
GOR	SHAD	HATH	HEWS	**HOD**
GORA	HADE	HATS	**HEY**	SHOD
GORE	HADJ	**HAW**	THEY	HODS
GORI	HADS	CHAW	WHEY	**HOE**
GORM	**HAE**	SHAW	HEYS	SHOE
GORP	THAE	THAW	**HIC**	HOED
GORY	WHAE	HAWK	CHIC	HOER
GOS	HAED	HAWM	HICK	HOES
EGOS	HAEM	HAWS	**HID**	**HOG**
GOSH	HAEN	**HAY**	CHID	CHOG
GOSS	HAES	CHAY	WHID	SHOG
GOT	HAET	SHAY	HIDE	HOGG
GOTH	**HAG**	HAYS	**HIE**	HOGH
GOV	SHAG	**HEH**	HIED	HOGS
GOVS	HAGG	HEHS	HIES	**HOH**
GOY	HAGS	**HEM**	**HIM**	PHOH
GOYS	**HAH**	AHEM	SHIM	HOHA
GUB	SHAH	THEM	WHIM	HOHS
GUBS	HAHA	HEME	HIMS	**HOI**
GUE	HAHS	HEMP	**HIN**	HOIK
AGUE	**HAJ**	HEMS	CHIN	**HOM**
GUES	HAJI	**HEN**	SHIN	WHOM
GUL	HAJJ	THEN	THIN	HOMA
GULA	**HAM**	WHEN	WHIN	HOME
GULE	CHAM	HEND	HIND	HOMO
GULF	SHAM	HENS	HING	HOMS
GULL	WHAM	HENT	HINS	HOMY
			HINT	

Hooks arranged by hook word

HON	CHUG	MICH	ZIFF	RINK	
CHON	THUG	RICH	IFFY	SINK	
PHON	HUGE	SICH	IFS	TINK	
THON	HUGS	TICH	DIFS	WINK	
HOND	HUGY	WICH	KIFS	INKS	
HONE	HUH	ICHS	RIFS	INKY	
HONG	HUHU	ICK	IGG	INN	
HONK	HUI	DICK	BIGG	GINN	
HONS	HUIA	HICK	MIGG	JINN	
HOO	HUIC	KICK	RIGG	LINN	
SHOO	HUIS	LICK	IGGS	WINN	
HOOD	HUM	MICK	ILK	INNS	
HOOF	CHUM	NICK	BILK	INS	
HOOK	HUMA	PICK	MILK	AINS	
HOON	HUMF	RICK	SILK	BINS	
HOOP	HUMP	SICK	ILKA	DINS	
HOOT	HUMS	TICK	ILKS	FINS	
HOP	HUN	WICK	ILL	GINS	
CHOP	SHUN	ICKY	BILL	HINS	
SHOP	HUNG	ICY	CILL	JINS	
WHOP	HUNH	RICY	DILL	KINS	
HOPE	HUNK	IDE	FILL	LINS	
HOPS	HUNS	AIDE	GILL	PINS	
HOS	HUNT	BIDE	HILL	RINS	
MHOS	HUP	CIDE	JILL	SINS	
OHOS	WHUP	EIDE	KILL	TINS	
PHOS	HUPS	HIDE	LILL	VINS	
RHOS	HUT	NIDE	MILL	WINS	
ZHOS	BHUT	RIDE	NILL	YINS	
HOSE	CHUT	SIDE	PILL	ZINS	
HOSS	PHUT	TIDE	RILL	ION	
HOST	SHUT	VIDE	SILL	CION	
HOT	HUTS	WIDE	TILL	LION	
PHOT	HYE	IDEA	VILL	PION	
SHOT	HYED	IDEE	WILL	IONS	
WHOT	HYEN	IDEM	YILL	IOS	
HOTE	HYES	IDES	ZILL	BIOS	
HOTS	HYP	IDS	ILLS	GIOS	
HOW	HYPE	AIDS	ILLY	IRE	
CHOW	HYPO	BIDS	IMP	CIRE	
DHOW	HYPS	CIDS	DIMP	DIRE	
SHOW	ICE	FIDS	GIMP	FIRE	
WHOW	BICE	GIDS	JIMP	HIRE	
HOWE	DICE	KIDS	LIMP	LIRE	
HOWF	FICE	LIDS	PIMP	MIRE	
HOWK	LICE	MIDS	SIMP	SIRE	
HOWL	MICE	NIDS	WIMP	TIRE	
HOWS	NICE	RIDS	IMPI	VIRE	
HOY	PICE	TIDS	IMPS	WIRE	
AHOY	RICE	VIDS	INK	IRED	
HOYA	SICE	YIDS	BINK	IRES	
HOYS	TICE	IFF	DINK	IRK	
HUB	VICE	BIFF	FINK	BIRK	
CHUB	WICE	DIFF	GINK	DIRK	
HUBS	ICED	JIFF	JINK	FIRK	
HUE	ICER	KIFF	KINK	KIRK	
HUED	ICES	MIFF	LINK	LIRK	
HUER	ICH	NIFF	MINK	MIRK	
HUES	DICH	RIFF	OINK	YIRK	
HUG	LICH	TIFF	PINK	IRKS	

ISH	**JAP**	JOTS	KAYO	**KIS**
BISH	JAPE	**JOW**	KAYS	SKIS
DISH	JAPS	JOWL	**KEA**	KISH
EISH	**JAR**	JOWS	KEAS	KISS
FISH	AJAR	**JOY**	**KEB**	KIST
HISH	JARK	JOYS	KEBS	**KIT**
KISH	JARL	**JUD**	**KED**	SKIT
NISH	JARP	JUDO	AKED	KITE
PISH	JARS	JUDS	EKED	KITH
WISH	**JAW**	JUDY	KEDS	KITS
ISM	JAWS	**JUG**	**KEF**	**KOA**
GISM	**JAY**	JUGA	KEFS	KOAN
JISM	JAYS	JUGS	**KEG**	KOAP
ISMS	**JEE**	**JUN**	SKEG	KOAS
ISO	AJEE	JUNK	KEGS	**KOB**
MISO	JEED	**JUS**	**KEN**	KOBO
PISO	JEEL	GJUS	SKEN	KOBS
ISOS	JEEP	JUST	KENO	**KOI**
ITA	JEER	**JUT**	KENS	KOIS
DITA	JEES	JUTE	KENT	**KON**
PITA	JEEZ	JUTS	**KEP**	IKON
VITA	**JET**	**KAB**	SKEP	KOND
ITAS	JETE	KABS	KEPI	KONK
ITS	JETS	**KAE**	KEPS	KONS
AITS	**JEU**	KAED	KEPT	**KOP**
BITS	JEUX	KAES	**KET**	KOPH
CITS	**JEW**	**KAF**	SKET	KOPS
DITS	JEWS	KAFS	KETA	**KOR**
FITS	**JIB**	**KAI**	KETE	KORA
GITS	JIBB	KAID	KETO	KORE
HITS	JIBE	KAIE	KETS	KORO
KITS	JIBS	KAIF	**KEV**	KORS
LITS	**JIG**	KAIK	KEYS	KORU
NITS	JIGS	KAIL	**KHI**	**KOS**
PITS	**JIN**	KAIM	KHIS	KOSS
RITS	DJIN	KAIN	**KID**	**KOW**
SITS	JINK	KAIS	SKID	KOWS
TITS	JINN	**KAK**	KIDS	**KUE**
WITS	JINS	KAKA	**KIF**	KUEH
ZITS	JINX	KAKI	KIFF	KUES
IVY	**JIZ**	KAKS	KIFS	**KYE**
JIVY	JIZZ	**KAM**	**KIN**	KYES
TIVY	**JOB**	KAMA	AKIN	**KYU**
IWI	JOBE	KAME	SKIN	KYUS
KIWI	JOBS	KAMI	KINA	**LAB**
IWIS	**JOE**	**KAS**	KIND	BLAB
JAB	SJOE	OKAS	KINE	FLAB
JABS	JOES	SKAS	KING	SLAB
JAG	JOEY	**KAT**	KINK	LABS
JAGA	**JOG**	IKAT	KINO	**LAC**
JAGG	JOGS	SKAT	KINS	LACE
JAGS	**JOL**	KATA	**KIP**	LACK
JAI	JOLE	KATI	SKIP	LACS
JAIL	JOLL	KATS	KIPE	LACY
JAK	JOLS	**KAW**	KIPP	**LAD**
JAKE	JOLT	SKAW	KIPS	BLAD
JAKS	**JOR**	KAWA	**KIR**	CLAD
JAM	JORS	KAWS	KIRK	GLAD
JAMB	**JOT**	**KAY**	KIRN	LADE
JAMS	JOTA	OKAY	KIRS	LADS

LADY	CLAW	LEKE	**LIG**	LOOK
LAG	FLAW	LEKS	LIGS	LOOM
BLAG	SLAW	LEKU	**LIN**	LOON
CLAG	LAWK	**LEP**	BLIN	LOOP
FLAG	LAWN	LEPS	LIND	LOOR
SLAG	LAWS	LEPT	LINE	LOOS
LAGS	**LAX**	**LES**	LING	LOOT
LAH	FLAX	ALES	LINK	**LOP**
BLAH	**LAY**	OLES	LINN	CLOP
LAHS	ALAY	ULES	LINO	FLOP
LAM	BLAY	LESS	LINS	GLOP
BLAM	CLAY	LEST	LINT	PLOP
CLAM	FLAY	**LET**	LINY	SLOP
FLAM	PLAY	BLET	**LIP**	LOPE
GLAM	SLAY	LETS	BLIP	LOPS
SLAM	LAYS	**LEU**	CLIP	**LOR**
LAMA	**LEA**	LEUD	FLIP	FLOR
LAMB	FLEA	**LEV**	SLIP	LORD
LAME	ILEA	LEVA	LIPA	LORE
LAMP	OLEA	LEVE	LIPE	LORN
LAMS	PLEA	LEVO	LIPO	LORY
LAP	LEAD	LEVY	LIPS	**LOS**
ALAP	LEAF	**LEW**	**LIS**	LOSE
CLAP	LEAK	ALEW	LISK	LOSH
FLAP	LEAL	BLEW	LISP	LOSS
KLAP	LEAM	CLEW	LIST	LOST
PLAP	LEAN	FLEW	**LIT**	**LOT**
SLAP	LEAP	PLEW	ALIT	BLOT
LAPS	LEAR	SLEW	FLIT	CLOT
LAR	LEAS	LEWD	GLIT	PLOT
ALAR	LEAT	**LEX**	SLIT	SLOT
LARD	**LED**	FLEX	LITE	LOTA
LARE	BLED	ILEX	LITH	LOTE
LARI	FLED	PLEX	LITS	LOTH
LARK	GLED	ULEX	LITU	LOTI
LARN	PLED	**LEY**	**LOB**	LOTO
LARS	SLED	BLEY	BLOB	LOTS
LAS	**LEE**	FLEY	GLOB	**LOU**
ALAS	ALEE	GLEY	SLOB	CLOU
LASE	BLEE	SLEY	LOBE	LOUD
LASH	FLEE	LEYS	LOBI	LOUN
LASS	GLEE	**LEZ**	LOBO	LOUP
LAST	SLEE	LEZZ	LOBS	LOUR
LAT	LEED	**LIB**	**LOD**	LOUS
BLAT	LEEK	GLIB	ALOD	LOUT
CLAT	LEEP	LIBS	CLOD	**LOW**
FLAT	LEER	**LID**	PLOD	ALOW
PLAT	LEES	GLID	LODE	BLOW
SLAT	LEET	OLID	LODS	CLOW
LATE	**LEG**	SLID	**LOG**	FLOW
LATH	CLEG	LIDO	BLOG	GLOW
LATI	FLEG	LIDS	CLOG	PLOW
LATS	GLEG	**LIE**	FLOG	SLOW
LATU	LEGS	PLIE	SLOG	LOWE
LAV	**LEI**	LIED	LOGE	LOWN
LAVA	GLEI	LIEF	LOGO	LOWP
LAVE	VLEI	LIEN	LOGS	LOWS
LAVS	LEIR	LIER	LOGY	LOWT
LAW	LEIS	LIES	**LOO**	**LOY**
BLAW	**LEK**	LIEU	LOOF	CLOY

PLOY	MALA	**MED**	MICS	**MOE**
LOYS	MALE	MEDS	**MID**	MOER
LUD	MALI	**MEE**	AMID	MOES
LUDE	MALL	SMEE	IMID	**MOG**
LUDO	MALM	MEED	MIDI	SMOG
LUDS	MALS	MEEK	MIDS	MOGS
LUG	MALT	MEER	**MIG**	**MOI**
GLUG	**MAM**	MEES	MIGG	MOIL
PLUG	IMAM	MEET	MIGS	MOIT
SLUG	MAMA	**MEG**	**MIL**	**MOL**
LUGE	MAMS	MEGA	MILD	MOLA
LUGS	**MAN**	MEGS	MILE	MOLD
LUM	MANA	**MEL**	MILK	MOLE
ALUM	MAND	MELA	MILL	MOLL
GLUM	MANE	MELD	MILO	MOLS
PLUM	MANG	MELL	MILS	MOLT
SLUM	MANI	MELS	MILT	MOLY
LUMA	MANO	MELT	**MIM**	**MOM**
LUMP	MANS	**MEM**	MIME	MOME
LUMS	MANY	MEME	**MIR**	MOMI
LUR	**MAP**	MEMO	AMIR	MOMS
BLUR	MAPS	MEMS	EMIR	**MON**
SLUR	**MAR**	**MEN**	SMIR	MONA
LURE	MARA	AMEN	MIRE	MONG
LURK	MARC	OMEN	MIRI	MONK
LURS	MARD	MEND	MIRK	MONO
LUV	MARE	MENE	MIRO	MONS
LUVS	MARG	MENG	MIRS	MONY
LUX	MARK	MENO	MIRV	**MOO**
FLUX	MARL	MENT	MIRY	MOOD
LUXE	MARM	MENU	**MIS**	MOOI
LYE	MARS	**MES**	AMIS	MOOK
LYES	MART	EMES	MISE	MOOL
LYM	MARY	**MEN**	MISO	MOON
LYME	**MAS**	MESA	MISS	MOOP
LYMS	AMAS	MESE	MIST	MOOR
MAA	MASA	MESH	**MIX**	MOOS
MAAR	MASE	MESS	MIXT	MOOT
MAAS	MASH	**MET**	MIXY	**MOP**
MAC	MASK	META	**MIZ**	MOPE
MACE	MASS	METE	MIZZ	MOPS
MACH	MAST	METH	**MNA**	MOPY
MACK	MASU	METS	MNAS	**MOR**
MACS	**MAT**	**MEU**	**MOA**	MORA
MAD	MATE	EMEU	MOAI	MORE
MADE	MATH	**MEW**	MOAN	MORN
MADS	MATS	SMEW	MOAS	MORS
MAE	MATT	MEWL	MOAT	MORT
MAES	MATY	MEWS	**MOB**	**MOS**
MAG	**MAW**	**MHO**	MOBE	EMOS
MAGE	MAWK	MHOS	MOBS	MOSE
MAGG	MAWN	**MIB**	MOBY	MOSH
MAGI	MAWR	MIBS	**MOC**	MOSK
MAGS	MAWS	**MIC**	MOCH	MOSS
MAK	**MAX**	EMIC	MOCK	MOST
MAKE	MAXI	MICA	MOCS	**MOT**
MAKI	**MAY**	MICE	**MOD**	MOTE
MAKO	MAYA	MICH	MODE	MOTH
MAKS	MAYO	MICK	MODI	MOTI
MAL	MAYS	MICO	MODS	MOTS

MOTT	NAGS	**NID**	NOOP	OAKY
MOTU	**NAM**	NIDE	**NOR**	**OAR**
MOU	NAME	NIDI	NORI	BOAR
MOUE	NAMS	NIDS	NORK	HOAR
MOUP	NAMU	**NIE**	NORM	ROAR
MOUS	**NAN**	ONIE	**NOS**	SOAR
MOW	ANAN	NIED	ONOS	VOAR
MOWA	NANA	NIEF	NOSE	OARS
MOWN	NANE	NIES	NOSH	OARY
MOWS	NANS	**NIL**	NOSY	**OAT**
MOY	**NAP**	ANIL	**NOT**	BOAT
MOYA	KNAP	NILL	KNOT	COAT
MOYL	SNAP	NILS	SNOT	DOAT
MOYS	NAPA	**NIM**	NOTA	GOAT
MOZ	NAPE	NIMB	NOTE	MOAT
MOZE	NAPS	NIMS	NOTT	OATH
MOZO	**NAS**	**NIP**	**NOW**	OATS
MOZZ	ANAS	SNIP	ANOW	**OBA**
MUD	MNAS	NIPA	ENOW	BOBA
MUDS	**NAT**	NIPS	GNOW	SOBA
MUG	GNAT	**NIS**	KNOW	OBAS
SMUG	NATS	ANIS	SNOW	**OBE**
MUGG	**NAW**	UNIS	NOWL	JOBE
MUGS	GNAW	NISH	NOWN	LOBE
MUM	SNAW	NISI	NOWS	MOBE
MUMM	**NAY**	**NIT**	NOWT	ROBE
MUMP	NAYS	KNIT	NOWY	OBES
MUMS	**NEB**	SNIT	**NOY**	OBEY
MUMU	SNEB	UNIT	NOYS	**OBI**
MUN	NEBS	NITE	**NUB**	LOBI
MUNG	**NED**	NITS	KNUB	OBIA
MUNI	SNED	**NIX**	SNUB	OBIS
MUNS	NEDS	NIXE	NUBS	OBIT
MUNT	**NEE**	NIXY	**NUN**	**OBO**
MUS	KNEE	**NOB**	NUNS	GOBO
AMUS	SNEE	KNOB	**NUR**	HOBO
EMUS	NEED	SNOB	KNUR	KOBO
MUSE	NEEM	NOBS	NURD	LOBO
MUSH	NEEP	**NOD**	NURL	ZOBO
MUSK	**NEF**	SNOD	NURR	OBOE
MUSO	NEFS	NODE	NURS	OBOL
MUSS	**NEG**	NODI	**NUS**	OBOS
MUST	NEGS	NODS	ANUS	**OBS**
MUT	**NEK**	**NOG**	GNUS	BOBS
SMUT	NEKS	SNOG	ONUS	COBS
MUTE	**NEP**	NOGG	**NUT**	DOBS
MUTI	NEPS	NOGS	KNUT	FOBS
MUTS	**NET**	**NOM**	NUTS	GOBS
MUTT	NETE	NOMA	**NYE**	HOBS
MYC	NETS	NOME	SNYE	JOBS
MYCS	NETT	NOMS	NYED	KOBS
NAB	**NEW**	**NON**	NYES	LOBS
SNAB	ANEW	ANON	**OAF**	MOBS
NABE	ENEW	NONA	GOAF	NOBS
NABK	KNEW	NONE	LOAF	ROBS
NABS	NEWS	NONG	OAFS	SOBS
NAG	NEWT	NONI	**OAK**	YOBS
KNAG	**NIB**	**NOO**	BOAK	**OCA**
SNAG	SNIB	NOOK	SOAK	COCA
NAGA	NIBS	NOON	OAKS	LOCA

SOCA	OFFS	MOLD	EONS	OONS
OCAS	**OFT**	SOLD	FONS	OONT
OCH	COFT	TOLD	GONS	**OOP**
COCH	LOFT	WOLD	HONS	COOP
LOCH	SOFT	YOLD	IONS	GOOP
MOCH	TOFT	OLDS	KONS	HOOP
ROCH	**OHM**	OLDY	MONS	LOOP
OCHE	OHMS	**OLE**	OONS	MOOP
ODA	**OHO**	BOLE	PONS	NOOP
CODA	BOHO	COLE	SONS	POOP
SODA	COHO	DOLE	TONS	ROOP
ODAH	SOHO	GOLE	WONS	SOOP
ODAL	TOHO	HOLE	ONST	YOOP
ODAS	OHOS	JOLE	**ONY**	OOPS
ODD	**OHS**	MOLE	BONY	**OOR**
ODDS	BOHS	NOLE	CONY	BOOR
ODE	DOHS	POLE	MONY	DOOR
BODE	FOHS	ROLE	PONY	GOOR
CODE	HOHS	SOLE	TONY	LOOR
LODE	OOHS	TOLE	ONYX	MOOR
MODE	SOHS	VOLE	**OOF**	POOR
NODE	**OIK**	OLEA	COOF	**OOS**
RODE	HOIK	OLEO	GOOF	BOOS
YODE	OIKS	OLES	HOOF	COOS
ODEA	**OIL**	**OLM**	LOOF	DOOS
ODES	BOIL	HOLM	POOF	GOOS
ODS	COIL	OLMS	ROOF	LOOS
BODS	FOIL	**OMS**	WOOF	MOOS
CODS	MOIL	COMS	YOOF	POOS
DODS	NOIL	DOMS	OOFS	ROOS
GODS	ROIL	HOMS	OOFY	WOOS
HODS	SOIL	MOMS	**OOH**	ZOOS
LODS	TOIL	NOMS	BOOH	OOSE
MODS	OILS	OOMS	POOH	OOSY
NODS	OILY	POMS	OOHS	**OOT**
PODS	**OKA**	ROMS	**OOM**	BOOT
RODS	HOKA	SOMS	BOOM	COOT
SODS	OKAS	TOMS	COOM	FOOT
TODS	OKAY	**ONE**	DOOM	HOOT
YODS	**OKE**	BONE	LOOM	LOOT
ODSO	BOKE	CONE	ROOM	MOOT
OES	COKE	DONE	SOOM	POOT
DOES	HOKE	FONE	TOOM	ROOT
FOES	JOKE	GONE	ZOOM	SOOT
GOES	LOKE	HONE	OOMS	TOOT
HOES	MOKE	LONE	**OON**	WOOT
JOES	POKE	NONE	BOON	ZOOT
MOES	ROKE	PONE	COON	OOTS
NOES	SOKE	RONE	DOON	**OPE**
ROES	TOKE	SONE	GOON	COPE
TOES	WOKE	TONE	HOON	DOPE
VOES	YOKE	ZONE	LOON	HOPE
WOES	OKEH	ONER	MOON	LOPE
OFF	OKES	ONES	NOON	MOPE
BOFF	**OLD**	**ONO**	POON	NOPE
COFF	BOLD	MONO	ROON	POPE
DOFF	COLD	ONOS	SOON	ROPE
GOFF	FOLD	**ONS**	TOON	TOPE
KOFF	GOLD	CONS	WOON	OPED
TOFF	HOLD	DONS	ZOON	OPEN

Hooks arranged by hook word

OPES	TORE	MOUP	YOWL	PALL
OPS	WORE	NOUP	OWLS	PALM
BOPS	YORE	ROUP	OWLY	PALP
COPS	ORES	SOUP	**OWN**	PALS
DOPS	**ORF**	OUPA	DOWN	PALY
FOPS	CORF	OUPH	GOWN	**PAM**
HOPS	ORFE	OUPS	LOWN	SPAM
KOPS	ORFS	**OUR**	MOWN	PAMS
LOPS	**ORS**	COUR	NOWN	**PAN**
MOPS	BORS	DOUR	POWN	SPAN
OOPS	CORS	FOUR	SOWN	PAND
POPS	DORS	HOUR	TOWN	PANE
SOPS	HORS	JOUR	OWNS	PANG
TOPS	JORS	LOUR	**OWT**	PANS
WOPS	KORS	POUR	DOWT	PANT
OPT	MORS	SOUR	LOWT	**PAP**
OPTS	TORS	TOUR	NOWT	PAPA
ORA	VORS	YOUR	ROWT	PAPE
BORA	**ORT**	OURN	TOWT	PAPS
FORA	BORT	OURS	OWTS	**PAR**
GORA	DORT	**OUS**	**OXY**	SPAR
HORA	FORT	FOUS	BOXY	PARA
KORA	MORT	LOUS	COXY	PARD
MORA	PORT	MOUS	DOXY	PARE
SORA	RORT	NOUS	FOXY	PARK
TORA	SORT	SOUS	POXY	PARP
ORAD	TORT	YOUS	**OYE**	PARR
ORAL	WORT	OUST	OYER	PARS
ORB	ORTS	**OUT**	OYES	PART
DORB	**OSE**	BOUT	OYEZ	**PAS**
FORB	COSE	DOUT	**OYS**	SPAS
SORB	DOSE	GOUT	BOYS	UPAS
ORBS	HOSE	HOUT	COYS	PASE
ORBY	LOSE	LOUT	DOYS	PASH
ORC	MOSE	NOUT	FOYS	PASS
TORC	NOSE	POUT	GOYS	PAST
ORCA	OOSE	ROUT	HOYS	**PAT**
ORCS	POSE	SOUT	JOYS	SPAT
ORD	ROSE	TOUT	LOYS	PATE
BORD	TOSE	OUTS	MOYS	PATH
CORD	OSES	**OVA**	NOYS	PATS
FORD	**OUD**	NOVA	SOYS	PATU
LORD	FOUD	OVAL	TOYS	PATY
SORD	LOUD	**OWE**	**PAC**	**PAV**
WORD	OUDS	HOWE	PACA	PAVE
ORDO	**OUK**	LOWE	PACE	PAVS
ORDS	DOUK	YOWE	PACK	**PAW**
ORE	GOUK	OWED	PACO	SPAW
BORE	JOUK	OWER	PACS	PAWA
CORE	POUK	OWES	PACT	PAWK
DORE	SOUK	**OWL**	PACY	PAWL
FORE	TOUK	BOWL	**PAD**	PAWN
GORE	YOUK	COWL	PADI	PAWS
HORE	ZOUK	DOWL	PADS	**PAY**
KORE	OUKS	FOWL	**PAH**	APAY
LORE	**OUP**	GOWL	OPAH	SPAY
MORE	COUP	HOWL	PAHS	PAYS
PORE	DOUP	JOWL	**PAL**	**PEA**
RORE	LOUP	NOWL	OPAL	PEAG
SORE		SOWL	PALE	PEAK

PEAL	PEWS	**PIX**	**POZ**	**PUR**
PEAN	**PHI**	PIXY	POZZ	SPUR
PEAR	PHIS	**PLU**	**PRE**	PURE
PEAS	PHIZ	PLUE	PREE	PURI
PEAT	**PHO**	PLUG	PREM	PURL
PEC	PHOH	PLUM	PREP	PURR
SPEC	PHON	PLUS	PREX	PURS
PECH	PHOS	**POA**	PREY	**PUS**
PECK	PHOT	POAS	PREZ	OPUS
PECS	**PIA**	**POD**	**PRO**	PUSH
PED	PIAL	APOD	PROA	PUSS
APED	PIAN	SPOD	PROB	**PUT**
OPED	PIAS	PODS	PROD	PUTS
SPED	**PIC**	**POI**	PROF	PUTT
PEDS	EPIC	POIS	PROG	PUTZ
PEE	SPIC	**POL**	PROM	**PUY**
EPEE	PICA	POLE	PROO	PUYS
PEED	PICE	POLK	PROP	**PYA**
PEEK	PICK	POLL	PROS	PYAS
PEEL	PICS	POLO	PROW	PYAT
PEEN	**PIE**	POLS	**PRY**	**PYE**
PEEP	SPIE	POLT	SPRY	PYES
PEER	PIED	POLY	PRYS	PYET
PEES	PIER	**POM**	**PSI**	**QAT**
PEG	PIES	POME	PSIS	QATS
PEGH	PIET	POMO	**PUB**	**QUA**
PEGS	**PIG**	POMP	PUBE	AQUA
PEH	PIGS	POMS	PUBS	QUAD
PEHS	**PIN**	**POO**	**PUD**	QUAG
PEN	SPIN	POOD	SPUD	QUAI
OPEN	PINA	POOF	PUDS	QUAT
PEND	PINE	POOH	PUDU	QUAY
PENE	PING	POOK	**PUG**	**RAD**
PENI	PINK	POOL	SPUG	BRAD
PENK	PINS	POON	PUGH	DRAD
PENS	PINT	POOP	PUGS	GRAD
PENT	PINY	POOR	**PUH**	ORAD
PEP	**PIP**	POOS	PUHA	PRAD
PEPO	PIPA	POOT	**PUL**	TRAD
PEPS	PIPE	**POP**	PULA	RADE
PER	PIPI	POPE	PULE	RADS
APER	PIPS	POPS	PULI	**RAG**
PERE	PIPY	**POS**	PULK	BRAG
PERI	**PIR**	APOS	PULL	CRAG
PERK	PIRL	EPOS	PULP	DRAG
PERM	PIRN	POSE	PULS	FRAG
PERN	PIRS	POSH	PULU	RAGA
PERP	**PIS**	POSS	PULY	RAGE
PERT	PISE	POST	**PUN**	RAGG
PERV	PISH	POSY	SPUN	RAGI
PES	PISO	**POT**	PUNA	RAGS
APES	PISS	SPOT	PUNG	**RAH**
OPES	**PIT**	POTE	PUNK	RAHS
PESO	SPIT	POTS	PUNS	**RAI**
PEST	PITA	POTT	PUNT	RAIA
PET	PITH	**POW**	PUNY	RAID
SPET	PITS	POWN	**PUP**	RAIK
PETS	PITY	POWS	PUPA	RAIL
PEW	**PIU**	**POX**	PUPS	RAIN
SPEW	PIUM	POXY	PUPU	RAIS

RAIT	CRAY	GREN	GRID	ROBE
RAJ	DRAY	WREN	IRID	ROBS
RAJA	FRAY	REND	RIDE	**ROC**
RAM	GRAY	RENK	RIDS	CROC
CRAM	PRAY	RENS	**RIF**	ROCH
DRAM	TRAY	RENT	RIFE	ROCK
GRAM	RAYA	RENY	RIFF	ROCS
PRAM	RAYS	**REO**	RIFS	**ROD**
TRAM	**REB**	REOS	RIFT	BROD
RAMI	REBS	**REP**	**RIG**	PROD
RAMP	**REC**	PREP	BRIG	TROD
RAMS	RECK	REPO	FRIG	RODE
RAN	RECS	REPP	GRIG	RODS
BRAN	**RED**	REPS	PRIG	**ROE**
CRAN	ARED	**RES**	TRIG	FROE
GRAN	BRED	ARES	RIGG	ROED
RANA	CRED	ERES	RIGS	ROES
RAND	ERED	IRES	**RIM**	**ROK**
RANG	IRED	ORES	BRIM	GROK
RANI	REDD	TRES	CRIM	ROKE
RANK	REDE	URES	GRIM	ROKS
RANT	REDO	RESH	PRIM	ROKY
RAP	REDS	REST	TRIM	**ROM**
CRAP	**REE**	**RET**	RIMA	FROM
DRAP	BREE	ARET	RIME	PROM
FRAP	CREE	FRET	RIMS	ROMA
TRAP	DREE	TRET	RIMU	ROMP
WRAP	FREE	RETE	RIMY	ROMS
RAPE	GREE	RETS	**RIN**	**ROO**
RAPS	PREE	**REV**	BRIN	BROO
RAPT	TREE	EREV	GRIN	PROO
RAS	REED	REVS	TRIN	ROOD
BRAS	REEF	**REW**	RIND	ROOF
ERAS	REEK	AREW	RINE	ROOK
FRAS	REEL	BREW	RING	ROOM
RASE	REEN	CREW	RINK	ROON
RASH	REES	DREW	RINS	ROOP
RASP	**REF**	GREW	**RIP**	ROOS
RAST	TREF	TREW	DRIP	ROOT
RAT	REFS	REWS	GRIP	**ROT**
BRAT	REFT	**REX**	TRIP	GROT
DRAT	**REG**	GREX	RIPE	TROT
FRAT	AREG	PREX	RIPP	VROT
GRAT	DREG	**REZ**	RIPS	ROTA
PRAT	REGO	PREZ	RIPT	ROTE
TRAT	REGS	TREZ	**RIT**	ROTI
RATA	**REH**	**RHO**	BRIT	ROTL
RATE	REHS	RHOS	CRIT	ROTO
RATH	**REI**	**RIA**	FRIT	ROTS
RATO	BREI	ARIA	GRIT	**ROW**
RATS	REIF	RIAL	WRIT	AROW
RATU	REIK	RIAS	RITE	BROW
RAW	REIN	**RIB**	RITS	CROW
BRAW	REIS	CRIB	RITT	DROW
CRAW	**REM**	DRIB	RITZ	FROW
DRAW	CREM	FRIB	**RIZ**	GROW
RAWN	PREM	RIBA	FRIZ	PROW
RAWS	REMS	RIBS	RIZA	TROW
RAY	**REN**	**RID**	**ROB**	VROW
BRAY	BREN	ARID	PROB	ROWS

ROWT	SADO	SAYS	SEWS	ISIT
RUB	SADS	**SEA**	**SEX**	SITE
DRUB	**SAG**	ASEA	SEXT	SITH
GRUB	SAGA	SEAL	SEXY	SITS
RUBE	SAGE	SEAM	**SEV**	SITZ
RUBS	SAGO	SEAN	SEYS	**SKA**
RUBY	SAGS	SEAR	**SHA**	SKAG
RUC	SAGY	SEAS	SHAD	SKAS
RUCK	**SAI**	SEAT	SHAG	SKAT
RUCS	SAIC	**SEC**	SHAH	SKAW
RUD	SAID	SECH	SHAM	**SKI**
CRUD	SAIL	SECO	SHAN	SKID
RUDD	SAIM	SECS	SHAT	SKIM
RUDE	SAIN	SECT	SHAW	SKIN
RUDS	SAIR	**SED**	SHAY	SKIO
RUE	SAIS	USED	**SHE**	SKIP
CRUE	**SAL**	**SEE**	SHEA	SKIS
GRUE	SALE	SEED	SHED	SKIT
TRUE	SALL	SEEK	SHES	**SKY**
RUED	SALP	SEEL	SHET	ESKY
RUER	SALS	SEEM	SHEW	SKYF
RUES	SALT	SEEN	**SHY**	SKYR
RUG	**SAM**	SEEP	ASHY	**SNY**
DRUG	SAMA	SEER	**SIB**	SNYE
FRUG	SAME	SEES	SIBB	**SOB**
TRUG	SAMP	**SEG**	SIBS	SOBA
RUGA	SAMS	SEGO	**SIC**	SOBS
RUGS	**SAN**	SEGS	SICE	**SOC**
RUM	SAND	**SEI**	SICH	SOCA
ARUM	SANE	SEIF	SICK	SOCK
DRUM	SANG	SEIK	SICS	SOCS
GRUM	SANK	SEIL	**SIF**	**SOD**
RUME	SANS	SEIR	SIFT	SODA
RUMP	SANT	SEIS	**SIK**	SODS
RUMS	**SAP**	**SEL**	SIKA	**SOG**
RUN	SAPS	SELD	SIKE	SOGS
RUND	**SAR**	SELE	**SIM**	**SOH**
RUNE	ASAR	SELF	SIMA	SOHO
RUNG	KSAR	SELL	SIMI	SOHS
RUNS	OSAR	SELS	SIMP	**SOL**
RUNT	TSAR	**SEN**	SIMS	SOLA
RUT	SARD	SENA	**SIN**	SOLD
BRUT	SARI	SEND	SIND	SOLE
RUTH	SARK	SENE	SINE	SOLI
RUTS	SARS	SENS	SING	SOLO
RYA	**SAT**	SENT	SINH	SOLS
RYAL	SATE	**SER**	SINK	**SOM**
RYAS	SATI	SERA	SINS	SOMA
RYE	**SAU**	SERE	**SIP**	SOME
TRYE	SAUL	SERF	SIPE	SOMS
RYES	SAUT	SERK	SIPS	SOMY
SAB	**SAV**	SERR	**SIR**	**SON**
SABE	SAVE	SERS	SIRE	SONE
SABS	SAVS	**SET**	SIRI	SONG
SAC	**SAW**	SETA	SIRS	SONS
SACK	SAWN	SETS	**SIS**	**SOP**
SACS	SAWS	SETT	PSIS	SOPH
SAD	**SAX**	**SEW**	SISS	SOPS
SADE	SAXE	SEWN	SIST	**SOS**
SADI	**SAY**		**SIT**	DSOS

Hooks arranged by hook word

ISOS	SUMO	**TAN**	TEAL	THEW	
SOSS	SUMP	TANA	TEAM	THEY	
SOT	SUMS	TANE	TEAR	**THO**	
SOTH	SUMY	TANG	TEAS	THON	
SOTS	**SUN**	TANH	TEAT	THOU	
SOU	SUNG	TANK	**TEC**	**TIC**	
SOUK	SUNK	TANS	TECH	ETIC	
SOUL	SUNN	**TAO**	TECS	OTIC	
SOUM	SUNS	TAOS	**TED**	TICE	
SOUP	**SUP**	**TAP**	STED	TICH	
SOUR	SUPE	ATAP	TEDS	TICK	
SOUS	SUPS	STAP	TEDY	TICS	
SOUT	**SUQ**	TAPA	**TEE**	**TID**	
SOV	SUQS	TAPE	TEED	TIDE	
SOVS	**SUR**	TAPS	TEEK	TIDS	
SOW	SURA	TAPU	TEEL	TIDY	
SOWF	SURD	**TAR**	TEEM	**TIE**	
SOWL	SURE	STAR	TEEN	STIE	
SOWM	SURF	TARA	TEER	TIED	
SOWN	**SUS**	TARE	TEES	TIER	
SOWP	SUSS	TARN	**TEF**	TIES	
SOWS	SUSU	TARO	TEFF	**TIG**	
SOY	**SYE**	TARP	TEFS	TIGE	
SOYA	SYED	TARS	**TEG**	TIGS	
SOYS	SYEN	TART	TEGG	**TIL**	
SPA	SYES	**TAS**	TEGS	TILE	
SPAE	**SYN**	ETAS	TEGU	TILL	
SPAG	SYNC	ITAS	**TEL**	TILS	
SPAM	SYND	UTAS	TELA	TILT	
SPAN	SYNE	TASH	TELD	**TIN**	
SPAR	**TAB**	TASK	TELE	TIND	
SPAS	STAB	TASS	TELL	TINE	
SPAT	TABI	**TAT**	TELS	TING	
SPAW	TABS	ETAT	TELT	TINK	
SPAY	TABU	STAT	**TEN**	TINS	
SPAZ	**TAD**	TATE	ETEN	TINT	
SPY	TADS	TATH	STEN	TINY	
ESPY	**TAE**	TATS	TEND	**TIP**	
SRI	TAED	TATT	TENE	TIPI	
SRIS	TAEL	TATU	TENS	TIPS	
STY	TAES	**TAU**	TENT	TIPT	
STYE	**TAG**	TAUS	**TES**	**TIS**	
SUB	STAG	TAUT	ATES	UTIS	
SUBA	TAGS	**TAV**	UTES	**TIT**	
SUBS	**TAI**	TAVA	TEST	TITE	
SUD	TAIG	TAVS	**TET**	TITI	
SUDD	TAIL	**TAW**	STET	TITS	
SUDS	TAIN	STAW	TETE	**TOC**	
SUE	TAIS	TAWA	TETH	ATOC	
SUED	TAIT	TAWS	TETS	TOCK	
SUER	**TAK**	TAWT	**TEW**	TOCO	
SUES	TAKA	**TAX**	STEW	TOCS	
SUET	TAKE	TAXA	TEWS	**TOD**	
SUI	TAKI	TAXI	**TEX**	TODS	
SUID	TAKS	**TAY**	TEXT	TODY	
SUIT	TAKY	STAY	**THE**	**TOE**	
SUK	**TAM**	TAYS	ETHE	TOEA	
SUKH	TAME		THEE	TOED	
SUKS	TAMP	**TEA**	THEM	TOES	
SUM	TAMS	TEAD	THEN	TOEY	
		TEAK			

TOG	STUB	RUDS	GUMP	IURE
TOGA	TUBA	SUDS	HUMP	JURE
TOGE	TUBE	WUDS	JUMP	LURE
TOGS	TUBS	**UEY**	LUMP	MURE
TOM	**TUG**	QUEY	MUMP	PURE
ATOM	TUGS	UEYS	PUMP	SURE
TOMB	**TUI**	**UFO**	RUMP	UREA
TOME	ETUI	BUFO	SUMP	URES
TOMO	PTUI	UFOS	TUMP	**URN**
TOMS	TUIS	**UGH**	YUMP	BURN
TON	**TUM**	EUGH	UMPH	CURN
TONE	STUM	PUGH	UMPS	DURN
TONG	TUMP	SUGH	UMPY	GURN
TONK	TUMS	VUGH	**UMU**	OURN
TONS	**TUN**	UGHS	MUMU	TURN
TONY	STUN	**UGS**	**UNI**	URNS
TOO	TUNA	BUGS	MUNI	**URP**
TOOK	TUND	DUGS	UNIS	BURP
TOOL	TUNE	FUGS	UNIT	RURP
TOOM	TUNG	HUGS	**UNS**	URPS
TOON	TUNS	JUGS	BUNS	**USE**
TOOT	TUNY	LUGS	DUNS	FUSE
TOP	**TUP**	MUGS	FUNS	MUSE
ATOP	TUPS	PUGS	GUNS	RUSE
STOP	**TUT**	RUGS	HUNS	USED
TOPE	TUTS	TUGS	MUNS	USER
TOPH	TUTU	VUGS	NUNS	USES
TOPI	**TWA**	YUGS	PUNS	**UTA**
TOPO	TWAE	**UKE**	RUNS	KUTA
TOPS	TWAL	BUKE	SUNS	UTAS
TOR	TWAS	CUKE	TUNS	**UTE**
TORA	TWAT	DUKE	**UPO**	BUTE
TORC	TWAY	JUKE	UPON	CUTE
TORE	**TWO**	LUKE	**UPS**	JUTE
TORI	TWOS	NUKE	CUPS	LUTE
TORN	**TYE**	PUKE	DUPS	MUTE
TORO	STYE	YUKE	GUPS	UTES
TORR	TYED	UKES	HUPS	**UTS**
TORS	TYEE	**ULE**	OUPS	BUTS
TORT	TYER	DULE	PUPS	CUTS
TORY	TYES	GULE	SUPS	GUTS
TOT	**TYG**	HULE	TUPS	HUTS
STOT	TYGS	MULE	YUPS	JUTS
TOTE	**UDO**	PULE	UPSY	MUTS
TOTS	BUDO	RULE	**URB**	NUTS
TOW	JUDO	TULE	BURB	OUTS
STOW	KUDO	YULE	CURB	PUTS
TOWN	LUDO	ULES	URBS	RUTS
TOWS	UDON	ULEX	**URD**	TUTS
TOWT	UDOS	**ULU**	BURD	**UTU**
TOWY	**UDS**	LULU	CURD	KUTU
TOY	BUDS	PULU	NURD	TUTU
TOYO	CUDS	SULU	SURD	UTUS
TOYS	DUDS	ZULU	TURD	**UVA**
TRY	FUDS	ULUS	URDE	UVAE
TRYE	JUDS	**UMM**	URDS	UVAS
TRYP	LUDS	MUMM	URDY	**VAC**
TSK	MUDS	**UMP**	**URE**	VACS
TSKS	OUDS	BUMP	CURE	**VAE**
TUB	PUDS	DUMP	DURE	UVAE

Hooks arranged by hook word

VAES	**VIM**	HWAN	WEEL	WITE
VAG	VIMS	SWAN	WEEM	WITH
VAGI	**VIN**	WAND	WEEN	WITS
VAGS	VINA	WANE	WEEP	**WIZ**
VAN	VINE	WANG	WEER	SWIZ
VANE	VINO	WANK	WEES	**WOE**
VANG	VINS	WANS	WEET	WOES
VANS	VINT	WANT	**WEM**	**WOF**
VANT	VINY	WANY	WEMB	WOFS
VAR	**VIS**	**WAP**	WEMS	**WOG**
VARA	VISA	SWAP	**WEN**	WOGS
VARE	VISE	WAPS	WENA	**WOK**
VARS	**VOE**	**WAR**	WEND	WOKE
VARY	EVOE	WARB	WENS	WOKS
VAS	VOES	WARD	WENT	**WON**
AVAS	**VOL**	WARE	**WET**	WONK
KVAS	VOLA	WARK	WETA	WONS
UVAS	VOLE	WARM	WETS	WONT
VASA	VOLK	WARN	**WEX**	**WOO**
VASE	VOLS	WARP	WEXE	WOOD
VAST	VOLT	WARS	**WEY**	WOOF
VAT	**VOR**	WART	SWEY	WOOL
VATS	VORS	WARY	WEYS	WOON
VATU	**VOW**	**WAS**	**WHA**	WOOS
VAU	AVOW	TWAS	WHAE	WOOT
VAUS	VOWS	WASE	WHAM	**WOP**
VAUT	**VUG**	WASH	WHAP	SWOP
VAV	VUGG	WASM	WHAT	WOPS
VAVS	VUGH	WASP	**WHO**	**WOS**
VAW	VUGS	WAST	WHOA	TWOS
VAWS	**VUM**	**WAT**	WHOM	WOST
VEE	OVUM	SWAT	WHOP	**WOT**
VEEP	VUMS	TWAT	WHOT	SWOT
VEER	**WAB**	WATE	WHOW	WOTS
VEES	SWAB	WATS	**WHY**	**WOW**
VEG	WABS	WATT	WHYS	WOWF
VEGA	**WAD**	**WAW**	**WIG**	WOWS
VEGO	SWAD	WAWA	SWIG	**WRY**
VET	WADD	WAWE	TWIG	AWRY
EVET	WADE	WAWL	WIGS	**WUD**
VETO	WADI	WAWS	**WIN**	WUDS
VETS	WADS	**WAX**	TWIN	WUDU
VEX	WADT	WAXY	WIND	**WUS**
VEXT	WADY	**WAY**	WINE	WUSS
VIA	**WAE**	AWAY	WING	**WYE**
VIAE	TWAE	SWAY	WINK	WYES
VIAL	WAES	TWAY	WINN	**WYN**
VIAS	**WAG**	WAYS	WINO	WYND
VID	SWAG	**WEB**	WINS	WYNN
AVID	WAGE	WEBS	WINY	WYNS
VIDE	WAGS	**WED**	**WIS**	**XIS**
VIDS	**WAI**	AWED	IWIS	AXIS
VIE	WAID	OWED	YWIS	**YAD**
VIED	WAIF	WEDS	WISE	DYAD
VIER	WAIL	**WEE**	WISH	YADS
VIES	WAIN	AWEE	WISP	**YAG**
VIEW	WAIR	SWEE	WISS	YAGI
VIG	WAIS	TWEE	WIST	YAGS
VIGA	WAIT	WEED	**WIT**	**YAH**
VIGS	**WAN**	WEEK	TWIT	AYAH

YAHS	EYEN	YIDS	**YUG**	ZEPS	
YAK	HYEN	**YIN**	YUGA	**ZHO**	
KYAK	SYEN	AYIN	YUGS	DZHO	
YAKS	YENS	PYIN	**YUK**	ZHOS	
YAM	**YEP**	TYIN	YUKE	**ZIG**	
LYAM	YEPS	YINS	YUKO	ZIGS	
YAMS	**YES**	**YIP**	YUKS	**ZIN**	
YAP	AYES	YIPE	YUKY	ZINC	
YAPP	BYES	YIPS	**YUM**	ZINE	
YAPS	DYES	**YOB**	YUMP	ZING	
YAR	EYES	YOBS	**YUP**	ZINS	
KYAR	HYES	**YOD**	YUPS	**ZIP**	
YARD	KYES	YODE	**YUS**	ZIPS	
YARE	LYES	YODH	AYUS	**ZIT**	
YARK	NYES	YODS	KYUS	ZITE	
YARN	OYES	**YOK**	ZAG	ZITI	
YARR	PYES	YOKE	ZAGS	ZITS	
YAW	RYES	YOKS	ZAP	**ZIZ**	
YAWL	SYES	**YOM**	ZAPS	ZIZZ	
YAWN	TYES	YOMP	ZEA	**ZOL**	
YAWP	WYES	**YON**	**ZEA**	ZOLS	
YAWS	YESK	YOND	ZEAL	**ZOO**	
YAWY	YEST	YONI	ZEAS	ZOOM	
YAY	PYET	YONT	**ZED**	ZOON	
YAYS	**YET**	**YOU**	ZEDS	ZOOS	
YEA	YETI	YOUK	**ZEE**	ZOOT	
YEAD	YETT	YOUR	MZEE	**ZOS**	
YEAH	**YEW**	YOUS	ZEES	DZOS	
YEAN	YEWS	**YOW**	**ZEK**	**ZZZ**	
YEAR	**YGO**	YOWE	ZEKS	ZZZS	
YEAS	YGOE	YOWL	**ZEL**		
YEN	**YID**	YOWS	ZELS		
			ZEP		

Four-letter root words

AALS	SABED	**ABYE**	ACERS	ACNES	
BAALS	**ABET**	ABYES	**ACES**	**ACRE**	
PAALS	ABETS	**ABYS**	DACES	NACRE	
TAALS	**ABID**	ABYSM	FACES	ACRED	
ABAC	RABID	ABYSS	LACES	ACRES	
ABACA	TABID	**ACAI**	MACES	**ACTA**	
ABACI	ABIDE	ACAIS	PACES	PACTA	
ABACK	**ABLE**	**ACCA**	RACES	**ACTS**	
ABACS	CABLE	BACCA	TACES	PACTS	
ABAS	FABLE	YACCA	**ACHE**	TACTS	
BABAS	GABLE	ACCAS	CACHE	**ACYL**	
CABAS	HABLE	**ACED**	MACHE	ACYLS	
ABASE	SABLE	FACED	NACHE	**ADAW**	
ABASH	TABLE	LACED	RACHE	ADAWS	
ABASK	ABLED	MACED	TACHE	**ADDS**	
ABBA	ABLER	PACED	ACHED	WADDS	
DABBA	ABLES	RACED	ACHES	**ADDY**	
YABBA	ABLET	**ACER**	**ACID**	BADDY	
ABBAS	**ABRI**	FACER	ACIDS	CADDY	
ABBE	ABRIM	LACER	ACIDY	DADDY	
ABBED	ABRIN	MACER	**ACME**	FADDY	
ABBES	ABRIS	PACER	ACMES	PADDY	
ABBEY	**ABUT**	RACER	**ACNE**	WADDY	
ABED	ABUTS	ACERB	ACNED		

ADIT	PAGES	RAILS	CAKED	**ALEF**
ADITS	RAGES	SAILS	FAKED	ALEFS
ADOS	SAGES	TAILS	LAKED	ALEFT
DADOS	WAGES	VAILS	NAKED	**ALES**
FADOS	**AGHA**	WAILS	OAKED	BALES
SADOS	AGHAS	**AIMS**	RAKED	DALES
ADZE	**AGIN**	KAIMS	WAKED	EALES
ADZED	FAGIN	MAIMS	**AKEE**	GALES
ADZES	AGING	SAIMS	RAKEE	HALES
AEON	**AGIO**	**AINE**	AKEES	KALES
PAEON	AGIOS	DAINE	**AKES**	MALES
AEONS	**AGLU**	FAINE	BAKES	PALES
AERO	AGLUS	RAINE	CAKES	RALES
AEROS	**AGMA**	SAINE	FAKES	SALES
AERY	MAGMA	AINEE	HAKES	TALES
FAERY	TAGMA	**AINS**	JAKES	VALES
AFAR	AGMAS	CAINS	LAKES	WALES
AFARA	**AGOG**	FAINS	MAKES	YALES
AFARS	AGOGE	GAINS	RAKES	**ALEW**
AFFY	**AGON**	HAINS	SAKES	ALEWS
BAFFY	WAGON	KAINS	TAKES	**ALFA**
DAFFY	AGONE	MAINS	WAKES	HALFA
TAFFY	AGONS	PAINS	**AKIN**	ALFAS
AFRO	AGONY	RAINS	LAKIN	**ALFS**
AFROS	**AGUE**	SAINS	TAKIN	CALFS
AGAR	VAGUE	TAINS	AKING	HALFS
AGARS	AGUED	WAINS	**ALAN**	**ALGA**
AGAS	AGUES	**AIRN**	ALAND	ALGAE
JAGAS	**AHED**	BAIRN	ALANE	ALGAL
NAGAS	AAHED	CAIRN	ALANG	ALGAS
RAGAS	RAHED	AIRNS	ALANS	**ALIF**
SAGAS	**AIAS**	**AIRS**	ALANT	CALIF
AGAST	RAIAS	FAIRS	**ALAP**	KALIF
AGED	**AIDE**	GAIRS	JALAP	ALIFS
CAGED	WAIDE	HAIRS	ALAPA	**ALKO**
GAGED	AIDED	LAIRS	ALAPS	ALKOS
PAGED	AIDER	MAIRS	**ALAR**	**ALKY**
RAGED	AIDES	PAIRS	MALAR	BALKY
WAGED	**AIDS**	SAIRS	TALAR	TALKY
AGEE	CAIDS	VAIRS	ALARM	ALKYD
RAGEE	GAIDS	WAIRS	ALARY	ALKYL
AGEN	KAIDS	**AIRT**	**ALAS**	**ALLS**
AGENE	LAIDS	AIRTH	BALAS	BALLS
AGENT	MAIDS	AIRTS	GALAS	CALLS
AGER	QAIDS	**AIRY**	MALAS	FALLS
CAGER	RAIDS	DAIRY	NALAS	GALLS
EAGER	SAIDS	FAIRY	PALAS	HALLS
GAGER	**AIGA**	HAIRY	TALAS	LALLS
JAGER	SAIGA	LAIRY	**ALAY**	MALLS
LAGER	TAIGA	VAIRY	PALAY	PALLS
PAGER	AIGAS	**AITS**	ALAYS	TALLS
RAGER	**AILS**	BAITS	**ALBA**	WALLS
SAGER	BAILS	GAITS	ALBAS	**ALLY**
WAGER	FAILS	RAITS	**ALBE**	BALLY
YAGER	HAILS	TAITS	ALBEE	DALLY
AGERS	JAILS	WAITS	**ALCO**	GALLY
AGES	KAILS	**AITU**	ALCOS	PALLY
CAGES	MAILS	AITUS	**ALEC**	RALLY
GAGES	NAILS	**AKED**	ALECK	SALLY
MAGES	PAILS	BAKED	ALECS	TALLY

WALLY	AMENS	LANAS	ANNOY	APERS
ALLYL	AMENT	MANAS	**ANNS**	APERT
ALMA	**AMIA**	NANAS	BANNS	APERY
HALMA	LAMIA	RANAS	CANNS	**APES**
TALMA	ZAMIA	TANAS	JANNS	CAPES
ALMAH	AMIAS	**ANCE**	**ANOA**	GAPES
ALMAS	**AMID**	DANCE	ANOAS	JAPES
ALME	AMIDE	HANCE	**ANON**	NAPES
ALMEH	AMIDO	LANCE	CANON	PAPES
ALMES	AMIDS	NANCE	FANON	RAPES
ALMS	**AMIE**	PANCE	**ANSA**	TAPES
BALMS	MAMIE	RANCE	HANSA	**APOD**
CALMS	RAMIE	**ANDS**	SANSA	APODE
HALMS	AMIES	BANDS	ANSAE	APODS
MALMS	**AMIN**	FANDS	**ANTA**	**APOS**
PALMS	GAMIN	HANDS	MANTA	CAPOS
ALOD	RAMIN	LANDS	ANTAE	GAPOS
ALODS	TAMIN	PANDS	ANTAR	**APPS**
ALOE	AMINE	RANDS	ANTAS	YAPPS
ALOED	AMINO	SANDS	**ANTE**	**APSE**
ALOES	AMINS	WANDS	ZANTE	LAPSE
ALOW	**AMIR**	**ANES**	ANTED	APSES
ALOWE	AMIRS	BANES	ANTES	**APSO**
ALPS	**AMIS**	CANES	**ANTI**	APSOS
CALPS	CAMIS	FANES	TANTI	**AQUA**
PALPS	KAMIS	JANES	ANTIC	AQUAE
SALPS	RAMIS	KANES	ANTIS	AQUAS
ALTO	TAMIS	LANES	**ANTS**	**ARAK**
SALTO	AMISS	MANES	BANTS	ARAKS
ALTOS	**AMLA**	PANES	CANTS	**ARAR**
ALTS	AMLAS	SANES	DANTS	ARARS
DALTS	**AMMO**	VANES	GANTS	**ARBA**
HALTS	AMMON	WANES	HANTS	ARBAS
MALTS	AMMOS	**ANGA**	KANTS	**ARBS**
SALTS	**AMOK**	FANGA	LANTS	BARBS
ALUM	AMOKS	KANGA	PANTS	CARBS
ALUMS	**AMPS**	MANGA	RANTS	DARBS
AMAH	CAMPS	PANGA	SANTS	GARBS
AMAHS	DAMPS	SANGA	VANTS	WARBS
AMAS	GAMPS	TANGA	WANTS	**ARCH**
CAMAS	LAMPS	ANGAS	ANTSY	LARCH
GAMAS	RAMPS	**ANIL**	**ANUS**	MARCH
KAMAS	SAMPS	ANILE	MANUS	PARCH
LAMAS	TAMPS	ANILS	**APAY**	**ARCO**
MAMAS	VAMPS	**ANIS**	APAYD	NARCO
SAMAS	**AMUS**	MANIS	APAYS	YARCO
AMASS	CAMUS	RANIS	**APED**	**ARCS**
AMBO	RAMUS	ANISE	CAPED	MARCS
GAMBO	WAMUS	**ANKH**	GAPED	NARCS
JAMBO	AMUSE	ANKHS	JAPED	**ARDS**
MAMBO	**AMYL**	**ANNA**	NAPED	BARDS
SAMBO	AMYLS	CANNA	RAPED	CARDS
ZAMBO	**ANAL**	MANNA	TAPED	EARDS
AMBOS	BANAL	NANNA	**APER**	FARDS
AMEN	CANAL	TANNA	CAPER	HARDS
RAMEN	FANAL	WANNA	GAPER	LARDS
SAMEN	**ANAN**	ANNAL	JAPER	NARDS
YAMEN	ANANA	ANNAS	PAPER	PARDS
AMEND	**ANAS**	ANNAT	RAPER	SARDS
AMENE	KANAS	**ANNO**	TAPER	WARDS

Hooks arranged by hook word

YARDS	ARISH	WARTS	ATOKS	JAVEL
AREA	**ARKS**	ARTSY	**ATOM**	NAVEL
AREAD	BARKS	**ARTY**	ATOMS	RAVEL
AREAE	CARKS	PARTY	ATOMY	AVELS
AREAL	DARKS	TARTY	**ATOP**	**AVER**
AREAR	HARKS	WARTY	ATOPY	CAVER
AREAS	JARKS	**ARUM**	**ATUA**	FAVER
ARED	KARKS	GARUM	ATUAS	HAVER
BARED	LARKS	LARUM	**AUFS**	LAVER
CARED	MARKS	ARUMS	HAUFS	PAVER
DARED	NARKS	**ARVO**	LAUFS	RAVER
EARED	PARKS	PARVO	**AUKS**	SAVER
FARED	RARKS	ARVOS	BAUKS	TAVER
HARED	SARKS	**ARYL**	CAUKS	WAVER
OARED	WARKS	ARYLS	JAUKS	AVERS
PARED	YARKS	**ASAR**	WAUKS	AVERT
RARED	**ARLE**	TASAR	**AULA**	**AVES**
SARED	CARLE	**ASCI**	AULAS	CAVES
TARED	FARLE	FASCI	**AULD**	EAVES
WARED	MARLE	**ASHY**	CAULD	FAVES
AREDD	PARLE	DASHY	FAULD	HAVES
AREDE	ARLED	HASHY	HAULD	LAVES
ARES	ARLES	MASHY	TAULD	NAVES
BARES	**ARMS**	WASHY	YAULD	OAVES
CARES	BARMS	**ASKS**	**AUNE**	PAVES
DARES	FARMS	BASKS	AUNES	RAVES
FARES	HARMS	CASKS	**AUNT**	SAVES
HARES	MARMS	HASKS	DAUNT	WAVES
LARES	WARMS	MASKS	GAUNT	**AVID**
MARES	**ARMY**	TASKS	HAUNT	PAVID
NARES	BARMY	**ASPS**	JAUNT	**AVOW**
PARES	**ARNA**	GASPS	NAUNT	AVOWS
RARES	VARNA	HASPS	SAUNT	**AWAY**
TARES	ARNAS	JASPS	TAUNT	AWAYS
VARES	**ARPA**	RASPS	VAUNT	**AWDL**
WARES	ARPAS	WASPS	AUNTS	AWDLS
ARET	**ARSE**	**ATAP**	AUNTY	**AWED**
CARET	CARSE	WATAP	**AURA**	CAWED
ARETE	FARSE	ATAPS	LAURA	DAWED
ARETS	MARSE	**ATES**	AURAE	HAWED
ARETT	PARSE	BATES	AURAL	JAWED
ARFS	ARSED	CATES	AURAR	KAWED
BARFS	ARSES	DATES	AURAS	LAWED
ZARFS	ARSEY	FATES	**AUTO**	MAWED
ARIA	**ARSY**	GATES	AUTOS	PAWED
MARIA	KARSY	HATES	**AVAL**	SAWED
VARIA	**ARTI**	MATES	NAVAL	TAWED
ARIAS	AARTI	NATES	AVALE	YAWED
ARID	PARTI	PATES	**AVAS**	**AWEE**
MARID	ARTIC	RATES	CAVAS	AWEEL
ARIL	ARTIS	SATES	FAVAS	**AWES**
ARILS	**ARTS**	TATES	JAVAS	WAWES
ARIS	CARTS	YATES	KAVAS	**AWLS**
DARIS	DARTS	**ATMA**	LAVAS	BAWLS
GARIS	FARTS	ATMAN	TAVAS	PAWLS
LARIS	HARTS	ATMAS	AVAST	WAWLS
NARIS	KARTS	**ATOC**	**AVEL**	YAWLS
PARIS	MARTS	ATOCS	CAVEL	**AWNS**
SARIS	PARTS	**ATOK**	FAVEL	BAWNS
ARISE	TARTS	ATOKE	GAVEL	DAWNS

FAWNS	GAZON	**BALM**	KBARS	BEAKY
LAWNS	AZONS	BALMS	**BASE**	**BEAM**
PAWNS	**AZYM**	BALMY	ABASE	ABEAM
RAWNS	AZYME	**BALS**	BASED	BEAMS
YAWNS	AZYMS	BALSA	BASER	BEAMY
AWNY	**BAAL**	**BALU**	BASES	**BEAN**
FAWNY	BAALS	BALUN	**BASH**	BEANO
LAWNY	**BABA**	BALUS	ABASH	BEANS
TAWNY	BABAS	**BANC**	BASHO	BEANY
YAWNY	**BABE**	BANCO	**BASK**	**BEAR**
AWOL	BABEL	BANCS	ABASK	ABEAR
AWOLS	BABES	**BAND**	BASKS	BEARD
AXED	**BABU**	ABAND	**BASS**	BEARE
FAXED	BABUL	BANDA	BASSE	BEARS
MAXED	BABUS	BANDH	BASSI	**BEAT**
RAXED	**BACH**	BANDS	BASSO	BEATH
TAXED	BACHA	BANDY	BASSY	BEATS
WAXED	BACHS	**BANE**	**BAST**	BEATY
AXEL	**BACK**	BANED	BASTA	**BEAU**
AXELS	ABACK	BANES	BASTE	BEAUS
AXES	BACKS	**BANG**	BASTI	BEAUT
FAXES	**BACS**	OBANG	BASTO	BEAUX
LAXES	ABACS	BANGS	BASTS	**BECK**
MAXES	**BAEL**	**BANI**	**BATE**	BECKE
PAXES	BAELS	BANIA	ABATE	BECKS
RAXES	**BAFF**	**BANK**	BATED	**BEDE**
SAXES	BAFFS	BANKS	BATES	BEDEL
TAXES	BAFFY	**BANT**	**BATH**	BEDES
WAXES	**BAFT**	BANTS	BATHE	BEDEW
ZAXES	ABAFT	BANTU	BATHS	**BEEF**
AXIL	BAFTS	BANTY	**BATT**	BEEFS
AXILE	**BAGH**	**BAPU**	BATTA	BEEFY
AXILS	BAGHS	BAPUS	BATTS	**BEEP**
AXIS	**BAHT**	**BARB**	BATTU	BEEPS
MAXIS	BAHTS	BARBE	BATTY	**BEER**
TAXIS	**BAIL**	BARBS	**BAUD**	BEERS
AXLE	BAILS	**BARD**	BAUDS	BEERY
AXLED	**BAIT**	BARDE	**BAUK**	**BEET**
AXLES	BAITH	BARDO	BAUKS	BEETS
AXON	BAITS	BARDS	**BAUR**	**BEGO**
CAXON	**BAJU**	BARDY	BAURS	BEGOT
TAXON	BAJUS	**BARE**	**BAWD**	**BEIN**
AXONE	**BAKE**	BARED	BAWDS	BEING
AXONS	BAKED	BARER	BAWDY	**BELL**
AYAH	BAKEN	BARES	**BAWL**	BELLE
RAYAH	BAKER	**BARF**	BAWLS	BELLS
AYAHS	BAKES	BARFS	**BAWN**	BELLY
AYES	**BALD**	**BARK**	BAWNS	**BELT**
BAYES	BALDS	BARKS	**BAWR**	BELTS
AYIN	BALDY	BARKY	BAWRS	**BEMA**
LAYIN	**BALE**	**BARM**	**BAYE**	BEMAD
ZAYIN	BALED	BARMS	BAYED	BEMAS
AYINS	BALER	BARMY	BAYES	**BEND**
AYRE	BALES	**BARN**	**BAYT**	BENDS
FAYRE	**BALK**	BARNS	BAYTS	BENDY
AYRES	BALKS	BARNY	**BEAD**	**BENE**
AZAN	BALKY	**BARP**	BEADS	BENES
HAZAN	**BALL**	BARPS	BEADY	BENET
AZANS	BALLS	**BARS**	**BEAK**	**BENI**
AZON	BALLY		BEAKS	BENIS

Hooks arranged by hook word

BENT	BIKE	BIZE	BLOWN	OBOLE	
BENTO	BIKED	BIZES	BLOWS	BOLES	
BENTS	BIKER	**BLAB**	BLOWY	**BOLL**	
BENTY	BIKES	BLABS	**BLUB**	BOLLS	
BERE	**BILE**	**BLAD**	BLUBS	**BOLO**	
BERES	BILED	BLADE	**BLUE**	BOLOS	
BERET	BILES	BLADS	BLUED	**BOLT**	
BERG	**BILK**	BLADY	BLUER	BOLTS	
BERGS	BILKS	**BLAE**	BLUES	**BOMA**	
BERK	**BILL**	BLAER	BLUET	ABOMA	
BERKO	BILLS	BLAES	BLUEY	BOMAS	
BERKS	BILLY	**BLAG**	**BLUR**	**BOMB**	
BERM	**BIMA**	BLAGS	BLURB	BOMBE	
BERME	BIMAH	**BLAH**	BLURS	BOMBO	
BERMS	BIMAS	BLAHS	BLURT	BOMBS	
BEST	**BIND**	**BLAM**	**BOAB**	**BOND**	
BESTI	BINDI	BLAME	BOABS	BONDS	
BESTS	BINDS	BLAMS	**BOAK**	**BONE**	
BETA	**BINE**	**BLAT**	BOAKS	BONED	
BETAS	BINER	BLATE	**BOAR**	BONER	
BETE	BINES	BLATS	BOARD	BONES	
BETED	**BING**	BLATT	BOARS	BONEY	
BETEL	BINGE	**BLAW**	BOART	**BONG**	
BETES	BINGO	BLAWN	**BOAS**	BONGO	
BETH	BINGS	BLAWS	BOAST	BONGS	
BETHS	BINGY	**BLAY**	**BOAT**	**BONK**	
BETS	**BINK**	BLAYS	BOATS	BONKS	
ABETS	BINKS	**BLEB**	**BOBA**	**BONY**	
BEYS	**BINT**	BLEBS	BOBAC	EBONY	
OBEYS	BINTS	**BLED**	BOBAK	**BOOB**	
BHEL	**BIOG**	ABLED	BOBAS	BOOBS	
BHELS	BIOGS	**BLEE**	**BOCK**	BOOBY	
BHUT	**BIRD**	BLEED	BOCKS	**BOOH**	
BHUTS	BIRDS	BLEEP	**BODE**	BOOHS	
BIAS	**BIRK**	BLEES	ABODE	**BOOK**	
OBIAS	BIRKS	**BLET**	BODED	EBOOK	
BIBB	**BIRL**	ABLET	BODES	BOOKS	
BIBBS	BIRLE	BLETS	**BOEP**	BOOKY	
BICE	BIRLS	**BLEY**	BOEPS	**BOOL**	
BICEP	**BIRO**	BLEYS	**BOET**	BOOLS	
BICES	BIROS	**BLIN**	BOETS	**BOOM**	
BIDE	**BIRR**	BLIND	**BOFF**	BOOMS	
ABIDE	BIRRS	BLING	BOFFO	BOOMY	
BIDED	**BISE**	BLINI	BOFFS	**BOON**	
BIDER	BISES	BLINK	**BOHO**	ABOON	
BIDES	**BISK**	BLINS	BOHOS	BOONG	
BIDET	BISKS	BLINY	**BOIL**	BOONS	
BIDI	**BITE**	**BLIP**	ABOIL	**BOOR**	
BIDIS	BITER	BLIPS	BOILS	BOORD	
BIER	BITES	**BLOB**	**BOKE**	BOORS	
BIERS	**BITO**	BLOBS	BOKED	**BOOS**	
BIFF	BITOS	**BLOC**	BOKES	BOOSE	
BIFFO	BITOU	BLOCK	**BOKO**	BOOST	
BIFFS	**BITS**	BLOCS	BOKOS	**BOOT**	
BIFFY	OBITS	**BLOG**	**BOLA**	BOOTH	
BIGA	BITSY	BLOGS	BOLAR	BOOTS	
BIGAE	**BITT**	**BLOT**	BOLAS	BOOTY	
BIGG	BITTE	BLOTS	**BOLD**	**BORA**	
BIGGS	BITTS	**BLOW**	BOLDS	BORAK	
BIGGY	BITTY	ABLOW	**BOLE**	BORAL	

BORAS	BOYSY	**BRIM**	**BUDO**	BURAS
BORAX	**BOZO**	ABRIM	BUDOS	**BURB**
BORD	BOZOS	BRIMS	**BUFF**	BURBS
ABORD	**BRAD**	**BRIN**	BUFFA	**BURD**
BORDE	BRADS	ABRIN	BUFFE	BURDS
BORDS	**BRAE**	BRINE	BUFFI	**BURG**
BORE	BRAES	BRING	BUFFO	BURGH
ABORE	**BRAG**	BRINK	BUFFS	BURGS
YBORE	BRAGS	BRINS	BUFFY	**BURK**
BORED	**BRAK**	BRINY	**BUFO**	BURKA
BOREE	BRAKE	**BRIO**	BUFOS	BURKE
BOREL	BRAKS	BRIOS	**BUHL**	BURKS
BORER	BRAKY	**BRIS**	BUHLS	**BURL**
BORES	**BRAN**	ABRIS	**BUHR**	BURLS
BORK	BRAND	BRISE	BUHRS	BURLY
BORKS	BRANK	BRISK	**BUIK**	**BURN**
BORM	BRANS	BRISS	BUIKS	BURNS
BORMS	BRANT	**BRIT**	**BUKE**	BURNT
BORN	**BRAS**	BRITH	BUKES	**BURP**
BORNA	BRASH	BRITS	**BULB**	BURPS
BORNE	BRASS	BRITT	BULBS	**BURR**
BORT	BRAST	**BROD**	**BULK**	BURRO
ABORT	**BRAT**	BRODS	BULKS	BURRS
BORTS	BRATS	**BROG**	BULKY	BURRY
BORTY	**BRAW**	BROGH	**BULL**	**BURS**
BORTZ	BRAWL	BROGS	BULLA	BURSA
BOSK	BRAWN	**BROO**	BULLS	BURSE
BOSKS	BRAWS	BROOD	BULLY	BURST
BOSKY	**BRAY**	BROOK	**BUMF**	**BUSH**
BOSS	ABRAY	BROOL	BUMFS	BUSHY
BOSSY	BRAYS	BROOM	**BUMP**	**BUSK**
BOTA	**BRED**	BROOS	BUMPH	BUSKS
BOTAS	BREDE	**BROS**	BUMPS	BUSKY
BOTH	BREDS	BROSE	BUMPY	**BUSS**
BOTHY	**BREE**	BROSY	**BUNA**	BUSSU
BOTT	BREED	**BROW**	ABUNA	**BUST**
BOTTE	BREEM	BROWN	BUNAS	BUSTI
BOTTS	BREER	BROWS	**BUND**	BUSTS
BOTTY	BREES	**BRUS**	BUNDE	BUSTY
BOUK	**BREI**	BRUSH	BUNDH	**BUTE**
BOUKS	BREID	BRUSK	BUNDS	BUTEO
BOUN	BREIS	BRUST	BUNDT	BUTES
BOUND	**BREN**	**BRUT**	BUNDU	**BUTS**
BOUNS	BRENS	BRUTE	BUNDY	ABUTS
BOUT	BRENT	BRUTS	**BUNG**	**BUTT**
ABOUT	**BRER**	**BUAT**	BUNGS	BUTTE
BOUTS	BRERE	BUATS	BUNGY	BUTTS
BOWL	BRERS	**BUBA**	**BUNK**	BUTTY
BOWLS	**BREW**	BUBAL	BUNKO	**BUZZ**
BOWR	BREWS	BUBAS	BUNKS	ABUZZ
BOWRS	**BREY**	**BUBU**	**BUNN**	BUZZY
BOWS	BREYS	BUBUS	BUNNS	**BYDE**
BOWSE	**BRIE**	**BUCK**	BUNNY	BYDED
BOYF	BRIEF	BUCKO	**BUNT**	BYDES
BOYFS	BRIER	BUCKS	BUNTS	**BYES**
BOYG	BRIES	BUCKU	BUNTY	ABYES
BOYGS	**BRIG**	**BUDA**	**BUOY**	**BYKE**
BOYO	BRIGS	BUDAS	BUOYS	BYKED
BOYOS	**BRIK**	**BUDI**	**BURA**	BYKES
BOYS	BRIKS	BUDIS	BURAN	**BYRE**

Hooks arranged by hook word

BYRES	**CAMA**	CARDS	CAVAS	**CHAM**
BYRL	CAMAN	CARDY	**CAVE**	CHAMP
BYRLS	CAMAS	**CARE**	CAVED	CHAMS
BYTE	**CAME**	SCARE	CAVEL	**CHAO**
BYTES	CAMEL	CARED	CAVER	CHAOS
CABA	CAMEO	CARER	CAVES	**CHAP**
CABAL	CAMES	CARES	**CAWK**	CHAPE
CABAS	**CAMO**	CARET	CAWKS	CHAPS
CABS	CAMOS	CAREX	**CAWS**	CHAPT
SCABS	**CAMP**	**CARK**	SCAWS	**CHAR**
CACA	SCAMP	CARKS	**CEAS**	CHARA
CACAO	CAMPI	**CARL**	CEASE	CHARD
CACAS	CAMPO	CARLE	**CECA**	CHARE
CADE	CAMPS	CARLS	CECAL	CHARK
CADEE	CAMPY	**CARN**	**CEDE**	CHARM
CADES	**CAMS**	CARNS	CEDED	CHARR
CADET	SCAMS	CARNY	CEDER	CHARS
CADI	**CANE**	**CARP**	CEDES	CHART
CADIE	CANED	SCARP	**CEDI**	CHARY
CADIS	CANEH	CARPI	CEDIS	**CHAS**
CADS	CANER	CARPS	**CEIL**	CHASE
ECADS	CANES	**CARR**	CEILI	CHASM
SCADS	**CANG**	CARRS	CEILS	**CHAT**
CAFE	CANGS	CARRY	**CELL**	CHATS
CAFES	**CANN**	**CARS**	CELLA	**CHAV**
CAFF	CANNA	SCARS	CELLI	SCHAV
SCAFF	CANNS	CARSE	CELLO	CHAVE
CAFFS	CANNY	**CART**	CELLS	CHAVS
CAGE	**CANS**	SCART	**CELT**	**CHAW**
CAGED	SCANS	CARTA	CELTS	CHAWK
CAGER	CANSO	CARTE	**CENS**	CHAWS
CAGES	CANST	CARTS	CENSE	**CHAY**
CAGEY	**CANT**	**CASA**	**CENT**	CHAYA
CAGS	SCANT	CASAS	SCENT	CHAYS
SCAGS	CANTO	**CASE**	CENTO	**CHEF**
CAID	CANTS	CASED	CENTS	CHEFS
CAIDS	CANTY	CASES	CENTU	**CHER**
CAIN	**CAPA**	**CASK**	**CEPE**	OCHER
CAINS	SCAPA	CASKS	CEPES	CHERE
CAKE	CAPAS	CASKY	**CERE**	CHERT
CAKED	**CAPE**	**CAST**	CERED	**CHEW**
CAKES	SCAPE	CASTE	CERES	CHEWS
CAKEY	CAPED	CASTS	**CERO**	CHEWY
CALF	CAPER	**CATE**	CEROS	**CHIA**
CALFS	CAPES	CATER	**CERT**	CHIAO
CALK	**CAPH**	CATES	CERTS	CHIAS
CALKS	CAPHS	**CATS**	**CESS**	**CHIB**
CALL	**CAPI**	SCATS	CESSE	CHIBS
SCALL	SCAPI	**CAUK**	**CETE**	**CHIC**
CALLA	CAPIZ	CAUKS	CETES	CHICA
CALLS	**CAPO**	**CAUL**	**CHAD**	CHICH
CALM	CAPON	CAULD	CHADO	CHICK
CALMS	CAPOS	CAULK	CHADS	CHICO
CALMY	CAPOT	CAULS	**CHAI**	CHICS
CALO	**CARB**	**CAUM**	CHAIN	**CHID**
CALOS	CARBO	CAUMS	CHAIR	CHIDE
CALP	CARBS	**CAUP**	CHAIS	**CHIK**
SCALP	CARBY	SCAUP	**CHAL**	CHIKS
CALPA	**CARD**	CAUPS	CHALK	**CHIN**
CALPS	CARDI	**CAVA**	CHALS	CHINA

CHINE	**CIST**	**CLOU**	**COIN**	CONIN
CHINK	CISTS	CLOUD	COINS	**CONK**
CHINO	**CITE**	CLOUR	**COIR**	CONKS
CHINS	CITED	CLOUS	COIRS	CONKY
CHIP	CITER	CLOUT	**COIT**	**CONN**
CHIPS	CITES	**CLOW**	COITS	CONNE
CHIT	**CIVE**	CLOWN	**COKE**	CONNS
CHITS	CIVES	CLOWS	COKED	**CONS**
CHIV	CIVET	**CLOY**	COKES	ICONS
CHIVE	**CLAD**	CLOYE	**COLA**	**COOF**
CHIVS	YCLAD	CLOYS	COLAS	COOFS
CHIVY	CLADE	**CLUB**	**COLD**	**COOK**
CHIZ	CLADS	CLUBS	ACOLD	COOKS
CHIZZ	**CLAG**	**CLUE**	SCOLD	COOKY
CHOC	CLAGS	CLUED	COLDS	**COOL**
CHOCK	**CLAM**	CLUES	**COLE**	COOLS
CHOCO	CLAME	**COAL**	COLED	COOLY
CHOCS	CLAMP	COALA	COLES	**COOM**
CHOG	CLAMS	COALS	COLEY	COOMB
CHOGS	**CLAN**	COALY	**COLL**	COOMS
CHON	CLANG	**COAT**	COLLS	COOMY
CHONS	CLANK	COATE	COLLY	**COON**
CHOP	CLANS	COATI	**COLT**	COONS
CHOPS	**CLAP**	COATS	COLTS	**COOP**
CHOU	CLAPS	**COBB**	**COMA**	SCOOP
CHOUT	CLAPT	COBBS	COMAE	COOPS
CHOUX	**CLAT**	COBBY	COMAL	COOPT
CHOW	ECLAT	**COCA**	COMAS	**COOS**
CHOWK	CLATS	COCAS	**COMB**	COOST
CHOWS	**CLAW**	**COCK**	COMBE	**COOT**
CHUB	CLAWS	ACOCK	COMBI	SCOOT
CHUBS	**CLAY**	COCKS	COMBO	COOTS
CHUG	CLAYS	COCKY	COMBS	**COPE**
CHUGS	**CLEF**	**COCO**	COMBY	SCOPE
CHUM	CLEFS	COCOA	**COME**	COPED
CHUMP	CLEFT	COCOS	COMER	COPEN
CHUMS	**CLEG**	**CODA**	COMES	COPER
CHUT	CLEGS	CODAS	COMET	COPES
CHUTE	**CLEM**	**CODE**	**COMM**	**COPS**
CIAO	CLEMS	CODEC	COMMA	SCOPS
CIAOS	**CLEW**	CODED	COMMO	COPSE
CIDE	CLEWS	CODEN	COMMS	COPSY
CIDED	**CLIP**	CODER	COMMY	**CORD**
CIDER	CLIPE	CODES	**COMP**	CORDS
CIDES	CLIPS	CODEX	COMPO	**CORE**
CIDS	CLIPT	**COED**	COMPS	SCORE
ACIDS	**CLOD**	COEDS	COMPT	CORED
CIEL	CLODS	**COFF**	**COND**	CORER
CIELS	**CLOG**	SCOFF	YCOND	CORES
CILL	CLOGS	COFFS	CONDO	COREY
CILLS	**CLON**	**COGS**	**CONE**	**CORK**
CINE	CLONE	SCOGS	SCONE	CORKS
CINES	CLONK	**COHO**	CONED	CORKY
CION	CLONS	COHOE	CONES	**CORM**
SCION	**CLOP**	COHOG	CONEY	CORMS
CIONS	CLOPS	COHOS	**CONF**	**CORN**
CIRE	**CLOT**	**COIF**	CONFS	ACORN
CIRES	CLOTE	COIFS	**CONI**	SCORN
CIRL	CLOTH	**COIL**	CONIA	CORNI
CIRLS	CLOTS	COILS	CONIC	CORNO

CORNS	COZES	CRITS	**CURB**	DACES
CORNU	COZEY	**CROC**	CURBS	**DACK**
CORNY	**CRAB**	CROCI	**CURD**	DACKS
CORS	SCRAB	CROCK	CURDS	**DADA**
CORSE	CRABS	CROCS	CURDY	DADAH
CORSO	**CRAG**	**CROG**	**CURE**	DADAS
COSE	SCRAG	SCROG	CURED	**DADO**
COSEC	CRAGS	CROGS	CURER	DADOS
COSED	**CRAM**	**CROP**	CURES	**DAFF**
COSES	SCRAM	CROPS	CURET	DAFFS
COSET	CRAME	**CROW**	**CURF**	DAFFY
COSEY	CRAMP	SCROW	SCURF	**DAGO**
COST	CRAMS	CROWD	CURFS	DAGOS
COSTA	**CRAN**	CROWN	**CURL**	**DAHL**
COSTE	SCRAN	CROWS	CURLI	DAHLS
COSTS	CRANE	**CRUD**	CURLS	**DAHS**
COTE	CRANK	CRUDE	CURLY	ODAHS
COTED	CRANS	CRUDS	**CURN**	**DAIS**
COTES	**CRAP**	CRUDY	CURNS	DAISY
COTH	SCRAP	**CRUE**	CURNY	**DALE**
COTHS	CRAPE	CRUEL	**CURR**	DALED
COTS	CRAPS	CRUES	CURRS	DALES
SCOTS	CRAPY	CRUET	CURRY	**DALI**
COTT	**CRAW**	**CRUS**	**CURS**	DALIS
COTTA	SCRAW	ECRUS	SCURS	**DALS**
COTTS	CRAWL	CRUSE	CURSE	ODALS
COUP	CRAWS	CRUSH	CURSI	UDALS
SCOUP	**CRAY**	CRUST	CURST	**DALT**
COUPE	SCRAY	CRUSY	**CUSH**	DALTS
COUPS	CRAYS	**CUBE**	CUSHY	**DAME**
COUR	**CRED**	CUBEB	**CUSK**	DAMES
SCOUR	ACRED	CUBED	CUSKS	**DAMN**
COURB	CREDO	CUBER	**CUSP**	DAMNS
COURD	CREDS	CUBES	CUSPS	**DAMP**
COURE	**CREE**	**CUDS**	**CUSS**	DAMPS
COURS	SCREE	SCUDS	CUSSO	DAMPY
COURT	CREED	**CUFF**	**CUTE**	**DANG**
COVE	CREEK	SCUFF	ACUTE	DANGS
COVED	CREEL	CUFFO	SCUTE	**DANK**
COVEN	CREEP	CUFFS	CUTER	DANKS
COVER	CREES	**CUIF**	CUTES	**DANT**
COVES	**CREM**	CUIFS	CUTEY	IDANT
COVET	CREME	**CUIT**	**CUTS**	DANTS
COVEY	CREMS	CUITS	SCUTS	**DARB**
COWK	**CREW**	**CUKE**	**CYAN**	DARBS
COWKS	SCREW	CUKES	CYANO	**DARE**
COWL	CREWE	**CULL**	CYANS	DARED
SCOWL	CREWS	SCULL	**CYMA**	DARER
COWLS	**CRIB**	CULLS	CYMAE	DARES
COWP	CRIBS	CULLY	CYMAR	**DARG**
SCOWP	**CRIM**	**CULM**	CYMAS	DARGA
COWPS	SCRIM	CULMS	**CYME**	DARGS
COWS	CRIME	**CULT**	CYMES	**DARI**
SCOWS	CRIMP	CULTI	**CYST**	DARIC
COXA	CRIMS	CULTS	CYSTS	DARIS
COXAE	**CRIS**	CULTY	**CYTE**	**DARK**
COXAL	CRISE	**CUNT**	CYTES	DARKS
COZE	CRISP	CUNTS	**CZAR**	DARKY
COZED	**CRIT**	**CUPS**	CZARS	**DARN**
COZEN	CRITH	SCUPS	**DACE**	DARNS

DART	**DECK**	**DENE**	**DIFF**	DITAS
DARTS	DECKO	DENES	DIFFS	**DITE**
DASH	DECKS	DENET	**DIKA**	DITED
DASHI	**DECO**	**DENI**	DIKAS	DITES
DASHY	DECOR	DENIM	**DIKE**	**DITS**
DATA	DECOS	DENIS	DIKED	ADITS
DATAL	DECOY	**DENS**	DIKER	EDITS
DATE	**DEED**	DENSE	DIKES	DITSY
DATED	DEEDS	**DENT**	DIKEY	**DITT**
DATER	DEEDY	IDENT	**DILL**	DITTO
DATES	**DEEM**	DENTS	DILLI	DITTS
DATO	ADEEM	**DERE**	DILLS	DITTY
DATOS	DEEMS	DERED	DILLY	**DITZ**
DAUB	**DEEN**	DERES	**DIME**	DITZY
DAUBE	DEENS	**DERM**	DIMER	**DIVA**
DAUBS	**DEEP**	DERMA	DIMES	DIVAN
DAUBY	DEEPS	DERMS	**DIMP**	DIVAS
DAUD	**DEER**	**DERN**	DIMPS	**DIVE**
DAUDS	DEERE	DERNS	**DINE**	DIVED
DAUR	DEERS	**DERO**	DINED	DIVER
DAURS	**DEES**	DEROS	DINER	DIVES
DAUT	IDEES	**DERV**	DINES	**DIVI**
DAUTS	**DEET**	DERVS	**DING**	DIVIS
DAWD	DEETS	**DESK**	DINGE	**DIXI**
DAWDS	**DEEV**	DESKS	DINGO	DIXIE
DAWK	DEEVE	**DEVA**	DINGS	DIXIT
DAWKS	DEEVS	DEVAS	DINGY	**DJIN**
DAWN	**DEFI**	**DHAK**	**DINK**	DJINN
DAWNS	DEFIS	DHAKS	DINKS	DJINS
DAWS	**DEID**	**DHAL**	DINKY	**DOAB**
ADAWS	DEIDS	DHALS	**DINO**	DOABS
DAWT	**DEIF**	**DHOL**	DINOS	**DOAT**
DAWTS	DEIFY	DHOLE	**DINT**	DOATS
DAYS	**DEIL**	DHOLL	DINTS	**DOCK**
ADAYS	DEILS	DHOLS	**DIOL**	DOCKS
DAZE	**DEKE**	**DHOW**	DIOLS	**DOCO**
DAZED	DEKED	DHOWS	**DIPS**	DOCOS
DAZER	DEKES	**DIAL**	DIPSO	**DODO**
DAZES	**DELE**	DIALS	**DIRE**	DODOS
DEAD	DELED	**DICE**	DIRER	**DOEK**
DEADS	DELES	DICED	**DIRK**	DOEKS
DEAL	**DELF**	DICER	DIRKE	**DOER**
IDEAL	DELFS	DICES	DIRKS	DOERS
DEALS	DELFT	DICEY	**DIRL**	**DOES**
DEALT	**DELI**	**DICH**	DIRLS	DOEST
DEAN	DELIS	DICHT	**DIRT**	**DOFF**
DEANS	**DELL**	**DICK**	DIRTS	DOFFS
DEAR	DELLS	DICKS	DIRTY	**DOGE**
DEARE	DELLY	DICKY	**DISA**	DOGES
DEARN	**DELO**	**DICT**	DISAS	DOGEY
DEARS	DELOS	EDICT	**DISC**	**DOIT**
DEARY	**DELT**	DICTA	DISCI	DOITS
DEAW	DELTA	DICTS	DISCO	**DOJO**
DEAWS	DELTS	DICTY	DISCS	DOJOS
DEAWY	**DEME**	**DIDO**	**DISH**	**DOLE**
DEBE	DEMES	DIDOS	DISHY	DOLED
DEBEL	**DEMO**	**DIEB**	**DISK**	DOLES
DEBES	DEMOB	DIEBS	DISKS	**DOLL**
DEBT	DEMON	**DIET**	**DITA**	DOLLS
DEBTS	DEMOS	DIETS	DITAL	DOLLY

Hooks arranged by hook word

DOLS	**DORSA**	**DRAC**	DUCES	**DURO**
IDOLS	DORSE	DRACK	**DUCK**	DUROC
DOLT	**DORT**	DRACO	DUCKS	DUROS
DOLTS	DORTS	**DRAD**	DUCKY	DUROY
DOME	DORTY	ADRAD	**DUCT**	**DURR**
DOMED	**DOSE**	YDRAD	EDUCT	DURRA
DOMES	DOSED	**DRAG**	DUCTS	DURRS
DONA	DOSEH	DRAGS	**DUDE**	DURRY
DONAH	DOSER	**DRAM**	DUDED	**DUSK**
DONAS	DOSES	DRAMA	DUDES	DUSKS
DONE	**DOTE**	DRAMS	**DUEL**	DUSKY
DONEE	DOTED	**DRAP**	DUELS	**DUST**
DONER	DOTER	DRAPE	**DUET**	ADUST
DONG	DOTES	DRAPS	DUETS	DUSTS
DONGA	**DOUC**	**DRAT**	DUETT	DUSTY
DONGS	DOUCE	DRATS	**DUFF**	**DWAM**
DONS	DOUCS	**DRAW**	DUFFS	DWAMS
UDONS	**DOUK**	DRAWL	**DUIT**	**DYAD**
DONSY	DOUKS	DRAWN	DUITS	DYADS
DOOB	**DOUM**	DRAWS	**DUKA**	**DYER**
DOOBS	DOUMA	**DRAY**	DUKAS	DYERS
DOOK	DOUMS	DRAYS	**DUKE**	**DYKE**
DOOKS	**DOUP**	**DREE**	DUKED	DYKED
DOOL	DOUPS	DREED	DUKES	DYKES
DOOLE	**DOUR**	DREES	**DULE**	DYKEY
DOOLS	ODOUR	**DREG**	DULES	**DYNE**
DOOLY	DOURA	DREGS	**DULL**	DYNEL
DOOM	**DOUT**	**DREK**	DULLS	DYNES
DOOMS	DOUTS	DREKS	DULLY	**DZHO**
DOOMY	**DOVE**	**DREY**	**DUMA**	DZHOS
DOON	DOVED	DREYS	DUMAS	**EACH**
DOONA	DOVEN	**DRIB**	**DUMB**	BEACH
DOOR	DOVER	DRIBS	DUMBO	LEACH
DOORN	DOVES	**DRIP**	DUMBS	PEACH
DOORS	**DOWD**	DRIPS	**DUMP**	REACH
DOPA	DOWDS	DRIPT	DUMPS	TEACH
DOPAS	DOWDY	**DROP**	DUMPY	**EALE**
DOPE	**DOWL**	DROPS	**DUNE**	VEALE
DOPED	DOWLE	DROPT	DUNES	EALES
DOPER	DOWLS	**DROW**	**DUNG**	**EANS**
DOPES	DOWLY	DROWN	DUNGS	BEANS
DOPEY	**DOWN**	DROWS	DUNGY	DEANS
DORB	ADOWN	**DRUB**	**DUNK**	GEANS
DORBA	DOWNA	DRUBS	DUNKS	JEANS
DORBS	DOWNS	**DRUG**	**DUNS**	LEANS
DORE	DOWNY	DRUGS	DUNSH	MEANS
ADORE	**DOWP**	**DRUM**	**DUNT**	PEANS
DOREE	DOWPS	DRUMS	DUNTS	REANS
DORK	**DOWS**	**DSOS**	**DUPE**	SEANS
DORKS	DOWSE	ODSOS	DUPED	WEANS
DORKY	**DOWT**	**DUAD**	DUPER	YEANS
DORM	DOWTS	DUADS	DUPES	**EARD**
DORMS	**DOZE**	**DUAL**	**DURA**	BEARD
DORMY	ADOZE	DUALS	DURAL	HEARD
DORP	DOZED	**DUAN**	DURAS	YEARD
DORPS	DOZEN	DUANS	**DURE**	EARDS
DORR	DOZER	**DUAR**	DURED	**EARL**
DORRS	DOZES	DUARS	DURES	PEARL
DORS	**DRAB**	**DUCE**	**DURN**	EARLS
ODORS	DRABS	EDUCE	DURNS	EARLY

EARN	BEAUS	REECH	**EINE**	FEMES
DEARN	**EAUX**	**EELS**	SEINE	HEMES
LEARN	BEAUX	FEELS	**EISH**	LEMES
YEARN	**EAVE**	HEELS	LEISH	MEMES
EARNS	DEAVE	JEELS	**EKED**	SEMES
EARS	HEAVE	KEELS	DEKED	TEMES
BEARS	LEAVE	PEELS	REKED	**EMEU**
DEARS	REAVE	REELS	**EKES**	EMEUS
FEARS	WEAVE	SEELS	DEKES	**EMIC**
GEARS	EAVED	TEELS	PEKES	DEMIC
HEARS	EAVES	WEELS	REKES	HEMIC
LEARS	**EBON**	**EELY**	**EKKA**	**EMIR**
NEARS	EBONS	DEELY	MEKKA	EMIRS
PEARS	EBONY	JEELY	EKKAS	**EMIT**
REARS	**ECAD**	SEELY	**ELAN**	DEMIT
SEARS	DECAD	**EERY**	ELAND	REMIT
TEARS	ECADS	BEERY	ELANS	EMITS
WEARS	**ECCE**	LEERY	**ELDS**	**EMMA**
YEARS	RECCE	PEERY	GELDS	GEMMA
EARST	**ECCO**	VEERY	MELDS	LEMMA
EASE	RECCO	**EEVN**	VELDS	EMMAS
CEASE	SECCO	EEVNS	WELDS	**EMMY**
FEASE	**ECHE**	**EFFS**	**ELFS**	FEMMY
LEASE	ECHED	JEFFS	DELFS	GEMMY
MEASE	ECHES	MEFFS	PELFS	JEMMY
PEASE	**ECHO**	TEFFS	SELFS	EMMYS
SEASE	ECHOS	**EFTS**	**ELKS**	**EMOS**
TEASE	**ECHT**	HEFTS	WELKS	DEMOS
EASED	FECHT	LEFTS	YELKS	MEMOS
EASEL	HECHT	WEFTS	**ELLS**	**EMPT**
EASER	WECHT	**EGAD**	BELLS	DEMPT
EASES	**ECOS**	BEGAD	CELLS	KEMPT
EAST	DECOS	EGADS	DELLS	NEMPT
BEAST	**ECRU**	**EGAL**	FELLS	TEMPT
FEAST	ECRUS	LEGAL	HELLS	EMPTS
HEAST	**EDDY**	REGAL	JELLS	EMPTY
LEAST	NEDDY	**EGER**	KELLS	**EMYD**
REAST	REDDY	LEGER	MELLS	EMYDE
YEAST	TEDDY	EGERS	PELLS	EMYDS
EASTS	**EDGE**	**EGGS**	SELLS	**ENDS**
EATH	HEDGE	TEGGS	TELLS	BENDS
BEATH	KEDGE	YEGGS	VELLS	FENDS
DEATH	LEDGE	**EGGY**	WELLS	HENDS
HEATH	SEDGE	LEGGY	YELLS	LENDS
MEATH	WEDGE	PEGGY	**ELMS**	MENDS
NEATH	EDGED	**EGIS**	HELMS	PENDS
EATHE	EDGER	AEGIS	YELMS	RENDS
EATS	EDGES	**EGMA**	**ELTS**	SENDS
BEATS	**EDGY**	REGMA	BELTS	TENDS
FEATS	HEDGY	EGMAS	CELTS	VENDS
GEATS	KEDGY	**EGOS**	DELTS	WENDS
HEATS	LEDGY	REGOS	FELTS	**ENES**
JEATS	SEDGY	SEGOS	GELTS	BENES
LEATS	WEDGY	VEGOS	KELTS	DENES
MEATS	**EDIT**	**EIDE**	MELTS	GENES
NEATS	EDITS	EIDER	PELTS	LENES
PEATS	**EECH**	**EIKS**	WELTS	MENES
SEATS	BEECH	REIKS	YELTS	NENES
TEATS	KEECH	**EILD**	**EMES**	PENES
EAUS	LEECH	EILDS	DEMES	TENES

Hooks arranged by hook word

ENEW	**ERIC**	FESSE	EUROS	**EXON**
RENEW	CERIC	GESSE	**EVEN**	EXONS
ENEWS	SERIC	JESSE	EEVEN	**EXPO**
ENGS	XERIC	ESSES	SEVEN	EXPOS
LENGS	ERICA	**ESTS**	YEVEN	**EXUL**
MENGS	ERICK	BESTS	EVENS	EXULS
ENOL	ERICS	FESTS	EVENT	EXULT
ENOLS	**ERKS**	GESTS	**EVER**	**EYAS**
ENOW	BERKS	HESTS	BEVER	EYASS
ENOWS	JERKS	JESTS	FEVER	**EYED**
ENVY	MERKS	KESTS	LEVER	FEYED
SENVY	NERKS	LESTS	NEVER	HEYED
EONS	PERKS	NESTS	SEVER	KEYED
AEONS	SERKS	PESTS	EVERT	**EYEN**
NEONS	YERKS	RESTS	EVERY	SEYEN
PEONS	ZERKS	TESTS	**EVES**	**EYER**
EORL	**ERNE**	VESTS	MEVES	FEYER
CEORL	CERNE	WESTS	NEVES	GEYER
EORLS	GERNE	YESTS	YEVES	EYERS
EPEE	KERNE	ZESTS	**EVET**	**EYOT**
TEPEE	TERNE	**ETAS**	REVET	EYOTS
EPEES	ERNED	BETAS	EVETS	**EYRA**
EPHA	ERNES	FETAS	**EVIL**	EYRAS
EPHAH	**ERNS**	GETAS	DEVIL	**EYRE**
EPHAS	DERNS	KETAS	KEVIL	EYRES
EPIC	FERNS	WETAS	EVILS	**FACE**
SEPIC	HERNS	ZETAS	**EWER**	FACED
EPICS	KERNS	**ETAT**	FEWER	FACER
EPOS	PERNS	ETATS	HEWER	FACES
PEPOS	TERNS	**ETCH**	NEWER	FACET
REPOS	**EROS**	FETCH	SEWER	**FACT**
ERAS	AEROS	KETCH	EWERS	FACTS
TERAS	CEROS	LETCH	**EWES**	**FADE**
ERASE	DEROS	RETCH	EWEST	FADED
ERED	HEROS	VETCH	**EWTS**	FADER
CERED	KEROS	**ETEN**	NEWTS	FADES
DERED	WEROS	ETENS	**EXAM**	**FADO**
LERED	ZEROS	**ETHE**	EXAMS	FADOS
MERED	EROSE	LETHE	**EXEC**	**FAFF**
SERED	**ERRS**	ETHER	EXECS	FAFFS
ERES	SERRS	**ETHS**	**EXED**	**FAIK**
BERES	**ERST**	BETHS	HEXED	FAIKS
CERES	PERST	HETHS	SEXED	**FAIL**
DERES	VERST	METHS	VEXED	FAILS
FERES	**ERUV**	TETHS	WEXED	**FAIN**
GERES	ERUVS	**ETIC**	YEXED	FAINE
HERES	**ESES**	METIC	**EXES**	FAINS
LERES	BESES	**ETNA**	DEXES	FAINT
MERES	LESES	ETNAS	HEXES	**FAIR**
PERES	MESES	**ETUI**	KEXES	FAIRS
SERES	RESES	ETUIS	LEXES	FAIRY
TERES	YESES	**EUGH**	REXES	**FAKE**
EREV	**ESKY**	HEUGH	SEXES	FAKED
EREVS	PESKY	LEUGH	TEXES	FAKER
ERGO	**ESNE**	TEUGH	VEXES	FAKES
ERGON	MESNE	EUGHS	WEXES	FAKEY
ERGOS	ESNES	**EUKS**	YEXES	**FALL**
ERGOT	**ESSE**	NEUKS	ZEXES	FALLS
ERGS	CESSE	YEUKS	**EXIT**	**FAME**
BERGS	DESSE	**EURO**	EXITS	FAMED

FAMES	FAZES	FESTY	FINES	FLAWS
FAND	**FEAL**	**FETA**	**FINI**	FLAWY
FANDS	FEALS	FETAL	FINIS	**FLAX**
FANE	**FEAR**	FETAS	**FINK**	FLAXY
FANES	AFEAR	**FETE**	FINKS	**FLAY**
FANG	FEARE	FETED	**FINO**	FLAYS
FANGA	FEARS	FETES	FINOS	**FLEA**
FANGO	**FEAT**	**FETT**	**FIRE**	FLEAM
FANGS	FEATS	FETTA	AFIRE	FLEAS
FANK	**FECK**	FETTS	FIRED	**FLEE**
FANKS	FECKS	**FEUD**	FIRER	FLEER
FANO	**FEEB**	FEUDS	FIRES	FLEES
FANON	FEEBS	**FIAR**	**FIRK**	FLEET
FANOS	**FEED**	FIARS	FIRKS	**FLEG**
FARD	FEEDS	**FIAT**	**FIRM**	FLEGS
FARDS	**FEEL**	FIATS	FIRMS	FLEW
FARE	FEELS	**FICE**	**FIRN**	FLEWS
FARED	**FEEN**	FICES	FIRNS	**FLEX**
FARER	FEENS	**FICO**	**FIRS**	FLEXO
FARES	**FEER**	FICOS	FIRST	**FLEY**
FARL	FEERS	**FIDO**	**FISC**	FLEYS
FARLE	**FEES**	FIDOS	FISCS	**FLIC**
FARLS	FEESE	**FIEF**	**FISH**	FLICK
FARM	FEHM	FIEFS	FISHY	FLICS
FARMS	FEHME	**FIER**	**FISK**	**FLIM**
FARO	**FEIS**	FIERE	FISKS	FLIMP
FAROS	FEIST	FIERS	**FIST**	FLIMS
FARS	**FELL**	FIERY	FISTS	**FLIP**
AFARS	FELLA	**FIFE**	FISTY	FLIPS
FARSE	FELLS	FIFED	**FITT**	**FLIR**
FART	FELLY	FIFER	FITTE	FLIRS
FARTS	**FELT**	FIFES	FITTS	FLIRT
FAST	FELTS	**FIGO**	**FIVE**	**FLIT**
FASTI	FELTY	FIGOS	FIVER	FLITE
FASTS	**FEME**	**FIKE**	FIVES	FLITS
FATE	FEMES	FIKED	**FIZZ**	FLITT
FATED	**FEND**	FIKES	FIZZY	**FLOC**
FATES	FENDS	**FILA**	**FLAB**	FLOCK
FATS	FENDY	FILAR	FLABS	FLOCS
FATSO	**FENI**	**FILE**	**FLAG**	**FLOE**
FAUN	FENIS	FILED	OFLAG	FLOES
FAUNA	**FENT**	FILER	FLAGS	**FLOG**
FAUNS	FENTS	FILES	**FLAK**	FLOGS
FAUR	**FEOD**	FILET	FLAKE	**FLOP**
FAURD	FEODS	**FILL**	FLAKS	FLOPS
FAUT	**FERE**	FILLE	FLAKY	**FLOR**
FAUTS	YFERE	FILLO	**FLAM**	FLORA
FAVA	FERER	FILLS	FLAME	FLORS
FAVAS	FERES	FILLY	FLAMM	FLORY
FAVE	**FERM**	**FILM**	FLAMS	**FLOW**
FAVEL	FERMI	FILMI	FLAMY	FLOWN
FAVER	FERMS	FILMS	**FLAN**	FLOWS
FAVES	**FERN**	FILMY	FLANK	**FLUB**
FAWN	FERNS	**FILO**	FLANS	FLUBS
FAWNS	FERNY	FILOS	**FLAP**	**FLUE**
FAWNY	**FESS**	**FIND**	FLAPS	FLUED
FAYS	FESSE	FINDS	**FLAT**	FLUES
OFAYS	**FEST**	**FINE**	FLATS	FLUEY
FAZE	FESTA	FINED	**FLAW**	**FLUS**
FAZED	FESTS	FINER	FLAWN	FLUSH

Hooks arranged by hook word

FOAL	FOSSE	FROST	FUZZY	GAMEY
FOALS	**FOUD**	**FROW**	**FYCE**	**GAMP**
FOAM	FOUDS	FROWN	FYCES	GAMPS
FOAMS	**FOUL**	FROWS	**FYKE**	**GAMS**
FOAMY	AFOUL	FROWY	FYKED	OGAMS
FOHN	FOULE	**FRUG**	FYKES	**GANE**
FOHNS	FOULS	FRUGS	**FYLE**	GANEF
FOID	**FOUR**	**FUBS**	FYLES	GANEV
FOIDS	FOURS	FUBSY	**FYRD**	**GANG**
FOIL	**FOWL**	**FUCK**	FYRDS	GANGS
FOILS	FOWLS	FUCKS	**GADE**	**GANT**
FOIN	**FRAB**	**FUEL**	GADES	GANTS
FOINS	FRABS	FUELS	**GADI**	**GAOL**
FOLD	**FRAG**	**FUFF**	GADID	GAOLS
FOLDS	FRAGS	FUFFS	GADIS	**GAPE**
FOLK	**FRAP**	FUFFY	**GADS**	AGAPE
FOLKS	FRAPE	**FUGU**	EGADS	GAPED
FOLKY	FRAPS	FUGUE	GADSO	GAPER
FOND	**FRAS**	FUGUS	**GAFF**	GAPES
FONDA	FRASS	**FUJI**	GAFFE	**GAPO**
FONDS	**FRAT**	FUJIS	GAFFS	IGAPO
FONDU	FRATE	**FULL**	**GAGE**	GAPOS
FONT	FRATI	FULLS	GAGED	**GARB**
FONTS	FRATS	FULLY	GAGER	GARBE
FOOD	**FRAU**	**FUME**	GAGES	GARBO
FOODS	FRAUD	FUMED	**GAID**	GARBS
FOODY	FRAUS	FUMER	GAIDS	**GARI**
FOOL	**FRAY**	FUMES	**GAIN**	GARIS
FOOLS	FRAYS	FUMET	AGAIN	**GARS**
FOOT	**FREE**	**FUND**	GAINS	AGARS
AFOOT	FREED	FUNDI	**GAIR**	**GART**
FOOTS	FREER	FUNDS	GAIRS	GARTH
FOOTY	FREES	FUNDY	**GAIT**	**GASP**
FORA	FREET	**FUNG**	GAITS	GASPS
FORAM	**FRET**	FUNGI	GAITT	GASPY
FORAY	FRETS	FUNGO	**GAJO**	**GAST**
FORB	**FRIB**	FUNGS	GAJOS	AGAST
FORBS	FRIBS	**FUNK**	**GALA**	GASTS
FORBY	**FRIG**	FUNKS	GALAH	**GATE**
FORD	FRIGS	FUNKY	GALAS	AGATE
FORDO	**FRIS**	**FURL**	GALAX	GATED
FORDS	FRISE	FURLS	**GALE**	GATER
FORE	FRISK	**FURR**	GALEA	GATES
AFORE	FRIST	FURRS	GALES	**GATH**
FOREL	**FRIT**	FURRY	**GALL**	GATHS
FORES	AFRIT	**FUSE**	GALLS	**GAUD**
FOREX	FRITH	FUSED	GALLY	GAUDS
FORK	FRITS	FUSEE	**GAMA**	GAUDY
FORKS	FRITT	FUSEL	AGAMA	**GAUM**
FORKY	FRITZ	FUSES	GAMAS	GAUMS
FORM	**FRIZ**	**FUSS**	GAMAY	GAUMY
FORME	FRIZE	FUSSY	**GAMB**	**GAUN**
FORMS	FRIZZ	**FUST**	GAMBA	GAUNT
FORT	**FROE**	FUSTS	GAMBE	**GAUP**
FORTE	FROES	FUSTY	GAMBO	GAUPS
FORTH	**FROG**	**FUZE**	GAMBS	**GAUR**
FORTS	FROGS	FUZED	**GAME**	GAURS
FORTY	**FROS**	FUZEE	GAMED	**GAUS**
FOSS	AFROS	FUZES	GAMER	GAUSS
FOSSA	FROSH	**FUZZ**	GAMES	**GAVE**

AGAVE	**GEST**	GIRTS	**GLOP**	GOLPS
GAVEL	EGEST	**GISM**	GLOPS	**GONE**
GAWD	GESTE	AGISM	**GLOW**	AGONE
GAWDS	GESTS	GISMO	AGLOW	GONEF
GAWK	**GETA**	GISMS	GLOWS	GONER
GAWKS	GETAS	**GIST**	**GLUE**	GONG
GAWKY	**GEUM**	AGIST	GLUED	GONGS
GAWP	GEUMS	GISTS	GLUER	**GONK**
GAWPS	**GHAT**	**GITE**	GLUES	GONKS
GAZE	GHATS	GITES	GLUEY	**GONS**
AGAZE	**GHEE**	**GIVE**	**GLUG**	AGONS
GAZED	GHEES	OGIVE	GLUGS	**GOOD**
GAZER	**GIBE**	GIVED	**GLUM**	AGOOD
GAZES	GIBED	GIVEN	GLUME	GOODS
GEAL	GIBEL	GIVER	GLUMS	GOODY
GEALS	GIBER	GIVES	**GLUT**	**GOOF**
GEAN	GIBES	**GLAD**	GLUTE	GOOFS
GEANS	**GIFT**	GLADE	GLUTS	GOOFY
GEAR	GIFTS	GLADS	**GNAR**	**GOOG**
GEARE	**GIGA**	GLADY	GNARL	GOOGS
GEARS	GIGAS	**GLAM**	GNARR	**GOOK**
GEAT	**GILA**	GLAMS	GNARS	GOOKS
GEATS	AGILA	**GLED**	**GNAT**	GOOKY
GECK	GILAS	OGLED	GNATS	**GOOL**
GECKO	**GILD**	GLEDE	**GNAW**	GOOLD
GECKS	GILDS	GLEDS	GNAWN	GOOLS
GEEK	**GILL**	**GLEE**	GNAWS	GOOLY
GEEKS	GILLS	AGLEE	**GNOW**	**GOON**
GEEKY	GILLY	GLEED	GNOWS	GOONS
GEEP	**GILT**	GLEES	**GOAD**	GOONY
GEEPS	GILTS	GLEET	GOADS	**GOOP**
GEES	**GIMP**	**GLEI**	**GOAF**	GOOPS
OGEES	GIMPS	GLEIS	GOAFS	GOOPY
GEESE	GIMPY	**GLEN**	**GOAL**	**GOOR**
GEEST	**GING**	GLENS	GOALS	GOORS
GEIT	AGING	GLENT	**GOAT**	GOORY
GEITS	GINGE	**GLEY**	GOATS	**GOOS**
GELD	GINGS	AGLEY	GOATY	GOOSE
GELDS	**GINK**	GLEYS	**GOBO**	GOOSY
GELT	GINKS	**GLIA**	GOBOS	**GORA**
GELTS	**GINN**	GLIAL	**GODS**	AGORA
GENA	GINNY	GLIAS	GODSO	GORAL
GENAL	**GIOS**	**GLIB**	**GOEL**	GORAS
GENAS	AGIOS	GLIBS	GOELS	**GORE**
GENE	**GIPS**	**GLID**	**GOER**	GORED
AGENE	GIPSY	GLIDE	GOERS	GORES
GENES	**GIRD**	**GLIM**	**GOFF**	**GORI**
GENET	GIRDS	GLIME	GOFFS	GORIS
GENT	**GIRL**	GLIMS	**GOGO**	**GORM**
AGENT	GIRLS	**GLIT**	GOGOS	GORMS
GENTS	GIRLY	GLITS	**GOLD**	GORMY
GENTY	**GIRN**	GLITZ	GOLDS	**GORP**
GENU	GIRNS	**GLOB**	GOLDY	GORPS
GENUA	**GIRO**	GLOBE	**GOLE**	**GOSH**
GENUS	GIRON	GLOBI	GOLEM	GOSHT
GERE	GIROS	GLOBS	GOLES	**GOSS**
GERES	**GIRR**	GLOBY	**GOLF**	GOSSE
GERM	GIRRS	**GLOM**	GOLFS	**GOTH**
GERMS	**GIRT**	GLOMS	**GOLP**	GOTHS
GERMY	GIRTH		GOLPE	**GOUK**

Hooks arranged by hook word

GOUKS	AGRIN	GULAS	**HAAF**	HAJJI
GOUT	GRIND	**GULE**	HAAFS	**HAKA**
GOUTS	GRINS	GULES	**HAAR**	HAKAM
GOUTY	**GRIP**	**GULF**	HAARS	HAKAS
GOWD	GRIPE	GULFS	**HABU**	**HAKE**
GOWDS	GRIPS	GULFY	HABUS	SHAKE
GOWF	GRIPT	**GULL**	**HACK**	HAKEA
GOWFS	GRIPY	GULLS	CHACK	HAKES
GOWK	**GRIS**	GULLY	SHACK	**HAKU**
GOWKS	GRISE	**GULP**	THACK	HAKUS
GOWL	GRIST	GULPH	WHACK	**HALE**
GOWLS	GRISY	GULPS	HACKS	SHALE
GOWN	**GRIT**	GULPY	**HADE**	WHALE
GOWNS	GRITH	**GUMP**	SHADE	HALED
GRAB	GRITS	GUMPS	HADED	HALER
GRABS	**GROG**	**GUNG**	HADES	HALES
GRAD	GROGS	GUNGE	**HADJ**	**HALF**
GRADE	**GROK**	GUNGY	HADJI	HALFA
GRADS	GROKS	**GUNK**	**HADS**	HALFS
GRAM	**GROT**	GUNKS	CHADS	**HALL**
GRAMA	GROTS	GUNKY	SHADS	SHALL
GRAME	**GROW**	**GURL**	HADST	HALLO
GRAMP	GROWL	GURLS	**HAEM**	HALLS
GRAMS	GROWN	GURLY	HAEMS	**HALM**
GRAN	GROWS	**GURN**	**HAET**	SHALM
GRANA	**GRUB**	GURNS	HAETS	HALMA
GRAND	GRUBS	**GURS**	**HAFF**	HALMS
GRANS	GRUE	GURSH	CHAFF	**HALO**
GRANT	GRUED	**GURU**	HAFFS	HALON
GRAT	GRUEL	GURUS	**HAFT**	HALOS
GRATE	GRUES	**GUSH**	CHAFT	**HALT**
GRAV	**GRUM**	GUSHY	SHAFT	SHALT
GRAVE	GRUME	**GUST**	HAFTS	HALTS
GRAVS	GRUMP	GUSTO	**HAGG**	**HAME**
GRAVY	**GUAN**	GUSTS	HAGGS	SHAME
GRAY	GUANA	GUSTY	**HAGS**	HAMED
GRAYS	GUANO	**GUTS**	SHAGS	HAMES
GREE	GUANS	GUTSY	**HAHA**	**HAMS**
AGREE	**GUAR**	**GUYS**	HAHAS	CHAMS
GREED	GUARD	GUYSE	**HAHS**	SHAMS
GREEK	GUARS	**GYAL**	SHAHS	WHAMS
GREEN	**GUCK**	GYALS	**HAIK**	**HAND**
GREES	GUCKS	**GYBE**	HAIKA	SHAND
GREET	GUCKY	GYBED	HAIKS	HANDS
GREN	**GUDE**	GYBES	HAIKU	HANDY
GRENS	GUDES	**GYMP**	**HAIL**	**HANG**
GRENZ	**GUES**	GYMPS	HAILS	BHANG
GREW	AGUES	**GYPS**	HAILY	CHANG
GREWS	GUESS	GYPSY	**HAIN**	PHANG
GREY	GUEST	**GYRE**	CHAIN	WHANG
GREYS	**GUFF**	GYRED	HAINS	HANGI
GRID	GUFFS	GYRES	HAINT	HANGS
GRIDE	**GUGA**	**GYRO**	**HAIR**	**HANK**
GRIDS	GUGAS	GYRON	CHAIR	CHANK
GRIG	**GUID**	GYROS	HAIRS	SHANK
GRIGS	GUIDE	**GYTE**	HAIRY	THANK
GRIM	GUIDS	GYTES	**HAJI**	HANKS
GRIME	**GULA**	**GYVE**	BHAJI	HANKY
GRIMY	GULAG	GYVED	HAJIS	**HANT**
GRIN	GULAR	GYVES	**HAJJ**	CHANT

HANTS	**HATS**	HEARD	**HEMP**	SHEWN	
HAPS	CHATS	HEARE	HEMPS	**HEWS**	
CHAPS	GHATS	HEARS	HEMPY	CHEWS	
SHAPS	KHATS	HEART	**HEND**	SHEWS	
WHAPS	WHATS	**HEAT**	SHEND	THEWS	
HAPU	**HAUD**	CHEAT	HENDS	WHEWS	
HAPUS	HAUDS	WHEAT	**HENS**	**HEYS**	
HARD	**HAUF**	HEATH	THENS	WHEYS	
CHARD	HAUFS	HEATS	WHENS	**HICK**	
SHARD	**HAUL**	**HEBE**	**HENT**	CHICK	
HARDS	SHAUL	THEBE	AHENT	THICK	
HARDY	HAULD	HEBEN	SHENT	HICKS	
HARE	HAULM	HEBES	HENTS	**HIDE**	
CHARE	HAULS	**HECH**	**HERB**	CHIDE	
PHARE	HAULT	HECHT	HERBS	HIDED	
SHARE	**HAUT**	**HECK**	HERBY	HIDER	
WHARE	GHAUT	CHECK	**HERD**	HIDES	
HARED	HAUTE	HECKS	SHERD	**HIED**	
HAREM	**HAVE**	**HEED**	HERDS	SHIED	
HARES	CHAVE	THEED	**HERE**	**HIES**	
HARK	SHAVE	HEEDS	CHERE	RHIES	
CHARK	HAVEN	HEEDY	SHERE	SHIES	
SHARK	HAVER	**HEEL**	THERE	**HIGH**	
HARKS	HAVES	SHEEL	WHERE	AHIGH	
HARL	**HAWK**	WHEEL	HERES	THIGH	
HARLS	CHAWK	HEELS	**HERL**	HIGHS	
HARM	HAWKS	**HEFT**	HERLS	HIGHT	
CHARM	**HAWM**	THEFT	**HERM**	**HIKE**	
THARM	SHAWM	WHEFT	THERM	HIKED	
HARMS	HAWMS	HEFTE	HERMA	HIKER	
HARN	**HAWS**	HEFTS	HERMS	HIKES	
SHARN	CHAWS	HEFTY	**HERN**	**HILA**	
HARNS	SHAWS	**HEID**	HERNS	HILAR	
HARO	THAWS	HEIDS	**HERO**	**HILD**	
HAROS	HAWSE	**HEIL**	HEROE	CHILD	
HARP	**HAYS**	HEILS	HERON	**HILI**	
SHARP	CHAYS	**HEIR**	HEROS	CHILI	
HARPS	SHAYS	THEIR	**HERS**	**HILL**	
HARPY	**HAZE**	HEIRS	HERSE	CHILL	
HART	HAZED	**HELE**	**HERY**	SHILL	
CHART	HAZEL	HELED	HERYE	THILL	
HARTS	HAZER	HELES	**HESP**	HILLO	
HASH	HAZES	**HELL**	THESP	HILLS	
SHASH	**HEAD**	SHELL	HESPS	HILLY	
HASHY	AHEAD	HELLO	**HEST**	**HILT**	
HASK	HEADS	HELLS	CHEST	HILTS	
HASKS	HEADY	**HELM**	GHEST	**HIMS**	
HASP	**HEAL**	WHELM	HESTS	SHIMS	
HASPS	SHEAL	HELMS	**HETE**	WHIMS	
HAST	WHEAL	**HELO**	THETE	**HIND**	
GHAST	HEALD	HELOS	HETES	AHIND	
HASTA	HEALS	HELOT	**HETH**	HINDS	
HASTE	**HEAP**	**HELP**	CHETH	**HING**	
HASTY	AHEAP	CHELP	KHETH	AHING	
HATE	CHEAP	WHELP	HETHS	EHING	
HATED	HEAPS	HELPS	**HETS**	OHING	
HATER	HEAPY	**HEME**	KHETS	THING	
HATES	**HEAR**	RHEME	SHETS	HINGE	
HATH	SHEAR	THEME	WHETS	HINGS	
HATHA	WHEAR	HEMES	**HEWN**	HINS	

Hooks arranged by hook word

CHINS	HOERS	HONEY	**HORS**	**HOYA**
SHINS	**HOES**	**HONG**	KHORS	HOYAS
THINS	SHOES	THONG	HORSE	**HUBS**
WHINS	**HOGG**	HONGI	HORST	CHUBS
HINT	HOGGS	HONGS	HORSY	**HUCK**
AHINT	**HOGH**	**HONK**	**HOSE**	CHUCK
HINTS	HOGHS	HONKS	CHOSE	SHUCK
HIOI	**HOGS**	HONKY	THOSE	HUCKS
HIOIS	CHOGS	**HONS**	WHOSE	**HUER**
HIPS	SHOGS	CHONS	HOSED	HUERS
CHIPS	**HOHS**	PHONS	HOSEL	**HUFF**
SHIPS	PHOHS	**HOOD**	HOSEN	CHUFF
WHIPS	**HOIK**	HOODS	HOSER	HUFFS
HIPT	HOIKS	HOODY	HOSES	HUFFY
WHIPT	**HOKE**	**HOOF**	HOSEY	**HUGE**
HIRE	CHOKE	CHOOF	**HOST**	HUGER
SHIRE	HOKED	WHOOF	GHOST	**HUGS**
HIRED	HOKES	HOOFS	HOSTA	CHUGS
HIREE	HOKEY	**HOOK**	HOSTS	THUGS
HIRER	**HOKI**	CHOOK	**HOTE**	**HUHU**
HIRES	HOKIS	SHOOK	SHOTE	HUHUS
HISH	**HOLD**	HOOKA	HOTEL	**HUIA**
SHISH	AHOLD	HOOKS	HOTEN	HUIAS
WHISH	HOLDS	HOOKY	**HOTS**	**HULA**
HISS	**HOLE**	**HOON**	PHOTS	HULAS
WHISS	DHOLE	SHOON	SHOTS	**HULE**
HISSY	THOLE	HOONS	**HOUF**	SHULE
HIST	WHOLE	**HOOP**	HOUFF	HULES
SHIST	HOLED	WHOOP	HOUFS	**HULK**
WHIST	HOLES	HOOPS	**HOUR**	HULKS
HISTS	HOLEY	**HOOT**	HOURI	HULKY
HITS	HOLK	BHOOT	HOURS	**HULL**
CHITS	HOLKS	SHOOT	**HOUT**	AHULL
SHITS	**HOLM**	WHOOT	CHOUT	HULLO
WHITS	HOLMS	HOOTS	SHOUT	HULLS
HIVE	**HOLS**	HOOTY	HOUTS	HULLY
CHIVE	DHOLS	**HOPE**	**HOVE**	**HUMA**
SHIVE	**HOLT**	SHOPE	SHOVE	HUMAN
HIVED	HOLTS	HOPED	HOVEA	HUMAS
HIVER	**HOMA**	HOPER	HOVED	**HUMF**
HIVES	HOMAS	HOPES	HOVEL	HUMFS
HIZZ	**HOME**	**HOPS**	HOVEN	**HUMP**
CHIZZ	HOMED	CHOPS	HOVER	CHUMP
WHIZZ	HOMER	SHOPS	HOVES	THUMP
HOAR	HOMES	WHOPS	**HOWE**	WHUMP
HOARD	HOMEY	**HORA**	HOWES	HUMPH
HOARS	**HOMO**	HORAH	**HOWF**	HUMPS
HOARY	ZHOMO	HORAL	HOWFF	HUMPY
HOAS	HOMOS	HORAS	HOWFS	**HUMS**
HOAST	**HOND**	**HORE**	**HOWK**	CHUMS
HOBO	HONDA	CHORE	CHOWK	**HUNK**
HOBOS	HONDS	SHORE	HOWKS	CHUNK
HOCK	**HONE**	WHORE	**HOWL**	THUNK
CHOCK	OHONE	**HORI**	THOWL	HUNKS
SHOCK	PHONE	HORIS	HOWLS	HUNKY
HOCKS	RHONE	**HORN**	**HOWS**	HUNS
HOED	SHONE	SHORN	CHOWS	SHUNS
SHOED	HONED	THORN	DHOWS	**HUNT**
HOER	HONER	HORNS	SHOWS	SHUNT
SHOER	HONES	HORNY	HOWSO	HUNTS

HUPS	ICERS	**IKON**	DIMPS	PIONS
WHUPS	**ICES**	EIKON	GIMPS	**IOTA**
HURL	BICES	IKONS	LIMPS	BIOTA
CHURL	DICES	**ILEA**	NIMPS	DIOTA
THURL	FICES	PILEA	PIMPS	IOTAS
HURLS	RICES	ILEAC	SIMPS	**IRED**
HURLY	SICES	ILEAL	TIMPS	AIRED
HURT	TICES	**ILEX**	WIMPS	FIRED
HURTS	VICES	SILEX	**INBY**	HIRED
HUSH	**ICKY**	**ILIA**	INBYE	MIRED
SHUSH	DICKY	CILIA	**INCH**	SIRED
HUSHY	KICKY	MILIA	CINCH	TIRED
HUSK	MICKY	ILIAC	FINCH	VIRED
HUSKS	NICKY	ILIAD	LINCH	WIRED
HUSKY	PICKY	ILIAL	PINCH	**IRES**
HUSO	TICKY	**ILKS**	WINCH	CIRES
HUSOS	WICKY	BILKS	**INFO**	FIRES
HUSS	**ICON**	MILKS	INFOS	HIRES
HUSSY	ICONS	SILKS	**INGO**	MIRES
HUTS	**IDEA**	**ILLS**	BINGO	SIRES
BHUTS	IDEAL	BILLS	DINGO	TIRES
PHUTS	IDEAS	CILLS	JINGO	VIRES
SHUTS	**IDEE**	DILLS	LINGO	WIRES
HWYL	IDEES	FILLS	PINGO	**IRID**
HWYLS	**IDES**	GILLS	INGOT	VIRID
HYEN	AIDES	HILLS	**INKS**	IRIDS
HYENA	BIDES	JILLS	BINKS	**IRIS**
HYENS	CIDES	KILLS	DINKS	SIRIS
HYKE	HIDES	LILLS	FINKS	**IRKS**
HYKES	NIDES	MILLS	GINKS	BIRKS
HYLA	RIDES	NILLS	JINKS	DIRKS
PHYLA	SIDES	PILLS	KINKS	FIRKS
HYLAS	TIDES	RILLS	LINKS	KIRKS
HYLE	WIDES	SILLS	MINKS	LIRKS
CHYLE	**IDLE**	TILLS	OINKS	MIRKS
PHYLE	SIDLE	VILLS	PINKS	YIRKS
HYLEG	IDLED	WILLS	RINKS	**IRON**
HYLES	IDLER	YILLS	SINKS	GIRON
HYMN	IDLES	ZILLS	TINKS	IRONE
HYMNS	**IDOL**	**ILLY**	WINKS	IRONS
HYPE	IDOLA	BILLY	**INKY**	IRONY
HYPED	IDOLS	DILLY	DINKY	**ISBA**
HYPER	**IDYL**	FILLY	HINKY	ISBAS
HYPES	IDYLL	GILLY	KINKY	**ISIT**
HYPO	IDYLS	HILLY	LINKY	VISIT
HYPOS	**IFFY**	SILLY	PINKY	**ISLE**
IAMB	BIFFY	TILLY	SINKY	AISLE
IAMBI	JIFFY	WILLY	ZINKY	LISLE
IAMBS	MIFFY	**IMAM**	**INNS**	ISLED
IBEX	NIFFY	IMAMS	JINNS	ISLES
VIBEX	**IGGS**	**IMID**	LINNS	ISLET
ICED	BIGGS	TIMID	WINNS	**ISMS**
DICED	MIGGS	IMIDE	**INTI**	GISMS
RICED	RIGGS	IMIDO	INTIL	JISMS
TICED	**IGLU**	IMIDS	INTIS	**ISNA**
VICED	IGLUS	**IMMY**	**INTO**	ISNAE
ICER	**IKAN**	JIMMY	PINTO	**ISOS**
DICER	IKANS	**IMPI**	**IONS**	MISOS
NICER	**IKAT**	IMPIS	CIONS	PISOS
RICER	IKATS	**IMPS**	LIONS	**ITAS**

Hooks arranged by hook word

DITAS	JARKS	JIFFY	JOTAS	KAIKA
LITAS	**JARL**	**JILL**	**JOUK**	KAIKS
PITAS	JARLS	JILLS	JOUKS	**KAIL**
VITAS	**JARP**	**JILT**	**JOUR**	SKAIL
ITCH	JARPS	JILTS	JOURS	KAILS
AITCH	**JASP**	**JIMP**	**JOWL**	**KAIM**
BITCH	JASPE	JIMPY	JOWLS	KAIMS
DITCH	JASPS	**JINK**	JOWLY	**KAIN**
FITCH	**JATO**	JINKS	**JUBA**	KAING
HITCH	JATOS	**JINN**	JUBAS	KAINS
MITCH	**JAUK**	DJINN	**JUBE**	**KAKA**
PITCH	JAUKS	JINNE	JUBES	KAKAS
TITCH	**JAUP**	JINNI	**JUCO**	**KAKI**
WITCH	JAUPS	JINNS	JUCOS	KAKIS
ITCHY	**JAVA**	**JINS**	**JUDO**	KALE
ITEM	JAVAS	DJINS	JUDOS	KALES
ITEMS	**JAZZ**	**JIRD**	**JUGA**	**KALI**
IWIS	JAZZY	JIRDS	AJUGA	KALIF
KIWIS	**JEAN**	**JISM**	JUGAL	KALIS
IXIA	JEANS	JISMS	**JUJU**	**KAMA**
IXIAS	**JEAT**	**JIVE**	JUJUS	KAMAS
IZAR	JEATS	JIVED	**JUKE**	**KAME**
SIZAR	**JEDI**	JIVER	JUKED	KAMES
IZARD	JEDIS	JIVES	JUKES	**KAMI**
IZARS	**JEEL**	JIVEY	**JUKU**	KAMIK
JAAP	JEELS	**JOBE**	JUKUS	KAMIS
JAAPS	JEELY	JOBED	**JUMP**	**KANA**
JACK	**JEEP**	JOBES	JUMPS	KANAE
JACKS	JEEPS	**JOCK**	JUMPY	KANAS
JACKY	**JEER**	JOCKO	**JUNK**	**KANE**
JADE	JEERS	JOCKS	JUNKS	KANEH
JADED	**JEFE**	**JOEY**	JUNKY	KANES
JADES	JEFES	JOEYS	**JUPE**	**KANG**
JAFA	**JEFF**	**JOHN**	JUPES	KANGA
JAFAS	JEFFS	JOHNS	**JURA**	KANGS
JAGA	**JEHU**	**JOIN**	JURAL	**KANS**
JAGAS	JEHUS	JOINS	JURAT	IKANS
JAGG	**JELL**	JOINT	**JURE**	**KANT**
JAGGS	JELLO	**JOKE**	JUREL	KANTS
JAGGY	JELLS	JOKED	**JUST**	**KAON**
JAIL	JELLY	JOKER	JUSTS	KAONS
JAILS	**JERK**	JOKES	**JUTE**	**KAPA**
JAKE	JERKS	JOKEY	JUTES	KAPAS
JAKES	JERKY	**JOLE**	**JUVE**	**KAPH**
JAKEY	**JESS**	JOLED	JUVES	KAPHS
JAMB	JESSE	JOLES	**KADE**	**KARA**
JAMBE	**JEST**	**JOLL**	KADES	KARAS
JAMBO	JESTS	JOLLS	**KADI**	KARAT
JAMBS	**JETE**	JOLLY	KADIS	**KARK**
JAMBU	JETES	**JOLT**	**KAGO**	KARKS
JANE	**JIAO**	JOLTS	KAGOS	**KARN**
JANES	JIAOS	JOLTY	**KAGU**	KARNS
JANN	**JIBB**	**JOMO**	KAGUS	**KARO**
JANNS	JIBBS	JOMON	**KAID**	KAROO
JANNY	**JIBE**	JOMOS	KAIDS	**KART**
JAPE	JIBED	**JONG**	**KAIE**	SKART
JAPED	JIBER	JONGS	KAIES	KARTS
JAPER	JIBES	**JOOK**	**KAIF**	KATA
JAPES	**JIFF**	JOOKS	KAIFS	KATAS
JARK	JIFFS	**JOTA**	**KAIK**	KATI

KATIS	KENOS	**KILN**	**KLIK**	**KOOK**
KATS	**KENS**	KILNS	KLIKS	KOOKS
IKATS	SKENS	**KILO**	**KNAG**	KOOKY
SKATS	**KENT**	KILOS	KNAGS	**KOPH**
KAVA	KENTE	**KILP**	**KNAP**	KOPHS
KAVAS	KENTS	KILPS	KNAPS	**KORA**
KAWA	**KEPI**	**KILT**	**KNAR**	KORAI
KAWAS	KEPIS	KILTS	KNARL	KORAS
KAWAU	**KEPS**	KILTY	KNARS	KORAT
KAWS	SKEPS	**KINA**	**KNEE**	**KORE**
SKAWS	**KERB**	KINAS	KNEED	KORES
KAYO	KERBS	**KIND**	KNEEL	**KORU**
KAYOS	**KERF**	KINDA	KNEES	KORUN
KAYS	KERFS	KINDS	**KNIT**	KORUS
OKAYS	**KERN**	KINDY	KNITS	**KOTO**
KAZI	KERNE	**KINE**	**KNOB**	KOTOS
KAZIS	KERNS	KINES	KNOBS	KOTOW
KBAR	**KERO**	**KING**	**KNOP**	**KRAB**
KBARS	KEROS	AKING	KNOPS	KRABS
KECK	**KEST**	EKING	**KNOT**	**KSAR**
KECKS	KESTS	KINGS	KNOTS	KSARS
KEEF	**KETA**	**KINK**	**KNOW**	**KUDO**
SKEEF	KETAS	SKINK	KNOWE	KUDOS
KEEFS	**KETO**	KINKS	KNOWN	**KUDU**
KEEK	KETOL	KINKY	KNOWS	KUDUS
KEEKS	**KETS**	**KINO**	**KNUB**	**KUFI**
KEEL	SKETS	KINOS	KNUBS	KUFIS
KEELS	**KHAF**	**KINS**	**KNUR**	**KUIA**
KEEN	KHAFS	SKINS	KNURL	KUIAS
SKEEN	**KHAN**	**KIPE**	KNURR	**KUKU**
KEENO	KHANS	KIPES	KNURS	KUKUS
KEENS	**KHAT**	**KIPP**	**KNUT**	**KULA**
KEEP	KHATS	KIPPA	KNUTS	KULAK
KEEPS	**KHET**	KIPPS	**KOAN**	KULAN
KEET	KHETH	**KIPS**	KOANS	KULAS
SKEET	KHETS	SKIPS	**KOAP**	**KURI**
KEETS	**KHOR**	**KIRK**	KOAPS	KURIS
KEGS	KHORS	KIRKS	**KOBO**	**KURU**
SKEGS	**KHUD**	**KIRN**	KOBOS	KURUS
KEIR	KHUDS	KIRNS	**KOEL**	**KUTA**
KEIRS	**KIBE**	**KISS**	KOELS	KUTAS
KELL	KIBEI	KISSY	**KOFF**	**KUTI**
SKELL	KIBES	**KIST**	SKOFF	KUTIS
KELLS	**KICK**	KISTS	KOFFS	**KUTU**
KELLY	KICKS	**KITE**	**KOHA**	KUTUS
KELP	KICKY	SKITE	KOHAS	**KUZU**
SKELP	**KIDS**	KITED	**KOHL**	KUZUS
KELPS	SKIDS	KITER	KOHLS	**KVAS**
KELPY	**KIEF**	KITES	**KOJI**	KVASS
KELT	KIEFS	**KITH**	KOJIS	**KYAK**
KELTS	**KIER**	KITHE	**KOLA**	KYAKS
KELTY	SKIER	KITHS	KOLAS	**KYAR**
KEMB	KIERS	**KITS**	**KOLO**	KYARS
KEMBO	**KIFF**	SKITS	KOLOS	**KYAT**
KEMBS	SKIFF	**KIVA**	**KOND**	KYATS
KEMP	**KIKE**	KIVAS	KONDO	**KYBO**
KEMPS	KIKES	**KIWI**	**KONK**	KYBOS
KEMPT	**KILL**	KIWIS	KONKS	**KYLE**
KEMPY	SKILL	**KLAP**	**KONS**	KYLES
KENO	KILLS	KLAPS	IKONS	**KYND**

KYNDE	**LAIK**	**LANE**	GLASS	PLAYS
KYNDS	GLAIK	ALANE	LASSI	SLAYS
KYPE	LAIKA	PLANE	LASSO	**LAZE**
KYPES	LAIKS	SLANE	LASSU	BLAZE
KYTE	**LAIN**	LANES	**LAST**	GLAZE
SKYTE	BLAIN	**LANG**	BLAST	LAZED
KYTES	ELAIN	ALANG	CLAST	LAZES
LABS	PLAIN	CLANG	PLAST	**LAZO**
BLABS	SLAIN	KLANG	LASTS	LAZOS
FLABS	**LAIR**	SLANG	**LATE**	**LAZY**
SLABS	FLAIR	**LANK**	ALATE	GLAZY
LACE	GLAIR	BLANK	BLATE	**LEAD**
GLACE	LAIRD	CLANK	ELATE	PLEAD
PLACE	LAIRS	FLANK	PLATE	LEADS
LACED	LAIRY	PLANK	SLATE	LEADY
LACER	**LAKE**	SLANK	LATED	**LEAF**
LACES	FLAKE	LANKS	LATEN	LEAFS
LACET	SLAKE	LANKY	LATER	LEAFY
LACEY	LAKED	**LANT**	LATEX	**LEAK**
LACK	LAKER	ALANT	**LATH**	BLEAK
ALACK	LAKES	PLANT	LATHE	LEAKS
BLACK	**LAKH**	SLANT	LATHI	LEAKY
CLACK	LAKHS	LANTS	LATHS	**LEAL**
FLACK	**LAKY**	**LAPS**	LATHY	ILEAL
PLACK	FLAKY	ALAPS	**LATS**	**LEAM**
SLACK	**LALL**	CLAPS	BLATS	FLEAM
LACKS	LALLS	FLAPS	CLATS	GLEAM
LADE	**LAMA**	KLAPS	FLATS	LEAMS
BLADE	LLAMA	PLAPS	PLATS	**LEAN**
CLADE	ULAMA	SLAPS	SLATS	CLEAN
GLADE	LAMAS	LAPSE	**LAUD**	GLEAN
SLADE	**LAMB**	**LARD**	BLAUD	LEANS
LADED	LAMBS	LARDS	LAUDS	LEANT
LADEN	LAMBY	LARDY	**LAUF**	LEANY
LADER	**LAME**	**LARE**	LAUFS	**LEAP**
LADES	BLAME	BLARE	**LAVA**	LEAPS
LADS	CLAME	FLARE	LAVAS	LEAPT
BLADS	FLAME	GLARE	**LAVE**	**LEAR**
CLADS	LAMED	LAREE	CLAVE	BLEAR
GLADS	LAMER	LARES	SLAVE	CLEAR
LADY	LAMES	**LARI**	LAVED	LEARE
BLADY	**LAMP**	LARIS	LAVER	LEARN
GLADY	CLAMP	**LARK**	LAVES	LEARS
LAER	LAMPS	LARKS	**LAWK**	LEARY
BLAER	**LAMS**	LARKY	LAWKS	**LEAS**
LAERS	BLAMS	**LARN**	**LAWN**	FLEAS
LAGS	CLAMS	LARNS	BLAWN	PLEAS
BLAGS	FLAMS	**LASE**	FLAWN	LEASE
CLAGS	GLAMS	BLASE	LAWNS	LEASH
FLAGS	SLAMS	LASED	LAWNY	LEAST
SLAGS	**LANA**	LASER	**LAWS**	**LEAT**
LAHS	LANAI	LASES	BLAWS	BLEAT
BLAHS	LANAS	**LASH**	CLAWS	CLEAT
LAIC	**LAND**	BLASH	FLAWS	PLEAT
LAICH	ALAND	CLASH	SLAWS	LEATS
LAICS	BLAND	FLASH	**LAYS**	**LEED**
LAID	ELAND	PLASH	ALAYS	BLEED
PLAID	GLAND	SLASH	BLAYS	GLEED
SLAID	LANDE	**LASS**	CLAYS	**LEEK**
LAIDS	LANDS	CLASS	FLAYS	CLEEK

GLEEK	LENTO	**LIEN**	LIMOS	LIPOS
SLEEK	**LEPT**	ALIEN	**LIMP**	**LIPS**
LEEKS	CLEPT	LIENS	BLIMP	BLIPS
LEEP	SLEPT	**LIER**	FLIMP	CLIPS
BLEEP	LEPTA	FLIER	LIMPA	FLIPS
CLEEP	**LERE**	PLIER	LIMPS	SLIPS
SLEEP	LERED	SLIER	**LIMY**	**LIRA**
LEEPS	LERES	LIERS	BLIMY	LIRAS
LEER	**LERP**	**LIES**	SLIMY	**LIRK**
FLEER	LERPS	CLIES	**LIND**	LIRKS
SLEER	**LESS**	FLIES	BLIND	**LISK**
LEERS	BLESS	PLIES	LINDS	FLISK
LEERY	**LEST**	VLIES	LINDY	GLISK
LEES	BLEST	**LIEU**	**LINE**	LISKS
BLEES	LESTS	LIEUS	ALINE	**LISP**
FLEES	**LETS**	**LIFE**	CLINE	LISPS
GLEES	BLETS	LIFER	LINED	**LIST**
LEESE	**LEUD**	LIFES	LINEN	ALIST
LEET	LEUDS	**LIFT**	LINER	BLIST
FLEET	**LEVE**	CLIFT	LINES	LISTS
GLEET	CLEVE	GLIFT	LINEY	**LITE**
SLEET	LEVEE	LIFTS	**LING**	BLITE
LEETS	LEVEL	**LIKE**	BLING	ELITE
LEFT	LEVER	ALIKE	CLING	FLITE
ALEFT	**LEYS**	GLIKE	FLING	LITED
CLEFT	BLEYS	YLIKE	PLING	LITER
LEFTE	FLEYS	LIKED	SLING	LITES
LEFTS	GLEYS	LIKEN	LINGA	**LITH**
LEFTY	SLEYS	LIKER	LINGO	LITHE
LEGS	**LEZZ**	LIKES	LINGS	LITHO
CLEGS	LEZZA	**LILL**	LINGY	LITHS
FLEGS	LEZZY	LILLS	**LINK**	LITS
LEHR	**LIAR**	**LILO**	BLINK	FLITS
LEHRS	LIARD	LILOS	CLINK	GLITS
LEIR	LIARS	**LILT**	PLINK	SLITS
LEIRS	LIART	LILTS	SLINK	**LIVE**
LEIS	**LIAS**	**LILY**	LINKS	ALIVE
GLEIS	ALIAS	SLILY	LINKY	BLIVE
VLEIS	GLIAS	**LIMA**	**LINN**	OLIVE
LEISH	**LIBS**	LIMAN	LINNS	SLIVE
LEME	GLIBS	LIMAS	LINNY	LIVED
FLEME	**LICE**	LIMAX	**LINO**	LIVEN
LEMED	SLICE	**LIMB**	LINOS	LIVER
LEMEL	**LICH**	CLIMB	**LINS**	LIVES
LEMES	LICHI	LIMBA	BLINS	**LOAD**
LEND	LICHT	LIMBI	**LINT**	LOADS
BLEND	**LICK**	LIMBO	CLINT	**LOAF**
LENDS	CLICK	LIMBS	ELINT	LOAFS
LENG	FLICK	LIMBY	FLINT	**LOAM**
LENGS	KLICK	**LIME**	GLINT	CLOAM
LENO	SLICK	CLIME	LINTS	GLOAM
LENOS	LICKS	GLIME	LINTY	LOAMS
LENS	**LIDO**	SLIME	**LINY**	LOAMY
GLENS	LIDOS	LIMED	BLINY	**LOAN**
LENSE	**LIED**	LIMEN	**LION**	SLOAN
LENT	CLIED	LIMES	LIONS	LOANS
BLENT	FLIED	LIMEY	**LIPE**	**LOBE**
GLENT	PLIED	**LIMN**	CLIPE	GLOBE
OLENT	**LIEF**	LIMNS	SLIPE	LOBED
LENTI	LIEFS	**LIMO**	**LIPO**	LOBES

Hooks arranged by hook word

LOBI	LOLLS	FLOPS	**LOUR**	LUCKS
GLOBI	LOLLY	GLOPS	CLOUR	LUCKY
LOBO	**LOMA**	PLOPS	FLOUR	**LUDE**
LOBOS	LOMAS	SLOPS	LOURE	BLUDE
LOBS	**LOME**	**LORD**	LOURS	ELUDE
BLOBS	LOMED	LORDS	LOURY	LUDES
GLOBS	LOMES	LORDY	**LOUS**	**LUDO**
SLOBS	**LONE**	**LORE**	CLOUS	LUDOS
LOCA	ALONE	BLORE	LOUSE	**LUES**
LOCAL	CLONE	LOREL	LOUSY	BLUES
LOCH	LONER	LORES	**LOUT**	CLUES
LOCHS	**LONG**	**LORY**	CLOUT	FLUES
LOCK	ALONG	FLORY	FLOUT	GLUES
BLOCK	FLONG	GLORY	GLOUT	PLUES
CLOCK	KLONG	**LOSE**	LOUTS	SLUES
FLOCK	PLONG	CLOSE	**LOVE**	**LUFF**
LOCKS	LONGA	LOSED	CLOVE	BLUFF
LOCO	LONGE	LOSEL	GLOVE	FLUFF
LOCOS	LONGS	LOSEN	SLOVE	PLUFF
LODE	**LOOF**	LOSER	LOVED	SLUFF
GLODE	ALOOF	LOSES	LOVER	LUFFA
LODEN	KLOOF	**LOSH**	LOVES	LUFFS
LODES	LOOFA	FLOSH	LOVEY	**LUGE**
LODS	LOOFS	SLOSH	**LOWE**	KLUGE
ALODS	**LOOK**	**LOSS**	ALOWE	LUGED
CLODS	PLOOK	FLOSS	LOWED	LUGER
PLODS	LOOKS	GLOSS	LOWER	LUGES
LOFT	**LOOM**	LOSSY	LOWES	**LUGS**
ALOFT	BLOOM	**LOST**	**LOWN**	GLUGS
LOFTS	GLOOM	GLOST	BLOWN	PLUGS
LOFTY	SLOOM	**LOTA**	CLOWN	SLUGS
LOGE	LOOMS	LOTAH	FLOWN	**LUIT**
ELOGE	**LOON**	LOTAS	LOWND	SLUIT
LOGES	LOONS	**LOTE**	LOWNE	**LUKE**
LOGO	LOONY	CLOTE	LOWNS	FLUKE
LOGOI	**LOOP**	FLOTE	**LOWP**	**LULL**
LOGON	BLOOP	ZLOTE	LOWPS	LULLS
LOGOS	CLOOP	LOTES	**LOWS**	**LULU**
LOGS	GLOOP	**LOTH**	BLOWS	LULUS
BLOGS	SLOOP	CLOTH	CLOWS	**LUMA**
CLOGS	LOOPS	SLOTH	FLOWS	LUMAS
FLOGS	LOOPY	**LOTI**	GLOWS	**LUMP**
SLOGS	**LOOR**	LOTIC	PLOWS	CLUMP
LOGY	FLOOR	**LOTO**	SLOWS	FLUMP
ELOGY	LOORD	LOTOS	LOWSE	PLUMP
OLOGY	**LOOS**	**LOTS**	**LOWT**	SLUMP
LOID	LOOSE	BLOTS	LOWTS	LUMPS
SLOID	**LOOT**	CLOTS	**LOYS**	LUMPY
LOIDS	CLOOT	PLOTS	CLOYS	**LUMS**
LOIN	SLOOT	SLOTS	PLOYS	ALUMS
ALOIN	LOOTS	**LOUD**	**LUAU**	GLUMS
ELOIN	**LOPE**	ALOUD	LUAUS	PLUMS
LOINS	ELOPE	CLOUD	**LUBE**	SLUMS
LOIR	SLOPE	**LOUN**	LUBED	**LUNA**
LOIRS	LOPED	LOUND	LUBES	LUNAR
LOKE	LOPER	LOUNS	**LUCE**	LUNAS
BLOKE	LOPES	**LOUP**	LUCES	**LUNE**
CLOKE	**LOPS**	LOUPE	**LUCK**	LUNES
LOKES	CLOPS	LOUPS	CLUCK	LUNET
LOLL	ELOPS	LOUPS	PLUCK	**LUNG**

CLUNG	**LYSE**	MALAM	MARES	AMAUT
FLUNG	LYSED	MALAR	**MARG**	MAUTS
SLUNG	LYSES	MALAS	MARGE	**MAWK**
LUNGE	**LYTE**	MALAX	MARGS	MAWKS
LUNGI	FLYTE	**MALE**	**MARK**	MAWKY
LUNGS	LYTED	MALES	MARKA	**MAWR**
LUNK	LYTES	**MALI**	MARKS	MAWRS
BLUNK	**MAAR**	MALIC	**MARL**	**MAXI**
CLUNK	MAARE	MALIK	MARLE	MAXIM
FLUNK	MAARS	MALIS	MARLS	MAXIS
PLUNK	**MABE**	**MALL**	MARLY	**MAYA**
SLUNK	MABES	SMALL	**MARM**	MAYAN
LUNKS	**MACE**	MALLS	SMARM	MAYAS
LUNT	MACED	**MALM**	MARMS	**MAYO**
BLUNT	MACER	SMALM	**MARS**	MAYOR
LUNTS	MACES	MALMS	MARSE	MAYOS
LURE	**MACH**	MALMY	MARSH	**MAYS**
ALURE	MACHE	**MALT**	**MART**	MAYST
LURED	MACHI	SMALT	SMART	**MAZE**
LURER	MACHO	MALTS	MARTS	AMAZE
LURES	MACHS	MALTY	**MASA**	SMAZE
LUREX	**MACK**	**MAMA**	OMASA	MAZED
LURK	SMACK	MAMAS	MASAS	MAZER
LURKS	MACKS	**MAMS**	**MASE**	MAZES
LURS	**MACS**	IMAMS	MASED	MAZEY
BLURS	EMACS	**MANA**	MASER	**MEAD**
SLURS	**MAGE**	MANAS	MASES	MEADS
LUSH	IMAGE	MANAT	**MASH**	**MEAL**
BLUSH	MAGES	**MAND**	SMASH	MEALS
FLUSH	**MAGG**	MANDI	MASHY	MEALY
PLUSH	MAGGS	**MANE**	**MASK**	**MEAN**
SLUSH	**MAGI**	MANED	MASKS	MEANE
LUSHY	MAGIC	MANEH	**MASS**	MEANS
LUSK	**MAID**	MANES	AMASS	MEANT
LUSKS	MAIDS	MANET	MASSA	MEANY
LUST	**MAIK**	**MANG**	MASSE	**MEAT**
LUSTS	SMAIK	MANGA	MASSY	MEATH
LUSTY	MAIKO	MANGE	**MAST**	MEATS
LUTE	MAIKS	MANGO	MASTS	MEATY
ELUTE	**MAIL**	MANGS	MASTY	**MECK**
FLUTE	EMAIL	MANGY	**MASU**	MECKS
GLUTE	MAILE	**MANI**	MASUS	**MEED**
LUTEA	MAILL	MANIA	**MATE**	MEEDS
LUTED	MAILS	MANIC	AMATE	**MEEK**
LUTER	**MAIM**	MANIS	MATED	SMEEK
LUTES	MAIMS	**MANO**	MATER	**MEER**
LUTZ	**MAIN**	MANOR	MATES	AMEER
KLUTZ	AMAIN	MANOS	MATEY	EMEER
LUXE	MAINS	**MANS**	**MATH**	MEERS
LUXES	**MAIR**	MANSE	MATHS	**MEES**
LWEI	MAIRE	**MARA**	**MATT**	SMEES
LWEIS	MAIRS	MARAE	MATTE	**MEET**
LYAM	**MAKE**	MARAH	MATTS	MEETS
LYAMS	MAKER	MARAS	**MAUD**	**MEFF**
LYME	MAKES	**MARC**	MAUDS	MEFFS
LYMES	**MAKI**	MARCH	**MAUL**	**MEGA**
LYNE	MAKIS	MARCS	MAULS	OMEGA
LYNES	**MAKO**	**MARD**	**MAUN**	**MEIN**
LYRE	MAKOS	MARDY	MAUND	MEINS
LYRES	**MALA**	**MARE**	**MAUT**	MEINT

MEINY	MESEL	**MILD**	MIRIN	SMOGS
MELA	MESES	MILDS	**MIRK**	**MOHR**
MELAS	**MESH**	**MILE**	SMIRK	MOHRS
MELD	MESHY	SMILE	MIRKS	**MOIL**
MELDS	**MESS**	MILER	MIRKY	MOILS
MELL	MESSY	MILES	**MIRS**	**MOIT**
SMELL	**META**	**MILK**	AMIRS	MOITS
MELLS	METAL	MILKO	EMIRS	**MOJO**
MELT	**METE**	MILKS	SMIRS	MOJOS
SMELT	METED	MILKY	**MIRV**	**MOKE**
MELTS	METER	**MILL**	MIRVS	SMOKE
MELTY	METES	MILLE	**MISE**	MOKES
MEME	**METH**	MILLS	MISER	**MOKI**
MEMES	METHO	**MILO**	MISES	MOKIS
MEMO	METHS	MILOR	**MISO**	**MOKO**
MEMOS	**MEUS**	MILOS	MISOS	SMOKO
MEND	EMEUS	**MILT**	**MISS**	MOKOS
AMEND	MEUSE	MILTS	AMISS	**MOLA**
EMEND	**MEVE**	MILTY	MISSA	MOLAL
MENDS	MEVED	MILTZ	MISSY	MOLAR
MENE	MEVES	**MIME**	**MIST**	MOLAS
AMENE	**MEWL**	MIMED	MISTS	**MOLD**
MENED	MEWLS	MIMEO	MISTY	MOLDS
MENES	**MEWS**	MIMER	**MITE**	MOLDY
MENG	SMEWS	MIMES	SMITE	**MOLE**
MENGE	**MEZE**	**MINA**	MITER	AMOLE
MENGS	MEZES	MINAE	MITES	MOLES
MENT	**MEZZ**	MINAR	**MITT**	**MOLL**
AMENT	MEZZE	MINAS	MITTS	MOLLA
MENTA	MEZZO	**MIND**	**MITY**	MOLLS
MENTO	**MICA**	MINDS	AMITY	MOLLY
MENU	MICAS	**MINE**	**MIXT**	**MOLT**
MENUS	**MICE**	AMINE	MIXTE	SMOLT
MEOU	AMICE	IMINE	**MIZZ**	YMOLT
MEOUS	**MICH**	MINED	MIZZY	MOLTO
MEOW	MICHE	MINER	**MOAN**	MOLTS
MEOWS	MICHT	MINES	MOANS	**MOME**
MERC	**MICK**	**MING**	**MOAT**	MOMES
MERCH	MICKS	MINGE	MOATS	**MONA**
MERCS	MICKY	MINGS	**MOBE**	MONAD
MERCY	**MICO**	MINGY	MOBES	MONAL
MERE	MICOS	**MINI**	**MOCH**	MONAS
MERED	**MIDI**	MINIM	MOCHA	**MONG**
MEREL	MIDIS	MINIS	MOCHS	AMONG
MERER	**MIDS**	**MINK**	MOCHY	EMONG
MERES	AMIDS	MINKE	**MOCK**	MONGO
MERI	IMIDS	MINKS	SMOCK	MONGS
MERIL	MIDST	**MINO**	MOCKS	**MONK**
MERIS	**MIEN**	AMINO	**MODE**	MONKS
MERIT	MIENS	IMINO	MODEL	**MONO**
MERK	**MIFF**	MINOR	MODEM	MONOS
SMERK	MIFFS	MINOS	MODER	**MOOD**
MERKS	MIFFY	**MINT**	MODES	MOODS
MERL	**MIGG**	MINTS	**MODI**	MOODY
MERLE	MIGGS	MINTY	MODII	**MOOK**
MERLS	**MIHI**	**MIRE**	**MOER**	MOOKS
MESA	MIHIS	MIRED	MOERS	**MOOL**
MESAL	**MIKE**	MIRES	**MOFO**	MOOLA
MESAS	MIKED	MIREX	MOFOS	MOOLI
MESE	MIKES	**MIRI**	**MOGS**	MOOLS

MOOLY	MOTEY	**MUIR**	**MUSK**	NAIFS
MOON	**MOTH**	MUIRS	MUSKS	**NAIK**
MOONS	MOTHS	**MULE**	MUSKY	NAIKS
MOONY	MOTHY	EMULE	**MUSO**	**NAIL**
MOOP	MOTI	MULED	MUSOS	SNAIL
MOOPS	MOTIF	MULES	**MUSS**	NAILS
MOOR	MOTIS	MULEY	MUSSE	**NALA**
SMOOR	**MOTT**	**MULL**	MUSSY	NALAS
MOORS	MOTTE	MULLA	**MUST**	**NAME**
MOORY	MOTTO	MULLS	MUSTH	NAMED
MOOS	MOTTS	**MUMM**	MUSTS	NAMER
MOOSE	MOTTY	MUMMS	MUSTY	NAMES
MOOT	MOTU	MUMMY	**MUTE**	**NANA**
SMOOT	MOTUS	**MUMP**	MUTED	ANANA
MOOTS	**MOUE**	MUMPS	MUTER	JNANA
MOPE	MOUES	**MUMS**	MUTES	NANAS
MOPED	**MOUP**	MUMSY	**MUTI**	**NANE**
MOPER	MOUPS	**MUMU**	MUTIS	INANE
MOPES	**MOUS**	MUMUS	**MUTS**	**NAPA**
MOPEY	MOUSE	**MUNG**	SMUTS	NAPAS
MOPS	MOUST	MUNGA	**MUTT**	**NAPE**
MOPSY	MOUSY	MUNGO	MUTTS	NAPED
MORA	**MOVE**	MUNGS	**MUZZ**	NAPES
MORAE	AMOVE	**MUNI**	MUZZY	**NAPS**
MORAL	EMOVE	MUNIS	**MYAL**	KNAPS
MORAS	MOVED	**MUNT**	MYALL	SNAPS
MORAT	MOVER	MUNTS	**MYNA**	**NARC**
MORAY	MOVES	MUNTU	MYNAH	NARCO
MORE	**MOWA**	**MUON**	MYNAS	NARCS
SMORE	MOWAS	MUONS	**MYTH**	**NARD**
MOREL	**MOXA**	**MURA**	MYTHI	NARDS
MORES	MOXAS	MURAL	MYTHS	**NARE**
MORN	**MOYA**	MURAS	MYTHY	SNARE
MORNE	MOYAS	**MURE**	**MYXO**	NARES
MORNS	**MOYL**	EMURE	MYXOS	**NARK**
MORS	MOYLE	MURED	**MZEE**	SNARK
MORSE	MOYLS	MURES	MZEES	NARKS
MORT	**MOZE**	MUREX	**NAAM**	NARKY
AMORT	MOZED	**MURK**	NAAMS	**NARY**
MORTS	MOZES	MURKS	**NAAN**	SNARY
MOSE	**MOZO**	MURKY	NAANS	UNARY
MOSED	MOZOS	**MURL**	**NABE**	**NATS**
MOSES	**MUCH**	MURLS	NABES	GNATS
MOSEY	MUCHO	MURLY	**NABK**	**NAVE**
MOSK	**MUCK**	**MURR**	NABKS	KNAVE
MOSKS	AMUCK	MURRA	**NABS**	NAVEL
MOSS	MUCKS	MURRE	SNABS	NAVES
MOSSO	MUCKY	MURRI	**NACH**	NAVEW
MOSSY	**MUFF**	MURRS	NACHE	**NAZE**
MOST	MUFFS	MURRY	NACHO	NAZES
MOSTE	**MUGG**	**MUSE**	**NADA**	**NAZI**
MOSTS	MUGGA	AMUSE	NADAS	NAZIR
MOTE	MUGGS	MUSED	**NAFF**	NAZIS
EMOTE	MUGGY	MUSER	NAFFS	**NEAL**
SMOTE	**MUGS**	MUSES	**NAGA**	NEALS
MOTED	SMUGS	MUSET	NAGAS	**NEAP**
MOTEL	**MUID**	**MUSH**	**NAGS**	SNEAP
MOTEN	MUIDS	SMUSH	KNAGS	NEAPS
MOTES	**MUIL**	MUSHA	SNAGS	**NEAR**
MOTET	MUILS	MUSHY	**NAIF**	ANEAR

Hooks arranged by hook word

NEARS	NEXTS	**NOBS**	**NORM**	NUMBS
NEAT	**NIBS**	KNOBS	ENORM	**NURD**
NEATH	SNIBS	SNOBS	NORMA	NURDS
NEATS	**NICE**	**NOCK**	NORMS	NURDY
NEBS	NICER	KNOCK	**NOSE**	**NURL**
SNEBS	**NICK**	NOCKS	NOSED	KNURL
NECK	SNICK	**NODE**	NOSER	NURLS
SNECK	NICKS	ANODE	NOSES	**NURR**
NECKS	NICKY	NODES	NOSEY	KNURR
NEDS	**NIDE**	**NODS**	**NOTA**	NURRS
SNEDS	SNIDE	SNODS	NOTAL	**NURS**
NEED	NIDED	**NOEL**	**NOTE**	KNURS
KNEED	NIDES	NOELS	NOTED	NURSE
SNEED	**NIEF**	**NOGG**	NOTER	**NUTS**
NEEDS	NIEFS	NOGGS	NOTES	KNUTS
NEEDY	**NIES**	**NOGS**	**NOUL**	NUTSO
NEEM	SNIES	SNOGS	NOULD	NUTSY
NEEMB	**NIFE**	**NOIL**	NOULE	**NYES**
NEEMS	KNIFE	NOILS	NOULS	SNYES
NEEP	NIFES	NOILY	**NOUN**	**OAFS**
NEEPS	**NIFF**	**NOIR**	NOUNS	GOAFS
NEIF	SNIFF	NOIRS	NOUNY	LOAFS
NEIFS	NIFFS	**NOLE**	**NOUP**	**OAKS**
NEMA	NIFFY	ANOLE	NOUPS	BOAKS
ENEMA	**NIGH**	NOLES	**NOUT**	SOAKS
NEMAS	ANIGH	**NOLL**	KNOUT	**OARS**
NEMN	NIGHS	KNOLL	SNOUT	BOARS
NEMNS	NIGHT	NOLLS	**NOVA**	HOARS
NENE	**NILL**	**NOLO**	NOVAE	ROARS
NENES	NILLS	NOLOS	NOVAS	SOARS
NEON	**NILS**	**NOMA**	**NOWL**	VOARS
NEONS	ANILS	NOMAD	NOWLS	**OARY**
NERD	**NIMB**	NOMAS	**NOWN**	GOARY
NERDS	NIMBI	**NOME**	KNOWN	HOARY
NERDY	NIMBS	GNOME	**NOWS**	ROARY
NERK	**NINE**	NOMEN	ENOWS	**OAST**
NERKA	NINES	NOMES	GNOWS	BOAST
NERKS	**NIPA**	**NONA**	KNOWS	COAST
NEST	NIPAS	NONAS	SNOWS	HOAST
NESTS	**NIPS**	**NONE**	**NOWT**	LOAST
NETE	SNIPS	NONES	NOWTS	ROAST
NETES	**NIRL**	NONET	NOWTY	TOAST
NETT	NIRLS	**NONG**	**NOWY**	OASTS
NETTS	NIRLY	NONGS	SNOWY	**OATH**
NETTY	**NISH**	**NONI**	**NUBS**	LOATH
NEUK	KNISH	NONIS	KNUBS	OATHS
NEUKS	**NITE**	**NOOK**	SNUBS	**OATS**
NEUM	UNITE	SNOOK	**NUDE**	BOATS
NEUME	NITER	**NOOKS**	NUDER	COATS
NEUMS	NITES	NOOKY	NUDES	DOATS
NEVE	**NITS**	**NOON**	**NUFF**	GOATS
NEVEL	KNITS	NOONS	SNUFF	MOATS
NEVER	SNITS	**NOOP**	NUFFS	**OBAS**
NEVES	UNITS	SNOOP	**NUKE**	BOBAS
NEWS	**NIXE**	NOOPS	NUKED	SOBAS
ENEWS	NIXED	**NORI**	NUKES	**OBES**
NEWSY	NIXER	NORIA	**NULL**	JOBES
NEWT	NIXES	NORIS	NULLA	LOBES
NEWTS	**NOAH**	**NORK**	NULLS	MOBES
NEXT	NOAHS	NORKS	**NUMB**	ROBES

OBESE	ODYLE	**OKEH**	**OLPE**	CONTO
OBEY	ODYLS	OKEHS	GOLPE	**ONUS**
OBEYS	**OFAY**	**OKES**	OLPES	BONUS
OBIA	OFAYS	BOKES	**OMBU**	CONUS
COBIA	**OFFS**	COKES	KOMBU	TONUS
OBIAS	BOFFS	HOKES	OMBUS	**OOFS**
OBIT	COFFS	JOKES	**OMEN**	COOFS
OOBIT	DOFFS	LOKES	NOMEN	GOOFS
OBITS	GOFFS	MOKES	WOMEN	HOOFS
OBOE	KOFFS	POKES	OMENS	LOOFS
OBOES	TOFFS	ROKES	**OMER**	POOFS
OBOL	**OGAM**	SOKES	COMER	ROOFS
BOBOL	OGAMS	TOKES	GOMER	WOOFS
OBOLE	**OGEE**	YOKES	HOMER	YOOFS
OBOLI	YOGEE	**OKRA**	VOMER	**OOFY**
OBOLS	OGEES	KOKRA	OMERS	BOOFY
OBOS	**OGLE**	OKRAS	**OMIT**	GOOFY
GOBOS	BOGLE	**OKTA**	VOMIT	POOFY
HOBOS	FOGLE	OKTAS	OMITS	ROOFY
KOBOS	OGLED	**OLDS**	**OMOV**	WOOFY
LOBOS	OGLER	BOLDS	OMOVS	**OOHS**
ZOBOS	OGLES	COLDS	**ONCE**	BOOHS
OCAS	**OGRE**	FOLDS	BONCE	POOHS
COCAS	OGRES	GOLDS	NONCE	**OOMS**
SOCAS	**OHED**	HOLDS	PONCE	BOOMS
OCHE	HOHED	MOLDS	SONCE	COOMS
BOCHE	OOHED	SOLDS	ONCER	DOOMS
OCHER	**OHIA**	WOLDS	ONCES	LOOMS
OCHES	OHIAS	**OLDY**	ONCET	ROOMS
OCTA	**OHOS**	GOLDY	**ONER**	SOOMS
OCTAD	BOHOS	MOLDY	BONER	TOOMS
OCTAL	COHOS	**OLEO**	DONER	ZOOMS
OCTAN	TOHOS	OLEOS	GONER	**OONS**
OCTAS	**OIKS**	**OLES**	HONER	BOONS
ODAH	HOIKS	BOLES	LONER	COONS
ODAHS	**OILS**	COLES	MONER	GOONS
ODAL	BOILS	DOLES	TONER	HOONS
MODAL	COILS	GOLES	ZONER	LOONS
NODAL	FOILS	HOLES	ONERS	MOONS
PODAL	MOILS	JOLES	ONERY	NOONS
ODALS	NOILS	MOLES	**ONES**	POONS
ODAS	ROILS	NOLES	BONES	ROONS
CODAS	SOILS	POLES	CONES	TOONS
SODAS	TOILS	ROLES	HONES	WOONS
ODES	**OILY**	SOLES	JONES	ZOONS
BODES	DOILY	TOLES	NONES	**OONT**
CODES	NOILY	VOLES	PONES	OONTS
LODES	ROILY	**OLID**	RONES	**OOPS**
MODES	SOILY	SOLID	SONES	COOPS
NODES	**OINK**	**OLIO**	TONES	GOOPS
RODES	BOINK	FOLIO	ZONES	HOOPS
ODIC	OINKS	POLIO	**ONIE**	LOOPS
IODIC	**OINT**	OLIOS	BONIE	MOOPS
SODIC	JOINT	**OLLA**	MONIE	NOOPS
ODOR	NOINT	HOLLA	**ONLY**	POOPS
ODORS	POINT	MOLLA	FONLY	ROOPS
ODSO	OINTS	OLLAS	SONLY	SOOPS
GODSO	**OKAY**	OLLAV	**ONOS**	WOOPS
ODSOS	TOKAY	**OLMS**	MONOS	YOOPS
ODYL	OKAYS	HOLMS	**ONTO**	**OOSE**

Hooks arranged by hook word

BOOSE	**OPUS**	BORTS	LOUMA	COVER
GOOSE	MOPUS	DORTS	OUMAS	DOVER
LOOSE	**ORAD**	FORTS	**OUPA**	HOVER
MOOSE	DORAD	MORTS	OUPAS	LOVER
NOOSE	**ORAL**	PORTS	**OUPH**	MOVER
ROOSE	BORAL	RORTS	OUPHE	ROVER
WOOSE	CORAL	SORTS	OUPHS	OVERS
OOSES	GORAL	TORTS	**OUPS**	OVERT
OOSY	HORAL	WORTS	COUPS	**OVUM**
GOOSY	LORAL	**ORZO**	DOUPS	NOVUM
OOTS	MORAL	ORZOS	LOUPS	**OWED**
BOOTS	PORAL	**OSES**	MOUPS	BOWED
COOTS	RORAL	COSES	NOUPS	COWED
FOOTS	SORAL	DOSES	ROUPS	DOWED
HOOTS	ORALS	HOSES	SOUPS	JOWED
LOOTS	**ORBS**	KOSES	**OURN**	LOWED
MOOTS	DORBS	LOSES	BOURN	MOWED
POOTS	FORBS	MOSES	MOURN	NOWED
ROOTS	SORBS	NOSES	YOURN	ROWED
SOOTS	**ORBY**	OOSES	**OURS**	SOWED
TOOTS	CORBY	POSES	COURS	TOWED
OOZE	FORBY	ROSES	FOURS	VOWED
BOOZE	**ORCA**	TOSES	HOURS	WOWED
COOZE	ORCAS	**OSSA**	JOURS	YOWED
OOZED	**ORCS**	FOSSA	LOURS	**OWER**
OOZES	TORCS	**OTIC**	POURS	BOWER
OOZY	**ORDO**	LOTIC	SOURS	COWER
BOOZY	FORDO	**OTTO**	TOURS	DOWER
DOOZY	SORDO	LOTTO	YOURS	LOWER
WOOZY	ORDOS	MOTTO	**OUST**	MOWER
OPAH	**ORDS**	POTTO	JOUST	POWER
OPAHS	BORDS	OTTOS	MOUST	ROWER
OPAL	CORDS	**OUCH**	ROUST	SOWER
COPAL	FORDS	COUCH	OUSTS	TOWER
NOPAL	LORDS	MOUCH	**OUTS**	VOWER
OPALS	SORDS	POUCH	BOUTS	**OWES**
OPED	WORDS	TOUCH	DOUTS	BOWES
COPED	**ORES**	VOUCH	GOUTS	HOWES
DOPED	BORES	OUCHT	HOUTS	LOWES
HOPED	CORES	**OUDS**	LOUTS	YOWES
LOPED	FORES	FOUDS	POUTS	**OWLS**
MOPED	GORES	**OUKS**	ROUTS	BOWLS
OOPED	KORES	BOUKS	SOUTS	COWLS
ROPED	LORES	DOUKS	TOUTS	DOWLS
TOPED	MORES	GOUKS	**OUZO**	FOWLS
OPEN	PORES	JOUKS	OUZOS	GOWLS
COPEN	RORES	POUKS	**OVAL**	HOWLS
OPENS	SORES	SOUKS	OVALS	JOWLS
OPES	TORES	TOUKS	**OVEL**	NOWLS
COPES	YORES	YOUKS	HOVEL	SOWLS
DOPES	**ORFE**	ZOUKS	NOVEL	YOWLS
HOPES	ORFES	**OULD**	OVELS	**OWLY**
LOPES	**ORGY**	COULD	**OVEN**	DOWLY
MOPES	PORGY	MOULD	COVEN	JOWLY
POPES	**ORLE**	NOULD	DOVEN	LOWLY
ROPES	ORLES	WOULD	HOVEN	**OWNS**
TOPES	**ORRA**	**OULK**	ROVEN	DOWNS
OPPO	MORRA	OULKS	WOVEN	GOWNS
ZOPPO	SORRA	**OUMA**	OVENS	LOWNS
OPPOS	**ORTS**	DOUMA	**OVER**	POWNS

TOWNS	PACOS	**PANE**	**PASE**	PEAKS	
OWRE	**PACT**	SPANE	PASEO	PEAKY	
HOWRE	EPACT	PANED	PASES	**PEAL**	
POWRE	PACTA	PANEL	**PASH**	SPEAL	
OWRES	PACTS	PANES	PASHA	PEALS	
OWSE	**PACY**	**PANG**	PASHM	**PEAN**	
BOWSE	SPACY	SPANG	**PASS**	SPEAN	
DOWSE	**PADI**	PANGA	PASSE	PEANS	
LOWSE	PADIS	PANGS	**PAST**	**PEAR**	
SOWSE	**PAGE**	**PANS**	PASTA	SPEAR	
TOWSE	APAGE	SPANS	PASTE	PEARE	
OWSEN	PAGED	PANSY	PASTS	PEARL	
OWTS	PAGER	**PANT**	PASTY	PEARS	
DOWTS	PAGES	PANTO	**PATE**	PEART	
LOWTS	**PAHS**	PANTS	SPATE	**PEAS**	
NOWTS	OPAHS	PANTY	PATED	PEASE	
ROWTS	**PAID**	**PAPA**	PATEN	**PEAT**	
TOWTS	APAID	PAPAL	PATER	SPEAT	
OXEN	**PAIK**	PAPAS	PATES	PEATS	
BOXEN	PAIKS	PAPAW	**PATH**	PEATY	
WOXEN	**PAIL**	**PAPE**	PATHS	**PEBA**	
OXER	SPAIL	PAPER	**PATS**	PEBAS	
BOXER	PAILS	PAPES	SPATS	**PECH**	
OXERS	**PAIN**	**PARA**	PATSY	PECHS	
OXES	SPAIN	PARAE	**PATU**	**PECK**	
BOXES	PAINS	PARAS	PATUS	SPECK	
COXES	PAINT	**PARD**	**PAUA**	PECKE	
FOXES	**PAIR**	SPARD	PAUAS	PECKS	
GOXES	PAIRE	PARDI	**PAUL**	PECKY	
HOXES	PAIRS	PARDS	SPAUL	**PECS**	
LOXES	**PAIS**	PARDY	PAULS	SPECS	
NOXES	PAISA	**PARE**	**PAVE**	**PEED**	
POXES	PAISE	SPARE	PAVED	SPEED	
OXID	**PALE**	PARED	PAVEN	**PEEK**	
OXIDE	SPALE	PAREO	PAVER	APEEK	
OXIDS	PALEA	PARER	PAVES	PEEKS	
OXIM	PALED	PARES	**PAWA**	**PEEL**	
OXIME	PALER	PAREU	PAWAS	SPEEL	
OXIMS	PALES	PAREV	PAWAW	PEELS	
OYER	PALET	**PARK**	**PAWK**	**PEEN**	
COYER	**PALL**	SPARK	PAWKS	PEENS	
FOYER	SPALL	PARKA	PAWKY	**PEEP**	
TOYER	PALLA	PARKI	**PAWL**	PEEPE	
OYERS	PALLS	PARKS	SPAWL	PEEPS	
OYES	PALLY	PARKY	PAWLS	**PEER**	
NOYES	**PALM**	**PARP**	**PAWN**	SPEER	
PAAL	PALMS	PARPS	SPAWN	PEERS	
PAALS	PALMY	**PARR**	PAWNS	PEERY	
PACA	**PALP**	PARRA	**PAWS**	PEES	
PACAS	PALPI	PARRS	SPAWS	EPEES	
PACE	PALPS	PARRY	**PAYS**	**PEGH**	
APACE	**PALS**	**PARS**	APAYS	PEGHS	
SPACE	OPALS	SPARS	SPAYS	**PEIN**	
PACED	PALSY	PARSE	PAYSD	PEINS	
PACER	**PAMS**	**PART**	**PEAG**	**PEKE**	
PACES	SPAMS	APART	PEAGE	PEKES	
PACEY	**PAND**	SPART	PEAGS	**PELA**	
PACK	PANDA	PARTI	**PEAK**	PELAS	
PACKS	PANDS	PARTS	APEAK	**PELE**	
PACO	PANDY	PARTY	SPEAK	PELES	

PELF
PELFS
PELL
SPELL
PELLS
PELT
SPELT
PELTA
PELTS
PEND
SPEND
UPEND
PENDS
PENDU
PENE
PENED
PENES
PENI
PENIE
PENIS
PENK
PENKS
PENS
OPENS
PENT
SPENT
PENTS
PEON
PEONS
PEONY
PEPO
PEPOS
PERE
PEREA
PERES
PERI
PERIL
PERIS
PERK
PERKS
PERKY
PERM
SPERM
PERMS
PERN
PERNS
PERP
PERPS
PERT
APERT
PERTS
PERV
PERVE
PERVS
PESO
PESOS
PEST
PESTO
PESTS
PESTY

PETS
SPETS
PEWS
SPEWS
PHIS
APHIS
PHOH
PHOHS
PHON
PHONE
PHONO
PHONS
PHONY
PHOT
PHOTO
PHOTS
PHUT
PHUTS
PIAL
SPIAL
PIAN
APIAN
PIANO
PIANS
PICA
SPICA
PICAL
PICAS
PICE
SPICE
PICK
SPICK
PICKS
PICKY
PICS
EPICS
SPICS
PIED
SPIED
PIER
SPIER
PIERS
PIERT
PIES
SPIES
PIET
PIETA
PIETS
PIETY
PIKA
PIKAS
PIKAU
PIKE
SPIKE
PIKED
PIKER
PIKES
PIKEY
PIKI
PIKIS

PILA
PILAF
PILAO
PILAR
PILAU
PILAW
PILE
SPILE
PILEA
PILED
PILEI
PILER
PILES
PILI
PILIS
PILL
SPILL
PILLS
PIMA
PIMAS
PIMP
PIMPS
PINA
SPINA
PINAS
PINE
OPINE
SPINE
PINED
PINES
PINEY
PING
APING
OPING
PINGO
PINGS
PINK
SPINK
PINKO
PINKS
PINKY
PINS
SPINS
PINT
PINTA
PINTO
PINTS
PINY
SPINY
PION
PIONS
PIONY
PIOY
PIOYE
PIOYS
PIPA
PIPAL
PIPAS
PIPE
PIPED

PIPER
PIPES
PIPET
PIPI
PIPIS
PIPIT
PIRL
PIRLS
PIRN
PIRNS
PISE
PISES
PISH
APISH
PISO
PISOS
PITA
PITAS
PITH
PITHS
PITHY
PITS
SPITS
PIUM
OPIUM
PIUMS
PIZE
PIZED
PIZES
PLAN
PLANE
PLANK
PLANS
PLANT
PLAP
PLAPS
PLAT
SPLAT
PLATE
PLATS
PLATY
PLAY
SPLAY
UPLAY
PLAYA
PLAYS
PLEA
PLEAD
PLEAS
PLEAT
PLEB
PLEBE
PLEBS
PLED
UPLED
PLEW
PLEWS
PLIE
PLIED
PLIER

PLIES
PLIM
PLIMS
PLOD
PLODS
PLOP
PLOPS
PLOT
PLOTS
PLOTZ
PLOW
PLOWS
PLOY
PLOYS
PLUE
PLUES
PLUG
PLUGS
PLUM
PLUMB
PLUME
PLUMP
PLUMS
PLUMY
PLUS
PLUSH
POCK
POCKS
POCKY
PODS
APODS
SPODS
POEM
POEMS
POEP
POEPS
POET
POETS
POGO
POGOS
POIS
POISE
POKE
SPOKE
POKED
POKER
POKES
POKEY
POLE
POLED
POLER
POLES
POLEY
POLK
POLKA
POLKS
POLL
POLLS
POLLY
POLO

POLOS	SPORE	SPRAD	PROOF	PULKA
POLT	PORED	PRADS	**PROP**	PULKS
POLTS	PORER	**PRAM**	PROPS	**PULL**
POLY	PORES	PRAMS	**PROS**	PULLI
POLYP	**PORK**	**PRAO**	PROSE	PULLS
POLYS	PORKS	PRAOS	PROSO	**PULP**
POME	PORKY	**PRAT**	PROSS	PULPS
POMES	**PORN**	SPRAT	PROST	PULPY
POMO	PORNO	PRATE	PROSY	**PULS**
POMOS	PORNS	PRATS	**PROW**	PULSE
POMP	PORNY	PRATT	PROWL	**PULU**
POMPS	**PORT**	PRATY	PROWS	PULUS
POND	APORT	**PRAU**	**PRYS**	**PUMA**
PONDS	SPORT	PRAUS	PRYSE	PUMAS
PONE	PORTA	**PRAY**	**PSIS**	**PUMP**
PONES	PORTS	SPRAY	APSIS	PUMPS
PONEY	PORTY	PRAYS	**PUBE**	**PUMY**
PONG	**POSE**	**PREE**	PUBES	SPUMY
PONGA	POSED	SPREE	**PUCE**	**PUNA**
PONGO	POSER	PREED	PUCER	PUNAS
PONGS	POSES	PREEN	PUCES	**PUNG**
PONGY	POSEY	PREES	**PUCK**	PUNGA
PONK	**POSH**	**PREM**	PUCKA	PUNGS
PONKS	SPOSH	PREMS	PUCKS	**PUNK**
PONT	POSHO	PREMY	**PUDS**	SPUNK
PONTS	**POSS**	**PREP**	SPUDS	PUNKA
PONTY	POSSE	PREPS	PUDSY	PUNKS
POOD	**POST**	**PREX**	**PUDU**	PUNKY
POODS	POSTS	PREXY	PUDUS	**PUNT**
POOF	**POTE**	**PREY**	**PUER**	PUNTO
SPOOF	POTED	PREYS	SPUER	PUNTS
POOFS	POTES	**PRIG**	PUERS	PUNTY
POOFY	**POTS**	SPRIG	**PUFF**	**PUPA**
POOH	SPOTS	PRIGS	PUFFS	PUPAE
POOHS	POTSY	**PRIM**	PUFFY	PUPAL
POOK	**POTT**	PRIMA	**PUGS**	PUPAS
SPOOK	POTTO	PRIME	SPUGS	**PUPU**
POOKA	POTTS	PRIMI	**PUHA**	PUPUS
POOKS	POTTY	PRIMO	PUHAS	**PURE**
POOL	**POUF**	PRIMP	**PUJA**	PURED
SPOOL	POUFF	PRIMS	PUJAH	PUREE
POOLS	POUFS	PRIMY	PUJAS	PURER
POON	**POUK**	**PROA**	**PUKE**	PURES
SPOON	POUKE	PROAS	PUKED	**PURI**
POONS	POUKS	**PROB**	PUKER	PURIM
POOP	**POUR**	PROBE	PUKES	PURIN
APOOP	POURS	PROBS	**PUKU**	PURIS
POOPS	**POUT**	**PROD**	PUKUS	**PURL**
POOR	SPOUT	SPROD	**PULA**	PURLS
SPOOR	POUTS	PRODS	PULAO	**PURR**
POORI	POUTY	**PROF**	PULAS	PURRS
POORT	**POWN**	PROFS	**PULE**	**PURS**
POOT	POWND	**PROG**	SPULE	SPURS
SPOOT	POWNS	SPROG	PULED	PURSE
POOTS	POWNY	PROGS	PULER	PURSY
POPE	**POXY**	**PROM**	PULES	**PUSH**
POPES	EPOXY	EPROM	**PULI**	PUSHY
POPS	**POZZ**	PROMO	PULIK	**PUSS**
POPSY	POZZY	PROMS	PULIS	PUSSY
PORE	**PRAD**	**PROO**	**PULK**	PUTT

PUTTI	QUIPO	RAGED	**RAKU**	TRAPE
PUTTO	QUIPS	RAGEE	RAKUS	RAPED
PUTTS	QUIPU	RAGER	**RALE**	RAPER
PUTTY	**QUIT**	RAGES	RALES	RAPES
PYAT	SQUIT	**RAGG**	**RAMI**	**RAPS**
PYATS	QUITE	RAGGA	RAMIE	CRAPS
PYET	QUITS	RAGGS	RAMIN	DRAPS
PYETS	**QUIZ**	RAGGY	RAMIS	FRAPS
PYIN	SQUIZ	**RAGI**	**RAMP**	TRAPS
PYINS	**QUOD**	TRAGI	CRAMP	WRAPS
PYNE	QUODS	RAGIS	GRAMP	**RAPT**
PYNED	**QUOP**	**RAGS**	TRAMP	TRAPT
PYNES	QUOPS	BRAGS	RAMPS	WRAPT
PYOT	**RABI**	CRAGS	**RAMS**	YRAPT
PYOTS	RABIC	DRAGS	CRAMS	**RARE**
PYRE	RABID	FRAGS	DRAMS	CRARE
SPYRE	RABIS	**RAIA**	GRAMS	URARE
PYRES	**RACE**	RAIAS	PRAMS	RARED
PYREX	BRACE	**RAID**	TRAMS	RAREE
PYRO	GRACE	BRAID	**RANA**	RARER
PYROS	TRACE	RAIDS	GRANA	RARES
QADI	RACED	**RAIK**	PRANA	**RARK**
QADIS	RACER	TRAIK	RANAS	RARKS
QAID	RACES	RAIKS	**RAND**	**RASE**
QAIDS	**RACH**	**RAIL**	BRAND	ERASE
QOPH	BRACH	BRAIL	GRAND	PRASE
QOPHS	ORACH	DRAIL	RANDS	URASE
QUAD	RACHE	FRAIL	RANDY	RASED
SQUAD	**RACK**	GRAIL	**RANG**	RASER
QUADS	BRACK	RAILE	KRANG	RASES
QUAG	CRACK	RAILS	ORANG	**RASH**
QUAGS	DRACK	**RAIN**	PRANG	BRASH
QUAI	FRACK	BRAIN	WRANG	CRASH
QUAIL	TRACK	DRAIN	RANGE	TRASH
QUAIR	WRACK	GRAIN	RANGI	**RASP**
QUAIS	RACKS	TRAIN	RANGY	GRASP
QUAT	**RACY**	RAINE	**RANI**	RASPS
SQUAT	ORACY	RAINS	RANID	RASPY
QUATE	**RADE**	RAINY	RANIS	**RAST**
QUATS	GRADE	**RAIS**	**RANK**	BRAST
QUAY	IRADE	RAISE	BRANK	WRAST
QUAYD	TRADE	**RAIT**	CRANK	RASTA
QUAYS	**RADS**	KRAIT	DRANK	**RATA**
QUEY	BRADS	TRAIT	FRANK	RATAL
QUEYN	GRADS	RAITA	PRANK	RATAN
QUEYS	PRADS	RAITS	TRANK	RATAS
QUID	TRADS	**RAJA**	RANKE	**RATE**
EQUID	**RAFF**	RAJAH	RANKS	CRATE
SQUID	DRAFF	RAJAS	**RANT**	FRATE
QUIDS	GRAFF	**RAKE**	BRANT	GRATE
QUIM	RAFFS	BRAKE	DRANT	IRATE
QUIMS	**RAFT**	CRAKE	GRANT	ORATE
QUIN	CRAFT	DRAKE	ORANT	PRATE
QUINA	DRAFT	RAKED	TRANT	URATE
QUINE	GRAFT	RAKEE	RANTS	WRATE
QUINO	KRAFT	RAKER	**RAPE**	RATED
QUINS	RAFTS	RAKES	CRAPE	RATEL
QUINT	**RAGA**	**RAKI**	DRAPE	RATER
QUIP	RAGAS	RAKIS	FRAPE	RATES
EQUIP	**RAGE**		GRAPE	**RATH**

WRATH	OREAD	FREED	TREND	DRIBS	
RATHA	TREAD	GREED	RENDS	FRIBS	
RATHE	READD	PREED	**RENS**	**RICE**	
RATHS	READS	TREED	BRENS	DRICE	
RATO	READY	REEDE	GRENS	GRICE	
RATOO	**REAK**	REEDS	WRENS	PRICE	
RATOS	BREAK	REEDY	**RENT**	TRICE	
RATS	CREAK	**REEF**	BRENT	RICED	
BRATS	FREAK	REEFS	DRENT	RICER	
DRATS	WREAK	REEFY	PRENT	RICES	
FRATS	REAKS	**REEK**	URENT	RICEY	
PRATS	**REAL**	CREEK	YRENT	**RICH**	
TRATS	AREAL	GREEK	RENTE	RICHT	
RATU	UREAL	REEKS	RENTS	**RICK**	
RATUS	REALM	REEKY	**REPO**	BRICK	
RAUN	REALO	**REEL**	REPOS	CRICK	
RAUNS	REALS	CREEL	REPOT	ERICK	
RAVE	**REAM**	REELS	**REPP**	PRICK	
BRAVE	BREAM	**REEN**	REPPS	TRICK	
CRAVE	CREAM	GREEN	**REPS**	WRICK	
DRAVE	DREAM	PREEN	PREPS	RICKS	
GRAVE	REAME	TREEN	**RESH**	**RICY**	
TRAVE	REAMS	REENS	FRESH	PRICY	
RAVED	REAMY	**REES**	**REST**	**RIDE**	
RAVEL	**REAN**	BREES	CREST	BRIDE	
RAVEN	REANS	CREES	DREST	GRIDE	
RAVER	**REAP**	DREES	PREST	PRIDE	
RAVES	REAPS	FREES	TREST	TRIDE	
RAWN	**REAR**	GREES	WREST	RIDER	
BRAWN	AREAR	PREES	RESTO	RIDES	
DRAWN	DREAR	TREES	RESTS	**RIDS**	
PRAWN	REARM	REEST	RESTY	GRIDS	
RAWNS	REARS	**REGO**	RETE	IRIDS	
RAWS	**RECK**	GREGO	ARETE	**RIEL**	
BRAWS	DRECK	REGOS	RETEM	ARIEL	
CRAWS	TRECK	**REGS**	RETES	ORIEL	
DRAWS	WRECK	DREGS	**RETS**	RIELS	
RAYA	RECKS	**REIF**	ARETS	**RIEM**	
RAYAH	**REDD**	PREIF	FRETS	RIEMS	
RAYAS	AREDD	TREIF	TRETS	**RIFE**	
RAYS	REDDS	REIFS	**REVS**	RIFER	
BRAYS	REDDY	REIFY	EREVS	**RIFF**	
CRAYS	**REDE**	**REIK**	**REWS**	GRIFF	
DRAYS	AREDE	REIKI	BREWS	TRIFF	
FRAYS	BREDE	REIKS	CREWS	RIFFS	
GRAYS	REDED	**REIN**	GREWS	**RIFT**	
PRAYS	REDES	GREIN	TREWS	DRIFT	
TRAYS	**REDO**	REINK	**RHEA**	GRIFT	
RAZE	CREDO	REINS	RHEAS	RIFTE	
BRAZE	UREDO	**REIS**	**RIAL**	RIFTS	
CRAZE	REDON	BREIS	PRIAL	RIFTY	
GRAZE	REDOS	REIST	TRIAL	**RIGG**	
RAZED	REDOX	**REKE**	URIAL	RIGGS	
RAZEE	**REDS**	REKED	RIALS	**RIGS**	
RAZER	BREDS	REKES	**RIAS**	BRIGS	
RAZES	CREDS	REKEY	ARIAS	FRIGS	
READ	**REED**	**REMS**	**RIBA**	GRIGS	
AREAD	BREED	CREMS	RIBAS	PRIGS	
BREAD	CREED	PREMS	**RIBS**	TRIGS	
DREAD	DREED	**REND**	CRIBS	**RILE**	

Hooks arranged by hook word

RILED	ARIOT	DRIVE	ROINS	**ROOK**
RILES	GRIOT	RIVED	**ROJI**	BROOK
RILEY	RIOTS	RIVEL	ROJIS	CROOK
RILL	**RIPE**	RIVEN	**ROKE**	DROOK
BRILL	CRIPE	RIVER	BROKE	ROOKS
DRILL	GRIPE	RIVES	PROKE	ROOKY
FRILL	TRIPE	RIVET	TROKE	**ROOM**
GRILL	RIPED	**RIVO**	WROKE	BROOM
KRILL	RIPEN	RIVOS	ROKED	GROOM
PRILL	RIPER	**RIZA**	ROKER	VROOM
TRILL	RIPES	RIZAS	ROKES	ROOMS
RILLE	**RIPP**	**ROAD**	**ROKS**	ROOMY
RILLS	RIPPS	BROAD	GROKS	**ROON**
RIMA	**RIPS**	TROAD	**ROLE**	CROON
PRIMA	DRIPS	ROADS	DROLE	KROON
RIMAE	GRIPS	**ROAM**	PROLE	ROONS
RIME	TRIPS	ROAMS	ROLES	**ROOP**
CRIME	**RIPT**	**ROAN**	**ROLF**	DROOP
GRIME	DRIPT	GROAN	ROLFS	TROOP
PRIME	GRIPT	ROANS	**ROLL**	ROOPS
RIMED	**RISE**	**ROAR**	DROLL	ROOPY
RIMER	ARISE	ROARS	PROLL	**ROOS**
RIMES	BRISE	ROARY	TROLL	BROOS
RIMS	CRISE	**ROBE**	ROLLS	ROOSA
BRIMS	FRISE	PROBE	**ROMA**	ROOSE
CRIMS	GRISE	ROBED	AROMA	ROOST
PRIMS	PRISE	ROBES	GROMA	**ROOT**
TRIMS	RISEN	**ROBS**	ROMAL	WROOT
RIMU	RISER	PROBS	ROMAN	ROOTS
RIMUS	RISES	**ROCH**	ROMAS	ROOTY
RIMY	**RISK**	BROCH	**ROMP**	**ROPE**
GRIMY	BRISK	**ROCK**	TROMP	GROPE
PRIMY	FRISK	BROCK	ROMPS	TROPE
RIND	RISKS	CROCK	**ROMS**	ROPED
GRIND	RISKY	FROCK	PROMS	ROPER
RINDS	**RISP**	TROCK	**RONE**	ROPES
RINDY	CRISP	ROCKS	CRONE	ROPEY
RINE	RISPS	ROCKY	DRONE	**RORE**
BRINE	**RITE**	**ROCS**	GRONE	CRORE
CRINE	TRITE	CROCS	IRONE	FRORE
TRINE	URITE	**RODE**	KRONE	PRORE
URINE	WRITE	ERODE	PRONE	RORES
RINES	RITES	TRODE	TRONE	**RORT**
RING	**RITS**	RODED	RONEO	RORTS
BRING	BRITS	RODEO	RONES	RORTY
ERING	CRITS	RODES	**RONG**	**RORY**
IRING	FRITS	**RODS**	PRONG	FRORY
WRING	GRITS	BRODS	WRONG	**ROSE**
RINGS	WRITS	PRODS	**RONT**	AROSE
RINK	**RITT**	TRODS	FRONT	BROSE
BRINK	BRITT	**ROES**	RONTE	EROSE
DRINK	FRITT	FROES	RONTS	PROSE
PRINK	RITTS	**ROIL**	**ROOD**	ROSED
RINKS	**RITZ**	BROIL	BROOD	ROSES
RINS	FRITZ	DROIL	ROODS	ROSET
BRINS	RITZY	ROILS	**ROOF**	**ROST**
GRINS	**RIVA**	ROILY	GROOF	CROST
TRINS	RIVAL	**ROIN**	PROOF	FROST
RINSE	RIVAS	GROIN	ROOFS	PROST
RIOT	**RIVE**	PROIN	ROOFY	ROSTI

ROSTS	TROWS	BRUME	BRUTS	SAKER
ROSY	VROWS	GRUME	**RYAL**	SAKES
BROSY	**ROWT**	RUMEN	RYALS	**SAKI**
PROSY	ROWTH	RUMES	**RYKE**	SAKIA
ROTA	ROWTS	**RUMP**	GRYKE	SAKIS
ROTAL	**RUBE**	CRUMP	TRYKE	**SALE**
ROTAN	RUBEL	FRUMP	RYKED	SALEP
ROTAS	RUBES	GRUMP	RYKES	SALES
ROTE	**RUBS**	TRUMP	**RYND**	SALET
WROTE	DRUBS	RUMPO	RYNDS	**SALL**
ROTED	GRUBS	RUMPS	**RYOT**	SALLE
ROTES	**RUCK**	RUMPY	RYOTS	SALLY
ROTI	CRUCK	**RUMS**	**RYPE**	**SALP**
ROTIS	TRUCK	ARUMS	GRYPE	SALPA
ROTL	RUCKS	DRUMS	RYPER	SALPS
ROTLS	**RUDD**	**RUND**	**SABE**	**SALS**
ROTO	RUDDS	RUNDS	SABED	SALSA
ROTON	RUDDY	**RUNE**	SABER	SALSE
ROTOR	**RUDE**	PRUNE	SABES	**SALT**
ROTOS	CRUDE	RUNED	**SACK**	SALTO
ROTS	PRUDE	RUNES	SACKS	SALTS
GROTS	RUDER	**RUNG**	**SADE**	SALTY
TROTS	RUDES	BRUNG	TSADE	**SAMA**
ROUE	**RUDS**	WRUNG	SADES	SAMAN
ROUEN	CRUDS	RUNGS	**SADI**	SAMAS
ROUES	**RUED**	**RUNT**	TSADI	**SAME**
ROUL	GRUED	BRUNT	SADIS	YSAME
PROUL	TRUED	GRUNT	**SADO**	SAMEK
ROULE	**RUER**	PRUNT	SADOS	SAMEL
ROULS	TRUER	RUNTS	**SAFE**	SAMEN
ROUM	RUERS	RUNTY	SAFED	SAMES
ROUMS	**RUES**	**RURP**	SAFER	SAMEY
ROUP	CRUES	RURPS	SAFES	**SAMP**
CROUP	GRUES	**RURU**	**SAGA**	SAMPI
GROUP	TRUES	RURUS	SAGAS	SAMPS
ROUPS	**RUFF**	**RUSA**	**SAGE**	**SAND**
ROUPY	GRUFF	RUSAS	USAGE	SANDS
ROUT	RUFFE	**RUSE**	SAGER	SANDY
CROUT	RUFFS	CRUSE	SAGES	**SANE**
GROUT	**RUGA**	DRUSE	**SAGO**	SANED
TROUT	RUGAE	RUSES	SAGOS	SANER
ROUTE	RUGAL	**RUSH**	**SAIC**	SANES
ROUTH	**RUGS**	BRUSH	SAICE	**SANG**
ROUTS	DRUGS	CRUSH	SAICK	SANGA
ROVE	FRUGS	FRUSH	SAICS	SANGH
DROVE	TRUGS	RUSHY	**SAID**	SANGO
GROVE	**RUIN**	**RUSK**	SAIDS	SANGS
PROVE	BRUIN	BRUSK	**SAIL**	**SANK**
TROVE	RUING	RUSKS	SAILS	SANKO
ROVED	RUINS	**RUST**	**SAIM**	**SANS**
ROVEN	**RUKH**	BRUST	SAIMS	SANSA
ROVER	RUKHS	CRUST	**SAIN**	**SANT**
ROVES	**RULE**	FRUST	SAINE	SANTO
ROWS	BRULE	TRUST	SAINS	SANTS
BROWS	RULED	RUSTS	**SAINT**	**SARD**
CROWS	RULER	RUSTY	**SAIR**	SARDS
DROWS	RULES	**RUTH**	SAIRS	**SARI**
FROWS	**RULY**	TRUTH	**SAIS**	SARIN
GROWS	TRULY	RUTHS	SAIST	SARIS
PROWS	**RUME**	**RUTS**	**SAKE**	**SARK**

Hooks arranged by hook word

SARKS	SCOP	SEEL	SERED	ASHES
SARKY	SCOPA	SEELD	SERER	ISHES
SARS	SCOPE	SEELS	SERES	SHET
KSARS	SCOPS	SEELY	SERF	ASHET
TSARS	SCOT	SEEM	SERFS	SHETS
SASS	ASCOT	SEEMS	SERK	SHEW
SASSE	ESCOT	SEEP	SERKS	SHEWN
SASSY	SCOTS	SEEPS	SERR	SHEWS
SATE	SCOW	SEEPY	SERRA	SHIM
SATED	SCOWL	SEER	SERRE	SHIMS
SATEM	SCOWP	SEERS	SERRS	SHIN
SATES	SCOWS	SEGO	SERRY	SHINE
SATI	SCUD	SEGOL	SERS	SHINS
SATIN	SCUDI	SEGOS	USERS	SHINY
SATIS	SCUDO	SEIF	SESE	SHIP
SAUL	SCUDS	SEIFS	SESEY	SHIPS
SAULS	SCUG	SEIL	SESS	SHIR
SAULT	SCUGS	SEILS	SESSA	SHIRE
SAUT	SCUL	SEIR	SETA	SHIRK
SAUTE	SCULK	SEIRS	SETAE	SHIRR
SAUTS	SCULL	SEIS	SETAL	SHIRS
SAVE	SCULP	SEISE	SETT	SHIRT
SAVED	SCULS	SEISM	SETTS	SHIT
SAVER	SCUM	SEKT	SEXT	SHITE
SAVES	SCUMS	SEKTS	SEXTO	SHITS
SAVEY	SCUP	SELE	SEXTS	SHIV
SAXE	SCUPS	SELES	SHAD	SHIVA
SAXES	SCUR	SELF	SHADE	SHIVE
SAYS	SCURF	SELFS	SHADS	SHIVS
SAYST	SCURS	SELL	SHADY	SHOE
SCAB	SCUT	SELLA	SHAG	SHOED
SCABS	SCUTA	SELLE	SHAGS	SHOER
SCAD	SCUTE	SELLS	SHAH	SHOES
SCADS	SCUTS	SEME	SHAHS	SHOG
SCAG	SCYE	SEMEE	SHAM	SHOGI
SCAGS	SCYES	SEMEN	SHAMA	SHOGS
SCAM	SEAL	SEMES	SHAME	SHOO
SCAMP	SEALS	SEMI	SHAMS	SHOOK
SCAMS	SEAM	SEMIE	SHAN	SHOOL
SCAN	SEAME	SEMIS	SHAND	SHOON
SCAND	SEAMS	SENA	SHANK	SHOOS
SCANS	SEAMY	SENAS	SHANS	SHOOT
SCANT	SEAN	SEND	SHAW	SHOP
SCAR	SEANS	SENDS	PSHAW	SHOPE
ESCAR	SEAR	SENS	SHAWL	SHOPS
OSCAR	SEARE	SENSA	SHAWM	SHOT
SCARE	SEARS	SENSE	SHAWN	SHOTE
SCARF	SEAS	SENSI	SHAWS	SHOTS
SCARP	SEASE	SENT	SHAY	SHOTT
SCARS	SEAT	SENTE	SHAYA	SHOW
SCART	SEATS	SENTI	SHAYS	SHOWD
SCARY	SECH	SENTS	SHEA	SHOWN
SCAT	SECHS	SEPT	SHEAF	SHOWS
SCATH	SECT	SEPTA	SHEAL	SHOWY
SCATS	SECTS	SEPTS	SHEAR	SHRI
SCATT	SEED	SERA	SHEAS	SHRIS
SCAW	SEEDS	SERAC	SHED	SHUL
SCAWS	SEEDY	SERAI	ASHED	SHULE
SCOG	SEEK	SERAL	SHEDS	SHULN
SCOGS	SEEKS	SERE	SHES	SHULS

SHUN	SILLS	**SKAW**	**SLAG**	SLUGS
SHUNS	SILLY	SKAWS	SLAGS	**SLUM**
SHUNT	**SILO**	**SKEE**	**SLAM**	SLUMP
SHUT	SILOS	SKEED	SLAMS	SLUMS
SHUTE	**SILT**	SKEEF	**SLAP**	**SLUR**
SHUTS	SILTS	SKEEN	SLAPS	SLURB
SHWA	SILTY	SKEER	**SLAT**	SLURP
SHWAS	**SIMA**	SKEES	SLATE	SLURS
SIAL	SIMAR	SKEET	SLATS	**SLUT**
SIALS	SIMAS	**SKEG**	SLATY	SLUTS
SIBB	**SIMI**	SKEGG	**SLAW**	**SMEE**
SIBBS	SIMIS	SKEGS	SLAWS	SMEEK
SICE	**SIMP**	**SKEN**	**SLAY**	SMEES
SICES	SIMPS	SKENE	SLAYS	**SMEW**
SICH	**SIND**	SKENS	**SLED**	SMEWS
SICHT	SINDS	**SKEO**	ISLED	**SMIR**
SICK	**SINE**	SKEOS	SLEDS	SMIRK
SICKO	SINED	**SKEP**	**SLEE**	SMIRR
SICKS	SINES	SKEPS	SLEEK	SMIRS
SIDA	SINEW	**SKER**	SLEEP	**SMIT**
SIDAS	**SING**	ASKER	SLEER	SMITE
SIDE	USING	ESKER	SLEET	SMITH
ASIDE	SINGE	SKERS	**SLEW**	SMITS
SIDED	SINGS	**SKET**	SLEWS	**SMOG**
SIDER	**SINH**	SKETS	**SLEY**	SMOGS
SIDES	SINHS	**SKEW**	SLEYS	**SMUG**
SIDH	**SINK**	ASKEW	**SLID**	SMUGS
SIDHA	SINKS	SKEWS	SLIDE	**SMUR**
SIDHE	SINKY	**SKID**	**SLIM**	SMURS
SIEN	**SIPE**	SKIDS	SLIME	**SMUT**
SIENS	SIPED	**SKIM**	SLIMS	SMUTS
SIENT	SIPES	SKIMO	SLIMY	**SNAB**
SIFT	**SIRE**	SKIMP	**SLIP**	SNABS
SIFTS	SIRED	SKIMS	SLIPE	**SNAG**
SIGH	SIREE	**SKIN**	SLIPS	SNAGS
SIGHS	SIREN	SKINK	SLIPT	**SNAP**
SIGHT	SIRES	SKINS	**SLIT**	SNAPS
SIGN	**SIRI**	SKINT	SLITS	**SNAR**
SIGNA	SIRIH	**SKIO**	**SLOB**	SNARE
SIGNS	SIRIS	SKIOS	SLOBS	SNARF
SIJO	**SISS**	**SKIP**	**SLOE**	SNARK
SIJOS	SISSY	SKIPS	SLOES	SNARL
SIKA	**SIST**	**SKIT**	**SLOG**	SNARS
SIKAS	SISTS	SKITE	SLOGS	SNARY
SIKE	**SITE**	SKITS	**SLOP**	**SNAW**
SIKER	SITED	**SKOL**	SLOPE	SNAWS
SIKES	SITES	SKOLS	SLOPS	**SNEB**
SILD	**SITH**	**SKUA**	SLOPY	SNEBS
SILDS	SITHE	SKUAS	**SLOT**	**SNED**
SILE	**SIZE**	**SKUG**	SLOTH	SNEDS
ESILE	SIZED	SKUGS	SLOTS	**SNEE**
SILED	SIZEL	**SKYF**	**SLOW**	SNEED
SILEN	SIZER	SKYFS	SLOWS	SNEER
SILER	SIZES	**SKYR**	**SLUB**	SNEES
SILES	**SKAG**	SKYRE	SLUBB	**SNIB**
SILEX	SKAGS	SKYRS	SLUBS	SNIBS
SILK	**SKAT**	**SLAB**	**SLUE**	**SNIG**
SILKS	SKATE	SLABS	SLUED	SNIGS
SILKY	SKATS	**SLAE**	SLUES	**SNIP**
SILL	SKATT	SLAES	**SLUG**	SNIPE

SNIPS	SOLDE	SORNS	**SPAT**	SPOTS
SNIPY	**SORT**	**SORT**	SPATE	**SPUD**
SNIT	SOLDO	SORTA	SPATS	SPUDS
SNITS	SOLDS	SORTS	**SPAW**	**SPUE**
SNOB	**SOLE**	**SOTH**	SPAWL	SPUED
SNOBS	SOLED	SOTHS	SPAWN	SPUER
SNOD	SOLEI	**SOUK**	SPAWS	SPUES
SNODS	SOLER	SOUKS	**SPAY**	**SPUG**
SNOG	SOLES	**SOUL**	SPAYD	SPUGS
SNOGS	**SOLI**	SOULS	SPAYS	**SPUN**
SNOT	SOLID	**SOUM**	**SPAZ**	SPUNK
SNOTS	**SOLO**	SOUMS	SPAZA	**SPUR**
SNOW	SOLON	**SOUP**	SPAZZ	SPURN
SNOWK	SOLOS	SOUPS	**SPEC**	SPURS
SNOWS	**SOMA**	SOUPY	SPECK	SPURT
SNOWY	SOMAN	**SOUR**	SPECS	**STAB**
SNUB	SOMAS	SOURS	**SPEK**	STABS
SNUBS	**SONE**	**SOUS**	SPEKS	**STAG**
SNUG	SONES	SOUSE	**SPET**	STAGE
SNUGS	**SONG**	**SOUT**	SPETS	STAGS
SNYE	SONGS	SOUTH	**SPEW**	STAGY
SNYES	**SONS**	SOUTS	SPEWS	**STAP**
SOAK	SONSE	**SOWF**	SPEWY	STAPH
SOAKS	SONSY	SOWFF	**SPIC**	STAPS
SOAP	**SOOK**	SOWFS	ASPIC	**STAR**
SOAPS	SOOKS	**SOWL**	SPICA	STARE
SOAPY	**SOOL**	SOWLE	SPICE	STARK
SOAR	SOOLE	SOWLS	SPICK	STARN
SOARE	SOOLS	**SOWM**	SPICS	STARR
SOARS	**SOOM**	SOWMS	SPICY	STARS
SOBA	SOOMS	**SOWN**	**SPIE**	START
SOBAS	**SOOP**	SOWND	SPIED	**STAT**
SOCA	SOOPS	SOWNE	SPIEL	STATE
SOCAS	**SOOT**	**SOWP**	SPIER	STATS
SOCK	SOOTE	SOWPS	SPIES	**STAW**
SOCKO	SOOTH	**SOWS**	**SPIF**	STAWS
SOCKS	SOOTS	SOWSE	SPIFF	**STAY**
SODA	SOOTY	**SOYA**	SPIFS	STAYS
SODAS	**SOPH**	SOYAS	**SPIK**	**STED**
SOFA	SOPHS	**SPAE**	SPIKE	STEDD
SOFAR	SOPHY	SPAED	SPIKS	STEDE
SOFAS	**SORA**	SPAER	SPIKY	STEDS
SOFT	PSORA	SPAES	**SPIM**	**STEM**
SOFTA	SORAL	**SPAG**	SPIMS	STEME
SOFTS	SORAS	SPAGS	**SPIN**	STEMS
SOFTY	**SORB**	**SPAM**	SPINA	**STEN**
SOIL	SORBO	SPAMS	SPINE	STEND
SOILS	SORBS	**SPAN**	SPINK	STENO
SOILY	**SORD**	SPANE	SPINS	STENS
SOJA	SORDA	SPANG	SPINY	STENT
SOJAS	SORDO	SPANK	**SPIT**	**STEP**
SOKE	SORDS	SPANS	SPITE	STEPS
SOKEN	**SORE**	**SPAR**	SPITS	STEPT
SOKES	SORED	SPARD	SPITZ	**STET**
SOLA	SOREE	SPARE	**SPIV**	STETS
SOLAH	SOREL	SPARK	SPIVS	**STEW**
SOLAN	SORER	SPARS	**SPOD**	STEWS
SOLAR	SORES	SPART	SPODE	STEWY
SOLAS	SOREX	**SPAS**	SPODS	**STIE**
SOLD	**SORN**	SPASM	**SPOT**	STIED

STIES	SUEDE	SWAMP	**SYPE**	TAKIN
STIM	**SUER**	SWAMY	SYPED	TAKIS
STIME	SUERS	**SWAN**	SYPES	**TALA**
STIMS	**SUET**	SWANG	**SYPH**	TALAK
STIMY	SUETS	SWANK	SYPHS	TALAQ
STIR	SUETY	SWANS	**TAAL**	TALAR
ASTIR	**SUGH**	**SWAP**	TAALS	TALAS
STIRE	SUGHS	SWAPS	**TABI**	**TALC**
STIRK	**SUID**	SWAPT	TABID	TALCS
STIRP	SUIDS	**SWAT**	TABIS	TALCY
STIRS	**SUIT**	SWATH	**TABS**	**TALE**
STOA	SUITE	SWATS	STABS	STALE
STOAE	SUITS	**SWAY**	**TABU**	TALEA
STOAI	**SUKH**	ASWAY	TABUN	TALER
STOAS	SUKHS	SWAYL	TABUS	TALES
STOAT	**SULK**	SWAYS	**TACE**	**TALK**
STOB	SULKS	**SWEE**	TACES	STALK
STOBS	SULKY	SWEED	TACET	TALKS
STOP	**SULU**	SWEEL	**TACH**	TALKY
ESTOP	SULUS	SWEEP	TACHE	**TALL**
STOPE	**SUMO**	SWEER	TACHO	STALL
STOPS	SUMOS	SWEES	TACHS	TALLS
STOPT	**SUMP**	SWEET	**TACK**	TALLY
STOT	SUMPH	**SWEY**	STACK	**TAME**
STOTS	SUMPS	SWEYS	TACKS	TAMED
STOTT	**SUNK**	**SWIG**	TACKY	TAMER
STOW	SUNKS	SWIGS	**TACO**	TAMES
STOWN	**SUNN**	**SWIM**	TACOS	**TAMP**
STOWP	SUNNA	ASWIM	**TACT**	STAMP
STOWS	SUNNS	SWIMS	TACTS	TAMPS
STUB	SUNNY	**SWIZ**	**TAEL**	**TANA**
STUBS	**SUPE**	SWIZZ	TAELS	TANAS
STUD	SUPER	**SWOB**	**TAGS**	TANE
STUDS	SUPES	SWOBS	STAGS	STANE
STUDY	**SURA**	**SWOP**	**TAHA**	**TANG**
STUM	SURAH	SWOPS	TAHAS	STANG
STUMM	SURAL	SWOPT	**TAHR**	TANGA
STUMP	SURAS	**SWOT**	TAHRS	TANGI
STUMS	SURAT	SWOTS	**TAIG**	TANGO
STUN	**SURD**	**SYBO**	STAIG	TANGS
ASTUN	SURDS	SYBOE	TAIGA	TANGY
STUNG	**SURE**	SYBOW	TAIGS	**TANH**
STUNK	USURE	**SYCE**	**TAIL**	TANHS
STUNS	SURED	SYCEE	TAILS	**TANK**
STUNT	SURER	SYCES	**TAIN**	STANK
STYE	SURES	**SYEN**	STAIN	TANKA
STYED	**SURF**	SYENS	TAINS	TANKS
STYES	SURFS	**SYKE**	TAINT	TANKY
SUBA	SURFY	SYKER	**TAIS**	**TANS**
TSUBA	**SUSU**	SYKES	TAISH	TANSY
SUBAH	SUSUS	**SYLI**	**TAIT**	**TAPA**
SUBAS	**SWAB**	SYLIS	TAITS	TAPAS
SUCK	SWABS	**SYNC**	**TAKA**	**TAPE**
SUCKS	**SWAD**	SYNCH	TAKAS	ETAPE
SUCKY	SWADS	SYNCS	**TAKE**	TAPED
SUDD	**SWAG**	**SYND**	STAKE	TAPEN
SUDDS	SWAGE	SYNDS	TAKEN	TAPER
SUDS	SWAGS	**SYNE**	TAKER	TAPES
SUDSY	**SWAM**	SYNED	TAKES	TAPET
SUED	SWAMI	SYNES	**TAKI**	**TAPS**

ATAPS	**TAXI**	TEILS	TETES	TIARA
STAPS	**TELA**	**TELA**	**TETH**	TIARS
TAPU	**TAYS**	STELA	TETHS	**TICE**
TAPUS	STAYS	TELAE	**TETS**	TICED
TARA	**TEAD**	**TELE**	STETS	TICES
TARAS	STEAD	STELE	**TEWS**	**TICH**
TARE	TEADE	TELES	STEWS	STICH
STARE	TEADS	TELEX	**TEXT**	TICHY
TARED	**TEAK**	**TELL**	TEXTS	**TICK**
TARES	STEAK	STELL	**THAN**	STICK
TARN	TEAKS	TELLS	THANA	TICKS
STARN	**TEAL**	TELLY	THANE	TICKY
TARNS	STEAL	**TEME**	THANK	**TIDE**
TARO	TEALS	STEME	THANS	TIDED
TAROC	**TEAM**	TEMED	**THAR**	TIDES
TAROK	STEAM	TEMES	THARM	**TIED**
TAROS	TEAMS	**TEMP**	THARS	STIED
TAROT	**TEAR**	TEMPI	**THAW**	**TIER**
TARP	STEAR	TEMPO	THAWS	TIERS
TARPS	TEARS	TEMPS	THAWY	**TIES**
TARS	TEARY	TEMPT	**THEE**	STIES
STARS	**TEAS**	**TEMS**	THEED	**TIFF**
TARSI	TEASE	ITEMS	THEEK	STIFF
TART	**TEAT**	STEMS	THEES	TIFFS
START	TEATS	TEMSE	**THEM**	**TIFT**
TARTS	**TECH**	**TEND**	THEMA	TIFTS
TARTY	TECHS	STEND	THEME	**TIGE**
TASH	TECHY	TENDS	**THEN**	TIGER
STASH	**TEDS**	TENDU	THENS	TIGES
TASK	STEDS	**TENE**	**THEW**	**TIKA**
TASKS	**TEED**	CTENE	THEWS	TIKAS
TASS	STEED	TENES	THEWY	**TIKE**
TASSE	**TEEK**	TENET	**THIG**	TIKES
TATE	STEEK	**TENS**	THIGH	**TIKI**
STATE	**TEEL**	ETENS	THIGS	TIKIS
TATER	STEEL	STENS	**THIN**	**TILE**
TATES	TEELS	TENSE	THINE	STILE
TATH	**TEEM**	**TENT**	THING	UTILE
TATHS	STEEM	STENT	THINK	TILED
TATS	TEEMS	TENTH	THINS	TILER
ETATS	**TEEN**	TENTS	**THIO**	TILES
STATS	STEEN	TENTY	THIOL	**TILL**
TATT	TEEND	**TEPA**	**THIR**	STILL
TATTS	TEENE	TEPAL	THIRD	TILLS
TATTY	TEENS	TEPAS	THIRL	TILLY
TATU	TEENY	**TERF**	**THON**	**TILT**
TATUS	**TEER**	TERFE	THONG	ATILT
TAUT	STEER	TERFS	**THOU**	STILT
TAUTS	TEERS	**TERM**	THOUS	TILTH
TAVA	**TEFF**	TERMS	**THRO**	TILTS
TAVAH	TEFFS	**TERN**	THROB	**TIME**
TAVAS	**TEGG**	STERN	THROE	STIME
TAWA	TEGGS	TERNE	THROW	TIMED
TAWAI	**TEGU**	TERNS	**THRU**	TIMER
TAWAS	TEGUA	**TEST**	THRUM	TIMES
TAWS	TEGUS	TESTA	**THUD**	**TIND**
STAWS	**TEHR**	TESTE	THUDS	TINDS
TAWSE	TEHRS	TESTS	**THUG**	**TINE**
TAWT	**TEIL**	TESTY	THUGS	TINEA
TAWTS	STEIL	**TETE**	**TIAR**	TINED

TINES	**TOHO**	STOOK	TOSAS	**TRAY**
TING	TOHOS	**TOOL**	**TOSE**	STRAY
STING	**TOIL**	STOOL	TOSED	TRAYS
TINGE	TOILE	TOOLS	TOSES	**TREE**
TINGS	TOILS	**TOOM**	**TOSH**	TREED
TINK	**TOIT**	TOOMS	TOSHY	TREEN
STINK	STOIT	**TOON**	**TOSS**	TREES
TINKS	TOITS	TOONS	STOSS	**TREF**
TINT	**TOKE**	**TOOT**	TOSSY	TREFA
STINT	ATOKE	TOOTH	**TOST**	**TREK**
TINTS	STOKE	TOOTS	YTOST	TREKS
TINTY	TOKED	**TOPE**	**TOTE**	**TRES**
TIPI	TOKEN	STOPE	TOTED	TRESS
TIPIS	TOKER	TOPED	TOTEM	TREST
TIPS	TOKES	TOPEE	TOTER	**TRET**
TIPSY	**TOKO**	TOPEK	TOTES	TRETS
TIRE	TOKOS	TOPER	**TOTS**	**TREW**
STIRE	**TOLA**	TOPES	STOTS	STREW
TIRED	TOLAN	**TOPH**	**TOUK**	TREWS
TIRES	TOLAR	TOPHE	TOUKS	**TREY**
TIRL	TOLAS	TOPHI	**TOUN**	TREYS
TIRLS	**TOLE**	TOPHS	TOUNS	**TRIE**
TIRO	STOLE	**TOPI**	**TOUR**	TRIED
TIROS	TOLED	TOPIC	STOUR	TRIER
TIRR	TOLES	TOPIS	TOURS	TRIES
TIRRS	**TOLL**	**TOPO**	**TOUT**	**TRIG**
TITE	ATOLL	TOPOI	STOUT	STRIG
TITER	TOLLS	TOPOS	TOUTS	TRIGO
TITI	TOLLY	**TOPS**	**TOWN**	TRIGS
TITIS	**TOLT**	STOPS	STOWN	**TRIM**
TIVY	TOLTS	**TORA**	TOWNS	TRIMS
STIVY	**TOLU**	TORAH	TOWNY	**TRIN**
TIZZ	TOLUS	TORAN	**TOWS**	TRINE
TIZZY	**TOMB**	TORAS	STOWS	TRINS
TOAD	TOMBS	**TORC**	TOWSE	**TRIO**
TOADS	**TOME**	TORCH	TOWSY	TRIOL
TOADY	TOMES	TORCS	**TOWT**	TRIOR
TOCK	**TOMO**	**TORE**	TOWTS	TRIOS
STOCK	TOMOS	STORE	**TOYO**	**TRIP**
TOCKS	**TOMS**	TORES	TOYON	ATRIP
TOCKY	ATOMS	**TORI**	TOYOS	STRIP
TOCO	**TONE**	TORIC	**TOZE**	TRIPE
TOCOS	ATONE	TORII	TOZED	TRIPS
TOCS	STONE	**TORO**	TOZES	TRIPY
ATOCS	TONED	TOROS	**TRAD**	**TROD**
TOEA	TONER	TOROT	STRAD	TRODE
TOEAS	TONES	**TORR**	TRADE	TRODS
TOFF	TONEY	TORRS	TRADS	**TROG**
TOFFS	**TONG**	**TORS**	**TRAM**	TROGS
TOFFY	STONG	TORSE	TRAMP	**TRON**
TOFT	TONGA	TORSI	TRAMS	TRONA
TOFTS	TONGS	TORSK	**TRAP**	TRONC
TOFU	**TONK**	TORSO	STRAP	TRONE
TOFUS	STONK	**TORT**	TRAPE	TRONK
TOGA	TONKA	TORTA	TRAPS	TRONS
TOGAE	TONKS	TORTE	TRAPT	**TROP**
TOGAS	**TONY**	TORTS	**TRAT**	STROP
TOGE	ATONY	**TORY**	TRATS	TROPE
TOGED	STONY	STORY	TRATT	**TROT**
TOGES	**TOOK**	**TOSA**		TROTH

Hooks arranged by hook word

TROTS	**TUNE**	STYES	ULANS	UNAUS
TROW	TUNED	**TYIN**	**ULES**	**UNBE**
STROW	TUNER	TYING	DULES	UNBED
TROWS	TUNES	**TYKE**	GULES	**UNCE**
TROY	**TUNG**	TYKES	HULES	BUNCE
STROY	STUNG	**TYMP**	MULES	DUNCE
TROYS	TUNGS	TYMPS	PULES	OUNCE
TRUE	**TUNS**	**TYND**	RULES	PUNCE
TRUED	STUNS	TYNDE	TULES	UNCES
TRUER	**TURD**	**TYNE**	YULES	**UNCI**
TRUES	TURDS	TYNED	**ULEX**	UNCIA
TRUG	**TURF**	TYNES	CULEX	**UNCO**
TRUGO	TURFS	**TYPE**	**ULNA**	BUNCO
TRUGS	TURFY	TYPED	ULNAD	JUNCO
TRYE	**TURK**	TYPES	ULNAE	UNCOS
TRYER	TURKS	TYPEY	ULNAR	UNCOY
TRYP	**TURM**	**TYPO**	ULNAS	**UNDE**
TRYPS	TURME	TYPOS	**ULUS**	BUNDE
TSAR	TURMS	**TYPP**	LULUS	UNDEE
TSARS	**TURN**	TYPPS	PULUS	UNDER
TUAN	TURNS	**TYRE**	SULUS	**UNDY**
TUANS	**TUSH**	STYRE	ZULUS	BUNDY
TUBA	TUSHY	TYRED	**ULVA**	CUNDY
TUBAE	**TUSK**	TYRES	VULVA	FUNDY
TUBAL	TUSKS	**TYRO**	ULVAS	GUNDY
TUBAR	TUSKY	TYROS	**UMBO**	OUNDY
TUBAS	**TUTU**	**TYTE**	BUMBO	**UNIS**
TUBE	TUTUS	STYTE	DUMBO	MUNIS
TUBED	**TWAE**	**TZAR**	GUMBO	**UNIT**
TUBER	TWAES	TZARS	JUMBO	UNITE
TUBES	**TWAL**	**UDAL**	RUMBO	UNITS
TUBS	TWALS	UDALS	UMBOS	UNITY
STUBS	**TWAT**	**UDON**	**UMPH**	**UNTO**
TUCK	TWATS	UDONS	BUMPH	JUNTO
STUCK	**TWAY**	**UDOS**	HUMPH	PUNTO
TUCKS	TWAYS	BUDOS	SUMPH	**UPAS**
TUFA	**TWEE**	JUDOS	**UMPS**	OUPAS
TUFAS	ETWEE	KUDOS	BUMPS	PUPAS
TUFF	TWEED	LUDOS	DUMPS	ZUPAS
STUFF	TWEEL	**UEYS**	GUMPS	**UPBY**
TUFFE	TWEEN	QUEYS	HUMPS	UPBYE
TUFFS	TWEER	**UFOS**	JUMPS	**UPDO**
TUFT	TWEET	BUFOS	LUMPS	UPDOS
TUFTS	**TWIG**	**UGHS**	MUMPS	**UPON**
TUFTY	TWIGS	EUGHS	PUMPS	JUPON
TUIS	**TWIN**	SUGHS	RUMPS	YUPON
ETUIS	TWINE	VUGHS	SUMPS	**UPTA**
TUISM	TWINK	**UGLY**	TUMPS	UPTAK
TULE	TWINS	FUGLY	YUMPS	**URAO**
TULES	TWINY	**UKES**	**UMPY**	URAOS
TUMP	**TWIT**	BUKES	BUMPY	**URBS**
STUMP	TWITE	CUKES	DUMPY	BURBS
TUMPS	TWITS	DUKES	HUMPY	CURBS
TUMPY	**TYED**	JUKES	JUMPY	**URDE**
TUMS	STYED	NUKES	LUMPY	URDEE
STUMS	**TYEE**	PUKES	RUMPY	**URDS**
TUNA	TYEES	YUKES	TUMPY	BURDS
TUNAS	**TYER**	**ULAN**	**UNAI**	CURDS
TUND	TYERS	KULAN	UNAIS	HURDS
TUNDS	**TYES**	YULAN	**UNAU**	NURDS

SURDS	WUSES	**VAST**	EVERT	VIOLS
TURDS	**UTAS**	AVAST	OVERT	**VIRE**
URDY	KUTAS	VASTS	VERTS	VIRED
CURDY	**UTES**	VASTY	VERTU	VIREO
NURDY	BUTES	**VATU**	**VERY**	VIRES
UREA	CUTES	VATUS	EVERY	**VIRL**
UREAL	JUTES	**VAUT**	**VEST**	VIRLS
UREAS	LUTES	VAUTE	VESTA	**VISA**
URES	MUTES	VAUTS	VESTS	VISAS
AURES	**UTIS**	**VEAL**	**VETS**	**VISE**
CURES	CUTIS	UVEAL	EVETS	AVISE
DURES	KUTIS	VEALE	**VIAL**	VISED
LURES	MUTIS	VEALS	VIALS	VISES
MURES	**UTUS**	VEALY	**VIBE**	**VITA**
PURES	KUTUS	**VEEP**	VIBES	VITAE
SURES	TUTUS	VEEPS	VIBEX	VITAL
URGE	**UVEA**	**VEER**	VIBEY	VITAS
GURGE	UVEAL	VEERS	**VICE**	**VITE**
PURGE	UVEAS	VEERY	VICED	EVITE
SURGE	**VADE**	**VEGA**	VICES	VITEX
URGED	EVADE	VEGAN	**VIDE**	**VIVA**
URGER	VADED	VEGAS	VIDEO	VIVAS
URGES	VADES	**VEGO**	**VIED**	VIVAT
URIC	**VAIL**	VEGOS	IVIED	**VIVE**
AURIC	AVAIL	**VEHM**	**VIER**	VIVER
URNS	VAILS	VEHME	VIERS	VIVES
BURNS	**VAIR**	**VEIL**	**VIES**	**VLEI**
CURNS	VAIRE	VEILS	IVIES	VLEIS
DURNS	VAIRS	VEILY	**VIEW**	**VOAR**
GURNS	VAIRY	**VEIN**	VIEWS	VOARS
TURNS	**VALE**	VEINS	VIEWY	**VOID**
URPS	AVALE	VEINY	**VIGA**	AVOID
BURPS	VALES	**VELA**	VIGAS	OVOID
RURPS	VALET	VELAR	**VILD**	VOIDS
TURPS	**VALI**	**VELD**	VILDE	**VOLA**
URSA	VALID	VELDS	**VILE**	VOLAE
BURSA	VALIS	VELDT	VILER	VOLAR
URSAE	**VAMP**	**VELE**	**VILL**	**VOLE**
URUS	VAMPS	VELES	VILLA	VOLED
GURUS	VAMPY	**VELL**	VILLI	VOLES
KURUS	**VANE**	KVELL	VILLS	VOLET
RURUS	VANED	VELLS	**VINA**	**VOLK**
URVA	VANES	**VENA**	VINAL	VOLKS
MURVA	**VANG**	VENAE	VINAS	**VOLT**
URVAS	VANGS	VENAL	**VINE**	VOLTA
USED	**VANT**	**VEND**	AVINE	VOLTE
BUSED	AVANT	VENDS	OVINE	VOLTI
FUSED	VANTS	**VENT**	VINED	VOLTS
MUSED	**VARA**	EVENT	VINER	**VOTE**
USER	VARAN	VENTS	VINES	VOTED
LUSER	VARAS	**VERB**	VINEW	VOTER
MUSER	**VARE**	VERBS	**VINO**	VOTES
USERS	VAREC	**VERS**	VINOS	**VOWS**
USES	VARES	AVERS	**VINT**	AVOWS
BUSES	**VARY**	OVERS	VINTS	**VRIL**
FUSES	OVARY	VERSE	**VINY**	VRILS
MUSES	**VASA**	VERSO	VINYL	**VROU**
PUSES	VASAL	VERST	**VIOL**	VROUS
RUSES	**VASE**	**VERT**	VIOLA	VROUW
SUSES	VASES	AVERT	VIOLD	**VROW**

VROWS	WAIST	**WAQF**	AWAVE	WEETS
VUGG	**WAIT**	WAQFS	WAVED	**WEFT**
VUGGS	AWAIT	**WARB**	WAVER	WEFTE
VUGGY	WAITE	WARBS	WAVES	WEFTS
VUGH	WAITS	WARBY	WAVEY	**WEID**
VUGHS	**WAKA**	**WARD**	**WAWA**	WEIDS
VUGHY	WAKAS	AWARD	WAWAS	**WEIL**
VULN	**WAKE**	SWARD	**WAWE**	WEILS
VULNS	AWAKE	WARDS	WAWES	**WEIR**
WAAC	WAKED	**WARE**	**WAWL**	SWEIR
WAACS	WAKEN	AWARE	WAWLS	WEIRD
WABS	WAKER	SWARE	**WAYS**	WEIRS
SWABS	WAKES	WARED	AWAYS	**WEKA**
WACK	**WAKF**	WARES	SWAYS	WEKAS
SWACK	WAKFS	WAREZ	TWAYS	**WELD**
WACKE	**WALD**	**WARK**	**WEAK**	WELDS
WACKO	WALDO	WARKS	TWEAK	**WELK**
WACKS	WALDS	**WARM**	**WEAL**	WELKE
WACKY	**WALE**	SWARM	SWEAL	WELKS
WADD	DWALE	WARMS	WEALD	WELKT
WADDS	SWALE	**WARN**	WEALS	**WELL**
WADDY	WALED	AWARN	**WEAN**	DWELL
WADE	WALER	WARNS	WEANS	SWELL
WADED	WALES	**WARP**	**WEAR**	WELLS
WADER	**WALI**	WARPS	SWEAR	WELLY
WADES	WALIS	**WARS**	WEARS	**WELT**
WADI	**WALK**	WARST	WEARY	DWELT
WADIS	WALKS	**WART**	**WEED**	SWELT
WADS	**WALL**	SWART	SWEED	WELTS
SWADS	WALLA	WARTS	TWEED	**WEMB**
WADT	WALLS	WARTY	WEEDS	WEMBS
WADTS	WALLY	**WASE**	WEEDY	**WEND**
WAES	**WALY**	WASES	**WEEK**	WENDS
TWAES	SWALY	**WASH**	WEEKE	**WENT**
WAFF	**WAME**	AWASH	WEEKS	WENTS
WAFFS	WAMED	SWASH	**WEEL**	**WEPT**
WAFT	WAMES	WASHY	AWEEL	SWEPT
WAFTS	**WAND**	**WASM**	SWEEL	**WERO**
WAGE	WANDS	WASMS	TWEEL	WEROS
SWAGE	**WANE**	**WASP**	WEELS	**WEST**
WAGED	WANED	WASPS	**WEEM**	EWEST
WAGER	WANES	WASPY	WEEMS	WESTS
WAGES	WANEY	**WAST**	**WEEN**	**WETA**
WAGS	**WANG**	WASTE	TWEEN	WETAS
SWAGS	DWANG	WASTS	WEENS	**WEXE**
WAID	SWANG	**WATE**	WEENY	WEXED
WAIDE	TWANG	WATER	**WEEP**	WEXES
WAIF	WANGS	**WATS**	SWEEP	**WEYS**
WAIFS	**WANK**	SWATS	WEEPS	SWEYS
WAIFT	SWANK	TWATS	WEEPY	**WHAM**
WAIL	TWANK	**WATT**	**WEER**	WHAMO
SWAIL	WANKS	WATTS	SWEER	WHAMS
WAILS	WANKY	**WAUK**	TWEER	**WHAP**
WAIN	**WANS**	WAUKS	**WEES**	WHAPS
SWAIN	SWANS	**WAUL**	SWEES	**WHAT**
TWAIN	**WANT**	WAULK	WEEST	WHATA
WAINS	WANTS	WAULS	**WEET**	WHATS
WAIR	WANTY	**WAUR**	SWEET	**WHEE**
WAIRS	**WAPS**	WAURS	TWEET	WHEEL
WAIS	SWAPS	**WAVE**	WEETE	WHEEN

WHEEP	WILDS	**WISE**	WOOLS	**YAAR**
WHEN	**WILE**	WISED	WOOLY	YAARS
WHENS	DWILE	WISER	**WOON**	**YACK**
WHET	WILED	WISES	WOONS	KYACK
WHETS	WILES	**WISH**	SWOON	YACKA
WHEW	**WILI**	SWISH	**WOOS**	YACKS
WHEWS	WILIS	WISHA	WOOSE	**YADS**
WHEY	**WILL**	WISHT	WOOSH	DYADS
WHEYS	SWILL	**WISP**	**WOOT**	**YAFF**
WHID	TWILL	WISPS	WOOTZ	NYAFF
WHIDS	WILLS	WISPY	**WOPS**	YAFFS
WHIG	WILLY	**WISS**	SWOPS	**YAGI**
WHIGS	**WILT**	SWISS	**WORD**	YAGIS
WHIM	TWILT	**WIST**	SWORD	**YAHS**
WHIMS	WILTS	TWIST	WORDS	AYAHS
WHIN	**WIMP**	WISTS	WORDY	**YAKS**
WHINE	WIMPS	**WITE**	**WORE**	KYAKS
WHINS	WIMPY	TWITE	SWORE	**YALE**
WHINY	**WIND**	WITED	**WORK**	YALES
WHIP	WINDS	WITES	AWORK	**YAMS**
WHIPS	WINDY	**WITH**	WORKS	LYAMS
WHIPT	**WINE**	SWITH	**WORM**	**YANG**
WHIR	DWINE	WITHE	WORMS	KYANG
WHIRL	GWINE	WITHS	WORMY	YANGS
WHIRR	SWINE	WITHY	**WORN**	**YANK**
WHIRS	TWINE	**WITS**	SWORN	YANKS
WHIT	WINED	SWITS	**WORT**	**YAPP**
WHITE	WINES	TWITS	WORTH	YAPPS
WHITS	WINEY	**WIVE**	WORTS	YAPPY
WHITY	**WING**	SWIVE	**WOTS**	**YARD**
WHIZ	AWING	WIVED	SWOTS	LYARD
WHIZZ	OWING	WIVER	**WOVE**	YARDS
WHOM	SWING	WIVES	WOVEN	**YARE**
WHOMP	WINGE	**WOAD**	**WRAP**	YARER
WHOP	WINGS	WOADS	WRAPS	**YARK**
WHOPS	WINGY	**WOCK**	WRAPT	YARKS
WHOW	**WINK**	WOCKS	**WREN**	**YARN**
EWHOW	SWINK	**WOKE**	WRENS	YARNS
WHUP	TWINK	AWOKE	**WRIT**	**YARR**
WHUPS	WINKS	WOKEN	WRITE	YARRS
WICE	**WINN**	**WOLD**	WRITS	**YATE**
TWICE	WINNA	WOLDS	**WUDU**	YATES
WICK	WINNS	**WOLF**	WUDUS	**YAUD**
WICKS	**WINO**	WOLFS	**WULL**	YAUDS
WICKY	WINOS	**WOMB**	WULLS	**YAUP**
WIDE	**WINS**	WOMBS	**WUSS**	YAUPS
WIDEN	TWINS	WOMBY	WUSSY	**YAWL**
WIDER	**WINY**	**WONK**	**WYLE**	YAWLS
WIDES	TWINY	WONKS	WYLED	**YAWN**
WIEL	**WIPE**	WONKY	WYLES	YAWNS
WIELD	SWIPE	**WONT**	**WYND**	YAWNY
WIELS	WIPED	WONTS	WYNDS	**YAWP**
WIFE	WIPER	**WOOD**	**WYNN**	YAWPS
WIFED	WIPES	WOODS	WYNNS	**YEAD**
WIFES	**WIRE**	WOODY	**WYTE**	YEADS
WIFEY	SWIRE	**WOOF**	WYTED	**YEAH**
WIGS	TWIRE	WOOFS	WYTES	YEAHS
SWIGS	WIRED	WOOFY	**XYST**	**YEAN**
TWIGS	WIRER	**WOOL**	XYSTI	YEANS
WILD	WIRES	WOOLD	XYSTS	**YEAR**

Hooks arranged by hook word

YEARD	YIRDS	YOUSE	**ZIFF**	ZURFS
YEARN	**YIRK**	**YOWE**	ZIFFS	**ZYGA**
YEARS	YIRKS	YOWED	**ZILA**	ZYGAL
YEAS	**YIRR**	YOWES	ZILAS	**ZYME**
YEAST	YIRRS	**YOWL**	**ZILL**	AZYME
YECH	**YITE**	YOWLS	ZILLA	ZYMES
YECHS	YITES	**YUAN**	ZILLS	
YECHY	**YLEM**	YUANS	**ZIMB**	
YEDE	XYLEM	**YUCA**	ZIMBI	
YEDES	YLEMS	YUCAS	ZIMBS	
YEED	**YLKE**	**YUCK**	**ZINC**	
YEEDS	YLKES	YUCKO	ZINCO	
YEGG	**VMPE**	YUCKS	ZINCS	
YEGGS	VMPES	YUCKY	ZINCY	
YELD	**YOCK**	**YUFT**	**ZINE**	
GYELD	YOCKS	YUFTS	AZINE	
YELK	**YODE**	**YUGA**	ZINEB	
YELKS	YODEL	YUGAS	ZINES	
YELL	**YODH**	**YUKE**	**ZING**	
YELLS	YODHS	YUKED	ZINGS	
YELM	**YOGA**	YUKES	ZINGY	
YELMS	YOGAS	**YUKO**	**ZITI**	
YELP	**YOGH**	YUKOS	ZITIS	
AYELP	YOGHS	**YULE**	**ZOBO**	
YELPS	**YOGI**	YULES	ZOBOS	
YELT	YOGIC	**YUMP**	**ZOBU**	
YELTS	YOGIN	YUMPS	ZOBUS	
YENS	YOGIS	**YURT**	**ZOEA**	
HYENS	**YOKE**	YURTA	ZOEAE	
SYENS	YOKED	YURTS	ZOEAL	
YERD	YOKEL	**YUZU**	ZOEAS	
YERDS	YOKER	YUZUS	**ZOIC**	
YERK	YOKES	**ZACK**	AZOIC	
YERKS	**YOLK**	ZACKS	**ZONA**	
YESK	YOLKS	**ZARF**	ZONAE	
YESKS	YOLKY	ZARFS	ZONAL	
YEST	**YOMP**	**ZATI**	**ZONE**	
YESTS	YOMPS	ZATIS	OZONE	
YESTY	**YONI**	**ZEAL**	ZONED	
YETI	YONIC	ZEALS	ZONER	
YETIS	YONIS	**ZEBU**	ZONES	
YETT	**YONT**	ZEBUB	**ZONK**	
YETTS	AYONT	ZEBUS	ZONKS	
YEUK	**YOOF**	**ZEES**	**ZOOM**	
YEUKS	YOOFS	MZEES	ZOOMS	
YEUKY	**YOOP**	**ZEIN**	**ZOON**	
YEVE	YOOPS	ZEINS	ZOONS	
YEVEN	**YORE**	**ZERK**	**ZOOT**	
YEVES	YORES	ZERKS	ZOOTY	
YIKE	**YORK**	**ZERO**	**ZORI**	
YIKED	YORKS	ZEROS	ZORIL	
YIKES	**YORP**	**ZEST**	ZORIS	
YILL	YORPS	ZESTS	**ZOUK**	
YILLS	**YOUK**	ZESTY	ZOUKS	
YINS	YOUKS	**ZETA**	**ZULU**	
AYINS	**YOUR**	ZETAS	ZULUS	
PYINS	YOURN	**ZEZE**	**ZUPA**	
YIPE	YOURS	ZEZES	ZUPAN	
YIPES	YOURT	**ZHOS**	ZUPAS	
YIRD	**YOUS**	DZHOS	**ZURF**	

Hooks arranged by hook letter

This set of lists contains hooks of two to eight letters, arranged alphabetically by hook letter rather than by the hook word. Front-hooks and end-hooks are shown for each letter in turn. Inflected words that end in -S have been omitted, as these words are both obvious and numerous.

A – Front-hooks

Two letters to three

A-AH	A-DO	A-IT	A-NE	A-WE
A-AL	A-GO	A-KA	A-NY	A-YE
A-AS	A-HA	A-LA	A-PE	A-YU
A-BA	A-HI	A-MA	A-PO	A-ZO
A-BO	A-ID	A-MI	A-RE	
A-BY	A-IN	A-MU	A-SH	
A-CH	A-IS	A-NA	A-TE	

Three letters to four

A-AHS	A-GAS	A-LAS	A-NOW	A-TAP
A-ALS	A-GED	A-LAY	A-NUS	A-TES
A-BAC	A-GEE	A-LEE	A-PAY	A-TOC
A-BAS	A-GEN	A-LES	A-PED	A-TOM
A-BED	A-GIN	A-LEW	A-PER	A-TOP
A-BET	A-GIO	A-LIT	A-PES	A-VAS
A-BID	A-GON	A-LOD	A-POD	A-VID
A-BOS	A-GUE	A-LOW	A-POS	A-VOW
A-BUT	A-HEM	A-LUM	A-QUA	A-WAY
A-BYE	A-HIS	A-MAS	A-RED	A-WED
A-BYS	A-HOY	A-MEN	A-REG	A-WEE
A-CHE	A-IDE	A-MID	A-RES	A-WRY
A-CID	A-IDS	A-MIR	A-RET	A-XIS
A-DAW	A-INS	A-MIS	A-REW	A-YAH
A-DIT	A-ITS	A-MUS	A-RIA	A-YES
A-DOS	A-JAR	A-NAN	A-RID	A-YIN
A-DRY	A-JEE	A-NAS	A-ROW	A-YUS
A-EON	A-KED	A-NEW	A-RUM	
A-FAR	A-KIN	A-NIL	A-SAR	
A-FRO	A-LAP	A-NIS	A-SEA	
A-GAR	A-LAR	A-NON	A-SHY	

Four letters to five

A-AHED	A-BEAR	A-BORE	A-CIDS	A-DOWN
A-ARTI	A-BETS	A-BORT	A-COCK	A-DOZE
A-BACK	A-BIDE	A-BOUT	A-COLD	A-DRAD
A-BACS	A-BLED	A-BRAY	A-CORN	A-DUST
A-BAFT	A-BLET	A-BRIM	A-CRED	A-EGIS
A-BAND	A-BLOW	A-BRIN	A-CUTE	A-EONS
A-BASE	A-BODE	A-BRIS	A-DAWS	A-EROS
A-BASH	A-BOIL	A-BUNA	A-DAYS	A-FARS
A-BASK	A-BOMA	A-BUTS	A-DEEM	A-FEAR
A-BATE	A-BOON	A-BUZZ	A-DITS	A-FIRE
A-BEAM	A-BORD	A-BYES	A-DORE	A-FOOT

A-FORE	A-HOLD	A-MAUT	A-PISH	A-TOMS
A-FOUL	A-HULL	A-MAZE	A-PODS	A-TONE
A-FRIT	A-IDES	A-MEER	A-POOP	A-TONY
A-FROS	A-IRED	A-MEND	A-PORT	A-TRIP
A-GAIN	A-ISLE	A-MENE	A-PSIS	A-URES
A-GAMA	A-ITCH	A-MENT	A-READ	A-URIC
A-GAPE	A-JUGA	A-MICE	A-REAL	A-VAIL
A-GARS	A-KING	A-MIDS	A-REAR	A-VALE
A-GAST	A-LACK	A-MINE	A-REDD	A-VANT
A-GATE	A-LAND	A-MINO	A-REDE	A-VAST
A-GAVE	A-LANE	A-MIRS	A-RETE	A-VERS
A-GAZE	A-LANG	A-MISS	A-RETS	A-VERT
A-GENE	A-LANT	A-MITY	A-RIAS	A-VINE
A-GENT	A-LAPS	A-MOLE	A-RIEL	A-VISE
A-GILA	A-LATE	A-MONG	A-RIOT	A-VOID
A-GING	A-LAYS	A-MORT	A-RISE	A-VOWS
A-GIOS	A-LEFT	A-MOVE	A-ROMA	A-WAIT
A-GISM	A-LIAS	A-MUCK	A-ROSE	A-WAKE
A-GIST	A-LIEN	A-MUSE	A-RUMS	A-WARD
A-GLEE	A-LIKE	A-NANA	A-SCOT	A-WARE
A-GLEY	A-LINE	A-NEAR	A-SHED	A-WARN
A-GLOW	A-LIST	A-NIGH	A-SHES	A-WASH
A-GONE	A-LIVE	A-NILS	A-SHET	A-WAVE
A-GONS	A-LODS	A-NODE	A-SIDE	A-WAYS
A-GOOD	A-LOFT	A-NOLE	A-SKER	A-WEEL
A-GORA	A-LOIN	A-PACE	A-SKEW	A-WING
A-GREE	A-LONE	A-PAGE	A-SPIC	A-WOKE
A-GRIN	A-LONG	A-PAID	A-STIR	A-WORK
A-GUES	A-LOOF	A-PART	A-STUN	A-YAHS
A-HEAD	A-LOUD	A-PAYS	A-SWAY	A-YELP
A-HEAP	A-LOWE	A-PEAK	A-SWIM	A-YINS
A-HENT	A-LUMS	A-PEEK	A-TAPS	A-YONT
A-HIGH	A-LURE	A-PERT	A-TILT	A-ZINE
A-HIND	A-MAIN	A-PHIS	A-TOCS	A-ZOIC
A-HING	A-MASS	A-PIAN	A-TOKE	A-ZYME
A-HINT	A-MATE	A-PING	A-TOLL	

Five letters to six

A-AHING	A-BLUSH	A-CATES	A-FIELD	A-GLARE
A-ARTIS	A-BOARD	A-CETYL	A-FLAME	A-GLEAM
A-BANDS	A-BODED	A-CIDER	A-FLOAT	A-GOING
A-BASED	A-BODES	A-CORNS	A-FREET	A-GORAS
A-BASER	A-BOMAS	A-CRAWL	A-FRESH	A-GOUTY
A-BASES	A-BORAL	A-CROSS	A-FRITS	A-GREED
A-BATED	A-BORDS	A-CUTER	A-FRONT	A-GREES
A-BATES	A-BORNE	A-CUTES	A-GAMAS	A-GREGE
A-BATTU	A-BORTS	A-DAWED	A-GAMIC	A-GRISE
A-BEARS	A-BOUND	A-DEEMS	A-GAPES	A-GRIZE
A-BIDED	A-BOUTS	A-DOORS	A-GATES	A-GUISE
A-BIDER	A-BRAID	A-DREAD	A-GAZED	A-HOLDS
A-BIDES	A-BRAYS	A-DRIFT	A-GEIST	A-HORSE
A-BLATE	A-BRINS	A-DROIT	A-GENES	A-IDANT
A-BLAZE	A-BROAD	A-DUSTS	A-GENTS	A-IRING
A-BLEST	A-BUNAS	A-EDILE	A-GHAST	A-ISLED
A-BLETS	A-BURST	A-EMULE	A-GILAS	A-ISLES
A-BLING	A-BUSED	A-ERUGO	A-GINGS	A-KIMBO
A-BLINS	A-BUSES	A-ETHER	A-GISMS	A-LANDS
A-BLOOM	A-CATER	A-FEARS	A-GISTS	A-LANTS

A-LARUM	A-MUCKS	A-ROUND	A-STONY	A-VENGE
A-LATED	A-MUSED	A-ROUSE	A-STOOP	A-VENUE
A-LAYED	A-MUSER	A-SCEND	A-STRAY	A-VERSE
A-LEGGE	A-MUSES	A-SCENT	A-STRUT	A-VERTS
A-LEVIN	A-NANAS	A-SCOTS	A-STUNS	A-VISED
A-LIENS	A-NEARS	A-SEITY	A-SWARM	A-VISES
A-LIGHT	A-NEATH	A-SHAKE	A-SWING	A-VITAL
A-LINED	A-NIGHT	A-SHAME	A-SWIRL	A-VOIDS
A-LINER	A-NODAL	A-SHETS	A-SWOON	A-VOUCH
A-LINES	A-NODES	A-SHIER	A-TAATA	A-VOWED
A-LOGIA	A-NOINT	A-SHINE	A-TELIC	A-VOWER
A-LOINS	A-NOLES	A-SHORE	A-THROB	A-WAITS
A-LURES	A-NOMIC	A-SIDES	A-TOKES	A-WAKED
A-MATED	A-PHONY	A-SKERS	A-TOLLS	A-WAKEN
A-MATES	A-PICAL	A-SLAKE	A-TONAL	A-WAKES
A-MAUTS	A-PIECE	A-SLANT	A-TONED	A-WARDS
A-MAZED	A-PODAL	A-SLEEP	A-TONER	A-WARNS
A-MAZES	A-RABIC	A-SLOPE	A-TONES	A-WATCH
A-MEERS	A-RABIS	A-SLOSH	A-TONIC	A-WEARY
A-MENDS	A-RAISE	A-SMEAR	A-TOPIC	A-WEIGH
A-MENED	A-REACH	A-SPICK	A-TRIAL	A-WHEEL
A-MENTA	A-READS	A-SPICS	A-TWAIN	A-WHILE
A-MIDST	A-REDES	A-SPINE	A-TWEEL	A-WHIRL
A-MINES	A-RETES	A-SPIRE	A-TWEEN	A-WOKEN
A-MISES	A-RIDER	A-SPORT	A-TWIXT	A-WRACK
A-MOLES	A-RIELS	A-SPOUT	A-TYPIC	A-WRONG
A-MOOVE	A-RIGHT	A-SQUAT	A-UNTIE	A-XENIC
A-MORAL	A-RILED	A-STARE	A-URATE	A-ZINES
A-MOUNT	A-RISEN	A-START	A-VAILS	A-ZONAL
A-MOVED	A-RISES	A-STERN	A-VALES	A-ZYMES
A-MOVES	A-ROMAS	A-STONE	A-VAUNT	

Six letters to seven

A-BANDED	A-BUTTER	A-ERUGOS	A-LEVINS	A-MOUNTS
A-BASHED	A-BYSSAL	A-ETHERS	A-LIASES	A-MOVING
A-BASHES	A-CANTHI	A-FEARED	A-LIGHTS	A-MUSERS
A-BASING	A-CATERS	A-FREETS	A-LINERS	A-MUSING
A-BATING	A-CAUDAL	A-GAINST	A-LINING	A-MUSIVE
A-BETTED	A-CERATE	A-GAMETE	A-LONELY	A-NEARED
A-BETTER	A-CEROUS	A-GEISTS	A-LUMINA	A-NOESES
A-BETTOR	A-CETYLS	A-GENTRY	A-LUMINE	A-NOESIS
A-BIDDEN	A-CHIRAL	A-GINNER	A-MASSED	A-NOETIC
A-BIDERS	A-CLINIC	A-GRASTE	A-MASSES	A-NOINTS
A-BIDING	A-CORNED	A-GRISED	A-MATING	A-NOTHER
A-BIOTIC	A-CUTELY	A-GRISES	A-MAZING	A-PAYING
A-BLINGS	A-CUTEST	A-GRIZES	A-MENAGE	A-PHASIC
A-BODING	A-CYCLIC	A-GROUND	A-MENDED	A-PHESES
A-BOUGHT	A-DAWING	A-GUISED	A-MENDER	A-PHONIC
A-BOUNDS	A-DEEMED	A-GUISES	A-MENING	A-PHOTIC
A-BRAIDS	A-DHARMA	A-HEIGHT	A-MENTAL	A-PLENTY
A-BRAYED	A-DREADS	A-HUNGRY	A-MENTUM	A-POSTIL
A-BREAST	A-DUSTED	A-ISLING	A-MERCER	A-PTERIA
A-BRIDGE	A-EDILES	A-ITCHES	A-MERCES	A-PTOTIC
A-BROACH	A-EGISES	A-LARUMS	A-MISSES	A-QUIVER
A-BROADS	A-EMULED	A-LAYING	A-MONGST	A-RACHIS
A-BUBBLE	A-EMULES	A-LEGGED	A-MOOVED	A-RAISED
A-BUSING	A-EOLIAN	A-LEGGES	A-MOOVES	A-RAISES
A-BUTTED	A-EONIAN	A-LENGTH	A-MOTION	A-REALLY

A-REDING	A-SHAMES	A-STARTS	A-THRILL	A-VERTED
A-RETTED	A-SHIEST	A-STATIC	A-THWART	A-VIATIC
A-RIPPLE	A-SHIVER	A-STELIC	A-TINGLE	A-VIATOR
A-RISING	A-SKLENT	A-STONED	A-TONERS	A-VISING
A-ROUSED	A-SLAKED	A-STONES	A-TONICS	A-VOIDED
A-ROUSER	A-SLAKES	A-STOUND	A-TONIES	A-VOIDER
A-ROUSES	A-SOCIAL	A-STRAND	A-TONING	A-VOWERS
A-RUGOLA	A-SPERSE	A-STRICT	A-TROPHY	A-VOWING
A-SCARED	A-SPICKS	A-STRIDE	A-TROPIN	A-WAITED
A-SCENDS	A-SPINES	A-STYLAR	A-UNTIES	A-WAITER
A-SCENTS	A-SPIRED	A-SUDDEN	A-URATES	A-WAKENS
A-SCONCE	A-SPIRES	A-SUNDER	A-VAILED	A-WAKING
A-SCRIBE	A-SPORTS	A-TAATAS	A-VAUNTS	A-WARDED
A-SEPSES	A-SPRAWL	A-TACTIC	A-VENGED	A-WARDER
A-SEPSIS	A-SPREAD	A-TAXIES	A-VENGER	A-WARNED
A-SEPTIC	A-SPROUT	A-THEISM	A-VENGES	A-WHEELS
A-SEXUAL	A-SQUINT	A-THEIST	A-VENTRE	A-ZYMITE
A-SHAMED	A-STABLE	A-THIRST	A-VENUES	

Seven letters to eight

A-BANDING	A-ESTIVAL	A-MIDSHIP	A-SEISMIC	A-TROPINS
A-BASHING	A-ETHERIC	A-MISSING	A-SEITIES	A-TROPISM
A-BATABLE	A-FEARING	A-MITOSES	A-SEPTATE	A-TWITTER
A-BEARING	A-FEBRILE	A-MITOSIS	A-SEPTICS	A-TYPICAL
A-BEGGING	A-FLUTTER	A-MITOTIC	A-SHAMING	A-VAILING
A-BETTERS	A-GAMETES	A-MOOVING	A-SHINESS	A-VARICES
A-BETTING	A-GENESES	A-MORALLY	A-SLAKING	A-VAUNTED
A-BETTORS	A-GENESIS	A-MORTISE	A-SOCIALS	A-VENGERS
A-BIDINGS	A-GENETIC	A-MOTIONS	A-SPARKLE	A-VENGING
A-BOUNDED	A-GINNERS	A-MOUNTED	A-SPERSED	A-VENTAIL
A-BRACHIA	A-GLIMMER	A-MUSETTE	A-SPERSES	A-VENTRED
A-BRAIDED	A-GLITTER	A-NEARING	A-SPHERIC	A-VENTRES
A-BRAYING	A-GLOSSAL	A-NEURISM	A-SPIRANT	A-VENTURE
A-BRIDGED	A-GNOSTIC	A-NODALLY	A-SPIRING	A-VERSION
A-BRIDGES	A-GRAPHIC	A-NOINTED	A-SPORTED	A-VERTING
A-BROOKED	A-GREEING	A-NOINTER	A-STARTED	A-VIATORS
A-BUTMENT	A-GRISING	A-PHONICS	A-STERNAL	A-VOIDERS
A-BUTTALS	A-GUISING	A-PHONIES	A-STEROID	A-VOIDING
A-BUTTERS	A-KINESES	A-PIARIST	A-STHENIA	A-VOUCHED
A-BUTTING	A-KINESIS	A-PLASTIC	A-STHENIC	A-VOUCHER
A-CANTHUS	A-KINETIC	A-POSTILS	A-STONIED	A-VOUCHES
A-CAUDATE	A-LEGGING	A-PRACTIC	A-STONIES	A-WAITERS
A-CAULINE	A-LIGHTED	A-PYRETIC	A-STONING	A-WAITING
A-CENTRIC	A-LOGICAL	A-PYREXIA	A-STONISH	A-WAKENED
A-CERATED	A-LUMINES	A-RAISING	A-STOUNDS	A-WAKENER
A-CHROMIC	A-MASSING	A-REACHED	A-STUNNED	A-WAKINGS
A-COSMISM	A-MAZEDLY	A-REACHES	A-SYNERGY	A-WANTING
A-COSMIST	A-MEIOSES	A-READING	A-SYSTOLE	A-WARDERS
A-DEEMING	A-MEIOSIS	A-RETTING	A-TECHNIC	A-WARDING
A-DHARMAS	A-MENAGED	A-ROUSERS	A-THEISMS	A-WARNING
A-DREADED	A-MENAGES	A-ROUSING	A-THEISTS	A-WEARIED
A-DUSTING	A-MENDERS	A-RUGOLAS	A-TONALLY	A-WEATHER
A-DYNAMIC	A-MENDING	A-SCENDED	A-TREMBLE	A-ZYGOSES
A-EMULING	A-MERCERS	A-SCRIBED	A-TROPHIC	A-ZYMITES
A-ESTHETE	A-MIDMOST	A-SCRIBES	A-TROPINE	

Eight letters to nine

A-BASEMENT	A-ETIOLOGY	A-MOROSITY	A-SEXUALLY	A-TEMPORAL
A-BASHLESS	A-FOREHAND	A-MORTISED	A-SKEWNESS	A-THEISTIC
A-BATEMENT	A-FORESAID	A-MORTISES	A-SMOULDER	A-THEMATIC
A-BIOGENIC	A-FORETIME	A-MOUNTING	A-SPERSING	A-THEOLOGY
A-BODEMENT	A-GELASTIC	A-MUSETTES	A-SPIRANTS	A-TONALITY
A-BOUNDING	A-GENTRIES	A-MUSINGLY	A-SPIRATED	A-TONICITY
A-BRAIDING	A-GNOSTICS	A-MYOTONIA	A-SPLENIUM	A-TROPHIED
A-BRIDGING	A-HISTORIC	A-NEURISMS	A-SPORTING	A-TROPHIES
A-BROOKING	A-HUNGERED	A-NOINTERS	A-STARTING	A-TROPINES
A-BUILDING	A-ISLELESS	A-NOINTING	A-STEROIDS	A-TROPISMS
A-BUTMENTS	A-LACKADAY	A-NUCLEATE	A-STHENIAS	A-VASCULAR
A-CELLULAR	A-LIENABLE	A-PATHETIC	A-STOMATAL	A-VAUNTING
A-CEPHALIC	A-LIGHTING	A-PERIODIC	A-STONYING	A-VENGEFUL
A-CHROMOUS	A-LIKENESS	A-PERTNESS	A-STOUNDED	A-VENTAILE
A-COSMISMS	A-LITERACY	A-PETALOUS	A-STRADDLE	A-VENTAILS
A-COSMISTS	A-LITERATE	A-PHERESES	A-STRINGED	A-VENTRING
A-CRITICAL	A-LIVENESS	A-PHERESIS	A-STRINGER	A-VENTURES
A-CUTENESS	A-LONENESS	A-PIARISTS	A-STUNNING	A-VERSIONS
A-DREADING	A-LUMINOUS	A-PLANETIC	A-SYLLABIC	A-VIRULENT
A-EOLIPILE	A-MAZEMENT	A-PRIORITY	A-SYMMETRY	A-VOCATION
A-ESTHESES	A-MENAGING	A-PYREXIAS	A-SYNAPSES	A-VOIDABLE
A-ESTHESIA	A-MENDABLE	A-RACHISES	A-SYNAPSIS	A-VOIDANCE
A-ESTHESIS	A-MIDSHIPS	A-REACHING	A-SYNDETIC	A-VOUCHERS
A-ESTHETES	A-MORALISM	A-RHYTHMIC	A-SYNDETON	A-VOUCHING
A-ESTHETIC	A-MORALIST	A-SCENDING	A-SYNERGIA	A-WAKENERS
A-ESTIVATE	A-MORALITY	A-SCRIBING	A-SYSTOLES	A-WAKENING
A-ETHEREAL	A-MORNINGS	A-SEPALOUS	A-SYSTOLIC	

A – End-hooks

Two letters to three

AB-A	AW-A	GO-A	OD-A	UT-A
AG-A	BA-A	HO-A	OR-A	YE-A
AH-A	BO-A	IT-A	PE-A	ZO-A
AI-A	CH-A	KO-A	PI-A	
AL-A	ER-A	MA-A	PO-A	
AM-A	ET-A	MO-A	SH-A	
AN-A	FA-A	OB-A	TE-A	

Three letters to four

ABB-A	BUB-A	DIV-A	HOH-A	KIN-A
ACT-A	BUD-A	DON-A	HOM-A	KOR-A
ALB-A	BUN-A	DOP-A	HOY-A	LAM-A
ALF-A	BUR-A	FET-A	HUI-A	LAV-A
AMI-A	CAB-A	FIL-A	HUM-A	LEV-A
ANN-A	CAM-A	FOR-A	IDE-A	LIP-A
ANT-A	CAP-A	GAG-A	ILK-A	LOT-A
ARB-A	CHI-A	GAL-A	JAG-A	LUM-A
ARE-A	COD-A	GAM-A	JOT-A	MAL-A
BET-A	COL-A	GEN-A	JUG-A	MAM-A
BIG-A	COX-A	GET-A	KAK-A	MAN-A
BOB-A	DAD-A	GIG-A	KAM-A	MAR-A
BON-A	DEV-A	GOR-A	KAT-A	MAS-A
BOR-A	DIS-A	GUL-A	KAW-A	MAY-A
BOT-A	DIT-A	HAH-A	KET-A	MEG-A

A – Front-hooks

MEL-A	OLE-A	RAJ-A	SOB-A	TOR-A
MES-A	ORC-A	RAN-A	SOC-A	TUB-A
MET-A	OUP-A	RAT-A	SOD-A	TUN-A
MIC-A	PAC-A	RAY-A	SOL-A	URE-A
MOL-A	PAP-A	RIB-A	SOM-A	VAR-A
MON-A	PAR-A	RIM-A	SOY-A	VAS-A
MOR-A	PAW-A	RIZ-A	SUB-A	VEG-A
MOW-A	PIC-A	ROM-A	SUR-A	VIG-A
MOY-A	PIN-A	ROT-A	TAK-A	VIN-A
NAG-A	PIP-A	RUG-A	TAN-A	VIS-A
NAN-A	PIT-A	SAG-A	TAP-A	VOL-A
NAP-A	PRO-A	SAM-A	TAR-A	WAW-A
NIP-A	PUH-A	SEN-A	TAV-A	WEN-A
NOM-A	PUL-A	SER-A	TAW-A	WET-A
NON-A	PUN-A	SET-A	TAX-A	WHO-A
NOT-A	PUP-A	SHE-A	TEL-A	YUG-A
OBI-A	RAG-A	SIK-A	TOE-A	
ODE-A	RAI-A	SIM-A	TOG-A	

Four letters to five

ABAC-A	DORS-A	KIPP-A	PASH-A	SHIV-A
AFAR-A	DOUM-A	LAIK-A	PAST-A	SIDH-A
ALAP-A	DOUR-A	LEPT-A	PELT-A	SIGN-A
ANAN-A	DOWN-A	LEZZ-A	PERE-A	SOFT-A
BACH-A	DRAM-A	LIMB-A	PIET-A	SORD-A
BALS-A	DURR-A	LIMP-A	PILE-A	SORT-A
BAND-A	ERIC-A	LING-A	PINT-A	SPAZ-A
BANI-A	FANG-A	LONG-A	PLAY-A	SPIC-A
BAST-A	FAUN-A	LOOF-A	POLK-A	SPIN-A
BATT-A	FELL-A	LUFF-A	PONG-A	SUNN-A
BORN-A	FEST-A	LUTE-A	POOK-A	TAIG-A
BUFF-A	FETT-A	MANG-A	PORT-A	TALE-A
BULL-A	FLOR-A	MANI-A	PRIM-A	TANG-A
BURK-A	FOND-A	MARK-A	PUCK-A	TANK-A
BURS-A	FOSS-A	MASS-A	PULK-A	TEGU-A
CALL-A	GALE-A	MENT-A	PUNG-A	TEST-A
CALP-A	GAMB-A	MISS-A	PUNK-A	THAN-A
CANN-A	GENU-A	MOCH-A	QUIN-A	THEM-A
CART-A	GRAM-A	MOLL-A	RAGG-A	TIAR-A
CELL-A	GRAN-A	MOOL-A	RAIT-A	TINE-A
CHAR-A	GUAN-A	MUGG-A	RAST-A	TONG-A
CHAY-A	HAIK-A	MULL-A	RATH-A	TONK-A
CHIC-A	HAKE-A	MUNG-A	ROOS-A	TORT-A
CHIN-A	HALF-A	MURR-A	SAKI-A	TREF-A
COAL-A	HALM-A	MUSH-A	SALP-A	TRON-A
COCO-A	HAST-A	NERK-A	SALS-A	UNCI-A
COMM-A	HATH-A	NORI-A	SANG-A	VEST-A
CONI-A	HERM-A	NORM-A	SANS-A	VILL-A
COST-A	HOND-A	NULL-A	SCOP-A	VIOL-A
COTT-A	HOOK-A	PACT-A	SCUT-A	VOLT-A
DARG-A	HOST-A	PAIS-A	SELL-A	WALL-A
DELT-A	HOVE-A	PALE-A	SENS-A	WHAT-A
DERM-A	HYEN-A	PALL-A	SEPT-A	WINN-A
DICT-A	IDOL-A	PAND-A	SERR-A	WISH-A
DONG-A	KAIK-A	PANG-A	SESS-A	YACK-A
DOON-A	KANG-A	PARK-A	SHAM-A	YURT-A
DORB-A	KIND-A	PARR-A	SHAY-A	ZILL-A

Five letters to six

AMENT-A	CORNU-A	HALAL-A	ORBIT-A	SENOR-A
AMRIT-A	CRACK-A	HALLO-A	ORGAN-A	SHIRR-A
ANTAR-A	CREST-A	HEDER-A	PAGOD-A	SHISH-A
ARGAL-A	CRUST-A	HEMIN-A	PARER-A	SOLER-A
BERTH-A	CUBIC-A	HILLO-A	PATER-A	SPIRE-A
BILBO-A	CUTCH-A	HOLLO-A	PATIN-A	STELL-A
BOCCI-A	EGEST-A	HULLO-A	PENNI-A	STERN-A
BOONG-A	EJECT-A	KAING-A	PETAR-A	STRIG-A
CABAL-A	ENTER-A	KORUN-A	PLANT-A	STRUM-A
CAMIS-A	EPOCH-A	KUTCH-A	PLASM-A	TALUK-A
CARDI-A	EXACT-A	LORIC-A	QUANT-A	TAPET-A
CHANG-A	FASCI-A	MAXIM-A	QUINO-A	TARSI-A
CHARK-A	FAVEL-A	MIASM-A	QUINT-A	TORAN-A
CHART-A	FIEST-A	MINIM-A	QUOTH-A	TREIF-A
CHICH-A	FRISK-A	MONER-A	RHUMB-A	TUNIC-A
CHORD-A	FRUST-A	NYMPH-A	SAHIB-A	VALET-A
CHORE-A	GLOSS-A	OBELI-A	SATYR-A	YOJAN-A
CONCH-A	GRAMP-A	OCHRE-A	SCARP-A	

Six letters to seven

ABOMAS-A	CHRISM-A	GALLET-A	MICELL-A	SELECT-A
ACANTH-A	CODEIN-A	GALLIC-A	MOMENT-A	SENHOR-A
ADDEND-A	CORTIN-A	GERMIN-A	NANDIN-A	SEQUEL-A
ALUMIN-A	COTING-A	GRAVID-A	OSMUND-A	SERING-A
ANALOG-A	CROTAL-A	GUNNER-A	PAISAN-A	SHEIKH-A
ANONYM-A	CURIOS-A	INFANT-A	PERSON-A	SIGNOR-A
ARABIC-A	CYATHI-A	INGEST-A	PLACIT-A	SQUILL-A
ASHRAM-A	DEJECT-A	KHALIF-A	POTASS-A	SULTAN-A
BUZUKI-A	DEODAR-A	LAVOLT-A	PROPYL-A	TAMBUR-A
CANDID-A	DRACHM-A	LOCUST-A	QUININ-A	TARTAN-A
CANTAL-A	EMBLEM-A	LOMENT-A	ROBUST-A	TAVERN-A
CEMENT-A	EROTIC-A	MADRAS-A	ROSACE-A	TEMPER-A
CHIASM-A	EXOTIC-A	MANDIR-A	ROTUND-A	TRISUL-A
CHIMER-A	FAVELL-A	MANIOC-A	SCHISM-A	TYMPAN-A
CHOLER-A	FORMIC-A	MARKKA-A	SECRET-A	VIATIC-A

Seven letters to eight

ABSCISS-A	BROUGHT-A	FASCIST-A	MRIDANG-A	STROBIL-A
AMYGDAL-A	CHAMPAC-A	HEPATIC-A	NYMPHAE-A	SYNTAGM-A
ANAPHOR-A	CHARISM-A	JAVELIN-A	PERFECT-A	TAMANDU-A
ANGELIC-A	CISTERN-A	MANDIOC-A	PIGNOLI-A	TAMBOUR-A
ANTEFIX-A	CONSULT-A	MARCHES-A	QUILLAI-A	THERIAC-A
ARBORET-A	DEMENTI-A	MARINER-A	RAKSHAS-A	TORMENT-A
AUTOMAT-A	DIASTEM-A	MATADOR-A	SALICET-A	TOURIST-A
BASILIC-A	DULCIAN-A	MELODIC-A	SARMENT-A	UNGUENT-A
BOTANIC-A	EPITHEM-A	MOLLUSC-A	SCIATIC-A	
BRONCHI-A	EXCERPT-A	MONSTER-A	SIGNORI-A	

Eight letters to nine

AQUATINT-A	BOUZOUKI-A	DIDRACHM-A	EXANTHEM-A	HIERATIC-A
ARGUMENT-A	CALYPTER-A	DIPLOMAT-A	FANFARON-A	HYPODERM-A
BOUSOUKI-A	CANEPHOR-A	ESOTERIC-A	HARMONIC-A	HYPOTHEC-A

A – End-hooks

JAMBOLAN-A   NICOTIAN-A   PHILOMEL-A   SLIVOVIC-A
MAIASAUR-A   PARAMENT-A   POZZOLAN-A   SOUVLAKI-A
MATACHIN-A   PHANTASM-A   PRINCIPI-A

B – Front-hooks

Two letters to three

B-AA	B-AT	B-IN	B-OO	B-UN
B-AD	B-AY	B-IO	B-OP	B-UR
B-AG	B-ED	B-IS	B-OR	B-US
B-AH	B-EE	B-IT	B-OS	B-UT
B-AL	B-EL	B-OB	B-OW	B-YE
B-AM	B-EN	B-OD	B-OX	
B-AN	B-ES	B-OH	B-OY	
B-AR	B-ET	B-OI	B-UG	
B-AS	B-ID	B-ON	B-UM	

Three letters to four

B-AAL	B-AWL	B-INK	B-ODS	B-RAW
B-AAS	B-AWN	B-INS	B-OFF	B-RAY
B-ABA	B-AYE	B-IOS	B-OHO	B-RED
B-ABY	B-AYS	B-IRK	B-OHS	B-REE
B-ACH	B-EAN	B-ISH	B-OIL	B-REI
B-ADS	B-EAR	B-ITS	B-OKE	B-REN
B-AFF	B-EAT	B-LAB	B-OLD	B-REW
B-AFT	B-EAU	B-LAD	B-OLE	B-RIG
B-AGS	B-EDS	B-LAG	B-ONE	B-RIM
B-AIL	B-EEN	B-LAH	B-ONY	B-RIN
B-AIT	B-EGO	B-LAM	B-OOH	B-RIT
B-AKE	B-ELL	B-LAT	B-OOM	B-ROD
B-ALE	B-ELS	B-LAW	B-OON	B-ROO
B-ALL	B-ELT	B-LAY	B-OOR	B-ROW
B-ALS	B-END	B-LED	B-OOS	B-RUT
B-AND	B-ENE	B-LEE	B-OOT	B-UDO
B-ANE	B-ENS	B-LET	B-OPS	B-UDS
B-ANI	B-ERE	B-LEW	B-ORA	B-UFO
B-ANT	B-ERG	B-LEY	B-ORD	B-UGS
B-ARB	B-ERK	B-LIN	B-ORE	B-UKE
B-ARD	B-EST	B-LIP	B-ORS	B-UMP
B-ARE	B-ETA	B-LOB	B-ORT	B-UNS
B-ARF	B-ETH	B-LOG	B-OUK	B-URB
B-ARK	B-HAT	B-LOT	B-OUT	B-URD
B-ARM	B-HUT	B-LOW	B-OWL	B-URN
B-ARS	B-ICE	B-LUR	B-OXY	B-URP
B-ASH	B-IDE	B-OAK	B-OYS	B-UTE
B-ASK	B-IDS	B-OAR	B-RAD	B-UTS
B-ASS	B-IFF	B-OAT	B-RAG	B-YES
B-ATE	B-IGG	B-OBA	B-RAN	
B-ATT	B-ILK	B-OBS	B-RAS	
B-AUK	B-ILL	B-ODE	B-RAT	

Four letters to five

B-AALS	B-ADDY	B-AIRN	B-AKES	B-ALKY
B-ABAS	B-AFFY	B-AITS	B-ALAS	B-ALLS
B-ACCA	B-AILS	B-AKED	B-ALES	B-ALLY

B-ALMS	B-IGGS	B-LINY	B-ORAL	B-RINE
B-ANAL	B-ILKS	B-LIPS	B-ORDS	B-RING
B-ANDS	B-ILLS	B-LIST	B-ORES	B-RINK
B-ANES	B-ILLY	B-LITE	B-ORTS	B-RINS
B-ANNS	B-INGO	B-LIVE	B-OUKS	B-RISE
B-ANTS	B-INKS	B-LOBS	B-OURN	B-RISK
B-ARBS	B-IOTA	B-LOCK	B-OUTS	B-RITS
B-ARDS	B-IRKS	B-LOGS	B-OWED	B-RITT
B-ARED	B-ITCH	B-LOKE	B-OWER	B-ROAD
B-ARES	B-LABS	B-LOOM	B-OWES	B-ROCH
B-ARFS	B-LACK	B-LOOP	B-OWLS	B-ROCK
B-ARKS	B-LADE	B-LORE	B-OWSE	B-RODS
B-ARMS	B-LADS	B-LOTS	B-OXEN	B-ROIL
B-ARMY	B-LADY	B-LOWN	B-OXER	B-ROKE
B-ASKS	B-LAER	B-LOWS	B-OXES	B-ROOD
B-ATES	B-LAGS	B-LUDE	B-RACE	B-ROOK
B-AUKS	B-LAHS	B-LUES	B-RACH	B-ROOM
B-AWLS	B-LAIN	B-LUFF	B-RACK	B-ROOS
B-AWNS	B-LAME	B-LUNK	B-RADS	B-ROSE
B-AYES	B-LAMS	B-LUNT	B-RAGS	B-ROSY
B-EACH	B-LAND	B-LURS	B-RAID	B-ROWS
B-EANS	B-LANK	B-LUSH	B-RAIL	B-RUIN
B-EARD	B-LARE	B-OAKS	B-RAIN	B-RULE
B-EARS	B-LASE	B-OARS	B-RAKE	B-RUME
B-EAST	B-LASH	B-OAST	B-RAND	B-RUNG
B-EATH	B-LAST	B-OATS	B-RANK	B-RUNT
B-EATS	B-LATE	B-OBAS	B-RANT	B-RUSH
B-EAUS	B-LATS	B-OBOL	B-RASH	B-RUSK
B-EAUX	B-LAUD	B-OCHE	B-RAST	B-RUST
B-EECH	B-LAWN	B-ODES	B-RATS	B-RUTS
B-EERY	B-LAWS	B-OFFS	B-RAVE	B-UDOS
B-EGAD	B-LAYS	B-OGLE	B-RAWN	B-UFOS
B-ELLS	B-LAZE	B-OHOS	B-RAWS	B-UKES
B-ELTS	B-LEAK	B-OILS	B-RAYS	B-UMBO
B-ENDS	B-LEAR	B-OINK	B-RAZE	B-UMPH
B-ENES	B-LEAT	B-OKES	B-READ	B-UMPS
B-ERES	B-LEED	B-OLDS	B-REAK	B-UMPY
B-ERGS	B-LEEP	B-OLES	B-REAM	B-UNCE
B-ERKS	B-LEES	B-ONCE	B-REDE	B-UNCO
B-ESES	B-LEND	B-ONER	B-REDS	B-UNDE
B-ESTS	B-LENT	B-ONES	B-REED	B-UNDY
B-ETAS	B-LESS	B-ONIE	B-REES	B-URBS
B-ETHS	B-LEST	B-ONUS	B-REIS	B-URDS
B-EVER	B-LETS	B-OOFY	B-RENS	B-URNS
B-HAJI	B-LEYS	B-OOHS	B-RENT	B-URPS
B-HANG	B-LIMP	B-OOMS	B-REWS	B-URSA
B-HOOT	B-LIMY	B-OONS	B-RICK	B-USED
B-HUTS	B-LIND	B-OOSE	B-RIDE	B-USES
B-ICES	B-LING	B-OOTS	B-RIGS	B-UTES
B-IDES	B-LINK	B-OOZE	B-RILL	
B-IFFY	B-LINS	B-OOZY	B-RIMS	

Five letters to six

B-ABIES	B-ACKER	B-AGGIE	B-ALLOT	B-ANKER
B-ABOON	B-ADDER	B-AILED	B-ALLOW	B-ANTED
B-ACCAS	B-ADMAN	B-AIRNS	B-ANANA	B-ARISH
B-ACHED	B-ADMEN	B-AKING	B-ANGER	B-ARKED
B-ACHES	B-AGGER	B-ALDER	B-ANGLE	B-ARRAS

B – Front-hooks

B-ARRET	B-LANKY	B-OASTS	B-RANDS	B-RISKS
B-ARROW	B-LARES	B-OATER	B-RANDY	B-RISKY
B-ASHED	B-LASTS	B-OBOLS	B-RANKS	B-RITTS
B-ASHES	B-LATER	B-OCHES	B-RANTS	B-ROACH
B-ASKED	B-LAUDS	B-OFFED	B-RASES	B-ROADS
B-ASSES	B-LAWED	B-OGLES	B-RATTY	B-ROCKS
B-ASSET	B-LAZED	B-OILED	B-RAVED	B-ROGUE
B-ASTER	B-LAZES	B-OILER	B-RAVER	B-ROILS
B-ATMAN	B-LEACH	B-OINKS	B-RAVES	B-ROKED
B-EAGLE	B-LEAKS	B-OLDEN	B-RAWER	B-ROKER
B-EANED	B-LEAKY	B-OLDER	B-RAWLY	B-ROKES
B-EARDS	B-LEARS	B-OMBER	B-RAWNS	B-ROMAL
B-EARED	B-LEARY	B-ONCES	B-RAYED	B-ROODS
B-EASTS	B-LEATS	B-ONERS	B-RAZED	B-ROOKS
B-EATEN	B-LEEPS	B-OOHED	B-RAZER	B-ROOMS
B-EATER	B-LENDS	B-OOSES	B-RAZES	B-ROOMY
B-EGGAR	B-LIGHT	B-OOZED	B-REACH	B-ROOSE
B-EGGED	B-LIMEY	B-OOZES	B-READS	B-ROSES
B-EIGNE	B-LIMPS	B-ORALS	B-READY	B-ROUGH
B-ELATE	B-LINDS	B-ORATE	B-REAKS	B-ROWED
B-ENDED	B-LINGS	B-ORDER	B-REAMS	B-RUINS
B-ENDER	B-LINKS	B-OTHER	B-REAST	B-RULES
B-HAJIS	B-LITES	B-OUGHT	B-REDED	B-RUMAL
B-HANGS	B-LITHE	B-OUNCE	B-REDES	B-RUMES
B-HOOTS	B-LOBBY	B-OVATE	B-REECH	B-RUNCH
B-ICKER	B-LOCKS	B-OVINE	B-REEDS	B-RUNTS
B-IDENT	B-LOKES	B-OWING	B-REEKS	B-RUSHY
B-IGGED	B-LOOEY	B-OWLED	B-REEST	B-RUSTS
B-ILLER	B-LOOIE	B-OWLER	B-REGMA	B-UDDER
B-INGLE	B-LOOMS	B-OWNED	B-REIST	B-UGGED
B-INNED	B-LOOPS	B-OXERS	B-RENNE	B-UMBLE
B-IONIC	B-LORES	B-RACED	B-RENTS	B-UMBOS
B-IOTAS	B-LOTTO	B-RACER	B-REVET	B-UMPED
B-ISHES	B-LOUSE	B-RACES	B-REWED	B-UNCES
B-ITCHY	B-LOUSY	B-RACKS	B-RIBES	B-UNCOS
B-LACKS	B-LOWED	B-RAGGY	B-RICHT	B-UNION
B-LADED	B-LOWER	B-RAIDS	B-RICKS	B-UNKED
B-LADER	B-LOWSE	B-RAILS	B-RIDES	B-URGER
B-LADES	B-LUDES	B-RAINS	B-RIDGE	B-URIAL
B-LAMED	B-LUFFS	B-RAINY	B-RIGHT	B-URNED
B-LAMER	B-LUNGE	B-RAIRD	B-RILLS	B-URPED
B-LAMES	B-LUNKS	B-RAISE	B-RINES	B-URSAE
B-LANCH	B-LUNTS	B-RAKED	B-RINGS	B-USHER
B-LANDS	B-LURRY	B-RAKES	B-RINKS	B-USING
B-LANKS	B-OAKED	B-RANCH	B-RISES	B-UTTER

Six letters to seven

B-ABYING	B-ALLONS	B-ARKING	B-EAGLES	B-ELATED
B-ACHING	B-ALLOTS	B-ARRACK	B-EANING	B-ELATES
B-ACKERS	B-ALLOWS	B-ARRETS	B-EARDED	B-ENDERS
B-ADDIES	B-ANALLY	B-ARROWS	B-EARING	B-ENDING
B-ADLAND	B-ANANAS	B-ASHING	B-EATERS	B-HISTIE
B-AFFIES	B-ANGERS	B-ASKING	B-EATING	B-ICKERS
B-AGGERS	B-ANGLED	B-ASSETS	B-EECHES	B-IDENTS
B-AGGIES	B-ANGLES	B-ASSIST	B-EERIER	B-IGGING
B-AILING	B-ANKERS	B-ASTERS	B-EERILY	B-INGLES
B-ALLIES	B-ANTING	B-ATONED	B-EGGARS	B-INGOES
B-ALLIUM	B-ARISTA	B-EAGLED	B-EGGING	B-INNING

B-IONICS	B-LISTER	B-ONDING	B-RAKING	B-ROCHES
B-ITCHED	B-LITHER	B-ONEYER	B-RAMBLE	B-ROCKED
B-ITCHES	B-LOBBED	B-ONUSES	B-RANDED	B-ROCKET
B-LACKED	B-LOCKED	B-OODLES	B-RANKED	B-RODDED
B-LACKER	B-LOCKER	B-OOFIER	B-RASHED	B-ROGUES
B-LADDER	B-LOGGER	B-OOHING	B-RASHER	B-ROILED
B-LADERS	B-LOOMED	B-OOZIER	B-RASHES	B-ROKERS
B-LADING	B-LOOPED	B-OOZILY	B-RASHLY	B-ROKING
B-LAGGED	B-LOOPER	B-OOZING	B-RASSES	B-ROMALS
B-LAGGER	B-LOTTED	B-ORATED	B-RATTLE	B-RONZER
B-LAMING	B-LOTTER	B-ORATES	B-RAUNCH	B-ROOKED
B-LANDER	B-LOUSED	B-ORDERS	B-RAVERS	B-ROOKIE
B-LANKED	B-LOUSES	B-ORDURE	B-RAVING	B-ROOMED
B-LANKER	B-LOWERS	B-OTHERS	B-RAWEST	B-ROOSES
B-LANKLY	B-LOWING	B-OUCHES	B-RAYING	B-ROTHER
B-LARNEY	B-LOWSED	B-OUGHTS	B-RAZERS	B-ROUGHS
B-LASHES	B-LOWSES	B-OULDER	B-RAZING	B-ROUGHT
B-LASTED	B-LUBBER	B-OUNCES	B-REAMED	B-RUCKLE
B-LASTER	B-LUFFED	B-OVATES	B-REASTS	B-RUMMER
B-LATEST	B-LUNGED	B-OVINES	B-REDING	B-RUNTED
B-LATHER	B-LUNGER	B-OWLERS	B-REEDER	B-RUSHED
B-LATTER	B-LUNGES	B-OWLING	B-REESTS	B-RUSHER
B-LAUDED	B-LUNKER	B-OWNING	B-REISTS	B-RUSHES
B-LAWING	B-LUNTED	B-OXLIKE	B-RENNES	B-UCKERS
B-LAZING	B-LUSHED	B-RABBLE	B-RENTER	B-UDDERS
B-LEAKER	B-LUSHER	B-RACERS	B-REVETS	B-UGGING
B-LEARED	B-LUSHES	B-RACHES	B-RICKED	B-ULLING
B-LEEPED	B-LUSTER	B-RACHET	B-RICKLE	B-UMBLES
B-LENDER	B-OATERS	B-RACING	B-RIDGED	B-UMPING
B-LESSER	B-OBECHE	B-RACKET	B-RIDGES	B-UNDIES
B-LESSES	B-OCCIES	B-RADDED	B-RIDING	B-UNIONS
B-LETTED	B-OFFING	B-RAGGED	B-RIGHTS	B-UNKING
B-LIGHTS	B-OILERS	B-RAIDED	B-RIMING	B-URGERS
B-LINGER	B-OILERY	B-RAIDER	B-RIMMED	B-URIALS
B-LINKED	B-OILING	B-RAILED	B-RIMMER	B-URNING
B-LINKER	B-OINKED	B-RAINED	B-RINDED	B-URPING
B-LINNED	B-OLDENS	B-RAIRDS	B-RINGER	B-USHERS
B-LIPPED	B-OLDEST	B-RAISED	B-RISKED	B-UTTERS
B-LISSES	B-OMBERS	B-RAISES	B-RISKER	

Seven letters to eight

B-ADLANDS	B-EERIEST	B-LANCHES	B-LIGHTED	B-LOOPERS
B-AILMENT	B-ELATING	B-LANKEST	B-LIGHTER	B-LOOPING
B-ALLIUMS	B-ENDINGS	B-LANKING	B-LIMBING	B-LOTTERS
B-ANALITY	B-ENDWAYS	B-LARNEYS	B-LINKERS	B-LOTTING
B-ANTINGS	B-ENDWISE	B-LASTERS	B-LINKING	B-LOUSIER
B-ARISTAS	B-ESPOUSE	B-LASTING	B-LINNING	B-LOUSILY
B-ARRACKS	B-ETACISM	B-LATHERS	B-LIPPING	B-LOUSING
B-ARTISAN	B-ITCHIER	B-LAUDING	B-LISTERS	B-LOWBALL
B-ASHLESS	B-ITCHILY	B-LEACHED	B-LITHELY	B-LOWDOWN
B-ASSISTS	B-ITCHING	B-LEACHER	B-LITHEST	B-LUBBERS
B-ATONING	B-LACKING	B-LEACHES	B-LOBBING	B-LUFFING
B-EAGLING	B-LADDERS	B-LEARIER	B-LOCKAGE	B-LUNGERS
B-EARDING	B-LADDERY	B-LEARING	B-LOCKERS	B-LUNGING
B-EARINGS	B-LADINGS	B-LEEPING	B-LOCKING	B-LUNKERS
B-EARLIKE	B-LAGGERS	B-LENDERS	B-LOGGERS	B-LUNTING
B-EATABLE	B-LAGGING	B-LENDING	B-LOGGING	B-LUSHERS
B-EATINGS	B-LANCHED	B-LETTING	B-LOOMING	B-LUSHING

B-LUSTERS	B-RACINGS	B-RASHEST	B-REGMATA	B-RODDING
B-OARFISH	B-RACKETS	B-RASHING	B-RENNING	B-ROGUERY
B-OATLIKE	B-RADDING	B-RATCHET	B-REVISES	B-ROGUISH
B-OBECHES	B-RAGGIER	B-RATLING	B-RICHTER	B-ROILING
B-OINKING	B-RAGGING	B-RATPACK	B-RICKING	B-RONZERS
B-OLDENED	B-RAIDERS	B-RATTIER	B-RICKLES	B-ROOKIES
B-OLDNESS	B-RAIDING	B-RATTISH	B-RIDGING	B-ROOKING
B-ONDINGS	B-RAILING	B-RATTLED	B-RIGHTEN	B-ROOMIER
B-OOFIEST	B-RAINIER	B-RATTLES	B-RIGHTER	B-ROOMING
B-OOZIEST	B-RAINILY	B-REACHED	B-RIGHTLY	B-ROTHERS
B-ORATING	B-RAINING	B-REACHER	B-RIMLESS	B-RUMMERS
B-ORDERED	B-RAISING	B-REACHES	B-RIMMERS	B-RUNCHES
B-ORDERER	B-RAMBLED	B-READING	B-RIMMING	B-RUSHERS
B-ORDURES	B-RAMBLES	B-REAKING	B-RINGERS	B-RUSHIER
B-OWLLIKE	B-RANCHED	B-REAMING	B-RINGING	B-RUSHING
B-RABBLED	B-RANCHER	B-REASTED	B-RISKING	B-RUSTING
B-RABBLER	B-RANCHES	B-REECHED	B-ROACHED	B-ULLINGS
B-RABBLES	B-RANDIES	B-REECHES	B-ROACHES	B-UNDYING
B-RACHETS	B-RANDING	B-REEDERS	B-ROADWAY	B-URNINGS
B-RACHIAL	B-RANKING	B-REEDING	B-ROCKETS	B-UTTERED

Eight letters to nine

B-AILMENTS	B-LATHERER	B-LUSTROUS	B-RANCHERS	B-RICHTEST
B-ARTISANS	B-LEACHERS	B-OILERIES	B-RANCHING	B-RICKYARD
B-EASTINGS	B-LEACHING	B-OLDENING	B-RASHNESS	B-RIDGINGS
B-EERINESS	B-LEARIEST	B-OOZINESS	B-RATCHETS	B-RIGHTENS
B-ELATEDLY	B-LENDINGS	B-ORDERERS	B-RATLINGS	B-RIGHTEST
B-ESPOUSED	B-LIGHTERS	B-ORDERING	B-RATPACKS	B-RIGHTISH
B-ESPOUSES	B-LIGHTING	B-RABBLERS	B-RATTIEST	B-RINGINGS
B-ETACISMS	B-LINDWORM	B-RABBLING	B-RATTLING	B-ROACHING
B-ITCHIEST	B-LOCKABLE	B-RACKETED	B-RAUNCHED	B-ROADSIDE
B-LACKLAND	B-LOCKAGES	B-RAGGIEST	B-RAUNCHES	B-ROADWAYS
B-LADDERED	B-LOCKINGS	B-RAGGINGS	B-REACHERS	B-ROOMIEST
B-LAGGINGS	B-LOGGINGS	B-RAIDINGS	B-REACHING	B-RUSHIEST
B-LANCHING	B-LOUSIEST	B-RAINIEST	B-REASTING	B-RUSHINGS
B-LANKNESS	B-LOWBALLS	B-RAINLESS	B-REECHING	B-RUSHLIKE
B-LASTINGS	B-LOWDOWNS	B-RAINWASH	B-REEDINGS	B-URSIFORM
B-LATHERED	B-LUSTERED	B-RAMBLING	B-REVETTED	B-UTTERING

B – End-hooks

Two letters to three

AB-B	DI-B	JA-B	MI-B	RE-B
AL-B	DO-B	JO-B	MO-B	SI-B
AR-B	FA-B	KA-B	NA-B	SO-B
BI-B	GI-B	KO-B	NE-B	TA-B
BO-B	GO-B	LA-B	NO-B	UR-B
DA-B	GU-B	LI-B	NU-B	WE-B
DE-B	HO-B	LO-B	OR-B	YO-B

Three letters to four

BAR-B	BUR-B	CUR-B	FEE-B	GAM-B
BIB-B	CAR-B	DIE-B	FLU-B	GAR-B
BOA-B	CHI-B	DOO-B	FOR-B	HER-B
BOO-B	COB-B	DOR-B	FRA-B	JAM-B

JIB-B	NIM-B	SIB-B	WAR-B
LAM-B	PRO-B	TOM-B	WEM-B

Four letters to five

ACER-B	COUR-B	NEEM-B	SLUR-B	ZINE-B
BLUR-B	CUBE-B	PLUM-B	THRO-B	
COOM-B	DEMO-B	SLUB-B	ZEBU-B	

Five letters to six

SCRAM-B
SUPER-B

Six letters to seven

POTHER-B	REPLUM-B
PROVER-B	

C – Front-hooks

Two letters to three

C-AA	C-AT	C-HI	C-OO	C-UM
C-AB	C-AW	C-ID	C-OP	C-UP
C-AD	C-AY	C-IS	C-OR	C-UR
C-AG	C-EE	C-IT	C-OS	C-UT
C-AM	C-EL	C-OB	C-OW	
C-AN	C-HA	C-OD	C-OX	
C-AR	C-HE	C-ON	C-OY	

Three letters to four

C-AAS	C-ARS	C-HER	C-LAM	C-OIL
C-ABA	C-ART	C-HEW	C-LAP	C-OKE
C-ABS	C-ASH	C-HIC	C-LAT	C-OLD
C-ADS	C-ASK	C-HID	C-LAW	C-OLE
C-AFF	C-ATE	C-HIN	C-LAY	C-OMS
C-AGE	C-AUF	C-HIP	C-LEG	C-ONE
C-AGS	C-AUK	C-HIS	C-LEW	C-ONS
C-AID	C-AVA	C-HIT	C-LIP	C-ONY
C-AIN	C-AVE	C-HOC	C-LOD	C-OOF
C-AKE	C-AYS	C-HOG	C-LOG	C-OOM
C-ALF	C-EAS	C-HON	C-LOP	C-OON
C-ALL	C-ELL	C-HOP	C-LOT	C-OOP
C-ALP	C-ELS	C-HOW	C-LOU	C-OOS
C-AMA	C-ELT	C-HUB	C-LOW	C-OOT
C-AMP	C-ENS	C-HUG	C-LOY	C-OPE
C-ANE	C-ERE	C-HUM	C-OAT	C-OPS
C-ANN	C-ESS	C-HUT	C-OBS	C-ORD
C-ANT	C-HAD	C-IDE	C-OCA	C-ORE
C-ANY	C-HAM	C-IDS	C-OCH	C-ORF
C-APE	C-HAO	C-ILL	C-ODA	C-ORS
C-APO	C-HAP	C-ION	C-ODE	C-OSE
C-ARB	C-HAS	C-IRE	C-ODS	C-OUP
C-ARD	C-HAT	C-ITS	C-OFF	C-OUR
C-ARE	C-HAW	C-LAD	C-OFT	C-OWL
C-ARK	C-HAY	C-LAG	C-OHO	C-OXY

B – End-hooks

C-OYS C-RAY C-RIM C-UDS C-URN
C-RAG C-RED C-RIT C-UKE C-UTE
C-RAM C-REE C-ROC C-UPS C-UTS
C-RAN C-REM C-ROW C-URB
C-RAP C-REW C-RUD C-URD
C-RAW C-RIB C-RUE C-URE

Four letters to five

C-ABAS C-EASE C-HOGS C-LEPT C-OLDS
C-ABLE C-ELLS C-HOKE C-LEVE C-OLES
C-ACHE C-ELTS C-HONS C-LICK C-OMER
C-ADDY C-EORL C-HOOF C-LIED C-ONES
C-AGED C-ERED C-HOOK C-LIES C-ONTO
C-AGER C-ERES C-HOPS C-LIFT C-ONUS
C-AGES C-ERIC C-HORE C-LIMB C-OOFS
C-AIDS C-ERNE C-HOSE C-LIME C-OOMS
C-AINS C-EROS C-HOUT C-LINE C-OONS
C-AIRN C-ESSE C-HOWK C-LING C-OOPS
C-AKED C-HACK C-HOWS C-LINK C-OOTS
C-AKES C-HADS C-HUBS C-LINT C-OOZE
C-ALFS C-HAFF C-HUCK C-LIPE C-OPAL
C-ALIF C-HAFT C-HUFF C-LIPS C-OPED
C-ALLS C-HAIN C-HUGS C-LOAM C-OPEN
C-ALMS C-HAIR C-HUMP C-LOCK C-OPES
C-ALPS C-HAMS C-HUMS C-LODS C-ORAL
C-AMAS C-HANG C-HUNK C-LOGS C-ORBY
C-AMIS C-HANK C-HURL C-LOKE C-ORDS
C-AMPS C-HANT C-HYLE C-LONE C-ORES
C-AMUS C-HAPS C-IDES C-LOOP C-OSES
C-ANAL C-HARD C-ILIA C-LOOT C-OUCH
C-ANES C-HARE C-ILLS C-LOPS C-OULD
C-ANNA C-HARK C-INCH C-LOSE C-OUPS
C-ANNS C-HARM C-IONS C-LOTE C-OURS
C-ANON C-HART C-IRES C-LOTH C-OVEN
C-ANTS C-HATS C-LACK C-LOTS C-OVER
C-APED C-HAVE C-LADE C-LOUD C-OWED
C-APER C-HAWK C-LADS C-LOUR C-OWER
C-APES C-HAWS C-LAGS C-LOUS C-OWLS
C-APOS C-HAYS C-LAME C-LOUT C-OXES
C-ARBS C-HEAP C-LAMP C-LOVE C-OYER
C-ARDS C-HEAT C-LAMS C-LOWN C-RACK
C-ARED C-HECK C-LANG C-LOWS C-RAFT
C-ARES C-HELP C-LANK C-LOYS C-RAGS
C-ARET C-HERE C-LAPS C-LUCK C-RAKE
C-ARKS C-HEST C-LASH C-LUES C-RAMP
C-ARLE C-HETH C-LASS C-LUMP C-RAMS
C-ARSE C-HEWS C-LAST C-LUNG C-RANK
C-ARTS C-HICK C-LATS C-LUNK C-RAPE
C-ASKS C-HIDE C-LAVE C-OAST C-RAPS
C-ATES C-HILD C-LAWS C-OATS C-RARE
C-AUKS C-HILI C-LAYS C-OBIA C-RASH
C-AULD C-HILL C-LEAN C-OCAS C-RATE
C-AVAS C-HINS C-LEAR C-ODAS C-RAVE
C-AVEL C-HIPS C-LEAT C-ODES C-RAWS
C-AVER C-HITS C-LEEK C-OFFS C-RAYS
C-AVES C-HIVE C-LEEP C-OHOS C-RAZE
C-AWED C-HIZZ C-LEFT C-OILS C-REAK
C-AXON C-HOCK C-LEGS C-OKES C-REAM

C-REDO	C-RICK	C-RONE	C-RUDS	C-URBS
C-REDS	C-RIME	C-ROOK	C-RUES	C-URDS
C-REED	C-RIMS	C-ROON	C-RUMP	C-URDY
C-REEK	C-RINE	C-RORE	C-RUSE	C-URES
C-REEL	C-RIPE	C-ROST	C-RUSH	C-URNS
C-REES	C-RISE	C-ROUP	C-RUST	C-UTES
C-REMS	C-RISP	C-ROUT	C-TENE	C-UTIS
C-REST	C-RITS	C-ROWS	C-UKES	
C-REWS	C-ROCK	C-RUCK	C-ULEX	
C-RIBS	C-ROCS	C-RUDE	C-UNDY	

Five letters to six

C-ABBED	C-ENTER	C-HILLS	C-LAWER	C-LUNKS
C-ABLED	C-ENTRY	C-HILLY	C-LAYED	C-LYING
C-ABLER	C-EORLS	C-HINKY	C-LEANS	C-OASTS
C-ABLES	C-ERING	C-HINTS	C-LEARS	C-OATER
C-ABLET	C-ERNED	C-HIPPY	C-LEATS	C-OBIAS
C-ACHED	C-ERNES	C-HIVED	C-LEAVE	C-OCHES
C-ACHES	C-ESSES	C-HIVES	C-LEEKS	C-OCKER
C-AGERS	C-HACKS	C-HOCKS	C-LEEPS	C-ODDER
C-AGING	C-HAFFS	C-HOKED	C-LEFTS	C-ODIST
C-AIRNS	C-HAFTS	C-HOKES	C-LEUCH	C-OFFED
C-AKING	C-HAINS	C-HOKEY	C-LEUGH	C-OFFER
C-ALIFS	C-HAIRS	C-HOLLA	C-LEVER	C-OILED
C-ALLEE	C-HAMMY	C-HOOFS	C-LEVIS	C-OILER
C-ALLOW	C-HANCE	C-HOOKS	C-LICKS	C-OLDER
C-AMASS	C-HANGS	C-HOPPY	C-LIFTS	C-OLDIE
C-AMBER	C-HANKS	C-HORAL	C-LIMAX	C-OLLIE
C-AMPED	C-HANTS	C-HOSEN	C-LIMBS	C-OMBER
C-AMPLE	C-HAPPY	C-HOSES	C-LIMES	C-OMERS
C-AMPLY	C-HARDS	C-HOUGH	C-LINCH	C-ONIUM
C-ANGLE	C-HARED	C-HOUSE	C-LINES	C-ONNED
C-ANKER	C-HARES	C-HOUTS	C-LINGS	C-OOPED
C-ANNAS	C-HARKS	C-HOWKS	C-LINGY	C-OORIE
C-ANTAR	C-HARMS	C-HUBBY	C-LINKS	C-OOZES
C-ANTED	C-HARRY	C-HUCKS	C-LINTS	C-OPALS
C-ANTIC	C-HARTS	C-HUFFS	C-LOAMS	C-OPENS
C-ANYON	C-HASTE	C-HUFFY	C-LOCKS	C-OPING
C-APERS	C-HAUNT	C-HUMPS	C-LOGGY	C-OPTER
C-APING	C-HAWED	C-HUNKS	C-LOKES	C-ORALS
C-ARETS	C-HAWKS	C-HUNKY	C-LONER	C-ORDER
C-ARKED	C-HAZAN	C-HURLS	C-LOOPS	C-OSIER
C-ARLES	C-HEAPS	C-HYLES	C-LOOTS	C-OSMIC
C-ARSES	C-HEAPY	C-ILIUM	C-LOSED	C-OTTAR
C-ARSEY	C-HEATS	C-ITHER	C-LOSER	C-OTTER
C-ARTEL	C-HECKS	C-IVIES	C-LOSES	C-OUPED
C-ASHED	C-HEDER	C-LACKS	C-LOTES	C-OURIE
C-ASHES	C-HELPS	C-LADES	C-LOUGH	C-OUTER
C-ASKED	C-HEMIC	C-LAMES	C-LOURS	C-OVARY
C-ASTER	C-HERRY	C-LAMMY	C-LOUTS	C-OVENS
C-AUDAD	C-HESTS	C-LAMPS	C-LOVER	C-OVERS
C-AUGHT	C-HETHS	C-LANKS	C-LOVES	C-OVERT
C-AVELS	C-HEWED	C-LANKY	C-LOWNS	C-OWING
C-AVERS	C-HEWER	C-LASTS	C-LUCKS	C-OWLED
C-AWING	C-HICKS	C-LATCH	C-LUCKY	C-OWRIE
C-AXONS	C-HIDED	C-LAVER	C-LUMPS	C-RACKS
C-EASED	C-HIDER	C-LAVES	C-LUMPY	C-RAFTS
C-EASES	C-HIDES	C-LAWED	C-LUNCH	C-RAGGY

C – Front-hooks

C-RAKED	C-RAVES	C-RIANT	C-ROUPY	C-RUSES
C-RAKES	C-RAWLY	C-RICKS	C-ROUSE	C-RUSTS
C-RAMPS	C-RAYON	C-RIMED	C-ROUTE	C-RUSTY
C-RANCH	C-RAZED	C-RIMES	C-ROUTS	C-TENES
C-RANKS	C-RAZES	C-RINES	C-ROWDY	C-UMBER
C-RANTS	C-REACH	C-RIPES	C-ROWED	C-UPPED
C-RAPED	C-REAKS	C-RISES	C-ROWER	C-UPPER
C-RAPES	C-REAMS	C-RISPS	C-RUCKS	C-URARE
C-RARES	C-REAMY	C-ROCKS	C-RUDDY	C-URARI
C-RASES	C-REATE	C-RONES	C-RUDER	C-URATE
C-RATCH	C-REDOS	C-ROOKS	C-RUDES	C-URIAL
C-RATED	C-REEDS	C-ROONS	C-RUMEN	C-URITE
C-RATER	C-REEKS	C-RORES	C-RUMMY	C-UTTER
C-RATES	C-REEKY	C-ROTAL	C-RUMPS	C-YCLED
C-RAVED	C-REELS	C-ROTCH	C-RUMPY	C-YESES
C-RAVEN	C-RESTS	C-ROTON	C-RUNCH	
C-RAVER	C-REWED	C-ROUPS	C-RURAL	

Six letters to seven

C-ABLETS	C-HACKED	C-HIPPER	C-LAMMED	C-LOBBER
C-ABLING	C-HAINED	C-HIPPIE	C-LAMMER	C-LOCKED
C-ACHING	C-HAIRED	C-HITTER	C-LAMPED	C-LOCKER
C-ACUMEN	C-HALLAH	C-HIVING	C-LAMPER	C-LOGGED
C-ADDIES	C-HALLAN	C-HIZZED	C-LANGER	C-LOGGER
C-AIRNED	C-HALLOT	C-HIZZES	C-LANKED	C-LONERS
C-ALLEES	C-HALUTZ	C-HOCKED	C-LAPPED	C-LOPPED
C-ALLOWS	C-HAMLET	C-HOCKER	C-LAPPER	C-LOSERS
C-AMBERS	C-HAMPER	C-HOKIER	C-LASHED	C-LOSING
C-AMELIA	C-HANCES	C-HOKING	C-LASHER	C-LOTTED
C-AMISES	C-HANGED	C-HOLLAS	C-LASHES	C-LOTTER
C-AMPING	C-HANGER	C-HOOFED	C-LASSES	C-LOUGHS
C-AMUSES	C-HANTED	C-HOOKED	C-LASSIS	C-LOURED
C-ANGLED	C-HAPPED	C-HOPPED	C-LATTER	C-LOUTED
C-ANGLES	C-HARING	C-HOPPER	C-LAVERS	C-LOVERS
C-ANKERS	C-HARKED	C-HORDED	C-LAWING	C-LOWNED
C-ANTARS	C-HARMED	C-HOUGHS	C-LAYING	C-LUBBER
C-ANTING	C-HARMER	C-HOUSED	C-LEANED	C-LUCKED
C-ANYONS	C-HASTEN	C-HOUSER	C-LEANER	C-LUMBER
C-ARABIN	C-HATTED	C-HOUSES	C-LEANLY	C-LUMPED
C-ARIOSE	C-HATTER	C-HUCKLE	C-LEARED	C-LUMPER
C-ARKING	C-HAUNTS	C-HUFFED	C-LEAVED	C-LUNKER
C-ARLING	C-HAWING	C-HUFFER	C-LEAVER	C-LUSTER
C-AROUSE	C-HAZANS	C-HUGGED	C-LEAVES	C-OATERS
C-ARRACK	C-HAZZAN	C-HUGGER	C-LEEPED	C-OCKERS
C-ARRECT	C-HEAPED	C-HUMMED	C-LICHES	C-ODISTS
C-ARTELS	C-HEAPER	C-HUMPED	C-LICKED	C-OFFERS
C-ARTFUL	C-HEATED	C-HUNTER	C-LICKER	C-OFFING
C-ASHIER	C-HEATER	C-HUPPAH	C-LIFTED	C-OILERS
C-ASHING	C-HEDERS	C-HUTZPA	C-LIMBED	C-OILING
C-ASKING	C-HELPED	C-ILICES	C-LIMBER	C-OLDEST
C-ASTERS	C-HEWERS	C-INCHED	C-LINGER	C-OLDIES
C-ASTRAL	C-HEWING	C-INCHES	C-LINKED	C-OLDISH
C-AULDER	C-HIDDEN	C-LACKED	C-LINKER	C-OLLIES
C-EASING	C-HIDERS	C-LACKER	C-LIPPED	C-OMBERS
C-ENSURE	C-HIDING	C-LADDER	C-LIPPER	C-ONIUMS
C-ENTERS	C-HILLED	C-LADDIE	C-LIPPIE	C-ONNING
C-ERNING	C-HILLER	C-LAGGED	C-LITTER	C-OOPING
C-EROTIC	C-HIPPED	C-LAMBER	C-LIVERS	C-OPTERS

C-ORACLE	C-RAKING	C-RAVING	C-RITTER	C-RUMPED
C-ORDERS	C-RAMMED	C-RAYONS	C-ROCHES	C-RUMPLE
C-OSIERS	C-RAMMER	C-RAZING	C-ROCHET	C-RUMPLY
C-OTTARS	C-RAMPED	C-REAKED	C-ROCKED	C-RUNKLE
C-OTTERS	C-RAMPER	C-REAMED	C-ROCKET	C-RUSHED
C-OUCHED	C-RANKED	C-REAMER	C-ROOKED	C-RUSHER
C-OUCHES	C-RANKER	C-REATES	C-ROQUET	C-RUSHES
C-OUPING	C-RANKLE	C-REELED	C-ROSIER	C-RUSTED
C-OURIER	C-RANKLY	C-REMATE	C-ROSSER	C-ULEXES
C-OUTERS	C-RAPIER	C-RESTED	C-ROTONS	C-ULLING
C-OUTHER	C-RAPING	C-RIBBED	C-ROUPED	C-UMBERS
C-OUVERT	C-RAPPED	C-RIBBER	C-ROUTES	C-UNDIES
C-OVERED	C-RAPPER	C-RICKED	C-ROWERS	C-UPPERS
C-OWLING	C-RASHED	C-RICKEY	C-ROWING	C-UPPING
C-RACKED	C-RASHER	C-RIMING	C-RUDDED	C-URARES
C-RACKER	C-RASHES	C-RIMMER	C-RUDDLE	C-URARIS
C-RACKET	C-RATERS	C-RIMPLE	C-RUDELY	C-URATES
C-RACKLE	C-RATING	C-RINGED	C-RUDEST	C-URITES
C-RAFTED	C-RAUNCH	C-RINGER	C-RUMBLE	C-UTISES
C-RAFTER	C-RAVENS	C-RIPPLE	C-RUMBLY	C-UTTERS
C-RAGGED	C-RAVERS	C-RISPED	C-RUMENS	

Seven letters to eight

C-ABLINGS	C-HANDLER	C-HINKIER	C-LADDERS	C-LINKING
C-AMASSES	C-HANGERS	C-HIPPIER	C-LADDIES	C-LIPPERS
C-AMBERED	C-HANGING	C-HIPPIES	C-LAGGING	C-LIPPIES
C-AMELIAS	C-HANTING	C-HIPPING	C-LAMBERS	C-LIPPING
C-ANGLING	C-HAPLESS	C-HIRLING	C-LAMMERS	C-LITORAL
C-ANNULAR	C-HAPPIER	C-HITTERS	C-LAMMING	C-LITTERS
C-ANTINGS	C-HAPPIES	C-HITTING	C-LAMPERS	C-LOBBERS
C-APSIDAL	C-HAPPING	C-HIZZING	C-LAMPING	C-LOCKERS
C-ARABINS	C-HARKING	C-HOCKING	C-LANGERS	C-LOCKING
C-AROUSAL	C-HARMERS	C-HOKIEST	C-LANKIER	C-LOGGERS
C-AROUSED	C-HARMFUL	C-HOLLERS	C-LANKING	C-LOGGIER
C-AROUSER	C-HARMING	C-HOOFING	C-LAPPERS	C-LOGGING
C-AROUSES	C-HAROSET	C-HOOKIES	C-LAPPING	C-LOPPING
C-ARRACKS	C-HARPIES	C-HOOKING	C-LASHERS	C-LOSABLE
C-ARRIAGE	C-HARRIER	C-HOPPERS	C-LASHING	C-LOSINGS
C-ASHLESS	C-HASTENS	C-HOPPIER	C-LATCHED	C-LOTTERS
C-ASTABLE	C-HATTERS	C-HOPPING	C-LATCHES	C-LOTTING
C-ASTEISM	C-HATTING	C-HORDING	C-LAWLESS	C-LOURING
C-AULDEST	C-HAUNTED	C-HOUSERS	C-LAWLIKE	C-LOUTING
C-ENSURED	C-HAUNTER	C-HOUSING	C-LEANERS	C-LOVERED
C-ENSURER	C-HAZANIM	C-HUCKLES	C-LEANEST	C-LOWNING
C-ENSURES	C-HAZZANS	C-HUFFIER	C-LEANING	C-LUBBERS
C-ENTERED	C-HEAPING	C-HUFFING	C-LEARING	C-LUCKIER
C-ENTRIES	C-HEATERS	C-HUGGERS	C-LEAVERS	C-LUCKING
C-ENTRISM	C-HEATING	C-HUGGING	C-LEAVING	C-LUMBERS
C-ENTRIST	C-HELPING	C-HUMMING	C-LEEPING	C-LUMPERS
C-HACKING	C-HERRIED	C-HUMPING	C-LEMMING	C-LUMPIER
C-HADARIM	C-HERRIES	C-HUNKIER	C-LICKERS	C-LUMPING
C-HAINING	C-HEWABLE	C-HUNTERS	C-LICKING	C-LUMPISH
C-HAIRING	C-HICKORY	C-HUPPAHS	C-LIMBERS	C-LUNCHES
C-HALLAHS	C-HIDINGS	C-HUTZPAH	C-LIMBING	C-LUNKERS
C-HALLANS	C-HILDING	C-HUTZPAS	C-LINCHES	C-LUSTERS
C-HALLOTH	C-HILLERS	C-INCHING	C-LINGERS	C-OCREATE
C-HAMLETS	C-HILLIER	C-LACKERS	C-LINGIER	C-OFFERED
C-HAMPERS	C-HILLING	C-LACKING	C-LINKERS	C-OLDNESS

C – Front-hooks

C-ORACLES	C-RAMPING	C-REEKIER	C-RITTERS	C-RUMBLED
C-OSMOSES	C-RANCHED	C-REELING	C-ROCHETS	C-RUMBLES
C-OTTERED	C-RANCHES	C-REMAINS	C-ROCKERY	C-RUMMIER
C-OUCHING	C-RANKEST	C-REMATED	C-ROCKETS	C-RUMMIES
C-OULDEST	C-RANKING	C-REMATES	C-ROCKING	C-RUMPING
C-OVARIES	C-RANKISH	C-RESTING	C-ROOKERY	C-RUMPLED
C-OVERAGE	C-RANKLED	C-RIBBERS	C-ROOKING	C-RUMPLES
C-OVERALL	C-RANKLES	C-RIBBING	C-ROQUETS	C-RUNCHES
C-OVERING	C-RAPPERS	C-RIBWORK	C-ROSIERS	C-RUNKLED
C-OVERLET	C-RAPPING	C-RICKETS	C-ROSSERS	C-RUNKLES
C-OVERTLY	C-RASHERS	C-RICKING	C-ROTCHES	C-RUSHERS
C-RACKERS	C-RASHING	C-RIMMERS	C-ROUCHES	C-RUSHING
C-RACKETS	C-RATCHES	C-RIMPLED	C-ROUPIER	C-RUSTIER
C-RACKING	C-RAUNCHY	C-RIMPLES	C-ROUPILY	C-RUSTILY
C-RAFTERS	C-RAVENED	C-RINGERS	C-ROUPING	C-RUSTING
C-RAFTING	C-RAVINGS	C-RINGING	C-ROWDIES	C-ULLINGS
C-RAGGIER	C-REAKING	C-RIPPLED	C-RUDDIER	C-UMBERED
C-RAMMERS	C-REAMERS	C-RIPPLER	C-RUDDING	C-UMBROUS
C-RAMMING	C-REAMIER	C-RIPPLES	C-RUDDLED	C-UNIFORM
C-RAMPERS	C-REAMING	C-RISPING	C-RUDDLES	C-UPPINGS

Eight letters to nine

C-AMPHORIC	C-HATTERED	C-LASHINGS	C-OVERTURE	C-RINGINGS
C-ANNULATE	C-HAUNTERS	C-LATCHING	C-RACKINGS	C-RIPPLERS
C-AROUSALS	C-HAUNTING	C-LAVATION	C-RAFTSMAN	C-RIPPLING
C-AROUSERS	C-HAZZANIM	C-LEANINGS	C-RAFTSMEN	C-ROCKETED
C-AROUSING	C-HEATABLE	C-LEANNESS	C-RAGGIEST	C-ROQUETED
C-ARRIAGES	C-HEATINGS	C-LEAVINGS	C-RANCHING	C-ROQUETTE
C-ASTEISMS	C-HEMOSTAT	C-LICKINGS	C-RANKLING	C-ROUPIEST
C-AVIARIES	C-HERRYING	C-LINGIEST	C-RANKNESS	C-RUDDIEST
C-EASELESS	C-HIDLINGS	C-LIPPINGS	C-RAUNCHED	C-RUDDLING
C-ENSURERS	C-HILLIEST	C-LITTERED	C-RAUNCHES	C-RUDENESS
C-ENSURING	C-HINKIEST	C-LOCKINGS	C-RAVENING	C-RUMBLIER
C-ENTERING	C-HIPPIEST	C-LOGGIEST	C-REAMIEST	C-RUMBLING
C-ENTRISMS	C-HIPPINGS	C-LOGGINGS	C-REEKIEST	C-RUMMIEST
C-ENTRISTS	C-HOPPIEST	C-LUCKIEST	C-REMASTER	C-RUMPLIER
C-HALUTZIM	C-HOPPINGS	C-LUMPIEST	C-REMATING	C-RUMPLING
C-HANDLERS	C-HOROLOGY	C-LUSTERED	C-RENATURE	C-RUNKLING
C-HANUKIAH	C-HUFFIEST	C-OFFERING	C-RESTINGS	C-RUSTIEST
C-HAPPIEST	C-HUNKIEST	C-OTTERING	C-RESTLESS	C-RUSTLESS
C-HARMLESS	C-HUTZPAHS	C-OVERABLE	C-RETINOID	C-UMBERING
C-HAROSETH	C-LANKIEST	C-OVERAGES	C-RIBBINGS	C-UNIFORMS
C-HAROSETS	C-LAPBOARD	C-OVERALLS	C-RIBWORKS	C-UPBEARER
C-HASTENED	C-LAPPERED	C-OVERLETS	C-RIMELESS	
C-HASTENER	C-LAPPINGS	C-OVERSLIP	C-RIMPLING	

C – End-hooks

Two letters to three

AR-C	HO-C	MO-C	PE-C	SO-C
BA-C	LA-C	MY-C	PI-C	TE-C
DO-C	MA-C	OR-C	RE-C	TI-C
HI-C	MI-C	PA-C	SI-C	TO-C

Three letters to four

ABA-C	CHI-C	MAR-C	TOR-C
ALE-C	DIS-C	SAI-C	ZIN-C
BAN-C	HUI-C	SYN-C	

Four letters to five

ANTI-C	COSE-C	LOTI-C	SERA-C	VARE-C
ARTI-C	DARI-C	MAGI-C	TARO-C	YOGI-C
BOBA-C	DURO-C	MALI-C	TOPI-C	YONI-C
CODE-C	ILEA-C	MANI-C	TORI-C	
CONI-C	ILIA-C	RABI-C	TRON-C	

Five letters to six

ACINI-C	CHOLI-C	FUNDI-C	LENTI-C	ORGIA-C
AGAMI-C	COCCI-C	FUNGI-C	LIMBI-C	PARSE-C
BUSTI-C	CULTI-C	IAMBI-C	MANIA-C	THYMI-C
CALPA-C	FILMI-C	KALPA-C	MYTHI-C	TRAGI-C

Six letters to seven

ALKALI-C	EMBOLI-C	NUCLEI-C	PYLORI-C	THALLI-C
CARDIA-C	EPHEBI-C	PHALLI-C	RHOMBI-C	TROPHI-C
COLONI-C	ISTHMI-C	PRIAPI-C	SCORIA-C	

Seven letters to eight

AMMONIA-C	CHIASMI-C	ELENCHI-C	RHYTHMI-C	TYMPANI-C
AMNESIA-C	CHORAGI-C	EPIGONI-C	SYLLABI-C	
APHASIA-C	CHOREGI-C	NURAGHI-C	THALAMI-C	
BULIMIA-C	DACTYLI-C	OMPHALI-C	TSUNAMI-C	

Eight letters to nine

EGOMANIA-C	MACARONI-C	PRODROMI-C	VIRTUOSI-C
FASCISTI-C	PARANOIA-C	SYMPOSIA-C	ZOOPHORI-C
INSOMNIA-C	PAROEMIA-C	TROCHILI-C	

D – Front-hooks

Two letters to three

D-AB	D-AW	D-IN	D-ON	D-UH
D-AD	D-AY	D-IS	D-OO	D-UN
D-AE	D-EE	D-IT	D-OP	D-UP
D-AG	D-EF	D-OB	D-OR	D-YE
D-AH	D-EL	D-OD	D-OS	D-ZO
D-AL	D-EN	D-OE	D-OW	
D-AM	D-EX	D-OF	D-OY	
D-AN	D-ID	D-OH	D-SO	
D-AS	D-IF	D-OM	D-UG	

C – End-hooks

Three letters to four

D-ABS	D-EAR	D-INK	D-ORB	D-RIB
D-ACE	D-ECO	D-INS	D-ORE	D-RIP
D-ADO	D-EEK	D-IRE	D-ORS	D-ROW
D-ADS	D-EEN	D-IRK	D-ORT	D-RUB
D-AFF	D-EFT	D-ISH	D-OSE	D-RUG
D-AFT	D-EKE	D-ITA	D-OUK	D-RUM
D-AGO	D-ELF	D-ITS	D-OUP	D-SOS
D-AGS	D-ELL	D-JIN	D-OUR	D-UDS
D-AHS	D-ELS	D-OAT	D-OUT	D-UGS
D-AIS	D-ELT	D-OBS	D-OWL	D-UKE
D-ALE	D-EME	D-ODS	D-OWN	D-ULE
D-ALS	D-EMO	D-OES	D-OWT	D-UMP
D-ALT	D-ENE	D-OFF	D-OXY	D-UNS
D-AMP	D-ENS	D-OHS	D-OYS	D-UPS
D-ANT	D-ERE	D-OLE	D-RAD	D-URE
D-ARB	D-ERN	D-OMS	D-RAG	D-URN
D-ARE	D-HOW	D-ONE	D-RAM	D-YAD
D-ARK	D-ICE	D-ONS	D-RAP	D-YES
D-ART	D-ICH	D-OOM	D-RAT	D-ZHO
D-ASH	D-ICK	D-OON	D-RAW	D-ZOS
D-ATE	D-IFF	D-OOR	D-RAY	
D-AWN	D-IFS	D-OOS	D-REE	
D-AYS	D-ILL	D-OPE	D-REG	
D-EAN	D-IMP	D-OPS	D-REW	

Four letters to five

D-ABBA	D-EKED	D-IRKS	D-RAFF	D-RIVE
D-ACES	D-EKES	D-ITAS	D-RAFT	D-ROIL
D-ADDY	D-ELFS	D-ITCH	D-RAGS	D-ROLE
D-ADOS	D-ELLS	D-JINN	D-RAIL	D-ROLL
D-AFFY	D-ELTS	D-JINS	D-RAIN	D-RONE
D-AINE	D-EMES	D-OATS	D-RAKE	D-ROOK
D-AIRY	D-EMIC	D-OFFS	D-RAMS	D-ROOP
D-ALES	D-EMIT	D-OILY	D-RANK	D-ROVE
D-ALLY	D-EMOS	D-OLES	D-RANT	D-ROWS
D-ALTS	D-EMPT	D-ONER	D-RAPE	D-RUBS
D-AMPS	D-ENES	D-OOMS	D-RAPS	D-RUGS
D-ANCE	D-ERED	D-OOZY	D-RATS	D-RUMS
D-ANTS	D-ERES	D-OPED	D-RAVE	D-RUSE
D-ARBS	D-ERNS	D-OPES	D-RAWN	D-UKES
D-ARED	D-EROS	D-ORAD	D-RAWS	D-ULES
D-ARES	D-ESSE	D-ORBS	D-RAYS	D-UMBO
D-ARIS	D-EVIL	D-ORTS	D-READ	D-UMPS
D-ARKS	D-EXES	D-OSES	D-REAM	D-UMPY
D-ARTS	D-HOLE	D-OUKS	D-REAR	D-UNCE
D-ASHY	D-HOLS	D-OUMA	D-RECK	D-URES
D-ATES	D-HOWS	D-OUPS	D-REED	D-URNS
D-AUNT	D-ICED	D-OUTS	D-REES	D-WALE
D-AWED	D-ICER	D-OVEN	D-REGS	D-WANG
D-AWNS	D-ICES	D-OVER	D-RENT	D-WELL
D-EANS	D-ICKY	D-OWED	D-REST	D-WELT
D-EARN	D-ILLS	D-OWER	D-RIBS	D-WILE
D-EARS	D-ILLY	D-OWLS	D-RICE	D-WINE
D-EATH	D-IMPS	D-OWLY	D-RIFT	D-YADS
D-EAVE	D-INGO	D-OWNS	D-RILL	D-ZHOS
D-ECAD	D-INKS	D-OWSE	D-RINK	
D-ECOS	D-INKY	D-OWTS	D-RIPS	
D-EELY	D-IOTA	D-RACK	D-RIPT	

Five letters to six

D-ABBAS	D-EDUCE	D-INNER	D-RAGEE	D-RONES
D-ABBED	D-EDUCT	D-IOTAS	D-RAGGY	D-ROOKS
D-ACKER	D-EGGED	D-IRKED	D-RAILS	D-ROOPS
D-ADDED	D-EIDER	D-ISHES	D-RAINS	D-ROOPY
D-ADDLE	D-EJECT	D-ITHER	D-RAKES	D-ROUTH
D-AFTER	D-EKING	D-JEBEL	D-RANTS	D-ROVED
D-AGGER	D-ELATE	D-JEMBE	D-RAPED	D-ROVER
D-AMPED	D-ELOPE	D-JINNI	D-RAPER	D-ROVES
D-AMPLY	D-ELUDE	D-JINNS	D-RAPES	D-ROWND
D-ANGER	D-ELVER	D-OATER	D-RAWER	D-RUGGY
D-ANGLE	D-ELVES	D-OCKER	D-RAWLY	D-RUMLY
D-ANKER	D-EMITS	D-ODDER	D-RAYED	D-RUMMY
D-ANTED	D-EMOTE	D-OFFED	D-READS	D-RUSES
D-APPLE	D-EMURE	D-OFFER	D-REAMS	D-UDDER
D-ARGLE	D-ERING	D-OILED	D-REAMY	D-UMBER
D-ARKED	D-ESSES	D-OLENT	D-REARS	D-UMBOS
D-ASHED	D-EVILS	D-ONNED	D-RECKS	D-UMPED
D-ASHES	D-EXIES	D-OPING	D-RICES	D-UNCES
D-AUNTS	D-HOLES	D-ORMER	D-RIFTS	D-UNDER
D-AVENS	D-HOOLY	D-OTTER	D-RIFTY	D-UNITE
D-AWING	D-HURRA	D-OUGHT	D-RILLS	D-UNKED
D-AWNED	D-ICERS	D-OUMAS	D-RINKS	D-UPPED
D-AWNER	D-ICIER	D-OUTED	D-RIVEL	D-URNED
D-EANED	D-ICING	D-OUTER	D-RIVEN	D-WALES
D-EARED	D-ICKER	D-OVENS	D-RIVER	D-WANGS
D-EARLY	D-IGGED	D-OVERS	D-RIVES	D-WELLS
D-EARNS	D-IMPLY	D-OWING	D-ROGER	D-WILES
D-EARTH	D-INGLE	D-OWNED	D-ROGUE	D-WINED
D-EAVED	D-INKED	D-OWNER	D-ROILS	D-WINES
D-EAVES	D-INKER	D-RAFFS	D-ROLES	
D-ECADS	D-INNED	D-RAFTS	D-ROLLS	

Six letters to seven

D-ACKERS	D-AWNERS	D-EMOTED	D-ITCHES	D-RABBET
D-ADDIES	D-AWNING	D-EMOTES	D-IZZARD	D-RABBLE
D-ADDING	D-EANING	D-EMURED	D-JEBELS	D-RAFTED
D-ADDLED	D-EARING	D-EMURES	D-JEMBES	D-RAFTER
D-ADDLES	D-EARTHS	D-EPOSES	D-JIBBAH	D-RAGEES
D-AFFIES	D-EATHLY	D-EVOLVE	D-OATERS	D-RAGGED
D-AGGERS	D-EDUCED	D-HURRAS	D-OCKERS	D-RAGGLE
D-ALLIED	D-EDUCES	D-ICIEST	D-OFFERS	D-RAILED
D-ALLIES	D-EDUCTS	D-ICINGS	D-OFFING	D-RAINED
D-AMPING	D-EFTEST	D-ICKERS	D-OLLIES	D-RAMMED
D-ANGERS	D-EGGING	D-ICKIER	D-ONNING	D-RANTED
D-ANGLED	D-EJECTA	D-IGGING	D-OODLES	D-RAPERS
D-ANGLER	D-EJECTS	D-IGNIFY	D-ORMERS	D-RAPIER
D-ANGLES	D-ELAPSE	D-IMPLED	D-OTTERS	D-RAPING
D-ANTING	D-ELATED	D-INGLES	D-OUCHED	D-RAPPED
D-APPLES	D-ELATES	D-INGOES	D-OUCHES	D-RATTED
D-ARGLES	D-ELOPED	D-INKIER	D-OUTERS	D-RAUGHT
D-ARKING	D-ELOPES	D-INKING	D-OUTING	D-RAWING
D-ARLING	D-ELUDED	D-INNERS	D-OVENED	D-RAYING
D-ASHIER	D-ELUDER	D-INNING	D-OVERED	D-READER
D-ASHING	D-ELUDES	D-IREFUL	D-OWLIER	D-REAMED
D-AUDING	D-ELVERS	D-IRKING	D-OWNERS	D-REAMER
D-AUNTER	D-EMERGE	D-ITCHED	D-OWNING	D-REARER

D – Front-hooks

D-RIBBED	D-ROGERS	D-ROVING	D-UDDERS	D-UPPING
D-RIBBER	D-ROGUES	D-ROWNDS	D-ULLING	D-URNING
D-RIBLET	D-ROILED	D-RUBBED	D-ULOSES	D-WELLED
D-RIFTED	D-ROLLED	D-RUBBER	D-ULOSIS	D-WINDLE
D-RILLED	D-ROLLER	D-RUGGED	D-UMPIES	D-WINING
D-RIPPED	D-ROOKED	D-RUGGER	D-UMPING	D-YESTER
D-RIPPER	D-ROOPED	D-RUMBLE	D-UNITES	
D-RIVELS	D-ROUGHT	D-RUMMER	D-UNKING	
D-RIVERS	D-ROUTHS	D-UBIETY	D-UNNEST	
D-RIVING	D-ROVERS	D-UCKERS	D-UNSHED	

Seven letters to eight

D-ADDLING	D-ELUSORY	D-JELLABA	D-RAMMING	D-RIPPING
D-ALLYING	D-EMERGED	D-JIBBAHS	D-RANTING	D-ROILING
D-ANGERED	D-EMERGES	D-OLOROSO	D-RAPIERS	D-ROLLING
D-ANGLERS	D-EMERSED	D-ONENESS	D-RAPPING	D-ROOKING
D-ANGLING	D-EMITTED	D-OUCHING	D-RATTING	D-ROOPIER
D-ARRAIGN	D-EMOTING	D-OVENING	D-RAWINGS	D-ROOPING
D-ASHIEST	D-EMOTION	D-OVERING	D-READERS	D-ROVINGS
D-AUNTERS	D-EMURING	D-OWLIEST	D-READING	D-ROWNDED
D-AWNINGS	D-ENOUNCE	D-RABBETS	D-REAMERS	D-RUBBERS
D-ECURIES	D-EPILATE	D-RABBLED	D-REAMIER	D-RUBBING
D-EDUCING	D-EPURATE	D-RABBLER	D-REAMING	D-RUGGERS
D-EJECTED	D-ESCRIBE	D-RABBLES	D-REARING	D-RUGGIER
D-ELAPSED	D-EVOLVED	D-RAFFISH	D-RIBBERS	D-RUGGING
D-ELAPSES	D-EVOLVES	D-RAFTERS	D-RIBBING	D-RUMBLED
D-ELATING	D-HOOLIES	D-RAFTING	D-RIBLETS	D-RUMBLES
D-ELATION	D-HURRIES	D-RAGGIER	D-RIFTIER	D-RUMMERS
D-ELOPING	D-ICKIEST	D-RAGGING	D-RIFTING	D-RUMMIES
D-ELUDERS	D-INGOING	D-RAGGLED	D-RILLING	D-UPLYING
D-ELUDING	D-INKIEST	D-RAGGLES	D-RINKING	D-WELLING
D-ELUSION	D-ITCHING	D-RAILING	D-RIPPERS	D-WINDLED
D-ELUSIVE	D-IZZARDS	D-RAINING	D-RIPPIER	D-WINDLES

Eight letters to nine

D-ALLIANCE	D-ELATIONS	D-EPILATED	D-IREFULLY	D-RIFTLESS
D-ANGERING	D-ELUSIONS	D-EPILATES	D-JELLABAH	D-RIVELLED
D-ANGLINGS	D-EMERGING	D-EPILATOR	D-JELLABAS	D-ROLLINGS
D-ARRAIGNS	D-EMERSION	D-EPURATED	D-RABBLERS	D-ROOPIEST
D-EBAUCHES	D-EMISSION	D-EPURATES	D-RABBLING	D-ROUTHIER
D-ECAUDATE	D-EMISSIVE	D-ESCRIBED	D-RAFTINGS	D-ROWNDING
D-EDUCIBLE	D-EMITTING	D-ESCRIBES	D-RAFTSMAN	D-RUBBINGS
D-EDUCTION	D-EMOTIONS	D-EVALUATE	D-RAFTSMEN	D-RUGGIEST
D-EDUCTIVE	D-EMULSIFY	D-EVOLVING	D-RAGGIEST	D-RUMBLING
D-EJECTING	D-ENERVATE	D-EXTRORSE	D-RAGGLING	D-UBIETIES
D-EJECTION	D-ENOUNCED	D-IGNIFIED	D-REAMIEST	D-WELLINGS
D-ELAPSING	D-ENOUNCES	D-IGNIFIES	D-RIFTIEST	D-WINDLING

D – End-hooks

Two letters to three

AD-D	BE-D	DO-D	GI-D	KI-D
AI-D	BI-D	EL-D	GO-D	LA-D
AN-D	BO-D	EN-D	HA-D	LI-D
AR-D	DA-D	FA-D	HI-D	LO-D
BA-D	DI-D	FE-D	HO-D	MA-D

ME-D	NO-D	PE-D	TE-D	YA-D
MI-D	OD-D	PO-D	TI-D	YO-D
MO-D	OR-D	RE-D	TO-D	
MU-D	OU-D	SO-D	UR-D	
NE-D	PA-D	TA-D	WE-D	

Three letters to four

ACE-D	DIE-D	HOE-D	NYE-D	SKI-D
AGE-D	DOW-D	HON-D	OPE-D	SOL-D
AKE-D	DUE-D	HOO-D	ORA-D	SUD-D
AMI-D	DYE-D	HUE-D	OWE-D	SUE-D
APE-D	EAR-D	HYE-D	PAN-D	SUI-D
APO-D	ECO-D	ICE-D	PAR-D	SUR-D
ARE-D	EKE-D	IRE-D	PEE-D	SYE-D
AWE-D	ERE-D	JEE-D	PEN-D	SYN-D
AXE-D	EYE-D	KAE-D	PIE-D	TAE-D
BAL-D	FAN-D	KAI-D	POO-D	TEA-D
BAN-D	FAR-D	KIN-D	PRO-D	TEE-D
BAR-D	FEE-D	KON-D	QUA-D	TEL-D
BEN-D	FEN-D	LAR-D	RAI-D	TEN-D
BIN-D	FEU-D	LEA-D	RAN-D	TIE-D
BON-D	FIN-D	LEE-D	RED-D	TIN-D
BOR-D	FON-D	LEU-D	REE-D	TOE-D
BRA-D	FOR-D	LEW-D	REN-D	TUN-D
BRO-D	FOU-D	LIE-D	RIN-D	TYE-D
BUN-D	FUN-D	LIN-D	ROE-D	USE-D
BUR-D	GAE-D	LOR-D	ROO-D	VIE-D
CAR-D	GAU-D	LOU-D	RUD-D	WAD-D
CHA-D	GEE-D	MAN-D	RUE-D	WAI-D
CHI-D	GEL-D	MAR-D	RUN-D	WAN-D
COL-D	GIE-D	MEE-D	SAI-D	WAR-D
CON-D	GOA-D	MEL-D	SAN-D	WEE-D
COR-D	GOO-D	MEN-D	SAR-D	WEN-D
CRU-D	HAE-D	MIL-D	SEE-D	WIN-D
CUE-D	HAN-D	MOL-D	SEL-D	WOO-D
CUR-D	HEN-D	MOO-D	SEN-D	WYN-D
DAW-D	HER-D	NEE-D	SHA-D	YAR-D
DEE-D	HIE-D	NIE-D	SHE-D	YEA-D
DEI-D	HIN-D	NUR-D	SIN-D	YON-D

Four letters to five

ABBE-D	ARED-D	BIKE-D	BROO-D	CITE-D
ABLE-D	ARLE-D	BILE-D	BYDE-D	CLOU-D
ACHE-D	ARSE-D	BLEE-D	BYKE-D	CLUE-D
ACNE-D	AXLE-D	BLIN-D	CAGE-D	CODE-D
ACRE-D	BAKE-D	BLUE-D	CAKE-D	COKE-D
ADZE-D	BALE-D	BOAR-D	CANE-D	COLE-D
AGUE-D	BANE-D	BODE-D	CAPE-D	CONE-D
AIDE-D	BARE-D	BOKE-D	CARE-D	COPE-D
ALAN-D	BASE-D	BONE-D	CASE-D	CORE-D
ALKY-D	BATE-D	BOOR-D	CAUL-D	COSE-D
ALOE-D	BAYE-D	BORE-D	CAVE-D	COTE-D
AMEN-D	BEAR-D	BOUN-D	CEDE-D	COUR-D
ANTE-D	BEMA-D	BRAN-D	CERE-D	COVE-D
APAY-D	BETE-D	BREE-D	CHAR-D	COZE-D
AREA-D	BIDE-D	BREI-D	CIDE-D	CREE-D

CROW-D	GAZE-D	LAZE-D	PACE-D	SATE-D
CUBE-D	GIBE-D	LEME-D	PAGE-D	SAVE-D
CURE-D	GIVE-D	LERE-D	PALE-D	SCAN-D
DALE-D	GLEE-D	LIAR-D	PANE-D	SEEL-D
DARE-D	GLUE-D	LIKE-D	PARE-D	SERE-D
DATE-D	GOOL-D	LIME-D	PATE-D	SHAN-D
DAZE-D	GORE-D	LINE-D	PAVE-D	SHOE-D
DEKE-D	GRAN-D	LITE-D	PAYS-D	SHOW-D
DELE-D	GREE-D	LIVE-D	PENE-D	SIDE-D
DERE-D	GRIN-D	LOBE-D	PIKE-D	SILE-D
DICE-D	GRUE-D	LOME-D	PILE-D	SINE-D
DIKE-D	GUAR-D	LOOR-D	PINE-D	SIPE-D
DINE-D	GYBE-D	LOPE-D	PIPE-D	SIRE-D
DITE-D	GYRE-D	LOSE-D	PIZE-D	SITE-D
DIVE-D	GYVE-D	LOUN-D	PLEA-D	SIZE-D
DOLE-D	HADE-D	LOVE-D	PLIE-D	SKEE-D
DOME-D	HALE-D	LOWE-D	POKE-D	SLUE-D
DOPE-D	HAME-D	LOWN-D	POLE-D	SNEE-D
DOSE-D	HARE-D	LUBE-D	PORE-D	SOLE-D
DOTE-D	HATE-D	LUGE-D	POSE-D	SOLI-D
DOVE-D	HAUL-D	LURE-D	POTE-D	SORE-D
DOZE-D	HAZE-D	LUTE-D	POWN-D	SOWN-D
DREE-D	HEAL-D	LYSE-D	PREE-D	SPAE-D
DUDE-D	HEAR-D	LYTE-D	PUKE-D	SPAR-D
DUKE-D	HELE-D	MACE-D	PULE-D	SPAY-D
DUPE-D	HIDE-D	MANE-D	PURE-D	SPIE-D
DURE-D	HIKE-D	MASE-D	PYNE-D	SPUE-D
DYKE-D	HIRE-D	MATE-D	QUAY-D	STED-D
EASE-D	HIVE-D	MAUN-D	RABI-D	STEN-D
EAVE-D	HOAR-D	MAZE-D	RACE-D	STIE-D
ECHE-D	HOKE-D	MENE-D	RAGE-D	STYE-D
EDGE-D	HOLE-D	MERE-D	RAKE-D	SURE-D
ELAN-D	HOME-D	METE-D	RANI-D	SWEE-D
ERNE-D	HONE-D	MEVE-D	RAPE-D	SYNE-D
FACE-D	HOPE-D	MIKE-D	RARE-D	SYPE-D
FADE-D	HOSE-D	MIME-D	RASE-D	TABI-D
FAKE-D	HOVE-D	MINE-D	RATE-D	TAME-D
FAME-D	HYPE-D	MIRE-D	RAVE-D	TAPE-D
FARE-D	IDLE-D	MONA-D	RAZE-D	TARE-D
FATE-D	ILIA-D	MOPE-D	READ-D	TEEN-D
FAUR-D	ISLE-D	MOSE-D	REDE-D	TEME-D
FAZE-D	IZAR-D	MOTE-D	REKE-D	THEE-D
FETE-D	JADE-D	MOVE-D	RICE-D	THIR-D
FIFE-D	JAPE-D	MOZE-D	RILE-D	TICE-D
FIKE-D	JIBE-D	MULE-D	RIME-D	TIDE-D
FILE-D	JIVE-D	MURE-D	RIPE-D	TILE-D
FINE-D	JOBE-D	MUSE-D	RIVE-D	TIME-D
FIRE-D	JOKE-D	MUTE-D	ROBE-D	TINE-D
FLUE-D	JOLE-D	NAME-D	RODE-D	TIRE-D
FRAU-D	JUKE-D	NAPE-D	ROKE-D	TOGE-D
FREE-D	KITE-D	NIDE-D	ROPE-D	TOKE-D
FUME-D	KNEE-D	NIXE-D	ROSE-D	TOLE-D
FUSE-D	LACE-D	NOMA-D	ROTE-D	TONE-D
FUZE-D	LADE-D	NOSE-D	ROVE-D	TOPE-D
FYKE-D	LAIR-D	NOTE-D	RULE-D	TOSE-D
GADI-D	LAKE-D	NOUL-D	RUNE-D	TOTE-D
GAGE-D	LAME-D	NUKE-D	RYKE-D	TOZE-D
GAME-D	LASE-D	OCTA-D	SABE-D	TREE-D
GAPE-D	LATE-D	OGLE-D	SAFE-D	TRIE-D
GATE-D	LAVE-D	OOZE-D	SANE-D	TRUE-D

TUBE-D	VALI-D	WAGE-D	WIEL-D	WYLE-D
TUNE-D	VANE-D	WAKE-D	WIFE-D	WYTE-D
TWEE-D	VICE-D	WALE-D	WILE-D	YEAR-D
TYNE-D	VINE-D	WAME-D	WINE-D	YIKE-D
TYPE-D	VIOL-D	WANE-D	WIPE-D	YOKE-D
TYRE-D	VIRE-D	WARE-D	WIRE-D	YOWE-D
ULNA-D	VISE-D	WAVE-D	WISE-D	YUKE-D
UNBE-D	VOLE-D	WEAL-D	WITE-D	ZONE-D
URGE-D	VOTE-D	WEIR-D	WIVE-D	
VADE-D	WADE-D	WEXE-D	WOOL-D	

Five letters to six

ABASE-D	BEARE-D	BUTTE-D	COZIE-D	EMCEE-D
ABATE-D	BECKE-D	CABLE-D	CRAKE-D	EMOTE-D
ABIDE-D	BEDYE-D	CACHE-D	CRANE-D	EMOVE-D
ABODE-D	BELEE-D	CADGE-D	CRAPE-D	EMULE-D
ABUSE-D	BELIE-D	CALVE-D	CRATE-D	EMURE-D
ACARI-D	BELLE-D	CANOE-D	CRAVE-D	ENDUE-D
ADDLE-D	BERME-D	CARTE-D	CRAZE-D	ENSUE-D
ADORE-D	BILGE-D	CARVE-D	CREPE-D	ENURE-D
AERIE-D	BINGE-D	CASTE-D	CREWE-D	ERASE-D
AFEAR-D	BIRLE-D	CAUDA-D	CRIME-D	ERODE-D
AGAMI-D	BITTE-D	CAUSE-D	CRINE-D	ETTLE-D
AGAZE-D	BLADE-D	CEASE-D	CROME-D	EVADE-D
AGREE-D	BLAME-D	CEAZE-D	CURSE-D	EVITE-D
AISLE-D	BLARE-D	CENSE-D	CURVE-D	EVOKE-D
ALATE-D	BLAZE-D	CERNE-D	CYCLE-D	EXEME-D
ALEYE-D	BLUME-D	CESSE-D	DAINE-D	EXILE-D
ALINE-D	BODGE-D	CHACE-D	DAMME-D	EXTOL-D
AMATE-D	BOGIE-D	CHAFE-D	DANCE-D	EXUDE-D
AMAZE-D	BOMBE-D	CHARE-D	DARRE-D	FABLE-D
AMBLE-D	BOOSE-D	CHASE-D	DAUBE-D	FADGE-D
AMENE-D	BOOZE-D	CHIDE-D	DEARE-D	FAINE-D
AMOVE-D	BOTTE-D	CHIEL-D	DEAVE-D	FALSE-D
AMUSE-D	BOUGE-D	CHIME-D	DEEVE-D	FARCE-D
ANELE-D	BOUSE-D	CHINE-D	DEICE-D	FARSE-D
ANGLE-D	BOWNE-D	CHIVE-D	DELVE-D	FAYNE-D
ANKLE-D	BOWSE-D	CHOKE-D	DEMAN-D	FEARE-D
APPAY-D	BOYAR-D	CHORE-D	DEUCE-D	FEASE-D
ARGAN-D	BRACE-D	CHUTE-D	DINGE-D	FEAZE-D
ARGLE-D	BRAKE-D	CLEPE-D	DIRKE-D	FEESE-D
ARGUE-D	BRAVE-D	CLIPE-D	DODGE-D	FEEZE-D
ATONE-D	BRAZE-D	CLOKE-D	DONNE-D	FENCE-D
AVALE-D	BREDE-D	CLONE-D	DORSA-D	FESSE-D
AVISE-D	BRIAR-D	CLOSE-D	DOUSE-D	FIBRE-D
AVIZE-D	BRIBE-D	CLOYE-D	DOWSE-D	FIDGE-D
AVYZE-D	BRIDE-D	CLYPE-D	DRAPE-D	FILLE-D
AWAKE-D	BRINE-D	COATE-D	DRONE-D	FITTE-D
AZOTE-D	BROKE-D	COCCI-D	DROVE-D	FLAKE-D
BADGE-D	BRUTE-D	COMBE-D	DROWN-D	FLAME-D
BAIZE-D	BUDGE-D	CONGE-D	DWINE-D	FLARE-D
BARBE-D	BUFFE-D	CONNE-D	EAGLE-D	FLITE-D
BARDE-D	BUGLE-D	COOEE-D	EDUCE-D	FLUKE-D
BARGE-D	BULGE-D	COPSE-D	ELATE-D	FLUME-D
BARRE-D	BUNCE-D	COSIE-D	ELIDE-D	FLUTE-D
BASSE-D	BUNDE-D	COSTE-D	ELOPE-D	FLYPE-D
BASTE-D	BURKE-D	COUPE-D	ELUDE-D	FLYTE-D
BATHE-D	BUTLE-D	COURE-D	ELUTE-D	FORCE-D

D – End-hooks

FORGE-D	HEEZE-D	MAILE-D	PEEVE-D	RAZEE-D
FORME-D	HEFTE-D	MANGE-D	PEISE-D	REAME-D
FORTE-D	HELVE-D	MARLE-D	PEIZE-D	REAVE-D
FOSSE-D	HERSE-D	MASSE-D	PENNE-D	RECCE-D
FOULE-D	HERYE-D	MATTE-D	PERCE-D	REDYE-D
FOYLE-D	HINGE-D	MEANE-D	PERVE-D	REEDE-D
FOYNE-D	HOISE-D	MEASE-D	PETAR-D	REEVE-D
FRAME-D	HOOVE-D	MEDIA-D	PEYSE-D	REGAR-D
FRIZE-D	HORDE-D	MEDLE-D	PHASE-D	REIVE-D
FUDGE-D	HORSE-D	MENGE-D	PHESE-D	RELIE-D
FUGLE-D	HOUSE-D	MENSE-D	PHONE-D	REMAN-D
FUGUE-D	IMAGE-D	MERGE-D	PIECE-D	REMEN-D
GABLE-D	IMBUE-D	METHO-D	PIQUE-D	RENNE-D
GAFFE-D	INDUE-D	METRE-D	PLACE-D	RENTE-D
GAMME-D	INKLE-D	MEUSE-D	PLANE-D	RESEE-D
GARBE-D	INURE-D	MICHE-D	PLATE-D	RETIE-D
GARRE-D	IRONE-D	MIEVE-D	PLONG-D	RETRO-D
GAUGE-D	ISSUE-D	MILLE-D	PLUME-D	REUSE-D
GEARE-D	JAMBE-D	MILOR-D	POISE-D	REVIE-D
GERNE-D	JESSE-D	MINCE-D	PONCE-D	REWIN-D
GESSE-D	JOULE-D	MINGE-D	PORGE-D	RHYME-D
GLARE-D	JUDGE-D	MITRE-D	POSSE-D	RIDGE-D
GLAZE-D	JUICE-D	MOBLE-D	POUPE-D	RIFLE-D
GLIDE-D	KEDGE-D	MODGE-D	POWRE-D	RIFTE-D
GLIME-D	KENTE-D	MONIE-D	POYSE-D	RILLE-D
GLOBE-D	KERNE-D	MOOVE-D	PRATE-D	RINSE-D
GLOVE-D	KERVE-D	MORNE-D	PREVE-D	ROATE-D
GLOZE-D	KITHE-D	MOUSE-D	PRICE-D	ROGUE-D
GOOSE-D	KLUGE-D	MOYLE-D	PRIDE-D	ROOSE-D
GORGE-D	KNIFE-D	MUDGE-D	PRIME-D	ROTTE-D
GOSSE-D	KNIVE-D	MUSSE-D	PRISE-D	ROUGE-D
GOUGE-D	KYNDE-D	NACRE-D	PRIZE-D	ROUSE-D
GRACE-D	KYTHE-D	NAPPE-D	PROBE-D	ROUTE-D
GRADE-D	LADLE-D	NEESE-D	PROKE-D	ROYNE-D
GRAPE-D	LANCE-D	NEEZE-D	PROLE-D	RUCHE-D
GRATE-D	LANDE-D	NERVE-D	PROSE-D	RUFFE-D
GRAVE-D	LAPSE-D	NICHE-D	PROVE-D	RYMME-D
GRAZE-D	LATHE-D	NOISE-D	PRUNE-D	SABLE-D
GRICE-D	LEARE-D	NOOSE-D	PRYSE-D	SABRE-D
GRIDE-D	LEASE-D	NUDGE-D	PULSE-D	SAINE-D
GRIME-D	LEAVE-D	NURSE-D	PUNCE-D	SALUE-D
GRIPE-D	LEDGE-D	OCHRE-D	PUREE-D	SALVE-D
GRISE-D	LEGGE-D	OPINE-D	PURGE-D	SASSE-D
GRONE-D	LENSE-D	ORATE-D	PURSE-D	SAUCE-D
GROPE-D	LEVEE-D	OUTRE-D	PUSLE-D	SAUTE-D
GROVE-D	LIGAN-D	OVATE-D	QUAKE-D	SCALE-D
GRYDE-D	LIGGE-D	PAIRE-D	QUEME-D	SCAPE-D
GUIDE-D	LITHE-D	PANNE-D	QUEUE-D	SCARE-D
GUILE-D	LOAVE-D	PARGE-D	QUIRE-D	SCENE-D
GUISE-D	LODGE-D	PARLE-D	QUITE-D	SCOPE-D
GUNGE-D	LONGE-D	PARSE-D	QUOTE-D	SCORE-D
GURGE-D	LOOSE-D	PASSE-D	QUYTE-D	SCREE-D
GUYLE-D	LOTTE-D	PASTE-D	RAILE-D	SCUSE-D
HALSE-D	LOUPE-D	PATTE-D	RAINE-D	SEAME-D
HALVE-D	LOURE-D	PAUSE-D	RAISE-D	SEARE-D
HASTE-D	LOUSE-D	PEACE-D	RANCE-D	SEASE-D
HAUSE-D	LOWNE-D	PEASE-D	RANGE-D	SEAZE-D
HAWSE-D	LOWSE-D	PEAZE-D	RANKE-D	SEDGE-D
HEAVE-D	LUNGE-D	PECKE-D	RAPPE-D	SEGUE-D
HEDGE-D	MACLE-D	PEEPE-D	RAYLE-D	SEINE-D

SEISE-D	SLIPE-D	STANE-D	TEASE-D	VALUE-D
SEIZE-D	SLIVE-D	STARE-D	TEAZE-D	VALVE-D
SEMEE-D	SLOPE-D	STATE-D	TEENE-D	VARVE-D
SENSE-D	SMILE-D	STAVE-D	TEMSE-D	VAUTE-D
SENTE-D	SMOKE-D	STEAR-D	TENSE-D	VAWTE-D
SERGE-D	SMORE-D	STEDE-D	TERNE-D	VEALE-D
SERRE-D	SNAKE-D	STEEL-D	TESTE-D	VENGE-D
SERVE-D	SNARE-D	STEME-D	TETRA-D	VERGE-D
SHADE-D	SNIDE-D	STILE-D	THEME-D	VERSE-D
SHAKE-D	SNIPE-D	STIME-D	THOLE-D	VISIE-D
SHALE-D	SNOKE-D	STIPE-D	THROE-D	VOGUE-D
SHAME-D	SNORE-D	STIRE-D	TINGE-D	VOICE-D
SHAPE-D	SOARE-D	STIVE-D	TITHE-D	VOLVE-D
SHARE-D	SOLAN-D	STOKE-D	TITLE-D	WAITE-D
SHAVE-D	SOLVE-D	STOLE-D	TOAZE-D	WAIVE-D
SHIEL-D	SOOLE-D	STONE-D	TODDE-D	WANZE-D
SHINE-D	SOOTE-D	STOPE-D	TOGAE-D	WARRE-D
SHIRE-D	SOUCE-D	STORE-D	TOILE-D	WASTE-D
SHITE-D	SOUSE-D	STOUN-D	TOUSE-D	WEAVE-D
SHORE-D	SOWCE-D	STOVE-D	TOUZE-D	WEDGE-D
SHOVE-D	SOWLE-D	STOWN-D	TOWSE-D	WEETE-D
SHREW-D	SOWSE-D	STUPE-D	TOWZE-D	WEFTE-D
SHROW-D	SPACE-D	STYLE-D	TRACE-D	WEISE-D
SHULE-D	SPADE-D	STYME-D	TRADE-D	WEIZE-D
SHUTE-D	SPANE-D	STYRE-D	TRAPE-D	WELKE-D
SIDLE-D	SPARE-D	STYTE-D	TRICE-D	WHALE-D
SIEGE-D	SPAUL-D	SUEDE-D	TRINE-D	WHILE-D
SIEVE-D	SPICE-D	SUITE-D	TROKE-D	WHINE-D
SINGE-D	SPIKE-D	SURGE-D	TROPE-D	WHITE-D
SITHE-D	SPILE-D	SWAGE-D	TRUCE-D	WHORE-D
SKATE-D	SPINE-D	SWALE-D	TWINE-D	WINCE-D
SKITE-D	SPIRE-D	SWEAR-D	TWIRE-D	WINGE-D
SKIVE-D	SPITE-D	SWIPE-D	TYTHE-D	WITHE-D
SKYRE-D	SPOKE-D	SWIVE-D	UNCLE-D	WOLVE-D
SKYTE-D	SPORE-D	SWOUN-D	UNITE-D	WORSE-D
SLAKE-D	SPRED-D	TABER-D	UNTIE-D	YODLE-D
SLATE-D	SPREE-D	TABLE-D	UPTIE-D	ZINKE-D
SLAVE-D	SPUME-D	TARGE-D	URINE-D	
SLICE-D	STAGE-D	TARRE-D	USURE-D	
SLIDE-D	STAKE-D	TASTE-D	VAGUE-D	
SLIME-D	STALE-D	TAWSE-D	VALSE-D	

Six letters to seven

ABDUCE-D	AERATE-D	ALLURE-D	ASPIRE-D	BANGLE-D
ABJURE-D	AFFEAR-D	AMENDE-D	ASSIZE-D	BASQUE-D
ABLATE-D	AFFINE-D	AMERCE-D	ASSUME-D	BATTLE-D
ABRADE-D	AGNAME-D	AMOOVE-D	ASSURE-D	BEAGLE-D
ACCEDE-D	AGNISE-D	ANNEXE-D	ASTONE-D	BEDAZE-D
ACCITE-D	AGNIZE-D	ANSATE-D	ATTIRE-D	BEETLE-D
ACCRUE-D	AGRISE-D	APPOSE-D	ATTUNE-D	BEGAZE-D
ACCUSE-D	AGRIZE-D	ARAISE-D	AURATE-D	BEHAVE-D
ADDUCE-D	AGRYZE-D	ARAYSE-D	AVAILE-D	BEHOVE-D
ADHERE-D	AGUISE-D	ARCADE-D	AVENGE-D	BEJADE-D
ADJURE-D	AGUIZE-D	AROUSE-D	AVIATE-D	BELACE-D
ADMIRE-D	ALCOVE-D	ARRIDE-D	AVULSE-D	BELATE-D
ADVENE-D	ALEGGE-D	ARRIVE-D	AWHAPE-D	BELOVE-D
ADVISE-D	ALLEGE-D	ASHAME-D	BABBLE-D	BEMETE-D
AEMULE-D	ALLUDE-D	ASLAKE-D	BAFFLE-D	BEMIRE-D

D – End-hooks

BEMUSE-D	CASQUE-D	DABBLE-D	DISPLE-D	ESCAPE-D
BENAME-D	CASTLE-D	DADDLE-D	DISUSE-D	ESTATE-D
BERAKE-D	CAUDLE-D	DAGGLE-D	DIVIDE-D	EUCHRE-D
BERATE-D	CENTRE-D	DAIDLE-D	DIVINE-D	EVINCE-D
BERIME-D	CERATE-D	DAMAGE-D	DONATE-D	EVOLVE-D
BERTHE-D	CESTOI-D	DANDLE-D	DOODLE-D	EVULSE-D
BETIDE-D	CHAINE-D	DANGLE-D	DORISE-D	EXCIDE-D
BETIME-D	CHANCE-D	DAPPLE-D	DORIZE-D	EXCISE-D
BEWARE-D	CHANGE-D	DARKLE-D	DOTTLE-D	EXCITE-D
BEZZLE-D	CHARGE-D	DARTLE-D	DOUBLE-D	EXCUSE-D
BINGLE-D	CHASSE-D	DAWDLE-D	DOUCHE-D	EXHALE-D
BIRDIE-D	CHAUFE-D	DAZZLE-D	DREDGE-D	EXHUME-D
BIRSLE-D	CHEESE-D	DEBASE-D	DROMON-D	EXPIRE-D
BISTRE-D	CHILDE-D	DEBATE-D	DROWSE-D	EXPOSE-D
BLENDE-D	CHIRRE-D	DEBONE-D	DRUDGE-D	FACETE-D
BLOUSE-D	CHOUSE-D	DECIDE-D	DUMPLE-D	FADDLE-D
BLOWSE-D	CHOWSE-D	DECKLE-D	ECLOSE-D	FANGLE-D
BLOWZE-D	CHROME-D	DECODE-D	EFFACE-D	FANKLE-D
BLUDGE-D	CIRCLE-D	DECOKE-D	EFFERE-D	FARCIE-D
BLUNGE-D	CLEAVE-D	DECREE-D	EFFUSE-D	FEAGUE-D
BOBBLE-D	CLICHE-D	DEDUCE-D	ELANCE-D	FEEBLE-D
BOGGLE-D	CLIQUE-D	DEFACE-D	ELAPSE-D	FERLIE-D
BOODIE-D	CLOTHE-D	DEFAME-D	EMBALE-D	FERULE-D
BOODLE-D	COBBLE-D	DEFILE-D	EMBASE-D	FETTLE-D
BOOGIE-D	COCKLE-D	DEFINE-D	EMBRUE-D	FEUTRE-D
BORATE-D	CODDLE-D	DEFUSE-D	EMERGE-D	FICKLE-D
BOTTLE-D	COERCE-D	DEFUZE-D	EMMOVE-D	FIDDLE-D
BOUNCE-D	COFFLE-D	DEGREE-D	EMPALE-D	FIGURE-D
BRAIDE-D	COGGLE-D	DELATE-D	EMPARE-D	FISSLE-D
BRAISE-D	COHERE-D	DELETE-D	EMULGE-D	FIXATE-D
BREEZE-D	COIFFE-D	DELIME-D	EMUNGE-D	FIZZLE-D
BRIDGE-D	COIGNE-D	DELOPE-D	ENABLE-D	FLANGE-D
BRIDLE-D	COLLAR-D	DELUDE-D	ENCAGE-D	FLEDGE-D
BRIGUE-D	COLLIE-D	DELUGE-D	ENCASE-D	FLEECE-D
BROCHE-D	COLOBI-D	DEMISE-D	ENCAVE-D	FLENSE-D
BRONZE-D	CONCHE-D	DEMODE-D	ENCODE-D	FLOUSE-D
BROWSE-D	CONGEE-D	DEMOTE-D	ENCORE-D	FONDLE-D
BRUISE-D	CONJEE-D	DEMURE-D	ENDITE-D	FONDUE-D
BUBBLE-D	COORIE-D	DENOTE-D	ENDURE-D	FOOTLE-D
BUCKLE-D	CORPSE-D	DENUDE-D	ENERVE-D	FOOZLE-D
BUDDLE-D	COSTAR-D	DEPONE-D	ENFACE-D	FORAGE-D
BUMBLE-D	COTISE-D	DEPOSE-D	ENFIRE-D	FOUTRE-D
BUMMLE-D	COUCHE-D	DEPUTE-D	ENFREE-D	FRAISE-D
BUNDLE-D	COUPLE-D	DERATE-D	ENGAGE-D	FRAPPE-D
BUNGLE-D	COURIE-D	DERIDE-D	ENGINE-D	FRIDGE-D
BURBLE-D	COURSE-D	DERIVE-D	ENGORE-D	FRIEZE-D
BUSTLE-D	CRADLE-D	DESINE-D	ENISLE-D	FRINGE-D
BUTTLE-D	CREASE-D	DESIRE-D	ENLACE-D	FUDDLE-D
BYLINE-D	CREATE-D	DESYNE-D	ENMOVE-D	FUMBLE-D
CACKLE-D	CREESE-D	DETUNE-D	ENNUYE-D	FUZZLE-D
CADDIE-D	CRINGE-D	DEVISE-D	ENRACE-D	GABBLE-D
CAJOLE-D	CROSSE-D	DEVOTE-D	ENRAGE-D	GAGGLE-D
CALQUE-D	CROUPE-D	DIBBLE-D	ENROBE-D	GAMBLE-D
CAMPLE-D	CRUISE-D	DIDDLE-D	ENSILE-D	GARAGE-D
CANDIE-D	CUDDLE-D	DILATE-D	ENSURE-D	GARBLE-D
CANDLE-D	CUFFLE-D	DILUTE-D	ENTAME-D	GARGLE-D
CANGLE-D	CURATE-D	DIMPLE-D	ENTICE-D	GAROTE-D
CANTLE-D	CURDLE-D	DINDLE-D	ENZONE-D	GELATE-D
CARNIE-D	CURRIE-D	DINNLE-D	EQUATE-D	GENTLE-D
	CUTTLE-D	DISMAY-D	ERMINE-D	GHESSE-D

GIGGLE-D	IGNORE-D	KINDLE-D	MUDDLE-D	PERUKE-D
GILLIE-D	ILLUDE-D	KIRTLE-D	MUFFLE-D	PERUSE-D
GIRDLE-D	ILLUME-D	KITTLE-D	MUMBLE-D	PESTLE-D
GLAIRE-D	IMBASE-D	KLUDGE-D	MUNITE-D	PETTLE-D
GLAIVE-D	IMBIBE-D	KREESE-D	MUSCLE-D	PHEESE-D
GLANCE-D	IMBRUE-D	LAIPSE-D	MUTATE-D	PHEEZE-D
GLEDGE-D	IMMURE-D	LALLAN-D	MUTINE-D	PHRASE-D
GOATEE-D	IMPALE-D	LANATE-D	MUZZLE-D	PIAFFE-D
GOBBLE-D	IMPAVE-D	LANGUE-D	NANNIE-D	PICKLE-D
GOGGLE-D	IMPEDE-D	LAUNCE-D	NATURE-D	PICOTE-D
GOITRE-D	IMPONE-D	LEAGUE-D	NEEDLE-D	PIDDLE-D
GOLLAN-D	IMPOSE-D	LEGATE-D	NEGATE-D	PIERCE-D
GOOGLE-D	IMPUTE-D	LENITE-D	NESTLE-D	PIFFLE-D
GOWLAN-D	INCAGE-D	LIAISE-D	NETTLE-D	PIMPLE-D
GRAINE-D	INCASE-D	LIBATE-D	NIBBLE-D	PINGLE-D
GREASE-D	INCAVE-D	LIGATE-D	NICKLE-D	PIRATE-D
GREAVE-D	INCEDE-D	LOATHE-D	NIDATE-D	PLAGUE-D
GREETE-D	INCISE-D	LOBATE-D	NIGGLE-D	PLEASE-D
GRIECE-D	INCITE-D	LOCATE-D	NIPPLE-D	PLEDGE-D
GRIEVE-D	INCUSE-D	LOCULE-D	NOBBLE-D	PLODGE-D
GRILLE-D	INDITE-D	LOUNGE-D	NODDLE-D	PLONGE-D
GRIPPE-D	INDUCE-D	LOUVRE-D	NODULE-D	PLUNGE-D
GROOVE-D	INFAME-D	LUMINE-D	NONAGE-D	PODDLE-D
GROUSE-D	INFUSE-D	LUNATE-D	NOODGE-D	POINTE-D
GRUDGE-D	INHALE-D	LUSTRE-D	NOODLE-D	POLICE-D
GUDDLE-D	INHERE-D	LUXATE-D	NOTATE-D	POLYPE-D
GUGGLE-D	INHUME-D	LYRATE-D	NOTICE-D	POMADE-D
GUIMPE-D	INISLE-D	MACKLE-D	NOUSLE-D	POONCE-D
GURGLE-D	INJURE-D	MACULE-D	NUANCE-D	POOTLE-D
GUSSIE-D	INLACE-D	MADAME-D	NUBBLE-D	POPPLE-D
GUTTLE-D	INSURE-D	MALGRE-D	NURDLE-D	POTCHE-D
GUZZLE-D	INTONE-D	MALICE-D	NURSLE-D	POUFFE-D
GYRATE-D	INVADE-D	MANAGE-D	NUTATE-D	POUNCE-D
HACKLE-D	INVITE-D	MANEGE-D	NUZZLE-D	PRAISE-D
HAGGLE-D	INVOKE-D	MANGLE-D	OBDURE-D	PRANCE-D
HAMBLE-D	IODATE-D	MANTLE-D	OBJURE-D	PREACE-D
HANDLE-D	IODISE-D	MANURE-D	OBLIGE-D	PREASE-D
HASSLE-D	IODIZE-D	MARBLE-D	OPAQUE-D	PREEVE-D
HEARSE-D	IONISE-D	MASCLE-D	OPIATE-D	PREVUE-D
HECKLE-D	IONIZE-D	MATURE-D	OPPOSE-D	PRIEVE-D
HEDDLE-D	JABBLE-D	MAUGRE-D	ORACLE-D	PRINCE-D
HIGGLE-D	JANGLE-D	MEASLE-D	OSMOSE-D	PROINE-D
HIRPLE-D	JAUNCE-D	MEDDLE-D	OUGLIE-D	PROTEI-D
HIRSLE-D	JAUNSE-D	MEGARA-D	OUTLIE-D	PROVEN-D
HOBBLE-D	JEELIE-D	MENACE-D	OUTVIE-D	PROYNE-D
HOCKLE-D	JERQUE-D	MENAGE-D	OUTWAR-D	PSYCHE-D
HODDLE-D	JIGGLE-D	METTLE-D	OUTWIN-D	PUDDLE-D
HOGTIE-D	JIMMIE-D	MICATE-D	PADDLE-D	PUGGLE-D
HOMAGE-D	JINGLE-D	MIDDLE-D	PALACE-D	PUMICE-D
HONDLE-D	JIRBLE-D	MINGLE-D	PALATE-D	PUNGLE-D
HOPPLE-D	JOGGLE-D	MINUTE-D	PARADE-D	PUPATE-D
HOWDIE-D	JOSTLE-D	MISCUE-D	PAROLE-D	PURFLE-D
HUDDLE-D	JOUNCE-D	MISTLE-D	PARPEN-D	PURPLE-D
HUMBLE-D	JUGGLE-D	MISUSE-D	PATINE-D	PURSUE-D
HURDLE-D	JUMBLE-D	MIZZLE-D	PEARCE-D	PUTTIE-D
HURTLE-D	JUNGLE-D	MOBBLE-D	PEBBLE-D	PUZZLE-D
HUSTLE-D	JUSTLE-D	MOTIVE-D	PEDDLE-D	QUAERE-D
ICICLE-D	KECKLE-D	MOTTLE-D	PEENGE-D	QUICHE-D
IDEATE-D	KIBBLE-D	MOUSLE-D	PEOPLE-D	RABBLE-D
IGNITE-D	KIDDIE-D	MOUSSE-D	PERSUE-D	RACEME-D

D – End-hooks

RADDLE-D	RESUME-D	SEDUCE-D	SPLICE-D	TICKLE-D
RAFFLE-D	RETAPE-D	SEETHE-D	SPLINE-D	TIDDLE-D
RAGGLE-D	RETILE-D	SEMBLE-D	SPONGE-D	TIERCE-D
RAMBLE-D	RETIME-D	SERENE-D	SPOUSE-D	TINGLE-D
RANKLE-D	RETIRE-D	SETTLE-D	SPRUCE-D	TINKLE-D
RASSLE-D	RETUNE-D	SEVERE-D	SPULYE-D	TIPPLE-D
RATTLE-D	RETYPE-D	SHEAVE-D	SPURNE-D	TIPTOE-D
RAUNGE-D	REURGE-D	SHELVE-D	SQUARE-D	TISSUE-D
RAVAGE-D	REVERE-D	SHINNE-D	SQUIRE-D	TITTLE-D
RAVINE-D	REVILE-D	SHOOLE-D	STABLE-D	TITULE-D
REBATE-D	REVISE-D	SHOPPE-D	STAPLE-D	TODDLE-D
REBORE-D	REVIVE-D	SHOTTE-D	STARVE-D	TOGATE-D
REBUKE-D	REVOKE-D	SHRIKE-D	STATUE-D	TOGGLE-D
RECANE-D	REVOTE-D	SHRINE-D	STAYNE-D	TONGUE-D
RECEDE-D	REWAKE-D	SHRIVE-D	STEALE-D	TOOTLE-D
RECITE-D	REWIRE-D	SHROVE-D	STEANE-D	TOPPLE-D
RECODE-D	REZONE-D	SICKLE-D	STEARE-D	TORQUE-D
RECULE-D	RIDDLE-D	SIFFLE-D	STEDDE-D	TOUCHE-D
RECURE-D	RIFFLE-D	SILAGE-D	STEEVE-D	TOUSLE-D
RECUSE-D	RIMPLE-D	SIMPLE-D	STEMME-D	TOUZLE-D
REDATE-D	RIPPLE-D	SINGLE-D	STEPPE-D	TOWMON-D
REDDLE-D	ROOTLE-D	SIPPLE-D	STERVE-D	TRANCE-D
REDUCE-D	ROTATE-D	SIZZLE-D	STIFLE-D	TRAYNE-D
REFACE-D	RUBBLE-D	SKLATE-D	STIMIE-D	TREBLE-D
REFILE-D	RUCKLE-D	SKRIKE-D	STIRRE-D	TRIAGE-D
REFINE-D	RUDDLE-D	SLEAVE-D	STODGE-D	TRIFLE-D
REFIRE-D	RUFFLE-D	SLEDGE-D	STONNE-D	TRIPLE-D
REFUGE-D	RUMBLE-D	SLEEVE-D	STOOGE-D	TROMPE-D
REFUSE-D	RUMPLE-D	SLUDGE-D	STOOPE-D	TROULE-D
REFUTE-D	RUNDLE-D	SLUICE-D	STRAFE-D	TROUPE-D
REGALE-D	RUNKLE-D	SMOILE-D	STRAKE-D	TRUDGE-D
REGLUE-D	RUSTLE-D	SMOOGE-D	STRIPE-D	TRYSTE-D
REHEAR-D	RUSTRE-D	SMOUSE-D	STRIVE-D	TUMBLE-D
REHIRE-D	SADDLE-D	SMOYLE-D	STROBE-D	TURBAN-D
RELACE-D	SAGGAR-D	SMUDGE-D	STROKE-D	TURTLE-D
RELATE-D	SALUTE-D	SNEBBE-D	STYMIE-D	TUSSLE-D
RELINE-D	SAMPLE-D	SNEEZE-D	SUBDUE-D	TWEEZE-D
RELIVE-D	SAPPLE-D	SNOOZE-D	SUCKLE-D	TWINGE-D
RELUME-D	SAVAGE-D	SNUBBE-D	SUDATE-D	ULLAGE-D
REMATE-D	SCARRE-D	SNUDGE-D	SUPPLE-D	UMPIRE-D
REMBLE-D	SCATHE-D	SOLACE-D	SUTTLE-D	UNBALE-D
REMEDE-D	SCERNE-D	SOLATE-D	SUTURE-D	UNBARE-D
REMISE-D	SCHEME-D	SOMBRE-D	SWARVE-D	UNBONE-D
REMOVE-D	SCLATE-D	SOOGEE-D	SWATHE-D	UNCAGE-D
RENAME-D	SCONCE-D	SOOGIE-D	SWERVE-D	UNCAKE-D
RENEGE-D	SCORSE-D	SOOTHE-D	SWINGE-D	UNCAPE-D
REPAVE-D	SCRAPE-D	SOPITE-D	SWOUNE-D	UNCASE-D
REPINE-D	SCRIBE-D	SORTIE-D	TACKLE-D	UNCOPE-D
REPONE-D	SCRIKE-D	SOUPLE-D	TAIGLE-D	UNDATE-D
REPOSE-D	SCRIVE-D	SOURCE-D	TAMMIE-D	UNEDGE-D
REPURE-D	SCROME-D	SOWSSE-D	TANGLE-D	UNFREE-D
REPUTE-D	SCRUZE-D	SOZZLE-D	TATTLE-D	UNGLUE-D
RESCUE-D	SCULLE-D	SPALLE-D	TEAGLE-D	UNGYVE-D
RESHOE-D	SCUNGE-D	SPARGE-D	TEAZLE-D	UNHELE-D
RESIDE-D	SCYTHE-D	SPARKE-D	TEETHE-D	UNHIVE-D
RESILE-D	SDAINE-D	SPARRE-D	TEMPLE-D	UNLACE-D
RESITE-D	SEARCE-D	SPATHE-D	TENURE-D	UNLADE-D
RESIZE-D	SECEDE-D	SPERRE-D	THIEVE-D	UNLIKE-D
RESKUE-D	SECURE-D	SPERSE-D	THRIVE-D	UNLIME-D
RESOLE-D	SEDATE-D	SPHERE-D	THRONE-D	UNLINE-D

UNLIVE-D	UNWIVE-D	VENTRE-D	WANGLE-D	WINDLE-D
UNLOVE-D	UNYOKE-D	VISAGE-D	WARBLE-D	WINKLE-D
UNPILE-D	UPDATE-D	VISITE-D	WARRAN-D	WINTLE-D
UNPOPE-D	UPDIVE-D	VITTLE-D	WARSLE-D	WOBBLE-D
UNRAKE-D	UPGAZE-D	VIZZIE-D	WATTLE-D	WRAXLE-D
UNROBE-D	UPPILE-D	VOLUME-D	WEEWEE-D	WRETHE-D
UNROPE-D	UPRATE-D	VOLUTE-D	WHEEZE-D	WRITHE-D
UNRULE-D	UPSIZE-D	VOYAGE-D	WHINGE-D	WUZZLE-D
UNSHOE-D	VACATE-D	WABBLE-D	WIBBLE-D	YABBIE-D
UNSURE-D	VALETE-D	WADDIE-D	WIDDLE-D	ZIZZLE-D
UNTAME-D	VAMOSE-D	WADDLE-D	WIGGLE-D	ZONATE-D
UNTILE-D	VAUNCE-D	WAFFLE-D	WILLIE-D	
UNTUNE-D	VELATE-D	WAGGLE-D	WIMBLE-D	
UNWIRE-D	VELURE-D	WAMBLE-D	WIMPLE-D	

Seven letters to eight

ABRIDGE-D	APPRISE-D	BECURSE-D	BROMIZE-D	COLLIDE-D
ABROOKE-D	APPRIZE-D	BEDRAPE-D	BUMBAZE-D	COLLUDE-D
ABSCISE-D	APPROVE-D	BEDUNCE-D	CABBAGE-D	COLOGNE-D
ABSOLVE-D	ARABISE-D	BEELINE-D	CADENCE-D	COMBINE-D
ACCINGE-D	ARABIZE-D	BEGRIME-D	CALCINE-D	COMMOVE-D
ACCRETE-D	ARCHIVE-D	BEGUILE-D	CALIBRE-D	COMMUNE-D
ACCURSE-D	ARCUATE-D	BEHOOVE-D	CALYCLE-D	COMMUTE-D
ACERATE-D	ARRANGE-D	BEKNAVE-D	CAPSIZE-D	COMPARE-D
ACETATE-D	ARTICLE-D	BELIEVE-D	CAPSULE-D	COMPERE-D
ACHIEVE-D	ASCRIBE-D	BEPROSE-D	CAPTIVE-D	COMPETE-D
ACQUIRE-D	ASKANCE-D	BEREAVE-D	CAPTURE-D	COMPILE-D
ACTUATE-D	ASPERGE-D	BERHYME-D	CAPUCHE-D	COMPOSE-D
ACYLATE-D	ASPERSE-D	BESHAME-D	CARCASE-D	COMPUTE-D
ADJUDGE-D	ASSIEGE-D	BESIEGE-D	CAROUSE-D	CONACRE-D
ADONISE-D	ASSUAGE-D	BESLAVE-D	CASCADE-D	CONCAVE-D
ADONIZE-D	ASSWAGE-D	BESLIME-D	CASEATE-D	CONCEDE-D
ADULATE-D	ATHEISE-D	BESMILE-D	CAUDATE-D	CONCISE-D
ADVANCE-D	ATHEIZE-D	BESMOKE-D	CAYENNE-D	CONDOLE-D
AFFEARE-D	ATOMISE-D	BESPICE-D	CENSURE-D	CONDONE-D
AFFORCE-D	ATOMIZE-D	BETEEME-D	CHALICE-D	CONDUCE-D
AGATISE-D	ATTACHE-D	BETITLE-D	CHARQUI-D	CONFIDE-D
AGATIZE-D	ATTRITE-D	BEWHORE-D	CHAUNCE-D	CONFINE-D
AGENISE-D	ATTUITE-D	BICYCLE-D	CHAUNGE-D	CONFUSE-D
AGENIZE-D	AUDIBLE-D	BIVALVE-D	CHELATE-D	CONFUTE-D
AGGRACE-D	AUREOLE-D	BLOOSME-D	CHICANE-D	CONGREE-D
AGGRADE-D	AURICLE-D	BRABBLE-D	CHORTLE-D	CONGRUE-D
AGGRATE-D	AVENTRE-D	BRAILLE-D	CHUCKLE-D	CONJURE-D
AGITATE-D	AVERAGE-D	BRAMBLE-D	CILIATE-D	CONNIVE-D
AGONISE-D	AZOTISE-D	BRANGLE-D	CITRATE-D	CONNOTE-D
AGONIZE-D	AZOTIZE-D	BRATTLE-D	CLAVATE-D	CONSOLE-D
ALLEDGE-D	BACCATE-D	BREATHE-D	CLEANSE-D	CONSUME-D
ALLEGGE-D	BACKHOE-D	BREENGE-D	CLIMATE-D	CONTUSE-D
AMENAGE-D	BAGPIPE-D	BREINGE-D	CLOSURE-D	CONVENE-D
ANALYSE-D	BALANCE-D	BREVETE-D	CLOTURE-D	CONVIVE-D
ANALYZE-D	BALLADE-D	BRIGADE-D	COALISE-D	CONVOKE-D
ANIMATE-D	BANDAGE-D	BRINDLE-D	COALIZE-D	COPPICE-D
ANODISE-D	BAPTISE-D	BRISTLE-D	COCKADE-D	CORNICE-D
ANODIZE-D	BAPTIZE-D	BRITTLE-D	COCKEYE-D	CORNUTE-D
ANTICKE-D	BARBATE-D	BROCADE-D	COGNISE-D	CORRADE-D
ANTIQUE-D	BARRAGE-D	BRODDLE-D	COGNIZE-D	CORRODE-D
APANAGE-D	BAUCHLE-D	BROMATE-D	COLLAGE-D	COSTATE-D
APPEASE-D	BECRIME-D	BROMISE-D	COLLATE-D	COSTUME-D

COTTAGE-D	DESERVE-D	EGOTIZE-D	EVOLUTE-D	GESTURE-D
COTTISE-D	DESPISE-D	ELEGISE-D	EXAMINE-D	GHILLIE-D
COWHIDE-D	DESPITE-D	ELEGIZE-D	EXAMPLE-D	GLIMPSE-D
CRACKLE-D	DESTINE-D	ELEVATE-D	EXCLUDE-D	GLOBATE-D
CRANKLE-D	DETERGE-D	ELOCUTE-D	EXCRETE-D	GOLOSHE-D
CREMATE-D	DETRUDE-D	EMANATE-D	EXCURSE-D	GRABBLE-D
CRENATE-D	DEVALUE-D	EMBATHE-D	EXECUTE-D	GRADATE-D
CREVICE-D	DEVIATE-D	EMBLAZE-D	EXPENSE-D	GRANNIE-D
CRIBBLE-D	DEVOICE-D	EMBOGUE-D	EXPIATE-D	GRAPPLE-D
CRIMPLE-D	DEVOLVE-D	EMBRACE-D	EXPLODE-D	GRECISE-D
CRINATE-D	DIALYSE-D	EMBRAVE-D	EXPLORE-D	GRECIZE-D
CRINKLE-D	DIALYZE-D	EMBRUTE-D	EXPULSE-D	GRIDDLE-D
CRIPPLE-D	DIARISE-D	EMICATE-D	EXPUNGE-D	GRIMACE-D
CROODLE-D	DIARIZE-D	EMPAIRE-D	EXPURGE-D	GRIZZLE-D
CRUDDLE-D	DICTATE-D	EMPAYRE-D	EXTRUDE-D	GRUBBLE-D
CRUMBLE-D	DIFFUSE-D	EMPERCE-D	FALCATE-D	GRUMBLE-D
CRUMPLE-D	DISABLE-D	EMPLACE-D	FANFARE-D	GRUNTLE-D
CRUNKLE-D	DISCAGE-D	EMPLANE-D	FATIGUE-D	GUMSHOE-D
CRUSADE-D	DISCASE-D	EMPLOYE-D	FEATURE-D	GUTTATE-D
CUITTLE-D	DISCIDE-D	EMPLUME-D	FELLATE-D	HACHURE-D
CULTURE-D	DISCURE-D	EMULATE-D	FENAGLE-D	HALTERE-D
CUNEATE-D	DISEASE-D	ENCHAFE-D	FERRULE-D	HAMBONE-D
CURETTE-D	DISEDGE-D	ENCHASE-D	FIBROSE-D	HASTATE-D
CURVATE-D	DISHOME-D	ENCLAVE-D	FILIATE-D	HERBAGE-D
CUSPATE-D	DISLIKE-D	ENCLOSE-D	FINAGLE-D	HEROISE-D
CYANIDE-D	DISPACE-D	ENDORSE-D	FINANCE-D	HEROIZE-D
CYANISE-D	DISPONE-D	ENFLAME-D	FINESSE-D	HOGNOSE-D
CYANIZE-D	DISPOSE-D	ENFORCE-D	FISSURE-D	HYDRATE-D
CYCLISE-D	DISPUTE-D	ENFRAME-D	FLAMBEE-D	ICONISE-D
CYCLIZE-D	DISRATE-D	ENGLOBE-D	FLOUNCE-D	ICONIZE-D
DEALATE-D	DISROBE-D	ENGORGE-D	FOLIAGE-D	IDOLISE-D
DEBRIDE-D	DISSAVE-D	ENGRACE-D	FOLIATE-D	IDOLIZE-D
DECEASE-D	DISTUNE-D	ENGRAVE-D	FORBODE-D	ILLAPSE-D
DECEIVE-D	DISYOKE-D	ENHANCE-D	FORMATE-D	IMAGINE-D
DECLARE-D	DIVERGE-D	ENLARGE-D	FORPINE-D	IMBATHE-D
DECLINE-D	DIVERSE-D	ENNOBLE-D	FORSLOE-D	IMBLAZE-D
DECUPLE-D	DIVORCE-D	ENOUNCE-D	FORTUNE-D	IMBRUTE-D
DECURVE-D	DIVULGE-D	ENPLANE-D	FOVEATE-D	IMBURSE-D
DEFENCE-D	DIVULSE-D	ENQUIRE-D	FRAZZLE-D	IMITATE-D
DEFENSE-D	DOCKISE-D	ENRANGE-D	FRECKLE-D	IMMERGE-D
DEFLATE-D	DOCKIZE-D	ENSLAVE-D	FRIBBLE-D	IMMERSE-D
DEFORCE-D	DOGGONE-D	ENSNARE-D	FRIZZLE-D	IMPASTE-D
DEGLAZE-D	DRABBLE-D	ENSTYLE-D	FROGEYE-D	IMPINGE-D
DEGRADE-D	DRAGGLE-D	ENTAYLE-D	FROUNCE-D	IMPLATE-D
DEHISCE-D	DRIBBLE-D	ENTHUSE-D	FRUMPLE-D	IMPLETE-D
DELAPSE-D	DRIZZLE-D	ENTITLE-D	FULMINE-D	IMPLODE-D
DELEAVE-D	DRUMBLE-D	ENTWINE-D	FURCATE-D	IMPLORE-D
DELOUSE-D	DUALISE-D	EPILATE-D	FURNACE-D	IMPROVE-D
DEMEANE-D	DUALIZE-D	EPISTLE-D	GABELLE-D	IMPULSE-D
DEMERGE-D	DWINDLE-D	EPURATE-D	GALEATE-D	INCENSE-D
DEMERSE-D	EBONISE-D	EROTISE-D	GALLISE-D	INCHASE-D
DENTATE-D	EBONIZE-D	EROTIZE-D	GALLIZE-D	INCLINE-D
DEPLANE-D	EBRIATE-D	ESCRIBE-D	GALOCHE-D	INCLOSE-D
DEPLETE-D	ECHOISE-D	ESLOYNE-D	GALOSHE-D	INCLUDE-D
DEPLORE-D	ECHOIZE-D	ESPOUSE-D	GAROTTE-D	INCURVE-D
DEPLUME-D	ECLIPSE-D	ESQUIRE-D	GARROTE-D	INDORSE-D
DEPRAVE-D	EDUCATE-D	ESTREPE-D	GAVOTTE-D	INDULGE-D
DEPRIVE-D	EFFORCE-D	EVIRATE-D	GAZETTE-D	INFLAME-D
DERANGE-D	EFFULGE-D	EVITATE-D	GEMMATE-D	INFLATE-D
DESCALE-D	EGOTISE-D	EVOCATE-D	GESTATE-D	INFORCE-D

INGLOBE-D	MESSAGE-D	OUTGAZE-D	PHILTRE-D	PROLATE-D
INHERCE-D	MIDSIZE-D	OUTHEAR-D	PHONATE-D	PROMISE-D
INNERVE-D	MIDWIFE-D	OUTHIRE-D	PICKAXE-D	PROMOTE-D
INQUERE-D	MIDWIVE-D	OUTHYRE-D	PICRATE-D	PRONATE-D
INQUIRE-D	MIGRATE-D	OUTLINE-D	PICTURE-D	PROPAGE-D
INSNARE-D	MINIATE-D	OUTLIVE-D	PILEATE-D	PROPALE-D
INSPIRE-D	MISCITE-D	OUTLOVE-D	PILLAGE-D	PROPINE-D
INSTATE-D	MISCODE-D	OUTMODE-D	PINNATE-D	PROPONE-D
INTERNE-D	MISDATE-D	OUTMOVE-D	PIPETTE-D	PROPOSE-D
INTITLE-D	MISFARE-D	OUTNAME-D	PISTOLE-D	PRORATE-D
INTRUDE-D	MISFILE-D	OUTPACE-D	PLACATE-D	PROVIDE-D
INTWINE-D	MISFIRE-D	OUTRACE-D	PLANCHE-D	PROVINE-D
INVERSE-D	MISHEAR-D	OUTRAGE-D	PLICATE-D	PROVOKE-D
INVOICE-D	MISLIKE-D	OUTRATE-D	PLUMAGE-D	PULSATE-D
INVOLVE-D	MISLIVE-D	OUTRAVE-D	POETISE-D	PURPOSE-D
INWEAVE-D	MISMATE-D	OUTSIZE-D	POETIZE-D	PUSTULE-D
IRIDISE-D	MISMOVE-D	OUTVOTE-D	POLEAXE-D	QUACKLE-D
IRIDIZE-D	MISNAME-D	OUTWILE-D	POLLUTE-D	QUIBBLE-D
IRISATE-D	MISPAGE-D	OVERAGE-D	POMMELE-D	QUIDDLE-D
IRONISE-D	MISRATE-D	OVERAWE-D	PORTAGE-D	QUIESCE-D
IRONIZE-D	MISRULE-D	OVERDYE-D	POSTURE-D	QUINCHE-D
ISOLATE-D	MISTIME-D	OVEREYE-D	POTHOLE-D	RABATTE-D
ITEMISE-D	MISTUNE-D	OVERSEE-D	POURSUE-D	RADIATE-D
ITEMIZE-D	MISTYPE-D	OVERUSE-D	PRAIRIE-D	RAILCAR-D
ITERATE-D	MISYOKE-D	OVULATE-D	PRANCKE-D	RAMPAGE-D
JALOUSE-D	MONOCLE-D	OXALATE-D	PRANKLE-D	RAMPIRE-D
JAWBONE-D	MONTAGE-D	OXIDATE-D	PRATTLE-D	RAPTURE-D
KEYNOTE-D	MORTICE-D	OXIDISE-D	PRAUNCE-D	RAWBONE-D
KNAPPLE-D	MORTISE-D	OXIDIZE-D	PREASSE-D	RAWHIDE-D
KNOBBLE-D	MULTURE-D	OZONATE-D	PREBAKE-D	REALISE-D
KNUBBLE-D	MURIATE-D	OZONISE-D	PRECEDE-D	REALIZE-D
KNUCKLE-D	MYTHISE-D	OZONIZE-D	PRECISE-D	REALLIE-D
KYANISE-D	MYTHIZE-D	PACKAGE-D	PRECODE-D	REARGUE-D
KYANIZE-D	NARRATE-D	PALMATE-D	PRECURE-D	REAWAKE-D
LABIATE-D	NECROSE-D	PALPATE-D	PREDATE-D	REBADGE-D
LACTATE-D	NICTATE-D	PANCAKE-D	PREFACE-D	REBRACE-D
LAICISE-D	NITRATE-D	PANICLE-D	PREFADE-D	RECEIVE-D
LAICIZE-D	NITRIDE-D	PANTILE-D	PREFILE-D	RECENSE-D
LAIRISE-D	NOURSLE-D	PARABLE-D	PREFIRE-D	RECLINE-D
LAIRIZE-D	NURTURE-D	PARBAKE-D	PRELUDE-D	RECLOSE-D
LARVATE-D	OBELISE-D	PASSAGE-D	PREMISE-D	RECOUPE-D
LATTICE-D	OBELIZE-D	PASTURE-D	PREMOVE-D	RECOURE-D
LEASOWE-D	OBLIQUE-D	PATINAE-D	PREPARE-D	RECOYLE-D
LECTURE-D	OBSCURE-D	PECTISE-D	PREPAVE-D	RECRATE-D
LEISURE-D	OBSERVE-D	PECTIZE-D	PREPONE-D	RECUILE-D
LIBRATE-D	OBTRUDE-D	PEDICLE-D	PREPOSE-D	RECURVE-D
LICENCE-D	OBVIATE-D	PENANCE-D	PRESAGE-D	RECYCLE-D
LICENSE-D	OCCLUDE-D	PENNATE-D	PRESIDE-D	REDLINE-D
LINEATE-D	OCTUPLE-D	PENTICE-D	PRESUME-D	REEVOKE-D
LIONISE-D	OCULATE-D	PENTISE-D	PRETAPE-D	REFENCE-D
LIONIZE-D	ODORISE-D	PEPTISE-D	PRETYPE-D	REFEREE-D
LIQUATE-D	ODORIZE-D	PEPTIZE-D	PREVENE-D	REFLATE-D
LOZENGE-D	OPERATE-D	PERDURE-D	PREVISE-D	REFORGE-D
MACHINE-D	OUTBAKE-D	PERFUME-D	PREWIRE-D	REFRAME-D
MANACLE-D	OUTCROW-D	PERFUSE-D	PRICKLE-D	REGAUGE-D
MANDATE-D	OUTDARE-D	PERJURE-D	PROBATE-D	REGLAZE-D
MASSAGE-D	OUTDATE-D	PERMUTE-D	PROCURE-D	REGORGE-D
MAULGRE-D	OUTDURE-D	PERTUSE-D	PRODUCE-D	REGRADE-D
MEASURE-D	OUTFACE-D	PERVADE-D	PROFANE-D	REGRATE-D
MEDIATE-D	OUTFIRE-D	PETIOLE-D	PROFILE-D	REGREDE-D

D – End-hooks

REHINGE-D	REVOICE-D	SIGMATE-D	SUFFICE-D	TWATTLE-D
REHOUSE-D	REVOLVE-D	SILENCE-D	SUFFUSE-D	TWEEDLE-D
REIMAGE-D	REWEAVE-D	SINUATE-D	SUICIDE-D	TWIDDLE-D
REISSUE-D	RHOMBOI-D	SIRNAME-D	SULCATE-D	TWINKLE-D
REJOICE-D	RIPOSTE-D	SITUATE-D	SULFATE-D	TWIZZLE-D
REJUDGE-D	ROMANCE-D	SKELLIE-D	SUMMATE-D	TYRANNE-D
RELAPSE-D	ROSETTE-D	SKIFFLE-D	SUNBAKE-D	ULULATE-D
RELEASE-D	RUINATE-D	SKITTLE-D	SUPPOSE-D	UMBRAGE-D
RELIEVE-D	RUMMAGE-D	SKUTTLE-D	SURBASE-D	UNAWAKE-D
REMERGE-D	RUPTURE-D	SKYDIVE-D	SURBATE-D	UNBRACE-D
RENAGUE-D	SALTATE-D	SMOODGE-D	SURFACE-D	UNBRAKE-D
RENEGUE-D	SALVAGE-D	SMUGGLE-D	SURMISE-D	UNCHOKE-D
REPIQUE-D	SARDINE-D	SNABBLE-D	SURNAME-D	UNCLOSE-D
REPLACE-D	SATIATE-D	SNAFFLE-D	SURVIVE-D	UNCRATE-D
REPLATE-D	SCABBLE-D	SNIFFLE-D	SUSPIRE-D	UNCURSE-D
REPLETE-D	SCAMBLE-D	SNIGGLE-D	SWADDLE-D	UNDERGO-D
REPRICE-D	SCANTLE-D	SNIRTLE-D	SWINDGE-D	UNDRAPE-D
REPRIME-D	SCAPPLE-D	SNOOZLE-D	SWINDLE-D	UNFENCE-D
REPRISE-D	SCEDULE-D	SNUFFLE-D	SWINGLE-D	UNGLOVE-D
REPRIVE-D	SCEPTRE-D	SNUGGLE-D	SWIZZLE-D	UNHINGE-D
REPRIZE-D	SCHAPPE-D	SNUZZLE-D	SYMBOLE-D	UNHORSE-D
REPROBE-D	SCHOOLE-D	SOLVATE-D	SYNAPSE-D	UNHOUSE-D
REPROVE-D	SCIENCE-D	SOUFFLE-D	SYRINGE-D	UNITISE-D
REPRYVE-D	SCOURGE-D	SPACKLE-D	TALLAGE-D	UNITIZE-D
REPULSE-D	SCOURSE-D	SPAIRGE-D	TAMARIN-D	UNLOOSE-D
REQUERE-D	SCREEVE-D	SPANGLE-D	TAPPICE-D	UNMITRE-D
REQUIRE-D	SCRIEVE-D	SPARKLE-D	TARTANE-D	UNNERVE-D
REQUITE-D	SCROOGE-D	SPECKLE-D	TEENAGE-D	UNNOBLE-D
REQUOTE-D	SCROUGE-D	SPICATE-D	TERRACE-D	UNPLACE-D
RERAISE-D	SCROWLE-D	SPINDLE-D	TEXTURE-D	UNPLUME-D
REROUTE-D	SCRUPLE-D	SPLODGE-D	THIMBLE-D	UNPURSE-D
RESCALE-D	SCUDDLE-D	SPLURGE-D	TITRATE-D	UNQUOTE-D
RESCORE-D	SCUFFLE-D	SPREAZE-D	TONSURE-D	UNREAVE-D
RESEIZE-D	SCUMBLE-D	SPREEZE-D	TOPLINE-D	UNREEVE-D
RESERVE-D	SCUTTLE-D	SPRINGE-D	TORTURE-D	UNSCALE-D
RESHAPE-D	SDEIGNE-D	SPULYIE-D	TRACHLE-D	UNSENSE-D
RESHAVE-D	SECLUDE-D	SPULZIE-D	TRADUCE-D	UNSHALE-D
RESHINE-D	SECONDE-D	SQUEEZE-D	TRAIPSE-D	UNSHAPE-D
RESLATE-D	SECRETE-D	SQUIDGE-D	TRAMPLE-D	UNSTATE-D
RESOLVE-D	SELVAGE-D	STARTLE-D	TRAPEZE-D	UNTRACE-D
RESPACE-D	SENSATE-D	STATURE-D	TREACLE-D	UNTWINE-D
RESPADE-D	SERIATE-D	STEEPLE-D	TREADLE-D	UNVAILE-D
RESPIRE-D	SERRATE-D	STICKLE-D	TREDDLE-D	UNVOICE-D
RESPITE-D	SERUEWE-D	STIDDIE-D	TREMBLE-D	UPCLOSE-D
RESTAGE-D	SERVEWE-D	STIPPLE-D	TRICKLE-D	UPCURVE-D
RESTATE-D	SERVICE-D	STIPULE-D	TRILOBE-D	UPGRADE-D
RESTOKE-D	SHACKLE-D	STOPPLE-D	TRINDLE-D	UPHEAVE-D
RESTORE-D	SHAMBLE-D	STRAYVE-D	TRIPPLE-D	UPRAISE-D
RESTYLE-D	SHEATHE-D	STRIATE-D	TROUBLE-D	UPROUSE-D
RESURGE-D	SHINGLE-D	STRODLE-D	TROUNCE-D	UPSCALE-D
RETASTE-D	SHMOOSE-D	STUBBLE-D	TRUCKLE-D	UPSTAGE-D
RETINUE-D	SHMOOZE-D	STUMBLE-D	TRUFFLE-D	UPSTARE-D
RETITLE-D	SHOGGLE-D	STYLISE-D	TRUNDLE-D	UPSURGE-D
RETRACE-D	SHOOGIE-D	STYLIZE-D	TRUSTEE-D	UPVALUE-D
RETRATE-D	SHOOGLE-D	SUBDUCE-D	TUILYIE-D	URINATE-D
REUNITE-D	SHRIEVE-D	SUBLATE-D	TUILZIE-D	UTILISE-D
REVALUE-D	SHUFFLE-D	SUBLIME-D	TUMESCE-D	UTILIZE-D
REVENGE-D	SHUTTLE-D	SUBSIDE-D	TURBINE-D	VACUATE-D
REVENUE-D	SIAMESE-D	SUBSUME-D	TWADDLE-D	VALANCE-D
REVERSE-D	SIAMEZE-D	SUBVENE-D	TWANGLE-D	VALUATE-D

VAMOOSE-D	VICIATE-D	WHAISLE-D	WHISTLE-D	WREATHE-D
VAMPIRE-D	VINTAGE-D	WHAIZLE-D	WHITTLE-D	WRESTLE-D
VANDYKE-D	VIOLATE-D	WHEEDLE-D	WHOMBLE-D	WRIGGLE-D
VANTAGE-D	VITIATE-D	WHEENGE-D	WHOMMLE-D	WRINKLE-D
VARIATE-D	WALLEYE-D	WHEEPLE-D	WHUMMLE-D	YCLEEPE-D
VENTURE-D	WARFARE-D	WHEEZLE-D	WOODBIN-D	
VERDURE-D	WARSTLE-D	WHEMMLE-D	WRANGLE-D	
VESTURE-D	WAYFARE-D	WHIFFLE-D	WRASSLE-D	
VIBRATE-D	WELCOME-D	WHIMPLE-D	WRASTLE-D	

Eight letters to nine

ABDICATE-D	APHORISE-D	BEDABBLE-D	CANULATE-D	COMANAGE-D
ABERRATE-D	APHORIZE-D	BEDAGGLE-D	CAPITATE-D	COMEDDLE-D
ABNEGATE-D	APPANAGE-D	BEDAZZLE-D	CAPONISE-D	COMINGLE-D
ABROGATE-D	APPETISE-D	BEDIMPLE-D	CAPONIZE-D	COMMENCE-D
ABSTERGE-D	APPETIZE-D	BEFRINGE-D	CAPRIOLE-D	COMMERCE-D
ACCOLADE-D	APPLIQUE-D	BEFUDDLE-D	CARACOLE-D	COMMERGE-D
ACCORAGE-D	APPRAISE-D	BEGIRDLE-D	CARAPACE-D	COMPESCE-D
ACCOUTRE-D	APRICATE-D	BEGRUDGE-D	CARINATE-D	COMPLETE-D
ACERBATE-D	ARBORISE-D	BEJUMBLE-D	CASEMATE-D	COMPRISE-D
ACIERATE-D	ARBORIZE-D	BELITTLE-D	CASTRATE-D	COMPRIZE-D
ACTIVATE-D	ARCHAISE-D	BEMINGLE-D	CATALYSE-D	COMPULSE-D
ACTIVISE-D	ARCHAIZE-D	BEMUDDLE-D	CATALYZE-D	CONCEIVE-D
ACTIVIZE-D	AREOLATE-D	BEMUFFLE-D	CATENATE-D	CONCLUDE-D
ACULEATE-D	ARILLATE-D	BEMUZZLE-D	CAVITATE-D	CONCRETE-D
ADUNCATE-D	ARMATURE-D	BENEFICE-D	CENTUPLE-D	CONDENSE-D
ADVOCATE-D	ARROGATE-D	BEPIMPLE-D	CHASTISE-D	CONFLATE-D
AFFIANCE-D	ASPERATE-D	BEPRAISE-D	CHIVAREE-D	CONGLOBE-D
AFFRONTE-D	ASPIRATE-D	BESMUDGE-D	CHROMISE-D	CONSERVE-D
AFTEREYE-D	ASSEMBLE-D	BESOOTHE-D	CHROMIZE-D	CONSPIRE-D
AGGRIEVE-D	ASSONATE-D	BESPOUSE-D	CICERONE-D	CONSTATE-D
ALBITISE-D	ASTRINGE-D	BILOBATE-D	CINCTURE-D	CONSTRUE-D
ALBITIZE-D	ATCHIEVE-D	BIRDLIME-D	CIVILISE-D	CONTINUE-D
ALIENATE-D	ATHETISE-D	BLOCKADE-D	CIVILIZE-D	CONTRIVE-D
ALKALISE-D	ATHETIZE-D	BLONDINE-D	CLODPATE-D	CONVERGE-D
ALKALIZE-D	ATMOLYSE-D	BLOVIATE-D	COADMIRE-D	CONVERSE-D
ALKYLATE-D	ATMOLYZE-D	BLUENOSE-D	COALESCE-D	CONVINCE-D
ALLIGATE-D	ATTICISE-D	BOLDFACE-D	COASSUME-D	CONVOLVE-D
ALLOCATE-D	ATTICIZE-D	BOMBARDE-D	COCREATE-D	CONVULSE-D
AMBULATE-D	AUTOLYSE-D	BOTANISE-D	CODERIVE-D	COPULATE-D
AMORTISE-D	AUTOLYZE-D	BOTANIZE-D	COENDURE-D	COQUETTE-D
AMORTIZE-D	AUTOMATE-D	BRATTICE-D	COEQUATE-D	CORDELLE-D
AMPUTATE-D	AUTOTYPE-D	BRETTICE-D	COEVOLVE-D	CORELATE-D
ANGULATE-D	AVIANISE-D	BROMELIA-D	COGITATE-D	CORONATE-D
ANKYLOSE-D	AVIANIZE-D	BULLDOZE-D	COGNOSCE-D	COROTATE-D
ANNALISE-D	BACKBONE-D	BURNOOSE-D	COHOBATE-D	CORVETTE-D
ANNALIZE-D	BACKDATE-D	BURNOUSE-D	COIFFURE-D	CREASOTE-D
ANNOTATE-D	BACKFIRE-D	BUTYLATE-D	COINCIDE-D	CRENELLE-D
ANNOUNCE-D	BADINAGE-D	CALAMINE-D	COINHERE-D	CREOLISE-D
ANNULATE-D	BALDPATE-D	CALCEATE-D	COINSURE-D	CREOLIZE-D
ANTECEDE-D	BANALISE-D	CALORISE-D	COLLAPSE-D	CREOSOTE-D
ANTEDATE-D	BANALIZE-D	CALORIZE-D	COLLOGUE-D	CREVASSE-D
ANTICISE-D	BARBECUE-D	CANALISE-D	COLLOQUE-D	CRISPATE-D
ANTICIZE-D	BARBEQUE-D	CANALIZE-D	COLOCATE-D	CRISTATE-D
ANTIDOTE-D	BAREBONE-D	CANONISE-D	COLONISE-D	CRITIQUE-D
APERTURE-D	BARNACLE-D	CANONIZE-D	COLONIZE-D	CROSSTIE-D
APHETISE-D	BECHANCE-D	CANOODLE-D	COLORISE-D	CRUSTATE-D
APHETIZE-D	BECLOTHE-D	CANTHARI-D	COLORIZE-D	CULTRATE-D

D – End-hooks

CUMULATE-D	DISGRACE-D	EMPLONGE-D	EVALUATE-D	GRADUATE-D
CURARISE-D	DISGRADE-D	EMPURPLE-D	EVANESCE-D	GRAECISE-D
CURARIZE-D	DISGUISE-D	ENCHARGE-D	EVIDENCE-D	GRAECIZE-D
CURLICUE-D	DISHABLE-D	ENCIRCLE-D	EVULGATE-D	GRATINEE-D
CUTINISE-D	DISHORSE-D	ENCLOTHE-D	EXCAVATE-D	GUNKHOLE-D
CUTINIZE-D	DISHOUSE-D	ENCRADLE-D	EXCHANGE-D	HARANGUE-D
DARRAINE-D	DISINURE-D	ENCREASE-D	EXECRATE-D	HARDNOSE-D
DATABASE-D	DISLEAVE-D	ENDAMAGE-D	EXERCISE-D	HARDWIRE-D
DATELINE-D	DISLODGE-D	ENERGISE-D	EXHUMATE-D	HEADLINE-D
DEADLINE-D	DISPENCE-D	ENERGIZE-D	EXORCISE-D	HEBETATE-D
DEAERATE-D	DISPENSE-D	ENERVATE-D	EXORCIZE-D	HEBRAISE-D
DEBOUCHE-D	DISPERSE-D	ENFEEBLE-D	EXPEDITE-D	HEBRAIZE-D
DEBRUISE-D	DISPLACE-D	ENFIERCE-D	EXTUBATE-D	HEMOLYSE-D
DECENTRE-D	DISPLODE-D	ENFILADE-D	EXUVIATE-D	HEMOLYZE-D
DECIMATE-D	DISPLUME-D	ENGIRDLE-D	FABULATE-D	HEPATISE-D
DECLASSE-D	DISPONGE-D	ENGRIEVE-D	FABULISE-D	HEPATIZE-D
DECORATE-D	DISPRIZE-D	ENGROOVE-D	FABULIZE-D	HERNIATE-D
DECOUPLE-D	DISPROVE-D	ENHEARSE-D	FANTASIE-D	HESITATE-D
DECREASE-D	DISPUNGE-D	ENKINDLE-D	FARADISE-D	HOMINISE-D
DEDICATE-D	DISPURSE-D	ENLUMINE-D	FARADIZE-D	HOMINIZE-D
DEFECATE-D	DISSEISE-D	ENRAUNGE-D	FASCIATE-D	HOOKNOSE-D
DEFILADE-D	DISSEIZE-D	ENSAMPLE-D	FASCICLE-D	HOTHOUSE-D
DEGREASE-D	DISSERVE-D	ENSCONCE-D	FATIGATE-D	HUMANISE-D
DEIONISE-D	DISSOLVE-D	ENSHRINE-D	FEDERATE-D	HUMANIZE-D
DEIONIZE-D	DISSUADE-D	ENSILAGE-D	FEMINISE-D	IDEALISE-D
DELEGATE-D	DISTANCE-D	ENSPHERE-D	FEMINIZE-D	IDEALIZE-D
DELIBATE-D	DISTASTE-D	ENSWATHE-D	FIBERISE-D	ILLUMINE-D
DEMONISE-D	DISUNITE-D	ENTANGLE-D	FIBERIZE-D	IMMANTLE-D
DEMONIZE-D	DISVALUE-D	ENTHRONE-D	FILAGREE-D	IMMINGLE-D
DENATURE-D	DIVAGATE-D	ENTRANCE-D	FILIGREE-D	IMMOLATE-D
DENOTATE-D	DIVINISE-D	ENVEIGLE-D	FILTRATE-D	IMMUNISE-D
DENOUNCE-D	DIVINIZE-D	ENVELOPE-D	FINALISE-D	IMMUNIZE-D
DENUDATE-D	DOMICILE-D	ENVISAGE-D	FINALIZE-D	IMPLEDGE-D
DEPEOPLE-D	DOMINATE-D	EPILOGUE-D	FLATLINE-D	IMPLUNGE-D
DEPILATE-D	DOWNSIZE-D	EQUALISE-D	FLUIDISE-D	IMPRESSE-D
DEPURATE-D	DOWNZONE-D	EQUALIZE-D	FLUIDIZE-D	IMPURPLE-D
DEPUTISE-D	DUBITATE-D	EQUIPAGE-D	FOCALISE-D	INCHOATE-D
DEPUTIZE-D	DUCHESSE-D	ERADIATE-D	FOCALIZE-D	INCORPSE-D
DEROGATE-D	DUNGAREE-D	ERGOTISE-D	FOOTNOTE-D	INCREASE-D
DESCRIBE-D	DYNAMISE-D	ERGOTIZE-D	FOREBODE-D	INCUBATE-D
DESCRIVE-D	DYNAMITE-D	ERUCTATE-D	FOREDATE-D	INDAGATE-D
DESOLATE-D	DYNAMIZE-D	ESCALADE-D	FORENAME-D	INDICATE-D
DETHRONE-D	EBIONISE-D	ESCALATE-D	FORHAILE-D	INDURATE-D
DETONATE-D	EBIONIZE-D	ESCALOPE-D	FORHOOIE-D	INFAMISE-D
DEVELOPE-D	ECHINATE-D	ESTIMATE-D	FORJUDGE-D	INFAMIZE-D
DIAGNOSE-D	EFFIERCE-D	ESTIVATE-D	FORWASTE-D	INFRINGE-D
DIALOGUE-D	ELONGATE-D	ESTRANGE-D	FRACTURE-D	INGROOVE-D
DIAPAUSE-D	ELUVIATE-D	ETERNISE-D	FRANCISE-D	INHEARSE-D
DIGITATE-D	EMACIATE-D	ETERNIZE-D	FRANCIZE-D	INHUMATE-D
DIGITISE-D	EMBATTLE-D	ETHERISE-D	FREEBASE-D	INITIATE-D
DIGITIZE-D	EMBEZZLE-D	ETHERIZE-D	FUMIGATE-D	INNOVATE-D
DIMERISE-D	EMBOLISE-D	ETHICISE-D	GANGRENE-D	INSCONCE-D
DIMERIZE-D	EMBOLIZE-D	ETHICIZE-D	GARGOYLE-D	INSCRIBE-D
DISABUSE-D	EMENDATE-D	ETHYLATE-D	GARROTTE-D	INSHRINE-D
DISAGREE-D	EMIGRATE-D	ETIOLATE-D	GEFUFFLE-D	INSOLATE-D
DISBURSE-D	EMMARBLE-D	EULOGISE-D	GEMINATE-D	INSPHERE-D
DISCIPLE-D	EMPEOPLE-D	EULOGIZE-D	GENERATE-D	INSTANCE-D
DISCLOSE-D	EMPERISE-D	EUPHUISE-D	GESNERIA-D	INSULATE-D
DISCOURE-D	EMPERIZE-D	EUPHUIZE-D	GLACIATE-D	INSWATHE-D
DISGORGE-D	EMPIERCE-D	EVACUATE-D	GLISSADE-D	INTHRONE-D

INTIMATE-D	LOGICISE-D	MISSPACE-D	ORDINATE-D	OVERTIRE-D
INTITULE-D	LOGICIZE-D	MISSTATE-D	ORGANISE-D	OVERTURE-D
INTONATE-D	LOOPHOLE-D	MISSTYLE-D	ORGANIZE-D	OVERTYPE-D
INTRIGUE-D	LORICATE-D	MISTITLE-D	OSCITATE-D	OVERURGE-D
INTUBATE-D	LUNULATE-D	MISTRACE-D	OSCULATE-D	OVERVOTE-D
INUNDATE-D	LUSTRATE-D	MISVALUE-D	OUTARGUE-D	PAGANISE-D
INVEAGLE-D	LYOPHILE-D	MITIGATE-D	OUTBLAZE-D	PAGANIZE-D
INVEIGLE-D	LYRICISE-D	MOBILISE-D	OUTBRAVE-D	PAGINATE-D
INVOCATE-D	LYRICIZE-D	MOBILIZE-D	OUTBRIBE-D	PALISADE-D
INVOLUTE-D	MACARISE-D	MODERATE-D	OUTBULGE-D	PALLIATE-D
IODINATE-D	MACARIZE-D	MODULATE-D	OUTCASTE-D	PAPALISE-D
IRRIGATE-D	MACERATE-D	MONETISE-D	OUTCHIDE-D	PAPALIZE-D
IRRITATE-D	MACULATE-D	MONETIZE-D	OUTCURSE-D	PARALYSE-D
JACULATE-D	MADERISE-D	MONOTONE-D	OUTDANCE-D	PARALYZE-D
JALOUSIE-D	MADERIZE-D	MOONFACE-D	OUTDODGE-D	PATINATE-D
JAPANISE-D	MAINLINE-D	MORALISE-D	OUTFABLE-D	PATINISE-D
JAPANIZE-D	MALAXATE-D	MORALIZE-D	OUTFENCE-D	PATINIZE-D
JAROVISE-D	MALLEATE-D	MORTGAGE-D	OUTGLARE-D	PATRIATE-D
JAROVIZE-D	MANICURE-D	MOTIVATE-D	OUTGUIDE-D	PECULATE-D
JAUNDICE-D	MARINADE-D	MOTORISE-D	OUTPLACE-D	PEDICURE-D
JEALOUSE-D	MARINATE-D	MOTORIZE-D	OUTPRICE-D	PEDIGREE-D
JOINTURE-D	MASSACRE-D	MUCKRAKE-D	OUTPRIZE-D	PEDUNCLE-D
JUBILATE-D	MATURATE-D	MURICATE-D	OUTQUOTE-D	PEJORATE-D
JUGULATE-D	MAXIMISE-D	MUSTACHE-D	OUTRAISE-D	PENALISE-D
JULIENNE-D	MAXIMIZE-D	MUTILATE-D	OUTRANGE-D	PENALIZE-D
JUMBOISE-D	MEDICATE-D	NASALISE-D	OUTSCORE-D	PENSIONE-D
JUMBOIZE-D	MEDICINE-D	NASALIZE-D	OUTSERVE-D	PERCEIVE-D
KEELHALE-D	MEDITATE-D	NAUSEATE-D	OUTSHAME-D	PERMEATE-D
KEFUFFLE-D	MELANISE-D	NAVIGATE-D	OUTSHINE-D	PERORATE-D
KEYSTONE-D	MELANIZE-D	NEBULISE-D	OUTSKATE-D	PEROXIDE-D
KLONDIKE-D	MELODISE-D	NEBULIZE-D	OUTSMILE-D	PERSPIRE-D
KLONDYKE-D	MELODIZE-D	NECKLACE-D	OUTSMOKE-D	PERSUADE-D
KREASOTE-D	MEMBRANE-D	NEGATIVE-D	OUTSNORE-D	PERSWADE-D
KREOSOTE-D	MEMORISE-D	NICKNAME-D	OUTSTARE-D	PERVIATE-D
LACERATE-D	MEMORIZE-D	NICOTINE-D	OUTSTATE-D	PHYSIQUE-D
LAMBASTE-D	METALISE-D	NODALISE-D	OUTTRADE-D	PICOWAVE-D
LAMINATE-D	METALIZE-D	NODALIZE-D	OUTVALUE-D	PINAFORE-D
LANGUAGE-D	MICROCAR-D	NOMADISE-D	OUTVOICE-D	PINNACLE-D
LAPIDATE-D	MILITATE-D	NOMADIZE-D	OUTWASTE-D	PINTSIZE-D
LATERISE-D	MINIMISE-D	NOMINATE-D	OVERBAKE-D	PIPELINE-D
LATERIZE-D	MINIMIZE-D	NOSEDIVE-D	OVERCROW-D	PIRLICUE-D
LATINISE-D	MISATONE-D	NOTARISE-D	OVERCURE-D	PLEASURE-D
LATINIZE-D	MISFRAME-D	NOTARIZE-D	OVERDARE-D	POLARISE-D
LAUREATE-D	MISGAUGE-D	NOVELISE-D	OVERDOSE-D	POLARIZE-D
LEGALISE-D	MISGRADE-D	NOVELIZE-D	OVERHALE-D	POLEMISE-D
LEGALIZE-D	MISGUIDE-D	NUCLEATE-D	OVERHATE-D	POLEMIZE-D
LEVERAGE-D	MISJUDGE-D	NUMERATE-D	OVERHEAR-D	POLONISE-D
LEVIGATE-D	MISLEEKE-D	OBDURATE-D	OVERHOPE-D	POLONIZE-D
LEVITATE-D	MISLODGE-D	OBLIGATE-D	OVERHYPE-D	POPULATE-D
LIBERATE-D	MISMETRE-D	OBSOLETE-D	OVERLADE-D	PORPOISE-D
LIGATURE-D	MISPARSE-D	OBTURATE-D	OVERLIVE-D	PORTIERE-D
LIGULATE-D	MISPLACE-D	OBVOLUTE-D	OVERLOVE-D	POSTCODE-D
LINOTYPE-D	MISPOISE-D	OCCUPATE-D	OVERMINE-D	POSTDATE-D
LIQUESCE-D	MISPRICE-D	OCELLATE-D	OVERNAME-D	POSTPONE-D
LITIGATE-D	MISPRISE-D	OPALESCE-D	OVERRAKE-D	POSTPOSE-D
LOBULATE-D	MISPRIZE-D	OPPILATE-D	OVERRATE-D	POULTICE-D
LOCALISE-D	MISQUOTE-D	OPSONISE-D	OVERRULE-D	POURTRAY-D
LOCALIZE-D	MISRAISE-D	OPSONIZE-D	OVERSAVE-D	PRACTICE-D
LOCOMOTE-D	MISROUTE-D	OPTIMISE-D	OVERSIZE-D	PRACTISE-D
LOCULATE-D	MISSHAPE-D	OPTIMIZE-D	OVERTIME-D	PREAMBLE-D

D – End-hooks

PRECLUDE-D	RECHANGE-D	REREVISE-D	SELVEDGE-D	SQUIGGLE-D
PREGUIDE-D	RECHARGE-D	RESADDLE-D	SEMIDOME-D	SQUILGEE-D
PREJUDGE-D	RECIRCLE-D	RESALUTE-D	SEMINATE-D	STAGNATE-D
PREMIERE-D	RECLOTHE-D	RESAMPLE-D	SEMINOMA-D	STAMPEDE-D
PRENTICE-D	RECOUPLE-D	RESECURE-D	SENTENCE-D	STARGAZE-D
PREPASTE-D	RECOURSE-D	RESEMBLE-D	SEPARATE-D	STELLATE-D
PREPENSE-D	RECREATE-D	RESETTLE-D	SEPTUPLE-D	STOCKADE-D
PREPLACE-D	REDAMAGE-D	RESINATE-D	SEQUENCE-D	STRADDLE-D
PREPRICE-D	REDARGUE-D	RESINISE-D	SERENADE-D	STRAGGLE-D
PRERINSE-D	REDECIDE-D	RESINIZE-D	SEROTYPE-D	STRANGLE-D
PRESCORE-D	REDEFINE-D	RESONATE-D	SEXTUPLE-D	STRAVAGE-D
PRESERVE-D	REDIVIDE-D	RESOURCE-D	SHAUCHLE-D	STREIGNE-D
PRESHAPE-D	REDOUBLE-D	RESPLICE-D	SHIVAREE-D	STRICKLE-D
PRESLICE-D	REEMERGE-D	RESTABLE-D	SHOWCASE-D	STRIDDLE-D
PRESOLVE-D	REENGAGE-D	RETACKLE-D	SHUNPIKE-D	STRINKLE-D
PRESSURE-D	REEXPOSE-D	RETRIEVE-D	SIBILATE-D	STRODDLE-D
PRESTORE-D	REFIGURE-D	RIDICULE-D	SIDELINE-D	STRUGGLE-D
PRETASTE-D	REFRINGE-D	RIGIDISE-D	SIDERATE-D	STUPRATE-D
PREUNITE-D	REGELATE-D	RIGIDIZE-D	SILICATE-D	SUBERISE-D
PREVALUE-D	REGROOVE-D	RIVALISE-D	SIMILISE-D	SUBERIZE-D
PRIMROSE-D	REGULATE-D	RIVALIZE-D	SIMILIZE-D	SUBITISE-D
PRODNOSE-D	REGULISE-D	ROBOTISE-D	SIMONISE-D	SUBITIZE-D
PROGNOSE-D	REGULIZE-D	ROBOTIZE-D	SIMONIZE-D	SUBLEASE-D
PROGRADE-D	REHANDLE-D	ROMANISE-D	SIMULATE-D	SUBMERGE-D
PROLAPSE-D	REHEARSE-D	ROMANIZE-D	SINICISE-D	SUBMERSE-D
PROLOGUE-D	REIGNITE-D	ROSTRATE-D	SINICIZE-D	SUBSERVE-D
PROLONGE-D	REILLUME-D	ROTAVATE-D	SIRENISE-D	SUBTITLE-D
PROMULGE-D	REIMPOSE-D	ROTOVATE-D	SIRENIZE-D	SUBTRUDE-D
PROROGUE-D	REINCITE-D	ROULETTE-D	SIRONISE-D	SUBVERSE-D
PROTRUDE-D	REINDUCE-D	ROYALISE-D	SIRONIZE-D	SUFFLATE-D
PTYALISE-D	REINFUSE-D	ROYALIZE-D	SLIPCASE-D	SULPHATE-D
PTYALIZE-D	REINJURE-D	RUMINATE-D	SNOWSHOE-D	SUNBATHE-D
PULVILLE-D	REINSURE-D	RURALISE-D	SOBERISE-D	SUPERATE-D
PUMICATE-D	REINVADE-D	RURALIZE-D	SOBERIZE-D	SUPINATE-D
PUNCTATE-D	REINVITE-D	SABOTAGE-D	SODOMISE-D	SURCEASE-D
PUNCTURE-D	REINVOKE-D	SAGINATE-D	SODOMIZE-D	SURPLICE-D
PURCHASE-D	REJUGGLE-D	SALINISE-D	SOLARISE-D	SURPRISE-D
PURLICUE-D	REKINDLE-D	SALINIZE-D	SOLARIZE-D	SURPRIZE-D
PYRITISE-D	RELEGATE-D	SALIVATE-D	SOLECISE-D	SYLLABLE-D
PYRITIZE-D	RELOCATE-D	SANGUINE-D	SOLECIZE-D	TABULATE-D
PYROLISE-D	RELUMINE-D	SANITATE-D	SOLIDATE-D	TAILGATE-D
PYROLIZE-D	REMARQUE-D	SANITISE-D	SOMNIATE-D	TAILPIPE-D
PYROLYSE-D	REMIGATE-D	SANITIZE-D	SONICATE-D	TALLIATE-D
PYROLYZE-D	RENATURE-D	SAPPHIRE-D	SORORISE-D	TARTRATE-D
QUADRATE-D	RENEGADE-D	SATIRISE-D	SORORIZE-D	TELETYPE-D
QUAGMIRE-D	RENFORCE-D	SATIRIZE-D	SPECIATE-D	TELEVISE-D
QUANTISE-D	RENOUNCE-D	SATURATE-D	SPECTATE-D	TENTACLE-D
QUANTIZE-D	RENOVATE-D	SCAVENGE-D	SPOLIATE-D	TETANISE-D
RACEMISE-D	RENVERSE-D	SCHEDULE-D	SPRACKLE-D	TETANIZE-D
RACEMIZE-D	REOPPOSE-D	SCHMOOSE-D	SPRADDLE-D	THEORISE-D
RADICATE-D	REPARTEE-D	SCHMOOZE-D	SPRANGLE-D	THEORIZE-D
RAMPAUGE-D	REPEOPLE-D	SCLEROSE-D	SPRATTLE-D	THRAPPLE-D
REACCEDE-D	REPERUSE-D	SCRABBLE-D	SPREATHE-D	THROPPLE-D
REACCUSE-D	REPHRASE-D	SCRAMBLE-D	SPREETHE-D	THROTTLE-D
READVISE-D	REPLEDGE-D	SCRATTLE-D	SPRINGAL-D	TIDIVATE-D
REAROUSE-D	REPLUNGE-D	SCRIBBLE-D	SPRINKLE-D	TINCTURE-D
REASSUME-D	REPREEVE-D	SCRIGGLE-D	SPUILZIE-D	TINPLATE-D
REASSURE-D	REPRIEVE-D	SCROUNGE-D	SQUABBLE-D	TIPPYTOE-D
REBOTTLE-D	REPURSUE-D	SCROWDGE-D	SQUATTLE-D	TITIVATE-D
RECENTRE-D	REQUOYLE-D	SCRUMPLE-D	SQUEEGEE-D	TITUBATE-D

TOLERATE-D	TUTORISE-D	UNIONIZE-D	URBANIZE-D	VIRILIZE-D
TORQUATE-D	TUTORIZE-D	UNIVALVE-D	URTICATE-D	VITALISE-D
TOTALISE-D	ULCERATE-D	UNMANTLE-D	VAGINATE-D	VITALIZE-D
TOTALIZE-D	ULTIMATE-D	UNMINGLE-D	VALIDATE-D	VOCALISE-D
TRABEATE-D	UNBOTTLE-D	UNMUFFLE-D	VALORISE-D	VOCALIZE-D
TRAMLINE-D	UNBRIDLE-D	UNMUZZLE-D	VALORIZE-D	VOLITATE-D
TRANSUDE-D	UNBUCKLE-D	UNPEOPLE-D	VAMBRACE-D	VOLPLANE-D
TRANSUME-D	UNBUNDLE-D	UNPRAISE-D	VAPORISE-D	VOLUMISE-D
TRAUCHLE-D	UNCHARGE-D	UNPUZZLE-D	VAPORIZE-D	VOLUMIZE-D
TRAVERSE-D	UNCINATE-D	UNRETIRE-D	VAPULATE-D	VOUTSAFE-D
TREASURE-D	UNCLOTHE-D	UNRIDDLE-D	VARICOSE-D	VOWELISE-D
TREPHINE-D	UNCOUPLE-D	UNRUFFLE-D	VARITYPE-D	VOWELIZE-D
TRESSURE-D	UNCREATE-D	UNSADDLE-D	VEGETATE-D	WARDROBE-D
TRIANGLE-D	UNDAZZLE-D	UNSETTLE-D	VELARISE-D	WHEYFACE-D
TRICYCLE-D	UNDERAGE-D	UNSLUICE-D	VELARIZE-D	WOMANISE-D
TRITIATE-D	UNDERUSE-D	UNSPHERE-D	VENENATE-D	WOMANIZE-D
TRIVALVE-D	UNDOUBLE-D	UNSWATHE-D	VENERATE-D	WORMHOLE-D
TRUNCATE-D	UNDULATE-D	UNTACKLE-D	VERJUICE-D	
TUBERCLE-D	UNHEARSE-D	UNTANGLE-D	VESICATE-D	
TUBULATE-D	UNICYCLE-D	UNTHRONE-D	VIGNETTE-D	
TUNICATE-D	UNIONISE-D	URBANISE-D	VIRILISE-D	

E – Front-hooks

Two letters to three

E-AN	E-CH	E-ME	E-ON	E-WE
E-AR	E-EL	E-MO	E-RE	E-YE
E-AS	E-EN	E-MU	E-ST	
E-AT	E-GO	E-NE	E-TA	

Three letters to four

E-ACH	E-CRU	E-KED	E-PEE	E-TAT
E-ALE	E-DIT	E-MES	E-PIC	E-TEN
E-ARD	E-ECH	E-MEU	E-POS	E-THE
E-ARS	E-ELS	E-MIC	E-RAS	E-TIC
E-AVE	E-GAD	E-MIR	E-RED	E-TUI
E-BON	E-GAL	E-MOS	E-RES	E-UGH
E-CAD	E-GIS	E-MUS	E-REV	E-VET
E-CHE	E-GOS	E-NEW	E-SKY	E-VOE
E-COD	E-IDE	E-NOW	E-SPY	E-YEN
E-COS	E-ISH	E-ONS	E-TAS	E-YES

Four letters to five

E-AGER	E-DUCE	E-LITE	E-MEUS	E-PEES
E-ALES	E-DUCT	E-LOGE	E-MIRS	E-PICS
E-ARDS	E-EVEN	E-LOGY	E-MONG	E-POXY
E-ARED	E-GADS	E-LOIN	E-MOTE	E-PROM
E-AVES	E-GEST	E-LOPE	E-MOVE	E-QUID
E-BONY	E-HING	E-LOPS	E-MULE	E-QUIP
E-BOOK	E-IKON	E-LUDE	E-MURE	E-RASE
E-CADS	E-KING	E-LUTE	E-NEMA	E-REVS
E-CLAT	E-LAIN	E-MACS	E-NEWS	E-RICK
E-CRUS	E-LAND	E-MAIL	E-NORM	E-RING
E-DICT	E-LATE	E-MEER	E-NOWS	E-RODE
E-DITS	E-LINT	E-MEND	E-PACT	E-ROSE

D – End-hooks

E-SCAR	E-STOP	E-TUIS	E-VENT	E-VITE
E-SCOT	E-TAPE	E-TWEE	E-VERT	E-WEST
E-SILE	E-TATS	E-UGHS	E-VERY	E-WHOW
E-SKER	E-TENS	E-VADE	E-VETS	

Five letters to six

E-AGERS	E-LANDS	E-MOTES	E-QUIDS	E-SPRIT
E-AGLET	E-LAPSE	E-MOVED	E-QUINE	E-STATE
E-ASTER	E-LATED	E-MOVES	E-QUIPS	E-STEEM
E-BOOKS	E-LATER	E-MULED	E-RASED	E-STOPS
E-CARTE	E-LEGIT	E-MULES	E-RASER	E-STRAY
E-CHARD	E-LICIT	E-MURED	E-RASES	E-STRUM
E-CLATS	E-LINTS	E-MURES	E-RICKS	E-TALON
E-CLOSE	E-LITES	E-NATES	E-RODED	E-TAMIN
E-CURIE	E-LOGES	E-NEMAS	E-RODES	E-TAPES
E-DICTS	E-LOINS	E-NERVE	E-ROSES	E-TERNE
E-DITED	E-LOPED	E-NEWED	E-SCAPE	E-THANE
E-DUCES	E-LOPER	E-NODAL	E-SCARP	E-TOILE
E-DUCTS	E-LOPES	E-NOSES	E-SCARS	E-TRIER
E-ECHED	E-LUDES	E-PACTS	E-SCOTS	E-TYPIC
E-ECHES	E-LUTED	E-PARCH	E-SCROW	E-VADED
E-EVENS	E-LUTES	E-PERDU	E-SCUDO	E-VADES
E-GALLY	E-MAILS	E-PICAL	E-SILES	E-VENTS
E-GESTS	E-MEERS	E-POSES	E-SKERS	E-VERTS
E-IDENT	E-MENDS	E-PRISE	E-SKIES	E-VILER
E-IDOLA	E-MERGE	E-PROMS	E-SPIAL	E-VOLVE
E-IKONS	E-MESES	E-PULIS	E-SPIED	
E-ITHER	E-METIC	E-QUANT	E-SPIER	
E-LANCE	E-MOTED	E-QUATE	E-SPIES	

Six letters to seven

E-AGLETS	E-LECTOR	E-MULING	E-SCAPES	E-TALONS
E-ASTERN	E-LEGIST	E-MUNGED	E-SCARPS	E-TAMINE
E-ASTERS	E-LEGITS	E-MURING	E-SCRIBE	E-TAMINS
E-BAYING	E-LICHES	E-NATION	E-SCROLL	E-TERNAL
E-BONIST	E-LOGIES	E-NERVED	E-SCROWS	E-THANES
E-CARTES	E-LOPERS	E-NERVES	E-SERINE	E-TOILES
E-CHARDS	E-LOPING	E-NEWING	E-SPIALS	E-TRIERS
E-CLOSED	E-LUTING	E-PERDUE	E-SPIERS	E-UPHROE
E-CLOSES	E-MAILED	E-PICENE	E-SPOUSE	E-VADING
E-COTYPE	E-MENDED	E-QUANTS	E-SPRITS	E-VANISH
E-CURIES	E-MENDER	E-QUINES	E-SPYING	E-VENTED
E-DENTAL	E-MERGED	E-QUITES	E-SQUIRE	E-VENTER
E-DITING	E-MERGES	E-RASERS	E-STATED	E-VERTED
E-ECHING	E-METICS	E-RASING	E-STATES	E-VICTOR
E-IRENIC	E-MICATE	E-RASURE	E-STEEMS	E-VILEST
E-LANCED	E-MONGST	E-RECTOR	E-STOVER	E-VOLUTE
E-LANCES	E-MOTION	E-RODENT	E-STRAYS	E-VOLVED
E-LAPSED	E-MOTIVE	E-RODING	E-STRICH	E-VOLVES
E-LAPSES	E-MOVING	E-SCAPED	E-STRUMS	

Seven letters to eight

E-BONISTS	E-CLOSING	E-COTYPES	E-LANCING	E-LECTION
E-CAUDATE	E-COSTATE	E-DENTATE	E-LAPSING	E-LECTORS

E-LEGISTS	E-MISSION	E-RECTION	E-SPOUSAL	E-VACUATE
E-LEVATOR	E-MISSIVE	E-RECTORS	E-SPOUSED	E-VALUATE
E-MAILING	E-MOTIONS	E-RODENTS	E-SPOUSES	E-VENTERS
E-MENDERS	E-MUNGING	E-SCALADE	E-SQUIRED	E-VENTING
E-MENDING	E-NATIONS	E-SCALADO	E-SQUIRES	E-VERSION
E-MERGING	E-NERVATE	E-SCALIER	E-STATING	E-VERTING
E-MERSION	E-NERVING	E-SCALLOP	E-STEEMED	E-VICTORS
E-METICAL	E-PHORATE	E-SCAPING	E-STOPPED	E-VOCABLE
E-MICATED	E-PICENES	E-SCARPED	E-STOVERS	E-VOLUTED
E-MICATES	E-QUALITY	E-SCRIBED	E-STRANGE	E-VOLUTES
E-MICTION	E-QUIPPED	E-SCRIBES	E-STRAYED	E-VOLVING
E-MIGRANT	E-QUIPPER	E-SCROLLS	E-TAMINES	E-VULGATE
E-MIGRATE	E-RADIATE	E-SERINES	E-TYPICAL	
E-MISSILE	E-RASURES	E-SPECIAL	E-UPHROES	

Eight letters to nine

E-CARINATE	E-MICATING	E-RADIATED	E-STEEMING	E-VANISHED
E-COMMERCE	E-MICTIONS	E-RADIATES	E-STOPPAGE	E-VANISHES
E-GRESSING	E-MIGRANTS	E-RADICANT	E-STOPPING	E-VENTINGS
E-IRENICAL	E-MIGRATED	E-RADICATE	E-STRANGER	E-VENTLESS
E-IRENICON	E-MIGRATES	E-RECTIONS	E-STRANGES	E-VERSIONS
E-JACULATE	E-MISSIONS	E-ROSTRATE	E-STRAYING	E-VINCIBLE
E-LATERITE	E-MOTIONAL	E-SCALADES	E-STRICHES	E-VINCIBLY
E-LECTIONS	E-MOTIVITY	E-SCALLOPS	E-THIONINE	E-VOCATION
E-LECTRESS	E-NUCLEATE	E-SCARPING	E-VACUATED	E-VOCATIVE
E-LEVATORS	E-NUMERATE	E-SCRIBING	E-VACUATES	E-VOLUTION
E-LOCUTION	E-PHORATES	E-SPOUSALS	E-VAGINATE	E-VULGATES
E-LOCUTORY	E-PICRITIC	E-SPOUSING	E-VALUABLE	
E-MENDABLE	E-PISTOLET	E-SQUIRESS	E-VALUATED	
E-MERGENCE	E-QUIPPERS	E-SQUIRING	E-VALUATES	
E-MERSIONS	E-QUIPPING	E-STABLISH	E-VALUATOR	

E – End-hooks

Two letters to three

AG-E	DE-E	HI-E	NY-E	SH-E
AL-E	DI-E	HO-E	OB-E	TA-E
AN-E	DO-E	ID-E	OD-E	TE-E
AR-E	EM-E	JO-E	ON-E	TI-E
AT-E	EN-E	KA-E	OP-E	TO-E
AW-E	ER-E	KY-E	OR-E	UR-E
AX-E	FA-E	LI-E	OS-E	US-E
AY-E	FE-E	MA-E	OW-E	UT-E
BE-E	GI-E	ME-E	OY-E	WE-E
BY-E	GO-E	MO-E	PE-E	WO-E
CH-E	GU-E	NA-E	PI-E	YA-E
DA-E	HA-E	NE-E	RE-E	

Three letters to four

ABB-E	AIN-E	ANT-E	BAR-E	BET-E
ABY-E	AKE-E	ARS-E	BAS-E	BID-E
ACH-E	ALA-E	AWE-E	BAT-E	BIN-E
ADZ-E	ALB-E	BAD-E	BAY-E	BIS-E
AGE-E	ALE-E	BAL-E	BED-E	BIT-E
AID-E	AMI-E	BAN-E	BEN-E	BIZ-E

E – Front-hooks

BOD-E	FER-E	LAT-E	NON-E	SAX-E
BOK-E	FET-E	LAV-E	NOS-E	SEL-E
BON-E	FIL-E	LEK-E	NOT-E	SEN-E
BOR-E	FIN-E	LEV-E	OBO-E	SER-E
BRA-E	FIR-E	LIN-E	OCH-E	SIC-E
BUT-E	FLU-E	LIP-E	OOS-E	SIK-E
CAD-E	FON-E	LIT-E	ORF-E	SIN-E
CAG-E	FOR-E	LOB-E	PAC-E	SIP-E
CAM-E	FRA-E	LOD-E	PAL-E	SIR-E
CAN-E	FRO-E	LOG-E	PAN-E	SIT-E
CAP-E	FUM-E	LOP-E	PAP-E	SNY-E
CAR-E	GAD-E	LOR-E	PAR-E	SOL-E
CAT-E	GAG-E	LOS-E	PAS-E	SOM-E
CEP-E	GAL-E	LOT-E	PAT-E	SON-E
CID-E	GAM-E	LOW-E	PAV-E	SPA-E
CIT-E	GAN-E	LUD-E	PEN-E	STY-E
COD-E	GAP-E	LUG-E	PER-E	SUP-E
COL-E	GAR-E	LUR-E	PIC-E	SUR-E
CON-E	GAT-E	LUX-E	PIN-E	SYN-E
COP-E	GEN-E	LYM-E	PIP-E	TAK-E
COR-E	GIB-E	MAC-E	PIS-E	TAM-E
COS-E	GIT-E	MAD-E	PLU-E	TAN-E
COT-E	GON-E	MAG-E	POL-E	TAP-E
COZ-E	GOR-E	MAK-E	POM-E	TAR-E
CRU-E	GUL-E	MAL-E	POP-E	TAT-E
CUB-E	HAD-E	MAN-E	POS-E	TEL-E
CUR-E	HAM-E	MAR-E	POT-E	TEN-E
CUT-E	HAT-E	MAS-E	PRE-E	TET-E
DAL-E	HEM-E	MAT-E	PUB-E	THE-E
DAM-E	HER-E	MEM-E	PUL-E	TIC-E
DEB-E	HET-E	MEN-E	PUR-E	TID-E
DEL-E	HID-E	MES-E	RAD-E	TIG-E
DEN-E	HOM-E	MET-E	RAG-E	TIL-E
DIM-E	HON-E	MIC-E	RAP-E	TIN-E
DIN-E	HOP-E	MIL-E	RAS-E	TIT-E
DIT-E	HOS-E	MIM-E	RAT-E	TOG-E
DIV-E	HOT-E	MIR-E	RED-E	TOM-E
DOG-E	HOW-E	MIS-E	RET-E	TON-E
DOL-E	HUG-E	MOB-E	RID-E	TOP-E
DOM-E	HYP-E	MOD-E	RIF-E	TOR-E
DON-E	IDE-E	MOL-E	RIM-E	TOT-E
DOP-E	JAK-E	MOM-E	RIN-E	TRY-E
DOR-E	JAP-E	MOP-E	RIP-E	TUB-E
DOS-E	JET-E	MOR-E	RIT-E	TUN-E
DOT-E	JIB-E	MOS-E	ROB-E	TWA-E
DUD-E	JOB-E	MOT-E	ROD-E	TYE-E
DUN-E	JOL-E	MOU-E	ROK-E	URD-E
DUP-E	JUT-E	MOZ-E	ROT-E	UVA-E
EAS-E	KAI-E	MUS-E	RUB-E	VAN-E
ECH-E	KAM-E	MUT-E	RUD-E	VAR-E
ELS-E	KET-E	NAB-E	RUM-E	VAS-E
ERN-E	KIN-E	NAM-E	RUN-E	VIA-E
ESS-E	KIP-E	NAN-E	SAB-E	VID-E
ETH-E	KIT-E	NAP-E	SAD-E	VIN-E
EVO-E	KOR-E	NET-E	SAG-E	VIS-E
FAD-E	LAC-E	NID-E	SAL-E	VOL-E
FAN-E	LAD-E	NIT-E	SAM-E	WAD-E
FAR-E	LAM-E	NIX-E	SAN-E	WAG-E
FAT-E	LAR-E	NOD-E	SAT-E	WAN-E
FEM-E	LAS-E	NOM-E	SAV-E	WAR-E

WAS-E	WHA-E	WOK-E	YOD-E	ZIN-E
WAT-E	WIN-E	YAR-E	YOK-E	ZIT-E
WAW-E	WIS-E	YGO-E	YOW-E	
WEX-E	WIT-E	YIP-E	YUK-E	

Four letters to five

ABAS-E	BRED-E	CRUS-E	GING-E	LEES-E
ABID-E	BRER-E	CURS-E	GLAD-E	LEFT-E
AGEN-E	BRIN-E	CYMA-E	GLED-E	LENS-E
AGOG-E	BRIS-E	DAUB-E	GLID-E	LEVE-E
AGON-E	BROS-E	DEAR-E	GLIM-E	LITH-E
AINE-E	BRUT-E	DEER-E	GLOB-E	LONG-E
ALAN-E	BUFF-E	DEEV-E	GLUM-E	LOOS-E
ALBE-E	BUND-E	DENS-E	GLUT-E	LOUP-E
ALGA-E	BURK-E	DHOL-E	GOLP-E	LOUR-E
ALOW-E	BURS-E	DING-E	GOOS-E	LOUS-E
AMEN-E	BUTT-E	DIRK-E	GOSS-E	LOWN-E
AMID-E	CADE-E	DIXI-E	GRAD-E	LOWS-E
AMIN-E	CADI-E	DONE-E	GRAM-E	LUNG-E
AMUS-E	CARL-E	DOOL-E	GRAT-E	MAAR-E
ANIL-E	CARS-E	DORE-E	GRAV-E	MACH-E
ANIS-E	CART-E	DORS-E	GRID-E	MAIL-E
ANSA-E	CAST-E	DOUC-E	GRIM-E	MAIR-E
ANTA-E	CEAS-E	DOWL-E	GRIP-E	MANG-E
APOD-E	CENS-E	DOWS-E	GRIS-E	MANS-E
AQUA-E	CESS-E	DRAP-E	GRUM-E	MARA-E
AREA-E	CHAP-E	EATH-E	GUID-E	MARG-E
ARED-E	CHAR-E	EMYD-E	GUNG-E	MARL-E
ARET-E	CHAS-E	ERAS-E	GUYS-E	MARS-E
ARIS-E	CHAV-E	EROS-E	HAST-E	MASS-E
ATOK-E	CHER-E	FAIN-E	HAUT-E	MATT-E
AURA-E	CHID-E	FARL-E	HAWS-E	MEAN-E
AVAL-E	CHIN-E	FARS-E	HEAR-E	MENG-E
AXIL-E	CHIV-E	FEAR-E	HEFT-E	MERL-E
AXON-E	CHUT-E	FEES-E	HERO-E	MEUS-E
AZYM-E	CLAD-E	FEHM-E	HERS-E	MEZZ-E
BARB-E	CLAM-E	FESS-E	HERY-E	MICH-E
BARD-E	CLIP-E	FIER-E	HING-E	MILL-E
BASS-E	CLON-E	FILL-E	HIRE-E	MINA-E
BAST-E	CLOT-E	FITT-E	HORS-E	MING-E
BATH-E	CLOY-E	FLAK-E	IMID-E	MINK-E
BEAR-E	COAT-E	FLAM-E	INBY-E	MIXT-E
BECK-E	COHO-E	FLIT-E	IRON-E	MOOS-E
BELL-E	COMA-E	FORM-E	ISNA-E	MORA-E
BERM-E	COMB-E	FORT-E	JAMB-E	MORN-E
BIGA-E	CONN-E	FOSS-E	JASP-E	MORS-E
BING-E	COPS-E	FOUL-E	JESS-E	MOST-E
BIRL-E	CORS-E	FRAP-E	JINN-E	MOTT-E
BITT-E	COST-E	FRAT-E	KANA-E	MOUS-E
BLAD-E	COUP-E	FRIS-E	KENT-E	MOYL-E
BLAM-E	COUR-E	FRIZ-E	KERN-E	MURR-E
BLAT-E	COXA-E	FUGU-E	KITH-E	MUSS-E
BOMB-E	CRAM-E	FUSE-E	KNOW-E	NACH-E
BOOS-E	CRAN-E	FUZE-E	KYND-E	NEUM-E
BORD-E	CRAP-E	GAFF-E	LAND-E	NOUL-E
BORE-E	CREM-E	GAMB-E	LAPS-E	NOVA-E
BORN-E	CREW-E	GARB-E	LARE-E	NURS-E
BOTT-E	CRIM-E	GEAR-E	LATH-E	OBES-E
BOWS-E	CRIS-E	GEES-E	LEAR-E	OBOL-E
BRAK-E	CRUD-E	GEST-E	LEAS-E	ODYL-E

E – End-hooks

OUPH-E	RAKE-E	SHIN-E	STAG-E	TROD-E
OXID-E	RAMI-E	SHIR-E	STAR-E	TRON-E
OXIM-E	RANG-E	SHIT-E	STAT-E	TROP-E
PAIR-E	RANK-E	SHIV-E	STED-E	TUBA-E
PAIS-E	RARE-E	SHOP-E	STEM-E	TUFF-E
PARA-E	RATH-E	SHOT-E	STIM-E	TURM-E
PARS-E	RAZE-E	SHUL-E	STIR-E	TWIN-E
PASS-E	REAM-E	SHUT-E	STOA-E	TWIT-E
PAST-E	REED-E	SIDH-E	STOP-E	TYND-E
PEAG-E	RENT-E	SING-E	SUED-E	ULNA-E
PEAR-E	RIFT-E	SIRE-E	SUIT-E	UNDE-E
PEAS-E	RILL-E	SITH-E	SWAG-E	UNIT-E
PECK-E	RIMA-E	SKAT-E	SYBO-E	UPBY-E
PEEP-E	RINS-E	SKEN-E	SYCE-E	URDE-E
PENI-E	RONT-E	SKIT-E	TACH-E	URSA-E
PERV-E	ROOS-E	SKYR-E	TASS-E	VAIR-E
PHON-E	ROUL-E	SLAT-E	TAWS-E	VAUT-E
PIOY-E	ROUT-E	SLID-E	TEAD-E	VEAL-E
PLAN-E	RUFF-E	SLIM-E	TEAS-E	VEHM-E
PLAT-E	RUGA-E	SLIP-E	TEEN-E	VENA-E
PLEB-E	SAIC-E	SLOP-E	TELA-E	VERS-E
PLUM-E	SAIN-E	SMIT-E	TEMS-E	VILD-E
POIS-E	SALL-E	SNAR-E	TENS-E	VITA-E
POSS-E	SALS-E	SNIP-E	TERF-E	VOLA-E
POUK-E	SASS-E	SOAR-E	TERN-E	VOLT-E
PRAT-E	SAUT-E	SOLD-E	TEST-E	WACK-E
PRIM-E	SCAR-E	SONS-E	THAN-E	WAID-E
PROB-E	SCOP-E	SOOL-E	THEM-E	WAIT-E
PROS-E	SCUT-E	SOOT-E	THIN-E	WAST-E
PRYS-E	SEAM-E	SORE-E	THRO-E	WEEK-E
PULS-E	SEAR-E	SOUS-E	TING-E	WEET-E
PUPA-E	SEAS-E	SOWL-E	TOGA-E	WEFT-E
PURE-E	SEIS-E	SOWN-E	TOIL-E	WELK-E
PURS-E	SELL-E	SOWS-E	TOPE-E	WHIN-E
QUAT-E	SEME-E	SPAN-E	TOPH-E	WHIT-E
QUIN-E	SEMI-E	SPAR-E	TORS-E	WING-E
QUIT-E	SENS-E	SPAT-E	TORT-E	WITH-E
RACH-E	SENT-E	SPIC-E	TOWS-E	WOOS-E
RAGE-E	SERR-E	SPIK-E	TRAD-E	WRIT-E
RAIL-E	SETA-E	SPIN-E	TRAP-E	YOUS-E
RAIN-E	SHAD-E	SPIT-E	TRIN-E	ZOEA-E
RAIS-E	SHAM-E	SPOD-E	TRIP-E	ZONA-E

Five letters to six

AGORA-E	BARGE-E	BROOS-E	CELLA-E	COLON-E
ALLEL-E	BATTU-E	BROWS-E	CHAIN-E	COMIC-E
ALMUD-E	BERTH-E	BUBAL-E	CHAIS-E	CONCH-E
ALULA-E	BETID-E	BULLA-E	CHANG-E	CONGE-E
AMEBA-E	BLEND-E	BUNJE-E	CHELA-E	CONIN-E
AMEND-E	BLOND-E	BURSA-E	CHILD-E	COOMB-E
AMPUL-E	BLOWS-E	CAMES-E	CHIRR-E	CORPS-E
ANCON-E	BOCCI-E	CAMIS-E	CHORE-E	COSTA-E
ANNEX-E	BOORD-E	CANNA-E	CHOWS-E	COTTA-E
ANYON-E	BOURN-E	CAPOT-E	CLAVI-E	COUCH-E
AORTA-E	BRAID-E	CARAT-E	CLOTH-E	COUPE-E
AVAIL-E	BREES-E	CARDI-E	CNIDA-E	COURS-E
AVERS-E	BRIBE-E	CAUDA-E	COATE-E	CREES-E
BACCA-E	BROCH-E	CAUSA-E	COIGN-E	CROSS-E

CROUP-E	GRILL-E	OCTAN-E	RESID-E	TALPA-E
CROUT-E	GROSZ-E	OLEIN-E	RESIT-E	TAMAL-E
CULPA-E	GUIMP-E	OPPOS-E	ROTCH-E	TAMIN-E
CURAT-E	GUTTA-E	ORACH-E	RUBIN-E	TAMIS-E
CURIA-E	GYROS-E	ORANG-E	SABIN-E	TANGI-E
CUTTO-E	HALID-E	ORCIN-E	SAITH-E	TEETH-E
DECAD-E	HEARS-E	ORPIN-E	SALAD-E	TENIA-E
DEMUR-E	HEAST-E	OSMOL-E	SALLE-E	TERRA-E
DERAT-E	HERMA-E	OUTBY-E	SALPA-E	TESTA-E
DEVOT-E	HEXAD-E	PALEA-E	SAROD-E	TESTE-E
DILDO-E	HOARS-E	PALLA-E	SASIN-E	THECA-E
DONNE-E	HORST-E	PARDI-E	SAVIN-E	THEIN-E
DOOLE-E	HUMAN-E	PAREV-E	SCALA-E	THERM-E
DORIS-E	HYDRA-E	PARKI-E	SCATH-E	THORP-E
DREAR-E	HYPHA-E	PAROL-E	SCHMO-E	THROW-E
DROWS-E	IMPED-E	PASSE-E	SCOPA-E	TIBIA-E
ENZYM-E	INCUS-E	PATIN-E	SCRAP-E	TOLAN-E
EOSIN-E	INDOL-E	PATTE-E	SCRAY-E	TOROS-E
EPRIS-E	INFER-E	PAVAN-E	SCULL-E	TOUCH-E
EQUIP-E	IODID-E	PAVIS-E	SELLA-E	TOXIN-E
EXPOS-E	IODIN-E	PELTA-E	SERIN-E	TRANS-E
FACET-E	JAMBE-E	PENNA-E	SERRA-E	TRIOS-E
FACIA-E	JINNE-E	PERDU-E	SEVER-E	TRIST-E
FARCI-E	KARAT-E	PETIT-E	SHOOL-E	TROAD-E
FASTI-E	KINAS-E	PHEER-E	SHOTT-E	TROMP-E
FAUNA-E	LAMIA-E	PHOCA-E	SILEN-E	TRYST-E
FEMAL-E	LARVA-E	PHYLA-E	SILVA-E	TUYER-E
FERIA-E	LASSI-E	PICOT-E	SITHE-E	TWYER-E
FILOS-E	LATHE-E	PINNA-E	SKEAN-E	ULNAR-E
FINAL-E	LAURA-E	PLAST-E	SKRIK-E	UMBRA-E
FITCH-E	LAWIN-E	PLEAS-E	SNATH-E	UNBAR-E
FLORA-E	LETHE-E	PLICA-E	SOOTH-E	UNCAP-E
FONDU-E	LIBRA-E	PLONG-E	SOURS-E	UNCIA-E
FORBY-E	LIPID-E	POINT-E	SOZIN-E	UNCUT-E
FORME-E	LOATH-E	POLYP-E	SPALL-E	UNRIP-E
FOSSA-E	LOBOS-E	POTCH-E	SPARK-E	UNTIL-E
FOVEA-E	LOCAL-E	POUFF-E	SPARS-E	UPTAK-E
FRISE-E	LUNGE-E	POULP-E	SPICA-E	URBAN-E
FRORN-E	LUNGI-E	PREIF-E	SPINA-E	UREAS-E
FUNDI-E	LUPIN-E	PRIEF-E	SPRIT-E	UVULA-E
FURAN-E	LYSIN-E	PROIN-E	SPURN-E	VALET-E
FURCA-E	LYTTA-E	PROYN-E	STEAL-E	VALIS-E
FUROL-E	MADAM-E	PSYCH-E	STEAN-E	VENIN-E
FUROR-E	MALIC-E	PURIN-E	STEAR-E	VERST-E
FUSIL-E	MAMMA-E	PUTTI-E	STEDD-E	VERTU-E
GALEA-E	MEATH-E	QUART-E	STELA-E	VILLA-E
GAMIN-E	MEDIA-E	QUICH-E	STONN-E	VIRTU-E
GEMMA-E	MENSA-E	QUINT-E	STOOP-E	VISIT-E
GEMOT-E	MERGE-E	RALLY-E	STOUR-E	VITTA-E
GENOM-E	MISER-E	RAPPE-E	STRIA-E	VOLVA-E
GLAIR-E	MISSA-E	RAVIN-E	STRIP-E	VULVA-E
GLEBA-E	MONGO-E	REBIT-E	STYLI-E	WALIS-E
GOURD-E	MORAL-E	RECIT-E	SUMMA-E	WATAP-E
GRAIL-E	MURRE-E	RECUR-E	SWATH-E	WHEAR-E
GRAIN-E	MUSCA-E	REDIA-E	SWING-E	ZOAEA-E
GRAND-E	NOMAD-E	REDON-E	SWITH-E	ZOMBI-E
GREES-E	NOULD-E	REGAL-E	SWOUN-E	ZOOEA-E
GREET-E	NUCHA-E	REPIN-E	SYLVA-E	
GRIFF-E	OCREA-E	REPOS-E	TALEA-E	

E – End-hooks

Six letters to seven

ABOLLA-E	CAPRIC-E	DOLENT-E	HYDRAS-E	NEURON-E
ACQUIT-E	CARDIA-E	DOMAIN-E	HYDRIA-E	NITRID-E
ADONIS-E	CARINA-E	DOMINE-E	HYDRID-E	NITRIL-E
ADVISE-E	CARLIN-E	DURESS-E	IMPING-E	NOVENA-E
AFFAIR-E	CAROCH-E	EMETIN-E	IMPROV-E	NYMPHA-E
AFFEAR-E	CARPAL-E	EMPLOY-E	INFANT-E	OBLIGE-E
ALANIN-E	CASERN-E	ENGAGE-E	INFULA-E	OCHREA-E
ALEXIN-E	CATENA-E	ENNUYE-E	INGENU-E	OCTETT-E
ALIDAD-E	CAVIAR-E	ENTETE-E	INSULA-E	OLEFIN-E
ALSOON-E	CELLOS-E	EPERDU-E	INTERN-E	ORIGAN-E
ALTERN-E	CESURA-E	EPIGON-E	INTIMA-E	OUVERT-E
ALUMIN-E	CHAETA-E	EPIMER-E	INULAS-E	PAIOCK-E
ALUMNA-E	CHIMER-E	EPUISE-E	INVITE-E	PAJOCK-E
AMIDIN-E	CHINES-E	ESCAPE-E	ISATIN-E	PALAMA-E
AMOEBA-E	CHOANA-E	ETAMIN-E	ISOBAR-E	PANGEN-E
ANATAS-E	CHOPIN-E	EUCAIN-E	ISOGON-E	PAPULA-E
ANILIN-E	CHORAL-E	EXEDRA-E	ISOMER-E	PARDAL-E
ANTICK-E	CHORDA-E	EXTERN-E	JAGHIR-E	PAROLE-E
ANTLIA-E	CICADA-E	EXUVIA-E	JASMIN-E	PARVIS-E
APHTHA-E	CINEOL-E	FACULA-E	JUBILE-E	PATERA-E
ARABIS-E	CITRIN-E	FASCIA-E	KAGOUL-E	PATINA-E
ARCSIN-E	CLEANS-E	FECULA-E	KAINIT-E	PENSIL-E
AREOLA-E	CLOACA-E	FERULA-E	KAOLIN-E	PEPSIN-E
ARISTA-E	COCAIN-E	FETICH-E	LACUNA-E	PEPTID-E
ARSHIN-E	CODEIN-E	FIANCE-E	LADRON-E	PESANT-E
ARTIST-E	COELOM-E	FIBROS-E	LAMINA-E	PICKAX-E
ASPERS-E	COMMER-E	FIBULA-E	LEASOW-E	PICOTE-E
ATTACH-E	COMMOT-E	FITCHE-E	LEGATE-E	PILULA-E
ATTRIT-E	COMPER-E	FLAMBE-E	LEUCIN-E	PINKEY-E
AUGUST-E	COMPOS-E	FLAVIN-E	LIGULA-E	PISTOL-E
AURORA-E	COMPOT-E	FOLIOS-E	LINGUA-E	PLANCH-E
AXILLA-E	CONCHA-E	FORBAD-E	LISSOM-E	PLANTA-E
BAGASS-E	CONSOL-E	FOREBY-E	LORICA-E	PLATAN-E
BAILLI-E	COPULA-E	FORMAT-E	LUCERN-E	PLEDGE-E
BALLAD-E	CORNEA-E	FRAPPE-E	LUNULA-E	PLEURA-E
BEGRIM-E	CORONA-E	FRIAND-E	LURDAN-E	POLEAX-E
BEGUIN-E	COSMIN-E	FRIJOL-E	MACULA-E	POMMEL-E
BELDAM-E	COUCHE-E	GALOSH-E	MARLIN-E	PONTIL-E
BENZIN-E	CRISTA-E	GANOIN-E	MARQUE-E	PRANCK-E
BENZOL-E	CRUSTA-E	GARROT-E	MATRIC-E	PRECIS-E
BERLIN-E	CUPULA-E	GENTIL-E	MAUVIN-E	PRISER-E
BESPAT-E	CYANID-E	GERMAN-E	MEDUSA-E	PROTYL-E
BETEEM-E	CYANIN-E	GLOSSA-E	MEGASS-E	PURLIN-E
BHISTI-E	DEFAST-E	GLYCIN-E	MESTOM-E	PYRROL-E
BICORN-E	DEMAIN-E	GOLOSH-E	MICELL-E	QUININ-E
BLINTZ-E	DEMEAN-E	GOODBY-E	MODERN-E	RADIAL-E
BOTONE-E	DENTIN-E	GOUGER-E	MODIST-E	RADULA-E
BOUCHE-E	DETENT-E	GRADIN-E	MONTAN-E	RATLIN-E
BOUCLE-E	DETENU-E	GRANDE-E	MOOLVI-E	RECOUP-E
BREATH-E	DEVISE-E	GRATIN-E	MORULA-E	REFUGE-E
BREVET-E	DEVOTE-E	GUANAS-E	MOUSME-E	REGINA-E
BROMID-E	DHOOTI-E	GUANIN-E	MUCOSA-E	REGULA-E
BROMIN-E	DIAMIN-E	HALTER-E	MURRIN-E	REQUIT-E
BRUCIN-E	DIAZIN-E	HAPTEN-E	MYELIN-E	RETINA-E
BUGGAN-E	DILUTE-E	HARMIN-E	NANDIN-E	RETIRE-E
CAGOUL-E	DIOXAN-E	HERNIA-E	NARCOS-E	REVERS-E
CAMERA-E	DIOXID-E	HEROIN-E	NATURA-E	RIPOST-E
CANULA-E	DIVERS-E	HYALIN-E	NEBULA-E	ROSIER-E

ROTULA-E	SIGNOR-E	STATIC-E	TARTAN-E	UNGULA-E
SAFROL-E	SITULA-E	STRANG-E	TARTAR-E	UNLAST-E
SAVANT-E	SIXAIN-E	STRIGA-E	TEGULA-E	UNVAIL-E
SCALAR-E	SKATOL-E	STROOK-E	TIMBAL-E	VAGINA-E
SCHOOL-E	SODAIN-E	STRUMA-E	TOLUID-E	VERDIT-E
SCLERA-E	SOIGNE-E	SUBTIL-E	TOLUOL-E	VERSIN-E
SCORIA-E	SPARTH-E	SUCCOS-E	TONNAG-E	VESICA-E
SCOURS-E	SPHAER-E	SULFID-E	TORULA-E	VISITE-E
SCROWL-E	SPHEAR-E	SUMMAT-E	TRITON-E	VOLANT-E
SDEIGN-E	SPIREM-E	SYLVIN-E	TROCHE-E	VOMICA-E
SECOND-E	SPREDD-E	SYMBOL-E	TROPIN-E	WREATH-E
SECRET-E	SPRING-E	SYNURA-E	TUNICA-E	ZONULA-E
SEROSA-E	SQUAMA-E	TABULA-E	TUSSOR-E	
SHEATH-E	STAITH-E	TAENIA-E	UNBORN-E	

Seven letters to eight

ABSCISS-E	CAFFEIN-E	EMPLOYE-E	HEGUMEN-E	MAXILLA-E
ABSINTH-E	CANNULA-E	EMPRESS-E	HEMATIN-E	MEDULLA-E
ACALEPH-E	CAPELIN-E	ENDORSE-E	HEMIPOD-E	MEGAPOD-E
ACANTHA-E	CARABIN-E	ENVELOP-E	HETAERA-E	MESQUIN-E
ACICULA-E	CARACOL-E	ESCALOP-E	HOLESOM-E	MESQUIT-E
ACKNOWN-E	CARDECU-E	ETATISM-E	HOLYDAM-E	METAMER-E
ACQUIRE-E	CERESIN-E	ETATIST-E	IMPRESS-E	MEZQUIT-E
ACRIDIN-E	CHALAZA-E	ETOURDI-E	INCONNU-E	MICELLA-E
ACTINIA-E	CHLORID-E	EULOGIA-E	INDAMIN-E	MINUTIA-E
AFFRONT-E	CHLORIN-E	EXAMINE-E	INDIGEN-E	MISWRIT-E
AGACANT-E	CINEAST-E	EXCLUDE-E	INDORSE-E	MONDAIN-E
AGLYCON-E	COCHLEA-E	EXHEDRA-E	INDULIN-E	MONOPOD-E
ALEURON-E	COLICIN-E	FALCULA-E	INERTIA-E	MORPHIN-E
ALKALIN-E	COMPLIN-E	FAUNULA-E	INFAUNA-E	MUSICAL-E
ALKALIS-E	CONTRAT-E	FILARIA-E	INHUMAN-E	NARCEIN-E
AMPHORA-E	CONTROL-E	FIMBRIA-E	INTERNE-E	NARWHAL-E
AMPULLA-E	CORYPHE-E	FINALIS-E	ISOCHOR-E	NEBBISH-E
AMYGDAL-E	COURANT-E	FISTULA-E	JACINTH-E	NEGLIGE-E
ANCILLA-E	CRANNOG-E	FLORULA-E	JEALOUS-E	NEURULA-E
ANETHOL-E	CREATIN-E	FLUORID-E	KERMESS-E	NICOTIN-E
ANTENNA-E	CROCEIN-E	FLUORIN-E	LACINIA-E	NOCTURN-E
ANTIGEN-E	CURARIS-E	FOLKMOT-E	LAMBAST-E	NOTITIA-E
ARMILLA-E	CYPSELA-E	FORMULA-E	LAMELLA-E	NOVELLA-E
ATABRIN-E	CYSTEIN-E	FOSSULA-E	LANOLIN-E	ONCOGEN-E
ATROPIN-E	DARRAIN-E	FOVEOLA-E	LARGESS-E	OOTHECA-E
AUREOLA-E	DAUPHIN-E	FRACTUR-E	LICENCE-E	OUTCAST-E
AUTOMAT-E	DEBOUCH-E	FUCHSIN-E	LICENSE-E	OUTCHID-E
AVELLAN-E	DECIDUA-E	FURCULA-E	LIGROIN-E	OUTRANG-E
BACKBIT-E	DECLASS-E	FUSAROL-E	LINGULA-E	OUTWRIT-E
BALADIN-E	DEVELOP-E	GELATIN-E	LIVEYER-E	OUVRIER-E
BALISTA-E	DEXTRIN-E	GENERAL-E	LOCUSTA-E	OXYPHIL-E
BARCHAN-E	DISPONE-E	GERMAIN-E	LUPULIN-E	PAENULA-E
BARGEES-E	DIVORCE-E	GINGIVA-E	LYOPHIL-E	PAPILLA-E
BARYTON-E	DOMICIL-E	GIRASOL-E	MALEFIC-E	PARVENU-E
BENEFIC-E	DOVECOT-E	GLIADIN-E	MAMILLA-E	PATELLA-E
BESTRID-E	DRACHMA-E	GRAMARY-E	MARCHES-E	PENSION-E
BIOPHOR-E	DUCHESS-E	GRANDAM-E	MARQUIS-E	PERIDOT-E
BOMBARD-E	DUVETYN-E	GRAPLIN-E	MASTICH-E	PERIGON-E
BROADAX-E	DYSODIL-E	GRATINE-E	MATADOR-E	PEROXID-E
BURNOUS-E	ECDYSON-E	GRAVIDA-E	MATELOT-E	PERSONA-E
CABEZON-E	ECHIDNA-E	HALIDOM-E	MAUVAIS-E	PFENNIG-E
CAESURA-E	EMERITA-E	HALIMOT-E	MAUVEIN-E	PIANIST-E

PICOLIN-E	PROTEID-E	SCHMOOZ-E	STROBIL-E	TRACHEA-E
PINNULA-E	PTERYLA-E	SCISSIL-E	SUCCUBA-E	TRAVOIS-E
PISCINA-E	PTOMAIN-E	SCOPULA-E	SULPHID-E	TRIAZIN-E
PLACCAT-E	QUADRAT-E	SCURRIL-E	SUNBATH-E	TRICORN-E
PLANULA-E	RATTLIN-E	SECONDE-E	SUSPENS-E	TRIOXID-E
PLAUDIT-E	REHEARS-E	SELVAGE-E	SYLPHID-E	TRIPTAN-E
PLIMSOL-E	RELEASE-E	SEQUELA-E	SYMBIOT-E	URETHAN-E
PLUMULA-E	RETRAIT-E	SERPULA-E	SYMITAR-E	URETHRA-E
PORPESS-E	RHABDOM-E	SESTETT-E	SYNONYM-E	VACCINE-E
PORTESS-E	RIBSTON-E	SEXTETT-E	TABORIN-E	VALVULA-E
PORTIER-E	ROCKABY-E	SILICON-E	TACHISM-E	VENTAIL-E
POTLACH-E	RUSSULA-E	SILIQUA-E	TACHIST-E	VERRUCA-E
POULARD-E	SALICIN-E	SKYBORN-E	TEREBRA-E	VITAMIN-E
PRACTIC-E	SALVAGE-E	SMARAGD-E	TESSERA-E	WANNABE-E
PRECAVA-E	SAPHENA-E	SOLANIN-E	THERMIT-E	WOODBIN-E
PREMIER-E	SAPONIN-E	SPICULA-E	THIAMIN-E	XANTHIN-E
PREPUPA-E	SARCINA-E	SPINULA-E	THIAZIN-E	XYLIDIN-E
PROLONG-E	SAUTOIR-E	SPIRULA-E	THIAZOL-E	ZECCHIN-E
PROMISE-E	SCAPULA-E	SQUILLA-E	THIONIN-E	ZOOGLEA-E
PROTEAS-E	SCHMELZ-E	STAMPED-E	TOLIDIN-E	ZYMOGEN-E
PROTEGE-E	SCHMOOS-E	STEARIN-E	TORCHER-E	

Eight letters to nine

ABORIGIN-E	CAPSOMER-E	DISTRAIT-E	HEPATICA-E	PALPEBRA-E
ABSCISSA-E	CARTOUCH-E	DISULFID-E	HISTAMIN-E	PANTALON-E
ACANTHIN-E	CATHEDRA-E	ECCLESIA-E	HISTIDIN-E	PARAFFIN-E
ACETAMID-E	CERCARIA-E	ECSTASIS-E	HOSPITAL-E	PAROCHIN-E
AFFRONTE-E	CHAPERON-E	EMPHASIS-E	INSHEATH-E	PARVOLIN-E
ALIZARIN-E	CHLORDAN-E	ENDAMEBA-E	INTERESS-E	PASTORAL-E
ALTERNAT-E	CIRRIPED-E	ENDOSMOS-E	INTERVAL-E	PATHOGEN-E
AMYGDALA-E	CISTERNA-E	ENSHEATH-E	INTIMIST-E	PENTOSAN-E
ANGUIPED-E	CLAUSULA-E	ENSHRINE-E	ISOCHRON-E	PENUMBRA-E
ANTEFIXA-E	COCHLEAR-E	ENTAMEBA-E	KHALIFAT-E	PEREGRIN-E
ANTISTAT-E	COMATULA-E	ENWREATH-E	LANDSLID-E	PERIODID-E
APOLOGIA-E	CONCOURS-E	EPHEDRIN-E	LAVALIER-E	PETECHIA-E
APPRAISE-E	CONFERVA-E	EPHEMERA-E	LODICULA-E	PHENAZIN-E
ASPIRATA-E	CONFRONT-E	EPIFAUNA-E	MAGDALEN-E	PHENETOL-E
AURICULA-E	CORPORAL-E	EPITHECA-E	MAMMILLA-E	PHOSPHID-E
AVENTAIL-E	CROSSBIT-E	ETRANGER-E	MANDARIN-E	PHOSPHIN-E
AVIFAUNA-E	CURCUMIN-E	EUCARYOT-E	MANDOLIN-E	PHOSPHOR-E
BACCHANT-E	CURTALAX-E	EUKARYOT-E	MARGARIN-E	PHOTOGEN-E
BACKSLID-E	CUSPIDOR-E	EXIGEANT-E	MESCALIN-E	PINNIPED-E
BALLADIN-E	CUTICULA-E	FENESTRA-E	METHADON-E	PLACENTA-E
BALLISTA-E	CYANAMID-E	FIBRILLA-E	MILLEPED-E	PLEONAST-E
BANDEROL-E	DANCETTE-E	FIGURANT-E	MILLIPED-E	POLYPHON-E
BASILICA-E	DARRAIGN-E	FISSIPED-E	MISCEGEN-E	PONTIFIC-E
BASOPHIL-E	DEBONAIR-E	FROSTBIT-E	MORTGAGE-E	POSTCAVA-E
BAUDRICK-E	DEBUTANT-E	FURFUROL-E	MULTIPED-E	PRETERIT-E
BENZIDIN-E	DECLASSE-E	GAILLARD-E	MULTITON-E	PRINCESS-E
BERBERIN-E	DEDICATE-E	GARAGIST-E	MUSCADIN-E	PROLAMIN-E
BLASTULA-E	DELEGATE-E	GASTNESS-E	MYXAMEBA-E	PROTAMIN-E
BOUTONNE-E	DEMIVOLT-E	GASTRULA-E	NIGROSIN-E	PROTOXID-E
BRANCHIA-E	DESPOTAT-E	GLABELLA-E	NUBECULA-E	PROVEDOR-E
BRASSIER-E	DETRAQUE-E	GLYCERIN-E	OENOPHIL-E	PUERPERA-E
BRUCELLA-E	DIPLOMAT-E	GRANDSIR-E	OSTRACOD-E	QUADRIGA-E
CACOMIXL-E	DIRIGISM-E	GUANIDIN-E	OVERBORN-E	QUARTETT-E
CANEPHOR-E	DISSEISE-E	HANDWRIT-E	PALESTRA-E	QUINOLIN-E
CAPONIER-E	DISSEIZE-E	HARMALIN-E	PALMIPED-E	QUINTETT-E

RACHILLA-E	SAFRANIN-E	SLUGHORN-E	THYROXIN-E	VERTEBRA-E
RATIONAL-E	SARABAND-E	SNAKEBIT-E	TOLUIDIN-E	VESICULA-E
REAEDIFY-E	SCELERAT-E	SQUADRON-E	TORCHIER-E	VIBRISSA-E
REFORMAT-E	SCLEREID-E	STROBILA-E	TRACHEID-E	VIGILANT-E
RELOCATE-E	SEMIMATT-E	STRONGYL-E	TRICHINA-E	VISAGIST-E
REMEDIAT-E	SEMUNCIA-E	SUBCOSTA-E	TRITICAL-E	VITELLIN-E
REPLICAS-E	SENSILLA-E	SYNOPSIS-E	TROCHLEA-E	VULSELLA-E
RESTRING-E	SERAPHIN-E	SYPHILIS-E	TURQUOIS-E	WHEREFOR-E
RETINULA-E	SHEEPCOT-E	TESSELLA-E	TYRANNIS-E	XYLOIDIN-E
RHEOPHIL-E	SHIGELLA-E	TETROXID-E	UNDERBIT-E	YERSINIA-E
RHODAMIN-E	SILICULA-E	THEREFOR-E	VAGINULA-E	ZOOGLOEA-E
RICERCAR-E	SIMPLIST-E	THIOPHEN-E	VERATRIN-E	

F – Front-hooks

Two letters to three

F-AA	F-AS	F-EM	F-OB	F-OY
F-AB	F-AT	F-EN	F-OE	F-UG
F-AD	F-AW	F-ER	F-OH	F-UM
F-AE	F-AX	F-ES	F-ON	F-UN
F-AG	F-AY	F-ET	F-OP	F-UR
F-AH	F-ED	F-ID	F-OR	
F-AN	F-EE	F-IN	F-OU	
F-AR	F-EH	F-IT	F-OX	

Three letters to four

F-AAS	F-AVA	F-ILL	F-LIT	F-OWL
F-ABS	F-AVE	F-INK	F-LOG	F-OXY
F-ACE	F-AWN	F-INS	F-LOP	F-OYS
F-ACT	F-AYS	F-IRE	F-LOR	F-RAG
F-ADO	F-EAR	F-IRK	F-LOW	F-RAP
F-ADS	F-EAT	F-ISH	F-LUX	F-RAS
F-AFF	F-EDS	F-ITS	F-OBS	F-RAT
F-AGS	F-EEL	F-LAB	F-OES	F-RAY
F-AHS	F-EEN	F-LAG	F-OHS	F-REE
F-AIL	F-EHS	F-LAM	F-OIL	F-RET
F-AIN	F-ELL	F-LAP	F-OLD	F-RIB
F-AIR	F-ELT	F-LAT	F-ONE	F-RIG
F-AKE	F-EME	F-LAW	F-ONS	F-RIT
F-ALL	F-EMS	F-LAX	F-OOT	F-RIZ
F-AND	F-END	F-LAY	F-OPS	F-ROE
F-ANE	F-ENS	F-LEA	F-ORA	F-ROM
F-ARD	F-ERE	F-LED	F-ORB	F-ROW
F-ARE	F-ERN	F-LEE	F-ORD	F-RUG
F-ARM	F-ESS	F-LEG	F-ORE	F-UDS
F-ARS	F-EST	F-LEW	F-ORT	F-UGS
F-ART	F-ETA	F-LEX	F-OUD	F-UNS
F-ASH	F-ICE	F-LEY	F-OUR	F-USE
F-ATE	F-IDS	F-LIP	F-OUS	

Four letters to five

F-ABLE	F-ACTS	F-AGIN	F-AIRS	F-ALLS
F-ACED	F-ADDY	F-AILS	F-AIRY	F-ANAL
F-ACER	F-ADOS	F-AINE	F-AKED	F-ANDS
F-ACES	F-AERY	F-AINS	F-AKES	F-ANES

E – End-hooks

F-ANGA	F-ERNS	F-LAYS	F-LOWS	F-RAPS
F-ANON	F-ESSE	F-LEAM	F-LUES	F-RATE
F-ARDS	F-ESTS	F-LEAS	F-LUFF	F-RATS
F-ARED	F-ETAS	F-LEER	F-LUKE	F-RAYS
F-ARES	F-ETCH	F-LEES	F-LUMP	F-REAK
F-ARLE	F-EVER	F-LEET	F-LUNG	F-REED
F-ARMS	F-EWER	F-LEGS	F-LUNK	F-REES
F-ARSE	F-EYED	F-LEME	F-LUSH	F-RESH
F-ARTS	F-EYER	F-LEYS	F-LUTE	F-RETS
F-ASCI	F-ICES	F-LICK	F-LYTE	F-RIBS
F-ATES	F-ILLS	F-LIED	F-OGLE	F-RIGS
F-AULD	F-ILLY	F-LIER	F-OILS	F-RILL
F-AVAS	F-INCH	F-LIES	F-OLDS	F-RISE
F-AVEL	F-INKS	F-LIMP	F-OLIO	F-RISK
F-AVER	F-IRED	F-LING	F-ONLY	F-RITS
F-AVES	F-IRES	F-LINT	F-OOTS	F-RITT
F-AWNS	F-IRKS	F-LIPS	F-ORBS	F-RITZ
F-AWNY	F-ITCH	F-LISK	F-ORBY	F-ROCK
F-AXED	F-LABS	F-LITE	F-ORDO	F-ROES
F-AXES	F-LACK	F-LITS	F-ORDS	F-RONT
F-AYRE	F-LAGS	F-LOCK	F-ORES	F-RORE
F-EARS	F-LAIR	F-LOGS	F-ORTS	F-RORY
F-EASE	F-LAKE	F-LONG	F-OSSA	F-ROST
F-EAST	F-LAKY	F-LOOR	F-OUDS	F-ROWS
F-EATS	F-LAME	F-LOPS	F-OURS	F-RUGS
F-ECHT	F-LAMS	F-LORY	F-OWLS	F-RUMP
F-EELS	F-LANK	F-LOSH	F-OXES	F-RUSH
F-ELLS	F-LAPS	F-LOSS	F-OYER	F-RUST
F-ELTS	F-LARE	F-LOTA	F-RACK	F-UGLY
F-EMES	F-LASH	F-LOTE	F-RAGS	F-UNDY
F-EMMY	F-LATS	F-LOUR	F-RAIL	F-USED
F-ENDS	F-LAWN	F-LOUT	F-RANK	F-USES
F-ERES	F-LAWS	F-LOWN	F-RAPE	

Five letters to six

F-ABLED	F-ARROW	F-ICHES	F-LANKS	F-LINGS
F-ABLER	F-ARSED	F-ICKLE	F-LARES	F-LINTS
F-ABLES	F-ARSES	F-IGGED	F-LASER	F-LINTY
F-ACERS	F-ASHED	F-ILIAL	F-LAWED	F-LIPPY
F-ACING	F-ASHES	F-ILLER	F-LAWNS	F-LISKS
F-ACTOR	F-ASTER	F-INGAN	F-LAXES	F-LITED
F-ADDLE	F-AWNED	F-INKED	F-LAYED	F-LITES
F-AERIE	F-AWNER	F-INNED	F-LAYER	F-LOCKS
F-AILED	F-AXING	F-INNER	F-LEAMS	F-LONGS
F-AIRED	F-AYRES	F-IRING	F-LEDGE	F-LOOEY
F-AIRER	F-EARED	F-IRKED	F-LEDGY	F-LOOIE
F-AKING	F-EASED	F-ISHES	F-LEECH	F-LOPPY
F-ALLOW	F-EASES	F-ITCHY	F-LEERS	F-LORAL
F-ALTER	F-EASTS	F-LACKS	F-LEETS	F-LOSSY
F-AMINE	F-EATER	F-LAIRS	F-LEMES	F-LOTAS
F-ANGAS	F-EERIE	F-LAKED	F-LENSE	F-LOTES
F-ANGLE	F-ENDED	F-LAKER	F-LETCH	F-LOURS
F-ANION	F-ENDER	F-LAKES	F-LEXES	F-LOURY
F-ANKLE	F-ESSES	F-LAMED	F-LICKS	F-LOUSE
F-ARCED	F-ESTER	F-LAMER	F-LIERS	F-LOUTS
F-ARLES	F-ETTLE	F-LAMES	F-LIGHT	F-LOWED
F-ARMED	F-EWEST	F-LANCH	F-LIMPS	F-LOWER
F-ARMER	F-EYING	F-LANES	F-LINCH	F-LUFFS

F-LUMPS	F-OGLES	F-OYERS	F-RICHT	F-ROSTS
F-LUNKS	F-OILED	F-RAILS	F-RIDGE	F-RUGAL
F-LURRY	F-OLDER	F-RAISE	F-RIGHT	F-RUMPS
F-LUSHY	F-OLIOS	F-RANKS	F-RIGID	F-RUMPY
F-LUTED	F-ONNED	F-RAPPE	F-RILLS	F-RUSTS
F-LUTER	F-ORMER	F-RATCH	F-RISES	F-UGGED
F-LUTES	F-OTHER	F-RATER	F-RISKS	F-UMBLE
F-LUXES	F-OUGHT	F-RAYED	F-RISKY	F-UNDER
F-LYING	F-OUTER	F-REAKS	F-RITES	F-UNKED
F-LYTED	F-OUTRE	F-REEST	F-RITTS	F-USING
F-LYTES	F-OWLED	F-REMIT	F-ROCKS	F-UTILE
F-ODDER	F-OWLER	F-RENNE	F-RONTS	

Six letters to seven

F-ABLING	F-ENDERS	F-LAYERS	F-LUSHES	F-RESHES
F-ACTION	F-ENDING	F-LAYING	F-LUSTER	F-RETTED
F-ACTIVE	F-ERNING	F-LECHES	F-LUTERS	F-RICHTS
F-ACTORS	F-ESTERS	F-LEDGED	F-LUTING	F-RIDGED
F-ACTUAL	F-ETCHED	F-LEDGES	F-LUTIST	F-RIDGES
F-ACTURE	F-ETCHER	F-LEEING	F-LYINGS	F-RIGGED
F-ADDLED	F-ETCHES	F-LEERED	F-LYTING	F-RIGGER
F-ADDLES	F-ETTLED	F-LEGGED	F-OILING	F-RIGHTS
F-AERIES	F-ETTLES	F-LEMING	F-OLLIES	F-RILLED
F-AILING	F-ICKLER	F-LENSED	F-ONDING	F-RINGED
F-AIREST	F-IGGING	F-LENSES	F-ONNING	F-RIPPER
F-AIRILY	F-INCHED	F-LICKED	F-ORGONE	F-RISKED
F-AIRING	F-INCHES	F-LICKER	F-ORMERS	F-RISKER
F-AIRWAY	F-INGANS	F-LIGHTS	F-ORPINE	F-RITTED
F-ALCADE	F-INKING	F-LIMPED	F-OTHERS	F-RITTER
F-ALLOWS	F-INNERS	F-LINGER	F-OULDER	F-RITZES
F-ALTERS	F-INNING	F-LINTED	F-OUTERS	F-RIZZER
F-AMINES	F-IRKING	F-LIPPED	F-OUTRED	F-ROCKED
F-ANGLED	F-ITCHES	F-LIPPER	F-OWLERS	F-ROMAGE
F-ANGLES	F-LACKED	F-LITING	F-OWLING	F-RONTES
F-ANIONS	F-LACKER	F-LITTER	F-OXLIKE	F-ROSTED
F-ANKLED	F-LAGGED	F-LOCKED	F-OXTAIL	F-ROTHER
F-ANKLES	F-LAGGER	F-LOGGED	F-RABBIT	F-ROUGHY
F-ARCING	F-LAKERS	F-LOGGER	F-RAGGED	F-ROUNCE
F-ARMERS	F-LAKIER	F-LOOSIE	F-RAILER	F-RUGGED
F-ARMING	F-LAKING	F-LOPPED	F-RAILLY	F-RUMPED
F-ARRANT	F-LAMING	F-LOPPER	F-RAISED	F-RUMPLE
F-ARROWS	F-LAMMED	F-LOSSES	F-RAISES	F-RUSHED
F-ARSING	F-LANGER	F-LOURED	F-RANGER	F-RUSHES
F-ASHERY	F-LANKED	F-LOUSED	F-RANKED	F-UCKERS
F-ASHING	F-LANKER	F-LOUSES	F-RANKER	F-UGGING
F-ASTERS	F-LAPPED	F-LOUTED	F-RANKLY	F-UGLIER
F-ATTEST	F-LAPPER	F-LOWERS	F-RAPPED	F-ULLAGE
F-AWNERS	F-LASERS	F-LOWERY	F-RAPPEE	F-ULLING
F-AWNIER	F-LASHED	F-LOWING	F-RAPPES	F-UMBLES
F-AWNING	F-LASHER	F-LUBBER	F-RASSES	F-UNDIES
F-EARFUL	F-LASHES	F-LUFFED	F-RATERS	F-UNFAIR
F-EARING	F-LASKET	F-LUMMOX	F-RAUGHT	F-UNKING
F-EASING	F-LATTEN	F-LUMPED	F-RAYING	F-UNNEST
F-EASTED	F-LATTER	F-LUNKER	F-RAZZLE	
F-EASTER	F-LAUNCH	F-LUSHED	F-REAKED	
F-EATING	F-LAWING	F-LUSHER	F-REMITS	

Seven letters to eight

F-ABLINGS	F-LAGGING	F-LINTIER	F-LUTINGS	F-RINGING
F-ACTIONS	F-LAKIEST	F-LINTING	F-LUTISTS	F-RIPPERS
F-ACTURES	F-LAMMING	F-LIPPERS	F-ORPINES	F-RISKERS
F-ADDLING	F-LANCHED	F-LIPPING	F-OUTRING	F-RISKFUL
F-AIRINGS	F-LANCHES	F-LITTERS	F-OXTAILS	F-RISKIER
F-AIRWAYS	F-LANGERS	F-LOCKING	F-RACKING	F-RISKILY
F-ALCADES	F-LANKING	F-LOGGERS	F-RAGGING	F-RISKING
F-ALLOWED	F-LAPPERS	F-LOGGING	F-RAGMENT	F-RITTERS
F-ALTERED	F-LAPPING	F-LOOSIES	F-RAISING	F-RITTING
F-ALTERER	F-LASHERS	F-LOPPERS	F-RANGERS	F-RIZZERS
F-ANGLING	F-LASHING	F-LOPPIER	F-RANKERS	F-ROCKING
F-ANKLING	F-LASKETS	F-LOPPIES	F-RANKEST	F-ROMAGES
F-ARCINGS	F-LATTENS	F-LOPPING	F-RANKING	F-ROSTING
F-ARMINGS	F-LAWLESS	F-LOSSIER	F-RAPPING	F-ROTHERS
F-ARROWED	F-LECTION	F-LOUNDER	F-RATCHES	F-ROUNCES
F-AWNIEST	F-LEDGIER	F-LOURIER	F-RAZZLES	F-RUGGING
F-AWNINGS	F-LEECHED	F-LOURING	F-REAKING	F-RUMPING
F-EARLESS	F-LEECHES	F-LOUSING	F-REEDMAN	F-RUMPLED
F-EASTERS	F-LEERING	F-LOUTING	F-REEDMEN	F-RUMPLES
F-EASTING	F-LEGGING	F-LOWERED	F-RETTING	F-RUSHING
F-ESTIVAL	F-LENSING	F-LUBBERS	F-RICHTED	F-UGLIEST
F-ETCHERS	F-LETCHED	F-LUFFING	F-RICKING	F-ULLAGES
F-ETCHING	F-LETCHES	F-LUMPING	F-RIDGING	F-UNCTION
F-ETTLING	F-LICHTER	F-LUNKERS	F-RIGGERS	F-UNFAIRS
F-ICKLEST	F-LICKERS	F-LURRIES	F-RIGGING	F-UNHOUSE
F-IRELESS	F-LICKING	F-LUSHERS	F-RIGHTED	F-USELESS
F-LABELLA	F-LIGHTED	F-LUSHEST	F-RIGHTEN	F-UTILITY
F-LACKERS	F-LIMPING	F-LUSHIER	F-RIGIDER	
F-LACKING	F-LINCHES	F-LUSHING	F-RIGIDLY	
F-LAGGERS	F-LINGERS	F-LUSTERS	F-RILLING	

Eight letters to nine

F-ACTUALLY	F-LAPPINGS	F-LITTERED	F-LUSTERED	F-RIGHTFUL
F-ALLOWING	F-LASHINGS	F-LOCKINGS	F-LUSTRATE	F-RIGHTING
F-ALTERERS	F-LAUGHTER	F-LOGGINGS	F-LUXMETER	F-RIGIDEST
F-ALTERING	F-LAUNCHED	F-LOPPIEST	F-RACKINGS	F-RIGIDITY
F-ARROWING	F-LAUNCHES	F-LOSSIEST	F-RAGGINGS	F-RISKIEST
F-ASHERIES	F-LECTIONS	F-LOUNDERS	F-RAGMENTS	F-ROCKINGS
F-EASTINGS	F-LEDGIEST	F-LOURIEST	F-RANKNESS	F-ROCKLESS
F-IBERISES	F-LEECHING	F-LOWERIER	F-RATCHING	F-RUMPLING
F-LABELLUM	F-LEERINGS	F-LOWERING	F-RECKLING	F-UNCTIONS
F-LACKERED	F-LETCHING	F-LUMMOXES	F-RICHTING	F-UNHOUSES
F-LAGGINGS	F-LIGHTING	F-LUSHIEST	F-RIGGINGS	
F-LANCHING	F-LINTIEST	F-LUSHNESS	F-RIGHTENS	

F – End-hooks

Two letters to three

AL-F	DO-F	GI-F	NE-F	RE-F
AR-F	EF-F	IF-F	OF-F	SI-F
DE-F	EL-F	KA-F	OO-F	TE-F
DI-F	ER-F	KI-F	OR-F	WO-F

Three letters to four

ALE-F	CUR-F	GUL-F	NIE-F	SER-F
BAR-F	DEI-F	HOO-F	POO-F	SKY-F
BEE-F	DEL-F	HOW-F	PRO-F	SOW-F
BOY-F	DIF-F	HUM-F	REE-F	SUR-F
BUM-F	DOF-F	KAI-F	REI-F	TEF-F
CHE-F	DOW-F	KIF-F	RIF-F	WAI-F
CON-F	FIE-F	LEA-F	ROO-F	WOO-F
COO-F	GOA-F	LIE-F	SEI-F	WOW-F
COR-F	GOO-F	LOO-F	SEL-F	

Four letters to five

BRIE-F	HOWF-F	POUF-F	SHEA-F	SPIF-F
GANE-F	KALI-F	PROO-F	SKEE-F	
GONE-F	MOTI-F	SCAR-F	SNAR-F	
HOUF-F	PILA-F	SCUR-F	SOWF-F	

Five letters to six

BELIE-F	GONIF-F	RELIE-F
DECAF-F	PILAF-F	

Six letters to seven

SHERIF-F

G – Front-hooks

Two letters to three

G-AB	G-AS	G-ET	G-NU	G-OX
G-AD	G-AT	G-HI	G-OB	G-OY
G-AE	G-AY	G-ID	G-OD	G-UM
G-AG	G-ED	G-IF	G-OE	G-UN
G-AL	G-EE	G-IN	G-ON	G-UP
G-AM	G-EL	G-IO	G-OO	G-UR
G-AN	G-EM	G-IS	G-OR	G-US
G-AR	G-EN	G-IT	G-OS	G-UT

Three letters to four

G-ABS	G-ALL	G-ASP	G-ENE	G-IOS
G-ABY	G-ALS	G-ATE	G-ENS	G-ISM
G-ADS	G-AMA	G-AVE	G-ERE	G-ITS
G-AFF	G-AMP	G-AYS	G-EST	G-JUS
G-AGA	G-ANE	G-EAN	G-ETA	G-LAD
G-AGE	G-ANT	G-EAR	G-HAT	G-LAM
G-AGS	G-APE	G-EAT	G-HIS	G-LED
G-AID	G-APO	G-EDS	G-IDS	G-LEE
G-AIN	G-ARB	G-EEK	G-ILL	G-LEG
G-AIR	G-ARE	G-ELD	G-IMP	G-LEI
G-AIT	G-ARS	G-ELS	G-INK	G-LEY
G-ALA	G-ART	G-ELT	G-INN	G-LIB
G-ALE	G-ASH	G-EMS	G-INS	G-LID

F – End-hooks

G-LIT	G-OBO	G-OOR	G-RAT	G-ROK
G-LOB	G-OBS	G-OOS	G-RAY	G-ROT
G-LOP	G-ODS	G-ORA	G-REE	G-ROW
G-LOW	G-OES	G-ORE	G-REN	G-RUB
G-LUG	G-OFF	G-OUK	G-REW	G-RUE
G-LUM	G-OLD	G-OUT	G-REX	G-RUM
G-NAT	G-OLE	G-OWL	G-RID	G-ULE
G-NAW	G-ONE	G-OWN	G-RIG	G-UMP
G-NOW	G-ONS	G-OYS	G-RIM	G-UNS
G-NUS	G-OOF	G-RAD	G-RIN	G-UPS
G-OAF	G-OON	G-RAM	G-RIP	G-URN
G-OAT	G-OOP	G-RAN	G-RIT	G-UTS

Four letters to five

G-ABLE	G-ETAS	G-LISK	G-ORAL	G-RIMY
G-AGED	G-EYER	G-LITS	G-ORES	G-RIND
G-AGER	G-HAST	G-LOAM	G-OUKS	G-RINS
G-AGES	G-HATS	G-LOBE	G-OUTS	G-RIOT
G-AIDS	G-HAUT	G-LOBI	G-OWLS	G-RIPE
G-AINS	G-HEST	G-LOBS	G-OWNS	G-RIPS
G-AIRS	G-HOST	G-LODE	G-OXES	G-RIPT
G-AITS	G-ILLS	G-LOOM	G-RACE	G-RISE
G-ALAS	G-ILLY	G-LOOP	G-RADE	G-RITS
G-ALES	G-IMPS	G-LOPS	G-RADS	G-ROAN
G-ALLS	G-INKS	G-LORY	G-RAFF	G-ROIN
G-ALLY	G-IRON	G-LOSS	G-RAFT	G-ROKS
G-AMAS	G-ISMS	G-LOST	G-RAIL	G-ROMA
G-AMBO	G-LACE	G-LOUT	G-RAIN	G-RONE
G-AMIN	G-LADE	G-LOVE	G-RAMP	G-ROOF
G-AMPS	G-LADS	G-LOWS	G-RAMS	G-ROOM
G-ANTS	G-LADY	G-LUES	G-RANA	G-ROPE
G-APED	G-LAIK	G-LUGS	G-RAND	G-ROTS
G-APER	G-LAIR	G-LUMS	G-RANT	G-ROUP
G-APES	G-LAMS	G-LUTE	G-RAPE	G-ROUT
G-APOS	G-LAND	G-NATS	G-RASP	G-ROVE
G-ARBS	G-LARE	G-NOME	G-RATE	G-ROWS
G-ARIS	G-LASS	G-NOWS	G-RAVE	G-RUBS
G-ARUM	G-LAZE	G-OAFS	G-RAYS	G-RUED
G-ASPS	G-LAZY	G-OARY	G-RAZE	G-RUES
G-ATES	G-LEAM	G-OATS	G-REED	G-RUFF
G-AUNT	G-LEAN	G-OBOS	G-REEK	G-RUME
G-AVEL	G-LEED	G-ODSO	G-REEN	G-RUMP
G-AZON	G-LEEK	G-OFFS	G-REES	G-RUNT
G-EANS	G-LEES	G-OLDS	G-REGO	G-RYKE
G-EARS	G-LEET	G-OLDY	G-REIN	G-RYPE
G-EATS	G-LEIS	G-OLES	G-RENS	G-ULES
G-ELDS	G-LENS	G-OLPE	G-REWS	G-UMBO
G-ELTS	G-LENT	G-OMER	G-RICE	G-UMPS
G-EMMA	G-LEYS	G-ONER	G-RIDE	G-UNDY
G-EMMY	G-LIAS	G-OOFS	G-RIDS	G-URGE
G-ENES	G-LIBS	G-OOFY	G-RIFF	G-URNS
G-ERES	G-LIFT	G-OONS	G-RIFT	G-URUS
G-ERNE	G-LIKE	G-OOPS	G-RIGS	G-WINE
G-ESSE	G-LIME	G-OOSE	G-RILL	G-YELD
G-ESTS	G-LINT	G-OOSY	G-RIME	

Five letters to six

G-ABBED	G-ERNES	G-LOSSY	G-RAMPS	G-RIPES
G-ABIES	G-ESSES	G-LOUTS	G-RANDS	G-RISES
G-ABLED	G-HARRY	G-LOVED	G-RANGE	G-RIVET
G-ABLES	G-HAZEL	G-LOVER	G-RANTS	G-ROANS
G-ABLET	G-HOSTS	G-LOVES	G-RAPED	G-ROINS
G-ABOON	G-IGGED	G-LOWED	G-RAPES	G-ROMAS
G-ADDED	G-ILLER	G-LOWER	G-RASPS	G-RONES
G-ADDER	G-IMPED	G-LUMPS	G-RATED	G-ROOFS
G-AGERS	G-INGLE	G-LUMPY	G-RATER	G-ROOMS
G-AGGER	G-INNED	G-LUNCH	G-RATES	G-ROPED
G-AGING	G-INNER	G-LUTES	G-RAVED	G-ROPER
G-ALANT	G-IRONS	G-NAMMA	G-RAVEL	G-ROPES
G-ALLEY	G-LACES	G-NATTY	G-RAVEN	G-ROSET
G-ALLOW	G-LADES	G-NOMES	G-RAVER	G-ROUGH
G-AMBIT	G-LAIKS	G-NOMIC	G-RAVES	G-ROUND
G-AMBLE	G-LAIRS	G-NOSES	G-RAYED	G-ROUPS
G-AMBOS	G-LAIRY	G-OBANG	G-RAYLE	G-ROUPY
G-AMINE	G-LANCE	G-OBOES	G-RAZED	G-ROUSE
G-AMINS	G-LANDS	G-ODSOS	G-RAZER	G-ROUTS
G-AMMON	G-LARES	G-OFFED	G-RAZES	G-ROVED
G-ANGER	G-LAZED	G-OFFER	G-REAVE	G-ROVES
G-ANTED	G-LAZES	G-OLDEN	G-REEDS	G-ROWER
G-APERS	G-LEAMS	G-OLDER	G-REEDY	G-ROWTH
G-APING	G-LEANS	G-OLLER	G-REENS	G-ROYNE
G-ARGLE	G-LEAVE	G-OLPES	G-REGOS	G-RUBBY
G-ARISH	G-LEDGE	G-OMERS	G-REINS	G-RUFFS
G-ARRET	G-LEEKS	G-ONERS	G-RESES	G-RUING
G-ARUMS	G-LEETS	G-ONION	G-REWED	G-RUMES
G-ASHED	G-LIFTS	G-ONIUM	G-REXES	G-RUMLY
G-ASHES	G-LIKES	G-OORIE	G-RICED	G-RUMPS
G-ASPER	G-LIMED	G-OOSES	G-RICER	G-RUMPY
G-ASSES	G-LIMES	G-ORALS	G-RICES	G-RUNTS
G-ASTER	G-LINTS	G-ORGIA	G-RIDES	G-RYKES
G-AUGER	G-LINTY	G-OWLED	G-RIEVE	G-UMBOS
G-AUNTS	G-LISKS	G-OWNED	G-RIFFS	G-UMPED
G-AVELS	G-LOAMS	G-RACED	G-RIFTS	G-UNITE
G-AZONS	G-LOBBY	G-RACES	G-RILLE	G-UNMAN
G-EARED	G-LOBED	G-RAFFS	G-RILLS	G-URGED
G-ELATE	G-LOBES	G-RAFTS	G-RIMED	G-URGES
G-ELDER	G-LOBUS	G-RAILE	G-RIMES	G-URNED
G-EMOTE	G-LOOMS	G-RAILS	G-RINDS	G-USHER
G-ENDER	G-LOOPS	G-RAINE	G-RIOTS	G-UTTER
G-ENTRY	G-LOOPY	G-RAINS	G-RIPED	
G-ERNED	G-LOPPY	G-RAINY	G-RIPER	

Six letters to seven

G-ABLETS	G-ALLOWS	G-ARGLES	G-AUNTER	G-ERNING
G-ABLING	G-AMBITS	G-ARRETS	G-AUNTLY	G-ESTATE
G-ADDERS	G-AMBLED	G-ASEITY	G-EARING	G-HASTED
G-ADDING	G-AMBLER	G-ASHING	G-ELATED	G-HAZELS
G-AGGERS	G-AMBLES	G-ASKING	G-ELATES	G-HOSTED
G-ALLEYS	G-AMINES	G-ASPERS	G-ELDERS	G-HOSTLY
G-ALLIED	G-AMMONS	G-ASTERS	G-ELDING	G-IGGING
G-ALLIES	G-ANGERS	G-ASTRAL	G-EMOTES	G-IMMIES
G-ALLIUM	G-ANTING	G-AUDING	G-ENDERS	G-IMPING
G-ALLONS	G-ARGLED	G-AUGERS	G-ENLOCK	G-INGLES

G – Front-hooks

G-INNERS	G-LOBING	G-RAILES	G-RIDDLE	G-ROUTED
G-INNING	G-LOBOSE	G-RAINED	G-RIDING	G-ROUTER
G-IRONIC	G-LOBULE	G-RAINES	G-RIEVER	G-ROWERS
G-IZZARD	G-LOOMED	G-RANGER	G-RIEVES	G-ROWING
G-LACIER	G-LOOPED	G-RANGES	G-RIFTED	G-ROWTHS
G-LADDER	G-LOPPED	G-RANTED	G-RIGGED	G-ROYNES
G-LADDIE	G-LORIES	G-RANTER	G-RILLED	G-RUBBED
G-LAIRED	G-LOSSES	G-RAPIER	G-RILLES	G-RUBBER
G-LANCED	G-LOUTED	G-RAPING	G-RIMIER	G-RUBBLE
G-LANCER	G-LOVERS	G-RASPED	G-RIMING	G-RUEING
G-LANCES	G-LOVING	G-RASPER	G-RIMMER	G-RUFFED
G-LANDES	G-LOWERS	G-RASSES	G-RINDED	G-RUFFLY
G-LASSES	G-LOWING	G-RATERS	G-RIPERS	G-RUMBLE
G-LASSIE	G-LUGGED	G-RATIFY	G-RIPING	G-RUMBLY
G-LAZIER	G-LUTEAL	G-RATINE	G-RIPPED	G-RUMMER
G-LAZILY	G-OBANGS	G-RATING	G-RIPPER	G-RUMPED
G-LAZING	G-OFFERS	G-RAUNCH	G-RIPPLE	G-RUNTED
G-LEAMED	G-OFFING	G-RAVELS	G-RISING	G-ULLING
G-LEANED	G-OLDENS	G-RAVERS	G-RITTED	G-UMPING
G-LEANER	G-OLDEST	G-RAVING	G-RITTER	G-UNDIES
G-LEAVES	G-OLDISH	G-RAYING	G-RIVETS	G-UNITES
G-LEDGED	G-OLLERS	G-RAYLES	G-ROINED	G-UNLESS
G-LEDGES	G-OLLIES	G-RAZERS	G-ROOMED	G-UNLOCK
G-LEEING	G-OOFIER	G-RAZING	G-ROOMER	G-UNSHIP
G-LEGGER	G-OOSIER	G-REAVED	G-ROPERS	G-UNSHOT
G-LIBBED	G-ORGIAS	G-REAVES	G-ROPING	G-URGING
G-LIBBER	G-OUTFLY	G-REEKED	G-ROSETS	G-URNING
G-LIMING	G-OWLING	G-REGALE	G-ROSSER	G-USHERS
G-LIMMER	G-OWNING	G-REINED	G-ROUGHS	G-UTTERS
G-LINTED	G-RABBLE	G-RENNED	G-ROUNDS	G-YMPING
G-LISTEN	G-RACING	G-RICERS	G-ROUPED	
G-LISTER	G-RACKLE	G-RICING	G-ROUSED	
G-LITTER	G-RAFTED	G-RIDDED	G-ROUSER	
G-LOBATE	G-RAFTER	G-RIDDER	G-ROUSES	

Seven letters to eight

G-ALLISES	G-HOSTING	G-LITTERY	G-OFFERED	G-RAVINGS
G-ALLIUMS	G-INNINGS	G-LOAMING	G-OLDENED	G-RAYLING
G-ALLOWED	G-IZZARDS	G-LOBATED	G-ONENESS	G-REAVING
G-ALLYING	G-LABELLA	G-LOBULAR	G-OOFIEST	G-REEDIER
G-AMBLERS	G-LADDIES	G-LOBULES	G-OOSIEST	G-REEDILY
G-AMBLING	G-LAIRIER	G-LOOMING	G-OUTWEED	G-REEKING
G-ANGLING	G-LAIRING	G-LOOPIER	G-RABBLED	G-REGALES
G-ARGLING	G-LANCERS	G-LOOPING	G-RABBLER	G-REINING
G-ARISHES	G-LANCING	G-LOPPIER	G-RABBLES	G-RENNING
G-ASKINGS	G-LANDERS	G-LOPPING	G-RAFTERS	G-RIDDERS
G-EARINGS	G-LASSIES	G-LOSSIER	G-RAFTING	G-RIDDLED
G-EARLESS	G-LAZIEST	G-LOUTING	G-RAINIER	G-RIDDLES
G-ELASTIC	G-LEAMING	G-LOVINGS	G-RAINING	G-RIEVERS
G-ELATING	G-LEANERS	G-LOWERED	G-RANGERS	G-RIEVING
G-ELATION	G-LEANING	G-LUGGING	G-RANTERS	G-RIFTING
G-ELDINGS	G-LIBBING	G-LUMPIER	G-RANTING	G-RIGGING
G-ENLOCKS	G-LIMMERS	G-LUMPILY	G-RANULAR	G-RILLING
G-ENTRIES	G-LINTIER	G-LUMPISH	G-RASPERS	G-RIMIEST
G-ESTATED	G-LINTING	G-LUNCHED	G-RASPING	G-RINDING
G-ESTATES	G-LISTENS	G-LUNCHES	G-RATINGS	G-RINNING
G-HARRIES	G-LISTERS	G-NATTIER	G-RAVELED	G-RIPPERS
G-HASTING	G-LITTERS	G-OATLIKE	G-RAVELLY	G-RIPPIER

G-RIPPING	G-ROUCHES	G-ROWABLE	G-RUMBLER	G-UNPAPER
G-RIPPLES	G-ROUNDED	G-ROWINGS	G-RUMBLES	G-UNSHIPS
G-RITTERS	G-ROUNDER	G-RUBBERS	G-RUMMEST	G-UNSTICK
G-RITTING	G-ROUPING	G-RUBBING	G-RUMNESS	G-UNSTOCK
G-ROINING	G-ROUSERS	G-RUBBLED	G-RUMPING	G-UTTERED
G-ROOMERS	G-ROUSING	G-RUBBLES	G-UNHOUSE	
G-ROOMING	G-ROUTERS	G-RUFFING	G-UNLOCKS	
G-ROSSERS	G-ROUTING	G-RUMBLED	G-UNMAKER	

Eight letters to nine

G-ALLOWING	G-LISTENED	G-NATTIEST	G-RATIFIER	G-ROUTINGS
G-AMBLINGS	G-LITTERED	G-OFFERING	G-RATIFIES	G-RUBBLING
G-ANTELOPE	G-LOOPIEST	G-OLDENING	G-RAUNCHED	G-RUMBLERS
G-ASEITIES	G-LOPPIEST	G-OUTFLIES	G-RAUNCHES	G-RUMBLIER
G-ELATIONS	G-LOSSIEST	G-OUTWEEDS	G-RAVELING	G-RUMBLING
G-ESTATING	G-LOSSLESS	G-RABBLERS	G-RAVELLED	G-UNFOUGHT
G-HOSTINGS	G-LOVELESS	G-RABBLING	G-REEDIEST	G-UNHOUSES
G-LAIRIEST	G-LOWERING	G-RAFTINGS	G-REENGAGE	G-UNMAKERS
G-LANDLESS	G-LUGGABLE	G-RAINIEST	G-RIDDLING	G-UNPAPERS
G-LAZINESS	G-LUMPIEST	G-RAINLESS	G-RIMINESS	G-UNSTICKS
G-LEANINGS	G-LUNCHING	G-RAPESEED	G-ROUNDERS	G-UNSTOCKS
G-LINTIEST	G-MELINITE	G-RATIFIED	G-ROUNDING	G-UTTERING

G – End-hooks

Two letters to three

BA-G	EN-G	JO-G	MU-G	TA-G
BE-G	ER-G	LA-G	NA-G	TE-G
BI-G	FA-G	LI-G	NE-G	TI-G
BO-G	FE-G	LO-G	NO-G	TO-G
DA-G	GI-G	MA-G	PE-G	WO-G
DE-G	HA-G	ME-G	PI-G	YA-G
DI-G	HO-G	MI-G	RE-G	YU-G
DO-G	JA-G	MO-G	SO-G	ZA-G

Three letters to four

AGO-G	DON-G	HON-G	PAN-G	SKA-G
ARE-G	DUN-G	HUN-G	PEA-G	SON-G
BAN-G	FAN-G	JAG-G	PIN-G	SPA-G
BIG-G	FRA-G	KIN-G	PLU-G	SUN-G
BIN-G	FRO-G	LIN-G	PRO-G	TAI-G
BIO-G	FUN-G	MAG-G	PUN-G	TAN-G
BON-G	GAN-G	MAN-G	QUA-G	TEG-G
BOY-G	GIN-G	MAR-G	RAG-G	TIN-G
BRA-G	GON-G	MEN-G	RAN-G	TON-G
BRO-G	GOO-G	MIG-G	RIG-G	TUN-G
BUN-G	GUN-G	MON-G	RIN-G	VAN-G
BUR-G	HAG-G	MUG-G	RUN-G	VUG-G
CAN-G	HAN-G	MUN-G	SAN-G	WAN-G
DAN-G	HIN-G	NOG-G	SHA-G	WIN-G
DIN-G	HOG-G	NON-G	SIN-G	ZIN-G

G – Front-hooks

Four letters to five

AGIN-G	BLIN-G	COHO-G	RUIN-G	SWAN-G
AKIN-G	BOON-G	GULA-G	SKEG-G	THIN-G
ALAN-G	BRIN-G	HYLE-G	SPAN-G	THON-G
BEIN-G	CLAN-G	KAIN-G	STUN-G	TYIN-G

Five letters to six

ACTIN-G	GAMIN-G	LYSIN-G	RAVIN-G	SERIN-G
BARON-G	GOBAN-G	MATIN-G	RAWIN-G	SEWIN-G
BASIN-G	KOBAN-G	MIRIN-G	RICIN-G	SPAIN-G
BELON-G	LAKIN-G	PAVIN-G	ROBIN-G	TAKIN-G
CONIN-G	LAWIN-G	PHOTO-G	ROSIN-G	TAMIN-G
COVIN-G	LAYIN-G	POTIN-G	SARIN-G	ZAMAN-G
ELDIN-G	LIKIN-G	PROLE-G	SATIN-G	
ELFIN-G	LININ-G	PURIN-G	SAVIN-G	

Six letters to seven

BIFFIN-G	DOBBIN-G	HOGGIN-G	OUTSIN-G	RUFFIN-G
BIGGIN-G	DUBBIN-G	HOISIN-G	OUTWIN-G	SEISIN-G
BOBBIN-G	FARCIN-G	JERKIN-G	OVERDO-G	SEIZIN-G
BOFFIN-G	FECKIN-G	LAGGIN-G	PARKIN-G	STATIN-G
BUGGIN-G	FEERIN-G	LEGGIN-G	PERFIN-G	TANNIN-G
BUSKIN-G	FIRKIN-G	MARLIN-G	PERKIN-G	TELLIN-G
CALKIN-G	GASKIN-G	MARTIN-G	PICKIN-G	TIFFIN-G
CARLIN-G	GERMIN-G	MATTIN-G	PIGGIN-G	TREPAN-G
CATALO-G	GITTIN-G	MERLIN-G	PIPPIN-G	TROPIN-G
CATLIN-G	GLOBIN-G	MINGIN-G	POSTIN-G	UNAKIN-G
CODLIN-G	GRADIN-G	MUFFIN-G	PUFFIN-G	VERSIN-G
COFFIN-G	GRATIN-G	MUNTIN-G	PURLIN-G	WASHIN-G
COPPIN-G	HARMIN-G	MURLIN-G	RAISIN-G	WELKIN-G
CUFFIN-G	HARPIN-G	NOGGIN-G	RATLIN-G	WITHIN-G
CYCLIN-G	HENNIN-G	NUBBIN-G	RENNIN-G	
CYMLIN-G	HIPPIN-G	OUTRAN-G	RIGLIN-G	
DENTIN-G	HODDIN-G	OUTRUN-G	ROBBIN-G	

Seven letters to eight

ASPIRIN-G	GALOPIN-G	MAHJONG-G	RELAXIN-G	TABORIN-G
CHITLIN-G	GELATIN-G	MORPHIN-G	RESILIN-G	UNDERDO-G
CREATIN-G	GLAIRIN-G	PEARLIN-G	SCULPIN-G	
CRISPIN-G	HALFLIN-G	PUMPKIN-G	SPELDIN-G	
EASTLIN-G	LITTLIN-G	RATTLIN-G	SPONGIN-G	
FINIKIN-G	MAFFLIN-G	RAVELIN-G	STEARIN-G	

Eight letters to nine

ABSCISIN-G	DAMASKIN-G	INVERTIN-G	SNEESHIN-G	WARFARIN-G
BALLADIN-G	FINICKIN-G	LICHENIN-G	SPELDRIN-G	
BULLETIN-G	GOLLIWOG-G	SECRETIN-G	TABOURIN-G	

H – Front-hooks

Two letters to three

H-AD	H-AY	H-IN	H-OM	H-UH
H-AE	H-EH	H-IS	H-ON	H-UM
H-AG	H-EM	H-IT	H-OO	H-UN
H-AH	H-EN	H-MM	H-OP	H-UP
H-AM	H-ER	H-OB	H-OS	H-UT
H-AN	H-ES	H-OD	H-OW	H-YE
H-AS	H-ET	H-OE	H-OX	
H-AT	H-EX	H-OH	H-OY	
H-AW	H-ID	H-OI	H-UG	

Three letters to four

H-ADS	H-ARK	H-EME	H-ODS	H-ORE
H-AFF	H-ARM	H-EMS	H-OES	H-ORS
H-AFT	H-ART	H-END	H-OHS	H-OSE
H-AGS	H-ASH	H-ENS	H-OIK	H-OUR
H-AHA	H-ASK	H-ERE	H-OKA	H-OUT
H-AHS	H-ASP	H-ERN	H-OKE	H-OWE
H-AIL	H-ATE	H-ERS	H-OLD	H-OWL
H-AIN	H-AUF	H-EST	H-OLE	H-OYS
H-AIR	H-AVE	H-ETH	H-OLM	H-UGS
H-AKA	H-AYS	H-ICK	H-OMS	H-ULE
H-AKE	H-EAR	H-IDE	H-ONE	H-UMP
H-ALE	H-EAT	H-ILL	H-ONS	H-UNS
H-ALF	H-ECH	H-INS	H-OOF	H-UPS
H-ALL	H-EEL	H-IRE	H-OON	H-UTS
H-ALT	H-EFT	H-ISH	H-OOP	H-WAN
H-AND	H-EHS	H-ITS	H-OOT	H-YEN
H-ANT	H-ELD	H-OAR	H-OPE	H-YES
H-ARD	H-ELL	H-OBO	H-OPS	
H-ARE	H-ELM	H-OBS	H-ORA	

Four letters to five

H-ABLE	H-ARMS	H-EDGY	H-INKY	H-OOTS
H-AILS	H-ARTS	H-EELS	H-IRED	H-OPED
H-AINS	H-ASHY	H-EFTS	H-IRES	H-OPES
H-AIRS	H-ASKS	H-ELLS	H-ITCH	H-ORAL
H-AIRY	H-ASPS	H-ELMS	H-OARS	H-OSES
H-AKES	H-ATES	H-EMES	H-OARY	H-OURS
H-ALES	H-AUFS	H-EMIC	H-OAST	H-OUTS
H-ALFA	H-AULD	H-ENDS	H-OBOS	H-OVEL
H-ALFS	H-AUNT	H-ERES	H-OHED	H-OVEN
H-ALLS	H-AVER	H-ERNS	H-OIKS	H-OVER
H-ALMA	H-AVES	H-EROS	H-OKES	H-OWES
H-ALMS	H-AWED	H-ESTS	H-OLDS	H-OWLS
H-ALTS	H-AZAN	H-ETHS	H-OLES	H-OWRE
H-ANCE	H-EARD	H-EUGH	H-OLLA	H-OXES
H-ANDS	H-EARS	H-EWER	H-OLMS	H-ULES
H-ANSA	H-EAST	H-EXED	H-OMER	H-UMPH
H-ANTS	H-EATH	H-EXES	H-ONER	H-UMPS
H-ARDS	H-EATS	H-EYED	H-ONES	H-UMPY
H-ARED	H-EAVE	H-IDES	H-OOFS	H-URDS
H-ARES	H-ECHT	H-ILLS	H-OONS	H-YENS
H-ARKS	H-EDGE	H-ILLY	H-OOPS	

Five letters to six

H-ACKEE	H-ARBOR	H-EATER	H-IRING	H-OSIER
H-ACKER	H-ARISH	H-EAVED	H-ISHES	H-OTTER
H-AFTER	H-ARKED	H-EAVES	H-ITCHY	H-OUSEL
H-AGLET	H-ARLED	H-EDGED	H-ITHER	H-OUTED
H-AILED	H-ARMED	H-EDGER	H-OARED	H-OVELS
H-AIRED	H-ARMER	H-EDGES	H-OASTS	H-OVERS
H-ALFAS	H-ARROW	H-EIGHT	H-OBOES	H-OWLED
H-ALLEL	H-ARTAL	H-ELVES	H-OCKER	H-OWLER
H-ALLOT	H-ASHED	H-EMMER	H-OGGIN	H-OWLET
H-ALLOW	H-ASHES	H-ENDED	H-OHING	H-OWRES
H-ALMAS	H-AUGHT	H-ERSES	H-OLDEN	H-UGGED
H-ALOED	H-AUNTS	H-ETHER	H-OLDER	H-UMBLE
H-ALOES	H-AVENS	H-EUGHS	H-OLLAS	H-UMPED
H-ALTER	H-AVERS	H-EWERS	H-OLLER	H-UMPTY
H-AMATE	H-AWING	H-EXACT	H-OMBRE	H-UPPED
H-AMBLE	H-AZANS	H-EXING	H-OMERS	H-USHER
H-ANGER	H-EARDS	H-EYING	H-ONERS	
H-ANKER	H-EARTH	H-ILLER	H-OOPED	
H-ANTED	H-EASTS	H-INTER	H-OPING	

Six letters to seven

H-ABDABS	H-AMBLED	H-AUDING	H-EXACTS	H-OSIERY
H-ACKEES	H-AMBLES	H-AUNTER	H-EXARCH	H-OSTLER
H-ACKERS	H-ANGERS	H-AUTEUR	H-IDLING	H-OTTERS
H-ADDIES	H-ANKERS	H-EARING	H-INKIER	H-OUSELS
H-ADDING	H-ANTING	H-EARTHS	H-INTERS	H-OUTING
H-AFTERS	H-APLITE	H-EATERS	H-ITCHED	H-OVERED
H-AGGADA	H-ARBORS	H-EATING	H-ITCHES	H-OWLERS
H-AGLETS	H-ARBOUR	H-EDGERS	H-OARIER	H-OWLETS
H-AILING	H-ARKING	H-EDGIER	H-OARING	H-OWLING
H-AIRIER	H-ARLING	H-EDGING	H-OCKERS	H-UGGING
H-AIRING	H-ARMERS	H-EIGHTH	H-OGGINS	H-ULLING
H-ALBERT	H-ARMFUL	H-EIGHTS	H-OLLERS	H-UMBLES
H-ALLELS	H-ARMING	H-EMMERS	H-OLLIES	H-UMPIES
H-ALLOWS	H-ARROWS	H-ENDING	H-OMBRES	H-UMPING
H-ALTERS	H-ASHIER	H-ERRING	H-OOPING	H-UPPING
H-AMATES	H-ASHING	H-EUREKA	H-OSIERS	H-USHERS

Seven letters to eight

H-AGGADAH	H-ALBERTS	H-ARROWED	H-EIGHTHS	H-OROLOGY
H-AGGADAS	H-ALLOWED	H-ARUSPEX	H-ERRINGS	H-OSTLERS
H-AGGADIC	H-ALTERED	H-ASHIEST	H-EUREKAS	H-OTTERED
H-AGGADOT	H-AMBLING	H-AUNTERS	H-EXAMINE	H-OUTINGS
H-AIRIEST	H-AMBONES	H-AUTEURS	H-EXARCHY	H-OVERFLY
H-AIRLESS	H-APLITES	H-EARINGS	H-INKIEST	H-OVERING
H-AIRLIKE	H-APLITIC	H-EATABLE	H-ITCHIER	H-USHERED
H-AIRLINE	H-ARBORED	H-EATINGS	H-ITCHILY	
H-AIRLOCK	H-ARBOURS	H-EDGIEST	H-ITCHING	
H-ALATION	H-ARMLESS	H-EDGINGS	H-OARIEST	

Eight letters to nine

H-AGGADAHS	H-AIRLOCKS	H-ARBOURED	H-EXAMINES	H-OOLACHAN
H-AGGADOTH	H-ALATIONS	H-ARMONICA	H-ITCHIEST	H-OSIERIES
H-AIRBRUSH	H-ALLOWING	H-ARQUEBUS	H-ODOGRAPH	H-OTTERING
H-AIRINESS	H-ALTERING	H-ARROWING	H-ODOMETER	H-USHERING
H-AIRLINES	H-ARBOROUS	H-ESSONITE	H-ODOMETRY	

H – End-hooks

Two letters to three

AA-H	ED-H	HO-H	PA-H	UG-H
AS-H	ET-H	IS-H	PE-H	YA-H
BA-H	FA-H	LA-H	PO-H	YE-H
BO-H	FE-H	NA-H	RE-H	
DA-H	HA-H	NO-H	SH-H	
DO-H	HE-H	OO-H	SO-H	

Three letters to four

AMA-H	EAT-H	LIT-H	PAS-H	SIN-H
ARC-H	FAS-H	LOS-H	PAT-H	SIT-H
BAC-H	GAS-H	LOT-H	PEC-H	SOP-H
BAG-H	GAT-H	MAC-H	PEG-H	SOT-H
BAS-H	GOS-H	MAS-H	PHO-H	SUK-H
BAT-H	GOT-H	MAT-H	PIS-H	TAN-H
BET-H	GUS-H	MES-H	PIT-H	TAS-H
BIS-H	HAS-H	MET-H	POO-H	TAT-H
BOO-H	HAT-H	MIC-H	POS-H	TEC-H
BOS-H	HET-H	MOC-H	PUG-H	TET-H
BOT-H	HIS-H	MOS-H	PUS-H	TIC-H
BUS-H	HOG-H	MOT-H	RAS-H	TOP-H
CAP-H	HUN-H	MUS-H	RAT-H	UMP-H
COS-H	KIS-H	NIS-H	RES-H	VUG-H
COT-H	KIT-H	NOS-H	ROC-H	WAS-H
DAS-H	KOP-H	OAT-H	RUT-H	WIS-H
DIS-H	KUE-H	ODA-H	SEC-H	WIT-H
DOS-H	LAS-H	OKE-H	SHA-H	YEA-H
DOT-H	LAT-H	OUP-H	SIC-H	YOD-H

Four letters to five

ABAS-H	BUND-H	FROS-H	LOTA-H	ROWT-H
AIRT-H	BURG-H	GALA-H	MANE-H	SANG-H
ALMA-H	CANE-H	GART-H	MARA-H	SCAT-H
ALME-H	CHIC-H	GIRT-H	MARC-H	SIRI-H
ARIS-H	CLOT-H	GRIT-H	MARS-H	SLOT-H
BAIT-H	CRIT-H	GULP-H	MEAT-H	SMIT-H
BAND-H	CRUS-H	GURS-H	MERC-H	SOLA-H
BEAT-H	DADA-H	HEAT-H	MUST-H	SOOT-H
BIMA-H	DONA-H	HORA-H	MYNA-H	SOUT-H
BOOT-H	DOSE-H	HUMP-H	NEAT-H	STAP-H
BRAS-H	DUNS-H	KANE-H	PLUS-H	SUBA-H
BRIT-H	EPHA-H	KHET-H	PUJA-H	SUMP-H
BROG-H	FLUS-H	LAIC-H	RAJA-H	SURA-H
BRUS-H	FORT-H	LEAS-H	RAYA-H	SWAT-H
BUMP-H	FRIT-H	LEIS-H	ROUT-H	SYNC-H

H – Front-hooks

TAIS-H   THIG-H   TORA-H   WOOS-H
TAVA-H   TILT-H   TORC-H   WORT-H
TENT-H   TOOT-H   TROT-H

Five letters to six

ALIYA-H	FINIS-H	KIBLA-H	POOJA-H	STOUT-H
ANKUS-H	GALUT-H	KYBOS-H	PRUTA-H	SUMAC-H
ARRIS-H	GAMAS-H	LAMED-H	PUNKA-H	SUNNA-H
ASPIS-H	GANJA-H	LAVAS-H	PURDA-H	SWART-H
CAMAS-H	GARIS-H	LIROT-H	RAKIS-H	TANNA-H
COHOS-H	GRUMP-H	LOOFA-H	RUPIA-H	THANA-H
COMET-H	HALVA-H	MATZA-H	SAMEK-H	TOROT-H
COPRA-H	HAMZA-H	MATZO-H	SCARP-H	TREFA-H
COSEC-H	HEART-H	MINIS-H	SCART-H	VAREC-H
CREES-H	HIGHT-H	MOLLA-H	SCOUT-H	WAIRS-H
DALED-H	HIJRA-H	MOOLA-H	SHEIK-H	WALLA-H
DARGA-H	HOOKA-H	MULLA-H	SHIVA-H	WIRRA-H
DELIS-H	HURRA-H	NALLA-H	SIRRA-H	ZIBET-H
DOURA-H	HUZZA-H	NULLA-H	SKART-H	ZILLA-H
DUKKA-H	IMPIS-H	PALLA-H	SMOOT-H	ZIZIT-H
EIGHT-H	INWIT-H	PARIS-H	SNEES-H	
FATWA-H	KHEDA-H	PERIS-H	SPART-H	
FELLA-H	KIBBE-H	POLIS-H	SPILT-H	

Six letters to seven

AARRGH-H	CHUPPA-H	MATZOT-H	QABALA-H	SUCCOT-H
AGGADA-H	FILMIS-H	MEGILP-H	SABBAT-H	SUKKOT-H
AGOROT-H	GRAMAS-H	MEZUZA-H	SABKHA-H	TALLIS-H
ALIYOT-H	HAGGIS-H	MIKVOT-H	SAHIBA-H	TALLIT-H
BABOOS-H	HALALA-H	MISSIS-H	SHANTI-H	TEREFA-H
BILLYO-H	HALLOT-H	OUTWIT-H	SHARIA-H	THANNA-H
BUSHWA-H	HEIGHT-H	PARKIS-H	SHIKSE-H	TURBIT-H
CADDIS-H	HUTZPA-H	PITARA-H	SIMURG-H	UNGIRT-H
CHALLA-H	LUCHOT-H	POORIS-H	STEALT-H	
CHALOT-H	MASTIC-H	PRUTOT-H	STIRRA-H	

Seven letters to eight

AGGADOT-H	GENIZOT-H	JELLABA-H	MESHUGA-H	SHAMMAS-H
AMARANT-H	HAFTARA-H	KABBALA-H	MEZUZOT-H	SHEHITA-H
BEGORRA-H	HAGGADA-H	KASHRUT-H	NARGILE-H	TZITZIT-H
CABBALA-H	HALAKHA-H	KETUBOT-H	OCTOPUS-H	VERANDA-H
CHALLOT-H	HAROSET-H	KHALIFA-H	PEISHWA-H	YESHIVA-H
CHUTZPA-H	HOSANNA-H	MADRASA-H	RABBITO-H	
GALABEA-H	HYDRANT-H	MASTABA-H	SAVANNA-H	
GALABIA-H	JAMBIYA-H	MEGILLA-H	SCAMPIS-H	

Eight letters to nine

ALLELUIA-H	GALLABIA-H	HAPHTARA-H	PARASHOT-H	TELESTIC-H
CHAROSET-H	HAFTAROT-H	INTIFADA-H	SANDARAC-H	YESHIVOT-H
DAHABIYA-H	HAFTOROT-H	KHANSAMA-H	SHAMIANA-H	
DJELLABA-H	HAGGADOT-H	MADRASSA-H	SHECHITA-H	
GALABIYA-H	HALACHOT-H	MAHARAJA-H	SHILLALA-H	
GALLABEA-H	HALAKHOT-H	MESHUGGA-H	TALLITOT-H	

I – Front-hooks

Two letters to three

I-CH	I-ON	I-RE	I-SO
I-DE	I-OS	I-SH	I-TA

Three letters to four

I-BIS	I-GAD	I-LEX	I-RED	I-SOS
I-CON	I-KAT	I-MAM	I-RES	I-TAS
I-DEE	I-KON	I-MID	I-RID	I-URE
I-DOL	I-LEA	I-ONS	I-SIT	I-WIS

Four letters to five

I-CONS	I-GAPO	I-MAMS	I-RADE	I-SLED
I-DANT	I-KANS	I-MIDS	I-RATE	I-TEMS
I-DEAL	I-KATS	I-MINE	I-RIDS	I-VIED
I-DEES	I-KONS	I-MINO	I-RING	I-VIES
I-DENT	I-LEAL	I-NANE	I-RONE	
I-DOLS	I-MAGE	I-ODIC	I-SHES	

Five letters to six

I-BICES	I-DEALS	I-MAGES	I-ONIUM	I-SATIN
I-BISES	I-DENTS	I-MINES	I-RATER	I-SLING
I-CONES	I-GAPOS	I-NERTS	I-RIDES	I-TEMED
I-CONIC	I-GUANA	I-NYALA	I-RISES	
I-DANTS	I-LEXES	I-ODISM	I-RONES	

Six letters to seven

I-GUANAS	I-NYALAS	I-ONIUMS	I-SATINS
I-MAGISM	I-ODISMS	I-RISING	I-SOLATE

Seven letters to eight

I-CONICAL	I-SABELLA	I-SOLATED	I-SOLATES
I-MAGISMS	I-SLANDER		

Eight letters to nine

I-CONICITY	I-SABELLAS	I-SOLATING	I-SOLATION
I-ODOMETRY	I-SLANDERS		

I – End-hooks

Two letters to three

AH-I	CH-I	KA-I	PO-I
AM-I	DE-I	KO-I	RE-I
AN-I	HO-I	MO-I	TA-I
BO-I	JA-I	OB-I	UN-I

Three letters to four

ANT-I	FIN-I	MAL-I	NOR-I	SIR-I
ART-I	GAD-I	MAN-I	PAD-I	SOL-I
BAN-I	GAR-I	MAX-I	PEN-I	TAB-I
BEN-I	GOR-I	MID-I	PER-I	TAK-I
BID-I	HAJ-I	MIR-I	PIP-I	TAX-I
BUD-I	IMP-I	MOA-I	PUL-I	TIP-I
CAD-I	KAK-I	MOD-I	PUR-I	TIT-I
CAP-I	KAM-I	MOM-I	QUA-I	TOP-I
CHA-I	KAT-I	MOO-I	RAG-I	TOR-I
CON-I	KEP-I	MOT-I	RAM-I	VAG-I
DAL-I	LAR-I	MUN-I	RAN-I	WAD-I
DEF-I	LAT-I	MUT-I	RAN-I	YAG-I
DEL-I	LOB-I	NID-I	ROT-I	YET-I
DEN-I	LOT-I	NIS-I	SAD-I	YON-I
DIV-I	MAG-I	NOD-I	SAR-I	ZIT-I
FEN-I	MAK-I	NON-I	SAT-I	
			SIM-I	

Four letters to five

ABAC-I	CURL-I	JINN-I	OBOL-I	SHOG-I
BASS-I	CURS-I	KIBE-I	PALP-I	SOLD-I
BAST-I	DASH-I	KORA-I	PARD-I	SOLE-I
BEST-I	DILL-I	LANA-I	PARK-I	STOA-I
BIND-I	DISC-I	LASS-I	PART-I	SWAM-I
BLIN-I	FAST-I	LATH-I	PILE-I	TANG-I
BUFF-I	FERM-I	LENT-I	POOR-I	TARS-I
BUST-I	FILM-I	LICH-I	PRIM-I	TAWA-I
CAMP-I	FRAT-I	LIMB-I	PULL-I	TEMP-I
CARD-I	FUND-I	LOGO-I	PUTT-I	TOPH-I
CARP-I	FUNG-I	LUNG-I	RANG-I	TOPO-I
CEIL-I	GLOB-I	MACH-I	REIK-I	TORI-I
CELL-I	HADJ-I	MAND-I	ROST-I	TORS-I
COAT-I	HAJJ-I	MODI-I	SAMP-I	VILL-I
COMB-I	HANG-I	MOOL-I	SCUD-I	VOLT-I
CORN-I	HONG-I	MURR-I	SENS-I	XYST-I
CROC-I	HOUR-I	MYTH-I	SENT-I	ZIMB-I
CULT-I	IAMB-I	NIMB-I	SERA-I	

Five letters to six

ANNUL-I	DENAR-I	HAIKA-I	MOIRA-I	SMALT-I
ARGAL-I	DEWAN-I	HERMA-I	NEROL-I	SOLID-I
AVANT-I	DJINN-I	JEHAD-I	PIROG-I	STELA-I
CAROL-I	DUETT-I	JIHAD-I	POLYP-I	TAPET-I
CHICH-I	EPHOR-I	JOWAR-I	RHOMB-I	YOGIN-I
CHILL-I	EQUAL-I	KAIKA-I	SCAMP-I	
CLYPE-I	FRACT-I	KROON-I	SENSE-I	
COLON-I	GARDA-I	KULAK-I	SHALL-I	
CUBIT-I	GLUTE-I	MANAT-I	SILEN-I	

Six letters to seven

ABOMAS-I	BANDAR-I	DAKOIT-I	ELENCH-I	HALLAL-I
ACANTH-I	CHIASM-I	DEMENT-I	EPIGON-I	HELLER-I
AFGHAN-I	DACTYL-I	DENARI-I	GRADIN-I	JAMPAN-I

MARTIN-I	PAESAN-I	REVERS-I	SECOND-I	SIGNOR-I
OBLAST-I	QAWWAL-I	RHYTHM-I	SHIKAR-I	TYMPAN-I

Seven letters to eight

BRAHMAN-I	CONDUCT-I	FASCISM-I	PARCHES-I	TROCHIL-I
CALAMAR-I	CORNETT-I	FASCIST-I	PERFECT-I	ZECCHIN-I
CAPITAN-I	COTHURN-I	HETAIRA-I	SIGNIOR-I	
CONCEPT-I	DRACHMA-I	KOFTGAR-I	STROBIL-I	
CONCERT-I	DUUMVIR-I	MARCHES-I	TANDOOR-I	

Eight letters to nine

ASTRAGAL-I	EUCALYPT-I	PASTORAL-I	QUARTETT-I	TRIUMVIR-I
CANNELON-I	LEYLANDI-I	PEDIPALP-I	QUINTETT-I	ZAMINDAR-I
CHORIAMB-I	MATACHIN-I	PHOSPHOR-I	RICERCAR-I	ZEMINDAR-I
DECEMVIR-I	MOSASAUR-I	PORTOLAN-I	STRELITZ-I	

J – Front-hooks

Two letters to three

J-AB	J-AR	J-ET	J-OR	J-UN
J-AG	J-AW	J-IN	J-OW	J-US
J-AI	J-AY	J-OB	J-OY	J-UT
J-AM	J-EE	J-OE	J-UG	

Three letters to four

J-ABS	J-ASP	J-EON	J-ISM	J-OWL
J-AGA	J-ASS	J-ERK	J-IVY	J-OYS
J-AGS	J-AUK	J-ESS	J-OBE	J-UDO
J-AIL	J-AVA	J-EST	J-OBS	J-UDS
J-AKE	J-AYS	J-IFF	J-OES	J-UGS
J-ANE	J-EAN	J-ILL	J-OKE	J-UKE
J-ANN	J-EAT	J-IMP	J-OLE	J-UMP
J-APE	J-EEL	J-INK	J-ORS	J-URE
J-ARK	J-EFF	J-INN	J-OUK	J-UTE
J-ARS	J-ELL	J-INS	J-OUR	J-UTS

Four letters to five

J-AGAS	J-ASPS	J-EMMY	J-OBES	J-UKES
J-AGER	J-AUKS	J-ERKS	J-OINT	J-UMBO
J-AILS	J-AUNT	J-ESSE	J-OKES	J-UMPS
J-AKES	J-AVAS	J-ESTS	J-OLES	J-UMPY
J-ALAP	J-AVEL	J-IFFY	J-ONES	J-UNCO
J-AMBO	J-AWED	J-ILLS	J-OUKS	J-UNTO
J-ANES	J-EANS	J-IMMY	J-OURS	J-UPON
J-ANNS	J-EATS	J-INGO	J-OUST	J-UTES
J-APED	J-EELS	J-INKS	J-OWED	
J-APER	J-EELY	J-INNS	J-OWLS	
J-APES	J-EFFS	J-ISMS	J-OWLY	
J-ARKS	J-ELLS	J-NANA	J-UDOS	

Five letters to six

J-ABBED	J-APERS	J-AVELS	J-INKER	J-UGGED
J-ACKER	J-APERY	J-AWING	J-NANAS	J-UMBLE
J-AGERS	J-APING	J-EANED	J-OINTS	J-UMBOS
J-AGGER	J-ARGON	J-EFFED	J-OTTER	J-UMPED
J-AILED	J-ARRAH	J-ESSES	J-OUNCE	J-UNCOS
J-ALAPS	J-ASPER	J-ESTER	J-OUSTS	J-UNCUS
J-AMBER	J-ASPIS	J-IGGED	J-OWING	J-UNKED
J-AMBOS	J-ASSES	J-IMPLY	J-OWLED	J-UNKET
J-ANGLE	J-AUNTS	J-INGLE	J-OWLER	
J-ANKER	J-AUNTY	J-INKED	J-UDDER	

Six letters to seven

J-ACKERS	J-ANKERS	J-IMMIES	J-OSTLER	J-UDDERS
J-AGGERS	J-ARGONS	J-INGLES	J-OTTERS	J-UGGING
J-AGGIES	J-ASPERS	J-INGOES	J-OUNCES	J-UMBLES
J-AILING	J-AUNTIE	J-INKERS	J-OUSTED	J-UMPING
J-AMBERS	J-AWLESS	J-INKING	J-OUSTER	J-UNCATE
J-ANGLED	J-EFFING	J-OCULAR	J-OWLERS	J-UNCOES
J-ANGLER	J-ESTERS	J-OINTED	J-OWLIER	J-UNKING
J-ANGLES	J-IGGING	J-OLLIES	J-OWLING	

Seven letters to eight

J-AMBONES	J-APERIES	J-OINTING	J-OUSTING	J-UNCTION
J-ANGLERS	J-ASPISES	J-OSTLERS	J-OWLIEST	
J-ANGLING	J-AUNTIES	J-OUSTERS	J-UDDERED	

Eight letters to nine

J-ANGLINGS	J-OCULARLY
J-ASPEROUS	J-UNCTIONS

J – End-hooks

Two letters to three

HA-J
TA-J

Three letters to four

BEN-J	HAJ-J
HAD-J	

K – Front-hooks

Two letters to three

K-AB	K-AW	K-ET	K-IS	K-OR
K-AE	K-AY	K-EX	K-IT	K-OS
K-AI	K-EA	K-HI	K-OB	K-OW
K-AM	K-ED	K-ID	K-OI	K-YE
K-AS	K-EF	K-IF	K-ON	K-YU
K-AT	K-EN	K-IN	K-OP	

Three letters to four

K-AAL	K-ARK	K-ERN	K-ITS	K-OFF
K-AAS	K-ART	K-EST	K-IWI	K-ONS
K-ABS	K-AVA	K-ETA	K-LAP	K-OPS
K-AGO	K-AWA	K-HAN	K-NAG	K-ORA
K-AID	K-AYS	K-HAT	K-NAP	K-ORE
K-AIL	K-BAR	K-HET	K-NEE	K-ORS
K-AIM	K-EAS	K-HIS	K-NEW	K-SAR
K-AIN	K-EDS	K-ICK	K-NIT	K-UDO
K-AIS	K-EEK	K-IDS	K-NOB	K-UTA
K-AKA	K-EEL	K-IFF	K-NOT	K-UTU
K-ALE	K-EEN	K-IFS	K-NOW	K-VAS
K-AMA	K-EFS	K-ILL	K-NUB	K-YAK
K-AMI	K-ELL	K-INK	K-NUR	K-YAR
K-ANA	K-ELT	K-INS	K-NUT	K-YES
K-ANE	K-ENS	K-IRK	K-OBO	K-YUS
K-ANT	K-ERF	K-ISH	K-OBS	

Four letters to five

K-AIDS	K-EDGY	K-ICKY	K-NITS	K-RAIT
K-AILS	K-EECH	K-ILLS	K-NOBS	K-RANG
K-AIMS	K-EELS	K-INKS	K-NOCK	K-RILL
K-AINS	K-ELLS	K-INKY	K-NOLL	K-RONE
K-ALES	K-ELTS	K-IRKS	K-NOUT	K-ROON
K-ALIF	K-EMPT	K-IWIS	K-NOWN	K-SARS
K-AMAS	K-ERNE	K-LANG	K-NOWS	K-UDOS
K-AMIS	K-ERNS	K-LAPS	K-NUBS	K-ULAN
K-ANAS	K-EROS	K-LICK	K-NURL	K-URUS
K-ANES	K-ESTS	K-LONG	K-NURR	K-UTAS
K-ANGA	K-ETAS	K-LOOF	K-NURS	K-UTIS
K-ANTS	K-ETCH	K-LUGE	K-NUTS	K-UTUS
K-ARKS	K-EVIL	K-LUTZ	K-OBOS	K-VELL
K-ARSY	K-EXES	K-NAGS	K-OFFS	K-YACK
K-ARTS	K-EYED	K-NAPS	K-OKRA	K-YAKS
K-AVAS	K-HATS	K-NAVE	K-OMBU	K-YANG
K-AWED	K-HETH	K-NEED	K-ORES	
K-BARS	K-HETS	K-NIFE	K-OSES	
K-EDGE	K-HORS	K-NISH	K-RAFT	

Five letters to six

K-ABAKA	K-EBBED	K-HETHS	K-LUGED	K-OKRAS
K-ABAYA	K-EDGED	K-HODJA	K-LUGES	K-OMBUS
K-ABELE	K-EDGER	K-ICKER	K-NAGGY	K-RAFTS
K-AINGA	K-EDGES	K-ILLER	K-NAVES	K-RAITS
K-ALIFS	K-EGGED	K-INDIE	K-NICKS	K-RATER
K-ALONG	K-EGGER	K-INGLE	K-NIFES	K-RILLS
K-ANGAS	K-EIGHT	K-INKED	K-NIGHT	K-RISES
K-ANTAR	K-EMBED	K-INKLE	K-NOBBY	K-ROONS
K-ANTED	K-ENTIA	K-IRKED	K-NOCKS	K-ULANS
K-ARKED	K-ERNED	K-ISHES	K-NOLLS	K-VASES
K-ARRIS	K-ERNES	K-LATCH	K-NUBBY	K-VELLS
K-ARSEY	K-ETTLE	K-LICKS	K-NURLS	K-VETCH
K-AURIS	K-EVILS	K-LONGS	K-NURRS	K-YACKS
K-AWING	K-EYING	K-LOOFS	K-OBANG	K-YANGS

Six letters to seven

K-ABAKAS	K-EDGING	K-ICKERS	K-LINKER	K-NUBBLE
K-ABAYAS	K-EECHES	K-ICKIER	K-LISTER	K-NUBBLY
K-ABELES	K-EGGERS	K-IDLING	K-LUGING	K-NURLED
K-AINGAS	K-EGGING	K-INDIES	K-LUTZES	K-OBANGS
K-AMISES	K-ENOSES	K-INGLES	K-NAPPED	K-ONNING
K-ANTARS	K-ENOSIS	K-INKIER	K-NAPPER	K-RATERS
K-ANTING	K-ERNING	K-INKING	K-NICKER	K-RIMMER
K-ARKING	K-ETCHES	K-INKLES	K-NIGHTS	K-RISING
K-EBBING	K-ETTLES	K-INSHIP	K-NISHES	K-VETCHY
K-EDGERS	K-HANJAR	K-IRKING	K-NOBBLE	
K-EDGIER	K-HODJAS	K-LAPPED	K-NOCKED	

Seven letters to eight

K-ALEWIFE	K-INKIEST	K-NAGGIER	K-NOBBIER	K-NUBBLES
K-EDGIEST	K-INSHIPS	K-NAPPERS	K-NOBBLED	K-NURLING
K-ETAMINE	K-LAPPING	K-NAPPING	K-NOBBLES	K-OSMOSES
K-ETCHING	K-LATCHES	K-NICKERS	K-NOCKING	K-RIMMERS
K-HANJARS	K-LINKERS	K-NIGHTED	K-NUBBIER	K-VETCHES
K-ICKIEST	K-LISTERS	K-NIGHTLY	K-NUBBLED	

Eight letters to nine

K-ALEWIVES	K-INKINESS	K-NICKERED	K-NUBBIEST	K-VETCHIER
K-ENOSISES	K-NAGGIEST	K-NOBBIEST	K-NUBBLIER	
K-ETAMINES	K-NEVELLED	K-NOBBLING	K-NUBBLING	

K – End-hooks

Two letters to three

AR-K	EE-K	JA-K	OI-K	WO-K
AS-K	EL-K	KA-K	OU-K	YA-K
BO-K	ER-K	MA-K	SI-K	YO-K
DA-K	IN-K	NE-K	TA-K	YU-K

Three letters to four

BAC-K	CAW-K	FIN-K	HOW-K	LUR-K
BAL-K	CHI-K	FIR-K	HUN-K	MAC-K
BAN-K	CON-K	FOR-K	JAR-K	MAR-K
BAR-K	COO-K	FUN-K	JIN-K	MAS-K
BAS-K	COR-K	GEE-K	JUN-K	MAW-K
BIN-K	COW-K	GIN-K	KAI-K	MEE-K
BIS-K	DAN-K	GON-K	KIN-K	MIC-K
BOA-K	DAW-K	GOO-K	KIR-K	MIL-K
BON-K	DEE-K	GUN-K	KON-K	MIR-K
BOO-K	DIN-K	HAN-K	LAC-K	MOC-K
BOR-K	DIS-K	HAS-K	LAR-K	MON-K
BOS-K	DOC-K	HAW-K	LAW-K	MOO-K
BRA-K	DOE-K	HIC-K	LEA-K	MOS-K
BUN-K	DOO-K	HOC-K	LEE-K	MUS-K
BUR-K	DOR-K	HOI-K	LIN-K	NAB-K
BUS-K	DUN-K	HON-K	LIS-K	NOO-K
CAR-K	FAN-K	HOO-K	LOO-K	NOR-K

PAC-K	POO-K	ROO-K	SOU-K	VOL-K
PAR-K	PUL-K	RUC-K	SUN-K	WAN-K
PAW-K	PUN-K	SAC-K	TAN-K	WAR-K
PEA-K	RAI-K	SAN-K	TAS-K	WEE-K
PEC-K	RAN-K	SAR-K	TEA-K	WIN-K
PEE-K	REC-K	SEE-K	TEE-K	WON-K
PEN-K	REE-K	SEI-K	TIC-K	YAR-K
PER-K	REI-K	SER-K	TIN-K	YES-K
PIC-K	REN-K	SIC-K	TOC-K	YOU-K
PIN-K	RIN-K	SIN-K	TON-K	
POL-K	ROC-K	SOC-K	TOO-K	

Four letters to five

ABAC-K	CHAW-K	FRIS-K	SKIN-K	SWAN-K
ABAS-K	CHIC-K	GLEE-K	SLEE-K	TALA-K
ALEC-K	CHIN-K	GREE-K	SMEE-K	TARO-K
BLIN-K	CHOC-K	KAMI-K	SMIR-K	THAN-K
BLOC-K	CHOW-K	KULA-K	SNAR-K	THEE-K
BOBA-K	CLAN-K	MALI-K	SNOW-K	THIN-K
BORA-K	CLON-K	PLAN-K	SPAN-K	TOPE-K
BRAN-K	CRAN-K	PULI-K	SPAR-K	TORS-K
BRIN-K	CREE-K	REIN-K	SPEC-K	TRON-K
BRIS-K	CROC-K	SAIC-K	SPIC-K	TWIN-K
BROO-K	DRAC-K	SAME-K	SPIN-K	UPTA-K
BRUS-K	ERIC-K	SCUL-K	SPUN-K	WAUL-K
CAUL-K	FLAN-K	SHAN-K	STAR-K	
CHAL-K	FLIC-K	SHIR-K	STIR-K	
CHAR-K	FLOC-K	SHOO-K	STUN-K	

Five letters to six

ANTIC-K	EMBAR-K	MEDIC-K	PANIC-K	UMIAC-K
ASPIC-K	IMBAR-K	MELIC-K	REBEC-K	UNBAR-K
BEGUN-K	JAMBO-K	MUSIC-K	RESEE-K	ZEBEC-K
DEBAR-K	KALPA-K	PACHA-K	SQUAW-K	

Six letters to seven

AMTRAC-K	DISBAR-K	LIMBEC-K	OUTRAN-K
BOOBOO-K	FINNAC-K	OOMIAC-K	TIETAC-K
CALPAC-K	GWEDUC-K	OUTBAR-K	TOMBAC-K

Seven letters to eight

ALMANAC-K	BAUDRIC-K	OVERRAN-K	PRACTIC-K	SHOEPAC-K
BALDRIC-K	FORERAN-K	POLITIC-K	SHELLAC-K	TAMARIS-K

Eight letters to nine

BERGAMAS-K
OVERTHIN-K

K – End-hooks

L – Front-hooks

Two letters to three

L-AB	L-AT	L-ES	L-OB	L-OW
L-AD	L-AW	L-ET	L-OD	L-OX
L-AG	L-AX	L-EX	L-OO	L-OY
L-AH	L-AY	L-ID	L-OP	L-UG
L-AM	L-EA	L-IN	L-OR	L-UM
L-AR	L-ED	L-IS	L-OS	L-UR
L-AS	L-EE	L-IT	L-OU	L-YE

Three letters to four

L-ABS	L-ASS	L-ESS	L-OBS	L-OUP
L-ACE	L-ATE	L-EST	L-OCA	L-OUR
L-ADS	L-AUF	L-EVE	L-OCH	L-OUS
L-AGS	L-AVA	L-EVO	L-ODE	L-OUT
L-AHS	L-AVE	L-ICE	L-ODS	L-OWE
L-AID	L-AWN	L-ICH	L-OFT	L-OWN
L-AIN	L-AYS	L-ICK	L-OKE	L-OWT
L-AIR	L-AZO	L-IDS	L-ONE	L-OYS
L-AKE	L-EAN	L-ILL	L-OOF	L-UDO
L-ALL	L-EAR	L-IMP	L-OOM	L-UDS
L-AMA	L-EAS	L-INK	L-OON	L-UGS
L-AMP	L-EAT	L-INN	L-OOP	L-UKE
L-ANA	L-ECH	L-INS	L-OOR	L-ULU
L-AND	L-EEK	L-ION	L-OOS	L-UMP
L-ANE	L-EFT	L-IRE	L-OOT	L-URE
L-ANT	L-EKE	L-IRK	L-OPE	L-UTE
L-ARD	L-EME	L-ITS	L-OPS	L-YAM
L-ARE	L-END	L-OAF	L-ORD	L-YES
L-ARK	L-ENG	L-OBE	L-ORE	
L-ARS	L-ENS	L-OBI	L-OSE	
L-ASH	L-ERE	L-OBO	L-OUD	

Four letters to five

L-ACED	L-ARCH	L-EASE	L-ESES	L-OAST
L-ACER	L-ARDS	L-EAST	L-ESTS	L-OATH
L-ACES	L-ARES	L-EATS	L-ETCH	L-OBES
L-AGER	L-ARIS	L-EAVE	L-ETHE	L-OBOS
L-AIDS	L-ARKS	L-EDGE	L-EUGH	L-ODES
L-AIRS	L-ARUM	L-EDGY	L-EVER	L-OKES
L-AIRY	L-AUFS	L-EECH	L-EXES	L-ONER
L-AKED	L-AURA	L-EERY	L-ILLS	L-OOFS
L-AKES	L-AVAS	L-EFTS	L-IMPS	L-OOMS
L-AKIN	L-AVER	L-EGAL	L-INCH	L-OONS
L-ALLS	L-AVES	L-EGER	L-INGO	L-OOPS
L-AMAS	L-AWED	L-EGGY	L-INKS	L-OOSE
L-AMIA	L-AWNS	L-EISH	L-INKY	L-OOTS
L-AMPS	L-AWNY	L-EMES	L-INNS	L-OPED
L-ANAS	L-AXES	L-EMMA	L-IONS	L-OPES
L-ANCE	L-AYIN	L-ENDS	L-IRKS	L-ORAL
L-ANDS	L-EACH	L-ENES	L-ISLE	L-ORDS
L-ANES	L-EANS	L-ENGS	L-ITAS	L-ORES
L-ANTS	L-EARN	L-ERED	L-LAMA	L-OSES
L-APSE	L-EARS	L-ERES	L-OAFS	L-OTIC

L-OTTO	L-OVER	L-OWNS	L-ULUS	L-UTES
L-OUMA	L-OWED	L-OWSE	L-UMPS	L-YAMS
L-OUPS	L-OWER	L-OWTS	L-UMPY	L-YARD
L-OURS	L-OWES	L-OXES	L-URES	
L-OUTS	L-OWLY	L-UDOS	L-USER	

Five letters to six

L-ACERS	L-ARVAL	L-ECHED	L-INGLE	L-ORATE
L-ACHES	L-ASHED	L-ECHES	L-INGOT	L-OTHER
L-ACING	L-ASHES	L-EDGED	L-INKED	L-OTTER
L-ACKER	L-ASSES	L-EDGER	L-INKER	L-OTTOS
L-ADDER	L-ASTER	L-EDGES	L-INNED	L-OUMAS
L-AGERS	L-ATRIA	L-EGERS	L-INTEL	L-OUPED
L-AGGER	L-AURAE	L-EGGED	L-INTER	L-OURIE
L-AIDED	L-AURAS	L-EGGER	L-IRKED	L-OUTED
L-AIRED	L-AURIC	L-EMMAS	L-ISLES	L-OVERS
L-AKING	L-AVERS	L-ENDER	L-ITHER	L-OWING
L-ALANG	L-AWFUL	L-ENVOY	L-IZARD	L-OWNED
L-AMBER	L-AWING	L-ERING	L-LAMAS	L-OWRIE
L-AMENT	L-AYINS	L-ESSES	L-OAVES	L-UGGED
L-AMIAS	L-EANED	L-ETHAL	L-OCKER	L-UMBER
L-AMPED	L-EARED	L-EVITE	L-OCULI	L-UMPED
L-ANGER	L-EARNS	L-EXEME	L-OFTER	L-UNARY
L-ANKER	L-EASED	L-ICHES	L-OLLER	L-USERS
L-APPEL	L-EASER	L-ICKER	L-ONELY	L-USHER
L-APSES	L-EASES	L-IGGED	L-ONERS	
L-ARKED	L-EASTS	L-IMBED	L-OOPED	
L-AROID	L-EAVED	L-IMPED	L-OOSES	
L-ARUMS	L-EAVES	L-IMPLY	L-OPING	

Six letters to seven

L-ACKERS	L-AWLESS	L-EGGIER	L-INDIES	L-OLLIES
L-ADDERS	L-AWNIER	L-EGGING	L-INGLES	L-OMENTA
L-ADDIES	L-EANING	L-EMURES	L-INGOES	L-OOPING
L-AGGERS	L-EARING	L-ENDERS	L-INGOTS	L-OTTERS
L-AIDING	L-EARNED	L-ENDING	L-INKERS	L-OUPING
L-AIRIER	L-EARNER	L-ENVOYS	L-INKING	L-OURIER
L-AIRING	L-EASERS	L-ETCHED	L-INNING	L-OUTING
L-ALANGS	L-EASING	L-ETCHES	L-INTELS	L-OVERED
L-AMBERS	L-ECHING	L-ETHALS	L-INTERS	L-OVERLY
L-AMENTS	L-EDGERS	L-EUGHEN	L-IONISE	L-OWLIER
L-AMPING	L-EDGIER	L-EVITES	L-IONIZE	L-OWNING
L-ANGERS	L-EECHED	L-EXEMES	L-IRKING	L-OXYGEN
L-APPELS	L-EECHES	L-ICKERS	L-IZARDS	L-UGGING
L-ARCHES	L-EERIER	L-IGGING	L-OBELIA	L-ULLING
L-ARKING	L-EERILY	L-IGNIFY	L-OCKERS	L-UMBERS
L-ASHING	L-EFTEST	L-IGNITE	L-OCULAR	L-UMPING
L-ASTERS	L-EGALLY	L-IMPING	L-OCULUS	L-USHERS
L-AUDING	L-EGGERS	L-INCHES	L-OLLERS	

Seven letters to eight

L-ABILITY	L-AMBLING	L-AUREATE	L-AZURITE	L-EDGIEST
L-ACERATE	L-ANGERED	L-AWFULLY	L-EARNERS	L-EECHING
L-AIRIEST	L-ANGUISH	L-AWNIEST	L-EARNING	L-EERIEST

L – Front-hooks

L-EGALITY	L-EVITATE	L-IONISER	L-OBELIAS	L-OXYGENS
L-EGGIEST	L-IGNEOUS	L-IONISES	L-OCULATE	L-UMBERED
L-ENDINGS	L-IGNITES	L-IONIZED	L-OMENTUM	
L-EPIDOTE	L-IMPINGS	L-IONIZER	L-ONENESS	
L-ETCHING	L-INCHPIN	L-IONIZES	L-OURIEST	
L-EVIRATE	L-IONISED	L-ITERATE	L-OWLIEST	

Eight letters to nine

L-ACERATED	L-EPIDOTES	L-IGNIFIED	L-IONISING	L-OCULATED
L-AMBLINGS	L-ETCHINGS	L-IGNIFIES	L-IONIZERS	L-OMENTUMS
L-AZURITES	L-EVIRATES	L-IMITABLE	L-IONIZING	L-UMBERING
L-EARNINGS	L-EVITATED	L-INCHPINS	L-ITERATES	
L-EERINESS	L-EVITATES	L-IONISERS	L-OCELLATE	

L – End-hooks

Two letters to three

AA-L	BE-L	EL-L	MI-L	PO-L
AI-L	DA-L	GU-L	MO-L	SO-L
AL-L	DE-L	JO-L	OI-L	TE-L
AW-L	DO-L	MA-L	OW-L	TI-L
BA-L	EE-L	ME-L	PA-L	ZO-L

Three letters to four

ANA-L	DEI-L	JAI-L	ORA-L	SEE-L
ANI-L	DEL-L	JAR-L	OVA-L	SEI-L
ARY-L	DIE-L	JEE-L	PAL-L	SEL-L
AVA-L	DOL-L	JOL-L	PAW-L	SOU-L
AVE-L	DOO-L	JOW-L	PEA-L	SOW-L
AXE-L	DOW-L	KAI-L	PEE-L	TAE-L
BAA-L	DUE-L	LEA-L	PIA-L	TAI-L
BAL-L	EAR-L	MAL-L	PIR-L	TEA-L
BEL-L	FAR-L	MAR-L	POL-L	TEE-L
BOI-L	FEE-L	MEL-L	POO-L	TEL-L
BOO-L	FIL-L	MEW-L	PUL-L	TIL-L
BOW-L	FOU-L	MIL-L	PUR-L	TOO-L
BUR-L	FUR-L	MOI-L	RAI-L	TWA-L
CAR-L	GAL-L	MOL-L	REE-L	VIA-L
CEL-L	GOA-L	MOO-L	RIA-L	WAI-L
CHA-L	GOE-L	MOY-L	ROT-L	WAW-L
COL-L	GOO-L	NIL-L	RYA-L	WEE-L
COO-L	GUL-L	NOW-L	SAI-L	WOO-L
COW-L	GUR-L	NUR-L	SAL-L	YAW-L
CUR-L	HER-L	OBO-L	SAU-L	YOW-L
DAH-L	HOW-L	ODA-L	SEA-L	ZEA-L

Four letters to five

ALGA-L	AWEE-L	BORE-L	CAVE-L	CRUE-L
ALKY-L	BABE-L	BRAW-L	CECA-L	DATA-L
ALLY-L	BABU-L	BROO-L	COMA-L	DEBE-L
ANNA-L	BEDE-L	BUBA-L	COXA-L	DHOL-L
AREA-L	BETE-L	CABA-L	CRAW-L	DITA-L
AURA-L	BORA-L	CAME-L	CREE-L	DRAW-L

DURA-L	ILIA-L	MORA-L	ROMA-L	THIO-L
DYNE-L	INTI-L	MORE-L	ROTA-L	THIR-L
EASE-L	JUGA-L	MOTE-L	RUBE-L	TRIO-L
FAVE-L	JURA-L	MURA-L	RUGA-L	TUBA-L
FETA-L	JURE-L	MYAL-L	SAME-L	TWEE-L
FORE-L	KETO-L	NAVE-L	SCOW-L	UREA-L
FUSE-L	KNAR-L	NEVE-L	SCUL-L	UVEA-L
GAVE-L	KNEE-L	NOTA-L	SEGO-L	VASA-L
GENA-L	KNUR-L	OCTA-L	SERA-L	VENA-L
GIBE-L	LEME-L	PANE-L	SETA-L	VINA-L
GLIA-L	LEVE-L	PAPA-L	SHAW-L	VINY-L
GNAR-L	LOCA-L	PEAR-L	SHEA-L	VITA-L
GORA-L	LORE-L	PERI-L	SHOO-L	WHEE-L
GROW-L	LOSE-L	PICA-L	SIZE-L	WHIR-L
GRUE-L	MAIL-L	PIPA-L	SNAR-L	YODE-L
HAZE-L	MERE-L	PROW-L	SORA-L	YOKE-L
HORA-L	MERI-L	PUPA-L	SORE-L	ZOEA-L
HOSE-L	MESA-L	QUAI-L	SPAW-L	ZONA-L
HOTE-L	MESE-L	RATA-L	SPIE-L	ZORI-L
HOVE-L	META-L	RATE-L	SURA-L	ZYGA-L
IDEA-L	MODE-L	RAVE-L	SWAY-L	
IDYL-L	MOLA-L	RIVA-L	SWEE-L	
ILEA-L	MONA-L	RIVE-L	TEPA-L	

Five letters to six

ACETA-L	DORSA-L	MAMMA-L	QUINO-L	SWIVE-L
AECIA-L	DORSE-L	MANGA-L	RANCE-L	TASSE-L
AMIDO-L	DRIVE-L	MANGE-L	RAPPE-L	TEASE-L
ANIMA-L	DRUPE-L	MEDIA-L	RECAL-L	TEAZE-L
ANTRA-L	EISEL-L	MENSA-L	RECTA-L	TECTA-L
AORTA-L	ENROL-L	MENTA-L	REDIA-L	TELIA-L
APNEA-L	EXTOL-L	MEREL-L	REFEL-L	TERCE-L
APPAL-L	FACIA-L	MISSA-L	REGNA-L	TERGA-L
ASSAI-L	FAUNA-L	MONGO-L	RETIA-L	THECA-L
ATRIA-L	FAVEL-L	MORAL-L	RIDGE-L	TIBIA-L
BABOO-L	FERIA-L	MORSE-L	RIGOL-L	TINEA-L
BARBE-L	FESTA-L	MUSSE-L	RONDE-L	TOMIA-L
BARRE-L	FLORA-L	NEWEL-L	RONNE-L	TORSE-L
BEDEL-L	FLOTE-L	NITRY-L	RUSSE-L	TRAVE-L
BEIGE-L	FOVEA-L	NORMA-L	SACRA-L	UMBRA-L
BORDE-L	FURCA-L	NUCHA-L	SAMBA-L	UMBRE-L
BUFFE-L	GAMBO-L	OMASA-L	SANTO-L	UNCIA-L
BURSA-L	GRAVE-L	OSTIA-L	SCRAW-L	VANDA-L
CAECA-L	GROVE-L	PALEA-L	SCROW-L	VARVE-L
CARTE-L	HANSE-L	PARRA-L	SCUTA-L	VERVE-L
CARVE-L	HOUSE-L	PASSE-L	SEPTA-L	VESTA-L
CAUDA-L	HYPHA-L	PASTE-L	SERAI-L	VISTA-L
CAUSA-L	JAMBU-L	PENCE-L	SHOVE-L	VULVA-L
CHAPE-L	KERNE-L	PENNA-L	SIGNA-L	WASTE-L
CORBE-L	KHAYA-L	PETRE-L	SOREL-L	WOOSE-L
COSTA-L	KNAWE-L	PINNA-L	SORTA-L	XENIA-L
CREWE-L	LABIA-L	PLICA-L	SPINA-L	ZOOEA-L
CRURA-L	LARVA-L	PODIA-L	SPINE-L	
CURIA-L	LENTI-L	PORTA-L	STIPE-L	
DERMA-L	LUTEA-L	PRIMA-L	STOMA-L	

Six letters to seven

ADNEXA-L	COLONE-L	FULFIL-L	MUCHEL-L	SHRIVE-L
ALODIA-L	CONCHA-L	GENERA-L	MUCOSA-L	STADIA-L
AMENTA-L	CORNEA-L	GINGAL-L	MULMUL-L	STERNA-L
ANGINA-L	CORNUA-L	GLOSSA-L	NATURA-L	STIGMA-L
APNOEA-L	CORONA-L	HEDERA-L	NOMINA-L	STRATA-L
AURORA-L	CORYZA-L	HERNIA-L	NYMPHA-L	STROMA-L
BARBEL-L	CRANIA-L	INSTAL-L	OMENTA-L	TAPETA-L
BORREL-L	CRESTA-L	INSTIL-L	OPTIMA-L	TASSEL-L
BURREL-L	CRISSA-L	INTIMA-L	ORBITA-L	TERTIA-L
CAMBIA-L	CRUSTA-L	ISCHIA-L	PALLIA-L	THERME-L
CAMERA-L	CUBICA-L	JEJUNA-L	PLEURA-L	TIERCE-L
CAPITA-L	DISMAY-L	JINGAL-L	POINTE-L	TIMBRE-L
CARINA-L	DISTIL-L	LACUNA-L	QUANTA-L	TOPFUL-L
CARREL-L	ELUVIA-L	LAMINA-L	QUINTA-L	TRAMEL-L
CENTRA-L	ELYTRA-L	LEXICA-L	REGINA-L	TRIVIA-L
CESURA-L	ENCINA-L	LIMINA-L	RETINA-L	TROCHI-L
CHAETA-L	ENTERA-L	LINGUA-L	ROSTRA-L	TWIBIL-L
CHANCE-L	EPOCHA-L	LOCHIA-L	RUMINA-L	UREDIA-L
CHORDA-L	ESCROL-L	LUMINA-L	SALIVA-L	VAGINA-L
CHOREA-L	ETHOXY-L	LUSTRA-L	SATYRA-L	VESICA-L
CHORIA-L	EXUVIA-L	MAXIMA-L	SCLERA-L	VIMINA-L
CHROME-L	FANNEL-L	MEDUSA-L	SCROTA-L	WADMOL-L
CHROMY-L	FASCIA-L	MIASMA-L	SEMINA-L	WOOSEL-L
CLOACA-L	FEMORA-L	MINIMA-L	SEROSA-L	ZOARIA-L

Seven letters to eight

ABOMASA-L	CHIASMA-L	GALANGA-L	MINUTIA-L	RESIDUA-L
ACHENIA-L	CHRISMA-L	GANGLIA-L	MONILIA-L	SABURRA-L
ACROMIA-L	CINEREA-L	GERMINA-L	MYCELIA-L	SAGITTA-L
AECIDIA-L	COMITIA-L	GINGIVA-L	NOUMENA-L	SOREDIA-L
ALLODIA-L	CONARIA-L	GONIDIA-L	OOGONIA-L	SPECTRA-L
ALLUVIA-L	CONIDIA-L	HYDROXY-L	OOTHECA-L	SPLENIA-L
AMPHORA-L	CORPORA-L	HYMENIA-L	PATAGIA-L	STAMINA-L
ANTENNA-L	CRIMINA-L	HYPOGEA-L	PERIDIA-L	STOMATA-L
APPERIL-L	CROPFUL-L	ILLUVIA-L	PERINEA-L	SULFURY-L
AQUARIA-L	DECIDUA-L	IMPERIA-L	PERSONA-L	SYNOVIA-L
ARCHAEA-L	DIHEDRA-L	INDICIA-L	PESSIMA-L	TEGMINA-L
BASIDIA-L	DILUVIA-L	INDUSIA-L	PISCINA-L	TESSERA-L
BIENNIA-L	DIPTERA-L	INERTIA-L	PLIMSOL-L	TESTRIL-L
BORSTAL-L	DUODENA-L	INFAUNA-L	PODAGRA-L	TORMINA-L
BRACHIA-L	DYSPNEA-L	INTHRAL-L	PRECAVA-L	TRACHEA-L
BRECCIA-L	ENTHRAL-L	KHEDIVA-L	PREPUPA-L	TYMPANA-L
BRIMFUL-L	ENTOZOA-L	LIXIVIA-L	PRONOTA-L	URETHRA-L
CAESURA-L	EROTICA-L	LOCUSTA-L	PROSOMA-L	VACCINA-L
CANDIDA-L	EXCRETA-L	MALARIA-L	PUDENDA-L	VIATICA-L
CAROUSE-L	EXORDIA-L	MANDRIL-L	PUPARIA-L	VISCERA-L
CEREBRA-L	EXTREMA-L	MARSHAL-L	PYGIDIA-L	ZOOGLEA-L
CHALAZA-L	FILARIA-L	METAZOA-L	PYREXIA-L	
CHAMISA-L	FIMBRIA-L	METHOXY-L	REPOSAL-L	

Eight letters to nine

ABDOMINA-L	ANECDOTA-L	ASPHYXIA-L	BLASTEMA-L	CACUMINA-L
AGNOMINA-L	ANGELICA-L	AVIFAUNA-L	BOTANICA-L	CALCANEA-L
AMBROSIA-L	ANTEFIXA-L	BACTERIA-L	BRANCHIA-L	CALVARIA-L
ANAPHORA-L	ANTIMONY-L	BASILICA-L	BRONCHIA-L	CATHEDRA-L

CENTINEL-L	ENDOSTEA-L	MESOGLEA-L	PYCNIDIA-L	SYMPOSIA-L
CENTONEL-L	ENSORCEL-L	MESOPHYL-L	PYORRHEA-L	SYNCYTIA-L
CERCARIA-L	EPENDYMA-L	MILIARIA-L	REDISTIL-L	SYNEDRIA-L
CHOCKFUL-L	EPHEMERA-L	MISENROL-L	REINSTAL-L	TEGMENTA-L
CISTERNA-L	EPICEDIA-L	MOSCHATE-L	RHIZOBIA-L	TENTORIA-L
CLAUSTRA-L	EPIFAUNA-L	OCCIPITA-L	RITORNEL-L	THERIACA-L
COLLEGIA-L	ERYTHEMA-L	PALESTRA-L	SACRARIA-L	TRAPEZIA-L
COLLUVIA-L	FENESTRA-L	PALPEBRA-L	SCIATICA-L	TRICHINA-L
CONFERVA-L	FORAMINA-L	PANNIKEL-L	SEMUNCIA-L	TRIENNIA-L
CONTINUA-L	FORESTAL-L	PAROEMIA-L	SENSORIA-L	TRIFORIA-L
CRITERIA-L	GYMNASIA-L	PENUMBRA-L	SIGNORIA-L	TRIHEDRA-L
DECENNIA-L	HEPATICA-L	PETECHIA-L	SPORIDIA-L	UNDERSEA-L
DEMENTIA-L	HERBARIA-L	PICKADIL-L	SPOROZOA-L	UREDINIA-L
DIARRHEA-L	HYPOGAEA-L	PLACENTA-L	STOMODEA-L	UROPYGIA-L
DICHASIA-L	LISTERIA-L	POSTCAVA-L	SUBCOSTA-L	VACCINIA-L
DYSPNOEA-L	MAGNESIA-L	PRESIDIA-L	SUBMENTA-L	VERTEBRA-L
DYSTOCIA-L	MANUBRIA-L	PROTOZOA-L	SUDAMINA-L	VESTIGIA-L
ECCLESIA-L	MARSUPIA-L	PTERYGIA-L	SULPHURY-L	VIBRISSA-L
EFFLUVIA-L	MENSTRUA-L	PUERPERA-L	SYMPODIA-L	ZOOGLOEA-L

M – Front-hooks

Two letters to three

M-AA	M-AT	M-ES	M-OI	M-OY
M-AD	M-AW	M-ET	M-OM	M-UG
M-AE	M-AX	M-HO	M-ON	M-UM
M-AG	M-AY	M-ID	M-OO	M-UN
M-AL	M-ED	M-IS	M-OP	M-US
M-AM	M-EE	M-NA	M-OR	M-UT
M-AN	M-EL	M-OB	M-OS	
M-AR	M-EM	M-OD	M-OU	
M-AS	M-EN	M-OE	M-OW	

Three letters to four

M-AAS	M-ARD	M-EMO	M-NAS	M-ORE
M-ACE	M-ARE	M-EMS	M-OAT	M-ORS
M-ACH	M-ARK	M-END	M-OBE	M-ORT
M-ADS	M-ARM	M-ENE	M-OBS	M-OSE
M-AGE	M-ARS	M-ENG	M-OCH	M-OUP
M-AGS	M-ART	M-ERE	M-ODE	M-OUS
M-AID	M-ARY	M-ERK	M-ODS	M-OWN
M-AIL	M-ASH	M-ESS	M-OES	M-OYS
M-AIM	M-ASK	M-ETA	M-OIL	M-UDS
M-AIN	M-ASS	M-ETH	M-OKE	M-UGS
M-AIR	M-ATE	M-EVE	M-OLD	M-ULE
M-AKE	M-ATT	M-HOS	M-OLE	M-UMM
M-ALA	M-AWN	M-ICE	M-OMS	M-UMP
M-ALE	M-AYS	M-ICH	M-ONO	M-UMU
M-ALL	M-EAN	M-ICK	M-ONS	M-UNI
M-ALS	M-EAT	M-IDS	M-ONY	M-UNS
M-ALT	M-EDS	M-IFF	M-OON	M-URE
M-AMA	M-EEK	M-IGG	M-OOP	M-USE
M-ANA	M-EFF	M-ILK	M-OOR	M-UTE
M-AND	M-ELD	M-ILL	M-OOS	M-UTS
M-ANE	M-ELL	M-INK	M-OOT	M-ZEE
M-ANI	M-ELS	M-IRE	M-OPE	
M-ANY	M-ELT	M-IRK	M-OPS	
M-ARC	M-EME	M-ISO	M-ORA	

Four letters to five

M-ACED	M-ANNA	M-EKKA	M-IRES	M-ORES
M-ACER	M-ANTA	M-ELDS	M-IRKS	M-ORRA
M-ACES	M-ANUS	M-ELLS	M-ISOS	M-ORTS
M-ACHE	M-ARCH	M-ELTS	M-ITCH	M-OSES
M-AGES	M-ARCS	M-EMES	M-OATS	M-OTTO
M-AGMA	M-ARES	M-EMOS	M-OBES	M-OUCH
M-AIDS	M-ARIA	M-ENDS	M-ODAL	M-OULD
M-AILS	M-ARID	M-ENES	M-ODES	M-OUPS
M-AIMS	M-ARKS	M-ENGS	M-OILS	M-OURN
M-AINS	M-ARLE	M-ERED	M-OKES	M-OUST
M-AIRS	M-ARMS	M-ERES	M-OLDS	M-OVER
M-AKES	M-ARSE	M-ERKS	M-OLDY	M-OWED
M-ALAR	M-ARTS	M-ESES	M-OLES	M-OWER
M-ALAS	M-ASHY	M-ESNE	M-OLLA	M-ULES
M-ALES	M-ASKS	M-ETHS	M-ONER	M-UMPS
M-ALLS	M-ATES	M-ETIC	M-ONIE	M-UNIS
M-ALMS	M-AWED	M-EVES	M-ONOS	M-URES
M-ALTS	M-AXED	M-ICKY	M-OONS	M-URVA
M-AMAS	M-AXES	M-IFFY	M-OOPS	M-USED
M-AMBO	M-AXIS	M-IGGS	M-OOSE	M-USER
M-AMIE	M-EANS	M-ILIA	M-OOTS	M-USES
M-ANAS	M-EASE	M-ILKS	M-OPED	M-UTES
M-ANES	M-EATH	M-ILLS	M-OPES	M-UTIS
M-ANGA	M-EATS	M-INKS	M-OPUS	M-ZEES
M-ANIS	M-EFFS	M-IRED	M-ORAL	

Five letters to six

M-ACERS	M-ANGAS	M-AUGER	M-ICHED	M-ORRIS
M-ACHES	M-ANGEL	M-AURIS	M-ICHES	M-OTHER
M-ACING	M-ANGER	M-AVENS	M-ICKLE	M-OTTOS
M-ADDED	M-ANGLE	M-AWING	M-ILIUM	M-OUGHT
M-ADDER	M-ANNAS	M-AXING	M-ILLER	M-OUPED
M-ADMAN	M-ANTAS	M-EAGER	M-IMBAR	M-OUSTS
M-ADMEN	M-ANTES	M-EAGRE	M-INGLE	M-OUTER
M-AGGIE	M-ANTIC	M-EANED	M-INION	M-OVERS
M-AGISM	M-ANTIS	M-EASED	M-INTER	M-OWING
M-AGMAS	M-ANTRA	M-EASES	M-IRING	M-OZZIE
M-AIDED	M-ARISH	M-EASLE	M-ISLED	M-UDDER
M-AILED	M-ARKED	M-EATHE	M-ISTLE	M-UGGED
M-AIMED	M-ARLED	M-EKKAS	M-ITHER	M-UMBLE
M-AIMER	M-ARLES	M-ELDER	M-OCKER	M-UMPED
M-AKING	M-ARRIS	M-EMBER	M-ODALS	M-UNIFY
M-ALATE	M-ARROW	M-ENDED	M-ODIST	M-UNITE
M-ALIGN	M-ARSES	M-ENDER	M-OILED	M-UNTIN
M-ALINE	M-ARTEL	M-ERING	M-OILER	M-URENA
M-ALIST	M-ASCOT	M-ERSES	M-OLDER	M-URINE
M-ALLEE	M-ASHED	M-ESNES	M-OLLAS	M-URVAS
M-ALLOW	M-ASHES	M-ESSES	M-OLLIE	M-USERS
M-AMBOS	M-ASKED	M-ESTER	M-OOPED	M-USHER
M-AMIES	M-ASKER	M-ETAGE	M-OPING	M-USING
M-AMMON	M-ASSES	M-ETHOS	M-ORALS	M-UTTER
M-ANANA	M-ASTER	M-ETHYL	M-ORGAN	
M-ANENT	M-ATOKE	M-ETTLE	M-ORGUE	

Six letters to seven

M-ADDERS	M-ARCHED	M-EASING	M-ITCHED	M-OUSTED
M-ADDING	M-ARCHER	M-EASLES	M-ITCHES	M-OUTERS
M-AGGIES	M-ARCHES	M-ELDERS	M-OCCIES	M-OUTHER
M-AGISMS	M-ARGENT	M-ELDING	M-OCKERS	M-OZZIES
M-AGNATE	M-ARKING	M-EMBERS	M-ODISTS	M-UCKERS
M-AIDING	M-ARLING	M-ENDERS	M-OILERS	M-UDDERS
M-AILING	M-ARROWS	M-ENDING	M-OILING	M-UGGING
M-AIMERS	M-ARROWY	M-ESTERS	M-OLLIES	M-ULLING
M-AIMING	M-ARTELS	M-ETAGES	M-OMENTA	M-UMBLES
M-ALATES	M-ASCOTS	M-ETHANE	M-ONEYER	M-UMPING
M-ALIGNS	M-ASHIER	M-ETHOXY	M-OOPING	M-UNITED
M-ALINES	M-ASHING	M-ETHYLS	M-OORIER	M-UNITES
M-ALISON	M-ASHMAN	M-ETTLED	M-OPUSES	M-UNTINS
M-ALLEES	M-ASHMEN	M-ETTLES	M-ORALLY	M-URENAS
M-ALLOWS	M-ASKERS	M-ICHING	M-ORGANS	M-URINES
M-AMMONS	M-ASKING	M-ICKLER	M-ORGUES	M-USEFUL
M-ANANAS	M-ASTERS	M-IFFIER	M-ORPHIC	M-USHERS
M-ANGELS	M-ATOKES	M-IMBARS	M-ORRICE	M-UTASES
M-ANGERS	M-AVISES	M-INGLES	M-OTHERS	M-UTTERS
M-ANGLED	M-AXILLA	M-INIONS	M-OUCHED	
M-ANGLER	M-EAGRES	M-INTERS	M-OUCHES	
M-ANGLES	M-EANING	M-IRITIS	M-OULDER	
M-ARABIS	M-EARING	M-ISTLES	M-OUPING	

Seven letters to eight

M-ACERATE	M-ARCHERS	M-EAGERLY	M-IFFIEST	M-ORRICES
M-ADWOMAN	M-ARCHING	M-EMETICS	M-ISOGAMY	M-ORRISES
M-ADWOMEN	M-ARGENTS	M-ENDINGS	M-ITCHING	M-OUCHING
M-AGISTER	M-ARISHES	M-ENOLOGY	M-OATLIKE	M-OUSTING
M-AGNATES	M-ARRIAGE	M-ERISTIC	M-OMENTUM	M-UNIFIED
M-AIDLESS	M-ARROWED	M-ETHANAL	M-ONEYERS	M-UNIFIES
M-ALIGNED	M-ASHIEST	M-ETHANES	M-OORIEST	M-UNITING
M-ALIGNER	M-ASKINGS	M-ETHANOL	M-ORALISM	M-UNITION
M-ALISONS	M-AXILLAE	M-ETHOXYL	M-ORALIST	M-UTTERED
M-ANGLERS	M-AXILLAR	M-ETHYLIC	M-ORALITY	M-UTTERER
M-ANGLING	M-AXILLAS	M-ICKLEST	M-ORATORY	

Eight letters to nine

M-ACERATED	M-ANGULATE	M-ETHANOIC	M-ISOGAMIC	M-USEFULLY
M-ACRODONT	M-ARRIAGES	M-ETHANOLS	M-OMENTUMS	M-UTTERERS
M-AGISTERS	M-ARROWING	M-ETHOXIDE	M-ORALISMS	M-UTTERING
M-ALIGNERS	M-AXILLARY	M-ETHYLATE	M-ORALISTS	
M-ALIGNING	M-ENARCHES	M-ETHYLENE	M-UNIFYING	
M-AMMONITE	M-ETHANALS	M-IFFINESS	M-UNITIONS	

M – End-hooks

Two letters to three

AI-M	DO-M	HE-M	JA-M	MI-M
AR-M	EL-M	HI-M	KA-M	MO-M
BA-M	FE-M	HM-M	LA-M	MU-M
DA-M	GU-M	HO-M	MA-M	NA-M
DI-M	HA-M	IS-M	ME-M	NO-M

M – Front-hooks

OH-M	PO-M	SO-M	UM-M	YO-M
OO-M	RE-M	TA-M	WE-M	YU-M
PA-M	SI-M	TO-M	YA-M	

Three letters to four

BAL-M	FER-M	KAI-M	PRE-M	TEE-M
BAR-M	FIL-M	LEA-M	PRO-M	THE-M
BOO-M	FIR-M	LOO-M	ROO-M	TOO-M
BOR-M	FOR-M	MAL-M	SAI-M	WAR-M
CHA-M	FRO-M	MAR-M	SEA-M	WAS-M
COO-M	GAU-M	MUM-M	SEE-M	WEE-M
COR-M	GIS-M	NEE-M	SHA-M	WHA-M
DEE-M	GOR-M	NOR-M	SKI-M	WHO-M
DOO-M	HAE-M	PAL-M	SOU-M	ZOO-M
DOR-M	HAW-M	PER-M	SOW-M	
FAR-M	HER-M	PIU-M	SPA-M	
FEH-M	IDE-M	PLU-M	TEA-M	

Four letters to five

ABRI-M	DENI-M	HAUL-M	REAL-M	STUM-M
ABYS-M	FLAM-M	MALA-M	REAR-M	THAR-M
ALAR-M	FLEA-M	MAXI-M	RETE-M	THRU-M
BREE-M	FORA-M	MINI-M	SATE-M	TOTE-M
BROO-M	GOLE-M	MODE-M	SEIS-M	TUIS-M
CHAR-M	HAKA-M	PASH-M	SHAW-M	
CHAS-M	HARE-M	PURI-M	SPAS-M	

Five letters to six

BALSA-M	COPAL-M	MESTO-M	PURIS-M	TELES-M
BESEE-M	DODGE-M	MONTE-M	SADIS-M	YOGIS-M
CENTU-M	LINGA-M	MURRA-M	SCRAW-M	
CHIAS-M	MALIS-M	MUTIS-M	SHTUM-M	
CONDO-M	MERIS-M	PARTI-M	SPIRE-M	

Six letters to seven

ANIMIS-M	FASCIS-M	MANTRA-M	MISTER-M	SENSIS-M
BUCKRA-M	GOPURA-M	MISSEE-M	PREWAR-M	

Seven letters to eight

CLASSIS-M	FINALIS-M	JIHADIS-M
CYMBALO-M	JEHADIS-M	TITANIS-M

Eight letters to nine

LITERATI-M	MRIDANGA-M
MEPHITIS-M	

N – Front-hooks

Two letters to three

N-AB	N-AT	N-ID	N-ON	N-UN
N-AE	N-AW	N-IS	N-OO	N-UR
N-AG	N-AY	N-IT	N-OR	N-US
N-AH	N-ED	N-OB	N-OS	N-UT
N-AM	N-EE	N-OD	N-OW	N-YE
N-AN	N-EF	N-OH	N-OX	
N-AS	N-ET	N-OM	N-OY	

Three letters to four

N-ABS	N-ARC	N-ERK	N-ITS	N-OUP
N-ACH	N-ARD	N-ESS	N-OBS	N-OUS
N-ADS	N-ARE	N-EST	N-ODE	N-OUT
N-AFF	N-ARK	N-EUK	N-ODS	N-OVA
N-AGA	N-ARY	N-EVE	N-OES	N-OWL
N-AGS	N-AVE	N-EWT	N-OIL	N-OWN
N-AIL	N-AYS	N-ICE	N-OLE	N-OWT
N-AIN	N-EAR	N-ICK	N-OMS	N-OYS
N-ALA	N-EAT	N-IDE	N-ONE	N-UKE
N-AMU	N-EDS	N-IDS	N-OON	N-UNS
N-ANA	N-EFS	N-IFF	N-OOP	N-URD
N-ANE	N-ENE	N-ILL	N-OPE	N-UTS
N-APE	N-EON	N-ISH	N-OSE	N-YES

Four letters to five

N-ACHE	N-ARES	N-EONS	N-ODAL	N-OULD
N-ACRE	N-ARIS	N-ERKS	N-ODES	N-OUPS
N-AGAS	N-ARKS	N-ESTS	N-OILS	N-OVEL
N-AILS	N-ATES	N-EUKS	N-OILY	N-OVUM
N-AKED	N-AUNT	N-EVER	N-OINT	N-OWED
N-ALAS	N-AVAL	N-EVES	N-OLES	N-OWLS
N-ANAS	N-AVEL	N-EWER	N-OMEN	N-OWTS
N-ANCE	N-AVES	N-EWTS	N-ONCE	N-OXES
N-ANNA	N-EARS	N-ICER	N-ONES	N-OYES
N-APED	N-EATH	N-ICKY	N-OONS	N-UKES
N-APES	N-EATS	N-IDES	N-OOPS	N-URDS
N-ARCO	N-EDDY	N-IFFY	N-OOSE	N-URDY
N-ARCS	N-EMPT	N-ILLS	N-OPAL	N-YAFF
N-ARDS	N-ENES	N-IMPS	N-OSES	

Five letters to six

N-ABBED	N-APRON	N-EATER	N-ICKLE	N-OSIER
N-ACHES	N-ARKED	N-EBBED	N-IMBED	N-OTARY
N-ACRED	N-ARRAS	N-ESSES	N-ISHES	N-OTHER
N-ACRES	N-ARROW	N-ESTER	N-ITHER	N-OUGHT
N-AGGER	N-AUGHT	N-ETHER	N-ODDER	N-OVELS
N-AILED	N-AUNTS	N-ETTLE	N-OGGIN	N-UMBER
N-AIVER	N-AVELS	N-EWEST	N-OINTS	N-UMPTY
N-ANNAS	N-EARED	N-ICHED	N-ONCES	N-UNCLE
N-APERY	N-EARLY	N-ICHES	N-OOSES	N-UTTER
N-APING	N-EATEN	N-ICKER	N-OPALS	N-YAFFS

Six letters to seven

N-AGGERS	N-AYWORD	N-EOLITH	N-ONUSES	N-UNCLES
N-AILING	N-EARING	N-ESTERS	N-OODLES	N-UNDINE
N-APHTHA	N-EBBING	N-ETTLED	N-OOLOGY	N-UNHOOD
N-APRONS	N-EDDIES	N-ETTLES	N-OUGHTS	N-UNLIKE
N-ARKING	N-EDDISH	N-ICHING	N-OVATED	N-UNSHIP
N-ARROWS	N-EGRESS	N-ICKERS	N-OYESES	N-UTTERS
N-ASCENT	N-EITHER	N-IFFIER	N-ULLING	N-YAFFED
N-ATRIUM	N-EMESES	N-OGGINS	N-UMBERS	
N-AUGHTS	N-EMESIS	N-OINTED	N-UMBLES	

Seven letters to eight

N-AINSELL	N-ATRIUMS	N-ETTLING	N-OVATION	N-UNHOODS
N-APERIES	N-AYWORDS	N-IFFIEST	N-ULLINGS	N-UNSHIPS
N-ARRASES	N-EARLIER	N-OINTING	N-UMBERED	N-YAFFING
N-ARROWED	N-EOLITHS	N-OTARIES	N-UNDINES	

Eight letters to nine

N-AINSELLS	N-AVICULAR	N-EGRESSES	N-OOLOGIES	N-UMBERING
N-APHTHOUS	N-AVIGATOR	N-EOLITHIC	N-OOSPHERE	
N-ARROWING	N-EARLIEST	N-EVERMORE	N-OVATIONS	

N – End-hooks

Two letters to three

AI-N	EA-N	HO-N	NO-N	TE-N
AN-N	EE-N	IN-N	NU-N	TI-N
AW-N	ER-N	IO-N	OO-N	TO-N
BA-N	FA-N	KI-N	OW-N	UR-N
BE-N	FE-N	KO-N	PA-N	WE-N
BI-N	GI-N	LI-N	PE-N	WO-N
BO-N	GO-N	MA-N	PI-N	YE-N
DA-N	GU-N	ME-N	RE-N	YO-N
DE-N	HA-N	MO-N	SI-N	
DI-N	HE-N	MU-N	SO-N	
DO-N	HI-N	NA-N	TA-N	

Three letters to four

AGE-N	CAN-N	EVE-N	GOO-N	LEA-N
AGO-N	CAR-N	EXO-N	GUR-N	LIE-N
AIR-N	CHI-N	EYE-N	HAE-N	LIN-N
ALA-N	CON-N	FAA-N	HER-N	LOO-N
AMI-N	COO-N	FAW-N	HEW-N	LOR-N
ANA-N	COR-N	FEE-N	HIS-N	LOU-N
AZO-N	CUR-N	FER-N	HOO-N	LOW-N
BAR-N	DAM-N	FIR-N	HYE-N	MAW-N
BEE-N	DAW-N	FOE-N	JIN-N	MOA-N
BOO-N	DEE-N	FOH-N	KAI-N	MOO-N
BOR-N	DOE-N	GAE-N	KIR-N	MOR-N
BRA-N	DOO-N	GAU-N	KOA-N	MOW-N
BUN-N	DOW-N	GIE-N	LAR-N	NOO-N
BUR-N	EAR-N	GIN-N	LAW-N	NOW-N

OPE-N	POW-N	SEW-N	THE-N	WIN-N
OUR-N	RAI-N	SHA-N	THO-N	WOO-N
PAW-N	RAW-N	SKI-N	TOO-N	WYN-N
PEA-N	REE-N	SOW-N	TOR-N	YAR-N
PEE-N	REI-N	SPA-N	TOW-N	YAW-N
PER-N	ROO-N	SUN-N	UDO-N	YEA-N
PHO-N	SAI-N	SYE-N	UPO-N	ZOO-N
PIA-N	SAW-N	TAI-N	WAI-N	
PIR-N	SEA-N	TAR-N	WAR-N	
POO-N	SEE-N	TEE-N	WEE-N	

Four letters to five

ABRI-N	DOZE-N	LADE-N	RIPE-N	SPAW-N
AMMO-N	DRAW-N	LATE-N	RISE-N	SPUR-N
ATMA-N	DROW-N	LEAR-N	RIVE-N	STAR-N
BAKE-N	ERGO-N	LIKE-N	ROMA-N	STOW-N
BALU-N	FANO-N	LIMA-N	ROTA-N	TABU-N
BLAW-N	FLAW-N	LIME-N	ROTO-N	TAKE-N
BLOW-N	FLOW-N	LINE-N	ROUE-N	TAKI-N
BRAW-N	FROW-N	LIVE-N	ROVE-N	TAPE-N
BROW-N	GIRO-N	LODE-N	RUME-N	TOKE-N
BURA-N	GIVE-N	LOGO-N	SAMA-N	TOLA-N
CAMA-N	GNAW-N	LOSE-N	SAME-N	TORA-N
CAPO-N	GREE-N	MAYA-N	SARI-N	TOYO-N
CHAI-N	GROW-N	MIRI-N	SATI-N	TREE-N
CLOW-N	GYRO-N	MOTE-N	SEME-N	TWEE-N
CODE-N	HALO-N	NOME-N	SHAW-N	VARA-N
CONI-N	HAVE-N	OCTA-N	SHEW-N	VEGA-N
COPE-N	HEBE-N	OWSE-N	SHOO-N	WAKE-N
COVE-N	HERO-N	PATE-N	SHOW-N	WHEE-N
COZE-N	HOSE-N	PAVE-N	SHUL-N	WIDE-N
CROW-N	HOTE-N	PREE-N	SILE-N	WOKE-N
DEAR-N	HOVE-N	PURI-N	SIRE-N	WOVE-N
DEMO-N	HUMA-N	QUEY-N	SKEE-N	YEAR-N
DIVA-N	JOMO-N	RAMI-N	SOKE-N	YEVE-N
DJIN-N	KNOW-N	RATA-N	SOLA-N	YOGI-N
DOOR-N	KORU-N	RAVE-N	SOLO-N	YOUR-N
DOVE-N	KULA-N	REDO-N	SOMA-N	ZUPA-N

Five letters to six

ALDER-N	CALLA-N	FARCI-N	INTRO-N	MODER-N
ALTER-N	CANTO-N	FLAME-N	JOTUN-N	MURRE-N
AMEBA-N	CARBO-N	FRORE-N	KRONE-N	MURRI-N
AMNIO-N	CARVE-N	FROZE-N	LARGE-N	NORMA-N
ARISE-N	CAUSE-N	GAZOO-N	LATHE-N	PAISA-N
ASTER-N	CAVER-N	GEMMA-N	LATTE-N	PANTO-N
AWAKE-N	CEDAR-N	GLAZE-N	LEAVE-N	PARKI-N
AWOKE-N	CHICO-N	GLOBI-N	LIGGE-N	PATTE-N
BABOO-N	CHOSE-N	GLUTE-N	LOIPE-N	PEASE-N
BANIA-N	CLOVE-N	GODSO-N	LONGA-N	PERCE-N
BARRE-N	COMMO-N	GRAVE-N	LOOSE-N	PHONO-N
BESEE-N	CRAVE-N	HASTE-N	LOUPE-N	PHOTO-N
BITTE-N	CRIME-N	HAUSE-N	MACRO-N	PIECE-N
BOREE-N	DOGMA-N	HEAVE-N	MANNA-N	PLATE-N
BRAZE-N	DOLMA-N	HOOVE-N	MEDIA-N	POLEY-N
BROKE-N	DRIVE-N	INTER-N	MICRO-N	PROVE-N

N – End-hooks

RABBI-N	SANTO-N	SITHE-N	TAVER-N	WARRE-N
RAPPE-N	SCHUL-N	SLIVE-N	THORO-N	WEDEL-N
RATIO-N	SCREE-N	SLOVE-N	THRAW-N	WEETE-N
RATOO-N	SEAME-N	SOLEI-N	THROW-N	WHITE-N
REEDE-N	SERRA-N	SPOKE-N	TORTE-N	WICCA-N
REPLA-N	SEXTO-N	STOLE-N	TRIGO-N	WIVER-N
RESAW-N	SHAKE-N	STONE-N	UNDER-N	WORSE-N
RESEE-N	SHAMA-N	STRAW-N	UNSEW-N	WROKE-N
RESEW-N	SHAPE-N	STREW-N	VERVE-N	
RESOW-N	SHAVE-N	STROW-N	VILLA-N	
ROTTE-N	SILVA-N	SYLVA-N	VODOU-N	

Six letters to seven

ABELIA-N	ENVIRO-N	PATTER-N	RIPSAW-N	UNDRAW-N
ACKNOW-N	EPIZOA-N	PHALLI-N	SALTER-N	UNLADE-N
ALKALI-N	GELATI-N	POSTER-N	SHIPPO-N	UNROVE-N
AMOEBA-N	GODDAM-N	PREWAR-N	SHOTTE-N	UNWOVE-N
ANLAGE-N	HOARSE-N	PROTEA-N	SHRIVE-N	UPBLOW-N
BETAKE-N	HOMELY-N	PROTEI-N	SIERRA-N	UPDRAW-N
BITTER-N	INWOVE-N	QUINTA-N	SILVER-N	UPGROW-N
BRAHMA-N	JIGSAW-N	REDRAW-N	SMIDGE-N	UPRISE-N
BRONZE-N	LAMPER-N	REFLOW-N	SOLITO-N	UPTAKE-N
CAPITA-N	LETTER-N	REGIME-N	STONER-N	URANIA-N
CHALLA-N	MEDUSA-N	REGIVE-N	STRIVE-N	UTOPIA-N
CHASTE-N	MISSEE-N	REGROW-N	STROKE-N	VIBRIO-N
CHIRRE-N	MONERA-N	RERISE-N	TAMARI-N	VOUDOU-N
CITHER-N	NUCLEI-N	RESHOW-N	TERTIA-N	WESTER-N
COARSE-N	ORARIA-N	RETAKE-N	TESTER-N	WRITHE-N
CRYPTO-N	OUTSEE-N	REWAKE-N	THRIVE-N	YESTER-N
EASTER-N	PAPAYA-N	REWOKE-N	TORULI-N	ZITHER-N
EMBRYO-N	PASTER-N	REWOVE-N	TRUDGE-N	

Seven letters to eight

ACANTHI-N	DILUVIA-N	HYPOGEA-N	OVERSEW-N	RESPOKE-N
ACTINIA-N	DIPTERA-N	LEATHER-N	OVERSOW-N	ROSARIA-N
ALFAQUI-N	DISLIKE-N	MAGNETO-N	PANACEA-N	RUBELLA-N
ALIZARI-N	ECTOZOA-N	MALARIA-N	PARAZOA-N	SLATTER-N
APHELIA-N	ELECTRO-N	METAZOA-N	PARTAKE-N	SOUTHER-N
AQUARIA-N	ENFROZE-N	MISDRAW-N	PELORIA-N	SPREDDE-N
ARCADIA-N	ENGRAVE-N	MISGIVE-N	PERTAKE-N	STROOKE-N
ARCHAEA-N	ENLARGE-N	MISGROW-N	PIMENTO-N	THROMBI-N
ASCIDIA-N	ENTOZOA-N	MISKNOW-N	POLYZOA-N	UNBROKE-N
AURELIA-N	FEDAYEE-N	MISTAKE-N	PRESHOW-N	UNFROZE-N
BEREAVE-N	FILARIA-N	MYCELIA-N	PUNALUA-N	UNLOOSE-N
BESPOKE-N	FLITTER-N	NORTHER-N	QUARTER-N	UNSHAPE-N
BESTREW-N	FLYBLOW-N	OPHIURA-N	REARISE-N	UNSPOKE-N
BESTROW-N	FORESEE-N	OUTDRAW-N	REAWAKE-N	UPBROKE-N
BOHEMIA-N	FORFAIR-N	OUTFLOW-N	REAWOKE-N	UPSPOKE-N
CHONDRI-N	FORGIVE-N	OUTGIVE-N	RECHOSE-N	UPTHROW-N
CODRIVE-N	FORSAKE-N	OUTGNAW-N	REDRIVE-N	VITELLI-N
COLLAGE-N	GALLICA-N	OUTGROW-N	REFROZE-N	WHIPSAW-N
CONIDIA-N	HACKSAW-N	OUTTAKE-N	REGALIA-N	WREATHE-N
DEFROZE-N	HISTRIO-N	OVERSEE-N	RESHAVE-N	

Eight letters to nine

AMBROSIA-N	EPICEDIA-N	MISCHOSE-N	OVERGIVE-N	SANNYASI-N
AMPHIBIA-N	FELLATIO-N	MISDRIVE-N	OVERGROW-N	SCHLIERE-N
BACTERIA-N	FOREKNOW-N	MISSHAPE-N	OVERLADE-N	SCHNECKE-N
BASILICA-N	FORESHEW-N	MISSPOKE-N	OVERRIPE-N	SEPTARIA-N
CALCANEA-N	FORESHOW-N	MISTHROW-N	OVERTAKE-N	SIGHTSEE-N
CALVARIA-N	FORSPOKE-N	MOLLUSCA-N	PANDEMIA-N	SPATLESE-N
CARETAKE-N	HERBARIA-N	OUTBROKE-N	PLANARIA-N	SPOROZOA-N
CASTELLA-N	HYDROZOA-N	OUTDRIVE-N	PRECHOSE-N	STRONTIA-N
CERCARIA-N	HYPOGAEA-N	OUTSPOKE-N	PREFROZE-N	SUBTOPIA-N
COLLEGIA-N	MAGNESIA-N	OUTTHROW-N	PROTOZOA-N	WINDBLOW-N
DEMERARA-N	MALVASIA-N	OVERBLOW-N	REPTILIA-N	WIREDRAW-N
DISPROVE-N	MARSUPIA-N	OVERDRAW-N	RESTRIVE-N	WITHDRAW-N
DYSTOPIA-N	MAUSOLEA-N	OVERFLOW-N	ROUGHHEW-N	

O – Front-hooks

Two letters to three

O-AR	O-DA	O-NO	O-OR	O-UT
O-AT	O-DE	O-NY	O-OS	O-WE
O-BA	O-ES	O-OF	O-PE	O-YE
O-BE	O-HM	O-OH	O-RE	
O-BI	O-HO	O-OM	O-UP	
O-BO	O-KA	O-ON	O-UR	
O-CH	O-NE	O-OP	O-US	

Three letters to four

O-ARS	O-DAL	O-KAY	O-ONS	O-RES
O-ARY	O-DAS	O-LEA	O-OPS	O-SAR
O-BAS	O-DOR	O-LES	O-OSE	O-TIC
O-BES	O-DSO	O-LID	O-PAH	O-UDS
O-BEY	O-FAY	O-MEN	O-PAL	O-UPS
O-BIS	O-GAM	O-NIE	O-PED	O-URN
O-BIT	O-GEE	O-NOS	O-PEN	O-UTS
O-BOS	O-HOS	O-NUS	O-PES	O-VUM
O-CHE	O-INK	O-OHS	O-PUS	O-WED
O-DAH	O-KAS	O-OMS	O-RAD	O-YES

Four letters to five

O-AKED	O-DOUR	O-LENT	O-PINE	O-UNDY
O-ARED	O-DSOS	O-LIVE	O-PING	O-UPAS
O-AVES	O-FAYS	O-LOGY	O-PIUM	O-VARY
O-BANG	O-FLAG	O-MASA	O-RACH	O-VERS
O-BEYS	O-GAMS	O-MEGA	O-RACY	O-VERT
O-BIAS	O-GEES	O-OBIT	O-RANG	O-VINE
O-BITS	O-GIVE	O-OHED	O-RANT	O-VOID
O-BOLE	O-GLED	O-OPED	O-RATE	O-WING
O-CHER	O-HING	O-OSES	O-READ	O-ZONE
O-DAHS	O-HONE	O-PAHS	O-RIEL	
O-DALS	O-INKS	O-PALS	O-SCAR	
O-DORS	O-KAYS	O-PENS	O-UNCE	

N – End-hooks

Five letters to six

O-BANGS	O-GIVES	O-OSIER	O-RANGY	O-URALI
O-BENTO	O-INKED	O-PALED	O-RANTS	O-URARI
O-BITER	O-LINGO	O-PENED	O-RATED	O-VINES
O-BLAST	O-LIVER	O-PINED	O-RATES	O-VOIDS
O-BLATE	O-LIVES	O-PINES	O-READS	O-WRIER
O-BOLES	O-MENED	O-PIUMS	O-RIELS	O-YESES
O-BOLUS	O-MENTA	O-PULUS	O-SCARS	O-ZONES
O-CELLI	O-OBITS	O-PUSES	O-STEAL	
O-EDEMA	O-OHING	O-RACHE	O-STENT	
O-FLAGS	O-OLOGY	O-RALLY	O-TITIS	
O-GAMIC	O-OPING	O-RANGE	O-UNCES	

Six letters to seven

O-BENTOS	O-ESTRAL	O-MENTUM	O-RANGER	O-URALIS
O-BLASTS	O-ESTRIN	O-MICRON	O-RANGES	O-URARIS
O-BOVATE	O-ESTRUM	O-MIKRON	O-RATING	O-UTMOST
O-CARINA	O-ESTRUS	O-NANISM	O-RATION	O-VARIES
O-CELLAR	O-INKING	O-PACIFY	O-ROTUND	O-VERBID
O-CREATE	O-KIMONO	O-PENING	O-STENTS	O-VERSET
O-DONATE	O-LIVERS	O-PINING	O-STRICH	O-WRIEST
O-DORISE	O-LOGIES	O-PINION	O-UAKARI	O-YESSES
O-DORIZE	O-MENING	O-POSSUM	O-UGLIED	O-ZONATE
O-EDEMAS	O-MENTAL	O-RACHES	O-UGLIES	

Seven letters to eight

O-CARINAS	O-EDEMATA	O-KIMONOS	O-OLOGIST	O-UROLOGY
O-DONATES	O-ENOLOGY	O-MICRONS	O-PINIONS	O-VARIOLE
O-DORISED	O-ESTRINS	O-MIKRONS	O-POSSUMS	O-VARIOUS
O-DORISES	O-ESTRIOL	O-MISSION	O-RANGIER	O-VERBIDS
O-DORIZED	O-ESTRONE	O-MISSIVE	O-RATIONS	O-VERSETS
O-DORIZES	O-ESTROUS	O-NANISMS	O-STOMATE	O-ZONATED
O-ECOLOGY	O-ESTRUMS	O-OLOGIES	O-UAKARIS	

Eight letters to nine

O-DORISING	O-ESTRIOLS	O-OLOGISTS	O-RANGIEST	O-VERMINED
O-DORIZING	O-ESTROGEN	O-PACIFIED	O-STOMATES	O-ZONATION
O-ECUMENIC	O-ESTRONES	O-PACIFIER	O-STRICHES	
O-ENOPHILE	O-ESTRUSES	O-PACIFIES	O-UROSCOPY	
O-ESOPHAGI	O-MISSIONS	O-PINIONED	O-VARIOLES	

O – End-hooks

Two letters to three

AB-O	EM-O	IS-O	ON-O	UP-O
AD-O	EX-O	LO-O	OX-O	WO-O
AG-O	GI-O	MO-O	PO-O	ZO-O
BI-O	GO-O	NO-O	RE-O	
BO-O	HA-O	OB-O	TA-O	
DO-O	HO-O	OH-O	TO-O	

Three letters to four

ALS-O	DIN-O	KEN-O	MIR-O	SAD-O
ALT-O	DOC-O	KET-O	MIS-O	SAG-O
ANN-O	DOD-O	KIN-O	MON-O	SEC-O
ARC-O	ECH-O	KOB-O	MOZ-O	SEG-O
BEG-O	ERG-O	KOR-O	MUS-O	SKI-O
BIT-O	FAD-O	LEV-O	ODS-O	SOH-O
BOH-O	FAN-O	LID-O	OLE-O	SOL-O
BOK-O	FAR-O	LIN-O	ORD-O	SUM-O
BOY-O	FID-O	LIP-O	PAC-O	TAR-O
BRO-O	FIG-O	LOB-O	PEP-O	TOC-O
BUB-O	FIL-O	LOG-O	PES-O	TOM-O
BUD-O	FIN-O	LOT-O	PIS-O	TOP-O
CAM-O	GAP-O	LUD-O	POL-O	TOR-O
CAP-O	GOB-O	MAK-O	POM-O	TOY-O
CHA-O	HER-O	MAN-O	PRO-O	VEG-O
CIT-O	HOB-O	MAY-O	RAT-O	VET-O
DAD-O	HOM-O	MEM-O	RED-O	VIN-O
DAG-O	HYP-O	MEN-O	REG-O	WIN-O
DEL-O	JUD-O	MIC-O	REP-O	YUK-O
DID-O	KAY-O	MIL-O	ROT-O	

Four letters to five

AMID-O	CHIN-O	GUAN-O	MOTT-O	REST-O
AMIN-O	CHOC-O	GUST-O	MUCH-O	RODE-O
BANC-O	COMB-O	HALL-O	MUNG-O	RONE-O
BARD-O	COMM-O	HELL-O	NACH-O	RUMP-O
BASH-O	COMP-O	HILL-O	NARC-O	SALT-O
BASS-O	COND-O	HOWS-O	NUTS-O	SANG-O
BAST-O	CORN-O	HULL-O	PANT-O	SANK-O
BEAN-O	CORS-O	IMID-O	PARE-O	SANT-O
BENT-O	CRED-O	JAMB-O	PASE-O	SCUD-O
BERK-O	CUFF-O	JELL-O	PEST-O	SEXT-O
BIFF-O	CUSS-O	JOCK-O	PHON-O	SICK-O
BING-O	CYAN-O	KARO-O	PHOT-O	SKIM-O
BOFF-O	DECK-O	KEEN-O	PIAN-O	SOCK-O
BOMB-O	DING-O	KEMB-O	PILA-O	SOLD-O
BONG-O	DIPS-O	KOND-O	PING-O	SORB-O
BUCK-O	DISC-O	LASS-O	PINK-O	SORD-O
BUFF-O	DITT-O	LENT-O	PINT-O	STEN-O
BUNK-O	DRAC-O	LIMB-O	PONG-O	TACH-O
BURR-O	DUMB-O	LING-O	PORN-O	TANG-O
BUTE-O	FANG-O	LITH-O	POSH-O	TEMP-O
CACA-O	FATS-O	MACH-O	POTT-O	TORS-O
CAME-O	FILL-O	MAIK-O	PRIM-O	TRIG-O
CAMP-O	FLEX-O	MANG-O	PROM-O	TRUG-O
CANS-O	FORD-O	MENT-O	PROS-O	VERS-O
CANT-O	FUNG-O	METH-O	PULA-O	VIDE-O
CARB-O	GADS-O	MEZZ-O	PUNT-O	VIRE-O
CELL-O	GAMB-O	MILK-O	PUTT-O	WACK-O
CENT-O	GARB-O	MIME-O	QUIN-O	WALD-O
CHAD-O	GECK-O	MOLT-O	QUIP-O	WHAM-O
CHIA-O	GISM-O	MONG-O	RATO-O	YUCK-O
CHIC-O	GODS-O	MOSS-O	REAL-O	ZINC-O

O – End-hooks

Five letters to six

AMMON-O	CRYPT-O	LIVED-O	REECH-O	THICK-O
BILLY-O	DINER-O	MEDIC-O	RIGHT-O	TOLED-O
BRILL-O	DORAD-O	MORPH-O	ROMAN-O	TRILL-O
BROCH-O	DUETT-O	NYMPH-O	SHACK-O	VIGOR-O
BRONC-O	ERING-O	PEDAL-O	SHEEP-O	VOMIT-O
CARDI-O	FASCI-O	PLONK-O	SMALT-O	WEIRD-O
CHARR-O	FRANC-O	PREST-O	SOLAN-O	WHACK-O
CHEAP-O	GIUST-O	PSEUD-O	SPEED-O	WHATS-O
CHEER-O	HALLO-O	PSYCH-O	STALK-O	
CHOCK-O	HOLLO-O	QUART-O	STERE-O	
CHURR-O	HULLO-O	RABAT-O	STING-O	
CONCH-O	LIBER-O	RANCH-O	STINK-O	

Six letters to seven

BANDIT-O	CYMBAL-O	PAESAN-O	PUMMEL-O	TAMARA-O
BATTER-O	GRADIN-O	PAISAN-O	RABBIT-O	TYMPAN-O
BRACER-O	MAGNET-O	PAMPER-O	REVERS-O	VERISM-O
BUDGER-O	MOMENT-O	PIMENT-O	SECOND-O	WHERES-O
CANTIC-O	NITROS-O	PRIMER-O	SERRAN-O	

Seven letters to eight

ARMIGER-O	CORNETT-O	INTAGLI-O	POLITIC-O	STAMPED-O
CAPITAN-O	COURANT-O	LEGGIER-O	PRELUDI-O	VIGOROS-O
CLASSIC-O	EXPRESS-O	MONTANT-O	RANCHER-O	ZECCHIN-O
COMMAND-O	FASCISM-O	PEEKABO-O	SESTETT-O	
CONCERT-O	FLAMING-O	PERFECT-O	SOMBRER-O	

Eight letters to nine

CABALLER-O	MAGNIFIC-O	PORTOLAN-O	QUINTETT-O
CAPRICCI-O	MANIFEST-O	PULVILLI-O	SOLFEGGI-O
DESTRUCT-O	PASTICCI-O	QUARTETT-O	

P – Front-hooks

Two letters to three

P-AD	P-AX	P-ET	P-OM	P-UG
P-AH	P-AY	P-HI	P-OO	P-UH
P-AL	P-EA	P-HO	P-OP	P-UN
P-AM	P-ED	P-IN	P-OS	P-UP
P-AN	P-EE	P-IS	P-OW	P-UR
P-AR	P-EH	P-IT	P-OX	P-US
P-AS	P-EN	P-OD	P-RE	P-UT
P-AT	P-ER	P-OH	P-SI	P-YA
P-AW	P-ES	P-OI	P-ST	P-YE

Three letters to four

P-AAL	P-ADS	P-AID	P-AIR	P-ALL
P-ACE	P-AGE	P-AIL	P-AIS	P-ALP
P-ACT	P-AHS	P-AIN	P-ALE	P-ALS

P-AND	P-EEN	P-INK	P-ONE	P-REP
P-ANE	P-EHS	P-INS	P-ONS	P-REX
P-ANT	P-EKE	P-ION	P-ONY	P-REZ
P-APE	P-ELF	P-ISH	P-OOF	P-RIG
P-ARD	P-ELL	P-ISO	P-OOH	P-RIM
P-ARE	P-ELT	P-ITA	P-OON	P-ROB
P-ARK	P-END	P-ITS	P-OOP	P-ROD
P-ARS	P-ENE	P-LAP	P-OOR	P-ROM
P-ART	P-ENS	P-LAT	P-OOS	P-ROO
P-ASH	P-EON	P-LAY	P-OOT	P-ROW
P-ASS	P-ERE	P-LEA	P-OPE	P-SIS
P-ATE	P-ERK	P-LED	P-OPS	P-TUI
P-AUA	P-ERN	P-LEW	P-ORE	P-UDS
P-AVE	P-EST	P-LEX	P-ORT	P-UGH
P-AWA	P-HAT	P-LIE	P-OSE	P-UGS
P-AWL	P-HEW	P-LOD	P-OUK	P-UKE
P-AWN	P-HIS	P-LOP	P-OUR	P-ULE
P-AYS	P-HOH	P-LOT	P-OUT	P-ULU
P-EAN	P-HON	P-LOW	P-OWN	P-UMP
P-EAR	P-HOS	P-LOY	P-OXY	P-UNS
P-EAS	P-HOT	P-LUG	P-RAD	P-UPS
P-EAT	P-HUT	P-LUM	P-RAM	P-URE
P-ECH	P-ICE	P-ODS	P-RAT	P-UTS
P-EDS	P-ICK	P-OKE	P-RAY	P-YES
P-EEK	P-ILL	P-OLE	P-REE	P-YET
P-EEL	P-IMP	P-OMS	P-REM	P-YIN

Four letters to five

P-AALS	P-ARED	P-ELTS	P-ISOS	P-LOYS
P-ACED	P-ARES	P-ENDS	P-ITAS	P-LUCK
P-ACER	P-ARIS	P-ENES	P-ITCH	P-LUES
P-ACES	P-ARKS	P-EONS	P-LACE	P-LUFF
P-ACTA	P-ARLE	P-EPOS	P-LACK	P-LUGS
P-ACTS	P-ARSE	P-ERES	P-LAID	P-LUMP
P-ADDY	P-ARTI	P-ERKS	P-LAIN	P-LUMS
P-AEON	P-ARTS	P-ERNS	P-LANE	P-LUNK
P-AGED	P-ARTY	P-ERST	P-LANK	P-LUSH
P-AGER	P-ARVO	P-ESKY	P-LANT	P-ODAL
P-AGES	P-ATES	P-ESTS	P-LAPS	P-OINT
P-AILS	P-AVER	P-HANG	P-LASH	P-OKES
P-AINS	P-AVES	P-HARE	P-LAST	P-OLES
P-AIRS	P-AVID	P-HOHS	P-LATE	P-OLIO
P-ALAS	P-AWED	P-HONE	P-LATS	P-ONCE
P-ALAY	P-AWLS	P-HONS	P-LAYS	P-ONES
P-ALES	P-AWNS	P-HOTS	P-LEAD	P-OOFS
P-ALLS	P-AXES	P-HUTS	P-LEAS	P-OOFY
P-ALLY	P-EACH	P-HYLA	P-LEAT	P-OOHS
P-ALMS	P-EANS	P-HYLE	P-LIED	P-OONS
P-ALPS	P-EARL	P-ICKY	P-LIER	P-OOPS
P-ANCE	P-EARS	P-ILEA	P-LIES	P-OOTS
P-ANDS	P-EASE	P-ILLS	P-LING	P-OPES
P-ANES	P-EATS	P-IMPS	P-LINK	P-ORAL
P-ANGA	P-EELS	P-INCH	P-LODS	P-ORES
P-ANTS	P-EERY	P-INGO	P-LONG	P-ORGY
P-APER	P-EGGY	P-INKS	P-LOOK	P-ORTS
P-APES	P-EKES	P-INKY	P-LOPS	P-OSES
P-ARCH	P-ELFS	P-INTO	P-LOTS	P-OTTO
P-ARDS	P-ELLS	P-IONS	P-LOWS	P-OUCH

P – Front-hooks

P-OUKS	P-RAWN	P-RIGS	P-ROMS	P-SORA
P-OURS	P-RAYS	P-RILL	P-RONE	P-UKES
P-OUTS	P-REED	P-RIMA	P-RONG	P-ULES
P-OWER	P-REEN	P-RIME	P-ROOF	P-ULUS
P-OWNS	P-REES	P-RIMS	P-RORE	P-UMPS
P-OWRE	P-REIF	P-RIMY	P-ROSE	P-UNCE
P-OXES	P-REMS	P-RINK	P-ROST	P-UNTO
P-RADS	P-RENT	P-RISE	P-ROSY	P-UPAS
P-RAMS	P-REPS	P-ROBE	P-ROUL	P-URES
P-RANA	P-REST	P-ROBS	P-ROVE	P-URGE
P-RANG	P-RIAL	P-RODS	P-ROWS	P-USES
P-RANK	P-RICE	P-ROIN	P-RUDE	P-YINS
P-RASE	P-RICK	P-ROKE	P-RUNE	
P-RATE	P-RICY	P-ROLE	P-RUNT	
P-RATS	P-RIDE	P-ROLL	P-SHAW	

Five letters to six

P-ACERS	P-AWNER	P-IRATE	P-LUMMY	P-REARM
P-ACING	P-EANED	P-ISHES	P-LUMPS	P-REBID
P-ACKER	P-EARLS	P-ITCHY	P-LUMPY	P-REBUY
P-ADDED	P-EARLY	P-LACED	P-LUNGE	P-RECUT
P-ADDER	P-EARST	P-LACER	P-LUNKS	P-REDRY
P-ADDLE	P-EASED	P-LACES	P-LURRY	P-REENS
P-AEONS	P-EASES	P-LACET	P-LUSHY	P-REEVE
P-AGERS	P-ECHED	P-LACKS	P-LYING	P-REFER
P-AGING	P-EERIE	P-LAIDS	P-ODIUM	P-REFIX
P-AIRED	P-EGGED	P-LANCH	P-OINTS	P-REIFS
P-AIRER	P-ELITE	P-LANES	P-OLDER	P-REMAN
P-ALAPA	P-ELVES	P-LANKS	P-OLIOS	P-REMEN
P-ALATE	P-ENDED	P-LANTS	P-OLLER	P-REMIX
P-ALAYS	P-ERSES	P-LATED	P-ONCES	P-RENTS
P-ALTER	P-ESTER	P-LATEN	P-ONTIC	P-REPAY
P-ANGAS	P-ETHER	P-LATER	P-OOHED	P-RESES
P-ANTED	P-ETTLE	P-LAYED	P-OOPED	P-RESET
P-APERS	P-HANGS	P-LAYER	P-OPERA	P-RESTO
P-APERY	P-HARES	P-LEACH	P-OSIER	P-RESTS
P-APISH	P-HAROS	P-LEADS	P-OTHER	P-RETAX
P-APISM	P-HEEZE	P-LEASE	P-OTTER	P-REVUE
P-ARISH	P-HONED	P-LEATS	P-OTTOS	P-REXES
P-ARKED	P-HONER	P-LEDGE	P-OUNCE	P-RIALS
P-ARLED	P-HONES	P-LEUCH	P-OUPED	P-RICED
P-ARLES	P-HONEY	P-LEUGH	P-OURIE	P-RICER
P-ARPEN	P-HOOEY	P-LEXES	P-OUTED	P-RICES
P-ARRAS	P-HYLIC	P-LIERS	P-OUTER	P-RICEY
P-ARSED	P-ICKER	P-LIGHT	P-OWRES	P-RICKS
P-ARSES	P-ICKLE	P-LINGS	P-RAISE	P-RIDES
P-ARSON	P-IGGED	P-LINKS	P-RANAS	P-RIEVE
P-ARTIS	P-ILEUM	P-LODGE	P-RANCE	P-RILLS
P-ARVOS	P-ILEUS	P-LONGE	P-RANKS	P-RIMED
P-ASHED	P-IMPED	P-LONGS	P-RASES	P-RIMER
P-ASHES	P-IMPLY	P-LOOKS	P-RATED	P-RIMES
P-ASSES	P-INGLE	P-LOUGH	P-RATER	P-RIMUS
P-ASTER	P-INION	P-LOVER	P-RATES	P-RINKS
P-AVENS	P-INKED	P-LOWED	P-RAWNS	P-RISER
P-AVERS	P-INKER	P-LOWER	P-RAXES	P-RISES
P-AVISE	P-INNED	P-LUCKS	P-RAYED	P-RIVET
P-AWING	P-INNER	P-LUCKY	P-REACH	P-ROBED
P-AWNED	P-IONIC	P-LUFFS	P-REACT	P-ROBES

P-ROINS	P-ROPER	P-ROVEN	P-RUNTS	P-UPPED
P-ROKED	P-RORES	P-ROVER	P-SHAWS	P-URGED
P-ROKER	P-ROSED	P-ROVES	P-SORAS	P-URGER
P-ROKES	P-ROSES	P-ROWER	P-TOSES	P-URGES
P-ROLES	P-ROSIT	P-ROYNE	P-UDDER	P-URINE
P-ROLLS	P-ROTON	P-RUDES	P-UGGED	P-USHER
P-RONES	P-ROULS	P-RUNED	P-UMPED	P-UTTER
P-ROOFS	P-ROVED	P-RUNES	P-UNCES	

Six letters to seven

P-ACKERS	P-ENATES	P-LAIDED	P-LUMPER	P-REARMS
P-ACTION	P-ENDING	P-LANATE	P-LUNGED	P-REAVER
P-ADDERS	P-ENFOLD	P-LANKED	P-LUNGER	P-REBIDS
P-ADDIES	P-ENSILE	P-LANNER	P-LUNGES	P-REBILL
P-ADDING	P-ENTICE	P-LAPPED	P-LUNKER	P-REBIND
P-ADDLED	P-EONISM	P-LASHED	P-LUSHER	P-REBOIL
P-ADDLES	P-ESTERS	P-LASHER	P-LUSHES	P-REBOOK
P-AEONIC	P-ETHERS	P-LASHES	P-LUSHLY	P-REBORN
P-AGINGS	P-ETTLED	P-LASTER	P-LUTEAL	P-REBUYS
P-AIREST	P-ETTLES	P-LATENS	P-ODIUMS	P-RECAST
P-AIRING	P-HANGED	P-LATINA	P-OINTED	P-RECEDE
P-ALAPAS	P-HATTER	P-LATTER	P-OLLERS	P-RECENT
P-ALATED	P-HEEZED	P-LAYERS	P-OLLIES	P-RECEPT
P-ALATES	P-HEEZES	P-LAYING	P-ONDING	P-RECESS
P-ALLIUM	P-HIZZES	P-LAYOFF	P-OODLES	P-RECIPE
P-ALTERS	P-HONERS	P-LEADED	P-OOFIER	P-RECODE
P-ANELED	P-HONEYS	P-LEADER	P-OOHING	P-RECOOK
P-ANTHER	P-HONIED	P-LEASED	P-OOPING	P-RECOUP
P-ANTING	P-HONING	P-LEASER	P-OPERAS	P-RECURE
P-ANTLER	P-HUTTED	P-LEASES	P-ORCINE	P-RECUTS
P-APISMS	P-ICKERS	P-LEDGED	P-ORGIES	P-REDATE
P-APPOSE	P-ICKIER	P-LEDGER	P-ORTHOS	P-REDIAL
P-ARABLE	P-ICKILY	P-LEDGES	P-OTHERS	P-REEDIT
P-ARCHED	P-ICKLER	P-LESSOR	P-OTTERS	P-REEVED
P-ARCHES	P-IGGING	P-LIABLE	P-OUCHED	P-REEVES
P-ARISES	P-IMPING	P-LIGHTS	P-OUCHES	P-REFACE
P-ARKING	P-IMPLED	P-LINKED	P-OULDER	P-REFECT
P-ARLING	P-INCASE	P-LINKER	P-OUNCES	P-REFERS
P-ARPENS	P-INCHED	P-LISSES	P-OUPING	P-REFILE
P-ARPENT	P-INCHER	P-LODGED	P-OUTERS	P-REFIRE
P-ARSING	P-INCHES	P-LODGES	P-OUTHER	P-REFORM
P-ARSONS	P-INFALL	P-LONGED	P-OUTING	P-REFUND
P-ARTIER	P-INFOLD	P-LONGES	P-OZZIES	P-REHEAT
P-ARTIES	P-INGLES	P-LOPPED	P-RABBLE	P-RELATE
P-ASHING	P-INGOES	P-LOTTED	P-RAISED	P-RELOAD
P-ASTERN	P-ININONS	P-LOTTER	P-RAISER	P-REMADE
P-ASTERS	P-INKERS	P-LOUGHS	P-RAISES	P-REMEET
P-ATRIAL	P-INKIER	P-LOVERS	P-RANCED	P-REMISE
P-AVISES	P-INKING	P-LOWBOY	P-RANCES	P-REMISS
P-AWNERS	P-INNATE	P-LOWERS	P-RANGED	P-REMIXT
P-AWNING	P-INNERS	P-LOWING	P-RANKED	P-REMOLD
P-EANING	P-INNING	P-LUCKED	P-RANKLE	P-REMOVE
P-EASING	P-INWORK	P-LUFFED	P-RATERS	P-RENAME
P-EATERY	P-ITCHED	P-LUGGED	P-RATING	P-RENTED
P-ECHING	P-ITCHES	P-LUGGER	P-RATTED	P-REPACK
P-EERIER	P-LACERS	P-LUMBER	P-RATTLE	P-REPAID
P-EGGING	P-LACETS	P-LUMPED	P-RAYING	P-REPAVE
P-ELITES	P-LACING	P-LUMPEN	P-REACTS	P-REPAYS

P-REPLAN	P-RETAPE	P-RICKED	P-RODDED	P-RUNTED
P-REPONE	P-RETELL	P-RICKER	P-ROINED	P-SALTER
P-REPOSE	P-RETEST	P-RICKLE	P-ROKERS	P-SHAWED
P-REPPED	P-RETOLD	P-RICKLY	P-ROKING	P-UBERTY
P-RESALE	P-RETRIM	P-RIDING	P-ROLLED	P-UCKERS
P-RESELL	P-RETYPE	P-RIEVES	P-ROLLER	P-UDDERS
P-RESENT	P-REVERB	P-RIGGED	P-ROOFED	P-UGGING
P-RESETS	P-REVIEW	P-RIGGER	P-ROOFER	P-ULLING
P-RESHIP	P-REVISE	P-RILLED	P-ROPERS	P-UMPING
P-RESHOW	P-REVUES	P-RIMERS	P-ROSIER	P-UNTIES
P-RESIDE	P-REWARM	P-RIMING	P-ROSILY	P-UPPING
P-RESIFT	P-REWASH	P-RIMMED	P-ROSING	P-URANIC
P-RESOAK	P-REWIRE	P-RIMMER	P-ROTONS	P-URGERS
P-RESOLD	P-REWORK	P-RINKED	P-ROVERS	P-URGING
P-RESORT	P-REWORN	P-RISERS	P-ROVING	P-URINES
P-RESTED	P-REWRAP	P-RISING	P-ROYNED	P-USHERS
P-RESTER	P-RICERS	P-RIVETS	P-ROYNES	P-UTTERS
P-RESTOS	P-RICIER	P-ROBAND	P-RUDERY	
P-RESUME	P-RICING	P-ROBING	P-RUDISH	

Seven letters to eight

P-ACTIONS	P-HONEYED	P-LESSORS	P-OTTERED	P-REBUILT
P-ADDLING	P-HUTTING	P-LIGHTED	P-OUCHING	P-RECASTS
P-AIRINGS	P-ICKIEST	P-LIGHTER	P-OUTINGS	P-RECEDED
P-AIRWISE	P-INCASES	P-LINKERS	P-RABBLES	P-RECEDES
P-ALIFORM	P-INCHERS	P-LINKING	P-RAISERS	P-RECEPTS
P-ALIMONY	P-INCHING	P-LODGING	P-RAISING	P-RECHECK
P-ALLIUMS	P-INFALLS	P-LONGING	P-RANCING	P-RECHOSE
P-ALTERED	P-INFOLDS	P-LOPPING	P-RANGING	P-RECIPES
P-ALTERER	P-INKIEST	P-LOTTERS	P-RANKING	P-RECITED
P-ANELING	P-INNINGS	P-LOTTING	P-RANKISH	P-RECLEAN
P-ANTHERS	P-INWORKS	P-LOWBOYS	P-RANKLED	P-RECODED
P-ANTINGS	P-ITCHIER	P-LOWLAND	P-RANKLES	P-RECODES
P-ANTLERS	P-ITCHILY	P-LUCKIER	P-RATINGS	P-RECOOKS
P-ARABLES	P-ITCHING	P-LUCKILY	P-RATTING	P-RECURED
P-ARCHING	P-LACINGS	P-LUCKING	P-RATTLED	P-RECURES
P-ARISHES	P-LAIDING	P-LUFFING	P-RATTLER	P-REDATED
P-ARPENTS	P-LANCHED	P-LUGGERS	P-RATTLES	P-REDATES
P-ARTICLE	P-LANCHES	P-LUGGING	P-REACHED	P-REDIALS
P-ARTISAN	P-LANKING	P-LUGHOLE	P-REACHER	P-REDRAFT
P-ARTWORK	P-LANNERS	P-LUMBAGO	P-REACHES	P-REDRIED
P-EARLIER	P-LAPPING	P-LUMBERS	P-REACTED	P-REDRIES
P-EARLIES	P-LASHERS	P-LUMMIER	P-READAPT	P-REDRILL
P-ECTASES	P-LASHING	P-LUMPENS	P-READMIT	P-REEDITS
P-EERIEST	P-LASTERS	P-LUMPERS	P-READOPT	P-REELECT
P-ENCHANT	P-LATINAS	P-LUMPIER	P-REALLOT	P-REENACT
P-ENFOLDS	P-LAYBACK	P-LUMPING	P-REALTER	P-REERECT
P-ENLIGHT	P-LAYOFFS	P-LUMPISH	P-REAPPLY	P-REEVING
P-ENOLOGY	P-LAYTIME	P-LUNGERS	P-REARMED	P-REFACED
P-ENTICED	P-LEACHED	P-LUNGING	P-REAVERS	P-REFACES
P-ENTICES	P-LEACHES	P-LUNKERS	P-REBILLS	P-REFECTS
P-ENTOMIC	P-LEADERS	P-LUSHEST	P-REBINDS	P-REFIGHT
P-EONISMS	P-LEADING	P-LUSHIER	P-REBIRTH	P-REFILED
P-ETTLING	P-LEASERS	P-LYINGLY	P-REBOARD	P-REFILES
P-HANGING	P-LEASING	P-OINTING	P-REBOILS	P-REFIRED
P-HARMING	P-LEASURE	P-OOFIEST	P-REBOOKS	P-REFIRES
P-HEEZING	P-LEATHER	P-ORTOLAN	P-REBOUND	P-REFIXED
P-HISHING	P-LEDGERS	P-OSTMARK	P-REBUILD	P-REFIXES

P-REFOCUS	P-REPLACE	P-RESIFTS	P-REUNITE	P-RIMMERS
P-REFORMS	P-REPLANS	P-RESOAKS	P-REVALUE	P-RIMMING
P-REFROZE	P-REPLANT	P-RESOLVE	P-REVERBS	P-RINKING
P-REFUNDS	P-REPONED	P-RESORTS	P-REVIEWS	P-ROBANDS
P-REGNANT	P-REPONES	P-RESPLIT	P-REVISED	P-RODDING
P-REHEATS	P-REPOSED	P-RESTAMP	P-REVISES	P-ROINING
P-REJUDGE	P-REPOSES	P-RESTERS	P-REVISIT	P-ROLLERS
P-RELATES	P-REPPING	P-RESTING	P-REVISOR	P-ROLLING
P-RELIVES	P-REPRESS	P-RESTORE	P-REWARMS	P-ROOFERS
P-RELOADS	P-REPRICE	P-RESUMED	P-REWEIGH	P-ROOFING
P-REMISED	P-REPRINT	P-RESUMER	P-REWIRED	P-ROSIEST
P-REMISES	P-RESALES	P-RESUMES	P-REWIRES	P-ROVINGS
P-REMIXED	P-RESCIND	P-RETAPED	P-REWORKS	P-ROYNING
P-REMIXES	P-RESCORE	P-RETAPES	P-REWRAPS	P-SALTERS
P-REMOLDS	P-RESELLS	P-RETASTE	P-RICIEST	P-SHAWING
P-REMORSE	P-RESENTS	P-RETELLS	P-RICKERS	P-UDDERED
P-REMOVED	P-RESERVE	P-RETESTS	P-RICKETS	P-UNITION
P-REMOVES	P-RESHAPE	P-RETRAIN	P-RICKING	P-UNITIVE
P-RENAMES	P-RESHIPS	P-RETREAT	P-RICKLES	P-URGINGS
P-RENTING	P-RESHOWN	P-RETRIAL	P-RIEVING	P-UTTERED
P-REORDER	P-RESHOWS	P-RETRIMS	P-RIGGERS	P-UTTERER
P-REPACKS	P-RESIDED	P-RETYPED	P-RIGGING	
P-REPAVED	P-RESIDER	P-RETYPES	P-RIGGISH	
P-REPAVES	P-RESIDES	P-REUNION	P-RILLING	

Eight letters to nine

P-ACTIONED	P-LEASINGS	P-READMITS	P-REDEFINE	P-REINSERT
P-ALTERERS	P-LEASURES	P-READOPTS	P-REDESIGN	P-REINVITE
P-ALTERING	P-LEATHERS	P-REALLOTS	P-REDIGEST	P-REJUDGED
P-ARTICLES	P-LIGHTERS	P-REALTERS	P-REDRILLS	P-REJUDGES
P-ARTISANS	P-LIGHTFUL	P-REARMING	P-REDRYING	P-RELATION
P-ARTWORKS	P-LIGHTING	P-REASSIGN	P-REEDITED	P-RELAUNCH
P-EARLIEST	P-LOWLANDS	P-REASSURE	P-REELECTS	P-RELOADED
P-EATERIES	P-LUCKIEST	P-REBIDDEN	P-REENACTS	P-RELOCATE
P-ENCHANTS	P-LUGHOLES	P-REBILLED	P-REERECTS	P-REMARKET
P-ENLIGHTS	P-LUMBAGOS	P-REBIRTHS	P-REEXPOSE	P-REMISING
P-ENTANGLE	P-LUMMIEST	P-REBOARDS	P-REFACING	P-REMIXING
P-ENTICING	P-LUMPIEST	P-REBOILED	P-REFERRED	P-REMODIFY
P-ETIOLATE	P-LUSHIEST	P-REBOOKED	P-REFERRER	P-REMOLDED
P-HONEYING	P-LUSHNESS	P-REBOUGHT	P-REFIGURE	P-REMOTION
P-ICKINESS	P-NEUMATIC	P-REBUILDS	P-REFILING	P-REMOVING
P-INFOLDED	P-OENOLOGY	P-REBUTTAL	P-REFILLED	P-RENOTIFY
P-INKINESS	P-ORTHOSES	P-REBUYING	P-REFIRING	P-RENUMBER
P-INNATELY	P-ORTOLANS	P-RECEDING	P-REFIXING	P-REOBTAIN
P-INSETTER	P-OSTMARKS	P-RECENSOR	P-REFORMAT	P-REOCCUPY
P-ITCHIEST	P-OTTERING	P-RECEPTOR	P-REFORMED	P-REORDAIN
P-ITCHINGS	P-RAISINGS	P-RECESSED	P-REFREEZE	P-REORDERS
P-LACELESS	P-RANKINGS	P-RECESSES	P-REFROZEN	P-REPACKED
P-LANCHING	P-RANKLING	P-RECHARGE	P-REFUNDED	P-REPASTED
P-LASHINGS	P-RATTLERS	P-RECHECKS	P-REGNANCY	P-REPAVING
P-LATINISE	P-RATTLING	P-RECHOOSE	P-REGROWTH	P-REPAYING
P-LATINIZE	P-REABSORB	P-RECHOSEN	P-REHANDLE	P-REPLACED
P-LATITUDE	P-REACCUSE	P-RECISION	P-REHARDEN	P-REPLACES
P-LAYBACKS	P-REACHERS	P-RECLEANS	P-REHEATED	P-REPONING
P-LAYTIMES	P-REACHING	P-RECODING	P-REHEATER	P-REPOSING
P-LEACHING	P-REACTING	P-RECOOKED	P-REHIRING	P-REPRICED
P-LEADINGS	P-READAPTS	P-RECURING	P-REIMPOSE	P-REPRICES
P-LEASABLE	P-READJUST	P-REDATING	P-REINFORM	P-REPRINTS

P-RERECORD	P-RESETTLE	P-RESTRESS	P-REUNITES	P-RIGGINGS
P-REREVIEW	P-RESHAPED	P-RESTRIKE	P-REVALUED	P-ROOFINGS
P-RESCHOOL	P-RESHAPES	P-RESUMERS	P-REVALUES	P-ROOFLESS
P-RESCINDS	P-RESHOWED	P-RESUMING	P-REVIEWED	P-ROSELIKE
P-RESCORED	P-RESIDENT	P-RESURVEY	P-REVIEWER	P-ROSINESS
P-RESCORES	P-RESIDERS	P-RETAPING	P-REVISING	P-ROSTRATE
P-RESCREEN	P-RESIDING	P-RETASTED	P-REVISION	P-RUDERIES
P-RESCRIPT	P-RESIFTED	P-RETASTES	P-REVISITS	P-UBERTIES
P-RESEASON	P-RESOAKED	P-RETESTED	P-REVISORS	P-UNGENTLY
P-RESELECT	P-RESOLVED	P-RETRAINS	P-REWARMED	P-UNITIONS
P-RESENTED	P-RESOLVES	P-RETREATS	P-REWASHED	P-USTULATE
P-RESENTER	P-RESORTED	P-RETRIALS	P-REWASHES	P-UTTERERS
P-RESERVED	P-RESTAMPS	P-RETYPING	P-REWEIGHS	P-UTTERING
P-RESERVER	P-RESTORED	P-REUNIONS	P-REWIRING	
P-RESERVES	P-RESTORES	P-REUNITED	P-REWORKED	

P – End-hooks

Two letters to three

AL-P	GI-P	LA-P	PA-P	TO-P
AM-P	GU-P	LI-P	PE-P	UM-P
AS-P	HA-P	LO-P	PI-P	UR-P
BA-P	HE-P	MA-P	PO-P	WO-P
BO-P	HI-P	MO-P	RE-P	YA-P
DA-P	HO-P	NA-P	SI-P	YE-P
DI-P	JA-P	NE-P	SO-P	YU-P
DO-P	KI-P	OO-P	TA-P	ZA-P
FA-P	KO-P	OU-P	TI-P	

Three letters to four

ALA-P	GAS-P	LEA-P	PRE-P	TAM-P
BAR-P	GAU-P	LEE-P	PRO-P	TAR-P
BEE-P	GEE-P	LIS-P	PUL-P	TRY-P
BUM-P	GOO-P	LOO-P	RAM-P	TUM-P
BUR-P	GOR-P	LOU-P	RAS-P	VEE-P
CAM-P	GUL-P	LOW-P	REP-P	WAR-P
CAR-P	GUM-P	LUM-P	RIP-P	WAS-P
CHA-P	GYM-P	MOO-P	ROM-P	WEE-P
CHI-P	HAS-P	MOU-P	ROO-P	WHA-P
COO-P	HEM-P	MUM-P	RUM-P	WHO-P
COW-P	HES-P	NEE-P	SAL-P	WIS-P
DAM-P	HOO-P	NOO-P	SAM-P	YAP-P
DEE-P	HUM-P	PAL-P	SEE-P	YAW-P
DIM-P	JAR-P	PAR-P	SIM-P	YOM-P
DOR-P	JEE-P	PEE-P	SKI-P	YUM-P
DOW-P	KIP-P	PER-P	SOU-P	
FRA-P	KOA-P	POM-P	SOW-P	
GAM-P	LAM-P	POO-P	SUM-P	

Four letters to five

BICE-P	CRIM-P	PRIM-P	SLEE-P	SWEE-P
BLEE-P	CRIS-P	SALE-P	SLUM-P	TRAM-P
CHAM-P	FLIM-P	SCAM-P	SLUR-P	WHEE-P
CHUM-P	GRAM-P	SCAR-P	STIR-P	WHOM-P
CLAM-P	GRUM-P	SCOW-P	STOW-P	
CRAM-P	PLUM-P	SCUL-P	STUM-P	
CREE-P	POLY-P	SKIM-P	SWAM-P	

Five letters to six

ESCAR-P	SCRIM-P	SHLEP-P	TRICE-P
SCRAW-P	SCRUM-P	THREE-P	

Six letters to seven

BEDLAM-P	SCHLEP-P
MANTRA-P	

Seven letters to eight

AUTOCAR-P
MINICAM-P

Q – Front-hooks

Two letters to three

Q-AT
Q-IS

Three letters to four

Q-AID
Q-UEY

Four letters to five

Q-AIDS
Q-UEYS

Q – End-hooks

Four letters to five

TALA-Q

R – Front-hooks

Two letters to three

R-AD	R-AW	R-EN	R-IT	R-UM
R-AG	R-AX	R-ES	R-OB	R-UN
R-AH	R-AY	R-ET	R-OD	R-UT
R-AI	R-ED	R-EX	R-OE	R-YA
R-AM	R-EE	R-HO	R-OM	R-YE
R-AN	R-EF	R-ID	R-OO	
R-AS	R-EH	R-IF	R-OW	
R-AT	R-EM	R-IN	R-UG	

Three letters to four

R-ACE	R-AND	R-EFT	R-INK	R-OOT
R-ACH	R-ANI	R-EGO	R-INS	R-OPE
R-ADS	R-ANT	R-EHS	R-ITS	R-ORE
R-AFF	R-APE	R-EIK	R-OAR	R-ORT
R-AFT	R-APT	R-EKE	R-OBE	R-OSE
R-AGA	R-ARE	R-EMS	R-OBS	R-OUP
R-AGE	R-ARK	R-END	R-OCH	R-OUT
R-AGS	R-ASH	R-ENS	R-ODE	R-OWT
R-AHS	R-ASP	R-EST	R-ODS	R-UDS
R-AIA	R-ATE	R-HOS	R-OES	R-UGS
R-AID	R-AVE	R-ICE	R-OIL	R-ULE
R-AIL	R-AWN	R-ICH	R-OKE	R-UMP
R-AIN	R-AYS	R-ICK	R-OLE	R-UNS
R-AIS	R-EAN	R-ICY	R-OMS	R-URP
R-AIT	R-EAR	R-IDE	R-ONE	R-USE
R-AKE	R-EDS	R-IDS	R-OOF	R-UTS
R-ALE	R-EEK	R-IFF	R-OOM	R-YES
R-AMI	R-EEL	R-IFS	R-OON	
R-AMP	R-EEN	R-IGG	R-OOP	
R-ANA	R-EFS	R-ILL	R-OOS	

Four letters to five

R-ABID	R-AMIS	R-EARS	R-HONE	R-OPED
R-ACED	R-AMPS	R-EAST	R-ICED	R-OPES
R-ACER	R-AMUS	R-EAVE	R-ICER	R-ORAL
R-ACES	R-ANAS	R-ECCE	R-ICES	R-ORES
R-ACHE	R-ANCE	R-ECCO	R-IDES	R-ORTS
R-AGAS	R-ANDS	R-EDDY	R-IGGS	R-OSES
R-AGED	R-ANIS	R-EECH	R-ILLS	R-OUPS
R-AGEE	R-ANTS	R-EELS	R-INKS	R-OUST
R-AGER	R-APED	R-EGAL	R-OARS	R-OUTS
R-AGES	R-APER	R-EGMA	R-OARY	R-OVEN
R-AHED	R-APES	R-EGOS	R-OAST	R-OVER
R-AIAS	R-ARED	R-EIKS	R-OBES	R-OWED
R-AIDS	R-ARES	R-EKED	R-ODES	R-OWER
R-AILS	R-ARKS	R-EKES	R-OILS	R-OWTS
R-AINE	R-ASPS	R-EMIT	R-OILY	R-ULES
R-AINS	R-ATES	R-ENDS	R-OKES	R-UMBO
R-AITS	R-AVEL	R-ENEW	R-OLES	R-UMPS
R-AKED	R-AVER	R-EPOS	R-ONES	R-UMPY
R-AKEE	R-AVES	R-ESES	R-OOFS	R-URPS
R-AKES	R-AWNS	R-ESTS	R-OOFY	R-URUS
R-ALES	R-AXED	R-ETCH	R-OOMS	R-USES
R-ALLY	R-AXES	R-EVET	R-OONS	
R-AMEN	R-AYAH	R-EXES	R-OOPS	
R-AMIE	R-EACH	R-HEME	R-OOSE	
R-AMIN	R-EANS	R-HIES	R-OOTS	

Five letters to six

R-ABIES	R-ADDED	R-AGERS	R-AILED	R-AMENS
R-ACERS	R-ADDER	R-AGING	R-AKEES	R-AMIES
R-ACHES	R-ADDLE	R-AHING	R-AKING	R-AMINS
R-ACING	R-ADIOS	R-AIDED	R-AMATE	R-AMPED
R-ACKER	R-AFTER	R-AIDER	R-AMBLE	R-ANCHO

R-ANGER	R-AXING	R-EMOTE	R-ICHES	R-OTARY
R-ANKER	R-AYAHS	R-EMOVE	R-ICIER	R-OTHER
R-ANKLE	R-AZURE	R-ENDED	R-ICING	R-OTTER
R-ANTED	R-EALES	R-ENDER	R-ICKER	R-OUGHT
R-APERS	R-EARED	R-ENEWS	R-ICKLE	R-OUNCE
R-APHIS	R-EARLY	R-ENTER	R-ICTAL	R-OUPED
R-APING	R-EASTS	R-ENVOI	R-ICTUS	R-OUSTS
R-APPEL	R-EAVED	R-ENVOY	R-IDENT	R-OUTED
R-APTLY	R-EAVES	R-EROSE	R-IGGED	R-OUTER
R-AREFY	R-EBOOK	R-ESILE	R-INKED	R-OVERS
R-ARKED	R-EDUCE	R-ESTER	R-IZARD	R-OWING
R-ASHED	R-EFFED	R-ETAPE	R-OARED	R-UDDER
R-ASHES	R-EGEST	R-EVERT	R-OASTS	R-UGGED
R-ASPER	R-EGRET	R-EVERY	R-OCHES	R-UMBLE
R-ASSES	R-EJECT	R-EVETS	R-OCKER	R-UMBOS
R-ASTER	R-EKING	R-EVOKE	R-OILED	R-UMPED
R-AUGHT	R-ELAND	R-EXINE	R-OLLER	R-UNLET
R-AVELS	R-ELATE	R-HEMES	R-ONION	R-UNRIG
R-AVENS	R-ELIDE	R-HEXES	R-OOPED	R-URBAN
R-AVERS	R-EMAIL	R-HONES	R-OOSES	R-USHER
R-AVINE	R-EMEND	R-ICERS	R-OPING	R-UTILE
R-AWING	R-EMITS	R-ICHED	R-OSIER	R-UTTER

Six letters to seven

R-ABIDER	R-APPORT	R-ELANDS	R-ETCHES	R-OOFIER
R-ACKERS	R-ARKING	R-ELAPSE	R-EVERTS	R-OOPING
R-ADDING	R-ASHING	R-ELATED	R-EVILER	R-OSIERS
R-ADDLED	R-ASPERS	R-ELATER	R-EVOKED	R-OTHERS
R-ADDLES	R-ASPISH	R-ELATES	R-EVOKER	R-OTTERS
R-AFTERS	R-ASTERS	R-EMAILS	R-EVOKES	R-OUCHES
R-AGGIES	R-ATTRAP	R-EMENDS	R-EVOLVE	R-OUGHLY
R-AGINGS	R-AZURES	R-EMERGE	R-EXINES	R-OUNCES
R-AIDERS	R-EARING	R-EMOTER	R-HACHIS	R-OUPING
R-AIDING	R-EASTED	R-EMOTES	R-ICHING	R-OUSTED
R-AILING	R-EBOOKS	R-EMOVED	R-ICIEST	R-OUSTER
R-ALLIED	R-ECLOSE	R-EMOVES	R-ICKERS	R-OUTERS
R-ALLIES	R-EDDISH	R-ENDERS	R-IGGING	R-OUTING
R-AMBLED	R-EDUCED	R-ENDING	R-IMPLED	R-OYSTER
R-AMBLER	R-EDUCES	R-ENEWED	R-INKING	R-UDDERS
R-AMBLES	R-EECHED	R-ENTERS	R-INNING	R-UGGING
R-AMENTA	R-EECHES	R-ENVOIS	R-IZARDS	R-UMBLES
R-AMPING	R-EFFING	R-ENVOYS	R-OARIER	R-UMPIES
R-ANCHOS	R-EGALLY	R-EPOSES	R-OARING	R-UMPING
R-ANGERS	R-EGENCE	R-EPRISE	R-OCKERS	R-UNLESS
R-ANKERS	R-EGENCY	R-ESILES	R-OILIER	R-UNRIGS
R-ANKLED	R-EGESTS	R-ESTATE	R-OILING	R-USHERS
R-ANKLES	R-EGRESS	R-ESTERS	R-OLLERS	R-UTTERS
R-ANTING	R-EGRETS	R-ETAPES	R-ONIONS	
R-APPELS	R-EJECTS	R-ETCHED	R-ONNING	

Seven letters to eight

R-ABIETIC	R-AMBLING	R-APPORTS	R-EASTING	R-EECHING
R-ADDLING	R-AMENTUM	R-APTNESS	R-ECLOSED	R-EGALITY
R-ADULATE	R-ANKLING	R-AREFIED	R-ECLOSES	R-EGENCES
R-ALLYING	R-ANTINGS	R-AREFIES	R-EDUCING	R-EJECTED
R-AMBLERS	R-APHIDES	R-ATTRAPS	R-EDUCTOR	R-EJECTOR

R – Front-hooks

R-ELAPSED	R-EMERGES	R-ESTATED	R-EVOLVES	R-OUSTING
R-ELAPSES	R-EMITTED	R-ESTATES	R-EVULSED	R-OUTINGS
R-ELATERS	R-EMITTER	R-ETCHING	R-HEMATIC	R-OYSTERS
R-ELATING	R-EMOTION	R-EVERTED	R-ICTUSES	R-UNROUND
R-ELATION	R-EMOVING	R-EVOKERS	R-OARIEST	R-URALITE
R-ELATIVE	R-ENEWING	R-EVOKING	R-OILIEST	
R-EMAILED	R-ENFORCE	R-EVOLUTE	R-OOFIEST	
R-EMENDED	R-ENOUNCE	R-EVOLVED	R-OTARIES	
R-EMERGED	R-EQUITES	R-EVOLVER	R-OUSTERS	

Eight letters to nine

R-AMBLINGS	R-EGRESSES	R-EMENDING	R-ENOUNCED	R-EVULSION
R-ANTIPOLE	R-EJECTING	R-EMERGING	R-ENOUNCES	R-OYSTERED
R-AREFYING	R-EJECTION	R-EMIGRATE	R-ERADIATE	R-OYSTERER
R-ECLOSING	R-EJECTIVE	R-EMISSION	R-ESTATING	R-UNCINATE
R-EDUCIBLE	R-EJECTORS	R-EMISSIVE	R-EVALUATE	R-UNROUNDS
R-EDUCTION	R-ELAPSING	R-EMITTERS	R-EVERSION	R-URALITES
R-EDUCTIVE	R-ELATEDLY	R-EMITTING	R-EVERTING	
R-EDUCTORS	R-ELATIONS	R-EMOTIONS	R-EVOCABLE	
R-EGENCIES	R-ELATIVES	R-ENFORCED	R-EVOLVERS	
R-EGRESSED	R-EMAILING	R-ENFORCES	R-EVOLVING	

R – End-hooks

Two letters to three

AI-R	FE-R	KO-R	NU-R	TA-R
BA-R	GO-R	LA-R	OO-R	TO-R
BO-R	GU-R	LO-R	OU-R	YA-R
DO-R	HE-R	MA-R	PA-R	
EA-R	JA-R	MI-R	PE-R	
ER-R	JO-R	MO-R	PI-R	
FA-R	KI-R	NO-R	SI-R	

Three letters to four

ACE-R	DEE-R	HUE-R	OYE-R	TEA-R
AGA-R	DOE-R	ICE-R	PAR-R	TEE-R
AGE-R	DOO-R	JEE-R	PEA-R	TIE-R
ALA-R	DOR-R	LEA-R	PEE-R	TOR-R
AMI-R	DYE-R	LEE-R	PIE-R	TYE-R
APE-R	EVE-R	LEI-R	POO-R	USE-R
AVE-R	EWE-R	LIE-R	PUR-R	VEE-R
BEE-R	EYE-R	LOO-R	RUE-R	VIE-R
BOA-R	FEE-R	LOU-R	SAI-R	WAI-R
BOO-R	FIE-R	MAA-R	SEA-R	WEE-R
BOW-R	FOU-R	MAW-R	SEE-R	YAR-R
BRR-R	FUR-R	MEE-R	SEI-R	YEA-R
BUR-R	GAU-R	MOE-R	SER-R	YOU-R
CAR-R	GOE-R	MOO-R	SKY-R	
CHA-R	GOO-R	NUR-R	SOU-R	
CHE-R	HOA-R	ONE-R	SPA-R	
CUR-R	HOE-R	OWE-R	SUE-R	

Four letters to five

ABLE-R	EDGE-R	LEVE-R	PILA-R	SPAE-R
AIDE-R	EIDE-R	LIFE-R	PILE-R	SPIE-R
ANTA-R	ETHE-R	LIKE-R	PIPE-R	SPUE-R
AREA-R	FACE-R	LINE-R	PLIE-R	STAR-R
AURA-R	FADE-R	LITE-R	POKE-R	SUPE-R
BAKE-R	FAKE-R	LIVE-R	POLE-R	SURE-R
BALE-R	FARE-R	LONE-R	PORE-R	SWEE-R
BARE-R	FAVE-R	LOPE-R	POSE-R	SYKE-R
BASE-R	FERE-R	LOSE-R	PUCE-R	TAKE-R
BIDE-R	FIFE-R	LOVE-R	PUKE-R	TALA-R
BIKE-R	FILA-R	LOWE-R	PULE-R	TALE-R
BINE-R	FILE-R	LUGE-R	PURE-R	TAME-R
BITE-R	FINE-R	LUNA-R	QUAI-R	TAPE-R
BLAE-R	FIRE-R	LURE-R	RACE-R	TATE-R
BLUE-R	FIVE-R	LUTE-R	RAGE-R	TIGE-R
BOLA-R	FLEE-R	MACE-R	RAKE-R	TILE-R
BONE-R	FREE-R	MAKE-R	RAPE-R	TIME-R
BORE-R	FUME-R	MALA-R	RARE-R	TITE-R
BREE-R	GAGE-R	MANO-R	RASE-R	TOKE-R
BRIE-R	GAME-R	MASE-R	RATE-R	TOLA-R
CAGE-R	GAPE-R	MATE-R	RAVE-R	TONE-R
CANE-R	GATE-R	MAYO-R	RAZE-R	TOPE-R
CAPE-R	GAZE-R	MAZE-R	RICE-R	TOTE-R
CARE-R	GIBE-R	MERE-R	RIDE-R	TRIE-R
CATE-R	GIVE-R	METE-R	RIFE-R	TRIO-R
CAVE-R	GLUE-R	MILE-R	RIME-R	TRUE-R
CEDE-R	GNAR-R	MILO-R	RIPE-R	TRYE-R
CHAI-R	GONE-R	MIME-R	RISE-R	TUBA-R
CHAR-R	GULA-R	MINA-R	RIVE-R	TUBE-R
CIDE-R	HALE-R	MINE-R	ROKE-R	TUNE-R
CITE-R	HATE-R	MINO-R	ROPE-R	TWEE-R
CLOU-R	HAVE-R	MISE-R	ROTO-R	ULNA-R
CODE-R	HAZE-R	MITE-R	ROVE-R	UNDE-R
COME-R	HIDE-R	MODE-R	RUDE-R	URGE-R
COPE-R	HIKE-R	MOLA-R	RULE-R	VELA-R
CORE-R	HILA-R	MOPE-R	RYPE-R	VILE-R
COVE-R	HIRE-R	MOVE-R	SABE-R	VINE-R
CUBE-R	HIVE-R	MUSE-R	SAFE-R	VIVE-R
CURE-R	HOME-R	MUTE-R	SAGE-R	VOLA-R
CUTE-R	HONE-R	NAME-R	SAKE-R	VOTE-R
CYMA-R	HOPE-R	NAZI-R	SANE-R	WADE-R
DARE-R	HOSE-R	NEVE-R	SAVE-R	WAGE-R
DATE-R	HOVE-R	NICE-R	SERE-R	WAKE-R
DAZE-R	HUGE-R	NITE-R	SHEA-R	WALE-R
DECO-R	HYPE-R	NIXE-R	SHIR-R	WATE-R
DICE-R	IDLE-R	NOSE-R	SHOE-R	WAVE-R
DIKE-R	JAPE-R	NOTE-R	SIDE-R	WHIR-R
DIME-R	JIBE-R	NUDE-R	SIKE-R	WIDE-R
DINE-R	JIVE-R	OCHE-R	SILE-R	WIPE-R
DIRE-R	JOKE-R	OGLE-R	SIMA-R	WIRE-R
DIVE-R	KITE-R	ONCE-R	SIZE-R	WISE-R
DONE-R	KNUR-R	PACE-R	SKEE-R	WIVE-R
DOPE-R	LACE-R	PAGE-R	SLEE-R	YARE-R
DOSE-R	LADE-R	PALE-R	SMIR-R	YOKE-R
DOTE-R	LAKE-R	PAPE-R	SNEE-R	ZONE-R
DOVE-R	LAME-R	PARE-R	SOFA-R	
DOZE-R	LASE-R	PATE-R	SOLA-R	
DUPE-R	LATE-R	PAVE-R	SOLE-R	
EASE-R	LAVE-R	PIKE-R	SORE-R	

R – End-hooks

Five letters to six

ABASE-R	CANOE-R	DROVE-R	HEFTE-R	MUDGE-R
ABATE-R	CANTO-R	EERIE-R	HINGE-R	MUGGA-R
ABIDE-R	CARTE-R	ELATE-R	HITHE-R	NAIVE-R
ABUSE-R	CARVE-R	ELOPE-R	HOMIE-R	NAPPE-R
ACUTE-R	CASTE-R	ELUDE-R	HOOVE-R	NERVE-R
ADORE-R	CAUSE-R	EMOTE-R	HOUSE-R	NICHE-R
AERIE-R	CAVIE-R	ERASE-R	ICKLE-R	NOBLE-R
AGILE-R	CELLA-R	EVADE-R	IMAGE-R	NOOSE-R
ALINE-R	CENSE-R	EVOKE-R	INANE-R	NUDGE-R
ALULA-R	CESSE-R	EXILE-R	IRATE-R	NURSE-R
AMBLE-R	CHADO-R	FABLE-R	IRONE-R	OBESE-R
AMPLE-R	CHAFE-R	FAINE-R	ISSUE-R	OLIVE-R
AMUSE-R	CHASE-R	FALSE-R	JAMBE-R	OORIE-R
ANCHO-R	CHIDE-R	FARCE-R	JASPE-R	OURIE-R
ANGLE-R	CHIME-R	FEARE-R	JUDGE-R	OWRIE-R
ARGUE-R	CHINA-R	FENCE-R	JUICE-R	PAIRE-R
ATONE-R	CHOKE-R	FILLE-R	KEDGE-R	PANDA-R
AWARE-R	CIRCA-R	FITTE-R	KNIFE-R	PANNE-R
BADGE-R	CLAVE-R	FLAKE-R	KNOWE-R	PARSE-R
BANDA-R	CLEVE-R	FLAME-R	KRONE-R	PASSE-R
BARBE-R	CLONE-R	FLEXO-R	LADLE-R	PASTE-R
BASSE-R	CLOSE-R	FLUTE-R	LANCE-R	PATTE-R
BASTE-R	CLOVE-R	FOLIA-R	LANDE-R	PAUSE-R
BATHE-R	COATE-R	FORCE-R	LAPSE-R	PECKE-R
BEARE-R	COMBE-R	FORGE-R	LARGE-R	PEEPE-R
BELIE-R	CONDO-R	FORME-R	LATHE-R	PEEVE-R
BESTI-R	CONGE-R	FOULE-R	LATTE-R	PENNE-R
BINGE-R	CONNE-R	FOXIE-R	LEASE-R	PHONE-R
BIRLE-R	COSIE-R	FRAME-R	LEAVE-R	PHYLA-R
BITTE-R	COSTA-R	FRATE-R	LEDGE-R	PIECE-R
BLADE-R	COSTE-R	FRIZE-R	LEFTE-R	PLACE-R
BLAME-R	COTTA-R	GAFFE-R	LEGGE-R	PLANE-R
BLATE-R	COUPE-R	GAMME-R	LENTO-R	PLATE-R
BLAZE-R	COZIE-R	GAUGE-R	LIEGE-R	POISE-R
BODGE-R	CRATE-R	GIMME-R	LIEVE-R	POKIE-R
BOMBE-R	CRAVE-R	GINGE-R	LIGGE-R	POSSE-R
BONIE-R	CROZE-R	GLAZE-R	LITHE-R	PRATE-R
BONZE-R	CRUDE-R	GLIDE-R	LODGE-R	PRICE-R
BOOZE-R	CURSE-R	GLOVE-R	LOGIE-R	PRIME-R
BORDE-R	CYCLE-R	GORGE-R	LONGE-R	PRISE-R
BOWSE-R	DAMME-R	GOUGE-R	LOOSE-R	PRIZE-R
BRACE-R	DANCE-R	GRADE-R	LOTTE-R	PROBE-R
BRAVE-R	DAUBE-R	GRATE-R	LOUSE-R	PROKE-R
BRAZE-R	DEARE-R	GRAVE-R	LOWSE-R	PROLE-R
BRIBE-R	DEICE-R	GRAZE-R	LUNGE-R	PRONE-R
BRINE-R	DELVE-R	GRICE-R	MACHE-R	PROSE-R
BROKE-R	DENSE-R	GRIPE-R	MAILE-R	PROVE-R
BRUTE-R	DINGE-R	GROPE-R	MANDI-R	PRUNE-R
BUDGE-R	DODGE-R	GUIDE-R	MANGE-R	PULSE-R
BUFFE-R	DORSE-R	GUILE-R	MATTE-R	PURGE-R
BUGLE-R	DOUCE-R	GUISE-R	MAUVE-R	PURSE-R
BULGE-R	DOUSE-R	GUSLA-R	MEANE-R	QUAKE-R
BURKE-R	DOVIE-R	GUYLE-R	MENTO-R	QUARE-R
BURSA-R	DOWIE-R	HALSE-R	MERGE-R	QUEUE-R
BUTLE-R	DOWSE-R	HALVE-R	MICHE-R	QUOTE-R
BUTTE-R	DRAPE-R	HAWSE-R	MILLE-R	RADGE-R
CABLE-R	DRIVE-R	HEARE-R	MINCE-R	RAILE-R
CADGE-R	DROLE-R	HEAVE-R	MINGE-R	RAISE-R
CALVE-R	DRONE-R	HEDGE-R	MOUSE-R	RANGE-R

RANKE-R	SEARE-R	SMOKE-R	SUMMA-R	VEALE-R
RAPPE-R	SEINE-R	SNARE-R	SURGE-R	VENGE-R
RATHE-R	SEISE-R	SNIDE-R	SWAGE-R	VERGE-R
REAME-R	SEIZE-R	SNIPE-R	SWIPE-R	VERSE-R
REAVE-R	SELLE-R	SNORE-R	TASTE-R	VILLA-R
RECTO-R	SERGE-R	SOARE-R	TAWIE-R	VIRGE-R
REEDE-R	SERVE-R	SOLDE-R	TEASE-R	VISIE-R
REIVE-R	SHADE-R	SOLVE-R	TEENE-R	VOGIE-R
RELIE-R	SHAKE-R	SONDE-R	TENNE-R	VOGUE-R
RENTE-R	SHAME-R	SORDO-R	TENSE-R	VOICE-R
RHYME-R	SHAPE-R	SPACE-R	TERSE-R	VULVA-R
RIDGE-R	SHARE-R	SPADE-R	TESTE-R	WACKE-R
RIEVE-R	SHAVE-R	SPARE-R	TITHE-R	WAITE-R
RIFLE-R	SHINE-R	SPICE-R	TITLE-R	WAIVE-R
RINSE-R	SHIVE-R	SPIDE-R	TOILE-R	WASTE-R
ROOSE-R	SHORE-R	SPIKE-R	TONNE-R	WEAVE-R
RORIE-R	SHOVE-R	SPINA-R	TOUSE-R	WEETE-R
ROTTE-R	SIDLE-R	STAGE-R	TOWIE-R	WHALE-R
ROUSE-R	SIEGE-R	STALE-R	TOWSE-R	WHINE-R
ROUTE-R	SINGE-R	STARE-R	TRACE-R	WHITE-R
SALVE-R	SKATE-R	STATE-R	TRADE-R	WINCE-R
SALVO-R	SKIVE-R	STELA-R	TRITE-R	WINGE-R
SAMBA-R	SLAKE-R	STIVE-R	TROVE-R	WITHE-R
SANGA-R	SLATE-R	STOKE-R	TWICE-R	WOLVE-R
SANSA-R	SLAVE-R	STONE-R	TWINE-R	WORSE-R
SAUCE-R	SLICE-R	STOPE-R	UNITE-R	WRITE-R
SCALA-R	SLIDE-R	STORE-R	USAGE-R	YODLE-R
SCALE-R	SLIVE-R	STOVE-R	USURE-R	
SCARE-R	SLOPE-R	STYLE-R	UVULA-R	
SCORE-R	SMILE-R	SUAVE-R	VAGUE-R	
SEAME-R	SMITE-R	SUITE-R	VALUE-R	

Six letters to seven

ABJURE-R	BABBLE-R	BOTTLE-R	CHARGE-R	COUPLE-R
ABRADE-R	BAFFLE-R	BOUNCE-R	CHASTE-R	COURIE-R
ACCEDE-R	BAGGIE-R	BRAIDE-R	CHAUFE-R	COURSE-R
ACCUSE-R	BARDIE-R	BRIDLE-R	CHEQUE-R	CRADLE-R
ADDUCE-R	BARMIE-R	BRONZE-R	CHEWIE-R	CREASE-R
ADHERE-R	BARRIE-R	BROWSE-R	CHILDE-R	CRINGE-R
ADJURE-R	BATTLE-R	BRUISE-R	CHOICE-R	CROSSE-R
ADMIRE-R	BEAGLE-R	BUBBLE-R	CHOOSE-R	CROUPE-R
ADVISE-R	BEETLE-R	BUCKLE-R	CHOUSE-R	CRUISE-R
ALLEGE-R	BEHAVE-R	BUMBLE-R	CHUKKA-R	CUDDLE-R
ALLURE-R	BIRKIE-R	BUNDLE-R	CIRCLE-R	CUISSE-R
ALNAGE-R	BITTIE-R	BUNGLE-R	CLAMBE-R	CUPOLA-R
AMENDE-R	BLAGUE-R	BURBLE-R	CLAQUE-R	CUPULA-R
AMERCE-R	BLENDE-R	BUSHIE-R	CLAVIE-R	CURDLE-R
APPOSE-R	BLITHE-R	BUSTLE-R	CLEAVE-R	CURRIE-R
AREOLA-R	BLONDE-R	BYLINE-R	COARSE-R	CUSHIE-R
AROUSE-R	BLOWIE-R	CACKLE-R	COBBLE-R	DABBLE-R
ARRIVE-R	BLUDGE-R	CAJOLE-R	COCKLE-R	DAMAGE-R
ASPIRE-R	BLUDIE-R	CANDLE-R	CODDLE-R	DANDLE-R
ASSIZE-R	BLUNGE-R	CANNIE-R	COERCE-R	DANGLE-R
ASSUME-R	BODGIE-R	CANULA-R	COHERE-R	DAWDLE-R
ASSURE-R	BOGGLE-R	CARNIE-R	COLLIE-R	DAZZLE-R
ASTUTE-R	BONNIE-R	CATTIE-R	COMAKE-R	DEBASE-R
AVENGE-R	BOODLE-R	CHANCE-R	COPULA-R	DEBATE-R
AXILLA-R	BOOKIE-R	CHANGE-R	COUCHE-R	DEBONE-R

DECIDE-R	FIGURE-R	HOPPLE-R	LOGGIE-R	ORANGE-R
DECODE-R	FLANGE-R	HUDDLE-R	LOONIE-R	ORNATE-R
DECREE-R	FLEECE-R	HUMANE-R	LOUNGE-R	OSCULA-R
DEFACE-R	FLENSE-R	HUMBLE-R	LOURIE-R	OUTLIE-R
DEFAME-R	FOLKIE-R	HUNKIE-R	LUCKIE-R	PADDLE-R
DEFILE-R	FONDLE-R	HURDLE-R	LUNULA-R	PALMIE-R
DEFINE-R	FOOTIE-R	HUSTLE-R	MACULA-R	PAPULA-R
DEFUSE-R	FOOTLE-R	IGNITE-R	MANAGE-R	PARADE-R
DELUDE-R	FOOZLE-R	IGNORE-R	MANGLE-R	PARKIE-R
DEMURE-R	FORAGE-R	IMBIBE-R	MANURE-R	PASTIE-R
DENUDE-R	FREEZE-R	IMPALE-R	MARBLE-R	PAVISE-R
DEPOSE-R	FROWIE-R	IMPEDE-R	MARINE-R	PEDDLE-R
DERIDE-R	FUDDLE-R	IMPOSE-R	MASHIE-R	PEERIE-R
DERIVE-R	FUMBLE-R	IMPURE-R	MASQUE-R	PEOPLE-R
DESIRE-R	FUTILE-R	IMPUTE-R	MATURE-R	PERUSE-R
DEVISE-R	GABBLE-R	INCITE-R	MEAGRE-R	PHRASE-R
DIBBLE-R	GAMBLE-R	INCOME-R	MEALIE-R	PIAFFE-R
DICKIE-R	GARBLE-R	INDITE-R	MEDDLE-R	PICKLE-R
DIDDLE-R	GARGLE-R	INDUCE-R	MENACE-R	PIDDLE-R
DILATE-R	GAUCHE-R	INFUSE-R	MICKLE-R	PIERCE-R
DILUTE-R	GAUCIE-R	INHALE-R	MIDDLE-R	PIFFLE-R
DINKIE-R	GAWSIE-R	INHUME-R	MIDGIE-R	PIGGIE-R
DIVIDE-R	GENTLE-R	INJURE-R	MILLIE-R	PILULA-R
DIVINE-R	GIGGLE-R	INSANE-R	MINGLE-R	PINGLE-R
DOCILE-R	GIRDLE-R	INSIDE-R	MINUTE-R	PINKIE-R
DOGGIE-R	GIRLIE-R	INSULA-R	MISUSE-R	PLAGUE-R
DONSIE-R	GIRNIE-R	INSURE-R	MOCHIE-R	PLANTA-R
DOODLE-R	GLANCE-R	INTONE-R	MOROSE-R	PLASTE-R
DOTTLE-R	GOBBLE-R	INVADE-R	MORULA-R	PLEASE-R
DOUBLE-R	GOGGLE-R	INVITE-R	MOSSIE-R	PLEDGE-R
DREARE-R	GOODIE-R	INVOKE-R	MOTTLE-R	PLUNGE-R
DREDGE-R	GOONIE-R	IODISE-R	MOUSIE-R	PODDIE-R
DRUDGE-R	GRAINE-R	IODIZE-R	MUDDLE-R	POINTE-R
DUCKIE-R	GRAMMA-R	IONISE-R	MUFFLE-R	POLICE-R
DUDDIE-R	GRANDE-R	IONIZE-R	MUMBLE-R	POLITE-R
EFFACE-R	GRANGE-R	JANGLE-R	MUSKIE-R	POTAGE-R
EMPALE-R	GREASE-R	JERQUE-R	MUZZLE-R	POTCHE-R
ENABLE-R	GREETE-R	JINGLE-R	NAPPIE-R	POUNCE-R
ENCODE-R	GRIEVE-R	JOGGLE-R	NEBULA-R	PRAISE-R
ENDURE-R	GRILLE-R	JOSTLE-R	NEEDLE-R	PRANCE-R
ENGAGE-R	GRIPPE-R	JUGGLE-R	NEGATE-R	PREMIE-R
ENGINE-R	GROOVE-R	JUGULA-R	NESTLE-R	PUDDLE-R
ENROBE-R	GROUSE-R	JUMBLE-R	NETTIE-R	PUGGIE-R
ENSURE-R	GRUDGE-R	JUNKIE-R	NETTLE-R	PUMICE-R
ENTICE-R	GRUNGE-R	KIDDIE-R	NEWSIE-R	PUNKIE-R
ESCAPE-R	GUSTIE-R	KIDGIE-R	NIBBLE-R	PURFLE-R
EVOLVE-R	GUTTLE-R	KINDLE-R	NIGGLE-R	PURPLE-R
EXCITE-R	GUZZLE-R	KITTLE-R	NIMBLE-R	PURSUE-R
EXCUSE-R	HACKLE-R	KOOKIE-R	NIRLIE-R	PUTTIE-R
EXHUME-R	HAGGLE-R	LACUNA-R	NOBBLE-R	PUZZLE-R
EXPIRE-R	HANDLE-R	LAMBIE-R	NONUSE-R	QUARTE-R
EXPOSE-R	HECKLE-R	LAMINA-R	NOOKIE-R	QUINTA-R
FACULA-R	HEMPIE-R	LEAGUE-R	NOTICE-R	RABBLE-R
FEEBLE-R	HIGGLE-R	LEGATO-R	NUZZLE-R	RADULA-R
FERLIE-R	HIPPIE-R	LIGULA-R	OBLIGE-R	RAFFLE-R
FETTLE-R	HOARSE-R	LINTIE-R	OBTUSE-R	RAMBLE-R
FIBULA-R	HOBBLE-R	LIPPIE-R	OFFICE-R	RANDIE-R
FICKLE-R	HOMAGE-R	LITTLE-R	ONLINE-R	RANULA-R
FIDDLE-R	HOODIE-R	LOATHE-R	OPAQUE-R	RATTLE-R
FIERCE-R	HOOLIE-R	LOCATE-R	OPPOSE-R	RAUCLE-R

RAVAGE-R	SALTIE-R	SOMBRE-R	SWATHE-R	UNGULA-R
REBATE-R	SALUTE-R	SONSIE-R	SWERVE-R	UNIQUE-R
REBUKE-R	SAMPLE-R	SOOTHE-R	SWINGE-R	UNMAKE-R
RECITE-R	SAVAGE-R	SPALLE-R	SWITHE-R	UNRIPE-R
REDUCE-R	SCARCE-R	SPARGE-R	TABULA-R	UNSAFE-R
REEKIE-R	SCHEME-R	SPARKE-R	TACKLE-R	UNSURE-R
REFINE-R	SCORSE-R	SPARRE-R	TALKIE-R	UNTRUE-R
REFUSE-R	SCOUSE-R	SPARSE-R	TANGIE-R	UNWISE-R
REFUTE-R	SCRAPE-R	SPENCE-R	TANGLE-R	UPDATE-R
REGALE-R	SCRIBE-R	SPLICE-R	TATTIE-R	UPMAKE-R
REGULA-R	SCULLE-R	SPONGE-R	TATTLE-R	UPRISE-R
RELATE-R	SCYTHE-R	SPRUCE-R	TAWTIE-R	URBANE-R
RELIVE-R	SECEDE-R	SPURNE-R	TECHIE-R	VISITE-R
REMAKE-R	SECURE-R	SQUARE-R	TEETHE-R	VOYAGE-R
REMOTE-R	SEDATE-R	STABLE-R	TEGULA-R	WABBLE-R
REMOVE-R	SEDUCE-R	STAPLE-R	TENTIE-R	WADDLE-R
RENEGE-R	SEELIE-R	STARVE-R	THRIVE-R	WAFFLE-R
REPINE-R	SEETHE-R	STEALE-R	THROWE-R	WAGGLE-R
REPOSE-R	SEMINA-R	STEEVE-R	TICKLE-R	WALLIE-R
RESCUE-R	SEMPLE-R	STELLA-R	TIDDLE-R	WANGLE-R
RESIDE-R	SERENE-R	STEMME-R	TINGLE-R	WARBLE-R
RESUME-R	SETTLE-R	STEPPE-R	TINKLE-R	WARSLE-R
RETAKE-R	SEVERE-R	STIEVE-R	TINNIE-R	WASPIE-R
RETIRE-R	SHELVE-R	STIFLE-R	TIPPLE-R	WEBBIE-R
REVERE-R	SHOPPE-R	STIRRE-R	TODDLE-R	WEDGIE-R
REVILE-R	SHRIVE-R	STODGE-R	TOGGLE-R	WEENIE-R
REVISE-R	SILKIE-R	STOOPE-R	TOOTLE-R	WEEPIE-R
REVIVE-R	SIMPLE-R	STRAFE-R	TORQUE-R	WHEEZE-R
REVOKE-R	SIZZLE-R	STRIDE-R	TOTTIE-R	WHINGE-R
RIDDLE-R	SKIVIE-R	STRIKE-R	TOUCHE-R	WIGGLE-R
RIFFLE-R	SLEDGE-R	STRIPE-R	TOUTIE-R	WINKLE-R
RIPPLE-R	SLEEVE-R	STRIVE-R	TOWNIE-R	WOBBLE-R
ROARIE-R	SMOUSE-R	STROKE-R	TRIFLE-R	WOODIE-R
ROOFIE-R	SMUDGE-R	STYLIE-R	TROUPE-R	WOOLIE-R
ROOKIE-R	SNEEZE-R	SUBDUE-R	TROUSE-R	WRITHE-R
ROOMIE-R	SNOOZE-R	SUBTLE-R	TRUDGE-R	YAPPIE-R
RUFFLE-R	SNUBBE-R	SUCKLE-R	TRYSTE-R	ZONULA-R
RUMBLE-R	SOAPIE-R	SUPPLE-R	TUMBLE-R	
RUSTLE-R	SOCAGE-R	SURFIE-R	TURTLE-R	
SADDLE-R	SOLACE-R	SVELTE-R	TWEEZE-R	

Seven letters to eight

ABRIDGE-R	APPRISE-R	BAPTISE-R	BRAILLE-R	CHINKIE-R
ABSOLVE-R	APPRIZE-R	BAPTIZE-R	BRASSIE-R	CHIPPIE-R
ACHIEVE-R	APPROVE-R	BEARDIE-R	BRAWLIE-R	CHORTLE-R
ACICULA-R	ARRANGE-R	BEGINNE-R	BREATHE-R	CHUCKLE-R
ACQUIRE-R	ASPERGE-R	BEGUILE-R	BRICKIE-R	CINGULA-R
ADVANCE-R	ASPERSE-R	BELIEVE-R	BRITTLE-R	CLEANSE-R
ADVERSE-R	ASSUAGE-R	BEREAVE-R	BROWNIE-R	COCHLEA-R
AGITATO-R	ATOMISE-R	BESIEGE-R	BRUSQUE-R	CODRIVE-R
AIRLINE-R	ATOMIZE-R	BESLAVE-R	CANNULA-R	COGNISE-R
AMPULLA-R	ATTACHE-R	BICYCLE-R	CAPABLE-R	COGNIZE-R
ANALYSE-R	AUGUSTE-R	BLASTIE-R	CAPTURE-R	COLLEGE-R
ANALYZE-R	AULNAGE-R	BLOCKIE-R	CAROUSE-R	COLLIDE-R
ANIMATE-R	AUSTERE-R	BOLSHIE-R	CENSURE-R	COLLUDE-R
ANIMATO-R	BAGPIPE-R	BONDAGE-R	CHAPPIE-R	COMBINE-R
ANTIQUE-R	BALANCE-R	BOOKSIE-R	CHARLIE-R	COMMUNE-R
APPEASE-R	BANDAGE-R	BRABBLE-R	CHICANE-R	COMMUTE-R

R – End-hooks

COMPARE-R	DRABBLE-R	GRUMBLE-R	NURTURE-R	PROFANE-R
COMPILE-R	DRIBBLE-R	HAGRIDE-R	OBLIQUE-R	PROFILE-R
COMPOSE-R	DRUGGIE-R	HEXAPLA-R	OBSCENE-R	PROFUSE-R
COMPUTE-R	ECLIPSE-R	IDOLISE-R	OBSCURE-R	PROMISE-R
CONCEDE-R	EMBLAZE-R	IDOLIZE-R	OBSERVE-R	PROMOTE-R
CONCISE-R	EMBRACE-R	IGNOBLE-R	OBTRUDE-R	PROPOSE-R
CONDOLE-R	EMPLOYE-R	IMAGINE-R	OCCLUDE-R	PROVIDE-R
CONDONE-R	ENCHASE-R	IMMENSE-R	OFFSIDE-R	PROVISO-R
CONDUCE-R	ENCLOSE-R	IMMERSE-R	OUTLINE-R	PROVOKE-R
CONFIDE-R	ENDORSE-R	IMPINGE-R	OUTLIVE-R	QUEENIE-R
CONFINE-R	ENFORCE-R	IMPLORE-R	OUTRIDE-R	QUIBBLE-R
CONFUTE-R	ENGRAVE-R	IMPROVE-R	OUTROPE-R	QUIDDLE-R
CONJURE-R	ENHANCE-R	INCENSE-R	OUTSIDE-R	RAGTIME-R
CONNIVE-R	ENLARGE-R	INCLINE-R	OUTVOTE-R	RAMPAGE-R
CONSOLE-R	ENNOBLE-R	INCLOSE-R	OVERDYE-R	REALISE-R
CONSUME-R	ENQUIRE-R	INDORSE-R	OVERLIE-R	REALIZE-R
CONVENE-R	ENSLAVE-R	INDULGE-R	OVERSEE-R	RECEIVE-R
CONVOKE-R	ENSNARE-R	INFLAME-R	OXIDISE-R	RECLINE-R
CORRODE-R	EPISTLE-R	INFLATE-R	OXIDIZE-R	RECYCLE-R
COSTUME-R	ESPOUSE-R	INQUIRE-R	OZONISE-R	REDLINE-R
COTTAGE-R	EXAMINE-R	INSNARE-R	OZONIZE-R	REECHIE-R
COUTHIE-R	EXCLUDE-R	INSPIRE-R	PACKAGE-R	REGRATE-R
COWRITE-R	EXCRETE-R	INTENSE-R	PAPILLA-R	REISSUE-R
CRAPPIE-R	EXECUTE-R	INTRUDE-R	PARTAKE-R	REJOICE-R
CREEPIE-R	EXEMPLA-R	INVOLVE-R	PASSAGE-R	RELAPSE-R
CRIPPLE-R	EXPLODE-R	ITEMISE-R	PASTURE-R	RELEASE-R
CRUMMIE-R	EXPLORE-R	ITEMIZE-R	PATELLA-R	RELIEVE-R
CRUSADE-R	EXPUNGE-R	JAUNTIE-R	PECULIA-R	RENEGUE-R
CUTESIE-R	EXTREME-R	JAWBONE-R	PEPTISE-R	REPLACE-R
DAYTALE-R	EXTRUDE-R	JOYRIDE-R	PEPTIZE-R	REPROVE-R
DECEIVE-R	FERTILE-R	JUSTICE-R	PERFUME-R	REPULSE-R
DECLARE-R	FINAGLE-R	KEYNOTE-R	PERJURE-R	REQUIRE-R
DECLINE-R	FINESSE-R	KILLDEE-R	PERVADE-R	REQUITE-R
DEFLATE-R	FISTULA-R	KNUCKLE-R	PILLAGE-R	RESERVE-R
DEFORCE-R	FLEECIE-R	LAMELLA-R	PINNULA-R	RESHAPE-R
DEGRADE-R	FLOSSIE-R	LECTURE-R	PLACATE-R	RESOLVE-R
DEJEUNE-R	FORESEE-R	LICENCE-R	PLANULA-R	RESTORE-R
DELOUSE-R	FORGIVE-R	LICENSE-R	PLOOKIE-R	RETRACE-R
DEMERGE-R	FORMULA-R	LINGULA-R	PLOTTIE-R	REUNITE-R
DEPLETE-R	FORSAKE-R	LIONISE-R	PLOUKIE-R	REVENGE-R
DEPLORE-R	FOVEOLA-R	LIONIZE-R	PLUMPIE-R	REVENUE-R
DEPRAVE-R	FRAGILE-R	LOWLIFE-R	PLUMULA-R	REVERSE-R
DEPRIVE-R	FRENULA-R	MAMILLA-R	POETISE-R	REVOLVE-R
DERANGE-R	FRIBBLE-R	MASSAGE-R	POETIZE-R	REWRITE-R
DESERVE-R	FRIZZLE-R	MAXILLA-R	POLLUTE-R	ROMANCE-R
DESPISE-R	FULSOME-R	MEASURE-R	POSTURE-R	ROSEOLA-R
DETERGE-R	FURCULA-R	MEDULLA-R	POTHOLE-R	ROUTHIE-R
DIALYSE-R	GABELLE-R	MICELLA-R	PRATTLE-R	RUBEOLA-R
DIALYZE-R	GANGLIA-R	MIDLIFE-R	PRECISE-R	RUMMAGE-R
DIFFUSE-R	GAROTTE-R	MILLINE-R	PREFACE-R	SALVAGE-R
DISABLE-R	GARROTE-R	MISLIKE-R	PRELUDE-R	SANDBUR-R
DISLIKE-R	GESTURE-R	MISTAKE-R	PREPARE-R	SCAMBLE-R
DISPONE-R	GLASSIE-R	MODERNE-R	PREPPIE-R	SCAPULA-R
DISPOSE-R	GLIMPSE-R	MORTICE-R	PRESAGE-R	SCAVAGE-R
DISPUTE-R	GOSPODA-R	MORTISE-R	PRESIDE-R	SCOURGE-R
DISROBE-R	GRABBLE-R	MULTURE-R	PRESUME-R	SCREEVE-R
DIVORCE-R	GRAPPLE-R	MUNDANE-R	PRIMSIE-R	SCROUGE-R
DIVULGE-R	GREENIE-R	NARRATE-R	PRIVATE-R	SCRUPLE-R
DOGGONE-R	GRIMACE-R	NEURULA-R	PROCURE-R	SCUFFLE-R
DOMINEE-R	GRIZZLE-R	NEWCOME-R	PRODUCE-R	SCUTTLE-R

SECONDE-R	SPICULA-R	SUPPOSE-R	TRIPPLE-R	VAUNTIE-R
SECRETE-R	SPINDLE-R	SUPREME-R	TROUBLE-R	VENTURE-R
SERVICE-R	SPLURGE-R	SURFACE-R	TROUNCE-R	VERBOSE-R
SHACKLE-R	SPOTTIE-R	SURMISE-R	TRUCKLE-R	VERDITE-R
SHEATHE-R	SPRINGE-R	SURNAME-R	TRUNDLE-R	VESTURE-R
SHEENIE-R	SPUNKIE-R	SURVIVE-R	TWADDLE-R	VEXILLA-R
SHINGLE-R	SQUEEZE-R	SWADDLE-R	TWANGLE-R	VIBRATO-R
SHUFFLE-R	STAGGIE-R	SWANKIE-R	TWATTLE-R	VILLAGE-R
SHUTTLE-R	STARTLE-R	SWANNIE-R	TWEEDLE-R	VINTAGE-R
SILENCE-R	STEAMIE-R	SWINDLE-R	TWIDDLE-R	VIOLATE-R
SINCERE-R	STEELIE-R	SWIZZLE-R	TWINKLE-R	WARFARE-R
SKELLIE-R	STIBBLE-R	TEENAGE-R	UNITISE-R	WARSTLE-R
SKYDIVE-R	STICKLE-R	TOASTIE-R	UNITIZE-R	WAYFARE-R
SMUGGLE-R	STIPPLE-R	TONTINE-R	UNWARIE-R	WELCOME-R
SNIFFLE-R	STOURIE-R	TOPLINE-R	UPGRADE-R	WHEEDLE-R
SNIGGLE-R	STRANGE-R	TOPSIDE-R	UPHEAVE-R	WHEELIE-R
SNOTTIE-R	STUBBIE-R	TORTURE-R	UPRAISE-R	WHIFFLE-R
SNUFFLE-R	STUMBLE-R	TOUSTIE-R	UPSTAGE-R	WHISTLE-R
SPAMMIE-R	STYLISE-R	TRADUCE-R	UPSTATE-R	WHITTLE-R
SPANGLE-R	STYLIZE-R	TRAMPLE-R	UTILISE-R	WINSOME-R
SPARKIE-R	SUBLIME-R	TREADLE-R	UTILIZE-R	WRANGLE-R
SPARKLE-R	SUBSIDE-R	TREMBLE-R	VALVULA-R	WREATHE-R
SPATULA-R	SUBTILE-R	TRIBUTE-R	VARIOLA-R	WRESTLE-R
SPECULA-R	SUFFICE-R	TRICKIE-R	VASCULA-R	WRIGGLE-R

Eight letters to nine

ABSOLUTE-R	CANONIZE-R	CONVERSE-R	DYNAMITE-R	FRACTURE-R
ABSTRUSE-R	CANOODLE-R	CONVINCE-R	EMBEZZLE-R	FREEBASE-R
ALKALISE-R	CAPITULA-R	CRIBELLA-R	ENERGISE-R	FRONTAGE-R
ALKALIZE-R	CARABINE-R	CRUNCHIE-R	ENERGIZE-R	GARROTTE-R
ANNOUNCE-R	CARACOLE-R	CUTICULA-R	ENFEEBLE-R	GASTRULA-R
ANTILIFE-R	CARETAKE-R	DECOUPLE-R	ENKINDLE-R	GLABELLA-R
ANTINUKE-R	CASTRATE-R	DEGREASE-R	ENTANGLE-R	GLADIOLA-R
APHORISE-R	CASTRATO-R	DEIONISE-R	ENVELOPE-R	GLADSOME-R
APHORIZE-R	CATALYSE-R	DEIONIZE-R	EQUALISE-R	GLISSADE-R
APPETISE-R	CATALYZE-R	DENOUNCE-R	EQUALIZE-R	GREWSOME-R
APPETIZE-R	CHASTISE-R	DESCRIBE-R	ESCALADE-R	GRUESOME-R
APPRAISE-R	CIVILISE-R	DESOLATE-R	ESTRANGE-R	HANDSOME-R
ARCHAISE-R	CIVILIZE-R	DETHRONE-R	ETHERISE-R	HARANGUE-R
ARCHAIZE-R	CLAUSULA-R	DEVELOPE-R	ETHERIZE-R	HARDLINE-R
ARTIFICE-R	CLITELLA-R	DIALOGUE-R	EULOGISE-R	HEADLINE-R
ASSEMBLE-R	COALMINE-R	DIGITISE-R	EULOGIZE-R	HESITATE-R
ASTRINGE-R	COINSURE-R	DIGITIZE-R	EXCHANGE-R	HOROLOGE-R
AURICULA-R	COLONISE-R	DISBURSE-R	EXERCISE-R	HUMANISE-R
BACKBITE-R	COLONIZE-R	DISCLOSE-R	EXORCISE-R	HUMANIZE-R
BARBECUE-R	COLORISE-R	DISCRETE-R	EXORCIZE-R	IDEALISE-R
BARRETTE-R	COLORIZE-R	DISGORGE-R	EXPEDITE-R	IDEALIZE-R
BASELINE-R	COMANAGE-R	DISGRACE-R	FARADISE-R	ILLUMINE-R
BEGRUDGE-R	COMMENCE-R	DISGUISE-R	FARADIZE-R	IMMUNISE-R
BELITTLE-R	COMPLETE-R	DISPENSE-R	FIBRILLA-R	IMMUNIZE-R
BLASTULA-R	CONCEIVE-R	DISPERSE-R	FINALISE-R	IMPOLITE-R
BLOCKADE-R	CONCLUDE-R	DISPLACE-R	FINALIZE-R	IMPRESSE-R
BLUELINE-R	CONDENSE-R	DISPROVE-R	FLAGELLA-R	INCREASE-R
BOMBARDE-R	CONSERVE-R	DISSOLVE-R	FLATLINE-R	INFRINGE-R
BOTANISE-R	CONSPIRE-R	DISSUADE-R	FLEXTIME-R	INSCRIBE-R
BOTANIZE-R	CONSTRUE-R	DISUNITE-R	FLUIDISE-R	INTIMATE-R
BULLDOZE-R	CONTINUE-R	DOWNCOME-R	FLUIDIZE-R	INTRIGUE-R
CANONISE-R	CONTRIVE-R	DRICKSIE-R	FOREBODE-R	INVEIGLE-R

KLONDIKE-R	NEBBISHE-R	POSSIBLE-R	SCAVENGE-R	TELEVISE-R
KLONDYKE-R	NEBULISE-R	POSTPONE-R	SCHEDULE-R	TESSELLA-R
LEGALISE-R	NEBULIZE-R	PRACTICE-R	SCHMOOZE-R	THEORISE-R
LEGALIZE-R	NICKNAME-R	PRACTISE-R	SCRABBLE-R	THEORIZE-R
LINOTYPE-R	NONDANCE-R	PREJUDGE-R	SCRAMBLE-R	THROTTLE-R
LITERATO-R	NOVELISE-R	PRESBYTE-R	SCRIBBLE-R	TOTALISE-R
LOCALISE-R	NOVELIZE-R	PRESERVE-R	SCROGGIE-R	TOTALIZE-R
LOCALIZE-R	NUISANCE-R	PROLONGE-R	SCROUNGE-R	TRAVERSE-R
MACERATE-R	OBLIGATO-R	PUNCTURE-R	SCRUMMIE-R	TREASURE-R
MAINLINE-R	OPERCULA-R	PURCHASE-R	SCUTELLA-R	TREPHINE-R
MASSACRE-R	OPTIMISE-R	PYROLYSE-R	SENSIBLE-R	TRICYCLE-R
MAXIMISE-R	OPTIMIZE-R	PYROLYZE-R	SENTENCE-R	TROCHLEA-R
MAXIMIZE-R	OPUSCULA-R	QUANTISE-R	SEQUENCE-R	UNBUNDLE-R
MEDICINE-R	ORGANISE-R	QUANTIZE-R	SERENADE-R	UNCHASTE-R
MELODISE-R	ORGANIZE-R	REASSURE-R	SHUNPIKE-R	UNCOUPLE-R
MELODIZE-R	OUTPLACE-R	RECHARGE-R	SIDELINE-R	UNDERLIE-R
MEMORISE-R	OVERCOME-R	REDOUBLE-R	SIGHTSEE-R	UNIONISE-R
MEMORIZE-R	OVERRIDE-R	REHEARSE-R	SKYWRITE-R	UNIONIZE-R
MINIBIKE-R	OVERRULE-R	REINSURE-R	SNOWSHOE-R	UNRIDDLE-R
MINIMISE-R	OVERTIME-R	RENOUNCE-R	SPIRILLA-R	UNSTABLE-R
MINIMIZE-R	PAGANISE-R	REPRIEVE-R	SPRINKLE-R	VAPORISE-R
MISGUIDE-R	PAGANIZE-R	RESEMBLE-R	SQUABBLE-R	VAPORIZE-R
MISJUDGE-R	PARALYSE-R	RESOLUTE-R	SQUIGGLE-R	VESICULA-R
MISPRIZE-R	PARALYZE-R	RESPONSE-R	STAMPEDE-R	VIGNETTE-R
MISQUOTE-R	PENDICLE-R	RETICULA-R	STARGAZE-R	VITALISE-R
MISSHAPE-R	PENSIONE-R	RETINULA-R	STRADDLE-R	VITALIZE-R
MOBILISE-R	PERCEIVE-R	RETRIEVE-R	STRAGGLE-R	VOCALISE-R
MOBILIZE-R	PERFECTO-R	RIDICULE-R	STRANGLE-R	VOCALIZE-R
MODERATO-R	PERSUADE-R	RINGSIDE-R	STROBILA-R	WARDROBE-R
MORALISE-R	PERVERSE-R	ROSTELLA-R	STRUGGLE-R	WOMANISE-R
MORALIZE-R	PHALANGE-R	SANITISE-R	SUBPHYLA-R	WOMANIZE-R
MORTGAGE-R	PLEASURE-R	SANITIZE-R	SUNBATHE-R	
MUCKRAKE-R	POLARISE-R	SATIRISE-R	SURPRISE-R	
MULTIUSE-R	POLARIZE-R	SATIRIZE-R	SUSPENSE-R	
NAVICULA-R	POSITIVE-R	SATURATE-R	TAILGATE-R	

S – Front-hooks

Two letters to three

S-AB	S-AW	S-EX	S-MA	S-OW
S-AD	S-AX	S-HA	S-NY	S-OX
S-AE	S-AY	S-HE	S-OB	S-OY
S-AG	S-EA	S-IF	S-OD	S-PA
S-AI	S-ED	S-IN	S-OH	S-UM
S-AL	S-EE	S-IS	S-OM	S-UN
S-AM	S-EL	S-IT	S-ON	S-UP
S-AN	S-EN	S-KA	S-OP	S-UR
S-AR	S-ER	S-KI	S-OS	S-US
S-AT	S-ET	S-KY	S-OU	S-YE

Three letters to four

S-ABS	S-AGO	S-AIR	S-ALS	S-ANT
S-ADO	S-AGS	S-AIS	S-ALT	S-ARD
S-ADS	S-AID	S-AKE	S-AMA	S-ARK
S-AFT	S-AIL	S-ALE	S-AMP	S-ARS
S-AGA	S-AIM	S-ALL	S-AND	S-ASH
S-AGE	S-AIN	S-ALP	S-ANE	S-ASS

S-ATE	S-ETA	S-LAB	S-OCA	S-PUD
S-AVE	S-HAD	S-LAG	S-ODA	S-PUG
S-AWN	S-HAG	S-LAM	S-ODS	S-PUN
S-AXE	S-HAH	S-LAP	S-OFT	S-PUR
S-AYS	S-HAM	S-LAT	S-OHO	S-TAB
S-CAB	S-HAN	S-LAW	S-OHS	S-TAG
S-CAD	S-HAT	S-LAY	S-OIL	S-TAP
S-CAG	S-HAW	S-LED	S-OKE	S-TAR
S-CAM	S-HAY	S-LEE	S-OLD	S-TAT
S-CAN	S-HES	S-LEW	S-OLE	S-TAW
S-CAR	S-HET	S-LEY	S-OMS	S-TAY
S-CAT	S-HEW	S-LID	S-ONE	S-TED
S-CAW	S-HIM	S-LIP	S-ONS	S-TEN
S-COG	S-HIN	S-LIT	S-OOM	S-TET
S-COP	S-HIP	S-LOB	S-OON	S-TEW
S-COT	S-HIT	S-LOG	S-OOP	S-TIE
S-COW	S-HOD	S-LOP	S-OOT	S-TOP
S-CRY	S-HOE	S-LOT	S-OPS	S-TOT
S-CUD	S-HOG	S-LOW	S-ORA	S-TOW
S-CUM	S-HOO	S-LUG	S-ORB	S-TUB
S-CUP	S-HOP	S-LUM	S-ORD	S-TUM
S-CUR	S-HOT	S-LUR	S-ORE	S-TUN
S-CUT	S-HOW	S-MEE	S-ORT	S-TYE
S-EAN	S-HUN	S-MEW	S-OUK	S-UDS
S-EAR	S-HUT	S-MIR	S-OUP	S-UGH
S-EAS	S-ICE	S-MOG	S-OUR	S-ULU
S-EAT	S-ICH	S-MUG	S-OUS	S-UMP
S-ECH	S-ICK	S-MUT	S-OUT	S-UNS
S-ECO	S-IDE	S-NAB	S-OWL	S-UPS
S-EEK	S-ILK	S-NAG	S-OWN	S-URD
S-EEL	S-ILL	S-NAP	S-OYS	S-URE
S-EEN	S-IMP	S-NAW	S-PAM	S-WAB
S-EGO	S-INK	S-NEB	S-PAN	S-WAD
S-EIK	S-INS	S-NED	S-PAR	S-WAG
S-ELD	S-IRE	S-NEE	S-PAS	S-WAN
S-ELF	S-ITS	S-NIB	S-PAT	S-WAP
S-ELL	S-JOE	S-NIP	S-PAW	S-WAT
S-ELS	S-KAS	S-NIT	S-PAY	S-WAY
S-EME	S-KAT	S-NOB	S-PEC	S-WEE
S-END	S-KAW	S-NOD	S-PED	S-WEY
S-ENE	S-KEG	S-NOG	S-PET	S-WIG
S-ENS	S-KEN	S-NOT	S-PEW	S-WIZ
S-ERA	S-KEP	S-NOW	S-PIC	S-WOP
S-ERE	S-KET	S-NUB	S-PIE	S-WOT
S-ERF	S-KID	S-NYE	S-PIN	S-YEN
S-ERK	S-KIN	S-OAK	S-PIT	S-YES
S-ERR	S-KIP	S-OAR	S-POD	
S-ERS	S-KIS	S-OBA	S-POT	
S-ESS	S-KIT	S-OBS	S-PRY	

Four letters to five

S-ABED	S-AIGA	S-ALES	S-AMEN	S-ARDS
S-ABLE	S-AILS	S-ALLY	S-AMPS	S-ARED
S-ADOS	S-AIMS	S-ALPS	S-ANDS	S-ARIS
S-AGAS	S-AINE	S-ALTO	S-ANES	S-ARKS
S-AGER	S-AINS	S-ALTS	S-ANGA	S-ATES
S-AGES	S-AIRS	S-AMAS	S-ANSA	S-AUNT
S-AIDS	S-AKES	S-AMBO	S-ANTS	S-AVER

S – Front-hooks

S-AVES	S-CUTE	S-HELL	S-KAWS	S-LOGS
S-AWED	S-CUTS	S-HEND	S-KEEF	S-LOID
S-AXES	S-EANS	S-HENT	S-KEEN	S-LOOM
S-CABS	S-EARS	S-HERD	S-KEET	S-LOOP
S-CADS	S-EASE	S-HERE	S-KEGS	S-LOOT
S-CAFF	S-EATS	S-HETS	S-KELL	S-LOPE
S-CAGS	S-ECCO	S-HEWN	S-KELP	S-LOPS
S-CALL	S-EDGE	S-HEWS	S-KENS	S-LOSH
S-CALP	S-EDGY	S-HIED	S-KEPS	S-LOTH
S-CAMP	S-EELS	S-HIES	S-KETS	S-LOTS
S-CAMS	S-EELY	S-HILL	S-KIDS	S-LOVE
S-CANS	S-EGOS	S-HIMS	S-KIER	S-LOWS
S-CANT	S-EINE	S-HINS	S-KIFF	S-LUES
S-CAPA	S-ELFS	S-HIPS	S-KILL	S-LUFF
S-CAPE	S-ELLS	S-HIRE	S-KINK	S-LUGS
S-CAPI	S-EMES	S-HISH	S-KINS	S-LUIT
S-CARE	S-ENDS	S-HIST	S-KIPS	S-LUMP
S-CARP	S-ENVY	S-HITS	S-KITE	S-LUMS
S-CARS	S-EPIC	S-HIVE	S-KITS	S-LUNG
S-CART	S-ERED	S-HOCK	S-KOFF	S-LUNK
S-CATS	S-ERES	S-HOED	S-KYTE	S-LURS
S-CAUP	S-ERIC	S-HOER	S-LABS	S-LUSH
S-CAWS	S-ERKS	S-HOES	S-LACK	S-MACK
S-CENT	S-ERRS	S-HOGS	S-LADE	S-MAIK
S-CHAV	S-EVEN	S-HONE	S-LAGS	S-MALL
S-CION	S-EVER	S-HOOK	S-LAID	S-MALM
S-COFF	S-EWER	S-HOON	S-LAIN	S-MALT
S-COGS	S-EXED	S-HOOT	S-LAKE	S-MARM
S-COLD	S-EXES	S-HOPE	S-LAMS	S-MART
S-CONE	S-EYEN	S-HOPS	S-LANE	S-MASH
S-COOP	S-HACK	S-HORE	S-LANG	S-MAZE
S-COOT	S-HADE	S-HORN	S-LANK	S-MEEK
S-COPE	S-HADS	S-HOTE	S-LANT	S-MEES
S-COPS	S-HAFT	S-HOTS	S-LAPS	S-MELL
S-CORE	S-HAGS	S-HOUT	S-LASH	S-MELT
S-CORN	S-HAHS	S-HOVE	S-LATE	S-MERK
S-COTS	S-HAKE	S-HOWS	S-LATS	S-MEWS
S-COUP	S-HALE	S-HUCK	S-LAVE	S-MILE
S-COUR	S-HALL	S-HULE	S-LAWS	S-MIRK
S-COWL	S-HALM	S-HUNS	S-LAYS	S-MIRS
S-COWP	S-HALT	S-HUNT	S-LEEK	S-MITE
S-COWS	S-HAME	S-HUSH	S-LEEP	S-MOCK
S-CRAB	S-HAMS	S-HUTS	S-LEER	S-MOGS
S-CRAG	S-HAND	S-ICES	S-LEET	S-MOKE
S-CRAM	S-HANK	S-IDES	S-LEPT	S-MOKO
S-CRAN	S-HAPS	S-IDLE	S-LEYS	S-MOLT
S-CRAP	S-HARD	S-ILEX	S-LICE	S-MOOR
S-CRAW	S-HARE	S-ILKS	S-LICK	S-MOOT
S-CRAY	S-HARK	S-ILLS	S-LIER	S-MORE
S-CREE	S-HARN	S-ILLY	S-LILY	S-MOTE
S-CREW	S-HARP	S-IMPS	S-LIME	S-MUGS
S-CRIM	S-HASH	S-INKS	S-LIMY	S-MUSH
S-CROG	S-HAUL	S-INKY	S-LING	S-MUTS
S-CROW	S-HAVE	S-IRED	S-LINK	S-NABS
S-CUDS	S-HAWM	S-IRES	S-LIPE	S-NAGS
S-CUFF	S-HAWS	S-IRIS	S-LIPS	S-NAIL
S-CULL	S-HAYS	S-IZAR	S-LITS	S-NAPS
S-CUPS	S-HEAL	S-KAIL	S-LIVE	S-NARE
S-CURF	S-HEAR	S-KART	S-LOAN	S-NARK
S-CURS	S-HEEL	S-KATS	S-LOBS	S-NARY

S-NEAP	S-PALE	S-POOR	S-TEEN	S-TUFF
S-NEBS	S-PALL	S-POOT	S-TEER	S-TUMP
S-NECK	S-PAMS	S-PORE	S-TEIL	S-TUMS
S-NEDS	S-PANE	S-PORT	S-TELA	S-TUNG
S-NEED	S-PANG	S-POSH	S-TELE	S-TUNS
S-NIBS	S-PANS	S-POTS	S-TELL	S-TYED
S-NICK	S-PARD	S-POUT	S-TEME	S-TYES
S-NIDE	S-PARE	S-PRAD	S-TEMS	S-TYRE
S-NIES	S-PARK	S-PRAT	S-TEND	S-TYTE
S-NIFF	S-PARS	S-PRAY	S-TENS	S-UGHS
S-NIPS	S-PART	S-PREE	S-TENT	S-ULUS
S-NITS	S-PATE	S-PRIG	S-TERN	S-UMPH
S-NOBS	S-PATS	S-PROD	S-TETS	S-UMPS
S-NODS	S-PAUL	S-PROG	S-TEWS	S-URDS
S-NOGS	S-PAWL	S-PUDS	S-TICH	S-URES
S-NOOK	S-PAWN	S-PUER	S-TICK	S-URGE
S-NOOP	S-PAWS	S-PUGS	S-TIED	S-USES
S-NOUT	S-PAYS	S-PULE	S-TIES	S-WABS
S-NOWS	S-PEAK	S-PUMY	S-TIFF	S-WACK
S-NOWY	S-PEAL	S-PUNK	S-TILE	S-WADS
S-NUBS	S-PEAN	S-PURS	S-TILL	S-WAGE
S-NUFF	S-PEAR	S-PYRE	S-TILT	S-WAGS
S-NYES	S-PEAT	S-QUAD	S-TIME	S-WAIL
S-OAKS	S-PECK	S-QUAT	S-TING	S-WAIN
S-OARS	S-PECS	S-QUID	S-TINK	S-WALE
S-OBAS	S-PEED	S-QUIT	S-TINT	S-WALY
S-OCAS	S-PEEL	S-QUIZ	S-TIRE	S-WANG
S-ODAS	S-PEER	S-TABS	S-TIVY	S-WANK
S-ODIC	S-PELL	S-TACK	S-TOCK	S-WANS
S-OILS	S-PELT	S-TAGS	S-TOIT	S-WAPS
S-OILY	S-PEND	S-TAIG	S-TOKE	S-WARD
S-OKES	S-PENT	S-TAIN	S-TOLE	S-WARE
S-OLDS	S-PERM	S-TAKE	S-TONE	S-WARM
S-OLES	S-PETS	S-TALE	S-TONG	S-WART
S-OLID	S-PEWS	S-TALK	S-TONK	S-WASH
S-ONCE	S-PIAL	S-TALL	S-TONY	S-WATS
S-ONES	S-PICA	S-TAMP	S-TOOK	S-WAYS
S-ONLY	S-PICE	S-TANE	S-TOOL	S-WEAL
S-OOMS	S-PICK	S-TANG	S-TOPE	S-WEAR
S-OOPS	S-PICS	S-TANK	S-TOPS	S-WEED
S-OOTS	S-PIED	S-TAPS	S-TORE	S-WEEL
S-ORAL	S-PIER	S-TARE	S-TORY	S-WEEP
S-ORBS	S-PIES	S-TARN	S-TOSS	S-WEER
S-ORDO	S-PIKE	S-TARS	S-TOTS	S-WEES
S-ORDS	S-PILE	S-TART	S-TOUN	S-WEET
S-ORES	S-PILL	S-TASH	S-TOUR	S-WEIR
S-ORRA	S-PINA	S-TATE	S-TOUT	S-WELL
S-ORTS	S-PINE	S-TATS	S-TOWN	S-WELT
S-OUKS	S-PINK	S-TAWS	S-TOWS	S-WEPT
S-OUPS	S-PINS	S-TAYS	S-TRAD	S-WEYS
S-OURS	S-PINY	S-TEAD	S-TRAP	S-WIGS
S-OUTS	S-PITS	S-TEAK	S-TRAY	S-WILL
S-OWED	S-PLAT	S-TEAL	S-TREW	S-WINE
S-OWER	S-PLAY	S-TEAM	S-TRIG	S-WING
S-OWLS	S-PODS	S-TEAR	S-TRIP	S-WINK
S-OWSE	S-POKE	S-TEDS	S-TROP	S-WIPE
S-PACE	S-POOF	S-TEED	S-TROW	S-WIRE
S-PACY	S-POOK	S-TEEK	S-TROY	S-WISH
S-PAIL	S-POOL	S-TEEL	S-TUBS	S-WISS
S-PAIN	S-POON	S-TEEM	S-TUCK	S-WITH

S – Front-hooks

S-WITS	S-WOON	S-WORD	S-WORN	S-YENS
S-WIVE	S-WOPS	S-WORE	S-WOTS	

Five letters to six

S-ABBED	S-CARTS	S-CUFFS	S-HARKS	S-IDLER
S-ABLED	S-CATCH	S-CULCH	S-HARNS	S-IDLES
S-ABLES	S-CATTY	S-CULLS	S-HARPS	S-ILLER
S-ACKER	S-CAUPS	S-CURFS	S-HARPY	S-IMPLY
S-ACRED	S-CENTS	S-CURRY	S-HAUGH	S-INGLE
S-ADDED	S-CERNE	S-CURVY	S-HAULS	S-INKER
S-ADDER	S-CHAVS	S-CUTCH	S-HAVEN	S-INNED
S-ADDLE	S-CHOUT	S-CUTES	S-HAVER	S-INNER
S-AFTER	S-CIONS	S-DAINE	S-HAVES	S-INTER
S-AGENE	S-CLAVE	S-DEIGN	S-HAWED	S-IRING
S-AGGER	S-CLIFF	S-EANED	S-HAWMS	S-IZARS
S-AIGAS	S-COFFS	S-EARED	S-HEALS	S-KAILS
S-AILED	S-COLDS	S-EASED	S-HEARS	S-KARTS
S-AIRED	S-CONES	S-EASES	S-HEATH	S-KEENS
S-AIRER	S-COOCH	S-EATER	S-HEAVE	S-KEETS
S-ALARY	S-COOPS	S-EDGED	S-HEELS	S-KELLS
S-ALINE	S-COOTS	S-EDGES	S-HELLS	S-KELLY
S-ALLEE	S-COPED	S-EDILE	S-HELVE	S-KELPS
S-ALLOW	S-COPES	S-EDUCE	S-HENDS	S-KERRY
S-ALTER	S-CORED	S-EGGAR	S-HERDS	S-KETCH
S-ALTOS	S-CORER	S-ELECT	S-HERRY	S-KIDDY
S-AMBOS	S-CORES	S-ELFED	S-HEUCH	S-KIERS
S-AMPLE	S-CORIA	S-ELVES	S-HEUGH	S-KILLS
S-ANCHO	S-CORNS	S-ENATE	S-HEWED	S-KINKS
S-ANGAS	S-CORSE	S-ENDED	S-HEWER	S-KITED
S-ANGER	S-COUPS	S-ENDER	S-HILLS	S-KITES
S-APPLE	S-COURS	S-ENTRY	S-HINNY	S-KOFFS
S-ARGUS	S-COUTH	S-ERING	S-HIPPO	S-KRANS
S-ASHED	S-COWED	S-ERRED	S-HIRED	S-KYTES
S-ASHES	S-COWLS	S-ESSES	S-HIRES	S-LACKS
S-ASSES	S-COWPS	S-ETTLE	S-HISTS	S-LADES
S-AUGER	S-CRABS	S-EVENS	S-HIVER	S-LAKED
S-AUNTS	S-CRAGS	S-EVERY	S-HIVES	S-LAKER
S-AVANT	S-CRAMS	S-EWERS	S-HOCKS	S-LAKES
S-AVERS	S-CRANS	S-EXING	S-HOERS	S-LANES
S-AVINE	S-CRAPE	S-EXIST	S-HONKY	S-LANTS
S-AWING	S-CRAPS	S-HACKS	S-HOOKS	S-LATCH
S-CABBY	S-CRAWL	S-HADED	S-HOOTS	S-LATED
S-CAFFS	S-CRAWS	S-HADES	S-HOPPY	S-LATER
S-CALLS	S-CRAYS	S-HAFTS	S-HOUGH	S-LAVED
S-CALPS	S-CREAK	S-HAKES	S-HOUSE	S-LAVER
S-CAMEL	S-CREAM	S-HALED	S-HOUTS	S-LAVES
S-CAMPI	S-CREED	S-HALES	S-HOVED	S-LAYED
S-CAMPS	S-CREES	S-HALMS	S-HOVEL	S-LAYER
S-CANTS	S-CREWS	S-HAMBA	S-HOVER	S-LEAVE
S-CANTY	S-CRIED	S-HAMED	S-HOVES	S-LEAZE
S-CAPAS	S-CRIES	S-HAMES	S-HUCKS	S-LEDGE
S-CAPED	S-CRIMP	S-HAMMY	S-HUGGY	S-LEECH
S-CAPES	S-CRIMS	S-HANDS	S-HULES	S-LEEKS
S-CARED	S-CRINE	S-HANDY	S-HUNTS	S-LEEPS
S-CARER	S-CROGS	S-HANKS	S-HYING	S-LEETS
S-CARES	S-CROME	S-HARDS	S-ICKER	S-LICKS
S-CARPS	S-CROWS	S-HARED	S-ICKLE	S-LIEVE
S-CARRY	S-CRUMP	S-HARES	S-IDLED	S-LIGHT

S-LIMED	S-MOOCH	S-OWLED	S-PINNY	S-TAIGS
S-LIMES	S-MOORS	S-PACED	S-PINTO	S-TAINS
S-LINGS	S-MOOTS	S-PACER	S-PLASH	S-TAKES
S-LINKS	S-MORES	S-PACES	S-PLATS	S-TALER
S-LINKY	S-MOUCH	S-PACEY	S-PLAYS	S-TALES
S-LIPPY	S-MOUSE	S-PAILS	S-PODDY	S-TALKS
S-LIVED	S-MOYLE	S-PAINS	S-POKED	S-TALKY
S-LIVEN	S-MUDGE	S-PALES	S-POKES	S-TALLS
S-LIVER	S-MURRY	S-PALLS	S-PONGY	S-TAMPS
S-LIVES	S-MUTCH	S-PANED	S-POOFS	S-TANGS
S-LOANS	S-NAGGY	S-PANES	S-POOFY	S-TANKS
S-LOBBY	S-NAILS	S-PANGS	S-POOKS	S-TAPES
S-LOGAN	S-NAKED	S-PARED	S-POOLS	S-TARED
S-LOIDS	S-NAPPY	S-PARER	S-POONS	S-TARES
S-LOOMS	S-NARES	S-PARES	S-POOTS	S-TARNS
S-LOOPS	S-NARKS	S-PARGE	S-PORAL	S-TARRY
S-LOOTS	S-NARKY	S-PARKS	S-PORED	S-TARTS
S-LOPED	S-NATCH	S-PARKY	S-PORES	S-TATER
S-LOPER	S-NEAPS	S-PARRY	S-PORTS	S-TATES
S-LOPES	S-NEATH	S-PARSE	S-PORTY	S-TATUS
S-LOPPY	S-NECKS	S-PARTS	S-POTTY	S-TAWED
S-LOUGH	S-NEEZE	S-PATES	S-POUTS	S-TEADS
S-LOWED	S-NELLY	S-PAULS	S-POUTY	S-TEAKS
S-LOWER	S-NICKS	S-PAVIN	S-PRANG	S-TEALS
S-LOWLY	S-NIDED	S-PAWLS	S-PRATS	S-TEAMS
S-LUFFS	S-NIDES	S-PAWNS	S-PRAYS	S-TEARS
S-LUMMY	S-NIFFS	S-PAYED	S-PREED	S-TEDDY
S-LUMPS	S-NIFFY	S-PEAKS	S-PREES	S-TEELS
S-LUMPY	S-NIFTY	S-PEALS	S-PRENT	S-TEEMS
S-LURRY	S-NIPPY	S-PEANS	S-PRIER	S-TEENS
S-LUSHY	S-NOBBY	S-PEARS	S-PRIGS	S-TEERS
S-MACKS	S-NOOKS	S-PEATS	S-PRINT	S-TEILS
S-MAIKS	S-NOOPS	S-PECKS	S-PRODS	S-TELAE
S-MALLS	S-NOWED	S-PECKY	S-PROGS	S-TELES
S-MALMS	S-NUBBY	S-PEELS	S-PRONG	S-TELIC
S-MALMY	S-NUDGE	S-PEERS	S-PRYER	S-TELLS
S-MALTS	S-NUFFS	S-PEISE	S-PUDDY	S-TEMED
S-MARMS	S-OAKED	S-PELLS	S-PUERS	S-TEMES
S-MARTS	S-OAKEN	S-PELTS	S-PUGGY	S-TENCH
S-MATCH	S-OAKER	S-PENCE	S-PULES	S-TENDS
S-MAZES	S-OARED	S-PENDS	S-PUNKS	S-TENTS
S-MEATH	S-OAVES	S-PERMS	S-PUNKY	S-TERES
S-MELLS	S-OBOLE	S-PERSE	S-PURGE	S-TERNS
S-MELTS	S-ODIUM	S-PERST	S-PYRES	S-TEWED
S-MERKS	S-OFTEN	S-PHENE	S-QUADS	S-TICKS
S-MEUSE	S-OFTER	S-PICAS	S-QUAIL	S-TICKY
S-MIDDY	S-OILED	S-PICKS	S-QUARE	S-TIFFS
S-MIDGE	S-OLDER	S-PIERS	S-QUARK	S-TILED
S-MIGHT	S-OLEIN	S-PIGHT	S-QUASH	S-TILES
S-MILER	S-OLIVE	S-PIKED	S-QUATS	S-TILLS
S-MILES	S-OLLER	S-PIKER	S-QUIDS	S-TILLY
S-MIRKS	S-OMBER	S-PIKES	S-QUIFF	S-TILTS
S-MIRKY	S-OMBRE	S-PIKEY	S-QUILL	S-TIMED
S-MITER	S-ONCES	S-PILED	S-QUINT	S-TIMES
S-MITES	S-OOPED	S-PILES	S-QUIRE	S-TINGS
S-MOCKS	S-ORBED	S-PILLS	S-QUIRT	S-TINKS
S-MOGGY	S-OUGHT	S-PINAS	S-QUITS	S-TINTS
S-MOKES	S-OUPED	S-PINED	S-TABLE	S-TINTY
S-MOKOS	S-OUTER	S-PINES	S-TACKS	S-TIRED
S-MOLTS	S-OWING	S-PINKS	S-TAGGY	S-TIRES

S – Front-hooks

S-TITCH	S-TOWED	S-TROWS	S-UTILE	S-WEIRS
S-TOCKS	S-TOWER	S-TROYS	S-WADDY	S-WELLS
S-TOCKY	S-TRADS	S-TRUCK	S-WAGED	S-WELTS
S-TOITS	S-TRAIK	S-TUBBY	S-WAGER	S-WIFTY
S-TOKED	S-TRAIN	S-TUCKS	S-WAGES	S-WILLS
S-TOKER	S-TRAIT	S-TUFFS	S-WAILS	S-WINES
S-TOKES	S-TRAMP	S-TUMPS	S-WAINS	S-WINGE
S-TOLED	S-TRAPS	S-TUMPY	S-WALED	S-WINGS
S-TOLES	S-TRASS	S-TYING	S-WALES	S-WINGY
S-TOMIA	S-TRAYS	S-TYLER	S-WANKS	S-WINKS
S-TONED	S-TRESS	S-TYRED	S-WANKY	S-WIPED
S-TONER	S-TREWS	S-TYRES	S-WARDS	S-WIPER
S-TONES	S-TRICK	S-UDDER	S-WARMS	S-WIPES
S-TONEY	S-TRIDE	S-UNBED	S-WARTY	S-WIRES
S-TONKS	S-TRIGS	S-UNDER	S-WASHY	S-WITCH
S-TONNE	S-TRIKE	S-UNHAT	S-WATCH	S-WITHE
S-TOOLS	S-TRIPE	S-UNKET	S-WAYED	S-WIVED
S-TOPED	S-TRIPS	S-UNLIT	S-WEALS	S-WIVES
S-TOPER	S-TRIPY	S-UNSET	S-WEARS	S-WOONS
S-TOPES	S-TRODE	S-UPPED	S-WEELS	S-WOOPS
S-TORES	S-TROKE	S-UPPER	S-WEENY	S-WOOSH
S-TOUNS	S-TROLL	S-URGED	S-WEEPS	S-WORDS
S-TOURS	S-TROUT	S-URGER	S-WEEPY	S-WOUND
S-TOUTS	S-TROVE	S-URGES	S-WEETS	

Six letters to seven

S-ABLING	S-CAMPER	S-CORNED	S-CROMES	S-EELIER
S-ACKERS	S-CANNED	S-CORNER	S-CROTAL	S-EGGARS
S-ADDING	S-CANNER	S-CORSES	S-CRUMMY	S-ELECTS
S-ADDLED	S-CANTED	S-COUPED	S-CRUMPS	S-ELFING
S-ADDLES	S-CANTER	S-COURED	S-CRUMPY	S-ELFISH
S-AGENES	S-CANTLE	S-COURIE	S-CRUNCH	S-ENATES
S-AGGERS	S-CAPING	S-COURSE	S-CRYING	S-ENDERS
S-AILING	S-CARERS	S-COUTER	S-CUDDLE	S-ENDING
S-AIREST	S-CARING	S-COUTHS	S-CUFFED	S-ENSATE
S-AIRING	S-CARPED	S-COWING	S-CUFFLE	S-ENSILE
S-ALINES	S-CARPER	S-COWLED	S-CULLED	S-ENVIES
S-ALLEES	S-CARTED	S-COWPED	S-CULLER	S-ERRING
S-ALLIED	S-CARVES	S-COWRIE	S-CULTCH	S-ETTLED
S-ALLIES	S-CATTED	S-CRAGGY	S-CUMBER	S-ETTLES
S-ALLOWS	S-CERNED	S-CRANCH	S-CUMMER	S-EXISTS
S-ALTERN	S-CERNES	S-CRANNY	S-CUNNER	S-EXPERT
S-ALTERS	S-CHOUTS	S-CRAPED	S-CUPPER	S-EXTANT
S-AMPLER	S-CLAVES	S-CRAPES	S-CURRED	S-HACKED
S-ANCHOS	S-CLIFFS	S-CRAPPY	S-CUTTER	S-HACKLE
S-ANGERS	S-COFFED	S-CRATCH	S-CUTTLE	S-HADING
S-APPLES	S-COFFER	S-CRAWLS	S-CUZZES	S-HAFTED
S-ARKING	S-COGGED	S-CRAWLY	S-DAINED	S-HAFTER
S-ARMIES	S-COLDER	S-CREAKS	S-DAINES	S-HAGGED
S-ASHING	S-COLLOP	S-CREAKY	S-DEIGNS	S-HALING
S-AUGERS	S-COOPED	S-CREAMS	S-EANING	S-HALLOT
S-AUNTER	S-COOPER	S-CREEDS	S-EARING	S-HALLOW
S-CABBED	S-COOTCH	S-CREWED	S-EASING	S-HAMBLE
S-CALLED	S-COOTER	S-CRIMPS	S-EATERS	S-HAMING
S-CALLOP	S-COPING	S-CRIMPY	S-EATING	S-HAMMED
S-CAMELS	S-COPULA	S-CRINES	S-EDGIER	S-HAMMER
S-CAMMED	S-CORERS	S-CROGGY	S-EDUCED	S-HANKED
S-CAMPED	S-CORING	S-CROMED	S-EDUCES	S-HARING

S-HARKED	S-IMPLED	S-LINGER	S-MOYLED	S-PANNER
S-HARPED	S-IMPLEX	S-LINKED	S-MOYLES	S-PARERS
S-HARPER	S-INGLES	S-LINKER	S-MUDGED	S-PARGED
S-HASHED	S-INKERS	S-LINTER	S-MUDGER	S-PARGES
S-HASHES	S-INKIER	S-LIPPED	S-MUDGES	S-PARING
S-HATTER	S-INKING	S-LIPPER	S-MUGGED	S-PARKED
S-HAUGHS	S-INNERS	S-LITHER	S-MUGGER	S-PARKER
S-HAULED	S-INNING	S-LITTER	S-MUSHED	S-PARKIE
S-HAVERS	S-INTERS	S-LIVERS	S-MUSHES	S-PARKLY
S-HAVING	S-IRENIC	S-LIVING	S-NAGGED	S-PARRED
S-HAWING	S-JAMBOK	S-LOBBER	S-NAILED	S-PARSER
S-HEALED	S-KEGGER	S-LOGANS	S-NAPPED	S-PARTAN
S-HEARER	S-KELPED	S-LOGGED	S-NAPPER	S-PATHED
S-HEATHS	S-KELTER	S-LOGGER	S-NEAPED	S-PATHIC
S-HEATHY	S-KENNED	S-LOOMED	S-NEBBED	S-PATTED
S-HEAVED	S-KEPPED	S-LOPERS	S-NECKED	S-PATTEE
S-HEAVES	S-KIDDED	S-LOPING	S-NEEZED	S-PATTER
S-HEELED	S-KIDDER	S-LOPPED	S-NEEZES	S-PAVINS
S-HELLED	S-KILLED	S-LOTTED	S-NIBBED	S-PAWNED
S-HELLER	S-KIMMER	S-LOTTER	S-NICKED	S-PAWNER
S-HELVED	S-KINKED	S-LOUGHS	S-NICKER	S-PAYING
S-HELVES	S-KIPPED	S-LOWEST	S-NIDING	S-PEANED
S-HEUCHS	S-KIPPER	S-LOWING	S-NIFFED	S-PECKED
S-HEUGHS	S-KITING	S-LOWISH	S-NIFFER	S-PEELED
S-HEWERS	S-KITTLE	S-LUBBER	S-NIGGER	S-PEELER
S-HEWING	S-LACKED	S-LUFFED	S-NIGGLE	S-PEERED
S-HIDDER	S-LACKER	S-LUGGED	S-NIPPED	S-PEISES
S-HILLED	S-LAGGED	S-LUGGER	S-NIPPER	S-PELTER
S-HIPPED	S-LAKERS	S-LUMBER	S-NODDED	S-PENCES
S-HIPPEN	S-LAKING	S-LUMPED	S-NODDER	S-PERSES
S-HIPPER	S-LAMMED	S-LUSHED	S-NOGGED	S-PHENES
S-HIPPIE	S-LAMMER	S-LUSHES	S-NUBBED	S-PHENIC
S-HIPPOS	S-LANDER	S-MALLED	S-NUDGED	S-PICKER
S-HIRING	S-LANGER	S-MARTED	S-NUDGES	S-PIGHTS
S-HIVERS	S-LAPPED	S-MARTEN	S-NUZZLE	S-PIKERS
S-HOCKED	S-LAPPER	S-MASHED	S-OAKERS	S-PIKING
S-HOCKER	S-LASHED	S-MASHER	S-OARING	S-PILING
S-HODDEN	S-LASHER	S-MASHES	S-OBOLES	S-PILLED
S-HOEING	S-LASHES	S-MASHUP	S-ODIUMS	S-PINIER
S-HOGGED	S-LATHER	S-MATTER	S-OFTEST	S-PINNER
S-HOOTER	S-LATTER	S-MEATHS	S-OILIER	S-PINNET
S-HOPPED	S-LAVERS	S-MELLED	S-OILING	S-PINTOS
S-HOPPER	S-LAVING	S-MELTED	S-OLIVES	S-PITTED
S-HOTTED	S-LAVISH	S-MELTER	S-OLLERS	S-PITTEN
S-HOUGHS	S-LAYERS	S-MEUSES	S-OMBERS	S-PITTER
S-HOUSES	S-LAYING	S-MIDGES	S-OMBRES	S-PLASHY
S-HOUTED	S-LEAVED	S-MIGHTS	S-OOPING	S-PLAYED
S-HOVELS	S-LEAVES	S-MILERS	S-ORBING	S-PLODGE
S-HOVERS	S-LEAZES	S-MIRKER	S-OUPING	S-PODIUM
S-HOVING	S-LEDGED	S-MITERS	S-OUTERS	S-POKING
S-HUNTED	S-LEDGER	S-MITTEN	S-OUTHER	S-PONGED
S-HUNTER	S-LEDGES	S-MOCKED	S-OWLING	S-POOLED
S-HUSHED	S-LENDER	S-MOILED	S-PACERS	S-POOLER
S-HUSHER	S-LICKED	S-MOLDER	S-PACIER	S-POORER
S-HUSHES	S-LICKER	S-MOORED	S-PACING	S-PORING
S-IDLERS	S-LIGHTS	S-MOOTED	S-PAINED	S-PORTED
S-IDLING	S-LIMIER	S-MOTHER	S-PALLED	S-PORTER
S-IGNIFY	S-LIMING	S-MOUSED	S-PANGED	S-POSHES
S-IGNORE	S-LIMMER	S-MOUSER	S-PANING	S-POTTED
S-ILEXES	S-LIMPSY	S-MOUSES	S-PANNED	S-POTTER

S – Front-hooks

S-POUTED	S-TARTER	S-TOMIUM	S-TUSHIE	S-WATTER
S-POUTER	S-TARTLY	S-TONERS	S-TYLERS	S-WAYING
S-PRANGS	S-TASHED	S-TONIER	S-TYRING	S-WEARER
S-PRAYED	S-TASHES	S-TONIES	S-UCKERS	S-WEEING
S-PRAYER	S-TATERS	S-TONING	S-UDDERS	S-WEEPER
S-PRIEST	S-TATUED	S-TONISH	S-UGGING	S-WEETED
S-PRINTS	S-TAWING	S-TONKED	S-ULLAGE	S-WEETEN
S-PUDDER	S-TEAMED	S-TONKER	S-UNBEDS	S-WEETER
S-PUDDLE	S-TEAMER	S-TONNES	S-UNBELT	S-WEIRED
S-PUNKIE	S-TEARED	S-TOOLED	S-UNDECK	S-WELLED
S-PURGES	S-TEDDED	S-TOPERS	S-UNHATS	S-WELTED
S-PURRED	S-TEEMED	S-TOPING	S-UNLESS	S-WELTER
S-PUTTER	S-TEENED	S-TOPPED	S-UNLIKE	S-WIGGED
S-QUAILS	S-TEERED	S-TOPPER	S-UNROOF	S-WIGGER
S-QUARER	S-TELLAR	S-TOPPLE	S-UNSETS	S-WILLED
S-QUARKS	S-TEMPLE	S-TORIES	S-UNSUIT	S-WILLER
S-QUELCH	S-TENDED	S-TOSSES	S-UNWISE	S-WINDLE
S-QUILLS	S-TENTED	S-TOTTED	S-UPPERS	S-WINERY
S-QUINTS	S-TERNAL	S-TOTTER	S-UPPING	S-WINGED
S-QUIRED	S-TERNED	S-TOTTIE	S-URGENT	S-WINGER
S-QUIRES	S-TEWING	S-TOURIE	S-URGERS	S-WINGES
S-QUIRTS	S-TIBIAL	S-TOUTER	S-URGING	S-WINISH
S-QUITCH	S-TICKED	S-TOWAGE	S-WADDIE	S-WINKED
S-TABBED	S-TICKER	S-TOWERS	S-WADDLE	S-WINKER
S-TABLED	S-TICKLE	S-TOWING	S-WAGERS	S-WIPERS
S-TABLES	S-TIFFED	S-TRAIKS	S-WAGGED	S-WIPING
S-TACKED	S-TILING	S-TRAINS	S-WAGGER	S-WISHED
S-TACKER	S-TILLED	S-TRAITS	S-WAGING	S-WISHER
S-TACKET	S-TILLER	S-TRAMPS	S-WALIER	S-WISHES
S-TAGGED	S-TILTED	S-TRAPPY	S-WALING	S-WISSES
S-TAGGER	S-TILTER	S-TRICKS	S-WALLET	S-WITCHY
S-TAKING	S-TIMING	S-TRIKES	S-WALLOW	S-WITHER
S-TALKED	S-TINGED	S-TRIPES	S-WANKED	S-WIVING
S-TALKER	S-TINKER	S-TRIPEY	S-WANKER	S-WIZZES
S-TAMPED	S-TINTED	S-TROKED	S-WANNED	S-WOONED
S-TAMPER	S-TINTER	S-TROKES	S-WAPPED	S-WOPPED
S-TANGED	S-TIPPLE	S-TROLLS	S-WAPPER	S-WORDED
S-TANKED	S-TIRING	S-TROUTS	S-WARDED	S-WOTTED
S-TANNIC	S-TIRRED	S-TROWED	S-WARMED	S-WOUNDS
S-TAPPED	S-TOCKED	S-TUBBED	S-WARMER	
S-TARING	S-TOITED	S-TUMBLE	S-WASHED	
S-TARRED	S-TOKERS	S-TUMPED	S-WASHER	
S-TARTED	S-TOKING	S-TUNNED	S-WASHES	

Seven letters to eight

S-ADDLING	S-CANNERS	S-CARRIER	S-COLLOPS	S-COURSED
S-ALLOWED	S-CANNING	S-CARTING	S-COOCHES	S-COURSES
S-ALLYING	S-CANTEST	S-CATCHES	S-COOPERS	S-COUTERS
S-ANGUINE	S-CANTIER	S-CATTERY	S-COOPING	S-COUTHER
S-ARGUSES	S-CANTILY	S-CATTIER	S-COOTERS	S-COWLING
S-ASHLESS	S-CANTING	S-CATTILY	S-COPULAE	S-COWPING
S-AUNTERS	S-CANTLED	S-CATTING	S-COPULAS	S-COWRIES
S-CABBING	S-CANTLES	S-CERNING	S-CORIOUS	S-CRABBED
S-CALLOPS	S-CARIOSE	S-CHAPPED	S-CORNERS	S-CRAGGED
S-CAMMING	S-CARIOUS	S-CHILLER	S-CORNING	S-CRAMMED
S-CAMPERS	S-CARLESS	S-COFFERS	S-COUPING	S-CRAPING
S-CAMPING	S-CARPERS	S-COFFING	S-COURIES	S-CRAPPED
S-CANDENT	S-CARPING	S-COGGING	S-COURING	S-CRAPPER

S-CRAWLED	S-HACKLES	S-INKIEST	S-LOGGING	S-NAGGING
S-CRAWLER	S-HADDOCK	S-IRONISE	S-LOOMING	S-NAILERY
S-CREAKED	S-HAFTERS	S-IRONIZE	S-LOPPIER	S-NAILING
S-CREAMED	S-HAFTING	S-JAMBOKS	S-LOPPING	S-NAPLESS
S-CREAMER	S-HAGGING	S-KEGGERS	S-LOTTERS	S-NAPPERS
S-CREWING	S-HALLOWS	S-KELLIES	S-LOTTING	S-NAPPIER
S-CRIBBLE	S-HAMBLED	S-KELPING	S-LOWDOWN	S-NAPPING
S-CRIMPED	S-HAMBLES	S-KELTERS	S-LOWINGS	S-NARKIER
S-CRIMPER	S-HAMMERS	S-KENNING	S-LOWNESS	S-NATCHES
S-CROMING	S-HAMMING	S-KEPPING	S-LUBBERS	S-NEAPING
S-CRUMMIE	S-HANKING	S-KERRIES	S-LUFFING	S-NEBBING
S-CRUMPED	S-HARKING	S-KETCHES	S-LUGGERS	S-NECKING
S-CRUMPLE	S-HARPERS	S-KIDDERS	S-LUGGING	S-NEEZING
S-CRUNCHY	S-HARPIES	S-KIDDIER	S-LUMBERS	S-NIBBING
S-CRYINGS	S-HARPING	S-KIDDING	S-LUMMIER	S-NICKERS
S-CUDDLED	S-HASHING	S-KILLIES	S-LUMPIER	S-NICKING
S-CUDDLES	S-HATTERS	S-KILLING	S-LUMPING	S-NIFFERS
S-CUFFING	S-HAULING	S-KIMMERS	S-LURRIES	S-NIFFIER
S-CUFFLED	S-HAVINGS	S-KINKING	S-LUSHIER	S-NIFFING
S-CUFFLES	S-HEADING	S-KINLESS	S-LUSHING	S-NIFTIER
S-CULCHES	S-HEALING	S-KIPPERS	S-MALLING	S-NIGGERS
S-CULLERS	S-HEARERS	S-KIPPING	S-MARTENS	S-NIGGLED
S-CULLING	S-HEARING	S-KITTLED	S-MARTING	S-NIGGLER
S-CULLION	S-HEATHER	S-KITTLES	S-MASHERS	S-NIGGLES
S-CUMBERS	S-HEAVING	S-LACKERS	S-MASHING	S-NIPPERS
S-CUMMERS	S-HEELING	S-LACKING	S-MASHUPS	S-NIPPIER
S-CUNNERS	S-HEILING	S-LAGGING	S-MATCHED	S-NIPPILY
S-CUPPERS	S-HELLERS	S-LAMMERS	S-MATCHES	S-NIPPING
S-CURRIED	S-HELLIER	S-LAMMING	S-MATTERS	S-NOBBIER
S-CURRIER	S-HELLING	S-LANDERS	S-MEARING	S-NOBBILY
S-CURRIES	S-HELVING	S-LANGERS	S-MELLING	S-NODDING
S-CURRING	S-HENDING	S-LAPPERS	S-MELTERS	S-NOGGING
S-CURVIER	S-HERRIES	S-LAPPING	S-MELTING	S-NUBBIER
S-CUTCHES	S-HIDDERS	S-LASHERS	S-MIDDIES	S-NUBBING
S-CUTTERS	S-HILLING	S-LASHING	S-MIRKIER	S-NUDGING
S-CUTTLED	S-HINNIED	S-LATCHES	S-MIRKILY	S-NUZZLED
S-CUTTLES	S-HINNIES	S-LATHERS	S-MITHERS	S-NUZZLES
S-CUTWORK	S-HIPLESS	S-LEAVING	S-MOCKING	S-OFTENER
S-DAINING	S-HIPPENS	S-LEDGERS	S-MOILING	S-OILIEST
S-DEIGNED	S-HIPPIES	S-LEECHES	S-MOLDERS	S-OMNIFIC
S-EARINGS	S-HIPPING	S-LEEPING	S-MOOCHED	S-ORDINES
S-EATINGS	S-HITLESS	S-LICKERS	S-MOOCHER	S-PACIEST
S-EDGIEST	S-HITTING	S-LICKING	S-MOOCHES	S-PAINING
S-EDITION	S-HOCKERS	S-LIGHTED	S-MOORING	S-PALLING
S-EDUCING	S-HOCKING	S-LIGHTER	S-MOOTING	S-PANGING
S-EDUCTOR	S-HOGGING	S-LIGHTLY	S-MOTHERS	S-PANNERS
S-EELIEST	S-HOOTERS	S-LIMIEST	S-MOTHERY	S-PANNING
S-ELECTED	S-HOOTING	S-LIMMERS	S-MOUCHED	S-PARABLE
S-ELECTEE	S-HOPPERS	S-LINGERS	S-MOUCHES	S-PARGING
S-ELECTOR	S-HOPPIER	S-LINKERS	S-MOULDER	S-PARKERS
S-ELFHOOD	S-HOPPING	S-LINKING	S-MOUSERS	S-PARKIER
S-ENDINGS	S-HOTTING	S-LINTERS	S-MOUSING	S-PARKIES
S-ENTRIES	S-HOUTING	S-LIPLESS	S-MOYLING	S-PARKING
S-ETTLING	S-HOVELED	S-LIPPERS	S-MUDGERS	S-PARKISH
S-EXPERTS	S-HUNTERS	S-LIPPIER	S-MUDGING	S-PARLING
S-FORZATI	S-HUNTING	S-LIPPING	S-MUGGING	S-PARRIER
S-FORZATO	S-HUSHERS	S-LITTERS	S-MUSHING	S-PARRING
S-HACKING	S-HUSHING	S-LIVERED	S-MUTCHED	S-PARTANS
S-HACKLED	S-HUTTING	S-LOBBERS	S-MUTCHES	S-PATTERS
S-HACKLER	S-IGNORES	S-LOGGERS	S-NAGGIER	S-PATTING

S-PAWNERS	S-PRAYERS	S-TEDDING	S-TOWAWAY	S-WALLETS
S-PAWNING	S-PRAYING	S-TEEMING	S-TOWINGS	S-WALLOWS
S-PEAKING	S-PREEING	S-TEENING	S-TRAIKED	S-WAMPISH
S-PEANING	S-PRIGGED	S-TEERING	S-TRAINED	S-WANKERS
S-PECKIER	S-PRIGGER	S-TELLING	S-TRAINER	S-WANKIER
S-PECKING	S-PRINTED	S-TEMPLES	S-TRAMMEL	S-WANKING
S-PECTATE	S-PRINTER	S-TENCHES	S-TRAMPED	S-WANNING
S-PEELERS	S-PUDDERS	S-TENDING	S-TRANGLE	S-WAPPERS
S-PEELING	S-PUDDING	S-TENTING	S-TRAPPED	S-WAPPING
S-PEERING	S-PUDDLES	S-TERNING	S-TRAPPER	S-WARDING
S-PELTERS	S-PUGGIES	S-TICKERS	S-TRASSES	S-WARMERS
S-PENDING	S-PUNKIER	S-TICKIES	S-TRESSED	S-WARMING
S-PERSING	S-PUNKIES	S-TICKING	S-TRESSES	S-WASHERS
S-PETTING	S-PURLING	S-TICKLED	S-TRICKLE	S-WASHIER
S-PIGHTED	S-PURRING	S-TICKLER	S-TRIDENT	S-WASHING
S-PIKELET	S-PUTTERS	S-TICKLES	S-TRIGGED	S-WATCHES
S-PILINGS	S-QUADDED	S-TIDDIES	S-TRIPIER	S-WEARERS
S-PILLAGE	S-QUAILED	S-TIFFING	S-TRIPPED	S-WEARING
S-PILLING	S-QUAREST	S-TILLAGE	S-TRIPPER	S-WEENIES
S-PINIEST	S-QUASHED	S-TILLERS	S-TROKING	S-WEEPERS
S-PINNERS	S-QUASHER	S-TILLIER	S-TROLLED	S-WEEPIER
S-PINNETS	S-QUASHES	S-TILLING	S-TROLLER	S-WEEPING
S-PINNIES	S-QUINIES	S-TILTERS	S-TROPHIC	S-WEETEST
S-PINNING	S-QUIRING	S-TILTING	S-TROWING	S-WEETING
S-PIRATED	S-QUIRTED	S-TINGING	S-TRUMPET	S-WEIRING
S-PITCHER	S-QUIZZES	S-TINKERS	S-TUBBIER	S-WELLING
S-PITTERS	S-TABBING	S-TINKING	S-TUBBING	S-WELTERS
S-PITTING	S-TABLING	S-TINTERS	S-TUMBLED	S-WELTING
S-PLASHED	S-TACKERS	S-TINTIER	S-TUMBLER	S-WIGGERS
S-PLASHER	S-TACKETS	S-TINTING	S-TUMBLES	S-WIGGING
S-PLASHES	S-TACKING	S-TIPPLED	S-TUMPIER	S-WILLERS
S-PLATTED	S-TAGGERS	S-TIPPLER	S-TUMPING	S-WILLING
S-PLATTER	S-TAGGIER	S-TIPPLES	S-TUNNING	S-WINDLED
S-PLAYING	S-TAGGING	S-TIRRING	S-TUSHIES	S-WINDLES
S-PLODGED	S-TAKEOUT	S-TITCHES	S-UBEROUS	S-WINGERS
S-PLODGES	S-TALKERS	S-TOCCATA	S-ULLAGES	S-WINGIER
S-PODDIER	S-TALKIER	S-TOCKIER	S-UNBAKED	S-WINGING
S-PODIUMS	S-TALKING	S-TOCKING	S-UNBELTS	S-WINGMAN
S-PONGIER	S-TALLAGE	S-TOITING	S-UNBLIND	S-WINGMEN
S-PONGING	S-TAMPERS	S-TONIEST	S-UNBLOCK	S-WINKERS
S-PONTOON	S-TAMPING	S-TONINGS	S-UNBURNT	S-WINKING
S-POOKING	S-TANGING	S-TONKERS	S-UNCHOKE	S-WISHERS
S-POOLERS	S-TANKING	S-TONKING	S-UNDECKS	S-WISHING
S-POOLING	S-TANNATE	S-TOOLING	S-UNDRESS	S-WISSING
S-PORTERS	S-TAPPING	S-TOOSHIE	S-UNROOFS	S-WITCHED
S-PORTIER	S-TARINGS	S-TOPLESS	S-UNSUITS	S-WITCHES
S-PORTING	S-TARRIER	S-TOPPERS	S-URGINGS	S-WITHERS
S-POTTERS	S-TARRING	S-TOPPING	S-WADDIES	S-WOONING
S-POTTIER	S-TARTING	S-TOPPLED	S-WADDLED	S-WOOSHED
S-POTTIES	S-TARTISH	S-TOPPLES	S-WADDLER	S-WOOSHES
S-POTTING	S-TASHING	S-TOTTERS	S-WADDLES	S-WOPPING
S-POUTERS	S-TEAMERS	S-TOTTIES	S-WAGGERS	S-WORDING
S-POUTIER	S-TEAMING	S-TOTTING	S-WAGGING	S-WOTTING
S-POUTING	S-TEARING	S-TOWABLE	S-WAINING	S-WOUNDED
S-PRATTLE	S-TEDDIES	S-TOWAGES	S-WALIEST	

Eight letters to nine

S-ALLOWING	S-EDUCTION	S-LIGHTEST	S-PLATTERS	S-TINTLESS
S-ARCOLOGY	S-EDUCTIVE	S-LIGHTING	S-PLATTING	S-TIPPLERS
S-CAMPINGS	S-EDUCTORS	S-LIGHTISH	S-PLODGING	S-TIPPLING
S-CANNINGS	S-ELECTEES	S-LIMINESS	S-PODDIEST	S-TOCCATAS
S-CANTIEST	S-ELECTING	S-LIMPSIER	S-PONGIEST	S-TOCKIEST
S-CANTLING	S-ELECTION	S-LIPPERED	S-PONTOONS	S-TONELESS
S-CARPINGS	S-ELECTIVE	S-LIPPIEST	S-PORTABLE	S-TOPPINGS
S-CATTIEST	S-ELECTORS	S-LIVERING	S-PORTANCE	S-TOPPLING
S-CHILLERS	S-ELFHOODS	S-LOPPIEST	S-PORTIEST	S-TOTTERED
S-CHILLING	S-ELFISHLY	S-LOWDOWNS	S-PORTLESS	S-TOWAWAYS
S-COOTCHED	S-EXERCISE	S-LUMBERED	S-POTTIEST	S-TRAIKING
S-COOTCHES	S-FORZANDI	S-LUMBERER	S-POUTIEST	S-TRAINERS
S-COPULATE	S-FORZANDO	S-LUMMIEST	S-POUTINGS	S-TRAINING
S-CORELESS	S-FORZATOS	S-LUMPIEST	S-PRATTLED	S-TRAMMELS
S-COURSING	S-GRAFFITI	S-LUSHIEST	S-PRATTLES	S-TRAMPING
S-CRABBING	S-GRAFFITO	S-MASHINGS	S-PRAYINGS	S-TRANGLES
S-CRAGGIER	S-HACKLERS	S-MATCHING	S-PRIGGERS	S-TRAPLINE
S-CRAGGILY	S-HACKLING	S-MATTERED	S-PRIGGING	S-TRAPPERS
S-CRAMMING	S-HADDOCKS	S-MELTINGS	S-PRINTERS	S-TRAPPIER
S-CRANCHED	S-HALLOWED	S-MIRKIEST	S-PRINTING	S-TRAPPING
S-CRANCHES	S-HALLOWER	S-MOCKINGS	S-PUDDINGS	S-TRESSING
S-CRAPPERS	S-HAMBLING	S-MOLDERED	S-PURLINGS	S-TRICKLED
S-CRAPPIER	S-HARPINGS	S-MOOCHERS	S-PURRINGS	S-TRICKLES
S-CRAPPING	S-HATTERED	S-MOOCHING	S-PUTTERED	S-TRIGGING
S-CRATCHES	S-HEADINGS	S-MOTHERED	S-PUTTERER	S-TRIPIEST
S-CRAWLERS	S-HEALINGS	S-MOUCHING	S-QUADDING	S-TRIPLING
S-CRAWLIER	S-HEARINGS	S-MOULDERS	S-QUAILING	S-TRIPPERS
S-CRAWLING	S-HEATHERS	S-MUTCHING	S-QUASHERS	S-TRIPPING
S-CREAKIER	S-HEATHIER	S-NAGGIEST	S-QUASHING	S-TROLLERS
S-CREAKING	S-HELLFIRE	S-NAPPIEST	S-QUELCHED	S-TROLLING
S-CREAMERS	S-HINNYING	S-NARKIEST	S-QUELCHES	S-TROSSERS
S-CREAMING	S-HIPPINGS	S-NICKERED	S-QUINCHED	S-TROUTING
S-CRIBBLED	S-HOPPIEST	S-NIFFIEST	S-QUINCHES	S-TRUMPETS
S-CRIBBLES	S-HOPPINGS	S-NIFTIEST	S-QUIRTING	S-TUBBIEST
S-CRIMPERS	S-HOUTINGS	S-NIGGERED	S-QUITCHES	S-TUMBLERS
S-CRIMPIER	S-HOVELING	S-NIGGLERS	S-TABLINGS	S-TUMBLING
S-CRIMPING	S-HOVELLED	S-NIGGLING	S-TACKINGS	S-TUMPIEST
S-CRUMMIER	S-HOVELLER	S-NIPPIEST	S-TACKLESS	S-TUNNINGS
S-CRUMMIES	S-HUNTINGS	S-NOBBIEST	S-TAGGIEST	S-UNBATHED
S-CRUMPING	S-IGNIFIED	S-NUBBIEST	S-TAKEOUTS	S-UNBEATEN
S-CRUMPLED	S-IGNIFIES	S-NUZZLING	S-TALKIEST	S-UNBLINDS
S-CRUMPLES	S-IMPLEXES	S-OILINESS	S-TALKINGS	S-UNBLOCKS
S-CRUNCHED	S-IRONISED	S-PARABLES	S-TALLAGES	S-UNBONNET
S-CRUNCHES	S-IRONISES	S-PARKIEST	S-TAMPINGS	S-UNBRIGHT
S-CRUNCHIE	S-IRONIZED	S-PATTERED	S-TANNATES	S-UNBURNED
S-CUDDLING	S-IRONIZES	S-PECKIEST	S-TARRIEST	S-UNCHOKES
S-CUFFLING	S-KETCHING	S-PECTATES	S-TARRINGS	S-UNSTRUCK
S-CULLINGS	S-KILLINGS	S-PECULATE	S-TEAMINGS	S-UNTANNED
S-CULLIONS	S-KIPPERED	S-PIGHTING	S-TICKINGS	S-WADDLERS
S-CULTCHES	S-KITTLING	S-PIKELETS	S-TICKLERS	S-WADDLING
S-CUMBERED	S-LAGGINGS	S-PILLAGES	S-TICKLING	S-WALLOWED
S-CURRIERS	S-LAMMINGS	S-PILLINGS	S-TICKSEED	S-WALLOWER
S-CURRYING	S-LANGUAGE	S-PINDLING	S-TILLAGES	S-WANKIEST
S-CURVIEST	S-LASHINGS	S-PINELIKE	S-TILLIEST	S-WARMINGS
S-CUTTLING	S-LATHERED	S-PINNINGS	S-TILLINGS	S-WASHIEST
S-CUTWORKS	S-LAUGHTER	S-PITTINGS	S-TILTINGS	S-WASHINGS
S-DEIGNING	S-LAVISHLY	S-PLASHERS	S-TINTIEST	S-WEARINGS
S-EDITIONS	S-LICKINGS	S-PLASHIER	S-TINTINGS	S-WEEPIEST
S-EDUCIBLE	S-LIGHTERS	S-PLASHING	S-TINTINGS	S-WEEPINGS

S – Front-hooks

S-WELLHEAD	S-WINERIES	S-WISHINGS	S-WOOSHING
S-WELLINGS	S-WINGBEAT	S-WITCHIER	S-WORDLESS
S-WELTERED	S-WINGEING	S-WITCHING	S-WORDPLAY
S-WINDLING	S-WINGIEST	S-WITHERED	S-WOUNDING

S – End-hooks

Because almost every noun and verb in English can form a new word by the addition of S, it would not helpful to supply a complete list of the end-hooks for S. However, three useful lists of end-hooks for S are provided in chapter 9 of this book: one shows words that already end in S but which can form another word by the addition of a second S; the second lists words ending in -ED which form valid words when an S is added; the third lists words ending in a consonant followed by Y which form valid words when an S is added.

T – Front-hooks

Two letters to three

T-AB	T-AT	T-EN	T-IT	T-OY
T-AD	T-AW	T-ES	T-OD	T-UG
T-AE	T-AX	T-ET	T-OE	T-UM
T-AG	T-AY	T-EX	T-OM	T-UN
T-AI	T-EA	T-HE	T-ON	T-UP
T-AM	T-ED	T-HO	T-OO	T-UT
T-AN	T-EE	T-ID	T-OP	T-WO
T-AR	T-EF	T-IN	T-OR	T-YE
T-AS	T-EL	T-IS	T-OW	

Three letters to four

T-AAL	T-ASK	T-ENE	T-INK	T-ORE
T-ABS	T-ASS	T-ENS	T-INS	T-ORS
T-ACE	T-ATE	T-ERF	T-IRE	T-ORT
T-ACH	T-ATT	T-ERN	T-ITS	T-OSE
T-ACT	T-AVA	T-EST	T-IVY	T-OUK
T-ADS	T-AWA	T-ETH	T-ODS	T-OUR
T-AGS	T-AYS	T-HAE	T-OES	T-OUT
T-AHA	T-EAR	T-HAN	T-OFF	T-OWN
T-AIL	T-EAS	T-HAT	T-OFT	T-OWT
T-AIN	T-EAT	T-HAW	T-OHO	T-OYS
T-AIS	T-ECH	T-HEM	T-OIL	T-RAD
T-AIT	T-EDS	T-HEN	T-OKE	T-RAM
T-AKA	T-EEK	T-HEW	T-OLD	T-RAP
T-AKE	T-EEL	T-HEY	T-OLE	T-RAT
T-ALA	T-EEN	T-HIN	T-OMS	T-RAY
T-ALE	T-EFF	T-HIS	T-ONE	T-REE
T-ALL	T-EFS	T-HON	T-ONS	T-REF
T-AMP	T-EGG	T-HUG	T-ONY	T-RES
T-ANA	T-ELD	T-ICE	T-OOM	T-RET
T-ANE	T-ELL	T-ICH	T-OON	T-REW
T-APE	T-ELS	T-ICK	T-OOT	T-REZ
T-ARE	T-ELT	T-IDE	T-OPE	T-RIG
T-ARS	T-EME	T-IDS	T-OPS	T-RIM
T-ART	T-EMS	T-IFF	T-ORA	T-RIN
T-ASH	T-END	T-ILL	T-ORC	T-RIP

T-ROD	T-SAR	T-URD	T-WAT	T-WOS
T-ROT	T-UGS	T-URN	T-WAY	T-YES
T-ROW	T-ULE	T-UTS	T-WEE	T-YIN
T-RUE	T-UMP	T-UTU	T-WIG	
T-RUG	T-UNS	T-WAE	T-WIN	
T-RYE	T-UPS	T-WAS	T-WIT	

Four letters to five

T-AALS	T-EARS	T-HURL	T-RAIN	T-ROWS
T-ABID	T-EASE	T-ICED	T-RAIT	T-RUCK
T-ABLE	T-EATS	T-ICES	T-RAMP	T-RUED
T-ACES	T-EDDY	T-ICKY	T-RAMS	T-RUER
T-ACHE	T-EELS	T-IDES	T-RANK	T-RUES
T-ACTS	T-EFFS	T-ILLS	T-RANT	T-RUGS
T-AFFY	T-EGGS	T-ILLY	T-RAPE	T-RULY
T-AGMA	T-ELLS	T-IMID	T-RAPS	T-RUMP
T-AIGA	T-EMES	T-IMPS	T-RAPT	T-RUST
T-AILS	T-EMPT	T-INKS	T-RASH	T-RUTH
T-AINS	T-ENDS	T-IRED	T-RATS	T-RYKE
T-AITS	T-ENES	T-IRES	T-RAVE	T-SADE
T-AKES	T-EPEE	T-ITCH	T-RAYS	T-SADI
T-AKIN	T-ERAS	T-OAST	T-READ	T-SARS
T-ALAR	T-ERES	T-OFFS	T-RECK	T-SUBA
T-ALAS	T-ERNE	T-OHOS	T-REED	T-ULES
T-ALES	T-ERNS	T-OILS	T-REEN	T-UMPS
T-ALKY	T-ESTS	T-OKAY	T-REES	T-UMPY
T-ALLS	T-ETHS	T-OKES	T-REIF	T-URDS
T-ALLY	T-EUGH	T-OLES	T-REND	T-URNS
T-ALMA	T-EXES	T-ONER	T-REST	T-URPS
T-AMIN	T-HACK	T-ONES	T-RETS	T-UTUS
T-AMIS	T-HANK	T-ONUS	T-REWS	T-WAES
T-AMPS	T-HARM	T-OOMS	T-RIAL	T-WAIN
T-ANAS	T-HAWS	T-OONS	T-RICE	T-WANG
T-ANGA	T-HEBE	T-OOTS	T-RICK	T-WANK
T-ANNA	T-HEED	T-OPED	T-RIDE	T-WATS
T-ANTI	T-HEFT	T-OPES	T-RIFF	T-WAYS
T-APED	T-HEIR	T-ORCS	T-RIGS	T-WEAK
T-APER	T-HEME	T-ORES	T-RILL	T-WEED
T-APES	T-HENS	T-ORTS	T-RIMS	T-WEEL
T-ARED	T-HERE	T-OSES	T-RINE	T-WEEN
T-ARES	T-HERM	T-OUCH	T-RINS	T-WEER
T-ARTS	T-HESP	T-OUKS	T-RIPE	T-WEET
T-ARTY	T-HETE	T-OURS	T-RIPS	T-WICE
T-ASAR	T-HEWS	T-OUTS	T-RITE	T-WIGS
T-ASKS	T-HICK	T-OWED	T-ROAD	T-WILL
T-ATES	T-HIGH	T-OWER	T-ROCK	T-WILT
T-AULD	T-HILL	T-OWNS	T-RODE	T-WINE
T-AUNT	T-HING	T-OWSE	T-RODS	T-WINK
T-AVAS	T-HINS	T-OWTS	T-ROKE	T-WINS
T-AVER	T-HOLE	T-OYER	T-ROLL	T-WINY
T-AWED	T-HONG	T-RACE	T-ROMP	T-WIRE
T-AWNY	T-HORN	T-RACK	T-RONE	T-WIST
T-AXED	T-HOSE	T-RADE	T-ROOP	T-WITE
T-AXES	T-HOWL	T-RADS	T-ROPE	T-WITS
T-AXIS	T-HUGS	T-RAGI	T-ROTS	
T-AXON	T-HUMP	T-RAIK	T-ROUT	
T-EACH	T-HUNK	T-RAIL	T-ROVE	

T – Front-hooks

Five letters to six

T-ABBED	T-AXMEN	T-HORNY	T-RAINS	T-ROWTH
T-ABLED	T-AXONS	T-HOUGH	T-RAITS	T-RUCKS
T-ABLES	T-CHICK	T-HOWLS	T-RAMPS	T-RUFFE
T-ABLET	T-EAGLE	T-HUMPS	T-RANCE	T-RUING
T-ACHES	T-EARED	T-HUNKS	T-RANKS	T-RUMPS
T-ACKER	T-EASED	T-HURLS	T-RANTS	T-RUSTS
T-AGGER	T-EASEL	T-ICHES	T-RAPED	T-RUSTY
T-AIGAS	T-EASER	T-ICING	T-RAPES	T-RUTHS
T-AILED	T-EASES	T-ICKER	T-RAVEL	T-RYKES
T-AIVER	T-ECHED	T-ICKLE	T-RAVES	T-SADES
T-AKING	T-EMPTS	T-IGGED	T-RAYNE	T-SADIS
T-ALANT	T-ENDED	T-ILLER	T-READS	T-SAMBA
T-ALKIE	T-ENDER	T-INGLE	T-RECKS	T-SORES
T-ALLIS	T-ENTER	T-INKED	T-REENS	T-SUBAS
T-ALLOT	T-ENURE	T-INKER	T-RENDS	T-UGGED
T-ALLOW	T-EPEES	T-INKLE	T-RESTS	T-UMBLE
T-ALMAS	T-ERBIA	T-INNED	T-REVET	T-UMPED
T-ALMUD	T-ERNED	T-INNER	T-RIALS	T-UPPED
T-AMBER	T-ERNES	T-INTER	T-RIBES	T-URBAN
T-AMINE	T-ERROR	T-IRADE	T-RICED	T-URNED
T-AMINS	T-ESTER	T-IRING	T-RICES	T-WAINS
T-AMPED	T-ETHER	T-ISSUE	T-RICKS	T-WAITE
T-ANGAS	T-HACKS	T-ITCHY	T-RIFLE	T-WANGS
T-ANGLE	T-HALER	T-ITHER	T-RILLS	T-WANKS
T-ANKER	T-HANKS	T-MESES	T-RIMER	T-WANKY
T-ANNAS	T-HARMS	T-OASTS	T-RINES	T-WEEDS
T-ANNOY	T-HATCH	T-OCHER	T-RIPES	T-WEEDY
T-ANTRA	T-HAWED	T-OILED	T-RITES	T-WEELS
T-APERS	T-HEAVE	T-OILER	T-RIVET	T-WEENS
T-APING	T-HEBES	T-OKAYS	T-ROADS	T-WEENY
T-ARRAS	T-HEFTS	T-OLLER	T-ROCKS	T-WEEST
T-ARROW	T-HEIRS	T-OLLIE	T-RODES	T-WEETS
T-ASHED	T-HEIST	T-ONERS	T-ROKED	T-WIGGY
T-ASHES	T-HEMES	T-OORIE	T-ROKES	T-WIGHT
T-ASKED	T-HENCE	T-OPING	T-ROLLS	T-WILLS
T-ASKER	T-HERES	T-OTHER	T-ROMPS	T-WILLY
T-ASSES	T-HERMS	T-OTTER	T-RONES	T-WILTS
T-ASSET	T-HESPS	T-OURIE	T-ROOPS	T-WINED
T-ASTER	T-HETES	T-OUTED	T-ROPED	T-WINES
T-AUGHT	T-HEWED	T-OUTER	T-ROPES	T-WINGE
T-AUNTS	T-HICKS	T-OWING	T-ROUGH	T-WINKS
T-AURIC	T-HIGHS	T-OYERS	T-ROULE	T-WIRED
T-AVERS	T-HILLS	T-RACED	T-ROUSE	T-WIRES
T-AVERT	T-HINGS	T-RACER	T-ROUTS	T-WISTS
T-AWING	T-HOLED	T-RACES	T-ROVER	T-WITCH
T-AXING	T-HOLES	T-RACKS	T-ROVES	T-WITES
T-AXITE	T-HONGS	T-RAIKS	T-ROWED	
T-AXMAN	T-HORNS	T-RAILS	T-ROWEL	

Six letters to seven

T-ABLETS	T-AFFIES	T-ALLIED	T-AMISES	T-ANTARA
T-ABLING	T-AGGERS	T-ALLIES	T-AMPING	T-ANTRUM
T-ACKERS	T-AILING	T-ALLOTS	T-ANGLED	T-ARROWS
T-ACNODE	T-AIVERS	T-ALLOWS	T-ANGLER	T-ARSIER
T-ACTION	T-ALANTS	T-ALMUDS	T-ANGLES	T-ARTIER
T-ACTUAL	T-ALIPED	T-AMBERS	T-ANKERS	T-ARTILY
T-ADDIES	T-ALKIES	T-AMINES	T-ANNOYS	T-ASHING

T-ASKERS	T-HEREIN	T-OUCHES	T-RICKLY	T-RUNDLE
T-ASKING	T-HEREOF	T-OUGHLY	T-RIDENT	T-RUNNEL
T-ASSETS	T-HEREON	T-OUTERS	T-RIFLED	T-RUSTED
T-ASTERS	T-HERETO	T-OUTING	T-RIFLER	T-SAMBAS
T-AUNTER	T-HERMAE	T-RACERS	T-RIFLES	T-UCKERS
T-AWNIER	T-HERMIT	T-RACING	T-RIGGED	T-UGGING
T-AXITES	T-HETHER	T-RACKED	T-RIGGER	T-UMBLES
T-CHICKS	T-HICKIE	T-RACKER	T-RILLED	T-UMBREL
T-EAGLED	T-HIGHED	T-RAIKED	T-RIMERS	T-UMBRIL
T-EAGLES	T-HILLER	T-RAILED	T-RIMMED	T-UMPING
T-EARFUL	T-HITHER	T-RAILER	T-RIMMER	T-UNABLE
T-EARING	T-HOLING	T-RAINED	T-RIPPED	T-UPPING
T-EASELS	T-HORNED	T-RAMMED	T-RIPPER	T-URGENT
T-EASERS	T-HUMPED	T-RAMMEL	T-RIPPLE	T-URNING
T-EASING	T-HUMPER	T-RAMPED	T-RIVETS	T-WADDLE
T-EDDIES	T-ICKERS	T-RAMPER	T-ROATED	T-WADDLY
T-EMPTED	T-ICKLER	T-RANCED	T-ROCHES	T-WAITES
T-ENABLE	T-IGGING	T-RANCES	T-ROCKED	T-WANGLE
T-ENDERS	T-ILLITE	T-RANSOM	T-ROKING	T-WATTLE
T-ENDING	T-INGLES	T-RANTED	T-ROLLED	T-WEAKER
T-ENFOLD	T-INKERS	T-RANTER	T-ROLLER	T-WEENIE
T-ENSILE	T-INKING	T-RAPING	T-ROMPED	T-WEETED
T-ENTERS	T-INKLED	T-RAPPED	T-ROOPED	T-WEETER
T-ENURED	T-INKLES	T-RAPPER	T-ROPING	T-WIDDLE
T-ENURES	T-INNERS	T-RASHED	T-ROTTED	T-WIGGED
T-ERBIAS	T-INNING	T-RASHER	T-ROTTER	T-WIGGER
T-ERBIUM	T-INTERS	T-RASHES	T-ROUBLE	T-WIGHTS
T-ERNING	T-INWORK	T-RASSES	T-ROUGHS	T-WILLED
T-ERRORS	T-IRADES	T-RAVELS	T-ROULES	T-WILTED
T-ESTATE	T-IRITIS	T-RAYNES	T-ROUNCE	T-WINGED
T-ESTERS	T-IRONIC	T-READER	T-ROUPED	T-WINGES
T-ETCHED	T-ISSUED	T-REASON	T-ROUSER	T-WINIER
T-ETHERS	T-ISSUES	T-RECKED	T-ROUSES	T-WINING
T-HACKED	T-ITCHES	T-REDDLE	T-ROUTER	T-WINKED
T-HALERS	T-OCHERS	T-REMBLE	T-ROVERS	T-WINKLE
T-HANKED	T-OFFISH	T-RENAIL	T-ROWELS	T-WINNED
T-HANKER	T-OILERS	T-RENDED	T-ROWING	T-WINTER
T-HAWING	T-OILING	T-RENTAL	T-ROWTHS	T-WIRING
T-HEATER	T-OLLERS	T-REVETS	T-RUCKED	T-WISTED
T-HEAVES	T-OLLIES	T-RIBLET	T-RUCKLE	T-WITCHY
T-HEISTS	T-OMENTA	T-RICING	T-RUEING	T-WITTED
T-HELVES	T-ONUSES	T-RICKED	T-RUFFES	T-WITTER
T-HEREAT	T-OTTERS	T-RICKER	T-RUFFLE	T-ZADDIK
T-HEREBY	T-OUCHED	T-RICKLE	T-RUMPED	

Seven letters to eight

T-ABLINGS	T-ANGLING	T-AUNTERS	T-ESTATES	T-HILLERS
T-ACNODES	T-ANNATES	T-AUTONYM	T-HACKING	T-HIRLING
T-ACONITE	T-ANNOYED	T-AWNIEST	T-HANKERS	T-HORNIER
T-ACTIONS	T-ANTARAS	T-EAGLING	T-HANKING	T-HORNILY
T-ADVANCE	T-ANTRUMS	T-EARDROP	T-HATCHED	T-HORNING
T-AILERON	T-APELIKE	T-EARLESS	T-HATCHER	T-HUMPERS
T-ALIPEDS	T-ARRASES	T-EASELED	T-HATCHES	T-HUMPING
T-ALLISES	T-ARROWED	T-EMPTING	T-HEATERS	T-ILLITES
T-ALLNESS	T-ARTIEST	T-ENFOLDS	T-HEMATIC	T-INKLING
T-ALLOWED	T-ASKINGS	T-ENTERED	T-HERMITS	T-INNINGS
T-ALLYING	T-ASSWAGE	T-ENURING	T-HICKIES	T-INWORKS
T-ANGLERS	T-ASTABLE	T-ERBIUMS	T-HICKISH	T-IRELESS

T – Front-hooks

T-ISSUING	T-RAVELED	T-RIPPIER	T-RUCKMEN	T-WEETING
T-ITCHIER	T-RAVELER	T-RIPPING	T-RUFFLED	T-WIDDLED
T-OCHERED	T-REACHER	T-RIPPLED	T-RUFFLES	T-WIDDLES
T-OMENTUM	T-READERS	T-RIPPLER	T-RUMPING	T-WIGGERS
T-OTTERED	T-READING	T-RIPPLES	T-RUNDLED	T-WIGGIER
T-OUCHING	T-REASONS	T-ROATING	T-RUNDLES	T-WIGGING
T-RACINGS	T-RECKING	T-ROCKING	T-RUNNELS	T-WIGHTED
T-RACKERS	T-REDDLED	T-ROLLERS	T-RUNNION	T-WIGLESS
T-RACKING	T-REDDLES	T-ROLLING	T-RUSTIER	T-WIGLIKE
T-RAIKING	T-REMBLED	T-ROMPING	T-RUSTILY	T-WILLIES
T-RAILERS	T-REMBLES	T-ROOPING	T-RUSTING	T-WILLING
T-RAILING	T-RENAILS	T-ROSSERS	T-RUTHFUL	T-WILTING
T-RAINING	T-RENDING	T-ROTTERS	T-UBEROUS	T-WINGING
T-RAMMELS	T-RENTALS	T-ROTTING	T-UMBRELS	T-WINIEST
T-RAMMIES	T-REVISES	T-ROUBLES	T-UMBRILS	T-WINKING
T-RAMMING	T-RIBLETS	T-ROUCHES	T-URGENCY	T-WINKLED
T-RAMPERS	T-RICKERS	T-ROUGHED	T-URNINGS	T-WINKLER
T-RAMPING	T-RICKING	T-ROUNCES	T-WADDLED	T-WINKLES
T-RANCHES	T-RICKLES	T-ROUPING	T-WADDLER	T-WINNING
T-RANCING	T-RIFLERS	T-ROUSERS	T-WADDLES	T-WINTERS
T-RANSOMS	T-RIFLING	T-ROUTERS	T-WANGLED	T-WISTING
T-RANTERS	T-RIGGERS	T-ROUTING	T-WANGLER	T-WITCHED
T-RANTING	T-RIGGING	T-ROWELED	T-WANGLES	T-WITCHES
T-RAPPERS	T-RILLING	T-RUCKING	T-WATTLED	T-WITTERS
T-RAPPING	T-RIMMERS	T-RUCKLED	T-WATTLES	T-WITTING
T-RASHERS	T-RIMMING	T-RUCKLES	T-WEEDIER	T-ZADDIKS
T-RASHING	T-RIPPERS	T-RUCKMAN	T-WEENIES	

Eight letters to nine

T-ACONITES	T-HEREAWAY	T-RAILHEAD	T-RIPPLING	T-WANGLERS
T-ACTUALLY	T-HEREFROM	T-RAILLESS	T-ROLLINGS	T-WANGLING
T-AILERONS	T-HEREINTO	T-RAINBAND	T-ROUGHING	T-WATTLING
T-ALLIABLE	T-HERENESS	T-RAINLESS	T-ROUSSEAU	T-WEEDIEST
T-ALLOWING	T-HEREUNTO	T-RAMPINGS	T-ROUTINGS	T-WIDDLING
T-ANGLINGS	T-HEREUPON	T-RANSOMED	T-ROWELING	T-WIGGIEST
T-ANNOYING	T-HEREWITH	T-RAPPINGS	T-ROWELLED	T-WIGHTING
T-ARROWING	T-HITHERTO	T-RAVELERS	T-RUCKLING	T-WINGEING
T-ARTINESS	T-HORNBILL	T-RAVELING	T-RUFFLING	T-WINKLERS
T-AURIFORM	T-HORNIEST	T-RAVELLED	T-RUMPLESS	T-WINKLING
T-AUTOLOGY	T-HORNLESS	T-RAVELLER	T-RUNNIONS	T-WINNINGS
T-AUTONYMS	T-HORNLIKE	T-REACHERS	T-RUSTABLE	T-WITCHIER
T-EARDROPS	T-HUMBLING	T-READINGS	T-RUSTIEST	T-WITCHING
T-EMPTINGS	T-INKLINGS	T-REDDLING	T-RUSTLESS	T-WITTERED
T-ENTERING	T-ITCHIEST	T-REMBLING	T-RUTHLESS	T-WITTINGS
T-ERRORIST	T-OCHERING	T-RIFLINGS	T-URGENTLY	T-ZADDIKIM
T-HATCHERS	T-OTTERING	T-RIMESTER	T-WADDLERS	
T-HATCHING	T-RACHITIS	T-RIMMINGS	T-WADDLIER	
T-HEMATICS	T-RACKINGS	T-RIPPLERS	T-WADDLING	

T – End-hooks

Two letters to three

AI-T	BA-T	DO-T	FA-T	HA-T
AL-T	BE-T	EA-T	FE-T	HE-T
AN-T	BI-T	EF-T	GI-T	HI-T
AR-T	BO-T	EL-T	GO-T	HO-T
AT-T	DI-T	ES-T	GU-T	JO-T

KA-T	MO-T	OO-T	PI-T	TI-T
KI-T	MU-T	OP-T	PO-T	TO-T
LA-T	NA-T	OR-T	RE-T	WE-T
LI-T	NE-T	OU-T	SI-T	WO-T
LO-T	NO-T	OW-T	SO-T	YE-T
MA-T	NU-T	PA-T	TA-T	
ME-T	OF-T	PE-T	TE-T	

Three letters to four

AIR-T	DOL-T	KEN-T	PEA-T	SUI-T
ARE-T	DOR-T	KEP-T	PEN-T	TAI-T
BAH-T	DOS-T	KIS-T	PER-T	TAR-T
BAN-T	DOW-T	LAS-T	PES-T	TAT-T
BAS-T	DUE-T	LEA-T	PHO-T	TAU-T
BAT-T	DUI-T	LEE-T	PIE-T	TAW-T
BAY-T	DUN-T	LEP-T	PIN-T	TEA-T
BEE-T	EAS-T	LES-T	POL-T	TEL-T
BEL-T	ECH-T	LIN-T	POO-T	TEN-T
BEN-T	ERS-T	LIS-T	POS-T	TES-T
BES-T	ETA-T	LOO-T	POT-T	TEX-T
BIN-T	EVE-T	LOS-T	PUN-T	TIL-T
BIS-T	FAR-T	LOU-T	PUT-T	TIN-T
BIT-T	FAS-T	LOW-T	PYA-T	TIP-T
BOA-T	FEE-T	MAL-T	PYE-T	TOO-T
BOO-T	FEN-T	MAR-T	QUA-T	TOR-T
BOR-T	FES-T	MAS-T	RAI-T	TOW-T
BOT-T	FET-T	MAT-T	RAN-T	TWA-T
BRA-T	FIT-T	MEE-T	RAP-T	UNI-T
BRU-T	FIX-T	MEL-T	RAS-T	VAN-T
BUN-T	FON-T	MEN-T	REF-T	VAS-T
BUS-T	FOR-T	MIL-T	REN-T	VAU-T
BUT-T	FRA-T	MIS-T	RES-T	VEX-T
CAN-T	GAN-T	MIX-T	RIF-T	VIN-T
CAR-T	GAR-T	MOA-T	RIP-T	VOL-T
CEL-T	GAS-T	MOI-T	RIT-T	WAD-T
CHA-T	GEL-T	MOL-T	ROO-T	WAI-T
CHI-T	GEN-T	MOO-T	ROW-T	WAN-T
CIS-T	GIF-T	MOR-T	RUN-T	WAR-T
COL-T	GIS-T	MOS-T	SAL-T	WAS-T
COO-T	GOA-T	MOT-T	SAN-T	WAT-T
COS-T	GUS-T	MUN-T	SAU-T	WEE-T
COT-T	HAE-T	MUS-T	SEA-T	WEN-T
CUR-T	HAN-T	MUT-T	SEC-T	WHA-T
DAL-T	HAS-T	NET-T	SEN-T	WHO-T
DAN-T	HEN-T	NEW-T	SET-T	WIS-T
DAW-T	HEP-T	NOT-T	SEX-T	WON-T
DEB-T	HES-T	NOW-T	SHA-T	WOO-T
DEE-T	HIN-T	OBI-T	SHE-T	WOS-T
DEF-T	HIP-T	ONS-T	SIF-T	YES-T
DEL-T	HIS-T	OON-T	SIS-T	YET-T
DEN-T	HOO-T	OUS-T	SKA-T	YON-T
DIE-T	HOS-T	PAC-T	SKI-T	ZOO-T
DIN-T	HUN-T	PAN-T	SOU-T	
DIP-T	JOL-T	PAR-T	SPA-T	
DIT-T	JUS-T	PAS-T	SUE-T	

Four letters to five

ABLE-T	COME-T	GLEE-T	NIGH-T	SLIP-T
AGAS-T	COMP-T	GLEN-T	NONE-T	SPAR-T
AGEN-T	COOP-T	GOSH-T	ONCE-T	SPUR-T
ALAN-T	COOS-T	GRAN-T	OUCH-T	STAR-T
ALEF-T	COSE-T	GREE-T	OVER-T	STEN-T
AMEN-T	COUR-T	GRIP-T	PAIN-T	STEP-T
ANNA-T	COVE-T	GRIS-T	PALE-T	STOA-T
APER-T	CRUE-T	GUES-T	PEAR-T	STOP-T
ARET-T	CRUS-T	HADS-T	PIER-T	STOT-T
AVAS-T	CURE-T	HAIN-T	PIPE-T	STUN-T
AVER-T	CURS-T	HAUL-T	PIPI-T	SURA-T
BEAU-T	DEAL-T	HEAR-T	PLAN-T	SWAP-T
BEGO-T	DELF-T	HECH-T	PLEA-T	SWEE-T
BENE-T	DENE-T	HELO-T	POOR-T	SWOP-T
BERE-T	DICH-T	HIGH-T	PRAT-T	TACE-T
BIDE-T	DIXI-T	HOAS-T	PROS-T	TAIN-T
BLAT-T	DOES-T	HORS-T	QUIN-T	TAPE-T
BLUE-T	DRIP-T	INGO-T	REES-T	TARO-T
BLUR-T	DROP-T	ISLE-T	REIS-T	TEMP-T
BOAR-T	DUET-T	JOIN-T	REPO-T	TENE-T
BOAS-T	EARS-T	JURA-T	RICH-T	TORO-T
BOOS-T	ERGO-T	KARA-T	RIVE-T	TRAP-T
BRAN-T	EVEN-T	KEMP-T	ROOS-T	TRAT-T
BRAS-T	EVER-T	KORA-T	ROSE-T	TRES-T
BREN-T	EWES-T	LACE-T	SAIN-T	TWEE-T
BRIT-T	EXUL-T	LEAN-T	SAIS-T	VALE-T
BRUS-T	FACE-T	LEAP-T	SALE-T	VELD-T
BUND-T	FAIN-T	LEAS-T	SAUL-T	VERS-T
BURN-T	FEIS-T	LIAR-T	SAYS-T	VIVA-T
BURS-T	FILE-T	LICH-T	SCAN-T	VOLE-T
CADE-T	FIRS-T	LUNE-T	SCAR-T	WAIF-T
CANS-T	FLEE-T	MANA-T	SCAT-T	WAIS-T
CAPO-T	FLIR-T	MANE-T	SHIR-T	WARS-T
CARE-T	FLIT-T	MAYS-T	SHOO-T	WEES-T
CHAP-T	FREE-T	MEAN-T	SHOT-T	WELK-T
CHAR-T	FRIS-T	MEIN-T	SHUN-T	WHIP-T
CHER-T	FRIT-T	MERI-T	SICH-T	WISH-T
CHOU-T	FROS-T	MICH-T	SIEN-T	WRAP-T
CIVE-T	FUME-T	MIDS-T	SIGH-T	YEAS-T
CLAP-T	GAIT-T	MORA-T	SKAT-T	YOUR-T
CLEF-T	GAUN-T	MOTE-T	SKEE-T	
CLIP-T	GEES-T	MOUS-T	SKIN-T	
CLOU-T	GENE-T	MUSE-T	SLEE-T	

Five letters to six

ABLES-T	BARBE-T	BONNE-T	CAPLE-T	CRUSE-T
ADMIX-T	BARES-T	BOUGE-T	CATCH-T	CURIE-T
AGHAS-T	BARRA-T	BOUGH-T	CHARE-T	CURVE-T
AMIDS-T	BARRE-T	BREES-T	CLASP-T	CUTES-T
ANIGH-T	BASAL-T	BREIS-T	CLOSE-T	DELIS-T
ANKLE-T	BASES-T	BREVE-T	COHOS-T	DIKAS-T
APPLE-T	BASSE-T	BROWS-T	COMMO-T	DIVER-T
ARPEN-T	BECKE-T	BUDGE-T	COMPO-T	DIVES-T
ARTIS-T	BEMIX-T	BUFFE-T	CORSE-T	DONNA-T
ASSOT-T	BENNE-T	BUGLE-T	COVEN-T	DOUCE-T
ASTER-T	BLAES-T	CABLE-T	COVER-T	DOUGH-T
AURIS-T	BLUES-T	CACHE-T	CRONE-T	DOWSE-T

DRAPE-T	HEIGH-T	PALES-T	ROUGH-T	SWIVE-T
DREAM-T	HONES-T	PARGE-T	RUDES-T	TABLE-T
DRIES-T	IDLES-T	PATEN-T	RUSSE-T	TAMES-T
DUPLE-T	JUMAR-T	PEARS-T	SADIS-T	TAPIS-T
EAGLE-T	KAPUT-T	PIERS-T	SAFES-T	TARGE-T
FAVES-T	LAMES-T	PIQUE-T	SAGES-T	TASSE-T
FERES-T	LANCE-T	PLACE-T	SAIDS-T	TAVER-T
FIDGE-T	LATEN-T	PLAIN-T	SALLE-T	TERCE-T
FILLE-T	LAXES-T	PLANE-T	SANES-T	TOILE-T
FINES-T	LEARN-T	POSSE-T	SCEAT-T	TOQUE-T
FLIES-T	LIKES-T	PRESE-T	SCREE-T	TRIAC-T
FORES-T	LINGO-T	PRIES-T	SCRIP-T	TRUES-T
FORGE-T	LIVES-T	PUCES-T	SCULP-T	TUFFE-T
FORGO-T	LOCUS-T	PURES-T	SERES-T	TURBO-T
FREES-T	LOWES-T	PURIS-T	SHIES-T	TYRAN-T
FROWS-T	MALIS-T	RABBI-T	SILEN-T	UNFIX-T
GABLE-T	MATZO-T	RACHE-T	SMILE-T	UNMIX-T
GADGE-T	MERES-T	RARES-T	SONNE-T	UNPEN-T
GAINS-T	MIDGE-T	RAYLE-T	SORES-T	UNWON-T
GAMBE-T	MILLE-T	REDIP-T	SOUGH-T	VERSE-T
GAMES-T	MODES-T	REFEL-T	SPINE-T	VERVE-T
GAMMA-T	MOLES-T	REGES-T	SPOIL-T	WAUGH-T
GARRE-T	MONGS-T	RELIC-T	STEAL-T	WAURS-T
GORGE-T	MOTET-T	REMIX-T	STILE-T	WEIGH-T
GROVE-T	MUSCA-T	RENNE-T	STRIP-T	WHISH-T
HAIRS-T	MUTES-T	REPOS-T	STYLE-T	WIDES-T
HALES-T	NUDES-T	RETES-T	SUMMA-T	WISES-T
HALLO-T	OCTAN-T	RILLE-T	SURES-T	WORSE-T
HAUGH-T	OCTET-T	RIPES-T	SWEER-T	WRIES-T
HAULS-T	OLIVE-T	ROQUE-T	SWEIR-T	

Six letters to seven

ACUTES-T	CANTLE-T	EASIES-T	LONGES-T	PERCEN-T
ADJOIN-T	CHEVRE-T	EPAULE-T	LOOSES-T	PINIES-T
AERIES-T	CIRCLE-T	FAINES-T	LOWSES-T	PLEDGE-T
ALKANE-T	CLOSES-T	FALSES-T	LUNIES-T	POKIES-T
ANIMIS-T	COMMIX-T	FASCIS-T	LUSHES-T	POLLEN-T
ARCHES-T	COMPAS-T	FITCHE-T	MANCHE-T	POSHES-T
ARTIES-T	COMPOS-T	FITTES-T	MANTLE-T	POSIES-T
ATTAIN-T	CONGES-T	FOULES-T	MATIES-T	POUNCE-T
ATTASK-T	CONSUL-T	FOXIES-T	MAUVES-T	PREMIX-T
BABIES-T	CONTES-T	GASHES-T	MEANES-T	PRONES-T
BALLAN-T	CONTRA-T	GRAVES-T	MEDIAN-T	QUARTE-T
BARGES-T	CORNET-T	GROSER-T	MIGHTS-T	QUINTE-T
BASSES-T	COSIES-T	GURGLE-T	MISHAP-T	RACKET-T
BASSET-T	COUPLE-T	HACKLE-T	MISKEN-T	RADGES-T
BEDROP-T	COZIES-T	HOLIES-T	MOLINE-T	RADIAN-T
BEIGNE-T	CROCHE-T	HOMIES-T	MONTAN-T	RAGMEN-T
BELEAP-T	CRUDES-T	INANES-T	NAIVES-T	RANKES-T
BEMEAN-T	CULVER-T	JINGLE-T	NOBLES-T	RASHES-T
BEWRAP-T	CURRAN-T	KENNET-T	NOSIES-T	REALES-T
BORSCH-T	DEARES-T	KINGLE-T	OAKIES-T	REDEAL-T
BOSQUE-T	DECREE-T	LAMBER-T	ORGIAS-T	REPLAN-T
BOSSES-T	DEWLAP-T	LANGUE-T	OVERGO-T	REWRAP-T
BRAVES-T	DIPLON-T	LARGES-T	PAIRES-T	RICHES-T
BROUGH-T	DOUBLE-T	LAZIES-T	PALMIE-T	RIPPLE-T
BUSIES-T	DROGUE-T	LITHES-T	PARPEN-T	RIZZAR-T
CALLAN-T	DROLES-T	LOGIES-T	PELTAS-T	ROOTLE-T

T – End-hooks

ROSIES-T	SINGLE-T	TENNIS-T	TRITES-T	WARRAN-T
RUBIES-T	SLEIGH-T	TENSES-T	TURBAN-T	WAVIES-T
RUNDLE-T	SNIDES-T	THATCH-T	UGLIES-T	WHEESH-T
SABKHA-T	SPARES-T	THOUGH-T	UNCLIP-T	WHITES-T
SEAWAN-T	SPAVIE-T	TIDIES-T	UNCOES-T	WOULDS-T
SENSIS-T	SPRAIN-T	TIERCE-T	UPLEAN-T	ZANIES-T
SESTET-T	STALES-T	TINIES-T	UPLEAP-T	ZONULE-T
SEXTAN-T	STRAIN-T	TONIES-T	VAGUES-T	
SEXTET-T	SUBPAR-T	TOWIES-T	WACKES-T	
SHARIA-T	TAIVER-T	TOWMON-T	WADSET-T	
SHERIA-T	TEMPLE-T	TRIPLE-T	WALIES-T	

Seven letters to eight

ANGRIES-T	DANDIES-T	GIDDIES-T	LINTIES-T	OUTLEAP-T
ARTSIES-T	DEBBIES-T	GIRLIES-T	LIPPIES-T	PALMIES-T
BACCARA-T	DEMURES-T	GLOBULE-T	LITTLES-T	PALSIES-T
BAGGIES-T	DICKIES-T	GOODIES-T	LOATHES-T	PAPPIES-T
BALDIES-T	DIDDIES-T	GOONIES-T	LOOBIES-T	PARKIES-T
BANDIES-T	DILLIES-T	GOOSIES-T	LOONIES-T	PASSMEN-T
BARDIES-T	DINGIES-T	GROSSES-T	LOPPIES-T	PASTIES-T
BARRIES-T	DINKIES-T	GROUSES-T	LOURIES-T	PEERIES-T
BASEMEN-T	DIPLOMA-T	GUMMIES-T	LUCKIES-T	PERSICO-T
BAWDIES-T	DIRTIES-T	GUTTIES-T	MARABOU-T	PETTIES-T
BIRKIES-T	DIVINES-T	HABITAN-T	MARDIES-T	PHONIES-T
BITTIES-T	DIZZIES-T	HANDCAR-T	MARMOSE-T	PIGGIES-T
BLONDES-T	DODDIES-T	HAPPIES-T	MASHIES-T	PINKIES-T
BLOWIES-T	DOGGIES-T	HARDIES-T	MATURES-T	PISTOLE-T
BODGIES-T	DOTTLES-T	HEAVIES-T	MEAGRES-T	PLANCHE-T
BONNIES-T	DOWDIES-T	HEMPIES-T	MEALIES-T	PLATIES-T
BOOKIES-T	DREARES-T	HENNIES-T	MERRIES-T	PLUSHES-T
BOSSIES-T	DRIBBLE-T	HIPPIES-T	MICKLES-T	POCKIES-T
BRASHES-T	DUCKIES-T	HISSIES-T	MIDGIES-T	PODDIES-T
BRINIES-T	DUMMIES-T	HOODIES-T	MINUTES-T	POPPIES-T
BUDDIES-T	DUMPIES-T	HOOKIES-T	MISDEAL-T	PORKIES-T
BUGGIES-T	DUNNIES-T	HOOLIES-T	MISPLAN-T	POTTIES-T
BULLIES-T	EARLIES-T	HUMBLES-T	MISSIES-T	PREPLAN-T
BUSHIES-T	EMONGES-T	HUMPIES-T	MOODIES-T	PRIVIES-T
BUTCHES-T	EMPTIES-T	HUNKIES-T	MOONIES-T	PUGGIES-T
CANZONE-T	FANCIES-T	HUSKIES-T	MOSSIES-T	PUNKIES-T
CARNIES-T	FATTIES-T	INDICAN-T	MOTTIES-T	PURPLES-T
CASEMEN-T	FEEBLES-T	INDIGEN-T	MOUSIES-T	PUSSIES-T
CATTIES-T	FENNIES-T	INSCULP-T	MOWBURN-T	QUARTET-T
CHEWIES-T	FERLIES-T	INTERNE-T	MUDDIES-T	QUINTET-T
CHOICES-T	FICKLES-T	IRONIES-T	MUSKIES-T	RAGGIES-T
CHOKIES-T	FINALIS-T	JAGGIES-T	MYLODON-T	RAMMIES-T
CISSIES-T	FLAKIES-T	JAMMIES-T	NAPPIES-T	RANDIES-T
CLASSIS-T	FLASHES-T	JANTIES-T	NASTIES-T	READIES-T
COCKIES-T	FLUSHES-T	JEHADIS-T	NEDDIES-T	REDREAM-T
COMBIES-T	FOLKIES-T	JEMMIES-T	NETTIES-T	REGIMEN-T
CONGREE-T	FOOTIES-T	JERKIES-T	NEWSIES-T	RELEARN-T
CONJOIN-T	FOVEOLE-T	JETTIES-T	NIFTIES-T	REMOTES-T
CONTRAS-T	FRESHES-T	JIHADIS-T	NODDIES-T	RETRAIT-T
CRAZIES-T	FUNNIES-T	JOLLIES-T	NONUPLE-T	ROOFIES-T
CROSSES-T	FURRIES-T	JUNGLIS-T	NOOKIES-T	ROOKIES-T
CURLIES-T	GAUDIES-T	JUNKIES-T	OCTUPLE-T	ROOMIES-T
CUSHIES-T	GAWKIES-T	KHALIFA-T	OPAQUES-T	ROOTIES-T
CUTTIES-T	GENTLES-T	KITTLES-T	ORANGES-T	ROUNDLE-T
DAFFIES-T		LAMBIES-T	OUTBURN-T	ROWDIES-T

RUDDIES-T	SIMPLES-T	SUNBURN-T	TELETEX-T	WEARIES-T
RUMMIES-T	SISSIES-T	SUNNIES-T	TIDDIES-T	WEBBIES-T
SAFARIS-T	SMOKIES-T	SUPPLES-T	TINNIES-T	WEDGIES-T
SALTIES-T	SOAPIES-T	SURFIES-T	TOFFIES-T	WEENIES-T
SASSIES-T	SODDIES-T	SWISHES-T	TOTTIES-T	WEEPIES-T
SAVAGES-T	SOMBRES-T	SYMBION-T	TOWNIES-T	WHITIES-T
SAVVIES-T	SOOTHES-T	TACKIES-T	TRANCHE-T	WITHIES-T
SECURES-T	SPANGLE-T	TALKIES-T	TRICKLE-T	WOODIES-T
SEDATES-T	SPARKLE-T	TANGIES-T	UNIQUES-T	WOOLIES-T
SEMIMAT-T	SPRUCES-T	TARDIES-T	UNLEARN-T	WUSSIES-T
SERENES-T	SQUARES-T	TARRIES-T	UTOPIAS-T	YAPPIES-T
SHINIES-T	STABLES-T	TATTIES-T	VEINULE-T	YUMMIES-T
SHIPMEN-T	STEEVES-T	TAWNIES-T	VETIVER-T	
SILKIES-T	STONIES-T	TECHIES-T	WALLIES-T	
SILLIES-T	SULKIES-T	TEGUMEN-T	WASPIES-T	

Eight letters to nine

AUGUSTES-T	CRUSTIES-T	MASTODON-T	SECRETES-T	STICKIES-T
BACKDROP-T	DAINTIES-T	MISLEARN-T	SEPTUPLE-T	STINGIES-T
BEARDIES-T	DAYDREAM-T	MODERNES-T	SEXTUPLE-T	STRANGES-T
BLASTIES-T	DISCOVER-T	MULTIPLE-T	SHEENIES-T	STUBBIES-T
BLOCKIES-T	DISTRAIN-T	NEUROMAS-T	SHODDIES-T	STUMPIES-T
BLOODIES-T	DOGGONES-T	OBLIQUES-T	SICKLIES-T	STURDIES-T
BOLSHIES-T	DREARIES-T	OBSCURES-T	SKELLIES-T	SUBLIMES-T
BRASSIES-T	DRUGGIES-T	OUTDREAM-T	SKILLIES-T	SUPREMES-T
BRICKIES-T	EXTREMES-T	OUTLEARN-T	SLUSHIES-T	SWANKIES-T
BRITTLES-T	FLEECIES-T	OVERBURN-T	SMELLIES-T	SWANNIES-T
BROWNIES-T	FLIMSIES-T	OVERLEAP-T	SMOOTHES-T	TAWDRIES-T
BUBBLIES-T	FLOPPIES-T	OVERPLAN-T	SNOTTIES-T	THINGIES-T
CABRIOLE-T	FLOSSIES-T	OVERSLIP-T	SPAMMIES-T	TIDDLIES-T
CHAPPIES-T	FOREMEAN-T	PEARLIES-T	SPARKIES-T	TOASTIES-T
CHATTIES-T	FRILLIES-T	PLACEMEN-T	SPIFFIES-T	TRANSFIX-T
CHERRIES-T	FRIZZIES-T	PLOTTIES-T	SPOONIES-T	TRENDIES-T
CHILLIES-T	GLASSIES-T	POLYGLOT-T	SPORTIES-T	TRUSTIES-T
CHINKIES-T	GLOSSIES-T	PRECISES-T	SPOTTIES-T	UNTIDIES-T
CHIPPIES-T	GREASIES-T	PREPPIES-T	SPRINGLE-T	VIDEOTEX-T
CHITTIES-T	GREENIES-T	PRETTIES-T	SPUNKIES-T	WHEELIES-T
CHOCCIES-T	GRISLIES-T	PRISSIES-T	SPURRIES-T	WHIMSIES-T
CHUMMIES-T	HARTBEES-T	PRIVATES-T	STAGGIES-T	WHINNIES-T
COMPLAIN-T	HEARTIES-T	QUEENIES-T	STANCHES-T	WHIRLIES-T
CONCISES-T	JAUNTIES-T	RESTRAIN-T	STEADIES-T	WINDBURN-T
CRAPPIES-T	LANDDROS-T	SAVORIES-T	STEAMIES-T	WOBBLIES-T
CREEPIES-T	LAVISHES-T	SCANTIES-T	STEELIES-T	WOOLLIES-T
CRUMMIES-T	LOVELIES-T	SCURVIES-T	STEGODON-T	WORTHIES-T

U – Front-hooks

Two letters to three

U-DO	U-MU	U-RE	U-TE
U-MM	U-PO	U-TA	

Three letters to four

U-DAL	U-LEX	U-RES	U-TES
U-DON	U-NIS	U-SED	U-TIS
U-DOS	U-NIT	U-SER	U-VAE
U-LES	U-PAS	U-TAS	U-VAS

T – End-hooks

Four letters to five

U-DALS	U-NITS	U-RASE	U-RIAL	U-SING
U-DONS	U-PEND	U-RATE	U-RINE	U-SURE
U-LAMA	U-PLAY	U-REAL	U-RITE	U-TILE
U-NARY	U-PLED	U-REDO	U-SAGE	U-VEAL
U-NITE	U-RARE	U-RENT	U-SERS	

Five letters to six

U-LAMAS	U-PENDS	U-PREST	U-REDOS	U-SABLE
U-LEXES	U-PHANG	U-PRISE	U-RESES	U-SAGER
U-LOSES	U-PLAID	U-PROLL	U-RIALS	U-SAGES
U-NEATH	U-PLAYS	U-PROSE	U-RINES	U-SURED
U-NITER	U-PLEAD	U-RARES	U-RITES	U-SURER
U-NITES	U-PLINK	U-RASES	U-ROSES	U-SURES
U-NOWED	U-PLOOK	U-RATES	U-RUBUS	U-SWARD
U-PASES	U-PRATE	U-REDIA	U-RUSES	

Six letters to seven

U-NEARED	U-PLEADS	U-PRAISE	U-PRISER	U-SWARDS
U-NEATEN	U-PLIGHT	U-PRATED	U-PRISES	
U-NITERS	U-PLINKS	U-PRATES	U-PROLLS	
U-PENDED	U-PLOOKS	U-PREACH	U-REDIAL	
U-PHANGS	U-PLYING	U-PRESTS	U-SURING	

Seven letters to eight

U-PENDING	U-PLINKED	U-PRAISES	U-PRISING
U-PLAYING	U-PRAISED	U-PRATING	U-PROLLED
U-PLIGHTS	U-PRAISER	U-PRISERS	

Eight letters to nine

U-PHANGING	U-PLIGHTED	U-PLINKING	U-PRAISING	U-PREACHES
U-PLEADING	U-PLIGHTER	U-PRAISERS	U-PREACHED	U-PROLLING

U – End-hooks

Two letters to three

AM-U	EM-U	LO-U	PI-U	UM-U
AY-U	FE-U	ME-U	SO-U	UT-U
EA-U	KY-U	MO-U	TA-U	YO-U

Three letters to four

AIT-U	GEN-U	LIT-U	PUL-U	TEG-U
BAL-U	GUR-U	MAS-U	PUP-U	THO-U
BAP-U	HAP-U	MEN-U	RAT-U	TUT-U
BED-U	HUH-U	MOT-U	RIM-U	VAT-U
BUB-U	KOR-U	MUM-U	SUS-U	WUD-U
EME-U	LAT-U	NAM-U	TAB-U	
FRA-U	LEK-U	PAT-U	TAP-U	
FUG-U	LIE-U	PUD-U	TAT-U	

Four letters to five

BANT-U	BUSS-U	JAMB-U	PEND-U	VERT-U
BATT-U	CENT-U	KAWA-U	PIKA-U	
BITO-U	CORN-U	LASS-U	PILA-U	
BUCK-U	FOND-U	MUNT-U	QUIP-U	
BUND-U	HAIK-U	PARE-U	TEND-U	

Five letters to six

CONGO-U	MANAT-U
HALER-U	

Six letters to seven

MANITO-U	TAMARA-U
SUBMEN-U	TURACO-U

V – Front-hooks

Two letters to three

V-AE	V-AS	V-ET	V-IS	V-OX
V-AG	V-AT	V-EX	V-OE	V-UG
V-AN	V-AW	V-ID	V-OR	V-UM
V-AR	V-EE	V-IN	V-OW	

Three letters to four

V-AGS	V-ANT	V-END	V-ILL	V-OLE
V-AIL	V-ARE	V-ERA	V-INS	V-ORS
V-AIN	V-ARS	V-ERS	V-IRE	V-ROT
V-AIR	V-ARY	V-EST	V-ITA	V-ROW
V-ALE	V-EGO	V-ICE	V-LEI	V-UGH
V-AMP	V-ELD	V-IDE	V-OAR	V-UGS
V-ANE	V-ELL	V-IDS	V-OES	

Four letters to five

V-AGUE	V-ARIA	V-ERST	V-IRED	V-OMER
V-AILS	V-ARNA	V-ESTS	V-IRES	V-OMIT
V-AIRS	V-AUNT	V-ETCH	V-IRID	V-OUCH
V-AIRY	V-EALE	V-EXED	V-ISIT	V-OWED
V-ALES	V-EERY	V-EXES	V-ITAS	V-OWER
V-AMPS	V-EGOS	V-IBEX	V-LEIS	V-ROOM
V-ANES	V-ELDS	V-ICED	V-LIES	V-ROWS
V-ANTS	V-ELLS	V-ICES	V-OARS	V-UGHS
V-ARES	V-ENDS	V-ILLS	V-OLES	V-ULVA

Five letters to six

V-AGILE	V-ALINE	V-ARNAS	V-AUNTY	V-ELATE
V-AGUED	V-ALLEY	V-ASTER	V-AWARD	V-ENDED
V-AGUES	V-AMPED	V-ATMAN	V-EALES	V-ENDER
V-AILED	V-ARIAS	V-AUNTS	V-EGGED	V-ENDUE

U – End-hooks

V-ENTER	V-EXING	V-IZARD	V-ORANT	V-ROOMS
V-ERSES	V-ICING	V-OMERS	V-OTARY	V-ULVAS
V-ERVEN	V-IRING	V-OMITS	V-OWING	

Six letters to seven

V-ACATES	V-ALINES	V-AWARDS	V-ENDING	V-IBICES
V-ACUATE	V-ALLEYS	V-EGGING	V-ENDUES	V-IZARDS
V-ACUITY	V-AMPING	V-ELATED	V-ENTAIL	V-OCULAR
V-AILING	V-ASSAIL	V-ELITES	V-ENTERS	V-OUCHED
V-AIRIER	V-AUNTER	V-ENATIC	V-ESTRAL	V-OUCHES
V-ALGOID	V-AUNTIE	V-ENDERS	V-ETCHES	V-ROOMED

Seven letters to eight

V-AGILITY	V-AUNTERS	V-ENTAILS	V-ICELESS	V-OUCHING
V-AIRIEST	V-ENATION	V-ENTAYLE	V-ICELIKE	V-ROOMING
V-ALLEYED	V-ENDINGS	V-ERISTIC	V-IRIDIAN	
V-ASSAILS	V-ENOLOGY	V-ERMINED	V-OTARIES	

Eight letters to nine

V-ACUITIES	V-ENTAYLES	V-INDICATE
V-ENATIONS	V-IDEOGRAM	

V – End-hooks

Two letters to three

DE-V	GO-V	LA-V	RE-V	TA-V
DI-V	GU-V	PA-V	SO-V	

Three letters to four

CHA-V	DEE-V	MIR-V
CHI-V	ERE-V	PER-V

Four letters to five

GANE-V	PARE-V
OLLA-V	

W – Front-hooks

Two letters to three

W-AB	W-AS	W-EM	W-IS	W-OS
W-AD	W-AT	W-EN	W-IT	W-OW
W-AE	W-AW	W-ET	W-OE	W-OX
W-AG	W-AX	W-EX	W-OF	W-US
W-AI	W-AY	W-HA	W-ON	W-YE
W-AN	W-ED	W-HO	W-OO	
W-AR	W-EE	W-IN	W-OP	

Three letters to four

W-ABS	W-ARB	W-EEK	W-HEY	W-IRE
W-ADD	W-ARD	W-EEL	W-HID	W-ISH
W-ADS	W-ARE	W-EEN	W-HIM	W-ITS
W-AFF	W-ARK	W-EFT	W-HIN	W-OES
W-AFT	W-ARM	W-ELD	W-HIP	W-OKE
W-AGE	W-ARS	W-ELK	W-HIT	W-OLD
W-AGS	W-ART	W-ELL	W-HOA	W-ONS
W-AID	W-ARY	W-ELT	W-HOM	W-OOF
W-AIL	W-ASH	W-EMS	W-HOP	W-OON
W-AIN	W-ASP	W-END	W-HOT	W-OOS
W-AIR	W-ATE	W-ENS	W-HOW	W-OOT
W-AIS	W-ATT	W-ERE	W-HUP	W-OPS
W-AIT	W-AUK	W-EST	W-ICE	W-ORD
W-AKA	W-AVE	W-ETA	W-ICH	W-ORE
W-AKE	W-AWA	W-HAE	W-ICK	W-ORT
W-ALE	W-AWE	W-HAM	W-IDE	W-RAP
W-ALL	W-AWL	W-HAP	W-ILL	W-REN
W-AND	W-AYS	W-HAT	W-IMP	W-RIT
W-ANE	W-EAN	W-HEN	W-INK	W-UDS
W-ANT	W-EAR	W-HET	W-INN	W-YES
W-ANY	W-EDS	W-HEW	W-INS	

Four letters to five

W-ADDS	W-ARTY	W-EXES	W-HIZZ	W-OOZY
W-ADDY	W-ASHY	W-HACK	W-HOLE	W-ORDS
W-AGED	W-ASPS	W-HALE	W-HOOF	W-ORTS
W-AGER	W-ATAP	W-HAMS	W-HOOP	W-OULD
W-AGES	W-AUKS	W-HANG	W-HOOT	W-OVEN
W-AGON	W-AVER	W-HAPS	W-HOPS	W-OWED
W-AIDE	W-AVES	W-HARE	W-HORE	W-OXEN
W-AILS	W-AWES	W-HATS	W-HOSE	W-RACK
W-AINS	W-AWLS	W-HEAL	W-HUMP	W-RANG
W-AIRS	W-AXED	W-HEAR	W-HUPS	W-RAPS
W-AITS	W-AXES	W-HEAT	W-ICKY	W-RAPT
W-AKED	W-EANS	W-HEEL	W-IDES	W-RAST
W-AKES	W-EARS	W-HEFT	W-ILLS	W-RATE
W-ALES	W-EAVE	W-HELM	W-ILLY	W-RATH
W-ALLS	W-ECHT	W-HELP	W-IMPS	W-REAK
W-ALLY	W-EDGE	W-HENS	W-INCH	W-RECK
W-AMUS	W-EDGY	W-HERE	W-INKS	W-RENS
W-ANDS	W-EELS	W-HETS	W-INNS	W-REST
W-ANES	W-EFTS	W-HEWS	W-IRED	W-RICK
W-ANNA	W-ELDS	W-HEYS	W-IRES	W-RING
W-ANTS	W-ELKS	W-HIMS	W-ITCH	W-RITE
W-ARBS	W-ELLS	W-HINS	W-OLDS	W-RITS
W-ARDS	W-ELTS	W-HIPS	W-OMEN	W-ROKE
W-ARED	W-ENDS	W-HIPT	W-OOFS	W-RONG
W-ARES	W-EROS	W-HISH	W-OOFY	W-ROOT
W-ARKS	W-ESTS	W-HISS	W-OONS	W-ROTE
W-ARMS	W-ETAS	W-HIST	W-OOPS	W-RUNG
W-ARTS	W-EXED	W-HITS	W-OOSE	W-USES

Five letters to six

W-ACKER	W-ADDER	W-AFTER	W-AGGER	W-AGONS
W-ADDED	W-ADDLE	W-AGERS	W-AGING	W-AILED

W – Front-hooks

W-AIRED	W-AXING	W-HARES	W-HOOFS	W-IZARD
W-AIVER	W-EANED	W-HEALS	W-HOOPS	W-ONNED
W-AKING	W-EARED	W-HEARE	W-HOOSH	W-OOSES
W-ALLOW	W-EASEL	W-HEATS	W-HOOTS	W-ORMER
W-AMBLE	W-EAVED	W-HEELS	W-HUMPS	W-OUBIT
W-ANGLE	W-EAVES	W-HEEZE	W-ICHES	W-OUNDY
W-ANION	W-EBBED	W-HEFTS	W-ICKER	W-OVENS
W-ANKER	W-EDGED	W-HELMS	W-IGGED	W-OWING
W-ANKLE	W-EDGES	W-HELPS	W-ILLER	W-RACKS
W-ANTED	W-EIGHT	W-HENCE	W-IMPED	W-RASSE
W-ARKED	W-ELDER	W-HERES	W-INDOW	W-RATHS
W-ARMED	W-ENDED	W-HERRY	W-INKED	W-REAKS
W-ARMER	W-ESTER	W-HEUGH	W-INKER	W-RECKS
W-ARRAY	W-ETHER	W-HEWED	W-INKLE	W-RESTS
W-ASHED	W-EXING	W-HILLY	W-INNED	W-RETCH
W-ASHEN	W-HACKS	W-HINGE	W-INNER	W-RICKS
W-ASHES	W-HALED	W-HINNY	W-INTER	W-RIGHT
W-ASTER	W-HALER	W-HIPPY	W-IRING	W-RINGS
W-ATAPS	W-HALES	W-HISTS	W-ISHES	W-RITES
W-AUGHT	W-HAMMY	W-HOLES	W-ITCHY	W-ROOTS
W-AVERS	W-HANGS	W-HOLLY	W-ITHER	

Six letters to seven

W-ACKERS	W-ARTIER	W-HEELED	W-HOLISM	W-ITCHES
W-ADDERS	W-ASHERY	W-HEELER	W-HOLIST	W-IZARDS
W-ADDIES	W-ASHIER	W-HEEZED	W-HOOFED	W-OLLIES
W-ADDING	W-ASHING	W-HEEZES	W-HOOPED	W-ONNING
W-ADDLED	W-ASPISH	W-HELMED	W-HOOPER	W-OOFIER
W-ADDLES	W-ASSAIL	W-HELPED	W-HOOPLA	W-OOZIER
W-AFFIES	W-ASTERS	W-HEREAT	W-HOOTED	W-OOZILY
W-AFTERS	W-ATTEST	W-HEREBY	W-HOPPED	W-ORMERS
W-AGGERS	W-AUGHTS	W-HEREIN	W-HOPPER	W-OUBITS
W-AILING	W-AXLIKE	W-HEREOF	W-HUMPED	W-OURALI
W-AIRING	W-EANING	W-HEREON	W-HUPPED	W-RACKED
W-AIVERS	W-EARING	W-HERETO	W-ICKERS	W-RANGED
W-ALLIES	W-EASELS	W-HETHER	W-IGGING	W-RAPPED
W-ALLOWS	W-EBBING	W-HEUGHS	W-ILLEST	W-RAPPER
W-AMBLED	W-EDGIER	W-HEWING	W-IMPING	W-RASSES
W-AMBLES	W-EDGING	W-HIDDER	W-IMPISH	W-RASSLE
W-AMUSES	W-EIGHTS	W-HINGED	W-IMPLED	W-REAKED
W-ANGLED	W-EIGHTY	W-HINGER	W-INCHED	W-RECKED
W-ANGLER	W-ELDERS	W-HINGES	W-INCHER	W-RESTED
W-ANGLES	W-ELDING	W-HIPPED	W-INCHES	W-RESTER
W-ANIONS	W-ENDING	W-HIPPER	W-INDIGO	W-RICKED
W-ANKERS	W-ESTERS	W-HISHED	W-INDOWS	W-RIGHTS
W-ANTING	W-ETHERS	W-HISHES	W-INKERS	W-RINGED
W-APPEND	W-HACKED	W-HISSED	W-INKING	W-RINGER
W-ARKING	W-HACKER	W-HISSES	W-INKLED	W-ROOTED
W-ARLING	W-HALERS	W-HISTED	W-INKLES	W-ROUGHT
W-ARMERS	W-HALING	W-HITHER	W-INNERS	W-ULLING
W-ARMING	W-HAMMED	W-HITTER	W-INNING	
W-ARRANT	W-HANGED	W-HIZZED	W-INTERS	
W-ARRAYS	W-HAPPED	W-HIZZES	W-ITCHED	

Seven letters to eight

W-ADDLING	W-EDGIEST	W-HINNIES	W-HOOSHES	W-OULDEST
W-AGELESS	W-EDGINGS	W-HIPLIKE	W-HOOTING	W-OURALIS
W-ALLEYED	W-ELDINGS	W-HIPPIER	W-HOPPERS	W-RACKFUL
W-ALLOWED	W-HACKERS	W-HIPPING	W-HOPPING	W-RACKING
W-AMBLING	W-HACKING	W-HIPSTER	W-HUMPING	W-RANGING
W-ANGLERS	W-HAMMING	W-HIRLING	W-HUPPING	W-RAPPERS
W-ANGLING	W-HANGING	W-HISHING	W-INCHERS	W-RAPPING
W-ANTHILL	W-HAPPING	W-HISSING	W-INCHING	W-RASSLED
W-ANTINGS	W-HEELERS	W-HISTING	W-INDIGOS	W-RASSLES
W-ARMINGS	W-HEELING	W-HITHERS	W-INDOWED	W-REAKING
W-ARRAYED	W-HEEZING	W-HITTERS	W-INKLING	W-RECKING
W-ARTIEST	W-HELMING	W-HIZZING	W-INNARDS	W-RESTERS
W-ARTLESS	W-HELPING	W-HOLISMS	W-INNINGS	W-RESTING
W-ASHIEST	W-HERRIED	W-HOLISTS	W-IRELESS	W-RETCHED
W-ASSAILS	W-HERRIES	W-HOOFING	W-ITCHIER	W-RETCHES
W-ASTABLE	W-HIDDERS	W-HOOPERS	W-ITCHING	W-RICKING
W-EANLING	W-HINGERS	W-HOOPING	W-OOFIEST	W-RINGERS
W-EARINGS	W-HINGING	W-HOOPLAS	W-OORALIS	W-RINGING
W-EASELED	W-HINNIED	W-HOOSHED	W-OOZIEST	W-ROOTING

Eight letters to nine

W-ALLOWING	W-EANLINGS	W-HERENESS	W-HIRLINGS	W-ITCHINGS
W-AMBLINGS	W-EDGEWISE	W-HEREUNTO	W-HITHERED	W-ITCHWEED
W-ANGLINGS	W-HACKINGS	W-HEREUPON	W-HOLESOME	W-OOZINESS
W-ANTHILLS	W-HEATLESS	W-HEREWITH	W-HOLISTIC	W-RAPPINGS
W-ARRAYING	W-HEELINGS	W-HERRYING	W-HOOSHING	W-RASSLING
W-ASHERIES	W-HEELLESS	W-HINNYING	W-HOPPINGS	W-RINGINGS
W-ASHINESS	W-HELPLESS	W-HIPPIEST	W-IMPISHLY	
W-ASSAILED	W-HEREFROM	W-HIPPINGS	W-INDOWING	
W-ASSAILER	W-HEREINTO	W-HIPSTERS	W-ITCHIEST	

W – End-hooks

Two letters to three

BO-W	HE-W	LO-W	PA-W	TO-W
DA-W	HO-W	MA-W	PE-W	WO-W
DE-W	JA-W	ME-W	PO-W	YA-W
DO-W	JO-W	MO-W	RE-W	YE-W
FA-W	KA-W	NA-W	SO-W	YO-W
FE-W	KO-W	NE-W	TA-W	
HA-W	LA-W	NO-W	TE-W	

Three letters to four

ALE-W	BRA-W	ENE-W	SHE-W	VIE-W
ANE-W	BRO-W	FRO-W	SKA-W	WHO-W
ARE-W	CHA-W	PRO-W	SPA-W	
AVO-W	CHE-W	SHA-W	THE-W	

Four letters to five

BEDE-W	PAPA-W	SINE-W	VINE-W
KOTO-W	PAWA-W	SYBO-W	VROU-W
NAVE-W	PILA-W	THRO-W	

W – Front-hooks

Five letters to six

BARRO-W	HOLLO-W	MORRO-W	REVIE-W	
BURRO-W	MATLO-W	OUTRO-W	UNCLE-W	
HALLO-W	MISSA-W	PURSE-W		

Six letters to seven

DAYGLO-W
FITCHE-W

Seven letters to eight

BUDGERO-W
RICKSHA-W

Eight letters to nine

KABELJOU-W

X – Front-hooks

Two letters to three

X-IS

Four letters to five

X-ERIC
X-YLEM

Five letters to six

X-YLEMS

Six letters to seven

X-EROSES
X-EROTIC

Eight letters to nine

X-ENOPHILE

X – End-hooks

Two letters to three

BO-X	HO-X	MU-X	RE-X	TI-X
DE-X	LA-X	NO-X	SI-X	WE-X
FA-X	LO-X	PA-X	SO-X	WO-X
GO-X	MA-X	PI-X	TA-X	YE-X
HE-X	MI-X	PO-X	TE-X	ZA-X

Three letters to four

APE-X	EAU-X	JEU-X	PRE-X
BRU-X	FLU-X	JIN-X	ULE-X
CRU-X	HOA-X	ONY-X	

Four letters to five

BEAU-X	CODE-X	LIMA-X	MURE-X	SORE-X
BORA-X	FORE-X	LURE-X	PYRE-X	TELE-X
CARE-X	GALA-X	MALA-X	REDO-X	VIBE-X
CHOU-X	LATE-X	MIRE-X	SILE-X	VITE-X

Five letters to six

ADIEU-X	BOYAU-X
BIJOU-X	DUPLE-X

Six letters to seven

BATEAU-X	CADEAU-X	GATEAU-X	MINIMA-X	SIMPLE-X
BUREAU-X	COTEAU-X	MILIEU-X	RESEAU-X	TRIPLE-X

Seven letters to eight

BANDEAU-X	CHAPEAU-X	JAMBEAU-X	OCTUPLE-X	ROULEAU-X
BATTEAU-X	CHATEAU-X	MANTEAU-X	PLATEAU-X	TABLEAU-X
BERCEAU-X	COUTEAU-X	MORCEAU-X	PONCEAU-X	TONNEAU-X
CAMAIEU-X	FABLIAU-X	NOUVEAU-X	RONDEAU-X	TRUMEAU-X

Eight letters to nine

ABOIDEAU-X	FLAMBEAU-X	PRIEDIEU-X
ABOITEAU-X	MULTIPLE-X	

Y – Front-hooks

Two letters to three

Y-AD	Y-AW	Y-ET	Y-OD	Y-UG
Y-AE	Y-AY	Y-EX	Y-OM	Y-UM
Y-AG	Y-EA	Y-GO	Y-ON	Y-UP
Y-AH	Y-EH	Y-ID	Y-OS	Y-US
Y-AM	Y-EN	Y-IN	Y-OU	
Y-AR	Y-ES	Y-OB	Y-OW	

Three letters to four

Y-ABA	Y-APP	Y-AWN	Y-ECH	Y-ELT
Y-ADS	Y-ARD	Y-AYS	Y-EGG	Y-ENS
Y-AFF	Y-ARE	Y-BET	Y-ELD	Y-ERK
Y-AGS	Y-ARK	Y-EAN	Y-ELK	Y-EST
Y-AHS	Y-ATE	Y-EAR	Y-ELL	Y-EUK
Y-ALE	Y-AWL	Y-EAS	Y-ELM	Y-EVE

X – End-hooks

Y-GOE	Y-OBS	Y-OOF	Y-OUS	Y-ULE
Y-IDS	Y-ODE	Y-OOP	Y-OWE	Y-UMP
Y-ILL	Y-ODS	Y-ORE	Y-OWL	Y-UPS
Y-INS	Y-OKE	Y-OUK	Y-UGS	Y-WIS
Y-IRK	Y-OLD	Y-OUR	Y-UKE	

Four letters to five

Y-ABBA	Y-AWNS	Y-ELLS	Y-IRKS	Y-OWLS
Y-ACCA	Y-AWNY	Y-ELMS	Y-LIKE	Y-RAPT
Y-AGER	Y-BORE	Y-ELTS	Y-MOLT	Y-RENT
Y-ALES	Y-CLAD	Y-ERKS	Y-OGEE	Y-SAME
Y-AMEN	Y-COND	Y-ESES	Y-OKES	Y-TOST
Y-APPS	Y-DRAD	Y-ESTS	Y-OOFS	Y-UKES
Y-ARCO	Y-EANS	Y-EUKS	Y-OOPS	Y-ULAN
Y-ARDS	Y-EARD	Y-EVEN	Y-ORES	Y-ULES
Y-ARKS	Y-EARN	Y-EVES	Y-OUKS	Y-UMPS
Y-ATES	Y-EARS	Y-EXED	Y-OURN	Y-UPON
Y-AULD	Y-EAST	Y-EXES	Y-OURS	
Y-AWED	Y-EGGS	Y-FERE	Y-OWED	
Y-AWLS	Y-ELKS	Y-ILLS	Y-OWES	

Five letters to six

Y-ABBAS	Y-ARKED	Y-EANED	Y-EXING	Y-SHEND
Y-ACCAS	Y-ARROW	Y-EARDS	Y-ICKER	Y-SHENT
Y-ACKER	Y-AWING	Y-EARLY	Y-IRKED	Y-ULANS
Y-AGERS	Y-AWNED	Y-EARNS	Y-OGEES	Y-UMPED
Y-AGGER	Y-AWNER	Y-EASTS	Y-OWING	Y-UMPIE
Y-AKKAS	Y-BLENT	Y-EMMER	Y-OWLED	Y-WROKE
Y-AMENS	Y-BOUND	Y-ESSES	Y-OWLER	
Y-ANKER	Y-BRENT	Y-ESTER	Y-PIGHT	
Y-ANTRA	Y-CLEPT	Y-EUKED	Y-PLAST	

Six letters to seven

Y-ACKERS	Y-AWNIER	Y-EARNER	Y-MOLTEN	Y-UCKERS
Y-AGGERS	Y-AWNING	Y-EASTED	Y-OWLERS	Y-UMPIES
Y-ANKERS	Y-CLEPED	Y-EMMERS	Y-OWLING	Y-UMPING
Y-ARKING	Y-EANING	Y-EUKING	Y-PLIGHT	
Y-ARROWS	Y-EARDED	Y-ICKERS	Y-SHENDS	
Y-AWNERS	Y-EARNED	Y-IRKING	Y-SLAKED	

Seven letters to eight

Y-ATAGHAN	Y-BOUNDEN	Y-EARDING	Y-EARNING
Y-AWNIEST	Y-CLEEPED	Y-EARLIES	Y-EASTING
Y-AWNINGS	Y-EANLING	Y-EARNERS	Y-OURSELF

Eight letters to nine

Y-ATAGHANS	Y-EANLINGS	Y-RAVISHED
Y-CLEEPING	Y-EARNINGS	Y-SHENDING

Y – End-hooks

Two letters to three

AB-Y	DE-Y	HE-Y	MA-Y	SH-Y
AN-Y	DO-Y	HO-Y	MO-Y	SO-Y
AR-Y	FA-Y	JA-Y	NA-Y	ST-Y
BA-Y	FE-Y	JO-Y	NO-Y	TA-Y
BE-Y	GO-Y	KA-Y	ON-Y	TO-Y
BO-Y	GU-Y	LA-Y	OX-Y	WE-Y
DA-Y	HA-Y	LO-Y	PA-Y	YA-Y

Three letters to four

ACH-Y	COX-Y	GUL-Y	OAR-Y	SHA-Y
ADD-Y	COZ-Y	HER-Y	OBE-Y	SOM-Y
AFF-Y	DEF-Y	HOM-Y	OIL-Y	SPA-Y
AIR-Y	DEN-Y	HUG-Y	OKA-Y	SUM-Y
ALA-Y	DEW-Y	ICK-Y	OLD-Y	TAK-Y
ALL-Y	DEX-Y	IFF-Y	OOF-Y	TED-Y
ARM-Y	DID-Y	ILL-Y	OOS-Y	THE-Y
ARS-Y	DOB-Y	INK-Y	ORB-Y	TID-Y
ART-Y	DOG-Y	JOE-Y	OWL-Y	TIN-Y
ASH-Y	DOM-Y	JUD-Y	PAC-Y	TOD-Y
AWA-Y	DOP-Y	LAC-Y	PAL-Y	TOE-Y
AWN-Y	DOR-Y	LAD-Y	PAT-Y	TON-Y
BOD-Y	DOT-Y	LEV-Y	PIN-Y	TOR-Y
BOG-Y	EAS-Y	LIN-Y	PIP-Y	TOW-Y
BON-Y	EEL-Y	LOG-Y	PIT-Y	TUN-Y
BOX-Y	EGG-Y	LOR-Y	PIX-Y	TWA-Y
BRA-Y	ELM-Y	MAN-Y	POL-Y	UMP-Y
BUR-Y	FAD-Y	MAR-Y	POS-Y	UPS-Y
BUS-Y	FOG-Y	MAT-Y	POX-Y	URD-Y
CAG-Y	FOX-Y	MIR-Y	PRE-Y	VAR-Y
CAN-Y	FRA-Y	MIX-Y	PUL-Y	VIN-Y
CHA-Y	FUM-Y	MOB-Y	PUN-Y	WAD-Y
CIT-Y	FUR-Y	MOL-Y	QUA-Y	WAN-Y
COL-Y	GAB-Y	MON-Y	REN-Y	WAR-Y
CON-Y	GAM-Y	MOP-Y	RIM-Y	WAX-Y
COP-Y	GAP-Y	NIX-Y	ROK-Y	WIN-Y
COR-Y	GOB-Y	NOS-Y	RUB-Y	YAW-Y
COS-Y	GOE-Y	NOW-Y	SAG-Y	YUK-Y
COW-Y	GOR-Y	OAK-Y	SEX-Y	

Four letters to five

ABBE-Y	BAFF-Y	BASS-Y	BENT-Y	BOOB-Y
ACID-Y	BALD-Y	BATT-Y	BIFF-Y	BOOK-Y
AGON-Y	BALK-Y	BAWD-Y	BIGG-Y	BOOM-Y
ALAR-Y	BALL-Y	BEAD-Y	BILL-Y	BOOT-Y
ANNO-Y	BALM-Y	BEAK-Y	BING-Y	BORT-Y
ANTS-Y	BAND-Y	BEAM-Y	BITS-Y	BOSK-Y
APER-Y	BANT-Y	BEAN-Y	BITT-Y	BOSS-Y
ARSE-Y	BARB-Y	BEAT-Y	BLAD-Y	BOTH-Y
ARTS-Y	BARD-Y	BEEF-Y	BLIN-Y	BOTT-Y
ATOM-Y	BARK-Y	BEER-Y	BLOW-Y	BOYS-Y
ATOP-Y	BARM-Y	BELL-Y	BLUE-Y	BRAK-Y
AUNT-Y	BARN-Y	BEND-Y	BONE-Y	BRIN-Y

BROS-Y	DAFF-Y	FISH-Y	GRIS-Y	JIMP-Y
BUFF-Y	DAIS-Y	FIST-Y	GUCK-Y	JIVE-Y
BULK-Y	DAMP-Y	FIZZ-Y	GULF-Y	JOKE-Y
BULL-Y	DARK-Y	FLAK-Y	GULL-Y	JOLL-Y
BUMP-Y	DASH-Y	FLAM-Y	GULP-Y	JOLT-Y
BUND-Y	DAUB-Y	FLAW-Y	GUNG-Y	JOWL-Y
BUNG-Y	DEAR-Y	FLAX-Y	GUNK-Y	JUMP-Y
BUNN-Y	DEAW-Y	FLOR-Y	GURL-Y	JUNK-Y
BUNT-Y	DECO-Y	FLUE-Y	GUSH-Y	KELL-Y
BURL-Y	DEED-Y	FOAM-Y	GUST-Y	KELP-Y
BURR-Y	DEIF-Y	FOLK-Y	GUTS-Y	KELT-Y
BUSH-Y	DELL-Y	FOOD-Y	GYPS-Y	KEMP-Y
BUSK-Y	DICE-Y	FOOT-Y	HAIL-Y	KICK-Y
BUST-Y	DICK-Y	FORA-Y	HAIR-Y	KILT-Y
BUTT-Y	DICT-Y	FORB-Y	HAND-Y	KIND-Y
BUZZ-Y	DIKE-Y	FORK-Y	HANK-Y	KINK-Y
CAGE-Y	DILL-Y	FORT-Y	HARD-Y	KISS-Y
CAKE-Y	DING-Y	FROW-Y	HARP-Y	KOOK-Y
CALM-Y	DINK-Y	FUBS-Y	HASH-Y	LACE-Y
CAMP-Y	DIRT-Y	FUFF-Y	HAST-Y	LAIR-Y
CANN-Y	DISH-Y	FULL-Y	HEAD-Y	LAMB-Y
CANT-Y	DITS-Y	FUND-Y	HEAP-Y	LANK-Y
CARB-Y	DITT-Y	FUNK-Y	HEED-Y	LARD-Y
CARD-Y	DITZ-Y	FURR-Y	HEFT-Y	LARK-Y
CARN-Y	DOGE-Y	FUSS-Y	HEMP-Y	LATH-Y
CARR-Y	DOLL-Y	FUST-Y	HERB-Y	LAWN-Y
CASK-Y	DONS-Y	FUZZ-Y	HILL-Y	LEAD-Y
CHAR-Y	DOOL-Y	GALL-Y	HISS-Y	LEAF-Y
CHEW-Y	DOOM-Y	GAMA-Y	HOAR-Y	LEAK-Y
CHIV-Y	DOPE-Y	GAME-Y	HOKE-Y	LEAN-Y
COAL-Y	DORK-Y	GASP-Y	HOLE-Y	LEAR-Y
COBB-Y	DORM-Y	GAUD-Y	HOME-Y	LEER-Y
COCK-Y	DORT-Y	GAUM-Y	HONE-Y	LEFT-Y
COLE-Y	DOWD-Y	GAWK-Y	HONK-Y	LEZZ-Y
COLL-Y	DOWL-Y	GEEK-Y	HOOD-Y	LIMB-Y
COMB-Y	DOWN-Y	GENT-Y	HOOK-Y	LIME-Y
COMM-Y	DUCK-Y	GERM-Y	HOOT-Y	LIND-Y
CONE-Y	DULL-Y	GILL-Y	HORN-Y	LINE-Y
CONK-Y	DUMP-Y	GIMP-Y	HORS-Y	LING-Y
COOK-Y	DUNG-Y	GINN-Y	HOSE-Y	LINK-Y
COOL-Y	DURO-Y	GIPS-Y	HUFF-Y	LINN-Y
COOM-Y	DURR-Y	GIRL-Y	HULK-Y	LINT-Y
COPS-Y	DUSK-Y	GLAD-Y	HULL-Y	LOAM-Y
CORE-Y	DUST-Y	GLOB-Y	HUMP-Y	LOFT-Y
CORK-Y	DYKE-Y	GLUE-Y	HUNK-Y	LOLL-Y
CORN-Y	EARL-Y	GOAT-Y	HURL-Y	LOON-Y
COSE-Y	EBON-Y	GOLD-Y	HUSH-Y	LOOP-Y
COVE-Y	EMPT-Y	GOOD-Y	HUSK-Y	LORD-Y
COZE-Y	EVER-Y	GOOF-Y	HUSS-Y	LOSS-Y
CRAP-Y	FAIR-Y	GOOK-Y	IRON-Y	LOUR-Y
CRUD-Y	FAKE-Y	GOOL-Y	ITCH-Y	LOUS-Y
CRUS-Y	FAWN-Y	GOON-Y	JACK-Y	LOVE-Y
CULL-Y	FELL-Y	GOOP-Y	JAGG-Y	LUCK-Y
CULT-Y	FELT-Y	GOOR-Y	JAKE-Y	LUMP-Y
CURD-Y	FEND-Y	GOOS-Y	JANN-Y	LUSH-Y
CURL-Y	FERN-Y	GORM-Y	JAZZ-Y	LUST-Y
CURN-Y	FEST-Y	GOUT-Y	JEEL-Y	MALM-Y
CURR-Y	FIER-Y	GRAV-Y	JELL-Y	MALT-Y
CUSH-Y	FILL-Y	GRIM-Y	JERK-Y	MANG-Y
CUTE-Y	FILM-Y	GRIP-Y	JIFF-Y	MARD-Y

MARL-Y	NICK-Y	PRAT-Y	SEEL-Y	TINT-Y
MASH-Y	NIFF-Y	PREM-Y	SEEP-Y	TIPS-Y
MASS-Y	NIRL-Y	PREX-Y	SERR-Y	TIZZ-Y
MAST-Y	NOIL-Y	PRIM-Y	SESE-Y	TOAD-Y
MATE-Y	NOOK-Y	PROS-Y	SHAD-Y	TOCK-Y
MAWK-Y	NOSE-Y	PUDS-Y	SHIN-Y	TOFF-Y
MAZE-Y	NOUN-Y	PUFF-Y	SHOW-Y	TOLL-Y
MEAL-Y	NOWT-Y	PULP-Y	SILK-Y	TONE-Y
MEAN-Y	NURD-Y	PUNK-Y	SILL-Y	TOSH-Y
MEAT-Y	NUTS-Y	PUNT-Y	SILT-Y	TOSS-Y
MEIN-Y	ONER-Y	PURS-Y	SINK-Y	TOWN-Y
MELT-Y	PACE-Y	PUSH-Y	SISS-Y	TOWS-Y
MERC-Y	PALL-Y	PUSS-Y	SLAT-Y	TRIP-Y
MESH-Y	PALM-Y	PUTT-Y	SLIM-Y	TUFT-Y
MESS-Y	PALS-Y	RAGG-Y	SLOP-Y	TUMP-Y
MICK-Y	PAND-Y	RAIN-Y	SNAR-Y	TURF-Y
MIFF-Y	PANS-Y	RAND-Y	SNIP-Y	TUSH-Y
MILK-Y	PANT-Y	RANG-Y	SNOW-Y	TUSK-Y
MILT-Y	PARD-Y	RASP-Y	SOAP-Y	TWIN-Y
MING-Y	PARK-Y	READ-Y	SOFT-Y	TYPE-Y
MINT-Y	PARR-Y	REAM-Y	SOIL-Y	UNCO-Y
MIRK-Y	PART-Y	REDD-Y	SONS-Y	UNIT-Y
MISS-Y	PAST-Y	REED-Y	SOOT-Y	VAIR-Y
MIST-Y	PATS-Y	REEF-Y	SOPH-Y	VAMP-Y
MIZZ-Y	PAWK-Y	REEK-Y	SOUP-Y	VAST-Y
MOCH-Y	PEAK-Y	REIF-Y	SPEW-Y	VEAL-Y
MOLD-Y	PEAT-Y	REKE-Y	SPIC-Y	VEER-Y
MOLL-Y	PECK-Y	REST-Y	SPIK-Y	VEIL-Y
MOOD-Y	PEER-Y	RICE-Y	SPIN-Y	VEIN-Y
MOOL-Y	PEON-Y	RIFT-Y	STAG-Y	VIBE-Y
MOON-Y	PERK-Y	RILE-Y	STEW-Y	VIEW-Y
MOOR-Y	PEST-Y	RIND-Y	STIM-Y	VUGG-Y
MOPE-Y	PHON-Y	RISK-Y	STUD-Y	VUGH-Y
MOPS-Y	PICK-Y	RITZ-Y	SUCK-Y	WACK-Y
MORA-Y	PIET-Y	ROAR-Y	SUDS-Y	WADD-Y
MOSE-Y	PIKE-Y	ROCK-Y	SUET-Y	WALL-Y
MOSS-Y	PINE-Y	ROIL-Y	SULK-Y	WANE-Y
MOTE-Y	PINK-Y	ROOF-Y	SUNN-Y	WANK-Y
MOTH-Y	PION-Y	ROOK-Y	SURF-Y	WANT-Y
MOTT-Y	PITH-Y	ROOM-Y	SWAM-Y	WARB-Y
MOUS-Y	PLAT-Y	ROOP-Y	TACK-Y	WART-Y
MUCK-Y	PLUM-Y	ROOT-Y	TALC-Y	WASH-Y
MUGG-Y	POCK-Y	ROPE-Y	TALK-Y	WASP-Y
MULE-Y	POKE-Y	RORT-Y	TALL-Y	WAVE-Y
MUMM-Y	POLE-Y	ROUP-Y	TANG-Y	WEAR-Y
MUMS-Y	POLL-Y	RUDD-Y	TANK-Y	WEED-Y
MURK-Y	PONE-Y	RUMP-Y	TANS-Y	WEEN-Y
MURL-Y	PONG-Y	RUNT-Y	TART-Y	WEEP-Y
MURR-Y	PONT-Y	RUSH-Y	TATT-Y	WELL-Y
MUSH-Y	POOF-Y	RUST-Y	TEAR-Y	WHIN-Y
MUSK-Y	POPS-Y	SALL-Y	TECH-Y	WHIT-Y
MUSS-Y	PORK-Y	SALT-Y	TEEN-Y	WICK-Y
MUST-Y	PORN-Y	SAME-Y	TELL-Y	WIFE-Y
MUZZ-Y	PORT-Y	SAND-Y	TENT-Y	WILL-Y
MYTH-Y	POSE-Y	SARK-Y	TEST-Y	WIMP-Y
NARK-Y	POTS-Y	SASS-Y	THAW-Y	WIND-Y
NEED-Y	POTT-Y	SAVE-Y	THEW-Y	WINE-Y
NERD-Y	POUT-Y	SCAR-Y	TICH-Y	WING-Y
NETT-Y	POWN-Y	SEAM-Y	TICK-Y	WISP-Y
NEWS-Y	POZZ-Y	SEED-Y	TILL-Y	WITH-Y

Y – End-hooks

WOMB-Y	WOOL-Y	YAPP-Y	YEUK-Y	ZINC-Y
WONK-Y	WORD-Y	YAWN-Y	YOLK-Y	ZING-Y
WOOD-Y	WORM-Y	YECH-Y	YUCK-Y	ZOOT-Y
WOOF-Y	WUSS-Y	YEST-Y	ZEST-Y	

Five letters to six

AMBER-Y	BROWS-Y	CRANK-Y	FAULT-Y	GLOSS-Y
ANGST-Y	BRUSH-Y	CRAWL-Y	FEIST-Y	GNARL-Y
APPLE-Y	BUNCH-Y	CREAK-Y	FELON-Y	GOOSE-Y
ARMOR-Y	CAIRN-Y	CREAM-Y	FILTH-Y	GOURD-Y
ARROW-Y	CARBO-Y	CREEK-Y	FINER-Y	GOWAN-Y
AUGUR-Y	CARSE-Y	CREEP-Y	FITCH-Y	GRAIN-Y
BAKER-Y	CATCH-Y	CREPE-Y	FIXIT-Y	GRAPE-Y
BALLS-Y	CAUSE-Y	CRESS-Y	FLAKE-Y	GRASS-Y
BARON-Y	CEDAR-Y	CRICK-Y	FLASH-Y	GREED-Y
BAULK-Y	CHAFF-Y	CRIMP-Y	FLECK-Y	GREEN-Y
BEACH-Y	CHALK-Y	CRISP-Y	FLESH-Y	GRIPE-Y
BEARD-Y	CHAMP-Y	CROAK-Y	FLIMS-Y	GROSZ-Y
BEAUT-Y	CHANT-Y	CROUP-Y	FLINT-Y	GROUP-Y
BEECH-Y	CHARR-Y	CROWD-Y	FLIRT-Y	GROUT-Y
BENCH-Y	CHASM-Y	CRUMB-Y	FLISK-Y	GROWL-Y
BETON-Y	CHEAP-Y	CRUMP-Y	FLOAT-Y	GRUFF-Y
BIELD-Y	CHECK-Y	CRUST-Y	FLOCK-Y	GRUMP-Y
BITCH-Y	CHEEK-Y	CURVE-Y	FLOSS-Y	GUANA-Y
BLANK-Y	CHEER-Y	CUTES-Y	FLOUR-Y	GUILT-Y
BLASH-Y	CHERT-Y	DAINT-Y	FLUFF-Y	HAULM-Y
BLAST-Y	CHEST-Y	DANCE-Y	FLUKE-Y	HEARS-Y
BLEAK-Y	CHILL-Y	DEATH-Y	FLUNK-Y	HEART-Y
BLEAR-Y	CHINK-Y	DENAR-Y	FLURR-Y	HEATH-Y
BLOCK-Y	CHIRP-Y	DIMPS-Y	FLUSH-Y	HERES-Y
BLOKE-Y	CHOKE-Y	DINGE-Y	FLUTE-Y	HITCH-Y
BLOOD-Y	CHUCK-Y	DJINN-Y	FOLKS-Y	HORSE-Y
BLOOM-Y	CHUFF-Y	DOUGH-Y	FOOTS-Y	HOUSE-Y
BLOWS-Y	CHUNK-Y	DOWER-Y	FORTH-Y	HUMUS-Y
BLUES-Y	CIDER-Y	DRAFF-Y	FREAK-Y	HURRA-Y
BLUID-Y	CLANK-Y	DRAFT-Y	FREET-Y	JACKS-Y
BOOKS-Y	CLART-Y	DRAPE-Y	FREIT-Y	JALOP-Y
BOOZE-Y	CLASS-Y	DRAWL-Y	FRIAR-Y	JAPER-Y
BOSOM-Y	CLECK-Y	DREAM-Y	FRILL-Y	JAUNT-Y
BOTCH-Y	CLIFF-Y	DREAR-Y	FRISK-Y	KECKS-Y
BOWER-Y	CLIFT-Y	DRECK-Y	FRIZZ-Y	KLUTZ-Y
BOWSE-Y	CLING-Y	DRESS-Y	FROST-Y	KNACK-Y
BRAIN-Y	CLOUD-Y	DRIFT-Y	FROTH-Y	KNARL-Y
BRAND-Y	CLUCK-Y	DROLL-Y	FROWS-Y	KNOLL-Y
BRANK-Y	CLUMP-Y	DROOL-Y	FRUIT-Y	KNURL-Y
BRASH-Y	CLUNK-Y	DROOP-Y	FRUMP-Y	KORUN-Y
BRASS-Y	COACH-Y	DROPS-Y	GALAX-Y	LAUGH-Y
BRAWL-Y	COCKS-Y	DROSS-Y	GAMES-Y	LEACH-Y
BRAWN-Y	COLON-Y	DROWS-Y	GHOST-Y	LEMON-Y
BREAD-Y	COLOR-Y	DUPER-Y	GLAIR-Y	LIMPS-Y
BRIAR-Y	CONCH-Y	DWEEB-Y	GLASS-Y	LINEN-Y
BRICK-Y	CONVO-Y	EARTH-Y	GLAUR-Y	LIVER-Y
BRIER-Y	CORSE-Y	EATER-Y	GLEAM-Y	LOATH-Y
BRISK-Y	COUNT-Y	EGGER-Y	GLEET-Y	LOWER-Y
BROOD-Y	COUTH-Y	EIGHT-Y	GLINT-Y	LUNAR-Y
BROOM-Y	CRACK-Y	EMBUS-Y	GLITZ-Y	MANGE-Y
BROTH-Y	CRAFT-Y	FAINT-Y	GLOOM-Y	MARSH-Y
BROWN-Y	CRAMP-Y	FAKER-Y	GLOOP-Y	MAUND-Y

MEDLE-Y	QUEEN-Y	SLEEK-Y	STEED-Y	TREND-Y
MEREL-Y	QUINS-Y	SLEEP-Y	STEEL-Y	TRESS-Y
MIGHT-Y	QUIRK-Y	SLEET-Y	STEEP-Y	TRICK-Y
MISER-Y	RAKER-Y	SLIMS-Y	STEER-Y	TRIPE-Y
MISSA-Y	RATAN-Y	SLINK-Y	STICK-Y	TROLL-Y
MONOS-Y	REAST-Y	SLOOM-Y	STIFF-Y	TROUT-Y
MOPER-Y	REECH-Y	SLOSH-Y	STILL-Y	TRUST-Y
MOTOR-Y	REEST-Y	SLUBB-Y	STILT-Y	TRUTH-Y
MOULD-Y	REPLA-Y	SLUMP-Y	STING-Y	TWANG-Y
MOUSE-Y	RESIN-Y	SLUSH-Y	STINK-Y	TWANK-Y
MOUTH-Y	RHEUM-Y	SMALM-Y	STINT-Y	TWEAK-Y
MURRA-Y	RIGHT-Y	SMARM-Y	STOCK-Y	TWEED-Y
MURRE-Y	RIVER-Y	SMART-Y	STONE-Y	TWEEL-Y
NIGHT-Y	ROOTS-Y	SMEAR-Y	STORE-Y	TWEEN-Y
NITER-Y	ROPER-Y	SMELL-Y	STORM-Y	TWERP-Y
NOMAD-Y	ROSET-Y	SMILE-Y	STOUR-Y	TWILL-Y
NOTCH-Y	ROSIN-Y	SMIRK-Y	STRAW-Y	TWIRL-Y
OCCAM-Y	ROUGH-Y	SMIRR-Y	STRIP-Y	TWIRP-Y
OCHER-Y	RUDER-Y	SMITH-Y	STUFF-Y	TWIST-Y
OCHRE-Y	SAMEL-Y	SMOKE-Y	STUMP-Y	UMBER-Y
OILER-Y	SATIN-Y	SNAIL-Y	SUGAR-Y	UNRED-Y
ONION-Y	SAUGH-Y	SNAKE-Y	SWAMP-Y	UNSEX-Y
ORANG-Y	SAVOR-Y	SNARK-Y	SWANK-Y	VAPOR-Y
ORBIT-Y	SCALL-Y	SNARL-Y	SWARD-Y	VAULT-Y
OSIER-Y	SCANT-Y	SNEAK-Y	SWART-Y	VAUNT-Y
OWLER-Y	SCARE-Y	SNEER-Y	SWASH-Y	VETCH-Y
PAEON-Y	SCATT-Y	SNELL-Y	SWATH-Y	VICAR-Y
PAINT-Y	SCAUR-Y	SNIDE-Y	SWEAT-Y	VINER-Y
PAPER-Y	SCREW-Y	SNIFF-Y	SWEEP-Y	VOGUE-Y
PARLE-Y	SCURF-Y	SNIFT-Y	SWEET-Y	VOLAR-Y
PATCH-Y	SCUZZ-Y	SNOOP-Y	SWIFT-Y	WAFER-Y
PEACH-Y	SEVER-Y	SNOOT-Y	SWING-Y	WARRE-Y
PEARL-Y	SHALE-Y	SNORT-Y	SWIPE-Y	WATER-Y
PETAR-Y	SHAND-Y	SNOUT-Y	SWIRL-Y	WAVER-Y
PHONE-Y	SHARN-Y	SNUFF-Y	SWISH-Y	WEENS-Y
PITCH-Y	SHARP-Y	SODOM-Y	SWOON-Y	WEIRD-Y
PLASH-Y	SHEAF-Y	SOREL-Y	SWOOP-Y	WHACK-Y
PLONK-Y	SHEEN-Y	SPACE-Y	SYLPH-Y	WHEAT-Y
PLOOK-Y	SHEEP-Y	SPARK-Y	SYRUP-Y	WHEEL-Y
PLOUK-Y	SHEET-Y	SPAWN-Y	TAWER-Y	WHELK-Y
PLUCK-Y	SHELF-Y	SPEAR-Y	TEENS-Y	WHIFF-Y
PLUFF-Y	SHELL-Y	SPECK-Y	THICK-Y	WHIMS-Y
PLUMP-Y	SHIFT-Y	SPEED-Y	THING-Y	WHINE-Y
PLUNK-Y	SHIRT-Y	SPEND-Y	THORN-Y	WHIRL-Y
PLUSH-Y	SHOAL-Y	SPICE-Y	THUMB-Y	WHIRR-Y
POACH-Y	SHORT-Y	SPIFF-Y	THYME-Y	WHISK-Y
POINT-Y	SHOUT-Y	SPIKE-Y	TIGER-Y	WHITE-Y
PONCE-Y	SINEW-Y	SPOOF-Y	TILER-Y	WHIZZ-Y
POUCH-Y	SIRUP-Y	SPOOK-Y	TITCH-Y	WIELD-Y
POUFF-Y	SKANK-Y	SPOON-Y	TITUP-Y	WINCE-Y
PRANK-Y	SKEAR-Y	SPORT-Y	TOAST-Y	WITCH-Y
PRICE-Y	SKEER-Y	SPOSH-Y	TOOTH-Y	WOODS-Y
PRICK-Y	SKELL-Y	SPOUT-Y	TOOTS-Y	WORTH-Y
PRIOR-Y	SKILL-Y	SPUNK-Y	TORCH-Y	WOUND-Y
PRISM-Y	SKIMP-Y	STAGE-Y	TOUCH-Y	WRATH-Y
PRISS-Y	SKUNK-Y	STALK-Y	TOUGH-Y	WRIST-Y
PUNCH-Y	SLANG-Y	STARR-Y	TOWER-Y	YEAST-Y
PUSLE-Y	SLANT-Y	STEAD-Y	TRAMP-Y	YOUTH-Y
QUACK-Y	SLATE-Y	STEAM-Y	TRASH-Y	
QUALM-Y	SLAVE-Y	STEDD-Y	TREAT-Y	

Y – End-hooks

Six letters to seven

ALMOND-Y	CYCLER-Y	HACKER-Y	NUGGET-Y	SHADOW-Y
ANALOG-Y	DACOIT-Y	HAUGHT-Y	NURSER-Y	SHEATH-Y
ANARCH-Y	DAKOIT-Y	HEALTH-Y	NUTTER-Y	SHINNE-Y
APOLOG-Y	DAUBER-Y	HELLER-Y	ORANGE-Y	SHIVER-Y
ARCHER-Y	DEANER-Y	HENNER-Y	ORATOR-Y	SHLOCK-Y
ARMOUR-Y	DIARCH-Y	HERBAR-Y	OROGEN-Y	SHLUMP-Y
AUTUMN-Y	DIDDLE-Y	HICCUP-Y	OVULAR-Y	SHOWER-Y
BALSAM-Y	DITHER-Y	HOGGER-Y	PALMAR-Y	SHRIEK-Y
BATTER-Y	DODDER-Y	HONEST-Y	PANICK-Y	SHRILL-Y
BEAVER-Y	DODGER-Y	HOSIER-Y	PARROT-Y	SHRIMP-Y
BEGGAR-Y	DOGGER-Y	IMAGER-Y	PASTIL-Y	SHROUD-Y
BIBBER-Y	DOUGHT-Y	ISOGON-Y	PAUNCH-Y	SHTICK-Y
BILLOW-Y	DOWLNE-Y	JAGGER-Y	PEDLAR-Y	SIGNOR-Y
BINDER-Y	DRAPER-Y	JARGON-Y	PEDLER-Y	SILVER-Y
BIOGEN-Y	DROICH-Y	JASPER-Y	PEPPER-Y	SINTER-Y
BLIGHT-Y	DROUTH-Y	JITTER-Y	PHLEGM-Y	SKETCH-Y
BLOTCH-Y	DUDDER-Y	JOBBER-Y	PICKER-Y	SLAVER-Y
BOBBER-Y	DYNAST-Y	JOINER-Y	PILFER-Y	SLEECH-Y
BOCKED-Y	DYVOUR-Y	KITSCH-Y	PILLOW-Y	SLOUCH-Y
BOILER-Y	EPARCH-Y	KITTEN-Y	PIZAZZ-Y	SLOUGH-Y
BRANCH-Y	EPONYM-Y	KLUDGE-Y	PLAGUE-Y	SLUTCH-Y
BRAVER-Y	EUPHON-Y	KOLHOZ-Y	PLOVER-Y	SMOOCH-Y
BREATH-Y	EXARCH-Y	KOLKOZ-Y	POTHER-Y	SMOOTH-Y
BREWER-Y	FACTOR-Y	KVETCH-Y	POTTER-Y	SMUTCH-Y
BRIBER-Y	FAGGOT-Y	LADDER-Y	POWDER-Y	SNATCH-Y
BROKER-Y	FARMER-Y	LATHER-Y	PREACH-Y	SNITCH-Y
BUGGER-Y	FERRET-Y	LECHER-Y	PROBIT-Y	SPICER-Y
BURSAR-Y	FIBBER-Y	LENGTH-Y	PUCKER-Y	SPIDER-Y
BUTLER-Y	FIDDLE-Y	LITTER-Y	PUFFER-Y	SPIKER-Y
BUTTER-Y	FIDGET-Y	LOLLOP-Y	QUARTZ-Y	SPIRIT-Y
BUTTON-Y	FISHER-Y	LOTTER-Y	QUAVER-Y	SPLASH-Y
CANKER-Y	FLAUNT-Y	MAGGOT-Y	QUEACH-Y	SPLEEN-Y
CANNER-Y	FLAVOR-Y	MAPPER-Y	QUIVER-Y	SPRAWL-Y
CARROT-Y	FLIGHT-Y	MARROW-Y	RABBIT-Y	SPRING-Y
CARVER-Y	FLOWER-Y	MARTYR-Y	RACKET-Y	SQUALL-Y
CASTOR-Y	FORGER-Y	MASTER-Y	RAGGED-Y	SQUASH-Y
CAUTER-Y	FOUGHT-Y	MATTER-Y	RAISIN-Y	SQUAWK-Y
CHANCE-Y	FRATCH-Y	MEADOW-Y	RATTER-Y	SQUEAK-Y
CHINCH-Y	FRATER-Y	MELLOW-Y	RAUNCH-Y	SQUIFF-Y
CHINTZ-Y	FROWST-Y	MENSCH-Y	RECTOR-Y	SQUINT-Y
CHOOSE-Y	FULLER-Y	MERCER-Y	RIBBON-Y	SQUIRM-Y
CHURCH-Y	FURROW-Y	MILDEW-Y	RIFLER-Y	SQUISH-Y
CINDER-Y	GADGET-Y	MISTER-Y	ROBBER-Y	STAGER-Y
CIRCUS-Y	GAGGER-Y	MOCKER-Y	ROCKER-Y	STARCH-Y
CITRUS-Y	GALANT-Y	MODEST-Y	RUBBER-Y	STARTS-Y
CLIQUE-Y	GARGET-Y	MONGER-Y	RUBBIT-Y	STATUS-Y
CLOVER-Y	GEODES-Y	MORALL-Y	RUSSET-Y	STENCH-Y
CLUTCH-Y	GINGER-Y	MORASS-Y	SALLOW-Y	STREAK-Y
COLOUR-Y	GINNER-Y	MORTAR-Y	SATRAP-Y	STREAM-Y
COOKER-Y	GLITCH-Y	MOTHER-Y	SAVOUR-Y	STREET-Y
COOPER-Y	GOSSIP-Y	MOUSER-Y	SCRAWL-Y	STRING-Y
COPPER-Y	GRAVEL-Y	MUMMER-Y	SCREAK-Y	STRIPE-Y
COSHER-Y	GROCER-Y	MUTTON-Y	SCRIMP-Y	SUCCOR-Y
COTTON-Y	GROUCH-Y	NAILER-Y	SCRUFF-Y	SULFUR-Y
CRAMES-Y	GROWTH-Y	NATTER-Y	SCRUMP-Y	SUMMAR-Y
CREESH-Y	GRUMPH-Y	NAUGHT-Y	SCRUNT-Y	SUMMER-Y
CRUNCH-Y	GULLER-Y	NECTAR-Y	SEALER-Y	SURGER-Y
CURSOR-Y	GUNNER-Y	NIGGER-Y	SENSOR-Y	SUTLER-Y
CUTLER-Y	GUTTER-Y	NOSHER-Y	SERVER-Y	SWARTH-Y

SWITCH-Y	THROAT-Y	TURNER-Y	VICTOR-Y	WIGGER-Y
TACKET-Y	TIDDLE-Y	TWITCH-Y	VILLAN-Y	WILLOW-Y
TALLOW-Y	TIMBER-Y	TYMPAN-Y	WAGGER-Y	WINDOW-Y
TANNER-Y	TINDER-Y	UNHAND-Y	WASHER-Y	WINTER-Y
TATTER-Y	TISSUE-Y	UNREAD-Y	WASTER-Y	WORMER-Y
THATCH-Y	TITTUP-Y	UNTENT-Y	WEALTH-Y	WREATH-Y
THIRST-Y	TOGGER-Y	VALLAR-Y	WEASEL-Y	YELLOW-Y
THREAD-Y	TOTTER-Y	VAPOUR-Y	WEEDER-Y	
THRIFT-Y	TRACER-Y	VELVET-Y	WEEVIL-Y	
THRILL-Y	TRICKS-Y	VERMIL-Y	WEIGHT-Y	
THRIST-Y	TRIPOD-Y	VERMIN-Y	WHALER-Y	

Seven letters to eight

ACTRESS-Y	CITATOR-Y	FLUTTER-Y	LACUNAR-Y	QUIZZER-Y
ADVISOR-Y	CLATTER-Y	FRIPPER-Y	LAMINAR-Y	RAINBOW-Y
ANTILOG-Y	CLERUCH-Y	FROTHER-Y	LEATHER-Y	RECOVER-Y
ANTIQUE-Y	CLUSTER-Y	FRUITER-Y	LYSOGEN-Y	REFINER-Y
ANTONYM-Y	CLUTTER-Y	FURRIER-Y	MERONYM-Y	REVISOR-Y
APOCARP-Y	COBBLER-Y	GARBAGE-Y	METONYM-Y	RHUBARB-Y
APOPLEX-Y	COLLIER-Y	GEALOUS-Y	MILITAR-Y	ROLLICK-Y
AUDITOR-Y	CONCEIT-Y	GIMMICK-Y	MONARCH-Y	ROTATOR-Y
AUTARCH-Y	COSTUME-Y	GLAZIER-Y	MONITOR-Y	RUBBISH-Y
AXILLAR-Y	COTTAGE-Y	GLIBBER-Y	MONOLOG-Y	SACRIST-Y
BASILAR-Y	CRAUNCH-Y	GLIDDER-Y	MONOPOD-Y	SADDLER-Y
BASTARD-Y	CREAMER-Y	GLIMMER-Y	MULLOCK-Y	SAFFRON-Y
BISCUIT-Y	CROOKER-Y	GLITTER-Y	MUSTARD-Y	SAMPLER-Y
BLADDER-Y	CRYOGEN-Y	GLUTTON-Y	NAVARCH-Y	SAVAGER-Y
BLANKET-Y	CURATOR-Y	GOLIARD-Y	NEBBISH-Y	SAWDUST-Y
BLISTER-Y	CURRANT-Y	GREENER-Y	NEGATOR-Y	SCATTER-Y
BLOOMER-Y	CURRIER-Y	GRILLER-Y	NITPICK-Y	SCHLEPP-Y
BLOSSOM-Y	CUSHION-Y	GRINDER-Y	NOMARCH-Y	SCHLOCK-Y
BLUBBER-Y	CUSTARD-Y	GROWLER-Y	ORANGER-Y	SCHLUMP-Y
BLUSTER-Y	DASTARD-Y	GYRATOR-Y	ORDINAR-Y	SCHMALZ-Y
BOTCHER-Y	DELIVER-Y	HAPLOID-Y	OUTWEAR-Y	SCHMOOZ-Y
BOULDER-Y	DEMAGOG-Y	HARMOST-Y	OVERMAN-Y	SCRATCH-Y
BRAZIER-Y	DILATOR-Y	HASSOCK-Y	PARADOX-Y	SCREECH-Y
BROIDER-Y	DIPLOID-Y	HATCHER-Y	PARONYM-Y	SCRUNCH-Y
BULLOCK-Y	DONATOR-Y	HATCHET-Y	PATCHER-Y	SCULLER-Y
BULRUSH-Y	DRAUGHT-Y	HEATHER-Y	PEACOCK-Y	SEMINAR-Y
BURGLAR-Y	DREAMER-Y	HEGEMON-Y	PEASANT-Y	SHATTER-Y
BUTCHER-Y	DROLLER-Y	HEGUMEN-Y	PEDAGOG-Y	SHELTER-Y
CABBAGE-Y	DROUGHT-Y	HEXAPOD-Y	PEDDLER-Y	SHIMMER-Y
CACONYM-Y	DRUDGER-Y	HEXARCH-Y	PERCHER-Y	SHUDDER-Y
CAJOLER-Y	ENACTOR-Y	HILLOCK-Y	PHANTOM-Y	SIGNIOR-Y
CALAMAR-Y	ENDARCH-Y	HOMOLOG-Y	PIZZAZZ-Y	SKITTER-Y
CANTICO-Y	ENDOGEN-Y	HOMONYM-Y	PLASTER-Y	SLABBER-Y
CARTOON-Y	ENGINER-Y	HUMMOCK-Y	PLUMBER-Y	SLATTER-Y
CENTAUR-Y	ENTREAT-Y	HYDROPS-Y	POLYGAM-Y	SLEEPER-Y
CHAFFER-Y	EUPLOID-Y	HYPONYM-Y	POLYGON-Y	SLIDDER-Y
CHANCER-Y	EVANGEL-Y	INCISOR-Y	POLYMER-Y	SLIPPER-Y
CHATTER-Y	FARRIER-Y	INTRADA-Y	POLYPOD-Y	SLITHER-Y
CHEATER-Y	FASHION-Y	JANIZAR-Y	PRIGGER-Y	SLOBBER-Y
CHEDDAR-Y	FEATHER-Y	JEALOUS-Y	PRINTER-Y	SLUMBER-Y
CHEVRON-Y	FLACKER-Y	JEOPARD-Y	PSALTER-Y	SMELTER-Y
CHIEFER-Y	FLATTER-Y	JUGGLER-Y	PUDDING-Y	SMOTHER-Y
CHIFFON-Y	FLAVOUR-Y	KNACKER-Y	PUPILAR-Y	SMUGGER-Y
CHIRRUP-Y	FLICKER-Y	KOLKHOS-Y	QUACKER-Y	SNICKER-Y
CIRCUIT-Y	FLUSTER-Y	KOLKHOZ-Y	QUIDDIT-Y	

SNIPPET-Y	SQUELCH-Y	SYNONYM-Y	TRIARCH-Y	UNWATER-Y
SNOTTER-Y	SQUOOSH-Y	TABLOID-Y	TRICKER-Y	UNWORTH-Y
SNUGGER-Y	STAGGER-Y	TASSELL-Y	TRIFFID-Y	VARNISH-Y
SOLDIER-Y	STEALTH-Y	THEOLOG-Y	TRIPPER-Y	VAUNTER-Y
SOLICIT-Y	STEMMER-Y	THICKET-Y	TROLLOP-Y	VAVASOR-Y
SOVKHOZ-Y	STOMACH-Y	THUNDER-Y	TUMULAR-Y	VILLAIN-Y
SPINACH-Y	STRETCH-Y	TITULAR-Y	TUSSOCK-Y	VINEGAR-Y
SPINNER-Y	STUDENT-Y	TOPARCH-Y	TUTELAR-Y	WARRANT-Y
SPLOTCH-Y	SULPHUR-Y	TOPONYM-Y	TWITTER-Y	WHISKER-Y
SPOOFER-Y	SUNBEAM-Y	TOURIST-Y	UNCLOUD-Y	WHISPER-Y
SPUTTER-Y	SYNCARP-Y	TRASHER-Y	UNTRUST-Y	

Eight letters to nine

ADULATOR-Y	DAYDREAM-Y	IMMODEST-Y	PAPILLAR-Y	SLAISTER-Y
ALLOPATH-Y	DEMOCRAT-Y	IMPLICIT-Y	PARAFFIN-Y	SOAPSUDS-Y
ALLOTTER-Y	DEVIATOR-Y	INCENSOR-Y	PATHOGEN-Y	SPLINTER-Y
AMPULLAR-Y	DICTATOR-Y	INVENTOR-Y	PEDERAST-Y	SPLUTTER-Y
ANAGLYPH-Y	DIRECTOR-Y	JEWELLER-Y	PENTARCH-Y	SQUEAKER-Y
ANTIPHON-Y	DISCOVER-Y	LAUDATOR-Y	PERFUMER-Y	SQUIRREL-Y
ASPERSOR-Y	EDUCATOR-Y	LOGOMACH-Y	PERIPTER-Y	STIPULAR-Y
ASSERTOR-Y	ELEVATOR-Y	MAGISTER-Y	PHOTOGEN-Y	STITCHER-Y
AUXILIAR-Y	EMANATOR-Y	MALINGER-Y	PHYLARCH-Y	SUBAHDAR-Y
BACILLAR-Y	EMBRACER-Y	MAMILLAR-Y	PISCATOR-Y	SUBLIMIT-Y
BIOGRAPH-Y	ENGRAVER-Y	MANDATOR-Y	POLYARCH-Y	SUBLUNAR-Y
BLEACHER-Y	EPIGRAPH-Y	MAXILLAR-Y	POLYMATH-Y	TAUTONYM-Y
BLIZZARD-Y	ETHNARCH-Y	MEDIATOR-Y	POLYONYM-Y	TELEPATH-Y
BOUTIQUE-Y	EUDAEMON-Y	MEDULLAR-Y	POLYPHON-Y	TETRAPOD-Y
BRANCHER-Y	EVOCATOR-Y	MIGRATOR-Y	PREDATOR-Y	TETRARCH-Y
BRIMFULL-Y	EXECUTOR-Y	MILLINER-Y	PRODITOR-Y	THEOSOPH-Y
BUSINESS-Y	EXEMPLAR-Y	MOUNTAIN-Y	PROVISOR-Y	TREACHER-Y
CALCULAR-Y	EXPIATOR-Y	MYOGRAPH-Y	PULSATOR-Y	TRIPLOID-Y
CAPSULAR-Y	FLOURISH-Y	MYSTAGOG-Y	PUPILLAR-Y	TRIUMVIR-Y
CHANDLER-Y	FOOTWEAR-Y	NARRATOR-Y	RADIATOR-Y	UNHEALTH-Y
CHARCOAL-Y	FORMULAR-Y	NONSTICK-Y	RAKEHELL-Y	UNTHRIFT-Y
CHICANER-Y	FREEBOOT-Y	NUMMULAR-Y	SCAPULAR-Y	VEXILLAR-Y
CINNAMON-Y	GOSSAMER-Y	OENOPHIL-Y	SCHMALTZ-Y	VIBRATOR-Y
COLOPHON-Y	GRANULAR-Y	OKEYDOKE-Y	SCOUTHER-Y	VILLAGER-Y
CONNIVER-Y	HAWTHORN-Y	OLIGARCH-Y	SECRETOR-Y	VISCOUNT-Y
CONTRAST-Y	HEADACHE-Y	OPSIMATH-Y	SEIGNEUR-Y	WHIFFLER-Y
COSTUMER-Y	HEPTARCH-Y	ORTHODOX-Y	SEIGNIOR-Y	WHIPCORD-Y
CREMATOR-Y	HIERARCH-Y	OSTEOGEN-Y	SERGEANT-Y	ZAMINDAR-Y
CROTCHET-Y	HISTOGEN-Y	OUTDOORS-Y	SERJEANT-Y	ZEMINDAR-Y
CURSITOR-Y	HUCKSTER-Y	OVERWEAR-Y	SINGSONG-Y	ZOOMORPH-Y
DANDRUFF-Y	HYPERNYM-Y	PALPATOR-Y	SINGULAR-Y	

Z – Front-hooks

Two letters to three

Z-AG	Z-EA	Z-EL	Z-IN	Z-OS
Z-AS	Z-ED	Z-EX	Z-IT	
Z-AX	Z-EE	Z-HO	Z-OO	

Three letters to four

Z-AGS	Z-ARF	Z-EDS	Z-ERK	Z-ETA
Z-ANY	Z-EAS	Z-ELS	Z-EST	Z-HOS

Z-IFF	Z-ITS	Z-OOM	Z-OOT
Z-ILL	Z-OBO	Z-OON	Z-OUK
Z-INS	Z-ONE	Z-OOS	Z-ULU

Four letters to five

Z-AMBO	Z-AYIN	Z-EXES	Z-OBOS	Z-OPPO
Z-AMIA	Z-ERKS	Z-HOMO	Z-ONER	Z-OUKS
Z-ANTE	Z-EROS	Z-ILLS	Z-ONES	Z-ULUS
Z-ARFS	Z-ESTS	Z-INKY	Z-OOMS	Z-UPAS
Z-AXES	Z-ETAS	Z-LOTE	Z-OONS	

Five letters to six

Z-AMBOS	Z-ANTES	Z-HOMOS	Z-ITHER
Z-AMIAS	Z-AYINS	Z-IGGED	Z-ONERS
Z-ANANA	Z-ESTER	Z-INKED	

Six letters to seven

Z-ANANAS	Z-INCITE	Z-OOGAMY	Z-OOLITE	Z-ORBING
Z-ESTERS	Z-INKIER	Z-OOGENY	Z-OOLITH	
Z-IGGING	Z-INKING	Z-OOIDAL	Z-OOLOGY	

Seven letters to eight

Z-INCITES	Z-ONETIME	Z-OOLITHS	Z-OOLOGIC	Z-OOSPERM
Z-INKIEST	Z-OOLITES	Z-OOLITIC	Z-OOPHYTE	Z-OOSPORE

Eight letters to nine

Z-OOGAMETE	Z-OOGENIES	Z-OOPHYTES	Z-OOSPORES
Z-OOGAMIES	Z-OOLOGIES	Z-OOPHYTIC	Z-OOSPORIC
Z-OOGAMOUS	Z-OOLOGIST	Z-OOSPERMS	

Z – End-hooks

Two letters to three

AD-Z	BI-Z	MI-Z	PO-Z
BE-Z	FE-Z	MO-Z	RE-Z

Three letters to four

CHE-Z	GEE-Z	MIZ-Z	POZ-Z	SIT-Z
CHI-Z	JEE-Z	MOZ-Z	PRE-Z	SPA-Z
DIT-Z	JIZ-Z	OYE-Z	PUT-Z	ZIZ-Z
FIZ-Z	LEZ-Z	PHI-Z	RIT-Z	

Four letters to five

BORT-Z	FRIT-Z	GREN-Z	SPAZ-Z	WARE-Z
CAPI-Z	FRIZ-Z	MILT-Z	SPIT-Z	WHIZ-Z
CHIZ-Z	GLIT-Z	PLOT-Z	SWIZ-Z	WOOT-Z

Z – Front-hooks

Five letters to six

PIZZA-Z   SPELT-Z
QUART-Z   SPRIT-Z

Six letters to seven

PIZZAZ-Z
SCHNOZ-Z

Blockers

Blockers are the opposite of hooks. They are words which cannot have a letter added at the beginning or end. These are extremely useful to know, as they allow you to close down whole sections of the board to your opponents. The following lists show blockers of two to six letters in length. Not included in the five and six-letter lists are words with endings that obviously preclude a single letter being added at the end: -ED, -J, -S, -X, -Y and -Z.

Two-letter words

FY
XU

Three-letter words

AUE	FRY	NOX	SAE	TWP
BEZ	GEY	NTH	SAZ	VLY
CAZ	GOX	NYS	SEZ	VOX
CLY	HEX	OXO	SHH	WOX
CUZ	HMM	PAX	SIX	YAE
DUH	HOX	PHT	SLY	YEH
DUX	KEX	PLY	SMA	YEX
FAE	LOX	POH	SOX	YOS
FAP	LUZ	PST	SWY	ZAS
FAX	MUX	PYX	TAJ	ZAX
FEW	NAE	QIS	THY	ZEX
FEZ	NAH	RAX	TIX	ZOA
FLY	NOH	RHY	TUX	ZUZ

Four-letter words

AAHS	AJEE	AROW	BANS	BEVY
ABBS	ALAE	ASEA	BAPS	BHAT
ABLY	ALBS	AVOS	BATS	BIBS
ABOS	ALEE	AWRY	BAYS	BIDS
ACHY	ALIT	AXAL	BEDS	BIEN
ADRY	ALSO	AYUS	BEDU	BIGS
AESC	ANEW	BAAS	BEEN	BINS
AGLY	ANOW	BABY	BEES	BIOS
AHEM	APEX	BADE	BEGS	BISH
AHIS	APTS	BADS	BELS	BIST
AHOY	AREG	BAGS	BENJ	BLEW
AJAR	AREW	BAMS	BENS	BOBS

BODS	COXY	DOPY	FAHS	GAGS
BODY	COYS	DORY	FAIX	GALS
BOGS	COZY	DOSH	FALX	GAMY
BOGY	CRUX	DOSS	FANS	GANS
BOHS	CUBS	DOST	FASH	GAPS
BOIS	CUED	DOTH	FAUX	GAPY
BOKS	CUES	DOTS	FAWS	GARE
BONA	CURT	DOTY	FEDS	GASH
BOPS	CWMS	DOUN	FEET	GATS
BORS	DABS	DOUX	FEGS	GAYS
BOSH	DADS	DOWF	FEHS	GAZY
BOTS	DAES	DOXY	FEMS	GEDS
BOXY	DAFT	DOYS	FENS	GEED
BRRR	DAGS	DOZY	FETS	GEEZ
BRUX	DAKS	DREW	FEUS	GELS
BUBO	DAMS	DRYS	FEYS	GEMS
BUBS	DANS	DUBS	FIBS	GENS
BUDS	DAPS	DUCI	FIDS	GEOS
BUGS	DAVY	DUDS	FIFI	GERT
BUMS	DEAF	DUED	FIGS	GETS
BUNS	DEBS	DUES	FIKY	GHIS
BURY	DEEK	DUGS	FILS	GIBS
BUSY	DEFT	DULY	FINS	GIDS
BUYS	DEFY	DUOS	FITS	GIED
CAAS	DEGS	DUPS	FIXT	GIEN
CAGY	DELS	DUSH	FLED	GIES
CAKY	DEMY	DUTY	FLIX	GIGS
CALX	DENY	DYED	FLUX	GINS
CANY	DESI	DYES	FOBS	GITS
CAPS	DEUS	DZOS	FOCI	GIZZ
CASH	DEVS	EASY	FOEN	GJUS
CAUF	DEWS	EBBS	FOES	GLEG
CAVY	DEWY	ECOD	FOGS	GNUS
CAYS	DEXY	ECUS	FOGY	GOAS
CEES	DEYS	EDDO	FOHS	GOBS
CELS	DIBS	EDHS	FONE	GOBY
CEPS	DIDY	EHED	FONS	GOES
CHEZ	DIED	EINA	FOPS	GOEY
CHIS	DIEL	ELHI	FOUS	GORY
CIGS	DIES	ELMY	FOXY	GOVS
CITO	DIFS	ELSE	FOYS	GOYS
CITS	DIGS	EMUS	FOZY	GREX
CITY	DIMS	EMYS	FRAE	GUBS
COAX	DINS	ENUF	FROM	GULS
COBS	DIPT	EOAN	FUCI	GULY
COCH	DISS	ESPY	FUDS	GUMS
CODS	DIVS	EUGE	FUGS	GUNS
COFT	DIXY	EUOI	FUMS	GUPS
COKY	DOBS	EVOE	FUMY	GUVS
COLS	DOBY	EVOS	FUNS	GYMS
COLY	DOCS	EWKS	FURS	GYNY
COMS	DODS	EYES	FURY	GYRI
CONY	DOEN	EYNE	FUSC	HAED
COPY	DOGS	EYRY	FUTZ	HAEN
CORF	DOGY	FAAN	GABS	HAES
CORY	DOHS	FAAS	GABY	HAZY
COSH	DOMS	FABS	GAED	HEHS
COSS	DOMY	FADS	GAEN	HELD
COSY	DOOS	FADY	GAES	HEMS
COWY	DOPS	FAGS	GAGA	HEPS

Blockers

HEPT	JOBS	LANX	MIRO	NUNS
HISN	JOCO	LARS	MIRY	NYAS
HIYA	JOES	LATI	MIXY	NYED
HOAX	JOGS	LATU	MNAS	OAKY
HOBS	JOKY	LAVS	MOAI	OBIS
HODS	JOLS	LECH	MOAS	OCCY
HOHA	JORS	LEKE	MOBS	ODDS
HOKA	JOSH	LEKS	MOBY	ODEA
HOLP	JOSS	LEKU	MOCS	OHMS
HOLY	JOTS	LEPS	MODS	OKAS
HOMS	JOWS	LEVA	MOES	OLEA
HOMY	JOYS	LEVO	MOLS	ONST
HOSS	JUDS	LEVY	MOLY	ONYX
HOYS	JUDY	LEWD	MOMI	OPTS
HUED	JUGS	LIDS	MOMS	ORFS
HUES	JURY	LIGS	MONS	ORYX
HUGY	JUTS	LIPA	MONY	OSAR
HUIC	JYNX	LIRE	MOOI	OYEZ
HUIS	KAAL	LIRI	MOPY	PACS
HUNG	KAAS	LITU	MOSH	PADS
HUNH	KABS	LOCI	MOTS	PALY
HWAN	KAED	LORN	MOWN	PAPS
HYED	KAES	LUDS	MOWS	PATY
HYES	KAFS	LUNY	MOYS	PAVS
HYPS	KAIS	LUVS	MOZZ	PEDS
HYTE	KAKS	LYCH	MUDS	PEGS
IBIS	KEAS	LYES	MUNS	PEHS
ICHS	KEBS	LYMS	MYCS	PEPS
IDEM	KEDS	LYNX	NADS	PFFT
IDLY	KEFS	LYRA	NAIN	PFUI
IGAD	KEKS	MAAS	NAMS	PHAT
ILKA	KEPT	MADE	NAMU	PHEW
INIA	KESH	MADS	NANS	PHIZ
INLY	KETE	MAES	NAOI	PHOS
INRO	KEWL	MAGS	NAOS	PIAS
IURE	KEYS	MAKS	NAVY	PIGS
JABS	KHIS	MALS	NAYS	PILY
JAGS	KIFS	MANY	NEFS	PIPS
JAKS	KILD	MAPS	NEGS	PIPY
JAMS	KIRS	MARY	NEKS	PIRS
JAPS	KISH	MATS	NEPS	PISS
JARS	KNEW	MATY	NESH	PITY
JASS	KOAS	MAWN	NESS	PIXY
JASY	KOBS	MAWS	NETS	PLEX
JAWS	KOIS	MAZY	NEVI	POAS
JAXY	KOPS	MEDS	NIDI	POCO
JAYS	KORO	MEGS	NIDS	POGY
JAZY	KORS	MELS	NIED	POKY
JEED	KOSS	MEMS	NIMS	POLS
JEES	KOWS	MENO	NISI	POMS
JEEZ	KRIS	METS	NIXY	PONS
JEON	KUEH	MHOS	NODI	PONY
JETS	KUES	MIBS	NOES	POOS
JEUX	KUNA	MICS	NOMS	PORY
JEWS	KUNE	MIGS	NOPE	POSY
JIBS	KYES	MIHA	NOSH	POWS
JIGS	KYNE	MILS	NOSY	PREZ
JINX	KYUS	MINX	NOTT	PRUH
JIVY	LACS	MINY	NOUS	PSST
JIZZ	LACY	MIPS	NOYS	PTUI

PUBS	SEIK	SUSS	TYGS	WIRY
PUGH	SELD	SWUM	TYPY	WOES
PUIR	SELS	SYED	UNDO	WOFS
PUKA	SENE	SYES	UPGO	WOGS
PULY	SEPS	TADS	UPSY	WOKS
PUNS	SESH	TAED	UVAE	WONS
PUNY	SETS	TAES	UVAS	WOST
PUPS	SEWN	TAKS	VACS	WOWF
PUTS	SEWS	TAKY	VAES	WOWS
PUTZ	SEXY	TALI	VAGI	WUDS
PUYS	SEYS	TAMS	VAGS	WYCH
PYAS	SHAT	TAOS	VAIN	WYES
PYES	SHMO	TAUS	VANS	WYNS
PYIC	SHOD	TAVS	VARS	YABA
QATS	SIBS	TAXA	VATS	YAGS
QUEP	SICS	TECS	VAUS	YALD
RACA	SIES	TEDY	VAVS	YAPS
RAHS	SIMS	TEES	VAWS	YAWS
RAZZ	SINS	TEFS	VEES	YAWY
REBS	SIPS	TEGS	VERA	YAYS
RECS	SIRS	TELD	VERD	YBET
REFS	SITS	TELS	VETO	YEBO
REFT	SITZ	TELT	VEXT	YEPS
REHS	SIZY	THAE	VIAE	YEWS
RELY	SJOE	THAT	VIAS	YGOE
RENK	SKAS	THEY	VIBS	YIDS
RENY	SKIS	THIS	VIDS	YIPS
REOS	SKRY	THUS	VIGS	YMPT
RHOS	SOBS	TICS	VIMS	YOBS
RHUS	SOCS	TIDS	VINS	YODS
RIFS	SODS	TIDY	VIVO	YOKS
ROED	SOGS	TIGS	VIZY	YOLD
ROKY	SOHO	TILS	VOES	YOND
ROPY	SOHS	TINS	VOLS	YOWS
ROUX	SOLS	TINY	VORS	YUCH
RUBY	SOME	TIPT	VROT	YUGS
RUCS	SOMS	TITS	VUGS	YUKS
RUNS	SOMY	TOBY	VUMS	YUKY
RYAS	SOON	TODS	WADY	YUNX
RYES	SOPS	TODY	WANY	YUPS
RYFE	SORI	TOED	WARY	YUTZ
SABS	SOSS	TOES	WAVY	YWIS
SACS	SOTS	TOEY	WAWS	ZAGS
SADS	SOVS	TOGS	WAXY	ZANY
SAFT	SOYS	TOLD	WEBS	ZAPS
SAGS	SPED	TONS	WEDS	ZEAS
SAGY	SPRY	TORN	WEMS	ZEDS
SAMS	SRIS	TOWY	WENA	ZEKS
SAPS	STEY	TOYS	WENS	ZELS
SASH	SUBS	TREZ	WERE	ZEPS
SAVS	SUCH	TSKS	WERT	ZIGS
SAWN	SUES	TUGS	WETS	ZINS
SAWS	SUKS	TUNY	WHAE	ZIPS
SCRY	SUMS	TUPS	WHIO	ZITE
SECO	SUMY	TUTS	WHOA	ZITS
SECS	SUNG	TUZZ	WHOT	ZIZZ
SEEN	SUNS	TWAS	WHYS	ZOLS
SEES	SUPS	TWOS	WICH	ZOOS
SEGS	SUQS	TYDE	WILY	ZZZS

Five-letter words

(The list does not include words ending in -ED, -J, -S, -X, -Y, -Z.)

AARGH	ALIKE	AWATO	BRUSK	CROST
ABACI	ALIVE	AWAVE	BUFFA	CRUSH
ABACK	ALOFT	AWEEL	BUFFI	CUFFO
ABAFT	ALONE	AWORK	BUILT	CUING
ABASH	ALOOF	AXIAL	BURNT	CUISH
ABASK	ALOUD	AXILE	BUTCH	CUNEI
ABEAM	ALOWE	AYELP	BUXOM	CURCH
ABLOW	ALTHO	AYGRE	BYSSI	CURLI
ABOIL	AMAIN	AYONT	CABRE	CURSI
ABORE	AMICI	AZIDO	CACTI	CURST
ABRAM	AMINO	AZOIC	CAESE	CWTCH
ABRIM	AMNIA	AZURN	CAJON	CYANO
ABUNE	AMNIC	BAITH	CAJUN	CYBER
ACERB	AMONG	BAKEN	CALID	CYMAE
ACHOO	AMORT	BANAL	CANST	DAWEN
ACMIC	ANILE	BARER	CAPUT	DAYCH
ACOCK	ANSAE	BARIC	CARPI	DAYNT
ACOLD	ANTAE	BASHO	CECAL	DEALT
ACRID	APACE	BASSI	CECUM	DEASH
ADOWN	APAGE	BASTA	CERIC	DEDAL
ADOZE	APAID	BATCH	CESTI	DEERE
ADRAD	APART	BEDAD	CHAPT	DEFFO
ADSUM	APAYD	BEEDI	CHAVE	DEMIC
ADUNC	APEAK	BEGAD	CHERE	DEMPT
ADYTA	APEEK	BEGAN	CHIAO	DESHI
AESIR	APERT	BEGAT	CHIMO	DIACT
AFALD	APGAR	BEGOT	CHODE	DICTA
AFIRE	APIAN	BELCH	CHOTA	DIDST
AFOOT	APOOP	BERKO	CHYND	DINGO
AFORE	APORT	BESAT	CILIA	DINNA
AFOUL	APTER	BESAW	CINCH	DIRER
AGAIN	AQUAE	BIFID	CINCT	DISCI
AGAST	AREAE	BIGAE	CIPPI	DITCH
AGGRI	AREAL	BINAL	CIRRI	DOCHT
AGLEE	AREAR	BIRCH	CIVIL	DOEST
AGLOW	AREDD	BITOU	CLAPT	DOETH
AGOOD	AREIC	BIVIA	CLASH	DOGGO
AGRIN	ARERE	BLAER	CLIPT	DOILT
AHEAD	ARIKI	BLASE	CLOMB	DOLCI
AHEAP	ARIOT	BLAWN	CLUNG	DOLIA
AHENT	AROSE	BLIST	COMAE	DOMAL
AHIGH	ARUHE	BLIVE	COMAL	DOMIC
AHIND	ASKEW	BLOWN	COOST	DONER
AHINT	ASKOI	BLUER	CORAM	DORIC
AHULL	ASTIR	BOEUF	CORNI	DOTAL
AHURU	ASWIM	BOLAR	CORNO	DOWNA
AIDOI	ASYLA	BONZA	COUDE	DRACK
AINEE	ATILT	BOREL	COULD	DRACO
AITCH	ATRIP	BORIC	COURD	DRANK
ALACK	AULIC	BORNA	COXAE	DRAVE
ALANE	AULOI	BOWIE	COXAL	DRAWN
ALBEE	AURAL	BOXEN	COYER	DRENT
ALEFT	AURAR	BRAVI	CRASH	DREST
ALGAE	AUREI	BREEM	CREPT	DRIPT
ALGAL	AVAST	BREME	CROCI	DROPT
ALGID	AWASH	BRUNG	CRONK	DUCAL

DUING	GAYER	HOVEN	LEAPT	MOOSE
DUMKA	GEESE	HOWBE	LEASH	MORAE
DUNCH	GELID	HOWSO	LEISH	MOSSO
DUNNO	GENAL	HUGER	LEPID	MOSTE
DUNSH	GENIC	HUMIC	LEPTA	MOTEN
DUOMI	GENII	HUMID	LEUCO	MUCHO
DURST	GENUA	HUNCH	LIART	MUCIC
DUTCH	GESSO	HUTCH	LIBRI	MUCID
DWELT	GEYAN	ICTIC	LITAI	MULCH
EHING	GEYER	ILEAC	LIVID	MULSH
ELMEN	GHEST	ILEAL	LOACH	MUNCH
EMONG	GIGHE	ILIAC	LOAST	MUSHA
ENLIT	GINZO	IMIDO	LOBAR	MUTER
ENORM	GIRSH	IMINO	LOGOI	MYOID
ETYMA	GLIAL	IMSHI	LOSEN	NAEVI
EVHOE	GLODE	INAPT	LOTIC	NANUA
EVOHE	GNASH	INBYE	LOYAL	NARIC
EWHOW	GNAWN	INCUT	LUACH	NARRE
EYRIR	GOBBI	INEPT	LUCID	NATAL
FATAL	GOBBO	INERM	LUDIC	NAUCH
FAUGH	GOIER	INFRA	LUMME	NAVAL
FAURD	GONIA	INTIL	LURCH	NEGRO
FAVER	GONNA	INTRA	LURID	NEIST
FAYER	GONZO	INUST	LYARD	NEMPT
FECAL	GOPIK	IODIC	LYART	NEVER
FECIT	GOTTA	ISNAE	LYCEA	NEWER
FEHME	GOYIM	JEUNE	LYNCH	NGWEE
FERER	GRANA	JINGO	LYTIC	NICER
FETAL	GREEK	JIRRE	MAARE	NIDAL
FETCH	GRIPT	JOKOL	MACHI	NIMBI
FETID	GROWN	JOMON	MADID	NITID
FEWER	GRYPT	JURAL	MANET	NIVAL
FEYER	GULAR	KACHA	MAPAU	NOHOW
FILAR	GULCH	KAMME	MARCH	NOMEN
FILCH	GURSH	KANAE	MARIA	NOMOI
FILUM	GWINE	KASME	MAYAN	NOOIT
FINCH	GYRAL	KAURU	MAYST	NOTAL
FLITT	HABLE	KAWAU	MEANT	NOTUM
FLOSH	HADAL	KEECH	MEDII	NOVAE
FLOWN	HADST	KEMPT	MEINT	NOXAL
FLUNG	HAITH	KENCH	MENSH	NUDER
FOCAL	HANCH	KIDGE	MERCH	NUDZH
FOLIC	HARSH	KINDA	MERER	NUGAE
FORDO	HASTA	KIORE	MESAL	NUMEN
FORZA	HATHA	KLIEG	MESIC	NUTSO
FORZE	HAULT	KNELT	MEYNT	NYING
FOUER	HAUTE	KNISH	MICRA	OATEN
FRACK	HEAME	KORAI	MIKRA	OBIIT
FRAPE	HEMAL	KOTCH	MILCH	OBOLI
FRATI	HEWGH	KOURA	MILIA	OGMIC
FRENA	HIANT	KRONA	MINAE	OHMIC
FROSH	HILAR	KYDST	MISCH	OHONE
FRUSH	HILCH	LABRA	MISDO	OIDIA
FUBAR	HILUM	LAEVO	MISGO	OLEIC
FUGAL	HINAU	LAITH	MITCH	OLPAE
FUNGO	HOING	LARCH	MIXTE	ONCET
FURTH	HOKKU	LAXER	MODII	ORGIC
GADJO	HOOCH	LAZZI	MOHUA	OSSIA
GANCH	HOTCH	LAZZO	MOLAL	OTAKU
GARNI	HOTEN	LEANT	MOLTO	OUTDO

Blockers

OUTGO	PYOID	SESSA	STAID	TONDI
OVOLI	PYRAL	SETAE	STASH	TONKA
OWSEN	PYRIC	SETAL	STEPT	TOPHI
PACTA	QUALE	SHAKT	STOAE	TOPOI
PADRI	QUASI	SHALT	STOAI	TORII
PAISE	QUAYD	SHASH	STOLN	TORSI
PAKKA	QUOAD	SHAWN	STONG	TRAPT
PALER	QURSH	SHERE	STOOD	TRIFF
PALPI	RABID	SHEWN	STOPT	TRILD
PAOLI	RADII	SHIUR	STUMM	TRUER
PAOLO	RAGDE	SHONE	STUNG	TRYMA
PAPAL	RAMAL	SHOON	STUNK	TUBAE
PAPPI	RAREE	SHOPE	STURE	TUBAL
PARAE	RARER	SHORN	SUCCI	TUBAR
PARVE	RASTA	SHOWN	SUENT	TUMID
PAVID	RAUPO	SHULN	SULCI	TYIYN
PAYSD	RECTI	SHUSH	SULFO	TYNDE
PEART	REDID	SIDHE	SUPRA	TYPAL
PELON	REJON	SIELD	SURAL	ULNAD
PENAL	RELIT	SIKER	SWACK	ULNAE
PENDU	REMET	SINCE	SWANG	ULPAN
PEPLA	RENAL	SITKA	SWAPT	UNAPT
PERCH	RERAN	SKEEF	SWARE	UNBID
PEREA	RESAT	SKINT	SWEPT	UNDEE
PETTI	REWAN	SKOSH	SWOLN	UNDID
PETTO	REWON	SLAID	SWOPT	UNDUE
PHPHT	RHYTA	SLAIN	SWORE	UNDUG
PHYLE	RIFER	SLANK	SWORN	UNETH
PIEZO	RIMAE	SLASH	SWUNG	UNGOT
PIING	RORAL	SLEER	SYKER	UNHIP
PILAR	RORIC	SLEPT	TABID	UNKID
PILCH	RORID	SLIER	TACIT	UNMET
PILEI	RUBAI	SLIPT	TAGMA	UNRID
PILUM	RUGAE	SLISH	TAISH	UNSOD
PINCH	RUNIC	SLUNG	TAKEN	UNWET
PLENA	RYPER	SLUNK	TANTI	UPBYE
PLESH	SAFER	SLYER	TANTO	UPLIT
POOCH	SAGUM	SMASH	TAPEN	UPRAN
PORAE	SAIST	SMOTE	TARDO	UPTER
PORCH	SALIC	SMUSH	TAULD	URAEI
POUPT	SAMEN	SNASH	TAZZE	URDEE
PRESA	SANER	SNOEP	TEACH	UREAL
PRIMI	SAPID	SNUCK	TELOI	UREIC
PROST	SATEM	SNUSH	TEMPI	URENT
PROUD	SAYNE	SOCKO	TEPID	URNAL
PSOAE	SAYST	SODIC	TEUCH	UTERI
PSOAI	SCAND	SOLDI	TEUGH	UVEAL
PUBIC	SCAPI	SOLDO	THAIM	VACUA
PUCER	SCUDI	SOPRA	THELF	VAGAL
PUCKA	SEELD	SORAL	THEMA	VAIRE
PUDIC	SEFER	SORBO	THIEF	VALID
PUKKA	SEGNI	SORDA	THILK	VAPID
PULIK	SENGI	SORER	THINE	VASAL
PULLI	SENSA	SOUCT	THOLI	VATIC
PULMO	SENTI	SPAKE	THOSE	VAUCH
PUPAE	SENZA	SPARD	THRAE	VEHME
PUPAL	SEPIC	SPAZA	THREW	VELUM
PURER	SERAL	SPENT	TICCA	VENAE
PUTID	SERER	SPRAD	TIDAL	VENAL
PUTTO	SERIC	SPUTA	TIMID	VERRA

VILDE	WAXEN	WOFUL	YCLAD	YTOST
VILLI	WELCH	WOKKA	YCOND	YUCCH
VIMEN	WELKT	WOMEN	YDRAD	YUCKO
VINIC	WELSH	WOMYN	YEVEN	YUMMO
VIOLD	WENCH	WOWEE	YEWEN	ZILCH
VIRAL	WERSH	WOXEN	YFERE	ZLOTE
VIRID	WHAMO	WRAPT	YINCE	ZOEAE
VITAE	WHICH	WRATE	YLIKE	ZOEAL
VIVID	WHILK	WROTE	YMOLT	ZONAE
VOILA	WHIPT	WROTH	YOGIC	ZOPPA
VOLAE	WHOSE	WRUNG	YOKUL	ZOPPO
VOLTA	WHOSO	WRYER	YOMIM	ZOWIE
VOLTI	WIDER	XERIC	YONIC	ZUZIM
VOULU	WILCO	XOANA	YOURN	ZYGAL
VULGO	WINCH	XYLIC	YOUSE	ZYGON
WAIDE	WINNA	XYSTI	YRAPT	ZYMIC
WANLE	WISER	YARER	YRENT	
WANNA	WISHA	YAULD	YRIVD	
WARST	WISHT	YBORE	YSAME	

Six-letter words

(The list does not include words ending in -ED, -J, -S, -X, -Y, -Z.)

AAHING	AFAWLD	ALEXIC	ANOUGH	ASHAKE
ABATTU	AFEARD	ALIBLE	ANOXIC	ASHINE
ABEIGH	AFFYDE	ALLYOU	ANTRAL	ASHORE
ABLAZE	AFIELD	ALMOST	ANURAL	ASHRAF
ABLEST	AFLAME	ALULAE	ANURIC	ASLANT
ABLOOM	AFLOAT	ALULAR	ANYHOW	ASLEEP
ABLUSH	AFRAID	ALUMNI	AORTAE	ASLOPE
ABOARD	AFRESH	ALVINE	AORTAL	ASLOSH
ABORAL	AFRONT	AMARNA	AORTIC	ASMEAR
ABORNE	AGAMIC	AMBACH	APEMAN	ASPOUT
ABULIC	AGAPAE	AMBUSH	APEMEN	ASQUAT
ABURST	AGAPAI	AMEBAE	APIECE	ASSOTT
ACETIC	AGHAST	AMEBAN	APNEAL	ASTARE
ACETUM	AGILER	AMEBIC	APNEIC	ASTOOP
ACHIER	AGLARE	AMIDIC	APODAL	ASTRUT
ACIDER	AGLEAM	AMIDST	APPAID	ASWARM
ACIDIC	AGOING	AMINIC	APPAYD	ASWING
ACINAR	AGONAL	AMMINO	APTEST	ASWIRL
ACINIC	AGONIC	AMMONO	APTING	ASWOON
ACKNEW	AGORAE	AMORAL	ARCANE	ATAVIC
ACRAWL	AGUISH	AMYLIC	ARCHEI	ATELIC
ACULEI	AHCHOO	ANCILE	ARDENT	ATHROB
ACUTER	AHORSE	ANCORA	AREACH	ATOKAL
ADIPIC	AIDANT	ANEATH	ARGULI	ATONAL
ADMIXT	AIDFUL	ANEMIC	ARGUTE	ATOPIC
ADNATE	AIDMAN	ANENST	ARIDER	ATWAIN
ADRIFT	AIDMEN	ANETIC	ARIGHT	ATWEEL
ADROIT	AIKONA	ANGOLA	ARILLI	ATWEEN
ADYTUM	AIMFUL	ANIGHT	ARIOSI	ATWIXT
ADZING	AIRMAN	ANISIC	ARISEN	ATYPIC
AECIAL	AIRMEN	ANKUSH	AROUND	AUDIAL
AECIUM	AKATEA	ANNULI	ARRIBA	AVANTI
AEDINE	AKIMBO	ANODAL	ARRISH	AVERSE
AEFALD	ALBEIT	ANODIC	ARSENO	AVIDER
AERIER	ALDERN	ANOMIC	ARSINO	AVITAL

Blockers

AVOUCH	BEHALF	BRAWER	CAUGHT	COSTAE
AWARER	BEHELD	BREACH	CAUSAE	COTTAE
AWATCH	BELIKE	BREECH	CAUSEN	COWIER
AWEIGH	BELIVE	BREGMA	CEDARN	COWISH
AWEING	BEMATA	BRICHT	CEDING	COWMAN
AWHATO	BEMIXT	BROKEN	CELLAE	COWMEN
AWHETO	BENIGN	BROMIC	CENDRE	COXIER
AWHILE	BEREFT	BROOCH	CENTAI	COXING
AWHIRL	BESANG	BRUMAL	CERCAL	COYEST
AWOKEN	BESEEN	BRUNCH	CERING	COYING
AWRACK	BESTAD	BRUTAL	CERULE	COYISH
AWRONG	BESUNG	BUCCAL	CHADRI	COZING
AWSOME	BETING	BUFFEL	CHANGA	CREANT
AXEMAN	BETOOK	BULBAR	CHELAE	CREDAL
AXEMEN	BETROD	BULLAE	CHEVAL	CRIANT
AXENIC	BEWENT	BUMALO	CHICER	CRIBLE
AXONAL	BEWEPT	BURSAE	CHOLIC	CRIMEN
AXONIC	BIAXAL	BURSAL	CHORIC	CRINAL
AZONAL	BIFOLD	BUSIER	CHOSEN	CRISIC
AZONIC	BIFORM	BUSMAN	CHOUSH	CROTCH
AZOTIC	BIGGER	BUSMEN	CHYLDE	CROUCH
BAALIM	BILING	BUYING	CICALE	CROUSE
BABIER	BIMBLE	BYDING	CIDING	CRUDER
BACCAE	BINATE	BYKING	CILIUM	CRURAL
BACULA	BINMAN	BYLIVE	CISTIC	CRUTCH
BADDER	BINMEN	BYPAST	CITING	CUBING
BADMAN	BIRKEN	CAAING	CITRIC	CUBITI
BADMEN	BISSON	CABMAN	CLASPT	CUEING
BAGMAN	BITTEN	CABMEN	CLATCH	CULPAE
BAGMEN	BIVIUM	CADENT	CLECHE	CULTIC
BALDER	BLAEST	CADMIC	CLENCH	CUMULI
BALING	BLAISE	CAECAL	CLEVER	CUNEAL
BANING	BLAIZE	CAECUM	CLINAL	CUPMAN
BANISH	BLANCH	CAGIER	CLINCH	CUPMEN
BARBAL	BLATER	CAGING	CLONAL	CUPRIC
BARDIC	BLEACH	CAKIER	CLONIC	CURIAE
BAREST	BLENCH	CALAMI	CLOVEN	CURIAL
BARFUL	BLOOIE	CALASH	CLUING	CURING
BARING	BLOTTO	CALCIC	CLUNCH	CURSAL
BARISH	BLUEST	CALLID	CLYING	CURTER
BARMAN	BLUIER	CALMER	CLYPEI	CURULE
BARMEN	BLUISH	CAMASH	CNIDAE	CUSPAL
BASEST	BOGMAN	CAMSHO	COAXAL	CUTCHA
BASSER	BOGMEN	CANIER	COBRIC	CYANIC
BATMAN	BOKING	CANNAE	COCCAL	CYMOID
BATMEN	BOLDER	CANNOT	COCCIC	CYMOSE
BAYMAN	BOLETI	CARDAN	COGENT	CYSTIC
BAYMEN	BOLLEN	CARDIO	COHOSH	CYTISI
BEATEN	BONIER	CARMAN	COITAL	CYTOID
BECAME	BONZER	CARMEN	COKIER	DADGUM
BEDASH	BOOING	CAROLI	COKING	DAEDAL
BEDIDE	BOREAL	CARRON	COMADE	DAEING
BEDRID	BOSHTA	CARTOP	COMETH	DAFTER
BEDYDE	BOSKER	CARVEN	COMODO	DAIMEN
BEFELD	BOSSER	CASEIC	COMOSE	DAMMIT
BEFELL	BOWMAN	CASINI	CONGII	DANISH
BEFORE	BOWMEN	CATCHT	CONING	DANKER
BEGILT	BOXIER	CATTLE	COOCOO	DARKER
BEGIRT	BOYING	CAUDAD	COSING	DAWISH
BEGONE	BOYISH	CAUDAE	COSMIC	DAYLIT

DAZING	DOURER	ENGILT	FAZING	FOETAL
DEAFER	DOVIER	ENGIRT	FEATER	FOETID
DEARER	DOVING	ENLEVE	FECUND	FOGASH
DEAWIE	DOVISH	ENMESH	FEEING	FOGMAN
DEBILE	DOWIER	ENODAL	FEHMIC	FOGMEN
DEBOSH	DOWING	ENOLIC	FEIRIE	FOLIAR
DECANI	DOZIER	ENRAPT	FELSIC	FONDER
DECENT	DREAMT	ENRICH	FENMAN	FONTAL
DEEDER	DREICH	EOCENE	FENMEN	FOOBAR
DEEING	DREIGH	EOTHEN	FEODAL	FORANE
DEEPER	DRENCH	EPHORI	FEREST	FORBYE
DEFFER	DRIEGH	EPICAL	FERIAE	FORDID
DEFTER	DRIEST	EPODIC	FERIAL	FOREDO
DEGAGE	DRIVEN	EQUALI	FERINE	FOREGO
DEIDER	DROLER	EREMIC	FERRIC	FORGAT
DEIFER	DROMIC	ERENOW	FERVID	FORGOT
DEIFIC	DROMOI	ERUCIC	FETING	FORMEE
DEKING	DRYEST	ERUVIM	FETISH	FORRAD
DELISH	DRYISH	ERUVIN	FEUDAL	FORREN
DELTIC	DUCTAL	ETERNE	FEUING	FORRIT
DELUXE	DUDING	ETYMIC	FEWEST	FOSSAE
DENSER	DUDISH	ETYPIC	FEYEST	FOUEST
DERING	DUEFUL	EURIPI	FEYING	FOULER
DERMAL	DUELLI	EWGHEN	FIFING	FOVEAE
DERMIC	DUETTI	EWKING	FIKIER	FOVEAL
DETACH	DUKING	EXEUNT	FIKING	FOXIER
DEVOID	DULLER	EXILIC	FIKISH	FOZIER
DEVOUT	DUMBER	EXODIC	FILIAL	FRACTI
DEWIER	DUMELA	EXODOI	FILMIC	FRAENA
DEWING	DUMOSE	EXONIC	FILOSE	FRANCO
DEXTRO	DUNNER	EXTOLD	FINEST	FREEST
DIAMYL	DUPING	EYEING	FINISH	FRENCH
DICIER	DURING	FAAING	FINITO	FRENNE
DIEING	DUSKER	FABBER	FINSKO	FRIGID
DIKIER	DYABLE	FACEUP	FISTIC	FROREN
DIKING	DYKIER	FACIAE	FITFUL	FRORNE
DINFUL	DYKING	FACILE	FIXIVE	FROZEN
DINING	EADISH	FADIER	FLANCH	FRUGAL
DINKER	EASIER	FAECAL	FLAXEN	FRUSTA
DIREST	EASSEL	FAINER	FLEECH	FULCRA
DISCAL	EASSIL	FAIRER	FLEMIT	FULGID
DISTAL	ECESIC	FAKING	FLENCH	FULVID
DITTIT	ECHINI	FALLEN	FLETCH	FUMIER
DJINNI	ECHOIC	FAMING	FLIEST	FUMING
DOABLE	EDENIC	FAMISH	FLINCH	FUMULI
DOGMAN	EFFETE	FAMULI	FLITCH	FUNDIC
DOGMEN	EGESTA	FARAND	FLOCCI	FUNEST
DOITIT	EIDENT	FARFET	FLOOIE	FUNGIC
DOLING	EIDOLA	FARING	FLORAE	FUNNER
DOLIUM	EIKING	FASCIO	FLORID	FURCAE
DOMIER	EKUELE	FATING	FLOUSH	FURCAL
DOMING	ELDEST	FATTER	FLUIER	FURDER
DOPIER	ELMIER	FAUNAE	FLUISH	FUSILE
DORMIE	ELVISH	FAUNAL	FLYEST	FUSING
DORSAD	EMBOST	FAURER	FLYMAN	FUSUMA
DORSUM	EMDASH	FAVEST	FLYMEN	FUZING
DOSING	EMMESH	FAVOSE	FLYSCH	FYKING
DOTIER	ENARCH	FAXING	FODGEL	GAEING
DOTISH	ENCASH	FAYEST	FOEMAN	GAGING
DOUCER	ENDASH	FAYING	FOEMEN	GAGMAN

GAGMEN	GREEBO	HOAING	INLAID	KIPPEN
GAIJIN	GREYER	HODMAN	INMESH	KIRSCH
GALEAE	GRINCH	HODMEN	INMOST	KLATCH
GAMASH	GRIPLE	HOHING	INRUSH	KLOOCH
GAMEST	GROSZE	HOLDEN	INTACT	KNITCH
GAMIER	GRUING	HOLIER	INTIME	KOKIRI
GAPIER	GRUTCH	HOLMIC	INTIRE	KOKOPU
GARDAI	GRYSIE	HOLPEN	INTOWN	KONAKI
GARISH	GUNMAN	HOMIER	INWITH	KONEKE
GASHER	GUNMEN	HOOROO	INWORN	KONINI
GASLIT	GUNNEN	HOOTCH	IRATER	KORARI
GASMAN	GUTTAE	HOOVEN	IRIDAL	KOTARE
GASMEN	GUYING	HOPING	IRIDIC	KOTUKU
GATVOL	GYBING	HORMIC	IRITIC	KOUROI
GAUNCH	GYLDEN	HORRID	IRREAL	KRONEN
GAYEST	GYMNIC	HOSING	ITERUM	KRONER
GAZIER	GYRANT	HOWZAT	ITSELF	KRONOR
GEASON	GYRING	HOWZIT	JACENT	KRONUR
GEDDIT	GYROSE	HOXING	JADING	KROONI
GEEING	GYVING	HOYING	JADISH	KULAKI
GEMINI	HABILE	HUDDEN	JANTEE	KUTCHA
GEMMAE	HADDEN	HUDDUP	JEEING	KYBOSH
GEMMAN	HAEING	HUGEST	JEJUNE	LABARA
GEMMEN	HAEMAL	HUMERI	JEWING	LABILE
GENIAL	HAEMIC	HUPIRO	JIBING	LABIUM
GEODIC	HAIKAI	HYDRAE	JIMPER	LACTIC
GESTIC	HAINCH	HYDRIC	JIMSON	LAESIE
GEYEST	HAKARI	HYEING	JINGKO	LAICAL
GIBING	HALERU	HYENIC	JINNEE	LAKISH
GIDDAP	HALEST	HYETAL	JIVIER	LAMEST
GIDDUP	HALFEN	HYMNIC	JIVING	LAMIAE
GIEING	HAMOSE	HYPHAE	JOBING	LAMISH
GIGMAN	HAMULI	HYPHAL	JOCOSE	LANOSE
GIGMEN	HANGUL	HYPOID	JOCUND	LARGER
GILDEN	HANIWA	IATRIC	JOKIER	LARINE
GIUSTO	HARDER	IBIDEM	JOKING	LAROID
GLAZEN	HARISH	ICEMAN	JOLING	LARVAE
GLEBAE	HATING	ICEMEN	JOVIAL	LARVAL
GLOBAL	HAULST	ICONIC	JOWING	LATHEN
GLUIER	HAUNCH	IDEATA	JOYFUL	LATISH
GLUING	HAWKIT	IDLEST	JOYING	LAURAE
GLUISH	HAZIER	IDOLUM	JUBATE	LAURIC
GLUNCH	HEARIE	IMIDIC	JUGATE	LAVASH
GLUTEI	HEISHI	IMMANE	JUKING	LAWEST
GNAMMA	HELIAC	IMMESH	JYMOLD	LAWFUL
GNOMAE	HELING	INANER	KAEING	LAWMAN
GNOMIC	HEMOID	INARCH	KAMAHI	LAWMEN
GOETIC	HEMPEN	INBENT	KANUKA	LAXEST
GOIEST	HEPPER	INBORN	KAONIC	LAYMAN
GOLDER	HERMAI	INCAVI	KAPUKA	LAYMEN
GONION	HETING	INCAVO	KAPUTT	LEALER
GONIUM	HEYING	INCUBI	KARMIC	LEARNT
GOOIER	HIATAL	INCULT	KAWING	LEETLE
GORIER	HIEING	INDIGN	KEIGHT	LEFTER
GOTTEN	HIEMAL	INFELT	KEKENO	LEGMAN
GOWDER	HIKING	INFERE	KEPPEN	LEGMEN
GOYISH	HIPPIC	INFIMA	KEPPIT	LEKKER
GRANUM	HISPID	INGRAM	KERERU	LENGER
GRAVEN	HITMAN	INGRUM	KEWLER	LENTEN
GRAYER	HITMEN	INKJET	KIBOSH	LENTIC

LERING	MACING	MIRCHI	NEANIC	OGRISH
LESBIC	MADMAN	MIRIER	NEARER	OIDIUM
LEWDER	MADMEN	MIRING	NEATER	OILMAN
LIBANT	MAGYAR	MISATE	NEBISH	OILMEN
LIBRAE	MAINER	MISDID	NEFAST	OMASAL
LIEDER	MAKUTA	MISLIT	NERVAL	OMASUM
LIEFER	MALEIC	MISMET	NESHER	OMIGOD
LIENAL	MALIBU	MISSAE	NETHER	ONAGRI
LIEVER	MALIST	MISSAW	NEUMIC	ONIRIC
LIFULL	MALLEI	MISUST	NEVOID	ONRUSH
LIGGEN	MALOTI	MITIER	NEWEST	OPTING
LIKEST	MAMAKO	MITRAL	NEWISH	ORBIER
LIKUTA	MAMAKU	MIXIER	NICEST	ORGANA
LIMBIC	MAMMAE	MIXING	NICISH	ORGIAC
LIMNIC	MANAIA	MNEMIC	NIELLI	ORIHOU
LIMPID	MANATU	MODICA	NIGHER	OSTEAL
LIMULI	MANENT	MODISH	NIOBIC	OSTIAL
LINEAL	MANFUL	MODULI	NIRLIT	OSTIUM
LINEAR	MANQUE	MODULO	NITRIC	OTIOSE
LINIER	MANTIC	MOIRAI	NIXING	OTITIC
LINISH	MAOMAO	MOKIHI	NOBBUT	OUTATE
LIPOIC	MARISH	MONACT	NOBLER	OUTBYE
LIROTH	MASING	MONISH	NODOSE	OUTDID
LITHIC	MATATA	MONOAO	NOGAKU	OUTSAT
LITTEN	MATIER	MOOING	NONFAT	OUTSAW
LIVEST	MAUGER	MOPIER	NONMAN	OUTWON
LOBULI	MAUNNA	MOPING	NONMEN	OWLISH
LOCULI	MAUVER	MOPISH	NONPAR	OWRIER
LOGIER	MAWGER	MORBID	NORDIC	OXALIC
LOIPEN	MAWING	MORISH	NOSIER	OXIDIC
LOMATA	MAXING	MORSAL	NOSTOI	OZONIC
LOMING	MAYEST	MORYAH	NOSTRO	PACTUM
LOOING	MAYHAP	MOSHAV	NOTING	PAINCH
LOOSER	MAZIER	MOSING	NOTOUR	PAIRER
LOOTEN	MEAGER	MOTIER	NOULDE	PALEAE
LORATE	MEATAL	MOUGHT	NOUNAL	PALEAL
LOREAL	MEDIAD	MOZING	NOWISE	PALEST
LOTHER	MEDIAE	MUCOSE	NOYING	PALIER
LOUCHE	MEEKER	MULISH	NUBILE	PALISH
LOUDER	MEIKLE	MUONIC	NUCHAE	PALLAE
LOUING	MENSAE	MURKER	NUDEST	PALLID
LOUPEN	MENSAL	MUSCAE	NUKING	PALPAL
LOUPIT	MEREST	MUTEST	NUMINA	PANINI
LOWSER	MERMAN	MUTING	NUTANT	PANINO
LOWSIT	MERMEN	MUXING	OAFISH	PAPISH
LOXING	MESIAD	MYSELF	OAKIER	PAPYRI
LUBING	MESIAL	MYTHIC	OBESER	PARDEE
LUBRIC	MESIAN	MYTHOI	OBIING	PARDIE
LUCENT	METING	MYXOID	OBITAL	PARERA
LUCKEN	MEVING	NAFFER	OBITER	PAREVE
LUITEN	MEWING	NAIANT	OBTECT	PARISH
LUNIER	MIDCAP	NAIFER	OCELLI	PARORE
LUPPEN	MIKING	NAIVER	OCHONE	PARTIM
LURING	MILDER	NAPING	OCREAE	PASSEE
LUTEUM	MILIUM	NARIAL	OCTOPI	PASSIM
LUTTEN	MILKEN	NARINE	ODDEST	PATAKA
LYFULL	MIMING	NASIAL	ODDISH	PATIKI
LYSING	MIMMER	NASTIC	OGAMIC	PAUSAL
LYTTAE	MINIER	NATANT	OGIVAL	PAWING
MAAING	MINISH	NAUTCH		PEARST

PEASEN	PLEXAL	PYEMIC	RELAID	SAFING
PEASON	PLIANT	PYNING	RELATA	SAFTER
PECTIC	PLICAE	PYXING	RELIDE	SAGEST
PEDATE	PLICAL	QUAINT	RELISH	SAGIER
PEEING	PLONGD	QUALIA	REMOUD	SAIDST
PELTAE	PLUTEI	QUATCH	RENKER	SAIRER
PENIAL	PODIAL	QUEINT	REPAND	SAKKOI
PENILE	POISHA	QUENCH	REROSE	SALEWD
PENILL	POKIER	QUETCH	RESAID	SALPAE
PENMAN	POLISH	QUINIC	RESAWN	SALWAR
PENMEN	POLYPI	QUOOKE	RESEEN	SAMIER
PENNAE	POMATO	QUOTHA	RESEWN	SANCTA
PENNIA	POMMEE	QURUSH	RESHOD	SANEST
PEPFUL	PONENT	RACIAL	RESHOT	SANING
PERAEA	PONTAL	RACIER	RESOWN	SAPEGO
PERDIE	PONTIC	RADDER	RETIAL	SAPFUL
PEREIA	POOING	RADGER	RETOOK	SARING
PERFET	POOKIT	RADISH	RETORE	SATING
PERISH	POPISH	RAHING	RETORN	SATIVE
PERITI	PORIER	RAKISH	RETRAL	SAYEST
PERNIO	POSHER	RAMATE	RETROD	SBIRRI
PEROXO	POSIER	RAMEAL	RETUSE	SBIRRO
PERTER	POTASH	RAMOSE	REWORE	SCALAE
PHAEIC	POTATO	RAMULI	RHINAL	SCATCH
PHATIC	POTING	RANCID	RHIZIC	SCEATT
PHOCAE	POTMAN	RANINE	RHODIC	SCHULN
PHONAL	POTMEN	RAPHAE	RHOTIC	SCIENT
PHYLAE	POUKIT	RAPINI	RICHER	SCOLIA
PHYLAR	POWWAW	RAPPEN	RICTAL	SCOOCH
PHYLIC	POXIER	RAREST	RIDDEN	SCOOSH
PHYLON	POXING	RARING	RIFEST	SCOPAE
PHYLUM	PRELAW	RATHER	RILIER	SCORCH
PIANIC	PREMAN	RAUCID	RILING	SCOTCH
PIAZZE	PREMEN	RAVISH	RIMOSE	SCRYDE
PICINE	PREMIA	RAWARU	RIPEST	SCULCH
PICRIC	PRIMAL	RAWISH	RODMAN	SCUTAL
PIEING	PROGUN	RAXING	RODMEN	SCUTCH
PIEMAN	PRONER	REALER	ROKIER	SCUTUM
PIEMEN	PRONTO	REALIA	ROOPIT	SCYPHI
PIERST	PROSIT	RECHIE	ROPIER	SEAMAN
PILEUM	PROWAR	RECKAN	RORIER	SEAMEN
PILOSE	PROWER	RECTAL	ROSCID	SEARCH
PINETA	PRUTAH	REDIAE	ROSEAL	SEARER
PINNAE	PSORIC	REDIPT	ROTING	SECESH
PINNAL	PUCEST	REDONE	ROUPET	SECUND
PINXIT	PUDENT	REDREW	ROUPIT	SEDENT
PINYIN	PUIRER	REECHO	RUBATI	SEDILE
PIONIC	PUKING	REEDEN	RUBBET	SEIKER
PIOPIO	PULIER	REFELL	RUBIER	SEJANT
PIPIER	PULPAL	REFELT	RUEFUL	SELDOM
PIRNIT	PUNCTA	REFLEW	RUGATE	SELLAE
PIROGI	PUNIER	REGAVE	RUGOSE	SEMEIA
PITHOI	PUNISH	REGILT	RULIER	SEMPER
PITMEN	PUREST	REGNAL	RURBAN	SEMPRE
PIZING	PURING	REGNUM	RUSHEN	SENITI
PLACID	PUTRID	REGREW	RUSINE	SENRYU
PLAGAL	PUTSCH	REGULI	RYKING	SENSUM
PLANAR	PUTTEN	REHASH	SACCOI	SEPMAG
PLEACH	PYCNIC	REHUNG	SADDER	SEPTAL
PLENCH	PYEING	REKING	SAFEST	SEREST

SERRAE	SLYEST	STELAR	TAVERT	TOMBAL
SETOSE	SLYISH	STERIC	TAWIER	TOMBIC
SEXFID	SMALTI	STEYER	TAXMAN	TOMIAL
SEXIER	SMATCH	STINKO	TAXMEN	TONANT
SEXING	SMEECH	STITCH	TEAING	TOOMER
SHAKEN	SMIRCH	STOLEN	TECTAL	TOPMAN
SHAPEN	SMOOSH	STOLID	TEDIER	TOPMEN
SHARON	SMOUCH	STOMAL	TEEING	TOROSE
SHAVEN	SNEESH	STOMIA	TEGMEN	TOROTH
SHAZAM	SNIDER	STONEN	TELIAL	TORRID
SHEESH	SOAKEN	STOUSH	TELIUM	TORTEN
SHOULD	SOBEIT	STRATI	TEMENE	TOSING
SHRANK	SOBFUL	STRAWN	TENIAE	TOSSEN
SHREWD	SOCMAN	STREWN	TENSER	TOTHER
SHROWD	SOCMEN	STRIAE	TENUTI	TOTING
SHRUNK	SODAIC	STRIPT	TERAPH	TOWIER
SHTOOM	SOEVER	STRODE	TERATA	TOYISH
SHTUMM	SOFTER	STRONG	TERBIC	TOYMAN
SHYEST	SOLEIN	STROVE	TERGAL	TOYMEN
SHYING	SOLEMN	STROWN	TERGUM	TOZING
SHYISH	SOLGEL	STRUCK	TERRAE	TRAGAL
SIALIC	SOLIDI	STRUNG	TERSER	TREFAH
SICCAN	SOLING	STYING	TESTAE	TREIFA
SICCAR	SOMATA	SUABLE	THECAE	TRENCH
SICKER	SOMONI	SUAVER	THECAL	TREPID
SIFREI	SORBIC	SUBITO	THENAL	TRIACT
SIGLOI	SORDID	SUBMAN	THENCE	TRIFID
SIGLUM	SOREST	SUBSEA	THETCH	TRILLO
SILENI	SOUGHT	SULCAL	THETIC	TRINAL
SILING	SOURER	SUMMAE	THOLOI	TRISTE
SILVAE	SPEECH	SUNKEN	THORIC	TRITER
SIMIAL	SPERST	SUNLIT	THRASH	TROPPO
SINFUL	SPETCH	SUPERB	THRAWN	TROUCH
SINING	SPICAE	SURBET	THRESH	TRUEST
SIPING	SPINAE	SUREST	THRICE	TRUING
SIRING	SPLOSH	SUTILE	THROVE	TRYPAN
SISTRA	SPOILT	SWATCH	THROWN	TSKING
SITHEE	SPOKEN	SWEERT	THRUSH	TUATUA
SITING	SPORAL	SWEIRT	THYINE	TUBATE
SITTEN	SPRACK	SWOOSH	THYMIC	TUFOLI
SIWASH	SPRAID	SYEING	THYRSI	TUMULI
SIZIER	SPRENT	SYLVAE	TIBIAE	TUNIER
SKEIGH	SPRIER	SYNING	TICING	TURBID
SKITCH	SPRONG	SYPING	TIEING	TURFEN
SKOLIA	SPRUNG	TAEING	TIFOSI	TURGID
SKOOSH	SPRUSH	TAIHOA	TIFOSO	TUSSAL
SKYIER	SPRYER	TAISCH	TIGLIC	TUTMAN
SKYING	SPUING	TAKIER	TINEAL	TUTMEN
SKYISH	SPUTUM	TALEAE	TINIER	TWEEST
SKYLIT	SQUUSH	TALLER	TINING	TWILIT
SKYMAN	STALER	TALPAE	TINMAN	TYEING
SKYMEN	STALKO	TAMEST	TINMEN	TYKISH
SLATCH	STANCH	TAPING	TITMAN	TYNING
SLEAZO	STANCK	TAPPIT	TITMEN	TYPIER
SLEEST	STATAL	TARNAL	TITULI	UBIQUE
SLIEST	STATIM	TAUGHT	TOEIER	UGSOME
SLIVEN	STEARD	TAUHOU	TOEING	ULNARE
SLOOSH	STEELD	TAURIC	TOFORE	ULTIMO
SLOWER	STELAE	TAUTER	TOLUIC	UMBRAE
SLUING	STELAI	TAUTIT	TOMATO	UMBRAL

Blockers

UNBEEN	UNREAL	USABLE	VULVAL	XENIAL
UNBENT	UNRENT	UVULAE	VULVAR	XENIUM
UNBORE	UNRUDE	VACANT	WABBIT	XOANON
UNCAST	UNSAID	VADOSE	WAEFUL	XYLOID
UNCHIC	UNSAWN	VAGILE	WAIRSH	XYSTOI
UNCIAE	UNSENT	VAGROM	WANDLE	YAKUZA
UNCINI	UNSEWN	VAGUER	WANIER	YAREST
UNCLAD	UNSHOD	VAINER	WANKLE	YAWING
UNCOER	UNSOFT	VALVAL	WANNEL	YBLENT
UNCOOL	UNSOLD	VALVAR	WANNER	YBOUND
UNCUTE	UNSOWN	VANMAN	WARIER	YBRENT
UNDEAD	UNSPUN	VANMEN	WARING	YCLEPT
UNDEAR	UNSUNG	VARSAL	WARMAN	YEDING
UNDONE	UNSUNK	VASTER	WARMEN	YEOMAN
UNDREW	UNTOLD	VATMAN	WASHEN	YEOMEN
UNEATH	UNTORN	VATMEN	WASSUP	YEVING
UNEVEN	UNTROD	VEDUTA	WAURST	YEXING
UNFELT	UNVEXT	VEDUTE	WAVIER	YIKING
UNFINE	UNWELL	VEGETE	WAXIER	YIPPEE
UNFIRM	UNWEPT	VEHMIC	WEXING	YITTEN
UNFIXT	UNWISH	VEINAL	WEYARD	YOWING
UNFOND	UNWIST	VELOCE	WHATEN	YPIGHT
UNGAIN	UNWONT	VENIAL	WHATNA	YPLAST
UNGILT	UNWORN	VENOSE	WHATSO	YSHENT
UNGLAD	UPBLEW	VERIER	WHEARE	YTTRIC
UNGORD	UPBORE	VERLIG	WHILOM	YUKIER
UNGUAL	UPDOVE	VERMAL	WHILST	YUKING
UNHEWN	UPDREW	VERNAL	WHITER	YWROKE
UNHUNG	UPGIRT	VIABLE	WHOMSO	ZAFTIG
UNHURT	UPGONE	VIBIER	WHOOSH	ZANIER
UNIFIC	UPGREW	VICING	WIDEST	ZAPATA
UNITAL	UPGUSH	VIDUAL	WIDISH	ZELOSO
UNJUST	UPHAND	VILLAE	WIFING	ZEROTH
UNKEND	UPHELD	VILLAR	WILFUL	ZINCIC
UNKENT	UPHILD	VINEAL	WILIER	ZIPTOP
UNKEPT	UPHOVE	VINIER	WILING	ZIZITH
UNKIND	UPHUNG	VINING	WIMMIN	ZOAEAE
UNLAID	UPLAID	VIRENT	WIRIER	ZOECIA
UNLASH	UPMOST	VIRILE	WISEST	ZOETIC
UNLEAL	UPPISH	VIRING	WISING	ZOFTIG
UNLICH	UPROSE	VISCID	WITHAL	ZONOID
UNLOST	UPRUSH	VISIVE	WITING	ZOOEAE
UNMADE	UPRYST	VISTAL	WOEFUL	ZOOEAL
UNMARD	UPSENT	VITTAE	WORSER	ZOOIER
UNMEEK	UPTOOK	VOGIER	WOWFER	ZOONAL
UNMEET	UPTORE	VOLAGE	WOWING	ZOONIC
UNMESH	UPTORN	VOLING	WRENCH	ZUFOLI
UNMIXT	UPWENT	VOLVAE	WRETCH	ZUFOLO
UNMOWN	URACHI	VORAGO	WROKEN	ZYGOID
UNOPEN	URATIC	VORANT	WRYEST	ZYMOID
UNPAID	UREMIC	VORPAL	WRYING	
UNPENT	URETIC	VOSTRO	WYLING	
UNPURE	URSINE	VULVAE	WYTING	

Chapter 9: Miscellaneous Lists

This section contains a variety of short lists that don't really have a home elsewhere in the book. Not all these lists are of great importance to Scrabble but they may appeal to some players. The section includes lists of words according to their frequency of play over one million simulated computer games, compound words whose two halves can be transposed, lists of place names and personal names that happen to be allowed words, and a fascinating list of words that unexpectedly take an -S hook. Finally there are lists of allowable words whose origins are in overseas English-speaking regions of the world. Most of these lists do not aim to be exhaustive but the contents have been selected in order to maintain some relevance to Scrabble.

Unexpected -S hooks

In a game of Scrabble, it can be a great advantage to be able to surprise the opponent by making a play using an S that unexpectedly hooks an existing word that looks as if it is unextendable. There are three categories of such words selected here: words that have already been pluralized with an S but which can then take a further S hook (eg CITES-S); words that are past tenses in -ED that can be treated as a noun and therefore take an -S hook (e.g. MARRIED-S); those words that end in consonant followed by Y where the plural can be a straight -S, breaking the standard rule of converting Y to I and adding ES (eg TRILBY-S).

Words ending in -S that take another S

ABBES-S	COSINES-S	INKLES-S	PROCURES-S	SUCKLES-S
ABYS-S	CUFFLES-S	KAVAS-S	PROS-S	TACKLES-S
AMAS-S	DURES-S	KINDLES-S	RANKLES-S	TAILLES-S
AMIS-S	ESQUIRES-S	KINGLES-S	RAYLES-S	TARTINES-S
BIBLES-S	FAINNES-S	LARGES-S	ROOTLES-S	TREADLES-S
BRAS-S	FANGLES-S	LOWNES-S	RUMPLES-S	TRICKLES-S
BULGINES-S	FOGLES-S	MAPLES-S	RUSTLES-S	TYRANNES-S
CAMAS-S	FOOTLES-S	MARQUES-S	SAGENES-S	USURES-S
CAPLES-S	FRAS-S	MORAS-S	SALTINES-S	WATTLES-S
CARES-S	GAMINES-S	NEEDLES-S	SHINES-S	WINDLES-S
CARLES-S	GARBLES-S	NERVINES-S	SKIFFLES-S	ZEBRAS-S
CAVAS-S	GAUS-S	OGRES-S	SOUPLES-S	
CHAPES-S	GUES-S	POSSES-S	SPARKLES-S	
CITES-S	HANDLES-S	PRELATES-S	SPECKLES-S	
COMBLES-S	HURTLES-S	PRINCES-S	SQUIRES-S	

Words ending in -ED that take an S

ASSURED-S	COMBINED-S	INBRED-S	LIMITED-S	PUREBRED-S
BELOVED-S	ELEVATED-S	INSURED-S	MALTED-S	UNLEADED-S
COLORED-S	FROSTED-S	INTENDED-S	MARRIED-S	UNWASHED-S
COLOURED-S	HOMEBRED-S	LAMED-S	MOPED-S	WICKED-S

Words ending in consonant plus Y that take an S

ABHENRY-S	COLBY-S	GOODBY-S	POLY-S	TELLY-S
ABY-S	DARCY-S	HENRY-S	QWERTY-S	TREVALLY-S
BIALY-S	DROSTDY-S	JANSKY-S	SHINDY-S	TRILBY-S
BLOWBY-S	EMMY-S	NY-S	STANDBY-S	WHY-S
BY-S	FLYBY-S	PLATY-S	SWINGBY-S	ZLOTY-S

Transposals

Some words consist of two elements (compound words) which can be transposed to give a different word. These give you two words for the price of one and it may be that only one of them will fit on a board during a game. This list focuses on transposals where the two halves are equal in length (for example, DOGWATCH and WATCHDOG are omitted) and ignores those that are not compound words (for example, TRYPAN and PANTRY are omitted).

BACKFALL	FALLBACK	HEADRAIL	RAILHEAD
BACKFIRE	FIREBACK	HILLSIDE	SIDEHILL
BACKLIFT	LIFTBACK	HOLDOVER	OVERHOLD
BACKSEAT	SEATBACK	HOMETOWN	TOWNHOME
BIRDCAGE	CAGEBIRD	HUNGOVER	OVERHUNG
BIRDSONG	SONGBIRD	JAYVEE	VEEJAY
BOILOVER	OVERBOIL	JOYPOP	POPJOY
BONEFISH	FISHBONE	LAYOUT	OUTLAY
BOOKCASE	CASEBOOK	LOCKPICK	PICKLOCK
BOOKWORK	WORKBOOK	LOOKOVER	OVERLOOK
BOOTJACK	JACKBOOT	MATESHIP	SHIPMATE
BUSHFIRE	FIREBUSH	OFFPUT	PUTOFF
BUYOUT	OUTBUY	OFFSET	SETOFF
COATTAIL	TAILCOAT	OUTPUT	PUTOUT
COMEDOWN	DOWNCOME	OUTRIG	RIGOUT
COMEOVER	OVERCOME	OUTRUN	RUNOUT
CUTOFF	OFFCUT	OUTSET	SETOUT
DOVERING	RINGDOVE	OVERPASS	PASSOVER
DOWNPLAY	PLAYDOWN	OVERSLIP	SLIPOVER
DOWNTURN	TURNDOWN	OVERTAKE	TAKEOVER
FLOODWATER	WATERFLOOD	OVERTURN	TURNOVER
FORTEPIANO	PIANOFORTE	OVERWING	WINGOVER
FRYPAN	PANFRY	PARSEC	SECPAR
GEARHEAD	HEADGEAR	PITSAW	SAWPIT
GUESTHOUSE	HOUSEGUEST	RAGTAG	TAGRAG
GUTROT	ROTGUT	ROADSIDE	SIDEROAD
HANDOVER	OVERHAND	ROOTWORM	WORMROOT
HANGOVER	OVERHANG	WOODWORM	WORMWOOD
HEADLONG	LONGHEAD		

Placenames

Some placenames can also be valid Scrabble words, either because the word has a meaning related to that place or just through sheer coincidence. Here is selection that may be of interest. The list is by no means exhaustive but represents a selection of words up to eight-letters in length that have some value to the Scrabble player. (The assistance of David Sutton is acknowledged in generating this list.)

ACTON	a stuffed jacket worn under mail
ALAMO	a kind of poplar
ALASKA	a heavy fabric
AMAZON	a tall, powerful woman
AMMAN	a district magistrate
ANGOLA	relating to a fabric made from the wool of the Angora goat
ARMAGNAC	a kind of brandy
ASCOT	a type of necktie with broad ends
ASSAM	in Malaysia, tamarind as used in cooking
BABEL	a scene of confusion
BALBOA	the monetary unit of Panama
BALMORAL	a flat Scottish bonnet
BANGKOK	a straw hat
BARBICAN	an outer defensive work; esp a tower at a gate or bridge
BEDLAM	an asylum
BERLIN	a type of carriage
BLARNEY	to talk persuasively
BOHEMIA	a community of bohemians
BOLIVIA	a type of fabric
BOLOGNA	a kind of sausage
BOSTON	a card game
BOURBON	a kind of whisky
BOWERY	any area frequented by drunks
BRAZIL	a dyewood
BRENT	a kind of goose
BRISTOL	a smooth cardboard
CAMELOT	a strong waterproof fabric
CANADA	a narrow canyon
CHAD	a punched out piece of paper
CHANTILLY	as in chantilly lace
CHEDDAR	a type of cheese
CHESHIRE	a kind of pig
CHILE	chili
CHINA	fine porcelain ware
COLOGNE	a perfumed liquid
COLORADO	refers to a medium strength cigar
CONGO	a kind of black Chinese tea
CORBY	a crow, a raven
CORDOBA	the standard monetary unit of Nicaragua
CREMONA	an ancient wind instrument
CREWE	a pot
DERBY	a kind of hat
DERRY	a dislike
DEVON	a breed of cattle from Devon
DOVER	to doze
ETNA	a vessel for heating liquids
FLORENCE	a former gold coin of Europe
FUJI	a silk fabric
FULHAM	a loaded die
GALILEE	a small chapel or porch at the western end of some medieval English churches
GAMBIA	the inspissated juice of a plant growing in Malacca
GENEVA	a spirit distilled from gin
GENOA	a large jib which overlaps the mainsail
GOA	a kind of Tibetan gazelle with backward-curving horns
GOSPORT	a communication device in an aeroplane
GREECE	a flight of steps
GUERNSEY	a woollen jersey
HACKNEY	a kind of cab
HAMBURG	a patty of ground beef

Placenames

HARROW	a spiked frame for breaking up ground
HASTINGS	early fruit or vegetables
HAVERING	present participle of 'to haver'
HENLEY	a type of sweater
HOLLAND	a coarse cotton or linen
HOMBURG	a man's felt hat
JAPAN	to coat with glossy, black lacquer
JAVA	a kind of coffee
JERSEY	a close-fitting, knitted shirt
JORDAN	a chamber-pot
KASHMIR	a soft twilled fabric of goat's wool
KENT	to punt or pole
LABRADOR	a breed of dog
LANGLEY	a unit of illumination used to measure the temperature of a star
LEVANT	to abscond
LEWIS	a dovetailed iron tenon made to fit into a stone so that it can be hoisted
LIMA	a kind of bean
LUCERNE	a fodder plant
MACON	smoked salted mutton
MADEIRA	a white wine
MADISON	a type of cycle race, first staged in Madison Square Gardens
MADRAS	a cotton fabric
MALI	one of the gardener class in India
MANILA	a fibre used in making rope
MAYO	mayonnaise
MEDINA	in N. African cities, the ancient native quarter
MINORCA	a type of domestic fowl
MODENA	a dark purple colour
MOLDOVA	a green tektite found in the Czech republic, thought to be the product of an ancient meteorite impact in Germany
MOROCCO	a kind of leather
MUSCAT	muscatel wine; a musky variety of grape or its vine
NATAL	relating to birth
NELSON	a wrestling hold
NIGER	a negro
NOME	a province or department esp. in ancient Greece
ORLEANS	a variety of plum
OXFORD	a type of shoe
PAISLEY	a patterned fabric
PANAMA	a kind of straw hat
PARIS	a European herb
PENNINE	a mineral of the chlorite group
PHOENIX	a mythological bird
PINNER	one who impounds cattle
POLISH	to make smooth and lustrous by rubbing
POPLAR	a kind of tree
PORTLAND	a kind of cement, having the color of the Portland stone
RABAT	to rotate into coincidence with another plane
RHINE	a drainage channel
RHONE	a roof-gutter
RIALTO	a theatrical district; a marketplace
RIOJA	a Spanish red wine
RIVIERA	any warm coastal district reminiscent of the Riviera
RUBICON	the winning of a game in piquet before one's opponent scores
RUSSIA	a kind of leather
SARK	a shirt, a chemise
SAUTERNE	a white wine
SEINE	to fish with a certain kind of net

SILESIA	a thin twilled cotton or linen
SODOM	any place notorious for vice
SOHO	a hunting cry
SOMERSET	a somersault
SPAIN	to wean
STEPNEY	a spare wheel
STROUD	a kind of coarse blanket made at Stroud
SUMATRA	a short, violent squall in or near the Straits of Malacca
SURREY	a horse-drawn carriage
TELFORD	a road made of stones
TEXAS	the uppermost structure on a steamboat
THEBES	plural of 'thebe', a monetary unit of Botswana
TILBURY	a light open two-wheeled carriage
TOLEDO	a sword made at Toledo
TONGA	a light two-wheeled Indian vehicle
TRIPOLI	an earthy substance originally brought from Tripoli, used in polishing stones and metals
TUPELO	a North American tree
TYNE	to lose
ULSTER	a kind of overcoat
VALENCIA	a kind of woven fabric
VICHY	a kind of mineral water
VICTORIA	a kind of open carriage
VIRGINIA	a type of flue-cured tobacco grown originally in Virginia
VOLTA	a lively dance in 3/4 time
WALES	weals
WALLSEND	a kind of coal
WANTAGE	a deficiency, a shortage
WARSAW	a kind of fish
WATERLOO	a decisive defeat or setback
WIGAN	a stiff plain-woven cotton
WOOMERA	a stick for launching a spear with greater force
WORTHING	present participle of 'worth', to be, to happen
YORK	to bowl a batsman with a YORKER
ZAIRE	a monetary unit of Zaire

Personal names

Similarly, some personal names can also be valid Scrabble words, either because the familiar personal name has itself been derived from a word (such as girls' names that come from flowers) or because something has been named after someone, or just out of coincidence. Here is selection that may be of interest. The list is by no means exhaustive but represents a selection of words up to eight-letters in length that have some value to the Scrabble player. (The assistance of David Sutton is acknowledged in generating this list.)

ABIGAIL	a lady's maid
ALAN	a large hunting dog
ALBERT	a short kind of watch-chain
ALMA	Egyptian dancing girl
ANNA	a former coin of India
BASIL	an aromatic herb
BEN	a mountain peak
BENEDICT	a newly married man
BENJAMIN	benzoine, a gum resin
BENNY	an amphetamine tablet
BERTHA	a woman's deep collar
BETH	a Hebrew letter

Placenames

BILL	to present for payment
BILLY	a metal container for cooking outdoors
BOBBY	a policeman
BONNIE	bonny (pretty)
BRAD	a thin nail
BUSTER	something large
CARL	a miser
CAROL	to sing joyously
CELESTE	a keyboard instrument
CHAD	a scrap of paper
CHARLEY	a fool
CHARLIE	a fool
CHUCK	to throw
CICERO	a typeface
CLARENCE	a closed carriage
CLEMENT	merciful
CLIFF	a high steep face of rock
CRISPIN	poetic for a shoemaker
DAISY	a flowering plant
DAPHNE	a flowering shrub
DAVY	a miner's safety lamp
DEXTER	situated on the right
DICK	a detective
DICKENS	a devil
DOLLY	a wheeled platform
DONNA	an Italian lady
DOTTY	crazy
DUSTY	full of dust
ERICA	a shrub of the heath family
FAGIN	one who trains young thieves
FANNY	the buttocks
FAY	to join closely
FELICITY	happiness
FLORENCE	a durable silk fabric
FLOSSIE	a floozy
FRANK	to mark for postage
FRITZ	a state of disrepair
GABBY	talkative
GILBERT	an electromagnetic unit of force
GILLY	to act as a hunting attendant
GLEN	a small valley
GLORIA	a halo
GRAHAM	wholewheat flour
GUY	chap, fellow
HANSEL	to inaugurate with a gift
HECTOR	to bully
HENRY	a unit of inductance
HERBY	abounding in herbs
HOMER	to hit a home run
HYACINTH	a type of flower
JACK	to raise with a type of lever
JACKY	a sailor
JADE	to weary
JAKE	a yokel
JANE	a girl or woman
JEAN	a durable cotton fabric
JEMIMA	an elastic-sided boot
JENNY	a travelling crane
JERRY	a builder of flimsy houses
JESS	to strap the legs of a hawk

JILL	a cart for carrying timber
JIMMY	to pry open with a crowbar
JO	a sweetheart
JOE	a sweetheart
JOEY	a young kangaroo
JOHNNY	a sleeveless hospital gown
JORDAN	a type of chamberpot
JOSEPH	a woman's long cloak
JOSH	to tease
JUDAS	a spyhole in a door
KELLY	a specialist drilling pipe
KELVIN	the SI unit of temperature
KEN	to know
KERRY	one of an Irish breed of cattle
KITTY	a fund of money
LANCE	to pierce with a lance
LAURA	a type of monastery
LOUIE	a lieutenant
LOUIS	a former gold coin of France
LUCIFER	a friction match
MARC	residue after pressing grapes
MARCEL	to give soft waves to hair with heated tongs
MARGE	margarine
MARIA	dark areas of the Moon or Mars
MARINA	a berthing area for yachts
MARTIN	a small bird
MARYJANE	marijuana
MATILDA	a hobo's bundle
MAXWELL	a unit of magnetic flux
MICKEY	to drug someone's drink
MOLLY	a tropical fish
MORGAN	a type of saddle horse
MORRIS	an English folk dance
NANCY	an effeminate young man
NAPOLEON	a old French gold coin
NELLIE	a weak or foolish person
NELLY	a weak or foolish person
NEWTON	a unit of force
NOAH	a shark (Australian slang)
NOEL	any Christmas carol
OLIVE	a small fruit
OSCAR	cash
PAM	a type of card game
PATSY	one who is easily fooled
PATTY	a thin, flat cake of food
PETER	to diminish gradually
RALPH	to vomit
REG	a regulation
REX	a king
ROMEO	a swain, a beau
RUTH	compassion
SALLY	to rush out suddenly
SANDY	covered with sand
SHAW	a small wood
SHEILA	a young girl or a woman
SHELLY	abounding in seashells
SHERLOCK	a detective
SHYLOCK	a ruthless creditor
SIBYL	a female prophet
SONNY	a small boy

Personal names

SPENCER	a short double-breasted overcoat
TAMMY	a fabric of mixed fibres
TEDDY	a furry, stuffed toy bear.
TERRY	an absorbent fabric
TIFFANY	a thin, mesh fabric
TIMOTHY	a kind of grass
TITAN	anything gigantic
TOBY	a type of drinking mug
TOMMY	to oppress by paying in goods instead of money
TONY	stylish
TROY	a system of weights
VERA	very
VERONICA	a type of herb
VICTORIA	a gigantic water lily
WALDO	a remote control gadget
WALLY	something visually pleasing
WARREN	a place where rabbits live
WEBSTER	a weaver

Playability lists

The lists of words given here represent those that have occurred most often in a million Scrabble games played by a computer against itself. So, by definition, all these words are certainly worth knowing because they naturally crop up on a regular basis. To assist, the words have been split into word-length and the most frequent words have been listed for each length. It is perhaps not surprising to see a lot of JQXZ words among these lists. To give a flavour of how the words without JQXZ sit within the most-frequently played words, a list of the top 500 irrespective of length is also included.

The 250 most frequently played 3-letter words

QAT	AZO	BEZ	JAY	HUI
QIS	JIN	JEU	OOF	ZAP
QUA	OAF	FIZ	LEZ	JOR
JOE	ZED	RIZ	FOE	JOY
ZEE	JIZ	ZIN	OWE	KEX
OXO	YEX	JIG	JOG	ZOL
EXO	ZEX	ZIT	TAX	JOB
AXE	GOX	EAU	WOE	FOH
JAI	WAX	FOX	RAX	JAG
IWI	HEX	WOF	BOX	WUD
SUQ	TIX	HOX	JOT	ZIP
AIA	ADZ	FEW	ZEL	GOV
JEE	VAW	JOW	LUZ	WEB
VEX	FAX	DEX	JAM	HOI
VOX	NIX	UEY	ZHO	FEH
ZEA	JAW	HAJ	ZEP	VIM
WEX	OYE	ZOO	JAB	UFO
TAJ	ZAG	WAI	REX	AWA
FEZ	REZ	ZIG	JIB	JUT
JET	ZAX	RAJ	FAW	POZ
JEW	AUA	WOO	BIZ	MIZ
ZOA	YOU	DZO	FIX	FAA
WIZ	NOX	TEX	AYU	OXY
WOX	VOW	AUE	EYE	JAP

MOZ	TUX	VAG	JAK	WYE
PIX	DUX	JOL	FEM	WEY
YAE	IVY	VUG	WIT	NEF
JUN	PAV	WAE	VIA	SIX
AYE	UVA	FOP	VUM	MEW
PAX	DOF	HOE	DUI	GIO
MAX	GIF	POX	FAY	VAT
YEA	FEG	FAP	VAU	HOO
FOU	FIB	DEV	DIF	VAV
VEG	GJU	FOY	YID	GOO
FAB	DIV	HOA	VAN	HAW
FOB	VOE	EVO	FUB	YIN
VIG	YOW	OHO	VIE	VLY
FIE	FEE	WEE	FAG	AHA
ZEK	EWE	GUV	YEW	NTH
VID	LOX	LAX	PEW	WAW
JUD	CAZ	VET	COZ	KOI
AVO	MIX	HAO	TWP	OAK
FEU	LEX	FEY	WAG	HOW
FAH	AWE	SAZ	WEM	FID
JAR	OOH	VOR	WIN	HAE
WIG	VIN	HUE	AAH	YEH
AHI	SEZ	BOW	XIS	YAW
HIE	WOG	JUG	FIG	AVA
OVA	CUZ	WAB	TAV	BEE
AUF	FAE	FOG	HEW	KEF

The 250 most frequently played 4-letter words

QADI	QUEY	WAIF	FRIZ	WOVE
QAID	JUVE	JEAN	IOTA	ZOIC
EUOI	QUAD	VIAE	AGIO	ZOOT
QATS	VIEW	JIRD	JEER	JAIL
JIAO	FIVE	QUIM	JILT	FAZE
ZOEA	JOEY	GREX	WIVE	ZEBU
QUAI	ZORI	FUJI	VEGO	JOLE
WAQF	OYEZ	WIFE	QUIP	ETUI
QUOD	RITZ	ANOA	FAVA	DOUX
IXIA	IBEX	ZONE	VROW	JEST
AJEE	BENJ	JAVA	JOBE	JEEL
JIVE	QUID	ROJI	ZONA	JEUX
JEDI	JETE	OGEE	HAJI	ZUPA
QUAG	OHIA	FAIX	JOTA	ZANY
QOPH	OUZO	AWEE	JEHU	OFAY
GEEZ	QUIT	VEXT	WEXE	NEXT
HIOI	QUOP	JATO	GAJO	PREZ
JEFE	QUAY	JOIN	ZARF	AEON
ZEIN	ZERO	JEEP	DOJO	DIXI
AQUA	ZINE	HUIA	JIVY	OBOE
EAUX	JEAT	HOAX	ZEAL	VROT
ZITE	JEED	JINX	EXIT	VIZY
ZETA	QUIN	ODEA	ZILA	GOAF
ZATI	QUAT	EVOE	OXID	TZAR
DITZ	JEON	JIBE	JUDO	TOEA
JEEZ	JANE	VIBE	INIA	ONIE
QUIZ	AVOW	JUTE	VIVO	VINO
TREZ	DJIN	FAVE	OBIA	ZINC
QUEP	ZEST	OOZE	APEX	YOWE
ZITI	JADE	JAFA	JAPE	ILEX

IZAR	BEEF	MOAI	FAUX	AXON
NAZI	YEVE	RIZA	JURA	OUPA
EOAN	ZOON	PERV	MZEE	BEVY
AZAN	YUTZ	PUTZ	YONI	VATU
VOID	KIVA	HIVE	WINO	OXER
UVAE	FADO	TIVY	AXED	MEOW
UVEA	AGEE	EXON	JISM	AITU
OXEN	YETI	YEAH	NAOI	PREX
LUTZ	EINE	HADJ	SWIZ	JAGA
VERB	CIAO	FEEB	HOOF	ROUX
FUTZ	FUZE	LANX	DERV	SITZ
MIRV	JONG	EUGE	ZOBU	WADI
VINT	WOOF	IDEE	EAVE	FIDO
JUPE	JURE	ZING	AZON	PIZE
VINY	DIVI	VETO	KOJI	KAZI
JOHN	JANN	TAXI	WEFT	FEOD
FOID	BIZE	BEAU	YOGI	HOVE
HAZE	TOZE	JOUR	WAVE	HAAF
FIGO	NIXE	YAGI	KIWI	VIGA
VEEP	JINN	JARL	MOOI	VEHM

The 250 most frequently played 5-letter words

TRANQ	EQUID	JEUNE	EQUIP	HELIX
QANAT	TOQUE	FAUVE	FOGIE	ORIXA
FAQIR	QUIET	JERID	MIAOU	ABOVE
NIQAB	QUARE	JIGOT	OJIME	JIRGA
QORMA	AIDOI	XOANA	VIGIA	TEAZE
TALAQ	JAXIE	QUEST	AZIDE	EXINE
ZOEAE	QUEME	ZOOID	VIEWY	ZONER
OUIJA	XENIA	VINEW	OGIVE	WEAVE
QIBLA	JIVED	ZOOEY	VEZIR	FEDEX
QUEEN	QUIRE	QUBIT	OURIE	JINGO
QUOTE	QAIDS	COOEE	VIBEX	PIVOT
ZOAEA	QUAIR	QUALE	VIZOR	ZANJA
AQUAE	UMIAQ	DIAZO	QUAIL	TOUZE
NERTZ	OORIE	EQUAL	QUART	NEEZE
ZAIRE	YOWIE	WIFIE	JAVEL	ZOEAL
QUOIF	AUDIO	BIVIA	GLITZ	ZOIST
ZOWIE	OIDIA	WAIVE	MIAOW	IXORA
QUOTA	WAREZ	VIFDA	SQUEG	ZAYIN
ZOOEA	FOVEA	JOINT	ZONDA	QUILT
QUENA	QUINA	ZINEB	WUXIA	BOWIE
QUERN	ZANTE	ZONAE	ZIBET	VEGIE
QUOAD	QUITE	QUOTH	EXEAT	RADIX
QUEER	VARIX	FRITZ	VROUW	FOXIE
QUEAN	RIOJA	DETOX	JINNE	JOULE
ROQUE	AINEE	ZERDA	QUANT	AZURE
YITIE	EEJIT	QUYTE	AZIDO	REJIG
QUOIT	JETON	QUEUE	INDEX	QUINT
GRENZ	QUINE	VOGIE	AVOID	WALTZ
AVIZE	JIRRE	BURQA	LOOIE	FUGIO
JEWIE	ADIEU	AJIVA	AXONE	WOOTZ
QUINO	QUIPO	QUERY	FEAZE	JUICE
QADIS	AIOLI	AZINE	AERIE	FOREX
FIQUE	HERTZ	QUIRT	QUEYN	QUASI
QUOIN	WEIZE	EERIE	AULOI	VENOM
VITEX	JIVER	JIVEY	AXITE	VOEMA
QUATE	ZLOTE	ZONED	JAWED	BOVID

AXOID	AWETO	AZOTE	POOVE	PIQUE
VIDEO	IVIED	RETAX	HAFIZ	VEINY
HOVEA	XENON	ADOZE	JOBED	TOWZE
URAEI	JEELY	JOYED	OZEKI	BEVUE
LOUIE	QUAKE	AVION	WAIDE	AREAE
TROOZ	VOWED	MILTZ	AXION	GAUJE
DURZI	AUREI	OXIDE	ZAMIA	JABOT
ZORIL	JIBED	TOPAZ	EXODE	HIVED
ANNEX	AIERY	YOGEE	WAITE	VIREO
WIVED	IVORY	ZIGAN	AALII	EJECT
WINZE	AECIA	JAGER	WIFEY	ADVEW
OVOID	DIVOT	QUODS	QURSH	FJORD
BORTZ	PIEZO	TOZIE	NAVEW	GAVOT
OBEAH	WANZE	JOWED	JIBER	QUONK

The 250 most frequently played 6-letter words

QINTAR	QUETHE	QUININ	CIRQUE	ZOFTIG
QINDAR	ADIEUX	ZORINO	WIZIER	GOODIE
EUOUAE	QUOTER	JEEING	ZANDER	ADJIGO
YAQONA	JOINER	ZENITH	VERNIX	BOATIE
QIVIUT	QUELEA	JAEGER	VIRAGO	EXTINE
ZOAEAE	FOOTIE	AZOTED	GIDJEE	AGOUTI
ZOOEAE	ZOOIER	JITTER	AVIZED	TOITOI
FEIJOA	QUINIE	EPIZOA	WAIRUA	JEZAIL
EQUATE	WIENIE	MANQUE	JOWARI	AGRIZE
QUIVER	QUEINT	FOODIE	SAIQUE	UPDIVE
ZOUAVE	ZOECIA	REQUIT	BINIOU	AUGITE
QUINOA	QUOTED	JOVIAL	JARINA	VAUDOO
QUAERE	JIVIER	QUIRED	ADAGIO	VEGETE
HAIQUE	EQUANT	QUARTZ	WEENIE	FAJITA
AZIONE	INJERA	QUALIA	JEANED	WOOLIE
QUAVER	IODIZE	ELUVIA	DZEREN	UNWOVE
ZEATIN	REQUIN	HAVIOR	FAQUIR	JUNIOR
QWERTY	EVZONE	EQUIPE	TWELVE	EXOGEN
ENTREZ	JILTED	ZOETIC	INJECT	DORIZE
QUANGO	UNVEXT	WOOPIE	ZELANT	COQUET
TRANQS	TAJINE	QUINCE	TOEBIE	ZEROED
EQUINE	QUARTO	OPIATE	BEANIE	DENTEX
TAUIWI	EVEJAR	TOQUET	JITNEY	ZINGED
OUTVIE	VOIDEE	OXGATE	QUANTA	VIZARD
SHEQEL	CAIQUE	JAILED	FRIEZE	WILTJA
QASIDA	ZANIER	EXODOI	TOONIE	VIZIED
QUINZE	QUITED	JINNEE	FEIRIE	VENEWE
EXUVIA	AVOURE	QANATS	DEAWIE	VIRINO
ZOARIA	JANTEE	QUARER	ENZIAN	UNHIVE
QIGONG	DIQUAT	TINAJA	ZEALOT	HEJIRA
EQUITY	JERQUE	QUOTHA	QUOOKE	ACQUIT
HOAGIE	JILTER	YAUTIA	AVENUE	AZOTIC
AGUIZE	TORQUE	IODINE	REVIEW	EURIPI
IONIZE	UNWIVE	QABALA	JENNET	OOZIER
EQUALI	AVIATE	BOVINE	VOYAGE	APOGEE
JARVIE	JOINED	JAILER	EVOVAE	TWEEZE
OZAENA	INWOVE	WOODIE	HEARIE	SUIVEZ
FOVEAE	JORDAN	IODATE	JURIED	GUIZER
HEINIE	FANJET	QUINOL	JILGIE	TIBIAE
LIQUOR	ZONURE	FERVID	ZANIED	VOTIVE
OPAQUE	AZERTY	GOATEE	FEAGUE	JAILOR
JEELIE	ZONATE	KEAVIE	QUINTE	TOETOE

CODEIA	QUEENY	QUINIC	VIZIER	ZINCED
REJOIN	ADJOIN	EJECTA	ERSATZ	ENZONE
TRIJET	VIGOUR	OARAGE	VIROID	EOCENE
INJURE	JUGATE	JAYGEE	VAHINE	ETOILE
VIRION	JETLAG	MARQUE	BEDAZE	ZINGEL
ANOXIA	ZINGER	WURLIE	WAIFED	BOUGIE
REAVOW	IOLITE	LOQUAT	FOULIE	ROQUET
NIQABS	FAQIRS	JIVING	QUIDAM	WEEPIE

The 250 most frequently played 7-letter words

ETAERIO	ENOLASE	SLINTER	EERIEST	GOATIER
ERASION	ELATION	LAITIES	ALINERS	AUREOLE
ETESIAN	IRISATE	AUSTERE	NORTENA	STINGER
OTARINE	RETINAE	AGENISE	IRONIST	EQUINIA
ATONIES	LENTORS	TERSION	SANTERA	EULOGIA
INERTIA	TANNERS	TRAINEE	STERILE	PERINEA
EROTISE	IDEATES	AENEOUS	OESTRAL	NITRIDE
AIERIES	OLEINES	AROINTS	ASTERIA	TOADIES
ORIGANE	ARANEID	ALUNITE	LENTIGO	ORATION
TAENIAE	TEENIER	ONSTAGE	ETOILES	ODONATE
SERIATE	DETRAIN	AREOLES	EUGENIA	DIETINE
INOSITE	LOERIES	LADRONE	SARDINE	TARSEAL
OTARIES	DARIOLE	SOUTANE	SNORTED	EGALITE
ROSEATE	URINOSE	TEARIER	OVARIES	NEUTRAL
SEALINE	SEQUOIA	AIRIEST	RETSINA	SNORTER
SENARII	LAIRISE	LINEAGE	DENTALS	AMNIOTE
ANISOLE	ENTASIA	EARLIES	GRANITA	ATONERS
ISATINE	AEONIAN	AUNTIES	OUTEARN	ACETONE
ESTRONE	DENARII	ESERINE	DENTILS	ANEURIN
OLEARIA	RATLINS	ANTIRED	INGRATE	SOAPIER
RIOTISE	ENTRAIN	ANESTRA	TOENAIL	ONLIEST
ANEROID	AERIALS	ATELIER	REALTIE	INSURED
AERIEST	RETINOL	ROADIES	AILERON	ELOINER
ARENITE	ACINOSE	ATEBRIN	ALERION	EVASION
ISOLATE	ERINITE	ARSENAL	RODENTS	SENATOR
TINDERS	ORDINEE	URALITE	RETILES	ROASTER
OARIEST	NAIADES	INDARTS	AURATES	SNAILED
EROTICA	TAENIAS	ETIOLIN	GODETIA	NAILERS
ALIENER	ENATION	ESTOILE	SOLERET	DOULEIA
EATERIE	ANTLIAE	OLESTRA	SIDERAL	ETALONS
ANISEED	SITULAE	SANTERO	LEANERS	BETAINE
REGINAE	ANERGIA	SODAINE	ROUTINE	TINNIER
ARENOSE	EROSION	SERRANO	ANEARED	RELINES
OLEATES	SUETIER	IODATES	EUGARIE	AREOLAS
LINEATE	EASTERN	TALONED	ATONIAS	IODISER
TORNADE	AUDITEE	ENDARTS	OREGANO	SOILIER
NEROLIS	NITERIE	ENROOTS	AEROBIA	DIORITE
ESTRIOL	ALIENEE	DITONES	AGONIES	LATRONS
AIRLINE	SNIFTER	RATIONS	SINTERY	SILTIER
AEOLIAN	RATEENS	STONIER	STONIED	OESTRIN
OREADES	NEGATOR	ARIETTA	RESILED	TRENISE
SINUATE	SOCIATE	NOSTRIL	OUTSEEN	NARCIST
SOREDIA	GENITOR	RONNIES	ARENOUS	TARAIRE
SIENITE	AERATES	RANDIES	SEALANT	OILIEST
SNIRTLE	LINTERS	NARTJIE	STEARIC	LEISTER
INEDITA	EPINAOI	ANESTRI	QINTARS	RESIDUA
AEROSAT	TROELIE	AGNISED	ELOINED	ISLETED
AREOLAE	TRANNIE	EVIRATE	NEONATE	ENTICES

RESILIN	LEADIER	ENRAGES	AILETTE	LARNIER
SENECIO	STERNED	OILSEED	LIAISON	ANOESIS
REALISE	LIGNITE	SNARIER	SYENITE	ISOBARE
TORSIVE	DIARIST	TANNIES	ISOLEAD	INSULAE
DEITIES	TROOLIE	ELUSION	STOITER	DEARIES
STRIVEN	SOSATIE	NUTRIAS	ODORATE	OBELIAS
ARISTAE	AUDIENT	ANSATED	ORNATER	ENTRAIL
CRETINS	RENTALS	BEANIES	NIOBATE	DELAINE
RESINED	DAUTIES	TENTIGO	BAINITE	TAILERS
RUNLETS	TAURINE	ELODEAS	OUTLIES	ABORTEE
STANINE	AUDITOR	ANTLERS	ROSETTE	RELENTS
TSARINA	EUCAINE	IRONERS	TOEBIES	INSNARE
EROTEMA	ASTROID	ANOETIC	ISOTONE	TENSION
EROSIVE	NETTIES	GENOISE	ROSACEA	NATURES
TOLANES	DENOTES	STANDEE	STARNIE	EUTEXIA
TINNERS	TRIDENT	AUREATE	LINNETS	INVERTS
ACEROSE	INSTATE	UNITAGE	AMIRATE	DELIRIA
GREISEN	ALIENED	NEATEST	TORANAS	NOVATED
NERINES	SALTIRE	AGISTED	STATION	ESTIVAL
SIERRAN	ENDEARS	LORRIES	ACETINS	WARISON
TOASTIE	SNIDIER	ONLINER	SIGNORE	EBRIOSE
DARTLES	EDITION	AWAITER	ANTIAIR	RUINATE
NITRILE	NEAREST	ENTRIST	EARNEST	ORATING
SAUTOIR	DISTAIN	RELICTS	MARTINS	NOURSLE
RAVELIN	DONATES	AIRWISE	ADENINE	TARRIED
PEATIER	ATRESIA	GENTILE	REMANIE	EBONITE
INJERAS	OREIDES	READIES	DEASOIL	RETINAL
ARAISED	DECIARE	NATTERS	APTERIA	GRIESIE
STANNEL	NEGATES	STANGED	LATRINE	DOLENTE
GANOINE	SLANTED	AEROGEL	AIRHOLE	DANCERS
AURELIA	STINTER	ROSIERE	PENTISE	ANTSIER
AGONISE	RAINOUT	ANTIQUE	NESTLER	TANGELO
ENACTOR	MOINEAU	TRITONE	SOLATIA	TONSURE
RETINAS	LINIEST	LEASURE	SOIGNEE	ELYSIAN
SEELIER	IOLITES	STARNED	NEATENS	NAEVOID
LIERNES	FESTIER	INSIDER	RATINES	TENNIES
ERODENT	OSIERED	DOUANES	RADIALE	ENDORSE
RILIEST	SATINET	ALTERNE	RAVINES	NITRILS
LINTIES	CORNEAE	LARGEST	ERRANTS	ALSOONE
NAIVETE	SAUNTER	OSTIATE	DIANOIA	DEANERS
SANDIER	ALIENOR	STRANGE	SOOTIER	LOONIER
RENAILS	TREASON	RETAINS	AGEUSIA	STIBINE
ONETIME	TUNICAE	HERNIAE	NORITES	OSTIARY
NARDINE	ATTIRED	DENIALS	ANOTHER	ANODISE
EUPNOEA	ACONITE	STEARIN	STEANED	RESIANT
AVENIRS	ALDRINS	INLIERS	ORIOLES	AEDILES
TRIUNES	DILATES	LEIPOAS	ENTROLD	OPIATED
OPERATE	SNARLER	OCREATE	RESTING	REAROSE
TESTIER	LAETARE	ONERIER	SECTION	RATLINE
CINEREA	SERRATI	NUTSIER	PETUNIA	TOXINES
TANAGER	INTERNE	AMARONE	INTERNS	NAILSET
REALIST	TRAINED	BORNITE	SEMEION	PERSONA

The 500 most frequently played 8-letter words

AERATION	AEROTONE	INERTIAL	DENTARIA	ETIOLATE
INERTIAE	ETAERIOS	DETAINEE	DOUANIER	ALIENATE
ERIONITE	AEGIRINE	DAINTIER	TENORITE	LITERATO
AEROLITE	ANTERIOR	ERADIATE	TAENIATE	ANTIHERO

TENTORIA	EURONOTE	EARSTONE	ORANGIER	DURATIVE
AREOLATE	REANOINT	INTERLAY	LITERATI	TAGAREEN
RENAILED	ORGANDIE	PEARLITE	AEROFOIL	RURALITE
AEGIRITE	OLEFIANT	OTTERING	ENTOILED	RATOONED
TREENAIL	EULOGIAE	CLARINET	REGENTAL	EROTETIC
RETAILOR	EQUATION	ANOREXIA	TETRONAL	INTEGRAL
RETAINER	DENTALIA	STOVAINE	NITERIES	OVARIOLE
AERATING	ENDOSTEA	ERINITES	AERODYNE	PRIORATE
ELATERIN	ARENITIC	TOLERATE	DATURINE	UNTAILED
RETAINED	DERACINE	YEASTIER	ANOINTER	INTRIGUE
ORIENTED	UREDINIA	ANOESTRA	RETIRANT	TAURINES
INTERNAL	AIRLINER	NOSELITE	INVESTOR	UINTAITE
AURELIAN	ACIERATE	SAUTOIRE	SOTERIAL	ANOESTRI
DELATION	DELETION	ALIENERS	VIOLATER	AUREOLED
INAURATE	NONELITE	CERATOID	EGOITIES	TRITONIA
OLEARIAS	EATERIES	EROGENIC	NEOTERIC	STONERAW
ELOIGNER	CAROTENE	NEGATRON	TONSILAR	REGAINED
NOTITIAE	PAEONIES	OUTEATEN	TINWARES	RETICENT
ALIENAGE	RELATION	APERIENT	NOTARIZE	SAGENITE
INTERIOR	NEARLIER	DENTINAL	ANTIGENE	IDEATIVE
UNEASIER	ATROPINE	DIGERATI	DOLERITE	VIROGENE
DETAINER	SERENATE	TOLEWARE	ROYALISE	PINDAREE
INTERVAL	REGIONAL	GERANIOL	MEIONITE	DIPTERAN
ETOURDIE	ONERIEST	AGENESIA	IRONWARE	ANTRORSE
RITORNEL	AEQUORIN	DEROGATE	DRAISINE	AIRBORNE
ANTLERED	GAIETIES	TONALITE	ETERNISE	LORINERS
RETINOID	RATIONED	IDOLATER	INDENTOR	ERGATIVE
OEDIPEAN	ORDAINER	NETTLIER	FREDAINE	ANEARING
AERONAUT	ITERATED	TOLERANT	URINATOR	ERECTION
TAENIOID	ALEURONE	INTARSIA	ALIENEES	TRIAZINE
REORIENT	ANTIMERE	REGAINER	FETATION	DRONIEST
INLANDER	TENURIAL	IDEATING	TETRAGON	IRONIEST
FOEDARIE	GOITERED	REIGNITE	AROINTED	VALERIAN
ADROITER	DEAERATE	DATELINE	AUNTLIER	ARANEIDS
IODINATE	IRENICAL	LOITERER	ANSERINE	TRENDIER
INTERAGE	ASTONIED	ANTIWEED	SELENIAN	GLADIATE
IDEATION	INERTIAS	ANTIDOTE	ERIGERON	ANTEATER
ERGATOID	LINGERIE	RENOVATE	SARTORII	HEADNOTE
TERATOID	TENEBRIO	GAINLIER	RAISONNE	ANTHERID
ENTAILER	EGESTION	IBOGAINE	RAVIGOTE	SCENARIO
THIOUREA	ASTEROID	ORDINATE	DIALOGER	TOASTIER
DRAGONET	RETINULA	RETIARII	IRONWEED	BENITIER
RIGATONI	ARANEOUS	OUTRAISE	TAINTURE	AUREOLAE
DEVIATOR	DONATIVE	TAILERON	JETLINER	OUTRANGE
INTORTED	LATEENER	METANOIA	GERONTIC	GALENOID
TRIENNIA	DIRIGENT	ANORETIC	ELUVIATE	RECOINED
DERATION	PAINTIER	FARINOSE	REASONED	ITERANCE
ORIENTAL	NITRATED	RATTLINE	INDAGATE	DELETING
GRATINEE	FLOATIER	RETAILER	RITENUTO	REINVITE
INFERIAE	INERRANT	TROTLINE	ANURETIC	BIDENTAL
TRIOLEIN	TREELAWN	RAINIEST	AEROLITH	INVERITY
ANTIWEAR	ACTINIAE	RAINDATE	SENORITA	TAQUERIA
REINVADE	ENTRESOL	RELOANED	FAINTIER	AGENETIC
ELOINERS	INORNATE	NONIDEAL	SEAFRONT	DEAIRING
TAILORED	RENATURE	UNDERLIE	WINTERED	HERNIATE
ORIENTER	ELATERID	NEGATION	OUTLINER	ANTELOPE
SIDENOTE	SEROTINE	NEONATES	VERATRIN	DICENTRA
OVERLAIN	SEDATION	NONRATED	TOENAILS	ENAUNTER
ARTERIAL	YERSINIA	RESONATE	JAROSITE	CRINATED
ELONGATE	GENITURE	ANTIDORA	HOTELIER	ANTIRAPE

RETIEING	AGOUTIES	PAINTURE	AIRWOMEN	DESYATIN
TRINODAL	ROILIEST	CREATINE	EVERSION	RATICIDE
RONDELET	DELICATE	GRAINIER	OILERIES	ERECTILE
OLEANDER	LINEATED	ARSENATE	AIRPLANE	SNAILIER
RENEGADO	DOCTRINE	TRIPTANE	VAUNTIER	AURELIAS
CINEASTE	ACOEMETI	RETINTED	INTRANET	ACRIDINE
INDARTED	ONIONIER	TREADLER	LIGATURE	TEAHOUSE
RETINOLS	OBLIGATE	REASONER	ANTLIATE	SIDERITE
REORDAIN	SAUTERNE	OPTIONEE	DILIGENT	PERINEAL
DISENROL	AUROREAN	GREENLIT	REATTAIN	AUDITION
OUTLEARN	TOWERING	TRAINMEN	GRIEVANT	GAUNTREE
ERGOTISE	AILETTES	ENTRAINS	ANTIPOLE	SIRENIAN
LEPORINE	RIVERAIN	ANTIRIOT	NITROGEN	LATERITE
NEUTRINO	DISTRAIN	INTERLAP	JOINTERS	NEATENED
DENOTIVE	TETANOID	EVIRATES	RELEARNT	VENETIAN
INITIATE	DENDRITE	ERINGOES	LITERATE	INTONATE
ATTAINER	TILERIES	EROTISED	ENDORSEE	RADIOMEN
NAUSEATE	ENGAOLED	WAITERED	OUTREIGN	RETIRING
INTERBED	STRAINED	REINETTE	JAUNTIER	NARTJIES
LENTOIDS	TEENTIER	RARITIES	TENEBRAE	GASOLINE
ABOITEAU	STRINGED	ENROOTED	OUTGLARE	SNARLIER
RATOONER	FLANERIE	DARRAINE	ETHERIAL	GNARLIER
TOWNLIER	ALLERION	RENTABLE	TOLIDINE	ENDEAVOR
ABOIDEAU	DEUTERON	WATERING	ANTIARIN	ROGATION
TRENDOID	FOETIDER	RELISTED	GELATION	INTERROW
VAURIENS	ATTORNED	MEDIATOR	ROTATIVE	ROSINATE
THIONATE	EUGENIAS	EOLIENNE	RANCIDER	ICTERINE
OEILLADE	COTELINE	ANTILIFE	NOTIFIER	UNRETIRE
TRAVOISE	LECANORA	DISAGREE	INTERTIE	UNDERLIT
AERIFIED	CORONATE	REVOTING	LITEROSE	DEIONISE
EUGARIES	ALGERINE	STOLIDER	RETRAITE	INSOLATE
UNTIDIER	ANEROIDS	LARIATED	TAILBONE	VINTAGED
METAIRIE	PELORIAN	LABORITE	RINGTONE	ETHERION
ANETHOLE	AVENTAIL	FAVORITE	ANTIQUER	ANAEROBE
LUNARIES	ELATIONS	ERUPTION	DEATHIER	IRRIGATE
LANNERET	ANISETTE	ATRAZINE	VENTAILE	TENDRILS

The 1000 most frequently played 2-to-8-letter words

QI	YO	JAI	JET	ADZ
QAT	OI	IWI	JEW	VAW
XI	EUOI	FE	ZOA	FAX
OX	OY	QATS	TRANQ	NIX
ZA	OW	SUQ	WIZ	JAW
EX	WO	AI	WOX	OYE
QIS	YU	HI	AZO	AE
AX	FY	AA	JIN	EA
ZO	EE	AIA	OAF	BI
JO	JOE	AY	ZED	NY
JA	AW	YA	JIZ	HE
XU	WE	JEE	YEX	ZAG
QADI	ZEE	VEX	ZEX	REZ
QAID	OXO	UH	EH	ZAX
OF	EXO	VOX	JIAO	KO
OO	AXE	OH	GOX	AUA
IF	YE	ZEA	HM	HO
OE	FA	WEX	WAX	YOU
IO	OU	TAJ	HEX	NOX
QUA	EF	FEZ	TIX	VOW

BEZ	AJEE	OD	PE	JAK
JEU	ID	VIG	SEZ	ZINE
FIZ	FAQIR	FIE	WOG	JEAT
RIZ	KA	ZITE	CUZ	FEM
ZIN	FIX	TALAQ	AD	WIT
JIG	NIQAB	ZETA	FAE	JEED
ZIT	AYU	ZATI	GU	NE
EAU	EYE	MI	VIEW	QUIN
FOX	HUI	PI	EM	PO
WOF	ZAP	DITZ	VAG	ME
BY	JIVE	ZEK	FIVE	VIA
HOX	JOR	ZOEAE	AG	VUM
FEW	JOY	VID	JOL	DUI
JOW	KEX	JUD	VUG	FAY
DEX	ZOL	AVO	WAE	QUAT
UEY	JOB	FEU	KY	JEON
HAJ	FOH	FAH	FOP	UN
AH	JAG	JAR	HOE	VAU
ZOO	WUD	JEEZ	EN	DA
WAI	JEDI	WIG	POX	JANE
ZIG	ZIP	AHI	JOEY	ED
RAJ	GOV	HIE	TI	DIF
WOO	WEB	QUIZ	FAP	YID
QANAT	QUAG	OVA	ZORI	VAN
DZO	HOI	AUF	OYEZ	FUB
TEX	FEH	TREZ	DEV	VIE
KI	QOPH	TUX	FOY	AVOW
AUE	VIM	DUX	HOA	DJIN
BE	GO	QUEP	RITZ	FAG
JAY	BO	IVY	IBEX	QUEEN
OOF	UFO	PAV	BENJ	MO
LEZ	AWA	UVA	EVO	YEW
MY	JUT	DOF	QUID	PEW
ZOEA	POZ	GIF	LI	ZEST
FOE	MIZ	FEG	OHO	COZ
OWE	FAA	FIB	WEE	ER
JOG	IT	GJU	OUIJA	AR
GI	DI	DIV	GUV	NO
QUAI	AB	OP	JETE	TWP
TAX	GEEZ	VOE	UR	JADE
HA	HIOI	YOW	LAX	WAG
WOE	OXY	ZITI	VET	WAIF
RAX	JAP	UP	HAO	WEM
BOX	JEFE	QUEY	OHIA	AN
JOT	MOZ	BA	OUZO	MU
WAQF	PIX	UG	DO	WIN
IN	YAE	FEE	FEY	AAH
OB	JUN	OM	NU	XIS
ZEL	AYE	OR	QUIT	FIG
QUOD	PAX	EWE	SAZ	JEAN
LUZ	QORMA	LOX	VOR	QUOTE
JAM	ZEIN	ON	QUOP	VIAE
ZHO	MAX	CAZ	HUE	UT
ZEP	YEA	MIX	BOW	JIRD
JAB	AQUA	JUVE	JUG	QUIM
REX	FOU	LEX	QIBLA	ZOAEA
JIB	EAUX	AWE	WAB	TAV
IXIA	VEG	OOH	QUAY	GREX
FAW	FAB	VIN	FOG	UM
BIZ	FOB	QUAD	ZERO	HEW

DE	KEF	QUEAN	BOH	TEW
FUJI	FAVE	OIK	QUOIN	ONIE
WIFE	ZOOEA	OFT	ETUI	FIN
ANOA	AM	MM	GEE	POW
ZONE	QUENA	LUV	DOUX	NEW
WYE	LO	ROQUE	FUG	YAH
WEY	OOZE	TUI	VITEX	QUIET
NEF	EGO	ZARF	GOA	EVE
JAVA	GIE	DOJO	JEST	VINO
ROJI	FAD	JIVY	WAY	ZINC
OGEE	VEE	POI	WED	YOWE
SIX	FON	LUX	JEEL	WOK
FAIX	PIU	WEN	FEN	DOW
AWEE	JAFA	ZEAL	ABO	HOB
RE	ST	YITIE	ERASION	KUE
AQUAE	QUERN	ADO	MA	QUARE
MEW	QINTAR	BAP	GOE	AIDOI
NERTZ	FRIZ	QUOIT	TEF	GOY
ET	OBE	BAH	YIP	HEN
GIO	IOTA	AGO	WAP	ILEX
VEXT	AGIO	ZAS	JEUX	SEX
ZAIRE	JEER	EXIT	AERATION	IZAR
VAT	OBI	FIT	RIF	JAXIE
PA	JILT	AT	OBO	SI
QUOIF	TE	ZILA	ZUPA	QUEME
JATO	WIVE	OXID	ONO	KOW
JOIN	WOW	JUDO	QUATE	NOH
JEEP	VAE	INIA	ZANY	XENIA
HOO	VEGO	VIVO	WYN	QINDAR
VAV	MUX	OBIA	OFAY	REV
GOO	KAF	BOP	OKA	AUK
HUIA	OUK	KEG	PAW	NAZI
HAW	QUIP	GRENZ	FUN	EOAN
YIN	GEY	KIF	HID	EWT
VLY	QUOAD	YOD	EQUID	JIVED
AHA	FAVA	AVIZE	HOG	SOV
NTH	SH	APEX	ETESIAN	HIN
HOAX	MOW	UTU	TOQUE	AZAN
JINX	ETAERIO	JAPE	NEXT	PEG
EL	VROW	WOVE	DUH	QUIRE
CH	WOP	ZOIC	BIO	VOID
ZOWIE	KOA	ZOOT	WET	UVAE
WAW	COX	DEF	PREZ	UVEA
NA	BOI	JAIL	WOT	OXEN
KOI	JOBE	VAR	WHO	LUTZ
ODEA	ZONA	SOX	AEON	VERB
OAK	HAJI	YAY	AL	ONE
EVOE	ODA	JEWIE	DIXI	QAIDS
TO	FUD	QUINO	OBOE	FED
JIBE	IS	QADIS	OBA	OTARINE
HOW	JOTA	FAZE	VROT	FUTZ
FID	HOY	FIQUE	DEW	QUAIR
HAE	JEHU	DOO	MOI	MIRV
YEH	BEG	VOL	VIZY	ATONIES
QUOTA	ZOS	ZEBU	VAC	UMIAQ
YAW	QUEER	SAX	TYG	EUK
AVA	WEXE	JOLE	GOAF	VINT
VIBE	GAJO	OKE	TZAR	APO
BEE	MAW	UNI	TOEA	HYE
JUTE	GEO	HEY	WON	INERTIAE

JUPE	AINEE	FAUX	AITU	EDH
CWM	DIVI	JURA	JEUNE	GUE
JUS	BOA	MZEE	PREX	HOD
OOP	JANN	YONI	POO	ION
IRE	BIZE	HAG	JAGA	YITE
FAN	TOZE	ADIEU	FAUVE	TAXA
YOB	OOT	TAW	DAK	GAZE
TA	EEJIT	WINO	LAV	NAZE
KAW	NIXE	AXED	OWT	QUALE
VINY	KEB	JISM	ROUX	WAT
EEK	JINN	NAOI	EON	GAY
FUM	MOAI	HIP	SITZ	YEP
JOHN	GHI	YUM	WADI	IDEA
OORIE	JETON	SWIZ	JERID	RIN
FOID	RIZA	LEV	HIM	DIAZO
HAZE	UPO	QUIPO	GEM	VAGI
FIGO	PERV	HOOF	FIR	AIGA
YOWIE	EFT	GIB	JIGOT	VEND
EIK	PUTZ	AIOLI	OUD	ICE
WHA	QUINE	WHY	AEROLITE	GOD
VEEP	HIVE	DERV	AVE	HAY
ODE	TIVY	HERTZ	FIDO	PIA
WRY	DAW	YGO	PIZE	NEB
AUDIO	EXON	NOO	XOANA	MINX
BEEF	ERIONITE	ZOBU	KAZI	IDE
YEVE	DUO	EAVE	FEOD	ROO
WAD	YEAH	PUB	WAN	AWN
OIDIA	HADJ	BEY	QUEST	GIP
ZOON	CAW	HEH	UMU	WOAD
LA	EMO	AKA	US	ENVY
WAREZ	TOY	OOR	HOVE	EQUAL
AFT	NAW	NOW	HAAF	ERUV
YUTZ	FEEB	YAD	VIGA	REI
KIVA	JIRRE	BIG	VEHM	VOTE
FADO	LANX	AZON	TIE	EME
FOVEA	ONY	KOJI	GAB	ZURF
AGEE	EWK	WEFT	ZEES	OUP
DOY	OOM	YOGI	ZOOID	ZOOM
QUINA	INERTIA	WAVE	VINEW	VENT
YETI	EUGE	KIWI	EIDE	WHIO
BOO	YAG	YEN	ICY	VIS
WUS	UKE	BAA	AGA	JOLT
HUB	FET	ENE	ZOOEY	WIFIE
EINE	FAT	MOOI	OMOV	JUBE
CIAO	IDEE	HIT	QUBIT	OAR
OON	YON	AXON	EKE	IURE
ZANTE	GOB	WEIZE	BUY	WUDU
QUITE	ZING	NAH	COOEE	JOWL
FUZE	VETO	MIB	TOO	ZEDS
UDO	TAXI	PHT	KUIA	TOE
OPE	PIE	COW	ULU	AUTO
POA	DOH	JIVER	WAVY	DAVY
VARIX	ABA	YOM	PEH	ONYX
JONG	YET	OUPA	TWIG	DIG
TWO	BEAU	KAI	VUGH	KHI
TOW	YUG	BEVY	HUN	HIYA
WOOF	GUY	VATU	WHIZ	DAH
RIOJA	JOUR	OXER	FINI	MOU
PYX	YAGI	MEOW	FOAM	DEI
JURE	JARL	ZLOTE	KAIE	AEROTONE

The 1000 most frequently played 2-to-8-letter words without J, Q, X, or Z

OF	MY	FIB	PO	VLY
OO	FOE	DIV	ME	AHA
IF	OWE	OP	VIA	NTH
OE	GI	VOE	VUM	EL
IO	HA	YOW	DUI	CH
YO	WOE	UP	FAY	WAW
OI	IN	BA	UN	NA
EUOI	OB	UG	VAU	KOI
OY	FAW	FEE	DA	ODEA
OW	ID	OM	ED	OAK
WO	KA	OR	DIF	EVOE
YU	AYU	EWE	YID	TO
FY	EYE	ON	VAN	HOW
EE	HUI	AWE	FUB	FID
AW	FOH	OOH	VIE	HAE
WE	WUD	VIN	AVOW	YEH
YE	GOV	PE	FAG	YAW
FA	WEB	WOG	MO	AVA
OU	HOI	AD	YEW	VIBE
EF	FEH	FAE	PEW	BEE
IWI	VIM	GU	ER	KEF
FE	GO	VIEW	AR	FAVE
AI	BO	EM	NO	AM
HI	UFO	VAG	TWP	LO
AA	AWA	FIVE	WAG	EGO
AIA	FAA	AG	WAIF	GIE
AY	IT	VUG	WEM	FAD
YA	DI	WAE	AN	VEE
UH	AB	KY	MU	FON
OH	HIOI	FOP	WIN	PIU
OAF	YAE	HOE	AAH	ST
EH	AYE	EN	FIG	OBE
HM	YEA	TI	VIAE	IOTA
VAW	FOU	FAP	UT	AGIO
OYE	VEG	DEV	TAV	OBI
AE	FAB	FOY	UM	TE
EA	FOB	HOA	HEW	WIVE
BI	OD	EVO	DE	WOW
NY	VIG	LI	WIFE	VAE
HE	FIE	OHO	ANOA	VEGO
KO	MI	WEE	WYE	KAF
AUA	PI	GUV	WEY	OUK
HO	VID	UR	NEF	GEY
YOU	AVO	VET	OGEE	FAVA
VOW	FEU	HAO	AWEE	SH
EAU	FAH	OHIA	RE	MOW
WOF	WIG	DO	MEW	ETAERIO
BY	AHI	FEY	ET	VROW
FEW	HIE	NU	GIO	WOP
UEY	OVA	VOR	VAT	KOA
AH	AUF	HUE	PA	BOI
WAI	IVY	BOW	HOO	ODA
WOO	PAV	WAB	VAV	FUD
KI	UVA	FOG	GOO	IS
AUE	DOF	FEM	HUIA	HOY
BE	GIF	WIT	HAW	BEG
OOF	FEG	NE	YIN	MAW

GEO	BIO	YOB	FEEB	YOM
OIK	WET	TA	ONY	OUPA
OFT	WOT	KAW	EWK	KAI
MM	WHO	VINY	OOM	BEVY
LUV	AEON	EEK	INERTIA	VATU
TUI	AL	FUM	EUGE	MEOW
POI	OBOE	OORIE	YAG	AITU
WEN	OBA	FOID	UKE	POO
YITIE	VROT	FIGO	FET	FAUVE
ADO	DEW	YOWIE	FAT	DAK
BAP	MOI	EIK	IDEE	LAV
BAH	VAC	WHA	YON	OWT
AGO	TYG	VEEP	GOB	EON
FIT	GOAF	ODE	VETO	WADI
AT	TOEA	WRY	PIE	HIM
INIA	WON	AUDIO	DOH	GEM
VIVO	TEW	BEEF	ABA	FIR
OBIA	ONIE	YEVE	YET	OUD
BOP	FIN	WAD	BEAU	AEROLITE
KEG	POW	OIDIA	YUG	AVE
KIF	NEW	LA	GUY	FIDO
YOD	YAH	AFT	YAGI	FEOD
UTU	EVE	KIVA	YONI	WAN
WOVE	VINO	FADO	HAG	UMU
DEF	YOWE	FOVEA	ADIEU	US
VAR	WOK	AGEE	TAW	HOVE
YAY	DOW	DOY	WINO	HAAF
DOO	HOB	YETI	NAOI	VIGA
VOL	KUE	BOO	HIP	VEHM
OKE	AIDOI	WUS	YUM	TIE
UNI	GOY	HUB	LEV	GAB
HEY	HEN	EINE	HOOF	VINEW
BOH	SI	CIAO	GIB	EIDE
ETUI	KOW	OON	AIOLI	ICY
GEE	NOH	UDO	WHY	AGA
FUG	REV	OPE	DERV	OMOV
GOA	AUK	POA	YGO	EKE
WAY	EOAN	TWO	NOO	BUY
WED	EWT	TOW	EAVE	COOEE
FEN	SOV	WOOF	PUB	TOO
ABO	HIN	AINEE	BEY	KUIA
ERASION	PEG	DIVI	HEH	ULU
MA	VOID	BOA	AKA	WAVY
GOE	UVAE	OOT	OOR	PEH
TEF	UVEA	KEB	NOW	TWIG
YIP	VERB	MOAI	YAD	VUGH
WAP	ONE	GHI	BIG	HUN
AERATION	FED	UPO	WEFT	FINI
RIF	OTARINE	PERV	YOGI	FOAM
OBO	MIRV	EFT	WAVE	KAIE
ONO	ATONIES	HIVE	KIWI	EDH
WYN	EUK	TIVY	YEN	GUE
OFAY	VINT	DAW	BAA	HOD
OKA	APO	ERIONITE	ENE	ION
PAW	HYE	DUO	MOOI	YITE
FUN	INERTIAE	YEAH	HIT	WAT
HID	CWM	CAW	NAH	GAY
HOG	OOP	EMO	MIB	YEP
ETESIAN	IRE	TOY	PHT	IDEA
DUH	FAN	NAW	COW	RIN

VAGI	HOWE	ANOW	VANT	DID
AIGA	ANY	AIERIES	MOB	GAD
VEND	WAGE	THY	SERIATE	DAG
ICE	APE	DEY	HAVE	AERIE
GOD	BID	GED	WRIT	FOHN
HAY	VIVA	FOGIE	MIAOW	SENARII
PIA	FAWN	KEA	VRIL	ANISOLE
NEB	INN	AKE	YODE	FIND
IDE	PHI	HOUF	FLEW	AULOI
ROO	GAU	TAO	INOSITE	MHO
AWN	ETAERIOS	MIAOU	MOY	BOK
GIP	UTE	FRY	YIPE	ISATINE
WOAD	KID	WIRY	HUT	ESTRONE
ENVY	DOE	VIGIA	UNAU	LOY
ERUV	ES	GRAV	VULN	GUB
REI	VEGA	PIG	PUH	WIS
VOTE	GYVE	EPEE	ANE	NAY
EME	DOWF	HAN	VADE	FADY
OUP	BOY	VIED	BIDI	ADAW
VENT	DIB	PFUI	WAR	RAH
WHIO	VITA	VIEWY	FANO	KET
VIS	PIOY	HON	TYE	FEME
WIFIE	WIPE	MOA	HUG	HAH
OAR	UNAI	AEGIRINE	FOIN	WITE
IURE	GID	MOG	BOD	TOYO
WUDU	OLEO	KAB	NEE	AIM
TOE	LEW	ORIGANE	BAFT	ABOVE
AUTO	ANA	NAVY	TEG	ORE
DAVY	VOGIE	KAE	HEM	BRR
DIG	HOH	GOWF	TAY	GYP
KHI	BAY	OLIO	OTARIES	KEY
HIYA	MOE	OGIVE	WAUR	OLEARIA
DAH	COO	DOB	ROSEATE	TAK
MOU	HAD	GET	ECO	DUG
DEI	OVUM	GAE	PEA	TOG
AEROTONE	ILIA	NOB	FOEN	KIT
OAT	TOEY	DAY	NON	OHM
EROTISE	REW	BUFO	VROUW	DOD
REH	VANG	ODAH	AHOY	SO
AERO	CEE	OURIE	FIAT	BOEP
NOY	AID	EUOUAE	AMU	GREW
VIVE	ROW	BAG	KAVA	OIL
BIVIA	YOK	NIE	RIVO	WEAVE
GOEY	SUI	RAW	WAID	PST
KOP	BYE	ANI	AIDE	GOT
WAIVE	BIN	NIB	AS	YAUD
YOOF	BEN	MOO	WEEP	LEI
VIFDA	DOG	REF	DEAF	LOO
WEEM	MEU	NOVA	PAUA	YAK
TWA	YUP	GYM	AVOID	URAO
EEN	MEOU	WEID	HEBE	OUR
BOG	PEE	MIG	RHY	GOOF
OWN	ITA	VITE	HOM	RID
HAUF	AGE	DEG	LOW	ENUF
OS	EERIE	HEP	DIP	KIP
MEG	GAP	CIG	SEALINE	PIVOT
VROU	EMU	WICE	LOOIE	PUY
FOR	TEE	ABY	KIEF	LAW
WILI	MEE	TAENIAE	FONE	BON
ORA	FUR	NYE	NEK	ANTERIOR

BIT	KED	DIM	ISOLATE	PED
KEP	EINA	DETAINEE	TIG	KAY
WAFT	PYE	LOU	WAWE	COG
WIDE	DEIF	DUE	AMIE	AIR
KOB	ENOW	VOAR	AGUE	UTA
DAB	NOR	DEE	FIL	NIEF
FRIB	AVID	ATUA	LIEU	VAMP
YAP	BOWIE	TOD	NIM	VENOM
VILD	ARENITE	BAM	BEEP	VOEMA
RIOTISE	FAR	GIT	FOUD	COY
FER	SPIV	WINY	WEMB	YGOE
AMI	FOOD	WOOT	FUGIO	BOVID
YEBO	NAB	YAM	VIDE	FINO
OUT	VIBS	GIVE	KEEF	KON
ANEROID	BUG	BET	PAH	BREW
HUP	POH	HOWF	ORF	VERY
HOYA	FEHM	MEVE	NAN	OOFY
POUF	VEGIE	YOGA	EGG	VIDEO
EMEU	ECU	COB	HEFT	FOOT
AERIEST	INERTIAL	AWAY	OUMA	HOVEA
BED	OCA	VOWS	NOD	URAEI
DYE	OBEY	OLEA	DIE	HET
FRO	DEB	DOM	HOT	NEP

Words from World English

One method of dealing with the awkward tile combinations that inevitably appear on your rack at some point in a game is to memorize a wide selection of words outside the core vocabulary of English. As the most widely spoken language in the world, English is rich in loan-words from other languages, and the versatility of the Roman alphabet and of English pronunciation means that these words tend to be assimilated without much corruption of their original sound. This means that there are many word in English that use 'foreign' letter combinations, which are ideal for Scrabble players. The following lists contain words from Australia, Canada, New Zealand and South Africa, as well as words from the main languages of the Indian Subcontinent - Hindi and Urdu - which have entered British English.

Australian words

Australian English is distinguished not only by the numerous Aboriginal terms for Australia's flora and fauna, but also by a great many shortened forms of commonplace English words. The Australian propensity to slang and short informal words is extremely useful to Scrabble players, especially as many of these words end in O, one of the most common tiles in the game. If you spot an O on the board when you have a difficult set of letters on your rack, there's a good chance that you'll be able to form an informal Aussie word. Native Australian words provide a range of unusual letter combinations, as well as a tendency to include double Os - ideal for rack balancing. Double Rs are also common in Australian English, as are Ks and Ys, so it's well worth acquiring some Antipodean vocabulary.

ADJIGO	yam plant
ALF	uncultivated Australian
ARVO	afternoon
ASPRO	associate professor
BARRO	embarrassing
BAUERA	small evergreen shrub
BEAUT	outstanding person or thing
BELAH	casuarina tree
BERKO	berserk
BIFFO	fighting or aggressive behaviour
BILBY	burrowing marsupial
BIZZO	empty and irrelevant talk
BOAB	baobab tree
BODGIE	unruly or uncouth man
BOGAN	fool
BOOBOOK	small spotted brown owl
BOOFY	strong but stupid
BOONG	offensive word for a Black person
BOOSHIT	very good
BORA	native Australian coming-of-age ceremony
BORAK	rubbish or nonsense
BRASCO	lavatory
BROLGA	large grey crane with red-and-green head
BRUMBY	wild horse
BUNYA	tall dome-shaped coniferous tree
BUNYIP	legendary monster
CADAGI	tropical eucalyptus tree
CARBY	carburettor
CHEWIE	chewing gum
CHIACK	tease or banter
CHOCO	conscript or militiaman
CHOOK	hen or chicken
CHOOM	Englishman
COMMO	communist
COMPO	compensation
CORREA	evergreen shrub
COUCAL	long-legged bird
COUGAN	rowdy person
CRONK	unfit or unsound
CROOL	spoil
CROWEA	pink-flowered shrub
DACK	forcibly remove someone's trousers
DADAH	illegal drugs
DAGGY	untidy or dishevelled
DASYURE	small carnivorous marsupial
DELO	delegate
DERRO	vagrant
DINKUM	genuine or right
DOCO	documentary
DONGA	steep-sided gully
DORBA	stupid, inept, or clumsy person
DRACK	unattractive
DRONGO	slow-witted person
DROOB	pathetic person
DUBBO	stupid
DUGITE	venomous snake
DURRY	cigarette
EARBASH	talk incessantly
EUMUNG	type of acacia
EVO	evening

EXO	excellent
FASTIE	deceitful act
FESTY	dirty or smelly
FIBRO	house built of fibrocement
FIGJAM	very conceited person
FIZGIG	frivolous or flirtatious girl
FOULIE	bad mood
FRIB	short heavy-conditioned piece of wool
FUNDIE	fundamentalist Christian
FURPHY	rumour or fictitious story
GALAH	grey-and-pink cockatoo
GARBO	dustman
GEEBUNG	tree with edible but tasteless fruit
GIDGEE	small acacia tree that sometimes emits an unpleasant smell
GILGAI	natural water hole
GING	child's catapult
GNOW	ground-dwelling bird
GOANNA	monitor lizard
GOOG	egg
GOOLIE	stone or pebble
GUNYAH	bush hut or shelter
GYMPIE	tall tree with stinging hairs on its leaves
HAKEA	type of shrub or tree
HOSTIE	air hostess
HOVEA	plant with purple flowers
HUTCHIE	groundsheet draped over an upright stick as a shelter
JARRAH	type of eucalyptus tree
JEFF	downsize or close down an organization
JUMBUCK	sheep
KARRI	type of eucalyptus tree
KOORI	native Australian
KYBO	temporary lavatory
KYLIE	boomerang that is flat on one side and convex on the other
LOPPY	man employed to do maintenance work on a ranch
LOWAN	ground-dwelling bird
LUBRA	Aboriginal woman
MALLEE	low shrubby eucalyptus tree
MARRI	type of eucalyptus
MIDDY	middle-sized glass of beer
MILKO	milkman
MOLOCH	spiny lizard
MOPOKE	small spotted owl
MOZ	hoodoo or hex
MUGGA	eucalyptus tree with pink flowers and dark bark
MULGA	acacia shrub
MULLOCK	waste material from a mine
MURREE	native Australian
MURRI	native Australian
MYALL	native Australian living independently of society
MYXO	myxomatosis
NANA	head
NARDOO	cloverlike fern
NEDDY	horse
NOAH	shark
NONG	stupid or incompetent person
NORK	female breast
NUMBAT	small marsupial with long snout
OCKER	uncultivated or boorish Australian
PIKER	wild bullock
PINDAN	desert region of Western Australia

PITURI	shrub with narcotic leaves
PLONKO	alcoholic, especially one who drinks wine
PLURRY	euphemism for bloody
PODDY	handfed calf or lamb
POKIE	poker machine
POON	stupid or ineffectual person
POONCE	male homosexual
POSSIE	position
PRELOVED	second-hand
QUOKKA	small wallaby
QUOLL	native cat
RAZOO	imaginary coin
REFFO	offensive term for a European refugee after World War Two
REGO	registration of a motor vehicle
RESTO	restored antique, vintage car, etc
ROO	kangaroo
ROUGHIE	something unfair, especially a trick
SANGER	sandwich
SANGO	sandwich
SCOZZA	rowdy person
SCUNGY	miserable, sordid or dirty
SHARPIE	member of a teenage group with short hair and distinctive clothes
SHERANG	boss
SHYPOO	liquor of poor quality
SITELLA	small black-and-white bird
SKEG	rear fin on the underside of a surfboard
SKITE	boast
SMOKO	cigarette break
SMOODGE	smooch
SPAG	offensive term for an Italian
SPRUIK	speak in public
SWAGGIE	vagrant worker
SWAGMAN	vagrant worker
SWY	gambling game
TONK	effeminate man
TOOSHIE	angry or upset
TRIELLA	three horse races nominated for a bet
TROPPO	mentally affected by a tropical climate
TRUCKIE	truck driver
TRUGO	game similar to croquet
TUAN	flying phalanger
TUART	type of eucalyptus tree
UMPIE	umpire
UNCO	awkward or clumsy
UPTA	of poor quality
UPTER	of poor quality
UTE	utility
VAG	vagrant
VEGO	vegetarian
VIGORO	women's game similar to cricket
WADDY	heavy wooden club used by native Australians
WAGGA	blanket made of sacks stitched together
WANDOO	eucalyptus tree with white bark
WARATAH	shrub with dark green leaves and crimson flowers
WARB	dirty or insignificant person
WHARFIE	wharf labourer
WIDGIE	female bodgie
WILGA	small drought-resistant tree
WIRILDA	acacia tree with edible seeds

WIRRAH	saltwater fish with bright blue spots
WOF	fool or idiot
WOOMERA	spear-throwing stick
WURLEY	Aboriginal hut
YABBER	talk or jabber
YABBY	small freshwater crayfish
YACCA	grass tree
YACKA	grass tree
YARRAN	small hardy tree
YATE	small eucalyptus tree
YIKE	argument, squabble or fight
YUCKO	disgusting
YUMMO	delicious
ZAMBUCK	St John ambulance attendant
ZIFF	beard

Canadian words

Canadian English combines a broad range of British and US terms with words derived from Inuit, as well as from other Native American languages such as Algonquin. Canadian English incorporates many Canadian French words from Quebec, and there are also a number of recently coined Canadian terms. Inuit words can be helpful to Scrabble players because they tend to be quite vowel-heavy. K occurs frequently in Inuit terms, and sometimes appears twice. Such words require a blank tile for the second K if they are to be played during a game.

AGLOO	breathing hole made in ice by a seal
AGLU	breathing hole made in ice by a seal
AMAUT	hood on an Inuit woman's parka for carrying a child
AMOWT	hood on an Inuit woman's parka for carrying a child
ATIGI	Inuit parka
BABICHE	thongs or lacings of rawhide
BARACHOIS	shallow lagoon formed by a sand bar
BATEAU	light flat-bottomed boat
BEIGNET	deep-fried pastry
BOGAN	sluggish side stream
BREWIS	Newfoundland cod stew
BUTTE	isolated steep-sided flat-topped hill
CANOLA	cooking oil extracted from a variety of rapeseed developed in Canada
CAYUSE	small Native American pony used by cowboys
COULEE	dry stream valley
CUSK	gadoid food fish
DEKE	act or instance of feinting in ice hockey
HOSER	unsophisticated rural person
ICEWINE	dessert wine made from frozen grapes
JOUAL	nonstandard Canadian French dialect
KAMIK	Inuit boot made of caribou hide or sealskin
KLOOCH	North American Indian woman
KLOOTCH	North American Indian woman
KUDLIK	Inuit soapstone seal-oil lamp
LOGAN	backwater
LOONIE	Canadian dollar coin with loon bird on one face
MUCKAMUCK	food
MUKTUK	beluga skin used as food
NANOOK	polar bear

PARFLECHE	dried rawhide
PARKADE	building used as a car park
PARKETTE	small public park
PLEW	beaver skin used as standard unit in fur trading
POGEY	financial relief for the unemployed
POGY	financial relief for the unemployed
POKELOGAN	backwater
POUTINE	chipped potatoes topped with curd cheese and tomato sauce
PUNG	horse-drawn sleigh
REDEYE	drink incorporating beer and tomato juice
RUBABOO	soup made by boiling pemmican
RUBBY	rubbing alcohol mixed with cheap wine for drinking
SKOOKUM	strong or brave
SNYE	side channel of a river
SPLAKE	hybrid trout bred by Canadian zoologists
SWILER	seal hunter
TILLICUM	friend
TOONIE	Canadian two-dollar coin
TULLIBEE	whitefish found in the Great Lakes
TUPEK	Inuit tent of animal skins
TUPIK	Inuit tent of animal skins
TWONIE	Canadian two-dollar coin
WAWA	speech or language
WENDIGO	evil spirit or cannibal

Hindi words

After Chinese, Hindi, the dominant language of India, is the most widely spoken language in the world. Many Hindi words entered British English during the Raj, and some have become everyday terms – BUNGALOW and PUNDIT, for example. Others are less common, but are useful to Scrabble players because they provide unusual letter combinations and thus solutions to difficult racks. Combinations such as BH, DH and KH are common in Hindi-derived words, and the preponderance of As, Is and Us can be very helpful in trying to balance a vowel-heavy rack. Above all, Hindi words are useful because they are quite unusual, and so provide a range of options for Scrabble players that aren't immediately obvious - fronthooking onto hang with a B, for example, or end-hooking onto PUNK with an A. Committing some Hindi-derived words to memory will help to keep your opponents on their toes.

AKHARA	gymnasium
ALAP	vocal music without words
AMBARY	tropical plant
ANKUS	elephant goad
ANNA	old copper coin
ARTI	Hindu ritual
AYAH	maidservant or nursemaid
BABU	Mr
BAEL	spiny tree
BAHADUR	title for distinguished Indians during the Raj
BANDH	general strike
BANYAN	tree with aerial roots
BHAJI	deep-fried vegetable savoury
BHANG	psychoactive drug made of hemp
BHANGRA	music combining traditional Punjabi music with Western pop
BHAVAN	large house or building

BHEESTY	water-carrier
BHINDI	okra used in cooking
BHISHTI	water-carrier
BINDI	decorative dot in middle of forehead
BOBBERY	mixed pack of hunting dogs
BUND	embankment
CHAI	tea, especially with added spices
CHAMPAC	tree with fragrant yellow flowers
CHAPATI	flat coarse unleavened bread
CHAPPAL	sandal
CHARAS	hashish
CHARKHA	spinning wheel
CHELA	disciple of a religious teacher
CHICHI	person of mixed British and Indian descent
CHILLUM	pipe for smoking cannabis
CHITAL	the axis deer
CHOLI	short-sleeved bodice
CHOWK	marketplace
CHUDDAR	large shawl or veil
CHUDDIES	underpants
CHUKAR	Indian partridge
COWAGE	tropical climbing plant with stinging pods
COWHAGE	tropical climbing plant with stinging pods
CRORE	ten million
DACOIT	member of a gang of armed robbers
DACOITY	robbery by an armed gang
DAK	system of mail delivery
DAL	split grain
DATURA	plant with trumpet-shaped flowers
DEODAR	Himalayan cedar
DEWAN	chief minister of an Indian princedom
DHAK	tropical tree with red flowers
DHAL	curry made from lentils
DHARNA	method of obtaining justice by fasting
DHOBI	washerman
DHOTI	loincloth
DUPATTA	scarf
DURBAR	court of an Indian ruler
DURRIE	cotton carpet
DURZI	Indian tailor
GANJA	potent form of cannabis
GAUR	large wild cow
GARIAL	fish-eating crocodilian with long slender snout
GAVIAL	fish-eating crocodilian with long slender snout
GHARIAL	fish-eating crocodilian with long slender snout
GHARRI	horse-drawn vehicle for hire
GHARRY	horse-drawn vehicle for hire
GHAT	stairs or passage leading down to a river
GHEE	clarified butter
GHERAO	industrial action in which workers imprison their employers
GINGILI	oil obtained from sesame seeds
GORAL	small goat antelope
GUAR	plant that produces gum
GUNNY	coarse fabric used for sacks
HARTAL	act of closing shop or stopping work as a political protest
HOWDAH	seat for riding on an elephant's back
JAGGERY	coarse brown sugar
JAI	victory
KHADDAR	cotton cloth
KHEDA	enclosure for captured elephants

KHEDAH	enclosure for captured elephants
KHEDDAH	enclosure for captured elephants
KOEL	parasitic cuckoo
KOS	Indian unit of distance
KRAIT	brightly coloured venomous snake
KUKRI	Ghurka knife
KULFI	Indian dessert
KURTA	long loose garment like a shirt without a collar
LAC	resinous substance secreted by insects
LAKH	100,000
LANGUR	arboreal monkey
LASSI	yoghurt drink
LATHI	long heavy stick used as a weapon
LUNGI	long piece of cloth worn as loincloth or turban
MACHAN	platform used in tiger hunting
MAHOUT	elephant driver
MAHSEER	large freshwater fish
MANDI	big market
MANDIR	Hindu or Jain temple
MAUND	unit of weight
MEHNDI	practice of painting designs on the hands and feet using henna
MELA	cultural or religious festival
MOHUR	old gold coin
MONAL	Asian pheasant
MORCHA	hostile demonstration against the government
MRIDANG	drum used in Indian music
NAUCH	intricate Indian dance
NAUTCH	intricate Indian dance
NAWAB	Muslim prince in India
NEEM	large tree
NILGAI	large Indian antelope
NULLAH	stream or drain
NUMDAH	coarse felt
OONT	camel
PACHISI	game resembling backgammon
PAISA	one hundredth of a rupee
PAKORA	dish of deep-fried chicken or vegetables
PANEER	soft white cheese
PARATHA	flat unleavened bread
PEEPUL	tree similar to the banyan
PUNKA	fan made of palm leaves
PUNKAH	fan made of palm leaves
PURDA	custom of keeping women secluded
PURDAH	custom of keeping women secluded
PURI	unleavened flaky bread
PUTTEE	strip of cloth wound around the leg
RAGGEE	cereal grass
RAGI	cereal grass
RAITA	yoghurt-and-vegetable dish served with curry
RAJ	government
RAJAH	ruler or landlord
RAMTIL	African plant grown in India
RANEE	queen or princess
RANI	queen or princess
RATHA	four-wheeled carriage drawn by horses or bullocks
ROTI	type of unleavened bread
RUPEE	standard monetary unit of India
RYOT	peasant or tenant farmer
SAMBAR	deer with three-tined antlers

SAMITI	political association
SAMOSA	triangular pastry containing spiced vegetables or meat
SARANGI	stringed instrument played with a bow
SARDAR	Sikh title
SARI	traditional dress of Indian women
SAROD	Indian stringed instrument
SWAMI	title for a Hindu saint or religious teacher
TABLA	pair of drums whose pitches can be varied
THALI	meal consisting of several small dishes
TIL	sesame
TOLA	unit of weight
TONGA	light two-wheeled vehicle
TOPEE	pith helmet
TOPI	pith helmet
URD	bean plant
VAHANA	vehicle in Indian myth
VANDA	type of orchid
VINA	stringed musical instrument
WALLAH	person in charge of a specific thing
ZENANA	part of a house reserved for women and girls
ZILA	administrative district in India
ZILLA	administrative district in India
ZILLAH	administrative district in India

New Zealand words

While New Zealand and Australian English have many words in common, the Kiwi lexicon is greatly enriched by New Zealand's Maori heritage. Maori-derived words are a marvellous resource for the Scrabble player, providing a wealth of unusual vowel combinations, and frequently using consonants that are rarer in European words, such as K, W and H. Maori words are especially good for balancing vowel-heavy racks, as many words use several As, Us or Is – sometimes with three vowels in a row. Relatively high-scoring consonants are also very common, especially K and H. Unfortunately, there is only one K in Scrabble, so many Maori words with two Ks are less useful than they might initially appear. Don't forget blank tiles, however: if you have a blank, a K and a couple of vowels on your rack, there's a good chance that you can find a New Zealand word to play profitably. There are also some unusual words that have entered the vocabulary of New Zealanders from European or Asian languages.

ATUA	spirit or demon
BOOHAI	thoroughly lost
COOTIE	body louse
GOORIE	mongrel dog
GRAUNCH	crush or destroy
HAKA	war dance
HANGI	open-air cooking pit
HAPU	subtribe
HAPUKA	large fish
HAPUKU	large fish
HEITIKI	neck ornament
HIKOI	protest march
HOKONUI	illicit whisky
HONGI	nose-touching greeting
HUHU	hairy beetle

HUI	conference or meeting
HUIA	extinct New Zealand bird
JAFA	offensive term for someone from Auckland
JANOLA	household bleach
KAHAWAI	large fish
KAI	food
KAIK	village
KAINGA	village
KAKA	long-billed parrot
KAKAPO	ground-dwelling parrot
KARAKIA	prayer
KARANGA	call or chant of welcome
KATIPO	small venomous spider
KAUPAPA	strategy, policy or cause
KAURI	coniferous tree
KAWA	protocol or etiquette
KIEKIE	climbing bush plant
KOHA	gift or donation
KOKAKO	long-tailed crow
KONEKE	farm vehicle
KORU	curved pattern
KOWHAI	small tree
KUIA	female elder
KURI	mongrel dog
KUTU	body louse
MANUKA	myrtaceous tree
MATAI	evergreen tree
MIHI	ceremonial greeting
MOA	extinct large flightless bird
MOKI	edible sea fish
MOKO	Maori tattoo or tattoo pattern
MOOLOO	person from Waikato
MOPOKE	small spotted owl
MUNGA	army canteen
NGAIO	small tree
NGATI	tribe or clan
NIKAU	palm tree
PAKAHI	acid soil or land
PAKAPOO	Chinese lottery
PAKOKO	small freshwater fish
PAUA	edible abalone
PERFING	early retirement from the police force with financial compensation
PIKAU	rucksack
PIPI	shellfish
PIUPIU	leaf skirt
POI	ball of woven flax
PONGA	tall tree fern
PORAE	edible sea fish
PORANGI	crazy
PORINA	moth larva
POTAE	hat
POWHIRI	welcoming ceremony
PUGGY	sticky
PUHA	sow thistle
PUKEKO	wading bird
PURIRI	forest tree
RAHUI	Maori prohibition
RATA	myrtaceous forest tree
RAUPATU	seizure of land

RAURIKI	sow thistle
SHEEPO	person who brings sheep to the catching pen for shearing
TAIAHA	ceremonial fighting staff
TAIHOA	hold on!
TAKAHE	rare flightless bird
TANGI	Maori funeral ceremony
TANIWHA	legendary monster
TAONGA	treasure
TAPU	sacred or forbidden
TARSEAL	bitumen surface of a road
TAUIWI	non-Maori people of New Zealand
TIKANGA	Maori customs
TOETOE	type of tall grass
TOITOI	type of tall grass
TWINK	white correction fluid
WAKA	Maori canoe
WEKA	flightless bird
WERO	warrior's challenge
WETA	long-legged wingless insect
WHANAU	family
WHENAU	native land

South African words

South African English includes words from Nguni languages such as Xhosa and Zulu, as well as Afrikaans, amongst other languages. For Scrabble players, South African English offers a host of useful words for balancing vowel-heavy racks. Many Afrikaans-derived words contain a double A, while Nguni words often contain two or three As. It's a good idea, therefore, to have some South African words up your sleeve for when you find yourself with two or more As on your rack. There are also a lot of K words in South African English. As K can be an awkward letter to use effectively, these can come in very handy, as can the Afrikaans-derived words containing V, which are most helpful in trying to use a difficult tile.

AMADODA	grown men
AMANDLA	politcal slogan calling for power to the Black population
BAAS	boss
BABALAS	drunk or hungover
BAKKIE	small truck
BRAAI	grill or roast meat
BRAAIVLEIS	barbecue
BUNDU	wild, remote region
DAGGA	marijuana
DWAAL	state of befuddlement
GEELBEK	yellow-jawed fish
HAMBA	go away
JA	yes
JAAP	simpleton
JEREPIGO	heavy desert wine
JONG	friend
KAAL	naked
KEREL	chap or fellow
KRAAL	stockaded village
KWAITO	type of pop music
LEGUAAN	large monitor lizard

MEERKAT	sociable mongoose
MENEER	Mr or sir
MEVROU	Mrs or madam
MOOI	pleasing
MUTI	herbal medicine
NAARTJIE	tangerine
NEK	mountain pass
NKOSI	master or chief
OKE	man
OOM	title of respect
OUBAAS	person senior in rank or years
PADKOS	snacks for a long journey
PLAAS	farm
ROOIKAT	lynx
SCAMTO	argot of urban South African Blacks
SKOLLY	hooligan
SNOEK	edible marine fish
SPEK	bacon, fat or fatty pork
STEEN	variety of white grape
STOKVEL	savings pool or syndicate
VLEI	area of marshy ground
VOEMA	vigour or energy
VOETSEK	expression of dismissal or rejection
VROU	woman or wife
YEBO	yes

Urdu words

Urdu, the official language of Pakistan and one of the official languages of India, is closely related to Hindi. Urdu, however, contains many more words derived from Arabic and Persian, and also uses a different system of writing from Hindi, lending a different character to the words that have entered English. Many Urdu culinary terms will be familiar to British Scrabble players from Indian restaurants, while most Anglo-Indian military vocabulary also derives from Urdu rather than Hindi. As with Hindi, the variant spellings of many Urdu words provide opportunities for Scrabble players, as does the frequency of the letter K.

BAGH	garden
BALTI	spicy Indian dish stewed until most liquid has evaporated
BASTI	slum
BEGUM	woman of high rank
BIRIANI	Indian dish of highly flavoured rice mixed with meat or fish
BIRYANI	Indian dish of highly flavoured rice mixed with meat or fish
BUSTEE	slum
BUSTI	slum
CHARPAI	bedstead of woven webbing on a wooden frame
CHARPOY	bedstead of woven webbing on a wooden frame
DAROGHA	manager
DHANSAK	Indian dish of meat or vegetables braised with lentils
INQILAB	revolution
IZZAT	honour or prestige
JACONET	light cotton fabric
JEMADAR	officer in the Indian police
KAMEEZ	long tunic
KHARIF	crop harvested at beginning of winter
KHAYAL	kind of Indian classical vocal music
KINCOB	fine silk fabric embroidered with gold or silver threads

KOFTA	Indian dish of seasoned minced meat shaped into balls
KOFTGAR	person skilled in inlaying steel with gold
KOFTGARI	art of inlaying steel with gold
KORMA	Indian dish of meat or vegetables braised with yoghurt or cream
LASCAR	sailor from the East Indies
MAIDAN	open space used for meetings and sports
MASALA	mixed spices ground into a paste
MOOLVI	Muslim doctor of the law
MOOLVIE	Muslim doctor of the law
MURDABAD	down with; death to
MUSTH	frenzied sexual excitement in male elephants
NUMDAH	coarse felt
QORMA	Indian dish of meat or vegetables braised with yoghurt or cream
RABI	crop harvested at the end of winter
SAHIB	title placed after a man's name
SAICE	servant who looks after horses
SARPANCH	head of a village council
SEPOY	Indian soldier in the service of the British
SHALWAR	loose-fitting trousers
SHIKAR	hunting
SHIKAREE	hunter
SHIKARI	hunter
SICE	servant who looks after horses
SUBADAH	chief native office in a company of sepoys
SUBADAR	chief native office in a company of sepoys
SUBAH	chief native office in a company of sepoys
SYCE	servant who looks after horses
TAHSIL	administrative division
TALOOKA	subdivision of a district
TALUK	subdivision of a district
TALUKA	subdivision of a district
TAMASHA	show or entertainment
TANDOORI	method of cooking on a spit in a clay oven

Chapter 10: Anagrams

A vital skill for the keen Scrabble player is the ability to find words (or anagrams) from given sets of letters. This is the real essence of Scrabble, which, after all, is about rearranging letters on your rack to find the highest scoring combination to place on the board. The most useful words, of course, are those of seven and eight letters, as these are essential for scoring 50-point bonuses. Having the component letters of a bonus word is great – but you still have to be able to get it onto the board to obtain the bonus. And even if there are useful hooks in place on the board, you need these to be in the right place – words already on the board and the limits of board space may well keep your bonus word out of the game. This is where anagrams are so useful. The lists presented in the remainder of this book will enable you to determine if there is a word which can be made from a particular set of letters. For example, is there a valid word that can be made from the letters AEILOPR? How about AEILOPT? (Respectively, yes and no.) If you have the letters for one bonus word, it's invaluable to know if the same letters will work in a different combination which will slot onto the board somewhere. For example, with the letters AEILNST on your rack, you may have spotted SALIENT, but if SALIENT won't fit on the board, have you considered the other eight words which can be made from its letters? A good knowledge of bonus-length anagrams allows you to adapt a good rack to the situation on the board. This enables you to play bonus words more easily - or at the very least, to avoid wasting time hunting for combinations that aren't there. These lists are particularly useful when you are trying to learn from your mistakes after a game or tournament. If you had a rack which you were sure could yield a bonus word, but couldn't find it, you can check the anagram lists to find whether you were on the right lines. The letter sets (so-called 'alphagrams') are listed alphabetically, according to the alphabetical order of their component letters. So, for example, the anagrams of AEINRST all appear together, and these are listed immediately before the anagrams of AEINRSV, and so on.

Seven-letter anagrams

AAAADNP	APADANA	**AAABCTW**	CATAWBA	**AAABKLW**	BAKLAWA
AAAALTY	ATALAYA	**AAABDFR**	ABFARAD	**AAABKPS**	BAASKAP
AAAARRS	ARAARAS	**AAABDGS**	DAGABAS	**AAABKSY**	KABAYAS
AAAASTT	ATAATAS	**AAABDHS**	BAHADAS	**AAABLLW**	WALLABA
AAABBCL	CABBALA	**AAABDJS**	BAJADAS	**AAABLMT**	TAMBALA
AAABBKL	KABBALA	**AAABDLM**	LAMBADA	**AAABLPR**	PALABRA
AAABBLS	BABALAS	**AAABDNN**	BANDANA	**AAABLQS**	QABALAS
AAABCCR	BACCARA	**AAABEGL**	GALABEA	**AAABLST**	ALBATAS
AAABCIR	ARABICA	**AAABFLL**	FALBALA		ATABALS
AAABCLO	BACALAO	**AAABGIL**	GALABIA		BALATAS
AAABCLS	CABALAS	**AAABHLQ**	QABALAH	**AAABMOS**	ABOMASA
AAABCLV	BACLAVA	**AAABILX**	ABAXIAL	**AAABMST**	MASTABA
AAABCMR	CARAMBA	**AAABIPS**	PIASABA	**AAABNNR**	RABANNA
AAABCNR	BARACAN	**AAABISS**	ABASIAS	**AAABNNS**	BANANAS
AAABCNS	CABANAS	**AAABITV**	BATAVIA	**AAABORR**	ARAROBA
AAABCOR	CARABAO	**AAABKKS**	KABAKAS	**AAABRST**	BRAATAS
AAABCSS	CASABAS	**AAABKLS**	KABALAS	**AAABRSX**	ABRASAX
	CASSABA	**AAABKLV**	BAKLAVA		ABRAXAS

AAABRSZ	BARAZAS	AAADHMR	ADHARMA	AAAGNTY	YATAGAN
	BAZAARS		HARAMDA	AAAHHKL	HALAKAH
AAABSTT	BATATAS	AAADHMS	HAMADAS		HALAKHA
AAACCIS	ACACIAS	AAADHNS	SADHANA	AAAHHLL	HALALAH
AAACCLM	MALACCA	AAADHWY	HADAWAY	AAAHHLV	HALAVAH
AAACCLP	ALPACCA	AAADILX	ADAXIAL	AAAHIKP	APHAKIA
AAACCLR	CARACAL	AAADIMN	DAMIANA	AAAHIKW	KAHAWAI
AAACCRS	CASCARA	AAADIRT	DATARIA	AAAHINR	HARIANA
AAACDGS	CADAGAS		RADIATA	AAAHIPS	APHASIA
AAACDIR	ARCADIA	AAADJMR	JAMADAR	AAAHIST	TAIAHAS
AAACDLU	ACAUDAL	AAADKNW	WAKANDA	AAAHJKW	KAJAWAH
AAACDMM	MACADAM	AAADLMN	AMANDLA	AAAHKRS	AKHARAS
AAACDNS	CANADAS		MANDALA	AAAHLLS	HALALAS
AAACEHR	ARCHAEA	AAADLMW	WADMAAL	AAAHLMR	HARMALA
AAACENP	PANACEA	AAADMNT	ADAMANT	AAAHLNN	ALANNAH
AAACGNT	AGACANT	AAADMPP	PAPADAM	AAAHLSW	HAWALAS
AAACHHL	HALACHA	AAADMRS	ARMADAS	AAAHMMT	MAHATMA
AAACHLZ	CHALAZA		MADRASA	AAAHMRS	ASHRAMA
AAACHNT	ACANTHA		RAMADAS	AAAHMST	TAMASHA
AAACHRY	ACHARYA	AAADNPS	PANADAS	AAAHNSV	VAHANAS
AAACILM	MALACIA	AAADNRS	SARDANA	AAAHPRT	PARATHA
AAACIMR	CARIAMA	AAADNRT	TANADAR	AAAHRTW	WARATAH
AAACINP	ACAPNIA	AAADWYY	AWAYDAY	AAAIKKR	KARAKIA
AAACINR	ACARIAN	AAAEGLT	GALATEA	AAAIKLT	LATAKIA
AAACIRS	ACRASIA	AAAEGNP	APANAGE	AAAIKRS	AKRASIA
AAACJMR	JACAMAR	AAAEHLT	ALTHAEA	AAAILLS	ALALIAS
AAACJNS	JACANAS	AAAEIMN	ANAEMIA	AAAILMR	MALARIA
AAACLLV	CAVALLA	AAAELMP	PALAMAE	AAAILNX	ANAXIAL
AAACLMN	ALMANAC	AAAELSZ	AZALEAS	AAAILPS	APLASIA
	MANCALA	AAAEMRT	TARAMEA	AAAILRS	ARALIAS
AAACLMR	CALAMAR	AAAENST	ANATASE	AAAILRT	TALARIA
AAACLNT	CANTALA	AAAERWY	AREAWAY	AAAIMNT	AMANITA
AAACLPS	ALPACAS	AAAFFLL	ALFALFA	AAAINPS	PAISANA
AAACLPT	CATALPA	AAAFHRT	HAFTARA	AAAIPRX	APRAXIA
AAACLRZ	ALCAZAR	AAAFIRT	RATAFIA	AAAIPSV	PIASAVA
AAACMNP	CAMPANA	AAAFNRS	SARAFAN	AAAIQRU	AQUARIA
AAACMRS	MARACAS	AAAFRWY	FARAWAY	AAAISST	ASTASIA
	MARASCA	AAAGGLN	GALANGA	AAAISTW	WAIATAS
	MASCARA	AAAGHIP	APHAGIA	AAAISTX	ATAXIAS
AAACNNR	CARANNA	AAAGHLN	LANGAHA	AAAJKST	JATAKAS
AAACNPT	CATAPAN	AAAGHNT	ATAGHAN	AAAJMPS	PAJAMAS
AAACNRS	ARCANAS	AAAGHPR	AGRAPHA	AAAJMSU	UJAMAAS
AAACNRT	NACARAT	AAAGILN	ANALGIA	AAAKKMR	MARKKAA
AAACNRU	CARAUNA	AAAGINR	ANGARIA	AAAKKNS	KANAKAS
AAACNRV	CARAVAN	AAAGINZ	GAZANIA	AAAKKRS	KARAKAS
AAACNST	CANASTA	AAAGIPT	PATAGIA	AAAKLMS	KAMALAS
AAACNTT	CANTATA	AAAGISS	ASSAGAI	AAAKLMY	YAMALKA
AAACPRX	CARAPAX	AAAGJMU	MAJAGUA	AAAKLSS	ALASKAS
AAACPST	PATACAS	AAAGKNR	KARANGA	AAAKMMU	MAMAKAU
AAACRWY	CARAWAY	AAAGLMM	AMALGAM	AAAKNST	KATANAS
AAACSST	CASSATA	AAAGLMN	MALANGA	AAAKPPU	KAUPAPA
AAACSSV	CASAVAS		NAGMAAL	AAALLPT	PALATAL
	CASSAVA	AAAGLNO	ANALOGA	AAALMPT	TAMPALA
AAACSTT	CATASTA	AAAGLNS	LASAGNA	AAALMRS	MARSALA
AAADDMO	AMADODA	AAAGLRS	ARGALAS	AAALMSS	MASALAS
AAADELM	ALAMEDA	AAAGMMT	MAGMATA		SALAAMS
AAADFRY	FARADAY	AAAGMNR	ANAGRAM	AAALNNT	LANTANA
AAADGGH	AGGADAH	AAAGMNS	SAGAMAN	AAALNPT	APLANAT
	HAGGADA	AAAGMTT	TAGMATA	AAALPPS	PALAPAS
AAADGGS	AGGADAS	AAAGNNS	NAGANAS	AAALRRY	ARRAYAL
AAADGIL	ADAGIAL	AAAGNPR	PARGANA	AAALWYY	LAYAWAY
AAADGRS	SAGRADA	AAAGNRR	NGARARA	AAAMMPR	MAMPARA
AAADHHS	SHAHADA	AAAGNRT	TANAGRA	AAAMMNS	MANANAS
AAADHMM	HAMMADA	AAAGNRU	GUARANA	AAAMNNT	ANATMAN

AAAMNPS	PANAMAS	AABCEKR	BACKARE	AABDEMN	BEADMAN
AAAMNRT	AMARANT	AABCELN	BALANCE	AABDEMS	SAMBAED
	MARANTA	AABCELP	CAPABLE	AABDENU	BANDEAU
AAAMNSS	SAMAANS		PACABLE	AABDERR	ABRADER
AAAMNST	ATAMANS	AABCELT	ACTABLE	AABDERS	ABRADES
AAAMNSW	MANAWAS	AABCEMR	MACABER	AABDERY	ABRAYED
AAAMNTY	MANYATA		MACABRE	AABDESU	AUBADES
AAAMORT	TAMARAO	AABCEMS	AMBSACE	AABDGHN	HANDBAG
AAAMPPU	PAPAUMA	AABCEOS	COBAEAS	AABDGHR	HARDBAG
AAAMPRT	PATAMAR	AABCERR	BARRACE	AABDGMO	GAMBADO
AAAMRRZ	ZAMARRA	AABCERT	ABREACT	AABDGNS	SANDBAG
AAAMRSS	ASRAMAS		BEARCAT	AABDGOS	DAGOBAS
	SAMARAS		CABARET	AABDHMS	BADMASH
	SAMSARA	AABCFKT	FATBACK	AABDHNT	HATBAND
AAAMRST	TAMARAS	AABCHHR	BRACHAH	AABDHNY	HAYBAND
	TARAMAS	AABCHIR	BRACHIA	AABDHRS	BARDASH
AAAMRTU	TAMARAU	AABCHMT	AMBATCH	AABDHRU	BAHADUR
AAANNSV	SAVANNA	AABCHNR	BARCHAN	AABDIIS	BASIDIA
AAANNSZ	ZANANAS	AABCHOR	ABROACH	AABDIKR	BIDARKA
AAANNTT	ANNATTA	AABCHSS	CASBAHS	AABDILN	BALADIN
AAANPPY	PAPAYAN	AABCILM	CAMBIAL	AABDIMR	BARMAID
AAANRST	ANTARAS	AABCINR	CARABIN	AABDINR	BANDARI
AAANRTT	TANTARA	AABCIOP	COPAIBA	AABDINS	INDABAS
	TARTANA	AABCITX	TAXICAB	AABDINT	TABANID
AAANSTT	ANATTAS	AABCKLY	LAYBACK	AABDIOT	BIODATA
AAAOPRZ	PARAZOA	AABCKNN	CANBANK	AABDIRS	ABRAIDS
AAAPPRT	APPARAT	AABCKPY	BACKPAY	AABDLLS	BALLADS
AAAPPSY	PAPAYAS		PAYBACK	AABDLMS	LAMBDAS
AAAPRSS	APSARAS	AABCKRR	BARRACK	AABDLNS	SALBAND
AAAPSST	PASSATA	AABCKRS	BACKRAS	AABDLRW	BRADAWL
AAAPTTU	TAUPATA	AABCKSW	BACKSAW	AABDMNR	ARMBAND
AAARSST	SATARAS	AABCLMU	CALUMBA	AABDNNO	ABANDON
AAARSTV	AVATARS	AABCLPY	CAPABLY	AABDNOR	BANDORA
AAARTTT	RATATAT	AABCLSY	SCYBALA	AABDNRS	BANDARS
AAARTTU	TUATARA	AABCMMU	MACUMBA		SANDBAR
AAARTXY	ATARAXY	AABCMST	TAMBACS	AABDNRU	BANDURA
AABBBOS	BAOBABS	AABCMSU	SAMBUCA	AABDNSW	BANDSAW
AABBCEG	CABBAGE	AABCNRR	CARBARN	AABDORS	ABROADS
AABBCGY	CABBAGY	AABCORR	CARBORA	AABDORV	BRAVADO
AABBCMO	CABOMBA	AABCORT	ABACTOR	AABDORX	BROADAX
AABBCOS	BABACOS		ACROBAT	AABDRRS	DARBARS
AABBDGR	GABBARD	AABCOTT	CATBOAT	AABDRRW	DRAWBAR
AABBDHS	HABDABS	AABCRSS	SCARABS	AABDRST	BASTARD
AABBEGN	BEANBAG	AABCSUU	AUCUBAS		TABARDS
AABBEIS	BABESIA	AABCTTU	CATTABU	AABDRSU	SUBADAR
AABBELT	BATABLE	AABDDEL	ADDABLE	AABDRSY	BAYARDS
AABBERT	BARBATE	AABDDEN	ABANDED	AABDSTU	DATABUS
AABBGRT	GABBART	AABDDER	ABRADED	AABEELT	EATABLE
AABBHLS	BABLAHS	AABDDIK	KABADDI	AABEEMN	AMEBEAN
AABBHST	SABBATH	AABDDIN	BANDAID	AABEEMO	AMOEBAE
AABBLLS	LABLABS	AABDDLN	BADLAND	AABEERZ	ZAREEBA
AABBLOR	BARBOLA	AABDDNS	SANDDAB	AABEFFL	AFFABLE
AABBLOS	BALBOAS	AABDEFL	FADABLE	AABEFFN	BEFFANA
AABBSST	SABBATS	AABDEGM	GAMBADE	AABEFGL	FLEABAG
AABBSSU	BABASSU	AABDEGN	BANDAGE	AABEFGU	AUFGABE
AABBSTY	BABYSAT	AABDEHS	ABASHED	AABEFNS	BEFANAS
AABCCEL	ACCABLE	AABDEIR	BRAAIED		FANBASE
AABCCER	BACCARE	AABDEIS	DIABASE	AABEGGG	BAGGAGE
AABCCET	BACCATE	AABDEKW	DAWBAKE	AABEGGR	GARBAGE
AABCCHH	BACHCHA	AABDELL	BALLADE	AABEGLR	ALGEBRA
AABCCIR	BRACCIA	AABDELT	ABLATED	AABEGMR	BERGAMA
AABCDIM	DICAMBA		DATABLE		MEGABAR
AABCDIR	CARABID	AABDELW	WADABLE	AABEGMS	AMBAGES
AABCEFR	FACEBAR	AABDEMM	BEMADAM	AABEGRR	BAGARRE

Seven-letter anagrams

	BARRAGE	**AABERRW**	BARWARE	**AABIKNS**	BANKSIA
AABEGSS	BAGASSE	**AABERSS**	ABASERS	**AABILLN**	ALBINAL
	SEABAGS	**AABERST**	ABATERS	**AABILLR**	BARILLA
AABEGST	ATABEGS		ABREAST	**AABILLS**	LABIALS
AABEGSU	ABUSAGE	**AABERSU**	BAUERAS	**AABILMN**	BIMANAL
AABEHLT	HATABLE		SUBAREA	**AABILMS**	BAALISM
AABEHNT	ABTHANE	**AABERSZ**	ZAREBAS	**AABILMY**	AMIABLY
AABEHRS	EARBASH	**AABERTT**	RABATTE	**AABILNS**	BASINAL
AABEHSS	ABASHES		TABARET	**AABILOU**	ABOULIA
AABEIKN	IKEBANA	**AABERTU**	ABATURE	**AABILRS**	BASILAR
AABEILM	AMABILE	**AABESTZ**	ZABETAS	**AABILST**	BALISTA
	AMIABLE	**AABETTU**	BATTEAU	**AABILSU**	ABULIAS
AABEILN	ABELIAN	**AABETUX**	BATEAUX	**AABIMMR**	MARIMBA
AABEILS	ABELIAS	**AABFFLY**	AFFABLY	**AABIMNO**	AMBOINA
AABEILT	LABIATE	**AABFILU**	FABLIAU		BONAMIA
AABEILX	ABAXILE	**AABFLRU**	FABULAR	**AABIMOS**	ABOMASI
AABEIOR	AEROBIA	**AABGGRS**	RAGBAGS	**AABIMRS**	AMBARIS
AABEIRS	AIRBASE	**AABGGRY**	GARBAGY		MARABIS
	ARABISE	**AABGGSS**	GASBAGS	**AABIMST**	BASMATI
AABEIRZ	ARABIZE	**AABGHNR**	BHANGRA	**AABINNS**	BANIANS
AABEJLL	JELLABA	**AABGHNS**	GABNASH	**AABINOU**	OUABAIN
AABEJMU	JAMBEAU		NASHGAB	**AABINRS**	ARABINS
AABEKLM	MAKABLE	**AABGHSW**	BAGWASH	**AABINRT**	ATABRIN
AABEKLT	TAKABLE	**AABGIIL**	ABIGAIL	**AABINST**	ABSTAIN
AABEKNS	SEABANK	**AABGILM**	MAILBAG	**AABINSW**	WABAINS
AABEKPR	PARBAKE	**AABGIMS**	GAMBIAS	**AABINSZ**	BANZAIS
AABEKRS	ARABESK	**AABGINR**	BARGAIN	**AABIORS**	ABROSIA
AABEKRY	KERBAYA	**AABGINS**	ABASING	**AABIORT**	AIRBOAT
AABEKST	ATABEKS		BAAINGS	**AABIPUX**	PAXIUBA
AABELLL	LABELLA		BISNAGA	**AABIRST**	BARISTA
AABELLN	BALNEAL	**AABGINT**	ABATING		BARTSIA
AABELLO	ABOLLAE	**AABGINZ**	BIZNAGA	**AABIRSZ**	ZARIBAS
AABELLR	EARBALL	**AABGIRS**	AIRBAGS	**AABISSW**	WASABIS
AABELLS	SABELLA	**AABGMNY**	MANGABY	**AABISTT**	ABATTIS
	SALABLE	**AABGOSZ**	GAZABOS	**AABJMRT**	JAMBART
AABELMN	NAMABLE	**AABGRST**	RATBAGS	**AABKMST**	TAMBAKS
AABELMS	MABELAS	**AABHHIS**	SAHIBAH	**AABKNNS**	KANBANS
AABELMT	TAMABLE	**AABHHKS**	SABKHAH	**AABKNRS**	BARKANS
AABELNO	ABALONE	**AABHHRU**	BRUHAHA	**AABKNRT**	TANBARK
AABELNR	BANALER	**AABHHSS**	SHABASH	**AABKOOZ**	BAZOOKA
AABELNS	BANSELA	**AABHINS**	HASBIAN	**AABKRST**	TASKBAR
AABELPP	PAPABLE	**AABHINT**	HABITAN	**AABLLNS**	BALLANS
AABELPR	PARABLE	**AABHISS**	SAHIBAS	**AABLLNT**	BALLANT
AABELPY	PAYABLE	**AABHITT**	HABITAT	**AABLLNY**	BANALLY
AABELRS	ARABLES	**AABHJNS**	BHAJANS	**AABLLOR**	ALLOBAR
AABELRT	RATABLE	**AABHKNR**	BARKHAN	**AABLLOS**	ABOLLAS
AABELSS	BALASES	**AABHKSS**	KASBAHS	**AABLLPT**	PATBALL
AABELST	ABLATES		SABKHAS	**AABLLST**	BALLAST
	ASTABLE	**AABHKST**	BHAKTAS		BALLATS
AABELSV	SAVABLE		SABKHAT	**AABLLSY**	BASALLY
AABELSY	SAYABLE	**AABHLRS**	BHARALS		SALABLY
AABELTT	ABETTAL	**AABHLTY**	BATHYAL	**AABLLWY**	WALLABY
AABELTU	TABLEAU	**AABHMNR**	BRAHMAN	**AABLMRS**	RAMBLAS
	TABULAE	**AABHMRS**	BRAHMAS	**AABLMRU**	LABARUM
AABELTV	VATABLE		SAMBHAR	**AABLMSS**	BALSAMS
AABELTX	TAXABLE	**AABHMSS**	SHAMBAS		SAMBALS
AABELWX	WAXABLE	**AABHMTT**	BATHMAT	**AABLMST**	LAMBAST
AABEMNO	AMOEBAN	**AABHNSV**	BHAVANS	**AABLMSY**	ABYSMAL
AABEMNS	BASEMAN	**AABHNSW**	BHAWANS		BALSAMY
AABEMOS	AMOEBAS	**AABHSSW**	BASHAWS	**AABLNTT**	BLATANT
AABENNW	WANNABE	**AABIILX**	BIAXIAL	**AABLORT**	ABLATOR
AABENRT	ANTBEAR	**AABIILZ**	ALBIZIA	**AABLOSV**	LAVABOS
AABENTY	ABEYANT	**AABIJMY**	JAMBIYA	**AABLPRU**	PABULAR
AABEORT	AEROBAT	**AABIKLM**	KALIMBA	**AABLPYY**	PAYABLY

AABLRST	ARBLAST	
AABLRSU	SUBALAR	
AABLRTU	TABULAR	
AABLRTY	RATABLY	
AABLSST	BASALTS	
AABLSSY	ABYSSAL	
AABLSTU	ABLAUTS	
AABLTTU	ABUTTAL	
AABLTXY	TAXABLY	
AABMNOT	BOATMAN	
AABMNOY	AMBOYNA	
AABMNST	BANTAMS	
	BATSMAN	
AABMORU	MARABOU	
AABMOSY	BAYAMOS	
AABMRSS	SAMBARS	
AABMRTU	TAMBURA	
AABMSST	TSAMBAS	
AABMSSY	AMBASSY	
AABNNOZ	BONANZA	
AABNNSY	BANYANS	
AABNOST	SABATON	
AABNOSY	SABAYON	
AABNSYY	BAYYANS	
AABORRS	ARROBAS	
	RASBORA	
AABORST	ABATORS	
	RABATOS	
AABORSZ	ABRAZOS	
AABOTTY	ATTABOY	
AABQSUU	SUBAQUA	
AABRRST	BARRATS	
AABRRSU	SABURRA	
AABRRUV	BRAVURA	
AABRSTY	BARYTAS	
AABSSSY	SASSABY	
AABSTTW	ABWATTS	
AABSTUX	SAXTUBA	
	SUBTAXA	
AABTTTU	BATTUTA	
AACCDEI	CICADAE	
AACCDEM	MEDACCA	
AACCDES	CASCADE	
	SACCADE	
AACCDII	ACCIDIA	
AACCDIR	CARDIAC	
AACCDIS	CICADAS	
AACCDSU	CADUACS	
AACCEFT	CATFACE	
AACCEKR	CARCAKE	
AACCELO	CLOACAE	
AACCENV	VACANCE	
AACCERS	CARCASE	
AACCEST	SACCATE	
AACCHHK	CHACHKA	
	KACHCHA	
AACCHIM	MACCHIA	
AACCHIN	CHICANA	
AACCHIR	ARCHAIC	
AACCHKS	KACCHAS	
AACCHLN	CLACHAN	
AACCHMP	CHAMPAC	
AACCHMS	CHACMAS	
AACCHNN	CANNACH	
AACCHNS	CANCHAS	
AACCHOR	CAROACH	
AACCHRT	CHARACT	
AACCILM	ACCLAIM	
AACCILS	ALCAICS	
	CICALAS	
AACCILU	ACICULA	
AACCIMS	CAIMACS	
AACCIMT	ACMATIC	
AACCINS	ANICCAS	
AACCINV	VACCINA	
AACCIOR	CARIOCA	
AACCIPT	PICCATA	
AACCIRT	ACRATIC	
AACCITT	ATACTIC	
AACCJKR	CARJACK	
AACCKLP	CALPACK	
AACCKRR	CARRACK	
AACCKRS	CARACKS	
	CRACKAS	
AACCLLO	CLOACAL	
AACCLLT	CATCALL	
AACCLOP	POLACCA	
AACCLOR	CARACOL	
AACCLOS	CLOACAS	
AACCLPS	CALPACS	
AACCLPT	PLACCAT	
AACCLRS	CALCARS	
AACCLRU	ACCRUAL	
	CARACUL	
AACCLSU	ACCUSAL	
AACCLTW	CATCLAW	
AACCMOS	MACACOS	
AACCNNS	CANCANS	
AACCNVY	VACANCY	
AACCORU	CURACAO	
	CURACOA	
AACCOST	ACCOAST	
AACCOTT	TOCCATA	
AACCRRT	CARRACT	
AACCRSS	CARCASS	
AACCRST	CARACTS	
AACDDEL	DECADAL	
AACDDER	ARCADED	
AACDDHR	CHADDAR	
AACDDIN	CANDIDA	
AACDDRW	CRAWDAD	
AACDEEM	ACADEME	
AACDEFL	FALCADE	
AACDEFS	FACADES	
AACDEHM	CHAMADE	
AACDEHR	CHARADE	
AACDEHT	CATHEAD	
AACDEII	AECIDIA	
AACDEIL	ALCAIDE	
AACDEIN	AIDANCE	
AACDEIR	CARDIAE	
AACDEIS	ACEDIAS	
AACDELL	ALCALDE	
AACDELN	CANALED	
	CANDELA	
	DECANAL	
AACDELP	PALACED	
AACDELR	CALDERA	
	CRAALED	
AACDELS	ALCADES	
	SCALADE	
AACDELY	ALCAYDE	
AACDEMY	ACADEMY	
AACDENR	DRACENA	
AACDENV	ADVANCE	
AACDENZ	CADENZA	
AACDEPS	SCAPAED	
AACDERS	ARCADES	
	ASCARED	
AACDERV	CADAVER	
AACDERY	DAYCARE	
AACDETU	CAUDATE	
AACDETV	VACATED	
AACDEUX	CADEAUX	
AACDFIR	FARADIC	
AACDFRS	CAFARDS	
AACDGGI	AGGADIC	
AACDGHI	HAGADIC	
AACDGIS	CADAGIS	
AACDHMR	DRACHMA	
AACDHNR	HANDCAR	
AACDHRS	CHADARS	
AACDHST	DATCHAS	
AACDIIS	ASCIDIA	
AACDILR	RADICAL	
AACDINS	SCANDIA	
AACDINT	ANTACID	
AACDINV	VANADIC	
AACDIOR	ACAROID	
AACDIRS	ACARIDS	
	ASCARID	
	CARDIAS	
AACDJKW	JACKDAW	
AACDKSY	DAYSACK	
AACDLNO	ACNODAL	
	CALANDO	
AACDLNS	SCANDAL	
AACDLOR	CARLOAD	
AACDLOS	SCALADO	
AACDLPR	PLACARD	
AACDMPS	MADCAPS	
AACDNRS	CADRANS	
	CANARDS	
AACDOOV	AVOCADO	
AACDPRU	CRAPAUD	
AACDRSS	CSARDAS	
AACDRSZ	CZARDAS	
AACEEGR	ACREAGE	
AACEEHR	EARACHE	
AACEEHT	CHAETAE	
AACEEKT	TEACAKE	
AACEELN	ANELACE	
AACEEMR	CAMERAE	
AACEEMS	AMESACE	
AACEENT	CATENAE	
AACEERT	ACERATE	
AACEESS	CASEASE	
AACEEST	CASEATE	
AACEETT	ACETATE	
AACEFIS	FASCIAE	
AACEFLT	FALCATE	
AACEFLU	FACULAE	

AACEFMN	FACEMAN	**AACELPS**	PALACES	GLACIAL
AACEFRR	CARFARE	**AACELPT**	PLACATE	**AACGILM**	MAGICAL
AACEFRS	CARAFES	**AACELRS**	SCALARE	**AACGILS**	SCAGLIA
AACEGGR	AGGRACE	**AACELRV**	CARAVEL	**AACGINT**	AGNATIC
AACEGHN	GANACHE	**AACELSS**	CALESAS	**AACGIRS**	AGARICS
AACEGHS	ACHAGES	**AACELST**	ACETALS	**AACGIRV**	AGRAVIC
AACEGIP	AGAPEIC		LACTASE	**AACGISU**	GUAIACS
AACEGKP	PACKAGE	**AACELTT**	LACTATE	**AACGJNT**	CATJANG
AACEGKS	SACKAGE	**AACELTV**	CLAVATE	**AACGLOT**	CATALOG
AACEGLS	SCALAGE	**AACELTY**	ACYLATE	**AACGLOU**	COAGULA
AACEGNR	CAGANER	**AACEMMR**	MACRAME	**AACGLSY**	GALYACS
	CARNAGE	**AACEMNS**	CASEMAN	**AACGNOU**	GUANACO
	CRANAGE	**AACEMNV**	CAVEMAN	**AACHHKR**	CHARKHA
AACEGRT	CARTAGE	**AACEMOS**	CAEOMAS	**AACHHLL**	CHALLAH
AACEGSV	SCAVAGE	**AACEMPR**	PARACME	**AACHHLS**	CHALAHS
AACEHIN	ACHENIA	**AACEMQU**	MACAQUE	**AACHIKL**	HALAKIC
AACEHIR	ARCHAEI	**AACEMRS**	CAMERAS	**AACHIKN**	KACHINA
AACEHKS	ASHCAKE	**AACEMSS**	CAMASES	**AACHIKR**	CHIKARA
AACEHLP	ACALEPH	**AACENPS**	CANAPES	**AACHILO**	ACHOLIA
AACEHLR	ALCHERA	**AACENRT**	CATERAN	**AACHILR**	ACHIRAL
AACEHLT	CHAETAL	**AACENSS**	CASSENA		RACHIAL
AACEHNO	CHOANAE	**AACENST**	CATENAS	**AACHILT**	CALATHI
AACEHNP	PANACHE	**AACENTT**	CANTATE	**AACHIMR**	MACHAIR
AACEHNR	ACHARNE	**AACENTY**	CYANATE	**AACHIMS**	CHAMISA
	ARCHEAN	**AACEOPT**	PEACOAT		CHIASMA
AACEHPP	APPEACH	**AACEORS**	ROSACEA	**AACHINT**	ACANTHI
AACEHPS	APACHES	**AACEPRT**	CAPRATE		TACHINA
AACEHPU	CHAPEAU	**AACEPRU**	CAPUERA	**AACHIPR**	CHARPAI
AACEHRT	TRACHEA	**AACEPRV**	PRECAVA		HAIRCAP
AACEHST	ACHATES	**AACEPWY**	PACEWAY	**AACHIPS**	APHASIC
AACEHTT	ATTACHE	**AACERSS**	CAESARS	**AACHIPT**	CHAPATI
AACEHTU	CHATEAU	**AACERST**	ACATERS	**AACHIRS**	ARACHIS
AACEILM	CAMELIA		CARATES	**AACHIRT**	CITHARA
AACEIMN	ANAEMIC	**AACERSU**	CAESURA	**AACHITY**	CYATHIA
AACEIMU	CAMAIEU	**AACERSZ**	SAZERAC	**AACHKMN**	HACKMAN
AACEINR	ACARINE	**AACERTT**	TEACART	**AACHKMP**	CHAMPAK
	CARINAE	**AACERTU**	ARCUATE	**AACHKNS**	ACHKANS
AACEIQU	ACEQUIA	**AACERWY**	RACEWAY	**AACHKPS**	CHAPKAS
AACEIRV	AVARICE	**AACESTV**	CAVEATS		PACHAKS
	CAVIARE		VACATES	**AACHKRS**	CHAKRAS
AACEIST	ECTASIA	**AACESTX**	EXACTAS		CHARKAS
AACEJLS	JACALES	**AACETTU**	ACTUATE	**AACHKRT**	HATRACK
AACEJRS	JACARES	**AACETUV**	VACUATE	**AACHKRY**	HAYRACK
AACEKNP	PANCAKE	**AACFFIL**	CAFFILA	**AACHKSW**	HACKSAW
AACEKNS	ASKANCE	**AACFILS**	CAFILAS		KWACHAS
AACEKOT	OATCAKE		FACIALS	**AACHLLN**	CHALLAN
AACELLN	CANELLA		FASCIAL	**AACHLLS**	CHALLAS
AACELLS	SACELLA	**AACFILU**	FAUCIAL	**AACHLMS**	CHASMAL
AACELLT	LACTEAL	**AACFINT**	FANATIC	**AACHLNS**	CHALANS
AACELMN	MANACLE	**AACFISS**	FASCIAS	**AACHLNT**	CANTHAL
AACELMR	CAMERAL	**AACFLLT**	CATFALL	**AACHLPP**	CHAPPAL
	CARAMEL	**AACFLLU**	FALCULA	**AACHLPS**	PASCHAL
	CERAMAL	**AACFLLY**	FALLACY	**AACHLPU**	CHALUPA
	MACERAL	**AACFLPT**	FLATCAP	**AACHLST**	CALTHAS
AACELMU	MACULAE	**AACFLRT**	FLATCAR	**AACHLSU**	ACUSHLA
AACELNP	CAPELAN		FRACTAL	**AACHMNP**	CHAPMAN
AACELNS	ANLACES	**AACFLRU**	FACULAR	**AACHMNS**	MACHANS
AACELNT	LACTEAN	**AACFLSU**	FAUCALS	**AACHMSY**	YASHMAC
AACELNU	CANULAE	**AACFLTU**	FACTUAL	**AACHNOP**	PANOCHA
	LACUNAE	**AACFNST**	CAFTANS	**AACHNOU**	HUANACO
AACELNV	VALANCE	**AACFRRU**	FARRUCA	**AACHNPX**	PANCHAX
AACELOR	ACEROLA	**AACGGMS**	CAGMAGS	**AACHNRS**	ANARCHS
AACELOV	COAEVAL	**AACGHNS**	CHAGANS	**AACHNRV**	NAVARCH
AACELPR	CARPALE	**AACGILL**	GALLICA	**AACHNRY**	ANARCHY

AACHNSS	ASHCANS
AACHNST	ACANTHS
AACHNSU	ANCHUSA
AACHNSZ	CHAZANS
AACHNZZ	CHAZZAN
AACHRRT	CATARRH
AACHRST	CHARTAS
AACHRSW	CARWASH
AACHRTU	AUTARCH
AACHRWY	ARCHWAY
AACHSSW	CASHAWS
AACHSTT	CHATTAS
AACIILN	ANCILIA
	LACINIA
AACIIMS	CAMISIA
AACIINP	APICIAN
AACIINT	ACTINIA
AACIITV	AVIATIC
	VIATICA
AACIJLP	JALAPIC
AACIJMS	JICAMAS
AACIKLL	ALKALIC
AACIKLR	CLARKIA
AACIKNN	CANAKIN
AACIKNT	KATCINA
AACIKRT	AKRATIC
AACILLN	ANCILLA
AACILLS	CALLAIS
AACILMR	MAILCAR
AACILMS	CALIMAS
	CAMAILS
AACILNP	CALPAIN
AACILNR	CARINAL
	CLARAIN
	CRANIAL
AACILNT	ACTINAL
	ALICANT
	ANTICAL
AACILOS	ASOCIAL
AACILOX	COAXIAL
AACILPS	APICALS
	SPACIAL
AACILPT	CAPITAL
	PLACITA
AACILRR	RAILCAR
AACILTT	CATTAIL
AACILTV	VATICAL
AACIMMR	MACRAMI
AACIMNO	MANIOCA
AACIMNS	CAIMANS
	MANIACS
AACIMNY	ANIMACY
AACIMOR	ACROMIA
AACIMPR	PICAMAR
AACIMSS	CAMISAS
AACIMTY	CYMATIA
AACINNT	CANTINA
AACINOR	CONARIA
	OCARINA
AACINPT	CAPITAN
	CAPTAIN
AACINRS	ACRASIN
	ARNICAS
	CARINAS
	SARCINA
AACINRT	ANTICAR
AACINRZ	CZARINA
AACINSS	ASCIANS
	CASSINA
	SANCAIS
AACINST	SATANIC
AACIOPT	TAPIOCA
AACIOPV	COPAIVA
AACIOST	ATOCIAS
	COAITAS
AACIPPR	PAPRICA
AACIPRS	PICARAS
AACIPRX	APRAXIC
AACIQTU	AQUATIC
AACIRSS	ASCARIS
AACIRST	CARITAS
AACIRSV	CAVIARS
AACISSS	CASSIAS
AACISST	CASITAS
AACISTT	ASTATIC
AACISTX	ATAXICS
AACJKLS	JACKALS
AACJKMN	JACKMAN
	MANJACK
AACJKSS	JACKASS
AACJOSU	ACAJOUS
AACJPTU	CAJAPUT
AACKLPS	KALPACS
AACKLTW	CATWALK
AACKMNP	MANPACK
	PACKMAN
AACKMRT	AMTRACK
AACKNRS	RANSACK
AACKPRR	CARPARK
AACKPRT	RATPACK
AACKPSZ	CZAPKAS
AACKPWX	PACKWAX
AACKPWY	PACKWAY
AACKRRS	ARRACKS
AACKSTT	ATTACKS
AACLLNS	CALLANS
AACLLNT	CALLANT
AACLLNU	CALLUNA
	LACUNAL
AACLLOO	CALALOO
AACLLOR	CORALLA
AACLLSU	CALALUS
	CLAUSAL
AACLLVY	CAVALLY
AACLMNO	COALMAN
AACLMNT	CALMANT
	CLAMANT
AACLMRU	MACULAR
AACLMST	LACTAMS
AACLMSU	CALAMUS
	MACULAS
AACLNNO	ANCONAL
AACLNNU	CANNULA
AACLNOS	CANOLAS
AACLNPY	CLAYPAN
AACLNRS	CARNALS
AACLNRU	CANULAR
	LACUNAR
AACLNST	CANTALS
AACLNSU	CANULAS
	LACUNAS
AACLOPR	CAPORAL
	CRAPOLA
AACLOPT	OCTAPLA
AACLORT	COALTAR
	CROTALA
AACLORZ	ALCORZA
AACLOST	CATALOS
	COASTAL
AACLOTT	CATTALO
AACLOTV	OCTAVAL
AACLPRS	CARPALS
AACLPRT	CALTRAP
AACLPSS	PASCALS
AACLPSU	PASCUAL
	PAUCALS
	SCAPULA
AACLPTY	PLAYACT
AACLRSS	LASCARS
	RASCALS
	SACRALS
	SCALARS
AACLRST	CASTRAL
AACLRTY	LACTARY
AACLRVY	CALVARY
	CAVALRY
AACLSSU	CASUALS
	CAUSALS
AACLSTT	SALTCAT
AACLSTU	ACTUALS
AACLSUV	VASCULA
AACLTTU	TACTUAL
AACMMOT	COMMATA
AACMNOR	CAMARON
	NARCOMA
AACMNRU	ARCANUM
AACMNSY	CAYMANS
AACMORR	CAMORRA
AACMORS	SARCOMA
AACMORT	MARCATO
AACMOSY	MACOYAS
AACMRRT	TRAMCAR
AACMRSS	SARCASM
AACMRST	AMTRACS
	RAMCATS
	TARMACS
AACNNOZ	CANZONA
AACNOST	SACATON
AACNOTZ	ZACATON
AACNPRT	CANTRAP
AACNPST	CAPSTAN
	CAPTANS
	CATNAPS
AACNRST	ARCTANS
	CANTARS
AACNRTU	CURTANA
AACNSSV	CANVASS
AACNSTT	ACTANTS
AACNSTU	ASCAUNT
AACOPPR	APOCARP
AACORST	OSTRACA
AACORTU	ACATOUR

Seven-letter anagrams

	AUTOCAR	**AADEGMS**	DAMAGES	**AADEMNS**	ANADEMS
AACOTUV	AUTOVAC	**AADEGNS**	AGENDAS		MAENADS
AACPRSS	SCARPAS	**AADEGRT**	GRADATE	**AADEMNT**	MANDATE
AACPSTW	CATSPAW	**AADEGRV**	RAVAGED	**AADEMRY**	DAYMARE
AACRRST	CARRATS	**AADEGRY**	DRAYAGE	**AADEMSS**	AMASSED
AACRRSU	CURARAS		YARDAGE	**AADENNT**	ANDANTE
AACRSTV	CRAVATS	**AADEGSV**	SAVAGED	**AADENRV**	VERANDA
AACRTTT	ATTRACT	**AADEHIR**	AIRHEAD	**AADENRW**	AWARNED
AACRTUV	VACATUR	**AADEHJR**	JARHEAD	**AADENST**	ANSATED
AACRTUY	ACTUARY	**AADEHKS**	AKEDAHS	**AADENSU**	SAUNAED
AACRTWY	CARTWAY	**AADEHMN**	HEADMAN	**AADENSW**	WEASAND
AACTUWY	CUTAWAY	**AADEHMS**	ASHAMED	**AADENWZ**	WEAZAND
AADDDEN	ADDENDA	**AADEHPS**	SAPHEAD	**AADEPRR**	PARADER
AADDEGM	DAMAGED	**AADEHPW**	AWHAPED	**AADEPRS**	ASPREAD
AADDEHH	HADEDAH	**AADEHRW**	RAWHEAD		PARADES
AADDEIL	ALIDADE		WARHEAD	**AADEPRT**	ADAPTER
AADDEMM	MADAMED	**AADEHWY**	HEADWAY		READAPT
AADDEMN	DEADMAN	**AADEIKK**	KAIAKED	**AADEPSS**	ESPADAS
AADDENP	DEADPAN	**AADEILR**	RADIALE		PASSADE
AADDEOR	DEODARA	**AADEILV**	AVAILED	**AADEPWW**	PAWAWED
AADDEPR	PARADED		VEDALIA	**AADERRS**	ARRASED
AADDEPT	ADAPTED	**AADEIMR**	MADEIRA	**AADERRW**	AWARDER
AADDERS	ADREADS	**AADEIMS**	AMIDASE	**AADERRY**	ARRAYED
AADDERW	AWARDED		SEAMAID	**AADERSW**	ADWARES
AADDESX	ADDAXES	**AADEINR**	ARANEID		SEAWARD
AADDGNR	GRADDAN	**AADEINS**	NAIADES	**AADERSY**	ARAYSED
	GRANDAD	**AADEINZ**	ZENAIDA		DARESAY
AADDHKR	KHADDAR	**AADEIPS**	DIAPASE	**AADERTU**	AURATED
AADDHRS	SRADDHA	**AADEIRS**	ARAISED	**AADESSY**	ASSAYED
AADDIIK	DIDAKAI	**AADEIRT**	AIRDATE	**AADFLTW**	TWAFALD
AADDIIV	DAVIDIA		RADIATE	**AADFMSU**	MADAFUS
AADDILS	ALIDADS		TIARAED	**AADFNRR**	FARRAND
AADDIMS	DADAISM	**AADEITV**	AVIATED	**AADFNST**	FANTADS
AADDIST	DADAIST	**AADEITW**	AWAITED	**AADFRST**	DAFTARS
AADDLNS	ADLANDS	**AADEJMR**	JEMADAR	**AADGGHR**	HAGGARD
AADDMRY	DRAMADY	**AADEKKY**	KAYAKED	**AADGGLR**	LAGGARD
AADDNVV	DVANDVA	**AADEKLR**	KRAALED	**AADGGOT**	AGGADOT
AADDOSU	AOUDADS	**AADEKLS**	ASLAKED	**AADGGRS**	SAGGARD
AADDRST	DASTARD	**AADEKMR**	KAMERAD	**AADGHIL**	HIDALGA
AADDRSW	ADWARDS	**AADEKMS**	MEDAKAS	**AADGHOR**	DAROGHA
AADDSST	STADDAS		SMAAKED	**AADGHRS**	DARGAHS
AADEEFR	AFEARED	**AADEKPR**	PARKADE	**AADGIIR**	GIARDIA
AADEEGH	HEADAGE	**AADELLP**	PADELLA	**AADGIMM**	DIGAMMA
AADEELT	DEALATE	**AADELLY**	ALLAYED	**AADGIMO**	AGAMOID
AADEEMT	EDEMATA	**AADELMN**	LEADMAN	**AADGIMR**	DIAGRAM
AADEENR	ANEARED	**AADELMO**	ALAMODE	**AADGIMS**	AGAMIDS
AADEERT	AERATED	**AADELMR**	ALARMED	**AADGINW**	ADAWING
AADEERW	AWARDEE	**AADELMX**	MALAXED	**AADGIOS**	ADAGIOS
AADEFFR	AFFEARD	**AADELNR**	ADRENAL	**AADGIOT**	AGATOID
AADEFGL	FALDAGE	**AADELNT**	LANATED	**AADGIRV**	GRAVIDA
AADEFGR	FARDAGE	**AADELNW**	DANELAW	**AADGLLW**	GADWALL
AADEFHT	FATHEAD	**AADELNX**	ADNEXAL	**AADGLMY**	AMYGDAL
AADEFIS	FADAISE	**AADELPR**	PARDALE	**AADGLNO**	GONADAL
AADEFLU	AEFAULD	**AADELPT**	PALATED	**AADGLNR**	GARLAND
AADEFNZ	FAZENDA	**AADELRT**	LATERAD	**AADGLNS**	SLADANG
AADEFTW	FATWAED	**AADELRU**	RADULAE	**AADGLRU**	GRADUAL
AADEGGR	AGGRADE	**AADELRY**	ALREADY	**AADGMNR**	GRANDAM
	GARAGED	**AADELSS**	SALADES		GRANDMA
AADEGHR	RAGHEAD		SALSAED	**AADGMNS**	GADSMAN
AADEGLS	GELADAS	**AADELTU**	ADULATE	**AADGMOT**	DOGMATA
AADEGMN	AGNAMED	**AADELTY**	DAYTALE	**AADGMRS**	SMARAGD
	MANAGED	**AADEMMN**	MANMADE	**AADGNPR**	GRANDPA
AADEGMR	DAMAGER	**AADEMMS**	MADAMES	**AADGNPS**	PADANGS
	MEGARAD	**AADEMNO**	ADENOMA		PADNAGS

AADGNRS	ARGANDS	**AADINRS**	RADIANS	**AADMRRY**	YARDARM
AADGNRT	GARDANT	**AADINRT**	INTRADA	**AADMRSU**	MARAUDS
AADGNRV	YARDANG		RADIANT	**AADMRSZ**	MAZARDS
AADGOPR	PODAGRA	**AADINRV**	VIRANDA	**AADMRZZ**	MAZZARD
AADGOPS	PAGODAS	**AADINRW**	WARDIAN	**AADMSYY**	MAYDAYS
AADGRSU	GARUDAS	**AADINSV**	NAVAIDS	**AADNNOT**	NOTANDA
AADGRSV	GAYDARS	**AADINSY**	NAYSAID	**AADNNRS**	RANDANS
AADHHPS	PADSHAH	**AADIOPZ**	DOPIAZA	**AADNOPR**	PANDORA
AADHHRT	HARDHAT	**AADIPTX**	TAXPAID	**AADNORT**	ONDATRA
AADHILS	DAHLIAS	**AADIQSS**	QASIDAS	**AADNORY**	ANYROAD
AADHIMR	HADARIM	**AADIRRW**	AIRWARD	**AADNPRS**	PANDARS
	HARAMDI	**AADIRSU**	SUDARIA	**AADNPRU**	PANDURA
AADHIMS	SAMADHI	**AADISST**	STADIAS	**AADNRRW**	WARRAND
AADHINP	DAPHNIA	**AADJLNS**	JANDALS	**AADNRRY**	DARRAYN
AADHJNR	HANDJAR	**AADKMRY**	DAYMARK	**AADNRSS**	NASARDS
AADHKNS	DHANSAK	**AADKMSS**	DAMASKS	**AADNRST**	ASTRAND
	KHANDAS	**AADKNRT**	TANKARD		TARANDS
AADHKNY	YAKHDAN	**AADKPSU**	PADAUKS	**AADNRTY**	TANYARD
AADHLRY	HALYARD	**AADKRWW**	AWKWARD	**AADNRVW**	VANWARD
AADHMMS	DHAMMAS	**AADLLLN**	LALLAND	**AADNRWY**	NAYWARD
AADHMNR	HARDMAN	**AADLLMR**	MALLARD	**AADOPRR**	PARADOR
AADHMRS	DHARMAS	**AADLLNW**	LAWLAND	**AADOPRS**	PARADOS
AADHNPR	HARDPAN	**AADLLPU**	PALUDAL	**AADOPRT**	ADAPTOR
AADHNRS	DARSHAN	**AADLLSS**	SALLADS	**AADOPRX**	PARADOX
	DHARNAS	**AADLMNN**	LANDMAN	**AADOPSS**	PASSADO
AADHNSW	HANDSAW	**AADLMNO**	MANDOLA		POSADAS
AADHPRS	PARDAHS		MONADAL	**AADOPTT**	DOPATTA
AADHRSS	HARDASS	**AADLMNU**	LADANUM	**AADORWY**	ROADWAY
	SRADHAS	**AADLMOR**	ARMLOAD	**AADOSTT**	TOSTADA
AADHRSZ	HAZARDS	**AADLMPS**	LAMPADS	**AADOWWX**	WOADWAX
AADHRWY	HAYWARD	**AADLMSW**	WADMALS	**AADPSSW**	PADSAWS
AADHSWY	WASHDAY	**AADLNOP**	DALAPON	**AADPSSY**	SPAYADS
AADIILR	DIARIAL	**AADLNOV**	VANLOAD	**AADPSYY**	PAYDAYS
AADIINO	DIANOIA	**AADLNOZ**	DANAZOL	**AADPTTU**	DUPATTA
AADIINR	DIARIAN	**AADLNRY**	LANYARD	**AADQRTU**	QUADRAT
AADIIPS	ADIPSIA	**AADLNSS**	SANDALS	**AADRRSS**	SARDARS
	ASPIDIA	**AADLNSU**	LANDAUS	**AADRSTU**	DATURAS
AADIJMN	JAMDANI	**AADLNSV**	VANDALS	**AADRSTY**	DAYSTAR
AADIKLY	ILKADAY	**AADLOPY**	PAYLOAD	**AADRSVW**	VAWARDS
AADILLO	ALLODIA	**AADLPPU**	APPLAUD	**AADRWWY**	WAYWARD
	ALODIAL	**AADLPRS**	PARDALS	**AAEEFFR**	AFFEARE
AADILMR	ADMIRAL	**AADLPYY**	PLAYDAY	**AAEEFGL**	LEAFAGE
	AMILDAR	**AADLRRU**	RADULAR	**AAEEFRT**	RATAFEE
AADILMT	MATILDA	**AADLRSU**	RADULAS	**AAEEGKL**	LEAKAGE
AADILNP	PALADIN	**AADMMRS**	DAMMARS	**AAEEGLT**	ETALAGE
AADILNR	LANIARD	**AADMNNO**	MADONNA		GALEATE
	NADIRAL	**AADMNNS**	SANDMAN	**AAEEGMN**	AMENAGE
AADILPS	APSIDAL	**AADMNOR**	MADRONA	**AAEEGMT**	AGAMETE
AADILRS	RADIALS		MANDORA		AGEMATE
AADILRT	TAILARD		MONARDA	**AAEEGRV**	AVERAGE
AADILSS	DALASIS		ROADMAN	**AAEEGST**	EATAGES
AADILST	STADIAL	**AADMNOW**	ADWOMAN	**AAEEHRT**	HETAERA
AADILTV	DATIVAL	**AADMNRS**	MANSARD	**AAEEINT**	TAENIAE
AADILWY	WAYLAID	**AADMNRW**	MANWARD	**AAEEKKS**	AKEAKES
AADIMNR	MANDIRA	**AADMNRY**	DRAYMAN	**AAEEKLS**	SEAKALE
AADIMNS	MAIDANS		YARDMAN	**AAEEKRW**	REAWAKE
AADIMNY	DAYANIM	**AADMNSY**	DAYSMAN	**AAEELMT**	MALEATE
AADIMOR	DIORAMA	**AADMNTU**	MUTANDA	**AAEELOR**	AREOLAE
AADIMOT	DOMATIA		TAMANDU	**AAEELPT**	PALEATE
AADIMRS	ARAMIDS	**AADMOPP**	PAPADOM	**AAEELRT**	LAETARE
AADINNN	NANDINA	**AADMOQU**	MADOQUA	**AAEEMNT**	EMANATE
AADINNP	PANDANI	**AADMORT**	MATADOR		ENEMATA
AADINPT	PINTADA	**AADMOSU**	AMADOUS		MANATEE
AADINRR	DARRAIN	**AADMPPU**	PAPADUM	**AAEEMRT**	AMREETA

Seven-letter anagrams

AAEEMTX	MEATAXE				GALENAS	
AAEEPPS	APPEASE				LAGENAS	
AAEEPRT	PATERAE				LASAGNE	
AAEERST	AERATES	AAEGLNU	AULNAGE	AAEHHPR	RHAPHAE
AAEERSW	SEAWARE		LEGUAAN	AAEHHPT	APHTHAE
AAEERTU	AUREATE	AAEGLOP	APOGEAL	AAEHILP	APHELIA
AAEERTW	TEAWARE	AAEGLRR	REALGAR	AAEHIRT	HETAIRA
AAEERTX	EXARATE	AAEGLRS	ALEGARS	AAEHKNT	KHANATE
AAEFFGR	AGRAFFE		LAAGERS	AAEHKPS	PAKEHAS
AAEFFIR	AFFAIRE	AAEGLST	AGELAST	AAEHKST	TAKAHES
AAEFFLL	FALAFEL		ALGATES	AAEHKSW	SEAHAWK
AAEFFNR	FANFARE		LASTAGE	AAEHLLL	ALLHEAL
AAEFFRS	AFFEARS	AAEGLSV	LAVAGES	AAEHLMT	HEMATAL
AAEFFTT	TAFFETA		SALVAGE	AAEHLNT	ETHANAL
AAEFGNS	FANEGAS	AAEGLSX	GALAXES	AAEHLPS	PHASEAL
AAEFGRS	AGRAFES	AAEGMNO	MANGEAO	AAEHLPX	HEXAPLA
AAEFGTW	WAFTAGE	AAEGMNR	MANAGER	AAEHLRT	TREHALA
AAEFIRR	AIRFARE	AAEGMNS	AGNAMES	AAEHLST	ALTHEAS
AAEFKLO	OAKLEAF		MANAGES	AAEHLTT	ATHLETA
AAEFLLV	FAVELLA		SAGAMEN	AAEHMSS	ASHAMES
AAEFLPR	EARFLAP	AAEGMNT	GATEMAN	AAEHMST	ATHAMES
	PARAFLE		MAGENTA		HAMATES
AAEFLRS	RAFALES		MAGNATE	AAEHMTT	THEMATA
AAEFLSV	FAVELAS		NAMETAG	AAEHNPR	HANAPER
AAEFMRT	FERMATA	AAEGMPR	RAMPAGE	AAEHNPS	SAPHENA
AAEFQRU	AQUAFER	AAEGMRT	REGMATA	AAEHNSY	HYAENAS
AAEFRRW	WARFARE	AAEGMSS	MASSAGE	AAEHPRZ	PHEAZAR
AAEFRWY	WAYFARE	AAEGMTT	METATAG	AAEHPSW	AWHAPES
AAEGGLS	GALAGES	AAEGNNP	PANNAGE	AAEHPSX	HAPAXES
AAEGGNO	ANAGOGE	AAEGNNT	TANNAGE	AAEHRSY	HEARSAY
AAEGGOP	APAGOGE	AAEGNOP	APOGEAN	AAEHSTT	HASTATE
AAEGGRS	GARAGES	AAEGNPT	PAGEANT	AAEIKLN	AKENIAL
AAEGGRT	AGGRATE	AAEGNPW	PAWNAGE	AAEILLX	AXILLAE
AAEGGSV	GAVAGES	AAEGNRR	ARRANGE	AAEILMN	LAMINAE
AAEGHLU	HAULAGE	AAEGNRT	TANAGER	AAEILMS	AMELIAS
AAEGHLY	HAYLAGE	AAEGNST	AGNATES		MALAISE
AAEGHNT	THANAGE	AAEGNSU	GUANASE	AAEILNN	ALANINE
AAEGILR	LAIRAGE	AAEGNTV	VANTAGE	AAEILNO	AEOLIAN
	REGALIA	AAEGNTW	WANTAGE	AAEILNT	ANTLIAE
AAEGILS	ALGESIA	AAEGORS	AGAROSE	AAEILOR	OLEARIA
AAEGINP	NAGAPIE		OARAGES	AAEILPX	EPAXIAL
AAEGINR	ANERGIA	AAEGPRR	PARERGA	AAEILRS	AERIALS
AAEGINV	VAGINAE	AAEGPRS	PARAGES	AAEILRU	AURELIA
AAEGINW	WAINAGE	AAEGPRW	WARPAGE	AAEILRV	REAVAIL
AAEGIPR	IGARAPE	AAEGPSS	PASSAGE		VELARIA
AAEGIRR	ARRIAGE	AAEGPSV	PAVAGES	AAEILSS	ALIASES
AAEGISS	ASSEGAI	AAEGPSY	PAYSAGE	AAEILSV	AVAILES
AAEGIST	AGATISE	AAEGQUY	QUAYAGE	AAEILSX	ALEXIAS
AAEGISU	AGEUSIA	AAEGRRV	RAVAGER	AAEIMMT	IMAMATE
AAEGITT	AGITATE	AAEGRST	AGRASTE	AAEIMNS	AMNESIA
AAEGITZ	AGATIZE		GASTREA		ANEMIAS
AAEGJTU	AJUTAGE		TEARGAS	AAEIMNT	AMENTIA
AAEGKNT	TANKAGE	AAEGRSV	RAVAGES		ANIMATE
AAEGKOS	SOAKAGE		SAVAGER	AAEIMPY	PYAEMIA
AAEGLLR	GLAREAL	AAEGRTT	REGATTA	AAEIMRT	AMIRATE
AAEGLLT	GALLATE	AAEGSSU	ASSUAGE	AAEIMRU	URAEMIA
	GALLETA		SAUSAGE	AAEIMTV	AMATIVE
	TALLAGE	AAEGSSV	AVGASES	AAEINNO	AEONIAN
AAEGLMN	GAMELAN		SAVAGES	AAEINPS	PAESANI
AAEGLMT	GAMETAL	AAEGSSW	ASSWAGE	AAEINPT	PATINAE
AAEGLNN	ANLAGEN	AAEGSTU	GATEAUS	AAEINST	ENTASIA
AAEGLNR	ALNAGER	AAEGSTW	WASTAGE		TAENIAS
AAEGLNS	ALNAGES	AAEGTTW	WATTAGE	AAEIPPS	APEPSIA
	ANLAGES	AAEGTUX	GATEAUX	AAEIPRR	PAREIRA
				AAEIPRS	SPIRAEA

AAEIPRT	APTERIA	**AAELNPR**	PREANAL	**AAEMRST**	AMEARST
AAEIPTT	APATITE	**AAELNPT**	PLANATE		RETAMAS
AAEIRRT	TARAIRE		PLANTAE	**AAEMRTU**	AMATEUR
AAEIRSS	ARAISES		PLATANE	**AAEMSSS**	AMASSES
AAEIRST	ARISTAE	**AAELNPU**	PAENULA	**AAENNNT**	ANTENNA
	ASTERIA	**AAELNRS**	ARSENAL	**AAENNST**	ANNATES
	ATRESIA	**AAELNSS**	ANLASES	**AAENNSZ**	ZENANAS
AAEIRSX	XERASIA	**AAELNST**	SEALANT	**AAENNTT**	TANNATE
AAEIRTT	ARIETTA	**AAELNSY**	ANALYSE	**AAENNTV**	VENTANA
AAEIRTV	VARIATE	**AAELNTT**	TETANAL	**AAENOPS**	APNOEAS
AAEIRTW	AWAITER	**AAELNTY**	ANALYTE		PAESANO
AAEIRVW	AIRWAVE	**AAELNTZ**	ZEALANT	**AAENOSZ**	OZAENAS
AAEISTT	SATIATE	**AAELNWY**	LANEWAY	**AAENPPR**	PARPANE
AAEISTV	AVIATES	**AAELNYZ**	ANALYZE	**AAENPSS**	PAESANS
AAEISTX	ATAXIES	**AAELORR**	AREOLAR	**AAENPST**	ANAPEST
AAEITUX	EUTAXIA	**AAELORS**	AREOLAS		PEASANT
AAEJMST	MAATJES	**AAELORU**	AUREOLA	**AAENPSV**	PAVANES
AAEJNRT	NAARTJE	**AAELOTX**	OXALATE	**AAENPSX**	PANAXES
AAEJOPR	APAREJO	**AAELPPR**	APPAREL	**AAENPTT**	EPATANT
AAEKKOR	KARAOKE	**AAELPPS**	APPEALS	**AAENRRT**	NARRATE
AAEKKRY	KAYAKER	**AAELPPT**	PALPATE	**AAENRSS**	NARASES
AAEKLMS	KAMELAS	**AAELPPU**	PAPULAE	**AAENRST**	ANESTRA
AAEKLNS	ALKANES	**AAELPRS**	EARLAPS		SANTERA
AAEKLNT	ALKANET	**AAELPRT**	APTERAL	**AAENRTT**	TARTANE
	KANTELA	**AAELPRV**	PALAVER	**AAENRTU**	NATURAE
AAEKLSS	ASLAKES	**AAELPSS**	PALASES		TAUREAN
AAEKMNW	WAKEMAN		PASELAS	**AAENRTV**	TAVERNA
AAEKMRR	EARMARK		PLAASES	**AAENRUW**	UNAWARE
AAEKMRS	SEAMARK	**AAELPST**	PALATES	**AAENRUZ**	AZUREAN
AAEKMSW	WAKAMES	**AAELPTT**	TAPETAL	**AAENSSU**	NAUSEAS
AAEKNNS	ANANKES	**AAELPTU**	PLATEAU	**AAENSSV**	VANESSA
AAEKNSW	AWAKENS	**AAELPTY**	APETALY	**AAENSSW**	SEAWANS
	WAKANES	**AAELRST**	TARSEAL	**AAENSTV**	SAVANTE
AAEKNUW	UNAWAKE	**AAELRTV**	LARVATE	**AAENSTW**	SEAWANT
AAEKPRT	PARTAKE	**AAELRTZ**	LAZARET	**AAEOPTZ**	ZAPATEO
AAEKPTU	PUKATEA	**AAELRVY**	ALVEARY	**AAEORRT**	AERATOR
AAEKRSS	KEASARS	**AAELSST**	ATLASES	**AAEORRU**	AURORAE
AAEKRST	KARATES	**AAELSTT**	SALTATE	**AAEORST**	AEROSAT
AAELLLM	LAMELLA	**AAELSTV**	VALETAS	**AAEPPRS**	APPEARS
AAELLNV	AVELLAN	**AAELSTZ**	ALTEZAS	**AAEPPRT**	PARAPET
AAELLNZ	ZANELLA	**AAELSUX**	ASEXUAL	**AAEPRSS**	PASEARS
AAELLPR	PARELLA	**AAELSWX**	SEALWAX		SARAPES
AAELLPS	PAELLAS	**AAELTUV**	VALUATE	**AAEPRST**	PETARAS
AAELLPT	PATELLA	**AAELTVV**	VALVATE	**AAEPRSY**	APYRASE
AAELLRT	LATERAL	**AAELTZZ**	ALTEZZA	**AAEPRSZ**	ZARAPES
AAELLRY	ALLAYER	**AAELWWY**	WELAWAY	**AAEPRTY**	PEATARY
	AREALLY	**AAEMMMR**	MAREMMA	**AAEPSTW**	WATAPES
AAELLSW	SEAWALL	**AAEMMMT**	MAMMATE	**AAEPTTW**	WATTAPE
AAELLTV	VALLATE	**AAEMMNT**	MEATMAN	**AAERRRS**	ARREARS
AAELMMR	ALMEMAR	**AAEMMNU**	MANUMEA	**AAERRRY**	ARRAYER
AAELMMT	LEMMATA	**AAEMMOT**	OMMATEA	**AAERRSS**	ARRASES
AAELMNT	AMENTAL	**AAEMNNT**	EMANANT	**AAERRST**	ERRATAS
AAELMNU	ALUMNAE	**AAEMNOR**	AMARONE	**AAERRTT**	TARTARE
AAELMOT	OATMEAL	**AAEMNPP**	PAMPEAN	**AAERSST**	SEARATS
AAELMPT	PALMATE	**AAEMNPS**	SPAEMAN	**AAERSSY**	ARAYSES
AAELMRW	MALWARE	**AAEMNPT**	PEATMAN		ASSAYER
AAELMST	MALATES	**AAEMNRT**	RAMENTA	**AAERSTU**	AURATES
	MALTASE	**AAEMNRU**	MURAENA	**AAERSTW**	AWAREST
	TAMALES	**AAEMNST**	NAMASTE	**AAERTTU**	TUATERA
AAELMSX	MALAXES	**AAEMNTU**	MANTEAU	**AAESSTV**	SAVATES
AAELMSY	AMYLASE	**AAEMOTY**	ATEMOYA	**AAESSWY**	SEAWAYS
AAELNNS	ANNEALS	**AAEMOTZ**	METAZOA	**AAFFILN**	AFFINAL
AAELNOP	APNOEAL	**AAEMQSU**	SQUAMAE	**AAFFILX**	AFFIXAL
AAELNOV	VALONEA	**AAEMRSS**	AMASSER	**AAFFIMS**	MAFFIAS

Seven-letter anagrams

AAFFINS	SAFFIAN	AAGGNTT	TAGGANT	AAGINRZ	ZINGARA
AAFFINT	AFFIANT	AAGGNWY	GANGWAY	AAGINST	AGAINST
AAFFIRS	AFFAIRS	AAGGQSU	QUAGGAS		AGITANS
	RAFFIAS	AAGGRSS	SAGGARS		ANTISAG
AAFFIST	TAFFIAS	AAGGRST	RAGTAGS		GITANAS
AAFFLRS	FARFALS		TAGRAGS	AAGINSU	IGUANAS
AAFFPRS	AFFRAPS	AAGHHRR	AARRGHH	AAGINSV	VAGINAS
AAFFRSY	AFFRAYS	AAGHILR	GHARIAL	AAGINSY	GAINSAY
AAFFRSZ	ZAFFARS	AAGHINN	ANHINGA	AAGINTY	ANTIGAY
AAFGHIN	AFGHANI	AAGHJNS	GANJAHS	AAGINWW	WAWAING
AAFGHNS	AFGHANS	AAGHKNS	KANGHAS	AAGIOSS	ASIAGOS
AAFGLMN	FLAGMAN		KHANGAS	AAGIOTT	AGITATO
AAFGORR	FARRAGO	AAGHKNT	THANGKA	AAGIPRS	AIRGAPS
AAFHIKL	KHALIFA	AAGHLNT	GNATHAL	AAGIPRU	PIRAGUA
AAFHINR	FARINHA	AAGHLOS	GASAHOL	AAGIRRY	ARGYRIA
AAFHLLS	ASHFALL	AAGHLSZ	GHAZALS	AAGIRSW	WARAGIS
AAFHLWY	HALFWAY	AAGHMNN	HANGMAN	AAGISTT	SAGITTA
AAFHSTW	FATWAHS	AAGHMNU	MAHUANG	AAGJNRS	GARJANS
AAFIILR	FILARIA	AAGHMNW	WHANGAM	AAGJRSU	JAGUARS
AAFIJST	FAJITAS	AAGHMRS	GRAHAMS	AAGKKNO	ANGAKOK
AAFIKLS	ALFAKIS		GRAMASH	AAGKLSY	GALYAKS
	KAFILAS	AAGHNRS	ARGHANS	AAGKOOZ	GAZOOKA
AAFIKSS	SIFAKAS		HANGARS	AAGKORT	KATORGA
AAFILNT	FANTAIL	AAGHNST	SANGHAT	AAGLLNS	LALANGS
	TAILFAN	AAGHQUU	QUAHAUG	AAGLLNT	GALLANT
AAFILQU	ALFAQUI	AAGHRSW	WASHRAG	AAGLLVY	VAGALLY
AAFINNT	INFANTA	AAGHSTY	SAGATHY	AAGLMMS	MALMAGS
AAFINNU	INFAUNA	AAGIINT	IGNATIA	AAGLMNS	MANGALS
AAFINRS	FARINAS	AAGIKNS	KAINGAS	AAGLNOR	GRANOLA
AAFINTT	ANTIFAT	AAGIKNT	TIKANGA	AAGLNOS	ANALOGS
AAFIPRT	PARFAIT	AAGIKNW	AWAKING	AAGLNOY	ANALOGY
AAFIRSS	SAFARIS	AAGIKNZ	ZIGANKA	AAGLNPS	LAPSANG
AAFIRSU	FUSARIA	AAGILMY	MYALGIA	AAGLNRS	LANGARS
AAFIRUY	RUFIYAA	AAGILNN	ANGINAL		RAGLANS
AAFIRWY	FAIRWAY	AAGILNO	LOGANIA	AAGLNRU	ANGULAR
AAFISST	FATSIAS	AAGILNP	PAGINAL	AAGLNSU	LAGUNAS
AAFJLLW	JAWFALL	AAGILNS	AGNAILS	AAGLNTY	GALANTY
AAFJLOR	ALFORJA	AAGILNV	AVALING	AAGLORU	ARUGOLA
AAFKNST	KAFTANS		VAGINAL	AAGLRST	GASTRAL
AAFLLLS	FALLALS	AAGILNY	ALAYING	AAGLRUU	ARUGULA
AAFLLTY	FATALLY	AAGILOS	ALOGIAS		AUGURAL
AAFLMPR	FRAMPAL		LAOGAIS	AAGLRVX	GRAVLAX
AAFLNOR	FORLANA	AAGILOT	OTALGIA	AAGLSST	STALAGS
AAFLNRU	FURLANA	AAGILPS	PALAGIS	AAGMMNS	MAGSMAN
AAFLNUU	FAUNULA	AAGILRS	ARGALIS	AAGMMRR	GRAMMAR
AAFLSTU	FLAUTAS		GARIALS	AAGMMRS	GRAMMAS
AAFLWYY	FLYAWAY	AAGILSV	GAVIALS	AAGMMST	GAMMATS
AAFMNRT	RAFTMAN	AAGILTW	WAGTAIL	AAGMMTU	GUMMATA
AAFMNST	FANTASM	AAGIMNO	ANGIOMA	AAGMMUY	MAMAGUY
AAFNRRT	FARRANT	AAGIMNS	MAGIANS	AAGMNNR	GRANNAM
AAFNSTT	FANTAST		SIAMANG	AAGMNOS	SANGOMA
AAFNSTY	FANTASY	AAGIMNT	AMATING	AAGMNOT	AGAMONT
AAFOSST	AFTOSAS	AAGIMNZ	AMAZING	AAGMNPR	PANGRAM
AAGGHNT	HANGTAG	AAGINNS	ANGINAS	AAGMNPY	PANGAMY
AAGGIJN	JAGAING		INANGAS	AAGMNRS	RAGMANS
AAGGILN	GANGLIA	AAGINNW	WANIGAN	AAGMNRT	TANGRAM
AAGGJRY	JAGGARY	AAGINOS	AGNOSIA		TRANGAM
AAGGKSU	GAGAKUS	AAGINPY	APAYING	AAGMNSW	SWAGMAN
AAGGLMO	MAGALOG	AAGINRR	ARRAIGN	AAGMNSZ	ZAMANGS
AAGGLOS	GALAGOS	AAGINRS	NAGARIS	AAGMOPY	APOGAMY
AAGGLRY	GRAYLAG		SANGRIA	AAGMORS	MARGOSA
AAGGMNS	MGANGAS		SARANGI	AAGMOSU	AGAMOUS
AAGGNOY	ANAGOGY	AAGINRT	GRANITA	AAGMPRS	GRAMPAS
AAGGNST	GANGSTA	AAGINRU	GUARANI	AAGMRRY	GRAMARY

AAGMRSY	MARGAYS	AAHIRST	SHARIAT	AAHNORV	NAVARHO
AAGNNOS	GOANNAS	AAHIRSV	VIHARAS	AAHNRTX	ANTHRAX
AAGNNRU	RUNANGA	AAHIRTV	HAVARTI	AAHNRTY	RHATANY
AAGNNSW	WANGANS	AAHISTW	TAWHAIS	AAHNSUW	WHANAUS
AAGNOPR	PARAGON	AAHJKNR	KHANJAR	AAHNSZZ	HAZZANS
AAGNORS	ANGORAS	AAHJKST	JHATKAS	AAHORSU	SAHUARO
AAGNORZ	ORGANZA	AAHJNRS	HANJARS	AAHPPRS	PARAPHS
AAGNOST	TAONGAS		RHANJAS	AAHPRSY	YARPHAS
AAGNPRS	PARANGS	AAHJRRS	JARRAHS	AAHPRTW	WARPATH
AAGNRRS	GARRANS	AAHKKST	KATHAKS	AAHPTWY	PATHWAY
AAGNRRY	GRANARY	AAHKLRS	LASHKAR	AAHRSSS	HASSARS
AAGNRSS	SANGARS	AAHKLST	KHALATS	AAHRSST	SHASTRA
AAGNRTV	VAGRANT	AAHKLSY	KHAYALS	AAHRSTY	ASHTRAY
AAGNSST	SATANGS	AAHKMSY	YASHMAK	AAHRTTW	ATHWART
AAGNSTU	TAGUANS	AAHKNST	KANTHAS	AAHSSSY	SASHAYS
AAGNSUY	GUANAYS	AAHKNSU	KAHUNAS	AAIIKKS	KAIKAIS
AAGOPRU	GAROUPA	AAHKPSS	PASHKAS	AAIIKSZ	ZAIKAIS
AAGOPSS	SAPSAGO	AAHKPSU	HAPUKAS	AAIILMR	AIRMAIL
AAGORSU	SAGUARO	AAHKRSS	RAKSHAS	AAIILPR	PAIRIAL
AAGOSTU	AGOUTAS	AAHLLLS	HALLALS	AAIILPT	TILAPIA
AAGPPRS	GRAPPAS	AAHLLNS	HALLANS	AAIILRZ	ALIZARI
AAGRRSY	GARRYAS		NALLAHS	AAIINNZ	ANZIANI
AAGRSUV	AVRUGAS	AAHLLOS	HALLOAS	AAIINRT	ANTIAIR
AAGTTUU	TAUTAUG	AAHLLPS	PALLAHS	AAIINTT	TITANIA
AAHHIRS	SHARIAH	AAHLLSW	WALLAHS	AAIINZZ	ZIZANIA
AAHHJJS	HAJJAHS	AAHLLWY	HALLWAY	AAIIRVV	VIVARIA
AAHHLLS	HALLAHS	AAHLMMS	HAMMALS	AAIJLNP	JALAPIN
AAHHLSV	HALVAHS		MAHMALS	AAIJMNP	JAMPANI
AAHHMSZ	HAMZAHS		MASHLAM	AAIJMNT	ANTIJAM
AAHHNNT	THANNAH	AAHLMRS	MARSHAL	AAIJNRS	JARINAS
AAHHNPT	NAPHTHA	AAHLMRU	HAMULAR	AAIJNRZ	JANIZAR
AAHHNST	THANAHS	AAHLMST	MALTHAS	AAIJNST	TINAJAS
AAHHOPR	PHARAOH	AAHLMSU	HAMAULS	AAIJPPY	JIPYAPA
AAHIIMT	HIMATIA	AAHLNPX	PHALANX	AAIJRSW	JAWARIS
AAHIJNR	HARIJAN	AAHLNRW	NARWHAL	AAIKLLN	ALKALIN
AAHIKOR	AKIRAHO	AAHLPRS	PHRASAL	AAIKLLS	ALKALIS
AAHIKPS	PAKAHIS	AAHLPST	ASPHALT	AAIKLMS	KALMIAS
AAHIKRT	KITHARA		SPATHAL		KAMILAS
AAHILLL	HALLALI		TAPLASH	AAIKLNP	PALINKA
AAHILLN	HALLIAN	AAHLRSS	ASHLARS	AAIKLNS	KALIANS
AAHILMR	ALMIRAH	AAHLRST	HARTALS	AAIKLPR	PALIKAR
AAHILMS	SHIMAAL	AAHLRSW	SHALWAR	AAIKMNN	MANAKIN
AAHILMT	THALAMI	AAHMMMS	HAMMAMS	AAIKMNR	RAMAKIN
AAHILNT	THALIAN	AAHMMNS	MASHMAN	AAIKMOR	ROMAIKA
AAHILPV	PAHLAVI	AAHMMSS	SHAMMAS	AAIKMRS	KARAISM
AAHILSW	SAHIWAL	AAHMNNU	HANUMAN	AAIKNRS	KINARAS
AAHILSY	ALIYAHS	AAHMNRS	HARMANS	AAIKNST	TANKIAS
AAHIMNO	MAHONIA	AAHMNSS	SHAMANS	AAIKORU	OUAKARI
AAHIMNS	SHAMINA	AAHMNTX	XANTHAM	AAIKOSY	SOKAIYA
AAHIMNZ	HAZANIM	AAHMOPR	AMPHORA	AAIKPPR	PAPRIKA
AAHIMSS	AHIMSAS	AAHMPRS	PHARMAS	AAIKPRR	AIRPARK
AAHINOP	APHONIA	AAHMQSU	QUAMASH	AAIKRSS	ASKARIS
AAHINPP	PAPHIAN	AAHMRSS	ASHRAMS	AAIKRST	KARAITS
AAHINPR	PIRANHA	AAHMSST	ASTHMAS	AAIKRSU	UAKARIS
AAHINST	SHAITAN		MATSAHS	AAIKSTT	ASTATKI
	TAHINAS	AAHMSSU	MASHUAS	AAIKTVV	AKVAVIT
AAHINTW	TANIWHA	AAHMSTZ	HAZMATS	AAILLLP	PALLIAL
AAHIPRS	PARIAHS		MATZAHS	AAILLLT	LATILLA
	RAPHIAS	AAHNNOS	HOSANNA	AAILLMM	MAMILLA
AAHIPRT	PITARAH	AAHNNST	TANNAHS	AAILLMN	LAMINAL
AAHIPTZ	ZAPTIAH		THANNAS		MANILLA
AAHIRRS	HARIRAS	AAHNNTX	XANTHAN	AAILLMR	ARMILLA
AAHIRSS	HARISSA	AAHNOPR	ANAPHOR	AAILLMX	MAXILLA
	SHARIAS	AAHNORT	ATHANOR	AAILLNT	LANITAL

AAILLNV	VANILLA	**AAILSSV**	SALIVAS	**AAINTTU**	TUTANIA
AAILLPP	PAPILLA		SALVIAS	**AAINTTX**	ANTITAX
AAILLRX	AXILLAR		VASSAIL	**AAIOPRS**	APORIAS
AAILLSV	SALIVAL	**AAILSSW**	WASSAIL	**AAIOPRT**	ATROPIA
AAILLSX	AXILLAS	**AAILTTT**	LATITAT	**AAIOPRV**	OVIPARA
AAILLUV	ALLUVIA	**AAIMMMT**	MAMMATI	**AAIORRS**	ROSARIA
AAILLXY	AXIALLY	**AAIMMNO**	AMMONIA	**AAIORSU**	SAOUARI
AAILMMN	MAILMAN	**AAIMMSS**	MIASMAS	**AAIORTV**	AVIATOR
AAILMMR	AMMIRAL	**AAIMNNO**	OMNIANA	**AAIPPRS**	APPAIRS
AAILMMS	MIASMAL	**AAIMNNT**	ANTIMAN	**AAIPPRU**	PUPARIA
AAILMMX	MAXIMAL	**AAIMNOS**	ANOSMIA	**AAIPPTT**	PITAPAT
AAILMNR	LAMINAR	**AAIMNOT**	AMATION	**AAIPRST**	PITARAS
	RAILMAN		ANIMATO	**AAIPRSY**	PIRAYAS
AAILMNS	ALMAINS	**AAIMNPT**	TIMPANA	**AAIPRTT**	PARTITA
	ANIMALS	**AAIMNRS**	MARINAS	**AAIPSTY**	PITAYAS
	LAMINAS	**AAIMNRT**	MARTIAN	**AAIPSZZ**	PIAZZAS
	MANILAS		TAMARIN	**AAIQSSU**	QUASSIA
AAILMNT	MATINAL	**AAIMNST**	MANATIS	**AAIQTUV**	AQUAVIT
AAILMNU	ALUMINA		STAMINA	**AAIRSST**	ARISTAS
AAILMNV	MAILVAN	**AAIMNSV**	VIMANAS		TARSIAS
AAILMPS	IMPALAS	**AAIMNTX**	TAXIMAN	**AAIRSTT**	STRIATA
AAILMQU	MAQUILA	**AAIMRRS**	MARARIS	**AAIRSTY**	RAIYATS
AAILMRT	MARITAL	**AAIMRST**	AMRITAS	**AAIRSUW**	WAIRUAS
	MARTIAL		TAMARIS	**AAIRSWY**	AIRWAYS
AAILMSS	ALISMAS	**AAIMRSU**	SAMURAI	**AAIRSZZ**	RAZZIAS
	SALAMIS	**AAIMRTU**	TIMARAU	**AAISTTV**	ATAVIST
AAILMSU	AUMAILS	**AAIMSST**	STASIMA	**AAISTUY**	YAUTIAS
AAILNNS	ALANINS	**AAIMSSU**	AMUSIAS	**AAITWXY**	TAXIWAY
AAILNOT	AILANTO	**AAIMSTT**	TATAMIS	**AAJJMRS**	JAMJARS
	ALATION	**AAIMSTV**	ATAVISM	**AAJKLWY**	JAYWALK
AAILNOV	NOVALIA	**AAIMSUV**	MAUVAIS	**AAJKMNR**	JARKMAN
	VALONIA	**AAINNRU**	URANIAN	**AAJKNSS**	SANJAKS
AAILNPS	SALPIAN	**AAINNRV**	NAVARIN	**AAJMNPS**	JAMPANS
AAILNPT	PLATINA		NIRVANA	**AAJMNZZ**	JAZZMAN
AAILNRU	ULNARIA	**AAINOPS**	ANOPIAS	**AAJMORR**	MOJARRA
AAILNRY	LANIARY		ANOPSIA	**AAJMORT**	MAJORAT
AAILNSS	SALINAS		PAISANO	**AAJMPSY**	PYJAMAS
AAILNST	LATINAS	**AAINORR**	ORARIAN	**AAJNNOS**	JOANNAS
AAILNSY	INYALAS	**AAINORV**	OVARIAN	**AAJNOSW**	AJOWANS
AAILNTV	VALIANT	**AAINOST**	ATONIAS	**AAJNOSY**	YOJANAS
AAILNTY	ANALITY	**AAINOSX**	ANOXIAS	**AAJNPRS**	PRAJNAS
AAILORS	ROSALIA	**AAINPPS**	PAPAINS	**AAJOPSU**	SAPAJOU
	SOLARIA	**AAINPRS**	PARIANS	**AAKKLPS**	KALPAKS
AAILORU	RAOULIA		PIRANAS	**AAKKLRU**	KARAKUL
AAILORV	OVARIAL	**AAINPSS**	PAISANS	**AAKKMOT**	TOKAMAK
	VARIOLA	**AAINPST**	PASTINA	**AAKKMRS**	MARKKAS
AAILORZ	ZOARIAL		PATINAS	**AAKKOPS**	KAKAPOS
AAILOST	SOLATIA		PINATAS	**AAKKSUZ**	ZAKUSKA
AAILPPT	APPALTI		TAIPANS	**AAKLMPU**	LAMPUKA
AAILPRS	PARIALS	**AAINRST**	ANTIARS	**AAKLMRV**	MALARKY
AAILPRT	PARTIAL		ARTISAN	**AAKLMUY**	YAMULKA
	PATRIAL		TSARINA	**AAKLNOO**	OOLAKAN
AAILPRY	AIRPLAY	**AAINRSU**	ANURIAS	**AAKLNOU**	OULAKAN
AAILPST	SPATIAL		SAURIAN	**AAKLOOP**	PALOOKA
AAILPTT	TALIPAT		URANIAS	**AAKLOOT**	TALOOKA
AAILPZZ	PALAZZI	**AAINRSV**	SAVARIN	**AAKLRSU**	KURSAAL
AAILQWW	QAWWALI	**AAINRTV**	VARIANT		RUSALKA
AAILRRV	ARRIVAL	**AAINRTW**	ANTIWAR	**AAKLSSU**	SAKSAUL
AAILRST	LARIATS	**AAINRTZ**	TZARINA	**AAKLSTU**	TALUKAS
	LATRIAS	**AAINSST**	ISTANAS	**AAKLWWY**	WALKWAY
AAILRTT	RATTAIL	**AAINSSY**	SANYASI	**AAKMMNR**	MARKMAN
AAILRTV	TRAVAIL	**AAINSTT**	ATTAINS	**AAKMNSU**	MANUKAS
AAILRWY	RAILWAY	**AAINSTV**	VANITAS	**AAKMORU**	AMOKURA
AAILSSS	ASSAILS	**AAINTTT**	ATTAINT	**AAKMOSU**	MOUSAKA

AAKMRSU	KARAMUS		PLATANS	AAMNOSZ	AMAZONS
	KUMARAS		SALTPAN	AAMNOTU	AUTOMAN
AAKMRUZ	MAZURKA	AALNPUU	PUNALUA	AAMNOTY	ANATOMY
AAKMRWY	WAYMARK	AALNQTU	QUANTAL	AAMNPRT	MANTRAP
AAKMSSY	YASMAKS	AALNRRU	RANULAR		RAMPANT
AAKNNTU	NUNATAK	AALNRSU	RANULAS	AAMNPRY	PARANYM
AAKNORS	ANORAKS	AALNRSW	NARWALS	AAMNPSS	PASSMAN
AAKNRST	KANTARS	AALNRTT	LATRANT		SAMPANS
AAKNSST	ASKANTS	AALNRTU	NATURAL	AAMNPST	TAMPANS
AAKNSTW	WANKSTA	AALNSST	SANTALS		TAPSMAN
AAKNSWZ	KWANZAS	AALNSTT	SALTANT	AAMNPTY	TYMPANA
AAKNTWY	TWANKAY		TALANTS	AAMNRST	ARTSMAN
AAKOOPP	PAKAPOO	AALNSTU	SULTANA		MANTRAS
AAKOPRS	PAKORAS	AALNSTY	ANALYST	AAMNRUY	MANUARY
AAKORST	OSTRAKA	AALNTTU	TALAUNT	AAMNSTU	MANTUAS
AAKPRWY	PARKWAY	AALOPPT	APPALTO		TAMANUS
AAKRSTU	KATSURA	AALOPRS	PARASOL	AAMOORS	AMOROSA
AAKRTUY	AUTARKY	AALOPST	TAPALOS	AAMOPRS	PARAMOS
AAKSSTT	ATTASKS	AALOPSY	PAYOLAS	AAMORRZ	ZAMARRO
AAKSTTT	ATTASKT	AALOPVV	PAVLOVA	AAMORSV	SAMOVAR
AAKSTUY	YUKATAS	AALOPZZ	PALAZZO	AAMORTY	AMATORY
AALLLNS	LALLANS	AALORRU	AURORAL	AAMOSSS	SAMOSAS
AALLLSS	SALLALS	AALORST	ALASTOR	AAMOSTT	STOMATA
AALLMMS	MALLAMS	AALORSU	AROUSAL	AAMOTTU	AUTOMAT
AALLMPU	AMPULLA	AALORTX	LAXATOR	AAMPRRT	RAMPART
AALLNOX	ALLOXAN	AALOSTT	SALTATO	AAMPSSY	AMPASSY
AALLNPU	PLANULA	AALOSVW	AVOWALS	AAMRSST	MATRASS
AALLNSY	ALANYLS	AALOTTY	TALAYOT	AAMRSSU	ASARUMS
	NASALLY	AALPPRU	PAPULAR	AAMRSTU	SUMATRA
AALLNVY	NAVALLY	AALPPRY	PAPYRAL		TRAUMAS
AALLORS	AROLLAS	AALPRRS	PARRALS	AAMRTTY	TRYMATA
AALLOSZ	AZOLLAS	AALPRSW	ASPRAWL	AAMRTWY	TRAMWAY
AALLOTV	LAVOLTA	AALPRSY	PARLAYS	AAMSSTU	SATSUMA
AALLPPS	APPALLS	AALPRTY	LAPTRAY	AANNNOS	ANNONAS
AALLPPY	PAPALLY	AALPSTU	SPATULA	AANNOTT	ANNATTO
AALLRUY	AURALLY	AALQSWW	QAWWALS	AANNPSS	SANPANS
AALLRVY	VALLARY	AALRSST	ASTRALS	AANNPSW	SWANPAN
AALLSTT	ATLATLS		TARSALS	AANNRSU	ANURANS
	TALLATS	AALRSTT	STRATAL	AANNSYZ	NYANZAS
AALLUVV	VALVULA	AALRSTU	AUSTRAL	AANOQSY	YAQONAS
AALMMMS	MAMMALS	AALRSTY	ASTYLAR	AANORST	TORANAS
AALMMNO	AMMONAL		SATYRAL	AANORTT	ARNATTO
AALMMNS	ALMSMAN	AALSSSV	VASSALS	AANOSST	SONATAS
AALMMNT	MALTMAN	AALSSTU	ASSAULT	AANOSTT	ANATTOS
AALMNOS	SALAMON	AALSSUX	SAXAULS	AANPPSS	SAPPANS
AALMNOY	ANOMALY	AALSTUV	VALUTAS	AANPRST	PARTANS
AALMNPS	NAPALMS	AALSWYY	WAYLAYS		SPARTAN
AALMNSU	MANUALS	AAMMMRY	MAMMARY		TARPANS
AALMORT	ALAMORT	AAMMNRT	MANTRAM		TRAPANS
AALMORY	MAYORAL	AAMMNST	AMTMANS	AANPRSU	PURANAS
AALMOST	AMATOLS	AAMMOTY	MYOMATA	AANPSST	PASSANT
AALMPRY	PALMARY	AAMMRRS	MARRAMS	AANQRTU	QUARTAN
	PALMYRA	AAMMRST	RAMSTAM	AANRRSW	WARRANS
AALMPSS	PLASMAS		TAMMARS	AANRRSY	YARRANS
AALMRRU	RAMULAR	AAMMSUZ	MAZUMAS	AANRRTW	WARRANT
AALMRSU	ALARUMS	AAMNNNS	MANNANS	AANRSSS	SANSARS
AALMSSU	MASULAS	AAMNNOY	ANONYMA	AANRSTT	RATTANS
AALMSTY	AMYTALS	AAMNOOS	MANOAOS		TANTRAS
AALMTTU	MULATTA	AAMNORR	MARRANO		TARTANS
AALNNRU	ANNULAR		ORRAMAN	AANRSTY	YANTRAS
AALNNSU	ANNUALS	AAMNORS	OARSMAN	AANRSTZ	TARZANS
AALNPRT	PLANTAR		RAMONAS	AANRUWY	RUNAWAY
AALNPRU	LUPANAR	AAMNORT	AMORANT	AANSSTT	TSANTSA
AALNPST	PLANTAS	AAMNORZ	ROMANZA	AANSSTV	SAVANTS

Seven-letter anagrams

AANSSTZ	STANZAS	ABBDEGR	GRABBED	ABBEMUZ	BUMBAZE
AANSSYY	NAYSAYS	ABBDEIT	TABBIED	ABBENRS	NABBERS
AANSTTT	STATANT	ABBDEIY	YABBIED	ABBEORS	EARBOBS
AANSTUV	AVAUNTS	ABBDEJL	JABBLED	ABBEOTX	BEATBOX
AANSWYY	ANYWAYS	ABBDELR	DABBLER	ABBERRS	BARBERS
AAOORRW	WOORARA		DRABBLE	ABBERST	BARBETS
AAOPSST	POTASSA		RABBLED		RABBETS
	SAPOTAS	ABBDELS	DABBLES		STABBER
AAOQSSU	OQUASSA		SLABBED	ABBERSW	SWABBER
AAORRSU	AURORAS	ABBDELW	WABBLED	ABBERSY	YABBERS
AAORRSV	VARROAS	ABBDERR	DRABBER	ABBESSU	SUBBASE
AAORSTT	TOTARAS	ABBDERS	DABBERS	ABBFIRT	FRABBIT
AAORSVV	VAVASOR	ABBDERT	DRABBET	ABBGGIN	GABBING
AAOSTTV	OTTAVAS	ABBDEST	STABBED	ABBGHSU	GUBBAHS
AAOTTUY	TATOUAY		TEBBADS	ABBGIJN	JABBING
AAOTWWY	TOWAWAY	ABBDESU	BEDAUBS	ABBGINN	NABBING
AAPPSWW	PAWPAWS	ABBDESW	SWABBED	ABBGINR	BARBING
AAPRRSU	PARURAS	ABBDGIN	DABBING	ABBGINS	SABBING
AAPRRTT	RATTRAP	ABBDHIJ	DJIBBAH	ABBGINT	TABBING
AAPRSST	SATRAPS	ABBDILR	LIBBARD	ABBGINU	BUBINGA
AAPRSTT	ATTRAPS	ABBDINR	RIBBAND	ABBGINY	BABYING
AAPRSTY	SATRAPY	ABBDITY	DABBITY	ABBGMSU	BUMBAGS
AAPRTUU	RAUPATU	ABBDLRU	LUBBARD	ABBGOOU	BUGABOO
AAPRTWY	PARTWAY	ABBDMOR	BOMBARD	ABBGORS	GABBROS
AAPZZZZ	PAZZAZZ	ABBDMOU	BABUDOM	ABBHIJS	JIBBAHS
AAQRSSU	QUASARS	ABBDNOX	BANDBOX	ABBHISY	BABYISH
AARRSSS	SARSARS	ABBEESU	BAUBEES	ABBHJSU	JUBBAHS
AARRSTT	TARTARS	ABBEESW	BAWBEES	ABBHOOS	HABOOBS
AARRSWY	WARRAYS	ABBEFST	FABBEST	ABBHRRU	RHUBARB
AARSSST	ASSARTS	ABBEGIR	GABBIER	ABBHTTU	BATHTUB
	SASTRAS	ABBEGLR	GABBLER	ABBIIMN	BAMBINI
AARSSTT	ASTARTS		GRABBLE	ABBIJLS	JILBABS
	STRATAS	ABBEGLS	GABBLES	ABBILLS	LIBLABS
AARSSTY	SATYRAS	ABBEGNO	BOGBEAN	ABBILOR	BILOBAR
AARSSWW	WARSAWS	ABBEGNU	BUGBANE	ABBILOS	BILBOAS
AASSTTU	STATUAS	ABBEGRR	GRABBER	ABBILOT	BOBTAIL
ABBBDEL	BABBLED	ABBEGRS	GABBERS	ABBILSU	BUBALIS
	BLABBED	ABBEGRU	BUGBEAR	ABBIMNO	BAMBINO
ABBBELR	BABBLER	ABBEHLS	SHABBLE	ABBIMSU	BABUISM
	BLABBER	ABBEILT	BITABLE	ABBINOR	RABBONI
	BRABBLE	ABBEIRS	BARBIES	ABBINRS	RABBINS
ABBBELS	BABBLES		RABBIES	ABBIORT	RABBITO
ABBBELU	ABUBBLE	ABBEIST	BABIEST	ABBIRST	RABBITS
ABBBITT	BABBITT		TABBIES	ABBIRTY	RABBITY
ABBCDER	CRABBED	ABBEISW	SWABBIE	ABBISTY	BABYSIT
ABBCDES	SCABBED	ABBEISY	YABBIES	ABBKLOU	BLAUBOK
ABBCEHI	BABICHE	ABBEJLS	JABBLES	ABBLLOX	BOXBALL
ABBCEHU	BABUCHE	ABBEJRS	JABBERS	ABBLLRU	BULLBAR
ABBCEIS	CABBIES	ABBELLR	BARBELL	ABBLLTU	BULLBAT
ABBCELR	CLABBER	ABBELMR	BRAMBLE	ABBLMRY	BRAMBLY
ABBCELS	SCABBLE	ABBELNS	SNABBLE	ABBLOOS	BABOOLS
ABBCERR	CRABBER	ABBELOR	BELABOR	ABBMOOR	BOMBORA
ABBCGIN	CABBING	ABBELPR	PRABBLE	ABBMOOS	BAMBOOS
ABBCIIS	BIBASIC	ABBELRR	RABBLER	ABBMOST	BOMBAST
ABBCIKT	BACKBIT	ABBELRS	BARBELS	ABBMOTU	BUMBOAT
ABBCIRS	BICARBS		RABBLES	ABBNOOS	BABOONS
ABBCKUY	BUYBACK		SLABBER	ABBOORU	RUBABOO
ABBCOST	BOBCATS	ABBELRU	BARBULE	ABBORSS	ABSORBS
ABBCOTY	ABBOTCY	ABBELRW	WABBLER	ABBOSTY	BATBOYS
ABBCRYY	CRYBABY	ABBELSU	BAUBLES		BOBSTAY
ABBDDEL	DABBLED		BUBALES	ABBQSUY	SQUABBY
ABBDDER	DRABBED	ABBELSW	BAWBLES	ABBRSSU	BUSBARS
ABBDEFR	FRABBED		WABBLES	ABBRSTU	BARBUTS
ABBDEGL	GABBLED	ABBELUY	BUYABLE		

ABBSSSU	SUBBASS	**ABCEERR**	ACERBER	**ABCELLU**	BULLACE
ABCCCHI	BACCHIC		CEREBRA	**ABCELMO**	CEMBALO
ABCCEIR	ACERBIC		REBRACE	**ABCELMR**	CAMBREL
	BRECCIA	**ABCEERU**	BERCEAU		CLAMBER
ABCCEIS	BACCIES	**ABCEESS**	BECASSE	**ABCELMS**	BECALMS
	SEBACIC	**ABCEESU**	BECAUSE		SCAMBLE
ABCCEOS	BACCOES	**ABCEFIS**	BIFACES	**ABCELOP**	PLACEBO
ABCCHII	BACCHII	**ABCEGIR**	RIBCAGE	**ABCELOV**	VOCABLE
ABCCHTY	BYCATCH	**ABCEGMO**	CAMBOGE	**ABCELPS**	BECLASP
ABCCILU	CUBICAL	**ABCEGOR**	BROCAGE	**ABCELPU**	BLUECAP
ABCCIMR	CAMBRIC	**ABCEGOS**	BOCAGES	**ABCELPY**	BYPLACE
ABCCINU	BUCCINA		BOSCAGE	**ABCELRS**	CABLERS
ABCCIOR	BORACIC	**ABCEGSU**	CUBAGES	**ABCELRU**	CURABLE
	BRACCIO	**ABCEHKL**	BECHALK	**ABCELRW**	BECRAWL
ABCCIOS	BOCCIAS	**ABCEHKO**	BACKHOE	**ABCELST**	CABLETS
ABCCISU	CUBICAS	**ABCEHLO**	CHAEBOL	**ABCELSU**	BASCULE
ABCCKOW	BAWCOCK	**ABCEHLU**	BAUCHLE	**ABCEMRS**	CAMBERS
ABCCKTU	CUTBACK	**ABCEHMR**	BECHARM		CEMBRAS
ABCCOOR	BAROCCO		BRECHAM		CRAMBES
ABCCOOT	TOBACCO		CHAMBER	**ABCEMSW**	WEBCAMS
ABCCSUU	SUCCUBA		CHAMBRE	**ABCEMSX**	EXCAMBS
ABCDDEU	ABDUCED	**ABCEHNR**	BRECHAN	**ABCENOR**	BACONER
ABCDEEH	BEACHED	**ABCEHOS**	BASOCHE	**ABCENOS**	BEACONS
ABCDEEL	BELACED	**ABCEHRS**	BRACHES	**ABCENOW**	COWBANE
	DEBACLE	**ABCEHRT**	BATCHER	**ABCENOZ**	CABEZON
ABCDEHT	BATCHED		BRACHET	**ABCENRU**	UNBRACE
ABCDEHU	DEBAUCH	**ABCEHST**	BATCHES	**ABCENSU**	CUBANES
ABCDEIK	DIEBACK	**ABCEIIT**	ABIETIC	**ABCEOOS**	CABOOSE
ABCDEIN	CABINED	**ABCEIKS**	BACKIES	**ABCEORR**	BRACERO
ABCDEIP	PEDICAB	**ABCEIKT**	TIEBACK	**ABCEORS**	BORACES
ABCDEIR	CARBIDE	**ABCEILL**	ICEBALL	**ABCEORU**	CORBEAU
ABCDEKL	BLACKED	**ABCEILM**	ALEMBIC	**ABCEORV**	CABOVER
ABCDEKR	REDBACK		CEMBALI	**ABCERRS**	BRACERS
ABCDELO	CODABLE	**ABCEILR**	CALIBER	**ABCERSU**	RUBACES
ABCDEOR	BROCADE		CALIBRE		SUBRACE
ABCDERS	DECARBS	**ABCEILT**	CITABLE	**ABCESSS**	ABSCESS
ABCDERT	BRACTED	**ABCEIMO**	AMOEBIC	**ABCESTW**	WEBCAST
ABCDERU	CUDBEAR	**ABCEINR**	CARBINE	**ABCFIKN**	FINBACK
ABCDESU	ABDUCES	**ABCEINT**	CABINET	**ABCFIKT**	BACKFIT
	SCUBAED	**ABCEIOR**	AEROBIC	**ABCFILO**	BIFOCAL
ABCDHIO	ICHABOD	**ABCEIOT**	ICEBOAT	**ABCFIOT**	BIOFACT
ABCDHOR	CHOBDAR	**ABCEIRS**	ASCRIBE	**ABCFIRS**	FABRICS
ABCDHOS	BODACHS		CABRIES	**ABCFKLY**	FLYBACK
ABCDIIS	DIBASIC		CARBIES	**ABCFLOO**	COBLOAF
ABCDILO	CABILDO		CARIBES	**ABCFNOS**	CONFABS
ABCDILR	BALDRIC	**ABCEIRZ**	ZEBRAIC	**ABCGHIN**	BACHING
ABCDINS	ABSCIND	**ABCEISS**	ABSCISE	**ABCGHKO**	HOGBACK
ABCDIRS	SCABRID		SCABIES	**ABCGIKN**	BACKING
ABCDIRT	CATBIRD		SEBASIC	**ABCGILN**	CABLING
ABCDIRU	BAUDRIC	**ABCEITT**	TABETIC	**ABCGINR**	BRACING
ABCDIRW	BAWDRIC	**ABCEJST**	ABJECTS	**ABCGKLO**	BACKLOG
ABCDISU	SUBACID	**ABCEKLN**	BLACKEN	**ABCGMSU**	SCUMBAG
ABCDNOS	ABSCOND	**ABCEKLO**	BECLOAK	**ABCHHII**	HIBACHI
ABCDOOR	CORDOBA	**ABCEKLR**	BLACKER	**ABCHILS**	CHABLIS
ABCDORR	BROCARD	**ABCEKNR**	BRACKEN	**ABCHIMT**	BATHMIC
ABCDSTU	ABDUCTS	**ABCEKRS**	BACKERS	**ABCHIOT**	COHABIT
ABCEEHS	BEACHES		REBACKS	**ABCHKOU**	CHABOUK
ABCEEHU	EBAUCHE	**ABCEKRT**	BRACKET	**ABCHKSU**	CHABUKS
ABCEELS	BELACES	**ABCEKST**	BACKETS	**ABCHKTU**	HACKBUT
ABCEEMR	EMBRACE		BACKSET	**ABCHKUW**	HAWBUCK
ABCEEMS	EMBACES		SETBACK	**ABCHNOR**	BROCHAN
ABCEENR	CARBEEN	**ABCEKSY**	BACKSEY	**ABCHNRU**	BRAUNCH
	CARBENE	**ABCEKTW**	WETBACK	**ABCHNRY**	BRANCHY
ABCEENS	ABSENCE	**ABCELLS**	BECALLS	**ABCHOSX**	CASHBOX

ABCHOTT	CHATBOT
ABCHPSU	HUBCAPS
ABCIILL	BACILLI
ABCIILN	ALBINIC
ABCIILS	BASILIC
ABCIILT	ALBITIC
ABCIIMN	MINICAB
ABCIIMS	IAMBICS
ABCIIOR	CIBORIA
ABCIIOT	ABIOTIC
ABCIJNO	JACOBIN
ABCIKLT	BACKLIT
ABCIKPS	BIPACKS
ABCIKSY	SICKBAY
ABCILNO	COALBIN
ABCILOU	ABOULIC
ABCILRS	SCRIBAL
ABCILTU	CUBITAL
ABCIMMS	CAMBISM
ABCIMMU	CAMBIUM
ABCIMST	CAMBIST
ABCIMSU	CUMBIAS
ABCINOR	CORBINA
ABCINOS	BONACIS
ABCINOT	BOTANIC
ABCIORR	BARRICO
ABCIORS	CABRIOS
ABCIORU	CARIBOU
ABCIOUV	BIVOUAC
ABCIRST	CABRITS
ABCIRTY	BARYTIC
ABCISSS	ABSCISS
ABCJOSU	JACOBUS
ABCKLLY	BLACKLY
ABCKLOT	BACKLOT
ABCKMOT	TOMBACK
ABCKMRU	BUCKRAM
ABCKMUZ	ZAMBUCK
ABCKNNO	BANNOCK
ABCKNRU	RUNBACK
ABCKNSU	SUNBACK
ABCKNTU	CUTBANK
ABCKORS	BAROCKS
ABCKORY	ROCKABY
ABCKOSW	SOWBACK
ABCKOTU	BACKOUT
	OUTBACK
ABCKPSU	BACKUPS
ABCKRSU	BUCKRAS
ABCKSTU	SACKBUT
	SUBTACK
ABCKSUW	BUCKSAW
	SAWBUCK
ABCLLOY	CALLBOY
ABCLMNU	CLUBMAN
ABCLMOY	CYMBALO
ABCLMSY	CYMBALS
ABCLMUU	BACULUM
ABCLNOS	BLANCOS
ABCLNOY	BALCONY
ABCLNSU	SUBCLAN
ABCLOOX	COALBOX
ABCLOST	COBALTS
ABCLOVY	VOCABLY
ABCLRUY	CURABLY
ABCMOPS	MOBCAPS
ABCMORS	COMARBS
	CRAMBOS
ABCMOST	COMBATS
	TOMBACS
ABCMRSS	SCRAMBS
ABCNORS	CARBONS
	CORBANS
ABCORRW	CROWBAR
ABCORSS	BRASCOS
ABCORSX	BOXCARS
ABCORSY	CARBOYS
ABCOSSU	BASUCOS
ABCSSTU	SACBUTS
	SUBACTS
ABDDDEL	BLADDED
ABDDDER	BRADDED
ABDDEEJ	BEJADED
ABDDEER	BEARDED
	BREADED
	DEBEARD
ABDDEES	DEBASED
ABDDEET	DEBATED
ABDDEEZ	BEDAZED
ABDDEIL	ADDIBLE
ABDDEIN	ABIDDEN
	BANDIED
ABDDEIR	BRAIDED
ABDDEIS	BADDIES
ABDDELR	BLADDER
ABDDELU	BLAUDED
ABDDENR	BRANDED
ABDDEOR	ABORDED
	BOARDED
	ROADBED
ABDDEOY	DEADBOY
ABDDERW	BEDWARD
ABDDEST	BADDEST
ABDDESY	DAYBEDS
ABDDHIS	BADDISH
ABDDHSU	BUDDHAS
ABDDINS	DISBAND
ABDDLLO	ODDBALL
ABDDMOR	DAMBROD
ABDEEFG	FEEDBAG
ABDEEFL	FEELBAD
ABDEEGL	BEAGLED
ABDEEGR	REBADGE
ABDEEGZ	BEGAZED
ABDEEHO	OBEAHED
ABDEEHS	BEHEADS
ABDEEHT	BEATHED
ABDEEHV	BEHAVED
ABDEEIR	BEADIER
	BEARDIE
ABDEEJS	BEJADES
ABDEEJT	JETBEAD
ABDEEKL	LAKEBED
ABDEEKR	BERAKED
ABDEEKS	DEBEAKS
ABDEELL	LABELED
ABDEELM	BELDAME
	BEMEDAL
	EMBALED
ABDEELN	ENABLED
ABDEELR	BEDERAL
	BLEARED
ABDEELS	BEADLES
ABDEELT	BELATED
	BLEATED
ABDEELY	BELAYED
	DYEABLE
ABDEEMN	BEADMEN
	BEDEMAN
	BENAMED
ABDEEMR	AMBERED
	BREAMED
	EMBREAD
ABDEEMS	EMBASED
ABDEEMT	BEDMATE
ABDEEMY	EMBAYED
ABDEEMZ	BEMAZED
ABDEEPR	BEDRAPE
	PREBADE
ABDEERR	BARREED
ABDEERS	BEADERS
	DEBASER
	SABERED
ABDEERT	BERATED
	BETREAD
	DEBATER
	REBATED
	TABERED
ABDEERW	BEWARED
ABDEERY	BEEYARD
	BERAYED
ABDEESS	DEBASES
	SEABEDS
ABDEEST	BESTEAD
	DEBATES
ABDEESZ	BEDAZES
ABDEETT	ABETTED
ABDEETX	BETAXED
ABDEFFL	BAFFLED
ABDEFLT	FLATBED
ABDEFLU	LEAFBUD
ABDEFOR	FORBADE
ABDEFOS	SOFABED
ABDEFRW	BEDWARF
ABDEFST	BEDFAST
ABDEGGL	BLAGGED
ABDEGGR	BRAGGED
ABDEGHI	BIGHEAD
ABDEGHR	BEGHARD
ABDEGIN	BEADING
ABDEGIR	ABRIDGE
	BRIGADE
ABDEGLM	GAMBLED
ABDEGLN	BANGLED
ABDEGLR	BELGARD
	GARBLED
ABDEGLS	BEGLADS
ABDEGNO	BONDAGE
	DOGBANE
ABDEGOS	BODEGAS
ABDEGRS	BADGERS
ABDEHIL	HIDABLE

ABDEHIT	HABITED	**ABDELNU**	UNBALED	**ABDERSY**	REDBAYS
ABDEHLM	HAMBLED	**ABDELOR**	LABORED	**ABDERTY**	DRYBEAT
ABDEHLR	HALBERD	**ABDELOS**	ALBEDOS	**ABDERUY**	DAUBERY
ABDEHOW	BOWHEAD	**ABDELOT**	BLOATED	**ABDETTU**	ABUTTED
ABDEHRS	BERDASH		LOBATED	**ABDFIRT**	FATBIRD
	BRASHED	**ABDELOW**	DOWABLE	**ABDGGIN**	BADGING
ABDEHRT	BREADTH	**ABDELPU**	DUPABLE	**ABDGGOR**	BOGGARD
ABDEHSU	SUBHEAD	**ABDELPY**	PYEBALD	**ABDGIIN**	ABIDING
ABDEIIL	ALIBIED	**ABDELRR**	DRABLER	**ABDGILN**	BALDING
ABDEIKT	BATIKED	**ABDELRS**	BEDRALS		BLADING
ABDEILP	BIPEDAL		BLADERS	**ABDGINN**	BANDING
	PIEBALD	**ABDELRT**	BLARTED	**ABDGINO**	ABODING
ABDEILR	BALDIER	**ABDELRU**	DURABLE	**ABDGINR**	BARDING
	BEDRAIL	**ABDELRW**	BRAWLED		BRIGAND
	BRAILED		WARBLED	**ABDGINT**	DINGBAT
	RAILBED	**ABDELRY**	DRYABLE	**ABDGINU**	DAUBING
	RIDABLE	**ABDELST**	BALDEST	**ABDGINW**	WINDBAG
ABDEILS	BALDIES		BLASTED	**ABDGIRT**	DIRTBAG
	DIABLES		STABLED	**ABDGLNO**	BOGLAND
	DISABLE	**ABDELSU**	BELAUDS	**ABDGLUY**	LADYBUG
ABDEILT	LIBATED	**ABDELTT**	BATTLED	**ABDGNOS**	BANDOGS
ABDEILU	AUDIBLE		BLATTED	**ABDGORS**	BODRAGS
ABDEILY	BEADILY	**ABDELTU**	ABLUTED	**ABDHHOS**	DOBHASH
ABDEIMO	AMEBOID	**ABDEMMO**	MAMBOED	**ABDHIIT**	ADHIBIT
ABDEIMR	EMBRAID	**ABDEMNO**	ABDOMEN	**ABDHILS**	BALDISH
ABDEIMS	IMBASED	**ABDEMNS**	BEDAMNS	**ABDHMOR**	RHABDOM
ABDEINR	BANDIER	**ABDEMRU**	RUMBAED	**ABDHMSU**	BUDMASH
	BRAINED	**ABDENNR**	BRANNED	**ABDHMTU**	MUDBATH
ABDEINS	BANDIES	**ABDENOR**	BANDORE	**ABDHNOR**	BODHRAN
	BASINED		BROADEN	**ABDHNSU**	HUSBAND
ABDEINW	BEDAWIN	**ABDENOT**	BATONED	**ABDHOSY**	HOBDAYS
ABDEIRR	BARDIER	**ABDENOY**	NAEBODY	**ABDHRSU**	BURDASH
	BRAIDER	**ABDENPS**	BEDPANS		RHABDUS
	BRIARED	**ABDENRR**	BRANDER	**ABDIINO**	ANOBIID
	RABIDER		REBRAND	**ABDIJRY**	JAYBIRD
ABDEIRS	ABIDERS	**ABDENRS**	BANDERS	**ABDIKNW**	BAWDKIN
	BARDIES	**ABDENRT**	BARTEND	**ABDIKRS**	DISBARK
	BRAISED	**ABDENRU**	UNBARED	**ABDILMO**	BIMODAL
	DARBIES	**ABDENRW**	BRAWNED	**ABDILOO**	DIABOLO
	SEABIRD	**ABDENSS**	BADNESS	**ABDILOR**	LABROID
	SIDEBAR	**ABDENSU**	SUBDEAN	**ABDILOT**	TABLOID
ABDEIRT	REDBAIT		UNBASED	**ABDILRS**	BRIDALS
	TRIBADE	**ABDENSY**	BENDAYS		LABRIDS
ABDEIRU	DAUBIER	**ABDENTU**	UNBATED		RIBALDS
ABDEIRW	BAWDIER	**ABDEOOT**	TABOOED	**ABDILRW**	AWLBIRD
ABDEIRX	AXEBIRD	**ABDEORR**	ARBORED	**ABDILRY**	RABIDLY
ABDEISS	BIASSED		BOARDER	**ABDILUY**	AUDIBLY
ABDEIST	BASTIDE		BROADER	**ABDILWY**	BAWDILY
ABDEISU	SUBIDEA		REBOARD	**ABDIMNR**	BIRDMAN
ABDEISW	BAWDIES	**ABDEORT**	ABORTED	**ABDIMOR**	AMBROID
ABDEJRU	ABJURED		BORATED	**ABDIMRS**	BARDISM
ABDEKLN	BLANKED		TABORED	**ABDIMRY**	MAYBIRD
ABDEKLU	BAULKED	**ABDEORV**	BRAVOED	**ABDINOR**	INBOARD
ABDEKNR	BRANKED	**ABDEOST**	BOASTED	**ABDINOT**	BANDITO
ABDEKNU	UNBAKED	**ABDEOTU**	BOUTADE	**ABDINRS**	RIBANDS
ABDEKRS	DEBARKS	**ABDEQSU**	BASQUED	**ABDINRT**	ANTBIRD
ABDELMP	BEDLAMP	**ABDERSS**	BRASSED	**ABDINRU**	UNBRAID
ABDELMR	MARBLED		SERDABS	**ABDINST**	BANDITS
	RAMBLED	**ABDERST**	DABSTER	**ABDIOSU**	BADIOUS
ABDELMS	BEDLAMS		TABERDS	**ABDIPRU**	UPBRAID
	BELDAMS	**ABDERSU**	DAUBERS	**ABDIRRS**	BRAIRDS
ABDELMW	WAMBLED		EARBUDS		BRIARDS
ABDELMY	EMBAYLD		SUBEDAR	**ABDIRSS**	DISBARS
ABDELNR	BLANDER	**ABDERSV**	ADVERBS	**ABDIRSU**	RIBAUDS

	SUBARID	
ABDIRTY	TRIBADY	
ABDKNOO	BANDOOK	
ABDKOOY	DAYBOOK	
ABDLLNY	BLANDLY	
ABDLLOR	BOLLARD	
ABDLNOR	BANDROL	
ABDLORY	BROADLY	
ABDLOSU	BUSLOAD	
ABDLOYY	LADYBOY	
ABDLRUY	DURABLY	
ABDLRYY	BYRLADY	
ABDLSUU	SUBDUAL	
ABDMNNO	BONDMAN	
ABDMRUY	MARYBUD	
ABDNOOR	BRADOON	
	ONBOARD	
ABDNOPR	PROBAND	
ABDNORS	ROBANDS	
ABDNOSU	ABOUNDS	
	BAUSOND	
ABDNOSX	SANDBOX	
ABDNOSY	SANDBOY	
ABDNOVY	ANYBODY	
ABDNRSU	SANDBUR	
ABDNRTU	TURBAND	
ABDNSTY	STANDBY	
ABDOORW	BARWOOD	
ABDOOWY	BAYWOOD	
ABDORRS	BORDARS	
ABDORSS	ADSORBS	
ABDORSY	BOYARDS	
	BYROADS	
ABDOSYY	DAYBOYS	
ABDRRSU	DURBARS	
ABDRSSU	ABSURDS	
ABDRSTU	BUSTARD	
ABDRUZZ	BUZZARD	
ABEEEGR	BEERAGE	
ABEEELS	SEEABLE	
ABEEELY	EYEABLE	
ABEEEMY	EYEBEAM	
ABEEERV	BEREAVE	
ABEEFFL	EFFABLE	
ABEEFLM	FLAMBEE	
ABEEFLO	BEEFALO	
ABEEFLS	BEFLEAS	
ABEEFTU	BEAUFET	
ABEEGGS	GEEBAGS	
ABEEGHR	HERBAGE	
ABEEGHS	BEEGAHS	
	BHAGEES	
ABEEGLL	GABELLE	
	GELABLE	
ABEEGLR	BEAGLER	
ABEEGLS	BEAGLES	
ABEEGLT	GETABLE	
ABEEGNR	REBEGAN	
ABEEGPW	WEBPAGE	
ABEEGRR	GERBERA	
ABEEGRS	ABREGES	
	BAREGES	
	BARGEES	
ABEEGRU	AUBERGE	

ABEEGRW	BREWAGE	
ABEEGSZ	BEGAZES	
ABEEHJS	BHAJEES	
ABEEHLW	HEWABLE	
ABEEHMS	BESHAME	
ABEEHMT	EMBATHE	
ABEEHNN	HENBANE	
ABEEHNS	BANSHEE	
	BEENAHS	
	SHEBEAN	
ABEEHNT	BENEATH	
ABEEHRT	BREATHE	
ABEEHRV	BEHAVER	
ABEEHSV	BEHAVES	
ABEEHTY	EYEBATH	
ABEEIKR	BEAKIER	
ABEEILS	BAILEES	
ABEEIMR	BEAMIER	
ABEEINS	BEANIES	
ABEEINT	BETAINE	
ABEEIRT	BEATIER	
	EBRIATE	
ABEEIST	BEASTIE	
ABEEJMS	JAMBEES	
ABEEJRS	BAJREES	
ABEEKLR	BLEAKER	
ABEEKLS	KABELES	
ABEEKNT	BETAKEN	
ABEEKNV	BEKNAVE	
ABEEKNY	EYEBANK	
ABEEKOP	PEEKABO	
ABEEKPR	BARKEEP	
	PREBAKE	
ABEEKPS	BESPAKE	
	BESPEAK	
ABEEKRR	BREAKER	
ABEEKRS	BEAKERS	
	BERAKES	
ABEEKST	BETAKES	
ABEELLR	LABELER	
	RELABEL	
ABEELLY	EYEBALL	
ABEELMM	EMBLEMA	
ABEELMS	EMBALES	
ABEELMT	BEAMLET	
ABEELMZ	EMBLAZE	
ABEELNP	PLEBEAN	
ABEELNR	ENABLER	
ABEELNS	BALEENS	
	ENABLES	
ABEELNT	TENABLE	
ABEELNU	NEBULAE	
ABEELOR	EARLOBE	
ABEELPR	BEPEARL	
ABEELPS	BELEAPS	
ABEELPT	BELEAPT	
ABEELQU	EQUABLE	
ABEELRR	BLEARER	
	ERRABLE	
ABEELRT	BLEATER	
	RETABLE	
ABEELRY	BELAYER	
ABEELST	BELATES	
ABEELSU	SUEABLE	

	USEABLE	
ABEELSV	BESLAVE	
ABEELSW	SEWABLE	
ABEEMNS	BASEMEN	
	BEMEANS	
	BENAMES	
ABEEMNT	BEMEANT	
ABEEMRS	AMBEERS	
	BEAMERS	
	BESMEAR	
ABEEMRV	EMBRAVE	
ABEEMSS	EMBASES	
ABEEMST	EMBASTE	
ABEENNW	BAWNEEN	
ABEENRV	VERBENA	
ABEENRY	BEANERY	
ABEEORS	AEROBES	
ABEEORT	ABORTEE	
ABEEPST	BESPATE	
ABEERRS	BEARERS	
	BREARES	
ABEERRT	REBATER	
	TABRERE	
	TEREBRA	
ABEERST	BEATERS	
	BERATES	
	REBATES	
ABEERSV	BEAVERS	
ABEERSW	BEWARES	
ABEERSY	EBAYERS	
	EYEBARS	
ABEERSZ	ZEREBAS	
ABEERTT	ABETTER	
	BERETTA	
ABEERVY	BEAVERY	
ABEERWY	BEWEARY	
ABEESST	SEBATES	
ABEESWX	BEESWAX	
ABEETXY	EXABYTE	
ABEFFIS	BAFFIES	
ABEFFLR	BAFFLER	
ABEFFLS	BAFFLES	
ABEFFOT	OFFBEAT	
ABEFGIL	FILABEG	
ABEFGLS	BEFLAGS	
ABEFGST	GABFEST	
ABEFILN	FINABLE	
ABEFILR	FRIABLE	
ABEFILS	FAIBLES	
ABEFILU	FIBULAE	
ABEFILX	FIXABLE	
ABEFINU	BEAUFIN	
ABEFIRT	BAREFIT	
ABEFITY	BEATIFY	
ABEFLLS	BEFALLS	
ABEFLLU	BALEFUL	
ABEFLLY	FLYABLE	
ABEFLMS	FLAMBES	
ABEFLNU	BANEFUL	
ABEFLNY	FLYBANE	
ABEFLRS	FABLERS	
ABEFLRY	FRYABLE	
ABEFMOS	BEFOAMS	
ABEFMRS	FERBAMS	

ABEFORR	FORBARE	**ABEGOUY**	BUOYAGE	**ABEILMR**	BALMIER
	FORBEAR	**ABEGRRU**	GARBURE		LAMBIER
ABEFORX	FAREBOX	**ABEGRST**	BARGEST		MIRABLE
ABEFORY	FOREBAY	**ABEGSTU**	BAGUETS		REMBLAI
ABEFPRS	PREFABS		TUBAGES	**ABEILMS**	ABLEISM
ABEGGIR	BAGGIER	**ABEHILR**	HIRABLE		EMBAILS
ABEGGIS	BAGGIES	**ABEHIMO**	BOHEMIA		LAMBIES
ABEGGLR	BLAGGER	**ABEHIMS**	BEAMISH	**ABEILMT**	BIMETAL
ABEGGMO	GAMBOGE	**ABEHIMT**	IMBATHE		LIMBATE
ABEGGNU	BUGGANE	**ABEHINS**	BANSHIE		TIMBALE
ABEGGRR	BRAGGER	**ABEHIRS**	BEARISH	**ABEILMU**	BUMELIA
ABEGGRS	BAGGERS	**ABEHISU**	BEAUISH	**ABEILMW**	WEBMAIL
	BEGGARS	**ABEHITU**	HABITUE	**ABEILMX**	MIXABLE
ABEGGRU	BURGAGE	**ABEHITZ**	ZABTIEH	**ABEILMY**	BEAMILY
ABEGGRY	BEGGARY	**ABEHKLS**	KEBLAHS	**ABEILMZ**	IMBLAZE
ABEGHNS	SHEBANG	**ABEHKNT**	BETHANK	**ABEILNP**	BIPLANE
ABEGHOR	BEGORAH	**ABEHKRU**	HAUBERK	**ABEILNS**	LESBIAN
ABEGHRU	BEARHUG	**ABEHKTU**	KETUBAH	**ABEILOS**	OBELIAS
ABEGIKL	BAGLIKE	**ABEHLMS**	HAMBLES	**ABEILPT**	PATIBLE
ABEGILV	GIVABLE		SHAMBLE	**ABEILRS**	BAILERS
ABEGIMN	BEAMING	**ABEHLNT**	BENTHAL	**ABEILRT**	LIBRATE
ABEGIMR	GAMBIER	**ABEHLNU**	UNHABLE		TABLIER
ABEGIMT	MEGABIT	**ABEHLRS**	HERBALS		TRIABLE
ABEGINN	BEANING	**ABEHLRT**	BLATHER	**ABEILRW**	BRAWLIE
ABEGINO	BEGONIA		HALBERT		WIRABLE
ABEGINR	BEARING	**ABEHLSS**	BLASHES	**ABEILRY**	BILAYER
ABEGINS	SABEING	**ABEHMNO**	HAMBONE	**ABEILSS**	ABSEILS
ABEGINT	BEATING	**ABEHNOS**	HEBONAS		ISABELS
ABEGINY	ABYEING	**ABEHNRY**	ABHENRY		LABISES
	EBAYING	**ABEHRRS**	BRASHER	**ABEILST**	ABLEIST
ABEGIPP	BAGPIPE		HERBARS		ALBITES
ABEGKLU	BULKAGE	**ABEHRRY**	HERBARY		ASTILBE
ABEGKOR	BROKAGE	**ABEHRSS**	BASHERS		BASTILE
ABEGKOS	BOSKAGE		BRASHES		BESTIAL
ABEGLLS	BEGALLS	**ABEHRST**	BATHERS		BLASTIE
ABEGLMR	GAMBLER		BERTHAS		LIBATES
	GAMBREL		BREATHS		STABILE
ABEGLMS	GAMBLES	**ABEHRTY**	BREATHY	**ABEILSW**	BEWAILS
ABEGLNR	BRANGLE	**ABEIILL**	BAILLIE	**ABEILSY**	BAILEYS
ABEGLNS	BANGLES	**ABEIILS**	ALIBIES	**ABEILSZ**	SIZABLE
ABEGLOR	ALBERGO		BAILIES	**ABEILVV**	BIVALVE
ABEGLOT	GLOBATE		BIALIES	**ABEIMNP**	PEMBINA
ABEGLRR	GARBLER	**ABEIINN**	BIENNIA	**ABEIMNR**	MIRBANE
ABEGLRS	GARBLES	**ABEIINT**	BAINITE	**ABEIMNT**	AMBIENT
ABEGLRU	BLAGUER	**ABEIJMR**	JAMBIER	**ABEIMRR**	BARMIER
ABEGLSS	BAGLESS	**ABEIJNS**	BASENJI	**ABEIMRS**	AMBRIES
ABEGLST	GABLETS	**ABEIKKS**	BAKKIES	**ABEIMSS**	IMBASES
ABEGLSU	BELUGAS	**ABEIKLL**	LIKABLE	**ABEIMSU**	MAUBIES
	BLAGUES	**ABEIKLR**	BALKIER	**ABEINOT**	NIOBATE
ABEGMOR	EMBARGO	**ABEIKLS**	SKIABLE	**ABEINPT**	BEPAINT
ABEGMRU	UMBRAGE	**ABEIKLT**	BATLIKE	**ABEINRR**	BARNIER
ABEGMST	GAMBETS	**ABEIKNR**	INBREAK	**ABEINRT**	ATEBRIN
ABEGNNT	BANTENG	**ABEIKNT**	BEATNIK	**ABEINRW**	WEBINAR
ABEGNOR	BEGROAN	**ABEIKRR**	BARKIER	**ABEINRZ**	ZEBRINA
ABEGNOS	NOSEBAG		BRAKIER	**ABEINSS**	SABINES
ABEGNRS	BANGERS	**ABEIKWY**	BIKEWAY	**ABEINST**	BANTIES
	GRABENS	**ABEILLN**	LINABLE		BASINET
ABEGNSW	BEGNAWS	**ABEILLO**	LOBELIA		BESAINT
ABEGOPY	PAGEBOY	**ABEILLP**	PLIABLE		BESTAIN
ABEGORR	BEGORRA	**ABEILLR**	BRAILLE	**ABEINTT**	TABINET
ABEGORS	BORAGES		LIBERAL	**ABEIORS**	ISOBARE
ABEGORX	GEARBOX	**ABEILLS**	BALLIES	**ABEIOSS**	ABIOSES
ABEGOSZ	GAZEBOS	**ABEILLV**	LIVABLE		ISOBASE
ABEGOTT	BOTTEGA	**ABEILMN**	MINABLE	**ABEIOST**	BOATIES

ABEIOTV	OBVIATE	**ABEKRRS**	BARKERS	**ABELPRU**	PUBERAL
ABEIPST	BAPTISE	**ABEKSST**	BASKETS	**ABELPTY**	TYPABLE
ABEIPTZ	BAPTIZE	**ABELLMN**	BELLMAN	**ABELQUY**	EQUABLY
ABEIRRR	BARRIER	**ABELLMS**	EMBALLS	**ABELRRS**	BARRELS
ABEIRRS	BARRIES	**ABELLNT**	NETBALL	**ABELRRW**	BRAWLER
	BRASIER	**ABELLOS**	LOSABLE		WARBLER
ABEIRRT	ARBITER	**ABELLOV**	LOVABLE	**ABELRSS**	BARLESS
	RAREBIT		VOLABLE		BRALESS
ABEIRRW	WARBIER	**ABELLRS**	BALLERS	**ABELRST**	ALBERTS
ABEIRRZ	BIZARRE	**ABELLRU**	RUBELLA		BATLERS
	BRAZIER		RULABLE		BLASTER
ABEIRSS	BASSIER	**ABELLST**	BALLETS		LABRETS
	BRAISES	**ABELLTU**	BALLUTE		STABLER
	BRASSIE		BULLATE	**ABELRSV**	VERBALS
ABEIRST	BAITERS	**ABELMMR**	MEMBRAL	**ABELRSW**	BAWLERS
	BARITES	**ABELMMS**	EMBALMS		WARBLES
	REBAITS	**ABELMNT**	BELTMAN	**ABELRSY**	BARLEYS
	TERBIAS		LAMBENT	**ABELRSZ**	BLAZERS
ABEIRSX	BRAXIES	**ABELMNU**	ALBUMEN	**ABELRTT**	BATTLER
ABEIRSZ	BRAIZES	**ABELMOV**	MOVABLE		BLATTER
	ZERIBAS	**ABELMRR**	MARBLER		BRATTLE
ABEIRTT	BATTIER		RAMBLER	**ABELRTW**	BLEWART
	BIRETTA	**ABELMRS**	AMBLERS	**ABELRUZ**	ZEBRULA
	RATBITE		BLAMERS	**ABELRVY**	BRAVELY
ABEIRTV	VIBRATE		LAMBERS	**ABELSST**	BASTLES
ABEIRUX	EXURBIA		MARBLES		STABLES
ABEISSS	BIASSES		RAMBLES	**ABELSSU**	SUBSALE
ABEISTT	BATISTE	**ABELMRT**	LAMBERT	**ABELSTT**	BATLETS
	BISTATE	**ABELMSU**	BEMAULS		BATTELS
ABEISTW	BAWTIES	**ABELMSW**	WAMBLES		BATTLES
ABEISUV	ABUSIVE	**ABELMTU**	MUTABLE		BLATEST
ABEITUX	BAUXITE	**ABELNOS**	BONSELA		TABLETS
ABEJLUY	BLUEJAY	**ABELNOT**	NOTABLE	**ABELSTU**	SUBLATE
ABEJMNO	JAMBONE	**ABELNOW**	OWNABLE	**ABELSTY**	BAETYLS
	JOBNAME	**ABELNOY**	BALONEY		BEASTLY
ABEJMNS	ENJAMBS	**ABELNRS**	BRANLES	**ABELSUY**	USEABLY
ABEJMRS	JAMBERS		BRANSLE	**ABELSWY**	BAWLEYS
ABEJMUX	JAMBEUX	**ABELNRT**	BRANTLE		BYELAWS
ABEJNOS	BANJOES	**ABELNRU**	NEBULAR	**ABELTWY**	BELTWAY
ABEJNOW	JAWBONE	**ABELNRY**	BLARNEY	**ABEMMOS**	MAMBOES
ABEJNST	BEJANTS	**ABELNSU**	NEBULAS	**ABEMMRS**	BAMMERS
ABEJORS	JERBOAS		UNBALES	**ABEMNOS**	AMBONES
ABEJRRU	ABJURER	**ABELNSY**	BYLANES		BEMOANS
ABEJRSU	ABJURES	**ABELNSZ**	BENZALS	**ABEMNOT**	BOATMEN
ABEKKKU	BUKKAKE	**ABELNTU**	ABLUENT	**ABEMNRY**	BYREMAN
ABEKLLY	BLEAKLY		TUNABLE		MYRBANE
ABEKLMS	KEMBLAS	**ABELNTY**	TENABLY	**ABEMNST**	BATSMEN
ABEKLNR	BLANKER	**ABELOPR**	ROPABLE	**ABEMNSU**	SUNBEAM
ABEKLNT	BLANKET	**ABELOPS**	POSABLE	**ABEMNSY**	BYNAMES
ABEKLOP	POKABLE	**ABELOPT**	POTABLE	**ABEMORT**	BROMATE
ABEKLRS	BALKERS	**ABELORR**	LABORER	**ABEMOTU**	OUTBEAM
ABEKLRU	BAULKER	**ABELORS**	LABROSE	**ABEMRST**	TAMBERS
ABEKMNS	EMBANKS	**ABELORT**	BLOATER	**ABEMRSW**	BESWARM
ABEKMRS	EMBARKS	**ABELORU**	RUBEOLA	**ABEMSSY**	EMBASSY
ABEKMSU	SAMBUKE	**ABELORW**	ROWABLE	**ABENNOR**	BARONNE
ABEKNRS	BANKERS	**ABELOSS**	BOLASES	**ABENNOS**	NANOBES
	BARKENS	**ABELOST**	BOATELS	**ABENNRR**	BRANNER
ABEKNRU	UNBRAKE		OBLATES	**ABENNRS**	BANNERS
ABEKNST	BANKETS	**ABELOSV**	ABSOLVE	**ABENNST**	BANNETS
ABEKNSU	SUNBAKE	**ABELOSW**	SOWABLE	**ABENORS**	BORANES
ABEKOOR	ABROOKE	**ABELOTT**	TOTABLE	**ABENORT**	BARONET
ABEKOTU	OUTBAKE	**ABELOTV**	VOTABLE		REBOANT
ABEKPRU	BREAKUP	**ABELOTW**	TEABOWL	**ABENORW**	RAWBONE
	UPBREAK		TOWABLE	**ABENORZ**	ZEBRANO

ABENOST	ONBEATS		BRASSET	ABGHHSU	HAGBUSH
ABENOSY	SOYBEAN		BREASTS	ABGHILN	BLAHING
ABENOTY	BAYONET	ABERSSU	ABUSERS	ABGHINS	BASHING
ABENPSU	SUBPENA		BUSERAS	ABGHINT	BATHING
ABENQTU	BANQUET		RUBASSE	ABGHLOT	HAGBOLT
ABENRRS	BARRENS		SURBASE	ABGHLRU	BURGHAL
ABENRRU	URBANER	ABERSSZ	ZEBRASS	ABGHMOO	GOOMBAH
ABENRST	BANTERS	ABERSTT	BATTERS	ABGHMRU	HAMBURG
	BARNETS		TABRETS	ABGHNOR	HAGBORN
ABENRSU	UNBARES	ABERSTU	ARBUTES		HORNBAG
	UNBEARS		BURSATE	ABGHOTU	ABOUGHT
ABENRSY	BARNEYS		SURBATE	ABGHSSU	BUGSHAS
ABENRSZ	BRAZENS	ABERSTV	BRAVEST	ABGHSTU	HAGBUTS
ABENRUX	EXURBAN	ABERSTW	BRAWEST	ABGIILN	BAILING
ABENSST	ABSENTS		WABSTER	ABGIINS	BIASING
	BASNETS	ABERSTX	BAXTERS	ABGIINT	BAITING
ABENSTT	BATTENS	ABERSTY	BARYTES	ABGIINZ	BAIZING
ABENSTU	BUTANES		BETRAYS	ABGIJMN	JAMBING
	SUNBEAT	ABERSUU	BUREAUS	ABGIJOO	JIGABOO
ABENSTZ	BEZANTS	ABERSWY	BEWRAYS	ABGIKLN	BALKING
ABENTZZ	BEZZANT	ABERTTU	ABUTTER	ABGIKNN	BANKING
ABEOOST	SEABOOT	ABERTTY	BATTERY	ABGIKNO	BOAKING
ABEOOTV	OBOVATE	ABERUUX	BUREAUX	ABGIKNR	BARKING
ABEOPRS	SAPROBE	ABESSST	BASSEST		BRAKING
ABEOPRT	PROBATE		BASSETS	ABGIKNS	BAKINGS
ABEOQRU	BAROQUE	ABESSSY	ABYSSES		BASKING
ABEORRS	ARBORES	ABESSTT	BASSETT	ABGIKNU	BAUKING
	BRASERO	ABESTTU	BATTUES	ABGIKST	KITBAGS
ABEORRT	ABORTER	ABEZZZZ	BEZZAZZ	ABGILLN	BALLING
	ARBORET	ABFFGIN	BAFFING	ABGILMN	AMBLING
	TABORER	ABFFIIL	BAILIFF		BALMING
ABEORST	BOASTER	ABFFINO	BANOFFI		BLAMING
	BOATERS	ABFFLOO	BOFFOLA		LAMBING
	BORATES	ABFFLOU	BUFFALO	ABGILMS	GIMBALS
	REBATOS	ABFGILN	FABLING	ABGILNR	BLARING
	SORBATE	ABFGINR	BARFING	ABGILNS	ABLINGS
ABEORSU	AEROBUS	ABFGLSU	BAGFULS		SABLING
ABEORSV	BRAVOES		BAGSFUL	ABGILNT	TABLING
ABEORSX	BORAXES	ABFGOOT	FOOTBAG	ABGILNW	BAWLING
ABEORSY	ROSEBAY	ABFHIST	BATFISH		BLAWING
ABEORSZ	BEZOARS	ABFHLSU	BASHFUL	ABGILNZ	BLAZING
ABEORTT	ABETTOR	ABFIILR	BIFILAR	ABGILOR	GARBOIL
	BATTERO	ABFIIMR	FIMBRIA	ABGILRT	BATGIRL
	TABORET	ABFILRU	FIBULAR	ABGIMMN	BAMMING
ABEOSTV	BOVATES	ABFILSU	FIBULAS	ABGIMRS	GAMBIRS
ABEPRSU	UPBEARS	ABFIMOR	FIBROMA	ABGIMST	GAMBIST
ABEPRSW	BEWRAPS	ABFLOTU	BOATFUL		GAMBITS
ABEPRTW	BEWRAPT	ABFLOTW	BATFOWL	ABGINNN	BANNING
ABEPRTY	TYPEBAR	ABFLOTY	FLYBOAT	ABGINNR	BARNING
ABEPSTU	UPBEATS	ABFOORT	FOOTBAR	ABGINNT	BANTING
ABEQRSU	BARQUES	ABFOOTY	FOYBOAT	ABGINOS	BAGNIOS
ABEQSSU	BASQUES	ABFSTTU	TUBFAST		GABIONS
ABERRST	BARRETS	ABGGGIN	BAGGING	ABGINOT	BOATING
	BARTERS	ABGGIIT	GIGABIT	ABGINRR	BARRING
ABERRSU	BURSERA	ABGGILN	GABLING	ABGINRS	SABRING
	SABREUR	ABGGILY	BAGGILY	ABGINRV	BRAVING
ABERRSV	BRAVERS	ABGGINN	BANGING	ABGINRY	BRAYING
ABERRSY	BRAYERS	ABGGINR	BARGING	ABGINRZ	BRAZING
ABERRSZ	BRAZERS		GARBING	ABGINSS	BASSING
ABERRUV	BRAVURE	ABGGIST	BAGGITS	ABGINST	BASTING
ABERRVY	BRAVERY	ABGGISW	BAGWIGS	ABGINSU	ABUSING
ABERSSS	BRASSES	ABGGNOS	GOBANGS	ABGINTT	BATTING
ABERSST	BASTERS	ABGGNSU	BUGGANS	ABGINTU	ANTIBUG
	BESTARS	ABGGORT	BOGGART		TABUING

ABGINTW	BATWING
ABGINTY	BAYTING
ABGIOPT	PIGBOAT
ABGIOSU	BAGUIOS
ABGKKNO	BANGKOK
ABGKNOS	KOBANGS
ABGKOOS	BOGOAKS
ABGKORW	WORKBAG
ABGLLMU	GUMBALL
ABGLMNU	LUMBANG
ABGLMOS	GAMBOLS
ABGLMOU	LUMBAGO
ABGLMSY	GYMBALS
ABGLNOO	BOLOGNA
ABGLOOT	TOOLBAG
ABGLORS	BROLGAS
ABGLORT	RAGBOLT
ABGLOSU	ALBUGOS
	SUBGOAL
ABGLRRU	BURGLAR
ABGMNOY	BOGYMAN
ABGMOOY	GOOMBAY
ABGMORW	BAGWORM
ABGNOOR	BARGOON
ABGNOOS	BOONGAS
	GABOONS
ABGNOPR	PROBANG
ABGNORS	BARONGS
	BROGANS
ABGNOTU	GUNBOAT
ABGNOWY	BOWYANG
ABGOORT	BOTARGO
ABGOPST	POSTBAG
ABGORRU	GOBURRA
ABGORST	BOGARTS
ABGORTU	OUTBRAG
ABGOTTU	TUGBOAT
ABGSSTU	SAGBUTS
ABHHISS	SHIBAHS
ABHHJSU	JUBHAHS
ABHHKOT	KHOTBAH
ABHHKTU	KHUTBAH
ABHHSUW	BUSHWAH
ABHHSUY	HUSHABY
ABHIINT	INHABIT
ABHIKLS	BASHLIK
	KIBLAHS
ABHIKST	BHAKTIS
ABHIKTW	HAWKBIT
ABHILNO	HOBNAIL
ABHILOS	ABOLISH
ABHILTU	HALIBUT
ABHIMNR	BRAHMIN
ABHIMRS	MIHRABS
ABHIMSZ	MAZHBIS
ABHINST	ABSINTH
ABHIOOS	BOOHAIS
ABHIOPS	PHOBIAS
ABHIORS	BOARISH
ABHIORT	BOTHRIA
ABHIOST	ISOBATH
ABHIOSU	HAUBOIS
ABHISTU	HABITUS
ABHKLSY	BASHLYK

ABHKORU	BOURKHA
ABHKRSU	KURBASH
ABHLMSY	SHAMBLY
ABHLOUX	BOXHAUL
ABHLRSY	BRASHLY
ABHLRTU	HURLBAT
ABHMNOS	BONHAMS
ABHMNSU	BUSHMAN
ABHMRSU	RHUMBAS
	SAMBHUR
ABHMSUY	MAYBUSH
ABHNOST	BOTHANS
ABHNSTU	SUNBATH
ABHOPRS	BARHOPS
ABHORRS	HARBORS
ABHORRU	HARBOUR
ABHOTUY	HAUTBOY
ABHPSTY	BYPATHS
ABHQSSU	BUQSHAS
ABHRSTU	TARBUSH
ABHSSUW	BUSHWAS
ABHSTUW	WASHTUB
ABIIINR	BIRIANI
ABIIKKS	KABIKIS
ABIIKKT	KIBITKA
ABIILLS	BAILLIS
ABIILMN	MINILAB
ABIILMU	BULIMIA
ABIILNQ	INQILAB
ABIILNS	AIBLINS
	BILIANS
ABIILOV	BOLIVIA
ABIILRY	BILIARY
ABIILST	STIBIAL
ABIILTY	ABILITY
ABIIMNR	MINIBAR
ABIIMSS	MISBIAS
ABIIMST	IAMBIST
ABIINNS	BAININS
ABIINOR	ROBINIA
ABIINRY	BIRYANI
ABIIOSS	ABIOSIS
ABIJLNR	BRINJAL
ABIJNOT	ABJOINT
ABIJRSU	JABIRUS
ABIKKSU	KABUKIS
ABIKLLY	BALKILY
ABIKLMN	LAMBKIN
ABIKLOR	KILOBAR
ABIKLOS	KOLBASI
ABIKMNR	BARMKIN
ABIKMRS	IMBARKS
ABIKNST	BANKITS
ABIKOUZ	BAZOUKI
ABIKRST	BRITSKA
ABIKRTZ	BRITZKA
ABIKSTT	BATTIKS
ABIKUUZ	BUZUKIA
ABILLMN	BILLMAN
ABILLMU	BALLIUM
ABILLMY	BALMILY
ABILLNP	PINBALL
ABILLPY	PLIABLY
ABILLSW	SAWBILL

ABILLSY	SYLLABI
ABILLTT	BATTILL
ABILLWX	WAXBILL
ABILLWY	WAYBILL
ABILMMS	IMBALMS
ABILMNU	ALBUMIN
ABILMOX	MAILBOX
ABILMRT	TIMBRAL
ABILMST	TIMBALS
ABILNOS	ALBINOS
ABILNOT	BITONAL
ABILNOZ	BIZONAL
ABILNRY	BAIRNLY
ABILOPR	BIPOLAR
	PARBOIL
ABILORS	BAILORS
ABILORT	ORBITAL
ABILORV	BOLIVAR
ABILOST	OBLASTI
ABILOTU	BAILOUT
	OBITUAL
	TABOULI
ABILRRY	LIBRARY
ABILRSS	BRASILS
ABILRST	TRIBALS
ABILRSU	BURIALS
	RAILBUS
ABILRSZ	BRAZILS
ABILSTU	TABULIS
ABILSYZ	SIZABLY
ABIMMRS	MIMBARS
ABIMMTU	MITUMBA
ABIMNRS	MINBARS
ABIMOSS	BIOMASS
ABIMPST	BAPTISM
	BITMAPS
ABIMRSS	BISMARS
ABIMRST	IMBRAST
ABIMRSU	BARIUMS
ABIMRTT	TRIMTAB
ABIMTTY	AMBITTY
ABINNSU	BUNNIAS
ABINOOR	BORONIA
ABINOOT	BONIATO
ABINORT	TABORIN
ABINORW	RAINBOW
ABINOSS	BASIONS
	BONSAIS
ABINOST	BASTION
	BONITAS
	OBTAINS
ABINOSU	ABUSION
ABINRST	BRISANT
ABINRTV	VIBRANT
ABIOORR	ARBORIO
ABIORRS	BARRIOS
ABIORRZ	BIZARRO
ABIORSS	ISOBARS
ABIORST	ORBITAS
ABIORTV	VIBRATO
ABIPRTY	BIPARTY
ABIPSTT	BAPTIST
ABIRTTY	TRAYBIT
ABISSST	BASSIST

ABISTTU	TUBAIST	ABLOPYY	PLAYBOY
ABJJOOS	JOJOBAS	ABLORST	BORSTAL
ABJKMOS	JAMBOKS	ABLORSU	LABOURS
	SJAMBOK		SUBORAL
ABJLMOO	JAMBOOL	ABLORSW	BARLOWS
ABJLMSU	JAMBULS	ABLORTW	BLAWORT
	JUMBALS	ABLORUW	BOURLAW
ABJOSZZ	JAZZBOS	ABLOSST	OBLASTS
ABKLLNY	BLANKLY	ABLOSTT	TALBOTS
ABKLOOW	LAWBOOK	ABLOSTV	ABVOLTS
ABKLOTX	TALKBOX	ABLOSTX	SALTBOX
ABKLRUW	BULWARK	ABLOSUV	SUBOVAL
ABKLSSY	SKYLABS	ABLOTUW	OUTBAWL
ABKLSTY	BYTALKS	ABLPRSU	BURLAPS
ABKMNOO	BOOKMAN	ABLPSUY	PLAYBUS
ABKMOST	TOMBAKS	ABLPSYY	BYPLAYS
ABKMSUZ	ZAMBUKS	ABLRSWY	BYRLAWS
ABKNNNO	NONBANK	ABLRTUU	TUBULAR
ABKNRSU	UNBARKS	ABLRTUY	BUTYRAL
ABKNRUU	BUNRAKU	ABLSTTU	BUTTALS
ABKOORS	BOORKAS	ABMMNOS	MOBSMAN
ABKORTU	OUTBARK	ABMNSTU	NUMBATS
ABKSSTU	SUBTASK	ABMNSUY	YNAMBUS
ABLLLOW	LOWBALL	ABMOORR	BARROOM
ABLLLUY	LULLABY	ABMOOSW	WABOOMS
ABLLNOO	BALLOON	ABMOOSZ	BAZOOMS
ABLLNOS	BALLONS	ABMOPST	BAMPOTS
ABLLOOS	LOBOLAS		SPAMBOT
ABLLOPR	PROBALL	ABMORTU	TAMBOUR
ABLLORR	ROLLBAR	ABMOSTU	SUBATOM
ABLLORT	TOLLBAR	ABMOSTW	WOMBATS
ABLLORU	LOBULAR	ABMRSSU	SAMBURS
ABLLOST	BALLOTS	ABMRSTU	TAMBURS
ABLLOSU	BULLOSA	ABNOORS	SOROBAN
ABLLOSW	BALLOWS	ABNOORZ	BORAZON
ABLLOTY	TALLBOY	ABNOOSS	BASSOON
ABLLOVY	LOVABLY	ABNOOST	BATOONS
ABLLPSU	BALLUPS	ABNORST	BARTONS
ABLLRUY	BULLARY	ABNORSY	BARYONS
ABLMMOU	BUMMALO	ABNORTY	BARYTON
ABLMNOU	UMBONAL	ABNOSSU	BONASUS
ABLMOOT	TOMBOLA	ABNOTUY	BUOYANT
ABLMOPS	APLOMBS	ABNRSTU	TURBANS
ABLMORS	BROMALS	ABNRSUU	AUBURNS
ABLMOSY	LAMBOYS	ABNRTTU	TURBANT
ABLMOVY	MOVABLY	ABNSTUW	BAWSUNT
ABLMPSU	PABLUMS	ABNSTYZ	BYZANTS
ABLMPUU	PABULUM	ABOOPSX	SOAPBOX
ABLMRSU	LABRUMS	ABOORTW	ROWBOAT
	LUMBARS	ABOOTTW	TOWBOAT
ABLMSTY	TYMBALS	ABORRSU	ARBOURS
ABLMTUY	MUTABLY	ABORRSW	BARROWS
ABLNOOP	POBLANO	ABORSTU	OUTBARS
ABLNOSZ	BLAZONS		ROBUSTA
ABLNOTU	BUTANOL		RUBATOS
ABLNOTY	NOTABLY		TABOURS
ABLNRSU	SLURBAN	ABORSTW	TOWBARS
ABLNSTU	BUNTALS	ABORSTY	TARBOYS
	TULBANS	ABOSSUU	AUSUBOS
ABLNTUY	TUNABLY	ABOSSHW	BOWSAWS
ABLOORS	BAROLOS	ABOSTUU	AUTOBUS
	ROBALOS	ABPRSTU	ABRUPTS
ABLOORT	TOOLBAR		SUBPART
ABLOORY	OBOLARY		

	UPBRAST
ABPRSUY	UPBRAYS
ABRRSSU	BURSARS
ABRRSUY	BURSARY
ABRRTUY	TURBARY
ABRSTUU	ARBUTUS
ABSSUWY	SUBWAYS
ACCCILY	ACYCLIC
ACCDDEE	ACCEDED
ACCDDEI	CADDICE
ACCDEEN	CADENCE
ACCDEER	ACCEDER
ACCDEES	ACCEDES
ACCDEHK	CHACKED
ACCDEHN	CHANCED
ACCDEHO	COACHED
ACCDEHT	CATCHED
ACCDEII	ACCIDIE
ACCDEIO	ACCOIED
ACCDEIT	ACCITED
ACCDEIU	CADUCEI
ACCDEKL	CACKLED
	CLACKED
ACCDEKO	COCKADE
ACCDEKR	CRACKED
ACCDENS	ACCENDS
ACCDENY	CADENCY
ACCDEOT	COACTED
ACCDEOV	ACCOYED
ACCDERU	ACCRUED
	CARDECU
ACCDESU	ACCUSED
	SUCCADE
ACCDFIL	FLACCID
ACCDHIL	CHALCID
ACCDILS	SCALDIC
ACCDINS	SCANDIC
ACCDIOT	CACTOID
	OCTADIC
ACCDKNO	CANDOCK
ACCDKOW	DAWCOCK
ACCDLOY	ACCOYLD
	CACODYL
ACCDORS	ACCORDS
ACCEEHL	CALECHE
ACCEEHO	COACHEE
ACCEELN	CENACLE
ACCEENR	CREANCE
ACCEERT	ACCRETE
ACCEFIT	FACTICE
ACCEFLU	FELUCCA
ACCEGIN	ACCINGE
ACCEGOS	SOCCAGE
ACCEHHI	CHECHIA
ACCEHIL	CALICHE
	CHALICE
ACCEHIM	MACCHIE
ACCEHIN	CHICANE
ACCEHLN	CHANCEL
ACCEHLO	COCHLEA
ACCEHNO	CONCHAE
ACCEHNR	CHANCER
	CHANCRE
ACCEHNS	CHANCES

ACCEHNT	CATCHEN
ACCEHNU	CHAUNCE
ACCEHNY	CHANCEY
ACCEHOR	CAROCHE
	COACHER
ACCEHOS	CHACOES
	COACHES
ACCEHPU	CAPUCHE
ACCEHRS	CREACHS
ACCEHRT	CATCHER
	RECATCH
ACCEHST	CACHETS
	CATCHES
ACCEHTT	CATHECT
ACCEHTU	CATECHU
ACCEHXY	CACHEXY
ACCEIKP	ICEPACK
ACCEIKR	CACKIER
ACCEILL	CALICLE
ACCEILN	CALCINE
ACCEILO	COELIAC
ACCEILS	CALICES
	CELIACS
ACCEILT	CALCITE
ACCEIMR	CERAMIC
	RACEMIC
ACCEINO	COCAINE
	OCEANIC
ACCEINV	VACCINE
ACCEIPR	CAPRICE
ACCEIPS	ICECAPS
	IPECACS
ACCEIPV	PECCAVI
ACCEIQU	CACIQUE
ACCEIRS	CARICES
ACCEIRT	CREATIC
ACCEIST	ACCITES
	ASCETIC
ACCEITT	ECTATIC
ACCEKLR	CACKLER
	CLACKER
	CRACKLE
ACCEKLS	CACKLES
ACCEKMO	MEACOCK
ACCEKOP	PEACOCK
ACCEKOS	SEACOCK
ACCEKPU	CUPCAKE
ACCEKRR	CRACKER
ACCEKRT	CRACKET
ACCELLY	CALYCLE
	CECALLY
ACCELNO	CONCEAL
ACCELNS	CANCELS
ACCELOR	CORACLE
ACCELOT	CACOLET
ACCELRS	CARCELS
ACCELSU	SACCULE
ACCELSY	CALYCES
	CYCLASE
ACCEMNU	CACUMEN
ACCENOR	CONACRE
ACCENOS	ASCONCE
ACCENOT	COENACT
ACCENOV	CONCAVE

ACCENPT	PECCANT
ACCENRS	CANCERS
ACCENST	ACCENTS
ACCEOPY	CACOEPY
ACCEORW	CRACOWE
ACCEOTT	TOCCATE
ACCEPRY	PECCARY
ACCEPST	ACCEPTS
ACCERRS	SCARCER
ACCERRT	CARRECT
ACCERSS	ARCSECS
ACCERSU	ACCRUES
	ACCURSE
	ACCUSER
ACCERSW	ACCREWS
ACCESSU	ACCUSES
ACCESSY	CYCASES
ACCFIIP	PACIFIC
ACCFILY	CALCIFY
ACCGHIN	CACHING
	CHACING
ACCGNOS	COGNACS
ACCHHIS	CHICHAS
ACCHHKU	KUCHCHA
ACCHIKS	CHIACKS
ACCHIMS	CHASMIC
ACCHINO	CHICANO
ACCHIOP	PICACHO
ACCHIOR	COCHAIR
ACCHIOT	CHAOTIC
ACCHIOU	ACOUCHI
ACCHIRS	SCRAICH
ACCHJSU	JACCHUS
ACCHKOY	HAYCOCK
ACCHKSY	CHYACKS
ACCHLNO	CONCHAL
ACCHLTU	CLAUCHT
ACCHNOS	CONCHAS
ACCHNRS	SCRANCH
ACCHNRU	CRAUNCH
ACCHOPU	CAPOUCH
	PACHUCO
ACCHORR	CARROCH
ACCHOSU	CACHOUS
ACCHOTW	CHOCTAW
ACCHOUY	ACOUCHY
ACCHPTU	CATCHUP
	UPCATCH
ACCHRRU	CURRACH
ACCHRST	SCRATCH
ACCHRSU	SCRAUCH
ACCHSSU	SUCCAHS
ACCIILN	ACLINIC
ACCIINT	ACTINIC
ACCIIST	ASCITIC
	SCIATIC
ACCIKRR	CARRICK
ACCIKRS	CARSICK
ACCILLU	CALCULI
ACCILMO	COMICAL
ACCILMU	CALCIUM
ACCILNO	CONICAL
	LACONIC
ACCILNY	CYNICAL

ACCILOR	CALORIC
ACCILOS	ACCOILS
	CALICOS
ACCILOV	VOCALIC
ACCILRU	CRUCIAL
ACCILRY	ACRYLIC
ACCILSS	CLASSIC
ACCILST	CLASTIC
ACCILSU	SACCULI
ACCIMOT	COMATIC
ACCIMOZ	ZIMOCCA
ACCIMRU	CUMARIC
ACCINNO	CANONIC
ACCINOP	CANOPIC
ACCINOR	ACRONIC
ACCINOS	COCAINS
ACCINOT	CANTICO
ACCINRU	CRUCIAN
ACCINSW	WICCANS
ACCINSY	CYCASIN
ACCIOPR	CAPROIC
ACCIORS	SCORIAC
ACCIORT	ACROTIC
ACCIOST	OCICATS
ACCIPRT	PRACTIC
ACCIRRS	CIRCARS
	RICRACS
ACCIRST	ARCTICS
ACCISTT	TACTICS
	TICTACS
ACCISTU	CAUSTIC
	CICUTAS
ACCKLOR	CARLOCK
ACCKLRY	CRACKLY
ACCKMOR	CROMACK
ACCKOPR	CAPROCK
ACCKOSS	CASSOCK
	COSSACK
ACCKOST	CASTOCK
ACCKPRU	CRACKUP
ACCLOSU	COUCALS
ACCLOSY	ACCLOYS
ACCMNOY	CACONYM
ACCMOOT	COCOMAT
ACCMOOY	COCOYAM
ACCMOPT	ACCOMPT
	COMPACT
ACCMRUU	CURCUMA
ACCNNOO	COONCAN
ACCNOOP	COCOPAN
ACCNOOR	RACCOON
ACCNOOS	CACOONS
ACCNOTT	CONTACT
ACCNOTU	ACCOUNT
ACCOORT	COACTOR
ACCOPTY	COPYCAT
ACCOQSU	SQUACCO
ACCORSS	CORCASS
	CORSACS
ACCORTU	ACCOURT
ACCOSST	ACCOSTS
ACCRSTU	ACCURST
ACDDDEI	CADDIED
ACDDDEL	CLADDED

ACDDDEU	ADDUCED
ACDDDKO	DADDOCK
ACDDEEF	DEFACED
ACDDEEL	DECALED
ACDDEER	CEDARED
ACDDEES	DECADES
ACDDEEY	DECAYED
ACDDEHR	CHEDDAR
ACDDEHY	DAYCHED
ACDDEIL	CLADDIE
ACDDEIN	CANDIED
ACDDEIS	CADDIES
ACDDEIU	DECIDUA
ACDDELN	CANDLED
ACDDELO	CLADODE
ACDDELR	CLADDER
	CRADLED
ACDDELS	SCALDED
ACDDELU	CAUDLED
ACDDEMU	DUCDAME
ACDDEOP	DECAPOD
ACDDERU	ADDUCER
ACDDESU	ADDUCES
	SCAUDED
ACDDHHU	CHUDDAH
ACDDHIS	CADDISH
ACDDHKO	HADDOCK
ACDDHOR	CHADDOR
ACDDHRU	CHUDDAR
ACDDIIS	DIACIDS
ACDDIKZ	ZADDICK
ACDDINS	CANDIDS
ACDDIRS	DISCARD
ACDDIRY	DRYADIC
ACDDIST	ADDICTS
	DIDACTS
ACDDISY	DYADICS
ACDDKMO	MADDOCK
ACDDKOP	PADDOCK
ACDDSSY	CADDYSS
ACDDSTU	ADDUCTS
ACDEEES	DECEASE
ACDEEFF	EFFACED
ACDEEFN	ENFACED
ACDEEFR	DEFACER
	REFACED
ACDEEFS	DEFACES
ACDEEFT	FACETED
ACDEEGL	GLACEED
ACDEEGN	ENCAGED
ACDEEHL	LEACHED
ACDEEHP	CHEAPED
	PEACHED
ACDEEHR	REACHED
ACDEEHT	CHEATED
ACDEEIR	DECIARE
ACDEEJT	DEJECTA
ACDEEKR	CREAKED
ACDEELL	CADELLE
ACDEELN	CLEANED
	ELANCED
	ENLACED
ACDEELR	CLEARED
	CREEDAL
	DECLARE
	RELACED
ACDEELS	DESCALE
ACDEELT	CLEATED
ACDEELV	CLEAVED
ACDEEMN	MENACED
ACDEEMO	CAMEOED
ACDEEMR	AMERCED
	CREAMED
	RACEMED
ACDEEMV	MEDEVAC
ACDEENR	ENRACED
	RECANED
ACDEENS	DECANES
	ENCASED
ACDEENT	ENACTED
ACDEENV	ENCAVED
	VENDACE
ACDEEPR	CAPERED
	PEARCED
	PREACED
ACDEEPS	ESCAPED
ACDEERS	CREASED
	DECARES
	SEARCED
ACDEERT	CATERED
	CEDRATE
	CERATED
	CREATED
	REACTED
ACDEERY	DECAYER
ACDEEST	TEDESCA
ACDEETU	EDUCATE
ACDEETX	EXACTED
ACDEFFH	CHAFFED
ACDEFFS	DECAFFS
ACDEFGO	DOGFACE
ACDEFHU	CHAUFED
ACDEFIN	FACIEND
	FANCIED
ACDEFIR	FARCIED
ACDEFKL	FLACKED
ACDEFRS	SCARFED
ACDEFRT	CRAFTED
	FRACTED
ACDEGGL	CLAGGED
ACDEGGR	CRAGGED
ACDEGGS	SCAGGED
ACDEGHN	CHANGED
	GANCHED
ACDEGHR	CHARGED
ACDEGIN	INCAGED
ACDEGIR	CADGIER
ACDEGIS	DISCAGE
ACDEGKO	DOCKAGE
ACDEGLN	CANGLED
	CLANGED
	GLANCED
ACDEGLO	DECALOG
ACDEGNO	CONGAED
	DECAGON
ACDEGNU	UNCAGED
ACDEGOR	CARGOED
	CORDAGE
ACDEGRS	CADGERS
ACDEGST	GEDACTS
ACDEHHN	HANCHED
ACDEHHT	HATCHED
ACDEHIN	CHAINED
	ECHIDNA
ACDEHIP	EDAPHIC
ACDEHIR	CHAIRED
ACDEHIX	HEXADIC
ACDEHKL	CHALKED
	HACKLED
ACDEHKR	CHARKED
ACDEHKS	SHACKED
ACDEHKT	THACKED
ACDEHKW	WHACKED
ACDEHLN	LANCHED
ACDEHLR	CHALDER
ACDEHLS	CLASHED
ACDEHLT	LATCHED
ACDEHMP	CHAMPED
ACDEHMR	CHARMED
	MARCHED
ACDEHMS	CHASMED
ACDEHMT	MATCHED
ACDEHNR	ENDARCH
	RANCHED
ACDEHNT	CHANTED
ACDEHOP	POACHED
ACDEHOR	CHORDAE
	ROACHED
ACDEHOS	COHEADS
ACDEHOT	CATHODE
ACDEHPP	CHAPPED
ACDEHPR	PARCHED
ACDEHPT	PATCHED
ACDEHPU	CUPHEAD
ACDEHRR	CHARRED
ACDEHRS	CRASHED
	ECHARDS
ACDEHRT	CHARTED
	RATCHED
ACDEHSS	CHASSED
ACDEHST	SCATHED
ACDEHSY	DAYCHES
ACDEHTT	CHATTED
ACDEHTW	WATCHED
ACDEHTY	YACHTED
ACDEHUV	VAUCHED
ACDEIIR	ACIDIER
ACDEILL	CEDILLA
ACDEILM	CAMELID
	CLAIMED
	DECIMAL
	DECLAIM
	MALICED
	MEDICAL
ACDEILN	INLACED
ACDEILR	DECRIAL
	RADICEL
	RADICLE
ACDEILS	SCAILED
ACDEILT	CITADEL
	DELTAIC
	DIALECT

Seven-letter anagrams

	EDICTAL	**ACDELNU**	LAUNCED			PEASCOD
ACDEILV	CAVILED		UNLACED	**ACDEOPT**	COAPTED
ACDEIMT	MICATED	**ACDELOP**	PEDOCAL	**ACDEORR**	CORRADE
ACDEIMV	MEDIVAC	**ACDELOR**	CAROLED	**ACDEORS**	SARCODE
ACDEIMY	MEDIACY		ORACLED	**ACDEORT**	CORDATE
ACDEINO	CODEINA	**ACDELOS**	COLEADS		REDCOAT
	OCEANID		SOLACED	**ACDEOST**	COASTED
ACDEINR	CAIRNED	**ACDELOT**	LOCATED	**ACDEOTT**	CODETTA
	CARNIED	**ACDELOV**	ALCOVED	**ACDEOUV**	COUVADE
	DANCIER	**ACDELPP**	CLAPPED	**ACDEPPR**	CRAPPED
ACDEINS	CANDIES	**ACDELPS**	CLASPED	**ACDEPRS**	REDCAPS
	INCASED		SCALPED		SCARPED
ACDEINV	INCAVED	**ACDELQU**	CALQUED		SCRAPED
ACDEINY	CYANIDE	**ACDELRR**	CRADLER	**ACDEPSU**	SCAUPED
ACDEIOS	CODEIAS	**ACDELRS**	CRADLES	**ACDEQSU**	CASQUED
ACDEIPR	EPACRID		RECLADS	**ACDERRS**	CARDERS
	PERACID		SCALDER		SCARRED
ACDEIPS	DISPACE	**ACDELRT**	CLARTED	**ACDERST**	REDACTS
ACDEIRR	ACRIDER	**ACDELRU**	CAULDER		SCARTED
	CARRIED	**ACDELRW**	CRAWLED	**ACDERSU**	CRUSADE
ACDEIRS	CARDIES	**ACDELSS**	CLASSED		SCAURED
	DARCIES		DECLASS	**ACDERTT**	DETRACT
	RADICES	**ACDELST**	CASTLED		TRACTED
	SIDECAR		SCLATED	**ACDERTU**	CURATED
ACDEIRU	DECURIA	**ACDELSU**	CAUDLES		TRADUCE
ACDEISS	DISCASE		CEDULAS	**ACDESTT**	SCATTED
ACDEIST	ACIDEST	**ACDELSW**	DECLAWS	**ACDESTV**	ADVECTS
	DACITES	**ACDELTT**	CLATTED	**ACDFIIT**	FATIDIC
ACDEISV	ADVICES	**ACDELTU**	CLAUTED	**ACDFIIY**	ACIDIFY
ACDEITT	DICTATE	**ACDELWW**	DEWCLAW	**ACDFIOT**	FACTOID
ACDEITY	EDACITY	**ACDEMMR**	CRAMMED	**ACDGGIN**	CADGING
ACDEJLO	CAJOLED	**ACDEMMS**	SCAMMED	**ACDGIIM**	DIGICAM
ACDEJNU	JAUNCED	**ACDEMNU**	DECUMAN	**ACDGIKN**	DACKING
ACDEKKN	KNACKED	**ACDEMOR**	CAROMED	**ACDGINN**	DANCING
ACDEKLM	MACKLED		COMRADE	**ACDGINO**	GONADIC
ACDEKLN	CLANKED	**ACDEMPR**	CRAMPED	**ACDGINR**	CARDING
ACDEKLO	CLOAKED	**ACDEMPS**	DECAMPS	**ACDGKLO**	DAGLOCK
ACDEKLS	SLACKED		SCAMPED	**ACDGNOT**	CANTDOG
ACDEKLT	TACKLED	**ACDENNS**	SCANNED	**ACDGORT**	DOGCART
	TALCKED	**ACDENNT**	CANDENT	**ACDHIIL**	CHILIAD
ACDEKLU	CAULKED	**ACDENNU**	NUANCED	**ACDHIMR**	DHARMIC
ACDEKMS	SMACKED	**ACDENOR**	ACORNED	**ACDHIOP**	PHACOID
ACDEKNR	CRANKED		DRACONE	**ACDHIRV**	DIARCHY
ACDEKNS	SNACKED	**ACDENOS**	ACNODES	**ACDHLOR**	CHORDAL
ACDEKNU	UNCAKED		DEACONS		DORLACH
ACDEKOR	CROAKED	**ACDENOT**	TACNODE	**ACDHMRS**	DRACHMS
ACDEKQU	QUACKED	**ACDENPR**	PRANCED	**ACDHNOW**	COWHAND
ACDEKRS	DACKERS	**ACDENPT**	PANDECT	**ACDHOOT**	CATHOOD
ACDEKRT	TRACKED	**ACDENPU**	UNCAPED	**ACDHOPR**	POCHARD
ACDEKRW	WRACKED		UNPACED	**ACDHORR**	ORCHARD
ACDEKRY	KEYCARD	**ACDENRS**	DANCERS	**ACDHORS**	CHADORS
ACDEKST	STACKED	**ACDENRT**	CANTRED	**ACDHRUY**	DUARCHY
ACDEKSW	SWACKED		TRANCED	**ACDHRVY**	DYARCHY
ACDELLS	SCALLED	**ACDENRU**	DURANCE	**ACDIIIN**	INDICIA
ACDELMM	CLAMMED		UNRACED	**ACDIIJT**	JADITIC
ACDELMP	CAMPLED	**ACDENRY**	ARDENCY	**ACDIINN**	INDICAN
	CLAMPED	**ACDENSS**	ASCENDS	**ACDIINO**	CONIDIA
ACDELMS	MASCLED	**ACDENST**	DECANTS	**ACDIINR**	ACRIDIN
ACDELMU	MACULED		DESCANT	**ACDIIOS**	ISODICA
ACDELNO	CELADON		SCANTED	**ACDIIRS**	CIDARIS
ACDELNR	CANDLER	**ACDENSU**	UNCASED		SCIARID
ACDELNS	CALENDS	**ACDENTU**	UNACTED	**ACDIIRT**	ARCTIID
	CANDLES	**ACDENUV**	VAUNCED		TRIACID
ACDELNT	CANTLED	**ACDEOPS**	PEACODS		TRIADIC

ACDIITY	ACIDITY	ACDMORZ	CZARDOM		RETEACH
ACDIKLS	SKALDIC	ACDMPSU	MUDCAPS		TEACHER
ACDILLO	CODILLA	ACDMSTU	MUDCATS	ACEEHST	EATCHES
ACDILMO	DOMICAL	ACDNOOR	CARDOON		ESCHEAT
ACDILMS	CLADISM	ACDNORS	CANDORS		TEACHES
ACDILNO	NODICAL		CARDONS	ACEEHTT	THECATE
ACDILNU	DULCIAN		DACRONS	ACEEHTX	EXCHEAT
	INCUDAL	ACDNORU	CANDOUR	ACEEILP	CALIPEE
ACDILOP	PLACOID		CAUDRON	ACEEIMT	EMICATE
	PODALIC	ACDOPST	PODCAST	ACEEINR	CINEREA
ACDILOR	CORDIAL	ACDORST	COSTARD	ACEEINU	EUCAINE
ACDILOT	COTIDAL	ACDORSU	CRUSADO	ACEEIRR	CARIERE
ACDILPU	PALUDIC	ACDORSW	COWARDS	ACEEISV	VESICAE
ACDILRT	TRICLAD	ACDORUZ	CRUZADO	ACEEJKN	JACKEEN
ACDILRY	ACRIDLY	ACDRSTU	CUSTARD	ACEEKNP	KNEECAP
ACDILST	CLADIST	ACDRSUU	CARDUUS	ACEELLN	NACELLE
ACDILTW	WILDCAT	ACEEEPS	ESCAPEE	ACEELLS	CALLEES
ACDILTY	DACTYLI	ACEEEUV	EVACUEE	ACEELMP	EMPLACE
ACDIMMU	CADMIUM	ACEEFFR	EFFACER	ACEELMR	RECLAME
ACDIMNO	MANDIOC	ACEEFFS	EFFACES	ACEELNR	CLEANER
	MONACID	ACEEFHN	ENCHAFE		RECLEAN
	MONADIC	ACEEFIN	FAIENCE	ACEELNS	CLEANSE
	NOMADIC		FIANCEE		ELANCES
ACDIMNY	DYNAMIC	ACEEFLU	FECULAE		ENLACES
ACDIMOO	CAMOODI	ACEEFMN	FACEMEN		SCALENE
ACDIMOT	COADMIT	ACEEFNS	ENFACES	ACEELNT	LATENCE
ACDINNO	NONACID	ACEEFNY	FAYENCE	ACEELNV	ENCLAVE
ACDINRU	IRACUND	ACEEFPR	PREFACE		VALENCE
ACDINST	DISCANT	ACEEFRS	REFACES	ACEELPR	PERCALE
ACDINSW	WINDACS	ACEEGIL	ELEGIAC		REPLACE
ACDINSY	CYANIDS	ACEEGNR	ENGRACE	ACEELPT	CAPELET
ACDIOPR	PARODIC	ACEEGNS	ENCAGES	ACEELRR	CLEARER
	PICADOR	ACEEGNT	CENTAGE	ACEELRS	ALERCES
ACDIORR	CORRIDA	ACEEGOT	ECOTAGE		CEREALS
ACDIORS	SARCOID	ACEEGSU	ESCUAGE		RELACES
ACDIORT	ARCTOID	ACEEHHT	CHEETAH		RESCALE
	CAROTID	ACEEHIP	CHEAPIE		SCLERAE
ACDIOST	DACOITS	ACEEHIT	HICATEE	ACEELRT	TREACLE
ACDIOSZ	ZODIACS		TEACHIE	ACEELRU	CAERULE
ACDIOTY	DACOITY	ACEEHIV	ACHIEVE	ACEELRV	CLEAVER
ACDIOXY	OXYACID	ACEEHKO	HOECAKE	ACEELST	CELESTA
ACDIPRS	CAPRIDS	ACEEHKS	HACKEES		SELECTA
ACDIPSS	CAPSIDS	ACEEHLR	LEACHER	ACEELSU	EUCLASE
ACDIPTY	DIPTYCA		RELACHE	ACEELSV	CLEAVES
ACDIQRU	QUADRIC	ACEEHLS	LEACHES	ACEELVX	EXCLAVE
ACDIRST	DRASTIC	ACEEHLT	CHELATE	ACEEMNR	MENACER
ACDIRTU	DATURIC	ACEEHMP	EMPEACH	ACEEMNS	CASEMEN
ACDISST	DICASTS	ACEEHMR	MACHREE		EMACSEN
ACDITUV	VIADUCT	ACEEHMT	MACHETE		MENACES
ACDJNTU	ADJUNCT	ACEEHNN	ENHANCE	ACEEMNT	CEMENTA
ACDKLOP	PADLOCK	ACEEHNP	CHEAPEN	ACEEMNV	CAVEMEN
ACDKLSY	SKYCLAD	ACEEHNS	ACHENES	ACEEMRR	AMERCER
ACDKMOO	MOCKADO		ENCHASE		CREAMER
ACDKMPU	MUDPACK	ACEEHOR	OCHREAE	ACEEMRS	AMERCES
ACDKOPR	POCKARD	ACEEHPP	ECHAPPE		CAREMES
ACDLLOR	COLLARD	ACEEHPR	CHEAPER		RACEMES
ACDLLUY	DUCALLY		PEACHER	ACEEMRT	CREMATE
ACDLNOR	CALDRON	ACEEHPS	PEACHES		MEERCAT
ACDLNOT	COTLAND	ACEEHRR	REACHER	ACEEMSS	CAMESES
ACDLOWY	LADYCOW	ACEEHRS	REACHES	ACEEMSZ	ECZEMAS
ACDLSTY	DACTYLS	ACEEHRT	CHEATER	ACEENNP	PENANCE
ACDMMNO	COMMAND		HECTARE	ACEENNR	NARCEEN
ACDMNOP	COMPAND		RECHATE	ACEENNT	CANTEEN
ACDMOOW	CAMWOOD		RECHEAT	ACEENNY	CAYENNE

Seven-letter anagrams

ACEENOR	CORNEAE	ACEFHRU	CHAUFER	ACEGINS	CEASING
ACEENOT	ACETONE	ACEFHSU	CHAUFES		INCAGES
ACEENRS	CAREENS	ACEFIIL	FELICIA	ACEGINV	VEGANIC
	CASERNE	ACEFILL	ICEFALL	ACEGINY	GYNECIA
	ENRACES	ACEFILM	MALEFIC	ACEGINZ	CEAZING
	RECANES	ACEFILR	FILACER	ACEGIOP	APOGEIC
ACEENRT	CENTARE	ACEFILS	FECIALS	ACEGIRT	CIGARET
	CRENATE	ACEFINN	FINANCE	ACEGIRU	GAUCIER
	REENACT	ACEFINR	FANCIER	ACEGIRW	GAWCIER
ACEENSS	CASSENE	ACEFINS	FANCIES	ACEGIST	CAGIEST
	ENCASES		FASCINE	ACEGJKL	JACKLEG
	SEANCES		FIANCES	ACEGKLO	LOCKAGE
	SENECAS	ACEFINU	UNIFACE	ACEGKLR	GRACKLE
ACEENST	CETANES	ACEFIRS	FARCIES	ACEGKMO	MOCKAGE
	TENACES		FIACRES	ACEGKOR	CORKAGE
ACEENSV	ENCAVES	ACEFITV	FACTIVE	ACEGLLO	COLLAGE
ACEENTU	CUNEATE	ACEFITY	ACETIFY	ACEGLNO	CONGEAL
ACEEORS	ACEROSE	ACEFKLR	FLACKER	ACEGLNR	CLANGER
ACEEORT	OCREATE	ACEFKLT	FLACKET		GLANCER
ACEEOSS	CASEOSE	ACEFLRU	CAREFUL	ACEGLNS	CANGLES
ACEEOST	ACETOSE	ACEFLSU	FECULAS		GLANCES
	COATEES	ACEFNNO	FACONNE	ACEGLOT	CATELOG
ACEEOTV	EVOCATE	ACEFNRT	CANTREF	ACEGLOU	CAGOULE
ACEEPRR	CAPERER	ACEFNRU	FURNACE	ACEGLPS	GELCAPS
	PRERACE	ACEFOPR	PROFACE	ACEGMOP	COMPAGE
ACEEPRS	ESCAPER	ACEFORR	FORECAR	ACEGNOR	ACROGEN
	PEARCES	ACEFOTU	OUTFACE		CORNAGE
	PERCASE	ACEFRRS	FARCERS	ACEGNOT	COAGENT
	PREACES		SCARFER		COGNATE
	RESPACE	ACEFRRT	CRAFTER	ACEGNSU	CANGUES
ACEEPSS	ESCAPES		REFRACT		UNCAGES
ACEEPST	PECTASE	ACEFRRU	FARCEUR	ACEGORS	CARGOES
ACEEPTT	PECTATE	ACEFRSU	SURFACE		CORSAGE
ACEERRS	CAREERS	ACEFRTU	FACTURE		SOCAGER
	CREASER		FURCATE	ACEGORU	COURAGE
ACEERRT	CATERER	ACEFSTU	FAUCETS	ACEGOSS	SOCAGES
	RECRATE	ACEGHLO	GALOCHE	ACEGOSW	COWAGES
	RETRACE	ACEGHNR	CHANGER	ACEGOTT	COTTAGE
	TERRACE	ACEGHNS	CHANGES	ACEGRTU	TRUCAGE
ACEERSS	CREASES		GANCHES	ACEGSTU	SCUTAGE
	SEARCES	ACEGHNU	CHAUNGE	ACEGTTU	CUTTAGE
ACEERST	CERATES	ACEGHOU	GOUACHE	ACEHHLS	CHALEHS
	CREATES	ACEGHOW	COWHAGE	ACEHHLT	HATCHEL
	ECARTES	ACEGHRR	CHARGER	ACEHHNS	HANCHES
	SECRETA	ACEGHRS	CHARGES	ACEHHRT	HATCHER
ACEERSU	CESURAE		CREAGHS	ACEHHRU	HACHURE
ACEERTX	EXACTER	ACEGHRT	GERTCHA	ACEHHRX	HEXARCH
	EXCRETA	ACEGHRU	GAUCHER	ACEHHST	CHETAHS
ACEERVZ	CERVEZA	ACEGILL	ELLAGIC		HATCHES
ACEESSS	ASCESES	ACEGILN	ANGELIC	ACEHHTT	HATCHET
ACEESST	ECTASES		ANGLICE	ACEHIKR	KACHERI
ACEESTT	CASETTE		GALENIC	ACEHIKS	HACKIES
ACEFFHI	AFFICHE	ACEGILP	PELAGIC	ACEHILL	CHALLIE
ACEFFHR	CHAFFER	ACEGILR	GLACIER		HELICAL
ACEFFIN	CAFFEIN		GRACILE	ACEHILM	LECHAIM
ACEFFIS	SCAFFIE	ACEGILS	ALGESIC	ACEHILR	CHARLIE
ACEFFOR	AFFORCE	ACEGILT	ALGETIC	ACEHILT	ALETHIC
ACEFFST	AFFECTS	ACEGIMO	CAMOGIE		ETHICAL
ACEFGIP	PIGFACE	ACEGIMR	GRIMACE	ACEHIMN	MACHINE
ACEFGLU	CAGEFUL	ACEGIMT	GAMETIC	ACEHIMP	IMPEACH
ACEFGOT	GEOFACT	ACEGINO	COINAGE	ACEHIMR	CHIMERA
ACEFHMR	CHAMFER	ACEGINP	PEACING	ACEHIMS	CHAMISE
ACEFHOR	ARCHFOE	ACEGINR	ANERGIC	ACEHIMT	HEMATIC
ACEFHRS	CHAFERS		GRECIAN	ACEHINN	ENCHAIN

ACEHINR	ARCHINE		SATCHEL	**ACEHPST**	HEPCATS
ACEHINS	CHAINES	**ACEHLTT**	CHATTEL		PATCHES
	INCHASE		LATCHET	**ACEHQUV**	QUEACHY
ACEHINT	CHANTIE	**ACEHMNP**	CHAPMEN	**ACEHRRS**	ARCHERS
ACEHINV	HYACINE	**ACEHMNR**	ENCHARM		CRASHER
	HYAENIC		MARCHEN	**ACEHRRT**	CHARTER
ACEHIOT	ACHIOTE	**ACEHMNS**	MANCHES		RECHART
ACEHIPP	CHAPPIE	**ACEHMNT**	MANCHET	**ACEHRRV**	CHARVER
ACEHIPR	CHARPIE	**ACEHMPR**	CHAMPER	**ACEHRRX**	XERARCH
ACEHIPT	APHETIC	**ACEHMRR**	CHARMER	**ACEHRRY**	ARCHERY
	HEPATIC		MARCHER	**ACEHRSS**	CHASERS
ACEHIRR	CHARIER	**ACEHMRS**	MACHERS		CRASHES
ACEHIRS	CAHIERS		MARCHES		ESCHARS
	CASHIER		MESARCH	**ACEHRST**	ARCHEST
	ERIACHS		SCHMEAR		CHARETS
ACEHIRT	THERIAC	**ACEHMRT**	MATCHER		CHASTER
ACEHIRV	ARCHIVE		REMATCH		RACHETS
ACEHISS	CHAISES	**ACEHMRU**	CHAUMER		RATCHES
ACEHIST	ACHIEST	**ACEHMSS**	SACHEMS	**ACEHRSU**	ARCHEUS
	AITCHES		SAMECHS	**ACEHRSV**	VARECHS
ACEHITV	YACHTIE		SCHEMAS	**ACEHRSW**	CHAWERS
ACEHITZ	ZAITECH	**ACEHMST**	MATCHES	**ACEHRSX**	EXARCHS
ACEHKLR	HACKLER	**ACEHMTT**	MATCHET	**ACEHRSY**	HYRACES
ACEHKLS	HACKLES	**ACEHMTY**	ECTHYMA	**ACEHRTT**	CHATTER
	SHACKLE	**ACEHMTZ**	CHAMETZ		RATCHET
ACEHKLT	HACKLET	**ACEHNNR**	CHANNER	**ACEHRTW**	WATCHER
ACEHKMN	HACKMEN	**ACEHNNT**	ENCHANT	**ACEHRTY**	YACHTER
ACEHKNV	HACKNEY	**ACEHNOP**	PANOCHE	**ACEHRXY**	EXARCHY
ACEHKOT	HOTCAKE	**ACEHNPS**	PECHANS	**ACEHSSS**	CHASSES
ACEHKRS	HACKERS	**ACEHNRR**	RANCHER	**ACEHSST**	SACHETS
ACEHKRW	WHACKER	**ACEHNRS**	CHENARS		SCATHES
ACEHKRY	HACKERY		RANCHES	**ACEHSSW**	CASHEWS
ACEHLLP	PELLACH	**ACEHNRT**	CHANTER	**ACEHSTW**	WATCHES
ACEHLLS	SHELLAC		TRANCHE	**ACEHSTX**	HEXACTS
ACEHLLT	HELLCAT	**ACEHNSS**	SCHANSE	**ACEHSUV**	VAUCHES
ACEHLMT	CHAMLET	**ACEHNST**	CHASTEN	**ACEHTTU**	TEUCHAT
ACEHLMY	ALCHEMY		NATCHES	**ACEHTTW**	WATCHET
ACEHLNN	CHANNEL	**ACEHNSU**	NAUCHES	**ACEIILM**	CIMELIA
ACEHLNO	CHALONE	**ACEHNSZ**	SCHANZE	**ACEIILS**	LAICISE
ACEHLNP	PLANCHE	**ACEHNTT**	ETCHANT	**ACEIILT**	CILIATE
ACEHLNR	CHARNEL	**ACEHNTU**	UNTEACH	**ACEIILZ**	LAICIZE
	LARCHEN	**ACEHNTY**	CHANTEY	**ACEIIPS**	EPISCIA
ACEHLNS	LANCHES	**ACEHNZZ**	CHAZZEN	**ACEIITV**	CAITIVE
ACEHLOP	EPOCHAL	**ACEHOOT**	OOTHECA		VICIATE
ACEHLOR	CHOLERA	**ACEHOPR**	POACHER	**ACEIJKS**	JACKIES
	CHORALE	**ACEHOPS**	CHEAPOS		JACKSIE
	CHOREAL		EPOCHAS	**ACEIKLS**	SACLIKE
ACEHLOS	LOACHES		POACHES	**ACEIKLT**	CATLIKE
	OSCHEAL		SHOEPAC	**ACEIKMR**	KERAMIC
ACEHLOT	CATHOLE	**ACEHORS**	CHOREAS	**ACEIKNT**	ANTICKE
	CHOLATE		ORACHES	**ACEIKOP**	PAIOCKE
ACEHLPS	CHAPELS		ROACHES	**ACEIKPR**	EARPICK
ACEHLPT	CHAPLET	**ACEHOSS**	CHAOSES	**ACEIKPW**	WICKAPE
ACEHLPY	CHEAPLY	**ACEHOTY**	CHAYOTE	**ACEIKPX**	PICKAXE
ACEHLRS	CLASHER	**ACEHPPS**	SCHAPPE	**ACEIKRS**	EIRACKS
	LARCHES	**ACEHPRS**	EPARCHS	**ACEIKRT**	TACKIER
	RASCHEL		PARCHES	**ACEIKRW**	WACKIER
ACEHLRT	ARCHLET	**ACEHPRT**	CHAPTER	**ACEIKSS**	SEASICK
	TRACHLE		PATCHER	**ACEIKST**	CAKIEST
ACEHLRY	CHARLEY		REPATCH		TACKIES
ACEHLSS	CLASHES	**ACEHPRU**	UPREACH	**ACEIKTT**	TIETACK
	SEALCHS	**ACEHPRY**	EPARCHY	**ACEILLL**	ALLELIC
ACEHLST	CHALETS		PREACHY	**ACEILLM**	LIMACEL
	LATCHES	**ACEHPSS**	CHAPESS		MICELLA

Seven-letter anagrams

ACEILLS	ALLICES	ACEIMNO	ENCOMIA	ACEINTZ	ZINCATE
	CAILLES	ACEIMNP	PEMICAN	ACEINYZ	CYANIZE
ACEILLX	LEXICAL	ACEIMNR	CARMINE	ACEIOOZ	ZOOECIA
ACEILMN	CNEMIAL	ACEIMNS	AMNESIC	ACEIOPT	ECTOPIA
	MELANIC		CINEMAS	ACEIORS	CARIOSE
ACEILMR	CALMIER	ACEIMNT	EMICANT		ORACIES
	CLAIMER		NEMATIC		SCORIAE
	MIRACLE	ACEIMOR	COREMIA	ACEIORT	EROTICA
	RECLAIM	ACEIMOV	VOMICAE	ACEIOST	SOCIATE
ACEILMS	LIMACES	ACEIMPR	CAMPIER	ACEIOTX	EXOTICA
	MALICES	ACEIMPY	PYAEMIC	ACEIPPR	CRAPPIE
ACEILMT	CLIMATE	ACEIMRT	MATRICE		EPICARP
	METICAL	ACEIMRU	URAEMIC	ACEIPPT	TAPPICE
ACEILMX	EXCLAIM	ACEIMSS	CAMISES	ACEIPRR	CRAPIER
ACEILMY	MYCELIA	ACEIMST	ACMITES	ACEIPRS	EPACRIS
ACEILNN	ENCINAL		ETACISM		SCRAPIE
ACEILNP	CAPELIN		MICATES		SPACIER
	PANICLE		SEMATIC	ACEIPRT	PARETIC
	PELICAN	ACEIMSU	CAESIUM		PICRATE
ACEILNR	CARLINE	ACEIMTX	TAXEMIC	ACEIPST	ASEPTIC
ACEILNS	INLACES	ACEINNP	PINNACE		PACIEST
	SANICLE	ACEINNR	CANNIER		SPICATE
	SCALENI		NARCEIN	ACEIPSU	AUSPICE
ACEILNU	CAULINE	ACEINNS	CANINES	ACEIPSZ	CAPIZES
ACEILOR	CALORIE		ENCINAS		CAPSIZE
	CARIOLE		NANCIES	ACEIPTV	CAPTIVE
	COALIER	ACEINNT	ANCIENT	ACEIQRU	ACQUIRE
	LORICAE	ACEINNY	CYANINE	ACEIQSU	CAIQUES
ACEILOS	CELOSIA	ACEINOP	APNOEIC	ACEIQTU	ACQUITE
	COALISE		PAEONIC	ACEIQUZ	CAZIQUE
ACEILOT	ALOETIC	ACEINOS	ACINOSE	ACEIRRR	CARRIER
ACEILOZ	COALIZE	ACEINOT	ACONITE	ACEIRRS	CARRIES
ACEILPR	CALIPER		ANOETIC		SCARIER
	REPLICA	ACEINPR	CAPRINE	ACEIRRT	CIRRATE
ACEILPS	PLAICES	ACEINPS	INSCAPE		ERRATIC
	SPECIAL		PINCASE	ACEIRRW	AIRCREW
ACEILPT	PLICATE	ACEINPT	PICANTE	ACEIRRZ	CRAZIER
ACEILPU	PECULIA	ACEINRR	CARNIER	ACEIRST	ATRESIC
ACEILRR	CERRIAL	ACEINRS	ARCSINE		CRISTAE
ACEILRS	CLARIES		ARSENIC		RACIEST
	ECLAIRS		CARNIES		STEARIC
	SCALIER		CERASIN	ACEIRSU	SAUCIER
ACEILRT	ARTICLE	ACEINRT	CANTIER		URICASE
	RECITAL		CERATIN	ACEIRSV	CARVIES
	TALCIER		CERTAIN		CAVIERS
ACEILRU	AURICLE		CREATIN		VARICES
ACEILRV	CALIVER		CRINATE		VISCERA
	CAVILER		NACRITE	ACEIRSZ	CRAZIES
	CLAVIER		TACRINE	ACEIRTT	ATRETIC
	VALERIC	ACEINSS	CASEINS		CATTIER
	VELARIC		CASSINE		CITRATE
ACEILRY	CLAYIER		INCASES	ACEISSS	ASCESIS
ACEILSS	SALICES	ACEINST	ACETINS	ACEISST	ASCITES
ACEILST	ASTELIC		CANIEST		ECTASIS
	ELASTIC		CINEAST	ACEISTT	CATTIES
	LACIEST	ACEINSU	EUCAINS		STATICE
	LATICES	ACEINSV	INCAVES		TIETACS
	SALICET	ACEINSY	CYANISE	ACEISTV	ACTIVES
ACEILSV	CLAVIES	ACEINTT	NICTATE	ACEISVV	VIVACES
	VESICAL		TETANIC	ACEITTV	CAVETTI
ACEILTT	LATTICE	ACEINTU	TUNICAE	ACEITTX	EXTATIC
	TACTILE	ACEINTV	VENATIC	ACEITUX	AUXETIC
ACEILVW	WAVICLE	ACEINTX	INEXACT	ACEJKMN	JACKMEN
ACEIMMS	CAMMIES	ACEINTY	CYANITE	ACEJKOP	PAJOCKE

ACEJKRS	JACKERS	ACEKSTT	STACKET	ACELNST	CANTLES
ACEJKST	JACKETS		TACKETS		CENTALS
ACEJLOR	CAJOLER	ACEKSTW	WACKEST		LANCETS
ACEJLOS	CAJOLES	ACEKSUW	WAESUCK		SCANTLE
ACEJNOS	CAJONES	ACEKTTY	TACKETY	ACELNSU	CENSUAL
ACEJNOT	JACONET	ACELLMO	CALOMEL		LACUNES
ACEJNOY	JOYANCE	ACELLMY	MYCELLA		LAUNCES
ACEJNSU	JAUNCES	ACELLNU	NUCLEAL		UNLACES
ACEJNTU	JUNCATE	ACELLNY	CLEANLY		UNSCALE
ACEJPTU	CAJEPUT	ACELLOR	CORELLA	ACELNTT	CANTLET
ACEJRTT	TRAJECT		OCELLAR	ACELNTY	LATENCY
ACEKKNR	KNACKER	ACELLOS	CALLOSE	ACELNVY	VALENCY
ACEKLLP	PELLACK		LOCALES	ACELOPR	POLACRE
ACEKLMS	MACKLES	ACELLOT	COLLATE	ACELOPS	ESCALOP
ACEKLNR	CRANKLE	ACELLPS	SCALPEL	ACELOPT	POLECAT
ACEKLNS	SLACKEN	ACELLPY	CLYPEAL	ACELOPU	COPULAE
ACEKLOR	EARLOCK	ACELLRR	CARRELL	ACELOQU	COEQUAL
ACEKLPS	SPACKLE	ACELLRS	CALLERS	ACELORR	CAROLER
ACEKLPT	PLACKET		CELLARS	ACELORS	CLAROES
ACEKLQU	QUACKLE		RECALLS		COALERS
ACEKLRS	CALKERS		SCLERAL		ESCOLAR
	LACKERS	ACELLRY	CLEARLY		ORACLES
	SLACKER	ACELLST	CALLETS		RECOALS
ACEKLRT	TACKLER	ACELMMR	CLAMMER		SOLACER
ACEKLRU	CAULKER	ACELMNO	COALMEN	ACELORT	LOCATER
ACEKLST	TACKLES	ACELMNS	ENCALMS	ACELORY	CALOYER
ACEKLSY	LACKEYS	ACELMOR	CAROMEL	ACELOSS	SOLACES
ACEKMNP	PACKMEN	ACELMOT	CAMELOT	ACELOST	ALECOST
ACEKMOR	COMAKER	ACELMOU	CAULOME		LACTOSE
ACEKMOS	COMAKES		LEUCOMA		LOCATES
ACEKMRS	SMACKER	ACELMPR	CLAMPER		SCATOLE
ACEKNOS	NOCAKES	ACELMPS	CAMPLES		TALCOSE
ACEKNPR	PRANCKE	ACELMRS	MARCELS	ACELOSV	ALCOVES
ACEKNRR	CRANKER	ACELMRY	CAMELRY		COEVALS
ACEKNRS	CANKERS	ACELMSS	MASCLES	ACELOTT	CALOTTE
	SNACKER		MESCALS	ACELOTU	OCULATE
ACEKNRY	CANKERY		SCAMELS	ACELOTY	ACOLYTE
ACEKNST	NACKETS	ACELMST	CALMEST		COTYLAE
ACEKNSU	UNCAKES		CAMLETS	ACELOUV	VACUOLE
ACEKORR	CROAKER	ACELMSU	ALMUCES	ACELPPR	CLAPPER
ACEKPPR	PREPACK		MACULES	ACELPPS	SCAPPLE
ACEKPRS	PACKERS	ACELMSZ	MEZCALS	ACELPRS	CARPELS
	REPACKS	ACELMTU	CALUMET		CLASPER
ACEKPST	PACKETS	ACELNNO	ALENCON		CRAPLES
ACEKQRU	QUACKER	ACELNNS	CANNELS		PARCELS
ACEKRRS	RACKERS	ACELNNU	UNCLEAN		PLACERS
	RERACKS	ACELNNY	LYNCEAN		RECLASP
ACEKRRT	RETRACK	ACELNOP	NOPLACE		SCALPER
	TRACKER	ACELNOR	CORNEAL	ACELPRT	PLECTRA
ACEKRSS	SACKERS	ACELNOS	SECONAL	ACELPRY	PRELACY
	SCREAKS	ACELNOT	LACTONE	ACELPSS	CAPLESS
ACEKRST	RACKETS	ACELNOZ	CALZONE	ACELPST	CAPLETS
	RESTACK	ACELNPS	ENCLASP		PLACETS
	RETACKS		SPANCEL	ACELPSU	CAPSULE
	STACKER	ACELNPT	CLAPNET		SCALEUP
	TACKERS	ACELNPU	CLEANUP		SPECULA
ACEKRSU	CAUKERS		UNPLACE		UPSCALE
ACEKRSW	CAWKERS	ACELNRS	LANCERS	ACELPSY	CYPSELA
	WACKERS		RANCELS	ACELPTY	ECTYPAL
ACEKRSY	SCREAKY	ACELNRT	CENTRAL	ACELPUU	CUPULAE
	YACKERS	ACELNRU	LUCARNE	ACELQRU	CLAQUER
ACEKRTT	RACKETT		NUCLEAR		LACQUER
ACEKRTY	RACKETY		UNCLEAR	ACELQSU	CALQUES
ACEKSST	CASKETS	ACELNRY	LARCENY		CLAQUES

ACELQUY	LACQUEY	**ACEMSTT**	METCAST	**ACENSSU**	UNCASES
ACELRRS	CARRELS	**ACEMSTU**	MUCATES		USANCES
ACELRRU	RAUCLER	**ACEMSUX**	EXACUMS	**ACENSTT**	CANTEST
ACELRRW	CRAWLER	**ACENNOS**	ANCONES	**ACENSTU**	NUTCASE
ACELRSS	CARLESS		SONANCE	**ACENSUU**	USAUNCE
	CLASSER	**ACENNOT**	CONNATE	**ACENSUV**	VAUNCES
	SCALERS	**ACENNOX**	COANNEX	**ACEOOPP**	APOCOPE
	SCLERAS	**ACENNOY**	NOYANCE	**ACEOOTZ**	ECTOZOA
ACELRST	CARTELS	**ACENNOZ**	CANZONE	**ACEOPRX**	EXOCARP
	CLARETS	**ACENNRS**	CANNERS	**ACEOPSS**	SCAPOSE
	CRESTAL		SCANNER	**ACEOPST**	CAPOTES
	SCARLET	**ACENNRY**	CANNERY		SCOPATE
	TARCELS	**ACENNST**	NASCENT		TOECAPS
ACELRSU	CESURAL	**ACENNSU**	NUANCES	**ACEOPSW**	COWPEAS
	RECUSAL	**ACENNTY**	TENANCY	**ACEOPTU**	OUTPACE
	SECULAR	**ACENOOR**	CORONAE	**ACEORRS**	COARSER
ACELRSV	CALVERS	**ACENOPT**	PATONCE		CORREAS
	CARVELS	**ACENOPU**	PONCEAU	**ACEORRT**	ACROTER
	CLAVERS	**ACENORS**	CANOERS		CREATOR
ACELRSW	CLAWERS		CARNOSE		REACTOR
ACELRTT	CLATTER		COARSEN	**ACEORSS**	ROSACES
ACELRTY	TREACLY		CORNEAS	**ACEORST**	COASTER
ACELSSS	CLASSES		EARCONS		COATERS
	SACLESS		NARCOSE		RECOATS
ACELSST	CASTLES	**ACENORT**	ENACTOR	**ACEORSU**	ACEROUS
	SCLATES	**ACENOSS**	CASSONE		CAROUSE
ACELSSU	CLAUSES	**ACENOST**	COSTEAN	**ACEORSW**	CROWEAS
ACELSSV	SCLAVES		OCTANES	**ACEORSX**	COAXERS
ACELSTU	CAUTELS	**ACENOTT**	ATTONCE	**ACEORTU**	OUTRACE
	SULCATE	**ACENOTV**	CENTAVO	**ACEORTV**	OVERACT
ACELSTY	ACETYLS	**ACENPRR**	PRANCER	**ACEORTX**	EXACTOR
	SCYTALE	**ACENPRS**	PRANCES	**ACEOSSU**	CASEOUS
ACELSUU	ACULEUS	**ACENPRU**	PRAUNCE	**ACEOSTT**	COSTATE
ACELSUX	EXCUSAL	**ACENPST**	CATNEPS	**ACEOSTU**	ACETOUS
ACELSXY	CALYXES	**ACENPSU**	PAUNCES	**ACEOSTV**	AVOCETS
ACELTUY	ACUTELY		UNCAPES		OCTAVES
ACELTXY	EXACTLY	**ACENPSW**	PAWNCES	**ACEOTTV**	CAVETTO
ACEMMRR	CRAMMER	**ACENPTT**	PENTACT	**ACEOTUU**	AUTOCUE
ACEMMRS	SCAMMER	**ACENPTY**	PATENCY		COUTEAU
ACEMNOR	CREMONA	**ACENRRY**	ERRANCY	**ACEOTUX**	COTEAUX
	ROMANCE	**ACENRSS**	ANCRESS	**ACEPPRR**	CRAPPER
ACEMNOS	ANCOMES		CASERNS	**ACEPPRS**	CAPPERS
ACEMNPS	ENCAMPS	**ACENRST**	CANTERS	**ACEPRRS**	CARPERS
ACEMNRT	CREMANT		CARNETS		SCARPER
ACEMNRW	CREWMAN		NECTARS		SCRAPER
ACEMNSU	ACUMENS		RECANTS	**ACEPRSS**	ESCARPS
ACEMOPR	COMPARE		SCANTER		PARSECS
	COMPEAR		TANRECS		SCRAPES
ACEMOPS	POMACES		TRANCES		SECPARS
ACEMORS	AMORCES	**ACENRSU**	SURANCE		SPACERS
ACEMORU	MORCEAU	**ACENRSV**	CAVERNS	**ACEPRST**	CARPETS
ACEMOSS	COSMEAS		CRAVENS		PREACTS
ACEMOST	CAMOTES	**ACENRSY**	CARNEYS		PRECAST
	COMATES		SCENARY		SPECTRA
ACEMOSU	MUCOSAE	**ACENRSZ**	ZARNECS	**ACEPRSU**	APERCUS
ACEMPRR	CRAMPER	**ACENRTT**	TRANECT		SCAUPER
ACEMPRS	CAMPERS	**ACENRTU**	CENTAUR	**ACEPRTU**	CAPTURE
	SCAMPER		UNCRATE	**ACEPSST**	ASPECTS
ACEMPRT	CRAMPET		UNTRACE	**ACEPSTU**	CUSPATE
ACEMPST	CAMPEST	**ACENRTY**	ENCRATY		TEACUPS
ACEMRSS	SCREAMS		NECTARY	**ACEQRTU**	RACQUET
ACEMRST	MERCATS	**ACENSST**	ASCENTS	**ACEQSSU**	CASQUES
ACEMRSY	CRAMESY		SECANTS		SACQUES
ACEMSSU	CAMUSES		STANCES	**ACEQSTU**	ACQUEST

ACERRRY	RECARRY	**ACFGINR**	FARCING	**ACGHIKN**	HACKING
ACERRSS	CRASSER	**ACFGINS**	FACINGS	**ACGHIMO**	OGHAMIC
	SCARERS	**ACFHIIS**	FIASCHI	**ACGHINR**	ARCHING
	SCARRES	**ACFHIST**	CATFISH		CHAGRIN
ACERRST	CARTERS	**ACFHISU**	FUCHSIA		CHARING
	CRATERS	**ACFHLNU**	FLAUNCH	**ACGHINS**	ACHINGS
	TRACERS	**ACFHNOU**	FAUCHON		CASHING
ACERRSU	CURARES	**ACFHRTU**	FUTHARC		CHASING
ACERRSV	CARVERS	**ACFHRTY**	FRATCHY	**ACGHINT**	GNATHIC
	CRAVERS	**ACFIILN**	FINICAL	**ACGHINW**	CHAWING
ACERRSY	CRAYERS	**ACFIKNN**	FINNACK		CHINWAG
ACERRTT	RETRACT	**ACFIKTY**	TACKIFY	**ACGHIOR**	CHORAGI
ACERRTU	TRACEUR	**ACFILNO**	FOLACIN	**ACGHIPR**	GRAPHIC
ACERRTY	TRACERY	**ACFILNY**	FANCILY	**ACGHIRS**	SCRAIGH
ACERRUV	VERRUCA	**ACFILOY**	COALIFY	**ACGHLTU**	CLAUGHT
ACERRVY	CARVERY	**ACFILRY**	CLARIFY	**ACGHNRU**	GRAUNCH
ACERSST	ACTRESS	**ACFILSS**	FISCALS	**ACGHOST**	GOTCHAS
	CASTERS	**ACFIMOR**	ACIFORM	**ACGHOSU**	GAUCHOS
	RECASTS		FORMICA	**ACGHRRU**	CURRAGH
ACERSSU	ARCUSES	**ACFIMRU**	FUMARIC	**ACGHRSU**	CURAGHS
	CAUSERS	**ACFIMSS**	FASCISM		SCRAUGH
	CESURAS	**ACFINNS**	FINNACS	**ACGIILN**	ALGINIC
	SAUCERS	**ACFINNY**	INFANCY	**ACGIITU**	AUGITIC
	SUCRASE	**ACFINOT**	FACTION	**ACGIJKN**	JACKING
ACERSSV	SCARVES	**ACFINRS**	FARCINS	**ACGIKLN**	CALKING
ACERSSY	CARSEYS	**ACFINRT**	FRANTIC		LACKING
	SCRAYES		INFARCT	**ACGIKNP**	PACKING
ACERSTT	SCATTER		INFRACT	**ACGIKNR**	ARCKING
ACERSTU	ACTURES	**ACFINRY**	CARNIFY		CARKING
	CAUTERS	**ACFIOPY**	OPACIFY		CRAKING
	CRUSTAE	**ACFIOSS**	FIASCOS		RACKING
	CURATES	**ACFIPRY**	CAPRIFY	**ACGIKNS**	CAKINGS
ACERSTY	SECTARY	**ACFIRSY**	SACRIFY		CASKING
ACERTTT	TETRACT		SCARIFY		SACKING
ACERTTU	CURTATE	**ACFISST**	FASCIST	**ACGIKNT**	TACKING
ACERTTX	EXTRACT	**ACFKLRU**	RACKFUL	**ACGIKNV**	VACKING
ACERTTY	CATTERY	**ACFKLSU**	SACKFUL	**ACGIKNY**	YACKING
ACERTUV	CURVATE	**ACFLLOY**	FOCALLY	**ACGILLN**	CALLING
ACERTUX	CURTAXE	**ACFLNOS**	FALCONS	**ACGILLO**	LOGICAL
ACERTUY	CAUTERY		FLACONS	**ACGILMN**	CALMING
ACESSTT	STACTES	**ACFLNSU**	CANFULS	**ACGILMY**	MYALGIC
ACESSTU	CAESTUS		CANSFUL	**ACGILNN**	LANCING
	CUESTAS	**ACFLOPW**	COWFLAP	**ACGILNO**	COALING
ACESSTY	CYTASES	**ACFLOST**	OLFACTS	**ACGILNP**	PLACING
	ECSTASY	**ACFLPSU**	CAPFULS	**ACGILNR**	CARLING
ACESSUY	CAUSEYS	**ACFLRSU**	CARFULS	**ACGILNS**	LACINGS
	CAYUSES	**ACFLRTU**	CARTFUL		SCALING
ACESTTU	ACUTEST	**ACFLRUU**	FURCULA	**ACGILNT**	CATLING
	SCUTATE	**ACFLTTU**	TACTFUL		TALCING
ACESTTY	TESTACY	**ACFLTUY**	FACULTY	**ACGILNU**	CINGULA
ACESTUY	EUSTACY	**ACFMSTU**	FACTUMS		GLUCINA
ACFFHSU	CHAUFFS	**ACFNNOT**	NONFACT	**ACGILNV**	CALVING
ACFFIIT	CAITIFF	**ACFNNUY**	UNFANCY	**ACGILNW**	CLAWING
ACFFIKM	MAFFICK	**ACFNRTU**	FRUCTAN	**ACGILNY**	CLAYING
ACFFILT	AFFLICT	**ACFNSTU**	UNFACTS	**ACGILOS**	CALIGOS
ACFFINS	FANFICS	**ACFORST**	FACTORS	**ACGILOT**	OTALGIC
ACFFINY	FANCIFY		FORCATS	**ACGILRS**	GARLICS
ACFFIRT	TRAFFIC	**ACFORTY**	FACTORY	**ACGIMMN**	CAMMING
ACFFIRY	FARCIFY	**ACFRRTU**	FRACTUR	**ACGIMNO**	COAMING
ACFFLSS	SCLAFFS	**ACFRSTU**	FRACTUS	**ACGIMNP**	CAMPING
ACFFLTU	FACTFUL	**ACGGHIS**	CHIGGAS	**ACGIMNU**	CAUMING
ACFFOST	CASTOFF	**ACGGINR**	GRACING	**ACGINNN**	CANNING
	OFFCAST	**ACGGIOS**	AGOGICS	**ACGINNR**	CRANING
ACFGHIN	CHAFING	**ACGGRSY**	SCRAGGY		RANCING

ACGINNS	CANINGS	**ACHIIKM**	KAMICHI	**ACHIRTY**	CHARITY
ACGINNT	CANTING	**ACHIILS**	ISCHIAL	**ACHISSS**	CHASSIS
ACGINOR	ORGANIC	**ACHIIMS**	CHIASMI	**ACHISST**	SCAITHS
ACGINOS	AGNOSIC	**ACHIINT**	CHIANTI	**ACHISTT**	CATTISH
	ANGICOS	**ACHIIPS**	PACHISI		CHATTIS
ACGINOT	COATING	**ACHIIRV**	CHIVARI		TACHIST
	COTINGA	**ACHIJKS**	HIJACKS	**ACHKKRU**	CHUKKAR
ACGINOX	COAXING	**ACHIJNT**	JACINTH	**ACHKKSU**	CHUKKAS
ACGINPP	CAPPING	**ACHIKOS**	KOCHIAS	**ACHKLST**	KLATSCH
ACGINPR	CARPING	**ACHIKRS**	RICKSHA	**ACHKMMO**	HAMMOCK
	CRAPING	**ACHIKRY**	HAYRICK	**ACHKOPS**	HOPSACK
ACGINPS	SCAPING	**ACHIKSS**	SHICKSA	**ACHKORS**	CHOKRAS
	SPACING	**ACHILLO**	LOCHIAL	**ACHKOSS**	HASSOCK
ACGINRS	ARCINGS	**ACHILLP**	PHALLIC		SHACKOS
	RACINGS	**ACHILLS**	CHALLIS	**ACHKOSW**	WHACKOS
	SACRING	**ACHILLT**	THALLIC	**ACHKOTT**	HATTOCK
	SCARING	**ACHILMO**	MALICHO	**ACHKRSU**	CHUKARS
ACGINRT	CARTING		MOCHILA	**ACHKSTW**	THWACKS
	CRATING	**ACHILMS**	CHIMLAS	**ACHLLOO**	ALCOHOL
	TRACING	**ACHILOR**	CHORIAL	**ACHLLOR**	CHLORAL
ACGINRV	CARVING	**ACHILOS**	SCHOLIA	**ACHLLOS**	CHOLLAS
	CRAVING	**ACHILPS**	CALIPHS	**ACHLLOT**	CHALLOT
ACGINRZ	CRAZING	**ACHILRS**	ARCHILS	**ACHLMOP**	CAMPHOL
ACGINSS	CASINGS		CARLISH	**ACHLMSY**	CHLAMYS
ACGINST	ACTINGS	**ACHILRY**	CHARILY	**ACHLMSZ**	SCHMALZ
	CASTING	**ACHILST**	CHITALS	**ACHLMYY**	ALCHYMY
ACGINSU	CAUSING	**ACHILSY**	CLAYISH	**ACHLNOS**	LOCHANS
	SAUCING	**ACHILWY**	LICHWAY	**ACHLNOY**	HALCYON
ACGINSV	CAVINGS	**ACHIMNO**	MANIHOC	**ACHLNSU**	NUCHALS
ACGINSW	CAWINGS		MOHICAN	**ACHLNTU**	TULCHAN
ACGINTT	CATTING	**ACHIMOS**	CHAMISO		UNLATCH
ACGINUV	VICUGNA		CHAMOIS	**ACHLOPR**	RAPLOCH
ACGIORT	ARGOTIC	**ACHIMOX**	CHAMOIX	**ACHLOPT**	POTLACH
ACGIRST	GASTRIC	**ACHIMRS**	CHARISM	**ACHLORS**	CHORALS
	TRAGICS		CHIMARS		LORCHAS
ACGKLLO	GALLOCK		CHRISMA		SCHOLAR
ACGKMMO	GAMMOCK	**ACHIMSS**	CHIASMS	**ACHLORT**	TROCHAL
ACGKORV	GARVOCK		SCHISMA	**ACHLOSW**	SALCHOW
ACGLLPU	CUPGALL	**ACHIMST**	MASTICH	**ACHLOTY**	ACOLYTH
ACGLNOR	CLANGOR		TACHISM	**ACHLPST**	SPLATCH
ACGLNOY	AGLYCON	**ACHINNU**	UNCHAIN	**ACHLTUZ**	CHALUTZ
ACGLNSU	GLUCANS	**ACHINOP**	APHONIC	**ACHMNOR**	MONARCH
ACGLNSY	GLYCANS	**ACHINOY**	ONYCHIA		NOMARCH
ACGLOSU	CAGOULS	**ACHINPS**	SPINACH	**ACHMNOU**	UNMACHO
ACGLOXY	COXALGY	**ACHINRS**	CHINARS	**ACHMNRU**	UNCHARM
ACGMNOP	CAMPONG	**ACHINRU**	UNCHAIR	**ACHMOPR**	CAMPHOR
ACGNNOR	CRANNOG	**ACHINRZ**	ZARNICH	**ACHMORS**	CHROMAS
ACGNOOT	OCTAGON	**ACHINTX**	XANTHIC		MORCHAS
ACGNORS	GARCONS	**ACHINUV**	CHAUVIN	**ACHMORZ**	MACHZOR
ACGNOSS	GASCONS	**ACHIOPS**	ISOPACH	**ACHMOST**	STOMACH
ACGNOSU	COUGANS	**ACHIOPT**	APHOTIC	**ACHMPTU**	MATCHUP
ACGORRY	GYROCAR	**ACHIORT**	CHARIOT	**ACHMSSU**	SUMACHS
ACGORSU	COUGARS		HARICOT	**ACHMSUW**	CUMSHAW
ACGORUU	COUGUAR	**ACHIOST**	ISOTACH	**ACHNNOS**	CHANSON
ACGOSWY	COGWAYS	**ACHIPPS**	SAPPHIC		NONCASH
ACGSTTU	CATGUTS	**ACHIPST**	HAPTICS	**ACHNOOY**	CHANOYO
ACHHIRS	RHACHIS		PATHICS	**ACHNORS**	ANCHORS
ACHHISV	CHAVISH		SPATHIC		ARCHONS
ACHHLOT	CHALOTH	**ACHIPTU**	CHUPATI		RANCHOS
ACHHMSU	CHUMASH	**ACHIPTW**	WHIPCAT	**ACHNORT**	CHANTOR
ACHHOST	TOSHACH	**ACHIQRU**	CHARQUI	**ACHNOSS**	SANCHOS
ACHHPPU	CHUPPAH	**ACHIQSU**	QUAICHS	**ACHNOST**	CHATONS
ACHHTTT	THATCHT	**ACHIRRT**	TRIARCH	**ACHNOSY**	ONYCHAS
ACHHTTY	THATCHY	**ACHIRTU**	HAIRCUT	**ACHNOTY**	TACHYON

ACHNOUY	CHANOYU
ACHNOVY	ANCHOVY
ACHNPSS	SCHNAPS
ACHNPUY	PAUNCHY
ACHNRTY	CHANTRY
ACHNRUY	RAUNCHY
	UNCHARY
ACHNSTU	CANTHUS
	CHAUNTS
	STAUNCH
ACHNSTY	SNATCHY
ACHOOSS	CASHOOS
ACHOOST	CAHOOTS
ACHOPRS	CARHOPS
	COPRAHS
ACHOPRT	TOPARCH
ACHOPRY	CHARPOY
ACHOPSY	POCHAYS
ACHORRS	CHARROS
ACHORRT	TROCHAR
ACHORST	ORCHATS
ACHORSU	AUROCHS
ACHPPSU	CHUPPAS
ACHPRSS	SCARPHS
ACHPTUZ	CHUTZPA
ACHRSST	SCARTHS
ACHRSTY	STARCHY
ACHRSUU	URACHUS
ACHSSTU	CUSHATS
ACHSSTY	STACHYS
ACHSSUW	CUSHAWS
ACHSTUW	WAUCHTS
ACHSTUY	CYATHUS
ACIIKNN	CANIKIN
ACIIKRS	AIRSICK
ACIILLN	ALLICIN
ACIILMM	MIMICAL
ACIILMS	LAICISM
ACIILNR	CLARINI
ACIILNS	INCISAL
	SALICIN
	SINICAL
ACIILNV	VICINAL
ACIILOV	VILIACO
ACIILPT	APLITIC
ACIILPU	APICULI
ACIILRY	CILIARY
ACIILSS	SILICAS
ACIILST	ITALICS
ACIILSU	ILIACUS
ACIILSV	CLIVIAS
ACIILTY	LAICITY
ACIIMMN	MINICAM
ACIIMMS	MIASMIC
ACIIMNR	CRIMINA
	MINICAR
ACIIMOT	COMITIA
ACIIMST	ISMATIC
	ITACISM
	SIMATIC
ACIINNO	ANIONIC
ACIINNS	NIACINS
ACIINOS	ASINICO
ACIINOV	AVIONIC
ACIINPS	PISCINA
ACIINTT	TITANIC
ACIINUX	AUXINIC
ACIIPPR	PRIAPIC
ACIIPRT	PIRATIC
ACIIRST	SATIRIC
ACIIRTT	TRIATIC
ACIITTX	TAXITIC
ACIJUZZ	JACUZZI
ACIKLLY	ALKYLIC
ACIKLNS	CALKINS
ACIKLOR	AIRLOCK
ACIKLTY	TACKILY
ACIKLWY	WACKILY
ACIKMOO	OOMIACK
ACIKMOT	COMATIK
ACIKMPR	RAMPICK
ACIKMPW	PICKMAW
ACIKMSU	UMIACKS
ACIKNNP	PANNICK
ACIKNPS	PANICKS
ACIKNPY	PANICKY
ACIKNRS	NICKARS
ACIKNST	ANTICKS
	CATKINS
	CATSKIN
ACIKNTT	TINTACK
ACIKOPS	PAIOCKS
ACIKORS	ARKOSIC
ACIKPRT	PATRICK
	TRIPACK
ACIKPSS	ASPICKS
ACIKRST	KARSTIC
ACILLLY	ALLYLIC
ACILLMS	MISCALL
ACILLRY	LYRICAL
ACILLSS	SCILLAS
ACILMNO	LIMACON
	MALONIC
ACILMOP	OILCAMP
ACILMOT	COMITAL
ACILMPS	PLASMIC
	PSALMIC
ACILMPY	CAMPILY
ACILMSU	MUSICAL
ACILNNO	CANNOLI
ACILNNU	UNCINAL
ACILNNY	CANNILY
ACILNOR	CLARINO
	CLARION
ACILNOS	ALNICOS
	OILCANS
ACILNOU	INOCULA
ACILNOY	ACYLOIN
ACILNOZ	CALZONI
ACILNPS	CAPLINS
	INCLASP
ACILNPY	PLIANCY
ACILNRS	CARLINS
ACILNST	CATLINS
	TINCALS
ACILNSU	UNCIALS
ACILNTU	LUNATIC
ACILNTY	ANTICLY
	CANTILY
ACILNUV	VINCULA
ACILOPT	CAPITOL
	COALPIT
	OPTICAL
	TOPICAL
ACILORR	RACLOIR
ACILORV	CORIVAL
ACILOSS	SOCIALS
ACILOST	CITOLAS
	STOICAL
ACILOTV	VOLATIC
	VOLTAIC
ACILOTX	TOXICAL
ACILPRT	CLIPART
ACILPST	PLACITS
	PLASTIC
ACILPSU	SPICULA
ACILPTY	TYPICAL
ACILRSS	CRISSAL
ACILRST	CITRALS
ACILRSU	URACILS
ACILRSY	SCARILY
ACILRTU	CURTAIL
	TRUCIAL
ACILRTY	CLARITY
ACILRVY	VICARLY
ACILRYZ	CRAZILY
ACILSSS	CLASSIS
ACILSSU	CLUSIAS
ACILSUY	SAUCILY
ACILTTY	CATTILY
	TACITLY
ACILTUV	VICTUAL
ACIMMNO	AMMONIC
ACIMNOP	CAMPION
ACIMNOR	MARCONI
	MINORCA
ACIMNOS	ANOSMIC
	CAMIONS
	CONIMAS
	MANIOCS
	MASONIC
ACIMNPU	PANICUM
ACIMNRS	ARCMINS
	NARCISM
ACIMNRT	MANTRIC
ACIMNRU	CRANIUM
	CUMARIN
ACIMNTT	CATMINT
ACIMOOS	OOMIACS
ACIMOPT	APOMICT
	POTAMIC
ACIMOSS	MOSAICS
ACIMOST	ATOMICS
	MATICOS
	OSMATIC
	SOMATIC
ACIMOSV	VOMICAS
ACIMPRT	CRAMPIT
	PTARMIC
ACIMPRY	PRIMACY
ACIMPSS	SCAMPIS
	SPASMIC

Seven-letter anagrams

ACIMPST	IMPACTS	ACIORTT	CITATOR		UNTACKS		
ACIMRSS	RACISMS		RICOTTA	ACKOPRR	PARROCK		
ACIMRST	MATRICS	ACIOSST	SCOTIAS	ACKOPSY	YAPOCKS		
ACIMRSY	MYRICAS	ACIOSSV	OVISACS	ACKORRT	TARROCK		
ACIMRSZ	CZARISM	ACIPRSS	CASSPIR	ACKOSTW	TOWSACK		
ACIMSST	MASTICS	ACIPRSY	PISCARY	ACKOWZZ	WAZZOCK		
	MISACTS	ACIPRTT	TIPCART	ACKPSSY	SKYCAPS		
	MISCAST	ACIPRVV	PRIVACY	ACKPSTU	STACKUP		
ACIMSTT	TACTISM	ACIPSST	SPASTIC	ACLLLOY	LOCALLY		
ACINNOT	ACTINON	ACIPSTT	TIPCATS	ACLLOOR	COROLLA		
	CANTION	ACIPTUY	PAUCITY	ACLLOOS	ALCOOLS		
	CONTAIN	ACIQRTU	QUARTIC	ACLLOPS	CALLOPS		
ACINNOZ	CANZONI	ACIQSTU	ACQUIST		SCALLOP		
ACINNST	INCANTS		ACQUITS	ACLLORS	COLLARS		
	STANNIC	ACIRRSS	SIRCARS	ACLLORU	LOCULAR		
ACINNSY	CYANINS	ACIRRST	TRICARS	ACLLOSU	CALLOUS		
ACINNTU	ANNICUT	ACIRRSU	CURARIS	ACLLOSW	CALLOWS		
ACINOPT	CAPTION	ACIRSST	RACISTS	ACLLOTU	OUTCALL		
	PACTION		SACRIST	ACLLOVY	VOCALLY		
ACINOQU	COQUINA	ACIRSSU	CUIRASS	ACLLRYY	ACRYLYL		
ACINORR	CARRION	ACIRSTT	ASTRICT	ACLLSUY	CULLAYS		
ACINORS	SARONIC	ACIRSTU	URTICAS	ACLMNOO	LOCOMAN		
ACINORT	CAROTIN	ACIRSTW	TWISCAR	ACLMNPU	UNCLAMP		
	CORTINA	ACIRSTY	SATYRIC	ACLMNUY	CALUMNY		
ACINORV	CORVINA	ACIRSTZ	CZARIST	ACLMOPS	COPALMS		
ACINOSS	CAISSON	ACIRTUY	RAUCITY	ACLMORS	CLAMORS		
	CASINOS	ACISSTT	STATICS	ACLMORU	CLAMOUR		
	CASSINO	ACISSTU	CASUIST	ACLMOSU	MUCOSAL		
ACINOST	ACTIONS	ACISTTU	CATSUIT	ACLMSTU	TALCUMS		
	ATONICS	ACISTUV	VACUIST	ACLMSUU	LUCUMAS		
	CATIONS	ACITUVY	VACUITY	ACLMSUY	MASCULY		
ACINOSU	ACINOUS	ACJKKSY	SKYJACK	ACLNNOO	NONCOLA		
ACINOSY	SYCONIA	ACJKLOW	LOCKJAW	ACLNOOR	CORONAL		
ACINOTT	TACTION	ACJKNNO	JANNOCK	ACLNOOT	COOLANT		
ACINOTU	AUCTION	ACJKOPS	PAJOCKS		OCTANOL		
	CAUTION	ACJKOPT	JACKPOT	ACLNOOV	VOLCANO		
ACINPRT	CANTRIP	ACJLORU	JOCULAR	ACLNORU	CORNUAL		
ACINPRU	PURANIC	ACJMNTU	MUNTJAC		COURLAN		
ACINPRY	CYPRIAN	ACJPTUU	CAJUPUT	ACLNOSS	CLASSON		
ACINPSS	PANISCS	ACKKLOY	KOLACKY	ACLNOST	COLTANS		
ACINPST	CATNIPS	ACKLLOP	POLLACK	ACLNOSX	CLAXONS		
ACINQTU	QUANTIC	ACKLLOY	LAYLOCK	ACLNOUV	UNVOCAL		
ACINRSS	ARCSINS	ACKLLSY	SLACKLY	ACLNPSU	UNCLASP		
ACINRST	NARCIST	ACKLMNO	LOCKMAN	ACLNRTU	TRUNCAL		
ACINRSU	CRUSIAN	ACKLMOR	ARMLOCK	ACLNSTY	SCANTLY		
ACINRTT	TANTRIC		LOCKRAM	ACLNSUV	VULCANS		
ACINRTU	CURTAIN	ACKLNOU	UNCLOAK	ACLOOPP	ALCOPOP		
	TURACIN	ACKLNRY	CRANKLY	ACLOOPR	CARPOOL		
ACINSTU	ANICUTS	ACKLOOR	OARLOCK	ACLOORT	LOCATOR		
	NAUTICS	ACKLORV	LAVROCK	ACLOOSZ	ZOCALOS		
ACINSUV	VICUNAS	ACKLORW	WARLOCK	ACLOPRT	CALTROP		
ACIOPRS	PICAROS	ACKLORY	ROCKLAY		PROCTAL		
	PROSAIC	ACKLOSS	LASSOCK	ACLOPRU	COPULAR		
ACIOPRT	APRICOT	ACKMMMO	MAMMOCK		CUPOLAR		
	APROTIC	ACKMNOS	SOCKMAN	ACLOPSU	COPULAS		
	PAROTIC	ACKMNRU	RUCKMAN		CUPOLAS		
	PATRICO	ACKMOST	STOMACK		SCOPULA		
ACIOPST	COPITAS	ACKMOTT	MATTOCK	ACLOPSY	CALYPSO		
	PSOATIC	ACKNNOW	ACKNOWN	ACLOPTY	POLYACT		
ACIOPTT	APTOTIC	ACKNOSW	ACKNOWS	ACLORRS	CORRALS		
ACIOPTY	OPACITY	ACKNPRS	PRANCKS	ACLORST	CARLOTS		
ACIORRS	CORSAIR	ACKNPSU	UNPACKS		CROTALS		
ACIORSU	CARIOUS	ACKNRTU	UNTRACK		SCROTAL		
	CURIOSA	ACKNSTU	UNSTACK	ACLORSU	CAROLUS		

	OCULARS	ACNORSU	NACROUS		READDED
	OSCULAR	ACNORSY	CRAYONS	ADDDEFL	FADDLED
	RUCOLAS	ACNORTT	CONTRAT	ADDDEGL	GLADDED
ACLORTY	ACTORLY	ACNORTU	COURANT	ADDDEIL	DAIDLED
ACLORUV	VOCULAR	ACNOSSZ	SCAZONS	ADDDEIS	DADDIES
ACLORYZ	CORYZAL	ACNOSTT	OCTANTS	ADDDEIW	WADDIED
ACLOSST	COSTALS	ACNOSTU	CONATUS	ADDDELN	DANDLED
ACLOSTU	LOCUSTA		NOCTUAS	ADDDELP	PADDLED
	TALCOUS		TOUCANS	ADDDELR	RADDLED
ACLOSTW	COTWALS	ACNOSTW	SNOWCAT	ADDDELS	DADDLES
ACLPRTY	CRYPTAL	ACNPRSY	SYNCARP		SADDLED
ACLPRUU	CUPULAR	ACNRRSU	CURRANS	ADDDELW	DAWDLED
ACLRSSW	SCRAWLS	ACNRRTU	CURRANT		WADDLED
ACLRSSY	CRASSLY	ACNRSTU	UNCARTS	ADDDELY	ADDEDLY
ACLRSTU	CRUSTAL	ACNRSUY	UNSCARY	ADDDENO	DEODAND
	CURTALS	ACNRSWY	SCRAWNY	ADDDENS	ADDENDS
ACLRSTY	CRYSTAL	ACNRTUY	TRUANCY	ADDDENU	UNADDED
ACLRSWY	SCRAWLY	ACNRUYZ	UNCRAZY	ADDDEQU	QUADDED
ACLSSTU	CUTLASS	ACOOPRR	CORPORA	ADDDGIN	DADDING
ACMNOPR	CRAMPON	ACOOPRT	ROOTCAP	ADDDHOY	HODADDY
ACMNOPY	COMPANY	ACOOPSU	OPACOUS	ADDDOOS	DOODADS
ACMNORS	MACRONS	ACOOPTT	TOPCOAT	ADDEEEM	ADEEMED
ACMNORY	ACRONYM	ACOORTU	TOURACO	ADDEEEY	DEADEYE
ACMNOSS	MASCONS	ACOOSTV	OCTAVOS	ADDEEFM	DEFAMED
ACMNSTU	SANCTUM	ACOPPRR	PROCARP	ADDEEGR	DEGRADE
ACMOOST	SCOTOMA	ACOPPRS	COPPRAS	ADDEEHL	HEALDED
ACMOPRT	COMPART	ACOPRRT	CARPORT	ADDEEHN	HEADEND
ACMOPSS	COMPASS	ACOPRST	CAPTORS	ADDEEHR	ADHERED
ACMOPST	COMPAST	ACOPSTU	UPCOAST		REDHEAD
ACMOPTU	CAMPOUT	ACOPSTW	COWPATS	ADDEEHS	DEASHED
ACMORRS	CARROMS	ACORRST	CARROTS	ADDEEIR	DEAIRED
ACMORST	COMARTS		TROCARS		READIED
ACMORTW	CATWORM	ACORRTT	TRACTOR	ADDEEIT	IDEATED
ACMOSST	MASCOTS	ACORRTU	CURATOR	ADDEEKN	KNEADED
	SCAMTOS	ACORRTY	CARROTY	ADDEEKR	DAKERED
ACMOSSU	MUCOSAS	ACORSST	CASTORS	ADDEELM	MEDALED
ACMOSTT	TOMCATS		COSTARS	ADDEELN	DELENDA
ACMOSTU	MOTUCAS	ACORSSU	SARCOUS		LADENED
ACMQTUU	CUMQUAT		SOUCARS	ADDEELP	PEDALED
ACMRSSU	SACRUMS	ACORSSW	SOWCARS		PLEADED
ACMRSSW	SCRAWMS	ACORSTT	COTTARS	ADDEELS	DELEADS
ACMSSTU	MUSCATS	ACORSTU	CUATROS	ADDEELT	DELATED
ACMSTUU	MUTUCAS		SURCOAT	ADDEELY	DELAYED
ACMSUUV	VACUUMS		TURACOS	ADDEEMN	AMENDED
ACNNNOS	CANNONS	ACORSTV	CAVORTS		DEADMEN
ACNNNUY	UNCANNY	ACORSTX	OXCARTS	ADDEEMR	DREAMED
ACNNORY	CANONRY	ACORSTY	CASTORY	ADDEEMS	ADDEEMS
ACNNOST	CANTONS	ACORSUU	RAUCOUS	ADDEENS	DEADENS
ACNNOSY	CANYONS	ACORSYZ	CORYZAS	ADDEENV	ADVENED
	SONANCY	ACORTUU	TURACOU		DAVENED
ACNNRSY	SCRANNY	ACOSSZZ	SCOZZAS	ADDEENY	DENAYED
ACNOOPS	POONACS	ACOSTTU	OUTACTS	ADDEEOT	DEODATE
ACNOORS	CORONAS		OUTCAST	ADDEERR	DREADER
	RACOONS	ACOSUUV	VACUOUS	ADDEERS	DEADERS
ACNOORT	CARTOON	ACPPRSY	SCRAPPY	ADDEERT	DERATED
	CORANTO	ACPRSSW	SCRAWPS		REDATED
ACNOPSW	SNOWCAP	ACPSSTU	CATSUPS		TREADED
ACNORRS	RANCORS		UPCASTS	ADDEERY	DERAYED
ACNORRU	RANCOUR	ACPSTUU	USUCAPT		YEARDED
ACNORRY	CARRYON	ACRRSTU	CRATURS	ADDEEST	DEADEST
ACNORST	CANTORS	ACRSTTU	TRACTUS		SEDATED
	CARTONS	ADDDDEL	DADDLED		STEADED
	CONTRAS	ADDDDOR	DODDARD	ADDEEVW	ADVEWED
	CRATONS	ADDDEER	DREADED	ADDEEWX	DEWAXED

Seven-letter anagrams

ADDEFHN	HANDFED	**ADDEISY**	DAYSIDE	**ADDERST**	ADDREST
ADDEFIR	FADDIER	**ADDEITU**	AUDITED		RADDEST
ADDEFLS	FADDLES	**ADDEJLY**	JADEDLY	**ADDERSW**	SWARDED
ADDEFLY	FADEDLY	**ADDEJNU**	UNJADED		WADDERS
ADDEFNU	UNFADED	**ADDEJRU**	ADJURED	**ADDERSY**	DRYADES
ADDEFRT	DRAFTED	**ADDEKLR**	DARKLED	**ADDERTT**	DRATTED
ADDEFRU	DEFRAUD	**ADDELLU**	ALLUDED	**ADDESST**	SADDEST
ADDEFRW	DWARFED		DUALLED	**ADDESTU**	ADUSTED
ADDEGGL	DAGGLED	**ADDELMW**	DWALMED		SUDATED
ADDEGGR	DRAGGED	**ADDELNR**	DANDLER	**ADDFHIS**	FADDISH
ADDEGHO	GODHEAD	**ADDELNS**	DANDLES	**ADDFIMS**	FADDISM
ADDEGIL	GLADDIE	**ADDELNU**	UNLADED	**ADDFINY**	DANDIFY
ADDEGIN	DEADING	**ADDELPP**	DAPPLED	**ADDFIST**	FADDIST
ADDEGJU	ADJUDGE	**ADDELPR**	PADDLER	**ADDGGIN**	GADDING
ADDEGLN	DANGLED	**ADDELPS**	PADDLES	**ADDGHIN**	HADDING
	GLADDEN	**ADDELRS**	LADDERS	**ADDGIIR**	DIAGRID
ADDEGLR	GLADDER		RADDLES	**ADDGILN**	ADDLING
ADDEGRS	GADDERS		SADDLER	**ADDGIMN**	MADDING
ADDEGRU	GUARDED	**ADDELRT**	DARTLED	**ADDGINO**	DADOING
ADDEHIR	DIEHARD	**ADDELRW**	DAWDLER	**ADDGINP**	PADDING
	DIHEDRA		DRAWLED	**ADDGINR**	RADDING
ADDEHIS	HADDIES		WADDLER	**ADDGINS**	SADDING
ADDEHKS	KEDDAHS	**ADDELRY**	DREADLY	**ADDGINU**	DAUDING
ADDEHLN	HANDLED		LADDERY	**ADDGINW**	DAWDING
ADDEHLS	DALEDHS	**ADDELSS**	SADDLES		WADDING
ADDEHOR	HOARDED	**ADDELST**	STADDLE	**ADDGIOS**	GADOIDS
ADDEHRS	SHARDED	**ADDELSW**	DAWDLES	**ADDGIPY**	GIDDYAP
ADDEHST	HADDEST		SWADDLE	**ADDGLNO**	GLADDON
ADDEIIK	DIDAKEI		WADDLES	**ADDGMNO**	GODDAMN
ADDEIIM	DIAMIDE	**ADDELTW**	TWADDLE	**ADDGMOS**	GODDAMS
ADDEIIS	DAISIED	**ADDELTY**	DATEDLY	**ADDGOOS**	OGDOADS
ADDEILL	DALLIED	**ADDELYZ**	DAZEDLY	**ADDGOOW**	DAGWOOD
	DIALLED	**ADDELZZ**	DAZZLED	**ADDGORW**	GODWARD
ADDEILP	PLAIDED	**ADDEMMR**	DRAMMED	**ADDGOSY**	DOGDAYS
ADDEILR	DIEDRAL	**ADDEMMW**	DWAMMED	**ADDHIKS**	KADDISH
	DRAILED	**ADDEMNS**	DEMANDS	**ADDHILS**	LADDISH
ADDEILS	DAIDLES		MADDENS	**ADDHIMS**	MADDISH
	LADDIES	**ADDEMNU**	MAUNDED	**ADDHINP**	DAPHNID
ADDEILT	DILATED	**ADDEMOP**	POMADED	**ADDHISS**	SADDISH
ADDEIMR	ADMIRED	**ADDEMRS**	MADDERS		SIDDHAS
	MARDIED	**ADDEMRY**	DRAMEDY	**ADDHITY**	HYDATID
ADDEIMS	DIADEMS	**ADDEMST**	MADDEST	**ADDHLOO**	LADHOOD
ADDEIMX	ADMIXED	**ADDEMUW**	DWAUMED	**ADDHOOS**	DOODAHS
ADDEINO	ADENOID	**ADDENOR**	ADORNED	**ADDHOTY**	ATHODYD
ADDEINP	PANDIED	**ADDENOT**	DONATED	**ADDHSSU**	SADDHUS
ADDEINR	DANDIER		NODATED	**ADDIINS**	DISDAIN
	DRAINED	**ADDENOU**	DUODENA	**ADDIIPS**	DIAPSID
ADDEINS	DANDIES	**ADDENPU**	PUDENDA	**ADDIKST**	TSADDIK
	SDAINED	**ADDENRS**	DANDERS	**ADDIKSZ**	ZADDIKS
ADDEINT	NIDATED	**ADDENRT**	DRANTED	**ADDIKTY**	KATYDID
ADDEINU	UNAIDED	**ADDENRU**	DAUNDER	**ADDIKTZ**	TZADDIK
ADDEINV	INVADED	**ADDENSS**	DESANDS	**ADDILMN**	MIDLAND
	VIDENDA		SADDENS	**ADDILNY**	DANDILY
ADDEIOR	RADIOED	**ADDENSU**	ASUDDEN	**ADDILOS**	DISLOAD
ADDEIOT	IODATED	**ADDENSY**	SDAYNED	**ADDIMNO**	DIAMOND
	TOADIED	**ADDENTU**	DAUNTED	**ADDIMOR**	DIADROM
ADDEIOV	AVOIDED		UNDATED	**ADDIMRS**	DIRDAMS
ADDEIPS	PADDIES	**ADDEOPT**	ADOPTED	**ADDIMSS**	MISADDS
ADDEIRR	ARRIDED	**ADDEORS**	DEODARS	**ADDIMSY**	DISMAYD
ADDEIRT	TARDIED	**ADDEOSS**	SADDOES		MIDDAYS
ADDEIST	TADDIES	**ADDEPPR**	DRAPPED	**ADDINOR**	ANDROID
ADDEISV	ADVISED	**ADDEPRS**	PADDERS	**ADDINRY**	DIANDRY
ADDEISW	SWADDIE	**ADDEPTU**	UPDATED	**ADDIPRS**	DISPRAD
	WADDIES	**ADDERSS**	ADDRESS	**ADDIQST**	TSADDIQ

ADDIQTZ	TZADDIQ	ENRAGED	SEASIDE
ADDIRZZ	DIZZARD	GRANDEE	**ADEEIST** IDEATES
ADDLLRU	DULLARD	GRENADE	**ADEEISV** ADVISEE
ADDLNRY	DRYLAND	**ADEEGNT** AGENTED	**ADEEITU** AUDITEE
ADDLOOS	SOLDADO	NEGATED	**ADEEITV** DEVIATE
ADDLTWY	TWADDLY	**ADEEGNV** AVENGED	**ADEEJSY** DEEJAYS
ADDMNOS	DODMANS	VENDAGE	**ADEEKNP** KNEEPAD
	ODDSMAN	**ADEEGOT** DOGEATE	**ADEEKNR** KNEADER
ADDMOOS	ADDOOMS	GOATEED	NAKEDER
ADDNNOR	DONNARD	**ADEEGPR** PREAGED	**ADEEKNS** SNEAKED
ADDOORS	DORADOS	**ADEEGRR** REGRADE	**ADEEKNW** WAKENED
ADDOPSY	DASYPOD	**ADEEGRS** DRAGEES	**ADEEKRS** DEKARES
ADDORST	DOTARDS	GREASED	SKEARED
ADDOSTU	OUTADDS	**ADEEGRU** GUARDEE	**ADEEKRW** REWAKED
ADDQSUY	SQUADDY	**ADEEGRV** GREAVED	WREAKED
ADEEEFY	FEDAYEE	**ADEEGRW** RAGWEED	**ADEEKTW** TWEAKED
ADEEELS	EASELED	WAGERED	**ADEEKWY** WEEKDAY
ADEEELV	DELEAVE	**ADEEGSS** DEGASES	**ADEELLP** LAPELED
ADEEEMN	DEMEANE	**ADEEHIR** HEADIER	**ADEELLS** ALLSEED
ADEEERR	ARREEDE	**ADEEHJS** HADJEES	**ADEELLY** ALLEYED
ADEEERX	EXEDRAE	**ADEEHLR** HEDERAL	**ADEELMM** MELAMED
ADEEESW	SEAWEED	**ADEEHLS** LEASHED	**ADEELMN** LEADMEN
ADEEFGU	FEAGUED	SHEALED	**ADEELMP** EMPALED
ADEEFHS	SHEAFED	**ADEEHLX** EXHALED	**ADEELMR** EMERALD
ADEEFIR	AREFIED	**ADEEHMN** HEADMEN	**ADEELMS** MEASLED
	FEDARIE	**ADEEHNN** HENNAED	**ADEELMT** MEDALET
ADEEFKR	FREAKED	**ADEEHNS** DASHEEN	METALED
ADEEFLN	ENDLEAF	**ADEEHNT** NETHEAD	**ADEELMU** AEMULED
ADEEFLR	FEDERAL	**ADEEHNV** HAVENED	**ADEELMY** YEALMED
ADEEFLS	DEFLEAS	**ADEEHPR** EPHEDRA	**ADEELNP** DEPLANE
ADEEFLT	DEFLATE	**ADEEHRR** ADHERER	PANELED
ADEEFMR	DEFAMER	REHEARD	**ADEELNR** LEARNED
ADEEFMS	DEFAMES	**ADEEHRS** ADHERES	**ADEELNS** LEADENS
ADEEFNS	DEAFENS	HEADERS	**ADEELNT** EDENTAL
ADEEFPR	PREFADE	HEARSED	LATENED
ADEEFRT	DRAFTEE	HEDERAS	**ADEELOS** ELODEAS
ADEEFRW	WAFERED	SHEARED	**ADEELPR** PEARLED
ADEEFST	DEAFEST	**ADEEHRT** EARTHED	PEDALER
	DEFASTE	HEARTED	PLEADER
	DEFEATS	**ADEEHRV** HAVERED	REPLEAD
	FEASTED	**ADEEHRX** EXHEDRA	**ADEELPS** DELAPSE
ADEEGGH	EGGHEAD	**ADEEHSS** DEASHES	ELAPSED
ADEEGGL	ALEGGED	**ADEEHST** HEADSET	PLEASED
ADEEGGN	ENGAGED	**ADEEHSV** SHEAVED	SEPALED
ADEEGLL	ALLEDGE	**ADEEHSX** HEXADES	**ADEELPT** PETALED
	ALLEGED	**ADEEHSY** HAYSEED	PLEATED
ADEEGLM	GLEAMED	**ADEEIJT** JADEITE	**ADEELQU** EQUALED
ADEEGLN	ANGELED	**ADEEILM** EMAILED	**ADEELRS** DEALERS
	GELANDE	LIMEADE	LEADERS
	GLEANED	**ADEEILN** ALIENED	REDEALS
ADEEGLR	LAGERED	DELAINE	**ADEELRT** ALERTED
	REGALED	**ADEEILR** LEADIER	ALTERED
ADEEGLT	GELATED	**ADEEILS** AEDILES	REDEALT
	LEGATED	DEISEAL	RELATED
	TEAGLED	**ADEEILY** EYELIAD	TREADLE
ADEEGLU	LEAGUED	**ADEEIMN** DEMAINE	**ADEELRV** RAVELED
ADEEGLV	GAVELED	**ADEEIMT** MEDIATE	**ADEELRW** LEEWARD
ADEEGLZ	DEGLAZE	**ADEEINN** ADENINE	**ADEELRX** RELAXED
ADEEGMN	ENDGAME	**ADEEINS** ANISEED	**ADEELRY** DELAYER
	MANEGED	**ADEEIRR** READIER	LAYERED
	MENAGED	**ADEEIRS** DEARIES	RELAYED
ADEEGMS	DEGAMES	READIES	**ADEELST** DELATES
ADEEGNR	ANGERED	**ADEEIRW** WEARIED	STEALED
	DERANGE	**ADEEISS** DISEASE	**ADEELSV** SLEAVED

Seven-letter anagrams

ADEELSW	SWEALED		REPAVED	**ADEFGGL**	FLAGGED
ADEELTT	LADETTE	**ADEEPSS**	PESADES	**ADEFGGR**	FRAGGED
ADEELTV	VALETED	**ADEEPTX**	EXAPTED	**ADEFGLN**	FANGLED
	VELATED	**ADEEQRU**	QUAERED		FLANGED
ADEELTX	EXALTED	**ADEEQTU**	EQUATED	**ADEFGNS**	DEFANGS
ADEELTZ	TEAZLED	**ADEERRR**	DREARER	**ADEFGOR**	FORAGED
ADEELUV	DEVALUE	**ADEERRS**	DREARES	**ADEFGOT**	FAGOTED
ADEELYZ	LAYDEEZ		READERS	**ADEFGOU**	FOUGADE
ADEEMNR	AMENDER		REDEARS	**ADEFGRS**	DEFRAGS
	ENARMED		REDSEAR	**ADEFGRT**	GRAFTED
	MEANDER		REREADS	**ADEFHIS**	DEAFISH
	REAMEND	**ADEERRT**	RETREAD	**ADEFHIT**	FAITHED
	REEDMAN		TREADER	**ADEFHLS**	FLASHED
	RENAMED	**ADEERRV**	AVERRED	**ADEFHLU**	HEADFUL
ADEEMNS	AMENDES	**ADEERRW**	REDWARE	**ADEFHRW**	WHARFED
	DEMEANS	**ADEERSS**	RESEDAS	**ADEFHST**	SHAFTED
	SEEDMAN	**ADEERST**	DEAREST	**ADEFIKL**	FADLIKE
ADEEMNT	ENTAMED		DERATES	**ADEFILL**	FLAILED
ADEEMNY	DEMAYNE		ESTRADE	**ADEFILS**	DISLEAF
ADEEMOS	OEDEMAS		REASTED	**ADEFIMN**	INFAMED
ADEEMPR	EMPARED		REDATES	**ADEFIMS**	DISFAME
	PREMADE		SEDATER	**ADEFINR**	FRIANDE
ADEEMRR	DREAMER		STEARED	**ADEFINS**	FADEINS
	REARMED		TASERED	**ADEFINT**	DEFIANT
	REDREAM	**ADEERSV**	ADVERSE		FAINTED
ADEEMRS	REMADES		EVADERS	**ADEFIRS**	FARSIDE
	REMEADS	**ADEERSW**	DRAWEES		FRAISED
	SMEARED		RESAWED	**ADEFIST**	DAFTIES
ADEEMRT	REMATED	**ADEERTT**	ARETTED		FADIEST
ADEEMST	STEAMED		TREATED	**ADEFITX**	FIXATED
ADEEMSU	MEDUSAE	**ADEERTV**	AVERTED	**ADEFKLN**	FANKLED
ADEEMSW	MAWSEED		TAVERED		FLANKED
ADEEMTW	MATWEED	**ADEERTW**	DEWATER	**ADEFKNR**	FRANKED
ADEEMWY	MAYWEED		TARWEED	**ADEFKNU**	UNFAKED
ADEENNS	ENNEADS		WATERED	**ADEFLLN**	ELFLAND
ADEENNX	ANNEXED	**ADEERTX**	RETAXED	**ADEFLLW**	DEWFALL
ADEENPS	SNEAPED	**ADEERVW**	WAVERED	**ADEFLMM**	FLAMMED
	SPEANED	**ADEERWX**	REWAXED	**ADEFLNN**	FENLAND
ADEENRS	DEANERS	**ADEESST**	SEDATES	**ADEFLOR**	ALFREDO
	ENDEARS	**ADEESSX**	AXSEEDS	**ADEFLOT**	FLOATED
ADEENRU	UNEARED	**ADEESSY**	ESSAYED	**ADEFLPP**	FLAPPED
ADEENRV	RAVENED	**ADEESTT**	ESTATED	**ADEFLRS**	FARDELS
ADEENRY	DEANERY	**ADEESTU**	SAUTEED	**ADEFLRU**	DAREFUL
	RENAYED	**ADEESTW**	SWEATED	**ADEFLTT**	FLATTED
	YEAREND	**ADEESTY**	YEASTED	**ADEFLTU**	DEFAULT
	YEARNED	**ADEESVY**	SAVEYED		FAULTED
ADEENST	STANDEE	**ADEESWX**	DEWAXES	**ADEFMNU**	UNFAMED
	STEANED	**ADEETUX**	EXUDATE	**ADEFMOS**	DEFOAMS
ADEENSV	ADVENES	**ADEEWWX**	WAXWEED	**ADEFNRS**	FARDENS
ADEENSW	DEEWANS	**ADEFFFL**	FLAFFED		SNARFED
ADEENTT	DENTATE	**ADEFFGR**	GRAFFED	**ADEFNSU**	SNAFUED
ADEEOPT	ADOPTEE	**ADEFFIN**	AFFINED		UNDEAFS
ADEEORS	OREADES	**ADEFFIP**	PIAFFED	**ADEFNUZ**	UNFAZED
ADEEORW	OARWEED	**ADEFFIR**	DAFFIER	**ADEFOOS**	SEAFOOD
ADEEPPR	PAPERED	**ADEFFIS**	DAFFIES	**ADEFORS**	FEDORAS
ADEEPRS	PREASED	**ADEFFIX**	AFFIXED	**ADEFORV**	FAVORED
	RESPADE	**ADEFFLM**	MAFFLED	**ADEFORY**	FEODARY
	SPEARED	**ADEFFLO**	LEADOFF		FORAYED
ADEEPRT	ADEPTER	**ADEFFLR**	RAFFLED	**ADEFOTU**	FADEOUT
	PREDATE	**ADEFFLW**	WAFFLED	**ADEFPPR**	FRAPPED
	RETAPED	**ADEFFNY**	NYAFFED	**ADEFPRR**	PREFARD
	TAPERED	**ADEFFQU**	QUAFFED	**ADEFRRT**	DRAFTER
ADEEPRV	DEPRAVE	**ADEFFST**	STAFFED		REDRAFT
	PERVADE	**ADEFFUW**	WAUFFED	**ADEFRRW**	DWARFER

ADEFRST	STRAFED		GRAINED	ADEGNRT	DRAGNET
ADEFRSU	FADEURS		READING		GRANTED
ADEFRSW	SWARFED	ADEGINS	AGNISED	ADEGNRU	ENGUARD
ADEFRSY	DEFRAYS	ADEGINV	DEAVING		RAUNGED
ADEFRUY	FEUDARY		EVADING	ADEGNRW	WRANGED
ADEFSTT	DAFTEST	ADEGINW	WINDAGE	ADEGNST	STANGED
ADEGGGL	GAGGLED	ADEGINY	YEADING	ADEGNSU	AUGENDS
ADEGGHL	HAGGLED	ADEGINZ	AGNIZED	ADEGNTU	GAUNTED
ADEGGHS	SHAGGED	ADEGIOT	GODETIA		UNGATED
ADEGGIR	DAGGIER	ADEGIRS	AGRISED	ADEGNTW	TWANGED
ADEGGIS	GADGIES	ADEGIRT	TRIAGED	ADEGNUW	UNWAGED
ADEGGIU	GAUDGIE	ADEGIRU	GAUDIER	ADEGORS	DOGEARS
	GUIDAGE	ADEGIRZ	AGRIZED	ADEGORT	GAROTED
ADEGGLR	DRAGGLE	ADEGIST	AGISTED	ADEGORW	DOWAGER
	GARGLED	ADEGISU	AGUISED		WORDAGE
	RAGGLED		GAUDIES	ADEGOSS	DOSAGES
ADEGGLS	DAGGLES	ADEGISV	VISAGED		SEADOGS
	SLAGGED	ADEGIUV	VIDUAGE	ADEGOST	DOGATES
ADEGGLW	WAGGLED	ADEGIUZ	AGUIZED		DOTAGES
ADEGGMO	DEMAGOG	ADEGJLN	JANGLED	ADEGOTT	TOGATED
ADEGGNS	SNAGGED	ADEGLLU	ULLAGED	ADEGOVY	VOYAGED
ADEGGOP	PEDAGOG	ADEGLMN	MANGLED	ADEGPRS	GRASPED
ADEGGPS	SPAGGED	ADEGLMR	MALGRED		SPADGER
ADEGGRR	DRAGGER	ADEGLMU	GLAUMED		SPARGED
ADEGGRS	DAGGERS	ADEGLNN	ENDLANG	ADEGPRU	UPGRADE
ADEGGRY	RAGGEDY	ADEGLNR	DANGLER	ADEGPUZ	UPGAZED
ADEGGST	GADGETS		GNARLED	ADEGRRS	GRADERS
	STAGGED	ADEGLNS	DANGLES		REGARDS
ADEGGSW	SWAGGED		GLANDES	ADEGRRU	GUARDER
ADEGGTY	GADGETY		LAGENDS	ADEGRSS	GRASSED
ADEGHIN	HEADING		SLANGED	ADEGRST	RADGEST
ADEGHIR	HAGRIDE	ADEGLNT	TANGLED	ADEGRSU	DESUGAR
	HEADRIG	ADEGLNU	LANGUED		SUGARED
ADEGHIS	HIDAGES	ADEGLNW	WANGLED	ADEGRTY	GYRATED
ADEGHJU	JUGHEAD	ADEGLOP	GALOPED		TRAGEDY
ADEGHLU	LAUGHED	ADEGLOT	GLOATED	ADEGRUU	AUGURED
ADEGHMO	HOMAGED	ADEGLPU	PLAGUED	ADEGRUY	GAUDERY
ADEGHNP	PHANGED	ADEGLRS	DARGLES	ADEGRYZ	AGRYZED
ADEGHNS	GNASHED	ADEGLRU	RAGULED	ADEGSSU	DEGAUSS
	HAGDENS	ADEGLRY	GRADELY	ADEHHKS	KHEDAHS
ADEGHNW	WHANGED	ADEGLSS	GLASSED	ADEHHOP	HOPHEAD
ADEGHOR	HAGRODE	ADEGLTY	DALGYTE	ADEHHOT	HOTHEAD
ADEGHPR	GRAPHED	ADEGMNS	GADSMEN	ADEHHSS	SHASHED
ADEGHST	GHASTED	ADEGMNU	AGENDUM	ADEHIJS	JEHADIS
ADEGHUW	WAUGHED		GUDEMAN	ADEHIKS	DASHEKI
ADEGILL	GALLIED	ADEGMOP	MEGAPOD	ADEHIKV	KHEDIVA
ADEGILN	ALIGNED	ADEGMRU	MAUGRED	ADEHILN	HIELAND
	DEALING	ADEGNNO	NONAGED		INHALED
	LEADING	ADEGNNU	DUNNAGE	ADEHILP	HELIPAD
ADEGILO	GEOIDAL	ADEGNOP	PONDAGE	ADEHILS	HALIDES
ADEGILR	GLADIER	ADEGNOR	GROANED	ADEHILY	HEADILY
	GLAIRED	ADEGNOS	SONDAGE	ADEHIMO	HAEMOID
ADEGILS	SILAGED	ADEGNOT	TANGOED	ADEHINP	HEADPIN
ADEGILT	LIGATED	ADEGNOV	DOGVANE		PINHEAD
	TAIGLED	ADEGNOW	GOWANED	ADEHINR	HANDIER
ADEGILV	GLAIVED		WAGONED	ADEHIPP	HAPPIED
ADEGIMP	MEDIGAP	ADEGNPR	PRANGED	ADEHIPR	RAPHIDE
ADEGIMS	DEGAMIS	ADEGNPS	SPANGED	ADEHIPS	APHIDES
ADEGINN	DEANING	ADEGNPU	UNPAGED		DIPHASE
ADEGINR	AREDING	ADEGNRR	GNARRED	ADEHIPT	PITHEAD
	DEARING		GRANDER	ADEHIRR	HARDIER
	DERAIGN	ADEGNRS	DANGERS		HARRIED
	EARDING		GANDERS	ADEHIRS	AIRSHED
	GRADINE		GARDENS		DASHIER

	HARDIES		HARDEST		SNAILED
	SHADIER		HARDSET	ADEILNU	ALIUNDE
ADEHIRT	AIRTHED		HATREDS		UNIDEAL
ADEHIRW	RAWHIDE		THREADS	ADEILNV	ANDVILE
ADEHIRY	HAYRIDE		TRASHED		ANVILED
	HYDRIAE	ADEHRSY	HYDRASE	ADEILNX	INDEXAL
ADEHKNS	SHANKED	ADEHRTW	THRAWED	ADEILOP	OEDIPAL
ADEHKNT	THANKED		WRATHED	ADEILOR	DARIOLE
ADEHKOR	HARDOKE	ADEHRTY	HYDRATE	ADEILOS	DEASOIL
ADEHKOT	KATHODE		THREADY		ISOLEAD
ADEHKRS	SHARKED	ADEHSST	STASHED	ADEILOU	DOULEIA
ADEHLLO	HALLOED	ADEHSSW	SWASHED	ADEILOZ	DIAZOLE
	HOLLAED	ADEHSTW	SWATHED	ADEILPP	APPLIED
ADEHLLP	LAPHELD	ADEHSYY	HEYDAYS	ADEILPR	LIPREAD
ADEHLMS	LAMEDHS	ADEHUZZ	HUZZAED		PEDRAIL
ADEHLNR	HANDLER	ADEIILR	DELIRIA		PREDIAL
ADEHLNS	HANDLES		IRIDEAL	ADEILPS	ALIPEDS
	HANDSEL	ADEIILS	DAILIES		ELAPIDS
ADEHLOS	SHOALED		LIAISED		LAIPSED
ADEHLOT	LOATHED		SEDILIA		LAPIDES
ADEHLPR	RALPHED	ADEIIMN	AMIDINE		PAIDLES
ADEHLPS	PLASHED		DIAMINE		PALSIED
ADEHLRS	HARELDS	ADEIINR	DENARII		PLEIADS
	HERALDS	ADEIINT	INEDITA	ADEILPT	PLAITED
ADEHLSS	HASSLED	ADEIINZ	DIAZINE		TALIPED
	SLASHED	ADEIIPR	PERIDIA	ADEILQU	QUAILED
ADEHLST	DALETHS	ADEIIRS	AIRSIDE	ADEILRR	LARDIER
ADEHLSU	SHAULED		DAIRIES	ADEILRS	DERAILS
ADEHLSW	SHAWLED		DIARIES		DIALERS
ADEHLTY	DEATHLY		DIARISE		REDIALS
ADEHMMS	SHAMMED	ADEIIRZ	DIARIZE		SIDERAL
ADEHMMW	WHAMMED	ADEIISS	DAISIES	ADEILRT	DILATER
ADEHMNR	HARDMEN	ADEIJMR	JEMIDAR		REDTAIL
	HERDMAN	ADEIKLN	KNAIDEL		TRAILED
ADEHMOP	MOPHEAD	ADEIKLS	SKAILED	ADEILRU	UREDIAL
ADEHMOR	HADROME	ADEIKLY	KAYLIED	ADEILRV	RIVALED
ADEHMRS	DERHAMS	ADEIKNS	KANDIES		VALIDER
ADEHMSS	SMASHED	ADEIKRS	DAIKERS	ADEILRY	READILY
ADEHNPS	DAPHNES		DARKIES	ADEILSS	AIDLESS
ADEHNRS	HANDERS	ADEIKRT	TRAIKED		DEASILS
	HARDENS	ADEILLL	DIALLEL	ADEILST	DETAILS
ADEHNRU	UNHEARD	ADEILLR	DALLIER		DILATES
ADEHNSS	SNASHED		DIALLER	ADEILSU	AUDILES
ADEHNST	HANDSET		RALLIED		DEASIUL
ADEHNSU	UNHEADS	ADEILLS	DALLIES		DUALISE
ADEHNTU	HAUNTED		DISLEAL	ADEILSV	DEVISAL
ADEHOOP	APEHOOD		LALDIES	ADEILSY	DIALYSE
ADEHOPT	POTHEAD		SALLIED		EYLIADS
ADEHOPX	HEXAPOD	ADEILLT	TALLIED	ADEILUZ	DUALIZE
ADEHORR	HOARDER	ADEILLV	VIALLED	ADEILYZ	DIALYZE
ADEHOST	HOASTED	ADEILLY	IDEALLY	ADEIMMR	MERMAID
ADEHOSX	OXHEADS	ADEILMM	DILEMMA	ADEIMMS	MISMADE
ADEHOTW	TOWHEAD	ADEILMO	MELODIA	ADEIMMT	TAMMIED
ADEHPPW	WHAPPED	ADEILMP	IMPALED	ADEIMNO	AMIDONE
ADEHPRS	PHRASED		IMPLEAD		DOMAINE
	SHARPED	ADEILMS	MAELIDS	ADEIMNR	ADERMIN
ADEHPST	HEPTADS		MEDIALS		INARMED
	SPATHED		MISDEAL	ADEIMNS	DEMAINS
ADEHPSW	PSHAWED		MISLEAD		MAIDENS
ADEHQSU	QUASHED	ADEILMU	MIAULED		MEDIANS
ADEHRRU	HURRAED	ADEILNN	ANNELID		MEDINAS
ADEHRSS	DASHERS		LINDANE		SIDEMAN
	SHADERS	ADEILNP	PLAINED	ADEIMNT	MEDIANT
ADEHRST	DEARTHS	ADEILNS	DENIALS	ADEIMNU	UNAIMED

ADEIMOU	MIAOUED	ADEINTV	DEVIANT	ADEISTW	DAWTIES
ADEIMOW	MIAOWED	ADEINVV	NAVVIED		WAISTED
ADEIMPR	DAMPIER	ADEIOPS	ADIPOSE	ADEISVV	SAVVIED
ADEIMPV	IMPAVED	ADEIOPT	OPIATED	ADEISWY	SIDEWAY
ADEIMRR	ADMIRER	ADEIORS	ROADIES		WAYSIDE
	MARDIER		SOREDIA	ADEITUZ	DEUTZIA
	MARRIED	ADEIORV	AVODIRE	ADEITWY	TIDEWAY
ADEIMRS	ADMIRES		AVOIDER	ADEJMOR	MAJORED
	MARDIES	ADEIORX	EXORDIA	ADEJMRU	JUMARED
	MISREAD	ADEIOST	IODATES		MUDEJAR
	SEDARIM		TOADIES	ADEJNSU	JAUNSED
	SIDEARM	ADEIOSX	OXIDASE	ADEJNTU	JAUNTED
ADEIMRT	READMIT	ADEIOSZ	DIAZOES	ADEJOPR	JEOPARD
ADEIMRY	MIDYEAR	ADEIOTX	OXIDATE	ADEJRRU	ADJURER
ADEIMST	DIASTEM	ADEIOVV	VAIVODE	ADEJRSU	ADJURES
	MISDATE	ADEIOVW	WAIVODE	ADEJSSU	JUDASES
ADEIMSV	VIDAMES	ADEIOWW	WAIWODE	ADEKKNS	SKANKED
ADEIMSX	ADMIXES	ADEIPPR	DRAPPIE	ADEKLNP	PLANKED
ADEIMTU	IDEATUM		PREPAID	ADEKLNR	RANKLED
	TAEDIUM	ADEIPPU	APPUIED	ADEKLNS	KALENDS
ADEIMTY	DAYTIME	ADEIPRR	DRAPIER	ADEKLNY	NAKEDLY
ADEINNN	NANDINE		PARRIED	ADEKLOP	POLKAED
	NANNIED		RAPIDER	ADEKLOS	SKOALED
ADEINNR	NARDINE	ADEIPRS	ASPIRED	ADEKLPP	KLAPPED
ADEINNS	DANNIES		DESPAIR	ADEKLRS	DARKLES
ADEINOR	ANEROID		DIAPERS	ADEKLST	SKLATED
ADEINOS	ADONISE		PRAISED		STALKED
	ANODISE	ADEIPRT	DIPTERA	ADEKLSY	YSLAKED
	SODAINE		PARTIED	ADEKLUW	WAULKED
ADEINOV	NAEVOID		PIRATED	ADEKMNS	DESKMAN
ADEINOX	DIOXANE	ADEIPRV	VAPIDER	ADEKMRS	DEMARKS
ADEINOZ	ADONIZE	ADEIPSS	APSIDES	ADEKNPP	KNAPPED
	ANODIZE	ADEIQRU	QUERIDA	ADEKNPR	PRANKED
ADEINPR	PARDINE	ADEIRRS	ARRIDES	ADEKNPS	SPANKED
ADEINPS	PANDIES		RAIDERS	ADEKNRR	KNARRED
	PANSIED	ADEIRRT	TARDIER	ADEKNRS	DARKENS
	SPAINED		TARRIED	ADEKNRU	UNRAKED
ADEINPT	DEPAINT	ADEIRRV	ARRIVED	ADEKNSS	SANDEKS
	PAINTED	ADEIRST	ARIDEST	ADEKNST	DANKEST
	PATINED		ASTERID		STANKED
ADEINRR	DRAINER		ASTRIDE	ADEKNSU	UNASKED
	RANDIER		DIASTER	ADEKNSW	SWANKED
ADEINRS	RANDIES		DISRATE	ADEKNUW	UNWAKED
	SANDIER		STAIDER	ADEKNVY	VANDYKE
	SARDINE		STAIRED	ADEKORT	TROAKED
ADEINRT	ANTIRED		TARDIES	ADEKPRS	SPARKED
	DETRAIN		TIRADES	ADEKPSY	KEYPADS
	TRAINED	ADEIRSU	RESIDUA	ADEKRST	DARKEST
ADEINRU	UNAIRED	ADEIRSV	ADVISER		STARKED
	URANIDE		VARDIES		STRAKED
ADEINRV	INVADER	ADEIRSX	RADIXES	ADEKRSY	DARKEYS
	RAVINED	ADEIRTT	ATTIRED	ADELLMS	SMALLED
ADEINSS	SDAINES	ADEIRTV	TARDIVE	ADELLMU	MEDULLA
ADEINST	DESTAIN	ADEIRTY	DIETARY	ADELLNR	LANDLER
	DETAINS	ADEISSS	DASSIES	ADELLNW	ELLWAND
	INSTEAD	ADEISST	DISSEAT	ADELLOR	ODALLER
	NIDATES		SAIDEST	ADELLOW	ALLOWED
	SAINTED	ADEISSV	ADVISES	ADELLOY	ALLOYED
	SATINED		DISSAVE	ADELLPS	SPALLED
	STAINED	ADEISSZ	ASSIZED	ADELLRS	LADLERS
ADEINSV	INVADES	ADEISTU	DAUTIES	ADELLRU	ALLURED
ADEINSW	DEWANIS	ADEISTV	AVIDEST		UDALLER
ADEINTT	TAINTED		DATIVES	ADELLST	STALLED
ADEINTU	AUDIENT		VISTAED	ADELLSU	ALLUDES

	ALUDELS		SOLATED		WOMANED
ADELLSV	DEVALLS	ADELOSV	SALVOED	ADEMNPS	DAMPENS
ADELMMS	SLAMMED	ADELOSW	WALDOES	ADEMNRS	DAMNERS
	SMALMED	ADELOTT	TOTALED		MANREDS
	LANDMEN	ADELOTU	OUTLEAD		RANDEMS
ADELMNN	MANDREL	ADELPPP	PLAPPED		REMANDS
ADELMNR	MANTLED	ADELPPS	DAPPLES	ADEMNRU	DURAMEN
ADELMNT	EARLDOM		SAPPLED		MANURED
ADELMOR	DAMOSEL		SLAPPED		MAUNDER
ADELMOS	DAMOZEL	ADELPRS	PEDLARS		UNARMED
ADELMOZ	PSALMED	ADELPRY	PEDLARY	ADEMNRY	DRAYMEN
ADELMPS	SAMPLED	ADELPST	SPALTED		YARDMEN
	MEDLARS		STAPLED	ADEMNSS	DESMANS
ADELMRS	MURALED	ADELPSU	UPLEADS		MADNESS
ADELMRU	DAMSELS	ADELPSW	DEWLAPS	ADEMNST	TANDEMS
ADELMSS	MALTEDS		SPAWLED	ADEMNSU	MEDUSAN
ADELMST	ALMUDES	ADELPSY	SPLAYED		SUDAMEN
ADELMSU	MEDUSAL	ADELPTT	PLATTED	ADEMNSY	DAYSMEN
ADELMSW	WADMELS	ADELPTW	DEWLAPT	ADEMNTU	UNMATED
ADELMYZ	MAZEDLY	ADELPTY	ADEPTLY		UNTAMED
ADELNNP	PLANNED	ADELRRS	LARDERS	ADEMOOV	AMOOVED
ADELNNU	UNLADEN	ADELRRU	RUDERAL	ADEMOPS	APEDOMS
ADELNOR	LADRONE	ADELRRW	DRAWLER		POMADES
ADELNOS	LOADENS	ADELRSS	RASSLED	ADEMORR	ARMORED
ADELNOT	TALONED		SARDELS	ADEMORS	RADOMES
ADELNOY	YEALDON	ADELRST	DARTLES	ADEMOSV	VAMOSED
ADELNPT	PLANTED		SLARTED	ADEMOSW	MEADOWS
ADELNPY	ENDPLAY	ADELRSU	LAUDERS	ADEMOSY	SAMOYED
ADELNRS	DARNELS	ADELRSW	WARSLED		SOMEDAY
	ENLARDS	ADELRSZ	DRAZELS	ADEMOWY	MEADOWY
	LANDERS	ADELRTT	RATTLED	ADEMPRS	DAMPERS
	RELANDS	ADELRTW	TRAWLED	ADEMPRT	TRAMPED
	SLANDER	ADELRTX	DEXTRAL	ADEMPSS	SPASMED
	SNARLED	ADELRTY	LYRATED	ADEMPST	DAMPEST
ADELNRU	LAUNDER	ADELRWW	WRAWLED		STAMPED
	LURDANE	ADELRWX	WRAXLED	ADEMPSW	SWAMPED
	RUNDALE	ADELRZZ	DAZZLER	ADEMRRU	EARDRUM
ADELNRY	DEARNLY	ADELSST	DESALTS	ADEMRST	SMARTED
ADELNSS	SENDALS	ADELSTT	SLATTED	ADEMRSU	REMUDAS
ADELNST	DENTALS	ADELSTU	AULDEST	ADEMRSW	SWARMED
	SLANTED		SALUTED	ADEMRTU	MATURED
ADELNSU	UNLADES	ADELSUV	AVULSED	ADEMSST	DEMASTS
	UNLEADS	ADELSWY	SWAYLED	ADEMSSU	ASSUMED
ADELNSY	ADENYLS	ADELSZZ	DAZZLES		MEDUSAS
ADELNTU	LUNATED	ADELTTT	TATTLED	ADEMTTU	MUTATED
	UNDEALT	ADELTTW	WATTLED	ADENNOY	ANNOYED
ADELNTW	WETLAND	ADELTUV	VAULTED		ANODYNE
ADELNUW	UNLAWED	ADELTUX	LUXATED	ADENNPS	SPANNED
ADELOPR	LEOPARD	ADELTWZ	WALTZED	ADENNPT	PENDANT
	PAROLED	ADEMMPS	SPAMMED	ADENNST	STANDEN
	PRELOAD	ADEMMRS	DAMMERS	ADENNSU	DUENNAS
ADELOPS	DEPOSAL		SMARMED	ADENNSW	SWANNED
	PEDALOS	ADEMMRT	TRAMMED	ADENNWY	DEWANNY
ADELOPT	PLOATED	ADEMNNS	SANDMEN	ADENOOP	NAPOOED
	TADPOLE	ADEMNNU	MUNDANE	ADENOOT	ODONATE
ADELORS	LOADERS		UNNAMED	ADENOOZ	ENDOZOA
	ORDEALS	ADEMNOR	MADRONE	ADENOPR	APRONED
	RELOADS		ROADMEN		OPERAND
ADELORT	DELATOR	ADEMNOS	DAEMONS		PADRONE
	LEOTARD		MASONED		PANDORE
ADELORU	ROULADE		MODENAS	ADENOPS	DAPSONE
ADELOSS	ALDOSES		MONADES	ADENOPT	NOTEPAD
	LASSOED		NOMADES		TONEPAD
ADELOST	SALTOED	ADEMNOW	ADWOMEN	ADENORR	ADORNER

	READORN	**ADENSTU**	SAUNTED		PETARDS
ADENORT	TORNADE		UNSATED	**ADEPRSY**	SPRAYED
ADENORU	RONDEAU	**ADENSTV**	ADVENTS	**ADEPRTT**	PRATTED
ADENOST	ASTONED	**ADENSTY**	STAYNED	**ADEPRTU**	UPDATER
	DONATES	**ADENSUV**	UNSAVED		UPRATED
	ONSTEAD	**ADENSUW**	UNSAWED	**ADEPSTT**	SPATTED
ADENOSU	DOUANES	**ADENSWY**	ENDWAYS	**ADEPSTU**	UPDATES
ADENOSY	NOYADES	**ADENSWZ**	WEZANDS	**ADEPSZZ**	SPAZZED
ADENOTT	NOTATED	**ADENTTU**	ATTUNED	**ADEQRSU**	SQUARED
ADENOTV	NOVATED		NUTATED	**ADERRST**	DARTERS
ADENOTZ	ZONATED		TAUNTED		DARTRES
ADENPPR	PARPEND	**ADENTUV**	VAUNTED		RETARDS
ADENPPS	APPENDS	**ADENTUX**	UNTAXED		STARRED
	SNAPPED	**ADENUWX**	UNWAXED		TRADERS
ADENPPW	WAPPEND	**ADENUWY**	UNWAYED	**ADERRSW**	DRAWERS
ADENPRR	PARDNER	**ADEOORS**	ROADEOS		REDRAWS
ADENPRS	PANDERS	**ADEOORT**	ODORATE		REWARDS
ADENPRU	UNDRAPE	**ADEOPPS**	APPOSED		WARDERS
	UNPARED		PEAPODS	**ADERRSY**	YARDERS
ADENPRW	PRAWNED	**ADEOPQU**	OPAQUED	**ADERSSU**	ASSURED
	PREDAWN	**ADEOPRR**	EARDROP		RUDASES
ADENPST	PEDANTS	**ADEOPRT**	ADOPTER	**ADERSSW**	SAWDERS
	PENTADS		READOPT		SWEARDS
ADENPSW	SPAWNED	**ADEOPRV**	VAPORED	**ADERSTT**	STARTED
ADENPSX	EXPANDS	**ADEOPSS**	SPADOES		TETRADS
	SPANDEX	**ADEOPST**	PODESTA	**ADERSTV**	ADVERTS
ADENPSY	DYSPNEA	**ADEORRS**	ADORERS		STARVED
ADENPTU	UNADEPT		DROSERA	**ADERSTW**	STEWARD
ADENPUV	UNPAVED	**ADEORRW**	ARROWED		STRAWED
ADENQTU	QUANTED	**ADEORRZ**	RAZORED		WRASTED
ADENRRS	DARNERS	**ADEORSS**	SARODES	**ADERSTY**	STRAYED
	ERRANDS	**ADEORST**	DOATERS	**ADERSUV**	DASYURE
	SNARRED		ROASTED	**ADERSVW**	DWARVES
ADENRRW	REDRAWN		TORSADE		SWARVED
ADENRRY	REYNARD		TROADES	**ADERWWY**	WEYWARD
ADENRSS	SANDERS	**ADEORSU**	AROUSED	**ADESSTU**	SUDATES
	SARSDEN	**ADEORSV**	OVERSAD	**ADESSTW**	WADSETS
ADENRST	ENDARTS		SAVORED	**ADESTTU**	STATUED
	STANDER	**ADEORSW**	REDOWAS	**ADESTTW**	SWATTED
	STARNED	**ADEORTT**	ROTATED		WADSETT
ADENRSU	ASUNDER		TROATED	**ADFFGIN**	DAFFING
	DANSEUR	**ADEORTU**	OUTDARE	**ADFFHNO**	HANDOFF
	DAUNERS		OUTREAD		OFFHAND
ADENRSW	DAWNERS		READOUT	**ADFFILY**	DAFFILY
	WANDERS	**ADEORWY**	RODEWAY	**ADFFIST**	DISTAFF
	WARDENS	**ADEORYZ**	ZEDOARY	**ADFFLNO**	FANFOLD
ADENRSZ	ZANDERS	**ADEOSTT**	TOASTED	**ADFFLOO**	OFFLOAD
ADENRTT	TRANTED	**ADEOTTU**	OUTDATE	**ADFFOOR**	AFFOORD
ADENRTU	DAUNTER	**ADEOWWY**	WAYWODE	**ADFFORS**	AFFORDS
	NATURED	**ADEPPRS**	DAPPERS	**ADFGGIN**	FADGING
	UNRATED	**ADEPPRT**	TRAPPED	**ADFGINN**	FANDING
	UNTREAD	**ADEPPRW**	WRAPPED	**ADFGINR**	FARDING
ADENRTV	VERDANT	**ADEPPST**	STAPPED	**ADFGINS**	FADINGS
ADENRTX	DEXTRAN	**ADEPPSW**	SWAPPED	**ADFGLLU**	GLADFUL
ADENRTY	DENTARY	**ADEPPTU**	PUPATED	**ADFHLNU**	HANDFUL
	TRAYNED	**ADEPPUY**	APPUYED	**ADFHLNY**	FLYHAND
	TYRANED	**ADEPRRS**	DRAPERS	**ADFHLSY**	SHADFLY
ADENRUY	UNREADY		SPARRED	**ADFHOOS**	SHADOOF
ADENRUZ	UNRAZED	**ADEPRRY**	DRAPERY	**ADFHSSU**	SHADUFS
ADENSSS	SADNESS	**ADEPRSS**	ADPRESS	**ADFILLU**	FLUIDAL
ADENSSU	SUNDAES		SPADERS	**ADFIMNR**	FINDRAM
ADENSSW	WESANDS		SPREADS	**ADFIMNY**	DAMNIFY
	WESSAND	**ADEPRST**	DEPARTS	**ADFINRS**	FRIANDS
ADENSTT	ATTENDS		DRAPETS	**ADFINRT**	INDRAFT

Seven-letter anagrams

ADFIORS	FORSAID		LIGANDS
ADFLLVY	LADYFLY	ADGILNU	LANGUID
ADFLMOO	DAMFOOL		LAUDING
ADFLMPU	MUDFLAP	ADGILOR	GOLIARD
ADFLMTU	MUDFLAT	ADGILOS	DIALOGS
ADFLNOP	PLAFOND	ADGILOV	VALGOID
ADFLNSY	SANDFLY	ADGILSU	GLADIUS
ADFLORU	FOULARD	ADGILUY	GAUDILY
ADFMNOS	FANDOMS	ADGIMMN	DAMMING
ADFMOSU	FUMADOS	ADGIMNN	DAMNING
ADFNNOT	FONDANT	ADGIMNP	DAMPING
ADFNOST	FANTODS	ADGIMNR	MRIDANG
ADFOOPT	FOOTPAD	ADGINNR	DARNING
ADFOOTW	FATWOOD		NARDING
ADFORRW	FORWARD		RANDING
	FROWARD	ADGINNS	SANDING
ADFPRTU	UPDRAFT	ADGINNT	DANTING
ADGGGIN	DAGGING	ADGINNW	DAWNING
ADGGHNO	HANGDOG	ADGINOR	ADORING
ADGGILN	GADLING		GRADINO
ADGGILR	RIGGALD		ROADING
ADGGINN	DANGING	ADGINOS	GANOIDS
ADGGINO	GOADING	ADGINOT	DOATING
ADGGINR	GRADING	ADGINPP	DAPPING
	NIGGARD	ADGINPR	DRAPING
ADGGINU	GAUDING	ADGINPS	SPADING
ADGHILO	HIDALGO	ADGINRR	DARRING
ADGHINN	HANDING	ADGINRS	DARINGS
ADGHINS	DASHING		GRADINS
	SHADING	ADGINRT	DARTING
ADGHINU	HAUDING		TRADING
ADGHIPR	DIGRAPH	ADGINRU	DAURING
ADGHIRR	ARDRIGH	ADGINRW	DRAWING
ADGHIRS	DISHRAG		WARDING
ADGHNNU	HANDGUN	ADGINRY	DRAYING
ADGHNOS	HAGDONS		YARDING
	SANDHOG	ADGINST	DATINGS
ADGHNOW	HAGDOWN	ADGINSU	AUDINGS
ADGHORW	HOGWARD	ADGINSW	WADINGS
ADGHRSU	DURGAHS	ADGINTU	DAUTING
ADGHRTU	DRAUGHT	ADGINTW	DAWTING
ADGIILN	DIALING	ADGINWY	GWYNIAD
	GLIADIN	ADGIORT	GORDITA
	LAIDING	ADGIPRU	PAGURID
ADGIILT	DIGITAL	ADGIRSU	GUISARD
ADGIIMN	MAIDING	ADGIRZZ	GIZZARD
ADGIINN	DAINING	ADGLLNO	GOLLAND
ADGIINO	GONIDIA	ADGLMNO	MANGOLD
ADGIINR	GRADINI	ADGLNOO	DONGOLA
	RAIDING		GONDOLA
ADGIINS	SIGANID	ADGLNOR	GOLDARN
ADGIINU	IGUANID	ADGLNOW	GOWLAND
ADGIINW	GWINIAD	ADGLNOY	DAYLONG
ADGIIPY	PYGIDIA	ADGLNRY	GRANDLY
ADGIJOS	ADJIGOS	ADGLOPS	LAPDOGS
ADGIKNR	DARKING	ADGLOWY	DAYGLOW
ADGILLN	LADLING	ADGMNOO	GOODMAN
ADGILMN	MADLING	ADGMNOR	GORMAND
ADGILNN	LANDING	ADGNOOR	DRAGOON
ADGILNO	DIGONAL		GADROON
	LOADING	ADGNOOS	GOONDAS
ADGILNR	DARLING	ADGNOPS	DOGNAPS
	LARDING	ADGNORS	DRAGONS
ADGILNS	LADINGS	ADGNORU	AGROUND

ADGNORY	ORGANDY
ADGNRRU	GURNARD
ADGNRSU	DURGANS
ADGNRUU	UNGUARD
ADGOOPS	GOSPODA
ADGORSW	WARDOGS
ADGORTU	OUTDRAG
ADGPRSU	UPDRAGS
ADGRSTU	DUSTRAG
ADHHIRS	HARDISH
ADHHIST	HADITHS
ADHHISW	WHIDAHS
ADHHKSU	DUHKHAS
ADHHMOS	SHAHDOM
ADHHOSU	HOUDAHS
ADHHOSW	HOWDAHS
ADHHSWY	WHYDAHS
ADHIIJS	JIHADIS
ADHIIJT	IJTIHAD
ADHIIKS	DASHIKI
ADHIIMS	MAIDISH
ADHIKNS	DANKISH
ADHIKOP	HAPKIDO
ADHIKRS	DARKISH
ADHIKSU	HAIDUKS
ADHILMO	HALIDOM
ADHILNY	HANDILY
ADHILOP	HAPLOID
ADHILOS	HALOIDS
ADHILOY	HOLIDAY
	HYALOID
	HYOIDAL
ADHILRY	HARDILY
ADHILSY	LADYISH
	SHADILY
ADHIMNS	HANDISM
ADHIMPS	DAMPISH
	PHASMID
ADHIMRS	DIRHAMS
	MIDRASH
ADHINOT	ANTHOID
ADHINPS	DISHPAN
ADHINPU	DAUPHIN
ADHINSS	SANDHIS
ADHIOOS	HOODIAS
ADHIORS	HAIRDOS
ADHIOST	TOADISH
ADHIRSS	SHAIRDS
ADHJKOS	KHODJAS
ADHKKSU	DUKKAHS
	DUKKHAS
ADHKORW	DORHAWK
ADHKOSU	SHAKUDO
ADHLLLO	HOLDALL
ADHLLNO	HOLLAND
ADHLMOY	HOLYDAM
ADHLMPY	LYMPHAD
ADHLORS	HOLARDS
ADHLOYY	HOLYDAY
ADHMNOO	HOODMAN
	MANHOOD
ADHMNSU	NUMDAHS
ADHMORY	HYDROMA
ADHNNSU	NHANDUS

	UNHANDS	**ADIJMSS**	MASJIDS	**ADILPST**	PLASTID
ADHNNUY	UNHANDY	**ADIJNOS**	ADJOINS	**ADILPSY**	DISPLAY
ADHNOOS	DAHOONS	**ADIJNOT**	ADJOINT	**ADILPTU**	PLAUDIT
ADHNORS	HADRONS	**ADIJSSS**	JASSIDS	**ADILPVY**	VAPIDLY
ADHNORU	UNHOARD	**ADIKLNY**	LADYKIN	**ADILQSU**	SQUALID
ADHNOSU	HOUDANS	**ADIKLOR**	KILORAD	**ADILRSZ**	LIZARDS
ADHNOTU	HANDOUT	**ADIKLOS**	ODALISK	**ADILRTY**	TARDILY
ADHNRSU	DHURNAS	**ADIKLPS**	KLIPDAS	**ADILSTU**	DUALIST
ADHNRSY	SHANDRY	**ADIKMNN**	MANKIND		TULADIS
ADHNRTY	HYDRANT	**ADIKMOS**	MIKADOS	**ADILSTY**	STAIDLY
ADHNRUY	UNHARDY	**ADIKMOU**	DAIMOKU	**ADILTUY**	DUALITY
ADHOOPT	HOPTOAD	**ADIKMSS**	DISMASK	**ADIMNNO**	MONDAIN
ADHOORR	RHODORA	**ADIKNOS**	DAKOINS	**ADIMNOS**	DAIMONS
ADHOORS	DHOORAS	**ADIKNPS**	KIDNAPS		DOMAINS
ADHOPRU	UPHOARD		SKIDPAN		MADISON
ADHOPST	DASHPOT	**ADIKNRS**	DISRANK	**ADIMNRS**	MANDIRS
ADHORRU	DHOURRA	**ADIKOST**	DAKOITS	**ADIMNSS**	DISMANS
ADHORSU	DOURAHS	**ADIKOTY**	DAKOITY	**ADIMNST**	MANTIDS
ADHOSSW	SHADOWS	**ADIKPRS**	DISPARK	**ADIMOOS**	ISODOMA
ADHOSWY	SHADOWY	**ADIKQRU**	DIQUARK	**ADIMORR**	MIRADOR
ADHPRSU	PURDAHS	**ADIKSST**	DIKASTS	**ADIMOST**	DIATOMS
ADHPSUU	UPHAUDS	**ADIKSSU**	ADSUKIS		MASTOID
ADHRRSU	DHURRAS	**ADIKSTT**	DIKTATS	**ADIMOSY**	DAIMYOS
ADIIILR	IRIDIAL	**ADIKSUZ**	ADZUKIS	**ADIMOTT**	MATTOID
ADIIINR	IRIDIAN	**ADIKSWY**	SKIDWAY	**ADIMPRY**	PYRAMID
ADIIKOS	AIKIDOS	**ADILLMM**	MILLDAM	**ADIMQSU**	QUIDAMS
ADIIKOT	DAKOITI	**ADILLRY**	LAIRDLY	**ADIMRSS**	DISARMS
ADIIKSY	YIDAKIS	**ADILLSY**	DISALLY	**ADIMRSU**	RADIUMS
ADIILLS	ILLIADS	**ADILLTY**	TIDALLY	**ADIMRSW**	MISDRAW
ADIILMS	MILADIS	**ADILLVY**	VALIDLY	**ADIMRSY**	MYRIADS
	MISDIAL	**ADILLYY**	DAYLILY	**ADIMSSS**	SADISMS
	MISLAID	**ADILMNO**	MONDIAL	**ADIMSST**	DISMAST
ADIILNO	LIANOID	**ADILMNR**	MANDRIL	**ADIMSSY**	DISMAYS
ADIILNV	INVALID		RIMLAND	**ADIMSTU**	DUMAIST
ADIILOS	SIALOID	**ADILMNU**	MAUDLIN		STADIUM
ADIILRW	WIRILDA	**ADILMOP**	DIPLOMA		
ADIILSS	SIALIDS	**ADILMOS**	AMIDOLS	**ADIMSWY**	MIDWAYS
ADIILST	DIALIST	**ADILMOU**	ALODIUM	**ADINNNS**	NANDINS
ADIILUV	DILUVIA	**ADILMOY**	AMYLOID	**ADINNOP**	DIPNOAN
ADIIMMS	MAIDISM	**ADILMPS**	PLASMID		NONPAID
ADIIMNN	INDAMIN	**ADILMSS**	DISMALS	**ADINNOR**	ANDIRON
ADIIMNS	AMIDINS	**ADILMSU**	DUALISM	**ADINNPS**	PINDANS
	DIAMINS	**ADILMSY**	DISMAYL	**ADINNRS**	INNARDS
ADIIMOS	DAIMIOS		LADYISM	**ADINNRW**	INDRAWN
ADIIMPV	IMPAVID	**ADILNNS**	INLANDS		WINNARD
ADIIMRS	MIDAIRS	**ADILNOR**	ORDINAL	**ADINNRY**	INNYARD
ADIIMRU	MUDIRIA	**ADILNOS**	DOLINAS	**ADINNSU**	INDUNAS
ADIIMSS	MISSAID		LADINOS	**ADINOOP**	POINADO
ADIINPR	PINDARI	**ADILNRS**	ALDRINS	**ADINOPP**	OPPIDAN
	PRIDIAN	**ADILNRU**	DIURNAL	**ADINOPR**	PADRONI
ADIINST	DISTAIN	**ADILNRY**	RANDILY		PONIARD
ADIINSU	INDUSIA	**ADILNSS**	ISLANDS	**ADINOPT**	PINTADO
	SUIDIAN	**ADILNST**	TINDALS	**ADINORR**	ORDINAR
ADIINSV	AVIDINS	**ADILNSU**	DUALINS	**ADINORS**	INROADS
ADIINSZ	DIAZINS		SUNDIAL		ORDAINS
	DIZAINS	**ADILOOV**	OVOIDAL		SADIRON
ADIIPRS	DIAPIRS	**ADILOOZ**	ZOOIDAL	**ADINORT**	DIATRON
ADIIPXY	PYXIDIA	**ADILOPR**	DIPOLAR	**ADINORV**	VIRANDO
ADIIQRU	DAQUIRI	**ADILORT**	DILATOR	**ADINOSX**	DIAXONS
ADIIRST	DIARIST	**ADILOSZ**	OZALIDS		DIOXANS
ADIIRTY	ARIDITY	**ADILOTU**	OUTLAID	**ADINOTX**	OXIDANT
ADIISSY	SAIYIDS	**ADILPRV**	PYRALID	**ADINPST**	PANDITS
ADIITVY	AVIDITY		RAPIDLY		SANDPIT
		ADILPSS	SALPIDS	**ADINQRS**	QINDARS
				ADINRRT	TRIDARN

Seven-letter anagrams

ADINRST	INDARTS	ADLMNOY	ALMONDY		MUSTARD
ADINRSU	DURIANS	ADLMOOR	LORDOMA	ADNNOOS	NANDOOS
	SUNDARI		MALODOR	ADNNOOT	NANODOT
ADINRSW	INWARDS	ADLMORU	MODULAR	ADNNOOV	NOONDAY
ADINRTU	TRIDUAN	ADLMOSW	WADMOLS	ADNNORS	RANDONS
	UNITARD	ADLMSTU	TALMUDS	ADNNORT	DONNART
ADINSTT	DISTANT	ADLNNOR	NORLAND	ADNNOST	DANTONS
ADINSTU	UNSTAID	ADLNNSU	SUNLAND		DONNATS
ADINTTY	DITTANY	ADLNOOR	LARDOON	ADNNOSU	ADNOUNS
ADINWWY	WINDWAY	ADLNOOS	DOOLANS	ADNNOTU	DAUNTON
ADIOOPR	PARODOI		ONLOADS	ADNNRTU	DUNNART
ADIOOSW	WOODSIA	ADLNOPU	POUNDAL	ADNNRUW	UNDRAWN
ADIOPRR	AIRDROP	ADLNORS	LADRONS	ADNOOPR	PANDOOR
ADIOPRS	SPAROID		LARDONS	ADNOORS	NARDOOS
ADIOPRT	PAROTID	ADLNORT	TROLAND	ADNOORT	DONATOR
ADIOPRV	PRIVADO	ADLNORU	NODULAR		ODORANT
ADIOPSU	ADIPOUS	ADLNOSS	SOLANDS		TANDOOR
ADIORST	ASTROID		SOLDANS		TORNADO
ADIORSU	SAUROID	ADLNOST	DALTONS	ADNOOSW	WANDOOS
ADIORSV	ADVISOR		SANDLOT	ADNOPRS	PARDONS
ADIORTU	AUDITOR	ADLNOSU	SOULDAN	ADNOPRU	PANDOUR
ADIOSTU	OUTSAID		UNLOADS	ADNOPRV	PROVAND
ADIOSVW	DISAVOW	ADLNOSX	OXLANDS	ADNOPST	DOPANTS
ADIPRSS	SPARIDS	ADLNOSY	SYNODAL	ADNORRW	NORWARD
ADIPRST	DISPART	ADLNOTU	OUTLAND	ADNORSW	ONWARDS
ADIQSTU	DIQUATS	ADLNPSU	UPLANDS	ADNORTU	ROTUNDA
ADIRRSS	SIRDARS	ADLNRSU	LURDANS	ADNORTY	TARDYON
ADIRRST	RITARDS	ADLNRUU	UNDULAR	ADNORWY	NAYWORD
ADIRRSZ	RIZARDS	ADLNRUY	LAUNDRY	ADNOSSU	SOUDANS
ADIRSSU	SARDIUS	ADLNSSU	SULDANS	ADNOSTT	DOTANTS
ADIRSSV	VISARDS	ADLNTUU	UNADULT	ADNOSTU	ASTOUND
ADIRSSW	WISARDS	ADLOPRU	POULARD	ADNPRUW	UPDRAWN
ADIRSTY	SATYRID	ADLOPSU	UPLOADS	ADNPSTU	DUSTPAN
ADIRSUY	DYSURIA	ADLORRW	WARLORD		STANDUP
ADIRSVZ	VIZARDS	ADLORSS	DORSALS		UPSTAND
ADIRSWZ	WIZARDS	ADLORSU	SUDORAL	ADNRSST	STRANDS
ADIRSZZ	IZZARDS	ADLOSSS	DOSSALS	ADNRSSU	SUNDRAS
ADISSST	SADISTS	ADLPSSU	SPAULDS	ADNRSTU	DRAUNTS
ADISSYY	SAYYIDS	ADMMNOS	MANDOMS		DURANTS
ADISTTY	DITTAYS	ADMMNSU	SUMMAND		TUNDRAS
ADJKOSU	JUDOKAS	ADMMOST	MADTOMS	ADNRSUW	SUNWARD
ADJLMOR	JARLDOM	ADMNOOR	DOORMAN		UNDRAWS
ADJLUUW	WUDJULA		MADRONO	ADNSSTY	DYNASTS
ADJNORS	JORDANS	ADMNOOW	WOODMAN	ADNSTYY	DYNASTY
ADJNORU	ADJOURN	ADMNOOZ	MADZOON	ADOOPRS	PARODOS
ADJORRU	ADJUROR	ADMNOQU	QUONDAM	ADOOPSU	APODOUS
ADJSSTU	ADJUSTS	ADMNORS	RANDOMS	ADOOPSW	SAPWOOD
ADKKLOY	KAKODYL		RODSMAN	ADOORSS	DOOSRAS
ADKLMRU	MUDLARK	ADMNORT	DORMANT	ADOORWY	DOORWAY
ADKOPSU	PADOUKS		MORDANT	ADOOSTT	TOSTADO
ADKORWY	DAYWORK	ADMNOSS	DAMSONS	ADOOSUV	VAUDOOS
	WORKDAY	ADMNOSU	OSMUNDA	ADOOWWX	WOODWAX
ADKRSWY	SKYWARD	ADMNOSY	DYNAMOS	ADOPRRW	WARDROP
ADLLMOW	WADMOLL	ADMNSTU	DUSTMAN	ADORRSU	ARDOURS
ADLLMOY	MODALLY	ADMOORT	DOORMAT	ADORSTW	TOWARDS
ADLLNOW	LOWLAND	ADMOORY	DAYROOM	ADORSUU	ARDUOUS
ADLLNOY	NODALLY	ADMOPPU	POPADUM	ADORSWY	AYWORDS
ADLLOPR	POLLARD	ADMORRS	RAMRODS	ADORTUW	OUTDRAW
ADLLOPS	DALLOPS	ADMORST	STARDOM		OUTWARD
ADLLORS	DOLLARS		TSARDOM	ADOUUVX	VAUDOUX
ADLLRWY	DRYWALL	ADMORSU	MADUROS	ADPRSTU	UPDARTS
ADLLTUY	ADULTLY	ADMORTW	MADWORT	ADPRSUW	UPDRAWS
ADLMNOS	ALMONDS	ADMORTZ	TZARDOM		UPWARDS
	DOLMANS	ADMRSTU	DURMAST	ADRSSUW	USWARDS

ADSSTUW	SAWDUST
AEEEFLR	EELFARE
AEEEGGN	ENGAGEE
AEEEGKL	KEELAGE
AEEEGLT	LEGATEE
AEEEGNT	TEENAGE
AEEEGPR	PEERAGE
AEEEGPS	SEEPAGE
AEEEGRR	EAGERER
AEEEGRT	ETAGERE
AEEEHLS	HEALEES
AEEEILN	ALIENEE
AEEEIRT	EATERIE
AEEELRS	RELEASE
AEEELTV	ELEVATE
AEEERVW	REWEAVE
AEEERWY	EYEWEAR
AEEFFLL	FELAFEL
AEEFFNS	NEAFFES
AEEFFRS	AFFEERS
AEEFGLN	FENAGLE
AEEFGNR	FREEGAN
AEEFGNT	FANTEEG
AEEFGRS	SERFAGE
AEEFGSU	FEAGUES
AEEFGTW	WEFTAGE
AEEFHRT	FEATHER, TEREFAH
AEEFILR	FILAREE, LEAFIER
AEEFILW	ALEWIFE
AEEFIRS	AREFIES, FAERIES, FREESIA
AEEFISW	SEAWIFE
AEEFKRS	FAKEERS
AEEFLLT	FELLATE, LEAFLET
AEEFLMN	ENFLAME
AEEFLMS	FEMALES
AEEFLRT	REFLATE
AEEFLRU	FERULAE
AEEFLRW	WELFARE
AEEFLRY	LEAFERY
AEEFLRZ	ALFEREZ
AEEFLSU	EASEFUL
AEEFLTX	TELEFAX
AEEFMNR	ENFRAME, FREEMAN
AEEFMRR	REFRAME
AEEFMRT	FERMATE
AEEFOTV	FOVEATE
AEEFPPR	FRAPPEE
AEEFRRS	FEARERS
AEEFRRT	FERRATE
AEEFRST	AFREETS, FEASTER
AEEFRTU	FEATURE
AEEFRWY	FREEWAY
AEEFSTT	FEATEST
AEEGGLL	ALLEGGE
AEEGGLR	GREGALE
AEEGGLS	ALEGGES
AEEGGLT	GATELEG
AEEGGNR	ENGAGER
AEEGGNS	ENGAGES
AEEGGOP	EPAGOGE
AEEGGRS	AGREGES, RAGGEES, REGGAES
AEEGGRU	REGAUGE
AEEGGST	TAGGEES
AEEGGSW	GEEGAWS
AEEGHIR	HIREAGE
AEEGHNT	THENAGE
AEEGHNW	WHANGEE
AEEGHSZ	GEEZAHS
AEEGILL	GALILEE
AEEGILM	MILEAGE
AEEGILN	LINEAGE
AEEGILP	EPIGEAL
AEEGILT	EGALITE
AEEGILW	WEIGELA
AEEGIMR	REIMAGE
AEEGINP	EPIGEAN
AEEGINR	REGINAE
AEEGINS	AGENISE
AEEGINU	EUGENIA
AEEGINZ	AGENIZE
AEEGIPP	PIPEAGE
AEEGIPR	PIERAGE
AEEGIRU	EUGARIE
AEEGISS	AEGISES, ASSIEGE
AEEGJRS	JAEGERS
AEEGJSY	JAYGEES
AEEGKLL	KLEAGLE
AEEGLLR	ALLEGER
AEEGLLS	ALLEGES
AEEGLLZ	GAZELLE
AEEGLMN	GLEEMAN, MELANGE
AEEGLMR	GLEAMER
AEEGLMT	MELTAGE
AEEGLNR	ENLARGE, GENERAL, GLEANER
AEEGLNT	ELEGANT
AEEGLNU	EUGLENA
AEEGLNV	EVANGEL
AEEGLOR	AEROGEL
AEEGLPR	PEREGAL
AEEGLPS	PELAGES
AEEGLRR	REGALER
AEEGLRS	GALERES, REGALES
AEEGLRU	LEAGUER, REGULAE
AEEGLRW	LEGWEAR
AEEGLRY	EAGERLY
AEEGLRZ	REGLAZE
AEEGLSS	AGELESS, ALGESES
AEEGLST	EAGLETS, GELATES, LEGATES, SEGETAL, TEAGLES, TELEGAS
AEEGLSU	LEAGUES
AEEGLSV	GLEAVES, SELVAGE
AEEGLTT	GALETTE
AEEGLTU	TEGULAE
AEEGLTV	VEGETAL
AEEGMMT	GEMMATE, TAGMEME
AEEGMNR	GERMANE
AEEGMNS	MANEGES, MENAGES
AEEGMNT	GATEMEN
AEEGMPR	PREGAME
AEEGMRR	MEAGRER
AEEGMRS	MEAGRES
AEEGMRU	REMUAGE
AEEGMSS	MEGASSE, MESSAGE
AEEGMST	GAMETES, METAGES
AEEGNNP	PANGENE
AEEGNNR	ENRANGE
AEEGNNS	ENNAGES
AEEGNOP	PEONAGE
AEEGNPP	GENAPPE
AEEGNRS	ENRAGES
AEEGNRT	GRANTEE, GREATEN, NEGATER, REAGENT
AEEGNRU	RENAGUE, UNEAGER
AEEGNRV	AVENGER, ENGRAVE
AEEGNSS	SAGENES, SENEGAS
AEEGNST	NEGATES
AEEGNSV	AVENGES, GENEVAS
AEEGNTT	TENTAGE
AEEGNTV	VENTAGE
AEEGOPS	APOGEES
AEEGORV	OVERAGE
AEEGOST	GOATEES
AEEGPRS	ASPERGE, PRESAGE
AEEGPRU	PUGAREE
AEEGPST	SEPTAGE
AEEGRRS	GREASER, REGEARS
AEEGRRT	GREATER, REGRATE
AEEGRRU	REARGUE
AEEGRRW	WAGERER
AEEGRSS	GREASES
AEEGRST	ERGATES, RESTAGE
AEEGRSV	GREAVES
AEEGRTU	TREAGUE
AEEGRUZ	GUEREZA
AEEGSSW	SEWAGES
AEEGSTT	GESTATE, TAGETES

AEEGTTZ	GAZETTE	AEEHRSW	WHEREAS				RETINAE
AEEHHNT	HEATHEN	AEEHRTT	THEATER				TRAINEE
AEEHHRT	HEATHER		THEATRE	AEEINST	ETESIAN
AEEHHST	SHEATHE		THEREAT	AEEINTV	NAIVETE
AEEHHSW	HEEHAWS	AEEHRTV	THREAVE	AEEINVW	INWEAVE
AEEHINR	HERNIAE	AEEHRTW	WEATHER	AEEIORT	ETAERIO
AEEHIPR	HEAPIER		WHEREAT	AEEIPRR	PEREIRA
AEEHIRV	HEAVIER		WREATHE	AEEIPRS	APERIES
AEEHIST	ATHEISE	AEEHSST	HEASTES		EPEIRAS
AEEHISV	HEAVIES	AEEHSSV	SHEAVES	AEEIPRT	PEATIER
AEEHITZ	ATHEIZE	AEEHSTV	THEAVES	AEEIPSV	PEAVIES
AEEHKMS	HAKEEMS	AEEHSWY	EYEWASH	AEEIPTX	EXPIATE
AEEHKNR	HEARKEN	AEEIIRS	AIERIES	AEEIRRR	ARRIERE
AEEHKNT	THANKEE	AEEIKLP	APELIKE	AEEIRRS	REARISE
AEEHKRT	HEKTARE		PEALIKE		RERAISE
AEEHKRU	HEUREKA	AEEIKLR	EARLIKE	AEEIRRT	TEARIER
AEEHLNT	LETHEAN		LEAKIER	AEEIRRW	WEARIER
AEEHLPT	HEELTAP	AEEIKLT	TEALIKE	AEEIRST	AERIEST
AEEHLRS	HEALERS	AEEIKPR	PEAKIER		SERIATE
AEEHLRT	HALTERE	AEEIKSV	KEAVIES	AEEIRSW	WEARIES
	LEATHER	AEEILLR	REALLIE	AEEIRTT	ARIETTE
AEEHLRV	HAVEREL	AEEILMR	MEALIER		ITERATE
AEEHLSS	LEASHES	AEEILMS	MEALIES	AEEIRTV	EVIRATE
AEEHLST	LATHEES	AEEILNP	ALEPINE	AEEISST	EASIEST
AEEHLSW	AWHEELS		ELAPINE	AEEISVV	EVASIVE
AEEHLSX	EXHALES	AEEILNR	ALIENER	AEEITTV	AVIETTE
AEEHLSY	EYELASH	AEEILNS	SEALINE		EVITATE
AEEHLTT	ATHLETE	AEEILNT	LINEATE	AEEITUX	EUTEXIA
AEEHMNT	METHANE	AEEILNX	ALEXINE	AEEIUVX	EXUVIAE
AEEHMRS	HAREEMS	AEEILPT	EPILATE	AEEJKSS	JAKESES
	MAHSEER		PILEATE	AEEJMSS	JAMESES
AEEHMRT	ERATHEM	AEEILRR	EARLIER	AEEJNST	SEJEANT
	THERMAE		LEARIER	AEEJNTU	JAUNTEE
AEEHMST	MEATHES	AEEILRS	EARLIES	AEEJRSV	EVEJARS
AEEHMSU	HEAUMES		REALISE	AEEJSVY	JAYVEES
AEEHNPS	PEAHENS	AEEILRT	ATELIER		VEEJAYS
AEEHNPT	HAPTENE		REALTIE	AEEKKNO	KOKANEE
	HEPTANE	AEEILRV	LEAVIER	AEEKKOO	KOEKOEA
	PHENATE		VEALIER	AEEKLLT	LAKELET
AEEHNRS	ARSHEEN	AEEILRZ	REALIZE	AEEKLMN	KEELMAN
AEEHNRT	EARTHEN	AEEILTT	AILETTE	AEEKLNS	ALKENES
	HEARTEN	AEEILTV	ELATIVE	AEEKLNT	KANTELE
AEEHNST	ETHANES	AEEIMNN	ENAMINE	AEEKLPS	PALKEES
AEEHNSV	HEAVENS	AEEIMNR	REMANIE	AEEKLRS	LEAKERS
AEEHNSX	HEXANES	AEEIMNS	MEANIES	AEEKLSV	VAKEELS
AEEHNTW	WHEATEN		NEMESIA	AEEKMNS	KAMSEEN
AEEHPRS	HEAPERS	AEEIMNT	ETAMINE	AEEKMNW	WAKEMEN
	RESHAPE		MATINEE	AEEKMRR	REMAKER
	SPHAERE	AEEIMNX	EXAMINE	AEEKMRS	REMAKES
	SPHEARE	AEEIMPR	EMPAIRE	AEEKMRT	MEERKAT
AEEHPRT	PREHEAT	AEEIMRR	REAMIER	AEEKNNN	NANKEEN
AEEHPSS	APHESES		REREMAI	AEEKNNP	KNEEPAN
	SPAHEES	AEEIMRS	SEAMIER	AEEKNRS	SNEAKER
AEEHPUV	UPHEAVE		SERIEMA	AEEKNRT	RETAKEN
AEEHQSU	QUASHEE	AEEIMRT	EMERITA	AEEKNRW	REWAKEN
AEEHRRS	HEARERS		EMIRATE		WAKENER
	REHEARS		MEATIER	AEEKNSS	SKEANES
	SHEARER	AEEIMSS	MISEASE	AEEKNSW	WEAKENS
AEEHRSS	HEARSES		SIAMESE	AEEKORW	REAWOKE
AEEHRST	AETHERS	AEEIMST	STEAMIE	AEEKPRS	PARKEES
	HEATERS	AEEIMSZ	SIAMEZE		RESPEAK
	REHEATS	AEEIMTT	TEATIME		SPEAKER
AEEHRSV	HEAVERS	AEEINPR	PERINEA	AEEKPRT	PERTAKE
	RESHAVE	AEEINRT	ARENITE	AEEKRRT	RETAKER

AEEKRRW	WREAKER	AEELPRS	LEAPERS	AEELTTY	LAYETTE
AEEKRST	RETAKES		PLEASER	AEELTVW	WAVELET
	SAKERET		PRESALE	AEEMMMR	MAREMME
AEEKRSU	EUREKAS		RELAPSE	AEEMMMS	MAMMEES
AEEKRSW	REWAKES		REPEALS	AEEMMNT	MEATMEN
AEEKRTW	TWEAKER	AEELPRT	PETRALE	AEEMMPY	EMPYEMA
AEEKSSS	ASKESES		PLEATER	AEEMMRT	AMMETER
AEEKSTW	WEAKEST		PRELATE		METAMER
AEELLLS	ALLELES		REPLATE	AEEMMSY	MAMEYES
AEELLMS	MALLEES	AEELPRU	PLEURAE	AEEMNNO	ANEMONE
AEELLOV	ALVEOLE	AEELPSS	ELAPSES	AEEMNNP	PENNAME
AEELLPR	PARELLE		PLEASES	AEEMNOX	AXONEME
AEELLSS	SALLEES		SAPELES	AEEMNPR	PRENAME
AEELLST	LEALEST	AEELPSU	EPAULES	AEEMNPS	SPAEMEN
AEELLWY	WALLEYE	AEELPTT	PALETTE	AEEMNPT	PEATMEN
AEELMNP	EMPANEL		PELTATE	AEEMNRS	MEANERS
	EMPLANE	AEELPTU	EPAULET		RENAMES
AEELMNR	REELMAN	AEELQRU	LEQUEAR	AEEMNRT	REMANET
AEELMNS	ENAMELS	AEELQSU	QUELEAS	AEEMNSS	ENSEAMS
	MELENAS		SEQUELA	AEEMNST	ENTAMES
AEELMNT	MANTEEL	AEELRRT	ALERTER		MEANEST
	TELEMAN		ALTERER	AEEMNSX	EXAMENS
AEELMNV	VELAMEN		REALTER	AEEMOPT	METOPAE
AEELMNY	AMYLENE		RELATER	AEEMORT	EROTEMA
AEELMPR	EMPALER	AEELRRV	RAVELER	AEEMOSW	AWESOME
	PREMEAL	AEELRRX	RELAXER		WAESOME
AEELMPS	EMPALES	AEELRSS	EARLESS	AEEMPRS	AMPERES
AEELMPX	EXAMPLE		LEASERS		EMPARES
	EXEMPLA		RESALES	AEEMPRT	TEMPERA
AEELMRS	MEALERS		RESEALS	AEEMPRY	EMPAYRE
AEELMRT	LAMETER		SEALERS	AEEMPST	METEPAS
AEELMSS	MEASLES	AEELRST	ELATERS	AEEMPSW	WAMPEES
AEELMSU	AEMULES		REALEST	AEEMPTU	AMPUTEE
AEELMSZ	MEAZELS		RELATES	AEEMQRU	MARQUEE
AEELMTU	EMULATE		RESLATE	AEEMRRS	REAMERS
AEELNNP	ENPLANE		STEALER		SMEARER
AEELNNR	LERNEAN	AEELRSU	LEASURE	AEEMRSS	SEAMERS
AEELNOS	ENOLASE	AEELRSV	LAVEERS	AEEMRST	REMATES
AEELNPR	REPANEL		LEAVERS		RETEAMS
AEELNPS	ALPEENS		REVEALS		STEAMER
	SPELEAN		SEVERAL		TEAMERS
AEELNRR	LEARNER		VEALERS	AEEMRSU	MEASURE
	RELEARN	AEELRSX	RELAXES	AEEMRTX	EXTREMA
AEELNRS	LEANERS	AEELRSY	SEALERY	AEEMRTY	METAYER
AEELNRT	ALTERNE	AEELRTX	EXALTER	AEEMSSS	SESAMES
	ENTERAL	AEELRUV	REVALUE	AEEMSST	MESETAS
	ETERNAL	AEELSST	ALTESSE		SEAMSET
	TELERAN		STEALES	AEEMSTT	METATES
AEELNRW	RENEWAL		TEASELS	AEEMSTX	TAXEMES
AEELNSS	ENSEALS	AEELSSV	SLEAVES	AEENNOT	NEONATE
AEELNST	ELANETS	AEELSSW	AWELESS	AEENNOV	NOVENAE
	LATEENS		WEASELS	AEENNPT	PENNATE
	LEANEST	AEELSSZ	SLEAZES		PENTANE
AEELNSV	ENSLAVE	AEELSTU	ELUATES	AEENNRS	ENSNARE
	LEAVENS		SETUALE		RENNASE
AEELNSW	WEANELS	AEELSTV	SALVETE	AEENNRX	REANNEX
AEELNTY	ENTAYLE		VALETES	AEENNST	NEATENS
AEELOPR	PAROLEE		VELETAS	AEENNSX	ANNEXES
AEELOPX	POLEAXE	AEELSTX	LATEXES	AEENNTU	UNEATEN
AEELORS	AREOLES	AEELSTY	EYALETS	AEENOPR	PERAEON
AEELORU	AUREOLE	AEELSTZ	TEAZELS	AEENOPU	EUPNOEA
AEELOST	OLEATES		TEAZLES	AEENORS	ARENOSE
AEELOSW	LEASOWE	AEELSWY	LEEWAYS	AEENOSS	ANOESES
AEELPRR	PEARLER		WEASELY	AEENOSU	AENEOUS

AEENPRS	PANEERS			PREASSE	AEESSUX	AUXESES
AEENPST	NEPETAS			SERAPES	AEESTTT	TESTATE
	PENATES	AEEPRST		REPEATS	AEESWXY	WAXEYES
	PESANTE			RETAPES	AEFFFLR	FLAFFER
AEENPSU	EUPNEAS	AEEPRSV		REPAVES	AEFFGIR	GIRAFFE
AEENPSW	PAWNEES	AEEPRSZ		SPREAZE		RIFFAGE
AEENPSX	EXPANSE	AEEPRTU		EPURATE	AEFFGNR	ENGRAFF
AEENRRS	EARNERS	AEEPRTY		PEATERY	AEFFGRS	GAFFERS
	REEARNS	AEEPRTZ		TRAPEZE	AEFFGRU	GAUFFER
AEENRRT	TERRANE	AEEPSSS		ASEPSES	AEFFHST	HAFFETS
AEENRRV	RAVENER	AEEPSST		PESETAS	AEFFINS	AFFINES
AEENRRY	YEARNER	AEEPSSW		PESEWAS	AEFFIPR	PIAFFER
AEENRSS	ENSEARS	AEEPSTT		SEPTATE	AEFFIPS	PIAFFES
AEENRST	EARNEST			SPATTEE	AEFFIRX	AFFIXER
	EASTERN	AEEPSVY		PEAVEYS		REAFFIX
	NEAREST	AEEQRSU		QUAERES	AEFFIST	TAFFIES
	RATEENS	AEEQSTU		EQUATES	AEFFISW	WAFFIES
AEENRSW	WEANERS	AEERRRS		REARERS	AEFFISX	AFFIXES
AEENRTT	ENTREAT	AEERRSS		ERASERS	AEFFKOP	OFFPEAK
	RATTEEN	AEERRST		RETEARS	AEFFKOR	RAKEOFF
	TERNATE			SERRATE	AEFFKOT	OFFTAKE
AEENRTV	AVENTRE			TEARERS		TAKEOFF
	NERVATE	AEERRSU		ERASURE	AEFFLLY	FLYLEAF
	VETERAN	AEERRSV		REAVERS	AEFFLMW	FLAMFEW
AEENRUV	UNREAVE	AEERRSW		REWEARS	AEFFLNS	SNAFFLE
AEENSST	ENTASES			SWEARER	AEFFLRR	RAFFLER
	SATEENS			WEARERS	AEFFLRS	FARFELS
	SENATES	AEERRTT		RETRATE		RAFFLES
	SENSATE			RETREAT	AEFFLRU	FEARFUL
	STEANES			TREATER	AEFFLRW	WAFFLER
AEENSSU	UNEASES	AEERRTV		AVERTER	AEFFLSW	WAFFLES
AEENSSV	AVENSES	AEERRTW		WATERER	AEFFLSY	YAFFLES
AEENSSW	WAENESS	AEERRVW		WAVERER	AEFFLTU	FATEFUL
AEENSTT	NEATEST	AEERSST		EASTERS	AEFFMRU	EARMUFF
AEENSUV	AVENUES			RESEATS	AEFFNST	NAFFEST
AEENSWZ	WEAZENS			SAETERS	AEFFOVW	WAVEOFF
AEENTTV	NAVETTE			SEAREST	AEFFQRU	QUAFFER
AEENUVW	UNWEAVE			SEATERS	AEFFRST	AFFRETS
AEEOPRT	OPERATE			STEARES		RESTAFF
AEEOPTZ	EPAZOTE			TEASERS		STAFFER
AEEORRS	REAROSE			TESSERA	AEFFRSY	EFFRAYS
AEEORSS	SEROSAE	AEERSSU		RESEAUS	AEFFRSZ	ZAFFERS
AEEORST	ROSEATE			SEASURE		ZAFFRES
AEEORSV	OVERSEA			UREASES	AEFFTTY	TAFFETY
AEEORTV	OVERATE	AEERSSV		ASSEVER	AEFGGGO	FOGGAGE
	OVEREAT	AEERSSY		ESSAYER	AEFGGIR	FAGGIER
AEEORVW	OVERAWE	AEERSTT		ESTREAT	AEFGGLR	FLAGGER
AEEOSUU	EUOUAES			RESTATE	AEFGGMO	MEGAFOG
AEEOSVV	EVOVAES			RETASTE	AEFGGRY	FAGGERY
AEEPPRR	PAPERER	AEERSTU		AUSTERE	AEFGILN	FEALING
	PREPARE	AEERSTW		SWEATER		FINAGLE
	REPAPER	AEERSTX		RETAXES		LEAFING
AEEPPRS	RAPPEES	AEERSUV		VAREUSE	AEFGILO	FOLIAGE
AEEPPRT	PRETAPE	AEERSUX		RESEAUX	AEFGILR	FRAGILE
AEEPPRV	PREPAVE	AEERSVW		WEAVERS	AEFGINR	FEARING
AEEPPRS	REAPERS	AEERSWX		REWAXES	AEFGINS	FEASING
	SPEARER	AEERTTX		EXTREAT	AEFGINT	FEATING
AEEPRRT	PEARTER	AEERTWW		WETWARE	AEFGINZ	FEAZING
	TAPERER	AEERTWX		TREEWAX	AEFGIRT	FRIGATE
AEEPRRV	PREAVER	AEESSSW		SEESAWS	AEFGIRU	REFUGIA
AEEPRSS	ASPERSE	AEESSSY		EYASSES	AEFGITU	FATIGUE
	PARESES	AEESSTT		ESTATES	AEFGLLU	FULLAGE
	PRAESES	AEESSTU		SAUTEES	AEFGLMN	FLAGMEN
	PREASES	AEESSTX		TEXASES	AEFGLNR	FLANGER

Code	Word(s)	Code	Word(s)	Code	Word(s)
AEFGLNS	FANGLES		FILASSE	AEFLNOV	FLAVONE
	FLANGES	AEFILST	FETIALS	AEFLNRS	SALFERN
AEFGLOT	FLOTAGE		SEALIFT	AEFLNRU	FLANEUR
AEFGLOW	FLOWAGE	AEFILTT	FLATTIE		FRENULA
AEFGLPU	PAGEFUL	AEFILWY	LIFEWAY		FUNERAL
AEFGLRS	REFLAGS	AEFIMNR	FIREMAN	AEFLNSU	FLAUNES
AEFGLRU	RAGEFUL	AEFIMNS	FAMINES	AEFLNTT	FLATTEN
AEFGLUZ	GAZEFUL		INFAMES	AEFLNUU	FAUNULE
AEFGMOR	FROMAGE	AEFIMOR	FOAMIER	AEFLOOV	FOVEOLA
AEFGMSU	FUMAGES	AEFIMRR	FIREARM	AEFLOPW	PEAFOWL
AEFGNRR	FRANGER	AEFIMRS	MISFARE	AEFLORS	LOAFERS
	GRANFER	AEFINNS	FAINNES		SAFROLE
AEFGNRT	ENGRAFT		FANNIES	AEFLORT	FLOATER
AEFGOOT	FOOTAGE	AEFINNT	INFANTE		FLOREAT
AEFGORR	FORAGER	AEFINNZ	FANZINE		REFLOAT
AEFGORS	FORAGES	AEFINPR	FIREPAN	AEFLORY	FORELAY
AEFGORT	FAGOTER	AEFINRR	REFRAIN	AEFLOST	FOLATES
AEFGORV	FORGAVE	AEFINRS	INFARES	AEFLOSW	SEAFOWL
AEFGRRT	GRAFTER		SERAFIN	AEFLPPR	FLAPPER
	REGRAFT	AEFINRT	FAINTER	AEFLPRS	FELSPAR
AEFGRSU	GAUFERS		FENITAR	AEFLPRU	FLAREUP
	GAUFRES	AEFINRW	FAWNIER	AEFLPRY	PALFREY
AEFHIRT	FAITHER	AEFINRX	XERAFIN	AEFLRSS	FALSERS
AEFHIRW	WHARFIE	AEFINST	FAINEST		FLASERS
AEFHISZ	HAFIZES		NAIFEST	AEFLRST	FALTERS
AEFHLLS	FELLAHS	AEFINSW	FANWISE	AEFLRSU	EARFULS
AEFHLOR	FAHLORE	AEFINTX	ANTEFIX		FERULAS
AEFHLRS	FLASHER	AEFIQRU	AQUIFER		REFUSAL
AEFHLRT	FARTHEL	AEFIRRR	FARRIER	AEFLRSY	FLAYERS
AEFHLRZ	FAHLERZ	AEFIRSS	FRAISES	AEFLRTT	FLATTER
AEFHLSS	FLASHES	AEFIRST	FAIREST	AEFLRTU	REFUTAL
AEFHLTU	HATEFUL	AEFIRTT	FATTIER		TEARFUL
AEFHRRT	FARTHER	AEFISST	FASTIES	AEFLRZZ	FRAZZLE
AEFHRST	FATHERS		FIESTAS	AEFLSST	FALSEST
	HAFTERS		FISSATE		FATLESS
	SHAFTER	AEFISTT	FATTIES		FESTALS
AEFHRSY	FASHERY	AEFISTX	FIXATES	AEFLSTU	FLUATES
AEFIILT	FILIATE	AEFJNST	FANJETS		SULFATE
AEFIIRS	FAIRIES	AEFKLNN	FLANKEN	AEFMNOR	FORAMEN
AEFIJLO	JEOFAIL	AEFKLNR	FLANKER		FOREMAN
AEFIJOS	FEIJOAS	AEFKLNS	FANKLES	AEFMNRT	RAFTMEN
AEFIKLN	FANLIKE	AEFKLOS	SEAFOLK	AEFMNRU	FRAENUM
AEFIKLR	FLAKIER	AEFKLRS	FLAKERS	AEFMORR	FOREARM
AEFIKLS	FLAKIES	AEFKLRT	FARTLEK	AEFMORS	FOAMERS
AEFIKLT	FATLIKE	AEFKLST	FLASKET	AEFMORT	FORMATE
AEFILLM	FAMILLE	AEFKLUW	WAKEFUL	AEFMOUW	WAMEFOU
AEFILLS	FAILLES	AEFKNRR	FRANKER	AEFMRRS	FARMERS
AEFILMN	FEMINAL	AEFKORS	FORSAKE		FRAMERS
	INFLAME	AEFLLNN	FANNELL	AEFMRRY	FARMERY
AEFILMR	FLAMIER		FLANNEL	AEFNNRS	FANNERS
AEFILNS	FINALES	AEFLLOT	FLOATEL	AEFNNST	ENFANTS
AEFILNT	INFLATE	AEFLLRS	FALLERS	AEFNOPR	PROFANE
AEFILNU	INFULAE		REFALLS	AEFNOPY	PAYFONE
AEFILNV	FLAVINE	AEFLLSY	FALSELY	AEFNORR	FORERAN
AEFILOT	FOLIATE	AEFLLTT	FLATLET	AEFNRRS	FARRENS
AEFILPT	FLEAPIT	AEFLLTU	TALEFUL	AEFNRSS	FARNESS
AEFILRR	FLARIER	AEFLLUZ	ZEALFUL	AEFNRSU	FURANES
	FRAILER	AEFLMNS	FLAMENS		UNSAFER
AEFILRU	FAILURE	AEFLMOR	FEMORAL	AEFNRSW	FAWNERS
AEFILRV	FAVRILE	AEFLMRS	FLAMERS	AEFNSST	FASTENS
AEFILRW	FLAWIER	AEFLMUW	WAMEFUL		FATNESS
AEFILRX	FLAXIER	AEFLMUZ	MAZEFUL	AEFNSTT	FATTENS
AEFILRZ	FILAZER	AEFLNNN	FLANNEN	AEFOPRW	FOREPAW
AEFILSS	FALSIES	AEFLNNS	FANNELS	AEFORRV	FAVORER

	OVERFAR	**AEGGMNY**	YEGGMAN	**AEGHORS**	GHERAOS
AEFORRY	FORAYER	**AEGGMSS**	EGGMASS	**AEGHOSS**	SEAHOGS
AEFORSW	FORESAW	**AEGGNNU**	GUNNAGE	**AEGHOST**	HOSTAGE
AEFORSY	FORESAY	**AEGGNRR**	GRANGER	**AEGHPRS**	SPREACH
AEFORTV	OVERFAT	**AEGGNRS**	GANGERS	**AEGHPST**	HATPEGS
AEFOSST	FATSOES		GRANGES	**AEGHRST**	GATHERS
	FOSSATE		NAGGERS	**AEGHSST**	GASHEST
AEFOSTU	FEATOUS	**AEGGNSU**	GANGUES	**AEGIIMN**	IMAGINE
AEFPPRS	FRAPPES	**AEGGRRY**	RAGGERY	**AEGIKLN**	LEAKING
AEFRRST	FRATERS	**AEGGRSS**	AGGRESS		LINKAGE
	RAFTERS		SAGGERS	**AEGIKLT**	GLAIKET
	STRAFER		SEGGARS		TAGLIKE
AEFRRTY	FRATERY	**AEGGRST**	GAGSTER	**AEGIKNP**	PEAKING
AEFRSSS	FRASSES		GARGETS	**AEGIKNR**	REAKING
AEFRSST	FASTERS		STAGGER	**AEGIKNS**	SINKAGE
	STRAFES		TAGGERS	**AEGIKPP**	KIPPAGE
AEFRSTU	FAUREST	**AEGGRSU**	GAUGERS	**AEGIKPR**	GARPIKE
AEFRSTW	FRETSAW	**AEGGRSW**	SWAGGER	**AEGIKRW**	GAWKIER
	WAFTERS		WAGGERS	**AEGIKSW**	GAWKIES
AEFRTTU	TARTUFE	**AEGGRSY**	YAGGERS	**AEGILLL**	ILLEGAL
AEFRTUW	WAFTURE	**AEGGRTY**	GARGETY	**AEGILLM**	MEGILLA
AEFRWYZ	FRAWZEY	**AEGGRWY**	WAGGERY		MILLAGE
AEFSSTT	FASTEST	**AEGGSWW**	GEWGAWS	**AEGILLN**	GALLEIN
	SAFTEST	**AEGHHIT**	AHEIGHT		NIGELLA
AEFSSUV	FAVUSES	**AEGHIJR**	JAGHIRE	**AEGILLP**	PILLAGE
AEFSTTT	FATTEST	**AEGHIKL**	HAGLIKE	**AEGILLS**	GALLIES
AEGGGLS	GAGGLES	**AEGHILN**	HEALING		GALLISE
AEGGGLU	LUGGAGE	**AEGHILR**	LAIGHER	**AEGILLT**	TILLAGE
AEGGGRS	GAGGERS	**AEGHIMT**	MEGAHIT	**AEGILLU**	LIGULAE
AEGGGRY	GAGGERY	**AEGHINP**	HEAPING	**AEGILLV**	VILLAGE
AEGGHLR	HAGGLER	**AEGHINR**	HEARING	**AEGILLY**	AGILELY
AEGGHLS	HAGGLES	**AEGHINT**	GAHNITE	**AEGILLZ**	GALLIZE
AEGGHMO	HEMAGOG		HEATING	**AEGILMN**	GEMINAL
AEGGHSW	EGGWASH	**AEGHINV**	HEAVING		LEAMING
AEGGIJR	JAGGIER	**AEGHINZ**	GENIZAH		MEALING
AEGGIJS	JAGGIES	**AEGHIOS**	HOAGIES	**AEGILMR**	GREMIAL
AEGGILN	EAGLING	**AEGHIRS**	HEGARIS		LAMIGER
	GEALING		HEGIRAS	**AEGILMS**	MILAGES
	LIGNAGE		HIRAGES	**AEGILNN**	ANELING
AEGGIMS	MAGGIES	**AEGHISS**	GEISHAS		EANLING
AEGGINR	GEARING	**AEGHISZ**	GHAZIES		LEANING
	NAGGIER	**AEGHLNO**	HALOGEN		NEALING
AEGGINS	AGEINGS	**AEGHLNT**	ALENGTH	**AEGILNP**	LEAPING
	SIGNAGE	**AEGHLOS**	GALOSHE		PEALING
AEGGIOS	ISAGOGE	**AEGHLRU**	LAUGHER		PLEAING
AEGGIRR	RAGGIER	**AEGHLSS**	SEALGHS	**AEGILNR**	ALIGNER
AEGGIRS	RAGGIES	**AEGHLST**	HAGLETS		ENGRAIL
	SAGGIER	**AEGHLSZ**	GHAZELS		LAERING
AEGGIRT	TAGGIER	**AEGHLTW**	THALWEG		LEARING
AEGGIRU	GARIGUE	**AEGHMNN**	HANGMEN		NARGILE
AEGGIST	STAGGIE	**AEGHMNO**	HOGMANE		REALIGN
AEGGISW	SWAGGIE	**AEGHMOR**	HOMAGER		REGINAL
AEGGJRS	JAGGERS	**AEGHMOS**	HOMAGES	**AEGILNS**	LEASING
AEGGJRY	JAGGERY		OHMAGES		LINAGES
AEGGLNO	AGELONG	**AEGHMSU**	MESHUGA		SEALING
AEGGLNR	GANGREL	**AEGHNOX**	HEXAGON	**AEGILNT**	ATINGLE
AEGGLNS	LAGGENS	**AEGHNRS**	GNASHER		ELATING
AEGGLRR	GARGLER		HANGERS		GELATIN
AEGGLRS	GARGLES		REHANGS		GENITAL
	LAGGERS		SHERANG		TAGLINE
	RAGGLES	**AEGHNRU**	NURAGHE	**AEGILNU**	LINGUAE
AEGGLRW	WAGGLER	**AEGHNSS**	GNASHES		UNAGILE
AEGGLRY	GREYLAG	**AEGHNST**	STENGAH	**AEGILNV**	LEAVING
AEGGLSW	WAGGLES	**AEGHOPY**	HYPOGEA		VEALING

AEGILNV	ALEYING		NEARING		TZIGANE
	YEALING	**AEGINNS**	INNAGES	**AEGINVW**	WEAVING
AEGILOS	GOALIES		SEANING	**AEGIORT**	GOATIER
	SOILAGE	**AEGINNT**	ANTEING	**AEGIPPR**	GAPPIER
AEGILOU	EULOGIA		ANTIGEN	**AEGIPPS**	PIPAGES
AEGILPS	PAIGLES		GENTIAN	**AEGIPRR**	GRAPIER
AEGILRR	GLARIER	**AEGINNU**	ANGUINE	**AEGIPRS**	GASPIER
AEGILRS	GLAIRES		GUANINE		PRISAGE
	GRAILES	**AEGINNW**	WEANING		SPAIRGE
AEGILRZ	GLAZIER	**AEGINNY**	YEANING	**AEGIPST**	GAPIEST
AEGILSS	ALGESIS	**AEGINOR**	ORIGANE	**AEGIRRZ**	GRAZIER
	GLASSIE	**AEGINOS**	AGONIES	**AEGIRSS**	AGRISES
	LIGASES		AGONISE		GASSIER
	SILAGES	**AEGINOZ**	AGONIZE	**AEGIRST**	AGISTER
AEGILST	AGILEST	**AEGINPP**	GENIPAP		AIGRETS
	AIGLETS	**AEGINPR**	REAPING		GAITERS
	GELATIS	**AEGINPS**	PEASING		SEAGIRT
	LIGATES		SPAEING		STAGIER
	TAIGLES		SPINAGE		STRIGAE
AEGILSV	GLAIVES	**AEGINPZ**	PEAZING		TIRAGES
AEGILTU	GLUTAEI	**AEGINRR**	ANGRIER		TRIAGES
AEGILTY	EGALITY		EARRING	**AEGIRSV**	GARVIES
AEGIMMR	GAMMIER		GRAINER		GRAVIES
AEGIMNN	AMENING		RANGIER		RIVAGES
	MEANING		REARING	**AEGIRSW**	EARWIGS
AEGIMNP	PIGMEAN	**AEGINRS**	ANGRIES		GAWSIER
AEGIMNR	GERMAIN		EARINGS	**AEGIRSZ**	AGRIZES
	GERMINA		ERASING	**AEGIRTV**	VIRGATE
	MANGIER		GAINERS		VITRAGE
	MEARING		GRAINES	**AEGIRUY**	YUGARIE
	REAMING		REAGINS	**AEGIRUZ**	GAUZIER
AEGIMNS	ENIGMAS		REGAINS	**AEGISST**	AGEISTS
	GAMINES		REGINAS		SAGIEST
	MEASING		SEARING	**AEGISSU**	AGUISES
	SEAMING		SERINGA	**AEGISSV**	VISAGES
AEGIMNT	MINTAGE	**AEGINRT**	GRANITE	**AEGISTU**	AUGITES
	TEAMING		GRATINE	**AEGISTY**	GASEITY
	TEGMINA		INGRATE	**AEGISTZ**	GAZIEST
AEGIMOS	IMAGOES		TANGIER	**AEGISUZ**	AGUIZES
AEGIMPR	EPIGRAM		TEARING	**AEGISYZ**	AZYGIES
	PRIMAGE	**AEGINRV**	REAVING	**AEGJLNR**	JANGLER
AEGIMPS	MAGPIES		VINEGAR	**AEGJLNS**	JANGLES
	MISPAGE	**AEGINRW**	WEARING	**AEGJLSS**	JAGLESS
AEGIMPT	PIGMEAT	**AEGINRZ**	ZINGARE	**AEGJLST**	JETLAGS
AEGIMRR	ARMIGER	**AEGINSS**	AGNISES	**AEGKKNO**	ANGEKOK
AEGIMRS	GISARME		SEASING	**AEGKLOU**	KAGOULE
	IMAGERS	**AEGINST**	EASTING	**AEGKLRS**	GRAKLES
	MAIGRES		EATINGS	**AEGKMRY**	KERYGMA
	MIRAGES		GAINEST	**AEGKMSS**	MASKEGS
AEGIMRT	MIGRATE		GENISTA	**AEGKNOR**	KARENGO
	RAGTIME		INGATES	**AEGKNRS**	SKANGER
AEGIMRU	GAUMIER		INGESTA	**AEGKRSW**	GAWKERS
AEGIMRY	IMAGERY		SEATING	**AEGKSST**	GASKETS
AEGIMSS	AGEISMS		TAGINES	**AEGLLLY**	LEGALLY
AEGIMST	GAMIEST		TANGIES	**AEGLLNO**	ALLONGE
	SIGMATE		TEASING		GALLEON
AEGIMSV	MISGAVE		TSIGANE	**AEGLLNR**	LANGREL
AEGINNO	GANOINE	**AEGINSU**	GUINEAS	**AEGLLNS**	LEGLANS
AEGINNP	NEAPING	**AEGINSY**	EASYING	**AEGLLNT**	GELLANT
	PEANING	**AEGINSZ**	AGNIZES	**AEGLLNY**	LANGLEY
AEGINNR	AGINNER		SEAZING	**AEGLLOR**	ALLEGRO
	EARNING	**AEGINTU**	UNITAGE	**AEGLLOT**	TOLLAGE
	ENGRAIN	**AEGINTV**	VINTAGE	**AEGLLRY**	ALLERGY
	GRANNIE	**AEGINTZ**	TEAZING		GALLERY

Seven-letter anagrams

	LARGELY		GRAUPEL		TONNAGE
	REGALLY		PLAGUER	**AEGNNOW**	NONWAGE
AEGLLST	GALLETS	**AEGLPSS**	GAPLESS	**AEGNNPS**	PANGENS
AEGLLSU	SEAGULL	**AEGLPSU**	PLAGUES		PENANGS
	SULLAGE		PLUSAGE	**AEGNNRT**	REGNANT
	ULLAGES	**AEGLPUY**	PLAGUEY	**AEGNNRU**	GUNNERA
AEGLLSY	GALLEYS	**AEGLRRU**	REGULAR	**AEGNNST**	GANNETS
AEGLLTU	GLUTEAL	**AEGLRSS**	LARGESS	**AEGNNTT**	TANGENT
AEGLMNR	MANGLER	**AEGLRSV**	GRAVELS	**AEGNNTU**	TUNNAGE
AEGLMNS	MANGELS		VERGLAS	**AEGNOOR**	OREGANO
	MANGLES	**AEGLRSY**	ARGYLES	**AEGNOPT**	PONTAGE
AEGLMOR	GLOMERA		GRAYLES	**AEGNORR**	GROANER
	GOMERAL				ORANGER
AEGLMOU	MOULAGE	**AEGLRSZ**	GLAZERS	**AEGNORS**	ONAGERS
AEGLMPU	PLUMAGE	**AEGLRTU**	GAULTER		ORANGES
AEGLMRS	MALGRES		TEGULAR	**AEGNORT**	NEGATOR
AEGLMRU	MAULGRE		TRAGULE	**AEGNORW**	WAGONER
AEGLMSV	MAGLEVS	**AEGLRTY**	GREATLY	**AEGNORY**	ORANGEY
AEGLMSY	MYGALES	**AEGLRVY**	GRAVELY	**AEGNOST**	ONSTAGE
AEGLNOS	ENGAOLS	**AEGLSSS**	GASLESS	**AEGNOSY**	NOSEGAY
AEGLNOT	TANGELO		GLASSES	**AEGNOWY**	WAYGONE
AEGLNPR	GRAPNEL	**AEGLSSU**	SAULGES	**AEGNPRS**	ENGRASP
AEGLNPS	SPANGLE	**AEGLSTT**	GESTALT	**AEGNPRT**	TREPANG
AEGLNRS	ANGLERS	**AEGLSTW**	TALWEGS	**AEGNRRS**	GARNERS
	ERLANGS	**AEGLTUV**	VULGATE		RANGERS
	LANGERS	**AEGLUUY**	GUAYULE	**AEGNRRT**	GRANTER
	LARGENS	**AEGLUVY**	VAGUELY		REGRANT
	SLANGER	**AEGMMNS**	MAGSMEN	**AEGNRSS**	SANGERS
AEGLNRT	TANGLER	**AEGMMRS**	GAMMERS		SERANGS
	TRANGLE		GRAMMES	**AEGNRST**	ARGENTS
AEGLNRU	GRANULE	**AEGMMRU**	RUMMAGE		GARNETS
AEGLNRW	WANGLER	**AEGMMSS**	SMEGMAS		STRANGE
	WRANGLE	**AEGMNNO**	AGNOMEN	**AEGNRSU**	RAUNGES
AEGLNRV	ANGERLY		NONGAME		UNGEARS
AEGLNSS	GLASSEN	**AEGMNOR**	MARENGO	**AEGNRSW**	GNAWERS
AEGLNST	GELANTS		MEGARON	**AEGNRTU**	GAUNTER
	LANGEST	**AEGMNOS**	GAMONES	**AEGNRTW**	TWANGER
	TANGLES		MANGOES	**AEGNRTY**	AGENTRY
AEGLNSU	ANGELUS	**AEGMNOT**	GEOMANT	**AEGNSSY**	GANSEYS
	LAGUNES		MAGNETO		GAYNESS
	LANGUES		MEGATON	**AEGNSTT**	GESTANT
AEGLNSW	WANGLES		MONTAGE	**AEGNTTU**	TUTENAG
AEGLNSY	LYNAGES	**AEGMNPY**	PYGMEAN	**AEGOORT**	ROOTAGE
AEGLNTT	GANTLET	**AEGMNRS**	ENGRAMS	**AEGOPPR**	PROPAGE
AEGLNTU	LANGUET		GERMANS	**AEGOPRT**	PORTAGE
AEGLNTW	TWANGLE		MANGERS		POTAGER
AEGLNUU	UNGULAE	**AEGMNRT**	GARMENT	**AEGOPST**	GESTAPO
AEGLNUW	GUNWALE		MARGENT		POSTAGE
AEGLOOZ	ZOOGLEA		RAGMENT		POTAGES
AEGLOPR	PERGOLA	**AEGMNST**	MAGNETS	**AEGOPTT**	POTTAGE
AEGLORS	GALORES	**AEGMNSW**	SWAGMEN	**AEGORRT**	GARROTE
	GAOLERS	**AEGMNTU**	AUGMENT	**AEGORSS**	SORAGES
AEGLORT	GLOATER		MUTAGEN	**AEGORST**	GAROTES
	LEGATOR	**AEGMOOR**	MOORAGE		ORGEATS
AEGLORV	VORLAGE	**AEGMORS**	ROMAGES		STORAGE
AEGLOSS	GLOSSAE	**AEGMOSW**	WAGSOME		TOERAGS
AEGLOST	GELATOS	**AEGMOSY**	GAYSOME	**AEGORSU**	AERUGOS
	LEGATOS	**AEGMOXY**	EXOGAMY	**AEGORTT**	GAROTTE
AEGLOSU	GEALOUS	**AEGMRSU**	MAUGRES	**AEGORTU**	OUTRAGE
AEGLOSV	LOVAGES		MURAGES	**AEGORUV**	OUVRAGE
AEGLOTV	VOLTAGE	**AEGMSUY**	MAGUEYS	**AEGORVY**	VOYAGER
AEGLPPR	GRAPPLE	**AEGMSUZ**	ZEUGMAS	**AEGOSSU**	GASEOUS
AEGLPRS	GRAPLES	**AEGNNOS**	NONAGES	**AEGOSTU**	OUTAGES
AEGLPRU	EARPLUG	**AEGNNOT**	NEGATON	**AEGOSTW**	STOWAGE

	TOWAGES
AEGOSTX	OXGATES
AEGOSVY	VOYAGES
AEGOTTU	OUTGATE
AEGOTTV	GAVOTTE
AEGOTUV	OUTGAVE
AEGOTUZ	OUTGAZE
AEGPPRS	GAPPERS
AEGPRRS	GRASPER
	SPARGER
AEGPRRY	GRAPERY
AEGPRSS	GASPERS
	SPARGES
AEGPRST	PARGETS
AEGPRSU	GAUPERS
AEGPRSW	GAWPERS
AEGPSSU	PEGASUS
AEGPSTU	UPSTAGE
AEGPSUZ	UPGAZES
AEGRRSS	GRASSER
AEGRRST	GARRETS
	GARTERS
	GRATERS
AEGRRSU	ARGUERS
	SUGARER
AEGRRSV	GRAVERS
AEGRRSZ	GRAZERS
AEGRRUU	AUGURER
AEGRRUV	GRAVURE
	VERRUGA
AEGRSSS	GASSERS
	GRASSES
AEGRSST	GASTERS
	STAGERS
AEGRSSU	ARGUSES
	SAUGERS
	USAGERS
AEGRSSW	SWAGERS
AEGRSSY	GYRASES
AEGRSTT	TARGETS
AEGRSTV	GRAVEST
AEGRSTY	GRAYEST
	GYRATES
	STAGERY
AEGRSUV	SEVRUGA
AEGRSVY	GARVEYS
AEGRSYZ	AGRYZES
AEGSSSU	GAUSSES
AEGSTUU	AUGUSTE
AEGSTUV	VAGUEST
AEGTTTU	GUTTATE
AEHHIKS	SHEIKHA
AEHHIRS	HASHIER
AEHHIST	SHEHITA
AEHHLST	HEALTHS
AEHHLTY	HEALTHY
AEHHNRS	HARSHEN
AEHHPRS	RHAPHES
AEHHRRS	HARSHER
AEHHRST	HEARTHS
AEHHSSS	SHASHES
AEHHSST	SHEATHS
AEHHSTY	SHEATHY
AEHIILR	HAILIER
AEHIIRR	HAIRIER
AEHIJRS	HEJIRAS
AEHIKLT	HATLIKE
AEHIKNS	HANKIES
AEHIKPS	PEAKISH
AEHIKRS	SHAKIER
AEHIKSS	SAKIEHS
AEHIKST	SHITAKE
AEHIKSW	HAWKIES
	WEAKISH
AEHIKSY	SAKIYEH
AEHILMN	HELIMAN
AEHILMO	HEMIOLA
AEHILMS	LEHAIMS
AEHILMY	LEHAYIM
AEHILNR	HERNIAL
	INHALER
AEHILNS	INHALES
AEHILNY	HYALINE
AEHILOR	AIRHOLE
AEHILPR	HARELIP
AEHILPT	HAPLITE
AEHILRS	HAILERS
	SHALIER
AEHILRT	LATHIER
AEHILRU	HAULIER
AEHILSS	SHEILAS
AEHILST	HALITES
	HELIAST
AEHILSW	SHAWLIE
	WHAISLE
AEHILTT	LITHATE
AEHILTY	HYALITE
AEHILUV	VIHUELA
AEHILVY	HEAVILY
AEHILWZ	WHAIZLE
AEHIMMR	HAMMIER
AEHIMMS	MAIHEMS
AEHIMNR	HARMINE
AEHIMNS	HAEMINS
	HEMINAS
AEHIMNT	HEMATIN
AEHIMNY	HYMENIA
AEHIMPS	PHAEISM
AEHIMRS	MASHIER
	MISHEAR
AEHIMSS	MASHIES
	MESSIAH
AEHIMST	ATHEISM
AEHINPR	HEPARIN
AEHINPS	INPHASE
AEHINPT	PENTHIA
AEHINRS	ARSHINE
	HERNIAS
AEHINRT	HAIRNET
	INEARTH
	THERIAN
AEHINSS	HESSIAN
AEHINST	SHEITAN
	STHENIA
AEHINSV	EVANISH
	VAHINES
AEHINSW	WAHINES
AEHIORR	HOARIER
AEHIPPR	HAPPIER
AEHIPPS	HAPPIES
AEHIPPT	EPITAPH
AEHIPRS	HARPIES
	SHARPIE
AEHIPSS	APHESIS
AEHIPSW	PEISHWA
AEHIPTZ	ZAPTIEH
AEHIQSU	HAIQUES
	QUASHIE
AEHIRRR	HARRIER
AEHIRRS	HARRIES
AEHIRSS	ARISHES
	RASHIES
	SHERIAS
AEHIRST	HASTIER
	SHERIAT
AEHIRSV	ASHIVER
AEHIRSW	WASHIER
	WEARISH
AEHIRTW	THAWIER
AEHIRWY	HAYWIRE
AEHISST	ASHIEST
	SAITHES
	STASHIE
	TAISHES
AEHISSV	SHAVIES
AEHISTT	ATHEIST
	STAITHE
AEHISTZ	HAZIEST
AEHISVY	YESHIVA
AEHITTW	THWAITE
AEHJLOW	JAWHOLE
AEHKMSS	SAMEKHS
AEHKNRS	HANKERS
	HARKENS
AEHKNRT	THANKER
AEHKNSZ	KHAZENS
AEHKOOR	HOROEKA
AEHKOSS	SHAKOES
AEHKPRS	PHREAKS
AEHKPSU	SHAKEUP
AEHKRRS	SHARKER
AEHKRSS	KASHERS
	SHAKERS
AEHKRSW	HAWKERS
AEHKSSY	ASHKEYS
AEHKSWY	HAWKEYS
AEHLLLS	HALLELS
AEHLLOS	HALLOES
AEHLLOV	HELLOVA
AEHLLRS	HERSALL
AEHLLST	LETHALS
AEHLLUV	HELLUVA
AEHLLYZ	HAZELLY
AEHLMNO	MANHOLE
AEHLMNY	HYMENAL
AEHLMOR	ARMHOLE
AEHLMPS	PELHAMS
AEHLMPW	WHAMPLE
AEHLMRS	HARMELS
AEHLMRT	THERMAL
AEHLMRU	HUMERAL
AEHLMST	HAMLETS

AEHLNOS	ENHALOS	**AEHMOPT**	APOTHEM	**AEHORTX**	OXHEART
AEHLNOT	ANETHOL	**AEHMORT**	TERAOHM	**AEHORUV**	HAVEOUR
	ETHANOL	**AEHMPRS**	HAMPERS	**AEHORUW**	WAREHOU
AEHLNRT	ENTHRAL	**AEHMPTY**	EMPATHY	**AEHOSTU**	ATHEOUS
AEHLNSS	HANSELS	**AEHMRRS**	HARMERS	**AEHPPRS**	PERHAPS
AEHLNST	HANTLES	**AEHMRSS**	MARSHES	**AEHPPRW**	WHAPPER
AEHLNSU	UNHEALS		MASHERS	**AEHPPSU**	SHAPEUP
	UNLEASH		SHAMERS		UPHEAPS
	UNSHALE		SHMEARS	**AEHPRRS**	HARPERS
AEHLOPR	EPHORAL		SMASHER		PHRASER
AEHLOPT	TAPHOLE	**AEHMRST**	HAMSTER		SHARPER
AEHLORS	SHOALER	**AEHMRTU**	MAUTHER	**AEHPRSS**	PHRASES
AEHLORT	LOATHER	**AEHMRTW**	MAWTHER		SERAPHS
	RATHOLE	**AEHMSSS**	SMASHES		SHAPERS
AEHLOSS	ASSHOLE	**AEHMSST**	SMEATHS		SHERPAS
AEHLOST	LOATHES	**AEHMSTT**	SHMATTE		SPHAERS
AEHLPRS	PLASHER	**AEHMSTU**	HUMATES		SPHEARS
	SPHERAL	**AEHMSUW**	MAHEWUS	**AEHPRST**	SPARTHE
AEHLPSS	HAPLESS	**AEHMUZZ**	MEZUZAH		TEPHRAS
	PLASHES	**AEHNNTU**	UNNEATH		THREAPS
AEHLPST	PLASHET	**AEHNNWY**	ANYWHEN	**AEHPRSW**	PREWASH
AEHLPSY	SHAPELY	**AEHNOPT**	PHAETON	**AEHPRTT**	PHATTER
AEHLRSS	ASHLERS		PHONATE	**AEHPRTY**	THERAPY
	HALSERS	**AEHNOPW**	WANHOPE	**AEHPSST**	SPATHES
	LASHERS	**AEHNOPY**	HYPONEA	**AEHPSSW**	PESHWAS
	SLASHER	**AEHNORS**	HOARSEN	**AEHPSTY**	HYPATES
AEHLRST	HALTERS		SENHORA	**AEHQRSU**	QUASHER
	HARSLET	**AEHNORT**	ANOTHER	**AEHQSSU**	QUASHES
	LATHERS	**AEHNOSX**	HEXOSAN	**AEHRRSS**	RASHERS
	SLATHER	**AEHNPPS**	HAPPENS		SHARERS
	THALERS	**AEHNPRS**	SHARPEN	**AEHRRST**	TRASHER
AEHLRSU	HAULERS	**AEHNPRT**	PANTHER	**AEHRRTU**	URETHRA
AEHLRSV	HALVERS	**AEHNPST**	HAPTENS	**AEHRSST**	RASHEST
AEHLRSW	WHALERS	**AEHNPSU**	UNSHAPE		SHASTER
AEHLRTY	EARTHLY	**AEHNPTY**	PHYTANE		SHATTER
	HARTELY	**AEHNRSS**	HARNESS		THREATS
	HEARTLY	**AEHNRST**	ANTHERS	**AEHRSSV**	SHAVERS
	LATHERY		HARTENS	**AEHRSSW**	HAWSERS
AEHLRWY	WHALERY		THENARS		SWASHER
AEHLSSS	ASHLESS	**AEHNRTU**	HAUNTER		WASHERS
	HASSELS		UNEARTH	**AEHRSTT**	HATTERS
	HASSLES		UNHEART		RATHEST
	SLASHES		URETHAN		SHATTER
AEHLSST	HASLETS	**AEHNRTX**	NARTHEX		THREATS
	HATLESS	**AEHNSSS**	SNASHES	**AEHRSTV**	HARVEST
	SHELTAS	**AEHNSST**	HASTENS		THRAVES
AEHLSSY	HAYSELS		SNATHES	**AEHRSTW**	SWATHER
AEHLSTT	STEALTH		SNEATHS		THAWERS
AEHLSTW	WEALTHS	**AEHNSSU**	HAUSENS		WREATHS
AEHLSWY	SHAWLEY	**AEHNSSZ**	SAZHENS	**AEHRSVW**	WHARVES
AEHLTWY	WEALTHY	**AEHNSTY**	ASTHENY	**AEHRSWY**	WASHERY
AEHMMNS	MASHMEN		SHANTEY	**AEHRSXY**	HYRAXES
AEHMMRS	HAMMERS	**AEHNSUW**	WHENUAS	**AEHRTUU**	HAUTEUR
	SHAMMER	**AEHNSUY**	HAUYNES	**AEHRTWY**	WREATHY
AEHMMSS	SHAMMES	**AEHNTTW**	WHATTEN	**AEHSSST**	STASHES
AEHMMSY	MAYHEMS	**AEHOORT**	TOHEROA	**AEHSSSW**	SWASHES
AEHMNOR	MENORAH	**AEHOPRT**	PHORATE	**AEHSSTW**	SWATHES
AEHMNOS	HOSEMAN	**AEHOPST**	TEASHOP	**AEHSTUX**	EXHAUST
AEHMNOT	NATHEMO	**AEHORRS**	HOARSER	**AEIIKLR**	AIRLIKE
AEHMNOY	HAEMONY	**AEHORST**	ASTHORE	**AEIIKNT**	KAINITE
AEHMNPY	NYMPHAE		EARSHOT	**AEIIKSS**	SAIKEIS
AEHMNRU	HUMANER		HAROSET	**AEIILLT**	TAILLIE
AEHMNST	ANTHEMS	**AEHORSX**	HOAXERS	**AEIILMP**	LIPEMIA
	HETMANS	**AEHORTU**	OUTHEAR	**AEIILMR**	RAMILIE
				AEIILNN	ANILINE

AEIILNR	AIRLINE	**AEIKLNO**	KAOLINE	**AEIKSSS**	ASKESIS
AEIILNX	EXILIAN	**AEIKLNR**	LANKIER	**AEIKSTT**	TAKIEST
AEIILRR	LAIRIER	**AEIKLNS**	ALKINES	**AEILLMN**	MANILLE
AEIILRS	LAIRISE	**AEIKLNT**	ANTLIKE	**AEILLNR**	RALLINE
AEIILRV	VIRELAI	**AEIKLNU**	UNALIKE	**AEILLNS**	AINSELL
AEIILRZ	LAIRIZE	**AEIKLOR**	OARLIKE	**AEILLNU**	UILLEAN
AEIILSS	LIAISES	**AEIKLOT**	KEITLOA	**AEILLNY**	ALIENLY
	SILESIA		OATLIKE	**AEILLOV**	ALVEOLI
AEIILST	LAITIES	**AEIKLRR**	LARKIER	**AEILLPR**	PALLIER
AEIILSW	LEWISIA	**AEIKLRS**	LAIKERS		PERILLA
AEIILTZ	TAILZIE		SERKALI	**AEILLPS**	ILLAPSE
AEIIMNT	INTIMAE	**AEIKLRT**	RATLIKE	**AEILLPU**	PILULAE
	MINIATE		TALKIER	**AEILLPY**	EPYLLIA
AEIIMPR	IMPERIA	**AEIKLRV**	KLAVIER	**AEILLQU**	LALIQUE
AEIIMRT	AIRTIME	**AEIKLRW**	WARLIKE	**AEILLRR**	RALLIER
AEIIMRV	VIREMIA	**AEIKLRY**	RAYLIKE	**AEILLRS**	RALLIES
AEIIMST	AMITIES	**AEIKLSS**	ALSIKES		SALLIER
	ATIMIES		ASSLIKE	**AEILLRT**	LITERAL
AEIIMTT	IMITATE	**AEIKLST**	LAKIEST		TALLIER
AEIINNS	ASININE		TALKIES		TRIELLA
	INSANIE	**AEIKLSW**	SAWLIKE	**AEILLRU**	RUELLIA
AEIINOP	EPINAOI	**AEIKLWX**	WAXLIKE	**AEILLRW**	WALLIER
AEIINQU	EQUINIA	**AEIKMMS**	MISMAKE	**AEILLSS**	ALLISES
AEIINNR	RAINIER	**AEIKMNP**	PIKEMAN		SALLIES
AEIINRS	SENARII	**AEIKMNR**	MANKIER	**AEILLST**	SITELLA
AEIINRT	INERTIA		RAMEKIN		TAILLES
AEIINST	ISATINE	**AEIKMNS**	KINEMAS		TALLIES
AEIINSX	SIXAINE	**AEIKMPR**	RAMPIKE	**AEILLSW**	WALLIES
AEIINTX	AXINITE	**AEIKMRW**	MAWKIER	**AEILLUV**	ELUVIAL
AEIIPRR	PRAIRIE	**AEIKMSS**	KAMISES	**AEILLVX**	VEXILLA
AEIIRRV	RIVIERA	**AEIKMST**	KETMIAS	**AEILMMN**	MAILMEN
	VAIRIER		MISTAKE	**AEILMMR**	MALMIER
AEIIRST	AIRIEST	**AEIKNNT**	NEATNIK	**AEILMMS**	LAMMIES
	IRISATE	**AEIKNPR**	RANPIKE		MELISMA
AEIIRSW	AIRWISE	**AEIKNRR**	NARKIER	**AEILMNN**	LINEMAN
AEIITTV	VITIATE	**AEIKNRS**	SNAKIER		MELANIN
AEIJKLM	JAMLIKE	**AEIKNRT**	KERATIN	**AEILMNO**	MINEOLA
AEIJKLW	JAWLIKE	**AEIKNRW**	WANKIER	**AEILMNP**	IMPANEL
AEIJLNV	JAVELIN	**AEIKNSS**	KINASES		MANIPLE
AEIJLNW	JAWLINE	**AEIKNST**	INTAKES	**AEILMNR**	MANLIER
AEIJLRS	JAILERS		KENTIAS		MARLINE
AEIJLSZ	JEZAILS		TANKIES		MINERAL
AEIJMMR	JAMMIER	**AEIKNSW**	SWANKIE		RAILMEN
AEIJMMS	JAMMIES	**AEIKNSY**	KYANISE	**AEILMNS**	ISLEMAN
	JEMIMAS		YANKIES		MALINES
AEIJMNS	JASMINE	**AEIKNSZ**	KAIZENS		MENIALS
AEIJNNS	JANNIES	**AEIKNTU**	UNAKITE		SEMINAL
AEIJNRS	INJERAS	**AEIKNTY**	KYANITE	**AEILMNT**	AILMENT
AEIJNRT	JANTIER	**AEIKNYZ**	KYANIZE		ALIMENT
	NARTJIE	**AEIKOST**	OAKIEST	**AEILMNU**	ALUMINE
AEIJNST	JANTIES	**AEIKPRR**	PARKIER	**AEILMOR**	LOAMIER
	TAJINES	**AEIKPRS**	PARKIES	**AEILMPR**	IMPALER
AEIJNTU	JAUNTIE		SPARKIE		IMPEARL
AEIJRSV	JARVIES	**AEIKPRW**	PAWKIER		LEMPIRA
AEIJRZZ	JAZZIER	**AEIKQRU**	QUAKIER		PALMIER
AEIJSSV	JIVEASS	**AEIKRRS**	KERRIAS	**AEILMPS**	IMPALES
AEIKKLO	OAKLIKE		SARKIER		PALMIES
AEIKKPS	PIKAKES	**AEIKRSS**	KAISERS	**AEILMPT**	IMPLATE
AEIKKST	TAKKIES		KARSIES		PALMIET
AEIKLLW	LAWLIKE	**AEIKRST**	ARKITES	**AEILMRR**	LARMIER
AEIKLLY	LEAKILY		KARITES		MARLIER
AEIKLMN	MANLIKE	**AEIKRSU**	KAURIES	**AEILMRS**	MAILERS
AEIKLMP	MAPLIKE	**AEIKRSW**	SKIWEAR		REALISM
AEIKLMR	ARMLIKE	**AEIKRSZ**	KARZIES		REMAILS

AEILMRT	LAMITER	**AEILNTV**	VENTAIL	**AEILSSV**	VALISES
	MALTIER	**AEILNUV**	UNALIVE		VESSAIL
	MARLITE		UNVAILE	**AEILSSW**	WALISES
AEILMSS	AIMLESS	**AEILNUW**	LAUWINE	**AEILSTU**	SITULAE
	MESAILS	**AEILNVY**	NAIVELY	**AEILSTV**	ESTIVAL
	SAMIELS	**AEILOPR**	PELORIA	**AEILSTW**	WALIEST
	SEISMAL	**AEILOPS**	LEIPOAS	**AEILSTY**	TAILYES
AEILMSZ	MEZAILS	**AEILORV**	VARIOLE	**AEILSTZ**	LAZIEST
AEILMTY	LAYTIME	**AEILOST**	ISOLATE	**AEILTVY**	VILAYET
	MEATILY	**AEILOTV**	VIOLATE	**AEILUVX**	EXUVIAL
AEILNNY	INANELY	**AEILPPR**	APPERIL	**AEIMMMS**	MAMMIES
AEILNOP	OPALINE		APPLIER	**AEIMMNS**	AMMINES
AEILNOR	AILERON		ARIPPLE		MISNAME
	ALERION	**AEILPPS**	APPLIES	**AEIMMPS**	SPAMMIE
	ALIENOR		LAPPIES	**AEIMMRR**	RAMMIER
AEILNOS	ANISOLE	**AEILPRS**	PALSIER	**AEIMMRS**	MAIMERS
AEILNOT	ELATION		PARLIES		RAMMIES
	TOENAIL	**AEILPRT**	PLAITER	**AEIMMRT**	MARMITE
AEILNPR	PEARLIN		PLATIER		TRAMMIE
	PLAINER	**AEILPRV**	PREVAIL	**AEIMMSS**	SAMMIES
	PRALINE	**AEILPSS**	ESPIALS	**AEIMMST**	MISMATE
AEILNPS	ALPINES		LAIPSES		SEMIMAT
	PINEALS		LAPISES		TAMMIES
	SPANIEL		LIPASES	**AEIMMZZ**	MIZMAZE
	SPLENIA		PALSIES	**AEIMNNT**	MANNITE
AEILNPT	PANTILE	**AEILPST**	APLITES	**AEIMNOR**	MORAINE
AEILNPW	PINWALE		PALIEST		ROMAINE
AEILNPX	EXPLAIN		PLATIES	**AEIMNOS**	ANOMIES
AEILNQU	EQUINAL		TALIPES	**AEIMNOT**	AMNIOTE
	QUINELA	**AEILPSY**	PAISLEY	**AEIMNOU**	MOINEAU
AEILNRR	LARNIER	**AEILQTU**	LIQUATE	**AEIMNPR**	PERMIAN
AEILNRS	ALINERS		TEQUILA	**AEIMNRR**	MARINER
	NAILERS	**AEILRRS**	RAILERS	**AEIMNRS**	MARINES
	RENAILS		RERAILS		REMAINS
AEILNRT	ENTRAIL	**AEILRRT**	RETIRAL		SEMINAR
	LATRINE		RETRIAL		SIRNAME
	RATLINE		TRAILER	**AEIMNRT**	MERANTI
	RELIANT	**AEILRSS**	AIRLESS		MINARET
	RETINAL		RESAILS		RAIMENT
	TRENAIL		SAILERS	**AEIMNRV**	VERMIAN
AEILNRV	RAVELIN		SERAILS	**AEIMNRW**	WIREMAN
AEILNRW	LAWNIER		SERIALS	**AEIMNSS**	INSEAMS
AEILNRX	RELAXIN	**AEILRST**	REALIST		SAMISEN
AEILNRY	INLAYER		RETAILS	**AEIMNST**	ETAMINS
	NAILERY		SALTIER		INMATES
AEILNSS	SALINES		SALTIRE		MAINEST
	SILANES		SLATIER		MANTIES
AEILNST	EASTLIN		TAILERS		TAMEINS
	ELASTIN	**AEILRSV**	REVISAL		TAMINES
	ENTAILS	**AEILRSW**	SWALIER	**AEIMNSW**	MANWISE
	NAILSET		WAILERS	**AEIMNTX**	TAXIMEN
	SALIENT	**AEILRTT**	TERTIAL	**AEIMNTY**	AMENITY
	SALTINE	**AEILRTU**	URALITE		ANYTIME
	SLAINTE	**AEILRTW**	WALTIER	**AEIMNUV**	MAUVEIN
	STANIEL	**AEILRTY**	IRATELY		MAUVINE
	TENAILS		REALITY	**AEIMOOP**	IPOMOEA
AEILNSU	INSULAE		TEARILY	**AEIMOPR**	EMPORIA
	INULASE	**AEILRVV**	REVIVAL		MEROPIA
AEILNSV	ALEVINS	**AEILRVY**	VIRELAY	**AEIMORR**	ARMOIRE
	VALINES	**AEILRWY**	WEARILY	**AEIMOST**	AMOSITE
AEILNSW	LAWINES	**AEILSSS**	LAISSES		ATOMIES
AEILNSX	ALEXINS		LASSIES		ATOMISE
AEILNSY	ELYSIAN	**AEILSST**	SALTIES		OSMIATE
AEILNTU	ALUNITE	**AEILSSU**	SAULIES	**AEIMOTX**	TOXEMIA

AEIMOTZ	ATOMIZE	AEINNRU	ANEURIN		NITRATE
AEIMPRR	RAMPIRE	AEINNSS	SANNIES		TARTINE
AEIMPRS	IMPRESA		SIENNAS		TERTIAN
	SAMPIRE	AEINNST	INANEST	AEINRTU	RUINATE
AEIMPRT	PRIMATE		STANINE		TAURINE
AEIMPRV	VAMPIER		TANNIES		URANITE
	VAMPIRE	AEINNSW	SWANNIE		URINATE
AEIMPSS	IMPASSE	AEINNSZ	ENZIANS	AEINRTW	TAWNIER
	PESSIMA	AEINNTT	ANTIENT		TINWARE
AEIMPST	IMPASTE	AEINOPS	EPINAOS	AEINRUV	VAURIEN
	PASTIME		SENOPIA	AEINRUW	UNWARIE
AEIMPSV	IMPAVES	AEINOPZ	EPIZOAN	AEINRUZ	AZURINE
AEIMPSW	MAPWISE	AEINORS	ERASION	AEINRVV	VERVAIN
AEIMPSY	PYEMIAS	AEINORT	OTARINE	AEINRWY	YAWNIER
	YAMPIES	AEINOSS	ANOESIS	AEINSSS	SANSEIS
AEIMRRR	MARRIER	AEINOST	ATONIES		SASINES
AEIMRRS	MARRIES	AEINOSV	EVASION	AEINSST	ENTASIS
	SIMARRE	AEINOSZ	AZIONES		NASTIES
AEIMRSS	MASSIER	AEINOXZ	OXAZINE		SEITANS
	SARMIES	AEINPPP	PANPIPE		SESTINA
AEIMRST	IMARETS	AEINPPR	NAPPIER		TANSIES
	MAESTRI	AEINPPS	NAPPIES		TISANES
	MAISTER		PINESAP	AEINSSV	SAVINES
	MASTIER	AEINPRS	PANIERS		VINASSE
	MISRATE		RAPINES	AEINSTT	INSTATE
	SEMITAR	AEINPRT	PAINTER		SATINET
	SMARTIE		PERTAIN	AEINSTU	AUNTIES
AEIMRSU	UREMIAS		REPAINT		SINUATE
AEIMRSV	MISAVER	AEINPSS	ASPINES	AEINSTV	NAIVEST
AEIMRSW	AWMRIES		PANSIES		NATIVES
	SEMIRAW		SAPIENS		VAINEST
AEIMRSY	RIMAYES	AEINPST	PANTIES	AEINSTW	AWNIEST
AEIMRTU	MURIATE		PATINES		TAWNIES
AEIMRTV	VITAMER		SAPIENT		WANIEST
AEIMRTW	WARTIME		SPINATE		WANTIES
AEIMSSS	AMISSES	AEINPSW	WINESAP	AEINSTX	ANTISEX
	MESSIAS	AEINPTT	PATIENT		SEXTAIN
AEIMSST	ASTEISM	AEINPTU	PETUNIA	AEINSTZ	ZANIEST
	MISEATS	AEINPTY	PANEITY		ZEATINS
	MISSEAT	AEINQTU	ANTIQUE	AEINSVV	NAVVIES
	SAMIEST		QUINATE	AEINSWY	ANYWISE
	SAMITES	AEINRRS	SIERRAN	AEINTUV	VAUNTIE
	TAMISES		SNARIER	AEINTVW	VAWNTIE
AEIMSSV	MASSIVE	AEINRRT	RETRAIN	AEINTVY	NAIVETY
	MAVISES		TERRAIN	AEINTXY	ANXIETY
AEIMSSW	SWAMIES		TRAINER	AEIOPRS	SOAPIER
AEIMSSY	MYIASES	AEINRSS	ARSINES	AEIOPSS	SOAPIES
AEIMSTT	ETATISM		SARNIES	AEIOPST	ATOPIES
	MATIEST	AEINRST	ANESTRI		OPIATES
	MATTIES		ANTSIER	AEIOQSU	SEQUOIA
AEIMSTZ	MAZIEST		NASTIER	AEIORRR	ARRIERO
	MESTIZA		RATINES		ROARIER
AEIMSUV	AMUSIVE		RESIANT	AEIORST	OARIEST
AEIMSXX	MAXIXES		RETAINS		OTARIES
AEIHTYZ	AZYMITE		RETINAS	AEIORSV	OVARIES
AEINNNS	NANNIES		RETSINA	AEIOSST	SOSATIE
AEINNOT	ENATION		STAINER	AEIOSTT	OSTIATE
AEINNPR	PANNIER		STARNIE		TOASTIE
AEINNPT	PANTINE		STEARIN	AEIOSTZ	AZOTISE
	PINNATE	AEINRSV	AVENIRS	AEIOTZZ	AZOTIZE
AEINNRS	INSANER		RAVINES	AEIPPPR	PAPPIER
	INSNARE	AEINRTT	INTREAT	AEIPPPS	PAPPIES
AEINNRT	ENTRAIN		ITERANT	AEIPPRS	APPRISE
	TRANNIE		NATTIER		SAPPIER

Seven-letter anagrams

AEIPPRT	PERIAPT	AEIRRSV	ARRIVES	AEJJLNU	JEJUNAL
AEIPPRY	YAPPIER		VARIERS	AEJKMNR	JARKMEN
AEIPPRZ	APPRIZE	AEIRRTT	RATTIER	AEJKNRS	JANKERS
	ZAPPIER		RETRAIT	AEJKPTU	KAJEPUT
AEIPPSS	PASPIES		TARTIER	AEJLNUV	JUVENAL
AEIPPSY	YAPPIES	AEIRRTW	WARTIER	AEJLOSU	JALOUSE
AEIPRRR	PARRIER	AEIRRTY	RETIARY		JEALOUS
AEIPRRS	ASPIRER	AEIRRVV	VIVERRA	AEJLOUZ	AZULEJO
	PARRIES	AEIRSSS	SASSIER	AEJLSSW	JAWLESS
	PRAISER	AEIRSST	ARSIEST	AEJMMRS	JAMMERS
	RAPIERS		ARTSIES	AEJMNZZ	JAZZMEN
	RASPIER		SAIREST	AEJMRST	RAMJETS
	REPAIRS		SATIRES	AEJMSST	JETSAMS
AEIPRRT	PARTIER		TIRASSE	AEJMSSY	JESSAMY
AEIPRSS	ASPIRES	AEIRSSU	SAURIES	AEJMSTY	MAJESTY
	PARESIS	AEIRSSZ	ASSIZER	AEJNNOS	JOANNES
	PARISES	AEIRSTT	ARTIEST	AEJNORZ	ZANJERO
	PRAISES		ARTISTE	AEJNSST	JESSANT
	SPIREAS		ATTIRES	AEJNSSU	JAUNSES
AEIPRST	PAIREST		IRATEST	AEJPRSS	JASPERS
	PARTIES		RATITES	AEJPRSY	JASPERY
	PASTIER		STRIATE	AEJRSVY	JARVEYS
	PIASTER		TASTIER	AEJRSZZ	JAZZERS
	PIASTRE		TERTIAS	AEJSTWY	JETWAYS
	PIRATES	AEIRSTV	TAIVERS	AEKKNRS	KRAKENS
	PRATIES		VASTIER		SKANKER
	TRAIPSE		VERITAS	AEKKRSY	YAKKERS
AEIPRSU	SPURIAE	AEIRSTW	WAISTER	AEKLLTU	KELLAUT
	UPRAISE		WAITERS	AEKLMOU	LEUKOMA
AEIPRSV	PARVISE		WARIEST	AEKLNPP	KNAPPLE
	PAVISER		WASTRIE	AEKLNPR	PRANKLE
AEIPRSW	WASPIER	AEIRSVV	SAVVIER	AEKLNRS	RANKLES
AEIPRTT	PARTITE	AEIRSVW	WAIVERS	AEKLNRV	KLAVERN
AEIPRTV	PRIVATE	AEIRTTT	ATTRITE	AEKLNST	ANKLETS
AEIPRTW	WIRETAP		TATTIER		ASKLENT
AEIPRXY	PYREXIA		TITRATE		LANKEST
AEIPSSS	ASEPSIS	AEIRTTV	TAIVERT	AEKLNSW	KNAWELS
	ASPISES	AEIRTTW	TAWTIER	AEKLNSY	ALKYNES
AEIPSST	PASTIES	AEIRTTX	EXTRAIT	AEKLORY	ROKELAY
	PATSIES	AEIRTUY	AUREITY	AEKLOST	SKATOLE
	PETSAIS	AEIRTUZ	AZURITE	AEKLOVZ	ZELKOVA
	TAPISES	AEIRTVY	VARIETY	AEKLPPT	PEPTALK
AEIPSSV	PASSIVE	AEIRWWY	WIREWAY	AEKLPRS	SPARKLE
	PAVISES	AEISSSS	SASSIES	AEKLPSS	SPLAKES
	PAVISSE	AEISSST	SIESTAS	AEKLPSY	KEYPALS
	SPAVIES		TASSIES	AEKLRRS	LARKERS
AEIPSSW	WASPIES	AEISSSW	WISEASS	AEKLRSS	SLAKERS
AEIPSTT	PATTIES	AEISSSZ	ASSIZES	AEKLRST	STALKER
	TAPETIS	AEISSUV	SUASIVE		TALKERS
AEIPSTU	TAUPIES	AEISSUX	AUXESIS	AEKLRSV	LEKVARS
AEIPSTV	SPAVIET	AEISSVV	SAVVIES	AEKLRSW	WALKERS
AEIPSTW	TAWPIES	AEISTTT	ETATIST	AEKLRUW	WAULKER
AEIPTXY	EPITAXY		TATTIES	AEKLSST	LASKETS
AEIQRUV	AQUIVER	AEISTTU	SITUATE		SKLATES
AEIQSSU	SAIQUES	AEISTTV	STATIVE	AEKLSTU	AUKLETS
AEIRRRT	TARRIER	AEISTTW	TAWIEST	AEKMMNR	MARKMEN
AEIRRRV	ARRIVER		TWAITES	AEKMNOS	SOKEMAN
AEIRRSS	ARRISES	AEISTTX	TAXITES	AEKMNRU	UNMAKER
	RAISERS	AEISTTY	SATIETY	AEKMNSU	UNMAKES
	SIERRAS	AEISTVW	WAVIEST	AEKMOOT	MATOOKE
AEIRRST	ARTSIER	AEISTWX	TAXWISE	AEKMOST	MATOKES
	SERRATI		WAXIEST	AEKMPRU	UPMAKER
	TARRIES	AEITTTU	ATTUITE	AEKMPSU	MAKEUPS
	TARSIER	AEITTTV	VITTATE		UPMAKES

AEKMRRS	MARKERS	**AELLMSU**	MALLEUS	**AELMMST**	STAMMEL
	REMARKS	**AELLMSY**	MELLAYS	**AELMMSY**	MALMSEY
AEKMRSS	MASKERS		MESALLY	**AELMNNS**	LENSMAN
AEKMRST	MARKETS	**AELLMTY**	METALLY	**AELMNOR**	ALMONER
AEKMRSU	KUMERAS	**AELLMWX**	MAXWELL		NEMORAL
AEKNNOP	NONPEAK	**AELLNOP**	PALLONE	**AELMNOS**	MELANOS
AEKNNRS	ENRANKS		PLEONAL	**AELMNOT**	LOMENTA
AEKNNST	KANTENS	**AELLNOR**	LLANERO		OMENTAL
AEKNNTU	UNTAKEN	**AELLNOV**	NOVELLA		TELAMON
AEKNOSW	WEAKONS	**AELLNOY**	ALONELY	**AELMNPR**	LAMPERN
AEKNPPR	KNAPPER	**AELLNPY**	PENALLY	**AELMNRS**	ALMNERS
AEKNPRS	SPANKER	**AELLNRT**	ENTRALL	**AELMNRU**	NUMERAL
AEKNPSU	UNSPEAK	**AELLNSS**	ALLNESS	**AELMNSS**	MANLESS
AEKNPTU	UPTAKEN	**AELLNSW**	ENWALLS	**AELMNST**	LAMENTS
AEKNRRS	RANKERS	**AELLNTT**	TALLENT		MANTELS
AEKNRSS	KRANSES	**AELLNUU**	LUNULAE		MANTLES
AEKNRST	RANKEST	**AELLNVY**	VENALLY	**AELMNSU**	MENSUAL
	STARKEN	**AELLORS**	ROSELLA	**AELMNTT**	MANTLET
	TANKERS	**AELLORT**	REALLOT	**AELMNTU**	NUTMEAL
AEKNRSU	UNRAKES	**AELLORV**	ALLOVER	**AELMOPR**	PLEROMA
AEKNRSW	SWANKER		OVERALL		RAMPOLE
	WANKERS	**AELLORY**	LOYALER	**AELMOPU**	AMPOULE
	YANKERS	**AELLOSS**	LOESSAL	**AELMOPY**	MAYPOLE
AEKNRSZ	KRANZES	**AELLPPS**	LAPPELS	**AELMORS**	MORALES
AEKNRVY	KNAVERY	**AELLPRS**	SPALLER	**AELMORT**	MOLERAT
AEKNSSU	ANKUSES	**AELLPRU**	PLEURAL	**AELMORU**	MORULAE
AEKNSWY	SWANKEY	**AELLPSS**	SPALLES	**AELMORV**	REMOVAL
AEKOPRS	PRESOAK	**AELLPST**	PALLETS	**AELMOSS**	MOLASSE
AEKORRS	ROSAKER	**AELLPTU**	PLUTEAL	**AELMOST**	MALTOSE
AEKORSS	ARKOSES	**AELLPTY**	PLAYLET	**AELMOSY**	AMYLOSE
	RESOAKS	**AELLQUY**	EQUALLY	**AELMOTT**	MATELOT
	SOAKERS	**AELLRRU**	ALLURER	**AELMPRS**	EMPARLS
AEKOSTV	VOETSAK	**AELLRST**	STELLAR		LAMPERS
AEKOTTU	OUTTAKE		TELLARS		PALMERS
	TAKEOUT	**AELLRSU**	ALLURES		SAMPLER
AEKPPSU	UPSPAKE		LAURELS	**AELMPRT**	TEMPLAR
	UPSPEAK	**AELLRSW**	WALLERS		TRAMPLE
AEKPRRS	PARKERS	**AELLRSY**	RALLYES	**AELMPRY**	LAMPREY
	REPARKS	**AELLRTY**	ALERTLY	**AELMPSS**	MAPLESS
	SPARKER		ELYTRAL		SAMPLES
AEKPRSS	SPARKES		RETALLY	**AELMPST**	AMPLEST
AEKPSSY	PASSKEY	**AELLRVY**	RAVELLY	**AELMPSU**	AMPULES
AEKPSTU	TAKEUPS	**AELLSST**	SALLETS	**AELMPTU**	PLUMATE
	UPTAKES		STELLAS	**AELMRRS**	MARRELS
AEKQRSU	QUAKERS		TASSELL	**AELMRSS**	ARMLESS
AEKQSSU	SQUEAKS	**AELLSSW**	LAWLESS	**AELMRST**	ARMLETS
AEKQSUY	SQUEAKY	**AELLSTT**	TALLEST		LAMSTER
AEKRRST	KARTERS		TALLETS		MARTELS
	KRATERS	**AELLSTW**	SETWALL		TRAMELS
	STARKER		SWALLET	**AELMRSU**	MAULERS
AEKRSST	SKATERS		WALLETS		SERUMAL
	STRAKES	**AELLSTY**	STALELY	**AELMRSV**	MARVELS
	STREAKS	**AELLSVY**	VALLEYS	**AELMRTT**	MARTLET
	TASKERS	**AELLTUU**	ULULATE	**AELMRTU**	RELATUM
AEKRSSY	KARSEYS	**AELLUVV**	VALVULE	**AELMSST**	MATLESS
AEKRSTY	STREAKY	**AELMMNO**	MAMELON		SAMLETS
AEKRSUW	WAUKERS	**AELMMNS**	ALMSMEN	**AELMSTU**	AMULETS
AEKSSSV	KVASSES	**AELMMNT**	MALTMEN		MULETAS
AEKSSTT	TSATSKE	**AELMMOY**	MYELOMA	**AELNNPR**	PLANNER
AEKSWYY	KEYWAYS	**AELMMRS**	LAMMERS	**AELNNPS**	PENNALS
AELLMNU	LUMENAL		RAMMELS	**AELNNPU**	UNPANEL
AELLMRS	SMALLER		RAMMLES	**AELNNRS**	ENSNARL
AELLMRT	TRAMELL		SLAMMER		LANNERS
AELLMST	MALLETS	**AELMMRT**	TRAMMEL	**AELNNRT**	LANTERN

Seven-letter anagrams

AELNNRU	UNLEARN	AELNSUW	UNWEALS		PERSALT
AELNNST	STANNEL	AELNTUV	ENVAULT		PLASTER
AELNNTU	ANNULET	AELOORS	AEROSOL		PLATERS
AELNOOS	ALSOONE		ROSEOLA		PSALTER
AELNOPS	ESPANOL	AELOPPR	PROPALE		STAPLER
	NOPALES	AELOPPX	APOPLEX	AELPRSU	PERUSAL
AELNOPT	POLENTA	AELOPRR	PERORAL		PLEURAS
AELNOPU	APOLUNE		PREORAL		SERPULA
AELNORS	LOANERS	AELOPRS	PAROLES	AELPRSW	PRAWLES
	ORLEANS		REPOSAL	AELPRSY	PARLEYS
	RELOANS	AELOPRT	PROLATE		PARSLEY
AELNORU	ALEURON	AELOPRV	OVERLAP		PLAYERS
AELNORV	VERONAL	AELOPST	APOSTLE		REPLAYS
AELNOST	ETALONS		PELOTAS		SPARELY
	TOLANES	AELOPSX	EXPOSAL	AELPRTT	PARTLET
AELNOTV	VOLANTE	AELOPTT	PALETOT		PLATTER
AELNOTY	ANOLYTE	AELOPTU	OUTLEAP		PRATTLE
AELNOUZ	ZONULAE	AELORRT	REALTOR	AELPRTY	PEARTLY
AELNPPR	PREPLAN		RELATOR		PEYTRAL
AELNPPY	PLAYPEN	AELORSS	LASSOER		PRELATY
AELNPRS	PLANERS		OARLESS		PTERYLA
	REPLANS		SEROSAL	AELPRUY	EPULARY
AELNPRT	PANTLER		SOLERAS	AELPSSS	PASSELS
	PLANTER	AELORST	OESTRAL		SAPLESS
	REPLANT		OLESTRA	AELPSST	PASTELS
AELNPRY	PLENARY	AELORTT	RETOTAL		STAPLES
AELNPSS	NAPLESS	AELORTU	ROTULAE	AELPSTT	PATTLES
AELNPST	PLANETS		TORULAE		PELTAST
	PLATENS	AELORTV	LEVATOR	AELPSTU	PULSATE
AELNPSU	UPLEANS	AELORTY	ROYALET		PUTEALS
AELNPTU	UPLEANT	AELORTZ	ZELATOR		SPATULE
AELNPTX	EXPLANT	AELORUU	ROULEAU	AELPSTZ	SPATZLE
AELNPTY	APLENTY	AELORVX	OVERLAX	AELPUUV	UPVALUE
	PENALTY	AELORVY	LAYOVER	AELQRRU	QUARREL
AELNQUU	UNEQUAL		OVERLAY	AELQSSU	LASQUES
AELNRRS	SNARLER	AELORWY	OWRELAY		SQUEALS
AELNRSS	RANSELS	AELOSSS	LASSOES	AELQSUZ	QUEZALS
AELNRST	ANTLERS	AELOSST	SOLATES	AELQTUZ	QUETZAL
	RENTALS	AELOSSV	SALVOES	AELRRSU	SURREAL
	SALTERN	AELOSSW	LEASOWS	AELRRSW	WARSLER
	SLANTER	AELOSTV	SOLVATE	AELRRTT	RATTLER
	STERNAL	AELOSTZ	ZEALOTS	AELRRTW	TRAWLER
AELNRSV	VERLANS	AELOSUZ	ZEALOUS	AELRSSS	RASSLES
AELNRSY	LARNEYS	AELOSVY	SAVELOY	AELRSST	ARTLESS
AELNRSZ	RANZELS	AELOTTU	TOLUATE		LASTERS
AELNRTT	TRENTAL	AELOTUV	OVULATE		SALTERS
AELNRTU	NEUTRAL	AELOTVV	VOLVATE		SLATERS
AELNRTV	VENTRAL	AELOTVY	OVATELY		TARSELS
AELNRUU	NEURULA	AELPPRS	LAPPERS	AELRSSU	SAURELS
AELNRUV	UNRAVEL		RAPPELS	AELRSSV	SALVERS
	VENULAR		SLAPPER		SERVALS
AELNSSU	SENSUAL	AELPPRY	REAPPLY		SLAVERS
	UNSEALS	AELPPSS	SAPPLES		VERSALS
AELNSSW	AWNLESS	AELPPST	APPLETS	AELRSSW	WARLESS
AELNSSX	LAXNESS		LAPPETS		WARSLES
AELNSTT	LATENTS		STAPPLE		WRASSLE
	LATTENS	AELPPSU	APPULSE	AELRSSY	RAYLESS
	TALENTS		PAPULES		SLAYERS
AELNSTU	ELUANTS		UPLEAPS	AELRSTT	RATTLES
	LUNATES	AELPPTU	UPLEAPT		SLATTER
	UNLASTE	AELPQSU	PLAQUES		STARLET
AELNSTV	LEVANTS	AELPRRS	PARRELS		STARTLE
AELNSTY	STANYEL	AELPRSS	LAPSERS		TATLERS
AELNSTZ	ZELANTS	AELPRST	PALTERS	AELRSTU	ESTRUAL

	SALUTER
AELRSTV	TRAVELS
	VARLETS
	VESTRAL
AELRSTW	WARSTLE
	WASTREL
	WRASTLE
AELRSTY	RAYLETS
AELRSUV	VALUERS
AELRSVV	VARVELS
AELRSVY	SLAVERY
AELRSWX	WRAXLES
AELRSWY	LAWYERS
AELRSZZ	RAZZLES
AELRTTT	TARTLET
	TATTLER
AELRTTU	TUTELAR
AELRTUV	VAULTER
AELRTWY	TRAWLEY
AELRTWZ	WALTZER
AELSSST	TASSELS
AELSSTT	LATESTS
	SALTEST
	STALEST
	TASLETS
AELSSTU	SALUTES
	TALUSES
AELSSTV	VESTALS
AELSSTW	WASTELS
AELSSTX	TAXLESS
AELSSTY	LYSATES
AELSSUV	AVULSES
AELSSVY	SLAVEYS
AELSSWY	WAYLESS
AELSTTT	TATTLES
AELSTTW	WATTLES
AELSTTY	STATELY
	STYLATE
AELSTUX	LUXATES
AELSTWZ	WALTZES
AELSUVY	SUAVELY
AELSWZZ	SWAZZLE
AELTTTW	TWATTLE
AELTTUX	TEXTUAL
AELTUVV	VULVATE
AEMMMRS	MAMMERS
AEMMMST	MAMMETS
AEMMMSY	MAMMEYS
AEMMNOT	MOMENTA
AEMMNSS	MESSMAN
AEMMNTU	AMENTUM
AEMMOPR	MAMPOER
AEMMORS	MARMOSE
AEMMORW	WOMMERA
AEMMPRS	SPAMMER
AEMMRRS	RAMMERS
AEMMRST	STAMMER
AEMMRSY	YAMMERS
AEMMRSZ	MAMZERS
AEMMSST	STEMMAS
AEMMSTU	MAUMETS
	SUMMATE
AEMMSTW	MAWMETS
AEMNNOR	MONERAN
AEMNNOS	MANNOSE
AEMNNOT	MONTANE
	NONMEAT
AEMNNOU	NOUMENA
AEMNNOZ	MENAZON
AEMNNRS	MANNERS
AEMNNRT	MANRENT
	REMNANT
AEMNNSW	NEWSMAN
AEMNNTU	UNMEANT
AEMNOPP	PAMPOEN
AEMNOPR	MANROPE
	REPOMAN
AEMNOPS	MOPANES
AEMNOPZ	ZAMPONE
AEMNORR	ORRAMEN
AEMNORS	ENAMORS
	MOANERS
	OARSMEN
AEMNORT	TONEARM
AEMNORU	ENAMOUR
	NEUROMA
AEMNORV	OVERMAN
AEMNORY	ANYMORE
	ROMNEYA
AEMNOSS	MONASES
AEMNOST	MANTOES
AEMNOTT	TOMENTA
AEMNOTU	AUTOMEN
	NOTAEUM
	OUTNAME
AEMNPSS	PASSMEN
AEMNPST	ENSTAMP
	TAPSMEN
AEMNPSU	PNEUMAS
AEMNPTU	PUTAMEN
AEMNPTY	PAYMENT
AEMNRRU	MANURER
AEMNRST	ARTSMEN
	MARTENS
	SARMENT
	SMARTEN
AEMNRSU	MANURES
	MURENAS
	SURNAME
AEMNRTU	TRUEMAN
AEMNRTV	VARMENT
AEMNSSS	MESSANS
AEMNSST	STAMENS
AEMNSSU	UNSEAMS
AEMNSTU	UNTAMES
	UNTEAMS
AEMNSTY	AMNESTY
AEMNTTU	NUTMEAT
AEMNTWY	WAYMENT
AEMOORT	TEAROOM
AEMOORW	WOOMERA
AEMOOST	OSTEOMA
AEMOOSV	AMOOVES
	VAMOOSE
AEMOPPR	PAMPERO
AEMOPSZ	APOZEMS
AEMORRR	ARMORER
AEMORRS	REMORAS
	ROAMERS
AEMORRV	OVERARM
AEMORRW	EARWORM
AEMORST	AMORETS
	MAESTRO
	OMERTAS
AEMORSU	RAMEOUS
AEMORSW	SEAWORM
	WOMERAS
AEMORSX	XEROMAS
AEMOSST	OSMATES
AEMOSSV	VAMOSES
AEMOSTT	STOMATE
AEMOSTW	TWASOME
AEMOSUZ	ZAMOUSE
AEMOSWY	SOMEWAY
AEMOTTZ	MOZETTA
AEMPPRS	MAPPERS
	PAMPERS
	PREAMPS
AEMPPRY	MAPPERY
AEMPRRS	PREARMS
	RAMPERS
AEMPRRT	TRAMPER
AEMPRRW	PREWARM
AEMPRST	EMPARTS
	RESTAMP
	STAMPER
	TAMPERS
AEMPRSV	REVAMPS
	VAMPERS
AEMPRSW	SWAMPER
AEMPRTT	TRAMPET
AEMPRTU	TEMPURA
AEMPSSU	EMPUSAS
AEMPTTT	ATTEMPT
AEMPTTU	TAPETUM
AEMQRSU	MARQUES
	MASQUER
AEMQSSU	MASQUES
	SQUAMES
AEMRRRS	MARRERS
AEMRRRY	REMARRY
AEMRRST	ARMREST
	SMARTER
AEMRRSU	ARMURES
AEMRRSV	MARVERS
AEMRRSW	REWARMS
	SWARMER
	WARMERS
AEMRRTU	ERRATUM
	MATURER
AEMRSST	MASTERS
	STREAMS
AEMRSSU	AMUSERS
	ASSUMER
	MASSEUR
AEMRSTT	MATTERS
	SMATTER
AEMRSTU	MATURES
	STRUMAE
AEMRSTW	WARMEST
AEMRSTY	MASTERY
	MAYSTER

Seven-letter anagrams

	STREAMY		NOTATES		WANTERS
AEMRTTX	MARTEXT	AENOSTU	SOUTANE	AENRSTY	TRAYNES
AEMRTTY	MATTERY	AENOSVW	WAVESON	AENRSUW	UNSWEAR
AEMRTUU	TRUMEAU	AENOUUV	NOUVEAU		UNWARES
AEMSSSU	ASSUMES	AENPPRS	NAPPERS	AENRSUY	SYNURAE
AEMSSTU	MUTASES		PARPENS	AENRSWY	YAWNERS
AEMSSUW	WAMUSES		PARSNEP	AENRTTU	TAUNTER
AEMSSYZ	ZYMASES		SNAPPER	AENRTTY	NATTERY
AEMSTTU	MUTATES	AENPPRT	PARPENT	AENRTUV	VAUNTER
AEMSTUV	MAUVEST	AENPPRU	UNPAPER	AENRTUW	UNWATER
AEMSTVZ	ZEMSTVA	AENPPST	PETNAPS	AENRUWY	UNWEARY
AEMSUZZ	MEZUZAS	AENPRRT	PARTNER	AENSSST	ASSENTS
AENNNOS	NONANES	AENPRRW	PRAWNER		SNASTES
AENNNPT	PENNANT		PREWARN	AENSSTU	NASUTES
AENNOPS	PANNOSE	AENPRST	ARPENTS		UNSEATS
AENNORT	NORTENA		ENTRAPS	AENSSTX	SEXTANS
AENNORY	ANNOYER		PANTERS	AENSSTY	STAYNES
AENNOSS	NOSEANS		PARENTS	AENSSTZ	STANZES
AENNOSV	NOVENAS		PASTERN	AENSSWY	SAWNEYS
AENNOSY	ANYONES		PERSANT	AENSSXY	SYNAXES
AENNOTU	TONNEAU		TREPANS	AENSTTT	ATTENTS
AENNPRS	PANNERS	AENPRSW	ENWRAPS	AENSTTU	ATTUNES
	SPANNER		PAWNERS		NUTATES
AENNQTU	QUANNET		SPAWNER		TAUTENS
AENNRST	TANNERS	AENPRSZ	PANZERS		TETANUS
AENNRSV	VANNERS	AENPRTT	PATTERN		UNSTATE
AENNRTT	ENTRANT		REPTANT	AENSTTX	SEXTANT
AENNRTV	VERNANT	AENPRUV	PARVENU	AENSTUX	UNTAXES
AENNRTY	TANNERY	AENPSST	APTNESS	AENSTWY	TAWNEYS
	TYRANNE		PATNESS	AENTTTU	ATTUENT
AENNSSW	WANNESS		PESANTS	AEOOPPS	PAPOOSE
AENNSTT	TANNEST	AENPSSY	SYNAPSE	AEOOPRS	OROPESA
	TENANTS	AENPSTT	PATENTS	AEOPPPS	PAPPOSE
AENNSTW	WANNEST		PATTENS	AEOPPRS	APPOSER
AENOOTZ	ENTOZOA	AENPSTU	PEANUTS		POPERAS
	OZONATE		PESAUNT	AEOPPRV	APPROVE
AENOPPR	PROPANE	AENPSTW	STEWPAN	AEOPPSS	APPOSES
AENOPRS	PERSONA	AENPSTY	SYNAPTE	AEOPQRU	OPAQUER
AENOPRT	OPERANT	AENPSTZ	PEZANTS	AEOPQSU	OPAQUES
	PRONATE	AENQSTU	EQUANTS	AEOPRRT	PRAETOR
	PROTEAN	AENRRSS	SERRANS		PRORATE
AENOPST	TEOPANS		SNARERS	AEOPRRV	VAPORER
AENOPSU	POSAUNE	AENRRST	ERRANTS	AEOPRSS	SOAPERS
AENOPSV	PAVONES		RANTERS	AEOPRST	ESPARTO
AENOPSW	WEAPONS	AENRRSW	WARNERS		PROTEAS
AENOPTU	AUTOPEN		WARRENS		SEAPORT
AENORRS	SERRANO	AENRRSY	YARNERS	AEOPRTT	PORTATE
AENORRT	ORNATER	AENRRTT	TRANTER	AEOPRTV	OVERAPT
AENORRV	OVERRAN	AENRRTY	TERNARY	AEOPRVY	OVERPAY
AENORSS	REASONS	AENRSSS	SARSENS	AEOPRWY	ROPEWAY
	SENORAS	AENRSST	SARSNET	AEOPSSS	PSOASES
AENORST	ATONERS		TRANSES	AEOPSST	PETASOS
	SANTERO	AENRSSW	ANSWERS		SAPOTES
	SENATOR		RAWNESS	AEOPSTT	APTOTES
	TREASON	AENRSSY	SARNEYS		TEAPOTS
AENORSU	ARENOUS	AENRSTT	NATTERS	AEOPSTY	TEAPOYS
AENORTU	OUTEARN		RATTENS	AEOPSTZ	TOPAZES
AENORTV	VENATOR	AENRSTU	AUNTERS	AEOQRTU	EQUATOR
AENORWZ	WARZONE		NATURES		QUORATE
AENORXY	ANOREXY		SAUNTER	AEOQRUV	VAQUERO
AENOSSS	SEASONS	AENRSTV	SERVANT	AEOQSUU	AQUEOUS
AENOSST	ASTONES		TAVERNS	AEORRRS	ROARERS
AENOSSW	WEASONS		VERSANT	AEORRSS	SOARERS
AENOSTT	ATTONES	AENRSTW	STRAWEN	AEORRST	ROASTER

AEORRSU	AROUSER		SPAREST		TARTEST
AEORRSV	SAVORER	**AEPRSSU**	PAUSERS		TATTERS
	SEROVAR	**AEPRSSY**	PESSARY	**AERSTTU**	ASTUTER
AEORSSS	SAROSES	**AEPRSTT**	PATTERS		STATURE
	SEROSAS		SPATTER	**AERSTTV**	VATTERS
AEORSST	OSETRAS		TAPSTER	**AERSTTW**	SWATTER
	OSSETRA	**AEPRSTU**	PASTURE		TEWARTS
AEORSSU	AROUSES		UPRATES	**AERSTTY**	YATTERS
AEORSTT	ROTATES		UPSTARE	**AERSTTZ**	STARETZ
	TOASTER		UPTEARS	**AERSTUU**	AUTEURS
AEORSUV	AVOURES	**AEPRSTY**	YAPSTER	**AERSTUY**	ESTUARY
AEORSVW	AVOWERS	**AEPRSTZ**	PATZERS	**AERSTVY**	STRAYVE
	OVERSAW	**AEPRSUX**	ARUSPEX	**AERSTWY**	WASTERY
	REAVOWS	**AEPRSUY**	YAUPERS	**AERTTTY**	TATTERY
AEORSVY	AVOYERS	**AEPRSWY**	SPYWARE	**AERTTUV**	VETTURA
AEORTTU	OUTRATE		YAWPERS	**AESSSTT**	TASSETS
AEORTUV	OUTRAVE	**AEPRSYY**	SPRAYEY	**AESSTTT**	ATTESTS
AEORTUW	OUTWEAR	**AEPRTXY**	APTERYX	**AESSTTU**	STATUES
AEORTVX	OVERTAX	**AEPSSTU**	PETASUS	**AESSTTV**	VASTEST
AEOSSTV	AVOSETS	**AEPSSZZ**	SPAZZES	**AESSTUV**	SUAVEST
AEOSTTU	OUTEATS	**AEPSTTU**	UPSTATE	**AESSTUY**	EUSTASY
AEOSUVZ	ZOUAVES	**AEPSZZZ**	PZAZZES	**AESSVVY**	SAVVEYS
AEPPPRU	PREPUPA	**AEQRRSU**	SQUARER	**AESTTTU**	STATUTE
AEPPRRS	RAPPERS	**AEQRRTU**	QUARTER		TAUTEST
AEPPRRT	TRAPPER	**AEQRSSU**	SQUARES	**AESTTTW**	WATTEST
AEPPRRW	PREWRAP	**AEQRSTU**	QUAREST	**AFFFGIN**	FAFFING
	WRAPPER		QUARTES	**AFFFLLO**	FALLOFF
AEPPRSS	APPRESS		QUATRES	**AFFGGIN**	GAFFING
	SAPPERS	**AEQRSUV**	QUAVERS	**AFFGINN**	NAFFING
AEPPRST	TAPPERS	**AEQRTTU**	QUARTET	**AFFGINW**	WAFFING
AEPPRSU	PAUPERS	**AEQRUVY**	QUAVERY	**AFFGINY**	AFFYING
	UPSPEAR	**AEQSSSU**	QUASSES		YAFFING
AEPPRSW	SWAPPER	**AERRSST**	ARRESTS	**AFFGSUW**	GUFFAWS
	WAPPERS		RASTERS	**AFFHILN**	HAFFLIN
AEPPRSY	PREPAYS		STARERS	**AFFHIRS**	RAFFISH
	YAPPERS	**AERRSSU**	ASSURER	**AFFHIST**	HAFFITS
AEPPRSZ	ZAPPERS		RASURES	**AFFIITX**	FIXATIF
AEPPSTT	TAPPETS	**AERRSTT**	RATTERS	**AFFIKRS**	KAFFIRS
AEPPSTU	PASTEUP		RESTART	**AFFILMN**	MAFFLIN
	PUPATES		STARTER	**AFFILOR**	RIFFOLA
AEPQRTU	PARQUET	**AERRSTV**	STARVER	**AFFILPS**	PILAFFS
AEPRRRS	SPARRER	**AERRSTY**	STRAYER	**AFFILSY**	FALSIFY
AEPRRSS	PARSERS	**AERRSUZ**	RAZURES	**AFFIMRS**	AFFIRMS
	RASPERS	**AERRSWY**	WARREYS	**AFFIMST**	MASTIFF
	SPARERS	**AERRTTY**	RATTERY	**AFFINRU**	FUNFAIR
	SPARRES	**AERSSST**	ASSERTS		RUFFIAN
	SPARSER		TRASSES	**AFFINTY**	TIFFANY
AEPRRST	PARTERS	**AERSSSU**	ASSURES	**AFFIORR**	FORFAIR
	PRATERS		SARUSES	**AFFIRRU**	FURFAIR
AEPRRSU	PARURES	**AERSSSW**	WRASSES	**AFFIRST**	TARIFFS
	UPREARS	**AERSSTT**	ASTERTS	**AFFIRSU**	SUFFARI
AEPRRSW	REWRAPS		STARETS	**AFFIRSZ**	ZAFFIRS
	WARPERS		STATERS	**AFFLOPY**	PLAYOFF
AEPRRSY	PRAYERS		TASTERS	**AFFLOSY**	LAYOFFS
	RESPRAY	**AERSSTV**	STARVES	**AFFMOPR**	OFFRAMP
	SPRAYER	**AERSSTW**	WASTERS	**AFFNORS**	SAFFRON
AEPRRTU	PARTURE	**AERSSTY**	ESTRAYS	**AFFNORT**	AFFRONT
	RAPTURE		STAYERS	**AFFOPSY**	PAYOFFS
AEPRRTW	REWRAPT		STAYRES	**AFFRSST**	STRAFFS
AEPRRTY	PARTYER	**AERSSUV**	VARUSES	**AFGGGIN**	FAGGING
	PETRARY	**AERSSVW**	SWARVES	**AFGGINN**	FANGING
AEPRSSS	PASSERS	**AERSSWY**	SAWYERS	**AFGGOST**	FAGGOTS
AEPRSST	PASTERS		SWAYERS	**AFGGOTY**	FAGGOTY
	REPASTS	**AERSTTT**	STRETTA	**AFGHHIS**	HAGFISH

AFGHINS	FASHING	AFHIKUY	KUFIYAH	AFILQUY	QUALIFY
AFGHINT	HAFTING	AFHILLN	HALFLIN	AFILRRY	FRIARLY
AFGHIRS	GARFISH	AFHILSS	FALSISH	AFILRSZ	FRAZILS
AFGHLSU	GASHFUL	AFHILTW	HALFWIT	AFILRTY	FRAILTY
AFGHLTU	FLAUGHT	AFHIMNU	HAFNIUM	AFILSSY	SALSIFY
AFGHRTU	FRAUGHT	AFHINOS	FASHION	AFILSTU	FISTULA
AFGIIKN	FAIKING	AFHINPS	PANFISH	AFILSTY	FALSITY
AFGIILN	FAILING	AFHINTU	UNFAITH	AFILTTY	FATTILY
AFGIINN	FAINING	AFHIORS	OARFISH	AFIMNRS	FIRMANS
AFGIINR	FAIRING	AFHIRSS	SHARIFS	AFIMOOS	MAFIOSO
AFGIINT	FIATING	AFHIRST	RATFISH	AFIMORV	AVIFORM
AFGIINW	WAIFING	AFHISST	FASTISH	AFIMRST	MAFTIRS
AFGIJMS	FIGJAMS	AFHISSW	SAWFISH	AFIMSSS	MASSIFS
AFGIKLN	FLAKING	AFHISTT	FATTISH	AFIMSSV	FAVISMS
AFGILLN	FALLING	AFHISHY	FISHWAY	AFIMSTT	FATTISM
AFGILMN	FLAMING	AFHKORY	HAYFORK	AFIMSUV	FAUVISM
AFGILNO	FOALING	AFHKRTU	FUTHARK	AFIMSUZ	UMFAZIS
	LOAFING	AFHLMRU	HARMFUL	AFIMTTY	MATTIFY
AFGILNR	FLARING	AFHLMSU	FULHAMS	AFINNNS	FINNANS
AFGILNS	FALSING	AFHLOOS	LOOFAHS	AFINNOR	FRANION
AFGILNT	FATLING	AFHLOTY	HAYLOFT	AFINNOS	FANIONS
AFGILNU	GAINFUL	AFHLSTU	HATFULS	AFINNOT	FONTINA
AFGILNW	FLAWING		HATSFUL	AFINNST	INFANTS
AFGILNY	ANGLIFY	AFHMOST	FATHOMS	AFINORS	INSOFAR
	FLAYING	AFHOOPT	POOFTAH	AFINRSU	UNFAIRS
AFGILRU	FIGURAL	AFHOPTU	POUFTAH	AFINRTU	ANTIFUR
AFGIMNO	FOAMING	AFHORSS	SHOFARS	AFINSSU	FUSAINS
AFGIMNR	FARMING	AFIILNS	FINALIS	AFINSTU	FAUNIST
	FRAMING		FINIALS		FIAUNTS
AFGIMNY	MAGNIFY	AFIILNT	TAILFIN		FUSTIAN
AFGINNN	FANNING	AFIILOR	AIRFOIL		INFAUST
AFGINNS	FINGANS	AFIILRT	AIRLIFT	AFIORST	FAITORS
AFGINNW	FAWNING	AFIILRY	FAIRILY	AFIORTU	FAITOUR
AFGINNY	FAYNING	AFIIMOS	MAFIOSI	AFIORTZ	FORZATI
AFGINOT	ANTIFOG	AFIJNNS	FINJANS	AFIQRSU	FAQUIRS
AFGINRR	FARRING	AFIKLLY	FLAKILY	AFISSTT	SITFAST
AFGINRS	FARSING	AFIKLOT	FLOKATI	AFISSTY	SATISFY
AFGINRT	FARTING	AFIKMNR	FINMARK	AFISTTT	FATTIST
	INGRAFT	AFIKNRT	RATFINK	AFISTUV	FAUVIST
	RAFTING	AFIKNSU	FUNKIAS	AFITTUY	FATUITY
AFGINRY	FRAYING	AFIKRSS	FRISKAS	AFJLRSU	JARFULS
AFGINST	FASTING	AFILLMS	MISFALL		JARSFUL
AFGINTT	FATTING	AFILLNP	PINFALL	AFKLNRY	FRANKLY
AFGINTU	FAUTING	AFILLNS	INFALLS	AFKLNTU	TANKFUL
AFGINTW	WAFTING	AFILLNY	FINALLY	AFKLOWY	FOLKWAY
AFGIOTT	FAGOTTI	AFILLPT	PITFALL	AFKRRTU	FRAKTUR
AFGIRTY	GRATIFY	AFILLPU	PAILFUL	AFLLMPU	PALMFUL
AFGKNOP	PAKFONG	AFILLRV	FRAILLY	AFLLMSU	FULLAMS
AFGKORT	KOFTGAR	AFILLTY	TAILFLY	AFLLNOS	ONFALLS
AFGLLLY	GALLFLY	AFILLUV	FLUVIAL	AFLLNSU	FULLANS
AFGLLUY	FUGALLY		VIALFUL	AFLLOOY	ALOOFLY
AFGLNOS	FLAGONS	AFILLUW	WAILFUL	AFLLORS	FLORALS
AFGLNSU	FUNGALS	AFILMNT	LIFTMAN	AFLLORU	FLORULA
AFGLRYY	GRAYFLY	AFILMOR	ALIFORM	AFLLOSW	FALLOWS
AFGMNOR	FROGMAN	AFILMOY	FOAMILY	AFLLOTU	FALLOUT
AFGMORS	FOGRAMS	AFILMPY	AMPLIFY		OUTFALL
AFGOOTT	FAGOTTO	AFILMSS	FALSISM	AFLLPSU	LAPFULS
AFGORRS	FRAGORS	AFILNPU	PAINFUL	AFLLPUY	PLAYFUL
AFGOSTU	FUGATOS	AFILNSV	FLAVINS	AFLLUWY	AWFULLY
AFHIIRS	FAIRISH	AFILNTU	ANTIFLU	AFLMNOU	MOANFUL
	HAIRIFS		FLUTINA	AFLMORS	FORMALS
AFHIISW	WAIFISH	AFILNTY	FAINTLY	AFLMORU	FORMULA
AFHIKLS	KHALIFS	AFILORW	AIRFLOW	AFLMORW	WOLFRAM
AFHIKRS	KHARIFS	AFILOTX	FOXTAIL	AFLMOST	FLOTSAM

AFLMRSU	ARMFULS	AGGGIJN	JAGGING	AGGINRU	ARGUING
	ARMSFUL	AGGGILN	LAGGING	AGGINRV	GRAVING
	FULMARS	AGGGIMN	MAGGING	AGGINRY	GRAYING
AFLMSTU	MASTFUL	AGGGINN	GANGING	AGGINRZ	GRAZING
AFLMSUU	FAMULUS		NAGGING	AGGINSS	GASSING
AFLNORT	FRONTAL	AGGGINR	RAGGING	AGGINST	GASTING
AFLNOTT	FLOTANT	AGGGINS	SAGGING		GATINGS
AFLNPSU	PANFULS	AGGGINT	TAGGING		STAGING
AFLNRTU	RUNFLAT	AGGGINU	GAUGING	AGGINSW	SWAGING
AFLNSTU	FLAUNTS	AGGGINV	VAGGING	AGGINSZ	GAZINGS
AFLNTUY	FLAUNTY	AGGGINW	WAGGING	AGGINUV	VAGUING
AFLOOTW	WOOLFAT	AGGGINZ	ZAGGING	AGGIORS	GORGIAS
AFLOPTT	FLATTOP	AGGHHIS	HAGGISH	AGGISWW	WIGWAGS
AFLORSS	SAFROLS	AGGHIIL	GHILGAI	AGGISZZ	ZIGZAGS
AFLORSU	FUSAROL	AGGHIMN	GINGHAM	AGGLOST	LOGGATS
AFLORSV	FLAVORS	AGGHINN	HANGING	AGGMNOS	MOGGANS
AFLORUV	FLAVOUR	AGGHINS	GASHING	AGGMORR	GROGRAM
AFLORVY	FLAVORY	AGGHISW	WAGGISH	AGGMOST	MAGGOTS
AFLORWW	WARWOLF	AGGIIJJ	JIGAJIG	AGGMOTY	MAGGOTY
AFLOSSU	FOSSULA	AGGIILS	GILGAIS	AGGMRSU	MUGGARS
AFLPRTY	FLYTRAP	AGGIIMN	IMAGING	AGGNOSU	GUANGOS
AFLPSTY	FLYPAST	AGGIINN	GAINING	AGGNOSW	WAGGONS
AFLRTUU	FUTURAL	AGGIINT	GAITING	AGGNOSX	OXGANGS
AFLRTUY	TRAYFUL	AGGIINV	GINGIVA	AGGNOSY	SYNAGOG
AFLSSTU	FUTSALS	AGGIJJO	JIGAJOG	AGGNPSU	UPGANGS
AFLSTUV	VATFULS	AGGIKNS	GASKING	AGGNRSU	NUGGARS
AFLSUWY	SWAYFUL	AGGIKNW	GAWKING	AGGPRSY	PYGARGS
AFLSWYY	FLYWAYS	AGGILLN	GALLING	AGHHIMN	HIGHMAN
AFMNNOR	NONFARM		GINGALL	AGHHINS	HASHING
AFMNOOT	FOOTMAN	AGGILNN	ANGLING	AGHHIWY	HIGHWAY
AFMNORT	FORMANT	AGGILNO	GAOLING	AGHHOSW	HOGWASH
AFMNOST	FANTOMS		GOALING	AGHHSSU	SHAUGHS
AFMNRSU	SURFMAN	AGGILNR	ARGLING	AGHHTUY	HAUGHTY
AFMNRTU	TURFMAN		GLARING	AGHIILN	HAILING
AFMOOSS	SAMFOOS	AGGILNS	GINGALS		NILGHAI
AFMORST	FARMOST		LAGGINS	AGHIINN	HAINING
	FORMATS	AGGILNZ	GLAZING	AGHIINR	HAIRING
AFMORSU	AUSFORM	AGGILOS	LOGGIAS	AGHIJRS	JAGHIRS
AFMORTU	FOUMART	AGGIMMN	GAMMING	AGHIKNN	HANKING
AFMOSTT	AFTMOST	AGGIMNN	MANGING	AGHIKNR	HARKING
AFMOSTU	SFUMATO	AGGIMNS	GAMINGS	AGHIKNS	SHAKING
AFNNNOS	NONFANS	AGGIMNU	GAUMING	AGHIKNW	HAWKING
AFNORRW	FORWARN	AGGINNN	GANNING	AGHIKSU	KIAUGHS
AFNORTW	FANWORT	AGGINNP	PANGING	AGHIKSW	GAWKISH
AFNOTUW	OUTFAWN	AGGINNR	RANGING	AGHILLN	HALLING
AFNPRSY	FRYPANS	AGGINNT	GANTING	AGHILNO	HALOING
AFNSSTU	SUNFAST		TANGING	AGHILNR	HARLING
AFOOPPR	APPROOF	AGGINNU	UNAGING	AGHILNS	HALSING
AFOORST	FOOTRAS	AGGINNW	GNAWING		LASHING
AFOORTZ	FORZATO	AGGINOT	GIGATON		SHALING
AFOOTWY	FOOTWAY	AGGINPP	GAPPING	AGHILNT	HALTING
AFORRSW	FARROWS	AGGINPR	GRAPING		LATHING
AFORRSY	FORRAYS		PARGING	AGHILNU	HAULING
	ORFRAYS	AGGINPS	GAPINGS		NILGHAU
AFORSSY	FORSAYS		GASPING	AGHILNV	HALVING
AFORSTU	FAUTORS		PAGINGS	AGHILNW	WHALING
	FOUTRAS	AGGINPU	GAUPING	AGHILNY	NYLGHAI
AFORSUV	FAVOURS	AGGINPW	GAWPING	AGHILOT	GOLIATH
AFOSSSU	FOUSSAS	AGGINRR	GARRING	AGHILRS	LARGISH
AFOSTTU	OUTFAST	AGGINRS	GRINGAS	AGHILRT	ALRIGHT
AFOSTUU	FATUOUS		RAGINGS	AGHILST	ALIGHTS
AFPSTUW	UPWAFTS		SIRGANG	AGHIMMN	HAMMING
AGGGGIN	GAGGING	AGGINRT	GRATING	AGHIMNR	HARMING
AGGGHIN	HAGGING		TARGING	AGHIMNS	MASHING

	SHAMING	**AGHNTUY**	NAUGHTY	**AGIJNPP**	JAPPING
AGHIMNW	HAWMING	**AGHOORT**	AGOROTH	**AGIJNPR**	JARPING
AGHIMPS	GAMPISH	**AGHOQSU**	QUAHOGS	**AGIJNPS**	JAPINGS
AGHINNO	NIHONGA	**AGHORTW**	WARTHOG	**AGIJNPU**	JAUPING
AGHINNT	HANTING	**AGHPTUY**	PAUGHTY	**AGIJNRR**	JARRING
	TANGHIN	**AGHRRSU**	GURRAHS	**AGIJNSW**	JAWINGS
AGHINOR	HOARING	**AGHRSTU**	TUGHRAS		JIGSAWN
AGHINOX	HOAXING	**AGHRSTY**	GYTRASH	**AGIJNZZ**	JAZZING
AGHINPP	HAPPING	**AGHSTUW**	WAUGHTS	**AGIJSSW**	JIGSAWS
AGHINPR	HARPING	**AGIIJLN**	JAILING	**AGIKKNR**	KARKING
AGHINPS	HASPING	**AGIIKLN**	LAIKING	**AGIKKNY**	YAKKING
	PASHING	**AGIIKLT**	GLAIKIT	**AGIKLNN**	ANKLING
	PHASING	**AGIIKNP**	PAIKING		LANKING
	SHAPING	**AGIIKNR**	RAIKING	**AGIKLNO**	OAKLING
AGHINPT	PATHING	**AGIILMN**	MAILING	**AGIKLNR**	LARKING
AGHINRS	GARNISH	**AGIILNN**	ALINING	**AGIKLNS**	LAKINGS
	RASHING		NAILING		SLAKING
	SHARING	**AGIILNR**	GLAIRIN	**AGIKLNT**	TALKING
AGHINRU	NURAGHI		LAIRING	**AGIKLNW**	WALKING
AGHINSS	SASHING		RAILING	**AGIKLWY**	GAWKILY
AGHINST	HASTING	**AGIILNS**	AISLING	**AGIKMNR**	MARKING
	TASHING		NILGAIS	**AGIKMNS**	MAKINGS
AGHINSU	ANGUISH		SAILING		MASKING
	HAUSING	**AGIILNT**	INTAGLI	**AGIKNNR**	NARKING
AGHINSV	HAVINGS		TAILING		RANKING
	SHAVING	**AGIILNV**	VAILING	**AGIKNNS**	SNAKING
AGHINSW	HAWSING		VIALING	**AGIKNNT**	KANTING
	SHAWING	**AGIILNW**	WAILING		TANKING
	WASHING	**AGIILOV**	VILIAGO	**AGIKNNU**	UNAKING
AGHINSY	HAYINGS	**AGIILPT**	PIGTAIL	**AGIKNNW**	WANKING
AGHINSZ	HAZINGS	**AGIILTY**	AGILITY	**AGIKNNY**	YANKING
AGHINTT	HATTING	**AGIIMMN**	MAIMING	**AGIKNOS**	SOAKING
	TATHING	**AGIIMMS**	IMAGISM	**AGIKNOY**	KAYOING
AGHINTW	THAWING	**AGIIMNN**	MAINING		OKAYING
AGHIOST	GOATISH	**AGIIMOR**	ORIGAMI	**AGIKNPR**	PARKING
AGHIPSW	PIGWASH	**AGIIMST**	IMAGIST	**AGIKNQU**	QUAKING
AGHIQSU	QUAIGHS	**AGIINNP**	PAINING	**AGIKNRR**	RARKING
AGHIRRS	GHARRIS	**AGIINNR**	AIRNING	**AGIKNRS**	RAKINGS
AGHIRST	GRAITHS		INGRAIN		SARKING
AGHIRSU	GUARISH		RAINING	**AGIKNRT**	KARTING
AGHIRSY	GRAYISH	**AGIINNS**	SAINING	**AGIKNRW**	WARKING
AGHJMNO	MAHJONG	**AGIINNW**	WAINING	**AGIKNRY**	YARKING
AGHKOSW	GOSHAWK	**AGIINNZ**	ZINGANI	**AGIKNSS**	ASKINGS
AGHLMPU	GALUMPH	**AGIINPR**	PAIRING		GASKINS
AGHLMSU	MUGHALS	**AGIINRS**	AIRINGS	**AGIKNST**	SKATING
AGHLNUV	NYLGHAU		ARISING		STAKING
AGHLOOS	GASOHOL		RAGINIS		TAKINGS
AGHLOSU	GOULASH		RAISING		TASKING
AGHLSTU	GALUTHS		SAIRING	**AGIKNSW**	WAKINGS
AGHLSTY	GHASTLY	**AGIINRT**	AIRTING	**AGIKNUW**	WAUKING
AGHMORY	HYGROMA		RAITING	**AGILLLN**	LALLING
AGHMRRU	MURRAGH	**AGIINRW**	WAIRING	**AGILLMN**	MALLING
AGHNNOU	HOUNGAN	**AGIINRZ**	ZINGARI	**AGILLMU**	GALLIUM
AGHNNSU	HUNGANS	**AGIINSV**	AVISING	**AGILLNP**	PALLING
	UNHANGS		VISAING	**AGILLNU**	LINGUAL
AGHNOTU	HANGOUT	**AGIINTW**	WAITING		LINGULA
	TOHUNGA	**AGIINTX**	TAXIING	**AGILLNW**	WALLING
AGHNPSU	HANGUPS	**AGIINVV**	VIVAING	**AGILLNY**	ALLYING
	UPHANGS	**AGIINVW**	WAIVING	**AGILLOR**	GORILLA
AGHNRST	THRANGS	**AGIINVZ**	AVIZING	**AGILLOT**	GALLIOT
AGHNRSU	NURHAGS	**AGIJKNU**	JAUKING	**AGILLRU**	LIGULAR
AGHNRUY	AHUNGRY	**AGIJLLN**	JINGALL	**AGILLSU**	LIGULAS
AGHNSTU	NAUGHTS	**AGIJLNS**	JINGALS		LUGSAIL
AGHNSUY	GUNYAHS	**AGIJMMN**	JAMMING	**AGILLYZ**	GLAZILY

AGILMMN	LAMMING	AGILNWY	YAWLING	AGINNRT	RANTING
AGILMMS	GIMMALS	AGILNYZ	LAZYING	AGINNRW	WARNING
AGILMNO	LOAMING	AGILOPT	GALIPOT	AGINNRY	YARNING
AGILMNP	LAMPING	AGILORS	GIRASOL	AGINNST	ANTINGS
	PALMING		GLORIAS		STANING
AGILMNR	MARLING	AGILORW	AIRGLOW	AGINNSU	GUANINS
AGILMNS	LINGAMS	AGILOST	GALIOTS	AGINNSW	AWNINGS
	MALIGNS		LATIGOS		SNAWING
AGILMNT	MALTING		SALIGOT		WANINGS
AGILMNU	MAULING	AGILRSS	SLAIRGS	AGINNTU	ANTIGUN
AGILMNY	MANGILY	AGILSSY	GASSILY	AGINNTW	WANTING
AGILMOS	GLIOMAS	AGILSTY	STAGILY	AGINNWY	YAWNING
AGILMPS	MAGILPS	AGILUYZ	GAUZILY	AGINNWZ	WANZING
AGILMPU	PLAGIUM	AGIMMNR	RAMMING	AGINNYZ	ZANYING
AGILMST	STIGMAL	AGIMMNS	SAMMING	AGINOOO	OOGONIA
AGILMNO	LOANING	AGIMMSS	MAGISMS	AGINOOP	POGONIA
AGILNNP	PLANING	AGIMNNN	MANNING	AGINOPR	PIGNORA
AGILNNR	LARNING	AGIMNNO	MOANING		PORANGI
AGILNNS	LIGNANS	AGIMNNR	RINGMAN	AGINOPS	SOAPING
	LINSANG	AGIMNNS	NAMINGS	AGINORR	ROARING
AGILNNT	TANLING	AGIMNNW	WINGMAN	AGINORS	IGNAROS
AGILNOP	GALOPIN	AGIMNOR	ROAMING		ORIGANS
AGILNOR	RANGOLI	AGIMNOT	MOATING		SIGNORA
AGILNOT	ANTILOG	AGIMNOV	AMOVING		SOARING
AGILNOV	LOAVING	AGIMNPP	MAPPING	AGINORT	ORATING
AGILNOZ	LAZOING	AGIMNPR	GRIPMAN		ROATING
AGILNPP	LAPPING		RAMPING	AGINORZ	ZINGARO
	PALPING	AGIMNPT	TAMPING	AGINOSS	SAGOINS
AGILNPR	GRAPLIN	AGIMNPV	VAMPING	AGINOST	AGONIST
	PARLING	AGIMNRR	MARRING		GITANOS
AGILNPS	LAPSING	AGIMNRS	ARMINGS	AGINOSU	SAGOUIN
	PALINGS		MARGINS	AGINOTU	AUTOING
	SAPLING	AGIMNRT	MARTING		OUTGAIN
AGILNPT	PLATING		MIGRANT	AGINOTV	OVATING
AGILNPW	LAPWING	AGIMNRW	WARMING	AGINOTZ	TOAZING
AGILNPY	PLAYING	AGIMNRY	MYRINGA	AGINOVW	AVOWING
AGILNRT	RATLING	AGIMNSS	MASSING	AGINPPP	PAPPING
AGILNRW	WARLING	AGIMNST	MASTING	AGINPPR	PARPING
AGILNRY	ANGRILY		MATINGS		RAPPING
	NARGILY		TAMINGS	AGINPPS	SAPPING
	RANGILY	AGIMNSU	AMUSING	AGINPPT	TAPPING
	RAYLING	AGIMNSY	MAYINGS	AGINPPW	WAPPING
AGILNSS	LASINGS	AGIMNTT	MATTING	AGINPPY	YAPPING
	SIGNALS	AGIMORS	ISOGRAM	AGINPPZ	ZAPPING
AGILNST	ANGLIST	AGIMORU	GOURAMI	AGINPRR	PARRING
	LASTING	AGIMOSY	ISOGAMY	AGINPRS	PARINGS
	SALTING	AGIMRRT	TRIGRAM		PARSING
	SLATING	AGIMRSU	GURAMIS		RASPING
	STALING	AGIMRTY	TRIGAMY		SPARING
AGILNSU	LINGUAS	AGIMSST	STIGMAS	AGINPRT	PARTING
	NILGAUS	AGIMSWW	WIGWAMS		PRATING
	SALUING	AGINNNP	PANNING		TRAPING
AGILNSV	SALVING	AGINNNT	TANNING	AGINPRW	WARPING
	SLAVING	AGINNNV	VANNING	AGINPRY	PRAYING
	VALSING	AGINNNW	WANNING	AGINPSS	PASSING
AGILNSW	LAWINGS	AGINNOS	GANOINS		SPAINGS
	SWALING	AGINNOT	ATONING	AGINPST	PASTING
AGILNSY	LAYINGS	AGINNOZ	ZINGANO	AGINPSU	PAUSING
	SLAYING	AGINNPP	NAPPING	AGINPSV	PAVINGS
AGILNTY	GIANTLY	AGINNPS	PINANGS	AGINPSY	PAYINGS
AGILNUV	VALUING		SPANING		SPAYING
AGILNUW	WAULING	AGINNPT	PANTING	AGINPTT	PATTING
AGILNVV	VALVING	AGINNPW	PAWNING	AGINPTU	TAPUING
AGILNWW	WAWLING	AGINNRS	SNARING	AGINPUY	YAUPING

AGINPWY	YAWPING	AGJLMOS	LOGJAMS	AGLSYYZ	SYZYGAL
AGINRRT	TARRING	AGJLRUU	JUGULAR	AGMMNOS	GAMMONS
AGINRRW	WARRING	AGJNOOR	JARGOON	AGMMNSU	MAGNUMS
AGINRST	GASTRIN	AGJNORS	JARGONS	AGMMORY	MYOGRAM
	GRATINS	AGJNORY	JARGONY	AGMMNNOR	GRANNOM
	RATINGS	AGJSTTY	GYTTJAS	AGMMNNOS	MAGNONS
	STARING	AGKLNNO	ANKLONG		SONGMAN
	TARINGS	AGKLNNU	ANKLUNG	AGMNNOT	TONGMAN
AGINRSV	RAVINGS	AGKLNOS	KALONGS	AGMNNOW	GOWNMAN
AGINRSW	RAWINGS	AGKLOOS	KAGOOLS	AGMNORS	MORGANS
AGINRSY	SIGNARY	AGKLOST	KGOTLAS	AGMNORU	ORGANUM
	SYRINGA	AGKLOSU	KAGOULS	AGMNOST	AMONGST
AGINRTT	RATTING	AGKMNOP	KAMPONG	AGMNSSU	MUSANGS
	TARTING	AGKMPRU	PUGMARK	AGMNSTU	MUSTANG
AGINRTW	RINGTAW	AGKNOPT	PAKTONG	AGMNSTY	GYMNAST
AGINRTY	GIANTRY	AGKNRSU	KURGANS		SYNTAGM
AGINRUW	WAURING	AGKORRW	RAGWORK	AGMNSYY	SYNGAMY
AGINRVY	VARYING	AGLLNOO	GALLOON	AGMOOYZ	ZOOGAMY
AGINRWY	RINGWAY	AGLLNOS	GALLONS	AGMOPRR	PROGRAM
AGINRZZ	RAZZING		GOLLANS	AGMOPRU	GOPURAM
AGINSSS	ASSIGNS	AGLLNTU	GALLNUT	AGMORRW	RAGWORM
	SASSING		NUTGALL	AGMORSS	ORGASMS
AGINSSU	SAGUINS	AGLLOOR	ROGALLO	AGMORSY	MORGAYS
AGINSSV	SAVINGS	AGLLOOT	GALLOOT	AGMOSYZ	ZYGOMAS
AGINSSW	SAWINGS	AGLLOPS	GALLOPS	AGMPRSU	GRAMPUS
AGINSSY	SAYINGS	AGLLOPU	PLUGOLA	AGMPSUZ	GAZUMPS
AGINSTT	STATING	AGLLORS	GOLLARS	AGMRSSU	GRASSUM
	TASTING	AGLLOSS	GLOSSAL	AGNNNOO	NONAGON
AGINSTU	SAUTING	AGLLOSU	GALLOUS	AGNNOOR	ARGONON
AGINSTV	STAVING	AGLLOSW	GALLOWS		ORGANON
AGINSTW	STAWING	AGLLOTT	GLOTTAL	AGNNOST	TONNAGS
	TAWINGS	AGLLPTY	GLYPTAL	AGNNOSY	NONGAYS
	TAWSING	AGLLRSY	ARGYLLS	AGNNSSU	UNSNAGS
	WASTING	AGLLRYY	GYRALLY	AGNNSTU	TANGUNS
AGINSTX	TAXINGS	AGLMMSY	GYMMALS	AGNNSUW	WANGUNS
AGINSTY	STAYING	AGLMOPY	POLYGAM	AGNOOSZ	GAZOONS
	STYGIAN	AGLMORS	GLAMORS	AGNOQSU	QUANGOS
AGINSUX	GUANXIS	AGLMORU	GLAMOUR	AGNORRS	GARRONS
AGINSVW	WAVINGS	AGLNNOS	LONGANS	AGNORRT	GRANTOR
AGINSWX	WAXINGS	AGLNNSU	LUNGANS	AGNORSS	SARONGS
AGINSWY	SWAYING	AGLNOOO	OLOGOAN	AGNORSU	OURANGS
AGINTTT	TATTING	AGLNOOS	LAGOONS	AGNORTU	OUTRANG
AGINTTU	TATUING	AGLNORU	LANGUOR	AGNOSSS	GOSSANS
	TAUTING	AGLNOSS	SLOGANS	AGNOSST	SONTAGS
AGINTTV	VATTING	AGLNOST	ALONGST	AGNOSTU	NOUGATS
AGINTTW	TAWTING	AGLNOSU	LANUGOS		OUTSANG
AGINTUV	VAUTING	AGLNOSW	GOWLANS	AGNOSZZ	GOZZANS
AGINTVW	VAWTING	AGLNPSY	SPANGLY	AGNOTUW	OUTGNAW
AGINTXY	TAXYING	AGLNPUY	GUNPLAY	AGNPRSS	SPRANGS
AGINTYZ	TZIGANY	AGLNRSU	LANGURS	AGNRSSU	SUNGARS
AGINVYZ	AVYZING	AGLNRUU	UNGULAR	AGNRTUY	GAUNTRY
AGINWWX	WAXWING	AGLNTUY	GAUNTLY	AGOPPST	STOPGAP
AGIOPPT	AGITPOP	AGLOOPS	APOLOGS	AGOPRST	RAGTOPS
AGIOPSS	GAPOSIS	AGLOOPY	APOLOGY	AGOPRSU	GOPURAS
AGIORST	AGISTOR	AGLOORS	GOORALS	AGORRST	GARROTS
	ORGIAST	AGLOOST	GALOOTS	AGORRTW	RAGWORT
AGIORSU	GIAOURS	AGLORSU	RUGOLAS	AGORRTY	GYRATOR
AGIORSV	VIRAGOS	AGLOSSS	GLOSSAS	AGORSSU	RUGOSAS
AGIOSTU	AGOUTIS	AGLOSSW	SAWLOGS	AGORSTU	RAGOUTS
AGIOUUV	OUGUIYA	AGLOSUV	VALGOUS	AGORTUY	GRAYOUT
AGIRSTU	GUITARS	AGLOSWY	LOGWAYS	AGOSTTU	TAUTOGS
AGIRTVY	GRAVITY	AGLRSSU	GUSLARS	AGOSUYZ	AZYGOUS
AGISTTW	WITGATS	AGLRSUU	ARGULUS	AGSSTUU	AUGUSTS
AGISTUV	VAGITUS	AGLRSUV	VULGARS	AHHHISS	HASHISH

AHHIIMS	HAIMISH	AHILLTY	LAITHLY	AHINRSS	ARSHINS
AHHIJRS	HIJRAHS	AHILMMO	MOHALIM		SHAIRNS
AHHIKKR	KHIRKAH	AHILMMS	MASHLIM	AHINRST	TARNISH
AHHIKSS	SHAIKHS	AHILMMY	HAMMILY	AHINRSU	UNHAIRS
AHHIKSW	HAWKISH	AHILMNS	MASHLIN	AHINRSV	VARNISH
AHHIMNU	HAHNIUM	AHILMOP	OMPHALI	AHINRTY	RHYTINA
AHHINST	SHANTIH	AHILMOS	HOLMIAS	AHINRVY	HRYVNIA
AHHIPRS	RHAPHIS	AHILMOT	HALIMOT	AHINSST	SHANTIS
AHHISSS	SHISHAS	AHILMOU	HALOUMI	AHINSSW	WASHINS
AHHISSV	SHIVAHS	AHILMSU	ALUMISH	AHINSTU	INHAUST
AHHISTT	SHITTAH	AHILNPS	PLANISH	AHINSYZ	ZANYISH
AHHKOOS	HOOKAHS	AHILNRS	SHRINAL	AHINTUU	TAUHINU
AHHLLOT	HALLOTH	AHILNRT	INTHRAL	AHIOOST	ATISHOO
AHHLRSY	HARSHLY	AHILNSS	LASHINS	AHIOPRU	OPHIURA
AHHMPRU	HARUMPH	AHILNSU	INHAULS	AHIOPXY	HYPOXIA
AHHOORS	HOORAHS	AHILNSY	HYALINS	AHIORSS	ORISSAS
AHHOPRS	SHOPHAR		LINHAYS	AHIORST	AIRSHOT
AHHPPSU	HUPPAHS	AHILORY	HOARILY		SHORTIA
AHHPTUZ	HUTZPAH	AHILOTY	ALIYOTH		THORIAS
AHHRRSU	HURRAHS	AHILOTZ	THIAZOL	AHIORSV	HAVIORS
AHHSUZZ	HUZZAHS	AHILPPS	PALSHIP	AHIORSW	AIRSHOW
AHIIKPS	PAKIHIS		SHIPLAP	AHIORUV	HAVIOUR
AHIIKRS	RIKISHA	AHILPPY	HAPPILY	AHIPRSS	RASPISH
	SHIKARI	AHILPRT	PHILTRA	AHIPRST	HARPIST
AHIILPS	SILPHIA	AHILPSY	APISHLY	AHIPRSU	RUPIAHS
AHIILST	LITHIAS	AHILSST	SALTISH	AHIPRSW	WARSHIP
AHIIMNT	THIAMIN		TAHSILS	AHIPRWY	WHIPRAY
AHIIMSS	SASHIMI	AHILSSV	SLAVISH	AHIPSSW	WASPISH
AHIIMST	SAMITHI	AHILSTU	HALITUS	AHIPSWW	WHIPSAW
AHIINPR	HAIRPIN		THULIAS	AHIPSWY	SHIPWAY
AHIINST	TAHINIS	AHILSTY	HASTILY	AHIRRSS	SHIRRAS
AHIINTU	HUITAIN	AHILSWY	WASHILY		SIRRAHS
AHIINTZ	THIAZIN	AHILSYZ	LAZYISH	AHIRRST	STIRRAH
AHIIPRS	AIRSHIP	AHIMMRS	RAMMISH	AHIRRSW	WIRRAHS
AHIIRTW	TAWHIRI	AHIMNNS	MANNISH	AHIRSST	HAIRSTS
AHIKKSS	KISHKAS	AHIMNNU	INHUMAN	AHIRSTT	ATHIRST
AHIKLPS	KALIPHS	AHIMNOT	MANIHOT		RATTISH
AHIKLRS	LARKISH	AHIMNPS	SHIPMAN		TARTISH
AHIKLSS	SHASLIK	AHIMNRS	HARMINS	AHIRSTW	TRISHAW
AHIKLST	KHILATS	AHIMOPR	MORPHIA		WRAITHS
AHIKLSY	SHAKILY	AHIMORS	MOHAIRS	AHISSTT	STAITHS
AHIKMNS	KHAMSIN	AHIMORZ	RHIZOMA	AHISSTU	SHIATSU
AHIKMRS	KASHMIR	AHIMOSS	SHAMOIS		THIASUS
AHIKMSV	MIKVAHS	AHIMPSS	MISHAPS	AHISSTW	WHATSIS
AHIKMSW	MAWKISH		PASHIMS	AHISTTW	WHATSIT
AHIKNRS	RANKISH	AHIMPST	MISHAPT	AHISTUZ	SHIATZU
AHIKNSS	SNAKISH	AHIMPSV	VAMPISH	AHITTWW	WHITTAW
AHIKNSV	KNAVISH	AHIMPSW	WAMPISH	AHJOOPS	POOJAHS
AHIKORS	KAROSHI	AHIMRSS	MAHSIRS	AHKKSSU	SUKKAHS
AHIKOSW	KOWHAIS	AHIMRST	THAIRMS	AHKLOOS	KOOLAHS
AHIKPRS	PARKISH		THIRAMS	AHKLPSU	PULKHAS
AHIKRSS	SHIKARS		THRIMSA	AHKMNSU	KHANUMS
AHIKRSW	RIKSHAW	AHIMRSW	WARMISH	AHKMORR	MARKHOR
AHIKSSS	SHIKSAS	AHIMSSU	HASSIUM	AHKMOSS	MOKSHAS
AHIKSST	SKAITHS	AHIMSTV	MITSVAH	AHKMOSW	MOHAWKS
AHILLNO	HALLION	AHIMTUZ	AZIMUTH	AHKMRTU	MUKHTAR
AHILLNP	PHALLIN	AHIMTVZ	MITZVAH	AHKNPSU	PUNKAHS
AHILLNT	ANTHILL	AHINNST	TANNISH	AHKPSUU	HAPUKUS
AHILLOS	HILLOAS	AHINNSW	WANNISH	AHKRSST	SKARTHS
AHILLRT	ATHRILL	AHINNTX	XANTHIN	AHKRSSU	KASHRUS
AHILLSS	SHALLIS	AHINORT	ORTHIAN	AHKRSTU	KASHRUT
AHILLST	TALLISH	AHINOTZ	HOATZIN		KHURTAS
AHILLSZ	ZILLAHS	AHINPRS	HARPINS		TUSHKAR
AHILLTT	TALLITH	AHINPST	HATPINS	AHLLMOS	MOLLAHS

Seven-letter anagrams

	OLLAMHS	AHMOSTU	MAHOUTS
AHLLMSU	MULLAHS	AHMOSTZ	MATZOHS
AHLLNOS	SHALLON	AHMOSWY	HAYMOWS
AHLLNOY	HALLYON	AHMOTTZ	MATZOTH
AHLLNSU	NULLAHS	AHMPSSU	MASHUPS
AHLLOOS	HALLOOS		SMASHUP
	HOLLOAS	AHMRRSU	MURRHAS
AHLLOPS	SHALLOP	AHMRSTW	WARMTHS
AHLLOST	SHALLOT	AHMRSTY	THRYMSA
AHLLOSU	HULLOAS	AHMSSSU	SAMSHUS
AHLLOSW	HALLOWS	AHNNSSU	SUNNAHS
	SHALLOW	AHNOOPR	HARPOON
AHLLOTY	LOATHLY	AHNOPRS	ORPHANS
	TALLYHO	AHNORSS	SHORANS
AHLLPSU	PHALLUS	AHNORSX	SAXHORN
AHLLPSY	ALPHYLS	AHNOTTW	WHATNOT
AHLLPYY	APHYLLY	AHNPPSS	SHNAPPS
AHLLRST	THRALLS	AHNPPUU	PUPUNHA
AHLLSTU	THALLUS	AHNPPUY	UNHAPPY
AHLMMSU	MASHLUM	AHNPRSU	UNSHARP
AHLMNPY	NYMPHAL	AHNPRXY	PHARYNX
AHLMNSY	HYMNALS	AHNPSSU	UNHASPS
AHLMNUY	HUMANLY	AHNRSVY	HRYVNAS
AHLMOOS	MOOLAHS	AHNRVYY	HRYVNYA
AHLMORU	HUMORAL	AHNSSTU	SUNHATS
AHLMOSS	SHALOMS	AHNSTUW	UNTHAWS
AHLMSTZ	SHMALTZ	AHNSTUY	UNHASTY
AHLMSUU	HAMULUS	AHOORSS	SHOORAS
AHLNOPR	ALPHORN	AHOORSY	HOORAYS
AHLNOPT	HAPLONT	AHOPRSS	PHASORS
	NAPHTOL	AHOPRTY	ATROPHY
AHLNORT	ALTHORN	AHOPSTW	WASHPOT
AHLOOPS	HOOPLAS	AHOPTTW	TOWPATH
AHLOOPW	WHOOPLA	AHORRSW	HARROWS
AHLOOTW	WOOLHAT	AHORSTT	THROATS
AHLORST	HARLOTS	AHORSTU	AUTHORS
AHLOSST	SHALOTS	AHORSTW	WROATHS
AHLOSTU	OUTLASH	AHORTTY	THROATY
AHLOTUU	OUTHAUL	AHOSTUW	OUTWASH
AHLPRSY	SHARPLY		WASHOUT
AHLPRUY	HYPURAL	AHPRRTY	PHRATRY
AHLPSSU	SULPHAS	AHPRSST	SPARTHS
AHLPSSY	SPLASHY	AHPSSUW	WASHUPS
AHMMMOT	MAMMOTH	AHPSTUZ	HUTZPAS
AHMMMUU	HUMMAUM	AHPSXYY	ASPHYXY
AHMMOSS	SHAMMOS	AHQSSUY	SQUASHY
AHMMOSW	WHAMMOS	AHRRSUY	HURRAYS
AHMNNSU	NUMNAHS	AHRSSSU	HUSSARS
AHMNNTU	MANHUNT	AHRSSTT	STRATHS
AHMNNUU	UNHUMAN	AHRSSTW	SWARTHS
AHMNOPS	SHOPMAN	AHRSTTW	THWARTS
AHMNOPT	PHANTOM	AHRSTWY	SWARTHY
AHMNORY	HARMONY	AHRTUWY	THRUWAY
AHMNOSS	HANSOMS	AHSSSTU	TUSSAHS
AHMNOSW	SHOWMAN	AIIILMT	MILITIA
AHMNRSU	RHAMNUS	AIIILNT	INITIAL
AHMNRYY	HYMNARY	AIIILVX	LIXIVIA
AHMOOPS	OOMPAHS	AIIIMRS	SAIMIRI
	SHAMPOO	AIIKKSW	WAKIKIS
AHMOOSS	SAMSHOO	AIIKMMS	SKIMMIA
AHMORRU	MORRHUA	AIIKMNN	MANIKIN
AHMORST	HARMOST	AIIKNNT	TANKINI
AHMORSZ	MAHZORS	AIIKNST	KAINITS
AHMOSSY	SHAMOYS	AIIKRRU	RAURIKI
AIIKRTT	TRAIKIT
AIILLLP	LAPILLI
AIILLMN	LIMINAL
AIILLMS	LIMAILS
AIILLMW	WILLIAM
AIILLNV	VILLAIN
AIILLQU	QUILLAI
AIILLUV	ILLUVIA
AIILMMN	MINIMAL
AIILMNN	LAMININ
AIILMNO	MONILIA
AIILMNS	MISLAIN
AIILMNT	INTIMAL
AIILMNV	VIMINAL
AIILMRS	SIMILAR
AIILMRT	MILITAR
AIILMRY	MILIARY
AIILNNS	ANILINS
AIILNOS	LIAISON
AIILNPT	PINTAIL
AIILNPU	NAUPLII
AIILNRY	RAINILY
AIILNTU	NAUTILI
AIILNTV	INVITAL
AIILNTY	ANILITY
AIILOPP	PAPILIO
AIILORV	RAVIOLI
AIILPRU	LIPURIA
AIILQSU	SILIQUA
AIILRST	LIATRIS
AIILRTV	TRIVIAL
	VITRAIL
AIIMMNS	ANIMISM
AIIMMNX	MAXIMIN
	MINIMAX
AIIMMSS	MISAIMS
AIIMNNV	MINIVAN
AIIMNOR	AMORINI
AIIMNPS	PAINIMS
	PIANISM
AIIMNPT	IMPAINT
	TIMPANI
AIIMNRT	MARTINI
AIIMNSS	SAIMINS
	SIMIANS
AIIMNST	ANIMIST
	INTIMAS
	SANTIMI
AIIMNTT	IMITANT
AIIMNTU	MINUTIA
AIIMNTV	VITAMIN
AIIMNTY	AMINITY
AIIMPRS	IMPAIRS
AIIMPSS	SIMPAIS
AIIMRST	SIMITAR
AIIMSST	SAMITIS
AIIMSSY	MYIASIS
AIINNOP	PIANINO
AIINNQU	QUININA
AIINNSZ	ZINNIAS
AIINNTY	INANITY
AIINOPS	SINOPIA
AIINOTT	NOTITIA
AIINPPR	RAPPINI

AIINPRS	ASPIRIN	AIKOORW	KOROWAI	AILMPRU	PRIMULA
AIINPST	PIANIST	AIKOPST	KATIPOS	AILMPST	PALMIST
AIINRSS	RAISINS	AIKORST	TROIKAS	AILMPSY	MISPLAY
AIINRSY	RAISINY	AIKOSTW	KWAITOS	AILMRST	MISTRAL
AIINRTV	VITRAIN	AIKRRSS	SIRKARS		RAMTILS
AIINRTZ	TRIAZIN	AIKRSST	STRAIKS	AILMRSU	SIMULAR
AIINSST	ISATINS	AIKRTUZ	ZIKURAT	AILMSSS	MISSALS
AIINSSX	SIXAINS	AILLLNO	LINALOL	AILMSST	MISTALS
AIINSTT	TITANIS	AILLMNU	LUMINAL	AILMSSX	LAXISMS
	TITIANS	AILLMNY	MANLILY	AILMSSY	MISLAYS
AIINSTV	NAIVIST	AILLMOT	MAILLOT	AILMSTU	ULTIMAS
AIIPRST	PIARIST	AILLMPU	PALLIUM	AILMSTY	MYALIST
AIIPSTW	WAPITIS	AILLMSU	ALLIUMS	AILMSUV	MAULVIS
AIIPTTU	PITUITA	AILLMSW	SAWMILL	AILNNOS	SOLANIN
AIISTUW	TAUIWIS	AILLMSY	MISALLY	AILNNOT	ANTLION
AIJJMMS	JIMJAMS	AILLNNO	LANOLIN	AILNNPU	PINNULA
AIJLORS	JAILORS	AILLNOP	PAILLON	AILNNSU	UNNAILS
AIJLORT	TOLARJI	AILLNPY	PLAINLY		UNSLAIN
AIJLSTW	WILTJAS	AILLNST	INSTALL	AILNOPY	POLYNIA
AIJLYZZ	JAZZILY	AILLNSV	VILLANS	AILNOQU	AQUILON
AIJMNSS	JASMINS	AILLNSW	INWALLS	AILNOSS	ALISONS
AIJMORS	ROMAJIS	AILLNVY	VILLANY		SIALONS
AIJNORT	JANITOR	AILLORT	LITORAL	AILNOST	LATINOS
AIJORSW	JOWARIS	AILLORZ	ZORILLA		TALIONS
AIJPSTU	JUPATIS	AILLPRS	PILLARS	AILNOTU	OUTLAIN
AIKKMNR	KIRKMAN	AILLPRU	PILULAR	AILNPRW	PRAWLIN
AIKKMOT	KOMATIK	AILLPSU	PILLAUS	AILNPSS	SPINALS
AIKKOOW	KOKOWAI		PILULAS	AILNPST	PLAINTS
AIKKOPY	KOPIYKA	AILLPUV	PLUVIAL	AILNPSU	PAULINS
AIKKSUZ	ZAKUSKI	AILLQSU	SQUILLA		SPINULA
AIKLLNY	LANKILY	AILLRSU	ARILLUS	AILNPSX	SALPINX
AIKLMMN	MILKMAN	AILLRVY	VIRALLY	AILNPTU	NUPTIAL
AIKLMNN	LINKMAN	AILLSTT	TALLITS		PATULIN
AIKLMNS	MALKINS	AILLSTY	SALTILY		UNPLAIT
AIKLMPU	LAMPUKI	AILLSUZ	LAZULIS	AILNPTY	INAPTLY
AIKLMSS	MISKALS	AILLTVY	VITALLY		PTYALIN
AIKLMSU	KALIUMS	AILLTWW	WITWALL	AILNPUV	PLUVIAN
AIKLNOS	KAOLINS	AILMMOR	IMMORAL	AILNQTU	QUINTAL
AIKLNSY	SNAKILY	AILMMSS	MALISMS	AILNRST	RATLINS
AIKLPWY	PAWKILY	AILMMSY	MYALISM	AILNRSU	INSULAR
AIKLQUY	QUAKILY	AILMMUU	ALUMIUM		URINALS
AIKLRTT	TITLARK	AILMMUW	MWALIMU	AILNRTT	RATTLIN
AIKLSSU	SALUKIS	AILMNNO	NOMINAL	AILNRTY	RIANTLY
AIKLSSY	SKYSAIL	AILMNOP	LAMPION	AILNSST	INSTALS
AIKMMRS	MISMARK	AILMNOS	MALISON	AILNSSU	INSULAS
AIKMMSS	IMMASKS		MONIALS	AILNSSV	SILVANS
AIKMNNS	KINSMAN		SOMNIAL	AILNSTT	LATTINS
AIKMNRS	RANKISM	AILMNOY	ALIMONY	AILNSTU	UNALIST
AIKMNSS	KAMSINS	AILMNPS	MISPLAN	AILNSTY	NASTILY
AIKMNSW	MAWKINS		PLASMIN		SAINTLY
AIKMOOS	OOMIAKS	AILMNPT	IMPLANT	AILNSUV	UNVAILS
AIKMPRS	IMPARKS	AILMNPU	ULPANIM	AILNTTY	NATTILY
AIKMRSU	KUMARIS	AILMNRS	MARLINS	AILNTUV	UNVITAL
	RUMAKIS	AILMNRU	MURLAIN	AILNTWY	TAWNILY
AIKMSST	KISMATS		RUMINAL	AILOORS	OORALIS
AIKNNNS	NANKINS	AILMNSS	MASLINS		OORIALS
AIKNNPS	NAPKINS	AILMNSU	ALUMINS	AILOORW	WOORALI
AIKNOST	KATIONS	AILMOOV	MOVIOLA	AILOPST	APOSTIL
AIKNPRS	KIRPANS	AILMOPS	LIPOMAS		TOPSAIL
	PARKINS	AILMOPT	OPTIMAL	AILOPSY	SOAPILY
AIKNPSS	PANISKS	AILMORS	ORALISM	AILOPTT	TALIPOT
AIKNRST	KIRTANS	AILMOST	SOMITAL	AILOPTV	PIVOTAL
AIKNSTU	TANUKIS	AILMOSY	ISOAMYL	AILOQTU	ALIQUOT
AIKOORT	ROOIKAT	AILMPRS	IMPARLS	AILORSS	SAILORS

Seven-letter anagrams

AILORST	ORALIST		MANSION	**AIMSSTU**	AUTISMS
	RIALTOS		ONANISM	**AINNNST**	TANNINS
	SLIOTAR	**AIMNNSS**	NANISMS	**AINNOPS**	SAPONIN
	TAILORS	**AIMNNSY**	MINYANS	**AINNOPT**	PINTANO
AILORSU	OURALIS	**AIMNOOR**	AMORINO	**AINNOSS**	NASIONS
AILORTY	ORALITY	**AIMNOOT**	AMOTION	**AINNOST**	ANOINTS
AILORUW	WOURALI	**AIMNOPR**	RAMPION		NATIONS
AILORUX	UXORIAL	**AIMNOPS**	MOPANIS		ONANIST
AILORVY	OLIVARY	**AIMNOPT**	MAINTOP	**AINNOSW**	WANIONS
AILOSSS	ASSOILS		PTOMAIN	**AINNPSS**	INSPANS
AILOSTT	ALTOIST		TAMPION	**AINNPST**	SNAPTIN
AILOSTU	OUTSAIL		TIMPANO	**AINNPTU**	UNPAINT
AILOSTX	OXTAILS	**AIMNOPZ**	ZAMPONI	**AINNQTU**	QUINNAT
AILOSWY	OILWAYS	**AIMNORS**	MAINORS		QUINTAN
AILOTVY	OVALITY	**AIMNORT**	TORMINA	**AINNRSU**	URANINS
AILPPRU	PUPILAR	**AIMNORU**	MAINOUR	**AINNRTT**	INTRANT
AILPPSU	SUIPLAP	**AIMNOST**	MANITOS	**AINNRTU**	URINANT
AILPPSY	PAYSLIP		STAMNOI	**AINNSTT**	INSTANT
	SAPPILY	**AIMNOTU**	MANITOU	**AINNSTU**	UNSAINT
AILPPTY	PLATYPI		TINAMOU	**AINNTUY**	ANNUITY
AILPQSU	PASQUIL	**AIMNPST**	PITMANS	**AINOOPR**	PRONAOI
AILPRSS	SPIRALS	**AIMNPSW**	IMPAWNS	**AINOORR**	ORARION
AILPRSU	PARULIS	**AIMNPSY**	PAYNIMS	**AINOORT**	ORATION
	SPIRULA	**AIMNPTY**	TYMPANI	**AINOOTV**	OVATION
	UPRISAL	**AIMNRRU**	MURRAIN	**AINOPPT**	APPOINT
AILPRSY	PYRALIS	**AIMNRST**	MARTINS	**AINOPRS**	PARISON
AILPSST	PASTILS	**AIMNRSU**	SURAMIN		PORINAS
	SPITALS		URANISM		SOPRANI
AILPSTU	TIPULAS	**AIMNRTU**	NATRIUM	**AINOPRT**	ATROPIN
AILPSTY	PASTILY	**AIMNRTV**	VARMINT	**AINOPSS**	PASSION
AILPSWY	SLIPWAY	**AIMNRUU**	URANIUM	**AINOPTT**	ANTIPOT
	WASPILY	**AIMNSST**	SANTIMS	**AINOPTU**	OPUNTIA
AILQSSU	SQUAILS	**AIMNSTT**	MATTINS		UTOPIAN
AILQTTU	QUITTAL	**AIMNSTU**	MANITUS	**AINOQSU**	QUINOAS
AILQTUY	QUALITY		SANTIMU	**AINORST**	AROINTS
AILRRVY	RIVALRY		TSUNAMI		RATIONS
AILRSTT	STARLIT	**AIMNSUV**	MAUVINS	**AINORSW**	WARISON
AILRSTU	RITUALS	**AIMNSUZ**	MIZUNAS	**AINORTU**	RAINOUT
	TRISULA	**AIMNSVY**	MAYVINS	**AINORTW**	WAITRON
AILRSTY	TRYSAIL	**AIMNSYZ**	ZANYISM	**AINORTX**	TRIAXON
AILRTTU	TITULAR	**AIMOPST**	IMPASTO	**AINOSSU**	SANIOUS
AILRTTY	RATTILY		MATIPOS		SUASION
	TARTILY	**AIMOPSY**	MYOPIAS	**AINOSTT**	STATION
AILRTUV	VIRTUAL	**AIMORRU**	ORARIUM	**AINOSUX**	ANXIOUS
	VITULAR	**AIMORST**	AMORIST	**AINOSVY**	SYNOVIA
AILSSSY	SASSILY	**AIMORTT**	TRITOMA	**AINPPRS**	PARSNIP
AILSSTU	TISSUAL	**AIMORUZ**	ZOARIUM	**AINPQTU**	PIQUANT
AILSSTX	LAXISTS	**AIMOSTT**	ATOMIST	**AINPRSS**	SPINARS
AILSSUV	VISUALS	**AIMPPSS**	PAPISMS		SPRAINS
AILSSVY	SYLVIAS	**AIMPPST**	MAPPIST	**AINPRST**	SPIRANT
AILSSVZ	VIZSLAS	**AIMPRRY**	PRIMARY		SPRAINT
AILSTTY	TASTILY	**AIMPRST**	ARMPITS	**AINPRSU**	PRUINAS
AILSTUW	LAWSUIT		IMPARTS	**AINPRSW**	INWRAPS
AILSVVY	SAVVILY		MISPART		RIPSAWN
AILTTTY	TATTILY	**AIMPRSY**	PYRAMIS	**AINPRTT**	TRIPTAN
AIMMMSU	MUMMIAS	**AIMQRSU**	MARQUIS	**AINPRTU**	PURITAN
AIMMMUX	MAXIMUM	**AIMRSST**	TSARISM		UPTRAIN
AIMMNTU	MANUMIT	**AIMRSTU**	ATRIUMS	**AINPSST**	PISSANT
AIMMORS	AMORISM		MATSURI		PTISANS
AIMMOSS	MIMOSAS	**AIMRSTY**	MAISTRY	**AINPSSV**	SPAVINS
AIMMOST	ATOMISM		SYMITAR	**AINPSTU**	TIPUNAS
AIMMSUX	MAXIMUS	**AIMRSTZ**	TZARISM	**AINQRST**	QINTARS
AIMNNOR	IRONMAN	**AIMSSSY**	MISSAYS	**AINQRTU**	QUINTAR
AIMNNOS	AMNIONS	**AIMSSTT**	STATISM	**AINQRUY**	QUINARY

AINQSSU	QUASSIN
AINQSTU	ASQUINT
	QUINTAS
AINQSUY	YANQUIS
AINRRTY	TRINARY
AINRRUY	URINARY
AINRSST	INSTARS
	SANTIRS
	STRAINS
AINRSTT	STRAINT
	TRANSIT
AINRSTU	NUTRIAS
AINRTTT	TITRANT
AINRTUY	UNITARY
AINSSTT	STATINS
	TANISTS
AINSSTU	ISSUANT
	SUSTAIN
AINSSXY	SYNAXIS
AINTTVY	TANTIVY
AIOORRW	WOORARI
AIOORSS	ARIOSOS
AIOPPRR	PROPRIA
AIOPRRT	AIRPORT
	PARITOR
AIOPRST	AIRPOST
	AIRSTOP
	PAROTIS
AIOPRSV	PAVIORS
AIOPRTT	PATRIOT
AIOPRTY	TOPIARY
AIOPRUV	PAVIOUR
AIOPSTU	UTOPIAS
AIORRRW	WARRIOR
AIORRSU	OURARIS
AIORRTT	TRAITOR
AIORRTX	ORATRIX
AIORSST	AORISTS
	ARISTOS
	SATORIS
AIORSSU	SOUARIS
AIORSSV	SAVIORS
AIORSTU	SAUTOIR
AIORSTV	TRAVOIS
	VIATORS
AIORSTY	OSTIARY
AIORSUV	SAVIOUR
	VARIOUS
AIOSSTT	TATSOIS
AIOSSYZ	ZOYSIAS
AIOTTUW	OUTWAIT
AIPPRRS	RIPRAPS
AIPPRSU	PRIAPUS
AIPPSST	PAPISTS
AIPRRTT	TRIPART
AIPRSST	RAPISTS
AIPRSSW	RIPSAWS
AIPRSTU	UPSTAIR
AIPRSUY	PYURIAS
AIPRTVV	PRAVITY
AIPSSTT	TAPISTS
AIPSSTW	PITSAWS
	SAWPITS
AIPYZZZ	PIZAZZY
AIPZZZZ	PIZZAZZ
AIRRSST	RISTRAS
	STIRRAS
AIRRSZZ	RIZZARS
AIRRTZZ	RIZZART
AIRSSSU	RUSSIAS
AIRSSTT	ARTISTS
	SITTARS
	STRAITS
	TSARIST
AIRSSTU	AURISTS
AIRSTTT	ATTRIST
	ATTRITS
AIRSTTU	TURISTA
AIRSTTY	YTTRIAS
AIRSTTZ	TZARIST
AIRSTVY	VARSITY
AIRTUVX	VITRAUX
AISSSST	ASSISTS
AISSTTT	STATIST
AISSTTU	AUTISTS
AISTTVY	VASTITY
AISTUVY	SUAVITY
AJKMNNU	JUNKMAN
AJKMNTU	MUNTJAK
AJKNSSY	JANSKYS
AJLLRUY	JURALLY
AJLMORY	MAJORLY
AJLNORU	JOURNAL
AJLOORS	JAROOLS
AJLOPPY	JALOPPY
AJMNRUY	JURYMAN
AJMOPST	JAMPOTS
AJMRSTU	JUMARTS
AJNRSTU	JURANTS
AKKKOOS	KOKAKOS
AKKKORU	ROKKAKU
AKKLRSY	SKYLARK
AKKLSWY	SKYWALK
AKKMOOT	TOKOMAK
AKKNNRSU	KUNKARS
AKKOOPS	PAKOKOS
AKKOQSU	QUOKKAS
AKLMMSU	MAMLUKS
AKLNOSU	KOULANS
AKLNOSX	KLAXONS
AKLOPRW	LAPWORK
AKLOSST	SKATOLS
AKLOSTW	KOTWALS
AKLOTTU	OUTTALK
AKLOTUW	OUTWALK
	WALKOUT
AKLPRSY	SPARKLY
AKLPSTU	UPTALKS
AKLPSUW	WALKUPS
AKLRSTY	STARKLY
AKLRSVY	VALKYRS
AKMNORW	WORKMAN
AKMNRTU	TRANKUM
AKMNSSU	UNMASKS
AKMOORT	MOOKTAR
AKMOOSS	OAKMOSS
AKMORST	OSTMARK
AKMPRSU	MARKUPS
AKMQTUU	KUMQUAT
AKMRSTU	MUSKRAT
AKMSTUU	MAKUTUS
AKNNOOS	NANOOKS
AKNORSU	KORUNAS
AKNORSY	KARYONS
	RYOKANS
AKNORTU	OUTRANK
AKOOPRT	PARTOOK
AKOORRS	KAROROS
	KARROOS
	KORORAS
AKOOSTU	ATOKOUS
AKOPRRU	PARKOUR
AKORRTW	ARTWORK
AKORRWW	WARWORK
AKORWWX	WAXWORK
AKOSSTU	OUTASKS
AKOSTTU	OUTTASK
AKOSTWY	TOWKAYS
AKQRSSU	SQUARKS
AKQSSUW	SQUAWKS
AKQSUWY	SQUAWKY
AKRSSTU	TUSKARS
AKSSWYY	SKYWAYS
ALLLOST	TALLOLS
ALLLOYY	LOYALLY
ALLMNOP	POLLMAN
ALLMNOT	TOLLMAN
ALLMNOY	ALLONYM
ALLMNPU	PULLMAN
ALLMOOS	OSMOLAL
ALLMORS	MORALLS
ALLMORY	MORALLY
ALLMOSS	SLALOMS
ALLMOST	MALTOLS
ALLMOSW	MALLOWS
ALLMPUU	PLUMULA
ALLMSUV	VALLUMS
ALLNOPS	POLLANS
ALLNOTY	TONALLY
ALLNOYZ	ZONALLY
ALLNRUU	LUNULAR
ALLNSTY	SLANTLY
ALLNTUU	ULULANT
ALLOOPS	APOLLOS
	PALOLOS
ALLOOST	LATOSOL
ALLOOTX	AXOLOTL
ALLOPRS	PALLORS
ALLOPRY	PAYROLL
ALLOPSW	WALLOPS
ALLORSS	SOLLARS
ALLORWY	ROLLWAY
ALLORYY	ROYALLY
ALLOSSW	SALLOWS
ALLOSTT	TALLOTS
ALLOSTV	LAVOLTS
ALLOSTW	TALLOWS
ALLOSWW	SWALLOW
	WALLOWS
ALLOSWY	SALLOWY
ALLOTTY	TOTALLY
ALLOTWY	TALLOWY

Seven-letter anagrams

	TOLLWAY	ALNOPYY	POLYNYA	ALRSTTY	STARTLY
ALLOTYY	LOYALTY	ALNORST	LATRONS	ALRSTUU	SUTURAL
ALLPRSU	PLURALS	ALNORSU	SOLUNAR	ALRSTUW	TULWARS
ALLPSSY	PSYLLAS	ALNORUV	UNROYAL	ALRSUUV	UVULARS
ALLQSSU	SQUALLS	ALNORUZ	ZONULAR	AMMMNOS	MAMMONS
ALLQSUY	SQUALLY	ALNOSST	SANTOLS	AMMMOSU	AMOMUMS
ALLRRUY	RURALLY		STANOLS	AMMNOOR	MOORMAN
ALLRSTU	LUSTRAL	ALNOSUZ	ZONULAS	AMMNOOT	MOOTMAN
ALLRSUY	LAURYLS	ALNPRUY	PLANURY	AMMNOPS	PSAMMON
ALLSUUY	USUALLY	ALNPSTU	PULSANT	AMMNRUY	NUMMARY
ALMMSUW	WAMMULS		PULTANS	AMMOORR	MAORMOR
ALMMSUY	AMYLUMS	ALNPTUY	UNAPTLY		MORMAOR
ALMNNUY	UNMANLY	ALNPTXY	PLANXTY	AMMOPTU	POMATUM
ALMNOOP	LAMPOON	ALNRSUY	URANYLS	AMMORST	MARMOTS
ALMNOOT	TOOLMAN	ALNSSTU	SULTANS	AMMOSXY	MYXOMAS
ALMNOOW	WOOLMAN	ALNSSVY	SYLVANS	AMMPSUW	WAMPUMS
ALMNOPS	PLASMON	ALNSTUW	WALNUTS	AMMRRSU	MARRUMS
ALMNOPW	PLOWMAN	ALNSUUU	UNUSUAL		MURRAMS
ALMNORS	NORMALS	ALOOPSS	SALOOPS	AMMRSUY	SUMMARY
ALMNORU	UNMORAL	ALOOPYZ	POLYZOA	AMMSSTU	SUMMATS
ALMNORY	ALMONRY	ALOORRS	SORORAL	AMNNOOX	MONAXON
ALMNOSS	SALMONS	ALOPPRS	POPLARS	AMNNORS	NORMANS
ALMNOSU	MONAULS	ALOPPRU	POPULAR	AMNNOSW	SNOWMAN
	SOLANUM	ALOPPRY	PROPYLA	AMNNOSY	ANONYMS
ALMNOWY	WOMANLY	ALOPPST	LAPTOPS	AMNNOTT	MONTANT
ALMNPSU	SUNLAMP	ALOPRRS	PARLORS	AMNNOTY	ANTONYM
ALMNRSU	MURLANS	ALOPRRU	PARLOUR	AMNNOUW	UNWOMAN
ALMNSUU	ALUMNUS	ALOPRST	PATROLS	AMNNSTU	STANNUM
ALMOOPY	POLYOMA		PORTALS	AMNOOPP	POMPANO
ALMOORS	OSMOLAR	ALOPRSU	PARLOUS	AMNOORS	MAROONS
ALMOPPT	PALMTOP	ALOPRSY	PYROLAS		ROMANOS
ALMOPRT	MARPLOT	ALOPSST	POSTALS	AMNOOTT	OTTOMAN
ALMORRU	MORULAR	ALOPSSU	SPOUSAL	AMNOOTZ	MATZOON
ALMORSS	SAMLORS	ALOPSUV	VOLUSPA	AMNOPPR	PROPMAN
ALMORST	MORTALS	ALOPTUY	OUTPLAY	AMNOPRT	PORTMAN
	STROMAL	ALOQRRU	RORQUAL	AMNOPRY	PARONYM
ALMORSU	MORULAS	ALOQRSU	SQUALOR	AMNOPST	POSTMAN
ALMORTU	TUMORAL	ALOQSTU	LOQUATS		TAMPONS
ALMOSST	SMALTOS	ALORRST	ROSTRAL		TOPSMAN
ALMOSTW	MATLOWS	ALORRSW	WORRALS	AMNOPTU	PANTOUM
ALMOSXY	XYLOMAS	ALORSST	SORTALS	AMNOPTY	TYMPANO
ALMOTTU	MULATTO	ALORSSU	ROSULAS	AMNORRS	MARRONS
ALMRSTY	SMARTLY	ALORSSV	SALVORS	AMNORSS	RAMSONS
ALMRSUU	RAMULUS	ALORSTU	ROTULAS		RANSOMS
ALMRTUU	MUTULAR		TORULAS	AMNORST	MATRONS
	TUMULAR	ALORSUV	LOUVARS		TRANSOM
ALMSSUY	ALYSSUM		VALOURS	AMNORSY	MASONRY
	ASYLUMS	ALORTWW	AWLWORT		MORNAYS
ALMSTUU	MUTUALS	ALORTYY	ROYALTY	AMNORTU	ROMAUNT
	UMLAUTS	ALORUVY	OVULARY	AMNOSST	STAMNOS
ALNNOOR	NONORAL	ALOSTTU	OUTLAST	AMNOSTU	AMOUNTS
ALNNOPY	NONPLAY	ALOSTUW	OUTLAWS		MOUTANS
ALNNRSU	UNSNARL	ALOSTUY	LAYOUTS		OUTMANS
ALNNSUU	ANNULUS		OUTLAYS	AMNOSYZ	ZYMOSAN
ALNOOPR	POLARON	ALOSTXY	OXYSALT	AMNOTUY	AUTONYM
ALNOOPT	PLATOON	ALPRRSU	LARRUPS	AMNPSTY	TYMPANS
ALNOOPV	VANPOOL	ALPRSSU	PULSARS	AMNPTYY	TYMPANY
ALNOORT	ORTOLAN	ALPRSSW	SPRAWLS	AMNQTUU	QUANTUM
ALNOOSS	SALOONS	ALPRSTY	PSALTRY	AMNRRUY	UNMARRY
	SOLANOS	ALPRSUU	PURSUAL	AMNRSTU	ANTRUMS
ALNOPPY	PANOPLY	ALPRSUW	PULWARS		UNSMART
ALNOPRS	PROLANS	ALPRSWY	SPRAWLY	AMNRTTU	TANTRUM
ALNOPSS	SPONSAL	ALQSTUY	SQUATLY	AMNSTTU	MUTANTS
ALNOPTU	OUTPLAN	ALRSSUU	RUSSULA	AMNSTUU	AUTUMNS

AMNTUUY	AUTUMNY
AMOOORS	AMOROSO
AMOOPRS	PROSOMA
AMOOPRT	TAPROOM
AMOORSU	AMOROUS
AMOORSV	MOORVAS
	VAROOMS
AMOORXY	OXYMORA
AMOPPSY	MAYPOPS
AMOPSTT	TOPMAST
AMORRST	MORTARS
AMORRSU	ARMOURS
AMORRSW	MARROWS
AMORRTY	MORTARY
AMORRUY	ARMOURY
AMORRWY	MARROWY
AMORSST	MATROSS
	STROAMS
AMORSSY	MORASSY
AMORWWX	WAXWORM
AMOSTUW	OUTSWAM
AMOSTUZ	MAZOUTS
AMOSUYZ	AZYMOUS
AMPRSST	STRAMPS
AMPRSUW	UPSWARM
	WARMUPS
AMRRSTU	RASTRUM
AMRRSTY	MARTYRS
AMRRSUY	MURRAYS
AMRRTYY	MARTYRY
AMRSSTU	STRUMAS
AMRSTTU	STRATUM
ANNNOSY	SYNANON
ANNOPRS	NAPRONS
ANNOPTY	POYNANT
ANNORST	NATRONS
	NONARTS
ANNORSW	NONWARS
ANNOSST	SANTONS
	SONANTS
ANNOSTW	WANTONS
ANNOSTY	TANNOYS
ANNOTTY	TANTONY
ANNPSSU	SANNUPS
	UNSNAPS
ANNPSTU	PANTUNS
ANNRTYY	TYRANNY
ANNSSTU	SUNTANS
ANNSSTY	SYNTANS
ANOOPRS	PRONAOS
	SOPRANO
ANOOPRT	PATROON
	PRONOTA
ANOORST	RATOONS
	SANTOOR
ANOORTT	ARNOTTO
	RATTOON
ANOPRRS	SPORRAN
ANOPRSS	PARSONS
	SANPROS
ANOPRST	PARTONS
	PATRONS
	TARPONS
ANOPRSW	PAWNORS
ANOPRTV	PROVANT
ANOPSTT	OPTANTS
ANOPSTU	OUTSPAN
ANOPSUY	YAUPONS
ANORRSW	NARROWS
ANORRWW	WARWORN
ANORSSV	SOVRANS
ANORSTT	ATTORNS
	RATTONS
	ROTTANS
ANORSTU	ROUSANT
	SANTOUR
ANORSTY	AROYNTS
ANORSUU	ANUROUS
	URANOUS
ANORWWY	WAYWORN
ANOSSTZ	STANZOS
ANOSTTU	TOTANUS
ANPPSUW	SUPPAWN
ANPRSSU	UNSPARS
ANPRSTU	SUNTRAP
	UNSTRAP
ANPRSUW	UNWRAPS
ANPRSUY	UNPRAYS
ANPSSUW	SUPAWNS
ANPSTUU	TUPUNAS
ANRSSTU	SANTURS
	SUNSTAR
ANRSSUY	SUNRAYS
ANRSTTU	TRUANTS
ANRSTTY	TYRANTS
ANRSUWY	RUNWAYS
ANSSTTU	TUTSANS
AOOPPRS	APROPOS
AOOPRTT	TAPROOT
AOORRST	ORATORS
AOORRSY	ARROYOS
AOORRTT	ROTATOR
AOORRTU	OUTROAR
AOORRTY	ORATORY
AOORSTT	TOOARTS
AOORSTU	OUTSOAR
AOORSTV	OVATORS
AOOSTTT	TATTOOS
AOOSTUZ	AZOTOUS
AOOTXYZ	ZOOTAXY
AOPPPSU	PAPPOUS
AOPPRRT	RAPPORT
AOPPRST	APPORTS
AOPRRST	PARROTS
	RAPTORS
AOPRRSU	UPROARS
AOPRRSW	SPARROW
AOPRRTY	PARROTY
	PORTRAY
AOPRSST	ASPORTS
	PASTORS
AOPRSSU	SAPOURS
	UPSOARS
AOPRSTU	ASPROUT
AOPRSTW	POSTWAR
AOPRSUV	VAPOURS
AOPRTTU	OUTPART
AOPRTUY	OUTPRAY
AOPRUVY	VAPOURY
AOPSSTU	OUTPASS
	PASSOUT
AOPSTTX	POSTTAX
AOPSTUY	AUTOPSY
	PAYOUTS
AOPSTWY	WAYPOST
AOPTTUU	AUTOPUT
AOQRSTU	QUARTOS
AORRSST	SARTORS
AORRSSU	ASSUROR
AORRSTW	TARROWS
AORRSWY	SOWARRY
	YARROWS
AORSSST	ASSORTS
AORSSTT	STATORS
AORSSTU	SOUTARS
AORSSUV	SAVOURS
AORSSUY	OSSUARY
	SUASORY
AORSTUW	OUTWARS
AORSTUY	YAOURTS
AORSUVY	SAVOURY
AORTUVY	AVOUTRY
AORUVVY	VOUVRAY
AOSSTUY	OUTSAYS
AOSTTTW	TATTOWS
AOSTTUY	OUTSTAY
APPRRUU	PURPURA
APPRSTY	STRAPPY
APPRSUW	UPWRAPS
APPRSUY	PAPYRUS
APRSSSU	SURPASS
APRSSWY	PSYWARS
APRSTTU	STARTUP
	UPSTART
APRSTTY	TAPSTRY
APRSUWY	SPURWAY
APSSTUY	UPSTAYS
APSSUWY	UPSWAYS
AQRTUYZ	QUARTZY
AQSTTUY	SQUATTY
ARSSSTU	TUSSARS
ARSSTTU	STRATUS
ARSSTTY	STARTSY
ASSTTUY	STATUSY
AVYYZZZ	ZYZZYVA
BBBDELO	BLOBBED
	BOBBLED
BBBDELU	BLUBBED
	BUBBLED
BBBEILS	BIBBLES
BBBEIOS	BOBBIES
BBBEIRS	BIBBERS
BBBEIRY	BIBBERY
BBBEISU	BUBBIES
BBBELOS	BOBBLES
BBBELRU	BLUBBER
	BUBBLER
BBBELSU	BUBBLES
BBBEORS	BOBBERS

Seven-letter anagrams

BBBEORY	BOBBERY	**BBDELNU**	NUBBLED	**BBEHLOR**	HOBBLER
BBBGIIN	BIBBING	**BBDELOO**	BEBLOOD	**BBEHLOS**	HOBBLES
BBBGINO	BOBBING	**BBDELOS**	BOBSLED	**BBEHMTU**	BETHUMB
BBBHIOS	BOBBISH	**BBDELOW**	WOBBLED	**BBEHORS**	HOBBERS
BBBHSUU	HUBBUBS	**BBDELRU**	BLURBED	**BBEIIKL**	BIBLIKE
BBBINOS	BOBBINS		BURBLED	**BBEIILR**	RIRIBLE
BBBIOTT	BOBBITT		RUBBLED	**BBEIILS**	BILBIES
BBCCIKO	BIBCOCK	**BBDELSU**	SLUBBED	**BBEIIMR**	IMBIBER
BBCDEHI	CHIBBED	**BBDEMSU**	BEDUMBS	**BBEIIMS**	IMBIBES
BBCDEIR	CRIBBED	**BBDENSU**	SNUBBED	**BBEIIRR**	RIBBIER
BBCDELO	COBBLED	**BBDEORS**	DOBBERS	**BBEIIRS**	RIBIBES
BBCDELU	CLUBBED	**BBDEOST**	STOBBED	**BBEIJOS**	JOBBIES
BBCEEHO	BOBECHE	**BBDEOSW**	SWOBBED	**BBEIJRS**	JIBBERS
BBCEEIR	BERBICE	**BBDERRU**	DRUBBER	**BBEIKLS**	KIBBLES
BBCEHIN	NEBBICH	**BBDERSU**	DUBBERS	**BBEILNR**	NIBBLER
BBCEILR	CRIBBLE	**BBDESSU**	SUBDEBS	**BBEILNS**	NIBBLES
BBCEIOR	COBBIER	**BBDESTU**	STUBBED	**BBEILOS**	BILBOES
BBCEIRR	CRIBBER	**BBDFLUU**	FLUBDUB		LOBBIES
BBCEISU	CUBBIES	**BBDGIIN**	DIBBING	**BBEILOT**	BIBELOT
BBCEKKO	KEBBOCK	**BBDGINO**	DOBBING	**BBEILPR**	PRIBBLE
BBCEKKU	KEBBUCK	**BBDGINU**	DUBBING	**BBEILQU**	QUIBBLE
BBCELOR	CLOBBER	**BBDIKSU**	DIBBUKS	**BBEILRS**	LIBBERS
	COBBLER	**BBDILRY**	DRIBBLY	**BBEILRT**	TRIBBLE
BBCELOS	COBBLES	**BBDINOS**	DOBBINS	**BBEILSS**	BIBLESS
BBCELRU	CLUBBER	**BBDINSU**	DUBBINS	**BBEILST**	STIBBLE
BBCEORS	COBBERS	**BBDIOOR**	BOOBIRD	**BBEILSW**	WIBBLES
BBCEOSW	COBWEBS	**BBDIRUY**	RUBBIDY	**BBEILSY**	YIBBLES
BBCGINO	COBBING	**BBDKSUY**	DYBBUKS	**BBEIMOS**	BIMBOES
BBCGINU	CUBBING	**BBEEEES**	BEEBEES		MOBBIES
BBCHISU	CUBBISH	**BBEEERR**	BERBERE	**BBEINOR**	NOBBIER
BBCINOU	BUBONIC	**BBEEERU**	BEBEERU	**BBEINRU**	NUBBIER
BBCRSUY	SCRUBBY	**BBEEIKS**	KEBBIES	**BBEIOOS**	BOOBIES
BBDDEIL	DIBBLED	**BBEEIRS**	BRIBEES	**BBEIOOT**	BOBOTIE
BBDDEIR	DRIBBED	**BBEEIRW**	WEBBIER	**BBEIRRS**	BRIBERS
BBDDERU	DRUBBED	**BBEEISW**	WEBBIES		RIBBERS
BBDEEIR	DEBBIER	**BBEEKLS**	LEBBEKS	**BBEIRRY**	BRIBERY
BBDEEIS	DEBBIES	**BBEELPS**	PEBBLES	**BBEIRSU**	RUBBIES
BBDEEIT	EBBTIDE	**BBEELSS**	EBBLESS	**BBEIRTU**	TUBBIER
BBDEELP	PEBBLED	**BBEENSS**	SNEBBES	**BBEISSU**	BUSBIES
BBDEENS	SNEBBED	**BBEFILR**	FRIBBLE		SUBBIES
BBDEEOR	BEROBED	**BBEFIRS**	FIBBERS	**BBEISTU**	STUBBIE
BBDEFLU	FLUBBED	**BBEFIRU**	FUBBIER	**BBEJORS**	JOBBERS
BBDEGIL	GLIBBED	**BBEFIRY**	FIBBERY	**BBEJORY**	JOBBERY
BBDEGLO	GOBBLED	**BBEFLRU**	FLUBBER	**BBEKLNO**	KNOBBLE
BBDEGRU	GRUBBED	**BBEFRUY**	FUBBERY	**BBEKLNU**	KNUBBLE
BBDEGSU	BEDBUGS	**BBEGIKN**	KEBBING	**BBEKLOS**	BLESBOK
BBDEHLO	HOBBLED	**BBEGILR**	GLIBBER	**BBEKLUU**	BUBUKLE
BBDEIIM	IMBIBED		GRIBBLE	**BBEKNOR**	KNOBBER
BBDEIKL	KIBBLED	**BBEGINN**	NEBBING	**BBEKNSU**	NEBBUKS
BBDEILN	NIBBLED	**BBEGINW**	WEBBING	**BBELLOY**	BELLBOY
BBDEILO	BILOBED	**BBEGIOR**	GOBBIER	**BBELLSU**	BULBELS
	LOBBIED	**BBEGIOS**	GIBBOSE	**BBELLTU**	BULBLET
BBDEILR	DIBBLER	**BBEGIRS**	GIBBERS	**BBELMOS**	MOBBLES
	DRIBBLE	**BBEGIST**	GIBBETS	**BBELMOT**	BOMBLET
BBDEILS	DIBBLES	**BBEGLOR**	GOBBLER	**BBELMRU**	BUMBLER
BBDEILW	WIBBLED	**BBEGLOS**	GOBBLES	**BBELMSU**	BUMBLES
BBDEINS	SNIBBED	**BBEGLRU**	GRUBBLE	**BBELNOR**	NOBBLER
BBDEIOS	DOBBIES	**BBEGNSU**	BEBUNGS	**BBELNOS**	NOBBLES
BBDEIRR	DRIBBER	**BBEGOST**	GOBBETS	**BBELNSU**	NUBBLES
BBDEIRS	DIBBERS	**BBEGRRU**	GRUBBER	**BBELNSY**	NYBBLES
BBDEKNO	KNOBBED	**BBEHIKS**	KIBBEHS	**BBELORS**	LOBBERS
BBDELMO	MOBBLED	**BBEHINS**	NEBBISH		SLOBBER
BBDELMU	BUMBLED	**BBEHIOS**	HOBBIES	**BBELORU**	BOERBUL
BBDELNO	NOBBLED	**BBEHISU**	HUBBIES	**BBELORW**	WOBBLER

BBELORY	LOBBYER	BBHOOUW	WHOOBUB	BCDEHOU	DEBOUCH
BBELOST	BOBLETS	BBHRSUY	SHRUBBY	BCDEIIO	BIOCIDE
BBELOSW	WOBBLES	BBIIILM	BILIMBI	BCDEIKR	BRICKED
BBELRRU	BURBLER	BBIIKTZ	KIBBITZ	BCDEIKS	SICKBED
BBELRSU	BURBLES	BBIILST	BIBLIST	BCDEIKT	BEDTICK
	LUBBERS	BBIISUU	BUIBUIS	BCDEILM	CLIMBED
	RUBBLES	BBIJMOO	JIBBOOM	BCDEILO	DOCIBLE
	SLUBBER	BBIJNOS	JIBBONS	BCDEIOS	BODICES
BBELSTU	STUBBLE	BBIKOSS	SKIBOBS		CEBOIDS
BBEMNSU	BENUMBS	BBIKTUZ	KIBBUTZ	BCDEIRS	SCRIBED
BBEMORS	BOMBERS	BBILLSU	BULBILS	BCDEKLO	BLOCKED
	MOBBERS	BBILLUU	LULIBUB	BCDEKLU	BUCKLED
BBENOTW	BOWBENT	BBILNOY	NOBBILY	BCDEKOR	BEDROCK
BBENRSU	SNUBBER	BBIMMOS	MOBBISM		BROCKED
BBENSSU	SNUBBES	BBIMOSY	YOBBISM	BCDEKOY	BOCKEDY
BBEOOSY	YOBBOES	BBINNSU	NUBBINS	BCDEKSU	BEDUCKS
BBEORRS	ROBBERS	BBINORS	RIBBONS	BCDELOU	BECLOUD
BBEORRY	ROBBERY		ROBBINS	BCDEMOR	CROMBED
BBEORSS	SOBBERS	BBINORY	RIBBONY	BCDEMRU	CRUMBED
BBEORSW	SWOBBER	BBIRTUY	RUBBITY	BCDENOU	BOUNCED
BBEORYY	YOBBERY	BBJLOOW	BLOWJOB		BUNCOED
BBEPRUW	BREWPUB	BBKLNOY	KNOBBLY	BCDEORU	COURBED
BBERRSU	RUBBERS	BBKLNUY	KNUBBLY	BCDEORW	BECROWD
BBERRUY	RUBBERY	BBKLOOU	BLOUBOK	BCDEOSU	SUBCODE
BBERSTU	TUBBERS	BBKOOOO	BOOBOOK	BCDESUU	SUBDUCE
BBFGIIN	FIBBING	BBKOOSS	BOSBOKS	BCDHIOR	BICHORD
BBFGINO	FOBBING	BBLLSUU	BULBULS	BCDHIRU	BRUCHID
BBFGINU	FUBBING	BBLOSUU	BULBOUS	BCDHOOU	CUBHOOD
BBGGIIN	GIBBING	BBLOSWY	BLOWBYS	BCDIIRU	RUBIDIC
BBGGINO	GOBBING	BBLSTUY	STUBBLY	BCDILOO	COLOBID
BBGHINO	HOBBING	BBMOOOX	BOOMBOX	BCDINOW	COWBIND
BBGIIJN	JIBBING	BBNNOOS	BONBONS	BCDIORW	COWBIRD
BBGIILN	LIBBING	BBNOOOS	BONOBOS	BCDIOSU	CUBOIDS
BBGIINN	NIBBING	BBNOORU	BOURBON	BCDIRSY	CYBRIDS
BBGIINR	BRIBING	BBOOOOS	BOOBOOS	BCDKORU	BURDOCK
	RIBBING	BBOOSSY	BOSSBOY	BCDNOSU	BONDUCS
BBGIJNO	JOBBING	BBOOSUU	BOUBOUS	BCDSTUU	SUBDUCT
BBGILLU	BILLBUG	BBORSTU	BURBOTS	BCEEEHN	BEECHEN
BBGILNO	LOBBING	BBOSSUY	BUSBOYS	BCEEEHS	BEECHES
BBGILNU	BULBING	BBRSSUU	SUBURBS		BESEECH
BBGIMNO	BOMBING	BCCEEHS	CHEBECS	BCEEFIN	BENEFIC
	MOBBING	BCCEIIS	BICCIES	BCEEFKL	BEFLECK
BBGINNU	NUBBING	BCCEILO	ECBOLIC	BCEEGIR	ICEBERG
BBGINOO	BOOBING	BCCEILU	CUBICLE	BCEEHIP	EPHEBIC
BBGINOR	ROBBING	BCCEILY	BICYCLE	BCEEHIT	HEBETIC
BBGINOS	GIBBONS	BCCEIOS	BOCCIES	BCEEHLR	BELCHER
	SOBBING	BCCEMOR	CROMBEC	BCEEHLS	BELCHES
BBGINPU	PUBBING	BCCILOU	BUCOLIC	BCEEHNR	BENCHER
BBGINRU	RUBBING	BCCILUY	CUBICLY	BCEEHNS	BENCHES
BBGINSU	GUBBINS	BCCINOO	OBCONIC	BCEEHOS	OBECHES
	SUBBING	BCCISUU	SUCCUBI	BCEEHOU	BOUCHEE
BBGINTU	TUBBING	BCCMOOX	COXCOMB	BCEEIMR	BECRIME
BBGIOSU	GIBBOUS	BCCMSUU	SUCCUMB	BCEEIPS	BESPICE
BBGIOSW	BOBWIGS	BCCNOOR	CORNCOB	BCEEIRS	ESCRIBE
BBHHIOS	HOBBISH	BCDEEHL	BELCHED	BCEEIRT	TEREBIC
BBHIMOS	MOBBISH	BCDEEHN	BENCHED	BCEEKNS	NEBECKS
BBHIOOS	BOOBISH	BCDEEIL	DECIBEL	BCEEKNU	BUCKEEN
BBHIOST	HOBBITS	BCDEEKS	BEDECKS	BCEEKRS	REBECKS
BBHIOSY	YOBBISH	BCDEENU	BEDUNCE	BCEEKST	BECKETS
BBHIRSU	RUBBISH	BCDEHIR	BIRCHED	BCEEKSZ	ZEBECKS
BBHISTU	TUBBISH	BCDEHIT	BITCHED	BCEEKUY	BUCKEYE
BBHJOOS	HOBJOBS	BCDEHNU	BUNCHED	BCEELOS	ECBOLES
BBHKOOS	BOSHBOK	BCDEHOR	BROCHED	BCEELOU	BOUCLEE
BBHNOOS	HOBNOBS	BCDEHOT	BOTCHED	BCEEMOS	BECOMES

Seven-letter anagrams

BCEENOS	OBSCENE	BCEKLOR	BLOCKER	BCHOORS	BROCHOS
BCEENRU	CRUBEEN	BCEKLRU	BRUCKLE	BCHORST	BORSCHT
BCEERSU	BECURSE		BUCKLER		BORTSCH
BCEFIIS	SEBIFIC	BCEKLSU	BUCKLES	BCIIKLN	NIBLICK
BCEGIKN	BECKING	BCEKMOS	BEMOCKS	BCIILMU	BULIMIC
BCEGLOS	BECLOGS	BCEKNOS	BECKONS	BCIILOR	COLIBRI
BCEHINR	BIRCHEN	BCEKORT	BROCKET	BCIILSY	SIBYLIC
BCEHINT	BENTHIC	BCEKORU	ROEBUCK	BCIINOS	BIONICS
	BITCHEN	BCEKOSU	BUCKOES	BCIINOT	BIONTIC
BCEHIOR	BRIOCHE	BCEKOTY	BYCOKET	BCIIOPS	BIOPICS
BCEHIOT	BIOTECH	BCEKRSU	BUCKERS		BIOPSIC
BCEHIRS	BIRCHES	BCEKSTU	BESTUCK	BCIIOPT	BIOPTIC
BCEHIST	BITCHES		BUCKETS	BCIIOST	BIOTICS
BCEHITW	BEWITCH	BCELLOW	COWBELL	BCIISTU	BISCUIT
BCEHLRU	BLUCHER	BCELLSU	SUBCELL	BCIKKOX	KICKBOX
BCEHNSU	BUNCHES	BCELMNU	CLUBMEN	BCIKNOS	KINCOBS
BCEHORS	BROCHES	BCELMOS	COMBLES	BCIKORT	BROCKIT
BCEHORT	BOTCHER	BCELMRU	CLUMBER	BCIKOTT	BITTOCK
BCEHORW	COWHERB		CRUMBLE	BCILMPU	PLUMBIC
BCEHOSS	BOSCHES	BCELMSU	SCUMBLE		UPCLIMB
BCEHOST	BOTCHES	BCELNOW	BECLOWN	BCILOOR	BICOLOR
BCEHOSU	BOUCHES	BCELORS	CORBELS		BROCOLI
	SUBECHO	BCELOSU	BOUCLES	BCILPSU	PUBLICS
BCEHRSU	CHERUBS	BCELRSU	BECURLS	BCIMNOU	UMBONIC
BCEHRTU	BUTCHER	BCELSSU	CUBLESS	BCIMSSU	CUBISMS
BCEHSTU	BUTCHES	BCEMNTU	CUMBENT	BCINOOR	BORONIC
BCEIIKR	BRICKIE	BCEMOOS	COOMBES	BCINOOS	BOSONIC
BCEIIKS	BICKIES	BCEMORS	COMBERS	BCINORS	BICORNS
BCEIISV	VIBICES		RECOMBS		BICRONS
BCEIKLM	LIMBECK	BCEMRRU	CRUMBER	BCINORU	RUBICON
BCEIKLO	BLOCKIE	BCEMRSU	CUMBERS	BCINRSU	BRUCINS
BCEIKLR	BRICKLE		SCUMBER	BCINSUU	INCUBUS
BCEIKNR	BRICKEN	BCENORU	BOUNCER	BCIOORT	ROBOTIC
BCEIKRS	BICKERS	BCENOSU	BOUNCES	BCIORSS	BORSICS
BCEIKST	BESTICK	BCEORSS	SCROBES	BCIORST	STROBIC
BCEIKSU	BUCKIES	BCEORSU	BESCOUR	BCIOSTY	SYBOTIC
BCEILMO	EMBOLIC		OBSCURE	BCIRRSU	RUBRICS
BCEILMR	CLIMBER	BCERRSU	CURBERS	BCIRTUY	BUTYRIC
	RECLIMB	BCERSTU	BECRUST	BCISSTU	BUSTICS
BCEILMS	EMBLICS		BECURST		CUBISTS
	LIMBECS	BCESSTU	SUBSECT	BCISTUU	CUBITUS
BCEILNO	BINOCLE	BCFSSUU	SUBFUSC	BCJKMUU	JUMBUCK
BCEILOR	BRICOLE	BCGIKNO	BOCKING	BCKLLOO	BOLLOCK
	CORBEIL	BCGIKNU	BUCKING	BCKLLOU	BULLOCK
BCEILOS	COLBIES	BCGIMNO	COMBING	BCKLNOU	UNBLOCK
BCEILOU	CIBOULE	BCGINNU	BUNCING	BCKLOOX	LOCKBOX
BCEILSY	BEYLICS	BCGINRU	CURBING	BCKMMOU	BUMMOCK
BCEIMNO	COMBINE	BCGORSU	COBURGS	BCKMOSU	BUCKSOM
BCEIMOR	COMBIER	BCGORSY	CYBORGS	BCKNNOO	BONNOCK
	MICROBE	BCHHORS	BORSHCH	BCKNSUU	NUBUCKS
BCEIMOS	COMBIES	BCHIIOP	BIOCHIP	BCKOTTU	BUTTOCK
BCEINOR	BICORNE	BCHIIOT	COHIBIT	BCLMOOU	COULOMB
BCEINOS	EBONICS	BCHIKOU	CHIBOUK	BCLMRUY	CRUMBLY
BCEINOZ	BENZOIC	BCHIKOY	BOYCHIK	BCLOOSU	COLOBUS
BCEINRU	BRUCINE	BCHIKSU	BUCKISH		SUBCOOL
BCEIORS	CORBIES	BCHILMY	CHIMBLY	BCLORTU	CLOTBUR
BCEIRRS	SCRIBER	BCHILOS	CHIBOLS	BCLSTUU	SUBCULT
BCEIRSS	SCRIBES	BCHIMOR	RHOMBIC	BCMMRUU	CRUMBUM
BCEIRSU	SUBERIC	BCHINOR	BRONCHI	BCMOOST	TOMBOCS
BCEIRTU	BRUCITE	BCHIOPR	PIBROCH	BCMORSY	CORYMBS
BCEISST	BISECTS	BCHIOPS	PHOBICS	BCMOSTU	COMBUST
BCEJOST	OBJECTS	BCHLOTY	BLOTCHY	BCNOORS	BRONCOS
BCEJSTU	SUBJECT	BCHLSSU	SCHLUBS	BCNOSTU	COBNUTS
BCEKLLO	BELLOCK	BCHNOOR	BRONCHO	BCNRSUU	UNCURBS

BCOOOOS	BOOCOOS	BDEEEPS	BESPEED	BDEENOR	DEBONER
BCOOPYY	COPYBOY	BDEEERR	BREEDER		ENROBED
BCOOSWY	COWBOYS		BREERED		REDBONE
BCOOTTY	BOYCOTT		REBREED	BDEENOS	DEBONES
BCTUUZZ	BUZZCUT	BDEEERZ	BREEZED	BDEENPR	PREBEND
BDDDEIU	BUDDIED	BDEEEST	DEBTEES	BDEENRS	BENDERS
BDDDELU	BUDDLED	BDEEFIR	BRIEFED	BDEEORR	REBORED
BDDDEOR	BRODDED		DEBRIEF	BDEEORS	BEDSORE
BDDEEER	REEDBED		FIBERED		SOBERED
BDDEEES	SEEDBED	BDEEFOX	FEEDBOX	BDEEORV	OVERBED
BDDEEEW	BEDEWED	BDEEGOR	BEGORED	BDEEORW	BOWERED
BDDEEIL	BIELDED	BDEEGOY	BOGEYED	BDEEOSX	SEEDBOX
BDDEEIR	DEBRIDE	BDEEGSU	BUGSEED	BDEERSU	BURSEED
BDDEEIS	BEDSIDE	BDEEHOV	BEHOVED	BDEERUW	BURWEED
BDDEEIT	BETIDED	BDEEHRT	BERTHED	BDEESSU	DEBUSES
	DEBITED	BDEEIKL	BEDLIKE	BDEFFLU	BLUFFED
BDDEELN	BLENDED	BDEEIKN	BEINKED	BDEFILR	FILBERD
BDDEENO	DEBONED	BDEEILL	BELLIED	BDEFLMU	FUMBLED
BDDEERS	BEDDERS		DELIBLE	BDEFLOU	BODEFUL
BDDEESU	DEBUSED		LIBELED	BDEFOOR	FORBODE
BDDEETU	DEBUTED	BDEEILS	EDIBLES	BDEGGLO	BOGGLED
BDDEGIN	BEDDING	BDEEILV	BEDEVIL	BDEGGOR	BROGGED
BDDEGIR	BRIDGED	BDEEIMR	BEMIRED	BDEGHIT	BEDIGHT
BDDEGLU	BLUDGED		BERIMED		BIGHTED
BDDEIIR	BIRDIED	BDEEIMT	BEDTIME	BDEGHOU	BOUGHED
BDDEIIS	BIDDIES		BETIMED	BDEGILN	BINGLED
BDDEILN	BLINDED	BDEEIMX	BEMIXED	BDEGILO	OBLIGED
BDDEILR	BRIDLED	BDEEINR	BENDIER	BDEGILS	BEGILDS
BDDEILU	BUILDED		INBREED	BDEGINN	BENDING
BDDEINR	BRINDED	BDEEINZ	BEDIZEN	BDEGINO	BOINGED
BDDEINU	BUNDIED	BDEEIRR	BERRIED	BDEGINR	BREDING
BDDEIOO	BOODIED		BRIERED	BDEGIOO	BOOGIED
BDDEIRR	REDBIRD	BDEEIRS	BREDIES	BDEGIOR	BODGIER
BDDEIRS	BIDDERS		DERBIES	BDEGIOS	BODGIES
BDDEIRU	BUDDIER	BDEEISS	BESIDES	BDEGIOT	BIGOTED
BDDEISU	BUDDIES	BDEEIST	BETIDES	BDEGIRS	BEGIRDS
BDDELNU	BUNDLED	BDEEIVV	BEVVIED		BRIDGES
BDDELOO	BLOODED	BDEEJLS	DJEBELS	BDEGIRU	BRIGUED
	BOODLED	BDEEJMS	DJEMBES	BDEGISU	BUDGIES
BDDELOR	BRODDLE	BDEEKMO	KEMBOED	BDEGLNU	BLUNGED
BDDELOS	BODDLES	BDEEKRU	REBUKED		BUNGLED
BDDELOU	DOUBLED	BDEELLS	BEDELLS	BDEGLRU	BLUDGER
BDDELSU	BUDDLES	BDEELMR	REMBLED		BURGLED
BDDENOU	BOUNDED	BDEELMS	SEMBLED	BDEGLSU	BLUDGES
BDDEOOR	BROODED	BDEELMU	UMBELED	BDEGNOW	BEDGOWN
BDDEORU	OBDURED	BDEELNR	BLENDER	BDEGNSU	BEDUNGS
BDDEOTU	DOUBTED		REBLEND	BDEGOOY	GOODBYE
BDDERSU	BUDDERS	BDEELNS	BLENDES	BDEGORS	BODGERS
	REDBUDS	BDEELNT	BENDLET	BDEGORU	BUDGERO
BDDESUU	SUBDUED	BDEELOV	BELOVED	BDEGRSU	BEDRUGS
BDDGIIN	BIDDING	BDEELOW	BOWELED		BUDGERS
BDDGINU	BUDDING		ELBOWED		REDBUGS
BDDGIOR	BIRDDOG	BDEELRT	TREBLED	BDEGSTU	BUDGETS
BDDISSU	DISBUDS	BDEELSS	BEDLESS	BDEHINS	BEHINDS
BDEEEFL	FEEBLED		BLESSED	BDEHIRT	BIRTHED
BDEEEIS	BEEDIES	BDEELTT	BLETTED	BDEHLMU	HUMBLED
BDEEELL	DELEBLE	BDEELZZ	BEZZLED	BDEHLOS	BEHOLDS
BDEEELP	BLEEPED	BDEEMOS	BESOMED	BDEHLSU	BLUSHED
BDEEELR	BLEEDER	BDEEMOW	EMBOWED	BDEHMTU	THUMBED
BDEEELT	BEETLED	BDEEMOX	EMBOXED	BDEHORY	HERDBOY
BDEEELV	BEVELED	BDEEMRU	EMBRUED	BDEHOST	HOTBEDS
BDEEEMN	BEDEMEN		UMBERED	BDEHRSU	BRUSHED
BDEEEMT	BEMETED	BDEEMSU	BEMUSED	BDEIIRS	BIRDIES
BDEEENS	BENDEES		EMBUSED		BRIDIES

BDEIIVV	BIVVIED	**BDEIRTY**	BEDIRTY	**BDENORU**	BOUNDER
BDEIJLR	JIRBLED	**BDEISST**	BEDSITS		REBOUND
BDEIKLN	BLINKED	**BDEISSU**	SUBSIDE		UNROBED
BDEIKLU	BUDLIKE	**BDEISTU**	BUISTED	**BDENORW**	BROWNED
BDEIKMO	KIMBOED		SUBEDIT	**BDENORZ**	BRONZED
BDEIKNO	BOINKED	**BDEITUY**	DUBIETY	**BDENOST**	OBTENDS
BDEIKRS	BRISKED	**BDEJLMU**	JUMBLED	**BDENOSY**	BEYONDS
BDEILLU	BULLIED	**BDEJORU**	OBJURED	**BDENOUW**	UNBOWED
BDEILMS	DIMBLES	**BDEKLNU**	BLUNKED	**BDENOUX**	UNBOXED
BDEILMW	WIMBLED	**BDEKNOO**	BOOKEND	**BDENRSU**	BURDENS
BDEILNN	BLINNED	**BDEKNOU**	BUNKOED	**BDENRTU**	BRUNTED
BDEILNR	BLINDER	**BDEKNSU**	DEBUNKS	**BDENSSU**	SUNBEDS
	BRINDLE	**BDEKOOR**	BROOKED	**BDENSTU**	SUBTEND
BDEILNS	BINDLES	**BDELLOR**	BEDROLL	**BDENSUY**	SEBUNDY
BDEILNY	BYLINED	**BDELMMU**	BUMMLED	**BDEOORR**	BROODER
BDEILOP	LOBIPED		MUMBLED	**BDEOORS**	BOORDES
BDEILOR	BROILED	**BDELMOO**	BLOOMED	**BDEOOST**	BOOSTED
BDEILOS	BOLIDES	**BDELMPU**	PLUMBED	**BDEOPRS**	BEDROPS
BDEILOX	BOLIXED	**BDELMRU**	DRUMBLE	**BDEOPRT**	BEDROPT
BDEILPP	BLIPPED		RUMBLED	**BDEOPST**	BEDPOST
BDEILRR	BRIDLER	**BDELMTU**	TUMBLED	**BDEORRS**	BORDERS
BDEILRS	BIRSLED	**BDELNOR**	BLONDER	**BDEORRU**	BORDURE
	BRIDLES	**BDELNOS**	BLONDES		BOURDER
BDEILRT	DRIBLET		BOLDENS	**BDEORSS**	DESORBS
BDEILRU	BLUDIER	**BDELNOU**	UNLOBED	**BDEORST**	DEBTORS
	BUILDER	**BDELNRU**	BLUNDER		STROBED
	REBUILD		BUNDLER	**BDEORSU**	OBDURES
BDEILSS	BLISSED	**BDELNSU**	BUNDLES		ROSEBUD
BDEILST	BILSTED	**BDELNTU**	BLUNTED	**BDEORSW**	BROWSED
BDEILTZ	BLITZED	**BDELOOP**	BLOOPED	**BDEORTU**	DOUBTER
BDEIMMR	BRIMMED	**BDELOOR**	BOODLER		OBTRUDE
BDEIMNR	BIRDMEN	**BDELOOS**	BOODLES		OUTBRED
BDEIMOR	BROMIDE	**BDELORS**	BORDELS		REDOUBT
BDEIMRU	IMBRUED	**BDELORU**	BOULDER	**BDEORUV**	OVERDUB
BDEIMTU	BITUMED		DOUBLER	**BDERRSU**	DEBURRS
BDEINOR	INORBED	**BDELORW**	BOWLDER	**BDERSSU**	SURBEDS
BDEINOU	BEDOUIN		LOWBRED	**BDERSTU**	BURSTED
BDEINPR	PREBIND	**BDELOST**	BOLDEST	**BDERSUU**	SUBDUER
BDEINRS	BINDERS	**BDELOSU**	BLOUSED	**BDERSUY**	RUDESBY
	INBREDS		DOUBLES	**BDESSTU**	BEDUSTS
	REBINDS	**BDELOSW**	BLOWSED		BESTUDS
BDEINRY	BINDERY	**BDELOTT**	BLOTTED	**BDESSUU**	SUBDUES
BDEINST	BIDENTS		BOTTLED	**BDESSUW**	SUBDEWS
BDEINSU	BEDUINS	**BDELOTU**	BOULTED	**BDFIILY**	BIFIDLY
	BUNDIES		DOUBLET	**BDFIIOR**	FIBROID
BDEIOOS	BOODIES	**BDELOWZ**	BLOWZED	**BDFIISU**	FIDIBUS
	DOOBIES	**BDELRRU**	BLURRED	**BDFIORS**	FORBIDS
BDEIORR	BROIDER	**BDELRTU**	BLURTED	**BDGGINO**	BODGING
BDEIORS	BORIDES	**BDELSSU**	BUDLESS	**BDGGINU**	BUDGING
	DISROBE	**BDELSTU**	BUSTLED	**BDGGLOU**	GOLDBUG
BDEIORT	DEBITOR	**BDELSWY**	LEWDSBY	**BDGIINN**	BINDING
	DEORBIT	**BDELTTU**	BUTTLED	**BDGIINR**	BIRDING
	ORBITED	**BDEMNNO**	BONDMEN		BRIDING
BDEIORV	OVERBID	**BDEMNOU**	EMBOUND	**BDGIINS**	BIDINGS
BDEIORZ	ZEBROID	**BDEMOOR**	BEDROOM	**BDGIIOO**	GOBIOID
BDEIOSY	DISOBEY		BOREDOM	**BDGIIOS**	GOBIIDS
BDEIPRS	PREBIDS		BROOMED	**BDGILOO**	GLOBOID
BDEIRRS	BIRDERS	**BDEMOOS**	BOSOMED	**BDGIMNU**	DUMBING
BDEIRST	BESTRID	**BDEMORS**	SOMBRED	**BDGINNO**	BONDING
	BISTRED	**BDEMSTU**	DUMBEST	**BDGINNU**	BUNDING
BDEIRSU	BRUISED	**BDENNOU**	BOUNDEN	**BDGINOS**	BODINGS
	BURDIES		UNBONED	**BDGINOY**	BODYING
BDEIRSV	VERBIDS	**BDENNSU**	UNBENDS	**BDGLLOU**	BULLDOG
BDEIRTU	BRUITED	**BDENORS**	BONDERS	**BDGLOOT**	DOGBOLT

BDGMSUU	MUDBUGS	BDNORUW	RUBDOWN	BEEGIMR	BEGRIME
BDGOOOW	BOGWOOD	BDNOSTU	OBTUNDS	BEEGINN	BEGINNE
BDGOOSY	GOODBYS	BDOOOWX	BOXWOOD	BEEGINP	BEEPING
BDGORSU	DORBUGS		WOODBOX	BEEGINR	BIGENER
BDHIINS	BHINDIS	BDORSWY	BYWORDS		BREINGE
	BINDHIS	BEEEEFR	FREEBEE		REBEGIN
BDHINOP	HOPBIND	BEEEEKS	BESEEKE	BEEGINS	BEIGNES
BDHIOSU	BUSHIDO	BEEEEMT	BETEEME	BEEGINT	BEETING
BDHIRSY	HYBRIDS	BEEEENP	PEEBEEN		BEIGNET
BDHMOOO	HOBODOM	BEEEFIR	BEEFIER	BEEGINU	BEGUINE
BDHNSUU	BUHUNDS		FREEBIE	BEEGISY	BIGEYES
BDHOOOY	BOYHOOD	BEEEFLR	FEEBLER	BEEGLNO	ENGLOBE
BDIIKNO	BODIKIN	BEEEFLS	FEEBLES	BEEGMNO	GOMBEEN
BDIILMS	DISLIMB	BEEEFTW	WEBFEET	BEEGMOU	EMBOGUE
BDIILOR	OILBIRD	BEEEGIS	BESIEGE	BEEGNOO	GOBONEE
BDIILOS	LIBIDOS	BEEEGKL	GEELBEK	BEEGNOS	ENGOBES
BDIIMNS	MISBIND	BEEEGNR	BREENGE	BEEGNRS	BERGENS
BDIIMRS	MIDRIBS	BEEEGRR	BERGERE	BEEGNRU	REBEGUN
BDIISTT	TIDBITS	BEEEHIV	BEEHIVE	BEEGNSU	BUNGEES
BDIKNOR	BRODKIN	BEEEHNS	SHEBEEN	BEEGNTU	UNBEGET
BDIKNOS	BODKINS	BEEEHPS	EPHEBES	BEEGRSU	BURGEES
BDILLNY	BLINDLY	BEEEIKL	BEELIKE	BEEGSUY	BUGEYES
BDILNNU	UNBLIND	BEEEILL	LIBELEE	BEEHINS	BESHINE
BDILNUU	UNBUILD	BEEEILN	BEELINE	BEEHIOP	EPHEBOI
BDILOOS	DIOBOLS	BEEEILV	BELIEVE	BEEHIRR	HERBIER
BDILPUU	BUILDUP	BEEEIRR	BEERIER	BEEHIST	BHISTEE
	UPBUILD	BEEEJLW	BEJEWEL	BEEHKSU	BUKSHEE
BDILRUY	BUIRDLY	BEEEJLZ	JEZEBEL	BEEHLRT	BLETHER
BDILTUY	DIBUTYL	BEEEKLL	BELLEEK		HERBLET
BDIMNPU	DUMPBIN	BEEEKLS	KEBELES	BEEHLST	BETHELS
BDIMNUU	DUBNIUM	BEEELPR	BLEEPER	BEEHMRY	BERHYME
BDIMORS	BROMIDS	BEEELRT	BEETLER	BEEHNNO	HEBENON
BDINNOU	INBOUND	BEEELRV	BEVELER	BEEHNOS	BESHONE
BDINNSU	UNBINDS	BEEELST	BEETLES	BEEHOOV	BEHOOVE
BDINOOR	BRIDOON	BEEEMOS	BEESOME	BEEHOPS	EPHEBOS
BDINOOW	WOODBIN	BEEEMRS	BERSEEM		PHOEBES
BDINOSU	BOUDINS	BEEEMSS	BESEEMS	BEEHORS	HERBOSE
BDINOUY	UNIBODY	BEEEMST	BEMETES	BEEHORW	BEWHORE
BDINPSU	UPBINDS		BETEEMS	BEEHOST	BEHOTES
BDINRSU	SUNBIRD	BEEENNZ	BENZENE	BEEHOSV	BEHOVES
BDINSTU	BUNDIST	BEEENTW	BETWEEN	BEEHPSU	EPHEBUS
	DUSTBIN	BEEEPRS	BEEPERS	BEEHRST	BERTHES
BDIOOOV	OBOVOID	BEEEPSW	BEWEEPS		SHERBET
BDIOORU	BOUDOIR	BEEERSS	BREESES	BEEHRSW	BESHREW
BDIOOST	BIODOTS	BEEERSZ	BEEZERS	BEEHRTY	THEREBY
BDIORSW	WOSBIRD		BREEZES	BEEHRWY	WHEREBY
BDIOSSY	BYSSOID	BEEERTV	BREVETE	BEEHSST	BEHESTS
BDIOSTU	OUTBIDS	BEEFGIN	BEEFING	BEEHSTY	BHEESTY
BDIOSUU	DUBIOUS	BEEFGIT	BIGFEET	BEEIJLU	JUBILEE
BDIRSTU	DISTURB	BEEFILR	FEBRILE	BEEIKLW	WEBLIKE
BDISSUY	SUBSIDY	BEEFILS	BELIEFS	BEEILLR	LIBELER
BDKLOOS	KOBOLDS	BEEFILY	BEEFILY	BEEILLS	BELLIES
BDKNOOU	BUNDOOK	BEEFINT	BENEFIT	BEEILLV	BILEVEL
BDLNOOS	DOBLONS	BEEFIRR	BRIEFER	BEEILMP	EPIBLEM
BDLOOOX	OXBLOOD	BEEFIRS	FRISBEE	BEEILMS	BESLIME
BDMOOSS	BOSSDOM	BEEFLTY	BEETFLY		BESMILE
BDMORUW	BUDWORM	BEEFNRU	FUNEBRE	BEEILNR	BERLINE
BDNNOOY	NONBODY	BEEFORY	FOREBYE	BEEILOS	OBELISE
BDNNOUU	UNBOUND	BEEFRST	BEFRETS	BEEILOZ	OBELIZE
BDNOORU	BOURDON	BEEGGNU	GEEBUNG	BEEILRS	BELIERS
BDNOOSS	DOBSONS	BEEGILL	LEGIBLE	BEEILRV	VERBILE
BDNOOWW	DOWNBOW	BEEGILO	OBLIGEE	BEEILRY	BEERILY
BDNOPUU	UPBOUND	BEEGILS	BEIGELS	BEEILTT	BETITLE
BDNORTU	TURBOND	BEEGILU	BEGUILE	BEEIMRS	BEMIRES

	BERIMES
	BIREMES
BEEIMST	BETIMES
BEEIMSX	BEMIXES
BEEINNS	BENNIES
BEEINNZ	BENZINE
BEEINOS	EBONIES
	EBONISE
BEEINOT	EBONITE
BEEINOZ	EBONIZE
BEEINPR	PEBRINE
BEEINRT	BENTIER
BEEINRZ	ZEBRINE
BEEINSW	NEWBIES
BEEIORS	EBRIOSE
BEEIOST	TOEBIES
BEEIQUZ	BEZIQUE
BEEIRRS	BERRIES
BEEIRRV	BREVIER
BEEIRST	REBITES
BEEIRTY	EBRIETY
BEEISST	BETISES
BEEISTT	BETTIES
BEEISTW	WEBSITE
BEEISVV	BEVVIES
BEEJNSU	BUNJEES
BEEJSSU	BEJESUS
BEEKMOS	BESMOKE
BEEKNOT	BETOKEN
BEEKOPS	BESPOKE
BEEKORS	REEBOKS
BEEKRRS	BERSERK
BEEKRRU	REBUKER
BEEKRSU	REBUKES
BEELLMN	BELLMEN
BEELLOT	LOBELET
BEELMMS	EMBLEMS
BEELMNT	BELTMEN
BEELMOW	EMBOWEL
BEELMRS	REMBLES
BEELMRT	TREMBLE
BEELMSS	SEMBLES
BEELNNO	ENNOBLE
BEELNOZ	BENZOLE
BEELNRT	REBLENT
BEELNSU	NEBULES
BEELOST	BOLETES
BEELOSV	BELOVES
BEELOSY	OBESELY
BEELOTY	EYEBOLT
BEELPST	BEPELTS
BEELRSS	BLESSER
BEELRST	BELTERS
	TREBLES
BEELRSY	BERLEYS
BEELRUZ	ZEBRULE
BEELSSS	BLESSES
BEELSSW	WEBLESS
BEELSZZ	BEZZLES
BEELTTU	BLUETTE
BEEMMRS	MEMBERS
BEEMNPT	BENEMPT
BEEMNRY	BYREMEN
BEEMORW	EMBOWER
BEEMOSS	MEBOSES
BEEMOSX	EMBOXES
BEEMRRU	UMBRERE
BEEMRSU	EMBRUES
BEEMRTU	EMBRUTE
BEEMSSU	BEMUSES
	EMBUSES
BEENNRS	BRENNES
BEENNST	BENNETS
BEENOOT	BOTONEE
BEENORR	ENROBER
BEENORS	BOREENS
	ENROBES
BEENORY	BONEYER
BEENOST	BEENTOS
	BONESET
BEENRRT	BRENTER
BEENSTU	BUTENES
	SUBTEEN
BEENSUV	SUBVENE
BEEOOST	BOOTEES
BEEOPPS	BOPEEPS
BEEOPRR	REPROBE
BEEOPRS	BEPROSE
BEEORRS	REBORES
	SOBERER
BEEORRU	BOURREE
BEEORSV	OBSERVE
	OBVERSE
	VERBOSE
BEEORSY	OBEYERS
BEEORTV	OVERBET
BEEORWY	EYEBROW
BEEOSST	OBESEST
BEEPRRV	PREVERB
BEEPRSU	BURPEES
BEEQSTU	BEQUEST
BEERRST	BERRETS
BEERRSU	BEURRES
BEERRSV	REVERBS
BEERRSW	BREWERS
BEERRWY	BREWERY
BEERSST	BREESTS
BEERSSU	REBUSES
	SUBSERE
BEERSTT	BETTERS
BEERSTV	BREVETS
BEERSTW	BESTREW
	WEBSTER
BEERTTU	BURETTE
BEESSTU	BUSTEES
BEETTUV	BUVETTE
BEFFIIS	BIFFIES
BEFFIRS	BIFFERS
BEFFIRU	BUFFIER
BEFFLRU	BLUFFER
BEFFOSU	BOUFFES
BEFFPSU	BEPUFFS
BEFFRSU	BUFFERS
	REBUFFS
BEFFSTU	BUFFEST
	BUFFETS
BEFGIIL	FILIBEG
BEFGIRU	FIREBUG
BEFGIST	BEGIFTS
BEFGLSU	BEGULFS
BEFHOOS	BEHOOFS
BEFILMS	FIMBLES
BEFILNO	LOBEFIN
BEFILNU	BLUEFIN
BEFILOS	FOIBLES
BEFILOU	BIOFUEL
BEFILPY	PLEBIFY
BEFILRT	FILBERT
BEFILRY	BRIEFLY
BEFILSU	FUSIBLE
	SUBFILE
BEFINOR	BONFIRE
BEFIOOR	BOOFIER
BEFIORS	FIBROSE
BEFIORX	FIREBOX
BEFIRST	BIFTERS
	FIBSTER
BEFIRSU	FUBSIER
BEFIRVY	VERBIFY
BEFITUX	TUBIFEX
BEFLLTY	FLYBELT
BEFLLWY	FLYBLEW
BEFLMRU	FUMBLER
BEFLMSU	BEFLUMS
	FUMBLES
BEFLOOS	BEFOOLS
BEFLOSU	BEFOULS
BEFLTUU	TUBEFUL
BEFOORR	FORBORE
BEFOOTW	WEBFOOT
BEFSSUU	SUBFEUS
BEGGINN	BEGGING
BEGGIIS	BIGGIES
BEGGINO	BEGOING
BEGGIOR	BOGGIER
BEGGIRU	BUGGIER
BEGGIST	BIGGEST
BEGGISU	BUGGIES
BEGGITY	BIGGETY
BEGGLOR	BLOGGER
	BOGGLER
BEGGLOS	BOGGLES
BEGGORS	BOGGERS
BEGGRSU	BUGGERS
BEGGRUY	BUGGERY
BEGHHIT	BEHIGHT
BEGHINT	BENIGHT
BEGHISS	BESIGHS
BEGHITT	BETIGHT
BEGHRRU	BURGHER
BEGIILR	BILGIER
BEGIIMT	BIGTIME
BEGIINN	INBEING
BEGIINR	BREIING
BEGIINS	BINGIES
BEGIKMN	KEMBING
BEGIKNR	KERBING
BEGILLN	BELLING
BEGILLY	LEGIBLY
BEGILNO	IGNOBLE
	INGLOBE
BEGILNR	BLINGER

BEGILNS	BINGLES	BEGNOSY	BYGONES	BEHNORT	BETHORN
BEGILNT	BELTING	BEGNOTT	BETTONG	BEHNOST	BENTHOS
BEGILNU	BLUEING	BEGNOTU	UNBEGOT	BEHNRTU	BURTHEN
	BULGINE	BEGNRSU	BUNGERS	BEHOORT	THEORBO
BEGILNY	BELYING	BEGNSUY	BUNGEYS	BEHOOSX	SHOEBOX
BEGILOR	OBLIGER	BEGOORS	BOOGERS	BEHOPRT	POTHERB
BEGILOS	OBLIGES		GOOBERS	BEHOPSU	PHOEBUS
BEGILRS	GERBILS	BEGOOSY	BOOGEYS	BEHORRT	BROTHER
BEGILRT	GILBERT	BEGORSU	BROGUES	BEHORST	BOSHTER
BEGILRU	BULGIER	BEGOSTU	BOUGETS		BOTHERS
BEGILST	GIBLETS		OUTBEGS	BEHORSU	HERBOUS
BEGIMNR	BERMING	BEGOSTW	BOWGETS	BEHORTT	BETROTH
BEGIMRS	BEGRIMS	BEGRRSU	BURGERS	BEHOSTU	BESHOUT
BEGINNU	UNBEING	BEGRSSU	BURGESS	BEHRRSU	BRUSHER
BEGINOS	BINGOES	BEHHKOT	KHOTBEH	BEHRSSU	BRUSHES
	BIOGENS	BEHIIST	BHISTIE		BUSHERS
BEGINOY	BIOGENY	BEHIITX	EXHIBIT	BEHRTTU	TURBETH
	OBEYING	BEHIKLO	HOBLIKE	BEIIKKS	BIKKIES
BEGINRR	BRINGER	BEHIKNT	BETHINK	BEIIKLN	NIBLIKE
BEGINRS	BINGERS	BEHIKRS	KIRBEHS	BEIIKLR	RIBLIKE
BEGINRV	VERBING	BEHILMS	BLEMISH	BEIIKRR	BIRKIER
BEGINRW	BREWING	BEHILMT	THIMBLE	BEIIKRS	BIRKIES
BEGINRY	BREYING	BEHILOS	BOLSHIE	BEIILLS	BILLIES
BEGINSS	BESINGS	BEHILRT	BLITHER	BEIILMR	LIMBIER
	BIGNESS	BEHILST	THIBLES	BEIILMX	MIXIBLE
BEGINST	BESTING	BEHILSU	BLUEISH	BEIILRS	RISIBLE
BEGINSU	BEGUINS		HELIBUS	BEIILSV	VISIBLE
	BUNGIES	BEHILSW	WEBLISH	BEIINOT	NIOBITE
BEGINTT	BETTING	BEHIMOR	BIOHERM	BEIINRR	BRINIER
BEGIOOS	BOOGIES	BEHIMOV	YOHIMBE	BEIINRS	BRINIES
	GOOBIES	BEHINOP	HIPBONE	BEIINST	STIBINE
BEGIORV	OVERBIG		HOPBINE	BEIIOTT	BIOTITE
BEGIOSS	BIGOSES	BEHINST	HENBITS	BEIIRRS	BIRSIER
BEGIOSU	BOUGIES	BEHIOST	BOTHIES		RIBIERS
BEGIRSU	BRIGUES	BEHIOTW	HOWBEIT	BEIIRST	BITSIER
	RUGBIES	BEHIRRT	REBIRTH	BEIIRTT	BITTIER
BEGISSU	GIBUSES	BEHIRST	HERBIST	BEIISTT	BITTIES
BEGKMOS	GEMSBOK	BEHIRSU	BUSHIER	BEIISTV	VIBIEST
BEGKNSU	BEGUNKS	BEHISSU	BUSHIES	BEIISVV	BIVVIES
BEGLLOU	GLOBULE	BEHISTT	THIBETS	BEIISZZ	BIZZIES
BEGLMOO	BEGLOOM	BEHISTZ	ZIBETHS	BEIJLRS	JERBILS
BEGLMRU	GRUMBLE	BEHKKOO	KOKOBEH		JIRBLES
BEGLMUU	BLUEGUM	BEHKORS	RHEBOKS	BEIJLSU	JUBILES
BEGLNOS	BELONGS	BEHLLOP	BELLHOP	BEIJMSU	JUMBIES
BEGLNRU	BLUNGER	BEHLLOX	HELLBOX	BEIJNSU	BUNJIES
	BUNGLER	BEHLMOW	WHOMBLE	BEIKLMS	BLIKSEM
BEGLNSU	BLUNGES	BEHLMRU	HUMBLER	BEIKLNR	BLINKER
	BUNGLES	BEHLMSU	HUMBLES	BEIKLNS	LIBKENS
BEGLOOS	GLOBOSE	BEHLOOT	BOTHOLE	BEIKLOR	BLOKIER
BEGLOOT	BOOTLEG	BEHLORT	BROTHEL	BEIKLOS	OBELISK
BEGLOST	GOBLETS	BEHLOSW	BEHOWLS	BEIKLOW	BOWLIKE
BEGLOSU	GLEBOUS	BEHLRRU	BURRHEL	BEIKLOX	BOXLIKE
BEGLOSW	BOWLEGS	BEHLRSU	BLUSHER	BEIKLRS	BILKERS
	WEBLOGS		BURHELS	BEIKLRU	BULKIER
BEGLOUV	LOVEBUG	BEHLSSU	BLUSHES	BEIKLSY	BEYLIKS
BEGLRSU	BUGLERS		BUSHELS	BEIKLTU	TUBLIKE
	BULGERS	BEHLSTU	BLUSHET	BEIKNRS	BRISKEN
	BURGLES	BEHMNSU	BUSHMEN	BEIKOOR	BOOKIER
BEGLRTY	BERGYLT	BEHMOOY	HOMEBOY		BROOKIE
BEGLSTU	BUGLETS	BEHMORS	HOMBRES	BEIKOOS	BOOKIES
BEGMNOY	BOGYMEN	BEHMOTU	BEMOUTH		BOOKSIE
BEGNNUU	UNBEGUN	BEHMPTU	BETHUMP	BEIKORS	BOSKIER
BEGNOOS	BONGOES	BEHNNOT	BENTHON	BEIKORT	REITBOK
BEGNORU	BURGEON	BEHNORS	BREHONS	BEIKRRS	BRISKER

BEIKRST	BRISKET	BEILSTU	BLUIEST		RIBOSES
BEIKRSW	BREWSKI		SUBTILE	BEIORST	ORBIEST
BEIKRTU	BURKITE	BEILSTW	BLEWITS		SORBITE
BEILLMN	BILLMEN	BEILSTZ	BLITZES	BEIORSU	BOUSIER
BEILLPR	PREBILL	BEILTTU	BLUETIT		OUREBIS
BEILLRR	BRILLER	BEIMMOS	BOMMIES	BEIORSY	BOYSIER
BEILLRS	BILLERS	BEIMMRR	BRIMMER	BEIORUV	BOUVIER
	REBILLS	BEIMNOR	BROMINE	BEIOSSS	BOSSIES
BEILLRU	BULLIER	BEIMNTU	BITUMEN	BEIOSSU	SOUBISE
BEILLST	BESTILL	BEIMOOR	BOOMIER	BEIOSSW	BOWSIES
	BILLETS	BEIMORS	BROMISE	BEIOSTT	BOTTIES
BEILLSU	BULLIES	BEIMORW	IMBOWER	BEIOSTX	BOXIEST
BEILMNR	NIMBLER		WOMBIER	BEIOSTY	OBESITY
BEILMNS	MILNEBS	BEIMORZ	BROMIZE	BEIPPSU	BUPPIES
BEILMOR	EMBROIL	BEIMOSS	OBEISMS	BEIPSST	BESPITS
BEILMOS	BEMOILS	BEIMOSZ	ZOMBIES	BEIPSSU	PUBISES
	EMBOILS	BEIMOTV	BEVOMIT	BEIQRTU	BRIQUET
	MOBILES	BEIMPRU	BUMPIER	BEIQSSU	BISQUES
	OBELISM	BEIMRST	BETRIMS	BEIRRRU	BURRIER
BEILMRS	LIMBERS		TIMBERS	BEIRRSU	BRISURE
BEILMRT	TIMBREL		TIMBRES		BRUISER
BEILMRW	WIMBREL	BEIMRSU	ERBIUMS		BURIERS
BEILMSU	SUBLIME		IMBRUES	BEIRRTU	BRUITER
BEILMSW	WIMBLES		IMBURSE	BEIRSSS	BRISSES
BEILNOO	OBELION	BEIMRTU	IMBRUTE	BEIRSST	BESTIRS
BEILNOS	BOLINES		TERBIUM		BISTERS
BEILNOW	BOWLINE	BEIMRTY	TIMBERY		BISTRES
BEILNRS	BERLINS	BEIMSST	BEMISTS		BITSERS
BEILNRY	BYLINER	BEIMSTU	SUBITEM		BREISTS
BEILNSU	SUBLINE	BEINNOP	PINBONE	BEIRSSU	BRUISES
BEILNSY	BYLINES	BEINNOR	BONNIER	BEIRSTT	BITTERS
BEILNSZ	BENZILS	BEINNOS	BENISON	BEIRSTU	BUSTIER
BEILNTZ	BLINTZE		BONNIES		RUBIEST
BEILOOR	LOOBIER	BEINNOZ	BENZOIN	BEIRTTU	TRIBUTE
BEILOOS	LOOBIES	BEINNSU	BUNNIES	BEIRTTY	TREYBIT
BEILOPR	PREBOIL	BEINNSZ	BENZINS	BEIRTVY	BREVITY
BEILOPY	EPIBOLY	BEINOOS	BOONIES	BEIRUZZ	BUZZIER
BEILOQU	OBLIQUE	BEINOOT	EOBIONT	BEISSTU	BUSIEST
BEILORR	BROILER	BEINORT	BORNITE		SUBSITE
BEILORS	BOILERS	BEINORW	BROWNIE	BEISTTU	BUTTIES
	LIBEROS	BEINOSS	BESOINS	BEITTWX	BETWIXT
	REBOILS	BEINOST	BONIEST	BEJJSUU	JUJUBES
BEILORT	TRILOBE		EBONIST	BEJKOUX	JUKEBOX
BEILORW	BLOWIER	BEINOSV	BOVINES	BEJLMRU	JUMBLER
BEILORY	BOILERY	BEINOSX	BONXIES	BEJLMSU	JUMBLES
BEILOST	BETOILS	BEINOSZ	BIZONES	BEJLOSS	JOBLESS
BEILOSW	BLOWIES	BEINOTT	BOTTINE	BEJORSU	OBJURES
BEILOSX	BOLIXES	BEINRRS	BRINERS	BEKLNRU	BLUNKER
BEILRRS	BIRLERS	BEINRSU	BURNIES	BEKLOOT	BOOKLET
BEILRRU	BURLIER		RUBINES	BEKLRSU	BULKERS
BEILRSS	BIRSLES		SUBERIN		BURLESK
	RIBLESS	BEINRSY	BYRNIES	BEKMNOO	BOOKMEN
BEILRST	BLISTER	BEINRTT	BITTERN	BEKMOSS	EMBOSKS
	BRISTLE	BEINRTU	BUNTIER	BEKMOST	STEMBOK
	RIBLETS		TRIBUNE	BEKNNOW	BEKNOWN
BEILRTT	BRITTLE		TURBINE	BEKNORS	BONKERS
	TRIBLET	BEINSSY	BYSSINE	BEKNORU	UNBROKE
BEILRTU	REBUILT	BEIOOPT	BIOTOPE	BEKNOST	BEKNOTS
BEILRTY	LIBERTY	BEIOORZ	BOOZIER	BEKNRSU	BUNKERS
BEILRTZ	BLITZER	BEIOOST	BOOTIES	BEKOOPR	PREBOOK
BEILRUY	BRULYIE	BEIOPTY	BIOTYPE	BEKOORS	BOOKERS
BEILRUZ	BRULZIE	BEIORRT	BORTIER		REBOOKS
BEILSSS	BLISSES		ORBITER	BEKOPRU	UPBROKE
BEILSST	BITLESS	BEIORSS	BOSSIER	BEKORRS	BROKERS

BEKORRY	BROKERY	BELOPSU	PUEBLOS	BEMPRSU	BUMPERS
BEKORWW	WEBWORK	BELORSS	ORBLESS	BEMSSTU	BESMUTS
BEKOSST	BOSKETS	BELORST	BOLSTER	BEMSSUU	SUBSUME
BEKOTTU	KETUBOT		BOLTERS	BEMSTUW	STEWBUM
BEKRRSU	BRUSKER		LOBSTER	BENNORU	UNBORNE
	BURKERS	BELORSU	ROUBLES	BENNORW	NEWBORN
BEKRSSU	BUSKERS	BELORSW	BLOWERS	BENNORZ	BRONZEN
BEKSSTU	BUSKETS		BOWLERS	BENNOST	BONNETS
BELLLMU	BLELLUM	BELORSY	SOBERLY	BENNOSU	UNBONES
BELLNPU	BULLPEN	BELORTT	BLOTTER	BENNSSU	BUNSENS
BELLORR	BORRELL		BOTTLER	BENNSTU	BUNNETS
BELLOSU	BOULLES	BELORTU	BOULTER	BENOORS	BOONERS
	LOBULES		TROUBLE	BENOOST	OBENTOS
	SOLUBLE	BELOSSU	BLOUSES	BENOPRR	PREBORN
BELLOSW	BELLOWS		BOLUSES	BENOPRU	UPBORNE
BELLOUV	VOLUBLE	BELOSSW	BLOWSES	BENORRW	BROWNER
BELLRRU	BURRELL		BOWLESS	BENORRZ	BRONZER
BELLRSU	BULLERS	BELOSTT	BOTTLES	BENORST	BRETONS
BELLSTU	BULLETS	BELOSTU	BOLETUS		SORBENT
BELMMOO	EMBLOOM	BELOSWZ	BLOWZES	BENORSU	BOURNES
BELMMRU	MUMBLER	BELRRSU	BURLERS		UNROBES
BELMMSU	BUMMELS		BURRELS		UNSOBER
	BUMMLES	BELRRTU	BLURTER	BENORSZ	BRONZES
	MUMBLES	BELRSTU	BLUSTER	BENORWY	BYWONER
BELMNOS	NOMBLES		BUSTLER	BENOSSU	BONUSES
BELMNOU	NELUMBO		BUTLERS	BENOSSW	BESNOWS
BELMNOY	BENOMYL		SUBTLER	BENOSTT	BOTNETS
BELMNSU	NUMBLES	BELRSUU	SUBRULE	BENOSTU	SUBTONE
BELMOOR	BLOOMER	BELRSUY	BURLEYS	BENOSUX	UNBOXES
	REBLOOM	BELRTUY	BRUTELY	BENOSUZ	SUBZONE
BELMOOS	BLOOSME		BUTLERY	BENOSWY	NEWSBOY
BELMOOT	BOOMLET	BELSSTU	BUSTLES	BENRRSU	BURNERS
BELMOPR	PROBLEM		SUBLETS	BENRSSU	BRUSSEN
BELMORT	TEMBLOR	BELSTTU	BUTTLES	BENRSTU	BRUNETS
BELMOSU	EMBOLUS	BELSTUU	TUBULES		BUNTERS
BELMOSY	SYMBOLE	BEMMNOS	MOBSMEN		BURNETS
BELMPRU	PLUMBER	BEMMOOS	EMBOSOM		BURSTEN
	REPLUMB	BEMMORR	BROMMER		SUBRENT
BELMRRU	RUMBLER	BEMMRRU	BRUMMER	BENSSTU	SUBNETS
BELMRSU	LUMBERS	BEMMRSU	BUMMERS	BEOORSS	BROOSES
	RUMBLES	BEMMSTU	BUMMEST		SORBOSE
	SLUMBER	BEMNORW	EMBROWN	BEOORST	BOOSTER
	UMBRELS	BEMNORY	EMBRYON		REBOOTS
BELMRTU	TUMBLER	BEMNOST	ENTOMBS	BEOORSZ	BOOZERS
	TUMBREL	BEMNOSU	UMBONES		REBOZOS
BELMRTY	TREMBLY	BEMNOSW	ENWOMBS	BEOORTY	BOOTERY
BELMSTU	STUMBLE	BEMNPTY	BYNEMPT	BEOPPRS	BOPPERS
	TUMBLES	BEMNRSU	NUMBERS	BEOPRRS	PROBERS
BELNNOU	UNNOBLE	BEMNSTU	NUMBEST	BEOPRRV	PROVERB
BELNNTU	UNBLENT	BEMNSUU	SUBMENU	BEOPRST	BESPORT
BELNOOR	BORNEOL	BEMNTTU	BUTMENT	BEOPSST	BESPOTS
BELNOOY	BOLONEY	BEMOOPR	PREBOOM	BEOPSTU	BESPOUT
BELNOST	NOBLEST	BEMOORS	BOOMERS	BEOQSSU	BOSQUES
BELNOSZ	BENZOLS	BEMORRS	SOMBRER	BEOQSTU	BOSQUET
BELNOYZ	BENZOYL	BEMORSS	SOMBERS	BEOQSUY	OBSEQUY
BELNRTU	BLUNTER		SOMBRES	BEOQTUU	BOUQUET
BELNSSU	UNBLESS	BEMORST	BESTORM	BEORRSS	RESORBS
BELNSTU	SUNBELT		MOBSTER	BEORRSW	BROWSER
	UNBELTS	BEMORSU	UMBROSE	BEORRWY	BEWORRY
	UNBLEST	BEMORSW	BEWORMS	BEORSST	BESORTS
BELNSYZ	BENZYLS	BEMORSY	EMBRYOS		SORBETS
BELOOPR	BLOOPER	BEMORUX	BUXOMER		STROBES
BELOORS	BOLEROS	BEMORWW	WEBWORM	BEORSSU	BOURSES
BELOOSS	SOBOLES	BEMOTUV	MYOTUBE	BEORSSW	BOWSERS

	BROWSES	BFIRTUY	BRUTIFY	**BGIINRT**	RINGBIT
BEORSTT	BETTORS	**BFKLOOU**	BOOKFUL	**BGIINST**	BITINGS
BEORSTU	OBTUSER	**BFKLOOY**	FLYBOOK	**BGIINTT**	BITTING
BEORSTV	OBVERTS	**BFKSSUU**	SUBFUSK	**BGIKLNU**	BULKING
BEORSTW	BESTROW	**BFLLOUW**	BOWLFUL	**BGIKNNO**	BONKING
BEORSTZ	BORTZES	**BFLLOWY**	BLOWFLY	**BGIKNNU**	BUNKING
BEORSUU	UBEROUS		FLYBLOW	**BGIKNOO**	BOOKING
BEORSUZ	BROUZES	**BFLOSUX**	BOXFULS	**BGIKNOR**	BORKING
	SUBZERO	**BFLOSYY**	FLYBOYS		BROKING
BEORSVV	BOVVERS	**BFLSTUU**	TUBFULS	**BGIKNRU**	BURKING
BEORSWY	BOWYERS	**BFOOOTY**	FOOTBOY	**BGIKNSU**	BUSKING
BEORUVY	OVERBUY	**BGGGIIN**	BIGGING	**BGILLNO**	BOLLING
BEOSSST	BOSSEST	**BGGGINO**	BOGGING	**BGILLNU**	BULLING
	BOSSETS	**BGGGINU**	BUGGING	**BGILMNO**	MOBLING
BEOSSTT	OBTESTS	**BGGHIIS**	BIGGISH	**BGILMNU**	BLUMING
BEOSSTW	BESTOWS	**BGGHIOS**	BOGGISH	**BGILMOU**	GUMBOIL
BEOSSWY	BOWSEYS	**BGGIILN**	BILGING	**BGILNOO**	BOOLING
BEPRRTU	PERTURB	**BGGIINN**	BINGING	**BGILNOS**	GLOBINS
BEPRSUY	PREBUYS	**BGGIINS**	BIGGINS		GOBLINS
BEPRTUY	PUBERTY	**BGGIISW**	BIGWIGS		LOBINGS
BEPSTUY	SUBTYPE	**BGGIITY**	BIGGITY	**BGILNOT**	BILTONG
BEQRSUU	BRUSQUE	**BGGILNO**	GLOBING		BOLTING
BEQSTUY	QUBYTES	**BGGILNU**	BUGLING	**BGILNOW**	BLOWING
BERRRSU	BURRERS		BULGING		BOWLING
BERRSTU	BRUTERS	**BGGINNO**	BONGING	**BGILNOY**	IGNOBLY
	BURSTER	**BGGINNU**	BUNGING	**BGILNRU**	BURLING
BERSSTU	BUSTERS	**BGGINOS**	BIGGONS	**BGILNRY**	BYRLING
BERSTTU	BUTTERS	**BGGINOU**	BOUGING	**BGILNSU**	BLUINGS
BERSTUV	SUBVERT	**BGGINSU**	BUGGINS	**BGILNTU**	BUTLING
BERSUZZ	BUZZERS	**BGGNOOS**	BOGONGS	**BGILOOR**	OBLIGOR
BERTTUY	BUTTERY	**BGGNOSU**	BUGONGS	**BGILOOY**	BIOLOGY
BESSSTU	SUBSETS	**BGHHIOY**	HIGHBOY	**BGILRSU**	BUSGIRL
BESSTTU	SUBTEST	**BGHIILS**	GHIBLIS	**BGIMMNU**	BUMMING
BESTTUX	SUBTEXT	**BGHIINS**	BINGHIS	**BGIMNNU**	NUMBING
BFFGIIN	BIFFING	**BGHILST**	BLIGHTS	**BGIMNOO**	BOOMING
BFFGINO	BOFFING	**BGHILTY**	BLIGHTY	**BGIMNOR**	BORMING
BFFGINU	BUFFING	**BGHINOO**	BOOHING	**BGIMNOT**	TOMBING
BFFIINS	BIFFINS		HOBOING	**BGIMNOW**	WOMBING
BFFILOO	BOILOFF	**BGHINOR**	BIGHORN	**BGIMNPU**	BUMPING
BFFINOS	BOFFINS	**BGHINSU**	BUSHING	**BGIMOSY**	BOGYISM
BFFLLUY	BLUFFLY	**BGHIPSU**	BUSHPIG	**BGINNOS**	BONINGS
BFFLOOW	BLOWOFF	**BGHIRST**	BRIGHTS	**BGINNOU**	BOUNING
BFFNOOU	BUFFOON	**BGHLRUU**	BULGHUR	**BGINNOW**	BOWNING
BFFORSU	RUBOFFS		BURGHUL	**BGINNRU**	BURNING
BFFOSUY	BUYOFFS	**BGHMORU**	HOMBURG	**BGINNTU**	BUNTING
BFGIOOT	BIGFOOT	**BGHMSUU**	HUMBUGS	**BGINOOS**	BOOSING
BFGIORT	FROGBIT	**BGHNORU**	HORNBUG	**BGINOOT**	BOOTING
BFGOOSW	FOGBOWS	**BGHOORU**	BOROUGH	**BGINOOZ**	BOOZING
BFHILSU	LUBFISH	**BGHORSU**	BROUGHS	**BGINOPP**	BOPPING
BFHIOSX	BOXFISH	**BGHORTU**	BROUGHT	**BGINOPR**	PROBING
BFHIRSU	FURBISH	**BGHOSTU**	BOUGHTS	**BGINORS**	BORINGS
BFHISTU	TUBFISH	**BGIIKLN**	BILKING		ROBINGS
BFHLSUY	BUSHFLY	**BGIIKNS**	BIKINGS		SORBING
BFIILMO	BIOFILM	**BGIILLN**	BILLING	**BGINORZ**	ZORBING
BFIILRS	FIBRILS	**BGIILMN**	LIMBING	**BGINOSS**	BOSSING
BFIINOR	FIBROIN	**BGIILNO**	BOILING		GIBSONS
BFIINRS	FIBRINS	**BGIILNR**	BIRLING		OBSIGNS
BFILMRU	BRIMFUL	**BGIILNS**	SIBLING	**BGINOSU**	BOUSING
BFILOTY	LIFTBOY	**BGIIMNR**	BRIMING	**BGINOSW**	BOWINGS
BFILSUY	FUSIBLY	**BGIIMNU**	IMBUING		BOWSING
BFIMOYZ	ZOMBIFY	**BGIINNN**	BINNING	**BGINOSX**	BOXINGS
BFINOSW	BOWFINS	**BGIINNR**	BRINING	**BGINOTT**	BOTTING
BFIORSS	ROSBIFS		INBRING	**BGINOUY**	BUOYING
BFIORSU	FIBROUS	**BGIINRR**	BIRRING	**BGINOWW**	WINGBOW

BGINPRU	BURPING	BHIOORS	BOORISH	BILLOSW	BILLOWS
	UPBRING	BHIOOST	BOOSHIT	BILLOSY	BILLYOS
BGINRRU	BURRING	BHIOPSS	BISHOPS	BILLOUV	VOLUBIL
BGINRSU	SUBRING	BHIOPST	PHOBIST	BILLOWY	BILLOWY
BGINRTU	BRUTING	BHIOSWZ	SHOWBIZ	BILLRUY	BURLILY
BGINRUX	BRUXING	BHIRSTU	BRUTISH	BILLRWY	WRYBILL
BGINRUY	BURYING	BHIRTTU	TURBITH	BILMNOR	NOMBRIL
	RUBYING	BHISTTU	BUSHTIT	BILMOSU	LIMBOUS
BGINSSU	BUSINGS	BHKNOSU	BOHUNKS	BILMPUY	BUMPILY
	BUSSING	BHLRSUU	BULRUSH	BILMRSU	UMBRILS
BGINSTU	BUSTING	BHMOORS	RHOMBOS	BILMRTU	TUMBRIL
	TUBINGS	BHMORSU	RHOMBUS	BILMSUU	BULIMUS
BGINSUY	BUSYING	BHMUUZZ	HUMBUZZ	BILNNOY	BONNILY
BGINSWY	SWINGBY	BHOOOOS	BOOHOOS	BILNOTU	BOTULIN
BGINTTU	BUTTING	BHOOPSY	SHOPBOY	BILNTUU	TUBULIN
BGINUZZ	BUZZING	BHOOSTW	BOWSHOT		UNBUILT
BGIORSU	RUBIGOS	BHOOSWX	SHOWBOX	BILOOPT	POTBOIL
BGIORTY	BIGOTRY	BHORSST	BORSHTS	BILOOYZ	BOOZILY
BGIOSSS	GOSSIBS	BHPRSUU	BRUSHUP	BILOPSU	UPBOILS
BGIUWZZ	BUZZWIG	BIIIKNS	BIKINIS	BILORST	BRISTOL
BGKLOOO	LOGBOOK	BIIKLOT	KILOBIT		STROBIL
BGKORSY	GRYSBOK	BIILLMS	MISBILL	BILOSSU	SUBSOIL
BGLMOOS	MOBLOGS	BIILLNO	BILLION	BILOSSY	BOSSILY
BGLMRUY	GRUMBLY	BIILLOU	BOUILLI	BILPTUU	UPBUILT
BGLNOOS	OBLONGS	BIILLTW	TWIBILL	BILRSTY	BRISTLY
BGLNOUW	BLOWGUN	BIILNNR	BIRLINN		TRILBYS
BGLOOSU	GLOBOUS	BIILNQU	QUIBLIN	BILRTTY	BRITTLY
BGLOSSU	BUGLOSS	BIILNTU	INBUILT	BILRTUY	TILBURY
BGLOSUY	BOGUSLY	BIILNVY	BIVINYL	BIMMOOS	IMBOSOM
BGLRSUU	BULGURS	BIILOSU	BILIOUS		MIOMBOS
BGMOORS	GOMBROS	BIILRSY	RISIBLY	BIMMORS	BROMISM
BGMOOTU	GUMBOOT	BIILSTW	TWIBILS	BIMNOOY	BIONOMY
BGMSSUU	SUBGUMS	BIILSVY	VISIBLY	BIMNORS	BROMINS
BGNOOWY	GOWNBOY	BIIMNOU	NIOBIUM		MISBORN
BGNOSSU	SUBSONG	BIIMNSU	MINIBUS	BIMNORW	IMBROWN
BGOORSU	BURGOOS	BIIMOSS	OBIISMS	BIMNOSS	BONISMS
BGORTUU	BURGOUT	BIIMOSZ	IMBIZOS	BIMNOST	INTOMBS
BGORTUW	BUGWORT	BIIMPRS	BIPRISM	BIMNOSU	OMNIBUS
BGOSTUU	BUGOUTS	BIIMSTU	STIBIUM	BIMNOSY	SYMBION
BHHIIST	BHISHTI	BIINORV	VIBRION	BIMOSSS	BOSSISM
BHHIKSU	BHIKHUS	BIINOST	BIOTINS	BIMOSTW	MISTBOW
BHIIINN	INHIBIN	BIINOSU	BINIOUS	BIMOSTY	SYMBIOT
BHIIINT	INHIBIT	BIIORSV	VIBRIOS	BIMRSTU	BRUTISM
BHIINRS	BRINISH	BIIOSUV	BIVIOUS	BIMRSUX	BRUXISM
BHIIPSS	SIBSHIP	BIIRSTU	BURITIS	BIMSSSU	SUBMISS
BHIISST	BHISTIS	BIISSTV	VIBISTS	BIMSSTU	SUBMITS
BHIKLOS	BLOKISH	BIISTTT	TITBITS	BINNOSU	BUNIONS
BHIKOOS	BOOKISH	BIJNOSU	SUBJOIN	BINOORS	BONSOIR
BHIKSSU	BUKSHIS	BIKLLUV	BULKILY	BINOORT	BIOTRON
BHILLOY	BILLYOH	BIKLNOT	INKBLOT	BINOOST	BONITOS
BHILLSU	BULLISH	BIKLNOY	LINKBOY	BINOOSU	NIOBOUS
BHILOTU	HOLIBUT	BIKLRSY	BRISKLY	BINORST	RIBSTON
BHILPSU	PUBLISH	BIKMNOO	BOOMKIN	BINORSU	BOURSIN
BHILSUY	BUSHILY	BIKMNPU	BUMPKIN	BINORUW	UNIBROW
BHIMOOR	RHOMBOI	BIKMNSU	BUMKINS	BINOSST	BONISTS
BHIMOOS	HOBOISM	BIKMOSS	IMBOSKS	BINPSUY	BUNYIPS
BHIMOPR	BIMORPH	BIKNSSU	BUSKINS	BINRSTU	INBURST
BHIMOPS	PHOBISM	BIKORRW	RIBWORK	BINRTUY	BUTYRIN
BHIMORT	THROMBI	BIKSUUZ	BUZUKIS	BINSTTU	UNBITTS
BHIMORU	BOHRIUM	BILLNOS	BILLONS	BINSTUU	SUBUNIT
BHIMSTU	BISMUTH	BILLNOU	BULLION	BIOOORS	ROOIBOS
BHINRSU	BURNISH	BILLOOY	LOOBILY	BIOORSZ	BORZOIS
BHIOOPR	BIOPHOR	BILLOPX	PILLBOX	BIOOSST	OBOISTS
		BILLORS	BRILLOS	BIOOSUV	OBVIOUS

BIOPRST	PROBITS	BMNOSTU	UNTOMBS	CCDEIIT	DEICTIC
BIOPRTY	PROBITY	BMOOORX	BOXROOM	CCDEIKL	CLICKED
BIORRTU	BURRITO	BMOORSY	BYROOMS	CCDEIKR	CRICKED
BIORRTW	RIBWORT	BMOOSTT	BOTTOMS	CCDEILR	CIRCLED
BIORSST	BISTROS	BMOOSTY	TOMBOYS	CCDEIMO	COMEDIC
BIORSTT	BISTORT	BMORSST	STROMBS	CCDEIOS	CODICES
	BITTORS	BMORSUU	BRUMOUS	CCDEIOT	DOCETIC
BIORSUU	RUBIOUS		UMBROUS	CCDEKLO	CLOCKED
BIORTTU	BITTOUR	BNNRSUU	SUNBURN		COCKLED
BIOSTUW	WOUBITS	BNNRTUU	UNBURNT	CCDEKLU	CLUCKED
BIRSTTU	BITTURS	BNOOSST	BOSTONS	CCDEKOR	CROCKED
	TURBITS	BNOOSTU	BOUTONS	CCDELOU	OCCLUDE
BISSSTU	SUBSIST		UNBOOTS	CCDENOO	CONCEDO
BISSTTU	TUBISTS	BNOOTTY	BOTTONY	CCDENOS	SCONCED
BISTUUU	BUSUUTI	BNORSSU	SUBORNS	CCDENOU	CONDUCE
BJMOOSU	BOOJUMS	BNORSTU	BURTONS	CCDEOST	DECOCTS
BJNOORU	BONJOUR	BNORSUU	BURNOUS	CCDHIIL	CICHLID
BKLNUUY	UNBULKY	BNORTUU	BURNOUT	CCDIILO	CODICIL
BKLOTUU	OUTBULK		OUTBURN	CCDIILU	CULICID
BKMNSUU	BUNKUMS	BNOSSUW	SUNBOWS	CCDIIOR	CRICOID
BKNNOOO	NONBOOK	BNOSTTU	BUTTONS	CCDILOY	CYCLOID
BKNOOTW	BOWKNOT	BNOTTUY	BUTTONY	CCDILYY	DICYCLY
BKNORSY	SKYBORN	BOOPSTW	BOWPOTS	CCDKLOU	CUCKOLD
BKOOOOS	BOOKOOS	BOOPSTX	POSTBOX	CCDNOOR	CONCORD
BKOORWX	WORKBOX	BOOPSTY	POSTBOY	CCDNOTU	CONDUCT
BKORSWY	BYWORKS		POTBOYS	CCEEGNO	COGENCE
BKRSTUU	KRUBUTS	BOORRSW	BORROWS	CCEEHIK	CHICKEE
BLLNTUY	BLUNTLY	BOORRTY	ROBOTRY	CCEEHIV	CEVICHE
BLLOOOS	LOBOLOS	BOOSTUW	WOOBUTS	CCEEHKR	CHECKER
BLLOSUU	BULLOUS	BOOSWWW	BOWWOWS		RECHECK
	LOBULUS	BOPSSTU	POSTBUS	CCEEHOR	ECORCHE
BLLOSUV	SOLUBLY	BORRSUW	BURROWS	CCEEHOU	COUCHEE
BLLOUVV	VOLUBLY	BORSSTW	BROWSTS	CCEEHRS	CRECHES
BLMMPUU	PLUMBUM	BORSTTU	TURBOTS		SCREECH
BLMNPUU	UNPLUMB	BORSTUU	RUBOUTS	CCEEILN	LICENCE
BLMOOOT	TOMBOLO	BORSTXY	BOSTRYX	CCEEILS	LECCIES
BLMOORW	LOBWORM	BOSTUUY	BUYOUTS	CCEEINR	ECCRINE
BLMOOSS	BLOSSOM		OUTBUYS	CCEEINS	SCIENCE
BLMOSSY	SYMBOLS	BPRSTUU	UPBURST	CCEEIOR	CICOREE
BLMOUXY	BUXOMLY	CCCDIOO	COCCOID	CCEEIRS	RECCIES
BLMRSUY	SLUMBRY	CCCDIOS	COCCIDS	CCEEIRV	CREVICE
BLMSTUY	STUMBLY	CCCNOOT	CONCOCT	CCEEKOY	COCKEYE
BLNNOUW	UNBLOWN	CCCOOSU	COCCOUS	CCEELNU	LUCENCE
BLNOORW	LOWBORN	CCDEEER	RECCEED	CCEELRY	RECYCLE
BLNOOSS	BOLSONS	CCDEEHK	CHECKED	CCEENRY	RECENCY
BLNOOSU	BLOUSON	CCDEEIM	ECDEMIC	CCEEORR	COERCER
BLNOPUW	UPBLOWN	CCDEEIO	ECOCIDE	CCEEORS	COERCES
BLNORSY	BORNYLS	CCDEEIR	RECCIED	CCEEORT	COERECT
BLNOSTU	UNBOLTS	CCDEEIS	DECCIES	CCEERSY	SECRECY
BLOOOTX	TOOLBOX	CCDEEKL	CLECKED	CCEFHRU	CURCHEF
BLOOPWY	PLOWBOY	CCDEENO	CONCEDE	CCEFNOT	CONFECT
BLOOQUY	OBLOQUY	CCDEENY	DECENCY	CCEGINY	GYNECIC
BLOORWW	LOWBROW	CCDEEOR	COERCED	CCEGNOY	COGENCY
BLOOSWY	LOWBOYS	CCDEEPS	SPECCED	CCEHHIS	CHICHES
BLOOTUW	BLOWOUT	CCDEESU	SUCCEED	CCEHIKN	CHICKEN
BLOPSTU	SUBPLOT	CCDEFLO	FLOCCED	CCEHIKU	CHUCKIE
BLOPSUW	BLOWUPS	CCDEHIL	CLICHED	CCEHILS	CHICLES
	UPBLOWS	CCDEHIN	CINCHED		CLICHES
BLORSTU	BRULOTS	CCDEHKO	CHOCKED	CCEHILU	CULCHIE
BLOSSTU	SUBLOTS	CCDEHKU	CHUCKED	CCEHIMS	CHEMICS
BLRTUYY	BUTYRYL	CCDEHNO	CONCHED	CCEHINO	CONCHIE
BMNOOOW	MOONBOW	CCDEHOU	COUCHED	CCEHINS	CINCHES
BMNOOSU	UNBOSOM	CCDEHTW	CWTCHED	CCEHINT	TECHNIC
BMNORUW	MOWBURN	CCDEIIL	ICICLED	CCEHINZ	ZECCHIN

CCEHIOR	CHOICER	CCEIOPT	ECTOPIC	CCHIMOR	CHROMIC
	CHOREIC	CCEIORS	CICEROS	CCHIMSY	CHYMICS
CCEHIOS	CHOICES	CCEIORT	CEROTIC	CCHINOR	CHRONIC
CCEHIRS	SCREICH		ORECTIC	CCHINOS	CHICONS
	SCRIECH	CCEIOSS	CISCOES		COCHINS
CCEHIST	CHICEST	CCEIPST	SCEPTIC	CCHINSU	SCUCHIN
	HECTICS	CCEIRST	CRETICS	CCHIORY	CHICORY
CCEHKLU	CHUCKLE	CCEISSU	SUCCISE	CCHIOTW	COWITCH
CCEHKMS	SCHMECK	CCEJNOT	CONJECT	CCHIPSU	HICCUPS
CCEHKNU	UNCHECK	CCEKLOR	CLOCKER	CCHIPSY	PSYCHIC
CCEHKOR	CHOCKER		COCKLER	CCHIPUY	HICCUPY
CCEHKPU	CHECKUP	CCEKLOS	COCKLES	CCHIRST	SCRITCH
CCEHKRU	CHUCKER	CCEKNOT	CONTECK	CCHKLOS	SCHLOCK
CCEHLOS	CLOCHES	CCEKNOY	COCKNEY	CCHKMOS	SCHMOCK
CCEHLRU	CLERUCH	CCEKOPS	COPECKS	CCHKMSU	SCHMUCK
CCEHLSU	CLEUCHS	CCEKOPT	PETCOCK	CCHKOOS	CHOCKOS
	CULCHES	CCEKORS	COCKERS	CCHKOSY	COCKSHY
CCEHNOS	CONCHES		RECOCKS	CCHKPUU	UPCHUCK
CCEHOOS	COOCHES	CCEKORT	CROCKET	CCHKSTU	SCHTUCK
CCEHORS	CROCHES	CCEKOST	COCKETS	CCHLSTU	SCULTCH
CCEHORT	CROCHET	CCELLOT	COLLECT	CCHLTUY	CLUTCHY
CCEHORU	COUCHER	CCELNOY	CYCLONE	CCHNOOS	CONCHOS
CCEHOSS	COSECHS	CCELNUY	LUCENCY	CCHNRSU	SCRUNCH
CCEHOSU	COUCHES	CCELRSY	CYCLERS	CCHNRUY	CRUNCHY
CCEHRSU	CURCHES	CCELRYY	CYCLERY	CCHOORS	SCROOCH
CCEHSTU	CUTCHES	CCENNOR	CONCERN	CCHOOST	SCOOTCH
CCEHSTW	CWTCHES	CCENNOT	CONCENT	CCHOSTU	SUCCOTH
CCEIILS	CILICES		CONNECT	CCIIILS	SILICIC
	ICICLES	CCENOPT	CONCEPT	CCIILNO	COLICIN
CCEIIMS	CIMICES	CCENORT	CONCERT	CCIILNS	CLINICS
CCEIIPS	PICCIES	CCENORW	CONCREW	CCIILOT	COLITIC
CCEIIRT	ICTERIC	CCENOSS	SCONCES	CCIILPR	CIRCLIP
CCEIIST	CECITIS	CCENOTV	CONVECT	CCIILST	CLITICS
CCEIKLR	CLICKER	CCEOOTT	COCOTTE	CCIINPS	PICNICS
CCEIKLT	CLICKET	CCEOPRT	PERCOCT	CCIIRST	CRITICS
CCEIKOR	COCKIER	CCEORRT	CORRECT	CCIIRTU	CIRCUIT
CCEIKOS	COCKIES	CCEORRU	REOCCUR	CCIISTY	SICCITY
CCEIKRT	CRICKET	CCEORSS	ESCROCS	CCIKLOW	COWLICK
CCEIKRY	CRICKEY		SOCCERS	CCIKLOY	COCKILY
CCEILMO	CELOMIC	CCEORTW	TWOCCER		COLICKY
CCEILNU	NUCLEIC	CCEOSSU	SUCCOSE	CCIKOPT	COCKPIT
CCEILOT	COCTILE	CCERTUW	CREWCUT	CCILNOO	COLONIC
CCEILRR	CIRCLER	CCESSSU	SUCCESS	CCILNOU	COUNCIL
CCEILRS	CIRCLES	CCFIRUY	CRUCIFY	CCILNSY	CYCLINS
	CLERICS	CCFLOSU	FLOCCUS	CCILOOP	PICCOLO
CCEILRT	CIRCLET	CCGHINO	GNOCCHI	CCILSTY	CYCLIST
CCEILSU	CULICES	CCGIINS	SICCING	CCIMNOU	UNCOMIC
CCEILSY	CYCLISE	CCGIINT	TICCING	CCIMOTY	MYCOTIC
	CYLICES	CCGIKNO	COCKING	CCINOOT	COCTION
CCEILTU	CUTICLE	CCGIKNU	CUCKING	CCINORY	CRYONIC
CCEILVZ	CYCLIZE	CCGILNY	CYCLING	CCINOTV	CONVICT
CCEIMNO	MECONIC	CCGKOOR	GORCOCK	CCIOORS	SIROCCO
CCEIMOS	COMICES	CCHHIIS	CHICHIS	CCIOPTU	OCCIPUT
	MOCCIES	CCHHIIT	ICHTHIC	CCIORSS	SCIROCS
CCEIMOT	COMETIC	CCHHILS	SCHLICH	CCIOSTT	TICTOCS
CCEIMST	SMECTIC	CCHHINY	CHINCHY	CCIPRTY	CRYPTIC
CCEINOR	CORNICE	CCHHOOS	CHOCHOS	CCIRSUY	CIRCUSY
	CROCEIN	CCHHRUY	CHURCHY	CCKMOOS	MOCOCKS
	CROCINE	CCHIIST	STICHIC	CCKMOSU	MOCUCKS
CCEINOS	CONCISE	CCHIKMS	SCHMICK	CCKNOSU	UNCOCKS
CCEINOT	CONCEIT	CCHIKOS	COCKISH	CCKOOSU	CUCKOOS
CCEINRT	CENTRIC	CCHIKST	SCHTICK	CCKOPSU	COCKUPS
CCEINSS	SCENICS		TCHICKS	CCKOSTU	CUSTOCK
CCEIOPP	COPPICE	CCHILOR	CHLORIC	CCLMSUU	MUCLUCS

CCLOOOZ	ZOCCOLO	CDDELOU	CLOUDED	CDEEHIS	DEHISCE
CCLOPSY	CYCLOPS	CDDELRU	CRUDDLE	CDEEHIT	CHEDITE
CCLOSTU	OCCULTS		CUDDLER	CDEEHIV	CHEVIED
CCMOOOR	MOROCCO		CURDLED	CDEEHKL	HECKLED
CCNOOOS	COCOONS	CDDELSU	CUDDLES	CDEEHLP	CHELPED
CCNOOPU	PUCCOON		SCUDDLE	CDEEHLT	LETCHED
CCNOOTU	COCONUT	CDDENOU	UNCODED	CDEEHLW	WELCHED
CCNOPUY	CONCUPY	CDDENSU	CUDDENS	CDEEHMS	SCHEMED
CCNORSU	CONCURS	CDDEORS	CODDERS	CDEEHNW	WENCHED
CCNOSSU	CONCUSS	CDDEORW	CROWDED	CDEEHOR	CHORDEE
CCOOORS	ROCOCOS	CDDERSU	SCUDDER		COHERED
CCORSSU	SUCCORS	CDDESTU	DEDUCTS		OCHERED
CCORSUU	SUCCOUR	CDDGINO	CODDING	CDEEHPR	PERCHED
CCORSUY	SUCCORY	CDDHIOR	DICHORD	CDEEHRS	CHEDERS
CCOSSTU	STUCCOS	CDDIIIO	DIDICOI	CDEEHRT	RETCHED
CCOSSUU	SUCCOUS	CDDIIKN	NIDDICK	CDEEHRU	EUCHRED
CCSSSUU	SUCCUSS	CDDIIOP	DIPODIC	CDEEHST	CHESTED
CDDDEEI	DECIDED	CDDIIOS	DISCOID	CDEEHTT	TETCHED
CDDDEEO	DECODED	CDDIIOY	DIDICOY	CDEEIIT	EIDETIC
CDDDEEU	DEDUCED	CDDIIRU	DRUIDIC	CDEEILN	DECLINE
CDDDELO	CLODDED	CDDIKOP	PIDDOCK	CDEEILP	PEDICEL
	CODDLED	CDDINSU	CUDDINS		PEDICLE
CDDDELU	CUDDLED	CDDIORS	DISCORD	CDEEILS	DECILES
CDDDERU	CRUDDED	CDDKOPU	PUDDOCK		DELICES
CDDDESU	SCUDDED	CDDKORU	RUDDOCK	CDEEIMN	ENDEMIC
CDDEEER	DECREED	CDEEEFL	FLEECED	CDEEIMS	DECIMES
	RECEDED	CDEEEFN	DEFENCE	CDEEINO	CODEINE
CDDEEES	SECEDED	CDEEEHK	CHEEKED	CDEEINR	CEDRINE
CDDEEII	DEICIDE	CDEEEHL	LEECHED	CDEEINS	INCEDES
CDDEEIN	INCEDED	CDEEEHP	CHEEPED	CDEEINT	ENTICED
CDDEEIR	DECIDER		DEPECHE	CDEEINV	EVINCED
	DECRIED	CDEEEHR	CHEERED	CDEEIOS	DIOCESE
CDDEEIS	DECIDES		REECHED	CDEEIOV	DEVOICE
CDDEEIX	EXCIDED	CDEEEHS	CHEESED	CDEEIPR	PIERCED
CDDEEKL	DECKLED	CDEEEIP	EPICEDE	CDEEIPT	PEDETIC
CDDEEKO	DECKOED	CDEEEIV	DECEIVE	CDEEIRR	DECRIER
	DECOKED	CDEEEJT	EJECTED	CDEEIRS	DECRIES
CDDEENO	ENCODED	CDEEEKL	CLEEKED		DEICERS
CDDEENS	DESCEND	CDEEELP	CLEEPED	CDEEIRT	RECITED
	SCENDED	CDEEELR	CREELED		TIERCED
CDDEENU	UNCEDED	CDEEELT	ELECTED	CDEEIST	DECEITS
CDDEEOR	DECODER	CDEEEPR	CREEPED	CDEEISV	DEVICES
	RECODED		PRECEDE	CDEEISX	EXCIDES
CDDEEOS	DECODES	CDEEERR	DECREER		EXCISED
CDDEEOY	DECOYED	CDEEERS	CREESED	CDEEITV	EVICTED
CDDEERU	REDUCED		DECREES	CDEEITX	EXCITED
CDDEESU	DEDUCES		RECEDES	CDEEJNO	CONJEED
	SEDUCED		SECEDER	CDEEJST	DEJECTS
CDDEEUW	CUDWEED	CDEEERT	DECREET	CDEEKKL	KECKLED
CDDEHIL	CHILDED		ERECTED	CDEEKLR	CLERKED
CDDEHIN	CHIDDEN	CDEEESS	SECEDES	CDEEKLS	DECKELS
CDDEHIT	DICHTED	CDEEESX	EXCEEDS		DECKLES
	DITCHED	CDEEFFH	CHEFFED	CDEEKNR	REDNECK
CDDEHNU	DUNCHED	CDEEFHT	FETCHED	CDEEKNS	SNECKED
CDDEHOR	CHORDED	CDEEFII	EDIFICE	CDEEKOS	DECOKES
CDDEHOU	DOUCHED	CDEEFKL	FLECKED	CDEEKPS	SPECKED
CDDEHRU	CHUDDER	CDEEFLT	CLEFTED	CDEEKRS	DECKERS
CDDEIIS	DISCIDE		DEFLECT	CDEEKRT	TRECKED
CDDEINU	INDUCED	CDEEFOR	DEFORCE	CDEEKRW	WRECKED
CDDEIOS	DISCOED	CDEEFST	DEFECTS	CDEELMM	CLEMMED
CDDEISU	CUDDIES	CDEEGIR	GRIECED	CDEELOS	ECLOSED
CDDELOR	CODDLER	CDEEGKT	GEDECKT	CDEELPU	CUPELED
CDDELOS	CODDLES	CDEEGNO	CONGEED		DECUPLE
	SCOLDED	CDEEHIP	CEPHEID	CDEELPY	YCLEPED

Key	Word(s)
CDEELRU	RECULED, ULCERED
CDEELSU	SCEDULE, SECLUDE
CDEELUX	EXCLUDE
CDEENOR	ENCODER, ENCORED
CDEENOS	ENCODES, SECONDE
CDEENOZ	COZENED
CDEENRS	DECERNS, SCERNED
CDEENRT	CENTRED, CREDENT
CDEENST	DESCENT, SCENTED
CDEEOOY	COOEYED
CDEEOPR	COPERED, PRECODE, PROCEED
CDEEORS	RECODES
CDEEORV	COVERED
CDEEORW	COWERED
CDEEORY	DECOYER
CDEEOST	CESTODE, ESCOTED, TEDESCO
CDEEOTV	COVETED
CDEERRU	RECURED, REDUCER
CDEERSS	SCREEDS
CDEERST	CRESTED
CDEERSU	RECUSED, REDUCES, RESCUED, SECURED, SEDUCER
CDEERSW	DECREWS, SCREWED
CDEERTU	ERUCTED
CDEERUV	DECURVE
CDEESSU	SEDUCES
CDEESSY	ECDYSES
CDEESTT	DECTETS, DETECTS
CDEESUX	EXCUSED
CDEFFHU	CHUFFED
CDEFFIL	CLIFFED
CDEFFIO	COIFFED
CDEFFLO	COFFLED
CDEFFLU	CUFFLED
CDEFFOS	SCOFFED
CDEFFSU	SCUFFED
CDEFHIL	FILCHED
CDEFHIN	FINCHED
CDEFHMO	CHEFDOM
CDEFHOO	CHOOFED
CDEFIIT	DEFICIT
CDEFIKL	FICKLED, FLICKED
CDEFILT	CLIFTED
CDEFINO	CONFIDE
CDEFKLO	FLOCKED
CDEFKOR	DEFROCK, FROCKED
CDEFNOR	CORNFED
CDEFNTU	DEFUNCT
CDEFOSU	DEFOCUS, FOCUSED
CDEFRTU	FRUCTED
CDEFSUU	FUCUSED
CDEGGHU	CHUGGED
CDEGGLO	CLOGGED, COGGLED
CDEGGOR	CROGGED
CDEGGOS	SCOGGED
CDEGGSU	SCUGGED
CDEGHLU	GULCHED
CDEGHOU	COUGHED
CDEGIIN	DEICING
CDEGIKN	DECKING
CDEGILN	CLINGED
CDEGILU	CLUDGIE
CDEGINO	COIGNED
CDEGINR	CRINGED
CDEGINU	DEUCING, EDUCING
CDEGIOR	ERGODIC
CDEGKOU	GEODUCK
CDEGKUW	GWEDUCK
CDEGLSU	CUDGELS
CDEGNSU	SCUNGED
CDEGOOS	SCOOGED
CDEGORS	CODGERS
CDEGOSU	SCOUGED
CDEGSUW	GWEDUCS
CDEHHIL	HILCHED
CDEHHIT	HITCHED
CDEHHNU	HUNCHED
CDEHHOT	HOTCHED
CDEHHTU	HUTCHED
CDEHIIL	CEILIDH
CDEHIIV	CHIVIED
CDEHIKN	CHINKED
CDEHIKO	HOICKED
CDEHIKR	CHIRKED
CDEHIKT	THICKED
CDEHILL	CHILLED
CDEHILO	CHELOID, HELCOID
CDEHILP	DELPHIC
CDEHILR	CHILDER, CHIRLED, ELDRICH
CDEHILS	CHIELDS, CHILDES
CDEHILT	LICHTED
CDEHIMR	CHIRMED
CDEHIMT	MITCHED
CDEHINN	CHINNED
CDEHINO	HEDONIC
CDEHINP	PINCHED
CDEHINW	WINCHED
CDEHIOR	CHOIRED
CDEHIOW	COWHIDE
CDEHIPP	CHIPPED
CDEHIPR	CHIRPED
CDEHIPT	PITCHED
CDEHIQU	QUICHED
CDEHIRR	CHIRRED
CDEHIRS	CHIDERS, HERDICS
CDEHIRT	CHIRTED, DITCHER, RICHTED
CDEHIST	DITCHES, SICHTED
CDEHISU	DUCHIES
CDEHITT	CHITTED
CDEHITW	WITCHED
CDEHIVV	CHIVVED
CDEHIZZ	CHIZZED
CDEHKLO	HOCKLED
CDEHKNU	CHUNKED
CDEHKOO	CHOOKED
CDEHKOS	SHOCKED
CDEHKOT	KOTCHED
CDEHKSU	SHUCKED
CDEHKUY	HEYDUCK
CDEHLMU	MULCHED
CDEHLNU	LUNCHED
CDEHLNY	LYNCHED
CDEHLOT	CLOTHED
CDEHLRU	LURCHED
CDEHMMU	CHUMMED
CDEHMNU	MUNCHED
CDEHMOO	MOOCHED
CDEHMOP	CHOMPED
CDEHMOR	CHROMED
CDEHMOU	MOUCHED
CDEHMPU	CHUMPED
CDEHMTU	MUTCHED
CDEHNOR	CHONDRE
CDEHNOT	NOTCHED
CDEHNPU	PUNCHED
CDEHNRU	CHUNDER, CHURNED
CDEHNSU	DUNCHES
CDEHNSY	SYNCHED
CDEHOOP	POOCHED
CDEHOPP	CHOPPED
CDEHOPT	POTCHED
CDEHOPU	POUCHED
CDEHORT	TORCHED
CDEHORW	CHOWDER, COWHERD
CDEHOSU	CHOUSED, DOUCHES, HOCUSED
CDEHOSW	CHOWSED, COWSHED
CDEHOTU	TOUCHED
CDEHOUV	VOUCHED
CDEHPSY	PSYCHED
CDEHRRU	CHURRED
CDEHRSU	CRUSHED
CDEHSSU	DUCHESS
CDEHSTU	DUTCHES
CDEHSTY	SCYTHED
CDEIIKR	DICKIER
CDEIIKS	DICKIES
CDEIILO	EIDOLIC

Seven-letter anagrams

CDEIIMR	DIMERIC		MISCODE
CDEIINR	DINERIC	CDEIMOT	DEMOTIC
CDEIINS	INCISED	CDEIMPR	CRIMPED
	INDICES	CDEIMPU	PUMICED
CDEIINT	IDENTIC	CDEIMSU	MISCUED
	INCITED	CDEINOS	CODEINS
CDEIIOR	ERICOID		CONDIES
CDEIIOV	OVICIDE		SECONDI
CDEIIRT	DICTIER	CDEINOT	CTENOID
	ICTERID		DEONTIC
CDEIIRV	VERIDIC		NOTICED
CDEIIST	DEISTIC	CDEINOU	DOUCINE
	DICIEST	CDEINOZ	ZINCODE
CDEIISU	SUICIDE	CDEINPR	PRINCED
CDEIJST	DISJECT	CDEINRS	CINDERS
CDEIKLN	CLINKED		DISCERN
	NICKLED		RESCIND
CDEIKLP	PICKLED	CDEINRU	INDUCER
CDEIKLS	SICKLED	CDEINRY	CINDERY
	SLICKED	CDEINSU	CUNDIES
CDEIKLT	TICKLED		INCUDES
CDEIKMS	MEDICKS		INCUSED
CDEIKNS	DICKENS		INDUCES
	SNICKED	CDEINSX	EXSCIND
CDEIKNZ	ZINCKED	CDEINSZ	DEZINCS
CDEIKOS	DOCKISE	CDEINTT	TINCTED
CDEIKOV	YOICKED	CDEINTU	UNCITED
CDEIKOZ	DOCKIZE	CDEIOOR	COORIED
CDEIKPR	PRICKED	CDEIOPR	PERCOID
CDEIKRR	DERRICK	CDEIOPT	PICOTED
CDEIKRS	DICKERS	CDEIORS	DISCOER
	SCRIKED		SCODIER
CDEIKRT	TRICKED	CDEIORT	CORDITE
CDEIKRU	DUCKIER	CDEIORU	COURIED
CDEIKRW	WRICKED	CDEIORV	CODRIVE
CDEIKST	DETICKS		DIVORCE
	STICKED	CDEIORW	CROWDIE
CDEIKSU	DUCKIES	CDEIOST	CESTOID
CDEIKSW	WICKEDS		COEDITS
CDEIKSY	DICKEYS		COTISED
CDEILLO	CODILLE	CDEIPRS	CRISPED
	COLLIDE		DISCERP
	COLLIED	CDEIPRT	PREDICT
CDEILLU	CULLIED	CDEIPST	DEPICTS
CDEILMO	MELODIC		DISCEPT
CDEILNU	INCLUDE	CDEIRRU	CURDIER
	NUCLIDE		CURRIED
CDEILOO	OCELOID	CDEIRST	CREDITS
CDEILOP	POLICED		DIRECTS
CDEILOR	DOCILER	CDEIRSU	CRUISED
CDEILOS	COLDIES		DISCURE
CDEILPP	CLIPPED	CDEIRSV	CERVIDS
CDEILPS	SPLICED		SCRIVED
CDEILPU	CLUPEID	CDEIRTV	VERDICT
CDEILQU	CLIQUED	CDEISST	DISSECT
CDEILRS	CLERIDS	CDEISSY	ECDYSIS
CDEILRU	LUCIDER	CDEITUX	EXCUDIT
CDEILST	DELICTS	CDEJNOU	JOUNCED
CDEILSU	SLUICED	CDEKKNO	KNOCKED
CDEILTU	DUCTILE	CDEKLNO	CLONKED
	DULCITE	CDEKLNU	CLUNKED
CDEIMNO	DEMONIC	CDEKLOW	WEDLOCK
CDEIMOR	DORMICE	CDEKLPU	PLUCKED
CDEIMOS	MEDICOS	CDEKLRU	RUCKLED

CDEKLSU	SCULKED
	SUCKLED
CDEKMOS	SMOCKED
CDEKNOR	DORNECK
CDEKNOS	DOCKENS
CDEKNRU	DRUCKEN
CDEKNSU	SUNDECK
	UNDECKS
CDEKOOR	CROOKED
CDEKORS	DOCKERS
	REDOCKS
CDEKORT	TROCKED
CDEKOST	DESTOCK
	DOCKETS
	STOCKED
CDEKRSU	DUCKERS
CDEKRTU	TRUCKED
CDELLOU	COLLUDE
	LOCULED
CDELLSU	SCULLED
CDELMOP	CLOMPED
CDELMPU	CLUMPED
CDELMSU	MUSCLED
CDELMTU	MULCTED
CDELNOO	CONDOLE
CDELNOU	ENCLOUD
CDELNOW	CLOWNED
CDELNOY	CONDYLE
CDELOOR	COLORED
	CROODLE
	CROOLED
	DECOLOR
CDELOPP	CLOPPED
CDELOPU	COUPLED
CDELORS	SCOLDER
CDELORU	CLOURED
CDELORW	CLOWDER
CDELOST	COLDEST
CDELOSU	DULCOSE
CDELOSW	SCOWLED
CDELOTT	CLOTTED
CDELOTU	CLOUTED
CDELOUY	DOUCELY
CDELOWY	COWEDLY
CDELPSU	SCULPED
CDELRRU	CURDLER
CDELRSU	CURDLES
	SCUDLER
CDELRUY	CRUDELY
CDELSTU	DULCETS
CDELTTU	CUTTLED
CDELTUU	DUCTULE
CDEMMNO	COMMEND
CDEMMOO	COMMODE
CDEMMSU	SCUMMED
CDEMNNO	CONDEMN
CDEMNOP	COMPEND
CDEMOOS	COMEDOS
CDEMOPT	COMPTED
CDEMORS	SCROMED
CDEMORU	DECORUM
CDEMPRU	CRUMPED
CDENNOO	CONDONE
CDENNOT	CONTEND

CDENOOP	POONCED	CDFIOOT	OCTOFID	CDIKNOW	WINDOCK
CDENOOR	CROONED	CDFIOSU	FUCOIDS	CDIKNPU	DUCKPIN
CDENOOS	CONDOES	CDFNOOU	COFOUND	CDILLOO	COLLOID
	SECONDO	CDGHIIN	CHIDING	CDILLUY	LUCIDLY
CDENOPU	POUNCED	CDGHILO	GLOCHID	CDILMTU	MIDCULT
	UNCOPED	CDGIIKN	DICKING	CDILNOS	CODLINS
CDENORS	CONDERS	CDGIINO	GONIDIC	CDILOTU	DULOTIC
	CORSNED	CDGIINS	DICINGS	CDILOTY	DICOTYL
	SCORNED		DISCING	CDIMMOU	MODICUM
CDENORU	CRUNODE	CDGIINT	DICTING	CDIMNOO	MONODIC
CDENORW	CROWNED	CDGIKNO	DOCKING	CDIMNSU	MUNDICS
	DECROWN	CDGIKNU	DUCKING	CDIMOOR	CORMOID
CDENOSS	SECONDS	CDGILNO	CODLING	CDIMOOS	COSMOID
CDENOST	DOCENTS		LINGCOD	CDIMOSS	COSMIDS
CDENOSY	ECDYSON	CDGINNO	CONDIGN	CDIMOSU	MUCOIDS
CDENOTU	COUNTED	CDGINOR	CORDING		MUSCOID
CDENPUY	PUDENCY	CDGINOS	CODINGS	CDIMSSU	MUSCIDS
CDENRUU	UNCURED	CDGINRU	CURDING	CDIMSTU	DICTUMS
CDENRUY	DUNCERY	CDGINTU	DUCTING	CDINOOS	CONOIDS
CDEOOPP	COPEPOD	CDGNOOO	COONDOG	CDINOOT	ODONTIC
CDEOOPS	OPCODES	CDGOOSY	COYDOGS	CDINOSY	SYNODIC
	SCOOPED	CDHIIMO	DOCHMII	CDINOTU	CONDUIT
CDEOOPT	COOPTED	CDHIINT	CHINDIT		NOCTUID
CDEOORR	CORRODE	CDHIIST	DISTICH	CDINSSY	SYNDICS
CDEOORV	CODROVE	CDHILLY	CHILDLY	CDINSTU	INDUCTS
	VOCODER	CDHILNU	UNCHILD	CDIOOTT	COTTOID
CDEOOST	SCOOTED	CDHILOR	CHLORID	CDIOPRR	RIPCORD
CDEOOTV	DOVECOT	CDHILOS	COLDISH	CDIOPSS	PSOCIDS
CDEOOPR	CROPPED	CDHINOR	CHONDRI	CDIORSV	CORVIDS
CDEOPRS	CORPSED	CDHINSU	DUNCISH	CDIOSST	CODISTS
CDEOPRU	CROUPED	CDHIOOR	CHOROID	CDIOSTT	COTTIDS
	PRODUCE		OCHROID	CDIOSTY	CYSTOID
CDEOPSU	SCOUPED	CDHIORS	DROICHS	CDIOTUV	OVIDUCT
CDEOPSW	SCOWPED		ORCHIDS	CDIPRSY	CYPRIDS
CDEOQTU	DOCQUET	CDHIORY	DROICHY	CDIPSSU	CUSPIDS
CDEORRS	CORDERS	CDHIOTU	OUTCHID	CDIRSUY	DYSURIC
	RECORDS	CDHIPTY	DIPTYCH	CDIRTUY	CRUDITY
CDEORRW	CROWDER	CDHIRTY	CHYTRID	CDISSSU	DISCUSS
CDEORSS	CROSSED	CDHKOOR	HORDOCK	CDISSTY	CYSTIDS
	SCORSED	CDHORSS	SCHRODS	CDKMORU	MUDROCK
CDEORSU	COURSED	CDIIILP	LIPIDIC	CDKNNOU	DUNNOCK
	SCOURED	CDIIIOT	IDIOTIC	CDKNOOR	DORNOCK
	SOURCED	CDIIJRU	JURIDIC	CDKNOSU	UNDOCKS
CDEORSW	SCOWDER	CDIILLY	IDYLLIC	CDLNOUU	UNCLOUD
CDEORTU	COURTED	CDIILMO	DOMICIL	CDLOOPY	LYCOPOD
	EDUCTOR	CDIILNY	DICLINY	CDLOSTU	COULDST
CDEORUU	DOUCEUR	CDIILOP	DIPLOIC	CDMMOOO	COMMODO
CDEOSSU	ESCUDOS	CDIIMOS	DISOMIC	CDMNOOS	CONDOMS
CDEOSTU	CUSTODE	CDIINOR	CRINOID	CDMNSUU	CUNDUMS
	DOUCEST	CDIINOT	DICTION	CDMOOST	DOTCOMS
	DOUCETS	CDIINOV	VIDICON		TOMCODS
	SCOUTED	CDIINOZ	ZINCOID	CDMOSUW	MUDSCOW
CDEOSTY	CYTODES	CDIINST	INDICTS	CDNNOTU	CONTUND
CDEOSYZ	ZYDECOS	CDIINTU	DUNITIC	CDNOORS	CONDORS
CDEPRSU	SPRUCED	CDIIOPT	PODITIC		CORDONS
CDEPRTY	DECRYPT	CDIIORS	CIRSOID	CDNORSU	UNCORDS
CDERRSU	SCURRED	CDIIORX	CORIXID	CDNOTUW	CUTDOWN
CDERSTU	CRUDEST	CDIIOSS	CISSOID	CDOOOPT	OCTOPOD
	CRUSTED	CDIIOSV	VISCOID	CDOOOST	DOOCOTS
CDERSUZ	SCRUZED	CDIIOTY	IDIOTCY	CDOOPST	POSTDOC
CDFHIOS	CODFISH	CDIIPRY	PYRIDIC	CDOORRY	CORRODY
CDFIILU	FLUIDIC	CDIIRSU	SCIURID	CDOORST	DOCTORS
CDFIJOR	FJORDIC	CDIKNNU	NUDNICK	CDOOTUW	WOODCUT
CDFILUY	DULCIFY	CDIKNOR	DORNICK	CDOPRTU	PRODUCT

Seven-letter anagrams

CDOSTUY	CUSTODY		PREFECT		LECHERY
CEEEEGH	GEECHEE	CEEFRST	REFECTS	CEEHLSS	CHESSEL
CEEEEHL	LEECHEE	CEEFSSU	FESCUES	CEEHLST	LETCHES
CEEEELT	ELECTEE	CEEGHIN	EECHING	CEEHLSW	LECHWES
CEEEFIL	FLEECIE	CEEGHOS	CHEGOES		WELCHES
CEEEFLR	FLEECER	CEEGIIP	EPIGEIC	CEEHLSY	LYCHEES
CEEEFLS	FLEECES	CEEGINR	CREEING		SLEECHY
CEEEFNR	REFENCE		ENERGIC	CEEHMRS	MERCHES
CEEEGNR	REGENCE		GENERIC		SCHEMER
CEEEGNS	EGENCES	CEEGINT	GENETIC		SCHMEER
CEEEGRS	GREECES	CEEGINU	EUGENIC	CEEHMRT	MERCHET
CEEEHIR	REECHIE	CEEGIRS	CIERGES	CEEHMSS	SCHEMES
CEEEHKS	KEECHES		GRECISE	CEEHNOP	PENOCHE
CEEEHLL	ECHELLE		GRIECES	CEEHNPU	PENUCHE
CEEEHLS	ELCHEES	CEEGIRZ	GRECIZE	CEEHNRW	WENCHER
	LEECHES	CEEGKOS	GECKOES	CEEHNST	CHENETS
CEEEHNR	ENCHEER	CEEGLLO	COLLEGE		TENCHES
CEEEHPR	CHEEPER	CEEGLNT	NEGLECT	CEEHNSV	CHEVENS
CEEEHRR	CHEERER	CEEGLOU	ECLOGUE	CEEHNSW	WENCHES
CEEEHRS	REECHES	CEEGNOR	COGENER		WHENCES
CEEEHSS	CHEESES		CONGREE	CEEHNTU	CHUTNEE
CEEEINP	EPICENE	CEEGNOS	CONGEES	CEEHORR	COHERER
CEEEIPR	CREEPIE	CEEGNRU	URGENCE	CEEHORS	CHEEROS
CEEEIRV	RECEIVE	CEEGNRY	REGENCY		CHOREES
CEEEITV	EVICTEE	CEEGORT	CORTEGE		COHERES
CEEEJRT	REEJECT	CEEGQRU	GRECQUE		ECHOERS
CEEELLU	ECUELLE	CEEHHSW	WHEECHS		RECHOSE
CEEELPY	YCLEEPE	CEEHIKM	KIMCHEE	CEEHORT	TROCHEE
CEEELRT	REELECT	CEEHILN	ELENCHI	CEEHOUV	VOUCHEE
CEEELST	CELESTE	CEEHILS	ELICHES	CEEHPRR	PERCHER
CEEELSV	CLEEVES		HELICES	CEEHPRS	PERCHES
CEEEMPR	EMPERCE		LICHEES	CEEHPRU	UPCHEER
CEEENRS	RECENSE	CEEHILV	VEHICLE	CEEHQRU	CHEQUER
CEEENSS	ESSENCE	CEEHIMR	CHIMERE	CEEHQSU	CHEQUES
CEEEPRR	CREEPER	CEEHIMS	CHEMISE	CEEHQUY	QUEECHY
CEEERRT	ERECTER		SCHEMIE	CEEHRST	ETCHERS
	REERECT	CEEHINR	INHERCE		RETCHES
CEEERSS	CREESES	CEEHINS	CHINESE	CEEHRSU	EUCHRES
CEEERST	SECRETE	CEEHIOR	CHEERIO	CEEHRSV	CHEVRES
CEEERSV	SCREEVE	CEEHIOS	ECHOISE	CEEHRSW	CHEWERS
CEEERTX	EXCRETE	CEEHIOZ	ECHOIZE		RECHEWS
CEEETUX	EXECUTE	CEEHIRT	ERETHIC	CEEHRSY	CREESHY
CEEFFNO	OFFENCE		ETHERIC	CEEHRTU	TEUCHER
CEEFFOR	EFFORCE		HERETIC	CEEHRTV	CHEVRET
CEEFFOS	COFFEES		TECHIER	CEEHSSS	CHESSES
CEEFFST	EFFECTS	CEEHIRW	CHEWIER	CEEHSSW	ESCHEWS
CEEFHIR	CHIEFER	CEEHISS	SEICHES	CEEHSTV	CHEVETS
CEEFHIT	FETICHE	CEEHIST	TECHIES		VETCHES
	FITCHEE	CEEHISV	CHEVIES	CEEHSTW	CHEWETS
CEEFHLS	FLECHES		SEVICHE	CEEIIKL	ICELIKE
CEEFHRT	FECHTER	CEEHISW	CHEWIES	CEEIINR	EIRENIC
	FETCHER	CEEHKLR	HECKLER	CEEIINW	ICEWINE
CEEFHST	FETCHES	CEEHKLS	HECKLES	CEEIIPR	EPEIRIC
CEEFINV	VENEFIC	CEEHKNP	HENPECK		EPICIER
CEEFIRR	FIERCER	CEEHKNS	KENCHES	CEEIJOR	REJOICE
CEEFKLR	FLECKER	CEEHKST	KETCHES	CEEIKLT	CLEEKIT
	FRECKLE	CEEHLNO	CHELONE	CEEIKNT	NECKTIE
CEEFLNU	FLUENCE		ECHELON	CEEIKPR	PECKIER
CEEFLRT	REFLECT	CEEHLNS	ELENCHS		PICKEER
CEEFNNS	FENNECS	CEEHLNU	LEUCHEN	CEEIKSS	SICKEES
CEEFNNU	UNFENCE	CEEHLOW	COWHEEL	CEEILLM	MICELLE
CEEFNOR	ENFORCE	CEEHLRS	LECHERS	CEEILMX	LEXEMIC
CEEFNRS	FENCERS	CEEHLRW	WELCHER	CEEILNO	CINEOLE
CEEFPRT	PERFECT	CEEHLRY	CHEERLY	CEEILNR	RECLINE

CEEILNS	LICENSE	CEEIRTT	TIERCET	CEEMNOW	NEWCOME
	SELENIC	CEEIRTU	EUCRITE	CEEMNRU	CERUMEN
	SILENCE	CEEIRTX	EXCITER	CEEMNRW	CREWMEN
CEEILNT	CENTILE	CEEISSX	EXCISES	CEEMNST	CEMENTS
	LICENTE	CEEISTU	CUTESIE	CEEMNSY	CYMENES
CEEILNU	LEUCINE	CEEISTX	EXCITES	CEEMOPR	COMPEER
CEEILPS	ECLIPSE	CEEITTT	TECTITE		COMPERE
CEEILPX	EXCIPLE	CEEITTZ	ZETETIC	CEEMOPT	COMPETE
CEEILRS	CEILERS	CEEJNOS	CONJEES	CEEMRRS	MERCERS
CEEILRT	RETICLE	CEEJORT	EJECTOR	CEEMRRY	MERCERY
	TIERCEL	CEEJRST	REJECTS		REMERCY
CEEILRU	RECUILE	CEEKKLS	KECKLES	CEEMRST	CERMETS
CEEILSS	ICELESS	CEEKKSS	KECKSES	CEEMSTU	TUMESCE
	SIECLES	CEEKLNT	NECKLET	CEEMSTY	MYCETES
CEEILST	SECTILE	CEEKLPS	SPECKLE	CEENNOU	ENOUNCE
CEEILSV	VESICLE	CEEKLSS	SECKELS	CEENNOV	CONVENE
CEEILTU	LEUCITE		SECKLES	CEENNRT	CENTNER
CEEIMMS	SEMEMIC	CEEKLST	TECKELS	CEENOOT	ECOTONE
CEEIMNO	MIOCENE	CEEKNRS	NECKERS	CEENOPT	POTENCE
CEEIMNT	CENTIME	CEEKOSS	COKESES	CEENORS	ENCORES
CEEIMRS	MERCIES	CEEKOSY	SOCKEYE		NECROSE
CEEIMRX	EXCIMER	CEEKPRS	PECKERS	CEENORU	COENURE
CEEIMST	EMETICS	CEEKPRY	RYEPECK	CEENORZ	COZENER
CEEINNS	INCENSE	CEEKRRW	WRECKER	CEENOST	CENOTES
CEEINOS	SENECIO	CEELLLU	CELLULE	CEENPRS	SPENCER
CEEINPR	PERCINE	CEELLNO	COLLEEN	CEENPRT	PERCENT
CEEINPS	PICENES	CEELLOS	CELLOSE		PRECENT
	PIECENS	CEELLPU	PUCELLE	CEENPSS	SPENCES
CEEINPT	PENTICE	CEELMNT	CLEMENT	CEENPST	PECTENS
CEEINPU	EUPNEIC	CEELMOO	COELOME	CEENRSS	CENSERS
CEEINRS	CERESIN	CEELMOS	CLEOMES		SCERNES
	SCRIENE	CEELMOT	TELECOM		SCREENS
	SINCERE	CEELMOW	WELCOME		SECERNS
CEEINRT	ENTERIC	CEELMSY	MYCELES	CEENRST	CENTERS
	ENTICER	CEELNOS	ENCLOSE		CENTRES
CEEINRV	CERVINE	CEELNPS	PENCELS		TENRECS
CEEINST	ENTICES	CEELNRS	CRENELS	CEENRSU	CENSURE
CEEINSV	EVINCES	CEELNRT	LECTERN	CEENRSY	SCENERY
CEEIOPT	PICOTEE	CEELNRU	LUCERNE	CEENTTU	CUNETTE
CEEIORT	COTERIE	CEELORS	CREOLES	CEEOPRU	RECOUPE
CEEIORV	REVOICE		RECLOSE	CEEOPST	PECTOSE
CEEIOST	COESITE	CEELORT	ELECTOR	CEEOPSU	COUPEES
CEEIPPR	PRECIPE		ELECTRO	CEEOPTY	ECOTYPE
CEEIPRR	CREPIER	CEELORY	RECOYLE	CEEORRS	RESCORE
	PIERCER	CEELOSS	ECLOSES	CEEORRT	ERECTOR
	REPRICE	CEELOSU	COULEES	CEEORRU	RECOURE
CEEIPRS	PIECERS	CEELOTU	ELOCUTE	CEEORRV	COVERER
	PIERCES	CEELOTV	COVELET		RECOVER
	PRECISE	CEELOTX	CELOTEX	CEEORRW	RECOWER
	RECIPES	CEELPRT	PLECTRE	CEEORSU	CEREOUS
CEEIPRT	RECEIPT		PRELECT	CEEORSV	CORVEES
CEEIPRU	EPICURE	CEELPRU	CUPELER	CEEORTV	COVETER
CEEIPSS	SPECIES	CEELRRU	CRUELER	CEEORTW	COWTREE
CEEIPST	PECTISE	CEELRSS	SCLERES	CEEORTX	COEXERT
CEEIPTZ	PECTIZE	CEELRST	TERCELS	CEEOTTT	OCTETTE
CEEIQSU	QUIESCE	CEELRSU	RECLUSE	CEEPPRT	PERCEPT
CEEIRRT	RECITER		RECULES		PRECEPT
CEEIRSS	CERISES	CEELRSW	CREWELS	CEEPPRU	PREPUCE
CEEIRST	CERITES	CEELRTU	LECTURE	CEEPRRU	PRECURE
	RECITES	CEELRTY	ERECTLY	CEEPRSS	PRECESS
	TIERCES	CEELSST	SELECTS	CEEPRST	RECEPTS
CEEIRSU	ECURIES	CEELSUX	CULEXES		RESPECT
CEEIRSV	SCRIEVE	CEELTTU	LETTUCE		SCEPTER
	SERVICE	CEEMMOR	COMMERE		SCEPTRE

	SPECTER		LUCIFER	CEGIKKN	KECKING
	SPECTRE	CEFIMOR	COMFIER	CEGIKNN	NECKING
CEEPRTX	EXCERPT	CEFIMRY	MERCIFY	CEGIKNP	PECKING
CEEPSTX	EXCEPTS	CEFINNO	CONFINE	CEGIKNR	RECKING
	EXPECTS	CEFINOR	COINFER	CEGIKRU	GUCKIER
CEEPSTY	ECTYPES		CONIFER	CEGILLN	CELLING
CEEPSUY	EYECUPS		INFORCE	CEGILMP	GEMCLIP
CEERRSU	RECURES	CEFINST	INFECTS	CEGILNP	CLEPING
	RESCUER	CEFIPSY	SPECIFY	CEGILNR	CLINGER
	SECURER	CEFIRSS	SFERICS		CRINGLE
CEERRSW	SCREWER	CEFIRTY	CERTIFY	CEGILNU	CLUEING
CEERRUV	RECURVE		RECTIFY		LUCIGEN
CEERSSS	CESSERS	CEFISSU	FICUSES	CEGILNW	CLEWING
	CRESSES	CEFKLLO	ELFLOCK	CEGILNY	GLYCINE
CEERSST	CRESSET	CEFKLOT	FETLOCK	CEGIMNO	GENOMIC
	RESECTS	CEFKLRY	FRECKLY	CEGIMNU	MUCIGEN
	SCREETS	CEFKRSU	FUCKERS	CEGINNR	CERNING
	SECRETS	CEFLNOU	FLOUNCE	CEGINNS	CENSING
CEERSSU	CERUSES	CEFLNTU	UNCLEFT		SCENING
	CESURES	CEFLNUY	FLUENCY	CEGINOR	COREIGN
	RECUSES	CEFMORY	COMFREY	CEGINOS	COGNISE
	RESCUES	CEFNORS	CONFERS		COIGNES
	SECURES	CEFNORU	FROUNCE	CEGINOZ	COGNIZE
CEERSTT	TERCETS	CEFNOSS	CONFESS	CEGINPR	CREPING
CEERSUX	EXCURSE	CEFNOST	CONFEST		PERCING
	EXCUSER	CEFNOSU	CONFUSE	CEGINRR	CRINGER
CEERTTU	CURETTE	CEFNOTU	CONFUTE	CEGINRS	CRINGES
CEESSTX	EXSECTS	CEFOPRS	FORCEPS	CEGINRW	CREWING
CEESSUX	EXCUSES	CEFORRS	FORCERS	CEGINSS	CESSING
CEETTUV	CUVETTE	CEFORRT	CROFTER	CEGIORT	ERGOTIC
CEFFHRU	CHUFFER	CEFORSS	FRESCOS	CEGIRRS	GRICERS
CEFFIOR	OFFICER	CEFORSU	FOCUSER	CEGKLNO	GENLOCK
CEFFIOS	COIFFES		REFOCUS	CEGKLOR	GROCKLE
	OFFICES	CEFOSSU	FOCUSES	CEGLNOO	COLOGNE
CEFFISU	SUFFICE		FUCOSES	CEGLOOY	ECOLOGY
CEFFLOS	COFFLES	CEFRSUW	CURFEWS	CEGLOSU	GLUCOSE
CEFFLSU	CUFFLES	CEFSSUU	FUCUSES	CEGLOSY	GLYCOSE
	SCUFFLE	CEGGHIR	CHIGGER	CEGNNOO	ONCOGEN
CEFFORS	COFFERS	CEGGHRU	CHUGGER	CEGNOOS	CONGOES
	SCOFFER	CEGGIIS	CIGGIES	CEGNORS	CONGERS
CEFFORT	COFFRET	CEGGIKN	GECKING	CEGNORU	CONGRUE
CEFFRSU	SCUFFER	CEGGIOR	GEORGIC	CEGNORY	CRYOGEN
CEFFSTU	SUFFECT	CEGGIOS	COGGIES	CEGNOST	CONGEST
CEFGHIN	CHEFING	CEGGLOR	CLOGGER	CEGNRUY	URGENCY
CEFGIKN	FECKING	CEGGLOS	COGGLES	CEGNSSU	SCUNGES
CEFGINN	FENCING	CEGGORS	COGGERS	CEGNSTY	CYGNETS
CEFHILR	FILCHER	CEGGPSU	EGGCUPS	CEGOORS	SCROOGE
CEFHILS	FILCHES	CEGHILN	LECHING	CEGORRS	GROCERS
CEFHILY	CHIEFLY	CEGHINO	ECHOING	CEGORRY	GROCERY
CEFHINS	FINCHES	CEGHINP	PECHING	CEGORSU	SCOURGE
CEFHIRY	CHIEFRY	CEGHINT	ETCHING		SCROUGE
CEFHIST	FITCHES	CEGHINW	CHEWING	CEHHILS	HILCHES
CEFHITT	FITCHET	CEGHIOR	CHOREGI	CEHHIOO	HOOCHIE
CEFHITW	FITCHEW	CEGHIOS	CHIGOES	CEHHIRS	CHERISH
CEFHLTU	FUTCHEL	CEGHIRS	CHIGRES		SHRIECH
CEFIILT	FICTILE		SCREIGH	CEHHIRT	HITCHER
CEFIIOR	ORIFICE	CEGHITU	GUICHET	CEHHIST	HITCHES
CEFIITV	FICTIVE	CEGHLSU	CLEUGHS	CEHHITU	HUTCHIE
CEFIKLR	FICKLER		GULCHES	CEHHNSU	HUNCHES
	FLICKER	CEGHORU	COUGHER	CEHHOOS	HOOCHES
CEFIKLS	FICKLES	CEGHRTU	GUTCHER	CEHHOST	HOTCHES
CEFILNT	INFLECT	CEGIILN	CEILING		SHOCHET
CEFILNU	FUNICLE		CIELING	CEHHSSU	SHEUCHS
CEFILRU	FLUERIC	CEGIINP	PIECING	CEHHSTU	HUTCHES

CEHIIKN	CHINKIE	CEHINOP	CHOPINE	CEHKNOU	UNCHOKE
CEHIIKS	HICKIES		PHOCINE	CEHKNSU	KUCHENS
CEHIIKT	THICKIE	CEHINOR	CHORINE	CEHKOOR	KERCHOO
CEHIILS	CHILIES	CEHINOT	HENOTIC	CEHKORS	CHOKERS
CEHIINR	HIRCINE	CEHINOX	CHOENIX		HOCKERS
CEHIINS	NICEISH	CEHINPR	NEPHRIC		SHOCKER
CEHIINT	ICHNITE		PHRENIC	CEHKOST	KOTCHES
	NITCHIE		PINCHER	CEHKOSY	CHOKEYS
CEHIIPP	CHIPPIE	CEHINPS	PINCHES		HOCKEYS
CEHIIRT	ITCHIER		SPHENIC	CEHKPTU	KETCHUP
	TICHIER	CEHINPU	PENUCHI	CEHKRSU	SHUCKER
CEHIISV	CHIVIES	CEHINQU	QUINCHE	CEHKRUY	HUCKERY
	VICHIES	CEHINRR	CHIRREN	CEHKSTU	KUTCHES
CEHIKNT	CHETNIK	CEHINRS	INCHERS	CEHKSTY	SKETCHY
	KITCHEN		NICHERS	CEHKTVY	KVETCHY
	THICKEN		RICHENS	CEHLLMO	MOCHELL
CEHIKNW	CHEWINK	CEHINRT	CITHERN	CEHLLMU	MUCHELL
CEHIKOO	CHOOKIE		CITHREN	CEHLLNS	SCHNELL
CEHIKOR	CHOKIER	CEHINRW	WINCHER	CEHLLOY	YELLOCH
CEHIKOS	CHOKIES	CEHINST	ETHNICS	CEHLLPU	CHELLUP
CEHIKPS	PECKISH		STHENIC	CEHLMOR	CHROMEL
CEHIKRR	CHIRKER	CEHINSU	ECHINUS	CEHLMSS	SCHELMS
CEHIKRS	SHICKER	CEHINSV	CHEVINS	CEHLMSU	MUCHELS
	SKRIECH	CEHINSW	WINCHES		MULCHES
CEHIKRT	THICKER	CEHINSZ	ZECHINS	CEHLMSZ	SCHMELZ
CEHIKRW	WHICKER	CEHINTW	WITCHEN	CEHLMUY	CHUMLEY
CEHIKST	CHEKIST	CEHIOPS	HOSPICE	CEHLNNU	CHUNNEL
CEHIKSY	HICKEYS	CEHIOPT	POTICHE	CEHLNOS	NOCHELS
CEHIKTT	THICKET	CEHIOPU	COPIHUE	CEHLNOT	CHOLENT
CEHILLR	CHILLER	CEHIORR	CHORRIE		NOTCHEL
CEHILMY	CHIMLEY	CEHIORS	COHEIRS	CEHLNRU	LUNCHER
CEHILNO	CHOLINE		HEROICS	CEHLNRY	LYNCHER
	HELICON	CEHIORT	ROTCHIE	CEHLNSU	LUNCHES
CEHILNS	LICHENS		THEORIC	CEHLNSY	LYNCHES
	LINCHES	CEHIOST	ECHOIST	CEHLNTY	LYNCHET
CEHILNT	LINCHET		TOISECH	CEHLOOS	SCHOOLE
	TINCHEL	CEHIOTU	COUTHIE	CEHLORS	CHOLERS
CEHILPR	PILCHER	CEHIOTV	CHEVIOT		ORCHELS
CEHILPS	PILCHES	CEHIPPR	CHIPPER	CEHLORT	CHORTLE
CEHILRT	LICHTER	CEHIPRR	CHIRPER	CEHLOST	CLOTHES
CEHILRV	CHERVIL	CEHIPRS	CERIPHS	CEHLPPS	SCHLEPP
CEHILSS	CHESILS		CIPHERS	CEHLPSS	SCHLEPS
	CHISELS		SPHERIC	CEHLPSU	PLEUCHS
CEHILST	ELTCHIS	CEHIPRT	PITCHER	CEHLQSU	SQUELCH
CEHILSZ	ZILCHES	CEHIPST	CHIPSET	CEHLRRU	LURCHER
CEHILTY	ETHYLIC		PITCHES	CEHLRSU	LURCHES
	LECYTHI	CEHIQSU	QUICHES	CEHMNRU	MUNCHER
	TECHILY	CEHIRRS	CHIRRES	CEHMNSU	MUNCHES
CEHILXY	HEXYLIC	CEHIRRT	RICHTER	CEHMNSY	MENSCHY
CEHIMMO	CHOMMIE	CEHIRST	CITHERS	CEHMOOR	MOOCHER
CEHIMMS	CHEMISM		ESTRICH	CEHMOOS	MOOCHES
CEHIMNY	CHIMNEY		RICHEST	CEHMOPR	CHOMPER
CEHIMOR	HOMERIC	CEHIRSU	CUSHIER	CEHMORS	CHROMES
	MOCHIER	CEHIRSZ	SCHERZI	CEHMORU	MOUCHER
	MORICHE	CEHIRTT	CHITTER	CEHMOSS	SCHMOES
CEHIMOS	ECHOISM	CEHISSU	CUISHES	CEHMOSU	MOUCHES
CEHIMRS	CHIMERS		CUSHIES	CEHMOTZ	CHOMETZ
	MICHERS	CEHISTT	TITCHES	CEHMRTU	CHETRUM
CEHIMRT	THERMIC	CEHISTW	WITCHES	CEHMSTU	HUMECTS
CEHIMRU	RHEUMIC	CEHISZZ	CHIZZES		MUTCHES
CEHIMST	CHEMIST	CEHKKRU	CHUKKER	CEHNNRU	CHUNNER
	MITCHES	CEHKLMO	HEMLOCK	CEHNOOP	HENCOOP
CEHIMSU	ECHIUMS	CEHKLOS	HOCKLES	CEHNOOR	COEHORN
CEHINNO	CHINONE	CEHKLSU	HUCKLES	CEHNORT	CHORTEN

Seven-letter anagrams

	NOTCHER	**CEIIJRU**	JUICIER	**CEIIRSS**	CISSIER
CEHNORV	CHEVRON	**CEIIKKR**	KICKIER	**CEIIRST**	ERISTIC
CEHNOST	NOTCHES	**CEIIKLS**	SICLIKE		RICIEST
	TECHNOS	**CEIIKMS**	MICKIES	**CEIIRSU**	CRUISIE
CEHNOSU	COHUNES	**CEIIKNS**	KINESIC	**CEIIRUZ**	CRUIZIE
CEHNPRU	PUNCHER	**CEIIKNT**	KINETIC	**CEIISSS**	CISSIES
	UNPERCH	**CEIIKPR**	PICKIER	**CEIISVV**	CIVVIES
CEHNPST	PSCHENT	**CEIIKQU**	QUICKIE	**CEIITUV**	UVEITIC
CEHNPSU	PUNCHES	**CEIIKRT**	TRICKIE	**CEIJNST**	INJECTS
CEHNRRU	CHURNER	**CEIIKSS**	SICKIES	**CEIJRSU**	JUICERS
CEHNRSU	RUNCHES	**CEIIKST**	EKISTIC	**CEIJSTU**	JUSTICE
CEHNRTU	CHUNTER		ICKIEST	**CEIKKNR**	KNICKER
CEHNSTU	CHESNUT		TICKIES	**CEIKKRS**	KICKERS
CEHNSTY	STENCHY	**CEIIKSW**	WICKIES	**CEIKLMR**	MICKLER
CEHNSUU	EUNUCHS	**CEIILLS**	SILICLE	**CEIKLMS**	MELICKS
CEHNTUY	CHUTNEY	**CEIILNN**	INCLINE		MICKLES
CEHOOPS	POOCHES	**CEIILNP**	PENICIL	**CEIKLNR**	CLINKER
CEHOORS	CHOOSER	**CEIILPP**	CLIPPIE		CRINKLE
	SOROCHE	**CEIILPT**	PELITIC	**CEIKLNS**	NICKELS
CEHOORT	CHEROOT	**CEIILST**	ELICITS		NICKLES
CEHOOSS	CHOOSES	**CEIILTV**	LEVITIC		SLICKEN
CEHOOSY	CHOOSEY	**CEIIMMT**	MIMETIC	**CEIKLPR**	PICKLER
CEHOOTU	OUTECHO	**CEIIMNR**	CREMINI		PRICKLE
CEHOPPR	CHOPPER		CRIMINE	**CEIKLPS**	PICKLES
CEHOPRS	PORCHES		MINCIER	**CEIKLPU**	CUPLIKE
CEHOPRT	POTCHER	**CEIIMNS**	MENISCI	**CEIKLRS**	LICKERS
CEHOPRY	CORYPHE	**CEIIMOT**	MEIOTIC		RICKLES
CEHOPST	POTCHES	**CEIIMPR**	EMPIRIC		SLICKER
CEHOPSU	POUCHES	**CEIIMPS**	EPICISM	**CEIKLRT**	TICKLER
CEHORRT	TORCHER	**CEIIMRS**	CIMIERS		TRICKLE
CEHORSS	COSHERS	**CEIIMRV**	VIREMIC	**CEIKLRU**	LUCKIER
CEHORST	HECTORS	**CEIIMSS**	SEISMIC	**CEIKLSS**	SICKLES
	ROCHETS	**CEIIMST**	MISCITE	**CEIKLST**	ICKLEST
	ROTCHES	**CEIIMTT**	TITMICE		STICKLE
	TOCHERS	**CEIINNO**	CONIINE		TICKLES
	TORCHES		INCONIE	**CEIKLSU**	LUCKIES
	TROCHES	**CEIINNR**	CINERIN	**CEIKLSY**	KYLICES
CEHORSU	CHOREUS	**CEIINOR**	ONEIRIC	**CEIKMRS**	SMICKER
	CHOUSER	**CEIINOS**	EOSINIC	**CEIKMRU**	MUCKIER
	ROUCHES		ICONISE	**CEIKMST**	SMICKET
CEHORSY	COSHERY		NICOISE	**CEIKMSY**	MICKEYS
CEHORSZ	SCHERZO	**CEIINOV**	INVOICE	**CEIKNOR**	CONKIER
CEHORTU	COUTHER	**CEIINOZ**	ICONIZE	**CEIKNOT**	KENOTIC
	RETOUCH	**CEIINPS**	PISCINE		KETONIC
	TOUCHER	**CEIINRS**	IRENICS	**CEIKNQU**	QUICKEN
CEHORTW	WOTCHER		SERICIN	**CEIKNRS**	NICKERS
CEHORUV	VOUCHER		SIRENIC		SNICKER
CEHOSSU	CHOUSES	**CEIINRT**	CITRINE	**CEIKNSS**	SICKENS
	HOCUSES		CRINITE	**CEIKNST**	SNICKET
CEHOSSW	CHOWSES		INCITER		TICKENS
CEHOSTU	TOUCHES		NERITIC	**CEIKNSW**	WICKENS
CEHOSUV	VOUCHES	**CEIINRZ**	ZINCIER	**CEIKOOS**	COOKIES
CEHPRSU	CHERUPS	**CEIINSS**	ICINESS	**CEIKOPR**	POCKIER
CEHPRSY	CHYPRES		INCISES	**CEIKOPS**	POCKIES
	CYPHERS	**CEIINST**	INCITES	**CEIKORR**	CORKIER
CEHPRTU	PUTCHER	**CEIINSU**	CUISINE		ROCKIER
CEHPSSY	PSYCHES	**CEIINTZ**	CITIZEN	**CEIKORT**	TOCKIER
CEHQSTU	QUETSCH		ZINCITE	**CEIKOST**	COKIEST
CEHRRSU	CRUSHER	**CEIIOPZ**	EPIZOIC	**CEIKOTT**	KETOTIC
CEHRSSU	CRUSHES	**CEIIPPR**	PIPERIC	**CEIKPRR**	PRICKER
CEHRSTT	STRETCH	**CEIIPRR**	PRICIER	**CEIKPRS**	PICKERS
CEHRSTY	SCYTHER	**CEIIPRS**	SPICIER		RIPECKS
CEHSSTU	TUSCHES	**CEIIPRT**	PICRITE		SPICKER
CEHSSTY	SCYTHES	**CEIIPST**	EPICIST	**CEIKPRT**	PRICKET

CEIKPRY	PICKERY	**CEILPSS**	SPLICES		NEPOTIC
CEIKPST	PICKETS	**CEILPSU**	SPICULE	**CEINORR**	CORNIER
	SKEPTIC	**CEILPSV**	PELVICS	**CEINORS**	COINERS
CEIKQRU	QUICKER	**CEILQSU**	CLIQUES		CRINOSE
CEIKRRS	RICKERS	**CEILQUY**	CLIQUEY		CRONIES
CEIKRRT	TRICKER	**CEILRRU**	CURLIER		ORCEINS
CEIKRSS	SCRIKES	**CEILRSS**	SLICERS		ORCINES
CEIKRST	RICKETS	**CEILRST**	RELICTS		RECOINS
	STICKER	**CEILRSU**	CURLIES		SERICON
	TICKERS	**CEILRSV**	CLIVERS	**CEINORT**	COINTER
CEIKRSU	SUCKIER	**CEILRSY**	CLERISY		NOTICER
CEIKRSW	WICKERS	**CEILRTT**	CLITTER		RECTION
CEIKRSY	RICKEYS	**CEILRTU**	CULTIER	**CEINORU**	COENURI
	YICKERS		UTRICLE		NOURICE
CEIKRTU	TRUCKIE	**CEILSSS**	SCISSEL	**CEINORV**	CORVINE
CEIKRTY	RICKETY	**CEILSSU**	SLUICES	**CEINORY**	ORIENCY
CEIKRUY	YUCKIER	**CEILSTU**	LUCITES	**CEINOSS**	CESSION
CEIKSST	SICKEST		LUETICS		COSINES
CEIKSTT	TICKETS	**CEILTTU**	CUITTLE		OSCINES
CEIKSTW	WICKETS	**CEIMMOS**	COMMIES	**CEINOST**	NOTICES
CEIKSTY	TICKEYS	**CEIMMRR**	CRIMMER		SECTION
CEILLMS	MICELLS	**CEIMMRU**	CRUMMIE	**CEINOSV**	NOVICES
CEILLNO	LIONCEL	**CEIMNNO**	MECONIN	**CEINOTT**	ENTOTIC
CEILLNU	NUCELLI	**CEIMNOR**	INCOMER		TONETIC
CEILLOR	COLLIER	**CEIMNOS**	COSMINE	**CEINOTX**	EXCITON
CEILLOS	COLLIES		INCOMES	**CEINOUV**	UNVOICE
CEILLST	CELLIST		MESONIC	**CEINOVV**	CONVIVE
CEILLSU	CULLIES	**CEIMNOT**	CENTIMO	**CEINPRS**	CRISPEN
CEILMOP	COMPILE		ENTOMIC		PINCERS
	POLEMIC		TONEMIC		PRINCES
CEILMOT	TELOMIC	**CEIMNRS**	CREMSIN	**CEINPRY**	CYPRINE
CEILMPR	CRIMPLE		MINCERS	**CEINPST**	INCEPTS
CEILNNU	NUCLEIN	**CEIMNRU**	MINCEUR		INSPECT
CEILNOP	PINOCLE		NUMERIC		PECTINS
	PLEONIC	**CEIMNYZ**	ENZYMIC		PEINCTS
CEILNOS	CINEOLS	**CEIMOOR**	COOMIER	**CEINPTY**	PYCNITE
	CONSEIL	**CEIMOPR**	MEROPIC	**CEINQSU**	CINQUES
	INCLOSE	**CEIMOPT**	METOPIC		QUINCES
CEILNOT	LECTION	**CEIMOQU**	COMIQUE	**CEINRRU**	CURNIER
CEILNOX	LEXICON	**CEIMORR**	MORRICE		REINCUR
CEILNPS	PENCILS	**CEIMORT**	MORTICE	**CEINRSS**	SCRINES
	SPLENIC	**CEIMOSX**	EXOSMIC	**CEINRST**	CISTERN
CEILNST	CLIENTS	**CEIMOTT**	TOTEMIC		CRETINS
	LECTINS	**CEIMOTV**	VICOMTE	**CEINRSV**	CRIVENS
	STENCIL	**CEIMOTX**	TOXEMIC	**CEINRSW**	WINCERS
CEILNSU	LEUCINS	**CEIMOUZ**	ZOECIUM	**CEINRTT**	CITTERN
CEILNTU	CUTLINE	**CEIMPRR**	CRIMPER	**CEINRUV**	INCURVE
	LINECUT	**CEIMPRS**	SPERMIC	**CEINSST**	INCESTS
	TUNICLE	**CEIMPRU**	PUMICER		INSECTS
CEILOOS	COOLIES	**CEIMPSU**	PUMICES	**CEINSSU**	INCUSES
CEILOPR	PELORIC	**CEIMRST**	CRETISM	**CEINSTU**	NEUSTIC
	POLICER		METRICS	**CEINSTY**	CYSTEIN
CEILOPS	POLICES	**CEIMRSU**	CERIUMS		CYSTINE
CEILOPT	TOECLIP		MURICES	**CEINSWY**	WINCEYS
CEILORS	COILERS	**CEIMSSU**	CESIUMS	**CEINTTX**	EXTINCT
	RECOILS		MISCUES	**CEINVVY**	VIVENCY
CEILORT	CORTILE	**CEINNOS**	CONINES	**CEIOOPR**	OPORICE
CEILORU	URCEOLI	**CEINNOV**	CONNIVE	**CEIOORS**	COORIES
CEILOSS	OSSICLE	**CEINNST**	INCENTS	**CEIOOST**	COOTIES
CEILOST	CITOLES	**CEINOOT**	COONTIE	**CEIOPPR**	CROPPIE
CEILOTT	COLETIT	**CEINOPR**	PERICON	**CEIOPPS**	COPPIES
CEILPPR	CLIPPER		PONCIER	**CEIOPRS**	COPIERS
	CRIPPLE		PORCINE		COPSIER
CEILPRS	SPLICER	**CEINOPT**	ENTOPIC		PERSICO

CEIOPST	POETICS	**CEIRRUV**	CURVIER	**CEKNOST**	NOCKETS
CEIOPSU	PICEOUS	**CEIRSSU**	CRUISES	**CEKNRWY**	WRYNECK
CEIOPSW	COWPIES		CRUSIES	**CEKNSSU**	SUCKENS
CEIORRS	CIRROSE		CUISSER	**CEKOOPR**	PRECOOK
	CORRIES	**CEIRSSV**	SCRIVES	**CEKOOPW**	COWPOKE
	CROSIER	**CEIRSTT**	TRISECT	**CEKOORR**	CROOKER
	ORRICES	**CEIRSTU**	CUITERS	**CEKOORS**	COOKERS
CEIORRU	COURIER		CURIETS		RECOOKS
CEIORRZ	CROZIER		CURITES	**CEKOORY**	COOKERY
CEIORSS	COSIERS		ICTERUS	**CEKOOSY**	COOKEYS
	CRIOSES	**CEIRSTW**	TWICERS	**CEKOPRR**	PREROCK
CEIORST	EROTICS	**CEIRSUV**	CRUIVES	**CEKOPST**	POCKETS
	TERCIOS		CURSIVE	**CEKORRS**	CORKERS
CEIORSU	COURIES	**CEIRSUZ**	CRUZIES		RECORKS
	SCOURIE	**CEIRTTU**	CUTTIER		ROCKERS
CEIORSV	CORSIVE	**CEIRTTX**	TECTRIX	**CEKORRY**	ROCKERY
	VOICERS	**CEISSSU**	CUISSES	**CEKORST**	RESTOCK
CEIORSW	COWRIES	**CEISSTU**	CESTUIS		ROCKETS
	SCOWRIE		CUEISTS		STOCKER
CEIORSZ	COZIERS		CUTISES	**CEKORTW**	TWOCKER
CEIORTT	COTTIER		ICTUSES	**CEKOSST**	SOCKETS
CEIORTV	EVICTOR	**CEISTTU**	CUTTIES	**CEKPRSU**	PUCKERS
CEIORTW	COWRITE	**CEJKNOY**	JOCKNEY	**CEKPRSY**	RYPECKS
CEIORTX	EXCITOR	**CEJKOSY**	JOCKEYS	**CEKPRUY**	PUCKERY
	XEROTIC	**CEJNOOS**	COJONES	**CEKRRTU**	TRUCKER
CEIORVY	VICEROY	**CEJNORU**	CONJURE	**CEKRSSU**	SUCKERS
CEIOSSS	COSSIES	**CEJNOSU**	JOUNCES	**CEKRSTU**	TUCKERS
CEIOSST	COSIEST		JUNCOES	**CEKRSUY**	YUCKERS
	COTISES	**CEJOPRT**	PROJECT	**CEKSSTU**	SUCKETS
	OECISTS	**CEKKLNU**	KNUCKLE	**CEKSTTU**	TUCKETS
CEIOSSU	CESIOUS	**CEKKNOR**	KNOCKER	**CELLMOU**	COLUMEL
CEIOSSV	VISCOSE	**CEKKOPS**	KOPECKS	**CELLNOO**	COLONEL
CEIOSTT	COTTISE	**CEKLLOP**	PELLOCK	**CELLORS**	ESCROLL
	SCOTTIE	**CEKLLRY**	CLERKLY	**CELLOST**	COLLETS
CEIOSTV	COSTIVE	**CEKLMNO**	LOCKMEN	**CELLOSU**	LOCULES
CEIOSTW	COWIEST	**CEKLMSU**	MUCKLES		OCELLUS
CEIOSTX	COEXIST	**CEKLNOS**	ENLOCKS	**CELLOSY**	CLOSELY
	COXIEST		SLOCKEN	**CELLRRU**	CRULLER
	EXOTICS	**CEKLNRU**	CLUNKER	**CELLRSU**	CRUELLS
CEIOSTY	SOCIETY		CRUNKLE		CULLERS
CEIOSTZ	COZIEST	**CEKLORS**	LOCKERS		SCULLER
CEIPPRU	CUPPIER		RELOCKS	**CELLRUY**	CRUELLY
CEIPPST	PEPTICS	**CEKLOST**	LOCKETS	**CELLSSU**	SCULLES
CEIPQTU	PICQUET		LOCKSET	**CELLSTU**	CULLETS
CEIPRRS	CRISPER	**CEKLOTY**	TOCKLEY	**CELMMSU**	MESCLUM
	PRICERS	**CEKLPRU**	PLUCKER	**CELMNOO**	LOCOMEN
CEIPRSS	SPICERS	**CEKLPSU**	PUCKLES		MONOCLE
CEIPRST	TRICEPS	**CEKLRSU**	RUCKLES	**CELMNSU**	CULMENS
CEIPRSY	SPICERY		SCULKER		MESCLUN
CEIPRTU	CUPRITE		SUCKLER	**CELMOOS**	COELOMS
	PICTURE	**CEKLRTU**	TRUCKLE	**CELMOPS**	COMPELS
CEIPRTY	PYRETIC	**CEKLSSU**	SUCKLES	**CELMOPX**	COMPLEX
CEIPRXY	PYREXIC	**CEKMNOS**	SOCKMEN	**CELMORS**	CORMELS
CEIPSSS	SCEPSIS	**CEKMNOY**	MOCKNEY	**CELMPRU**	CLUMPER
CEIPSST	CESSPIT	**CEKMNRU**	RUCKMEN		CRUMPLE
	SEPTICS	**CEKMORS**	MOCKERS	**CELMSSU**	MUSCLES
CEIQRSU	CIRQUES	**CEKMORY**	MOCKERY	**CELMSUU**	SECULUM
CEIRRRU	CURRIER	**CEKMRSU**	MUCKERS	**CELMSUY**	LYCEUMS
CEIRRSU	CRUISER	**CEKNNSU**	UNSNECK	**CELMTUU**	CUMULET
	CURRIES	**CEKNOOV**	CONVOKE	**CELNNOU**	NUCLEON
	SUCRIER	**CEKNORR**	CRONKER	**CELNNSU**	NUNCLES
CEIRRTT	CRITTER	**CEKNORS**	CONKERS	**CELNOOR**	CORONEL
CEIRRTU	RECRUIT		RECKONS	**CELNOOS**	COLONES
CEIRRTX	RECTRIX	**CEKNORT**	TROCKEN		CONSOLE

CELNORS	CLONERS		RELUCTS	**CENOORS**	CEROONS
	CORNELS	**CELRSTY**	CLYSTER	**CENOORT**	CORONET
CELNOSU	COUNSEL	**CELRSUV**	CULVERS	**CENOOSS**	COOSENS
	UNCLOSE	**CELRSUW**	CURLEWS	**CENOPRS**	CREPONS
CELNOTU	NOCTULE	**CELRTTU**	CLUTTER	**CENOPRU**	POUNCER
CELNRSU	LUCERNS	**CELRTUU**	CULTURE	**CENOPSU**	POUNCES
CELNRTU	LECTURN	**CELRTUV**	CULVERT		UNCOPES
CELNSUU	NUCLEUS	**CELRTUY**	CRUELTY	**CENOPSY**	SYNCOPE
	NUCULES		CUTLERY	**CENOPTU**	POUNCET
CELNSUW	UNCLEWS	**CELSTTU**	CUTLETS	**CENOPTY**	POTENCY
CELOOPR	PRECOOL		CUTTLES	**CENOQRU**	CONQUER
CELOORR	COLORER		SCUTTLE	**CENORRS**	CORNERS
	RECOLOR	**CEMMNOT**	COMMENT		SCORNER
CELOORS	COOLERS	**CEMMNOU**	COMMUNE	**CENORRW**	CROWNER
	CREOSOL	**CEMMOOT**	COMMOTE		RECROWN
CELOOST	COOLEST	**CEMMOOV**	COMMOVE	**CENORSS**	CENSORS
	OCELOTS	**CEMMORS**	COMMERS	**CENORST**	CONSTER
CELOPPS	COPPLES	**CEMMOTU**	COMMUTE		CORNETS
CELOPRU	COUPLER	**CEMMRSU**	CUMMERS		CRESTON
CELOPSU	CLOSEUP		SCUMMER		CRONETS
	COUPLES	**CEMNNOT**	CONTEMN	**CENORSU**	CONURES
	OPUSCLE	**CEMNOOP**	COMPONE		ROUNCES
	UPCLOSE	**CEMNOOS**	ONCOMES	**CENORTT**	CORNETT
CELOPTU	COUPLET	**CEMNOOY**	ECONOMY	**CENORTU**	CORNUTE
	OCTUPLE		MONOECY		COUNTER
CELOQSU	CLOQUES	**CEMNOSU**	CONSUME		RECOUNT
CELORRU	CORULER		MUSCONE		TROUNCE
CELORSS	CLOSERS	**CEMNRSU**	CRUMENS	**CENORTV**	CONVERT
	CRESOLS	**CEMNRTU**	CENTRUM	**CENORTW**	CROWNET
	ESCROLS	**CEMNSTU**	CENTUMS	**CENORUV**	UNCOVER
CELORST	COLTERS	**CEMOOPS**	COMPOSE	**CENOSSY**	COYNESS
	CORSLET	**CEMOOPT**	COMPOTE	**CENOSTT**	CONTEST
	COSTREL	**CEMOOTU**	OUTCOME	**CENOSTU**	CONTUSE
	LECTORS	**CEMOPRS**	COMPERS		ECONUTS
CELORSU	CLOSURE	**CEMOPRT**	COMPTER		UNCOEST
	COLURES	**CEMOPST**	COEMPTS	**CENOSTV**	COVENTS
CELORSV	CLOVERS	**CEMOPSU**	UPCOMES	**CENOSVY**	CONVEYS
	VELCROS	**CEMOPTU**	COMPUTE		COVYNES
CELORSW	SCOWLER	**CEMORRS**	CREMORS	**CENOTTX**	CONTEXT
	SCROWLE	**CEMORSS**	SCROMES	**CENPRTY**	ENCRYPT
CELORSY	SCROYLE	**CEMOSSU**	COMUSES	**CENPTUX**	EXPUNCT
CELORTT	CLOTTER		MUSCOSE	**CENRRTU**	CURRENT
	CROTTLE	**CEMOSSY**	MYCOSES	**CENRSSY**	SCRYNES
CELORTU	CLOTURE	**CEMOSTU**	COSTUME	**CENRSTU**	ENCRUST
	CLOUTER	**CEMPRRU**	CRUMPER	**CENRSUU**	UNCURSE
	COULTER	**CEMPRTU**	CRUMPET	**CENRSUW**	UNSCREW
CELORVY	CLOVERY	**CEMRRUY**	MERCURY	**CENRTUV**	CENTURY
CELOSST	CLOSEST	**CEMRSTU**	RECTUMS	**CENSSTY**	ENCYSTS
	CLOSETS	**CEMSSUU**	MUCUSES	**CEOOPRS**	COOPERS
CELOSSU	OSCULES	**CEMSTTU**	TECTUMS		SCOOPER
CELOSSX	COXLESS	**CENNOOR**	NONCORE	**CEOOPRY**	COOPERY
CELOSTY	COTYLES	**CENNOOS**	NEOCONS	**CEOORSS**	COOSERS
CELOSUV	VOCULES	**CENNOOT**	CONNOTE		ROSCOES
CELOTTU	CULOTTE	**CENNORS**	CONNERS	**CEOORST**	COOTERS
CELPRSU	CURPELS	**CENNOST**	CONSENT		SCOOTER
	SCRUPLE		NOCENTS	**CEOORSV**	CROOVES
CELPSUU	CUPULES	**CENNOTT**	CONTENT	**CEOORTU**	ECOTOUR
CELPSUY	CLYPEUS	**CENNOTV**	CONVENT	**CEOORTW**	COWROTE
CELRRSU	CURLERS	**CENNRSU**	CUNNERS	**CEOORVY**	OVERCOY
CELRSSY	CRESYLS		SCUNNER	**CEOOSTY**	COYOTES
CELRSTU	CLUSTER	**CENOOPS**	POCOSEN		OOCYTES
	CULTERS		POONCES	**CEOPPRR**	CROPPER
	CUSTREL	**CENOORR**	CORONER	**CEOPPRS**	COPPERS
	CUTLERS		CROONER	**CEOPPRU**	PRECOUP

CEOPPRY	COPPERY	**CEPPRRU**	CRUPPER	**CFILORS**	FROLICS
CEOPRRS	SCORPER	**CEPPRSU**	CUPPERS	**CFILORU**	FLUORIC
CEOPRRT	PORRECT		SCUPPER	**CFIMNOR**	CONFIRM
CEOPRRU	CROUPER	**CEPRRSU**	SPRUCER	**CFIMOST**	COMFITS
	PROCURE	**CEPRSSU**	PERCUSS	**CFINORY**	CORNIFY
CEOPRSS	CORPSES		SPRUCES	**CFINOST**	CONFITS
	PROCESS	**CEPRSSY**	CYPRESS	**CFIORST**	FICTORS
CEOPRST	COPTERS	**CEPRSTU**	PRECUTS	**CFIORSY**	SCORIFY
	PROSECT	**CEPRSTY**	SCEPTRY	**CFIRSTU**	FRUICTS
CEOPRSU	COUPERS	**CEPRSUW**	SCREWUP	**CFISSTU**	FUSTICS
	CROUPES	**CEPRUUV**	UPCURVE	**CFKLLOU**	LOCKFUL
	RECOUPS	**CEPSSTU**	SUSPECT	**CFKNORU**	UNFROCK
CEOPRTT	PROTECT	**CERRSSU**	CURSERS	**CFKOTTU**	FUTTOCK
CEOPRUU	COUPURE	**CERRSSY**	SCRYERS	**CFKPSUU**	FUCKUPS
CEOPRUV	COVERUP	**CERRSSU**	CUSSERS	**CFLMRUU**	FULCRUM
CEOPSTY	COTYPES	**CERRSTU**	CRUSETS	**CFLNORY**	CORNFLY
CEOQRTU	CROQUET	**CERRSUZ**	SCRUZES	**CFLNOOU**	CONFLUX
	ROCQUET	**CERSTTU**	CURTEST	**CFLNOUY**	FLOUNCY
CEOQSTU	COQUETS		CUTTERS	**CFLOOPW**	COWFLOP
CEORRSS	CROSSER		SCUTTER	**CFLOPRU**	CROPFUL
	RECROSS	**CERSTUV**	CURVETS	**CFLPSUU**	CUPFULS
	SCORERS	**CERSTUY**	CURTESY		CUPSFUL
	SCORSER		CURTSEY	**CFMNOOR**	CONFORM
CEORRST	RECTORS	**CESSUZZ**	SCUZZES	**CFMOORT**	COMFORT
CEORRSU	COURSER	**CFFFKOU**	FUCKOFF	**CFNORTU**	FUNCTOR
	CRUORES	**CFFGINO**	COFFING	**CFOSSTU**	FUSTOCS
	SCOURER	**CFFGINU**	CUFFING	**CFOSSUU**	FUSCOUS
CEORRSW	CROWERS	**CFFHINO**	CHIFFON	**CGGGINO**	COGGING
	SCOWRER	**CFFIIRT**	TRIFFIC	**CGGIINR**	GRICING
CEORRSY	SORCERY	**CFFIKKO**	KICKOFF	**CGGORSY**	SCROGGY
CEORRSZ	CROZERS	**CFFIKOP**	PICKOFF	**CGHHOSU**	CHOUGHS
CEORRTU	COURTER	**CFFILSS**	SCLIFFS	**CGHIILM**	MILCHIG
CEORRTY	RECTORY	**CFFINOS**	COFFINS	**CGHIIMN**	CHIMING
CEORSSS	CROSSES	**CFFINSU**	CUFFINS		MICHING
	SCORSES	**CFFKOOO**	COOKOFF	**CGHIINN**	CHINING
CEORSST	CORSETS	**CFFMOSU**	OFFSCUM		INCHING
	COSTERS	**CFFNSUU**	UNCUFFS		NICHING
	ESCORTS	**CFFOSTU**	CUTOFFS	**CGHIINR**	RICHING
	SCOTERS		OFFCUTS	**CGHIINT**	ITCHING
	SCROTES	**CFFRSSU**	SCRUFFS	**CGHIINV**	CHIVING
	SECTORS	**CFFRSUY**	SCRUFFY	**CGHIKNO**	CHOKING
CEORSSU	COURSES	**CFGIINO**	COIFING		HOCKING
	SCOURSE	**CFGIKNU**	FUCKING	**CGHILPY**	GLYPHIC
	SCOUSER	**CFGINOR**	FORCING	**CGHILTY**	GLITCHY
	SOURCES	**CFHILYY**	CHYLIFY	**CGHINNO**	CHIGNON
	SUCROSE	**CFHIMYY**	CHYMIFY	**CGHINOR**	CHORING
CEORSSW	ESCROWS	**CFHINSU**	FUCHSIN		OCHRING
CEORSSY	CORSEYS	**CFHIOSW**	COWFISH	**CGHINOS**	COSHING
CEORSTT	COTTERS	**CFHIRST**	FRICHTS	**CGHINOU**	OUCHING
CEORSTU	COUTERS	**CFHORTU**	FUTHORC	**CGHINOW**	CHOWING
	CROUTES	**CFIIIMR**	MIRIFIC	**CGHINRU**	RUCHING
	SCOUTER	**CFIIIVV**	VIVIFIC	**CGHINSU**	CHUSING
CEORSTV	CORVETS	**CFIIKNY**	FINICKY	**CGHINTU**	CHUTING
	COVERTS	**CFIILNT**	INFLICT	**CGHIOST**	GOTHICS
	VECTORS	**CFIIMNO**	OMNIFIC	**CGHIOSY**	GOYISCH
CEORTUU	COUTURE	**CFIIMOT**	MOTIFIC	**CGHLNOS**	SCHLONG
CEORTUV	COUVERT	**CFIIMRY**	MICRIFY	**CGHLOSU**	CLOUGHS
	CUTOVER	**CFIINOT**	FICTION	**CGHOORT**	TORGOCH
	OVERCUT	**CFIINOY**	ICONIFY	**CGHORUY**	GROUCHY
CEOSSST	COSSETS	**CFIINYZ**	ZINCIFY	**CGIIJNU**	JUICING
CEOSSSU	SCOUSES	**CFIIOSS**	OSSIFIC	**CGIIKKN**	KICKING
CEOSSSY	SYCOSES	**CFIKNNO**	FINNOCK	**CGIIKLN**	LICKING
CEOSTTT	OCTETTS	**CFIKOSS**	FOSSICK	**CGIIKMM**	GIMMICK
CEOSTTU	CUTTOES	**CFIKTUW**	FUCKWIT	**CGIIKNN**	NICKING

CGIIKNP	PICKING	CGIMNOP	COMPING	CHHRTTU	THRUTCH
CGIIKNR	RICKING	CGIMNOR	CROMING	CHIIILO	CHILIOI
CGIIKNS	SICKING	CGIMNOS	COMINGS	CHIIKLM	MILCHIK
CGIIKNT	TICKING	CGINNNO	CONNING	CHIIKMS	KIMCHIS
CGIIKNW	WICKING	CGINNNU	CUNNING	CHIIKNN	KINCHIN
CGIILLO	ILLOGIC	CGINNOP	PONCING	CHIIKSS	SICKISH
CGIILNO	COILING	CGINNOR	CORNING	CHIILLS	CHILLIS
CGIILNP	CLIPING	CGINNOS	CONSIGN	CHIILNT	CHITLIN
CGIILNS	SLICING	CGINNPU	PUNCING	CHIILOT	THIOLIC
CGIIMNN	MINCING	CGINNSY	SYNCING	CHIILST	LITCHIS
CGIIMNR	CRIMING	CGINOOP	COOPING	CHIILTY	ITCHILY
CGIINNO	COINING	CGINOOS	COOINGS	CHIIMST	ISTHMIC
CGIINNR	CRINING	CGINOPP	COPPING	CHIIMSU	ISCHIUM
CGIINNW	WINCING	CGINOPS	COPINGS	CHIINNP	INCHPIN
CGIINNZ	ZINCING		COPSING	CHIINOT	THIONIC
CGIINOR	GIRONIC		PICONGS	CHIINST	CHITINS
CGIINOV	VOICING		SCOPING	CHIIOPT	OPHITIC
CGIINPR	PRICING	CGINOPU	COUPING	CHIIOST	STICHOI
CGIINPS	SPICING	CGINOPW	COWPING	CHIIRRS	SCIRRHI
CGIINRT	TRICING	CGINOPY	COPYING	CHIKLLO	HILLOCK
CGIINSS	CISSING	CGINORS	SCORING	CHIKLTY	THICKLY
CGIKLNO	CLOKING	CGINORU	COURING	CHIKNOO	CHINOOK
	LOCKING	CGINORW	CROWING	CHIKORS	CHIKORS
CGIKLNU	LUCKING	CGINORY	GYRONIC		CHOKRIS
CGIKMNO	MOCKING	CGINOSS	COSIGNS	CHIKORY	HICKORY
CGIKMNU	MUCKING	CGINOST	COSTING	CHIKOST	THICKOS
CGIKNNO	CONKING		GNOSTIC	CHIKPSU	PUCKISH
	NOCKING	CGINOSU	CONGIUS	CHIKRSS	SCHRIKS
CGIKNOO	COOKING		SOUCING	CHIKSST	SCHTIKS
CGIKNOP	POCKING	CGINOSV	COVINGS		SHTICKS
CGIKNOR	CORKING	CGINOSW	SCOWING	CHIKSTY	KITSCHY
	ROCKING		SOWCING		SHTICKY
CGIKNOS	SOCKING	CGINOSY	COSYING	CHILLMU	CHILLUM
CGIKNOT	TOCKING	CGINOTT	COTTING	CHILLTY	LICHTLY
CGIKNOW	COWKING	CGINOYZ	COZYING	CHILNOO	HOLONIC
CGIKNOY	YOCKING	CGINPPU	CUPPING	CHILNOR	CHLORIN
CGIKNPU	KINGCUP	CGINRRU	CURRING	CHILNSY	LYCHNIS
	PUCKING	CGINRSU	CURSING	CHILOOS	COOLISH
CGIKNRU	RUCKING	CGINRSY	CRYINGS	CHILORS	ORCHILS
CGIKNSU	SUCKING		SCRYING	CHILORT	TROCHIL
CGIKNTU	TUCKING	CGINRTU	TRUCING	CHILOST	COLTISH
CGIKNUY	YUCKING	CGINRUV	CURVING	CHILPSY	SYLPHIC
CGILLNO	COLLING	CGINSSU	CUSSING	CHILSTU	CULTISH
CGILLNU	CULLING		SCUSING	CHILSUY	CUSHILY
CGILMNU	CULMING	CGINTTU	CUTTING	CHIMMOR	MICROHM
CGILMNY	CYMLING	CGIOOOS	GIOCOSO	CHIMNPY	NYMPHIC
CGILNNO	CLONING	CGIOOST	COGITOS	CHIMOPR	MORPHIC
CGILNNU	UNCLING	CGIOTYZ	ZYGOTIC	CHIMORS	CHORISM
CGILNOO	COOLING	CGKLNOU	GUNLOCK		CHRISOM
	LOCOING	CGLLOSY	GLYCOLS	CHIMRRY	MYRRHIC
CGILNOS	CLOSING	CGLLSYY	GLYCYLS	CHIMRSS	CHRISMS
CGILNOT	COLTING	CGLNOSU	UNCLOGS	CHIMSSS	SCHISMS
CGILNOW	COWLING	CGLOOSU	COLUGOS	CHIMSTY	CHYMIST
CGILNOY	CLOYING	CGNOOSU	CONGOUS		TYCHISM
CGILNPY	CLYPING	CGOORRW	GORCROW	CHINOOR	CHORION
CGILNRU	CURLING	CHHIIKS	HICKISH	CHINOPS	CHOPINS
CGILNSY	GLYCINS	CHHIKOR	CHIKHOR		PHONICS
CGILOOO	OOLOGIC	CHHINOR	RHONCHI	CHINOPY	CIPHONY
CGILORW	COWGIRL	CHHINTU	UNHITCH	CHINORS	CRONISH
CGILOTT	GLOTTIC	CHHIRST	SHRITCH	CHINOST	CHITONS
CGILPSU	GILCUPS	CHHISST	SHTCHIS	CHINOSU	CUSHION
CGILPTU	GILTCUP	CHHISTY	ICHTHYS	CHINPSY	HYPNICS
CGILPTY	GLYPTIC	CHHLOTU	LUCHOTH	CHINQSU	SQUINCH
CGIMNOO	COOMING	CHHNOOS	HONCHOS	CHINRSU	URCHINS

CHINSTY	SNITCHY	CHNOORT	TORCHON		MISTICO
CHINTUW	UNWITCH	CHNORRS	SCHNORR		SOMITIC
CHINTYZ	CHINTZY	CHNORSY	SYNCHRO	CIIMOTT	MITOTIC
CHIOOPR	POCHOIR	CHNORTU	COTHURN	CIIMOTV	MOTIVIC
CHIOORS	ISOCHOR	CHNOSZZ	SCHNOZZ	CIIMRST	TRISMIC
CHIOORZ	CHORIZO	CHNOTUU	UNCOUTH	CIIMSSV	CIVISMS
CHIOPRT	TROPHIC	CHNSTUU	TUCHUNS	CIIMSTV	VICTIMS
CHIOPST	PHOTICS	CHOOPPS	COPSHOP	CIINNOT	NICOTIN
CHIOPXY	HYPOXIC	CHOORST	COHORTS	CIINNTU	TUNICIN
CHIORST	CHORIST	CHOORSU	OCHROUS	CIINOOT	COITION
	OSTRICH	CHOOSST	COHOSTS	CIINOPR	PORCINI
CHIORSW	CHOWRIS	CHOPSSY	PSYCHOS	CIINOPS	PSIONIC
CHIOSST	STICHOS	CHOPTUU	TOUCHUP	CIINORS	INCISOR
CHIOSSZ	SCHIZOS	CHORRSU	CHURROS	CIINORT	NORITIC
CHIPRRU	CHIRRUP	CHORSTU	TROCHUS		TIRONIC
CHIPRRY	PYRRHIC	CHOSSTU	SCHOUTS	CIINPRS	CRISPIN
CHIPSSY	PHYSICS		SCOUTHS	CIINQTU	QUINTIC
CHIQSTU	SQUITCH	CHOSSTW	SCOWTHS	CIINRST	CITRINS
CHIRRSU	CURRISH	CHPSSUY	SCYPHUS	CIINRSU	RICINUS
CHIRSTY	CHRISTY	CHRRSUU	CHURRUS	CIINSSV	VISCINS
CHISSST	SCHISTS	CHSSTUY	SCHUYTS	CIINTUV	UNICITY
CHISSTU	SCHUITS	CIIILLT	ILLICIT	CIIORST	SORITIC
CHISTTU	CHUTIST		ILLITIC	CIIOSTX	COXITIS
CHISTWY	SWITCHY	CIIILNV	INCIVIL	CIIOSUV	VICIOUS
CHISYZZ	SCHIZZY	CIIIMNR	CRIMINI	CIIPRSS	SPIRICS
CHITTWY	TWITCHY	CIIINPT	INCIPIT	CIIPRTY	PYRITIC
CHKLOOO	HOOLOCK	CIIJLUY	JUICILY	CIIRSTV	VITRICS
CHKLOOT	KLOOTCH	CIIKKLL	KILLICK	CIIRTVX	VICTRIX
CHKLOSS	SHLOCKS	CIIKKMS	MISKICK	CIJKORS	CROJIKS
CHKLOSY	SHLOCKY	CIIKLPY	PICKILY	CIJNNOO	CONJOIN
	SHYLOCK	CIIKMMM	MIMMICK	CIJNNTU	INJUNCT
CHKMMOO	HOMMOCK	CIIKMNN	MINNICK	CIJNOOS	COJOINS
CHKMMOU	HUMMOCK	CIIKNPS	PICKINS	CIKKLLO	KILLOCK
CHKMOSS	SHMOCKS	CIIKNPT	NITPICK	CIKKOPT	TOPKICK
CHKMSSU	SHMUCKS	CIIKNSW	INWICKS	CIKKOTU	OUTKICK
CHKNOOS	SCHNOOK	CIIKNTU	CUTIKIN	CIKKPSU	KICKUPS
CHKOOST	SCHTOOK	CIIKPUW	WICKIUP	CIKLLOP	PILLOCK
CHKORSU	CHUKORS	CIIKSST	TISICKS	CIKLLOR	ROLLICK
CHKPTUU	PUTCHUK	CIIKSTT	STICKIT	CIKLLOS	SILLOCK
CHKSSTU	SHTUCKS	CIILLTY	LICITLY	CIKLLOW	KILLCOW
CHLMOOS	MOLOCHS	CIILLVY	CIVILLY	CIKLLSY	SLICKLY
CHLMORV	CHROMYL	CIILNOP	CIPOLIN	CIKLLUY	LUCKILY
CHLMPSU	SCHLUMP		PICOLIN	CIKLMSU	MISLUCK
CHLOOSS	SCHOOLS	CIILNOS	SILICON	CIKLMSY	SMICKLY
CHLOOST	COOLTHS	CIILNPS	INCLIPS	CIKLMUY	MUCKILY
CHLOPST	SPLOTCH	CIILNUV	UNCIVIL	CIKLNOS	INLOCKS
CHLORSS	SCHORLS	CIILNVY	VINYLIC	CIKLNRY	CRINKLY
CHLORTY	CHOLTRY	CIILOOT	OOLITIC	CIKLNSU	UNSLICK
CHLOSSS	SCHLOSS	CIILOPT	POLITIC	CIKLOOO	OLICOOK
CHLOSUY	CHYLOUS	CIILORT	CORTILI	CIKLOPY	POCKILY
	SLOUCHY	CIILOST	COLITIS	CIKLOPZ	ZIPLOCK
CHLOTYZ	ZLOTYCH		SOLICIT	CIKLORY	ROCKILY
CHLSTUY	SLUTCHY	CIILOTT	LITOTIC	CIKLPRY	PRICKLY
CHMOORS	CHROMOS	CIILPRY	PRICILY	CIKLQUY	QUICKLY
CHMOOSS	SCHMOOS	CIILPSY	SPICILY	CIKLRTY	TRICKLY
CHMOOST	SCHTOOM	CIILSSS	SCISSIL	CIKLSTU	LUSTICK
CHMOOSY	SMOOCHY	CIILSSV	SILVICS	CIKMNNO	MINNOCK
CHMOOSZ	SCHMOOZ	CIIMMNO	MINICOM	CIKMNSU	NICKUMS
CHMOSUY	CHYMOUS	CIIMMRY	MIMICRY	CIKMOOS	MISCOOK
CHMSTUY	SMUTCHY	CIIMNNO	NIMONIC	CIKMORR	RIMROCK
CHNNOOR	CHRONON	CIIMNOS	MISCOIN	CIKMSSU	MUSICKS
CHNNOSU	NONSUCH	CIIMNOT	MICTION	CIKMSTU	STICKUM
CHNOOPS	PONCHOS	CIIMNRY	CRIMINY	CIKNNOP	PINNOCK
CHNOORS	COHORNS	CIIMOST	MIOTICS	CIKNNOW	WINNOCK

CIKNOSW	COWSKIN	**CIMNOOR**	MORONIC	**CIOQRSU**	CROQUIS
CIKNPSU	UNPICKS		OMICRON	**CIORRSU**	CIRROUS
CIKNPSY	PYKNICS	**CIMNORS**	CRIMSON	**CIORSSS**	SCISSOR
CIKNPTU	NUTPICK		MICRONS	**CIORSTT**	TRICOTS
CIKNSTU	UNSTICK	**CIMNOSS**	COSMINS	**CIORSTU**	CITROUS
CIKOPPT	POCKPIT	**CIMNOSU**	CONIUMS	**CIORSTV**	VICTORS
CIKORRS	CORKIRS	**CIMNRSU**	CRINUMS	**CIORSUU**	CURIOUS
CIKOSTU	SICKOUT	**CIMOORS**	MORISCO	**CIORTVY**	VICTORY
CIKOTUW	OUTWICK	**CIMOORT**	MOTORIC	**CIOSSSY**	SYCOSIS
CIKPPSU	PICKUPS	**CIMOOST**	OSMOTIC	**CIOSSUV**	VISCOUS
CIKPSTU	STICKUP	**CIMOPSY**	COPYISM	**CIOTTUY**	OUTCITY
	UPTICKS		MISCOPY	**CIPRSST**	SCRIPTS
CIKPUWY	WICKYUP		MYOPICS	**CIPRSSU**	PRUSSIC
CIKRSST	STRICKS	**CIMORSU**	CORIUMS	**CIPRTTY**	TRYPTIC
CIKRSTY	TRICKSY	**CIMOSST**	COSMIST	**CIPRUVY**	PYRUVIC
CILLNOS	COLLINS		SITCOMS	**CIPSTTY**	STYPTIC
CILLNOU	CULLION	**CIMOSSY**	MYCOSIS	**CIRRTTU**	CRITTUR
CILLOOR	CRIOLLO	**CIMOSTY**	MYOTICS	**CIRSSTU**	RUSTICS
CILLOPY	POLLICY	**CIMOTYZ**	ZYMOTIC	**CIRSTUY**	CITRUSY
CILLRUY	CURLILY	**CIMPRSS**	SCRIMPS	**CIRTUVY**	CURVITY
CILMNOP	COMPLIN	**CIMPRSY**	SCRIMPY	**CISSTUY**	CYTISUS
CILMNOS	CLONISM	**CIMRSSU**	CRISSUM	**CJKNNOO**	JONNOCK
CILMNSY	CYMLINS	**CIMRSUU**	CURIUMS	**CJNORUY**	CONJURY
CILMOOS	LOCOISM	**CIMSSTU**	MISCUTS	**CKKLNUY**	KNUCKLY
CILMSTU	CULTISM	**CIMSSTY**	MYSTICS	**CKLLMOU**	MULLOCK
CILNOOR	ORCINOL	**CIMSSUV**	VISCUMS	**CKLLOOP**	POLLOCK
CILNOOS	CLOISON	**CINNNOU**	INCONNU	**CKLLOOR**	ROLLOCK
	SCOLION	**CINNORU**	UNICORN	**CKLLORU**	RULLOCK
CILNOPR	PILCORN	**CINNOSU**	NUNCIOS	**CKLNOSU**	UNLOCKS
CILNORY	CORNILY	**CINNOTU**	UNCTION	**CKLNOTU**	LOCKNUT
	LYRICON	**CINNSUU**	UNCINUS	**CKLNUUY**	UNLUCKY
CILNOSU	ULICONS	**CINOOPR**	PORCINO	**CKLOOOY**	OLYCOOK
	UNCOILS	**CINOOPS**	OPSONIC	**CKLOORW**	ROWLOCK
CILNOTU	LINOCUT		POCOSIN	**CKLOOTU**	LOCKOUT
CILNOXY	XYLONIC	**CINOORS**	CORONIS	**CKLOPSU**	LOCKUPS
CILNPSU	INSCULP	**CINOOSS**	COOSINS		UPLOCKS
	SCULPIN	**CINOOSV**	OVONICS	**CKLOPTU**	POTLUCK
	UNCLIPS	**CINOPPS**	COPPINS		PUTLOCK
CILNPTU	UNCLIPT	**CINOPRX**	PRINCOX	**CKMMMOU**	MUMMOCK
CILNSTU	LINCTUS	**CINORRT**	TRICORN	**CKMOPSU**	MOCKUPS
CILOOPT	COPILOT	**CINORSS**	INCROSS	**CKNOOOR**	ROCKOON
CILOORU	COULOIR	**CINORST**	CISTRON	**CKNORSU**	UNCORKS
CILOOSS	COLOSSI		CITRONS	**CKNOSTU**	UNSTOCK
CILOOST	SCIOLTO		CORNIST	**CKNSTUU**	UNSTUCK
CILOPRW	PILCROW		CORTINS		UNTUCKS
CILOPRY	PYLORIC	**CINORSZ**	ZIRCONS	**CKOOOPT**	COOKTOP
CILOPSU	OILCUPS	**CINORTU**	RUCTION	**CKOOOTU**	COOKOUT
	UPCOILS	**CINORTY**	TYRONIC		OUTCOOK
CILOPSW	COWSLIP	**CINOSST**	CONSIST	**CKOORSU**	SOUROCK
CILORST	LICTORS		TOCSINS	**CKOORTU**	OUTROCK
CILOSTU	COUTILS	**CINOSSU**	COUSINS	**CKOPTTU**	PUTTOCK
	OCULIST	**CINOSTU**	SUCTION	**CKORTUW**	CUTWORK
CILPRSY	CRISPLY	**CINOSUZ**	COUZINS	**CKOSSTU**	TUSSOCK
CILPRTU	CULPRIT		ZINCOUS	**CKSSTUU**	TUSSUCK
CILRRSU	SCURRIL	**CINOTXY**	OXYNTIC	**CLLMOSU**	MOLLUSC
CILRSUU	SURCULI	**CINRSTU**	INCRUST	**CLLOOPS**	COLLOPS
CILRSUY	CRUSILY	**CIOOPRT**	PORTICO		SCOLLOP
CILSTTU	CULTIST		PROOTIC	**CLLORSS**	SCROLLS
CIMMNSU	CUMMINS	**CIOOPSU**	COPIOUS	**CLLOSUU**	LOCULUS
CIMMOSS	COSMISM	**CIOOQTU**	COQUITO	**CLMNOSU**	COLUMNS
CIMMOST	COMMITS	**CIOORST**	OCTROIS	**CLMOOPT**	COMPLOT
CIMMOTX	COMMIXT	**CIOORSU**	CORIOUS	**CLMOPTU**	PLUMCOT
CIMNNOS	NINCOMS	**CIOPRST**	TROPICS	**CLMOSUU**	LUCUMOS
CIMNNSU	NINCUMS	**CIOPSTY**	COPYIST		OSCULUM

Seven-letter anagrams

CLMPRUY	CRUMPLY	CNOOSTY	TYCOONS	DDDEILN	DINDLED
CLMSUUU	CUMULUS	CNOOSUU	NOCUOUS	DDDEILP	PIDDLED
CLNOORT	CONTROL	CNOOSVY	CONVOYS	DDDEILR	DIDDLER
CLNOOSS	CONSOLS	CNOOTTW	COTTOWN		RIDDLED
CLNOOSU	COLONUS	CNOOTTY	COTTONY	DDDEILS	DIDDLES
CLNOSSU	CONSULS	CNOPRTY	CRYPTON	DDDEILT	TIDDLED
CLNOSTU	CONSULT	CNOPSTU	PUNCTOS	DDDEILW	WIDDLED
	UNCOLTS	CNORSSU	UNCROSS	DDDEILY	DIDDLEY
CLNOSUW	UNCOWLS	CNORSSY	SYNROCS	DDDEIMU	MUDDIED
CLNRSUU	UNCURLS	CNORTUY	COUNTRY	DDDEIOR	DODDIER
CLOOPPW	COWPLOP	CNRSSTU	SCRUNTS	DDDEIOS	DODDIES
CLOOPST	COPLOTS	CNRSTUY	SCRUNTY	DDDEIRS	DIDDERS
CLOOPTY	POLYCOT	COOORSZ	COROZOS	DDDEIRU	DUDDIER
CLOORSU	COLOURS	COOPRRT	PROCTOR		RUDDIED
CLOORUY	COLOURY	COOPRSS	SCROOPS	DDDELMU	MUDDLED
CLOOSTY	CYTOSOL	COOPRTU	OUTCROP	DDDELNO	NODDLED
CLOPTUY	OCTUPLY		OCTOPUS	DDDELOO	DOODLED
CLORSSW	SCROWLS	COOPSTU	COPOUTS	DDDELOP	PLODDED
CLORSSY	CROSSLY	COOPSUY	COYPOUS		PODDLED
CLORSUY	CORYLUS	COORSTU	OCTUORS	DDDELOS	DODDLES
CLORTUY	COURTLY	COORSUU	ROUCOUS	DDDELOT	TODDLED
CLOSSTU	LOCUSTS	COORTUW	OUTCROW	DDDELPU	PUDDLED
CLPRSUU	UPCURLS	COOSSTY	OOCYSTS	DDDELRU	RUDDLED
CLPSSTU	SCULPTS	COOSTTY	OTOCYST	DDDENOS	SNODDED
CMMNOOS	COMMONS	COPRRSS	SCRORPS	DDDEOPR	PRODDED
CMMOORS	ROMCOMS	COPRRTU	CORRUPT	DDDEOQU	QUODDED
CMMOOST	COMMOTS	COPRSTY	CRYPTOS	DDDEORS	DODDERS
CMMOPSY	COMSYMP	COPRSUU	CUPROUS	DDDEORY	DODDERY
CMMRSUY	SCRUMMY	COPRTUU	UPCOURT	DDDEPSU	SPUDDED
CMNNOOS	NONCOMS	CORRSSU	CURSORS	DDDERSU	DUDDERS
CMNOOOT	MONOCOT	CORRSUY	CURSORY	DDDERUY	DUDDERY
CMNOOPY	COMPONY	CORSSTU	SCRUTOS	DDDESTU	STUDDED
CMNOSSY	SYNCOMS	COSTTUU	CUTOUTS	DDDGINO	DODDING
CMNPTUU	PUNCTUM	DDDDEIL	DIDDLED	DDEEEFX	FEDEXED
CMOOPRT	COMPORT	DDDEEGR	DREDGED	DDEEEGR	DEGREED
CMOOPST	COMPOST	DDDEEHL	HEDDLED	DDEEEIR	DEEDIER
	COMPOTS	DDDEEHS	SHEDDED	DDEEELN	NEEDLED
CMOORSU	CORMOUS	DDDEEIR	DERIDED	DDEEELT	DELETED
CMOOSTY	SCOTOMY	DDDEELM	MEDDLED	DDEEELV	DEVELED
CMORSTU	SCROTUM	DDDEELP	PEDDLED	DDEEELW	WEDELED
CMORTUW	CUTWORM	DDDEELR	REDDLED	DDEEEMN	EMENDED
CMOSSTU	CUSTOMS	DDDEELS	SLEDDED	DDEEEMR	REMEDED
CMPRSSU	SCRUMPS	DDDEELU	DELUDED	DDEEENT	TEENDED
CMPRSUU	CUPRUMS	DDDEEMO	DEMODED	DDEEENW	ENDEWED
CMPRSUY	SCRUMPY	DDDEENS	SNEDDED	DDEEEPS	SPEEDED
CNNOPSY	PYCNONS	DDDEENU	DENUDED	DDEEEST	DEEDEST
CNNORTU	NOCTURN	DDDEERU	UDDERED		STEEDED
CNNORUW	UNCROWN	DDDEEST	STEDDED	DDEEESX	DESEXED
CNNOSUY	UNSONCY	DDDEFIL	FIDDLED	DDEEEWY	DYEWEED
CNOOOPS	POCOSON	DDDEFLU	FUDDLED	DDEEFGL	FLEDGED
CNOOPPR	POPCORN	DDDEGII	GIDDIED	DDEEFII	DEIFIED
CNOOPRU	CROUPON	DDDEGIR	GRIDDED		EDIFIED
CNOOPSU	COUPONS	DDDEGLU	GUDDLED	DDEEFIL	DEFILED
	SOUPCON	DDDEGRU	DRUDGED		FIELDED
CNOORRW	CORNROW	DDDEHIW	WHIDDED	DDEEFIN	DEFINED
CNOORST	CONSORT	DDDEHLO	HODDLED	DDEEFLU	DEEDFUL
	CROTONS	DDDEHLU	HUDDLED	DDEEFNS	DEFENDS
CNOORTT	CONTORT	DDDEHTU	THUDDED	DDEEFSU	DEFUSED
CNOORTU	CONTOUR	DDDEIIK	KIDDIED	DDEEFUZ	DEFUZED
	CORNUTO	DDDEIIR	DIDDIER	DDEEGGL	GLEDGED
	CROUTON	DDDEIIS	DIDDIES	DDEEGIN	DEEDING
CNOOSST	NOSTOCS	DDDEIIV	DIVIDED		DEIGNED
	ONCOSTS	DDDEIKS	SKIDDED	DDEEGIS	DISEDGE
CNOOSTT	COTTONS	DDDEILM	MIDDLED	DDEEGLP	PLEDGED

DDEEGLS	SLEDGED	**DDEELSU**	DELUDES		GRIDDLE
DDEEGLU	DELUGED	**DDEEMMO**	MODEMED	**DDEGIMO**	DEMIGOD
DDEEGNU	UNEDGED	**DDEEMOT**	DEMOTED	**DDEGINO**	DINGOED
DDEEGRR	DREDGER	**DDEEMRU**	DEMURED	**DDEGINR**	GRINDED
DDEEGRS	DREDGES	**DDEENNU**	UNENDED		REDDING
DDEEHLS	HEDDLES	**DDEENOP**	DEPONED	**DDEGINT**	TEDDING
DDEEHNU	DUDHEEN	**DDEENOT**	DENOTED	**DDEGINW**	WEDDING
DDEEHRS	SHEDDER	**DDEENOV**	DOVENED	**DDEGINY**	EDDYING
DDEEILM	DELIMED	**DDEENOW**	ENDOWED	**DDEGIOR**	DODGIER
DDEEILR	DREIDEL	**DDEENOZ**	DOZENED	**DDEGIRR**	GRIDDER
DDEEILS	SLEIDED	**DDEENPS**	DEPENDS	**DDEGKLU**	KLUDGED
DDEEILV	DEVILED	**DDEENPU**	UPENDED	**DDEGLOP**	PLODGED
DDEEILW	WIELDED	**DDEENRS**	REDDENS	**DDEGLOS**	DOGSLED
DDEEILY	DEEDILY	**DDEENRT**	TRENDED	**DDEGLSU**	GUDDLES
	YIELDED	**DDEENRU**	DENUDER		SLUDGED
DDEEIMN	DENIMED		ENDURED	**DDEGMOO**	DOGEDOM
DDEEIMP	IMPEDED	**DDEENST**	STENDED	**DDEGMOS**	DODGEMS
DDEEIMS	DEMISED	**DDEENSU**	DENUDES	**DDEGMSU**	SMUDGED
	MISDEED		DUDEENS	**DDEGNOO**	NOODGED
DDEEINR	NEDDIER		DUENDES	**DDEGNOS**	GODDENS
DDEEINS	DESINED	**DDEENSY**	DESYNED		GODSEND
	NEDDIES	**DDEENTU**	DETUNED	**DDEGNOU**	DUDGEON
	SDEINED	**DDEEOOR**	RODEOED	**DDEGNSU**	SNUDGED
DDEEINT	ENDITED	**DDEEOPS**	DEPOSED	**DDEGORS**	DODGERS
	TEINDED		SEEDPOD		GORSEDD
DDEEINW	INDEWED	**DDEEORR**	ORDERED	**DDEGORY**	DODGERY
	WIDENED	**DDEEORV**	DOVERED	**DDEGOSS**	GODDESS
DDEEINX	DEINDEX	**DDEEORW**	DOWERED	**DDEGOST**	STODGED
	INDEXED	**DDEEOTV**	DEVOTED	**DDEGRRU**	DRUDGER
DDEEINZ	DIZENED	**DDEEOTX**	DETOXED	**DDEGRSU**	DRUDGES
DDEEIOV	VIDEOED	**DDEEPRS**	PEDDERS	**DDEGRTU**	TRUDGED
DDEEIPR	PREDIED		SPREDDE	**DDEHINS**	NEDDISH
DDEEIPS	DEPSIDE	**DDEEPTU**	DEPUTED	**DDEHIOW**	HOWDIED
DDEEIRR	DERIDER	**DDEERRS**	REDDERS	**DDEHIRS**	HIDDERS
	REDDIER	**DDEERSS**	DRESSED		REDDISH
	REDRIED	**DDEERST**	REDDEST		SHIDDER
	RIDERED		TEDDERS	**DDEHIRT**	THIRDED
DDEEIRS	DERIDES	**DDEERSW**	WEDDERS	**DDEHIRW**	WHIDDER
	DESIRED	**DDEERTU**	DETRUDE	**DDEHIRY**	HYDRIDE
	DIEDRES	**DDEESST**	STEDDES	**DDEHLNO**	HONDLED
	RESIDED	**DDEETTU**	DUETTED	**DDEHLOS**	HODDLES
DDEEIRV	DERIVED	**DDEFGIR**	FRIDGED	**DDEHLRU**	HUDDLER
DDEEIRW	WEIRDED	**DDEFILR**	FIDDLER		HURDLED
DDEEIST	DEIDEST	**DDEFILS**	FIDDLES	**DDEHLSU**	HUDDLES
	TEDDIES	**DDEFILY**	FIDDLEY	**DDEHNOS**	HODDENS
DDEEISV	DEVISED	**DDEFIOR**	FOREDID		SHODDEN
DDEEKKO	DEKKOED	**DDEFIRT**	DRIFTED	**DDEHNOU**	HOUNDED
DDEELLU	DUELLED	**DDEFISU**	FUDDIES	**DDEHNRU**	HUNDRED
DDEELLW	DWELLED	**DDEFLNO**	FONDLED	**DDEHNSU**	DUNSHED
DDEELMO	MODELED	**DDEFLOO**	FLOODED	**DDEHNUZ**	NUDZHED
DDEELMR	MEDDLER	**DDEFLRU**	FUDDLER	**DDEHOSW**	SHOWDED
DDEELMS	MEDDLES	**DDEFLSU**	FUDDLES	**DDEHRSU**	SHUDDER
DDEELNO	OLDENED	**DDEFNOR**	FRONDED	**DDEHRSY**	SHREDDY
DDEELNS	LEDDENS	**DDEFNOU**	FONDUED	**DDEIIKR**	KIDDIER
DDEELOP	DELOPED		FOUNDED	**DDEIIKS**	KIDDIES
DDEELOW	DOWELED	**DDEFNSU**	DEFUNDS	**DDEIIMS**	MIDDIES
DDEELOY	YODELED	**DDEFORS**	FODDERS	**DDEIINT**	INDITED
DDEELPR	PEDDLER	**DDEGGRU**	DRUGGED	**DDEIINV**	DIVINED
DDEELPS	PEDDLES		GRUDGED	**DDEIIOS**	IODIDES
	SPELDED	**DDEGHIT**	DIGHTED		
DDEELRS	REDDLES	**DDEGIIR**	GIDDIER	**DDEIIOX**	DIOXIDE
	SLEDDER	**DDEGIIS**	GIDDIES	**DDEIIOZ**	IODIZED
DDEELRT	TREDDLE	**DDEGILR**	GIRDLED	**DDEIIRT**	DIRTIED
DDEELRU	DELUDER		GLIDDER		TIDDIER

Seven-letter anagrams

DDEIIRV	DIVIDER	**DDEINSW**	SWIDDEN		DONNERD
DDEIIST	STIDDIE	**DDEIOOS**	DOODIES	**DDENOOP**	ENDOPOD
	TIDDIES	**DDEIOPR**	PODDIER	**DDENOOS**	DESNOOD
DDEIISV	DIVIDES	**DDEIOPS**	PODDIES		SNOODED
DDEIISW	WIDDIES	**DDEIORS**	DORISED	**DDENOPS**	DESPOND
DDEIITT	DITTIED		SODDIER	**DDENOPU**	POUNDED
DDEIIVV	DIVVIED	**DDEIORV**	OVERDID	**DDENOPW**	POWNDED
DDEIIZZ	DIZZIED	**DDEIORW**	DOWDIER	**DDENORS**	DONDERS
DDEIKLN	KINDLED	**DDEIORZ**	DORIZED		NODDERS
DDEIKLS	KIDDLES	**DDEIOSS**	SODDIES		SNODDER
DDEIKNR	KINDRED	**DDEIOST**	TODDIES	**DDENORT**	TRODDEN
DDEIKOS	KIDDOES	**DDEIOSW**	DOWDIES	**DDENORU**	REDOUND
DDEIKRS	KIDDERS	**DDEIOTT**	DITTOED		ROUNDED
	SKIDDER	**DDEIOWW**	WIDOWED		UNDERDO
DDEILLO	DOLLIED	**DDEIPPR**	DRIPPED	**DDENORW**	DROWNED
DDEILLR	DRILLED	**DDEIPRS**	DISPRED		ROWNDED
DDEILLU	ILLUDED	**DDEIPRU**	UPDRIED		WONDRED
DDEILMP	DIMPLED	**DDEIPSU**	PUDDIES	**DDENOSS**	ODDNESS
DDEILMR	MIDDLER	**DDEIPUV**	UPDIVED		SODDENS
DDEILMS	MIDDLES	**DDEIRRS**	RIDDERS	**DDENOSU**	SOUNDED
DDEILNN	DINNLED	**DDEIRRU**	RUDDIER	**DDENOSW**	SOWNDED
DDEILNS	DINDLES	**DDEIRSU**	RUDDIES	**DDENOSY**	DYNODES
	SLIDDEN	**DDEIRSW**	WIDDERS	**DDENOUW**	WOUNDED
DDEILNW	DWINDLE	**DDEISSU**	DISUSED	**DDENPSU**	PUDDENS
	WINDLED	**DDEISTU**	STUDDIE	**DDENRSU**	DUNDERS
DDEILOR	DROILED		STUDIED	**DDENSSU**	SUDDENS
DDEILOS	DILDOES	**DDEJRSU**	JUDDERS	**DDENSTU**	STUDDEN
DDEILOT	DELTOID	**DDEKMOU**	DUKEDOM	**DDEOOPR**	DROOPED
DDEILPR	PIDDLER	**DDEKOOR**	DROOKED	**DDEOORU**	ODOURED
DDEILPS	DISPLED	**DDEKORU**	DROUKED	**DDEOORW**	REDWOOD
	PIDDLES	**DDELLOR**	DROLLED	**DDEOOWY**	DYEWOOD
DDEILPU	DUPLIED	**DDELMOU**	MOULDED	**DDEOPPR**	DROPPED
DDEILQU	QUIDDLE	**DDELMPU**	DUMPLED	**DDEOPRR**	PRODDER
DDEILRR	RIDDLER	**DDELMRU**	MUDDLER	**DDEOPRW**	DEWDROP
DDEILRS	DREIDLS	**DDELMSU**	MUDDLES	**DDEORSW**	DROWSED
	RIDDLES	**DDELNOO**	NOODLED		SWORDED
	SLIDDER	**DDELNOS**	NODDLES	**DDEPRSS**	SPREDDS
DDEILRT	TIDDLER	**DDELNOU**	LOUNDED	**DDEPRSU**	PUDDERS
DDEILST	TIDDLES		NODULED		SPUDDER
DDEILSW	WIDDLES	**DDELNOW**	LOWNDED	**DDERRSU**	RUDDERS
DDEILTU	DILUTED	**DDELNRU**	NURDLED	**DDERSSU**	SUDDERS
DDEILTW	TWIDDLE		RUNDLED	**DDGGINO**	DODGING
DDEILTY	LYDDITE	**DDELOOR**	DOODLER		GODDING
	TIDDLEY		DROOLED	**DDGHINO**	HODDING
DDEIMMU	DUMMIED	**DDELOOS**	DOODLES	**DDGHOOO**	GODHOOD
DDEIMNS	MIDDENS	**DDELOOW**	WOOLDED	**DDGIIKN**	KIDDING
DDEIMNU	MUEDDIN	**DDELOPR**	PLODDER	**DDGIILN**	LIDDING
DDEIMOO	MOODIED	**DDELOPS**	PODDLES	**DDGIILY**	GIDDILY
DDEIMOR	DERMOID	**DDELORT**	TODDLER	**DDGIINR**	RIDDING
DDEIMOS	DESMOID	**DDELORW**	WORLDED	**DDGIMNU**	MUDDING
DDEIMRU	MUDDIER	**DDELOST**	TODDLES	**DDGINNO**	NODDING
DDEIMSS	DESMIDS	**DDELOTT**	DOTTLED	**DDGINOP**	PODDING
DDEIMST	MIDDEST	**DDELPRU**	PUDDLER	**DDGINOR**	RODDING
DDEIMSU	DEDIMUS	**DDELPSU**	PUDDLES	**DDGINOS**	SODDING
	MUDDIES		SPUDDLE	**DDGINOT**	TODDING
DDEINOP	POINDED	**DDELRSU**	RUDDLES	**DDGINPU**	PUDDING
DDEINOR	NODDIER	**DDELSTU**	STUDDLE	**DDGINRU**	RUDDING
DDEINOS	NODDIES	**DDEMMRU**	DRUMMED	**DDGINUW**	WUDDING
DDEINOT	DENTOID	**DDEMMSU**	SMEDDUM	**DDGIPUY**	GIDDUPY
DDEINOW	INDOWED	**DDEMNOS**	ODDSMEN	**DDGMOOS**	DOGDOMS
DDEINPS	DISPEND	**DDEMNOT**	ODDMENT	**DDGOOOW**	DOGWOOD
DDEINRU	UNDRIED	**DDEMNOU**	MOUNDED	**DDHIIKS**	KIDDISH
DDEINST	DISTEND	**DDEMRSU**	MUDDERS	**DDHIISS**	SIDDHIS
DDEINSU	NUDDIES	**DDENNOR**	DENDRON	**DDHIKSU**	KIDDUSH

DDHINOS	HODDINS	**DEEEHPW**	WHEEPED		SNEERED
DDHIORY	HYDROID	**DEEEHPZ**	PHEEZED	**DEEENRT**	ENTERED
DDHIRSY	HYDRIDS	**DEEEHRS**	HEEDERS	**DEEENRV**	ENERVED
DDIIIOO	OIDIOID		HEREDES	**DEEENRW**	RENEWED
DDIIKKS	DIKDIKS		SHEERED	**DEEENRY**	RENEYED
DDIIKLS	SKIDLID	**DEEEHST**	SEETHED	**DEEENST**	STEENED
DDIIKSV	KIDVIDS		SHEETED	**DEEENSV**	VENDEES
DDIILOP	DIPLOID	**DEEEHTT**	TEETHED	**DEEENSW**	ENSEWED
DDIIOSX	DIOXIDS	**DEEEHWZ**	WHEEZED	**DEEENSZ**	SNEEZED
	IXODIDS	**DEEEIJL**	JEELIED	**DEEENTT**	DETENTE
DDIIQTU	QUIDDIT	**DEEEIMR**	EMERIED		NEDETTE
DDIKNOS	DODKINS	**DEEEINR**	NEEDIER	**DEEENTU**	DETENUE
DDIKOOS	SKIDDOO	**DEEEIPS**	DEEPIES	**DEEENTV**	EVENTED
DDILMUY	MUDDILY	**DEEEIRR**	REEDIER	**DEEEORW**	OREWEED
DDILNRS	DIRNDLS	**DEEEIRS**	SEEDIER	**DEEEOTV**	DEVOTEE
DDILOSY	DYSODIL	**DEEEIRW**	WEEDIER	**DEEEPRS**	SPEEDER
DDILOWY	DOWDILY	**DEEEISV**	DEVISEE		SPEERED
DDILRUY	RUDDILY	**DEEEJLW**	JEWELED	**DEEEPRT**	PETERED
DDILTWY	TWIDDLY	**DEEEJNU**	DEJEUNE	**DEEEPRU**	EPERDUE
DDIMOOS	DODOISM	**DEEEJRR**	JERREED	**DEEEPRV**	PREEVED
DDIMRSU	DIRDUMS	**DEEEJRS**	JEREEDS	**DEEEPSS**	PEDESES
DDIMSSU	DUDISMS	**DEEEKLN**	KNEELED	**DEEEPST**	DEEPEST
DDINOST	SNODDIT	**DEEEKLS**	SLEEKED		STEEPED
DDIORTU	TURDOID	**DEEEKMS**	SMEEKED	**DEEEQRU**	QUEERED
DDIRRUY	DRUIDRY	**DEEEKNW**	WEEKEND	**DEEERRS**	REEDERS
DDIRSSU	SIDDURS	**DEEEKRS**	KREESED	**DEEERRV**	REVERED
DDLLMOO	DOLLDOM		SKEERED	**DEEERSS**	RESEEDS
DDMMSUU	DUMDUMS	**DEEEKRY**	REKEYED		SEEDERS
DDMNOOR	DROMOND	**DEEEKST**	STEEKED	**DEEERST**	REESTED
DDMRSUU	DURDUMS	**DEEELLV**	LEVELED		STEERED
DDNORSW	DROWNDS	**DEEELMS**	MESELED	**DEEERSV**	DESERVE
DDOOOOS	DOODOOS	**DEEELNR**	NEEDLER		SEVERED
DDORSTY	DROSTDY	**DEEELNS**	NEEDLES	**DEEERSW**	RESEWED
DEEEEMX	EXEEMED	**DEEELPS**	SPEELED		SEWERED
DEEEEWW	WEEWEED	**DEEELPT**	DEPLETE		SWEERED
DEEEFFR	EFFERED	**DEEELRT**	DEERLET		WEEDERS
DEEEFLR	FLEERED	**DEEELRV**	LEVERED	**DEEERSY**	REDEYES
DEEEFLT	FLEETED		REVELED	**DEEERTV**	EVERTED
DEEEFNR	ENFREED	**DEEELST**	DELETES	**DEEERTW**	TWEERED
DEEEFNS	DEFENSE		SLEETED	**DEEERTX**	EXERTED
DEEEFRS	FEEDERS		STEELED	**DEEERWY**	WEEDERY
	REFEEDS	**DEEELSV**	SLEEVED	**DEEESSX**	DESEXES
DEEEFRV	FEVERED	**DEEELSW**	SWEELED	**DEEESTV**	STEEVED
DEEEFSX	FEDEXES	**DEEELTW**	TWEEDLE	**DEEESTW**	SWEETED
DEEEGKL	GLEEKED		TWEELED	**DEEETTV**	VEDETTE
DEEEGKR	GREEKED	**DEEELTX**	TELEXED	**DEEETTW**	TWEETED
DEEEGLP	PLEDGEE	**DEEEMMW**	EMMEWED	**DEEETWZ**	TWEEZED
DEEEGLT	GLEETED	**DEEEMNR**	EMENDER	**DEEFFFO**	FEOFFED
DEEEGMR	DEMERGE		REEDMEN	**DEEFFIN**	EFFENDI
	EMERGED	**DEEEMNS**	DEMESNE	**DEEFFOR**	OFFERED
DEEEGNP	PEENGED		SEEDMEN	**DEEFFST**	DEFFEST
DEEEGNR	GREENED	**DEEEMNW**	ENMEWED	**DEEFFSU**	EFFUSED
	RENEGED	**DEEEMRS**	DEMERSE	**DEEFGGL**	FLEGGED
DEEEGRR	REGREDE		EMERSED	**DEEFGIN**	FEEDING
DEEEGRS	DEGREES		MEDRESE		FEIGNED
DEEEGRT	DETERGE		REDEEMS	**DEEFGIP**	PIGFEED
	GREETED		REMEDES	**DEEFGLS**	FLEDGES
DEEEGST	EGESTED	**DEEEMRT**	METERED	**DEEFGRU**	REFUGED
DEEEHKT	THEEKED	**DEEEMST**	STEEMED	**DEEFHLS**	FLESHED
DEEEHLS	SHEELED	**DEEENPR**	PREENED		SHELFED
DEEEHLW	WHEEDLE	**DEEENPS**	DEEPENS	**DEEFHLU**	HEEDFUL
	WHEELED	**DEEENQU**	QUEENED	**DEEFHRS**	FRESHED
DEEEHNS	SHEENED	**DEEENRS**	NEEDERS	**DEEFIIR**	DEIFIER
DEEEHPS	PHEESED		SERENED		EDIFIER

	REIFIED	**DEEGILN**	DELEING	**DEEHIKV**	KHEDIVE
DEEFIIS	DEIFIES	**DEEGILR**	GELIDER	**DEEHILS**	SHIELED
	EDIFIES		LEDGIER	**DEEHILT**	LETHIED
DEEFILN	ENFILED		LEIDGER	**DEEHINR**	INHERED
DEEFILR	DEFILER	**DEEGIMN**	DEEMING	**DEEHIRR**	HERRIED
	FERLIED	**DEEGIMV**	DEMIVEG		REHIRED
	FIELDER	**DEEGINN**	ENGINED	**DEEHIRT**	DIETHER
	REFILED		NEEDING	**DEEHIST**	HEISTED
DEEFILS	DEFILES	**DEEGINR**	DREEING	**DEEHITV**	THIEVED
DEEFILT	FILETED		ENERGID	**DEEHKLW**	WHELKED
DEEFIMS	MISFEED		GREINED	**DEEHLLO**	HELLOED
DEEFINR	DEFINER		REEDING	**DEEHLLS**	SHELLED
	ENFIRED		REIGNED	**DEEHLMW**	WHELMED
	FENDIER	**DEEGINS**	SDEIGNE	**DEEHLNU**	UNHELED
	REFINED		SEEDING	**DEEHLOV**	HOVELED
DEEFINS	DEFINES	**DEEGINV**	DEEVING	**DEEHLPW**	WHELPED
DEEFINT	FEINTED	**DEEGINW**	WEEDING	**DEEHLSV**	SHELVED
DEEFINX	ENFIXED	**DEEGINY**	YEEDING	**DEEHLSW**	WELSHED
DEEFIRR	FERRIED	**DEEGIPW**	PIGWEED	**DEEHMNR**	HERDMEN
	REFIRED	**DEEGIRS**	SEDGIER	**DEEHMNS**	MENSHED
	REFRIED	**DEEGIRV**	DIVERGE	**DEEHMOR**	HOMERED
DEEFIRS	DEFIERS		GRIEVED	**DEEHMRU**	RHEUMED
	SERIFED	**DEEGIRW**	WEDGIER	**DEEHMUX**	EXHUMED
DEEFIRT	FETIDER	**DEEGIST**	EDGIEST	**DEEHNOY**	HONEYED
DEEFIRX	REFIXED	**DEEGISW**	WEDGIES	**DEEHNPR**	PREHEND
DEEFIRY	REEDIFY	**DEEGJRU**	REJUDGE	**DEEHNRS**	HERDENS
DEEFIRZ	FRIEZED	**DEEGKMO**	GEEKDOM	**DEEHNUY**	UNHEEDY
DEEFIST	DEIFEST	**DEEGKRS**	KEDGERS	**DEEHORS**	RESHOED
DEEFLLU	FUELLED	**DEEGLMU**	EMULGED	**DEEHORV**	HOVERED
DEEFLNS	FLENSED	**DEEGLNS**	LEGENDS	**DEEHOSY**	HOSEYED
DEEFLNU	NEEDFUL	**DEEGLNT**	GENTLED	**DEEHPRS**	SPHERED
DEEFLOT	FEEDLOT		GLENTED	**DEEHRRS**	HERDERS
DEEFLOY	EYEFOLD	**DEEGLOY**	GOLDEYE	**DEEHRSS**	HERDESS
DEEFLRU	FERULED	**DEEGLPR**	PLEDGER	**DEEHRSU**	USHERED
DEEFLRY	DEERFLY	**DEEGLPS**	PLEDGES	**DEEHRSW**	SHREWED
DEEFLSU	DEFUELS	**DEEGLPT**	PLEDGET	**DEEHRTW**	WRETHED
DEEFLTT	FETTLED	**DEEGLRS**	GELDERS	**DEEHSYY**	HEYDEYS
DEEFMOR	FREEDOM		LEDGERS	**DEEHTTW**	WHETTED
DEEFNRS	FENDERS		REDLEGS	**DEEIINT**	DIETINE
DEEFNRU	UNFREED		SLEDGER	**DEEIIPR**	EPEIRID
DEEFNUU	UNFEUED	**DEEGLRU**	GRUELED	**DEEIIRW**	WEIRDIE
DEEFORV	OVERFED		REGLUED	**DEEIIST**	DEITIES
DEEFORZ	DEFROZE	**DEEGLRW**	WERGELD	**DEEIJLL**	JELLIED
DEEFRSU	DEFUSER	**DEEGLSS**	SLEDGES	**DEEIJMM**	JEMMIED
	REFUSED	**DEEGLSU**	DELUGES	**DEEIJTT**	JETTIED
DEEFRSW	SWERFED	**DEEGMNU**	EMUNGED	**DEEIKLL**	KILLDEE
DEEFRTT	FRETTED		GUDEMEN	**DEEIKLN**	KNEIDEL
DEEFRTU	FEUTRED	**DEEGMRS**	DEGERMS		LIKENED
	REFUTED	**DEEGMUW**	GUMWEED	**DEEIKMW**	MIDWEEK
DEEFSSU	DEFUSES	**DEEGNNO**	ENDOGEN	**DEEIKNR**	REINKED
DEEFSTT	DEFTEST	**DEEGNNR**	GRENNED	**DEEIKNS**	ENSKIED
DEEFSUZ	DEFUZES	**DEEGNOR**	ENGORED		SKEINED
DEEGGIS	GIDGEES	**DEEGNRS**	GENDERS	**DEEIKOV**	DOVEKIE
DEEGGLS	GLEDGES	**DEEGNSU**	DENGUES	**DEEILLS**	DELLIES
DEEGHIN	HEEDING		UNEDGES	**DEEILMS**	DELIMES
	NEIGHED	**DEEGOOS**	SOOGEED	**DEEILNO**	ELOINED
DEEGHIR	HEDGIER	**DEEGORR**	ROGERED	**DEEILNR**	REDLINE
DEEGHIW	WEIGHED	**DEEGOSS**	GESSOED		RELINED
DEEGHOW	HOGWEED	**DEEGOSY**	GEODESY	**DEEILNS**	ENISLED
DEEGHRS	HEDGERS	**DEEGOTU**	OUTEDGE		ENSILED
DEEGHSS	GHESSED	**DEEGRRU**	REURGED		LINSEED
DEEGIJS	GIDJEES	**DEEGRSW**	SWEDGER	**DEEILNT**	LENITED
DEEGIKN	DEKEING	**DEEGSSU**	GUESSED	**DEEILNV**	LIVENED
DEEGIKR	KEDGIER	**DEEGSTU**	GUESTED	**DEEILNY**	DYELINE

	NEEDILY		RESINED		RESITED
DEEILOR	REOILED	DEEINRU	UREDINE	DEEIRSU	RESIDUE
DEEILOS	OILSEED	DEEINRW	REWIDEN		UREIDES
DEEILPR	PERILED		WIDENER	DEEIRSV	DERIVES
	REPLIED	DEEINRX	INDEXER		DEVISER
DEEILPS	SEEDLIP		REINDEX		DIVERSE
	SPEILED	DEEINSS	DESINES		REVISED
	SPIELED	DEEINST	DESTINE	DEEIRSW	SWEIRED
DEEILRS	RESILED		ENDITES	DEEIRSZ	RESIZED
DEEILRT	RETILED		STEINED	DEEIRTU	ERUDITE
DEEILRV	DELIVER	DEEINSV	DEVEINS	DEEIRTV	RIVETED
	LIVERED		ENDIVES		VERDITE
	RELIVED	DEEINSW	ENDWISE	DEEIRVV	REVIVED
	REVILED		SINEWED	DEEISSU	DISEUSE
DEEILRW	WIELDER	DEEINSX	INDEXES	DEEISSV	DEVISES
DEEILRY	REEDILY	DEEINTT	DINETTE	DEEISTT	TEDIEST
	YIELDER	DEEINTU	DETINUE	DEEISTW	DEWIEST
DEEILSS	DIESELS	DEEINTV	EVIDENT	DEEISTX	EXISTED
	IDLESSE	DEEINVW	VINEWED	DEEITTV	VIDETTE
	SEIDELS	DEEINVX	INVEXED	DEEJNOS	JONESED
DEEILST	ISLETED	DEEINWZ	WIZENED	DEEJNOY	ENJOYED
DEEILSY	EYELIDS	DEEIOPS	EPISODE	DEEJQRU	JERQUED
	SEEDILY		POESIED	DEEKKRT	TREKKED
DEEILTU	DILUTEE	DEEIOPT	EPIDOTE	DEEKLLN	KNELLED
DEEILTV	DEVILET	DEEIOPX	EPOXIDE	DEEKLLV	KVELLED
DEEILWY	WEEDILY		EPOXIED	DEEKLPS	SKELPED
DEEIMMO	MIMEOED	DEEIORS	OREIDES	DEEKLRS	SKELDER
DEEIMMS	MISDEEM		OSIERED	DEEKMNS	DESKMEN
DEEIMMW	IMMEWED	DEEIOSV	VOIDEES	DEEKMRS	SMERKED
DEEIMNO	DOMINEE	DEEIPPT	PEPTIDE	DEEKNNS	SKENNED
DEEIMNR	ERMINED	DEEIPRS	PREDIES	DEEKNOT	TOKENED
DEEIMNS	DESMINE		PRESIDE	DEEKNSY	ENSKYED
	SIDEMEN		SPEIRED	DEEKORV	REVOKED
DEEIMNT	DEMENTI		SPIERED	DEEKOVY	DOVEKEY
DEEIMOR	EMEROID	DEEIPRT	PREEDIT	DEEKPPS	SKEPPED
DEEIMPR	DEMIREP		TEPIDER	DEEKPRU	PERUKED
	EPIDERM	DEEIPRV	DEPRIVE	DEEKRRS	SKERRED
	IMPEDER		PREDIVE	DEEKRSU	RESKUED
DEEIMPS	IMPEDES		PRIEVED	DEEKSTT	SKETTED
	SEMIPED	DEEIPRX	EXPIRED	DEELLMS	SMELLED
DEEIMPT	EMPTIED	DEEIPSS	DESPISE	DEELLNS	SNELLED
DEEIMRS	REMEIDS		PEDESIS	DEELLPS	SPELLED
	REMISED	DEEIPST	DESPITE	DEELLQU	QUELLED
DEEIMRT	DEMERIT	DEEIQRU	QUERIED	DEELLRU	DUELLER
	DIMETER	DEEIQTU	QUIETED	DEELLRW	DWELLER
	MERITED	DEEIRRS	DERRIES	DEELLRY	ELDERLY
	MITERED		DESIRER	DEELLST	STELLED
	RETIMED		REDRIES	DEELLSW	SWELLED
DEEIMRX	REMIXED		RESIDER	DEELMNO	LEMONED
DEEIMSS	DEMISES		SERRIED	DEELMOR	MODELER
DEEIMTT	EMITTED	DEEIRRT	RETIRED		REMODEL
DEEINNP	PENNIED		RETRIED	DEELMPT	TEMPLED
DEEINNS	INDENES		TIREDER	DEELMPU	DEPLUME
DEEINNT	DENTINE	DEEIRRV	DERIVER	DEELMRS	MELDERS
DEEINNU	ENNUIED		REDRIVE	DEELMRU	RELUMED
DEEINNZ	DENIZEN		RIVERED	DEELMST	SMELTED
DEEINOR	ORDINEE	DEEIRRW	REWIRED	DEELMSU	MULESED
DEEINPR	REPINED		WEIRDER	DEELMSY	MEDLEYS
	RIPENED	DEEIRSS	DESIRES	DEELMTT	METTLED
DEEINPW	PINWEED		RESIDES	DEELNOT	DOLENTE
DEEINRR	DERNIER	DEEIRST	DIESTER	DEELNPU	PENDULE
	NERDIER		DIETERS	DEELNRS	LENDERS
DEEINRS	DENIERS		REEDITS		RELENDS
	NEREIDS		REISTED		SLENDER

Seven-letter anagrams

DEELNSS	ENDLESS	DEEMOSY	MOSEYED	DEEOPPY	POPEYED
DEELNST	DENTELS	DEEMPRS	DEPERMS	DEEOPRR	PEDRERO
	NESTLED		PREMEDS	DEEOPRS	DEPOSER
DEELNSW	WEDELNS	DEEMPTT	TEMPTED		REPOSED
DEELNSY	DENSELY	DEEMRRU	DEMURER	DEEOPRW	POWERED
DEELNTT	NETTLED	DEEMRSU	DEMURES	DEEOPSS	DEPOSES
DEELOOS	DOOLEES		RESUMED		SPEEDOS
DEELOPP	PEOPLED	DEEMSUY	MUDEYES	DEEOPSX	EXPOSED
DEELOPR	DEPLORE	DEENNOR	ENDERON		PODEXES
DEELOPS	DELOPES	DEENNOS	DONNEES	DEEOPXY	EPOXYED
DEELOPV	DEVELOP	DEENNOT	ENDNOTE	DEEORRR	ORDERER
DEELOPX	EXPLODE		TENONED		REORDER
DEELORS	RESOLED	DEENNOY	DOYENNE	DEEORRS	REREDOS
DEELORU	URODELE	DEENNOZ	ENZONED	DEEORRV	OVERRED
DEELORV	LOVERED	DEENNPT	PENDENT		REDROVE
DEELORW	LOWERED	DEENNST	DENNETS	DEEORST	OERSTED
	ROWELED		STENNED		ROSETED
DEELORY	YODELER	DEENNTZ	TENDENZ		TEREDOS
DEELOSU	DELOUSE	DEENNUY	ENNUYED	DEEORSV	DEVORES
DEELOTV	DOVELET	DEENOOR	RONEOED	DEEORSW	RESOWED
DEELOTW	TOWELED	DEENOPR	REPONED	DEEORSX	REDOXES
DEELOVV	DEVOLVE	DEENOPS	DEPONES	DEEORTT	OTTERED
	EVOLVED		SPONDEE		TETRODE
DEELPRS	PEDLERS	DEENOPT	PENTODE	DEEORTV	REVOTED
	SPELDER	DEENORS	ENDORSE	DEEORTW	TOWERED
DEELPRU	PRELUDE	DEENORT	ERODENT	DEEORTX	OXTERED
DEELPRY	PEDLERY	DEENORW	ENDOWER	DEEORTZ	ROZETED
DEELPST	PESTLED		REENDOW	DEEORUV	OVERDUE
DEELPTT	PETTLED	DEENORZ	REZONED	DEEORVY	OVERDYE
DEELRRU	RULERED	DEENOST	DENOTES	DEEORXX	XEROXED
DEELRSS	ELDRESS	DEENPPR	PERPEND	DEEOSTV	DEVOTES
DEELRSU	DUELERS	DEENPRS	SPENDER	DEEOSTX	DETOXES
	ELUDERS	DEENPRT	PRENTED	DEEOTUW	OUTWEED
DEELRSV	DELVERS		PRETEND	DEEPPPR	PREPPED
DEELRSW	REWELDS	DEENPSX	EXPENDS	DEEPPST	STEPPED
	WELDERS	DEENRRS	RENDERS	DEEPPSU	SPEEDUP
DEELRUV	VELURED	DEENRRU	ENDURER	DEEPRRS	SPERRED
DEELSSW	DEWLESS	DEENRSS	REDNESS	DEEPRRU	PERDURE
DEELSTT	SETTLED		RESENDS		REPURED
DEELSTU	TELEDUS		SENDERS	DEEPRSS	DEPRESS
DEELSTW	LEWDEST	DEENRST	STERNED		PRESSED
	SWELTED		TENDERS		SPERSED
DEELSUV	EVULSED		TENDRES	DEEPRST	PRESTED
DEELSVV	DEVVELS	DEENRSU	ENDURES	DEEPRSU	PERDUES
DEELTUX	EXULTED		ENSURED		PERSUED
DEELVXY	VEXEDLY	DEENRSV	VENDERS		PERUSED
DEEMMOV	EMMOVED	DEENRSZ	DZERENS		SUPERED
DEEMMST	STEMMED	DEENRTU	DENTURE	DEEPRTU	ERUPTED
DEEMNOR	MODERNE		RETUNED		REPUTED
DEEMNOT	DEMETON		TENURED	DEEPRTY	RETYPED
DEEMNOU	EUDEMON	DEENRTV	VENTRED	DEEPRUV	PREVUED
DEEMNOV	ENMOVED	DEENSST	DENSEST	DEEPSTU	DEPUTES
	VENOMED	DEENSSU	DUENESS	DEEQSTU	QUESTED
DEEMNOY	MONEYED	DEENSSY	DESYNES	DEERRSS	DRESSER
DEEMNRS	MENDERS		ENDYSES		REDRESS
	REMENDS	DEENSTT	DETENTS	DEERRUV	VERDURE
DEEMNST	DEMENTS		STENTED	DEERSSS	DRESSES
DEEMNTU	UNMETED	DEENSTU	DETENUS	DEERSST	DESERTS
DEEMNUW	UNMEWED		DETUNES		DESSERT
DEEMORS	EMERODS	DEENSTX	EXTENDS		TRESSED
DEEMORV	REMOVED	DEENSUV	VENDUES	DEERSSU	DURESSE
DEEMORX	EXODERM	DEENSUW	UNSEWED	DEERSTV	STERVED
DEEMOSS	DEMOSES	DEENSUX	UNSEXED		VERDETS
DEEMOST	DEMOTES	DEENUVX	UNVEXED	DEERSTW	STREWED

	WRESTED	**DEFHORT**	FROTHED	**DEFLNOP**	PENFOLD
DEERSTX	DEXTERS	**DEFHRSU**	FRUSHED	**DEFLNOR**	FONDLER
DEERSTY	DYESTER	**DEFIILM**	MIDLIFE		FORLEND
DEERSVW	SWERVED	**DEFIILN**	INFIDEL	**DEFLNOS**	ENFOLDS
DEERTTU	UTTERED		INFIELD		FONDLES
DEERTUX	EXTRUDE	**DEFIIMS**	FIDEISM	**DEFLNOT**	TENFOLD
DEESSTT	DETESTS	**DEFIIMW**	MIDWIFE	**DEFLNRU**	DERNFUL
DEESSTV	DEVESTS	**DEFIINU**	UNIFIED	**DEFLOOR**	FLOODER
DEESTTT	STETTED	**DEFIINX**	INFIXED		FLOORED
DEFFFLU	FLUFFED	**DEFIIST**	FIDEIST		REFLOOD
DEFFGRU	GRUFFED	**DEFIKLS**	FLISKED	**DEFLOOT**	FOOTLED
DEFFHIW	WHIFFED	**DEFIKRS**	FRISKED	**DEFLOOZ**	FOOZLED
DEFFHOU	HOUFFED	**DEFILLO**	FOLLIED	**DEFLOPP**	FLOPPED
DEFFHOW	HOWFFED	**DEFILLR**	FRILLED	**DEFLORS**	FOLDERS
DEFFIKS	SKIFFED	**DEFILMP**	FLIMPED		REFOLDS
DEFFILP	PIFFLED	**DEFILNR**	FLINDER	**DEFLORT**	TELFORD
DEFFILR	RIFFLED	**DEFILNT**	FLINTED	**DEFLORU**	FLOURED
DEFFILS	SIFFLED	**DEFILNU**	UNFILDE		FOULDER
DEFFIMO	FIEFDOM		UNFILED	**DEFLOSS**	FLOSSED
DEFFINS	SNIFFED	**DEFILOO**	FOLIOED	**DEFLOSU**	DEFOULS
DEFFIOS	DIEOFFS	**DEFILOW**	OLDWIFE		FLOUSED
	OFFSIDE	**DEFILPP**	FLIPPED	**DEFLOTU**	FLOUTED
DEFFIPS	SPIFFED	**DEFILPU**	UPFIELD	**DEFLPRU**	PURFLED
DEFFIRS	DIFFERS	**DEFILRT**	FLIRTED	**DEFLRRU**	FLURRED
DEFFIST	STIFFED		TRIFLED	**DEFLRUU**	DUREFUL
DEFFISU	DIFFUSE	**DEFILRU**	DIREFUL	**DEFLUZZ**	FUZZLED
DEFFKOS	SKOFFED	**DEFILSS**	FISSLED	**DEFMNUU**	UNFUMED
DEFFLMU	MUFFLED	**DEFILST**	STIFLED	**DEFMORS**	DEFORMS
DEFFLPU	PLUFFED	**DEFILSU**	SULFIDE		SERFDOM
DEFFLRU	RUFFLED	**DEFILTT**	FLITTED	**DEFMPRU**	FRUMPED
DEFFLSU	DUFFELS	**DEFILTY**	FETIDLY	**DEFNOOR**	FORDONE
	DUFFLES	**DEFILXY**	FIXEDLY	**DEFNORT**	FRONTED
	SLUFFED	**DEFILZZ**	FIZZLED	**DEFNORU**	FOUNDER
DEFFNOR	FORFEND	**DEFIMOR**	DEIFORM		REFOUND
DEFFNOS	OFFENDS	**DEFIMOW**	WIFEDOM	**DEFNORW**	FROWNED
	SENDOFF	**DEFINRS**	FINDERS	**DEFNOST**	FONDEST
DEFFNSU	SNUFFED		FRIENDS	**DEFNOSU**	FONDUES
DEFFOPU	POUFFED		REDFINS	**DEFNPRU**	PREFUND
DEFFORS	DOFFERS		REFINDS	**DEFNRSU**	FUNDERS
DEFFOSW	SOWFFED	**DEFINRU**	UNFIRED		REFUNDS
DEFFRSU	DUFFERS	**DEFINST**	SNIFTED	**DEFNSUU**	UNFUSED
DEFFSTU	DUFFEST	**DEFINSU**	FUNDIES	**DEFOOPR**	PROOFED
	STUFFED		INFUSED	**DEFOOPS**	SPOOFED
DEFGGIR	FRIGGED	**DEFINSY**	DENSIFY	**DEFOORS**	DOOFERS
DEFGGLO	FLOGGED	**DEFINUX**	UNFIXED		FORDOES
DEFGGOR	FROGGED	**DEFINUY**	UNDEIFY	**DEFOORT**	REDFOOT
DEFGGRU	FRUGGED	**DEFIOOS**	FOODIES	**DEFORST**	DEFROST
DEFGINN	FENDING	**DEFIOQU**	QUOIFED		FROSTED
DEFGINR	FRINGED	**DEFIORU**	FOUDRIE	**DEFORTU**	FOUTRED
DEFGINU	FEUDING	**DEFIOST**	FOISTED	**DEFSSUU**	DUFUSES
DEFGINY	DEFYING	**DEFIPRY**	PERFIDY	**DEGGGIL**	GIGGLED
DEFGIOR	FIREDOG	**DEFIRRT**	DRIFTER	**DEGGGIN**	DEGGING
DEFGIRS	FRIDGES	**DEFIRST**	FRISTED	**DEGGGIR**	GRIGGED
DEFGIRT	GRIFTED	**DEFIRTT**	FRITTED	**DEGGGLO**	GOGGLED
DEFGIRU	FIGURED	**DEFIRTU**	FRUITED	**DEGGGLU**	GLUGGED
DEFGIST	FIDGETS	**DEFIRZZ**	FRIZZED		GUGGLED
DEFGITY	FIDGETY	**DEFISTU**	FEUDIST	**DEGGGOR**	GROGGED
DEFGRTU	GRUFTED	**DEFISTW**	SWIFTED	**DEGGHIL**	HIGGLED
DEFHIRS	REDFISH	**DEFKLNU**	FLUNKED	**DEGGHIN**	HEDGING
DEFHIST	SHIFTED	**DEFLLOU**	DOLEFUL	**DEGGHIW**	WHIGGED
DEFHLOO	ELFHOOD	**DEFLLUW**	DEWFULL	**DEGGHOS**	SHOGGED
DEFHLSU	FLUSHED	**DEFLMOS**	SELFDOM	**DEGGIJL**	JIGGLED
	SHEDFUL	**DEFLMPU**	FLUMPED	**DEGGIKN**	KEDGING
DEFHOOW	WHOOFED	**DEFLNOO**	ONEFOLD	**DEGGILN**	GELDING

Seven-letter anagrams

	NIGGLED	**DEGIIKR**	KIDGIER	**DEGIMSS**	SMIDGES
DEGGILW	WIGGLED	**DEGIILL**	GILLIED	**DEGIMST**	MIDGETS
DEGGINS	EDGINGS	**DEGIILN**	EILDING	**DEGINNN**	DENNING
	SNIGGED		ELIDING	**DEGINNP**	PENDING
DEGGINW	WEDGING	**DEGIIMR**	MIDGIER	**DEGINNR**	GRINNED
DEGGIOR	DOGGIER	**DEGIIMS**	MIDGIES		RENDING
DEGGIOS	DOGGIES	**DEGIINN**	INDIGEN	**DEGINNS**	ENDINGS
DEGGIPR	PRIGGED	**DEGIINR**	DINGIER		SENDING
DEGGIRS	DIGGERS	**DEGIINS**	DINGIES	**DEGINNT**	DENTING
DEGGIRT	TRIGGED	**DEGIINT**	DIETING		TENDING
DEGGIRU	DRUGGIE		EDITING	**DEGINNU**	ENDUING
DEGGISW	SWIGGED		IGNITED	**DEGINNV**	VENDING
DEGGITW	TWIGGED	**DEGIIPS**	GIPSIED	**DEGINNW**	WENDING
DEGGJLO	JOGGLED	**DEGIIRR**	RIDGIER	**DEGINNY**	DENYING
DEGGJLU	JUGGLED		RIGIDER	**DEGINOP**	PIDGEON
DEGGKSU	SKUGGED	**DEGIIRS**	DIRIGES	**DEGINOR**	ERODING
DEGGLOO	GOOGLED	**DEGIISW**	WIDGIES		GROINED
DEGGLOR	DOGGREL	**DEGIJLN**	JINGLED		IGNORED
DEGGLOS	DOGLEGS	**DEGIKLO**	DOGLIKE		NEGROID
	SLOGGED		GODLIKE		REDOING
DEGGLOT	TOGGLED	**DEGILLO**	GOLLIED	**DEGINOS**	DINGOES
DEGGLPU	PLUGGED	**DEGILLR**	GRILLED	**DEGINOT**	INGOTED
	PUGGLED	**DEGILLU**	GULLIED	**DEGINOW**	WENDIGO
DEGGLRU	GURGLED	**DEGILLV**	GELIDLY		WIDGEON
DEGGLSU	SLUGGED	**DEGILMN**	MEDLING		WONGIED
DEGGMSU	SMUGGED		MELDING	**DEGINRR**	GRINDER
DEGGNOO	DOGGONE		MINGLED		REGRIND
DEGGNOS	SNOGGED	**DEGILMS**	MIDLEGS	**DEGINRS**	DINGERS
DEGGNOU	GUDGEON	**DEGILNN**	LENDING		ENGIRDS
DEGGNSU	SNUGGED	**DEGILNO**	GLENOID	**DEGINRU**	DUNGIER
DEGGOPR	PROGGED	**DEGILNP**	PINGLED	**DEGINRW**	REDWING
DEGGORS	DOGGERS	**DEGILNS**	DINGLES		WRINGED
DEGGORT	TROGGED		ELDINGS	**DEGINRY**	YERDING
DEGGORY	DOGGERY		ENGILDS	**DEGINSS**	DESIGNS
DEGGOSS	DOGGESS		SINGLED		SDEIGNS
DEGGRRU	DRUGGER	**DEGILNT**	GLINTED	**DEGINST**	NIDGETS
	GRUDGER		TINGLED		STEDING
DEGGRSU	GRUDGES	**DEGILNU**	DUELING		STINGED
DEGGRTU	DRUGGET		ELUDING	**DEGINSU**	GUNDIES
DEGHHIT	HIGHTED		INDULGE		SUEDING
	THIGHED	**DEGILNV**	DELVING	**DEGINSW**	SWINDGE
DEGHHOU	HOUGHED		DEVLING		SWINGED
DEGHILN	HINDLEG	**DEGILNW**	WELDING	**DEGINSY**	DINGEYS
DEGHILT	DELIGHT	**DEGILOR**	GLORIED		DYEINGS
	LIGHTED		GODLIER	**DEGINTU**	DUETING
DEGHINN	HENDING		GOLDIER	**DEGINTW**	TWINGED
DEGHINO	HONGIED	**DEGILOU**	OUGLIED	**DEGINUX**	EXUDING
DEGHINR	HERDING	**DEGILRR**	GIRDLER	**DEGIOOR**	GOODIER
DEGHINT	NIGHTED	**DEGILRS**	GILDERS	**DEGIOOS**	GOODIES
DEGHINW	WHINGED		GIRDLES		SOOGIED
DEGHIOT	HOGTIED		GLIDERS	**DEGIOPR**	PODGIER
DEGHIPT	PIGHTED		GRISLED	**DEGIORR**	GRODIER
DEGHIRT	GIRTHED		LIDGERS	**DEGIORT**	GOITRED
	RIGHTED		REGILDS	**DEGIPPR**	GRIPPED
DEGHIST	SIGHTED		RIDGELS	**DEGIPRU**	PUDGIER
DEGHITW	WIGHTED		RIDGELS	**DEGIPSY**	GYPSIED
DEGHLOO	DOGHOLE	**DEGILRU**	GUILDER	**DEGIQSU**	SQUIDGE
DEGHNOT	THONGED	**DEGILRW**	WERGILD	**DEGIRRS**	GIRDERS
DEGHORR	DROGHER	**DEGILTZ**	GLITZED		RIDGERS
DEGHORU	ROUGHED	**DEGILUV**	DIVULGE	**DEGIRRU**	DURGIER
DEGHOST	GHOSTED	**DEGIMNN**	MENDING	**DEGIRSS**	DIGRESS
DEGHOSU	SOUGHED	**DEGIMNO**	DEMOING	**DEGIRSU**	GUIDERS
DEGHOTU	OUGHTED		MENDIGO	**DEGIRTT**	GRITTED
	TOUGHED	**DEGIMNS**	SMIDGEN	**DEGISST**	DIGESTS
		DEGIMPU	GUIMPED		

	DISGEST		OVERDOG	DEHINUV	UNHIVED
DEGISSU	GUSSIED	DEGOOST	STOOGED	DEHIOOR	HOODIER
DEGISTU	DUGITES	DEGOPRU	GROUPED	DEHIOOS	HOODIES
	GIUSTED	DEGORRS	DROGERS	DEHIOOT	DHOOTIE
DEGISTW	WIDGETS	DEGORSS	GROSSED	DEHIORS	RHODIES
DEGJLNU	JUNGLED		SODGERS	DEHIORT	THEROID
DEGJRSU	JUDGERS	DEGORST	STODGER	DEHIOST	HOISTED
DEGKKOR	GROKKED	DEGORSU	DROGUES	DEHIOSU	HIDEOUS
DEGKLSU	KLUDGES		GOURDES	DEHIOSV	DOVEISH
DEGKLUY	KLUDGEY		GROUSED	DEHIOSW	HOWDIES
DEGLMMO	GLOMMED	DEGORTU	DROGUET	DEHIOSX	OXHIDES
DEGLMOO	GLOOMED		GROUTED	DEHIOTU	HIDEOUT
DEGLMOU	MOGULED	DEGOSST	STODGES	DEHIPPS	SHIPPED
DEGLNNO	ENDLONG	DEGOSTU	DEGOUTS	DEHIPPW	WHIPPED
DEGLNOP	PLONGED	DEGOSTW	GOWDEST	DEHIRRS	SHIRRED
DEGLNOS	DONGLES	DEGRRTU	TRUDGER	DEHIRRU	DHURRIE
	GOLDENS	DEGRSTU	TRUDGES		HURRIED
DEGLNOU	LOUNGED	DEGSSTU	DEGUSTS	DEHIRRW	WHIRRED
DEGLNPU	PLUNGED	DEHHISW	WHISHED	DEHIRST	DITHERS
	PUNGLED	DEHHMPU	HUMPHED		SHIRTED
DEGLNSU	GULDENS	DEHHOOS	HOOSHED	DEHIRSU	HURDIES
DEGLNUU	UNGLUED	DEHHSSU	SHUSHED	DEHIRSV	DERVISH
	UNGLUED	DEHIIKO	HIKOIED		SHRIVED
DEGLOOP	GLOOPED	DEHIINN	HINNIED	DEHIRTV	THRIVED
DEGLOPP	GLOPPED	DEHIIPS	PIEDISH	DEHIRTW	WRITHED
DEGLOPR	PLEDGOR	DEHIIRS	DISHIER	DEHIRTY	DITHERY
DEGLOPS	PLODGES	DEHIKRS	SHIRKED	DEHISSW	SWISHED
	SPLODGE		SHRIKED		WHISSED
DEGLORS	LODGERS	DEHIKSW	WHISKED	DEHISTT	SHITTED
DEGLORW	GROWLED	DEHILLO	HILLOED	DEHISTW	WHISTED
DEGLOSS	GLOSSED	DEHILLS	SHILLED	DEHISVV	SHIVVED
	GODLESS	DEHILMS	DISHELM	DEHIWZZ	WHIZZED
DEGLOST	GOLDEST	DEHILNP	DELPHIN	DEHKNTU	THUNKED
DEGLOTU	GLOUTED	DEHILOT	LITHOED	DEHLLOO	HOLLOED
DEGLSSU	SLUDGES	DEHILPR	HIRPLED	DEHLLOU	HULLOED
DEGLTTU	GLUTTED	DEHILRS	HIRSLED	DEHLMOU	MUDHOLE
	GUTTLED	DEHILRT	THIRLED	DEHLMSU	MULSHED
DEGLUZZ	GUZZLED	DEHILRW	WHIRLED	DEHLNOS	HONDLES
DEGMNOO	GOODMEN	DEHILSS	SHIELDS	DEHLOOS	SHOOLED
DEGMOOR	GROOMED	DEHILTY	DIETHYL	DEHLOOT	TOEHOLD
DEGMOOS	SMOODGE	DEHIMMS	SHIMMED	DEHLOPP	HOPPLED
	SMOOGED	DEHIMMW	WHIMMED	DEHLORS	HOLDERS
DEGMPRU	GRUMPED	DEHIMNS	MEHNDIS	DEHLORW	WHORLED
DEGMRSU	MUDGERS	DEHIMNU	INHUMED	DEHLOSS	SLOSHED
	SMUDGER	DEHIMOP	HEMIPOD	DEHLOST	SLOTHED
DEGMSSU	SMUDGES	DEHIMOR	HEIRDOM	DEHLRRU	HURDLER
DEGNNOU	DUNGEON	DEHIMOS	DISHOME	DEHLRSU	HURDLES
DEGNOOS	NOODGES	DEHIMOT	ETHMOID	DEHLRTU	HURTLED
DEGNOPR	PRONGED	DEHIMRS	DIRHEMS	DEHLSSU	SLUSHED
DEGNOPS	SPONGED	DEHIMRU	HUMIDER	DEHLSTU	HUSTLED
DEGNORU	GUERDON	DEHIMST	SMITHED	DEHMNOO	HOODMEN
	UNDERGO	DEHIMUX	HUMIDEX	DEHMNSU	MUDHENS
	UNGORED	DEHINNS	SHINNED	DEHMOPR	MORPHED
DEGNORW	WRONGED	DEHINNT	THINNED	DEHMOPW	WHOMPED
DEGNOTU	TONGUED	DEHINOP	DIPHONE	DEHMORU	HUMORED
DEGNRSU	DUNGERS		PHONIED	DEHMOST	METHODS
	GERUNDS	DEHINOR	HORDEIN	DEHMOTU	MOUTHED
	NUDGERS	DEHINOS	HOIDENS	DEHMPTU	THUMPED
DEGNRTU	GRUNTED	DEHINOV	HYENOID	DEHMPUW	WHUMPED
	TRUDGEN	DEHINPS	ENDSHIP	DEHMSSU	SMUSHED
DEGNRUU	UNURGED	DEHINRS	HINDERS	DEHNNSU	SHUNNED
DEGNSSU	SNUDGES		NERDISH	DEHNOOR	HONORED
DEGNUVY	UNGYVED		SHRINED	DEHNOOW	HOEDOWN
DEGOORV	GROOVED	DEHINRU	UNHIRED		WOODHEN

Seven-letter anagrams

DEHNOPU	UNHOPED	**DEIIMNO**	DOMINIE	**DEIKLLS**	DESKILL
DEHNORS	DEHORNS	**DEIIMRT**	TIMIDER		SKILLED
DEHNORT	NORTHED	**DEIIMST**	MISDIET	**DEIKLNP**	PLINKED
	THONDER		MISEDIT	**DEIKLNR**	KINDLER
	THORNED		STIMIED	**DEIKLNS**	KINDLES
	THRONED	**DEIIMSZ**	MIDSIZE		SLINKED
DEHNORU	HOUNDER	**DEIIMVW**	MIDWIVE	**DEIKLNT**	TINKLED
DEHNOSU	UNSHOED	**DEIINOS**	IODINES	**DEIKLNU**	UNLIKED
DEHNOSY	HOYDENS		IONISED	**DEIKLNW**	WINKLED
DEHNOTZ	DOZENTH	**DEIINOT**	EDITION	**DEIKLOP**	PODLIKE
DEHNRSU	HURDENS		TENIOID	**DEIKLOR**	RODLIKE
DEHNRTU	THUNDER	**DEIINOZ**	IONIZED	**DEIKLOS**	KELOIDS
DEHNSSU	DUNSHES	**DEIINNR**	RINDIER	**DEIKLRS**	SKIRLED
	SNUSHED	**DEIINRS**	INSIDER	**DEIKLRT**	KIRTLED
DEHNSSY	YSHENDS		SNIDIER	**DEIKLST**	KIDLETS
DEHNSTU	SHUNTED	**DEIINRT**	INDITER	**DEIKLTT**	KITTLED
DEHNSUZ	NUDZHES		NITRIDE	**DEIKMMS**	SKIMMED
DEHNSYY	HYDYNES	**DEIINRU**	URIDINE	**DEIKMPS**	SKIMPED
DEHOOPT	PHOTOED	**DEIINRV**	DIVINER	**DEIKMRS**	SMIRKED
DEHOOPW	WHOOPED	**DEIINRW**	WINDIER	**DEIKNNS**	SKINNED
DEHOOST	SOOTHED	**DEIINSS**	INSIDES	**DEIKNOS**	DOESKIN
DEHOOSW	WOOSHED	**DEIINST**	INDITES	**DEIKNOV**	INVOKED
DEHOOTT	TOOTHED		TINEIDS	**DEIKNPR**	PRINKED
DEHOOTW	WHOOTED	**DEIINSV**	DIVINES	**DEIKNRR**	DRINKER
DEHOPPS	SHOPPED	**DEIINTV**	INVITED	**DEIKNRS**	KINDERS
DEHOPPW	WHOPPED	**DEIIORS**	IODISER		KINREDS
DEHORSS	SHODERS	**DEIIORT**	DIORITE		REDSKIN
DEHORST	DEHORTS	**DEIIORV**	IVORIED	**DEIKNST**	DINKEST
	SHORTED	**DEIIORZ**	IODIZER		KINDEST
DEHORSV	SHROVED	**DEIIOSS**	IODISES	**DEIKNSW**	SWINKED
DEHORSW	SHROWED	**DEIIOSX**	OXIDISE	**DEIKNSY**	DINKEYS
DEHORTT	TROTHED	**DEIIOSZ**	IODIZES		KIDNEYS
DEHORTW	WORTHED	**DEIIOXZ**	OXIDIZE	**DEIKNSZ**	ZENDIKS
DEHOSTT	SHOTTED	**DEIIPPR**	DIPPIER	**DEIKNTT**	KNITTED
DEHOSTU	SHOUTED	**DEIIPRS**	PIERIDS	**DEIKNTW**	TWINKED
	SOUTHED	**DEIIPRT**	RIPTIDE	**DEIKORR**	DORKIER
DEHOSTW	SOWTHED		TIDERIP	**DEIKOSY**	DISYOKE
DEHPPUW	WHUPPED	**DEIIRRT**	DIRTIER	**DEIKPPS**	SKIPPED
DEHPSSY	PHYSEDS	**DEIIRST**	DIRTIES	**DEIKQRU**	QUIRKED
DEHPTTU	PHUTTED		DITSIER	**DEIKRRS**	SKIRRED
DEIIIRS	IRIDISE		TIDIERS	**DEIKRST**	SKIRTED
DEIIIRZ	IRIDIZE	**DEIIRTT**	TRITIDE	**DEIKRSU**	DUIKERS
DEIIJMM	JIMMIED	**DEIIRTX**	EDITRIX		DUSKIER
DEIIKKL	KIDLIKE	**DEIIRTZ**	DITZIER	**DEIKSTY**	DYKIEST
DEIIKLS	DISLIKE	**DEIIRVV**	VIVIDER	**DEIKSVY**	SKYDIVE
DEIIKNR	DINKIER	**DEIIRZZ**	DIZZIER	**DEILLMO**	MODELLI
DEIIKNS	DINKIES	**DEIISTT**	DIETIST	**DEILLMU**	ILLUMED
	KINDIES		DITTIES	**DEILLNW**	INDWELL
DEIIKST	DIKIEST		TIDIEST	**DEILLOR**	DOLLIER
DEIILLR	DILLIER	**DEIISTV**	VISITED	**DEILLOS**	DOLLIES
DEIILLS	DILLIES	**DEIISVV**	DIVVIES	**DEILLOV**	LIVELOD
DEIILLW	WILLIED	**DEIISZZ**	DIZZIES	**DEILLPR**	PRILLED
DEIILMN	MIDLINE	**DEIIVZZ**	VIZZIED	**DEILLPS**	SPILLED
DEIILMP	IMPLIED	**DEIJLLO**	JOLLIED	**DEILLQU**	QUILLED
DEIILMT	DELIMIT	**DEIJNOR**	JOINDER	**DEILLRR**	DRILLER
	LIMITED	**DEIJNOT**	JOINTED		REDRILL
DEIILNS	INISLED	**DEIJNRU**	INJURED	**DEILLRT**	TRILLED
	LINDIES	**DEIJNSU**	DISJUNE	**DEILLRU**	DULLIER
DEIILOS	DOILIES	**DEIJORY**	JOYRIDE	**DEILLRV**	DREVILL
	IDOLISE	**DEIJOST**	JOISTED	**DEILLSS**	LIDLESS
DEIILOZ	IDOLIZE	**DEIJRRS**	JERRIDS	**DEILLST**	STILLED
DEIILPS	LIPIDES	**DEIJTTU**	JUTTIED	**DEILLSU**	ILLUDES
DEIILRV	LIVIDER	**DEIKKNS**	SKINKED		SULLIED
DEIIMMX	IMMIXED	**DEIKKRS**	SKRIKED	**DEILLSW**	SWILLED

DEILLTW	TWILLED	**DEILOSY**	DOYLIES	**DEIMNRU**	UNRIMED
DEILMMP	PLIMMED	**DEILOTU**	OUTLIED	**DEIMNSS**	DIMNESS
DEILMMS	SLIMMED		TOLUIDE		MISSEND
DEILMNS	MILDENS	**DEILPPR**	RIPPLED	**DEIMNST**	MINDSET
DEILMNU	LUMINED	**DEILPPS**	SIPPLED		MISTEND
	UNLIMED		SLIPPED	**DEIMNSW**	MISWEND
DEILMOP	IMPLODE	**DEILPPT**	TIPPLED	**DEIMNTU**	MINUTED
DEILMOR	MOLDIER	**DEILPPU**	UPPILED		MUNITED
DEILMOS	MELOIDS	**DEILPRT**	TRIPLED		MUTINED
	MIDSOLE	**DEILPRU**	PRELUDI		UNTIMED
	SMOILED	**DEILPSS**	DISPELS	**DEIMNUX**	UNMIXED
DEILMOY	MYELOID		DISPLES	**DEIMOOR**	DOOMIER
DEILMPP	PIMPLED	**DEILPSU**	DUPLIES		MOIDORE
DEILMPR	RIMPLED	**DEILPTY**	TEPIDLY		MOODIER
DEILMPS	DIMPLES	**DEILQTU**	QUILTED	**DEIMOOS**	MOODIES
	MISPLED	**DEILRRU**	LURIDER	**DEIMOPR**	IMPEDOR
	SIMPLED	**DEILRSS**	SIDLERS	**DEIMOPS**	IMPOSED
DEILMPW	WIMPLED		SLIDERS	**DEIMORR**	REMORID
DEILMST	MILDEST	**DEILRSV**	DRIVELS	**DEIMORS**	MISDOER
	MISTLED	**DEILRSW**	SWIRLED		MOIDERS
DEILMSW	MILDEWS		WILDERS	**DEIMORU**	ERODIUM
DEILMWY	MILDEWY	**DEILRSY**	RIDLEYS	**DEIMOSS**	MISDOES
DEILMXY	MIXEDLY	**DEILRTU**	DILUTER	**DEIMOST**	DISTOME
DEILMZZ	MIZZLED	**DEILRTW**	TWIRLED		DOMIEST
DEILNNS	DINNLES	**DEILRTY**	TIREDLY		MODISTE
	LINDENS	**DEILRVY**	DEVILRY		MOISTED
DEILNNU	UNLINED	**DEILRWY**	WEIRDLY	**DEIMOSW**	MOWDIES
DEILNOO	EIDOLON	**DEILRWZ**	WRIZLED	**DEIMOTT**	OMITTED
DEILNOS	DOLINES	**DEILRZZ**	DRIZZLE	**DEIMOTV**	MOTIVED
	INDOLES	**DEILSST**	DELISTS		VOMITED
	SONDELI	**DEILSTT**	SLITTED	**DEIMPPR**	PRIMPED
DEILNOT	LENTOID		STILTED	**DEIMPRT**	DIREMPT
DEILNOU	UNOILED	**DEILSTU**	DILUTES	**DEIMPRU**	DUMPIER
DEILNPP	NIPPLED		DUELIST		UMPIRED
DEILNPS	SPELDIN	**DEILSTW**	WILDEST	**DEIMPSU**	DUMPIES
	SPINDLE	**DEILSTY**	DISTYLE	**DEIMPTU**	IMPUTED
	SPLINED	**DEILSUV**	DIVULSE	**DEIMRRS**	SMIRRED
DEILNPU	UNPILED	**DEILSZZ**	SIZZLED	**DEIMRSW**	MISDREW
DEILNRT	TENDRIL	**DEILTTT**	TITTLED	**DEIMRSY**	SEMIDRY
	TRINDLE	**DEILTTU**	TITULED	**DEIMRUU**	UREDIUM
DEILNST	DENTILS	**DEILTTV**	VITTLED	**DEIMSST**	DEMISTS
DEILNSW	SWINDLE	**DEILTTW**	TWILTED	**DEIMSSU**	MISUSED
	WINDLES	**DEILZZZ**	ZIZZLED	**DEIMSTT**	SMITTED
DEILNSY	SNIDELY	**DEIMMMU**	MUMMIED	**DEIMSTU**	MUISTED
DEILNTU	DILUENT	**DEIMMOT**	TOMMIED		TEDIUMS
	UNTILED	**DEIMMPR**	PRIMMED	**DEIMSTY**	STYMIED
DEILNTW	INDWELT	**DEIMMRS**	DIMMERS	**DEINNNU**	NUNDINE
	WINTLED	**DEIMMRT**	MIDTERM	**DEINNOO**	ONIONED
DEILNUV	UNLIVED		TRIMMED	**DEINNOP**	PINNOED
DEILOOS	DOOLIES	**DEIMMRU**	DUMMIER	**DEINNOR**	ENDIRON
DEILOPR	LEPORID		IMMURED	**DEINNOS**	DONNIES
DEILOPS	DESPOIL	**DEIMMST**	DIMMEST		ONDINES
	DIPLOES	**DEIMMSU**	DUMMIES	**DEINNOT**	INTONED
	DIPOLES		MEDIUMS		NOINTED
	PELOIDS	**DEIMNNU**	MINUEND	**DEINNRS**	DINNERS
	SOLIPED		UNMINED		ENDRINS
	SPOILED	**DEIMNOP**	IMPONED	**DEINNRU**	DUNNIER
DEILOPT	PILOTED	**DEIMNOR**	MINORED		INURNED
DEILOPU	EUPLOID	**DEIMNOS**	DOMINES	**DEINNST**	DENTINS
DEILORS	SOLDIER		EMODINS		INDENTS
	SOLIDER		MISDONE		INTENDS
DEILORT	DOILTER	**DEIMNPS**	IMPENDS	**DEINNSU**	DUNNIES
DEILORW	DOWLIER	**DEIMNRS**	MINDERS		UNDINES
DEILOSV	LIVEDOS		REMINDS	**DEINNSW**	ENWINDS

DEINNSY	DYNEINS	DEIOORS	ODORISE	DEIOSTW	DOWIEST
DEINNTU	DUNNITE		OROIDES	DEIOSTX	EXODIST
DEINNTW	TWINNED	DEIOORW	WOODIER	DEIOSTZ	DOZIEST
DEINOOZ	OZONIDE	DEIOORZ	ODORIZE	DEIOSUV	DEVIOUS
DEINOPR	POINDER	DEIOOSS	ISODOSE	DEIOTUV	OUTVIED
	PROINED	DEIOOST	OSTEOID	DEIOTUW	WIDEOUT
DEINOPS	DISPONE	DEIOOSW	WOODIES	DEIPPPU	PUPPIED
	SPINODE	DEIOOSZ	DOOZIES	DEIPPQU	QUIPPED
DEINOPT	POINTED	DEIOOVV	VOIVODE	DEIPPRR	DRIPPER
DEINOQU	QUOINED	DEIOOWW	WOIWODE	DEIPPRS	DIPPERS
DEINORR	DRONIER	DEIOPPP	POPPIED	DEIPPRT	TRIPPED
DEINORS	DINEROS	DEIOPPS	DOPPIES	DEIPPST	PEPTIDS
	DONSIER	DEIOPRS	PERIODS	DEIPPSU	DUPPIES
	INDORSE	DEIOPRT	DIOPTER	DEIPRSS	PRISSED
	ORDINES		DIOPTRE		SPIDERS
	ROSINED		PERIDOT	DEIPRST	SPIRTED
	SORDINE		PROTEID		STRIPED
DEINORU	DOURINE	DEIOPRV	PROVIDE	DEIPRSU	PUDSIER
	NEUROID	DEIOPRX	PEROXID		SIRUPED
DEINORW	DOWNIER	DEIOPSS	DISPOSE		UPDRIES
	WINDORE	DEIOPST	DEPOSIT	DEIPRSY	SPIDERY
DEINOSS	ONSIDES		DOPIEST	DEIPSSU	UPSIDES
DEINOST	DITONES		PODITES	DEIPSSV	VESPIDS
	STONIED		POSITED	DEIPSTT	SPITTED
DEINPPS	SNIPPED		SOPITED	DEIPSTU	DISPUTE
DEINPRS	PINDERS		TOPSIDE	DEIPSUV	UPDIVES
DEINPRT	PRINTED	DEIOPSV	VESPOID	DEIPSUZ	UPSIZED
DEINPST	DIPNETS	DEIOPTT	TIPTOED	DEIPSXY	PYXIDES
	STIPEND	DEIOPTV	PIVOTED	DEIPTTU	PUTTIED
DEINPSU	UNIPEDS	DEIOQTU	QUOITED		TITUPED
	UNSPIDE	DEIORRT	DORTIER	DEIQRSU	SQUIRED
	UNSPIED	DEIORRW	ROWDIER	DEIQRTU	QUIRTED
DEINPUW	UNWIPED		WORDIER	DEIQTTU	QUITTED
DEINRRU	NURDIER		WORRIED	DEIQUZZ	QUIZZED
DEINRST	TINDERS	DEIORSS	DORISES	DEIRRST	STIRRED
DEINRSU	INSURED		DOSSIER		STRIDER
DEINRSV	VERDINS	DEIORST	EDITORS	DEIRRSU	DRUSIER
DEINRSW	REWINDS		ROISTED		DURRIES
	WINDERS		ROSITED	DEIRRSV	DRIVERS
DEINRTT	TRIDENT		SORTIED	DEIRRUX	DRUXIER
DEINRTU	INTRUDE		STEROID	DEIRSST	DISSERT
	TURDINE		STORIED		STRIDES
	UNTIRED		TIERODS	DEIRSSU	DISEURS
	UNTRIDE		TRIODES		SUDSIER
	UNTRIED	DEIORSV	DEVISOR	DEIRSTU	DUSTIER
DEINRTX	DEXTRIN		DEVOIRS		REDUITS
DEINRTY	TINDERY		VISORED		STUDIER
DEINRUW	UNWIRED		VOIDERS	DEIRSTV	DIVERTS
DEINSST	DISNEST	DEIORSW	DOWRIES		STRIVED
	DISSENT		ROWDIES		VERDITS
	SNIDEST		WEIRDOS	DEISSST	DESISTS
DEINSSU	NIDUSES	DEIORSZ	DORIZES	DEISSSU	DISUSES
DEINSSV	VENDISS	DEIORTT	DOTTIER	DEISSTU	STUDIES
DEINSSW	WINDSES	DEIORTU	ETOURDI		TISSUED
DEINSSY	ENDYSIS		IODURET	DEISSTV	DIVESTS
DEINSTT	DENTIST		OUTRIDE	DEISTTW	DEWITTS
	DISTENT	DEIORTZ	ROZITED		TWISTED
	STINTED	DEIORVZ	VIZORED	DEISWZZ	SWIZZED
DEINSTU	DISTUNE	DEIORWW	WIDOWER	DEITTTW	TWITTED
	DUNITES	DEIOSTT	DOTIEST	DEJLOST	JOSTLED
DEINSTY	DENSITY		STOITED	DEJLSTU	JUSTLED
	DESTINY	DEIOSTU	OUTSIDE	DEJOORY	JOYRODE
DEINSUZ	UNSIZED		TEDIOUS	DEJOSTU	JOUSTED
DEINUVW	UNWIVED	DEIOSTV	DOVIEST	DEKKLSU	SKULKED

DEKKNSU	SKUNKED	**DELMOUV**	VOLUMED	**DELOPTZ**	PLOTZED
DEKLLNO	KNOLLED	**DELMPPU**	PLUMPED	**DELORRY**	ORDERLY
DEKLLOS	SKOLLED	**DELMPRU**	RUMPLED	**DELORSS**	DORSELS
DEKLLSU	SKULLED	**DELMPSU**	DUMPLES		RODLESS
DEKLNOP	PLONKED		SLUMPED		SOLDERS
DEKLNPU	PLUNKED	**DELMTUY**	MUTEDLY	**DELORST**	DROLEST
DEKLNRU	KNURLED	**DELMUZZ**	MUZZLED		OLDSTER
	RUNKLED	**DELNOOS**	NOODLES		STRODLE
DEKLRSU	SKUDLER		SNOOLED	**DELORSW**	WELDORS
DEKNNOS	NONSKED	**DELNORS**	RONDELS	**DELORSY**	YODLERS
DEKNNRU	DRUNKEN	**DELNORT**	ENTROLD	**DELORTT**	DOTTLER
DEKNOOS	SNOOKED	**DELNORU**	LOUNDER		DOTTREL
DEKNOPP	KNOPPED		ROUNDEL	**DELORTU**	TROULED
DEKNOPR	PRONKED		ROUNDLE	**DELORUV**	LOUVRED
DEKNOQU	QUONKED	**DELNOSS**	OLDNESS	**DELOSSS**	DOSSELS
DEKNOST	STONKED	**DELNOSU**	LOUDENS	**DELOSSU**	DULOSES
DEKNOSW	SNOWKED		NODULES	**DELOSTT**	DOTTELS
DEKNOSY	DONKEYS		NOUSLED		DOTTLES
DEKNOTT	KNOTTED	**DELNOSW**	DOWLNES		SLOTTED
DEKNOTU	KNOUTED	**DELNOSZ**	DONZELS	**DELOSTU**	LOUDEST
DEKNOUY	UNYOKED	**DELNOTW**	LETDOWN		OULDEST
DEKNPSU	SPUNKED	**DELNOTY**	NOTEDLY		TOUSLED
DEKNRRU	DRUNKER	**DELNOUV**	UNLOVED	**DELOSYY**	DOYLEYS
DEKNRSU	DUNKERS	**DELNOWY**	DOWLNEY	**DELOSZZ**	SOZZLED
DEKNRTU	TRUNKED	**DELNPRU**	PLUNDER	**DELOTUU**	OUTDUEL
DEKNSSU	DUSKENS	**DELNRSU**	LURDENS	**DELOTUV**	VOLUTED
DEKOOPS	SPOOKED		NURDLES	**DELOTUZ**	TOUZLED
DEKOOST	DOOKETS		NURSLED	**DELPPRU**	PURPLED
	STOOKED		RUNDLES	**DELPPSU**	SUPPLED
DEKOOTW	KOTOWED	**DELNRTU**	RUNDLET	**DELPRSU**	DRUPELS
DEKOPST	DESKTOP		TRUNDLE		SLURPED
DEKORST	STROKED	**DELNRUU**	UNRULED	**DELPSSU**	PLUSSED
DEKORWY	KEYWORD	**DELNSSU**	DULNESS	**DELPSTU**	DUPLETS
DEKOSSU	KUDOSES	**DELNUWY**	UNWELDY	**DELPSUY**	SPULYED
DEKOSVY	SKYDOVE	**DELNUZZ**	NUZZLED	**DELPUZZ**	PUZZLED
DEKPRSU	PREDUSK	**DELOOPP**	PLEOPOD	**DELRRSU**	SLURRED
DEKRSUY	DUYKERS	**DELOOPS**	POODLES	**DELRSTU**	LUSTRED
DEKSSTU	DUSKEST		SPOOLED		RUSTLED
DELLMOO	MODELLO	**DELOOPT**	POOTLED		STRUDEL
DELLOOW	WOOLLED	**DELOORT**	ROOTLED	**DELRTTU**	TURTLED
DELLOPR	PROLLED	**DELOORW**	WOOLDER	**DELSSTU**	TUSSLED
	REDPOLL	**DELOOSS**	DOLOSSE	**DELSTTU**	SUTTLED
DELLORR	DROLLER	**DELOOST**	STOOLED	**DELUWZZ**	WUZZLED
DELLORT	TROLLED		TOLEDOS	**DEMMRRU**	DRUMMER
DELLOSU	DUELLOS	**DELOOSW**	DEWOOLS	**DEMMSTU**	STUMMED
DELLOVW	LOWVELD	**DELOOTT**	TOOTLED	**DEMNOOR**	DOORMEN
DELLRWY	DRYWELL	**DELOPPP**	PLOPPED		MORENDO
DELLSTU	DULLEST		POPPLED	**DEMNOOW**	WOODMEN
DELMMSU	SLUMMED	**DELOPPR**	DROPPLE	**DEMNORS**	MODERNS
DELMNOS	DOLMENS	**DELOPPS**	SLOPPED		RODSMEN
DELMOOS	SLOOMED	**DELOPPT**	TOPPLED	**DEMNORT**	MORDENT
DELMOOW	ELMWOOD	**DELOPPY**	POLYPED	**DEMNORU**	MOURNED
DELMOPR	PREMOLD	**DELOPRS**	POLDERS	**DEMNORY**	DEMONRY
DELMORS	MOLDERS		PRESOLD	**DEMNOST**	ENDMOST
	REMOLDS	**DELOPRT**	DROPLET	**DEMNOSU**	MENUDOS
	SLORMED		PRETOLD	**DEMNOTU**	DEMOUNT
	SMOLDER	**DELOPRU**	POULDER		MOUNTED
DELMORU	MOULDER		POULDRE	**DEMNOUV**	UNMOVED
	REMOULD		PROULED	**DEMNSTU**	DUSTMEN
DELMOSU	MODULES	**DELOPRW**	PROWLED	**DEMOOPP**	POPEDOM
	MOUSLED	**DELOPSU**	SOUPLED	**DEMOOPR**	PREDOOM
DELMOSY	SMOYLED	**DELOPSY**	DEPLOYS		PROMOED
DELMOTT	MOTTLED		PODLEYS	**DEMOOPS**	SPOOMED
DELMOTU	MOULTED	**DELOPTT**	PLOTTED	**DEMOORS**	DROOMES

Seven-letter anagrams

	SMOORED	**DENOPUX**	EXPOUND	**DEOPRRS**	DORPERS
DEMOORT	MOTORED	**DENORRS**	DRONERS	**DEOPRRU**	PROUDER
DEMOORV	VROOMED	**DENORRU**	RONDURE	**DEOPRST**	DEPORTS
DEMOOSS	OSMOSED		ROUNDER		REDTOPS
DEMOOST	SMOOTED		UNORDER		SPORTED
DEMOOTT	MOTTOED	**DENORRW**	DROWNER	**DEOPRSU**	POUDERS
DEMOOTU	OUTMODE	**DENORSS**	SONDERS		POUDRES
DEMOPRT	TROMPED	**DENORST**	RODENTS	**DEOPRSW**	POWDERS
DEMOPST	STOMPED		SNORTED	**DEOPRTU**	TROUPED
DEMORRS	DORMERS	**DENORSU**	ENDUROS	**DEOPRWY**	POWDERY
DEMORRU	RUMORED		RESOUND	**DEOPSST**	DESPOTS
DEMORST	STORMED		SOUNDER	**DEOPSSU**	PSEUDOS
DEMORSW	DEWORMS		UNDOERS		SPOUSED
DEMOSSU	MOUSSED	**DENORSV**	VENDORS	**DEOPSTT**	SPOTTED
	SMOUSED	**DENORSW**	DOWNERS	**DEOPSTU**	OUTSPED
DEMOSTT	DOMETTS		WONDERS		SPOUTED
DEMOSTU	MOUSTED	**DENORSY**	YONDERS	**DEOPTTY**	TYPTOED
	SMOUTED	**DENORUW**	REWOUND	**DEOQRTU**	TORQUED
DEMOSTY	MODESTY		WOUNDER	**DEORRSS**	DORSERS
DEMPRSU	DUMPERS	**DENOSTT**	SNOTTED	**DEORRST**	DORTERS
DEMPRTU	TRUMPED	**DENOSTU**	DEUTONS		RODSTER
DEMPSTU	STUMPED		SNOUTED	**DEORRSU**	ORDURES
DEMRRSU	MURDERS	**DENOSUW**	SWOUNED	**DEORRSV**	DROVERS
	SMURRED		UNSOWED	**DEORRSW**	REWORDS
DEMSTTU	SMUTTED	**DENPRSU**	SPURNED		SWORDER
DENNORT	DONNERT	**DENPRTU**	PRUDENT	**DEORRVY**	OVERDRY
	TENDRON		PRUNTED	**DEORSSS**	DOSSERS
DENNORU	ENROUND		UPTREND		DROSSES
DENNOST	STONNED	**DENPSSU**	SENDUPS	**DEORSSU**	DOUSERS
	TENDONS		SUSPEND	**DEORSSW**	DOWSERS
DENNOTU	UNNOTED		UPSENDS		DROWSES
	UNTONED	**DENRSSU**	SUNDERS	**DEORSTT**	DETORTS
DENNOUW	ENWOUND		UNDRESS		DOTTERS
	UNOWNED	**DENRSSY**	DRYNESS	**DEORSTU**	DETOURS
DENNOUZ	UNZONED	**DENRSTU**	RETUNDS		DOUREST
DENNRSU	UNDERNS		UNDREST		DOUTERS
DENNSSU	DUNNESS	**DENRSUU**	UNSURED		OUTREDS
DENNSTU	DUNNEST	**DENSSTY**	SYNDETS		REDOUTS
	STUNNED	**DENSSUW**	SUNDEWS		ROUSTED
DENNTUU	UNTUNED	**DENSTTU**	STUDENT	**DEORSTW**	STROWED
DENOOPS	SNOOPED		STUNTED		WORSTED
	SPOONED	**DENTUVY**	DUVETYN	**DEORSTY**	DESTROY
DENOOSS	NOSODES	**DEOOPPS**	OPPOSED		ROYSTED
DENOOST	SNOOTED	**DEOOPRS**	SPOORED		STROYED
	STOODEN	**DEOOPRT**	TORPEDO	**DEORSUV**	DEVOURS
DENOOSW	SWOONED		TROOPED	**DEORTTT**	TROTTED
	WOODENS	**DEOOPST**	STOOPED	**DEORTTU**	TUTORED
DENOOSZ	SNOOZED	**DEOOPSW**	SWOOPED	**DEORTUU**	OUTDURE
DENOOTU	DUOTONE		WOOPSED	**DEORTUW**	OUTDREW
	OUTDONE	**DEOOPSX**	EXOPODS	**DEOSSSW**	SOWSSED
DENOOUW	UNWOOED	**DEOORRT**	REDROOT	**DEOSSTW**	DOWSETS
DENOPPR	PROPEND	**DEOORST**	ROOSTED	**DEOSSYY**	ODYSSEY
DENOPPU	UNPOPED	**DEOORSZ**	DOOZERS	**DEOSTTT**	STOTTED
DENOPRS	PERNODS	**DEOORTU**	OUTDOER	**DEOSTTU**	DUETTOS
	PONDERS		OUTRODE		TESTUDO
	RESPOND	**DEOORTW**	WROOTED	**DEOSTTW**	SWOTTED
DENOPRT	PORTEND	**DEOOSTT**	TOOTSED	**DEOSTUU**	DUTEOUS
	PROTEND	**DEOOSTU**	OUTDOES	**DEOSTUX**	TUXEDOS
DENOPRU	POUNDER	**DEOPPPR**	PROPPED	**DEOTTUY**	TUTOYED
	UNROPED	**DEOPPQU**	QUOPPED	**DEPRRSU**	SPURRED
DENOPRV	PROVEND	**DEOPPRR**	DROPPER	**DEPRRUY**	PRUDERY
DENOPRY	PROYNED	**DEOPPRS**	DOPPERS	**DEPRSTU**	SPURTED
DENOPSU	UNPOSED	**DEOPPST**	STOPPED	**DEPRSUU**	PURSUED
DENOPTY	POYNTED	**DEOPPSW**	SWOPPED		USURPED

DEPRSUY	SYRUPED
DERRSTU	RUSTRED
DERSSSU	SUDSERS
DERSSTU	DUSTERS
	TRUSSED
DERSTTU	STURTED
	TRUSTED
DERSTTY	TRYSTED
DERSTUU	SUTURED
DERSTUY	RESTUDY
DFFGINO	DOFFING
DFFGINU	DUFFING
DFFIIMR	MIDRIFF
DFFIIRT	TRIFFID
DFFIMOR	DIFFORM
DFFLOOU	FOODFUL
DFFOSTU	DUSTOFF
DFGGIIN	FIDGING
DFGGINU	FUDGING
DFGGOOS	FOGDOGS
DFGHIOS	DOGFISH
DFGIINN	FINDING
DFGIINY	DIGNIFY
DFGILNO	FOLDING
DFGINNO	FONDING
DFGINNU	FUNDING
DFGINOR	FORDING
DFGINOU	FUNGOID
DFGMOOY	FOGYDOM
DFHILSU	DISHFUL
DFHIMSU	MUDFISH
DFIKRSU	FURKIDS
DFILLUY	FLUIDLY
DFILMMO	FILMDOM
DFILMNU	MINDFUL
DFILNOP	PINFOLD
DFILNOS	INFOLDS
DFILORT	TRIFOLD
DFILORU	FLUORID
DFILOSX	SIXFOLD
DFILOTW	TWIFOLD
DFILSSU	SULFIDS
DFILTUU	DUTIFUL
DFIMNUY	MUNDIFY
DFIMOOS	FOODISM
DFIMORS	DISFORM
DFINOTU	OUTFIND
DFLMOOU	DOOMFUL
DFLMOUW	MUDFLOW
DFLNOSU	UNFOLDS
DFLOORU	ODORFUL
DFLOOTU	FOLDOUT
DFLOOTW	TWOFOLD
DFLOPRY	DROPFLY
DFLOPSU	FOLDUPS
	UPFOLDS
DFLOTWY	TWYFOLD
DFNNOOO	NONFOOD
DFNNOUU	UNFOUND
DFNORUY	FOUNDRY
DFOORSX	OXFORDS
DGGGIIN	DIGGING
DGGGINO	DOGGING
DGGHIOS	DOGGISH
DGGIILN	GILDING
	GLIDING
DGGIINN	DINGING
DGGIINR	GIRDING
	GRIDING
	RIDGING
DGGIINU	GUIDING
DGGIJNU	JUDGING
DGGILNO	GODLING
	LODGING
DGGIMNO	MODGING
DGGIMNU	MUDGING
DGGINNO	DONGING
DGGINNU	DUNGING
	NUDGING
DGGINRY	GRYDING
DGGNOSU	DUGONGS
	GUNDOGS
DGHHOOO	HOGHOOD
DGHIILN	HIDLING
	HILDING
DGHIINS	DISHING
	HIDINGS
	SHINDIG
DGHILNO	HOLDING
DGHILNY	HYLDING
DGHILOS	GOLDISH
DGHILPY	DIGLYPH
DGHINOO	HOODING
DGHINOR	HORDING
DGHINSU	DUSHING
DGHINTU	HINDGUT
	UNDIGHT
DGHIOOS	GOODISH
DGHIOPS	DOGSHIP
	GODSHIP
DGHOOPS	HOPDOGS
DGHOOST	HOTDOGS
DGHORTU	DROUGHT
DGHOTUY	DOUGHTY
DGIIKLN	KIDLING
DGIIKNN	DINKING
	KINDING
DGIIKNR	DIRKING
DGIIKNS	DISKING
DGIILLN	DILLING
DGIILMN	MILDING
DGIILNO	LOIDING
DGIILNR	DIRLING
DGIILNS	SIDLING
	SLIDING
DGIILNW	WILDING
DGIILNY	DINGILY
DGIILRS	RIDGILS
DGIILRY	RIGIDLY
DGIIMMN	DIMMING
DGIIMNN	MINDING
DGIIMNS	SMIDGIN
DGIIMOP	PIGMOID
DGIIMOS	SIGMOID
DGIINNN	DINNING
DGIINNR	RINDING
DGIINNS	NIDINGS
	SINDING
	SNIDING
DGIINNT	DINTING
	TINDING
DGIINNU	INDUING
DGIINNW	DWINING
	WINDING
DGIINOS	INDIGOS
DGIINOV	VOIDING
DGIINOW	WINDIGO
DGIINOX	DIGOXIN
DGIINPP	DIPPING
DGIINPR	PRIDING
DGIINPS	PIDGINS
DGIINPU	PINGUID
DGIINRS	RIDINGS
DGIINRT	DIRTING
DGIINRV	DRIVING
DGIINRY	YIRDING
DGIINSS	DISSING
	SIDINGS
DGIINST	TIDINGS
DGIINSV	DIVINGS
DGIINTT	DITTING
DGIINTY	DIGNITY
	TIDYING
DGIIORT	TIGROID
DGIJOSU	JUDOGIS
DGIKMNO	KINGDOM
DGIKNNU	DUNKING
DGIKNNY	KYNDING
DGIKNOO	DOOKING
DGIKNOS	DOGSKIN
DGIKNOU	DOUKING
DGIKNSU	DUSKING
DGILLNO	DOLLING
DGILLNU	DULLING
DGILLOY	GODLILY
DGILMNO	MOLDING
DGILNOR	GIRLOND
	LORDING
DGILNOY	YODLING
DGILNSU	UNGILDS
DGILNYY	DYINGLY
DGILOPY	PODGILY
DGILOST	DIGLOTS
DGILPUY	PUDGILY
DGILRUY	GUILDRY
DGIMNOO	DOOMING
DGIMNPU	DUMPING
DGIMOPY	PYGMOID
DGIMSTU	MIDGUTS
DGINNNO	DONNING
DGINNNU	DUNNING
DGINNOP	PONDING
DGINNOR	DRONING
DGINNOS	DONINGS
	ONDINGS
DGINNOU	UNDOING
DGINNOW	DOWNING
DGINNRU	DURNING
DGINNSY	SYNDING
DGINNTU	DUNTING
	TUNDING
DGINNUW	WINDGUN

Seven-letter anagrams

DGINNUY	UNDYING	DHILLOS	DOLLISH	DIILLST	DISTILL
DGINOOW	WOODING	DHILLPY	PHYLLID	DIILLVY	LIVIDLY
DGINOPP	DOPPING	DHILLSU	DULLISH	DIILMNS	DISLIMN
DGINOPS	DOPINGS	DHILMUY	HUMIDLY	DIILMOO	MODIOLI
	PONGIDS	DHILNOP	DOLPHIN	DIILMOS	IDOLISM
DGINORR	DORRING	DHILOST	DOLTISH	DIILMST	MIDLIST
DGINORS	RODINGS	DHILOSU	LOUDISH	DIILMTY	TIMIDLY
DGINORT	DORTING	DHILPSU	LUDSHIP	DIILNNU	INDULIN
DGINORV	DROVING		SULPHID	DIILNOT	TOLIDIN
DGINORW	WORDING	DHILPSY	SYLPHID	DIILNWY	WINDILY
DGINOSS	DOSSING	DHILRTY	THIRDLY	DIILNXY	XYLIDIN
DGINOST	DOTINGS	DHIMOPR	DIMORPH	DIILOPS	LIPOIDS
DGINOSU	DOUSING	DHIMORU	HUMIDOR	DIILOST	IDOLIST
	GUIDONS		RHODIUM	DIILQSU	LIQUIDS
DGINOSW	DISGOWN	DHIMOSS	MISSHOD	DIILRSU	SILURID
	DOWSING	DHIMPSU	DUMPISH	DIILRTY	DIRTILY
DGINOSZ	DOZINGS	DHINNOS	DONNISH	DIILSST	DISTILS
DGINOTT	DOTTING	DHINNSU	DUNNISH	DIILSTY	IDYLIST
DGINOTU	DOUTING	DHINOPS	DONSHIP	DIILVVY	VIVIDLY
DGINPPU	DUPPING	DHINOPY	HYPNOID	DIILYZZ	DIZZILY
DGINRSU	UNGIRDS	DHINORS	DISHORN	DIIMNOR	MIDIRON
DGINRSY	DRYINGS		DRONISH	DIIMNSU	INDIUMS
DGINSSU	SUDSING	DHINRSU	NURDISH	DIIMORS	DIORISM
DGINSTU	DUSTING	DHINSSY	SHINDYS	DIIMOSS	IODISMS
DGIOPRY	PRODIGY	DHINSTU	TUNDISH	DIIMSSS	DISMISS
DGIOSTW	GODWITS	DHIOOST	DHOOTIS	DIIMSTW	DIMWITS
DGIPRSU	UPGIRDS	DHIOPTY	PHYTOID	DIIMSUV	VIDIMUS
DGIQSUY	SQUIDGY		TYPHOID	DIINNOT	TONDINI
DGISSTU	DISGUST	DHIORSW	WORDISH	DIINNSW	INWINDS
DGLNORU	GOLDURN	DHIORTY	THYROID	DIINOQU	QUINOID
DGLNOUY	UNGODLY	DHIPRSU	PRUDISH	DIINORS	SORDINI
DGLOOOW	LOGWOOD	DHIPRSY	SYRPHID	DIINORT	DINITRO
DGLOOST	GODSLOT	DHJOPRU	JODHPUR	DIINOSX	DIOXINS
DGLOOSU	DUOLOGS	DHKMOOU	MUDHOOK	DIINRST	NITRIDS
DGLOPSY	SPLODGY	DHKORSY	DROSHKY	DIIOOPS	OPIOIDS
DGLOSYY	DYSLOGY	DHLMOOU	HOODLUM	DIIOPRS	SPIROID
DGMOOUW	GUMWOOD	DHLOOTU	HOLDOUT	DIIORSV	DIVISOR
DGMOPRU	GUMDROP	DHLOPSU	HOLDUPS		VIROIDS
DGMORUU	GURUDOM		UPHOLDS	DIIORTX	TRIOXID
DGNNORU	NONDRUG	DHMMRUU	HUMDRUM	DIIRSTX	DISTRIX
DGNOOOP	GONOPOD	DHMNOYY	HYMNODY	DIITUVY	VIDUITY
DGNOOOR	GODROON	DHNNOOU	NUNHOOD	DIJMSSU	MUSJIDS
DGNOORS	DRONGOS	DHNOOOS	SONHOOD	DIJOSTU	JUDOIST
DGNOOSS	GODSONS	DHNOOSU	UNHOODS	DIKKLSU	KUDLIKS
DGNOOSW	GODOWNS	DHOOOOS	HOODOOS	DIKKOPS	DIKKOPS
DGNOOTW	DOGTOWN	DHOOPRU	UPHOORD	DIKLNOR	LORDKIN
DGNORSU	GROUNDS	DHOORST	HOTRODS	DIKLSTU	KIDULTS
DGNOSSU	SUNDOGS	DHOORSU	RHODOUS	DIKLSUY	DUSKILY
DGOORTT	DOGTROT	DHOPRSU	PUSHROD	DIKMNSU	DINKUMS
DGOPRRU	PRODRUG	DHOPRSY	HYDROPS	DIKNNOS	NONSKID
DGOSTUU	DUGOUTS	DHORSSU	SHROUDS	DIKNNSU	NUDNIKS
DHIILNS	HIDLINS	DHORSTU	DROUTHS	DIKNOOW	INKWOOD
DHIILOT	DITHIOL	DHORSUV	HYDROUS	DIKNORV	DVORNIK
	LITHOID		SHROUDY	DIKOORT	DROOKIT
DHIILSW	WILDISH	DHORTUV	DROUTHY	DIKOOSS	SKIDOOS
DHIIMMS	DIMMISH	DHORXYY	HYDROXY	DIKORTU	DROUKIT
DHIIMNO	HOMINID	DIIIMOS	SIMIOID	DILLMSU	MUDSILL
DHIIMPS	MIDSHIP	DIIIMRU	IRIDIUM	DILLOSY	SOLIDLY
DHIINRU	HIRUDIN	DIIIMSV	DIVISIM	DILLPSY	PSYLLID
DHIIOPX	XIPHOID	DIIINPS	INSIPID	DILLRUY	LURIDLY
DHIIORZ	RHIZOID	DIIJNOS	DISJOIN	DILMNRU	DRUMLIN
DHIIOST	HISTOID	DIIKKNS	KIDSKIN	DILMOOY	DOOMILY
DHIIPST	DIPSHIT	DIIKLNS	DISLINK		MOODILY
DHIKSSU	DUSKISH	DIIKNOT	DOITKIN	DILMORS	MILORDS

DILMOST	MISTOLD	DINOSSW	DISOWNS	DMOOOQU	QUOMODO
DILMOSU	SOLIDUM	DINOSWW	WINDOWS	DMORTUW	MUDWORT
DILMOSY	ODYLISM	DINOTUW	OUTWIND	DNNOORW	NONWORD
DILMPUY	DUMPILY	DINOWWY	WINDOWY	DNNOOST	DONNOTS
DILMTUY	TUMIDLY	DINPSTU	PUNDITS	DNNORUU	UNROUND
DILNNSU	DUNLINS	DINPSUW	UPWINDS	DNNORUW	RUNDOWN
DILNOOS	OODLINS		WINDUPS	DNNOSUU	UNSOUND
DILNOPS	DIPLONS	DINRSSU	SUNDRIS	DNNOSUW	SUNDOWN
DILNOPT	DIPLONT	DINSSTU	NUDISTS	DNNOUUW	UNWOUND
DILNOQU	QUODLIN	DIOOPPS	DOPPIOS	DNNRTUU	TURNDUN
DILNORT	INTROLD	DIOOPRS	SPOROID	DNNSTUU	TUNDUNS
DILNOSU	UNSOLID	DIOOPSS	ISOPODS	DNOORTU	OROTUND
DILNOXY	INDOXYL	DIOORST	DISROOT	DNOOSUV	VODOUNS
DILNPSU	LISPUND		TOROIDS		VOUDONS
DILNPSY	SPINDLY	DIOORTT	RIDOTTO	DNOOTUW	NUTWOOD
DILNSTU	INDULTS	DIOOSTX	TOXOIDS	DNOOUUV	VOUDOUN
DILORTU	DILUTOR	DIOPRST	DISPORT	DNOPRUU	ROUNDUP
DILORWY	ROWDILY		TORPIDS	DNOPTUW	PUTDOWN
	WORDILY		TRIPODS	DNOPUUW	UPWOUND
DILOSSS	DOSSILS	DIOPRTY	TRIPODY	DNORSST	STRONDS
DILOSSU	DULOSIS	DIOPSST	DISPOST	DNORSTU	ROTUNDS
	SOLIDUS	DIORRST	STRIDOR	DNOSSTU	STOUNDS
DILOSTU	TOLUIDS	DIORSTT	DISTORT	DNOSSTW	STOWNDS
DILOSTY	STYLOID	DIOSSTU	STUDIOS	DNOSSUW	SWOUNDS
DILOTTY	DOTTILY	DIOSUUV	VIDUOUS	DNOSSWW	SWOWNDS
DILRYZZ	DRIZZLY	DIPRSTU	DISRUPT	DOOOOSV	VOODOOS
DILSTUY	DUSTILY	DIPSSTU	STUPIDS	DOOOPSW	DOOWOPS
DIMMOST	MIDMOST	DIRSTUY	SURDITY	DOOORSU	ODOROUS
DIMNNOO	MIDNOON	DJNNOOS	DONJONS	DOOORTU	OUTDOOR
DIMNNOS	DONNISM	DKNNRUU	UNDRUNK	DOOPRSU	UROPODS
DIMNNOT	DINMONT	DKNOOPS	PONDOKS	DOOPRSY	PROSODY
DIMNOOS	DOMINOS	DKOOOOS	KOODOOS	DOOPRTU	DROPOUT
DIMNOPU	IMPOUND	DKOOOSZ	ODZOOKS		OUTDROP
DIMNORS	DORMINS	DLLOOPS	DOLLOPS	DOOPSTU	UPSTOOD
	NIMRODS	DLLORWY	WORLDLY	DOORRSS	SORDORS
DIMNOTW	MIDTOWN	DLMNOOY	MYLODON	DOORRTU	DORTOUR
DIMNOWX	MIXDOWN	DLMNOSU	UNMOLDS	DOOSUUV	VOUDOUS
DIMNSSU	NUDISMS	DLMNOUU	UNMOULD	DORSSTU	STROUDS
DIMOPSU	PODIUMS	DLMOSUU	MODULUS	DORSUVY	DYVOURS
	SPODIUM	DLNOOWW	LOWDOWN	DORUVYY	DYVOURY
DIMORSW	MISWORD	DLNOPRU	PULDRON	DPSSTUU	DUSTUPS
DIMOSST	MODISTS	DLNOPSY	SPONDYL	EEEEFRR	REFEREE
DIMOSSU	SODIUMS	DLNORSU	UNLORDS	EEEEGTX	EXEGETE
DIMOSSW	WISDOMS	DLNORUY	ROUNDLY	EEEENTT	ENTETEE
DIMOSTU	DIMOUTS	DLNOSUY	SOUNDLY	EEEEPST	TEEPEES
DIMRTUU	TRIDUUM	DLOOOTW	WOODLOT	EEEEPSV	VEEPEES
DIMRUUV	DUUMVIR	DLOOPPY	POLYPOD	EEEEPSW	PEEWEES
DINNOOR	RONDINO	DLOOPSS	PODSOLS	EEEESWW	WEEWEES
DINNOOT	TONDINO	DLOOPSZ	PODZOLS	EEEFFFO	FEOFFEE
DINNOPR	NONDRIP	DLOOPTU	OUTPLOD	EEEFFOR	OFFEREE
DINNOPW	PINDOWN	DLOOPTY	TYLOPOD	EEEFFRS	EFFERES
DINNOSS	SINDONS	DLOOPUY	DUOPOLY	EEEFGRU	REFUGEE
DINNOUW	INWOUND	DLOOPWY	PLYWOOD	EEEFHRS	SHEREEF
DINNSUW	UNWINDS	DLOORSU	DOLOURS	EEEFIRR	REEFIER
DINOORS	INDOORS	DLOOSTU	OUTSOLD	EEEFIRS	FEERIES
	SORDINO	DLOOTTU	OUTTOLD	EEEFLRR	FLEERER
DINOORT	TORDION	DLOPRUY	PROUDLY	EEEFLRS	FEELERS
DINOOST	ISODONT	DLORSTY	DRYLOTS		REFEELS
DINOPSU	DUPIONS	DLOSTUW	WOULDST	EEEFLRT	FLEETER
	UNIPODS	DMMOORU	MUDROOM	EEEFLSS	FEELESS
DINORSU	DIURONS	DMNOOOP	MONOPOD	EEEFMNR	FREEMEN
	DURIONS	DMNOORS	DROMONS	EEEFNRS	ENFREES
DINORTU	TURDION	DMNOOTW	TOWMOND	EEEFNRV	ENFEVER
DINORWW	WINDROW	DMNOSSU	OSMUNDS	EEEFORS	FORESEE

Seven-letter anagrams

EEEFRRS	REEFERS	EEEIJLS	JEELIES	EEELLRV	LEVELER
EEEFRRZ	FREEZER	EEEIKLL	EELLIKE	EEELMNR	REELMEN
EEEFRSZ	FREEZES	EEEIKLS	KEELIES	EEELMNT	ELEMENT
EEEGHNW	WHEENGE	EEEIKLY	EYELIKE		TELEMEN
EEEGIKR	GEEKIER	EEEIKRR	REEKIER	EEELMPX	EXEMPLE
EEEGILN	GLEENIE	EEEILRR	LEERIER	EEELMSX	LEXEMES
EEEGILS	ELEGIES	EEEILRS	SEELIER	EEELNST	STELENE
	ELEGISE	EEEILRV	RELIEVE	EEELNSV	ELEVENS
EEEGILZ	ELEGIZE	EEEILST	EELIEST	EEELPRS	PEELERS
EEEGINP	EPIGENE		STEELIE		SLEEPER
EEEGINR	GREENIE				SPEELER
EEEGIPR	PERIGEE	EEEIMMS	MEEMIES	EEELPRT	REPLETE
EEEGKLR	KEGELER	EEEIMNS	ENEMIES	EEELPRX	REEXPEL
EEEGLMN	GLEEMEN	EEEIMNT	EMETINE	EEELPST	STEEPLE
EEEGLNT	GENTEEL	EEEIMPR	EPIMERE	EEELRRS	REELERS
EEEGMRR	REMERGE		PREEMIE	EEELRRV	REVELER
EEEGMRS	EMERGES	EEEIMRS	EMERIES	EEELRSV	RELEVES
	MERGEES	EEEIMRT	EREMITE		SLEEVER
EEEGNNO	NEOGENE	EEEINQU	QUEENIE	EEELRTV	LEVERET
EEEGNPR	EPERGNE	EEEINRS	ESERINE	EEELSSS	LESSEES
EEEGNPS	PEENGES	EEEINRT	TEENIER	EEELSST	TELESES
EEEGNRR	GREENER	EEEINRW	WEENIER	EEELSSV	SLEEVES
	REGREEN	EEEINSW	WEENIES	EEELSSY	EYELESS
	RENEGER	EEEINTW	TWEENIE	EEELSTU	EUSTELE
EEEGNRS	RENEGES	EEEIPRR	PEERIER	EEELSTX	TELEXES
EEEGNRU	RENEGUE	EEEIPRS	PEERIES	EEELSTY	EYELETS
EEEGNRV	REVENGE		SEEPIER	EEELTTX	TELETEX
EEEGNSS	GENESES	EEEIPRW	WEEPIER	EEEMMSS	MESEEMS
EEEGNTT	GENETTE	EEEIPST	EPEEIST		SEMEMES
EEEGRRT	GREETER	EEEIPSU	EPUISEE	EEEMNRS	MENEERS
	REGREET	EEEIPSW	WEEPIES	EEEMNSS	NEMESES
EEEGRSS	GREESES	EEEIRRT	RETIREE	EEEMNST	MENTEES
EEEGRST	GREETES	EEEIRRV	REVERIE	EEEMORT	EROTEME
EEEGRSZ	GEEZERS	EEEIRST	EERIEST	EEEMOSY	EYESOME
EEEGRUX	EXERGUE	EEEIRSV	VEERIES	EEEMPRT	PREMEET
EEEHILW	WHEELIE	EEEIRSZ	RESEIZE	EEEMRSS	SEEMERS
EEEHINS	SHEENIE	EEEISTW	SWEETIE	EEEMRST	MEETERS
EEEHIRX	HEXEREI	EEEJLRW	JEWELER		REMEETS
EEEHISZ	HEEZIES	EEEJNPY	JEEPNEY		TEEMERS
EEEHLNW	ENWHEEL	EEEJPRS	JEEPERS	EEEMRTX	EXTREME
EEEHLOY	EYEHOLE	EEEJRRS	JEERERS	EEEMSST	ESTEEMS
EEEHLPS	SHEEPLE	EEEJSST	JESTEES		MESTEES
EEEHLPW	WHEEPLE	EEEKKRS	KEEKERS	EEEMSTT	MEETEST
EEEHLRS	HEELERS	EEEKLLU	UKELELE	EEEMSTU	EMEUTES
	REHEELS	EEEKLMN	KEELMEN	EEENNPT	PENTENE
EEEHLRW	WHEELER	EEEKLNR	KNEELER	EEENNRT	ETRENNE
EEEHLST	LETHEES	EEEKLNS	SLEEKEN	EEENNSV	VENENES
EEEHLWZ	WHEEZLE	EEEKLNX	KLEENEX	EEENNTT	ENTENTE
EEEHNST	ETHENES	EEEKLPW	EKPWELE	EEENNUY	ENNUYEE
EEEHNSX	HEXENES	EEEKLRS	KEELERS	EEENPRR	PREENER
EEEHNSY	SHEENEY		SLEEKER	EEENPRT	PRETEEN
EEEHPRS	PHEERES	EEEKMNS	MEEKENS		TERPENE
EEEHPSS	PHEESES	EEEKMST	MEEKEST	EEENPRV	PREVENE
EEEHPSZ	PHEEZES	EEEKNPT	KEEPNET	EEENPSS	PENSEES
EEEHRRS	SHEERER	EEEKNRS	KEENERS	EEENPST	ENSTEEP
EEEHRST	SEETHER	EEEKNST	KEENEST		STEEPEN
	SHEETER		KETENES	EEENPSW	ENSWEEP
EEEHRTT	TEETHER	EEEKORV	REEVOKE	EEENPSX	EXPENSE
EEEHRWZ	WHEEZER	EEEKPRS	KEEPERS	EEENRRS	SERENER
EEEHSST	SEETHES	EEEKRRS	REEKERS		SNEERER
EEEHSSV	SHEEVES	EEEKRSS	KREESES	EEENRRT	ENTERER
EEEHSTT	ESTHETE		RESEEKS		REENTER
	TEETHES		SEEKERS		TERREEN
EEEHSWZ	WHEEZES	EEEKRST	KEESTER		TERRENE
			SKEETER		

EEENRRV	VENERER	EEFFGLU	EFFULGE	EEFILST	FELSITE
EEENRRW	RENEWER	EEFFINT	FIFTEEN		LEFTIES
EEENRSS	SERENES	EEFFIRS	EFFEIRS		LIEFEST
EEENRST	ENTREES	EEFFKLS	KEFFELS	EEFILTY	EYELIFT
	RETENES	EEFFNOS	OFFENSE	EEFIMMR	FEMMIER
	TEENERS	EEFFORR	OFFERER	EEFIMNR	FIREMEN
EEENRSV	ENERVES		REOFFER	EEFIMRT	FEMITER
	EVENERS	EEFFOST	TOFFEES	EEFINNR	FENNIER
	VENEERS	EEFFSSU	EFFUSES	EEFINNS	FENNIES
EEENRSZ	SNEEZER	EEFFSTU	SUFFETE	EEFINRR	FERNIER
EEENRTV	EVENTER	EEFGILN	FEELING		REFINER
	EVERNET		FLEEING	EEFINRS	ENFIRES
EEENRTW	TWEENER	EEFGILT	GEFILTE		FEERINS
EEENRTX	EXTERNE	EEFGINR	FEERING		FINEERS
EEENRUV	REVENUE		FEIGNER		REFINES
	UNREEVE		FREEING	EEFINRT	FEINTER
EEENSSZ	SNEEZES		REEFING	EEFINSS	FINESSE
EEENSTV	EVENEST	EEFGINS	FEESING	EEFINSX	ENFIXES
EEENSTW	SWEETEN	EEFGINZ	FEEZING	EEFIPRR	PREFIRE
EEENSTX	EXTENSE	EEFGIRR	GRIEFER	EEFIPRS	PREIFES
EEENSVW	VENEWES	EEFGIST	GIFTEES		PRIEFES
EEENSWY	SWEENEY	EEFGLLU	GLEEFUL	EEFIRRS	FERRIES
EEEOPPS	EPOPEES	EEFGLOR	FORELEG		REFIRES
EEEORSV	OVERSEE	EEFGLOS	SOLFEGE		REFRIES
EEEORSY	EYESORE	EEFGORR	REFORGE	EEFIRRT	FERRITE
EEEORVY	OVEREYE	EEFGORY	FROGEYE	EEFIRSS	FRISEES
EEEPPRS	PEEPERS	EEFGRSU	REFUGES	EEFIRST	FESTIER
EEEPRSS	PEERESS	EEFHIRS	FRESHIE	EEFIRSX	REFIXES
EEEPRST	ESTREPE		HEIFERS	EEFIRSZ	FRIEZES
	STEEPER	EEFHIRT	HEFTIER	EEFISTV	FESTIVE
EEEPRSV	PEEVERS	EEFHISY	FISHEYE	EEFLLOS	FELLOES
	PREEVES	EEFHLMN	FLEHMEN	EEFLLRS	FELLERS
EEEPRSW	SWEEPER	EEFHLNS	ENFLESH	EEFLLRU	FUELLER
	WEEPERS	EEFHLRS	FLESHER	EEFLLST	FELLEST
EEEPRSZ	SPREEZE		HERSELF	EEFLLTY	FLEETLY
EEEQRRU	QUEERER	EEFHLSS	FLESHES	EEFLMTU	TEEMFUL
	REQUERE	EEFHNRS	FRESHEN	EEFLNNO	ENFELON
EEEQSUZ	SQUEEZE	EEFHORT	THEREOF	EEFLNNS	FENNELS
EEERRRV	REVERER	EEFHORW	WHEREOF	EEFLNOS	ONESELF
EEERRST	RETREES	EEFHRRS	FRESHER	EEFLNRS	FLENSER
	STEERER		REFRESH		FRESNEL
EEERRSV	RESERVE	EEFHRRU	FUEHRER	EEFLNSS	FLENSES
	REVERES	EEFHRSS	FRESHES	EEFLNTU	TEENFUL
	REVERSE	EEFHRST	FRESHET	EEFLOOV	FOVEOLE
	SEVERER		HEFTERS	EEFLORS	FORLESE
EEERSSS	SEERESS	EEFIIMN	FEMINIE	EEFLOTU	OUTFEEL
EEERSTT	TEETERS	EEFIIRR	FIERIER	EEFLRRS	FERRELS
	TERETES		REIFIER	EEFLRRU	FERRULE
EEERSTV	STEEVER	EEFIIRS	REIFIES	EEFLRST	FELTERS
EEERSTW	SWEETER	EEFIKLL	ELFLIKE		REFLETS
EEERSUV	REVEUSE	EEFILLS	FELLIES		TELFERS
EEERSUW	SERUEWE	EEFILLX	FLEXILE	EEFLRSU	FERULES
EEERSVW	SERVEWE	EEFILNO	OLEFINE		FUELERS
	WEEVERS	EEFILNS	FELINES		REFUELS
EEERTTW	TWEETER	EEFILOR	FORELIE	EEFLRTT	FETTLER
EEERTWZ	TWEEZER	EEFILPR	PREFILE	EEFLRTU	FLEURET
EEESSTT	SETTEES		PRELIFE	EEFLRUX	FLEXURE
	TESTEES	EEFILRR	FERLIER	EEFLSTT	FETTLES
EEESSTV	STEEVES	EEFILRS	FERLIES		LEFTEST
	VESTEES		REFILES	EEFLSUY	EYEFULS
EEESTTW	WEETEST		REFLIES	EEFMNOR	FOREMEN
EEESTWZ	TWEEZES		RELIEFS	EEFMNRT	FERMENT
EEFFFNO	ENFEOFF	EEFILRT	FELTIER	EEFMOTT	MOFETTE
EEFFFOR	FEOFFER		FERTILE	EEFMPRU	PERFUME

Seven-letter anagrams

EEFMSTW	FEWMETS	EEGHNRT	GREENTH	EEGINNZ	NEEZING
EEFMTTU	FUMETTE	EEGHNRY	GREYHEN	EEGINOP	EPIGONE
EEFNORT	OFTENER	EEGHRTU	TEUGHER	EEGINOS	GENOISE
EEFNORZ	ENFROZE	EEGHSSS	GHESSES		SOIGNEE
EEFNRRY	FERNERY	EEGHSTZ	SHEGETZ	EEGINPP	PEEPING
EEFNRSS	ENSERFS	EEGIIRS	GRIESIE	EEGINPR	PEERING
EEFNRSU	UNFREES	EEGIJLN	JEELING		PREEING
EEFNRTV	FERVENT	EEGIJNP	JEEPING	EEGINPS	SEEPING
EEFNSSW	FEWNESS	EEGIJNR	JEERING	EEGINPV	PEEVING
EEFNSSY	FEYNESS	EEGIKKN	KEEKING	EEGINPW	WEEPING
EEFORRV	FOREVER	EEGIKLL	LEGLIKE	EEGINRS	GREISEN
EEFORRZ	REFROZE	EEGIKLM	GEMLIKE	EEGINRT	GENTIER
EEFORSX	FOREXES	EEGIKLN	KEELING		INTEGER
EEFOTTU	FOUETTE	EEGIKLP	PEGLIKE		TEERING
EEFPRRS	PREFERS	EEGIKNN	KEENING		TREEING
EEFPRSU	PERFUSE		KNEEING	EEGINRV	REEVING
EEFRRST	FERRETS	EEGIKNP	KEEPING		REGIVEN
EEFRRSU	REFUSER		PEEKING		VEERING
EEFRRTT	FRETTER	EEGIKNR	REEKING	EEGINSS	GENESIS
EEFRRTU	REFUTER	EEGIKNS	SEEKING		SEEINGS
EEFRRTY	FERRETY		SKEEING		SIGNEES
EEFRSST	FESTERS	EEGIKNT	KITENGE	EEGINSW	SEEWING
EEFRSSU	REFUSES	EEGILLS	GELLIES		SWEEING
EEFRSTT	FETTERS	EEGILNP	LEEPING	EEGINTV	VENTIGE
EEFRSTU	FEUTRES		PEELING	EEGINTW	WEETING
	REFUTES	EEGILNR	LEERING	EEGINTX	EXIGENT
EEFRSTW	FEWTERS		REELING	EEGIOST	EGOTISE
EEFSSTU	FETUSES	EEGILNS	LEESING		GOETIES
EEGGGIS	GEGGIES		SEELING	EEGIOTZ	EGOTIZE
EEGGGLR	GLEGGER	EEGILNT	GENTILE	EEGIRRV	GRIEVER
EEGGHTU	THUGGEE	EEGILOS	ELOGIES	EEGIRSS	SIEGERS
EEGGILN	GLEEING	EEGILPS	SPIEGEL	EEGIRSV	GRIEVES
	NEGLIGE	EEGILRS	LEIGERS		REGIVES
EEGGILR	LEGGIER		LIEGERS	EEGIRTT	TERGITE
EEGGINR	GREEING	EEGILRV	VELIGER	EEGIRTU	GUERITE
EEGGIPS	PEGGIES	EEGILST	ELEGIST	EEGISTV	VESTIGE
EEGGIRS	GREIGES		ELEGITS	EEGKLRS	KEGLERS
EEGGIST	EGGIEST	EEGIMMR	GEMMIER	EEGKNOR	KEROGEN
EEGGISV	VEGGIES		GREMMIE	EEGKNRU	GERENUK
EEGGKRS	KEGGERS		IMMERGE	EEGLLNS	LEGLENS
	SKEGGER	EEGIMNR	MEERING	EEGLLSS	LEGLESS
EEGGLRS	EGGLERS		REGIMEN	EEGLLST	LEGLETS
	LEGGERS	EEGIMNS	SEEMING	EEGLMMU	GEMMULE
EEGGLSS	EGGLESS	EEGIMNT	MEETING	EEGLMOR	GOMEREL
EEGGMNY	YEGGMEN		TEEMING	EEGLMSU	EMULGES
EEGGMSU	MUGGEES	EEGIMNX	EXEMING		LEGUMES
EEGGNNS	GENSENG	EEGIMRR	GERMIER	EEGLNNS	GENNELS
EEGGNOR	ENGORGE	EEGIMRS	EMIGRES	EEGLNOR	ERELONG
EEGGNOY	GEOGENY		REGIMES	EEGLNOU	EUGENOL
EEGGORR	REGORGE		REMIGES	EEGLNOZ	LOZENGE
EEGGORU	GOUGERE	EEGINNP	PEENING	EEGLNRT	GENTLER
EEGGORV	OVEREGG	EEGINNR	ENGINER	EEGLNRY	GREENLY
EEGGPRU	PUGGREE		INGENER	EEGLNST	GENTLES
EEGHILN	HEELING	EEGINNS	ENGINES		LENGEST
EEGHINR	REHINGE		GENNIES	EEGLNSU	LUNGEES
EEGHINT	THEEING		NEESING	EEGLOSS	EGOLESS
EEGHINY	HYGIENE		SNEEING	EEGLPSS	PEGLESS
EEGHINZ	HEEZING	EEGINNT	TEENING	EEGLRRU	GRUELER
EEGHIRW	REWEIGH	EEGINNU	GENUINE	EEGLRST	REGLETS
	WEIGHER		INGENUE	EEGLRSU	REGLUES
EEGHKRS	SKREEGH	EEGINNV	EEVNING	EEGLRTW	WERGELT
EEGHLNU	LEUGHEN		EVENING	EEGLRTY	TELERGY
EEGHMNO	HEGEMON	EEGINNW	ENEWING	EEGMMRY	GEMMERY
EEGHMNU	HEGUMEN		WEENING	EEGMNOS	EMONGES

	GENOMES	EEHIMPS	HEMPIES	EEHMNNO	NONHEME
EEGMNRS	GERMENS		IMPHEES	EEHMNNS	MENSHEN
EEGMNST	SEGMENT	EEHIMPT	EPITHEM	EEHMNOP	PHONEME
EEGMNSU	EMUNGES	EEHIMRS	MESHIER	EEHMNOS	HOSEMEN
EEGMNTU	TEGUMEN	EEHINNR	HENNIER	EEHMNRU	ENRHEUM
EEGMOST	GEMOTES	EEHINNS	HENNIES	EEHMNRY	MYNHEER
EEGMRRS	MERGERS	EEHINNY	HYENINE	EEHMNSS	MENSHES
EEGMRTU	GUMTREE	EEHINOR	HEROINE	EEHMORT	THEOREM
EEGNNST	GENNETS	EEHINRR	ERRHINE	EEHMPST	TEMPEHS
EEGNOPS	PONGEES	EEHINRS	HENRIES	EEHMRST	THERMES
EEGNORS	ENCORES		INHERES	EEHMRUX	EXHUMER
	NEGROES		RESHINE	EEHMSST	SMEETHS
EEGNOSX	EXOGENS	EEHINRT	NEITHER	EEHMSUV	HUMVEES
EEGNPUX	EXPUNGE		THEREIN	EEHMSUX	EXHUMES
EEGNRSS	NEGRESS	EEHINRW	WHEREIN	EEHNNOS	SHONEEN
EEGNRST	GERENTS	EEHINST	THEINES	EEHNNRS	HENNERS
	REGENTS	EEHIORS	HEROISE	EEHNNRY	HENNERY
EEGNRSV	VENGERS	EEHIORZ	HEROIZE	EEHNOOR	HONOREE
EEGNRSY	GYRENES	EEHIPRT	PRITHEE	EEHNOPT	POTHEEN
EEGNSSU	GENUSES	EEHIPSV	PEEVISH	EEHNORS	RESHONE
	NEGUSES	EEHIPTT	EPITHET	EEHNORT	THEREON
EEGNSTU	GUESTEN	EEHIRRS	HERRIES	EEHNORW	NOWHERE
EEGOOSS	SOOGEES		REHIRES		WHEREON
EEGOPRT	PROTEGE	EEHIRSS	HEIRESS	EEHNOSX	HEXONES
EEGORTV	OVERGET		HERISSE	EEHNPSS	SEPHENS
EEGOSSS	GESSOES	EEHIRST	HEISTER		SPHENES
EEGPPRR	PREPREG	EEHIRSV	SHRIEVE	EEHNPSW	NEPHEWS
EEGPRSU	PUGREES	EEHIRTW	THEWIER	EEHNRST	THRENES
EEGPRUX	EXPURGE	EEHIRWY	WHEYIER	EEHNSST	NESHEST
EEGRRSS	REGRESS	EEHISST	HESSITE	EEHNSTU	ENTHUSE
	SERGERS	EEHISTV	THIEVES	EEHNSTV	SEVENTH
EEGRRST	REGRETS	EEHKLOV	KEYHOLE	EEHNSTY	ETHYNES
EEGRRSU	RESURGE	EEHKLSS	SHEKELS	EEHNSWW	WHENWES
	REURGES	EEHKOOV	EYEHOOK	EEHOOPW	WHOOPEE
EEGRRSV	VERGERS	EEHKRSS	SHREEKS	EEHOOST	TOESHOE
EEGRRUY	GRUYERE	EEHLLMP	PHELLEM	EEHOPRU	EUPHROE
EEGRSST	REGESTS	EEHLLNS	ENSHELL	EEHOPSS	SHEEPOS
EEGRSSU	GUESSER	EEHLLOS	HELLOES	EEHOPST	HEPTOSE
EEGRSSY	GEYSERS	EEHLLOT	THEELOL	EEHORRV	HOVERER
EEGRSTT	GETTERS	EEHLLRS	HELLERS	EEHORSS	RESHOES
EEGRSTU	GESTURE		SHELLER	EEHORST	HETEROS
EEGRSTY	GREYEST	EEHLLRY	HELLERY	EEHORSU	REHOUSE
EEGSSSU	GUESSES	EEHLMMW	WHEMMLE	EEHORSW	WHERESO
EEHHORU	HOUHERE	EEHLMRS	HELMERS	EEHORTT	THERETO
EEHHRTT	THETHER	EEHLMRT	THERMEL	EEHORTW	WHERETO
EEHHRTW	WHETHER	EEHLMST	HELMETS	EEHORVW	HOWEVER
EEHHSTW	WHEESHT	EEHLNSU	UNHELES		WHOEVER
EEHIINS	HEINIES	EEHLNSY	HENLEYS	EEHOSST	ETHOSES
EEHIKLN	HENLIKE	EEHLORY	HOLEYER	EEHOSSX	HEXOSES
EEHIKLO	HOELIKE	EEHLPRS	HELPERS	EEHOSTW	TOWHEES
EEHILLR	HELLERI	EEHLPRT	TELPHER	EEHOSTY	EYESHOT
	HELLIER	EEHLPSS	PLESHES	EEHPPST	HEPPEST
EEHILMN	HELIMEN	EEHLQSS	SHEQELS	EEHPRSS	SPHERES
	HEMLINE	EEHLRST	SHELTER	EEHPRST	HEPSTER
EEHILNT	THEELIN	EEHLRSV	SHELVER		PETHERS
EEHILOP	PIEHOLE	EEHLRSW	WELSHER		SPERTHE
EEHILPS	EPHELIS	EEHLRSY	SHEERLY		THREEPS
EEHILRS	LEISHER	EEHLSSU	HUELESS	EEHPRTY	PRYTHEE
EEHILRW	WHILERE	EEHLSSV	SHELVES	EEHQSTU	QUETHES
EEHILST	SHELTIE	EEHLSSW	SHEWELS	EEHRRSW	WERSHER
EEHILSX	HELIXES		WELSHES	EEHRRTW	WHERRET
EEHIMMS	MISHMEE	EEHLSTT	SHTETEL	EEHRSSU	RUSHEES
EEHIMNO	HEMIONE	EEHLSTV	THELVES	EEHRSSW	SHEWERS
EEHIMPR	HEMPIER	EEHMMRS	HEMMERS	EEHRSTT	TETHERS

Seven-letter anagrams

EEHRSTW	WETHERS	EEIKRRS	KERRIES	EEILPRU	PUERILE
	WRETHES	EEIKRST	KEISTER	EEILPSS	PELISSE
EEHRSTZ	HERTZES		KIESTER	EEILPST	EPISTLE
EEHRSVW	WHERVES	EEIKRSY	SKIEYER		PELITES
EEHRTTW	WHETTER	EEIKSST	SEIKEST	EEILPWY	WEEPILY
EEHRVWY	WHYEVER	EEIKSTT	STEEKIT	EEILQRU	RELIQUE
EEHSTUV	SHUTEYE	EEIKTTT	TEKTITE	EEILRRS	RELIERS
EEIIKKS	KIEKIES	EEILLMT	MELLITE	EEILRRV	RELIVER
EEIIKRS	KIERIES	EEILLNS	NELLIES		REVILER
EEIILMS	MIELIES	EEILLPS	ELLIPSE	EEILRSS	IRELESS
EEIILRV	VEILIER	EEILLRS	LEISLER		RESILES
EEIIMNS	MEINIES		RELLIES	EEILRST	LEISTER
EEIIMPR	RIEMPIE	EEILLRT	TREILLE		RETILES
EEIIMRT	EMERITI	EEILLRV	EVILLER		STERILE
EEIIMST	ITEMISE	EEILLRY	LEERILY	EEILRSU	LEISURE
EEIIMTZ	ITEMIZE	EEILLSS	EISELLS	EEILRSV	LEVIERS
EEIINNS	NEINEIS	EEILLST	TELLIES		RELIVES
EEIINRT	ERINITE	EEILLSV	VIELLES		REVILES
	NITERIE	EEILLSW	WELLIES		SERVILE
EEIINRV	VEINIER	EEILMMT	MELTEMI		VEILERS
EEIINST	SIENITE	EEILMNN	LINEMEN	EEILRSX	EXILERS
EEIINSW	EISWEIN	EEILMNR	ERMELIN	EEILRTT	RETITLE
	WIENIES	EEILMNS	ISLEMEN	EEILRVY	LIVEYER
EEIINTV	INVITEE	EEILMNY	MYELINE	EEILSSS	SESELIS
EEIIPST	PIETIES	EEILMPT	IMPLETE		SESSILE
EEIIRRV	RIVIERE	EEILMRT	MELTIER	EEILSST	LISTEES
EEIIRVW	VIEWIER	EEILMRV	VERMEIL		TELESIS
EEIISST	SEITIES	EEILMST	ELMIEST		TIELESS
EEIISTV	VISITEE	EEILNNO	LEONINE	EEILSSU	ILEUSES
EEIJKLT	JETLIKE	EEILNNT	LENIENT	EEILSSV	SLIEVES
EEIJKRR	JERKIER	EEILNNV	ENLIVEN	EEILSSW	LEWISES
EEIJKRS	JERKIES	EEILNOR	ELOINER	EEILSSX	LEXISES
EEIJLLS	JELLIES	EEILNOS	OLEINES		SILEXES
EEIJMMR	JEMMIER	EEILNPS	PENSILE	EEILSTV	EVILEST
EEIJMMS	JEMMIES	EEILNPT	PENLITE		LEVITES
EEIJNNS	JENNIES	EEILNRS	LIERNES		LIEVEST
EEIJRRS	JERRIES		RELINES		VELITES
EEIJRTT	JETTIER	EEILNRV	LIVENER	EEILSTX	SEXTILE
EEIJSSS	JESSIES	EEILNSS	ENISLES	EEILSUV	ELUSIVE
EEIJSTT	JETTIES		ENSILES	EEILSVW	WEEVILS
EEIKKRR	KERKIER		SENILES	EEILSZZ	LEZZIES
EEIKKST	TEKKIES		SENSILE	EEILTTX	TEXTILE
EEIKLLS	KELLIES		SILENES	EEILTUX	ULEXITE
	SKELLIE	EEILNST	LENITES	EEILVWY	WEEVILY
EEIKLNT	NETLIKE		LISENTE	EEIMMNS	IMMENSE
EEIKLNY	KEYLINE		SETLINE	EEIMMRS	IMMERSE
EEIKLOT	TOELIKE		TENSILE	EEIMMSS	MIMESES
EEIKLPS	KELPIES	EEILNSY	YEELINS		MISSEEM
EEIKLPT	PIKELET	EEILNTT	ENTITLE	EEIMMST	MISMEET
EEIKLSS	SELKIES	EEILNTV	VEINLET	EEIMNNO	NOMINEE
EEIKLST	KELTIES	EEILNUV	VEINULE	EEIMNNT	EMINENT
	SLEEKIT	EEILOPT	PETIOLE	EEIMNOS	SEMEION
EEIKMNP	PIKEMEN	EEILORS	LOERIES	EEIMNOT	ONETIME
EEIKMPR	KEMPIER	EEILORT	TROELIE	EEIMNRS	ERMINES
EEIKMPS	MISKEEP	EEILORV	OVERLIE	EEIMNRV	MINEVER
EEIKNOS	EIKONES		RELIEVO	EEIMNRW	WIREMEN
EEIKNPY	PINKEYE	EEILOST	ESTOILE	EEIMNSS	INSEEMS
EEIKNRT	KERNITE		ETOILES		MISSEEN
EEIKNSS	ENSKIES	EEILOTZ	ZEOLITE		NEMESIS
	KINESES	EEILPRR	REPLIER		SIEMENS
EEIKNWY	EYEWINK	EEILPRS	REPLIES	EEIMNST	EMETINS
EEIKPRR	PERKIER		SPIELER	EEIMNSW	MISWEEN
EEIKPRS	PESKIER	EEILPRT	PERLITE	EEIMNSY	MEINEYS
EEIKPSW	KEWPIES		REPTILE		MENYIES

EEIMNTT	MINETTE	EEINPRR	REPINER	EEIORSS	SOIREES
EEIMOPS	EPISOME		RIPENER	EEIORST	EROTISE
EEIMOPT	EPITOME	EEINPRS	EREPSIN	EEIORSV	EROSIVE
EEIMORS	ISOMERE		REPINES	EEIORTZ	EROTIZE
EEIMOSS	MEIOSES	EEINPRT	INEPTER	EEIOSST	ISOETES
EEIMOTV	EMOTIVE	EEINPRZ	PRENZIE	EEIOSTT	TOEIEST
EEIMPRR	PREMIER	EEINPSS	PENISES	EEIPPPR	PEPPIER
	REPRIME	EEINPST	PENTISE		PREPPIE
EEIMPRS	EMPIRES	EEINPSV	PENSIVE	EEIPPST	PEPTISE
	EMPRISE		VESPINE		TIPPEES
	EPIMERS	EEINQRU	ENQUIRE	EEIPPTT	PIPETTE
	IMPRESE		INQUERE	EEIPPTZ	PEPTIZE
	PERMIES	EEINQSU	EQUINES	EEIPQRU	PERIQUE
	PREMIES	EEINQTU	QUIETEN		REEQUIP
	PREMISE	EEINQUY	QUEYNIE		REPIQUE
	SPIREME	EEINRRS	RERISEN	EEIPQSU	EQUIPES
EEIMPRT	EMPTIER		RESINER	EEIPRRR	PERRIER
EEIMPRZ	EMPRIZE	EEINRRT	INERTER	EEIPRRS	PERRIES
EEIMPST	EMPTIES		REINTER		PRISERE
	SEPTIME		RENTIER		REPRISE
EEIMQRU	REQUIEM		TERRINE		RESPIRE
EEIMRRR	MERRIER	EEINRRV	NERVIER	EEIPRRV	REPRIVE
EEIMRRS	MERRIES		VERNIER	EEIPRRW	PREWIRE
EEIMRRT	MITERER	EEINRSS	SEINERS	EEIPRRX	EXPIRER
	TRIREME		SEREINS	EEIPRRZ	REPRIZE
EEIMRRU	EREMURI		SERINES	EEIPRSS	ESPIERS
EEIMRSS	MERISES	EEINRST	ENTIRES		PRESSIE
	MESSIER		ENTRIES	EEIPRST	PESTIER
	MISERES		NERITES		RESPITE
	REMISES		RETINES	EEIPRSV	PREVISE
EEIMRST	MEISTER		TRENISE		PRIEVES
	METIERS		TRIENES	EEIPRSW	SPEWIER
	REEMITS	EEINRSV	ENVIERS	EEIPRSX	EXPIRES
	RETIMES		INVERSE		PREXIES
	TREMIES		VEINERS	EEIPRTT	PETTIER
	TRISEME		VENIRES	EEIPRTY	YPERITE
EEIMRSX	MIREXES		VERSINE	EEIPRVW	PREVIEW
	REMIXES	EEINRSW	NEWSIER	EEIPRZZ	PREZZIE
EEIMRTT	EMITTER		WEINERS	EEIPSSS	SPEISES
	TERMITE		WIENERS	EEIPSTT	PETITES
EEIMSSS	MISSEES	EEINRSX	REXINES		PETTIES
	SEMISES	EEINRTT	NETTIER	EEIPSTW	PEEWITS
EEIMSST	METISSE		TENTIER	EEIQRRU	QUERIER
EEINNNP	PENNINE	EEINRTU	NEURITE		REQUIRE
EEINNPS	PENNIES		RETINUE	EEIQRSU	ESQUIRE
	PINENES		REUNITE		QUERIES
EEINNRS	NERINES		UTERINE	EEIQRTU	QUIETER
EEINNRT	INTERNE	EEINSSS	SENSEIS		REQUITE
EEINNRU	NEURINE	EEINSST	SEITENS	EEIQSTU	EQUITES
EEINNRV	ENRIVEN		SESTINE	EEIRRRT	RETIRER
	INNERVE	EEINSSV	SENVIES		TERRIER
	NERVINE	EEINSSW	NEWSIES	EEIRRSS	RERISES
EEINNRW	WENNIER	EEINSTT	NETTIES		SERRIES
EEINNST	INTENSE	EEINSTV	TENSIVE		SIRREES
	TENNIES		VENITES	EEIRRST	ETRIERS
EEINNSV	VENINES	EEINSTX	EXTINES		REITERS
EEINNTW	ENTWINE		SIXTEEN		RESTIER
EEINNTZ	NETIZEN	EEINSTY	SYENITE		RETIRES
EEINOPR	PEREION	EEIOPPT	EPITOPE		RETRIES
	PIONEER	EEIOPSS	POESIES		TERRIES
EEINOPS	PEONIES	EEIOPST	POETISE	EEIRRSV	REIVERS
EEINORR	ONERIER	EEIOPSX	EPOXIES		REVERSI
EEINOSS	EOSINES	EEIOPTZ	POETIZE		REVISER
EEINPPS	PEPSINE	EEIORRS	ROSIERE		RIEVERS

Seven-letter anagrams

Code	Word(s)
EEIRRSW	REWIRES
	SWEIRER
EEIRRTV	RIVERET
	RIVETER
EEIRRTW	REWRITE
EEIRRVV	REVIVER
EEIRSSS	SEISERS
EEIRSST	RESITES
EEIRSSU	REISSUE
	SEISURE
EEIRSSV	IVRESSE
	REVISES
EEIRSSZ	RESIZES
	SEIZERS
EEIRSTT	TESTIER
EEIRSTU	SUETIER
EEIRSTV	RESTIVE
	SIEVERT
	STIEVER
	VERIEST
	VERITES
EEIRSTW	STEWIER
EEIRSTZ	ZESTIER
EEIRSUZ	SEIZURE
EEIRSVV	REVIVES
EEIRSVW	REVIEWS
	VIEWERS
EEIRTVV	VETIVER
EEISSSV	ESSIVES
EEISSTV	VITESSE
EEISSTW	WESTIES
EEISSTX	SEXIEST
EEISTTW	WETTIES
EEISTTY	YETTIES
EEISTVX	VITEXES
EEITUXZ	ZEUXITE
EEJKRRS	JERKERS
EEJLLMU	JUMELLE
EEJLRWY	JEWELRY
EEJNNST	JENNETS
EEJNOOR	REJONEO
EEJNORS	REJONES
EEJNORY	ENJOYER
	REENJOY
EEJNOSS	JONESES
EEJORST	RESOJET
EEJPRRU	PERJURE
EEJQRRU	JERQUER
EEJQRSU	JERQUES
EEJRSST	JESTERS
EEJRSSY	JERSEYS
EEKKOTV	VETKOEK
EEKKRRT	TREKKER
EEKKSSY	KEKSYES
EEKLLNV	KNEVELL
EEKLLSY	SLEEKLY
EEKLLUU	UKULELE
EEKLMPS	KEMPLES
EEKLMRZ	KLEZMER
EEKLNNS	KENNELS
EEKLNOS	KEELSON
EEKLNRS	KERNELS
EEKLPRS	KELPERS
EEKLRST	KELTERS
	KESTREL
	SKELTER
EEKLSSY	KEYLESS
EEKLSTT	KETTLES
EEKLSTW	KEWLEST
EEKMNOS	SOKEMEN
EEKMPRS	KEMPERS
EEKMRSS	KERMESS
EEKNNRS	KENNERS
EEKNNST	KENNETS
EEKNNTT	KENNETT
EEKNORW	REWOKEN
EEKNOSS	KENOSES
EEKNOST	KETONES
EEKNOTY	KEYNOTE
EEKNRSS	SKREENS
EEKNRST	RENKEST
EEKNSST	KNESSET
EEKNSTU	NETSUKE
EEKOOPP	PEKEPOO
EEKOPRS	RESPOKE
EEKOPTU	OUTKEEP
EEKORRV	REVOKER
EEKORST	RESTOKE
EEKORSV	EVOKERS
	REVOKES
EEKOSSS	SEKOSES
EEKOSST	KETOSES
EEKOSTV	VOETSEK
EEKPPSU	UPKEEPS
EEKPRRS	REPERKS
EEKPRSU	PERUKES
EEKRRUZ	KREUZER
EEKRSST	STREEKS
EEKRSSU	RESKUES
EEKRSSW	RESKEWS
	SKEWERS
EEKRSSY	KERSEYS
EEKRSTY	KEYSTER
EEKSSTW	SKEWEST
EEKSSTY	KEYSETS
EELLLVY	LEVELLY
EELLMOR	MORELLE
EELLMOS	MOSELLE
EELLMRS	MERELLS
	SMELLER
EELLMRV	VERMELL
EELLNOR	RELLENO
EELLNOV	NOVELLE
EELLNRS	SNELLER
EELLNST	TELLENS
EELLNSW	NEWELLS
EELLNUV	UNLEVEL
EELLOPS	POLLEES
EELLORS	ROSELLE
EELLORZ	ROZELLE
EELLPRS	PRESELL
	RESPELL
	SPELLER
EELLPRT	PRETELL
EELLPST	PELLETS
EELLQRU	QUELLER
EELLRSS	RESELLS
	SELLERS
EELLRST	RETELLS
	TELLERS
EELLRSU	RUELLES
EELLRSW	SWELLER
EELLRSY	YELLERS
EELLSTV	VELLETS
EELMMOP	POMMELE
EELMMPU	EMPLUME
EELMNNS	LENSMEN
EELMNOO	OENOMEL
EELMOPR	PLEROME
EELMOPT	LEPTOME
EELMOPY	EMPLOYE
EELMORW	EELWORM
EELMOST	OMELETS
	TELOMES
EELMPRS	SEMPLER
EELMPST	PELMETS
	STEMPEL
	STEMPLE
	TEMPLES
EELMPTT	TEMPLET
EELMRST	MELTERS
	REMELTS
	RESMELT
	SMELTER
EELMRSU	LEMURES
	RELUMES
EELMRSW	MEWLERS
EELMSST	TELESMS
EELMSSU	MULESES
EELMSTT	METTLES
	STEMLET
EELNNSV	VENNELS
EELNOPV	ENVELOP
EELNOPY	POLYENE
EELNOSV	ELEVONS
EELNOSY	ESLOYNE
EELNOTT	NOTELET
EELNOTU	TOLUENE
EELNPSS	PENSELS
	SPLEENS
EELNPST	PENTELS
EELNPSY	SPLEENY
EELNQUY	QUEENLY
EELNRST	NESTLER
	RELENTS
	SLENTER
EELNRSU	UNREELS
EELNRTT	LETTERN
	NETTLER
EELNRUV	NERVULE
EELNSSS	LESSENS
EELNSST	NESTLES
	NETLESS
EELNSSU	UNSEELS
EELNSTT	NETTLES
	TELNETS
EELNSTU	ELUENTS
	UNSTEEL
EELNSTY	ENSTYLE
	TENSELY
EELNSUV	VENULES
EELNSXY	XYLENES

EELNTTU	LUNETTE	EELRSUV	VELURES	EEMPRTT	TEMPTER
EELOPPR	PEOPLER	EELRSUX	LUREXES	EEMPRTU	PERMUTE
EELOPPS	PEOPLES	EELRSVV	VERVELS	EEMPSSU	EMPUSES
EELOPPZ	ZEPPOLE	EELSSSU	USELESS	EEMPSTT	TEMPEST
EELOPRS	ELOPERS	EELSSSV	VESSELS	EEMPSTX	EXEMPTS
	LEPROSE	EELSSSX	SEXLESS	EEMRRST	TERMERS
EELOPRX	EXPLORE	EELSSTT	SETTLES	EEMRRSU	MURREES
EELOPSS	ELOPSES	EELSSTU	SETULES		RESUMER
EELOPTU	EELPOUT	EELSSUV	EVULSES	EEMRRUU	REMUEUR
EELORSS	RESOLES	EELSTUY	EUSTYLE	EEMRSST	MESTERS
EELORST	SOLERET	EELSTVV	VELVETS		RESTEMS
EELORSV	RESOLVE	EELSTVW	TWELVES	EEMRSSU	RESUMES
EELORSY	EROSELY	EELSTWY	SWEETLY	EEMRSUX	MUREXES
EELORTT	LORETTE	EELTVVY	VELVETY	EEMSSSU	SMEUSES
EELORTV	OVERLET	EEMMNOS	MONEMES	EEMSSTU	MUSTEES
EELORVV	EVOLVER	EEMMNOT	MEMENTO	EEMSTTU	MUSETTE
	REVOLVE	EEMMNSS	MESSMEN	EENNORT	ENTERON
EELOSSS	LOESSES	EEMMORS	MEROMES		TENONER
EELOSST	OSSELET	EEMMOST	MESTOME	EENNORU	NEURONE
	TELOSES	EEMMOSU	MOUSMEE	EENNOSS	ONENESS
	TOELESS	EEMMOSV	EMMOVES	EENNOSZ	ENZONES
EELOSTT	TELEOST	EEMMRST	STEMMER	EENNOTT	NONETTE
EELOSUV	EVOLUES	EEMMRSY	YEMMERS	EENNOTY	NEOTENY
EELOSVV	EVOLVES	EEMMSST	SEMSEMS	EENNPRS	PENNERS
EELOTUV	EVOLUTE	EEMMSST	STEMMES	EENNQUU	UNQUEEN
	VELOUTE	EEMNNOV	ENVENOM	EENNRST	RENNETS
EELPPRX	PERPLEX	EEMNNSW	NEWSMEN		TENNERS
EELPPSU	PEEPULS	EEMNOOS	SOMEONE	EENNRUV	UNNERVE
EELPQRU	PREQUEL	EEMNOOY	MOONEYE	EENNSST	SENNETS
EELPRST	PELTERS	EEMNOPR	REPOMEN	EENNSSU	UNSEENS
	PETRELS	EEMNORS	MOREENS		UNSENSE
	RESPELT	EEMNORV	OVERMEN	EENNSSW	NEWNESS
	SPELTER		VENOMER	EENOPPR	PREPONE
EELPRSU	REPULSE	EEMNORY	MONEYER		PROPENE
EELPRSY	SLEEPRY	EEMNOST	TEMENOS	EENOPPT	PEPTONE
	YELPERS		TONEMES	EENOPRS	OPENERS
EELPRTY	PEYTREL	EEMNOSV	ENMOVES		PEREONS
EELPRTZ	PRETZEL	EEMNPRU	PREMUNE		PERONES
EELPRUX	PLEXURE	EEMNPTU	UMPTEEN		REOPENS
EELPRVY	REPLEVY	EEMNRTU	TRUEMEN		REPONES
EELPSST	PESTLES	EEMNSYZ	ENZYMES	EENOPST	OPENEST
EELPSTT	PETTLES	EEMOOSW	WOESOME		PENTOSE
EELPSTY	STEEPLY	EEMOPRR	EMPEROR		POSTEEN
EELPSUX	EXPULSE	EEMOPRT	TEMPORE		POTEENS
EELQRUY	QUEERLY	EEMOPRV	PREMOVE	EENOPTT	POTTEEN
EELQSSU	SEQUELS	EEMOPRW	EMPOWER	EENOPTY	NEOTYPE
EELRRSV	VERRELS	EEMOPST	METOPES	EENORRV	OVERREN
EELRRVY	REVELRY	EEMORRS	REMORSE	EENORSS	SENORES
EELRSST	STREELS		ROEMERS	EENORST	ESTRONE
	TRESSEL	EEMORRT	REMOTER	EENORSY	ONEYERS
EELRSSU	RULESSE	EEMORRU	UROMERE		ONEYRES
EELRSTT	LETTERS	EEMORRV	REMOVER	EENORSZ	REZONES
	LETTRES	EEMORST	EMOTERS	EENORTV	OVERNET
	SETTLER		METEORS	EENORVW	OVERNEW
	STERLET		REMOTES		REWOVEN
	TRESTLE	EEMORSV	REMOVES	EENOSSW	WOENESS
EELRSTV	SERVLET	EEMOSST	MESTESO	EENOSSY	ESSOYNE
	SVELTER	EEMOTTZ	MOZETTE		NOYESES
EELRSTW	SWELTER	EEMPPRT	PREEMPT	EENOSTU	OUTSEEN
	WELTERS	EEMPRRT	PRETERM	EENOSTV	VENTOSE
	WRESTLE	EEMPRSS	EMPRESS		VOTEENS
EELRSTY	RESTYLE	EEMPRST	TEMPERS	EENOSTW	TOWNEES
	TERSELY	EEMPRSU	PRESUME	EENOSVZ	EVZONES
EELRSTZ	SELTZER		SUPREME	EENOTTT	TONETTE

Seven-letter anagrams

EENPPRT	PERPENT		TREETOP	EEPRSTT	PERTEST
EENPRST	PENSTER	EEOPRTU	OUTPEER		PETTERS
	PRESENT	EEOPSSS	SPEOSES		PRETEST
	REPENTS	EEOPSST	POETESS	EEPRSTU	PERTUSE
	SERPENT	EEOPSSU	ESPOUSE		REPUTES
EENPRSY	PYRENES		POSEUSE	EEPRSTW	PEWTERS
EENPRTV	PREVENT	EEOPSSX	EXPOSES	EEPRSTX	EXPERTS
EENPRTY	PERENTY	EEOPSTU	TOUPEES		SEXPERT
EENPSSS	SPENSES	EEOPSTY	EYESPOT	EEPRSTY	RETYPES
EENPSTU	PUNTEES		PEYOTES	EEPRSUV	PREVUES
EENPSTW	ENSWEPT	EEOPTUW	OUTWEEP	EEPRSXY	PYREXES
EENPSTY	STEPNEY	EEOQRTU	REQUOTE	EEPRTTX	PRETEXT
EENQSTU	SEQUENT	EEORRST	RESTORE	EEPSSTT	SEPTETS
EENRRST	RENTERS	EEORRSV	REVERSO	EEPSTTU	PUTTEES
	RERENTS	EEORRSZ	REZEROS	EEPSTTY	TYPESET
	STERNER	EEORRTU	REROUTE	EEQRRUY	EQUERRY
EENRRSU	ENSURER	EEORRTV	EVERTOR	EEQRSTU	QUESTER
EENRRSV	NERVERS	EEORRTW	REWROTE		REQUEST
EENRRTY	REENTRY	EEORSST	OSSETER	EEQRSUU	QUEUERS
EENRRUV	NERVURE		STEREOS	EEQSSTU	QUEESTS
EENRSST	NESTERS	EEORSSX	SOREXES	EEQSUYZ	SQUEEZY
	RENESTS		XEROSES	EERRSST	RESTERS
	RESENTS	EEORSTT	ROSETTE	EERRSSV	SERVERS
	STRENES	EEORSTV	ESTOVER		VERSERS
EENRSSU	ENSURES		OVERSET	EERRSTT	TERRETS
EENRSTT	NETTERS		REVOTES	EERRSTU	URETERS
	TENTERS		VETOERS	EERRSTV	REVERTS
	TESTERN	EEORSTX	XEROTES	EERRSTW	STREWER
EENRSTU	NEUTERS	EEORSTY	ESOTERY		WRESTER
	RETUNES	EEORSUV	OEUVRES	EERRSUV	REVEURS
	TENURES		OVERUSE	EERRSVW	SWERVER
	TUREENS	EEORSVW	OVERSEW	EERRSVY	SERVERY
EENRSTV	VENTERS	EEORSXX	XEROXES	EERRTTU	REUTTER
	VENTRES	EEORTUV	OUVERTE		UTTERER
EENRSTW	WESTERN	EEORTVW	OVERWET	EERRTTY	RETTERY
EENRSTX	EXTERNS	EEOSSSY	OYESSES	EERSSST	TRESSES
EENRSTY	STYRENE	EEOSSTU	OUTSEES	EERSSTT	RETESTS
	YESTERN	EEPPPRS	PEPPERS		SETTERS
EENRSVV	VERVENS	EEPPPRY	PEPPERY		STREETS
EENRTUV	VENTURE	EEPPRST	STEPPER		TERSEST
EENSSST	SETNESS	EEPPRSX	PERSPEX		TESTERS
EENSSSY	SYNESES	EEPPRTY	PRETYPE	EERSSTV	REVESTS
EENSSTT	TENSEST	EEPPSST	STEPPES		STERVES
EENSSTV	STEVENS	EEPPSTU	STEEPUP		VERSETS
EENSSTW	WETNESS	EEPPSUW	UPSWEEP		VERSTES
EENSSUV	VENUSES	EEPPSUY	EUPEPSY	EERSSTW	STEWERS
EENSSUX	NEXUSES	EEPRRSS	PRESSER		WESTERS
	UNSEXES		REPRESS	EERSSTX	EXSERTS
EENSSVW	SWEVENS		SPERRES	EERSSTZ	ZESTERS
EENSTTX	EXTENTS	EEPRRST	PRESTER	EERSSUX	XERUSES
EENSTTY	TEENTSY	EEPRRSU	PERUSER	EERSSUY	SEYSURE
EENSTUW	UNSWEET		REPURES	EERSSVW	SWERVES
EENSTVY	SEVENTY	EEPRRSY	PREYERS	EERSTTT	STRETTE
EEOOPRS	OPEROSE	EEPRRTV	PERVERT		TETTERS
EEOOSTT	TOETOES	EEPRRVY	REPRYVE	EERSTTU	TRUSTEE
EEOPPRS	PREPOSE	EEPRSSS	PRESSES	EERSTTV	TREVETS
EEOPPTT	POPETTE		SPERSES		VETTERS
EEOPPTU	OUTPEEP	EEPRSST	PESTERS	EERSTTW	WETTERS
EEOPRRS	REPOSER		PRESETS	EERSTTX	TEXTERS
EEOPRRV	REPROVE	EEPRSSU	PERSUES	EERSTTY	STREETY
EEOPRRW	REPOWER		PERUSES		SYRETTE
EEOPRSS	REPOSES	EEPRSSV	VESPERS	EERSTUV	VERSUTE
EEOPRSX	EXPOSER	EEPRSSW	SPEWERS		VERTUES
EEOPRTT	PROETTE	EEPRSSX	EXPRESS		VESTURE

EERSTUY	TUYERES	EFFLMSU	MUFFLES	EFGIRSU	FIGURES
EERSTVV	VERVETS	EFFLNSU	SNUFFLE	EFGKOOP	OPGEFOK
EERSTWY	TWYERES	EFFLOPS	POFFLES	EFGLLSU	FLUGELS
EERTTUX	TEXTURE	EFFLOSU	SOUFFLE	EFGLNSU	ENGULFS
EESSSTT	SESTETS	EFFLRRU	RUFFLER	EFGLNTU	FULGENT
	TSETSES	EFFLRSU	RUFFLES	EFGLORS	GOLFERS
EESSTTT	SESTETT	EFFLRTU	FRETFUL	EFGLORT	FROGLET
EESSTTU	SUTTEES		TRUFFLE	EFGLOSS	FOGLESS
EESSTTX	SEXTETS	EFFNRSU	SNUFFER	EFGMNOR	FROGMEN
EESSTTY	STEYEST	EFFNRUU	UNRUFFE	EFGNOOR	FORGONE
EESSTTZ	TZETSES	EFFNSTU	FUNFEST	EFGNOSU	FUNGOES
EESTTTW	WETTEST	EFFOORR	OFFEROR	EFGOORR	FORGOER
EESTTTX	SEXTETT	EFFOPRR	PROFFER	EFGOORS	FORGOES
EESTTZZ	TZETZES	EFFOPSU	POUFFES	EFGORRS	FORGERS
EFFFINO	INFEOFF	EFFORRT	TROFFER	EFGORRU	FERRUGO
EFFFIRU	FUFFIER	EFFORST	EFFORTS	EFGORRY	FORGERY
EFFFLRU	FLUFFER	EFFORSW	SWOFFER	EFGORST	FORGETS
EFFFOOR	FEOFFOR	EFFOSST	OFFSETS	EFGORSW	GOWFERS
EFFGIJN	JEFFING		SETOFFS	EFGORTU	FOREGUT
EFFGINR	REFFING	EFFPRSU	PUFFERS	EFHIINS	FINEISH
EFFGINS	EFFINGS	EFFPRUY	PUFFERY	EFHIIRS	FISHIER
EFFGIRS	GRIFFES	EFFRSSU	SUFFERS	EFHIJSW	JEWFISH
EFFGISU	GUFFIES	EFFRSTU	RESTUFF	EFHILMS	FLEMISH
EFFGORS	GOFFERS		STUFFER		HIMSELF
EFFGRRU	GRUFFER		TRUFFES	EFHILSS	HISSELF
EFFHILW	WHIFFLE	EFFSSUU	SUFFUSE		SELFISH
EFFHIRS	SHERIFF	EFFSTTU	TUFFETS	EFHILST	LEFTISH
EFFHIRU	HUFFIER	EFGGIOR	FOGGIER	EFHILTY	HEFTILY
EFFHIRW	WHIFFER	EFGGIRR	FRIGGER	EFHINNS	FENNISH
EFFHITW	WHIFFET	EFGGIRU	FUGGIER	EFHINST	FISHNET
EFFHLSU	SHUFFLE	EFGGIRY	FIGGERY	EFHIRSS	FISHERS
EFFHRSU	HUFFERS	EFGGLOR	FLOGGER		SERFISH
EFFIIJS	JIFFIES	EFGGORS	FOGGERS		SHERIFS
EFFIIMR	MIFFIER	EFGHIMS	GEMFISH	EFHIRST	SHIFTER
EFFIINR	NIFFIER	EFGHINT	HEFTING	EFHIRSY	FISHERY
EFFIIST	FIFTIES	EFGHIRT	FIGHTER	EFHISUW	HUSWIFE
	IFFIEST		FREIGHT	EFHLLPU	HELPFUL
	STIFFIE		REFIGHT	EFHLLSY	FLESHLY
EFFIKLS	SKIFFLE	EFGIKNR	KERFING	EFHLNSU	UNFLESH
EFFILLU	LIFEFUL	EFGILLN	FELLING	EFHLOOX	FOXHOLE
EFFILNO	OFFLINE	EFGILMN	FLEMING	EFHLOPU	HOPEFUL
EFFILNS	SNIFFLE	EFGILNR	FLINGER	EFHLOSS	FLOSHES
EFFILPR	PIFFLER	EFGILNS	SELFING	EFHLRSU	FLUSHER
EFFILPS	PIFFLES	EFGILNT	FELTING	EFHLRSY	FRESHLY
EFFILRR	RIFFLER	EFGILNU	FUELING	EFHLSSU	FLUSHES
EFFILRS	RIFFLES	EFGILNX	FLEXING	EFHLSTY	THYSELF
EFFILRY	FIREFLY	EFGILNY	FLEYING	EFHLTTW	TWELFTH
EFFILSS	SIFFLES	EFGILRU	FUGLIER	EFHNORT	FORHENT
EFFIMOS	MOFFIES		GULFIER	EFHOORS	HOOFERS
EFFINRS	NIFFERS	EFGIMNT	FIGMENT	EFHORRT	FROTHER
	SNIFFER	EFGINNP	PFENNIG	EFHORSS	FROSHES
EFFINST	INFEFTS	EFGINNR	FERNING	EFHORST	FOTHERS
	STIFFEN	EFGINOR	FOREIGN	EFHRRSU	FUHRERS
EFFIOPR	PIFFERO	EFGINPR	PERFING	EFHRRTU	FURTHER
EFFIORT	FORFEIT	EFGINRS	FINGERS	EFHRSSU	FRUSHES
	TOFFIER		FRINGES	EFIIKLN	FINLIKE
EFFIORX	FOXFIRE	EFGINRU	GUNFIRE	EFIIKST	FIKIEST
EFFIOST	TOFFIES	EFGINSS	FESSING	EFIILLS	FILLIES
EFFIPRU	PUFFIER	EFGINTT	FETTING	EFIILMR	FILMIER
EFFIRRT	TRIFFER	EFGINTW	WEFTING	EFIILMS	MISFILE
EFFIRST	RESTIFF	EFGIOOR	GOOFIER	EFIILRT	FIRELIT
	STIFFER	EFGIORV	FORGIVE		FITLIER
EFFLLOS	SELLOFF	EFGIRRT	GRIFTER	EFIILRY	FIERILY
EFFLMRU	MUFFLER	EFGIRRU	FIGURER	EFIILSS	FISSILE

Code	Word(s)
EFIIMRR	RIMFIRE
EFIIMRS	MISFIRE
EFIIMST	SEMIFIT
EFIINNR	FINNIER
EFIINPV	FIVEPIN
EFIINRT	NIFTIER
EFIINRU	UNIFIER
EFIINSS	FINISES
EFIINST	FINITES
	NIFTIES
EFIINSU	UNIFIES
EFIINSX	INFIXES
EFIIRRR	FIRRIER
EFIIRRT	RIFTIER
EFIIRST	FISTIER
EFIIRTW	WIFTIER
EFIIRZZ	FIZZIER
EFIISSV	FISSIVE
EFIISTW	SWIFTIE
EFIJLLY	JELLIFY
EFIJLOR	FRIJOLE
EFIJLOT	JETFOIL
EFIKLNU	FLUNKIE
EFIKLOR	FOLKIER
EFIKLOS	FOLKIES
EFIKLOX	FOXLIKE
EFIKLRU	FLUKIER
EFIKNRS	KNIFERS
EFIKNRU	FUNKIER
EFIKORR	FORKIER
EFIKRRS	FRISKER
EFIKRST	FRISKET
EFILLMS	MISFELL
EFILLOO	FOLIOLE
EFILLOS	FOLLIES
EFILLOW	LOWLIFE
EFILLRR	FRILLER
EFILLRS	FILLERS
	REFILLS
EFILLST	FILLETS
EFILLUW	WILEFUL
EFILMNT	LIFTMEN
EFILMNU	FULMINE
EFILMOT	FILEMOT
EFILMRS	FILMERS
	REFILMS
EFILMSS	SELFISM
EFILMST	FILMSET
	LEFTISM
EFILNNO	NONLIFE
EFILNOS	OLEFINS
EFILNOX	FLEXION
EFILNSS	FINLESS
EFILOOS	FLOOSIE
	FOLIOSE
EFILOOZ	FLOOZIE
EFILOPR	PROFILE
EFILORR	FLORIER
EFILORT	LOFTIER
	TREFOIL
EFILOSS	FLOSSIE
EFILOSU	FOULIES
EFILOSX	SEXFOIL
EFILPPR	FLIPPER
EFILPPS	FIPPLES
EFILPPU	PIPEFUL
EFILPRS	PILFERS
EFILPRY	PILFERY
EFILQUY	LIQUEFY
EFILRRS	RIFLERS
EFILRRT	FLIRTER
	TRIFLER
EFILRRY	RIFLERY
EFILRST	FILTERS
	LIFTERS
	STIFLER
	TRIFLES
EFILRTT	FLITTER
EFILRTU	FLUTIER
	FUTILER
EFILRTY	FLYTIER
EFILRVV	FLIVVER
EFILRZZ	FRIZZLE
EFILSSS	FISSLES
EFILSST	SELFIST
	STIFLES
EFILSTT	LEFTIST
EFILSTU	FLUIEST
	SULFITE
EFILSZZ	FIZZLES
EFILUVX	FLUXIVE
EFIMMRU	FERMIUM
EFIMNOR	FERMION
EFIMNTT	FITMENT
EFIMOST	FOMITES
EFIMRRS	FIRMERS
EFIMRST	FIRMEST
	FREMITS
EFIMRTY	METRIFY
EFIMSTU	FUMIEST
EFIMTTU	FUMETTI
EFINNOR	INFERNO
EFINNRS	FINNERS
EFINNRU	FUNNIER
EFINNSU	FUNNIES
EFINOPR	FORPINE
EFINPRS	PERFINS
EFINRST	SNIFTER
EFINRSU	INFUSER
EFINRUY	REUNIFY
EFINSST	FITNESS
	INFESTS
EFINSSU	INFUSES
EFINSUX	UNFIXES
EFINSZZ	FIZZENS
EFIOOPR	POOFIER
EFIOORR	ROOFIER
EFIOORS	ROOFIES
EFIOORT	FOOTIER
EFIOORW	WOOFIER
EFIOOST	FOOTIES
	FOOTSIE
	OOFIEST
EFIOPRR	PORIFER
EFIOPRT	FIREPOT
	PIEFORT
EFIORRT	ROTIFER
EFIORRW	FROWIER
EFIORSS	FROISES
EFIORST	FOISTER
	FORTIES
EFIORTU	OUTFIRE
EFIORTV	OVERFIT
EFIOSST	SOFTIES
EFIOSTX	FOXIEST
EFIOSTZ	FOZIEST
EFIPPRR	FRIPPER
EFIPPRT	FRIPPET
EFIPRST	PRESIFT
EFIPRTY	PETRIFY
EFIRRRU	FURRIER
EFIRRSU	FRISEUR
	FRISURE
	FURRIES
	SURFIER
EFIRRSZ	FRIZERS
EFIRRTT	FRITTER
EFIRRTU	FRITURE
	FRUITER
	TURFIER
EFIRRTY	TERRIFY
EFIRRUZ	FURZIER
EFIRRZZ	FRIZZER
EFIRSST	RESIFTS
	SIFTERS
	STRIFES
EFIRSSU	FISSURE
	FUSSIER
	SURFIES
EFIRSTT	FITTERS
	TITFERS
EFIRSTU	FUSTIER
	SURFEIT
EFIRSTW	SWIFTER
EFIRSTZ	FRITZES
EFIRSUX	FIXURES
EFIRSVY	VERSIFY
EFIRSZZ	FIZZERS
	FRIZZES
EFIRTTU	TUFTIER
	TURFITE
EFIRTUV	FURTIVE
EFIRTUX	FIXTURE
EFIRUZZ	FUZZIER
EFISTTT	FITTEST
EFISTTY	TESTIFY
EFJLSTU	JESTFUL
EFKLMNO	MENFOLK
EFKLMOR	MERFOLK
EFKLNRU	FLUNKER
EFKLNUY	FLUNKEY
EFKLOPU	POKEFUL
EFKLPSU	SKEPFUL
EFKNRSU	FUNKERS
EFKORRS	FORKERS
EFLLORU	FLORULE
EFLLOST	FLOTELS
EFLLOSW	FELLOWS
EFLLRSU	FULLERS
EFLLRUY	FULLERY
EFLLSSY	FLYLESS
EFLLSTU	FULLEST

EFLMOSU	FULSOME		RESTFUL		FOUTRES
EFLMPRU	FRUMPLE	EFLRTTU	FLUTTER	EFORSTW	TWOFERS
EFLMSUU	MUSEFUL	EFLSSUU	USEFULS	EFOSSTT	SOFTEST
EFLNNOS	NONSELF	EFLSTUZ	ZESTFUL	EFOSTWW	WOWFEST
EFLNNOU	NONFUEL	EFLSUZZ	FUZZLES	EFPRTUY	PUTREFY
EFLNNSU	FUNNELS	EFMNOOT	FOOTMEN	EFPSTUY	STUPEFY
EFLNORT	FORLENT	EFMNORS	ENFORMS	EFRRSSU	SURFERS
EFLNORU	FLEURON	EFMNOST	FOMENTS	EFRRSTU	RETURFS
EFLNORW	REFLOWN	EFMNRSU	FRENUMS	EFRRSUU	FUREURS
EFLNORY	FELONRY		SURFMEN	EFRSSSU	FUSSERS
EFLNOST	TEFLONS	EFMNRTU	TURFMEN	EFRSTTU	TUFTERS
EFLNOSU	SULFONE	EFMOORZ	ZOEFORM	EFRSTUU	FUTURES
EFLNOTT	FLETTON	EFMOPRR	PERFORM	EFSSTTU	FUSTETS
	FONTLET		PREFORM	EGGGIKN	KEGGING
EFLNPSU	PENFULS	EFMOPRT	POMFRET	EGGGILN	LEGGING
EFLNPUX	FUNPLEX	EFMORRS	FORMERS	EGGGILR	GIGGLER
EFLNSSU	FULNESS		REFORMS	EGGGILS	GIGGLES
	UNSELFS	EFMOTTU	FUMETTO	EGGGINP	PEGGING
EFLNSTU	FLUENTS	EFMPRUY	PERFUMY	EGGGINV	VEGGING
	NESTFUL	EFMRRSU	FERRUMS	EGGGLOR	GOGGLER
	NETFULS	EFMRTUY	FURMETY	EGGGLOS	GOGGLES
EFLNSUY	SYNFUEL	EFNNORT	FORNENT	EGGGLSU	GUGGLES
EFLNTTU	TENTFUL	EFNNORU	FENURON	EGGGNOS	EGGNOGS
EFLNTUU	TUNEFUL	EFNNOTU	UNOFTEN	EGGHILR	HIGGLER
EFLOORR	FLOORER	EFNNSTU	FUNNEST	EGGHILS	HIGGLES
	FORLORE	EFNOOST	EFTSOON	EGGHINP	PEGHING
EFLOORS	FORSLOE		FESTOON	EGGHIRT	THIGGER
EFLOORT	FOOTLER	EFNORRT	FRONTER	EGGHIRU	HUGGIER
EFLOORY	FOOLERY		REFRONT	EGGHLOS	SHOGGLE
EFLOORZ	FOOZLER	EFNORRU	FORERUN	EGGHORS	HOGGERS
EFLOOST	FOOTLES	EFNORRW	FROWNER	EGGHORY	HOGGERY
EFLOOSZ	FOOZLES	EFNORST	FRONTES	EGGHOST	HOGGETS
EFLOPPR	FLOPPER	EFNORTU	FORTUNE	EGGHRSU	HUGGERS
EFLORRS	ROLFERS	EFNORTW	FORWENT	EGGIIJR	JIGGIER
EFLORSS	FLOSSER	EFNORUZ	UNFROZE	EGGIILN	GINGELI
EFLORST	FLORETS	EFNOSST	SOFTENS	EGGIILS	GILGIES
	LOFTERS	EFNRSTU	FUNSTER	EGGIINS	SIEGING
EFLORSU	FUROLES	EFOOPRR	PROOFER	EGGIIPR	PIGGIER
	OURSELF		REPROOF	EGGIIPS	PIGGIES
EFLORSW	FLOWERS	EFOOPRS	SPOOFER	EGGIIRW	WIGGIER
	FOWLERS	EFOOPRT	FORETOP	EGGIJLS	JIGGLES
	REFLOWS		POOFTER	EGGIJRS	JIGGERS
	WOLFERS	EFOORRS	REROOFS	EGGIKLN	KEGLING
EFLORSX	FLEXORS		ROOFERS	EGGILLN	GELLING
EFLORTT	FORTLET	EFOORST	FOETORS	EGGILMS	LEGGISM
EFLORTU	FLOUTER		FOOTERS		MIGGLES
EFLORTW	FELWORT		REFOOTS	EGGILNN	LENGING
EFLORVY	FLYOVER	EFOORSW	WOOFERS	EGGILNR	NIGGLER
	OVERFLY	EFOORTW	WOOFTER	EGGILNS	GINGLES
EFLORWW	WERWOLF	EFOPPRY	FOPPERY		LEGGINS
EFLORWY	FLOWERY	EFOPRSS	PROFESS		NIGGLES
EFLOSSS	FLOSSES	EFOPRST	FORPETS		SNIGGLE
EFLOSSU	FLOUSES	EFOPRSU	PROFUSE	EGGILNU	GLUEING
EFLOSTU	FOULEST	EFOPRTU	POUFTER		LUGEING
EFLOTTU	OUTFELT	EFOPRTY	TORPEFY	EGGILNY	GINGELY
EFLOTUW	OUTFLEW	EFORRSU	FERROUS		GLEYING
EFLPRRU	PURFLER		FURORES	EGGILOR	LOGGIER
EFLPRSU	PURFLES	EFORRSV	FERVORS	EGGILRS	LIGGERS
EFLPRUY	PREYFUL	EFORRTY	TORREFY	EGGILRW	WIGGLER
EFLPSTU	PESTFUL	EFORRUV	FERVOUR		WRIGGLE
EFLRRSU	FURLERS	EFORSST	FORESTS	EGGILST	GIGLETS
EFLRSSU	FURLESS		FOSTERS	EGGILSU	LUGGIES
EFLRSTU	FLUSTER	EFORSSU	FOURSES	EGGILSW	WIGGLES
	FLUTERS	EFORSTU	FOUTRES	EGGIMMN	GEMMING

Seven-letter anagrams

EGGIMNN	MENGING	EGGNRRU	GRUNGER	EGHINRY	HERYING
EGGIMNR	GERMING	EGGNRSU	GRUNGES	EGHINST	NIGHEST
	MERGING		SNUGGER	EGHINSW	HEWINGS
EGGIMOS	MOGGIES	EGGNSTU	NUGGETS		SHEWING
EGGIMRU	MUGGIER	EGGNTUY	NUGGETY		WHINGES
EGGINNN	GENNING	EGGOPRR	PROGGER	EGHINSX	HEXINGS
EGGINNR	GERNING	EGGORRS	GORGERS	EGHINTT	TIGHTEN
EGGINNS	GINSENG	EGGORST	GORGETS	EGHINWW	WHEWING
EGGINNV	VENGING		TOGGERS	EGHIOOS	SHOOGIE
EGGINRS	GINGERS	EGGORSU	GOUGERS	EGHIOPS	PISHOGE
	NIGGERS	EGGORTY	TOGGERY	EGHIORS	OGREISH
	SERGING	EGGPRUY	PUGGERY	EGHIORU	ROUGHIE
	SNIGGER	EGGRRSU	RUGGERS	EGHIOST	HOGTIES
EGGINRU	GRUEING	EGGRSTU	TUGGERS	EGHIOTT	GOTHITE
	GUNGIER	EGGSSTU	SUGGEST	EGHIOTU	TOUGHIE
EGGINRV	VERGING	EGHHHIT	HEIGHTH	EGHIOTV	EIGHTVO
EGGINRW	GREWING	EGHHIMN	HIGHMEN	EGHIRRT	RIGHTER
EGGINRY	GINGERY	EGHHIRS	HIGHERS	EGHIRSS	GIRSHES
	GREYING	EGHHIST	EIGHTHS		SIGHERS
	NIGGERY		HEIGHTS	EGHIRST	RESIGHT
EGGINSS	GESSING		HIGHEST		SIGHTER
EGGINTT	GETTING	EGHHOSW	SHOWGHE	EGHIRSU	GRUSHIE
EGGINTW	TWIGGEN	EGHHSSU	SHEUGHS		GUSHIER
EGGIORS	SOGGIER	EGHHSUW	WHEUGHS	EGHIRSY	GREYISH
EGGIPRR	PRIGGER	EGHIILL	GHILLIE	EGHIRTT	TIGHTER
EGGIPRU	PUGGIER	EGHIILN	HEILING	EGHIRUV	VUGHIER
EGGIPRY	PIGGERY	EGHIINR	HEIRING	EGHISTW	WEIGHTS
EGGIPSU	PUGGIES	EGHIINT	NIGHTIE	EGHISTY	HYGEIST
EGGIRRS	RIGGERS	EGHIINV	INVEIGH	EGHITWY	WEIGHTY
EGGIRRT	TRIGGER	EGHIKLO	HOGLIKE	EGHLLOU	LUGHOLE
EGGIRRU	RUGGIER	EGHIKNR	GHERKIN	EGHLMPS	PHLEGMS
EGGIRSW	SWIGGER	EGHIKRS	SKREIGH	EGHLMPY	PHLEGMY
	WIGGERS		SKRIEGH	EGHLNOR	LEGHORN
EGGIRTW	TWIGGER	EGHILLN	HELLING	EGHLNPU	ENGULPH
EGGIRUV	VUGGIER	EGHILMN	HELMING	EGHLNST	LENGTHS
EGGIRWY	WIGGERY	EGHILMP	MEGILPH	EGHLNTY	LENGTHY
EGGJLOR	JOGGLER	EGHILNP	HELPING		THEGNLY
EGGJLOS	JOGGLES	EGHILNR	HERLING	EGHLOOS	GOLOSHE
EGGJLRU	JUGGLER	EGHILNS	ENGLISH		SHOOGLE
EGGJLSU	JUGGLES		SHINGLE	EGHLOOT	THEOLOG
EGGJORS	JOGGERS	EGHILNT	ENLIGHT	EGHLOSS	SEGHOLS
EGGLMSU	SMUGGLE		LIGHTEN	EGHLPSU	PLEUGHS
EGGLNOS	LEGONGS	EGHILNV	HELVING	EGHLTUY	TEUGHLY
EGGLNSU	SNUGGLE	EGHILOU	GHOULIE	EGHMMOS	MEGOHMS
EGGLOOS	GOOGLES	EGHILPT	PIGHTLE	EGHMNOU	HUMOGEN
EGGLOOY	GEOLOGY	EGHILRT	LIGHTER	EGHMOSU	GUMSHOE
EGGLORS	LOGGERS		RELIGHT	EGHNOOS	HOGNOSE
	SLOGGER	EGHILSS	SLEIGHS	EGHNORS	GORHENS
EGGLORT	TOGGLER	EGHILST	SLEIGHT	EGHNORU	ENROUGH
EGGLOST	GOGLETS	EGHIMMN	HEMMING		ROUGHEN
	LOGGETS	EGHIMNS	MESHING	EGHNOSU	ENOUGHS
	TOGGLES	EGHIMNT	THEMING	EGHNOTU	TOUGHEN
EGGLOSW	WOGGLES	EGHIMPT	EMPIGHT	EGHNRSU	HUNGERS
EGGLPRU	PLUGGER	EGHINNN	HENNING	EGHOPRS	GOPHERS
EGGLPSU	PUGGLES	EGHINNT	HENTING	EGHORRU	ROUGHER
EGGLRSU	GLURGES	EGHINNU	UNHINGE	EGHORTU	TOUGHER
	GURGLES	EGHINOS	HONGIES	EGHOSTT	GHETTOS
	LUGGERS		SHOEING	EGHOSUU	HUGEOUS
	SLUGGER	EGHINPS	HESPING	EGHRSSU	GURSHES
EGGLRTU	GURGLET		PHESING		GUSHERS
EGGLSTU	GUGLETS	EGHINRR	HERRING	EGHRTUY	THEURGY
EGGMRSU	MUGGERS	EGHINRS	HINGERS	EGIIJKL	JIGLIKE
	SMUGGER	EGHINRT	RIGHTEN	EGIIJLS	JILGIES
EGGNOOY	GEOGONY	EGHINRW	WHINGER	EGIIKLP	PIGLIKE

Code	Word(s)
EGIIKLW	WIGLIKE
EGIILLS	GILLIES
EGIILMT	LEGITIM
EGIILNR	LEIRING
	LINGIER
EGIILNS	SEILING
EGIILNT	LIGNITE
EGIILNV	VEILING
EGIILNX	EXILING
EGIILPS	GILPIES
EGIILRR	GIRLIER
EGIILRS	GIRLIES
EGIIMMS	GIMMIES
EGIIMNN	MEINING
EGIIMNP	IMPINGE
EGIIMNR	MINGIER
EGIIMNT	ITEMING
EGIIMNV	MIEVING
EGIIMPR	GIMPIER
EGIIMPS	PIGMIES
EGIIMRR	GRIMIER
EGIIMSV	MISGIVE
EGIINNP	PEINING
EGIINNR	GINNIER
	REINING
EGIINNS	INGINES
	INSIGNE
	SEINING
EGIINNV	VEINING
EGIINOP	EPIGONI
EGIINPS	PEISING
	PIGSNIE
EGIINPZ	PEIZING
EGIINRR	GIRNIER
EGIINRT	IGNITER
	TIERING
	TIGRINE
EGIINRV	REIVING
	RIEVING
EGIINRW	WEIRING
	WINGIER
EGIINRZ	ZINGIER
EGIINSS	SEISING
EGIINST	IGNITES
EGIINSV	SIEVING
	VISEING
EGIINSW	WEISING
EGIINSZ	SEIZING
EGIINTV	EVITING
EGIINTX	EXITING
EGIINVW	VIEWING
EGIINWZ	WEIZING
EGIIOPR	PIEROGI
EGIIPPS	GIPPIES
EGIIPRR	GRIPIER
EGIIPRW	PERIWIG
EGIIPSS	GIPSIES
EGIJKNR	JERKING
EGIJLLN	JELLING
EGIJLNR	JINGLER
EGIJLNS	JINGLES
EGIJLNT	JINGLET
EGIJNOS	JINGOES
EGIJNSS	JESSING
EGIJNST	JESTING
EGIJNTT	JETTING
EGIKKLN	LEKKING
EGIKLMU	GUMLIKE
EGIKLNP	KELPING
EGIKLNR	ERLKING
EGIKLNS	KINGLES
EGIKLNT	KINGLET
EGIKLNW	WELKING
EGIKLRS	KILERGS
EGIKLRU	RUGLIKE
EGIKLTU	GUTLIKE
EGIKMNP	KEMPING
EGIKNNN	KENNING
EGIKNNR	KERNING
EGIKNNT	KENTING
EGIKNOV	EVOKING
EGIKNPP	KEPPING
EGIKNPR	PERKING
EGIKNRU	GUNKIER
EGIKNRV	KERVING
EGIKNRY	KEYRING
	YERKING
EGIKNST	KESTING
EGIKNSW	SKEWING
EGIKNSY	KEYINGS
	YESKING
EGIKNUY	YEUKING
EGILLMN	MELLING
EGILLNO	LOGLINE
EGILLNS	LEGLINS
	LINGELS
	LINGLES
	SELLING
EGILLNT	GILLNET
	TELLING
EGILLNW	WELLING
EGILLNY	YELLING
EGILLOR	GIROLLE
EGILLOS	GOLLIES
EGILLRR	GRILLER
EGILLRS	GILLERS
	GRILLES
EGILLST	GILLETS
EGILLSU	GULLIES
	LIGULES
EGILMMN	LEMMING
EGILMMR	GLIMMER
EGILMMY	GEMMILY
EGILMNR	GREMLIN
	MERLING
	MINGLER
EGILMNS	MINGLES
EGILMNT	MELTING
EGILMNU	EMULING
	GUMLINE
	LEGUMIN
EGILMNW	MEWLING
EGILMNY	YELMING
EGILMOR	GOMERIL
EGILMOS	SEMILOG
EGILMOU	ELOGIUM
EGILMPS	GLIMPSE
	MEGILPS
EGILMST	GIMLETS
EGILNNS	GINNELS
	LENSING
EGILNOP	ELOPING
EGILNOS	ELOIGNS
	LEGIONS
	LIGNOSE
	LINGOES
	LONGIES
EGILNOT	LENTIGO
EGILNPP	LEPPING
EGILNPR	PINGLER
EGILNPS	PINGLES
	SPIGNEL
EGILNPT	PELTING
EGILNPY	YELPING
EGILNRS	GIRNELS
	LINGERS
	SLINGER
EGILNRT	RINGLET
	TINGLER
	TRINGLE
EGILNRY	RELYING
EGILNSS	SINGLES
EGILNST	GLISTEN
	LESTING
	SINGLET
	SNIGLET
	TINGLES
EGILNSU	LUNGIES
	SLUEING
EGILNSW	SLEWING
	SWINGLE
EGILNSZ	ZINGELS
EGILNTT	ETTLING
	LETTING
EGILNTU	ELUTING
EGILNTW	WELTING
	WINGLET
EGILNUY	GUYLINE
EGILNVY	LEVYING
EGILOOS	GOOLIES
	OLOGIES
EGILOPS	EPILOGS
EGILORS	GLOIRES
	GLORIES
EGILOSS	GLIOSES
EGILOST	ELOGIST
	LOGIEST
EGILOSU	OUGLIES
EGILPPR	GRIPPLE
EGILPRU	GULPIER
EGILPST	PIGLETS
EGILPSY	GILPEYS
EGILRRU	GURLIER
EGILRSS	GRILSES
EGILRST	GLISTER
	GRISTLE
EGILRSU	GUILERS
	LIGURES
	LURGIES
EGILRSY	GREISLY
	GRIESLY
	GRISELY

Seven-letter anagrams

EGILRTT	GLITTER	EGINNRR	GRINNER		PIGSNEY
EGILRTY	TIGERLY	EGINNRS	ENRINGS	EGINPTT	PETTING
EGILRUV	VIRGULE		GINNERS	EGINPYY	EPIGYNY
EGILRZZ	GRIZZLE	EGINNRT	RENTING	EGINQUU	QUEUING
EGILSST	LEGISTS		RINGENT	EGINRRS	ERRINGS
EGILSSW	WIGLESS		TERNING		GIRNERS
EGILSTU	GLUIEST	EGINNRU	ENURING		RINGERS
	UGLIEST	EGINNRV	NERVING		SERRING
EGILSTW	WIGLETS	EGINNRY	GINNERY	EGINRRW	WRINGER
EGILSTZ	GLITZES		RENYING	EGINRSS	INGRESS
EGIMMRR	GRIMMER	EGINNSS	ENSIGNS		RESIGNS
EGIMMRS	GIMMERS		SENSING		SIGNERS
	MEGRIMS	EGINNST	NESTING		SINGERS
EGIMMRU	GUMMIER		SENTING	EGINRST	RESTING
EGIMMSU	GUMMIES		TENSING		STINGER
EGIMMTU	GUMMITE	EGINNSU	ENSUING	EGINRSU	REUSING
EGIMNNN	NEMNING		GUNNIES		RUEINGS
EGIMNNO	OMENING		INGENUS		SIGNEUR
EGIMNNR	RINGMEN	EGINNSW	NEWSING	EGINRSV	SERVING
EGIMNNS	MENSING	EGINNSY	GYNNIES		VERSING
EGIMNNW	WINGMEN	EGINNTT	NETTING	EGINRSW	SWINGER
EGIMNOR	MOERING		TENTING		WINGERS
EGIMNOS	MISGONE	EGINNTV	VENTING	EGINRSY	SYRINGE
EGIMNOT	EMOTING	EGINNVY	ENVYING	EGINRSZ	ZINGERS
	MITOGEN	EGINOOR	GOONIER	EGINRTT	GITTERN
EGIMNOU	MEOUING	EGINOOS	GOONIES		RETTING
EGIMNOV	EMOVING		ISOGONE	EGINRTU	TRUEING
EGIMNOW	MEOWING		NOOGIES	EGINRTV	VERTING
EGIMNPR	GRIPMEN	EGINOPR	PERIGON	EGINRTY	RETYING
	IMPREGN		PIROGEN	EGINRVV	REVVING
	PERMING		PONGIER	EGINRVY	REVYING
EGIMNPT	EMPTING	EGINOPS	EPIGONS	EGINSST	INGESTS
	PIGMENT		PIGEONS		SIGNETS
	TEMPING		PINGOES	EGINSSW	SEWINGS
EGIMNQU	QUEMING	EGINORR	IGNORER		SWINGES
EGIMNRS	GERMINS	EGINORS	ERINGOS	EGINSSY	YESSING
	MERINGS		IGNORES	EGINSTT	SETTING
	MINGERS		REGIONS		TESTING
EGIMNRT	METRING		SIGNORE	EGINSTU	GUNITES
	TERMING	EGINORT	GENITOR	EGINSTV	VESTING
EGIMNRU	EMURING	EGINORV	OVERING	EGINSTW	STEWING
EGIMNSS	MESSING	EGINORZ	ZEROING		TWINGES
EGIMNST	STEMING	EGINOSU	IGNEOUS		WESTING
	TEMSING	EGINOSW	WIGEONS	EGINSTZ	ZESTING
EGIMNSU	MEUSING	EGINOSY	ISOGENY	EGINSVX	VEXINGS
EGIMNSW	MEWSING	EGINOSZ	GINZOES	EGINSWY	SWEYING
EGIMORR	GORMIER	EGINOTT	TENTIGO	EGINSZZ	GIZZENS
EGIMORS	OGREISM	EGINOTV	VETOING	EGINTTV	VETTING
EGIMOSS	EGOISMS	EGINOTZ	GENIZOT	EGINTTW	WETTING
	MISGOES	EGINPPP	PEPPING	EGINTTX	TEXTING
EGIMOST	EGOTISM	EGINPPR	REPPING	EGIOOPR	GOOPIER
EGIMPSU	GUIMPES	EGINPPS	PIGPENS	EGIOORS	GOORIES
EGIMPSY	GYMPIES	EGINPRS	PERSING		GOOSIER
	PYGMIES		PINGERS	EGIOOSS	GOOSIES
EGIMRSW	MISGREW		SPRINGE		SOOGIES
EGIMSST	STIGMES	EGINPRU	PUERING	EGIOOST	GOOIEST
EGINNNP	PENNING	EGINPRV	PERVING	EGIOPPS	GIPPOES
EGINNNR	RENNING		PREVING	EGIOPRS	PORGIES
EGINNNY	YENNING	EGINPRY	PREYING		SERPIGO
EGINNOO	IONOGEN	EGINPSS	GIPSENS	EGIOPRU	GROUPIE
EGINNOP	OPENING	EGINPSU	SPUEING		PIROGUE
EGINNOR	NEGRONI	EGINPSW	SPEWING	EGIORRS	GORSIER
EGINNOV	OVENING	EGINPSY	ESPYING	EGIORST	GOITERS
EGINNPU	PENGUIN		PEYSING		GOITRES

	GORIEST	EGLNPRU	PLUNGER	EGMORSU	GRUMOSE
EGIORTU	GOUTIER	EGLNPSU	PLUNGES		MORGUES
EGIORTV	VERTIGO		PUNGLES	EGMORTU	GOURMET
EGIORTZ	ZORGITE	EGLNRSU	LUNGERS	EGNNOOS	NONEGOS
EGIORUV	VOGUIER	EGLNRTU	GRUNTLE	EGNNORT	RONTGEN
EGIOSST	EGOISTS	EGLNSSU	GUNLESS	EGNNOSU	GUENONS
	STOGIES		GUNSELS	EGNNPTU	PUNGENT
EGIOSTT	EGOTIST	EGLNSTU	ENGLUTS	EGNNRSU	GUNNERS
EGIOSTV	VOGIEST		GLUTENS	EGNNRUY	GUNNERY
EGIOTUV	OUTGIVE	EGLNSUU	UNGLUES	EGNNSYY	GYNNEYS
EGIPPRR	GRIPPER	EGLOORS	REGOSOL	EGNNTUU	UNGUENT
EGIPPRS	GIPPERS	EGLOOSY	GOOLEYS	EGNOOPS	PONGOES
	GRIPPES	EGLOPRS	PROLEGS	EGNOORS	ORGONES
EGIPPSU	GUPPIES	EGLOPSS	GOSPELS		OROGENS
EGIPPSY	GYPPIES	EGLOPTU	GLUEPOT	EGNOORY	OROGENY
EGIPRRS	GRIPERS	EGLORRW	GROWLER	EGNOOST	GENTOOS
EGIPRUU	GUIPURE	EGLORSS	GLOSSER	EGNOOSY	GOONEYS
EGIPSSY	GYPSIES		REGLOSS	EGNOOTU	OUTGONE
EGIRRRU	GURRIER	EGLORSU	REGULOS	EGNOOYZ	ZOOGENY
EGIRRST	GRISTER	EGLORSV	GLOVERS	EGNOPRS	PRESONG
EGIRRSU	GURRIES		GROVELS		SPONGER
	SURGIER	EGLORSW	GLOWERS	EGNOPRY	PROGENY
EGIRRSV	VIRGERS		REGLOWS		PYROGEN
EGIRRTT	GRITTER	EGLOSSS	GLOSSES	EGNOPSS	SPONGES
EGIRSST	TIGRESS	EGLOSST	GOSLETS	EGNOPSW	GOWPENS
EGIRSSU	GUISERS	EGLOSUV	VOULGES	EGNORRW	REGROWN
EGIRSTU	GUSTIER	EGLPRSU	GULPERS		WRONGER
	GUTSIER		SPLURGE	EGNORSS	ENGROSS
EGIRSTV	GRIVETS	EGLPRUY	GYPLURE	EGNORST	TONGERS
EGIRSUZ	GUIZERS	EGLRSTU	GURLETS	EGNORSU	SURGEON
EGIRTTU	GUTTIER	EGLRSUU	REGULUS	EGNORSV	GOVERNS
	TURGITE	EGLRSUY	GUYLERS	EGNORSY	ERYNGOS
EGISSSU	GUSSIES	EGLRSYY	GRYSELY		GROYNES
EGISTTU	GUTTIES	EGLRTTU	GUTTLER	EGNORUY	YOUNGER
EGISUWY	WISEGUY	EGLRUZZ	GUZZLER	EGNOSSY	GONYSES
EGJLNSU	JUNGLES	EGLSSTU	GUTLESS	EGNOSTU	TONGUES
EGJLSTU	JUGLETS		TUGLESS	EGNOSXY	OXYGENS
EGJOSTT	GJETOST	EGLSTTU	GUTTLES	EGNPRSU	REPUGNS
EGKLORW	LEGWORK	EGLSTUU	GLUTEUS	EGNPSSU	SPUNGES
EGKMSSU	MUSKEGS	EGLSUZZ	GUZZLES	EGNPSUX	EXPUGNS
EGKNOSY	KYOGENS	EGMMORT	GROMMET	EGNRRTU	GRUNTER
EGLLORS	GOLLERS	EGMMOSU	GUMMOSE	EGNRSTU	GUNTERS
EGLLRSU	GULLERS	EGMMRRU	GRUMMER		GURNETS
EGLLRUY	GULLERY	EGMMRSU	GUMMERS		SURGENT
EGLLSTU	GULLETS	EGMMRTU	GRUMMET	EGNRSUY	GURNEYS
EGLLSUY	GULLEYS	EGMNNOS	SONGMEN	EGNRSYY	SYNERGY
EGLMMRU	GLUMMER	EGMNNOT	TONGMEN	EGNRTTU	GRUTTEN
EGLMNOO	ENGLOOM	EGMNNOW	GOWNMEN		TURGENT
EGLMNOR	MONGREL	EGMNOOS	MONGOES	EGNSUVY	UNGYVES
EGLMOOR	LEGROOM	EGMNORS	MONGERS	EGOOPRS	POGOERS
EGLMSSU	GUMLESS		MORGENS	EGOOPSY	POOGYES
EGLNNSU	GUNNELS	EGMNORU	MURGEON	EGOORRV	GROOVER
EGLNOOY	ENOLOGY	EGMNORY	MONGERY	EGOORSV	GROOVES
	NEOLOGY	EGMNOST	EMONGST	EGOORSY	GOOSERY
EGLNOPS	PLONGES	EGMNOSU	EUMONGS	EGOORTU	OUTGOER
EGLNORS	LONGERS		MUNGOES	EGOORTV	OVERGOT
EGLNORU	LOUNGER	EGMNOSY	MYOGENS	EGOOSST	STOOGES
EGLNOST	LONGEST	EGMNOYZ	ZYMOGEN	EGOOSSY	GOOSEYS
EGLNOSU	LOUNGES	EGMNSTU	NUTMEGS	EGOOSTU	OUTGOES
EGLNOSY	LYSOGEN	EGMNSUU	EUMUNGS	EGOPRRS	GROPERS
EGLNOUV	UNGLOVE	EGMOORR	GROOMER	EGOPRRU	GROUPER
EGLNOXY	LOXYGEN		REGROOM		REGROUP
	XYLOGEN	EGMOOSS	SMOOGES	EGORRSS	GROSERS
EGLNOYZ	LOZENGY	EGMORST	GROMETS		GROSSER

EGORRST	GROSERT	EHIIPPS	HIPPIES	EHILNSS	ELSHINS
EGORRSU	GROUSER		SHIPPIE	EHILNTY	ETHINYL
EGORRSW	GROWERS	EHIIPRT	PITHIER	EHILOOR	HOOLIER
	REGROWS	EHIIRSS	HISSIER	EHILOOS	HOOLIES
EGORRTU	GROUTER	EHIIRST	HIRSTIE	EHILOPT	HOPLITE
EGORRUY	ROGUERY	EHIIRTW	WHITIER	EHILOSS	ISOHELS
EGORSSS	GROSSES		WITHIER	EHILOST	EOLITHS
EGORSST	GOSTERS	EHIISSS	HISSIES		HOLIEST
	GROSETS	EHIISST	STISHIE		HOSTILE
	STORGES	EHIISTW	WHITIES	EHILPRS	HIRPLES
EGORSSU	GROUSES		WITHIES	EHILPRT	PHILTER
EGORSTV	GROVETS	EHIJNNO	JOHNNIE		PHILTRE
EGORSUV	VOGUERS	EHIKKRS	SHIKKER	EHILPSS	HIPLESS
EGORTUW	OUTGREW	EHIKKSS	KISHKES	EHILRRW	WHIRLER
EGOSSTU	GUSTOES	EHIKLRU	HULKIER	EHILRSS	HIRSELS
EGOSSTY	STOGEYS	EHIKLTU	HUTLIKE		HIRSLES
EGOSSYZ	ZYGOSES	EHIKLTY	LEKYTHI	EHILRST	SLITHER
EGOSTTU	GOUTTES	EHIKMNT	METHINK	EHILRSU	HURLIES
EGOSTYZ	ZYGOTES	EHIKMSV	MIKVEHS		LUSHIER
EGPPRSY	GYPPERS	EHIKNOS	HONKIES	EHILRSV	SHRIVEL
EGPRRSU	PURGERS	EHIKNRS	KERNISH	EHILRTU	LUTHIER
EGPRSSU	SPURGES	EHIKNRT	RETHINK	EHILRTW	WHIRTLE
EGPRSTY	GYPSTER		THINKER	EHILSSS	SLISHES
EGPRSUU	UPSURGE	EHIKNRU	HUNKIER	EHILSST	HITLESS
EGRRSSU	SURGERS	EHIKNSS	KNISHES	EHILSTT	LISTETH
EGRRSUY	SURGERY	EHIKNSU	HUNKIES		LITHEST
EGRSSTU	GUTSERS	EHIKOOR	HOOKIER		THISTLE
EGRSSUY	GYRUSES	EHIKOOS	HOOKIES	EHILSTV	THIVELS
EGRSTTU	GUTTERS	EHIKOST	HOKIEST	EHILSTW	WHISTLE
EGRSTUZ	GUTZERS	EHIKPRS	KEPHIRS	EHILTTU	THULITE
EGRTTUY	GUTTERY		PERKISH	EHILTTW	WHITTLE
EGSSSTU	GUSSETS	EHIKRRS	SHIRKER	EHILTWY	WHITELY
EHHIIMS	HEIMISH	EHIKRSS	SHREIKS	EHIMMRS	SHIMMER
EHHIKSS	SHEIKHS		SHRIEKS	EHIMMSY	SHIMMEY
	SHIKSEH		SHRIKES	EHIMNOS	HOMINES
EHHILLS	HELLISH	EHIKRSU	HUSKIER	EHIMNPS	SHIPMEN
EHHINNS	HENNISH	EHIKRSW	WHISKER	EHIMNRS	MENHIRS
EHHIPRS	HERSHIP	EHIKRSY	SHRIEKY	EHIMNRU	INHUMER
EHHIRST	HITHERS	EHIKSSS	SHIKSES		RHENIUM
EHHIRSU	HUSHIER	EHIKSSU	HUSKIES	EHIMNSU	INHUMES
EHHIRTT	THITHER	EHIKSTW	WHISKET	EHIMNTY	THYMINE
EHHIRTW	WHITHER	EHIKSWY	WHISKEY	EHIMORS	HEROISM
EHHISSW	WHISHES	EHIKRSW	WHISKER		MOREISH
EHHISWY	WHEYISH	EHILLMN	HILLMEN	EHIMORT	MOITHER
EHHNPSY	HYPHENS	EHILLNO	HELLION		MOTHIER
EHHOOSS	HOOSHES	EHILLNS	INSHELL	EHIMORZ	RHIZOME
EHHORTT	THOTHER	EHILLOO	OILHOLE	EHIMOST	HOMIEST
EHHRSSU	HUSHERS	EHILLOS	HILLOES	EHIMPPX	PEMPHIX
	SHUSHER		HOLLIES	EHIMPRU	HUMPIER
EHHSSSU	SHUSHES	EHILLRS	HILLERS	EHIMPRW	WHIMPER
EHIIIKT	HEITIKI		RELLISH	EHIMPSU	HUMPIES
EHIIKLP	HIPLIKE	EHILLRT	THILLER	EHIMRST	HERMITS
EHIIKNR	HINKIER	EHILLRU	HULLIER		MITHERS
EHIILLR	HILLIER	EHILLTY	LITHELY	EHIMRSU	HEURISM
EHIILNP	HIPLINE	EHILMMO	MOHELIM		MUSHIER
EHIILTT	LITHITE	EHILMPW	WHIMPLE	EHIMRTT	THERMIT
EHIIMSS	MEISHIS	EHILMSU	HELIUMS	EHIMRTY	MYTHIER
EHIINNS	HINNIES		HUMLIES		THYMIER
EHIINRS	SHINIER		MUHLIES	EHIMSST	THEISMS
EHIINRT	INHERIT	EHILMTT	MELTITH	EHIMSTU	HUMITES
EHIINRW	WHINIER	EHILMUW	UMWHILE		TUMSHIE
EHIINRZ	RHIZINE	EHILNOP	PINHOLE	EHIMSTY	MYTHISE
EHIINSS	SHINIES	EHILNOT	HOTLINE	EHIMSWY	WHIMSEY
EHIIPPR	HIPPIER		NEOLITH	EHIMTYZ	MYTHIZE
		EHILNPS	PLENISH		

EHINNNS	HENNINS		SERIPHS	EHLLNSU	UNSHELL
EHINNRT	THINNER	EHIPRST	HIPSTER	EHLLOOS	HOLLOES
EHINNSS	SHINNES	EHIPRSU	PUSHIER	EHLLORS	HOLLERS
EHINNSW	WENNISH	EHIPRSW	WHISPER	EHLLOSU	HULLOES
EHINNSY	SHINNEY	EHIPSTT	PETTISH	EHLLRSU	HULLERS
EHINOPR	PHONIER	EHIPSZZ	PHIZZES	EHLMMOW	WHOMMLE
EHINOPS	PHONIES	EHIRRRU	HURRIER	EHLMMSU	HUMMELS
EHINOPX	PHOENIX	EHIRRSS	SHERRIS	EHLMMUW	WHUMMLE
EHINORR	HORNIER	EHIRRSU	HURRIES	EHLMNOT	MENTHOL
EHINORS	HEROINS		RUSHIER	EHLMNOY	HOMELYN
	INSHORE	EHIRRSV	SHRIVER	EHLMNSU	UNHELMS
EHINOST	ETHIONS	EHIRRTV	THRIVER	EHLMOOS	HOLESOM
	HISTONE	EHIRRTW	WHERRIT	EHLMOPS	PHLOEMS
EHINOSU	HEINOUS		WHIRRET	EHLMSSU	MULSHES
EHINPPS	HIPPENS		WRITHER	EHLMSTY	METHYLS
	SHIPPEN	EHIRSSS	HISSERS	EHLNOPS	PHENOLS
EHINPSS	HIPNESS	EHIRSSV	SHIVERS	EHLNORT	HORNLET
EHINRSS	SHINERS		SHRIVES	EHLNPSY	PHENYLS
	SHRINES	EHIRSSW	SWISHER	EHLNRTU	LUTHERN
EHINRST	HINTERS		WISHERS	EHLNTTY	TENTHLY
	NITHERS	EHIRSTT	HITTERS	EHLNTYY	ETHYNYL
EHINRSV	SHRIVEN		TITHERS	EHLOOPT	POTHOLE
EHINRSW	WHINERS	EHIRSTU	HIRSUTE	EHLOOSS	SHOOLES
EHINRTV	THRIVEN	EHIRSTV	THRIVES	EHLOOSY	HOOLEYS
EHINRTW	WRITHEN	EHIRSTW	SWITHER	EHLOPPR	HOPPLER
EHINRTZ	ZITHERN		WITHERS	EHLOPPS	HOPPLES
EHINSSS	SHINESS		WRITHES	EHLOPSX	PHLOXES
EHINSST	SITHENS	EHIRSTZ	ZITHERS	EHLOPSY	SPYHOLE
EHINSTW	WHITENS	EHIRSVY	SHIVERY	EHLORST	HOLSTER
EHINSTZ	ZENITHS	EHIRTTW	WHITRET		HOSTLER
EHINSUV	UNHIVES		WHITTER	EHLORSW	HOWLERS
EHINTUW	UNWHITE	EHIRWZZ	WHIZZER	EHLORTW	WHORTLE
EHIOOPW	WHOOPIE	EHISSSU	HUSSIES	EHLORTY	HELOTRY
EHIOORT	HOOTIER	EHISSSW	SWISHES	EHLOSSS	SLOSHES
EHIOOST	TOOSHIE		WHISSES	EHLOSST	HOSTELS
EHIOPPR	HOPPIER	EHISSTT	THEISTS	EHLOSSU	HOUSELS
EHIOPRS	ROSEHIP	EHISSTU	STUSHIE	EHLOSSV	SHOVELS
EHIOPSS	SOPHIES		TUSHIES	EHLOSTT	LOTHEST
EHIOPST	ETHIOPS	EHISTTW	TEWHITS		SHOTTLE
	OPHITES		WETTISH	EHLOSTW	HOWLETS
EHIORRS	HORSIER		WHITEST		THOWELS
EHIORRT	HERITOR	EHISTWY	WHITEYS	EHLOSTY	THYLOSE
EHIORSS	HOSIERS	EHISUZZ	HUZZIES	EHLOTXY	ETHOXYL
EHIORST	HERIOTS	EHISWZZ	WHIZZES	EHLPPSS	SHLEPPS
	HOISTER	EHJOPSS	JOSEPHS	EHLPRSU	PLUSHER
	SHORTIE	EHJORSS	JOSHERS	EHLPSSU	PLUSHES
	TOSHIER	EHKLNOS	LOKSHEN	EHLRRSU	HURLERS
EHIORSU	HOUSIER	EHKLOOT	HOOKLET	EHLRSSU	LUSHERS
EHIORSW	SHOWIER	EHKLPST	KLEPHTS	EHLRSTU	HURTLES
EHIORSY	HOSIERY	EHKMOOS	SMOKEHO		HUSTLER
EHIORTT	THORITE	EHKMOSY	SKYHOME	EHLRSUY	HURLEYS
EHIORTU	OUTHIRE	EHKNORS	HONKERS	EHLSSSU	SLUSHES
	ROUTHIE	EHKNOSY	HONKEYS	EHLSSTT	SHTETLS
EHIORTV	OVERHIT	EHKNRSU	HUNKERS	EHLSSTU	HUSTLES
EHIOSST	HOSTIES	EHKNSSU	HUNKSES		LUSHEST
EHIOSTT	HOTTIES	EHKNSUY	HUNKEYS		SLUSHES
EHIOSTY	ISOHYET	EHKOORS	HOOKERS	EHLSTTU	SHUTTLE
EHIPPRS	PRESHIP	EHKOOSY	HOOKEYS	EHMMRSU	HUMMERS
	SHIPPER	EHKORSS	KOSHERS	EHMNNOO	NONHOME
EHIPPRW	WHIPPER	EHKORSW	HOWKERS	EHMNOOR	HORMONE
EHIPPST	HIPPEST	EHKORSY	HORKEYS		MOORHEN
EHIPPTW	WHIPPET	EHKOSSS	SKOSHES	EHMNOPS	PHENOMS
EHIPRSS	PISHERS	EHKRSSU	HUSKERS		SHOPMEN
	RESHIPS	EHKRSTU	TUSHKER	EHMNOST	MONETHS

EHMNOSW	SHOWMEN			EHQRSSU	QURSHES
EHMNPSU	HUMPENS	EHNRTWY	WRYTHEN	EHRRSSU	RUSHERS
EHMNPTY	NYMPHET	EHNSSSU	SNUSHES	EHRRSTU	HURTERS
EHMNTTU	HUTMENT	EHNSSSY	SHYNESS	EHRSSTY	SHYSTER
EHMOOSS	SHMOOSE	EHOOOPS	HOOPOES		THYRSES
EHMOOSW	SOMEHOW	EHOOPRS	HOOPERS	EHRSTTU	SHUTTER
EHMOOSX	HOMOSEX	EHOOPRW	WHOOPER	EHRSTTW	STREWTH
EHMOOSZ	SHMOOZE	EHOOPTY	OOPHYTE	EHRSTUW	WUTHERS
EHMOPRW	MORPHEW	EHOORST	HOOTERS	EHRSTUY	TUSHERY
EHMORSS	MOSHERS		RESHOOT	EHRTTTY	THRETTY
EHMORST	MOTHERS		SHEROOT	EHSSSTU	TUSSEHS
	SMOTHER		SHOOTER	EIIILRV	RILIEVI
	THERMOS		SOOTHER	EIIILST	ILEITIS
EHMORTU	MOUTHER	EHOORSV	HOOVERS	EIIINPR	RIPIENI
EHMORTY	MOTHERY	EHOORTV	OVERHOT	EIIJMMS	JIMMIES
EHMOSWY	SOMEWHY	EHOOSST	SOOTHES	EIIJMPR	JIMPIER
EHMOTXY	METHOXY	EHOOSSW	WOOSHES	EIIJSTV	JIVIEST
EHMPRSU	HUMPERS	EHOPPRS	HOPPERS	EIIKKLN	INKLIKE
EHMPRTU	THUMPER		SHOPPER	EIIKKNR	KINKIER
EHMRRSY	RHYMERS	EHOPPRT	PROPHET	EIIKLLP	LIPLIKE
EHMRRTU	MURTHER	EHOPPRW	WHOPPER	EIIKLLS	KILLIES
EHMRSSU	MUSHERS	EHOPPSS	SHOPPES	EIIKLMR	MILKIER
EHMRSUU	HUMERUS	EHOPRRY	ORPHREY	EIIKLMS	MISLIKE
EHMRTUV	VERMUTH	EHOPRST	POTHERS	EIIKLNT	TINLIKE
EHMSSSU	SMUSHES		STROPHE	EIIKLPS	PLISKIE
EHMSSUU	HUMUSES		THORPES	EIIKLRS	SILKIER
EHNNOOR	NONHERO	EHOPRSU	UPHROES	EIIKLSS	SILKIES
EHNNOPR	NEPHRON	EHOPRSW	PRESHOW	EIIKLST	KILTIES
EHNNOPY	HYPNONE	EHOPRSY	PHORESY	EIIKLVY	IVYLIKE
EHNNRSU	SHUNNER	EHOPRTU	POUTHER	EIIKMRR	MIRKIER
EHNNSTU	UNSHENT	EHOPRTY	POTHERY	EIIKNNT	KINETIN
EHNNSUW	UNSHEWN	EHOPRUY	EUPHORY	EIIKNPR	PINKIER
EHNOORR	HONORER	EHOPSSS	SPOSHES	EIIKNPS	PINKIES
EHNOORS	HEROONS	EHOPSST	POSHEST	EIIKNRS	SINKIER
	ONSHORE	EHOPSTY	TYPHOSE	EIIKNRZ	ZINKIER
	SOREHON	EHORRSS	SHORERS	EIIKNSS	KINESIS
EHNOPRS	PHONERS	EHORRST	RHETORS	EIIKNST	INKIEST
EHNOPRY	HYPERON		ROTHERS	EIIKNTW	TWINKIE
EHNOPSU	EUPHONS		SHORTER	EIIKPRS	SPIKIER
EHNOPSY	PHONEYS	EHORRTW	THROWER	EIIKPSS	PISKIES
EHNOPUY	EUPHONY	EHORSST	HORSTES	EIIKRRS	RISKIER
EHNOPXY	PHENOXY		TOSHERS	EIIKRSV	SKIVIER
EHNORRS	HORNERS	EHORSSU	HOUSERS	EIIKSTT	KITTIES
EHNORRT	HORRENT	EHORSSV	SHOVERS	EIILLMM	MILLIME
	NORTHER		SHROVES	EIILLMN	MILLINE
EHNORRY	HERONRY	EHORSSW	RESHOWS	EIILLMR	MILLIER
EHNORSS	NOSHERS		SHOWERS	EIILLMS	MILLIES
	SENHORS	EHORSTT	HOTTERS	EIILLMT	LIMELIT
EHNORST	HORNETS	EHORSTU	SHOUTER	EIILLNV	VILLEIN
	SHORTEN		SOUTHER	EIILLPS	ILLIPES
	THRENOS	EHORSTW	THROWES		PILLIES
	THRONES	EHORSTX	EXHORTS	EIILLRS	SILLIER
EHNORSU	UNHORSE	EHORSWY	SHOWERY	EIILLRT	TILLIER
EHNORSW	RESHOWN	EHORTUY	OUTHYRE	EIILLSS	SILLIES
EHNORSY	NOSHERY	EHOSSST	HOSTESS	EIILLST	ILLITES
EHNOSST	HOTNESS	EHOSSSU	SHOUSES	EIILLSW	WILLIES
EHNOSSU	UNSHOES	EHOSSTT	SHOTTES	EIILLTT	LITTLIE
EHNOSTT	SHOTTEN	EHOSTTT	HOTTEST		TILLITE
EHNOSTY	HONESTY	EHOTTTW	WOTTETH	EIILLTV	VITELLI
EHNOSUU	UNHOUSE	EHPRSSU	PUSHERS	EIILMNV	MILVINE
EHNOTUY	YOUTHEN	EHPRSSY	SYPHERS	EIILMPR	IMPERIL
EHNPRSY	PHRENSY	EHPRSYZ	ZEPHYRS	EIILMPS	IMPLIES
EHNRSTU	HUNTERS	EHPRTTU	TURPETH	EIILMPT	LIMEPIT
	SHUNTER	EHPRTUW	UPTHREW	EIILMRR	MIRLIER

EIILMRS	MILREIS	**EIIMNST**	MINIEST	**EIINSSZ**	SEIZINS
	SLIMIER	**EIIMNTV**	MINIVET	**EIINSTT**	SITTINE
EIILMRT	LIMITER	**EIIMNTY**	NIMIETY		TINIEST
	MILTIER	**EIIMOSS**	MEIOSIS	**EIINSTU**	UNITIES
EIILMSS	MISLIES	**EIIMPRS**	PISMIRE		UNITISE
	MISSILE		PRIMSIE	**EIINSTV**	INVITES
	SIMILES	**EIIMPRW**	WIMPIER		VINIEST
EIILMST	ELITISM	**EIIMPST**	PIETISM	**EIINSTW**	WINIEST
	LIMIEST	**EIIMPTY**	IMPIETY	**EIINSUZ**	UNISIZE
	LIMITES	**EIIMRSS**	MERISIS	**EIINTUV**	UNITIVE
EIILMSU	MILIEUS		MISSIER	**EIINTUZ**	UNITIZE
EIILMSV	MISLIVE	**EIIMRST**	MIRIEST	**EIIORST**	RIOTISE
EIILMUX	MILIEUX		MISTIER	**EIIORSV**	IVORIES
EIILNNS	LINNIES		RIMIEST	**EIIORTZ**	RIOTIZE
EIILNOS	ELISION	**EIIMSSS**	MISSIES	**EIIOSTZ**	ZOISITE
	ISOLINE	**EIIMSST**	MITISES	**EIIPPPR**	PIPPIER
	LIONISE		STIMIES	**EIIPPRR**	RIPPIER
EIILNOT	ETIOLIN	**EIIMSSV**	MISSIVE	**EIIPPRT**	TIPPIER
EIILNOV	OLIVINE	**EIIMSSZ**	SIZEISM	**EIIPPRZ**	ZIPPIER
EIILNOZ	LIONIZE	**EIIMSTT**	MITIEST	**EIIPPST**	PIPIEST
EIILNPS	SPLENII	**EIIMSTX**	MIXIEST	**EIIPPSY**	YIPPIES
EIILNRR	NIRLIER	**EIINNNP**	NINEPIN	**EIIPRRS**	SPIRIER
EIILNRS	INLIERS	**EIINNNS**	NINNIES	**EIIPRRT**	TRIPIER
	RESILIN	**EIINNOS**	INOSINE	**EIIPRRV**	PRIVIER
EIILNRT	LINTIER	**EIINNPS**	PINNIES	**EIIPRST**	PITIERS
	NITRILE	**EIINNQU**	QUININE		TIPSIER
EIILNSS	INISLES	**EIINNRT**	TINNIER	**EIIPRSV**	PRIVIES
EIILNST	LINIEST	**EIINNST**	INTINES	**EIIPRSW**	SWIPIER
	LINTIES		TINNIES		WISPIER
EIILNTT	INTITLE	**EIINNSW**	INSINEW	**EIIPSTT**	PIETIST
EIILNTU	INUTILE	**EIINNTV**	INVENIT	**EIIPTTT**	PITTITE
EIILOPR	LIRIOPE	**EIINNTW**	INTWINE	**EIIPTTU**	PITUITE
EIILORR	ROILIER	**EIINOPR**	RIPIENO	**EIIRRTZ**	RITZIER
EIILORS	SOILIER	**EIINOPS**	PIONIES	**EIIRSSS**	SISSIER
EIILORV	RILIEVO		SINOPIE	**EIIRSSV**	VISIERS
EIILOST	IOLITES	**EIINORR**	IRONIER	**EIIRSTV**	REVISIT
	OILIEST	**EIINORS**	IONISER		STIVIER
EIILPPR	LIPPIER		IRONIES		VISITER
EIILPPS	LIPPIES		IRONISE	**EIIRSTW**	WIRIEST
EIILPST	SPILITE		NOISIER	**EIIRSVZ**	VIZIERS
EIILQSU	SILIQUE	**EIINORZ**	IONIZER	**EIIRSWZ**	WIZIERS
EIILRST	RILIEST		IRONIZE	**EIIRTTW**	WITTIER
	SILTIER	**EIINOSS**	IONISES	**EIISSSS**	SISSIES
EIILRSV	LIVIERS	**EIINOST**	INOSITE	**EIISSTV**	VISITES
EIILRSX	ELIXIRS	**EIINOSZ**	IONIZES	**EIISSTX**	SIXTIES
EIILSSV	VISILES	**EIINPPR**	NIPPIER	**EIISSTZ**	SIZEIST
EIILSTT	ELITIST	**EIINPRS**	INSPIRE		SIZIEST
EIILSTU	UTILISE		PIRNIES	**EIISTTT**	TITTIES
EIILSTW	WILIEST		SNIPIER	**EIISTUV**	UVEITIS
EIILSZZ	LIZZIES		SPINIER	**EIISTZZ**	TIZZIES
EIILTUY	TUILYIE	**EIINPST**	PINIEST	**EIISVZZ**	VIZZIES
EIILTUZ	TUILZIE		PINITES	**EIJKKSU**	JUKSKEI
	UTILIZE		TIEPINS	**EIJKLRY**	JERKILY
EIILTXY	EXILITY	**EIINPTT**	PENTITI	**EIJKNPR**	PERJINK
EIIMMRS	MIMSIER	**EIINQRU**	INQUIRE		PREJINK
EIIMMSS	MIMESIS	**EIINQSU**	QUINIES	**EIJKNRS**	JERKINS
EIIMMST	MISTIME	**EIINQTU**	INQUIET		JINKERS
EIIMMSX	IMMIXES	**EIINRTT**	NITRITE	**EIJKNRU**	JUNKIER
EIIMNNS	MINNIES		NITTIER	**EIJKNSU**	JUNKIES
EIIMNPR	PRIMINE		TINTIER	**EIJKOST**	JOKIEST
EIIMNRT	INTERIM	**EIINRTV**	INVITER	**EIJLLNY**	INJELLY
	MINTIER		VITRINE	**EIJLLOR**	JOLLIER
	TERMINI	**EIINRTW**	TWINIER	**EIJLLOS**	JOLLIES
EIIMNRV	MINIVER	**EIINSSS**	SEISINS	**EIJLLST**	JILLETS

EIJLORT	JOLTIER	EIKLNTT	KNITTLE	EIKNPSU	PUNKIES
EIJLORW	JOWLIER	EIKLNTU	NUTLIKE		SPUNKIE
EIJLRST	JILTERS	EIKLNTW	TWINKLE	EIKNPSY	PINKEYS
EIJMPRU	JUMPIER	EIKLOOP	PLOOKIE	EIKNRSS	SINKERS
EIJMPST	JIMPEST	EIKLOPT	POTLIKE	EIKNRST	REKNITS
EIJNNOS	ENJOINS	EIKLOPU	PLOUKIE		SKINTER
EIJNORS	JOINERS	EIKLORY	YOLKIER		STINKER
	REJOINS	EIKLOTY	TOYLIKE		TINKERS
EIJNORT	JOINTER	EIKLPRY	PERKILY	EIKNRSW	SWINKER
EIJNORY	JOINERY	EIKLPST	SKELPIT		WINKERS
EIJNOST	JONTIES	EIKLPSU	PUSLIKE	EIKNRTT	KNITTER
EIJNPRU	JUNIPER	EIKLPSY	PESKILY		TRINKET
EIJNRRU	INJURER	EIKLRST	KILTERS	EIKNSSU	SUNKIES
EIJNRSU	INJURES		KIRTLES	EIKNSTT	KITTENS
EIJNSTY	JITNEYS		KLISTER	EIKNTTY	KITTENY
EIJNTTW	TWINJET	EIKLRSU	SULKIER	EIKNTUZ	KUNZITE
EIJRSTT	JITTERS	EIKLRTT	KITTLER	EIKOORR	ROOKIER
	TRIJETS	EIKLSSS	KISSELS	EIKOORS	KOORIES
EIJRTTY	JITTERY	EIKLSSU	SULKIES		ROOKIES
EIJSSTU	JESUITS	EIKLSTT	KITTELS	EIKOOST	STOOKIE
EIJSSUV	JUSSIVE		KITTLES	EIKOPPR	PORKPIE
EIJSTTU	JUTTIES		SKITTLE	EIKOPPS	KOPPIES
EIKKLNR	KLINKER	EIKMMRR	KRIMMER	EIKOPRR	PORKIER
EIKKLNS	KINKLES	EIKMMRS	KIMMERS	EIKOPRS	PORKIES
EIKKLSY	KYLIKES		SKIMMER	EIKOPST	POKIEST
	SKYLIKE	EIKMNNS	KINSMEN	EIKORST	ROKIEST
EIKKMNR	KIRKMEN	EIKMNOR	MONIKER	EIKORSY	YORKIES
EIKKNRS	SKINKER	EIKMNRS	MERKINS	EIKOSST	KETOSIS
EIKKOOR	KOOKIER	EIKMNSS	MISKENS	EIKPPRS	KIPPERS
EIKKRSS	SKRIKES	EIKMNST	MISKENT		SKIPPER
EIKKRSY	YIKKERS	EIKMNSW	MISKNEW	EIKPPST	SKIPPET
EIKKRUY	YUKKIER	EIKMORS	IRKSOME	EIKPRSS	SPIKERS
EIKLLNW	INKWELL		SMOKIER	EIKPRSY	SPIKERY
EIKLLOS	SKOLLIE	EIKMOSS	SMOKIES	EIKPSSS	SKEPSIS
EIKLLOW	OWLLIKE	EIKMOSY	MISYOKE	EIKRRSS	RISKERS
EIKLLRS	KILLERS	EIKMPST	MISKEPT	EIKRRST	SKIRRET
	RESKILL	EIKMPSU	MUSPIKE		SKIRTER
EIKLLST	SKILLET	EIKMRRS	SMIRKER		STRIKER
EIKLMMN	MILKMEN	EIKMRRU	MURKIER	EIKRSSS	KISSERS
EIKLMNN	LINKMEN	EIKMRSS	KIRMESS	EIKRSST	STRIKES
EIKLMNR	KREMLIN	EIKMRST	MIRKEST	EIKRSSV	SKIVERS
EIKLMRS	MILKERS	EIKMRSU	MUSKIER	EIKRSTT	SKITTER
EIKLNNS	ENLINKS	EIKMSST	KISMETS	EIKRSTU	TURKIES
EIKLNNU	NUNLIKE	EIKMSSU	MUSKIES		TUSKIER
EIKLNOS	SONLIKE	EIKMSSY	MISKEYS	EIKSSTT	KITSETS
EIKLNPR	PLINKER	EIKMSTU	KUMITES	EIKSSTW	WESKITS
EIKLNRS	LINKERS		MISTEUK		WISKETS
	RELINKS	EIKNNOR	EINKORN	EIKSSTY	SKYIEST
	SLINKER	EIKNNOS	KINONES	EIKSTUY	YUKIEST
EIKLNRT	TINKLER	EIKNNPS	PINKENS	EILLLOS	LOLLIES
EIKLNRU	URNLIKE	EIKNNRS	SKINNER	EILLMNU	MULLEIN
EIKLNRW	WINKLER	EIKNOOR	NOOKIER	EILLMOS	MOLLIES
	WRINKLE		ROOINEK	EILLMOT	MELILOT
EIKLNSS	INKLESS	EIKNOOS	NOOKIES	EILLMOU	MOUILLE
	KINLESS	EIKNOPS	PINKOES	EILLMRS	MILLERS
	SILKENS	EIKNORV	INVOKER	EILLMST	MILLETS
EIKLNST	LENTISK	EIKNORW	WONKIER		MISTELL
	TINKLES	EIKNOSS	KENOSIS	EILLMSU	ILLUMES
EIKLNSU	SUNLIKE	EIKNOSV	INVOKES	EILLMTU	MULLITE
	UNLIKES	EIKNPRR	PRINKER	EILLNNP	PENNILL
EIKLNSV	KELVINS	EIKNPRS	PERKINS	EILLNOS	LIONELS
EIKLNSW	WELKINS		PINKERS		NIELLOS
	WINKLES	EIKNPRU	PUNKIER	EILLNSS	ILLNESS
EIKLNSY	SKYLINE	EIKNPST	PINKEST	EILLNST	LENTILS

	LINTELS
	TELLINS
EILLNUV	LEVULIN
EILLOPS	POLLIES
EILLORU	ROUILLE
EILLORW	LOWLIER
EILLORZ	ZORILLE
EILLOST	OILLETS
	TOLLIES
EILLOSV	VILLOSE
EILLOSW	WOLLIES
EILLPPR	PREPILL
EILLPRS	SPILLER
EILLPSS	LIPLESS
EILLPSU	PILULES
EILLQTU	QUILLET
EILLRRT	TRILLER
EILLRSS	SILLERS
EILLRST	RILLETS
	STILLER
	TILLERS
	TRELLIS
EILLRSW	SWILLER
	WILLERS
EILLRTT	LITTLER
EILLSST	LISTELS
EILLSSU	SULLIES
EILLSTT	LITTLES
EILLSTU	TUILLES
EILLSTW	WILLEST
	WILLETS
EILLSWY	WILLEYS
EILMMNO	MOLIMEN
EILMMRS	LIMMERS
	SLIMMER
EILMMRU	LUMMIER
EILMNOO	OINOMEL
EILMNOS	LOMEINS
	MOLINES
EILMNOT	MOLINET
EILMNPS	PLENISM
EILMNRS	LIMNERS
	MERLINS
EILMNSS	SIMNELS
EILMNSU	EMULSIN
	LUMINES
	UNLIMES
EILMNSY	MYELINS
EILMOOS	MOOLIES
EILMOOV	MOOLVIE
EILMOPR	IMPLORE
EILMORR	LORIMER
EILMORS	MOILERS
EILMORT	MOTLIER
EILMOSS	LIMOSES
	LISSOME
	SMOILES
EILMOST	MOTILES
EILMPPS	PIMPLES
EILMPPU	PLUMPIE
EILMPRS	LIMPERS
	PRELIMS
	RIMPLES
	SIMPLER
EILMPRU	LUMPIER
	PLUMIER
EILMPRY	PRIMELY
EILMPSS	SIMPLES
EILMPST	LIMPEST
	LIMPETS
EILMPSU	IMPULSE
EILMPSW	WIMPLES
EILMPSX	SIMPLEX
EILMPSY	LIMPSEY
EILMPTY	EMPTILY
EILMRRU	MURLIER
EILMRRY	MERRILY
EILMRSS	RIMLESS
	SMILERS
EILMRST	MILTERS
EILMRSU	MISRULE
EILMRSV	VERMILS
EILMRSY	MISERLY
	MISRELY
EILMRTY	LYMITER
EILMRVY	VERMILY
EILMSSS	MISSELS
EILMSST	MISTLES
	SMILETS
EILMSSU	MUESLIS
EILMSSY	MESSILY
	MILSEYS
	SMILEYS
EILMSTT	SMITTLE
EILMSTZ	MILTZES
EILMSZZ	MIZZLES
EILMUUV	ELUVIUM
EILNNOR	ONLINER
EILNNPU	PINNULE
EILNNRY	INNERLY
EILNNSS	INNLESS
EILNNST	LINNETS
EILNNSU	UNLINES
EILNNSW	WINNLES
EILNNSY	LINNEYS
EILNOOP	POLONIE
EILNOOR	LOONIER
EILNOOS	LOONIES
EILNOOV	VIOLONE
EILNOPP	PLENIPO
EILNOPR	PLERION
	PROLINE
EILNOPS	EPSILON
	PINOLES
EILNOPT	POINTEL
	PONTILE
	POTLINE
	TOPLINE
EILNORR	LORINER
EILNORS	NEROLIS
EILNORT	RETINOL
EILNOSS	ESLOINS
	INSOLES
	LESIONS
	LIONESS
EILNOST	ENTOILS
	LIONETS
	ONLIEST
EILNOSU	ELUSION
EILNOTU	ELUTION
	OUTLINE
EILNOTV	VIOLENT
EILNOTW	TOWLINE
EILNOVV	INVOLVE
EILNPPS	LIPPENS
	NIPPLES
EILNPRS	PILSNER
EILNPRU	PURLINE
EILNPSS	PENSILS
	SPINELS
	SPLINES
EILNPST	LEPTINS
	PINTLES
	PLENIST
EILNPSU	LINEUPS
	LUPINES
	SPINULE
	UNPILES
EILNPTY	INEPTLY
EILNPUV	VULPINE
EILNRST	LINTERS
	SLINTER
	SNIRTLE
EILNRSV	SILVERN
EILNRTY	INERTLY
EILNRVY	NERVILY
EILNSSS	SINLESS
EILNSST	ENLISTS
	LISTENS
	SILENTS
	TINSELS
EILNSSU	INSULSE
	SILENUS
EILNSSV	SNIVELS
EILNSSW	WINLESS
EILNSSY	LINSEYS
	LYSINES
EILNSTU	LUNIEST
	LUTEINS
	UNTILES
	UTENSIL
EILNSTV	VENTILS
EILNSTW	WESTLIN
	WINTLES
EILNSUV	UNLIVES
	UNVEILS
EILNSUX	LINUXES
EILNSUY	LUNYIES
EILNSVY	SYLVINE
EILNVXY	VIXENLY
EILOOPR	LOOPIER
EILOORS	ORIOLES
EILOORT	TROOLIE
EILOORW	WOOLIER
EILOOSS	LOOSIES
EILOOST	OOLITES
	OSTIOLE
	STOOLIE
EILOOSW	WOOLIES
EILOOTZ	ZOOLITE
EILOPPR	LOPPIER
EILOPPS	LOPPIES

EILOPPZ	ZEPPOLI
EILOPRS	SLOPIER
	SPOILER
EILOPRT	POITREL
	POLITER
EILOPST	PIOLETS
	PISTOLE
EILOPSU	PILEOUS
EILOPSV	PLOSIVE
EILOPTT	PLOTTIE
EILOPTX	EXPLOIT
EILORRS	LORRIES
EILORRU	LOURIER
EILORSS	LORISES
	LOSSIER
	RISSOLE
EILORST	ESTRIOL
	LOITERS
	TOILERS
EILORSU	LOURIES
	LOUSIER
	SOILURE
EILORSV	OLIVERS
	VIOLERS
EILORSW	LOWRIES
EILORTT	TORTILE
	TRIOLET
EILORTU	OUTLIER
EILORTV	OVERLIT
EILOSSV	SOLIVES
EILOSTT	LITOTES
	TOILETS
EILOSTU	OUTLIES
EILOSTV	OLIVETS
	VIOLETS
EILOSTW	OWLIEST
EILOSTZ	ZLOTIES
EILOTUV	OUTLIVE
EILOTUW	OUTWILE
EILPPPY	PEPPILY
EILPPRR	RIPPLER
EILPPRS	LIPPERS
	RIPPLES
	SLIPPER
EILPPRT	RIPPLET
	TIPPLER
	TRIPPLE
EILPPRU	PULPIER
EILPPSS	PIPLESS
	SIPPLES
EILPPST	STIPPLE
	TIPPLES
EILPPSU	PILEUPS
	UPPILES
EILPPSW	SWIPPLE
EILPRSS	LISPERS
EILPRST	RESPLIT
	SPIRTLE
	TRIPLES
EILPRTT	TRIPLET
EILPRTX	TRIPLEX
EILPRUU	PURLIEU
EILPSSS	PLISSES
EILPSST	STIPELS
	TIPLESS
EILPSSW	SWIPLES
EILPSSZ	ZIPLESS
EILPSTT	SPITTLE
EILPSTU	PULIEST
	PUTELIS
	STIPULE
EILPSUY	SPULYIE
EILPSUZ	SPULZIE
EILPSZZ	PIZZLES
EILPTTY	PETTILY
EILQRTU	QUILTER
EILQRUU	LIQUEUR
EILQTUY	QUIETLY
EILRRSU	LURRIES
	SURLIER
EILRRTW	TWIRLER
EILRSST	LISTERS
	RELISTS
EILRSSV	SILVERS
	SLIVERS
EILRSSW	SWILERS
EILRSTT	LITTERS
	SLITTER
	STILTER
	TESTRIL
	TILTERS
	TITLERS
EILRSTU	LUSTIER
	RULIEST
	RUTILES
EILRSTY	STYLIER
EILRSUV	SURVEIL
EILRSUW	WURLIES
EILRSVY	LIVYERS
	SILVERY
EILRSZZ	SIZZLER
EILRTTY	LITTERY
	TRITELY
EILRTUV	RIVULET
EILSSTT	STILETS
EILSSTW	WITLESS
EILSSTY	STYLISE
EILSSVW	SWIVELS
EILSSZZ	SIZZLES
EILSTTT	TITTLES
EILSTTU	LUTITES
	TITULES
EILSTTV	VITTLES
EILSTTY	STYLITE
	TESTILY
EILSTVY	SYLVITE
EILSTYZ	STYLIZE
	ZESTILY
EILSUVV	LUVVIES
EILSWZZ	SWIZZLE
EILSZZZ	ZIZZLES
EILTWZZ	TWIZZLE
EIMMMOS	MOMMIES
EIMMMST	MIMMEST
EIMMMSU	MUMMIES
EIMMNRS	NIMMERS
EIMMNSU	IMMUNES
EIMMOPS	POMMIES
EIMMORS	MEMOIRS
EIMMOST	TOMMIES
EIMMOSV	MISMOVE
EIMMPRR	PRIMMER
EIMMPRU	PREMIUM
EIMMRRS	RIMMERS
EIMMRRT	TRIMMER
EIMMRRU	RUMMIER
EIMMRSS	MERISMS
	SIMMERS
EIMMRST	MISTERM
EIMMRSU	IMMURES
	MUMSIER
	RUMMIES
EIMMRSW	SWIMMER
EIMMRSZ	ZIMMERS
EIMMRUY	YUMMIER
EIMMSST	SEMMITS
	TSIMMES
EIMMSTU	TUMMIES
EIMMSTZ	TZIMMES
EIMMSUY	YUMMIES
EIMNNOR	IRONMEN
EIMNNOT	MENTION
EIMNOOR	IONOMER
	MOONIER
EIMNOOS	ISONOME
	MOONIES
	NOISOME
EIMNOOT	EMOTION
EIMNOOX	EXOMION
EIMNOPR	PROMINE
EIMNOPS	IMPONES
	PEONISM
EIMNOPT	EMPTION
	PIMENTO
EIMNORS	MERINOS
	MERSION
EIMNOSS	EONISMS
EIMNOST	MESTINO
	MOISTEN
	MONTIES
	SENTIMO
EIMNOSW	WINSOME
EIMNOTY	OMNEITY
	OMNIETY
EIMNPSS	MISPENS
EIMNPST	EMPTINS
	PIMENTS
EIMNPTU	PINETUM
EIMNQSU	MESQUIN
EIMNRRU	MURRINE
EIMNRST	ENTRISM
	MINSTER
	MINTERS
	REMINTS
EIMNRSU	MUREINS
	MURINES
	NEURISM
EIMNRSV	VERMINS
EIMNRTU	MINUTER
	MUNTRIE
	UNMITER
	UNMITRE

EIMNRVY	VERMINY	EIMPRSS	IMPRESS	EINNOTT	NONETTI
EIMNSSS	SENSISM		PREMISS		TONTINE
EIMNSST	MISSENT		SIMPERS	EINNOVW	INWOVEN
EIMNSSU	MINUSES		SPIREMS	EINNPRS	PINNERS
EIMNSTT	MITTENS	EIMPRST	IMPREST		SPINNER
	SMITTEN		PERMITS	EINNPRT	ENPRINT
EIMNSTU	MINUETS	EIMPRSU	RUMPIES	EINNPRU	PUNNIER
	MINUTES		SPUMIER	EINNPST	PINNETS
	MISTUNE		UMPIRES		SPINNET
	MUNITES	EIMPRTU	IMPUTER		TENPINS
	MUTINES		TUMPIER	EINNPSY	SPINNEY
EIMNSTW	MISWENT	EIMPRTX	PREMIXT	EINNRRU	RUNNIER
EIMNSUX	UNMIXES	EIMPSST	MISSTEP	EINNRSS	SINNERS
EIMNSZZ	MIZZENS	EIMPSSU	SEPIUMS	EINNRST	INTERNS
EIMNUZZ	MUEZZIN	EIMPSTU	IMPETUS		TINNERS
EIMOORR	MOORIER		IMPUTES	EINNRSU	SUNNIER
	ROOMIER		UPTIMES		UNREINS
EIMOORS	ROOMIES	EIMPSTY	MISTYPE		UNRISEN
EIMOPPR	MOPPIER	EIMPSUY	YUMPIES	EINNRSW	WINNERS
	POMPIER	EIMQSTU	MESQUIT	EINNRTV	VINTNER
EIMOPRR	PRIMERO	EIMQTUZ	MEZQUIT	EINNRUV	UNRIVEN
EIMOPRS	IMPOSER	EIMRRST	RETRIMS	EINNSST	SENNITS
	PROMISE		TRIMERS		SINNETS
	SEMIPRO	EIMRRSU	MURRIES	EINNSSU	SUNNIES
EIMOPRV	IMPROVE	EIMRSST	MISTERS	EINNSSY	SINSYNE
EIMOPRW	IMPOWER		SMITERS	EINNSTT	INTENTS
EIMOPSS	IMPOSES	EIMRSSU	MISUSER		TENNIST
	MOPSIES		MUSSIER	EINNSTU	TUNNIES
EIMOPST	MOPIEST		SURMISE	EINNSTV	INVENTS
	OPTIMES	EIMRSSV	VERISMS	EINNSUW	UNSINEW
	STOMPIE	EIMRSTT	METRIST	EINNSWY	SWINNEY
EIMOPSY	MYOPIES	EIMRSTU	MUSTIER	EINNTUW	UNTWINE
EIMORRW	WORMIER	EIMRSTY	MISTERY	EINOOPZ	EPIZOON
EIMORSS	ISOMERS		SMYTRIE	EINOORS	EROSION
	MOISERS	EIMRTTU	TERTIUM	EINOOST	ISOTONE
	MOSSIER	EIMRTUV	VITREUM		TOONIES
EIMORST	EROTISM	EIMRTUX	MIXTURE	EINOOSZ	OZONISE
	MOISTER	EIMRUZZ	MUZZIER	EINOOTW	TWOONIE
	MORTISE	EIMSSST	MISSETS	EINOOTZ	ZOONITE
	TRISOME	EIMSSSU	MISUSES	EINOOZZ	OZONIZE
EIMORSU	MOUSIER	EIMSSSX	SEXISMS	EINOPPR	POPERIN
EIMORSV	VERISMO	EIMSSTY	STYMIES		PROPINE
EIMORTT	MOTTIER	EIMSTYZ	ZYMITES	EINOPPS	PEPINOS
	OMITTER	EIMUUVX	EXUVIUM	EINOPRR	PORNIER
EIMORTV	VOMITER	EINNNOS	NONNIES	EINOPRS	ORPINES
EIMORVX	OVERMIX	EINNNRS	RENNINS		PIONERS
EIMOSSS	MOSSIES	EINNOOS	IONONES		PROINES
EIMOSST	MITOSES	EINNOPS	PENSION	EINOPRT	POINTER
	SOMITES		PINONES		PROTEIN
EIMOSSU	MOUSIES		SPINONE		PTERION
EIMOSTT	MOTIEST	EINNOPT	PONTINE		REPOINT
	MOTTIES	EINNOQU	QUINONE		TROPINE
	TITMOSE	EINNORS	RONNIES	EINOPRV	PROVINE
EIMOSTU	TIMEOUS	EINNORT	INTONER	EINOPSS	SPINOSE
EIMOSTV	MOTIVES		NOINTER	EINOPST	PINTOES
EIMOSTX	EXOTISM		TERNION		POINTES
EIMOSTZ	MESTIZO	EINNORU	NOUNIER		PONTIES
EIMOSYZ	ISOZYME		REUNION	EINOPSW	POWNIES
EIMOSZZ	MOZZIES	EINNORV	ENVIRON		WINESOP
EIMOTTU	TIMEOUT	EINNOSS	SONNIES	EINOPSY	PIONEYS
EIMPRRS	PRIMERS	EINNOST	INTONES	EINOPTT	PENTITO
EIMPRRT	PRETRIM		TENSION	EINOPTU	POUTINE
EIMPRRU	IMPURER	EINNOSV	VENISON	EINOQUX	EQUINOX
	PRIMEUR	EINNOSY	YONNIES	EINORRS	IRONERS

Seven-letter anagrams

	ROSINER	**EINQRUU**	UNIQUER	**EIOOPSW**	WOOPIES
EINORSS	ORNISES	**EINQRUY**	ENQUIRY	**EIOORRT**	ROOTIER
	SENIORS	**EINQSSU**	SEQUINS	**EIOORST**	OORIEST
	SONERIS	**EINQSTU**	INQUEST		ROOTIES
	SONSIER		QUINTES		SOOTIER
EINORST	NORITES	**EINQSUU**	UNIQUES		TOORIES
	OESTRIN	**EINQSUZ**	QUINZES		TOORIES
	ORIENTS	**EINQTTU**	QUINTET	**EIOORTZ**	ZOOTIER
	STONIER	**EINQTUU**	UNQUIET	**EIOORWZ**	WOOZIER
	TERSION	**EINRRSS**	RINSERS	**EIOOSST**	OOSIEST
	TRIONES	**EINRRSU**	INSURER	**EIOOSTT**	TOOTSIE
EINORSU	URINOSE		RUINERS	**EIOOSTZ**	OOZIEST
EINORSV	ENVIROS	**EINRRTU**	RUNTIER		ZOOIEST
	RENVOIS	**EINRSST**	ESTRINS	**EIOPPPR**	POPPIER
	VERSION		INSERTS	**EIOPPPS**	POPPIES
EINORSW	SNOWIER		SINTERS	**EIOPPRS**	SOPPIER
EINORTT	TRITONE	**EINRSSU**	INSURES	**EIOPPSS**	POPSIES
EINORTU	ROUTINE		SUNRISE	**EIOPPST**	POTPIES
EINORTW	NOWTIER	**EINRSSV**	VERSINS	**EIOPQRU**	PIROQUE
	TOWNIER	**EINRSTT**	ENTRIST	**EIOPRRS**	PROSIER
EINORTZ	TRIZONE		RETINTS	**EIOPRRT**	PIERROT
EINOSSS	ESSOINS		STINTER		PORTIER
	OSSEINS		TINTERS		PRERIOT
	SESSION	**EINRSTU**	NUTSIER	**EIOPRRU**	ROUPIER
EINOSST	NOSIEST		TRIUNES	**EIOPRSS**	POISERS
	SONTIES		UNITERS		PROSSIE
	STONIES	**EINRSTV**	INVERTS	**EIOPRST**	PERIOST
EINOSSU	SINUOSE		STRIVEN		PORIEST
EINOSSZ	SOZINES	**EINRSTW**	TWINERS		PROSTIE
EINOSTT	SNOTTIE		WINTERS		REPOSIT
	TONIEST	**EINRSTY**	SINTERY		RIPOSTE
	TONITES	**EINRSUW**	UNWIRES		ROPIEST
EINOSTW	TOWNIES		UNWISER	**EIOPRSU**	POURIES
	TWONIES	**EINRSVW**	WIVERNS		SOUPIER
EINOSTX	TOXINES	**EINRSWY**	SWINERY	**EIOPRSX**	PROXIES
EINOSUV	ENVIOUS	**EINRTTU**	NUTTIER	**EIOPRTT**	POTTIER
	NIVEOUS	**EINRTTW**	TWINTER	**EIOPRTU**	POUTIER
	VEINOUS		WRITTEN	**EIOPRTV**	OVERTIP
EINOTTT	TOTIENT	**EINRTUV**	UNRIVET		PIVOTER
EINPPRS	NIPPERS		VENTURI	**EIOPSSS**	POSSIES
	SNIPPER	**EINRTUW**	UNWRITE	**EIOPSST**	POSIEST
EINPPSS	PEPSINS	**EINRTWY**	WINTERY		POSTIES
EINPPST	SNIPPET	**EINSSST**	SENSIST		POTSIES
EINPPSW	WIPPENS	**EINSSSU**	SINUSES		SEPIOST
EINPRRT	PRINTER	**EINSSSY**	SYNESIS		SOPITES
	REPRINT	**EINSSTU**	INTUSES	**EIOPSSU**	POUSSIE
EINPRRU	UNRIPER	**EINSSTV**	INVESTS	**EIOPSTT**	POTTIES
EINPRSS	SNIPERS	**EINSSTW**	WISENTS		SPOTTIE
EINPRST	NIPTERS		WITNESS		TIPTOES
	PTERINS	**EINSSTY**	TINSEYS	**EIOPSTU**	PITEOUS
EINPRSU	PRUINES	**EINSSUW**	SUNWISE	**EIOPSTX**	EXPOSIT
	PURINES	**EINSSWY**	WINSEYS		POXIEST
	UPRISEN	**EINSTTU**	TUNIEST	**EIOPSTY**	ISOTYPE
EINPRTU	REPUNIT	**EINSTTW**	ENTWIST	**EIOPSZZ**	POZZIES
EINPSST	INSTEPS		TWINSET	**EIOPTUW**	WIPEOUT
	SPINETS	**EINSTTY**	TENSITY	**EIOQRTU**	QUOITER
EINPSSU	PUISNES	**EINSTWY**	WITNEYS	**EIOQTUX**	QUIXOTE
	SUPINES	**EINSUVW**	UNWIVES	**EIORRRS**	SORRIER
EINPSTT	SPITTEN	**EINSWZZ**	WIZZENS	**EIORRRT**	RORTIER
EINPSTU	PUNIEST	**EINTTTW**	TWITTEN		TERROIR
	PUNTIES	**EINTTUY**	TENUITY	**EIORRRW**	WORRIER
EINPSTW	INSWEPT	**EIOOPRR**	ROOPIER	**EIORRSS**	ORRISES
EINPTTY	TINTYPE	**EIOOPRV**	POOVIER		ROSIERS
EINQRSU	REQUINS	**EIOOPST**	ISOTOPE	**EIORRST**	RIOTERS
					ROISTER

	RORIEST	**EIPRSSS**	PISSERS	**EIRSSUW**	WUSSIER
EIORRSV	REVISOR		PRISSES	**EIRSTTT**	STRETTI
EIORRSW	WORRIES	**EIPRSST**	ESPRITS		TITTERS
EIORRUV	OUVRIER		PERSIST		TRITEST
EIORRVV	REVIVOR		PRIESTS	**EIRSTTU**	TERTIUS
EIORSSS	SEISORS		SITREPS	**EIRSTTV**	TRIVETS
EIORSST	ROSIEST		SPRIEST	**EIRSTTW**	RETWIST
	SIROSET		SPRITES		TWISTER
	SORITES		STIRPES		WITTERS
	SORTIES		STRIPES	**EIRSTUV**	REVUIST
	STORIES		TRIPSES		STUIVER
	TOSSIER	**EIPRSSU**	PUSSIER		VIRTUES
	TRIOSES		SUSPIRE	**EIRSUVV**	SURVIVE
EIORSSU	SERIOUS		UPRISES	**EIRSUVW**	SURVIEW
EIORSSV	VIROSES	**EIPRSSW**	SWIPERS	**EIRTTTW**	TWITTER
EIORSSX	XEROSIS	**EIPRSTT**	PITTERS	**EIRTTUV**	VUTTIER
EIORSSZ	SEIZORS		SPITTER	**EISSSSW**	SWISSES
EIORSTT	STOITER		TIPSTER	**EISSSTU**	SITUSES
EIORSTU	OURIEST	**EIPRSTU**	PERITUS		TISSUES
	STOURIE		PUIREST	**EISSSTW**	SWITSES
	TOURIES	**EIPRSTV**	PRIVETS	**EISSSTX**	SEXISTS
	TOUSIER	**EIPRSTX**	EXTIRPS	**EISSSUW**	WUSSIES
EIORSTV	TORSIVE	**EIPRSTY**	PYRITES	**EISSTTY**	TYSTIES
EIORSTW	OWRIEST		STRIPEY	**EISSTUV**	TUSSIVE
	TOWSIER	**EIPRSUU**	EURIPUS	**EISSTUY**	TISSUEY
EIORTTT	TOTTIER	**EIPRTTU**	PUTTIER	**EISSTVW**	SWIVETS
EIORTTU	TOUTIER	**EIPRUVW**	PURVIEW	**EISSWZZ**	SWIZZES
EIORTTV	TORTIVE	**EIPSSSU**	PUSSIES	**EISTTTU**	TUTTIES
	VIRETOT	**EIPSSTZ**	SPITZES	**EISTTUW**	WETSUIT
EIORTUV	VOITURE	**EIPSSUZ**	UPSIZES	**EJJMNUU**	JEJUNUM
EIORTUZ	TOUZIER	**EIPSTTU**	PUTTIES	**EJKMNNU**	JUNKMEN
EIORTWZ	TOWZIER	**EIPSTTY**	TYPIEST	**EJKNRSU**	JUNKERS
EIOSSTU	SOUTIES	**EIQRSSU**	RISQUES	**EJKNSTU**	JUNKETS
EIOSSTV	SOVIETS		SQUIERS	**EJKOORY**	JOOKERY
	STOVIES		SQUIRES	**EJKORUY**	JOUKERY
EIOSTTT	STOTTIE	**EIQRSTU**	QUERIST	**EJLLORY**	JOLLYER
	TOTTIES		REQUITS	**EJLLOSY**	JOLLEYS
EIOSTTU	TOUSTIE	**EIQRSUV**	QUIVERS	**EJLORST**	JOLTERS
EIOSTTW	TOWIEST	**EIQRTTU**	QUITTER		JOSTLER
EIOSTUV	OUTVIES	**EIQRUVY**	QUIVERY	**EJLORSW**	JOWLERS
EIOSTUZ	OUTSIZE	**EIQRUZZ**	QUIZZER	**EJLOSST**	JOSTLES
EIOSTVV	VOTIVES	**EIQSTUU**	QUIETUS	**EJLOSSY**	JOYLESS
EIPPPSU	PUPPIES	**EIQSUZZ**	QUIZZES	**EJLSSTU**	JUSTLES
EIPPQRU	QUIPPER	**EIRRRST**	STIRRER	**EJMNRUY**	JURYMEN
EIPPRRS	RIPPERS	**EIRRSST**	STIRRES	**EJMOSST**	JETSOMS
EIPPRRT	TRIPPER	**EIRRSTT**	RITTERS	**EJMPRSU**	JUMPERS
EIPPRSS	SIPPERS		TERRITS	**EJNORRU**	REJOURN
EIPPRST	TIPPERS	**EIRRSTU**	RUSTIER	**EJNORUY**	JOURNEY
EIPPRSU	PURPIES	**EIRRSTV**	STRIVER	**EJNOSST**	JETSONS
EIPPRSY	YIPPERS	**EIRRSTW**	WRITERS	**EJNOSTT**	JETTONS
EIPPRSZ	ZIPPERS	**EIRRSZZ**	RIZZERS	**EJOORVY**	OVERJOY
EIPPRTT	TRIPPET	**EIRRTTU**	RUTTIER	**EJOOSSY**	SOOJEYS
EIPPSST	SIPPETS	**EIRSSST**	RESISTS	**EJOPPRT**	PROPJET
EIPPSTT	TIPPETS		SISTERS	**EJOPRST**	PROJETS
EIPPSUY	YUPPIES	**EIRSSSU**	ISSUERS	**EJOPRTT**	JETPORT
EIPQSTU	PIQUETS		RISUSES	**EJORSSS**	JOSSERS
EIPRRSS	PRISERS	**EIRSSTT**	SITTERS	**EJORSTT**	JOTTERS
EIPRRST	STRIPER	**EIRSSTU**	SUITERS	**EJORSTU**	JOUSTER
EIPRRSU	PURSIER	**EIRSSTV**	STIVERS	**EJOSTTU**	OUTJEST
	UPRISER		STRIVES		OUTJETS
EIPRRSZ	PRIZERS		TREVISS	**EJPRRUY**	PERJURY
EIPRRTU	PURTIER		VERISTS	**EJRSSTU**	JUSTERS
EIPRRTY	TRIPERY	**EIRSSUU**	USURIES	**EJSSTTU**	JUSTEST
EIPRRUV	UPRIVER	**EIRSSUV**	VIRUSES	**EKKLOOY**	OLYKOEK

Seven-letter anagrams

EKKLRSU	SKULKER	EKOPRRS	PORKERS	ELLORTY	TROLLEY
EKKOPSU	PUKEKOS		PROKERS	ELLORVV	LOVERLY
EKLLMSU	SKELLUM	EKOPRRW	PREWORK	ELLOSST	TOLSELS
EKLLNOR	KNOLLER	EKOPRUY	KOUPREY	ELLOSTU	OUTSELL
EKLLRRU	KRULLER	EKOPTTU	OUTKEPT		SELLOUT
EKLMMSU	KUMMELS	EKORRST	STROKER	ELLOSTX	EXTOLLS
EKLMSSU	MUSKLES	EKORRSW	REWORKS	ELLOSVY	VOLLEYS
	SKELUMS		WORKERS	ELLOSWY	YELLOWS
EKLNOPR	PLONKER	EKORRSY	YORKERS	ELLOTTU	OUTTELL
EKLNORS	SNORKEL	EKORSST	STOKERS	ELLOTUW	OUTWELL
EKLNOSS	KELSONS		STROKES	ELLOTUY	OUTYELL
	SLOKENS	EKORUYY	EURYOKY	ELLOVWY	VOWELLY
EKLNOSU	LEUKONS	EKPPSUU	SEPPUKU	ELLOWYY	YELLOWY
EKLNPRU	PLUNKER	EKPRSSY	KRYPSES	ELLPRSU	PULLERS
EKLNPSU	SPELUNK	EKRRSSY	SKRYERS	ELLPSTU	PULLETS
EKLNRSU	LUNKERS	EKRSSTU	TUSKERS	ELLPSUW	UPSWELL
	RUNKLES	EKRSTUY	TURKEYS		UPWELLS
EKLNSST	SKLENTS	EKRSUVY	KURVEYS	ELLPSUY	PULLEYS
EKLOORS	LOOKERS	ELLLORR	LORRELL	ELMMOPS	POMMELS
	RELOOKS	ELLLORS	LOLLERS	ELMMOPU	PUMMELO
EKLOPST	KLEPTOS	ELLLOSZ	LOZELLS	ELMMORT	TROMMEL
EKLOSTV	STOKVEL	ELLLRSU	LULLERS	ELMMPRU	PLUMMER
EKLRRSU	LURKERS	ELLMNOO	MOELLON	ELMMPSU	PUMMELS
EKLRSSU	SULKERS	ELLMNOP	POLLMEN	ELMMPTU	PLUMMET
EKLSTTU	SKUTTLE	ELLMNOT	TOLLMEN	ELMMRSU	SLUMMER
EKLSTUZ	KLUTZES	ELLMNSU	MULLENS	ELMMRTU	TUMMLER
EKMMRSU	SKUMMER	ELLMOOR	MORELLO	ELMMSTU	STUMMEL
EKMNORW	WORKMEN	ELLMORR	MORRELL	ELMNOOT	MOONLET
EKMNORY	MONKERY	ELLMOSW	MELLOWS		TOOLMEN
EKMNOSU	MUSKONE	ELLMOWY	MELLOWY	ELMNOOW	WOOLMEN
EKMNOSY	MONKEYS	ELLMPSU	PELLUMS	ELMNOPW	PLOWMEN
EKMNPTU	UNKEMPT	ELLMPUU	PLUMULE	ELMNORS	MERLONS
EKMOOPS	MOPOKES	ELLMRSU	MULLERS	ELMNOST	LOMENTS
EKMORSS	SMOKERS	ELLMSTU	MULLETS		MELTONS
EKMRSTU	MURKEST	ELLMSUV	VELLUMS	ELMNOSY	MYELONS
EKMSSTU	MUSKETS	ELLMSUY	MULLEYS	ELMNOTU	MOULTEN
EKMSSUY	KUMYSES	ELLNNOT	TONNELL	ELMNOTY	YMOLTEN
EKNNOST	NEKTONS	ELLNOOW	WOOLLEN	ELMNPPU	PLUMPEN
EKNOORS	SNOOKER	ELLNOPS	POLLENS	ELMNPSU	LUMPENS
EKNOPSU	UNSPOKE	ELLNOPT	POLLENT		PLENUMS
EKNORST	REKNOTS	ELLNORS	ENROLLS	ELMNPUU	UNPLUME
	STONKER	ELLNOST	STOLLEN	ELMOOPP	POMPELO
	STROKEN	ELLNOSU	NOUSELL	ELMOOPS	POMELOS
	TONKERS		VELLONS	ELMOORT	TREMOLO
EKNORSW	KNOWERS	ELLNOSW	SWOLLEN	ELMOOSS	OSMOLES
EKNORSY	YONKERS	ELLNOVY	NOVELLY	ELMOOSY	MOOLEYS
EKNORTT	KNOTTER	ELLNOXY	XYLENOL	ELMOPRT	PREMOLT
EKNORTW	NETWORK	ELLNPSU	UNSPELL	ELMOPRV	POLYMER
EKNORUY	YOUNKER	ELLNSSU	SULLENS	ELMOPSU	PLUMOSE
EKNOSTY	STENOKY		UNSELLS		PUMELOS
EKNOSUY	UNYOKES	ELLNSUU	LUNULES	ELMOPSY	EMPLOYS
EKNPRSU	PUNKERS	ELLOOSW	WOOSELL	ELMORSS	MORSELS
EKNPSTU	PUNKEST	ELLOOSY	LOOSELY	ELMORST	MERLOTS
EKNPSUY	PUNKEYS	ELLOOTU	TOLUOLE		MOLTERS
EKNRTUY	TURNKEY	ELLOPRR	PROLLER	ELMORSU	EMULSOR
EKNSSTU	SUNKETS	ELLOPRS	POLLERS	ELMORTT	MOTTLER
EKOOPRT	PERTOOK		REPOLLS	ELMORTU	MOULTER
EKOOPRV	PROVOKE	ELLOPTU	POLLUTE	ELMOSST	MOLESTS
EKOORRS	KOREROS	ELLORRS	REROLLS	ELMOSSU	MOUSLES
EKOORRY	ROOKERY		ROLLERS	ELMOSSY	SMOYLES
EKOORST	STOOKER	ELLORRT	TROLLER	ELMOSTT	MOTTLES
	STROOKE	ELLORSS	SOLLERS	ELMOSTY	MOTLEYS
EKOORTW	KOTOWER		SORELLS	ELMOSUU	EMULOUS
EKOPPSU	UPSPOKE	ELLORST	TOLLERS	ELMOSUV	VOLUMES

ELMOSXY	OXYMELS	ELNRUZZ	NUZZLER	ELOPSSU	SOUPLES
ELMOSZZ	MOZZLES	ELNSSSU	SUNLESS	ELOPSTT	POTTLES
ELMPPRU	PLUMPER	ELNSSSY	SELSYNS	ELOPSTU	TUPELOS
ELMPPSU	PEPLUMS		SLYNESS	ELOPSTY	PEYOTLS
ELMPRSU	LUMPERS	ELNSTTU	NUTLETS	ELOPSTZ	PLOTZES
	RUMPLES	ELNSUZZ	NUZZLES	ELOPTUY	OUTYELP
ELMPRUY	PLUMERY		SNUZZLE	ELORRSS	SORRELS
ELMRSTY	MYRTLES	ELOOPPS	POEPOLS	ELORRSW	WORRELS
ELMRTUU	MULTURE	ELOOPRS	LOOPERS	ELORSSS	LESSORS
ELMRTUY	ELYTRUM		POOLERS	ELORSST	OSTLERS
ELMRUZZ	MUZZLER		RESPOOL		STEROLS
ELMSSSU	MUSSELS		SPOOLER		TORSELS
	SUMLESS	ELOOPSS	POSOLES	ELORSSU	LOUSERS
ELMSTUU	MUTUELS	ELOOPST	POOTLES	ELORSSV	SOLVERS
	MUTULES	ELOOPSZ	POZOLES	ELORSTT	LOTTERS
ELMSTUW	UMWELTS	ELOORST	LOOTERS		SETTLOR
ELMSUZZ	MUZZLES		RETOOLS		SLOTTER
ELNNOPU	NONUPLE		ROOTLES		TOLTERS
ELNNORS	RONNELS		TOOLERS	ELORSTU	ELUTORS
ELNNOSS	NELSONS	ELOORSW	WOOLERS		OUTLERS
ELNNRSU	RUNNELS	ELOORTT	ROOTLET		TROULES
ELNNRTU	TRUNNEL		TOOTLER	ELORSTV	REVOLTS
ELNNSTU	TUNNELS	ELOOSST	LOOSEST	ELORSTW	TROWELS
ELNOOPT	PELOTON		LOTOSES		WORTLES
ELNOOSS	LOOSENS	ELOOSSW	WOOSELS	ELORSUV	LOUVERS
ELNOOSU	UNLOOSE	ELOOSTT	TOOLSET		LOUVRES
ELNOOSW	WOOLENS		TOOTLES		VELOURS
ELNOOSY	LOONEYS	ELOOSTU	OUTSOLE	ELORSUY	ELUSORY
ELNOOSZ	SNOOZLE	ELOOSWY	WOOLSEY	ELORSVW	WOLVERS
ELNOPRU	PLEURON	ELOOTUV	OUTLOVE	ELORSWY	YOWLERS
ELNOPRY	PRONELY	ELOPPPS	POPPLES	ELORTTY	LOTTERY
ELNOPST	LEPTONS	ELOPPRS	LOPPERS	ELORTVY	OVERTLY
ELNOPSY	POLEYNS		PROPELS	ELOSSTU	LOTUSES
ELNOPTU	OPULENT	ELOPPST	STOPPLE		SOLUTES
ELNORSS	NORSELS		TOPPLES		TOUSLES
ELNORST	LENTORS	ELOPPSU	POULPES	ELOSSTW	LOWSEST
ELNORSU	NOURSLE		UPSLOPE		SLOWEST
ELNORTY	ELYTRON	ELOPPSY	POLYPES	ELOSSTY	SYSTOLE
ELNOSSS	LESSONS	ELOPRRS	PROLERS		TOLSEYS
	SONLESS	ELOPRRU	PROULER		TOYLESS
ELNOSST	TELSONS	ELOPRRW	PROWLER		TYLOSES
ELNOSSU	ENSOULS	ELOPRRY	PYRROLE	ELOSSVW	VOWLESS
	NOUSLES	ELOPRSS	PLESSOR	ELOSSXY	XYLOSES
ELNOSSV	SLOVENS		SLOPERS	ELOSSZZ	SOZZLES
ELNOSSW	LOWNESS		SPLORES	ELOSTTU	OUTLETS
ELNOSTT	TONLETS	ELOPRST	PETROLS	ELOSTTY	TYLOTES
ELNOSTU	LENTOUS		REPLOTS	ELOSTUU	LUTEOUS
ELNOSTV	SOLVENT	ELOPRSU	LEPROUS	ELOSTUV	VOLUTES
ELNOSUV	UNLOVES		PELORUS	ELOSTUZ	TOUZLES
ELNOSUZ	ZONULES		PERLOUS	ELOSTYZ	TOLZEYS
ELNOSVY	LENVOYS		SPORULE	ELOSWYY	YOWLEYS
ELNOSZZ	NOZZLES	ELOPRSV	PLOVERS	ELOSWZZ	SWOZZLE
ELNOTTW	TOWNLET	ELOPRSW	PLOWERS	ELPPRRU	PURPLER
ELNOTUZ	ZONULET		REPLOWS	ELPPRSU	PULPERS
ELNOTVY	NOVELTY	ELOPRSX	PLEXORS		PURPLES
ELNPSST	SPLENTS	ELOPRSY	LEPROSY		REPULPS
ELNPSTU	PENULTS	ELOPRTT	PLOTTER		SUPPLER
ELNPSTV	PENTYLS	ELOPRTU	PLOUTER	ELPPSSU	SUPPLES
ELNRSSU	NURSLES		POULTER	ELPQSUU	PULQUES
	RUNLESS	ELOPRTW	PLOWTER	ELPRRSU	PURLERS
ELNRSTU	RUNLETS	ELOPRTY	PROTYLE		SLURPER
ELNRSTY	STERNLY	ELOPRVY	OVERPLY	ELPRSSU	PULSERS
ELNRSUU	UNRULES		PLOVERY	ELPRSTU	SPURTLE
ELNRSUZ	LUZERNS	ELOPSST	TOPLESS	ELPRSUV	PULVERS

Seven-letter anagrams

ELPRTUU	PULTURE
ELPRUZZ	PUZZLER
ELPSSSU	PLUSSES
	PUSSELS
ELPSSUU	LUPUSES
ELPSSUY	PUSLEYS
	PUSSLEY
	SPULYES
ELPSTUU	PLUTEUS
	PUSTULE
ELPSUZZ	PUZZELS
	PUZZLES
ELRRSTU	RUSTLER
ELRRTTU	TURTLER
ELRSSSU	RUSSELS
ELRSSTU	LUSTERS
	LUSTRES
	RESULTS
	RUSTLES
	SUTLERS
	ULSTERS
ELRSSTY	STYLERS
ELRSTTU	TURTLES
ELRSTTY	TETRYLS
ELRSTUY	SUTLERY
ELRSTWY	SWELTRY
ELRSUWY	WURLEYS
ELRSUWZ	WURZELS
ELRTTUY	UTTERLY
ELRTUUV	VULTURE
ELSSSTU	TUSSLES
ELSSSUU	LUSUSES
ELSSTTU	SUTTLES
ELSSTTY	STYLETS
ELSSTYY	SYSTYLE
ELSUWZZ	WUZZLES
EMMMOST	MOMMETS
EMMMRSU	MUMMERS
EMMMRUY	MUMMERY
EMMNNOS	MNEMONS
EMMNOOR	MONOMER
	MOORMEN
EMMNOOT	MOMENTO
	MOOTMEN
EMMNORY	MERONYM
EMMNOST	MOMENTS
	MONTEMS
EMMNOTU	OMENTUM
EMMNOTY	METONYM
EMMOOTY	MYOTOME
EMMOPRR	PROMMER
EMMORSS	MOMSERS
EMMORSZ	MOMZERS
EMMOSST	MESTOMS
EMMOSSU	MOMUSES
	MOUSMES
EMMOSYZ	ZYMOMES
EMMPRSU	MUMPERS
EMMPSTU	METUMPS
EMMRRSU	RUMMERS
EMMRSSU	SUMMERS
EMMRSTU	RUMMEST
EMMRSUY	SUMMERY
EMMSSUU	MUSEUMS

EMNNOOR	MONERON
EMNNOSW	SNOWMEN
EMNNOWW	NEWMOWN
EMNOOPT	METOPON
EMNOORS	MOONERS
EMNOORT	MONTERO
EMNOOSS	MONOSES
EMNOOST	MOONSET
EMNOOSY	NOYSOME
EMNOOTY	ENOMOTY
EMNOPPR	PROPMEN
EMNOPRT	PORTMEN
EMNOPST	POSTMEN
	TOPSMEN
EMNOPSU	SPUMONE
EMNOPSY	EPONYMS
EMNOPYY	EPONYMY
EMNORRU	MOURNER
EMNORSS	SERMONS
EMNORST	MENTORS
	MONSTER
	MONTRES
EMNORTT	TORMENT
EMNORTU	MONTURE
	MOUNTER
	REMOUNT
EMNOSST	STEMSON
EMNOSTU	UNSMOTE
EMNOSTY	ETYMONS
EMNOSXY	EXONYMS
EMNPSSU	PENSUMS
EMNRRSU	MURRENS
EMNRRUY	UNMERRY
EMNRSSU	RUMNESS
EMNRSTU	MUNSTER
	MUNTERS
	STERNUM
EMOOPRS	OOSPERM
EMOOPRT	PROMOTE
EMOOPRY	POMEROY
EMOORRS	MOROSER
	ROOMERS
EMOORST	MOOTERS
EMOORSU	UROSOME
EMOOSSS	OSMOSES
EMOOSTT	MOOTEST
	MOTTOES
	TOOMEST
EMOOSTW	TWOSOME
EMOOSTY	MYOSOTE
	TOYSOME
EMOOSXY	OXYSOME
EMOOTUV	OUTMOVE
EMOPPRS	MOPPERS
EMOPPST	MOPPETS
EMOPPSY	POMPEYS
EMOPPTU	UPTEMPO
EMOPRRS	ROMPERS
EMOPRST	STOMPER
	TROMPES
EMOPRSU	SUPREMO
EMOPSSU	MOPUSES
EMOPSSY	MYOPSES
EMOQSSU	MOSQUES

EMORRST	STORMER
	TERMORS
	TREMORS
EMORRSU	MORSURE
EMORRSW	WORMERS
EMORRWY	WORMERY
EMORSSS	MOSSERS
EMORSST	MOTSERS
EMORSSU	MOUSERS
	SMOUSER
EMORSTU	MOUTERS
	OESTRUM
EMORSUV	MEVROUS
EMORSUY	MOUSERY
EMOSSSU	MOUSSES
	SMOUSES
EMOSSTT	MOSTEST
EMOSSYZ	ZYMOSES
EMOSTTT	MOTETTS
EMOSTVZ	ZEMSTVO
EMOTTTU	TETOTUM
EMOTUZZ	MEZUZOT
EMPPRSU	PUMPERS
	REPUMPS
EMPPSTU	MUPPETS
EMPRSTU	RESTUMP
	STUMPER
	SUMPTER
EMPRTTU	TRUMPET
EMPSSTU	SEPTUMS
EMRRSTU	STURMER
EMRRSUY	MURREYS
EMRSSTU	ESTRUMS
	MUSTERS
	STUMERS
EMRSTTU	MUTTERS
EMRSTYY	MYSTERY
EMSSSTY	SYSTEMS
ENNNOPS	PENNONS
ENNNOSW	NONNEWS
ENNNRUY	NUNNERY
ENNOOPR	PRENOON
ENNOORS	NOONERS
ENNOORT	NORTENO
ENNOORZ	NONZERO
ENNOOTT	NONETTO
ENNORST	STONERN
	TONNERS
ENNORSU	NEURONS
	NONUSER
ENNORSW	RENOWNS
	WONNERS
ENNORTU	NEUTRON
ENNORUV	UNROVEN
ENNOSST	SONNETS
	STONNES
	TENSONS
ENNOSSU	NONUSES
ENNOSSW	NOWNESS
ENNOSTU	NEUSTON
ENNOSTW	NEWTONS
ENNOSTZ	TENZONS
ENNOUVW	UNWOVEN
ENNPRSU	PUNNERS

ENNPSTU	PUNNETS	ENORSTY	TYRONES	EOOPRSW	SWOOPER
	UNSPENT	ENORSUV	NERVOUS	EOOPRTU	OUTROPE
ENNRRSU	RUNNERS	ENORSUW	UNSWORE	EOOPRTV	OVERTOP
ENNRSTU	RUNNETS	ENORSUZ	ZONURES	EOOPRTW	TOWROPE
	STUNNER	ENORSVY	RENVOYS	EOOPRVY	POOVERY
ENNRSUW	WUNNERS	ENORSZZ	NOZZERS	EOOPRYZ	ZOOPERY
ENNSSTU	UNNESTS	ENORTUW	UNWROTE	EOOPSST	STOOPES
ENNSTTU	UNTENTS	ENORTUY	TOURNEY	EOOPSSW	WOOPSES
ENNSTUU	UNTUNES	ENOSSST	SESTONS	EOOPTYZ	ZOOTYPE
ENNSTYY	SYNTENY	ENOSSTT	OSTENTS	EOORRSS	ROOSERS
ENNTTUY	UNTENTY		STETSON	EOORRST	ROOSTER
ENOOPPR	PROPONE		TESTONS		ROOTERS
ENOOPRS	OPERONS	ENOSSTU	OUTNESS		TOREROS
	SNOOPER		TONUSES	EOORRVW	ROWOVER
ENOOPSY	SPOONEY	ENOSSTW	TWONESS	EOORSSS	SOROSES
ENOORSS	NOOSERS	ENOSSTX	SEXTONS	EOORSTT	TOOTERS
	SEROONS	ENOSSUW	SWOUNES	EOORSVW	OVERSOW
	SOONERS	ENOSSWW	SWOWNES	EOORTUW	OUTWORE
ENOORST	ENROOTS	ENOSTTU	STOUTEN	EOOSSST	OSTOSES
ENOORSU	ONEROUS		TENUTOS	EOOSSSU	OSSEOUS
ENOORSW	SWOONER	ENOSTUU	TENUOUS	EOOSSTT	TOOTSES
ENOORSZ	SNOOZER	ENOTTUW	OUTWENT	EOOSTWZ	WOOTZES
ENOOSST	SOONEST	ENPPRSU	PRENUPS	EOOTTUV	OUTVOTE
ENOOSSZ	SNOOZES	ENPRRSU	PRUNERS	EOPPPRS	POPPERS
ENOOSTT	TESTOON		SPURNER	EOPPPST	POPPETS
ENOOSTU	UNSOOTE	ENPRSSU	SPURNES	EOPPRRS	PROPERS
ENOOTXY	OXYTONE	ENPRSTU	PUNSTER		PROSPER
ENOPPSU	UNPOPES		PUNTERS	EOPPRSS	OPPRESS
ENOPRRS	PERRONS	ENPRSUU	UNPURSE		PORPESS
ENOPRRU	PRONEUR	ENPRSWY	PREWYNS	EOPPRST	POPSTER
ENOPRRW	PREWORN	ENPSSSU	SUSPENS		STOPPER
ENOPRSS	PERSONS	ENPSSTU	UNSTEPS		TOPPERS
ENOPRST	POSTERN	ENPSTTU	STUPENT	EOPPRSU	PURPOSE
	PRONEST	ENPSTUU	TUNEUPS	EOPPRSW	SWOPPER
ENOPRSU	UNROPES	ENPSTUW	UNSWEPT	EOPPRSY	PYROPES
ENOPRSY	PROYNES	ENRRSSU	NURSERS		YOPPERS
	PYONERS	ENRRSTU	RETURNS	EOPPSSU	SUPPOSE
	PYRONES		TURNERS	EOPRRSS	PRESSOR
ENOPRTT	PORTENT	ENRRSUU	UNSURER		PROSERS
ENOPRTY	ENTROPY	ENRRSUY	NURSERY	EOPRRST	PORTERS
ENOPSST	POSNETS	ENRRTUU	NURTURE		PRESORT
	STEPSON		UNTRUER		PRETORS
ENOPSTT	POTENTS	ENRRTUY	TURNERY		REPORTS
ENOPSUX	XENOPUS	ENRSSTU	UNRESTS		SPORTER
ENOPSWY	POWNEYS	ENRSSWY	WRYNESS	EOPRRSU	POURERS
ENOQTUU	UNQUOTE	ENRSTTU	ENTRUST		REPOURS
ENORRSS	SNORERS		NUTTERS	EOPRRSV	PROVERS
	SORNERS	ENRSUZZ	NUZZERS	EOPRRTU	TROUPER
ENORRST	SNORTER	ENRSVWY	WYVERNS	EOPRSSS	POSSERS
ENORRSZ	RONZERS	ENRTTUY	NUTTERY		PROSSES
ENORRTT	TORRENT	ENSSSTU	SUNSETS	EOPRSST	PORTESS
ENORRUV	OVERRUN	EOOOPRS	OOSPORE		POSTERS
	RUNOVER	EOOPPRS	OPPOSER		PRESTOS
ENORSSS	SENSORS		POOPERS		REPOSTS
ENORSST	NESTORS		PROPOSE		RESPOTS
	STONERS	EOOPPRV	POPOVER		STOPERS
	TENSORS	EOOPPSS	OPPOSES	EOPRSSU	POSEURS
ENORSSW	WORSENS	EOOPRRS	SPOORER		SEROPUS
ENORSSY	SENSORY	EOOPRRT	PROTORE		SOUPERS
ENORSTT	ROTTENS		TROOPER	EOPRSSW	PROWESS
	SNOTTER	EOOPRSS	POROSES	EOPRSSY	OSPREYS
	STENTOR	EOOPRST	POOREST		PYROSES
ENORSTU	TENOURS		POOTERS	EOPRSTT	POTTERS
	TONSURE		STOOPER		PROTEST

Seven-letter anagrams

	SPOTTER		SOUREST		TRUSTER
EOPRSTU	PETROUS		SOUTERS		TURRETS
	POSTURE		STOURES	ERRSTTY	TRYSTER
	POUTERS		TOUSERS	ERSSSTU	RUSSETS
	PROTEUS		TROUSES		TRUSSES
	SEPTUOR		TUSSORE		TUSSERS
	SPOUTER	EORSSTV	STOVERS	ERSSSUU	USURESS
	TROUPES	EORSSTW	SOWTERS	ERSSTTU	TUTRESS
EOPRSTW	POWTERS		STOWERS	ERSSTTY	TRYSTES
	PROWEST		TOWSERS	ERSSTUU	SUTURES
EOPRSTX	EXPORTS		WORSETS	ERSSTUY	RUSSETY
EOPRSTZ	POTZERS	EORSSTY	OYSTERS	ERSSTXY	XYSTERS
EOPRSUU	POURSUE		STOREYS	ERSSUVY	SURVEYS
	UPROUSE	EORSSTZ	ZOSTERS	ERSTTTU	STUTTER
EOPRSUV	OVERSUP	EORSSWW	WOWSERS	ERSTTUX	URTEXTS
EOPRSUW	POURSEW	EORSTTT	STOTTER	FFFGINU	FUFFING
EOPRTTY	POTTERY		STRETTO	FFFILOT	LIFTOFF
EOPRTUY	EUTROPY		TOTTERS	FFFLOSY	FLYOFFS
EOPRTVY	POVERTY	EORSTTU	OUTSERT	FFGGINO	GOFFING
EOPSSSS	POSSESS		STOUTER	FFGHINU	HUFFING
EOPSSST	POSSETS		TOUTERS	FFGIIMN	MIFFING
EOPSSSU	POUSSES	EORSTTW	SWOTTER	FFGIINN	NIFFING
	SPOUSES	EORSTTX	EXTORTS	FFGIINR	GRIFFIN
EOPSSTX	SEXPOTS	EORSTTY	ROSETTY		RIFFING
EOPSTTU	OUTSTEP	EORSTUX	SEXTUOR	FFGIINT	TIFFING
	TOUPETS	EORSUVY	VOYEURS	FFGILNU	LUFFING
EOPSTTW	STEWPOT	EORTTTY	TOTTERY	FFGIMNU	MUFFING
EOPTTUW	OUTWEPT	EORTTUY	TUTOYER	FFGINOR	GRIFFON
EOQRRTU	TORQUER	EOSSSST	STOSSES	FFGINOS	GONIFFS
EOQRSTU	QUESTOR	EOSSSSW	SOWSSES		OFFINGS
	QUOTERS	EOSSTTU	OUTSETS	FFGINPU	PUFFING
	ROQUETS		SETOUTS	FFGINRU	RUFFING
	TORQUES	EOSSUYZ	SOYUZES	FFGLOOS	LOGOFFS
EOQSTTU	TOQUETS	EOSTTTW	WOTTEST	FFGLRUY	GRUFFLY
EORRRST	RORTERS	EPPPSTU	PUPPETS	FFHHISU	HUFFISH
	TERRORS	EPPRRTU	PRERUPT	FFHIINS	FINFISH
EORRSSS	ROSSERS	EPPRRUU	PURPURE	FFHIISY	FISHIFY
EORRSST	RESORTS	EPPRSSU	SUPPERS	FFHIKNU	HUFFKIN
	ROSTERS	EPPSSTU	UPSTEPS	FFHILSU	FISHFUL
	SORTERS	EPPSTUW	UPSWEPT	FFHILTY	FIFTHLY
	STORERS	EPRRRSU	SPURRER	FFHILUV	HUFFILY
EORRSSU	ROUSERS	EPRRSSU	PURSERS	FFHIMSU	MUFFISH
EORRSTT	RETORTS	EPRRSTU	SPURTER	FFHIOST	TOFFISH
	ROTTERS	EPRRSUU	PURSUER	FFHIOSX	FOXFISH
	STERTOR		USURPER	FFHOOSW	SHOWOFF
	TORRETS	EPRRSUY	SPURREY	FFHORSS	SHROFFS
EORRSTU	RETOURS	EPRRTUU	RUPTURE	FFHOSTU	SHUTOFF
	ROUSTER	EPRSSSU	PUSSERS	FFIILMY	MIFFILY
	ROUTERS	EPRSSTU	UPRESTS	FFIINST	TIFFINS
	TOURERS	EPRSSTY	SPRYEST	FFIISUZ	ZIFFIUS
	TROUSER	EPRSSUU	PURSUES	FFIKLSS	SKLIFFS
EORRSTV	TROVERS	EPRSSUW	PURSEWS	FFILLLU	FULFILL
EORRSTW	STROWER	EPRSTTU	PUTTERS	FFILLSU	FULFILS
EORRSTY	ROYSTER		SPUTTER	FFILNSY	SNIFFLY
	STROYER	EPRSTUU	PUTURES	FFILOST	FILFOTS
EORRSZZ	ROZZERS	EPRSUVY	PURVEYS	FFILOUZ	ZUFFOLI
EORRTTT	TROTTER	EQRSTWY	QWERTYS	FFILPSS	SPLIFFS
EORRTTU	TORTURE	ERRSSTU	RUSTRES	FFILPUY	PUFFILY
	TROUTER		TRUSSER	FFILRTY	FRITFLY
EORSSST	TOSSERS	ERRSSUU	USURERS	FFILSTU	FISTFUL
EORSSSU	SOURESS	ERRSSUY	SURREYS	FFILSTY	STIFFLY
EORSSTU	ESTROUS	ERRSTTU	RUTTERS	FFIMNSU	MUFFINS
	OESTRUS			FFINNSU	NUFFINS
	OUSTERS			FFINOOT	FINFOOT

FFINOPS	SPINOFF	**FGIILNS**	FILINGS	**FGINRTU**	TURFING
FFINOPT	PONTIFF	**FGIILNT**	FLITING	**FGINSSU**	FUSSING
FFINPSU	PUFFINS		LIFTING	**FGINSTU**	FUSTING
FFINRSU	RUFFINS	**FGIILNX**	FLIXING	**FGINTTU**	TUFTING
FFIOPRS	RIPOFFS	**FGIILNY**	LIGNIFY	**FGINTUZ**	FUTZING
FFIOPST	TIPOFFS	**FGIIMNR**	FIRMING	**FGINUZZ**	FUZZING
FFIORTY	FORTIFY	**FGIINNN**	FINNING	**FGIORST**	FRIGOTS
FFIOSST	SOFFITS	**FGIINNO**	FOINING	**FGIORTW**	FIGWORT
FFIQSUY	SQUIFFY	**FGIINNS**	FININGS	**FGISTUU**	FUGUIST
FFIRTUY	FRUTIFY	**FGIINRR**	FIRRING	**FGJLSUU**	JUGFULS
FFJMOPU	JUMPOFF	**FGIINRS**	FIRINGS		JUGSFUL
FFKLORU	FORKFUL	**FGIINRT**	RIFTING	**FGLLNUU**	LUNGFUL
FFLLOOU	LOOFFUL	**FGIINRY**	NIGRIFY	**FGLLOWY**	GLOWFLY
FFLMORU	FORMFUL	**FGIINRZ**	FRIZING	**FGLMSUU**	MUGFULS
FFLNSUY	SNUFFLY	**FGIINST**	FISTING	**FGLNORU**	FURLONG
FFLOOUZ	ZUFFOLO		SIFTING	**FGLNOSU**	SONGFUL
FFLOSTY	FYLFOTS	**FGIINSX**	FIXINGS	**FGLNPUU**	UPFLUNG
FFNORSU	RUNOFFS	**FGIINSY**	SIGNIFY	**FGLOOUY**	UFOLOGY
FFNORTU	TURNOFF	**FGIINTT**	FITTING	**FGLORSU**	FULGORS
FFOOPST	STOPOFF		TIFTING	**FGLORUU**	FULGOUR
FFOPSTU	OFFPUTS	**FGIINZZ**	FIZZING	**FGLOTUY**	GOUTFLY
	PUTOFFS	**FGIKLNU**	FLUKING	**FGLSTUU**	GUSTFUL
FFRRSUU	FURFURS	**FGIKNNU**	FUNKING		GUTFULS
FGGGIIN	FIGGING	**FGIKNOR**	FORKING		GUTSFUL
FGGGINO	FOGGING	**FGIKNSY**	SKYFING	**FGNOORU**	FOURGON
FGGGINU	FUGGING	**FGILLNU**	FULLING	**FGNORSY**	GRYFONS
FGGHIIS	FISHGIG	**FGILMNU**	FLUMING	**FGNOSUU**	FUNGOUS
FGGIINT	GIFTING	**FGILNOO**	FOOLING	**FHHLSUU**	HUSHFUL
FGGIISS	FISGIGS	**FGILNOP**	FOPLING	**FHIILMS**	FILMISH
FGGIISZ	FIZGIGS	**FGILNOR**	ROLFING	**FHIILSY**	FISHILY
FGGIIZZ	FIZZGIG	**FGILNOT**	LOFTING	**FHIILTY**	LITHIFY
FGGILNO	GOLFING	**FGILNOU**	FOULING	**FHIINPS**	PINFISH
FGGILNU	FUGLING	**FGILNOW**	FLOWING	**FHIKLOS**	FOLKISH
	GULFING		FOWLING	**FHILLSU**	FULLISH
FGGILOY	FOGGILY		WOLFING	**FHILOOS**	FOOLISH
FGGILUY	FUGGILY	**FGILNOY**	FOYLING	**FHILOSW**	WOLFISH
FGGINOO	GOOFING	**FGILNPU**	UPFLING	**FHILPSU**	SHIPFUL
FGGINOR	FORGING	**FGILNPY**	FLYPING	**FHILPTU**	PITHFUL
FGGINOW	GOWFING	**FGILNRU**	FURLING	**FHILSUW**	WISHFUL
FGGINUU	FUGUING	**FGILNSU**	INGULFS	**FHINOSU**	FUSHION
FGHHIOS	HOGFISH	**FGILNSY**	FLYINGS	**FHINRSU**	FURNISH
FGHIINS	FISHING	**FGILNTU**	FLUTING	**FHINSSU**	SUNFISH
FGHIINT	INFIGHT	**FGILNTY**	FLYTING	**FHINSTU**	UNSHIFT
FGHIIPS	PIGFISH	**FGILNUX**	FLUXING	**FHIOOST**	OOFTISH
FGHILST	FLIGHTS	**FGILOOY**	GOOFILY	**FHIOPPS**	FOPPISH
FGHILSU	SIGHFUL	**FGILORY**	GLORIFY	**FHIOPSX**	FOXSHIP
FGHILTY	FLIGHTY	**FGIMNOR**	FORMING	**FHIORRY**	HORRIFY
FGHIMNU	HUMFING	**FGIMOSY**	FOGYISM	**FHIOSST**	SOFTISH
FGHINOO	HOOFING	**FGINNNO**	FONNING	**FHIOSTU**	OUTFISH
FGHINOU	HOUFING	**FGINNNU**	FUNNING	**FHIPPSU**	PUPFISH
FGHINOW	HOWFING	**FGINNOY**	FOYNING	**FHIPSTU**	UPSHIFT
FGHIOSY	FOGYISH	**FGINOOR**	ROOFING	**FHIRSST**	SHRIFTS
FGHIRST	FRIGHTS	**FGINOOT**	FOOTING	**FHIRSTT**	THRIFTS
FGHNOOR	FOGHORN	**FGINOOW**	WOOFING	**FHIRTTY**	THRIFTY
FGHORUY	FROUGHY	**FGINOPP**	FOPPING	**FHIRTUY**	THURIFY
FGHOTUY	FOUGHTY	**FGINOPU**	POUFING	**FHISSSU**	HUSSIFS
FGIIKNN	FINKING	**FGINORS**	FROINGS	**FHISSTU**	SHUFTIS
	KNIFING	**FGINORT**	FORTING	**FHKORTU**	FUTHORK
FGIIKNR	FIRKING	**FGINOST**	SOFTING	**FHLNORU**	HORNFUL
FGIIKNS	FISKING	**FGINOSW**	SOWFING	**FHLNSUU**	UNFLUSH
FGIILLN	FILLING	**FGINOSX**	FOXINGS	**FHLOOSY**	SHOOFLY
FGIILMN	FILMING	**FGINRRU**	FURRING	**FHLOPSU**	SHOPFUL
FGIILNO	FOILING	**FGINRSU**	SURFING	**FHLPSUU**	PUSHFUL
FGIILNR	RIFLING	**FGINRSY**	FRYINGS	**FHLRTUU**	HURTFUL

	RUTHFUL	**FILORSV**	FRIVOLS	**FLMOORU**	ROOMFUL
FHNOTUX	FOXHUNT	**FILORTU**	FLORUIT	**FLMORSY**	FORMYLS
FHOOORS	FORHOOS	**FILORTY**	TRIFOLY	**FLMORWY**	WORMFLY
FHOOORT	HOOFROT	**FILOSSS**	FOSSILS	**FLMSUUU**	FUMULUS
FHOOOTT	HOTFOOT	**FILPPUY**	PULPIFY	**FLNOORR**	FORLORN
FHOORSW	FORHOWS	**FILPSTU**	UPLIFTS	**FLNOOSU**	UNFOOLS
FHORSTU	FOURTHS	**FILRRUY**	FURRILY	**FLNOOSW**	ONFLOWS
FIIIKNN	FINIKIN	**FILRSTY**	FIRSTLY	**FLNRSUU**	UNFURLS
FIIKNRS	FIRKINS	**FILRYZZ**	FRIZZLY		URNFULS
FIIKNYZ	ZINKIFY	**FILSSUY**	FUSSILY	**FLOOOTU**	OUTFOOL
FIILLMO	MILFOIL	**FILSTTU**	FLUTIST	**FLOOPWX**	FOWLPOX
FIILLMY	FILMILY	**FILSTUW**	WISTFUL	**FLOORSW**	FORSLOW
FIILLNS	INFILLS	**FILSTUY**	FUSTILY	**FLOOTUW**	OUTFLOW
FIILLPS	FILLIPS	**FILSTWY**	SWIFTLY	**FLOPSTU**	POTFULS
FIILLSU	FUSILLI	**FILTTUY**	TUFTILY	**FLOPSUW**	UPFLOWS
FIILNOT	TINFOIL	**FILUYZZ**	FUZZILY	**FLOPTUU**	POUTFUL
FIILNTY	NIFTILY	**FIMMMUY**	MUMMIFY	**FLOSUUV**	FULVOUS
FIILPRS	RIFLIPS	**FIMMORS**	MISFORM	**FLPRSUU**	UPFURLS
FIILPTU	PITIFUL	**FIMNORS**	INFORMS	**FLRSSUU**	SULFURS
FIILQUY	LIQUIFY	**FIMNORU**	UNIFORM	**FLRSUUY**	SULFURY
FIIMMNU	INFIMUM	**FIMOORS**	ISOFORM	**FMNORSU**	UNFORMS
FIIMNRS	INFIRMS	**FIMOORV**	OVIFORM	**FMRSTUU**	FRUSTUM
FIIMSST	MISFITS	**FIMORRT**	TRIFORM	**FNNNUUY**	UNFUNNY
FIINORS	FIORINS	**FIMORTY**	MORTIFY	**FNNOORT**	FRONTON
FIINOSS	FISSION	**FIMRTUY**	FURMITY	**FNOORRW**	FORWORN
FIINRTY	NITRIFY	**FIMSTYY**	MYSTIFY	**FNOORSU**	SUNROOF
FIIOPST	POSITIF	**FINOOSS**	FOISONS		UNROOFS
FIIPSTY	TIPSIFY	**FINOPRS**	FRIPONS	**FNOPRTU**	UPFRONT
FIIRTVY	VITRIFY	**FINOPSU**	SOUPFIN	**FNRSTUU**	UNTURFS
FIJLLOY	JOLLIFY	**FINOPTY**	PONTIFY	**FNSSUUY**	UNFUSSY
FIJSTUY	JUSTIFY	**FINORSS**	FRISSON	**FNSTTUU**	UNSTUFT
FIKKLNO	KINFOLK	**FINORST**	FORINTS	**FOOOPRT**	ROOFTOP
FIKLLSU	SKILFUL	**FINORTY**	INTROFY	**FOOORTT**	FOOTROT
FIKLLUY	FLUKILY	**FINOSSU**	FUSIONS	**FOOOTTU**	OUTFOOT
FIKLNOW	WOLFKIN	**FIOORSU**	FURIOSO	**FOORSSS**	FOSSORS
FIKLNSU	SKINFUL	**FIOPRST**	FORPITS	**FOORTTX**	FOXTROT
FIKLNUY	FUNKILY		PROFITS	**FOPSSTU**	FUSSPOT
FIKLRSU	RISKFUL		SPORTIF	**FORRSUW**	FURROWS
FIKLSTU	KISTFUL	**FIOPRSY**	PROSIFY	**FORRUWY**	FURROWY
	LUTFISK	**FIOPSTX**	POSTFIX	**FORSSTW**	FROWSTS
FIKNNOS	FINNSKO	**FIORRTY**	TORRIFY	**FORSTWY**	FROWSTY
FIKNOSX	FOXSKIN	**FIORSSU**	FURIOUS	**GGGIINN**	GIGGING
FIKRSTU	TURFSKI	**FIOSTTU**	OUTFITS	**GGGHINO**	HOGGING
FILLLUW	WILLFUL	**FIOTTTU**	TOFUTTI	**GGGHINU**	HUGGING
FILLMOY	MOLLIFY	**FIPPUYY**	YUPPIFY	**GGGIIJN**	JIGGING
FILLNUY	NULLIFY	**FIRSSTT**	STRIFTS	**GGGIILN**	LIGGING
FILLOTU	TOILFUL	**FIRSSUY**	RUSSIFY	**GGGIINP**	PIGGING
FILLOTY	LOFTILY	**FKLMOOT**	FOLKMOT	**GGGIINR**	RIGGING
FILLPSU	UPFILLS	**FKLORUW**	WORKFUL	**GGGIINT**	TIGGING
FILLSTU	LISTFUL	**FKNOSTY**	KONFYTS	**GGGIINW**	WIGGING
FILMNOO	MONOFIL	**FKOOORS**	FORSOOK	**GGGIINZ**	ZIGGING
FILMOSU	FOLIUMS	**FKRSSUY**	SKYSURF	**GGGIIST**	GIGGITS
FILMSTU	MISTFUL	**FLLOOSW**	FOLLOWS	**GGGIJNO**	JOGGING
FILNNUY	FUNNILY	**FLLOPTU**	PLOTFUL	**GGGIJNU**	JUGGING
FILNORS	FLORINS		TOPFULL	**GGGILNO**	LOGGING
FILNORU	FLUORIN	**FLLOSSY**	LOSLYFS	**GGGILNU**	LUGGING
FILNOSW	INFLOWS	**FLLOSUU**	SOULFUL	**GGGIMNO**	MOGGING
FILNOUX	FLUXION	**FLLOUWY**	WOFULLY	**GGGIMNU**	MUGGING
FILNSTU	TINFULS	**FLLSTUU**	LUSTFUL	**GGGINNO**	GONGING
FILNTUY	UNFITLY	**FLMMOUX**	FLUMMOX		NOGGING
FILOOSU	FOLIOUS	**FLMNOOU**	MOUFLON	**GGGINNU**	GUNGING
FILOOTW	WITLOOF	**FLMNOSU**	MUFLONS	**GGGINOR**	GORGING
FILORST	FIRLOTS	**FLMOOOT**	TOMFOOL	**GGGINOS**	SOGGING
	FLORIST	**FLMOORS**	FORMOLS	**GGGINOT**	TOGGING

GGGINOU	GOUGING	GGILNNU	LUNGING	GHHIOPT	HIGHTOP
GGGINPU	PUGGING	GGILNOS	GOSLING	GHHIRST	SHRIGHT
GGGINRU	GURGING		OGLINGS	GHHORTU	THROUGH
	RUGGING	GGILNOV	GLOVING	GHHOSSU	SHOUGHS
GGGINSU	SUGGING	GGILNOW	GLOWING	GHHOTTU	THOUGHT
GGGINTU	TUGGING		GOWLING	GHIIIMN	MIHIING
GGHHIIN	HIGHING	GGILNOZ	GLOZING	GHIIKNO	HOIKING
GGHHIOS	HOGGISH	GGILNPU	GULPING	GHIIKNT	KITHING
GGHIIJS	JIGGISH	GGILNRU	GURLING	GHIILLN	HILLING
GGHIINN	HINGING	GGILNSU	LUGINGS	GHIILNR	HIRLING
	NIGHING	GGILNUY	GUYLING	GHIILNT	HILTING
GGHIINS	SIGHING		UGLYING		LITHING
GGHIIPS	PIGGISH	GGILOOS	GIGOLOS	GHIILNW	WHILING
GGHIIRS	RIGGISH	GGILOST	GIGLOTS	GHIILRS	GIRLISH
GGHIITT	THIGGIT	GGILOSY	SOGGILY	GHIINNS	SHINING
GGHILOS	LOGGISH	GGILRWY	WRIGGLY	GHIINNT	HINTING
GGHIMSU	MUGGISH	GGIMMNU	GUMMING		NITHING
GGHINNO	HONGING	GGIMNNU	MUNGING	GHIINNW	WHINING
GGHINOS	HOGGINS	GGIMNOR	GORMING	GHIINOS	HOISING
GGHINSU	GUSHING	GGIMNPU	GUMPING	GHIINPP	HIPPING
	SUGHING	GGIMNPY	GYMPING	GHIINPS	PISHING
GGHIOSW	WOGGISH	GGIMNSU	MUGGINS	GHIINPT	PITHING
GGHIPSU	PUGGISH	GGINNNU	GUNNING	GHIINRS	HIRINGS
GGHLOSY	SHOGGLY	GGINNOO	ONGOING		SHIRING
GGHORSU	GROUGHS	GGINNOP	PONGING	GHIINSS	HISSING
GGHOSTU	THUGGOS	GGINNOR	GRONING	GHIINST	HISTING
GGIIILN	GINGILI	GGINNOS	NOGGINS		INSIGHT
GGIIJJS	JIGJIGS	GGINNOT	TONGING		SHITING
GGIIKNN	KINGING	GGINNOW	GOWNING		SITHING
GGIILLN	GILLING	GGINNRU	GURNING	GHIINSW	WISHING
GGIILMN	GLIMING	GGINOOP	POGOING	GHIINTT	HITTING
GGIILNP	PIGLING	GGINOOS	GOOSING		TITHING
GGIILNR	RIGLING	GGINOPR	GORPING	GHIINTW	WHITING
GGIILNU	GUILING		GROPING		WITHING
GGIIMNN	MINGING		PORGING	GHIINZZ	HIZZING
GGIIMNP	GIMPING	GGINOPU	UPGOING	GHIIOPR	PIROGHI
GGIIMNR	GRIMING	GGINOQS	QIGONGS	GHIIRST	TIGRISH
GGIINNN	GINNING	GGINORS	GORINGS	GHIJNOS	JOSHING
GGIINNO	INGOING		GRINGOS	GHIKLNO	HOLKING
GGIINNP	PINGING	GGINORU	ROGUING	GHIKLNU	HULKING
GGIINNR	GIRNING		ROUGING	GHIKNNO	HONKING
	RINGING	GGINORW	GROWING	GHIKNOO	HOOKING
GGIINNS	SIGNING	GGINORZ	GROZING	GHIKNOW	HOWKING
	SINGING	GGINOSS	GOSSING	GHIKNST	KNIGHTS
GGIINNT	TINGING	GGINOUV	VOGUING	GHIKNSU	HUSKING
GGIINNW	WINGING	GGINPPY	GYPPING	GHIKNTY	KYTHING
GGIINNZ	ZINGING	GGINPRU	PURGING	GHIKRTU	TUGHRIK
GGIINPP	GIPPING	GGINRSU	SURGING	GHILLNU	HULLING
GGIINPR	GRIPING		URGINGS	GHILLSU	GULLISH
GGIINPS	PIGGINS	GGINSTU	GUSTING	GHILLTY	LIGHTLY
GGIINRS	GRISING		GUTSING	GHILNOS	HOLINGS
GGIINRT	GIRTING	GGINTTU	GUTTING		LONGISH
	RINGGIT	GGIOORS	GORGIOS	GHILNOT	THOLING
GGIINSU	GUISING	GGIPRSY	SPRIGGY	GHILNOW	HOWLING
GGIINSV	GIVINGS	GGLLOOS	LOGLOGS	GHILNPU	INGULPH
GGIINTT	GITTING	GGLOOOS	GOOGOLS	GHILNRU	HURLING
GGIIRRS	GRIGRIS	GGMRSUU	MUGGURS	GHILNSU	LUSHING
GGIJNSU	JUGGINS	GGNOORS	GORGONS		SHULING
GGIKLNU	KLUGING	GGNOOSY	GONGYOS	GHILNSY	SHINGLY
GGIKNOS	GINGKOS	GGRRSUU	GRUGRUS	GHILNTY	NIGHTLY
	GINKGOS	GHHHIIS	HIGHISH	GHILPST	PLIGHTS
GGILLNU	GULLING	GHHHIST	HIGHTHS	GHILPTU	UPLIGHT
GGILMUY	MUGGILY	GHHIINS	HISHING	GHILPTY	YPLIGHT
GGILNNO	LONGING	GHHINSU	HUSHING	GHILRTY	RIGHTLY

Seven-letter anagrams

GHILSST	SLIGHTS	GHIQSTU	QUIGHTS	GIIKNNZ	ZINKING
GHILSTY	SIGHTLY	GHIRSTW	WRIGHTS	GIIKNPP	KIPPING
GHILSUV	GUSHILY	GHISTTW	TWIGHTS	GIIKNPS	PIGSKIN
GHILTTY	TIGHTLY	GHLMOOO	HOMOLOG		PIKINGS
GHILTWY	WIGHTLY	GHLMOSU	MOGHULS		SPIKING
GHIMMNU	HUMMING	GHLOOSY	SHOOGLY	GIIKNRS	GIRKINS
GHIMNNY	HYMNING	GHLOPSU	PLOUGHS		GRISKIN
GHIMNOS	GNOMISH	GHLORUY	ROUGHLY		KRISING
	HOMINGS	GHLOSSU	SLOUGHS		RISKING
	MOSHING	GHLOSTY	GHOSTLY	GIIKNRY	YIRKING
GHIMNPU	HUMPING	GHLOSUY	SLOUGHY	GIIKNSS	KISSING
GHIMNRY	RHYMING	GHLOTUY	TOUGHLY		SKIINGS
GHIMNSU	MUSHING	GHMORSU	SORGHUM	GIIKNST	KISTING
GHIMRSU	SIMURGH	GHMOSTU	MUGSHOT		KITINGS
GHIMSST	SMIGHTS	GHMPRSU	GRUMPHS		SKITING
GHIMSTT	MIGHTST	GHMPRUY	GRUMPHY	GIIKNSV	SKIVING
GHINNOP	PHONING	GHNOOPS	GONOPHS		VIKINGS
GHINNOR	HORNING	GHNOPRY	GRYPHON	GIIKNTT	KITTING
GHINNOS	NOSHING	GHNORST	THRONGS	GIILLLN	LILLING
GHINNOT	NOTHING	GHNORUU	UNROUGH	GIILLMN	MILLING
GHINNTU	HUNTING	GHNOSSU	SHOGUNS	GIILLNN	NILLING
GHINOOP	HOOPING	GHNOSTU	GUNSHOT	GIILLNO	GILLION
	POOHING		HOGNUTS	GIILLNP	PILLING
GHINOOS	SHOOING		NOUGHTS	GIILLNR	RILLING
GHINOOT	HOOTING		SHOTGUN	GIILLNT	LILTING
GHINOOV	HOOVING	GHNOTUY	YOUNGTH		TILLING
GHINOPP	HOPPING	GHOOOSW	HOOSGOW	GIILLNW	WILLING
GHINOPS	GINSHOP	GHOOPST	PHOTOGS	GIILMNN	LIMNING
	POSHING	GHOOQSU	QUOHOGS	GIILMNO	MOILING
GHINOPY	HYPOING	GHOORSS	SORGHOS	GIILMNP	LIMPING
GHINORS	HORSING	GHORSTU	TROUGHS	GIILMNS	LIMINGS
	SHORING	GHORSTW	GROWTHS		SLIMING
GHINORW	WHORING	GHORTUW	WROUGHT		SMILING
GHINOST	HOSTING	GHORTUY	YOGHURT	GIILMNT	MILTING
	TOSHING	GHORTWY	GROWTHY	GIILMPR	PILGRIM
GHINOSU	HOUSING	GHOSTUU	OUTGUSH	GIILMRY	GRIMILY
GHINOSV	SHOVING	GIIIKNT	TIKIING	GIILNNN	LINNING
GHINOSW	SHOWING	GIIINRS	IRISING	GIILNNR	NIRLING
GHINOTT	HOTTING		NIGIRIS	GIILNNS	LIGNINS
	TONIGHT	GIIJKNN	JINKING		LININGS
GHINOTU	HOUTING	GIIJLNT	JILTING	GIILNNT	LINTING
	THOUING	GIIJNNO	JOINING	GIILNNY	INLYING
GHINPPU	HUPPING	GIIJNNX	JINXING	GIILNOP	PIGNOLI
GHINPPY	HYPPING	GIIKKNN	KINKING	GIILNOR	LIGROIN
GHINPSU	GUNSHIP	GIIKKNR	KIRKING		ROILING
	PUSHING	GIIKLLN	KILLING	GIILNOS	SILOING
GHINPSY	HYPINGS	GIIKLMN	MILKING		SOILING
GHINRSU	RUSHING	GIIKLNN	INKLING	GIILNOT	TOILING
GHINRTU	HURTING		KILNING	GIILNPP	LIPPING
	UNGIRTH		LINKING	GIILNPS	LISPING
	UNRIGHT	GIIKLNR	LIRKING		PILINGS
GHINSTU	SHUTING	GIIKLNS	LIKINGS		SLIPING
	TUSHING		SILKING		SPILING
	UNSIGHT	GIIKLNT	KILTING	GIILNRS	RIGLINS
GHINTTU	HUTTING		KITLING	GIILNRT	TIRLING
GHINTTY	TYTHING	GIIKNNO	OINKING	GIILNST	LISTING
GHIOPSZ	PHIZOGS	GIIKNNP	KINGPIN		SILTING
GHIORST	RIGHTOS		PINKING		STILING
GHIORSU	ROGUISH	GIIKNNR	KIRNING		TILINGS
GHIOSUV	VOGUISH		RINKING	GIILNSV	LIVINGS
GHIPRST	SPRIGHT	GIIKNNS	SINKING		SLIVING
GHIPRTU	UPRIGHT	GIIKNNT	TINKING	GIILNTT	TILTING
GHIPSST	SPIGHTS	GIIKNNV	KNIVING		TITLING
GHIPTTU	UPTIGHT	GIIKNNW	WINKING	GIILNTW	WILTING

	WITLING	**GIINPSS**	PISSING	**GIKNNOW**	KNOWING
GIILOSS	GLIOSIS	**GIINPST**	SPITING	**GIKNNOZ**	ZONKING
GIILOST	OLIGIST	**GIINPSW**	SWIPING	**GIKNNSU**	UNKINGS
GIILRST	STRIGIL		WIPINGS	**GIKNOOP**	POOKING
GIIMMNN	NIMMING		WISPING	**GIKNOOR**	ROOKING
GIIMMNR	RIMMING	**GIINPTT**	PITTING	**GIKNOOS**	SOOKING
GIIMNNS	MININGS	**GIINPTW**	WINGTIP	**GIKNOPR**	PORKING
GIIMNNT	MINTING	**GIINPTY**	PITYING		PROKING
GIIMNPP	PIMPING	**GIINQRU**	QUIRING	**GIKNOPS**	SPOKING
GIIMNPR	PRIMING	**GIINQTU**	QUITING	**GIKNOPU**	POUKING
GIIMNPS	IMPINGS	**GIINRRS**	SIRRING	**GIKNORT**	TROKING
GIIMNPW	WIMPING	**GIINRRT**	TIRRING	**GIKNORW**	WORKING
GIIMNRT	MITRING	**GIINRRY**	YIRRING	**GIKNORY**	YORKING
GIIMNRV	MIRVING	**GIINRSS**	RISINGS	**GIKNOST**	STOKING
GIIMNSS	MISSING	**GIINRST**	STIRING	**GIKNOSU**	SOUKING
GIIMNST	MISTING		TIRINGS	**GIKNOSY**	YOKINGS
	SMITING	**GIINRSV**	VIRGINS	**GIKNOTU**	TOUKING
	STIMING	**GIINRSW**	WIRINGS	**GIKNOUY**	YOUKING
	TIMINGS	**GIINRTT**	RITTING	**GIKNRSY**	SKRYING
GIINNNP	PINNING	**GIINRTW**	TWIRING		SKYRING
GIINNNR	RINNING		WRITING	**GIKNSTU**	TUSKING
GIINNNS	INNINGS	**GIINSST**	SISTING	**GIKNSTY**	SKYTING
	SINNING	**GIINSSU**	ISSUING	**GIKRSTU**	TUGRIKS
GIINNNT	TINNING	**GIINSSW**	WISSING	**GILLLNO**	LOLLING
GIINNNW	WINNING	**GIINSSZ**	SIZINGS	**GILLLNU**	LULLING
GIINNOP	OPINING	**GIINSTT**	SITTING	**GILLMNU**	MULLING
	PIONING	**GIINSTU**	SUITING	**GILLNNU**	NULLING
GIINNOR	IRONING	**GIINSTV**	STIVING	**GILLNOP**	POLLING
	ROINING	**GIINSTW**	WISTING	**GILLNOR**	ROLLING
GIINNOS	NOISING	**GIINSVW**	SWIVING	**GILLNOT**	TOLLING
GIINNOT	OINTING	**GIINTTT**	TITTING	**GILLNPU**	PULLING
GIINNPP	NIPPING	**GIINTTW**	WITTING	**GILLNSU**	ULLINGS
GIINNPS	SNIPING	**GIINVYZ**	VIZYING	**GILLNUW**	WULLING
GIINNPU	PINGUIN	**GIINZZZ**	ZIZZING	**GILLNYY**	LYINGLY
GIINNRS	RINSING	**GIIORSV**	ISOGRIV	**GILLOOS**	LOLIGOS
GIINNRT	TRINING	**GIJKNNU**	JUNKING	**GILLORS**	RIGOLLS
GIINNRU	INURING	**GIJKNOO**	JOOKING	**GILMMUY**	GUMMILY
	RUINING	**GIJKNOU**	JOUKING	**GILMNOO**	LOOMING
	URINING	**GIJLLNO**	JOLLING		MOOLING
GIINNSW	INSWING	**GIJLNOT**	JOLTING	**GILMNOR**	MORLING
GIINNTT	TINTING	**GIJLNOU**	JOULING	**GILMNOT**	MOLTING
GIINNTU	UNITING	**GIJLNOW**	JOWLING	**GILMNOY**	MOYLING
GIINNTV	VINTING	**GIJLNSU**	JUNGLIS	**GILMNPU**	LUMPING
GIINNTW	TWINING	**GIJMNPU**	JUMPING		PLUMING
GIINOPS	POISING	**GIJNOTT**	JOTTING	**GILMNRU**	MURLING
GIINORS	ORIGINS	**GIJNRUY**	JURYING	**GILMNSU**	LIGNUMS
	SIGNIOR	**GIJNSTU**	JUSTING	**GILMPSY**	GYMSLIP
	SIGNORI	**GIJNTTU**	JUTTING	**GILNNOO**	GLONOIN
GIINORT	IGNITOR	**GIKKNNO**	KONKING		LOONING
	RIOTING	**GIKKNOO**	KOOKING	**GILNNOU**	LOUNING
GIINOSY	YOGINIS	**GIKKNOY**	YOKKING	**GILNNOW**	LOWNING
GIINOTT	TOITING	**GIKKNUY**	YUKKING	**GILNNRU**	NURLING
GIINPPP	PIPPING	**GIKLNOO**	LOOKING	**GILNNSU**	UNSLING
GIINPPR	RIPPING	**GIKLNOP**	POLKING	**GILNNTU**	LUNTING
GIINPPS	PIPINGS	**GIKLNRU**	LURKING	**GILNNUV**	VULNING
	SIPPING	**GIKLNSU**	LUSKING	**GILNOOP**	LOOPING
GIINPPT	TIPPING		SULKING		POOLING
GIINPPY	YIPPING	**GIKMNOS**	SMOKING	**GILNOOS**	LOGIONS
GIINPPZ	ZIPPING	**GIKMNSU**	MUSKING		LOOSING
GIINPQU	PIQUING	**GIKNNNO**	KONNING		OLINGOS
GIINPRS	PRISING	**GIKNNOO**	KONGONI		SOLOING
	RISPING	**GIKNNOP**	PONKING		SOOLING
	SPIRING	**GIKNNOS**	SNOKING	**GILNOOT**	LOOTING
GIINPRZ	PRIZING	**GIKNNOT**	TONKING		TOOLING

Seven-letter anagrams

GILNOPP	LOPPING	GIMNNOR	MORNING		WONINGS
GILNOPR	PROLING	GIMNNOS	MIGNONS	GINNOSZ	ZONINGS
GILNOPS	POLINGS	GIMNNTU	MUNTING	GINNOTW	WONTING
	SLOPING	GIMNOOP	MOOPING	GINNPRU	PRUNING
GILNOPT	POLTING	GIMNOOR	MOORING	GINNPTU	PUNTING
GILNOPU	LOUPING		ROOMING	GINNRSU	NURSING
GILNOPW	LOWPING	GIMNOOS	SOOMING		URNINGS
	PLOWING	GIMNOOT	MOOTING	GINNRTU	TURNING
GILNOPY	PLOYING		TOOMING	GINNSTU	TUNINGS
GILNORS	LORINGS	GIMNOOV	MOOVING	GINNTTU	NUTTING
GILNORU	LOURING	GIMNOOZ	ZOOMING	GINNTUY	UNTYING
GILNOSS	LOSINGS	GIMNOPP	MOPPING	GINOOPP	POGONIP
GILNOST	LINGOTS	GIMNOPR	ROMPING		POOPING
	TIGLONS	GIMNOPU	MOUPING	GINOOPR	ROOPING
	TOLINGS	GIMNOPY	YOMPING	GINOOPS	SOOPING
GILNOSU	LOUSING	GIMNORS	SMORING	GINOOPT	POOTING
GILNOSV	LOVINGS	GIMNORU	ROUMING	GINOORS	ROOSING
	SOLVING	GIMNORW	WORMING	GINOORT	ROOTING
GILNOSW	LOWINGS	GIMNOSS	MOSSING	GINOOSS	ISOGONS
	LOWSING	GIMNOST	GNOMIST	GINOOST	SOOTING
	SLOWING	GIMNOSU	MOUSING	GINOOSW	WOOINGS
	SOWLING		SOUMING	GINOOSY	ISOGONY
GILNOTT	LOTTING	GIMNOSW	MOWINGS	GINOOTT	TOOTING
GILNOTU	LOUTING		SOWMING	GINOPPP	POPPING
GILNOTW	LOWTING	GIMNPPU	PUMPING	GINOPPS	SOPPING
GILNOVV	VOLVING	GIMNPRU	RUMPING	GINOPPT	TOPPING
GILNOVW	WOLVING	GIMNPSU	IMPUGNS	GINOPPU	POUPING
GILNOWY	YOWLING		SPUMING	GINOPPW	WOPPING
GILNPPU	PULPING	GIMNPTU	TUMPING	GINOPRS	PROIGNS
GILNPRU	PURLING	GIMNPUY	YUMPING		PROSING
GILNPSU	PLUSING	GIMNSSU	MUSINGS		ROPINGS
	PULINGS		MUSSING		SPORING
	PULSING	GIMNSTU	MUSTING	GINOPRT	PORTING
	PUSLING	GIMNSTY	STYMING		TROPING
GILNPUY	UPLYING	GIMNUZZ	MUZZING	GINOPRU	INGROUP
GILNRSU	RULINGS	GIMORSS	OGRISMS		POURING
GILNSSU	NISGULS		SIMORGS		ROUPING
GILNSTU	LUSTING	GIMORSW	MISGROW	GINOPRV	PROVING
	LUTINGS	GIMOSSY	YOGISMS	GINOPRW	POWRING
	SINGULT	GIMOSTU	GOMUTIS	GINOPRY	YORPING
GILNSTY	STYLING	GIMRSSU	SIMURGS	GINOPSS	POSINGS
GILNSUY	LUNGYIS	GIMRSUU	GURUISM		POSSING
GILNVYY	VYINGLY	GINNNOO	NOONING	GINOPST	POSTING
GILOORS	GIROSOL	GINNNOR	RONNING		STOPING
GILOOSS	ISOLOGS	GINNNOW	WONNING	GINOPSU	SOUPING
GILOOST	OLOGIST	GINNNPU	PUNNING	GINOPSY	POYSING
GILOOTW	TWIGLOO	GINNNRU	RUNNING	GINOPTT	POTTING
GILORTT	TRIGLOT	GINNNSU	SUNNING	GINOPTU	POUTING
GILORTY	TRILOGY	GINNNTU	TUNNING	GINOQTU	QUOTING
GILOSTT	GLOTTIS	GINNOOS	NOOSING	GINORRT	RORTING
GILOTUY	GOUTILY	GINNOOW	WOONING	GINORRV	VORRING
GILRSTY	GRISTLY	GINNOOZ	ZOONING	GINORSS	GRISONS
GILRTUY	LITURGY	GINNOPS	SPONGIN		INGROSS
GILRYZZ	GRIZZLY	GINNOPY	PONYING		SIGNORS
GILSTUY	GUSTILY	GINNORS	SNORING		SORINGS
	GUTSILY		SORNING	GINORST	ROSTING
GIMMMNU	MUMMING	GINNORU	GRUNION		SORTING
GIMMNOT	TOMMING	GINNORW	INGROWN		STORING
GIMMNPU	MUMPING	GINNORY	GIRONNY		TRIGONS
GIMMNRY	RYMMING		ROYNING	GINORSU	ROUSING
GIMMNSU	SUMMING	GINNOSS	NOSINGS		SOURING
GIMMNUV	VUMMING	GINNOST	STONING	GINORSV	ROVINGS
GIMMORS	GIMMORS		TONINGS	GINORSW	ROWINGS
GIMNNOO	MOONING	GINNOSW	SNOWING		WORSING

GINORSY	ROSYING	GIOOPRR	PORRIGO	GNNORUW	UNGROWN
	SIGNORY	GIOORSV	VIGOROS	GNNORYY	GYRONNY
GINORTT	ROTTING	GIOPRRU	PRURIGO	GNNOSUW	UNGOWNS
GINORTU	OUTGRIN	GIOPSSS	GOSSIPS	GNNOUUY	UNYOUNG
	OUTRING	GIOPSST	SPIGOTS	GNNRUUW	UNWRUNG
	ROUTING	GIOPSSY	GOSSIPY	GNNSTUU	UNSTUNG
	TOURING	GIOPSTU	PIGOUTS	GNOOORS	GORSOON
GINORTW	ROWTING	GIORRSU	RIGOURS	GNOOOSS	GOSSOON
	TROWING	GIORSTU	OUTRIGS	GNOOOYZ	ZOOGONY
GINOSSS	SOSSING		RIGOUTS	GNOORST	TROGONS
GINOSST	STINGOS	GIORSUV	VIGOURS	GNOPPSU	OPPUGNS
	TOSSING	GIOSSYZ	ZYGOSIS		POPGUNS
GINOSSU	SOUSING	GISWWYY	WYSIWYG	GNOPRTU	GUNPORT
GINOSSW	SOWINGS	GJLMUUU	JUGULUM	GNOPRUW	GROWNUP
	SOWSING	GJNOOSU	GOUJONS		UPGROWN
GINOSTT	SOTTING	GJNRSUU	GURJUNS	GNOPSTU	POTGUNS
GINOSTU	OUSTING	GJOORTT	JOGTROT	GNORTUU	OUTRUNG
	OUTINGS	GKKNOOS	SONGKOK	GNOSTUU	OUTGUNS
	OUTSING	GKMOOSU	GOMOKUS		OUTSUNG
	TOUSING	GLLLOOR	LOGROLL	GNPSUUW	UPSWUNG
GINOSTV	STOVING	GLLOOPS	GOLLOPS	GOOOORS	GOOROOS
	VOTINGS	GLMMSUU	SLUMGUM	GOOPRST	GOSPORT
GINOSTW	STOWING	GLMNOOO	MONOLOG	GOORSTT	GROTTOS
	TOWINGS	GLMNOOS	MONGOLS	GOORTUW	OUTGROW
	TOWSING	GLMNUUU	UMLUNGU	GOPRSUW	UPGROWS
GINOSTY	TOYINGS	GLMOOOR	MOORLOG	GORRSTU	TURGORS
GINOTTT	TOTTING	GLMOOYY	MYOLOGY	GORSTTU	GUTROTS
GINOTTU	TOUTING	GLMORUW	LUGWORM		ROTGUTS
GINOTTW	TOWTING	GLNNOOR	LORGNON	GORSTUY	YOGURTS
	WOTTING	GLNNSUU	UNSLUNG	HHIIPPS	HIPPISH
GINOTUW	OUTWING	GLNOOOS	OOLONGS	HHIISTW	WHITISH
GINOTUZ	TOUZING	GLNOOOY	NOOLOGY	HHIMRTY	RHYTHMI
GINOTWZ	TOWZING	GLNOOPR	PROLONG	HHINNSU	HUNNISH
GINPPPU	PUPPING	GLNOOPY	POLYGON	HHINORS	HORNISH
GINPPSU	SUPPING	GLNOOSU	OULONGS	HHIOPST	HIPSHOT
	UPPINGS	GLNORWY	WRONGLY	HHIORSW	WHORISH
GINPPTU	TUPPING	GLNOSUW	SUNGLOW	HHIOSTT	HOTTISH
GINPRRU	PURRING	GLNOTTU	GLUTTON	HHISSTW	WHISHTS
GINPRSS	SPRINGS	GLNOUYY	YOUNGLY	HHMMSUU	HUMHUMS
GINPRSU	PURSING	GLNPSUU	UNPLUGS	HHMRSTY	RHYTHMS
GINPRSY	PRYINGS	GLOOORY	OROLOGY	HHOOSTT	HOTSHOT
	PRYSING	GLOOOTY	OTOLOGY	HIIIKRS	RIKISHI
	SPRINGY	GLOOOYZ	ZOOLOGY	HIIISTV	SHIVITI
GINPSSY	SPYINGS	GLOOPRS	PROLOGS	HIIJKNS	HIJINKS
GINPSTU	PIGNUTS	GLOORUY	UROLOGY	HIIKLMS	KHILIMS
	STUPING	GLOOSTU	LOGOUTS	HIIKNNS	SHINKIN
GINPSTY	TYPINGS	GLOOTUW	OUTGLOW	HIIKNPS	KINSHIP
GINPSUW	UPSWING	GLOPSTU	PUTLOGS		PINKISH
GINPTTU	PUTTING	GLORSSY	GROSSLY	HIILMTU	LITHIUM
GINPTUY	UPTYING	GLPRSUY	SPLURGY	HIILNSY	SHINILY
GINPTUZ	PUTZING	GMMOSUU	GUMMOUS	HIILPST	SHILPIT
GINQTUY	QUYTING	GMMPUUW	MUGWUMP	HIILPSU	HUIPILS
GINRRSU	RUNRIGS	GMNNOOS	GNOMONS	HIILPTY	PITHILY
GINRSST	STRINGS	GMNOORU	GUNROOM	HIILRTT	TRILITH
GINRSTU	RUSTING	GMNOORW	MORWONG	HIIMMSS	MISHMIS
GINRSTY	STRINGY	GMNSTUU	GUMNUTS	HIIMNSX	MINXISH
	STYRING	GMNSUUZ	MZUNGUS	HIIMPSW	WIMPISH
	TRYINGS	GMOOPRS	POGROMS	HIIMRSU	SHIURIM
GINRSUU	USURING	GMOOSTU	GOMUTOS	HIIMSSS	MISSISH
GINRTTU	RUTTING	GMORSUU	GRUMOUS	HIIMSST	MISHITS
GINSSSU	SUSSING	GMORTUW	MUGWORT	HIIMSTT	SHITTIM
GINSTTU	TUTSING	GMPSSUY	GYPSUMS	HIINNOT	THIONIN
GINSTTY	STYTING	GMRUVYZ	ZYMURGY	HIINORS	NOIRISH
GINTTTU	TUTTING	GNNOORS	ROGNONS		ROINISH

Seven-letter anagrams

HIINOSS	HOISINS	HILPSST	SPILTHS	HIOSSTT	SOTTISH
HIINPPS	HIPPINS	HILPSUY	PUSHILY	HIOSTTU	OUTHITS
HIINPSS	INSHIPS	HILSSTY	HYLISTS	HIOSTUW	OUTWISH
HIINSSW	SWINISH		STYLISH	HIOTTUW	OUTWITH
HIINSTW	WITHINS	HILSTTY	THISTLY		WITHOUT
HIIOPRS	POHIRIS	HILSTWY	SWITHLY	HIQSSUY	SQUISHY
HIIOPRW	POWHIRI	HILSTXY	SIXTHLY	HIRSSTT	THIRSTS
HIIOPRZ	RHIZOPI	HIMMPSU	MUMPISH		THRISTS
HIIORST	HISTRIO	HIMMRSU	RUMMISH	HIRSTTU	RUTTISH
HIIPSSW	WISPISH	HIMMSTY	MYTHISM	HIRSTTY	THIRSTY
HIIPSXY	PIXYISH	HIMNOOS	MOONISH		THRISTY
HIISTTT	TITTISH	HIMNOPR	MORPHIN		
HIJNSSU	SHINJUS	HIMNSSU	MUNSHIS	HJNNOOS	JOHNSON
HIKLNOT	HOTLINK	HIMNSTU	HUMINTS	HKKLOOS	KOLKHOS
HIKLSSU	LUSKISH	HIMNSTY	HYMNIST	HKKLOOZ	KOLKHOZ
HIKLSUY	HUSKILY	HIMOORS	MOORISH	HKKOOSY	SKYHOOK
HIKMNOS	MONKISH	HIMOPRS	ORPHISM	HKKOSTU	SUKKOTH
HIKMOTV	MIKVOTH		ROMPISH	HKLOOYZ	KOLHOZY
HIKMRSU	MURKISH	HIMOPSS	SOPHISM	HKNOOSS	SHNOOKS
HIKMSUZ	MUZHIKS	HIMOPST	PHOTISM	HKNOOSU	UNHOOKS
HIKNNOR	INKHORN	HIMORST	RIMSHOT	HKNOOWW	KNOWHOW
HIKNNTU	UNTHINK	HIMORSW	WORMISH	HKNSSUU	UNHUSKS
HIKNOOU	HOKONUI	HIMORTU	THORIUM	HKOOOPT	POTHOOK
HIKNPSU	PUNKISH	HIMOTTY	TIMOTHY	HKOOPSU	HOOKUPS
HIKNRSS	SHRINKS	HIMPRSS	SHRIMPS	HKOOSST	SHTOOKS
HIKOORS	ROOKISH	HIMPRSY	SHRIMPY	HKOOSVZ	SOVKHOZ
HIKOPSY	SKYPHOI	HIMPRTU	TRIUMPH	HKOPSSY	SKYPHOS
HILLOPT	HILLTOP	HIMPTUY	PYTHIUM	HKORSWY	WORKSHY
HILLOPY	LYOPHIL	HIMRSTY	RHYMIST	HLLOOSS	HOLLOOS
HILLPSU	UPHILLS	HIMSSTU	ISTHMUS	HLLOOSU	HULLOOS
HILLRSS	SHRILLS	HIMSTTY	MYTHIST	HLLOOSW	HOLLOWS
HILLRST	THRILLS	HINNNSU	NUNNISH	HLLOPSY	PHYLLOS
HILLRSY	SHRILLY	HINNORT	TINHORN	HLLPSUY	PLUSHLY
HILLRTY	THRILLY	HINNOST	TONNISH	HLMNOTY	MONTHLY
HILMMOU	HOLMIUM	HINNPSU	NUNSHIP	HLMNPYY	NYMPHLY
HILMOPS	LOMPISH	HINOOPS	INHOOPS	HLMOOSS	SHOLOMS
	PHLOMIS	HINOORT	HORNITO	HLMORRY	MYRRHOL
HILMOSS	HOLISMS	HINOORZ	HORIZON	HLMOSTY	THYMOLS
HILMOSW	WHOLISM	HINOOST	INSOOTH	HLMPSSU	SHLUMPS
HILMPSU	LUMPISH	HINOPPS	SHIPPON	HLMPSUY	SHLUMPY
HILMSSY	HYLISMS	HINOPSS	SIPHONS	HLOOPSS	SPLOOSH
HILMSUY	MUSHILY		SONSHIP	HLOOSTY	SOOTHLY
HILMTUU	THULIUM	HINORST	HORNIST	HLOOTUW	OUTHOWL
HILNNTY	NINTHLY	HINORSU	NOURISH	HLOPRTY	PROTHYL
HILNOPY	PHONILY	HINORSY	ROYNISH	HLOPSTY	PHYTOLS
HILNORY	HORNILY	HINOSST	STONISH	HLORSTY	SHORTLY
HILNOTY	THIONYL	HINOSSW	SNOWISH	HLOTUYY	YOUTHLY
HILNPST	PLINTHS	HINOSTW	TOWNISH	HLPRSUU	SULPHUR
HILOOST	OOLITHS	HINPPSU	PUSHPIN		UPHURLS
HILOOTT	OTOLITH	HINPSSU	UNSHIPS	HMMMSUU	HUMMUMS
HILOOTZ	ZOOLITH	HINPSTY	PHYTINS	HMMNOOY	HOMONYM
HILOPST	LITHOPS	HINPTUW	UNWHIPT	HMMOOSU	HOUMMOS
HILOPXY	OXYPHIL	HINRSTU	RUNTISH	HMMRTUY	THRUMMY
HILORSY	HORSILY	HIOOPRS	POORISH	HMNOPSY	NYMPHOS
HILORTU	UROLITH	HIOOSSV	SHIVOOS	HMNOPYY	HYPONYM
HILOSST	HOLISTS	HIOOSSW	WHOOSIS	HMNPSUY	HYPNUMS
HILOSSW	SLOWISH	HIOPPPS	POPPISH	HMOOPRS	MORPHOS
HILOSTU	LOUTISH	HIOPPSS	SHIPPOS	HMOORSS	SHROOMS
HILOSTW	WHOLIST	HIOPRSW	WORSHIP	HMOOSST	SMOOTHS
HILOSTY	HYLOIST	HIOPSST	SOPHIST	HMOOSTY	SMOOTHY
HILOSVW	WOLVISH	HIOPSSY	PHYSIOS	HMOOSUU	HOUMOUS
HILOSWY	SHOWILY	HIOPSTU	UPHOIST	HMORSUU	HUMOURS
HILOTWW	WHITLOW	HIORSSU	SOURISH	HMSTUYZ	ZYTHUMS
HILPRUW	UPWHIRL	HIORSTY	HISTORY	HNNOOPS	PHONONS
				HNNORSU	UNSHORN

HNNOSTY	SYNTHON	IIKLLSY	SILKILY	IIMOSSU	SIMIOUS
HNNOSUW	UNSHOWN	IIKLMNP	LIMPKIN	IIMRSST	SMRITIS
HNOOPST	PHOTONS	IIKLMRY	MIRKILY	IIMRSSU	SURIMIS
HNOOPSU	UNHOOPS	IIKLNOS	OILSKIN	IIMRSTW	MISWRIT
HNOOPTY	TYPHOON	IIKLPSY	SPIKILY	IIMRTTU	TRITIUM
HNOORSS	HORSONS	IIKLRSY	RISKILY	IIMRTUV	TRIVIUM
HNOORST	THORONS	IIKMNOR	KIRIMON	IIMSSSZ	SIZISMS
HNOORSU	HONOURS	IIKMNPS	SIMPKIN	IIMSSTT	TIMISTS
HNOOSTU	UNSHOOT	IIKMNSS	SIMKINS	IIMSSTU	MISSUIT
HNOPSSY	SYPHONS	IIKNPPS	PIPKINS	IINNOOP	OPINION
HNOPSTY	PHYTONS	IIKNSSS	SISKINS	IINNOPS	PINIONS
	PYTHONS	IIKOSST	OIKISTS		SPINONI
	TYPHONS	IIKOSTT	TITOKIS	IINNOTU	UNITION
HNORSTY	RHYTONS	IIKPSUW	WIKIUPS	IINNQSU	QUININS
HNORTUW	UNWORTH	IILLLSY	SILLILY	IINNQTU	QUINTIN
HNOSTUU	UNSHOUT	IILLMNO	MILLION	IINOPSS	ISOSPIN
HNOSUWY	UNSHOWY	IILLMSY	SLIMILY		SINOPIS
HNOTTUU	OUTHUNT	IILLNOP	PILLION	IINOPST	POITINS
HNRTTUU	UNTRUTH	IILLNOZ	ZILLION	IINORST	IRONIST
HNSSTUU	UNSHUTS	IILLNST	INSTILL	IINORSV	VIRINOS
HOOOOPS	HOOPOOS	IILLNTT	LITTLIN		VIRIONS
HOOPPST	POTSHOP	IILLPSU	ILLUPIS	IINORTT	INTROIT
HOOPRST	PORTHOS	IILMNOS	LIONISM	IINOSSV	VISIONS
HOOPSSY	SHYPOOS	IILMNSS	SIMLINS	IINOSUV	INVIOUS
HOOPSTT	HOTPOTS	IILMORS	SIMILOR	IINOTTU	TUITION
	HOTSPOT	IILMOSS	LIMOSIS	IINPPPS	PIPPINS
	POTSHOT	IILMSTU	STIMULI	IINQRUY	INQUIRY
HOOPSTU	UPSHOOT	IILMSTY	MISTILY	IINRTTY	TRINITY
HOOPSTY	TOYSHOP	IILNNOT	NITINOL	IINSSST	INSISTS
HOOQSSU	SQUOOSH	IILNNSU	INSULIN	IINSTTU	INTUITS
HOORRRS	HORRORS		INULINS	IINSTTW	INTWIST
HOORRST	ORTHROS	IILNNTY	TINNILY		NITWITS
HOORSUZ	HUZOORS	IILNOPT	PINITOL	IIOOSTT	TOITOIS
HOOSTTU	OUTSHOT	IILNORS	SIRLOIN	IIOPRSS	PISSOIR
HOPRSTU	HOTSPUR	IILNOSV	VIOLINS	IIOPSTY	PIOSITY
HOPRTTU	PRUTOTH	IILNOSY	NOISILY	IIORSSV	VIROSIS
HOPRTUW	UPTHROW	IILNPPY	NIPPILY	IIORSTV	IVORIST
HOPSSSY	HYSSOPS	IILNPUV	PULVINI		VISITOR
HOPSSTU	UPSHOTS	IILNRST	NITRILS	IIOSTTU	OUSTITI
HOPSTTU	SHOTPUT	IILNRSV	RIVLINS	IIPPSUU	PIUPIUS
HOPSTUU	OUTPUSH	IILNSST	INSTILS	IIPRRSU	PURIRIS
HOPSTUY	TYPHOUS	IILOPRT	TRIPOLI	IIPRSST	SPIRITS
HORSTTW	TROWTHS	IILOPST	PILOTIS		TRIPSIS
HORSTUU	OUTRUSH	IILORTV	VITRIOL	IIPRSTU	PITURIS
HOSSTTU	STOUTHS	IILOSTV	VIOLIST	IIPRSTY	SPIRITY
HOSTTUU	SHUTOUT	IILPRVY	PRIVILY	IIPRTVY	PRIVITY
HPPSSUU	PUSHUPS	IILPSST	PISTILS	IIQSTUV	QIVIUTS
HPRTTUU	THRUPUT	IILPSTY	TIPSILY	IIRRSTT	TIRRITS
HRSSTTU	THRUSTS	IILPSWY	WISPILY	IISSSTZ	SIZISTS
HRSSTUY	THYRSUS	IILRTYZ	RITZILY	IISTTZZ	TZITZIS
IIIJJLN	JINJILI	IILSTTT	TITLIST	IITTTZZ	TZITZIT
IIIKMNN	MINIKIN	IILTTUY	UTILITY	IJJMSUU	JUJUISM
IIIKMNS	MINISKI	IILTTWY	WITTILY	IJJSTUU	JUJITSU
IIIMRST	MIRITIS	IIMMMNU	MINIMUM		JUJUIST
IIIRSTT	TIRITIS	IIMMNSU	MINIMUS	IJKLLOY	KILLJOY
IIISTTW	WISTITI		MINIUMS	IJKMOSU	MOUJIKS
IIJKOPR	PIROJKI	IIMNNOS	MINIONS	IJKMSUZ	MUZJIKS
IIJLLNO	JILLION	IIMNOSS	MISSION	IJKNOSS	JOSKINS
IIJMMNY	JIMMINY	IIMNOSU	IONIUMS	IJLLLOY	JOLLILY
IIJMNOS	MISJOIN		NIMIOUS	IJLLOTY	JOLLITY
IIJNNOT	INJOINT	IIMNOTX	MIXTION		JOLTILY
IIKKLNY	KINKILY	IIMNPRT	IMPRINT	IJLMPUY	JUMPILY
IIKKNPS	KIPSKIN	IIMOPSU	IMPIOUS	IJLNOQU	JONQUIL
IIKLLMV	MILKILY	IIMOSST	MITOSIS	IJLNOTY	JOINTLY

IJMOSSS	JISSOMS	IKPRSSY	KRYPSIS	ILNOOST	LOTIONS
IJNNOTU	UNJOINT	ILLLOWY	LOWLILY		SOLITON
IJNORSU	JUNIORS	ILLMNOU	MULLION	ILNOPPS	POPLINS
IJNOTUX	OUTJINX	ILLMNRU	MILLRUN	ILNOPRU	PURLOIN
IJRSSTU	JURISTS	ILLMOOR	MOORILL	ILNOPST	PONTILS
IKKMNOU	KIKUMON	ILLMOOT	TIMOLOL	ILNOPSU	PULSION
IKKNNSU	UNKINKS	ILLMOPS	PLIMSOL		UPSILON
IKKNORT	KIRKTON	ILLMOSU	LOLIUMS	ILNOPSY	YPSILON
IKKORRS	KORKIRS	ILLMPUY	LUMPILY	ILNOPYY	POLYNYI
IKKSUUY	KIKUYUS	ILLMSUU	LIMULUS	ILNOQSU	QUINOLS
IKLLOTU	OUTKILL	ILLNOOY	LOONILY	ILNORST	NOSTRIL
IKLLPSU	UPSKILL	ILLNOQU	QUILLON	ILNORSU	SURLOIN
IKLLSTU	KILLUTS	ILLNORU	RULLION	ILNORTU	TORULIN
IKLLSUY	SULKILY	ILLNOST	LINTOLS	ILNOSST	TONSILS
IKLMNPU	LUMPKIN	ILLNPUU	LUPULIN	ILNOSSU	INSOULS
IKLMOOS	LOOKISM	ILLNSUW	UNWILLS	ILNOSTU	OILNUTS
IKLMOPS	MILKSOP	ILLNTUY	NULLITY		ULTIONS
IKLMOSY	SMOKILY	ILLOOPY	LOOPILY	ILNOSTY	STONILY
	SOYMILK	ILLOORZ	ZORILLO		TYLOSIN
IKLMRUY	MURKILY	ILLOPRY	PILLORY	ILNOSWY	SNOWILY
IKLMSUY	MUSKILY	ILLOPST	POLLIST	ILNOTUV	VOLUTIN
IKLNNSU	UNLINKS	ILLOPSW	PILLOWS	ILNPRSU	PURLINS
IKLNOOS	SKOLION	ILLOPWY	PILLOWY	ILNPSST	SPLINTS
IKLNOOT	KILOTON	ILLOSUV	VILLOUS	ILNPSTU	UNSPILT
IKLNOSU	ULIKONS	ILLOSUY	LOUSILY		UNSPLIT
IKLNPSU	LINKUPS	ILLOSWW	WILLOWS	ILNRSTY	NITRYLS
	SKULPIN	ILLOTUW	OUTWILL	ILNSSTU	INSULTS
	UPLINKS	ILLOTXY	XYLITOL	ILNSSVY	SYLVINS
IKLNRWY	WRINKLY	ILLOUVV	VOLVULI	ILNTTUY	NUTTILY
IKLNTWY	TWINKLY	ILLOWWY	WILLOWY	ILOOORS	ROSOLIO
IKLOOST	LOOKIST	ILLPOUY	PULPILY	ILOOPST	POLOIST
IKLOOTT	TOOLKIT	ILLPSUV	PULVILS		TOPSOIL
IKLOSSU	SOUSLIK	ILLQSSU	SQUILLS	ILOORST	LORIOTS
IKLSSSU	SUSLIKS	ILLRSUY	SURLILY	ILOORTY	OLITORY
IKLSTTU	KITTULS	ILLSTUY	LUSTILY	ILOOSST	SOLOIST
IKMNOOO	OKIMONO	ILMMRUY	RUMMILY	ILOOSTY	SOOTILY
IKMNOOR	OMIKRON	ILMMSSU	SLUMISM	ILOOWYZ	WOOZILY
IKMNOOS	KIMONOS	ILMMSUU	MIMULUS	ILOPPSY	SOPPILY
	MONOSKI	ILMNOOT	MOONLIT	ILOPRRY	PRIORLY
IKMNORS	MIKRONS	ILMNOOY	MOONILY	ILOPRSY	PROSILY
	MORKINS	ILMNOSU	MOULINS	ILOPRUY	ROUPILY
IKMNOSW	MISKNOW	ILMNRSU	MURLINS	ILOPSST	PISTOLS
IKMNPPU	PUMPKIN	ILMNSSU	MUSLINS		POSTILS
IKMNRSU	RUMKINS	ILMOORY	ROOMILY	ILOPSSX	OXSLIPS
IKMNRTU	TRINKUM	ILMOOSS	MOLOSSI	ILOPSTT	SPOTLIT
IKMOOST	MISTOOK	ILMOOSV	MOOLVIS	ILOPSTU	SLIPOUT
IKMOSSU	KOUMISS	ILMORSW	WORMILS	ILOPSUY	PIOUSLY
IKMPRSS	SKRIMPS	ILMORTU	TURMOIL	ILOQRSU	LIQUORS
IKMSSTU	MUSKITS	ILMOSTY	MOISTLY	ILORRSY	SORRILY
IKNNPSU	PUNKINS	ILMOSUY	MOUSILY	ILORSTU	TROILUS
IKNNPTU	UNPINKT	ILMPSSY	SLIMPSY	ILOSSTY	TOSSILY
IKNNSTU	UNKNITS	ILMPSTU	PLUMIST		TYLOSIS
IKNOOST	ISOKONT	ILMRSSY	LYRISMS	ILOSTTW	WITTOLS
IKNOPRW	PINWORK	ILMSSUY	MUSSILY	ILPPSSU	SLIPUPS
IKNOPST	INKPOTS	ILMSTUY	MUSTILY	ILPPSTU	PULPITS
	INKSPOT	ILMUYZZ	MUZZILY	ILPRSUY	PURSILY
IKNORSW	INWORKS	ILNNOOY	NONOILY	ILPSTTU	UPTILTS
IKNORTW	TINWORK	ILNNOPS	NONSLIP	ILRSSTU	TRISULS
IKNPSTU	SPUTNIK	ILNNORU	LINURON	ILRSSTY	LYRISTS
	UPKNITS	ILNNSUY	SUNNILY	ILRSTUY	RUSTILY
IKORSTU	TURKOIS	ILNOOPS	PLOSION	ILRTTUY	RUTTILY
IKOSSTU	OUTKISS	ILNOOPV	VOLPINO	ILSSTTU	LUTISTS
IKPRSSU	PRUSIKS	ILNOORS	ROSINOL	ILSSTTY	STYLIST
	SPRUIKS	ILNOOSS	SOLIONS	ILSTTUU	TITULUS

IMMMOSS	MOMISMS	IMQRSSU	SQUIRMS	INRSTTU	INTRUST
IMMNOSS	MONISMS	IMQRSUY	SQUIRMY	INSSTUU	SUNSUIT
	NOMISMS	IMRSSTU	SISTRUM		UNSUITS
IMMNOSU	MUSIMON		TRISMUS	INSTTUW	UNTWIST
	OMNIUMS		TRUISMS	INTTUWY	UNWITTY
IMMNOUU	MUONIUM	IMRTTUY	YTTRIUM	IOOPRSS	POROSIS
IMMOOSS	SIMOOMS	INNNOOR	NONIRON	IOOPRSV	PROVISO
IMMOPTU	OPTIMUM	INNNORU	RUNNION	IOOPSTY	ISOTOPY
IMMOSSU	OSMIUMS	INNOOPS	OPSONIN	IOORSSS	SOROSIS
IMMOSTU	STOMIUM	INNOORS	RONIONS	IOORSST	TSOORIS
IMMOSTW	WOMMITS	INNOOST	NOTIONS	IOORSTT	RISOTTO
IMMSSTU	MUTISMS	INNOPSY	PINYONS	IOORSTU	RIOTOUS
	SUMMIST	INNORST	INTRONS	IOOSSSS	SISSOOS
	SUMMITS	INNOSSU	UNISONS	IOOSSST	OSTOSIS
IMNNNOU	MUNNION	INNOSTU	NONSUIT	IOPPPRT	PITPROP
IMNNOOR	NORIMON	INNOSUY	UNNOISY	IOPPPST	POPPITS
IMNNOSW	MINNOWS	INNOSWW	WINNOWS	IOPPRST	RIPSTOP
IMNNSTU	MUNTINS	INNQSUY	SQUINNY	IOPPSTT	TIPTOPS
IMNOOPP	POMPION	INNRSTU	INTURNS	IOPRSST	RIPOSTS
IMNOOPT	TOMPION	INOOPRT	PORTION	IOPRSSY	PYROSIS
IMNOORR	MORRION	INOOPSS	POISONS	IOPRSTT	PROTIST
IMNOORS	MORIONS		POISSON		TROPIST
IMNOORT	MONITOR	INOOPST	OPTIONS	IOPSSTU	PISTOUS
	TROMINO		POSITON	IOPSTTU	UTOPIST
IMNOOSS	MONOSIS		POTIONS	IOPTTUY	OUTPITY
	SIMOONS	INOORSS	ORISONS	IOQRTTU	QUITTOR
IMNOOST	MOTIONS	INOORST	ISOTRON	IOQSSTU	QUOISTS
IMNOOSU	OMINOUS		NITROSO	IORRSTW	WORRITS
IMNOOSY	ISONOMY		TORSION	IORRSZZ	RIZZORS
IMNOOUX	OXONIUM	INOORSZ	ZORINOS	IORRTTX	TORTRIX
IMNOPPU	PUMPION	INOORTT	TORTONI	IORSSTU	SUITORS
IMNOPRW	PINWORM	INOOSST	TOISONS		TSOURIS
IMNOPSU	SPUMONI	INOOSUX	NOXIOUS	IORSTTU	TOURIST
IMNORRU	MURRION	INOPPRS	POPRINS	IORSTTW	TWISTOR
IMNORTY	TRIONYM	INOPPST	TOPSPIN	IORTTUW	OUTWRIT
IMNOSST	MONISTS	INOPRSS	PRISONS	IOSSSTT	TSOTSIS
IMNOSSY	MYOSINS		SPINORS	IOSSTTU	OUTSITS
IMNOSVY	VISNOMY	INOPRST	TROPINS	IOSTTUW	OUTWITS
IMNRRSU	MURRINS	INOPRSU	INPOURS	IPPQSUU	QUIPPUS
IMNRSTU	UNTRIMS	INOPSST	PISTONS	IPRRSTU	IRRUPTS
IMOOPRX	PROXIMO		POSTINS		STIRRUP
IMOOSSS	OSMOSIS		SPINTOS	IPRSSTU	PURISTS
IMOOSSU	OSMIOUS	INOPSSU	POUSSIN		SPRUITS
IMOOSTV	VOMITOS		SPINOUS		UPRISTS
IMOPRSS	PORISMS	INOPSTT	TINPOTS		UPSTIRS
IMOPRST	IMPORTS	INOPSTU	SPINOUT	IPRSTUU	PURSUIT
	TROPISM	INORSTT	INTORTS	IPSSSTY	STYPSIS
IMOPRSV	IMPROVS		TRITONS	IPSSTTY	TYPISTS
IMOPRTU	PROTIUM	INORSTU	NITROUS	IPSTTTU	TITTUPS
IMOPSST	IMPOSTS		TURIONS	IPTTTUY	TITTUPY
	MISSTOP	INORSUU	RUINOUS	IQRRSSU	SQUIRRS
IMOPSTU	UTOPISM		URINOUS	IQRSSTU	SQUIRTS
IMORRRS	MIRRORS	INORSUV	UNVISOR	JJSTUUU	JUJUTSU
IMORSST	MISSORT	INOSSTT	STOTINS	JKNOOSU	KUNJOOS
IMORSTU	TOURISM	INOSSTU	OUTSINS	JLLOOPS	JOLLOPS
IMORSTY	TRISOMY		USTIONS	JMOPTUU	OUTJUMP
IMOSSTU	MISSOUT	INOSSUU	SINUOUS	JNNORUY	NONJURY
	SUMOIST	INOSTUW	OUTWINS	JNNOSTU	JOTUNNS
IMOSSYZ	ZYMOSIS	INPRSST	SPRINTS	JNOORSU	JOURNOS
IMOSTTT	TOMTITS	INPRSTU	TURNIPS		SOJOURN
IMOSTUV	VOMITUS		UNSTRIP	JOOPPSY	JOYPOPS
IMOSTUW	OUTSWIM	INPRSTY	TRYPSIN		POPJOYS
IMPRSSU	PURISMS	INQSSTU	SQUINTS	JOSTTUU	OUTJUTS
IMPSSTU	SUMPITS	INQSTUY	SQUINTY	KKLMSUU	MUKLUKS

Seven-letter anagrams

KKLOOYZ	KOLKOZY	LNNOPSU	NONPLUS	MOQSTUU	QUOTUMS
KKMOOSU	SKOOKUM	LNOOPSU	UNSPOOL	MORRSTU	ROSTRUM
KKMSTUU	MUKTUKS	LNOOPTU	PULTOON	MORRSUU	RUMOURS
KKNRSUU	KUNKURS	LNOOSST	STOLONS	MORSTUU	TUMOURS
KKSSSTT	TSKTSKS	LNOPSTU	PLUTONS	MOSSSTY	MYSOSTS
KLLMOSU	MOLLUSK		PULTONS	MOSSTTU	UTMOSTS
KLNOOPS	PLONKOS	LNOSSUU	UNSOULS	MOSSTUU	OUTSUMS
KLOOOTU	LOOKOUT	LNPSTUU	PULTUNS	MOSTUUW	OUTSWUM
	OUTLOOK	LNRTUUV	VULTURN	NNNSUUY	UNSUNNY
KLOOPSU	LOOKUPS	LNRTUUY	UNTRULY	NNOOOPR	NONPOOR
	UPLOOKS	LOOOORS	OLOROSO	NNOOOPT	PONTOON
KLOSTUU	OUTSULK	LOOORST	ROTOLOS	NNOOPRS	NONPROS
KLRSTUU	KULTURS	LOOPTTU	OUTPLOT	NNOOPRU	PRONOUN
KMOOORS	MOKOROS	LOOSSTV	VOLOSTS	NNOOPSS	SPONSON
KMOSSUY	KOUMYSS	LOPPRSY	PROPYLS	NNOOPST	NONSTOP
KMPRSSU	SKRUMPS	LOPPSUU	PULPOUS		PONTONS
KNNNOUW	UNKNOWN	LOPPSUY	POLYPUS	NNOORSY	RONYONS
KNNOORW	NONWORK	LOPRRSY	PYRROLS	NNOOSTW	WONTONS
KNNOSTU	UNKNOTS	LOPRSTY	PROTYLS	NNORSTU	TURNONS
KNOOPTT	TOPKNOT	LOPRSUY	PYLORUS	NNORSUW	UNSWORN
KNOPRTY	KRYPTON	LOPRTUY	POULTRY	NNOSSUY	UNSONSY
KNORRTY	KRYTRON	LOPSSTY	STYLOPS	NNOSTYY	SYNTONY
KNORSUW	UNWORKS	LORSTTY	TROTYLS	NNRSTUU	UNTURNS
KOOOTTU	OUTTOOK	LORSTUU	TORULUS	NOOOSUZ	OZONOUS
KOOPRTW	TOPWORK	LOSTTUY	STOUTLY	NOOOSVX	SONOVOX
	WORKTOP	LPRSSUU	SURPLUS	NOOPRSS	SPONSOR
KOORTUW	OUTWORK	MMNNOOV	MONONYM	NOOPRST	PROTONS
	WORKOUT	MMNOSSU	MUSMONS	NOOPSSY	POYSONS
KOOSSSU	KOUSSOS		SUMMONS	NOOPSUY	YOUPONS
KOOSSUU	SOUKOUS	MMOOPPS	POMPOMS	NOORSST	TONSORS
KOOSTTU	TUKTOOS	MMOOSTT	MOTMOTS	NOORSTU	UNROOST
KOOSTHW	KOWTOWS	MMOPSTY	SYMPTOM		UNROOTS
KOPRSUW	WORKUPS	MMRRSUU	MURMURS	NOORTUW	OUTWORN
KORTTUW	TUTWORK	MMSTUUU	MUTUUMS	NOOTTWY	TOYTOWN
LLLMMUU	MULMULL	MMSUUUU	MUUMUUS	NOPPRSU	UNPROPS
LLLOOPS	LOLLOPS	MNNOOOS	MONSOON	NOPSSTU	SUNSPOT
LLLOOPY	LOLLOPY	MNNOORU	MONURON		UNSTOPS
LLMMSUU	MULMULS	MNNOSYY	SYNONYM	NOPSTUW	UPTOWNS
LLMOOPR	ROLLMOP	MNNOTUU	UNMOUNT	NORSTUU	OUTRUNS
LLMPPUY	PLUMPLY	MNOOOPP	POMPOON		RUNOUTS
LLNORSU	UNROLLS	MNOOOYZ	ZOONOMY	NORTTUU	OUTTURN
LLOGPRT	ROLLTOP	MNOOPPS	POMPONS		TURNOUT
	TROLLOP	MNOOPST	TOMPONS	NOSSTUW	UNSTOWS
LLOOPSY	POLYOLS	MNOOPTY	TOPONYM	NPRSTUU	TURNUPS
LLOOPTU	OUTPOLL	MNOORSU	SUNROOM		UPTURNS
LLOORTU	OUTROLL		UNMOORS	NRSSTTU	STRUNTS
	ROLLOUT	MNOOSTU	MOUTONS	NRSSTUU	STURNUS
LLOOSTU	TOLUOLS	MNOOSTW	TOWMONS		UNTRUSS
LLOPRSU	UPROLLS	MNOOSUY	ONYMOUS	NRSTTUU	UNTRUST
LLOPTUU	OUTPULL	MNOOTTW	TOWMONT	OOOOPRT	POTOROO
	PULLOUT	MNORSTU	NOSTRUM	OOOOSZZ	ZOOZOOS
LLORSST	STROLLS	MNOSTTU	MUTTONS	OOOPRTU	OUTROOP
LLOSTUY	TOLUYLS	MNOTTUY	MUTTONY	OOORTTU	OUTROOT
LLPPSUU	PULLUPS	MOOOTYZ	ZOOTOMY	OOPPSST	POSTOPS
LMMSTUU	MULTUMS	MOOPPSU	POMPOUS	OOPRRST	TORPORS
LMOOOOS	MOOLOOS	MOOPRSY	POMROYS	OOPRSSU	SOURSOP
LMOORSU	ORMOLUS	MOOPSSU	OPOSSUM	OOPRSTU	PORTOUS
LMOOSTY	TOYLSOM	MOOPSTT	TOPMOST		UPROOTS
LMOPSUU	PLUMOUS	MOORRSW	MORROWS	OOPRSTV	PROVOST
LMORSSU	MUSROLS	MOOSTTU	OUTMOST	OOPRTTU	OUTPORT
LMRSTUU	LUSTRUM	MOPPRST	PROMPTS	OOPRTUU	OUTPOUR
LMSTTUU	TUMULTS	MOPSSSU	POSSUMS	OOPSSTT	TOSSPOT
LMSTUUU	TUMULUS	MOPSSUU	SPUMOUS	OOPSTTU	OUTPOST
LNNOOOW	NONWOOL	MOQRSUU	QUORUMS		OUTTOPS

OOPSWWW	POWWOWS	**OPPRSTY**	STROPPY	**ORRSTTU**	TRUSTOR
OORRSSW	SORROWS	**OPPRSUY**	PYROPUS	**ORSSSTU**	TUSSORS
OORSTUU	ROUTOUS	**OPRSSTU**	SPROUTS	**ORSSTTU**	STROUTS
OORSTUW	OUTROWS		STROUPS	**ORSSUUU**	USUROUS
OORTTTU	OUTTROT		STUPORS	**ORSTTUU**	SURTOUT
OPPPRSU	UPPROPS	**OPSSSTU**	TOSSUPS	**ORSTTUY**	TRYOUTS
OPPRRTU	PURPORT	**OPSTTUU**	OUTPUTS	**RSSSTUU**	TUSSURS
OPPRSTU	SUPPORT		PUTOUTS		

Eight-letter anagrams

AAAABCLZ	CALABAZA	**AAABDEHH**	DAHABEAH	**AAACCIMM**	CAIMACAM
AAAABENN	ANABAENA	**AAABDEST**	DATABASE	**AAACCLMS**	MALACCAS
AAAABKPS	BAASKAAP	**AAABDFRS**	ABFARADS	**AAACCLPS**	ALPACCAS
AAAACCRR	CARACARA	**AAABDHHI**	DAHABIAH	**AAACCLRS**	CARACALS
AAAACGNR	CARAGANA	**AAABDHHL**	HABDALAH	**AAACCRSS**	CASCARAS
AAAACJRR	JARARACA	**AAABDHIY**	DAHABIYA	**AAACCRTT**	CATARACT
AAAACLMT	CALAMATA	**AAABDIKR**	BAIDARKA	**AAACDDRT**	DATACARD
AAAACNRS	ANASARCA	**AAABDKNT**	DATABANK	**AAACDEIM**	ACADEMIA
AAAADMTV	AMADAVAT	**AAABDLMS**	LAMBADAS	**AAACDELM**	ACELDAMA
AAAADNPS	APADANAS	**AAABDNNN**	BANDANNA	**AAACDEMN**	ADAMANCE
AAAADTVV	AVADAVAT	**AAABDNNS**	BANDANAS	**AAACDENR**	DRACAENA
AAAAHJMR	MAHARAJA	**AAABDNRS**	SARABAND	**AAACDEQU**	AQUACADE
AAAAIKMN	KAMAAINA	**AAABDNRT**	ABRADANT	**AAACDETU**	ACAUDATE
AAAAIMPR	ARAPAIMA	**AAABEGHL**	GALABEAH	**AAACDFIR**	FARADAIC
AAAAIRTX	ATARAXIA	**AAABEGLL**	GALLABEA	**AAACDILR**	CALDARIA
AAAAJKRR	JARARAKA	**AAABEGLS**	GALABEAS	**AAACDINR**	ACARIDAN
AAAAKKMT	TAKAMAKA	**AAABEHNR**	HABANERA		ARCADIAN
AAAAKKNT	KATAKANA	**AAABEHRT**	BARATHEA	**AAACDIRS**	ARCADIAS
AAAAKKVV	KAVAKAVA	**AAABEMPR**	PARABEMA	**AAACDKLY**	LACKADAY
AAAAKKWW	KAWAKAWA	**AAABENSS**	ANABASES	**AAACDMMS**	MACADAMS
AAAAKLMT	KALAMATA	**AAABFLLS**	FALBALAS	**AAACDMNY**	ADAMANCY
AAAALLVV	LAVALAVA	**AAABGHIL**	GALABIAH	**AAACDNNO**	ANACONDA
AAAALSTY	ATALAYAS	**AAABGILL**	GALLABIA	**AAACDNRS**	SANDARAC
AAAAMMTT	MATAMATA	**AAABGILS**	GALABIAS	**AAACDOTV**	ADVOCAAT
AAAAPPRR	PARAPARA	**AAABGILY**	GALABIYA	**AAACEGNT**	AGACANTE
AAAARRSS	SASARARA	**AAABGLNY**	BANGALAY	**AAACEGTU**	AGUACATE
AAABBCHL	CABBALAH	**AAABGLOR**	ALGAROBA	**AAACEHIN**	ACHAENIA
AAABBCLS	CABBALAS	**AAABGMNQ**	MBAQANGA	**AAACEHLR**	ARCHAEAL
AAABBELT	ABATABLE	**AAABGRTU**	RUTABAGA	**AAACEHLT**	CALATHEA
AAABBHKL	KABBALAH	**AAABHLQS**	QABALAHS	**AAACEHLZ**	CHALAZAE
AAABBILT	ABBATIAL	**AAABHMST**	MASTABAH	**AAACEHNR**	ARCHAEAN
AAABBKLS	KABBALAS	**AAABILTT**	BATTALIA	**AAACEHNT**	ACANTHAE
AAABCCMW	MACCABAW	**AAABINSS**	ANABASIS	**AAACELNT**	ANALECTA
AAABCCRS	BACCARAS	**AAABIPSS**	PIASABAS	**AAACELST**	CATALASE
AAABCCRT	BACCARAT		PIASSABA	**AAACENNP**	PANACEAN
AAABCHIR	ABRACHIA	**AAABISTV**	BATAVIAS	**AAACENPS**	PANACEAS
AAABCHLS	CALABASH	**AAABKLSV**	BAKLAVAS	**AAACGHNR**	CHARANGA
AAABCHMU	MACAHUBA	**AAABKLSW**	BAKLAWAS	**AAACGINT**	CAATINGA
AAABCILP	ABAPICAL	**AAABKPSS**	BAASKAPS	**AAACGLSW**	SCALAWAG
AAABCINT	ANABATIC		BAASSKAP	**AAACGMNP**	CAMPAGNA
AAABCIRS	ARABICAS	**AAABLLSW**	WALLABAS	**AAACGMNR**	ARMAGNAC
AAABCITT	CIABATTA	**AAABLMOS**	ABOMASAL	**AAACHHLS**	HALACHAS
AAABCLOS	BACALAOS	**AAABLMST**	TAMBALAS	**AAACHILZ**	CHALAZIA
AAABCLSV	BACLAVAS	**AAABLOPR**	PARABOLA	**AAACHIPS**	APHASIAC
AAABCNRR	BARRACAN	**AAABLPRS**	PALABRAS	**AAACHLLZ**	CHALAZAL
	BARRANCA	**AAABMSST**	MASTABAS	**AAACHLNR**	ANARCHAL
AAABCNRS	BARACANS	**AAABNNRS**	RABANNAS	**AAACHLSZ**	CHALAZAS
AAABCNRU	CARNAUBA	**AAABORRS**	ARAROBAS	**AAACHNST**	ACANTHAS
AAABCORS	CARABAOS	**AAACCELN**	CALCANEA	**AAACHRSY**	ACHARYAS
AAABCPRY	CAPYBARA	**AAACCEPR**	CARAPACE	**AAACILMN**	MANIACAL
AAABCSSS	CASSABAS	**AAACCHMP**	CHAMPACA	**AAACILMR**	CALAMARI
AAABCSTW	CATAWBAS	**AAACCILR**	CALCARIA	**AAACILMS**	MALACIAS

AAACILOS	ALOCASIA
AAACILPR	CARPALIA
AAACILRV	CALVARIA
AAACILSY	CALISAYA
AAACIMRS	CARIAMAS
AAACINPS	ACAPNIAS
AAACINTV	CAVATINA
AAACIPSU	SAPUCAIA
AAACIRRS	SACRARIA
AAACIRSS	ACRASIAS
AAACIRTX	ATARAXIC
AAACJMRS	JACAMARS
AAACKLMN	ALMANACK
AAACKMRT	TAMARACK
AAACLLSV	CAVALLAS
AAACLMNS	ALMANACS
	MANCALAS
AAACLMRS	CALAMARS
AAACLMRY	CALAMARY
AAACLNST	CANTALAS
AAACLPST	CATALPAS
AAACLRST	ALCATRAS
AAACLRSZ	ALCAZARS
AAACMNPS	CAMPANAS
AAACMOST	ATAMASCO
AAACMRSS	MACASSAR
	MARASCAS
	MASCARAS
AAACMRSU	AMARACUS
AAACNNRS	CARANNAS
AAACNOPT	CAPONATA
AAACNPST	CATAPANS
AAACNRST	NACARATS
AAACNRSU	CARAUNAS
AAACNRSV	CARAVANS
AAACNSST	CANASTAS
AAACNSTT	CANTATAS
AAACRRWY	CARRAWAY
AAACRSWY	CARAWAYS
AAACSSST	CASSATAS
AAACSSSV	CASSAVAS
AAACSSTT	CATASTAS
AAACSTWY	CASTAWAY
AAADEFGN	FANEGADA
AAADEFHY	FADEAWAY
AAADEGNP	APANAGED
AAADEIHZ	MAZAEDIA
AAADEJMP	PAJAMAED
AAADELMS	ALAMEDAS
	SALAAMED
AAADEMNP	EMPANADA
AAADENTV	VANADATE
AAADEPRT	TAPADERA
AAADFRSY	FARADAYS
AAADGGHH	HAGGADAH
AAADGGHS	AGGADAHS
	HAGGADAS
AAADGIMM	GAMMADIA
AAADGLMY	AMYGDALA
AAADGLNS	SALADANG
AAADHHLV	HAVDALAH
AAADHHSS	SHAHADAS
AAADHMMS	HAMMADAS
AAADHMRS	ADHARMAS
	HARAMDAS
	MADRASAH
AAADHNRT	THANADAR
AAADHNSS	SADHANAS
AAADIILR	RADIALIA
AAADILLP	PALLADIA
AAADILRU	ADULARIA
AAADIMNS	DAMIANAS
AAADIMNY	ADYNAMIA
AAADIRST	DATARIAS
	RADIATAS
AAADJMRS	JAMADARS
AAADKLMN	KALAMDAN
AAADKNSW	WAKANDAS
AAADKRRV	AARDVARK
AAADLMNQ	QALAMDAN
AAADLMNS	AMANDLAS
	MANDALAS
AAADLMSW	WADMAALS
AAADMNST	ADAMANTS
AAADMNTU	TAMANDUA
AAADMORT	MATADORA
AAADMPPP	PAPPADAM
AAADMPPS	PAPADAMS
AAADMRSS	MADRASAS
	MADRASSA
AAADNRSS	SARDANAS
AAADNRST	TANADARS
AAADSWYY	AWAYDAYS
AAAEEKRR	KAREAREA
AAAEGISS	ASSEGAAI
AAAEGLMX	MALAXAGE
AAAEGLRT	ALTARAGE
AAAEGLST	GALATEAS
AAAEGNPP	APPANAGE
AAAEGNPS	APANAGES
AAAEGRST	GASTRAEA
AAAEHLMT	HAEMATAL
AAAEHLST	ALTHAEAS
AAAEHMNT	ANATHEMA
AAAEHNPS	ANAPHASE
AAAEHPTU	PAHAUTEA
AAAEIMNS	ANAEMIAS
AAAEKKRT	KARATEKA
AAAEKTWY	TAKEAWAY
AAAELMMN	ANALEMMA
AAAELMPT	PALAMATE
AAAELMTX	MALAXATE
AAAELNPT	PANATELA
AAAELRTV	LAVATERA
AAAEMRST	TARAMEAS
AAAENNSS	ANANASES
AAAENOPR	PARANOEA
AAAENPRV	PARAVANE
AAAENPST	ANAPAEST
AAAENSST	ANATASES
AAAEPRST	SEPARATA
AAAERSWY	AREAWAYS
AAAERTWY	TEARAWAY
AAAFFLLS	ALFALFAS
AAAFHHRT	HAFTARAH
AAAFHRST	HAFTARAS
AAAFINST	FANTASIA
AAAFINUV	AVIFAUNA
AAAFIRST	RATAFIAS
AAAFLLWY	FALLAWAY
AAAFMQRU	AQUAFARM
AAAFNRSS	SARAFANS
AAAFRSWY	FARAWAYS
AAAGGLLN	GALANGAL
AAAGGLNS	GALANGAS
AAAGGLOP	GALAPAGO
AAAGHINR	HIRAGANA
AAAGHIPR	AGRAPHIA
AAAGHIPS	APHAGIAS
AAAGHLNS	LANGAHAS
AAAGHNNT	AGNATHAN
AAAGHNSS	SAGANASH
AAAGHNST	ATAGHANS
AAAGHNTY	YATAGHAN
AAAGILMM	MAMALIGA
AAAGILNS	ANALGIAS
AAAGILPT	PATAGIAL
AAAGILRT	ALIGARTA
AAAGIMMT	GAMMATIA
AAAGINRR	AGRARIAN
AAAGINRS	ANGARIAS
AAAGINSZ	GAZANIAS
AAAGISSS	ASSAGAIS
AAAGJMSU	MAJAGUAS
AAAGKNRS	KARANGAS
AAAGLMMS	AMALGAMS
AAAGLMNS	MALANGAS
	NAGMAALS
AAAGLNSS	LASAGNAS
AAAGLNTV	GALAVANT
AAAGLRRW	WARRAGAL
AAAGLRST	ASTRAGAL
AAAGMNRS	ANAGRAMS
AAAGMPRR	PARAGRAM
AAAGNOPR	ARAPONGA
AAAGNPRS	PARASANG
	PARGANAS
AAAGNPRU	ARAPUNGA
AAAGNRST	TANAGRAS
AAAGNRSU	GUARANAS
AAAGNSTY	YATAGANS
AAAHHHKL	HALAKHAH
AAAHHKLS	HALAKAHS
	HALAKHAS
AAAHHLLS	HALALAHS
AAAHHLSV	HALAVAHS
AAAHHPRS	PARASHAH
AAAHHPRT	HAPHTARA
AAAHHSTT	TATAHASH
AAAHIKPS	APHAKIAS
AAAHIKSW	KAHAWAIS
AAAHIMNR	MAHARANI
AAAHIMNS	SHAMIANA
AAAHIMRT	HAMARTIA
AAAHINPR	RAPHANIA
AAAHINRS	HARIANAS
AAAHIPSS	APHASIAS
AAAHIPTY	PITAHAYA
AAAHJKSW	KAJAWAHS
AAAHKMNS	KHANSAMA
AAAHKRSS	RAKSHASA
AAAHLMRS	HARMALAS

AAAHLNNS	ALANNAHS	AAALRRSY	ARRAYALS	AABBELOS	BAALEBOS
AAAHMMST	MAHATMAS	AAALSWYY	LAYAWAYS	AABBELOT	BOATABLE
AAAHMNRT	AMARANTH	AAAMMPRS	MAMPARAS	AABBELRR	BARRABLE
AAAHMRSS	ASHRAMAS	AAAMNNST	ANATMANS	AABBELRY	BEARABLY
AAAHMSST	TAMASHAS	AAAMNOPR	PANORAMA	AABBELSU	ABUSABLE
AAAHNNSV	SAVANNAH	AAAMNRRY	YARRAMAN	AABBEORT	BAREBOAT
AAAHNOPR	ANAPHORA	AAAMNRST	AMARANTS	AABBGRST	GABBARTS
AAAHNSTY	ATHANASY		MARANTAS	AABBHKSU	BABUSHKA
AAAHPRST	PARATHAS	AAAMNSTY	MANYATAS	AABBHSST	SABBATHS
AAAHRSTW	WARATAHS	AAAMNTTY	MANYATTA	AABBIILL	BILABIAL
AAAHSWWY	WASHAWAY	AAAMORST	TAMARAOS	AABBILRT	BARBITAL
AAAHTTWY	THATAWAY	AAAMOTTU	AUTOMATA	AABBIRSU	BABIRUSA
AAAIIMNP	APIMANIA	AAAMPRST	PATAMARS	AABBLLMY	BLAMABLY
AAAIINPR	APIARIAN	AAAMPRTT	PATTAMAR	AABBLORS	BARBOLAS
AAAIKKMM	KAIMAKAM	AAAMRRSZ	ZAMARRAS	AABBLSSU	SUBBASAL
AAAIKKRS	KARAKIAS	AAAMRSSS	SAMSARAS	AABBMMOZ	ZAMBOMBA
AAAIKLST	LATAKIAS	AAAMRSTU	TAMARAUS	AABBSSSU	BABASSUS
AAAIKRSS	AKRASIAS	AAAMRTTU	TRAUMATA	AABCCCHI	BACCHIAC
AAAILLMR	MALARIAL	AAAMRTZZ	RAZMATAZ	AABCCDET	BACCATED
AAAILLPT	PALATIAL	AAANNSSV	SAVANNAS	AABCCEHK	BACKACHE
AAAILMNR	MALARIAN	AAANNSTT	ANNATTAS	AABCCELS	CASCABEL
AAAILMRS	MALARIAS	AAANOPRZ	PARAZOAN		CASCABLE
	RASMALAI	AAANORSY	SAYONARA	AABCCERT	BRACCATE
AAAILMSV	MALVASIA	AAANPRTV	PARAVANT	AABCCHHS	BACHCHAS
AAAILNPR	PLANARIA	AAANQTUU	AQUANAUT	AABCCHIN	BACCHIAN
AAAILNRU	AULARIAN	AAANRSTT	TANTARAS	AABCCHIS	BISCACHA
AAAILPRS	PARASAIL		TARANTAS	AABCCHIZ	BIZCACHA
AAAILPRV	PARAVAIL		TARTANAS	AABCCHKS	CASHBACK
AAAILPRX	PARAXIAL	AAAORSWY	SOARAWAY	AABCCHKT	BACKCHAT
AAAILPSS	APLASIAS	AAAPPRST	APPARATS	AABCCHNT	BACCHANT
AAAILQRU	AQUARIAL	AAAPQRTU	PARAQUAT	AABCCIMR	CARBAMIC
AAAILRST	SALARIAT	AAAPSSST	PASSATAS	AABCCINN	CANNABIC
AAAIMMQQ	QAIMAQAM	AAARSTTT	RATATATS	AABCCKKP	BACKPACK
AAAIMMST	MIASMATA	AAARSTTU	TUATARAS	AABCCKLL	CALLBACK
AAAIMNRR	MARINARA	AAASTWYY	STAYAWAY	AABCCKLP	BLACKCAP
AAAIMNST	AMANITAS	AABBBDEK	KABABBED	AABCCKLW	CLAWBACK
AAAIMRSU	MAIASAUR	AABBBELS	BABBELAS	AABCCKST	BACKCAST
AAAINNRR	RANARIAN	AABBCDEG	CABBAGED		SCATBACK
AAAINOPR	PARANOIA	AABBCDKN	BACKBAND	AABCCMOT	CATACOMB
AAAINPSS	PAISANAS	AABBCDRS	SCABBARD	AABCCMOY	MACCABOY
AAAINQRU	AQUARIAN	AABBCEGS	CABBAGES	AABCDEIN	ABIDANCE
AAAIPRST	ASPIRATA	AABBCEGY	CABBAGEY	AABCDEIT	ABDICATE
AAAIPRSX	APRAXIAS	AABBCEIS	ABBACIES	AABCDEKT	BACKDATE
AAAIPSSV	PIASAVAS	AABBCEKR	BAREBACK	AABCDELL	CABALLED
	PIASSAVA	AABBCEKT	BACKBEAT	AABCDELN	BALANCED
AAAISSST	ASTASIAS	AABBCINR	BARBICAN	AABCDHKN	BACKHAND
AAAKKTZZ	KAZATZKA	AABBCIRR	BARBARIC	AABCDHKR	HARDBACK
AAAKLMSV	YAMALKAS	AABBCIST	SABBATIC	AABCDIIS	DIABASIC
AAAKLWWY	WALKAWAY	AABBCKST	BACKSTAB	AABCDILL	BALLADIC
AAAKMNRS	NAMASKAR	AABBCMOS	CABOMBAS	AABCDILR	ALDICARB
AAAKMTUU	KAUMATUA	AABBCORS	BARBASCO	AABCDILU	BICAUDAL
AAAKOSWY	SOAKAWAY	AABBDENS	BASEBAND	AABCDIMS	DICAMBAS
AAAKPPSU	KAUPAPAS	AABBDERT	BARBATED	AABCDINT	ABDICANT
AAALLPRX	PARALLAX	AABBDGRS	GABBARDS	AABCDIRS	CARABIDS
AAALLPST	PALATALS	AABBEELR	BEARABLE	AABCDKLN	BACKLAND
AAALMMOR	MALAROMA	AABBEELT	BEATABLE	AABCDKLO	BACKLOAD
AAALMPST	TAMPALAS	AABBEGNS	BEANBAGS	AABCDKNR	BANKCARD
AAALMRSS	MARSALAS	AABBEILL	BAILABLE	AABCDKRW	BACKWARD
AAALNNPT	PLATANNA	AABBEISS	BABESIAS		DRAWBACK
AAALNNST	LANTANAS	AABBEKLN	BANKABLE	AABCDKRY	BACKYARD
AAALNPRT	RATAPLAN	AABBELLM	BLAMABLE	AABCDLNS	SCABLAND
AAALNPST	APLANATS	AABBELLN	BEANBALL	AABCDNRR	BRANCARD
AAALNRTT	TARLATAN	AABBELLS	BASEBALL	AABCDNST	CABSTAND
AAALPRST	SATRAPAL	AABBELNN	BANNABLE	AABCEEFL	FACEABLE

AABCEEHS	SEABEACH	AABCHKSW	BACKWASH	AABCSTTU	CATTABUS
AABCEENY	ABEYANCE	AABCHLOO	COOLABAH	AABDDEET	DEADBEAT
AABCEERS	SCARABEE	AABCHMRY	CHAMBRAY	AABDDEGN	BANDAGED
AABCEERT	ACERBATE	AABCHNRS	BARCHANS	AABDDEHL	BALDHEAD
AABCEFRS	FACEBARS	AABCIILR	BIRACIAL	AABDDEHN	HEADBAND
AABCEGOT	CABOTAGE	AABCIILS	BASILICA	AABDDEIR	ABRAIDED
AABCEHKL	HACKABLE	AABCIINR	BRAINIAC	AABDDELL	BALLADED
AABCEHLS	CASHABLE	AABCIKLT	TAILBACK	AABDDENR	BRANDADE
AABCEHMS	AMBACHES	AABCILLR	BACILLAR	AABDDERT	TABARDED
AABCEHNR	BARCHANE		CABRILLA	AABDDESS	BADASSED
AABCEILM	AMICABLE	AABCILMS	BALSAMIC	AABDDIKS	KABADDIS
AABCEIMN	AMBIANCE		CABALISM	AABDDINZ	ZINDABAD
AABCEINR	CARABINE	AABCILMY	AMICABLY	AABDDLNS	BADLANDS
AABCEIRT	BACTERIA	AABCILNN	CANNIBAL	AABDDMOR	DAMBOARD
AABCEITT	CIABATTE	AABCILNO	ANABOLIC	AABDDMRU	MURDABAD
AABCEKLM	CLAMBAKE	AABCILOR	BRACIOLA	AABDDNSS	SANDDABS
AABCEKLP	PACKABLE	AABCILST	BASALTIC	AABDEEHL	BEHEADAL
AABCEKLR	LACEBARK		CABALIST	AABDEEHR	BAREHEAD
AABCEKLS	SACKABLE	AABCINNN	CANNABIN	AABDEELR	READABLE
AABCEKST	BACKSEAT	AABCINNR	CINNABAR	AABDEELT	DATEABLE
	SEATBACK	AABCINNS	CANNABIS		DEALBATE
AABCELLL	CALLABLE	AABCINOT	BOTANICA	AABDEELV	EVADABLE
AABCELLP	PLACABLE	AABCINRS	CARABINS	AABDEELW	WADEABLE
AABCELLR	CABALLER	AABCINSU	BANAUSIC	AABDEEMN	ENDAMEBA
AABCELLS	SCALABLE	AABCIOPS	COPAIBAS	AABDEERT	TEABREAD
AABCELNR	BALANCER	AABCIOSS	SCABIOSA	AABDEERY	BAYADEER
	BARNACLE	AABCIRSS	BRASSICA		BAYADERE
AABCELNS	BALANCES	AABCISSS	ABSCISSA	AABDEGHN	HEADBANG
AABCELOR	ALBACORE	AABCISTX	TAXICABS	AABDEGIN	BADINAGE
AABCELPR	CAPABLER	AABCKKLT	TALKBACK	AABDEGIR	BIGARADE
AABCELPS	SPACELAB	AABCKLNO	LOANBACK	AABDEGLR	GRADABLE
AABCELRS	BERASCAL	AABCKLNY	CLAYBANK	AABDEGMS	GAMBADES
AABCELRT	BRACTEAL	AABCKLPS	BACKSLAP	AABDEGNR	BANDAGER
	CARTABLE	AABCKLPY	PLAYBACK	AABDEGNS	BANDAGES
AABCELST	CASTABLE	AABCKLSY	LAYBACKS	AABDEGRR	BARRAGED
AABCELSU	CAUSABLE	AABCKNNS	CANBANKS	AABDEHHI	DAHABIEH
AABCELWY	CABLEWAY	AABCKNPS	SNAPBACK	AABDEHKR	HARDBAKE
AABCEMRT	CRABMEAT	AABCKPRT	BRATPACK	AABDEHMR	HARDBEAM
AABCEMRV	VAMBRACE	AABCKPRW	BACKWRAP	AABDEHNR	BAREHAND
AABCEMSS	AMBSACES	AABCKPSY	BACKPAYS	AABDEILN	BALADINE
AABCENYY	ABEYANCY		PAYBACKS	AABDEILR	RADIABLE
AABCEORS	ACARBOSE	AABCKRRS	BARRACKS	AABDEILT	LABIATED
AABCERRS	BARRACES	AABCKSSW	BACKSAWS	AABDEIOU	ABOIDEAU
AABCERST	ABREACTS	AABCKSTY	BACKSTAY	AABDEIRS	ARABISED
	BEARCATS	AABCKSWY	SWAYBACK	AABDEIRZ	ARABIZED
	CABARETS	AABCLLLO	COALBALL	AABDEISS	DIABASES
	CABRESTA	AABCLLLY	BALLCLAY	AABDEJLL	DJELLABA
AABCERTT	CABRETTA	AABCLLPY	PLACABLY	AABDEJNX	BANJAXED
AABCESSU	ABACUSES	AABCLLSY	SCALABLY	AABDEKPR	PARBAKED
AABCFHKL	HALFBACK	AABCLMRY	CARBAMYL	AABDEKRV	DAYBREAK
AABCFIIL	BIFACIAL	AABCLMSU	CALUMBAS	AABDEKSW	DAWBAKES
AABCFKLL	BACKFALL	AABCLNTY	BLATANCY	AABDELLS	BALLADES
	FALLBACK	AABCLNUU	CUNABULA	AABDELLT	BALLATED
AABCFKLT	FLATBACK	AABCLRRY	CARBARYL	AABDELLU	LAUDABLE
AABCFKST	FASTBACK	AABCLRSU	LABRUSCA	AABDELMN	DAMNABLE
	FATBACKS	AABCMMSU	MACUMBAS	AABDELMS	BALSAMED
AABCGIMO	CAMBOGIA	AABCMSSU	SAMBUCAS	AABDELNS	SANDABLE
AABCGKRY	GRAYBACK	AABCNORR	BARRANCO	AABDELOR	ADORABLE
AABCHHRS	BRACHAHS	AABCNRRS	CARBARNS	AABDELPR	DRAPABLE
AABCHILR	BRACHIAL	AABCORRS	CARBORAS		PARABLED
AABCHINR	BRANCHIA	AABCORST	ABACTORS	AABDELPT	BALDPATE
AABCHKLS	BACKLASH		ACROBATS	AABDELRS	BASELARD
AABCHKLU	BACKHAUL	AABCOSTT	CATBOATS	AABDELRT	TRADABLE
AABCHKRS	SHABRACK	AABCRSTT	ABSTRACT	AABDELRW	DRAWABLE

AABDELRY	READABLY	AABDLRSW	BRADAWLS	AABEFHKL	HALFBEAK
AABDELSW	SAWBLADE	AABDMNNS	BANDSMAN	AABEFLLL	FLABELLA
AABDELSY	ABASEDLY	AABDMNNY	BANDYMAN	AABEFLMO	FOAMABLE
AABDEMMS	BEMADAMS	AABDMNOR	BOARDMAN	AABEFLMR	FARMABLE
AABDEMNS	BEADSMAN	AABDMNRS	ARMBANDS		FRAMABLE
AABDEMNT	BANDMATE	AABDNNOS	ABANDONS	AABEFLMU	FLAMBEAU
AABDENSU	BANDEAUS	AABDNNTU	ABUNDANT	AABEFLTU	FABULATE
AABDENTU	UNABATED	AABDNORS	BANDORAS	AABEFNSS	FANBASES
AABDENUX	BANDEAUX	AABDNPSS	PASSBAND	AABEGGGS	BAGGAGES
AABDENVW	WAVEBAND	AABDNRRY	BARNYARD	AABEGGLY	GAGEABLY
AABDEORS	SEABOARD	AABDNRSS	SANDBARS	AABEGGRS	GARBAGES
AABDEORT	TEABOARD	AABDNRSU	BANDURAS	AABEGGRY	GARBAGEY
AABDEORX	BROADAXE	AABDNSSW	BANDSAWS	AABEGHIL	GALABIEH
AABDERRS	ABRADERS	AABDORSV	BRAVADOS	AABEGHLN	HANGABLE
AABDERRT	TABERDAR	AABDORTY	BOATYARD	AABEGHNR	BERGHAAN
AABDERRW	BEARWARD	AABDORWY	BROADWAY	AABEGILN	GAINABLE
AABDERTT	RABATTED		WAYBOARD	AABEGILT	AGITABLE
AABDERTV	VARTABED	AABDRRSS	BRASSARD	AABEGINR	ABEARING
AABDERWY	WAYBREAD	AABDRRSW	DRAWBARS	AABEGLLL	GLABELLA
AABDESSS	BADASSES	AABDRSST	BASTARDS	AABEGLLM	BALLGAME
AABDFHLN	FAHLBAND	AABDRSSU	SUBADARS	AABEGLNW	GNAWABLE
AABDGHNS	HANDBAGS	AABDRSTY	BASTARDY	AABEGLRS	ALGEBRAS
AABDGHRS	HARDBAGS	AABEEFLN	FLEABANE	AABEGLRT	GLABRATE
AABDGINN	ABANDING	AABEEGGL	GAGEABLE	AABEGLRU	ARGUABLE
AABDGINR	ABRADING	AABEEGKR	BRAKEAGE	AABEGLRZ	GRAZABLE
AABDGLNR	LANDGRAB		BREAKAGE	AABEGMNR	BARGEMAN
AABDGMOS	GAMBADOS	AABEEGLT	ABLEGATE	AABEGMNY	MANGABEY
AABDGNOV	VAGABOND	AABEEGNT	ABNEGATE	AABEGMRS	BERGAMAS
AABDGNSS	SANDBAGS	AABEEHLL	HEALABLE		MEGABARS
AABDGORR	GARBOARD	AABEEHLR	HEARABLE	AABEGMRT	BREGMATA
AABDGORT	TAGBOARD	AABEEHLT	HATEABLE	AABEGMTT	GAMBETTA
AABDGOTU	GADABOUT		HEATABLE	AABEGNOR	BARONAGE
AABDHINR	HAIRBAND	AABEEHMR	HARAMBEE	AABEGORT	ABROGATE
AABDHLLN	HANDBALL	AABEEKLM	MAKEABLE	AABEGOST	SABOTAGE
AABDHLLR	HARDBALL	AABEEKLT	TAKEABLE	AABEGOSZ	GAZABOES
AABDHNST	HATBANDS	AABEEKMT	BAKEMEAT	AABEGRRS	BAGARRES
AABDHNSY	HAYBANDS		MAKEBATE		BARRAGES
AABDHRSU	BAHADURS	AABEEKRW	BAKEWARE	AABEGRSS	BRASSAGE
	SUBAHDAR	AABEELLS	LEASABLE	AABEGSSS	BAGASSES
AABDIILR	BIRADIAL		SALEABLE	AABEGSSU	ABUSAGES
AABDIILS	BASIDIAL		SEALABLE	AABEHIRR	HERBARIA
AABDIKRS	BIDARKAS	AABEELMN	AMENABLE	AABEHJLL	JELLABAH
AABDILLN	BALLADIN		NAMEABLE	AABEHKLS	SHAKABLE
AABDILNS	BALADINS	AABEELMT	TAMEABLE	AABEHLMS	SHAMABLE
AABDIMNO	ABDOMINA	AABEELPR	REAPABLE	AABEHLOT	OATHABLE
AABDIMNR	MADBRAIN	AABEELPT	TAPEABLE	AABEHLPS	SHAPABLE
AABDIMRS	BARMAIDS	AABEELRS	ERASABLE	AABEHLPT	ALPHABET
AABDINNR	RAINBAND	AABEELRT	RATEABLE	AABEHLRS	SHARABLE
AABDINRS	BANDARIS		TEARABLE	AABEHLRW	WARHABLE
AABDINST	TABANIDS	AABEELRW	WEARABLE	AABEHLSV	SHAVABLE
AABDKNNS	SANDBANK	AABEELST	EATABLES	AABEHLSW	WASHABLE
AABDLLRY	BALLADRY		TEASABLE	AABEHNOR	HABANERO
	BALLYARD	AABEELSV	SAVEABLE	AABEHNST	ABTHANES
AABDLLUY	LAUDABLY	AABEEMNO	AMOEBEAN	AABEIJLL	JAILABLE
AABDLMNU	LABDANUM	AABEEMNT	ENTAMEBA	AABEIKLS	KIELBASA
AABDLMNY	DAMNABLY	AABEEMPR	ABAMPERE	AABEIKNS	IKEBANAS
AABDLMRU	ADUMBRAL	AABEENNW	WANNABEE	AABEILLL	ALLIABLE
AABDLNPT	PLATBAND	AABEENOR	ANAEROBE	AABEILLM	MAILABLE
AABDLNSS	SALBANDS	AABEERRT	ABERRATE	AABEILLS	ISABELLA
AABDLOOT	BOATLOAD	AABEERSZ	ZAREEBAS		SAILABLE
AABDLOPR	LAPBOARD	AABEERTT	TRABEATE	AABEILNR	INARABLE
AABDLORR	LABRADOR	AABEFFNS	BEFFANAS	AABEILNS	BANALISE
	LARBOARD	AABEFGLS	FLEABAGS	AABEILNZ	BANALIZE
AABDLORY	ADORABLY	AABEFGSU	AUFGABES	AABEILRS	RAISABLE

AABEILRV	VARIABLE	AABELOVW	AVOWABLE	AABGLLLO	GOALBALL
AABEILST	BALISTAE	AABELPPR	PALPEBRA	AABGLLRY	BALLYRAG
	LABIATES	AABELPPT	TAPPABLE	AABGLMNU	GALBANUM
	SATIABLE	AABELPRS	PARABLES	AABGLNOW	BANGALOW
AABEILTV	ABLATIVE		PARSABLE	AABGLRUY	ARGUABLY
AABEIMNR	AMBERINA		PREBASAL	AABGMORR	BAROGRAM
AABEIMRS	AMBARIES		SPARABLE	AABGNORZ	GARBANZO
AABEINOZ	ZABAIONE	AABELPSS	PASSABLE	AABHHISS	SAHIBAHS
AABEINRT	ATABRINE	AABELPSY	PAYABLES	AABHHKSS	SABKHAHS
	RABATINE	AABELRST	ARBALEST	AABHHORU	BROUHAHA
AABEINST	BASANITE		RATABLES	AABHHRSU	BRUHAHAS
AABEIOTU	ABOITEAU	AABELRTY	BETRAYAL	AABHIIMP	AMPHIBIA
AABEIRSS	AIRBASES		RATEABLY	AABHIINU	BAUHINIA
	ARABISES	AABELSST	BASALTES	AABHIJMY	JAMBIYAH
AABEIRSV	ABRASIVE	AABELSTT	ABETTALS	AABHILLR	HAIRBALL
AABEIRSZ	ARABIZES		STATABLE	AABHILTU	HABITUAL
AABEIRTU	AUBRETIA		TASTABLE	AABHIMNR	BRAHMANI
	AUBRIETA	AABELSTU	TABLEAUS	AABHINSS	HASBIANS
AABEISST	ABATISES	AABELSTW	WASTABLE	AABHINST	HABITANS
AABEJLLS	JELLABAS	AABELSTX	TAXABLES	AABHINTT	HABITANT
AABEJLMM	JAMMABLE	AABELSWY	SWAYABLE	AABHIRST	TABASHIR
AABEJMUX	JAMBEAUX	AABELTTU	TABULATE	AABHISTT	HABITATS
AABEJNOZ	ZABAJONE	AABELTUX	TABLEAUX	AABHKLLW	BALLHAWK
AABEJNSX	BANJAXES	AABEMMXY	MYXAMEBA	AABHKNRS	BARKHANS
AABEKLLS	SLAKABLE	AABENNSW	WANNABES	AABHKSST	SABKHATS
AABEKLLT	TALKABLE	AABENRRT	ABERRANT	AABHLLSW	WASHBALL
AABEKLLW	WALKABLE	AABENRST	ANTBEARS	AABHLMSY	SHAMABLY
AABEKLMS	MASKABLE		RATSBANE	AABHMNRS	BRAHMANS
AABEKMNR	BRAKEMAN	AABENRTU	ARBUTEAN	AABHMRSS	SAMBHARS
AABEKNSS	SEABANKS	AABEORRT	ARBORETA	AABHMSTT	BATHMATS
AABEKPRR	PARBREAK	AABEORST	AEROBATS	AABHNOTU	AUTOBAHN
AABEKPRS	PARBAKES		RABATOES	AABHQSSU	SQUABASH
AABEKRRS	BARESARK	AABEOSSU	OUBAASES	AABHRRSU	SURBAHAR
AABEKRSS	ARABESKS	AABEQSUU	USQUABAE	AABIIJLT	JAILBAIT
AABEKRSY	KERBAYAS	AABERRRT	BARRATER	AABIILSZ	ALBIZIAS
AABELLMT	MEATBALL	AABERRSW	BARWARES	AABIILZZ	ALBIZZIA
AABELLNO	LOANABLE	AABERSSU	SUBAREAS	AABIINST	ANTIBIAS
AABELLPP	PALPABLE	AABERSTT	RABATTES	AABIIPST	BAPTISIA
AABELLPS	LAPSABLE		TABARETS	AABIJMSY	JAMBIYAS
AABELLPY	PLAYABLE	AABERSTU	ABATURES	AABIKLMS	KABALISM
AABELLRS	EARBALLS	AABESZZZ	BAZAZZES		KALIMBAS
AABELLSS	SABELLAS	AABETTUX	BATTEAUX	AABIKLST	KABALIST
AABELLSV	SALVABLE	AABFILUX	FABLIAUX	AABIKNSS	BANKSIAS
AABELLSY	SALEABLY	AABFLLST	FASTBALL	AABILLLY	LABIALLY
	SLAYABLE	AABFLOTT	FALTBOAT	AABILLRS	BARILLAS
AABELLUV	VALUABLE		FLATBOAT	AABILLST	BALLISTA
AABELMNY	AMENABLY			AABILMNS	BAILSMAN
AABELMPP	MAPPABLE	AABGGGNN	GANGBANG	AABILMNU	BIMANUAL
AABELMST	BLASTEMA	AABGGNOT	TABOGGAN	AABILMQS	QABALISM
	LAMBASTE	AABGGRRT	BRAGGART	AABILMSS	BAALISMS
AABELMSU	AMUSABLE	AABGHINS	ABASHING	AABILNNU	BIANNUAL
AABELMTU	AMBULATE	AABGHKRS	SHAGBARK	AABILNOR	BARONIAL
AABELNNT	TANNABLE	AABGHNRS	BHANGRAS	AABILNOT	ABLATION
AABELNOS	ABALONES	AABGHNSS	NASHGABS	AABILNRT	BRANTAIL
AABELNOT	ATONABLE	AABGIILS	ABIGAILS	AABILNRU	BINAURAL
AABELNPS	ANABLEPS	AABGIINR	BRAAIING	AABILNTY	BANALITY
AABELNPT	PANTABLE	AABGILMS	MAILBAGS	AABILOST	SAILBOAT
AABELNPW	PAWNABLE	AABGILNT	ABLATING	AABILOSU	ABOULIAS
			BANGTAIL	AABILOTT	BOATTAIL
AABELNRY	BALNEARY	AABGIMNS	SAMBAING	AABILQST	QABALIST
AABELNSS	BANSELAS	AABGIMSU	GAMBUSIA	AABILRRT	ARBITRAL
AABELNST	BANALEST	AABGINRS	BARGAINS	AABILRST	ARBALIST
AABELOPR	PARABOLE	AABGINRY	ABRAYING	AABILRSU	BALISAUR
AABELORR	ARBOREAL	AABGINSS	BISNAGAS	AABILRSY	BASILARY
AABELOSV	LAVABOES	AABGINSZ	BIZNAGAS		

AABILRVY	VARIABLY	AABMMOSU	ABOMASUM	AACCERSS	CARCASES
AABILSST	BALISTAS	AABMNNOO	BONAMANO	AACCERTU	ACCURATE
AABILSTY	SATIABLY	AABMNOST	BOATSMAN		CARUCATE
AABILSUX	SUBAXIAL	AABMNOSY	AMBOYNAS	AACCFGOO	CACAFOGO
AABIMMRS	MARIMBAS	AABMNOTW	BATWOMAN	AACCFILR	FARCICAL
AABIMNNO	BONAMANI	AABMNRTU	RAMBUTAN	AACCFLTU	CALCTUFA
AABIMNOS	AMBOINAS	AABMORSU	MARABOUS	AACCGILT	GALACTIC
	BONAMIAS	AABMORTU	MARABOUT	AACCHHIL	HALACHIC
AABIMNRU	MANUBRIA		TAMBOURA	AACCHHKS	CHACHKAS
AABIMORS	AMBROSIA	AABMOSSU	ABOMASUS	AACCHHKT	CHATCHKA
AABIMRSU	SIMARUBA	AABMRSTU	TAMBURAS	AACCHILL	CAILLACH
AABIMSST	BASMATIS	AABNNOST	ABSONANT	AACCHILP	PACHALIC
AABINNPR	BRAINPAN	AABNNOSZ	BONANZAS	AACCHINR	ANARCHIC
AABINORS	ABRASION	AABNOSST	SABATONS		CHARACIN
AABINOSU	OUABAINS	AABNOSSY	SABAYONS	AACCHINS	CHICANAS
AABINRST	ATABRINS	AABORRRT	BARRATOR	AACCHIOR	AIRCOACH
	BARTISAN	AABORRSS	RASBORAS	AACCHISV	VISCACHA
AABINRTZ	BARTIZAN	AABORRSU	BAROSAUR	AACCHIVZ	VIZCACHA
AABINSST	ABSTAINS	AABORSTT	BAROSTAT	AACCHLLT	CATCHALL
AABIORRS	SORBARIA	AABRRRTY	BARRATRY	AACCHLNS	CLACHANS
AABIORSS	ABROSIAS	AABRRSST	BRASSART	AACCHLOR	CHARCOAL
AABIORST	AIRBOATS	AABRRSSU	SABURRAS	AACCHLOT	CACHALOT
AABIORSV	BAVAROIS	AABRRSUV	BRAVURAS	AACCHLRS	CLARSACH
AABIORTT	ABATTOIR	AABSSTUX	SAXTUBAS	AACCHMNO	COACHMAN
AABIOSSY	BIOASSAY	AABSTTTU	BATTUTAS	AACCHMPS	CHAMPACS
AABIPSUX	PAXIUBAS	AACCCDIS	SACCADIC	AACCHNNS	CANNACHS
AABIRSST	BARISTAS	AACCCFIO	FOCACCIA	AACCHNOR	CORANACH
	BARTSIAS	AACCCHHU	CACHUCHA	AACCHRST	CHARACTS
AABIRTUY	RUBAIYAT	AACCCRUY	ACCURACY	AACCIINV	VACCINIA
AABISTUZ	ZAIBATSU	AACCDDES	CASCADED	AACCIIST	SCIATICA
AABJLMNO	JAMBOLAN	AACCDEIM	ACADEMIC	AACCILMS	ACCLAIMS
AABJMRST	JAMBARTS	AACCDELO	ACCOLADE	AACCILNV	VACCINAL
AABKLLPR	BALLPARK	AACCDEMS	MEDACCAS	AACCILRU	ACICULAR
AABKMNNS	BANKSMAN	AACCDENU	CADUCEAN	AACCILSU	ACICULAS
AABKNRST	TANBARKS	AACCDERR	RACECARD	AACCILTT	TACTICAL
AABKOOSZ	BAZOOKAS	AACCDERS	CARCASED	AACCIMNU	CACUMINA
AABKOPRS	SOAPBARK		CARDCASE	AACCINSV	VACCINAS
AABKRSST	TASKBARS	AACCDESS	CASCADES	AACCIORS	CARIOCAS
AABLLMOR	BALMORAL		SACCADES	AACCIORU	CARIACOU
AABLLNST	BALLANTS	AACCDHIR	CHARACID	AACCIPRT	APRACTIC
AABLLORS	ALLOBARS	AACCDIIS	ACCIDIAS	AACCIPTY	CAPACITY
AABLLORY	ABORALLY	AACCDIRS	CARDIACS	AACCIRTY	CARYATIC
AABLLPPY	PALPABLY	AACCDOVY	ADVOCACY	AACCISTT	STACCATI
AABLLPRT	TRAPBALL	AACCEELT	CALCEATE	AACCJKRS	CARJACKS
AABLLPST	PATBALLS	AACCEENT	CETACEAN	AACCJKRW	CRACKJAW
AABLLSST	BALLASTS	AACCEFLO	COALFACE	AACCJORU	CARCAJOU
AABLLSTU	BLASTULA	AACCEFST	CATFACES		CARJACOU
AABLLSVY	SALVABLY	AACCEGOR	ACCORAGE	AACCKKPS	PACKSACK
AABLLUVY	VALUABLY	AACCEGRU	CARUCAGE	AACCKLOS	COALSACK
AABLMNOR	ABNORMAL	AACCEHIX	CACHEXIA	AACCKLPS	CALPACKS
AABLMNTU	AMBULANT	AACCEILN	CALCANEI	AACCKORT	COATRACK
AABLMOST	BLASTOMA	AACCEILU	ACICULAE	AACCKRRS	CARRACKS
AABLMRSU	LABARUMS	AACCEIRR	CERCARIA	AACCLLRU	CALCULAR
AABLMSST	LAMBASTS	AACCEKRS	CARCAKES	AACCLLST	CATCALLS
AABLNSSU	SUBNASAL	AACCELLY	CAECALLY	AACCLMNY	CLAMANCY
AABLNTTT	BLATTANT		CALYCEAL	AACCLOPS	POLACCAS
AABLORST	ABLATORS	AACCELOR	CARACOLE	AACCLORS	CARACOLS
AABLOTUY	LAYABOUT	AACCELPT	PLACCATE	AACCLPRS	CALCSPAR
AABLOVWY	AVOWABLY	AACCELRR	CARCERAL	AACCLPST	PLACCATS
AABLPSSY	PASSABLY	AACCELTY	CALYCATE	AACCLRSU	ACCRUALS
AABLRRSU	SABURRAL	AACCEMNU	CUMACEAN		CARACULS
AABLRSST	ARBLASTS	AACCENRT	CARCANET		SACCULAR
AABLRSUU	SUBAURAL	AACCENSV	VACANCES	AACCLSSU	ACCUSALS
AABLSTTU	ABUTTALS	AACCENTU	ACUTANCE	AACCLSTW	CATCLAWS

AACCNSTU	ACCUSANT	**AACDEKNS**	ASKANCED	**AACDHNOW**	WAHCONDA
AACCOPRS	ASCOCARP	**AACDEKTT**	ATTACKED	**AACDHNRS**	HANDCARS
AACCORSU	CURACAOS	**AACDELLN**	CALENDAL	**AACDHNRT**	HANDCART
	CURACOAS		CANALLED	**AACDHPRS**	CRASHPAD
AACCOSST	ACCOASTS	**AACDELLS**	ALCALDES	**AACDIINS**	ASCIDIAN
AACCOSTT	STACCATO	**AACDELMN**	MANACLED	**AACDIIRU**	ACIDURIA
	STOCCATA	**AACDELNR**	CALENDAR	**AACDILLP**	PALLADIC
	TOCCATAS		LANDRACE	**AACDILMN**	MANDALIC
AACCRRST	CARRACTS	**AACDELNS**	CANDELAS	**AACDILMT**	DALMATIC
AACDDEHI	ACIDHEAD	**AACDELNV**	VALANCED	**AACDILMU**	CALADIUM
AACDDEIL	DAEDALIC	**AACDELOS**	CASELOAD	**AACDILNO**	DIACONAL
AACDDENV	ADVANCED		ESCALADO	**AACDILNR**	CARDINAL
AACDDETU	CAUDATED	**AACDELPT**	PLACATED	**AACDILNU**	DULCIANA
AACDDGHL	CLADDAGH	**AACDELRS**	CALDERAS	**AACDILNV**	VANDALIC
AACDDHRS	CHADDARS	**AACDELSS**	SCALADES	**AACDILOZ**	ZODIACAL
AACDDILN	CANDIDAL	**AACDELSY**	ALCAYDES	**AACDILPS**	CAPSIDAL
AACDDINR	RADICAND	**AACDELTT**	LACTATED	**AACDILRR**	RAILCARD
AACDDINS	CANDIDAS	**AACDELTV**	CLAVATED	**AACDILRS**	RADICALS
AACDDRSW	CRAWDADS	**AACDELTY**	ACYLATED	**AACDIMNO**	MANDIOCA
AACDEEHH	HEADACHE	**AACDENOT**	ANECDOTA	**AACDIMNY**	ADYNAMIC
AACDEEHR	AREACHED	**AACDENRS**	DRACENAS		CYANAMID
	HEADRACE	**AACDENRV**	ADVANCER	**AACDIMOS**	CAMISADO
AACDEEHS	HEADCASE	**AACDENSV**	ADVANCES	**AACDIMRT**	DRAMATIC
AACDEELS	ESCALADE		CANVASED	**AACDINRT**	RADICANT
AACDEEMS	ACADEMES	**AACDENSZ**	CADENZAS		TRIDACNA
AACDEEPS	ESCAPADE	**AACDENTU**	ADUNCATE	**AACDINRY**	RADIANCY
AACDEERT	ACERATED	**AACDENTV**	TADVANCE	**AACDINSS**	SCANDIAS
AACDEEST	CASEATED	**AACDEOPS**	ESCAPADO	**AACDINST**	ANTACIDS
	ESTACADE	**AACDEOTU**	AUTOCADE	**AACDIOTU**	AUTACOID
AACDEETT	ACETATED	**AACDEOTV**	ADVOCATE	**AACDIRSS**	ASCARIDS
AACDEETU	ECAUDATE	**AACDEPRS**	SCARPAED	**AACDIRTY**	CARYATID
AACDEETV	CAVEATED	**AACDEQUY**	ADEQUACY	**AACDITUY**	AUDACITY
AACDEFHR	HARDFACE	**AACDERST**	CADASTER	**AACDJKSW**	JACKDAWS
AACDEFLS	FALCADES		CADASTRE	**AACDJQRU**	JACQUARD
AACDEFLT	FALCATED	**AACDERSV**	CADAVERS	**AACDKLLN**	LACKLAND
AACDEFNT	CAFTANED	**AACDERSY**	DAYCARES	**AACDKPRT**	TRACKPAD
AACDEGGR	AGGRACED	**AACDERTU**	ARCUATED	**AACDKSSY**	DAYSACKS
AACDEGKP	PACKAGED	**AACDESTU**	CAUDATES	**AACDLLUY**	CAUDALLY
AACDEGMR	DECAGRAM	**AACDETTU**	ACTUATED	**AACDLNSS**	SCANDALS
AACDEHHY	HEADACHY	**AACDETUV**	VACUATED	**AACDLORS**	CARLOADS
AACDEHIN	HACIENDA	**AACDFLNR**	FLANCARD	**AACDLORT**	CARTLOAD
AACDEHLN	CHALANED	**AACDGGHI**	HAGGADIC	**AACDLORY**	COALYARD
AACDEHLP	CEPHALAD	**AACDGINR**	ARCADING	**AACDLOSS**	SCALADOS
AACDEHMR	DRACHMAE		CARANGID	**AACDLOSV**	CALVADOS
AACDEHMS	CHAMADES		CARDIGAN	**AACDLPRS**	PLACARDS
AACDEHRS	CHARADES	**AACDHHKR**	HARDHACK	**AACDLRTY**	DACTYLAR
	HARDCASE	**AACDHHNS**	SHADCHAN	**AACDMMOR**	CARDAMOM
AACDEHRT	CATHEDRA	**AACDHHRS**	SHADRACH	**AACDMMRU**	CARDAMUM
AACDEHST	CATHEADS	**AACDHIIS**	DICHASIA	**AACDMNNO**	MANCANDO
AACDEHTT	ATTACHED	**AACDHILL**	CHILLADA	**AACDMNOR**	CARDAMON
AACDEIIL	AECIDIAL	**AACDHILR**	DIARCHAL	**AACDOOSV**	AVOCADOS
AACDEIIM	ACIDEMIA	**AACDHIMR**	CHADARIM	**AACDORRT**	CARTROAD
AACDEILM	CAMAILED		DRACHMAI	**AACDPRSU**	CRAPAUDS
AACDEILS	ALCAIDES	**AACDHINP**	HANDICAP	**AACEEFIT**	FACETIAE
	SIDALCEA	**AACDHINR**	ARACHNID	**AACEEFLP**	PALEFACE
AACDEIMN	MAENADIC	**AACDHKPR**	HARDPACK	**AACEEFNS**	FEASANCE
AACDEIMS	CAMISADE	**AACDHKRT**	HARDTACK	**AACEEGIR**	ACIERAGE
AACDEIMT	ACETAMID	**AACDHLNP**	HANDCLAP		AGACERIE
AACDEINR	CANARIED	**AACDHLOT**	CATHODAL	**AACEEGLR**	CLEARAGE
	RADIANCE	**AACDHLRY**	CHARLADY	**AACEEGLV**	CLEAVAGE
AACDEINS	AIDANCES		DYARCHAL	**AACEEGNR**	CARAGEEN
AACDEIRT	RADICATE	**AACDHMMR**	DRAMMACH	**AACEEGNY**	GYNAECEA
AACDEJNT	ADJACENT	**AACDHMOP**	PACHADOM	**AACEEGRS**	ACREAGES
AACDEKNP	PANCAKED	**AACDHMRS**	DRACHMAS		GEARCASE

AACEEHLP	ACALEPHE
AACEEHLT	LEACHATE
AACEEHRS	AREACHES
	EARACHES
AACEEHRT	TRACHEAE
AACEEIMT	EMACIATE
AACEEINN	ENCAENIA
AACEEIRT	ACIERATE
AACEEKRT	CARETAKE
AACEEKST	TEACAKES
AACEELNS	ANELACES
AACEELRT	LACERATE
AACEELST	ESCALATE
AACEELTU	ACULEATE
AACEEMRT	MACERATE
	RACEMATE
AACEEMSS	AMESACES
AACEEMST	CASEMATE
AACEENNT	CATENANE
AACEENRS	CESAREAN
AACEENRW	CANEWARE
AACEENTT	CATENATE
AACEEPRV	PRECAVAE
AACEEPSS	SEASCAPE
AACEERSU	CAESURAE
AACEERTV	ACERVATE
AACEESSS	CASEASES
AACEESST	CASEATES
AACEESTT	ACETATES
AACEETUV	EVACUATE
AACEETVX	EXCAVATE
AACEFFIN	AFFIANCE
AACEFHLP	HALFPACE
AACEFILM	FACEMAIL
AACEFILT	CALIFATE
AACEFIST	FASCIATE
AACEFKMS	FACEMASK
AACEFLLU	FALCULAE
AACEFRRS	CARFARES
AACEFRRU	FURCRAEA
AACEFRSS	FRACASES
AACEFRST	SEACRAFT
AACEFRSX	CARFAXES
AACEFRTT	ARTEFACT
AACEGGRS	AGGRACES
AACEGHNS	GANACHES
AACEGHNT	CHANTAGE
AACEGILN	ANGELICA
AACEGILT	GLACIATE
AACEGINR	CANAIGRE
AACEGINY	GYNAECIA
AACEGIOP	APOGAEIC
AACEGIRR	CARRIAGE
AACEGIRV	VICARAGE
AACEGKPR	PACKAGER
AACEGKPS	PACKAGES
AACEGKRT	TRACKAGE
AACEGKSS	SACKAGES
AACEGLNY	LANCEGAY
AACEGLSS	SCALAGES
AACEGMNO	COMANAGE
AACEGMNP	CAMPAGNE
AACEGNRS	CAGANERS
	CARNAGES
	CRANAGES
AACEGRST	CARTAGES
AACEGRSV	SCAVAGER
AACEGSSV	SCAVAGES
AACEHHRU	HUARACHE
AACEHIKN	ICEKHANA
AACEHILL	ACHILLEA
	HELIACAL
AACEHILN	ACHENIAL
AACEHILP	PHACELIA
AACEHIMR	CHIMAERA
AACEHIMT	HAEMATIC
AACEHIPT	HEPATICA
AACEHIRS	ARCHAISE
AACEHIRT	THERIACA
AACEHIRZ	ARCHAIZE
AACEHKSS	ASHCAKES
AACEHLNT	CALANTHE
AACEHLNU	EULACHAN
AACEHLPS	ACALEPHS
AACEHLRS	ALCHERAS
AACEHLRT	TRACHEAL
AACEHLRX	EXARCHAL
AACEHLSS	CALASHES
AACEHLST	ALCAHEST
AACEHMNP	CAMPHANE
AACEHMRS	MARCHESA
AACEHMSS	CAMASHES
AACEHMST	SCHEMATA
AACEHNOR	ARCHAEON
AACEHNPS	PANACHES
AACEHPRT	RACEPATH
AACEHPSU	CHAPEAUS
AACEHPUX	CHAPEAUX
AACEHQTU	CHAQUETA
AACEHRSS	CHARASES
AACEHRST	TRACHEAS
AACEHRSU	ARCHAEUS
AACEHRTT	ATTACHER
	REATTACH
AACEHSTT	ATTACHES
AACEHSTU	CHATEAUS
AACEHTUX	CHATEAUX
AACEIILN	LACINIAE
AACEIINT	ACTINIAE
AACEIIRV	CAVIARIE
AACEIKMT	KAMACITE
AACEILLM	CAMELLIA
AACEILLN	ALLIANCE
	ANCILLAE
	CANAILLE
AACEILMN	ANALCIME
	CALAMINE
AACEILMS	CAMELIAS
AACEILMT	CALAMITE
AACEILNS	CANALISE
AACEILNT	ANALCITE
	LAITANCE
AACEILNU	ACAULINE
AACEILNV	VALENCIA
	VALIANCE
AACEILNZ	CANALIZE
AACEILOP	ALOPECIA
AACEILRT	TAILRACE
AACEILRV	CAVALIER
AACEILST	SALICETA
AACEIMNS	AMNESIAC
AACEIMRS	MACARISE
AACEIMRZ	MACARIZE
AACEIMTT	CATAMITE
AACEIMUX	CAMAIEUX
AACEINNT	ANTIACNE
AACEINRS	ACARINES
	CANARIES
	CESARIAN
	SARCINAE
AACEINRT	CARINATE
	CRANIATE
AACEINRV	VARIANCE
AACEINST	ESTANCIA
AACEINTV	CAVATINE
AACEIOPR	CAPOEIRA
AACEIPPS	PAPACIES
AACEIPRS	AIRSCAPE
	AIRSPACE
AACEIPRT	APRICATE
AACEIPSS	CAPIASES
AACEIPTT	APATETIC
	CAPITATE
AACEIQSU	ACEQUIAS
AACEIRSV	AVARICES
	CAVIARES
AACEIRTV	VICARATE
AACEISST	ECTASIAS
AACEITTV	ACTIVATE
	CAVITATE
AACEJLTU	JACULATE
AACEKKLW	CAKEWALK
AACEKLRW	RACEWALK
AACEKMPR	CAPMAKER
AACEKMRR	CARMAKER
AACEKNPS	PANCAKES
AACEKNSS	ASKANCES
AACEKOST	OATCAKES
AACEKRTT	ATTACKER
	REATTACK
AACELLMR	MARCELLA
AACELLNR	CANALLER
AACELLNS	CANELLAS
AACELLOT	ALLOCATE
AACELLST	CASTELLA
	LACTEALS
AACELLTY	ALLEYCAT
AACELMNP	PLACEMAN
AACELMNS	MANACLES
AACELMOT	CELOMATA
AACELMRS	CARAMELS
	CERAMALS
	MACERALS
AACELMTU	MACULATE
AACELNNO	ANCONEAL
AACELNNU	CANNULAE
AACELNOR	LECANORA
AACELNPR	PARLANCE
AACELNPS	CAPELANS
	SCALEPAN
AACELNPT	PLACENTA

Eight-letter anagrams

AACELNPY	ANYPLACE	AACEPRSU	CAPUERAS		PANGAMIC
AACELNRT	LACERANT	AACEPSWY	PACEWAYS	AACGIMOP	APOGAMIC
AACELNRY	ARCANELY	AACERRTU	ARCATURE	AACGIMRR	MARGARIC
AACELNST	ANALECTS	AACERSSS	RASCASSE	AACGIMUU	GUAIACUM
AACELNSV	VALANCES	AACERSSU	CAESURAS	AACGINOT	CONTAGIA
AACELNTU	CANULATE	AACERSSZ	SAZERACS	AACGINPS	SCAPAING
	LACUNATE	AACERSTT	CASTRATE	AACGINTV	VACATING
	TENACULA		TEACARTS	AACGISTY	SAGACITY
AACELORS	ACEROLAS	AACERSWY	RACEWAYS	AACGJNST	CATJANGS
AACELORV	CAVALERO	AACERTTT	TRACTATE	AACGLMOU	GLAUCOMA
AACELOST	CATALOES	AACESSSV	CAVASSES	AACGLOST	CATALOGS
AACELOSU	ACAULOSE	AACESSTT	SCEATTAS	AACGMNRS	CRAGSMAN
AACELOSV	COAEVALS	AACESTTU	ACTUATES	AACGNOSU	GUANACOS
AACELPRS	CARPALES	AACESTUV	VACUATES	AACGNRVY	VAGRANCY
AACELPRT	PLACATER	AACESUWY	CAUSEWAY	AACHHIKL	HALAKHIC
AACELPRV	PRECAVAL	AACFFILS	CAFFILAS	AACHHIKR	KACHAHRI
AACELPST	PLACATES	AACFGRST	CRAGFAST	AACHHILR	RHACHIAL
AACELPSU	SCAPULAE	AACFHMST	CAMSHAFT	AACHHIMS	MASHIACH
AACELRSS	SCALARES	AACFILLY	FACIALLY	AACHHKRS	CHARKHAS
AACELRSU	CAESURAL	AACFILOS	FASCIOLA	AACHHLLS	CHALLAHS
AACELRSV	CARAVELS	AACFINST	FANATICS	AACHHLOT	HALACHOT
AACELRTY	ACRYLATE	AACFIRRT	AIRCRAFT	AACHHORU	HUARACHO
AACELRWY	CLAYWARE	AACFIRST	FRASCATI	AACHHTWY	HATCHWAY
	CLEARWAY	AACFIRTT	ARTIFACT	AACHIIMR	MARIACHI
AACELSST	LACTASES	AACFISST	FASCISTA	AACHIKKZ	KAZACHKI
AACELSTT	LACTATES	AACFJKLP	FLAPJACK	AACHIKNR	CHINKARA
AACELSTY	ACYLATES	AACFKLPT	FLATPACK	AACHIKNS	KACHINAS
	CATALYSE	AACFLLST	CATFALLS	AACHIKNT	KATCHINA
AACELTTY	CATTLEYA	AACFLLSU	FALCULAS	AACHIKRS	CHIKARAS
AACELTYZ	CATALYZE	AACFLOPR	PARFOCAL	AACHILLP	CALIPHAL
AACEMMRS	MACRAMES	AACFLPST	FLATCAPS	AACHILLR	RACHILLA
AACEMNOR	AMORANCE	AACFLRST	FLATCARS	AACHILMS	CHAMISAL
AACEMNPS	SPACEMAN		FRACTALS		CHIASMAL
AACEMNST	CAMSTANE	AACFRRSU	FARRUCAS	AACHILMT	THALAMIC
AACEMPRS	PARACMES	AACFRRTW	WARCRAFT	AACHILNP	CHAPLAIN
AACEMQSU	MACAQUES	AACGGINO	ANAGOGIC	AACHILOS	ACHOLIAS
AACEMRSS	MASSACRE	AACGGIOP	APAGOGIC	AACHILPS	CALIPASH
AACEMSSS	CAMASSES	AACGHILT	TAIGLACH		PASHALIC
AACENOTU	OCEANAUT	AACGHIPR	AGRAPHIC	AACHILPT	HAPTICAL
AACENPRS	PANCREAS	AACGHIRR	CHIRAGRA	AACHILRV	ARCHIVAL
AACENPRT	CATNAPER	AACGHLLO	AGALLOCH	AACHIMNN	CHAINMAN
AACENPST	PASTANCE	AACGHLRU	RUGALACH		CHINAMAN
AACENPSU	SAUCEPAN	AACGHNOR	CHARANGO	AACHIMNP	CHINAMPA
AACENPTT	PANCETTA	AACGHOPZ	GAZPACHO	AACHIMNR	CHAIRMAN
AACENRST	CANASTER	AACGHORU	GUACHARO	AACHIMNS	SHAMANIC
	CATERANS	AACGIIMN	MAGICIAN	AACHIMNT	MATACHIN
AACENRSV	CANVASER	AACGIINR	GARCINIA	AACHIMNZ	CHAZANIM
AACENRTT	REACTANT	AACGILLN	GALLICAN	AACHIMRR	ARMCHAIR
AACENRTY	CATENARY	AACGILLO	ALOGICAL	AACHIMRS	ARCHAISM
AACENRVZ	CZAREVNA	AACGILLS	GALLICAS		CHARISMA
AACENSSS	CASSENAS		GLACIALS		MACHAIRS
AACENSSV	CANVASES	AACGILLU	ALGUACIL	AACHIMSS	CHAMISAS
AACENSTT	CANTATES	AACGILNN	CANALING		CHIASMAS
	CASTANET	AACGILNO	ANALOGIC	AACHIMST	CATHISMA
AACENSTY	CYANATES	AACGILNR	CRAALING	AACHINNT	ACANTHIN
AACENTUV	EVACUANT	AACGILNT	ANTALGIC	AACHINRT	CANTHARI
AACEOPPR	COAPPEAR	AACGILNV	GALVANIC	AACHINSW	CHAINSAW
AACEOPRT	CAPROATE	AACGILOU	GUAIACOL	AACHIPPT	CHAPPATI
AACEOPST	PEACOATS	AACGILOX	COXALGIA	AACHIPRS	CHARPAIS
AACEORSS	ROSACEAS	AACGILRT	TRAGICAL		HAIRCAPS
AACEORSU	ARACEOUS	AACGILSS	SCAGLIAS	AACHIPSS	APHASICS
AACEORTV	CAVEATOR	AACGIMMT	MAGMATIC	AACHIPST	CHAPATIS
AACEOSST	SEACOAST	AACGIMNN	MANGANIC	AACHIPTT	CHAPATTI
AACEPRST	CAPRATES	AACGIMNP	CAMPAIGN	AACHIRST	ARCHAIST

	CITHARAS
AACHIRTX	TAXIARCH
AACHKKOZ	KAZACHOK
AACHKMPS	CHAMPAKS
AACHKNSW	HACKSAWN
AACHKPSS	SCHAPSKA
AACHKRST	HATRACKS
AACHKRSY	HAYRACKS
AACHKSSW	HACKSAWS
AACHKSTY	HAYSTACK
AACHLLLU	HALLUCAL
AACHLLNS	CHALLANS
AACHLLOR	ALACHLOR
AACHLMNO	MONACHAL
AACHLMOS	CHLOASMA
AACHLNOO	OOLACHAN
AACHLORT	THORACAL
AACHLOST	CALATHOS
AACHLPPS	CHAPPALS
AACHLPSS	PASCHALS
AACHLPSU	CHALUPAS
AACHLSSU	ACUSHLAS
AACHLSTU	CALATHUS
AACHMMNR	MARCHMAN
AACHMNNR	RANCHMAN
AACHMNTW	WATCHMAN
AACHMNTY	YACHTMAN
AACHMNUY	NAUMACHY
AACHMORT	ACHROMAT
	TRACHOMA
AACHMPRT	CHAMPART
AACHMPRY	PHARMACY
AACHMSSY	YASHMACS
AACHNOPS	PANOCHAS
AACHNOSU	HUANACOS
AACHNPRS	SARPANCH
AACHNRST	TRASHCAN
AACHNRSV	NAVARCHS
AACHNRVY	NAVARCHY
AACHNSSU	ANCHUSAS
AACHNSTU	ACANTHUS
AACHNSZZ	CHAZZANS
AACHOPPR	APPROACH
AACHOPRR	PARACHOR
AACHORTU	RACAHOUT
AACHOTTU	TACAHOUT
AACHRRST	CATARRHS
AACHRSTU	AUTARCHS
AACHRSWY	ARCHWAYS
AACHRTUY	AUTARCHY
AACIILMN	ANIMALIC
AACIILMO	MAIOLICA
AACIILRT	IATRICAL
AACIILRV	VICARIAL
AACIILTV	VIATICAL
AACIIMNT	ANIMATIC
AACIIMSS	CAMISIAS
AACIINNT	ACTINIAN
AACIINPR	PICARIAN
AACIINPT	CAPITANI
AACIINST	ACTINIAS
AACIIRSV	VISCARIA
AACIJLMO	MAJOLICA
AACIJNOP	JAPONICA

AACIKLMS	MAILSACK
AACIKLRS	CLARKIAS
AACIKMNW	MACKINAW
AACIKNNS	CANAKINS
AACIKNST	KATCINAS
AACIKRTU	AUTARKIC
AACILLLY	LAICALLY
AACILLMR	LACRIMAL
AACILLMT	CLIMATAL
AACILLNS	ANCILLAS
AACILLPV	APICALLY
AACILLRY	RACIALLY
AACILMNT	CALAMINT
	CLAIMANT
AACILMOR	ACROMIAL
AACILMOT	ATOMICAL
AACILMRS	MAILCARS
AACILMTY	CALAMITY
AACILNOR	CONARIAL
AACILNPS	CALPAINS
AACILNRS	CLARAINS
AACILNRV	CARNIVAL
AACILNST	ALICANTS
	SANTALIC
AACILNTT	TANTALIC
AACILNTU	NAUTICAL
AACILNTY	ANALYTIC
AACILNUV	NAVICULA
AACILNVY	VALIANCY
AACILOSS	ASOCIALS
AACILOTT	COATTAIL
	TAILCOAT
AACILPRU	PIACULAR
AACILPST	APLASTIC
	CAPITALS
AACILPSZ	CAPSIZAL
AACILPTU	CAPITULA
AACILPTY	ATYPICAL
AACILQRU	ACQUIRAL
AACILRRS	RAILCARS
AACILRTY	ALACRITY
AACILRUU	AURICULA
AACILRUV	AVICULAR
AACILSTT	CATTAILS
	STATICAL
AACILSTY	SALACITY
AACIMMNO	AMMONIAC
AACIMMRS	MACARISM
	MACRAMIS
	MARASMIC
AACIMNOR	ARMONICA
	MACARONI
	MAROCAIN
AACIMNOS	MANIOCAS
AACIMNOT	ANATOMIC
AACIMORT	AROMATIC
AACIMOTX	MAXICOAT
AACIMPRS	PICAMARS
AACINNST	CANTINAS
AACINOPR	PARANOIC
AACINOPT	CAPITANO
	PACATION
AACINORS	OCARINAS
AACINORT	RAINCOAT

AACINOTV	VACATION
AACINPRT	CANTRAIP
AACINPST	CAPITANS
	CAPTAINS
AACINPTY	CAPITAYN
AACINQTU	ACQUAINT
AACINRSS	ACRASINS
	SARCINAS
AACINRST	ARCANIST
AACINRSZ	CZARINAS
AACINSSS	CASSINAS
AACINSTZ	STANZAIC
AACIOPST	TAPIOCAS
AACIOPSV	COPAIVAS
AACIPPRS	PAPRICAS
AACIPRST	ASPARTIC
AACIPRTY	RAPACITY
AACIQSTU	AQUATICS
AACIRRTT	TARTARIC
AACIRSTT	CASTRATI
AACIRSTZ	CZARITSA
AACIRTVY	CAVITARY
AACIRTZZ	CZARITZA
AACISSTW	SWASTICA
AACJKLPS	SLAPJACK
AACJKMNS	MANJACKS
AACJKOOR	JACKAROO
AACJKSTY	JACKSTAY
AACJPSTU	CAJAPUTS
AACKKNPS	KNAPSACK
AACKLOWY	LOCKAWAY
AACKLSTW	CATWALKS
AACKMNPS	MANPACKS
AACKMNRT	TRACKMAN
AACKMNST	TACKSMAN
AACKMRST	AMTRACKS
AACKNRSS	RANSACKS
AACKORWY	ROCKAWAY
AACKPRRS	CARPARKS
AACKPRST	RATPACKS
AACKPSWY	PACKWAYS
AACKRTWY	TRACKWAY
AACLLLOO	CALLALOO
AACLLMMU	MACALLUM
AACLLMRY	LACRYMAL
AACLLNRY	CARNALLY
AACLLNST	CALLANTS
AACLLNSU	CALLUNAS
AACLLOOS	CALALOOS
AACLLRRY	CARRYALL
AACLLRSY	RASCALLY
AACLLSUU	CLAUSULA
AACLLSUV	CASUALLY
	CAUSALLY
AACLLTUV	ACTUALLY
AACLMNNS	CLANSMAN
AACLMNSS	CLASSMAN
AACLMNST	CALMANTS
AACLMOTU	COMATULA
AACLMRRU	MACRURAL
AACLNNOT	CANTONAL
AACLNNRU	CANNULAR
AACLNNSU	CANNULAS
AACLNOPR	COPLANAR

AACLNOTT	OCTANTAL	AACORTTU	ACTUATOR	AADEEGLR	LAAGERED
AACLNPSY	CLAYPANS		AUTOCRAT	AADEEGLT	GALEATED
AACLNRSU	LACUNARS	AACOSTUV	AUTOVACS	AADEEGMN	AMENAGED
AACLNRUY	LACUNARY	AACPSSTW	CATSPAWS		ENDAMAGE
AACLNTVY	VACANTLY	AACRSTTT	ATTRACTS	AADEEGMR	REDAMAGE
AACLOOPT	TAPACOLO	AACRSTUV	VACATURS	AADEEGNR	GADARENE
AACLOPRS	CAPORALS	AACRSTWY	CARTWAYS	AADEEGRV	AVERAGED
	CRAPOLAS	AACSTUWY	CUTAWAYS	AADEEHMT	MEATHEAD
AACLOPST	OCTAPLAS	AADDDEEH	DEADHEAD	AADEEIRT	ERADIATE
AACLOPTU	TAPACULO	AADDDEER	ADREADED	AADEEIRW	AWEARIED
AACLORRU	ORACULAR	AADDDERW	ADWARDED	AADEEKNW	AWAKENED
AACLORST	COALTARS	AADDDGNR	GRANDDAD	AADEEKRW	REAWAKED
AACLORSU	CAROUSAL	AADDEELT	DEALATED	AADEELNN	ANNEALED
AACLORSZ	ALCORZAS	AADDEFLL	DEADFALL	AADEELPP	APPEALED
AACLORUV	VACUOLAR	AADDEGGR	AGGRADED	AADEELST	DEALATES
AACLOSTT	CATTALOS	AADDEGRT	GRADATED	AADEELTV	ALVEATED
AACLOSUU	ACAULOUS	AADDEHHR	HARDHEAD	AADEEMNS	MAENADES
AACLPPRT	CLAPTRAP	AADDEHHS	HADEDAHS	AADEEMNT	EMANATED
AACLPRST	CALTRAPS	AADDEHLN	HEADLAND	AADEEMOT	OEDEMATA
AACLPRSU	CAPSULAR	AADDEHMN	HANDMADE	AADEEMRR	DEMERARA
	SCAPULAR	AADDEHRW	HEADWARD	AADEENPT	TAPENADE
AACLPRTY	CALYPTRA	AADDEHRZ	HAZARDED	AADEENTT	ANTEDATE
AACLPSSU	SCAPULAS	AADDEILN	DEDALIAN	AADEEPPR	APPEARED
AACLPSTY	PLAYACTS	AADDEILS	ALIDADES	AADEEPPS	APPEASED
AACLPTTU	CATAPULT	AADDEIRT	RADIATED	AADEEPRS	PASEARED
AACLRSTU	CLAUSTRA	AADDEKMS	DAMASKED	AADEEQTU	ADEQUATE
AACLRSUV	VASCULAR	AADDELNS	SANDALED	AADEERSW	AWARDEES
AACLRTUX	CURTALAX	AADDELTU	ADULATED	AADEFFLT	AFFLATED
AACLRWWY	CRAWLWAY	AADDEMNT	MANDATED	AADEFFNR	FANFARED
AACLSSTT	SALTCATS	AADDEMRU	MARAUDED	AADEFFRY	AFFRAYED
AACLSTTY	CATALYST	AADDEMRY	DAYDREAM	AADEFGLS	FALDAGES
AACLSTUY	CASUALTY	AADDENPR	PANDARED	AADEFGRS	FARDAGES
AACMNOOR	MACAROON	AADDENPS	DEADPANS	AADEFHLT	FLATHEAD
AACMNORS	CAMARONS	AADDEORS	DEODARAS	AADEFHST	FATHEADS
	MASCARON	AADDGMNR	GRANDDAM		HEADFAST
	NARCOMAS	AADDGNRS	GRADDANS	AADEFHTW	FATWAHED
AACMNPRY	RAMPANCY		GRANDADS	AADEFILR	FAIRLEAD
AACMNRRU	MACRURAN	AADDGNRU	GRADUAND	AADEFIRS	FARADISE
AACMNRSU	ARCANUMS	AADDHHRS	SHRADDHA		SAFARIED
AACMORRS	CAMORRAS	AADDHIMN	HANDMAID	AADEFIRZ	FARADIZE
AACMORSS	SARCOMAS	AADDHKRS	KHADDARS	AADEFISS	FADAISES
AACMORST	MARCATOS	AADDHRSS	SRADDHAS	AADEFLLR	FALDERAL
AACMRRST	TRAMCARS	AADDIIKS	DIDAKAIS	AADEFLRY	DEFRAYAL
AACMRSSS	SARCASMS	AADDIISV	DAVIDIAS	AADEFLTT	FALDETTA
AACNNOSZ	CANZONAS	AADDILNO	DIANODAL	AADEFNSZ	FAZENDAS
AACNOSST	SACATONS	AADDIMSS	DADAISMS	AADEFRRW	WARFARED
AACNOSTZ	ZACATONS	AADDISST	DADAISTS	AADEFRWY	WAYFARED
AACNOTTY	CATATONY	AADDKMMO	MOKADDAM	AADEGGRS	AGGRADES
AACNPRST	CANTRAPS	AADDLLNY	LANDLADY		SAGGARED
AACNPSST	CAPSTANS	AADDLNRW	LANDWARD	AADEGGRT	AGGRATED
AACNRSTT	TRANSACT	AADDLNRY	YARDLAND	AADEGGRU	GUARDAGE
AACNRSTU	CURTANAS	AADDMMQU	MUQADDAM	AADEGHLN	DANELAGH
AACOORTX	TOXOCARA	AADDNRST	STANDARD	AADEGHNR	HANGARED
AACOPPRS	APOCARPS	AADDNRWY	YARDWAND	AADEGHRS	RAGHEADS
AACOPPRY	APOCARPY	AADDNSVV	DVANDVAS		RHAGADES
AACOPRSU	ACARPOUS	AADDRSST	DASTARDS	AADEGILL	DIALLAGE
AACOPRTU	AUTOCARP	AADDRSTY	DASTARDY	AADEGILT	GLADIATE
AACOPSTV	POSTCAVA	AADEEERT	DEAERATE	AADEGINR	AREADING
AACOPSTY	APOSTACY	AADEEFFR	AFFEARED		DRAINAGE
AACORRTV	VARACTOR	AADEEGHR	GEARHEAD		GARDENIA
AACORSSW	CARASSOW		HEADGEAR	AADEGINT	INDAGATE
AACORSTT	CASTRATO	AADEEGHS	HEADAGES	AADEGIRR	GERARDIA
AACORSTU	ACATOURS	AADEEGHT	HEADGATE	AADEGIRV	GRAVIDAE
	AUTOCARS	AADEEGLM	MEGADEAL	AADEGIST	AGATISED

AADEGITT	AGITATED	**AADEILPR**	PRAEDIAL	**AADELMPT**	PALMATED
AADEGITV	DIVAGATE	**AADEILPS**	PALISADE	**AADELMRU**	ALARUMED
AADEGITZ	AGATIZED	**AADEILPT**	LAPIDATE	**AADELMYZ**	AMAZEDLY
AADEGJTU	ADJUTAGE	**AADEILRS**	SALARIED	**AADELNPT**	PEATLAND
AADEGKMR	DEKAGRAM	**AADEILRT**	LARIATED	**AADELNRS**	ADRENALS
AADEGLLT	TALLAGED	**AADEILSS**	ASSAILED	**AADELNSW**	DANELAWS
AADEGLMN	MAGDALEN	**AADEILSV**	VEDALIAS	**AADELNSY**	ANALYSED
AADEGLMY	AMYGDALE	**AADEILTT**	DILATATE	**AADELNYZ**	ANALYZED
AADEGLNS	SELADANG	**AADEILTV**	VALIDATE	**AADELOTX**	OXALATED
AADEGLOP	GALOPADE	**AADEIMNN**	AMANDINE	**AADELPPT**	PALPATED
AADEGLSV	SALVAGED	**AADEIMNP**	PANDEMIA	**AADELPRS**	PARDALES
AADEGMNR	GRANDAME	**AADEIMNR**	MARINADE	**AADELPRY**	PARLAYED
AADEGMPR	RAMPAGED	**AADEIMNT**	ANIMATED	**AADELPTY**	PLAYDATE
AADEGMRS	DAMAGERS		DIAMANTE	**AADELQUU**	QUAALUDE
	MEGARADS	**AADEIMPZ**	DIAZEPAM	**AADELRSY**	SALEYARD
	SMARAGDE	**AADEIMRS**	MADEIRAS	**AADELRTU**	RADULATE
AADEGMSS	MASSAGED	**AADEIMRV**	MARAVEDI	**AADELRTV**	LARVATED
AADEGNRR	ARRANGED	**AADEIMSS**	AMIDASES	**AADELRTY**	DAYTALER
AADEGNTV	VANTAGED		SEAMAIDS	**AADELSTT**	SALTATED
AADEGPRV	PAYGRADE	**AADEIMST**	ADAMSITE	**AADELSTU**	ADULATES
AADEGPSS	PASSAGED		DIASTEMA	**AADELSTY**	DAYTALES
AADEGRST	GRADATES	**AADEINPT**	PATINAED	**AADELTUV**	VALUATED
AADEGRSV	SAVEGARD	**AADEINRR**	DARRAINE	**AADEMNOS**	ADENOMAS
AADEGRSY	DRAYAGES	**AADEINRS**	ARANEIDS	**AADEMNPS**	SPADEMAN
	YARDAGES	**AADEINRT**	DENTARIA	**AADEMNST**	MANDATES
AADEGRTU	GRADUATE		RAINDATE	**AADEMNUZ**	UNAMAZED
AADEGSSU	ASSUAGED	**AADEINSZ**	ZENAIDAS	**AADEMORT**	MATADORE
AADEGSSW	ASSWAGED	**AADEINTT**	ATTAINED	**AADEMRRU**	MARAUDER
AADEHHHS	HASHHEAD	**AADEIPPR**	APPAIRED	**AADEMRSS**	MADRASES
AADEHHOR	HOARHEAD	**AADEIPRS**	PARADISE	**AADEMRSY**	DAYMARES
AADEHILN	NAILHEAD	**AADEIPSS**	DIAPASES	**AADEMSSS**	ADMASSES
AADEHILR	HEADRAIL	**AADEIPSU**	DIAPAUSE	**AADEMWZZ**	ZAMZAWED
	RAILHEAD	**AADEIPTV**	ADAPTIVE	**AADENNST**	ANDANTES
AADEHILS	HEADSAIL	**AADEIRST**	AIRDATES	**AADENNRT**	NARRATED
AADEHIRR	DIARRHEA		DATARIES	**AADENRRW**	WARRANED
AADEHIRS	AIRHEADS		RADIATES	**AADENRSV**	VERANDAS
AADEHIWY	HIDEAWAY	**AADEIRTV**	VARIATED	**AADENRTT**	TARTANED
AADEHJRS	JARHEADS	**AADEISST**	DIASTASE	**AADENSSW**	WEASANDS
AADEHKMR	HEADMARK	**AADEISTT**	ASTATIDE	**AADENSTY**	ASYNDETA
AADEHLLL	HALALLED		SATIATED	**AADENSTZ**	STANZAED
AADEHLLO	HALLOAED	**AADEITVW**	VIEWDATA	**AADENSWZ**	WEAZANDS
AADEHLMP	HEADLAMP	**AADEJMPY**	PYJAMAED	**AADENTUV**	AVAUNTED
AADEHLNR	ANHEDRAL	**AADEJMRS**	JEMADARS	**AADEOPRT**	TAPADERO
AADEHLPS	SLAPHEAD	**AADEJNNP**	JAPANNED	**AADEOPST**	ADESPOTA
AADEHLRS	ASHLARED	**AADEKLLN**	LAKELAND	**AADEORRT**	AERODART
AADEHMNS	HEADSMAN	**AADEKLNR**	KALENDAR	**AADEPPRT**	PREADAPT
AADEHMST	MASTHEAD	**AADEKLRY**	KALEYARD	**AADEPRRS**	PARADERS
AADEHNPS	SANDHEAP	**AADEKMNR**	MANDRAKE	**AADEPRST**	ADAPTERS
AADEHNRV	VERANDAH	**AADEKMRS**	KAMERADS		READAPTS
AADEHNSX	HANDAXES	**AADEKNST**	ASKANTED	**AADEPSSS**	PASSADES
AADEHPPR	PARAPHED	**AADEKNUW**	UNAWAKED	**AADEQRTU**	QUADRATE
AADEHPSS	SAPHEADS	**AADEKPRS**	PARKADES	**AADERRRW**	REARWARD
AADEHRRW	HARDWARE	**AADEKSTT**	ATTASKED	**AADERRSW**	AWARDERS
AADEHRRZ	HAZARDER	**AADELLOS**	ALDOLASE	**AADERRWY**	WARRAYED
AADEHRSS	HARASSED	**AADELLPP**	APPALLED	**AADERSST**	ASSARTED
AADEHRSW	RAWHEADS	**AADELLPS**	PADELLAS	**AADERSSW**	SEAWARDS
	WARHEADS	**AADELLRT**	DATALLER	**AADERSTT**	ASTARTED
AADEHSSY	SASHAYED	**AADELLWY**	WELLADAY	**AADERSTW**	EASTWARD
AADEHSTT	HASTATED	**AADELMNP**	NAPALMED		RADWASTE
AADEHSTY	HEADSTAY	**AADELMNR**	ALDERMAN	**AADERUVY**	AYURVEDA
AADEHSWY	HEADWAYS		MALANDER	**AADFGNNO**	FANDANGO
AADEILMS	MALADIES	**AADELMNS**	DALESMAN	**AADFGRSU**	SAUFGARD
AADEILMU	AUMAILED		LEADSMAN	**AADFHMNR**	FARMHAND
AADEILNT	DENTALIA	**AADELMOS**	ALAMODES		

AADFHNST	HANDFAST		GRANDMAS	AADILMNO	DOMAINAL
AADFIINT	INTIFADA	AADGMRSS	SMARAGDS		DOMANIAL
AADFIMRS	FARADISM	AADGNNQU	QUANDANG	AADILMNP	PLAIDMAN
AADFINRU	UNAFRAID	AADGNPRS	GRANDPAS	AADILMRS	ADMIRALS
AADFLLLN	LANDFALL	AADGNRST	GARDANTS		AMILDARS
AADFLLNT	FLATLAND	AADGNRSY	YARDANGS	AADILMST	MATILDAS
AADFLMNR	FARMLAND	AADGNRTU	GUARDANT	AADILNOR	ORDALIAN
AADFLORW	AARDWOLF	AADGNRUV	VANGUARD	AADILNPR	PRANDIAL
AADFLOTW	DATAFLOW	AADGNRWY	DRANGWAY	AADILNPS	PALADINS
AADFLOTX	TOADFLAX	AADGOPRS	PODAGRAS	AADILNRS	LANIARDS
AADFLOWY	FOLDAWAY	AADGRRUW	GURDWARA	AADILNTT	DILATANT
AADFMRRY	FARMYARD	AADHHIPS	PADISHAH	AADILOPS	PALISADO
AADGGHOT	AGGADOTH	AADHHKNS	SHADKHAN	AADILORR	RAILROAD
	HAGGADOT	AADHHPRS	PADSHAHS	AADILPRS	PARDALIS
AADGGHRS	HAGGARDS	AADHHRST	HARDHATS	AADILPRY	LAPIDARY
AADGGIMN	DAMAGING	AADHIINP	APHIDIAN	AADILRRS	RISALDAR
AADGGLNN	GANGLAND	AADHILLR	HALLIARD	AADILRST	DIASTRAL
AADGGLRS	LAGGARDS	AADHILNR	HANDRAIL		TAILARDS
AADGGRSS	SAGGARDS	AADHILRV	HAVILDAR	AADILSST	STADIALS
AADGGRST	STAGGARD	AADHIMRS	HARAMDIS	AADIMNNR	MANDARIN
AADGHILS	HIDALGAS	AADHIMSS	SAMADHIS	AADIMNOR	RADIOMAN
AADGHIPR	DIAGRAPH	AADHINOT	ANTHODIA	AADIMNOT	MANATOID
AADGHIST	HAGADIST	AADHINPS	DAPHNIAS	AADIMNRS	MANDIRAS
AADGHORS	DAROGHAS	AADHINRR	HARRIDAN	AADIMNRT	TAMARIND
AADGHRTU	HATGUARD	AADHIPRS	PARISHAD	AADIMNRY	DAIRYMAN
AADGIINS	GAINSAID	AADHJNRS	HANDJARS		MAINYARD
AADGIIRS	GIARDIAS	AADHKLOT	KATHODAL	AADIMNRZ	ZAMINDAR
AADGILLO	GLADIOLA	AADHKNSS	DHANSAKS	AADIMNSS	DAMASSIN
AADGILLR	GAILLARD	AADHKNSY	YAKHDANS	AADIMNSU	SUDAMINA
	GALLIARD	AADHLMOY	DALMAHOY	AADIMNUV	VANADIUM
AADGILMR	MADRIGAL	AADHLNPY	HANDPLAY	AADIMORS	DIORAMAS
AADGILNO	DIAGONAL	AADHLNSW	WASHLAND	AADIMPST	MISADAPT
	GONADIAL	AADHLPSS	SLAPDASH	AADIMRSW	MISAWARD
AADGILNS	SALADING	AADHLRSY	HALYARDS	AADIMSTZ	SAMIZDAT
AADGIMMN	MADAMING	AADHLRUY	HAULYARD	AADINNNS	NANDINAS
AADGIMMS	DIGAMMAS	AADHMNNY	HANDYMAN	AADINNOT	ADNATION
AADGIMNR	MRIDANGA	AADHMNOU	OMADHAUN	AADINOPR	PARANOID
AADGIMOS	AGAMOIDS	AADHMOPS	PASHADOM	AADINOPS	DIAPASON
AADGIMPR	PARADIGM	AADHNPRS	HARDPANS	AADINOPT	ADAPTION
AADGIMRS	DIAGRAMS	AADHNRSS	DARSHANS	AADINORT	ANTIDORA
AADGIMRT	GRADATIM	AADHNSSW	HANDSAWS	AADINOTV	AVOIDANT
AADGINPR	PARADING	AADHNSTT	HATSTAND	AADINPST	PINTADAS
AADGINPT	ADAPTING	AADHRRTW	THRAWARD	AADINRRS	DARRAINS
AADGINRR	DARRAIGN	AADHRRYZ	HAZARDRY	AADINRRW	AIRDRAWN
AADGINRU	GUARDIAN	AADHRSWY	HAYWARDS	AADINRST	INTRADAS
AADGINRW	AWARDING	AADHSSWY	WASHDAYS		RADIANTS
AADGIQRU	QUADRIGA	AADIILNS	SIALIDAN	AADINRSV	VIRANDAS
AADGIRSV	GRAVIDAS	AADIINOS	DIANOIAS	AADINRTY	INTRADAY
AADGLLSW	GADWALLS	AADIIPSS	ADIPSIAS	AADIOPRS	DIASPORA
AADGLMOR	MALGRADO	AADIJMNS	JAMDANIS	AADIOPSZ	DOPIAZAS
AADGLMSY	AMYGDALS	AADIKLLO	ALKALOID	AADIORRT	RADIATOR
AADGLNOR	LARGANDO	AADIKLLR	KILLADAR	AADIPSUY	UPADAISY
AADGLNRS	GARLANDS	AADIKLRY	KAILYARD	AADIRRSW	AIRWARDS
AADGLNSS	SLADANGS	AADIKLSY	ILKADAYS	AADIRRSY	DISARRAY
AADGLOOW	AGALWOOD	AADIKMNS	DAMASKIN	AADISTXY	DYSTAXIA
AADGLOPR	PODAGRAL	AADIKNQR	QINDARKA	AADJNTTU	ADJUTANT
AADGLORW	GOALWARD	AADILLLO	ALLODIAL	AADJNTUV	ADJUVANT
AADGLPRW	GLADWRAP	AADILLNR	LANDRAIL	AADKLMNR	LANDMARK
AADGLRSU	GRADUALS	AADILLPR	PAILLARD	AADKLNPR	PARKLAND
AADGMNOP	PAGANDOM		PALLIARD	AADKLRTU	TALUKDAR
AADGMNOR	DRAGOMAN	AADILLRS	SILLADAR	AADKMNRS	DARKMANS
AADGMNOS	GOADSMAN	AADILLRY	RADIALLY	AADKMRSY	DAYMARKS
AADGMNRS	DRAGSMAN	AADILLSY	DYSLALIA	AADKNRST	TANKARDS
	GRANDAMS	AADILMNN	MAINLAND	AADKORWY	WORKADAY

AADKPRRW	PARKWARD	AADOPRRS	PARADORS	AAEELLMR	AMARELLE
AADLLLNS	LALLANDS	AADOPRST	ADAPTORS	AAEELLMT	MALLEATE
AADLLMPY	LADYPALM	AADOPRXY	PARADOXY	AAEELLNV	AVELLANE
AADLLMRS	MALLARDS	AADOPSSS	PASSADOS	AAEELLPT	PATELLAE
AADLLNOV	ANODALLY	AADOPSTT	DOPATTAS	AAEELMMT	METAMALE
AADLLNPY	PLAYLAND	AADOPSUV	PADUASOY	AAEELMST	MALEATES
AADLLNSW	LAWLANDS	AADORSVY	SAVOYARD	AAEELNNR	ANNEALER
AADLMNNS	LANDSMAN	AADORSWY	ROADWAYS		LERNAEAN
AADLMNOR	MANDORLA	AADOSSTT	TOSTADAS	AAEELNPS	SEAPLANE
AADLMNOS	MANDOLAS	AADPSTTU	DUPATTAS		SPELAEAN
AADLMNSS	LANDMASS	AADQRSTU	QUADRATS	AAEELNPT	PANETELA
AADLMNSU	LADANUMS	AADRSSTY	DAYSTARS	AAEELNPU	PAENULAE
AADLMNUU	LAUDANUM	AAEEEHRT	HETAERAE	AAEELNST	ELASTANE
AADLMORS	ARMLOADS	AAEEEMRT	AMEERATE	AAEELORT	AREOLATE
AADLNOPR	PARLANDO	AAEEFFRS	AFFEARES	AAEELORU	AUREOLAE
AADLNOPS	DALAPONS	AAEEFGLS	LEAFAGES	AAEELPPR	APPEALER
	SOAPLAND	AAEEFRRS	SEAFARER	AAEELRST	LAETARES
AADLNOST	SALTANDO	AAEEFRST	RATAFEES	AAEELRTU	LAUREATE
AADLNOSV	VANLOADS	AAEEGILN	ALIENAGE	AAEELRTV	VALERATE
AADLNOSZ	DANAZOLS	AAEEGILP	EPIGAEAL	AAEELSST	ELASTASE
AADLNRSY	LANYARDS	AAEEGINP	EPIGAEAN	AAEELTUV	EVALUATE
AADLOPSY	PAYLOADS	AAEEGINS	AGENESIA	AAEELVWY	WAYLEAVE
AADLORST	LOADSTAR	AAEEGKLS	LEAKAGES	AAEEMMTT	TEAMMATE
AADLORTU	ADULATOR	AAEEGLLN	ENALLAGE	AAEEMNPT	NAMETAPE
	LAUDATOR	AAEEGLRY	LAYERAGE	AAEEMNST	EMANATES
AADLPPRW	WALDRAPP	AAEEGLST	ETALAGES		MANATEES
AADLPPSU	APPLAUDS		STEALAGE	AAEEMPRS	PARAMESE
AADLPSYY	PLAYDAYS	AAEEGLSV	SALVAGEE	AAEEMRST	AMREETAS
AADMMNOW	MADWOMAN	AAEEGMNS	AMENAGES	AAEEMSTT	SEATMATE
AADMMNSU	MANDAMUS	AAEEGMPR	AMPERAGE	AAEEMSTX	MEATAXES
AADMNNOS	MADONNAS	AAEEGMST	AGAMETES	AAEENNNT	ANTENNAE
AADMNORS	MADRONAS		AGEMATES	AAEENPRT	PARANETE
	MANDORAS	AAEEGMTY	METAYAGE	AAEENRRS	ARRASENE
	MONARDAS	AAEEGNRS	SANGAREE	AAEENRST	ARSENATE
	ROADSMAN	AAEEGNRT	TAGAREEN		SERENATA
AADMNORT	MANDATOR	AAEEGRST	STEARAGE	AAEENRTT	ANTEATER
AADMNRSS	MANSARDS	AAEEGRSV	AVERAGES	AAEENSTU	NAUSEATE
AADMNRSW	MANWARDS	AAEEGRTW	WATERAGE	AAEEPPRR	APPEARER
AADMNSTU	TAMANDUS	AAEEHIMR	HAEREMAI		RAPPAREE
AADMOPPP	PAPPADOM	AAEEHKKR	HARAKEKE		REAPPEAR
AADMOPPS	PAPADOMS	AAEEHKRT	HEKETARA	AAEEPPRS	APPEASER
AADMOQSU	MADOQUAS	AAEEHLMR	AHEMERAL	AAEEPPSS	APPEASES
AADMORRT	TRAMROAD	AAEEHMNR	HERMAEAN	AAEEPRST	ASPERATE
AADMORST	MATADORS	AAEEHNPS	SAPHENAE		SEPARATE
AADMPPSU	PAPADUMS	AAEEHPRT	EARTHPEA	AAEEPSTT	ASEPTATE
AADMRRSY	YARDARMS		HEARTPEA	AAEERRWW	REWAREWA
AADMRSZZ	MAZZARDS	AAEEHRST	HETAERAS	AAEERSSW	SEAWARES
AADNNPSU	PANDANUS	AAEEHRTW	AWEATHER	AAEERSTT	STEARATE
AADNOPRS	PANDORAS		WHEATEAR	AAEERSTW	SEAWATER
AADNOPSS	SANDSOAP	AAEEHRWY	HEREAWAY		TEAWARES
AADNORST	ONDATRAS	AAEEILNT	ALIENATE	AAEERSWX	EARWAXES
AADNORTY	DONATARY	AAEEINTT	TAENIATE	AAEERSYY	YEASAYER
AADNOSUV	VANADOUS	AAEEJMNP	JAMPANEE	AAEFFGRS	AGRAFFES
AADNOSWY	NOWADAYS	AAEEKLSS	SEAKALES	AAEFFGST	STAFFAGE
AADNPRSU	PANDURAS	AAEEKLTW	LATEWAKE	AAEFFIRS	AFFAIRES
AADNPSTT	STANDPAT	AAEEKMNS	NAMESAKE	AAEFFLLR	FARFALLE
AADNQRSU	QUADRANS	AAEEKMRT	TEAMAKER	AAEFFLLS	FALAFELS
AADNQRTU	QUADRANT	AAEEKNRW	AWAKENER	AAEFFLPR	PARAFFLE
AADNQRUY	QUANDARY		REAWAKEN	AAEFFLRT	TAFFAREL
AADNRRSW	WARRANDS	AAEEKPRT	PARAKEET	AAEFFNRS	FANFARES
AADNRRSY	DARRAYNS	AAEEKPSS	SEASPEAK	AAEFFRRY	AFFRAYER
AADNRSTY	TANYARDS	AAEEKQSU	SEAQUAKE	AAEFFSTT	TAFFETAS
AADNRSWY	NAYWARDS	AAEEKRSW	REAWAKES	AAEFGGRT	GRAFTAGE
AADOPPRR	PARADROP	AAEELLLM	LAMELLAE	AAEFGHRW	WHARFAGE

Eight-letter anagrams

AAEFGINR	AFEARING	**AAEGILSS**	ALGESIAS	**AAEGLRST**	AGRESTAL
AAEFGITT	FATIGATE	**AAEGILSX**	GALAXIES	**AAEGLRSV**	SALVAGER
AAEFGLLL	FLAGELLA	**AAEGILTT**	TAILGATE	**AAEGLRTY**	LEGATARY
AAEFGLOT	FLOATAGE	**AAEGIMNO**	EGOMANIA	**AAEGLSST**	AGELASTS
AAEFGRTU	FRAUTAGE	**AAEGIMNP**	PIGMAEAN		LASTAGES
AAEFGSTW	WAFTAGES	**AAEGIMNS**	MAGNESIA	**AAEGLSSV**	SALVAGES
AAEFIILR	FILARIAE	**AAEGIMNT**	AGMINATE	**AAEGLSVY**	SAVAGELY
AAEFIKLT	KALIFATE		ENIGMATA	**AAEGLTUV**	VAULTAGE
AAEFILTY	FAYALITE	**AAEGIMNZ**	MAGAZINE	**AAEGMMNR**	ENGRAMMA
AAEFIMRR	AIRFRAME	**AAEGIMRR**	MARRIAGE	**AAEGMMNS**	GAMESMAN
AAEFINNT	FAINEANT	**AAEGIMRT**	GEMATRIA	**AAEGMNPY**	PYGMAEAN
AAEFINNU	INFAUNAE		MARITAGE	**AAEGMNRS**	MANAGERS
AAEFINPU	EPIFAUNA	**AAEGINNR**	ANEARING	**AAEGMNRT**	MAGNETAR
AAEFINST	FANTASIE	**AAEGINPS**	NAGAPIES	**AAEGMNRV**	GRAVAMEN
AAEFINTX	ANTEFIXA		PAGANISE	**AAEGMNST**	MAGENTAS
AAEFIRRS	AIRFARES	**AAEGINPT**	PAGINATE		MAGNATES
AAEFKMST	MAKEFAST	**AAEGINPZ**	PAGANIZE		NAMETAGS
AAEFLLSV	FAVELLAS	**AAEGINRS**	ANERGIAS	**AAEGMORR**	AEROGRAM
AAEFLMOT	MEATLOAF		ANGARIES	**AAEGMORS**	SAGAMORE
AAEFLMTT	FLATMATE		ARGINASE	**AAEGMPRR**	RAMPAGER
AAEFLNUU	FAUNULAE	**AAEGINRT**	AERATING	**AAEGMPRS**	RAMPAGES
AAEFLPRS	EARFLAPS	**AAEGINST**	SAGINATE	**AAEGMPRU**	RAMPAUGE
	PARAFLES	**AAEGINSW**	WAINAGES	**AAEGMRRV**	MARGRAVE
AAEFLRTW	FLATWARE	**AAEGINTV**	NAVIGATE	**AAEGMRRY**	GRAMARYE
AAEFMRST	FERMATAS		VAGINATE	**AAEGMRSS**	MASSAGER
AAEFMRSU	FUMARASE	**AAEGIPRS**	IGARAPES	**AAEGMRST**	MEGASTAR
AAEFMRTU	FUMARATE	**AAEGIPRU**	PERIAGUA	**AAEGMRTU**	AGERATUM
AAEFQRSU	AQUAFERS	**AAEGIRRS**	ARRIAGES	**AAEGMSSS**	MASSAGES
AAEFRRRW	WARFARER	**AAEGIRSV**	VAGARIES	**AAEGMSTT**	METATAGS
AAEFRRSW	WARFARES	**AAEGISSS**	ASSEGAIS	**AAEGMTTW**	MEGAWATT
AAEFRRWY	WAYFARER	**AAEGISST**	AGATISES	**AAEGNNOP**	NEOPAGAN
AAEFRSWY	WAYFARES	**AAEGISSU**	AGEUSIAS	**AAEGNNPS**	PANNAGES
AAEFRTTX	AFTERTAX	**AAEGISTT**	AGITATES	**AAEGNNST**	TANNAGES
AAEGGINR	GRAINAGE	**AAEGISTZ**	AGATIZES	**AAEGNPST**	PAGEANTS
AAEGGIOT	AGIOTAGE	**AAEGIVWY**	GIVEAWAY	**AAEGNPSW**	PAWNAGES
AAEGGLNR	LANGRAGE	**AAEGJSTU**	AJUTAGES	**AAEGNRRR**	ARRANGER
AAEGGLNU	LANGUAGE	**AAEGKNST**	TANKAGES	**AAEGNRRS**	ARRANGES
AAEGGMMR	GRAMMAGE	**AAEGKOSS**	SOAKAGES	**AAEGNRST**	STARAGEN
AAEGGNOS	ANAGOGES	**AAEGLLMS**	SMALLAGE		TANAGERS
AAEGGNOW	WAGONAGE	**AAEGLLPR**	PELLAGRA	**AAEGNRTU**	RUNAGATE
AAEGGNRY	GARGANEY	**AAEGLLSS**	GALLEASS	**AAEGNSSU**	GUANASES
AAEGGOPR	PARAGOGE	**AAEGLLST**	GALLATES	**AAEGNSTT**	STAGNATE
AAEGGOPS	APAGOGES		GALLETAS	**AAEGNSTV**	VANTAGES
AAEGGRST	AGGRATES		STALLAGE	**AAEGNSTW**	WANTAGES
AAEGHLNP	PHALANGE		TALLAGES	**AAEGNTUV**	VAUNTAGE
AAEGHLSU	HAULAGES	**AAEGLLTU**	GLUTAEAL	**AAEGORRT**	ARROGATE
AAEGHLSY	HAYLAGES	**AAEGLMNS**	GAMELANS	**AAEGORSS**	AGAROSES
AAEGHMRX	HEXAGRAM	**AAEGLMNV**	GAVELMAN	**AAEGORTT**	AEGROTAT
AAEGHMSS	GAMASHES	**AAEGLMPY**	GAMEPLAY	**AAEGPPRW**	WRAPPAGE
AAEGHNRU	HARANGUE	**AAEGLMST**	ALMAGEST	**AAEGPRSS**	PASSAGER
AAEGHNST	THANAGES	**AAEGLNOU**	ANALOGUE	**AAEGPRSW**	WARPAGES
AAEGHOPY	HYPOGAEA	**AAEGLNPP**	LAGNAPPE	**AAEGPSSS**	PASSAGES
AAEGILLP	PELAGIAL	**AAEGLNPT**	PLANTAGE	**AAEGPSSY**	PAYSAGES
AAEGILLR	GALLERIA	**AAEGLNRS**	ALNAGERS	**AAEGQSUY**	QUAYAGES
AAEGILLT	ALLIGATE	**AAEGLNRT**	ARGENTAL	**AAEGRRSV**	RAVAGERS
AAEGILMS	SEMIGALA	**AAEGLNRU**	AULNAGER	**AAEGRSST**	GASTREAS
AAEGILNP	PELAGIAN	**AAEGLNSS**	LASAGNES	**AAEGRSSU**	ASSUAGER
AAEGILNR	GERANIAL	**AAEGLNSU**	AULNAGES	**AAEGRSTT**	REGATTAS
	REGALIAN		LEGUAANS	**AAEGRSTV**	STRAVAGE
AAEGILNT	AGENTIAL	**AAEGLNTU**	ANGULATE	**AAEGRSTZ**	STARGAZE
	ALGINATE	**AAEGLOSV**	AASVOGEL	**AAEGRSVY**	SAVAGERY
AAEGILRS	GASALIER	**AAEGLRRS**	REALGARS	**AAEGSSSU**	ASSUAGES
	LAIRAGES		RESALGAR		SAUSAGES
	REGALIAS	**AAEGLRRW**	WARRAGLE	**AAEGSSSV**	AVGASSES

Code	Word(s)
AAEGSSSW	ASSWAGES
AAEGSSTV	SAVAGEST
AAEGSSTW	TASSWAGE
	WASTAGES
AAEGSTTW	WATTAGES
AAEGSTWY	GATEWAYS
	GETAWAYS
AAEHIIRT	HETAIRAI
	HETAIRIA
AAEHILMN	HIELAMAN
AAEHILNP	APHELIAN
AAEHILNT	ANTHELIA
AAEHILPR	PARHELIA
AAEHIMNT	ANTHEMIA
	HAEMATIN
AAEHIMRU	MAIREHAU
AAEHINPT	APHANITE
AAEHINST	ASTHENIA
AAEHIPST	APATHIES
AAEHIRST	HETAIRAS
AAEHIRTT	HATTERIA
AAEHKLST	ALKAHEST
AAEHKMRT	HATMAKER
AAEHKMRV	HAYMAKER
AAEHKNST	KHANATES
AAEHKSSW	SEAHAWKS
AAEHLLLS	ALLHEALS
AAEHLMNT	METHANAL
AAEHLMNW	WHALEMAN
AAEHLMSY	SEALYHAM
AAEHLMTU	HAMULATE
AAEHLNOZ	HALAZONE
AAEHLNRT	ANTHERAL
AAEHLNRW	NARWHALE
AAEHLNST	ETHANALS
AAEHLNTX	EXHALANT
AAEHLOPT	APHOLATE
AAEHLPRS	PEARLASH
AAEHLPRX	HEXAPLAR
AAEHLPSX	HEXAPLAS
AAEHLPUV	UPHEAVAL
AAEHLRST	TREHALAS
AAEHLRTT	THEATRAL
AAEHLSSV	LAVASHES
AAEHLSTT	ATHLETAS
AAEHMMOT	HEMATOMA
AAEHMNPT	PATHNAME
AAEHMNPY	NYMPHAEA
AAEHMNRS	SHAREMAN
	SHEARMAN
AAEHMNRT	EARTHMAN
AAEHMOPR	AMPHORAE
AAEHMOPT	HEPATOMA
AAEHMORT	ATHEROMA
AAEHNPRS	HANAPERS
AAEHNPSS	SAPHENAS
AAEHNPST	PHEASANT
AAEHNPSY	SYNAPHEA
AAEHNTTX	XANTHATE
AAEHPRSZ	PHEAZARS
AAEHRRSS	HARASSER
AAEHRSSS	HARASSES
AAEHRSSY	HEARSAYS
AAEHRSTU	ARETHUSA
AAEHRTWX	EARTHWAX
AAEIIKNS	AKINESIA
AAEIILMP	LIPAEMIA
AAEIIMRV	VIRAEMIA
AAEIINSV	AVIANISE
AAEIINVZ	AVIANIZE
AAEIIPRS	APIARIES
AAEIIRSV	AVIARIES
AAEIJLNV	JAVELINA
AAEIJNPS	JAPANISE
AAEIJNPZ	JAPANIZE
AAEIJNRT	NAARTJIE
AAEIKKMZ	KAMIKAZE
AAEIKLLN	ALKALINE
AAEIKLLS	ALKALIES
	ALKALISE
AAEIKLLV	LAVALIKE
AAEIKLLZ	ALKALIZE
AAEIKLNT	ANTILEAK
AAEIKMRR	KRAMERIA
AAEIKPRT	PARAKITE
AAEILLLU	ALLELUIA
AAEILLMM	MAMILLAE
AAEILLMR	ARMILLAE
AAEILLMX	MAXILLAE
AAEILLNT	ALLANITE
AAEILLPP	PAPILLAE
AAEILLPT	PALLIATE
AAEILLRT	ARILLATE
AAEILLRV	LAVALIER
AAEILLRY	AERIALLY
AAEILLTT	TALLIATE
AAEILLTV	ALLATIVE
AAEILMMX	AXILEMMA
AAEILMNN	MELANIAN
AAEILMNT	ALAIMENT
	ANTIMALE
	LAMINATE
AAEILMNV	VELAMINA
AAEILMRT	MATERIAL
AAEILMSS	MALAISES
AAEILNNS	ALANINES
	ANNALISE
AAEILNNZ	ANNALIZE
AAEILNPR	AIRPLANE
AAEILNPT	PALATINE
AAEILNRU	AURELIAN
AAEILNRV	VALERIAN
AAEILNSS	NASALISE
AAEILNSZ	NASALIZE
AAEILNTT	ANTLIATE
AAEILNTV	AVENTAIL
AAEILORS	OLEARIAS
AAEILPPS	PAPALISE
AAEILPPZ	PAPALIZE
AAEILPRT	PARIETAL
AAEILPRX	PREAXIAL
AAEILPST	STAPELIA
AAEILRRT	ARTERIAL
AAEILRSS	ASSAILER
	REASSAIL
	SALARIES
AAEILRSU	AURELIAS
AAEILRSV	REAVAILS
AAEILRTV	VARIETAL
AAEILSTV	AESTIVAL
	SALIVATE
AAEILSTX	SAXATILE
AAEILSWY	AISLEWAY
AAEILTVX	LAXATIVE
AAEIMMST	IMAMATES
AAEIMNOT	METANOIA
AAEIMNOX	ANOXEMIA
AAEIMNPR	PEARMAIN
AAEIMNPS	PAEANISM
AAEIMNPT	IMPANATE
AAEIMNRR	MARINERA
AAEIMNRT	ANIMATER
	MARINATE
AAEIMNRZ	MAZARINE
AAEIMNSS	AMNESIAS
AAEIMNST	AMENTIAS
	ANIMATES
AAEIMNTZ	NIZAMATE
AAEIMOPR	PAROEMIA
AAEIMOTX	TOXAEMIA
AAEIMOTZ	AZOTEMIA
AAEIMPRS	ASPERMIA
	SAPREMIA
AAEIMPSY	PYAEMIAS
AAEIMRST	AMIRATES
AAEIMRSU	URAEMIAS
AAEIMRTT	AMARETTI
AAEIMSUV	MAUVAISE
AAEINNTT	ANTENATI
AAEINORT	AERATION
AAEINORX	ANOREXIA
AAEINPPR	PRIAPEAN
AAEINPRS	PANARIES
AAEINPRT	ANTIRAPE
AAEINPTT	PATINATE
AAEINRRW	RAINWEAR
AAEINRST	ANTISERA
	ARTESIAN
	RATANIES
	RESINATA
	SANTERIA
	SEATRAIN
AAEINRTT	ATTAINER
	REATTAIN
AAEINRTU	INAURATE
AAEINRTW	ANTIWEAR
AAEINRTZ	ATRAZINE
AAEINSST	ENTASIAS
AAEINSTT	ASTATINE
	SANITATE
	TANAISTE
AAEINSTV	SANATIVE
AAEINTTT	TITANATE
AAEIPPRS	APPRAISE
AAEIPPSS	APEPSIAS
AAEIPRRS	PAREIRAS
AAEIPRSS	SPIRAEAS
AAEIPRST	ASPIRATE
	PARASITE
	SEPTARIA
AAEIPRTT	PATRIATE
AAEIPRTZ	TRAPEZIA

Eight-letter anagrams

AAEIPRXY	APYREXIA
AAEIPSTT	APATITES
AAEIQRTU	TAQUERIA
AAEIRRRT	TERRARIA
AAEIRRTV	VERATRIA
AAEIRSST	ASTERIAS
	ATRESIAS
AAEIRSSX	XERASIAS
AAEIRSTT	ARIETTAS
	ARISTATE
AAEIRSTV	VARIATES
AAEIRSTW	AWAITERS
AAEIRSVW	AIRWAVES
AAEIRTTZ	ZARATITE
AAEISSTT	SATIATES
AAEISTUX	EUTAXIAS
AAEITTVX	TAXATIVE
AAEJLNOP	JALAPENO
AAEJMNRY	MARYJANE
AAEJNNPR	JAPANNER
AAEJNRST	NAARTJES
AAEJNRTZ	JAZERANT
AAEJOPRS	APAREJOS
AAEJRSSV	SVARAJES
AAEJRSSW	SWARAJES
AAEKKORS	KARAOKES
AAEKKRSY	KAYAKERS
AAEKLLTY	ALKYLATE
AAEKLMRW	LAWMAKER
AAEKLMRY	MALARKEY
AAEKLNRS	LARNAKES
AAEKLNST	ALKANETS
	KANTELAS
AAEKLPRS	ASPARKLE
AAEKMMPR	MAPMAKER
AAEKMORT	KERATOMA
AAEKMRRS	EARMARKS
AAEKMRRW	WARMAKER
AAEKMRSS	SEAMARKS
AAEKNPRT	PARTAKEN
AAEKORTY	AKARYOTE
AAEKPRRT	PARTAKER
AAEKPRST	PARTAKES
AAEKPSTU	PUKATEAS
AAEKSSSV	KAVASSES
	VAKASSES
AAELLLMR	LAMELLAR
AAELLLMS	LAMELLAS
AAELLLPR	PARALLEL
AAELLMPU	AMPULLAE
AAELLNPU	PLANULAE
AAELLNSS	NASSELLA
AAELLNSZ	ZANELLAS
AAELLORV	ALVEOLAR
AAELLPRS	PARELLAS
AAELLPRT	PATELLAR
AAELLPST	PATELLAS
AAELLRST	LATERALS
AAELLRSY	ALLAYERS
AAELLSSW	SEAWALLS
AAELLUVV	VALVULAE
AAELLWWY	WELLAWAY
AAELLWYY	ALLEYWAY
AAELMMNO	MELANOMA
AAELMMOX	AXOLEMMA
AAELMMRS	ALMEMARS
AAELMMTU	MALAMUTE
AAELMNOT	MALONATE
AAELMNOX	AXONEMAL
AAELMNPT	PLATEMAN
AAELMNRT	MATERNAL
AAELMNSS	SALESMAN
AAELMNST	TALESMAN
AAELMNSW	WEALSMAN
AAELMNSY	SEAMANLY
AAELMOST	OATMEALS
AAELMOSU	MAUSOLEA
AAELMOTZ	METAZOAL
AAELMPPY	MAYAPPLE
AAELMPRT	MALAPERT
AAELMPRX	EXAMPLAR
AAELMPSS	LAMPASES
	LAMPASSE
AAELMPST	PLATEASM
AAELMPTV	VAMPLATE
AAELMPTY	PLAYMATE
AAELMRSW	MALWARES
AAELMRSY	LAMASERY
AAELMRTT	MALTREAT
AAELMSST	MALTASES
AAELMSSY	AMYLASES
AAELNNNT	ANTENNAL
AAELNNOT	NEONATAL
AAELNNTU	ANNULATE
AAELNOSS	SEASONAL
AAELNOSV	VALONEAS
AAELNPRS	PRENASAL
AAELNPRT	PARENTAL
	PARLANTE
	PATERNAL
	PRENATAL
AAELNPRW	WARPLANE
AAELNPST	PLATANES
	PLEASANT
AAELNPSU	PAENULAS
AAELNPTT	PANTALET
AAELNRSS	ARSENALS
AAELNRST	ASTERNAL
AAELNRSY	ANALYSER
AAELNRTT	ALTERANT
	ALTERNAT
	TARLETAN
AAELNRTX	RELAXANT
AAELNRYZ	ANALYZER
AAELNSST	SEALANTS
AAELNSSV	ENVASSAL
AAELNSSY	ANALYSES
AAELNSTT	ATLANTES
AAELNSTY	ANALYTES
AAELNSTZ	ZEALANTS
AAELNSWY	LANEWAYS
AAELNSYZ	ANALYZES
AAELOPRS	PSORALEA
AAELORSU	AUREOLAS
AAELORTY	ALEATORY
AAELOSTX	OXALATES
AAELPPRS	APPARELS
AAELPPST	PALPATES
AAELPPSU	APPLAUSE
AAELPRST	PALESTRA
AAELPRSV	PALAVERS
AAELPRSY	PARALYSE
AAELPRTT	TETRAPLA
AAELPRWY	PLAYWEAR
AAELPRYZ	PARALYZE
AAELPSTU	PLATEAUS
AAELPSTV	PALSTAVE
AAELPSWY	PALEWAYS
AAELPTUV	VAPULATE
AAELPTUX	PLATEAUX
AAELRSST	TARSEALS
AAELRSTZ	LAZARETS
AAELRTUV	VELATURA
AAELRUZZ	ZARZUELA
AAELRWYY	WAYLAYER
AAELSSTT	SALTATES
AAELSTUV	VALUATES
AAELSTZZ	ALTEZZAS
AAEMMMRS	MAREMMAS
AAEMMNOT	AMMONATE
AAEMMNRT	ARMAMENT
AAEMMNSU	MANUMEAS
AAEMMOST	METASOMA
AAEMMSTT	STEMMATA
AAEMNORS	AMARONES
AAEMNORT	EMANATOR
AAEMNOSW	SEAWOMAN
AAEMNOTZ	METAZOAN
AAEMNPPS	PAMPEANS
AAEMNPRS	PARMESAN
	SPEARMAN
AAEMNPRT	PARAMENT
AAEMNRRY	YARRAMEN
AAEMNRST	SARMENTA
	SEMANTRA
AAEMNRSU	MURAENAS
AAEMNRTT	ATRAMENT
AAEMNRTW	WATERMAN
AAEMNSST	NAMASTES
AAEMNSTU	MANTEAUS
AAEMNTUX	MANTEAUX
AAEMOPXZ	OXAZEPAM
AAEMORTT	AMARETTO
	TERATOMA
AAEMORTX	XEROMATA
AAEMOSTT	STEATOMA
AAEMOSTY	ATEMOYAS
AAEMOTTU	AUTOMATE
AAEMPPSS	PAMPASES
AAEMPTTU	AMPUTATE
AAEMQSTU	SQUAMATE
AAEMRRTU	ARMATURE
AAEMRSSS	AMASSERS
AAEMRSTU	AMATEURS
AAEMRTTU	MATURATE
AAENNNST	ANTENNAS
AAENNOTT	ANNOTATE
AAENNSTT	STANNATE
	TANNATES
AAENNSTU	NAUSEANT
AAENNSTV	VENTANAS
AAENOPSS	PAESANOS

AAENOQTU	AQUATONE	AAFFMNST	STAFFMAN	AAFLNOTT	FLOATANT
AAENORRU	AUROREAN	AAFFNNOR	FANFARON	AAFLNRSU	FURLANAS
AAENORST	ANOESTRA	AAFFOORW	FOOFARAW	AAFLSTWY	FLATWAYS
AAENORSU	ARANEOUS	AAFGHINS	AFGHANIS	AAFLSWYY	FLYAWAYS
AAENORTU	AERONAUT	AAFGHNRU	FRAUGHAN	AAFMNRST	RAFTSMAN
AAENOSST	ASSONATE	AAFGILNO	GOLFIANA	AAFMNSST	FANTASMS
AAENPPRS	PARPANES	AAFGINTW	FATWAING	AAFMOPRR	PARAFORM
AAENPPRT	APPARENT	AAFGLLNU	LANGLAUF	AAFNPPRT	FRAPPANT
	TRAPPEAN	AAFGLNRT	FLAGRANT	AAFNSSTT	FANTASTS
AAENPRTY	PRYTANEA	AAFGNRRT	FRAGRANT	AAGGGHNS	GANGSHAG
AAENPSST	ANAPESTS	AAFGORRS	FARRAGOS	AAGGGINR	GARAGING
	PEASANTS	AAFHHIKL	KHALIFAH	AAGGHNST	HANGTAGS
AAENPSTT	ANTEPAST	AAFHHORT	HAFTORAH	AAGGILLN	GANGLIAL
AAENPSTY	PEASANTY	AAFHIKLS	KHALIFAS	AAGGILNR	GANGLIAR
AAENRRRT	NARRATER	AAFHIKLT	KHALIFAT	AAGGIMNN	MANAGING
AAENRRSS	NARRASES		KHILAFAT	AAGGIMNR	MARAGING
AAENRRST	NARRATES	AAFHINRS	FARINHAS	AAGGINNT	ANTIGANG
AAENRSST	SANTERAS	AAFHIRST	AIRSHAFT	AAGGINRV	RAVAGING
AAENRSTT	TARTANES	AAFHLLSS	ASHFALLS	AAGGINSV	SAVAGING
AAENRSTV	TAVERNAS	AAFHLSTW	FLATWASH	AAGGIRST	GARAGIST
	TSAREVNA	AAFHLSTY	LAYSHAFT	AAGGITTW	GIGAWATT
AAENRSUW	UNAWARES	AAFHORTT	HAFTAROT	AAGGLLLY	LALLYGAG
AAENRSYY	NAYSAYER	AAFHRSUU	HAUSFRAU	AAGGLMOS	MAGALOGS
AAENRTVZ	TZAREVNA	AAFIILLM	FAMILIAL	AAGGLNOT	TAGALONG
AAENSSSV	VANESSAS	AAFIILLR	FILARIAL	AAGGLRSY	GRAYLAGS
AAENSSTV	SAVANTES	AAFIILMR	FAMILIAR	AAGGMNNS	GANGSMAN
AAENSSTW	SEAWANTS	AAFIILNR	FILARIAN	AAGGNNOO	ONGAONGA
AAENSSWY	AWAYNESS	AAFIILRS	FILARIAS	AAGGNSST	GANGSTAS
AAENTTTT	ATTENTAT	AAFIINST	FISTIANA	AAGGNSTT	TAGGANTS
AAEOPPSS	APOAPSES	AAFIKLLY	ALKALIFY	AAGGNSWY	GANGWAYS
AAEOPSTT	APOSTATE	AAFILLNR	RAINFALL	AAGGRSTT	STAGGART
AAEOPSTZ	ZAPATEOS	AAFILLUV	AVAILFUL	AAGHHIMS	MASHGIAH
AAEORRST	AERATORS	AAFILMST	FATALISM	AAGHHINS	SHANGHAI
AAEORSST	AEROSATS	AAFILNNU	INFAUNAL	AAGHHNOS	OANSHAGH
AAEORSTT	AEROSTAT	AAFILNQU	ALFAQUIN	AAGHILNN	HANGNAIL
AAEORTTV	ROTAVATE	AAFILNST	FANTAILS	AAGHILPY	HYPALGIA
AAEPPRRT	TARPAPER		TAILFANS	AAGHILRS	GHARIALS
AAEPPRST	PARAPETS	AAFILOPR	PARAFOIL		HARIGALS
AAEPPSTT	APPESTAT	AAFILQSU	ALFAQUIS	AAGHIMNS	ASHAMING
AAEPQRTU	PARAQUET	AAFILSTT	FATALIST	AAGHIMRT	TAGHAIRM
AAEPRSSY	APYRASES	AAFILTTY	FATALITY	AAGHINNS	ANHINGAS
AAEPRTXY	TAXPAYER	AAFIMNOR	FORAMINA	AAGHINPS	PAGANISH
AAEPSTTW	WATTAPES	AAFIMNOT	ANTIFOAM	AAGHINPW	AWHAPING
AAEPSWXX	PAXWAXES	AAFINNOV	FAVONIAN	AAGHIPRR	AIRGRAPH
AAEPSZZZ	PAZAZZES	AAFINNRS	SAFRANIN	AAGHIRSV	VAGARISH
AAERRRSY	ARRAYERS	AAFINNST	INFANTAS	AAGHKMNY	GYMKHANA
AAERRSST	TARRASES	AAFINNSU	INFAUNAS	AAGHKNST	THANGKAS
AAERRSTT	TARTARES	AAFINRRW	WARFARIN	AAGHLNNS	LANGSHAN
AAERRTTT	TARTRATE	AAFINSTU	FAUSTIAN	AAGHLNPY	ANAGLYPH
AAERSSSY	ASSAYERS	AAFIPRST	PARFAITS	AAGHLOSS	GASAHOLS
AAERSTTU	SATURATE	AAFIRSST	SAFARIST	AAGHMNOY	HOGMANAY
	TUATERAS	AAFIRSUY	RUFIYAAS		MAHOGANY
AAERTTTW	TERAWATT	AAFIRSWY	FAIRWAYS	AAGHMNSU	MAHUANGS
AAERTWWY	WATERWAY	AAFIRTTT	FRITTATA	AAGHMNSW	WHANGAMS
AAESTWWY	WASTEWAY	AAFJLLSW	JAWFALLS	AAGHNOPR	AGRAPHON
AAFFGILS	GAFFSAIL	AAFJLORS	ALFORJAS	AAGHNPRY	PHRYGANA
AAFFHIKY	KAFFIYAH	AAFLLNOV	FLAVANOL	AAGHNSST	SANGHATS
AAFFIILX	AFFIXIAL	AAFLLNUV	FAUNALLY	AAGHOPPR	APOGRAPH
AAFFILRT	TAFFRAIL	AAFLLPRT	PRATFALL	AAGHQSUU	QUAHAUGS
AAFFINPR	PARAFFIN	AAFLLPST	SPATFALL	AAGHRRTU	ARRAUGHT
AAFFINSS	SAFFIANS	AAFLMORV	LAVAFORM	AAGHRSSW	WASHRAGS
AAFFINST	AFFIANTS	AAFLNNOT	NONFATAL	AAGIIKKN	KAIAKING
AAFFLPST	PALSTAFF	AAFLNORS	FORLANAS	AAGIILMN	IMAGINAL
AAFFLSTU	AFFLATUS		SAFRONAL	AAGIILNS	ALIASING

Eight-letter anagrams

AAGIILNV	AVAILING	AAGINNSY	SYNANGIA	AAGMNSSW	SWAGSMAN
AAGIIMNN	MAGAININ	AAGINNTV	VAGINANT	AAGMNSTY	SYNTAGMA
AAGIIMST	ASTIGMIA	AAGINNTW	AWANTING	AAGMORSS	MARGOSAS
AAGIINNU	IGUANIAN	AAGINORR	RANGIORA	AAGMOTUY	AUTOGAMY
AAGIINRS	ARAISING	AAGINOSS	AGNOSIAS	AAGMOTYZ	ZYGOMATA
AAGIINST	IGNATIAS	AAGINPPY	APPAYING	AAGMRSST	MATGRASS
AAGIINTV	AVIATING	AAGINPRU	PAGURIAN	AAGNNNOP	NONPAGAN
AAGIINTW	AWAITING	AAGINPRW	PARAWING	AAGNNSTT	STAGNANT
AAGIKKNY	KAYAKING	AAGINPRY	AGRYPNIA	AAGNOPRS	PARAGONS
AAGIKLNO	KAOLIANG	AAGINPST	PAGANIST	AAGNOPRT	TRAGOPAN
AAGIKLNR	KRAALING	AAGINPWW	PAWAWING	AAGNORRT	ARROGANT
AAGIKLNS	ASLAKING	AAGINRRS	ARRAIGNS		TARRAGON
AAGIKMNS	SMAAKING	AAGINRRY	ARRAYING	AAGNORSZ	ORGANZAS
AAGIKMRS	SKIAGRAM	AAGINRSS	SANGRIAS	AAGNORTU	ARGONAUT
AAGIKNST	TIKANGAS		SARANGIS	AAGNRSTV	VAGRANTS
AAGIKNSW	AWAKINGS	AAGINRST	GRANITAS	AAGNRTUY	GUARANTY
AAGIKNSZ	ZIGANKAS	AAGINRSU	GUARANIS	AAGNRTYZ	ZYGANTRA
AAGILLNU	UNIALGAL	AAGINRSY	ARAYSING	AAGOPRSU	GAROUPAS
AAGILLNY	ALLAYING	AAGINSST	ASSIGNAT	AAGOPSSS	SAPSAGOS
AAGILLSS	GALLIASS	AAGINSSU	GAUSSIAN	AAGORSSS	SARGASSO
AAGILLTV	GALLIVAT	AAGINSSY	ASSAYING	AAGORSSU	SAGUAROS
AAGILLUZ	ALGUAZIL		GAINSAYS	AAGRRSSY	RAYGRASS
AAGILMMR	MAILGRAM	AAGIORTT	AGITATOR	AAGRSSTU	SASTRUGA
AAGILMNO	MAGNOLIA	AAGIORTV	AVIGATOR	AAGRSTUZ	ZASTRUGA
AAGILMNR	ALARMING	AAGIPRSU	PIRAGUAS	AAGSTTUU	TAUTAUGS
	MARGINAL	AAGIRRSY	ARGYRIAS	AAHHIIMM	MAHIMAHI
AAGILMNX	MALAXING	AAGIRSTV	GRAVITAS	AAHHIINN	HINAHINA
AAGILMOT	GLIOMATA		STRAVAIG	AAHHIKNU	HANUKIAH
AAGILMRY	GRAYMAIL	AAGISSTT	SAGITTAS	AAHHIRSS	SHARIAHS
AAGILMSY	MYALGIAS	AAGKKNOS	ANGAKOKS	AAHHKLOT	HALAKHOT
AAGILNOS	LOGANIAS	AAGKLRSV	GRAVLAKS		HALAKOTH
AAGILNOT	GALTONIA	AAGKNOOR	KANGAROO	AAHHKMRS	HASHMARK
AAGILNPT	PALATING	AAGKOOSZ	GAZOOKAS	AAHHKSWW	HAWKSHAW
AAGILNRR	LARRIGAN	AAGKORST	KATORGAS	AAHHMMSS	SHAMMASH
AAGILNSS	SALSAING	AAGLLMOV	ALLOGAMY	AAHHNNOS	HOSANNAH
AAGILNTV	GALIVANT	AAGLLNOO	LAGOONAL	AAHHNNST	THANNAHS
AAGILNUV	VAGINULA	AAGLLNRY	LARYNGAL	AAHHNPST	NAPHTHAS
AAGILOOP	APOLOGIA	AAGLLNST	GALLANTS	AAHHOPRS	PHARAOHS
AAGILOPT	TOPALGIA	AAGLLOOP	APOLOGAL	AAHIIKRT	TARAKIHI
AAGILOSS	AGLOSSIA	AAGLLOPY	POLYGALA	AAHIILRT	HAIRTAIL
AAGILOST	OTALGIAS	AAGLLOSS	AGLOSSAL	AAHIJNRS	HARIJANS
AAGILPRY	PLAGIARY	AAGLMNSS	GLASSMAN	AAHIJPRS	RAJASHIP
AAGILRRW	WARRIGAL	AAGLNNOO	ANALOGON	AAHIKLPS	PASHALIK
AAGILRTT	ATTAGIRL	AAGLNORS	GRANOLAS	AAHIKLST	HALAKIST
AAGILSTT	SAGITTAL	AAGLNPSS	LAPSANGS	AAHIKORW	WHAKAIRO
AAGILSTW	WAGTAILS	AAGLNQUU	AQUALUNG	AAHIKRST	KITHARAS
AAGIMMRR	MARIGRAM	AAGLNRRU	GRANULAR	AAHILLLS	HALLALIS
AAGIMNNN	MANGANIN	AAGLOPRY	PARALOGY		SHILLALA
AAGIMNNO	AGNOMINA	AAGLORSU	ARUGOLAS	AAHILLNS	HALLIANS
AAGIMNOS	ANGIOMAS	AAGLRRUW	WARRAGUL	AAHILMNR	HARMALIN
AAGIMNPS	PAGANISM	AAGLRSTU	GASTRULA	AAHILMRS	ALMIRAHS
AAGIMNRR	MARGARIN	AAGLRSUU	ARUGULAS	AAHILMSS	SHIMAALS
AAGIMNSS	AMASSING	AAGMMRRS	GRAMMARS	AAHILNNT	INHALANT
	SIAMANGS	AAGMMSUY	MAMAGUYS	AAHILNOT	HALATION
AAGIMNSY	GYMNASIA	AAGMNNOR	NANOGRAM	AAHILOPP	HAPLOPIA
AAGIMPTU	PATAGIUM	AAGMNNRS	GRANNAMS	AAHILPSV	PAHLAVIS
AAGIMSSV	SAVAGISM	AAGMNOPZ	ZAMPOGNA	AAHILPSY	PHYSALIA
AAGIMSTT	STIGMATA	AAGMNORT	MARTAGON	AAHILRRZ	ARRHIZAL
AAGINNNW	WANNIGAN	AAGMNOSS	SANGOMAS	AAHILSSW	SAHIWALS
AAGINNNY	NANNYGAI	AAGMNOST	AGAMONTS	AAHIMNOS	MAHONIAS
AAGINNOT	AGNATION	AAGMNPRS	PANGRAMS	AAHIMNPS	PASHMINA
AAGINNRW	AWARNING	AAGMNRST	TANGRAMS	AAHIMNSS	SHAMINAS
AAGINNSU	SAUNAING		TRANGAMS	AAHIMNZZ	HAZZANIM
AAGINNSW	WANIGANS	AAGMNRTU	ARMGAUNT	AAHIMRSW	RAWMAISH

AAHIMRTY	ARYTHMIA	**AAHRSSST**	SHASTRAS	**AAILLLSS**	SALSILLA
AAHINOPS	APHONIAS	**AAHRSSTY**	ASHTRAYS	**AAILLLST**	LATILLAS
AAHINPPS	PAPHIANS	**AAHRSTTW**	STRAWHAT	**AAILLLUV**	ALLUVIAL
AAHINPRS	PIRANHAS	**AAIIILMR**	MILIARIA	**AAILLMMM**	MAMMILLA
AAHINRSW	RAINWASH	**AAIIIMNR**	NIRAMIAI	**AAILLMMR**	MAMILLAR
AAHINRTU	HAURIANT	**AAIIJJPP**	JIPIJAPA	**AAILLMNS**	LAMINALS
AAHINSST	SHAITANS	**AAIIKKKR**	KAKARIKI		MANILLAS
AAHINSTW	TANIWHAS	**AAIIKKNN**	KINAKINA	**AAILLMNT**	MANTILLA
AAHIOPRT	ATROPHIA	**AAIILLQU**	QUILLAIA	**AAILLMNV**	ANIMALLY
AAHIPRST	PITARAHS	**AAIILMNS**	MAINSAIL	**AAILLMPT**	TAILLAMP
AAHIPSTZ	ZAPTIAHS	**AAIILMRS**	AIRMAILS	**AAILLMRS**	ARMILLAS
AAHIPSXY	ASPHYXIA	**AAIILNRZ**	ALIZARIN	**AAILLMRT**	RAMTILLA
AAHIRSSS	HARISSAS	**AAIILNUX**	UNIAXIAL	**AAILLMRX**	MAXILLAR
AAHIRSST	SHARIATS	**AAIILPRR**	RIPARIAL	**AAILLMSX**	MAXILLAS
AAHIRSTV	HAVARTIS	**AAIILPRS**	PAIRIALS	**AAILLNOV**	VALLONIA
AAHISTWY	THISAWAY	**AAIILPST**	TILAPIAS	**AAILLNPU**	NAUPLIAL
AAHJKNRS	KHANJARS	**AAIILRSZ**	ALIZARIS	**AAILLNST**	LANITALS
AAHKKOOR	HOROKAKA	**AAIILRTX**	TRIAXIAL	**AAILLNSV**	VANILLAS
AAHKLLMR	HALLMARK	**AAIILRUX**	AUXILIAR	**AAILLPPR**	PAPILLAR
AAHKLRSS	LASHKARS	**AAIILTXY**	AXIALITY	**AAILLRRY**	ARILLARY
AAHKMOTW	TOMAHAWK	**AAIIMNNT**	AMANITIN	**AAILLRSX**	AXILLARS
AAHKMSSY	YASHMAKS		MAINTAIN	**AAILLRXY**	AXILLARY
AAHKRSSW	SAWSHARK	**AAIIMNPX**	PANMIXIA	**AAILMMRS**	ALARMISM
AAHLLLOO	HALLALOO	**AAIINNRT**	ANTIARIN		AMMIRALS
AAHLLMRS	MARSHALL	**AAIINOTV**	AVIATION	**AAILMMSX**	MAXIMALS
AAHLLOPT	ALLOPATH	**AAIINPRR**	RIPARIAN	**AAILMNNT**	LAMANTIN
AAHLLSWY	HALLWAYS	**AAIINPZZ**	PIAZZIAN	**AAILMNOP**	PALAMINO
AAHLMMSS	MASHLAMS	**AAIINRST**	INTARSIA	**AAILMNOR**	MANORIAL
AAHLMOOS	MASOOLAH	**AAIINSTT**	TITANIAS		MORAINAL
AAHLMOPR	AMPHORAL	**AAIINSZZ**	ZIZANIAS	**AAILMNOX**	MONAXIAL
AAHLMRSS	MARSHALS	**AAIIOPST**	APOSITIA	**AAILMNPS**	PANISLAM
AAHLMSTU	THALAMUS	**AAIIORTZ**	ZOIATRIA	**AAILMNRU**	MANURIAL
AAHLNPST	ASHPLANT	**AAIIPRST**	APIARIST	**AAILMNRY**	LAMINARY
AAHLNRSW	NARWHALS	**AAIIPRVV**	VIVIPARA	**AAILMNSS**	NASALISM
AAHLPRRT	PHRATRAL	**AAIIRSTV**	AVIARIST	**AAILMNST**	STAMINAL
AAHLPSST	ASPHALTS	**AAIIRSTW**	WISTARIA		TALISMAN
AAHLRSSW	SHALWARS	**AAIIRTVX**	AVIATRIX	**AAILMNSU**	ALUMINAS
AAHMNNPU	PANHUMAN	**AAIJLLQU**	QUILLAJA	**AAILMNSV**	MAILVANS
AAHMNNSU	HANUMANS	**AAIJLNPS**	JALAPINS		NAVALISM
AAHMNORT	MARATHON	**AAIJMNPS**	JAMPANIS	**AAILMOPT**	LIPOMATA
AAHMNOST	HOASTMAN	**AAIJNRSY**	JANISARY	**AAILMORR**	ARMORIAL
AAHMNOTX	XANTHOMA	**AAIJNRSZ**	JANIZARS	**AAILMPPS**	PAPALISM
AAHMNPST	PHANTASM	**AAIJNRYZ**	JANIZARY	**AAILMPRT**	PRIMATAL
AAHMNRST	TRASHMAN	**AAIJPPSY**	JIPYAPAS	**AAILMQSU**	MAQUILAS
AAHMNSTX	XANTHAMS	**AAIKKNOS**	SKOKIAAN	**AAILMRST**	ALARMIST
AAHMOPRS	AMPHORAS	**AAIKKSTZ**	KAZATSKI		ALASTRIM
AAHMRSST	STRAMASH	**AAIKLNNN**	ALKANNIN		MARTIALS
AAHNNOSS	HOSANNAS	**AAIKLNPS**	PALINKAS	**AAILMTTU**	ULTIMATA
AAHNNPSW	SHWANPAN	**AAIKLNST**	NASTALIK	**AAILNNOT**	NATIONAL
AAHNNSTX	XANTHANS	**AAIKLPRS**	PALIKARS	**AAILNNPT**	PLAINANT
AAHNOPRS	ANAPHORS	**AAIKMNNS**	MANAKINS		PLANTAIN
AAHNORST	ATHANORS	**AAIKMNRS**	RAMAKINS	**AAILNNRU**	LUNARIAN
AAHNORSV	NAVARHOS	**AAIKMNST**	ANTIMASK	**AAILNNST**	ANNALIST
AAHNOSTT	THANATOS	**AAIKMORS**	ROMAIKAS		SANTALIN
AAHNPSTT	PHANTAST	**AAIKMRSS**	KARAISMS	**AAILNOPS**	SALOPIAN
AAHNPSTY	PHANTASY	**AAIKMRST**	TAMARISK	**AAILNOPT**	TALAPOIN
AAHNTUWY	HUNTAWAY	**AAIKNNTT**	ANTITANK	**AAILNORS**	ORINASAL
AAHOPRST	PARASHOT	**AAIKORSU**	OUAKARIS	**AAILNORT**	NOTARIAL
AAHOPRTU	AUTOHARP	**AAIKPPRS**	PAPRIKAS		RATIONAL
AAHOQSUW	AQUASHOW	**AAIKPRRS**	AIRPARKS	**AAILNOST**	AILANTOS
AAHORSSU	SAHUAROS	**AAIKSSTT**	ASTATKIS		ALATIONS
AAHPRSTW	WARPATHS	**AAIKSSTV**	SVASTIKA	**AAILNOSV**	VALONIAS
AAHPSTWY	PATHWAYS	**AAIKSSTW**	SWASTIKA	**AAILNOTV**	LAVATION
AAHRRTTW	THRAWART	**AAIKSTVV**	AKVAVITS	**AAILNOTX**	LAXATION

Eight-letter anagrams

AAILNPRU	PLANURIA	AAIMRSSU	SAMURAIS	AAISSTTV	ATAVISTS
AAILNPSS	SALPIANS	AAIMRSTU	TIMARAUS	AAISTWXY	TAXIWAYS
AAILNPST	PLATINAS	AAIMSSSY	MISASSAY	AAJKLSWY	JAYWALKS
AAILNQTU	ALIQUANT	AAIMSSTV	ATAVISMS	AAJMMORR	MARJORAM
AAILNSSY	ANALYSIS	AAINNOPV	PAVONIAN	AAJMORRS	MOJARRAS
AAILNSTV	VALIANTS	AAINNOST	SONATINA	AAJMORST	MAJORATS
AAILNSTY	NASALITY	AAINNOTT	NATATION	AAJOPSSU	SAPAJOUS
AAILNTTT	LATITANT	AAINNOTX	ANATOXIN	AAKKLRSU	KARAKULS
AAILNTTY	NATALITY	AAINNRSV	NAVARINS	AAKKMMOO	KAMOKAMO
AAILORRS	RASORIAL		NIRVANAS	AAKKMOST	TOKAMAKS
AAILORRV	VARIOLAR	AAINNRTU	NUTARIAN	AAKKOSUZ	ZAKOUSKA
AAILORSS	ROSALIAS	AAINNSST	NAISSANT	AAKKSTYZ	KAZATSKY
AAILORSU	RAOULIAS	AAINNSSY	SANNYASI	AAKLMPSU	LAMPUKAS
AAILORSV	VARIOLAS	AAINOOPS	ANOOPSIA	AAKLMRUY	YARMULKA
AAILPPRU	PUPARIAL	AAINOPSS	ANOPSIAS	AAKLMSUY	YAMULKAS
AAILPPST	PAPALIST		PAISANOS	AAKLNOOS	OOLAKANS
AAILPRST	PARTIALS	AAINORRS	ORARIANS	AAKLNOSU	OULAKANS
	PATRIALS		ROSARIAN	AAKLOOPS	PALOOKAS
	TRIAPSAL	AAINOTTX	TAXATION	AAKLOOST	TALOOKAS
AAILPRSY	AIRPLAYS	AAINPPRY	PAPYRIAN	AAKLPRTY	KALYPTRA
AAILPSTT	TALIPATS	AAINPRST	ASPIRANT	AAKLRSSU	KURSAALS
AAILQRSU	SQUARIAL		PARTISAN		RUSALKAS
AAILQSWW	QAWWALIS		SPARTINA	AAKLSSSU	SAKSAULS
AAILRRSV	ARRIVALS	AAINPRTZ	PARTIZAN	AAKLSWWY	WALKWAYS
AAILRSTT	RATTAILS	AAINPSST	PASTINAS	AAKMMNRS	MARKSMAN
AAILRSTV	TRAVAILS	AAINQRRU	QUARRIAN	AAKMORUZ	MAZOURKA
AAILRSVY	SALIVARY	AAINQRTU	QUATRAIN	AAKMOSSU	MOUSAKAS
AAILRSWY	RAILWAYS	AAINQTTU	AQUATINT		MOUSSAKA
AAILRTUY	AURALITY	AAINRRSS	SARRASIN	AAKMRSUZ	MAZURKAS
AAILSSSV	VASSAILS	AAINRRSZ	SARRAZIN	AAKMRSWY	WAYMARKS
AAILSSSW	WASSAILS	AAINRSST	ARTISANS	AAKNNSTU	NUNATAKS
AAILSSTY	STAYSAIL		TSARINAS	AAKNRSYY	SYNKARYA
AAILSTTT	LATITATS	AAINRSSU	SAURIANS	AAKNSSTW	WANKSTAS
AAIMMNOS	AMMONIAS	AAINRSSV	SAVARINS	AAKNSTWY	TWANKAYS
AAIMMNST	MAINMAST	AAINRSTV	VARIANTS	AAKOOPPS	PAKAPOOS
AAIMMRSU	SAMARIUM	AAINRSTY	SANITARY	AAKOPPRT	PORTAPAK
AAIMMNRT	TRAINMAN	AAINRSTZ	TZARINAS	AAKOPRSWY	PARKWAYS
AAIMNOOZ	ZOOMANIA	AAINRTWY	TRAINWAY	AAKRSSTU	KATSURAS
AAIMNORT	ANIMATOR	AAINSSSS	ASSASSIN	AALLLSTY	LAYSTALL
	MONTARIA	AAINSSSY	SANYASIS	AALLMNST	STALLMAN
	TAMANOIR	AAINSSTT	SATANIST	AALLMNTY	TALLYMAN
AAIMNORW	AIRWOMAN	AAINSTTT	ANTISTAT	AALLMNUY	MANUALLY
AAIMNOSS	ANOSMIAS		ATTAINTS	AALLMORY	AMORALLY
AAIMNOST	AMATIONS	AAINSTTU	TUTANIAS	AALLMPRU	AMPULLAR
AAIMNOTT	ANTIATOM	AAINSTTV	AVANTIST	AALLMSST	SMALLSAT
AAIMNPRZ	MARZIPAN	AAINSTTY	SATANITY	AALLNNUY	ANNUALLY
AAIMNPST	ANTISPAM	AAIOPPSS	APOAPSIS	AALLNOST	SANTALOL
AAIMNPTU	PUTAMINA	AAIOPRRT	TROPARIA	AALLNOSX	ALLOXANS
AAIMNRRT	TRIMARAN	AAIOPRST	ATROPIAS	AALLNOTY	ATONALLY
AAIMNRRU	RANARIUM	AAIOPRSU	PAROUSIA	AALLNPRU	PLANULAR
AAIMNRST	MARTIANS	AAIOPSTU	AUTOPSIA	AALLNRTY	TARNALLY
	TAMARINS	AAIORSSU	SAOUARIS	AALLOORW	WALLAROO
AAIMNSST	MANTISSA	AAIORSTV	AVIATORS	AALLORSU	ALLOSAUR
	SATANISM	AAIORTUZ	AZOTURIA	AALLORWY	ROLLAWAY
	STAMINAS	AAIPPSTT	PITAPATS	AALLOSTV	LAVOLTAS
AAIMNSTU	AMIANTUS	AAIPRSSX	SPARAXIS	AALLPRST	PLASTRAL
AAIMNSTY	MAINSTAY	AAIPRSTT	PARTITAS	AALLRSTY	ASTRALLY
AAIMOPRS	MARIPOSA	AAIQRSTU	AQUARIST	AALLRUVV	VALVULAR
	PAROSMIA	AAIQSSSU	QUASSIAS	AALMMNOS	AMMONALS
AAIMPRST	PASTRAMI	AAIQSTUV	AQUAVITS	AALMNORT	MATRONAL
AAIMPRSU	MARSUPIA	AAIRSSTT	TSARITSA	AALMNORU	MONAURAL
AAIMQRUU	AQUARIUM	AAIRSTTZ	TSARITZA	AALMNOSS	SALAMONS
AAIMRRSY	MISARRAY	AAIRSTWY	STAIRWAY	AALMNOWY	LAYWOMAN
AAIMRRTY	MARTYRIA	AAIRTTZZ	TZARITZA	AALMNPTY	TYMPANAL

AALMNTTU	TANTALUM	AAMMRSSU	MARASMUS	ABBBELMO	BOMBABLE
AALMNTUU	AUTUMNAL	AAMMNNORS	SONARMAN	ABBBELRR	BRABBLER
AALMOOSS	MASSOOLA	AAMNNOSY	ANONYMAS	ABBBELRS	BABBLERS
AALMOPPR	MALAPROP	AAMNGRRS	MARRANOS		BLABBERS
AALMOPSX	AXOPLASM	AAMNORSZ	ROMANZAS		BRABBLES
AALMOSTT	STOMATAL	AAMNPRST	MANTRAPS	ABBBELTU	TUBBABLE
AALMOTXY	XYLOMATA	AAMNPRSY	PARANYMS	ABBBGILN	BABBLING
AALMPPSU	PASPALUM	AAMNQSUW	SQUAWMAN		BLABBING
AALMPRSY	PALMYRAS	AAMOORSS	AMOROSAS	ABBBHSUY	BUSHBABY
AALMPSTY	PLATYSMA	AAMOPRRU	PARAMOUR	ABBBIRTY	BABBITRY
AALMQSUU	SQUAMULA	AAMORRSZ	ZAMARROS	ABBBISTT	BABBITTS
AALMSTTU	MULATTAS	AAMORSSU	MOSASAUR	ABBBOORU	RUBBABOO
AALNNNOS	NONNASAL	AAMORSSV	SAMOVARS	ABBBOSTU	SUBABBOT
AALNNNOV	NONNAVAL	AAMORSTT	STROMATA	ABBCCKMO	BACKCOMB
AALNNOPP	NONPAPAL	AAMOSTTU	AUTOMATS	ABBCDEKN	BACKBEND
AALNNOPT	PANTALON	AAMPRRST	RAMPARTS	ABBCDELS	SCABBLED
AALNNOST	SONANTAL	AAMRSSST	SMARTASS	ABBCDERS	SCRABBED
AALNNPUU	PUNALUAN	AAMRSSTT	MATTRASS	ABBCDKNO	BACKBOND
AALNNRSU	ANNULARS	AAMRSSTU	SUMATRAS	ABBCEERU	BARBECUE
AALNNTTY	NATANTLY	AAMRSTWY	TRAMWAYS	ABBCEGIR	CRIBBAGE
AALNNTUU	LUNANAUT	AAMSSSTU	SATSUMAS	ABBCEHIS	BABICHES
AALNOORS	ORONASAL	AANNOSST	ASSONANT	ABBCEHOU	BABOUCHE
AALNOPRT	PATRONAL	AANNOSTT	ANNATTOS	ABBCEHOY	BEACHBOY
AALNOPST	POSTANAL	AANNOTTW	NANOWATT	ABBCEHSU	BABUCHES
AALNORUV	ANOVULAR	AANNPSSW	SWANPANS	ABBCEHTU	BATHCUBE
AALNPRSU	LUPANARS	AANNRSTY	STANNARY	ABBCEIKT	BACKBITE
AALNPSST	SALTPANS	AANOOPPX	OPOPANAX	ABBCEILR	BARBICEL
AALNPSUU	PUNALUAS	AANOOPRZ	PARAZOON	ABBCEIRR	CRABBIER
AALNPTWX	WAXPLANT	AANOPRTY	ANATROPY	ABBCEIRS	SCABBIER
AALNRRTY	ARRANTLY	AANORRRT	NARRATOR	ABBCEKLU	BLUEBACK
AALNRSTU	NATURALS	AANORSTT	ARNATTOS	ABBCEKNO	BACKBONE
AALNSSTT	SALTANTS	AANORSTY	SANATORY	ABBCEKNU	BUCKBEAN
AALNSSTU	SULTANAS	AANORTTY	NATATORY	ABBCELLU	CLUBABLE
AALNSSTY	ANALYSTS	AANPPTTY	PATTYPAN	ABBCELRS	CLABBERS
AALNSTTU	TALAUNTS	AANPRSST	SPARTANS		SCRABBLE
	TANTALUS	AANQRSTU	QUARTANS	ABBCELRU	CURBABLE
AALOPPRT	PALPATOR	AANRRSTW	WARRANTS	ABBCELSS	SCABBLES
AALOPPRV	APPROVAL	AANRRTTY	TARTANRY	ABBCERRS	CRABBERS
AALOPPST	APOPLAST	AANRRTWY	WARRANTY	ABBCGINR	CRABBING
AALOPRSS	PARASOLS	AANRSTTU	SATURANT	ABBCGINS	SCABBING
AALOPRST	PASTORAL	AANRSUWY	RUNAWAYS	ABBCGIOR	GABBROIC
AALOPSVV	PAVLOVAS	AANSSSTT	TSANTSAS	ABBCIILL	BIBLICAL
AALOPSZZ	PALAZZOS	AAOORRSW	WOORARAS	ABBCIINR	RABBINIC
AALORSST	ALASTORS	AAOPSSST	POTASSAS	ABBCIKRT	BRICKBAT
AALORSSU	AROUSALS	AAOPSSTY	APOSTASY	ABBCILRV	CRABBILY
AALORSTX	LAXATORS	AAOQSSSU	OQUASSAS	ABBCILSY	SCABBILY
AALORTUV	VALUATOR	AAORSSTT	STAROSTA	ABBCKLOW	BLOWBACK
AALORTVY	LAVATORY	AAORSSVV	VAVASORS	ABBCKLOY	BLACKBOY
AALOSTTY	TALAYOTS		VAVASSOR	ABBCKNRU	BACKBURN
AALPRSTU	PASTURAL	AAORSUVV	VAVASOUR	ABBCKSUY	BUYBACKS
	SPATULAR	AAORSVVY	VAVASORY	ABBCLRSY	SCRABBLY
AALPRSTY	LAPTRAYS	AAOSTTUY	TATOUAYS	ABBDDEEL	BEDDABLE
AALPSSTU	SPATULAS	AAOSTWWY	STOWAWAY	ABBDDEEU	BEDAUBED
AALRRTTY	TARTARLY		TOWAWAYS	ABBDDEIL	BIDDABLE
AALRSSTU	AUSTRALS	AAPRRSTT	RATTRAPS	ABBDDELR	DRABBLED
AALRSSTY	SATYRALS	AAPRSTUU	RAUPATUS	ABBDDEOR	BEDBOARD
AALRSSVY	VASSALRY	AARSTTUY	STATUARY	ABBDDILY	BIDDABLY
AALRSTTW	STALWART	ABBBCDEO	CABOBBED	ABBDEEER	BEEBREAD
AALRSTUY	SALUTARY	ABBBDEEK	KEBABBED	ABBDEEHR	REHABBED
AALSSSTU	ASSAULTS	ABBBDEEL	BEDABBLE	ABBDEEJR	JABBERED
AAMMMSTU	MAMMATUS	ABBBDEKO	KABOBBED	ABBDEELN	BENDABLE
AAMMNPRS	RAMPSMAN	ABBBDELR	BRABBLED	ABBDEERR	BARBERED
AAMMNRST	MANTRAMS	ABBBEILR	BABBLIER	ABBDEERT	RABBETED
AAMMOTXY	MYXOMATA		BRIBABLE	ABBDEERY	YABBERED

Eight-letter anagrams

ABBDEGLR	GRABBLED	ABBEHLSS	SHABBLES	ABBGINSW	SWABBING
ABBDEHOO	BOOBHEAD	ABBEHORT	BATHROBE	ABBGINTY	TABBYING
ABBDEILN	BINDABLE	ABBEILLL	BILLABLE	ABBGINYY	YABBYING
ABBDEIRR	DRABBIER	ABBEILLO	BOILABLE	ABBGOOSU	BUGABOOS
ABBDEIRT	RABBITED	ABBEILMS	BABELISM	ABBHIIMS	BIMBASHI
ABBDELMO	BABELDOM	ABBEILNU	BUBALINE	ABBHILSY	SHABBILY
ABBDELMR	BRAMBLED	ABBEILOT	BILOBATE	ABBHINOS	NABOBISH
ABBDELNO	BONDABLE	ABBEILOV	OBVIABLE	ABBHIORT	RABBITOH
ABBDELNS	SNABBLED	ABBEILRS	SLABBIER	ABBHRRSU	RHUBARBS
ABBDELRR	DRABBLER	ABBEILRW	WABBLIER	ABBHRRUY	RHUBARBY
ABBDELRS	DABBLERS	ABBEILST	BISTABLE	ABBHSTTU	BATHTUBS
	DRABBLES	ABBEIMRU	BERIMBAU	ABBIINOT	BIBATION
ABBDEMOR	BOMBARDE	ABBEINTT	TABBINET	ABBILLOT	BOATBILL
ABBDEMUZ	BUMBAZED	ABBEIRRT	RABBITER	ABBILLSU	SILLABUB
ABBDENRU	UNBARBED	ABBEIRRW	BARBWIRE	ABBILOST	BIOBLAST
ABBDEORS	ABSORBED	ABBEISST	TABBISES		BOBTAILS
ABBDEORX	BREADBOX	ABBEISSW	SWABBIES	ABBILOTU	TABBOULI
ABBDEQSU	SQUABBED	ABBEKLOO	BOOKABLE	ABBIMNOS	BAMBINOS
ABBDERRS	DRABBERS	ABBELLLU	BLUEBALL		NABOBISM
ABBDERST	DRABBEST	ABBELLRS	BARBELLS	ABBIMSSU	BABUISMS
	DRABBETS	ABBELMRS	BRAMBLES	ABBINORS	RABBONIS
ABBDFOOY	BABYFOOD	ABBELNRU	BURNABLE	ABBINORX	BRAINBOX
ABBDGILN	DABBLING	ABBELNSS	SNABBLES	ABBINSSU	SUBBASIN
ABBDGINR	DRABBING	ABBELOOT	BOOTABLE	ABBIORST	RABBITOS
ABBDGIOR	GABBROID	ABBELOPR	PROBABLE	ABBIRRTY	RABBITRY
ABBDHIJS	DJIBBAHS	ABBELORS	BELABORS	ABBIRSUU	SUBURBIA
ABBDHIRS	DRABBISH		SORBABLE	ABBISSTY	BABYSITS
ABBDHIRT	BIRDBATH	ABBELORU	BELABOUR	ABBKKNOO	BANKBOOK
ABBDHOOY	BABYHOOD	ABBELPRS	PRABBLES	ABBKLOSU	BLAUBOKS
ABBDILNO	BAILBOND	ABBELQSU	SQUABBLE	ABBLLLOW	BLOWBALL
ABBDILRS	LIBBARDS	ABBELRRS	RABBLERS	ABBLLOSX	BOXBALLS
ABBDINRS	RIBBANDS	ABBELRSS	BARBLESS	ABBLLRSU	BULLBARS
ABBDLLOY	BABYDOLL		SLABBERS	ABBLLSTU	BULLBATS
ABBDLMOO	BOMBLOAD	ABBELRSU	BARBULES	ABBLLSUY	SYLLABUB
ABBDLRSU	LUBBARDS	ABBELRSW	WABBLERS	ABBLOPRY	PROBABLY
ABBDMORS	BOMBARDS	ABBELRSY	SLABBERY	ABBMOORS	BOMBORAS
ABBDMOSU	BABUDOMS	ABBELSUV	BUYABLES	ABBMOSST	BOMBASTS
ABBDNORW	BROWBAND	ABBEMOOR	AEROBOMB	ABBMOSTU	BUMBOATS
ABBDOORX	BOXBOARD	ABBEMOSX	BOMBAXES	ABBNNRSU	SUBURBAN
ABBDORRU	RUBBOARD	ABBEMSUZ	BUMBAZES	ABBOORSU	RUBABOOS
ABBEEHRR	REHABBER	ABBENORS	BASEBORN	ABBOSSTY	BOBSTAYS
ABBEEILT	BITEABLE	ABBENORY	NABOBERY	ABCCCIOO	BOCACCIO
ABBEEINR	BEARBINE	ABBENOSS	NABOBESS	ABCCDEHO	CABOCHED
ABBEEJRR	JABBERER	ABBEORRS	ABSORBER	ABCCDHIK	DABCHICK
ABBEEJRS	BEJABERS		REABSORB	ABCCEEHN	BECHANCE
ABBEELOY	OBEYABLE	ABBEORTW	BROWBEAT	ABCCEELP	PECCABLE
ABBEELTU	BLUEBEAT	ABBEQRSU	SQUABBER	ABCCEEOR	CABOCEER
ABBEENOR	BAREBONE	ABBERRRY	BARBERRY	ABCCEFLU	CLUBFACE
ABBEEQRU	BARBEQUE	ABBERRYY	BAYBERRY	ABCCEILR	BRECCIAL
ABBEERTT	BARBETTE	ABBERSST	STABBERS	ABCCEILY	CELIBACY
ABBEESSS	ABBESSES	ABBERSSW	SWABBERS	ABCCEIRS	BRECCIAS
ABBEFFLU	BUFFABLE	ABBESSSU	SUBBASES	ABCCEIRT	BACTERIC
ABBEFILR	FLABBIER	ABBFGINR	FRABBING	ABCCEKMO	COMEBACK
ABBEGIRR	GRABBIER	ABBFILLY	FLABBILY	ABCCESUU	SUCCUBAE
ABBEGIST	GABBIEST	ABBFLOOT	BOBFLOAT	ABCCHISU	BACCHIUS
ABBEGLRR	GRABBLER	ABBGGILN	GABBLING	ABCCHNOO	CABOCHON
ABBEGLRS	GABBLERS	ABBGGINR	GRABBING	ABCCHOSU	CHUBASCO
	GRABBLES	ABBGIJLN	JABBLING	ABCCIKKK	KICKBACK
ABBEGNOS	BOGBEANS	ABBGILNR	RABBLING	ABCCIKKP	PICKBACK
ABBEGNSU	BUGBANES	ABBGILNS	SLABBING	ABCCIKOR	ABRICOCK
ABBEGRRS	GRABBERS	ABBGILNU	BAUBLING	ABCCILOR	CARBOLIC
ABBEGRSU	BUGBEARS	ABBGILNW	WABBLING	ABCCILOT	COBALTIC
ABBEHILS	BABELISH	ABBGINST	STABBING	ABCCILUU	CUBICULA
ABBEHIRS	SHABBIER	ABBGINSU	BUBINGAS	ABCCIMRS	CAMBRICS

ABCCINOR	CARBONIC	ABCDEMRS	SCRAMBED	ABCEENOZ	CABEZONE
ABCCINSU	BUCCINAS	ABCDENRU	UNBRACED	ABCEENRS	CARBEENS
ABCCIORS	ASCORBIC	ABCDENSU	ABDUCENS		CARBENES
ABCCKLLO	BALLCOCK	ABCDENTU	ABDUCENT	ABCEENRT	CABERNET
ABCCKLOX	CLACKBOX	ABCDEORS	BROCADES	ABCEENSS	ABSENCES
ABCCKOOT	COCKBOAT	ABCDEORW	BECOWARD	ABCEEPRT	BECARPET
ABCCKOSW	BAWCOCKS	ABCDEORY	CARBOYED	ABCEERRS	REBRACES
ABCCKSTU	CUTBACKS	ABCDERSU	CUDBEARS	ABCEERST	ACERBEST
ABCCLLUY	BUCCALLY	ABCDESTU	SUBACTED	ABCEERUX	BERCEAUX
ABCCLOOO	COCOBOLA	ABCDFKLO	FOLDBACK	ABCEESSS	BECASSES
ABCCMOOY	MACCOBOY	ABCDGINU	ABDUCING	ABCEFIIT	BEATIFIC
ABCCOORS	BAROCCOS	ABCDHKLO	HOLDBACK	ABCEFIKL	BACKFILE
ABCCOOST	TOBACCOS	ABCDHLNU	CLUBHAND	ABCEFIKR	BACKFIRE
ABCCSSUU	SUCCUBAS	ABCDHORS	CHOBDARS		FIREBACK
ABCDDEER	DECARBED	ABCDIILO	BIOCIDAL	ABCEFINO	BONIFACE
ABCDDEOR	BROCADED		DIABOLIC	ABCEFLNO	BACLOFEN
ABCDDETU	ABDUCTED	ABCDIIMY	CYMBIDIA	ABCEGHIN	BEACHING
ABCDEEFK	FEEDBACK	ABCDIIRT	TRIBADIC	ABCEGIKV	GIVEBACK
ABCDEEHL	BLEACHED	ABCDIKLR	BALDRICK	ABCEGILN	BELACING
ABCDEEHR	BERDACHE	ABCDIKLS	BACKSLID	ABCEGIMN	EMBACING
	BREACHED	ABCDIKRU	BAUDRICK	ABCEGIRS	RIBCAGES
ABCDEEJT	ABJECTED	ABCDILLR	BIRDCALL	ABCEGKLL	BLACKLEG
ABCDEEKR	REBACKED	ABCDILOS	CABILDOS	ABCEGKLO	BLOCKAGE
ABCDEELL	BECALLED	ABCDILOU	CUBOIDAL	ABCEGKMU	MEGABUCK
ABCDEELM	BECALMED	ABCDILRS	BALDRICS	ABCEGKOR	BROCKAGE
ABCDEELS	DEBACLES	ABCDINOR	BRACONID	ABCEGKRY	GREYBACK
ABCDEELU	EDUCABLE	ABCDINSS	ABSCINDS	ABCEGMOS	CAMBOGES
ABCDEEMR	CAMBERED	ABCDIRST	CATBIRDS	ABCEGNOR	BONGRACE
	EMBRACED	ABCDIRSU	BAUDRICS	ABCEGORS	BROCAGES
ABCDEEMX	EXCAMBED		SUBACRID	ABCEGOSS	BOSCAGES
ABCDEENO	BEACONED	ABCDIRSW	BAWDRICS	ABCEHITT	BATHETIC
ABCDEEPP	BECAPPED	ABCDKNOW	BACKDOWN	ABCEHKLS	BECHALKS
ABCDEERR	REBRACED	ABCDKOOR	BACKDOOR	ABCEHKOS	BACKHOES
ABCDEETU	ABDUCTEE	ABCDKOOW	BACKWOOD	ABCEHKTW	BETHWACK
ABCDEFLO	BOLDFACE	ABCDKOPR	BACKDROP	ABCEHLNR	BLANCHER
ABCDEGIR	BIRDCAGE	ABCDKORW	BACKWORD	ABCEHLNS	BLANCHES
	CAGEBIRD	ABCDLLNU	CLUBLAND	ABCEHLOR	BACHELOR
ABCDEHIR	BEDCHAIR	ABCDNOSS	ABSCONDS	ABCEHLOS	CHAEBOLS
ABCDEHKO	BACKHOED	ABCDOORS	CORDOBAS	ABCEHLSU	BAUCHLES
ABCDEHLN	BLANCHED	ABCDOORW	CRABWOOD		CHASUBLE
ABCDEHLU	BAUCHLED	ABCDOPRU	CUPBOARD	ABCEHMOT	HECATOMB
	CLUBHEAD	ABCDORRS	BROCARDS	ABCEHMRS	BECHARMS
ABCDEHNR	BRANCHED	ABCDORTU	ABDUCTOR		BRECHAMS
ABCDEHOR	BROACHED	ABCDORUY	OBDURACY		CHAMBERS
ABCDEHOS	CABOSHED	ABCEEEFK	BEEFCAKE	ABCEHNRR	BRANCHER
ABCDEIIT	DIABETIC	ABCEEFNT	BENEFACT		REBRANCH
ABCDEIKS	BACKSIDE	ABCEEHIR	BEACHIER	ABCEHNRS	BRANCHES
	DIEBACKS	ABCEEHLM	BECHAMEL		BRECHANS
ABCDEILR	CALIBRED	ABCEEHLN	ALEBENCH	ABCEHOOT	COHOBATE
ABCDEIPS	PEDICABS	ABCEEHLR	BLEACHER	ABCEHOPU	PABOUCHE
ABCDEIRS	ASCRIBED	ABCEEHLS	BLEACHES	ABCEHORR	BROACHER
	CARBIDES	ABCEEHLW	CHEWABLE	ABCEHORS	BROACHES
ABCDEISS	ABSCISED	ABCEEHRR	BREACHER	ABCEHORU	BAROUCHE
ABCDEKLO	BLOCKADE	ABCEEHRS	BREACHES	ABCEHOSS	BASOCHES
ABCDEKLV	BACKVELD	ABCEEHSU	EBAUCHES	ABCEHRST	BATCHERS
ABCDEKNN	NECKBAND	ABCEEILT	CELIBATE		BRACHETS
ABCDEKNU	UNBACKED		CITEABLE	ABCEHRTT	BRATCHET
ABCDEKRS	REDBACKS	ABCEEIMN	AMBIENCE	ABCEIIRT	RABIETIC
ABCDELMS	SCAMBLED	ABCEEKLY	EYEBLACK	ABCEIKKL	KICKABLE
ABCDELNO	BLANCOED	ABCEELOV	EVOCABLE	ABCEIKLP	PICKABLE
ABCDELOO	CABOODLE	ABCEELRR	CEREBRAL	ABCEIKLR	CRABLIKE
ABCDELRU	BARLEDUC	ABCEELRT	BRACELET	ABCEIKLS	SCABLIKE
ABCDEMNU	DUMBCANE	ABCEEMRR	EMBRACER	ABCEIKST	TIEBACKS
ABCDEMOT	COMBATED	ABCEEMRS	EMBRACES	ABCEIKWZ	ZWIEBACK

Eight-letter anagrams

ABCEILLR	CRIBELLA	ABCEKSTW	WETBACKS		LIFTBACK
ABCEILLS	ICEBALLS	ABCELLOS	CLOSABLE	ABCFIKNS	FINBACKS
ABCEILLT	BALLETIC	ABCELLPU	CULPABLE	ABCFIKST	BACKFITS
ABCEILMS	ALEMBICS	ABCELLRU	BRUCELLA	ABCFILOS	BIFOCALS
ABCEILNN	BINNACLE	ABCELLSU	BUCELLAS	ABCFIOST	BIOFACTS
ABCEILNO	BIOCLEAN		BULLACES	ABCFKLLU	FULLBACK
	COINABLE	ABCELMNY	LAMBENCY	ABCFKLLY	BLACKFLY
ABCEILNU	BACULINE	ABCELMOR	BECLAMOR	ABCFKLOW	BACKFLOW
ABCEILOR	ALBICORE	ABCELMOS	CEMBALOS	ABCFKLSY	FLYBACKS
	BRACIOLE	ABCELMRS	CAMBRELS	ABCFKOST	SOFTBACK
	CABRIOLE		CLAMBERS	ABCGGIMO	GAMBOGIC
ABCEILOS	SOCIABLE		SCAMBLER	ABCGHINT	BATCHING
ABCEILRS	CALIBERS		SCRAMBLE	ABCGHKOS	HOGBACKS
	CALIBRES	ABCELMRY	CYMBALER	ABCGHNPU	PUNCHBAG
ABCEILST	BASILECT	ABCELMSS	SCAMBLES	ABCGIINN	CABINING
ABCEILTT	BITTACLE	ABCELNOT	BALCONET	ABCGIKLN	BLACKING
ABCEILTU	BACULITE	ABCELNUU	NUBECULA	ABCGIKNS	BACKINGS
ABCEILTY	BIACETYL	ABCELOOT	BOOTLACE	ABCGIKNW	WINGBACK
ABCEIMRW	MICAWBER	ABCELOPS	PLACEBOS	ABCGILNS	CABLINGS
ABCEIMST	BETACISM	ABCELOPY	COPYABLE	ABCGINRS	BRACINGS
ABCEINOO	COENOBIA	ABCELORT	BROCATEL	ABCGINSU	SCUBAING
ABCEINRS	BRISANCE	ABCELOST	OBSTACLE	ABCGKLMU	BLACKGUM
	CARBINES	ABCELOSV	VOCABLES	ABCGKLOS	BACKLOGS
ABCEINRT	BACTERIN	ABCELOTU	BLUECOAT	ABCGLNOX	CLANGBOX
ABCEINRV	VIBRANCE	ABCELPSS	BECLASPS	ABCGMSSU	SCUMBAGS
ABCEINST	BASCINET	ABCELPSU	BLUECAPS	ABCHHIIS	HIBACHIS
	CABINETS	ABCELPSY	BYPLACES	ABCHIIPS	BIPHASIC
ABCEINTU	INCUBATE	ABCELRSU	ARBUSCLE	ABCHIKLS	BLACKISH
ABCEIORS	AEROBICS	ABCELRSW	BECRAWLS	ABCHIKRS	BRACKISH
ABCEIORT	BORACITE		BESCRAWL	ABCHILMO	CHOLIAMB
ABCEIOST	ICEBOATS	ABCELRTT	BRACTLET	ABCHILOO	COOLIBAH
ABCEIRRT	CATBRIER	ABCELSSU	BASCULES	ABCHIMOR	CHORIAMB
	CRIBRATE		SUBSCALE	ABCHIMRU	BRACHIUM
ABCEIRSS	ASCRIBES	ABCELTTU	CUTTABLE	ABCHINOR	BRONCHIA
ABCEIRSW	CRABWISE	ABCEMOOS	CAMBOOSE	ABCHIOOR	BORACHIO
ABCEIRTT	BRATTICE	ABCEMORS	CRAMBOES	ABCHIOST	COHABITS
ABCEIRTY	ACERBITY	ABCEMORT	COMBATER	ABCHIRRT	TRIBRACH
ABCEISSS	ABSCISES	ABCENORS	BACONERS	ABCHKLOT	HACKBOLT
	ABSCISSE	ABCENOSU	SUBOCEAN	ABCHKLOW	HOWLBACK
ABCEISST	ASBESTIC	ABCENOSW	COWBANES	ABCHKMPU	HUMPBACK
ABCEISTT	TABETICS	ABCENOSZ	CABEZONS	ABCHKOOP	CHAPBOOK
ABCEJKLU	BLUEJACK	ABCENOUY	BUOYANCE	ABCHKOOS	CASHBOOK
ABCEJLTY	ABJECTLY	ABCENRSU	UNBRACES	ABCHKOSU	CHABOUKS
ABCEKKRU	BUCKRAKE	ABCENTUX	EXCUBANT	ABCHKRSU	BACKRUSH
ABCEKKSW	SKEWBACK	ABCEOOSS	CABOOSES	ABCHKSTU	HACKBUTS
ABCEKLLO	LOCKABLE	ABCEOPUU	BEAUCOUP	ABCHKSUW	HAWBUCKS
ABCEKLMO	MOCKABLE	ABCEORRS	BRACEROS	ABCHLLUU	CLUBHAUL
ABCEKLNS	BLACKENS	ABCEORST	CABESTRO	ABCHMOTX	MATCHBOX
ABCEKLOO	COOKABLE		CABRESTO	ABCHNORS	BROCHANS
ABCEKLOR	ROCKABLE	ABCEORSU	CORBEAUS	ABCHOORR	ROORBACH
ABCEKLOS	BECLOAKS	ABCEOSUX	SAUCEBOX	ABCHOSTT	CHATBOTS
ABCEKLPU	PALEBUCK	ABCEPSSU	SUBSPACE	ABCHOTWX	WATCHBOX
ABCEKLSS	BACKLESS	ABCERRTU	CARBURET	ABCIIKRR	AIRBRICK
ABCEKLST	BLACKEST	ABCERRWY	CYBERWAR	ABCIILMU	BULIMIAC
ABCEKNOT	BOATNECK	ABCERSSU	SUBRACES	ABCIILOT	BIOTICAL
ABCEKNRS	BRACKENS	ABCERTUU	CUBATURE	ABCIIMNS	MINICABS
ABCEKOOS	BOOKCASE	ABCESSTU	SUBCASTE	ABCIINOT	CIBATION
	CASEBOOK	ABCESSTW	WEBCASTS	ABCIINSS	ABSCISIN
ABCEKORY	ROCKABYE	ABCESSUU	SUBCAUSE	ABCIIORS	ISOBARIC
ABCEKRST	BACKREST	ABCESTUU	SUBACUTE	ABCIIRST	TRIBASIC
	BRACKETS	ABCFIKLL	BACKFILL	ABCIISTY	BASICITY
ABCEKSST	BACKSETS	ABCFIKLN	BLACKFIN	ABCIITUX	BAUXITIC
	SETBACKS	ABCFIKLP	BACKFLIP	ABCIJNOS	JACOBINS
ABCEKSSY	BACKSEYS	ABCFIKLT	BACKLIFT	ABCIKKLL	KICKBALL

ABCIKLST	BACKLIST	ABCKOSSW	SOWBACKS	ABDDELOT	DEADBOLT
ABCIKLTU	BUCKTAIL	ABCKOSTU	BACKOUTS	ABDDELRS	BLADDERS
ABCIKNPS	BACKSPIN		OUTBACKS	ABDDELRY	BLADDERY
ABCIKSSY	SICKBAYS	ABCKSSTU	SACKBUTS	ABDDENNU	UNBANDED
ABCILLNY	BILLYCAN		SUBTACKS	ABDDENOU	ABOUNDED
ABCILLRU	LUBRICAL	ABCKSSUW	BUCKSAWS	ABDDENST	BEDSTAND
ABCILLSU	BACILLUS		SAWBUCKS	ABDDEORS	ADSORBED
ABCILLSY	SYLLABIC	ABCLLNOR	CORNBALL		ROADBEDS
ABCILMMO	CIMBALOM	ABCLLOSY	CALLBOYS	ABDDEOSY	DEADBOYS
ABCILMSU	SUBCLAIM	ABCLLPUY	CULPABLY	ABDDERSW	BEDWARDS
ABCILNOR	CARBINOL	ABCLMMOY	CYMBALOM	ABDDGILN	BLADDING
ABCILNOS	COALBINS	ABCLMOOO	COLOBOMA	ABDDGINR	BRADDING
ABCILNPU	PUBLICAN	ABCLMOSY	CYMBALOS	ABDDHIOR	RHABDOID
ABCILOOR	COOLIBAR	ABCLMSUU	BACULUMS	ABDDILMO	LAMBDOID
ABCILOSY	SOCIABLY	ABCLMSUY	SCYBALUM	ABDDILRY	LADYBIRD
ABCILRRU	RUBRICAL	ABCLNORY	CARBONYL	ABDDIMNO	BONDMAID
ABCIMMSS	CAMBISMS	ABCLNSSU	SUBCLANS	ABDDINSS	DISBANDS
ABCIMMSU	CAMBIUMS	ABCLORXY	CARBOXYL	ABDDIRRY	YARDBIRD
ABCIMORR	MICROBAR	ABCLOSUV	SUBVOCAL	ABDDLLOS	ODDBALLS
ABCIMRTU	UMBRATIC	ABCLSSSU	SUBCLASS	ABDDLUWY	BULWADDY
ABCIMSST	CAMBISTS	ABCLSUUU	SUBUCULA	ABDDMORS	DAMBRODS
ABCINNOS	NONBASIC	ABCMOORT	MOBOCRAT	ABDEEEFL	BEFLEAED
ABCINORS	CORBINAS	ABCNNORU	CONURBAN		FEEDABLE
ABCINORU	CONURBIA	ABCNORTY	CORYBANT	ABDEEEFN	BEDEAFEN
ABCINORY	BARYONIC	ABCNOUYY	BUOYANCY	ABDEEEHR	BEHEADER
ABCINOST	BOTANICS	ABCORRSS	CROSSBAR	ABDEEELP	BELEAPED
ABCINRVY	VIBRANCY	ABCORRSW	CROWBARS	ABDEEEMN	BEMEANED
ABCIOPRS	SAPROBIC	ABCORRTU	TURBOCAR	ABDEEERV	BEAVERED
ABCIORRS	BARRICOS	ABCORSSU	SCABROUS		BEREAVED
ABCIORSU	CARIBOUS	ABCOSSTU	SUBCOSTA	ABDEEFGS	FEEDBAGS
ABCIOSSU	SCABIOUS	ABCOSTTU	COTTABUS	ABDEEFIT	TABEFIED
ABCIOSUV	BIVOUACS	ABCRSTTU	SUBTRACT	ABDEEFLM	FLAMBEED
ABCIRSTT	ABSTRICT	ABDDDEEM	BEMADDED	ABDEEFLS	FEELBADS
ABCIRSUV	SUBVICAR	ABDDDEET	ADDEBTED	ABDEEFMO	BEFOAMED
ABCJKOOT	BOOTJACK	ABDDEEEH	BEHEADED	ABDEEFMR	BEDFRAME
	JACKBOOT	ABDDEEEK	DEBEAKED	ABDEEGGL	BEDAGGLE
ABCKKOOR	BOOKRACK	ABDDEEGG	DEBAGGED	ABDEEGGR	BEGGARED
ABCKKORW	BACKWORK	ABDDEEGR	BADGERED	ABDEEGHR	HERBAGED
ABCKLLOR	ROLLBACK		REBADGED	ABDEEGLL	BEGALLED
ABCKLLOS	BALLOCKS	ABDDEEHS	BEDASHED		GABELLED
ABCKLLPU	PULLBACK	ABDDEEHT	DEATHBED	ABDEEGNW	BEGNAWED
ABCKLNNO	NONBLACK	ABDDEEIL	BELADIED	ABDEEGRS	REBADGES
ABCKLOPT	BLACKTOP	ABDDEEKR	DEBARKED	ABDEEGRU	BEDEGUAR
ABCKLOPW	PLOWBACK	ABDDEELU	BELAUDED	ABDEEHIR	BRAEHEID
ABCKLOST	BACKLOTS	ABDDEEMN	BEDAMNED	ABDEEHLS	SHEDABLE
	SLOTBACK		BEMADDEN	ABDEEHLU	BLUEHEAD
ABCKLOSW	SLOWBACK	ABDDEENY	BENDAYED	ABDEEHMS	BESHAMED
ABCKLOTU	BLACKOUT	ABDDEEPR	BEDRAPED	ABDEEHMT	EMBATHED
ABCKMOOR	BACKROOM	ABDDEERR	DEBARRED	ABDEEHNO	BONEHEAD
ABCKMORR	BROCKRAM	ABDDEERS	DEBEARDS	ABDEEHRT	BREATHED
ABCKMOSS	MOSSBACK	ABDDEEST	BEDSTEAD	ABDEEHSS	BEDASHES
ABCKMOST	BACKMOST		BESTADDE	ABDEEHST	BETHESDA
	TOMBACKS	ABDDEGIR	ABRIDGED	ABDEEHTT	BEHATTED
ABCKMRSU	BUCKRAMS		BRIGADED	ABDEEIKL	BEADLIKE
ABCKMSUZ	ZAMBUCKS	ABDDEHMO	HEBDOMAD	ABDEEIKR	BIDARKEE
ABCKNNOS	BANNOCKS	ABDDEHMU	DUMBHEAD	ABDEEILM	EMBAILED
ABCKNORY	CRYOBANK	ABDDEHOY	HOBDAYED	ABDEEILN	DENIABLE
ABCKNRSU	RUNBACKS	ABDDEILS	DISABLED	ABDEEILR	RIDEABLE
ABCKNRTU	TURNBACK	ABDDEILU	AUDIBLED	ABDEEILS	ABSEILED
ABCKNSTU	CUTBANKS		BUDDLEIA		BELADIES
ABCKOORR	ROORBACK	ABDDEINR	BRANDIED	ABDEEILT	DELIBATE
ABCKOORU	BUCKAROO	ABDDEINS	SIDEBAND		EDITABLE
ABCKOPST	BACKSTOP	ABDDEINW	WIDEBAND	ABDEEILV	EVADIBLE
ABCKORUY	BUCKAYRO	ABDDEIRR	BRAIRDED	ABDEEILW	BEWAILED

Eight-letter anagrams

ABDEEIPR	BEDIAPER	ABDEERSS	DEBASERS	ABDEHKLU	BULKHEAD
ABDEEIRR	BEARDIER	ABDEERST	BETREADS	ABDEHKNO	KNOBHEAD
ABDEEIRS	BEARDIES		BREASTED	ABDEHLLN	HANDBELL
ABDEEIRT	EBRIATED		DEBATERS	ABDEHLLO	HOLDABLE
	REBAITED	ABDEERSY	BEEYARDS	ABDEHLLU	BULLHEAD
ABDEEIST	BEADIEST	ABDEERTT	BATTERED	ABDEHLMS	SHAMBLED
	DIABETES		DRABETTE	ABDEHLOT	BOLTHEAD
ABDEEITU	BEAUTIED	ABDEERTW	WATERBED	ABDEHLRS	HALBERDS
ABDEEJMN	ENJAMBED	ABDEERTY	BETRAYED	ABDEHMNO	HAMBONED
ABDEEJST	JETBEADS	ABDEERWY	BEWRAYED	ABDEHMOR	RHABDOME
ABDEEKLS	LAKEBEDS	ABDEESST	BASSETED	ABDEHMRU	RHUMBAED
ABDEEKMN	EMBANKED		BESTEADS	ABDEHMSU	AMBUSHED
ABDEEKMR	BEDMAKER	ABDEFHOO	BOOFHEAD	ABDEHNTU	UNBATHED
	EMBARKED	ABDEFIIS	BASIFIED	ABDEHORR	ABHORRED
ABDEEKNR	BARKENED	ABDEFILN	FINDABLE		HARBORED
	BEDARKEN	ABDEFLLO	FOLDABLE	ABDEHOSW	BESHADOW
ABDEEKNV	BEKNAVED	ABDEFLNU	FUNDABLE		BOWHEADS
ABDEEKPR	PREBAKED		UNFABLED	ABDEHRST	BREADTHS
ABDEEKRR	DEBARKER	ABDEFLOR	FORDABLE	ABDEHSSU	SUBHEADS
ABDEELLL	LABELLED	ABDEFLST	FLATBEDS	ABDEHTTU	BUTTHEAD
ABDEELLM	EMBALLED	ABDEFLSU	LEAFBUDS	ABDEIIRT	DIATRIBE
ABDEELLN	LENDABLE	ABDEFNRU	FABURDEN	ABDEIKMR	IMBARKED
ABDEELLT	BALLETED	ABDEFOSS	SOFABEDS	ABDEIKNS	BANKSIDE
ABDEELLW	WELDABLE	ABDEFRRY	FRYBREAD	ABDEIKNU	BAUDEKIN
ABDEELMM	EMBALMED	ABDEFRSW	BEDWARFS	ABDEILLR	BRAILLED
ABDEELMN	MENDABLE	ABDEGGIL	DIGGABLE	ABDEILLS	SLIDABLE
ABDEELMS	BELDAMES	ABDEGGNU	UNBAGGED	ABDEILMM	DIMMABLE
	BEMEDALS	ABDEGHIS	BIGHEADS		IMBALMED
ABDEELMU	BEMAULED	ABDEGHRS	BEGHARDS	ABDEILMN	MANDIBLE
ABDEELMZ	EMBLAZED	ABDEGIJN	BEJADING	ABDEILMS	SEMIBALD
ABDEELNS	SENDABLE	ABDEGILM	GIMBALED	ABDEILMZ	IMBLAZED
ABDEELNT	BANDELET	ABDEGILN	BLINDAGE	ABDEILNR	BILANDER
ABDEELNV	VENDABLE	ABDEGILU	GUIDABLE	ABDEILNT	BIDENTAL
ABDEELOR	ERODABLE	ABDEGIMT	GAMBITED	ABDEILNW	WINDABLE
	LEEBOARD	ABDEGINO	GABIONED	ABDEILNY	DENIABLY
ABDEELOS	ALBEDOES	ABDEGINR	BEARDING	ABDEILOV	VOIDABLE
ABDEELPT	BEDPLATE		BREADING	ABDEILOX	OXIDABLE
ABDEELRR	BARRELED	ABDEGINS	BEADINGS	ABDEILPP	DIPPABLE
ABDEELRS	BEDERALS		DEBASING	ABDEILPS	PIEBALDS
ABDEELRV	DEVERBAL	ABDEGINT	DEBATING	ABDEILRS	BEDRAILS
ABDEELRZ	BLAZERED	ABDEGINZ	BEDAZING		DISABLER
ABDEELSV	BESLAVED	ABDEGIPP	BAGPIPED		RAILBEDS
ABDEELTT	BATTELED	ABDEGIRR	ABRIDGER	ABDEILRT	LIBRATED
	TABLETED	ABDEGIRS	ABRIDGES	ABDEILRV	DRIVABLE
ABDEELZZ	BEDAZZLE		BRIGADES	ABDEILRY	DIABLERY
ABDEEMNO	BEMOANED	ABDEGLMO	GAMBOLED	ABDEILSS	DISABLES
ABDEEMNS	BEADSMEN	ABDEGLNR	BRANGLED	ABDEILST	BALDIEST
	BEDESMAN	ABDEGLOT	GLOBATED	ABDEILSU	AUDIBLES
ABDEEMRR	EMBARRED	ABDEGLRS	BELGARDS	ABDEILSY	BIASEDLY
ABDEEMRS	EMBREADS	ABDEGLRY	BADGERLY	ABDEILTU	DUTIABLE
ABDEEMRV	EMBRAVED	ABDEGLSU	SLUGABED	ABDEILVV	BIVALVED
ABDEEMST	BEDMATES	ABDEGMRU	UMBRAGED	ABDEIMNR	BRIDEMAN
ABDEENNR	BANNERED	ABDEGNOR	BONDAGER	ABDEIMOO	AMOEBOID
ABDEENRT	BANTERED	ABDEGNOS	BONDAGES	ABDEIMOR	AMBEROID
ABDEENRU	UNBEARED		DOGBANES	ABDEIMRR	IMBARRED
ABDEENRY	BARNEYED	ABDEGNRU	UNGARBED	ABDEIMRS	EMBRAIDS
ABDEENRZ	BRAZENED	ABDEGOPR	PEGBOARD	ABDEINNR	ENDBRAIN
ABDEENST	ABSENTED	ABDEGORT	BOGARTED	ABDEINOR	DEBONAIR
ABDEENTT	BATTENED	ABDEGRSU	SUBGRADE	ABDEINOS	BEDSONIA
ABDEEPRS	BEDRAPES	ABDEHILL	BILLHEAD	ABDEINOT	OBTAINED
	BESPREAD	ABDEHILS	DISHABLE	ABDEINRS	BRANDIES
ABDEEPTT	BEPATTED	ABDEHIMT	IMBATHED		BRANDISE
ABDEERRT	BARTERED	ABDEHINS	BANISHED	ABDEINST	BANDIEST
ABDEERRY	RYEBREAD	ABDEHITU	HABITUDE	ABDEINSU	UNBIASED

ABDEINSW	BEDAWINS
ABDEINTU	UNBAITED
ABDEIOTV	OBVIATED
ABDEIPRT	BIPARTED
ABDEIPST	BAPTISED
ABDEIPTZ	BAPTIZED
ABDEIRRS	BRAIDERS
ABDEIRSS	SEABIRDS
	SIDEBARS
ABDEIRST	BARDIEST
	BRAIDEST
	RABIDEST
	REDBAITS
	TRIBADES
ABDEIRSU	DAUBRIES
ABDEIRSW	BAWDRIES
	DAWBRIES
ABDEIRSX	AXEBIRDS
ABDEIRTV	VIBRATED
ABDEISST	BASTIDES
ABDEISSU	DISABUSE
	SUBIDEAS
ABDEISTU	DAUBIEST
ABDEISTW	BAWDIEST
ABDEITTU	DUBITATE
ABDEJNOW	JAWBONED
ABDEKLSW	SKEWBALD
ABDEKNNU	UNBANKED
ABDEKNRU	UNBARKED
	UNBRAKED
ABDEKNSU	SUNBAKED
ABDEKOOR	ABROOKED
ABDEKOOT	DATEBOOK
ABDEKORW	BEADWORK
ABDEKORY	KEYBOARD
ABDEKOTU	OUTBAKED
ABDELLMO	MOLDABLE
ABDELLOR	BEADROLL
ABDELLOT	BALLOTED
ABDELMNU	UNBLAMED
ABDELMPS	BEDLAMPS
ABDELNOR	BANDEROL
ABDELNOU	UNDOABLE
ABDELNOZ	BLAZONED
ABDELNRY	BENADRYL
	BYLANDER
ABDELNSS	BALDNESS
ABDELNST	BLANDEST
ABDELORU	LABOURED
ABDELOSV	ABSOLVED
ABDELOSW	DOWSABEL
ABDELPSY	PYEBALDS
ABDELRRS	DRABLERS
ABDELRSU	DURABLES
ABDELRTT	BRATTLED
ABDELSTU	SUBLATED
ABDEMNNS	BANDSMEN
ABDEMNNY	BANDYMEN
ABDEMNOR	BOARDMEN
ABDEMNOS	ABDOMENS
ABDEMORT	BROMATED
ABDEMRSU	BERMUDAS
ABDEMRTU	DRUMBEAT
	UMBRATED
ABDENNNU	UNBANNED
ABDENNOS	NOSEBAND
ABDENOOT	BATOONED
ABDENORS	BANDORES
	BROADENS
ABDENORW	RAWBONED
ABDENORY	BONEYARD
ABDENOTW	DOWNBEAT
ABDENRRS	BRANDERS
	REBRANDS
ABDENRRU	UNBARRED
ABDENRSS	DRABNESS
ABDENRST	BANDSTER
	BARTENDS
ABDENRTU	BREADNUT
	TURBANED
ABDENSSU	SUBDEANS
ABDENSTU	UNBASTED
ABDENSUU	UNABUSED
ABDENSWY	BENDWAYS
ABDENTTU	DEBUTANT
ABDEOORW	BEARWOOD
ABDEOPRR	PREBOARD
ABDEOPRT	PROBATED
ABDEORRS	ADSORBER
	BOARDERS
	REBOARDS
ABDEORRU	ARBOURED
ABDEORRW	DRAWBORE
	WARDROBE
ABDEORST	BROADEST
ABDEORSW	SOWBREAD
ABDEORTU	OBDURATE
	TABOURED
ABDEORUX	BORDEAUX
ABDEOSTU	BOUTADES
ABDEPRSU	SUPERBAD
ABDEPRUY	UPBRAYED
ABDEPSSY	BYPASSED
ABDERRSU	ABSURDER
ABDERSST	DABSTERS
ABDERSSU	SUBEDARS
	SURBASED
ABDERSTU	SURBATED
ABDERSTW	BEDSTRAW
ABDERSTY	DRYBEATS
ABDERTUW	DRAWTUBE
ABDESUWY	SUBWAYED
ABDFILOR	FORBIDAL
ABDFIMRR	BIRDFARM
ABDFIRST	FATBIRDS
ABDFLOOT	FOLDBOAT
ABDFNORU	FUNBOARD
ABDFRSUW	SUBDWARF
ABDGGORS	BOGGARDS
ABDGHINR	HANGBIRD
ABDGIINR	BRAIDING
ABDGIINS	ABIDINGS
ABDGILNR	BARDLING
ABDGILNS	BLADINGS
ABDGILNU	BLAUDING
ABDGILOR	GAOLBIRD
ABDGIMRU	GUIMBARD
ABDGINNR	BRANDING
ABDGINNS	BANDINGS
ABDGINNY	BANDYING
ABDGINOR	ABORDING
	BOARDING
ABDGINRS	BRIGANDS
ABDGINST	DINGBATS
ABDGINSU	DAUBINGS
ABDGINSW	WINDBAGS
ABDGIRST	DIRTBAGS
ABDGLNOS	BOGLANDS
ABDGLOOR	LOGBOARD
ABDGLSUY	LADYBUGS
ABDHHSSU	SHADBUSH
ABDHIIST	ADHIBITS
ABDHILLN	HANDBILL
ABDHILNS	BLANDISH
ABDHINRS	BRANDISH
ABDHIORS	BROADISH
ABDHIPRS	BARDSHIP
ABDHIRTY	BIRTHDAY
ABDHKNOO	HANDBOOK
ABDHLNSU	BUSHLAND
ABDHLORW	BLOWHARD
ABDHLOSW	SHADBLOW
ABDHMORS	RHABDOMS
ABDHMOTU	BADMOUTH
ABDHMSTU	MUDBATHS
ABDHNORS	BODHRANS
ABDHNSSU	HUSBANDS
ABDHOORT	HARDBOOT
ABDIIJLR	JAILBIRD
ABDIILLR	BILLIARD
ABDIILRR	RAILBIRD
ABDIIMNR	MIDBRAIN
ABDIIMSU	BASIDIUM
ABDIINOS	ANOBIIDS
	OBSIDIAN
ABDIINRR	RAINBIRD
ABDIINTT	BANDITTI
ABDIIORT	ORIBATID
ABDIIRTY	RABIDITY
ABDIJRSY	JAYBIRDS
ABDIKLNR	BLINKARD
ABDIKLOU	KILOBAUD
ABDIKNSW	BAWDKINS
ABDIKRSS	DISBARKS
ABDILLRY	BRIDALLY
	RIBALDLY
ABDILOOS	DIABOLOS
ABDILORS	LABROIDS
ABDILOST	BLASTOID
	TABLOIDS
ABDILOTY	TABLOIDY
ABDILRRY	RIBALDRY
ABDILRSW	AWLBIRDS
ABDILRZZ	BLIZZARD
ABDILSTU	SUBTIDAL
ABDIMNRS	MISBRAND
ABDIMORS	AMBROIDS
ABDIMRSS	BARDISMS
ABDIMRSY	MAYBIRDS
ABDINORS	INBOARDS
ABDINORU	AIRBOUND

ABDINOST	BANDITOS	ABEEFILN	FINEABLE	ABEEIKRS	BAKERIES
ABDINOTY	ANTIBODY	ABEEFILR	AFEBRILE	ABEEIKRT	TIEBREAK
ABDINRST	ANTBIRDS		BALEFIRE	ABEEIKST	BEAKIEST
ABDINRSU	UNBRAIDS		FIREABLE	ABEEILLN	LIENABLE
ABDINRTY	BANDITRY	ABEEFILS	FEASIBLE		LINEABLE
ABDIOSUU	SUBAUDIO	ABEEFILT	FLEABITE	ABEEILLR	RELIABLE
ABDIPRSU	UPBRAIDS	ABEEFIRS	FIREBASE	ABEEILLV	LEVIABLE
ABDIRRUY	RIBAUDRY	ABEEFIST	TABEFIES		LIVEABLE
ABDJMOOR	DOORJAMB	ABEEFLLL	FELLABLE	ABEEILLX	EXILABLE
ABDKLNOO	BOOKLAND	ABEEFLLN	BEFALLEN	ABEEILMN	MINEABLE
ABDKNOOS	BANDOOKS	ABEEFLMS	FLAMBEES	ABEEILMS	BELAMIES
ABDKOOSY	DAYBOOKS	ABEEFLOS	BEEFALOS	ABEEILNN	BIENNALE
ABDKORSY	SKYBOARD	ABEEFORR	FOREBEAR	ABEEILNP	PLEBEIAN
ABDLLNOS	SLOBLAND	ABEEFSTU	BEAUFETS	ABEEILNS	BASELINE
ABDLLNUW	BUNDWALL	ABEEGHRS	HERBAGES	ABEEILNU	BANLIEUE
ABDLLORS	BOLLARDS	ABEEGHRT	BERTHAGE	ABEEILNV	ENVIABLE
ABDLNORS	BANDROLS	ABEEGILV	GIVEABLE	ABEEILPX	EXPIABLE
ABDLNOSU	SUBNODAL	ABEEGINR	BAREGINE	ABEEILRR	BLEARIER
ABDLOSSU	BUSLOADS		BERGENIA	ABEEILRT	LIBERATE
ABDLOSYY	LADYBOYS	ABEEGIRV	VERBIAGE	ABEEILRW	BEWAILER
ABDLRSUU	SUBDURAL	ABEEGLLR	GABELLER	ABEEILSS	SEISABLE
ABDLRSUY	ABSURDLY	ABEEGLLS	GABELLES	ABEEILST	SEABLITE
ABDLSSUU	SUBDUALS	ABEEGLRS	BEAGLERS	ABEEILSV	EVASIBLE
ABDLSTUU	SUBADULT	ABEEGLTT	GETTABLE	ABEEILSZ	SEIZABLE
ABDMNNOS	BONDSMAN	ABEEGMNR	BARGEMEN		SIZEABLE
ABDMNOUW	MAWBOUND	ABEEGMRT	BREGMATE	ABEEILTV	EVITABLE
ABDMOOPR	MOPBOARD	ABEEGMTY	MEGABYTE	ABEEILVW	VIEWABLE
ABDMRSUY	MARYBUDS	ABEEGNTT	BAGNETTE	ABEEIMRS	AMBERIES
ABDNNNOR	NONBRAND	ABEEGOSZ	GAZEBOES	ABEEIMRT	AMBERITE
ABDNOORS	BRADOONS	ABEEGPSW	WEBPAGES	ABEEIMST	BEAMIEST
ABDNORSU	BAUDRONS	ABEEGRRS	GERBERAS	ABEEINST	BETAINES
ABDNORUY	BOUNDARY	ABEEGRST	ABSTERGE	ABEEINTY	AYENBITE
ABDNOSSY	SANDBOYS	ABEEGRSU	AUBERGES	ABEEIPRS	BEPRAISE
ABDNRRSU	SANDBURR	ABEEGRSW	BREWAGES	ABEEIRTT	BATTERIE
ABDNRSSU	SANDBURS	ABEEGTTU	BAGUETTE	ABEEIRTV	BREVIATE
ABDNRSTU	TURBANDS	ABEEHILR	HIREABLE	ABEEISST	BEASTIES
ABDNSSTY	STANDBYS	ABEEHINT	THEBAINE	ABEEISSV	ABESSIVE
ABDNSTUU	BUTSUDAN	ABEEHIRS	HEBRAISE	ABEEISTT	BEATIEST
ABDOORSW	BARWOODS	ABEEHIRZ	HEBRAIZE	ABEEISTU	BEAUTIES
ABDOORTU	OUTBOARD	ABEEHLLL	HEELBALL	ABEEITUX	BEAUXITE
ABDOOSSW	BASSWOOD	ABEEHLLP	HELPABLE	ABEEJMOR	JAMBOREE
ABDOOSWY	BAYWOODS	ABEEHLLR	BEERHALL	ABEEKLOT	KEELBOAT
ABDRSSTU	BUSTARDS		HAREBELL	ABEEKLSS	BEAKLESS
ABDRSUZZ	BUZZARDS	ABEEHLSV	BEHALVES	ABEEKLST	BLEAKEST
ABEEEFLR	REEFABLE	ABEEHMSS	BESHAMES	ABEEKMNR	BRAKEMEN
ABEEEFRS	FREEBASE	ABEEHMST	EMBATHES		EMBANKER
ABEEEGRS	BARGEESE	ABEEHNNS	HENBANES	ABEEKMRR	REEMBARK
	BEERAGES	ABEEHNPP	BEHAPPEN	ABEEKNSV	BEKNAVES
ABEEEGRV	BEVERAGE	ABEEHNSS	BANSHEES	ABEEKNSY	EYEBANKS
ABEEEHTT	HEBETATE		SHEBEANS	ABEEKOOP	PEEKABOO
ABEEEKLP	KEEPABLE	ABEEHNTT	HEBETANT	ABEEKOPS	PEEKABOS
ABEEELLP	PEELABLE	ABEEHORS	RHEOBASE	ABEEKORV	OVERBAKE
ABEEELLR	REELABLE	ABEEHQTU	BEQUEATH	ABEEKPRS	BARKEEPS
ABEEEMSY	EYEBEAMS	ABEEHRRT	BREATHER		PREBAKES
ABEEENRT	TENEBRAE	ABEEHRST	BREATHES	ABEEKPSS	BESPEAKS
ABEEENRV	BEREAVEN		HARTBEES	ABEEKRRS	BREAKERS
ABEEENST	ABSENTEE	ABEEHRSV	BEHAVERS	ABEEKRST	BESTREAK
ABEEERRT	TEREBRAE	ABEEHSTY	EYEBATHS	ABEELLLR	LABELLER
ABEEERRV	BEREAVER	ABEEIKKL	BEAKLIKE	ABEELLLS	SELLABLE
ABEEERSV	BEREAVES	ABEEIKLL	LIKEABLE	ABEELLLT	TELLABLE
ABEEFFNO	BANOFFEE	ABEEIKLM	BEAMLIKE	ABEELLMT	MELTABLE
ABEEFFTU	BEAUFFET	ABEEIKLN	BEANLIKE	ABEELLOT	BALLOTEE
ABEEFILL	FILEABLE	ABEEIKLR	BEARLIKE	ABEELLOV	LOVEABLE
		ABEEIKLT	BAKELITE	ABEELLRS	LABELERS

	RELABELS	**ABEENNRU**	EBURNEAN	**ABEFILTT**	FITTABLE
ABEELLSY	EYEBALLS	**ABEENNSW**	BAWNEENS	**ABEFILUZ**	FABULIZE
ABEELLTT	LETTABLE	**ABEENNTU**	UNBEATEN	**ABEFINNR**	FIBRANNE
ABEELMMR	EMBALMER	**ABEENORS**	SEABORNE	**ABEFINSU**	BEAUFINS
	EMMARBLE	**ABEENOTZ**	BENZOATE	**ABEFIORT**	BIFORATE
ABEELMNO	BONEMEAL	**ABEENRRR**	BARRENER		FIREBOAT
ABEELMOV	MOVEABLE	**ABEENRRT**	BANTERER	**ABEFIRRT**	FIREBRAT
ABEELMPR	PREAMBLE	**ABEENRSS**	BARENESS	**ABEFITUY**	BEAUTIFY
ABEELMRT	ATREMBLE	**ABEENRST**	ABSENTER	**ABEFLLMU**	BLAMEFUL
ABEELMRZ	EMBLAZER	**ABEENRSV**	VERBENAS	**ABEFLLRU**	FURLABLE
ABEELMSS	ASSEMBLE	**ABEENRTT**	BATTENER	**ABEFLLTU**	TABLEFUL
	BEAMLESS	**ABEENSSS**	BASENESS	**ABEFLMOR**	FORMABLE
ABEELMST	BEAMLETS	**ABEENSTW**	NEWSBEAT	**ABEFLNRU**	FUNEBRAL
ABEELMSZ	EMBLAZES	**ABEEORRV**	OVERBEAR	**ABEFLNSY**	FLYBANES
ABEELMTT	EMBATTLE	**ABEEORRS**	BOREARES	**ABEFLOTU**	OUTFABLE
ABEELNOP	BEANPOLE	**ABEEORST**	ABORTEES	**ABEFLRSU**	SURFABLE
	OPENABLE		REBATOES	**ABEFMRSU**	SUBFRAME
ABEELNOV	OVENABLE	**ABEEORTV**	OVERBEAT	**ABEFOORT**	BAREFOOT
ABEELNRS	ENABLERS	**ABEEOSTX**	TEABOXES	**ABEFORRS**	FORBEARS
ABEELNRT	RENTABLE	**ABEEPRRU**	UPBEARER	**ABEFORSY**	FOREBAYS
ABEELNST	NESTABLE	**ABEEPRRY**	PEABERRY	**ABEGGGIN**	ABEGGING
ABEELNTT	NETTABLE	**ABEEPTTY**	PETABYTE	**ABEGGHLU**	HUGGABLE
ABEELNTU	TUNEABLE	**ABEEQSUU**	USQUEBAE	**ABEGGILN**	BEAGLING
ABEELOPR	OPERABLE	**ABEERRRT**	BARTERER	**ABEGGINZ**	BEGAZING
	ROPEABLE	**ABEERRST**	REBATERS	**ABEGGIRR**	BRAGGIER
ABEELOPS	POSEABLE		TABRERES	**ABEGGIST**	BAGGIEST
ABEELORS	EARLOBES		TEREBRAS	**ABEGGITY**	GIGABYTE
ABEELORV	OVERABLE	**ABEERRTT**	BARRETTE	**ABEGGLLU**	LUGGABLE
ABEELORX	EXORABLE		BATTENER	**ABEGGLRS**	BLAGGERS
ABEELOTT	TOTEABLE		BERRETTA	**ABEGGLRY**	BEGGARLY
ABEELOTV	VOTEABLE	**ABEERRTV**	VERTEBRA	**ABEGGMOS**	GAMBOGES
ABEELPRS	BEPEARLS	**ABEERRTY**	BETRAYER	**ABEGGNSU**	BUGGANES
ABEELPTT	PETTABLE		TEABERRY	**ABEGGRRS**	BRAGGERS
ABEELPTY	TYPEABLE	**ABEERRWY**	BEWRAYER	**ABEGGRST**	BRAGGEST
ABEELRST	ARBELEST	**ABEERSTT**	ABETTERS	**ABEGGRSU**	BURGAGES
	BLEAREST		BERETTAS	**ABEGHILP**	PHILABEG
	BLEATERS	**ABEERSTU**	SUBERATE	**ABEGHILR**	ALBERGHI
	RESTABLE	**ABEERTTT**	BETATTER	**ABEGHINO**	OBEAHING
	RETABLES	**ABEERTTY**	TERABYTE	**ABEGHINT**	BEATHING
ABEELRSU	REUSABLE	**ABEESTXY**	EXABYTES	**ABEGHINV**	BEHAVING
ABEELRSV	BESLAVER	**ABEESZZZ**	BEZAZZES	**ABEGHNSS**	SHEBANGS
	SERVABLE	**ABEETTUX**	EXTUBATE	**ABEGHORR**	BEGORRAH
ABEELRSY	BELAYERS	**ABEFFKOR**	BREAKOFF	**ABEGHOSU**	BAGHOUSE
ABEELRTT	BATTELER	**ABEFFLRS**	BAFFLERS	**ABEGHRRY**	HAGBERRY
ABEELRTU	BATELEUR	**ABEFFOST**	OFFBEATS	**ABEGHRST**	BARGHEST
	BLEUATRE	**ABEFGILS**	FILABEGS	**ABEGHRSU**	BEARHUGS
ABEELSSS	BASELESS	**ABEFGILT**	GIFTABLE	**ABEGIIMS**	BIGAMIES
ABEELSST	BATELESS	**ABEFGLLR**	BERGFALL	**ABEGIINO**	IBOGAINE
	BEATLESS	**ABEFGSST**	GABFESTS	**ABEGIJTU**	BIJUGATE
ABEELSSU	SUBLEASE	**ABEFHILS**	FISHABLE	**ABEGIKNR**	BERAKING
ABEELSSV	BESLAVES	**ABEFHOOT**	HOOFBEAT		BREAKING
ABEELSTT	SEATBELT	**ABEFIIMR**	FIMBRIAE	**ABEGIKNT**	BETAKING
	TESTABLE	**ABEFIIRS**	BASIFIER	**ABEGILLN**	LABELING
ABEELSTW	STEWABLE	**ABEFIISS**	BASIFIES	**ABEGILMN**	EMBALING
ABEELTTW	WETTABLE	**ABEFILLL**	FALLIBLE	**ABEGILNN**	ENABLING
ABEEMMNR	MEMBRANE		FILLABLE	**ABEGILNR**	BLEARING
ABEEMMRU	BUMMAREE	**ABEFILLM**	FILMABLE	**ABEGILNS**	SIGNABLE
ABEEMNOR	BEMOANER	**ABEFILLO**	FOILABLE		SINGABLE
ABEEMNST	BASEMENT	**ABEFILLR**	FIREBALL	**ABEGILNT**	BELATING
ABEEMNTT	ABETMENT	**ABEFILLT**	LIFTABLE		BLEATING
	BATEMENT	**ABEFILOT**	LIFEBOAT		TANGIBLE
ABEEMRSS	BESMEARS	**ABEFILRS**	BARFLIES	**ABEGILNY**	BELAYING
ABEEMRSV	EMBRAVES	**ABEFILSU**	FABULISE	**ABEGILOT**	OBLIGATE
ABEENNRT	BANNERET	**ABEFILSY**	FEASIBLY	**ABEGIMNN**	BENAMING

ABEGIMNR	BREAMING	ABEHILLR	HAIRBELL	ABEIILST	ALBITISE
ABEGIMNS	BEAMINGS	ABEHILNR	HIBERNAL		SIBILATE
	EMBASING	ABEHILRS	BLASHIER	ABEIILTV	VITIABLE
	MISBEGAN	ABEHILTT	HITTABLE	ABEIILTZ	ALBITIZE
ABEGIMNY	EMBAYING		TITHABLE	ABEIINRR	BRAINIER
ABEGIMRS	GAMBIERS	ABEHIMMS	MEMSAHIB	ABEIINRS	BINARIES
ABEGIMST	MEGABITS	ABEHIMNO	BOHEMIAN	ABEIINST	BAINITES
ABEGIMUX	GIAMBEUX	ABEHIMOS	BOHEMIAS	ABEIJLNO	JOINABLE
ABEGINOR	ABORIGEN		OBEAHISM	ABEIJLTU	JUBILATE
ABEGINOS	BEGONIAS	ABEHIMST	IMBATHES	ABEIJMNN	BENJAMIN
ABEGINRR	BARREING	ABEHINRS	BANISHER	ABEIJMRS	JAMBIERS
	BERRIGAN	ABEHINSS	BANISHES	ABEIJNSS	BASENJIS
ABEGINRS	BEARINGS		BANSHIES	ABEIKLLL	KILLABLE
	SABERING	ABEHINST	ABSINTHE	ABEIKLLM	BALMLIKE
ABEGINRT	BERATING	ABEHIOPU	EUPHOBIA		LAMBLIKE
	REBATING	ABEHIORV	BEHAVIOR	ABEIKLLN	BALKLINE
	TABERING	ABEHIRRS	BRASHIER		LINKABLE
ABEGINRW	BEWARING	ABEHISTU	HABITUES	ABEIKLLS	SLABLIKE
ABEGINRY	BERAYING	ABEHISTZ	ZABTIEHS	ABEIKLNR	BARNLIKE
ABEGINST	BEATINGS	ABEHJORS	JOBSHARE	ABEIKLNS	BLANKIES
ABEGINSY	EBAYINGS	ABEHKLLW	HAWKBELL		SINKABLE
ABEGINTT	ABETTING	ABEHKNOR	HORNBEAK	ABEIKLOS	KILOBASE
ABEGINTW	WINGBEAT	ABEHKNST	BETHANKS	ABEIKLOT	BOATLIKE
ABEGIOSS	BIOGASES	ABEHKOPS	BAKESHOP	ABEIKLRU	BAULKIER
ABEGIPPR	BAGPIPER	ABEHKRSU	HAUBERKS	ABEIKLSS	KISSABLE
ABEGIPPS	BAGPIPES	ABEHKSTU	KETUBAHS	ABEIKLST	BALKIEST
ABEGKLSU	BULKAGES	ABEHLLRT	BETHRALL	ABEIKLSY	KIELBASY
ABEGKORS	BROKAGES	ABEHLMMU	HUMMABLE	ABEIKNNR	NINEBARK
	GROSBEAK	ABEHLMSS	SHAMBLES	ABEIKNRR	BRANKIER
ABEGKOSS	BOSKAGES	ABEHLNOT	BENTHOAL	ABEIKNRS	BEARSKIN
ABEGLLLU	GULLABLE	ABEHLNTU	HUNTABLE		INBREAKS
ABEGLLOR	BARGELLO	ABEHLOSW	SHOWABLE	ABEIKNST	BEATNIKS
ABEGLMOR	BEGLAMOR	ABEHLOTU	TABOULEH		SNAKEBIT
ABEGLMRS	GAMBLERS	ABEHLOTY	HYLOBATE	ABEIKRST	BARKIEST
	GAMBRELS	ABEHLRST	BLATHERS		BRAKIEST
ABEGLMUY	MEALYBUG		HALBERTS		BREASKIT
ABEGLNRS	BRANGLES	ABEHLSSS	BASHLESS	ABEIKSWY	BIKEWAYS
ABEGLORW	GROWABLE	ABEHLSST	BATHLESS	ABEILLLM	MILLABLE
ABEGLRRS	GARBLERS	ABEHMNOR	HORNBEAM	ABEILLLT	TILLABLE
ABEGLRSS	GARBLESS	ABEHMNOS	HAMBONES	ABEILLLW	WILLABLE
ABEGLRSU	BLAGUERS	ABEHMOOR	REHOBOAM	ABEILLMM	LIMBMEAL
ABEGLRUU	BLAGUEUR	ABEHMRSU	AMBUSHER	ABEILLMS	MISLABEL
ABEGLSTU	GUSTABLE	ABEHMSSU	AMBUSHES	ABEILLNT	LIBELANT
ABEGMNOS	GAMBESON	ABEHMSTU	BUSHMEAT	ABEILLOS	ISOLABLE
ABEGMNOY	BOGEYMAN	ABEHNRSY	ABHENRYS		LOBELIAS
	MONEYBAG	ABEHNSTU	SUNBATHE	ABEILLOV	VIOLABLE
ABEGMORT	BERGAMOT	ABEHORRR	ABHORRER	ABEILLPS	LAPSIBLE
ABEGMRSU	UMBRAGES		HARBORER	ABEILLQU	LIQUABLE
ABEGNNST	BANTENGS	ABEHORST	BATHORSE	ABEILLRR	BRAILLER
ABEGNORS	BEGROANS	ABEHOSST	BATHOSES	ABEILLRS	BALLSIER
ABEGNOSS	NOSEBAGS	ABEHOSTX	HATBOXES		BRAILLES
ABEGNRST	BANGSTER	ABEHOSXY	HAYBOXES		LIBERALS
ABEGNRTU	BURGANET	ABEHPSSU	SUBPHASE	ABEILLRY	BERYLLIA
ABEGNSTU	SUBAGENT	ABEHRSST	BRASHEST		BLEARILY
ABEGOORS	BARGOOSE	ABEHRTUY	EURYBATH		RELIABLY
ABEGOPSY	PAGEBOYS	ABEIIKLS	KIELBASI	ABEILLST	BASTILLE
ABEGOSTT	BOTTEGAS	ABEIILLS	BAILLIES		LISTABLE
ABEGOSUY	BUOYAGES	ABEIILMT	IMITABLE	ABEILLTT	TILTABLE
ABEGRRSU	GARBURES	ABEIILNN	BIENNIAL	ABEILMMR	IMBALMER
ABEGRRUV	BURGRAVE	ABEIILNR	BILINEAR	ABEILMNS	BAILSMEN
ABEGRSST	BARGESTS	ABEIILNV	INVIABLE		BIMENSAL
ABEGRSTU	BARGUEST	ABEIILPT	PITIABLE	ABEILMNT	BAILMENT
ABEGSSTU	SUBSTAGE	ABEIILRR	LIBRAIRE	ABEILMOR	BROMELIA
ABEHIKLS	BLEAKISH	ABEIILRS	BISERIAL	ABEILMRR	MARBLIER

ABEILMRS	REMBLAIS	ABEIMRSU	AUMBRIES	ABEIRRYZ	BRAZIERY
ABEILMRW	WAMBLIER	ABEIMRTV	AMBIVERT	ABEIRSSS	BRASSIES
ABEILMSS	ABLEISMS		VERBATIM	ABEIRSSU	AIRBUSES
	MISSABLE	ABEIMSSU	IAMBUSES	ABEIRSTT	BIRETTAS
ABEILMST	BALMIEST	ABEINNOS	BESONIAN	ABEIRSTV	VIBRATES
	BIMETALS	ABEINNOZ	BEZONIAN	ABEIRSTW	WARBIEST
	LAMBIEST	ABEINNRR	BRANNIER	ABEIRSTY	BESTIARY
	TIMBALES	ABEINNRU	INURBANE		SYBARITE
ABEILMSU	BUMELIAS	ABEINORR	AIRBORNE	ABEIRSUX	EXURBIAS
ABEILMSW	WEBMAILS	ABEINORS	BARONIES	ABEIRTTY	YTTERBIA
ABEILMSZ	IMBLAZES		SEAROBIN	ABEISSST	BASSIEST
ABEILNNW	WINNABLE	ABEINORT	BARITONE	ABEISSTT	BATISTES
ABEILNOP	OPINABLE		OBTAINER	ABEISTTT	BATTIEST
ABEILNOT	TAILBONE		REOBTAIN	ABEISTUX	BAUXITES
ABEILNPS	BIPLANES		TABORINE	ABEISZZZ	BIZAZZES
ABEILNPT	PINTABLE	ABEINOST	BOTANIES	ABEITTTU	TITUBATE
ABEILNRS	RINSABLE		BOTANISE	ABEJKLOU	KABELJOU
ABEILNRU	RUINABLE		NIOBATES	ABEJLMPU	JUMPABLE
ABEILNSS	ALBINESS		OBEISANT	ABEJLSUY	BLUEJAYS
	LESBIANS	ABEINOTZ	BOTANIZE	ABEJMNOS	JAMBONES
ABEILNST	INSTABLE	ABEINPST	BEPAINTS		JOBNAMES
ABEILNSU	SABULINE	ABEINQSU	BASQUINE	ABEJMOOR	JEROBOAM
ABEILNTV	BIVALENT	ABEINRRW	BRAWNIER	ABEJNORW	JAWBONER
ABEILNTY	BINATELY	ABEINRST	ATEBRINS	ABEJNOSW	JAWBONES
ABEILNUV	UNVIABLE		BANISTER	ABEJOSWX	JAWBOXES
ABEILNVY	ENVIABLY		BARNIEST	ABEJRRSU	ABJURERS
ABEILORR	BORRELIA	ABEINRSU	ANBURIES	ABEKKKSU	BUKKAKES
ABEILORS	BOREALIS		URBANISE	ABEKLMOS	ABELMOSK
ABEILORT	LABORITE	ABEINRSW	WEBINARS		SMOKABLE
ABEILOTV	BLOVIATE	ABEINRSZ	ZEBRINAS	ABEKLNOW	KNOWABLE
ABEILPPR	RIPPABLE	ABEINRTU	BRAUNITE	ABEKLNRY	BANKERLY
ABEILPPT	TIPPABLE		URBANITE	ABEKLNST	BLANKEST
ABEILPRT	PARTIBLE	ABEINRUZ	URBANIZE		BLANKETS
ABEILPRZ	PRIZABLE	ABEINSSS	BIASNESS	ABEKLNTY	BLANKETY
ABEILPSS	PASSIBLE	ABEINSST	BASINETS	ABEKLORW	WORKABLE
ABEILPST	EPIBLAST		BASSINET	ABEKLRSS	BARKLESS
ABEILRRU	REBURIAL		BESAINTS	ABEKLRSU	BAULKERS
ABEILRRW	BRAWLIER		BESTAINS	ABEKMNNS	BANKSMEN
ABEILRST	BLASTIER	ABEINSSU	UNBIASES	ABEKMNTU	BUNKMATE
	LIBRATES	ABEINSTT	TABINETS	ABEKMSSU	SAMBUKES
	TABLIERS	ABEINTTU	INTUBATE	ABEKNNOT	BANKNOTE
ABEILRSY	BILAYERS	ABEIORRS	ARBORISE	ABEKNRSU	UNBRAKES
ABEILRTT	TITRABLE	ABEIORRZ	ARBORIZE	ABEKNSSU	SUNBAKES
ABEILRTW	WRITABLE	ABEIORSS	ISOBARES	ABEKNSSY	SNEAKSBY
ABEILRVY	BIYEARLY	ABEIORST	SABOTIER	ABEKOORS	ABROOKES
ABEILSST	ABLEISTS	ABEIORTV	ABORTIVE	ABEKOORY	YEARBOOK
	ASTILBES	ABEIOSSS	ISOBASES	ABEKORTU	BREAKOUT
	BASTILES	ABEIOSTV	OBVIATES		OUTBREAK
	BESTIALS	ABEIPRRS	SPARERIB	ABEKOSTU	OUTBAKES
	BLASTIES	ABEIPRST	BAPTISER	ABEKPRSU	BREAKUPS
	STABILES	ABEIPRTZ	BAPTIZER		UPBREAKS
ABEILSSU	ISSUABLE	ABEIPSST	BAPTISES	ABEKRSTY	BASKETRY
	SUASIBLE	ABEIPSTZ	BAPTIZES	ABELLLMU	LABELLUM
ABEILSTU	SUITABLE	ABEIRRRS	BARRIERS	ABELLLOR	ROLLABLE
ABEILSTY	BEASTILY	ABEIRRSS	BRASIERS	ABELLLOT	TOLLABLE
ABEILSUX	BISEXUAL		BRASSIER	ABELLLSY	SYLLABLE
ABEILSVV	BIVALVES	ABEIRRST	ARBITERS	ABELLMOR	OMBRELLA
ABEILSYZ	SIZEABLY		BARRIEST	ABELLMRU	UMBELLAR
ABEIMNPS	PEMBINAS		RAREBITS		UMBRELLA
ABEIMNRS	MIRBANES	ABEIRRSZ	BIZARRES	ABELLNNO	BALLONNE
ABEIMNST	AMBIENTS		BRAZIERS	ABELLNOS	BONSELLA
ABEIMORS	BIRAMOSE	ABEIRRTT	BIRRETTA	ABELLNOT	BALLONET
ABEIMORU	AEROBIUM		BRATTIER	ABELLNRU	RUBELLAN
ABEIMRST	BARMIEST	ABEIRRVY	BREVIARY	ABELLNST	NETBALLS

ABELLOPW	PLOWABLE	ABELORSV	ABSOLVER	ABENQSTU	BANQUETS
ABELLORT	BALLOTER	ABELOSSU	SABULOSE	ABENRRYZ	BRAZENRY
ABELLOSV	SOLVABLE	ABELOSSV	ABSOLVES	ABENRSTU	UNBRASTE
ABELLOTU	LOBULATE	ABELOSTU	ABSOLUTE		URBANEST
ABELLOTY	LOBATELY	ABELOSTW	BESTOWAL	ABENSSSS	BASSNESS
	OBLATELY		STOWABLE	ABENSTZZ	BEZZANTS
ABELLOVY	LOVEABLY		TEABOWLS	ABEOOSST	SEABOOTS
ABELLRSU	RUBELLAS	ABELOTTU	OUTBLEAT	ABEOPPRY	PAPERBOY
ABELLRVY	VERBALLY	ABELOTUZ	OUTBLAZE	ABEOPRSS	SAPROBES
ABELLSTU	BALLUTES	ABELPRTU	PUBERTAL	ABEOPRST	PROBATES
ABELMMSU	SUMMABLE	ABELQSUU	SUBEQUAL	ABEOPSST	POSTBASE
ABELMNNO	NOBLEMAN	ABELRRSW	BRAWLERS	ABEOQRSU	BAROQUES
ABELMNOZ	EMBLAZON		WARBLERS	ABEORRRT	BARRETOR
ABELMNST	SEMBLANT	ABELRRTU	BARRULET	ABEORRSS	BRASEROS
ABELMNSU	ALBUMENS	ABELRSST	BLASTERS	ABEORRST	ABORTERS
	BLUESMAN		STABLERS		ARBORETS
ABELMOOT	MOOTABLE	ABELRSSY	LABRYSES		TABORERS
ABELMOSU	ALBUMOSE	ABELRSTT	BATTLERS	ABEORRTU	TABOURER
ABELMOSV	MOVABLES		BLATTERS	ABEORSST	BOASTERS
ABELMOTY	METABOLY		BRATTLES		SORBATES
ABELMOVY	MOVEABLY	ABELRSTU	BALUSTER	ABEORSSY	ROSEBAYS
ABELMPTU	PLUMBATE		RUSTABLE	ABEORSTT	ABETTORS
ABELMRRS	MARBLERS	ABELRSTW	BLEWARTS		BATTEROS
	RAMBLERS	ABELRSUZ	ZEBRULAS		TABORETS
ABELMRST	LAMBERTS	ABELRTTU	BURLETTA	ABEORSTU	SABOTEUR
ABELMSSY	ASSEMBLY		REBUTTAL	ABEORTTU	OBTURATE
ABELNNOR	BANNEROL	ABELSSSU	SUBSALES		TABOURET
ABELNNRU	RUNNABLE	ABELSSTT	STABLEST	ABEORTUV	OUTBRAVE
ABELNORZ	BLAZONER	ABELSSTU	SUBLATES	ABEOSSST	ASBESTOS
ABELNOSS	BONSELAS	ABELSTUU	SUBULATE	ABEOSTUV	SUBOVATE
ABELNOST	NEOBLAST	ABELSTWY	BELTWAYS	ABEOSTWX	SWEATBOX
	NOTABLES	ABELTTUU	TUBULATE	ABEPRRTU	ABRUPTER
	STONABLE	ABELTTUY	BUTYLATE	ABEPRSSY	PASSERBY
ABELNOSY	BALONEYS	ABEMMNOO	MOONBEAM	ABEPRSTY	TYPEBARS
ABELNPRU	PRUNABLE	ABEMNOST	BOATSMEN	ABEPSSSY	BYPASSES
ABELNPSU	SUBPANEL	ABEMNOTU	UMBONATE	ABEQRSUU	ARQUEBUS
ABELNQTU	BLANQUET	ABEMNOTW	BATWOMEN	ABERRRTY	BARRETRY
ABELNRRY	BARRENLY	ABEMNPRU	PENUMBRA	ABERRSSU	SABREURS
ABELNRSS	BRANSLES	ABEMNRSY	MYRBANES	ABERRTYY	TAYBERRY
ABELNRST	BRANTLES	ABEMNSSU	SUNBEAMS	ABERRWXY	WAXBERRY
ABELNRSY	BLARNEYS	ABEMNSTU	SUBMENTA	ABERSSST	BRASSETS
ABELNRTU	TURNABLE	ABEMNSUY	SUNBEAMY	ABERSSSU	RUBASSES
ABELNRUY	URBANELY	ABEMNTTU	ABUTMENT		SURBASES
ABELNRYZ	BRAZENLY	ABEMORRS	EMBRASOR	ABERSSTU	ABSTRUSE
ABELNSTU	ABLUENTS	ABEMORST	BROMATES		SURBATES
	UNSTABLE	ABEMORSU	AMBEROUS	ABERSSTW	WABSTERS
ABELNSTY	ABSENTLY	ABEMORTZ	BAROMETZ	ABERSTTU	ABUTTERS
ABELNSUU	UNUSABLE	ABEMOSTU	OUTBEAMS	ABERSTUW	WATERBUS
ABELNTUY	TUNEABLY	ABEMRSSW	BESWARMS	ABERTTUY	BUTYRATE
ABELOOTY	TABOOLEY	ABENNORS	BARONNES	ABESSSTT	BASSETTS
ABELOPRT	PORTABLE	ABENNOTU	BUTANONE	ABESSSTU	ASBESTUS
ABELOPRU	POURABLE		NANOTUBE	ABESSTTU	SUBSTATE
ABELOPRV	PROVABLE	ABENNRRS	BRANNERS	ABFFGILN	BAFFLING
ABELOPRY	OPERABLY	ABENOPSU	SUBPOENA	ABFFIILS	BAILIFFS
ABELOPST	POTABLES	ABENORSS	BARONESS	ABFFINOS	BANOFFIS
ABELOPTT	TABLETOP	ABENORST	BARONETS	ABFFLLPU	PUFFBALL
ABELOQTU	QUOTABLE	ABENORSZ	ZEBRANOS	ABFFLOOS	BOFFOLAS
ABELORRS	LABORERS	ABENORTT	BETATRON	ABFFLOST	BLASTOFF
ABELORRU	LABOURER	ABENORTV	BEVATRON	ABFFLOSU	BUFFALOS
	RUBEOLAR	ABENORTY	BARYTONE	ABFFNOTU	BOUFFANT
ABELORST	BLOATERS	ABENOSSW	SAWBONES	ABFGILNS	FABLINGS
	SORTABLE	ABENOSSY	SOYBEANS	ABFGLLOO	GOOFBALL
	STORABLE	ABENOSTY	BAYONETS	ABFGOOST	FOOTBAGS
ABELORSU	RUBEOLAS	ABENPSSU	SUBPENAS	ABFGORUU	FAUBOURG

ABFHIIST	BAITFISH
ABFHILLS	FISHBALL
ABFHINNO	INFOBAHN
ABFHIORS	BOARFISH
ABFHOOTT	FOOTBATH
ABFHSSTU	SUBSHAFT
ABFIILLR	FIBRILLA
ABFIILMR	FIMBRIAL
ABFIILRR	FIBRILAR
ABFILLLY	FALLIBLY
ABFILNSU	BASINFUL
ABFILOTT	BOATLIFT
ABFILSTU	FABULIST
ABFIMORS	FIBROMAS
ABFJORSU	FRABJOUS
ABFKLLOR	FORKBALL
	KORFBALL
ABFLLOOS	FOOSBALL
ABFLLOOT	FOOTBALL
ABFLLORU	FOURBALL
ABFLLOST	SOFTBALL
ABFLMORY	FORMABLY
ABFLNSUU	BUSULFAN
ABFLOSTU	BOASTFUL
	BOATFULS
ABFLOSTW	BATFOWLS
ABFLOSTY	FLYBOATS
ABFLOSUU	FABULOUS
ABFNORTU	TURBOFAN
ABFOORST	FOOTBARS
ABFOOSTY	FOYBOATS
ABFORSTU	SURFBOAT
ABFSSTTU	TUBFASTS
ABGGGILN	BLAGGING
ABGGGINR	BRAGGING
ABGGGINS	BAGGINGS
ABGGIIST	GIGABITS
ABGGIJNN	JINGBANG
ABGGILMN	GAMBLING
ABGGILNR	GARBLING
ABGGINNS	BANGINGS
ABGGNNUY	GUNNYBAG
ABGGNOOT	TOBOGGAN
ABGGORST	BOGGARTS
ABGHHILL	HIGHBALL
ABGHIINT	HABITING
ABGHILMN	HAMBLING
ABGHINRS	BRASHING
ABGHINSS	BASHINGS
ABGHINWZ	WHIZBANG
ABGHIOPR	BIOGRAPH
ABGHLOST	HAGBOLTS
ABGHMOOS	GOOMBAHS
ABGHMORU	BROUGHAM
ABGHMRSU	HAMBURGS
ABGHNORS	HORNBAGS
ABGHORTU	BROUGHTA
ABGHOSTU	BUSHGOAT
ABGHPRSU	SUBGRAPH
ABGIIILN	ALIBIING
ABGIIKNT	BATIKING
ABGIILNR	BRAILING
ABGIILNS	SAIBLING
ABGIILNT	LIBATING
ABGIILOT	OBLIGATI
ABGIIMNS	IMBASING
ABGIIMST	BIGAMIST
ABGIINNO	BIGNONIA
ABGIINNR	BRAINING
ABGIINOR	ABORIGIN
ABGIINRS	BRAISING
ABGIINSS	BIASINGS
	BIASSING
ABGIINST	BAITINGS
ABGIJNRU	ABJURING
ABGIJOOS	JIGABOOS
ABGIKLNN	BLANKING
ABGIKLNS	BALKINGS
ABGIKLNU	BAULKING
ABGIKNNR	BRANKING
ABGIKNNS	BANKINGS
ABGIKNRR	RINGBARK
ABGILLMN	LAMBLING
ABGILLNS	BALLINGS
ABGILMNR	MARBLING
	RAMBLING
ABGILMNS	AMBLINGS
	LAMBINGS
ABGILMNW	WAMBLING
ABGILNNT	BANTLING
ABGILNNU	UNBALING
ABGILNOR	LABORING
ABGILNOT	BLOATING
	OBLIGANT
ABGILNRT	BLARTING
	BRATLING
ABGILNRW	BRAWLING
	WARBLING
ABGILNST	BLASTING
	STABLING
	TABLINGS
ABGILNSW	BAWLINGS
ABGILNTT	BATTLING
	BLATTING
ABGILNTY	TANGIBLY
ABGILOOT	OBLIGATO
ABGILORS	GARBOILS
ABGILORW	BRIGALOW
ABGILRST	BATGIRLS
ABGIMMNO	MAMBOING
ABGIMNRU	RUMBAING
ABGIMOSU	BIGAMOUS
	SUBIMAGO
ABGIMSST	GAMBISTS
ABGINNNR	BRANNING
ABGINNOR	ABORNING
ABGINNOT	BATONING
ABGINNRU	UNBARING
ABGINNRX	BANXRING
ABGINNST	BANTINGS
ABGINOOR	BIGAROON
ABGINOOT	TABOOING
ABGINORT	ABORTING
	BORATING
	TABORING
ABGINORV	BRAVOING
ABGINOST	BOASTING
	BOATINGS
	BOSTANGI
ABGINRRS	BARRINGS
ABGINRSS	BRASSING
ABGINRST	BRASTING
ABGINSST	BASTINGS
ABGINSTT	BATTINGS
ABGINSTW	BATSWING
ABGINTTU	ABUTTING
ABGIOPST	PIGBOATS
ABGIRRSS	RIBGRASS
ABGKKNOS	BANGKOKS
ABGKORSW	WORKBAGS
ABGLLLOY	GLOBALLY
ABGLLLUY	GULLABLY
ABGLLMSU	GUMBALLS
ABGLLNUW	BUNGWALL
ABGLLORU	GLOBULAR
ABGLLRUY	BULLYRAG
ABGLMNSU	LUMBANGS
ABGLMOPU	PLUMBAGO
ABGLMOSU	LUMBAGOS
ABGLNOOS	BOLOGNAS
ABGLNOOT	LONGBOAT
ABGLNOUW	BUNGALOW
ABGLOOST	TOOLBAGS
ABGLOOTY	BATOLOGY
ABGLORST	RAGBOLTS
ABGLORSU	GLABROUS
ABGLOSSU	SUBGOALS
ABGLRRSU	BURGLARS
ABGLRRUY	BURGLARY
ABGMNOOR	GAMBROON
ABGMNOOY	BOOGYMAN
ABGMOOSY	GOOMBAYS
ABGMORSW	BAGWORMS
ABGNOORS	BARGOONS
ABGNOORY	BOONGARY
ABGNOPRS	PROBANGS
ABGNORSU	OSNABURG
ABGNOSTU	GUNBOATS
ABGNOSWY	BOWYANGS
ABGOORST	BOTARGOS
ABGOPSST	POSTBAGS
ABGORRSU	GOBURRAS
ABGORSTU	OUTBRAGS
ABGOSTTU	TUGBOATS
ABHHIKSS	BAKSHISH
ABHHKOST	KHOTBAHS
ABHHKSTU	KHUTBAHS
ABHHRSTU	HATBRUSH
ABHHSSUW	BUSHWAHS
ABHIINRS	BAIRNISH
	BRAINISH
ABHIINST	INHABITS
ABHIIORZ	RHIZOBIA
ABHIKLLW	HAWKBILL
ABHIKLOR	KOHLRABI
ABHIKLSS	BASHLIKS
ABHIKSTW	HAWKBITS
ABHIKSUZ	BUZKASHI
ABHILLPT	PITHBALL
ABHILNOS	HOBNAILS
ABHILNOT	BIATHLON
ABHILOPS	BASOPHIL

ABHILRTW	WHIRLBAT	ABIIRSSV	VIBRISSA	ABILSTUY	SUITABLY
ABHILSST	STABLISH	ABIJLNRS	BRINJALS	ABIMMNOO	MAINBOOM
ABHILSTU	HALIBUTS	ABIJLNTU	JUBILANT	ABIMMSTU	MITUMBAS
ABHIMMST	BATHMISM	ABIJNOOT	JOBATION	ABIMNOSU	BIMANOUS
ABHIMNRS	BRAHMINS	ABIJNOST	ABJOINTS	ABIMNRSU	URBANISM
ABHINSST	ABSINTHS		BANJOIST	ABIMNRTU	TAMBURIN
ABHIOSST	ISOBATHS	ABIKLLLM	LAMBKILL	ABIMORSU	BIRAMOUS
ABHIOSTU	HAUTBOIS	ABIKLLUY	BAULKILY	ABIMORSY	BOYARISM
ABHIRRSU	AIRBRUSH	ABIKLMNS	LAMBKINS	ABIMPSST	BAPTISMS
ABHIRSSS	BRASSISH		LAMBSKIN	ABIMRSST	STRABISM
ABHIRSTT	BRATTISH	ABIKLMOU	KUMBALOI	ABIMRSTT	TRIMTABS
ABHJNOOT	JOHNBOAT	ABIKLNRY	BYRLAKIN	ABINNOST	ANTISNOB
ABHKLSSY	BASHLYKS	ABIKLORS	KILOBARS	ABINOORS	BORONIAS
ABHKLSUW	BUSHWALK	ABIKLOSS	KOLBASIS	ABINOORT	ABORTION
ABHKOOOT	BOATHOOK		KOLBASSI	ABINOOST	BONIATOS
ABHKORSU	BOURKHAS	ABIKLSSY	KISSABLY	ABINOPTX	PAINTBOX
	KOURBASH	ABIKMNNR	BRINKMAN	ABINORST	TABORINS
ABHKORSV	BOSHVARK	ABIKMNRS	BARMKINS	ABINORSW	RAINBOWS
ABHLLMOT	MOTHBALL	ABIKNORR	IRONBARK	ABINORTU	TABOURIN
ABHLLOOY	BALLYHOO	ABIKOSUZ	BAZOUKIS	ABINORWY	RAINBOWY
ABHLLPSU	PUSHBALL	ABIKRSST	BRITSKAS	ABINOSST	ANTIBOSS
ABHLLSTU	BULLSHAT	ABIKRSTZ	BRITZKAS		BASTIONS
ABHLORTW	WHORLBAT		BRITZSKA	ABINOSSU	ABUSIONS
ABHLOSUX	BOXHAULS	ABILLLPY	PLAYBILL	ABINOSTT	BOTANIST
ABHLOSWW	WASHBOWL	ABILLMSU	BALLIUMS	ABINRSTU	URBANIST
ABHLPSUY	SUBPHYLA	ABILLNPS	PINBALLS	ABINRSTV	VIBRANTS
ABHLRSTU	HURLBATS	ABILLORT	TRILOBAL	ABINRTUY	URBANITY
ABHLSSTU	SALTBUSH	ABILLOVY	VIOLABLY	ABINTTTU	TITUBANT
ABHMNOTY	BOTHYMAN	ABILLPST	SPITBALL	ABIOORTV	OBVIATOR
ABHMNSUU	SUBHUMAN	ABILLRTY	TRIBALLY	ABIOPRSU	BIPAROUS
ABHMOORT	BATHROOM	ABILLSSW	SAWBILLS	ABIOPSTU	SUBTOPIA
ABHMRSSU	SAMBHURS	ABILLSTT	BATTILLS	ABIORRST	ARBORIST
ABHNSSTU	SUNBATHS	ABILLSWX	WAXBILLS	ABIORRSZ	BIZARROS
ABHOORST	TARBOOSH	ABILLSWY	WAYBILLS	ABIORRTV	VIBRATOR
ABHOOSTW	SHOWBOAT	ABILMNOU	OLIBANUM	ABIORSTV	VIBRATOS
ABHORRSU	HARBOURS	ABILMNSU	ALBUMINS	ABIORTUY	OBITUARY
ABHORSTU	TARBOUSH	ABILMOPS	BIOPLASM	ABIPSSTT	BAPTISTS
ABHOSTUY	HAUTBOYS	ABILMORS	LABORISM	ABIRRSTU	AIRBURST
ABHSSTUW	WASHTUBS		MISLABOR	ABIRSSUZ	SUBSIZAR
ABIIINRS	BIRIANIS	ABILMOTU	BUMALOTI	ABIRSTTY	TRAYBITS
ABIIINRY	BIRIYANI	ABILNOOT	BOLTONIA	ABISSSST	BASSISTS
ABIIKKST	KIBITKAS		LOBATION	ABISSTTU	TUBAISTS
ABIIKLSS	BASILISK		OBLATION	ABJKMOSS	SJAMBOKS
ABIILLMR	MILLIBAR	ABILNOPR	PANBROIL	ABJLMOOS	JAMBOOLS
ABIILLTY	LABILITY	ABILNORU	UNILOBAR	ABKKMOOR	BOOKMARK
ABIILMNO	BINOMIAL	ABILNOTU	ABLUTION	ABKLLNOR	BANKROLL
ABIILMNS	ALBINISM		ABUTILON	ABKLOOPY	PLAYBOOK
	MINILABS	ABILNRTU	TRIBUNAL	ABKLOOSW	LAWBOOKS
ABIILMSU	BULIMIAS		TURBINAL	ABKLORTW	BLOWKART
ABIILNOT	LIBATION	ABILNRWY	BRAWNILY	ABKLORWY	WORKABLY
ABIILNQS	INQILABS	ABILOPRS	PARBOILS	ABKLRSUW	BULWARKS
ABIILNRS	BRASILIN	ABILOPST	BIOPLAST	ABKNNNOS	NONBANKS
ABIILNRY	BRAINILY	ABILORST	LABORIST	ABKNNOSW	SNOWBANK
ABIILNRZ	BRAZILIN		ORBITALS	ABKNOPST	STOPBANK
ABIILNST	SIBILANT		STROBILA	ABKNPRTU	BANKRUPT
ABIILNVY	INVIABLY	ABILORSV	BOLIVARS	ABKNRSUU	BUNRAKUS
ABIILOSV	BOLIVIAS	ABILORTY	LIBATORY	ABKOOPSS	PASSBOOK
ABIILPTY	PITIABLY	ABILORUV	BIOVULAR	ABKOORTW	WORKBOAT
ABIIMNOT	AMBITION	ABILOSTU	BAILOUTS	ABKOOSTT	KOTTABOS
ABIIMNRS	BINARISM		TABOULIS	ABKORSTU	OUTBARKS
	MINIBARS	ABILPSSY	PASSIBLY	ABKSSSTU	SUBTASKS
ABIIMSST	IAMBISTS	ABILRSSY	BRASSILY	ABLLLOSW	LOWBALLS
ABIINORS	ROBINIAS	ABILRSUV	SUBVIRAL	ABLLMOOR	BALLROOM
ABIINRSY	BIRYANIS	ABILSSUY	ISSUABLY	ABLLMOPW	BLOWLAMP

ABLLMOSY	SMALLBOY
ABLLNOOS	BALLOONS
ABLLNOSW	SNOWBALL
ABLLORRS	ROLLBARS
ABLLORST	BORSTALL
	TOLLBARS
ABLLORSU	SOURBALL
ABLLOSTY	TALLBOYS
ABLLRTUY	BRUTALLY
ABLLSSUY	SYLLABUS
ABLMMOSU	BUMMALOS
ABLMNRUU	ALBURNUM
	LABURNUM
ABLMOOST	TOMBOLAS
ABLMOSTY	MYOBLAST
ABLMPSUU	PABULUMS
ABLNNOOR	NONLABOR
ABLNOOPS	POBLANOS
ABLNORST	LASTBORN
ABLNORYZ	BLAZONRY
ABLNOSTU	BUTANOLS
ABLNOSUZ	SUBZONAL
ABLNRSUU	SUBLUNAR
ABLNSTUY	UNSTABLY
ABLNSUUY	UNUSABLY
ABLOOPRR	PROLABOR
ABLOORST	BARSTOOL
	TOOLBARS
ABLOORTY	OBLATORY
ABLOOSTT	BOOTLAST
ABLOOSTZ	ZOOBLAST
ABLOPRSU	SUBPOLAR
ABLOPRTY	PORTABLY
ABLOPRVY	PROVABLY
ABLOPSUU	PABULOUS
ABLOPSYY	PLAYBOYS
ABLOQTUY	QUOTABLY
ABLORSST	BORSTALS
ABLORSSU	SUBSOLAR
ABLORSTW	BLAWORTS
ABLORSTY	SORTABLY
ABLORSUW	BOURLAWS
ABLORTUW	OUTBRAWL
ABLOSSUU	SABULOUS
ABLOSTTU	SUBTOTAL
ABLOSTUW	OUTBAWLS
ABLPRTUY	ABRUPTLY
ABLRSTUY	BUTYRALS
ABMNTTUY	BUTTYMAN
ABMOORRS	BARROOMS
ABMOPSST	SPAMBOTS
ABMORSTU	TAMBOURS
ABMOSSTU	SUBATOMS
ABMRRSUY	BURRAMYS
ABNNNORU	NONURBAN
ABNOORRT	ROBORANT
ABNOORSS	SOROBANS
ABNOORSZ	BORAZONS
ABNOORYZ	BRYOZOAN
ABNOOSSS	BASSOONS
ABNORSTY	BARYTONS
ABNORTUU	RUNABOUT
ABNOSSSU	BONASSUS
ABNOSTUX	SUBTAXON

ABNRSTTU	TURBANTS
ABOORRSU	ARBOROUS
ABOORSTW	ROWBOATS
ABOOSTTU	OUTBOAST
ABOOSTTW	TOWBOATS
ABORSSTU	ROBUSTAS
ABPRSSTU	SUBPARTS
ACCCDIIO	COCCIDIA
ACCCEHIX	CACHEXIC
ACCCELRY	CYCLECAR
ACCCENPY	PECCANCY
ACCCFIIL	CALCIFIC
ACCCHILO	COLCHICA
ACCCHRTY	CATCHCRY
ACCCIILT	CALCITIC
ACCCIIPR	CAPRICCI
ACCCILLY	CYCLICAL
ACCCIOPU	CAPUCCIO
ACCDDEEN	ACCENDED
	CADENCED
ACCDDEIS	CADDICES
ACCDDEKO	COCKADED
ACCDDEOR	ACCORDED
ACCDDIII	DIACIDIC
ACCDDIIT	DIDACTIC
ACCDEEER	REACCEDE
ACCDEEHT	CACHETED
ACCDEELN	CANCELED
ACCDEENR	CANCERED
ACCDEENS	CADENCES
ACCDEENT	ACCENTED
ACCDEEPT	ACCEPTED
ACCDEERS	ACCEDERS
ACCDEERT	ACCRETED
ACCDEERU	CARDECUE
ACCDEERW	ACCREWED
ACCDEESS	ACCESSED
ACCDEGIN	ACCEDING
	ACCINGED
ACCDEHIK	CHIACKED
ACCDEHIL	CHALICED
ACCDEHIN	CHICANED
ACCDEHKY	CHYACKED
ACCDEHLT	CLATCHED
ACCDEHNR	CRANCHED
ACCDEHNU	CHAUNCED
ACCDEHPU	CAPUCHED
ACCDEIIS	ACCIDIES
ACCDEILN	CALCINED
ACCDEILO	ECOCIDAL
ACCDEILU	CAUDICLE
ACCDEILY	DELICACY
ACCDEINO	DECANOIC
ACCDEINT	ACCIDENT
ACCDEIRT	ACCREDIT
ACCDEISU	CAUDICES
ACCDEKLR	CRACKLED
ACCDEKOS	COCKADES
ACCDELLY	CALYCLED
ACCDELOY	ACCLOYED
ACCDENOR	CONACRED
ACCDENOV	CONCAVED
ACCDEORR	ACCORDER
ACCDEOST	ACCOSTED

ACCDERSU	ACCURSED
	CARDECUS
ACCDESSU	SUCCADES
ACCDESUU	CADUCEUS
	CAUCUSED
ACCDGHOO	COACHDOG
ACCDHIIR	DIARCHIC
ACCDHILS	CHALCIDS
ACCDHIMO	DOCHMIAC
ACCDHIOR	CHAORDIC
ACCDHIOT	CATHODIC
ACCDHIRY	DYARCHIC
ACCDHLOR	CLOCHARD
ACCDIINU	UNACIDIC
ACCDIIOT	ACIDOTIC
ACCDIIRT	CARDITIC
ACCDIIST	DICASTIC
ACCDIITY	DICACITY
ACCDILNU	DUNCICAL
ACCDILOY	CALYCOID
ACCDILTY	DACTYLIC
ACCDINOR	CANCROID
	DRACONIC
ACCDIOOR	CORACOID
ACCDIORS	SARCODIC
ACCDIOST	STICCADO
ACCDITUY	CADUCITY
ACCDKNOS	CANDOCKS
ACCDKOSW	DAWCOCKS
ACCDLOSY	CACODYLS
ACCDOOST	STOCCADO
ACCDOOXY	CACODOXY
ACCDOSUU	CADUCOUS
ACCEEEPT	ACCEPTEE
ACCEEHIT	HICCATEE
ACCEEHLO	COCHLEAE
ACCEEHLS	CALECHES
ACCEEHOS	COACHEES
ACCEEHRT	CETERACH
ACCEEHST	SEECATCH
ACCEEILR	CELERIAC
ACCEEILS	ECCLESIA
ACCEEINV	VACCINEE
ACCEEKLN	NECKLACE
ACCEELNO	COENACLE
ACCEELNR	CANCELER
	CLARENCE
ACCEELNS	CENACLES
ACCEELOS	COALESCE
ACCEELRT	CALCRETE
ACCEENNS	NASCENCE
ACCEENPR	CREPANCE
ACCEENRS	CREANCES
ACCEENRT	REACCENT
ACCEENST	ACESCENT
ACCEEORT	COCREATE
	CROCEATE
ACCEEPRT	ACCEPTER
	REACCEPT
ACCEERST	ACCRETES
ACCEERSU	REACCUSE
ACCEESSS	ACCESSES
ACCEFFIY	EFFICACY
ACCEFILS	FASCICLE

ACCEFIST	FACTICES		SCENICAL	ACCENOSU	CONCAUSE
ACCEFLSU	FELUCCAS	ACCEILNT	CANTICLE	ACCENOSV	CONCAVES
ACCEGINS	ACCINGES	ACCEILNV	CLAVECIN	ACCEOPRT	ACCEPTOR
ACCEGKMO	GAMECOCK	ACCEILNY	CALYCINE	ACCEOPTU	OCCUPATE
ACCEGNOY	COAGENCY	ACCEILOP	ALOPECIC	ACCEORSS	ARCCOSES
ACCEGOSS	SOCCAGES	ACCEILOS	CALICOES	ACCEORST	ECTOSARC
ACCEHHIS	CHECHIAS		COELIACS	ACCEORSW	CRACOWES
ACCEHHKO	CHECHAKO	ACCEILRV	CERVICAL	ACCEORTU	ACCOUTER
ACCEHHKT	CHATCHKE	ACCEILST	CALCITES		ACCOUTRE
	HATCHECK	ACCEILTY	ACETYLIC	ACCEOSSS	SACCOSES
ACCEHIKP	CHICKPEA	ACCEIMOS	OCCAMIES	ACCERRST	CARRECTS
ACCEHIKR	AIRCHECK	ACCEIMRS	CERAMICS	ACCERSST	SCARCEST
ACCEHILM	ALCHEMIC	ACCEINNR	CANCRINE	ACCERSSU	ACCURSES
	CHEMICAL	ACCEINOR	COCINERA		ACCUSERS
ACCEHILP	CEPHALIC	ACCEINOS	COCAINES	ACCESSTU	CACTUSES
ACCEHILS	CALICHES	ACCEINOT	ACETONIC	ACCESSUU	CAUCUSES
	CHALICES	ACCEINRT	ACENTRIC	ACCFFLTU	CALCTUFF
ACCEHILT	HECTICAL	ACCEINSV	VACCINES	ACCFHLTY	CATCHFLY
ACCEHIMN	MECHANIC	ACCEINTU	CUNEATIC	ACCFIILT	LACTIFIC
ACCEHIMS	SACHEMIC	ACCEIOPR	CECROPIA	ACCFIKLL	CALFLICK
ACCEHINO	ANECHOIC	ACCEIOTV	COACTIVE	ACCFLNOO	CONFOCAL
ACCEHINR	CHANCIER	ACCEIPRS	CAPRICES	ACCFOORT	COFACTOR
	CHICANER	ACCEIPRT	PRACTICE	ACCGHIKN	CHACKING
ACCEHINS	CHICANES	ACCEIPSV	PECCAVIS	ACCGHINN	CHANCING
ACCEHINT	ATECHNIC	ACCEIQSU	CACIQUES	ACCGHINO	COACHING
	CATECHIN	ACCEIRRR	RICERCAR	ACCGHINT	CATCHING
ACCEHIOS	COACHIES	ACCEIRSU	CAESURIC	ACCGHIOR	CHORAGIC
ACCEHIRT	CATCHIER		CURACIES	ACCGIINT	ACCITING
ACCEHKPY	PAYCHECK	ACCEIRTU	CRUCIATE	ACCGIKLN	CACKLING
ACCEHLNS	CHANCELS	ACCEISST	ASCETICS		CLACKING
ACCEHLOR	COCHLEAR	ACCEISTT	ECSTATIC	ACCGIKMR	GIMCRACK
ACCEHLOS	COCHLEAS	ACCEKLNR	CRACKNEL	ACCGIKNR	CRACKING
ACCEHLOT	CATECHOL	ACCEKLRS	CACKLERS	ACCGILOX	COXALGIC
ACCEHLST	CLATCHES		CLACKERS	ACCGINOT	COACTING
ACCEHMNO	COACHMEN		CRACKLES	ACCGINOY	ACCOYING
ACCEHNNO	CHACONNE	ACCEKMOS	MEACOCKS	ACCGINRU	ACCRUING
ACCEHNNY	CYNANCHE	ACCEKNOR	CORNCAKE	ACCGINSU	ACCUSING
ACCEHNOR	CHARNECO	ACCEKOPS	PEACOCKS	ACCGLOOY	CACOLOGY
	ENCROACH	ACCEKOPY	PEACOCKY	ACCHHITT	CHITCHAT
ACCEHNOT	CONCHATE	ACCEKOSS	SEACOCKS	ACCHHMOS	CAMSHOCH
ACCEHNRS	CHANCERS	ACCEKPSU	CUPCAKES	ACCHHMOU	MUCHACHO
	CHANCRES	ACCEKRRS	CRACKERS	ACCHIIMS	CHIASMIC
	CRANCHES	ACCEKRST	CRACKETS	ACCHIIRT	RACHITIC
ACCEHNRY	CHANCERY	ACCELLSY	CALYCLES	ACCHIIST	CHIASTIC
ACCEHNSU	CHAUNCES	ACCELLUV	CALYCULE	ACCHILNO	CHALONIC
ACCEHOPT	CACHEPOT	ACCELMNY	CYCLAMEN	ACCHILNY	CHANCILY
ACCEHORS	CAROCHES	ACCELNOS	CONCEALS	ACCHILOR	ORICHALC
	COACHERS	ACCELNOV	CONCLAVE	ACCHILOT	CATHOLIC
ACCEHPSU	CAPUCHES	ACCELNRU	CARUNCLE	ACCHIMOR	ACHROMIC
ACCEHRST	CATCHERS	ACCELOOT	COLOCATE	ACCHINNO	CINCHONA
	CRATCHES	ACCELORS	CORACLES	ACCHINOS	CHICANOS
ACCEHSST	SCATCHES	ACCELORT	ACROLECT	ACCHINPU	CAPUCHIN
ACCEHSTT	CATHECTS	ACCELOST	CACOLETS	ACCHIOPS	PICACHOS
ACCEHSTU	CATECHUS	ACCELRSY	SCARCELY	ACCHIORS	COCHAIRS
ACCEIIST	CAECITIS	ACCELRTU	CLEARCUT	ACCHIORT	THORACIC
ACCEIKLT	TICKLACE	ACCELSSU	SACCULES		TROCHAIC
ACCEIKPS	ICEPACKS	ACCELSSY	CYCLASES	ACCHIOSU	ACOUCHIS
ACCEIKST	CACKIEST	ACCELWYY	CYCLEWAY	ACCHIRRT	CARRITCH
ACCEILLN	CANCELLI	ACCENNSY	NASCENCY	ACCHIRSS	SCRAICHS
ACCEILLR	CLERICAL	ACCENORR	CORNACRE	ACCHKLOR	CHARLOCK
ACCEILLS	CALICLES	ACCENORS	CONACRES	ACCHKOSY	HAYCOCKS
ACCEILLU	CAULICLE	ACCENORT	ACCENTOR	ACCHLOOT	CACHOLOT
ACCEILLV	CLAVICLE	ACCENOST	COENACTS	ACCHLSTU	CLAUCHTS
ACCEILNS	CALCINES		COSECANT	ACCHMORS	CASCHROM

ACCHNNUY	UNCHANCY	ACCIMORR	MICROCAR	ACDDDEIS	CADDISED
ACCHNOOR	COANCHOR	ACCIMORU	COUMARIC	ACDDDEIT	ADDICTED
	CORONACH	ACCIMOSZ	ZIMOCCAS	ACDDDETU	ADDUCTED
ACCHNOTU	COUCHANT	ACCIMPSU	CAPSICUM	ACDDDKOS	DADDOCKS
ACCHNRUY	CRAUNCHY	ACCIMSTY	CYMATICS	ACDDEEES	DECEASED
ACCHNTUY	UNCATCHY	ACCINOOS	OCCASION	ACDDEEHO	COHEADED
ACCHOOTU	OUTCOACH	ACCINOOT	COACTION	ACDDEEHT	DETACHED
ACCHOPSU	PACHUCOS	ACCINORT	CRATONIC	ACDDEEIT	DEDICATE
ACCHORTU	CARTOUCH		NARCOTIC	ACDDEEIU	DECIDUAE
ACCHORTY	OCTARCHY	ACCINORV	CAVICORN	ACDDEEKR	DACKERED
ACCHOSTW	CHOCTAWS	ACCINOST	CANTICOS	ACDDEELL	DECALLED
ACCHOTTU	OUTCATCH	ACCINOTY	CANTICOY	ACDDEELR	DECLARED
ACCHPSTU	CATCHUPS		CYANOTIC	ACDDEELS	DESCALED
ACCHRRSU	CURRACHS	ACCINRSU	CRUCIANS	ACDDEELW	DECLAWED
ACCHRSSU	SCRAUCHS	ACCINSSY	CYCASINS	ACDDEEMP	DECAMPED
ACCHRSTY	SCRATCHY	ACCIOOPP	APOCOPIC	ACDDEENO	DEACONED
ACCHRTWY	WATCHCRY	ACCIOPST	SPICCATO	ACDDEENR	CREDENDA
ACCIIIOT	OITICICA	ACCIORST	ACROSTIC	ACDDEENS	ASCENDED
ACCIILLN	CLINICAL	ACCIORSY	ISOCRACY	ACDDEENT	DECADENT
ACCIILMT	CLIMATIC	ACCIOSTT	STICCATO		DECANTED
ACCIILNO	ICONICAL	ACCIOSTU	ACOUSTIC	ACDDEERT	REDACTED
ACCIILRT	CRITICAL	ACCIPRST	PRACTICS	ACDDEETU	EDUCATED
ACCIIMNN	CINNAMIC	ACCIRRTT	TRICTRAC	ACDDEETV	ADVECTED
ACCIINNO	ANICONIC	ACCIRSTY	SCARCITY	ACDDEGIS	DISCAGED
ACCIINNP	PICCANIN	ACCISSTU	CAUSTICS	ACDDEHIK	DICKHEAD
ACCIINOT	ACONITIC	ACCKKRSU	RUCKSACK	ACDDEHKN	DECKHAND
	CATIONIC	ACCKLLOO	ALCOLOCK	ACDDEHRS	CHEDDARS
	ITACONIC	ACCKLORS	CARLOCKS	ACDDEHRY	CHEDDARY
ACCIINPS	CAPSICIN	ACCKMMRU	CRUMMACK	ACDDEIIL	DEICIDAL
ACCIINTY	CYANITIC	ACCKMORS	CROMACKS	ACDDEIIM	MEDICAID
ACCIIOPT	OCCIPITA	ACCKOOOP	COCKAPOO	ACDDEILS	CLADDIES
ACCIIPST	PASTICCI	ACCKOOOT	COCKATOO	ACDDEILU	DECIDUAL
ACCIIRTX	CICATRIX	ACCKOPRS	CAPROCKS	ACDDEINR	CANDIDER
ACCIISST	SCIATICS	ACCKOPRT	CRACKPOT		RIDDANCE
ACCIJKMR	JIMCRACK	ACCKORST	STOCKCAR	ACDDEINT	DEDICANT
ACCIKKNN	NICKNACK	ACCKOSSS	CASSOCKS	ACDDEINY	CYANIDED
ACCIKKRR	RICKRACK		COSSACKS	ACDDEIPS	DISPACED
ACCIKKTT	TICKTACK	ACCKOSST	CASTOCKS	ACDDEIRT	READDICT
ACCIKLOT	COCKTAIL	ACCKPRSU	CRACKUPS	ACDDEISS	CADDISES
ACCIKNST	CANSTICK	ACCLLNOV	CYCLONAL		DISCASED
ACCIKOPR	APRICOCK	ACCLLOSU	OCCLUSAL	ACDDEISU	DECIDUAS
ACCIKPRT	PRACTICK	ACCLLSUU	CALCULUS	ACDDEITT	DICTATED
ACCILLUV	CALYCULI	ACCLSSUU	SACCULUS	ACDDEKLO	DEADLOCK
ACCILMOS	COSMICAL	ACCMNOSY	CACONYMS	ACDDEKOR	RADDOCKE
ACCILMOX	CACOMIXL	ACCMNOYY	CACONYMY	ACDDELOS	CLADODES
ACCILMSU	CALCIUMS	ACCMOOST	COCOMATS	ACDDELRS	CLADDERS
ACCILMUU	ACICULUM	ACCMOOSY	COCOYAMS	ACDDENRU	UNCARDED
ACCILNOT	CICLATON	ACCMOPST	ACCOMPTS	ACDDENTU	ADDUCENT
	LACTONIC		COMPACTS	ACDDEOPS	DECAPODS
ACCILNOV	VOLCANIC	ACCMOSTU	ACCUSTOM	ACDDEORR	CORRADED
ACCILNUV	VULCANIC	ACCMRSUU	CURCUMAS	ACDDEORW	COWARDED
ACCILORS	CALORICS	ACCNNOOS	COONCANS	ACDDERSU	ADDUCERS
ACCILORT	CORTICAL	ACCNOOPS	COCOPANS		CRUSADED
ACCILOSS	CLASSICO	ACCNOORS	RACCOONS	ACDDERTU	TRADUCED
ACCILOSV	VOCALICS	ACCNOOTU	COCOANUT	ACDDGILN	CLADDING
ACCILPRY	CAPRYLIC	ACCNOPTU	OCCUPANT	ACDDGINU	ADDUCING
ACCILRRU	CIRCULAR	ACCNORTT	CONTRACT	ACDDGINY	CADDYING
ACCILRSY	ACRYLICS	ACCNOSTT	CONTACTS	ACDDHHSU	CHUDDAHS
ACCILSSS	CLASSICS	ACCNOSTU	ACCOUNTS	ACDDHIIO	DIADOCHI
ACCILSST	CLASTICS	ACCOORST	COACTORS	ACDDHIMR	DIDRACHM
ACCILTUU	CUTICULA	ACCOPSTY	COPYCATS	ACDDHIOY	DIADOCHY
ACCIMNOS	MOCCASIN	ACCOQSSU	SQUACCOS	ACDDHIRY	HYDRACID
ACCIMNTU	CANTICUM	ACCORRTY	CARRYCOT	ACDDHKNO	DOCKHAND
ACCIMOPR	MICROCAP	ACCORSTU	ACCOURTS	ACDDHKOS	HADDOCKS

	SHADDOCK	**ACDEEINR**	DERACINE	**ACDEEOPS**	PEASECOD
ACDDHORS	CHADDORS	**ACDEEINU**	AUDIENCE	**ACDEEORT**	DECORATE
ACDDHRSU	CHUDDARS	**ACDEEINV**	DEVIANCE		RECOATED
ACDDIIOR	CARDIOID	**ACDEEIPS**	DISPEACE	**ACDEEOTV**	EVOCATED
ACDDILNY	CANDIDLY	**ACDEEIRS**	DECIARES	**ACDEEPPR**	RECAPPED
ACDDILRW	WILDCARD	**ACDEEJKT**	JACKETED	**ACDEEPRS**	ESCARPED
ACDDILTY	DIDACTYL	**ACDEEKLR**	LACKERED		RESPACED
ACDDINNU	UNCANDID	**ACDEEKLY**	LACKEYED	**ACDEEPRT**	CARPETED
ACDDINSY	DISCANDY	**ACDEEKNR**	CANKERED		PREACTED
ACDDIRSS	DISCARDS	**ACDEEKPR**	REPACKED	**ACDEEPST**	ASPECTED
ACDDKLNO	DOCKLAND	**ACDEEKPT**	PACKETED	**ACDEERRS**	SCAREDER
ACDDKMOS	MADDOCKS	**ACDEEKRR**	RERACKED	**ACDEERRT**	CRATERED
ACDDKOPS	PADDOCKS	**ACDEEKRS**	SCREAKED		RECRATED
ACDDKORY	DOCKYARD	**ACDEEKRT**	RACKETED		RETRACED
ACDDORTU	ADDUCTOR		RETACKED		TERRACED
ACDEEEFT	DEFECATE	**ACDEEKST**	CASKETED	**ACDEERSS**	CARESSED
ACDEEEKS	SEEDCAKE	**ACDEELLR**	CELLARED	**ACDEERST**	CEDRATES
ACDEEEMR	REEDMACE		RECALLED	**ACDEERSY**	DECAYERS
ACDEEENR	CAREENED	**ACDEELLS**	CADELLES	**ACDEESTU**	EDUCATES
ACDEEENT	ANTECEDE	**ACDEELMN**	ENCALMED	**ACDEESUX**	CAUDEXES
ACDEEERR	CAREERED	**ACDEELMP**	EMPLACED	**ACDEESUY**	CAUSEYED
ACDEEERS	DECREASE	**ACDEELNR**	CALENDER	**ACDEFFHU**	CHAUFFED
ACDEEESS	DECEASES		ENCRADLE	**ACDEFFLS**	SCLAFFED
	SEEDCASE	**ACDEELNS**	CLEANSED	**ACDEFFOR**	AFFORCED
ACDEEFFT	AFFECTED	**ACDEELNT**	LANCETED	**ACDEFGIN**	DEFACING
ACDEEFHN	ENCHAFED	**ACDEELNV**	ENCLAVED	**ACDEFGOS**	DOGFACES
ACDEEFIL	CALEFIED	**ACDEELOR**	COLEADER	**ACDEFHKU**	HEADFUCK
ACDEEFIN	DEFIANCE		RECOALED	**ACDEFHLN**	FLANCHED
ACDEEFIS	CASEFIED	**ACDEELPR**	PARCELED	**ACDEFIIL**	DEIFICAL
ACDEEFPR	PREFACED		REPLACED	**ACDEFIIP**	PACIFIED
ACDEEFRS	DEFACERS	**ACDEELRR**	DECLARER	**ACDEFILN**	CANFIELD
	FRESCADE	**ACDEELRS**	DECLARES	**ACDEFILR**	FILECARD
ACDEEFRY	FEDERACY		RESCALED		FRICADEL
ACDEEFTT	FACETTED	**ACDEELRT**	CLARETED	**ACDEFINN**	FINANCED
ACDEEGLY	DELEGACY		DECRETAL	**ACDEFINS**	FACIENDS
ACDEEGNR	ENGRACED		TREACLED	**ACDEFLOT**	OLFACTED
ACDEEHIN	ECHIDNAE	**ACDEELRV**	CALVERED	**ACDEFNOW**	FACEDOWN
ACDEEHIR	CHARIDEE		CLAVERED	**ACDEFNRU**	FURNACED
ACDEEHIV	ACHIEVED	**ACDEELSS**	DECLASSE	**ACDEFORT**	FACTORED
ACDEEHKO	COKEHEAD		DESCALES	**ACDEFOTU**	OUTFACED
ACDEEHLP	PLEACHED	**ACDEEMNO**	CODENAME	**ACDEFRSU**	SURFACED
ACDEEHLT	CHELATED	**ACDEEMNP**	ENCAMPED	**ACDEFRTU**	FURCATED
ACDEEHMR	DEMARCHE	**ACDEEMRS**	SCREAMED	**ACDEGGRS**	SCRAGGED
ACDEEHNN	ENHANCED	**ACDEEMRT**	CREMATED	**ACDEGHLO**	GALOCHED
ACDEEHNR	ENARCHED	**ACDEEMSV**	MEDEVACS	**ACDEGHNU**	CHAUNGED
ACDEEHNS	ENCASHED	**ACDEENNP**	PENANCED		GAUNCHED
	ENCHASED	**ACDEENNT**	TENDANCE	**ACDEGIIL**	ALGICIDE
ACDEEHPR	PREACHED	**ACDEENNY**	CAYENNED	**ACDEGIKM**	MAGICKED
ACDEEHRS	SEARCHED	**ACDEENOT**	ANECDOTE	**ACDEGILN**	DECALING
ACDEEHRT	DETACHER	**ACDEENRS**	ASCENDER	**ACDEGIMR**	DECIGRAM
	RACHETED		REASCEND		GRIMACED
ACDEEHSS	CHASSEED	**ACDEENRT**	CANTERED	**ACDEGINU**	GUIDANCE
ACDEEHST	DETACHES		CRENATED	**ACDEGINY**	DECAYING
	SACHETED		DECANTER	**ACDEGIRS**	DISGRACE
ACDEEIIP	EPICEDIA		NECTARED	**ACDEGISS**	DISCAGES
ACDEEILT	DELICATE		RECANTED	**ACDEGIST**	CADGIEST
ACDEEILU	AEDICULE	**ACDEENRV**	CAVERNED	**ACDEGKOS**	DOCKAGES
ACDEEIMR	CERAMIDE		CRAVENED	**ACDEGLLO**	COLLAGED
	MEDICARE	**ACDEENRY**	CARNEYED	**ACDEGLOS**	DECALOGS
ACDEEIMT	DECIMATE		DECENARY	**ACDEGLOU**	CLOUDAGE
	EMICATED	**ACDEENRZ**	CREDENZA	**ACDEGNOS**	DECAGONS
	MEDICATE	**ACDEENSV**	VENDACES	**ACDEGNRU**	UNGRACED
ACDEEINN	DECENNIA	**ACDEENTT**	DANCETTE	**ACDEGORS**	CORDAGES
	ENNEADIC	**ACDEENTU**	CUNEATED	**ACDEGOTT**	COTTAGED

ACDEHHIN	HAINCHED	**ACDEIINR**	ACRIDINE	**ACDEINNT**	INCANTED
ACDEHHNU	HAUNCHED	**ACDEIINS**	SCIAENID	**ACDEINOP**	CANOPIED
ACDEHHRU	HACHURED	**ACDEIINT**	ACTINIDE	**ACDEINOS**	CODEINAS
ACDEHHTT	DETHATCH		CTENIDIA		DIOCESAN
	THATCHED		DIACTINE		OCEANIDS
ACDEHIIP	APHICIDE		INDICATE	**ACDEINOT**	ACTIONED
ACDEHIJK	HIJACKED	**ACDEIINU**	INDUCIAE		CATENOID
ACDEHILR	HERALDIC	**ACDEIIRT**	RATICIDE	**ACDEINOV**	VOIDANCE
ACDEHILT	DITHECAL	**ACDEIIST**	ACIDIEST	**ACDEINPT**	PEDANTIC
ACDEHIMM	CHAMMIED	**ACDEIITV**	CAVITIED		PENTADIC
ACDEHIMN	MACHINED		VATICIDE	**ACDEINRR**	RANCIDER
ACDEHIMS	SCHIEDAM		VICIATED	**ACDEINRT**	CRINATED
ACDEHINR	INARCHED	**ACDEIJNU**	JAUNDICE		DICENTRA
ACDEHINS	ECHIDNAS	**ACDEIKNP**	PANICKED	**ACDEINSS**	ACIDNESS
	INCHASED	**ACDEIKNT**	ANTICKED	**ACDEINST**	DANCIEST
ACDEHIRS	RACHIDES	**ACDEIKPX**	PICKAXED		DISTANCE
ACDEHIRT	THRIDACE	**ACDEILLM**	MEDALLIC	**ACDEINSY**	CYANIDES
	TRACHEID	**ACDEILLN**	DECLINAL		CYANISED
ACDEHIRV	ARCHIVED	**ACDEILLS**	CEDILLAS	**ACDEINTT**	NICTATED
ACDEHIST	SCAITHED	**ACDEILLV**	CAVILLED	**ACDEINTU**	INCUDATE
ACDEHISU	CHIAUSED	**ACDEILMN**	MEDCINAL	**ACDEINVY**	DEVIANCY
ACDEHKLO	HEADLOCK	**ACDEILMO**	CAMELOID	**ACDEINYZ**	CYANIZED
ACDEHKLS	SHACKLED		MELODICA	**ACDEIOPS**	DIASCOPE
ACDEHKNU	UNHACKED	**ACDEILMS**	CAMELIDS	**ACDEIORS**	IDOCRASE
ACDEHKOV	HAVOCKED		DECIMALS	**ACDEIORT**	CERATOID
ACDEHKRU	ARCHDUKE		DECLAIMS	**ACDEIORV**	COVARIED
ACDEHKTW	THWACKED		MEDICALS	**ACDEIOSS**	ACIDOSES
ACDEHLNP	PLANCHED	**ACDEILMT**	CLIMATED	**ACDEIOSU**	EDACIOUS
ACDEHLNR	CHANDLER		MALEDICT	**ACDEIPPT**	TAPPICED
ACDEHLNU	LAUNCHED	**ACDEILMX**	CLIMAXED	**ACDEIPRS**	EPACRIDS
ACDEHLOS	COALSHED	**ACDEILNP**	PANICLED		PERACIDS
ACDEHLRS	CHALDERS	**ACDEILNU**	DULCINEA	**ACDEIPRT**	PICRATED
ACDEHLRT	TRACHLED	**ACDEILNY**	ADENYLIC	**ACDEIPSS**	DISPACES
ACDEHLSS	CHADLESS	**ACDEILOS**	COALISED		SPADICES
ACDEHMST	SMATCHED	**ACDEILOZ**	COALIZED	**ACDEIPST**	SPICATED
ACDEHNOR	ANCHORED	**ACDEILPR**	PLACIDER	**ACDEIPSZ**	CAPSIZED
	RONDACHE	**ACDEILPS**	DISPLACE	**ACDEIPTV**	CAPTIVED
ACDEHNPU	PAUNCHED	**ACDEILPT**	PLICATED	**ACDEIQRU**	ACQUIRED
ACDEHNRU	RAUNCHED	**ACDEILRS**	DECRIALS	**ACDEIRSS**	SIDECARS
	UNARCHED		RADICELS	**ACDEIRST**	ACRIDEST
ACDEHNRY	ENDARCHY		RADICLES	**ACDEIRSU**	DECURIAS
ACDEHNST	SNATCHED	**ACDEILRT**	ARTICLED	**ACDEIRTT**	CITRATED
	STANCHED		LACERTID		TETRACID
ACDEHNSU	UNCASHED	**ACDEILRU**	AURICLED		TETRADIC
ACDEHNTU	CHAUNTED		RADICULE	**ACDEISSS**	DISCASES
ACDEHORR	HARDCORE	**ACDEILST**	CITADELS	**ACDEISTT**	DICTATES
ACDEHORT	CHORDATE		DIALECTS	**ACDEKLNR**	CRANKLED
ACDEHORW	COWHEARD	**ACDEILSY**	ECDYSIAL	**ACDEKLPS**	SPACKLED
ACDEHOST	CATHODES	**ACDEILTT**	LATTICED	**ACDEKLQU**	QUACKLED
ACDEHOUV	AVOUCHED	**ACDEILTY**	DIACETYL	**ACDEKNPR**	PRANCKED
ACDEHPPS	SCHAPPED	**ACDEIMNO**	COMEDIAN	**ACDEKNPU**	UNPACKED
ACDEHPRS	SCARPHED		DAEMONIC	**ACDEKNRU**	UNRACKED
ACDEHPST	DESPATCH		DEMONIAC	**ACDEKNSU**	UNCASKED
ACDEHPSU	CUPHEADS	**ACDEIMNP**	PANDEMIC	**ACDEKNTU**	UNTACKED
ACDEHPTU	DEATHCUP	**ACDEIMNT**	MEDICANT	**ACDEKOST**	STOCKADE
ACDEHQTU	QUATCHED	**ACDEIMOR**	COADMIRE	**ACDEKRSY**	KEYCARDS
ACDEHRRS	CHRESARD		RACEMOID	**ACDELLNU**	UNCALLED
ACDEHRST	STARCHED	**ACDEIMPS**	MIDSPACE	**ACDELLOR**	CAROLLED
ACDEHTUW	WAUCHTED	**ACDEIMPT**	IMPACTED		COLLARED
ACDEIILN	ALCIDINE	**ACDEIMRT**	DERMATIC	**ACDELLOT**	COLLATED
ACDEIILS	LAICISED		TIMECARD	**ACDELLSU**	CALLUSED
ACDEIILT	CILIATED	**ACDEIMST**	MISACTED	**ACDELMOR**	CLAMORED
ACDEIILZ	LAICIZED	**ACDEIMSV**	MEDIVACS	**ACDELMSU**	MUSCADEL
ACDEIIMU	AECIDIUM	**ACDEINNR**	CRANNIED	**ACDELNOO**	CANOODLE

ACDELNOR	COLANDER		UNDERACT	ACDGNOST	CANTDOGS
	CONELRAD		UNTRACED	ACDGORST	DOGCARTS
ACDELNOS	CELADONS	ACDENRUV	UNCARVED	ACDHIILS	CHILIADS
ACDELNPU	UNPLACED	ACDENRVY	VERDANCY	ACDHIINT	TACHINID
ACDELNRS	CANDLERS	ACDENSST	DESCANTS	ACDHIIPS	DIPHASIC
ACDELNRY	CALENDRY	ACDENSUU	UNCAUSED	ACDHIKNP	HANDPICK
ACDELNST	SCANTLED	ACDENTTY	DANCETTY	ACDHIKOR	CHOKIDAR
ACDELNSU	UNSCALED	ACDEOORS	DOORCASE	ACDHIKOT	KATHODIC
ACDELNUW	UNCLAWED	ACDEOPRS	SCOREPAD	ACDHILNT	THINCLAD
ACDELOOW	LACEWOOD	ACDEOPRU	CROUPADE	ACDHILPR	PILCHARD
ACDELOPS	PEDOCALS	ACDEOPRY	COPYREAD	ACDHILPS	CLAPDISH
ACDELOPT	CLODPATE	ACDEOPSS	PEASCODS	ACDHIMTW	MIDWATCH
ACDELOPU	CUPOLAED	ACDEOPTT	CAPOTTED	ACDHINOR	HADRONIC
ACDELORV	OVERCLAD	ACDEOPTU	OUTPACED		RHODANIC
ACDELOTU	OCULATED	ACDEORRS	CORRADES	ACDHINRY	DINARCHY
ACDELPPS	SCAPPLED	ACDEORRT	REDACTOR	ACDHINSW	SANDWICH
ACDELPSU	CAPSULED	ACDEORSS	SARCODES	ACDHIOPS	SCAPHOID
	UPSCALED	ACDEORST	REDCOATS	ACDHIOPY	HYPOACID
ACDELRRS	CRADLERS	ACDEORSU	CAROUSED	ACDHIORY	HYRACOID
ACDELRSS	SCALDERS	ACDEORTU	AERODUCT	ACDHIPST	DISPATCH
ACDELRSW	SCRAWLED		EDUCATOR	ACDHIQRU	CHARQUID
ACDELRSY	SACREDLY		OUTRACED	ACDHIRRU	CHURIDAR
ACDELSTU	CAULDEST	ACDEORTV	CAVORTED	ACDHKORR	HARDROCK
	SULCATED	ACDEOSTT	CODETTAS	ACDHLNOR	CHALDRON
ACDELSWW	DEWCLAWS		COSTATED		CHLORDAN
ACDEMMRS	SCRAMMED	ACDEOSUV	COUVADES		CHONDRAL
ACDEMNOR	ROMANCED	ACDEOTTU	OUTACTED	ACDHLORS	DORLACHS
ACDEMNSU	DECUMANS	ACDEPPRS	SCRAPPED	ACDHMNTU	DUTCHMAN
ACDEMOPR	COMPADRE	ACDEPRSW	SCRAWPED	ACDHMORU	MOUCHARD
	COMPARED	ACDEPRTU	CAPTURED	ACDHNORW	CHAWDRON
ACDEMORR	CARROMED	ACDEPSTU	CUSPATED	ACDHNOSW	COWHANDS
ACDEMORS	COMRADES	ACDEQTUU	AQUEDUCT	ACDHOOST	CATHOODS
ACDEMORT	DEMOCRAT	ACDERRSU	CRUSADER	ACDHOOTW	WOODCHAT
ACDEMPSU	CAMPUSED	ACDERRTU	TRADUCER	ACDHOPRS	POCHARDS
ACDEMRSW	SCRAWMED	ACDERSSU	CRUSADES	ACDHOPTU	TOUCHPAD
ACDEMSTU	MUSCADET	ACDERSTT	DETRACTS	ACDHORRS	ORCHARDS
ACDEMUUV	VACUUMED		SCRATTED	ACDHORSY	DYSCHROA
ACDENNNO	CANNONED	ACDERSTU	TRADUCES	ACDIIILN	INDICIAL
	NONDANCE	ACDERTUV	CURVATED	ACDIIINS	INDICIAS
ACDENNNU	UNCANNED	ACDFFHNU	HANDCUFF	ACDIIIPR	DIAPIRIC
ACDENNOR	ORDNANCE	ACDFFIRT	DIFFRACT	ACDIIJLU	JUDICIAL
ACDENNOT	CANTONED	ACDFFLOS	SCAFFOLD	ACDIIKLP	PICKADIL
ACDENNST	SCANDENT	ACDFIILU	FIDUCIAL	ACDIILMS	DISCLAIM
ACDENOPR	ENDOCARP	ACDFILMR	FILMCARD	ACDIILNO	CONIDIAL
ACDENORR	RANCORED	ACDFILOU	FUCOIDAL	ACDIILNS	SCALDINI
ACDENORS	DRACONES	ACDFINOR	FRICANDO	ACDIILOV	OVICIDAL
	ENDOSARC	ACDFIOST	FACTOIDS	ACDIILSU	SUICIDAL
ACDENORT	CARTONED	ACDGHINY	DAYCHING	ACDIILTY	CALIDITY
	NOTECARD	ACDGHOTW	DOGWATCH		DIALYTIC
ACDENORY	CRAYONED		WATCHDOG	ACDIIMNO	DAIMONIC
	DEACONRY	ACDGIILO	DIALOGIC	ACDIIMOR	CORMIDIA
ACDENOST	ENDOCAST	ACDGIIMS	DIGICAMS		DIORAMIC
	TACNODES	ACDGILNN	CANDLING	ACDIIMOT	DIATOMIC
ACDENOSY	CYANOSED	ACDGILNR	CRADLING	ACDIIMSU	ASCIDIUM
ACDENOTT	COATTEND	ACDGILNS	SCALDING	ACDIINNO	CONIDIAN
ACDENOTU	OUTDANCE	ACDGILNU	CAUDLING	ACDIINNS	INDICANS
	UNCOATED	ACDGIMOT	DOGMATIC	ACDIINNT	INDICANT
ACDENPPU	UNCAPPED	ACDGINNS	DANCINGS	ACDIINOP	PINACOID
ACDENPRU	PRAUNCED	ACDGINNY	CANDYING	ACDIINOT	ACTINOID
ACDENPST	PANDECTS	ACDGINRS	CARDINGS		DIATONIC
ACDENRST	CANTREDS	ACDGINSU	SCAUDING	ACDIINPY	PYCNIDIA
ACDENRSU	DURANCES	ACDGIOPR	PODAGRIC	ACDIINRS	ACRIDINS
ACDENRTU	UNCARTED	ACDGKLOS	DAGLOCKS	ACDIIORV	VARICOID
	UNCRATED	ACDGLNOO	GOLCONDA	ACDIIOSS	ACIDOSIS

ACDIIOSX	OXIDASIC	ACDIORST	CAROTIDS	ACEEEFRR	CAREFREE
ACDIIRSS	SCIARIDS	ACDIORTT	DICTATOR	ACEEEGLN	ELEGANCE
ACDIIRST	ARCTIIDS	ACDIOSTX	DOXASTIC	ACEEEGPR	CREEPAGE
	CARDITIS	ACDIOSTY	DYSTOCIA	ACEEEGRS	CARGEESE
	TRIACIDS	ACDIOSXY	OXYACIDS	ACEEEIPR	EARPIECE
	TRIADICS	ACDIPRST	ADSCRIPT	ACEEEIPS	SEAPIECE
ACDIIRTY	ACRIDITY	ACDIPSTY	DIPTYCAS	ACEEEKNT	NECKATEE
ACDIISST	SADISTIC	ACDIQRSU	QUADRICS	ACEEELMR	CAMELEER
ACDIKLTU	DUCKTAIL	ACDIRSST	DRASTICS	ACEEENRR	CAREENER
ACDIKMOO	COOKMAID	ACDIRSTT	DISTRACT	ACEEENRS	ENCREASE
ACDIKRRY	RICKYARD	ACDIRTWY	CITYWARD	ACEEENSV	EVANESCE
ACDILLOS	CODILLAS	ACDISTUV	VIADUCTS	ACEEEPSS	ESCAPEES
ACDILLOU	CAUDILLO	ACDJNSTU	ADJUNCTS	ACEEERRR	CAREERER
	LODICULA	ACDKKLUW	DUCKWALK	ACEEERRT	RECREATE
ACDILLPY	PLACIDLY	ACDKLOPS	PADLOCKS	ACEEERTT	ETCETERA
ACDILMOR	DROMICAL	ACDKMMOR	DRAMMOCK	ACEEERTX	EXECRATE
ACDILMOU	MUCOIDAL	ACDKMPSU	MUDPACKS	ACEEESUV	EVACUEES
ACDILMSS	CLADISMS	ACDKOPRS	POCKARDS	ACEEFFIN	CAFFEINE
ACDILMTU	TALMUDIC	ACDLLORS	COLLARDS	ACEEFFOR	FOREFACE
ACDILNOO	CONOIDAL	ACDLNNOR	CORNLAND	ACEEFFRS	EFFACERS
ACDILNOR	IRONCLAD	ACDLNOPR	CROPLAND	ACEEFFRT	AFFECTER
ACDILNOS	SCALDINO	ACDLNORS	CALDRONS	ACEEFHNS	ENCHAFES
ACDILNOT	ANTICOLD	ACDLNORU	CAULDRON	ACEEFHWY	WHEYFACE
	DALTONIC		CRUNODAL	ACEEFILM	MALEFICE
ACDILNRY	RANCIDLY	ACDLNORY	CONDYLAR	ACEEFILR	LIFECARE
ACDILNSU	DULCIANS	ACDLNOST	COTLANDS	ACEEFILS	CALEFIES
ACDILNSY	SYNDICAL	ACDLNSSU	SUNSCALD	ACEEFINS	FAIENCES
ACDILNUU	NUDICAUL	ACDLOOOR	COLORADO		FIANCEES
ACDILOPS	PLACOIDS	ACDLOORT	DOCTORAL	ACEEFISS	CASEFIES
ACDILOPY	POLYACID	ACDLORWY	COWARDLY	ACEEFKOR	ECOFREAK
	POLYADIC	ACDLOSWY	LADYCOWS	ACEEFLPU	PEACEFUL
ACDILORS	CORDIALS	ACDLSTUY	DACTYLUS	ACEEFLSS	FACELESS
ACDILORT	DICROTAL	ACDMMNOO	COMMANDO	ACEEFLTY	FACETELY
ACDILOUV	OVIDUCAL	ACDMMNOS	COMMANDS	ACEEFNSY	FAYENCES
ACDILPSU	CUSPIDAL	ACDMNOPS	COMPANDS	ACEEFPRR	PREFACER
ACDILRST	TRICLADS	ACDMNORY	DORMANCY	ACEEFPRS	PREFACES
ACDILSST	CLADISTS		MORDANCY	ACEEFPRT	PERFECTA
ACDILSTW	WILDCATS	ACDMOOPR	MACROPOD		PRAEFECT
ACDIMMSU	CADMIUMS	ACDMOOSW	CAMWOODS	ACEEFPTY	TYPEFACE
ACDIMNOO	CODOMAIN	ACDMORSZ	CZARDOMS	ACEEFRSU	FARCEUSE
	MONODAIN	ACDMPRTU	DUMPCART	ACEEGHNR	ENCHARGE
ACDIMNOS	MANDIOCS	ACDNOORR	RONCADOR		RECHANGE
	MONACIDS	ACDNOORS	CARDOONS	ACEEGHNX	EXCHANGE
ACDIMNSU	MUSCADIN	ACDNOORT	ACRODONT	ACEEGHRR	RECHARGE
	SCANDIUM	ACDNOORV	CORDOVAN	ACEEGIKL	CAGELIKE
ACDIMNSY	DYNAMICS	ACDNOOTU	DUCATOON	ACEEGILS	ELEGIACS
ACDIMOOS	CAMOODIS	ACDNORRW	WARDCORN		LEGACIES
ACDIMOST	COADMITS	ACDNORSU	CANDOURS	ACEEGINS	AGENCIES
ACDIMOSY	DOCIMASY		CAUDRONS	ACEEGINT	AGENETIC
ACDINNOO	ANCONOID	ACDNOSTW	DOWNCAST	ACEEGIRS	GRAECISE
ACDINNOS	NONACIDS	ACDNOSUU	ADUNCOUS	ACEEGIRZ	GRAECIZE
ACDINNOY	ANODYNIC	ACDOOPPR	PODOCARP	ACEEGKNR	NECKGEAR
ACDINOPS	SPONDAIC	ACDOOPTY	OCTAPODY	ACEEGKRW	WRECKAGE
ACDINORS	SARDONIC	ACDOORST	OSTRACOD	ACEEGLNY	ELEGANCY
ACDINORT	TORNADIC		SCORDATO	ACEEGLPU	PUCELAGE
ACDINORW	CORDWAIN	ACDOPRST	POSTCARD	ACEEGNNT	TANGENCE
ACDINSST	DISCANTS	ACDOPSST	PODCASTS	ACEEGNOZ	COZENAGE
ACDINSTY	DYNASTIC	ACDORRWY	COWARDRY	ACEEGNRS	ENGRACES
ACDINTUY	ADUNCITY	ACDORSST	COSTARDS	ACEEGNRY	REAGENCY
ACDIOOTU	AUTOCOID	ACDORSSU	CRUSADOS	ACEEGNST	CENTAGES
ACDIOPRS	PICADORS	ACDORSUZ	CRUZADOS	ACEEGNSV	SCAVENGE
	SPORADIC	ACDRSSTU	CUSTARDS	ACEEGORR	RACEGOER
ACDIORRS	CORRIDAS	ACDRSTTU	DUSTCART	ACEEGORV	COVERAGE
ACDIORSS	SARCOIDS	ACDRSTUY	CUSTARDY	ACEEGOST	ECOTAGES

ACEEGSSU	ESCUAGES	**ACEEHSST**	ESCHEATS	**ACEEKNRW**	NECKWEAR
ACEEHHRU	HEUCHERA	**ACEEHSTX**	CATHEXES	**ACEEKRRT**	RACKETER
ACEEHHST	CHEETAHS		EXCHEATS	**ACEELLMT**	CELLMATE
ACEEHILR	LEACHIER	**ACEEHTTV**	CHAVETTE	**ACEELLNS**	NACELLES
ACEEHINT	ECHINATE	**ACEEHTWY**	WATCHEYE	**ACEELLNT**	LANCELET
ACEEHIPR	PEACHIER	**ACEEIKLL**	LACELIKE	**ACEELLOT**	OCELLATE
ACEEHIPS	CHEAPIES	**ACEEIKLV**	CAVELIKE	**ACEELLPT**	CAPELLET
ACEEHIPT	EPITHECA	**ACEEIKMR**	ICEMAKER	**ACEELLRR**	CELLARER
	PETECHIA	**ACEEIKNP**	PEACENIK		RECALLER
ACEEHIRT	AETHERIC	**ACEEIKRR**	CREAKIER	**ACEELLRT**	CELLARET
	HETAERIC	**ACEEILLM**	MICELLAE	**ACEELLRV**	CREVALLE
ACEEHIRV	ACHIEVER	**ACEEILLP**	CALLIPEE	**ACEELLSS**	LACELESS
	CHIVAREE	**ACEEILMN**	CAMELINE	**ACEELMNO**	CAMELEON
ACEEHIST	HICATEES	**ACEEILMT**	EMETICAL	**ACEELMNP**	PLACEMEN
ACEEHISV	ACHIEVES	**ACEEILMU**	LEUCEMIA	**ACEELMPS**	EMPLACES
ACEEHITV	ATCHIEVE	**ACEEILNP**	CAPELINE	**ACEELMRS**	RECLAMES
ACEEHKNS	SKEECHAN	**ACEEILNR**	CARELINE		SCLEREMA
ACEEHKOS	HOECAKES		CINEREAL	**ACEELNPR**	PRECLEAN
ACEEHKTT	HACKETTE		RELIANCE	**ACEELNPT**	PENTACLE
ACEEHLMP	EMPLEACH	**ACEEILNS**	SALIENCE	**ACEELNRR**	LARCENER
ACEEHLOS	SHOELACE	**ACEEILPS**	CALIPEES	**ACEELNRS**	CLEANERS
ACEEHLPS	PLEACHES		ESPECIAL		CLEANSER
ACEEHLRS	LEACHERS	**ACEEILRS**	ESCALIER		RECLEANS
	RELACHES	**ACEEILRV**	RECEIVAL	**ACEELNRU**	CERULEAN
ACEEHLSS	LACHESES	**ACEEIMOT**	ACOEMETI	**ACEELNRV**	VERNACLE
ACEEHLST	CHELATES	**ACEEIMRR**	CREAMIER	**ACEELNSS**	CLEANSES
ACEEHLSW	ESCHEWAL		REARMICE	**ACEELNST**	CLEANEST
ACEEHLTV	CHEVALET		RECAMIER		LATENCES
ACEEHMNP	CAMPHENE	**ACEEIMRS**	CASIMERE	**ACEELNSU**	NUCLEASE
ACEEHMNR	MENARCHE		RACEMISE	**ACEELNSV**	ENCLAVES
ACEEHMRS	CASHMERE	**ACEEIMRT**	CEMITARE		VALENCES
	MACHREES	**ACEEIMRZ**	RACEMIZE	**ACEELNTT**	TENTACLE
	MARCHESE	**ACEEIMST**	EMICATES	**ACEELNTU**	NUCLEATE
ACEEHMST	MACHETES	**ACEEINNR**	NARCEINE	**ACEELOPS**	ESCALOPE
ACEEHNNR	ENHANCER	**ACEEINPS**	SAPIENCE		OPALESCE
ACEEHNNS	ENHANCES	**ACEEINPT**	PATIENCE	**ACEELORS**	ESCAROLE
ACEEHNPS	CHEAPENS	**ACEEINRS**	CINEREAS	**ACEELORT**	CORELATE
ACEEHNRS	ENARCHES		INCREASE		RELOCATE
	ENCHASER		RESIANCE	**ACEELOSS**	SECALOSE
ACEEHNRV	REVANCHE	**ACEEINRT**	CENTIARE	**ACEELOSV**	VOCALESE
ACEEHNSS	ENCASHES		CREATINE	**ACEELPPR**	PREPLACE
	ENCHASES		INCREATE	**ACEELPRR**	PRECLEAR
ACEEHOOT	OOTHECAE		ITERANCE		REPLACER
ACEEHOPT	APOTHECE	**ACEEINST**	CINEASTE	**ACEELPRS**	PERCALES
ACEEHORT	OCHREATE	**ACEEINSU**	EUCAINES		REPLACES
ACEEHPPS	ECHAPPES	**ACEEINTV**	ENACTIVE	**ACEELPRT**	PRAELECT
ACEEHPRR	PREACHER	**ACEEINTX**	EXITANCE	**ACEELPST**	CAPELETS
ACEEHPRS	PEACHERS	**ACEEIPPR**	PRAECIPE	**ACEELPSY**	CYPSELAE
	PREACHES	**ACEEIPST**	SPECIATE	**ACEELPTU**	PECULATE
ACEEHPRT	ETHERCAP	**ACEEIQRU**	ACQUIREE	**ACEELPTY**	CLYPEATE
ACEEHPST	CHEAPEST	**ACEEIRRS**	CARIERES	**ACEELRRS**	CLEARERS
ACEEHQSU	QUEACHES		CREASIER	**ACEELRSS**	CARELESS
ACEEHRRS	REACHERS	**ACEEIRSU**	CAUSERIE		RESCALES
	RESEARCH	**ACEEIRSW**	WISEACRE	**ACEELRST**	CLEAREST
	SEARCHER	**ACEEIRTV**	CREATIVE		SCELERAT
ACEEHRRT	TREACHER		REACTIVE		TREACLES
ACEEHRSS	SEARCHES	**ACEEISTV**	VESICATE	**ACEELRSV**	CERVELAS
ACEEHRST	CHEATERS	**ACEEJKNS**	JACKEENS		CLEAVERS
	HECTARES	**ACEEJKRT**	REJACKET	**ACEELRTT**	RACLETTE
	RECHATES	**ACEEKLMR**	MACKEREL	**ACEELRTU**	ULCERATE
	RECHEATS	**ACEEKLRT**	RETACKLE	**ACEELRTV**	CERVELAT
	TEACHERS	**ACEEKLRW**	EELWRACK	**ACEELRTX**	EXCRETAL
ACEEHRTT	CATHETER	**ACEEKMPT**	EMPACKET	**ACEELSST**	CELESTAS
ACEEHRTY	CHEATERY	**ACEEKNPS**	KNEECAPS		SELECTAS

ACEELSSU	EUCLASES	ACEERRST	CATERERS	ACEFINRS	FANCIERS
ACEELSTT	TELECAST		RECRATES		FRANCISE
ACEELSVX	EXCLAVES		RETRACES	ACEFINRX	CARNIFEX
ACEEMMOT	AMMOCETE		TERRACES	ACEFINRZ	FRANCIZE
ACEEMNNS	SCENEMAN	ACEERRSU	ECRASEUR	ACEFINSS	FASCINES
ACEEMNOT	MECONATE	ACEERRTU	CREATURE	ACEFINST	FANCIEST
ACEEMNPS	SPACEMEN	ACEERRUV	VERRUCAE	ACEFINSU	UNIFACES
ACEEMNRS	MENACERS	ACEERSSS	CARESSES	ACEFIOSS	FIASCOES
ACEEMNST	CASEMENT	ACEERSST	CATERESS	ACEFIPRY	REPACIFY
ACEEMOPR	CAMPOREE		CERASTES	ACEFIRRT	CRAFTIER
ACEEMOPT	COPEMATE	ACEERSSU	SURCEASE	ACEFIRTT	TRIFECTA
ACEEMORS	RACEMOSE	ACEERSSV	CREVASSE	ACEFIRTY	FERACITY
ACEEMORV	OVERCAME	ACEERSTU	SECATEUR	ACEFISST	FACTISES
ACEEMRRS	AMERCERS	ACEERSTX	EXACTERS	ACEFKLRS	FLACKERS
	CREAMERS	ACEERSVZ	CERVEZAS	ACEFKLRY	FLACKERY
	SCREAMER	ACEERTTU	ERUCTATE	ACEFKLST	FLACKETS
ACEEMRRY	CREAMERY	ACEESSST	ECSTASES	ACEFLLSS	CALFLESS
ACEEMRST	CREMATES	ACEESSTT	CASETTES	ACEFLMNO	FLAMENCO
	MEERCATS		CASSETTE	ACEFLNOR	FALCONER
ACEEMRTW	CREWMATE	ACEESTTX	EXACTEST	ACEFLNOT	CONFLATE
ACEENNPS	PENANCES	ACEFFGIN	EFFACING		FALCONET
ACEENNRS	NARCEENS	ACEFFHIR	CHAFFIER	ACEFLNRY	CRANEFLY
ACEENNRT	ENTRANCE	ACEFFHIS	AFFICHES	ACEFLORS	ALFRESCO
ACEENNST	CANTEENS	ACEFFHRS	CHAFFERS	ACEFLRTU	CRATEFUL
ACEENNSY	CAYENNES	ACEFFHRU	CHAUFFER		FULCRATE
ACEENOPT	CONEPATE	ACEFFHRY	CHAFFERY	ACEFLRUU	FURCULAE
ACEENORT	CAROTENE	ACEFFILT	FACELIFT	ACEFMNOO	MOONFACE
ACEENOST	ACETONES	ACEFFIMS	CAFFEISM	ACEFNNOS	FACONNES
	NOTECASE	ACEFFINS	CAFFEINS	ACEFNORV	CONFERVA
ACEENPRR	PARCENER	ACEFFISS	SCAFFIES	ACEFNPRT	PENCRAFT
ACEENPRT	PERCEANT	ACEFFLLU	FULLFACE	ACEFNRST	CANTREFS
	PREENACT	ACEFFLRS	SCLAFFER	ACEFNRSU	FURNACES
ACEENRRT	RECANTER	ACEFFORS	AFFORCES	ACEFOOPT	FOOTPACE
	RECREANT	ACEFGINN	ENFACING	ACEFOORT	FOOTRACE
ACEENRSS	CASERNES	ACEFGINR	REFACING	ACEFOPST	POSTFACE
ACEENRST	CENTARES	ACEFGINT	FACETING	ACEFORRS	FORECARS
	ENCASTRE	ACEFGIPS	PIGFACES	ACEFORST	FORECAST
	REASCENT	ACEFGLRU	GRACEFUL	ACEFORSX	CARFOXES
	REENACTS	ACEFGLSU	CAGEFULS	ACEFOSTU	OUTFACES
	SARCENET	ACEFGOST	GEOFACTS	ACEFRRSS	SCARFERS
ACEENRTU	ENACTURE	ACEFHIKS	FISHCAKE	ACEFRRST	CRAFTERS
	UNCREATE	ACEFHISV	CAVEFISH		REFRACTS
ACEENSSS	CASSENES	ACEFHLNS	FLANCHES	ACEFRRSU	FARCEURS
ACEENSTX	EXSECANT	ACEFHMRS	CHAMFERS		SURFACER
ACEEOQTU	COEQUATE	ACEFHORS	ARCHFOES	ACEFRRTU	FRACTURE
ACEEORST	CREASOTE	ACEFHORU	FAROUCHE	ACEFRSSU	SURFACES
ACEEOSSS	CASEOSES	ACEFHRST	FRATCHES	ACEFRSTU	FACTURES
ACEEOSTT	ECOSTATE	ACEFHRSU	CHAUFERS		FURCATES
ACEEOSTV	EVOCATES	ACEFIILS	FELICIAS	ACEGGILN	CAGELING
ACEEPRRS	CAPERERS	ACEFIIPR	PACIFIER		GLACEING
ACEEPRRT	RECARPET	ACEFIIPS	PACIFIES	ACEGGILR	CLAGGIER
ACEEPRSS	ESCAPERS	ACEFIIRT	ARTIFICE	ACEGGINN	ENCAGING
	RESPACES	ACEFIKLL	CALFLIKE	ACEGGIOP	EPAGOGIC
ACEEPRTT	ETTERCAP	ACEFILLS	ICEFALLS	ACEGGIRR	CRAGGIER
ACEEPRTU	PERACUTE	ACEFILLY	FACILELY	ACEGHIIT	CHIGETAI
ACEEPRTX	EXCERPTA	ACEFILOP	EPIFOCAL	ACEGHILN	LEACHING
ACEEPSST	PECTASES	ACEFILOS	FASCIOLE	ACEGHILT	LICHGATE
ACEEPSSU	AUCEPSES		FOCALISE		TEIGLACH
ACEEPSTT	PECTATES	ACEFILOZ	FOCALIZE	ACEGHINP	CHEAPING
	SPECTATE	ACEFILRS	FILACERS		PEACHING
ACEEPSTY	TYPECASE	ACEFILRY	FIRECLAY	ACEGHINR	REACHING
ACEERRRT	RETRACER	ACEFIMNY	FEMINACY	ACEGHINT	CHEATING
ACEERRSS	CARESSER	ACEFIMPR	CAMPFIRE		TEACHING
	CREASERS	ACEFINNS	FINANCES	ACEGHLOS	GALOCHES

Eight-letter anagrams

ACEGHLRS	SCHLAGER
ACEGHLRU	RUGELACH
ACEGHLTY	LYCHGATE
ACEGHLUY	GAUCHELY
ACEGHMMU	CHUMMAGE
ACEGHMOR	ECHOGRAM
	GRAMOCHE
ACEGHNPU	CHANGEUP
ACEGHNRS	CHANGERS
ACEGHNRU	UNCHARGE
ACEGHNSU	CHAUNGES
	GAUNCHES
ACEGHOSU	GOUACHES
ACEGHOSW	COWHAGES
ACEGHRRS	CHARGERS
ACEGHRTU	RECAUGHT
ACEGHSTU	GAUCHEST
ACEGIIMP	EPIGAMIC
ACEGIINR	REAGINIC
ACEGIINV	VICINAGE
ACEGIKNR	CREAKING
ACEGILLO	COLLEGIA
ACEGILLR	ALLERGIC
ACEGILMU	MUCILAGE
ACEGILMY	GLYCEMIA
ACEGILNN	CLEANING
	ELANCING
	ENLACING
ACEGILNR	CLEARING
	RELACING
ACEGILNT	CLEATING
ACEGILNV	CLEAVING
ACEGILNW	LACEWING
ACEGILOS	CALIGOES
ACEGILPS	PELAGICS
ACEGILRS	GLACIERS
	GRACILES
ACEGILRV	CLAVIGER
ACEGILRY	GLYCERIA
ACEGILSS	GLACISES
ACEGILST	GELASTIC
	GESTICAL
ACEGIMMT	TAGMEMIC
ACEGIMNN	MENACING
ACEGIMNO	CAMEOING
ACEGIMNR	AMERCING
	CREAMING
	GERMANIC
ACEGIMNS	MAGNESIC
ACEGIMNT	MAGNETIC
ACEGIMOS	CAMOGIES
ACEGIMOX	EXOGAMIC
ACEGIMRR	GRIMACER
ACEGIMRS	GRIMACES
ACEGIMTY	MEGACITY
ACEGINNO	CANOEING
ACEGINNR	ENRACING
	RECANING
ACEGINNS	ENCASING
ACEGINNT	ENACTING
ACEGINNV	ENCAVING
ACEGINOS	COINAGES
ACEGINOY	GYNOECIA
ACEGINPR	CAPERING
	PEARCING
	PREACING
ACEGINPS	ESCAPING
ACEGINRS	CREASING
	GRECIANS
	SEARCING
ACEGINRT	ARGENTIC
	CATERING
	CITRANGE
	CREATING
	REACTING
ACEGINSS	CAGINESS
	CEASINGS
ACEGINTX	EXACTING
ACEGIOTT	COGITATE
ACEGIPRS	SPAGERIC
ACEGIRST	AGRESTIC
	CIGARETS
	ERGASTIC
ACEGISTU	GAUCIEST
ACEGISTW	GAWCIEST
ACEGJKLS	JACKLEGS
ACEGKLOS	LOCKAGES
ACEGKLOV	GAVELOCK
ACEGKLRS	GRACKLES
ACEGKMOS	MOCKAGES
ACEGKORS	CORKAGES
ACEGKORW	CAGEWORK
ACEGKOST	STOCKAGE
ACEGKRTU	TRUCKAGE
ACEGLLNO	COLLAGEN
ACEGLLOS	COLLAGES
ACEGLNOS	CONGEALS
	LONGCASE
ACEGLNOT	OCTANGLE
ACEGLNOY	AGLYCONE
ACEGLNRS	CLANGERS
	GLANCERS
ACEGLOST	CATELOGS
ACEGLOSU	CAGOULES
ACEGMNOY	GEOMANCY
ACEGMNRS	CRAGSMEN
ACEGMOPS	COMPAGES
ACEGMORS	SCARMOGE
ACEGMRRY	GRAMERCY
ACEGNNOR	CRANNOGE
ACEGNNOY	CYANOGEN
ACEGNNRY	REGNANCY
ACEGNNTY	TANGENCY
ACEGNORS	ACROGENS
	CORNAGES
ACEGNOST	COAGENTS
	COGNATES
ACEGNSSY	CAGYNESS
ACEGOORS	CARGOOSE
ACEGOPRY	GEOCARPY
ACEGORSS	CORSAGES
	SOCAGERS
ACEGORST	ESCARGOT
ACEGORSU	COURAGES
ACEGORTT	COTTAGER
ACEGORTY	CATEGORY
ACEGOSTT	COTTAGES
ACEGOTTY	COTTAGEY
ACEGRSTU	TRUCAGES
ACEGSSTU	SCUTAGES
ACEGSTTU	CUTTAGES
ACEHHINS	HAINCHES
ACEHHIPS	CHEAPISH
ACEHHIRR	HIERARCH
ACEHHIST	SHECHITA
ACEHHISU	HUISACHE
ACEHHLST	HATCHELS
ACEHHLSU	SHAUCHLE
ACEHHMNN	HENCHMAN
ACEHHNRT	ETHNARCH
ACEHHNSU	HAUNCHES
ACEHHPRT	HEPTARCH
ACEHHRST	HATCHERS
ACEHHRSU	HACHURES
ACEHHRTT	THATCHER
ACEHHRTY	HATCHERY
	THEARCHY
ACEHHRXY	HEXARCHY
ACEHHSTT	HATCHETS
	THATCHES
ACEHHTTY	HATCHETY
ACEHIIMS	ISCHEMIA
ACEHIINT	ETHICIAN
ACEHIIRT	HETAIRIC
	HIERATIC
ACEHIJKR	HIJACKER
ACEHIJNT	JACINTHE
ACEHIKLP	KEPHALIC
ACEHIKLR	CHALKIER
	HACKLIER
ACEHIKLW	LICHWAKE
ACEHIKRS	KACHERIS
ACEHIKRW	WHACKIER
ACEHILLS	CHALLIES
ACEHILLT	HELLICAT
ACEHILMN	INCHMEAL
ACEHILMO	CHOLEMIA
ACEHILMP	IMPLEACH
ACEHILMS	CAMELISH
	LECHAIMS
ACEHILMY	LECHAYIM
ACEHILNP	CEPHALIN
ACEHILNT	CHAINLET
	CHATLINE
	ETHNICAL
ACEHILOR	HALICORE
	HEROICAL
ACEHILPR	PARHELIC
ACEHILPY	PEACHILY
ACEHILRR	CHARLIER
ACEHILRS	CHARLIES
ACEHILST	ETHICALS
ACEHILTT	ATHLETIC
	THETICAL
ACEHIMMS	CHAMMIES
ACEHIMNN	CHAINMEN
	CHINAMEN
ACEHIMNP	CAMPHINE
ACEHIMNR	CHAIRMEN
ACEHIMNS	MACHINES
ACEHIMNT	ANTHEMIC
ACEHIMNU	ACHENIUM

ACEHIMPR	CAMPHIRE	ACEHISTY	YACHTIES		SLATCHES
ACEHIMPT	EMPATHIC	ACEHISTZ	ZAITECHS	ACEHLSTT	CHATTELS
	EMPHATIC	ACEHKLLS	SHELLACK		LATCHETS
ACEHIMRS	CHASMIER	ACEHKLOV	HAVELOCK	ACEHLSTY	CHASTELY
	CHIMERAS	ACEHKLPR	KREPLACH	ACEHMMNR	MARCHMEN
	MARCHESI	ACEHKLRS	HACKLERS	ACEHMNNR	RANCHMEN
ACEHIMRT	RHEMATIC		SHACKLER	ACEHMNOP	PHONECAM
ACEHIMSS	CHAMISES	ACEHKLSS	SHACKLES	ACEHMNOR	CHOREMAN
ACEHIMST	HEMATICS	ACEHKLST	HACKLETS	ACEHMNRS	ENCHARMS
	MASTICHE		KLATCHES	ACEHMNRT	MERCHANT
	MISTEACH	ACEHKLTY	LATCHKEY	ACEHMNSS	CHESSMAN
	TACHISME	ACEHKMPU	MUCKHEAP	ACEHMNST	MANCHETS
ACEHIMTT	THEMATIC	ACEHKNSY	HACKNEYS	ACEHMNTW	WATCHMEN
ACEHIMTZ	MECHITZA	ACEHKOPS	SHOEPACK	ACEHMNTY	YACHTMEN
ACEHINNS	ENCHAINS	ACEHKORV	HAVOCKER	ACEHMORT	CHROMATE
ACEHINOT	ETHANOIC	ACEHKOSS	SHACKOES	ACEHMOST	MOSCHATE
	INCHOATE	ACEHKOST	HOTCAKES	ACEHMPRS	CHAMPERS
ACEHINOX	HEXANOIC	ACEHKOSW	WHACKOES	ACEHMRRS	CHARMERS
ACEHINPS	PAINCHES	ACEHKOTU	TUCKAHOE		MARCHERS
ACEHINPT	HAPTENIC	ACEHKRSW	WHACKERS	ACEHMRSS	SCHMEARS
ACEHINRS	ARCHINES	ACEHKRTW	THWACKER	ACEHMRST	MATCHERS
	INARCHES	ACEHLLMO	MALLECHO	ACEHMRSU	CHAUMERS
ACEHINRV	VACHERIN	ACEHLLOO	COALHOLE	ACEHMSST	SMATCHES
ACEHINSS	ACHINESS	ACEHLLOR	ORCHELLA	ACEHMSTT	MATCHETS
	INCHASES	ACEHLLPS	PELLACHS		SCHMATTE
ACEHINST	ASTHENIC	ACEHLLSS	SHELLACS	ACEHMSTU	MUSTACHE
	CHANTIES	ACEHLLST	HELLCATS	ACEHMSTY	ECTHYMAS
ACEHINSY	HYACINES	ACEHLLSU	HALLUCES	ACEHNNOP	PANCHEON
	SYNECHIA	ACEHLMOT	CHAMELOT	ACEHNNOT	NANOTECH
ACEHIOPR	POACHIER	ACEHLMST	CHAMLETS	ACEHNNPT	PENCHANT
ACEHIOST	ACHIOTES	ACEHLNNS	CHANNELS	ACEHNNRS	CHANNERS
	TOISEACH	ACEHLNOS	CHALONES	ACEHNNST	ENCHANTS
ACEHIPPR	CHAPPIER	ACEHLNOU	EULACHON	ACEHNOPR	CANEPHOR
ACEHIPPS	CHAPPIES	ACEHLNPS	PLANCHES		CHAPERON
ACEHIPRS	ASPHERIC	ACEHLNPT	PLANCHET	ACEHNOPS	PANOCHES
	CHARPIES	ACEHLNRS	CHARNELS	ACEHNOPT	CENOTAPH
	PARCHESI	ACEHLNRU	LAUNCHER	ACEHNORR	RANCHERO
	SERAPHIC		RELAUNCH	ACEHNORT	ANCHORET
ACEHIPRT	CHAPITER	ACEHLNST	STANCHEL	ACEHNPRT	PENTARCH
	PATCHIER	ACEHLNSU	LAUNCHES	ACEHNPRU	UNPREACH
	PHREATIC	ACEHLOOT	OOTHECAL	ACEHNPSU	PAUNCHES
ACEHIPST	HEPATICS	ACEHLOPT	POTLACHE	ACEHNRRS	RANCHERS
	PASTICHE	ACEHLORS	CHOLERAS	ACEHNRSS	ARCHNESS
	PISTACHE		CHORALES	ACEHNRST	CHANTERS
ACEHIPTT	PATHETIC	ACEHLORT	CHELATOR		SNATCHER
ACEHIPTW	WHITECAP		CHLORATE		STANCHER
ACEHIQSU	QUAICHES		TROCHLEA		TRANCHES
ACEHIRRR	CHARRIER	ACEHLORU	LEACHOUR	ACEHNRSU	RAUNCHES
ACEHIRSS	CASHIERS	ACEHLOST	CATHOLES	ACEHNRSW	CRENSHAW
	RACHISES		CHOLATES	ACEHNRTT	TRANCHET
ACEHIRST	CHARIEST		ESCHALOT	ACEHNRTU	CHAUNTER
	STICHERA	ACEHLPRT	CHAPTREL	ACEHNSSS	SCHANSES
	THERIACS	ACEHLPRV	CHAPELRY	ACEHNSST	CHASTENS
ACEHIRSU	EUCHARIS	ACEHLPSS	CHAPLESS		SNATCHES
ACEHIRSV	ARCHIVES	ACEHLPST	CHAPLETS		STANCHES
ACEHIRSW	ARCHWISE	ACEHLRSS	CLASHERS	ACEHNSSZ	SCHANZES
ACEHIRTT	CHATTIER		RASCHELS	ACEHNSTT	ETCHANTS
	THEATRIC	ACEHLRST	ARCHLETS	ACEHNSTU	NAUTCHES
ACEHISST	CHASTISE		TRACHLES		UNCHASTE
	TAISCHES	ACEHLRSV	CHARLEYS	ACEHNSTY	CHANTEYS
ACEHISSU	CHIAUSES	ACEHLRTU	ARCHLUTE	ACEHNSTZ	SCHANTZE
ACEHISTT	CHATTIES		TRAUCHLE	ACEHNSZZ	CHAZZENS
	TACHISTE	ACEHLSSS	CASHLESS	ACEHOPPR	COPPERAH
ACEHISTX	CATHEXIS	ACEHLSST	SATCHELS	ACEHOPRR	REPROACH

Eight-letter anagrams

ACEHOPRS	POACHERS		CANITIES	**ACEILLSS**	SCALLIES
ACEHOPSS	SHOEPACS	**ACEIINTV**	INACTIVE	**ACEILMMO**	CAMOMILE
ACEHORRS	HORSECAR	**ACEIINTZ**	ANTICIZE	**ACEILMMR**	CLAMMIER
ACEHORRV	OVERARCH	**ACEIIPRS**	PIRACIES	**ACEILMNN**	CLINAMEN
ACEHORST	CHAROSET	**ACEIIPSS**	EPISCIAS	**ACEILMNO**	COALMINE
	THORACES	**ACEIIPTX**	EPITAXIC	**ACEILMNP**	MANCIPLE
ACEHORTT	THEOCRAT	**ACEIIRRT**	CRITERIA	**ACEILMNS**	MELANICS
ACEHORTU	OUTREACH	**ACEIIRSV**	VICARIES		MENISCAL
ACEHORUV	AVOUCHER	**ACEIISTT**	ATTICISE		MESCALIN
ACEHOSSW	SHOWCASE	**ACEIISTU**	ACUITIES	**ACEILMNY**	MYCELIAN
ACEHOSTU	CATHOUSE	**ACEIISTV**	ACTIVISE	**ACEILMOS**	CAMISOLE
	SOUTACHE		CAITIVES	**ACEILMPS**	MISPLACE
ACEHOSTY	CHAYOTES		CAVITIES	**ACEILMPT**	PELMATIC
ACEHOSUV	AVOUCHES		VICIATES	**ACEILMRS**	CLAIMERS
ACEHOTTU	OUTCHEAT	**ACEIITTV**	VITICETA		MIRACLES
ACEHPPSS	CHAPPESS	**ACEIITTZ**	ATTICIZE		RECLAIMS
	SCHAPPES	**ACEIITVZ**	ACTIVIZE	**ACEILMRT**	METRICAL
ACEHPRRS	PRECRASH	**ACEIJKSS**	JACKSIES	**ACEILMRY**	CREAMILY
ACEHPRST	CHAPTERS	**ACEIJMST**	MAJESTIC	**ACEILMST**	CALMIEST
	PATCHERS	**ACEIJNRR**	JERRICAN		CLEMATIS
ACEHPRSU	PURCHASE	**ACEIKKLS**	SACKLIKE		CLIMATES
ACEHPRTY	PATCHERY	**ACEIKKNR**	KNACKIER		METICALS
	PETCHARY	**ACEIKLLM**	CLAMLIKE	**ACEILMSU**	MUSICALE
ACEHPSTY	SCYPHATE		MILLCAKE	**ACEILMSX**	CLIMAXES
ACEHQSTU	QUATCHES	**ACEIKLLW**	CLAWLIKE		EXCLAIMS
ACEHRRSS	CRASHERS	**ACEIKLLY**	CLAYLIKE	**ACEILMTU**	AMULETIC
ACEHRRST	CHARTERS	**ACEIKLNR**	CLANKIER	**ACEILNNP**	PANNICLE
	RECHARTS	**ACEIKLRT**	TALCKIER		PINNACLE
	STARCHER	**ACEIKLRY**	CREAKILY	**ACEILNNR**	ENCRINAL
ACEHRRSV	CHARVERS	**ACEIKMNN**	NICKNAME	**ACEILNOR**	ACROLEIN
ACEHRRTT	TETRARCH	**ACEIKMRS**	KERAMICS		COLINEAR
ACEHRSST	STARCHES	**ACEIKMRV**	MAVERICK		CREOLIAN
ACEHRSSU	CHASSEUR	**ACEIKNPS**	CAPESKIN		LONICERA
ACEHRSTT	CHATTERS	**ACEIKNRR**	CRANKIER	**ACEILNPS**	CAPELINS
	RATCHETS	**ACEIKNRS**	SKINCARE		PANICLES
ACEHRSTW	WATCHERS	**ACEIKNSS**	CAKINESS		PELICANS
ACEHRSTY	YACHTERS	**ACEIKOPS**	PAIOCKES	**ACEILNPT**	PECTINAL
ACEHRTTY	CHATTERY	**ACEIKORR**	CROAKIER		PLANETIC
	TRACHYTE	**ACEIKPRS**	EARPICKS	**ACEILNRS**	CARLINES
ACEHSSSU	CHAUSSES	**ACEIKPSW**	WICKAPES		LANCIERS
ACEHSSTT	CHASTEST	**ACEIKPSX**	PICKAXES	**ACEILNRT**	CLARINET
ACEHSSTW	SWATCHES	**ACEIKQRU**	QUACKIER	**ACEILNSS**	LACINESS
ACEHSTTU	CATHETUS	**ACEIKRRV**	VRAICKER		SANICLES
	TEUCHATS	**ACEIKSTT**	TACKIEST	**ACEILNST**	CANISTEL
ACEHSTTW	WATCHETS		TIETACKS	**ACEILNSU**	AESCULIN
ACEHTTUZ	ZUCHETTA	**ACEIKSTW**	WACKIEST		LUNACIES
ACEIIKNT	AKINETIC	**ACEILLLT**	CLITELLA	**ACEILNSY**	SALIENCY
ACEIILMN	LIMACINE	**ACEILLMR**	MICELLAR	**ACEILOPR**	CAPRIOLE
ACEIILNR	IRENICAL		MILLRACE	**ACEILOPT**	POETICAL
ACEIILNS	SALICINE	**ACEILLMS**	LIMACELS	**ACEILORR**	CARRIOLE
ACEIILNX	ALEXINIC		MICELLAS	**ACEILORS**	CALORIES
ACEIILSS	LAICISES	**ACEILLMT**	METALLIC		CALORISE
ACEIILST	CILIATES	**ACEILLMY**	MYCELIAL		CARIOLES
	SILICATE	**ACEILLNT**	CLIENTAL	**ACEILORT**	EROTICAL
ACEIILSZ	LAICIZES	**ACEILLOP**	CALLIOPE		LORICATE
ACEIIMRS	CASIMIRE	**ACEILLOR**	ROCAILLE	**ACEILORV**	ARVICOLE
ACEIIMRV	VIRAEMIC	**ACEILLOS**	LOCALISE	**ACEILORZ**	CALORIZE
ACEIIMSS	ASEISMIC	**ACEILLOT**	LOCALITE	**ACEILOSS**	CELOSIAS
ACEIIMST	METICAIS		TEOCALLI		COALISES
ACEIIMTU	MAIEUTIC	**ACEILLOZ**	LOCALIZE	**ACEILOST**	ALOETICS
ACEIINPS	PISCINAE	**ACEILLPR**	CALLIPER		COALIEST
ACEIINRS	RIANCIES	**ACEILLPS**	ALLSPICE		SOCIETAL
ACEIINRT	ARENITIC	**ACEILLPY**	EPICALLY	**ACEILOSU**	EUSOCIAL
ACEIINST	ANTICISE	**ACEILLRV**	CAVILLER	**ACEILOSV**	VOCALISE

ACEILOSX	SAXICOLE	ACEIMOPR	COPREMIA	ACEINPSY	SAPIENCY
ACEILOSZ	COALIZES	ACEIMOPT	POEMATIC	ACEINPTT	PITTANCE
ACEILOTV	LOCATIVE	ACEIMOTX	TOXAEMIC	ACEINPUY	PICAYUNE
ACEILOVZ	VOCALIZE	ACEIMOTZ	AZOTEMIC	ACEINRRU	CURARINE
ACEILPPY	PIPECLAY		METAZOIC	ACEINRRY	CINERARY
ACEILPRS	CALIPERS	ACEIMPRR	CRAMPIER	ACEINRSS	ARCSINES
	REPLICAS		MERICARP		ARSENICS
	SPIRACLE	ACEIMPRS	PARECISM		CERASINS
ACEILPRT	PARTICLE		SAPREMIC		RACINESS
	PRELATIC	ACEIMPRT	IMPACTER	ACEINRST	CANISTER
ACEILPRU	PECULIAR	ACEIMPSS	ESCAPISM		CARNIEST
ACEILPSS	SLIPCASE		MISSPACE		CERATINS
	SPECIALS		SCAMPIES		CISTERNA
ACEILPST	PLICATES	ACEIMPST	CAMPIEST		CREATINS
	SEPTICAL		CAMPSITE		NACRITES
	TIECLASP	ACEIMPTU	PUMICATE		SCANTIER
ACEILPSU	SPICULAE	ACEIMRST	CERAMIST		TACRINES
ACEILPTY	ETYPICAL		MATRICES	ACEINRTT	INTERACT
ACEILPXY	EPICALYX		MISTRACE	ACEINRTU	ANURETIC
ACEILRRT	CLARTIER		SCIMETAR	ACEINRTV	NAVICERT
ACEILRRW	CRAWLIER	ACEIMRTT	TREMATIC	ACEINRTX	XERANTIC
ACEILRSS	CLASSIER	ACEIMRTU	MURICATE	ACEINRVY	VICENARY
ACEILRST	ALTRICES	ACEIMSST	CASTEISM	ACEINSSS	CASSINES
	ARTICLES		ETACISMS	ACEINSST	CINEASTS
	RECITALS	ACEIMSSU	CAESIUMS		SCANTIES
	SELICTAR	ACEIMSTU	AUTECISM	ACEINSSU	ISSUANCE
	STERICAL	ACEIMTTU	MUTICATE	ACEINSSY	CYANISES
ACEILRSU	AURICLES	ACEINNOS	CANONISE	ACEINSTT	CANTIEST
ACEILRSV	CALIVERS	ACEINNOT	ENACTION		ENTASTIC
	CAVILERS	ACEINNOZ	CANONIZE		NICTATES
	CLAVIERS	ACEINNPS	PINNACES		TETANICS
	VISCERAL	ACEINNRS	CRANNIES	ACEINSTV	CISTVAEN
ACEILRTT	TRACTILE		NARCEINS		VESICANT
ACEILRTU	RETICULA	ACEINNST	ANCIENTS	ACEINSTY	CYANITES
ACEILRTV	VERTICAL		CANNIEST	ACEINSTZ	ZINCATES
ACEILRTY	LITERACY		INSECTAN	ACEINSYZ	CYANIZES
ACEILRUV	ACERVULI		INSTANCE	ACEINTTU	TUNICATE
ACEILSST	ELASTICS	ACEINNSU	NUISANCE	ACEINTTX	EXCITANT
	SALICETS	ACEINNSY	CYANINES	ACEINTTY	TENACITY
	SCALIEST	ACEINNTU	UNCINATE	ACEINTUV	UNACTIVE
ACEILSTT	LATTICES	ACEINOPR	APOCRINE	ACEIOPRT	APORETIC
	TALCIEST		CAPONIER		OPERATIC
ACEILSTY	CLAYIEST		PROCAINE	ACEIOPST	ECTOPIAS
ACEILSUV	VESICULA	ACEINOPS	CANOPIES	ACEIOPVW	PICOWAVE
ACEILSVW	WAVICLES		CAPONISE	ACEIORSS	SCARIOSE
ACEILTVY	ACTIVELY		PAEONICS	ACEIORSV	COVARIES
ACEIMMNP	PEMMICAN	ACEINOPZ	CAPONIZE		VARICOSE
ACEIMMOS	SEMICOMA	ACEINORS	SCENARIO	ACEIOSST	SOCIATES
ACEIMMRS	RACEMISM	ACEINORT	ACTIONER	ACEIOSSU	CAESIOUS
ACEIMMTT	METAMICT		ANORETIC	ACEIOSTT	OSCITATE
ACEIMNNO	MONECIAN		CREATION	ACEIOTVV	VOCATIVE
ACEIMNOR	CORAMINE		REACTION	ACEIPPRR	CRAPPIER
ACEIMNOT	COINMATE	ACEINORV	VERONICA		PERICARP
ACEIMNOX	ANOXEMIC	ACEINORX	ANOREXIC	ACEIPPRS	CRAPPIES
ACEIMNPS	PEMICANS	ACEINOST	ACONITES		EPICARPS
ACEIMNRS	CARMINES		CANOEIST	ACEIPPST	TAPPICES
	CREMAINS		SONICATE	ACEIPRRS	PERISARC
ACEIMNRU	MANICURE	ACEINOTT	TACONITE	ACEIPRSS	SCRAPIES
ACEIMNSS	AMNESICS	ACEINOTV	CONATIVE	ACEIPRST	CRAPIEST
ACEIMNST	AMNESTIC		INVOCATE		CRISPATE
	SEMANTIC	ACEINOTX	EXACTION		PARETICS
ACEIMNSU	SEMUNCIA	ACEINPQU	PIQUANCE		PICRATES
ACEIMNSY	SYCAMINE	ACEINPSS	INSCAPES		PRACTISE
ACEIMNTU	NEUMATIC		PINCASES	ACEIPRTV	PRACTIVE

ACEIPRTY	APYRETIC
ACEIPSST	ASEPTICS
	ESCAPIST
	SPACIEST
ACEIPSSU	AUSPICES
ACEIPSSZ	CAPSIZES
ACEIPSTV	CAPTIVES
ACEIQRRU	ACQUIRER
ACEIQRSU	ACQUIRES
ACEIQSTU	ACQUITES
ACEIQSUZ	CAZIQUES
ACEIRRRS	CARRIERS
	SCARRIER
ACEIRRST	ERRATICS
ACEIRRSU	CURARISE
ACEIRRSW	AIRCREWS
	AIRCREW
ACEIRRTT	RETRAICT
ACEIRRTX	CREATRIX
ACEIRRTY	RETIRACY
ACEIRRUZ	CURARIZE
ACEIRSST	SCARIEST
ACEIRSSU	SAUCIERS
	SCAURIES
	URICASES
ACEIRSSV	VICARESS
ACEIRSTT	CITRATES
	CRISTATE
	SCATTIER
ACEIRSTU	SURICATE
ACEIRSTZ	CRAZIEST
ACEIRTTU	URTICATE
ACEIRTTV	TRACTIVE
ACEIRTUV	CURATIVE
ACEIRTVY	VERACITY
ACEISSSS	CASSISES
ACEISSST	ECSTASIS
ACEISSSU	SAUCISSE
ACEISSTT	STATICES
ACEISSTU	SAUCIEST
	SUITCASE
ACEISTTT	CATTIEST
ACEISTTU	EUSTATIC
ACEISTTW	SCAWTITE
ACEISTUX	AUXETICS
ACEJKOOR	JACKEROO
ACEJKOPS	PAJOCKES
ACEJLORS	CAJOLERS
ACEJLORY	CAJOLERY
ACEJMRST	SCRAMJET
ACEJNNOO	JONCANOE
ACEJNOST	JACONETS
ACEJNOSY	JOYANCES
ACEJNRRY	JERRYCAN
ACEJNSTU	JUNCATES
ACEJPSTU	CAJEPUTS
ACEJRSTT	TRAJECTS
ACEKKMRU	MUCKRAKE
ACEKKNRS	KNACKERS
ACEKKNRY	KNACKERY
ACEKLLPS	PELLACKS
ACEKLNRS	CRANKLES
ACEKLNSS	SLACKENS
ACEKLNTU	UNTACKLE
ACEKLORS	EARLOCKS
ACEKLORV	LAVEROCK
ACEKLORW	LACEWORK
ACEKLPRS	SPRACKLE
ACEKLPSS	SPACKLES
ACEKLPST	PLACKETS
ACEKLQSU	QUACKLES
ACEKLRSS	SLACKERS
ACEKLRST	TACKLERS
ACEKLRSU	CAULKERS
ACEKLSSS	SACKLESS
ACEKLSST	SLACKEST
	TACKLESS
ACEKMNRT	TRACKMEN
ACEKMNST	TACKSMEN
ACEKMORS	COMAKERS
ACEKMRSS	SMACKERS
ACEKNNOW	ACKNOWNE
ACEKNPRS	PRANCKES
ACEKNPRU	UNPACKER
ACEKNPSS	PACKNESS
ACEKNRSS	SNACKERS
ACEKNRST	CRANKEST
ACEKOORT	CARETOOK
ACEKOORW	COOKWARE
ACEKOPRV	OVERPACK
ACEKOPRW	CAPEWORK
ACEKORRS	CROAKERS
ACEKORRV	OVERRACK
ACEKORSW	CASEWORK
ACEKPPRS	PREPACKS
ACEKPSSY	SKYSCAPE
ACEKQRSU	QUACKERS
ACEKQRUY	QUACKERY
ACEKRRST	RETRACKS
	TRACKERS
ACEKRRTY	RACKETRY
ACEKRSST	RESTACKS
	STACKERS
ACEKRSTT	RACKETTS
ACEKRSTU	RUCKSEAT
ACEKSSTT	STACKETS
ACEKSSUW	WAESUCKS
ACELLLRU	CELLULAR
ACELLMOS	CALOMELS
ACELLMSU	SACELLUM
ACELLMSY	MYCELLAS
ACELLNRU	NUCELLAR
ACELLOPS	COLLAPSE
	ESCALLOP
ACELLORR	CAROLLER
ACELLORS	CORELLAS
ACELLORT	COLLARET
ACELLORV	COVERALL
	OVERCALL
ACELLORW	CALLOWER
ACELLOSS	CALLOSES
	COALLESS
ACELLOST	COLLATES
ACELLOSW	COLESLAW
ACELLOTU	LOCULATE
ACELLOVY	COEVALLY
ACELLPSS	SCALPELS
ACELLRRS	CARRELLS
ACELLRTY	RECTALLY
ACELLSSU	CALLUSES
ACELLSSW	CLAWLESS
ACELLSTU	SCUTELLA
ACELLTWY	CETYWALL
ACELMMOU	MAMELUCO
ACELMMRS	CLAMMERS
ACELMNNS	CLANSMEN
ACELMNOR	AMELCORN
	CORNMEAL
ACELMNOU	COLUMNEA
ACELMNRU	CRUMENAL
ACELMNSS	CALMNESS
	CLASSMEN
ACELMOPT	COMPLEAT
ACELMORR	CLAMORER
ACELMORS	CAROMELS
	SCLEROMA
ACELMORY	CLAYMORE
ACELMOST	CAMELOTS
	MOLECAST
ACELMOSU	CAULOMES
	LEUCOMAS
	MACULOSE
ACELMPRS	CLAMPERS
ACELMPSY	ECLAMPSY
ACELMSSU	LACMUSES
ACELMSTU	CALUMETS
	MUSCATEL
ACELMSUU	SAECULUM
ACELMTUU	CUMULATE
ACELNNNO	CANNELON
ACELNNOS	ALENCONS
ACELNNRS	SCRANNEL
ACELNOOT	ECOTONAL
ACELNOPT	CONEPATL
ACELNORV	NOVERCAL
ACELNOSS	SECONALS
ACELNOST	LACTONES
ACELNOSU	LACUNOSE
ACELNOSZ	CALZONES
ACELNOTV	COVALENT
ACELNOVY	CONVEYAL
ACELNPSS	ENCLASPS
	SPANCELS
ACELNPST	CLAPNETS
ACELNPSU	CLEANUPS
	UNPLACES
ACELNRST	CENTRALS
ACELNRSU	LUCARNES
ACELNRVY	CRAVENLY
ACELNSST	SCANTLES
ACELNSSU	SCALENUS
	UNSCALES
ACELNSTT	CANTLETS
ACELNSTY	SECANTLY
ACELOOSU	ACOELOUS
ACELOPPU	POPULACE
ACELOPRS	PARCLOSE
	POLACRES
ACELOPRT	PECTORAL
ACELOPRU	OPERCULA
ACELOPSS	ESCALOPS
ACELOPST	POLECATS

ACELOPSU	SCOPULAE	ACEMMRSS	SCAMMERS		OUTRANCE
ACELOPTU	COPULATE	ACEMNOOR	COENAMOR	ACENORTY	ENACTORY
	OUTPLACE	ACEMNORR	ROMANCER	ACENORUY	EUCARYON
ACELOPTY	CALOTYPE	ACEMNORS	CREMONAS	ACENOSSS	CASSONES
ACELOQSU	COEQUALS		ROMANCES	ACENOSST	CONTESSA
ACELORRS	CAROLERS	ACEMNORU	CUMARONE		COSTEANS
ACELORRT	RECTORAL	ACEMNOST	CAMSTONE	ACENOSSV	CAVESSON
ACELORSS	ESCOLARS	ACEMNPSS	CAMPNESS	ACENOSSY	CYANOSES
	LACROSSE	ACEMNRUY	NUMERACY	ACENOSTT	CONSTATE
	SOLACERS	ACEMNSSU	MANCUSES	ACENOSTV	CENTAVOS
ACELORST	LOCATERS	ACEMOORS	ACROSOME	ACENOTTU	TOUCANET
	SECTORAL	ACEMOOST	COMATOSE	ACENPRRS	PRANCERS
ACELORSU	CAROUSEL	ACEMOPRR	COMPARER	ACENPRSU	ENCARPUS
ACELORSY	CALOYERS	ACEMOPRS	CAPSOMER		PRAUNCES
	COARSELY		COMPARES	ACENPSTT	PENTACTS
ACELOSST	ALECOSTS		COMPEARS	ACENPTTU	PUNCTATE
	COATLESS		MESOCARP	ACENRSST	CRANTSES
	LACTOSES	ACEMOPRT	MERCAPTO	ACENRSSU	SURANCES
	SCATOLES	ACEMORRT	CREMATOR	ACENRSTT	TRANECTS
ACELOSTT	CALOTTES	ACEMORRV	OVERCRAM		TRANSECT
ACELOSTU	LACTEOUS	ACEMORSU	RACEMOUS	ACENRSTU	CENTAURS
	LOCUSTAE	ACEMORSW	CASEWORM		RECUSANT
	OSCULATE	ACEMORSY	SYCAMORE		UNCRATES
ACELOSTY	ACOLYTES	ACEMORTY	COMETARY		UNTRACES
ACELOSUV	VACUOLES	ACEMORUX	MORCEAUX	ACENRSTY	ANCESTRY
ACELOTTY	CATOLYTE	ACEMOSSU	COASSUME	ACENRTTU	TRUNCATE
ACELOTXY	ACETOXYL	ACEMPRRS	CRAMPERS	ACENRTUY	CENTAURY
ACELPPRS	CLAPPERS	ACEMPRSS	SCAMPERS		CYANURET
	SCRAPPLE	ACEMPRST	CRAMPETS	ACENSSTT	SCANTEST
ACELPPSS	SCAPPLES	ACEMPSSU	CAMPUSES	ACENSSTU	NUTCASES
ACELPRSS	CLASPERS	ACEMRSST	SCAMSTER	ACENSSTW	NEWSCAST
	RECLASPS	ACEMSSTT	METCASTS	ACENSSUU	USAUNCES
	SCALPERS	ACENNNOU	ANNOUNCE	ACEOOPPS	APOCOPES
ACELPRST	SCEPTRAL	ACENNOSS	CANONESS	ACEOOPSU	POACEOUS
	SPECTRAL		SONANCES	ACEOORTT	COROTATE
ACELPRSU	SPECULAR	ACENNOSY	NOYANCES	ACEOORTV	EVOCATOR
ACELPRTY	CALYPTER	ACENNOSZ	CANZONES		OVERCOAT
ACELPSSU	CAPSULES	ACENNOTT	COTENANT	ACEOPPRS	COPPERAS
	SCALEUPS	ACENNOTV	COVENANT	ACEOPRRT	RECAPTOR
	UPSCALES	ACENNOTZ	CANZONET	ACEOPRST	POSTRACE
ACELPTUU	CUPULATE	ACENNPRY	PERNANCY	ACEOPRSX	EXOCARPS
ACELPTUY	EUCALYPT	ACENNRSS	SCANNERS	ACEOPRTT	ATTERCOP
ACELQRSU	CLAQUERS	ACENNSUY	SEACUNNY	ACEOPRTU	OUTCAPER
	LACQUERS	ACENOORT	CORONATE	ACEOPSTU	OUTPACES
ACELQRUU	CLAQUEUR	ACENOOTZ	ECTOZOAN		SAUCEPOT
ACELQSUY	LACQUEYS	ACENOPRT	COPARENT	ACEORRST	ACROTERS
ACELRRSW	CRAWLERS		PORTANCE		CREATORS
	SCRAWLER	ACENOPST	CAPSTONE		REACTORS
ACELRSSS	CLASSERS		OPENCAST	ACEORRSU	CAROUSER
	SCARLESS	ACENOPSU	PONCEAUS	ACEORRTT	RETROACT
ACELRSST	SCARLETS	ACENOPUX	PONCEAUX	ACEORRTU	EUROCRAT
ACELRSSU	RECUSALS	ACENOQTU	COTQUEAN	ACEORRTV	CAVORTER
	SECULARS	ACENORRW	CAREWORN	ACEORRVW	OVERCRAW
ACELRSTT	CLATTERS	ACENORRY	CRAYONER	ACEORSST	COARSEST
	SCRATTLE	ACENORSS	COARSENS		COASTERS
ACELRSTU	RAUCLEST		NARCOSES	ACEORSSU	CAROUSES
ACELRTTU	CULTRATE	ACENORST	ANCESTOR	ACEORSTT	SECTATOR
ACELRTTY	CLATTERY		ENACTORS	ACEORSTU	OUTRACES
ACELSSTT	TACTLESS		SARCONET	ACEORSTV	OVERACTS
ACELSSTU	CUTLASES		SORTANCE		OVERCAST
ACELSSTY	SCYTALES	ACENORSU	CARNEOUS	ACEORSTX	EXACTORS
ACELSSUX	EXCUSALS		NACREOUS	ACEORTUY	EUCARYOT
ACEMMOTY	MYCETOMA	ACENORTT	CONTRATE	ACEOSSTU	SEASCOUT
ACEMMRRS	CRAMMERS	ACENORTU	COURANTE	ACEOSTTT	COATTEST

ACEOSTTU	OUTCASTE	**ACFHIRSW**	CRAWFISH	**ACGGGINS**	SCAGGING
ACEOSTTV	CAVETTOS	**ACFHIRSY**	CRAYFISH	**ACGGHINN**	CHANGING
ACEOSTUU	AUTOCUES	**ACFHISSU**	FUCHSIAS		GANCHING
ACEOTUUX	COUTEAUX	**ACFHLMRU**	CHARMFUL	**ACGGHINR**	CHARGING
ACEOTUXY	AUXOCYTE	**ACFHLTUW**	WATCHFUL	**ACGGHLUU**	CHUGALUG
ACEPPRRS	CRAPPERS	**ACFHMNOR**	CHAMFRON	**ACGGIINN**	INCAGING
	SCRAPPER	**ACFHNNOR**	CHANFRON	**ACGGIINT**	GIGANTIC
ACEPRRSS	SCARPERS	**ACFHNOSU**	FAUCHONS	**ACGGIIOS**	ISAGOGIC
	SCRAPERS	**ACFHRSTU**	FUTHARCS	**ACGGILNN**	CANGLING
ACEPRRSU	SUPERCAR	**ACFIILST**	FISTICAL		CLANGING
ACEPRRTU	CAPTURER	**ACFIILSV**	SALVIFIC		GLANCING
ACEPRSST	PRECASTS	**ACFIILTY**	FACILITY	**ACGGILRV**	CRAGGILY
ACEPRSSU	SCAUPERS	**ACFIIMPS**	PACIFISM	**ACGGINNO**	CONGAING
ACEPRSTU	CAPTURES	**ACFIIMSS**	FASCISMI	**ACGGINNU**	UNCAGING
	PRESCUTA	**ACFIIPST**	PACIFIST	**ACGGINOR**	CARGOING
ACEPSTTY	TYPECAST	**ACFIISST**	FASCISTI	**ACGGIOOR**	CORAGGIO
ACEQRSTU	RACQUETS		FASCITIS	**ACGGLNOU**	GLUCAGON
ACEQSSTU	ACQUESTS	**ACFIKLNS**	CALFSKIN	**ACGGLRSY**	SCRAGGLY
ACERRSTT	RETRACTS	**ACFIKNNS**	FINNACKS	**ACGHHIJK**	HIGHJACK
ACERRSTU	TRACEURS	**ACFILLSY**	FISCALLY	**ACGHHINN**	HANCHING
ACERRSUV	VERRUCAS	**ACFILNOR**	FORNICAL	**ACGHHINT**	HATCHING
ACERSSST	CRASSEST	**ACFILNOS**	FOLACINS	**ACGHIIMN**	MICHIGAN
ACERSSSU	SUCRASES	**ACFILNOT**	CALIFONT	**ACGHIINN**	CHAINING
ACERSSTT	SCATTERS	**ACFILORT**	TRIFOCAL	**ACGHIINR**	CHAIRING
ACERSSTY	ACTRESSY	**ACFILOTU**	CLAFOUTI	**ACGHIKLN**	CHALKING
ACERSTTT	TETRACTS	**ACFILRTY**	CRAFTILY		HACKLING
ACERSTTU	CRUSTATE	**ACFILSSY**	CLASSIFY	**ACGHIKNR**	CHARKING
ACERSTTX	EXTRACTS	**ACFILSTU**	SULFATIC	**ACGHIKNS**	HACKINGS
ACERSTTY	CYTASTER	**ACFIMNRU**	FRANCIUM		SHACKING
	SCATTERY	**ACFIMORR**	ARCIFORM	**ACGHIKNT**	THACKING
ACERSTUX	CURTAXES	**ACFIMORS**	FORMICAS	**ACGHIKNW**	WHACKING
ACERTTUW	CUTWATER	**ACFIMOSS**	FASCISMO	**ACGHILNN**	LANCHING
ACFFGHIN	CHAFFING	**ACFIMSSS**	FASCISMS	**ACGHILNS**	CLASHING
ACFFHNOR	CHAFFRON	**ACFINORT**	FRACTION	**ACGHILNT**	LATCHING
ACFFIILO	OFFICIAL	**ACFINOST**	FACTIONS	**ACGHILNU**	LAUCHING
ACFFIIST	CAITIFFS	**ACFINPRS**	SCARFPIN	**ACGHILNY**	ACHINGLY
ACFFIKMS	MAFFICKS	**ACFINRST**	INFARCTS	**ACGHILOR**	OLIGARCH
ACFFILNU	FANCIFUL		INFRACTS	**ACGHIMNP**	CHAMPING
ACFFILST	AFFLICTS	**ACFINSTY**	SANCTIFY	**ACGHIMNR**	CHARMING
ACFFIRST	TRAFFICS	**ACFIOSTU**	FACTIOUS		MARCHING
ACFFKORT	OFFTRACK	**ACFIRTUY**	FURACITY	**ACGHIMNT**	MATCHING
ACFFLOSW	SCOFFLAW	**ACFISSST**	FASCISTS	**ACGHINNR**	RANCHING
ACFFOSST	CASTOFFS	**ACFKLLOR**	ROCKFALL	**ACGHINNT**	CHANTING
	OFFCASTS	**ACFKLORS**	FORSLACK	**ACGHINNU**	UNACHING
ACFGHINU	CHAUFING	**ACFKLOST**	LOCKFAST	**ACGHINOP**	POACHING
ACFGHITT	CATFIGHT	**ACFKLRSU**	RACKFULS	**ACGHINOR**	ROACHING
ACFGIIMN	MAGNIFIC	**ACFKLRUW**	WRACKFUL	**ACGHINPP**	CHAPPING
ACFGIIPR	CAPRIFIG	**ACFKLSSU**	SACKFULS	**ACGHINPR**	PARCHING
ACFGIKLN	FLACKING		SACKSFUL	**ACGHINPT**	NIGHTCAP
ACFGIKNR	FRACKING	**ACFKOSTT**	FATSTOCK		PATCHING
ACFGINNY	FANCYING	**ACFLMNOO**	MOONCALF	**ACGHINRR**	CHARRING
ACFGINRS	FARCINGS	**ACFLNNOO**	NONFOCAL	**ACGHINRS**	ARCHINGS
	SCARFING	**ACFLNORY**	FALCONRY		CHAGRINS
ACFGINRT	CRAFTING	**ACFLOOPS**	FOOLSCAP		CRASHING
	FRACTING	**ACFLOPSW**	COWFLAPS	**ACGHINRT**	CHARTING
ACFGITUY	FUGACITY	**ACFLORSU**	SCROFULA		RATCHING
ACFGKNOP	PACKFONG	**ACFLOTTU**	FLOATCUT	**ACGHINRU**	CHURINGA
ACFGLNOR	CORNFLAG	**ACFLRRUU**	FURCULAR		NURAGHIC
ACFHHINW	HAWFINCH	**ACFLRSTU**	CARTFULS	**ACGHINSS**	CHASINGS
ACFHIJKS	JACKFISH	**ACFMOTTU**	FACTOTUM	**ACGHINST**	SCATHING
ACFHILNO	FALCHION	**ACFNNOST**	NONFACTS	**ACGHINSW**	CHINWAGS
ACFHILOS	COALFISH	**ACFNRSTU**	FRUCTANS	**ACGHINTT**	CHATTING
ACFHINOU	FAUCHION	**ACFRRSTU**	FRACTURS	**ACGHINTW**	WATCHING
ACFHIRSS	SCARFISH	**ACGGGILN**	CLAGGING	**ACGHINTY**	YACHTING

ACGHINUV	VAUCHING	**ACGILMNS**	CALMINGS		SCRAPING
ACGHIPRS	GRAPHICS	**ACGILMNU**	MACULING	**ACGINPSS**	SPACINGS
ACGHIQTU	ACQUIGHT	**ACGILMTU**	GLUTAMIC	**ACGINPSU**	SCAUPING
ACGHIRSS	SCRAIGHS	**ACGILNNT**	CANTLING	**ACGINRRS**	SCARRING
ACGHLLOR	GRALLOCH	**ACGILNNU**	LAUNCING	**ACGINRRY**	CARRYING
ACGHLMOO	LOGOMACH		UNLACING	**ACGINRSS**	SACRINGS
ACGHLOOY	CHAOLOGY	**ACGILNOR**	CAROLING	**ACGINRST**	SCARTING
ACGHLSTU	CLAUGHTS		ORACLING		TRACINGS
ACGHNRYY	GYNARCHY	**ACGILNOS**	SOLACING	**ACGINRSU**	SCAURING
ACGHNTUU	UNCAUGHT	**ACGILNOT**	LOCATING	**ACGINRSV**	CARVINGS
ACGHORSU	CHORAGUS	**ACGILNPP**	CLAPPING		CRAVINGS
ACGHPTUU	UPCAUGHT	**ACGILNPS**	CLASPING	**ACGINRTT**	TRACTING
ACGHRRSU	CURRAGHS		PLACINGS	**ACGINRTU**	CURATING
ACGHRSSU	SCRAUGHS		SCALPING	**ACGINSST**	CASTINGS
ACGIILMN	CLAIMING	**ACGILNQU**	CALQUING	**ACGINSTT**	SCATTING
	MALICING	**ACGILNRS**	CARLINGS	**ACGINSUV**	VICUGNAS
ACGIILNN	INLACING	**ACGILNRT**	CLARTING	**ACGIOORS**	GRACIOSO
ACGIILNO	LOGICIAN	**ACGILNRU**	CINGULAR	**ACGIORST**	ORGASTIC
ACGIILNS	SCAILING	**ACGILNRW**	CRAWLING	**ACGIORSU**	GRACIOUS
ACGIILNU	LINGUICA	**ACGILNSS**	CLASSING	**ACGIPRSY**	SPAGYRIC
ACGIILNV	CAVILING		SCALINGS	**ACGJLNOU**	CONJUGAL
ACGIILRS	GRACILIS	**ACGILNST**	CASTLING	**ACGKMMOS**	GAMMOCKS
ACGIIMNT	MICATING		CATLINGS	**ACGKORSV**	GARVOCKS
ACGIIMOS	ISOGAMIC		SCLATING	**ACGLLPSU**	CUPGALLS
ACGIIMST	SIGMATIC	**ACGILNSU**	GLUCINAS	**ACGLMOUU**	COAGULUM
ACGIINNS	INCASING	**ACGILNTT**	CLATTING	**ACGLNORS**	CLANGORS
ACGIINNV	INCAVING	**ACGILNTU**	CLAUTING	**ACGLNORU**	CLANGOUR
ACGIINRT	GRANITIC	**ACGILNUY**	GUANYLIC	**ACGLNOSY**	AGLYCONS
ACGIIPRS	SPAGIRIC	**ACGILRSU**	SURGICAL	**ACGLOORY**	ARCOLOGY
ACGIJJKO	JICKAJOG	**ACGIMMNR**	CRAMMING	**ACGLOSUU**	GLAUCOUS
ACGIJKNS	JACKINGS	**ACGIMMNS**	SCAMMING	**ACGLSSTU**	CUTGLASS
ACGIJLNO	CAJOLING	**ACGIMNOR**	CAROMING	**ACGMNOPS**	CAMPONGS
ACGIJNNU	JAUNCING	**ACGIMNOS**	COAMINGS	**ACGNNOOT**	CONTANGO
ACGIKKNN	KNACKING	**ACGIMNPR**	CRAMPING	**ACGNNORS**	CRANNOGS
ACGIKLMN	MACKLING	**ACGIMNPS**	CAMPINGS	**ACGNOOST**	OCTAGONS
ACGIKLNN	CLANKING		SCAMPING	**ACGNORST**	CONGRATS
ACGIKLNO	CLOAKING	**ACGIMNSY**	GYMNASIC	**ACGORRSY**	GYROCARS
ACGIKLNS	CALKINGS		SYNGAMIC	**ACGORSSW**	COWGRASS
	SLACKING	**ACGIMOPR**	PICOGRAM	**ACGORSUU**	COUGUARS
ACGIKLNT	TACKLING	**ACGIMORS**	ORGASMIC	**ACGPPSUU**	SCUPPAUG
	TALCKING	**ACGIMOUU**	GUAIOCUM	**ACGRSSTU**	CUTGRASS
ACGIKLNU	CAULKING	**ACGINNNS**	CANNINGS	**ACHHILPT**	PHTHALIC
ACGIKLRY	GARLICKY		SCANNING	**ACHHINTW**	WHINCHAT
ACGIKMNO	COMAKING	**ACGINNNU**	NUANCING	**ACHHINTY**	HYACINTH
ACGIKMNS	SMACKING	**ACGINNPR**	PRANCING	**ACHHIPPR**	HIPPARCH
ACGIKNNR	CRANKING	**ACGINNPU**	UNCAPING	**ACHHLLOT**	CHALLOTH
ACGIKNNS	SNACKING	**ACGINNRT**	TRANCING	**ACHHLMOS**	MASHLOCH
ACGIKNNU	UNCAKING	**ACGINNRU**	UNCARING	**ACHHLNOR**	RHONCHAL
ACGIKNOR	CROAKING	**ACGINNRY**	CARNYING	**ACHHLORY**	HOLARCHY
ACGIKNPS	PACKINGS	**ACGINNST**	CANTINGS	**ACHHLPRY**	PHYLARCH
ACGIKNQU	QUACKING		SCANTING	**ACHHLSUY**	SHAUCHLY
ACGIKNRS	ARCKINGS	**ACGINNSU**	UNCASING	**ACHHNTTU**	NUTHATCH
	RACKINGS	**ACGINNUV**	VAUNCING		UNTHATCH
ACGIKNRT	TRACKING	**ACGINOPT**	COAPTING	**ACHHOSST**	TOSHACHS
ACGIKNRW	WRACKING	**ACGINORS**	ORGANICS	**ACHHPPSU**	CHUPPAHS
ACGIKNSS	SACKINGS	**ACGINORY**	CONGIARY	**ACHHPTUZ**	CHUTZPAH
ACGIKNST	STACKING	**ACGINOST**	AGNOSTIC	**ACHIIKMS**	KAMICHIS
	TACKINGS		COASTING	**ACHIILMS**	CHILIASM
ACGIKPRS	GRIPSACK		COATINGS	**ACHIILPT**	HAPLITIC
ACGILLNS	CALLINGS		COTINGAS	**ACHIILST**	CHILIAST
ACGILMMN	CLAMMING	**ACGINPPR**	CRAPPING	**ACHIINRT**	TRICHINA
ACGILMNO	GNOMICAL	**ACGINPPS**	CAPPINGS	**ACHIINST**	CHIANTIS
ACGILMNP	CAMPLING	**ACGINPRS**	CARPINGS	**ACHIIPRS**	PARCHISI
	CLAMPING		SCARPING	**ACHIIPSS**	PACHISIS

ACHIIRST	RACHITIS	ACHINNOP	PANCHION	ACHMNORS	MONARCHS
ACHIIRSU	ISCHURIA	ACHINNSU	ANCHUSIN		NOMARCHS
ACHIJKPW	WHIPJACK		UNCHAINS	ACHMNORY	MONARCHY
ACHIJNST	JACINTHS	ACHINOPR	PAROCHIN		NOMARCHY
ACHIKKNS	KNACKISH		PROCHAIN	ACHMNRSU	UNCHARMS
ACHIKKSW	KICKSHAW	ACHINOPS	APHONICS	ACHMNRTU	TRUCHMAN
ACHIKLLW	HICKWALL	ACHINORT	ANORTHIC	ACHMOORT	CHATROOM
ACHIKLMY	HICKYMAL	ACHINOST	CHITOSAN	ACHMOPRS	CAMPHORS
ACHIKLOR	HAIRLOCK	ACHINOSY	ONYCHIAS	ACHMORSZ	MACHZORS
ACHIKLPT	CHALKPIT	ACHINOTZ	HOACTZIN	ACHMORTU	OUTCHARM
ACHIKNOP	PACHINKO	ACHINPSY	SPINACHY		OUTMARCH
ACHIKNRS	CRANKISH	ACHINRSU	UNCHAIRS	ACHMOSST	STOMACHS
ACHIKQSU	QUACKISH	ACHINRSZ	ZARNICHS	ACHMOSTY	STOMACHY
ACHIKRSS	RICKSHAS	ACHINSUV	CHAUVINS	ACHMOTTU	OUTMATCH
ACHIKRSW	RICKSHAW	ACHIOPRT	ATROPHIC	ACHMPSTU	MATCHUPS
ACHIKRSY	HAYRICKS	ACHIOPSS	ISOPACHS	ACHMSSUW	CUMSHAWS
ACHIKSSS	SHICKSAS	ACHIORSS	COARSISH	ACHNNORU	UNANCHOR
ACHILLOR	ORCHILLA	ACHIORST	ACTORISH	ACHNNOSS	CHANSONS
ACHILLRT	CLITHRAL		CHARIOTS	ACHNOOSY	CHANOYOS
ACHILMOP	OMPHALIC		HARICOTS	ACHNORST	CHANTORS
ACHILMOS	MALICHOS	ACHIORTV	TOVARICH	ACHNORXY	CHRONAXY
	MOCHILAS	ACHIOSST	ISOTACHS	ACHNOSTY	TACHYONS
ACHILMRS	CHRISMAL	ACHIPPSS	SAPPHICS	ACHNOSUY	CHANOYUS
ACHILMTY	MYTHICAL	ACHIPRRT	PARRITCH	ACHNPPSS	SCHNAPPS
ACHILNNS	CLANNISH		PHRATRIC	ACHNRSTU	UNSTARCH
ACHILNOO	HOOLICAN	ACHIPSTU	CHUPATIS	ACHNRSYY	SYNARCHY
ACHILNOS	LICHANOS	ACHIPSTW	WHIPCATS	ACHNRTUY	CHAUNTRY
ACHILNPS	CLANSHIP	ACHIPTTU	CHUPATTI	ACHOORTU	COAUTHOR
ACHILOPR	ORPHICAL	ACHIQRSU	CHARQUIS	ACHOORTY	CHAYROOT
	RHOPALIC	ACHIRRST	TRIARCHS	ACHOPRST	TOPARCHS
ACHILOPU	PACHOULI	ACHIRRTY	TRIARCHY	ACHOPRSY	CHARPOYS
ACHILORT	ACROLITH	ACHIRSTT	CHARTIST	ACHOPRTY	TOPARCHY
ACHILPSY	PHYSICAL		STRAICHT	ACHORRST	TROCHARS
ACHILPTY	PATCHILY	ACHIRSTU	HAIRCUTS	ACHOTTUW	OUTWATCH
ACHILRUV	CHYLURIA	ACHISSTT	TACHISTS		WATCHOUT
ACHILRVV	CHIVALRY	ACHISTTY	CHASTITY	ACHPRSTU	PUSHCART
ACHILSWY	LICHWAYS	ACHKKORW	HACKWORK	ACHPSTUZ	CHUTZPAS
ACHILTTY	CHATTILY	ACHKKRSU	CHUKKARS	ACHPTTUY	CHUPATTY
ACHIMMOS	MACHISMO	ACHKMMOS	HAMMOCKS	ACHRRTUY	CRAYTHUR
	MACHOISM	ACHKMORS	SHAMROCK	ACHRSTTU	STRAUCHT
ACHIMMST	MISMATCH	ACHKNNUU	NUNCHAKU	ACIIILMN	INIMICAL
ACHIMNNW	WINCHMAN	ACHKNOOT	CANTHOOK	ACIIILNV	CIVILIAN
ACHIMNOP	CHAMPION	ACHKOPSS	HOPSACKS	ACIIINST	ISATINIC
ACHIMNOR	CHOIRMAN	ACHKOSSS	HASSOCKS	ACIIKLNO	KAOLINIC
	HARMONIC	ACHKOSSY	HASSOCKY	ACIIKNNN	CANNIKIN
	OMNIARCH	ACHKOSTT	HATTOCKS	ACIIKNNS	CANIKINS
ACHIMNOS	MANIHOCS	ACHLLOOS	ALCOHOLS	ACIIKNTY	KYANITIC
	MOHICANS	ACHLLORS	CHLORALS	ACIIKPRT	PAITRICK
ACHIMNPT	PITCHMAN	ACHLLORY	CHORALLY	ACIILLNS	ALLICINS
ACHIMNSU	INASMUCH	ACHLMOPS	CAMPHOLS	ACIILLNV	VANILLIC
ACHIMOPR	AMPHORIC	ACHLMSTZ	SCHMALTZ	ACIILLSU	SILICULA
ACHIMOSS	CHAMISOS	ACHLMSYZ	SCHMALZY	ACIILLSV	SILVICAL
	ISOCHASM	ACHLNOOU	OULACHON	ACIILLTV	VILLATIC
ACHIMPSS	SCAMPISH	ACHLNOSY	HALCYONS	ACIILMMS	MISCLAIM
ACHIMPST	MISPATCH	ACHLNSTU	TULCHANS	ACIILMNR	CRIMINAL
ACHIMRSS	CHARISMS	ACHLNSTY	STANCHLY	ACIILMNU	ALUMINIC
ACHIMRST	CHARTISM	ACHLOPRS	RAPLOCHS	ACIILMOT	COMITIAL
ACHIMRTY	ARYTHMIC	ACHLOPRT	CALTHROP	ACIILMPT	PALMITIC
ACHIMSSS	SCHISMAS	ACHLOPRY	POLYARCH	ACIILMRT	MARLITIC
ACHIMSST	MASTICHS	ACHLOPTT	POTLATCH	ACIILMSS	LAICISMS
	TACHISMS	ACHLORSS	SCHOLARS	ACIILNOR	IRONICAL
ACHIMSSU	CHIASMUS	ACHLOSSW	SALCHOWS	ACIILNOT	TALIONIC
ACHIMTUY	CYATHIUM	ACHLOSTY	ACOLYTHS	ACIILNPS	PISCINAL
		ACHLOTWX	WAXCLOTH	ACIILNPT	PLATINIC

ACIILNSS	SALICINS	ACIJSUZZ	JACUZZIS	ACILNORT	CILANTRO
ACIILOSV	VILIACOS	ACIKLMOT	MOCKTAIL		CONTRAIL
ACIILRTT	TRITICAL	ACIKLMST	MALSTICK	ACILNOSU	UNSOCIAL
ACIILRTU	URALITIC	ACIKLNOT	ANTILOCK	ACILNOSY	ACYLOINS
ACIILSST	SILASTIC	ACIKLNRY	CRANKILY	ACILNOUV	UNIVOCAL
ACIILSTV	SILVATIC	ACIKLORS	AIRLOCKS	ACILNPSS	INCLASPS
ACIIMMNP	MINICAMP	ACIKLORY	CROAKILY		SCALPINS
ACIIMMNS	MINICAMS	ACIKMNST	STICKMAN	ACILNRSU	CISLUNAR
ACIIMNNO	AMNIONIC	ACIKMOOS	OOMIACKS	ACILNRUY	CULINARY
ACIIMNNT	MANNITIC	ACIKMOST	COMATIKS		URANYLIC
ACIIMNOR	MORAINIC	ACIKMPRS	RAMPICKS	ACILNSTU	LUNATICS
ACIIMNOS	SIMONIAC	ACIKMPST	MAPSTICK		SULTANIC
ACIIMNOT	AMNIOTIC	ACIKMPSW	PICKMAWS	ACILNSTY	SCANTILY
ACIIMNRS	MINICARS	ACIKMQSU	QUACKISM	ACILNTTU	ANTICULT
ACIIMNST	ACTINISM	ACIKNNPR	CRANKPIN	ACILNTTY	INTACTLY
ACIIMNSU	MUSICIAN	ACIKNNPS	PANNICKS	ACILOPRT	TROPICAL
ACIIMNTU	ACTINIUM	ACIKNORT	ANTIROCK	ACILOPRV	VALPROIC
ACIIMNTY	IMITANCY	ACIKNSST	CATSKINS	ACILOPST	CAPITOLS
	INTIMACY	ACIKNSTT	TINTACKS		COALPITS
	MINACITY	ACIKPRST	PATRICKS		POSTICAL
ACIIMOST	COMITIAS		TRIPACKS	ACILORRS	RACLOIRS
	IOTACISM	ACIKSTTY	STATICKY	ACILORRV	CORRIVAL
ACIIMOTT	AMITOTIC	ACILLLNY	CLINALLY	ACILORST	CALORIST
ACIIMPRT	PRIMATIC	ACILLLOP	POLLICAL	ACILORSV	CORIVALS
ACIIMPRV	VAMPIRIC	ACILLMMY	CLAMMILY	ACILORTV	VORTICAL
ACIIMRST	SCIMITAR	ACILLMOS	LOCALISM	ACILORYZ	ZIRCALOY
ACIIMRTU	MURIATIC	ACILLMSS	MISCALLS	ACILOSTV	VOCALIST
ACIIMSST	ITACISMS	ACILLNOO	COLONIAL	ACILOTUV	OUTCAVIL
ACIIMSTT	ATTICISM	ACILLNOR	CARILLON	ACILOTVY	VOCALITY
	MASTITIC	ACILLNOS	SCALLION	ACILPRST	CLIPARTS
ACIIMSTV	ACTIVISM	ACILLNUY	UNCIALLY	ACILPRSU	SPICULAR
ACIIMTUV	VIATICUM	ACILLOQU	COQUILLA	ACILPRTU	PICTURAL
ACIINNOT	INACTION	ACILLORT	CLITORAL	ACILPSST	PLASTICS
	NICOTIAN	ACILLORY	COLLYRIA	ACILPSUU	APICULUS
ACIINNQU	CINQUAIN	ACILLOST	LOCALIST	ACILRRTU	TURRICAL
ACIINNRV	NIRVANIC	ACILLOSY	SOCIALLY	ACILRSTU	CURTAILS
ACIINNTT	INCITANT	ACILLOTY	COITALLY		RUSTICAL
ACIINNTY	CANINITY		LOCALITY	ACILRTUV	CULTIVAR
ACIINOPT	OPTICIAN	ACILLOUV	COLLUVIA		CURVITAL
ACIINORZ	ZIRCONIA	ACILLSSY	CLASSILY	ACILSSST	CLASSIST
ACIINOSS	ASINICOS	ACILMNNY	CINNAMYL	ACILSTTY	SCATTILY
ACIINOSV	AVIONICS	ACILMNOP	COMPLAIN	ACILSTUV	VICTUALS
ACIINOTT	CITATION	ACILMNOS	LACONISM	ACILSTVY	SYLVATIC
ACIINPSS	PISCINAS		LIMACONS	ACIMMOSS	ACOSMISM
ACIINPTY	ANTIPYIC	ACILMOOS	SCOLIOMA	ACIMMTUY	CYMATIUM
ACIINRSS	NARCISSI	ACILMOPR	PICLORAM	ACIMNNNO	CINNAMON
ACIINRSU	URANISCI		PROCLAIM	ACIMNOOR	ACROMION
ACIINRTU	URANITIC	ACILMOPS	OILCAMPS	ACIMNOPS	CAMPIONS
ACIINTTY	ANTICITY	ACILMOPT	COMPITAL	ACIMNORS	MARCONIS
ACIIOPST	APOSITIC	ACILMOSV	VOCALISM		MINORCAS
ACIIORST	AORISTIC	ACILMPTU	PLACITUM	ACIMNORT	ROMANTIC
ACIIORTV	VICTORIA	ACILMRTU	MULTICAR	ACIMNORU	CONARIUM
ACIIPPST	PAPISTIC	ACILMSSS	CLASSISM		COUMARIN
ACIIRSST	TRIASSIC		MISCLASS	ACIMNORY	ACRIMONY
ACIIRSTT	ARTISTIC	ACILMSSU	MUSICALS	ACIMNOSS	MOCASSIN
	TRIATICS	ACILMSTY	MYSTICAL	ACIMNOST	MONASTIC
ACIISTTT	ATTICIST	ACILMTUY	ULTIMACY	ACIMNOTU	ACONITUM
ACIISTTU	AUTISTIC	ACILNNOS	CANNOLIS	ACIMNPSU	PANICUMS
ACIISTTV	ACTIVIST	ACILNOOT	LOCATION	ACIMNPTY	TYMPANIC
ACIITTVY	ACTIVITY	ACILNOOV	VOCALION	ACIMNRSS	NARCISMS
ACIITVVY	VIVACITY	ACILNOPS	SALPICON	ACIMNRSU	CRANIUMS
ACIJKKPS	SKIPJACK	ACILNOPT	PLATONIC		CUMARINS
ACIJKSTW	STICKJAW	ACILNORS	CLARINOS	ACIMNSTT	CATMINTS
ACIJRSSU	JURASSIC		CLARIONS	ACIMNSTU	TSUNAMIC

ACIMOOST	SCOTOMIA	ACINPRSY	CYPRIANS	ACKLMNOS	LOCKSMAN
ACIMOPRT	IMPACTOR	ACINPSTY	SYNAPTIC	ACKLMORS	ARMLOCKS
ACIMOPST	APOMICTS	ACINQSTU	QUANTICS		LOCKRAMS
ACIMORST	ACROTISM	ACINRSST	NARCISTS	ACKLNOSU	UNCLOAKS
ACIMORSY	CRAMOISY	ACINRSSU	CRUSIANS	ACKLOOPW	WOOLPACK
ACIMOSST	ACOSMIST	ACINRSTU	CURTAINS	ACKLOORS	OARLOCKS
	MASSICOT		SATURNIC	ACKLOOSW	WOOLSACK
ACIMOSTT	MASTICOT		TURACINS	ACKLORSV	LAVROCKS
	STOMATIC	ACINRTTU	TACITURN	ACKLORSW	WARLOCKS
ACIMPRST	CRAMPITS		URTICANT	ACKLORSY	ROCKLAYS
	PTARMICS	ACINSTTY	SANCTITY	ACKLOSSS	LASSOCKS
ACIMRRSY	MISCARRY		SCANTITY	ACKMMMOS	MAMMOCKS
ACIMRSSZ	CZARISMS	ACINSTYY	SYNCYTIA	ACKMNOST	STOCKMAN
ACIMSSST	MISCASTS	ACIOOPST	SCOTOPIA	ACKMNRTU	TRUCKMAN
ACIMSSTT	TACTISMS	ACIOOTYZ	ZOOCYTIA	ACKMOSST	STOMACKS
ACINNNOO	NONANOIC	ACIOPRST	APRICOTS	ACKMOSTT	MATTOCKS
ACINNOOT	CONATION		PISCATOR	ACKNOPSW	SNOWPACK
	INTONACO	ACIOPRTT	PROTATIC	ACKNORSU	CRANKOUS
ACINNOQU	CONQUIAN	ACIOPRTY	POTICARY	ACKNRSTU	UNTRACKS
ACINNORR	NARICORN	ACIOPSST	POTASSIC	ACKNSSTU	UNSTACKS
ACINNOSS	SCANSION	ACIOPSSU	SPACIOUS	ACKOPRRS	PARROCKS
ACINNOST	ACTINONS	ACIOPSTU	AUTOPSIC	ACKOPRRT	TRAPROCK
	CANONIST		CAPTIOUS	ACKORRST	TARROCKS
	CANTIONS	ACIOPTTU	AUTOPTIC	ACKORSTW	CATWORKS
	CONTAINS	ACIORRSS	CORSAIRS	ACKOSSTW	TOWSACKS
	SANCTION	ACIORSSU	SCARIOUS	ACKOSWZZ	WAZZOCKS
	SONANTIC	ACIORSTT	CITATORS	ACKPSSTU	STACKUPS
ACINNOTU	CONTINUA		RICOTTAS	ACLLLNOY	CLONALLY
	COUNTIAN	ACIORTTY	ATROCITY	ACLLMNOU	COLUMNAL
ACINNRTY	TYRANNIC		CITATORY	ACLLMORU	CORALLUM
ACINNSTU	ANNICUTS	ACIORTVY	VORACITY	ACLLMOSU	MOLLUSCA
ACINNSTY	INSTANCY	ACIOSSST	COASSIST	ACLLNNOO	NONLOCAL
ACINOOPR	PICAROON	ACIOSSTY	ISOSTACY	ACLLOORS	COROLLAS
ACINOOTV	VOCATION	ACIOSTUU	CAUTIOUS	ACLLOORT	COLLATOR
ACINOPPT	PANOPTIC	ACIPRRUU	PIRARUCU	ACLLOOSS	COLOSSAL
ACINOPRS	PARSONIC	ACIPRSSS	CASSPIRS	ACLLOPSS	SCALLOPS
ACINOPST	CAPTIONS	ACIPRSTT	TIPCARTS	ACLLORUY	OCULARLY
	PACTIONS	ACIPRTTY	TRIPTYCA	ACLLOSTU	LOCUSTAL
ACINOPTU	ACUPOINT	ACIPSSST	SPASTICS		OUTCALLS
ACINOQSU	COQUINAS	ACIQRSTU	QUARTICS	ACLLOSTY	COSTALLY
ACINORRS	CARRIONS	ACIQSSTU	ACQUISTS	ACLLRSYY	ACRYLYLS
ACINORRT	CARROTIN	ACIRRTTX	TRACTRIX	ACLLRTUU	CULTURAL
	CONTRAIR	ACIRRTUX	CURATRIX	ACLMMNOU	COMMUNAL
ACINORSS	NARCOSIS	ACIRSSST	SACRISTS	ACLMMORW	CLAMWORM
ACINORST	CANTORIS	ACIRSSTT	ASTRICTS	ACLMNOOO	COOLAMON
	CAROTINS	ACIRSSTW	TWISCARS	ACLMNOOR	COLORMAN
	CORTINAS	ACIRSSTY	SACRISTY	ACLMNORU	COLUMNAR
ACINORSV	CORVINAS	ACIRSSTZ	CZARISTS	ACLMNORY	NORMALCY
ACINORTT	TRACTION	ACISSSTU	CASUISTS	ACLMNPSU	UNCLAMPS
ACINORTU	NOCTURIA	ACISSTTU	CATSUITS	ACLMORSU	CLAMOURS
ACINORTY	CARYOTIN	ACISSTUV	VACUISTS	ACLMORTU	CROTALUM
ACINOSSS	CAISSONS	ACISTTUY	ASTUCITY	ACLMPRSU	SCALPRUM
	CASSINOS	ACJKKSSY	SKYJACKS	ACLMRSUU	MUSCULAR
ACINOSSY	CYANOSIS	ACJKLLOR	JACKROLL	ACLMSSTU	MASSCULT
ACINOSTT	OSCITANT	ACJKLOSW	LOCKJAWS	ACLMSTUU	CUSTUMAL
	TACTIONS	ACJKNNOS	JANNOCKS	ACLMSUUV	VASCULUM
ACINOSTU	ANTICOUS	ACJKOPST	JACKPOTS	ACLNNOOS	NONCOLAS
	AUCTIONS	ACJMNSTU	MUNTJACS	ACLNNOOV	NONVOCAL
	CAUTIONS	ACJPSTUU	CAJUPUTS	ACLNNOSS	NONCLASS
ACINOSTW	WAINSCOT	ACKKMOPR	POCKMARK	ACLNOORS	CORONALS
ACINOSWX	COXSWAIN	ACKKORRW	RACKWORK	ACLNOORT	COLORANT
ACINOTTX	TOXICANT	ACKLLOPS	POLLACKS	ACLNOOST	COOLANTS
ACINPQUY	PIQUANCY	ACKLLOSY	LAYLOCKS		OCTANOLS
ACINPRST	CANTRIPS	ACKLLPSU	SKULLCAP	ACLNOOSV	VOLCANOS

ACLNOPSY	SYNCOPAL	ACNORRTY	CONTRARY	ADDEEELV	DELEAVED
ACLNORSU	CONSULAR	ACNORSTT	CONTRAST	ADDEEEMN	DEMEANED
	COURLANS		CONTRATS	ADDEEEMR	REMEADED
ACLNORTU	CALUTRON	ACNORSTU	COURANTS	ADDEEENR	DEADENER
ACLNOSSS	CLASSONS	ACNORTTU	TURNCOAT		ENDEARED
ACLNOSTU	CONSULTA	ACNORTUY	NOCTUARY	ADDEEENW	DANEWEED
	OSCULANT	ACNOSSTW	SNOWCATS	ADDEEESY	DEADEYES
ACLNPSSU	UNCLASPS	ACNPRSSY	SYNCARPS	ADDEEFGN	DEFANGED
ACLNPTUU	PUNCTUAL	ACNPRSUY	SPRAUNCY	ADDEEFHN	HANDFEED
ACLNSSUY	UNCLASSY	ACNPRSYY	SYNCARPY	ADDEEFIL	DEFILADE
ACLOOPPS	ALCOPOPS	ACNRRSTU	CURRANTS	ADDEEFIM	MADEFIED
ACLOOPRR	CORPORAL	ACNRRTUY	CURRANTY	ADDEEFLT	DEFLATED
ACLOOPRS	CARPOOLS	ACOOPRRS	CORPORAS	ADDEEFMO	DEFOAMED
ACLOORST	LOCATORS	ACOOPRST	COPASTOR	ADDEEFNU	UNDEAFED
ACLOORWY	COLORWAY		ROOTCAPS	ADDEEFPR	PREFADED
ACLOPRRU	PROCURAL	ACOOPSTT	TOPCOATS	ADDEEFRY	DEFRAYED
ACLOPRST	CALTROPS	ACOORSTU	TOURACOS		FEEDYARD
ACLOPRXY	XYLOCARP	ACOPPRRS	PROCARPS	ADDEEFTT	DEFATTED
ACLOPSSU	SCOPULAS	ACOPRRST	CARPORTS	ADDEEGGR	DAGGERED
ACLOPSSY	CALYPSOS	ACOPRRTT	PROTRACT	ADDEEGHR	HARDEDGE
ACLOPSUU	OPUSCULA	ACORRSTT	TRACTORS	ADDEEGLL	ALLEDGED
ACLORRTU	TORCULAR	ACORRSTU	CURATORS	ADDEEGLN	DANEGELD
ACLORTUW	OUTCRAWL	ACORRTUY	CARRYOUT	ADDEEGLZ	DEGLAZED
ACLOSSTU	OUTCLASS		CURATORY	ADDEEGNR	DANGERED
ACLRSSTY	CRYSTALS	ACORSSTU	SURCOATS		DERANGED
ACMMNOSY	SCAMMONY	ACORSSUW	CURASSOW		GANDERED
ACMMNOYY	MYOMANCY	ACORSSWY	CROSSWAY		GARDENED
ACMNOOPR	CRAMPOON	ACORSTTY	CRYOSTAT	ADDEEGOR	DOGEARED
	MONOCARP	ACORSTUU	TURACOUS	ADDEEGRR	DEGRADER
ACMNOORR	CROMORNA	ACOSSTTU	OUTCASTS		REGARDED
ACMNOORT	MONOCRAT	ACPSSTUU	USUCAPTS		REGRADED
ACMNOOYZ	ZOOMANCY	ACPSSYCT	PUSSYCAT	ADDEEGRS	DEGRADES
ACMNOPRS	CORPSMAN	ADDDEEEL	DELEADED	ADDEEGSS	DEGASSED
	CRAMPONS	ADDDEEEM	ADDEEMED	ADDEEHLR	HERALDED
ACMNORSY	ACRONYMS	ADDDEEEN	DEADENED	ADDEEHLY	ALDEHYDE
ACMNSSTU	SANCTUMS	ADDDEEGR	DEGRADED	ADDEEHNR	ADHEREND
ACMOOORT	COATROOM	ADDDEEIM	DIADEMED		HARDENED
ACMOOPRS	COPROSMA	ADDDEELR	LADDERED	ADDEEHNS	HEADENDS
ACMOORRT	MOTORCAR	ADDDEEMN	DEMANDED	ADDEEHNU	UNHEADED
ACMOORUU	COUMAROU		MADDENED	ADDEEHOP	DOPEHEAD
ACMOOSST	SCOTOMAS	ADDDEENR	DANDERED	ADDEEHRS	REDHEADS
ACMOPRST	COMPARTS		REDDENDA	ADDEEHRT	THREADED
ACMOPSTU	CAMPOUTS	ADDDEENS	DESANDED	ADDEEIKR	DAIKERED
ACMORRSS	CROSSARM		SADDENED	ADDEEILN	DEADLINE
ACMORSTW	CATWORMS	ADDDEEPS	SEPADDED	ADDEEILR	DEADLIER
	WORMCAST	ADDDEGJU	ADJUDGED		DERAILED
ACMORSTY	COSTMARY	ADDDEIMS	MISADDED		REDIALED
ACMQSTUU	CUMQUATS	ADDDELSW	SWADDLED	ADDEEILT	DETAILED
ACNNNORY	CANNONRY	ADDDELTW	TWADDLED	ADDEEIMT	MEDIATED
ACNNOORT	NONACTOR	ADDDEMNU	ADDENDUM	ADDEEINT	DETAINED
ACNNOSTT	CONSTANT	ADDDEMOO	ADDOOMED	ADDEEINU	UNIDEAED
ACNOOORT	OCTAROON	ADDDENOS	DEODANDS	ADDEEIPR	DIAPERED
ACNOOPRT	COPATRON	ADDDENPU	UNPADDED	ADDEEISS	DISEASED
ACNOORRY	CORONARY	ADDDENRU	DEUDDARN	ADDEEIST	STEADIED
ACNOORST	CARTOONS	ADDDEOOW	DEADWOOD	ADDEEITV	DEVIATED
	CORANTOS	ADDDEORS	ADDORSED	ADDEEKMR	DEMARKED
	OSTRACON	ADDDEOTU	OUTADDED	ADDEEKNR	DARKENED
ACNOORSU	CANOROUS	ADDDEQSU	SQUADDED	ADDEELLM	MEDALLED
ACNOORTU	COURANTO	ADDDGILN	DADDLING	ADDEELLP	PEDALLED
ACNOORTY	CARTOONY	ADDEEEFL	DEFLEAED	ADDEELLV	DEVALLED
	OCTONARY	ADDEEEFN	DEAFENED	ADDEELNO	LOADENED
ACNOPSSW	SNOWCAPS	ADDEEEFT	DEFEATED	ADDEELNP	DEPLANED
ACNORRSU	RANCOURS	ADDEEEJY	DEEJAYED	ADDEELNR	ENLARDED
ACNORRSY	CARRYONS	ADDEEELN	LEADENED		RELANDED

Eight-letter anagrams

ADDEELNU	UNLEADED	ADDEHILR	DIHEDRAL	ADDELLOR	DOLLARED
ADDEELOR	RELOADED	ADDEHINW	HEADWIND	ADDELMOS	DOLMADES
ADDEELPS	DELAPSED	ADDEHIRS	DIEHARDS	ADDELNNU	DUNELAND
ADDEELRS	RESADDLE	ADDEHIRW	RAWHIDED	ADDELNOO	ONLOADED
ADDEELRT	TREADLED	ADDEHLOS	SHEDLOAD	ADDELNOU	DUODENAL
ADDEELST	DESALTED	ADDEHMRU	DRUMHEAD		UNLOADED
ADDEELUV	DEVALUED	ADDEHNNU	UNHANDED	ADDELNPU	PUDENDAL
ADDEEMNN	DEMANNED	ADDEHNSU	UNDASHED	ADDELNRS	DANDLERS
ADDEEMNP	DAMPENED		UNSHADED	ADDELNSU	UNSADDLE
ADDEEMNR	DAMNEDER	ADDEHOPR	DROPHEAD	ADDELOOR	ELDORADO
	DEMANDER	ADDEHORW	HEADWORD	ADDELOPU	UPLOADED
	REDEMAND	ADDEHOSW	SHADOWED	ADDELPRS	PADDLERS
	REMANDED	ADDEHPRU	PURDAHED		SPRADDLE
ADDEEMST	DEMASTED	ADDEHRTY	HYDRATED	ADDELRSS	SADDLERS
ADDEENPP	APPENDED	ADDEIIKS	DIDAKEIS	ADDELRST	STRADDLE
ADDEENPR	PANDERED	ADDEIIMS	DIAMIDES	ADDELRSW	DAWDLERS
ADDEENPX	EXPANDED	ADDEIINZ	DAIDZEIN		SWADDLER
ADDEENRR	DARNEDER	ADDEIIRS	DIARISED		WADDLERS
ADDEENRT	ENDARTED	ADDEIIRZ	DIARIZED	ADDELRSY	SADDLERY
ADDEENRU	DAUNERED	ADDEIITV	ADDITIVE	ADDELRTW	TWADDLER
ADDEENRW	DAWNERED	ADDEIJNO	ADJOINED	ADDELSST	STADDLES
	WANDERED	ADDEIKNP	KIDNAPED	ADDELSSW	SWADDLES
	WARDENED	ADDEILNS	ISLANDED	ADDELSTW	TWADDLES
ADDEENSS	DEADNESS		LANDSIDE	ADDEMMNU	UNDAMMED
ADDEENTT	ATTENDED	ADDEILNT	TIDELAND	ADDEMNNU	UNDAMNED
	DENTATED	ADDEILRS	DIEDRALS	ADDEMNPU	UNDAMPED
ADDEENTU	DENUDATE	ADDEILRW	WADDLIER	ADDEMNST	DAMNDEST
ADDEENUV	UNEVADED	ADDEILSU	DUALISED	ADDEMOSY	DOMESDAY
ADDEEOST	DEODATES	ADDEILSY	DIALYSED	ADDENNOT	DANTONED
ADDEEPRS	RESPADED	ADDEILUZ	DUALIZED	ADDENOPR	PARDONED
ADDEEPRT	DEPARTED	ADDEILYZ	DIALYZED	ADDENORU	UNADORED
	PREDATED	ADDEIMOS	SODAMIDE	ADDENPRU	UNDRAPED
ADDEEPRV	DEPRAVED	ADDEIMRS	DISARMED	ADDENRST	DARNDEST
	PERVADED		MISDREAD		STRANDED
ADDEERRS	DREADERS	ADDEIMST	MISDATED	ADDENRSU	DAUNDERS
ADDEERRT	RETARDED	ADDEIMSY	DISMAYED	ADDENRTU	DRAUNTED
ADDEERRW	REWARDED	ADDEIMTT	ADMITTED		UNTRADED
	WARDERED	ADDEINOR	ORDAINED	ADDENRUW	UNWARDED
ADDEERRY	DEERYARD	ADDEINOS	ADENOIDS	ADDEORTU	OUTDARED
ADDEERSW	SAWDERED		ADONISED	ADDEOTTU	OUTDATED
ADDEERTT	DERATTED		ANODISED	ADDEPRSU	SUPERADD
ADDEERTV	ADVERTED	ADDEINOZ	ADONIZED	ADDEPRTU	UPDARTED
ADDEFFOR	AFFORDED		ANODIZED	ADDFFILO	DAFFODIL
ADDEFIIL	LADIFIED	ADDEINPR	DREPANID	ADDFFINR	DANDRIFF
ADDEFILT	DEADLIFT	ADDEINRS	SARDINED	ADDFFNRU	DANDRUFF
ADDEFILY	LADYFIED	ADDEINRT	INDARTED	ADDFGILN	FADDLING
ADDEFIST	FADDIEST	ADDEINST	DANDIEST	ADDFIMSS	FADDISMS
ADDEFLRU	DREADFUL	ADDEIOPR	PARODIED	ADDFISST	FADDISTS
ADDEFRSU	DEFRAUDS	ADDEIORS	ROADSIDE	ADDGGILN	GLADDING
ADDEGGLR	DRAGGLED		SIDEROAD	ADDGGORU	GUARDDOG
ADDEGHOS	GODHEADS	ADDEIOTX	OXIDATED	ADDGIILN	DAIDLING
ADDEGILO	DIALOGED	ADDEIPPR	DIDAPPER	ADDGIIRS	DIAGRIDS
ADDEGILS	GLADDIES	ADDEIPRS	DISPREAD	ADDGIKNR	GRANDKID
ADDEGINR	DREADING	ADDEIPSS	DIPSADES	ADDGILNN	DANDLING
	READDING	ADDEIQSU	SQUADDIE	ADDGILNP	PADDLING
ADDEGIRS	DISGRADE	ADDEIRST	DISRATED	ADDGILNR	RADDLING
ADDEGJSU	ADJUDGES	ADDEIRSW	SIDEWARD	ADDGILNS	SADDLING
ADDEGLNS	GLADDENS	ADDEIRVZ	VIZARDED	ADDGILNW	DAWDLING
ADDEGLST	GLADDEST	ADDEISSU	DISSUADE		WADDLING
ADDEGNOP	DOGNAPED	ADDEISSV	DISSAVED	ADDGINPS	PADDINGS
ADDEGNRU	UNGRADED	ADDEISSW	SWADDIES	ADDGINQU	QUADDING
ADDEGPRU	UPGRADED	ADDEISSY	DAYSIDES	ADDGINSW	WADDINGS
ADDEHHIN	HINDHEAD	ADDEJSTU	ADJUSTED	ADDGINWY	WADDYING
ADDEHHLN	HANDHELD	ADDEKNVY	VANDYKED	ADDGLNOS	GLADDONS

ADDGMNOS	GODDAMNS			FEDERATE		ADEEFLLT	FELLATED
ADDGMRUU	MUDGUARD			REDEFEAT		ADEEFLMN	ENFLAMED
ADDGOOSW	DAGWOODS		ADEEEGLT	DELEGATE		ADEEFLNS	ENDLEAFS
ADDGOQSU	GODSQUAD		ADEEEGNR	RENEGADE		ADEEFLOR	FREELOAD
ADDGORSW	GODWARDS		ADEEEGNT	TEENAGED		ADEEFLPR	PEDALFER
ADDHHLNO	HANDHOLD		ADEEEGPS	GAPESEED		ADEEFLRR	DEFERRAL
ADDHIMOO	MAIDHOOD		ADEEEGRR	REGEARED		ADEEFLRS	FEDERALS
ADDHINPS	DAPHNIDS		ADEEEGRS	DEGREASE		ADEEFLRT	DEFLATER
ADDHINRW	HINDWARD		ADEEEGUW	AGUEWEED			FALTERED
ADDHINSY	DANDYISH		ADEEEHHW	HEEHAWED			REFLATED
ADDHIOTY	HYDATOID		ADEEEHRS	HAEREDES		ADEEFLSS	FADELESS
ADDHISTY	HYDATIDS		ADEEEHRT	REHEATED		ADEEFLST	DEFLATES
ADDHLOOS	LADHOODS		ADEEEHRX	EXHEDRAE		ADEEFLSX	FLAXSEED
ADDHLOOY	LADYHOOD		ADEEEHSY	EYESHADE		ADEEFMNR	ENFRAMED
ADDHOORW	HARDWOOD		ADEEEINT	DETAINEE			FREEDMAN
ADDHOSTY	ATHODYDS		ADEEEKNW	WEAKENED		ADEEFMOR	DEFOAMER
ADDIIKMZ	ZADDIKIM		ADEEELMN	ENAMELED		ADEEFMRR	REFRAMED
ADDIILUV	DIVIDUAL		ADEEELNS	ENSEALED		ADEEFMRS	DEFAMERS
ADDIINOT	ADDITION		ADEEELNV	LEAVENED		ADEEFNRU	UNFEARED
ADDIINSS	DISDAINS		ADEEELPR	REPEALED		ADEEFNSS	DEAFNESS
ADDIINTV	DIVIDANT		ADEEELRS	RELEASED		ADEEFNST	FASTENED
ADDIIPSS	DIAPSIDS			RESEALED		ADEEFNTT	FATTENED
ADDIKSST	TSADDIKS		ADEEELRV	LAVEERED		ADEEFORR	FOREREAD
ADDIKSTY	KATYDIDS			REVEALED		ADEEFORT	FOREDATE
ADDIKSTZ	TZADDIKS		ADEEELST	TEASELED		ADEEFOTV	FOVEATED
ADDILLNS	LANDSLID		ADEEELSV	DELEAVES		ADEEFPRS	PREFADES
ADDILLNW	WILDLAND		ADEEELSW	WEASELED		ADEEFRRT	RAFTERED
ADDILMNS	MIDLANDS		ADEEELTV	ELEVATED		ADEEFRRY	DEFRAYER
ADDILNNW	LANDWIND		ADEEELTZ	TEAZELED			FEDERARY
ADDILOSS	DISLOADS		ADEEEMNS	DEMEANES		ADEEFRST	DRAFTEES
ADDIMNOS	DIAMONDS			ENSEAMED		ADEEFRTU	FEATURED
ADDIMNSY	DANDYISM		ADEEEMNT	EMENDATE		ADEEGGHS	EGGHEADS
ADDIMNVY	DIDYNAMY		ADEEEMRT	RETEAMED		ADEEGGJR	JAGGEDER
ADDIMORS	DIADROMS		ADEEEMRU	EMERAUDE		ADEEGGLL	ALLEGGED
ADDINNOR	ORDINAND		ADEEENNT	NEATENED		ADEEGGRR	RAGGEDER
ADDINORS	ANDROIDS		ADEEENRR	REEARNED		ADEEGGRS	SAGGERED
	DISADORN		ADEEENRS	ENSEARED		ADEEGGRT	RETAGGED
ADDINQUY	QUIDDANY			SERENADE		ADEEGGRU	REGAUGED
ADDINRWW	WINDWARD		ADEEENTT	ATTENDEE		ADEEGGWW	GEWGAWED
ADDIORTY	ADDITORY			EDENTATE		ADEEGHNR	REHANGED
ADDIQSST	TSADDIQS		ADEEENWZ	WEAZENED		ADEEGHOR	GHERAOED
ADDIQSTZ	TZADDIQS		ADEEEPRS	RAPESEED		ADEEGHRT	GATHERED
ADDIRSZZ	DIZZARDS		ADEEEPRT	DEPARTEE		ADEEGIMN	ADEEMING
ADDKNRRU	DRUNKARD			REPEATED		ADEEGIMR	REIMAGED
ADDLLNOR	LANDLORD		ADEEERRS	ARREEDES		ADEEGINR	REGAINED
ADDLLRSU	DULLARDS		ADEEERST	RESEATED		ADEEGINS	AGENISED
ADDLNNOW	DOWNLAND		ADEEERVW	REWEAVED		ADEEGINZ	AGENIZED
ADDLNOOW	DOWNLOAD		ADEEESSW	SEAWEEDS		ADEEGIRS	DISAGREE
	WOODLAND			SEESAWED		ADEEGISS	ASSIEGED
ADDLNORR	RANDLORD		ADEEFFIR	EFFRAIDE		ADEEGLLS	ALLEDGES
ADDLNORS	LANDDROS		ADEEFGLN	FENAGLED		ADEEGLLT	GALLETED
ADDLOOSS	SOLDADOS		ADEEFHNR	FREEHAND		ADEEGLLV	GAVELLED
ADDLORTY	DOTARDLY		ADEEFHOR	FOREHEAD		ADEEGLNO	ENGAOLED
ADDMOOSY	DOOMSDAY		ADEEFHRT	FATHERED		ADEEGLNR	ENLARGED
ADDNOPWY	PANDOWDY		ADEEFIIR	AERIFIED			LANGERED
ADDNORWW	DOWNWARD		ADEEFILN	ENFILADE			LARGENED
	DRAWDOWN		ADEEFIMS	MADEFIES		ADEEGLNT	DANEGELT
ADDOORRY	DOORYARD			SEMIDEAF		ADEEGLRV	GRAVELED
ADDOORWW	WOODWARD		ADEEFINR	FREDAINE		ADEEGLRZ	REGLAZED
ADDOORWY	WOODYARD		ADEEFIOR	FOEDARIE		ADEEGLSV	SELVAGED
ADDOPSSY	DASYPODS		ADEEFIRR	RAREFIED		ADEEGLSZ	DEGLAZES
ADEEEFFR	AFFEERED		ADEEFIRS	FEDARIES		ADEEGMMO	GAMODEME
ADEEEFNY	FEDAYEEN		ADEEFIRY	REAEDIFY		ADEEGMMT	GEMMATED
ADEEEFRT	DEFEATER		ADEEFIST	SAFETIED		ADEEGMNR	GENDARME

Eight-letter anagrams

ADEEGMNS	ENDGAMES	ADEEHKWW	HAWKWEED	ADEEIKNP	KIDNAPEE
ADEEGMNY	GANYMEDE	ADEEHKWY	HAWKEYED	ADEEIKSW	WEAKSIDE
	MEGADYNE	ADEEHLLW	WELLHEAD	ADEEILLO	OEILLADE
ADEEGMOP	MEGAPODE	ADEEHLNO	ENHALOED	ADEEILLR	REALLIED
ADEEGMOS	MEGADOSE	ADEEHLNR	REHANDLE	ADEEILMN	ENDEMIAL
ADEEGMSS	MESSAGED	ADEEHLNS	HANSELED	ADEEILMR	REMAILED
ADEEGNNR	ENDANGER	ADEEHLNU	UNHEALED		REMEDIAL
	ENRANGED	ADEEHLRS	ASHLERED	ADEEILMS	LIMEADES
ADEEGNNV	VENDANGE	ADEEHLRT	HALTERED	ADEEILMV	MEDIEVAL
ADEEGNOR	RENEGADO		LATHERED	ADEEILNR	RENAILED
ADEEGNRR	DERANGER	ADEEHLSS	HEADLESS	ADEEILNS	DELAINES
	GARDENER	ADEEHLTY	HEATEDLY	ADEEILNT	DATELINE
	GARNERED	ADEEHMMO	HOMEMADE		ENTAILED
ADEEGNRS	DERANGES	ADEEHMMR	HAMMERED		LINEATED
	GRANDEES	ADEEHMNN	MENHADEN	ADEEILPR	PEDALIER
	GRENADES	ADEEHMNS	HEADSMEN	ADEEILPS	PLEIADES
ADEEGNRU	DUNGAREE	ADEEHMNT	ANTHEMED	ADEEILPT	DEPILATE
	RENAGUED	ADEEHMPR	HAMPERED		EPILATED
	UNAGREED	ADEEHMSS	EMDASHES		PILEATED
	UNDERAGE	ADEEHMST	STEMHEAD	ADEEILRR	DERAILER
	UNGEARED	ADEEHNOT	HEADNOTE		RERAILED
ADEEGNRV	ENGRAVED	ADEEHNPP	HAPPENED	ADEEILRS	REALISED
ADEEGNSS	AGEDNESS	ADEEHNRR	HARDENER		RESAILED
ADEEGNSV	VENDAGES		REHARDEN		SIDEREAL
ADEEGORT	DEROGATE	ADEEHNRT	ADHERENT	ADEEILRT	DETAILER
ADEEGORV	OVERAGED		HARTENED		ELATERID
ADEEGOST	DOGEATES		NEATHERD		RETAILED
ADEEGOTW	GOATWEED		THREADEN	ADEEILRZ	REALIZED
ADEEGPRS	ASPERGED	ADEEHNSS	DASHEENS	ADEEILSS	DEISEALS
	PRESAGED		ENDASHES		IDEALESS
ADEEGPRT	PARGETED	ADEEHNST	HASTENED	ADEEILST	LEADIEST
ADEEGRRR	REGARDER		NETHEADS	ADEEILSV	DISLEAVE
ADEEGRRS	REGRADES	ADEEHNTU	UNHEATED	ADEEILSY	EYELIADS
ADEEGRRT	GARRETED	ADEEHOPR	HEADROPE	ADEEIMNR	REMAINED
	GARTERED	ADEEHORS	SOREHEAD	ADEEIMNS	DEMAINES
	REGRATED	ADEEHORV	OVERHEAD		INSEAMED
ADEEGRRU	REARGUED	ADEEHPPU	UPHEAPED	ADEEIMNT	DEMENTIA
	REDARGUE	ADEEHPRS	EPHEDRAS	ADEEIMNX	EXAMINED
ADEEGRSS	DEGASSER		RESHAPED	ADEEIMPR	EMPAIRED
	DRESSAGE	ADEEHPRT	PREDEATH	ADEEIMRR	DREAMIER
ADEEGRST	RESTAGED		THREAPED	ADEEIMRS	MADERISE
ADEEGRSU	GUARDEES	ADEEHPUV	UPHEAVED	ADEEIMRT	DIAMETER
ADEEGRSW	RAGWEEDS	ADEEHRRS	ADHERERS		REMEDIAT
ADEEGRTT	TARGETED		REDSHARE	ADEEIMRZ	MADERIZE
ADEEGSSS	DEGASSES	ADEEHRRT	RETHREAD	ADEEIMSS	SIAMESED
ADEEGSTT	GESTATED		THREADER	ADEEIMST	MEDIATES
ADEEGSWY	EDGEWAYS	ADEEHRST	HEADREST	ADEEIMSZ	SIAMEZED
ADEEGTTZ	GAZETTED	ADEEHRSV	RESHAVED	ADEEIMTT	ADMITTEE
ADEEHHRS	REHASHED	ADEEHRSW	REWASHED		MEDITATE
ADEEHHST	SHEATHED		WASHERED	ADEEINNS	ADENINES
ADEEHIKL	HEADLIKE	ADEEHRTT	HATTERED		ANDESINE
ADEEHILN	HEADLINE		THREATED	ADEEINOP	OEDIPEAN
ADEEHILS	DEISHEAL	ADEEHRTW	WREATHED	ADEEINPR	PINDAREE
ADEEHIRT	DEATHIER	ADEEHSST	HEADSETS	ADEEINPT	DIAPENTE
ADEEHISS	EADISHES	ADEEHSSY	HAYSEEDS	ADEEINRS	ARSENIDE
ADEEHIST	ATHEISED	ADEEIILS	IDEALISE		DENARIES
	HEADIEST	ADEEIILZ	IDEALIZE		DRAISENE
ADEEHISV	ADHESIVE	ADEEIITV	IDEATIVE		NEARSIDE
ADEEHITZ	ATHEIZED	ADEEIJKL	JADELIKE	ADEEINRT	DETAINER
ADEEHKNR	DAKERHEN	ADEEIJMR	JEREMIAD		RETAINED
	HANKERED	ADEEIJRS	JADERIES	ADEEINRV	REINVADE
	HARKENED	ADEEIJST	JADEITES	ADEEINSS	ANISEEDS
ADEEHKPR	PHREAKED	ADEEIKLS	LAKESIDE	ADEEINST	ANDESITE
ADEEHKRS	KASHERED	ADEEIKMR	DIEMAKER	ADEEINTW	ANTIWEED

ADEEINVW	INWEAVED	ADEELMNP	EMPLANED	ADEELRSY	DELAYERS
ADEEIPRR	RAPIERED	ADEELMNR	ALDERMEN	ADEELRTV	TRAVELED
	REPAIRED	ADEELMNS	DALESMEN	ADEELRUV	REVALUED
ADEEIPRS	AIRSPEED		EMENDALS	ADEELRWY	LAWYERED
ADEEIPTX	EXPIATED		LEADSMEN	ADEELSST	DATELESS
ADEEIRRR	DREARIER	ADEELMNT	LAMENTED		DETASSEL
ADEEIRRS	DREARIES	ADEELMOR	REMOLADE		TASSELED
	RERAISED	ADEELMOS	SOMEDEAL	ADEELSTT	LADETTES
ADEEIRST	READIEST	ADEELMPR	EMPARLED	ADEELSTY	SEDATELY
	SERIATED	ADEELMPX	EXAMPLED	ADEELSUV	DEVALUES
	SIDERATE	ADEELMRS	DEMERSAL	ADEEMMMR	MAMMERED
	STEADIER		EMERALDS	ADEEMMRY	YAMMERED
ADEEIRSV	READVISE	ADEELMRT	TRAMELED	ADEEMMSS	MESDAMES
ADEEIRTT	ITERATED	ADEELMRV	MARVELED	ADEEMMXY	MYXEDEMA
ADEEIRTV	DERIVATE	ADEELMST	MEDALETS	ADEEMNNR	MANNERED
	EVIRATED	ADEELMTU	EMULATED		REMANNED
	TAIVERED	ADEELNNP	ENPLANED	ADEEMNOR	DEMEANOR
ADEEIRTW	WAITERED	ADEELNNU	UNANELED		ENAMORED
ADEEISSS	DISEASES	ADEELNOR	OLEANDER	ADEEMNOS	DAEMONES
	SEASIDES		RELOANED	ADEEMNOT	NEMATODE
ADEEISST	STEADIES	ADEELNPS	DEPLANES	ADEEMNOU	EUDAEMON
ADEEISSV	ADESSIVE		SPALDEEN	ADEEMNPR	DAMPENER
	ADVISEES	ADEELNPT	ENDPLATE	ADEEMNPS	SPADEMEN
ADEEISTU	AUDITEES	ADEELNPU	UPLEANED	ADEEMNPY	EPENDYMA
ADEEISTV	DEVIATES	ADEELNRT	ANTLERED	ADEEMNRS	AMENDERS
	SEDATIVE	ADEELNRV	LAVENDER		MEANDERS
ADEEITTV	EVITATED	ADEELNSU	UNLEASED		REAMENDS
ADEEITVW	TIDEWAVE		UNSEALED	ADEEMNSS	SEEDSMAN
ADEEKMRR	REMARKED	ADEELNSV	ENSLAVED	ADEEMNST	STAMENED
ADEEKMRT	DEMARKET	ADEELNTT	TALENTED	ADEEMNSU	UNSEAMED
	MARKETED	ADEELNTU	UNELATED	ADEEMNSY	DEMAYNES
ADEEKNNR	ENRANKED	ADEELNTV	LEVANTED	ADEEMNTU	UNTEAMED
ADEEKNPS	KNEEPADS	ADEELNTY	ENTAYLED	ADEEMNTW	METEWAND
ADEEKNPW	KNAPWEED	ADEELOPS	PEDALOES	ADEEMORS	SEADROME
ADEEKNRR	DARKENER	ADEELOPX	POLEAXED	ADEEMORT	MODERATE
ADEEKNRS	KNEADERS	ADEELORR	RELOADER	ADEEMPPR	PAMPERED
ADEEKNST	NAKEDEST	ADEELORU	AUREOLED		REMAPPED
ADEEKORS	RESOAKED	ADEELORV	OVERLADE	ADEEMPRR	PREARMED
ADEEKPRR	REPARKED	ADEELOST	DESOLATE	ADEEMPRT	EMPARTED
ADEEKQSU	SQUEAKED	ADEELOSW	LEASOWED		TAMPERED
ADEEKRST	STREAKED	ADEELPPR	LAPPERED	ADEEMPRV	REVAMPED
ADEEKSWY	WEEKDAYS		RAPPELED	ADEEMPRY	EMPAYRED
ADEELLLP	LAPELLED	ADEELPPT	LAPPETED	ADEEMPST	STAMPEDE
ADEELLMT	METALLED	ADEELPPU	UPLEAPED		STEPDAME
ADEELLMU	MEDULLAE	ADEELPRS	PEDALERS	ADEEMRRS	DREAMERS
ADEELLNP	PANELLED		PLEADERS		REDREAMS
ADEELLNW	ENWALLED		RELAPSED	ADEEMRRT	REDREAMT
ADEELLNY	LEADENLY		REPLEADS	ADEEMRRV	MARVERED
ADEELLPR	PEDALLER	ADEELPRT	PALTERED	ADEEMRRW	REWARMED
	PREDELLA		REPLATED	ADEEMRRY	DREAMERY
ADEELLPS	SEPALLED	ADEELPRY	PARLEYED	ADEEMRST	MASTERED
ADEELLPT	PALLETED		REPLAYED		STREAMED
	PETALLED	ADEELPSS	DELAPSES	ADEEMRSU	MEASURED
ADEELLQU	EQUALLED	ADEELPST	PEDESTAL	ADEEMRTT	MATTERED
ADEELLRS	SARDELLE	ADEELPTY	PEDATELY	ADEEMRTY	METEYARD
ADEELLRT	TELLARED	ADEELQSU	SQUEALED	ADEEMSSW	MAWSEEDS
ADEELLRU	LAURELED	ADEELRRR	LARDERER	ADEEMSTW	MATWEEDS
ADEELLRV	RAVELLED	ADEELRRT	TREADLER	ADEEMSWY	MAYWEEDS
ADEELLSS	ALLSEEDS	ADEELRRY	READERLY	ADEENNPT	PENNATED
	LEADLESS	ADEELRST	DESALTER	ADEENNRS	ENSNARED
ADEELLTY	ELATEDLY		RESLATED	ADEENNRU	UNEARNED
ADEELLVY	VALLEYED		TREADLES	ADEENNTT	TENANTED
ADEELLWY	WALLEYED	ADEELRSV	SLAVERED	ADEENNUW	UNWEANED
ADEELMNO	LEMONADE	ADEELRSW	LEEWARDS	ADEENNUY	UNYEANED

ADEENOPW	WEAPONED		REPASSED	ADEFGIIS	GASIFIED
ADEENORS	REASONED		RESPADES	ADEFGILN	FINAGLED
ADEENORV	ENDEAVOR	ADEEPRST	PEDERAST	ADEFGILO	FOLIAGED
ADEENORY	AERODYNE		PREDATES	ADEFGILS	GADFLIES
ADEENOSS	ADENOSES		REPASTED		GASFIELD
	SEASONED		TRAPESED	ADEFGIMN	DEFAMING
ADEENOST	ENDOSTEA	ADEEPRSU	PERSUADE	ADEFGIRT	DRIFTAGE
ADEENOTT	DENOTATE	ADEEPRSV	DEPRAVES	ADEFGIRU	ARGUFIED
	DETONATE		PERVADES	ADEFGITU	FATIGUED
ADEENPPR	ENDPAPER	ADEEPRSW	PERSWADE	ADEFGLOT	GATEFOLD
ADEENPPS	SANDPEEP	ADEEPRSZ	SPREAZED	ADEFGLRU	FELDGRAU
ADEENPRR	PANDERER	ADEEPRTT	PATTERED	ADEFGNOR	FRONDAGE
ADEENPRT	PARENTED	ADEEPRTU	DEPURATE	ADEFGOSU	FOUGADES
ADEENPRU	UNREAPED		EPURATED	ADEFHHIS	HEADFISH
ADEENPRX	EXPANDER	ADEEPRTZ	TRAPEZED	ADEFHILS	DEALFISH
ADEENPSW	SNAPWEED	ADEEPSST	STAPEDES	ADEFHILY	HAYFIELD
ADEENPTT	PATENTED	ADEEPSTT	ADEPTEST	ADEFHIMS	FAMISHED
	PATTENED	ADEEPSWY	SPEEDWAY	ADEFHKOR	FORKHEAD
ADEENRRW	WANDERER	ADEEQRTU	DETRAQUE	ADEFHLSU	HEADFULS
ADEENRSS	DEARNESS	ADEEQRUV	QUAVERED	ADEFHLTU	DEATHFUL
ADEENRSU	UNDERSEA	ADEERRRT	RETARDER	ADEFHMOT	FATHOMED
	UNERASED	ADEERRRW	REDRAWER	ADEFHNOR	FOREHAND
	UNSEARED		REREWARD	ADEFHOST	SOFTHEAD
ADEENRSW	ANSWERED		REWARDER	ADEFIILN	FINIALED
ADEENRSY	YEARENDS	ADEERRST	ARRESTED	ADEFIILR	AIRFIELD
ADEENRTT	ATTENDER		DREAREST	ADEFIILS	LADIFIES
	NATTERED		RASTERED		SALIFIED
	RATTENED		RETREADS	ADEFIILT	FILIATED
ADEENRTU	DENATURE		SERRATED	ADEFIIMR	RAMIFIED
	UNDERATE		TREADERS	ADEFIINS	SANIFIED
	UNDEREAT	ADEERRSV	ADVERSER	ADEFIINZ	NAZIFIED
ADEENRTV	AVENTRED	ADEERRSW	REDWARES	ADEFIIRR	RARIFIED
ADEENRUV	UNREAVED	ADEERRTT	RETRATED	ADEFIIRT	RATIFIED
ADEENSST	ASSENTED	ADEERRTW	REDWATER	ADEFIIRU	AURIFIED
	SENSATED	ADEERRWY	WARREYED	ADEFILMN	INFLAMED
	STANDEES	ADEERSST	ASSERTED	ADEFILNR	FILANDER
ADEENSSU	DANSEUSE		ESTRADES	ADEFILNT	INFLATED
ADEENSTU	UNSEATED	ADEERSTT	ASTERTED	ADEFILOR	FORELAID
ADEENSTY	ANDESYTE		RESTATED	ADEFILOT	FOLIATED
ADEENTTU	TAUTENED		RETASTED	ADEFILSS	DISLEAFS
ADEENTTV	VENDETTA	ADEERSTW	DEWATERS	ADEFILSY	DAYFLIES
ADEEOPRR	PADERERO		TARWEEDS		LADYFIES
ADEEOPRT	OPERATED		WASTERED	ADEFIMPR	FIREDAMP
ADEEOPST	ADOPTEES	ADEERSTY	ESTRAYED	ADEFIMRS	MISFARED
ADEEORRV	OVERDARE	ADEERTTT	TATTERED	ADEFIMSS	DISFAMES
	OVERDEAR	ADEERTTY	YATTERED	ADEFINPR	PANFRIED
	OVERREAD	ADEERTWW	WARTWEED	ADEFINRR	INFRARED
ADEEORSW	OARWEEDS	ADEERVYY	EVERYDAY	ADEFINRS	FRIANDES
ADEEORVW	OVERAWED	ADEESSSS	ASSESSED	ADEFINRU	UNFAIRED
	REAVOWED	ADEESSTT	SEDATEST	ADEFINYZ	DENAZIFY
ADEEPPRR	DAPPERER	ADEESTTT	ATTESTED	ADEFIORS	FORESAID
	PREPARED	ADEESTUX	EXUDATES	ADEFIRRT	DRAFTIER
ADEEPPRT	PRETAPED	ADEESVVY	SAVVEYED	ADEFIRSS	FARSIDES
ADEEPPRU	PAUPERED	ADEESWWX	WAXWEEDS	ADEFKSST	DESKFAST
ADEEPPRV	PREPAVED	ADEFFGUW	GUFFAWED	ADEFLLLU	LADLEFUL
ADEEPPRW	WAPPERED	ADEFFIMR	AFFIRMED	ADEFLLNS	ELFLANDS
ADEEPPRS	RESPREAD	ADEFFIRR	DRAFFIER	ADEFLLOR	FALDEROL
	SPREADER	ADEFFIRT	TARIFFED	ADEFLLOW	FALLOWED
ADEEPPRT	DEPARTER	ADEFFIST	DAFFIEST	ADEFLLRY	ALDERFLY
ADEEPPRU	UPREARED	ADEFFLNS	SNAFFLED	ADEFLLSW	DEWFALLS
ADEEPPRV	DEPRAVER	ADEFFLOS	LEADOFFS	ADEFLLUY	FEUDALLY
	PERVADER	ADEFFORT	TRADEOFF	ADEFLMRU	DREAMFUL
ADEEPRSS	ASPERSED	ADEFFRST	STRAFFED	ADEFLNNS	FENLANDS
	PREASSED	ADEFGGOT	FAGGOTED	ADEFLNOR	FORELAND

ADEFLNRU	DEARNFUL	**ADEGHIRR**	HAGRIDER	**ADEGIMRT**	MIGRATED
ADEFLNTU	FLAUNTED	**ADEGHIRS**	GARISHED	**ADEGIMST**	SIGMATED
ADEFLNUU	UNFEUDAL		HAGRIDES	**ADEGINNR**	GRANNIED
ADEFLNUW	UNFLAWED		HEADRIGS	**ADEGINNV**	ADVENING
ADEFLORT	DEFLATOR	**ADEGHIRT**	GRAITHED		DAVENING
ADEFLORV	FLAVORED	**ADEGHJSU**	JUGHEADS	**ADEGINNW**	AWNINGED
ADEFLORY	FORELADY	**ADEGHLNO**	HEADLONG	**ADEGINNY**	DENAYING
ADEFLPRS	FELDSPAR		LONGHEAD	**ADEGINOR**	ORGANDIE
ADEFLPSU	SPADEFUL	**ADEGHLOS**	GALOSHED	**ADEGINOS**	AGONISED
ADEFLRSW	SELFWARD	**ADEGHNNU**	UNHANGED		DIAGNOSE
ADEFLRTU	TRADEFUL	**ADEGHNRT**	THRANGED	**ADEGINOZ**	AGONIZED
ADEFLRTW	LEFTWARD	**ADEGHOOP**	PAGEHOOD	**ADEGINPU**	ANGUIPED
ADEFLRZZ	FRAZZLED	**ADEGHORT**	GOATHERD	**ADEGINRR**	DREARING
ADEFLSTU	DEFAULTS	**ADEGHRTU**	DAUGHTER	**ADEGINRS**	DERAIGNS
	SULFATED	**ADEGHTUW**	WAUGHTED		GRADINES
ADEFMNRU	UNFRAMED	**ADEGIILN**	GLIADINE		READINGS
ADEFMORT	FORMATED	**ADEGIILP**	DIPLEGIA	**ADEGINRT**	DERATING
ADEFMOSU	FAMOUSED	**ADEGIIMN**	IMAGINED		GRADIENT
	FUMADOES	**ADEGIIMS**	DIGAMIES		REDATING
ADEFNNNU	UNFANNED	**ADEGIINR**	DEAIRING		TREADING
ADEFNOPR	PROFANED	**ADEGIINT**	IDEATING	**ADEGINRY**	DERAYING
ADEFNSST	DAFTNESS	**ADEGIIRT**	DIGERATI		READYING
ADEFOOSS	SEAFOODS	**ADEGIITT**	DIGITATE		YEARDING
ADEFORRR	FORRADER	**ADEGIJSW**	JIGSAWED	**ADEGINSS**	ASSIGNED
ADEFORRW	FARROWED	**ADEGIKLO**	GOADLIKE	**ADEGINST**	SEDATING
	FOREWARD	**ADEGIKNN**	KNEADING		STEADING
ADEFORRY	FOREYARD	**ADEGIKNR**	DAKERING	**ADEGINSW**	WINDAGES
	FORRAYED	**ADEGILLO**	GLADIOLE	**ADEGINTV**	VINTAGED
ADEFORUV	FAVOURED	**ADEGILLP**	PILLAGED	**ADEGINVW**	ADVEWING
ADEFOSTU	FADEOUTS	**ADEGILLR**	GLADLIER	**ADEGINWX**	DEWAXING
ADEFPRRT	PREDRAFT		GRILLADE	**ADEGINYZ**	ZYGAENID
ADEFPTUW	UPWAFTED	**ADEGILLS**	GALLISED	**ADEGIORT**	ERGATOID
ADEFRRST	DRAFTERS	**ADEGILLZ**	GALLIZED	**ADEGIOST**	GODETIAS
	REDRAFTS	**ADEGILMN**	MALIGNED	**ADEGIPRR**	PARRIDGE
ADEFRSTW	DWARFEST		MEDALING	**ADEGIPRS**	SPAIRGED
ADEFSSTT	STEDFAST	**ADEGILNN**	LADENING	**ADEGIRWY**	RIDGEWAY
ADEGGGNU	UNGAGGED	**ADEGILNO**	GALENOID	**ADEGISSU**	DISUSAGE
ADEGGIRR	DRAGGIER	**ADEGILNP**	PEDALING	**ADEGISTU**	GAUDIEST
ADEGGIST	DAGGIEST		PLEADING	**ADEGISUV**	VIDUAGES
ADEGGISU	GAUDGIES	**ADEGILNR**	DANGLIER	**ADEGIUWY**	GUIDEWAY
	GUIDAGES		DEARLING	**ADEGJNOR**	JARGONED
ADEGGJLY	JAGGEDLY		DRAGLINE	**ADEGKLOY**	DEKALOGY
ADEGGLNU	ANGLEDUG	**ADEGILNS**	DEALINGS	**ADEGLLNU**	GLANDULE
ADEGGLRS	DRAGGLES		LEADINGS		UNGALLED
ADEGGLRY	RAGGEDLY		SIGNALED	**ADEGLLOP**	GALLOPED
ADEGGMOS	DEMAGOGS	**ADEGILNT**	DELATING	**ADEGLLOR**	GOLLARED
ADEGGMOY	DEMAGOGY	**ADEGILNY**	DELAYING	**ADEGLLOW**	GALLOWED
ADEGGNOW	WAGGONED	**ADEGILOR**	DIALOGER	**ADEGLLSU**	GALLUSED
ADEGGNTU	UNTAGGED	**ADEGILOS**	GOLIASED	**ADEGLMOR**	GLAMORED
ADEGGNUU	UNGAUGED	**ADEGILOU**	DIALOGUE	**ADEGLMOS**	GLADSOME
ADEGGOPS	PEDAGOGS	**ADEGILOY**	IDEALOGY	**ADEGLMPU**	PLUMAGED
ADEGGOPY	PEDAGOGY	**ADEGILRS**	SLAIRGED	**ADEGLMRU**	MAULGRED
ADEGGPRS	SPRAGGED	**ADEGILSS**	GLISSADE	**ADEGLMUY**	AMYGDULE
ADEGGRRS	DRAGGERS	**ADEGILST**	GLADIEST	**ADEGLNOP**	ANGLEPOD
ADEGGRTY	GADGETRY	**ADEGILSV**	DISGAVEL	**ADEGLNOY**	GONDELAY
ADEGHHOS	HOGSHEAD	**ADEGIMMN**	AMENDING	**ADEGLNPS**	SPANGLED
ADEGHILN	HEALDING	**ADEGIMNO**	AMIDOGEN	**ADEGLNRS**	DANGLERS
ADEGHILT	ALIGHTED	**ADEGIMNR**	DREAMING		GLANDERS
	GILTHEAD		MARGINED	**ADEGLNRW**	WRANGLED
ADEGHINR	ADHERING		MIDRANGE	**ADEGLNSS**	GLADNESS
	HEADRING	**ADEGIMOR**	IDEOGRAM	**ADEGLNTW**	TWANGLED
ADEGHINS	DEASHING	**ADEGIMPS**	MEDIGAPS	**ADEGLNUZ**	UNGLAZED
	HEADINGS		MISPAGED	**ADEGLOPP**	GALOPPED
	SHEADING	**ADEGIMRS**	MISGRADE	**ADEGLORV**	OVERGLAD

ADEGLPPR	GRAPPLED		HOTHEADS
ADEGLSTY	DALGYTES	ADEHHRRU	HURRAHED
ADEGMMNO	GAMMONED	ADEHHRST	THRASHED
ADEGMMRU	RUMMAGED	ADEHHUZZ	HUZZAHED
ADEGMNOR	DRAGOMEN	ADEHIITZ	THIAZIDE
ADEGMNOS	GOADSMEN	ADEHIJMS	JEHADISM
ADEGMNOT	MONTAGED	ADEHIJST	JEHADIST
ADEGMNOY	ENDOGAMY	ADEHIKLN	HANDLIKE
ADEGMNRS	DRAGSMEN	ADEHIKLV	KHEDIVAL
ADEGMNSU	AGENDUMS	ADEHIKNS	SKINHEAD
ADEGMOPS	MEGAPODS	ADEHIKSS	DASHEKIS
ADEGMORS	ORGASMED	ADEHIKST	SKAITHED
ADEGMORW	WORDGAME	ADEHIKSV	KHEDIVAS
ADEGMPUZ	GAZUMPED	ADEHILLO	HILLOAED
ADEGNNOR	ANDROGEN	ADEHILLP	PHIALLED
	DRAGONNE		PILLHEAD
ADEGNNPU	UNPANGED	ADEHILMO	HALIDOME
ADEGNNSU	DUNNAGES	ADEHILNR	HARDLINE
ADEGNOPR	DOGNAPER	ADEHILNU	UNHAILED
ADEGNOPS	PONDAGES	ADEHILPS	HELIPADS
ADEGNOPU	POUNDAGE	ADEHILSV	LAVISHED
ADEGNORT	DRAGONET	ADEHILSW	WHAISLED
ADEGNOSS	SONDAGES	ADEHILWZ	WHAIZLED
ADEGNOSV	DOGVANES	ADEHIMMS	SHAMMIED
ADEGNPUY	PYENGADU	ADEHIMOT	HEMATOID
ADEGNRRU	GRANDEUR	ADEHIMRS	MISHEARD
ADEGNRST	DRAGNETS		SEMIHARD
	GRANDEST	ADEHIMRY	HYDREMIA
ADEGNRSU	ENGUARDS	ADEHINOP	DIAPHONE
ADEGNRUU	UNARGUED	ADEHINOS	ADHESION
ADEGNRUZ	GAZUNDER	ADEHINOY	HYOIDEAN
	UNGRAZED	ADEHINPS	DEANSHIP
ADEGOORV	OVERGOAD		HEADPINS
ADEGOORY	GOODYEAR		PINHEADS
ADEGOPPR	PROPAGED	ADEHINPU	DAUPHINE
ADEGOPRR	DRAGROPE	ADEHINRT	ANTHERID
	PROGRADE	ADEHINRU	UNHAIRED
ADEGOPRT	PORTAGED	ADEHINSS	DANISHES
ADEGORRT	GARROTED		SHANDIES
ADEGORST	GOADSTER	ADEHINST	HANDIEST
ADEGORSW	DOWAGERS	ADEHINSV	VANISHED
	WORDAGES	ADEHIOTT	ATHETOID
ADEGORTT	GAROTTED	ADEHIPRS	RAPHIDES
ADEGORTU	OUTRAGED	ADEHIPSS	PISSHEAD
	RAGOUTED	ADEHIPST	PITHEADS
ADEGORTW	WATERDOG		SIDEPATH
ADEGOTTV	GAVOTTED	ADEHIRRT	TRIHEDRA
ADEGOTUZ	OUTGAZED	ADEHIRRW	HARDWIRE
ADEGPRRU	UPGRADER	ADEHIRSS	AIRSHEDS
ADEGPRSS	SPADGERS		RADISHES
ADEGPRSU	UPGRADES	ADEHIRST	HAIRSTED
ADEGPSTU	UPSTAGED		HARDIEST
ADEGRRST	DRAGSTER	ADEHIRSV	RAVISHED
ADEGRRSU	GUARDERS	ADEHIRSW	DISHWARE
ADEGRSSU	DESUGARS		RAWHIDES
	GRADUSES	ADEHIRSY	HAYRIDES
ADEGTTTU	GUTTATED	ADEHIRVW	HIVEWARD
ADEHHIPR	RHAPHIDE	ADEHISST	DASHIEST
ADEHHIPS	HEADSHIP		SHADIEST
ADEHHIST	SHITHEAD	ADEHISSW	SIWASHED
ADEHHNTU	HEADHUNT	ADEHJLOT	JOLTHEAD
ADEHHOOR	HOORAHED	ADEHKLNU	LUNKHEAD
ADEHHOPS	HOPHEADS	ADEHKNRS	REDSHANK
ADEHHOST	HEADSHOT	ADEHKNSU	UNSHAKED
ADEHKORS	HARDOKES
ADEHKORW	HEADWORK
ADEHKOST	KATHODES
ADEHLLOO	HALLOOED
	HOLLOAED
ADEHLLOU	HULLOAED
ADEHLLOW	HALLOWED
ADEHLLRT	THRALLED
ADEHLLRW	HELLWARD
ADEHLLSY	DAYSHELL
ADEHLMNO	HOMELAND
ADEHLMOY	HOLYDAME
ADEHLNRS	HANDLERS
ADEHLNSS	HANDLESS
	HANDSELS
ADEHLNST	SHETLAND
ADEHLNSU	UNHALSED
	UNLASHED
	UNSHALED
ADEHLNUV	UNHALVED
ADEHLOOR	HORDEOLA
ADEHLOOT	TOOLHEAD
ADEHLOPS	ASPHODEL
	PHOLADES
ADEHLOPW	PLOWHEAD
ADEHLPSS	SPLASHED
ADEHLRRY	HERALDRY
ADEHMNNY	HANDYMEN
ADEHMNOS	HANDSOME
ADEHMNOT	METHADON
	THANEDOM
ADEHMNRS	HERDSMAN
ADEHMNRU	UNHARMED
ADEHMNSU	UNSHAMED
ADEHMOOP	OOMPAHED
ADEHMOOR	HEADROOM
ADEHMOPS	MOPHEADS
ADEHMORS	HADROMES
ADEHMORW	HOMEWARD
ADEHMOST	HEADMOST
ADEHMOSU	MADHOUSE
ADEHMOSY	SHAMOYED
ADEHNNSW	HANDSEWN
ADEHNOPR	ORPHANED
ADEHNOPT	PHONATED
ADEHNORS	HARDNOSE
ADEHNORV	HANDOVER
	OVERHAND
ADEHNOSS	SANDSHOE
ADEHNOSU	SEAHOUND
ADEHNPSU	UNHASPED
	UNSHAPED
ADEHNPTU	UNPATHED
ADEHNRSS	HARDNESS
ADEHNRSU	UNSHARED
ADEHNRSW	SWANHERD
ADEHNRTU	UNTHREAD
ADEHNSST	HANDSETS
ADEHNSSU	SUNSHADE
	UNSASHED
ADEHNSUV	UNSHAVED
ADEHNSUW	UNWASHED
ADEHNTTU	UNHATTED
ADEHNTUW	UNTHAWED

ADEHOOPS	APEHOODS	ADEIKLLO	KELOIDAL	ADEILNOP	PALINODE
ADEHOORW	HAREWOOD	ADEIKLLR	LARDLIKE	ADEILNOS	NODALISE
ADEHOORY	HOORAYED	ADEIKLLY	LADYLIKE	ADEILNOT	DELATION
ADEHOPRS	RHAPSODE	ADEIKLNS	SANDLIKE	ADEILNOZ	NODALIZE
ADEHOPST	POTASHED	ADEIKLNW	DAWNLIKE	ADEILNPS	SANDPILE
	POTHEADS		WANDLIKE	ADEILNPT	PANTILED
ADEHOPSX	HEXAPODS	ADEIKLOT	TOADLIKE	ADEILNPU	PALUDINE
ADEHOPXY	HEXAPODY	ADEIKLOX	ALKOXIDE	ADEILNRS	ISLANDER
ADEHORRS	HOARDERS	ADEIKLRR	DARKLIER	ADEILNSU	UNSAILED
ADEHORRV	OVERHARD	ADEIKLSW	SIDEWALK	ADEILNSV	ANDVILES
ADEHORRW	HARROWED	ADEIKMMS	IMMASKED	ADEILNTU	UNTAILED
ADEHORSW	SHADOWER	ADEIKMPR	IMPARKED	ADEILNTV	DIVALENT
ADEHORTT	THROATED	ADEIKMRT	TIDEMARK	ADEILNUV	UNVAILED
ADEHORTU	AUTHORED	ADEIKNPR	KIDNAPER	ADEILOPS	EPISODAL
	OUTHEARD	ADEIKNSY	KYANISED		OPALISED
ADEHOSTW	TOWHEADS	ADEIKNYZ	KYANIZED		SEPALOID
ADEHPSTU	DUSTHEAP	ADEIKORT	KERATOID	ADEILOPT	PETALOID
ADEHQSSU	SQUASHED	ADEIKRST	STRAIKED	ADEILOPZ	OPALIZED
ADEHRRUY	HURRAYED	ADEILLMY	MEDIALLY	ADEILOQU	ODALIQUE
ADEHRSSY	HYDRASES	ADEILLNN	LANDLINE	ADEILORS	DARIOLES
ADEHRSTY	HYDRATES	ADEILLNU	UNALLIED		SOLIDARE
ADEHRTTW	THWARTED	ADEILLNV	ANVILLED		SOREDIAL
ADEIILMN	LIMNAEID	ADEILLNW	INWALLED	ADEILORT	IDOLATER
ADEIILMS	IDEALISM	ADEILLNY	LEYLANDI		TAILORED
	MILADIES	ADEILLOR	ARILLODE	ADEILORV	OVERLAID
ADEIILPR	PERIDIAL	ADEILLPR	PALLIDER	ADEILORX	EXORDIAL
ADEIILRS	LAIRISED		PILLARED	ADEILOSS	ASSOILED
ADEIILRZ	LAIRIZED	ADEILLPS	ILLAPSED		DEASOILS
ADEIILST	IDEALIST		SPADILLE		ISOLEADS
ADEIILTV	DILATIVE	ADEILLRS	DALLIERS	ADEILOST	DIASTOLE
ADEIILTY	IDEALITY		DIALLERS		ISOLATED
ADEIIMMS	MISAIMED	ADEILLRT	TRIALLED		SODALITE
ADEIIMNN	INDAMINE	ADEILLRV	RIVALLED		SOLIDATE
ADEIIMNR	MERIDIAN	ADEILLSW	SIDEWALL	ADEILOSU	DOULEIAS
ADEIIMNS	AMIDINES	ADEILMMM	MELAMDIM	ADEILOSZ	DIAZOLES
	DIAMINES	ADEILMMS	DILEMMAS		SLEAZOID
ADEIIMNT	MINIATED	ADEILMNO	MELANOID	ADEILOTT	DATOLITE
ADEIIMPR	IMPAIRED	ADEILMNP	PLAIDMEN	ADEILOTV	DOVETAIL
ADEIIMRS	SEMIARID	ADEILMNU	UNMAILED		VIOLATED
ADEIIMTT	IMITATED	ADEILMNY	MAIDENLY	ADEILPPP	PEDIPALP
ADEIINNS	SANIDINE		MEDIANLY	ADEILPRS	LIPREADS
ADEIINOT	IDEATION	ADEILMOS	DAMOISEL		PARSLIED
	IODINATE		MELODIAS		PEDRAILS
	TAENIOID	ADEILMOX	ALDOXIME		PREDIALS
ADEIINRS	DRAISINE	ADEILMPP	PALMIPED		SPIRALED
ADEIINRT	DAINTIER	ADEILMPR	IMPARLED	ADEILPRT	DIPTERAL
ADEIINRU	UREDINIA	ADEILMPS	IMPLEADS		TRIPEDAL
ADEIINST	ADENITIS		MISPLEAD	ADEILPRU	EPIDURAL
	DAINTIES	ADEILMPT	IMPLATED	ADEILPRV	DEPRIVAL
ADEIINSZ	DIAZINES	ADEILMRS	DISMALER	ADEILPSS	DESPISAL
ADEIINTV	VANITIED	ADEILMRY	DREAMILY	ADEILPST	TALIPEDS
ADEIINUV	INDUVIAE	ADEILMSS	MAIDLESS	ADEILPTU	PLAUDITE
ADEIIPRR	PERRADII		MISDEALS	ADEILQSU	SQUAILED
	PRAIRIED		MISLEADS	ADEILQTU	LIQUATED
ADEIIPRS	PRESIDIA	ADEILMST	MEDALIST	ADEILRRW	DRAWLIER
ADEIIPST	STAPEDII		MISDEALT	ADEILRRY	DREARILY
ADEIIRSS	AIRSIDES	ADEILMSY	DYSMELIA	ADEILRST	DILATERS
	DIARISES	ADEILNNO	NONIDEAL		LARDIEST
ADEIIRST	IRISATED	ADEILNNP	PINELAND		REDTAILS
ADEIIRSZ	DIARIZES	ADEILNNR	INLANDER	ADEILRSU	RESIDUAL
ADEIITTV	TIDIVATE	ADEILNNS	ANNELIDS	ADEILRSY	DIALYSER
	VITIATED		LINDANES	ADEILRTT	DETRITAL
ADEIITUV	AUDITIVE	ADEILNNT	DENTINAL	ADEILRTY	DIELYTRA
ADEIJMRS	JEMIDARS	ADEILNNU	UNNAILED	ADEILRVY	VARIEDLY

ADEILRYZ	DIALYZER		MISRATED	ADEINRTT	NITRATED
ADEILSSU	DEASIULS		READMITS	ADEINRTU	DATURINE
	DUALISES	ADEIMRSY	MIDYEARS		INDURATE
ADEILSSV	DEVISALS	ADEIMRTT	ADMITTER		RUINATED
ADEILSSY	DIALYSES	ADEIMRTU	MURIATED		URINATED
ADEILSTV	VALIDEST	ADEIMSST	DIASTEMS	ADEINRUV	UNVARIED
ADEILSTY	DIASTYLE		MISDATES	ADEINRVY	VINEYARD
	STEADILY	ADEIMSTU	TAEDIUMS	ADEINSST	DESTAINS
ADEILSUV	DISVALUE	ADEIMSTY	DAYTIMES		SANDIEST
ADEILSUZ	DUALIZES	ADEINNNS	NANDINES	ADEINSSV	AVIDNESS
ADEILSWY	SLIDEWAY	ADEINNOT	ANOINTED		VANESSID
ADEILSXY	DYSLEXIA		ANTINODE	ADEINSSW	WINDASES
ADEILSYZ	DIALYZES	ADEINNOV	DEVONIAN	ADEINSTT	INSTATED
ADEILTTU	ALTITUDE	ADEINNPT	PINNATED	ADEINSTU	AUDIENTS
	LATITUDE	ADEINNPU	UNPAINED		SINUATED
ADEILTVY	DATIVELY	ADEINNRS	INSNARED	ADEINSTV	DEVIANTS
ADEIMMNS	MISNAMED	ADEINNRZ	RENDZINA	ADEINSTY	DESYATIN
ADEIMMNU	UNMAIMED	ADEINNSU	UNSAINED	ADEIOPRR	PRERADIO
ADEIMMRS	MERMAIDS	ADEINNSX	DISANNEX	ADEIOPRS	DIASPORE
ADEIMMST	MISMATED	ADEINNTU	ANTIDUNE		PARODIES
ADEIMNNO	DEMONIAN		INUNDATE	ADEIOPRV	OVERPAID
	MONDAINE	ADEINOPP	PEPONIDA	ADEIOPSS	ADIPOSES
ADEIMNOP	DOPAMINE	ADEINOPT	ANTIPODE	ADEIOPST	DIOPTASE
ADEIMNOR	RADIOMEN	ADEINORR	ORDAINER	ADEIOPTV	ADOPTIVE
ADEIMNOS	AMIDONES		REORDAIN	ADEIORRT	ADROITER
	DAIMONES	ADEINORS	ANEROIDS	ADEIORST	ASTEROID
	DOMAINES		DONARIES	ADEIORSV	AVODIRES
	NOMADIES	ADEINORT	AROINTED		AVOIDERS
	NOMADISE		DERATION	ADEIORTT	TERATOID
ADEIMNOT	DOMINATE		ORDINATE	ADEIORTV	DEVIATOR
	NEMATOID		RATIONED	ADEIOSSX	OXIDASES
ADEIMNOU	EUDAIMON	ADEINORU	DOUANIER	ADEIOSTX	OXIDATES
ADEIMNOZ	NOMADIZE	ADEINOSS	ADENOSIS	ADEIOSTZ	AZOTISED
ADEIMNPW	IMPAWNED		ADONISES	ADEIOSVV	VAIVODES
ADEIMNRR	MANRIDER		ANODISES	ADEIOSVW	WAIVODES
ADEIMNRS	ADERMINS	ADEINOST	ASTONIED	ADEIOSWW	WAIWODES
	SIRNAMED		SEDATION	ADEIOTZZ	AZOTIZED
ADEIMNRU	MURAENID	ADEINOSX	DIOXANES	ADEIPPRS	APPRISED
ADEIMNRY	DAIRYMEN	ADEINOSZ	ADONIZES		DRAPPIES
ADEIMNRZ	ZEMINDAR		ANODIZES	ADEIPPRZ	APPRIZED
ADEIMNSS	SIDESMAN	ADEINOTT	ANTIDOTE	ADEIPRRS	DRAPIERS
ADEIMNST	MEDIANTS		TETANOID	ADEIPRSS	DESPAIRS
	TIDESMAN	ADEINOTV	DONATIVE	ADEIPRST	DIPTERAS
ADEIMNSU	MAUNDIES	ADEINPPX	APPENDIX		RAPIDEST
ADEIMNSY	DYNAMISE	ADEINPRS	SPRAINED		SPIRATED
ADEIMNTY	DYNAMITE	ADEINPRT	DIPTERAN		TARSIPED
ADEIMNYZ	DYNAMIZE	ADEINPRU	UNPAIRED		TRAIPSED
ADEIMORR	AIRDROME		UNREPAID	ADEIPRSU	UPRAISED
ADEIMORT	MEDIATOR	ADEINPST	DEPAINTS	ADEIPRSW	RIPSAWED
ADEIMOSS	SESAMOID	ADEINPSV	SPAVINED	ADEIPRTU	EUPATRID
ADEIMOST	ATOMISED	ADEINQTU	ANTIQUED		PREAUDIT
ADEIMOTZ	ATOMIZED	ADEINRRS	DRAINERS	ADEIPSSX	SPADIXES
ADEIMPRR	RAMPIRED		SERRANID	ADEIPSTV	VAPIDEST
ADEIMPRT	IMPARTED	ADEINRSS	ARIDNESS	ADEIPTTU	APTITUDE
	PREADMIT		SARDINES	ADEIQRRU	QUARRIED
ADEIMPRV	VAMPIRED	ADEINRST	DETRAINS	ADEIQRSU	QUERIDAS
ADEIMPST	DAMPIEST		RANDIEST	ADEIQSUY	QUAYSIDE
	IMPASTED		STRAINED	ADEIRRSW	SWARDIER
ADEIMRRS	ADMIRERS	ADEINRSU	DENARIUS	ADEIRRTW	TAWDRIER
	DISARMER		UNRAISED	ADEIRRWW	WIREDRAW
	MARRIEDS		URANIDES	ADEIRRZZ	RIZZARED
ADEIMRSS	MISREADS	ADEINRSV	INVADERS	ADEIRSST	ASTERIDS
	SIDEARMS		SANDIVER		DIASTERS
ADEIMRST	MARDIEST	ADEINRSY	SYNEDRIA		DISASTER

	DISRATES	**ADELLNSW**	ELLWANDS	**ADELOORV**	OVERLOAD
ADEIRSSU	RADIUSES		WALLSEND	**ADELOOTW**	LATEWOOD
	SUDARIES	**ADELLNTY**	DENTALLY	**ADELOOWW**	WOODWALE
ADEIRSSV	ADVISERS	**ADELLNUW**	UNWALLED	**ADELOPPR**	PROPALED
ADEIRSTT	STRAITED	**ADELLOPW**	WALLOPED	**ADELOPRS**	LEOPARDS
	STRIATED	**ADELLORS**	ODALLERS		PRELOADS
	TARDIEST	**ADELLOSW**	SALLOWED	**ADELOPRT**	PORTALED
ADEIRSTW	TAWDRIES	**ADELLOTT**	ALLOTTED		PROLATED
ADEIRTTT	ATTRITED		TOTALLED	**ADELOPRU**	POULARDE
	TITRATED	**ADELLOTV**	LAVOLTED	**ADELOPRW**	POLEWARD
ADEIRTUV	DURATIVE	**ADELLOTW**	TALLOWED	**ADELOPSS**	DEPOSALS
ADEIRVWY	DRIVEWAY	**ADELLOVY**	LADYLOVE	**ADELOPST**	TADPOLES
ADEISSST	ASSISTED	**ADELLOWW**	WALLOWED	**ADELOPSU**	PALUDOSE
	DISSEATS	**ADELLQSU**	SQUALLED	**ADELOPSY**	SEPALODY
ADEISSSV	DISSAVES	**ADELLRSU**	UDALLERS	**ADELOPTY**	PETALODY
ADEISSTT	DISTASTE	**ADELLTUU**	ULULATED	**ADELORRV**	OVERLARD
	STAIDEST	**ADELMNNS**	LANDSMEN	**ADELORSS**	ROADLESS
ADEISSTV	DISTAVES	**ADELMNOS**	LODESMAN	**ADELORST**	DELATORS
ADEISSWY	SIDEWAYS	**ADELMNRS**	MANDRELS		LEOTARDS
	WAYSIDES	**ADELMOOW**	WOODMEAL		LODESTAR
ADEISTTU	SITUATED	**ADELMOPS**	MALPOSED	**ADELORSU**	ROULADES
ADEISTUZ	DEUTZIAS	**ADELMORS**	EARLDOMS	**ADELORTW**	LEADWORT
ADEISTWY	TIDEWAYS	**ADELMOSS**	DAMOSELS	**ADELOSSS**	SODALESS
ADEITTTU	ATTITUDE	**ADELMOSZ**	DAMOZELS	**ADELOSST**	TOADLESS
	ATTUITED	**ADELMOTU**	MODULATE	**ADELOSSW**	DOWLASES
ADEJLOSU	JALOUSED	**ADELMPRT**	TRAMPLED	**ADELOSTU**	OUTLEADS
ADEJMMNU	UNJAMMED	**ADELMRRU**	DEMURRAL	**ADELOSTV**	SOLVATED
ADEJMRRU	JUMARRED	**ADELMSSY**	MASSEDLY	**ADELOTUV**	OVULATED
ADEJNRUW	UNDERJAW	**ADELMSUY**	AMUSEDLY	**ADELOTUW**	OUTLAWED
ADEJOPRS	JEOPARDS	**ADELMTTY**	MATTEDLY	**ADELOVWY**	AVOWEDLY
ADEJOPRY	JEOPARDY	**ADELMTUU**	UMLAUTED	**ADELPPRY**	DAPPERLY
ADEJRRSU	ADJURERS	**ADELNNTU**	UNNANELD	**ADELPQUX**	QUADPLEX
ADEJRSTU	ADJUSTER	**ADELNNOT**	LENTANDO	**ADELPRRU**	LARRUPED
	READJUST	**ADELNOPR**	PONDERAL	**ADELPRSW**	SPRAWLED
ADEKLMRY	MARKEDLY	**ADELNORS**	LADRONES	**ADELPRTT**	PRATTLED
ADEKLNOX	KLAXONED		SOLANDER	**ADELPRTU**	PREADULT
ADEKLNPP	KNAPPLED	**ADELNORU**	UNLOADER	**ADELPSTT**	SPLATTED
ADEKLNPR	PRANKLED		URODELAN	**ADELPSTU**	PULSATED
ADEKLNSU	UNSLAKED	**ADELNORV**	OVERLAND	**ADELPUUV**	UPVALUED
ADEKLORW	LEADWORK		RONDAVEL	**ADELRRSU**	RUDERALS
ADEKLPRS	SPARKLED	**ADELNOSY**	YEALDONS	**ADELRRSW**	DRAWLERS
ADEKLPTU	UPTALKED	**ADELNPRS**	SPANDREL	**ADELRRTU**	ULTRARED
ADEKMNRU	UNMARKED	**ADELNPRU**	PENDULAR	**ADELRSSW**	WARDLESS
ADEKMNSU	UNMASKED		UNDERLAP		WRASSLED
ADEKMORS	DARKSOME		UPLANDER	**ADELRSTT**	STARTLED
ADEKMTUU	MAKUTUED	**ADELNPRY**	PANDERLY	**ADELRSTW**	WARSTLED
ADEKNNRU	UNRANKED		REPANDLY		WRASTLED
ADEKNNSS	DANKNESS	**ADELNPSY**	DYSPNEAL	**ADELRSZZ**	DAZZLERS
ADEKNOSU	UNSOAKED		ENDPLAYS	**ADELRTUY**	ADULTERY
ADEKNOTW	TAKEDOWN	**ADELNPUY**	UNPLAYED	**ADELSTTY**	STATEDLY
ADEKNRSS	DARKNESS	**ADELNRSS**	SLANDERS	**ADELTTTW**	TWATTLED
ADEKNSVY	VANDYKES	**ADELNRSU**	LAUNDERS	**ADEMMNOW**	MADWOMEN
ADEKOOTW	TEAKWOOD		LURDANES	**ADEMMSTU**	SUMMATED
ADEKOSTU	OUTASKED		RUNDALES	**ADEMNNNU**	UNMANNED
ADEKQSUW	SQUAWKED	**ADELNRTU**	DENTURAL	**ADEMNNOR**	NORMANDE
ADELLMOR	MORALLED	**ADELNRTY**	ARDENTLY	**ADEMNNOU**	UNMOANED
ADELLMOS	SLALOMED	**ADELNRUY**	UNDERLAY	**ADEMNNRU**	MUNDANER
ADELLMRU	MEDULLAR	**ADELNSSS**	SANDLESS		UNDERMAN
	MURALLED	**ADELNSTU**	UNSALTED	**ADEMNOOR**	MAROONED
ADELLMSU	MEDULLAS	**ADELNSTW**	WETLANDS	**ADEMNOPR**	POMANDER
ADELLNNU	ANNULLED	**ADELNTUU**	UNDULATE	**ADEMNOPT**	TAMPONED
ADELLNPS	SPENDALL	**ADELNUUV**	UNVALUED	**ADEMNORS**	MADRONES
ADELLNRS	LANDLERS	**ADELNUZZ**	UNDAZZLE		RANSOMED
ADELLNSS	LANDLESS	**ADELOOPV**	LEVODOPA		ROADSMEN

Eight-letter anagrams

ADEMNOTU	AMOUNTED	ADENORST	TORNADES		READOPTS
	OUTNAMED	ADENORTT	ATTORNED	ADEOPRSU	UPSOARED
ADEMNPPU	UNMAPPED	ADENORTW	DANEWORT	ADEOPRTT	TETRAPOD
ADEMNPSS	DAMPNESS		TEARDOWN	ADEOPRUV	VAPOURED
ADEMNRRU	UNDERARM	ADENORTY	AROYNTED	ADEOPSST	PODESTAS
	UNMARRED	ADENORUX	RONDEAUX	ADEOPSTT	DESPOTAT
ADEMNRSU	DURAMENS	ADENOSST	ONSTEADS		POSTDATE
	MAUNDERS	ADENOTUY	AUTODYNE	ADEORRSS	DROSERAS
	SURNAMED	ADENOUVW	UNAVOWED	ADEORRST	ROADSTER
ADEMNRTU	UNDREAMT	ADENPPRS	PARPENDS	ADEORRTW	TARROWED
ADEMNRUW	UNWARMED	ADENPPSU	UNSAPPED	ADEORRVW	OVERDRAW
ADEMNSSU	MEDUSANS	ADENPPTU	UNTAPPED	ADEORSST	ASSORTED
ADEMNSUU	UNAMUSED	ADENPRRS	PARDNERS		TORSADES
ADEMNTTU	UNMATTED	ADENPRSU	UNDRAPES	ADEORSTU	OUTDARES
ADEMOORT	MODERATO		UNSPARED		OUTREADS
ADEMOORV	VAROOMED	ADENPRSW	PREDAWNS		READOUTS
ADEMOOST	STOMODEA	ADENPRTU	DEPURANT	ADEORSTX	EXTRADOS
ADEMOOSV	VAMOOSED		UNPARTED	ADEORSUV	SAVOURED
ADEMOPRY	PYODERMA	ADENPRTY	PEDANTRY	ADEORSWY	RODEWAYS
ADEMOPST	STAMPEDO	ADENPRUW	UNWARPED	ADEORTTU	OUTRATED
ADEMOPSU	MOUSEPAD	ADENPRUY	UNDERPAY		OUTTRADE
ADEMORRT	MORTARED		UNPRAYED	ADEORTUV	OUTRAVED
ADEMORRU	ARMOURED	ADENPSSY	DYSPNEAS	ADEOSSTT	ASSOTTED
ADEMORRW	MARROWED		SYNAPSED	ADEOSTTU	OUTDATES
ADEMORST	STROAMED	ADENQRSU	SQUANDER	ADEOSWWY	WAYWODES
ADEMORTU	OUTDREAM	ADENRRST	STRANDER	ADEOTTTW	TATTOWED
ADEMORTW	DAMEWORT	ADENRRSY	REYNARDS	ADEPPRST	STRAPPED
	WARDMOTE	ADENRRTU	UNTARRED	ADEPRRTU	RAPTURED
ADEMOSSY	SAMOYEDS	ADENRRWY	WARDENRY	ADEPRSTU	PASTURED
ADEMPRST	STRAMPED	ADENRSSS	SARSDENS		UPDATERS
ADEMRRSU	EARDRUMS	ADENRSST	STANDERS		UPSTARED
ADEMRRTY	MARTYRED	ADENRSSU	DANSEURS	ADEPSTUY	UPSTAYED
ADEMNNTU	UNTANNED	ADENRSTU	DAUNTERS	ADEPSUWY	UPSWAYED
ADENNORT	NONRATED		TRANSUDE	ADEQSTTU	SQUATTED
ADENNOSY	ANODYNES		UNTREADS	ADERRSSW	WARDRESS
ADENNOTU	UNATONED	ADENRSTX	DEXTRANS	ADERRSTT	REDSTART
ADENNOTW	WANTONED	ADENRSUY	UNDERSAY	ADERSSSU	ASSUREDS
ADENNOTY	TANNOYED	ADENRTTU	TRUANTED	ADERSSTW	STEWARDS
ADENNPST	PENDANTS	ADENRTTY	TYRANTED	ADERSSUY	DASYURES
ADENNRRU	UNDERRAN	ADENRTUX	UNDERTAX	ADERSTTU	STATURED
ADENNRTY	TYRANNED	ADENRUWY	UNDERWAY	ADERSTUX	SURTAXED
ADENNRUW	UNWARNED	ADENSSSW	WESSANDS	ADERSTVY	STRAYVED
ADENNSTU	ASTUNNED	ADENSTTU	UNSTATED	ADERSTWW	WESTWARD
ADENNTUW	UNWANTED		UNTASTED	ADESSTTW	WADSETTS
ADENOOPS	EPANODOS	ADENSTUW	UNWASTED	ADFFGIIR	GIRAFFID
ADENOORT	RATOONED	ADENSTUY	UNSTAYED	ADFFGINS	DAFFINGS
ADENOORW	WANDEROO		UNSTEADY	ADFFHIRS	DRAFFISH
ADENOOST	ODONATES	ADENSUWY	UNSWAYED	ADFFHNOS	HANDOFFS
ADENOOTZ	OZONATED	ADEOOPRW	PEARWOOD	ADFFISST	DISTAFFS
ADENOPRR	PARDONER	ADEOOPSS	APODOSES	ADFFLNOS	FANFOLDS
ADENOPRS	OPERANDS	ADEOORRT	TOREADOR	ADFFLOOS	OFFLOADS
	PADRONES	ADEOOTTT	TATTOOED	ADFFLRUU	FRAUDFUL
	PANDORES	ADEOPPRT	PREADOPT	ADFFNOST	STANDOFF
ADENOPRT	PRONATED	ADEOPPRV	APPROVED	ADFFOORS	AFFOORDS
ADENOPRX	EXPANDOR	ADEOPRRS	EARDROPS	ADFGINNU	UNFADING
ADENOPSS	DAPSONES	ADEOPRRT	PARROTED	ADFGINRS	FARDINGS
	SPADONES		PREDATOR	ADFGINRT	DRAFTING
ADENOPST	NOTEPADS		PRORATED	ADFGINRW	DWARFING
	TONEPADS		PROTRADE	ADFHILSY	LADYFISH
ADENOPSU	UNSOAPED		TEARDROP	ADFHINSS	SANDFISH
ADENOPSY	DYSPNOEA	ADEOPRRU	UPROARED	ADFHIOST	TOADFISH
ADENORRS	ADORNERS	ADEOPRST	ADOPTERS	ADFHIRSW	DWARFISH
	READORNS		ASPORTED	ADFHLNSU	HANDFULS
ADENORRW	NARROWED		PASTORED		HANDSFUL

ADFHLNSY	FLYHANDS	ADGHNNSU	HANDGUNS	ADGILORS	GOLIARDS
ADFHLOST	HOLDFAST	ADGHNOSS	SANDHOGS	ADGILORY	GOLIARDY
ADFHOOSS	SHADOOFS	ADGHNOSW	HAGDOWNS		GYROIDAL
ADFIIILR	FILARIID	ADGHOOPR	ODOGRAPH	ADGILRVY	GRAVIDLY
ADFIILPY	LAPIDIFY	ADGHORSW	HOGWARDS	ADGIMMNR	DRAMMING
ADFILLLN	LANDFILL	ADGHPSYY	DYSPHAGY	ADGIMMNW	DWAMMING
ADFILLMN	FILMLAND	ADGHRSTU	DRAUGHTS	ADGIMNNU	MAUNDING
ADFILLNO	NAILFOLD	ADGHRTUY	DRAUGHTY	ADGIMNOP	POMADING
ADFILLNW	WINDFALL	ADGIIIRT	TIGRIDIA	ADGIMNPS	DAMPINGS
ADFILMNO	MANIFOLD	ADGIILLN	DIALLING	ADGIMNRS	MRIDANGS
ADFILMRU	FLUIDRAM	ADGIILLO	GLADIOLI	ADGIMNRY	MARDYING
ADFILNWW	WINDFLAW	ADGIILNO	GONIDIAL	ADGIMNUW	DWAUMING
ADFILRTY	DRAFTILY	ADGIILNP	PLAIDING	ADGIMOSU	DIGAMOUS
ADFIMNRS	FINDRAMS	ADGIILNR	DRAILING	ADGINNOR	ADORNING
ADFIMORY	FAIRYDOM	ADGIILNS	DIALINGS	ADGINNOT	DONATING
ADFIMRSW	DWARFISM		GLIADINS	ADGINNPY	PANDYING
ADFINORZ	FORZANDI	ADGIILNT	DILATING	ADGINNRS	DARNINGS
ADFINRST	INDRAFTS	ADGIILPY	PYGIDIAL	ADGINNRT	DRANTING
ADFIORSV	DISFAVOR	ADGIILST	DIGITALS	ADGINNRU	UNDARING
ADFKLLNO	FOLKLAND	ADGIILTY	ALGIDITY	ADGINNSS	SANDINGS
ADFLLNOW	DOWNFALL	ADGIIMNR	ADMIRING	ADGINNST	STANDING
ADFLMNOR	LANDFORM	ADGIIMNX	ADMIXING	ADGINNSW	DAWNINGS
ADFLMNOY	MANYFOLD	ADGIIMOR	IDIOGRAM	ADGINNSY	SDAYNING
ADFLMOPR	FRAMPOLD	ADGIIMST	DIGAMIST	ADGINNTU	DAUNTING
ADFLMPSU	MUDFLAPS	ADGIINNR	DRAINING	ADGINOOP	POIGNADO
ADFLMSTU	MUDFLATS	ADGIINNS	SDAINING	ADGINOOR	RIGADOON
ADFLNOPS	PLAFONDS	ADGIINNT	NIDATING	ADGINOPT	ADOPTING
ADFLOOWY	FLOODWAY	ADGIINNU	GUANIDIN	ADGINORS	ROADINGS
ADFLORSU	FOULARDS	ADGIINNV	INVADING	ADGINORU	RIGAUDON
ADFMRSTU	STUDFARM	ADGIINNY	DIGYNIAN	ADGINOST	DOATINGS
ADFNNOST	FONDANTS	ADGIINOR	RADIOING	ADGINOTY	TOADYING
ADFNOORZ	FORZANDO	ADGIINOT	IODATING	ADGINPPR	DRAPPING
ADFOOPST	FOOTPADS	ADGIINOV	AVOIDING	ADGINPTU	UPDATING
ADFOOSTW	FATWOODS	ADGIINRR	ARRIDING	ADGINRRS	GRANDSIR
ADFOOSWY	FOODWAYS	ADGIINRS	RAIDINGS	ADGINRST	TRADINGS
ADFORRSW	FORWARDS	ADGIINRY	DAIRYING	ADGINRSW	DRAWINGS
	FROWARDS	ADGIINSS	SIGANIDS		SWARDING
ADFPRSTU	UPDRAFTS	ADGIINSU	IGUANIDS		WARDINGS
ADGGGILN	DAGGLING	ADGIINSV	ADVISING	ADGINRSY	YARDINGS
ADGGGINR	DRAGGING	ADGIINSW	GWINIADS	ADGINRTT	DRATTING
ADGGGINS	DAGGINGS	ADGIINTU	AUDITING	ADGINRTU	ANTIDRUG
ADGGHNOS	HANGDOGS	ADGIJNRU	ADJURING	ADGINRTY	TARDYING
ADGGHORY	HYDRAGOG	ADGIKLNR	DARKLING	ADGINSTU	ADUSTING
ADGGILNN	DANGLING	ADGILLNU	ALLUDING		SUDATING
ADGGILNS	GADLINGS		DUALLING	ADGINSWY	GWYNIADS
ADGGILRS	RIGGALDS	ADGILLNW	WINDGALL	ADGIORST	GORDITAS
ADGGINRS	NIGGARDS	ADGILLNY	DALLYING	ADGIPRSU	PAGURIDS
ADGGINRU	GUARDING	ADGILLOT	GOLDTAIL	ADGIRSSU	GUISARDS
ADGGLRSU	SLUGGARD	ADGILMNS	GILDSMAN	ADGIRSZZ	GIZZARDS
ADGHHILN	HIGHLAND		MADLINGS	ADGKOOSZ	GADZOOKS
ADGHHIOR	HIGHROAD	ADGILMNW	DWALMING	ADGLLNOS	GOLLANDS
ADGHILLL	GILDHALL	ADGILMOR	MARIGOLD	ADGLMNOS	MANGOLDS
ADGHILNN	HANDLING	ADGILNNS	LANDINGS	ADGLMNSU	GUMLANDS
ADGHILOS	HIDALGOS		SANDLING	ADGLNOOS	DONGOLAS
ADGHILPY	DIAGLYPH	ADGILNNU	UNLADING		GONDOLAS
ADGHILTY	DAYLIGHT	ADGILNOS	LOADINGS	ADGLNORS	GOLDARNS
ADGHINOR	HOARDING	ADGILNPP	DAPPLING	ADGLNOSW	GOWLANDS
ADGHINPR	HANDGRIP	ADGILNRS	DARLINGS	ADGLOORY	GARDYLOO
ADGHINSS	SHADINGS	ADGILNRT	DARTLING	ADGLOSWY	DAYGLOWS
ADGHIPRS	DIGRAPHS	ADGILNRW	DRAWLING	ADGMNOOR	ONDOGRAM
ADGHIRRS	ARDRIGHS	ADGILNRY	DARINGLY	ADGMNORS	GORMANDS
ADGHIRSS	DISHRAGS	ADGILNZZ	DAZZLING	ADGMNORU	GOURMAND
ADGHITTW	TIGHTWAD	ADGILOOS	SOLIDAGO	ADGNNOQU	QUANDONG
ADGHLNNO	LONGHAND	ADGILOPR	PRODIGAL	ADGNNORS	GRANDSON

ADGNNRYY	GYNANDRY	ADHLLLOS	HOLDALLS	ADIILRST	DISTRAIL
ADGNOORS	DRAGOONS	ADHLLNOR	HANDROLL	ADIILRSW	WIRILDAS
	GADROONS	ADHLLNOS	HOLLANDS	ADIILSST	DIALISTS
ADGNRRSU	GURNARDS	ADHLLNUV	VALLHUND	ADIILSSY	DIALYSIS
ADGNRSUU	UNGUARDS	ADHLMNOO	HANDLOOM	ADIILTVY	VALIDITY
ADGOOPRS	GOSPODAR	ADHLMORT	THRALDOM	ADIIMMSS	MAIDISMS
ADGOPRST	POSTGRAD	ADHLMOSY	HOLYDAMS	ADIIMNNS	INDAMINS
ADGOPRSU	PODARGUS	ADHLMPSY	LYMPHADS	ADIIMPSU	ASPIDIUM
ADGORSTU	OUTDRAGS	ADHLNORW	WALDHORN	ADIIMRST	TRIADISM
ADGORTUU	OUTGUARD	ADHLNOTU	DUATHLON	ADIIMRSU	MUDIRIAS
ADGRSSTU	DUSTRAGS	ADHLNOUW	DOWNHAUL	ADIINNOT	NIDATION
ADHHIPRS	HARDSHIP	ADHLOSYY	HOLYDAYS	ADIINNOZ	DIAZINON
ADHHLOOV	HAVDOLOH	ADHMNOOS	MANHOODS	ADIINOOT	IODATION
ADHHMOSS	SHAHDOMS	ADHMOPRS	DRAMSHOP	ADIINOTU	AUDITION
ADHHNRTY	HYDRANTH	ADHMORSY	HYDROMAS	ADIINPRS	PINDARIS
ADHIIIKS	DAISHIKI	ADHNNOOR	HONORAND	ADIINRST	DISTRAIN
ADHIIJMS	JIHADISM	ADHNNORY	NONHARDY	ADIINSST	DISTAINS
ADHIIJST	IJTIHADS	ADHNOOTU	AUNTHOOD	ADIINSSU	SUIDIANS
	JIHADIST	ADHNORSU	UNHOARDS	ADIIOPRS	SPORIDIA
ADHIIKSS	DASHIKIS	ADHNOSTU	HANDOUTS	ADIIOPRT	TAPIROID
ADHIIMPS	AMIDSHIP		THOUSAND	ADIIOPSS	ADIPOSIS
ADHIINOP	OPHIDIAN	ADHNOSUW	UNSHADOW	ADIIORST	TARSIOID
ADHIINRW	WHINIARD	ADHNOSWW	DOWNWASH	ADIIPRTU	TRIPUDIA
ADHIJLSY	JADISHLY	ADHNRSTY	HYDRANTS	ADIIPRTY	RAPIDITY
ADHIKOPS	HAPKIDOS	ADHOOPRS	HOSPODAR	ADIIPSTY	SAPIDITY
ADHILLMO	HOLLIDAM	ADHOOPST	HOPTOADS	ADIIPTVY	VAPIDITY
ADHILLNS	SANDHILL	ADHOORRS	RHODORAS	ADIIQRSU	DAQUIRIS
ADHILLOP	PHALLOID	ADHOORSW	ROADSHOW	ADIIRSST	DIARISTS
ADHILLOT	THALLOID	ADHOORYZ	HYDROZOA	ADIIRSTT	DISTRAIT
ADHILLRV	HYDRILLA	ADHOPRST	HARDTOPS		TRIADIST
ADHILMOO	HOMALOID		POTSHARD	ADIJNOST	ADJOINTS
ADHILMOS	HALIDOMS	ADHOPRSU	UPHOARDS	ADIKKRRW	KIRKWARD
ADHILNOR	RHODINAL	ADHOPRSY	RHAPSODY	ADIKKRRY	KIRKYARD
ADHILNST	HANDLIST	ADHOPSST	DASHPOTS	ADIKLLOR	ROADKILL
ADHILOPS	HAPLOIDS	ADHORRSU	DHOURRAS	ADIKLNPS	LANDSKIP
	SHIPLOAD	ADHORRTY	HYDRATOR	ADIKLNSY	LADYKINS
ADHILOPY	HAPLOIDY	ADHORSTU	TOADRUSH	ADIKLORS	KILORADS
ADHILOST	SHITLOAD	ADHORSWY	SHOWYARD	ADIKLOSS	ODALISKS
ADHILOSY	HOLIDAYS	ADHPSTYY	DYSPATHY	ADIKMNNS	MANKINDS
	HYALOIDS	ADIIINRV	VIRIDIAN	ADIKMOSU	DAIMOKUS
ADHILPSY	LADYSHIP	ADIIIQRU	DAIQUIRI	ADIKMSSS	DISMASKS
ADHIMNOR	RHODAMIN	ADIIKLLN	KALLIDIN	ADIKNNNU	DUNNAKIN
ADHIMNOS	ADMONISH	ADIIKLMM	MILKMAID	ADIKNNST	INKSTAND
ADHIMNOU	HUMANOID	ADIIKLST	TAILSKID	ADIKNOPY	PYINKADO
ADHIMNSS	HANDISMS	ADIIKNOP	PINAKOID	ADIKNPSS	SKIDPANS
ADHIMOPP	AMPHIPOD	ADIIKNST	ANTISKID	ADIKNRSS	DISRANKS
ADHIMPSS	PHASMIDS	ADIIKOST	DAKOITIS	ADIKNRST	STINKARD
ADHIMRTY	MYRIADTH	ADIILLMR	MILLIARD	ADIKPRSS	DISPARKS
ADHINOPY	DIAPHONY	ADIILLNY	IDYLLIAN	ADIKQRSU	DIQUARKS
ADHINPSS	DISHPANS	ADIILLOP	LIPOIDAL	ADIKSSWY	SKIDWAYS
ADHINPSU	DAUPHINS	ADIILLOR	ARILLOID	ADILLLPY	PALLIDLY
ADHINRTW	HANDWRIT	ADIILLST	DIALLIST	ADILLMMS	MILLDAMS
ADHINRWY	WHINYARD	ADIILLUV	DILUVIAL	ADILLMNR	MANDRILL
ADHINSST	STANDISH	ADIILMSS	MISDIALS	ADILLMOU	ALLODIUM
ADHINSTU	DIANTHUS	ADIILNOT	DILATION	ADILLMOV	VILLADOM
ADHIOSTY	TOADYISH	ADIILNSU	INDUSIAL	ADILLMSY	DISMALLY
ADHIPRSW	WARDSHIP	ADIILNSV	INVALIDS	ADILLNPS	LANDSLIP
ADHIPRSY	SHIPYARD	ADIILNSW	WINDSAIL	ADILLOOP	POLOIDAL
ADHIPSTY	DISPATHY	ADIILNTW	TAILWIND	ADILLOPS	SPADILLO
ADHIRTWW	WITHDRAW	ADIILNTY	DAINTILY	ADILLOSW	DISALLOW
ADHITWWY	WIDTHWAY	ADIILNUV	DILUVIAN	ADILLOSY	DISLOYAL
ADHKNORW	HANDWORK		INDUVIAL	ADILLRWY	WILLYARD
ADHKORSW	DORHAWKS	ADIILOPP	DIPLOPIA	ADILLSTY	DISTALLY
ADHKOSSU	SHAKUDOS	ADIILPST	LAPIDIST	ADILMMOS	MODALISM

ADILMNNO	MANDOLIN	**ADIMMNSY**	DYNAMISM	**ADIOOPRT**	PAROTOID
ADILMNOS	SALMONID	**ADIMMOST**	AMIDMOST	**ADIOOPSS**	APODOSIS
ADILMNRS	MANDRILS	**ADIMMOTU**	DOMATIUM	**ADIOOSSW**	WOODSIAS
	RIMLANDS	**ADIMNNOS**	MONDAINS	**ADIOPPST**	POSTPAID
ADILMOOR	MODIOLAR	**ADIMNNOT**	DOMINANT	**ADIOPRRS**	AIRDROPS
ADILMOPS	DIPLOMAS	**ADIMNOOR**	MAINDOOR	**ADIOPRSS**	SPAROIDS
	PLASMOID	**ADIMNOSS**	MADISONS	**ADIOPRST**	PARODIST
ADILMOPT	DIPLOMAT	**ADIMNOST**	DONATISM		PAROTIDS
ADILMOPV	OLYMPIAD		SAINTDOM	**ADIOPRSV**	PRIVADOS
ADILMORU	ORDALIUM	**ADIMNOWW**	WIDOWMAN	**ADIOPRTY**	PODIATRY
ADILMOST	MODALIST	**ADIMNRSW**	MISDRAWN	**ADIOPSTY**	DYSTOPIA
ADILMOSU	ALODIUMS	**ADIMNRSY**	MISANDRY	**ADIORRTT**	TRADITOR
ADILMOSY	AMYLOIDS	**ADIMNSSY**	SYSADMIN	**ADIORSST**	ASTROIDS
ADILMOTY	MODALITY	**ADIMNSTY**	DYNAMIST		SARODIST
ADILMPRY	LAMPYRID	**ADIMOPRY**	MYRIAPOD	**ADIORSSV**	ADVISORS
ADILMPSS	PLASMIDS	**ADIMOPSY**	SYMPODIA	**ADIORSTT**	STRADIOT
ADILMPSU	PALUDISM	**ADIMORRS**	MIRADORS	**ADIORSTU**	AUDITORS
ADILMSSU	DUALISMS	**ADIMOSST**	MASTOIDS	**ADIORSVY**	ADVISORY
ADILMSSY	DISMAYLS	**ADIMOSTT**	MATTOIDS	**ADIORTUY**	AUDITORY
	LADYISMS	**ADIMOSTY**	TOADYISM	**ADIOSSVW**	DISAVOWS
ADILMTUY	MULTIDAY	**ADIMPRSY**	PYRAMIDS	**ADIPRRTU**	PURTRAID
ADILNNNU	NUNDINAL	**ADIMRSSW**	MISDRAWS	**ADIPRSST**	DISPARTS
ADILNNOT	NONTIDAL	**ADIMRSUU**	SUDARIUM	**ADIRRWYZ**	WIZARDRY
ADILNNOV	NONVALID	**ADIMSSST**	DISMASTS	**ADIRSSTY**	SATYRIDS
ADILNNSU	DISANNUL	**ADIMSSTU**	DUMAISTS	**ADIRSSUY**	DYSURIAS
ADILNOOR	DOORNAIL		STADIUMS	**ADJKNRUY**	JUNKYARD
ADILNOOV	VINDALOO	**ADINNNTU**	INUNDANT	**ADJLMORS**	JARLDOMS
ADILNOPY	PALINODY	**ADINNOOT**	DONATION	**ADJLSUUW**	WUDJULAS
ADILNORS	ORDINALS		NODATION	**ADJNORSU**	ADJOURNS
ADILNORT	TRINODAL	**ADINNOPS**	DIPNOANS	**ADJORRSU**	ADJURORS
ADILNOTY	NODALITY	**ADINNORS**	ANDIRONS	**ADJORSTU**	ADJUSTOR
ADILNPRS	SPANDRIL	**ADINNORT**	ORDINANT	**ADKKLOSY**	KAKODYLS
ADILNPST	DISPLANT	**ADINNORY**	NONDAIRY	**ADKLMRSU**	MUDLARKS
ADILNRSU	DIURNALS	**ADINNOTU**	NUDATION	**ADKLNOPR**	DRONKLAP
ADILNRWY	INWARDLY	**ADINNRSW**	WINNARDS	**ADKLOORW**	WOODLARK
ADILNSSU	SUNDIALS	**ADINNRSY**	INNYARDS		WORKLOAD
ADILNSSW	WINDLASS	**ADINOOPS**	ISOPODAN	**ADKMNORW**	MARKDOWN
ADILOOPZ	DIPLOZOA	**ADINOOPT**	ADOPTION	**ADKMOORR**	DARKROOM
ADILOORT	IDOLATOR	**ADINOORT**	TANDOORI	**ADKNORTU**	OUTDRANK
	TOROIDAL	**ADINOOTT**	DOTATION	**ADKNRSTU**	STUNKARD
ADILOOSV	OVOIDALS	**ADINOPPS**	OPPIDANS	**ADKOORRW**	ROADWORK
ADILOPRT	DIOPTRAL	**ADINOPRR**	RAINDROP	**ADKORRWY**	YARDWORK
	TRIPODAL	**ADINOPRS**	PONIARDS	**ADKORSWY**	DAYWORKS
ADILOPSS	DISPOSAL	**ADINOPRY**	PYRANOID		WORKDAYS
ADILOQSU	SQUALOID	**ADINOPST**	PINTADOS	**ADKRSSWY**	SKYWARDS
ADILORST	DILATORS		SATINPOD	**ADLLLOOY**	DOOLALLY
ADILORSY	SOLIDARY	**ADINORRS**	ORDINARS	**ADLLMOSW**	WADMOLLS
ADILORTY	ADROITLY	**ADINORRY**	ORDINARY	**ADLLNOPW**	PLOWLAND
	DILATORY	**ADINORSS**	SADIRONS	**ADLLNOSW**	LOWLANDS
	IDOLATRY	**ADINORST**	DIATRONS	**ADLLOPRS**	POLLARDS
ADILOSST	SODALIST		INTRADOS	**ADLLORSY**	DORSALLY
ADILOSTY	SODALITY	**ADINORSU**	DINOSAUR	**ADLLRSWY**	DRYWALLS
ADILPPSY	DISAPPLY	**ADINORSV**	VIRANDOS	**ADLMNNOO**	NONMODAL
ADILPRSY	PYRALIDS	**ADINORTU**	DURATION	**ADLMNOOR**	MOORLAND
ADILPSST	PLASTIDS	**ADINOSTU**	SUDATION	**ADLMNORY**	RANDOMLY
ADILPSSY	DISPLAYS	**ADINOSTX**	OXIDANTS	**ADLMNOSS**	MOSSLAND
ADILPSTU	PLAUDITS	**ADINOSTY**	DYSTONIA	**ADLMOORS**	LORDOMAS
ADILRTTY	TILTYARD	**ADINPSST**	SANDPITS		MALODORS
ADILRTWY	TAWDRILY	**ADINPSSY**	SYNAPSID	**ADLMOORU**	MALODOUR
ADILRWYZ	WIZARDLY	**ADINRRST**	TRIDARNS	**ADLMOPRW**	MOLDWARP
ADILSSTU	DUALISTS	**ADINRSSU**	SUNDARIS	**ADLMOPSY**	PSALMODY
ADIMMNOO	AMMONOID	**ADINRSTU**	UNITARDS	**ADLMORSU**	MODULARS
ADIMMNOS	MONADISM	**ADINRUVZ**	UNVIZARD	**ADLNNORS**	NORLANDS
	NOMADISM	**ADINSWWY**	WINDWAYS	**ADLNNOSW**	SNOWLAND

ADLNNOTU	NONADULT
ADLNNOTW	TOWNLAND
ADLNNSSU	SUNLANDS
ADLNNTUU	UNDULANT
ADLNOORS	LARDOONS
ADLNOORW	LOANWORD
ADLNOPRT	PORTLAND
ADLNOPRU	PAULDRON
ADLNOPSU	POUNDALS
ADLNOPWY	DOWNPLAY
	PLAYDOWN
ADLNORST	TROLANDS
ADLNORWY	ONWARDLY
ADLNOSST	SANDLOTS
ADLNOSSU	SOULDANS
ADLNOSSY	SYNODALS
ADLNOSTU	OUTLANDS
ADLOOPRU	UROPODAL
ADLOORWW	WOOLWARD
ADLOPRSU	POULARDS
ADLOPRWY	WORDPLAY
ADLOPSUU	PALUDOUS
ADLOQSUW	OLDSQUAW
ADLORRSW	WARLORDS
ADLORTWY	TOWARDLY
ADLPRUWY	UPWARDLY
ADLRRTUY	ULTRADRY
ADMMNOOS	DOOMSMAN
ADMMNSSU	SUMMANDS
ADMMNTUU	MUTANDUM
ADMNNORY	MONANDRY
ADMNNOSU	SOUNDMAN
ADMNNOTU	NOTANDUM
ADMNOOOT	ODONTOMA
ADMNOORS	DOORSMAN
	MADRONOS
ADMNOORW	MOONWARD
ADMNOOST	MASTODON
ADMNOOSW	WOODSMAN
ADMNOOSZ	MADZOONS
ADMNORST	DORMANTS
	MORDANTS
ADMNORSW	SANDWORM
	SWORDMAN
ADMNOSSU	OSMUNDAS
ADMNPPSU	SANDPUMP
ADMOOPPP	POPPADOM
ADMOORRW	WARDROOM
ADMOORST	DOORMATS
ADMOORSY	DAYROOMS
ADMOPPPU	POPPADUM
ADMOPPSU	POPADUMS
ADMORSST	STARDOMS
	TSARDOMS
ADMORSTW	MADWORTS
ADMORSTZ	TZARDOMS
ADMRSSTU	DURMASTS
	MUSTARDS
ADMRSTUY	MUSTARDY
ADNNOOST	NANODOTS
ADNNOOSY	NOONDAYS
ADNNORTY	DYNATRON
ADNNOSTU	DAUNTONS
ADNNRSTU	DUNNARTS
ADNOOPRS	PANDOORS
	SPADROON
ADNOOQRU	QUADROON
ADNOORST	DONATORS
	ODORANTS
	TANDOORS
	TORNADOS
ADNOORTY	DONATORY
ADNOOSVW	ADVOWSON
ADNOPRSU	PANDOURS
ADNOPRSV	PROVANDS
ADNOQRSU	SQUADRON
ADNORRSW	NORWARDS
ADNORSTU	ROTUNDAS
ADNORSTW	SANDWORT
ADNORSTY	TARDYONS
ADNORSWY	NAYWORDS
ADNORSXY	SARDONYX
ADNORTUW	OUTDRAWN
	UNTOWARD
ADNORWWY	WANWORDY
ADNOSSTU	ASTOUNDS
ADNOSTTU	OUTSTAND
	STANDOUT
ADNPRSSU	SANDSPUR
ADNPSSTU	DUSTPANS
	STANDUPS
	UPSTANDS
ADNRSSUW	SUNWARDS
ADOOPPRU	PAUROPOD
ADOOPRRT	TRAPDOOR
ADOOPRSU	SAUROPOD
ADOOPSSW	SAPWOODS
ADOORSWY	DOORWAYS
ADOOSSSW	SASSWOOD
ADOOSSTT	TOSTADOS
ADOPRRSW	WARDROPS
ADOPRSSW	PASSWORD
ADOPSSSU	SOAPSUDS
ADORRSTU	DARTROUS
ADORSTUW	OUTDRAWS
	OUTWARDS
ADORSTUY	SUDATORY
ADORTUVY	ADVOUTRY
ADPRRTUY	PURTRAYD
ADRSSTTU	STARDUST
ADSSSTUW	SAWDUSTS
ADSSTUWY	SAWDUSTY
AEEEELRS	RELEASEE
AEEEEMRT	EMEERATE
AEEEFLRS	EELFARES
AEEEFRRW	FREEWARE
AEEEFRTY	AFTEREYE
AEEEGGNR	REENGAGE
AEEEGKLS	KEELAGES
AEEEGLLS	LEGALESE
AEEEGLNR	GENERALE
AEEEGLRT	EGLATERE
	REGELATE
	RELEGATE
AEEEGLRV	LEVERAGE
AEEEGLST	LEGATEES
AEEEGLSV	SELVAGEE
AEEEGLTV	VEGELATE
AEEEGMRT	METERAGE
AEEEGNRT	GENERATE
	RENEGATE
	TEENAGER
AEEEGNSS	AGENESES
AEEEGPRS	PEERAGES
AEEEGPSS	SEEPAGES
AEEEGRST	EAGEREST
	ETAGERES
	STEERAGE
AEEEGRSW	SEWERAGE
AEEEGTTV	VEGETATE
AEEEHKLL	KEELHALE
AEEEHLRT	ETHEREAL
AEEEHMPR	EPHEMERA
AEEEHNRS	ENHEARSE
AEEEHRRS	REHEARSE
AEEEHRRT	REHEATER
AEEEHSTT	AESTHETE
AEEEILNS	ALIENEES
AEEEIMNX	EXAMINEE
AEEEIMRT	EMERITAE
AEEEIRST	EATERIES
AEEEJNTT	JEANETTE
AEEEKKPS	KEEPSAKE
AEEEKMSS	KAMEESES
AEEEKMSZ	KAMEEZES
AEEEKNRW	WEAKENER
AEEELLPP	APPELLEE
AEEELLST	TELESALE
AEEELMNR	ENAMELER
AEEELNRT	LATEENER
AEEELNRV	VENEREAL
AEEELNST	SELENATE
AEEELPRR	REPEALER
AEEELQSU	SEQUELAE
AEEELRRS	RELEASER
AEEELRRV	REVEALER
AEEELRSS	RELEASES
AEEELRST	TEASELER
AEEELRSW	WEASELER
AEEELRTX	AXLETREE
AEEELSSS	EASELESS
AEEELSTV	ELEVATES
AEEEMMRT	METAMERE
AEEEMNST	EASEMENT
AEEEMPRS	PERMEASE
AEEEMPRT	PERMEATE
AEEENNRV	VENEREAN
AEEENNTV	VENENATE
AEEENPTT	PATENTEE
AEEENRST	SERENATE
AEEENRTT	ENTERATE
AEEENRTV	ENERVATE
	VENERATE
AEEEPRRT	REPARTEE
	REPEATER
	REREPEAT
AEEEPSTW	SWEETPEA
AEEERRST	ARRESTEE
AEEERRTW	TREEWARE
AEEERSST	ESTERASE
	TESSERAE
AEEERSVW	REWEAVES

AEEERTWY	EYEWATER	AEEFLRSW	WELFARES		GELATINE
AEEFFLLS	FELAFELS	AEEFLTTT	FLATETTE		LEGATINE
AEEFFLRT	TAFFEREL	AEEFMNOR	FOREMEAN	AEEGILNV	INVEAGLE
AEEFFLTT	FLATFEET		FORENAME	AEEGILOU	EULOGIAE
AEEFFNRT	AFFERENT	AEEFMNRS	ENFRAMES	AEEGILPR	PERIGEAL
AEEFGILR	FILAGREE	AEEFMORS	FEARSOME	AEEGILRS	GASELIER
AEEFGIRR	FERRIAGE	AEEFMRRS	REFRAMES	AEEGILST	EGALITES
AEEFGIRS	FEGARIES	AEEFMRTY	FEMETARY		ELEGIAST
AEEFGIRT	FIGEATER	AEEFNRST	FASTENER	AEEGILSW	WEIGELAS
AEEFGLNS	FENAGLES		FENESTRA	AEEGILTV	LEVIGATE
AEEFGLSU	FUSELAGE		REFASTEN	AEEGIMNR	GERMAINE
AEEFGNRS	FREEGANS	AEEFNRTT	FATTENER	AEEGIMNT	GEMINATE
AEEFGNST	FANTEEGS	AEEFNSSS	SAFENESS	AEEGIMRS	GAMESIER
AEEFGRSS	SERFAGES	AEEFORRV	OVERFEAR		REIMAGES
AEEFGSTW	WEFTAGES	AEEFOSTU	FEATEOUS	AEEGIMRT	EMIGRATE
AEEFHIRS	SHEAFIER	AEEFRRST	FERRATES		REMIGATE
AEEFHLLS	SELFHEAL	AEEFRSST	FEASTERS	AEEGINNT	ANTIGENE
AEEFHRST	FEATHERS	AEEFRSTU	FEATURES	AEEGINPR	PERIGEAN
AEEFHRTY	FEATHERY	AEEFRSWY	FREEWAYS	AEEGINRR	REGAINER
AEEFIINR	INFERIAE	AEEFTTUV	FAUVETTE	AEEGINRS	ANERGIES
AEEFIIRS	AERIFIES	AEEGGHIW	WEIGHAGE		GESNERIA
AEEFIKLL	LEAFLIKE	AEEGGINR	AGREEING	AEEGINRT	GRATINEE
AEEFIKLW	KALEWIFE	AEEGGIRV	AGGRIEVE		INTERAGE
AEEFIKRR	FREAKIER	AEEGGLLS	ALLEGGES	AEEGINRZ	RAZEEING
AEEFIKRS	FAKERIES	AEEGGLOU	AEGLOGUE	AEEGINSS	AGENESIS
AEEFIKRW	WAKERIFE	AEEGGLRS	GREGALES		AGENISES
AEEFILMN	FILENAME	AEEGGNNR	GANGRENE		ASSIGNEE
AEEFILNR	FLANERIE	AEEGGNOS	GASOGENE	AEEGINST	SAGENITE
AEEFILRS	FILAREES	AEEGGNOZ	GAZOGENE	AEEGINSU	EUGENIAS
	SERAFILE	AEEGGNRS	ENGAGERS	AEEGINSV	ENVISAGE
AEEFILRT	FEATLIER	AEEGGOPS	EPAGOGES	AEEGINSZ	AGENIZES
	FRAILTEE	AEEGGPRU	PUGGAREE	AEEGINTV	AGENTIVE
AEEFILST	FEALTIES	AEEGGRSU	REGAUGES		NEGATIVE
	FETIALES	AEEGHIRS	HIREAGES	AEEGINTX	EXIGEANT
	LEAFIEST	AEEGHIRT	HERITAGE	AEEGIPPS	PIPEAGES
AEEFIPSW	SPAEWIFE	AEEGHLOT	HELOTAGE	AEEGIPQU	EQUIPAGE
AEEFIRRR	RAREFIER	AEEGHLRS	SHEARLEG	AEEGIPRS	PIERAGES
AEEFIRRS	RAREFIES	AEEGHLRW	RAGWHEEL	AEEGIPVW	PAGEVIEW
AEEFIRSS	FREESIAS	AEEGHMOP	HOMEPAGE	AEEGIRRS	GREASIER
AEEFIRTT	FETERITA	AEEGHMPR	GRAPHEME	AEEGIRSS	GREASIES
AEEFISST	SAFETIES	AEEGHNRS	SHAGREEN	AEEGIRSU	EUGARIES
AEEFKMNT	FAKEMENT	AEEGHNST	THENAGES	AEEGIRTT	AIGRETTE
AEEFKOPR	FOREPEAK	AEEGHNSW	WHANGEES	AEEGIRTV	ERGATIVE
AEEFKRRY	FREAKERY	AEEGHORS	GHERAOES	AEEGISSS	ASSIEGES
AEEFLLMR	FEMERALL	AEEGHRRT	GATHERER	AEEGISTY	GAYETIES
AEEFLLMT	FLAMELET		REGATHER	AEEGKLLS	KLEAGLES
AEEFLLNR	REFALLEN	AEEGIILW	WEIGELIA	AEEGKMRR	REGMAKER
AEEFLLNV	EVENFALL	AEEGIINR	AEGIRINE	AEEGKNNR	GENNAKER
AEEFLLRW	FAREWELL	AEEGIIRT	AEGIRITE	AEEGLLNR	ALLERGEN
AEEFLLSS	LEAFLESS	AEEGIIST	GAIETIES	AEEGLLPR	PRELEGAL
AEEFLLST	FELLATES	AEEGIKLM	GAMELIKE	AEEGLLRS	ALLEGERS
	LEAFLETS	AEEGIKLT	GATELIKE	AEEGLLSZ	GAZELLES
AEEFLMNS	ENFLAMES	AEEGIKLU	AGUELIKE	AEEGLMNS	MELANGES
AEEFLMOS	FLEASOME	AEEGILLS	GALILEES	AEEGLMNV	GAVELMEN
AEEFLMPR	PREFLAME		LEGALISE	AEEGLMOS	MESOGLEA
AEEFLMSS	FAMELESS	AEEGILLZ	LEGALIZE	AEEGLMPX	MEGAPLEX
	SELFSAME	AEEGILMN	LIEGEMAN	AEEGLMRS	GLEAMERS
AEEFLNRU	FUNEREAL	AEEGILMR	GLEAMIER	AEEGLMRT	TELEGRAM
AEEFLOOV	FOVEOLAE	AEEGILMS	GELSEMIA	AEEGLMRY	MEAGERLY
AEEFLORV	OVERLEAF		MILEAGES		MEAGRELY
AEEFLRRR	REFERRAL	AEEGILNR	ALGERINE	AEEGLMST	MELTAGES
AEEFLRRT	FALTERER	AEEGILNS	ENSILAGE	AEEGLNNR	ENLARGEN
AEEFLRSS	FEARLESS		LINEAGES	AEEGLNNT	ENTANGLE
AEEFLRST	REFLATES	AEEGILNT	GALENITE	AEEGLNOS	GASOLENE

AEEGLNOT	ELONGATE		NEGATERS	AEEHIPRS	PHARISEE
AEEGLNRR	ENLARGER		REAGENTS		SPHAIREE
AEEGLNRS	ENLARGES		SEGREANT	AEEHIPST	APHETISE
	GENERALS		SERGEANT		HEAPIEST
	GLEANERS		STERNAGE		HEPATISE
AEEGLNRT	REGENTAL	AEEGNRSU	RENAGUES	AEEHIPTT	HEPATITE
AEEGLNSU	EUGLENAS	AEEGNRSV	AVENGERS	AEEHIPTZ	APHETIZE
AEEGLNSV	EVANGELS		ENGRAVES		HEPATIZE
AEEGLNVY	EVANGELY	AEEGNRTU	GAUNTREE	AEEHIRRS	HEARSIER
AEEGLOOZ	ZOOGLEAE	AEEGNRWY	GREENWAY	AEEHIRRT	EARTHIER
AEEGLORS	AEROGELS	AEEGNSSS	SAGENESS		HEARTIER
AEEGLOST	SEGOLATE	AEEGNSTT	TENTAGES	AEEHIRSS	ASHERIES
AEEGLPRS	PEREGALS	AEEGNSTV	VENTAGES	AEEHIRST	HEARTIES
AEEGLRRS	REGALERS	AEEGNTTV	VEGETANT	AEEHIRSV	SHIVAREE
AEEGLRSS	EELGRASS	AEEGOPRV	OVERPAGE	AEEHIRTW	WHEATIER
	GEARLESS	AEEGOPSS	SAPEGOES	AEEHISST	ATHEISES
	LARGESSE	AEEGORRV	OVERGEAR		ESTHESIA
AEEGLRSU	LEAGUERS	AEEGORSV	OVERAGES	AEEHISTT	ATHETISE
AEEGLRSW	LEGWEARS	AEEGORVV	OVERGAVE		HESITATE
AEEGLRSZ	REGLAZES	AEEGOSTX	GEOTAXES	AEEHISTV	HEAVIEST
AEEGLRTU	REGULATE	AEEGPRRS	ASPERGER	AEEHISTZ	ATHEIZES
AEEGLRUX	EXERGUAL		PRESAGER	AEEHITTZ	ATHETIZE
AEEGLSST	GATELESS	AEEGPRRT	PARGETER	AEEHKLLR	RAKEHELL
AEEGLSSV	SELVAGES	AEEGPRSS	ASPERGES	AEEHKLLU	KEELHAUL
AEEGLSSW	WAGELESS		PRESAGES	AEEHKMNS	KHAMSEEN
AEEGLSSY	EYEGLASS	AEEGPRSU	PUGAREES	AEEHKNRR	HANKERER
AEEGLSTT	GALETTES	AEEGPSST	SEPTAGES		HARKENER
AEEGLSTV	VEGETALS	AEEGRRRT	REGRATER	AEEHKNRS	HEARKENS
AEEGLTTU	TUTELAGE	AEEGRRSS	GREASERS	AEEHKPRR	PHREAKER
AEEGLTUV	EVULGATE	AEEGRRST	REGRATES	AEEHKRST	HEKTARES
AEEGMMNR	ENGRAMME	AEEGRRSU	REARGUES	AEEHKRSU	HEUREKAS
AEEGMMNS	GAMESMEN	AEEGRRSW	WAGERERS	AEEHLLSS	SEASHELL
AEEGMMOS	GAMESOME	AEEGRRTT	RETARGET	AEEHLMNW	WHALEMEN
AEEGMMST	GEMMATES	AEEGRSST	RESTAGES		WHEELMAN
	TAGMEMES	AEEGRSTT	GREATEST	AEEHLMNY	HYMENEAL
AEEGMNOR	ARGEMONE	AEEGRSTU	TREAGUES	AEEHLMOS	HEALSOME
AEEGMNRS	AGREMENS	AEEGRSTW	STREWAGE	AEEHLMPT	HELPMATE
AEEGMNRT	AGREMENT	AEEGRSUZ	GUEREZAS	AEEHLNOS	ENHALOES
AEEGMNSS	GAMENESS	AEEGSSTT	GESTATES	AEEHLNOT	ANETHOLE
	MAGNESES	AEEGSTTZ	GAZETTES	AEEHLNPT	ELEPHANT
AEEGMNTT	TEGMENTA	AEEHHHSS	HASHEESH	AEEHLNRT	LEATHERN
AEEGMNTZ	GAZEMENT	AEEHHIRT	HEATHIER	AEEHLNSS	HALENESS
AEEGMOOT	OOGAMETE	AEEHHLNZ	HAZELHEN	AEEHLNTX	EXHALENT
AEEGMOST	SOMEGATE	AEEHHNST	ENSHEATH	AEEHLNVY	HEAVENLY
AEEGMPRS	PREGAMES		HEATHENS	AEEHLORS	ARSEHOLE
AEEGMRST	GAMESTER	AEEHHOOP	PAHOEHOE		HALOSERE
	MEAGREST	AEEHHRSS	REHASHES	AEEHLORV	OVERHALE
AEEGMRSU	REMUAGES	AEEHHRST	HEATHERS	AEEHLOSU	ALEHOUSE
AEEGMSSS	MEGASSES		SHEATHER	AEEHLPRT	PLEATHER
	MESSAGES	AEEHHRTY	HEATHERY	AEEHLPST	HEELTAPS
AEEGMSSU	MESSUAGE	AEEHHSST	SHEATHES		PLEASETH
AEEGNNNO	ENNEAGON	AEEHIKLR	HARELIKE	AEEHLPTT	TELEPATH
AEEGNNPS	PANGENES	AEEHIKRS	SHIKAREE	AEEHLRRT	LATHERER
AEEGNNRS	ENRANGES	AEEHILNP	ELAPHINE	AEEHLRST	HALTERES
AEEGNNRT	GENERANT	AEEHILRS	SHIRALEE		LEATHERS
AEEGNNRU	ENRAUNGE	AEEHILRT	ETHERIAL	AEEHLRSV	HAVERELS
AEEGNNRV	ENGRAVEN	AEEHIMNT	HEMATEIN	AEEHLRTT	HEARTLET
AEEGNOPS	PEONAGES		HEMATINE	AEEHLRTY	LEATHERY
AEEGNPPS	GENAPPES	AEEHIMNX	HEXAMINE	AEEHLSST	HATELESS
AEEGNRRT	ETRANGER	AEEHIMPT	EPITHEMA		HEATLESS
AEEGNRRV	ENGRAVER	AEEHIMTT	HEMATITE	AEEHLSTT	ATHLETES
AEEGNRST	ESTRANGE	AEEHINRS	INHEARSE	AEEHLTTY	ETHYLATE
	GRANTEES	AEEHINRT	ATHERINE	AEEHMMRR	HAMMERER
	GREATENS		HERNIATE		REHAMMER

AEEHMNNY	HYMENEAN	AEEHRSTT	EARTHSET	AEEILNRT	ELATERIN
AEEHMNPS	SHEEPMAN		THEATERS		ENTAILER
AEEHMNRS	SHAREMEN		THEATRES		TREENAIL
	SHEARMEN	AEEHRSTV	THREAVES	AEEILNSS	SEALINES
AEEHMNRT	EARTHMEN	AEEHRSTW	WEATHERS	AEEILNSV	VASELINE
AEEHMNST	METHANES		WREATHES	AEEILNSX	ALEXINES
AEEHMNTU	ATHENEUM	AEEHRTVW	WHATEVER	AEEILNTV	ELVANITE
AEEHMNTX	EXANTHEM	AEEHRTXZ	EXAHERTZ		VENTAILE
AEEHMORW	HOMEWARE	AEEHSTTW	SAWTEETH	AEEILORT	AEROLITE
AEEHMPRR	HAMPERER	AEEHSTVY	HEAVYSET	AEEILOTT	ETIOLATE
AEEHMPSS	EMPHASES	AEEIIMRT	METAIRIE	AEEILPRR	PEARLIER
AEEHMRSS	MAHSEERS	AEEIINRT	INERTIAE	AEEILPRS	ESPALIER
AEEHMRST	ERATHEMS	AEEIISST	ASEITIES		PEARLIES
AEEHMRTY	ERYTHEMA	AEEIJPRS	JAPERIES	AEEILPRT	PEARLITE
AEEHMSST	MATHESES	AEEIKKLL	LAKELIKE	AEEILPST	EPILATES
AEEHMTUX	EXHUMATE	AEEIKKLP	PEAKLIKE	AEEILPSW	PALEWISE
AEEHNNSS	SNEESHAN	AEEIKKLW	LIKEWAKE	AEEILQSU	EQUALISE
AEEHNNTX	XANTHENE	AEEIKLLS	SEALLIKE	AEEILQUX	EXEQUIAL
AEEHNOPR	EARPHONE	AEEIKLMS	SEAMLIKE	AEEILQUZ	EQUALIZE
AEEHNPST	HAPTENES	AEEIKLMU	LEUKEMIA	AEEILRRS	REALISER
	HEPTANES	AEEIKLMZ	MAZELIKE	AEEILRRT	RETAILER
	PHENATES	AEEIKLPT	TAPELIKE	AEEILRRZ	REALIZER
	STEPHANE	AEEIKLRW	WEAKLIER	AEEILRSS	REALISES
AEEHNRSS	ARSHEENS	AEEIKLST	LEAKIEST	AEEILRST	ATELIERS
AEEHNRST	HASTENER	AEEIKLSV	VASELIKE		EARLIEST
	HEARTENS	AEEIKLVW	WAVELIKE		LATERISE
AEEHNRSU	UNHEARSE	AEEIKMMR	MERIMAKE		LEARIEST
AEEHNRSV	RESHAVEN	AEEIKMNT	KETAMINE		REALTIES
AEEHNRTT	HATERENT	AEEIKNRS	SNEAKIER	AEEILRSV	VELARISE
	THREATEN	AEEIKNRT	ANKERITE	AEEILRSY	YEARLIES
AEEHNRTU	URETHANE		KREATINE	AEEILRSZ	REALIZES
AEEHNRTW	ENWREATH	AEEIKNSS	AKINESES		SLEAZIER
	WATERHEN	AEEIKPST	PEAKIEST	AEEILRTT	LATERITE
	WREATHEN	AEEIKRRS	RAKERIES		LITERATE
AEEHNRWY	ANYWHERE		SKEARIER	AEEILRTV	LEVIRATE
AEEHNSST	ANTHESES	AEEIKRTW	TWEAKIER		RELATIVE
AEEHNSTU	UNEATHES	AEEILLNT	TENAILLE	AEEILRTZ	LATERIZE
AEEHNSTW	ENSWATHE	AEEILLRS	REALLIES	AEEILRVW	LIVEWARE
	WHEATENS	AEEILLRT	LAETRILE		REVIEWAL
AEEHOPRT	EPHORATE	AEEILLST	LEALTIES	AEEILRVZ	VELARIZE
AEEHOPRV	OVERHEAP	AEEILMMN	MELAMINE	AEEILSST	ASTELIES
AEEHORRV	OVERHEAR	AEEILMMT	MEALTIME	AEEILSTT	AILETTES
AEEHORSS	SEAHORSE	AEEILMNS	MELANISE	AEEILSTV	ELATIVES
	SEASHORE	AEEILMNT	MELANITE		LEAVIEST
AEEHORTV	OVERHATE	AEEILMNZ	MELANIZE		VEALIEST
	OVERHEAT	AEEILMRS	ALMERIES	AEEILSVW	ALEWIVES
AEEHOSTU	TEAHOUSE		MEASLIER	AEEILTTV	LEVITATE
AEEHPPRS	PRESHAPE	AEEILMRT	EREMITAL	AEEILTUV	ELUVIATE
AEEHPRRS	REPHRASE		MATERIEL	AEEIMMNT	MEANTIME
	RESHAPER		REALTIME	AEEIMNNS	ENAMINES
AEEHPRRT	THREAPER	AEEILMST	MEALIEST	AEEIMNRS	REMANIES
AEEHPRSS	RESHAPES		METALISE	AEEIMNRT	ANTIMERE
	SPHAERES	AEEILMSV	MALVESIE	AEEIMNRX	EXAMINER
	SPHEARES	AEEILMTZ	METALIZE	AEEIMNSS	NEMESIAS
AEEHPRST	PREHEATS	AEEILNNS	SELENIAN	AEEIMNST	ETAMINES
	SPREATHE	AEEILNPR	PERINEAL		MATINEES
AEEHPRUV	UPHEAVER	AEEILNPS	ALEPINES		MISEATEN
AEEHPSUV	UPHEAVES		PENALISE		SEMINATE
AEEHQSSU	QUASHEES		SEPALINE	AEEIMNSX	EXAMINES
AEEHRRSS	SHEARERS	AEEILNPT	PETALINE	AEEIMNUV	MAUVEINE
AEEHRRTU	URETHRAE		TAPELINE	AEEIMOSS	AMEIOSES
AEEHRRTW	WREATHER	AEEILNPZ	PENALIZE	AEEIMPRS	EMPAIRES
AEEHRSSV	RESHAVES	AEEILNRR	NEARLIER	AEEIMRRS	SMEARIER
AEEHRSSW	REWASHES	AEEILNRS	ALIENERS	AEEIMRSS	SERIEMAS

AEEIMRST	EMERITAS		RERAISES
	EMIRATES	**AEEIRRST**	ARTERIES
	REAMIEST		REASTIER
	STEAMIER	**AEEIRRTT**	RETRAITE
AEEIMRTV	VIAMETER	**AEEIRRTW**	WATERIER
AEEIMSSS	MISEASES	**AEEIRRVW**	WAVERIER
	SIAMESES	**AEEIRSST**	SERIATES
AEEIMSST	SEAMIEST	**AEEIRSTT**	ARIETTES
	STEAMIES		ITERATES
AEEIMSSZ	SIAMEZES		TEARIEST
AEEIMSTT	ESTIMATE		TREATIES
	ETATISME		TREATISE
	MEATIEST	**AEEIRSTV**	EVIRATES
	TEATIMES	**AEEIRSTW**	SWEATIER
AEEIMSTW	TEAMWISE		TAWERIES
AEEINNRS	ANSERINE		WASTERIE
AEEINNTV	VENETIAN		WEARIEST
AEEINOPS	PAEONIES	**AEEIRSTY**	YEASTIER
AEEINPRS	NAPERIES	**AEEIRSVV**	AVERSIVE
AEEINPRT	APERIENT	**AEEISSTX**	EXTASIES
AEEINPTT	PIANETTE	**AEEISSVW**	SEAWIVES
AEEINRRS	REARISEN	**AEEISTTT**	ETATISTE
AEEINRRT	RETAINER		STEATITE
AEEINRSS	SENARIES	**AEEISTTV**	AVIETTES
AEEINRST	ARENITES		ESTIVATE
	ARSENITE		EVITATES
	RESINATE	**AEEISTUX**	EUTAXIES
	STEARINE		EUTEXIAS
	TRAINEES	**AEEITTUX**	EUTAXITE
AEEINRSU	UNEASIER	**AEEITUVX**	EXUVIATE
AEEINSSS	EASINESS	**AEEJLNPT**	JETPLANE
AEEINSST	ETESIANS	**AEEJLOSU**	JEALOUSE
	TENIASES	**AEEJNRST**	SERJEANT
AEEINSSV	VAINESSE	**AEEJOPRT**	PEJORATE
AEEINSTT	ANISETTE	**AEEJRTTW**	WATERJET
	TETANIES	**AEEKKLWY**	LYKEWAKE
	TETANISE	**AEEKKNOS**	KOKANEES
AEEINSTV	NAIVETES	**AEEKKPSY**	KEEPSAKY
AEEINSVW	INWEAVES	**AEEKLLSS**	LEAKLESS
AEEINTTZ	TETANIZE	**AEEKLLST**	LAKELETS
AEEIOOPP	EPOPOEIA		SKELETAL
AEEIORST	ETAERIOS	**AEEKLMMU**	MAMELUKE
AEEIPPRR	PAPERIER	**AEEKLMRT**	TELEMARK
AEEIPPSS	APEPSIES	**AEEKLMRY**	YARMELKE
AEEIPPST	APPETISE	**AEEKLMSS**	MAKELESS
AEEIPPSU	EUPEPSIA	**AEEKLNST**	KANTELES
AEEIPPTT	APPETITE	**AEEKLPSS**	PEAKLESS
AEEIPPTZ	APPETIZE	**AEEKLSSW**	WAKELESS
AEEIPRRR	RARERIPE	**AEEKLSTY**	EYESTALK
	REPAIRER	**AEEKMNSS**	KAMSEENS
AEEIPRRS	PEREIRAS	**AEEKMORV**	MAKEOVER
	SPEARIER	**AEEKMOTY**	YOKEMATE
AEEIPRST	PARIETES	**AEEKMRRR**	REMARKER
	PETARIES	**AEEKMRRS**	REMAKERS
AEEIPRTV	PERVIATE	**AEEKMRRT**	MARKETER
AEEIPSST	EPITASES		REMARKET
AEEIPSTT	PEATIEST	**AEEKMRST**	MEERKATS
AEEIPSTX	EPITAXES	**AEEKNNNS**	NANKEENS
	EXPIATES	**AEEKNNPS**	KNEEPANS
AEEIPTVX	EXAPTIVE	**AEEKNORW**	REAWOKEN
AEEIQRSU	QUEASIER	**AEEKNPRT**	PERTAKEN
AEEIQRUZ	QUEAZIER	**AEEKNPST**	NETSPEAK
AEEIQSTU	EQUISETA	**AEEKNPSU**	SNEAKEUP
AEEIRRSS	REARISES	**AEEKNPSW**	NEWSPEAK

AEEKNRSS	SNEAKERS
AEEKNRSW	REWAKENS
	WAKENERS
AEEKNSSW	WEAKNESS
AEEKOOPP	PEEKAPOO
AEEKORRV	OVERRAKE
AEEKORST	KERATOSE
	KREASOTE
AEEKORTV	OVERTAKE
	TAKEOVER
AEEKORVW	OVERWEAK
AEEKPRSS	RESPEAKS
	SPEAKERS
AEEKPRST	PERTAKES
AEEKPRTT	PARKETTE
AEEKPRTU	REUPTAKE
AEEKQRSU	SQUEAKER
AEEKRRST	RETAKERS
	STREAKER
AEEKRRSW	WREAKERS
AEEKRSST	SAKERETS
AEEKRSTW	TWEAKERS
AEELLLPT	PELLETAL
AEELLLTT	TELLTALE
AEELLMMS	MAMSELLE
AEELLMSS	MEALLESS
AEELLNOV	NOVELLAE
AEELLOSV	ALVEOLES
AEELLOTT	ALLOTTEE
AEELLPRS	PARELLES
AEELLPTT	PALLETTE
	PLATELET
AEELLPTY	TELEPLAY
AEELLRRT	TERRELLA
AEELLRRV	RAVELLER
AEELLSST	SATELLES
	TESSELLA
AEELLSSZ	ZEALLESS
AEELLSTT	STELLATE
AEELLSWY	WALLEYES
	WEASELLY
AEELLTVV	VALVELET
AEELMMTU	MALEMUTE
AEELMNPS	EMPANELS
	EMPLANES
	ENSAMPLE
AEELMNPT	PLATEMEN
AEELMNRT	LAMENTER
AEELMNSS	LAMENESS
	MALENESS
	MANELESS
	NAMELESS
	SALESMEN
AEELMNST	MANTEELS
	STEELMAN
	TALESMEN
AEELMNSW	WEALSMEN
AEELMNSY	AMYLENES
AEELMNTT	MANTELET
AEELMNTV	LAVEMENT
AEELMOTT	MATELOTE
AEELMPRS	EMPALERS
	RESAMPLE
AEELMPRX	EXEMPLAR

AEELMPRY	EMPYREAL		PREALTER	**AEEMNNSS**	MEANNESS
AEELMPSX	EXAMPLES	**AEELPRRY**	PARLEYER	**AEEMNORV**	OVERNAME
AEELMPTT	PALMETTE	**AEELPRSS**	PLEASERS	**AEEMNORZ**	ARMOZEEN
	TEMPLATE		PRESALES	**AEEMNOSS**	ANEMOSES
AEELMRST	LAMETERS		RELAPSES	**AEEMNOSW**	SEAWOMEN
AEELMRTX	EXTREMAL	**AEELPRST**	PETRALES	**AEEMNOSX**	AXONEMES
AEELMSSS	SEAMLESS		PLEATERS	**AEEMNPRS**	PRENAMES
AEELMSST	MATELESS		PRELATES		SPEARMEN
	MEATLESS		REPLATES	**AEEMNPRT**	PERMEANT
	TAMELESS	**AEELPRSU**	PLEASURE		PETERMAN
AEELMSTU	EMULATES		SERPULAE	**AEEMNPRY**	EMPYREAN
AEELNNPS	ENPLANES	**AEELPRSV**	VESPERAL	**AEEMNPTV**	PAVEMENT
AEELNNRT	LANNERET	**AEELPRTY**	PTERYLAE	**AEEMNRST**	REMANETS
AEELNNSS	LEANNESS	**AEELPRUV**	PREVALUE	**AEEMNRSU**	USERNAME
AEELNOPR	PERONEAL	**AEELPSST**	SPATLESE	**AEEMNRSV**	VERSEMAN
AEELNOPT	ANTELOPE		TAPELESS	**AEEMNRSW**	MENSWEAR
AEELNORU	ALEURONE	**AEELPSTT**	PALETTES	**AEEMNRTU**	NUMERATE
AEELNOSS	ENOLASES	**AEELPSTU**	EPAULETS	**AEEMNRTV**	AVERMENT
AEELNPPS	SPALPEEN	**AEELPSTV**	SEPTLEVA	**AEEMNRTW**	WATERMEN
AEELNPRR	PRERENAL	**AEELPSTZ**	SPAETZLE	**AEEMNRUV**	MANEUVER
AEELNPRS	REPANELS	**AEELQRSU**	LEQUEARS	**AEEMNRVY**	EVERYMAN
AEELNPSS	PALENESS		SQUEALER	**AEEMNSSS**	SAMENESS
	PANELESS	**AEELQSUZ**	QUEZALES	**AEEMNSST**	TAMENESS
AEELNQSU	SQUALENE	**AEELRRST**	ALTERERS	**AEEMNSTU**	MANSUETE
AEELNRRS	LEARNERS		REALTERS	**AEEMNSTW**	SWEETMAN
	RELEARNS		RELATERS	**AEEMORST**	EROTEMAS
AEELNRRT	RELEARNT	**AEELRRSV**	RAVELERS	**AEEMORTV**	OVERTAME
AEELNRSS	REALNESS		REVERSAL	**AEEMPPRR**	PAMPERER
AEELNRST	ALTERNES		SLAVERER	**AEEMPRRT**	TAMPERER
	ETERNALS	**AEELRRSX**	RELAXERS	**AEEMPRRV**	REVAMPER
	TELERANS	**AEELRRTU**	URETERAL	**AEEMPRST**	TEMPERAS
AEELNRSV	ENSLAVER	**AEELRRTV**	TRAVELER	**AEEMPRSY**	EMPAYRES
AEELNRSW	RENEWALS	**AEELRSST**	RESLATES	**AEEMPRTT**	ATTEMPER
AEELNRTV	LEVANTER		STEALERS	**AEEMPSTU**	AMPUTEES
	RELEVANT		TEARLESS	**AEEMQRRU**	REMARQUE
AEELNRTW	TREELAWN		TESSERAL	**AEEMQRSU**	MARQUEES
AEELNRTX	EXTERNAL	**AEELRSSU**	LEASURES	**AEEMQTTU**	MAQUETTE
AEELNRUU	NEURULAE	**AEELRSSV**	SEVERALS	**AEEMRRSS**	SMEARERS
AEELNRUV	REVENUAL	**AEELRSSW**	WARELESS	**AEEMRRST**	REMASTER
AEELNSST	LATENESS	**AEELRSTT**	ALERTEST		STREAMER
AEELNSSV	ENSLAVES	**AEELRSTU**	RESALUTE	**AEEMRRSU**	MEASURER
	VANELESS	**AEELRSTX**	EXALTERS	**AEEMRRTT**	TETRAMER
AEELNSTY	ENTAYLES	**AEELRSTY**	EASTERLY	**AEEMRSST**	MASSETER
AEELNTUV	EVENTUAL	**AEELRSUV**	REVALUES		SEAMSTER
AEELNTVY	VENTAYLE	**AEELRSVY**	AVERSELY		STEAMERS
AEELOPRS	PAROLEES	**AEELSSST**	ALTESSES	**AEEMRSSU**	MEASURES
AEELOPRV	OVERLEAP		SATELESS		REASSUME
AEELOPSX	POLEAXES		SEATLESS	**AEEMRSTT**	TEAMSTER
AEELOPTT	TOEPLATE	**AEELSSTU**	SETUALES	**AEEMRSTW**	STEMWARE
AEELORRS	RELEASOR	**AEELSSTV**	SALVETES	**AEEMRSTY**	METAYERS
AEELORST	OLEASTER	**AEELSSVW**	WAVELESS	**AEEMRTWY**	YAWMETER
AEELORSU	AUREOLES	**AEELSTTT**	STATELET	**AEEMSSST**	SEAMSETS
AEELORSV	OVERSALE	**AEELSTTY**	LAYETTES	**AEEMSSSU**	MASSEUSE
AEELORTT	TOLERATE	**AEELSTVW**	WAVELETS	**AEEMSSTU**	MEATUSES
AEELORTV	ELEVATOR	**AEEMMNRS**	MERESMAN	**AEEMSTTU**	AMUSETTE
	OVERLATE	**AEEMMNTZ**	MAZEMENT	**AEENNOST**	NEONATES
AEELORTW	TOLEWARE	**AEEMMPSY**	EMPYEMAS	**AEENNPST**	PENTANES
AEELORVZ	OVERZEAL	**AEEMMRRY**	YAMMERER	**AEENNRRS**	ENSNARER
AEELOSSW	LEASOWES	**AEEMMRST**	AMMETERS	**AEENNRSS**	ENSNARES
AEELOSTV	LOVESEAT		METAMERS		NEARNESS
AEELOTTT	TEETOTAL	**AEEMMSST**	MESSMATE		RENNASES
AEELPRRS	PEARLERS	**AEEMNNOS**	ANEMONES	**AEENNRTU**	ENAUNTER
	RELAPSER	**AEEMNNPS**	PENNAMES	**AEENNRTV**	REVENANT
AEELPRRT	PALTERER	**AEEMNNRT**	REMANENT	**AEENNRUX**	ANNEXURE

Eight-letter anagrams

AEENNSSS	SANENESS	AEEORRTV	OVERRATE	AEERSSUU	URAEUSES
AEENNSST	NEATNESS	AEEORRVW	OVERWEAR	AEERSSUV	VAREUSES
AEENNSTT	SETENANT	AEEORRVY	OVERYEAR	AEERSTTT	ATTESTER
AEENOORT	AEROTONE	AEEORSSV	OVERSEAS	AEERSTTX	EXTREATS
AEENOPRS	PERAEONS	AEEORSTV	OVEREATS	AEERSTWW	WETWARES
	PERSONAE	AEEORSVW	OVERSAVE	AEERTTTZ	TERZETTA
AEENOPSU	EUPNOEAS	AEEORSVW	OVERAWES	AEERVWYY	EVERYWAY
AEENORRS	REASONER	AEEORSVY	OVEREASY	AEESSSSS	ASSESSES
AEENORRV	OVERNEAR	AEEPPPRU	PREPUPAE	AEESSTTT	TESTATES
AEENORSS	RESEASON	AEEPPRRR	PREPARER	AEFFFLRS	FLAFFERS
	SEASONER	AEEPPRRS	PAPERERS	AEFFGIIL	EFFIGIAL
AEENORST	EARSTONE		PREPARES	AEFFGINR	FIREFANG
	RESONATE		REPAPERS	AEFFGIRS	GIRAFFES
AEENORTV	OVERNEAT	AEEPPRRU	PUERPERA		RIFFAGES
	RENOVATE	AEEPPRST	PREPASTE	AEFFGNRS	ENGRAFFS
AEENORVW	OVENWARE		PRETAPES	AEFFGOST	OFFSTAGE
AEENOTTU	OUTEATEN	AEEPPRSV	PREPAVES	AEFFGRSU	GAUFFERS
AEENPPRT	PETNAPER	AEEPRRRT	PARTERRE		SUFFRAGE
AEENPPTT	APPETENT	AEEPRRSS	ASPERSER	AEFFHIKY	KAFFIYEH
AEENPQTU	PETANQUE		SPEARERS		KEFFIYAH
AEENPRUV	PARVENUE	AEEPRRST	TAPERERS	AEFFHILL	HALFLIFE
AEENPSSU	APNEUSES	AEEPRRSV	PREAVERS	AEFFILNY	AFFINELY
AEENPSSX	EXPANSES	AEEPRRTT	PATTERER	AEFFILRW	WAFFLIER
AEENPTTY	ANTETYPE		PRETREAT	AEFFILUV	EFFLUVIA
AEENRRRW	WARRENER	AEEPRRTU	APERTURE	AEFFIMRR	AFFIRMER
AEENRRSS	RARENESS	AEEPRSSS	ASPERSES		REAFFIRM
AEENRRST	TERRANES		PREASSES	AEFFIMRW	FARMWIFE
AEENRRSV	RAVENERS		REPASSES	AEFFIPRS	PIAFFERS
AEENRRSW	ANSWERER	AEEPRSST	TRAPESES	AEFFIRSX	AFFIXERS
	REANSWER	AEEPRSSZ	SPREAZES	AEFFKLRU	FREAKFUL
AEENRRSY	YEARNERS	AEEPRSTT	PEARTEST	AEFFKORS	RAKEOFFS
AEENRRTT	NATTERER		PRETASTE	AEFFKOST	OFFTAKES
	RATTENER	AEEPRSTU	EPURATES		TAKEOFFS
AEENRRTU	RENATURE		SUPERATE	AEFFLMSW	FLAMFEWS
AEENRRTV	TAVERNER	AEEPRSTZ	TRAPEZES	AEFFLNSS	SNAFFLES
AEENRSSS	SEARNESS	AEEPSSTT	SPATTEES	AEFFLNTU	AFFLUENT
AEENRSST	ASSENTER	AEEQRRUV	QUAVERER	AEFFLRRS	RAFFLERS
	EARNESTS	AEERRRST	ARRESTER	AEFFLRSW	WAFFLERS
	SARSENET		REARREST	AEFFLSTU	FEASTFUL
AEENRSSU	ANURESES	AEERRSST	ASSERTER		SUFFLATE
AEENRSSX	XERANSES		REASSERT	AEFFLSUX	AFFLUXES
AEENRSTT	ENTREATS		SERRATES	AEFFMMST	STAFFMEN
	RATTEENS		TERRASES	AEFFMRSU	EARMUFFS
AEENRSTU	SAUTERNE	AEERRSSU	ERASURES	AEFFNNSS	NAFFNESS
AEENRSTV	AVENTRES		REASSURE	AEFFNORT	AFFRONTE
	VETERANS	AEERRSSW	SWEARERS	AEFFORST	AFFOREST
AEENRSUV	UNREAVES	AEERRSTT	RETRATES	AEFFOSVW	WAVEOFFS
AEENRTTV	ANTEVERT		RETREATS	AEFFQRSU	QUAFFERS
AEENRTTX	EXTERNAT		TREATERS	AEFFRSST	RESTAFFS
	EXTRANET	AEERRSTU	AUSTERER		STAFFERS
AEENRTTY	ENTREATY		TREASURE	AEFFRTTU	TARTUFFE
AEENRTUV	AVENTURE	AEERRSTV	AVERTERS	AEFGGGOS	FOGGAGES
AEENRVWW	NEWWAVER		TRAVERSE	AEFGGILR	FLAGGIER
AEENSSST	SENSATES	AEERRSTW	WATERERS	AEFGGINU	FEAGUING
AEENSTTV	NAVETTES	AEERRSVW	WAVERERS	AEFGGIST	FAGGIEST
AEENSUVW	UNWEAVES	AEERSSSS	REASSESS	AEFGGLRS	FLAGGERS
AEEOPRRT	PATERERO	AEERSSSU	SEASURES	AEFGGMOS	MEGAFOGS
	PERORATE	AEERSSSV	ASSEVERS	AEFGHINR	HANGFIRE
AEEOPRST	OPERATES	AEERSSSY	ESSAYERS	AEFGHINS	SHEAFING
	PROTEASE	AEERSSTT	ESTREATS	AEFGHOSS	FOGASHES
AEEOPRTT	OPERETTA		RESTATES	AEFGHTTU	FUGHETTA
AEEOPSTZ	EPAZOTES		RETASTES	AEFGIIRS	GASIFIER
AEEORRSU	REAROUSE	AEERSSTW	SWEATERS	AEFGIISS	GASIFIES
AEEORRSW	SOWARREE	AEERSSTZ	ERSATZES	AEFGIKLN	FANGLIKE

AEFGIKNR	FREAKING	**AEFHILPP**	HALFPIPE	**AEFILMNT**	FILAMENT
AEFGILNR	FINAGLER	**AEFHILRS**	FLASHIER	**AEFILMST**	FLAMIEST
AEFGILNS	FINAGLES	**AEFHIMSS**	FAMISHES	**AEFILMSY**	MAYFLIES
AEFGILOS	FOLIAGES	**AEFHIRST**	FAITHERS	**AEFILMTY**	FEMALITY
AEFGILRR	FRAGILER	**AEFHIRSW**	WHARFIES	**AEFILNNR**	INFERNAL
AEFGILTT	LIFTGATE	**AEFHLMSU**	SHAMEFUL	**AEFILNOR**	FORELAIN
AEFGIMTU	FUMIGATE	**AEFHLNOT**	HALFTONE	**AEFILNOT**	OLEFIANT
AEFGINRW	WAFERING	**AEFHLNSS**	HALFNESS	**AEFILNPS**	LIFESPAN
AEFGINRY	AREFYING	**AEFHLORS**	FAHLORES	**AEFILNRT**	INFLATER
AEFGINST	FEASTING	**AEFHLPRS**	PARFLESH	**AEFILNRU**	FRAULEIN
AEFGINTU	FANTIGUE	**AEFHLRSS**	FLASHERS	**AEFILNST**	INFLATES
AEFGIORR	FAIRGOER	**AEFHLRST**	FARTHELS	**AEFILNSV**	FLAVINES
AEFGIRRU	ARGUFIER	**AEFHLRTY**	FATHERLY	**AEFILNTT**	ANTILEFT
AEFGIRST	FRIGATES	**AEFHLSST**	FLASHEST	**AEFILOOR**	AEROFOIL
AEFGIRSU	ARGUFIES	**AEFHLSTU**	HASTEFUL	**AEFILORS**	FORESAIL
AEFGIRTU	FIGURATE	**AEFHMNRS**	FRESHMAN	**AEFILORT**	FLOATIER
	FRUITAGE	**AEFHMORT**	FATHOMER	**AEFILOST**	FOLIATES
AEFGIRTW	GIFTWARE	**AEFHNRSW**	FERNSHAW	**AEFILPPR**	FLAPPIER
AEFGISTU	FATIGUES	**AEFHRSST**	SHAFTERS	**AEFILPRX**	PREFIXAL
AEFGLLNO	LONGLEAF	**AEFHRSTT**	FARTHEST	**AEFILPST**	FLEAPITS
AEFGLLOP	FLAGPOLE	**AEFIIKLW**	WAIFLIKE	**AEFILRST**	FLARIEST
AEFGLLSS	FLAGLESS	**AEFIILLN**	NAILFILE		FRAILEST
AEFGLLSU	FULLAGES	**AEFIILMS**	FAMILIES	**AEFILRSU**	FAILURES
AEFGLMNU	FUGLEMAN	**AEFIILNS**	FINALISE	**AEFILRSV**	FAVRILES
AEFGLMOP	MEGAFLOP	**AEFIILNT**	ANTILIFE	**AEFILRSZ**	FILAZERS
AEFGLNOX	FLEXAGON	**AEFIILNZ**	FINALIZE	**AEFILRTT**	FILTRATE
AEFGLNRS	FLANGERS	**AEFIILSS**	SALIFIES	**AEFILRTU**	FAULTIER
AEFGLNSS	FANGLESS	**AEFIILST**	FETIALIS		FILATURE
AEFGLOOR	FLOORAGE		FILIATES	**AEFILRUW**	WEARIFUL
AEFGLOPR	LEAPFROG	**AEFIIMNS**	INFAMIES	**AEFILSSS**	FILASSES
AEFGLORW	GAREFOWL		INFAMISE	**AEFILSST**	SEALIFTS
AEFGLOST	FLOTAGES	**AEFIIMNZ**	FEMINAZI	**AEFILSSW**	SAWFLIES
AEFGLOSW	FLOWAGES		INFAMIZE	**AEFILSTT**	FLATTIES
AEFGLPSU	PAGEFULS	**AEFIIMRS**	RAMIFIES	**AEFILSTU**	FISTULAE
AEFGLRTU	GRATEFUL	**AEFIINRT**	FAINTIER	**AEFILSTV**	FESTIVAL
AEFGLSTU	STAGEFUL	**AEFIINRV**	VINIFERA	**AEFILSTW**	FLATWISE
AEFGLTUX	FLUXGATE	**AEFIINSS**	SANIFIES		FLAWIEST
AEFGMNOR	FORGEMAN	**AEFIINST**	FAINITES	**AEFILSTX**	FLAXIEST
AEFGMNRT	FRAGMENT	**AEFIINSZ**	NAZIFIES	**AEFILSWY**	LIFEWAYS
AEFGMORS	FROMAGES	**AEFIIPRT**	APERITIF	**AEFILTUU**	FAUTEUIL
AEFGNNOT	FONTANGE	**AEFIIRRS**	FRIARIES	**AEFIMMMR**	MAMMIFER
AEFGNORT	FRONTAGE		RARIFIES	**AEFIMMRS**	MISFRAME
AEFGNRRS	FRANGERS	**AEFIIRRT**	RATIFIER	**AEFIMNST**	MANIFEST
	GRANFERS	**AEFIIRST**	RATIFIES	**AEFIMORR**	AERIFORM
AEFGNRST	ENGRAFTS	**AEFIIRSU**	AURIFIES	**AEFIMORT**	FORMIATE
AEFGOOPT	FOOTPAGE	**AEFIITVX**	FIXATIVE	**AEFIMOST**	FOAMIEST
AEFGOORT	FOOTGEAR	**AEFIJLOS**	JEOFAILS	**AEFIMRRS**	FIREARMS
AEFGOOST	FOOTAGES	**AEFIKLMO**	FOAMLIKE	**AEFIMRRW**	FIRMWARE
AEFGORRS	FORAGERS	**AEFIKLNU**	FAUNLIKE	**AEFIMRSS**	MISFARES
AEFGORST	FAGOTERS	**AEFIKLNW**	FAWNLIKE	**AEFINNSS**	FAINNESS
AEFGORTT	FROTTAGE	**AEFIKLRY**	FREAKILY		NAIFNESS
AEFGOSSU	FOUGASSE	**AEFIKLST**	FLAKIEST	**AEFINNST**	INFANTES
AEFGRRST	GRAFTERS	**AEFIKMNN**	KNIFEMAN	**AEFINNSZ**	FANZINES
	REGRAFTS	**AEFIKMRR**	FIREMARK	**AEFINOPR**	PINAFORE
AEFHIKRS	FREAKISH	**AEFIKRUW**	WAUKRIFE	**AEFINORS**	FARINOSE
AEFHIKSW	WEAKFISH	**AEFILLMS**	FAMILLES	**AEFINOTT**	FETATION
AEFHILLN	FELLAHIN	**AEFILLNT**	FLATLINE	**AEFINPRS**	FIREPANS
AEFHILLR	FIREHALL	**AEFILLOT**	FELLATIO		PANFRIES
AEFHILLT	TEFILLAH	**AEFILLRW**	FIREWALL	**AEFINRRS**	REFRAINS
AEFHILMS	FISHMEAL	**AEFILMNR**	INFLAMER	**AEFINRRU**	UNFAIRER
AEFHILMT	HALFTIME		RIFLEMAN	**AEFINRRZ**	FRANZIER
AEFHILNS	SHINLEAF	**AEFILMNS**	FLAMINES	**AEFINRSS**	FAIRNESS
AEFHILOR	FORHAILE		INFLAMES		SANSERIF
AEFHILOX	HEXAFOIL		MISFALNE		SERAFINS

AEFINRST	FAINTERS	AEFLNOPT	PANTOFLE	AEFNORRW	FOREWARN
	FENITARS	AEFLNORS	FARNESOL	AEFNORST	SEAFRONT
AEFINRSX	XERAFINS	AEFLNORT	FLOREANT	AEFNORSU	FURANOSE
AEFINSTT	FAINTEST	AEFLNOSV	FLAVONES	AEFNPRSU	SUPERFAN
AEFINSTW	FAWNIEST	AEFLNRRU	FRENULAR	AEFNRRST	TRANSFER
AEFIORTV	FAVORITE	AEFLNRRS	SALFERNS	AEFNRRUY	FUNERARY
AEFIPRRT	FIRETRAP	AEFLNRSU	FLANEURS	AEFNRSTU	AFTERSUN
AEFIQRSU	AQUIFERS		FUNERALS	AEFNSSST	FASTNESS
AEFIRRRS	FARRIERS	AEFLNRTU	FLAUNTER	AEFNSSTU	UNSAFEST
AEFIRRRY	FARRIERY	AEFLNSST	FLATNESS	AEFNSTUY	UNSAFETY
AEFIRRST	FRATRIES	AEFLNSTT	FLATTENS	AEFOORTW	FOOTWEAR
AEFIRSTW	WASTRIFE	AEFLNSUU	FAUNULES	AEFOPRRT	FOREPART
AEFIRTUX	FIXATURE	AEFLNSUY	UNSAFELY	AEFOPRST	FOREPAST
AEFISTTT	FATTIEST	AEFLOORS	SEAFLOOR	AEFOPRSW	FOREPAWS
AEFKLLOT	FOLKTALE	AEFLOORV	FOVEOLAR	AEFORRSV	FAVORERS
AEFKLMRY	FLYMAKER	AEFLOOSV	FOVEOLAS	AEFORRSW	FORSWEAR
AEFKLNRS	FLANKERS	AEFLOPRT	TERAFLOP	AEFORRSY	FORAYERS
AEFKLOSS	SEAFOLKS	AEFLOPRY	FOREPLAY	AEFORRUV	FAVOURER
AEFKLRST	FARTLEKS	AEFLOPSW	PEAFOWLS	AEFORRWY	FORWEARY
AEFKLRUW	WREAKFUL	AEFLORRV	FLAVORER	AEFORSSY	FORESAYS
AEFKLSST	FLASKETS	AEFLORSS	SAFROLES	AEFORSTV	OVERFAST
AEFKLSTT	TALKFEST	AEFLORST	FLOATERS	AEFORSTW	FORWASTE
AEFKNORR	FORERANK		FORESTAL		SOFTWARE
AEFKNORS	FORSAKEN		REFLOATS	AEFORSTY	FORESTAY
AEFKNPRR	PREFRANK	AEFLORSU	FUSAROLE	AEFOSTTU	OUTFEAST
AEFKNRRS	FRANKERS	AEFLORSY	FORELAYS	AEFOSTUU	FEATUOUS
AEFKNRST	FRANKEST	AEFLORTW	FLEAWORT	AEFOSTUV	VOUTSAFE
AEFKOPRS	FORSPEAK	AEFLOSSU	FOSSULAE	AEFPRSST	PRESSFAT
AEFKORRS	FORSAKER	AEFLOSSW	SEAFOWLS	AEFRRSST	STRAFERS
AEFKORRW	WORKFARE	AEFLOSTT	FALSETTO	AEFRSSTW	FRETSAWS
AEFKORSS	FORSAKES	AEFLPPRS	FLAPPERS	AEFRSTTU	TARTUFES
AEFKORTU	FREAKOUT	AEFLPPRY	FLYPAPER	AEFRSTUW	WAFTURES
AEFLLMMU	FLAMMULE	AEFLPRSS	FELSPARS	AEFRSWYZ	FRAWZEYS
AEFLLNNS	FANNELLS	AEFLPRSU	FLAREUPS	AEGGGILN	ALEGGING
	FLANNELS	AEFLPRSY	PALFREYS	AEGGGINN	ENGAGING
AEFLLNNU	UNFALLEN	AEFLPSUU	PAUSEFUL	AEGGGLSU	LUGGAGES
AEFLLORT	FELLATOR	AEFLRSSU	REFUSALS	AEGGHIRS	SHAGGIER
AEFLLORU	FLORULAE	AEFLRSTT	FATTRELS	AEGGHISS	HAGGISES
AEFLLORV	OVERFALL		FLATTERS	AEGGHJRY	JAGGHERY
AEFLLORW	FALLOWER	AEFLRSTU	REFUTALS	AEGGHLRS	HAGGLERS
AEFLLOST	FLOATELS	AEFLRSZZ	FRAZZLES	AEGGHMOS	HEMAGOGS
AEFLLPRT	PRATFELL	AEFLRRTU	AFLUTTER	AEGGHMSU	MESHUGGA
AEFLLPSS	FLAPLESS	AEFLRTTY	FLATTERY	AEGGHOPY	GEOPHAGY
AEFLLPTU	PLATEFUL	AEFLSSTU	FLATUSES	AEGGHORU	ROUGHAGE
AEFLLRUW	AWFULLER		SULFATES	AEGGIINV	GINGIVAE
AEFLLRUX	FLEXURAL	AEFLSTTT	FLATTEST	AEGGIJST	JAGGIEST
AEFLLSSW	FLAWLESS	AEFLSTTU	TASTEFUL	AEGGIKNR	KNAGGIER
AEFLLSTT	FLATLETS	AEFLSTUW	WASTEFUL	AEGGILLN	ALLEGING
AEFLLSTY	FESTALLY	AEFMNORS	FORAMENS	AEGGILLR	GRILLAGE
AEFLMNOT	MATFELON	AEFMNRRY	FERRYMAN	AEGGILMN	GLEAMING
AEFLMORU	FORMULAE	AEFMNRST	RAFTSMEN	AEGGILNN	ANGELING
	FUMAROLE	AEFMNRSU	FRAENUMS		GLEANING
AEFLMORW	LEAFWORM	AEFMORRS	FOREARMS	AEGGILNR	GANGLIER
AEFLMOSS	FOAMLESS	AEFMORRT	REFORMAT		LAGERING
AEFLMOSY	FLAYSOME	AEFMORST	FOREMAST		REGALING
AEFLMOTU	FLAMEOUT		FORMATES	AEGGILNS	LIGNAGES
AEFLMPRR	FRAMPLER		MORTSAFE	AEGGILNT	GELATING
AEFLMSUW	WAMEFULS	AEFMORVW	WAVEFORM		LEGATING
AEFLNNNS	FLANNENS	AEFMOSSU	FAMOUSES		TEAGLING
AEFLNNOT	FONTANEL	AEFMOSUW	WAMEFOUS	AEGGILNU	LEAGUING
AEFLNNOV	NONLEAFY	AEFNNSTU	UNFASTEN	AEGGILNV	GAVELING
AEFLNNTY	FENTANYL	AEFNOPRR	PROFANER	AEGGILOT	TALEGGIO
AEFLNOPR	FLAPERON	AEFNOPRS	PROFANES	AEGGILRS	SLAGGIER
	FOREPLAN	AEFNOPSY	PAYFONES	AEGGILRW	WAGGLIER

AEGGIMNN	MANEGING	AEGHILNX	EXHALING	AEGHPRTU	UPGATHER
	MENAGING	AEGHILPS	SHAGPILE	AEGHRTTU	RETAUGHT
AEGGIMRT	GREGATIM	AEGHILRT	LITHARGE	AEGIILLU	AIGUILLE
AEGGIMSU	MISGAUGE		THIRLAGE	AEGIILMN	EMAILING
AEGGINNR	ANGERING	AEGHILRU	LAUGHIER	AEGIILMO	OLIGEMIA
	ENRAGING	AEGHILST	LAIGHEST	AEGIILMR	REMIGIAL
AEGGINNT	AGENTING	AEGHIMNW	WEIGHMAN	AEGIILNN	ALIENING
	NEGATING	AEGHIMPS	MAGESHIP	AEGIILNR	GAINLIER
AEGGINNU	UNAGEING	AEGHIMST	MEGAHITS	AEGIILRR	GLAIRIER
AEGGINNV	AVENGING	AEGHINNN	HENNAING	AEGIILTT	LITIGATE
AEGGINOS	SEAGOING	AEGHINNT	NAETHING	AEGIILTV	LIGATIVE
AEGGINRS	GEARINGS	AEGHINNV	HAVENING	AEGIIMNR	IMAGINER
	GREASING	AEGHINRS	HEARINGS		MIGRAINE
	SNAGGIER		HEARSING	AEGIIMNS	IMAGINES
AEGGINRV	GREAVING		SHEARING	AEGIIMTT	MITIGATE
AEGGINRW	WAGERING	AEGHINRT	EARTHING	AEGIINNN	NENNIGAI
AEGGINSS	SIGNAGES		HEARTING	AEGIINNR	ARGININE
AEGGINST	NAGGIEST		INGATHER	AEGIINRR	GRAINIER
AEGGIOPR	ARPEGGIO	AEGHINRV	HAVERING	AEGIIRRT	IRRIGATE
	GEROPIGA	AEGHINST	GAHNITES	AEGIISTV	VESTIGIA
AEGGIOSS	ISAGOGES		HEATINGS	AEGIJLNR	JANGLIER
AEGGIQRU	QUAGGIER	AEGHINSV	HEAVINGS	AEGIKLNS	LINKAGES
AEGGIRRU	GARRIGUE		SHEAVING		SNAGLIKE
AEGGIRST	RAGGIEST	AEGHINSZ	GENIZAHS	AEGIKLNT	GNATLIKE
	STAGGIER	AEGHINTT	GNATHITE	AEGIKLNW	WEAKLING
AEGGIRSU	GARIGUES	AEGHIOPS	ESOPHAGI	AEGIKLOT	GOATLIKE
AEGGIRWY	EARWIGGY	AEGHIPPR	EPIGRAPH	AEGIKMNR	REMAKING
AEGGISST	SAGGIEST	AEGHIPRT	GRAPHITE	AEGIKMRW	WIGMAKER
	STAGGIES	AEGHIRRS	GHARRIES	AEGIKNNS	SNEAKING
AEGGISSW	SWAGGIES	AEGHIRSS	GARISHES	AEGIKNNW	WAKENING
AEGGISTT	TAGGIEST	AEGHLNOS	HALOGENS	AEGIKNPS	SPEAKING
AEGGLNPT	EGGPLANT	AEGHLNOV	HYALOGEN	AEGIKNRS	SKEARING
AEGGLNRS	GANGRELS	AEGHLOPY	HYPOGEAL	AEGIKNRT	RETAKING
AEGGLORY	GARGOYLE	AEGHLOSS	GALOSHES	AEGIKNRW	REWAKING
AEGGLOWY	WAYLEGGO	AEGHLOTX	HEXAGLOT		WREAKING
AEGGLRRS	GARGLERS	AEGHLRSU	LAUGHERS	AEGIKNSS	SINKAGES
AEGGLRST	STRAGGLE	AEGHLRTU	LAUGHTER	AEGIKNTW	TWEAKING
AEGGLRSW	WAGGLERS	AEGHLRTY	LETHARGY	AEGIKPPS	KIPPAGES
AEGGLRSY	GREYLAGS	AEGHLSTW	THALWEGS	AEGIKPRS	GARPIKES
AEGGMNNS	GANGSMEN	AEGHMNOP	PHENOGAM	AEGIKSTW	GAWKIEST
AEGGMNOR	GENOGRAM	AEGHMNOS	HOGMANES	AEGILLLS	ILLEGALS
AEGGMORR	ERGOGRAM	AEGHMNOY	HOGMENAY	AEGILLMS	LEGALISM
AEGGMORT	MORTGAGE	AEGHMOPT	APOTHEGM		MEGILLAS
AEGGNNSU	GUNNAGES	AEGHMORS	HOMAGERS		MILLAGES
AEGGNORV	OVERGANG	AEGHMORT	ETHOGRAM	AEGILLNR	ALLERGIN
AEGGNORW	WAGGONER	AEGHMSSU	MESHUGAS	AEGILLNS	GALLEINS
AEGGNRRS	GRANGERS	AEGHNNST	HANGNEST		NIGELLAS
AEGGNRST	GANGSTER	AEGHNOPT	HEPTAGON	AEGILLNU	LINGULAE
AEGGOPRU	GROUPAGE		PATHOGEN	AEGILLNY	GENIALLY
AEGGRSST	GAGSTERS	AEGHNOPY	HYPOGEAN	AEGILLPR	PILLAGER
	STAGGERS	AEGHNORV	HANGOVER	AEGILLPS	PILLAGES
AEGGRSSW	SWAGGERS		OVERHANG		SPILLAGE
AEGGRSTY	STAGGERY	AEGHNOSX	HEXAGONS	AEGILLRU	GUERILLA
AEGHHMSU	MESHUGAH	AEGHNPSW	SPANGHEW	AEGILLRV	VILLAGER
AEGHIJRS	JAGHIRES	AEGHNRSS	GNASHERS	AEGILLSS	GALLISES
AEGHILLM	MEGILLAH		SHERANGS	AEGILLST	LEGALIST
AEGHILLS	SHIGELLA	AEGHNSST	STENGAHS		STILLAGE
AEGHILMT	MEGALITH	AEGHOPPR	PROPHAGE		TILLAGES
AEGHILNR	NARGHILE	AEGHOPPY	APOPHYGE	AEGILLSV	VILLAGES
	NARGILEH	AEGHOPXY	EXOPHAGY	AEGILLSZ	GALLIZES
AEGHILNS	HEALINGS	AEGHORST	SHORTAGE	AEGILLTU	LIGULATE
	LEASHING	AEGHOSST	HOSTAGES	AEGILLTY	LEGALITY
	SHEALING	AEGHOSSU	GASHOUSE	AEGILMMR	AGLIMMER
AEGHILNT	ATHELING	AEGHPRSS	SPREAGHS		LAMMIGER

Eight-letter anagrams

AEGILMNP	EMPALING		TAGLINES		PRIMAGES
AEGILMNR	GERMINAL	**AEGILNSV**	LEAVINGS	**AEGIMPRU**	UMPIRAGE
	MALIGNER		SLEAVING	**AEGIMPSS**	MISPAGES
	MALINGER	**AEGILNSW**	SWEALING	**AEGIMPST**	PIGMEATS
AEGILMNS	MEASLING	**AEGILNSY**	YEALINGS	**AEGIMQRU**	QUAGMIRE
AEGILMNT	LIGAMENT	**AEGILNTV**	VALETING	**AEGIMRRS**	ARMIGERS
	METALING	**AEGILNTX**	EXALTING	**AEGIMRRT**	RAGTIMER
	TEGMINAL	**AEGILNTZ**	TEAZLING	**AEGIMRSS**	GISARMES
AEGILMNU	AEMULING	**AEGILNUV**	VAGINULE	**AEGIMRST**	MAGISTER
AEGILMNY	YEALMING	**AEGILOPS**	SPOILAGE		MIGRATES
AEGILMRS	GREMIALS	**AEGILOPT**	PILOTAGE		RAGTIMES
	LAMIGERS	**AEGILORS**	GASOLIER		STERIGMA
	REGALISM		GIRASOLE	**AEGIMSST**	SIGMATES
AEGILMRX	LEXIGRAM		SERAGLIO	**AEGIMSSU**	MISUSAGE
AEGILMTU	MULTIAGE	**AEGILOSS**	GOLIASES	**AEGIMSTU**	GAUMIEST
AEGILNNP	PANELING		OILGASES	**AEGINNNX**	ANNEXING
AEGILNNR	LEARNING		SOILAGES	**AEGINNOS**	ANGINOSE
AEGILNNS	EANLINGS	**AEGILOST**	LATIGOES		GANOINES
	LEANINGS		OTALGIES	**AEGINNOT**	NEGATION
AEGILNNT	GANTLINE	**AEGILOSU**	EULOGIAS	**AEGINNPS**	SNEAPING
	LATENING	**AEGILPPS**	SLIPPAGE		SPEANING
AEGILNNU	UNGENIAL	**AEGILPPU**	PUPILAGE	**AEGINNRS**	AGINNERS
AEGILNNW	WEANLING	**AEGILPRU**	PLAGUIER		EARNINGS
AEGILNNY	YEANLING	**AEGILRRU**	GLAURIER		ENGRAINS
AEGILNOR	GERANIOL	**AEGILRSS**	GLASSIER		GRANNIES
	REGIONAL	**AEGILRST**	GLARIEST	**AEGINNRV**	RAVENING
AEGILNOS	GASOLINE		REGALIST	**AEGINNRY**	RENAYING
AEGILNOT	GELATION	**AEGILRSY**	GREASILY		YEARNING
	LEGATION	**AEGILRSZ**	GLAZIERS	**AEGINNST**	ANTIGENS
AEGILNPR	GRAPLINE	**AEGILRTT**	AGLITTER		GENTIANS
	PEARLING	**AEGILRTU**	LIGATURE		STEANING
AEGILNPS	ELAPSING	**AEGILRTY**	REGALITY	**AEGINNSU**	GUANINES
	PLEASING	**AEGILRVW**	LAWGIVER		SANGUINE
AEGILNPT	PLEATING	**AEGILRYZ**	GLAZIERY	**AEGINNSW**	WEANINGS
AEGILNQU	EQUALING	**AEGILSSS**	GLASSIES	**AEGINORR**	ORANGIER
AEGILNRR	GNARLIER	**AEGILSTZ**	GLAZIEST	**AEGINORS**	IGNAROES
AEGILNRS	ALIGNERS	**AEGIMMST**	GAMMIEST		ORGANISE
	ENGRAILS	**AEGIMNNO**	NONIMAGE		ORIGANES
	NARGILES	**AEGIMNNR**	ENARMING	**AEGINORZ**	ORGANIZE
	REALIGNS		RENAMING	**AEGINOSS**	AGONISES
	SALERING	**AEGIMNNS**	MEANINGS	**AEGINOSZ**	AGONIZES
	SANGLIER	**AEGIMNNT**	ENTAMING	**AEGINPPR**	PAPERING
	SIGNALER	**AEGIMNPR**	EMPARING	**AEGINPPS**	GENIPAPS
	SLANGIER	**AEGIMNRR**	REARMING	**AEGINPRS**	PREASING
AEGILNRT	ALERTING	**AEGIMNRS**	GERMAINS		SPEARING
	ALTERING		SMEARING	**AEGINPRT**	RETAPING
	INTEGRAL	**AEGIMNRT**	EMIGRANT		TAPERING
	RELATING		REMATING	**AEGINPRV**	REPAVING
	TANGLIER	**AEGIMNRU**	GERANIUM	**AEGINPRY**	REPAYING
	TERAGLIN		MAUNGIER	**AEGINPSS**	SPAEINGS
	TRIANGLE	**AEGIMNSS**	GAMINESS		SPINAGES
AEGILNRV	RAVELING	**AEGIMNST**	MANGIEST	**AEGINPSY**	GYPSEIAN
AEGILNRX	RELAXING		MINTAGES	**AEGINPTY**	EGYPTIAN
AEGILNRY	LAYERING		MISAGENT	**AEGINQTU**	EQUATING
	RELAYING		STEAMING	**AEGINRRS**	EARRINGS
	YEARLING		TEAMINGS		GRAINERS
AEGILNSS	GAINLESS	**AEGIMNSV**	VEGANISM	**AEGINRRV**	AVERRING
	GLASSINE	**AEGIMNTU**	TEGUMINA	**AEGINRSS**	ASSIGNER
	LEASINGS		UMANGITE		REASSIGN
	SEALINGS	**AEGIMOOS**	OOGAMIES		SEARINGS
AEGILNST	EASTLING	**AEGIMORR**	ARMIGERO		SERINGAS
	GELATINS	**AEGIMORS**	GORAMIES	**AEGINRST**	ANGRIEST
	GENITALS	**AEGIMORW**	WAGMOIRE		ANGSTIER
	STEALING	**AEGIMPRS**	EPIGRAMS		ASTRINGE

	GANISTER	**AEGIRSST**	AGISTERS	**AEGLNPRS**	GRAPNELS
	GANTRIES	**AEGIRSTT**	STRIGATE		SPANGLER
	GRANITES	**AEGIRSTV**	VIRGATES		SPRANGLE
	INGRATES		VITRAGES	**AEGLNPSS**	PANGLESS
	RANGIEST	**AEGIRSUU**	AUGURIES		SPANGLES
	REASTING	**AEGIRSUY**	YUGARIES	**AEGLNPST**	SPANGLET
	STEARING	**AEGISSST**	GASSIEST	**AEGLNRRW**	WRANGLER
	TASERING	**AEGISSTT**	STAGIEST	**AEGLNRSS**	SLANGERS
AEGINRSV	VINEGARS	**AEGISSTW**	GAWSIEST	**AEGLNRST**	STRANGLE
AEGINRSW	RESAWING	**AEGISTUZ**	GAUZIEST		TANGLERS
	SWEARING	**AEGJLNOR**	JARGONEL		TRANGLES
	WEARINGS	**AEGJLNRS**	JANGLERS	**AEGLNRSU**	GRANULES
AEGINRSY	RESAYING	**AEGJLTUU**	JUGULATE	**AEGLNRSW**	WANGLERS
	SYNERGIA	**AEGKKKNO**	ANGEKKOK		WRANGLES
AEGINRTT	ARETTING	**AEGKKNOS**	ANGEKOKS	**AEGLNRSY**	LARYNGES
	GNATTIER	**AEGKLLOT**	LEKGOTLA	**AEGLNRTW**	TWANGLER
	TREATING	**AEGKLOSU**	KAGOULES	**AEGLNRUY**	GUNLAYER
AEGINRTV	AVERTING	**AEGKMNRU**	GUNMAKER	**AEGLNSTT**	GANTLETS
	GRIEVANT	**AEGKMRSY**	KERYGMAS	**AEGLNSTU**	LANGUETS
	TAVERING	**AEGKNORS**	KARENGOS	**AEGLNSTW**	TWANGLES
	VINTAGER	**AEGKNRSS**	SKANGERS	**AEGLNSUW**	GUNWALES
AEGINRTW	TWANGIER	**AEGLLLMU**	GLUMELLA	**AEGLNTTU**	GAUNTLET
	WATERING	**AEGLLNNO**	NONLEGAL	**AEGLNTUU**	UNGULATE
AEGINRTX	RETAXING	**AEGLLNOS**	ALLONGES	**AEGLOOOZ**	ZOOGLOEA
AEGINRVW	WAVERING		GALLEONS	**AEGLOOPU**	APOLOGUE
AEGINRVY	VINEGARY	**AEGLLNOV**	LONGEVAL	**AEGLOORY**	AEROLOGY
AEGINRWX	REWAXING	**AEGLLNPS**	LANGSPEL		AREOLOGY
AEGINRWY	WEARYING	**AEGLLNRS**	LANGRELS		
AEGINSST	EASTINGS	**AEGLLNST**	GELLANTS	**AEGLOOSZ**	ZOOGLEAS
	GENISTAS	**AEGLLNSY**	LANGLEYS	**AEGLOPRS**	PERGOLAS
	GIANTESS	**AEGLLOOZ**	ZOOGLEAL	**AEGLOPRY**	PLAYGOER
	SEATINGS	**AEGLLOPR**	GALLOPER	**AEGLOPTT**	PLOTTAGE
	TEASINGS	**AEGLLORS**	ALLEGROS	**AEGLORST**	GLOATERS
	TSIGANES	**AEGLLORV**	OVERGALL		LEGATORS
AEGINSSY	ESSAYING	**AEGLLORY**	ALLEGORY	**AEGLORSU**	GLAREOUS
AEGINSTT	ESTATING	**AEGLLOSS**	GAOLLESS	**AEGLORSV**	VORLAGES
	TANGIEST		GOALLESS	**AEGLORTU**	OUTGLARE
AEGINSTU	SAUTEING	**AEGLLOST**	TOLLAGES	**AEGLORTV**	TRAVELOG
	UNITAGES	**AEGLLOTT**	TOLLGATE	**AEGLORTW**	WATERLOG
AEGINSTV	VINTAGES	**AEGLLRVY**	GRAVELLY	**AEGLORTY**	GEOLATRY
AEGINSTW	SWEATING	**AEGLLSSU**	GALLUSES	**AEGLOSSW**	GALOWSES
AEGINSTY	YEASTING		SEAGULLS	**AEGLOSTV**	VOLTAGES
AEGINSTZ	TZIGANES		SULLAGES	**AEGLOSUY**	GEALOUSY
AEGINSVW	WEAVINGS	**AEGLMNNO**	MANGONEL	**AEGLPPRR**	GRAPPLER
AEGINSVY	SAVEYING	**AEGLMNOY**	AMYLOGEN	**AEGLPPRS**	GRAPPLES
AEGIOPRR	PROGERIA	**AEGLMNRS**	MANGLERS	**AEGLPRSU**	EARPLUGS
AEGIORSS	ARGOSIES	**AEGLMNSS**	GLASSMEN		GRAUPELS
AEGIORSV	VIRAGOES	**AEGLMNTU**	GUNMETAL		PLAGUERS
AEGIORTV	RAVIGOTE	**AEGLMOPS**	MEGALOPS	**AEGLPSSU**	PLUSAGES
AEGIOSTT	GOATIEST	**AEGLMORS**	GOMERALS		PLUSSAGE
AEGIOSTU	AGOUTIES	**AEGLMOSU**	MOULAGES		
AEGIOSTX	GEOTAXIS	**AEGLMOTU**	OUTGLEAM	**AEGLRRSU**	REGULARS
AEGIPPRT	GRIPTAPE	**AEGLMOTV**	MEGAVOLT	**AEGLRRUV**	VULGARER
AEGIPPST	GAPPIEST	**AEGLMPSU**	PLUMAGES	**AEGLRSTU**	GAULTERS
AEGIPRSS	PRISAGES	**AEGLMRSU**	MAULGRES		GESTURAL
	SPAIRGES	**AEGLMSSU**	GAUMLESS		TRAGULES
AEGIPRST	GRAPIEST	**AEGLNNOR**	NONGLARE	**AEGLRTUY**	ARGUTELY
AEGIPRTY	PTERYGIA	**AEGLNNPT**	PLANGENT	**AEGLSSTT**	GESTALTS
AEGIPSST	GASPIEST	**AEGLNNSY**	LANGSYNE	**AEGLSSUV**	VALGUSES
AEGIQRSU	SQUIRAGE	**AEGLNNTU**	UNTANGLE	**AEGLSTUU**	GLUTAEUS
AEGIRRSS	GRASSIER	**AEGLNOPT**	GANTLOPE	**AEGLSTUV**	VULGATES
AEGIRRSU	SUGARIER	**AEGLNORY**	YEARLONG	**AEGLSUUY**	GUAYULES
AEGIRRSZ	GRAZIERS	**AEGLNOST**	TANGELOS	**AEGMMNOR**	GAMMONER
AEGIRRTY	ARGYRITE	**AEGLNOSU**	ANGULOSE	**AEGMMRRU**	RUMMAGER
				AEGMMRSU	RUMMAGES
				AEGMNNOS	AGNOMENS

Eight-letter anagrams

AEGMNNOT	MAGNETON	AEGNRSSY	GRAYNESS	AEHHIMTW	HAMEWITH
AEGMNORR	RENOGRAM	AEGNRSTU	STRAUNGE	AEHHINST	INSHEATH
AEGMNORS	MEGARONS	AEGNRSTW	TWANGERS	AEHHIPSW	PEISHWAH
AEGMNORV	MANGROVE	AEGNRSYY	ASYNERGY	AEHHISST	HASHIEST
	VENOGRAM	AEGNSSST	GASTNESS		SHEHITAS
AEGMNOST	GEOMANTS	AEGNSSSY	SYNGASES	AEHHISVY	YESHIVAH
	MAGNETOS	AEGNSTTU	GAUNTEST	AEHHLNTU	UNHEALTH
	MEGATONS		TUTENAGS	AEHHNRSS	HARSHENS
	MONTAGES	AEGOORST	ROOTAGES	AEHHNRSW	HERNSHAW
AEGMNOSX	MAGNOXES	AEGOORSV	VORAGOES	AEHHORST	HAROSETH
AEGMNOXY	XENOGAMY	AEGOOSWY	WAYGOOSE	AEHHRRST	THRASHER
AEGMNRST	GARMENTS	AEGOPPRS	PROPAGES	AEHHRSST	HARSHEST
	MARGENTS	AEGOPPST	STOPPAGE		THRASHES
	RAGMENTS	AEGOPRST	PORTAGES		
AEGMNRTU	ARGENTUM		POTAGERS	AEHIIKLR	HAIRLIKE
	ARGUMENT	AEGOPRTU	PORTAGUE	AEHIIKRT	TERAKIHI
AEGMNSSW	SWAGSMEN	AEGOPSST	GESTAPOS	AEHIIKST	SHIITAKE
AEGMNSSY	GAMYNESS		POSTAGES	AEHIILMO	HEMIOLIA
AEGMNSTU	AUGMENTS	AEGOPSSU	SPOUSAGE	AEHIILMT	LITHEMIA
	MUTAGENS	AEGOPSTT	GATEPOST	AEHIILNR	HAIRLINE
AEGMOORS	MOORAGES		POTTAGES	AEHIILST	HAILIEST
AEGMOPRW	GAPEWORM	AEGORRRT	GARROTER	AEHIIMNT	THIAMINE
AEGMOPST	POSTGAME		REGRATOR	AEHIIMOP	HEMIOPIA
AEGMORRW	WORMGEAR	AEGORRST	GARROTES	AEHIINNT	IANTHINE
AEGMORSS	GOSSAMER	AEGORRTT	GAROTTER	AEHIINTZ	THIAZINE
AEGMPRUZ	GAZUMPER		GARROTTE	AEHIIRRW	WIREHAIR
AEGMPSTU	STUMPAGE	AEGORSSS	SARGOSES	AEHIIRST	HAIRIEST
AEGNNOPT	PENTAGON	AEGORSST	STORAGES	AEHIKKLW	HAWKLIKE
AEGNNORT	NEGATRON	AEGORSTT	GAROTTES	AEHIKLLO	HALOLIKE
AEGNNOST	NEGATONS	AEGORSTU	OUTRAGES	AEHIKLLT	LATHLIKE
	TONNAGES	AEGORSUV	OUVRAGES	AEHIKLMS	SHEKALIM
AEGNNPRT	PREGNANT	AEGORSVY	VOYAGERS	AEHIKLNP	KEPHALIN
AEGNNRSU	GUNNERAS	AEGORTTU	TUTORAGE	AEHIKLRS	RASHLIKE
AEGNNRTY	GANNETRY	AEGORTUU	OUTARGUE	AEHIKMNZ	KHAZENIM
AEGNNSTT	TANGENTS	AEGORUVY	VOYAGEUR	AEHIKNSS	SNEAKISH
AEGNNSTU	TUNNAGES	AEGOSSTU	OUTGASES	AEHIKSST	SHAKIEST
AEGNNTUU	UNGUENTA	AEGOSSTW	STOWAGES		SHITAKES
AEGNOORS	OREGANOS	AEGOSSYZ	AZYGOSES	AEHIKSSY	SAKIYEHS
AEGNOPRR	PARERGON	AEGOSTTU	OUTGATES	AEHILLNT	THALLINE
AEGNOPST	PONTAGES	AEGOSTTV	GAVOTTES	AEHILMNY	HYMENIAL
AEGNORRS	GROANERS	AEGOSTUZ	OUTGAZES	AEHILMOS	HEMIOLAS
AEGNORRY	ORANGERY	AEGPRRSS	GRASPERS	AEHILMOT	HALIMOTE
AEGNORST	ESTRAGON		SPARGERS	AEHILMQS	SHEQALIM
	NEGATORS	AEGPRSTU	UPSTAGER	AEHILMRU	HAULMIER
	ORANGEST	AEGPSSTU	UPSTAGES	AEHILMSW	LIMEWASH
	RAGSTONE	AEGPSSUU	GAUPUSES	AEHILMSY	LEHAYIMS
	STONERAG	AEGPSSUW	GAWPUSES	AEHILNOP	APHELION
AEGNORSW	WAGONERS	AEGQRTUU	TRUQUAGE		PHELONIA
AEGNORTT	TETRAGON	AEGRRSSS	GRASSERS	AEHILNRS	INHALERS
AEGNORTU	OUTRANGE	AEGRRSSU	SUGARERS	AEHILNRU	INHAULER
AEGNORTY	NEGATORY	AEGRRSSY	RYEGRASS	AEHILNSY	HYALINES
AEGNORUV	VARGUENO	AEGRRSUU	AUGURERS	AEHILNTX	ANTHELIX
AEGNOSSY	NOSEGAYS	AEGRRSUV	GRAVURES	AEHILNTZ	ZENITHAL
AEGNOTUY	AUTOGENY		VERRUGAS	AEHILORS	AIRHOLES
AEGNPPRU	GUNPAPER	AEGRSSSU	SARGUSES		SHOALIER
AEGNPRRS	RESPRANG	AEGRSSUV	SEVRUGAS	AEHILORT	AEROLITH
AEGNPRSS	ENGRASPS	AEGRSTTY	STRATEGY	AEHILOTZ	THIAZOLE
AEGNPRST	TREPANGS	AEGRSTUU	AUGUSTER	AEHILPRS	EARLSHIP
AEGNPRSU	SPEARGUN	AEGSSTUU	AUGUSTES		HARELIPS
AEGNPRYY	PANEGYRY	AEGSTTTU	GUTTATES		PLASHIER
AEGNRRST	GRANTERS	AEHHHIST	SHEHITAH	AEHILPST	HAPLITES
	REGRANTS	AEHHIKSS	SHEIKHAS	AEHILRSS	HAIRLESS
	STRANGER	AEHHIMPV	HYPHEMIA	AEHILRSU	HAULIERS
AEGNRSST	STRANGES			AEHILRSV	LAVISHER
					SHRIEVAL

AEHILRTY	EARTHILY	AEHINRTU	HAURIENT	AEHJNNOS	JOHANNES
	HEARTILY	AEHINRTW	TARWHINE	AEHKMOPW	MOPEHAWK
AEHILSST	HELIASTS	AEHINRUW	WHARENUI	AEHKNNSU	UNSHAKEN
	SHALIEST	AEHINSSS	ASHINESS	AEHKNOSW	HAWKNOSE
AEHILSSV	LAVISHES		HESSIANS	AEHKNRST	THANKERS
AEHILSSW	SHAWLIES	AEHINSST	ANTHESIS	AEHKNSSU	ANKUSHES
	WHAISLES		SHANTIES	AEHKNSWW	NEWSHAWK
AEHILSTT	LATHIEST		SHEITANS	AEHKOOPR	REAPHOOK
	LITHATES		STHENIAS	AEHKOSTU	SHAKEOUT
AEHILSTY	HYALITES	AEHINSSV	VANISHES	AEHKPSSU	SHAKEUPS
AEHILSUV	VIHUELAS	AEHINSSZ	HAZINESS	AEHKRRSS	SHARKERS
AEHILSWZ	WHAIZLES	AEHINSTT	HESITANT	AEHLLLTY	LETHALLY
AEHIMMSS	SHAMMIES	AEHINSTW	INSWATHE	AEHLLMOP	LAMPHOLE
AEHIMMST	HAMMIEST	AEHINTTT	ANTITHET	AEHLLMTY	METHYLAL
AEHIMMSW	WHAMMIES	AEHIOPRS	APHORISE	AEHLLNRT	ENTHRALL
AEHIMNNU	INHUMANE	AEHIOPRU	EUPHORIA	AEHLLNTU	UNLETHAL
AEHIMNRS	HARMINES	AEHIOPRZ	APHORIZE	AEHLLORW	HALLOWER
	SHIREMAN	AEHIOPTT	THIOTEPA	AEHLLRSS	HERSALLS
AEHIMNSS	SHAMISEN	AEHIORRV	OVERHAIR	AEHLLSST	HALTLESS
AEHIMNST	HEMATINS	AEHIORST	HOARIEST	AEHLMMNS	HELMSMAN
AEHIMNSU	HUMANISE	AEHIORTU	THIOUREA	AEHLMNOS	MANHOLES
AEHIMNTU	INHUMATE	AEHIPPRS	PAPISHER	AEHLMNOT	HOTELMAN
AEHIMNUZ	HUMANIZE		SAPPHIRE		METHANOL
AEHIMPRS	SAMPHIRE	AEHIPPSS	PAPISHES	AEHLMNUY	HUMANELY
	SERAPHIM	AEHIPPST	EPITAPHS	AEHLMORS	ARMHOLES
AEHIMPRT	TERAPHIM		HAPPIEST	AEHLMOSU	HAMULOSE
AEHIMPRX	XERAPHIM		PEATSHIP	AEHLMPPT	PAMPHLET
AEHIMPSS	EMPHASIS	AEHIPRRS	PHRASIER	AEHLMPSW	WHAMPLES
	MISSHAPE	AEHIPRRT	RATHRIPE	AEHLMRSS	HARMLESS
	PHAEISMS	AEHIPRSS	PARISHES	AEHLMRST	THERMALS
AEHIMPST	MATESHIP		SHARPIES	AEHLMRSU	HUMERALS
	SHIPMATE	AEHIPRST	TRIPHASE	AEHLNOST	ANETHOLS
AEHIMRRS	MARSHIER	AEHIPRTT	THREAPIT		ETHANOLS
AEHIMRSS	MARISHES	AEHIPSSW	PEISHWAS	AEHLNOTY	ETHANOYL
	MISHEARS	AEHIPSTZ	ZAPTIEHS	AEHLNPRS	SHRAPNEL
AEHIMSSS	MESSIAHS	AEHIPSWW	WASHWIPE	AEHLNPTY	ENTHALPY
AEHIMSST	ATHEISMS	AEHIQSSU	QUASHIES	AEHLNRST	ENTHRALS
	MASHIEST	AEHIRRRS	HARRIERS	AEHLNSST	NATHLESS
	MATHESIS	AEHIRRSS	ARRISHES	AEHLNSSU	UNLASHES
AEHIMTUY	EUTHYMIA	AEHIRRST	TRASHIER		UNSHALES
AEHINNPZ	PHENAZIN	AEHIRRSV	RAVISHER	AEHLNSTY	NAYTHLES
AEHINNSS	SHANNIES	AEHIRRSW	WAIRSHER	AEHLNTUZ	HAZELNUT
AEHINNTX	XANTHEIN	AEHIRRTW	WRATHIER	AEHLOPRT	PLETHORA
	XANTHINE	AEHIRSST	SHERIATS	AEHLOPSS	HAPLOSES
AEHINOPS	APHONIES	AEHIRSSV	RAVISHES	AEHLOPST	TAPHOLES
AEHINOPU	EUPHONIA	AEHIRSSW	SWASHIER	AEHLOPTT	HOTPLATE
AEHINORT	ANTIHERO	AEHIRSTU	THESAURI	AEHLORST	LOATHERS
AEHINOTT	THIONATE	AEHIRSTW	SWATHIER		RATHOLES
AEHINPPY	EPIPHANY		WATERISH	AEHLORSY	HOARSELY
AEHINPRS	HEPARINS	AEHIRSTY	HYSTERIA	AEHLORUV	OVERHAUL
	PARISHEN	AEHIRSWY	HAYWIRES	AEHLOSSS	ASSHOLES
	SERAPHIN	AEHIRTYZ	YAHRZEIT	AEHLOSST	SHOALEST
AEHINPRT	PERIANTH	AEHISSST	STASHIES	AEHLOSTT	LOATHEST
AEHINPST	PENTHIAS	AEHISSSW	SIWASHES	AEHLPPRT	THRAPPLE
	THESPIAN	AEHISSSY	ESSAYISH	AEHLPRSS	PLASHERS
AEHINRRS	SHARNIER	AEHISSTT	ATHEISTS		SPLASHER
AEHINRRU	UNHAIRER		HASTIEST	AEHLPSSS	SPLASHES
AEHINRSS	ARSHINES		STAITHES	AEHLPSST	PATHLESS
AEHINRST	HAIRNETS	AEHISSTU	HIATUSES		PLASHETS
	INEARTHS	AEHISSTW	WASHIEST	AEHLPSTU	SULPHATE
	THERIANS	AEHISSVY	YESHIVAS	AEHLRRTU	URETHRAL
AEHINRSV	ENRAVISH	AEHISTTW	THAWIEST	AEHLRSSS	SLASHERS
	VANISHER		THWAITES	AEHLRSST	HARSLETS
AEHINRSW	SHERWANI	AEHJLOSW	JAWHOLES		SLATHERS

Eight-letter anagrams

Code	Word	Code	Word	Code	Word
AEHLSSSS	SASHLESS	AEHNSSTT	THATNESS	AEIIKLNT	KALINITE
AEHLSSTT	STEALTHS	AEHNSSTW	WHATNESS	AEIIKNRS	KAISERIN
AEHLSSTW	THAWLESS	AEHNSSTY	SHANTEYS	AEIIKNSS	AKINESIS
AEHLSSWY	SHAWLEYS	AEHNSTUW	UNSWATHE	AEIIKNST	KAINITES
AEHLSTTY	STEALTHY	AEHOORST	TOHEROAS	AEIIKRTY	TERIYAKI
AEHMMRSS	SHAMMERS	AEHOPPRS	PROPHASE	AEIILLMR	MILLIARE
AEHMNNPY	NYMPHEAN	AEHOPRRY	PYORRHEA		RAMILLIE
AEHMNOPR	MORPHEAN	AEHOPRSS	PHAROSES	AEIILLRS	RAILLIES
AEHMNORS	HORSEMAN	AEHOPRST	PHORATES	AEIILLST	TAILLIES
	MENORAHS		POTSHARE	AEIILLTV	ILLATIVE
	RHAMNOSE	AEHOPSST	PATHOSES	AEIILMNN	MAINLINE
	SHOREMAN		POTASHES	AEIILMNS	ALIENISM
AEHMNOST	HOASTMEN		SPATHOSE		MILESIAN
AEHMNOSU	HOUSEMAN		TEASHOPS	AEIILMPR	IMPERIAL
AEHMNPRU	PREHUMAN	AEHOPSTT	HEATSPOT	AEIILMPS	LIPEMIAS
AEHMNRST	TRASHMEN		POSTHEAT	AEIILMRS	RAMILIES
AEHMNSTU	HUMANEST	AEHOPSTU	PHASEOUT	AEIILMTT	MILITATE
AEHMOPRT	METAPHOR		TAPHOUSE	AEIILNNS	ANILINES
AEHMOPST	APOTHEMS	AEHOQRUU	HUAQUERO	AEIILNQU	AQUILINE
AEHMORST	TERAOHMS	AEHORRRW	HARROWER		QUINIELA
AEHMOSTT	HEMOSTAT	AEHORRSV	OVERRASH	AEIILNRR	AIRLINER
AEHMOSTU	OUTSHAME	AEHORRSW	WARHORSE	AEIILNRS	AIRLINES
AEHMOSTW	SOMEWHAT	AEHORSST	ASTHORES		SNAILIER
AEHMOSTY	HOMESTAY		EARSHOTS	AEIILNRT	INERTIAL
AEHMPPRY	PAMPHREY		HAROSETS	AEIILNSS	SALINISE
AEHMPRST	HAMPSTER		HOARSEST	AEIILNST	ALIENIST
AEHMRSSS	SMASHERS	AEHORSSW	SAWHORSE		LATINISE
AEHMRSST	HAMSTERS	AEHORSTT	RHEOSTAT		LITANIES
AEHMRSTU	MAUTHERS	AEHORSTU	OUTHEARS	AEIILNSZ	SALINISE
AEHMRSTW	MAWTHERS		RATHOUSE	AEIILNTZ	LATINIZE
AEHMSSSU	SHAMUSES	AEHORSTX	OXHEARTS	AEIILPPT	TAILPIPE
AEHMSSTT	SHMATTES		THORAXES	AEIILPRT	LIPARITE
AEHMSTTY	AMETHYST	AEHORSUV	HAVEOURS		REPTILIA
AEHMSUZZ	MEZUZAHS	AEHORSVW	OVERWASH	AEIILQSU	SILIQUAE
AEHNNOPT	PANTHEON	AEHORSWY	HORSEWAY	AEIILRSS	LAIRISES
AEHNNOTX	XANTHONE	AEHOSSTU	HOUSESAT	AEIILRST	LAIRIEST
AEHNNPRU	NENUPHAR	AEHPPRSW	WHAPPERS		LISTERIA
AEHNNPSU	UNSHAPEN	AEHPPSSU	SHAPEUPS	AEIILRSV	RIVALISE
AEHNNSUV	UNSHAVEN	AEHPRRSS	PHRASERS		VIRELAIS
AEHNNSUW	UNWASHEN		SHARPERS	AEIILRSZ	LAIRIZES
AEHNOOPT	HANEPOOT	AEHPRSST	SHARPEST	AEIILRTT	LITERATI
AEHNOPPY	HYPOPNEA		SPARTHES	AEIILRVZ	RIVALIZE
	PAYPHONE	AEHPRSUX	HARUSPEX	AEIILSSS	SILESIAS
AEHNOPRT	HAPTERON	AEHPRSUY	EUPHRASY	AEIILSSW	LEWISIAS
AEHNOPST	PHAETONS	AEHPSTTT	PHATTEST	AEIILSTV	VITALISE
	PHONATES	AEHQRSSU	QUASHERS	AEIILSTX	LAXITIES
	STANHOPE		SQUASHER	AEIILSTZ	TAILZIES
AEHNOPSW	WANHOPES	AEHQSSSU	SQUASHES	AEIILTVZ	VITALIZE
AEHNOPSY	HYPONEAS	AEHRRSST	TRASHERS	AEIIMMRT	MARITIME
AEHNOPXY	XENOPHYA	AEHRRSTU	URETHRAS	AEIIMMSX	MAXIMISE
AEHNOQTU	HAQUETON	AEHRRSTY	TRASHERY	AEIIMMTX	MAXIMITE
AEHNORSS	HOARSENS	AEHRRTTW	THWARTER	AEIIMMXZ	MAXIMIZE
	SENHORAS	AEHRSSST	SHASTERS	AEIIMNNT	ANTIMINE
AEHNOSSX	HEXOSANS	AEHRSSSW	SWASHERS	AEIIMNRU	URINEMIA
AEHNPRSS	SHARPENS	AEHRSSTT	SHATTERS	AEIIMNST	MINIATES
AEHNPRST	PANTHERS	AEHRSSTV	HARVESTS	AEIIMNSZ	SIMAZINE
AEHNPSSU	UNSHAPES	AEHRSSTW	SWATHERS	AEIIMNTT	INTIMATE
AEHNPSTY	PHYTANES	AEHRSTTY	SHATTERY	AEIIMNTU	MINUTIAE
AEHNRSSS	RASHNESS	AEHRSTUU	HAUTEURS	AEIIMNTV	VITAMINE
AEHNRSTU	HAUNTERS	AEHRSTVZ	SHVARTZE	AEIIMOSS	AMEIOSIS
	UNEARTHS	AEHSSTUX	EXHAUSTS	AEIIMPRR	IMPAIRER
	UNHEARTS	AEIIINTT	INITIATE	AEIIMPSY	EPIMYSIA
	URETHANS	AEIIIRRT	RETIARII	AEIIMRSS	MISRAISE
AEHNRTTU	EARTHNUT	AEIIKLLT	TAILLIKE	AEIIMRST	AIRTIMES

	SERIATIM	**AEIJNRTU**	JAUNTIER	**AEIKNRST**	KERATINS
AEIIMRSV	VIREMIAS	**AEIJNSTT**	JANTIEST		NARKIEST
AEIIMSTT	IMITATES	**AEIJNSTU**	JAUNTIES	**AEIKNRSW**	SWANKIER
AEIINNRS	SIRENIAN	**AEIJORST**	JAROSITE	**AEIKNRTW**	KNITWEAR
AEIINNRT	TRIENNIA	**AEIJORSV**	JAROVISE	**AEIKNSST**	SNAKIEST
AEIINNSS	INSANIES	**AEIJORVZ**	JAROVIZE	**AEIKNSSW**	SWANKIES
AEIINNTV	INNATIVE	**AEIJPSSS**	JASPISES	**AEIKNSSY**	KYANISES
AEIINOTT	NOTITIAE	**AEIJSTZZ**	JAZZIEST	**AEIKNSTU**	UNAKITES
AEIINPRT	PAINTIER	**AEIKKLLW**	LIKEWALK	**AEIKNSTV**	KISTVAEN
AEIINPST	PATINISE	**AEIKKLMS**	MASKLIKE	**AEIKNSTW**	TWANKIES
	PIANISTE	**AEIKKLNT**	TANKLIKE		WANKIEST
AEIINPTZ	PATINIZE	**AEIKKLPR**	PARKLIKE	**AEIKNSTY**	KYANITES
AEIINQSU	EQUINIAS	**AEIKKMNO**	KAKIEMON	**AEIKNSYZ**	KYANIZES
AEIINRRV	RIVERAIN	**AEIKKNRS**	SKANKIER	**AEIKOSST**	STOKESIA
AEIINRSS	AIRINESS	**AEIKLLMP**	PALMLIKE	**AEIKPRRS**	SPARKIER
AEIINRST	INERTIAS	**AEIKLLMS**	SELAMLIK	**AEIKPRSS**	SPARKIES
	RAINIEST	**AEIKLLPY**	PLAYLIKE	**AEIKPRST**	PARKIEST
AEIINRSY	YERSINIA	**AEIKLLSS**	KILLASES	**AEIKPSTW**	PAWKIEST
AEIINRTZ	TRIAZINE	**AEIKLLST**	SALTLIKE	**AEIKQSTU**	QUAKIEST
AEIINSST	ISATINES	**AEIKLMOT**	MOATLIKE	**AEIKRSST**	ASTERISK
	SANITIES	**AEIKLMST**	MASTLIKE		SARKIEST
	SANITISE	**AEIKLNNP**	PANNIKEL	**AEIKRSTW**	WATERSKI
	TENIASIS	**AEIKLNOS**	KAOLINES	**AEILLLMO**	MALLEOLI
AEIINSSX	SIXAINES	**AEIKLNOV**	NOVALIKE	**AEILLLMS**	ALLELISM
AEIINSTV	VANITIES	**AEIKLNPS**	SKIPLANE	**AEILLLNY**	LINEALLY
AEIINSTX	AXINITES	**AEIKLNSS**	SEALSKIN	**AEILLMNS**	MANILLES
AEIINSTZ	SANITIZE	**AEIKLNST**	LANKIEST	**AEILLMNY**	MENIALLY
AEIINSVV	INVASIVE	**AEIKLNSW**	SWANLIKE	**AEILLMSS**	MAILLESS
AEIINTTT	TITANITE	**AEIKLNSY**	SNEAKILY	**AEILLMSY**	MESIALLY
AEIINTTU	UINTAITE	**AEIKLNTU**	AUNTLIKE	**AEILLNNO**	LANOLINE
AEIIPRRS	PRAIRIES	**AEIKLOPS**	SOAPLIKE	**AEILLNNS**	NAINSELL
AEIIPRST	PARITIES	**AEIKLOST**	KEITLOAS	**AEILLNNU**	UNLINEAL
AEIIPRSW	PAIRWISE	**AEIKLPRS**	SPARLIKE	**AEILLNOR**	ALLERION
AEIIPRTZ	TRAPEZII	**AEIKLPRT**	TRAPLIKE	**AEILLNPS**	SPLENIAL
AEIIPRZZ	PIZZERIA	**AEIKLPSS**	KALPISES	**AEILLNPY**	ALPINELY
AEIIPSST	EPITASIS	**AEIKLPSW**	WASPLIKE	**AEILLNQU**	QUINELLA
AEIIPSTX	EPITAXIS	**AEIKLQUY**	QUAYLIKE	**AEILLNRY**	LINEARLY
AEIIRRST	RARITIES	**AEIKLRSS**	SERKALIS	**AEILLNSS**	AINSELLS
AEIIRRSV	RIVIERAS	**AEIKLRST**	LARKIEST		NAILLESS
AEIIRRTT	IRRITATE		STALKER		SENSILLA
AEIIRSSS	SIRIASES		STARLIKE	**AEILLNUV**	LAEVULIN
AEIIRSST	IRISATES	**AEIKLRSV**	KLAVIERS	**AEILLNVY**	VENIALLY
	SATIRISE	**AEIKLRTW**	WARTLIKE	**AEILLOSS**	LOESSIAL
AEIIRSTV	VAIRIEST	**AEIKLRVY**	VALKYRIE	**AEILLOTV**	VOLATILE
AEIIRSTW	WISTERIA	**AEIKLRWY**	WALKYRIE	**AEILLPPR**	APPERILL
AEIIRSTX	SEXTARII	**AEIKLSSS**	SAIKLESS	**AEILLPRS**	PERILLAS
AEIIRSTZ	SATIRIZE	**AEIKLSTT**	TALKIEST	**AEILLPSS**	ILLAPSES
AEIIRSVV	VIVARIES	**AEIKMMSS**	MISMAKES	**AEILLPST**	PALLIEST
AEIIRTTT	TRITIATE	**AEIKMNRS**	RAMEKINS		PASTILLE
AEIIRTVZ	VIZIRATE	**AEIKMNST**	MANKIEST	**AEILLQSU**	LALIQUES
AEIISTTV	VITIATES		MISTAKEN		SQUILLAE
AEIISTVZ	IZVESTIA	**AEIKMPRS**	RAMPIKES	**AEILLQTU**	TEQUILLA
AEIITTTV	TITIVATE	**AEIKMPSS**	MISSPEAK	**AEILLRRS**	RALLIERS
AEIITTVV	VITATIVE	**AEIKMRST**	MISTAKER	**AEILLRRY**	RAILLERY
AEIJKLZZ	JAZZLIKE		SITKAMER	**AEILLRSS**	RAILLESS
AEIJLLSS	JAILLESS	**AEIKMSST**	MISTAKES		SALLIERS
AEIJLMSS	MAJLISES	**AEIKMSTW**	MAWKIEST	**AEILLRST**	LITERALS
AEIJLNSV	JAVELINS	**AEIKNNST**	NEATNIKS		TALLIERS
AEIJLNSW	JAWLINES	**AEIKNNTU**	ANTINUKE		TRIELLAS
AEIJLOPS	JALOPIES	**AEIKNPRR**	PRANKIER	**AEILLRSU**	RUELLIAS
AEIJLOSU	JALOUSIE	**AEIKNPRS**	RANPIKES	**AEILLRSY**	SERIALLY
AEIJMMST	JAMMIEST	**AEIKNPST**	SNAKEPIT	**AEILLRTU**	TAILLEUR
AEIJMNSS	JASMINES	**AEIKNRRR**	KNARRIER	**AEILLRVX**	VEXILLAR
AEIJNRST	NARTJIES	**AEIKNRRS**	SNARKIER	**AEILLSSS**	SAILLESS

Eight-letter anagrams

AEILLSST	SITELLAS	AEILMRSS	REALISMS		LARNIEST
	TAILLESS	AEILMRST	LAMISTER		LATRINES
	TALLISES		LAMITERS		RATLINES
AEILLSTT	SITTELLA		MARLIEST		REINSTAL
	TALLITES		MARLITES		RETINALS
AEILLSTW	WALLIEST		MISALTER		TRENAILS
AEILLSUV	ALLUSIVE	AEILMRSY	MISLAYER	AEILNRSU	LUNARIES
AEILLSYZ	SLEAZILY		SMEARILY	AEILNRSV	RAVELINS
AEILLTUZ	LAZULITE	AEILMRTT	REMITTAL	AEILNRSX	RELAXINS
AEILMMNS	MELANISM	AEILMRUV	VELARIUM	AEILNRSY	INLAYERS
AEILMMNS	IMMANTLE	AEILMSSX	SMILAXES		SNAILERY
AEILMMNY	IMMANELY	AEILMSTT	MALTIEST	AEILNRTT	RATTLINE
AEILMMOR	MEMORIAL		METALIST	AEILNRTU	AUNTLIER
AEILMMOT	IMMOLATE		SMALTITE		RETINULA
AEILMMRT	TRILEMMA	AEILMSTU	SIMULATE		TENURIAL
AEILMMSS	MELISMAS	AEILMSTY	LAYTIMES	AEILNRTV	INTERVAL
AEILMMST	MALMIEST		STEAMILY	AEILNRTY	INTERLAY
AEILMMTU	MALEMIUT		TALEYSIM	AEILNSST	EASTLINS
AEILMNNO	MINNEOLA	AEILMSUV	MISVALUE		ELASTINS
AEILMNNP	IMPANNEL	AEILMTTU	MUTILATE		NAILSETS
AEILMNNS	LINESMAN		ULTIMATE		SALIENTS
	MELANINS	AEILNNOS	SOLANINE		SALTINES
AEILMNOS	LAMINOSE	AEILNNPU	PINNULAE		STANIELS
	MINEOLAS	AEILNNRT	INTERNAL	AEILNSSU	INULASES
	SEMOLINA	AEILNNSY	INSANELY	AEILNSSZ	LAZINESS
AEILMNPS	IMPANELS	AEILNNTY	INNATELY	AEILNSTU	ALUNITES
	MANIPLES	AEILNOPR	PELORIAN		INSULATE
AEILMNRS	MARLINES	AEILNOPS	OPALINES	AEILNSTV	VENTAILS
	MINERALS	AEILNOPT	ANTIPOLE	AEILNSTW	LAWNIEST
	MISLEARN	AEILNOPU	POULAINE	AEILNSUV	UNVAILES
AEILMNRT	TERMINAL	AEILNORS	AILERONS	AEILNSUW	LAUWINES
	TRAMLINE		ALERIONS	AEILNSUY	UNEASILY
AEILMNRU	LEMURIAN		ALIENORS	AEILNTVY	NATIVELY
AEILMNSS	ISLESMAN	AEILNORT	ORIENTAL		VENALITY
AEILMNST	AILMENTS		RELATION	AEILNUVV	UNIVALVE
	ALIMENTS		TAILERON	AEILOORV	OVARIOLE
	MANLIEST	AEILNORV	OVERLAIN	AEILOPPR	OILPAPER
	MELANIST	AEILNOSS	ANISOLES	AEILOPPT	OPPILATE
	SMALTINE	AEILNOST	ELATIONS	AEILOPRS	PELORIAS
AEILMNSU	ALUMINES		INSOLATE		POLARISE
AEILMOOV	MOVIEOLA		TOENAILS	AEILOPRT	EPILATOR
AEILMOPR	PROEMIAL	AEILNOSX	SILOXANE		PETIOLAR
AEILMOPS	EPISOMAL	AEILNOTT	TONALITE	AEILOPRZ	POLARIZE
AEILMORS	MORALISE	AEILNPPT	PIEPLANT	AEILOPST	SPOLIATE
AEILMORT	AMITROLE	AEILNPRS	PEARLINS	AEILORRT	RETAILOR
	ROLAMITE		PRALINES	AEILORSS	SOLARISE
AEILMORZ	MORALIZE	AEILNPRT	INTERLAP	AEILORST	SOTERIAL
AEILMOST	LOAMIEST		TRAPLINE	AEILORSV	OVERSAIL
AEILMOSV	SEMIOVAL		TRIPLANE		VALORISE
AEILMOSW	WAILSOME	AEILNPSS	PAINLESS		VARIOLES
AEILMPRS	IMPALERS		SPANIELS		VOLARIES
	IMPEARLS	AEILNPST	PANELIST	AEILORSY	ROYALISE
	LEMPIRAS		PANTILES	AEILORSZ	SOLARIZE
AEILMPRU	PLUMERIA		PLAINEST	AEILORTT	LITERATO
AEILMPRV	PRIMEVAL	AEILNPSU	SPINULAE	AEILORTV	VIOLATER
AEILMPSS	PESSIMAL	AEILNPSW	PINWALES	AEILORTZ	TRIAZOLE
AEILMPST	IMPLATES	AEILNPSX	EXPLAINS	AEILORVZ	VALORIZE
	PALMIEST	AEILNPTT	TINPLATE	AEILORYZ	ROYALIZE
	PALMIETS	AEILNPTY	PENALITY	AEILOSST	ISOLATES
	PETALISM	AEILNQSU	QUINELAS	AEILOSSX	OXALISES
	SEPTIMAL	AEILNQTU	QUANTILE	AEILOSTT	TOTALISE
AEILMPTY	PLAYTIME	AEILNRRS	SNARLIER	AEILOSTV	VIOLATES
AEILMQRU	QUALMIER	AEILNRSS	RAINLESS	AEILOTTV	VOLITATE
AEILMRRS	LARMIERS	AEILNRST	ENTRAILS	AEILOTTZ	TOTALIZE

AEILPPQU	APPLIQUE	**AEIMMPRS**	SPAMMIER		ARMORIES
AEILPPRS	APPERILS	**AEIMMPSS**	SPAMMIES	**AEIMORST**	AMORTISE
	APPLIERS	**AEIMMPST**	PSAMMITE		ATOMISER
AEILPRRS	REPRISAL	**AEIMMRRS**	SMARMIER	**AEIMORTT**	AMORETTI
AEILPRRT	PALTRIER	**AEIMMRST**	MARMITES	**AEIMORTZ**	AMORTIZE
	PRETRIAL		RAMMIEST		ATOMIZER
AEILPRST	PILASTER		TRAMMIES	**AEIMOSST**	AMITOSES
	PLAISTER	**AEIMMRTU**	IMMATURE		AMOSITES
	PLAITERS	**AEIMMSST**	MISMATES		ATOMISES
AEILPRSU	SPIRULAE	**AEIMMSTT**	SEMIMATT		OSMIATES
AEILPRSV	PREVAILS	**AEIMMSZZ**	MIZMAZES	**AEIMOSTX**	TOXEMIAS
AEILPRSW	SLIPWARE	**AEIMNNOT**	ANTINOME	**AEIMOSTZ**	ATOMIZES
AEILPRTV	LIVETRAP		NOMINATE	**AEIMOTTV**	MOTIVATE
AEILPRXY	PYREXIAL	**AEIMNNRS**	REINSMAN	**AEIMPRRS**	RAMPIRES
AEILPSST	PALSIEST	**AEIMNNRT**	TRAINMEN	**AEIMPRRT**	IMPARTER
AEILPSSY	PAISLEYS	**AEIMNNST**	MANNITES		TRAMPIER
AEILPSTT	PLATIEST	**AEIMNOPT**	PTOMAINE	**AEIMPRSS**	IMPRESAS
AEILPSTY	PTYALISE	**AEIMNORS**	MORAINES		MISPARSE
AEILPSUV	PLAUSIVE		ROMAINES		SAMPIRES
AEILPTYZ	PTYALIZE		ROMANISE	**AEIMPRST**	APTERISM
AEILQRSU	SQUAILER	**AEIMNORW**	AIRWOMEN		PRIMATES
AEILQRTU	QUARTILE	**AEIMNORZ**	ARMOZINE	**AEIMPRSV**	VAMPIRES
	REQUITAL		ROMANIZE	**AEIMPRSW**	SWAMPIER
AEILQSTU	LIQUATES	**AEIMNOSS**	ANEMOSIS	**AEIMPRTU**	APTERIUM
	TEQUILAS	**AEIMNOST**	AMNIOTES	**AEIMPSSS**	IMPASSES
AEILQSUY	QUEASILY		MASONITE	**AEIMPSST**	IMPASTES
AEILQTUV	EQUALITY		MISATONE		PASTIMES
AEILRRST	RETIRALS		SOMNIATE		TIMEPASS
	RETRIALS	**AEIMNOSU**	MOINEAUS	**AEIMPSTV**	VAMPIEST
	TRAILERS	**AEIMNOSW**	WOMANISE	**AEIMQRSU**	MARQUISE
AEILRRSU	RURALISE	**AEIMNOTZ**	MONAZITE	**AEIMRRRS**	MARRIERS
AEILRRTT	RATTLIER	**AEIMNOUX**	EXONUMIA	**AEIMRRSS**	SIMARRES
AEILRRTU	RURALITE	**AEIMNOWZ**	WOMANIZE	**AEIMRSST**	ASTERISM
AEILRRTY	LITERARY	**AEIMNPRZ**	PRIZEMAN		MAISTERS
AEILRRUZ	RURALIZE	**AEIMNPSX**	PANMIXES		MISRATES
AEILRSST	REALISTS	**AEIMNQRU**	RAMEQUIN		SEMITARS
	SALTIERS	**AEIMNRRS**	MARINERS		SMARTIES
	SALTIRES	**AEIMNRRV**	RIVERMAN	**AEIMRSSV**	MISAVERS
	SLAISTER	**AEIMNRSS**	SEMINARS	**AEIMRSSY**	EMISSARY
AEILRSSV	REVISALS		SIRNAMES	**AEIMRSTT**	MISTREAT
	RIVALESS	**AEIMNRST**	MERANTIS		TERATISM
AEILRSTT	TERTIALS		MINARETS	**AEIMRSTU**	MURIATES
AEILRSTU	URALITES		RAIMENTS		SEMITAUR
AEILRSVV	REVIVALS	**AEIMNRSU**	ANEURISM	**AEIMRSTV**	VITAMERS
AEILRSVY	VIRELAYS	**AEIMNRSY**	SEMINARY	**AEIMRSTW**	WARTIMES
AEILRTTY	ALTERITY	**AEIMNRTT**	INTERMAT	**AEIMRSTX**	MATRIXES
AEILRTUV	VAULTIER		MARTINET	**AEIMRSTY**	SYMITARE
AEILRTUZ	LAZURITE	**AEIMNRTU**	RUMINATE	**AEIMRSWW**	SWIMWEAR
AEILRTVV	TRIVALVE	**AEIMNRTW**	WARIMENT	**AEIMSSST**	ASTEISMS
AEILRTWY	WATERILY	**AEIMNRTY**	TYRAMINE		MASSIEST
AEILRTXZ	ZELATRIX	**AEIMNSSS**	SAMISENS		MISSEATS
AEILSSSV	VESSAILS	**AEIMNSST**	MANTISES	**AEIMSSSV**	MASSIVES
AEILSSTT	SALTIEST		MATINESS	**AEIMSSTT**	ETATISMS
	SLATIEST	**AEIMNSSU**	ANIMUSES		MASTIEST
AEILSSTW	SWALIEST	**AEIMNSSZ**	MAZINESS		MISSTATE
AEILSTTW	WALTIEST	**AEIMNSUV**	MAUVEINS	**AEIMSSTX**	MASTIXES
AEILSTVY	VILAYETS		MAUVINES	**AEIMSSTZ**	MESTIZAS
AEILSTWY	SWEATILY	**AEIMNTTU**	MATUTINE	**AEIMSTYZ**	AZYMITES
AEILSTYY	YEASTILY	**AEIMNTVZ**	VIZAMENT	**AEIMTTUV**	MUTATIVE
AEIMMMRZ	MAMZERIM	**AEIMOOPS**	IPOMOEAS	**AEINNNOX**	ANNEXION
AEIMMNNT	IMMANENT	**AEIMOPRS**	MEROPIAS	**AEINNOPS**	SAPONINE
AEIMMNOS	SEMINOMA	**AEIMOPSX**	APOMIXES	**AEINNOPV**	PAVONINE
AEIMMNOT	AMMONITE	**AEIMOPTT**	OPTIMATE	**AEINNORS**	RAISONNE
AEIMMNSS	MISNAMES	**AEIMORRS**	ARMOIRES	**AEINNORT**	ANOINTER

	INORNATE
	REANOINT
AEINNOST	ENATIONS
	SONATINE
AEINNOTT	INTONATE
AEINNOTV	INNOVATE
	VENATION
AEINNPRS	PANNIERS
AEINNPST	PANTINES
AEINNRRS	INSNARER
AEINNRRT	INERRANT
AEINNRSS	INSNARES
AEINNRST	ENTRAINS
	TRANNIES
AEINNRSU	ANEURINS
	UNARISEN
AEINNRSW	SWANNIER
AEINNRTT	INTRANET
AEINNSST	INSANEST
	STANINES
AEINNSSV	VAINNESS
AEINNSSW	SWANNIES
AEINNSSZ	ZANINESS
AEINNSTT	ANTIENTS
	STANNITE
AEINNTUV	UNNATIVE
AEINOPPT	ANTIPOPE
AEINOPRT	ATROPINE
AEINOPSS	SENOPIAS
AEINOPST	SAPONITE
AEINOPSZ	EPIZOANS
AEINOPTZ	TOPAZINE
AEINOQRU	AEQUORIN
AEINOQTU	EQUATION
AEINORRT	ANTERIOR
AEINORRW	IRONWARE
AEINORSS	ERASIONS
	SENSORIA
AEINORST	ANOESTRI
	ARSONITE
	NOTARIES
	NOTARISE
	ROSINATE
	SENORITA
AEINORSV	AVERSION
AEINORTT	TENTORIA
AEINORTZ	NOTARIZE
AEINOSST	ASSIENTO
	ASTONIES
AEINOSSV	EVASIONS
AEINOSSX	SAXONIES
AEINOSTV	STOVAINE
AEINOSTX	SAXONITE
AEINOSXZ	OXAZINES
AEINOTVX	VEXATION
AEINPPPS	PANPIPES
AEINPPRS	SNAPPIER
AEINPPRY	PAPYRINE
AEINPPSS	PINESAPS
AEINPPST	NAPPIEST
AEINPRRT	PRETRAIN
	TERRAPIN
AEINPRRU	UNREPAIR
AEINPRST	PAINTERS
	PANTRIES
	PERTAINS
	PINASTER
	PRISTANE
	REPAINTS
AEINPRSU	UNPRAISE
AEINPRSW	SPAWNIER
AEINPRTT	TRIPTANE
AEINPRTU	PAINTURE
AEINPRTX	EXPIRANT
AEINPSST	SAPIENTS
	STEAPSIN
AEINPSSU	APNEUSIS
AEINPSSW	WINESAPS
AEINPSTT	PATIENTS
AEINPSTU	PETUNIAS
	SUPINATE
AEINPSTY	EPINASTY
AEINPTTY	ANTITYPE
AEINQRTU	ANTIQUER
	QUAINTER
AEINQSTU	ANTIQUES
	QUANTISE
AEINQTTU	EQUITANT
AEINQTUY	ANTIQUEY
AEINQTUZ	QUANTIZE
AEINRRST	RESTRAIN
	RETRAINS
	STRAINER
	TERRAINS
	TRAINERS
	TRANSIRE
AEINRRTT	RETIRANT
AEINRRTV	VERATRIN
AEINRRTW	INTERWAR
AEINRRUW	UNWARIER
AEINRSST	ARTINESS
	RESIANTS
	RETSINAS
	SNARIEST
	STAINERS
	STARNIES
	STEARINS
AEINRSSU	ANURESIS
	SENARIUS
AEINRSSW	WARINESS
AEINRSSX	XERANSIS
AEINRSTT	INTREATS
	NITRATES
	STRAITEN
	TARTINES
	TERTIANS
AEINRSTU	RUINATES
	TAURINES
	URANITES
	URINATES
AEINRSTW	TINWARES
AEINRSUV	VAURIENS
AEINRSUZ	AZURINES
	SUZERAIN
AEINRSVV	VERVAINS
AEINRSZZ	SNAZZIER
AEINRTTU	TAINTURE
AEINRTUV	VAUNTIER
AEINSSST	SAINTESS
	SESTINAS
AEINSSSV	VINASSES
AEINSSTT	ANTSIEST
	INSTATES
	NASTIEST
	SATINETS
	TITANESS
AEINSSTU	SINUATES
AEINSSTX	SEXTAINS
AEINSSVW	WAVINESS
AEINSSWX	WAXINESS
AEINSTTT	NATTIEST
AEINSTTV	TASTEVIN
AEINSTTW	TAWNIEST
AEINSTUV	SUIVANTE
AEINSTWY	YAWNIEST
AEINSUVV	VESUVIAN
AEINTTUU	AUTUNITE
AEIOOPTT	PATOOTIE
AEIOPPST	APPOSITE
AEIOPRRT	PRIORATE
AEIOPRRW	AIRPOWER
AEIOPRSV	VAPORISE
AEIOPRTX	EXPIATOR
AEIOPRVZ	VAPORIZE
AEIOPSST	SOAPIEST
AEIOPTTV	OPTATIVE
AEIOQSSU	SEQUOIAS
AEIORRRS	ARRIEROS
AEIORRSS	ROSARIES
AEIORRST	ROARIEST
	ROTARIES
AEIORRSV	SAVORIER
AEIORSSV	SAVORIES
AEIORSTT	TOASTIER
AEIORSTU	OUTRAISE
	SAUTOIRE
AEIORSTV	TRAVOISE
	VIATORES
	VOTARIES
AEIORSVW	AVOWRIES
AEIORTTV	ROTATIVE
AEIOSSST	SOSATIES
AEIOSSTT	TOASTIES
AEIOSSTZ	AZOTISES
AEIOSTZZ	AZOTIZES
AEIPPPST	PAPPIEST
AEIPPRRS	APPRISER
AEIPPRRT	TRAPPIER
AEIPPRRZ	APPRIZER
AEIPPRSS	APPRISES
AEIPPRST	PERIAPTS
AEIPPRSZ	APPRIZES
AEIPPSST	SAPPIEST
AEIPPSTY	YAPPIEST
AEIPPSTZ	ZAPPIEST
AEIPQRTU	PRATIQUE
AEIPRRRS	PARRIERS
	SPARRIER
AEIPRRSS	ASPIRERS
	PRAISERS
AEIPRRST	PARTIERS
AEIPRRSU	UPRAISER

AEIPRRSY	SPRAYIER	AEIRSWWY	WAYWISER	AEKMPRSU	UPMAKERS
AEIPRRTV	PRIVATER		WIREWAYS	AEKMPRTU	UPMARKET
AEIPRSST	PASTRIES	AEIRTTTW	ATWITTER	AEKNNRSS	RANKNESS
	PIASTERS	AEISSSST	SASSIEST	AEKNORRV	OVERRANK
	PIASTRES	AEISSSTW	TISWASES	AEKNORUY	EUKARYON
	RASPIEST	AEISSSTY	ESSAYIST	AEKNOTTU	OUTTAKEN
	TRAIPSES	AEISSTTT	TASTIEST	AEKNPPRS	KNAPPERS
AEIPRSSU	UPRAISES	AEISSTTU	SITUATES	AEKNPPSS	SPANSPEK
AEIPRSSV	PARVISES	AEISSTTV	STATIVES	AEKNPRSS	SPANKERS
	PAVISERS		VASTIEST	AEKNPSSU	UNSPEAKS
AEIPRSSX	PRAXISES	AEISSTVV	SAVVIEST	AEKNRSST	STARKENS
AEIPRSTV	PRIVATES	AEISSTWZ	TIZWASES	AEKNRSSW	SWANKERS
AEIPRSTW	WIRETAPS	AEISTTTT	TATTIEST	AEKNRSTZ	KRANTZES
AEIPRSTY	ASPERITY	AEISTTTU	ATTUITES	AEKNSSTW	SWANKEST
AEIPRSVY	VESPIARY	AEISTTTW	TAWTIEST	AEKNSSWY	SWANKEYS
AEIPRSWW	WARPWISE	AEJKPSTU	KAJEPUTS	AEKOORSV	OVERSOAK
AEIPRSXY	PYREXIAS	AEJLNSUV	JUVENALS	AEKOPRRT	PARROKET
AEIPRTVY	VARITYPE	AEJLORTV	TOLARJEV	AEKOPRSS	PRESOAKS
AEIPSSST	PASTISES	AEJLOSSU	JALOUSES	AEKOPSTU	OUTSPEAK
AEIPSSSV	PASSIVES	AEJLOSUY	JEALOUSY		SPEAKOUT
	PAVISSES	AEJLOSUZ	AZULEJOS	AEKORRSS	ROSAKERS
AEIPSSTT	PASTIEST	AEJNORSZ	ZANJEROS	AEKORRWW	WORKWEAR
AEIPSSTW	WASPIEST	AEKKKKMRU	KRUMKAKE	AEKORSSS	KAROSSES
AEIPSSTY	EPISTASY	AEKKLLWY	LYKEWALK	AEKORSTV	OVERTASK
AEIPSZZZ	PIZAZZES	AEKKMNOO	KAKEMONO		VOERTSAK
	PIZZAZES	AEKKNRSS	SKANKERS	AEKORSTW	SEATWORK
AEIPTTUV	PUTATIVE	AEKKOSSS	SAKKOSES	AEKORTUY	EUKARYOT
AEIQRRRU	QUARRIER	AEKLLSTU	KELLAUTS	AEKOSTTU	OUTSKATE
AEIQRRSU	QUARRIES	AEKLMORS	LARKSOME		OUTTAKES
AEIQRRTU	QUARTIER	AEKLMOSU	LEUKOMAS		STAKEOUT
AEIQRUZZ	QUAZZIER	AEKLMRUW	LUKEWARM		TAKEOUTS
AEIRRRST	STARRIER	AEKLMRUY	YARMULKE	AEKPPSSU	UPSPEAKS
	TARRIERS	AEKLNNSS	LANKNESS	AEKPRRSS	SPARKERS
AEIRRRSV	ARRIVERS	AEKLNOSY	ANKYLOSE	AEKPSSSY	PASSKEYS
AEIRRSST	TARSIERS	AEKLNPPS	KNAPPLES	AEKQRSUW	SQUAWKER
AEIRRSSY	SISERARY	AEKLNPRS	PRANKLES	AEKRRSST	STARKERS
AEIRRSTT	RETRAITS	AEKLNPRT	PLANKTER	AEKRSSTT	STARKEST
	STRAITER	AEKLNRSS	RANKLESS	AEKSSSTT	TSATSKES
	TARRIEST	AEKLNRSV	KLAVERNS	AELLLORY	LOYALLER
AEIRRSTW	STRAWIER	AEKLNSST	TANKLESS	AELLLRTU	TELLURAL
AEIRRSVV	VIVERRAS	AEKLOPRT	LAKEPORT	AELLLSUV	VULSELLA
AEIRRTTT	RETRAITT	AEKLOPRW	ROPEWALK	AELLMNOO	ALLOMONE
AEIRRTTY	TERTIARY	AEKLOPTY	KALOTYPE	AELLMNOZ	MANZELLO
AEIRRVWY	RIVERWAY	AEKLORSY	ROKELAYS	AELLMNST	STALLMEN
AEIRSSST	ASSISTER	AEKLORTV	OVERTALK	AELLMNTY	MENTALLY
	TIRASSES	AEKLORVW	WALKOVER		TALLYMEN
AEIRSSSZ	ASSIZERS	AEKLOSST	SKATOLES	AELLMORR	MORALLER
AEIRSSTT	ARTISTES		STALKOES	AELLMORS	SLALOMER
	ARTSIEST	AEKLOSVZ	ZELKOVAS	AELLMORT	MARTELLO
	STRIATES	AEKLPPST	PEPTALKS	AELLMOSS	LOAMLESS
AEIRSSTV	TRAVISES	AEKLPRRS	SPARKLER	AELLMOTY	TOMALLEY
AEIRSSTW	WAISTERS	AEKLPRSS	SPARKLES	AELLMOYZ	ALLOZYME
	WAITRESS	AEKLPRST	SPARKLET	AELLMPUU	PLUMULAE
	WASTRIES	AEKLRSST	STALKERS	AELLMRST	TRAMELLS
AEIRSTTT	ATTRITES	AEKLRSUW	WAULKERS	AELLMRSY	MERSALYL
	RATTIEST	AEKLSSST	TASKLESS	AELLMSST	SMALLEST
	TARTIEST	AEKMMNRS	MARKSMEN	AELLMSWX	MAXWELLS
	TITRATES	AEKMNRSU	UNMAKERS	AELLNOOT	ATENOLOL
	TRISTATE		UNMASKER	AELLNOPS	PALLONES
AEIRSTTW	WARTIEST	AEKMOOST	MATOOKES	AELLNOPV	VOLPLANE
AEIRSTTX	EXTRAITS	AEKMOPRT	TOPMAKER	AELLNORS	LLANEROS
AEIRSTTZ	TRISTEZA	AEKMORTW	TEAMWORK	AELLNOSV	NOVELLAS
AEIRSTUZ	AZURITES		WORKMATE	AELLNOWW	ENWALLOW
AEIRSTVY	VESTIARY	AEKMPRRV	VERKRAMP	AELLNPRU	PRUNELLA

AELLNPSS	PLANLESS	
AELLNPTT	PLANTLET	
AELLNPTU	PLANTULE	
AELLNRUY	NEURALLY	
	UNREALLY	
AELLNRVY	VERNALLY	
AELLNSST	TALLNESS	
AELLNSTT	TALLENTS	
AELLNTTY	LATENTLY	
AELLNTUU	LUNULATE	
AELLNTUY	LUNATELY	
AELLOOPS	PALEOSOL	
AELLOPPR	APPELLOR	
AELLOPRS	REPOSALL	
AELLOPRT	PREALLOT	
AELLOPRW	WALLOPER	
AELLOPTY	ALLOTYPE	
AELLORRY	ROYALLER	
AELLORSS	ROSELLAS	
AELLORST	REALLOTS	
	ROSTELLA	
AELLORSV	ALLOVERS	
	OVERALLS	
AELLORSW	SALLOWER	
AELLORTT	ALLOTTER	
AELLORWW	WALLOWER	
AELLOSTY	LOYALEST	
AELLOSUV	ALVEOLUS	
AELLPRSS	SPALLERS	
AELLPSSY	PLAYLESS	
AELLPSTY	PLAYLETS	
AELLQRSU	SQUALLER	
AELLRRSU	ALLURERS	
AELLRRTY	RETRALLY	
AELLRTTY	LATTERLY	
AELLRTVY	TREVALLY	
AELLRTYY	LYRATELY	
AELLRWYY	LAWYERLY	
AELLSSST	SALTLESS	
	TASSELLS	
AELLSSTW	SETWALLS	
	SWALLETS	
AELLSSTY	TASSELLY	
AELLSTUU	ULULATES	
AELLSTVY	VESTALLY	
AELLSUVV	VALVULES	
AELLSUXY	SEXUALLY	
AELMMNOS	MAMELONS	
AELMMORW	MEALWORM	
AELMMOSV	MYELOMAS	
AELMMRSS	SLAMMERS	
AELMMRST	STRAMMEL	
	TRAMMELS	
AELMMSST	STAMMELS	
AELMMSSY	MALMSEYS	
AELMNNOT	NONMETAL	
AELMNNOU	NOUMENAL	
AELMNNRV	MANNERLY	
AELMNNTU	UNMANTLE	
AELMNOPS	NEOPLASM	
	PLEONASM	
AELMNORS	ALMONERS	
AELMNOST	SALMONET	
	TELAMONS	

AELMNOSU	MELANOUS	
AELMNOWY	LAYWOMEN	
AELMNOVY	YEOMANLY	
AELMNPRS	LAMPERNS	
AELMNRSU	MENSURAL	
	NUMERALS	
AELMNSTT	MANTLETS	
AELMNSTU	NUTMEALS	
AELMNSTY	MESNALTY	
AELMOOPT	OMOPLATE	
AELMOORS	SALEROOM	
AELMOPRR	PREMOLAR	
	PREMORAL	
AELMOPRS	PLEROMAS	
	RAMPOLES	
AELMOPRT	PROMETAL	
	TEMPORAL	
AELMOPSU	AMPOULES	
AELMOPSX	EXOPLASM	
AELMOPSY	MAYPOLES	
	PLAYSOME	
AELMOPTT	METAPLOT	
	PALMETTO	
AELMORST	MOLERATS	
AELMORSU	RAMULOSE	
AELMORSV	REMOVALS	
AELMORSY	RAMOSELY	
AELMORTU	EMULATOR	
AELMORTZ	METRAZOL	
AELMOSSS	MOLASSES	
AELMOSST	MALTOSES	
AELMOSSY	AMYLOSES	
AELMOSTT	MATELOTS	
AELMOSTU	SOULMATE	
AELMOSTY	ATMOLYSE	
AELMOTVZ	MAZELTOV	
AELMOTYZ	ATMOLYZE	
AELMPRRT	TRAMPLER	
AELMPRRS	SAMPLERS	
AELMPRST	TEMPLARS	
	TRAMPLES	
AELMPRSV	LAMPREYS	
	SAMPLERY	
AELMPSUX	AMPLEXUS	
AELMQSUU	SQUAMULE	
AELMRSST	LAMSTERS	
	TRAMLESS	
AELMRSTT	MALTSTER	
	MARTLETS	
AELMRSTU	STAUMREL	
AELMRSTY	MASTERLY	
AELMRTUY	MATURELY	
AELMSSSS	MASSLESS	
AELMSSST	MASTLESS	
AELNNNPU	UNPANNEL	
AELNNOOP	NAPOLEON	
AELNNOOX	NALOXONE	
AELNNOPT	PENTANOL	
AELNNOQU	NONEQUAL	
AELNNORU	NEURONAL	
AELNNOSU	ANNULOSE	
AELNNPRS	PLANNERS	
AELNNPSU	UNPANELS	
AELNNRSS	ENSNARLS	

AELNNRST	LANTERNS	
AELNNRSU	UNLEARNS	
AELNNRTU	UNLEARNT	
AELNNSST	STANNELS	
AELNNSTU	ANNULETS	
AELNOOTZ	ENTOZOAL	
AELNOPPY	POLYPNEA	
AELNOPRS	PERSONAL	
	PSORALEN	
AELNOPRV	OVERPLAN	
AELNOPST	LAPSTONE	
	PLEONAST	
	POLENTAS	
AELNOPSU	APOLUNES	
AELNOPTW	TOWPLANE	
AELNORSU	ALEURONS	
	NEUROSAL	
AELNORSV	VERONALS	
AELNORTT	TETRONAL	
	TOLERANT	
AELNORTU	OUTLEARN	
AELNORTY	ORNATELY	
AELNOSSV	OVALNESS	
AELNOSTV	VOLANTES	
AELNOSTY	ANOLYTES	
AELNPPRS	PREPLANS	
AELNPPRT	PREPLANT	
AELNPPSY	PLAYPENS	
	SPYPLANE	
AELNPRST	PANTLERS	
	PLANTERS	
	REPLANTS	
AELNPRSU	PURSLANE	
	SUPERNAL	
AELNPRTY	PLENARTY	
AELNPSSS	SNAPLESS	
	SPANLESS	
AELNPSSU	SPANSULE	
AELNPSTX	EXPLANTS	
AELNPTTU	PATULENT	
	PETULANT	
AELNPTTY	PATENTLY	
AELNQSUU	UNEQUALS	
AELNRRSS	SNARLERS	
AELNRRTY	ERRANTLY	
AELNRRUU	NEURULAR	
AELNRRUV	NERVULAR	
AELNRSST	SALTERNS	
	SLANTERS	
AELNRSTT	SLATTERN	
	TRENTALS	
AELNRSTU	NEUTRALS	
AELNRSTV	VENTRALS	
AELNRSUU	NEURULAS	
AELNRSUV	UNRAVELS	
AELNRSVY	SYLVANER	
AELNRSXY	LARYNXES	
AELNRTTW	TRAWLNET	
AELNRUWY	UNWARELY	
AELNSSST	SALTNESS	
AELNSSTY	STANYELS	
AELNSTUV	ENVAULTS	
AELNSUUX	UNSEXUAL	
AELNTTUX	EXULTANT	

AELOOPRZ	ZOOPERAL	**AELPRRSW**	SPRAWLER	**AELSSTTW**	WATTLESS
AELOORRS	ROSEOLAR	**AELPRRTT**	PRATTLER	**AELSSWZZ**	SWAZZLES
AELOORSS	AEROSOLS	**AELPRSST**	PERSALTS	**AELSTTTW**	TWATTLES
	ROSEOLAS		PLASTERS	**AELSTTUU**	USTULATE
AELOORTW	WATERLOO		PSALTERS	**AELSTTUY**	ASTUTELY
AELOORTZ	ZOOLATER		STAPLERS	**AELUUVVZ**	VUVUZELA
AELOPPRS	PROLAPSE	**AELPRSSU**	PERUSALS	**AEMMMOTU**	OMMATEUM
	PROPALES	**AELPRSSY**	PARSLEYS	**AEMMMRTY**	MAMMETRY
	SAPROPEL		SPARSELY	**AEMMNNOY**	MONEYMAN
AELOPPSU	PAPULOSE	**AELPRSTT**	PARTLETS	**AEMMNPRS**	RAMPSMEN
AELOPPTU	POPULATE		PLATTERS	**AEMMNRRY**	MERRYMAN
AELOPPXY	APOPLEXY		PRATTLES	**AEMMNRTU**	RAMENTUM
AELOPQUY	OPAQUELY		SPLATTER	**AEMMOORT**	ROOMMATE
AELOPRRV	REPROVAL		SPRATTLE	**AEMMOPRS**	MAMPOERS
AELOPRSS	REPOSALS	**AELPRSTU**	APLUSTRE	**AEMMORSS**	MARMOSES
AELOPRST	PETROSAL	**AELPRSTY**	PEYTRALS	**AEMMORST**	MARMOSET
	POLESTAR		PLASTERY	**AEMMORSW**	WOMMERAS
	PROLATES		PSALTERY	**AEMMOSTU**	MOUSEMAT
AELOPRSU	LEAPROUS	**AELPRSUY**	SUPERLAY	**AEMMPRSS**	SPAMMERS
AELOPRSV	OVERLAPS	**AELPSSSS**	PASSLESS	**AEMMRSST**	STAMMERS
AELOPRVY	OVERPLAY	**AELPSSST**	PASTLESS	**AEMMRTUY**	MAUMETRY
AELOPRYZ	PYRAZOLE	**AELPSSTT**	PELTASTS	**AEMMRTWY**	MAWMETRY
AELOPSSS	SOAPLESS	**AELPSSTU**	PULSATES	**AEMMSSTU**	SUMMATES
AELOPSST	APOSTLES		SPATULES	**AEMMSSUW**	WAMMUSES
AELOPSSU	ESPOUSAL	**AELPSSTZ**	SPATZLES	**AEMNNOPW**	PENWOMAN
	SEPALOUS	**AELPSUUV**	UPVALUES	**AEMNNORS**	MONERANS
AELOPSSX	EXPOSALS	**AELQRRSU**	QUARRELS		SONARMEN
AELOPSTT	PALETOTS	**AELQRSUV**	SERVQUAL	**AEMNNORT**	ORNAMENT
AELOPSTU	OUTLEAPS	**AELQRSUY**	SQUARELY	**AEMNNOSS**	MANNOSES
	PETALOUS	**AELQSTTU**	SQUATTLE	**AEMNNOST**	MONTANES
AELOPTTU	OUTLEAPT	**AELQSTUZ**	QUETZALS	**AEMNNOSZ**	MENAZONS
AELORRST	REALTORS	**AELRRSSW**	WARSLERS	**AEMNNRST**	MANRENTS
	RELATORS	**AELRRSTT**	RATTLERS		REMNANTS
	RESTORAL		STARTLER	**AEMNOORR**	MAROONER
AELORSSS	LASSOERS	**AELRRSTW**	TRAWLERS	**AEMNOORT**	ANTEROOM
AELORSST	OLESTRAS		WARSTLER	**AEMNOORY**	AERONOMY
AELORSTT	RETOTALS	**AELRRTVY**	VARLETRY	**AEMNOOSZ**	MESOZOAN
AELORSTU	ROSULATE	**AELRSSST**	STARLESS	**AEMNOOTZ**	METAZOON
AELORSTV	LEVATORS	**AELRSSSW**	WRASSLES	**AEMNOPPS**	PAMPOENS
	OVERSALT	**AELRSSTT**	SLATTERS	**AEMNOPRS**	MANROPES
AELORSTY	ROYALETS		STARLETS		PROSEMAN
AELORSTZ	ZELATORS		STARTLES	**AEMNOPRT**	EMPATRON
AELORSUU	ROULEAUS	**AELRSSTU**	SALUTERS	**AEMNOPRW**	MANPOWER
AELORSVY	LAYOVERS	**AELRSSTW**	WARSTLES	**AEMNORRS**	RANSOMER
	OVERLAYS		WARTLESS	**AEMNORST**	MONSTERA
AELORSWY	OWRELAYS		WASTRELS		ONSTREAM
AELORTTV	VARLETTO		WRASTLES		STOREMAN
AELORTYZ	ZEALOTRY	**AELRSSUU**	RUSSULAE		TONEARMS
AELORUUX	ROULEAUX	**AELRSSUW**	WALRUSES	**AEMNORSU**	ENAMOURS
AELOSSTV	SOLVATES	**AELRSTTT**	TARTLETS		NEUROMAS
AELOSSTY	ASYSTOLE		TATTLERS	**AEMNORSV**	OVERMANS
AELOSSVY	SAVELOYS	**AELRSTTU**	LUSTRATE		OVERSMAN
AELOSTTU	TOLUATES		TUTELARS	**AEMNORSY**	ROMNEYAS
AELOSTTW	WASTELOT	**AELRSTTY**	SLATTERY	**AEMNORTT**	TORMENTA
AELOSTUV	OVULATES	**AELRSTUV**	VAULTERS	**AEMNORTU**	ROUTEMAN
AELOSTUY	AUTOLYSE		VESTURAL	**AEMNORTY**	MONETARY
AELOTUUV	OUTVALUE	**AELRSTWY**	TRAWLEYS	**AEMNORVY**	OVERMANY
AELOTUYZ	AUTOLYZE	**AELRSTWZ**	WALTZERS	**AEMNORYY**	YEOMANRY
AELPPPRU	PREPUPAL	**AELRSUVY**	SURVEYAL	**AEMNOSTU**	NOTAEUMS
AELPPPRY	PREAPPLY	**AELRTTTW**	TWATTLER		OUTNAMES
AELPPRSS	SLAPPERS	**AELRTTUX**	TEXTURAL		SEAMOUNT
AELPPSST	STAPPLES	**AELRTTUY**	TUTELARY	**AEMNPRSS**	PRESSMAN
AELPPSSU	APPULSES	**AELSSSTU**	SALTUSES	**AEMNPRSU**	SUPERMAN
AELPRRRU	LARRUPER	**AELSSSTY**	STAYLESS	**AEMNPSST**	ENSTAMPS

Eight-letter anagrams

	PASSMENT
AEMNPSTU	SPUMANTE
AEMNPSTY	PAYMENTS
AEMNQSUW	SQUAWMEN
AEMNRRSU	MANURERS
	SURNAMER
AEMNRRUY	NUMERARY
AEMNRSST	SARMENTS
	SMARTENS
AEMNRSSU	SURNAMES
AEMNRSSW	WARMNESS
AEMNRSTU	ANESTRUM
	MENSTRUA
	TRANSUME
AEMNRSTV	VARMENTS
AEMNRSTW	TRANSMEW
	TREWSMAN
AEMNRSUY	ANEURYSM
AEMNSTTU	NUTMEATS
AEMNSTWY	WAYMENTS
AEMOOPST	POMATOES
AEMOORRW	WAREROOM
AEMOORST	TEAROOMS
AEMOORSW	WOOMERAS
AEMOORTT	AMORETTO
AEMOOSST	MAESTOSO
	OSTEOMAS
AEMOOSSV	VAMOOSES
AEMOOSTT	OSTOMATE
	TOMATOES
AEMOOSTU	AUTOSOME
AEMOOTTY	TOMATOEY
AEMOPPRS	PAMPEROS
AEMOPRTW	POMWATER
	TAPEWORM
AEMOQSSU	SQUAMOSE
AEMORRRS	ARMORERS
AEMORRRU	ARMOURER
AEMORRST	REARMOST
AEMORRSV	OVERARMS
AEMORRSW	EARWORMS
AEMORRSY	ROSEMARY
AEMORRVW	OVERWARM
AEMORSSS	MORASSES
AEMORSST	MAESTROS
AEMORSSW	SEAWORMS
AEMORSSY	MAYORESS
AEMORSTV	OVERMAST
AEMORSVW	OVERSWAM
AEMORTTU	TAUTOMER
AEMOSSTT	EASTMOST
	STOMATES
AEMOSSTW	TWASOMES
AEMOSSUZ	ZAMOUSES
AEMOSSWY	SOMEWAYS
AEMOSTTZ	MOZETTAS
AEMOTTZZ	MOZZETTA
AEMPPRST	PRESTAMP
AEMPRRST	TRAMPERS
AEMPRRSW	PREWARMS
AEMPRRSY	SPERMARY
AEMPRSST	RESTAMPS
	STAMPERS
AEMPRSSW	SWAMPERS
AEMPRSTT	TRAMPETS
AEMPRSTU	TEMPURAS
	UPSTREAM
AEMPRSUX	SUPERMAX
AEMPSSUW	MAWPUSES
	WAMPUSES
AEMPSTTT	ATTEMPTS
AEMQRSSU	MARQUESS
	MASQUERS
AEMRRSST	ARMRESTS
AEMRRSSW	SWARMERS
AEMRRSTU	MATURERS
AEMRRTUV	VERATRUM
AEMRSSSU	ASSUMERS
	MASSEURS
AEMRSSTT	MATTRESS
	SMARTEST
	SMATTERS
AEMRSSTY	MAYSTERS
AEMRSTTU	MATUREST
	TESTAMUR
AEMRSTTX	MARTEXTS
AEMRTUUX	TRUMEAUX
AEMSTTTU	TESTATUM
AENNNPST	PENNANTS
AENNNTTU	UNTENANT
AENNOOTZ	ENTOZOAN
AENNOPRT	PATRONNE
AENNOPRX	NAPROXEN
AENNOPST	PENTOSAN
AENNOPUW	UNWEAPON
AENNORST	NORTENAS
	RESONANT
AENNORSU	UNREASON
AENNORSY	ANNOYERS
AENNORTU	UNORNATE
AENNORTW	WANTONER
AENNORUX	NEURAXON
AENNORVY	NOVENARY
AENNOSSU	UNSEASON
AENNOSTU	TONNEAUS
AENNOSTX	NONTAXES
AENNOTUX	TONNEAUX
AENNPRSS	SPANNERS
AENNPSSU	PANNUSES
AENNQSTU	QUANNETS
AENNRSTT	ENTRANTS
AENNRSTY	TYRANNES
AENNRSWY	SWANNERY
AENNRTTY	TENANTRY
AENOOPST	TEASPOON
AENOORRT	RATOONER
AENOOSTZ	OZONATES
AENOPPRS	PROPANES
AENOPRSS	PERSONAS
	RESPONSA
AENOPRST	OPERANTS
	PRONATES
	PROTEANS
AENOPRSY	PYRANOSE
AENOPRTT	PATENTOR
AENOPRWY	WEAPONRY
AENOPSSU	POSAUNES
AENOPSTU	AUTOPENS
AENORRRW	NARROWER
AENORRSS	SERRANOS
AENORRST	ANTRORSE
AENORSST	ASSENTOR
	SANTEROS
	SENATORS
	STARNOSE
	TREASONS
AENORSSU	ANSEROUS
	ARSENOUS
AENORSTT	ORNATEST
AENORSTU	OUTEARNS
AENORSTV	VENATORS
AENORSTW	STONERAW
AENORSUV	RAVENOUS
AENORSWZ	WARZONES
AENORTTV	TEVATRON
AENORTTX	TETRAXON
AENORTTY	ATTORNEY
AENORTWW	TOWNWEAR
AENOSSTU	SOUTANES
AENOSSTZ	STANZOES
AENOSSUU	NAUSEOUS
AENOSSVW	WAVESONS
AENOTTUU	AUTOTUNE
AENOUUVX	NOUVEAUX
AENPPRSS	PARSNEPS
	SNAPPERS
AENPPRST	PARPENTS
AENPPRSU	UNPAPERS
AENPRRST	PARTNERS
AENPRRSW	PRAWNERS
	PREWARNS
AENPRSST	PASTERNS
	RAPTNESS
AENPRSSW	SPAWNERS
AENPRSTT	PATTERNS
	TRANSEPT
	TRAPNEST
AENPRSTU	PERSAUNT
AENPRSUV	PARVENUS
AENPSSST	PASTNESS
AENPSSSY	SYNAPSES
AENPSSTU	PESAUNTS
AENPSSTW	STEWPANS
	WASPNEST
AENPSSTY	SYNAPTES
AENPSSTZ	SPETSNAZ
AENPSTZZ	SPETZNAZ
AENQRRTU	QUARTERN
AENQSTTU	QUESTANT
AENRRRTY	ERRANTRY
AENRRSTT	TRANTERS
AENRSSST	SARSNETS
AENRSSTT	TARTNESS
AENRSSTU	ANESTRUS
	SAUNTERS
AENRSSTV	SERVANTS
	VERSANTS
AENRSSUW	UNSWEARS
AENRSTTU	TAUNTERS
AENRSTUV	VAUNTERS
AENRSTUW	UNWATERS
AENRSTWY	STERNWAY

AENRTUVY	VAUNTERY	**AEORRTUV**	AVOUTRER		SQUATTER
AENRTUWY	UNWATERY	**AEORRTZZ**	TERRAZZO	**AEQRSTUZ**	QUARTZES
AENRTWYY	ENTRYWAY	**AEORRVWY**	OVERWARY	**AEQRTTTU**	QUARTETT
AENSSSTV	VASTNESS	**AEORSSSS**	ASSESSOR	**AERRSSSU**	ASSURERS
AENSSSTW	WASTNESS	**AEORSSST**	OSSETRAS	**AERRSSTT**	RESTARTS
AENSSTTU	TAUTNESS	**AEORSSTT**	STRATOSE		STARTERS
	UNSTATES		TOASTERS	**AERRSSTU**	SERRATUS
AENSSTTX	SEXTANTS	**AEORSSTU**	OSSATURE	**AERRSSTV**	STARVERS
AENSSTXY	SYNTAXES	**AEORSSTV**	VOTARESS	**AERRSSTY**	STRAYERS
AEOOPPPS	PAPPOOSE	**AEORSSTX**	STORAXES	**AERRSTUY**	TREASURY
AEOOPPSS	PAPOOSES	**AEORSSUU**	ROUSSEAU	**AERSSSST**	STRASSES
AEOOPRRT	OPERATOR	**AEORSTTT**	ATTESTOR	**AERSSSTY**	SATYRESS
AEOOPRSS	OROPESAS		TESTATOR	**AERSSTTT**	STRETTAS
AEOOPSTT	POTATOES	**AEORSTTU**	OUTRATES	**AERSSTTU**	STATURES
AEOORRST	SORORATE		OUTSTARE	**AERSSTTW**	SWATTERS
AEOORTTT	TATTOOER		SEATROUT	**AERSSTUX**	SURTAXES
AEOORTTV	ROTOVATE	**AEORSTUV**	OUTRAVES	**AERSSTVY**	STRAYVES
AEOPPRRV	APPROVER	**AEORSTUW**	OUTSWARE	**AERSSTXY**	STYRAXES
AEOPPRSS	APPOSERS		OUTSWEAR	**AERSTTUV**	VETTURAS
AEOPPRST	TRAPPOSE		OUTWEARS	**AERSTTVY**	TRAVESTY
AEOPPRSV	APPROVES	**AEORSTVY**	OVERSTAY	**AERTTUXY**	TEXTUARY
AEOPQRTU	PAROQUET	**AEORSUVW**	WAVEROUS	**AESSSTTU**	STATUSES
AEOPQSTU	OPAQUEST	**AEORSVWY**	OVERSWAY	**AESSTTTU**	ASTUTEST
AEOPRRRT	PARROTER	**AEORTUWY**	OUTWEARY		STATUTES
AEOPRRSS	ASPERSOR		ROUTEWAY	**AFFFFINN**	NIFFNAFF
AEOPRRST	PRAETORS	**AEORTVXY**	VEXATORY	**AFFFFIRR**	RIFFRAFF
	PRORATES	**AEOSTTTU**	OUTSTATE	**AFFFGILN**	FLAFFING
AEOPRRSV	VAPORERS	**AEOSTTUW**	OUTWASTE	**AFFFLLOS**	FALLOFFS
AEOPRRTV	OVERPART	**AEPPPRSU**	PREPUPAS	**AFFGGINR**	GRAFFING
AEOPRRUV	VAPOURER	**AEPPPSSU**	PAPPUSES	**AFFGGINS**	GAFFINGS
AEOPRRVW	WRAPOVER	**AEPPRRST**	STRAPPER	**AFFGHIRT**	AFFRIGHT
AEOPRRWW	WARPOWER		TRAPPERS	**AFFGIINP**	PIAFFING
AEOPRSST	ESPARTOS	**AEPPRRSW**	PREWRAPS	**AFFGIINX**	AFFIXING
	PORTASES		WRAPPERS	**AFFGIIRT**	GRAFFITI
	PROTASES	**AEPPRSSU**	UPSPEARS	**AFFGILMN**	MAFFLING
	SEAPORTS	**AEPPRSSW**	SWAPPERS	**AFFGILNR**	RAFFLING
AEOPRSSU	ASPEROUS	**AEPPSSTU**	PASTEUPS	**AFFGILNW**	WAFFLING
AEOPRSSV	OVERPASS	**AEPQRSTU**	PARQUETS	**AFFGIMRS**	MISGRAFF
	PASSOVER	**AEPRRRSS**	SPARRERS	**AFFGINNY**	NYAFFING
AEOPRSTT	PROSTATE	**AEPRRSSY**	RESPRAYS	**AFFGINQU**	QUAFFING
AEOPRSTU	APTEROUS		SPRAYERS	**AFFGINST**	STAFFING
AEOPRSTV	OVERPAST	**AEPRRSTU**	PARTURES	**AFFGINUW**	WAUFFING
AEOPRSVY	OVERPAYS		PASTURER	**AFFGIORT**	GRAFFITO
AEOPRSWY	ROPEWAYS		RAPTURES	**AFFHILLS**	FALLFISH
AEOPRTWX	WATERPOX	**AEPRRSTY**	PARTYERS	**AFFHILNS**	HAFFLINS
AEOPSSST	POTASSES	**AEPRSSST**	SPARSEST	**AFFHILST**	FLATFISH
AEOPTTUY	AUTOTYPE		TAPSTERS	**AFFHILTU**	FAITHFUL
AEOQRSTU	EQUATORS	**AEPRSSTT**	SPATTERS	**AFFIINTY**	AFFINITY
	QUAESTOR		TAPSTERS	**AFFIISTX**	FIXATIFS
AEOQRSUV	VAQUEROS	**AEPRSSTU**	PASTURES	**AFFILLMM**	FLIMFLAM
AEOQRTTU	TORQUATE		UPSTARES	**AFFILMNS**	MAFFLINS
AEOQRTUZ	QUATORZE	**AEPRSSTY**	YAPSTERS	**AFFILORS**	RIFFOLAS
AEORRRST	ARRESTOR	**AEPRSSWY**	SPYWARES	**AFFILSUX**	SUFFIXAL
AEORRSST	ASSERTOR	**AEPRSTTU**	STUPRATE	**AFFIMSST**	MASTIFFS
	ASSORTER		UPSTATER	**AFFINORR**	FORFAIRN
	ORATRESS	**AEPRSTTY**	TAPESTRY	**AFFINOSU**	AFFUSION
	REASSORT	**AEPRSTUX**	SUPERTAX	**AFFINRSU**	FUNFAIRS
	ROASTERS	**AEPRTUVY**	PYRUVATE		RUFFIANS
AEORRSSU	AROUSERS	**AEPSSSSU**	PASSUSES	**AFFIORRS**	FORFAIRS
AEORRSSV	SAVORERS	**AEPSSTTU**	UPSTATES	**AFFIPSTT**	TIPSTAFF
	SEROVARS	**AEQRRSSU**	SQUARERS	**AFFIRRSU**	FURFAIRS
AEORRSTT	ROSTRATE	**AEQRRSTU**	QUARTERS	**AFFIRSSU**	SUFFARIS
AEORRSUV	SAVOURER	**AEQRSSTU**	SQUAREST	**AFFLLOOT**	FOOTFALL
AEORRTTV	OVERTART	**AEQRSTTU**	QUARTETS	**AFFLLTUU**	FAULTFUL

Eight-letter anagrams

AFFLOOOT	FOALFOOT	AFGIMRST	MISGRAFT	AFHOORST	HAFTOROS
AFFLOOTT	FLATFOOT	AFGINNNS	FANNINGS	AFHOORTT	HAFTOROT
AFFLOPSY	PLAYOFFS	AFGINNRS	SNARFING	AFHOPSTU	POUFTAHS
AFFLORTU	FORFAULT	AFGINNSU	SNAFUING	AFIIKMRS	FAKIRISM
AFFLRRUU	FURFURAL	AFGINNSW	FAWNINGS	AFIILLLY	FILIALLY
AFFMOPRS	OFFRAMPS	AFGINORV	FAVORING	AFIILLNU	UNFILIAL
AFFNORSS	SAFFRONS	AFGINORY	FORAYING	AFIILMMS	FAMILISM
AFFNORST	AFFRONTS	AFGINPPR	FRAPPING	AFIILMNS	FINALISM
AFFNRONY	SAFFRONY	AFGINRST	INGRAFTS	AFIILNRU	UNIFILAR
AFFNRRUU	FURFURAN		RAFTINGS	AFIILNST	FINALIST
AFGGGILN	FLAGGING		STRAFING		TAILFINS
AFGGGINR	FRAGGING	AFGINRSW	SWARFING	AFIILNTY	FINALITY
AFGGGINS	FAGGINGS	AFGINRSY	FRAYINGS	AFIILORS	AIRFOILS
AFGGILNN	FANGLING	AFGINRTU	FIGURANT	AFIILRST	AIRLIFTS
	FLANGING	AFGINSST	FASTINGS	AFIIMNPR	RIFAMPIN
AFGGILOP	GIGAFLOP	AFGINSTW	WAFTINGS	AFIIMRSY	FAIRYISM
AFGGINOR	FORAGING	AFGINSUY	SANGUIFY	AFIINNOS	SAINFOIN
AFGGINOT	FAGOTING	AFGIORST	ISOGRAFT		SINFONIA
AFGGINRT	GRAFTING	AFGIPRTW	GIFTWRAP	AFIINOTX	FIXATION
AFGGORTY	FAGGOTRY	AFGKNOPS	PAKFONGS	AFIIORRT	TRIFORIA
AFGHIINT	FAITHING	AFGKORST	KOFTGARS	AFIJKRTU	JAKFRUIT
AFGHILLN	HALFLING	AFGLLNOT	FLATLONG	AFIJMNOR	JANIFORM
AFGHILNS	FLASHING	AFGLLRUU	FULGURAL	AFIKLNNR	FRANKLIN
AFGHILNT	FANLIGHT	AFGLLRUY	FRUGALLY	AFIKLORT	FORKTAIL
AFGHILPS	FLAGSHIP	AFGLLSSU	GLASSFUL	AFIKLOST	FLOKATIS
AFGHINRT	FARTHING	AFGLLSTU	GASTFULL	AFIKMNNR	FINNMARK
AFGHINRW	WHARFING	AFGLNNOO	GONFALON	AFIKMNRS	FINMARKS
AFGHINST	SHAFTING	AFGLNORU	GROANFUL	AFIKNRST	RATFINKS
AFGHIOST	GOATFISH	AFGLNOUW	WAGONFUL	AFIKRSTY	KARSTIFY
AFGHIRSY	GRAYFISH	AFGNNNOO	GONFANON	AFILLLOT	FLOTILLA
AFGHLLUU	LAUGHFUL	AFGOORTZ	ZOOGRAFT	AFILLMSS	MISFALLS
AFGHLNSU	FLASHGUN	AFHIILRS	FRAILISH	AFILLMUY	AIMFULLY
AFGHLSTU	FLAUGHTS	AFHIILSS	SAILFISH	AFILLNPS	PINFALLS
	GHASTFUL	AFHIILST	FISHTAIL	AFILLNPU	PLAINFUL
AFGHRSTU	FRAUGHTS	AFHIIMST	MISFAITH	AFILLPST	PITFALLS
AFGIILLN	FLAILING	AFHIINST	FAINTISH	AFILLPSU	PAILFULS
AFGIILNS	FAILINGS	AFHIKSUV	KUFIYAHS		PAILSFUL
AFGIIMNN	INFAMING	AFHILLNS	HALFLINS	AFILLSUV	VIALFULS
AFGIINNT	FAINTING	AFHILLSW	WALLFISH	AFILLTUY	FAULTILY
AFGIINRS	FAIRINGS	AFHILLSY	FLASHILY	AFILMNOR	FORMALIN
	FRAISING	AFHILOSY	OAFISHLY		INFORMAL
AFGIINTX	FIXATING	AFHILSST	SALTFISH	AFILMNOS	FOILSMAN
AFGIKLNN	FANKLING	AFHILSTT	FLATTISH	AFILMOPR	PALIFORM
	FLANKING	AFHILSTW	HALFWITS	AFILMSSS	FALSISMS
AFGIKNNR	FRANKING	AFHIMNST	MANSHIFT	AFILNNNO	NONFINAL
AFGIKORT	KOFTGARI	AFHIMNSU	HAFNIUMS	AFILNORT	FLATIRON
AFGILLNS	FALLINGS	AFHINOSS	FASHIONS		INFLATOR
AFGILLNT	FLATLING	AFHINOSY	FASHIONY	AFILNOSU	FUSIONAL
AFGILMMN	FLAMMING	AFHINSTU	UNFAITHS	AFILNPPT	FLIPPANT
AFGILMNO	FLAMINGO	AFHIOSSU	FASHIOUS	AFILNRTU	TRAINFUL
AFGILNOS	LOAFINGS	AFHIRSST	STARFISH	AFILNRUY	UNFAIRLY
AFGILNOT	FLOATING	AFHISSWY	FISHWAYS	AFILNSTU	FLUTINAS
AFGILNPP	FLAPPING	AFHKLNTU	THANKFUL		INFLATUS
AFGILNRU	INFRUGAL	AFHKORSX	FOXSHARK	AFILOORT	FAROLITO
AFGILNST	FATLINGS	AFHKORSY	HAYFORKS	AFILORSW	AIRFLOWS
AFGILNTT	FLATTING	AFHKRSTU	FUTHARKS	AFILORTY	FILATORY
AFGILNTU	FAULTING	AFHLLOTU	LOATHFUL	AFILOSTX	FOXTAILS
AFGILORW	GAIRFOWL	AFHLNSUY	UNFLASHY	AFILRSSU	FISSURAL
AFGILSSY	GLASSIFY	AFHLOSTU	OUTFLASH	AFILRSTU	FISTULAR
AFGIMNOS	FOAMINGS	AFHLOSTY	HAYLOFTS	AFILSSTU	FISTULAS
AFGIMNRS	FARMINGS	AFHLRTUW	WRATHFUL	AFILSTTU	FLAUTIST
	FRAMINGS	AFHNOOST	FANTOOSH	AFIMMNOR	MANIFORM
AFGIMNTU	FUMIGANT	AFHOOPST	POOFTAHS	AFIMMNOY	AMMONIFY
AFGIMORS	GASIFORM	AFHOOPTT	FOOTPATH	AFIMMORR	RAMIFORM

AFIMNOPR	NAPIFORM	**AFLNTUUY**	UNFAULTY	**AGGHINUW**	WAUGHING
AFIMNORR	RANIFORM	**AFLOOSTW**	WOOLFATS	**AGGHISTT**	GASTIGHT
AFIMNORT	NATIFORM	**AFLOOTTU**	OUTFLOAT	**AGGHJMNO**	MAHJONGG
AFIMNOSU	INFAMOUS	**AFLOPSTT**	FLATTOPS	**AGGHLOOT**	GOLGOTHA
AFIMOOSS	MAFIOSOS	**AFLORSSU**	FUSAROLS	**AGGIIJJS**	JIGAJIGS
AFIMORRU	AURIFORM	**AFLORSUV**	FLAVOURS	**AGGIILNN**	ALIGNING
AFIMORRV	VARIFORM	**AFLORUVY**	FLAVOURY	**AGGIILNR**	GLAIRING
AFIMORSV	VASIFORM	**AFLOSTUU**	FLATUOUS	**AGGIILNS**	SILAGING
AFIMRSUU	FUSARIUM	**AFLPRSTY**	FLYTRAPS	**AGGIILNT**	LIGATING
AFIMSSTT	FATTISMS	**AFLPSSTY**	FLYPASTS		TAIGLING
AFIMSSUV	FAUVISMS	**AFLRSTTU**	STARTFUL	**AGGIILNV**	GINGIVAL
AFINNORS	FRANIONS	**AFLRSTUY**	TRAYFULS	**AGGIIMNS**	IMAGINGS
AFINNOST	FONTINAS	**AFMNNNUY**	FUNNYMAN	**AGGIINNR**	GRAINING
AFINNOTU	FOUNTAIN	**AFMNNORT**	FRONTMAN	**AGGIINNS**	AGNISING
AFINNRTY	INFANTRY	**AFMNORST**	FORMANTS		GAININGS
AFINOPSY	SAPONIFY	**AFMNOSUU**	UNFAMOUS	**AGGIINNZ**	AGNIZING
AFINQTUY	QUANTIFY	**AFMOOPRR**	PROFORMA	**AGGIINRS**	AGRISING
AFINRSTX	TRANSFIX	**AFMORSSU**	AUSFORMS	**AGGIINRT**	TRIAGING
AFINSSTU	FAUNISTS	**AFMORSTU**	FOUMARTS	**AGGIINRZ**	AGRIZING
	FUSTIANS	**AFMORTUY**	FUMATORY	**AGGIINST**	AGISTING
AFIOOPRR	AIRPROOF	**AFMOSSTU**	SFUMATOS	**AGGIINSU**	AGUISING
AFIORSTU	FAITOURS	**AFNNOTTY**	NONFATTY	**AGGIINUZ**	AGUIZING
AFIORSTZ	SFORZATI	**AFNORRSW**	FORWARNS	**AGGIJJOS**	JIGAJOGS
AFIRSTTY	STRATIFY	**AFNORSTW**	FANWORTS	**AGGIJLNN**	JANGLING
AFISSSTT	SITFASTS	**AFNOSTUW**	OUTFAWNS	**AGGIKNSS**	GASKINGS
AFISSTTT	FATTISTS	**AFOOPPRS**	APPROOFS	**AGGILLNS**	GINGALLS
AFISSTUV	FAUVISTS	**AFOOPRRT**	RATPROOF	**AGGILLNU**	ULLAGING
AFKLNOTU	OUTFLANK	**AFOORSTZ**	FORZATOS	**AGGILLNV**	GALLYING
AFKLNPRU	PRANKFUL		SFORZATO	**AGGILMNN**	MANGLING
AFKLNSTU	TANKFULS	**AFOOSTWY**	FOOTWAYS	**AGGILMNO**	GLOAMING
AFKLORTW	FLATWORK	**AFORSTTW**	FORSWATT	**AGGILMNR**	MALGRING
AFKLOSWY	FOLKWAYS	**AFOSSTTU**	OUTFASTS	**AGGILMNU**	GLAUMING
AFKMOORT	FOOTMARK	**AFOSSTUU**	FASTUOUS	**AGGILNNO**	GANGLION
AFKMORRW	FARMWORK	**AGGGGILN**	GAGGLING	**AGGILNNR**	GNARLING
AFKRRSTU	FRAKTURS	**AGGGHILN**	HAGGLING	**AGGILNNS**	ANGLINGS
AFLLLORY	FLORALLY	**AGGGHINS**	SHAGGING		SLANGING
AFLLLUWY	LAWFULLY	**AGGGILNN**	GANGLING	**AGGILNNT**	GNATLING
AFLLMNUY	MANFULLY	**AGGGILNR**	GARGLING		TANGLING
AFLLMORY	FORMALLY		RAGGLING	**AGGILNNW**	WANGLING
AFLLMPSU	PALMFULS	**AGGGILNS**	LAGGINGS	**AGGILNOP**	GALOPING
AFLLNOOV	FLAVONOL		SLAGGING	**AGGILNOT**	GLOATING
AFLLNOSW	SNOWFALL	**AGGGILNW**	WAGGLING		GOATLING
AFLLNUUW	UNLAWFUL	**AGGGINNS**	GANGINGS	**AGGILNPU**	PLAGUING
AFLLOOTW	FOOTWALL		SNAGGING	**AGGILNPY**	GAPINGLY
AFLLOSTU	FALLOUTS	**AGGGINPS**	SPAGGING	**AGGILNRY**	GRAYLING
	OUTFALLS	**AGGGINRS**	RAGGINGS		RAGINGLY
AFLLRTUY	ARTFULLY	**AGGGINSS**	SAGGINGS	**AGGILNSS**	GLASSING
AFLLSTUW	WASTFULL	**AGGGINST**	STAGGING	**AGGILNSZ**	GLAZINGS
AFLMNNUU	UNMANFUL		TAGGINGS	**AGGIMNRU**	MAUGRING
AFLMNOPR	PLANFORM	**AGGGINSU**	GAUGINGS	**AGGINNOR**	GROANING
AFLMNORU	UNFORMAL	**AGGGINSW**	SWAGGING	**AGGINNOT**	TANGOING
AFLMNOST	LOFTSMAN	**AGGGIVZZ**	ZIGZAGGY	**AGGINNOW**	WAGONING
AFLMOPRT	PLATFORM	**AGGHIILS**	GHILGAIS	**AGGINNPR**	PRANGING
AFLMORRU	FORMULAR	**AGGHILNU**	LAUGHING	**AGGINNPS**	SPANGING
AFLMORSU	FORMULAS	**AGGHILST**	GASLIGHT	**AGGINNRR**	GNARRING
AFLMORSW	WOLFRAMS	**AGGHILSY**	SHAGGILY	**AGGINNRS**	RANGINGS
AFLMORTU	FOULMART	**AGGHIMNO**	HOMAGING	**AGGINNRT**	GRANTING
AFLMORTW	FLATWORM	**AGGHIMNS**	GINGHAMS	**AGGINNRU**	RAUNGING
AFLMOSST	FLOTSAMS	**AGGHINNP**	PHANGING	**AGGINNRW**	WRANGING
AFLMOSUY	FAMOUSLY	**AGGHINNS**	GNASHING	**AGGINNST**	STANGING
AFLNOPRU	APRONFUL		HANGINGS	**AGGINNSW**	GNAWINGS
AFLNORST	FRONTALS	**AGGHINNW**	WHANGING	**AGGINNTU**	GAUNTING
AFLNRTUU	UNARTFUL	**AGGHINPR**	GRAPHING	**AGGINNTW**	TWANGING
AFLNTUUV	VAUNTFUL	**AGGHINST**	GHASTING	**AGGINNUZ**	UNGAZING

Eight-letter anagrams

AGGINORT	GAROTING		LASHINGS	AGHLMOOR	HOLOGRAM
AGGINOST	GIGATONS		SLANGISH	AGHLMOOY	HOLOGAMY
AGGINOVY	VOYAGING		SLASHING	AGHLMPSU	GALUMPHS
AGGINOWY	WAYGOING	AGHILNST	HALTINGS	AGHLNOSU	SHOGUNAL
AGGINPRS	GRASPING		LATHINGS	AGHLNSUY	NYLGHAUS
	PARGINGS	AGHILNSU	LANGUISH	AGHLOOSS	GASOHOLS
	SPARGING		NILGHAUS	AGHLOTUU	OUTLAUGH
AGGINPSS	GASPINGS		SHAULING	AGHMMOOY	HOMOGAMY
AGGINPUZ	UPGAZING	AGHILNSW	SHAWLING	AGHMNPSU	SPHAGNUM
AGGINRSS	GRASSING		WHALINGS	AGHMOOPY	OMOPHAGY
	SIRGANGS	AGHILNSY	NYLGHAIS	AGHMOPRY	MYOGRAPH
AGGINRST	GRATINGS	AGHILOST	GOLIATHS	AGHMORSY	HYGROMAS
AGGINRSU	SUGARING	AGHILRSY	GARISHLY	AGHMRRSU	MURRAGHS
AGGINRSV	GRAVINGS	AGHILRTY	GRAITHLY	AGHNNOSU	HOUNGANS
AGGINRSZ	GRAZINGS	AGHILSUY	AGUISHLY	AGHNORST	STAGHORN
AGGINRTY	GYRATING	AGHIMMNS	SHAMMING	AGHNOSTU	HANGOUTS
AGGINRUU	AUGURING	AGHIMMNW	WHAMMING		TOHUNGAS
AGGINRYZ	AGRYZING	AGHIMNPR	PHARMING	AGHNPRSY	SYNGRAPH
AGGINSSS	GASSINGS	AGHIMNSS	MASHINGS	AGHNTTUU	UNTAUGHT
AGGINSST	STAGINGS		SMASHING	AGHOOPYZ	ZOOPHAGY
AGGINSWY	GAYWINGS	AGHIMNTY	THINGAMY	AGHOPSSW	SWAGSHOP
AGGIRTUZ	ZIGGURAT	AGHIMOST	OGHAMIST	AGHORSTW	WARTHOGS
AGGKLNNU	ANGKLUNG	AGHIMPRU	GRAPHIUM	AGHRSTTU	STRAUGHT
AGGLLLOY	LOLLYGAG	AGHINNOS	NIHONGAS	AGIIIKMR	KIRIGAMI
AGGLLOOV	ALGOLOGY	AGHINNOT	GNATHION	AGIIILNS	LIAISING
AGGLMOOR	LOGOGRAM	AGHINNSS	SNASHING	AGIIINNS	INSIGNIA
AGGLNOPW	GANGPLOW	AGHINNST	TANGHINS	AGIIINRV	VIRGINIA
AGGLOORY	AGROLOGY	AGHINNTU	HAUNTING	AGIIKLNS	SKAILING
AGGLRSTY	STRAGGLY	AGHINNTY	ANYTHING	AGIIKNNT	ANTIKING
AGGMORRS	GROGRAMS	AGHINORS	ORANGISH	AGIIKNRT	TRAIKING
AGGMOSTY	MYSTAGOG	AGHINOST	HOASTING	AGIILLLM	MILLIGAL
AGGNOSSY	SYNAGOGS	AGHINPPW	WHAPPING	AGIILLNV	VIALLING
AGGNUWZZ	ZUGZWANG	AGHINPPY	HAPPYING	AGIILLOV	VILLAGIO
AGHHIILT	HIGHTAIL	AGHINPRS	HARPINGS		VILLIAGO
AGHHINSS	SHASHING		PHRASING	AGIILMNP	IMPALING
AGHHISWY	HIGHWAYS		SHARPING	AGIILMNS	MAILINGS
AGHHLOTU	ALTHOUGH	AGHINPSS	PHASINGS		MISALIGN
AGHIILNN	INHALING		SHAPINGS	AGIILMNU	MIAULING
AGHIILNS	NILGHAIS	AGHINPSW	PSHAWING	AGIILNNP	PLAINING
AGHIINNS	HAININGS	AGHINQSU	QUASHING	AGIILNNS	NAILINGS
AGHIINRT	AIRTHING	AGHINRRU	HURRAING		SNAILING
AGHIIPRR	HAIRGRIP	AGHINRRY	HARRYING	AGIILNNU	INGUINAL
AGHIIRTT	AIRTIGHT	AGHINRSS	SHARINGS	AGIILNNV	ANVILING
AGHIJNRT	NIGHTJAR	AGHINRST	TRASHING	AGIILNNY	INLAYING
AGHIKNNS	SHANKING	AGHINRTW	THRAWING	AGIILNOP	PIGNOLIA
AGHIKNNT	THANKING		WRATHING	AGIILNOR	ORIGINAL
AGHIKNRS	SHARKING	AGHINSST	HASTINGS	AGIILNOT	INTAGLIO
AGHIKNSS	SHAKINGS		STASHING		LIGATION
AGHIKNSW	HAWKINGS	AGHINSSV	SHAVINGS		TAGLIONI
AGHILLNO	HALLOING	AGHINSSW	SWASHING	AGIILNOX	GLOXINIA
	HOLLAING		WASHINGS	AGIILNPS	LAIPSING
AGHILLNS	HALLINGS	AGHINSTT	HATTINGS	AGIILNPT	PLAITING
AGHILLNT	ALLNIGHT	AGHINSTW	SWATHING	AGIILNQU	QUAILING
AGHILMTY	ALMIGHTY		THAWINGS	AGIILNRS	GLAIRINS
AGHILNOO	HOOLIGAN	AGHINUZZ	HUZZAING		RAILINGS
AGHILNOR	LONGHAIR	AGHIOPRS	ISOGRAPH	AGIILNRT	RINGTAIL
AGHILNOS	SHOALING	AGHIPRRT	TRIGRAPH		TRAILING
AGHILNOT	LOATHING	AGHIRSTT	STRAIGHT	AGIILNRV	RIVALING
AGHILNPR	RALPHING	AGHISSTT	TIGHTASS		VIRGINAL
AGHILNPS	PLASHING	AGHISSTW	SIGHTSAW	AGIILNSS	AISLINGS
AGHILNRS	HARLINGS	AGHJMNOS	MAHJONGS		SAILINGS
	RINGHALS	AGHKNOPT	PAKTHONG	AGIILNST	TAILINGS
AGHILNRY	NARGHILY	AGHKOSSW	GOSHAWKS		
AGHILNSS	HASSLING	AGHLLMPU	GALLUMPH		

AGIILNSU	LINGUISA
AGIILNSW	WAILINGS
AGIILNTT	LITIGANT
AGIILNTV	VIGILANT
AGIILORU	OLIGURIA
AGIILOSV	VILIAGOS
AGIILPST	PIGTAILS
AGIILTVY	VAGILITY
AGIIMMNS	MAIMINGS
AGIIMMSS	IMAGISMS
AGIIMNNR	INARMING
AGIIMNOR	IGNORAMI
AGIIMNOU	MIAOUING
AGIIMNOW	MIAOWING
AGIIMNPV	IMPAVING
AGIIMNSS	AMISSING
AGIIMNST	GIANTISM
AGIIMNTT	MITIGANT
AGIIMORS	ORIGAMIS
AGIIMSST	IMAGISTS
AGIINNPS	SPAINING
AGIINNPT	PAINTING
	PATINING
AGIINNRS	INGRAINS
AGIINNRT	TRAINING
AGIINNRV	RAVINING
AGIINNST	SAINTING
	SATINING
	STAINING
AGIINNSW	SWAINING
AGIINNTT	TAINTING
AGIINOPT	OPIATING
AGIINORS	SIGNORIA
AGIINORT	RIGATONI
AGIINPRS	ASPIRING
	PAIRINGS
	PRAISING
AGIINPRT	PIRATING
AGIINRRV	ARRIVING
AGIINRSS	RAISINGS
AGIINRTT	ATTIRING
AGIINSSZ	ASSIZING
AGIINSTV	VISTAING
AGIINSTW	WAISTING
	WAITINGS
AGIISSTV	VISAGIST
AGIJLLNS	JINGALLS
AGIJLNPY	JAPINGLY
AGIJMMNS	JAMMINGS
AGIJMNOR	MAJORING
AGIJMNRU	JUMARING
AGIJNNSU	JAUNSING
AGIJNNTT	TJANTING
AGIJNNTU	JAUNTING
AGIJNRRS	JARRINGS
AGIKKNNS	SKANKING
AGIKLMOR	KILOGRAM
AGIKLNNP	PLANKING
AGIKLNNR	RANKLING
AGIKLNOP	POLKAING
AGIKLNOS	OAKLINGS
	SKOALING
AGIKLNPP	KLAPPING
AGIKLNST	SKLATING
	STALKING
	TALKINGS
AGIKLNSW	WALKINGS
AGIKLNTY	TAKINGLY
AGIKLNUW	WAULKING
AGIKLORY	KILOGRAY
AGIKMNNU	UNMAKING
AGIKMNPU	UPMAKING
AGIKMNRS	MARKINGS
AGIKMNSS	MASKINGS
AGIKNNPP	KNAPPING
AGIKNNPR	PRANKING
AGIKNNPS	SPANKING
AGIKNNRR	KNARRING
AGIKNNRS	RANKINGS
AGIKNNRU	UNRAKING
AGIKNNST	STANKING
	TANKINGS
AGIKNNSW	SWANKING
AGIKNORT	TROAKING
AGIKNOSS	SOAKINGS
AGIKNOST	GOATSKIN
AGIKNOSY	KAYOINGS
AGIKNPRS	PARKINGS
	SPARKING
AGIKNPTU	UPTAKING
AGIKNQSU	QUAKINGS
AGIKNRSS	SARKINGS
AGIKNRST	KARTINGS
	STARKING
AGIKNSST	SKATINGS
	TASKINGS
AGILLLNS	LALLINGS
AGILLMNS	MALLINGS
	SMALLING
AGILLMNU	MULLIGAN
AGILLMNY	MALIGNLY
AGILLMSU	GALLIUMS
AGILLNOW	ALLOWING
AGILLNOY	ALLOYING
AGILLNPS	SPALLING
AGILLNRU	ALLURING
	LINGULAR
AGILLNRY	RALLYING
AGILLNST	STALLING
AGILLNSU	LINGUALS
	LINGULAS
AGILLNSW	WALLINGS
AGILLNSY	SALLYING
	SIGNALLY
	SLANGILY
AGILLNTY	TALLYING
AGILLOOR	GILLAROO
AGILLOPT	GALLIPOT
AGILLORS	GORILLAS
AGILLOST	GALLIOTS
AGILLPRY	PLAYGIRL
AGILLPUY	PLAGUILY
AGILLSSU	LUGSAILS
AGILLSSY	GLASSILY
AGILMMNS	LAMMINGS
	SLAMMING
	SMALMING
AGILMNNT	MANTLING
AGILMNPS	LAMPINGS
	PSALMING
	SAMPLING
AGILMNQU	QUALMING
AGILMNRS	MARLINGS
AGILMNST	MALTINGS
AGILMOPR	LIPOGRAM
AGILMORS	ALGORISM
AGILMPSU	PLAGIUMS
AGILNNNP	PLANNING
AGILNNOP	PANGOLIN
AGILNNOS	LOANINGS
AGILNNPT	PLANTING
AGILNNRS	SNARLING
AGILNNSS	LINSANGS
AGILNNST	SLANTING
	TANLINGS
AGILNNUW	UNLAWING
AGILNNUY	UNGAINLY
	UNLAYING
AGILNOOO	OOGONIAL
AGILNOOS	ISOGONAL
AGILNOPR	PAROLING
AGILNOPS	GALOPINS
AGILNOPT	PLOATING
AGILNORS	RANGOLIS
AGILNORT	TRIGONAL
AGILNOSS	GLOSSINA
	LASSOING
AGILNOST	ANTILOGS
	SALTOING
	SOLATING
AGILNOSV	SALVOING
AGILNOTT	TOTALING
AGILNOTY	ANTILOGY
AGILNPPP	PLAPPING
AGILNPPS	LAPPINGS
	SAPPLING
	SLAPPING
AGILNPPY	APPLYING
AGILNPRS	GRAPLINS
	SPARLING
	SPRINGAL
AGILNPSS	SAPLINGS
AGILNPST	PLATINGS
	SPALTING
	STAPLING
AGILNPSW	LAPWINGS
	SPAWLING
AGILNPSY	PALSYING
	SPLAYING
AGILNPTT	PLATTING
AGILNPUY	UPLAYING
AGILNRSS	RASSLING
AGILNRST	RATLINGS
	SLARTING
	STARLING
AGILNRSU	SINGULAR
AGILNRSW	WARLINGS
	WARSLING
AGILNRTT	RATTLING
AGILNRTW	TRAWLING
AGILNRVY	RAVINGLY
AGILNRWW	WRAWLING

AGILNRWX	WRAXLING	**AGIMNRTU**	MATURING
AGILNSST	ANGLISTS	**AGIMNSSU**	ASSUMING
	LASTINGS	**AGIMNSTT**	MATTINGS
	SALTINGS	**AGIMNTTU**	MUTATING
	SLATINGS	**AGIMORRT**	MIGRATOR
AGILNSSV	SALVINGS	**AGIMORSS**	ISOGRAMS
AGILNSSW	SWALINGS	**AGIMORSU**	GOURAMIS
AGILNSTT	SLATTING	**AGIMQRUY**	QUAGMIRY
AGILNSTU	SALUTING	**AGIMRRST**	TRIGRAMS
AGILNSUV	AVULSING	**AGINNNNY**	NANNYING
AGILNSUW	WAULINGS	**AGINNNOY**	ANNOYING
AGILNSVY	SAVINGLY	**AGINNNPS**	PANNINGS
AGILNSWW	WAWLINGS		SPANNING
AGILNSWY	SWAYLING	**AGINNNST**	TANNINGS
AGILNTTT	TATTLING	**AGINNNSV**	VANNINGS
AGILNTTW	WATTLING	**AGINNNSW**	SWANNING
AGILNTUV	VAULTING	**AGINNNUW**	UNWANING
AGILNTUX	LUXATING	**AGINNOOP**	NAPOOING
AGILNTWZ	WALTZING	**AGINNOPR**	APRONING
AGILNTXY	TAXINGLY	**AGINNOPT**	POIGNANT
AGILOOPY	APIOLOGY	**AGINNORT**	IGNORANT
AGILOORS	GLORIOSA	**AGINNOST**	ASTONING
AGILOOXY	AXIOLOGY	**AGINNOSU**	ANGINOUS
AGILOPST	GALIPOTS	**AGINNOTT**	NOTATING
AGILORSS	GIRASOLS	**AGINNPPS**	SNAPPING
AGILORSW	AIRGLOWS	**AGINNPRW**	PRAWNING
AGILOSST	SALIGOTS	**AGINNPST**	PANTINGS
AGILRSSY	GRASSILY	**AGINNPSW**	SPAWNING
AGILSYYZ	SYZYGIAL		WINGSPAN
AGIMMNPS	SPAMMING	**AGINNPUY**	UNPAYING
AGIMMNRS	SMARMING	**AGINNQTU**	QUANTING
AGIMMNRT	TRAMMING	**AGINNRRS**	SNARRING
AGIMMNTY	TAMMYING	**AGINNRSS**	SNARINGS
AGIMMOSY	MISOGAMY	**AGINNRST**	RANTINGS
AGIMNNOS	MASONING		STARNING
	MOANINGS	**AGINNRSW**	WARNINGS
AGIMNNOW	WOMANING	**AGINNRTT**	TRANTING
AGIMNNRU	MANURING	**AGINNRTU**	NATURING
	UNARMING	**AGINNRTY**	TRAYNING
AGIMNNSW	SWINGMAN		TYRANING
AGIMNNTU	UNTAMING	**AGINNSTU**	SAUNTING
AGIMNOOV	AMOOVING		STAUNING
AGIMNORR	ARMORING		UNSATING
	ROARMING	**AGINNSTW**	WANTINGS
AGIMNORS	ORGANISM	**AGINNSTY**	STAYNING
	ROAMINGS	**AGINNSUY**	UNSAYING
AGIMNORU	ORIGANUM	**AGINNSWY**	YAWNINGS
AGIMNORY	AGRIMONY	**AGINNTTU**	ATTUNING
AGIMNOST	ANTISMOG		NUTATING
AGIMNOSV	VAMOSING		TAUNTING
AGIMNPPS	MAPPINGS	**AGINNTUV**	VAUNTING
AGIMNPRS	RAMPINGS	**AGINNTUX**	UNTAXING
AGIMNPRT	TRAMPING	**AGINNVVY**	NAVVYING
AGIMNPSS	SPASMING	**AGINOOPS**	POGONIAS
AGIMNPST	STAMPING	**AGINOORT**	ROGATION
	TAMPINGS	**AGINOPPS**	APPOSING
AGIMNPSV	VAMPINGS	**AGINOPQU**	OPAQUING
AGIMNPSW	SWAMPING	**AGINOPRV**	VAPORING
AGIMNRRY	MARRYING	**AGINORRS**	GARRISON
AGIMNRST	MIGRANTS		ROARINGS
	SMARTING	**AGINORRW**	ARROWING
AGIMNRSW	SWARMING	**AGINORRZ**	RAZORING
	WARMINGS	**AGINORSS**	ASSIGNOR
AGIMNRSY	MYRINGAS		SIGNORAS

	SOARINGS		
AGINORST	ORGANIST		
	ROASTING		
AGINORSU	AROUSING		
AGINORSV	SAVORING		
AGINORTT	ROTATING		
	TROATING		
AGINORTV	GRAVITON		
AGINORTY	GYRATION		
	ORGANITY		
AGINOSST	AGONISTS		
AGINOSSU	SAGOUINS		
AGINOSTT	TANGOIST		
	TOASTING		
AGINOSTU	OUTGAINS		
AGINPPRS	RAPPINGS		
AGINPPRT	TRAPPING		
AGINPPRW	WRAPPING		
AGINPPST	STAPPING		
	TAPPINGS		
AGINPPSW	SWAPPING		
AGINPPTU	PUPATING		
AGINPPUY	APPUYING		
AGINPRRS	SPARRING		
AGINPRRY	PARRYING		
AGINPRSS	PARSINGS		
	PINGRASS		
	RASPINGS		
AGINPRST	PARTINGS		
	PRATINGS		
AGINPRSW	WARPINGS		
AGINPRSY	PRAYINGS		
	SPRAYING		
AGINPRTT	PRATTING		
AGINPRTU	UPRATING		
AGINPRTY	PARTYING		
AGINPSSS	PASSINGS		
AGINPSST	PASTINGS		
AGINPSSU	PAUSINGS		
AGINPSTT	SPATTING		
AGINPSWY	YAWPINGS		
AGINPSZZ	SPAZZING		
AGINQRSU	SQUARING		
AGINRRST	STARRING		
	TARRINGS		
AGINRRTY	TARRYING		
AGINRSST	GASTRINS		
	STARINGS		
AGINRSSU	ASSURING		
AGINRSSY	SYRINGAS		
AGINRSTT	RATTINGS		
	STARTING		
AGINRSTV	STARVING		
AGINRSTW	RINGTAWS		
	STRAWING		
	WRASTING		
AGINRSTY	STINGRAY		
	STRAYING		
AGINRSVW	SWARVING		
AGINRSVY	VARYINGS		
AGINRSWY	RINGWAYS		
AGINRTYY	GYNIATRY		
AGINSSTT	TASTINGS		
AGINSSTW	WASTINGS		

AGINSSWY	SWAYINGS	AGMMORSY	MYOGRAMS		SHIKARIS
AGINSTTT	TATTINGS	AGMMORYZ	ZYMOGRAM	AHIILNPS	PLAINISH
AGINSTTW	SWATTING	AGMNNORS	GRANNOMS	AHIILOST	HALIOTIS
AGINSVVY	SAVVYING	AGMNNOSW	GOWNSMAN	AHIILPTW	WHIPTAIL
AGINSWWX	WAXWINGS	AGMNOOPR	PORNOMAG	AHIILRTY	HILARITY
AGIOORSU	ORAGIOUS	AGMNOORS	SONOGRAM	AHIIMNNO	HOMINIAN
AGIOORSZ	GRAZIOSO	AGMNOORY	AGRONOMY	AHIIMNOT	HIMATION
AGIOORTU	AUTOGIRO	AGMNORST	ANGSTROM	AHIIMNRU	MANUHIRI
AGIOPPRT	AGITPROP	AGMNORSU	ORGANUMS	AHIIMNST	HISTAMIN
AGIOPPST	AGITPOPS	AGMNSSTU	MUSTANGS		ISTHMIAN
AGIOPRUY	UROPYGIA	AGMNSSTY	GYMNASTS		THIAMINS
AGIORRTT	GRATTOIR		SYNTAGMS	AHIIMOPX	AMPHIOXI
AGIORSST	AGISTORS	AGMOOOSU	OOGAMOUS	AHIIMRST	ISARITHM
	ORGIASTS	AGMOOPRY	POROGAMY	AHIIMSSS	SASHIMIS
AGIOSUUY	OUGUIYAS	AGMOOTVY	VAGOTOMY	AHIIMSST	SAMITHIS
AGIRSSTU	SASTRUGI	AGMOPRRS	PROGRAMS	AHIINOPT	PHOTINIA
AGIRSTUZ	ZASTRUGI	AGMOPRSU	GOPURAMS	AHIINOTT	TITHONIA
AGIRTTUY	GRATUITY	AGMORRSW	RAGWORMS	AHIINPRS	HAIRPINS
AGJLRSUU	JUGULARS	AGMRSSSU	GRASSUMS	AHIINPST	ANTISHIP
AGJNOORS	JARGOONS	AGNNNOOS	NONAGONS	AHIINSST	SAINTISH
AGJNOPST	JOGPANTS	AGNNOOPT	POONTANG	AHIINSSW	SWAINISH
AGKLNNOS	ANKLONGS	AGNNOORS	ARGONONS	AHIINSTU	HUITAINS
AGKLNNSU	ANKLUNGS		ORGANONS	AHIINSTZ	THIAZINS
AGKMMORY	KYMOGRAM	AGNNOQTU	QUANTONG	AHIIOPST	HOSPITIA
AGKMNOPS	KAMPONGS	AGNNORSU	NONSUGAR	AHIIPRSS	AIRSHIPS
AGKMPRSU	PUGMARKS	AGNNOTUW	OUTGNAWN	AHIKLNRS	RINKHALS
AGKNOPST	PAKTONGS	AGNORRST	GRANTORS	AHIKLRSY	RAKISHLY
AGKORRSW	RAGWORKS	AGNORTUY	NUGATORY	AHIKLSSS	SHASLIKS
AGKORSSW	GASWORKS	AGNOSTUW	OUTGNAWS	AHIKMNSS	KHAMSINS
AGLLLNOW	LONGWALL	AGNPPRSU	UPSPRANG	AHIKMRSS	KASHMIRS
AGLLMOPW	GLOWLAMP	AGNRSSTU	NUTGRASS	AHIKNPRS	PRANKISH
AGLLNOOS	GALLOONS	AGOORRTY	ROGATORY	AHIKNPST	TANKSHIP
AGLLNSTU	GALLNUTS	AGOORTUY	AUTOGYRO	AHIKORRW	HAIRWORK
	NUTGALLS	AGOPPSST	STOPGAPS	AHIKORSS	KAROSHIS
AGLLOORS	ROGALLOS	AGORRSST	GROSSART	AHIKPRSS	SPARKISH
AGLLOOST	GALLOOTS		ROTGRASS	AHIKRSSW	RIKSHAWS
AGLLOPSU	PLUGOLAS	AGORRSTW	RAGWORTS	AHILLMOU	HALLOUMI
AGLLPRSU	SPURGALL	AGORRSTY	GYRATORS	AHILLMPS	PHALLISM
AGLLPSTY	GLYPTALS	AGORRTYY	GYRATORY	AHILLMSS	SMALLISH
AGLLRUVY	VULGARLY	AGORSTTY	GYROSTAT	AHILLMTU	THALLIUM
AGLMOOTY	ATMOLOGY	AGORSTUY	GRAYOUTS	AHILLNOS	HALLIONS
AGLMOPSY	POLYGAMS	AHHIKKRS	KHIRKAHS	AHILLNPS	PHALLINS
AGLMOPYY	POLYGAMY	AHHIKLSS	SHASHLIK	AHILLNRT	INTHRALL
AGLMORSU	GLAMOURS	AHHILNPT	PHTHALIN	AHILLNST	ANTHILLS
AGLNOOOS	OLOGOANS	AHHILOST	HAILSHOT	AHILLNTW	WANTHILL
AGLNORSU	LANGUORS	AHHILPSW	WHIPLASH	AHILLPST	PHALLIST
AGLNOSST	GLASNOST	AHHIMSS	MISHMASH	AHILLSTT	TALLITHS
AGLNOSUU	ANGULOUS	AHHIMNSU	HAHNIUMS	AHILLSVY	LAVISHLY
AGLNOSWY	LONGWAYS	AHHINNST	SHANTIHS	AHILMMSS	MASHLIMS
AGLNPSUY	GUNPLAYS	AHHIPRSS	SHARPISH	AHILMNSS	MASHLINS
AGLNRUUV	UNVULGAR	AHHISSTT	SHITTAHS	AHILMOPT	PHILAMOT
AGLNSSSU	SUNGLASS	AHHKMOTW	HAWKMOTH	AHILMOST	HALIMOTS
AGLNSTUY	YGLAUNST	AHHKRSTU	KASHRUTH		MAILSHOT
AGLOOPST	GOALPOST	AHHLMRTY	RHYTHMAL	AHILMOSU	HALOUMIS
AGLOOTUY	AUTOLOGY	AHHLNOPT	NAPHTHOL	AHILMQSU	QUALMISH
AGLOPRSS	LOPGRASS	AHHLNPTY	NAPHTHYL	AHILMTUZ	HALUTZIM
AGLORSSY	GLOSSARY	AHHMPRRU	HARRUMPH	AHILNOPS	SIPHONAL
AGLPSSSY	SPYGLASS	AHHMPRSU	HARUMPHS	AHILNOPT	OLIPHANT
AGLRTTUU	GUTTURAL	AHHNORTW	HAWTHORN	AHILNORT	HORNTAIL
AGLSTUUY	AUGUSTLY	AHHOPRSS	SHOPHARS	AHILNRST	INTHRALS
AGMMNOOR	MONOGRAM	AHHOPSTU	APHTHOUS	AHILOORT	LOTHARIO
	NOMOGRAM	AHHPSTUZ	HUTZPAHS	AHILOPSS	ALPHOSIS
AGMMNOOY	MONOGAMY	AHIIILMN	MALIHINI		HAPLOSIS
AGMMOORT	TOMOGRAM	AHIIKRSS	RIKISHAS	AHILOPST	HOSPITAL

AHILOSTU	HALITOUS	AHIPRSST	HARPISTS	AHMNORRS	RAMSHORN
AHILOSTZ	THIAZOLS		STARSHIP	AHMOOPPT	PHOTOMAP
AHILPPSS	PALSHIPS	AHIPRSSW	WARSHIPS	AHMOOPSS	SHAMPOOS
	SHIPLAPS	AHIPRSWY	WHIPRAYS	AHMOORSW	WASHROOM
AHILPRTU	ULTRAHIP	AHIPSSWW	WHIPSAWS	AHMOOSSS	SAMSHOOS
AHILPSSY	PHYSALIS	AHIPSSWY	SHIPWAYS	AHMOPTVY	MYOPATHY
AHILPSXY	PHYLAXIS	AHIQRSSU	SQUARISH	AHMORRST	SHORTARM
AHILRSTY	TRASHILY	AHIRRSST	STIRRAHS	AHMORRSU	MORRHUAS
AHILRTWY	WRATHILY	AHIRSSTT	STARTISH	AHMORSST	HARMOSTS
AHIMMNSU	HUMANISM	AHIRSSTW	TRISHAWS	AHMORSTY	HARMOSTY
AHIMMORZ	MAHZORIM	AHISSSTU	SHIATSUS	AHMORTTW	TAMWORTH
AHIMMOSS	SHAMOSIM	AHISSTTW	WHATSITS	AHMORTUW	WARMOUTH
AHIMMOSV	MOSHAVIM	AHISSTUZ	SHIATZUS	AHMOSTTW	MOSTWHAT
AHIMNOST	HOISTMAN	AHISTTWW	WHITTAWS	AHMPSSSU	SMASHUPS
	MANIHOTS	AHKLOPST	SHOPTALK	AHMPSTYY	SYMPATHY
AHIMNOSW	WOMANISH	AHKLORTW	LATHWORK	AHMQSSUU	MUSQUASH
AHIMNSTU	HUMANIST	AHKMOORR	MARKHOOR	AHMRSSTY	THRYMSAS
AHIMNSTX	XANTHISM	AHKMORRS	MARKHORS	AHNNSTYY	SYNANTHY
AHIMNTUY	HUMANITY	AHKMRSTU	MUKHTARS	AHNOOPPY	APOPHONY
AHIMOOSY	YAHOOISM	AHKNOTTU	OUTTHANK	AHNOOPRS	HARPOONS
AHIMOPRS	APHORISM	AHKNOTUY	THANKYOU	AHNOOPSU	APHONOUS
	MORPHIAS	AHKRSSTU	KASHRUTS	AHNOORRY	HONORARY
AHIMOPST	OPSIMATH		TUSHKARS	AHNOOPSW	PAWNSHOP
AHIMORRW	HAIRWORM	AHLLLOOP	POOLHALL	AHNOPPSY	PANSOPHY
AHIMPPSS	SAPPHISM	AHLLNOOS	SHALLOON	AHNOPSST	SNAPSHOT
AHIMPRST	TRAMPISH	AHLLNOSS	SHALLONS	AHNORSSX	SAXHORNS
AHIMPSSW	SWAMPISH	AHLLNOSY	HALLYONS	AHNORTWW	WANWORTH
AHIMRSST	SMARTISH	AHLLNOTW	TOWNHALL	AHNOSTTW	WHATNOTS
	THRIMSAS	AHLLNOUW	UNHALLOW	AHNOSTUX	XANTHOUS
AHIMSSSU	HASSIUMS	AHLLNRTU	TURNHALL	AHNPPSUU	PUPUNHAS
AHIMSSTV	MITSVAHS	AHLLOPPS	SHALLOPS	AHNRSVYY	HRYVNYAS
AHIMSTUZ	AZIMUTHS	AHLLOSST	SHALLOTS	AHOOPTYZ	ZOOPATHY
AHIMSTVZ	MITZVAHS	AHLLOSSW	SHALLOWS	AHOOSSTY	SOOTHSAY
AHINNNSY	NANNYISH	AHLLOSTU	THALLOUS	AHOOSTTW	SAWTOOTH
AHINNOPT	ANTIPHON	AHLLOSTY	TALLYHOS	AHOPSSTW	WASHPOTS
AHINNSTX	XANTHINS	AHLLPRVY	PHYLLARY	AHOPSSTW	TOWPATHS
AHINOOPY	HYPONOIA	AHLMMOPY	LYMPHOMA	AHOPSTUW	SOUTHPAW
AHINOPRU	OPHIURAN	AHLMMSSU	MASHLUMS	AHORTTUW	WATTHOUR
AHINORST	TRAHISON	AHLMNOOR	HORMONAL	AHOSSTUW	WASHOUTS
AHINOSST	ASTONISH	AHLMOOPS	OMPHALOS	AHOSSTUY	SOUTHSAY
AHINOSTZ	HOATZINS	AHLMOPTY	POLYMATH	AHRSTUWY	THRUWAYS
AHINPPSS	SNAPPISH	AHLMOSUU	HAMULOUS	AIIILLVX	LIXIVIAL
AHINPRST	TRANSHIP	AHLMSTYZ	SHMALTZY	AIIILMST	MILITIAS
AHINPRSY	SYRPHIAN	AHLNNORT	LANTHORN	AIIILNST	INITIALS
AHINPSWW	WHIPSAWN	AHLNOPRS	ALPHORNS	AIIILRVZ	VIZIRIAL
AHINQSUV	VANQUISH	AHLNOPST	HAPLONTS	AIIIMRSS	SAIMIRIS
AHINRSTY	RHYTINAS		NAPHTOLS	AIIIRSSS	SIRIASIS
AHINRSVY	HRYVNIAS	AHLNORST	ALTHORNS	AIIJKMOT	KOMITAJI
	VARNISHY	AHLNRTWY	THRAWNLY	AIIJNRTX	JANITRIX
AHINSSTU	INHAUSTS	AHLOOPSW	WHOOPLAS	AIIKKSUY	SUKIYAKI
AHINSTUU	TAUHINUS	AHLOOSTW	WOOLHATS	AIIKLLST	SILKTAIL
AHIOOPPT	PHOTOPIA	AHLOPSST	SLAPSHOT	AIIKLNRR	LARRIKIN
AHIOOSST	ATISHOOS	AHLORRTY	HARLOTRY	AIIKMMSS	SKIMMIAS
AHIOPRST	APHORIST	AHLORTTU	ULTRAHOT	AIIKMNNN	MANNIKIN
AHIOPRSU	OPHIURAS	AHLOSTUU	OUTHAULS	AIIKMNNS	MANIKINS
AHIOPRSV	VAPORISH	AHLRSTUY	LATHYRUS	AIIKMNPR	MINIPARK
AHIOPSXY	HYPOXIAS	AHLRTTWY	THWARTLY	AIIKNNNP	PANNIKIN
AHIORSST	AIRSHOTS	AHMMMOST	MAMMOTHS	AIIKNNST	TANKINIS
	SHORTIAS	AHMMMSUU	HUMMAUMS	AIIKORTY	YAKITORI
AHIORSSW	AIRSHOWS	AHMNNNOU	NONHUMAN	AIIKRRSU	RAURIKIS
AHIORSTV	TOVARISH	AHMNNSTU	HUNTSMAN	AIIKTTZZ	TZATZIKI
AHIORSUV	HAVIOURS		MANHUNTS	AIILLLMT	MILLTAIL
AHIOSTWY	HOISTWAY	AHMNOPST	PHANTOMS	AIILLLUV	ILLUVIAL
AHIPPSST	SAPPHIST	AHMNOPTY	PHANTOMY	AIILLMNO	MONILIAL

AIILLMRY	MILLIARY		MISTRAIN	AIKKRTUZ	ZIKKURAT
AIILLMST	TALLISIM	AIIMNSST	ANIMISTS	AIKLLLMW	WALKMILL
AIILLMSW	WILLIAMS		SAINTISM	AIKLLMRR	RILLMARK
AIILLMTT	TALLITIM		SAMNITIS	AIKLLMUW	WAUKMILL
AIILLNNV	VANILLIN	AIIMNSTT	IMITANTS	AIKLLSTY	STALKILY
AIILLNOP	POLLINIA		TITANISM	AIKLMNNS	LINKSMAN
AIILLNOT	ILLATION	AIIMNSTV	NATIVISM	AIKLMPSU	LAMPUKIS
AIILLNPT	ANTIPILL		VITAMINS	AIKLMPTU	KALUMPIT
AIILLNSV	VILLAINS	AIIMNTTU	TITANIUM	AIKLNNPS	SNAPLINK
AIILLNVY	VILLAINY	AIIMOPSX	APOMIXIS	AIKLNPST	LANTSKIP
AIILLPRS	SLIPRAIL	AIIMORTT	IMITATOR	AIKLNRSY	SNARKILY
	SPIRILLA		TIMARIOT	AIKLNSWY	SWANKILY
AIILLQSU	QUILLAIS	AIIMOSST	AMITOSIS	AIKLOSUV	SOUVLAKI
AIILLUWW	WILLIWAU	AIIMPPRS	PRIAPISM	AIKLOTTW	KILOWATT
AIILLWWW	WILLIWAW	AIIMPRTY	IMPARITY	AIKLPRSY	SPARKILY
AIILMMNS	MINIMALS	AIIMRSST	SIMITARS	AIKLRSTT	TITLARKS
AIILMNNS	LAMININS	AIIMRSTU	TIRAMISU	AIKLSSSY	SKYSAILS
AIILMNOS	MONILIAS	AIIMRUVV	VIVARIUM	AIKMMNOO	MAKIMONO
AIILMNOT	LIMATION	AIIMSSTT	MASTITIS	AIKMMRSS	MISMARKS
	MILTONIA	AIINNOPS	PIANINOS	AIKMNOOY	YAKIMONO
AIILMNPS	ALPINISM	AIINNOSV	INVASION	AIKMNRSS	RANKISMS
AIILMNPT	PALMITIN	AIINNOTV	NIVATION	AIKMORSS	KOMISSAR
AIILMNTT	MILITANT	AIINNQSU	QUININAS	AIKMRSTZ	SITZMARK
AIILMNTU	MINUTIAL	AIINNQTU	QUINTAIN	AIKNNOOS	NAINSOOK
AIILMPUV	IMPLUVIA	AIINNSTY	INSANITY	AIKNNSSW	SWANSKIN
AIILMRST	MISTRIAL	AIINOOSV	AVOISION	AIKNORST	SKIATRON
	TRIALISM	AIINOPSS	SINOPIAS	AIKNORTY	KARYOTIN
AIILMRTY	LIMITARY	AIINORTT	ANTIRIOT	AIKNOSTT	STOTINKA
	MILITARY		TRITONIA	AIKOORST	ROOIKATS
AIILMSTV	VITALISM	AIINOSTT	NOTITIAS	AIKPTTUU	PATUTUKI
AIILNOPV	PAVILION		OSTINATI	AIKRSSTY	SATYRISK
AIILNOSS	LIAISONS	AIINPRSS	ASPIRINS	AIKRSTUZ	ZIKURATS
AIILNOSV	VISIONAL	AIINPSST	PIANISTS	AILLLNOO	LINALOOL
AIILNPST	ALPINIST	AIINRRTT	IRRITANT	AILLLNOS	LINALOLS
	ANTISLIP	AIINRSTV	VITRAINS	AILLLPSU	LAPILLUS
	PINTAILS	AIINRSTZ	TRIAZINS	AILLMMSY	SMALMILY
	TAILSPIN	AIINSTTV	NATIVIST	AILLMNQU	QUILLMAN
AIILNRSU	SILURIAN		VISITANT	AILLMNST	STILLMAN
AIILNSTY	SALINITY	AIINTTVY	NATIVITY	AILLMOST	MAILLOTS
AIILNTTY	LATINITY	AIIORRST	SARTORII		MISALLOT
AIILOPPS	PAPILIOS	AIIORSTT	AORTITIS	AILLMOSY	LOYALISM
AIILORSV	RAVIOLIS	AIIORSTV	OVARITIS	AILLMOTY	MOLALITY
AIILPRSU	LIPURIAS	AIIORTTV	VITIATOR	AILLMPRY	PRIMALLY
AIILQSSU	SILIQUAS	AIIPRRST	AIRSTRIP	AILLMPSU	PALLIUMS
AIILRSTT	TRIALIST	AIIPRSST	PIARISTS	AILLMSSW	SAWMILLS
AIILRTTY	TRIALITY	AIIPRVVY	VIVIPARY	AILLMUUV	ALLUVIUM
AIILRTVY	RIVALITY	AIIPSTTU	PITUITAS	AILLNNOS	LANOLINS
AIILSTTV	VITALIST	AIIRSSTT	SATIRIST	AILLNOPP	PAPILLON
AIILSTTW	WAITLIST		SITARIST	AILLNOPS	PAILLONS
AIILTTVY	VITALITY	AIISSSTY	SYSSITIA	AILLNOPV	PAVILLON
AIIMMMST	MAMMITIS	AIJKKNOU	KINKAJOU	AILLNORT	ANTIROLL
AIIMMNNY	MINYANIM	AIJLLOOR	JILLAROO	AILLNOST	STALLION
AIIMMNSS	ANIMISMS	AIJLLOVY	JOVIALLY	AILLNOSU	ALLUSION
AIIMMNSX	MAXIMINS	AIJLNTUY	JAUNTILY	AILLNOUV	ALLUVION
AIIMMNTY	IMMANITY	AIJLOTVY	JOVIALTY	AILLNPSY	SPINALLY
AIIMMSTX	MAXIMIST	AIJMORTY	MAJORITY	AILLNPTY	PLIANTLY
AIIMNNOS	INSOMNIA	AIJNOPPY	POPINJAY	AILLNSST	INSTALLS
AIIMNNSV	MINIVANS	AIJNORST	JANITORS	AILLOQTU	TOQUILLA
AIIMNPSS	PIANISMS	AIKKMOOR	KORIMAKO	AILLORSY	SAILORLY
	SINAPISM	AIKKMOST	KOMATIKS	AILLORSZ	ZORILLAS
AIIMNPST	IMPAINTS	AIKKNOTY	KANTIKOY	AILLORTT	LITTORAL
	MISPAINT	AIKKOOSW	KOKOWAIS		TORTILLA
AIIMNPSX	PANMIXIS	AIKKOPSY	KOPIYKAS	AILLOSTY	LOYALIST
AIIMNRST	MARTINIS	AIKKOSUZ	ZAKOUSKI	AILLOTTT	TALLITOT

AILLPPRU	PUPILLAR	AILMPRSU	PRIMULAS	AILNSTTU	LUTANIST
AILLPPSU	SUPPLIAL	AILMPSST	PALMISTS	AILNSTUU	NAUTILUS
AILLPPTU	PULPITAL		PSALMIST	AILNSYZZ	SNAZZILY
AILLPRSY	SPIRALLY	AILMPSSY	MISPLAYS	AILOOPRT	TROOPIAL
AILLPRTY	PALTRILY	AILMPSTY	PTYALISM	AILOORRS	SORORIAL
AILLPSTY	PLAYLIST	AILMRSRU	RURALISM	AILOORST	ISOLATOR
AILLPSUV	PLUVIALS	AILMRSST	MISTRALS		OSTIOLAR
AILLPSWY	SPILLWAY	AILMRSSU	SIMULARS	AILOORSW	WOORALIS
AILLQSSU	SQUILLAS		SURMISAL	AILOORTV	VIOLATOR
AILLRSTY	RALLYIST	AILMRSTU	ALTRUISM	AILOPRRV	PROVIRAL
AILLRTUY	RITUALLY		MURALIST	AILOPRSU	PLIOSAUR
AILLRTWY	WILLYART		ULTRAISM	AILOPRTU	TROUPIAL
AILLSTWW	WITWALLS	AILMSSTY	MYALISTS	AILOPRTY	POLARITY
AILLSUVY	VISUALLY	AILNNOOT	NOTIONAL	AILOPRUY	POLYURIA
AILLWWWY	WILLYWAW	AILNNORV	NONRIVAL	AILOPSST	APOSTILS
AILMMNOO	MONOMIAL		NONVIRAL		TOPSAILS
AILMMNUU	ALUMINUM	AILNNOSS	SOLANINS	AILOPSTT	TALIPOTS
AILMMOOR	MAILROOM	AILNNOST	ANTLIONS	AILOQSTU	ALIQUOTS
AILMMORS	MORALISM	AILNNOSU	UNISONAL	AILORSST	ORALISTS
AILMMORT	IMMORTAL	AILNNOTU	LUNATION		SLIOTARS
AILMMRSY	SMARMILY	AILNNOTV	NONVITAL		SOLARIST
AILMMSSY	MYALISMS	AILNNPRU	PINNULAR	AILORSTU	SUTORIAL
AILMMSTU	SUMMITAL	AILNNPSU	PINNULAS	AILORSTY	ROYALIST
AILMMSUU	ALUMIUMS	AILNNPTY	UNPLIANT		SOLITARY
AILMMSUW	MWALIMUS	AILNNSTU	INSULANT	AILORSUW	WOURALIS
AILMNNOS	NOMINALS	AILNOOPT	NOPALITO	AILORSVY	SAVORILY
AILMNNOT	MANNITOL		OPTIONAL	AILORTTU	TUTORIAL
AILMNNTU	LUMINANT	AILNOOST	SOLATION	AILORTUV	OUTRIVAL
AILMNOOP	PALOMINO	AILNOPPT	OPPILANT	AILOSTT	ALTOISTS
AILMNOOR	MONORAIL	AILNOPRU	UNIPOLAR	AILOSSTU	OUTSAILS
AILMNOOS	MOONSAIL	AILNOPRV	PARVOLIN	AILOSTTT	TOTALIST
AILMNOOT	MOTIONAL	AILNOPSY	POLYNIAS	AILOTTTY	TOTALITY
AILMNOPR	PROLAMIN	AILNOPTV	ANVILTOP	AILPPRUY	PUPILARY
AILMNOPS	LAMPIONS	AILNOPTY	PONYTAIL	AILPPSSU	SUIPLAPS
AILMNOPT	PILOTMAN	AILNOQSU	AQUILONS	AILPPSSY	PAYSLIPS
AILMNOPY	PALIMONY	AILNORST	TONSILAR	AILPQSSU	PASQUILS
AILMNORT	TORMINAL	AILNORTZ	TRIZONAL	AILPRSSU	SPIRULAS
AILMNOSS	MALISONS	AILNOSSS	SASSOLIN		UPRISALS
AILMNOSU	LAMINOUS	AILNOSTY	LANOSITY	AILPRSTU	STIPULAR
AILMNPSS	MISPLANS	AILNOSUV	AVULSION	AILPSSWY	SLIPWAYS
	PLASMINS	AILNOSVY	SYNOVIAL	AILPSTUY	PLAYSUIT
AILMNPST	IMPLANTS	AILNOTTV	VOLITANT	AILQSTTU	QUITTALS
	MISPLANT	AILNOTTY	TONALITY	AILRRSTU	RURALIST
AILMNPTU	PLATINUM	AILNOTUX	LUXATION	AILRRSTY	STARRILY
AILMNRSU	MURLAINS	AILNPPSY	SNAPPILY	AILRRTUY	RURALITY
AILMNRUY	LUMINARY	AILNPRSU	PURSLAIN	AILRSSTU	TISSULAR
AILMNSTU	SIMULANT	AILNPRSW	PRAWLINS		TRISULAS
AILMOORS	SAILROOM	AILNPRUV	PULVINAR	AILRSSTY	TRYSAILS
AILMOORT	MOTORAIL	AILNPSTU	NUPTIALS	AILRSTTU	ALTRUIST
	MOTORIAL		PATULINS		TITULARS
AILMOOSV	MOVIOLAS		UNPLAITS		ULTRAIST
AILMOPRX	PROXIMAL	AILNPSTY	PTYALINS	AILRSTTY	STRAITLY
AILMORSS	ORALISMS	AILNPSUU	NAUPLIUS	AILRSUVV	SURVIVAL
	SOLARISM	AILNPTTU	TULIPANT	AILRTTUY	TITULARY
AILMORST	MORALIST	AILNQRTU	TRANQUIL	AILSSTUW	LAWSUITS
AILMORSU	SOLARIUM	AILNQSTU	QUINTALS	AIMMMNOU	AMMONIUM
AILMORSY	ROYALISM	AILNQTUY	QUAINTLY	AIMMMSUX	MAXIMUMS
AILMORTY	MOLARITY	AILNRSSU	INSULARS	AIMMNORT	MORTMAIN
	MORALITY	AILNRSTT	RATTLINS	AIMMNOSW	WOMANISM
AILMOSSY	ISOAMYLS	AILNRSTU	LUNARIST	AIMMNPTU	TIMPANUM
AILMOSTT	TOTALISM	AILNRTTU	RUTILANT	AIMMNSTU	MANUMITS
AILMOSTU	SOLATIUM	AILNRUWY	UNWARILY	AIMMORSS	AMORISMS
AILMOSTV	VOLTAISM	AILNSSTU	STUNSAIL	AIMMOSST	ATOMISMS
AILMPPSY	MISAPPLY		UNALISTS		SOMATISM

AIMMOSSU	MIASMOUS	**AIMRSSTT**	MISSTART	**AINPPRTT**	TRIPPANT
AIMMPSST	MISSTAMP	**AIMRSSTU**	MATSURIS	**AINPRSST**	SPIRANTS
AIMMRRSV	MISMARRY	**AIMRSSTY**	SYMITARS		SPRAINTS
AIMMRSUU	MASURIUM	**AIMRSSTZ**	TZARISMS	**AINPRSTT**	TRIPTANS
AIMNNOPT	POINTMAN	**AIMRSTTU**	STRIATUM	**AINPRSTU**	PURITANS
AIMNNOSS	MANSIONS	**AIMRTTUY**	MATURITY		UPTRAINS
	ONANISMS	**AIMSSSTT**	STATISMS	**AINPSSST**	PISSANTS
AIMNNOTU	ANTIMUON	**AINNNOST**	SANTONIN	**AINPSSSY**	SYNAPSIS
	MOUNTAIN	**AINNOOTT**	NOTATION	**AINPSSTU**	PUISSANT
AIMNNOTY	ANTIMONY	**AINNOOTV**	NOVATION	**AINPSTTU**	PANTSUIT
	ANTINOMY	**AINNOOTZ**	ZONATION	**AINQRSTU**	QUINTARS
AIMNNRTU	RUMINANT	**AINNOPRT**	ANTIPORN	**AINQSSSU**	QUASSINS
AIMNOOOZ	ZOONOMIA	**AINNOPSS**	SAPONINS	**AINQTTUY**	QUANTITY
AIMNOORV	OMNIVORA	**AINNOPST**	PINTANOS	**AINRSSTT**	STRAINTS
AIMNOOST	AMOTIONS	**AINNOSST**	ONANISTS		TRANSITS
AIMNOOTY	MYOTONIA	**AINNOTTU**	NUTATION	**AINRSTTT**	TITRANTS
AIMNOPRS	RAMPIONS	**AINNPSST**	SNAPTINS	**AINRSTTU**	ANTIRUST
AIMNOPRT	PROTAMIN	**AINNPSTU**	UNPAINTS		NATURIST
AIMNOPST	MAINTOPS	**AINNQSTU**	QUINNATS	**AINRSTTY**	TANISTRY
	PTOMAINS		QUINTANS	**AINSSSTU**	SUSTAINS
	TAMPIONS	**AINNRSTT**	INTRANTS	**AIOOORRT**	ORATORIO
AIMNOPTV	PIVOTMAN	**AINNRSTU**	INSURANT	**AIOORRSW**	WOORARIS
AIMNOQRU	MAROQUIN	**AINNRSTY**	TYRANNIS	**AIOORSUV**	OVARIOUS
AIMNORSU	MAINOURS	**AINNSSTT**	INSTANTS	**AIOPRRST**	AIRPORTS
AIMNORTY	MINATORY	**AINNSSTU**	UNSAINTS		PARITORS
AIMNOSST	STASIMON	**AINNSTTY**	NYSTATIN	**AIOPRRTT**	PORTRAIT
AIMNOSTU	MANITOUS	**AINOOPTT**	POTATION	**AIOPRSST**	AIRPOSTS
	TINAMOUS	**AINOORRS**	ORARIONS		AIRSTOPS
AIMNOSTW	WOMANIST	**AINOORST**	ORATIONS		PROSAIST
AIMNOTTU	MUTATION	**AINOORTT**	ROTATION		PROTASIS
AIMNPRVY	PAYNIMRY	**AINOOSTT**	OSTINATO	**AIOPRSTT**	PATRIOTS
AIMNPSTU	SUMPITAN	**AINOOSTV**	OVATIONS	**AIOPRSUV**	PAVIOURS
AIMNRRSU	MURRAINS	**AINOOTTV**	OTTAVINO	**AIOPSSTT**	PASTITSO
AIMNRSSU	SURAMINS	**AINOPPRT**	PARPOINT	**AIOPSTTU**	UTOPIAST
	URANISMS	**AINOPPST**	APPOINTS	**AIORRRSW**	WARRIORS
AIMNRSTT	TANTRISM	**AINOPPTU**	PUPATION	**AIORRSTT**	TRAITORS
	TRANSMIT	**AINOPRSS**	PARISONS	**AIORRSTV**	VARISTOR
AIMNRSTU	NATRIUMS	**AINOPRST**	ATROPINS	**AIORRTTT**	TITRATOR
	NATURISM	**AINOPRTV**	PROVIANT	**AIORRTWY**	RYOTWARI
AIMNRSTV	VARMINTS	**AINOPSSS**	PASSIONS	**AIORSSST**	ASSISTOR
AIMNRSUU	URANIUMS	**AINOPSTT**	POSTNATI	**AIORSSTU**	SAUTOIRS
AIMNSSTU	TSUNAMIS	**AINOPSTU**	OPUNTIAS	**AIORSSUV**	SAVIOURS
AIMNSSYZ	ZANYISMS		UTOPIANS	**AIORSTTU**	TOURISTA
AIMNSTTU	ANTISMUT	**AINOPSTW**	SWAPTION	**AIORSTTV**	VOTARIST
AIMOPRSS	PROSAISM	**AINOPTTU**	OUTPAINT	**AIORSTUV**	VIRTUOSA
AIMOPRST	ATROPISM	**AINOPTWY**	WAYPOINT	**AIOSSSTY**	ISOSTASY
	PASTROMI	**AINOQRRU**	QUARRION	**AIOSTTUW**	OUTWAITS
AIMOPSST	IMPASTOS	**AINOQRSU**	NARQUOIS	**AIPPRSTY**	PAPISTRY
AIMOPSSY	SYMPOSIA	**AINORRSW**	WARRISON	**AIPRSSTU**	UPSTAIRS
AIMORRST	ARMORIST	**AINORRTT**	NITRATOR	**AIPRSSTY**	SPARSITY
AIMORRSU	ORARIUMS	**AINORRTU**	URINATOR	**AIPYZZZZ**	PIZZAZZY
	ROSARIUM	**AINORSST**	ARSONIST	**AIRRSSTY**	ARTISTRY
AIMORRUV	VARIORUM	**AINORSSW**	WARISONS	**AIRRSTZZ**	RIZZARTS
AIMORSST	AMORISTS	**AINORSTT**	STRONTIA	**AIRSSSTT**	TSARISTS
AIMORSSU	OSSARIUM	**AINORSTU**	RAINOUTS	**AIRSSTTT**	ATTRISTS
AIMORSTT	TRITOMAS		SUTORIAN	**AIRSSTTU**	TURISTAS
AIMORSTY	RAMOSITY	**AINORSTW**	WAITRONS	**AIRSSTTZ**	TZARISTS
AIMOSSTT	ATOMISTS	**AINORSTX**	TRIAXONS	**AISSSTTT**	STATISTS
	SOMATIST	**AINORTVY**	VANITORY	**AJKMNSTU**	MUNTJAKS
AIMPPRUU	PUPARIUM	**AINOSSSU**	SUASIONS	**AJKNNOOU**	JUNKANOO
AIMPPSST	MAPPISTS	**AINOSSTT**	STATIONS	**AJLNORSU**	JOURNALS
AIMPRSST	MISPARTS	**AINOSSVY**	SYNOVIAS	**AJMNNOOR**	NONMAJOR
AIMPRSTY	PARTYISM	**AINOSTTU**	TITANOUS	**AJMRSTUY**	JURYMAST
AIMRSSST	TSARISMS	**AINPPRSS**	PARSNIPS	**AJORRTUY**	JURATORY

Eight-letter anagrams

AKKLRSSY	SKYLARKS	**ALMNOPSS**	PLASMONS	**ALOPSTUU**	PATULOUS
AKKLSSWY	SKYWALKS	**ALMNORTY**	MATRONLY	**ALOPSTUY**	OUTPLAYS
AKKMOOST	TOKOMAKS	**ALMNOSSU**	SOLANUMS	**ALOQRRSU**	RORQUALS
AKKORSTW	TASKWORK	**ALMNPSSU**	SUNLAMPS	**ALOQRRSU**	SQUALORS
AKKOSUVZ	KUVASZOK	**ALMOOPRS**	PROSOMAL	**ALORRSUY**	SURROYAL
AKLLMRUY	MULLARKY	**ALMOOPRY**	PLAYROOM	**ALORSTTW**	SALTWORT
AKLMNOOW	MOONWALK	**ALMOOPSY**	POLYOMAS	**ALORSTWW**	AWLWORTS
AKLNNOPT	PLANKTON	**ALMOORTU**	ALUMROOT	**ALORSUVY**	SAVOURLY
AKLOPRSW	LAPWORKS	**ALMOPPST**	LAMPPOST	**ALORTUWY**	OUTLAWRY
AKLORSTW	SALTWORK		PALMTOPS	**ALOSSTTU**	OUTLASTS
AKLOSTTU	OUTTALKS	**ALMOPRST**	MARPLOTS	**ALOSSTXY**	OXYSALTS
AKLOSTUW	OUTWALKS	**ALMORSUU**	RAMULOUS	**ALPPSTUY**	PLATYPUS
	WALKOUTS	**ALMORSUY**	RAMOUSLY	**ALPRSSUU**	PURSUALS
AKLPRRSU	LARKSPUR	**ALMOSTTU**	MULATTOS	**ALPRSTUU**	PUSTULAR
AKMMNOOR	MONOMARK	**ALMPRSTU**	PLASTRUM	**ALRSSSUU**	RUSSULAS
AKMNOOOT	TOKONOMA	**ALMPSSTY**	SYMPLAST	**AMMNOORT**	MOTORMAN
AKMNOOPU	MOKOPUNA	**ALMRRTYY**	MARTYRLY	**AMMNOPSS**	PSAMMONS
AKMNRSTU	TRANKUMS	**ALMRTUUY**	TUMULARY	**AMMNPTUY**	TYMPANUM
AKMOORST	MOOKTARS	**ALMSSSUY**	ALYSSUMS	**AMMOORRS**	MAORMORS
AKMOPRST	POSTMARK	**ALNNNOOT**	NONTONAL		MORMAORS
AKMORSST	OSTMARKS	**ALNNOOPR**	NONPOLAR	**AMMOPSTU**	POMATUMS
AKMQSTUU	KUMQUATS	**ALNNOORS**	NONSOLAR	**AMMORRWY**	ARMYWORM
AKMRSSTU	MUSKRATS	**ALNNOORY**	NONROYAL	**AMMNOOSX**	MONAXONS
AKNOORST	OSTRAKON	**ALNNOPSY**	NONPLAYS	**AMNNOOTT**	MONTANTO
AKNOOUYZ	YOKOZUNA	**ALNNORRU**	NONRURAL	**AMNNORSW**	MANSWORN
AKNOPSTW	SWANKPOT	**ALNNOTWY**	WANTONLY	**AMNNORSY**	MANSONRY
AKNORSTU	OUTRANKS	**ALNNRSSU**	UNSNARLS	**AMNNOSTT**	MONTANTS
AKOPRRSU	PARKOURS	**ALNOOPPR**	PROPANOL	**AMNNOSTW**	TOWNSMAN
AKOPRRTW	PARTWORK	**ALNOOPRS**	POLARONS	**AMNNOSTY**	ANTONYMS
AKORRSTW	ARTWORKS	**ALNOOPRT**	PORTOLAN	**AMNNOSUW**	UNWOMANS
AKORRSWW	WARWORKS		PRONOTAL	**AMNNOTTU**	MOUNTANT
AKORSWWX	WAXWORKS	**ALNOOPST**	PLATOONS	**AMNNOTYY**	ANTONYMY
AKOSSTTU	OUTTASKS	**ALNOOPSV**	VANPOOLS	**AMNNPSTU**	PUNTSMAN
ALLLOSWY	SALLOWLY	**ALNOOPXY**	POLYAXON	**AMNNSSTU**	STANNUMS
ALLLPPUY	PULPALLY	**ALNOOPYZ**	POLYZOAN	**AMNNSTTU**	STUNTMAN
ALLLPRUY	PLURALLY	**ALNOOPZZ**	POZZOLAN	**AMNOOPPS**	POMPANOS
ALLMNORY	NORMALLY	**ALNOORST**	ORTOLANS	**AMNOOSTT**	OTTOMANS
ALLMNOSY	ALLONYMS	**ALNOPRST**	PLASTRON	**AMNOOSTZ**	MATZOONS
ALLMNPSU	PULLMANS	**ALNOPRTU**	PORTULAN	**AMNOOTUY**	AUTONOMY
ALLMOPSX	SMALLPOX	**ALNOPRTY**	PATRONLY	**AMNOOTWY**	TOYWOMAN
ALLMORTY	MORTALLY	**ALNOPSTU**	OUTPLANS	**AMNOOTXY**	TAXONOMY
ALLMOUWY	MULLOWAY	**ALNOPSYY**	POLYNYAS	**AMNOPRSW**	SPANWORM
ALLMPRUU	PLUMULAR	**ALNORRWY**	NARROWLY	**AMNOPRSY**	PARONYMS
ALLMTUUY	MUTUALLY	**ALNORSVY**	SOVRANLY	**AMNOPRYY**	PARONYMY
ALLNNOOY	NONLOYAL	**ALNPPSTU**	SUPPLANT	**AMNOPSTU**	PANTOUMS
ALLNNOUY	NOUNALLY	**ALNRRTUU**	NURTURAL	**AMNORSST**	TRANSOMS
ALLNOOPS	PLANOSOL	**ALNRTTUY**	TRUANTLY	**AMNORSTU**	ROMAUNTS
ALLNORSS	LASSLORN	**ALOOPPRS**	PROPOSAL	**AMNORSTY**	STRAMONY
ALLOOSST	LATOSOLS	**ALOOPRST**	POSTORAL	**AMNOSSYZ**	ZYMOSANS
ALLOOSTX	AXOLOTLS	**ALOOPRTU**	UPROOTAL	**AMNOSTUY**	AUTONYMS
ALLOPRSY	PAYROLLS	**ALOORSUV**	VALOROUS	**AMNOTTUY**	TAUTONYM
ALLOPSTY	POSTALLY	**ALOORTYZ**	ZOOLATRY	**AMNRSTTU**	TANTRUMS
ALLOPTYY	ALLOTYPY	**ALOPPRSU**	POPULARS	**AMOOORSS**	AMOROSOS
ALLORSST	ALLSORTS	**ALOPPRYY**	POLYPARY	**AMOOPRSS**	PROSOMAS
ALLORSWY	ROLLWAYS	**ALOPPSSU**	SUPPOSAL	**AMOOPRST**	TAPROOMS
ALLORTUW	ULTRALOW	**ALOPPSUU**	PAPULOUS	**AMOORRTY**	MORATORY
ALLORTWW	WALLWORT	**ALOPRRSU**	PARLOURS	**AMOORSTZ**	SMORZATO
ALLOSSWW	SWALLOWS		SPORULAR	**AMOORTWY**	MOTORWAY
ALLOSTWY	TOLLWAYS	**ALOPRSTT**	PORTLAST	**AMOOSSTU**	ASTOMOUS
ALLRUUVY	UVULARLY	**ALOPRSTU**	POSTURAL	**AMOOSTVV**	VASOTOMY
ALMMNRUU	NUMMULAR		PULSATOR	**AMOOTTUY**	AUTOTOMY
ALMMORTW	MALTWORM	**ALOPRSTY**	PASTORLY	**AMOPRRST**	MARSPORT
ALMNNOOR	NONMORAL	**ALOPSSSU**	SPOUSALS	**AMOPRSXY**	PAROXYSM
ALMNOOPS	LAMPOONS	**ALOPSSUV**	VOLUSPAS	**AMOPSSTT**	TOPMASTS

AMOQSSUU	SQUAMOUS	AOPRRTUY	POURTRAY	BBCEMNOU	BUNCOMBE
AMORRTUY	MORTUARY	AOPRSSTT	STARSPOT	BBCERRSU	SCRUBBER
AMORSTTU	OUTSMART	AOPRSTTU	OUTPARTS	BBCGHIIN	CHIBBING
AMORSWWX	WAXWORMS	AOPRSTTY	PYROSTAT	BBCGIINR	CRIBBING
AMORTTUY	MUTATORY	AOPRSTUY	OUTPRAYS	BBCGILNO	COBBLING
AMPRSSUW	UPSWARMS	AOPSSSTU	PASSOUTS	BBCGILNU	CLUBBING
AMPRSTYY	SYMPATRY	AOPSSTWY	WAYPOSTS	BBCGINSU	CUBBINGS
AMRRSSTU	RASTRUMS	AOPSTTUU	AUTOPUTS	BBCHILSU	CLUBBISH
AMRSSTTU	STRATUMS	AOPTTUYY	AUTOTYPY	BBCHILUV	CHUBBILY
ANNNOSSY	SYNANONS	AORRSSSU	ASSURORS	BBCHKOOS	BOSCHBOK
ANNOOQTU	NONQUOTA	AORRSTTW	STARWORT	BBCHKSUU	BUSHBUCK
ANNOORST	SONORANT	AORRTTWW	WARTWORT	BBCILLUV	CLUBBILY
ANNOPRTY	NONPARTY	AORSSTTU	STRATOUS	BBCILMSU	CLUBBISM
ANNOPSST	NONPASTS	AORSSTTY	STAROSTY	BBCILRSY	SCRIBBLY
ANNOSSTU	STANNOUS	AORSTTTU	OUTSTART	BBCILSTU	CLUBBIST
ANNPRSUY	SPUNYARN	AORSUVVY	VOUVRAYS	BBCIPSUU	SUBPUBIC
ANOOPRRT	PRONATOR	AOSSTTUY	OUTSTAYS	BBCKLOSU	SUBBLOCK
ANOOPRSS	SOPRANOS	APPRRSUU	PURPURAS	BBDDEEMO	DEMOBBED
ANOOPRST	PATROONS	APRSSTTU	STARTUPS	BBDDEEMU	BEDUMBED
ANOORSST	SANTOORS		UPSTARTS	BBDDEERU	REDUBBED
ANOORSSU	ARSONOUS	APRSSUWY	SPURWAYS	BBDDEILR	DRIBBLED
ANOORSTT	ARNOTTOS	ASVYYZZZ	ZYZZYVAS	BBDDENUU	UNDUBBED
	RATTOONS	BBBCEOWY	COBWEBBY	BBDEEGIR	GIBBERED
ANOORSUU	ANOUROUS	BBBDEEKO	KEBOBBED	BBDEEGIT	GIBBETED
ANOPPPRT	PROPPANT	BBBDEEOR	BEROBBED	BBDEEIJR	JIBBERED
ANOPRRSS	SPORRANS	BBBDENOU	UNBOBBED	BBDEEIST	DEBBIEST
ANOPRSTU	STROUPAN	BBBEEILR	BLEBBIER		EBBTIDES
ANOPRTTU	TRAPUNTO	BBBEGILN	BLEBBING	BBDEEMNU	BENUMBED
ANOPSSTU	OUTSPANS	BBBEILOR	BLOBBIER	BBDEENUW	UNWEBBED
ANOQRSSU	SQUARSON		BOBBLIER	BBDEEOPP	BEBOPPED
ANORSSTU	SANTOURS	BBBEILRU	BUBBLIER	BBDEERRU	RUBBERED
ANORSTVY	SOVRANTY	BBBEILSU	BUBBLIES	BBDEERSU	SUBBREED
ANORSUVY	UNSAVORY	BBBEINOT	BOBBINET	BBDEFILR	FRIBBLED
ANOTTUUV	OUTVAUNT	BBBELRSU	BLUBBERS	BBDEGLRU	GRUBBLED
ANPPSSUW	SUPPAWNS		BUBBLERS	BBDEHORT	THROBBED
ANPRSSTU	SUNTRAPS	BBBELRUY	BLUBBERY	BBDEHRSU	SHRUBBED
	UNSTRAPS	BBBGILNO	BLOBBING	BBDEILLN	BELLBIND
ANPRSTUU	PURSUANT		BOBBLING	BBDEILLR	BELLBIRD
ANRRSTUY	UNSTARRY	BBBGILNU	BLUBBING	BBDEILQU	QUIBBLED
ANRRTTUY	TRUANTRY		BUBBLING	BBDEILRR	DRIBBLER
ANRSSSTU	SUNSTARS	BBBHNOOV	HOBNOBBY	BBDEILRS	DIBBLERS
ANRSSTYY	SYNASTRY	BBBHOOUU	HUBBUBOO		DRIBBLES
AOOOPRST	SOAPROOT	BBBIOSTT	BOBBITTS	BBDEILRT	DRIBBLET
AOOOPRSZ	SPOROZOA	BBBOOSXY	BOBBYSOX	BBDEILRU	BLUEBIRD
AOOOPRTZ	PROTOZOA	BBCCIKOS	BIBCOCKS	BBDEIMOV	DIVEBOMB
AOOPPRSY	APOSPORY	BBCDEILR	CRIBBLED	BBDEINOR	RIBBONED
AOOPRSSU	SAPOROUS	BBCDERSU	SCRUBBED	BBDEINRU	UNRIBBED
AOOPRSTT	TAPROOTS	BBCDIMOV	BOMBYCID	BBDEIQSU	SQUIBBED
AOOPRSTU	ATROPOUS	BBCEEHOS	BOBECHES	BBDEIRRS	DRIBBERS
AOOPRSTW	SOAPWORT	BBCEHINS	NEBBICHS	BBDEKLNO	KNOBBLED
AOOPRSUV	VAPOROUS	BBCEHIRU	CHUBBIER	BBDEKLNU	KNUBBLED
AOOPRTTY	POTATORY	BBCEILRS	CRIBBLES	BBDELLMU	DUMBBELL
AOORRSTT	ROTATORS		SCRIBBLE	BBDELLOO	BOBOLLED
AOORRSTU	OUTROARS	BBCEILRU	CLUBBIER	BBDELOOS	BEBLOODS
AOORRTTY	ROTATORY	BBCEIOST	COBBIEST	BBDELOSS	BOBSLEDS
AOORSSTU	OUTSOARS	BBCEIRRS	CRIBBERS	BBDELSTU	STUBBLED
AOORSSUV	SAVOROUS	BBCEKKOS	KEBBOCKS	BBDENRUU	UNRUBBED
AOORSTUV	OUTSAVOR	BBCEKKSU	KEBBUCKS	BBDERRSU	DRUBBERS
AOPPRRST	RAPPORTS	BBCEKLSU	BLESBUCK	BBDERSUU	SUBURBED
AOPPRSST	PASSPORT	BBCEKLUU	BLUEBUCK	BBDFLSUU	FLUBDUBS
AOPPRSTU	TRAPPOUS	BBCELORS	CLOBBERS	BBDGIILN	DIBBLING
AOPRRRTY	PARROTRY		COBBLERS	BBDGIINR	DRIBBING
AOPRRSSW	SPARROWS	BBCELORY	COBBLERY	BBDGINRU	DRUBBING
AOPRRSTY	PORTRAYS	BBCELRSU	CLUBBERS	BBDGINSU	DUBBINGS

Eight-letter anagrams

BBDIIKMU	DIBBUKIM	BBEILRST	STIBBLER	BBGILMNU	BUMBLING
BBDIKMUY	DYBBUKIM		TRIBBLES	BBGILNNO	NOBBLING
BBDIOORS	BOOBIRDS	BBEILRSU	SLUBBIER	BBGILNNU	NUBBLING
BBDOSUYY	BUSYBODY	BBEILSST	STIBBLES	BBGILNOW	WOBBLING
BBEEEMSX	BEMBEXES	BBEIMMOT	TIMEBOMB	BBGILNOY	LOBBYING
BBEEERRS	BERBERES	BBEIMNOS	BOMBESIN	BBGILNRU	BLURBING
BBEEERSU	BEBEERUS	BBEIMOST	BOMBSITE		BURBLING
BBEEHINS	NEBBISHE	BBEIMRSU	BRUMBIES		RUBBLING
BBEEHLOW	BOBWHEEL	BBEINORS	SNOBBIER	BBGILNSU	SLUBBING
BBEEIIRR	BERIBERI	BBEINOST	NOBBIEST	BBGILRUY	GRUBBILY
BBEEILPR	PEBBLIER	BBEINRSU	SNUBBIER	BBGIMNOS	BOMBINGS
	PLEBBIER	BBEINSTU	NUBBIEST		MOBBINGS
BBEEIMSX	BEMBIXES	BBEIOOST	BOBOTIES	BBGINNSU	SNUBBING
BBEEIMTT	BIMBETTE	BBEIORTU	OUTBRIBE	BBGINOSS	SOBBINGS
BBEEINRR	BERBERIN	BBEIRSTU	STUBBIER	BBGINOST	STOBBING
BBEEIRRS	BERBERIS		SUBTRIBE	BBGINOSW	SWOBBING
BBEEISTW	WEBBIEST	BBEISSTU	STUBBIES	BBGINRSU	RUBBINGS
BBEEJLMU	BEJUMBLE	BBEISTTU	TUBBIEST	BBGINSSU	SUBBINGS
BBEELLLU	BLUEBELL	BBEKLNOS	KNOBBLES	BBGINSTU	STUBBING
BBEEOPPR	BEBOPPER	BBEKLNSU	KNUBBLES		TUBBINGS
BBEFILRR	FRIBBLER	BBEKLOOU	BLUEBOOK	BBGLOOWY	LOBBYGOW
BBEFILRS	FRIBBLES	BBEKLOSS	BLESBOKS	BBHILOSS	SLOBBISH
BBEFILRT	FLIBBERT	BBEKLSUU	BUBUKLES	BBHIMOSY	HOBBYISM
BBEFIMOR	FIREBOMB	BBEKNOOT	BONTEBOK	BBHINOSS	SNOBBISH
BBEFISTU	FUBBIEST	BBEKNORS	KNOBBERS	BBHINSSU	SNUBBISH
BBEFLRSU	FLUBBERS	BBELLOSY	BELLBOYS	BBHIOOSY	BOOBYISH
BBEGIIST	GIBBSITE	BBELLRUY	LUBBERLY	BBHIORTY	HOBBITRY
BBEGILNP	PEBBLING	BBELLSTU	BULBLETS	BBHIOSTY	HOBBYIST
BBEGILOR	GLOBBIER	BBELMOST	BOMBLETS	BBHIRSUY	RUBBISHY
BBEGILRS	GRIBBLES	BBELMRSU	BUMBLERS	BBHKOOSS	BOSHBOKS
BBEGILRY	GLIBBERY	BBELNORS	NOBBLERS	BBHOOSUW	WHOOBUBS
BBEGILST	GLIBBEST	BBELOORW	BOBOWLER	BBHRSSUU	SUBSHRUB
BBEGINNS	SNEBBING	BBELORSS	SLOBBERS	BBIIILMS	BILIMBIS
BBEGINSW	WEBBINGS	BBELORSU	BOERBULS	BBIILLSU	SILLIBUB
BBEGIOST	GOBBIEST	BBELORSW	WOBBLERS	BBIILSST	BIBLISTS
BBEGIRRU	GRUBBIER	BBELORSY	LOBBYERS	BBIJMOOS	JIBBOOMS
BBEGLORS	GOBBLERS		SLOBBERY	BBIKLLOO	BILLBOOK
BBEGLRSU	GRUBBLES	BBELOTUW	BLOWTUBE	BBIKLNOO	BOBOLINK
BBEGRRSU	GRUBBERS	BBELRRSU	BURBLERS	BBILLOYY	BILLYBOY
BBEHINSY	NEBBISHY	BBELRSSU	SLUBBERS	BBILLSUU	LULIBUBS
BBEHIOTW	BOBWHITE	BBELSSTU	STUBBLES	BBILMOSY	LOBBYISM
BBEHLORS	HOBBLERS	BBEMOSXY	BOMBYXES	BBILNOSY	SNOBBILY
BBEHLSUU	BLUEBUSH	BBENORSY	SNOBBERY	BBILOSTY	LOBBYIST
BBEHMSTU	BETHUMBS	BBENRSSU	SNUBBERS	BBILOSUU	BIBULOUS
BBEHORRT	THROBBER	BBEORRXY	BOXBERRY	BBILRSTU	BLURBIST
BBEIILRS	RIBIBLES	BBEORSSW	SWOBBERS	BBILSTUY	STUBBILY
BBEIIMRS	IMBIBERS	BBEPRSUW	BREWPUBS	BBIMMOSS	MOBBISMS
BBEIIRST	RIBBIEST	BBFGILNU	FLUBBING	BBIMNOSS	SNOBBISM
BBEIKNOR	KNOBBIER	BBGGIILN	GLIBBING	BBIMOOSY	BOOBYISM
BBEIKNRU	KNUBBIER	BBGGILNO	GOBBLING	BBIMOSSY	YOBBISMS
BBEILLLU	BLUEBILL	BBGGINRU	GRUBBING	BBINORRY	RIBBONRY
BBEILLNO	BONIBELL	BBGHILNO	HOBBLING	BBJLOOSW	BLOWJOBS
BBEILNRS	NIBBLERS	BBGIIIMN	IMBIBING	BBKLOOSU	BLOUBOKS
BBEILNRU	NUBBLIER	BBGIIJNS	JIBBINGS	BBKOOOOS	BOOBOOKS
BBEILORS	SLOBBIER	BBGIIKLN	KIBBLING	BBLLNNUU	BULNBULN
BBEILORW	WOBBLIER	BBGIILMN	BLIMBING	BBLLOUYY	BULLYBOY
BBEILOST	BIBELOTS	BBGIILMN	NIBBLING	BBNOORSU	BOURBONS
BBEILOSW	WOBBLIES	BBGIILNW	WIBBLING	BBNORSTU	STUBBORN
BBEILPRS	PRIBBLES	BBGIINNS	SNIBBING	BBOOSSSY	BOSSBOYS
BBEILQRU	QUIBBLER	BBGIINRS	RIBBINGS	BCCIILY	BICYCLIC
BBEILQSU	QUIBBLES	BBGIJNOS	JOBBINGS	BCCDEILY	BICYCLED
BBEILRRU	BURBLIER	BBGIKNNO	KNOBBING	BCCDHIKO	DOBCHICK
	RUBBLIER	BBGILLSU	BILLBUGS	BCCDIKOR	COCKBIRD
BBEILRRY	BILBERRY	BBGILMNO	MOBBLING	BCCEEIRR	CEREBRIC

BCCEHIRU	CHERUBIC	BCDEHLOT	BLOTCHED	BCEEHOSU	BOUCHEES
BCCEHORS	BESCORCH	BCDEHNRU	BRUNCHED	BCEEIILM	IMBECILE
BCCEIIIS	CICISBEI	BCDEHOOR	BROOCHED	BCEEIKRR	BICKERER
BCCEIILO	LIBECCIO	BCDEIIOS	BIOCIDES	BCEEILNR	BERNICLE
BCCEIIOS	CICISBEO	BCDEIIRR	RICEBIRD	BCEEIMRS	BECRIMES
BCCEILOS	ECBOLICS	BCDEIITU	DECUBITI	BCEEINOT	CENOBITE
BCCEILOV	BIOCYCLE	BCDEIKRR	REDBRICK	BCEEIOSX	ICEBOXES
BCCEILRU	CRUCIBLE	BCDEIKSS	SICKBEDS	BCEEIPSS	BESPICES
BCCEILRY	BICYCLER	BCDEIKST	BEDTICKS		BICEPSES
BCCEILSU	CUBICLES	BCDEILRY	CREDIBLY	BCEEIRSS	ESCRIBES
BCCEILSY	BICYCLES	BCDEIMNO	COMBINED	BCEEIRTT	BRETTICE
BCCEMORS	CROMBECS	BCDEINOU	ICEBOUND	BCEEJORT	REOBJECT
BCCEMRUU	CUCUMBER	BCDEIRSU	CURBSIDE	BCEEKNOR	BECKONER
BCCHIKOY	BOYCHICK	BCDEKOOO	CODEBOOK	BCEEKNSU	BUCKEENS
BCCIIMOR	MICROBIC	BCDEKORS	BEDROCKS	BCEEKSUY	BUCKEYES
BCCIISTU	CUBISTIC	BCDEKOSS	BEDSOCKS	BCEELLOT	BELLCOTE
BCCIITUY	CUBICITY	BCDELMRU	CRUMBLED	BCEELOOR	BORECOLE
BCCIKLLO	COCKBILL	BCDELMSU	SCUMBLED	BCEELOSU	BOUCLEES
BCCILMOU	COLUMBIC	BCDELOSU	BECLOUDS	BCEELRTU	TUBERCLE
BCCILOOR	BROCCOLI	BCDEMNOU	UNCOMBED	BCEEMMOR	COMEMBER
BCCILOSU	BUCOLICS	BCDEMOOY	COEMBODY	BCEEMNRU	ENCUMBER
BCCINORR	CORNCRIB	BCDEMORY	CORYMBED	BCEEMRRU	CEREBRUM
BCCIRTUU	CUCURBIT	BCDENRUU	UNCURBED		CUMBERER
BCCLOOOO	COCOBOLO	BCDEOORT	CODEBTOR	BCEENORS	OBSCENER
BCCMOOSX	COXCOMBS	BCDEOOWY	COWBOYED	BCEENRSU	CRUBEENS
BCCMSSUU	SUCCUMBS	BCDEORSU	OBSCURED	BCEEPRTY	CYBERPET
BCCNOORS	CORNCOBS	BCDEORSW	BECROWDS	BCEERSSU	BECURSES
BCCSSUUU	SUCCUBUS	BCDEOSSU	SUBCODES	BCEERSTU	SUBERECT
BCDDEEEK	BEDECKED	BCDESSUU	SUBDUCES	BCEERSXY	CYBERSEX
BCDDEEKU	BEDUCKED	BCDHIRSU	BRUCHIDS	BCEERTVY	BREVETCY
BCDDEENU	BEDUNCED	BCDHOOSU	CUBHOODS	BCEFFIIR	FEBRIFIC
BCDDEHIL	CHILDBED	BCDHORSU	SUBCHORD	BCEFHISU	SUBCHIEF
BCDDESUU	SUBDUCED	BCDIIMOR	BROMIDIC	BCEFILOR	FORCIBLE
BCDEEEHR	BREECHED	BCDIIPSU	BICUSPID	BCEGHILN	BELCHING
BCDEEGLU	BECUDGEL	BCDIKLLU	DUCKBILL	BCEGHINN	BENCHING
BCDEEHLN	BLENCHED	BCDILMOY	MOLYBDIC	BCEGIINO	BIOGENIC
BCDEEHNR	BEDRENCH	BCDILORU	COLUBRID	BCEGIMNO	BECOMING
BCDEEHOU	DEBOUCHE	BCDIMOOR	COMORBID	BCEGKMSU	GEMSBUCK
BCDEEIKN	BENEDICK	BCDIMORS	SCOMBRID	BCEGLNOO	CONGLOBE
BCDEEIKR	BICKERED	BCDINOSW	COWBINDS	BCEHIIOT	BIOETHIC
BCDEEILR	CREDIBLE	BCDINRUU	RUBICUND	BCEHIIRT	BITCHIER
BCDEEILS	DECIBELS	BCDIORSW	COWBIRDS	BCEHILMY	CHIMBLEY
BCDEEILU	EDUCIBLE	BCDKNOOO	BOONDOCK	BCEHIMOR	BICHROME
BCDEEIMR	BECRIMED	BCDKORSU	BURDOCKS	BCEHIMRS	BESMIRCH
BCDEEINT	BENEDICT	BCDSSTUU	SUBDUCTS	BCEHIMRU	CHERUBIM
BCDEEIPS	BESPICED	BCEEEEFN	BENEFICE	BCEHINNO	CHINBONE
BCDEEIRS	DESCRIBE	BCEEEFKN	NECKBEEF	BCEHINRU	BUNCHIER
	ESCRIBED	BCEEEHIR	BEECHIER		CHERUBIN
BCDEEIST	BISECTED	BCEEEHRS	BREECHES	BCEHINSU	SUBNICHE
BCDEEJOT	OBJECTED	BCEEENRS	BESCREEN	BCEHIORS	BRIOCHES
BCDEEKMO	BEMOCKED	BCEEERSU	BERCEUSE	BCEHIORT	BOTCHIER
BCDEEKNO	BECKONED	BCEEFILN	FENCIBLE	BCEHIOST	BIOTECHS
BCDEEKRU	REEDBUCK	BCEEFKLS	BEFLECKS	BCEHIRRT	BRICHTER
BCDEEKTU	BUCKETED	BCEEFLTU	CLUBFEET	BCEHIRST	BRITCHES
BCDEELNU	BEUNCLED	BCEEGIRS	ICEBERGS	BCEHIRTY	BITCHERY
BCDEELOR	CORBELED	BCEEHINR	BENCHIER	BCEHLOST	BLOTCHES
BCDEELRU	BECURLED	BCEEHKSU	BUCKSHEE	BCEHLRSU	BLUCHERS
BCDEEMOR	RECOMBED	BCEEHLNR	BLENCHER	BCEHMSTU	BESMUTCH
BCDEEMRU	CUMBERED	BCEEHLNS	BLENCHES	BCEHNOPT	BENCHTOP
BCDEENSU	BEDUNCES	BCEEHLOT	BECLOTHE	BCEHNRRU	BRUNCHER
BCDEEORV	BEDCOVER	BCEEHLRS	BELCHERS	BCEHNRSU	BRUNCHES
BCDEEOTT	OBTECTED	BCEEHNRS	BENCHERS	BCEHOORS	BROOCHES
BCDEERSU	BECURSED	BCEEHNRU	UNBREECH	BCEHOPSU	SUBEPOCH
BCDEHINS	DISBENCH	BCEEHNTU	BEECHNUT	BCEHORRU	BROCHURE

BCEHORSS	BORSCHES	BCEKOSTY	BYCOKETS	BCHKNORU	BUCKHORN
BCEHORST	BOTCHERS	BCELLOSW	COWBELLS	BCHKOSTU	BUCKSHOT
BCEHORSW	COWHERBS	BCELLRUW	WELLCURB	BCHLNOUX	LUNCHBOX
BCEHORTY	BOTCHERY	BCELLSSU	SUBCELLS	BCHLRSUU	CLUBRUSH
BCEHRSTU	BUTCHERS	BCELMOSS	COMBLESS	BCHNOORS	BRONCHOS
BCEHRTUY	BUTCHERY	BCELMRSU	CLUMBERS	BCHNORSU	BRONCHUS
BCEHSTTU	BUTCHEST		CRUMBLES	BCHORSST	BORSCHTS
BCEIIKLN	ICEBLINK	BCELMSSU	SCUMBLES	BCIIILMU	UMBILICI
BCEIIKRR	BRICKIER	BCELNOSW	BECLOWNS	BCIIIOTT	BIOTITIC
BCEIIKRS	BRICKIES	BCELRSSU	CURBLESS	BCIIKLNS	NIBLICKS
BCEIILMS	MISCIBLE	BCEMRRSU	CRUMBERS	BCIILLSV	SIBYLLIC
BCEIILNV	VINCIBLE	BCEMRSSU	SCUMBERS	BCIILMRU	LUMBRICI
BCEIILOP	EPIBOLIC	BCENOOOX	ECONOBOX	BCIILMSU	BULIMICS
BCEIIMRS	IMBRICES	BCENORSU	BOUNCERS	BCIILNVY	VINCIBLY
BCEIINRS	INSCRIBE	BCEORRSU	OBSCURER	BCIILORS	COLIBRIS
BCEIKLMO	COMBLIKE	BCEORRWY	COWBERRY	BCIILOTY	BIOLYTIC
BCEIKLMS	LIMBECKS	BCEORSSU	BESCOURS	BCIIMNOO	BIONOMIC
BCEIKLOO	BOOKLICE		OBSCURES	BCIIMORU	CIBORIUM
BCEIKLOR	BLOCKIER	BCERSSTU	BECRUSTS	BCIIMRSS	SCRIBISM
BCEIKLOS	BLOCKIES	BCESSSTU	SUBSECTS	BCIINORT	BORNITIC
BCEIKLRS	BRICKLES	BCESSTUU	SUBCUTES	BCIINORV	VIBRONIC
BCEIKLTU	BLUETICK	BCFIIMOR	MORBIFIC	BCIIOPTY	BIOTYPIC
BCEIKSST	BESTICKS	BCFIIORT	FIBROTIC	BCIIORST	BISTROIC
BCEILMRS	CLIMBERS	BCFILORY	FORCIBLY		SORBITIC
	RECLIMBS	BCFIMORU	CUBIFORM	BCIIOSTT	BISCOTTI
BCEILNOS	BINOCLES	BCFLOOTU	CLUBFOOT	BCIISSTU	BISCUITS
BCEILNRU	RUNCIBLE	BCFSSSUU	SUBFUSCS	BCIISTUY	BISCUITY
BCEILNYZ	BENZYLIC	BCGHIINR	BIRCHING	BCIKKNSU	BUCKSKIN
BCEILORS	BRICOLES	BCGHIINT	BITCHING	BCIKLOOT	BOOTLICK
	CORBEILS	BCGHINNU	BUNCHING	BCIKLOST	LOBSTICK
BCEILOSU	CIBOULES	BCGHINOR	BROCHING	BCIKORRW	CRIBWORK
BCEILOTU	TUBICOLE	BCGHINOT	BOTCHING	BCIKOSTT	BITSTOCK
BCEILPRU	REPUBLIC	BCGHINPU	PINCHBUG		BITTOCKS
BCEIMNOR	COMBINER	BCGHINTU	BUTCHING	BCILLPUY	PUBLICLY
BCEIMNOS	COMBINES	BCGIIKNR	BRICKING	BCILMOSY	SYMBOLIC
BCEIMNRU	INCUMBER	BCGIIKST	BIGSTICK	BCILMOTU	OUTCLIMB
BCEIMORS	MICROBES	BCGIILMN	CLIMBING	BCILMPSU	UPCLIMBS
BCEIMOST	COMBIEST	BCGIILOO	BIOLOGIC	BCILNOUY	BOUNCILY
BCEIMOSW	COMBWISE	BCGIINRS	SCRIBING	BCILOORS	BICOLORS
BCEIMRRU	CRUMBIER	BCGIKLNO	BLOCKING		BROCOLIS
BCEINORS	BICORNES	BCGIKLNU	BUCKLING	BCILOORU	BICOLOUR
BCEINORU	BOUNCIER	BCGIKNSU	BUCKINGS	BCIMORSU	MICROBUS
BCEINOVX	BICONVEX	BCGILMNY	CYMBLING	BCINORSU	BURSICON
BCEINRSU	BRUCINES	BCGIMNOR	CROMBING		RUBICONS
BCEIOOPS	BIOSCOPE	BCGIMNOS	COMBINGS	BCINOSSU	SUBSONIC
BCEIOOSS	SCOOBIES	BCGIMNRU	CRUMBING	BCINOSTU	SUBTONIC
BCEIORRS	CRIBROSE	BCGIMNUU	CUMBUNGI	BCINOSUU	INCUBOUS
BCEIORST	BISECTOR	BCGINNOU	BOUNCING	BCINSTUU	SUBTUNIC
BCEIRRSS	SCRIBERS		BUNCOING	BCIOOPSY	BIOSCOPY
BCEIRSTU	BRUCITES	BCGINORU	COURBING	BCIOORST	ROBOTICS
BCEIRTTY	YTTERBIC	BCGINRSU	CURBINGS	BCIOOSTT	BISCOTTO
BCEJOORT	OBJECTOR	BCHIILTY	BITCHILY	BCIOPSTU	SUBOPTIC
BCEJSSTU	SUBJECTS	BCHIIOPS	BIOCHIPS		SUBTOPIC
BCEKLLNU	BULLNECK	BCHIIOST	COHIBITS	BCIORRSU	CRIBROUS
BCEKLLOS	BELLOCKS	BCHIISSU	HIBISCUS	BCIORSST	CROSSBIT
BCEKLNOT	BLONCKET	BCHIKLOS	BLOCKISH	BCISSTUU	SUBCUTIS
BCEKLNUU	UNBUCKLE	BCHIKOSU	CHIBOUKS	BCJKMSUU	JUMBUCKS
BCEKLORS	BLOCKERS	BCHIKOSY	BOYCHIKS	BCKKOOOO	COOKBOOK
BCEKLRSU	BUCKLERS	BCHILNUY	BUNCHILY	BCKLLOOS	BOLLOCKS
	SUBCLERK	BCHILOTY	BOTCHILY	BCKLLOSU	BULLOCKS
BCEKMSTU	STEMBUCK	BCHIOORY	CHOIRBOY	BCKLLOUY	BULLOCKY
BCEKOORU	BUCKEROO	BCHIOPRS	PIBROCHS	BCKLNOSU	SUNBLOCK
BCEKORST	BROCKETS	BCHIORRT	BIRROTCH		UNBLOCKS
BCEKORSU	ROEBUCKS	BCHIOTTU	OUTBITCH	BCKMMOSU	BUMMOCKS

BCKNNOOS	BONNOCKS	BDDEFOOR	FORBODED		REBUFFED
BCKOOOPY	COPYBOOK	BDDEGINS	BEDDINGS	BDEEFFTU	BUFFETED
BCKOSTTU	BUTTOCKS	BDDEIIMO	IMBODIED	BDEEFGGO	BEFOGGED
BCLMOORU	CLUBROOM	BDDEILNR	BRINDLED	BDEEFGIT	BEGIFTED
BCLMOOSU	COULOMBS	BDDEILOO	BLOODIED	BDEEFGLU	BEGULFED
BCLMOOTU	OUTCLOMB	BDDEINNU	UNBIDDEN	BDEEFILR	BELFRIED
BCLOORTU	CLUBROOT	BDDEINOU	UNBODIED	BDEEFINN	BEFINNED
BCLOOSSU	SUBCOOLS	BDDEINRU	UNDERBID	BDEEFINR	BEFRIEND
BCLORSTU	CLOTBURS	BDDEIORS	DISORBED	BDEEFIRS	DEBRIEFS
BCLSSTUU	SUBCULTS		DISROBED	BDEEFIRU	RUBEFIED
BCMMRSUU	CRUMBUMS	BDDEIOWY	WIDEBODY	BDEEFITT	BEFITTED
BCMORSUU	CUMBROUS	BDDEIRRS	REDBIRDS	BDEEFLOO	BEFOOLED
BCMOSSTU	COMBUSTS	BDDEISSU	SUBSIDED	BDEEFLOU	BEFOULED
BCNNOUUY	UNBOUNCY	BDDEISTU	BUDDIEST	BDEEFOOR	FOREBODE
BCOOORTW	CROWBOOT	BDDELMRU	DRUMBLED	BDEEFOOW	BEEFWOOD
BCOOPSYY	COPYBOYS	BDDELOOR	BLOODRED	BDEEFSUU	SUBFEUED
BCOORSSW	CROSSBOW	BDDELORS	BRODDLES	BDEEGGIW	BEWIGGED
BCOOSTTY	BOYCOTTS	BDDENNOU	UNBONDED	BDEEGGMO	EMBOGGED
BCORSTTU	OBSTRUCT	BDDENOTU	OBTUNDED	BDEEGGNU	UNBEGGED
BCRSSTUU	SUBCRUST	BDDENRUU	UNDERBUD	BDEEGGRU	BEGRUDGE
BCSTUUZZ	BUZZCUTS	BDDEORTU	OBTRUDED		BUGGERED
BDDDDEEU	DEBUDDED	BDDGIINS	BIDDINGS		DEBUGGER
BDDDEEEM	EMBEDDED	BDDGILNU	BUDDLING	BDEEGHIS	BESIGHED
BDDDEEIM	IMBEDDED	BDDGINOR	BRODDING	BDEEGILN	BLEEDING
BDDDEEIR	DEBRIDED	BDDGINSU	BUDDINGS	BDEEGILR	BEGIRDLE
BDDDEEMU	BEMUDDED	BDDGINUY	BUDDYING	BDEEGILU	BEGUILED
BDDDEENU	UNBEDDED	BDDGIORS	BIRDDOGS	BDEEGIMR	BEGRIMED
BDDDELOR	BRODDLED	BDDGOOSY	DOGSBODY	BDEEGINR	BERINGED
BDDDENUU	UNBUDDED	BDDHIIRY	DIHYBRID		BREEDING
BDDEEELL	DEBELLED	BDDINOOW	WOODBIND		BREINGED
BDDEEERS	REEDBEDS	BDDINOSU	DISBOUND	BDEEGINW	BEDEWING
BDDEEESS	SEEDBEDS	BDDINPUU	PUDIBUND		BEWINGED
BDDEEFIR	BIRDFEED	BDEEEEMS	BESEEMED	BDEEGINY	BEDYEING
BDDEEFLU	BEFUDDLE	BDEEEEMT	BETEEMED	BDEEGKNU	BEGUNKED
BDDEEGGU	DEBUGGED	BDEEEGIS	BESIEGED	BDEEGLNO	BELONGED
BDDEEGIL	BEGILDED	BDEEEGMM	BEGEMMED		ENGLOBED
BDDEEGIR	BEGIRDED	BDEEEGNO	EDGEBONE	BDEEGMOU	EMBOGUED
BDDEEGNU	BEDUNGED	BDEEEGNR	BREENGED	BDEEGMSU	BESMUDGE
BDDEEGTU	BUDGETED	BDEEEGRU	BUDGEREE	BDEEGOOY	BOOGEYED
BDDEEHOS	DEBOSHED	BDEEEHST	BEDSHEET	BDEEGORU	BEROUGED
BDDEEIMM	BEDIMMED	BDEEEHTU	HEBETUDE	BDEEGRSV	SVEDBERG
BDDEEIMO	EMBODIED	BDEEEILN	BEELINED	BDEEGRTU	BUDGETER
BDDEEINR	REBIDDEN	BDEEEILV	BELIEVED	BDEEGSSU	BUGSEEDS
BDDEEINT	INDEBTED	BDEEEINS	BENISEED	BDEEHISW	DWEEBISH
BDDEEINW	BINDWEED	BDEEEIRW	DWEEBIER	BDEEHLNO	BEHOLDEN
BDDEEIOR	REBODIED	BDEEELLR	REBELLED	BDEEHLOR	BEHOLDER
BDDEEIRR	REEDBIRD	BDEEELLV	BEVELLED	BDEEHLOW	BEHOWLED
BDDEEIRS	BIRDSEED	BDEEELMM	EMBLEMED	BDEEHLSU	BUSHELED
	DEBRIDES	BDEEELPT	BEPELTED	BDEEHMOR	HOMEBRED
BDDEEISS	BEDSIDES	BDEEELRS	BLEEDERS	BDEEHMRY	BERHYMED
BDDEEKNU	DEBUNKED	BDEEELRY	BERLEYED	BDEEHOOV	BEHOOVED
BDDEELMU	BEMUDDLE	BDEEELUW	BLUEWEED	BDEEHORT	BOTHERED
BDDEELNO	BOLDENED	BDEEEMMR	MEMBERED	BDEEHORW	BEWHORED
BDDEENNU	UNBENDED	BDEEEMNS	BEDESMEN	BDEEHOSS	DEBOSHES
BDDEENOT	OBTENDED	BDEEENTT	BENETTED	BDEEIILL	ELIDIBLE
BDDEENRU	BURDENED	BDEEEPSS	BESPEEDS	BDEEIILN	INEDIBLE
BDDEEORR	BORDERED	BDEEERRS	BREEDERS	BDEEIILR	BIELDIER
BDDEEORS	DESORBED		REBREEDS	BDEEIIPT	BEPITIED
BDDEEOSS	DEBOSSED	BDEEERRV	REVERBED	BDEEIKRS	KERBSIDE
BDDEEOTT	BEDOTTED	BDEEERTT	BETTERED	BDEEIKSS	BEKISSED
BDDEERRU	DEBURRED	BDEEERTV	BREVETED	BDEEILLL	LIBELLED
BDDEESSU	DEBUSSED	BDEEETTW	BEWETTED	BDEEILLR	REBILLED
BDDEESTU	BEDUSTED	BDEEFFPU	BEPUFFED	BDEEILLT	BILLETED
BDDEESUW	SUBDEWED	BDEEFFRU	BUFFERED	BDEEILLU	ELUDIBLE

Eight-letter anagrams

BDEEILMO	BEMOILED		REBLENDS	BDEFIORS	FIBROSED
	EMBOILED	BDEELNST	BENDLETS	BDEFOORS	FORBODES
BDEEILMP	BEDIMPLE	BDEELNTU	UNBELTED	BDEFOORY	FOREBODY
BDEEILMR	LIMBERED	BDEELORU	REDOUBLE	BDEGHHIR	HIGHBRED
BDEEILMS	BESLIMED	BDEELOSU	BESOULED	BDEGHILT	BLIGHTED
	BESMILED	BDEELOSV	BELOVEDS	BDEGHIRT	BEDRIGHT
BDEEILNR	LINEBRED	BDEELRTU	BUTLERED	BDEGHIST	BEDIGHTS
	RENDIBLE	BDEELRUY	BURLEYED	BDEGIILN	BIELDING
BDEEILNU	UNEDIBLE	BDEELSST	DEBTLESS	BDEGIINT	BETIDING
BDEEILNV	VENDIBLE	BDEEMNOT	BODEMENT		DEBITING
BDEEILOR	ERODIBLE		ENTOMBED	BDEGILNN	BLENDING
	REBOILED	BDEEMNOW	ENWOMBED	BDEGILNO	INGLOBED
BDEEILOS	OBELISED	BDEEMNRU	NUMBERED	BDEGINNO	DEBONING
BDEEILOT	BETOILED	BDEEMORR	EMBORDER	BDEGINNS	BENDINGS
BDEEILOZ	OBELIZED	BDEEMORS	SOMBERED	BDEGINOS	OBSIGNED
BDEEILRV	BEDRIVEL	BDEEMORW	BEWORMED	BDEGINSU	DEBUSING
BDEEILRW	BEWILDER	BDEEMORY	REEMBODY	BDEGINTU	DEBUTING
BDEEILSV	BEDEVILS	BDEEMOSS	EMBOSSED	BDEGIOST	BODGIEST
BDEEILTT	BETITLED	BDEEMPRU	BUMPERED	BDEGLMRU	GRUMBLED
BDEEIMNR	BRIDEMEN	BDEEMRTU	EMBRUTED	BDEGLNOU	BLUDGEON
BDEEIMOR	EMBODIER	BDEEMSSU	EMBUSSED	BDEGLRSU	BLUDGERS
BDEEIMOS	EMBODIES	BDEENNOT	BONNETED	BDEGNOSW	BEDGOWNS
BDEEIMRT	TIMBERED	BDEENORS	DEBONERS	BDEGOOSY	GOODBYES
BDEEIMST	BEDTIMES		REDBONES	BDEGORRY	DOGBERRY
	BEMISTED	BDEENOSW	BESNOWED	BDEGORSU	BUDGEROS
BDEEIMSU	EMBUSIED	BDEENOUV	UNOBEYED	BDEGORUW	BUDGEROW
BDEEINOS	EBONISED	BDEENPRS	PREBENDS	BDEHIKOS	KIBOSHED
BDEEINOT	OBEDIENT	BDEENRRU	BURDENER	BDEHILMT	THIMBLED
BDEEINOZ	EBONIZED	BDEENSUV	SUBVENED	BDEHIOPS	BISHOPED
BDEEINRS	INBREEDS	BDEEOORT	REBOOTED	BDEHKOSY	KYBOSHED
BDEEINRT	INTERBED	BDEEOPRR	REPROBED	BDEHLMOW	WHOMBLED
BDEEINST	BENDIEST	BDEEOPRS	BEPROSED	BDEHLSUV	BUSHVELD
BDEEINSW	BENDWISE	BDEEOPRW	BEPOWDER	BDEHMOOY	HOMEBODY
BDEEINSZ	BEDIZENS	BDEEORRR	BORDERER	BDEHOOOO	BOOHOOED
BDEEIORS	REBODIES	BDEEORRS	RESORBED	BDEHORSU	BESHROUD
BDEEIORU	BOUDERIE	BDEEORRV	OVERBRED	BDEHORSY	HERDBOYS
BDEEIRRU	REBURIED	BDEEORSS	BEDSORES	BDEIIIKN	BIKINIED
BDEEIRRV	RIVERBED	BDEEORST	BESORTED	BDEIIKLR	BIRDLIKE
BDEEIRST	BESTRIDE		BESTRODE	BDEIIKTZ	KIBITZED
	BISTERED	BDEEORSV	OBSERVED	BDEIILMR	BIRDLIME
BDEEIRSU	DEBRUISE	BDEEORTU	OUTBREED	BDEIILNY	INEDIBLY
BDEEIRSY	BIRDSEYE	BDEEORTV	OBVERTED	BDEIILRU	BLUIDIER
BDEEIRTT	BITTERED	BDEEOSSS	DEBOSSES	BDEIILTY	DEBILITY
BDEEISTU	BESUITED		OBSESSED	BDEIIMOS	IMBODIES
BDEEKMOS	BESMOKED	BDEEOSST	BETOSSED	BDEIINNZ	BENZIDIN
	EMBOSKED	BDEEOSTT	BESOTTED	BDEIIOPS	BIOPSIED
BDEEKNRU	BUNKERED		OBTESTED	BDEIKMOS	IMBOSKED
	DEBUNKER	BDEEOSTW	BESTOWED	BDEIKNOR	BRODEKIN
BDEEKOOR	REBOOKED	BDEEPRRU	PUREBRED	BDEIKNSU	BUSKINED
BDEEKORR	BROKERED	BDEERRTU	TRUEBRED	BDEILLMU	BDELLIUM
BDEELLMU	UMBELLED	BDEERRWY	DEWBERRY	BDEILLNU	UNBILLED
BDEELLOW	BELLOWED	BDEERSSU	BURSEEDS	BDEILLNW	WINDBELL
	BOWELLED	BDEERSUW	BURWEEDS	BDEILLOW	BILLOWED
BDEELLRU	BULLERED	BDEERTTU	BUTTERED	BDEILLOX	BOLLIXED
BDEELLRY	REDBELLY		REBUTTED	BDEILMNO	IMBOLDEN
BDEELLTU	BULLETED	BDEESSSU	DEBUSSES	BDEILMOS	SEMIBOLD
BDEELLUW	BULLWEED	BDEFIILR	BIRDLIFE	BDEILMSU	SUBLIMED
BDEELMNO	EMBOLDEN	BDEFIIRR	FIREBIRD	BDEILNNO	BLONDINE
BDEELMOR	REBELDOM	BDEFIIRU	RUBIFIED	BDEILNOU	UNBOILED
BDEELMPU	BEPLUMED	BDEFIKOR	BIFORKED		UNILOBED
BDEELMRT	TREMBLED	BDEFILRS	FILBERDS	BDEILNOY	BODYLINE
BDEELMRU	LUMBERED	BDEFILSU	SUBFIELD	BDEILNRS	BLINDERS
BDEELNNO	ENNOBLED	BDEFIMOR	BIFORMED		BRINDLES
BDEELNRS	BLENDERS	BDEFINRR	FERNBIRD	BDEILNRU	UNBRIDLE

BDEILNST	BLINDEST	BDEKNOOU	UNBOOKED	BDEOPSST	BEDPOSTS
BDEILNVY	VENDIBLY	BDELLOOR	BORDELLO	BDEOPSTU	SUBDEPOT
BDEILOOR	BLOODIER		DOORBELL	BDEORRSU	BORDURES
BDEILOOS	BLOODIES	BDELLOOX	BOLLOXED		BOURDERS
BDEILOPU	UPBOILED	BDELLORS	BEDROLLS		SUBORDER
BDEILOQU	OBLIQUED	BDELLOUZ	BULLDOZE	BDEORRTU	OBTRUDER
BDEILORT	TRILOBED	BDELMOOS	BLOOSMED	BDEORRUW	BURROWED
BDEILORV	LOVEBIRD	BDELMOSY	SYMBOLED	BDEORSSU	ROSEBUDS
BDEILOSS	BODILESS	BDELMRSU	DRUMBLES	BDEORSTU	DOUBTERS
BDEILOSW	DISBOWEL	BDELMRUU	DELUBRUM		OBTRUDES
BDEILPRU	PREBUILD	BDELMSTU	STUMBLED		REDOUBTS
BDEILQTU	BEDQUILT	BDELNNOU	UNNOBLED	BDEORSUV	OVERDUBS
BDEILRRS	BRIDLERS	BDELNNUU	UNBUNDLE	BDERSSUU	SUBDUERS
BDEILRRY	LYREBIRD	BDELNOOS	DOBLONES	BDERSTUU	SUBTRUDE
BDEILRST	BRISTLED	BDELNOSS	BOLDNESS	BDFFIPRU	PUFFBIRD
	DRIBLETS		BONDLESS	BDFGNOOU	FOGBOUND
BDEILRSU	BUILDERS	BDELNOST	BLONDEST	BDFIIITY	BIFIDITY
	REBUILDS	BDELNOTU	UNBOLTED	BDFIIORS	FIBROIDS
BDEILRTT	BRITTLED	BDELNOUU	UNDOUBLE	BDFILLLO	BILLFOLD
BDEILSST	BILSTEDS	BDELNOUW	UNBLOWED	BDFILNOO	BLOODFIN
BDEILSTU	BLUDIEST	BDELNRSU	BLUNDERS	BDFILSUU	SUBFLUID
BDEIMNOT	INTOMBED		BUNDLERS	BDFINORU	UNFORBID
BDEIMNSU	NIMBUSED	BDELOORS	BOODLERS	BDFINRUU	FURIBUND
BDEIMNUU	UNIMBUED	BDELOORV	OVERBOLD	BDFIRRSU	SURFBIRD
BDEIMORR	IMBORDER	BDELOOUW	BLUEWOOD	BDFLOTUU	DOUBTFUL
	MORBIDER	BDELORSU	BOULDERS	BDFORSUY	BODYSURF
BDEIMORS	BROMIDES		DOUBLERS	BDGGIINR	BRIDGING
	BROMISED	BDELORSW	BOWLDERS	BDGGILNU	BLUDGING
BDEIMORY	EMBRYOID	BDELORTU	TROUBLED	BDGGLOSU	GOLDBUGS
BDEIMORZ	BROMIZED	BDELORUU	DOUBLURE	BDGHOOUY	DOUGHBOY
BDEIMOSS	IMBOSSED	BDELORUY	BOULDERY	BDGIIKNR	KINGBIRD
BDEIMRSU	IMBURSED	BDELOSTU	DOUBLETS	BDGIILNN	BLINDING
BDEIMRTU	IMBRUTED	BDELPSUU	SUBDUPLE	BDGIILNR	BRIDLING
BDEINOOS	NOBODIES	BDEMNNOS	BONDSMEN	BDGIILNU	BUILDING
BDEINOOW	WOODBINE	BDEMNOSU	EMBOUNDS	BDGIINNS	BINDINGS
BDEINORV	OVENBIRD	BDEMNOTU	UNTOMBED	BDGIINRS	BIRDINGS
BDEINOSU	BEDOUINS	BDEMNSSU	DUMBNESS	BDGIINRW	BIRDWING
BDEINOTU	BOUNTIED	BDEMOORS	BEDROOMS	BDGIIOOS	GOBIOIDS
BDEINPRS	PREBINDS		BOREDOMS	BDGILNNO	BLONDING
BDEINRSU	BURNSIDE	BDEMOOSY	SOMEBODY	BDGILNNU	BUNDLING
BDEINRTU	TURBINED	BDEMOOTT	BOTTOMED	BDGILNOO	BLOODING
	UNDERBIT	BDEMSSUU	SUBSUMED		BOODLING
BDEINRUU	UNBURIED	BDENNOTU	DUBONNET	BDGILNOU	DOUBLING
BDEINSUX	SUBINDEX	BDENNOUY	YBOUNDEN	BDGILNOY	BODINGLY
BDEINTTU	UNBITTED	BDENNRUU	UNBURDEN	BDGILNTU	BLINDGUT
BDEIOORR	BROODIER		UNBURNED	BDGILOOS	GLOBOIDS
BDEIORRS	BROIDERS	BDENOORU	EUROBOND	BDGINNOS	BONDINGS
	DISROBER	BDENOOTU	UNBOOTED	BDGINNOU	BOUNDING
BDEIORRU	BOURRIDE	BDENOOTW	BENTWOOD		UNBODING
BDEIORRY	BROIDERY	BDENOPRU	PREBOUND	BDGINNUY	BUNDYING
BDEIORSS	DISROBES		UNPROBED	BDGINOOR	BROODING
BDEIORST	DEBITORS	BDENORSU	BOUNDERS	BDGINOOY	BOODYING
	DEORBITS		REBOUNDS	BDGINORS	BIRDSONG
BDEIORSV	OVERBIDS		SUBORNED		SONGBIRD
BDEIORTU	TUBEROID	BDENOTTU	BUTTONED	BDGINORU	OBDURING
BDEIOSSY	DISOBEYS	BDENRSTU	SUBTREND	BDGINOTU	DOUBTING
BDEIOSUX	SUBOXIDE	BDENRSUU	UNBRUSED	BDGINSUU	SUBDUING
BDEIRSSU	DISBURSE	BDENSSTU	SUBTENDS	BDGLLOSU	BULLDOGS
	SUBSIDER	BDENSTUU	UNBUSTED	BDGLOOST	DOGBOLTS
BDEISSSU	SUBSIDES	BDEOORRS	BROODERS	BDGNRUUY	BURGUNDY
BDEISSTU	SUBEDITS	BDEOORRW	BORROWED	BDGOOOSW	BOGWOODS
BDEKLLUV	BULLDYKE	BDEOORTU	OUTBOXED	BDHIIPRW	WHIPBIRD
BDEKLMOO	BLOKEDOM	BDEOOTUX	OUTBOXED	BDHILNOS	BLONDISH
BDEKNOOS	BOOKENDS	BDEOOWWW	BOWWOWED	BDHIMOOR	RHOMBOID

BDHIMORT	BIRTHDOM	BDLNOOUY	UNBLOODY	BEEEELPRS	BLEEPERS
BDHIMSTU	DUMBSHIT	BDLNOOWW	BLOWDOWN	BEEELRST	BEETLERS
BDHIMSUU	SUBHUMID	BDLOOOSX	OXBLOODS	BEEELRSV	BEVELERS
BDHINOPS	HOPBINDS	BDLORSUW	SUBWORLD	BEEEMMRR	REMEMBER
BDHIOPRST	BIRDSHOT	BDMOORRS	SMORBROD	BEEEMNSU	UNBESEEM
BDHIOSSU	BUSHIDOS	BDMOOSSS	BOSSDOMS	BEEEMRSS	BERSEEMS
BDHLOOOT	HOTBLOOD	BDMORSUW	BUDWORMS	BEEENNSZ	BENZENES
BDHMOOOS	HOBODOMS	BDNNOOTU	BUNODONT	BEEENNSST	SEBESTEN
BDHNNRSUU	UNSHRUBD	BDNOOPTU	POTBOUND	BEEENSTW	BETWEENS
BDHOOOSY	BOYHOODS	BDNOORSU	BOURDONS	BEEEPPPR	BEPEPPER
BDIIINRS	BRINDISI	BDNOOSUX	SOUNDBOX	BEEEPRST	BEPESTER
BDIIIORV	VIBRIOID	BDNOOSWW	DOWNBOWS	BEEERRST	BRETESSE
BDIIKNOS	BODIKINS	BDNOOTUU	OUTBOUND	BEEERSTT	BESETTER
BDIILLNW	WINDBILL	BDNORSTU	TURBONDS	BEEESSST	TSESSEBE
BDIILMSS	DISLIMBS	BDNORSUW	RUBDOWNS	BEEFFLMU	BEMUFFLE
BDIILMSU	MISBUILD	BDOOOSWX	BOXWOODS	BEEFFRTU	BUFFETER
BDIILOOS	BIOSOLID	BDORUWZZ	BUZZWORD	BEEFGILN	FEEBLING
BDIILOQU	OBLIQUID	BEEEEFLN	ENFEEBLE	BEEFGINR	BEFINGER
BDIILORS	OILBIRDS	BEEEEFRS	FREEBEES		BEFRINGE
BDIIMNSS	MISBINDS	BEEEEKSS	BESEEKES	BEEFHILS	FEEBLISH
BDIIMRUU	RUBIDIUM	BEEEEMST	BETEEMES	BEEFIIRS	FIBERISE
BDIKNORS	BRODKINS	BEEEENPS	PEEBEENS	BEEFIIRZ	FIBERIZE
BDILLOOY	BLOODILY	BEEEENRT	TEREBENE	BEEFILLT	LIFEBELT
BDILMORY	MORBIDLY	BEEEENRZ	EBENEZER	BEEFILLX	FLEXIBLE
BDILNNSU	SUNBLIND	BEEEFIRS	FREEBIES	BEEFILNU	UNBELIEF
	UNBLINDS	BEEEFIST	BEEFIEST	BEEFILRS	BELFRIES
BDILNOOO	DIOBOLON	BEEEFLSS	BEEFLESS	BEEFINST	BENEFITS
BDILNOWW	WINDBLOW		FEBLESSE	BEEFIRRS	BRIEFERS
BDILNPRU	PURBLIND	BEEEFLST	FEEBLEST	BEEFIRSS	FRISBEES
BDILNSUU	UNBUILDS	BEEEGILN	BELEEING	BEEFIRST	BRIEFEST
BDILOORY	BROODILY	BEEEGINS	BESEEING	BEEFIRSU	RUBEFIES
BDILOPRY	POLYBRID	BEEEGIRS	BESIEGER	BEEFLORU	BEFOULER
BDILOTUU	OUTBUILD	BEEEGISS	BESIEGES	BEEFLORW	BEFLOWER
BDILPSUU	BUILDUPS	BEEEGKLS	GEELBEKS	BEEFNORR	FREEBORN
	UPBUILDS	BEEEGNRS	BREENGES	BEEFNRTU	UNBEREFT
BDILRTUY	TURBIDLY	BEEEGORS	GREEBOES	BEEFOORT	FREEBOOT
BDIMNORU	MORIBUND	BEEEGRRS	BERGERES	BEEGGNRU	GREENBUG
BDIMNOSU	MISBOUND	BEEEGRTT	BEGETTER	BEEGGNSU	GEEBUNGS
BDIMNPSU	DUMPBINS	BEEEHIST	BHEESTIE	BEEGHLMR	BERGMEHL
BDIMNSUU	DUBNIUMS	BEEEHISV	BEEHIVES	BEEGIILL	ELIGIBLE
BDIMOOSS	DISBOSOM	BEEEHLRT	HERBELET	BEEGIILX	EXIGIBLE
BDIMOSTU	MISDOUBT	BEEEHLWW	WEBWHEEL	BEEGILLR	GERBILLE
BDINNOSU	INBOUNDS	BEEEHNOY	HONEYBEE	BEEGILMN	BEMINGLE
BDINNRUW	WINDBURN	BEEEHNSS	SHEBEENS	BEEGILNP	BLEEPING
BDINOORS	BRIDOONS	BEEEILLL	LIBELLEE	BEEGILNT	BEETLING
BDINOOSW	WOODBINS	BEEEILLS	LIBELEES	BEEGILNV	BEVELING
BDINORSW	SNOWBIRD	BEEEILLT	BILLETEE	BEEGILOS	OBLIGEES
BDINRSSU	SUNBIRDS	BEEEILNS	BEELINES	BEEGILRU	BEGUILER
BDINRTUU	UNTURBID	BEEEILRV	BELIEVER	BEEGILSU	BEGUILES
BDINSSTU	BUNDISTS	BEEEILSV	BELIEVES	BEEGIMNT	BEMETING
	DUSTBINS	BEEEINST	EBENISTE	BEEGIMRS	BEGRIMES
BDIOORSU	BOUDOIRS	BEEEIRRZ	BREEZIER	BEEGINNR	BEGINNER
BDIOORTY	BOTRYOID	BEEEIRST	BEERIEST		BENIGNER
BDIORSSW	WOSBIRDS	BEEEJLSW	BEJEWELS	BEEGINNS	BEGINNES
BDIORUZZ	BURDIZZO	BEEEJLSZ	JEZEBELS	BEEGINRR	BREERING
BDIOSTUY	BODYSUIT	BEEEJSUZ	BEJEEZUS	BEEGINRS	BIGENERS
BDIRSSTU	DISTURBS	BEEEKLLS	BELLEEKS		BREINGES
BDKNOOOR	DOORKNOB	BEEELLRR	REBELLER		REBEGINS
BDKNOOSU	BUNDOOKS	BEEELLRT	BELLETER	BEEGINRZ	BREEZING
BDKOOORW	WORDBOOK	BEEELLRV	BEVELLER	BEEGINST	BEIGNETS
BDKOORWY	BODYWORK	BEEELMNS	ENSEMBLE	BEEGINSU	BEGUINES
BDKOOSTU	STUDBOOK	BEEELMRS	RESEMBLE	BEEGINSW	BEESWING
BDLLSTUU	BULLDUST	BEEELMSY	BESEEMLY	BEEGKLUY	KEYBUGLE
BDLNOOOU	DOUBLOON	BEEELMZZ	EMBEZZLE	BEEGLNOR	BELONGER

BEEGLNOS	ENGLOBES
BEEGMNOS	GOMBEENS
BEEGMNOY	BOGEYMEN
BEEGMOSU	EMBOGUES
BEEGMRSU	SUBMERGE
BEEGNOOW	WOBEGONE
BEEGNOTT	BEGOTTEN
BEEGNRSU	SUBGENRE
	SUNGREBE
BEEGNSTU	UNBEGETS
BEEGOOPR	GEOPROBE
BEEGOPSX	PEGBOXES
BEEHHMOT	BEHEMOTH
BEEHIKLR	HERBLIKE
BEEHIMOT	BOEHMITE
BEEHINSS	BESHINES
	NEBISHES
BEEHIRST	HERBIEST
BEEHIRSV	BESHIVER
BEEHISST	BHISTEES
BEEHKSSU	BUKSHEES
BEEHLLNT	HELLBENT
BEEHLOOR	BOREHOLE
BEEHLOVY	BEHOVELY
BEEHLRSS	HERBLESS
BEEHLRST	BLETHERS
	HERBLETS
BEEHLRSU	BUSHELER
BEEHMORW	HOMEBREW
BEEHMRSY	BERHYMES
BEEHMSTU	SUBTHEME
BEEHNNOS	HEBENONS
BEEHNOOP	NEOPHOBE
BEEHNRRT	BRETHREN
BEEHOOST	BESOOTHE
BEEHOOSV	BEHOOVES
BEEHORSW	BEWHORES
BEEHRRST	SHERBERT
BEEHRSST	SHERBETS
BEEHRSSW	BESHREWS
BEEIILNZ	ZIBELINE
BEEIINOS	EBIONISE
BEEIINOZ	EBIONIZE
BEEIINRT	BENITIER
BEEIIORS	BOISERIE
BEEIIPST	BEPITIES
BEEIIRRR	BRIERIER
BEEIIRSS	IBERISES
BEEIISTU	UBIETIES
BEEIISTZ	BITESIZE
BEEIJLSU	JUBILEES
BEEIJORT	BOERTJIE
BEEIJSTU	BEJESUIT
BEEIKKRS	BREKKIES
BEEIKLNY	EYEBLINK
BEEIKLTU	TUBELIKE
BEEIKLWY	BIWEEKLY
BEEIKORS	BROEKIES
BEEIKSSS	BEKISSES
BEEILLLR	LIBELLER
BEEILLNO	LOBELINE
BEEILLNT	BELTLINE
BEEILLNU	BLUELINE
BEEILLRS	LIBELERS
BEEILLRT	BILLETER
BEEILLSV	BILEVELS
BEEILLTT	BELITTLE
BEEILLTU	TULLIBEE
BEEILMOS	EMBOLIES
	EMBOLISE
BEEILMOZ	EMBOLIZE
BEEILMPP	BEPIMPLE
BEEILMPR	PERIBLEM
BEEILMPS	EPIBLEMS
BEEILMRR	LIMBERER
BEEILMSS	BESLIMES
	BESMILES
BEEILNNS	BLENNIES
BEEILNRS	BERLINES
BEEILNRY	BERYLINE
BEEILNSS	SENSIBLE
BEEILNST	STILBENE
	TENSIBLE
BEEILNSU	NEBULISE
BEEILNUZ	NEBULIZE
BEEILORS	EROSIBLE
BEEILOSS	OBELISES
BEEILOSZ	OBELIZES
BEEILOTV	LOVEBITE
BEEILRRT	TERRIBLE
BEEILRSU	BLUESIER
BEEILRSV	VERBILES
BEEILRYZ	BREEZILY
BEEILSTT	BETITLES
BEEIMORT	BIOMETER
BEEIMRRU	UMBRIERE
BEEIMRST	BIMESTER
BEEIMRTT	EMBITTER
BEEIMSSU	EMBUSIES
BEEINNSS	BEINNESS
BEEINNSZ	BENZINES
BEEINORT	TENEBRIO
BEEINOSS	EBONISES
BEEINOST	BETONIES
	EBONITES
BEEINOSZ	EBONIZES
BEEINPRS	PEBRINES
BEEINRSS	NEBRISES
BEEINRSZ	ZEBRINES
BEEINRTT	REBITTEN
BEEINSTT	BENTIEST
BEEIOQSU	OBSEQUIE
BEEIORSS	SOBERISE
BEEIORSW	BOWERIES
BEEIORSZ	SOBERIZE
BEEIORTV	OVERBITE
BEEIQSUZ	BEZIQUES
BEEIRRSU	REBURIES
BEEIRRSV	BREVIERS
BEEIRRTT	BITTERER
BEEIRSSU	SUBERISE
BEEIRSSV	BREVISES
BEEIRSSW	BREWISES
BEEIRSTU	UBERTIES
BEEIRSUZ	SUBERIZE
BEEISSTW	WEBSITES
BEEKMOPR	PEMBROKE
BEEKMOSS	BESMOKES
BEEKNOPS	BESPOKEN
BEEKNOST	BETOKENS
	STEENBOK
BEEKRRSS	BERSERKS
BEEKRRSU	REBUKERS
BEELLMTU	UMBELLET
BEELLORW	BELLOWER
	REBELLOW
BEELLOST	LOBELETS
BEELLSST	BELTLESS
BEELLSUV	SUBLEVEL
BEELMMOP	BEPOMMEL
BEELMNNO	NOBLEMEN
BEELMNSU	BLUESMEN
BEELMOSW	EMBOWELS
BEELMRRT	TREMBLER
BEELMRRU	LUMBERER
BEELMRST	TREMBLES
BEELMSTU	BLUESTEM
BEELMUZZ	BEMUZZLE
BEELNNOR	ENNOBLER
BEELNNOS	ENNOBLES
BEELNOSS	BONELESS
	NOBLESSE
BEELNOSU	BLUENOSE
	NEBULOSE
BEELNOSZ	BENZOLES
BEELNSSU	BLUENESS
BEELNTTU	BETELNUT
BEELNTUY	BUTYLENE
BEELOOST	OBSOLETE
BEELOQRU	BRELOQUE
BEELORTT	REBOTTLE
BEELORVW	OVERBLEW
BEELOSTW	STEELBOW
BEELOSTY	EYEBOLTS
BEELPRSS	PREBLESS
BEELPRUV	BUPLEVER
BEELRSSS	BLESSERS
BEELRSSV	VERBLESS
BEELRSUZ	ZEBRULES
BEELRTUU	TRUEBLUE
BEELSSTU	TUBELESS
BEELSTTU	BLUETTES
BEEMNRRU	NUMBERER
	RENUMBER
BEEMOORS	BORESOME
BEEMOPRT	OBTEMPER
BEEMORRS	SOMBERER
BEEMORSS	EMBOSSER
BEEMORSW	EMBOWERS
BEEMOSSS	EMBOSSES
BEEMQSUU	EMBUSQUE
BEEMRRSU	UMBRERES
BEEMRSSU	SUBMERSE
BEEMRSTU	EMBRUTES
BEEMRTTU	UMBRETTE
BEEMRTUZ	ZERUMBET
BEEMSSSU	EMBUSSES
BEENNOOS	NONOBESE
BEENNOOT	BOTONNEE
BEENOPTY	TEENYBOP
BEENORRS	ENROBERS
BEENORTU	BOUNTREE

Eight-letter anagrams

BEENORTV	VERBOTEN	BEFILNSU	BLUEFINS	BEGIINTW	BITEWING
BEENOSST	BONESETS	BEFILOST	BOTFLIES	BEGIIOSS	SIGISBEO
BEENOSTU	TUBENOSE	BEFILOSU	BIOFUELS	BEGIKMNO	KEMBOING
BEENOSTY	BONEYEST	BEFILOUY	LIFEBUOY	BEGIKNRS	KERBINGS
BEENPRST	BESPRENT	BEFILRST	FILBERTS	BEGIKNRU	REBUKING
BEENRSTT	BRENTEST	BEFILSSU	SUBFILES	BEGILLLU	BLUEGILL
BEENRSTW	BESTREWN	BEFINORS	BONFIRES		GULLIBLE
BEENRTTU	BRUNETTE	BEFIOOST	BOOFIEST	BEGILLNS	BELLINGS
BEENSSSU	SUBSENSE	BEFIORSS	FIBROSES	BEGILLNU	BULLGINE
BEENSSTU	SUBTEENS	BEFIORTT	FOREBITT	BEGILLNY	BELLYING
	SUBTENSE	BEFIRSST	FIBSTERS	BEGILMNR	REMBLING
BEENSSUV	SUBVENES	BEFISSTU	FUBSIEST	BEGILMNS	SEMBLING
BEEOORRT	BOORTREE	BEFISSUX	SUBFIXES	BEGILNNY	BENIGNLY
BEEOORRV	OVERBORE	BEFLLLUY	BELLYFUL	BEGILNOR	IGNOBLER
BEEOORTT	BEETROOT	BEFLLSTY	FLYBELTS	BEGILNOS	INGLOBES
BEEOPRRS	REPROBES	BEFLMRSU	FUMBLERS	BEGILNOV	BELOVING
BEEOPRSS	BEPROSES	BEFLORUW	FURBELOW	BEGILNOW	BOWELING
BEEOPSSU	BESPOUSE	BEFLSTUU	TUBEFULS		ELBOWING
BEEORRSU	BOURREES	BEFMOOOR	FOREBOOM	BEGILNRT	TREBLING
BEEORRSV	OBSERVER	BEFNOORR	FORBORNE	BEGILNSS	BLESSING
	VERBOSER	BEFNOSSY	FYNBOSES		GLIBNESS
BEEORRTU	BOURTREE	BEFORRXY	FOXBERRY	BEGILNST	BELTINGS
BEEORSST	SOBEREST	BEGGGINS	BEGGINGS		BLINGEST
BEEORSSU	SUBEROSE	BEGGIINN	BINGEING	BEGILNSU	BLUEINGS
BEEORSSV	OBSERVES	BEGGIINO	BOGIEING		BULGINES
	OBVERSES	BEGGILRU	BLUGGIER	BEGILNTT	BLETTING
BEEORSTU	TUBEROSE	BEGGINOY	BOGEYING	BEGILNUW	BLUEWING
BEEORSTV	OVERBETS	BEGGIOST	BOGGIEST	BEGILNZZ	BEZZLING
BEEORSTW	BESTOWER	BEGGISTU	BUGGIEST	BEGILORS	OBLIGERS
BEEORSWY	EYEBROWS	BEGGLORS	BLOGGERS	BEGILRST	GILBERTS
BEEOSSSS	OBSESSES		BOGGLERS	BEGILSTU	BULGIEST
BEEOSSST	BETOSSES	BEGGOOOS	GOOSEGOB	BEGIMNOS	BESOMING
BEEPPRSU	PREPUBES	BEGHHIST	BEHIGHTS	BEGIMNOW	EMBOWING
BEEPRRSU	SUPERBER	BEGHIILP	PHILBEG	BEGIMNOX	EMBOXING
BEEPRRSV	PREVERBS	BEGHIKNT	BEKNIGHT	BEGIMNRU	EMBRUING
BEEPRSTY	PRESBYTE	BEGHILRT	BLIGHTER		UMBERING
BEEQSSTU	BEQUESTS		THERBLIG	BEGIMNSU	BEMUSING
BEERRSTW	BREWSTER	BEGHINOR	NEIGHBOR		EMBUSING
BEERRTTU	REBUTTER	BEGHINOT	BEHOTING		MISBEGUN
BEERSSSU	SUBSERES	BEGHINOV	BEHOVING	BEGIMOST	MISBEGOT
BEERSSTW	BESTREWS	BEGHINRT	BERTHING	BEGIMOSY	BOGEYISM
	WEBSTERS		BRIGHTEN	BEGINNNO	NONBEING
BEERSSUV	SUBSERVE	BEGHINST	BENIGHTS	BEGINNNR	BRENNING
	SUBVERSE	BEGHIOST	GOBSHITE	BEGINNNU	UNBENIGN
BEERSTTU	BURETTES	BEGHIRRT	BRIGHTER	BEGINNOR	ENROBING
BEERSTTY	BYSTREET	BEGHLNOU	BUNGHOLE		RINGBONE
BEESTTUV	BUVETTES	BEGHNOTU	BOUGHTEN	BEGINNSU	UNBEINGS
BEFFISTU	BUFFIEST	BEGHORTU	REBOUGHT	BEGINOOS	BESOGNIO
BEFFLRSU	BLUFFERS	BEGHOSTU	BESOUGHT	BEGINORR	REBORING
BEFFLSTU	BLUFFEST	BEGHOSUU	BUGHOUSE	BEGINORS	SOBERING
BEFGIILL	FILLIBEG	BEGHRRSU	BURGHERS	BEGINORW	BOWERING
BEFGIILS	FILIBEGS	BEGIIISS	SIGISBEI	BEGINRRS	BRINGERS
BEFGIINR	BRIEFING	BEGIILLN	LIBELING	BEGINRRY	BERRYING
BEFGILNU	FUNGIBLE	BEGIILLY	ELIGIBLY	BEGINRSV	VERBINGS
BEFGIRSU	FIREBUGS	BEGIILST	BILGIEST	BEGINRSW	BREWINGS
BEFHILSU	BLUEFISH	BEGIIMNR	BEMIRING	BEGINRUY	REBUYING
BEFHINOS	BONEFISH		BERIMING	BEGINSTT	BETTINGS
	FISHBONE	BEGIIMNS	MISBEGIN	BEGINVVY	BEVVYING
BEFHIRSU	BUSHFIRE	BEGIIMNT	BETIMING	BEGKMOSS	GEMSBOKS
	FIREBUSH	BEGIIMNX	BEMIXING	BEGLLORY	GORBELLY
BEFIIRSU	RUBIFIES	BEGIIMNY	BIGEMINY	BEGLLOSU	GLOBULES
BEFILLXY	FLEXIBLY	BEGIINNS	INBEINGS	BEGLLOTU	GLOBULET
BEFILMOR	FORELIMB	BEGIINRT	REBITING	BEGLMOOS	BEGLOOMS
BEFILNOS	LOBEFINS	BEGIINRZ	ZINGIBER	BEGLMRRU	GRUMBLER

BEGLMRSU	GRUMBLES	BEHLOOPY	HYPOBOLE	BEIIRSST	BIRSIEST
BEGLMSUU	BLUEGUMS		LYOPHOBE	BEIIISSTT	BITSIEST
BEGLNOUW	BLUEGOWN	BEHLOOST	BOTHOLES	BEIISSTU	SUBITISE
BEGLNRSU	BLUNGERS	BEHLORST	BROTHELS	BEIISTTT	BITTIEST
	BUNGLERS	BEHLOSSU	SLOEBUSH	BEIISTUZ	SUBITIZE
BEGLOOSS	GLOBOSES	BEHLRRSU	BURRHELS	BEIJLMRU	JUMBLIER
BEGLOOST	BOOTLEGS	BEHLRSSU	BLUSHERS	BEIJMOSU	JUMBOISE
BEGLOSUV	LOVEBUGS	BEHLSSSU	BUSHLESS	BEIJMOUZ	JUMBOIZE
BEGLOTUU	OUTBULGE	BEHLSSTU	BLUSHETS	BEIJNORW	BIJWONER
BEGLRSTY	BERGYLTS	BEHMNOTY	BOTHYMEN	BEIKKLNO	KNOBLIKE
BEGMNOOY	BOOGYMEN	BEHMOOOX	HOMEOBOX	BEIKLLOT	BOLTLIKE
BEGNOORU	BOURGEON	BEHMOOST	BESMOOTH	BEIKLLOW	BOWLLIKE
BEGNORSU	BURGEONS	BEHMOOSY	HOMEBOYS	BEIKLMOT	TOMBLIKE
BEGNORTU	BURGONET	BEHMOSTU	BEMOUTHS	BEIKLMOW	WOMBLIKE
BEGNOSTT	BETTONGS	BEHMPSTU	BETHUMPS	BEIKLNRS	BLINKERS
BEGNSSUU	SUBGENUS	BEHNNOST	BENTHONS	BEIKLOSS	OBELISKS
BEGORRUY	BROGUERY	BEHNNOUY	HONEYBUN	BEIKLOST	BLOKIEST
BEGPRSUU	SUPERBUG	BEHNORST	BETHORNS	BEIKLOTY	KILOBYTE
BEHHKOST	KHOTBEHS	BEHNRSTU	BURTHENS	BEIKLRUY	RUBYLIKE
BEHIISST	BHISTIES	BEHOOOPZ	ZOOPHOBE	BEIKLSTU	BULKIEST
BEHIISTX	EXHIBITS	BEHOOOST	BOOTHOSE	BEIKMNNR	BRINKMEN
BEHIKLOS	BLOKEISH	BEHOORST	THEORBOS	BEIKNOST	STEINBOK
BEHIKLSU	BUSHLIKE	BEHOORSX	HORSEBOX	BEIKNNRY	INKBERRY
BEHIKNST	BETHINKS	BEHOOSTX	HOTBOXES	BEIKNRSS	BRISKENS
BEHIKOSS	KIBOSHES	BEHOOSUY	HOUSEBOY	BEIKOORS	BOOKSIER
BEHILLOS	SHOEBILL	BEHOPRST	POTHERBS		BROOKIES
BEHILLTY	BLITHELY	BEHORRST	BROTHERS	BEIKOORT	BROOKITE
BEHILMRW	WHIMBREL	BEHORSSU	ROSEBUSH	BEIKOOST	BOOKIEST
BEHILMST	THIMBLES	BEHORSTT	BETROTHS	BEIKORST	REITBOKS
BEHILMTV	BIMETHYL	BEHOSSTU	BESHOUTS	BEIKOSST	BOSKIEST
BEHILNPY	BIPHENYL	BEHRRSSU	BRUSHERS	BEIKRSST	BRISKEST
BEHILORR	HORRIBLE	BEHRSTTU	TURBETHS		BRISKETS
BEHILORS	BOLSHIER	BEIIIKMN	MINIBIKE	BEIKRSSW	BREWSKIS
BEHILOSS	BOLSHIES	BEIIKRST	BIRKIEST	BEIKRSTU	BURKITES
BEHILRST	BLITHERS	BEIIKRTZ	KIBITZER	BEILLMRY	LIMBERLY
BEHILRTU	THURIBLE	BEIIKSTZ	KIBITZES	BEILLMSS	LIMBLESS
BEHILSTT	BLITHEST	BEIILLST	LIBELIST	BEILLMSU	SEMIBULL
BEHIMNOO	BONHOMIE	BEIILMMO	IMMOBILE	BEILLNTU	BULLETIN
BEHIMOOS	SEMIHOBO	BEIILMOS	MOBILISE	BEILLORS	BROLLIES
BEHIMORS	BIOHERMS	BEIILMOZ	MOBILIZE	BEILLORV	OVERBILL
BEHIMOSY	YOHIMBES	BEIILMST	LIMBIEST	BEILLOSU	LIBELOUS
BEHIMRTU	THUMBIER	BEIILMSU	BULIMIES	BEILLOSX	BOLLIXES
BEHINNOS	SHINBONE	BEIILNRS	RINSIBLE	BEILLPRS	PREBILLS
BEHINOPS	HIPBONES	BEIILOPR	PERIBOLI	BEILLRST	BRILLEST
	HOPBINES	BEIILRSS	RISIBLES	BEILLSST	BESTILLS
BEHINOSW	WISHBONE	BEIILRST	TRILBIES	BEILLSTU	BULLIEST
BEHIOOPR	BIOPHORE	BEIILRTT	LIBRETTI	BEILMMOS	EMBOLISM
BEHIPRRT	PREBIRTH	BEIILRUZ	BRUILZIE	BEILMNOR	BROMELIN
BEHIRRST	REBIRTHS	BEIILSSV	VISIBLES	BEILMNOU	NOBELIUM
BEHIRRSU	BRUSHIER	BEIILSTT	STILBITE	BEILMNRU	UNLIMBER
BEHIRSST	HERBISTS	BEIIMNNR	RENMINBI	BEILMNST	NIMBLEST
BEHIRSSU	HUBRISES	BEIIMNNU	BIENNIUM	BEILMNUU	NEBULIUM
BEHIRSSY	HYBRISES	BEIIMNOS	EBIONISM	BEILMOOR	BLOOMIER
BEHISSTU	BUSHIEST	BEIIMRTT	IMBITTER	BEILMORS	EMBROILS
BEHKOSSY	KYBOSHES	BEIINNRS	BRINNIES	BEILMOSS	OBELISMS
BEHKOTTU	KETUBOTH	BEIINORS	BRIONIES	BEILMPTU	PLUMBITE
BEHLLOOT	BOLTHOLE	BEIINOST	NIOBITES	BEILMRRU	RUMBLIER
BEHLLOOW	BLOWHOLE	BEIINQUU	BIUNIQUE	BEILMRSS	BRIMLESS
BEHLLOPS	BELLHOPS	BEIINRST	BRINIEST	BEILMRST	TIMBRELS
BEHLLPSU	BELLPUSH	BEIINSST	STIBINES	BEILMRSU	SUBLIMER
BEHLLSSU	SUBSHELL	BEIINSTT	STIBNITE	BEILMRSW	WIMBRELS
BEHLMOSW	WHOMBLES	BEIIOPSS	BIOPSIES	BEILMSSU	LIMBUSES
BEHLMRSU	HUMBLERS	BEIIORST	ORBITIES		SUBLIMES
BEHLMSTU	HUMBLEST	BEIIOSTT	BIOTITES	BEILNNTU	BUNTLINE

BEILNOPS	BONSPIEL	BEIMOSTW	WOMBIEST	BEIRSSTU	BUSTIERS
BEILNOSU	NUBILOSE	BEIMOSTY	SYMBIOTE	BEIRSTTU	TRIBUTES
BEILNOSW	BOWLINES	BEIMPSTU	BUMPIEST	BEIRSTTY	TREYBITS
BEILNOVY	BOVINELY	BEIMRSSU	IMBURSES	BEISSSTU	SUBSITES
BEILNRSY	BYLINERS	BEIMRSTU	IMBRUTES	BEISSTTU	BUSTIEST
BEILNSSU	SUBLINES		RESUBMIT	BEISTUZZ	BUZZIEST
BEILNSSY	SENSIBLY		TERBIUMS	BEJKOOST	JESTBOOK
BEILNSTU	BUSTLINE	BEIMSSTU	SUBITEMS	BEJLMRSU	JUMBLERS
BEILNSTY	TENSIBLY	BEINNOPS	PINBONES	BEJORTTU	TURBOJET
BEILNSTZ	BLINTZES	BEINNOSS	BENISONS	BEKLNORY	BROKENLY
BEILOORV	BOILOVER		BONINESS	BEKLNRSU	BLUNKERS
	OVERBOIL	BEINNOST	BONNIEST	BEKLOOOR	BOOKLORE
BEILOOST	LOOBIEST	BEINNOSZ	BENZOINS	BEKLOORT	BROOKLET
BEILOPPW	BLOWPIPE	BEINNRYZ	ZEBRINNY	BEKLOOSS	BOOKLESS
BEILOPRS	PREBOILS	BEINNTTU	UNBITTEN	BEKLOOST	BOOKLETS
BEILOPSS	POSSIBLE	BEINOOST	BONITOES	BEKLORUV	OVERBULK
BEILOQRU	BELIQUOR		EOBIONTS	BEKLRSSU	BURLESKS
	OBLIQUER	BEINORRW	BROWNIER	BEKMOOPS	SPEKBOOM
BEILOQSU	OBLIQUES	BEINORRZ	BRONZIER	BEKMOSST	STEMBOKS
BEILORRS	BROILERS	BEINORST	BORNITES	BEKNNORU	UNBROKEN
BEILORST	STROBILE		RIBSTONE	BEKNOOOT	NOTEBOOK
	TRILOBES	BEINORSW	BROWNIES	BEKNOPRU	UPBROKEN
BEILORSU	BLOUSIER	BEINORSY	BRYONIES	BEKNORSY	SKYBORNE
BEILORSW	BLOWSIER	BEINORTZ	BRONZITE	BEKOOORV	OVERBOOK
BEILORTT	BLOTTIER	BEINOSST	EBONISTS	BEKOOPRS	PREBOOKS
	LIBRETTO	BEINOSSX	BOXINESS	BEKOORST	BOOKREST
BEILORWZ	BLOWZIER	BEINOSTT	BOTTINES	BEKOORTU	OUTBROKE
BEILOSSY	BIOLYSES	BEINOSTU	BOUNTIES	BEKOOTTX	TEXTBOOK
BEILOSTW	BLOWIEST	BEINRRSY	NISBERRY	BEKORSWW	WEBWORKS
BEILPRTU	PREBUILT	BEINRSSU	SUBERINS	BEKORTUW	TUBEWORK
BEILPRTV	BLIPVERT	BEINRSTT	BITTERNS	BEKOSSXY	SKYBOXES
BEILRRRU	BLURRIER	BEINRSTU	TRIBUNES	BEKRSSTU	BRUSKEST
BEILRRTT	BRITTLER		TURBINES	BELLLLPU	BELLPULL
BEILRRTY	TERRIBLY	BEINRSUU	UNBURIES	BELLLMSU	BLELLUMS
BEILRSST	BLISTERS	BEINRTTU	UNBITTER	BELLMORT	MORTBELL
	BRISTLES	BEINSSSU	BUSINESS	BELLMORU	UMBRELLO
BEILRSTT	BRITTLES	BEINSTTU	BUNTIEST	BELLMRUY	LUMBERLY
	TRIBLETS	BEIOOPST	BIOTOPES	BELLNOPS	BONSPELL
BEILRSTU	BURLIEST	BEIOORST	ROBOTISE	BELLNORW	WELLBORN
	SUBTILER	BEIOORTZ	ROBOTIZE	BELLNOSU	BULLNOSE
BEILRSTY	BLISTERY	BEIOOSSV	OVIBOSES	BELLNOSW	SNOWBELL
BEILRSTZ	BLITZERS	BEIOOSTZ	BOOZIEST	BELLNPSU	BULLPENS
BEILRSUY	BRULYIES	BEIOPSTY	BIOTYPES	BELLNTUY	TUNBELLY
BEILRSUZ	BRULZIES	BEIOQTUU	BOUTIQUE	BELLOOSU	LOBULOSE
BEILRTTY	BITTERLY	BEIORRST	ORBITERS	BELLOOSX	BOLLOXES
BEILSTTU	BLUETITS	BEIORRSU	BOURSIER	BELLOPTY	POTBELLY
	SUBTITLE	BEIORRSW	BROWSIER	BELLORTW	BELLWORT
BEIMMRRS	BRIMMERS	BEIORRTU	ROBURITE	BELLOSST	BLOTLESS
BEIMNORS	BROMINES	BEIORSTT	SORBITES		BOLTLESS
BEIMNRUZ	BRUNIZEM	BEIORSTT	BORTIEST	BELLOSSU	SOLUBLES
BEIMNSSU	NIMBUSES	BEIORSTY	SOBRIETY	BELLOSWY	SOWBELLY
BEIMNSTU	BITUMENS	BEIORSUV	BOUVIERS	BELLRRSU	BURRELLS
BEIMOORR	BROOMIER	BEIOSSST	BOSSIEST	BELMMOOS	EMBLOOMS
BEIMOORS	BOSOMIER	BEIOSSSU	SOUBISES	BELMMRSU	MUMBLERS
	RIBOSOME	BEIOSSTU	BOUSIEST	BELMNOSU	NELUMBOS
BEIMOOST	BOOMIEST	BEIOSSTY	BOYSIEST	BELMNOSY	BENOMYLS
BEIMORRV	OVERBRIM	BEIOTTZZ	BOZZETTI	BELMOORS	BLOOMERS
BEIMORSS	BROMISES	BEIPPRSU	PREPUBIS		REBLOOMS
BEIMORSW	IMBOWERS	BEIQRSTU	BRIQUETS	BELMOORY	BLOOMERY
BEIMORSZ	BROMIZES	BEIRRSSU	BRISURES	BELMOOSS	BLOOSMES
BEIMORTY	BIOMETRY		BRUISERS	BELMOOST	BOOMLETS
BEIMORYZ	RIBOZYME	BEIRRSTU	BRUITERS	BELMOPRS	PROBLEMS
BEIMOSSS	IMBOSSES		BURRIEST	BELMORST	TEMBLORS
BEIMOSTV	BEVOMITS	BEIRRTTU	TRIBUTER	BELMORSY	SOMBERLY

	SOMBRELY	BEMNSTTU	BUTMENTS	BEORSUVY	OVERBUSY
BELMORUW	RUMBELOW	BEMNTTUY	BUTTYMEN		OVERBUYS
BELMOSST	TOMBLESS	BEMOORRS	SOMBRERO	BEOSSTTU	OBTUSEST
BELMOSSY	SYMBOLES	BEMOORTT	BOTTOMER	BEPRRSTU	PERTURBS
BELMPRSU	PLUMBERS	BEMORSST	BESTORMS	BEPSSTUY	SUBTYPES
	REPLUMBS		MOBSTERS	BEQRRSUU	BRUSQUER
BELMPRUY	PLUMBERY		SOMBREST	BERRSSTU	BURSTERS
BELMRRSU	RUMBLERS	BEMORSSU	MORBUSES	BERRSTUU	SURREBUT
BELMRRUY	MULBERRY	BEMORSWW	WEBWORMS	BERSSTTU	BUTTRESS
BELMRSSU	SLUMBERS	BEMORTUW	TUBEWORM	BERSSTUV	SUBVERST
BELMRSTU	STUMBLER	BEMOSTUX	BUXOMEST		SUBVERTS
	TUMBLERS	BEMOSTUY	MYOTUBES	BESSSSUY	BYSSUSES
	TUMBRELS	BEMRSSTU	BUMSTERS	BESSSTTU	SUBTESTS
BELMRSUY	SLUMBERY	BEMSSSUU	SUBSUMES	BESSTTUX	SUBTEXTS
BELMSSTU	STUMBLES	BEMSSTUW	STEWBUMS	BFFFLMUU	BUMFLUFF
BELNNNOO	NONNOBLE	BENNNOTU	UNBONNET	BFFGILNU	BLUFFING
BELNNOSU	UNNOBLES	BENNOOTU	BOUTONNE	BFFGINSU	BUFFINGS
BELNOORS	BORNEOLS	BENNOPYY	PENNYBOY	BFFHORSU	BRUSHOFF
BELNOOSS	BOONLESS	BENNORSW	NEWBORNS	BFFILOOS	BOILOFFS
BELNOOSY	BOLONEYS	BENNSSSU	SNUBNESS	BFFLOOSW	BLOWOFFS
BELNOSTW	SNOWBELT	BENOORRV	OVERBORN	BFFLOTUU	OUTBLUFF
BELNOSUU	NEBULOUS	BENOORSU	BURNOOSE	BFFNOOSU	BUFFOONS
BELNOSYZ	BENZOYLS	BENORRSU	SUBORNER	BFFNOSUX	SNUFFBOX
BELNOTTU	UNBOTTLE	BENORRSZ	BRONZERS	BFGHINTU	BUNFIGHT
BELNSSTU	SUNBELTS	BENORRTU	TRUEBORN	BFGILMNU	FUMBLING
BELNSTTU	BLUNTEST	BENORRUV	OVERBURN	BFGIOOST	BIGFOOTS
BELNSTUU	UNSUBLET	BENORSST	SORBENTS	BFGIORST	FROGBITS
BELOOOSX	LOOSEBOX	BENORSTU	BURSTONE	BFGLLORU	BULLFROG
BELOOPRS	BLOOPERS		RUBSTONE	BFHIILLS	BILLFISH
BELOOPRT	BOLTROPE	BENORSTW	BESTROWN	BFHILOST	FISHBOLT
BELOORSW	ROSEBOWL		BROWNEST	BFHILOSW	BLOWFISH
BELOORVW	OVERBLOW	BENORSUU	BURNOUSE		FISHBOWL
BELOOSST	BOOTLESS	BENORSWY	BYWONERS	BFHIMNSU	NUMBFISH
BELOOTUV	OBVOLUTE	BENORTTU	BUTTONER	BFHLLSUU	BLUSHFUL
BELORRTU	TROUBLER		REBUTTON	BFIILMOS	BIOFILMS
BELORSST	BOLSTERS	BENOSSTU	SUBTONES	BFIINORS	FIBROINS
	LOBSTERS	BENOSSUZ	SUBZONES	BFIIORSS	FIBROSIS
BELORSSW	BROWLESS	BENOSSWY	NEWSBOYS	BFIKLOOP	FLIPBOOK
BELORSTT	BLOTTERS	BENRRSUY	SUNBERRY	BFILLMRU	BRIMFULL
	BOTTLERS	BENRSSTU	SUBRENTS	BFILLSSU	BLISSFUL
BELORSTU	BOULTERS	BENRSTUY	SUBENTRY	BFILOSTY	LIFTBOYS
	TROUBLES	BENSSSUY	BUSYNESS	BFIMNORU	NUBIFORM
BELOSSTU	OUTBLESS	BEOOORTV	OVERBOOT	BFIMORTU	TUBIFORM
BELOSTUU	TUBULOSE	BEOORRRW	BORROWER	BFINORYZ	BRONZIFY
BELOSTUY	OBTUSELY		REBORROW	BFIORSTT	FROSTBIT
BELPRSUY	SUPERBLY	BEOORRVW	OVERBROW	BFKLOOSU	BOOKFULS
BELRRSTU	BLURTERS	BEOORSSS	OBSESSOR	BFKLOOSY	FLYBOOKS
BELRSSTU	BLUSTERS		SORBOSES	BFKSSSUU	SUBFUSKS
	BUSTLERS	BEOORSST	BOOSTERS	BFLLNOWY	FLYBLOWN
BELRSSUU	SUBRULES	BEOORSTY	BOTRYOSE	BFLLOSUW	BOWLFULS
BELRSTUY	BLUSTERY	BEOOSTUX	OUTBOXES	BFLLOSWY	FLYBLOWS
BELRTUUU	TUBULURE	BEOOTTZZ	BOZZETTO	BFLOORSU	SUBFLOOR
BELSSTTU	SUBTLEST	BEOPRRSV	PROVERBS	BFNOORTW	BOWFRONT
BELSSTUY	SUBSTYLE	BEOPRSST	BESPORTS	BFOOOSTY	FOOTBOYS
BELSTTUY	SUBTLETY	BEOPSSTU	BESPOUTS	BGGGIINS	BIGGINGS
BEMMOOSS	EMBOSOMS	BEOQSSTU	BOSQUETS	BGGGILNO	BLOGGING
BEMMORRS	BROMMERS	BEOQSTUU	BOUQUETS		BOGGLING
BEMMRRSU	BRUMMERS	BEORRRUW	BURROWER	BGGGINOR	BROGGING
BEMMRRUU	BEMURMUR	BEORRSSW	BROWSERS	BGGGINSU	BUGGINGS
BEMNNSSU	NUMBNESS	BEORRSTU	ROBUSTER	BGGHIINT	BIGHTING
BEMNOORT	TROMBONE	BEORSSSU	SORBUSES	BGGIILNN	BINGLING
BEMNORSW	EMBROWNS	BEORSSTW	BESTROWS		BLINGING
BEMNORSY	EMBRYONS	BEORSSUU	SUBEROUS	BGGIILNO	OBLIGING
BEMNSSUU	SUBMENUS	BEORSTUU	TUBEROUS	BGGIILNY	GIBINGLY

Eight-letter anagrams

BGGIINNO	BOINGING	**BGIJLMNU**	JUMBLING	**BGINORST**	STROBING
BGGIINNR	BRINGING	**BGIJNORU**	OBJURING	**BGINORSW**	BROWSING
BGGIINRU	BRIGUING	**BGIJOSUU**	BIJUGOUS	**BGINORSZ**	ZORBINGS
BGGILNNU	BLUNGING	**BGIKLNNU**	BLUNKING	**BGINOSWW**	WINGBOWS
	BUNGLING	**BGIKLNOT**	KINGBOLT	**BGINPRSU**	UPBRINGS
BGGILNRU	BURGLING	**BGIKMNNO**	BONKINGS	**BGINRSSU**	SUBRINGS
BGGINOOT	TOBOGGIN	**BGIKNNOU**	BUNKOING	**BGINRSTU**	BRUSTING
BGGINOOY	BOOGYING	**BGIKNOOR**	BROOKING		BRUTINGS
BGHHHISU	HIGHBUSH	**BGIKNOOS**	BOOKINGS		BURSTING
BGHHINOR	HIGHBORN	**BGIKNORS**	BROKINGS	**BGINSSSU**	BUSSINGS
BGHHIORW	HIGHBROW	**BGIKNSSU**	BUSKINGS	**BGINSSTU**	BUSTINGS
BGHHIOSY	HIGHBOYS	**BGIKNSTU**	STINKBUG	**BGINSSWY**	SWINGBYS
BGHIINRT	BIRTHING	**BGILLLUY**	GULLIBLY	**BGINSUZZ**	BUZZINGS
BGHILMNU	HUMBLING	**BGILLNOU**	GLOBULIN	**BGISUWZZ**	BUZZWIGS
BGHILNSU	BLUSHING	**BGILLNRU**	BULLRING	**BGKLOOOS**	LOGBOOKS
BGHILRTY	BRIGHTLY	**BGILLNSU**	BULLINGS	**BGKNOOOS**	SONGBOOK
BGHIMNTU	THUMBING	**BGILLNUY**	BULLYING	**BGKORSSY**	GRYSBOKS
BGHIMOTU	BIGMOUTH	**BGILMMNU**	BUMMLING	**BGLLNOOY**	OBLONGLY
BGHINORS	BIGHORNS		MUMBLING	**BGLNOOSW**	LONGBOWS
BGHINRSU	BRUSHING	**BGILMNOO**	BLOOMING	**BGLNOSUW**	BLOWGUNS
BGHINRTU	UNBRIGHT	**BGILMNPU**	PLUMBING	**BGLOORYY**	BRYOLOGY
BGHINSSU	BUSHINGS	**BGILMNRU**	RUMBLING	**BGMNOOOR**	GOMBROON
BGHIORSU	BROGUISH	**BGILMNTU**	TUMBLING	**BGMOOSTU**	GUMBOOTS
BGHIPSSU	BUSHPIGS	**BGILMORY**	GORBLIMY	**BGMORRUW**	GRUBWORM
BGHLRSUU	BULGHURS	**BGILMOSU**	GUMBOILS	**BGNOOSWY**	GOWNBOYS
	BURGHULS	**BGILMOTU**	GUMBOTIL	**BGNOSSSU**	SUBSONGS
BGHMORSU	HOMBURGS	**BGILNNOS**	SNOBLING	**BGOPRSUU**	SUBGROUP
BGHNORSU	HORNBUGS	**BGILNNTU**	BLUNTING	**BGORSTUU**	BURGOUTS
BGHNOTUU	UNBOUGHT	**BGILNOOP**	BLOOPING	**BGORSTUW**	BUGWORTS
BGHOOPTU	BOUGHPOT	**BGILNORT**	RINGBOLT	**BHHIISST**	BHISHTIS
BGHOORSU	BOROUGHS	**BGILNORY**	BORINGLY	**BHIIINNS**	INHIBINS
BGIIJLNR	JIRBLING	**BGILNOST**	BILTONGS	**BHIIINST**	INHIBITS
BGIIJLNY	JIBINGLY		BOLTINGS	**BHIIKRSS**	BRISKISH
BGIIKLNN	BLINKING	**BGILNOSU**	BLOUSING	**BHIILMPS**	BLIMPISH
BGIIKMNO	KIMBOING	**BGILNOSW**	BOWLINGS	**BHIIMRST**	MISBIRTH
BGIIKNNO	BOINKING	**BGILNOTT**	BLOTTING	**BHIIOPRT**	PROHIBIT
BGIIKNRS	BRISKING		BOTTLING	**BHIIPSSS**	SIBSHIPS
BGIILLNS	BILLINGS	**BGILNOTU**	BOULTING	**BHIKLLOO**	BILLHOOK
BGIILMNW	WIMBLING	**BGILNOWY**	BOWINGLY	**BHIKMNTU**	THUMBKIN
BGIILNNN	BLINNING	**BGILNRRU**	BLURRING	**BHILLNOR**	HORNBILL
BGIILNNY	BYLINING	**BGILNRTU**	BLURTING	**BHILLOSY**	BILLYOHS
BGIILNOR	BROILING	**BGILNSTU**	BUSTLING	**BHILLPUW**	BULLWHIP
BGIILNOS	BOILINGS	**BGILNTTU**	BUTTLING	**BHILLSTU**	BULLSHIT
BGIILNOX	BOLIXING	**BGILOORS**	OBLIGORS	**BHILNSTU**	BLUNTISH
BGIILNPP	BLIPPING	**BGILRSSU**	BUSGIRLS	**BHILORRY**	HORRIBLY
BGIILNRS	BIRLINGS	**BGIMNOOR**	BROOMING	**BHILORUY**	BIHOURLY
	BIRSLING	**BGIMNOOS**	BOOMINGS	**BHILOSTU**	HOLIBUTS
	BRISLING		BOSOMING	**BHILOSYY**	BOYISHLY
BGIILNSS	BLISSING	**BGIMNORS**	SOMBRING	**BHIMNORT**	THROMBIN
	SIBLINGS	**BGIMNORW**	RINGWOMB	**BHIMOOPR**	BIOMORPH
BGIILNTY	BITINGLY	**BGIMNPSU**	BUMPINGS	**BHIMOOSS**	HOBOISMS
BGIILNTZ	BLITZING	**BGIMOSSY**	BOGYISMS	**BHIMOPRS**	BIMORPHS
BGIIMMNR	BRIMMING	**BGINNNOU**	UNBONING	**BHIMOPSS**	PHOBISMS
BGIIMNRS	BRIMINGS	**BGINNORU**	UNROBING	**BHIMORSU**	BOHRIUMS
BGIIMNRU	IMBRUING	**BGINNORW**	BROWNING	**BHIMORTU**	BOTHRIUM
BGIINNOR	INORBING	**BGINNORZ**	BRONZING	**BHIMSSTU**	BISMUTHS
BGIINNRS	INBRINGS	**BGINNOUW**	UNBOWING	**BHINOPSU**	UNBISHOP
BGIINORT	ORBITING	**BGINNOUX**	UNBOXING	**BHINORSW**	BROWNISH
BGIINRST	RINGBITS	**BGINNRSU**	BURNINGS	**BHIOOPRS**	BIOPHORS
BGIINRSU	BRUISING	**BGINNRTU**	BRUNTING	**BHIOOPRT**	BIOTROPH
BGIINRTU	BRUITING	**BGINNSTU**	BUNTINGS	**BHIOPSST**	PHOBISTS
BGIINSTT	BITTINGS	**BGINOOST**	BONGOIST	**BHIRSTTU**	TURBITHS
BGIINSTU	BUISTING		BOOSTING	**BHISSTTU**	BUSHTITS
BGIINVVY	BIVVYING	**BGINOOSZ**	BOOZINGS	**BHKLORUW**	BUHLWORK

BHKMNOOY	HYMNBOOK	BILLOSUY	BLOUSILY	BKNNOOOS	NONBOOKS
BHKNOOOR	HORNBOOK	BILLOSWY	BLOWSILY	BKNOOSTW	BOWKNOTS
BHKOOOPS	BOOKSHOP	BILLOWYZ	BLOWZILY	BKORSUWY	BUSYWORK
BHLLNORU	BULLHORN	BILLRRUY	BLURRILY	BLLLLOOY	LOBLOLLY
BHLLOSTU	BULLSHOT	BILLRSWY	WRYBILLS	BLLMOORW	BOLLWORM
BHLLRSUU	BULLRUSH	BILMMPSU	PLUMBISM	BLLOPTUU	BULLPOUT
BHLOOOTT	TOLBOOTH	BILMNORS	NOMBRILS	BLLOTUUY	OUTBULLY
BHLOSTUU	OUTBLUSH	BILMOSTU	BOTULISM	BLMMPSUU	PLUMBUMS
BHLRSUUY	BULRUSHY	BILMRSTU	TUMBRILS	BLMNPSUU	UNPLUMBS
BHMNTTUU	THUMBNUT	BILNOSTU	BOTULINS	BLMOOOST	TOMBOLOS
BHMOPTTU	THUMBPOT	BILNOSUU	NUBILOUS	BLMOOOTU	OUTBLOOM
BHMORSTU	THROMBUS	BILNSTUU	TUBULINS	BLMOOOTY	LOBOTOMY
BHNOOOST	BOSTHOON	BILOOPST	POTBOILS	BLMOORSW	LOBWORMS
BHNOORTX	BOXTHORN	BILOORST	SORBITOL	BLMOOSSS	BLOSSOMS
BHNOSSUW	SNOWBUSH	BILOORTT	BORLOTTI	BLMOOSSY	BLOSSOMY
BHOOPSSY	SHOPBOYS	BILOPSSY	POSSIBLY	BLMOPSUU	PLUMBOUS
BHOORTTU	OUTTHROB	BILORSST	BRISTOLS	BLNOOSSU	BLOUSONS
BHOOSSTW	BOWSHOTS		STROBILS	BLNSTUUY	UNSUBTLY
BHPRSSUU	BRUSHUPS	BILOSSSU	SUBSOILS	BLOOPSWY	PLOWBOYS
BIIKLOST	KILOBITS	BILOSTUY	ISOBUTYL	BLOORSWW	LOWBROWS
BIIKNOOT	BOOTIKIN	BILOTTUU	OUTBUILT	BLOOSSTY	SLYBOOTS
BIILLMOR	MORBILLI	BILSTTUY	SUBTILTY	BLOOSTUW	BLOWOUTS
BIILLMSS	MISBILLS	BIMMOOSS	IMBOSOMS	BLOPSSTU	SUBPLOTS
BIILLNOS	BILLIONS	BIMMORSS	BROMISMS	BLORSTUY	ROBUSTLY
BIILLOSU	BOUILLIS	BIMNNUUU	UNUNBIUM	BLOSTUUU	TUBULOUS
BIILLSTW	TWIBILLS	BIMNORSW	IMBROWNS	BLRSTUYY	BUTYRYLS
BIILMOTY	MOBILITY	BIMNOSSY	SYMBIONS	BMNOOORW	MONOBROW
BIILMSTU	MISBUILT	BIMNOSTY	SYMBIONT	BMNOOOSW	MOONBOWS
	SUBLIMIT	BIMNRRUU	MUIRBURN	BMNOOOTW	BOOMTOWN
BIILNNRS	BIRLINNS	BIMNRUUV	VIBURNUM	BMNOORRU	MOORBURN
BIILNOOV	OBLIVION	BIMOORST	ROBOTISM	BMNOOSSU	UNBOSOMS
BIILNORU	UROBILIN	BIMOSSSS	BOSSISMS	BMNORSUW	MOWBURNS
BIILNOTY	NOBILITY	BIMOSSTW	MISTBOWS	BMNORTUW	MOWBURNT
BIILNQSU	QUIBLINS	BIMOSSTY	SYBOTISM	BMOOORSX	BOXROOMS
BIILNSTU	SUBTILIN		SYMBIOTS	BMOORSSU	SOMBROUS
BIILNSVY	BIVINYLS	BIMRSSTU	BRUTISMS	BMOORSTU	MOTORBUS
BIILNTUY	NUBILITY	BIMRSSUX	BRUXISMS	BMOORTTY	BOTTOMRY
BIILORST	STROBILI	BINNORTW	TWINBORN	BMORSSTU	STROMBUS
BIILOSSU	SIBILOUS	BINOORST	BIOTRONS	BNNORTUW	NUTBROWN
BIILOSSY	BIOLYSIS		ISOBRONT	BNNOTTUU	UNBUTTON
BIILSTTW	WITBLITS	BINORSST	RIBSTONS	BNNRSSUU	SUNBURNS
BIIMMNSY	NIMBYISM	BINORSSU	BOURSINS	BNNRSTUU	SUNBURNT
BIIMMOSZ	ZOMBIISM	BINORSUW	UNIBROWS	BNOOOSTW	SNOWBOOT
BIIMNOSU	NIOBIUMS	BINRSSTU	INBURSTS	BNOOOSUY	SONOBUOY
BIIMPRSS	BIPRISMS	BINRSTUY	BUTYRINS	BNOORTUW	BROWNOUT
BIIMSSTU	STIBIUMS	BINSSTUU	SUBUNITS	BNOPRSTU	POSTBURN
BIINOOTX	BIOTOXIN	BIOPRRSU	SUBPRIOR	BNORRUUW	UNBURROW
BIINORSV	VIBRIONS	BIOPRSTW	BOWSPRIT	BNORSTUU	BURNOUTS
BIINOTVY	BOVINITY	BIORRSTU	BURRITOS		OUTBURNS
BIINRSTU	BURINIST	BIORRSTW	RIBWORTS		
BIIQTUUY	UBIQUITY	BIORSSTT	BISTORTS	BNORTTUU	OUTBURNT
BIIRSSTU	BURSITIS	BIORSTTU	BITTOURS	BNRSSTUU	SUNBURST
BIJNOSSU	SUBJOINS	BIORSTTY	BOTRYTIS	BOOPSSTY	POSTBOYS
BIKLLSSU	SUBSKILL	BIORSTUY	BISTOURY	BORSTTUU	OUTBURST
BIKLNOST	INKBLOTS	BIOSTTUY	OBTUSITY	BORSTUUY	BUTYROUS
BIKLNOSY	LINKBOYS	BIRSSTTU	SUBTRIST	BPRSSTUU	UPBURSTS
BIKMNOOS	BOOMKINS	BIRSSUUV	SUBVIRUS	CCCDIILY	DICYCLIC
BIKMNPSU	BUMPKINS	BISSSSTU	SUBSISTS	CCCDIOOS	COCCOIDS
BIKOOSUU	BOUSOUKI	BISSTUUU	BUSUUTIS	CCCDKLOO	COLDCOCK
BIKOOUUZ	BOUZOUKI	BKKOOORW	BOOKWORK	CCCEEILT	ECLECTIC
BIKORRSW	RIBWORKS		WORKBOOK	CCCEGOSY	COCCYGES
BILLMSUY	BULLYISM	BKLOSTUU	OUTBULKS	CCCEHIOR	CHOCCIER
BILLNOOU	BOUILLON	BKMOOORW	BOOKWORM	CCCEHIOS	CHOCCIES
BILLNOSU	BULLIONS	BKMOORUZ	ZOMBORUK	CCCEIIRT	ECCRITIC
				CCCEILNY	ENCYCLIC

CCCEILUV	EUCYCLIC	CCDELOTU	OCCULTED		ECCRISES
CCCEOSXY	COCCYXES	CCDENOOO	COCOONED	CCEEIRSV	CERVICES
CCCHIORY	CHICCORY	CCDENORU	CONDUCER		CRESCIVE
CCCIINSU	SUCCINIC	CCDENOSU	CONDUCES		CREVICES
CCCILLYY	CYCLICLY	CCDEORRU	OCCURRED	CCEEITTU	EUTECTIC
CCCILNOV	CYCLONIC	CCDEORSU	SUCCORED	CCEEKLOR	COCKEREL
CCCILOPY	CYCLOPIC	CCDEOSTU	STUCCOED	CCEEKNRW	CREWNECK
CCCINSTU	SUCCINCT	CCDHIIKP	DIPCHICK	CCEEKOSY	COCKEYES
CCCIOORS	SCIROCCO	CCDHIILO	CICHLOID	CCEELMNY	CLEMENCY
CCCKOORW	COCKCROW	CCDHIILS	CICHLIDS	CCEELNSU	LUCENCES
CCCNOOST	CONCOCTS	CCDHIIOR	DICHROIC	CCEELOSS	SCOLECES
CCDDEENO	CONCEDED	CCDHIIOT	DICHOTIC	CCEELRRY	RECYCLER
CCDDEEOT	DECOCTED	CCDHINOO	CONCHOID	CCEELRSY	RECYCLES
CCDDELOU	OCCLUDED	CCDIILNU	NUCLIDIC	CCEEMMNO	COMMENCE
CCDDENOU	CONDUCED	CCDIILOS	CODICILS	CCEEMMOR	COMMERCE
CCDEEENR	CREDENCE	CCDIILSU	CULICIDS	CCEEMOPS	COMPESCE
CCDEEHIL	CLICHEED	CCDIINOO	CONOIDIC	CCEENNOS	ENSCONCE
CCDEEHLN	CLENCHED	CCDIINOS	SCINCOID	CCEENORT	CONCRETE
CCDEEILN	LICENCED	CCDIINST	DISCINCT	CCEENRST	CRESCENT
CCDEEINS	SCIENCED	CCDIIORS	CRICOIDS	CCEEORRS	COERCERS
CCDEEIOP	CODPIECE	CCDIIORT	DICROTIC	CCEEORST	COERECTS
CCDEEIOS	ECOCIDES	CCDILOSY	CYCLOIDS	CCEFFHKO	CHECKOFF
CCDEEIRV	CREVICED	CCDINOTU	CONDUCTI	CCEFHRSU	CURCHEFS
CCDEEKOR	COCKERED	CCDKLOSU	CUCKOLDS	CCEFIIPS	SPECIFIC
	RECOCKED	CCDKOOOW	WOODCOCK	CCEFINOT	COINFECT
CCDEEKOY	COCKEYED	CCDNOORS	CONCORDS	CCEFIRRU	CRUCIFER
CCDEELRY	RECYCLED	CCDNOSTU	CONDUCTS	CCEFLLOU	FLOCCULE
CCDEENOR	CONCEDER	CCEEEILN	LICENCEE	CCEFLOOS	FLOCCOSE
CCDEENOS	CONCEDES	CCEEFFOT	COEFFECT	CCEFNOST	CONFECTS
CCDEESSU	SUCCEEDS	CCEEGINR	RECCEING	CCEGHIKN	CHECKING
CCDEHHRU	CHURCHED	CCEEGNOS	COGENCES	CCEGHIOR	CHOREGIC
CCDEHIKT	TCHICKED	CCEEHIKS	CHICKEES	CCEGIKLN	CLECKING
CCDEHILN	CLINCHED	CCEEHILN	ELENCHIC	CCEGILMY	GLYCEMIC
CCDEHIPU	HICCUPED	CCEEHINZ	ZECCHINE	CCEGILOO	ECOLOGIC
CCDEHKLU	CHUCKLED	CCEEHISV	CEVICHES	CCEGILRY	GLYCERIC
CCDEHLTU	CLUTCHED	CCEEHKNS	SCHNECKE	CCEGINNO	CONGENIC
	DECLUTCH	CCEEHKPR	PRECHECK	CCEGINOR	COERCING
CCDEHNRU	CRUNCHED	CCEEHKRS	CHECKERS	CCEGINPS	SPECCING
CCDEHOOS	SCOOCHED		RECHECKS	CCEGINRY	RECCYING
CCDEHOOT	COOTCHED	CCEEHLNR	CLENCHER	CCEGNOOS	COGNOSCE
CCDEHORS	SCORCHED	CCEEHLNS	CLENCHES	CCEHHIIR	CHICHIER
CCDEHORT	CROTCHED	CCEEHORS	ECORCHES	CCEHHINS	CHINCHES
CCDEHORU	CROUCHED	CCEEHOSU	COUCHEES	CCEHHRSU	CHURCHES
CCDEHOST	SCOTCHED	CCEEHRSY	SCREECHY	CCEHIIMR	CHIMERIC
CCDEHRTU	CRUTCHED	CCEEIILS	CICELIES	CCEHIIMS	ISCHEMIC
CCDEHSTU	SCUTCHED	CCEEIIST	CECITIES	CCEHIINZ	ZECCHINI
CCDEIILO	CLEIDOIC	CCEEIKLR	CLECKIER	CCEHIKNP	PINCHECK
CCDEIINO	COINCIDE	CCEEILMU	LEUCEMIC	CCEHIKNS	CHICKENS
CCDEIIRT	CRICETID	CCEEILNR	ENCIRCLE	CCEHIKSU	CHUCKIES
CCDEIIST	DEICTICS		LICENCER	CCEHILNR	CLINCHER
CCDEILOS	SCOLECID	CCEEILNS	LICENCES	CCEHILNS	CLINCHES
CCDEILSY	CYCLISED	CCEEILNT	ELENCTIC	CCEHILOR	CHOLERIC
CCDEILYZ	CYCLIZED	CCEEILPY	EPICYCLE	CCEHILOV	CHOICELY
CCDEINOR	CORNICED	CCEEILRR	RECIRCLE	CCEHILSU	CULCHIES
CCDEINOS	CONCISED	CCEEILRT	ELECTRIC	CCEHILTY	HECTICLY
CCDEINOT	OCCIDENT	CCEEIMNU	ECUMENIC	CCEHINOR	CORNICHE
CCDEIOPP	COPPICED	CCEEINOR	CICERONE		ENCHORIC
CCDEIOPU	OCCUPIED		CROCEINE	CCEHINOS	CONCHIES
CCDEIORT	CODIRECT	CCEEINOV	CONCEIVE	CCEHINOZ	ZECCHINO
CCDEKNOU	UNCOCKED	CCEEINSS	SCIENCES	CCEHINRU	CRUNCHIE
CCDEKOOU	CUCKOOED	CCEEIORS	CICOREES	CCEHINSS	CHICNESS
CCDELNOU	CONCLUDE	CCEEIORV	COERCIVE	CCEHINST	TECHNICS
CCDELORU	OCCLUDER	CCEEIPSS	SPECCIES	CCEHINSZ	ZECCHINS
CCDELOSU	OCCLUDES	CCEEIRSS	CERCISES	CCEHIORT	RICOCHET

CCEHIOST	CHOICEST	**CCEILOSS**	SCOLICES	**CCENNORS**	CONCERNS
CCEHIRSS	SCREICHS	**CCEILRRS**	CIRCLERS	**CCENNOST**	CONCENTS
	SCRIECHS	**CCEILRRU**	CURRICLE		CONNECTS
CCEHKLRU	CHUCKLER	**CCEILRST**	CIRCLETS	**CCENOORT**	CONCERTO
CCEHKLSU	CHUCKLES	**CCEILRSY**	CRESYLIC	**CCENOOTT**	CONCETTO
CCEHKMSS	SCHMECKS	**CCEILRTY**	TRICYCLE	**CCENOPST**	CONCEPTS
CCEHKMSU	CHECKSUM	**CCEILRUU**	CURLICUE	**CCENORST**	CONCERTS
CCEHKNSU	UNCHECKS	**CCEILSSY**	CYCLISES	**CCENORSW**	CONCREWS
CCEHKORW	CHECKROW	**CCEILSTU**	CUTICLES	**CCENORTY**	CORNETCY
CCEHKOTU	CHECKOUT	**CCEILSYZ**	CYCLIZES	**CCENOSTV**	CONVECTS
CCEHKPSU	CHECKUPS	**CCEIMNOO**	ECONOMIC	**CCENRRUY**	CURRENCY
CCEHKRSU	CHUCKERS		ONCOMICE	**CCEOOORR**	COROCORE
CCEHLMOR	CROMLECH	**CCEIMOPR**	COPREMIC	**CCEOORSU**	CROCEOUS
CCEHLNNU	UNCLENCH	**CCEIMOST**	COSMETIC	**CCEOOSTT**	COCOTTES
CCEHLNSU	CLUNCHES	**CCEIMRRU**	MERCURIC	**CCEOPRUY**	REOCCUPY
CCEHLRSU	CLERUCHS	**CCEIMRUV**	CERVICUM	**CCEORRST**	CORRECTS
CCEHLRUY	CLERUCHY	**CCEINNOS**	INSCONCE	**CCEORRSU**	REOCCURS
CCEHLSSU	SCULCHES	**CCEINNOV**	CONVINCE		SUCCORER
CCEHLSTU	CLUTCHES	**CCEINOOR**	COERCION	**CCEORSSU**	CROCUSES
	CULTCHES	**CCEINOOZ**	CENOZOIC	**CCEORSTU**	STUCCOER
CCEHNRRU	CRUNCHER	**CCEINOPR**	COPRINCE	**CCEORSTW**	TWOCCERS
CCEHNRSU	CRUNCHES	**CCEINOPT**	CONCEPTI	**CCEOSSTU**	STUCCOES
CCEHOOSS	SCOOCHES	**CCEINORS**	CONCISER	**CCERSTUW**	CREWCUTS
CCEHOOST	COOTCHES		CORNICES	**CCESSSUU**	CUSCUSES
CCEHORRS	SCORCHER		CROCEINS	**CCFGILNO**	FLOCCING
CCEHORSS	SCORCHES	**CCEINORT**	CONCERTI	**CCFHKLOU**	CHOCKFUL
CCEHORST	CROCHETS		NECROTIC	**CCFIINOR**	CORNIFIC
	CROTCHES	**CCEINOSS**	CONCISES	**CCFIIRUX**	CRUCIFIX
CCEHORSU	COUCHERS	**CCEINOST**	CONCEITS	**CCFIKNOY**	COCKNIFY
	CROUCHES	**CCEINOTT**	CONCETTI	**CCFILLOU**	FLOCCULI
CCEHORTT	CROTCHET		TECTONIC	**CCFILNOT**	CONFLICT
CCEHOSST	SCOTCHES	**CCEINOTY**	CONCEITY	**CCFKLOOT**	COCKLOFT
CCEHRSTU	CRUTCHES	**CCEINPRT**	PRECINCT	**CCFLOOOO**	LOCOFOCO
	SCUTCHER	**CCEINRTU**	CINCTURE	**CCGHHIOU**	HICCOUGH
CCEHRTUY	CUTCHERY	**CCEINSTY**	SYNECTIC	**CCGHIINN**	CINCHING
CCEHSSTU	SCUTCHES	**CCEIOORT**	CROCOITE	**CCGHIKNO**	CHOCKING
CCEIIKLN	NICKELIC	**CCEIOOTX**	ECOTOXIC	**CCGHIKNU**	CHUCKING
CCEIILNO	COLICINE	**CCEIOOTZ**	ECTOZOIC	**CCGHINNO**	CONCHING
CCEIILNT	ENCLITIC	**CCEIOPPS**	COPPICES	**CCGHINOS**	GNOCCHIS
CCEIILNU	CULICINE	**CCEIOPRT**	ECTROPIC	**CCGHINOU**	COUCHING
CCEIILOR	LICORICE	**CCEIOPRU**	OCCUPIER	**CCGHINTW**	CWTCHING
CCEIILPT	ECLIPTIC	**CCEIOPSU**	OCCUPIES	**CCGIIKLN**	CLICKING
CCEIILST	SCILICET	**CCEIOPTY**	ECOTYPIC	**CCGIIKNR**	CRICKING
CCEIILTU	LEUCITIC	**CCEIORST**	CORTICES	**CCGIILNR**	CIRCLING
CCEIINNO	CONICINE	**CCEIOTXY**	EXOCYTIC	**CCGIILNU**	GLUCINIC
CCEIINNR	ENCRINIC	**CCEIPSST**	SCEPTICS	**CCGIKLNO**	CLOCKING
CCEIINOR	CICERONI	**CCEIRSSU**	CIRCUSES		COCKLING
CCEIINTU	CICUTINE	**CCEJNOST**	CONJECTS	**CCGIKLNU**	CLUCKING
CCEIIRRT	CIRCITER	**CCEKLORS**	CLOCKERS	**CCGIKNOR**	CROCKING
CCEIIRSS	ECCRISIS		COCKLERS	**CCGILLOV**	GLYCOLIC
CCEIIRST	ICTERICS	**CCEKNOST**	CONTECKS	**CCGILNOY**	GLYCONIC
CCEIIRTT	RECTITIC	**CCEKNOSY**	COCKNEYS	**CCGILNSY**	CYCLINGS
CCEIIRTU	EUCRITIC	**CCEKOPST**	PETCOCKS	**CCGILOSU**	GLUCOSIC
CCEIKKLO	COCKLIKE	**CCEKORRY**	CROCKERY	**CCGINNOS**	SCONCING
CCEIKLRS	CLICKERS	**CCEKORST**	CROCKETS	**CCGINOTW**	TWOCCING
CCEIKLRU	CLUCKIER	**CCEKORSU**	COCKSURE	**CCGKOORS**	GORCOCKS
CCEIKLST	CLICKETS	**CCELLOST**	COLLECTS	**CCHHIITY**	ICHTHYIC
CCEIKORS	COCKSIER	**CCELMOPT**	COMPLECT	**CCHHILSS**	SCHLICHS
CCEIKOST	COCKIEST	**CCELNOSY**	CYCLONES	**CCHHINOT**	CHTHONIC
CCEIKRST	CRICKETS	**CCELOPSY**	CYCLOPES	**CCHHLRUY**	CHURCHLY
CCEILMOO	COELOMIC	**CCELORTU**	OCCULTER	**CCHHNRUU**	UNCHURCH
CCEILMOP	COMPLICE	**CCELOSSY**	CYCLOSES	**CCHHOOWW**	CHOWCHOW
CCEILNOR	CORNICLE	**CCELRUUY**	CURLYCUE	**CCHIINUZ**	ZUCCHINI
CCEILNUY	UNICYCLE	**CCELSSUY**	CYCLUSES	**CCHIIORT**	ORCHITIC

Eight-letter anagrams

CCHIKMPU	CHIPMUCK	CCKKLMUU	MUCKLUCK	CDDEEKOT	DOCKETED
CCHIKORV	CHICKORY	CCKMMORU	CRUMMOCK	CDDEEKUW	DUCKWEED
CCHIKSST	SCHTICKS	CCKMOOOR	MOORCOCK	CDDEELMO	COMEDDLE
CCHILNNU	UNCLINCH	CCKNORTU	TURNCOCK	CDDEELPU	DECUPLED
CCHILNUY	UNCHICLY	CCKOOPRT	CROCKPOT	CDDEELSU	SCEDULED
CCHINORS	CHRONICS	CCKOOPST	STOPCOCK		SECLUDED
CCHINSSU	SCUCHINS	CCKOPRSU	COCKSPUR	CDDEELUX	EXCLUDED
CCHIPSSY	PSYCHICS	CCKOSSTU	CUSTOCKS	CDDEELUY	DEUCEDLY
CCHKLOSS	SCHLOCKS	CCLLOTUY	OCCULTLY	CDDEENOS	SECONDED
CCHKLOSY	SCHLOCKY	CCLMOOPU	COCOPLUM	CDDEENSS	DESCENDS
CCHKMNUU	NUMCHUCK	CCLNOOOR	CONCOLOR	CDDEEOPR	PRECODED
CCHKMOSS	SCHMOCKS	CCLOOOSZ	ZOCCOLOS	CDDEEORR	RECORDED
CCHKMSSU	SCHMUCKS	CCLOORSU	OCCLUSOR	CDDEEORS	DECODERS
CCHKOOST	COCKSHOT	CCMOOORS	MOROCCOS	CDDEERUV	DECURVED
CCHKOPTU	PUTCHOCK	CCNOOPSU	PUCCOONS	CDDEESUW	CUDWEEDS
CCHKOSTU	COCKSHUT	CCNOORSU	CONCOURS	CDDEFIIO	CODIFIED
CCHKPSUU	UPCHUCKS	CCNOOSTU	COCONUTS	CDDEFINO	CONFIDED
CCHKSSTU	SCHTUCKS	CCOOOORR	COROCORO	CDDEGIIN	DECIDING
CCHLNTUU	UNCLUTCH	CCOOSSUU	COUSCOUS	CDDEGINO	DECODING
CCHNRSUY	SCRUNCHY	CCOOTTUU	TUCOTUCO	CDDEGINU	DEDUCING
CCHOORST	SCROOTCH	CCORSSTU	CROSSCUT	CDDEHIOW	COWHIDED
CCIIIMSV	CIVICISM	CCORSSUU	SUCCOURS	CDDEHISU	CHUDDIES
CCIIIPRT	PICRITIC	CCOTTUUU	TUCUTUCO	CDDEHRSU	CHUDDERS
CCIIKKPW	PICKWICK	CCRSUUUU	SURUCUCU	CDDEIINT	INDICTED
CCIIKNPY	PICNICKY	CCTTUUUU	TUCUTUCU	CDDEIISS	DISCIDES
CCIILNOS	COLICINS	CDDDEETU	DEDUCTED	CDDEIISU	SUICIDED
CCIILORT	CLITORIC	CDDDEIIS	DISCIDED	CDDEIKOS	DOCKISED
CCIILPRS	CIRCLIPS	CDDDELRU	CRUDDLED		DOCKSIDE
CCIIMNSY	CYNICISM	CDDDELSU	SCUDDLED	CDDEIKOZ	DOCKIZED
CCIINNSU	CICINNUS	CDDDIIOV	DIDDICOY	CDDEILLO	COLLIDED
CCIINORZ	ZIRCONIC	CDDEEEEX	EXCEEDED	CDDEILNU	INCLUDED
CCIINOTY	CONICITY	CDDEEEFN	DEFENCED	CDDEILOR	CLODDIER
CCIIRSTU	CIRCUITS	CDDEEEFT	DEFECTED	CDDEILRU	CUDDLIER
CCIIRTUY	CIRCUITY	CDDEEEIR	REDECIDE	CDDEIMOS	MISCODED
CCIKKLOP	LOCKPICK	CDDEEEIV	DECEIVED	CDDEINTU	INDUCTED
	PICKLOCK	CDDEEEJT	DEJECTED	CDDEIORV	DIVORCED
CCIKKOTT	TICKTOCK	CDDEEENR	DECERNED	CDDEIRRU	CRUDDIER
CCIKLOSW	COWLICKS	CDDEEENT	DECEDENT	CDDEIRSU	DISCURED
CCIKNOPR	PRINCOCK	CDDEEEPR	PRECEDED	CDDEKNOU	UNDOCKED
CCIKOPRS	CROPSICK	CDDEEERS	SCREEDED	CDDELLOU	COLLUDED
CCIKOPST	COCKPITS	CDDEEERW	DECREWED	CDDELNOO	CONDOLED
CCILLOTY	CYCLITOL	CDDEEETT	DETECTED	CDDELOOR	CROODLED
CCILNOOS	COLONICS	CDDEEFOR	DEFORCED	CDDELORS	CODDLERS
CCILNOSU	COUNCILS	CDDEEGLU	CUDGELED	CDDELRSU	CRUDDLES
CCILNSUY	SUCCINYL	CDDEEHIS	DEHISCED		CUDDLERS
CCILOOPS	PICCOLOS	CDDEEHIT	CHEDDITE	CDDELSSU	SCUDDLES
CCILORUU	CURCULIO	CDDEEHNR	DRENCHED	CDDEMNOU	DUNCEDOM
CCILOSSY	CYCLOSIS	CDDEEIIM	MEDICIDE	CDDENNOO	CONDONED
CCILSSTY	CYCLISTS	CDDEEIIS	DEICIDES	CDDENOOR	CORDONED
CCIMNRUU	CURCUMIN	CDDEEIKR	DICKERED	CDDENORU	UNCORDED
CCINOORT	CROTONIC	CDDEEIKT	DETICKED	CDDEOORR	CORRODED
CCINOOST	COCTIONS	CDDEEILN	DECLINED	CDDEOORT	DOCTORED
CCINOPRT	PROCINCT	CDDEEILP	PEDICLED	CDDEOORW	CODEWORD
CCINOPSY	SYNCOPIC	CDDEEINR	CINDERED	CDDEOPRU	PRODUCED
CCINOPTY	PYCNOTIC	CDDEEINZ	DEZINCED	CDDERSSU	SCUDDERS
CCINORSY	CRYONICS	CDDEEIOT	COEDITED	CDDGHILO	GODCHILD
CCINOSTV	CONVICTS	CDDEEIOV	DEVOICED	CDDGILNO	CLODDING
CCIOOPST	SCOTOPIC	CDDEEIPT	DEPICTED		CODDLING
CCIOORSS	SIROCCOS	CDDEEIRS	DECIDERS	CDDGILNU	CUDDLING
CCIOOTXY	OXYTOCIC		DESCRIED	CDDGINRU	CRUDDING
CCIOPRST	COSCRIPT	CDDEEIRT	CREDITED	CDDGINSU	SCUDDING
CCIOPSTU	OCCIPUTS		DIRECTED	CDDHHISU	SHIDDUCH
CCIRSSUY	CIRCUSSY	CDDEEKNU	UNDECKED	CDDHIIRY	DIHYDRIC
CCJNNOTU	CONJUNCT	CDDEEKOR	REDOCKED	CDDHILOS	CLODDISH

CDDHIORS	DICHORDS		RESECTED	**CDEEHLPU**	PLEUCHED
CDDIIIOS	DIDICOIS		SCREETED	**CDEEHLQU**	QUELCHED
CDDIIKNS	NIDDICKS		SECRETED	**CDEEHLSU**	SCHEDULE
CDDIIOSS	DISCOIDS	**CDEEERSV**	SCREEVED	**CDEEHMTU**	HUMECTED
CDDIIOSY	DIDICOYS	**CDEEERTT**	DETECTER	**CDEEHNQU**	QUENCHED
CDDIISTY	DYTISCID	**CDEEERTX**	EXCRETED	**CDEEHNRR**	DRENCHER
CDDIKOPS	PIDDOCKS	**CDEEESSX**	EXCESSED	**CDEEHNRS**	DRENCHES
CDDIORSS	DISCORDS	**CDEEESTX**	EXSECTED	**CDEEHNRT**	TRENCHED
CDDKOPSU	PUDDOCKS	**CDEEETUX**	EXECUTED	**CDEEHNRW**	WRENCHED
CDDKORSU	RUDDOCKS	**CDEEFFOR**	COFFERED	**CDEEHNST**	STENCHED
CDDMMOUU	MOCUDDUM		EFFORCED	**CDEEHNUW**	UNCHEWED
CDDOOORW	CORDWOOD	**CDEEFHLN**	FLENCHED	**CDEEHORS**	CHORDEES
CDEEEERX	EXCEEDER	**CDEEFHLT**	FLETCHED		COSHERED
CDEEEFFT	EFFECTED	**CDEEFHNR**	FRENCHED	**CDEEHORT**	HECTORED
CDEEEFHL	FLEECHED	**CDEEFIIL**	ICEFIELD		TOCHERED
CDEEEFNR	REFENCED	**CDEEFIIS**	EDIFICES	**CDEEHPRU**	CHERUPED
CDEEEFNS	DEFENCES	**CDEEFIIT**	FETICIDE	**CDEEHPRY**	CYPHERED
CDEEEFRT	REDEFECT	**CDEEFINT**	INFECTED	**CDEEHQTU**	QUETCHED
	REFECTED	**CDEEFKLR**	FRECKLED	**CDEEHRTW**	WRETCHED
CDEEEHHW	WHEECHED	**CDEEFKOR**	FOREDECK	**CDEEHSSU**	DUCHESSE
CDEEEHLR	CHEERLED	**CDEEFLST**	DEFLECTS	**CDEEIILT**	ELICITED
	LECHERED	**CDEEFNNU**	UNFENCED	**CDEEIIMN**	MEDICINE
CDEEEHMS	SMEECHED	**CDEEFNOR**	ENFORCED	**CDEEIIMP**	EPIDEMIC
CDEEEHOR	REECHOED	**CDEEFORR**	DEFORCER	**CDEEIINT**	INDICTEE
CDEEEHPS	DEPECHES	**CDEEFORS**	DEFORCES	**CDEEIIOS**	DIOECIES
	SPEECHED		FRESCOED	**CDEEIIRT**	DIERETIC
CDEEEHRS	CREESHED	**CDEEFORT**	DEFECTOR	**CDEEIIST**	EIDETICS
CDEEEHRW	RECHEWED	**CDEEGIIR**	REGICIDE	**CDEEIISV**	DECISIVE
CDEEEHST	TEDESCHE	**CDEEGINO**	GENOCIDE	**CDEEIITT**	DIETETIC
CDEEEHSW	ESCHEWED	**CDEEGINR**	RECEDING	**CDEEIJNT**	INJECTED
CDEEEINP	PIECENED	**CDEEGINS**	SECEDING	**CDEEIJOR**	REJOICED
CDEEEINV	EVIDENCE	**CDEEGIOS**	GEODESIC	**CDEEIKLN**	NICKELED
CDEEEIPS	EPICEDES	**CDEEGIOT**	GEODETIC	**CDEEIKMY**	MICKEYED
CDEEEIRV	DECEIVER	**CDEEGIRS**	GRECISED	**CDEEIKNR**	NICKERED
	RECEIVED	**CDEEGIRU**	CUDGERIE	**CDEEIKNS**	SICKENED
CDEEEISV	DECEIVES	**CDEEGIRZ**	GRECIZED	**CDEEIKNV**	INVECKED
CDEEEJRT	REJECTED	**CDEEGKST**	GEDECKTS	**CDEEIKPT**	PICKETED
CDEEEKNW	NECKWEED	**CDEEGLRU**	CUDGELER	**CDEEIKRR**	DRECKIER
CDEEELLX	EXCELLED	**CDEEGNOR**	CONGREED	**CDEEIKRT**	DETICKER
CDEEELNR	CRENELED	**CDEEHHSU**	SHEUCHED	**CDEEIKRW**	WICKEDER
CDEEELOS	COLESEED	**CDEEHHTT**	THETCHED		WICKERED
CDEEELPY	YCLEEPED	**CDEEHIKL**	HELIDECK	**CDEEIKRY**	YICKERED
CDEEELST	DESELECT	**CDEEHILN**	LICHENED	**CDEEIKST**	TICKSEED
	SELECTED	**CDEEHILP**	CHELIPED	**CDEEIKTT**	TICKETED
CDEEELUX	EXCLUDEE	**CDEEHILS**	CHISELED	**CDEEILNP**	PENCILED
CDEEEMNT	CEMENTED	**CDEEHINR**	ENRICHED		PENDICLE
CDEEEMOR	COREDEEM		INHERCED	**CDEEILNR**	DECLINER
CDEEEMPR	EMPERCED		NICHERED		RECLINED
CDEEENNT	TENDENCE		RICHENED	**CDEEILNS**	DECLINES
CDEEENOS	SECONDEE	**CDEEHIOS**	ECHOISED		LICENSED
CDEEENRS	RECENSED	**CDEEHIOZ**	ECHOIZED		SILENCED
	SCREENED	**CDEEHIPR**	CIPHERED	**CDEEILNT**	DENTICLE
	SECERNED		DECIPHER	**CDEEILNU**	NUCLEIDE
CDEEENRT	CENTERED	**CDEEHIPS**	CEPHEIDS	**CDEEILOR**	RECOILED
	DECENTER	**CDEEHIRR**	CHERRIED	**CDEEILPS**	ECLIPSED
	DECENTRE		DREICHER		PEDICELS
CDEEEPRS	PRECEDES	**CDEEHIRW**	RICHWEED	**CDEEILRS**	SCLEREID
CDEEEPTX	EXCEPTED	**CDEEHISS**	DEHISCES	**CDEEILRT**	DERELICT
	EXPECTED	**CDEEHIST**	CHEDITES	**CDEEILRU**	RECUILED
CDEEERRS	DECREERS		TEDESCHI	**CDEEIMNR**	ENDERMIC
	SCREEDER	**CDEEHITW**	ITCHWEED	**CDEEIMNS**	CNEMIDES
CDEEERSS	RECESSED	**CDEEHKST**	SKETCHED		ENDEMICS
	SECEDERS	**CDEEHKTV**	KVETCHED	**CDEEIMOR**	MEDIOCRE
CDEEERST	DECREETS	**CDEEHLMO**	LEECHDOM		

Eight-letter anagrams

CDEEIMOS	COMEDIES	CDEEKOST	SOCKETED	CDEEOPPR	COPPERED
CDEEIMPR	PREMEDIC	CDEEKPRU	PUCKERED	CDEEOPRS	PRECODES
CDEEIMRS	MISCREED	CDEEKRSU	SUCKERED		PROCEEDS
CDEEIMRV	DECEMVIR	CDEEKRTU	TUCKERED	CDEEOPRU	RECOUPED
CDEEINNS	INCENSED	CDEELLOR	CORDELLE	CDEEORRR	RECORDER
CDEEINNT	INCENTED	CDEELLOT	COLLETED		RERECORD
	INDECENT	CDEELLPU	CUPELLED	CDEEORRS	RESCORED
CDEEINOR	RECOINED	CDEELMOW	WELCOMED	CDEEORRU	RECOURED
CDEEINOS	CODEINES	CDEELNOS	ENCLOSED	CDEEORST	CORSETED
CDEEINPR	PINCERED	CDEELNPU	PEDUNCLE		ESCORTED
CDEEINPS	DISPENCE	CDEELNTY	DECENTLY		SECTORED
CDEEINPT	DEPEINCT	CDEELNUW	UNCLEWED	CDEEORSV	COVERSED
	INCEPTED	CDEELOOW	LOCOWEED	CDEEORSW	ESCROWED
	PEINCTED	CDEELOPU	DECOUPLE	CDEEORSY	DECOYERS
	PENTICED	CDEELORS	RECLOSED	CDEEORTT	COTTERED
CDEEINRU	REINDUCE	CDEELORV	CLOVERED		DETECTOR
CDEEINTU	INDUCTEE	CDEELORY	RECOYLED	CDEEORTV	CORVETED
CDEEINTV	INVECTED	CDEELOSS	CODELESS		VECTORED
CDEEIOPR	RECOPIED	CDEELOST	CLOSETED	CDEEOSST	CESTODES
CDEEIORV	CODERIVE	CDEELOTU	ELOCUTED		COSSETED
	DIVORCEE	CDEELPRU	PRECLUDE	CDEEOSTT	ESCOTTED
	REVOICED	CDEELPSU	DECUPLES	CDEEPRRU	PRECURED
CDEEIOSS	DIOCESES	CDEELRTU	LECTURED	CDEEPRST	SCEPTRED
CDEEIOSV	DEVOICES		RELUCTED	CDEERRNU	RECURRED
CDEEIPRR	REPRICED			CDEERRSU	CURSEDER
CDEEIPRS	PRECISED	CDEELRUX	EXCLUDER		REDUCERS
CDEEIPRT	DECREPIT	CDEELSSU	SCEDULES	CDEERRUV	RECURVED
	DEPICTER		SECLUDES	CDEERSSU	SEDUCERS
	PRECITED	CDEELSUX	EXCLUDES	CDEERSUV	DECURVES
CDEEIPRU	PEDICURE	CDEEMOPR	COMPERED	CDEERSUX	EXCURSED
CDEEIPST	PECTISED	CDEEMOPT	COEMPTED	CDEERTTU	CURETTED
CDEEIPTZ	PECTIZED		COMPETED	CDEERTUV	CURVETED
CDEEIQSU	QUIESCED	CDEEMORT	ECTODERM	CDEFFINO	COFFINED
CDEEIRRS	DECRIERS	CDEEMSTU	TUMESCED	CDEFFISU	SUFFICED
	DESCRIER	CDEENNOR	RECONNED	CDEFFLSU	SCUFFLED
CDEEIRRT	DIRECTER	CDEENNOS	CONDENSE	CDEFFNUU	UNCUFFED
	REDIRECT	CDEENNOU	DENOUNCE	CDEFHILN	FLINCHED
CDEEIRSS	DESCRIES		ENOUNCED	CDEFHILT	FLITCHED
CDEEIRST	DESERTIC	CDEENNOV	CONVENED	CDEFHIMO	CHIEFDOM
	DISCREET	CDEENNPY	PENDENCY	CDEFHIRT	FRICHTED
	DISCRETE	CDEENNTU	UNDECENT	CDEFHMOS	CHEFDOMS
CDEEIRSU	DECURIES	CDEENNTY	TENDENCY	CDEFIIIL	FILICIDE
CDEEIRSV	DESCRIVE	CDEENOOS	COOSENED	CDEFIIIT	CITIFIED
	SCRIEVED	CDEENORR	CORNERED	CDEFIIOR	CODIFIER
	SERVICED	CDEENORS	CENSORED	CDEFIIOS	CODIFIES
CDEEIRTU	CUITERED		ENCODERS	CDEFIIST	DEFICITS
	DEUTERIC		NECROSED	CDEFIITY	CITYFIED
CDEEISUV	SEDUCIVE		SECONDER	CDEFINNO	CONFINED
CDEEITUV	EDUCTIVE	CDEENORT	CENTRODE	CDEFINNU	INFECUND
CDEEJKOY	JOCKEYED	CDEENORU	COENDURE	CDEFINOR	CONFIDER
CDEEKLNO	ENLOCKED	CDEENOSS	SECONDES		INFORCED
CDEEKLOR	RELOCKED	CDEENOSY	ECDYSONE	CDEFINOS	CONFIDES
CDEEKLPS	SPECKLED	CDEENOTU	DUECENTO	CDEFINOX	CONFIXED
CDEEKMOR	MOCKERED	CDEENOTX	COEXTEND	CDEFIORY	RECODIFY
CDEEKMRU	MUCKERED	CDEENOVX	CONVEXED	CDEFKORS	DEFROCKS
CDEEKNOR	RECKONED	CDEENOVY	CONVEYED	CDEFLNOU	FLOUNCED
CDEEKNRS	REDNECKS	CDEENPRU	PRUDENCE	CDEFLORY	FORCEDLY
CDEEKNRU	UNRECKED	CDEENRSU	CENSURED	CDEFNORU	FROUNCED
CDEEKOOR	RECOOKED	CDEENRUV	VERECUND		UNFORCED
CDEEKOPT	POCKETED	CDEENRUW	UNCREWED	CDEFNOSU	CONFUSED
CDEEKORR	RECORKED	CDEENSST	DESCENTS	CDEFNOTU	CONFUTED
CDEEKORT	ROCKETED	CDEENSSU	CENSUSED	CDEFNSTU	DEFUNCTS
CDEEKORV	OVERDECK	CDEENSTY	ENCYSTED	CDEFOSSU	FOCUSSED
CDEEKORW	ROCKWEED	CDEEOOPR	COOPERED	CDEGHLNU	GLUNCHED
		CDEEOOTV	DOVECOTE		

CDEGHORU	GROUCHED
CDEGHRTU	GRUTCHED
CDEGIILP	DIPLEGIC
CDEGIINN	INCEDING
CDEGIINX	EXCIDING
CDEGIKNO	DECKOING
	DECOKING
CDEGIKNS	DECKINGS
CDEGILSU	CLUDGIES
CDEGINNO	ENCODING
CDEGINNS	SCENDING
CDEGINOR	RECODING
CDEGINOS	CODESIGN
	COGNISED
	COSIGNED
CDEGINOY	DECOYING
	GYNECOID
CDEGINOZ	COGNIZED
CDEGINRU	REDUCING
CDEGINRY	DECRYING
CDEGINSU	SEDUCING
CDEGINSY	DYSGENIC
CDEGKOSU	GEODUCKS
CDEGKSUW	GWEDUCKS
CDEGLNOO	COLOGNED
CDEGNORU	CONGRUED
CDEGOORS	SCROOGED
CDEGORSU	SCOURGED
	SCROUGED
CDEGORSW	SCROWDGE
CDEHHNOO	HONCHOED
CDEHIILO	HELICOID
CDEHIILS	CEILIDHS
CDEHIIMO	HOMICIDE
CDEHIIMR	CHIMERID
CDEHIINO	ECHINOID
CDEHIIVV	CHIVVIED
CDEHIKOS	HOICKSED
CDEHIKRW	HERDWICK
CDEHIKST	SKITCHED
CDEHILMR	MERCHILD
CDEHILNR	CHILDREN
CDEHILOR	CHLORIDE
CDEHILOS	CHELOIDS
CDEHILRT	ELDRITCH
CDEHIMOR	CHROMIDE
CDEHIMOT	METHODIC
CDEHIMRS	SMIRCHED
CDEHINNR	INDRENCH
CDEHINOS	HEDONICS
CDEHINQU	QUINCHED
CDEHINST	SNITCHED
CDEHIOOR	CHOREOID
	OCHIDORE
CDEHIOSW	COWHIDES
CDEHIOTU	OUTCHIDE
CDEHIOTY	THEODICY
CDEHIQTU	QUITCHED
CDEHIRST	DITCHERS
CDEHISTT	STITCHED
CDEHISTW	SWITCHED
CDEHITTW	TWITCHED
CDEHKLSU	SHELDUCK
CDEHKNOU	UNCHOKED

CDEHKSUY	HEYDUCKS
CDEHLOOR	COHOLDER
CDEHLOOS	DESCHOOL
	SCHOOLED
CDEHLORT	CHORTLED
CDEHLOSU	SLOUCHED
CDEHMNTU	DUTCHMEN
CDEHMOOS	SMOOCHED
CDEHMOSU	SMOUCHED
CDEHMSTU	SMUTCHED
CDEHNOOP	CHENOPOD
	PONCHOED
CDEHNORS	CHONDRES
CDEHNRSU	CHUNDERS
CDEHOORR	RHEOCORD
CDEHOOSS	SCOOSHED
CDEHOOST	COHOSTED
CDEHORSU	CHORUSED
CDEHORSW	CHOWDERS
	COWHERDS
CDEHOSSU	HOCUSSED
CDEHOSSW	COWSHEDS
CDEHSSSU	SCHUSSED
CDEIIILS	SILICIDE
CDEIIIMT	MITICIDE
CDEIIIOS	IDIOCIES
CDEIIIRV	VIRICIDE
CDEIIITV	VITICIDE
CDEIIKKS	SIDEKICK
CDEIIKLS	DISCLIKE
	SICKLIED
CDEIIKMM	MIMICKED
CDEIIKNR	CIDERKIN
CDEIIKNW	INWICKED
CDEIIKRS	DRICKSIE
CDEIIKRT	DICKTIER
CDEIIKST	DICKIEST
	STICKIED
CDEIILMM	DILEMMIC
CDEIILMO	DOMICILE
CDEIILNN	INCLINED
CDEIILNO	INDOCILE
CDEIILOT	IDIOLECT
CDEIILPS	DISCIPLE
CDEIILPU	PEDICULI
	PULICIDE
CDEIILRU	RIDICULE
CDEIIMOS	DIOECISM
CDEIIMRT	DIMETRIC
CDEIIMST	MISCITED
CDEIINNT	INCIDENT
CDEIINOS	DECISION
	ICONISED
CDEIINOV	INVOICED
CDEIINOZ	ICONIZED
CDEIINRT	INDICTER
	INDIRECT
	REINDICT
CDEIINTY	CYTIDINE
CDEIIOPR	PERIODIC
CDEIIOPS	EPISODIC
CDEIIOPT	EPIDOTIC
CDEIIOSU	DIECIOUS
CDEIIOSV	OVICIDES

CDEIIPPT	PEPTIDIC
CDEIIPRR	CIRRIPED
CDEIIRST	ICTERIDS
CDEIIRTU	DIURETIC
CDEIIRUV	VIRUCIDE
CDEIISSU	SUICIDES
CDEIISTT	DICTIEST
CDEIITWY	CITYWIDE
CDEIJNOO	COJOINED
CDEIJSST	DISJECTS
CDEIKLNO	INLOCKED
CDEIKLNR	CRINKLED
CDEIKLNU	UNLICKED
CDEIKLOR	CORDLIKE
CDEIKLOS	SIDELOCK
CDEIKLPR	PRICKLED
CDEIKLRT	TRICKLED
CDEIKLRU	LUDERICK
CDEIKLST	STICKLED
CDEIKLWY	WICKEDLY
CDEIKMSU	MUSICKED
CDEIKNPU	UNPICKED
CDEIKNTU	TUNICKED
CDEIKOSS	DOCKISES
CDEIKOST	DIESTOCK
CDEIKOSY	YOICKSED
CDEIKOSZ	DOCKIZES
CDEIKRRS	DERRICKS
CDEIKSTU	DUCKIEST
CDEILLOR	COLLIDER
CDEILLOS	CODILLES
	COLLIDES
CDEILLOU	LODICULE
CDEILLOY	DOCILELY
CDEILLPU	PELLUCID
CDEILMMS	SCLIMMED
CDEILMNO	DOLMENIC
CDEILMOP	COMPILED
	COMPLIED
CDEILMOS	MELODICS
CDEILMOY	MYCELOID
CDEILMPR	CRIMPLED
CDEILMRU	DULCIMER
CDEILMSY	DYSMELIC
CDEILNOS	INCLOSED
CDEILNOU	NUCLEOID
	UNCOILED
	UNDOCILE
CDEILNRY	CYLINDER
CDEILNSU	INCLUDES
	NUCLIDES
	UNSLICED
CDEILOOW	WOODLICE
CDEILOPS	SCOPELID
CDEILOPU	CLUPEOID
	UPCOILED
CDEILORS	SCLEROID
CDEILORU	CLOUDIER
CDEILORV	COVERLID
CDEILOSS	DISCLOSE
CDEILOST	DOCILEST
CDEILPPR	CRIPPLED
CDEILPSU	CLUPEIDS
CDEILRTY	DIRECTLY

Eight-letter anagrams

CDEILSTU	DULCITES	CDEIPRSY	CYPRIDES	CDELORSS	CORDLESS
	LUCIDEST	CDEIPRTU	PICTURED		SCOLDERS
CDEILSXY	DYSLEXIC	CDEIPSST	DISCEPTS	CDELORSU	CLOSURED
CDEILTTU	CUITTLED	CDEIPSSU	CUSPIDES	CDELORSW	CLOWDERS
CDEIMMOT	DECOMMIT	CDEIRRSU	SCURRIED		SCROWLED
CDEIMMOX	COMMIXED	CDEIRSSU	DISCURES	CDELORTU	CLOTURED
CDEIMOOW	WOODMICE	CDEIRSTU	CRUDITES	CDELORZZ	CROZZLED
CDEIMORT	MORTICED		CURDIEST	CDELOSSU	DULCOSES
CDEIMOSS	MISCODES		CURTSIED	CDELOSTU	COULDEST
CDEIMOST	DEMOTICS	CDEIRSTV	VERDICTS		LOCUSTED
	DOMESTIC	CDEISSST	DISSECTS	CDELPRSU	SCRUPLED
CDEIMPRS	SCRIMPED	CDEISSSU	DISCUSES	CDELPRUU	UPCURLED
CDEINNOU	UNCOINED	CDEJNORU	CONJURED	CDELPSTU	SCULPTED
CDEINNOV	CONNIVED	CDEKKLNU	KNUCKLED	CDELRRSU	CURDLERS
CDEINOOS	COOSINED	CDEKLMOR	CLERKDOM	CDELRSSU	SCUDLERS
CDEINOOZ	ENDOZOIC	CDEKLMOU	DUCKMOLE	CDELRSUY	CURSEDLY
CDEINORR	CORDINER	CDEKLNOU	UNLOCKED	CDELRTUU	CULTURED
CDEINORS	CONSIDER	CDEKLNRU	CRUNKLED	CDELRUVY	CURVEDLY
CDEINORT	CENTROID	CDEKLOPU	UPLOCKED	CDELSSTU	DUCTLESS
	DOCTRINE	CDEKLORY	YELDROCK	CDELSSUY	CUSSEDLY
CDEINORU	DECURION	CDEKLOSW	WEDLOCKS	CDELSTTU	SCUTTLED
CDEINORV	CODRIVEN	CDEKLRTU	TRUCKLED	CDELSTUU	DUCTULES
CDEINOST	DEONTICS	CDEKNOOU	UNCOOKED	CDEMMNOO	COMMONED
CDEINOSU	DOUCINES	CDEKNOOV	CONVOKED	CDEMMNOS	COMMENDS
CDEINOSZ	ZINCODES	CDEKNORS	DORNECKS	CDEMMNOU	COMMUNED
CDEINOTU	EDUCTION	CDEKNORU	UNCORKED	CDEMMOOS	COMMODES
CDEINOUV	UNVOICED	CDEKNSSU	SUNDECKS	CDEMMOOV	COMMOVED
CDEINOVV	CONVIVED	CDEKNSUU	UNSUCKED	CDEMMOTU	COMMUTED
CDEINPRS	PRESCIND	CDEKNTUU	UNTUCKED	CDEMMRSU	SCRUMMED
CDEINPRU	UNPRICED	CDEKOPSY	COPYDESK	CDEMNNOS	CONDEMNS
CDEINPSY	DYSPNEIC	CDEKOSST	DESTOCKS	CDEMNOOW	COMEDOWN
CDEINRRU	INCURRED	CDELLNUU	UNCULLED		DOWNCOME
CDEINRSS	DISCERNS	CDELLOOP	CLODPOLE	CDEMNOPS	COMPENDS
	RESCINDS	CDELLORS	SCROLLED	CDEMNOSU	CONSUMED
CDEINRSU	INDUCERS	CDELLORU	COLLUDER	CDEMNOTU	DOCUMENT
CDEINRTU	REINDUCT	CDELLOSU	COLLUDES	CDEMNSUU	SECUNDUM
CDEINRUV	INCURVED	CDELLOTU	CLOUDLET	CDEMOOPS	COMPOSED
CDEINSSX	EXSCINDS	CDELLTUY	DULCETLY	CDEMOPTU	COMPUTED
CDEINSTY	SYNDETIC	CDELMNOO	MONOCLED	CDEMORSU	DECORUMS
CDEIOORS	CORODIES	CDELMNOU	COLUMNED	CDEMOSTU	COSTUMED
CDEIOORT	COEDITOR	CDELMPRU	CRUMPLED		CUSTOMED
CDEIOPRS	PERCOIDS	CDELNOOR	CONDOLER	CDEMPRSU	SCRUMPED
CDEIOPRT	DEPICTOR	CDELNOOS	CONDOLES	CDENNOOR	CONDONER
CDEIOPST	DESPOTIC		CONSOLED	CDENNOOS	CONDONES
CDEIOPTY	COPYEDIT	CDELNOOU	UNCOOLED	CDENNOOT	CONNOTED
CDEIORRT	CREDITOR	CDELNOSS	COLDNESS	CDENNOST	CONTENDS
	DIRECTOR	CDELNOSU	ENCLOUDS	CDENNOUY	UNCOYNED
CDEIORRV	CODRIVER		UNCLOSED	CDENOORS	CONDORES
	DIVORCER	CDELNOSY	CONDYLES	CDENOORT	CREODONT
CDEIORSS	DISCOERS		SECONDLY	CDENOOST	SECODONT
CDEIORST	CORDITES	CDELNOTU	UNCOLTED	CDENOOTT	COTTONED
CDEIORSU	DISCOURE	CDELNOUW	UNCOWLED	CDENOOVY	CONVOYED
CDEIORSV	CODRIVES	CDELNOUY	UNCLOYED	CDENORSS	CORSNEDS
	DISCOVER	CDELNRUU	UNCURLED	CDENORSU	CRUNODES
	DIVORCES	CDELNSUY	SECUNDLY	CDENORSW	DECROWNS
CDEIORSW	CROWDIES	CDELOORS	COLOREDS	CDENORTU	CORNUTED
CDEIORSY	DECISORY		CROODLES		TROUNCED
CDEIORTU	OUTCRIED		DECOLORS	CDENOSSY	ECDYSONS
CDEIOSST	CESTOIDS	CDELOORU	COLOURED	CDENOSTU	CONTUSED
	SCODIEST		DECOLOUR	CDENRSUU	UNCURSED
CDEIOSTT	COTTISED	CDELOORV	OVERCOLD	CDENRTUU	UNDERCUT
CDEIPRSS	DISCERPS	CDELOOTT	DOLCETTO	CDENRUUV	UNCURVED
CDEIPRST	PREDICTS	CDELOPSU	UPCLOSED	CDEOOPPS	COPEPODS
	SCRIPTED	CDELOPTU	OCTUPLED	CDEOOPRS	SCROOPED

CDEOOPST	POSTCODE	**CDHILOOS**	DOLICHOS		WINDSOCK
CDEOORRR	CORRODER	**CDHILORS**	CHLORIDS	**CDIKNOTW**	DOWNTICK
CDEOORRS	CORRODES	**CDHIMOSU**	DOCHMIUS	**CDIKNPSU**	DUCKPINS
CDEOORSU	DECOROUS	**CDHINNOR**	CHONDRIN	**CDILLOOS**	COLLOIDS
CDEOORSV	VOCODERS	**CDHINORY**	HYDRONIC	**CDILLOTU**	DULCITOL
CDEOOSTV	DOVECOTS	**CDHIOOPW**	WOODCHIP	**CDILLOUY**	CLOUDILY
CDEOPRRU	PROCURED	**CDHIOORS**	CHOROIDS	**CDILMSTU**	MIDCULTS
	PRODUCER	**CDHIOORT**	TROCHOID	**CDILOOPS**	PODSOLIC
CDEOPRSU	PRODUCES	**CDHIOPRW**	WHIPCORD	**CDILOOPZ**	PODZOLIC
CDEOQSTU	DOCQUETS	**CDHIOPRY**	HYDROPIC	**CDILOORS**	DISCOLOR
CDEORRSW	CROWDERS	**CDHIOPSY**	PSYCHOID	**CDILOORT**	LORDOTIC
CDEORRTU	REDUCTOR	**CDHIORRT**	TRICHORD	**CDILOOTY**	COTYLOID
CDEORSST	DOCTRESS	**CDHIOSUV**	DISVOUCH	**CDILOSST**	DISCLOST
CDEORSSU	SCOURSED	**CDHIPSTY**	DIPTYCHS	**CDILOSTY**	DICOTYLS
CDEORSSW	SCOWDERS	**CDHIRSTY**	CHYTRIDS		SCOLYTID
CDEORSTU	EDUCTORS	**CDHKOORS**	HORDOCKS	**CDIMMOSU**	MODICUMS
	SEDUCTOR	**CDHLOOPY**	COPYHOLD	**CDIMOORT**	MICRODOT
CDEORSUU	DOUCEURS	**CDHNORSU**	CHONDRUS	**CDINNQUU**	QUIDNUNC
CDEOSSTU	CUSTODES	**CDHOOOPW**	WOODCHOP	**CDINOOOR**	CORONOID
CDEPRSTY	DECRYPTS	**CDHOORRU**	UROCHORD	**CDINOOTU**	NOCTUOID
CDEPRUUV	UPCURVED	**CDIIIMNS**	MINIDISC	**CDINOPSY**	DYSPNOIC
CDERSTTU	DESTRUCT	**CDIIIMNU**	INDICIUM	**CDINORSW**	DISCROWN
CDFIILSU	FLUIDICS	**CDIIINSV**	INVISCID	**CDINORTU**	INDUCTOR
CDFIKMNU	MINDFUCK	**CDIIIORT**	DIORITIC	**CDINOSTU**	CONDUITS
CDFIKORS	DISFROCK	**CDIIKMNO**	DOMINICK		DISCOUNT
CDFKOOTU	DUCKFOOT	**CDIIKPST**	DIPSTICK		NOCTUIDS
CDFNNOOU	CONFOUND	**CDIILMOS**	DOMICILS	**CDINOSTY**	DYSTONIC
CDFNOOSU	COFOUNDS	**CDIILOPP**	DIPLOPIC	**CDIOOPPS**	PROSODIC
CDGHIILN	CHILDING	**CDIILOTY**	DOCILITY	**CDIOORRR**	CORRIDOR
CDGHIILO	CHILIDOG	**CDIILRUY**	URIDYLIC	**CDIOPRRS**	RIPCORDS
CDGHIINS	CHIDINGS	**CDIILSVY**	VISCIDLY	**CDIOPRSU**	CUSPIDOR
CDGHIINT	DICHTING	**CDIILTUY**	LUCIDITY	**CDIOSSTY**	CYSTOIDS
	DITCHING	**CDIIMNOU**	CONIDIUM	**CDIOSTUV**	OVIDUCTS
CDGHILOS	GLOCHIDS		MUCINOID	**CDJLNOUY**	JOCUNDLY
CDGHINNU	DUNCHING		ONCIDIUM	**CDKLNOOW**	LOCKDOWN
CDGHINOR	CHORDING	**CDIIMTUY**	MUCIDITY	**CDKLOOOS**	OCKODOLS
CDGHINOU	DOUCHING	**CDIINOOS**	ISODICON	**CDKMMORU**	DRUMMOCK
CDGIINNU	INDUCING		ONISCOID	**CDKMORSU**	MUDROCKS
CDGIINOS	DISCOING	**CDIINORT**	INDICTOR	**CDKNNOSU**	DUNNOCKS
CDGIKLNU	DUCKLING	**CDIINOST**	DICTIONS	**CDKNOORS**	DORNOCKS
CDGIKLOR	GRIDLOCK	**CDIINOSV**	VIDICONS	**CDKOOORW**	CORKWOOD
CDGIKNOS	DOCKINGS	**CDIINPRY**	CYPRINID	**CDKORTUW**	DUCTWORK
CDGIKNSU	DUCKINGS	**CDIINPTU**	PUNDITIC	**CDLLLOOP**	CLODPOLL
CDGILNOS	CODLINGS	**CDIINSTT**	DISTINCT	**CDLNOOOW**	COOLDOWN
	LINGCODS	**CDIIOORS**	SORICOID	**CDLNOSUU**	UNCLOUDS
	SCOLDING	**CDIIOOSU**	DIOICOUS	**CDLNOUUY**	UNCLOUDY
CDGILNOU	CLOUDING	**CDIIOPRT**	DIOPTRIC	**CDLOOOTW**	COLTWOOD
CDGILNRU	CURDLING		DIPROTIC	**CDLOOPSY**	LYCOPODS
CDGINORS	CORDINGS		TRIPODIC	**CDLOORTY**	DOCTORLY
CDGINORW	CROWDING	**CDIIORSU**	SCIUROID	**CDLOOSTU**	OUTSCOLD
CDGINSTU	DUCTINGS	**CDIIORSX**	CORIXIDS	**CDMNOOPU**	COMPOUND
CDGLOOOY	CODOLOGY	**CDIIOSSS**	CISSOIDS	**CDMNORUU**	CORUNDUM
CDGNOOOS	COONDOGS	**CDIIOSTY**	SODICITY	**CDMOSSUW**	MUDSCOWS
CDGNOOTU	GONODUCT	**CDIIPTUY**	CUPIDITY	**CDNNOOOT**	CONODONT
CDHHIILS	CHILDISH		PUDICITY	**CDNNOOTY**	CYNODONT
CDHIILTW	TWICHILD	**CDIIRSSU**	SCIURIDS	**CDNNOSTU**	CONTUNDS
CDHIINST	CHINDITS	**CDIIRSTT**	DISTRICT	**CDNOSTUW**	CUTDOWNS
CDHIIOOR	CHORIOID	**CDIJNSTU**	DISJUNCT	**CDOOOPST**	OCTOPODS
CDHIIORT	HIDROTIC	**CDIKKNOW**	KICKDOWN	**CDOOPSST**	POSTDOCS
	TRICHOID	**CDIKKOPR**	DROPKICK	**CDOORRUY**	CORDUROY
CDHIIOSZ	SCHIZOID	**CDIKNNSU**	NUDNICKS	**CDOORTUW**	OUTCROWD
CDHIISST	DISTICHS	**CDIKNORS**	DORNICKS	**CDOOSTUW**	WOODCUTS
CDHILNSU	UNCHILDS	**CDIKNOSW**	WINDOCKS	**CDOPRSTU**	PRODUCTS
CDHILOOP	CHILOPOD			**CDORSSUW**	CUSSWORD

Eight-letter anagrams

CEEEEGHS	GEECHEES
CEEEEHLS	LEECHEES
CEEEEIPY	EYEPIECE
CEEEEJRT	REJECTEE
CEEEELST	ELECTEES
	SELECTEE
CEEEEPRS	PRECEESE
CEEEFFIR	EFFIERCE
CEEEFFRT	EFFECTER
CEEEFHLS	FLEECHES
CEEEFILR	FLEECIER
CEEEFILS	FLEECIES
CEEEFINR	ENFIERCE
CEEEFLRS	FLEECERS
CEEEFNOR	CONFEREE
CEEEFNRS	REFENCES
CEEEGIMN	EMCEEING
CEEEGINS	EGENCIES
CEEEGINX	EXIGENCE
CEEEGITX	EXEGETIC
CEEEGMNR	MERGENCE
CEEEGNRS	REGENCES
CEEEGNRV	VERGENCE
CEEEHIKR	CHEEKIER
CEEEHIRR	CHEERIER
	REECHIER
CEEEHIRS	CHEESIER
CEEEHLLS	ECHELLES
CEEEHLRV	CHEVEREL
CEEEHLSS	SLEECHES
CEEEHMSS	SMEECHES
CEEEHNNP	PENNEECH
CEEEHNRS	ENCHEERS
CEEEHORS	REECHOES
CEEEHPRS	CHEEPERS
CEEEHPSS	SPEECHES
CEEEHRRS	CHEERERS
CEEEHRSS	CREESHES
	SECESHER
CEEEHRSW	ESCHEWER
CEEEHRVY	CHEVERYE
CEEEHSSS	SECESHES
CEEEIJTV	EJECTIVE
CEEEIKRR	CREEKIER
CEEEILNN	LENIENCE
CEEEILNS	LICENSEE
CEEEILNT	TELECINE
CEEEILRS	CELERIES
CEEEILRT	ERECTILE
CEEEILTV	CLEVEITE
	ELECTIVE
CEEEIMNN	EMINENCE
CEEEIMPR	EMPIERCE
CEEEIMRR	REREMICE
CEEEINNT	ENCEINTE
CEEEINPR	PIECENER
CEEEINPS	EPICENES
CEEEINRS	CERESINE
	SCREENIE
CEEEINSS	ESNECIES
CEEEIOPT	TOEPIECE
CEEEIPRR	CREEPIER
	CREPERIE
CEEEIPRS	CREEPIES

CEEEIPRV	PERCEIVE
CEEEIRRV	RECEIVER
CEEEIRSV	RECEIVES
CEEEIRSX	EXERCISE
CEEEIRTV	ERECTIVE
CEEEISSS	ECESISES
CEEEISTV	EVICTEES
CEEEJRRT	REJECTER
CEEEJRST	REEJECTS
CEEEKNNP	PENNEECK
CEEELLNR	CRENELLE
CEEELLSU	ECUELLES
CEEELOPR	OPERCELE
CEEELOSS	COLESSEE
CEEELPRT	PREELECT
CEEELPSY	YCLEEPES
CEEELRRV	CLEVERER
CEEELRST	REELECTS
	RESELECT
CEEELRTT	ELECTRET
	TERCELET
CEEELSST	CELESTES
CEEEMNNS	SCENEMEN
CEEEMNRT	CEMENTER
	CEREMENT
	RECEMENT
CEEEMORT	ECTOMERE
CEEEMPRS	EMPERCES
CEEEMRTY	CEMETERY
CEEENNPT	TENPENCE
CEEENNST	SENTENCE
CEEENPRS	PRESENCE
CEEENPRT	PRETENCE
CEEENQSU	SEQUENCE
CEEENRRS	RESCREEN
	SCREENER
CEEENRRT	RECENTER
	RECENTRE
CEEENRSS	RECENSES
CEEENSSS	ESSENCES
CEEENSST	CENTESES
CEEEPRRS	CREEPERS
CEEEPRRT	PREERECT
CEEEPRTX	EXPECTER
CEEERRST	ERECTERS
	REERECTS
	SECRETER
CEEERRSU	RESECURE
CEEERRSV	SCREEVER
CEEERRTX	EXCRETER
CEEERSSS	RECESSES
CEEERSST	SECRETES
	SESTERCE
CEEERSSU	CEREUSES
CEEERSSV	SCREEVES
CEEERSTX	EXCRETES
CEEERTTV	CREVETTE
CEEERTUX	EXECUTER
CEEESSSX	EXCESSES
CEEESTUX	EXECUTES
CEEFFNOS	OFFENCES
CEEFFORS	EFFORCES
CEEFFORT	EFFECTOR
CEEFGILN	FLEECING

CEEFHIKR	KERCHIEF
CEEFHIRY	CHIEFERY
CEEFHISS	CHIEFESS
CEEFHIST	CHIEFEST
	FETICHES
CEEFHKLU	CHEEKFUL
CEEFHLNR	FLENCHER
CEEFHLNS	FLENCHES
CEEFHLRT	FLETCHER
CEEFHLRU	CHEERFUL
CEEFHLST	FLETCHES
CEEFHNRS	FRENCHES
CEEFHORU	FOURCHEE
CEEFHRST	FECHTERS
	FETCHERS
CEEFIINT	INFICETE
CEEFILLY	FLEECILY
CEEFILRT	TELFERIC
CEEFILRY	FIERCELY
CEEFINPP	FIPPENCE
CEEFINRT	FRENETIC
	INFECTER
	REINFECT
CEEFIPRT	PERFECTI
CEEFIRST	FIERCEST
CEEFKLRS	FLECKERS
	FRECKLES
CEEFKLSS	FECKLESS
CEEFLNOR	FLORENCE
CEEFLNSU	FLUENCES
CEEFLNTU	FECULENT
CEEFLRST	REFLECTS
CEEFNNSU	UNFENCES
CEEFNORR	CONFRERE
	ENFORCER
	RECONFER
	RENFORCE
CEEFNORS	ENFORCES
CEEFNORW	FENCEROW
CEEFNOTU	OUTFENCE
CEEFNRVY	FERVENCY
CEEFOPRR	PERFORCE
CEEFOPRT	PERFECTO
CEEFORRS	FRESCOER
CEEFORSS	FRESCOES
CEEFORTW	CROWFEET
CEEFPRST	PERFECTS
	PREFECTS
CEEGHIKN	CHEEKING
CEEGHILN	LEECHING
CEEGHINP	CHEEPING
CEEGHINR	CHEERING
	REECHING
CEEGHINS	CHEESING
CEEGHLOW	COGWHEEL
CEEGIINP	EPIGENIC
CEEGIJNT	EJECTING
CEEGIKLN	CLEEKING
CEEGILNP	CLEEPING
CEEGILNR	CREELING
CEEGILNT	ELECTING
CEEGILOT	ECLOGITE
CEEGILRS	CLERGIES
CEEGILRT	TELERGIC

CEEGIMNS	MISCEGEN	**CEEHINST**	SITHENCE	**CEEHNQRU**	QUENCHER
CEEGINOO	COOEEING	**CEEHINSX**	CHENIXES	**CEEHNQSU**	QUENCHES
CEEGINOR	EROGENIC	**CEEHINTT**	ENTHETIC	**CEEHNRRT**	RETRENCH
CEEGINPR	CREEPING	**CEEHIORS**	CHEERIOS		TRENCHER
CEEGINRS	CREESING	**CEEHIOSS**	ECHOISES	**CEEHNRRW**	WRENCHER
	GENERICS	**CEEHIOSU**	ICEHOUSE	**CEEHNRST**	TRENCHES
CEEGINRT	ERECTING	**CEEHIOSV**	COHESIVE	**CEEHNRSW**	WENCHERS
	GENTRICE	**CEEHIOSZ**	ECHOIZES		WRENCHES
CEEGINST	GENETICS	**CEEHIPRR**	CIPHERER	**CEEHNSST**	STENCHES
CEEGINSU	EUGENICS	**CEEHIPRT**	HERPETIC	**CEEHNSTU**	CHUTNEES
CEEGINXY	EXIGENCY	**CEEHIRRR**	CHERRIER	**CEEHOOPR**	POECHORE
CEEGIORX	EXOERGIC	**CEEHIRRS**	CHERRIES	**CEEHOORS**	RECHOOSE
CEEGIRSS	GRECISES	**CEEHIRRT**	CHERTIER	**CEEHOPRS**	PRECHOSE
CEEGIRSZ	GRECIZES	**CEEHIRSS**	RICHESSE	**CEEHOPRY**	CORYPHEE
CEEGLLOR	COLLEGER	**CEEHIRST**	CHESTIER	**CEEHOPST**	SHEEPCOT
CEEGLLOS	COLLEGES		HERETICS	**CEEHOPTT**	POCHETTE
CEEGLNST	NEGLECTS	**CEEHIRTT**	TETCHIER	**CEEHORRS**	COHERERS
CEEGLOSU	ECLOGUES	**CEEHIRTU**	HEURETIC		COSHERER
CEEGMMOR	COMMERGE	**CEEHIRTV**	VETCHIER	**CEEHORRT**	HECTORER
CEEGMNOY	CYMOGENE	**CEEHISSV**	SEVICHES		TORCHERE
CEEGNNOO	ONCOGENE	**CEEHISTT**	ESTHETIC	**CEEHORSS**	ORCHESES
CEEGNNOR	CONGENER		TECHIEST	**CEEHORST**	TROCHEES
CEEGNNPU	PUNGENCE	**CEEHISTW**	CHEWIEST	**CEEHOSUV**	VOUCHEES
CEEGNORS	COGENERS	**CEEHKLPR**	KREPLECH	**CEEHPPRS**	PERCHERS
	CONGREES	**CEEHKLRS**	HECKLERS	**CEEHPRRY**	PERCHERY
CEEGNORT	CONGREET	**CEEHKNPS**	HENPECKS	**CEEHPRSU**	UPCHEERS
	COREGENT	**CEEHKRST**	RESKETCH	**CEEHPSST**	SPETCHES
CEEGNORV	CONVERGE		SKETCHER	**CEEHQRSU**	CHEQUERS
CEEGNOTY	ECTOGENY	**CEEHKRTV**	KVETCHER	**CEEHQSTU**	QUETCHES
CEEGNRSU	URGENCES	**CEEHKSST**	SKETCHES	**CEEHRSTV**	CHEVRETS
CEEGNRVY	VERGENCY	**CEEHKSTV**	KVETCHES	**CEEHRSTW**	WRETCHES
CEEGORST	CORTEGES	**CEEHLMOO**	HEMOCOEL	**CEEHRTTU**	TEUCHTER
CEEGQRSU	GRECQUES	**CEEHLMSZ**	SCHMELZE	**CEEHSTTU**	TEUCHEST
CEEHHIRS	CHESHIRE	**CEEHLNOO**	HOLOCENE	**CEEIIKLP**	EPICLIKE
CEEHHMNN	HENCHMEN	**CEEHLNOS**	CHELONES	**CEEIIKLV**	VICELIKE
CEEHHSTT	THETCHES		ECHELONS	**CEEIIMPR**	EPIMERIC
CEEHIIST	ETHICISE	**CEEHLNOT**	ENCLOTHE	**CEEIIMRT**	EREMITIC
CEEHIITZ	ETHICIZE	**CEEHLNPS**	PLENCHES	**CEEIINRT**	ICTERINE
CEEHIKLY	CHEEKILY	**CEEHLNPU**	PENUCHLE		REINCITE
CEEHIKMS	KIMCHEES	**CEEHLNSU**	ELENCHUS	**CEEIINST**	NICETIES
CEEHIKNW	CHEEWINK	**CEEHLORT**	RECLOTHE	**CEEIINSW**	ICEWINES
CEEHILLN	CHENILLE	**CEEHLOSS**	ECHOLESS	**CEEIINVV**	EVINCIVE
CEEHILLV	CHEVILLE	**CEEHLOSW**	COWHEELS	**CEEIIPRS**	EPICIERS
CEEHILRS	CHISELER	**CEEHLQSU**	QUELCHES	**CEEIIRST**	SERICITE
	SCHLIERE	**CEEHLRSU**	HERCULES	**CEEIJNOT**	EJECTION
CEEHILRT	TELECHIR	**CEEHLRSW**	WELCHERS	**CEEIJNRT**	REINJECT
CEEHILRV	CHEVERIL	**CEEHLSSS**	CHESSELS	**CEEIJORR**	REJOICER
CEEHILRW	CLERIHEW	**CEEHMNNS**	MENSCHEN	**CEEIJORS**	REJOICES
CEEHILRY	CHEERILY	**CEEHMNOR**	CHOREMEN	**CEEIJRUV**	VERJUICE
CEEHILSV	VEHICLES		CHROMENE	**CEEIKKLN**	NECKLIKE
CEEHILSW	SWELCHIE	**CEEHMNSS**	CHESSMEN	**CEEIKKLO**	COKELIKE
CEEHILSY	CHEESILY		MENSCHES	**CEEIKKSS**	KECKSIES
CEEHIMMS	CHEMMIES	**CEEHMORT**	COMETHER	**CEEIKLMU**	LEUKEMIC
CEEHIMRS	CHIMERES	**CEEHMOTY**	HEMOCYTE	**CEEIKLNN**	NECKLINE
CEEHIMRT	HERMETIC	**CEEHMRSS**	SCHEMERS	**CEEIKLPR**	PICKEREL
CEEHIMSS	CHEMISES		SCHMEERS	**CEEIKNRS**	SICKENER
	SCHEMIES	**CEEHMRST**	MERCHETS	**CEEIKNST**	NECKTIES
CEEHINOR	COINHERE	**CEEHNNOW**	NOWHENCE	**CEEIKPRS**	PICKEERS
CEEHINPR	ENCIPHER	**CEEHNNRT**	ENTRENCH		SPECKIER
CEEHINPT	PHENETIC	**CEEHNOPS**	PENOCHES	**CEEIKPRT**	PICKETER
CEEHINPU	EUPHENIC	**CEEHNORS**	RECHOSEN	**CEEIKPST**	PECKIEST
CEEHINRR	ENRICHER	**CEEHNORT**	COHERENT	**CEEILLLP**	PELLICLE
CEEHINRS	ENRICHES	**CEEHNORV**	CHEVERON	**CEEILLMS**	MICELLES
	INHERCES	**CEEHNPSU**	PENUCHES	**CEEILLNT**	LENTICEL

	LENTICLE	**CEEINNOT**	NEOTENIC	**CEEIPRUX**	PRECIEUX
CEEILMOR	COMELIER	**CEEINNRS**	INCENSER	**CEEIPSST**	PECTISES
CEEILMPS	SEMPLICE	**CEEINNRT**	INCENTER	**CEEIPSTZ**	PECTIZES
CEEILNNT	CENTINEL		INCENTRE	**CEEIQSSU**	QUIESCES
CEEILNNY	LENIENCY	**CEEINNSS**	INCENSES	**CEEIRRSS**	CERRISES
CEEILNOP	PLIOCENE		NICENESS	**CEEIRRST**	RECITERS
CEEILNOS	CINEOLES	**CEEINNST**	NESCIENT	**CEEIRRSV**	SERVICER
CEEILNOT	COTELINE	**CEEINOPU**	EUPNOEIC	**CEEIRRSW**	SCREWIER
	ELECTION	**CEEINORR**	ENCIERRO	**CEEIRRTU**	URETERIC
CEEILNOV	VIOLENCE	**CEEINORT**	ERECTION	**CEEIRSSV**	SCRIEVES
CEEILNPR	PENCILER		NEOTERIC		SERVICES
CEEILNPU	PULICENE	**CEEINORV**	OVERNICE	**CEEIRSTT**	TIERCETS
CEEILNPX	CINEPLEX	**CEEINORX**	EXOCRINE	**CEEIRSTU**	CERUSITE
CEEILNRR	RECLINER	**CEEINOSS**	SENECIOS		CUTESIER
CEEILNRS	LICENSER	**CEEINOST**	ICESTONE		EUCRITES
	RECLINES		SEICENTO	**CEEIRSTV**	VERTICES
	SILENCER	**CEEINOTV**	EVECTION	**CEEIRSTX**	EXCITERS
CEEILNRU	CERULEIN	**CEEINPRT**	PRENTICE	**CEEIRSVX**	CERVIXES
CEEILNRV	VERNICLE		TERPENIC	**CEEISSST**	CITESSES
CEEILNSS	ENCLISES	**CEEINPST**	PECTINES	**CEEISTTT**	TECTITES
	LICENSES		PENTICES	**CEEISTTZ**	ZETETICS
	SILENCES	**CEEINPSX**	SIXPENCE	**CEEISUVX**	EXCUSIVE
CEEILNST	CENTILES	**CEEINQRU**	QUERCINE	**CEEJKOTT**	JOCKETTE
CEEILNSU	LEUCINES	**CEEINRRS**	SINCERER	**CEEJORRT**	REJECTOR
CEEILORR	RECOILER	**CEEINRRSS**	CERESINS	**CEEJORST**	EJECTORS
CEEILORS	CREOLISE		SCRIENES	**CEEKKNOS**	KNEESOCK
CEEILORZ	CREOLIZE	**CEEINRST**	CENTRIES	**CEEKKNPS**	KENSPECK
CEEILOSS	SOLECISE		ENTERICS	**CEEKLNPU**	PENUCKLE
CEEILOSZ	SOLECIZE		ENTICERS	**CEEKLNSS**	NECKLESS
CEEILPRS	ECLIPSER		SCIENTER	**CEEKLNST**	NECKLETS
	PRESLICE		SECRETIN	**CEEKLPSS**	SPECKLES
	RESPLICE	**CEEINRSU**	INSECURE	**CEEKLRSS**	CLERKESS
CEEILPRY	CREEPILY		SINECURE		RECKLESS
CEEILPSS	ECLIPSES	**CEEINRTT**	RETICENT	**CEEKNORR**	RECKONER
CEEILPSX	EXCIPLES	**CEEINRTU**	CEINTURE	**CEEKNRSU**	SUCKENER
CEEILQSU	LIQUESCE		ENURETIC	**CEEKOPRT**	POCKETER
CEEILRST	RETICLES	**CEEINSST**	CENTESIS	**CEEKOPRX**	OXPECKER
	SCLERITE	**CEEINSTY**	CYSTEINE	**CEEKORRT**	CORKTREE
	TIERCELS	**CEEIOPPR**	PERICOPE		ROCKETER
	TRISCELE	**CEEIOPPS**	EPISCOPE	**CEEKOSSY**	SOCKEYES
CEEILRSU	CISELEUR	**CEEIOPRS**	RECOPIES	**CEEKOSTT**	SOCKETTE
	CISELURE	**CEEIOPST**	ECTOPIES	**CEEKPRRU**	PUCKERER
	RECUILES		PICOTEES	**CEEKPRSY**	RYEPECKS
CEEILRSV	VERSICLE	**CEEIORST**	COTERIES	**CEEKRRSW**	WRECKERS
CEEILRTU	RETICULE		ESOTERIC	**CEELLLSU**	CELLULES
CEEILRTY	CELERITY	**CEEIORSV**	REVOICES	**CEELLMOU**	MOLECULE
CEEILSSV	CLEVISES	**CEEIORSX**	EXORCISE	**CEELLNOS**	COLLEENS
	VESICLES	**CEEIORTT**	EROTETIC	**CEELLNOU**	NUCLEOLE
	VICELESS	**CEEIORTV**	ORECTIVE	**CEELLORT**	RECOLLET
CEEILSTT	TELESTIC	**CEEIORTX**	EXOTERIC	**CEELLOSS**	CELLOSES
	TESTICLE	**CEEIORXZ**	EXORCIZE	**CEELLPRU**	CUPELLER
CEEILSTU	LEUCITES	**CEEIOSST**	COESITES	**CEELLPSU**	PUCELLES
CEEIMMPY	EMPYEMIC	**CEEIOSTV**	COVETISE	**CEELLRRU**	CRUELLER
CEEIMMRS	MESMERIC	**CEEIPPRR**	PREPRICE	**CEELLRVY**	CLEVERLY
CEEIMMST	MEMETICS	**CEEIPPRS**	PRECIPES	**CEELLSSU**	CLUELESS
CEEIMNNY	EMINENCY	**CEEIPPRT**	PRECEPIT	**CEELLSTY**	SELECTLY
CEEIMNPS	SPECIMEN	**CEEIPPTU**	EUPEPTIC	**CEELMOOS**	COELOMES
CEEIMNST	CENTIMES	**CEEIPRRS**	PIERCERS	**CEELMOPT**	COMPLETE
	TENESMIC		PRECISER	**CEELMORW**	WELCOMER
CEEIMORT	METEORIC		REPRICES	**CEELMOST**	TELECOMS
CEEIMOTY	MEIOCYTE	**CEEIPRSS**	PRECISES	**CEELMOSW**	WELCOMES
CEEIMRSX	EXCIMERS	**CEEIPRST**	CREPIEST	**CEELMRTU**	ELECTRUM
CEEIMSTT	SMECTITE		RECEIPTS	**CEELNNOP**	PENONCEL
CEEINNOP	PINECONE	**CEEIPRSU**	EPICURES	**CEELNNOT**	CENTONEL

	NONELECT	**CEENNOSU**	ENOUNCES		SPECTERS
CEELNOPU	OPULENCE	**CEENNOSV**	CONVENES		SPECTRES
CEELNOPY	LYCOPENE	**CEENNRST**	CENTNERS	**CEEPRSSY**	CYPRESES
CEELNORS	ENCLOSER	**CEENOOST**	ECOTONES	**CEEPRSTX**	EXCERPTS
	ENSORCEL	**CEENOPST**	POTENCES	**CEERRSST**	RECTRESS
CEELNORT	ELECTRON	**CEENOPTW**	TWOPENCE	**CEERRSSU**	RESCUERS
CEELNORU	ENCOLURE	**CEENORRS**	RECENSOR		SECURERS
CEELNOSS	ENCLOSES	**CEENORSS**	NECROSES	**CEERRSSW**	SCREWERS
CEELNPTU	CENTUPLE	**CEENORSU**	COENURES	**CEERRSUV**	RECURVES
CEELNRST	LECTERNS	**CEENORSV**	CONSERVE	**CEERRTUZ**	CREUTZER
CEELNRSU	LUCERNES		CONVERSE	**CEERSSST**	CRESSETS
CEELNRTU	RELUCENT	**CEENORSZ**	COZENERS	**CEERSSTU**	SECUREST
CEELNRTY	RECENTLY	**CEENORTT**	TRECENTO	**CEERSSTW**	SETSCREW
CEELNSTU	ESCULENT	**CEENORVY**	CONVEYER	**CEERSSUX**	EXCUSERS
CEELOOVV	COEVOLVE		RECONVEY		EXCUSERS
CEELOPRU	OPERCULE	**CEENOSVX**	CONVEXES	**CEERSTTU**	CURETTES
	RECOUPLE	**CEENPPTU**	TUPPENCE	**CEERTUXY**	EXECUTRY
CEELORSS	CORELESS	**CEENPRSS**	SPENCERS	**CEESSSTU**	CESTUSES
	RECLOSES	**CEENPRST**	PERCENTS	**CEESTTUV**	CUVETTES
	SCLEROSE		PRECENTS	**CEFFGHIN**	CHEFFING
CEELORST	CORSELET	**CEENPSSU**	SUSPENCE	**CEFFHIRU**	CHUFFIER
	ELECTORS	**CEENQSUY**	SEQUENCY	**CEFFHSTU**	CHUFFEST
	ELECTROS	**CEENRRSU**	CENSURER	**CEFFIILR**	CLIFFIER
	SELECTOR	**CEENRSSU**	CENSURES	**CEFFIORS**	OFFICERS
CEELORSY	RECOYLES	**CEENRSTU**	UNSECRET	**CEFFIORU**	COIFFEUR
CEELORTV	COVERLET	**CEENSSSU**	CENSUSES		COIFFURE
CEELOSSU	COLEUSES	**CEENSSTU**	CUTENESS	**CEFFIRSU**	SUFFICER
CEELOSTU	ELOCUTES	**CEENSTTU**	CUNETTES	**CEFFISSU**	SUFFICES
CEELOSTV	COVELETS	**CEEOORST**	CREOSOTE	**CEFFLORU**	FORCEFUL
CEELPRST	PLECTRES	**CEEOPRRS**	PRESCORE	**CEFFLRSU**	SCUFFLER
	PRELECTS	**CEEOPRRT**	RECEPTOR	**CEFFLSSU**	CUFFLESS
CEELPRSU	CUPELERS	**CEEOPRTX**	EXCEPTOR		SCUFFLES
CEELRRTU	LECTURER	**CEEOPRTY**	CEROTYPE	**CEFFORSS**	SCOFFERS
CEELRSST	LECTRESS	**CEEOPSST**	PECTOSES	**CEFFORST**	COFFRETS
CEELRSSU	CURELESS	**CEEOPSTY**	ECOTYPES	**CEFFRSSU**	SCUFFERS
	RECLUSES	**CEEOQTTU**	COQUETTE	**CEFGHINT**	FECHTING
CEELRSSW	CREWLESS	**CEEORRRS**	SORCERER		FETCHING
CEELRSTU	CRUELEST	**CEEORRSS**	RESCORES	**CEFGIKLN**	FLECKING
	LECTURES	**CEEORRST**	ERECTORS	**CEFGILNT**	CLEFTING
CEELRSTY	SECRETLY		SECRETOR	**CEFGINNS**	FENCINGS
CEELRSUY	SECURELY	**CEEORRSU**	RECOURES	**CEFGLNUY**	FULGENCY
CEELSTTU	LETTUCES		RECOURSE	**CEFHIIMS**	MISCHIEF
CEEMMNTU	CEMENTUM		RESOURCE	**CEFHILNR**	FLINCHER
CEEMMORS	COMMERES	**CEEORRSV**	COVERERS	**CEFHILNS**	FLINCHES
CEEMNORR	CREMORNE		RECOVERS	**CEFHILRS**	FILCHERS
CEEMNORW	NEWCOMER	**CEEORRSW**	RECOWERS	**CEFHILRT**	FLICHTER
CEEMNORY	CEREMONY	**CEEORRUV**	OVERCURE	**CEFHILST**	FLITCHES
CEEMNOYZ	COENZYME	**CEEORRVY**	RECOVERY	**CEFHINSU**	FUCHSINE
CEEMNRSU	CERUMENS	**CEEORSTV**	COVETERS	**CEFHISTT**	FITCHETS
CEEMOORV	COMEOVER	**CEEORSTW**	COWTREES	**CEFHISTU**	FUCHSITE
	OVERCOME	**CEEORSTX**	COEXERTS	**CEFHISTW**	FITCHEWS
CEEMOORW	OWRECOME		CORTEXES	**CEFHKOOR**	FOREHOCK
CEEMOOTY	OOMYCETE	**CEEORTTV**	CORVETTE	**CEFHLSSY**	FLYSCHES
CEEMOPRS	COMPEERS	**CEEORTUX**	EXECUTOR	**CEFHLSTU**	CHESTFUL
	COMPERES	**CEEOSSST**	CESTOSES		FUTCHELS
CEEMOPST	COMPETES	**CEEOSTTT**	OCTETTES	**CEFIIIST**	CITIFIES
CEEMOSSS	COSMESES	**CEEPPRST**	PERCEPTS	**CEFIILLM**	MELLIFIC
CEEMSSTU	TUMESCES		PRECEPTS	**CEFIILNO**	OLEFINIC
CEENNOOS	CONENOSE	**CEEPPRSU**	PREPUCES	**CEFIILRT**	CLIFTIER
CEENNORS	ONSCREEN	**CEEPPRSU**	PRECURES	**CEFIILST**	FELSITIC
CEENNORT	CRETONNE		PRECURSE	**CEFIILTY**	FELICITY
CEENNORU	RENOUNCE	**CEEPRSST**	RESPECTS	**CEFIIOPR**	OPIFICER
CEENNORV	CONVENER		SCEPTERS	**CEFIIORS**	ORIFICES
CEENNOST	CENTONES		SCEPTRES	**CEFIIPRT**	PETRIFIC

CEFIIRRT	FERRITIC	CEGGIORS	CROGGIES		SPECKING
	TERRIFIC		GEORGICS	CEGIKNRT	TRECKING
CEFIISTY	CITYFIES		SCROGGIE	CEGIKNRW	WRECKING
CEFIKLOR	FIRELOCK	CEGGLNOY	GLYCOGEN	CEGIKSTU	GUCKIEST
	FLOCKIER	CEGGLORS	CLOGGERS	CEGILMMN	CLEMMING
CEFIKLRS	FLICKERS	CEGHHINT	HECHTING	CEGILMNO	COMINGLE
CEFIKLRY	FLICKERY	CEGHIINY	HYGIENIC	CEGILMPS	GEMCLIPS
CEFIKLST	FICKLEST	CEGHIKLN	HECKLING	CEGILNOO	NEOLOGIC
CEFILLLO	FOLLICLE	CEGHIKNT	KETCHING	CEGILNOS	ECLOSING
CEFILMRU	CRIMEFUL	CEGHILNP	CHELPING	CEGILNPU	CUPELING
	MERCIFUL	CEGHILNT	LETCHING	CEGILNRS	CLINGERS
CEFILNOT	FLECTION	CEGHILNW	WELCHING		CRINGLES
CEFILNST	INFLECTS	CEGHILST	GLITCHES	CEGILNRU	RECULING
CEFILNSU	FUNICLES	CEGHIMNS	SCHEMING		ULCERING
CEFILOUV	VOICEFUL	CEGHINNW	WENCHING	CEGILNRY	GLYCERIN
CEFILRSU	FLUERICS	CEGHINOR	COHERING	CEGILNSU	LUCIGENS
	LUCIFERS		OCHERING	CEGILNSY	GLYCINES
CEFIMOST	COMFIEST	CEGHINPR	PERCHING	CEGILNTU	CULTIGEN
CEFINNOR	CONFINER	CEGHINQU	CHEQUING	CEGILRSY	LYSERGIC
CEFINNOS	CONFINES	CEGHINRS	GRINCHES	CEGIMNOS	GENOMICS
CEFINORS	COINFERS	CEGHINRT	RETCHING	CEGIMNOY	MYOGENIC
	CONIFERS	CEGHINRU	EUCHRING	CEGIMNSU	MUCIGENS
	FORENSIC	CEGHINST	CHESTING	CEGIMNUY	GYNECIUM
	FORINSEC		ETCHINGS	CEGINNOR	ENCORING
	FORNICES	CEGHINVY	CHEVYING	CEGINNOZ	COZENING
	INFORCES	CEGHIRSS	SCREIGHS	CEGINNRS	SCERNING
CEFINORT	INFECTOR	CEGHIRTU	THEURGIC	CEGINNRT	CENTRING
CEFINOSX	CONFIXES	CEGHISTU	GUICHETS	CEGINNST	SCENTING
CEFINOTT	CONFETTI	CEGHLNSU	GLUNCHES	CEGINNSY	ENSIGNCY
CEFIOPRS	FORCIPES	CEGHMRUY	CHEMURGY		SYNGENIC
CEFIORTY	FEROCITY	CEGHNORS	GROSCHEN	CEGINOOP	GEOPONIC
CEFIRRSU	SCURFIER	CEGHORSU	CHOREGUS	CEGINOOR	OROGENIC
CEFIRSTU	FRUTICES		COUGHERS	CEGINOOV	COOEYING
CEFIRTUV	FRUCTIVE		GROUCHES	CEGINOOZ	ZOOGENIC
CEFKLLOS	ELFLOCKS	CEGHRSTU	GRUTCHES	CEGINOPR	COPERING
CEFKLOOR	FORELOCK		GUTCHERS	CEGINOPY	PYOGENIC
CEFKLOST	FETLOCKS	CEGIILMO	OLIGEMIC	CEGINORS	COGNISER
CEFKLPSY	FLYSPECK	CEGIILNR	CLINGIER		COREIGNS
CEFKLRUW	WRECKFUL	CEGIILNS	CEILINGS		COSIGNER
CEFLLOSU	FLOSCULE		CIELINGS	CEGINORT	GERONTIC
CEFLNOSU	FLOUNCES	CEGIILNT	GENTILIC	CEGINORV	COVERING
CEFLNRUU	FURUNCLE	CEGIILOP	EPILOGIC	CEGINORW	COWERING
CEFLNSTU	SCENTFUL	CEGIILOS	LOGICISE	CEGINORZ	COGNIZER
CEFLOPTY	COPYLEFT	CEGIILOZ	LOGICIZE	CEGINOSS	COGNISES
CEFMORSY	COMFREYS	CEGIINNT	ENTICING	CEGINOST	ESCOTING
CEFNOOTT	CONFETTO	CEGIINNV	EVINCING	CEGINOSZ	COGNIZES
CEFNORSU	FROUNCES	CEGIINOP	EPIGONIC	CEGINOTV	COVETING
CEFNORTU	CONFUTER	CEGIINOS	ISOGENIC	CEGINOXY	OXYGENIC
CEFNOSSU	CONFUSES	CEGIINPR	PIERCING	CEGINRRS	CRINGERS
CEFNOSTU	CONFUTES	CEGIINPS	PIECINGS	CEGINRRU	RECURING
CEFOORST	SOFTCORE	CEGIINRT	RECITING	CEGINRST	CRESTING
CEFOPRSU	PREFOCUS	CEGIINSS	GNEISSIC	CEGINRSU	RECUSING
CEFORRST	CROFTERS	CEGIINSX	EXCISING		RESCUING
CEFORSSU	FOCUSERS	CEGIINTV	EVICTING		SCUNGIER
CEFORSTU	FRUCTOSE	CEGIINTX	EXCITING		SECURING
CEFOSSSU	FOCUSSES	CEGIIOST	EGOISTIC	CEGINRSW	SCREWING
CEGGHIRS	CHIGGERS	CEGIJLOU	LOGJUICE	CEGINRSY	SYNERGIC
CEGGHRSU	CHUGGERS	CEGIKKLN	KECKLING	CEGINRTU	ERUCTING
CEGGILOO	GEOLOGIC	CEGIKLNR	CLERKING	CEGINSUX	EXCUSING
CEGGILOR	CLOGGIER		RECKLING	CEGIRSTU	SCUTIGER
	COGGLIER	CEGIKNNR	RINGNECK	CEGKLNNO	LONGNECK
CEGGILRS	SCRIGGLE	CEGIKNNS	NECKINGS	CEGKLNOS	GENLOCKS
CEGGINNO	CONGEING		SNECKING	CEGKLORS	GROCKLES
CEGGINOO	GEOGONIC	CEGIKNPS	PECKINGS	CEGLLOOU	COLLOGUE

Code	Word	Code	Word	Code	Word
CEGLLORY	GLYCEROL	CEHIIRTW	WITCHIER	CEHILTTY	TETCHILY
CEGLLRVY	GLYCERYL	CEHIISTT	CHITTIES	CEHIMMOS	CHOMMIES
CEGLNOOS	COLOGNES		ETHICIST	CEHIMMRU	CHUMMIER
CEGLNOTY	COGENTLY		ITCHIEST	CEHIMMSS	CHEMISMS
CEGLOOOY	OECOLOGY		THEISTIC	CEHIMMSU	CHUMMIES
CEGLOOTY	CETOLOGY		TICHIEST	CEHIMNNW	WINCHMEN
CEGLOSSU	GLUCOSES	CEHIISVV	CHIVVIES	CEHIMNOP	PHONEMIC
CEGLOSSY	GLYCOSES	CEHIKLPT	KLEPHTIC	CEHIMNOR	CHOIRMEN
CEGMNNOO	COGNOMEN	CEHIKLRS	CLERKISH	CEHIMNPT	PITCHMEN
CEGNNOOS	ONCOGENS	CEHIKLSU	SUCHLIKE	CEHIMNSU	MUNCHIES
CEGNNPUY	PUNGENCY	CEHIKMOS	HOMESICK	CEHIMNSY	CHIMNEYS
CEGNOOTY	GONOCYTE	CEHIKNRU	CHUNKIER	CEHIMOOT	HOMEOTIC
CEGNORSS	CONGRESS	CEHIKNST	CHETNIKS	CEHIMORR	CHROMIER
CEGNORSU	CONGRUES		KITCHENS	CEHIMORS	CHROMISE
	SCROUNGE		KNITCHES		MORICHES
CEGNORSY	CRYOGENS		THICKENS	CEHIMORT	CHROMITE
CEGNORVY	CRYOGENY	CEHIKNSW	CHEWINKS		TRICHOME
CEGNOSST	CONGESTS	CEHIKOOS	CHOOKIES	CEHIMORZ	CHROMIZE
CEGNOTYY	CYTOGENY	CEHIKOSS	HOICKSES	CEHIMOSS	ECHOISMS
CEGNRTUY	TURGENCY	CEHIKOST	CHOKIEST		MISCHOSE
CEGOORSS	SCROOGES		THICKOES	CEHIMOST	MOCHIEST
CEGORRSU	SCOURGER	CEHIKRSS	KIRSCHES	CEHIMOTW	CHOWTIME
	SCROUGER		SHICKERS	CEHIMRRS	SMIRCHER
CEGORSSU	SCOURGES		SKRIECHS	CEHIMRSS	SMIRCHES
	SCROUGES	CEHIKRST	CHIRKEST	CEHIMSST	CHEMISTS
CEHHIIRT	HITCHIER	CEHIKRSW	WHICKERS	CEHINNOS	CHINONES
CEHHINPY	HYPHENIC	CEHIKSST	CHEKISTS	CEHINNRT	INTRENCH
CEHHIOOS	HOOCHIES		KITSCHES	CEHINOOS	COHESION
CEHHIRST	HITCHERS		SKITCHES	CEHINOPR	PROCHEIN
CEHHISTU	HUTCHIES	CEHIKSTT	THICKEST	CEHINOPS	CHOPINES
CEHHNORU	HURCHEON		THICKETS	CEHINOPT	PHONETIC
CEHHOOSS	COHOSHES		THICKSET	CEHINOPU	EUPHONIC
CEHHOOST	HOOTCHES	CEHIKTTY	THICKETY	CEHINORS	CHORINES
CEHHOPTY	HYPOTHEC	CEHILLPR	PRECHILL	CEHINORT	NOTCHIER
CEHHOSST	SHOCHETS	CEHILLRS	CHILLERS	CEHINORU	UNHEROIC
CEHHOSSU	CHOUSHES		SCHILLER	CEHINOSY	HYOSCINE
CEHIIKNR	CHINKIER	CEHILLST	CHILLEST	CEHINOTY	ONYCHITE
CEHIIKNS	CHINKIES	CEHILMMS	SCHIMMEL	CEHINPRS	PINCHERS
CEHIIKST	THICKIES	CEHILMOU	HUMICOLE		PINSCHER
CEHIILLR	CHILLIER	CEHILMSY	CHIMLEYS	CEHINPRU	PUNCHIER
CEHIILLS	CHILLIES	CEHILMTY	METHYLIC		UNCIPHER
CEHIILMO	HEMIOLIC	CEHILNOP	PHENOLIC	CEHINPSU	PENUCHIS
CEHIILMT	LITHEMIC		PINOCHLE	CEHINQSU	QUINCHES
CEHIILNN	LICHENIN	CEHILNOR	CHLORINE	CEHINRSS	RICHNESS
CEHIILNT	LECITHIN	CEHILNOS	CHOLINES	CEHINRST	CHRISTEN
CEHIILOT	EOLITHIC		HELICONS		CITHERNS
CEHIILTY	HELICITY	CEHILNPY	PHENYLIC		CITHRENS
CEHIIMOP	HEMIOPIC	CEHILNSS	CHINLESS		SNITCHER
CEHIIMOS	ISOCHEME	CEHILNST	LINCHETS	CEHINRSW	WINCHERS
	ISOCHIME		TINCHELS	CEHINRTU	RUTHENIC
CEHIIMPT	MEPHITIC	CEHILOOS	SCHOOLIE	CEHINSST	CHINTSES
CEHIIMRT	HERMITIC	CEHILOPT	CHIPOTLE		SNITCHES
CEHIIMST	ETHICISM		HELICOPT	CEHINSTW	WITCHENS
CEHIINST	ICHNITES	CEHILORS	CEORLISH	CEHINSTZ	CHINTZES
	NITCHIES	CEHILORT	CHLORITE	CEHIOORS	CHOOSIER
CEHIIPPR	CHIPPIER		CLOTHIER		ISOCHORE
CEHIIPPS	CHIPPIES	CEHILORY	HEROICLY	CEHIOPPR	CHOPPIER
CEHIIPRR	CHIRPIER	CEHILPRS	PILCHERS	CEHIOPRS	SOPHERIC
CEHIIPRT	PITCHIER	CEHILPTY	PHYLETIC	CEHIOPRU	EUPHORIC
CEHIIRST	CHRISTIE	CEHILRSV	CHERVILS		POUCHIER
CEHIIRSZ	SCHIZIER	CEHILSTT	LICHTEST	CEHIOPSS	HOSPICES
CEHIIRTT	CHITTIER	CEHILSTW	SWITCHEL	CEHIOPST	POSTICHE
	TITCHIER	CEHILSTY	CHESTILY		POTICHES
	TRICHITE		LECYTHIS	CEHIOPSU	COPIHUES

Eight-letter anagrams

CEHIOPTU	EUPHOTIC	CEHLNOTU	UNCLOTHE	CEHOOSUW	COWHOUSE
CEHIORRS	CHORRIES	CEHLNPRU	PRELUNCH	CEHOPPRS	CHOPPERS
CEHIORRT	RHETORIC	CEHLNRSU	LUNCHERS	CEHOPPRY	PROPHECY
	TORCHIER	CEHLNRSY	LYNCHERS	CEHOPRST	POTCHERS
CEHIORRV	OVERRICH	CEHLNSTY	LYNCHETS	CEHOPRSY	CORYPHES
CEHIORSS	CHORISES	CEHLOORS	RESCHOOL	CEHORRST	TORCHERS
	ORCHESIS	CEHLOOSS	SCHOOLES	CEHORSSU	CHORUSES
	ORCHISES	CEHLORRT	CHORTLER		CHOUSERS
CEHIORST	ROTCHIES	CEHLORST	CHORTLES	CEHORSSZ	SCHERZOS
	THEORICS	CEHLORSU	SLOUCHER	CEHORSTU	SCOUTHER
CEHIORSW	CHOWRIES	CEHLORTY	HECTORLY		TOUCHERS
CEHIORTT	TROCHITE	CEHLOSSU	SLOUCHES		TROUCHES
CEHIORTU	COUTHIER	CEHLOSTU	SELCOUTH	CEHORSTW	SCOWTHER
	TOUCHIER	CEHLPPSS	SCHLEPPS	CEHORSUV	VOUCHERS
CEHIOSST	ECHOISTS	CEHLPPSY	SCHLEPPY	CEHOSSSU	HOCUSSES
	TOISECHS	CEHLQSUY	SQUELCHY	CEHOSTTU	COUTHEST
CEHIOSTV	CHEVIOTS	CEHLRRSU	LURCHERS	CEHOTTUZ	ZUCHETTO
CEHIPPRS	CHIPPERS	CEHLSSTU	SLUTCHES	CEHPRSTU	PUTCHERS
CEHIPRRS	CHIRPERS	CEHLSTUY	LECYTHUS	CEHPSSTU	PUTSCHES
CEHIPRSS	SPHERICS	CEHMNRSU	MUNCHERS	CEHRRSSU	CRUSHERS
CEHIPRST	PITCHERS	CEHMNRTU	TRUCHMEN	CEHRSSSU	SCHUSSER
	SPITCHER	CEHMNSSU	MUCHNESS	CEHRSSTY	SCYTHERS
CEHIPSST	CHIPSETS	CEHMOORS	MOOCHERS	CEHRSTTY	STRETCHY
CEHIQSTU	QUITCHES		SMOOCHER	CEHSSSSU	SCHUSSES
CEHIRSST	STRICHES	CEHMOOSS	SCHMOOSE	CEIIILSV	CIVILISE
CEHIRSTT	CHITTERS		SMOOCHES	CEIIILVZ	CIVILIZE
	RESTITCH	CEHMOOSZ	SCHMOOZE	CEIIIMNT	CIMINITE
	RICHTEST	CEHMOPRS	CHOMPERS	CEIIINNS	SINICISE
	STITCHER	CEHMORSU	MOUCHERS	CEIIINSV	INCISIVE
CEHIRSTW	SWITCHER	CEHMORUV	OVERMUCH	CEIIINSZ	SINICIZE
CEHIRSTY	HYSTERIC	CEHMOSSU	SMOUCHES	CEIIJSTU	JESUITIC
CEHIRTTW	TWITCHER	CEHMRSTU	CHETRUMS		JUICIEST
CEHIRTWY	WITCHERY	CEHMSSTU	SMUTCHES	CEIIKKST	KICKIEST
CEHISSTT	STITCHES	CEHNNNOU	NUNCHEON	CEIIKLMR	LIMERICK
CEHISSTU	CUSHIEST	CEHNNOPU	PUNCHEON	CEIIKLRS	SICKLIER
CEHISSTW	SWITCHES	CEHNNOSU	NONESUCH	CEIIKLRT	TICKLIER
CEHISSUW	SUCHWISE		UNCHOSEN	CEIIKLSS	SICKLIES
CEHISTTW	TWITCHES	CEHNNRSU	CHUNNERS	CEIIKMMR	MIMICKER
CEHKKRSU	CHUKKERS	CEHNOOPS	HENCOOPS	CEIIKMST	KISMETIC
CEHKLLOS	SKELLOCH	CEHNOORS	COEHORNS	CEIIKNRZ	ZINCKIER
CEHKLMOS	HEMLOCKS		SCHOONER	CEIIKNSS	ICKINESS
CEHKLOOS	KLOOCHES	CEHNOPTU	PUTCHEON		KINESICS
CEHKLORS	SHERLOCK	CEHNORST	CHORTENS	CEIIKNST	KINETICS
CEHKNOSU	SUNCHOKE		NOTCHERS	CEIIKPRR	PRICKIER
	UNCHOKES	CEHNORSV	CHEVRONS	CEIIKPST	PICKIEST
CEHKNPUY	KEYPUNCH	CEHNORTU	CHOUNTER	CEIIKQSU	QUICKIES
CEHKORSS	SHOCKERS	CEHNORVY	CHEVRONY	CEIIKRRT	TRICKIER
CEHKPSTU	KETCHUPS	CEHNOSSZ	SCHNOZES	CEIIKRST	STICKIER
CEHKRSSU	SHUCKERS	CEHNPPRU	PREPUNCH	CEIIKSST	EKISTICS
CEHKRSTU	HUCKSTER	CEHNPRSU	PUNCHERS		STICKIES
CEHLLMOS	MOCHELLS	CEHNPSST	PSCHENTS	CEIIKTTT	TEKTITIC
CEHLLMSU	MUCHELLS	CEHNRRSU	CHURNERS	CEIILLMT	MELLITIC
	SCHELLUM	CEHNRSTU	CHUNTERS	CEIILLNO	LINOLEIC
CEHLLORS	CHOLLERS	CEHNSSSU	SUCHNESS	CEIILLOP	POLLICIE
CEHLLOSY	YELLOCHS	CEHNSSTU	CHESNUTS	CEIILLPT	ELLIPTIC
CEHLLOUY	LOUCHELY	CEHNSTTU	CHESTNUT	CEIILLSS	SILICLES
CEHLLPSU	CHELLUPS	CEHNSTUY	CHUTNEYS	CEIILLSU	SILICULE
CEHLMNOU	HOMUNCLE	CEHOOORZ	ZOOCHORE	CEIILMNS	LEMNISCI
CEHLMORS	CHROMELS	CEHOORSS	CHOOSERS	CEIILMNT	LIMNETIC
CEHLMSUY	CHUMLEYS		SOROCHES	CEIILMNY	MYELINIC
CEHLNNOU	LUNCHEON	CEHOORST	CHEROOTS	CEIILMOT	CIMOLITE
CEHLNNSU	CHUNNELS	CEHOORSU	OCHEROUS	CEIILNNR	INCLINER
CEHLNOST	CHOLENTS		OCHREOUS	CEIILNNS	INCLINES
	NOTCHELS	CEHOOSSS	SCOOSHES	CEIILNOP	PICOLINE

CEIILNOS	ISOCLINE
	SILICONE
CEIILNPS	PENICILS
CEIILNQU	CLINIQUE
CEIILNSS	ENCLISIS
CEIILOPP	EPIPLOIC
	EPIPOLIC
CEIILOPS	POLICIES
CEIILORT	ELICITOR
CEIILOTZ	ZEOLITIC
CEIILPPS	CLIPPIES
CEIILPRT	PERLITIC
CEIILPRU	PIRLICUE
CEIILPSS	ECLIPSIS
CEIILPTX	EXPLICIT
CEIILPTY	PYELITIC
CEIILQRU	CLIQUIER
CEIILRSU	SLUICIER
CEIILRSY	LYRICISE
CEIILRTV	VERTICIL
CEIILRYZ	LYRICIZE
CEIILSSS	SCISSILE
CEIIMNOT	EMICTION
CEIIMNRS	CREMINIS
CEIIMNRU	URINEMIC
CEIIMNST	MINCIEST
CEIIMOPT	EPITOMIC
CEIIMORS	ISOMERIC
CEIIMOST	COMITIES
	SEMIOTIC
CEIIMPRR	CRIMPIER
CEIIMPRS	EMPIRICS
	MISPRICE
CEIIMPSS	EPICISMS
CEIIMPTU	PUMICITE
CEIIMRRT	TRIMERIC
CEIIMRST	MERISTIC
	SCIMITER
	TRISEMIC
CEIIMRTT	TERMITIC
CEIIMSST	MISCITES
CEIINNOP	NEPIONIC
CEIINNOR	IRENICON
CEIINNOS	CONINES
	OSCININE
CEIINNOT	COTININE
	NICOTINE
CEIINNRS	CINERINS
CEIINNRT	INTRINCE
CEIINNST	INSCIENT
CEIINOPR	PECORINI
CEIINOPS	EPINOSIC
CEIINOPT	EPITONIC
CEIINORS	RECISION
	SORICINE
CEIINOSS	ICONISES
CEIINOSV	INVOICES
CEIINOSX	EXCISION
CEIINOSZ	ICONIZES
CEIINOTV	EVICTION
CEIINPPR	PRINCIPE
CEIINPSS	PISCINES
CEIINRSS	SERICINS
CEIINRST	CITRINES
	CRINITES
	INCITERS
CEIINRSU	INCISURE
	SCIURINE
CEIINRTU	NEURITIC
CEIINSSU	CUISINES
CEIINSTU	CUTINISE
CEIINSTY	CYTISINE
	SYENITIC
CEIINSTZ	CITIZENS
	ZINCIEST
	ZINCITES
CEIINTUZ	CUTINIZE
CEIIOPRS	IRISCOPE
CEIIOPRT	PERIOTIC
CEIIOPSW	WICOPIES
CEIIOPTT	PICOTITE
CEIIOSTT	OSTEITIC
CEIIOSTV	SOVIETIC
CEIIPRRS	CRISPIER
CEIIPRST	PICRITES
	PRICIEST
CEIIPSST	EPICISTS
	SPICIEST
CEIIQRTU	CRITIQUE
CEIIRSST	ERISTICS
CEIIRSSU	CRUISIES
CEIIRSTT	RECTITIS
CEIIRSTV	VERISTIC
CEIIRSUZ	CRUIZIES
CEIISSST	CISSIEST
CEIISTVV	VIVISECT
CEIJMORT	MICROJET
CEIJNORT	INJECTOR
CEIJNORU	JOUNCIER
CEIJNOUV	CUNJEVOI
CEIJRSTU	JUSTICER
CEIJSSTU	JUSTICES
CEIKKLOR	CORKLIKE
	ROCKLIKE
CEIKKNRS	KNICKERS
CEIKKRRS	SKERRICK
CEIKLLTU	CULTLIKE
CEIKLMOR	CORMLIKE
CEIKLMST	MICKLEST
CEIKLMSU	SCUMLIKE
CEIKLNPS	SPICKNEL
CEIKLNRS	CLINKERS
	CRINKLES
CEIKLNRU	CLUNKIER
CEIKLNSS	SLICKENS
CEIKLOSV	LOVESICK
CEIKLOTU	LEUKOTIC
CEIKLPRS	PICKLERS
	PRICKLES
CEIKLPRU	PLUCKIER
CEIKLRSS	SLICKERS
CEIKLRST	STICKLER
	STRICKLE
	TICKLERS
	TRICKLES
CEIKLRSY	SICKERLY
CEIKLRTT	TRICKLET
CEIKLSST	SLICKEST
	STICKLES
CEIKLSSW	WICKLESS
CEIKLSTU	LUCKIEST
CEIKMNOR	MONICKER
CEIKMNST	STICKMEN
CEIKMOPT	IMPOCKET
CEIKMORS	OCKERISM
CEIKMRSS	SMICKERS
CEIKMRSU	MUSICKER
CEIKMSST	SMICKETS
CEIKMSTU	MUCKIEST
CEIKNNOT	NEKTONIC
CEIKNNSU	INSUCKEN
CEIKNOST	CONKIEST
	KENOTICS
CEIKNOTY	CYTOKINE
CEIKNQSU	QUICKENS
CEIKNRSS	SNICKERS
CEIKNRST	STRICKEN
CEIKNRSU	UNSICKER
CEIKNRSY	SNICKERY
CEIKNSSS	SICKNESS
CEIKNSST	SNICKETS
CEIKOPST	POCKIEST
CEIKORRS	ROCKIERS
CEIKORST	CORKIEST
	ROCKIEST
	STOCKIER
CEIKORSV	OVERSICK
CEIKOSSY	YOICKSES
CEIKOSTT	TOCKIEST
CEIKPRRS	PRICKERS
CEIKPRST	PRICKETS
CEIKPSST	SKEPTICS
	SPICKEST
CEIKQSTU	QUICKEST
	QUICKSET
CEIKRRST	TRICKERS
CEIKRRTY	TRICKERY
CEIKRSST	STICKERS
CEIKRSTU	TRUCKIES
CEIKRTTY	RICKETTY
CEIKSSTU	SUCKIEST
CEIKSTUY	YUCKIEST
CEILLMOY	COMELILY
CEILLNOS	LIONCELS
CEILLNOU	NUCLEOLI
CEILLOPS	POLLICES
CEILLOQU	COQUILLE
CEILLORS	COLLIERS
	ORSELLIC
CEILLORY	COLLIERY
CEILLOTU	COUTILLE
CEILLRTU	TELLURIC
CEILLSST	CELLISTS
CEILLSSU	CULLISES
CEILMMUY	MYCELIUM
CEILMNOP	COMPLINE
CEILMNOT	MONTICLE
CEILMOOP	PICOMOLE
CEILMOPR	COMPILER
	COMPLIER
CEILMOPS	COMPILES
	COMPLIES

POLEMICS
CEILMOSS SOLECISM
CEILMOSU COLISEUM
CEILMPRS CRIMPLES
CEILMPRU CLUMPIER
CEILMPUU PECULIUM
CEILMRSU CLUMSIER
MUSCLIER
CEILMTUU LUTECIUM
CEILNNOT CONTLINE
CEILNNSU NUCLEINS
CEILNNSY SYNCLINE
CEILNOOS COLONIES
COLONISE
ECLOSION
CEILNOOZ COLONIZE
CEILNOPR PERCOLIN
REPLICON
CEILNOPS PINOCLES
CEILNOPT LEPTONIC
CEILNOPY POLYENIC
CEILNORS INCLOSER
LICENSOR
CEILNOSS CONSEILS
INCLOSES
CEILNOST LECTIONS
TELSONIC
CEILNOSU LEUCOSIN
CEILNOSX LEXICONS
CEILNPRY PRINCELY
CEILNRTU LINCTURE
CEILNRUV CULVERIN
CEILNSST STENCILS
CEILNSTU CUTLINES
LINECUTS
TUNICLES
CEILNSUU UNSLUICE
CEILOORS COLORISE
CEILOORZ COLORIZE
CEILOPPS POPSICLE
CEILOPRS POLICERS
CEILOPRT LEPROTIC
PETROLIC
CEILOPRV PROCLIVE
CEILOPST TOECLIPS
CEILOPTU EPULOTIC
POULTICE
CEILOPTY EPICOTYL
LIPOCYTE
CEILORST CLOISTER
COISTREL
COSTLIER
CREOLIST
CEILORTT CLOTTIER
CEILORTY CRYOLITE
CEILOSSS OSSICLES
CEILOSST SOLECIST
SOLSTICE
CEILOSSU COULISSE
CEILOSTT COLETITS
CEILOTVY VELOCITY
CEILPPRR CRIPPLER
CEILPPRS CLIPPERS
CRIPPLES

CEILPRSS SPLICERS
CEILPRSU SURPLICE
CEILPRUU PURLICUE
CEILPSSU SPICULES
CEILRRSU SCURRILE
CEILRSTT CLITTERS
CEILRSTU CURLIEST
UTRICLES
CEILSSSS SCISSELS
CEILSTTU CUITTLES
CULTIEST
CEIMMNNO MNEMONIC
CEIMMNOU ENCOMIUM
MECONIUM
CEIMMORT RECOMMIT
CEIMMORU COREMIUM
CEIMMOSX COMMIXES
CEIMMRRS CRIMMERS
CEIMMRRU CRUMMIER
CEIMMRSU CRUMMIES
SCRUMMIE
SCUMMIER
CEIMMRSY MERYCISM
CEIMNNOO ENCOMION
CEIMNNOR NONCRIME
CEIMNNOS MECONINS
CEIMNNOT NEOMYCIN
CEIMNOOT EMOTICON
CEIMNOPT PENTOMIC
CEIMNOPY EPONYMIC
CEIMNORS CREMOSIN
INCOMERS
SERMONIC
CEIMNORT INTERCOM
CEIMNOSS COSMINES
CEIMNOST CENTIMOS
CEIMNRST CENTRISM
CEIMNRSU NUMERICS
CEIMNSSU MENISCUS
CEIMOOST COOMIEST
CEIMOOSZ MESOZOIC
CEIMOOUZ ZOOECIUM
CEIMOPRS COMPRISE
CEIMOPRX PROXEMIC
CEIMOPRZ COMPRIZE
CEIMOQSU COMIQUES
CEIMORRS MORRICES
CEIMORRT MORTICER
CEIMORST MORTICES
CEIMORSX EXORCISM
CEIMORSY ISOCRYME
CEIMORTY EMICTORY
CEIMOSSS COSMESIS
CEIMOSTV VICOMTES
CEIMPRRS CRIMPERS
SCRIMPER
CEIMPRRU CRUMPIER
CEIMPRSU PUMICERS
CEIMRRSU SCRIMURE
CEIMRRTU TURMERIC
CEIMRSST CRETISMS
CEIMSSTY SYSTEMIC
CEINNNOT INNOCENT
CEINNNOU INCONNUE

CEINNORS INCENSOR
CEINNORU NEURONIC
CEINNORV CONNIVER
CEINNORW COWINNER
CEINNOSV CONNIVES
CEINNOTU CONTINUE
CEINNOTV COINVENT
CEINNSTY SYNTENIC
CEINOOPR PECORINO
CEINOOSS CONIOSES
CEINOOST COONTIES
CEINOOTZ ENTOZOIC
ENZOOTIC
CEINOPPR CORNPIPE
CEINOPPT PEPTONIC
CEINOPRS CONSPIRE
INCORPSE
CEINOPRT ENTROPIC
INCEPTOR
PRETONIC
CEINOPRV PROVINCE
CEINOPST PONCIEST
CEINOPTT ENTOPTIC
CEINOPTU UNPOETIC
CEINORRS RESORCIN
CEINORRT TRICORNE
CEINORSS NECROSIS
SERICONS
CEINORST COINTERS
CORNIEST
NOTICERS
RECTIONS
CEINORSU COINSURE
NOURICES
ROUNCIES
CEINORTT CONTRITE
CORNETTI
CEINORTU NEUROTIC
UNEROTIC
CEINORTV CONTRIVE
CEINOSSS CESSIONS
COSINESS
CEINOSST SECTIONS
CEINOSSX COXINESS
CEINOSSZ COZINESS
CEINOSTT CENTOIST
STENOTIC
TONETICS
CEINOSTU COUNTIES
CEINOSTX EXCITONS
CEINOSTY CYTOSINE
CEINOSUV UNVOICES
CEINOSVV CONVIVES
CEINOTUX UNEXOTIC
CEINPRSS CRISPENS
PRINCESS
CEINPRST SPECTRIN
CEINPSST INSPECTS
CEINPSTY PYCNITES
CEINRRSU REINCURS
CEINRSST CISTERNS
CEINRSTT CENTRIST
CITTERNS
CEINRSTU CURNIEST

CEINRSUV	INCURVES	CEIRRSTT	CRITTERS	CEKNOSTU	UNSOCKET
CEINRSVV	CRIVVENS		RESTRICT	CEKNPRUU	UNPUCKER
CEINRTTU	INTERCUT		STRICTER	CEKNRSTU	STRUCKEN
	TINCTURE	CEIRRSTU	CRUSTIER	CEKNRSWY	WRYNECKS
CEINSSTY	CYSTEINS		RECRUITS	CEKOOORV	OVERCOOK
	CYSTINES	CEIRRSUV	SCURVIER	CEKOOPRS	PRECOOKS
CEINSTTX	EXTINCTS	CEIRSSSU	CUISSERS	CEKOOPSW	COWPOKES
CEIOOPRS	OPORICES		SCISSURE	CEKOORRS	ROCKROSE
CEIOOTUV	OUTVOICE	CEIRSSTT	TRISECTS	CEKOORRW	COWORKER
CEIOOTXX	EXOTOXIC	CEIRSSTU	CITRUSES	CEKOORRY	CROOKERY
CEIOPPRS	CROPPIES		CRUSTIES	CEKOORST	CROOKEST
CEIOPPSY	EPISCOPY		CURTSIES	CEKOPRST	SPROCKET
CEIOPRRU	CROUPIER		RICTUSES	CEKORRTY	ROCKETRY
CEIOPRSS	PERSICOS	CEIRSSTV	VICTRESS	CEKORSST	RESTOCKS
CEIOPRST	PERSICOT	CEIRSSUV	CURSIVES		STOCKERS
CEIOPRSU	PRECIOUS		SCURVIES	CEKORSTW	TWOCKERS
CEIOPRTU	EUTROPIC	CEIRSTTU	TUTRICES	CEKRRSTU	RESTRUCK
	OUTPRICE	CEIRSTUV	CURVIEST		TRUCKERS
CEIOPSST	COPSIEST	CEIRSTUY	SECURITY	CEKRSSUU	RUCKUSES
CEIOPSSU	SPECIOUS	CEIRSUZZ	SCUZZIER	CELLMOSU	COLUMELS
CEIORRSS	CROSIERS	CEISSSSU	CISSUSES	CELLNOOS	COLONELS
CEIORRSU	COURIERS	CEISSSTU	CISTUSES	CELLNORS	ENSCROLL
CEIORRSZ	CROZIERS	CEISTTTU	CUTTIEST	CELLNSUU	NUCELLUS
CEIORRTU	COURTIER	CEJKNOSY	JOCKNEYS	CELLNTUU	LUCULENT
CEIORRTW	COWRITER	CEJLOOSY	JOCOSELY	CELLNTUY	LUCENTLY
CEIORRUZ	CRUZEIRO	CEJNORRU	CONJURER	CELLOOQU	COLLOQUE
CEIORSST	CROSSTIE	CEJNORSU	CONJURES	CELLORSS	ESCROLLS
CEIORSSU	SCOURIES	CEJNRTUU	JUNCTURE	CELLOSSY	CLOYLESS
CEIORSSV	CORSIVES	CEJNSSUU	JUNCUSES	CELLRRSU	CRULLERS
CEIORSSW	SCOWRIES	CEJOPRST	PROJECTS	CELLRSSU	SCULLERS
CEIORSSX	SIXSCORE	CEKKLNRU	KNUCKLER	CELLRSUY	SCULLERY
CEIORSTT	COTTIERS	CEKKLNSU	KNUCKLES	CELMMSSU	MESCLUMS
CEIORSTU	CITREOUS	CEKKNORS	KNOCKERS	CELMNOOR	COLORMEN
	OUTCRIES	CEKLLNOR	ROLLNECK	CELMNOOS	MONOCLES
CEIORSTV	EVICTORS	CEKLLOOV	LOVELOCK	CELMNOTY	CLOYMENT
	VORTICES	CEKLLOPS	PELLOCKS	CELMNOUY	UNCOMELY
CEIORSTW	COWRITES	CEKLLSSU	LUCKLESS	CELMNSSU	MESCLUNS
CEIORSTX	EXCITORS	CEKLMNOS	LOCKSMEN	CELMNTUU	MUCULENT
	EXORCIST	CEKLNOSS	SLOCKENS	CELMOOOT	LOCOMOTE
CEIORSVY	VICEROYS	CEKLNOST	STENLOCK	CELMOOPY	COEMPLOY
CEIORTTU	TOREUTIC	CEKLNRSU	CLUNKERS	CELMOOSY	CLOYSOME
CEIOSSSV	VISCOSES		CRUNKLES	CELMOPSU	COMPULSE
CEIOSSTT	COTTISES	CEKLOORV	OVERLOCK	CELMOPSY	SYMPLOCE
	SCOTTIES	CEKLOOSS	COOKLESS	CELMOSUU	CUMULOSE
CEIOSSTU	COITUSES	CEKLOPST	LOCKSTEP	CELMOSYY	CYMOSELY
CEIOSSTX	COEXISTS	CEKLORSS	ROCKLESS	CELMPRSU	CLUMPERS
CEIPPSTU	CUPPIEST	CEKLOSSS	SOCKLESS		CRUMPLES
CEIPQSTU	PICQUETS	CEKLOSST	LOCKSETS		SCRUMPLE
CEIPRRSS	CRISPERS	CEKLOSTY	TOCKLEYS	CELMPRTU	PLECTRUM
CEIPRRST	RESCRIPT	CEKLPRSU	PLUCKERS	CELMPSUU	SPECULUM
	SCRIPTER	CEKLRRTU	TRUCKLER	CELMSSSU	SCUMLESS
CEIPRRSU	SPRUCIER	CEKLRSSU	SCULKERS	CELMSSUU	SECULUMS
CEIPRSST	CRISPEST		SUCKLERS	CELMSTUU	CUMULETS
CEIPRSTU	CREPITUS	CEKLRSTU	TRUCKLES	CELNNOSU	NUCLEONS
	CUPRITES	CEKLSSSU	SUCKLESS	CELNNOTY	NOCENTLY
	PICTURES	CEKMNOST	STOCKMEN	CELNNOUV	UNCLOVEN
	PIECRUST	CEKMNOSY	MOCKNEYS	CELNOORS	CONSOLER
CEIPSSST	CESSPITS	CEKMNRTU	TRUCKMEN		CORONELS
CEIRRRSU	CURRIERS	CEKNNSSU	UNSNECKS	CELNOORT	CONTROLE
	SCURRIER	CEKNOORV	CONVOKER	CELNOORU	ENCOLOUR
CEIRRRUY	CURRIERY	CEKNOOSV	CONVOKES	CELNOOSS	CONSOLES
CEIRRSSU	CRUISERS	CEKNOPST	PENSTOCK		COOLNESS
	SCURRIES	CEKNORST	CRONKEST	CELNOOVV	CONVOLVE
	SUCRIERS	CEKNORTU	COKERNUT	CELNOPRT	PLECTRON

Eight-letter anagrams

Code	Word(s)
CELNOPUU	UNCOUPLE
CELNOPUY	OPULENCY
CELNORTW	CROWNLET
CELNORWY	CLOWNERY
CELNOSSU	CLONUSES
	COUNSELS
	UNCLOSES
CELNOSTU	NOCTULES
CELNOSUV	CONVULSE
CELNOSVY	SOLVENCY
CELNOVXY	CONVEXLY
CELNPTUU	PUNCTULE
CELNRSTU	LECTURNS
CELOOORV	OVERCOOL
CELOOPRS	PRECOOLS
CELOOPSS	CESSPOOL
CELOORRS	COLORERS
	RECOLORS
CELOORRU	COLOURER
CELOORSS	COLESSOR
	CREOSOLS
CELOORTW	COLEWORT
CELOORVY	OVERCLOY
CELOOSTU	CLOSEOUT
CELOPRSS	CROPLESS
CELOPRSU	COUPLERS
CELOPSSU	CLOSEUPS
	OPUSCLES
	UPCLOSES
CELOPSTU	COUPLETS
	OCTUPLES
CELOPSUU	OPUSCULE
CELOPTTU	OCTUPLET
CELOPTUX	OCTUPLEX
CELORRSU	CORULERS
CELORSST	CORSLETS
	COSTRELS
	CROSSLET
CELORSSU	CLOSURES
	SCLEROUS
CELORSSW	SCOWLERS
	SCROWLES
CELORSSY	SCROYLES
CELORSTT	CLOTTERS
	CROTTLES
CELORSTU	CLOTURES
	CLOUTERS
	COULTERS
CELORSTY	COYSTREL
CELORSUU	ULCEROUS
	URCEOLUS
CELORSUY	CROUSELY
CELORTTU	COURTLET
CELORTVY	COVERTLY
CELOSSST	COSTLESS
CELOSTTU	CULOTTES
CELPRRSU	SCRUPLER
CELPRSSU	SCRUPLES
CELPRSTU	RESCULPT
CELPRSUY	SPRUCELY
CELRSSTU	CLUSTERS
	CUSTRELS
CELRSSTY	CLYSTERS
CELRSTTU	CLUTTERS
	SCUTTLER
CELRSTUU	CULTURES
CELRSTUV	CULVERTS
CELRSTUY	CLUSTERY
CELRTTUY	CLUTTERY
CELSSTTU	SCUTTLES
CELSSTUU	CULTUSES
CEMMNOOR	COMMONER
CEMMNOOS	CONSOMME
CEMMNOOY	COMMONEY
CEMMNORU	COMMUNER
CEMMNOST	COMMENTS
CEMMNOSU	COMMUNES
CEMMOOST	COMMOTES
CEMMOOSV	COMMOVES
CEMMORTU	COMMUTER
CEMMOSTU	COMMUTES
CEMMRSSU	SCUMMERS
CEMNNOST	CONTEMNS
CEMNOOPT	CONTEMPO
CEMNOORR	CROMORNE
CEMNOOTY	MONOCYTE
CEMNOPRS	CORPSMEN
CEMNOPTT	CONTEMPT
CEMNORSU	CONSUMER
	MUCRONES
CEMNOSSU	CONSUMES
	MUSCONES
CEMNRSTU	CENTRUMS
CEMOOPRS	COMPOSER
CEMOOPSS	COMPOSES
CEMOOPST	COMPOTES
CEMOOPSY	MYOSCOPE
CEMOORSY	SYCOMORE
CEMOOSSS	COSMOSES
CEMOOSTU	OUTCOMES
CEMOOSTY	CYTOSOME
CEMOPRSS	COMPRESS
CEMOPRST	COMPTERS
CEMOPRTU	COMPUTER
CEMOPSTU	COMPUTES
CEMORSSU	CORMUSES
CEMORSTU	COSTUMER
	CUSTOMER
CEMOSSTU	COSTUMES
CEMOSTUY	COSTUMEY
CEMOTXYY	MYXOCYTE
CEMPRSTU	CRUMPEST
	CRUMPETS
	SPECTRUM
CENNOOPR	CORNPONE
CENNOORV	CONVENOR
CENNOOST	CONNOTES
CENNORRT	CORNRENT
CENNORTU	NOCTURNE
CENNOSST	CONSENTS
CENNOSTT	CONTENTS
CENNOSTV	CONVENTS
CENNRSSU	SCUNNERS
CENOOOTZ	ECTOZOON
CENOOPSS	POCOSENS
CENOORRS	CORONERS
	CROONERS
CENOORST	CORONETS
CENOORSU	CORNEOUS
CENOORSV	CONVERSO
CENOORTT	CORNETTO
CENOORVY	CONVEYOR
CENOPRSU	POUNCERS
CENOPRSY	NECROPSY
CENOPSSY	PYCNOSES
	SYNCOPES
CENOPSTU	POUNCETS
CENOQRSU	CONQUERS
CENOQSTU	CONQUEST
CENORRSS	SCORNERS
CENORRSW	CROWNERS
	RECROWNS
CENORRTU	TROUNCER
CENORSST	CONSTERS
	CRESTONS
CENORSSU	CORNUSES
CENORSTT	CORNETTS
CENORSTU	CONSTRUE
	CORNUTES
	COUNTERS
	RECOUNTS
	TROUNCES
CENORSTV	CONVERTS
CENORSTW	CROWNETS
CENORSUU	CERNUOUS
	COENURUS
CENORSUV	UNCOVERS
CENORSUY	CYNOSURE
CENOSSTT	CONTESTS
CENOSSTU	CONTUSES
	COUNTESS
CENOSTTX	CONTEXTS
CENPRSTY	ENCRYPTS
CENPRTUU	PUNCTURE
CENPSTUX	EXPUNCTS
CENRRSTU	CURRENTS
CENRSSTU	CURTNESS
	ENCRUSTS
CENRSSUU	UNCURSES
CENRSSUW	UNSCREWS
CEOOOPST	OTOSCOPE
CEOOPRRV	OVERCROP
CEOOPRSS	SCOOPERS
CEOOPSWX	COWPOXES
CEOORRVW	OVERCROW
CEOORSST	SCOOTERS
CEOORSTU	ECOTOURS
	OUTSCORE
CEOOSTUV	COVETOUS
CEOPPRRS	CROPPERS
CEOPPRST	PROSPECT
CEOPPRSU	SUPERCOP
CEOPRRRU	PROCURER
CEOPRRSS	SCORPERS
CEOPRRST	PORRECTS
CEOPRRSU	CROUPERS
	PROCURES
CEOPRSST	PROSECTS
CEOPRSSU	CORPUSES
CEOPRSTT	PROTECTS
CEOPRSTW	CROWSTEP
	SCREWTOP

CEOPRSUU	COUPURES		FLICKING	**CFNNOORT**	CONFRONT
	CUPREOUS	**CFGIIKNR**	FRICKING	**CFNORSTU**	FUNCTORS
CEOPRSUV	COVERUPS	**CFGIKLNO**	FLOCKING	**CFOOORTW**	CROWFOOT
CEOPRSUW	SUPERCOW	**CFGIKNOR**	FROCKING	**CFRSTUUU**	USUFRUCT
CEOQRSTU	CROQUETS	**CFGIKNSU**	FUCKINGS	**CGGHHINU**	CHUGGING
	ROCQUETS	**CFGINORT**	CROFTING	**CGGGILNO**	CLOGGING
CEOQRTUY	COQUETRY	**CFGINOSU**	FOCUSING		COGGLING
CEORRSSS	CROSSERS	**CFHIINOO**	FINOCHIO	**CGGGINOR**	CROGGING
	SCORSERS	**CFHIIORR**	HORRIFIC	**CGGGINOS**	COGGINGS
CEORRSSU	COURSERS	**CFHIKORS**	ROCKFISH		SCOGGING
	CURSORES	**CFHIKSSU**	SUCKFISH	**CGGGINSU**	SCUGGING
	SCOURERS	**CFHILPTY**	FLYPITCH	**CGGHILNU**	GULCHING
CEORRSSW	SCOWRERS	**CFHIMOSS**	SCOMFISH	**CGGHINOU**	COUGHING
CEORRSTU	COURTERS	**CFHIMSSU**	SCUMFISH	**CGGIILNN**	CLINGING
CEORRSTY	CORSETRY	**CFHINSSU**	FUCHSINS	**CGGIINNO**	COIGNING
CEORSSST	CROSSEST	**CFHLOPUU**	POUCHFUL	**CGGIINNR**	CRINGING
CEORSSSU	SCOURSES	**CFHORSTU**	FUTHORCS	**CGGIINRS**	GRICINGS
	SUCROSES	**CFIIIKNN**	FINICKIN	**CGGILLOY**	CLOGGILY
CEORSSTU	CRUSTOSE	**CFIIILSY**	SILICIFY	**CGGILRSY**	SCRIGGLY
	SCOUTERS	**CFIIKNNY**	FINNICKY	**CGGINNSU**	SCUNGING
CEORSSUV	CORVUSES	**CFIIKNYZ**	ZINCKIFY	**CGGINOOS**	SCOOGING
CEORSTUU	COUTURES	**CFIILMNU**	FULMINIC	**CGGINORS**	SCROGGIN
	OUTCURSE	**CFIILNST**	INFLICTS	**CGGINOSU**	SCOUGING
CEORSTUV	COUVERTS	**CFIILNUU**	FUNICULI	**CGHHIILN**	HILCHING
	CUTOVERS	**CFIILOPR**	PROLIFIC	**CGHHIINT**	HITCHING
	OVERCUTS	**CFIILPSU**	PULSIFIC	**CGHHINNU**	HUNCHING
CEORSTUY	COURTESY	**CFIILSTU**	SULFITIC	**CGHHINOT**	HOTCHING
CEORTUUV	OUTCURVE	**CFIIMNOS**	SOMNIFIC	**CGHHINTU**	HUTCHING
CEOSSSTU	COSTUSES	**CFIIMOPR**	PICIFORM	**CGHIIKNN**	CHINKING
CEOSSTTU	COTTUSES	**CFIIMORT**	MORTIFIC	**CGHIIKNO**	HOICKING
CEPPRRSU	CRUPPERS	**CFIINOPT**	PONTIFIC	**CGHIIKNR**	CHIRKING
CEPPRSSU	SCUPPERS	**CFIINORT**	FRICTION	**CGHIIKNT**	THICKING
CEPPRTUU	UPPERCUT	**CFIINOST**	FICTIONS	**CGHIILLN**	CHILLING
CEPRSSTU	SPRUCEST	**CFIKLORY**	FROLICKY	**CGHIILNR**	CHIRLING
CEPRSSUW	SCREWUPS	**CFIKLSTU**	STICKFUL	**CGHIILNT**	CHITLING
CEPRSSUY	CYPRUSES	**CFIKNNOS**	FINNOCKS		LICHTING
CEPRSTUU	CUTPURSE	**CFIKOSSS**	FOSSICKS	**CGHIIMNR**	CHIRMING
CEPRSUUV	UPCURVES	**CFIKPSTU**	PUCKFIST	**CGHIIMNS**	MICHINGS
CEPSSSTU	SUSPECTS	**CFIKSTUW**	FUCKWITS	**CGHIIMNT**	MITCHING
CERSSSUU	RUSCUSES	**CFILMOOR**	COLIFORM	**CGHIINNN**	CHINNING
CERSSTTU	SCUTTERS	**CFILNOSU**	SULFONIC	**CGHIINNP**	PINCHING
CERSSTUY	CURTSEYS	**CFILRSUU**	SULFURIC	**CGHIINNW**	WINCHING
CERSSUUX	EXCURSUS	**CFIMNOOR**	CONIFORM	**CGHIINOR**	CHOIRING
CFFFKOSU	FUCKOFFS	**CFIMNORS**	CONFIRMS	**CGHIINPP**	CHIPPING
CFFGHINU	CHUFFING	**CFIMNORU**	CUNIFORM	**CGHIINPR**	CHIRPING
CFFGIINO	COIFFING		UNCIFORM	**CGHIINPT**	PITCHING
CFFGILNO	COFFLING	**CFIMOSSU**	MISFOCUS	**CGHIINQU**	QUICHING
CFFGILNU	CUFFLING	**CFINNOTU**	FUNCTION	**CGHIINRR**	CHIRRING
CFFGINOS	SCOFFING	**CFIOPRUY**	COPURIFY	**CGHIINRT**	CHIRTING
CFFGINSU	SCUFFING	**CFKLLOSU**	LOCKFULS		RICHTING
CFFHINOS	CHIFFONS	**CFKLRTUU**	TRUCKFUL	**CGHIINST**	ITCHINGS
CFFHINOY	CHIFFONY	**CFKNORSU**	UNFROCKS		SICHTING
CFFIKKOS	KICKOFFS	**CFKOSTTU**	FUTTOCKS	**CGHIINTT**	CHITTING
CFFIKLNU	CUFFLINK	**CFLLOORU**	COLORFUL	**CGHIINTW**	WITCHING
CFFIKOPS	PICKOFFS	**CFLLOPRU**	CROPFULL	**CGHIINVV**	CHIVVING
CFFINNOU	UNCOFFIN	**CFLMRSUU**	FULCRUMS	**CGHIINVY**	CHIVYING
CFFIRTUY	FRUCTIFY	**CFLMRUUU**	FURCULUM	**CGHIINZZ**	CHIZZING
CFFKKNOO	KNOCKOFF	**CFLNOORT**	CORNLOFT	**CGHIKLNO**	HOCKLING
CFFKOOOS	COOKOFFS	**CFLNORSU**	SCORNFUL	**CGHIKNNU**	CHUNKING
CFFMOSSU	OFFSCUMS	**CFLOOPSU**	SCOOPFUL	**CGHIKNOO**	CHOOKING
CFGHIILN	FILCHING	**CFLOOPSW**	COWFLOPS	**CGHIKNOS**	SHOCKING
CFGHINOO	CHOOFING	**CFLOPRSU**	CROPFULS	**CGHIKNOT**	KOTCHING
CFGIIKLN	FICKLING	**CFMNOORS**	CONFORMS	**CGHIKNSU**	SHUCKING
		CFMOORST	COMFORTS	**CGHILMNU**	MULCHING

CGHILNNU	LUNCHING	CGIILMOS	LOGICISM	CGILMNTU	MULCTING
CGHILNNY	LYNCHING	CGIILNOP	POLICING	CGILMNUU	CINGULUM
CGHILNOT	CLOTHING	CGIILNPP	CLIPPING		GLUCINUM
CGHILNRU	LURCHING	CGIILNPS	SPLICING	CGILMOOY	MYOLOGIC
CGHIMMNU	CHUMMING	CGIILNQU	CLIQUING	CGILNNNO	NONCLING
CGHIMNNU	MUNCHING	CGIILNSS	SLICINGS	CGILNNOS	CLONINGS
CGHIMNOO	MOOCHING	CGIILNSU	SLUICING	CGILNNOW	CLOWNING
CGHIMNOP	CHOMPING	CGIILOST	LOGICIST	CGILNOOR	COLORING
CGHIMNOR	CHROMING		LOGISTIC		CROOLING
CGHIMNOU	MOUCHING	CGIILRTU	LITURGIC	CGILNOOY	COOINGLY
CGHIMNPU	CHUMPING	CGIIMNNO	INCOMING	CGILNOPP	CLOPPING
CGHIMNTU	MUTCHING	CGIIMNNS	MINCINGS	CGILNOPU	COUPLING
CGHIMPSY	SPHYGMIC	CGIIMNPR	CRIMPING	CGILNORU	CLOURING
CGHINNOS	CHIGNONS	CGIIMNPU	PUMICING	CGILNOSS	CLOSINGS
CGHINNOT	NOTCHING	CGIIMNSU	MISCUING	CGILNOSW	COWLINGS
CGHINNPU	PUNCHING	CGIINNOS	COININGS		SCOWLING
CGHINNRU	CHURNING	CGIINNOT	NOTICING	CGILNOTT	CLOTTING
CGHINNSY	SYNCHING	CGIINNPR	PRINCING	CGILNOTU	CLOUTING
CGHINOOP	POOCHING	CGIINNSU	INCUSING	CGILNPSU	SCULPING
CGHINOOS	CHOOSING	CGIINNSW	WINCINGS	CGILNRSU	CURLINGS
CGHINOPP	CHOPPING	CGIINNTT	TINCTING	CGILNRYY	CRYINGLY
CGHINOPT	POTCHING	CGIINOOS	ISOGONIC	CGILNTTU	CUTTLING
CGHINOPU	POUCHING	CGIINOPT	PICOTING	CGILOOOZ	ZOOLOGIC
CGHINORT	TORCHING	CGIINORT	TRIGONIC	CGILOORU	UROLOGIC
CGHINOSU	CHOUSING	CGIINOST	COTISING	CGILOPRY	COPYGIRL
	HOCUSING	CGIINOSV	VOICINGS	CGILORSW	COWGIRLS
CGHINOSW	CHOWSING	CGIINPRS	CRISPING	CGILPSTU	GILTCUPS
CGHINOTU	TOUCHING		PRICINGS	CGILPSTY	GLYPTICS
CGHINOUV	VOUCHING	CGIINRSU	CRUISING	CGIMMNSU	SCUMMING
CGHINPSY	PSYCHING	CGIINRSV	SCRIVING	CGIMNNOO	GNOMONIC
CGHINPTU	PINCHGUT	CGIINSSS	CISSINGS		ONCOMING
CGHINRRU	CHURRING	CGIJNNOU	JOUNCING	CGIMNOPS	COMPINGS
CGHINRSU	CRUSHING	CGIKKNNO	KNOCKING	CGIMNOPT	COMPTING
	RUCHINGS	CGIKLNNO	CLONKING	CGIMNOPU	UPCOMING
CGHINSTY	SCYTHING	CGIKLNNU	CLUNKING	CGIMNORS	SCROMING
CGHLNOSS	SCHLONGS	CGIKLNOR	ROCKLING	CGIMNPRU	CRUMPING
CGHNOOOS	SOOCHONG	CGIKLNOS	LOCKINGS	CGIMRRUY	MICRURGY
CGHNOOSU	SOUCHONG	CGIKLNPU	PLUCKING	CGINNNOS	CONNINGS
CGHOORST	TORGOCHS	CGIKLNRU	RUCKLING	CGINNNSU	CUNNINGS
CGIIILNT	LIGNITIC	CGIKLNSU	SCULKING	CGINNOOP	POONCING
CGIIINNS	INCISING		SUCKLING	CGINNOOR	CROONING
CGIIINNT	INCITING	CGIKMNOS	MOCKINGS	CGINNOPU	POUNCING
CGIIKLNN	CLINKING		SMOCKING		UNCOPING
	NICKLING	CGIKNOOR	CROOKING	CGINNORS	SCORNING
CGIIKLNP	PICKLING	CGIKNOOS	COOKINGS	CGINNORW	CROWNING
CGIIKLNS	LICKINGS	CGIKNORS	ROCKINGS	CGINNOSS	CONSIGNS
	SICKLING	CGIKNORT	TROCKING	CGINNOTU	COUNTING
	SLICKING	CGIKNORW	CORKWING	CGINOOPS	SCOOPING
CGIIKLNT	TICKLING	CGIKNOST	STOCKING	CGINOOPT	COOPTING
CGIIKMMS	GIMMICKS	CGIKNOTW	TWOCKING	CGINOOST	SCOOTING
CGIIKMMY	GIMMICKY	CGIKNPSU	KINGCUPS	CGINOOTV	COGNOVIT
CGIIKNNS	SNICKING	CGIKNRTU	TRUCKING	CGINOPPR	CROPPING
CGIIKNNZ	ZINCKING	CGIKNSSU	SUCKINGS	CGINOPRS	CORPSING
CGIIKNOY	YOICKING	CGIKNSTU	GUNSTICK	CGINOPRU	CROUPING
CGIIKNPR	PRICKING	CGIKPSTU	PIGSTUCK	CGINOPSU	SCOUPING
CGIIKNPS	PICKINGS	CGILLNOS	COLLINGS	CGINOPSW	SCOWPING
CGIIKNRS	SCRIKING	CGILLNOY	COLLYING	CGINORSS	CROSSING
CGIIKNRT	TRICKING	CGILLNSU	CULLINGS		SCORINGS
CGIIKNRW	WRICKING		SCULLING		SCORSING
CGIIKNST	STICKING	CGILLNUY	CULLYING	CGINORSU	COURSING
	TICKINGS	CGILMNOP	CLOMPING		SCOURING
CGIIKNSW	WICKINGS	CGILMNPU	CLUMPING		SOURCING
CGIIKPST	PIGSTICK	CGILMNSU	MUSCLING	CGINORTU	COURTING
CGIILLOS	ILLOGICS	CGILMNSY	CYMLINGS	CGINOSST	GNOSTICS

CGINOSTU	SCOUTING	CHIKMNNU	MUNCHKIN	CHIOORSZ	CHORIZOS
CGINPPSU	CUPPINGS	CHIKMNPU	CHIPMUNK	CHIOORTT	ORTHOTIC
CGINPRSU	SPRUCING	CHIKMNTU	MUTCHKIN	CHIOPRST	STROPHIC
CGINRRSU	SCURRING	CHIKNNOP	PHINNOCK	CHIOPSTY	HYPOCIST
CGINRRUY	CURRYING	CHIKNOOS	CHINOOKS	CHIOPTTU	OUTPITCH
CGINRSSU	CURSINGS	CHIKOPTY	KYPHOTIC		PITCHOUT
CGINRSSY	SCRYINGS	CHIKORST	TROCHISK	CHIORSSS	CROSSISH
CGINRSTU	CRUSTING	CHIKOSST	STOCKISH	CHIORSST	CHORISTS
CGINRSUZ	SCRUZING	CHIKPSYY	PHYSICKY	CHIPRRSU	CHIRRUPS
CGINSTTU	CUTTINGS	CHILLMSU	CHILLUMS	CHIPRRSY	PYRRHICS
	TUNGSTIC	CHILLOOT	OILCLOTH	CHIPRRUY	CHIRRUPY
CGKLNOSU	GUNLOCKS	CHILMMUY	CHUMMILY	CHIPRTTY	TRIPTYCH
CGKNOSTU	GUNSTOCK	CHILMOPS	COMPLISH	CHIPSSTY	PSYCHIST
CGLLOSYY	GLYCOSYL	CHILMOSU	SCHOLIUM	CHIRRSSU	SCIRRHUS
CGLMOOYY	MYCOLOGY	CHILMPSU	CLUMPISH	CHISSTTU	CHUTISTS
CGLNOOOY	ONCOLOGY	CHILNNPY	LYNCHPIN	CHKLOOOS	HOOLOCKS
CGLOOOTY	TOCOLOGY	CHILNOOS	SCHOLION	CHKLOSSY	SHYLOCKS
CGLOOTYY	CYTOLOGY	CHILNORS	CHLORINS	CHKMMOOS	HOMMOCKS
CGMNNOOR	MONGCORN	CHILNOSW	CLOWNISH	CHKMMOSU	HUMMOCKS
CGMNNORU	MUNGCORN	CHILNPUY	PUNCHILY	CHKMMOUY	HUMMOCKY
CGNORSUY	SCROUNGY	CHILOOOZ	HOLOZOIC	CHKNOOSS	SCHNOOKS
CGOORRSW	GORCROWS	CHILOOPT	HOLOPTIC	CHKNORSU	CORNHUSK
CHHIIKST	THICKISH	CHILOOYZ	HYLOZOIC	CHKOOOPS	COOKSHOP
CHHIILTY	HITCHILY	CHILOPPY	CHOPPILY	CHKOOSST	SCHTOOKS
CHHIIPST	PHTHISIC	CHILORST	TROCHILS	CHKOPSTU	TUCKSHOP
CHHIKORS	CHIKHORS	CHILOSTT	CLOTTISH	CHKPSTUU	PUTCHUKS
CHHILRSU	CHURLISH	CHILOSYY	COYISHLY	CHLMORSY	CHROMYLS
CHHIMPSU	CHUMSHIP	CHILOTUY	TOUCHILY	CHLMPSSU	SCHLUMPS
CHHIMRTY	RHYTHMIC	CHIMMOOR	MICROMHO	CHLMPSUY	SCHLUMPY
CHHKOOPS	HOCKSHOP	CHIMMORS	MICROHMS	CHLNOOOP	COLOPHON
CHHNORSU	RHONCHUS	CHIMMORU	CHROMIUM	CHLOORSU	CHLOROUS
CHHOOPTT	HOTCHPOT	CHIMNNOO	NONOHMIC	CHLOPSTY	SPLOTCHY
CHIIILOS	CHILIOIS	CHIMNOOR	HORMONIC	CHLORTUY	CHOULTRY
CHIIINRT	RHINITIC	CHIMNORS	CHRISMON	CHMNOORT	CORNMOTH
CHIIKLST	TICKLISH	CHIMNORW	INCHWORM	CHMNORRU	CRUMHORN
CHIIKNNS	KINCHINS	CHIMNOSU	INSOMUCH	CHMOORSU	CHROMOUS
CHIIKRST	TRICKISH	CHIMNOSY	CHYMOSIN	CHMOOSYZ	SCHMOOZY
CHIIKRTW	WHITRICK	CHIMNOUY	ONYCHIUM	CHNNOORS	CHRONONS
CHIILLLY	CHILLILY	CHIMOORU	MOUCHOIR	CHNOOPTT	TOPNOTCH
CHIILMSY	HYLICISM	CHIMORSS	CHORISMS	CHNOORST	TORCHONS
CHIILNNP	LINCHPIN		CHRISOMS	CHNOPRSU	SUNPORCH
CHIILNST	CHITLINS	CHIMORST	CHRISTOM	CHNOPTUU	OUTPUNCH
CHIILOPT	HOPLITIC	CHIMOSTU	MISTOUCH	CHNORRSS	SCHNORRS
CHIILORT	TROCHILI	CHIMPSSY	PSYCHISM	CHNORSSY	SYNCHROS
CHIILOST	HOLISTIC	CHIMSSTY	CHYMISTS	CHNORSTU	COTHURNS
CHIILPRV	CHIRPILY		TYCHISMS	CHOOORYZ	ZOOCHORY
CHIILPTY	PITCHILY	CHINOOPT	PHOTONIC	CHOOPPSS	COPSHOPS
CHIILQSU	CLIQUISH	CHINOORS	CHORIONS	CHOOPSTU	OCTOPUSH
CHIILSTY	HYLICIST		ISOCHRON	CHOPSTUU	TOUCHUPS
CHIIMOPT	PHIMOTIC	CHINOORT	ORTHICON	CHORSTTU	SHORTCUT
CHIIMORZ	RHIZOMIC	CHINOPTY	HYPNOTIC	CIIIKNTU	CUITIKIN
CHIIMPRU	PICHURIM		PHYTONIC	CIIILMPT	IMPLICIT
CHIINNPS	INCHPINS		PYTHONIC	CIIILMSU	SILICIUM
CHIINOPS	SIPHONIC		TYPHONIC	CIIILNOV	OLIVINIC
CHIINORT	ORNITHIC	CHINORTU	COTHURNI	CIIILPST	SPILITIC
CHIIORSS	CHORISIS	CHINOSSU	CUSHIONS	CIIILSTV	CIVILIST
CHIIORST	HISTORIC	CHINOSTZ	SCHIZONT	CIIILTVY	CIVILITY
	ORCHITIS	CHINOSUY	CUSHIONY	CIIIMNRS	CRIMINIS
CHIIPPRU	HIPPURIC	CHINSTTU	UNSTITCH	CIIIMNSV	INCIVISM
CHIIRSTT	TRISTICH	CHIOOPPT	PHOTOPIC	CIIINNOS	INCISION
CHIKLLOS	HILLOCKS	CHIOOPRS	POCHOIRS	CIIINNRT	CITRININ
CHIKLLOY	HILLOCKY	CHIOOPTY	OOPHYTIC	CIIINOTY	IONICITY
CHIKLNUY	CHUNKILY	CHIOORSS	ISOCHORS	CIIINPPR	PRINCIPI
CHIKLORS	HORLICKS	CHIOORSU	ICHOROUS	CIIINPST	INCIPITS

Eight-letter anagrams

CIIINTVV	VICINITY	CIINNORU	UNIRONIC	CIKNNOSW	WINNOCKS
CIIJRSTU	JURISTIC	CIINNOST	NICOTINS	CIKNOPTY	PYKNOTIC
CIIKKLLS	KILLICKS	CIINNSTT	INSTINCT	CIKNOSSW	COWSKINS
CIIKKMSS	MISKICKS	CIINNSTU	TUNICINS	CIKNPSTU	NUTPICKS
CIIKLLSY	SICKLILY	CIINOOPP	CIOPPINO	CIKNSSTU	UNSTICKS
CIIKLOPT	POLITICK	CIINOOSS	CONIOSIS	CIKOPPST	POCKPITS
CIIKLPST	LICKSPIT	CIINOOST	COITIONS	CIKOPSTT	TIPSTOCK
	LIPSTICK		ISOTONIC	CIKORTTU	OUTTRICK
CIIKLRTY	TRICKILY	CIINOOTZ	ZOONITIC	CIKOSSTT	STOCKIST
CIIKLSTY	STICKILY	CIINOPRS	PORCINIS	CIKOSSTU	SICKOUTS
CIIKMMMS	MIMMICKS	CIINOPSS	PSIONICS	CIKOSTTU	STICKOUT
CIIKMNNS	MINNICKS	CIINOPSU	OPINICUS	CIKOSTUW	OUTWICKS
CIIKNOOT	COOTIKIN	CIINORSS	INCISORS	CIKPSSTU	STICKUPS
CIIKNPPR	PINPRICK	CIINORSS	CROSTINI	CIKPSUWY	WICKYUPS
CIIKNPST	NITPICKS	CIINORSY	INCISORY	CILLMNOR	CORNMILL
	STICKPIN	CIINOSSS	SCISSION	CILLMSUY	CLUMSILY
CIIKNPTY	NITPICKY	CIINOSTT	STICTION		CULLYISM
CIIKNSTU	CUTIKINS	CIINOTTY	TONICITY	CILLNOOT	COTILLON
CIIKPSUW	WICKIUPS	CIINPRSS	CRISPINS	CILLNORS	INSCROLL
CIILLMTU	TILLICUM	CIINPSTU	SINCIPUT	CILLNOSU	CULLIONS
CIILLNOP	POLLINIC	CIINQSTU	QUINTICS		SCULLION
CIILMOPY	IMPOLICY	CIIOOPST	ISOTOPIC	CILLOOOT	OCOTILLO
CIILMOSS	SCIOLISM	CIIOPRST	PORISTIC	CILLOORS	CRIOLLOS
CIILMQSU	CLIQUISM	CIIOPSTT	OPTICIST	CILMMSUY	SCUMMILY
CIILMRSY	LYRICISM	CIIOPSTY	ISOTYPIC	CILMNOPS	COMPLINS
CIILNOOT	NOCTILIO	CIIOQTUX	QUIXOTIC	CILMNOPU	PULMONIC
CIILNOPS	CIPOLINS	CIIORRWW	WIRRICOW	CILMNOSS	CLONISMS
	PICOLINS	CIIOTTXY	TOXICITY	CILMNOUU	INOCULUM
	PSILOCIN	CIIPRRTU	PRURITIC	CILMNUUV	VINCULUM
CIILNORT	NITROLIC	CIIPRSTU	PURISTIC	CILMOORS	COLORISM
CIILNOSS	SILICONS	CIIRSTTU	TRUISTIC		MISCOLOR
CIILNOST	COLISTIN	CIISSTTY	CYSTITIS	CILMOOSS	LOCOISMS
CIILOOPT	POLITICO	CIJKOSTY	JOYSTICK	CILMOPSY	OLYMPICS
CIILOOTZ	ZOOLITIC	CIJNNOOS	CONJOINS	CILMORUX	MICROLUX
CIILOPPT	POPLITIC	CIJNNOOT	CONJOINT	CILMPRSY	SCRIMPLY
CIILOPPT	COLPITIS	CIJNNOTU	JUNCTION	CILMPSUU	SPICULUM
	POLITICS	CIJNNSTU	INJUNCTS	CILMSSTU	CULTISMS
	PSILOTIC	CIJOOSTY	JOCOSITY	CILMSTYY	MYSTICLY
CIILORST	CLITORIS	CIKKLLOS	KILLOCKS	CILNNORY	NONLYRIC
	COISTRIL	CIKKOPST	TOPKICKS	CILNOORS	ORCINOLS
CIILOSST	SCIOLIST	CIKKOSTU	OUTKICKS	CILNOORU	UNICOLOR
	SOLICITS	CIKLLOPR	KILLCROP	CILNOOSS	CLOISONS
CIILOSTY	SOLICITY	CIKLLOPS	PILLOCKS	CILNOOST	COLONIST
CIILOSVV	SLIVOVIC	CIKLLORS	ROLLICKS		STOLONIC
CIILPRSY	CRISPILY	CIKLLORY	ROLLICKY	CILNOOTU	LOCUTION
CIILRSTY	LYRICIST	CIKLLOSS	SILLOCKS	CILNOPRS	PILCORNS
CIILRTUU	UTRICULI	CIKLLOSW	KILLCOWS	CILNOPTU	PLUTONIC
CIILSSSS	SCISSILS	CIKLLPUY	PLUCKILY	CILNORSY	LYRICONS
CIILSTTY	STYLITIC	CIKLMSSU	MISLUCKS	CILNOSTU	LINOCUTS
CIIMMNOS	MINICOMS	CIKLNOST	LINSTOCK	CILNOSUY	COUSINLY
CIIMNOOS	ISONOMIC	CIKLOOOS	OLICOOKS	CILNPSSU	INSCULPS
CIIMNOSS	MISCOINS	CIKLOPST	LOPSTICK		SCULPINS
CIIMNOST	MICTIONS	CIKLOPSU	LIPOSUCK	CILNPSTU	INSCULPT
	MONISTIC	CIKLOSTU	OUTSLICK	CILOOPST	COPILOTS
	NOMISTIC	CIKLOSTY	STOCKILY	CILOOPYZ	POLYZOIC
CIIMNOVY	VIOMYCIN	CIKMNNOS	MINNOCKS	CILOORRT	TRICOLOR
CIIMORST	TRISOMIC	CIKMOORS	SICKROOM	CILOORST	COLORIST
CIIMOSST	MISTICOS	CIKMOOSS	MISCOOKS		CORTISOL
	STOICISM	CIKMOPST	MOPSTICK	CILOORSU	COULOIRS
CIIMOSYZ	ISOZYMIC	CIKMORRS	RIMROCKS	CILOOSSU	SCIOLOUS
CIIMPRST	SCRIMPIT	CIKMSSTU	STICKUMS	CILOPPRY	PROPYLIC
CIIMRSTY	MYRISTIC	CIKNNOOS	COONSKIN	CILOPRRY	PYRROLIC
CIIMRTTU	TRITICUM	CIKNNOPS	PINNOCKS	CILOPRSW	PILCROWS
CIINNNOO	NONIONIC	CIKNNOST	NONSTICK	CILOPRUY	CROUPILY

	POLYURIC	CINRSTTU	INSTRUCT	CLMOPSTU	PLUMCOTS
CILOPSSW	COWSLIPS	CINRSTUY	SCRUTINY	CLMOSUUU	CUMULOUS
CILORSTY	COYSTRIL	CIOOOPRS	OOSPORIC	CLNNOOOR	NONCOLOR
CILOSSTU	OCULISTS	CIOOOTTX	OTOTOXIC	CLNOORST	CONTROLS
CILOSSTY	SYSTOLIC	CIOOOTXZ	ZOOTOXIC	CLNOORTU	CONTROUL
CILOSSUU	LUSCIOUS	CIOOPRST	PORTICOS		COUNTROL
CILPRSTU	CULPRITS		PROOTICS	CLNOSSTU	CONSULTS
CILPSSTU	SCULPSIT	CIOOPTYZ	ZOOTYPIC	CLNOSTUY	UNCOSTLY
CILRSTTY	STRICTLY	CIOOQSTU	COQUITOS	CLOOOPRT	PROTOCOL
CILRSTUY	CRUSTILY	CIOORRWW	WORRICOW	CLOOPPSW	COWPLOPS
	RUSTICLY	CIOORSSU	SCORIOUS	CLOOPSTY	POLYCOTS
CILRSUVY	SCURVILY	CIOOSSTU	STOCIOUS	CLOORTUY	LOCUTORY
CILSSTTU	CULTISTS	CIOPSSTY	COPYISTS	CLOOSSSU	COLOSSUS
CIMMOSSS	COSMISMS	CIORRSTU	CURSITOR	CLOOSSTY	CYTOSOLS
CIMNNOSU	NONMUSIC	CIORSSSS	SCISSORS	CLOPRSTU	SCULPTOR
CIMNOOOZ	ZOONOMIC	CIORSTUU	RUCTIOUS	CLRSSUUU	SURCULUS
CIMNOORS	OMICRONS	CIPPRRUU	PURPURIC	CMMNNOOU	UNCOMMON
CIMNOORU	CORONIUM	CIPSSTTY	STYPTICS	CMMOPSSY	COMSYMPS
CIMNOOTY	MYOTONIC	CIRRSTTU	CRITTURS	CMNOOOST	MONOCOTS
CIMNOPRT	COMPRINT	CIRSSTUY	CITRUSSY	CMNOOOTY	ONCOTOMY
CIMNORSS	CRIMSONS	CJNNOOTU	CONJUNTO	CMNOORRW	CORNWORM
CIMNORSY	CRONYISM	CJNOORRU	CONJUROR	CMNOPSTU	CONSUMPT
CIMNOSTU	MISCOUNT	CJRSUUUU	SUCURUJU	CMOOPRST	COMPORTS
CIMNOSSU	MUCINOUS	CKKNOOTU	KNOCKOUT	CMOOPSST	COMPOSTS
CIMNOSUY	SYCONIUM	CKKOORRW	ROCKWORK	CMOPRSUX	SCRUMPOX
CIMOOOTZ	ZOOTOMIC	CKLLMOSU	MULLOCKS	CMORSSTU	SCROTUMS
CIMOORSS	MORISCOS	CKLLMOUY	MULLOCKY	CMORSTUW	CUTWORMS
CIMOPSSY	COPYISMS	CKLLOOPS	POLLOCKS	CNNOOORT	CONTORNO
CIMOSSST	COSMISTS	CKLLOORS	ROLLOCKS	CNNORSTU	NOCTURNS
CIMOSTUU	MUTICOUS	CKLLORSU	RULLOCKS	CNNORSUW	UNCROWNS
CIMOSTUY	MUCOSITY	CKLMMOOS	SLOMMOCK	CNOOOORT	OCTOROON
CIMOSTYZ	ZYMOTICS	CKLMMOSU	SLUMMOCK	CNOOOPSS	POCOSONS
CINNNOOT	NONTONIC	CKLMNOSU	LOCKNUTS	CNOOPPRS	POPCORNS
CINNNOSU	INCONNUS	CKLOOOSY	OLYCOOKS	CNOOPRSU	CROUPONS
CINNOOSS	SCOINSON	CKLOORSW	ROWLOCKS	CNOOPSSU	SOUPCONS
CINNOOST	SCONTION	CKLOOSTU	LOCKOUTS	CNOORRSW	CORNROWS
CINNOOTU	CONTINUO	CKLOPSTU	POTLUCKS	CNOORRTY	CRYOTRON
CINNOOTX	NONTOXIC		PUTLOCKS	CNOORSST	CONSORTS
CINNORSU	UNICORNS	CKMMMOSU	MUMMOCKS	CNOORSTT	CONTORTS
CINNOSTU	UNCTIONS	CKMMORUW	MUCKWORM	CNOORSTU	CONTOURS
CINNOSTY	SYNTONIC	CKMNOOOR	MOONROCK		CORNUTOS
CINNQUUX	QUINCUNX	CKMOOOOR	COOKROOM		CROUTONS
CINOOOPT	COOPTION	CKNOOORS	ROCKOONS		OUTSCORN
CINOOOTZ	ZOONOTIC	CKNOSSTU	UNSTOCKS	CNOOSTTW	COTTOWNS
CINOOPRS	SCORPION	CKNRSTUU	UNSTRUCK	CNOOTTUU	OUTCOUNT
CINOOPRT	PROTONIC	CKOOOPST	COOKTOPS	CNOPRSTY	CRYPTONS
CINOOPSS	POCOSINS	CKOOOSTU	COOKOUTS	CNOPSSTY	POSTSYNC
CINOORST	CROSTINO		OUTCOOKS	CNOSTUUU	UNCTUOUS
CINOOSUV	COVINOUS	CKOOPSTT	STOCKPOT	COOOPSTU	OUTSCOOP
CINOOTXY	OXYTOCIN	CKOORSSU	SOUROCKS	COOOPSTY	OTOSCOPY
CINOPSSY	PYCNOSIS	CKOORSTU	OUTROCKS	COOOPSYZ	ZOOSCOPY
CINOPSTY	SYNOPTIC	CKOPSTTU	PUTTOCKS	COOPPSTU	POSTCOUP
CINORRST	TRICORNS	CKORSTUW	CUTWORKS	COOPRRST	PROCTORS
CINORSST	CISTRONS		SCUTWORK	COOPRSST	TOPCROSS
	CORNISTS	CKOSSSTU	TUSSOCKS	COOPRSTU	OUTCROPS
CINORSTT	CONTRIST	CKOSSTUY	TUSSOCKY	COOPRSUU	CROUPOUS
	STRONTIC	CKSSSTUU	TUSSUCKS	COOPRSUY	UROSCOPY
CINORSTU	RUCTIONS	CLLLOOPT	CLOTPOLL	COORRWWY	WORRYCOW
CINORSUY	COUSINRY	CLLMOSSU	MOLLUSCS	COORSSTU	OUTCROSS
CINORTUX	COTURNIX	CLLOOPSS	SCOLLOPS	COORSTUW	OUTCROWS
CINOSSST	CONSISTS	CLLOOQUY	COLLOQUY	COOSSTTY	OTOCYSTS
CINOSSTU	SUCTIONS	CLMMNOOY	COMMONLY	COPRRSTU	CORRUPTS
CINOSTUV	VISCOUNT	CLMOOOTY	COLOTOMY	DDDDEEIR	DIDDERED
CINRSSTU	INCRUSTS	CLMOOPST	COMPLOTS	DDDDEEOR	DODDERED

DDDEEEFN	DEFENDED	DDEEEHNU	UNHEEDED	DDEEGORS	SODGERED
DDDEEEENP	DEPENDED	DDEEEILS	DIESELED	DDEEGRRS	DREDGERS
DDDEEEENR	REDDENED	DDEEEIMR	REMEDIED	DDEEGSTU	DEGUSTED
DDDEEEENU	UNDEEDED		REMEIDED	DDEEHILS	SHIELDED
DDDEEEERT	TEDDERED	DDEEEINR	REDENIED	DDEEHINO	HOIDENED
DDDEEEERW	REWEDDED	DDEEEINV	DEVEINED	DDEEHINR	HINDERED
	WEDDERED	DDEEEIRT	REEDITED	DDEEHIRT	DITHERED
DDDEEFNU	DEFUNDED	DDEEEIST	DEEDIEST	DDEEHISS	EDDISHES
DDDEEFOR	FODDERED		STEEDIED	DDEEHNOR	DEHORNED
DDDEEGIS	DISEDGED	DDEEELLV	DEVELLED	DDEEHNOY	HOYDENED
DDDEEHRS	SHREDDED	DDEEELNW	WEDELNED	DDEEHNSU	DUDHEENS
DDDEEIST	STEDDIED	DDEEELPT	DEPLETED	DDEEHORT	DEHORTED
DDDEEJRU	JUDDERED	DDEEELRW	REWELDED	DDEEHRRS	SHREDDER
DDDEELRT	TREDDLED	DDEEELSS	DEEDLESS	DDEEHRSS	SHEDDERS
DDDEENOR	DONDERED	DDEEELTW	TWEEDLED	DDEEIINT	INEDITED
	REDDENDO	DDEEEMNR	REMENDED	DDEEIIRV	REDIVIDE
DDDEENOS	SODDENED	DDEEEMNT	DEMENTED	DDEEILLV	DEVILLED
DDDEENUW	UNWEDDED	DDEEEMPR	DEPERMED	DDEEILMN	MILDENED
DDDEEORR	DODDERER	DDEEEMRS	DEMERSED	DDEEILMW	MILDEWED
DDDEEORS	RESODDED	DDEEENNU	UNNEEDED	DDEEILNR	REDLINED
DDDEEPRU	PUDDERED	DDEEENPX	EXPENDED	DDEEILNT	DENTILED
DDDEERTU	DETRUDED	DDEEENNR	RENDERED	DDEEILRS	DREIDELS
DDDEGILR	GRIDDLED	DDEEENRT	TENDERED	DDEEILRV	DRIVELED
DDDEGNOU	UNGODDED	DDEEENSU	UNSEEDED	DDEEILRW	WILDERED
DDDEHIRT	THRIDDED	DDEEENTT	DENETTED	DDEEILST	DELISTED
DDDEIILS	DIDDLIES	DDEEENTX	EXTENDED	DDEEIMNP	IMPENDED
DDDEIIMS	SMIDDIED	DDEEENUW	UNWEEDED	DDEEIMNR	REMINDED
DDDEIINV	DIVIDEND	DDEEERRT	DETERRED	DDEEIMOR	MOIDERED
DDDEIIST	DIDDIEST	DDEEERRS	DESERTED	DDEEIMSS	MISDEEDS
	STIDDIED	DDEEERSV	DESERVED	DDEEIMST	DEMISTED
DDDEILNU	UNLIDDED	DDEEESTT	DETESTED	DDEEIMTT	DEMITTED
DDDEILNW	DWINDLED	DDEEESTV	DEVESTED	DDEEINNR	DINNERED
DDDEILQU	QUIDDLED	DDEEESWY	DYEWEEDS	DDEEINNT	INDENTED
DDDEILRS	DIDDLERS	DDEEFFIR	DIFFERED		INTENDED
DDDEILSY	DIDDLEYS	DDEEFFNO	OFFENDED	DDEEINNU	UNDENIED
DDDEILTW	TWIDDLED	DDEEFGGO	DEFOGGED	DDEEINRT	DENDRITE
DDDEIMOS	DISMODED	DDEEFGIT	FIDGETED	DDEEINRW	REWINDED
DDDEINOR	DENDROID	DDEEFINR	FRIENDED	DDEEINST	DESTINED
DDDEINRU	UNDERDID	DDEEFINU	UNDEFIDE		NEDDIEST
DDDEIOST	DODDIEST		UNDEFIED	DDEEINTU	UNEDITED
DDDEIQSU	SQUIDDED	DDEEFLNO	ENFOLDED	DDEEIOPR	PERIODED
DDDEISTU	DUDDIEST	DDEEFLOR	REFOLDED	DDEEIPPR	REDIPPED
DDDENORW	DROWNDED	DDEEFLOU	DEFOULED	DDEEIPRR	PREDRIED
DDDGIILN	DIDDLING	DDEEFMOR	DEFORMED	DDEEIPRS	PRESIDED
DDDIIOOR	DORIDOID	DDEEFNRU	REFUNDED	DDEEIPRV	DEPRIVED
DDEEEEMR	REDEEMED		UNDERFED	DDEEIPSS	DEPSIDES
DDEEEENP	DEEPENED	DDEEFORR	FODDERER		DESPISED
DDEEEERS	RESEEDED	DDEEGGIR	DERIGGED	DDEEIPST	DESPITED
DDEEEERW	DEERWEED	DDEEGGOR	DOGGEDER	DDEEIRRS	DERIDERS
DDEEEFIR	REDEFIED	DDEEGHNU	UNHEDGED	DDEEIRST	REDDIEST
DDEEEFLU	DEFUELED	DDEEGILN	ENGILDED	DDEEIRSV	DIVERSED
DDEEEFLX	DEFLEXED	DDEEGILR	REGILDED	DDEEIRTV	DIVERTED
DDEEEFNR	DEFENDER	DDEEGINR	ENGIRDED	DDEEISST	DESISTED
	FENDERED		ENRIDGED		STEDDIES
DDEEEFNS	DEFENSED	DDEEGINS	DESIGNED	DDEEISTV	DIVESTED
DDEEEFRR	DEFERRED		SDEIGNED	DDEEITTW	DEWITTED
DDEEEGLR	LEDGERED	DDEEGIRV	DIVERGED	DDEEJLLO	JODELLED
DDEEEGMR	DEGERMED	DDEEGISS	DISEDGES	DDEEKNSU	DUSKENED
	DEMERGED	DDEEGIST	DIGESTED	DDEEILMO	MODELLED
DDEEEGNR	DEGENDER	DDEEGJRU	REJUDGED	DDEEILLW	DOWELLED
	GENDERED	DDEEGLNO	GOLDENED	DDEEILLY	YODELLED
DDEEEGRR	REGREDED	DDEEGLNU	UNGELDED	DDEEILMOR	MOLDERED
DDEEEGRT	DETERGED	DDEEGMMU	DEGUMMED		REMOLDED
DDEEEHLW	WHEEDLED	DDEEGOPS	GODSPEED	DDEEILMPU	DEPLUMED

DDEELMRS	MEDDLERS	DDEFLNOU	UNFOLDED	DDEHNRSU	HUNDREDS
DDEELNOU	LOUDENED	DDEFLOPU	UPFOLDED	DDEHOOOO	HOODOOED
DDEELNUW	UNWELDED	DDEFLRSU	FUDDLERS	DDEHOOSW	WOODSHED
DDEELOOW	DEWOOLED	DDEFLRUU	UDDERFUL	DDEHORSU	SHROUDED
DDEELOPR	DEPLORED	DDEFNNUU	UNFUNDED	DDEHRSSU	SHUDDERS
	POLDERED	DDEGGINR	DREDGING	DDEHRSUY	SHUDDERY
DDEELOPX	EXPLODED	DDEGGLOY	DOGGEDLY	DDEIIIRS	IRIDISED
DDEELOPY	DEPLOYED	DDEGGNOO	DOGGONED	DDEIIIRZ	IRIDIZED
DDEELORS	SOLDERED	DDEGHILN	HEDDLING	DDEIIKLS	DISLIKED
DDEELOSU	DELOUSED	DDEGHINS	SHEDDING	DDEIIKRS	KIDDIERS
DDEELOVV	DEVOLVED	DDEGIINR	DERIDING		SKIDDIER
DDEELPRS	PEDDLERS	DDEGIIST	GIDDIEST	DDEIILNR	DIELDRIN
DDEELPRU	PRELUDED	DDEGILMN	MEDDLING	DDEIILOS	IDOLISED
DDEELPRY	PEDDLERY	DDEGILNP	PEDDLING	DDEIILOZ	IDOLIZED
DDEELPUX	DUPLEXED	DDEGILNR	REDDLING	DDEIILRT	TIDDLIER
DDEELRSS	SLEDDERS	DDEGILNS	SLEDDING	DDEIILST	TIDDLIES
DDEELRST	TREDDLES	DDEGILNU	DELUDING	DDEIIMSS	SMIDDIES
DDEELRSU	DELUDERS		INDULGED	DDEIIMSZ	MIDSIZED
DDEEMNNU	UNMENDED		UNGILDED	DDEIIMVW	MIDWIVED
DDEEMNOR	ENDODERM	DDEGILOS	DISLODGE	DDEIINRT	NITRIDED
DDEEMORR	DORMERED	DDEGILRS	GRIDDLES	DDEIINTU	UNTIDIED
DDEEMORW	DEWORMED	DDEGILRY	GLIDDERY	DDEIIOPR	PERIODID
DDEEMRRU	DEMURRED	DDEGILST	GLIDDEST	DDEIIOPS	DIOPSIDE
	MURDERED	DDEGILUV	DIVULGED		DIPODIES
DDEENNOR	DONNERED	DDEGIMOS	DEMIGODS	DDEIIOST	ODDITIES
	REDONNED	DDEGINNS	SNEDDING	DDEIIOSX	DIOXIDES
DDEENNOY	ENDODYNE	DDEGINNU	DENUDING		OXIDISED
DDEENNTU	UNDENTED	DDEGINRS	REDDINGS	DDEIIOXZ	OXIDIZED
	UNTENDED	DDEGINRU	UNGIRDED	DDEIIRSV	DIVIDERS
DDEENOOW	WOODENED	DDEGINST	STEDDING	DDEIIRUV	REDUVIID
DDEENOPR	PERDENDO	DDEGINSW	SWINDGED	DDEIISST	STIDDIES
	PONDERED		WEDDINGS	DDEIISTT	TIDDIEST
DDEENOPW	PONDWEED	DDEGINUU	UNGUIDED	DDEIKNRS	KINDREDS
DDEENORS	ENDORSED	DDEGIOST	DODGIEST	DDEIKOOS	SKIDOOED
DDEENORW	WONDERED	DDEGIPRU	UPGIRDED	DDEIKOSY	DISYOKED
DDEENOSS	ENDOSSED	DDEGIQSU	SQUIDGED	DDEIKRSS	SKIDDERS
DDEENPRS	SPREDDEN	DDEGIRRS	GRIDDERS	DDEIKSVY	SKYDIVED
DDEENRNU	DURNEDER	DDEGJNUU	UNJUDGED	DDEILMOP	IMPLODED
DDEENRSU	DENUDERS	DDEGLOPS	SPLODGED	DDEILMOV	DEVILDOM
	SUNDERED	DDEGLOSS	DOGSLEDS	DDEILMRS	MIDDLERS
DDEENRTU	RETUNDED	DDEGMOOS	DOGEDOMS	DDEILMRU	MUDDLIER
DDEEOPRT	DEPORTED		SMOODGED	DDEILMSU	MUDSLIDE
DDEEOPRW	POWDERED	DDEGNORU	GROUNDED	DDEILNPS	SPINDLED
DDEEOPSS	SEEDPODS		UNDERDOG		SPLENDID
DDEEORRW	REWORDED		UNDERGOD	DDEILNRT	TRINDLED
DDEEORTT	DETORTED	DDEGNOSS	GODSENDS	DDEILNRU	UNRIDDLE
DDEEORTU	DETOURED	DDEGNOSU	DUDGEONS	DDEILNSW	DWINDLES
DDEEORUV	DEVOURED	DDEGOOTU	OUTDODGE		SWINDLED
DDEEORVY	OVERDYED	DDEGORSS	GORSEDDS	DDEILOPS	DISPLODE
DDEEOTUX	TUXEDOED	DDEGRRSU	DRUDGERS		LOPSIDED
DDEEPRRU	PERDURED	DDEGRRUY	DRUDGERY	DDEILOST	DELTOIDS
DDEEPRSS	SPREDDES	DDEHILNY	HIDDENLY	DDEILOSY	DYSODILE
DDEERRUV	VERDURED	DDEHILOO	IDLEHOOD	DDEILPRS	PIDDLERS
DDEERSTU	DETRUDES	DDEHIMOS	DISHOMED	DDEILPRU	PUDDLIER
DDEERTUX	EXTRUDED	DDEHINNU	UNHIDDEN	DDEILQRU	QUIDDLER
DDEFFISU	DIFFUSED	DDEHINOR	DIHEDRON	DDEILQSU	QUIDDLES
DDEFIIIN	NIDIFIED	DDEHIORS	SHODDIER	DDEILRRS	RIDDLERS
DDEFIILM	MIDFIELD	DDEHIOSS	SHODDIES	DDEILRSS	SLIDDERS
DDEFIILR	FIDDLIER	DDEHIRSS	SHIDDERS	DDEILRST	STRIDDLE
DDEFIIMO	MODIFIED	DDEHIRSW	WHIDDERS		TIDDLERS
DDEFIIMW	MIDWIFED	DDEHIRSY	HYDRIDES	DDEILRSY	SLIDDERY
DDEFILNO	INFOLDED	DDEHLRSU	HUDDLERS	DDEILRTW	TWIDDLER
DDEFILRS	FIDDLERS	DDEHNOOU	UNHOODED	DDEILRZZ	DRIZZLED
DDEFILSY	FIDDLEYS	DDEHNPUU	UPHUDDEN	DDEILSTW	TWIDDLES

DDEILSTY	LYDDITES	DDEMMSSU	SMEDDUMS	DDGILNRU	RUDDLING
	TIDDLEYS	DDEMNOOU	UNDOOMED	DDGIMNUY	MUDDYING
DDEILSUV	DIVULSED	DDEMNOST	ODDMENTS	DDGIMRSU	DRUDGISM
DDEIMMNU	UNDIMMED	DDEMNOUU	DUODENUM	DDGINNOS	NODDINGS
DDEIMNNU	UNMINDED	DDEMNPUU	PUDENDUM		SNODDING
DDEIMNSU	MUEDDINS	DDEMOOTU	OUTMODED	DDGINOPR	PRODDING
DDEIMNUV	VIDENDUM	DDENNORS	DENDRONS	DDGINOQU	QUODDING
DDEIMORS	DERMOIDS	DDENNOSU	UNSODDEN	DDGINORS	RODDINGS
DDEIMOSS	DESMOIDS	DDENOOPS	ENDOPODS	DDGINPSU	PUDDINGS
DDEIMOSU	MEDUSOID	DDENOOSS	DESNOODS		SPUDDING
DDEIMSTU	MUDDIEST	DDENOOUW	UNWOODED	DDGINPUY	PUDDINGY
DDEINNRU	UNRIDDEN	DDENOPSS	DESPONDS	DDGINRUY	RUDDYING
DDEINNTU	UNDINTED	DDENORSU	REDOUNDS	DDGINSTU	STUDDING
DDEINOPS	DISPONED	DDENORTU	ROTUNDED	DDGLORRU	DRUGLORD
DDEINORS	INDORSED	DDENORUW	UNWORDED	DDGOOOSW	DOGWOODS
DDEINORT	TRENDOID	DDENOSST	SNODDEST	DDHILOSY	SHODDILY
DDEINOST	NODDIEST	DDENOSTU	STOUNDED	DDHILSUY	DUDISHLY
DDEINOSW	DISENDOW	DDENOSTW	STOWNDED	DDHIORSY	HYDROIDS
	DISOWNED	DDENOSUW	SWOUNDED	DDHIOSWY	DOWDYISH
	DOWNSIDE	DDENOTTU	DONUTTED	DDHLLOOO	DOLLHOOD
DDEINOWW	WINDOWED		UNDOTTED	DDHLMOOO	HOODMOLD
DDEINPPU	UNDIPPED	DDENRSTU	DURNDEST	DDHLNOOW	HOLDDOWN
DDEINPSS	DISPENDS	DDENSTUY	SUDDENTY	DDIIIIVV	DIVIDIVI
DDEINRST	STRIDDEN	DDEOOOSV	VOODOOED	DDIIKLSS	SKIDLIDS
DDEINRTU	INTRUDED	DDEOORSW	REDWOODS	DDIILOPS	DIPLOIDS
DDEINSST	DISTENDS	DDEOORWW	ROWDEDOW	DDIILOPY	DIPLOIDY
DDEINSSW	SWIDDENS	DDEOOSWY	DYEWOODS	DDIIMMUY	DIDYMIUM
DDEINSTU	DISTUNED	DDEOOUUV	VOUDOUED	DDIIMOSU	DISODIUM
DDEIOORS	ODORISED	DDEOPRRS	PRODDERS	DDIIMRSU	DRUIDISM
DDEIOORZ	ODORIZED	DDEOPRSW	DEWDROPS		SIDDURIM
DDEIOPRS	DROPSIED	DDEORTUU	OUTDURED	DDIINOPU	DUPONDII
	SPODDIER	DDEPRSSU	SPUDDERS	DDIIQSTU	QUIDDITS
DDEIOPRV	PROVIDED	DDFGIILN	FIDDLING	DDIIQTUY	QUIDDITY
DDEIOPSS	DISPOSED	DDFGILNU	FUDDLING	DDIKOOSS	SKIDDOOS
DDEIOPST	PODDIEST	DDFIILSU	DISULFID	DDILOOPP	DIPLOPOD
DDEIORRS	DISORDER	DDFIIOSU	FIDDIOUS	DDILOOWW	WILDWOOD
	SORDIDER	DDFMNOUU	DUMFOUND	DDILORSY	SORDIDLY
DDEIOSST	SODDIEST	DDGGIINY	GIDDYING	DDILOSSY	DYSODILS
DDEIOSTW	DOWDIEST	DDGGILNU	GUDDLING	DDIMOOSS	DODOISMS
DDEIPRSS	DISPREDS	DDGGINNO	DINGDONG	DDIMOSUY	DIDYMOUS
DDEIPRSU	SPUDDIER	DDGGINOS	DODGINGS	DDIMOSWY	DOWDYISM
DDEIPSTU	DISPUTED	DDGGINRU	DRUDGING	DDINNOWW	DOWNWIND
DDEIRSSU	DRUIDESS	DDGHIINW	WHIDDING	DDINOOOT	ODONTOID
DDEIRSTU	RUDDIEST	DDGHILNO	HODDLING	DDINOOWW	WOODWIND
	STURDIED	DDGHILNU	HUDDLING	DDLLMOOS	DOLLDOMS
DDEISSTU	STUDDIES	DDGHINTU	THUDDING	DDLMORSU	DOLDRUMS
DDEKMOSU	DUKEDOMS	DDGHOOOS	GODHOODS	DDMNOORS	DROMONDS
DDELLNUU	UNDULLED	DDGIIINO	INDIGOID	DDNOORTW	DOWNTROD
DDELLOOP	DOLLOPED	DDGIIINV	DIVIDING	DDOORWWY	ROWDYDOW
DDELMNOU	UNMOLDED	DDGIIKNS	SKIDDING	DDORSSTY	DROSTDYS
DDELMRSU	MUDDLERS	DDGIIKNY	KIDDYING	DEEEEFRR	REFEREED
DDELNORU	UNLORDED	DDGIILMN	MIDDLING	DEEEEFRZ	DEFREEZE
DDELNOSY	SODDENLY	DDGIILNN	DINDLING	DEEEEGKR	KEDGEREE
DDELNRTU	TRUNDLED	DDGIILNP	PIDDLING	DEEEEHLR	REHEELED
DDELNSUY	SUDDENLY	DDGIILNR	RIDDLING	DEEEEKMN	MEEKENED
DDELOORS	DOODLERS	DDGIILNT	TIDDLING	DEEEELTY	EYELETED
DDELOPRS	PLODDERS	DDGIILNW	WIDDLING	DEEEEMMS	MESEEMED
DDELORST	STRODDLE	DDGILMNU	MUDDLING	DEEEEMRR	REDEEMER
	STRODLED	DDGILNNO	NODDLING	DEEEEMST	ESTEEMED
	TODDLERS	DDGILNOO	DOODLING	DEEEENPR	DEEPENER
DDELOSYY	DYSODYLE	DDGILNOP	PLODDING	DEEEENRV	VENEERED
DDELPRSU	PUDDLERS		PODDLING	DEEEERTT	TEETERED
DDELPSSU	SPUDDLES	DDGILNOT	TODDLING	DEEEFFIR	EFFEIRED
DDELSSTU	STUDDLES	DDGILNPU	PUDDLING	DEEEFHLO	FEEDHOLE

DEEEFHST	SHEETFED
DEEEFINR	FINEERED
	NEEDFIRE
	REDEFINE
DEEEFIPT	TEPEFIED
DEEEFIRS	REDEFIES
DEEEFIRW	FIREWEED
DEEEFKST	KEFTEDES
DEEEFLLR	REFELLED
DEEEFLPT	DEEPFELT
DEEEFLRR	FERRELED
DEEEFLRT	FELTERED
	TELFERED
DEEEFLRU	REFUELED
DEEEFLRX	REFLEXED
DEEEFLSX	DEFLEXES
DEEEFMNR	FREEDMEN
DEEEFNRS	ENSERFED
DEEEFNRT	DEFERENT
DEEEFNSS	DEFENSES
DEEEFNST	ENFESTED
DEEEFORV	OVERFEED
DEEEFRRR	DEFERRER
	REFERRED
DEEEFRRT	FERRETED
DEEEFRST	FESTERED
DEEEFRTT	FETTERED
DEEEFRTW	FEWTERED
DEEEGGPR	REPEGGED
DEEEGHNW	WHEENGED
DEEEGILS	ELEGISED
DEEEGILZ	ELEGIZED
DEEEGINS	DESIGNEE
DEEEGIPR	PEDIGREE
DEEEGIRR	GREEDIER
DEEEGISS	DIEGESES
DEEEGISW	EDGEWISE
DEEEGLPR	REPLEDGE
DEEEGLPS	PLEDGEES
DEEEGLSS	EDGELESS
DEEEGLSV	SELVEDGE
DEEEGMRR	DEMERGER
	REMERGED
DEEEGMRS	DEMERGES
DEEEGNNR	ENGENDER
DEEEGNRU	RENEGUED
DEEEGNRV	REVENGED
DEEEGRRS	REGREDES
DEEEGRRT	DETERGER
DEEEGRSS	EGRESSED
DEEEGRST	DETERGES
DEEEGRTT	GETTERED
DEEEHHSW	WHEESHED
DEEEHKRS	SHREEKED
DEEEHLMT	HELMETED
DEEEHLPW	WHEEPLED
DEEEHLRW	WHEEDLER
DEEEHLSS	HEEDLESS
DEEEHLSW	WHEEDLES
DEEEHLWZ	WHEEZLED
DEEEHMMR	REHEMMED
DEEEHMMS	EMMESHED
DEEEHMNS	ENMESHED
DEEEHMPS	HEMPSEED
DEEEHMPW	HEMPWEED
DEEEHPRT	THREEPED
DEEEHRTT	TETHERED
DEEEIKLR	DEERLIKE
	REEDLIKE
DEEEIKLS	SEEDLIKE
DEEEIKLW	WEEDLIKE
DEEEILNR	NEEDLIER
DEEEILNS	SELENIDE
DEEEILRV	RELIEVED
DEEEILTV	DELETIVE
DEEEILVW	WEEVILED
DEEEIMNS	INSEEMED
DEEEIMRS	REMEDIES
DEEEIMST	SEEDTIME
DEEEINNX	ENDEXINE
DEEEINRR	REINDEER
DEEEINRS	NEREIDES
	REDENIES
DEEEINST	NEEDIEST
DEEEINSX	ENDEIXES
DEEEINTV	EVENTIDE
DEEEIPRS	SPEEDIER
DEEEIPTX	EXPEDITE
DEEEIRRR	DERRIERE
DEEEIRSS	DIERESES
DEEEIRST	REEDIEST
DEEEIRSZ	RESEIZED
DEEEIRTW	TWEEDIER
DEEEIRVW	REVIEWED
DEEEISST	SEEDIEST
	STEEDIES
DEEEISSV	DEVISEES
DEEEISTW	WEEDIEST
DEEEJLLW	JEWELLED
DEEEJNRU	DEJEUNER
DEEEJNSU	DEJEUNES
DEEEJRRS	JERREEDS
DEEEJRSY	JERSEYED
DEEEKLNN	KENNELED
DEEEKLNR	KERNELED
DEEEKLNU	UNKEELED
DEEEKNSW	WEEKENDS
DEEEKOPW	POKEWEED
DEEEKORV	REEVOKED
DEEEKPRR	REPERKED
DEEEKRST	STREEKED
DEEEKRSW	RESKEWED
	SKEWERED
DEEELLLV	LEVELLED
DEEELLNT	DENTELLE
DEEELLNV	NEVELLED
DEEELLNW	NEWELLED
DEEELLPR	PREDELLE
	REPELLED
DEEELLPT	PELLETED
DEEELLPX	EXPELLED
DEEELLRT	TELLERED
DEEELLRV	REVELLED
DEEELMOS	SOMEDELE
DEEELMRT	REMELTED
DEEELNPU	UNPEELED
DEEELNRS	NEEDLERS
DEEELNRT	RELENTED
DEEELNRU	UNREELED
DEEELNSS	LESSENED
	NEEDLESS
	SELDSEEN
DEEELNSU	UNSEELED
DEEELNTT	TELNETED
DEEELOPP	DEPEOPLE
DEEELOPV	DEVELOPE
DEEELPRT	DEPLETER
	PELTERED
	REPLETED
DEEELPST	DEPLETES
	STEEPLED
DEEELRSS	REDELESS
DEEELRST	DEERLETS
	STREELED
DEEELRTT	LETTERED
DEEELRTW	TWEEDLER
	WELTERED
DEEELSSS	SEEDLESS
DEEELSSV	VESSELED
DEEELSSW	WEEDLESS
DEEELSTW	TWEEDLES
DEEELTVV	VELVETED
DEEEMNNT	NEEDMENT
DEEEMNRS	EMENDERS
DEEEMNSS	DEMESNES
	SEEDSMEN
DEEEMPRT	TEMPERED
DEEEMPTX	EXEMPTED
DEEEMRRU	MURDEREE
DEEEMRSS	DEMERSES
	MEDRESES
DEEEMRST	DEEMSTER
DEEENNRT	ENTENDER
DEEENNUW	UNWEENED
DEEENOPR	REOPENED
DEEENORS	ENDORSEE
DEEENPRT	REPENTED
	REPETEND
DEEENPRU	UNPEERED
DEEENPRV	PREVENED
DEEENPRX	EXPENDER
DEEENPSS	DEEPNESS
DEEENPSX	EXPENSED
DEEENRRR	RENDERER
DEEENRRT	RERENTED
	TENDERER
DEEENRRV	REVEREND
DEEENRST	RENESTED
	RESENTED
DEEENRTT	TENTERED
DEEENRTU	NEUTERED
DEEENRTX	EXTENDER
DEEENRUV	REVENUED
	UNREEVED
DEEENSSS	SEEDNESS
DEEENSSY	EYEDNESS
DEEENSTT	DETENTES
	NEDETTES
DEEENSTU	DETENUES
DEEENSTX	DENTEXES
DEEENSUV	VENDEUSE
DEEEOPRR	PEDERERO

Eight-letter anagrams

DEEEOPRT	DEPORTEE	DEEFHLRS	FELDSHER	DEEFNSST	DEFTNESS
DEEEORRZ	REZEROED	DEEFHORT	FOTHERED	DEEFOORR	REROOFED
DEEEORST	STEREOED	DEEFIILN	FEDELINI	DEEFOORS	FOREDOES
DEEEORSV	OVERSEED		LENIFIED	DEEFOORT	FOOTERED
DEEEORSW	OREWEEDS	DEEFIINT	DEFINITE		REFOOTED
DEEEORVY	OVEREYED	DEEFIIRS	DEIFIERS	DEEFOORW	WOODFREE
DEEEOSTV	DEVOTEES		EDIFIERS	DEEFORST	DEFOREST
DEEEPPPR	PEPPERED		FIRESIDE		FORESTED
DEEEPRSS	SPEEDERS	DEEFIIRV	VERIFIED		FOSTERED
DEEEPRST	ESTREPED	DEEFILLR	REFILLED	DEEFORTU	FOUTERED
	PESTERED	DEEFILLT	FILLETED	DEEFORUY	FOUREYED
DEEEPRSZ	SPREEZED	DEEFILMR	REFILMED	DEEFPRSU	PERFUSED
DEEEPRTX	EXPERTED	DEEFILMS	MEDFLIES	DEEFRRTU	RETURFED
DEEEQRRU	REQUERED	DEEFILNX	INFLEXED	DEEFRSSU	DEFUSERS
DEEEQSUZ	SQUEEZED	DEEFILPR	PILFERED	DEEGGHHO	HEDGEHOG
DEEERRRT	DETERRER		PREFILED	DEEGGHIP	HEDGEPIG
DEEERRRV	VERDERER	DEEFILRS	DEFILERS	DEEGGIJR	JIGGERED
DEEERRST	DESERTER		FIELDERS		REJIGGED
DEEERRSV	DESERVER	DEEFILRT	FILTERED	DEEGGINR	GINGERED
	RESERVED	DEEFIMSS	MISFEEDS		NIGGERED
	REVERSED	DEEFIMTU	TUMEFIED		RENIGGED
DEEERRTV	REVERTED	DEEFINRR	INFERRED	DEEGGIRR	DREGGIER
DEEERSSV	DESERVES	DEEFINRS	DEFINERS		RERIGGED
DEEERSTT	DETESTER	DEEFINRZ	FRENZIED	DEEGGLOR	DOGGEREL
	RESETTED	DEEFINSS	FINESSED	DEEGGNOR	ENGORGED
	RETESTED	DEEFINST	FENDIEST	DEEGGNPU	UNPEGGED
	SETTERED		INFESTED	DEEGGNTU	NUGGETED
	STREETED	DEEFIORS	FORESIDE	DEEGGORR	REGORGED
DEEERSTV	REVESTED	DEEFIORT	FOETIDER	DEEGGORT	GORGETED
DEEERSTW	WESTERED	DEEFIPRR	PREFIRED		TOGGERED
DEEERSTX	EXSERTED	DEEFIPRX	PREFIXED	DEEGGQSU	SQUEGGED
DEEERSUW	SERUEWED	DEEFIRRV	FERVIDER	DEEGGRRU	RUGGEDER
DEEERSVW	SERVEWED	DEEFIRST	RESIFTED	DEEGHHIR	HIGHERED
DEEERTTT	TETTERED	DEEFIRTT	REFITTED	DEEGHHOP	HEDGEHOP
DEEERTTV	REVETTED	DEEFISTT	FETIDEST	DEEGHHSU	SHEUGHED
DEEERTTW	REWETTED	DEEFLLNU	UNFELLED	DEEGHHUW	WHEUGHED
DEEESTTU	SUEDETTE	DEEFLLOW	FELLOWED	DEEGHILS	SLEIGHED
DEEESTTV	VEDETTES	DEEFLLRU	FULLERED	DEEGHINR	REHINGED
DEEFFGLU	EFFULGED	DEEFLNNU	FUNNELED	DEEGHIST	HEDGIEST
DEEFFGOR	GOFFERED	DEEFLNOR	ENFOLDER	DEEGHITW	WEIGHTED
DEEFFINR	NIFFERED		FORELEND	DEEGHLPU	PLEUGHED
DEEFFINS	EFFENDIS	DEEFLNSU	NEEDFULS	DEEGHNRU	HUNGERED
DEEFFINT	INFEFTED		UNSELFED	DEEGHOPR	GOPHERED
DEEFFIRS	SERIFFED	DEEFLNTU	DEFLUENT	DEEGHOPS	SHEEPDOG
DEEFFNOR	FOREFEND		UNFELTED	DEEGHORW	HEDGEROW
	OFFENDER	DEEFLNUX	UNFLEXED	DEEGHOSW	HOGWEEDS
	REOFFEND	DEEFLORW	DEFLOWER	DEEGHOTT	DOGTEETH
DEEFFRSU	SUFFERED		FLOWERED		GHETTOED
DEEFGGOR	DEFOGGER		REFLOWED	DEEGIINN	INDIGENE
DEEFGILR	FLEDGIER	DEEFLOST	FEEDLOTS	DEEGIISS	DIEGESIS
DEEFGINR	FINGERED	DEEFLOSY	EYEFOLDS	DEEGIKST	KEDGIEST
DEEFGINS	FEEDINGS	DEEFLPSU	SPEEDFUL	DEEGILMO	LIEGEDOM
DEEFGINX	FEDEXING	DEEFLRRU	FERRULED	DEEGILMP	IMPLEDGE
DEEFGIPS	PIGFEEDS	DEEFLRUX	REFLUXED	DEEGILMT	GIMLETED
DEEFGIRT	FIDGETER	DEEFMNOR	ENFORMED	DEEGILNN	NEEDLING
DEEFGIUW	GUDEWIFE	DEEFMNOT	FOMENTED	DEEGILNO	ELOIGNED
DEEFGLNU	ENGULFED	DEEFMORR	DEFORMER		LEGIONED
DEEFGLOO	FEELGOOD		REFORMED	DEEGILNR	ENGIRDLE
DEEFGLUW	GULFWEED	DEEFMORS	FREEDOMS		LINGERED
DEEFGORR	REFORGED	DEEFMPRU	PERFUMED		REEDLING
DEEFGORY	FROGEYED	DEEFNOOR	FOREDONE	DEEGILNS	SEEDLING
DEEFHIMU	HUMEFIED	DEEFNORZ	DEFROZEN	DEEGILNT	DELETING
DEEFHINT	HINDFEET	DEEFNOST	SOFTENED	DEEGILNU	EUGLENID
DEEFHLOR	FREEHOLD	DEEFNRRU	REFUNDER	DEEGILNV	DEVELING

DEEGILNW	WEDELING	DEEGLRSW	WERGELDS	DEEHKNOS	KEESHOND
DEEGILRS	LEIDGERS	DEEGMNOR	MONGERED	DEEHKNRU	HUNKERED
DEEGILRW	WEREGILD	DEEGMNRU	DUNGMERE	DEEHKORS	KOSHERED
DEEGILRY	GREEDILY	DEEGMSUW	GUMWEEDS	DEEHLLOR	HOLLERED
DEEGILST	GELIDEST	DEEGNNOS	ENDOGENS	DEEHLLOV	HOVELLED
	LEDGIEST	DEEGNNOY	ENDOGENY	DEEHLMMW	WHEMMLED
DEEGIMMR	IMMERGED	DEEGNOPU	GEEPOUND	DEEHLMNU	UNHELMED
DEEGIMNN	EMENDING	DEEGNORV	GOVERNED	DEEHLMSW	WELDMESH
DEEGIMNR	REMEDING	DEEGNPRU	REPUGNED	DEEHLNPU	UNHELPED
DEEGIMRU	DEMIURGE	DEEGNPUX	EXPUGNED	DEEHLORV	OVERHELD
DEEGINNR	ENRINGED		EXPUNGED		VERDELHO
DEEGINNS	ENSIGNED	DEEGNRUY	UNGREEDY	DEEHLOST	HOSTELED
DEEGINNT	TEENDING	DEEGNSTU	NUTSEDGE	DEEHLOSU	HOUSELED
DEEGINNW	ENDEWING	DEEGORST	GOSTERED	DEEHLOSV	SHOVELED
DEEGINOP	PIGEONED	DEEGOSTU	OUTEDGES	DEEHLPPS	SHLEPPED
DEEGINPS	SPEEDING	DEEGOTUW	GOUTWEED	DEEHLSTU	SLEUTHED
DEEGINRR	DERINGER	DEEGPRUX	EXPURGED	DEEHMNRS	HERDSMEN
DEEGINRS	DESIGNER	DEEGRRSU	RESURGED	DEEHMNSU	UNMESHED
	ENERGIDS	DEEGRSSW	SWEDGERS	DEEHMORT	MOTHERED
	REDESIGN	DEEGRSTU	GESTURED	DEEHNOPY	PHONEYED
	REEDINGS	DEEGRTTU	GUTTERED	DEEHNORR	DEERHORN
	RESIGNED	DEEGSSTU	GUSSETED		DEHORNER
DEEGINRY	REDYEING	DEEHHIRT	HITHERED	DEEHNORT	DETHRONE
DEEGINSS	DINGESSE	DEEHHNPY	HYPHENED		THRENODE
	EDGINESS	DEEHHPRS	SHEPHERD	DEEHNOWY	HONEYDEW
	SDEIGNES	DEEHHRST	THRESHED	DEEHNPRS	PREHENDS
	SEEDINGS	DEEHHRSU	HUSHERED	DEEHNSTU	ENTHUSED
DEEGINST	INGESTED	DEEHIKLR	HERDLIKE	DEEHOORV	HOOVERED
	SIGNETED	DEEHIKLS	SHEDLIKE	DEEHOPRT	POTHERED
	STEEDING	DEEHIKRS	SHREIKED	DEEHORRS	REDHORSE
DEEGINSW	WEEDINGS		SHRIEKED	DEEHORRT	DEHORTER
DEEGINSX	DESEXING	DEEHIKSV	KHEDIVES	DEEHORSU	REHOUSED
DEEGINZZ	GIZZENED	DEEHILNS	ENSHIELD	DEEHORSW	RESHOWED
DEEGIORT	GOITERED	DEEHILRS	HIRSELED		SHOWERED
DEEGIOST	EGOTISED		RELISHED	DEEHORTT	HOTTERED
DEEGIOTZ	EGOTIZED		SHIELDER	DEEHORTX	EXHORTED
DEEGIPRU	PREGUIDE	DEEHILSS	HIDELESS	DEEHPRSY	SYPHERED
DEEGIPSW	PIGWEEDS	DEEHILSV	DISHEVEL	DEEHRRSW	SHREWDER
DEEGIRST	DIGESTER	DEEHIMMS	IMMESHED	DEEHRTUW	WUTHERED
	ESTRIDGE	DEEHIMNS	INMESHED	DEEIIKLT	TIDELIKE
	REDIGEST	DEEHIMOP	HEMIPODE	DEEIILNS	SIDELINE
DEEGIRSU	GUDESIRE	DEEHIMRT	MITHERED	DEEIILRV	LIVERIED
DEEGIRSV	DIVERGES	DEEHINPR	EPHEDRIN	DEEIILRW	WIELDIER
DEEGISST	SEDGIEST	DEEHINRR	HINDERER	DEEIIMRS	DIMERISE
DEEGISTW	WEDGIEST	DEEHINRS	DRISHEEN	DEEIIMRZ	DIMERIZE
DEEGJPRU	PREJUDGE		RESHINED	DEEIIMST	ITEMISED
DEEGJRSU	REJUDGES	DEEHINRT	NITHERED	DEEIIMTZ	ITEMIZED
DEEGKMOS	GEEKDOMS	DEEHINST	DISTHENE	DEEIINOS	DEIONISE
DEEGLLOR	GOLLERED	DEEHINTW	WHITENED	DEEIINOZ	DEIONIZE
DEEGLLRU	GRUELLED	DEEHIORS	HEROISED	DEEIINST	DIETINES
DEEGLLUY	GULLEYED	DEEHIORZ	HEROIZED	DEEIINSX	ENDEIXIS
DEEGLNOR	GOLDENER	DEEHIOTX	ETHOXIDE	DEEIIPRS	EPEIRIDS
DEEGLNOU	ENGOULED	DEEHIPRS	HESPERID	DEEIIPRU	PRIEDIEU
DEEGLNOZ	LOZENGED		PERISHED	DEEIIRSS	DIERESIS
DEEGLNRY	LEGENDRY	DEEHIRRS	REDSHIRE	DEEIIRST	SIDERITE
DEEGLOPR	PLEDGEOR	DEEHIRRT	DITHERER	DEEIIRSV	DERISIVE
DEEGLOPS	DOGSLEEP	DEEHIRRW	WHERRIED	DEEIIRSW	WEIRDIES
DEEGLORV	GROVELED	DEEHIRST	DIETHERS	DEEIISSS	DISSEISE
DEEGLORW	GLOWERED	DEEHIRSV	SHIVERED	DEEIISSW	SIDEWISE
	REGLOWED		SHRIEVED	DEEIISSX	DEIXISES
DEEGLOSY	GOLDEYES	DEEHIRSW	SHREWDIE	DEEIISSZ	DISSEIZE
DEEGLPRS	PLEDGERS	DEEHIRTW	WITHERED	DEEIJNNO	ENJOINED
DEEGLPST	PLEDGETS	DEEHIRTY	HEREDITY	DEEIJNOR	REJOINED
DEEGLRSS	SLEDGERS	DEEHKLPS	HELPDESK	DEEIJRTT	JITTERED

Eight-letter anagrams

DEEIKKRY YIKKERED	OVERIDLE	DIMETERS
DEEIKLLR KILLDEER	**DEEILOSS** OILSEEDS	MISTERED
DEEIKLLS KILLDEES	**DEEILOTT** TOILETED	**DEEIMRTT** REMITTED
SKELLIED	**DEEILPPR** LIPPERED	**DEEIMSSU** MEDIUSES
DEEIKLMO DOMELIKE	**DEEILPRX** DIPLEXER	**DEEINNPR** REPINNED
DEEIKLMW MILKWEED	**DEEILPSS** SEEDLIPS	**DEEINNRS** SINNERED
DEEIKLNN ENKINDLE	**DEEILPST** EPISTLED	**DEEINNRT** INDENTER
ENLINKED	**DEEILPSU** EPULIDES	INTENDER
DEEIKLNR REKINDLE	**DEEILPSY** SPEEDILY	INTERNED
RELINKED	**DEEILRRV** DRIVELER	**DEEINNRU** UNREINED
DEEIKLNS SILKENED	**DEEILRST** RELISTED	**DEEINNRV** INNERVED
DEEIKLNU DUNELIKE	**DEEILRSU** LEISURED	**DEEINNST** DENTINES
DEEIKLOV DOVELIKE	**DEEILRSV** DELIVERS	DESINENT
DEEIKLSW SILKWEED	DESILVER	**DEEINNSZ** DENIZENS
DEEIKMSW MIDWEEKS	SILVERED	**DEEINNTV** INVENTED
DEEIKMSY MISKEYED	SLIVERED	**DEEINNTW** ENTWINED
DEEIKNNP PINKENED	**DEEILRSW** WIELDERS	**DEEINNUV** UNENVIED
DEEIKNRS DEERSKIN	**DEEILRSY** YIELDERS	UNVEINED
DEEIKNRT TINKERED	**DEEILRTT** LITTERED	**DEEINOPS** DISPONEE
DEEIKNTT KITTENED	RETITLED	OPENSIDE
DEEIKOSV DOVEKIES	**DEEILRVY** DELIVERY	**DEEINORS** INDORSEE
DEEIKPPR KIPPERED	**DEEILSSS** IDLESSES	ORDINEES
DEEIKRSU DUKERIES	**DEEILSST** TIDELESS	**DEEINORT** ORIENTED
DEEIKRSV SKIVERED	**DEEILSSV** DEVILESS	**DEEINORW** IRONWEED
DEEIKSTT DISKETTE	**DEEILSTU** DILUTEES	**DEEINOST** SIDENOTE
DEEILLMP IMPELLED	**DEEILSTV** DEVILETS	**DEEINOSV** NOSEDIVE
MILLEPED	**DEEILSUV** DELUSIVE	**DEEINOTV** DENOTIVE
DEEILLNO NIELLOED	**DEEILSVW** SWIVELED	**DEEINPPR** NIPPERED
DEEILLOR ORIELLED	**DEEILTUY** YULETIDE	**DEEINPRS** SPENDIER
DEEILLPR PERILLED	**DEEIMMNS** ENDEMISM	**DEEINPSS** DISPENSE
DEEILLRT TILLERED	**DEEIMMOS** SEMIDOME	PIEDNESS
TREDILLE	**DEEIMMRS** IMMERSED	**DEEINPST** PENTISED
DEEILLRV RIVELLED	SIMMERED	**DEEINPSU** UNESPIED
DEEILLVY VEILEDLY	**DEEIMMSS** MISDEEMS	**DEEINPSW** PINWEEDS
DEEILLWY WILLEYED	**DEEIMNOR** DOMINEER	**DEEINQRU** ENQUIRED
DEEILMNU DEMILUNE	**DEEIMNOS** DEMONISE	INQUERED
DEEILMOS MELODIES	DOMINEES	**DEEINQSU** SEQUINED
MELODISE	**DEEIMNOZ** DEMONIZE	**DEEINRRT** INTERRED
DEEILMOZ MELODIZE	**DEEIMNPT** PEDIMENT	TRENDIER
DEEILMPT IMPLETED	**DEEIMNRR** REMINDER	**DEEINRRV** REDRIVEN
DEEILNOS ESLOINED	REREMIND	**DEEINRRW** REWINDER
LESIONED	**DEEIMNRT** REMINTED	**DEEINRSS** DIRENESS
DEEILNOT DELETION	**DEEIMNRV** VERMINED	**DEEINRST** INSERTED
ENTOILED	**DEEIMNSS** DESMINES	NERDIEST
DEEILNPP LIPPENED	SIDESMEN	RESIDENT
DEEILNRR REDLINER	**DEEIMNST** DEMENTIS	SINTERED
DEEILNRS REDLINES	SEDIMENT	TRENDIES
DEEILNRU UNDERLIE	TIDESMEN	**DEEINRSU** UREDINES
DEEILNSS IDLENESS	**DEEIMNSU** SEMINUDE	**DEEINRSV** INVERSED
LINSEEDS	**DEEIMNTT** MITTENED	**DEEINRSW** REWIDENS
DEEILNST ENLISTED	**DEEIMORS** EMEROIDS	WIDENERS
LINTSEED	**DEEIMOST** TEDISOME	**DEEINRSX** INDEXERS
LISTENED	**DEEIMPRR** PERIDERM	**DEEINRTT** RETINTED
TINSELED	REPRIMED	**DEEINRTU** RETINUED
DEEILNSV SNIVELED	**DEEIMPRS** DEMIREPS	REUNITED
DEEILNSY DYELINES	EPIDERMS	**DEEINRTV** INVERTED
DEEILNTT ENTITLED	IMPEDERS	**DEEINRTW** WINTERED
DEEILNUV UNLEVIED	PREMISED	**DEEINRTX** DEXTRINE
UNVEILED	SIMPERED	**DEEINSST** DESTINES
DEEILOPT LEPIDOTE	**DEEIMPRX** PREMIXED	**DEEINSSV** VENDISES
PETIOLED	**DEEIMPSS** SEMIPEDS	**DEEINSSW** DEWINESS
DEEILORT DOLERITE	**DEEIMRSS** DERMISES	WIDENESS
LOITERED	**DEEIMRST** DEMERITS	**DEEINSTT** DINETTES
DEEILORV EVILDOER	DEMISTER	INSETTED

DEEINSTU	DETINUES	**DEEIRRSS**	DERRISES	**DEELLOTX**	EXTOLLED
DEEINSTV	EVIDENTS		DESIRERS	**DEELLOVW**	VOWELLED
	INVESTED		DRESSIER	**DEELLOVY**	VOLLEYED
DEEINSUZ	UNSEIZED		RESIDERS	**DEELLOWY**	YELLOWED
DEEINTUV	DUVETINE	**DEEIRRST**	DESTRIER	**DEELLPUW**	UPWELLED
DEEINUVW	UNVIEWED	**DEEIRRSU**	RUDERIES	**DEELLRSU**	DUELLERS
DEEIOPRT	PERIDOTE	**DEEIRRSV**	DERIVERS	**DEELLRSW**	DWELLERS
	PROTEIDE		REDRIVES	**DEELLSSW**	WELDLESS
DEEIOPRX	PEROXIDE	**DEEIRRTV**	DIVERTER	**DEELLSUX**	DUXELLES
DEEIOPSS	EPISODES		VERDITER	**DEELMMOP**	POMMELED
DEEIOPST	EPIDOTES	**DEEIRRWW**	WIREDREW	**DEELMMPU**	EMPLUMED
	POETISED	**DEEIRRZZ**	RIZZERED		PUMMELED
DEEIOPSX	EPOXIDES	**DEEIRSST**	DIESTERS	**DEELMNOO**	MELODEON
DEEIOPTZ	POETIZED		EDITRESS	**DEELMNOS**	LODESMEN
DEEIORRV	OVERRIDE		RESISTED	**DEELMNTU**	UNMELTED
DEEIORST	EROTISED		SISTERED	**DEELMNTW**	WELDMENT
DEEIORSV	OVERSIDE	**DEEIRSSU**	DIURESES	**DEELMOOS**	DOLESOME
DEEIORSW	DOWERIES		REISSUED	**DEELMOPR**	EMPOLDER
	WEIRDOES		RESIDUES	**DEELMOPY**	EMPLOYED
DEEIORTU	ETOURDIE	**DEEIRSSV**	DEVISERS	**DEELMORS**	MODELERS
DEEIORTV	OVEREDIT		DISSERVE		MORSELED
DEEIORTZ	EROTIZED		DISSEVER		REMODELS
DEEIORVW	OVERWIDE		DIVERSES	**DEELMOST**	MOLESTED
DEEIOTVX	VIDEOTEX	**DEEIRSTT**	TIREDEST	**DEELMOSU**	DUELSOME
DEEIPPQU	EQUIPPED	**DEEIRSTU**	ERUDITES	**DEELMPPU**	PEPLUMED
DEEIPPRZ	ZIPPERED		SURETIED	**DEELMPSU**	DEPLUMES
DEEIPPST	PEPTIDES	**DEEIRSTV**	VERDITES	**DEELMRUY**	DEMURELY
	PEPTISED	**DEEIRSTW**	WEIRDEST	**DEELNNTU**	TUNNELED
DEEIPPTT	PIPETTED	**DEEIRTTT**	TITTERED	**DEELNOOS**	LOOSENED
DEEIPPTZ	PEPTIZED	**DEEIRTTV**	RIVETTED	**DEELNORT**	REDOLENT
DEEIPQRU	REPIQUED	**DEEIRTTW**	WITTERED		RONDELET
DEEIPQTU	PIQUETED	**DEEISSSU**	DISEUSES	**DEELNORV**	OVERLEND
DEEIPRRS	PREDRIES	**DEEISTTV**	VIDETTES	**DEELNOSS**	LESSONED
	PRESIDER	**DEEJKNTU**	JUNKETED	**DEELNOSU**	ENSOULED
	REPRISED	**DEEJPRRU**	PERJURED	**DEELNOSY**	ESLOYNED
	RESPIRED	**DEEJPTTU**	UPJETTED	**DEELNPRS**	RESPLEND
DEEIPRRV	DEPRIVER	**DEEKKOOY**	OKEYDOKE	**DEELNPRY**	DEPRENYL
	REPRIVED	**DEEKLNOS**	SLOKENED	**DEELNPSU**	PENDULES
DEEIPRRW	PREWIRED	**DEEKLNST**	SKLENTED	**DEELNRTU**	UNDERLET
DEEIPRRZ	REPRIZED	**DEEKLOOR**	RELOOKED	**DEELNRTY**	TENDERLY
DEEIPRSS	DESPISER	**DEEKLRSS**	SKELDERS	**DEELNSSW**	LEWDNESS
	DISPERSE	**DEEKMNOY**	MONKEYED	**DEELNSTY**	ENSTYLED
	PRESIDES	**DEEKNNNU**	UNKENNED	**DEELNTTU**	UNLETTED
DEEIPRST	PREEDITS	**DEEKNOST**	DESKNOTE	**DEELNWWY**	NEWLYWED
	PRIESTED	**DEEKNOTW**	KNOTWEED	**DEELOORT**	RETOOLED
	RESPITED	**DEEKNOTY**	KEYNOTED	**DEELOPPR**	LOPPERED
DEEIPRSU	DUPERIES	**DEEKNSSW**	NEWSDESK	**DEELOPRR**	DEPLORER
DEEIPRSV	DEPRIVES	**DEEKOORR**	KOREROED	**DEELOPRS**	DEPLORES
	PREVISED	**DEEKORRW**	REWORKED	**DEELOPRV**	PRELOVED
DEEIPRTT	PITTERED	**DEEKORST**	RESTOKED	**DEELOPRW**	REPLOWED
	PRETTIED	**DEEKOSVY**	DOVEKEYS	**DEELOPRX**	EXPLODER
DEEIPRTX	EXTIRPED	**DEEKRUVY**	KURVEYED		EXPLORED
DEEIPSSS	DESPISES	**DEELLMOR**	MODELLER	**DEELOPRY**	DEPLOYER
DEEIPSST	DESPITES	**DEELLMOW**	MELLOWED		REDEPLOY
	SIDESTEP	**DEELLMRU**	MULLERED	**DEELOPSV**	DEVELOPS
DEEIPSTT	TEPIDEST	**DEELLNOP**	POLLENED	**DEELOPSX**	EXPLODES
DEEIPSTU	DEPUTIES	**DEELLNOR**	ENROLLED	**DEELORRS**	RESOLDER
	DEPUTISE		RONDELLE		SOLDERER
DEEIPTUZ	DEPUTIZE	**DEELLOPR**	REPOLLED	**DEELORSU**	DELOUSER
DEEIQRRU	REQUIRED	**DEELLORR**	REROLLED		URODELES
DEEIQRSU	ESQUIRED	**DEELLORW**	ROWELLED	**DEELORSV**	RESOLVED
DEEIQRTU	REQUITED		WELLDOER	**DEELORSY**	YODELERS
DEEIQRUV	QUIVERED	**DEELLORY**	YODELLER	**DEELORTT**	DOTTEREL
DEEIQTUU	QUIETUDE	**DEELLOTW**	TOWELLED		TOLTERED

DEELORTV	REVOLTED	**DEEMRRRU**	DEMURRER	**DEENTTUV**	UNVETTED
DEELORTW	TROWELED		MURDERER	**DEENTTUW**	UNWETTED
DEELORTY	DELETORY	**DEEMRSTU**	DEMUREST	**DEENTUVY**	DUVETYNE
DEELORUV	LOUVERED		MUSTERED	**DEEOOPPR**	PEREOPOD
DEELORVV	REVOLVED	**DEEMRTTU**	MUTTERED	**DEEOORRV**	OVERDOER
DEELORVW	OVERLEWD	**DEEMSSTY**	SYSTEMED		OVERRODE
DEELOSSU	DELOUSES	**DEENNNOP**	PENNONED	**DEEOORSV**	OVERDOES
DEELOSTV	DOVELETS	**DEENNNPU**	UNPENNED		OVERDOSE
DEELOSVV	DEVOLVES	**DEENNOPT**	DEPONENT	**DEEOPPRS**	PREPOSED
DEELOTUV	EVOLUTED	**DEENNOPU**	UNOPENED	**DEEOPPST**	ESTOPPED
DEELPPRU	REPULPED	**DEENNORS**	ENDERONS	**DEEOPRRR**	PREORDER
DEELPRRU	PRELUDER	**DEENNORW**	RENOWNED	**DEEOPRRS**	PEDREROS
DEELPRSS	SPELDERS	**DEENNOSS**	DONENESS	**DEEOPRRT**	DEPORTER
DEELPRSU	PRELUDES	**DEENNOST**	ENDNOTES		PORTERED
	REPULSED		SONNETED		REPORTED
DEELPRTU	DRUPELET	**DEENNOSY**	DOYENNES	**DEEOPRRU**	REPOURED
DEELPRUV	PULVERED	**DEENNPST**	PENDENTS	**DEEOPRRV**	REPROVED
DEELPRUX	DUPLEXER	**DEENNRTU**	UNRENTED	**DEEOPRRW**	POWDERER
DEELPSUX	DUPLEXES		UNTENDER	**DEEOPRSS**	DEPOSERS
	EXPULSED	**DEENNRUV**	UNNERVED	**DEEOPRST**	DOPESTER
DEELPTTY	PETTEDLY	**DEENNSSU**	NUDENESS		POSTERED
DEELRSTU	DELUSTER		UNSENSED		REEDSTOP
	LUSTERED	**DEENNSTU**	UNNESTED		REPOSTED
	RESULTED	**DEENNTTU**	UNNETTED	**DEEOPRSY**	EYEDROPS
	ULSTERED		UNTENTED	**DEEOPRTT**	POTTERED
DEELRSTW	LEWDSTER	**DEENNTUV**	UNVENTED		REPOTTED
	WRESTLED	**DEENOORT**	ENROOTED	**DEEOPRTW**	POWTERED
DEELRSTY	RESTYLED	**DEENOORV**	OVERDONE	**DEEOPRTX**	EXPORTED
DEELRSUV	REVULSED	**DEENOORW**	WOODENER	**DEEOPRUZ**	DOUZEPER
DEEMMORS	MESODERM	**DEENOOSV**	NOSEDOVE	**DEEOPSST**	POSSETED
DEEMMRRU	DUMMERER	**DEENOPPR**	PREPONED	**DEEOPSSU**	ESPOUSED
DEEMMRSU	SUMMERED	**DEENOPRR**	PONDERER	**DEEOPSTU**	OUTSPEED
DEEMNNRU	UNDERMEN	**DEENOPRW**	PREOWNED	**DEEOQRTU**	REQUOTED
DEEMNNTU	TENENDUM	**DEENOPSS**	SPONDEES		ROQUETED
DEEMNOOS	ENDOSOME	**DEENOPST**	PENTODES	**DEEORRRS**	ORDERERS
	MOONSEED	**DEENORRS**	ENDORSER		REORDERS
DEEMNOQU	QUEENDOM	**DEENORRW**	WONDERER	**DEEORRRV**	VERDEROR
DEEMNORR	MODERNER	**DEENORSS**	ENDORSES	**DEEORRST**	RESORTED
DEEMNORS	MODERNES	**DEENORST**	ERODENTS		RESTORED
	SERMONED	**DEENORSW**	ENDOWERS		ROSTERED
DEEMNORT	ENTODERM		REENDOWS	**DEEORRSV**	OVERREDS
	MENTORED		WORSENED	**DEEORRTT**	RETORTED
DEEMNOSS	DEMONESS	**DEENORTU**	DEUTERON	**DEEORRTU**	REROUTED
	ENMOSSED	**DEENOSSS**	ENDOSSES		RETOURED
DEEMNOST	DEMETONS	**DEENOSST**	STENOSED	**DEEORRUV**	DEVOURER
DEEMNOSU	EUDEMONS	**DEENPPRS**	PERPENDS		OVERRUDE
DEEMOOPR	PODOMERE	**DEENPRSS**	SPENDERS	**DEEORRVW**	OVERDREW
DEEMOORT	ODOMETER	**DEENPRST**	PRETENDS	**DEEORRVY**	OVERDYER
DEEMOPPY	POMPEYED	**DEENRRSU**	ENDURERS	**DEEORSST**	DOSSERET
DEEMOPRV	PREMOVED		SUNDERER		OERSTEDS
DEEMOPST	DEEPMOST	**DEENRRTU**	RETURNED	**DEEORSTT**	ROSETTED
DEEMOQRU	QUEERDOM	**DEENRSSU**	RUDENESS		TETRODES
DEEMORRT	TREMORED	**DEENRSTU**	DENTURES	**DEEORSTX**	DEXTROSE
DEEMORRW	DEWORMER		SEDERUNT	**DEEORSTY**	OYSTERED
DEEMORST	MODESTER		UNDERSET		STOREYED
DEEMORSW	WORMSEED		UNDESERT	**DEEORSUV**	OVERUSED
DEEMORSX	EXODERMS		UNRESTED	**DEEORSVY**	OVERDYES
DEEMORTU	MOUTERED	**DEENRSUU**	UNDERUSE	**DEEORTTT**	TOTTERED
	UDOMETER	**DEENRSUV**	UNSERVED	**DEEORTTX**	EXTORTED
DEEMPPRU	REPUMPED		UNVERSED	**DEEORTUV**	DEVOUTER
DEEMPRST	DEMPSTER	**DEENRTUV**	VENTURED	**DEEOSSUX**	EXODUSES
DEEMPRSU	PRESUMED	**DEENSSSY**	SYNDESES	**DEEOSTUW**	OUTWEEDS
DEEMPRTU	PERMUTED	**DEENSTTU**	UNTESTED	**DEEOSTUX**	TUXEDOES
DEEMPSUW	SUMPWEED	**DEENSTUV**	UNVESTED	**DEEPPRSU**	SUPPERED

DEEPPRTY	PRETYPED	**DEFGIOOW**	GOODWIFE	**DEFILNNO**	NINEFOLD
DEEPPSSU	SPEEDUPS	**DEFGIORS**	FIREDOGS	**DEFILNOR**	INFOLDER
DEEPRRSU	PERDURES	**DEFGJORU**	FORJUDGE	**DEFILNOU**	UNFOILED
DEEPRRVY	REPRYVED	**DEFGMOOY**	FOGEYDOM	**DEFILNRS**	FLINDERS
DEEPRSTU	PERTUSED	**DEFGNORU**	UNFORGED	**DEFILNRU**	UNRIFLED
DEEPRSUW	PURSEWED	**DEFGOOSX**	DOGFOXES		URNFIELD
DEEPRSUY	PSEUDERY	**DEFHIIMU**	HUMIFIED	**DEFILNRY**	FRIENDLY
DEEPRTTU	PUTTERED	**DEFHIINS**	FIENDISH	**DEFILOPR**	PROFILED
DEEPRUVY	PURVEYED		FINISHED	**DEFILORR**	FLORIDER
DEERRSSS	DRESSERS	**DEFHILLO**	LIFEHOLD	**DEFILORU**	FLUORIDE
DEERRSUV	VERDURES	**DEFHILSS**	DISFLESH	**DEFILORV**	FRIVOLED
DEERRTTU	TURRETED	**DEFHINSU**	UNFISHED	**DEFILOTU**	OUTFIELD
DEERRTUX	EXTRUDER	**DEFHIOOW**	WIFEHOOD	**DEFILOTY**	FOETIDLY
DEERSSST	DESSERTS	**DEFHIRST**	REDSHIFT	**DEFILPRU**	PRIDEFUL
	STRESSED	**DEFHLOOS**	ELFHOODS	**DEFILPTU**	UPLIFTED
DEERSSSU	DURESSES		SELFHOOD	**DEFILRRU**	FLURRIED
DEERSSTU	RUSSETED	**DEFHLOSU**	FLOUSHED	**DEFILRVY**	FERVIDLY
DEERSSTY	DYESTERS	**DEFHLSSU**	SHEDFULS	**DEFILRZZ**	FRIZZLED
DEERSTTU	TRUSTEED	**DEFHOOOR**	FORHOOED	**DEFILSSU**	SULFIDES
DEERSTUV	VESTURED	**DEFHOORS**	SERFHOOD	**DEFIMNOR**	INFORMED
DEERSTUX	EXTRUDES	**DEFHOORW**	FORHOWED	**DEFIMOPR**	PEDIFORM
DEERSUVY	SURVEYED	**DEFIIILV**	VILIFIED	**DEFIMORY**	REMODIFY
DEERTTUX	TEXTURED	**DEFIIIMN**	MINIFIED	**DEFIMOSW**	WIFEDOMS
DEFFHILW	WHIFFLED	**DEFIIINS**	NIDIFIES	**DEFIMRRU**	DRUMFIRE
DEFFHLSU	SHUFFLED	**DEFIIINV**	VINIFIED	**DEFINNRU**	REINFUND
DEFFHORS	SHROFFED	**DEFIIIVV**	VIVIFIED		UNFRIEND
DEFFIINT	TIFFINED	**DEFIILLN**	INFILLED	**DEFINOPR**	FORPINED
DEFFIIPS	SPIFFIED	**DEFIILLO**	OILFIELD	**DEFINORW**	FOREWIND
DEFFIKLS	SKIFFLED	**DEFIILLP**	FILLIPED	**DEFINRTY**	TRENDIFY
DEFFILNS	SNIFFLED	**DEFIILLW**	WILDLIFE	**DEFINSTU**	UNSIFTED
DEFFILOV	FIVEFOLD	**DEFIILMR**	MIDLIFER	**DEFINTTU**	UNFITTED
DEFFIMOS	FIEFDOMS	**DEFIILMS**	MISFIELD	**DEFIOORW**	FIREWOOD
DEFFIORS	OFFSIDER		MISFILED	**DEFIOPRT**	PIEDFORT
DEFFIOSS	OFFSIDES	**DEFIILNO**	DIOLEFIN		PROFITED
DEFFIQSU	SQUIFFED	**DEFIILNS**	INFIDELS	**DEFIORRU**	FROIDEUR
DEFFIRSU	DIFFUSER		INFIELDS	**DEFIORSU**	FOUDRIES
DEFFISSU	DIFFUSES	**DEFIILOR**	OILFIRED	**DEFIORTU**	OUTFIRED
DEFFISUX	SUFFIXED	**DEFIILRW**	WILDFIRE	**DEFIOTXY**	DETOXIFY
DEFFLNSU	SNUFFLED	**DEFIILSU**	FLUIDISE	**DEFIRRST**	DRIFTERS
DEFFLOSU	SOUFFLED	**DEFIILTY**	FIDELITY	**DEFIRSSU**	FISSURED
DEFFLRTU	TRUFFLED	**DEFIILUZ**	FLUIDIZE		SURFSIDE
DEFFNORS	FORFENDS	**DEFIIMNO**	OMNIFIED	**DEFISSTU**	FEUDISTS
DEFFNOSS	SENDOFFS	**DEFIIMNR**	INFIRMED	**DEFKLORY**	FORKEDLY
DEFFSSUU	SUFFUSED	**DEFIIMNU**	MUNIFIED	**DEFKNORU**	UNFORKED
DEFFSTUY	DYESTUFF	**DEFIIMOR**	MODIFIER	**DEFLLOOR**	FOLDEROL
DEFGGILN	FLEDGING	**DEFIIMOS**	MODIFIES	**DEFLLOOW**	FOLLOWED
DEFGHILT	FLIGHTED	**DEFIIMRS**	MISFIRED	**DEFLMOSS**	SELFDOMS
DEFGHIRT	FRIGHTED	**DEFIIMSS**	FIDEISMS	**DEFLMPRU**	FRUMPLED
DEFGIIIN	IGNIFIED	**DEFIIMSW**	MIDWIFES	**DEFLNOOU**	UNFOOLED
DEFGIILN	DEFILING	**DEFIINOT**	NOTIFIED	**DEFLNOPS**	PENFOLDS
	FIELDING	**DEFIINTU**	FINITUDE	**DEFLNORS**	FONDLERS
DEFGIILU	UGLIFIED	**DEFIINTY**	IDENTIFY		FORLENDS
DEFGIINN	DEFINING	**DEFIIOSS**	OSSIFIED	**DEFLNORU**	FLOUNDER
DEFGIINY	DEIFYING	**DEFIIOTV**	VIDEOFIT		UNFOLDER
	EDIFYING	**DEFIIPRU**	PURIFIED	**DEFLNOST**	TENFOLDS
DEFGIIRR	FRIGIDER	**DEFIIPSS**	FISSIPED	**DEFLNRUU**	UNFURLED
DEFGIIST	DIGESTIF	**DEFIIPTY**	TYPIFIED	**DEFLNSSU**	FUNDLESS
DEFGILNU	INGULFED	**DEFIIRRT**	DRIFTIER	**DEFLNTUU**	UNFLUTED
DEFGILRU	DIRGEFUL	**DEFIISST**	FIDEISTS	**DEFLOORS**	FLOODERS
DEFGILTY	GIFTEDLY	**DEFIITTY**	FETIDITY		FORSLOED
DEFGINSU	DEFUSING	**DEFILLNU**	UNFILLED		REFLOODS
	FEUDINGS	**DEFILLPU**	UPFILLED	**DEFLOORT**	FORETOLD
DEFGINTU	UNGIFTED	**DEFILMNU**	FULMINED	**DEFLOORV**	OVERFOLD
DEFGINUZ	DEFUZING		UNFILMED	**DEFLOOSS**	FOODLESS

Eight-letter anagrams

DEFLOOUW	FUELWOOD	DEGGLORS	DOGGRELS	DEGIIMST	MIDGIEST
DEFLOPUW	UPFLOWED	DEGGLORY	GORGEDLY	DEGIIMSU	MISGUIDE
DEFLORSS	FORDLESS	DEGGLRUY	RUGGEDLY	DEGIINNR	NIDERING
DEFLORST	TELFORDS	DEGGNOOR	DOGGONER	DEGIINNS	DESINING
DEFLORSU	FOULDERS	DEGGNOOS	DOGGONES		INDIGENS
DEFLPRUU	UPFURLED	DEGGNORU	UNGORGED		SDEINING
DEFLRSUU	DESULFUR	DEGGNOSU	GUDGEONS	DEGIINNT	ENDITING
	SULFURED	DEGGRRSU	DRUGGERS		INDIGENT
DEFMNORU	UNFORMED		GRUDGERS		TEINDING
DEFMOOOR	FOREDOOM	DEGGRSTU	DRUGGETS	DEGIINNW	INDEWING
DEFMORSS	SERFDOMS	DEGHHILV	HIGHVELD		WIDENING
DEFNNORT	FRONDENT	DEGHIILL	GHILLIED	DEGIINNX	INDEXING
DEFNNOSS	FONDNESS	DEGHIINS	DINGHIES	DEGIINNZ	DIZENING
DEFNNOUW	NEWFOUND	DEGHIKNT	KNIGHTED	DEGIINOS	INDIGOES
DEFNOOPS	SPOONFED	DEGHILNS	HINDLEGS	DEGIINOV	VIDEOING
DEFNOORS	FRONDOSE		SHINGLED	DEGIINRS	DESIRING
DEFNOORU	UNROOFED	DEGHILOU	OUGHLIED		RESIDING
DEFNOORV	OVERFOND	DEGHILPT	PLIGHTED		RINGSIDE
DEFNOOTU	UNFOOTED	DEGHILST	DELIGHTS	DEGIINRT	DIRIGENT
DEFNOPRS	FORSPEND		SLIGHTED	DEGIINRV	DERIVING
DEFNORRU	FRONDEUR	DEGHINNS	SHENDING		VIRGINED
DEFNORSU	FOUNDERS	DEGHINNU	UNHINGED	DEGIINRW	WEIRDING
	REFOUNDS	DEGHIOOS	SHOOGIED	DEGIINST	DIETINGS
DEFNORTU	FORTUNED	DEGHIOPS	DOGESHIP		DINGIEST
DEFNORUV	OVERFUND	DEGHIORU	DOUGHIER		EDITINGS
DEFNOSSW	DOWFNESS	DEGHIPST	DESPIGHT		INDIGEST
DEFNPRSU	PREFUNDS		SPIGHTED	DEGIINSV	DEVISING
DEFNRRUU	UNDERFUR	DEGHIQTU	QUIGHTED	DEGIIRST	RIDGIEST
	UNFURRED	DEGHITTW	TWIGHTED		RIGIDEST
DEFNRTUU	UNTURFED	DEGHLNOR	HORNGELD	DEGIISSU	DISGUISE
DEFNTTUU	UNTUFTED	DEGHLOOS	DOGHOLES	DEGIJMSU	MISJUDGE
DEFOORRW	FOREWORD		GOLOSHED	DEGIKKNO	DEKKOING
DEFOORST	REDFOOTS		SHOOGLED	DEGIKLNU	DUKELING
DEFOOSSU	DOOFUSES	DEGHLOPU	PLOUGHED	DEGIKLOV	KIDGLOVE
DEFOOTUX	OUTFOXED	DEGHLORY	HYDROGEL	DEGIKLRU	KLUDGIER
DEFORRUW	FURROWED	DEGHLOSU	SLOUGHED	DEGIKNNU	UNKINGED
DEFORSST	DEFROSTS	DEGHMOSU	GUMSHOED	DEGILLNU	DUELLING
	FROSTEDS	DEGHMPRU	GRUMPHED	DEGILLNW	DWELLING
DEFORSTW	FROWSTED	DEGHNOOS	HOGNOSED	DEGILMNO	MODELING
DEGGGIIT	GIGGITED	DEGHNORT	THRONGED	DEGILMNS	GILDSMEN
DEGGGILN	GLEDGING	DEGHNORY	HYDROGEN	DEGILMOS	MISLODGE
DEGGHINS	HEDGINGS	DEGHOOSU	DOGHOUSE	DEGILMPS	GLIMPSED
DEGGHIRS	DREGGISH	DEGHORRS	DROGHERS	DEGILNNO	OLDENING
DEGGHLOS	SHOGGLED	DEGHORTU	TROUGHED	DEGILNNS	LENDINGS
DEGGHRSU	SHRUGGED	DEGHPSUU	UPGUSHED	DEGILNOP	DEPLOING
DEGGIINN	DEIGNING	DEGIIIRS	RIGIDISE		DIPLOGEN
DEGGILNP	PLEDGING	DEGIIIRZ	RIGIDIZE	DEGILNOS	GLENOIDS
DEGGILNS	GELDINGS	DEGIIIST	DIGITISE		SIDELONG
	SLEDGING	DEGIIITZ	DIGITIZE	DEGILNOW	DOWELING
	SNIGGLED	DEGIIKNS	KINGSIDE	DEGILNOY	YODELING
DEGGILNU	DELUGING	DEGIIKST	KIDGIEST	DEGILNPS	SPELDING
DEGGILRW	WRIGGLED	DEGIILMN	DELIMING	DEGILNRU	INDULGER
DEGGINNU	UNEDGING	DEGIILNR	GRIDELIN	DEGILNRY	YELDRING
DEGGINRU	UNRIGGED	DEGIILNS	EILDINGS	DEGILNSU	INDULGES
DEGGINSW	WEDGINGS		SIDELING	DEGILNSV	DEVLINGS
DEGGINUW	UNWIGGED	DEGIILNT	DILIGENT	DEGILNSW	SWINGLED
DEGGIORS	DISGORGE	DEGIILNV	DEVILING		WELDINGS
DEGGIOST	DOGGIEST	DEGIILNW	WIELDING	DEGILNWY	WINGEDLY
DEGGIPRS	SPRIGGED	DEGIILNY	YIELDING	DEGILOOR	GOODLIER
DEGGIRRU	DRUGGIER	DEGIILTU	DIGITULE	DEGILOOY	IDEOLOGY
DEGGIRST	STRIGGED	DEGIILTY	GELIDITY	DEGILORV	OVERGILD
DEGGIRSU	DRUGGIES	DEGIIMNP	IMPEDING	DEGILOST	GODLIEST
DEGGLMSU	SMUGGLED		IMPINGED		GOLDIEST
DEGGLNSU	SNUGGLED	DEGIIMNS	DEMISING	DEGILOSZ	GOLDSIZE

DEGILPSU	PULSIDGE	DEGINRSW	REDWINGS	DEHHILTW	WITHHELD
DEGILRRS	GIRDLERS	DEGINRSY	SYNERGID	DEHHISTW	WHISHTED
DEGILRSU	GUILDERS		SYRINGED	DEHHLSUY	HUSHEDLY
	SLUDGIER	DEGINSSU	DINGUSES	DEHHMRTY	RHYTHMED
DEGILRSW	WERGILDS	DEGINSSW	SWINDGES	DEHHOOSW	WHOOSHED
DEGILRUV	DIVULGER	DEGINSTU	DUNGIEST	DEHIIKLS	DISHLIKE
DEGILRZZ	GRIZZLED	DEGINTTU	DUETTING	DEHIILLS	HILLSIDE
DEGILSUV	DIVULGES	DEGIOORS	GOODSIRE		SIDEHILL
DEGIMMNO	MODEMING	DEGIOOST	GOODIEST	DEHIILLW	WHILLIED
DEGIMNNS	MENDINGS	DEGIOPRR	PORRIDGE	DEHIILNS	LINISHED
DEGIMNOS	MENDIGOS	DEGIOPRT	RIDGETOP	DEHIILSV	DEVILISH
	SMIDGEON	DEGIOPSS	GOSSIPED	DEHIIMMS	SHIMMIED
DEGIMNOT	DEMOTING	DEGIOPST	PODGIEST	DEHIIMNS	MINISHED
DEGIMNPU	IMPUGNED	DEGIORRU	GOURDIER	DEHIIMRU	MUDIRIEH
DEGIMNRU	DEMURING	DEGIORRV	OVERGIRD	DEHIIMST	DITHEISM
DEGIMNSS	SMIDGENS	DEGIORST	DIGESTOR		SMITHIED
DEGIMOOT	GOODTIME		GRODIEST	DEHIIMSW	WHIMSIED
DEGIMOOY	GEOMYOID		STODGIER	DEHIINNS	SHINNIED
DEGIMRSU	SMUDGIER	DEGIOTUU	OUTGUIDE	DEHIINNW	WHINNIED
DEGINNNU	UNENDING	DEGIPSTU	PUDGIEST	DEHIINSS	SHINDIES
DEGINNOP	DEPONING	DEGIQSSU	SQUIDGES	DEHIINST	SHINTIED
DEGINNOT	DENOTING	DEGIRRTU	TURGIDER	DEHIIPSS	SHIPSIDE
DEGINNOV	DOVENING	DEGIRSTU	DURGIEST	DEHIIRRW	WHIRRIED
DEGINNOW	ENDOWING	DEGISSST	DISGESTS	DEHIIRST	DISHERIT
DEGINNOZ	DOZENING	DEGJMNTU	JUDGMENT	DEHIISST	DISHIEST
DEGINNPS	SPENDING	DEGLLNOY	GOLDENLY	DEHIISTT	DITHEIST
DEGINNPU	UPENDING	DEGLLOOP	GOLLOPED		STITHIED
DEGINNRT	TRENDING	DEGLLOSS	GOLDLESS	DEHIJMNO	DEMIJOHN
DEGINNRU	ENDURING	DEGLMNOT	LODGMENT	DEHIKLMS	MILKSHED
	UNRINGED	DEGLMOOY	DEMOLOGY	DEHIKLOO	HOODLIKE
DEGINNSS	SENDINGS	DEGLNOOT	GOLDTONE	DEHIKMOS	SHEIKDOM
DEGINNST	STENDING	DEGLNOUV	UNGLOVED	DEHIKPSU	DUKESHIP
DEGINNSU	UNSIGNED	DEGLNRTU	GRUNTLED	DEHILLOP	PHELLOID
DEGINNSV	VENDINGS	DEGLOOPR	PROLOGED	DEHILLRS	SHRILLED
DEGINNSY	DESYNING	DEGLOOPY	PEDOLOGY	DEHILLRT	THRILLED
DEGINNTU	DETUNING	DEGLOOUU	DUOLOGUE	DEHILMOS	DEMOLISH
	UNTINGED	DEGLOPRS	PLEDGORS	DEHILMPW	WHIMPLED
	UNTINGED	DEGLOPSS	SPLODGES	DEHILMSS	DISHELMS
DEGINNUW	UNWINGED	DEGLPRSU	SPLURGED	DEHILMTY	DIMETHYL
DEGINOOR	RODEOING	DEGMMNUU	UNGUMMED	DEHILNOR	INHOLDER
DEGINOPR	PROIGNED	DEGMOOPR	POGROMED	DEHILNOY	HONIEDLY
DEGINOPS	DEPOSING	DEGMOOSS	SMOODGES	DEHILNPY	DIPHENYL
	DISPONGE	DEGMRSSU	SMUDGERS	DEHILOOR	HELIODOR
	PIDGEONS	DEGNNORU	GROUNDEN	DEHILOOS	DHOOLIES
DEGINORR	ORDERING	DEGNNOSU	DUNGEONS	DEHILOPS	DEPOLISH
DEGINORS	NEGROIDS	DEGNNOUW	UNGOWNED		POLISHED
DEGINORU	GUERIDON	DEGNOORS	DRONGOES	DEHILOTY	HOLYTIDE
DEGINORV	DOVERING	DEGNOOSS	GOODNESS	DEHILPRT	PHILTRED
	RINGDOVE	DEGNOOST	STEGODON	DEHILPSU	SULPHIDE
DEGINORW	DOWERING	DEGNOPPU	OPPUGNED	DEHILPSY	SYLPHIDE
DEGINOSW	WENDIGOS	DEGNORRU	GROUNDER	DEHILRTW	WRITHLED
	WIDGEONS		REGROUND	DEHILSTW	WHISTLED
DEGINOTV	DEVOTING	DEGNORSU	GUERDONS	DEHILSTY	DIETHYLS
DEGINOTX	DETOXING	DEGNORTU	TRUDGEON	DEHILTTW	WHITTLED
DEGINPRS	SPRINGED	DEGNORUU	UNROUGED	DEHIMNOS	HEDONISM
DEGINPRY	PREDYING	DEGNORYY	GYRODYNE		MONISHED
DEGINPSU	DISPUNGE	DEGNPRUU	UNPURGED	DEHIMOPS	HEMIPODS
DEGINPTU	DEPUTING	DEGNRSTU	TRUDGENS	DEHIMORS	HEIRDOMS
DEGINRRS	GRINDERS	DEGOORSV	OVERDOGS	DEHIMOSS	DISHOMES
	REGRINDS	DEGOORTT	GROTTOED	DEHIMOST	ETHMOIDS
DEGINRRY	GRINDERY	DEGORSST	STODGERS	DEHIMPRS	SHRIMPED
	REDRYING	DEGORSTU	DROGUETS	DEHIMPSY	DEMYSHIP
DEGINRSS	DRESSING	DEGPRSUU	UPSURGED	DEHIMSTU	HUMIDEST
DEGINRST	STRINGED	DEGRRSTU	TRUDGERS	DEHIMSTY	MYTHISED
DEGINRSU	GRUNDIES				

Eight-letter anagrams

DEHIMTYZ	MYTHIZED	DEHLSTTU	SHUTTLED	DEIILMRU	DELIRIUM
DEHINOOP	INHOOPED	DEHMMRTU	THRUMMED	DEIILMST	DELIMITS
DEHINOPR	NEPHROID	DEHMNOOY	HOMODYNE		LIMITEDS
DEHINOPS	DIPHONES	DEHMNRUY	UNRHYMED	DEIILMSU	SEDILIUM
	SIPHONED	DEHMOORS	SHROOMED	DEIILMSV	DEVILISM
	SPHENOID	DEHMOORW	WHOREDOM		MIDLIVES
DEHINORS	HORDEINS	DEHMOOSS	SHMOOSED		MISLIVED
DEHINOST	HEDONIST		SMOOSHED	DEIILMSW	SEMIWILD
DEHINPSS	ENDSHIPS	DEHMOOST	SMOOTHED	DEIILNNU	INDULINE
DEHINPSU	PUNISHED	DEHMOOSZ	SHMOOZED	DEIILNOS	LIONISED
DEHINSUW	UNWISHED	DEHMOPRY	HYPODERM	DEIILNOT	TOLIDINE
DEHIOOST	DHOOTIES	DEHMORUU	HUMOURED	DEIILNOZ	LIONIZED
	HOODIEST	DEHNNTUU	UNHUNTED	DEIILNPV	VILIPEND
DEHIOOVW	WIVEHOOD	DEHNOOPU	UNHOOPED	DEIILNTT	INTITLED
DEHIOPRS	SPHEROID	DEHNOORU	HONOURED	DEIILNVY	DIVINELY
DEHIOPRT	TROPHIED	DEHNOOSW	HOEDOWNS	DEIILNXY	XYLIDINE
DEHIORRR	HORRIDER		WOODHENS	DEIILOPS	PLOIDIES
DEHIORSS	DISHORSE	DEHNOPSY	SYPHONED	DEIILORS	IDOLISER
	HIDROSES	DEHNORSU	ENSHROUD	DEIILORZ	IDOLIZER
DEHIORTU	OUTHIRED		HOUNDERS	DEIILOSS	IDOLISES
DEHIORTW	WITHEROD		UNHORSED	DEIILOSZ	IDOLIZES
	WORTHIED	DEHNORSY	ENHYDROS	DEIILPRT	TRIPLIED
DEHIORTY	THYREOID	DEHNORTY	THRENODY	DEIILPSS	SIDESLIP
DEHIOSSU	DISHOUSE	DEHNOSSW	SNOWSHED	DEIILRST	REDISTIL
DEHIOSSW	SIDESHOW	DEHNOSTZ	DOZENTHS	DEIILSTU	UTILISED
DEHIOSTU	HIDEOUTS	DEHNOSUU	UNHOUSED	DEIILSTV	LIVIDEST
DEHIPSSU	PSEUDISH	DEHNRSTU	THUNDERS	DEIILTUV	DILUTIVE
DEHIQSSU	SQUISHED	DEHNRSUU	UNRUSHED	DEIILTUY	TUILYIED
DEHIRRST	REDSHIRT	DEHNRTUY	THUNDERY	DEIILTUZ	TUILZIED
DEHIRRSU	DHURRIES	DEHOOOPP	POPEHOOD		UTILIZED
DEHIRSTT	THIRSTED	DEHOOPRT	THEROPOD	DEIIMMRS	DIMERISM
	THRISTED	DEHOOSSW	SWOOSHED	DEIIMMST	MISTIMED
DEHIRTWW	WITHDREW	DEHOPRST	POTSHERD	DEIIMMTT	IMMITTED
DEHKLNOU	ELKHOUND	DEHORRST	REDSHORT	DEIIMNOS	DOMINIES
DEHKNOOU	UNHOOKED	DEHORTUY	OUTHYRED	DEIIMNRT	DIRIMENT
DEHKNSUU	UNHUSKED	DEHOSSTU	STOUSHED	DEIIMNTU	MUTINIED
DEHKOOSS	SKOOSHED	DEHPPSTU	SHTUPPED	DEIIMNUV	VENIDIUM
DEHLLOOO	HOLLOOED	DEHPRSSU	SPRUSHED	DEIIMOSS	DISOMIES
DEHLLOOU	HULLOOED	DEHPRSUU	UPRUSHED	DEIIMPRU	PERIDIUM
DEHLLOOW	HOLLOWED	DEHQSSUU	SQUUSHED	DEIIMPSS	DIMPSIES
DEHLLOPY	PHYLLODE	DEHRRSTU	DRUTHERS	DEIIMRSV	MISDRIVE
DEHLMMOW	WHOMMLED	DEHRSTTU	THRUSTED	DEIIMSST	MISDIETS
DEHLMMUW	WHUMMLED	DEIIIMST	DIMITIES		MISEDITS
DEHLMOOT	HOTELDOM	DEIIINSV	DIVINISE	DEIIMSTT	TIMIDEST
DEHLMORY	HYDROMEL	DEIIINVZ	DIVINIZE	DEIIMSVW	MIDWIVES
DEHLMOSU	MUDHOLES	DEIIIRSS	IRIDISES	DEIINNOP	PINIONED
DEHLMPSU	SHLUMPED	DEIIIRSZ	IRIDIZES	DEIINNPP	PINNIPED
DEHLNOOW	DOWNHOLE	DEIIIRTV	VIRIDITE	DEIINNTW	INTWINED
DEHLNTUY	HUNTEDLY	DEIIISVV	DIVISIVE	DEIINNUV	UNDIVINE
DEHLOOOW	WOODHOLE	DEIIKKLS	DISKLIKE	DEIINORS	DERISION
DEHLOOPT	POTHOLED	DEIIKLMS	MISLIKED		IRONISED
DEHLOORV	HOLDOVER	DEIIKLNR	KINDLIER		IRONSIDE
	OVERHOLD	DEIIKLNS	DISLIKEN		RESINOID
DEHLOOSS	HOODLESS	DEIIKLNV	DEVILKIN	DEIINORT	RETINOID
	SLOOSHED	DEIIKLRS	DISLIKER	DEIINORZ	IRONIZED
DEHLOOST	TOEHOLDS	DEIIKLSS	DISLIKES	DEIINOST	EDITIONS
	TOOLSHED	DEIIKNST	DINKIEST		SEDITION
DEHLOOSW	WOOLSHED	DEIIKSVV	SKIVVIED	DEIINOSV	VISIONED
DEHLOPRU	UPHOLDER	DEIILLMP	MILLIPED	DEIINOTY	IDONEITY
DEHLOPSS	SPLOSHED	DEIILLMT	TIDEMILL	DEIINPPW	WINDPIPE
DEHLORSU	SHOULDER	DEIILLST	DILLIEST	DEIINPRS	INSPIRED
DEHLPRUU	UPHURLED	DEIILMMS	SEMIMILD	DEIINPRT	INTREPID
DEHLRRSU	HURDLERS	DEIILMNS	MIDLINES	DEIINPRV	PYRIDINE
DEHLRSWY	SHREWDLY	DEIILMPR	DIMPLIER	DEIINPSS	SIDESPIN

DEIINPTU	UNPITIED	DEIKLLOR	LORDLIKE		MOULDIER
DEIINQRU	INQUIRED	DEIKLLSS	DESKILLS	DEILMORV	OVERMILD
DEIINQSU	QUINSIED	DEIKLMMS	SKLIMMED	DEILMOSS	MIDSOLES
	SQUINIED	DEIKLMNU	UNMILKED	DEILMOST	MELODIST
DEIINRSS	INDRISES	DEIKLMRU	DRUMLIKE		MODELIST
	INSIDERS	DEIKLNNU	UNLINKED		MOLDIEST
DEIINRST	DISINTER	DEIKLNOW	DOWNLIKE	DEILMOSU	EMULSOID
	INDITERS	DEIKLNPU	UPLINKED	DEILMOTV	DEMIVOLT
	NITRIDES	DEIKLNRS	KINDLERS	DEILMPPU	PLUMIPED
	RINDIEST	DEIKLNRW	WRINKLED	DEILMPSU	DISPLUME
DEIINRSU	DISINURE	DEIKLNSS	KINDLESS		IMPULSED
	URIDINES	DEIKLNTW	TWINKLED	DEILMPTU	MULTIPED
DEIINRSV	DIVINERS	DEIKLSSS	DISKLESS	DEILMRRU	DRUMLIER
DEIINRTU	UNTIDIER	DEIKLSTT	SKITTLED	DEILMRRU	MISRULED
DEIINSST	INSISTED	DEIKLSTU	DUSTLIKE	DEILMSSY	DEMISSLY
	SNIDIEST	DEIKMNOO	KIMONOED	DEILMSTU	MUSTELID
	TIDINESS	DEIKMOSY	MISYOKED	DEILNNOT	INDOLENT
DEIINSTU	DISUNITE	DEIKMPRS	SKRIMPED	DEILNOOS	EIDOLONS
	NUDITIES	DEIKNNOR	DONNIKER		SOLENOID
	UNITISED	DEIKNNPU	UNPINKED	DEILNOPT	TOPLINED
	UNTIDIES	DEIKNNRU	UNKINDER	DEILNORS	DISENROL
DEIINSTV	DIVINEST	DEIKNNSS	KINDNESS	DEILNOSS	SONDELIS
DEIINSTW	WINDIEST	DEIKNORV	OVERKIND	DEILNOST	LENTOIDS
DEIINTTU	INTUITED	DEIKNORW	INWORKED	DEILNOSU	DELUSION
DEIINTTY	IDENTITY	DEIKNOSS	DOESKINS		INSOULED
DEIINTUZ	UNITIZED	DEIKNRRS	DRINKERS		UNSOILED
DEIIOPRS	PRESIDIO	DEIKNRSS	REDSKINS	DEILNOTU	OUTLINED
DEIIOPRT	DIPTEROI	DEIKNSSU	UNKISSED	DEILNOVV	INVOLVED
DEIIOPTY	IDIOTYPE	DEIKORSS	DROSKIES	DEILNPRS	SPELDRIN
DEIIOPZZ	PEZIZOID	DEIKORST	DORKIEST		SPINDLER
DEIIORSS	IODISERS	DEIKOSSY	DISYOKES	DEILNPRU	UNDERLIP
DEIIORST	DIORITES	DEIKPRSU	PRUSIKED	DEILNPSS	SPELDINS
DEIIORSX	OXIDISER		SPRUIKED		SPINDLES
DEIIORSZ	IODIZERS	DEIKRRSU	SKURRIED	DEILNPST	SPLINTED
DEIIORTX	TRIOXIDE	DEIKRSVY	SKYDIVER	DEILNRSS	RINDLESS
DEIIORTY	IODYRITE	DEIKSSTU	DUSKIEST	DEILNRST	SNIRTLED
DEIIORXZ	OXIDIZER	DEIKSSVY	SKYDIVES		TENDRILS
DEIIOSSX	OXIDISES	DEILLMNU	UNMILLED		TRINDLES
DEIIOSTT	OTITIDES	DEILLNSW	INDWELLS	DEILNRSW	SWINDLER
DEIIOSXZ	OXIDIZES	DEILLNTU	UNTILLED	DEILNRTU	UNDERLIT
DEIIPPRR	DRIPPIER	DEILLNUW	UNWILLED	DEILNRTY	TRENDILY
DEIIPPST	DIPPIEST	DEILLOOV	LIVELOOD	DEILNSST	DINTLESS
DEIIPRST	RIPTIDES	DEILLOPW	PILLOWED	DEILNSSV	VILDNESS
	SPIRITED	DEILLORR	LORDLIER	DEILNSSW	SWINDLES
	TIDERIPS	DEILLORS	DOLLIERS		WILDNESS
DEIIPRSZ	DISPRIZE	DEILLORT	TROLLIED		WINDLESS
DEIIPTTY	TEPIDITY	DEILLORU	LOUDLIER	DEILNSTU	DILUENTS
DEIIQSTU	DISQUIET	DEILLOSV	LIVELODS		INSULTED
DEIIRRVV	VIVERRID	DEILLOWW	WILLOWED		UNLISTED
DEIIRSSU	DIURESIS	DEILLPRR	PREDRILL	DEILNTTU	UNTILTED
DEIIRSTT	DIRTIEST	DEILLRRS	DRILLERS		UNTITLED
	TRITIDES		REDRILLS	DEILNTUY	UNITEDLY
DEIISSTT	DIETISTS	DEILLRSV	DREVILLS	DEILNUWY	UNWIELDY
	DITSIEST	DEILLSTU	DUELLIST	DEILOOPS	POOLSIDE
DEIISTTZ	DITZIEST		DULLIEST	DEILOOPW	WOODPILE
DEIISTVV	VIVIDEST	DEILMNOO	MELODION	DEILOORR	DROOLIER
DEIISTZZ	DIZZIEST	DEILMNSS	MILDNESS	DEILOPPY	POLYPIDE
DEIJNNOU	UNJOINED		MINDLESS	DEILOPRS	LEPORIDS
DEIJNORS	JOINDERS	DEILMNSU	MUSLINED	DEILOPRU	PRELUDIO
DEIJNSSU	DISJUNES	DEILMOOT	DOLOMITE	DEILOPSS	DESPOILS
DEIJORRY	JOYRIDER	DEILMOPR	IMPLORED		DIPLOSES
DEIJORSY	JOYRIDES		IMPOLDER		SOLIPEDS
DEIKKLNO	KLONDIKE	DEILMOPS	IMPLODES	DEILOPST	PISTOLED
DEIKKNNU	UNKINKED	DEILMORU	LEMUROID		POSTILED

Eight-letter anagrams

DEILOPSU	EUPLOIDS	**DEIMNOPT**	PIEDMONT	**DEINNRUW**	UNWINDER
DEILOPUY	EUPLOIDY	**DEIMNORT**	DORMIENT	**DEINNSTU**	DUNNIEST
DEILOQRU	LIQUORED	**DEIMNOST**	DEMONIST		DUNNITES
DEILORRW	LOWRIDER	**DEIMNOTW**	DOWNTIME	**DEINNTUU**	UNUNITED
DEILORSS	SOLDIERS	**DEIMNOWW**	WIDOWMEN	**DEINNTUW**	UNTWINED
DEILORST	STOLIDER	**DEIMNPRU**	UNPRIMED	**DEINOOPS**	POISONED
DEILORSU	SOULDIER	**DEIMNPSS**	MISSPEND	**DEINOOPT**	OPTIONED
DEILORSY	SOLDIERY	**DEIMNPTU**	IMPUDENT	**DEINOOPW**	PINEWOOD
DEILORTY	ELYTROID	**DEIMNRTU**	RUDIMENT	**DEINOOSU**	IDONEOUS
DEILOSST	SOLIDEST		UNMITRED	**DEINOOSZ**	OZONIDES
DEILOSSV	DISSOLVE	**DEIMNSSS**	MISSENDS		OZONISED
DEILOSTT	DOILTEST	**DEIMNSST**	MINDSETS	**DEINOOTV**	DEVOTION
DEILOSTU	SOLITUDE		MISTENDS	**DEINOOZZ**	OZONIZED
	TOLUIDES	**DEIMNSSU**	UNMISSED	**DEINOPPR**	PROPINED
DEILOSTW	DOWLIEST	**DEIMNSSW**	MISWENDS	**DEINOPPW**	DOWNPIPE
DEILOSVW	OLDWIVES	**DEIMNSTU**	MISTUNED	**DEINOPRS**	DISPONER
DEILOTUV	OUTLIVED	**DEIMOORS**	MOIDORES		POINDERS
DEILOTUW	OUTWILED	**DEIMOOSS**	SODOMIES		PRISONED
DEILOTUY	OUTYIELD		SODOMISE	**DEINOPRT**	DIPTERON
DEILPPRT	TRIPPLED	**DEIMOOST**	DOOMIEST	**DEINOPRU**	INPOURED
DEILPPST	STIPPLED		MOODIEST	**DEINOPRV**	PROVINED
DEILPPSU	SUPPLIED		SODOMITE	**DEINOPRY**	PYRENOID
DEILPPTU	PULPITED	**DEIMOOSZ**	SODOMIZE	**DEINOPSS**	DISPONES
DEILPRSS	DRIPLESS	**DEIMOPRS**	IMPEDORS		DOPINESS
DEILPRSU	SERPULID		PROMISED		SPINODES
DEILPSTT	SPLITTED	**DEIMOPRT**	IMPORTED	**DEINOPSU**	UNPOISED
DEILPSTU	STIPULED	**DEIMOPRV**	IMPROVED	**DEINOPTW**	DEWPOINT
DEILPSUY	SPULYIED	**DEIMOPST**	IMPOSTED	**DEINORRS**	INDORSER
DEILPSUZ	SPULZIED	**DEIMORRR**	MIRRORED	**DEINORSS**	INDORSES
DEILPTTU	UPTILTED	**DEIMORRS**	MISORDER		SORDINES
DEILRRSU	SLURRIED		MORRISED	**DEINORST**	DRONIEST
DEILRSSY	DRESSILY	**DEIMORSS**	MISDOERS	**DEINORSU**	DOURINES
DEILRSTU	DILUTERS	**DEIMORST**	MORTISED		SOURDINE
	LURIDEST	**DEIMORSU**	DIMEROUS	**DEINORSW**	DISOWNER
	STUDLIER		ERODIUMS		WINDORES
DEILRSVY	DIVERSLY		SOREDIUM		WINDROSE
DEILRSZZ	DRIZZLES	**DEIMORSV**	MISDROVE	**DEINORTT**	INTORTED
DEILRTVY	DEVILTRY	**DEIMORUX**	EXORDIUM	**DEINORVW**	OVERWIND
DEILSSTU	DUELISTS	**DEIMOSST**	DISTOMES	**DEINOSST**	DONSIEST
DEILSSTY	DISTYLES		MODISTES	**DEINOSSV**	VOIDNESS
	STYLISED	**DEIMOSTT**	DEMOTIST	**DEINOSSZ**	DOZINESS
DEILSSUV	DIVULSES	**DEIMPRST**	DIREMPTS	**DEINOSTW**	DOWNIEST
DEILSTUY	SEDULITY	**DEIMPSTU**	DUMPIEST	**DEINOSWZ**	DOWNSIZE
DEILSTYZ	STYLIZED		DUMPSITE	**DEINOTTU**	DUETTINO
DEILSWZZ	SWIZZLED	**DEIMPSTY**	MISTYPED	**DEINOTUV**	INDEVOUT
DEILTWZZ	TWIZZLED	**DEIMQRSU**	SQUIRMED	**DEINPPRU**	UNRIPPED
DEIMMNOO	OMNIMODE	**DEIMRSSU**	SURMISED	**DEINPPTU**	UNTIPPED
DEIMMNOS	DEMONISM	**DEIMRSTU**	DIESTRUM	**DEINPPUZ**	UNZIPPED
DEIMMOOV	MOVIEDOM	**DEIMRSUU**	RESIDUUM	**DEINPRST**	SPRINTED
DEIMMOST	IMMODEST	**DEINNNOU**	INNUENDO	**DEINPRTU**	TURNIPED
DEIMMOSV	MISMOVED	**DEINNNPU**	UNPINNED	**DEINPRUZ**	UNPRIZED
DEIMMPST	MISDEMPT	**DEINNNSU**	NUNDINES	**DEINPSST**	STIPENDS
DEIMMRST	MIDTERMS	**DEINNNTU**	UNTINNED	**DEINPTTU**	INPUTTED
DEIMMRSU	DRUMMIES	**DEINNOOT**	NOONTIDE		UNPITTED
DEIMMSTU	DUMMIEST	**DEINNOPT**	ENDPOINT	**DEINQSTU**	SQUINTED
	SUMMITED	**DEINNORS**	ENDIRONS	**DEINRRTU**	INTRUDER
DEIMNNOS	MISDONNE	**DEINNORT**	INDENTOR	**DEINRSSU**	INSUREDS
DEIMNNOU	UNMONIED	**DEINNORU**	UNIRONED		SUNDRIES
DEIMNNSU	MINUENDS	**DEINNOWW**	WINNOWED	**DEINRSTT**	STRIDENT
DEIMNOOS	DOMINOES	**DEINNPRU**	UNDERPIN		TRIDENTS
	MONODIES	**DEINNRSU**	UNRINSED	**DEINRSTU**	INTRUDES
DEIMNOOT	DEMOTION	**DEINNRTU**	INTURNED		NURDIEST
	MOTIONED	**DEINNRUU**	UNINURED	**DEINRSTX**	DEXTRINS
DEIMNOOX	MONOXIDE	**DEINNRUV**	UNDRIVEN	**DEINRTUW**	UNDERWIT

DEINSSST	DISNESTS	DEIPPTTU	TITUPPED		STROLLED
	DISSENTS	DEIPRRTU	IRRUPTED	DELLOSTY	OLDSTYLE
DEINSSSY	SYNDESIS		PUTRIDER	DELLOSVW	LOWVELDS
DEINSSTT	DENTISTS	DEIPRSSU	DISPURSE	DELLOTUW	OUTDWELL
DEINSSTU	DISTUNES		SUSPIRED	DELLRSWY	DRYWELLS
DEINSSUU	UNISSUED	DEIPRSTU	DISPUTER	DELMNOOV	NOVELDOM
DEINSTUU	UNSUITED		STUPIDER	DELMNORY	MODERNLY
DEINTTUW	UNWITTED	DEIPRSTZ	SPRITZED	DELMNOSU	UNSELDOM
DEIOOPRR	DROOPIER	DEIPSSTU	DISPUTES	DELMNOTW	MELTDOWN
DEIOORSS	ODORISES		PUDSIEST	DELMNPUU	PENDULUM
DEIOORSW	WOODSIER	DEIPTTTU	TITTUPED		UNPLUMED
DEIOORSZ	ODORIZES	DEIQRRSU	SQUIRRED	DELMOOSW	ELMWOODS
DEIOOSSS	ISODOSES	DEIQRSTU	SQUIRTED	DELMOPRS	PREMOLDS
DEIOOSST	OSTEOIDS	DEIRRSST	STRIDERS	DELMORSS	SMOLDERS
DEIOOSTW	WOODIEST	DEIRRSTU	STURDIER	DELMORSU	MOULDERS
DEIOOSVV	VOIVODES	DEIRSSST	DISSERTS		REMOULDS
DEIOOSWW	WOIWODES		DISTRESS		SMOULDER
DEIOPRRV	PROVIDER	DEIRSSTU	DIESTRUS	DELMOSTY	MODESTLY
DEIOPRSS	DISPOSER		DRUSIEST	DELMRTUU	MULTURED
	DROPSIES		STUDIERS	DELMTTUU	TUMULTED
DEIOPRST	DIOPTERS		STURDIES	DELNOOSU	NODULOSE
	DIOPTRES	DEIRSSUY	DYSURIES		UNLOOSED
	DIPTEROS	DEIRSTTU	DETRITUS	DELNOOSZ	SNOOZLED
	PERIDOTS	DEIRSTUX	DRUXIEST	DELNOOWY	WOODENLY
	PORTSIDE	DEIRSUVV	SURVIVED	DELNOPPU	UNLOPPED
	PROTEIDS	DEISSSTU	SUDSIEST	DELNOPRS	SPLENDOR
	RIPOSTED	DEISSTTU	DUSTIEST	DELNOPUW	UNPLOWED
	TOPSIDER	DEISTTTU	DUETTIST	DELNORSU	LOUNDERS
DEIOPRSV	DISPROVE	DEJLOOOR	JORDELOO		NOURSLED
	PROVIDES	DEJOOPPY	POPJOYED		ROUNDELS
DEIOPRSW	DROPWISE	DEKKLNOY	KLONDYKE		ROUNDLES
DEIOPRSX	PEROXIDS	DEKKNSTU	STUKKEND		UNSOLDER
DEIOPSSS	DISPOSES	DEKKSSTT	TSKTSKED	DELNORTU	ROUNDLET
DEIOPSST	DEPOSITS	DEKLNOOU	UNLOOKED	DELNORYY	YONDERLY
	TOPSIDES	DEKLOOPU	UPLOOKED	DELNOSSU	LOUDNESS
DEIOPSTV	POSTDIVE	DEKLRSSU	SKUDLERS	DELNOSSW	DOWNLESS
DEIORRRT	TORRIDER	DEKLSTTU	SKUTTLED	DELNOSTW	LETDOWNS
DEIORRSS	DROSSIER	DEKMNOSU	UNSMOKED	DELNOSUU	UNDULOSE
DEIORRSW	DROWSIER	DEKMPRSU	SKRUMPED		UNSOULED
DEIORRSY	DERISORY	DEKNNOSS	NONSKEDS	DELNOSUV	UNSOLVED
DEIORRTU	OUTRIDER	DEKNORUW	UNWORKED	DELNOTWY	WONTEDLY
DEIORRTW	WORRITED	DEKNRSTU	DRUNKEST	DELNPRSU	PLUNDERS
DEIORRZZ	RIZZORED	DEKNRSUY	UNDERSKY	DELNRRTU	TRUNDLER
DEIORSSS	DOSSIERS	DEKNSSSU	DUSKNESS	DELNRSTU	RUNDLETS
DEIORSST	STEROIDS	DEKOOPRV	PROVOKED		TRUNDLES
DEIORSSU	DESIROUS	DEKOOTWW	KOWTOWED	DELNSUZZ	SNUZZLED
DEIORSSV	DEVISORS	DEKOPSST	DESKTOPS	DELOOORW	WOODLORE
DEIORSTT	DORTIEST	DEKORSWY	KEYWORDS	DELOOPPS	PLEOPODS
DEIORSTU	IODURETS	DEKPRSSU	PREDUSKS	DELOORRV	OVERLORD
	OUTRIDES	DELLLOOP	LOLLOPED	DELOORRW	WORDLORE
	OUTSIDER	DELLMOOS	MODELLOS	DELOORSS	DOORLESS
	SUITORED	DELLMOSW	SWELLDOM		LORDOSES
DEIORSTW	ROWDIEST	DELLMOSY	SELDOMLY		ODORLESS
	WORDIEST	DELLNOPU	UNPOLLED	DELOORSV	OVERSOLD
DEIORSWW	WIDOWERS	DELLNORU	UNROLLED	DELOORSW	WOOLDERS
DEIORTTX	TETROXID	DELLNORW	ROWNDELL	DELOORTY	ROOTEDLY
DEIORTUV	OUTDRIVE	DELLNPUU	UNPULLED	DELOORUV	OVERLOUD
DEIOSSTU	OUTSIDES	DELLNSSU	DULLNESS	DELOOSSW	WOODLESS
DEIOSSTX	EXODISTS	DELLOPRS	REDPOLLS	DELOOTUV	OUTLOVED
DEIOSTTT	DOTTIEST	DELLOPRU	UPROLLED	DELOPPRS	DROPPLES
DEIOSTUW	WIDEOUTS	DELLOPTU	POLLUTED	DELOPPST	STOPPLED
DEIOSTUZ	OUTSIZED	DELLORRY	DROLLERY	DELOPPSY	POLYPEDS
DEIPPRRS	DRIPPERS	DELLORSS	LORDLESS	DELOPRST	DROPLETS
DEIPPRST	STRIPPED	DELLORST	DROLLEST	DELOPRSU	POULDERS

	POULDRES
DELOPSTU	POSTLUDE
DELORSST	OLDSTERS
	STRODLES
DELORSSW	WORDLESS
DELORSTT	DOTTRELS
DELORSUY	DELUSORY
DELOSSUU	SEDULOUS
DELOSTTT	DOTTLEST
DELOSTTY	SOTTEDLY
DELOSTUU	OUTDUELS
DELOSTUW	WOULDEST
DELOTTUW	OUTDWELT
DELOTUVY	DEVOUTLY
DELPSTUU	PUSTULED
DELRSSTU	STRUDELS
DELSSSSU	SUDSLESS
DELSSSTU	DUSTLESS
DEMMNOOO	MONOMODE
DEMMNOOS	DOOMSMEN
DEMMNOSU	SUMMONED
DEMMNSUU	UNSUMMED
DEMMRRSU	DRUMMERS
DEMMRRUU	MURMURED
DEMMRSTU	STRUMMED
DEMNNOSU	SOUNDMEN
DEMNOOOP	MONOPODE
DEMNOOPT	TOMPONED
DEMNOORS	DOORSMEN
DEMNOORU	UNMOORED
DEMNOOSS	ENDOSMOS
DEMNOOSW	WOODSMEN
DEMNORST	MORDENTS
DEMNORSW	SWORDMEN
DEMNORSY	SYNDROME
DEMNORUW	UNWORMED
DEMNOSTU	DEMOUNTS
	MUDSTONE
DEMOOPPS	POPEDOMS
DEMOOPRR	PRODROME
DEMOOPRS	PREDOOMS
DEMOOPRT	PROMOTED
DEMOORST	DOOMSTER
DEMOORSU	DORMOUSE
DEMOORTY	ODOMETRY
DEMOOSTU	OUTMODES
DEMOOTUV	OUTMOVED
DEMOPPRT	PROMPTED
DEMOPSSU	POSSUMED
DEMORRUU	RUMOURED
DEMORTUY	UDOMETRY
DEMPRSTU	DUMPSTER
DENNOSUU	UNSUNNED
DENNOOOZ	ENDOZOON
DENNOOWZ	DOWNZONE
DENNORST	TENDRONS
DENNORSU	ENROUNDS
DENNOSTU	UNSTONED
DENNOSTY	SYNDETON
DENNOTUW	UNWONTED
DENNPRUU	UNPRUNED
DENNRRUU	UNDERRUN
DENNRTUU	UNTURNED
DENNRTUY	UNTRENDY
DENOOORT	OREODONT
DENOOOTW	WOODTONE
	WOODTONE
DENOOOVW	OVENWOOD
DENOOPPR	PROPONED
DENOOPRS	PRODNOSE
DENOOPSY	POYSONED
DENOORRS	ENDORSOR
DENOORTU	UNROOTED
DENOORTX	NEXTDOOR
DENOOSSW	WOODNESS
DENOOSTU	DUOTONES
DENOPPRS	PROPENDS
DENOPRSS	RESPONDS
DENOPRST	PORTENDS
	PROTENDS
DENOPRSU	POUNDERS
DENOPRSV	PROVENDS
DENOPRUV	UNPROVED
DENOPSTU	OUTSPEND
	UNPOSTED
DENOPSTW	STEWPOND
DENOPSUX	EXPOUNDS
DENOPTTU	UNPOTTED
DENOQTUU	UNQUOTED
DENORRSU	RONDURES
	ROUNDERS
	UNORDERS
DENORRSW	DROWNERS
DENORRTU	ROTUNDER
DENORRUU	ROUNDURE
DENORSSU	DOURNESS
	RESOUNDS
	SOUNDERS
DENORSTU	ROUNDEST
	TONSURED
	UNSORTED
DENORSTY	DRYSTONE
DENORSUU	UNROUSED
	UNSOURED
DENORSUW	WOUNDERS
DENORTTU	UNROTTED
DENORTUW	UNDERTOW
DENOSSTU	SOUNDEST
DENOSTUW	UNSTOWED
DENOTUUV	UNDEVOUT
DENPRSTU	UPTRENDS
DENPRSUU	UNPURSED
DENPRTUU	UPTURNED
DENPSSSU	SUSPENDS
DENRRTUU	NURTURED
DENRSSSU	SUNDRESS
DENRSTTU	STRUNTED
DENRSTUU	UNRUSTED
DENSSTTU	STUDENTS
DENSTTUY	STUDENTY
DENSTUVY	DUVETYNS
DEOOORSW	ROSEWOOD
DEOOOSWW	WOODWOSE
DEOOPPRS	PROPOSED
DEOOPPRT	PTEROPOD
DEOOPRRV	PROVEDOR
DEOOPRST	DOORSTEP
	TORPEDOS
DEOOPRTU	UPROOTED
DEOOPWWW	POWWOWED
DEOORRST	REDROOTS
DEOORRSW	SORROWED
DEOORRVW	OVERWORD
DEOORRWW	OWREWORD
DEOORSTU	OUTDOERS
DEOORTUV	OUTDROVE
DEOORTUW	OUTROWED
DEOOTTUV	OUTVOTED
DEOPPRRS	DROPPERS
DEOPPRST	STROPPED
DEOPPRSU	PURPOSED
DEOPPSSU	SUPPOSED
DEOPRRTU	PROTRUDE
DEOPRSTU	POSTURED
	PROUDEST
	SPROUTED
DEOPRSUU	POURSUED
	UPROUSED
DEOPSSTU	UPTOSSED
DEORRSST	RODSTERS
DEORRSSW	SWORDERS
DEORRTTU	TORTURED
DEORSSTU	OUTDRESS
DEORSSTW	WORSTEDS
DEORSSTY	DESTROYS
DEORSSUV	OVERSUDS
DEORSTTU	STROUTED
DEORSTUU	OUTDURES
DEORSTUV	OVERDUST
DEORSTUX	DEXTROUS
DEOSSSYY	ODYSSEYS
DEOSSTTU	TESTUDOS
DEPPSSYY	DYSPEPSY
DEPRRTUU	RUPTURED
DEQRSUUY	SURQUEDY
DERSTTTU	STRUTTED
DFFGINSU	DUFFINGS
DFFIILUV	FLUIDIFY
DFFIIMRS	MIDRIFFS
DFFIIRST	TRIFFIDS
DFFIIRTY	TRIFFIDY
DFFIORSU	DIFFUSOR
DFFLOORU	FOURFOLD
DFFOORUW	WOODRUFF
DFFOSSTU	DUSTOFFS
DFGGHIOT	DOGFIGHT
DFGGIINR	FRIDGING
DFGHILOS	GOLDFISH
DFGIIIRY	RIGIDIFY
DFGIILRY	FRIGIDLY
DFGIINNS	FINDINGS
DFGIINRT	DRIFTING
DFGILNNO	FONDLING
DFGILNOO	FLOODING
DFGILNOS	FOLDINGS
DFGINNOU	FONDUING
	FOUNDING
DFGINNSU	FUNDINGS
DFGINOOR	FORDOING
DFGINOSU	FUNGOIDS
DFGMOOSY	FOGYDOMS
DFHIIMUY	HUMIDIFY

DFHILSSU	DISHFULS	DGHHOOOS	HOGHOODS	DGIIMPUY	PYGIDIUM
DFHIMRSU	DRUMFISH	DGHIILNS	HIDLINGS	DGIINNOP	POINDING
DFHINOOT	HINDFOOT		HILDINGS	DGIINNOR	NONRIGID
DFHINOPS	FISHPOND	DGHIIMNT	MIDNIGHT	DGIINNOW	INDOWING
DFHISSTU	STUDFISH	DGHIIMST	MISDIGHT	DGIINNRW	WINDRING
DFHLOOOT	FOOTHOLD	DGHIINNW	HINDWING	DGIINNSS	SINDINGS
DFHNOOUX	FOXHOUND	DGHIINPS	SPHINGID	DGIINNSW	WINDINGS
DFIIINVY	DIVINIFY	DGHIINRT	THIRDING	DGIINORR	GRIDIRON
DFIILMTU	MULTIFID	DGHIINSS	DISHINGS	DGIINORS	DORISING
DFIILOSY	SOLIDIFY		SHINDIGS	DGIINORT	DIGITRON
DFIILTUY	FLUIDITY	DGHIISST	DISSIGHT	DGIINORZ	DORIZING
DFIINPRT	DRIFTPIN	DGHIKNOO	KINGHOOD	DGIINOSV	VOIDINGS
DFIKNOOS	SKINFOOD	DGHILLNU	DUNGHILL	DGIINOSW	WINDIGOS
DFILLOOT	FLOODLIT	DGHILNNO	HONDLING	DGIINOSX	DIGOXINS
DFILLORY	FLORIDLY	DGHILNOS	HOLDINGS	DGIINOTT	DITTOING
DFILLOWW	WILDFOWL	DGHILNRU	HURDLING	DGIINOWW	WIDOWING
DFILMMOS	FILMDOMS	DGHILNSY	HYLDINGS	DGIINPPR	DRIPPING
DFILNNOU	NONFLUID	DGHILOOR	GIRLHOOD	DGIINPPS	DIPPINGS
DFILNOPS	PINFOLDS	DGHILPSY	DIGLYPHS	DGIINPUV	UPDIVING
DFILORSU	FLUORIDS	DGHINNOU	HOUNDING	DGIINRST	STRIDING
DFIMOOOR	IODOFORM	DGHINNSU	DUNSHING	DGIINRSV	DRIVINGS
DFIMOOSS	FOODISMS	DGHINNUZ	NUDZHING	DGIINRTY	DIRTYING
DFIMORSS	DISFORMS	DGHINOSW	SHOWDING	DGIINSSU	DISUSING
DFINOSTU	OUTFINDS	DGHINOWY	HOWDYING	DGIINTTY	DITTYING
DFINRSUW	WINDSURF	DGHINSTU	HINDGUTS	DGIINVVY	DIVVYING
DFIOOPRS	DISPROOF		UNDIGHTS	DGIINYZZ	DIZZYING
DFKMMOPU	DUMMKOPF	DGHIOORS	DROOGISH	DGIKLOOY	KIDOLOGY
DFLMOSUW	MUDFLOWS	DGHIOPSS	DOGSHIPS	DGIKMNOS	KINGDOMS
DFLNOOWW	DOWNFLOW		GODSHIPS	DGIKNOOR	DROOKING
DFLOORUU	ODOURFUL	DGHNOTUU	DOUGHNUT	DGIKNOOW	KINGWOOD
DFLOOSTU	FOLDOUTS	DGHOOOTT	DOGTOOTH	DGIKNORU	DROUKING
DFLOOSTW	TWOFOLDS	DGHORRUY	ROUGHDRY	DGIKNOSS	DOGSKINS
DFLOPRUU	PROUDFUL	DGHORSTU	DROUGHTS	DGILLNOR	DROLLING
DFNOOPRU	PROFOUND	DGHORTUY	DROUGHTY		LORDLING
DFNOORSU	FRONDOUS	DGIIIMRS	DIRIGISM	DGILLNOY	DOLLYING
DFNOOTUU	OUTFOUND	DGIIINNT	INDITING	DGILLOOW	GOODWILL
DFOOOORW	WOODROOF	DGIIINNV	DIVINING	DGILMNOS	MOLDINGS
DFOOOSTW	SOFTWOOD	DGIIINOS	IODISING	DGILMNOU	MOULDING
DGGGIINS	DIGGINGS	DGIIINOZ	IODIZING	DGILMNPU	DUMPLING
DGGGINOS	DOGGINGS	DGIIIRTY	RIGIDITY	DGILMSUY	SMUDGILY
DGGGINRU	DRUGGING	DGIIKLNN	KINDLING	DGILNNOO	NOODLING
	GRUDGING	DGIIKLNS	KIDLINGS	DGILNNOU	LOUNDING
DGGHIINT	DIGHTING	DGIIKNNR	DRINKING	DGILNNOW	LOWNDING
DGGIILNR	GIRDLING	DGIILLNR	DRILLING	DGILNNRU	NURDLING
	RIDGLING	DGIILLNS	DILLINGS	DGILNOOR	DROOLING
DGGIILNS	GILDINGS	DGIILLNU	ILLUDING	DGILNOOW	WOOLDING
	GLIDINGS	DGIILLNW	WILDLING	DGILNORS	GIRLONDS
DGGIINNO	DINGOING	DGIILLOU	LIGULOID		LORDINGS
DGGIINNR	GRINDING	DGIILMNP	DIMPLING	DGILNORY	YOLDRING
DGGIINNW	WINGDING	DGIILNNN	DINNLING	DGILNOTY	DOTINGLY
DGGIINRS	GIRDINGS	DGIILNNP	PINDLING	DGILNPUY	DUPLYING
	RIDGINGS	DGIILNNW	WINDLING	DGILOOTW	GILTWOOD
DGGIINSU	GUIDINGS	DGIILNNY	INDIGNLY	DGILOPSU	SOLPUGID
DGGIKLNU	KLUDGING	DGIILNOR	DROILING	DGILOSTY	STODGILY
DGGILNOP	PLODGING	DGIILNOS	DISLOIGN	DGILRTUY	TURGIDLY
DGGILNOS	GODLINGS	DGIILNPS	DISPLING	DGIMMNRU	DRUMMING
	LODGINGS	DGIILNSS	SLIDINGS	DGIMMNUY	DUMMYING
DGGILNSU	SLUDGING	DGIILNSW	WILDINGS	DGIMNNOU	MOUNDING
DGGIMNSU	SMUDGING	DGIILNTU	DILUTING	DGIMNOOY	MOODYING
DGGINNOO	NOODGING	DGIIMNNS	MINDINGS	DGIMNPSU	DUMPINGS
DGGINNSU	SNUDGING	DGIIMNOS	MISDOING	DGIMOPSY	GIPSYDOM
DGGINOST	STODGING	DGIIMNOU	GONIDIUM	DGINNNSU	DUNNINGS
DGGINRTU	TRUDGING	DGIIMNSS	SMIDGINS	DGINNOOS	SNOODING
DGGIRSTU	DRUGGIST	DGIIMOSS	SIGMOIDS	DGINNOPU	POUNDING

Eight-letter anagrams

DGINNOPW	POWNDING	DHIINTWW	WITHWIND	DHNOPSUW	PUSHDOWN
DGINNORU	INGROUND	DHIIOPRU	OPHIURID	DHNORSUU	UNSHROUD
	ROUNDING	DHIIOPSX	XIPHOIDS	DHNORSUW	DOWNRUSH
DGINNORW	DROWNING	DHIIORSS	HIDROSIS	DHNOSTUW	SHUTDOWN
	ROWNDING	DHIIORSZ	RHIZOIDS	DHOOOPRT	ORTHOPOD
DGINNOSU	SOUNDING	DHIIPSST	DIPSHITS	DHOOORTX	ORTHODOX
	UNDOINGS	DHIKNOOW	HOODWINK	DHOOPRST	DROPSHOT
DGINNOSW	SOWNDING	DHIKORSY	HYDROSKI	DHOOPRSU	UPHOORDS
DGINNOUW	WOUNDING	DHILLNOW	DOWNHILL	DHOORSUW	WOODRUSH
DGINNSSY	SYNDINGS	DHILLOPY	PHYLLOID	DHOPRSSU	PUSHRODS
DGINNSUW	WINDGUNS	DHILLORS	DROLLISH	DHOPRSYY	HYDROPSY
DGINOOPR	DROOPING	DHILLOST	TOLLDISH	DIIIKMNS	MINIDISK
DGINOOPS	GOSPODIN	DHILLPSY	PHYLLIDS	DIIILLQU	ILLIQUID
	SPONGOID	DHILMOPY	LYMPHOID	DIIILTVY	LIVIDITY
DGINOOTU	OUTDOING	DHILMOSY	MODISHLY	DIIIMOST	IDIOTISM
DGINOPPR	DROPPING	DHILNOPS	DOLPHINS	DIIIMRSU	IRIDIUMS
DGINOPPS	DOPPINGS	DHILOPRS	LORDSHIP	DIIIMTTY	TIMIDITY
DGINORSV	DROVINGS	DHILOPSS	SLIPSHOD	DIIINOSV	DIVISION
DGINORSW	DROWSING	DHILORRY	HORRIDLY	DIIINTVY	DIVINITY
	SWORDING	DHILPSSU	LUDSHIPS	DIIIPRST	DISPIRIT
	WORDINGS		SULPHIDS	DIIIRTVY	VIRIDITY
DGINOSSW	DISGOWNS	DHILPSSY	SYLPHIDS	DIIITVVY	VIVIDITY
DGINOSUY	DIGYNOUS	DHIMMNOT	MIDMONTH	DIIJNOSS	DISJOINS
DGINPRUY	UPDRYING	DHIMNOST	HINDMOST	DIIJNOST	DISJOINT
DGINSSTU	DUSTINGS	DHIMNOSU	UNMODISH	DIIKKNSS	KIDSKINS
DGINSTUY	STUDYING	DHIMOOOV	OMOHYOID	DIIKLLNY	KINDLILY
DGIOOPRU	GROUPOID	DHIMOOSS	MISSHOOD	DIIKLNSS	DISLINKS
DGIOPRRY	PORRIDGY	DHIMOPPY	HIPPYDOM	DIIKNOST	DOITKINS
DGIOSUVZ	DIZYGOUS	DHIMOPRS	DIMORPHS	DIILLMNR	MILLRIND
DGISSSTU	DISGUSTS	DHIMORSU	HUMIDORS	DIILLMNW	WINDMILL
DGLNORSU	GOLDURNS		RHODIUMS	DIILLMOU	LIMULOID
DGLOOOPY	PODOLOGY	DHINNOTW	THINDOWN	DIILLMPY	LIMPIDLY
DGLOOOSW	LOGWOODS	DHINOOPR	PHORONID	DIILLQUY	LIQUIDLY
DGLOOOSY	DOSOLOGY	DHINOORS	DISHONOR	DIILLSST	DISTILLS
DGLOOOXY	DOXOLOGY	DHINOPSS	DONSHIPS	DIILLSTY	IDYLLIST
DGLOOSST	GODSLOTS	DHINORSS	DISHORNS	DIILMNSS	DISLIMNS
DGMNNOUU	MUNDUNGO	DHINORSU	ROUNDISH	DIILMOPP	POMPILID
DGMOOSUW	GUMWOODS	DHINOTUW	WHODUNIT	DIILMOSS	IDOLISMS
DGMOPRSU	GUMDROPS	DHINTUWY	WHYDUNIT		SOLIDISM
DGMOPSYY	GYPSYDOM	DHIOOOPR	IODOPHOR	DIILMOTY	MYTILOID
DGMORSUU	GURUDOMS	DHIOOPRZ	RHIZOPOD	DIILMSST	MIDLISTS
DGNNORUU	UNGROUND	DHIOPRSU	PROUDISH	DIILMUUV	DILUVIUM
DGNOOOPS	GONOPODS	DHIOPSTY	TYPHOIDS	DIILNNSU	INDULINS
DGNOOORS	GODROONS	DHIORSTY	THYROIDS	DIILNOST	TOLIDINS
DGNOOSTW	DOGTOWNS		THYRSOID	DIILNOTU	DILUTION
DGNOOTYZ	ZYGODONT	DHIORSWY	ROWDYISH		TOLUIDIN
DGOORSTT	DOGTROTS	DHIPRSSY	SYRPHIDS	DIILNOUV	DILUVION
DGOPRRSU	PRODRUGS	DHJOPRSU	JODHPURS	DIILNOXY	XYLOIDIN
DGOPRSTU	POSTDRUG	DHKMNOOO	MONKHOOD	DIILNSXY	XYLIDINS
DHHILOTW	WITHHOLD	DHKMOOSU	MUDHOOKS	DIILNTUY	UNTIDILY
DHHIOPPS	PHOSPHID	DHLLOPYY	PHYLLODY	DIILOPRT	TRIPLOID
DHIIIMNS	DIMINISH	DHLMOOSU	HOODLUMS	DIILOPSS	DIPLOSIS
	MINIDISH	DHLOOORT	ROOTHOLD	DIILOPSY	YPSILOID
DHIIINST	HISTIDIN	DHLOORSY	HYDROSOL	DIILOQSU	SOLIQUID
DHIIIOST	HISTIOID	DHLOOSTU	HOLDOUTS	DIILORSU	SILUROID
	IDIOTISH	DHLORXYY	HYDROXYL	DIILORTU	UTILIDOR
DHIILOSS	SOLIDISH	DHLOSSTU	SHOULDST	DIILOSST	IDOLISTS
DHIIMNOO	HOMINOID	DHMMRSUU	HUMDRUMS		SOLIDIST
DHIIMNOS	HOMINIDS	DHMNOOOT	HOMODONT	DIILOSTY	SOLIDITY
DHIIMOST	ISTHMOID	DHMOOPPU	PUMPHOOD	DIILPPRY	DRIPPILY
DHIIMPSS	MIDSHIPS	DHMORTUY	DRYMOUTH	DIILQSUU	LIQUIDUS
DHIIMTUY	HUMIDITY	DHNNOOSU	NUNHOODS	DIILRSSU	SILURIDS
DHIINPSW	WINDSHIP	DHNOOOSS	SONHOODS	DIILSSTY	IDYLISTS
DHIINRSU	HIRUDINS	DHNOOSWW	SHOWDOWN	DIIMMNOU	DOMINIUM

DIIMNNOO	DOMINION	DILPSTUY	STUPIDLY	DKORSTUW	STUDWORK
DIIMNNSU	UNDINISM	DILRSTUY	STURDILY	DLLMORRU	DRUMROLL
DIIMNOPT	MIDPOINT	DIMMNORY	MYRMIDON	DLLMORSU	SLUMLORD
DIIMNORS	MIDIRONS	DIMMOOSU	ISODOMUM	DLLNORUY	UNLORDLY
DIIMNSUU	INDUSIUM	DIMMOSST	MIDMOSTS	DLMNOOSW	SNOWMOLD
DIIMOPRS	PRISMOID	DIMNNOOS	MIDNOONS	DLMNOOSY	MYLODONS
DIIMORSS	DIORISMS	DIMMNOSS	DONNISMS	DLMNOOTY	MYLODONT
DIIMPUXY	PYXIDIUM	DIMNNOST	DINMONTS	DLMNOSUU	UNMOULDS
DIIMRUUV	DUUMVIRI	DIMNOOOS	ISODOMON	DLMORSUY	SMOULDRY
DIIMTTUY	TUMIDITY	DIMNOOST	MONODIST	DLNOOPRU	POULDRON
DIINNOSU	DISUNION	DIMNOPSU	IMPOUNDS	DLNOOSUU	NODULOUS
DIINOOPS	IODOPSIN	DIMNOSSU	MISSOUND	DLNOOSWW	LOWDOWNS
DIINOOPU	DOUPIONI	DIMNOSTU	DISMOUNT		SLOWDOWN
DIINOQSU	QUINOIDS	DIMNOSTW	MIDTOWNS	DLNOPRSU	PULDRONS
DIINOSSU	SINUSOID	DIMNOSUW	UNWISDOM	DLNOPSSY	SPONDYLS
DIINSTUY	DISUNITY	DIMNOSWX	MIXDOWNS	DLNORTUY	ROTUNDLY
DIIOPRTY	PITYROID	DIMOOPRR	PRODROMI	DLNOSUUU	UNDULOUS
DIIORSST	SISTROID	DIMOOPRV	MYRIOPOD	DLOOOORS	DOLOROSO
DIIORSSV	DIVISORS	DIMOORTW	MODIWORT	DLOOOPSS	SPODOSOL
DIIORSTX	TRIOXIDS	DIMOOSST	SODOMIST	DLOOORSU	DOLOROUS
DIIORSUV	VIRUSOID	DIMOPRSU	MISPROUD	DLOOOSTW	WOODLOTS
DIIPSTTY	TIDYTIPS	DIMOPSSU	SPODIUMS	DLOOPPSY	POLYPODS
DIJOSSTU	JUDOISTS	DIMORSSW	MISWORDS	DLOOPPUW	PULPWOOD
DIKLMOOW	MILKWOOD	DIMORSTY	MIDSTORY	DLOOPPYY	POLYPODY
DIKLNNOW	DOWNLINK	DIMORSWY	ROWDYISM	DLOOPSTU	OUTPLODS
DIKLNNUY	UNKINDLY	DIMOSTUY	DUMOSITY	DLOOPSTY	TYLOPODS
DIKLNORS	LORDKINS	DIMRSTUU	TRIDUUMS	DLOOPSWY	PLYWOODS
DIKLRUUU	DURUKULI	DIMRSUUV	DUUMVIRS	DMMOOORT	MOTORDOM
DIKNOOSW	INKWOODS	DINNOORS	RONDINOS	DMMOORSU	MUDROOMS
	WOODSKIN	DINNOOST	TONDINOS	DMMNOOOT	MONODONT
DIKNORSV	DVORNIKS	DINNOPSW	DOWNSPIN	DMNOOOPS	MONOPODS
DIKNORTU	OUTDRINK		PINDOWNS	DMNOOOPY	MONOPODY
DIKOOSTU	DITOKOUS	DINOOORW	IRONWOOD	DMNOOSTU	MOONDUST
DILLMNOP	MILLPOND	DINOOPSU	DIPNOOUS	DMNOOSTW	DOWNMOST
DILLMSSU	MUDSILLS	DINOORRS	INDORSOR		TOWMONDS
DILLOORS	DOORSILL	DINOORST	TORDIONS	DMOOOQSU	QUOMODOS
DILLOSTY	STOLIDLY	DINOORSU	NIDOROUS	DMOOORWW	WOODWORM
DILLPSSY	PSYLLIDS	DINOOSST	ISODONTS		WORMWOOD
DILMNOOS	SMILODON	DINOOSTT	ODONTIST	DMOPPPUU	PUPPODUM
DILMNORW	LINDWORM	DINOOSTY	NODOSITY	DMOPPPUY	PUPPYDOM
DILMNOSW	SLIMDOWN	DINOPRTY	DRYPOINT	DMORSTUW	MUDWORTS
DILMNRSU	DRUMLINS	DINORSTU	STURNOID	DMPPPUUY	MUDPUPPY
DILMOOSU	MODIOLUS		TURDIONS	DNNOOOWY	NONWOODY
DILMOSSU	SOLIDUMS	DINORSWW	WINDROWS	DNNOOPRU	PUNDONOR
DILMOSSY	ODYLISMS	DINOSTUW	OUTWINDS	DNNOORWS	NONWORDS
DILNNOOS	NONSOLID	DINPRTUY	PUNDITRY	DNNOOTWW	DOWNTOWN
DILNOPST	DIPLONTS	DINRSTUY	INDUSTRY	DNNORRUU	RUNROUND
DILNOPSU	LISPOUND	DIOOPRRT	PRODITOR	DNNORSUU	UNROUNDS
DILNOQSU	QUODLINS	DIOOPRRV	PROVIDOR	DNNORSUW	RUNDOWNS
DILNOSXY	INDOXYLS	DIOOPRTX	PROTOXID	DNNORTUW	DOWNTURN
DILNOUWY	WOUNDILY	DIOORSST	DISROOTS		TURNDOWN
DILNPSSU	LISPUNDS	DIOORSTT	RIDOTTOS	DNNOSSUW	SUNDOWNS
DILNRSUY	SUNDRILY	DIOPRSST	DISPORTS	DNNRSTUU	TURNDUNS
DILOOPPY	POLYPOID	DIOPSSST	DISPOSTS	DNOOPPRU	PROPOUND
DILOOPRY	DROOPILY	DIORRSST	STRIDORS	DNOOPRSW	SNOWDROP
DILOORSS	LORDOSIS	DIORSSTT	DISTORTS	DNOOPRUW	DOWNPOUR
DILOOSUY	ODIOUSLY	DIOSSTUU	STUDIOUS	DNOOPSUY	DUOPSONY
DILOOTUV	VOLUTOID	DIPRSSTU	DISRUPTS	DNOORSUW	WONDROUS
DILOPRTY	TORPIDLY	DIRSSTTU	DISTRUST	DNOOSTUW	NUTWOODS
DILORRTY	TORRIDLY	DKLNOOOW	LOOKDOWN	DNOOSTWW	STOWDOWN
DILORSTU	DILUTORS	DKMNOOOR	KOMONDOR	DNOOSUUV	VOUDOUNS
DILORSWY	DROWSILY	DKNORTUU	OUTDRUNK	DNOOTUUW	OUTWOUND
DILOSSTY	STYLOIDS	DKOOOPRW	PORKWOOD	DNOPRSSU	SUNDROPS
DILPRTUY	PUTRIDLY	DKOOORWW	WOODWORK	DNOPRSUU	ROUNDUPS

Eight-letter anagrams

DNOPSTUW	PUTDOWNS
DNORRSUU	SURROUND
DNORSSUY	UNDROSSY
DOOOPPRT	PROTOPOD
DOOOPRST	DOORPOST
	DOORSTOP
DOOORSTU	OUTDOORS
DOOORSUW	SOURWOOD
DOOOSTTU	OUTSTOOD
DOOPRRTW	DROPWORT
DOOPRSTU	DROPOUTS
	OUTDROPS
DOOPRSTW	STOPWORD
DOOPSWWY	POWSOWDY
DOORRSTU	DORTOURS
DOORRSUU	ORDUROUS
DOORSSUU	SUDOROUS
DOSTTUUY	OUTSTUDY
EEEEEFNRZ	ENFREEZE
EEEEFRRS	REFEREES
EEEEFRRZ	REFREEZE
EEEEGGRR	GREEGREE
EEEEGMRR	REEMERGE
EEEEGQSU	SQUEEGEE
EEEEGSSX	EXEGESES
EEEEGSTX	EXEGETES
EEEEHTTY	EYETEETH
EEEEELLPX	EXPELLEE
EEEEELLVY	EYELEVEL
EEEEELMST	TELESEME
EEEEELNSV	SLEEVEEN
EEEEENRRV	VENEERER
EEEEPPRR	REPEREPE
EEEEPPSW	PEESWEEP
EEEEPRRV	REPREEVE
EEEEPTTW	PEETWEET
EEEFFFOS	FEOFFEES
EEEFFLOR	FOREFEEL
EEEFFLTY	EFFETELY
EEEFFNRT	EFFERENT
EEEFFORS	OFFEREES
EEEFFORT	FOREFEET
EEEFFOTU	ETOUFFEE
EEEFFRVW	FEVERFEW
EEEFGMRR	GERMFREE
EEEFGRSU	REFUGEES
EEEFHRSS	SHEREEFS
EEEFIPRR	REPRIEFE
EEEFIPST	TEPEFIES
EEEFIRRT	FREETIER
EEEFIRST	REEFIEST
EEEFLRRS	FLEERERS
EEEFLRSX	REFLEXES
EEEFLSST	FEETLESS
EEEFLSTT	FLEETEST
EEEFNNPY	PENNYFEE
EEEFNORS	FORESEEN
EEEFNRRT	REFERENT
EEEFNRSS	FREENESS
EEEFNRSV	ENFEVERS
EEEFNRTT	ENFETTER
EEEFNRUZ	UNFREEZE
EEEFORRS	FORESEER
EEEFORRV	OVERFREE

EEEEFORSS	FORESEES
EEEEFRRRR	REFERRER
EEEEFRRRT	FERRETER
EEEEFRRSZ	FREEZERS
EEEFRRTT	FETTERER
EEEGGILN	NEGLIGEE
EEEGGIRS	EGGERIES
EEEGHINT	EIGHTEEN
EEEGHLRS	SHEERLEG
EEEGHMNU	HEGUMENE
EEEGHNSW	WHEENGES
EEEGIKST	GEEKIEST
EEEGILMN	LIEGEMEN
EEEGILNS	GLEENIES
EEEGILNV	ENVEIGLE
	LEVEEING
EEEGILPS	ESPIEGLE
EEEGILRT	GLEETIER
EEEGILSS	ELEGISES
EEEGILSZ	ELEGIZES
EEEGIMNX	EXEEMING
EEEGIMTV	VEGEMITE
EEEGINNR	ENGINEER
EEEGINRR	GREENIER
EEEGINRS	ENERGIES
	ENERGISE
	GREENIES
	RESEEING
EEEGINRV	ENGRIEVE
EEEGINRZ	ENERGIZE
EEEGIPRS	PERIGEES
EEEGIRTY	TIGEREYE
EEEGISSX	EXEGESIS
EEEGISTV	EGESTIVE
EEEGITVV	VEGETIVE
EEEGKLRS	KEGELERS
EEEGLMOS	GLEESOME
EEEGLNRT	GREENLET
EEEGMNOS	MONGEESE
EEEGMNRT	EMERGENT
EEEGMNRU	MERENGUE
EEEGMORT	GEOMETER
EEEGMRRS	REMERGES
EEEGNNRS	SENGREEN
EEEGNPRS	EPERGNES
EEEGNRRS	GREENERS
	REGREENS
	RENEGERS
EEEGNRRU	RENEGUER
EEEGNRRV	REVENGER
EEEGNRRY	GREENERY
EEEGNRST	GREENEST
EEEGNRSU	RENEGUES
EEEGNRSV	REVENGES
EEEGNSTT	GENETTES
EEEGOPRT	PROTEGEE
EEEGRRST	GREETERS
	REGREETS
EEEGRSSS	EGRESSES
EEEGRSUX	EXERGUES
EEEHHSSW	WHEESHES
EEEHILRW	EREWHILE
	WHEELIER
EEEHILSW	WHEELIES

EEEHINRS	SHEENIER
EEEHINSS	SHEENIES
EEEHINSY	EYESHINE
EEEHIPRS	SHEEPIER
EEEHIRSS	HERESIES
EEEHIRST	ETHERISE
	SHEETIER
EEEHIRSX	HEXEREIS
EEEHIRTZ	ETHERIZE
EEEHIRWZ	WHEEZIER
EEEHKLNO	KNEEHOLE
EEEHLLSS	HEELLESS
EEEHLMNW	WHEELMEN
EEEHLMPT	HELPMEET
EEEHLNSW	ENWHEELS
EEEHLNTV	ELEVENTH
EEEHLNTY	ETHYLENE
EEEHLNXY	HEXYLENE
EEEHLOPP	PEEPHOLE
EEEHLOPW	WEEPHOLE
EEEHLOSY	EYEHOLES
EEEHLPSW	WHEEPLES
EEEHLRSW	WHEELERS
EEEHLSWZ	WHEEZLES
EEEHMMSS	EMMESHES
EEEHMNNT	MENTHENE
EEEHMNPS	SHEEPMEN
EEEHMNSS	ENMESHES
EEEHMNTV	VEHEMENT
EEEHNNPT	NEPENTHE
EEEHNNQU	HENEQUEN
EEEHNPRS	ENSPHERE
EEEHNRSS	HERENESS
EEEHNRTV	REVEHENT
EEEHNRVW	WHENEVER
EEEHNSSS	SNEESHES
EEEHNSSY	SHEENEYS
EEEHORST	SHOETREE
EEEHPRRT	THREEPER
EEEHPRSS	HERPESES
	PHERESES
EEEHPRST	SPREETHE
EEEHRRVW	WHEREVER
EEEHRSST	SEETHERS
	SHEEREST
	SHEETERS
EEEHRSTT	TEETHERS
EEEHRSWZ	WHEEZERS
EEEHSSST	ESTHESES
EEEHSSTT	ESTHETES
EEEIKLMS	MISLEEKE
EEEIKLRS	SKEELIER
	SLEEKIER
EEEIKLRT	TREELIKE
EEEIKLSW	WEEKLIES
EEEIKNSS	KNEESIES
EEEIKNTX	EKTEXINE
EEEIKRRS	SKEERIER
EEEIKRST	REEKIEST
EEEILLRV	REVEILLE
EEEILMRS	SEEMLIER
EEEILNNO	EOLIENNE
EEEILNPR	PELERINE
EEEILNRY	EYELINER

EEEEILNST	ENLISTEE		REVIEWER		SPEELERS
	SELENITE	**EEEIRSST**	STEERIES	**EEELPRST**	REPLETES
EEEEILNSU	UNSEELIE	**EEEIRSSV**	SEVERIES	**EEELPRSX**	REEXPELS
EEEEILPRS	SLEEPIER	**EEEIRSSZ**	RESEIZES	**EEELPRSY**	SLEEPERY
EEEEILRRV	RELIEVER	**EEEIRTVX**	EXERTIVE	**EEELPSST**	STEEPLES
EEEEILRST	LEERIEST	**EEEISSTW**	SWEETIES	**EEELPTTY**	TELETYPE
	SLEETIER	**EEEJKKNR**	KNEEJERK	**EEELRRSV**	REVELERS
	STEELIER	**EEEJLLRW**	JEWELLER	**EEELRRTT**	LETTERER
EEEEILRSV	RELIEVES	**EEEJLRSW**	JEWELERS		RELETTER
EEEEILRSZ	SLEEZIER	**EEEJNPSY**	JEEPNEYS	**EEELRSST**	TREELESS
EEEEILRVY	LIVEYERE	**EEEKLLSS**	KEELLESS	**EEELRSSV**	SLEEVERS
EEEEILSST	SEELIEST	**EEEKLLSU**	UKELELES	**EEELRSTT**	RESETTLE
	STEELIES	**EEEKLNNR**	ENKERNEL	**EEELRSTV**	LEVERETS
EEEEILSSW	ELSEWISE	**EEEKLNRS**	KNEELERS		VERSELET
EEEEILSTV	TELEVISE	**EEEKLNSS**	SLEEKENS	**EEELRSVY**	SEVERELY
EEEEILTVW	TELEVIEW	**EEEKLPSW**	EKPWELES	**EEELRTVV**	VELVERET
EEEEIMNRU	MEUNIERE	**EEEKLRSS**	SLEEKERS	**EEELSSTU**	EUSTELES
EEEEIMNST	EMETINES	**EEEKLSST**	SLEEKEST	**EEELSSTW**	WEETLESS
EEEEIMPRR	PREMIERE	**EEEKMNSS**	MEEKNESS	**EEELSTVY**	STEEVELY
EEEEIMPRS	EMPERIES	**EEEKMORV**	OVERMEEK	**EEELTTTX**	TELETEXT
	EMPERISE	**EEEKMRSS**	KERMESSE	**EEEMMNRS**	MERESMEN
	EPIMERES	**EEEKNNSS**	KEENNESS	**EEEMMORS**	MESOMERE
	PREEMIES	**EEEKNORS**	KEROSENE	**EEEMMRUZ**	MEZEREUM
EEEEIMPRZ	EMPERIZE	**EEEKNORV**	OVERKEEN	**EEEMNNTT**	TENEMENT
EEEEIMRRS	MISERERE		OVERKNEE	**EEEMNORZ**	MEZEREON
EEEEIMRST	EREMITES	**EEEKNPST**	KEEPNETS	**EEEMNPRT**	PETERMEN
EEEEIMRTT	REMITTEE	**EEEKOPRV**	OVERKEEP	**EEEMNRST**	ENTREMES
EEEEINNNT	NINETEEN	**EEEKORSV**	REEVOKES	**EEEMNRSV**	VERSEMEN
EEEEINNRT	INTERNEE	**EEEKRRST**	STREEKER	**EEEMNRVY**	EVERYMEN
	RETINENE	**EEEKRSST**	KEESTERS	**EEEMNSST**	MEETNESS
EEEEINPRT	PERENTIE		SKEETERS	**EEEMNSTW**	SWEETMEN
EEEEINQRU	QUEENIER	**EEELLLRV**	LEVELLER	**EEEMORRV**	EVERMORE
EEEEINQSU	QUEENIES	**EEELLLSW**	SEWELLEL	**EEEMORST**	EROTEMES
EEEEINQTU	QUEENITE	**EEELLNOR**	ENROLLEE		STEREOME
EEEEINRRS	SNEERIER	**EEELLNQU**	QUENELLE	**EEEMORTV**	OVERTEEM
EEEEINRSS	EERINESS	**EEELLPRR**	REPELLER	**EEEMPRRT**	RETEMPER
	ESERINES	**EEELLPRX**	EXPELLER		TEMPERER
EEEEINRST	ETERNISE	**EEELLRRS**	RESELLER	**EEEMPRSS**	EMPRESSE
	TEENSIER	**EEELLRRT**	RETELLER	**EEEMPSSY**	EMPYESES
EEEEINRSV	VENERIES	**EEELLRRV**	REVELLER	**EEEMRRTX**	EXTREMER
EEEEINRSW	WEENSIER	**EEELLRSV**	LEVELERS	**EEEMRSST**	SEMESTER
EEEEINRSZ	SNEEZIER	**EEELMNST**	ELEMENTS	**EEEMRSTX**	EXTREMES
EEEEINRTT	REINETTE		STEELMEN	**EEENNOPR**	NEOPRENE
	TEENTIER	**EEELMOPP**	EMPEOPLE	**EEENNOSV**	VENENOSE
EEEEINRTZ	ETERNIZE	**EEELMOPY**	EMPLOYEE	**EEENNPST**	PENTENES
EEEEINSSW	SWEENIES	**EEELMORT**	TELOMERE	**EEENNRST**	ETRENNES
EEEEINSTT	TEENIEST	**EEELMOTT**	OMELETTE	**EEENNRUV**	UNEVENER
EEEEINSTW	TWEENIES	**EEELMPSX**	EXEMPLES	**EEENNSSV**	EVENNESS
	WEENIEST	**EEELMRTU**	MULETEER	**EEENNSTT**	ENTENTES
EEEEINTUX	EUXENITE	**EEELMSSS**	SEEMLESS	**EEENOPRR**	REOPENER
EEEEIPRRV	REPRIEVE	**EEELMSST**	TEEMLESS	**EEENORSV**	OVERSEEN
EEEEIPRST	PEERIEST	**EEELNOPV**	ENVELOPE	**EEENORVW**	OVERWEEN
	STEEPIER	**EEELNOSV**	NOVELESE	**EEENORVY**	EVERYONE
EEEEIPRSW	SWEEPIER	**EEELNQTU**	QUEENLET	**EEENOSTY**	EYESTONE
EEEEIPSST	EPEEISTS	**EEELNRRU**	UNREELER	**EEENPPRS**	PREPENSE
	SEEPIEST	**EEELNRSW**	NEWSREEL	**EEENPRRS**	PREENERS
EEEEIPSTW	WEEPIEST	**EEELNRSY**	SERENELY	**EEENPRRT**	REPENTER
EEEEIQSUX	EXEQUIES	**EEELNRTV**	NERVELET	**EEENPRST**	PRETEENS
EEEEIRRST	REESTIER	**EEELNRTY**	TERYLENE		PRETENSE
	RETIREES	**EEELOPPR**	REPEOPLE		TERPENES
EEEEIRRSV	REREVISE	**EEELORST**	SLOETREE	**EEENPRSV**	PREVENES
	REVERIES	**EEELPPRS**	PRESLEEP	**EEENPSST**	ENSTEEPS
EEEEIRRTV	RETRIEVE	**EEELPRSS**	PEERLESS		STEEPENS
EEEEIRRVW	REREVIEW		SLEEPERS	**EEENPSSW**	ENSWEEPS

Eight-letter anagrams

EEENPSSX	EXPENSES	**EEERSSUW**	SERUEWES	**EEFHISST**	FETISHES
EEENNRSS	SNEERERS	**EEERSSVW**	SERVEWES	**EEFHISSY**	FISHEYES
EEENRRST	ENTERERS	**EEERSTTW**	TWEETERS	**EEFHISTT**	HEFTIEST
	REENTERS	**EEERSTVX**	VERTEXES	**EEFHLLWY**	FLYWHEEL
	RESENTER	**EEERSTWZ**	TWEEZERS	**EEFHLMNS**	FLEHMENS
	TERREENS	**EEESSTTT**	SESTETTE	**EEFHLMOT**	HOMEFELT
	TERRENES	**EEESSTTV**	STEEVEST	**EEFHLMST**	THEMSELF
EEENRRSV	RENVERSE	**EEESSTTW**	SWEETEST	**EEFHLNSU**	SHEENFUL
	VENERERS	**EEESTTTX**	SEXTETTE	**EEFHLRSS**	FLESHERS
EEENRRSW	RENEWERS	**EEFFFGLU**	GEFUFFLE	**EEFHLSTY**	FLYSHEET
EEENRRTU	RETURNEE	**EEFFFKLU**	KEFUFFLE	**EEFHMNRS**	FRESHMEN
EEENRRTV	REVERENT	**EEFFFNOS**	ENFEOFFS	**EEFHMORR**	HEREFROM
EEENRRUV	REVENUER	**EEFFFORS**	FEOFFERS	**EEFHNORT**	FOREHENT
EEENRSST	SERENEST	**EEFFGIIS**	EFFIGIES	**EEFHNRSS**	FRESHENS
EEENRSSU	ENURESES	**EEFFGINR**	EFFERING	**EEFHORRT**	THEREFOR
EEENRSSZ	SNEEZERS	**EEFFGIRR**	GREFFIER	**EEFHORRW**	WHEREFOR
EEENRSTV	EVENTERS	**EEFFGLSU**	EFFULGES	**EEFHORSW**	FORESHEW
	EVERNETS	**EEFFHIKY**	KEFFIYEH	**EEFHRRSS**	FRESHERS
EEENRSTW	TWEENERS	**EEFFINST**	FIFTEENS	**EEFHRRSU**	FUEHRERS
EEENRSTX	EXTERNES	**EEFFISUV**	EFFUSIVE	**EEFHRSST**	FRESHEST
EEENRSTY	YESTREEN	**EEFFLNTU**	EFFLUENT		FRESHETS
EEENRSUV	REVENUES	**EEFFLORT**	FOREFELT		
	UNREEVES	**EEFFLSUX**	EFFLUXES	**EEFIIKLL**	LIFELIKE
EEENSSTW	SWEETENS	**EEFFMORR**	FREEFORM	**EEFIIKLW**	WIFELIKE
	TWEENESS	**EEFFMOTT**	MOFFETTE	**EEFIIKRS**	FIKERIES
EEENSSWY	SWEENEYS	**EEFFNOSS**	OFFENSES	**EEFIILLN**	LIFELINE
EEEOPPSY	POPESEYE	**EEFFORRS**	OFFERERS	**EEFIILMT**	LIFETIME
EEEOPRRV	OVERPEER		REOFFERS	**EEFIILNS**	LENIFIES
EEEOPRSX	REEXPOSE	**EEFFORSX**	FORFEXES	**EEFIILRW**	WIFELIER
EEEORRSV	OVERSEER	**EEFFRRSU**	SUFFERER	**EEFIIMNN**	FEMININE
EEEORRSX	XEROSERE	**EEFFSSTU**	SUFFETES	**EEFIIMNS**	FEMINISE
EEEORRSZ	REZEROES	**EEFGIILR**	FILIGREE	**EEFIIMNZ**	FEMINIZE
EEEORSST	EROTESES	**EEFGILNR**	FLEERING	**EEFIINRS**	FINERIES
EEEORSSV	OVERSEES	**EEFGILNS**	FEELINGS	**EEFIIRRS**	REIFIERS
EEEORSSY	EYESORES	**EEFGILNT**	FLEETING	**EEFIIRRT**	FREITIER
EEEORSVY	OVEREYES	**EEFGINNP**	PFENNIGE	**EEFIIRRV**	VERIFIER
EEEPPPRR	PEPPERER	**EEFGINRR**	FINGERER	**EEFIIRST**	FEISTIER
EEEPPSTU	STEEPEUP		REFRINGE		FERITIES
EEEPRRST	PESTERER	**EEFGINRS**	FEERINGS		FIERIEST
EEEPRRSU	REPERUSE		FEIGNERS	**EEFIIRSV**	VERIFIES
EEEPRRSV	PERVERSE		REEFINGS	**EEFIKLLT**	FELTLIKE
	PRESERVE	**EEFGINRV**	FEVERING	**EEFIKLMU**	FUMELIKE
EEEPRRTW	PEWTERER	**EEFGINRZ**	FREEZING	**EEFIKLNR**	FERNLIKE
EEEPRSST	ESTREPES	**EEFGIRRS**	GRIEFERS	**EEFIKLRS**	SERFLIKE
	STEEPERS	**EEFGIRRU**	REFIGURE	**EEFIKLSU**	FUSELIKE
EEEPRSSW	SWEEPERS	**EEFGLLTU**	GEFULLTE	**EEFIKMNN**	KNIFEMEN
EEEPRSSZ	SPREEZES	**EEFGLMNU**	FUGLEMEN	**EEFIKNNP**	PENKNIFE
EEEPSSTT	STEEPEST	**EEFGLNRY**	GREENFLY	**EEFILLMT**	TELEFILM
EEEPSTTT	SEPTETTE	**EEFGLNUV**	VENGEFUL	**EEFILLNY**	FELINELY
EEEQRRSU	REQUERES	**EEFGLORS**	FORELEGS	**EEFILLRW**	FREEWILL
EEEQRRUV	VERQUERE	**EEFGLOSS**	SOLFEGES	**EEFILLSS**	LIFELESS
EEEQRSTU	QUEEREST	**EEFGMNOR**	FORGEMEN	**EEFILMNR**	RIFLEMEN
EEEQRSUZ	SQUEEZER	**EEFGNOOR**	FOREGONE	**EEFILMOS**	LIFESOME
EEEQSSUZ	SQUEEZES	**EEFGOORR**	FOREGOER	**EEFILMST**	FISTMELE
EEERRRSV	RESERVER	**EEFGOORS**	FOREGOES	**EEFILMTX**	FLEXTIME
	REVERERS	**EEFGORRS**	REFORGES	**EEFILNOS**	FELONIES
	REVERSER	**EEFGORSY**	FROGEYES		OLEFINES
EEERRRTV	REVERTER	**EEFHILLR**	HELLFIRE	**EEFILNSS**	FINELESS
EEERRSST	STEERERS	**EEFHILRS**	FLESHIER	**EEFILNUV**	NIEVEFUL
EEERRSSV	RESERVES		SHELFIER	**EEFILORS**	FORELIES
	REVERSES	**EEFHIMSU**	HUMEFIES	**EEFILPRR**	PILFERER
EEERRSTT	RESETTER	**EEFHIRSS**	FRESHIES	**EEFILPRS**	PREFILES
EEERRSTV	SEVEREST	**EEFHIRSV**	FEVERISH	**EEFILRRT**	FERTILER
EEERSSUV	REVEUSES	**EEFHIRTY**	ETHERIFY		FILTERER
					REFILTER

EEFILRSS	FIRELESS	**EEFLOOSV**	FOVEOLES	**EEGGILNR**	LEGERING
EEFILRST	FERLIEST	**EEFLOOTV**	FOVEOLET	**EEGGILNS**	NEGLIGES
EEFILRSU	FUSILEER	**EEFLOPTT**	POLTFEET	**EEGGILNT**	GLEETING
EEFILSST	FELSITES	**EEFLORRW**	FLOWERER	**EEGGILNY**	GINGELEY
EEFILSSW	WIFELESS		REFLOWER	**EEGGILOR**	LEGGIERO
EEFILSTT	FELTIEST	**EEFLORSS**	FORLESES	**EEGGILST**	LEGGIEST
EEFILSTY	EYELIFTS	**EEFLORTV**	LEFTOVER	**EEGGIMNR**	EMERGING
EEFIMMST	FEMMIEST	**EEFLORTW**	FLOWERET	**EEGGINNP**	PEENGING
EEFIMORT	FORETIME	**EEFLORVW**	OVERFLEW	**EEGGINNR**	GREENING
EEFIMRRS	MISREFER	**EEFLORWW**	WEREWOLF		RENEGING
EEFIMRST	FEMITERS	**EEFLOSTU**	OUTFEELS	**EEGGINRS**	GREESING
EEFIMSTU	TUMEFIES	**EEFLOSTV**	LOVEFEST	**EEGGINRT**	GREETING
EEFINNSS	FINENESS	**EEFLOSUX**	FLEXUOSE	**EEGGINST**	EGESTING
EEFINNST	FENNIEST	**EEFLRRSU**	FERRULES	**EEGGINSU**	SEGUEING
EEFINORV	OVERFINE	**EEFLRSST**	FRETLESS	**EEGGIPRR**	PREGGIER
EEFINRRR	INFERRER	**EEFLRSTT**	FETTLERS	**EEGGJLRU**	REJUGGLE
EEFINRRS	REFINERS	**EEFLRSTU**	FLEURETS	**EEGGKRSS**	SKEGGERS
EEFINRRY	REFINERY	**EEFLRSUX**	FLEXURES	**EEGGLNSS**	GLEGNESS
EEFINRSS	FINESSER		REFLUXES	**EEGGLOOR**	GEOLOGER
	RIFENESS	**EEFLSSSU**	FUSELESS	**EEGGNNSS**	GENSENGS
EEFINRST	FERNIEST	**EEFMNORT**	FOMENTER	**EEGGNORS**	ENGORGES
	INFESTER	**EEFMNRRY**	FERRYMEN	**EEGGORRS**	REGORGES
EEFINRSU	REINFUSE	**EEFMNRST**	FERMENTS	**EEGGORSU**	GOUGERES
EEFINRSZ	FRENZIES	**EEFMORRR**	REFORMER	**EEGGORSV**	OVEREGGS
EEFINSSS	FINESSES	**EEFMORST**	FRETSOME	**EEGGPRRS**	PREGGERS
EEFINSTT	FEINTEST	**EEFMOSTT**	MOFETTES	**EEGGPRSU**	PUGGREES
EEFIORRV	OVERRIFE	**EEFMPRRU**	PERFUMER	**EEGGQRSU**	SQUEGGER
EEFIORSX	ORIFEXES	**EEFMPRSU**	PERFUMES	**EEGHHINT**	HEIGHTEN
EEFIPRRS	PREFIRES	**EEFMSTTU**	FUMETTES	**EEGHIIST**	EIGHTIES
EEFIPRSX	PREFIXES	**EEFNNORS**	ENFROSEN	**EEGHIKNT**	THEEKING
EEFIRRST	FERRITES	**EEFNNORZ**	ENFROZEN	**EEGHIKRS**	SKEIGHER
EEFIRRSU	SUREFIRE	**EEFNORRZ**	REFROZEN	**EEGHILNS**	HEELINGS
EEFIRRTT	FRETTIER	**EEFNORST**	ENFOREST		SHEELING
EEFIRRVY	REVERIFY		RESOFTEN	**EEGHILNW**	WHEELING
EEFIRSTT	FRISETTE		SOFTENER	**EEGHILRS**	SLEIGHER
EEFIRSTY	ESTERIFY	**EEFNORTU**	FOURTEEN	**EEGHIMNW**	WEIGHMEN
EEFIRTTZ	FRIZETTE	**EEFNORTW**	FOREWENT	**EEGHINNS**	SHEENING
EEFISSSW	FESSWISE	**EEFNOSTT**	OFTENEST	**EEGHINPS**	PHEESING
EEFISSTT	FESTIEST	**EEFNQRTU**	FREQUENT	**EEGHINPT**	PHENGITE
EEFISTWW	WEFTWISE	**EEFNRTTU**	UNFETTER	**EEGHINPW**	WHEEPING
EEFKNORW	FOREKNEW	**EEFOORRT**	ROOFTREE	**EEGHINPZ**	PHEEZING
EEFLLLNU	FLUELLEN	**EEFOPRRZ**	PREFROZE	**EEGHINRS**	GREENISH
EEFLLNSS	FELLNESS	**EEFORRST**	FORESTER		REHINGES
EEFLLORT	FORETELL		FOSTERER		SHEERING
EEFLLORV	OVERFELL		REFOREST	**EEGHINST**	SEETHING
EEFLLRSU	FUELLERS	**EEFORRSU**	FERREOUS		SHEETING
EEFLLRXY	REFLEXLY	**EEFORRSV**	FOREVERS	**EEGHINSY**	HYGIENES
EEFLLSSS	SELFLESS	**EEFORRTY**	FERETORY	**EEGHINTT**	TEETHING
EEFLMNSU	MENSEFUL	**EEFORSUV**	FEVEROUS	**EEGHINWZ**	WHEEZING
EEFLMORU	FUMEROLE	**EEFOSSTT**	FOSSETTE	**EEGHIOTT**	GOETHITE
EEFLMSSU	FUMELESS	**EEFOSSTU**	FOETUSES	**EEGHIPRW**	PREWEIGH
EEFLNNOS	ENFELONS	**EEFOSTTU**	FOUETTES	**EEGHIRSW**	REWEIGHS
EEFLNORT	FORELENT	**EEFPRSSU**	PERFUSES		WEIGHERS
EEFLNORU	FLUORENE	**EEFRRSSU**	REFUSERS	**EEGHIRTW**	WEIGHTER
EEFLNORW	ENFLOWER	**EEFRRSTT**	FRETTERS	**EEGHISST**	SIGHTSEE
EEFLNOST	FELSTONE	**EEFRRSTU**	REFUTERS	**EEGHISTY**	EYESIGHT
EEFLNRSS	FERNLESS	**EEGGGLST**	GLEGGEST	**EEGHKRSS**	SKREEGHS
	FLENSERS	**EEGGHLLS**	EGGSHELL	**EEGHLNNT**	LENGTHEN
	FRESNELS	**EEGGHLOR**	HOGGEREL	**EEGHMNOS**	HEGEMONS
EEFLNRSU	SNEERFUL	**EEGGHMSU**	MESHUGGE	**EEGHMNOY**	HEGEMONY
EEFLNRTU	REFLUENT	**EEGGHSTU**	THUGGEES	**EEGHMNSU**	HEGUMENS
EEFLNSSS	SELFNESS	**EEGGIJRR**	REJIGGER	**EEGHMNUY**	HEGUMENY
EEFLNSSU	SENSEFUL	**EEGGIKLN**	GLEEKING	**EEGHMORT**	GEOTHERM
EEFLNTUV	EVENTFUL	**EEGGIKNR**	GREEKING	**EEGHNNRU**	ENHUNGER

EEGHNOOP	GEOPHONE	
EEGHNOPS	PHOSGENE	
EEGHNOPY	HYPOGENE	
EEGHNRST	GREENTHS	
EEGHNRSY	GREYHENS	
EEGHNSSU	HUGENESS	
EEGHOPTY	GEOPHYTE	
EEGHORTT	TOGETHER	
EEGHOSTT	GHETTOES	
EEGHSTTU	TEUGHEST	
EEGIILNR	LINGERIE	
EEGIILNV	INVEIGLE	
EEGIIMNS	GEMINIES	
EEGIINRT	REIGNITE	
	RETIEING	
EEGIINTV	GENITIVE	
EEGIIOST	EGOITIES	
EEGIJLNW	JEWELING	
EEGIJLNY	JEELYING	
EEGIJNRS	JEERINGS	
EEGIJOPR	JEREPIGO	
EEGIKLLN	GLENLIKE	
EEGIKLLU	GLUELIKE	
EEGIKLMR	GERMLIKE	
EEGIKLNN	KNEELING	
EEGIKLNS	KEELINGS	
	SLEEKING	
EEGIKLOT	EKLOGITE	
EEGIKMNS	SMEEKING	
EEGIKNNS	KEENINGS	
EEGIKNPS	KEEPINGS	
EEGIKNRS	KREESING	
	SKEERING	
EEGIKNRY	REKEYING	
EEGIKNST	KITENGES	
	STEEKING	
EEGILLNV	LEVELING	
EEGILMOS	EGLOMISE	
EEGILNOR	ELOIGNER	
EEGILNPS	PEELINGS	
	SLEEPING	
	SPEELING	
EEGILNRR	LINGERER	
EEGILNRS	LEERINGS	
	REELINGS	
EEGILNRT	GREENLIT	
EEGILNRU	REGULINE	
EEGILNRV	LEVERING	
	REVELING	
EEGILNSS	SEELINGS	
EEGILNST	GENTILES	
	SLEETING	
	STEELING	
EEGILNSV	SLEEVING	
EEGILNSW	SWEELING	
EEGILNTW	TWEELING	
EEGILNTX	TELEXING	
EEGILOPU	EPILOGUE	
EEGILOSS	GELOSIES	
EEGILOSU	EULOGIES	
	EULOGISE	
EEGILOUZ	EULOGIZE	
EEGILPSS	SPIEGELS	
EEGILQSU	SQUILGEE	
EEGILRSU	REGULISE	
EEGILRSV	VELIGERS	
EEGILRTV	VERLIGTE	
EEGILRTY	LEGERITY	
EEGILRUZ	REGULIZE	
EEGILSST	ELEGISTS	
EEGIMMNW	EMMEWING	
EEGIMMRS	GREMMIES	
	IMMERGES	
EEGIMMST	GEMMIEST	
EEGIMNNS	MENINGES	
EEGIMNNW	ENMEWING	
EEGIMNRS	REGIMENS	
EEGIMNRT	METERING	
	REGIMENT	
EEGIMNRU	MERINGUE	
EEGIMNRY	EMERYING	
EEGIMNSS	SEEMINGS	
EEGIMNST	MEETINGS	
	STEEMING	
EEGIMNSU	EUGENISM	
EEGIMRST	GERMIEST	
EEGINNPR	PREENING	
EEGINNQU	QUEENING	
EEGINNRS	ENGINERS	
	INGENERS	
	SERENING	
	SNEERING	
EEGINNRT	ENTERING	
EEGINNRV	ENERVING	
EEGINNRW	RENEWING	
EEGINNRY	ENGINERY	
	RENEYING	
EEGINNST	STEENING	
EEGINNSU	INGENUES	
	UNSEEING	
EEGINNSV	EEVNINGS	
	EVENINGS	
EEGINNSW	ENSEWING	
EEGINNSZ	SNEEZING	
EEGINNTV	EVENTING	
EEGINOOS	OOGENIES	
EEGINOPR	PERIGONE	
EEGINOPS	EPIGONES	
EEGINORR	ERIGERON	
EEGINORS	ERINGOES	
EEGINORV	VIROGENE	
EEGINOSS	GENOISES	
EEGINOST	EGESTION	
EEGINPRR	PEREGRIN	
EEGINPRS	SPEERING	
	SPREEING	
EEGINPRT	PETERING	
EEGINPRU	PUREEING	
EEGINPRV	PREEVING	
EEGINPST	STEEPING	
EEGINPSW	SWEEPING	
	WEEPINGS	
EEGINQRU	QUEERING	
EEGINQUU	QUEUEING	
EEGINRRS	RESIGNER	
EEGINRRV	REVERING	
EEGINRSS	GREISENS	
EEGINRST	GENTRIES	
		INTEGERS
		REESTING
		STEERING
		STREIGNE
EEGINRSU		SEIGNEUR
EEGINRSV		SEVERING
		VEERINGS
EEGINRSW		RESEWING
		SEWERING
		SWEERING
EEGINRTU		GENITURE
EEGINRTV		EVERTING
EEGINRTW		TWEERING
EEGINRTX		EXERTING
		GENETRIX
EEGINSSS		GNEISSES
EEGINSSU		GENIUSES
EEGINSTT		GENTIEST
EEGINSTU		EUGENIST
EEGINSTV		STEEVING
		VENTIGES
EEGINSTW		SWEETING
EEGINSTX		EXIGENTS
EEGINTTV		VIGNETTE
EEGINTTW		TWEETING
EEGINTUX		TEGUEXIN
EEGINTWZ		TWEEZING
EEGIOPSU		EPIGEOUS
EEGIORST		ERGOTISE
EEGIORTZ		ERGOTIZE
EEGIORVV		OVERGIVE
EEGIOSST		EGOTISES
EEGIOSTZ		EGOTIZES
EEGIPRST		PRESTIGE
EEGIRRST		REGISTER
EEGIRRSV		GRIEVERS
EEGIRSTT		GRISETTE
		TERGITES
EEGIRSTU		GUERITES
EEGISSTV		VESTIGES
EEGISTTV		VEGETIST
EEGJORSU		GOUJEERS
EEGKLNOW		WEEKLONG
EEGKNORS		KEROGENS
EEGKNRSU		GERENUKS
EEGLLRRU		GRUELLER
EEGLMMSU		GEMMULES
EEGLMNOP		EMPLONGE
EEGLMNTU		EMULGENT
EEGLMORS		GOMERELS
EEGLMOSS		GLOSSEME
EEGLNNTU		UNGENTLE
EEGLNOPY		POLYGENE
EEGLNOSU		EUGENOLS
EEGLNOSZ		LOZENGES
EEGLNOTY		TELEGONY
EEGLNPRU		REPLUNGE
EEGLNSTT		GENTLEST
EEGLOPRS		GOSPELER
EEGLORRV		GROVELER
EEGLORVY		LEVOGYRE
EEGLRRSU		GRUELERS
EEGLRSTW		WERGELTS
EEGMMOSU		GEMMEOUS

EEGMNOST	EMONGEST
	GEMSTONE
EEGMNOYZ	ZYMOGENE
EEGMNSST	SEGMENTS
EEGMNTTU	TEGUMENT
EEGMORSU	GRUESOME
EEGMORSW	GREWSOME
EEGMORTY	GEOMETRY
EEGMRSTU	GUMTREES
EEGNNNOR	NONGREEN
EEGNNORT	ROENTGEN
EEGNNOSS	GONENESS
EEGNNOSV	EVENSONG
EEGNNOXY	XENOGENY
EEGNOORV	ENGROOVE
	OVERGONE
EEGNOOST	OSTEOGEN
EEGNOPTY	GENOTYPE
EEGNORST	ESTROGEN
EEGNORSU	GENEROUS
EEGNORSY	ERYNGOES
EEGNOTYZ	ZYGOTENE
EEGNPRUX	EXPUNGER
EEGNPSUX	EXPUNGES
EEGNRSSY	GREYNESS
EEGNRSUY	GUERNSEY
EEGNSSTU	GUESTENS
EEGOORRV	REGROOVE
EEGOORSV	OVERGOES
EEGOPRST	PROTEGES
EEGOPRSU	SUPEREGO
EEGORRST	OSTREGER
EEGORRUV	OVERURGE
EEGORRVW	OVERGREW
EEGORSSS	OGRESSES
EEGORSTU	UROSTEGE
EEGORSTV	OVERGETS
EEGPPRRS	PREPREGS
EEGPRSUX	EXPURGES
EEGRRSSU	RESURGES
EEGRRSTU	GESTURER
EEGRRSUY	GRUYERES
EEGRSSSU	GUESSERS
EEGRSSTU	GESTURES
EEHHIPSS	SHEEPISH
EEHHIRST	ETHERISH
EEHHIRTW	HEREWITH
EEHHKKOO	KOHEKOHE
EEHHLLLO	HELLHOLE
EEHHLRST	THRESHEL
EEHHNOPT	ETHEPHON
EEHHNOSU	HENHOUSE
EEHHRRST	THRESHER
EEHHRSST	THRESHES
EEHHSSTW	WHEESHTS
EEHHSSWW	SHWESHWE
EEHIIKLV	HIVELIKE
EEHIJMNR	MIJNHEER
EEHIKLLT	HELLKITE
EEHIKLMO	HOMELIKE
EEHIKLMP	HEMPLIKE
EEHIKLMS	SHEKELIM
EEHIKLOS	HOSELIKE
EEHIKLRW	WHELKIER
EEHIKLWY	WHEYLIKE
EEHIKRRS	SHRIEKER
EEHILLMS	SHLEMIEL
EEHILLNP	HELPLINE
EEHILLRS	HELLERIS
	HELLIERS
	SHELLIER
EEHILMNS	HEMLINES
EEHILMNU	HELENIUM
EEHILMOR	HOMELIER
EEHILNOP	ENOPHILE
	NEOPHILE
EEHILNPW	PINWHEEL
EEHILNST	THEELINS
EEHILOPS	PIEHOLES
EEHILORT	HOTELIER
EEHILOSS	HELIOSES
EEHILPRT	HERPTILE
EEHILRSS	HEIRLESS
	RELISHES
EEHILRSV	SHELVIER
EEHILSST	LEISHEST
	SHELTIES
EEHILSSV	HIVELESS
EEHILWYZ	WHEEZILY
EEHIMMSS	IMMESHES
	MISHMEES
EEHIMNOS	HEMIONES
EEHIMNRS	SHIREMEN
EEHIMNRT	THEREMIN
EEHIMNSS	INMESHES
EEHIMOST	HOMESITE
EEHIMPRS	EMPERISH
EEHIMPRT	HEMIPTER
EEHIMPST	EPITHEMS
	HEMPIEST
EEHIMQUV	VEHMIQUE
EEHIMRRU	RHEUMIER
EEHIMRST	ERETHISM
	ETHERISM
EEHIMRTT	THERMITE
EEHIMSST	MESHIEST
EEHINNQU	HENEQUIN
	HENIQUEN
EEHINNRS	ENSHRINE
EEHINNRT	INHERENT
EEHINNSS	SNEESHIN
EEHINNST	HENNIEST
EEHINORS	HEROINES
	NOSHERIE
EEHINORT	ETHERION
	HEREINTO
EEHINPRS	INSPHERE
EEHINPRT	NEPHRITE
	PREHNITE
	TREPHINE
EEHINPSX	PHENIXES
EEHINRRS	ERRHINES
EEHINRSS	RESHINES
EEHINRTT	THIRTEEN
EEHINRTW	WHITENER
EEHIOPPS	HOSEPIPE
EEHIORSS	HEROISES
EEHIORST	ISOTHERE
	THEORIES
	THEORISE
EEHIORSZ	HEROIZES
EEHIORTZ	THEORIZE
EEHIOSTX	ETHOXIES
EEHIPPST	PSEPHITE
EEHIPPTY	EPIPHYTE
EEHIPRRS	PERISHER
	SPHERIER
EEHIPRSS	PERISHES
	PHERESIS
EEHIPRST	TREESHIP
EEHIPRTT	PERTHITE
	TEPHRITE
	THREEPIT
EEHIPSST	STEEPISH
EEHIPSTT	EPITHETS
	TIPSHEET
EEHIPSUU	EUPHUISE
EEHIPUUZ	EUPHUIZE
EEHIQRSU	QUEERISH
EEHIRRSS	SHERRIES
EEHIRRSV	SHIVERER
EEHIRRSW	WHERRIES
EEHIRRTW	WITHERER
EEHIRRTX	HERETRIX
EEHIRSST	HEISTERS
EEHIRSSV	SHRIEVES
EEHIRSSX	RHEXISES
EEHIRSTT	ETHERIST
EEHIRTVY	THIEVERY
EEHISSST	ESTHESIS
	HESSITES
EEHISSTW	SWEETISH
EEHISTTW	THEWIEST
EEHISTWY	WHEYIEST
EEHKLOSY	KEYHOLES
EEHKOOSY	EYEHOOKS
EEHLLLOW	WELLHOLE
EEHLLMPS	PHELLEMS
EEHLLMSS	HELMLESS
EEHLLNSS	ENSHELLS
EEHLLORV	HOVELLER
EEHLLOSS	HOLELESS
EEHLLOST	THEELOLS
EEHLLPSS	HELPLESS
EEHLLRSS	SHELLERS
EEHLMMNS	HELMSMEN
EEHLMMSW	WHEMMLES
EEHLMNOT	HOTELMEN
EEHLMOOS	HOLESOME
EEHLMOSS	HOMELESS
EEHLMOSY	HEMOLYSE
EEHLMOYZ	HEMOLYZE
EEHLMRST	THERMELS
EEHLNOPT	PHENETOL
EEHLNOTT	TELETHON
EEHLOPSS	HOPELESS
EEHLOPST	HEELPOST
	PESTHOLE
	TELESHOP
EEHLORST	HOSTELER
EEHLORSV	SHOVELER
EEHLOSSS	SHOELESS

Eight-letter anagrams

EEHLOSTY	HOLEYEST	EEHORRSW	RESHOWER	EEIINORT	ERIONITE
EEHLPPRS	SHLEPPER		SHOWERER	EEIINPPR	PIPERINE
EEHLPRST	TELPHERS	EEHORRTX	EXHORTER	EEIINPRS	PINERIES
EEHLPRSU	SPHERULE	EEHORSSU	REHOUSES	EEIINPRV	VIPERINE
EEHLPSSY	PHYLESES	EEHORSVW	WHOSEVER	EEIINRRV	RIVERINE
EEHLRSST	SHELTERS	EEHORTTU	THEREOUT	EEIINRSS	RESINISE
EEHLRSSV	SHELVERS	EEHORTUW	WHEREOUT		SIRENISE
EEHLRSSW	WELSHERS	EEHOSSTY	EYESHOTS	EEIINRST	ERINITES
EEHLRSTY	SHELTERY	EEHPRSST	HEPSTERS		NITERIES
EEHLSSTT	SHTETELS		SPERTHES	EEIINRSV	VINERIES
EEHLSSTW	THEWLESS	EEHPRSTU	SUPERHET	EEIINRSW	SINEWIER
EEHMMOPR	MORPHEME	EEHPRSTY	HYPESTER		WINERIES
EEHMMORT	OHMMETER		PHYSETER	EEIINRSZ	RESINIZE
EEHMNOOS	MOONSHEE	EEHRRSTW	WHERRETS		SIRENIZE
EEHMNOPS	PHONEMES	EEHRSSSU	RHESUSES	EEIINRTT	INTERTIE
EEHMNORS	HORSEMEN		USHERESS		RETINITE
	SHOREMEN	EEHRSSTW	WERSHEST	EEIINRTV	REINVITE
EEHMNOSU	HOUSEMEN	EEHRSTTW	WHETTERS	EEIINSST	SIENITES
EEHMNOSW	SOMEWHEN	EEHSSTUY	SHUTEYES	EEIINSSV	INESSIVE
EEHMNRSU	ENRHEUMS	EEIIKKLT	KITELIKE	EEIINSSW	EISWEINS
EEHMNRSY	MYNHEERS	EEIIKLLN	LINELIKE	EEIINSTT	ENTITIES
EEHMNSSU	UNMESHES	EEIIKLLR	LIKELIER	EEIINSTV	INVITEES
EEHMNTTU	UMTEENTH	EEIIKLLT	TILELIKE		VEINIEST
EEHMOORT	RHEOTOME	EEIIKLLV	VEILLIKE	EEIIOPTZ	EPIZOITE
EEHMOOSS	HOMEOSES	EEIIKLNP	PINELIKE	EEIIORSS	OSIERIES
EEHMORST	THEOREMS	EEIIKLNV	VEINLIKE	EEIIPRSS	PIERISES
EEHMORVW	WHOMEVER		VINELIKE	EEIIPRSX	EXPIRIES
EEHMRSUX	EXHUMERS	EEIIKLPP	PIPELIKE	EEIIPRTT	EPITRITE
EEHMSSTY	METHYSES	EEIIKLRW	WIRELIKE	EEIIQSTU	EQUITIES
EEHNNOOT	ETHONONE	EEIIKLSV	VISELIKE	EEIIQTUV	QUIETIVE
EEHNNORT	ENTHRONE	EEIIKLSW	LIKEWISE	EEIIRRSV	RIVIERES
EEHNNOSS	SHONEENS	EEIILLMM	MILLIEME	EEIIRRTV	TIRRIVEE
EEHNNPPU	UNHEPPEN	EEIILLMT	MELILITE	EEIIRRTV	VERITIES
EEHNNSSS	NESHNESS	EEIILLOP	EOLIPILE	EEIISSTV	VISITEES
EEHNNSTU	UNNETHES	EEIILLRV	LIVELIER	EEIISTVW	VIEWIEST
EEHNOORS	HONOREES	EEIILMNT	ILMENITE	EEIJKLTU	JUTELIKE
EEHNOPRU	HEREUPON		MELINITE	EEIJKRST	JERKIEST
EEHNOPST	POSHTEEN		MENILITE	EEIJLMSS	MEJLISES
	POTHEENS		TIMELINE	EEIJLNNU	JULIENNE
EEHNOPTY	HYPNOTEE	EEIILMRT	TIMELIER	EEIJLNRT	JETLINER
	NEOPHYTE	EEIILMSS	EMISSILE	EEIJLNUV	JUVENILE
EEHNORSS	SENHORES	EEIILNPP	PIPELINE	EEIJMMST	JEMMIEST
EEHNORST	HONESTER	EEIILNST	LENITIES	EEIJNNOR	ENJOINER
EEHNORSW	HERONSEW	EEIILNTV	LENITIVE	EEIJNRRU	REINJURE
	NOWHERES	EEIILORS	OILERIES	EEIJSTTT	JETTIEST
EEHNORTU	HEREUNTO	EEIILRST	TILERIES	EEIKKRST	KERKIEST
EEHNORTV	OVERHENT	EEIILRSV	LIVERIES	EEIKLLRS	SKELLIER
EEHNOSST	ETHNOSES	EEIILRSW	WISELIER	EEIKLLRY	KYRIELLE
EEHNPRSU	UNSPHERE	EEIILSTV	LEVITIES	EEIKLLSS	SKELLIES
EEHNRTTU	UNTETHER		VEILIEST	EEIKLMST	STEMLIKE
EEHNSSTU	ENTHUSES	EEIILSTW	LEWISITE	EEIKLNOS	NOSELIKE
EEHNSSTV	SEVENTHS	EEIIMMTT	MIMETITE	EEIKLNOV	OVENLIKE
EEHOOPRS	OOSPHERE	EEIIMNOT	MEIONITE	EEIKLNRU	RUNELIKE
EEHOOPRV	OVERHOPE	EEIIMNST	ENMITIES	EEIKLNSS	LIKENESS
EEHOOPSW	WHOOPEES	EEIIMOST	MOIETIES	EEIKLNST	NESTLIKE
EEHOORSV	OVERSHOE	EEIIMPRS	RIEMPIES	EEIKLNSY	KEYLINES
EEHOOSST	TOESHOES	EEIIMRSS	MISERIES	EEIKLNTT	TENTLIKE
EEHOOTTY	EYETOOTH	EEIIMRST	ITEMISER	EEIKLOPP	POPELIKE
EEHOPPRY	HYPEROPE	EEIIMRTZ	ITEMIZER	EEIKLOPR	ROPELIKE
EEHOPPSW	PEEPSHOW	EEIIMSST	ITEMISES	EEIKLOPT	POETLIKE
EEHOPRSU	EUPHROES	EEIIMSSV	EMISSIVE	EEIKLORS	ROSELIKE
EEHOPRVY	OVERHYPE	EEIIMSTZ	ITEMIZES	EEIKLORT	LORIKEET
EEHOPSST	HEPTOSES	EEIINNST	EINSTEIN	EEIKLPST	PIKELETS
EEHORRSV	HOVERERS		NINETIES		SPIKELET

	STEPLIKE
EEIKLRST	TRISKELE
EEIKLSTV	VESTLIKE
EEIKMOOV	MOVIEOKE
EEIKMOTX	KETOXIME
EEIKMPSS	MISKEEPS
EEIKMPST	KEMPIEST
EEIKMRSS	KERMISES
EEIKNORS	KEROSINE
EEIKNORV	REINVOKE
EEIKNPSY	PINKEYES
EEIKNRRT	TINKERER
EEIKNRST	KERNITES
EEIKNSWY	EYEWINKS
EEIKOQUV	EQUIVOKE
EEIKORSU	EUROKIES
EEIKPPRR	KIPPERER
EEIKPRST	PERKIEST
EEIKPSST	PESKIEST
EEIKRSS	SKERRIES
EEIKRRST	RESTRIKE
EEIKRSST	KEISTERS
	KIESTERS
EEIKRSTU	KEIRETSU
EEIKSSTY	SKIEYEST
EEIKSTTT	TEKTITES
EEILLMPR	IMPELLER
EEILLMRS	SMELLIER
EEILLMRU	REILLUME
EEILLMSS	LIMELESS
	SMELLIES
EEILLMST	MELLITES
EEILLNOR	LONELIER
EEILLNPS	SPINELLE
EEILLNSS	LINELESS
EEILLNSV	SENILELY
EEILLNVV	VENVILLE
EEILLOOP	EOLOPILE
EEILLORS	ORSEILLE
EEILLORV	LOVELIER
EEILLOSV	LOVELIES
EEILLPSS	ELLIPSES
	PILELESS
EEILLPSY	SLEEPILY
EEILLPZZ	PIZZELLE
EEILLRSS	LEISLERS
EEILLRST	TREILLES
EEILLSSS	ISLELESS
EEILLSSV	VEILLESS
EEILLSTT	STELLITE
EEILLSTV	EVILLEST
EEILLSTW	WELLSITE
EEILLTVY	VELLEITY
EEILLVWY	WEEVILLY
EEILMMST	MELTEMIS
EEILMNNO	LIMONENE
EEILMNNS	LINESMEN
EEILMNNU	ENLUMINE
EEILMNOP	PEMOLINE
EEILMNOR	LEMONIER
EEILMNRS	ERMELINS
EEILMNRU	LEMURINE
	RELUMINE
EEILMNSS	ISLESMEN
EEILMNSU	SELENIUM
	SEMILUNE
EEILMNSY	MYELINES
EEILMOPS	POLEMISE
EEILMOPZ	POLEMIZE
EEILMORT	MOTELIER
EEILMOST	MESOLITE
	MISLETOE
EEILMPST	IMPLETES
EEILMPSX	IMPLEXES
EEILMQTU	MIQUELET
EEILMRSS	RIMELESS
EEILMRST	TERMLIES
EEILMRSV	VERMEILS
EEILMSST	TIMELESS
EEILMSTT	MELTIEST
EEILMSUV	EMULSIVE
EEILNNOT	NONELITE
EEILNNST	LENIENTS
	SENTINEL
EEILNNSV	ENLIVENS
EEILNOPR	LEPORINE
EEILNORS	ELOINERS
EEILNOST	NOSELITE
EEILNOSV	NOVELISE
EEILNOVV	LOVEVINE
EEILNOVZ	NOVELIZE
EEILNPPZ	ZEPPELIN
EEILNPRS	PILSENER
EEILNPRU	PERILUNE
EEILNPRV	REPLEVIN
EEILNPST	PENLITES
	PLENTIES
EEILNQUY	EQUINELY
EEILNRSS	REINLESS
EEILNRST	ENLISTER
	LISTENER
	REENLIST
	SILENTER
EEILNRSV	LIVENERS
	SNIVELER
EEILNRTT	NETTLIER
EEILNRTY	ENTIRELY
	LIENTERY
EEILNRUV	UNVEILER
EEILNSST	LITENESS
	SETLINES
EEILNSSV	EVILNESS
	LIVENESS
	VEINLESS
	VILENESS
	VINELESS
EEILNSSW	WINELESS
EEILNSTT	ENTITLES
EEILNSTV	VEINLETS
EEILNSUV	VEINULES
EEILNTUV	VEINULET
EEILOPRS	PELORIES
EEILOPST	PETIOLES
EEILORRT	LOITERER
EEILORRV	OVERLIER
EEILORRW	LOWERIER
EEILORST	LITEROSE
	TROELIES
EEILORSV	OVERLIES
	RELIEVOS
	VOLERIES
EEILORSW	OWLERIES
EEILORVV	OVERLIVE
	OVERVEIL
EEILOSST	ESTOILES
EEILOSSX	ISOLEXES
EEILOSTW	OWELTIES
EEILOSTZ	ZEOLITES
EEILOSVW	VOWELISE
EEILOTTT	TOILETTE
EEILOVWZ	VOWELIZE
EEILPPSS	PIPELESS
EEILPPSY	EPILEPSY
EEILPRRS	REPLIERS
EEILPRSS	SPIELERS
EEILPRST	EPISTLER
	PELTRIES
	PERLITES
	REPTILES
	SPIRELET
EEILPRSU	SUPERLIE
EEILPRSV	PRELIVES
EEILPSSS	PELISSES
EEILPSST	EPISTLES
EEILPSSU	EPULISES
EEILPSSV	PELVISES
EEILPSTY	EPISTYLE
EEILQRSU	RELIQUES
EEILRRSV	RELIVERS
	RESILVER
	REVILERS
	SILVERER
	SLIVERER
EEILRRTT	LITTERER
EEILRSST	LEISTERS
	RITELESS
	TIRELESS
EEILRSSU	LEISURES
EEILRSSV	SERVILES
EEILRSSW	WIRELESS
EEILRSTT	RETITLES
EEILRSVY	LIVEYERS
EEILSSTW	WITELESS
EEILSSTX	EXITLESS
	SEXTILES
EEILSSVW	VIEWLESS
EEILSSVX	SILVEXES
EEILSTTX	TEXTILES
EEILSTUX	ULEXITES
EEILSTVY	STIEVELY
EEIMMNRS	IMMENSER
EEIMMORS	MEMORIES
	MEMORISE
EEIMMORZ	MEMORIZE
EEIMMOST	SOMETIME
EEIMMRRS	IMMERSER
EEIMMRSS	IMMERSES
EEIMMRST	MERISTEM
	MIMESTER
	MISMETRE
	STEMMIER
EEIMMRSU	EUMERISM

EEIMMRTT	TERMTIME	EEIMPSSY	EMPYESIS	EEINPRSS	EREPSINS
EEIMMSSS	MISSEEMS	EEIMPSTT	EMPTIEST		RIPENESS
EEIMMSST	MISMEETS	EEIMQRSU	REQUIEMS	EEINPRSU	PENURIES
EEIMMSTU	SEMIMUTE	EEIMQSTU	MESQUITE		RESUPINE
EEIMNNOS	NOMINEES	EEIMQTUZ	MEZQUITE	EEINPRTU	PREUNITE
EEIMNNRS	REINSMEN	EEIMRRST	MERRIEST	EEINPRTX	INEXPERT
EEIMNOPS	EPISEMON		MITERERS	EEINPSST	PENTISES
	SEMIOPEN		RIMESTER	EEINPSTT	INEPTEST
EEIMNORS	EMERSION		TRIREMES		SPINETTE
EEIMNORT	TIMONEER	EEIMRRTT	REMITTER	EEINQRRU	ENQUIRER
EEIMNORV	OVERMINE		TRIMETER	EEINQRSU	ENQUIRES
	VOMERINE	EEIMRSST	MEISTERS		INQUERES
EEIMNOST	MONETISE		MISSTEER		SQUIREEN
	SEMITONE		TRISEMES	EEINQSTU	QUIETENS
EEIMNOTX	XENOTIME	EEIMRSTT	EMITTERS	EEINQSUY	QUEYNIES
EEIMNOTZ	MONETIZE		TERMITES	EEINRRSS	RESINERS
	ZONETIME	EEIMRSTU	EMERITUS	EEINRRST	INSERTER
EEIMNPRS	SPERMINE	EEIMRTTY	TEMERITY		REINSERT
EEIMNPRU	PERINEUM	EEIMSSST	MESSIEST		REINTERS
EEIMNPRZ	PRIZEMEN		METISSES		RENTIERS
EEIMNPST	SEPIMENT	EEINNNPS	PENNINES		TERRINES
EEIMNQSU	MESQUINE	EEINNOPS	PENSIONE	EEINRRSU	REINSURE
EEIMNRRT	TERMINER	EEINNPTT	PENITENT	EEINRRSV	VERNIERS
EEIMNRRV	RIVERMEN	EEINNRST	INTENSER	EEINRRTU	REUNITER
EEIMNRST	MISENTER		INTERNES		UNRETIRE
EEIMNRSV	MINEVERS	EEINNRSU	NEURINES	EEINRRTV	INVERTER
EEIMNRTU	MUTINEER	EEINNRSV	INNERVES	EEINRRTW	WINTERER
EEIMNRTV	VIREMENT		NERVINES	EEINRRTX	INTERREX
EEIMNSSS	MISSENSE	EEINNRTT	INTERNET	EEINRSST	INTERESS
EEIMNSSW	MISWEENS		RENITENT		SENTRIES
EEIMNSTT	MINETTES	EEINNRTV	INVENTER		TRENISES
EEIMNSTV	MISEVENT		REINVENT	EEINRSSU	ENURESIS
EEIMOPRS	MOPERIES	EEINNRUX	XENURINE		ERINUSES
	PROMISEE	EEINNSST	TENNISES	EEINRSSV	INVERSES
	REIMPOSE	EEINNSTT	SENTIENT		VERSINES
EEIMOPSS	EPISOMES	EEINNSTW	ENTWINES	EEINRSTT	INERTEST
EEIMOPST	EPISTOME		WENNIEST		INSETTER
	EPITOMES	EEINNSTZ	NETIZENS		INTEREST
	EPSOMITE	EEINOOPT	OPTIONEE		STERNITE
EEIMORSS	ISOMERES	EEINOPPR	PEPERINO		TRIENTES
EEIMORST	TIRESOME		PEPERONI	EEINRSTU	ESURIENT
EEIMORSZ	SIEROZEM		RONEPIPE		NEURITES
EEIMORTV	OVERTIME	EEINOPRS	ISOPRENE		RETINUES
EEIMORTX	OXIMETER		PEREIONS		REUNITES
EEIMOSSS	SEMIOSES		PIONEERS	EEINRSTV	NERVIEST
EEIMOSSW	SOMEWISE	EEINOPTY	EYEPOINT		REINVEST
EEIMOSSX	EXOMISES	EEINORRR	ORNERIER		SERVIENT
EEIMOTTT	TOTEMITE	EEINORRT	ORIENTER		SIRVENTE
EEIMPPRS	EPISPERM		REORIENT	EEINRSTX	INTERSEX
EEIMPPST	PIPESTEM	EEINORSS	ESSOINER	EEINRSTY	SERENITY
EEIMPRRS	PREMIERS	EEINORST	ONERIEST	EEINRSUV	UNIVERSE
	REPRIMES		SEROTINE	EEINRSVX	VERNIXES
	SIMPERER	EEINORSV	EVERSION	EEINRSWW	NEWSWIRE
EEIMPRSS	EMPRISES	EEINORTT	TENORITE	EEINRTTY	ENTIRETY
	IMPRESES	EEINORTX	EXERTION		ETERNITY
	IMPRESSE	EEINOSSS	ENOSISES	EEINSSST	SESTINES
	MESPRISE		NOESISES	EEINSSSW	WISENESS
	PREMISES	EEINOSST	ESSONITE	EEINSSSX	SEXINESS
	SPIREMES	EEINOSTT	NOISETTE	EEINSSTW	NEWSIEST
EEIMPRST	EMPTIERS		TEOSINTE	EEINSSTX	SIXTEENS
EEIMPRSX	PREMIXES	EEINPPSS	PEPSINES	EEINSSTY	SYENITES
EEIMPRSZ	EMPRIZES	EEINPRRS	PRERINSE	EEINSSUX	UNISEXES
	MESPRIZE		REPINERS	EEINSTTT	NETTIEST
EEIMPSST	SEPTIMES		RIPENERS		TENTIEST

EEINSTTW	TENTWISE	EEIPRSZZ	PREZZIES	EEJLLORY	JOLLEYER
	TWENTIES	EEIPRTUV	ERUPTIVE	EEJLPSTU	PULSEJET
EEINSTTX	EXISTENT	EEIPSSSS	SPEISSES	EEJNOORS	REJONEOS
EEIOPPRS	EPISPORE	EEIPSSTT	PESTIEST	EEJNORSY	ENJOYERS
	POPERIES	EEIPSSTW	SPEWIEST		REENJOYS
EEIOPPST	EPITOPES		STEPWISE	EEJORSST	RESOJETS
EEIOPRRS	ROPERIES	EEIPSTTT	PETTIEST	EEJPRRRU	PERJURER
EEIOPRRT	PORTIERE	EEIQRRRU	REQUIRER	EEJPRRSU	PERJURES
EEIOPRRV	OVERRIPE	EEIQRRSU	QUERIERS	EEJPRSTU	SUPERJET
EEIOPRST	POETISER		REQUIRES	EEJQRRSU	JERQUERS
	POETRIES	EEIQRRTU	REQUITER	EEKKORWW	WORKWEEK
EEIOPRTZ	POETIZER	EEIQRRUV	QUIVERER	EEKKOSTV	VETKOEKS
EEIOPSST	POETISES		VERQUIRE	EEKKRRST	TREKKERS
EEIOPSTZ	POETIZES	EEIQRSSU	ESQUIRES	EEKLLNRY	KERNELLY
EEIORRRS	ORRERIES	EEIQRSTU	QUIETERS	EEKLLNSV	KNEVELLS
EEIORRSS	ROSERIES		REQUITES	EEKLLSUU	UKULELES
	ROSIERES	EEIQRSTW	QWERTIES	EEKLMRSZ	KLEZMERS
EEIORRTV	OVERTIRE	EEIQRTUY	QUEERITY	EEKLNNNU	UNKENNEL
EEIORRTW	TOWERIER	EEIQSSSU	ESQUISSE	EEKLNOSS	KEELSONS
EEIORRTX	EXTERIOR	EEIQSTTU	QUIETEST	EEKLNOST	SKELETON
EEIORRUV	OUVRIERE	EEIRRRST	RETIRERS	EEKLNOSV	VELSKOEN
EEIORSST	EROTESIS		TERRIERS	EEKLOSSU	LEUKOSES
	EROTISES	EEIRRRTW	REWRITER	EEKLOSSY	YOKELESS
EEIORSSX	OREXISES	EEIRRRST	RESISTER	EEKLRSST	KESTRELS
EEIORSTZ	EROTIZES		TRESSIER		SKELTERS
EEIORSVW	OVERWISE	EEIRRRSU	REISSUER	EEKNNSTT	KENNETTS
EEIORSVZ	OVERSIZE	EEIRRRSV	REVERSIS	EEKNOPRS	RESPOKEN
EEIORVVW	OVERVIEW		REVISERS	EEKNORTY	KEYNOTER
EEIORVWW	WIREWOVE	EEIRRSSW	WERRISES	EEKNOSTY	KEYNOTES
EEIPPPRR	PREPPIER	EEIRRSTV	RESTRIVE		KEYSTONE
EEIPPPRS	PREPPIES		REVERIST	EEKNSSST	KNESSETS
EEIPPPST	PEPPIEST		RIVERETS	EEKNSSSW	SKEWNESS
EEIPPQRU	EQUIPPER		RIVETERS	EEKNSSTU	NETSUKES
EEIPPRRS	PERSPIRE	EEIRRSTW	REWRITES	EEKOOPPS	PEKEPOOS
EEIPPRRT	PERIPTER	EEIRRSVV	REVIVERS	EEKOORST	KREOSOTE
EEIPPRST	PEPTISER	EEIRRTTT	TITTERER	EEKOPRTV	OVERKEPT
EEIPPRTY	PERIPETY	EEIRSSSU	REISSUES	EEKOPSTU	OUTKEEPS
EEIPPRTZ	PEPTIZER		SEISURES	EEKORRSV	REVOKERS
EEIPPSST	PEPTISES	EEIRSSSV	IVRESSES	EEKORSST	RESTOKES
EEIPPSTT	PIPETTES	EEIRSSTT	RESTIEST	EEKORSTV	OVERKEST
EEIPPSTZ	PEPTIZES	EEIRSSTU	SURETIES		VOERTSEK
EEIPQRSU	PERIQUES	EEIRSSTV	SIEVERTS	EEKRRSUZ	KREUZERS
	REEQUIPS		TREVISES	EEKRRTUZ	KREUTZER
	REPIQUES		VESTRIES	EEKRSSTY	KEYSTERS
EEIPQSTU	PEQUISTE	EEIRSSTW	SWEIREST	EELLLLMP	PELLMELL
EEIPRRRS	PERRIERS	EEIRSSUZ	SEIZURES	EELLMORS	MORELLES
EEIPRRSS	PRISERES	EEIRSTTU	SUETTIER	EELLMORW	MELLOWER
	REPRISES	EEIRSTVV	VETIVERS	EELLMOSS	MOSELLES
	RESPIRES	EEIRSTVY	SEVERITY	EELLMPTU	PLUMELET
EEIPRRSV	REPRIVES	EEIRTTTZ	TERZETTI	EELLMRSS	SMELLERS
EEIPRRSW	PREWIRES	EEIRTTVV	VETIVERT	EELLMRSV	VERMELLS
EEIPRRSX	EXPIRERS	EEISSSTV	VITESSES	EELLNNOV	NONLEVEL
EEIPRRSZ	REPRIZES	EEISSTTT	TESTIEST	EELLNORR	ENROLLER
EEIPRRTT	PRETERIT	EEISSTTU	SUETIEST		REENROLL
	PRETTIER	EEISSTTV	STIEVEST	EELLNORS	RELLENOS
EEIPRRTW	TWERPIER	EEISSTTW	STEWIEST	EELLNOUV	NOUVELLE
EEIPRSSS	PRESSIES	EEISSTTZ	ZESTIEST	EELLNPRU	PRUNELLE
EEIPRSST	RESPITES	EEISTTTX	TETTIXES	EELLNRSU	SULLENER
EEIPRSSV	PREVISES	EEISTUXZ	ZEUXITES	EELLNSSS	LENSLESS
EEIPRSTT	PRETTIES	EEJJLNUY	JEJUNELY	EELLNSST	SNELLEST
EEIPRSTX	PREEXIST	EEJKMOOS	JOKESOME	EELLNSSW	WELLNESS
EEIPRSTY	PERSEITY	EEJKNRTU	JUNKETER	EELLNSTU	ENTELLUS
	YPERITES	EEJKORST	JOKESTER	EELLNSUV	UNLEVELS
EEIPRSVW	PREVIEWS	EEJLLMSU	JUMELLES	EELLOPSS	ELLOPSES

	POLELESS	EELNOPSV	ENVELOPS	EELOSSSU	SOLEUSES
EELLORRR	REROLLER	EELNOPSY	POLYENES	EELOSSTT	TELEOSTS
EELLORSS	ROSELLES	EELNOPTY	POLYTENE	EELOSSTU	SETULOSE
EELLORST	SOLLERET	EELNOQTU	ELOQUENT	EELOSSTV	VETOLESS
EELLORSV	OVERSELL	EELNORST	ENTRESOL		VOTELESS
EELLORSZ	ROZELLES	EELNORTT	TELETRON	EELOSTTX	SEXTOLET
EELLORTX	EXTOLLER	EELNORTV	OVERLENT	EELOSTUV	EVOLUTES
EELLORVY	VOLLEYER	EELNOSSS	NOSELESS		VELOUTES
EELLORWY	YELLOWER		SOLENESS	EELPPSSU	PEPLUSES
EELLOSSS	SOLELESS	EELNOSST	NOTELESS	EELPPSTU	SEPTUPLE
EELLOSSV	LOVELESS		TONELESS	EELPQRSU	PREQUELS
EELLOSUV	LEVULOSE	EELNOSSU	SELENOUS	EELPRRSU	REPULSER
EELLPRSS	PRESELLS	EELNOSSY	ESLOYNES	EELPRSST	SPELTERS
	RESPELLS	EELNOSSZ	ZONELESS	EELPRSSU	REPULSES
	SPELLERS	EELNOSTT	NOTELETS	EELPRSTY	PEYTRELS
EELLPRST	PRETELLS	EELNOSTU	TOLUENES	EELPRSTZ	PRETZELS
EELLPSST	PELTLESS	EELNOSUV	VENULOSE	EELPRSUX	PLEXURES
EELLQRSU	QUELLERS	EELNOTVV	EVOLVENT	EELPRTXY	EXPERTLY
EELLRSSU	RULELESS	EELNRSST	NESTLERS	EELPSSTZ	SPELTZES
EELLRSSW	SWELLERS		SLENTERS	EELPSSUX	EXPULSES
EELLSSTU	TELLUSES	EELNRSTT	LETTERNS		PLEXUSES
EELLSSTW	SWELLEST		NETTLERS		SUPLEXES
EELLSTVY	SVELTELY	EELNRSUV	NERVULES	EELPSTUX	SEXTUPLE
EELMMPSU	EMPLUMES	EELNSSSW	NEWSLESS	EELRRSTW	WRESTLER
EELMMPUX	EXEMPLUM	EELNSSTT	TENTLESS	EELRSSST	RESTLESS
EELMNOOS	LONESOME	EELNSSTU	TUNELESS		TRESSELS
	OENOMELS		UNSTEELS	EELRSSTT	SETTLERS
EELMNORS	SOLEMNER	EELNSSTV	VENTLESS		STERLETS
EELMNSUY	UNSEEMLY	EELNSSTY	ENSTYLES		TRESTLES
EELMNTTU	TEMULENT	EELNSSUV	UNSELVES	EELRSSTU	STREUSEL
EELMNTUY	UNMEETLY	EELNSTTU	LUNETTES	EELRSSTV	SERVLETS
EELMOOSV	LOVESOME		UNSETTLE	EELRSSTW	SWELTERS
EELMOPRS	PLEROMES	EELOORVV	OVERLOVE		WRESTLES
EELMOPRY	EMPLOYER	EELOPPRS	PEOPLERS	EELRSSTY	RESTYLES
	REEMPLOY	EELOPPSS	PEPLOSES		TYRELESS
EELMOPST	LEPTOMES		POPELESS	EELRSSTZ	SELTZERS
EELMOPSY	EMPLOYES	EELOPPST	ESTOPPEL	EELRSTWY	WESTERLY
	POLYSEME	EELOPPSZ	ZEPPOLES	EELSSSTV	VESTLESS
EELMORST	MOLESTER	EELOPRRX	EXPLORER	EELSSSTZ	ZESTLESS
EELMORSW	EELWORMS	EELOPRSV	PRESOLVE	EELSSTTV	SVELTEST
EELMORTV	OVERMELT	EELOPRSX	EXPLORES	EELSSTTX	TEXTLESS
EELMORTY	MOTLEYER	EELOPRTT	TELEPORT	EELSSTUY	EUSTYLES
	REMOTELY	EELOPSST	POETLESS		
EELMOSSV	MOVELESS	EELOPSTU	EELPOUTS		
EELMOTVW	TWELVEMO		OUTSLEEP		
EELMPPRU	EMPURPLE		SLEEPOUT		
EELMPSST	SEMPLEST	EELOQRUY	REQUOYLE		
	STEMPELS	EELORRSV	RESOLVER		
	STEMPLES	EELORRTV	REVOLTER		
EELMPSTT	TEMPLETS	EELORRTW	TROWELER		
EELMRRTU	MURRELET	EELORRUV	OVERRULE		
EELMRSST	RESMELTS	EELORRVV	REVOLVER		
	SMELTERS	EELORSSS	ROSELESS		
	TERMLESS	EELORSST	SOLERETS		
EELMRSTY	SMELTERY	EELORSSV	RESOLVES		
EELMRTUX	LUXMETER	EELORSTT	LORETTES		
EELMSSST	STEMLESS	EELORSTU	RESOLUTE		
EELMSSTT	STEMLETS	EELORSTV	OVERLETS		
EELNNOSS	LONENESS	EELORSVV	EVOLVERS		
EELNNRTU	TUNNELER		REVOLVES		
EELNNUVY	UNEVENLY	EELORTTU	ROULETTE		
EELNOORS	LOOSENER	EELORTUV	REVOLUTE		
EELNOPPU	UNPEOPLE		TRUELOVE		
EELNOPRT	PETRONEL	EELOSSST	OSSELETS		

EEMMNNOY	MONEYMEN
EEMMNOOP	MENOPOME
EEMMNOST	MEMENTOS
EEMMNOTV	MOVEMENT
EEMMNRRY	MERRYMEN
EEMMOORS	MEROSOME
EEMMOOSS	MESOSOME
EEMMOSST	MESTOMES
EEMMOSSU	MOUSMEES
EEMMRSST	STEMMERS
EEMMRSTY	STEMMERY
EEMMRTUX	EXTREMUM
EEMNNOPR	PRENOMEN
EEMNNOPW	PENWOMEN
EEMNNOSV	ENVENOMS
EEMNOOSS	SOMEONES
EEMNOOSY	MOONEYES
EEMNOPRS	PROSEMEN
EEMNORRS	SERMONER
EEMNORSS	MORENESS
EEMNORST	SERMONET
	STOREMEN

EEMNORSU	MOUNSEER	EENNQSUU	UNQUEENS	EEOOPRST	PROTEOSE
EEMNORSV	OVERSMEN	EENNRSUV	UNNERVES	EEOOPRSX	EXOSPORE
	VENOMERS	EENNSSSU	UNSENSES	EEOOPRTZ	ZOETROPE
EEMNORSY	MONEYERS	EENNSSTX	NEXTNESS	EEOORRVW	OVERWORE
EEMNORTU	ROUTEMEN	EENOORST	OESTRONE	EEOORTVV	OVERVOTE
EEMNPRSS	PRESSMEN		ROESTONE	EEOOSSST	OSTEOSES
EEMNPRSU	SUPERMEN	EENOORTU	EURONOTE	EEOPPRRR	PROPERER
EEMNPRTU	ERUMPENT	EENOORTV	OVERTONE	EEOPPRSS	PORPESSE
	UNTEMPER	EENOPPRS	PREPONES		PREPOSES
EEMNRSTU	MUENSTER		PROPENES	EEOPPSTT	POPETTES
EEMNRSTW	TREWSMEN		PROPENSE	EEOPPSTU	OUTPEEPS
EEMNSSTU	MUTENESS	EENOPPST	PEPTONES	EEOPRRRT	REPORTER
	TENESMUS	EENOPRSS	RESPONSE	EEOPRRRV	REPROVER
EEMNSTTV	VESTMENT	EENOPRST	PROTENSE	EEOPRRSS	REPOSERS
EEMOOPRT	PROTEOME	EENOPRSU	PERONEUS	EEOPRRST	PRESTORE
EEMOORRT	OROMETER	EENOPRTT	ENTREPOT	EEOPRRSU	REPOSURE
EEMOORRV	MOREOVER	EENOPRTU	OUTPREEN	EEOPRRSV	REPROVES
EEMOORTT	ROOMETTE	EENOPRXY	PYROXENE	EEOPRRSW	REPOWERS
EEMOOSSX	EXOSMOSE	EENOPSST	PENTOSES	EEOPRRTT	POTTERER
EEMOPRRS	EMPERORS		POSTEENS	EEOPRRTV	OVERPERT
	PREMORSE	EENOPSTT	POSTTEEN	EEOPRRTX	EXPORTER
EEMOPRSV	PREMOVES		POTTEENS		REEXPORT
EEMOPRSW	EMPOWERS	EENOPSTY	NEOTYPES	EEOPRSSS	ESPRESSO
EEMOQRSU	MORESQUE	EENORRSV	OVERRENS	EEOPRSST	PORTESSE
EEMOQTTU	MOQUETTE	EENORRTT	ROTTENER	EEOPRSSU	ESPOUSER
EEMORRSS	REMORSES	EENORSSS	SORENESS		REPOUSSE
EEMORRSU	UROMERES	EENORSST	ESTRONES	EEOPRSSX	EXPOSERS
EEMORRSV	REMOVERS	EENORSSU	NEUROSES		EXPRESSO
EEMORRTU	MOUTERER	EENORSTT	ONSETTER	EEOPRSTT	PROETTES
	OUTREMER	EENORSTV	OVERNETS		TREETOPS
EEMORSTT	SOMERSET	EENORSTX	EXTENSOR	EEOPRSTU	OUTPEERS
EEMORSTT	REMOTEST	EENORSVW	OVERSEWN	EEOPRSTV	OVERSTEP
EEMORSTU	TEMEROUS	EENORTVW	OVERWENT	EEOPRSTY	SEROTYPE
EEMOSSST	MESTESOS	EENOSSST	STENOSES	EEOPRSUX	EXPOSURE
EEMOTTTU	TEETOTUM	EENOSSSY	ESSOYNES	EEOPRTVY	OVERTYPE
EEMOTTZZ	MOZZETTE	EENOSTTT	TONETTES	EEOPSSSU	ESPOUSES
EEMPPRST	PREEMPTS	EENOSTUV	VENTOUSE		POSEUSES
EEMPRRST	PRETERMS	EENPPRST	PERPENTS	EEOPSSTW	SWEETSOP
EEMPRRSU	PRESUMER	EENPRSST	PENSTERS	EEOPSSTY	EYESPOTS
	SUPREMER		PERTNESS	EEOPSTUW	OUTSWEEP
EEMPRSST	SEMPSTER		PRESENTS		OUTWEEPS
EEMPRSSU	PRESUMES		SERPENTS	EEOQRSTU	REQUOTES
	SUPREMES	EENPRSSU	PURENESS	EEOQRTTU	ROQUETTE
EEMPRSTT	TEMPTERS	EENPRSTT	STREPENT	EEORRRST	RESORTER
EEMPRSTU	PERMUTES	EENPRSTV	PREVENTS		RESTORER
EEMPSSTT	TEMPESTS	EENPRTUX	UNEXPERT		RETRORSE
EEMPSSTY	EMPTYSES	EENPSSSU	SUSPENSE	EEORRRTT	RETORTER
EEMRRSSU	RESUMERS	EENPSSTY	STEPNEYS	EEORRSST	RESTORES
EEMRRSTU	MUSTERER	EENPSTTU	PETUNTSE	EEORRSSV	REVERSOS
EEMRRSUU	EREMURUS	EENPTTUZ	PETUNTZE	EEORRSTU	REROUTES
	REMUEURS	EENQSSTU	SEQUENTS	EEORRSTV	EVERTORS
EEMRRTTU	MUTTERER	EENRRRTU	RETURNER		RESTROVE
EEMSSTTU	MUSETTES	EENRRSSU	ENSURERS	EEORRSTX	EXTRORSE
EENNNOSS	NONSENSE	EENRRSTV	RENVERST	EEORRSTY	OYSTERER
EENNNOTV	NONEVENT	EENRRSUV	NERVURES	EEORRSUV	OVERSURE
EENNNPTY	TENPENNY	EENRRTUV	VENTURER	EEORRTTT	TOTTERER
EENNOORT	ROTENONE	EENRSSSU	SURENESS	EEORRTTX	EXTORTER
EENNOPSS	OPENNESS	EENRSSTT	STERNEST	EEORRTUV	OVERTURE
EENNOPTX	EXPONENT		TESTERNS		TROUVERE
EENNORRW	RENOWNER	EENRSSTU	TRUENESS	EEORSSST	OSSETERS
EENNORST	ENTERONS	EENRSSTW	WESTERNS	EEORSSTT	ROSETTES
	TENONERS	EENRSSTY	STYRENES	EEORSSTV	ESTOVERS
EENNORSU	NEURONES	EENRSTUV	VENTURES		OVERSETS
EENNOSTT	NONETTES	EEOOPPRS	REOPPOSE	EEORSSUV	OVERUSES

EEORSSVW	OVERSEWS	EFFHIITT	FIFTIETH	EFFSSSUU	SUFFUSES
EEORSTTU	OUTSTEER	EFFHILRW	WHIFFLER	EFGGGILN	FLEGGING
EEORSTUV	OUTSERVE	EFFHILSW	WHIFFLES	EFGGIINN	FEIGNING
EEORSTVW	OVERWETS	EFFHIRSS	SHERIFFS	EFGGILOS	SOLFEGGI
EEORSTVX	VORTEXES	EFFHIRSW	WHIFFERS	EFGGINRU	REFUGING
EEORTTTZ	TERZETTO	EFFHISTU	HUFFIEST	EFGGIORR	FROGGIER
EEOSSSVW	VOWESSES	EFFHISTW	WHIFFETS	EFGGIOST	FOGGIEST
EEOSSTTT	SESTETTO	EFFHLLSU	SHELFFUL	EFGGIRRS	FRIGGERS
EEPPRRSS	PREPRESS	EFFHLRSU	SHUFFLER	EFGGIRTU	EGGFRUIT
EEPPRSST	STEPPERS	EFFHLSSU	SHUFFLES	EFGGISTU	FUGGIEST
EEPPRSTY	PRETYPES	EFFHOOOR	FOREHOOF	EFGGLORS	FLOGGERS
EEPPSSUW	UPSWEEPS	EFFHOORS	OFFSHORE	EFGGORRY	FROGGERY
EEPQRRUU	PERRUQUE	EFFIIMST	MIFFIEST	EFGHHIIL	HIGHLIFE
EEPRRSSS	PRESSERS	EFFIINRS	SNIFFIER	EFGHIILS	FLEISHIG
EEPRRSST	PRESTERS	EFFIINSS	IFFINESS	EFGHILNS	FLESHING
EEPRRSSU	PERUSERS	EFFIINST	NIFFIEST		SHELFING
	PRESSURE	EFFIIPRS	SPIFFIER		FRESHING
EEPRRSTV	PERVERTS	EFFIIPSS	SPIFFIES	EFGHINRT	FRIGHTEN
EEPRRSUU	REPURSUE	EFFIISST	STIFFIES	EFGHIOSY	FOGEYISH
EEPRRSVY	REPRYVES	EFFIKLLO	FOLKLIFE	EFGHIPRT	PREFIGHT
EEPRRTTU	PUTTERER	EFFIKLRU	RUFFLIKE	EFGHIRST	FIGHTERS
EEPRSSTT	PRETESTS	EFFIKLSS	SKIFFLES		FREIGHTS
EEPRSSTX	SEXPERTS	EFFILNRS	SNIFFLER		REFIGHTS
EEPRSSUX	SUPERSEX	EFFILNSS	SNIFFLES	EFGHNOTU	FOUGHTEN
EEPRSTTU	UPSETTER	EFFILORT	FORELIFT	EFGHORTU	REFOUGHT
EEPRSTTX	PRETEXTS	EFFILPRS	PIFFLERS	EFGIIINS	IGNIFIES
EEPSSTTY	TYPESETS	EFFILPRU	PLUFFIER	EFGIILNR	REFILING
EEQRSSTU	QUESTERS	EFFILRRS	RIFFLERS	EFGIILNT	FILETING
	REQUESTS	EFFILRRU	RUFFLIER	EFGIILNU	FIGULINE
EERRSSST	RESTRESS	EFFILRSU	SIFFLEUR	EFGIILRU	UGLIFIER
EERRSSTU	TRESSURE	EFFINOSU	EFFUSION	EFGIILSU	UGLIFIES
EERRSSTW	STREWERS	EFFINRSS	SNIFFERS	EFGIIMNS	MISFEIGN
	WRESTERS	EFFINRSU	SNUFFIER	EFGIINNR	ENFIRING
EERRSSVW	SWERVERS	EFFINSST	STIFFENS		INFRINGE
EERRSTTU	REUTTERS	EFFIOPRS	PIFFEROS		REFINING
	UTTERERS	EFFIORST	FORFEITS	EFGIINNT	FEINTING
EERRSTUV	VESTURER	EFFIORSX	FOXFIRES	EFGIINNX	ENFIXING
EERRSTVY	REVESTRY	EFFIOSTT	TOFFIEST	EFGIINRR	FRINGIER
EERRSUVY	RESURVEY	EFFIPSTU	PUFFIEST		REFIRING
EERSSSST	STRESSES	EFFIQRSU	SQUIFFER	EFGIINRU	FIGURINE
EERSSSTU	ESTRUSES	EFFIRSTT	TRIFFEST	EFGIINRX	REFIXING
EERSSSUY	SEYSURES	EFFIRSTU	STUFFIER	EFGIINRY	REIFYING
EERSSTTU	TRUSTEES	EFFISSTT	STIFFEST	EFGIINRZ	FRIEZING
EERSSTTY	SYRETTES	EFFISSUX	SUFFIXES	EFGIITUV	FUGITIVE
EERSSTUU	UTERUSES	EFFLLOSS	SELLOFFS	EFGIKLLU	GULFLIKE
EERSSTUV	VESTURES	EFFLMNUU	UNMUFFLE	EFGIKLOR	FROGLIKE
EERSTTTU	UTTEREST	EFFLMRSU	MUFFLERS	EFGIKNOR	FOREKING
EERSTTUX	TEXTURES	EFFLNRSU	SNUFFLER	EFGILLNO	LIFELONG
EESSSTTT	SESTETTS	EFFLNRUU	UNRUFFLE	EFGILLNU	FUELLING
EESSTTTX	SEXTETTS	EFFLNSSU	SNUFFLES	EFGILLUU	GUILEFUL
EFFFGINO	FEOFFING	EFFLOSSU	SOUFFLES	EFGILMOR	FILMGOER
EFFFILRU	FLUFFIER	EFFLRRSU	RUFFLERS	EFGILNNS	FLENSING
EFFFINOS	INFEOFFS	EFFLRSTU	TRUFFLES	EFGILNOR	FLORIGEN
EFFFISTU	FUFFIEST	EFFNRSSU	SNUFFERS	EFGILNRS	FLINGERS
EFFFLRSU	FLUFFERS	EFFNSSTU	FUNFESTS	EFGILNRU	FERULING
EFFFOORS	FEOFFORS	EFFOOORT	FOREFOOT	EFGILNRY	FERLYING
EFFGILRU	GRIEFFUL	EFFOORRS	OFFERORS		REFLYING
EFFGINOR	OFFERING	EFFOPRRS	PROFFERS	EFGILNSS	SELFINGS
EFFGINSU	EFFUSING	EFFORRST	TROFFERS	EFGILNST	FELTINGS
EFFGIRRU	GRUFFIER	EFFORRUV	OVERRUFF	EFGILNTT	FETTLING
EFFGRSTU	GRUFFEST	EFFORSSW	SWOFFERS	EFGILNTW	LEFTWING
EFFHIILS	FILEFISH	EFFRRSUU	FURFURES	EFGILPRU	FIREPLUG
EFFHIIRW	WHIFFIER	EFFRSSTU	RESTUFFS	EFGILSST	GIFTLESS
EFFHIISW	FISHWIFE		STUFFERS	EFGILSTU	FUGLIEST

	GULFIEST	EFHIORSV	OVERFISH	EFIIMNRS	MISINFER
EFGIMNST	FIGMENTS	EFHIORTT	FORTIETH	EFIIMNST	FEMINIST
EFGIMOSY	FOGEYISM	EFHIPRSS	SERFSHIP	EFIIMNSU	MUNIFIES
EFGIMRUU	REFUGIUM	EFHIPRSU	FURPHIES	EFIIMNTY	FEMINITY
EFGINNNP	PFENNING	EFHIRRTU	THURIFER	EFIIMRRS	RIMFIRES
EFGINNPS	PFENNIGS	EFHIRSST	SHIFTERS	EFIIMRSS	MISFIRES
EFGINNRS	FERNINGS	EFHISSTU	SHUFTIES	EFIINNOS	SINFONIE
EFGINORV	FORGIVEN	EFHISSUW	HUSWIFES	EFIINNST	FINNIEST
EFGINORW	FOREWING	EFHKLNOU	FUNKHOLE	EFIINORR	INFERIOR
EFGINPRS	PERFINGS	EFHLLLSU	SHELLFUL	EFIINORT	NOTIFIER
EFGINPUY	PINGUEFY	EFHLNORS	HORNFELS	EFIINOST	NOTIFIES
EFGINRRY	FERRYING	EFHLNOUY	HONEYFUL	EFIINPSV	FIVEPINS
	REFRYING	EFHLOOSS	HOOFLESS	EFIINPSX	SPINIFEX
EFGINRSU	GUNFIRES	EFHLOOSX	FOXHOLES	EFIINRRT	FERRITIN
	REFUSING	EFHLOPST	FLESHPOT	EFIINRST	SNIFTIER
EFGINRSW	SWERFING	EFHLOPSU	HOPEFULS	EFIINRSU	UNIFIERS
EFGINRTT	FRETTING	EFHLORSY	HORSEFLY	EFIINRSY	RESINIFY
EFGINRTU	FEUTRING	EFHLORVY	HOVERFLY	EFIINSTT	NIFTIEST
	REFUTING	EFHLOSSU	FLOUSHES	EFIINSUV	INFUSIVE
EFGINRTY	GENTRIFY	EFHLOSUU	HOUSEFUL	EFIIORSS	OSSIFIER
EFGIOOST	GOOFIEST	EFHLOSUY	HOUSEFLY	EFIIOSSS	OSSIFIES
EFGIOPTT	PETTIFOG	EFHLRSSU	FLUSHERS	EFIIPRRU	PURIFIER
EFGIORRV	FORGIVER	EFHLSSTU	FLUSHEST	EFIIPRST	SPITFIRE
EFGIORSV	FORGIVES	EFHLSTTW	TWELFTHS	EFIIPRSU	PURIFIES
EFGIRRST	GRIFTERS	EFHNORST	FORHENTS	EFIIPRTY	TYPIFIER
EFGIRRSU	FIGURERS	EFHNOSUU	FUNHOUSE	EFIIPSTY	TYPIFIES
EFGLOOTY	FETOLOGY	EFHOORSW	FORESHOW	EFIIRRST	FIRRIEST
EFGLOOVX	FOXGLOVE	EFHORRST	FROTHERS	EFIIRRTU	FRUITIER
EFGLORST	FROGLETS	EFHORRTY	FROTHERY	EFIIRRZZ	FRIZZIER
EFGLRSUU	SURGEFUL	EFHRRSTU	FURTHERS	EFIIRSTT	RIFTIEST
EFGLSSTU	SLUGFEST	EFHRSTTU	FURTHEST	EFIIRSZZ	FRIZZIES
EFGNOSST	SONGFEST	EFIIILRV	VILIFIER	EFIIRTUV	FRUITIVE
EFGNSSUU	FUNGUSES	EFIIILSV	VILIFIES	EFIIRVVY	REVIVIFY
EFGOORRS	FORGOERS	EFIIIMNS	MINIFIES	EFIISSTT	FISTIEST
EFGORRSU	FERRUGOS	EFIIINNT	INFINITE	EFIISSTW	SWIFTIES
EFGORSTU	FOREGUTS	EFIIINSV	VINIFIES	EFIISTTW	WIFTIEST
EFHHIRSS	FRESHISH	EFIIIRVV	VIVIFIER	EFIISTZZ	FIZZIEST
EFHIIKLS	FISHLIKE	EFIIISTX	FIXITIES	EFIJLORS	FRIJOLES
	FLEISHIK	EFIIISVV	VIVIFIES	EFIJLOST	JETFOILS
EFHIILLT	HELILIFT	EFIIKLLM	FILMLIKE	EFIKKLLO	FOLKLIKE
EFHIILNS	FISHLINE	EFIIKLNT	FLINKITE	EFIKKLOR	FORKLIKE
EFHIILRT	FILTHIER	EFIIKLRS	FLISKIER	EFIKLLOT	LOFTLIKE
EFHIILST	TILEFISH	EFIIKNPR	FIREPINK	EFIKLLOW	WOLFLIKE
EFHIIMSU	HUMIFIES	EFIIKRRS	FRISKIER	EFIKLMOR	FOREMILK
EFHIINRS	FINISHER	EFIILLNT	TEFILLIN	EFIKLNSU	FLUNKIES
	REFINISH	EFIILLRR	FRILLIER	EFIKLOOR	ROOFLIKE
EFHIINSS	FINISHES	EFIILLRS	FRILLIES	EFIKLOOT	FOOTLIKE
EFHIIPPS	PIPEFISH	EFIILMRS	FLIMSIER	EFIKLORS	FOLKSIER
EFHIIPRS	FIRESHIP	EFIILMSS	FLIMSIES	EFIKLORW	LIFEWORK
EFHIIRST	SHIFTIER		MISFILES	EFIKLOST	FOLKIEST
EFHIISST	FISHIEST	EFIILMST	FILMIEST	EFIKLRSU	SURFLIKE
EFHIKLOO	HOOFLIKE	EFIILNRT	FLINTIER	EFIKLRTU	TURFLIKE
EFHILLSY	ELFISHLY	EFIILNTY	FELINITY	EFIKLSTU	FLUKIEST
	FLESHILY		FINITELY		LUTEFISK
EFHILOPS	FISHPOLE	EFIILOQU	FILIOQUE	EFIKNNOS	FINNESKO
EFHILRSU	FLUSHIER	EFIILRRT	FLIRTIER	EFIKNORS	FORESKIN
EFHILSSS	FISHLESS	EFIILRST	FILISTER	EFIKNRSU	REFUSNIK
EFHILTWY	WHITEFLY	EFIILRSU	FUSILIER	EFIKNSTU	FUNKIEST
EFHINNOT	FENTHION	EFIILSTT	FITLIEST	EFIKORRW	FIREWORK
EFHINSST	FISHNETS	EFIILSTY	FEISTILY	EFIKORST	FORKIEST
EFHIOOOR	FORHOOIE	EFIIMMNS	FEMINISM	EFIKRRSS	FRISKERS
EFHIOPRS	FORESHIP	EFIIMNOS	FISNOMIE	EFIKRSST	FRISKETS
EFHIORRT	FROTHIER		OMNIFIES	EFILLLNU	FLUELLIN
EFHIORSS	ROSEFISH	EFIIMNRR	INFIRMER	EFILLMSS	FILMLESS

Eight-letter anagrams

EFILLMSU	SMILEFUL	EFILSTTW	SWIFTLET	EFIRRRUY	FURRIERY
EFILLOOS	FOLIOLES	EFIMMRSU	FERMIUMS	EFIRRSSU	FRISEURS
EFILLORV	OVERFILL	EFIMNORR	INFORMER		FRISURES
EFILLORW	LOWLIFER		REINFORM	EFIRRSTT	FRITTERS
EFILLOSW	LOWLIFES		RENIFORM	EFIRRSTU	FRITURES
EFILLRRS	FRILLERS	EFIMNORS	ENSIFORM		FRUITERS
EFILLRUY	IREFULLY		FERMIONS		FURRIEST
EFILLSTY	STELLIFY	EFIMNRSS	FIRMNESS	EFIRRSZZ	FRIZZERS
EFILLTUY	FUTILELY	EFIMNRSTT	FITMENTS	EFIRRTUY	FRUITERY
EFILMNOS	FOILSMEN	EFIMOORR	FIREROOM	EFIRSSSU	FISSURES
EFILMNSU	FULMINES	EFIMORRT	RETIFORM	EFIRSSTU	SURFEITS
EFILMOST	FILEMOTS	EFIMORRW	FIREWORM		SURFIEST
EFILMRRS	FIRMLESS	EFIMORST	SETIFORM	EFIRSSTW	SWIFTERS
EFILMSSS	SELFISMS	EFIMOSST	SEMISOFT	EFIRSTTU	TURFIEST
EFILMSST	FILMSETS	EFIMOSTT	OFTTIMES		TURFITES
	LEFTISMS	EFIMPRRU	FRUMPIER	EFIRSTUX	FIXTURES
EFILMSUY	EMULSIFY	EFIMRSTU	FREMITUS	EFIRSTUZ	FURZIEST
EFILNNTU	INFLUENT	EFINNORS	INFERNOS	EFISSSTU	FUSSIEST
EFILNOOR	ROOFLINE	EFINNPSU	FINESPUN	EFISSTTU	FUSTIEST
EFILNORU	FLUORINE	EFINNRST	FERNINST	EFISSTTW	SWIFTEST
EFILNOSU	NOISEFUL	EFINNSTU	FUNNIEST	EFISTTTU	TUFTIEST
EFILNOSX	FLEXIONS	EFINOPRS	FORPINES	EFISTUZZ	FUZZIEST
EFILNRTT	FLITTERN	EFINOPTX	PONTIFEX	EFKLLOOR	FOLKLORE
EFILNRYZ	FRENZILY	EFINORRT	FRONTIER	EFKLMNOS	MENFOLKS
EFILNSUX	INFLUXES	EFINORSU	REFUSION	EFKLMOOT	FOLKMOTE
EFILNUWY	UNWIFELY	EFINORTY	RENOTIFY	EFKLMORS	MERFOLKS
EFILOOSS	FLOOSIES	EFINOSSX	FOXINESS	EFKLNRSU	FLUNKERS
EFILOOSZ	FLOOZIES	EFINOSSZ	FOZINESS	EFKLNSUY	FLUNKEYS
EFILOPPR	FLOPPIER	EFINOSTT	FISTNOTE	EFKLOPSU	POKEFULS
EFILOPPS	FLOPPIES	EFINRRRU	FURRINER	EFKLORSS	FORKLESS
EFILOPRR	PROFILER	EFINRRST	SNIFTERS	EFKLORUW	FLUEWORK
EFILOPRS	PROFILES	EFINRSSU	INFUSERS	EFKLPSSU	SKEPFULS
EFILORRU	FLOURIER	EFINRTTU	UNFITTER	EFKNOORW	FOREKNOW
EFILORRV	FRIVOLER	EFIOOPST	POOFIEST	EFKNRSTU	FUNKSTER
EFILORSS	FLOSSIER	EFIOORST	ROOFIEST	EFKOOPRS	FORSPOKE
EFILORST	FLORIEST	EFIOOSST	FOOTSIES	EFKORRTW	FRETWORK
	TREFOILS	EFIOOSTT	FOOTIEST	EFLLLOOW	WOOLFELL
EFILORTU	FLUORITE	EFIOOSTW	WOOFIEST	EFLLLOWY	FELLOWLY
EFILOSSS	FLOSSIES	EFIOOSTW	WOOFIEST	EFLLLPSU	SPELLFUL
EFILOSSX	SEXFOILS	EFIOPRRS	PORIFERS	EFLLNSSU	FULLNESS
EFILOSTT	LOFTIEST	EFIOPRRT	PORTFIRE	EFLLNTUY	FLUENTLY
EFILOSTU	OUTFLIES		PROFITER	EFLLOORW	FOLLOWER
EFILPPRS	FLIPPERS	EFIOPRST	FIREPOTS	EFLLOOTW	FOOTWELL
EFILPPST	FLIPPEST		PIEFORTS	EFLLORSU	FLORULES
EFILPPSU	PIPEFULS		POSTFIRE	EFLLORUV	OVERFULL
EFILPRTU	UPLIFTER	EFIORRST	FROSTIER	EFLLORUW	WOFULLER
EFILPSTU	SPITEFUL		ROTIFERS	EFLLOSST	LOFTLESS
EFILRRST	FLIRTERS	EFIORRSW	FROWSIER	EFLLOUWY	WOEFULLY
	TRIFLERS	EFIORRTT	RETROFIT	EFLLRUUY	RUEFULLY
EFILRRSU	FLURRIES	EFIORRUZ	FROUZIER	EFLLSUUY	USEFULLY
EFILRRZZ	FRIZZLER	EFIORRWZ	FROWZIER	EFLMMRUY	FLUMMERY
EFILRSST	RIFTLESS	EFIORSST	FOISTERS	EFLMNOOU	MONOFUEL
	STIFLERS	EFIORSTU	FOUSTIER	EFLMNOST	LOFTSMEN
EFILRSTT	FLITTERS		OUTFIRES	EFLMNRUU	FRENULUM
EFILRSTW	FEWTRILS	EFIORSTW	FROWIEST	EFLMORRY	FORMERLY
EFILRSTY	FLYTIERS	EFIORTTU	REOUTFIT	EFLMORSS	FORMLESS
EFILRSVV	FLIVVERS	EFIPPRRS	FRIPPERS	EFLMORSU	FULSOMER
EFILRSZZ	FRIZZLES	EFIPPRRY	FRIPPERY	EFLMOSTT	LEFTMOST
EFILRTTU	FRUITLET	EFIPPRST	FRIPPETS	EFLMPRSU	FRUMPLES
EFILSSST	SELFISTS	EFIPPRUY	REPURIFY	EFLNOOSU	FELONOUS
EFILSSTT	LEFTISTS	EFIPRSST	PRESIFTS	EFLNORSU	FLEURONS
EFILSSTU	SULFITES	EFIPRSTU	SUPERFIT	EFLNORTT	FRONTLET
EFILSTTU	FLUTIEST	EFIPRSUX	SUPERFIX	EFLNORYZ	FROZENLY
	FUTILEST	EFIPRTTY	PRETTIFY	EFLNOSSU	FOULNESS
		EFIRRRSU	FURRIERS		

	SULFONES
EFLNOSTT	FLETTONS
	FONTLETS
EFLNOSTY	STONEFLY
EFLNSSTU	NESTFULS
EFLNSSUY	SYNFUELS
EFLNSTTU	TENTFULS
EFLNSUUU	UNUSEFUL
EFLOOPRV	FLOPOVER
EFLOORRS	FLOORERS
EFLOORSS	FORSLOES
	ROOFLESS
EFLOORST	FOOTLERS
EFLOORSW	FORESLOW
EFLOORSZ	FOOZLERS
EFLOORTU	FOOTRULE
EFLOORUV	OVERFOUL
EFLOORVW	OVERFLOW
EFLOOSST	FOOTLESS
EFLOPPRS	FLOPPERS
EFLOPRUW	POWERFUL
EFLOPRUX	FOURPLEX
EFLORRUV	RYEFLOUR
EFLORSSS	FLOSSERS
EFLORSTT	FORTLETS
EFLORSTU	FLOUTERS
EFLORSTW	FELWORTS
EFLORSUY	YOURSELF
EFLORSVY	FLYOVERS
EFLOSUUX	FLEXUOUS
EFLPRRSU	PURFLERS
EFLPRSSU	PRESSFUL
EFLPRSUU	PURSEFUL
EFLRSSTU	FLUSTERS
	TURFLESS
EFLRSTTU	FLUTTERS
EFLRSTUU	FRUSTULE
	SULFURET
EFLRSTUY	FLUSTERY
EFLRTTUY	FLUTTERY
EFMNNUUV	FUNNYMEN
EFMNNORT	FRONTMEN
EFMNORTY	FROMENTY
EFMNRTUY	FRUMENTY
	FURMENTY
EFMOORST	FOREMOST
EFMOORSU	FOURSOME
EFMOPRRS	PERFORMS
	PREFORMS
EFMOPRST	POMFRETS
EFNNOOOR	FORENOON
EFNNORST	FORNENST
EFNNORSU	FENURONS
EFNNORUZ	UNFROZEN
EFNOOOTT	FOOTNOTE
EFNOOPRT	PENTROOF
EFNOORRW	FOREWORN
EFNOOSST	EFTSOONS
	FESTOONS
EFNOPRST	FORSPENT
EFNORRST	REFRONTS
	RENFORST
EFNORRSU	FORERUNS
EFNORRSW	FROWNERS
EFNORSTU	FORTUNES
EFNOSSST	SOFTNESS
EFNOTUZZ	FUZZTONE
EFNRSSTU	FUNSTERS
EFOOOPRT	FOOTROPE
EFOOORST	FOOTSORE
EFOOPRRS	PROOFERS
	REPROOFS
EFOOPRSS	SPOOFERS
EFOOPRST	FORETOPS
	POOFTERS
EFOOPRSY	SPOOFERY
EFOOPRTW	WETPROOF
EFOOPSTT	FOOTSTEP
EFOORRSW	FORSWORE
EFOORSTT	FOOTREST
EFOORSTV	OVERSOFT
EFOORSTW	WOOFTERS
EFOOSTUX	OUTFOXES
EFOPRRSU	PROFUSER
EFOPRSTU	POUFTERS
EFORRRUW	FURROWER
EFORRSST	FORTRESS
EFORRSTW	FROWSTER
EFORRSTY	FORESTRY
EFORRSUV	FERVOURS
EFORRTTU	FROTTEUR
EFORSSST	FOSTRESS
EGGGIILR	GIGGLIER
EGGGILNS	LEGGINGS
EGGGILOR	GOGGLIER
EGGGILRS	GIGGLERS
EGGGINPS	PEGGINGS
EGGGIORR	GROGGIER
EGGGLORS	GOGGLERS
EGGGNNOR	RONGGENG
EGGGOOOS	GOOSEGOG
EGGGORRY	GROGGERY
EGGHIINN	NEIGHING
EGGHIINW	WEIGHING
EGGHIKSW	EGGWHISK
EGGHILRS	HIGGLERS
EGGHINSS	GHESSING
EGGHIRST	THIGGERS
EGGHISSU	SHUGGIES
EGGHISTU	HUGGIEST
EGGHLORU	ROUGHLEG
EGGHLOSS	SHOGGLES
EGGHRTUY	THUGGERY
EGGIIJLR	JIGGLIER
EGGIIJST	JIGGIEST
EGGIILLN	GINGELLI
EGGIILNR	NIGGLIER
EGGIILNS	GINGELIS
EGGIILRW	WIGGLIER
EGGIINNN	ENGINING
EGGIINNR	GREINING
	REIGNING
EGGIINNS	SINGEING
EGGIINNT	TINGEING
EGGIINNW	WINGEING
EGGIINRV	GRIEVING
	REGIVING
EGGIIPST	PIGGIEST
EGGIIRTW	TWIGGIER
EGGIISTW	WIGGIEST
EGGIKLNO	GONGLIKE
EGGIKLNS	KEGLINGS
EGGIKNOS	GINGKOES
	GINKGOES
EGGILLNY	GINGELLY
EGGILMNU	EMULGING
EGGILMSS	LEGGISMS
EGGILNNO	LONGEING
EGGILNNT	GENTLING
	GLENTING
EGGILNNU	LUNGEING
EGGILNRS	NIGGLERS
	SNIGGLER
EGGILNRU	GRUELING
	REGLUING
EGGILNRY	GINGERLY
EGGILNSS	SNIGGLES
EGGILNSU	LUGEINGS
EGGILNSY	GLEYINGS
EGGILOOS	GOOGLIES
EGGILOST	LOGGIEST
EGGILQSU	SQUIGGLE
EGGILRRW	WRIGGLER
EGGILRSW	WIGGLERS
	WRIGGLES
EGGIMNNU	EMUNGING
EGGIMNRS	MERGINGS
EGGIMORS	SMOGGIER
EGGIMSTU	MUGGIEST
EGGINNNR	GRENNING
EGGINNOR	ENGORING
EGGINNSS	GINSENGS
EGGINORR	GORGERIN
	ROGERING
EGGINORU	ROGUEING
EGGINOUV	VOGUEING
EGGINRRU	GRUNGIER
	REURGING
EGGINRSS	GRESSING
	SERGINGS
	SNIGGERS
EGGINRSY	GREYINGS
EGGINSSU	GUESSING
	SNUGGIES
EGGINSTT	GETTINGS
EGGINSTU	GUESTING
	GUNGIEST
EGGIOSST	SOGGIEST
EGGIPRRS	PRIGGERS
	SPRIGGER
EGGIPRRY	PRIGGERY
EGGIPRSU	PUGGRIES
EGGIPSSU	SPUGGIES
EGGIPSTU	PUGGIEST
EGGIRRST	TRIGGERS
EGGIRSSW	SWIGGERS
EGGIRSTT	TRIGGEST
EGGIRSTU	RUGGIEST
	STUGGIER
EGGIRSTW	TWIGGERS
EGGISTUV	VUGGIEST
EGGJLORS	JOGGLERS

Eight-letter anagrams

EGGJLRSU	JUGGLERS
EGGJLRUY	JUGGLERY
EGGLMOOY	GEMOLOGY
EGGLMRSU	SMUGGLER
EGGLMSSU	SMUGGLES
EGGLNSSU	SNUGGLES
EGGLORSS	SLOGGERS
EGGLORST	TOGGLERS
EGGLORUY	GURGOYLE
EGGLPRSU	PLUGGERS
EGGLRSSU	SLUGGERS
EGGLRSTU	GURGLETS
	STRUGGLE
EGGMNTUY	NUTMEGGY
EGGMRSUY	SMUGGERY
EGGMSSTU	SMUGGEST
EGGNOOST	GEOGNOST
EGGNOOSY	GEOGNOSY
EGGNORST	GONGSTER
EGGNRRSU	GRUNGERS
EGGNRSUY	SNUGGERY
EGGNSSTU	SNUGGEST
EGGOORSU	GORGEOUS
EGGOPRRS	PROGGERS
EGGSSSTU	SUGGESTS
EGHHHIST	HEIGHTHS
EGHHIIMS	SEMIHIGH
EGHHIIRS	HIGHRISE
EGHHILTY	EIGHTHLY
EGHHINSS	HIGHNESS
EGHHIORV	OVERHIGH
EGHHORUW	ROUGHHEW
EGHHOSSW	SHOWGHES
EGHIIKLS	SIGHLIKE
EGHIILLS	GHILLIES
EGHIILNR	HIRELING
EGHIILNS	SHEILING
	SHIELING
EGHIIMRT	MIGHTIER
EGHIINNR	INHERING
EGHIINRR	REHIRING
EGHIINRT	THINGIER
EGHIINST	HEISTING
	NIGHTIES
	THINGIES
EGHIINSV	INVEIGHS
EGHIINTV	THIEVING
EGHIIRST	RIGHTIES
	TIGERISH
EGHIISTY	HYGIEIST
EGHIKNRS	GHERKINS
EGHIKRSS	SKREIGHS
	SKRIEGHS
EGHILLNO	HELLOING
EGHILLNS	SHELLING
EGHILMNW	WHELMING
EGHILMOR	HOMEGIRL
EGHILMPS	MEGILPHS
EGHILNNU	UNHELING
EGHILNOV	HOVELING
EGHILNPS	HELPINGS
EGHILNPT	PENLIGHT
EGHILNPW	WHELPING
EGHILNRS	HERLINGS
	SHINGLER
EGHILNSS	SHINGLES
EGHILNST	ENLIGHTS
	LIGHTENS
EGHILNSV	SHELVING
EGHILNSW	WELSHING
EGHILNUW	GLUHWEIN
EGHILORT	REGOLITH
EGHILOSU	GHOULIES
	OUGHLIES
EGHILPRT	PLIGHTER
EGHILPST	PIGHTLES
EGHILRST	LIGHTERS
	RELIGHTS
	SLIGHTER
EGHILSSS	SIGHLESS
EGHILSST	SLEIGHTS
EGHILSTT	LIGHTEST
EGHIMNNS	MENSHING
EGHIMNOR	HOMERING
EGHIMNSS	MESHINGS
EGHIMNUX	EXHUMING
EGHIMPRU	GRUMPHIE
EGHIMSTT	MIGHTEST
EGHINNOY	HONEYING
EGHINNSS	NIGHNESS
EGHINNST	SENNIGHT
EGHINNSU	UNHINGES
EGHINORT	THROEING
EGHINORV	HOVERING
EGHINOSS	SHOEINGS
EGHINOST	HISTOGEN
EGHINOSU	GINHOUSE
EGHINOSY	HOSEYING
EGHINOTZ	GENIZOTH
EGHINPRS	SPHERING
EGHINPSS	SPHINGES
EGHINQTU	QUETHING
EGHINRRS	HERRINGS
EGHINRRU	HUNGRIER
EGHINRRY	HERRYING
EGHINRST	RIGHTENS
EGHINRSU	USHERING
EGHINRSW	SHREWING
	WHINGERS
EGHINRTW	WRETHING
EGHINSTT	SHETTING
	TIGHTENS
EGHINTUW	UNWEIGHT
EGHIOOSS	SHOOGIES
EGHIOPSS	PISHOGES
EGHIOPSU	PISHOGUE
EGHIORST	GHOSTIER
EGHIORSU	ROUGHIES
EGHIOSTT	GOTHITES
EGHIOSTU	TOUGHIES
EGHIOSTV	EIGHTVOS
EGHIOTUW	OUTWEIGH
EGHIQRTU	REQUIGHT
EGHIRRST	RIGHTERS
EGHIRRUY	HIERURGY
EGHIRSST	RESIGHTS
	SIGHTERS
EGHIRSTT	RIGHTEST
	STREIGHT
EGHISSTU	GUSHIEST
EGHISSTY	HYGEISTS
EGHISTTT	TIGHTEST
EGHISTUV	VUGHIEST
EGHKLNOU	GUNKHOLE
EGHLLOPU	PLUGHOLE
EGHLLOSU	LUGHOLES
EGHLMNOP	PHLEGMON
EGHLNORS	LEGHORNS
EGHLNPSU	ENGULPHS
EGHLNRUY	HUNGERLY
EGHLOOOR	HOROLOGE
EGHLOORY	RHEOLOGY
EGHLOOSS	GOLOSHES
	SHOOGLES
EGHLOOST	THEOLOGS
EGHLOOTY	ETHOLOGY
	THEOLOGY
EGHLOPRU	PLOUGHER
EGHLOPRY	HYPERGOL
EGHMNOOY	HOMOGENY
EGHMNORS	GEMSHORN
EGHMNOSU	HUMOGENS
EGHMOPUY	HYPOGEUM
EGHMOSSU	GUMSHOES
EGHNOOPT	PHOTOGEN
EGHNOOSS	HOGNOSES
EGHNOOTY	THEOGONY
EGHNORSU	ENROUGHS
	ROUGHENS
EGHNORUV	HUNGOVER
	OVERHUNG
EGHNOSTU	TOUGHENS
EGHNOSUU	GUNHOUSE
EGHNRSTT	STRENGTH
EGHOOOSW	HOOSEGOW
EGHORRSU	ROUGHERS
EGHORRTW	REGROWTH
EGHORSTU	RESOUGHT
	ROUGHEST
EGHOSTTU	TOUGHEST
EGHPSSUU	UPGUSHES
EGIIINSV	VISIEING
EGIIJLNR	JINGLIER
EGIIKKLN	KINGLIKE
EGIIKLLO	KILLOGIE
EGIIKLNN	LIKENING
EGIIKLNR	KINGLIER
	RINGLIKE
EGIIKLNW	WINGLIKE
EGIIKLTW	TWIGLIKE
EGIIKNNR	REINKING
EGIIKNNS	SKEINING
EGIILMMN	IMMINGLE
EGIILMST	LEGITIMS
EGIILNNO	ELOINING
EGIILNNR	RELINING
EGIILNNS	ENISLING
	ENSILING
EGIILNNT	LENITING
EGIILNNU	LINGUINE
EGIILNNV	LIVENING

EGIILNOR	LIGROINE	EGIINRRS	RERISING	EGIKNRRS	SKERRING
	RELIGION	EGIINRRT	RETIRING	EGIKNRSU	RESKUING
	REOILING	EGIINRRW	REWIRING	EGIKNSTT	SKETTING
EGIILNPR	PERILING	EGIINRST	GIRNIEST	EGIKNSTU	GUNKIEST
EGIILNPS	SPEILING		IGNITERS	EGILLMNS	SMELLING
	SPIELING		REISTING	EGILLNNO	LONGLINE
EGIILNRS	RESILING		RESITING	EGILLNNS	SNELLING
	RIESLING		STINGIER	EGILLNOS	LOGLINES
EGIILNRT	GIRTLINE		STRIGINE	EGILLNOV	LIVELONG
	GLINTIER	EGIINRSU	SIGNIEUR	EGILLNPS	SPELLING
	RETILING	EGIINRSV	REVISING	EGILLNQU	QUELLING
	TINGLIER	EGIINRSW	RINGWISE	EGILLNST	GILLNETS
	TIRELING		SWEIRING		STELLING
EGIILNRV	LIVERING		SWINGIER		TELLINGS
	RELIVING	EGIINRSZ	RESIZING	EGILLNSW	SWELLING
	REVILING	EGIINRTU	INTRIGUE		WELLINGS
EGIILNST	LIGNITES	EGIINRTV	RIVETING	EGILLNSY	YELLINGS
	LINGIEST	EGIINRTX	GENITRIX	EGILLNTU	GLUTELIN
EGIILNSV	VEILINGS	EGIINRVV	REVIVING	EGILLOOR	GLORIOLE
EGIILNSW	WISELING	EGIINSSS	SEISINGS	EGILLORS	GIROLLES
EGIILRRS	GRISLIER	EGIINSST	STINGIES	EGILLRRS	GRILLERS
EGIILRSS	GRISLIES	EGIINSSZ	SEIZINGS	EGILLRRY	GRILLERY
EGIILRST	GIRLIEST	EGIINSTW	WINGIEST	EGILMMNS	LEMMINGS
EGIILRTU	GUILTIER	EGIINSTX	EXISTING	EGILMMRS	GLIMMERS
EGIILRTZ	GLITZIER	EGIINSTZ	ZINGIEST	EGILMMRY	GLIMMERY
EGIIMMNO	MIMEOING	EGIINSVW	VIEWINGS	EGILMNNO	LEMONING
EGIIMMNW	IMMEWING	EGIIOPRS	PIROGIES	EGILMNNU	UNMINGLE
EGIIMNNU	INGENIUM	EGIIPPRR	GRIPPIER	EGILMNOT	LONGTIME
EGIIMNOS	IGNOMIES	EGIIPRST	GRIPIEST	EGILMNPU	IMPLUNGE
EGIIMNPR	IMPINGER	EGIIPRSW	PERIWIGS	EGILMNRS	GREMLINS
EGIIMNPS	IMPINGES	EGIIPSST	PIGSTIES		MERLINGS
EGIIMNRS	REMISING	EGIIRRTT	GRITTIER		MINGLERS
EGIIMNRT	MERITING	EGIITUXY	EXIGUITY	EGILMNRU	RELUMING
	MITERING	EGIJKNOS	JINGKOES	EGILMNST	MELTINGS
	RETIMING	EGIJKNRS	JERKINGS		SMELTING
EGIIMNRX	REMIXING	EGIJLLNY	JELLYING	EGILMNSU	GUMLINES
EGIIMNST	MINGIEST	EGIJLNRS	JINGLERS		LEGUMINS
EGIIMNSV	MISGIVEN	EGIJLNRU	JUNGLIER		MULESING
EGIIMNTT	EMITTING	EGIJLNST	JINGLETS	EGILMOOR	GLOOMIER
EGIIMOPT	IMPETIGO	EGIJMMNY	JEMMYING		OLIGOMER
EGIIMORR	GRIMOIRE	EGIJNNOS	JONESING	EGILMORS	GOMERILS
EGIIMPST	GIMPIEST	EGIJNNOY	ENJOYING	EGILMOSU	ELOGIUMS
EGIIMRST	GRIMIEST	EGIJNQRU	JERQUING	EGILMOUU	EULOGIUM
	TIGERISM	EGIJNSST	JESTINGS	EGILMPRS	GLIMPSER
EGIIMSSV	MISGIVES	EGIJNTTY	JETTYING	EGILMPRU	GLUMPIER
EGIINNPR	REPINING	EGIKKLNS	LEKKINGS	EGILMPSS	GLIMPSES
	RIPENING	EGIKKNRT	TREKKING	EGILNNST	NESTLING
EGIINNRS	RESINING	EGIKLLNN	KNELLING	EGILNNTT	NETTLING
EGIINNSS	SEININGS	EGIKLLNV	KVELLING	EGILNNTU	GLUTENIN
EGIINNST	GINNIEST	EGIKLNOS	SONGLIKE	EGILNOPP	PEOPLING
	STEINING	EGIKLNPS	SKELPING		POPELING
EGIINNSV	VEININGS	EGIKLNRS	ERLKINGS	EGILNORS	RESOLING
EGIINNSW	SINEWING	EGIKLNSS	KINGLESS	EGILNORW	LOWERING
EGIINNTU	UNTIEING	EGIKLNST	KINGLETS		ROWELING
EGIINNVW	VINEWING	EGIKMNPS	KEMPINGS	EGILNOSS	LIGNOSES
EGIINNWZ	WIZENING	EGIKMNRS	SMERKING		LOGINESS
EGIINOPR	PEIGNOIR	EGIKNNNS	KENNINGS	EGILNOSU	LIGNEOUS
EGIINORS	SEIGNIOR		SKENNING	EGILNOSW	LONGWISE
EGIINPRS	SPEIRING	EGIKNNOT	TOKENING	EGILNOTW	TOWELING
	SPIERING	EGIKNNRS	KERNINGS	EGILNOVV	EVOLVING
EGIINPRV	PRIEVING	EGIKNNSY	ENSKYING	EGILNPRS	PINGLERS
EGIINPRX	EXPIRING	EGIKNORV	OVERKING		SPERLING
EGIINPSS	PIGSNIES		REVOKING		SPRINGLE
EGIINQTU	QUIETING	EGIKNPPS	SKEPPING	EGILNPRY	REPLYING

EGILNPSS	SPIGNELS	EGIMNNNO	MIGNONNE	EGINOOST	GOONIEST
EGILNPST	PELTINGS	EGIMNNOV	ENMOVING	EGINOPRS	PERIGONS
	PESTLING		VENOMING		REPOSING
EGILNPSY	YELPINGS	EGIMNNSW	SWINGMEN		SPONGIER
EGILNPTT	PETTLING	EGIMNNUW	UNMEWING	EGINOPRW	POWERING
EGILNRRU	RULERING	EGIMNOOR	GERONIMO	EGINOPRY	PIGEONRY
EGILNRRY	ERRINGLY	EGIMNORS	NEGROISM	EGINOPST	PONGIEST
EGILNRSS	RINGLESS	EGIMNORV	REMOVING	EGINOPSU	EPIGONUS
	SLINGERS	EGIMNOST	MITOGENS	EGINOPSX	EXPOSING
EGILNRST	LINGSTER	EGIMNOSU	GEMINOUS	EGINOPSY	POESYING
	RINGLETS	EGIMNOSY	MOSEYING	EGINOPXY	EPOXYING
	STERLING	EGIMNPRS	IMPREGNS	EGINORRS	IGNORERS
	TINGLERS	EGIMNPRU	IMPUGNER	EGINORSS	GORINESS
	TRINGLES	EGIMNPST	EMPTINGS		SIGNORES
EGILNRSW	NEWSGIRL		PIGMENTS	EGINORST	GENITORS
EGILNRUV	VELURING	EGIMNPTT	TEMPTING		ROSETING
EGILNSSS	SIGNLESS	EGIMNPTY	EMPTYING	EGINORSW	RESOWING
EGILNSST	GLISTENS	EGIMNRSS	GRIMNESS	EGINORSY	SEIGNORY
	SINGLETS	EGIMNRSU	RESUMING	EGINORTT	OTTERING
	SNIGLETS	EGIMNRUY	ERYNGIUM	EGINORTU	OUTREIGN
EGILNSSU	GLUINESS	EGIMORSS	OGREISMS		ROUTEING
	UGLINESS	EGIMORST	ERGOTISM	EGINORTV	REVOTING
EGILNSSW	SWINGLES		GORMIEST	EGINORTW	TOWERING
	WINGLESS	EGIMOSST	EGOTISMS	EGINORTX	OXTERING
EGILNSTT	LETTINGS	EGIMOSTW	TWIGSOME	EGINORTZ	ROZETING
	SETTLING	EGIMPRRU	GRUMPIER	EGINORVW	OVERWING
EGILNSTW	SWELTING	EGIMSSSU	MISGUESS		WINGOVER
	WELTINGS	EGINNNOT	TENONING	EGINORXX	XEROXING
	WINGLETS	EGINNNOZ	ENZONING	EGINOSTT	TENTIGOS
EGILNSUV	EVULSING	EGINNNRS	RENNINGS	EGINOTUV	OUTGIVEN
EGILNSUY	GUYLINES	EGINNNST	STENNING	EGINPPPR	PREPPING
EGILNTUX	EXULTING	EGINNNUY	ENNUYING	EGINPPRS	REPPINGS
EGILNVXY	VEXINGLY	EGINNOOR	RONEOING	EGINPPST	STEPPING
EGILOOOS	OOLOGIES	EGINNOOS	IONOGENS	EGINPRRS	RESPRING
EGILOOPR	GLOOPIER	EGINNOPR	REPONING		SPERRING
EGILOORR	GROOLIER	EGINNOPS	OPENINGS		SPRINGER
EGILOOSU	ISOLOGUE	EGINNORS	NEGRONIS	EGINPRRU	REPURING
EGILOOTY	ETIOLOGY	EGINNORT	NITROGEN	EGINPRSS	PRESSING
EGILOPPR	GLOPPIER		RINGTONE		SPERSING
EGILORRW	GROWLIER	EGINNORV	VIGNERON		SPRINGES
EGILORSS	GLOSSIER	EGINNORZ	REZONING	EGINPRST	PRESTING
EGILORTV	OVERGILT	EGINNOSU	ENGINOUS	EGINPRSU	PERSUING
EGILORTY	GYROLITE	EGINNPRT	PRENTING		PERUSING
EGILOSSS	GLOSSIES	EGINNPSU	PENGUINS		SUPERING
EGILOSST	ELOGISTS	EGINNRRS	GRINNERS	EGINPRTU	ERUPTING
EGILOSTU	EULOGIST	EGINNRRU	UNERRING		REPUTING
EGILPPRS	GRIPPLES	EGINNRST	RENTINGS	EGINPRTY	RETYPING
EGILPSTU	GULPIEST		STERNING	EGINPRUV	PREVUING
EGILRRZZ	GRIZZLER	EGINNRSU	ENSURING	EGINPRYY	PERIGYNY
EGILRSST	GLISTERS	EGINNRSV	NERVINGS	EGINPSSY	PIGSNEYS
	GRISTLES	EGINNRTU	RETUNING	EGINPSTT	PETTINGS
	GRITLESS		TENURING		SPETTING
EGILRSTT	GLITTERS	EGINNRTV	VENTRING	EGINQRUY	QUERYING
EGILRSTU	GURLIEST	EGINNSSS	SENSINGS	EGINQSTU	QUESTING
EGILRSTY	GREYLIST	EGINNSST	NESTINGS	EGINQSUU	QUEUINGS
EGILRSUV	VIRGULES	EGINNSTT	NETTINGS	EGINRRST	RESTRING
EGILRSZZ	GRIZZLES		STENTING		RINGSTER
EGILRTTY	GLITTERY		TENTINGS		STRINGER
EGILSSTW	TWIGLESS	EGINNSTV	VENTINGS	EGINRRSW	WRINGERS
EGIMMNOV	EMMOVING	EGINNSUW	UNSEWING	EGINRRSY	SERRYING
EGIMMNST	STEMMING	EGINNSUX	UNSEXING	EGINRRTY	RETRYING
EGIMMRST	GRIMMEST	EGINNSVY	ENVYINGS	EGINRSST	RESTINGS
EGIMMSTU	GUMMIEST	EGINOORV	INGROOVE		STINGERS
	GUMMITES	EGINOOSS	ISOGONES		TRESSING

Code	Word(s)
	TRIGNESS
EGINRRSV	SERVINGS
	VERSINGS
EGINRRSW	SWINGERS
EGINRSSY	SYRINGES
EGINRSTT	GITTERNS
EGINRSTV	STERVING
EGINRSTW	STREWING
	WRESTING
EGINRSVW	SWERVING
EGINRTTU	UTTERING
EGINSSTT	SETTINGS
	TESTINGS
EGINSSTV	VESTINGS
EGINSSTW	STEWINGS
	WESTINGS
EGINSTTT	STETTING
EGINSTTW	WETTINGS
EGIOOPST	GOOPIEST
EGIOORRV	GROOVIER
EGIOOSST	GOOSIEST
EGIOPRSS	GOSSIPER
	SERPIGOS
EGIOPRSU	GROUPIES
	PIROGUES
EGIOPRTU	PORTIGUE
EGIORRTT	GROTTIER
EGIORRTU	GROUTIER
EGIORRTV	OVERGIRT
EGIORSST	GORSIEST
	STRIGOSE
EGIORSSU	GRISEOUS
EGIORSTU	GOUSTIER
EGIORSTV	VERTIGOS
EGIORSTY	OYSTRIGE
EGIORSTZ	ZORGITES
EGIORSUV	GRIEVOUS
EGIOSSTT	EGOTISTS
EGIOSTTU	GOUTIEST
EGIOSTUV	OUTGIVES
	VOGUIEST
EGIOSUUX	EXIGUOUS
EGIPPRRS	GRIPPERS
EGIPRSUU	GUIPURES
EGIRRRSU	GURRIERS
EGIRRSST	GRISTERS
EGIRRSTT	GRITTERS
EGIRRSTY	REGISTRY
EGIRSSTU	SURGIEST
EGIRSTTT	GRITTEST
EGIRSTTU	TURGITES
EGISSTTU	GUSTIEST
	GUTSIEST
EGISSUWY	WISEGUYS
EGISSYYZ	SYZYGIES
EGISTTTU	GUTTIEST
EGJLNORU	JONGLEUR
EGJLNOTU	JELUTONG
EGJOSSTT	GJETOSTS
EGKLORSW	LEGWORKS
EGLLMORW	GROMWELL
EGLLOOPR	GOLLOPER
EGLLOOPY	PELOLOGY
EGLLOPSY	GOSPELLY
EGLLPSSU	PLUGLESS
EGLMMSTU	GLUMMEST
EGLMNOOS	ENGLOOMS
	LONGSOME
EGLMNOOY	MENOLOGY
EGLMNORS	MONGRELS
EGLMNSSU	GLUMNESS
EGLMOORS	LEGROOMS
EGLMOPRU	PROMULGE
EGLMORSS	GORMLESS
EGLMOSSS	SMOGLESS
EGLNNOOR	LONGERON
EGLNNOSS	LONGNESS
EGLNNTUY	UNGENTLY
EGLNOOOY	OENOLOGY
EGLNOOPR	PROLONGE
EGLNOOPY	PENOLOGY
EGLNOORV	OVERLONG
EGLNOOVY	VENOLOGY
EGLNOPYY	POLYGENY
EGLNORSU	LOUNGERS
EGLNORUU	LONGUEUR
EGLNOSSS	SONGLESS
EGLNOSSY	LYSOGENS
EGLNOSUV	UNGLOVES
EGLNOSXY	LOXYGENS
	XYLOGENS
EGLNOSYY	LYSOGENY
EGLNPRSU	PLUNGERS
EGLNRSSU	RUNGLESS
EGLNRSTU	GRUNTLES
EGLNRTUY	URGENTLY
EGLOOORY	OREOLOGY
EGLOOPRU	PROLOGUE
EGLOOPTY	LOGOTYPE
EGLOORSS	REGOSOLS
EGLOORSY	SEROLOGY
EGLOOSXY	SEXOLOGY
EGLOPRTU	GROUPLET
EGLOPSTU	GLUEPOTS
EGLORRSW	GROWLERS
EGLORRWY	GROWLERY
EGLORSSS	GLOSSERS
EGLORSSU	ROSESLUG
EGLORSUU	RUGULOSE
EGLORSUY	RUGOSELY
EGLPRRSU	SPLURGER
EGLPRSSU	SPLURGES
EGLPRSUY	GYPLURES
EGLRSTTU	GUTTLERS
EGLRSUZZ	GUZZLERS
EGLSSSTU	GUSTLESS
EGLSSUUV	VULGUSES
EGMMNOOR	MONOGERM
EGMMORST	GROMMETS
EGMMOSSU	GUMMOSES
EGMMRSTU	GRUMMEST
	GRUMMETS
EGMNNOOY	MONOGENY
	NOMOGENY
EGMNNOSW	GOWNSMEN
EGMNOOOS	GONOSOME
	MONGOOSE
EGMNOORY	MEROGONY
EGMNOOSU	MUNGOOSE
EGMNORSU	MURGEONS
EGMNOSYZ	ZYMOGENS
EGMNRSSU	GRUMNESS
EGMNSSSU	SMUGNESS
EGMOORRS	GROOMERS
	REGROOMS
EGMORSTU	GOURMETS
EGNNOOTY	ONTOGENY
EGNNORST	RONTGENS
EGNNOSTU	GUNSTONE
	NONGUEST
EGNNOTTU	UNGOTTEN
EGNNSSSU	SNUGNESS
EGNNSTTU	TUNGSTEN
EGNNSTUU	UNGUENTS
EGNOOOPR	GONOPORE
EGNOOPPU	OPPUGNER
EGNOOPRS	SPONGERS
EGNOPRSY	PYROGENS
EGNORRST	STRONGER
EGNORRSW	WRONGERS
EGNORSST	SONGSTER
EGNORSSU	SURGEONS
EGNORSTT	TONGSTER
EGNORSTU	STURGEON
EGNORSTW	WRONGEST
EGNORSUY	YOUNGERS
EGNOSTUY	YOUNGEST
EGNPRRSU	RESPRUNG
EGNPRSUU	SUPERGUN
EGNRRSTU	GRUNTERS
	RESTRUNG
EGOOPRRU	PROROGUE
EGOORRSV	GROOVERS
EGOORRVW	OVERGROW
EGOORSTT	GROTTOES
EGOORSTU	OUTGOERS
EGOPRRSS	PROGRESS
EGOPRRSU	GROUPERS
	REGROUPS
EGOPSSUY	GYPSEOUS
EGORRSSS	GROSSERS
EGORRSST	GROSERTS
EGORRSSU	GROUSERS
EGORRSTU	GROUTERS
EGORSSST	GROSSEST
EGORSSTU	GROUSEST
EGOSSTUU	OUTGUESS
EGPRSSTY	GYPSTERS
EGPRSSUU	UPSURGES
EHHIIPRS	HEIRSHIP
EHHIISTV	THIEVISH
EHHIKSSS	SHIKSEHS
EHHILMNT	HELMINTH
EHHILOPR	RHEOPHIL
EHHILOST	SHITHOLE
EHHINOPT	THIOPHEN
EHHIOPRS	HEROSHIP
EHHIORTT	HITHERTO
EHHIPRSS	HERSHIPS

EHHIPSST	PHTHISES	EHIIRSSU	HUISSIER	EHILNOOP	OENOPHIL
EHHIRSSW	SHREWISH	EHIIRSSW	SWISHIER	EHILNOPS	PINHOLES
EHHIRSTW	WHITHERS	EHIIRSTT	SHITTIER	EHILNOPT	THOLEPIN
EHHISSTU	HUSHIEST		THIRTIES	EHILNORU	UNHOLIER
EHHLOOST	SHOTHOLE	EHIIRWZZ	WHIZZIER	EHILNOSS	HOLINESS
EHHNOORS	SHOEHORN	EHIISSST	HISSIEST	EHILNOST	HOLSTEIN
EHHOOPST	THEOSOPH		STISHIES		HOTLINES
EHHOOSSW	WHOOSHES	EHIISSTT	STITHIES		NEOLITHS
EHHOOSTU	HOTHOUSE	EHIISTTW	WHITIEST	EHILNOSV	NOVELISH
EHHORSTU	SHOUTHER		WITHIEST	EHILNOTX	XENOLITH
EHHRSSSU	SHUSHERS	EHIISTTX	SIXTIETH	EHILNPSY	SYLPHINE
EHHRSSTU	THRUSHES	EHIJNNOS	JOHNNIES	EHILNSTY	ETHINYLS
EHIIIKST	HEITIKIS	EHIKKLOO	HOOKLIKE	EHILNSWY	NEWISHLY
EHIIIPSX	PIXIEISH	EHIKKLSU	HUSKLIKE	EHILOOPZ	ZOOPHILE
EHIIKLPT	PITHLIKE	EHIKKRSS	SHIKKERS	EHILOOST	HOOLIEST
EHIIKLPW	WHIPLIKE	EHIKLMNY	HYMNLIKE	EHILOPRS	POLISHER
EHIIKNST	HINKIEST	EHIKLMOT	MOTHLIKE		REPOLISH
EHIIKSSW	WHISKIES	EHIKLMPU	HUMPLIKE	EHILOPRT	HELIPORT
EHIILLST	HILLIEST	EHIKLNOR	HORNLIKE	EHILOPSS	POLISHES
EHIILLSW	WHILLIES	EHIKLNOS	SINKHOLE	EHILOPST	HELISTOP
EHIILMOS	HOMILIES	EHIKLOOP	HOOPLIKE		HOPLITES
EHIILNPS	HIPLINES	EHIKLOSY	YOKELISH		ISOPLETH
EHIILNRS	LINISHER	EHIKLOTY	LEKYTHOI	EHILOPXY	OXYPHILE
EHIILNSS	LINISHES	EHIKLRSU	RUSHLIKE	EHILORSS	SLOSHIER
EHIILOSS	HELIOSIS	EHIKLSTU	HULKIEST	EHILORSU	HOURLIES
EHIILPSU	HUIPILES	EHIKMNST	METHINKS	EHILORTY	RHYOLITE
EHIILRRW	WHIRLIER	EHIKNORS	SHONKIER	EHILOSST	HOSTILES
EHIILRSV	LIVERISH	EHIKNOSS	HOKINESS	EHILPRST	PHILTERS
EHIILRSW	WHIRLIES	EHIKNPSU	SHUNPIKE		PHILTRES
EHIILSTT	LITHITES	EHIKNRRS	SHRINKER	EHILPRSU	PLUSHIER
	THELITIS	EHIKNRST	RETHINKS	EHILPRSY	SYLPHIER
EHIIMMRW	WHIMMIER		THINKERS	EHILPSSS	SHIPLESS
EHIIMMSS	SHIMMIES	EHIKNSTU	HUNKIEST	EHILPSST	PITHLESS
EHIIMNNO	HOMININE	EHIKOOST	HOOKIEST		THLIPSES
EHIIMNOS	HOMINIES	EHIKOPRS	POKERISH	EHILPSSY	PHYLESIS
	HOMINISE	EHIKRRSS	SHIRKERS	EHILPSTU	SULPHITE
EHIIMNOZ	HOMINIZE	EHIKRRSW	SHIRKERS	EHILRRSW	WHIRLERS
EHIIMNSS	MINISHES	EHIKRSWY	WHISKERY	EHILRSST	SLITHERS
EHIIMPST	MEPHITIS	EHIKSSTU	HUSKIEST		THRISSEL
EHIIMRSW	WHIMSIER	EHIKSSTW	WHISKETS	EHILRSSU	SLUSHIER
EHIIMSST	SMITHIES	EHIKSSWY	WHISKEYS	EHILRSSV	SHRIVELS
EHIIMSSW	WHIMSIES	EHILLLMO	MOLEHILL	EHILRSTT	THRISTLE
EHIINNOS	INHESION	EHILLMOP	PHILOMEL	EHILRSTU	LUTHIERS
EHIINNOT	THIONINE	EHILLMOY	HOMELILY	EHILRSTW	WHIRTLES
EHIINNQU	HENIQUIN	EHILLNOS	HELLIONS		WHISTLER
EHIINNRS	INSHRINE	EHILLNSS	INSHELLS	EHILRSTY	SLITHERY
EHIINNRW	WHINNIER	EHILLOOS	OILHOLES	EHILRTTW	WHITTLER
EHIINNSS	SHINNIES	EHILLOPY	LYOPHILE	EHILRTTY	TRIETHYL
EHIINNSW	WHINNIES	EHILLPTY	PHYLLITE	EHILSSST	SHITLESS
EHIINRRT	HIRRIENT	EHILLRRS	SHRILLER	EHILSSSU	SLUSHIES
EHIINRST	INHERITS	EHILLRRT	THRILLER	EHILSSSW	WISHLESS
EHIINRSZ	RHIZINES	EHILLRST	THILLERS	EHILSSTT	THISTLES
EHIINSST	SHINIEST	EHILLRTY	LITHERLY	EHILSSTU	LUSHIEST
	SHINTIES	EHILLSST	HILTLESS	EHILSSTW	WHISTLES
EHIINSTW	WHINIEST	EHILLSSW	SWELLISH	EHILSTTU	THULITES
EHIINSVX	VIXENISH	EHILLSTU	HULLIEST	EHILSTTW	WHITTLES
EHIIPPRW	WHIPPIER	EHILLSVY	ELVISHLY	EHIMMNUY	HYMENIUM
EHIIPPSS	SHIPPIES	EHILMNOS	LEMONISH	EHIMMRSS	SHIMMERS
EHIIPPST	HIPPIEST	EHILMOOR	HEIRLOOM	EHIMMRSY	SHIMMERY
EHIIPRSV	VIPERISH	EHILMOST	HELOTISM	EHIMMSSY	SHIMMEYS
EHIIPSTT	PITHIEST	EHILMPSW	WHIMPLES	EHIMNOPR	MORPHINE
EHIIRRST	SHIRTIER	EHILMPSY	SYMPHILE	EHIMNORT	THERMION
EHIIRRSW	WHIRRIES	EHILMQUU	UMQUHILE	EHIMNOSS	HOMINESS
EHIIRRTX	HERITRIX	EHILMSTT	MELTITHS		MONISHES

EHIMNOST	HOISTMEN	EHINORTV	OVERTHIN	EHIPRSWY	WHISPERY
EHIMNOSU	HEMIONUS	EHINORZZ	HIZZONER	EHIPSSTU	PUSHIEST
EHIMNOTT	MONTEITH	EHINOSST	HISTONES	EHIPSTUU	EUPHUIST
EHIMNPRS	NEPHRISM	EHINOSTU	OUTSHINE	EHIQSSSU	SQUISHES
	PHRENISM	EHINPPRU	UNHIPPER	EHIRRRSU	HURRIERS
EHIMNPST	SHIPMENT	EHINPPSS	SHIPPENS	EHIRRRSV	SHRIVERS
EHIMNRRU	MURRHINE	EHINPRSU	PUNISHER	EHIRRSTT	THIRSTER
EHIMNRRY	MYRRHINE	EHINPSSU	PUNISHES	EHIRRSTV	THRIVERS
EHIMNRSU	INHUMERS	EHINPSSX	SPHINXES	EHIRRSTW	WHERRITS
	RHENIUMS	EHINRSSU	INRUSHES		WHIRRETS
EHIMNSTY	THYMINES	EHINRSTZ	ZITHERNS		WRITHERS
EHIMOOSS	HOMEOSIS	EHINSSST	THISNESS	EHIRRTTU	TRUTHIER
EHIMOOST	SMOOTHIE	EHINSSUW	UNWISHES	EHIRSSSW	SWISHERS
EHIMOPRS	SOPHERIM	EHIOOPST	ISOPHOTE	EHIRSSTU	RUSHIEST
EHIMOPSS	PHIMOSES	EHIOOPSW	WHOOPIES	EHIRSSTW	SWITHERS
EHIMORSS	HEROISMS		WHOOPSIE	EHIRSTTW	WHITRETS
EHIMORST	ISOTHERM	EHIOORTT	TOOTHIER		WHITSTER
	MOITHERS	EHIOOSST	STOOSHIE		WHITTERS
EHIMORSZ	RHIZOMES	EHIOOSTT	HOOTIEST	EHIRSWZZ	WHIZZERS
EHIMORTU	MOUTHIER	EHIOPPPS	POPESHIP	EHIRTTTW	WHITTRET
EHIMOSTT	MOTHIEST	EHIOPPRS	SHOPPIER	EHISSSTU	STUSHIES
EHIMOSTW	SHOWTIME	EHIOPPST	HOPPIEST	EHISSSTW	SWISHEST
EHIMPPSS	PSEPHISM		POETSHIP	EHISSTUW	THUSWISE
EHIMPRRS	SHRIMPER	EHIOPPSU	EOHIPPUS	EHISSUVW	HUSWIVES
EHIMPRSU	MURPHIES	EHIOPRSS	POSERISH	EHKLNOOT	KNOTHOLE
EHIMPRSW	WHIMPERS		ROSEHIPS	EHKLOOSS	HOOKLESS
EHIMPSTU	HUMPIEST		SPOSHIER	EHKLOOST	HOOKLETS
	HUMPTIES	EHIOPRST	TROPHIES	EHKLOOSZ	KOLHOZES
	TUMPHIES	EHIOPTTW	WHITEPOT	EHKLOSTY	LEKYTHOS
EHIMPSUU	EUPHUISM	EHIORRST	HERITORS	EHKLSTUY	LEKYTHUS
EHIMPTTU	UMPTIETH	EHIORRTU	ROUTHIER	EHKMOORW	HOMEWORK
EHIMRRTY	HERMITRY	EHIORRTW	WORTHIER	EHKMOOSS	SMOKEHOS
EHIMRSST	SMITHERS	EHIORSST	HOISTERS	EHKMORSU	HUMORESK
EHIMRSSU	HEURISMS		HORSIEST	EHKMORSW	MESHWORK
EHIMRSTT	THERMITS		HOSTRIES	EHKMOSSY	SKYHOMES
EHIMRSTW	MISTHREW		SHORTIES	EHKNNRSU	SHRUNKEN
EHIMRSTY	SMITHERY	EHIORSTT	THEORIST	EHKNOOOS	HOOKNOSE
EHIMRTUU	HUMITURE		THORITES	EHKNORSU	UNKOSHER
EHIMSSTU	MUSHIEST	EHIORSTU	OUTHIRES	EHKOOSSS	SKOOSHES
	TUMSHIES		SHOUTIER	EHKOPSSY	KYPHOSES
EHIMSSTY	METHYSIS	EHIORSTV	OVERHITS	EHKRSSTU	TUSHKERS
	MYTHISES	EHIORSTW	WORTHIES	EHLLMOPY	PHYLLOME
EHIMSSWY	WHIMSEYS	EHIORTUY	YOUTHIER	EHLLNSSU	UNSHELLS
EHIMSTTY	MYTHIEST	EHIORTWZ	HOWITZER	EHLLNSTU	NUTSHELL
	THYMIEST	EHIOSSSW	WHOSISES	EHLLOOOP	LOOPHOLE
EHIMSTYZ	MYTHIZES	EHIOSSTT	TOSHIEST	EHLLOORW	HOLLOWER
EHINNORT	INTHRONE	EHIOSSTU	HOUSESIT	EHLMMOSW	WHOMMLES
EHINNOTW	NONWHITE		HOUSIEST	EHLMMSUW	WHUMMLES
EHINNRST	THINNERS		STOUSHIE	EHLMNOST	MENTHOLS
EHINNRSY	SHINNERY	EHIOSSTW	SHOWIEST	EHLMNOSY	HOMELYNS
EHINNSST	THINNESS	EHIOSSTY	ISOHYETS	EHLMNOTU	MOLEHUNT
EHINNSSU	SUNSHINE	EHIOSTVY	YESHIVOT	EHLMNOUY	UNHOMELY
EHINNSSY	SHINNEYS	EHIOTTUW	WHITEOUT	EHLMNSSY	HYMNLESS
EHINNSTT	THINNEST	EHIPPRSS	PRESHIPS	EHLMOORW	WORMHOLE
EHINOOPS	ISOPHONE		SHIPPERS	EHLMOOST	LOTHSOME
EHINOPPR	HORNPIPE	EHIPPRSW	WHIPPERS	EHLMOPSY	MESOPHYL
EHINOPRT	TRIPHONE	EHIPPSSU	HIPPUSES	EHLMORTY	MOTHERLY
EHINOPST	PHONIEST	EHIPPSTW	WHIPPETS	EHLMOTXY	METHOXYL
	SIPHONET	EHIPQSUY	PHYSIQUE	EHLMPSSU	HUMPLESS
EHINOPSW	WINESHOP	EHIPRSST	HIPSTERS	EHLNNOPU	UNHOLPEN
EHINORRT	THORNIER		THRIPSES	EHLNOPSU	SULPHONE
EHINORSS	HERISSON	EHIPRSSW	WHISPERS	EHLNORSS	HORNLESS
EHINORST	HORNIEST	EHIPRSTU	SUPERHIT	EHLNORST	HORNLETS
	ORNITHES	EHIPRSTW	WHIPSTER	EHLNOSST	LOTHNESS

EHLNOSTY	HONESTLY	EHMORSTU	MOUTHERS	EHOPPRSS	SHOPPERS
EHLNRSTU	LUTHERNS	EHMORSTY	SMOTHERY	EHOPPRST	PROPHETS
EHLNSSSU	LUSHNESS	EHMORTUV	VERMOUTH	EHOPPRSW	WHOPPERS
	SHUNLESS	EHMOSSUU	HOUMUSES	EHOPPRSY	PROPHESY
EHLNSTYY	ETHYNYLS	EHMOTUZZ	MEZUZOTH	EHOPRRSY	ORPHREYS
EHLOOPRT	PORTHOLE	EHMPRSTU	THUMPERS	EHOPRSST	HOTPRESS
	POTHOLER	EHMRRSTU	MURTHERS		STROPHES
EHLOOPSS	HOOPLESS	EHMRSTUV	VERMUTHS	EHOPRSSW	PRESHOWS
EHLOOPST	POSTHOLE	EHMRTUYY	EURYTHMY	EHOPRSTU	POUTHERS
	POTHOLES	EHMSSTUY	THYMUSES		SUPERHOT
EHLOOPTY	HOLOTYPE	EHNNOPRS	NEPHRONS	EHOPRSTY	TROPHESY
EHLOORVY	OVERHOLY	EHNNOPSY	HYPNONES	EHOPRSUV	PUSHOVER
EHLOOSSS	SLOOSHES	EHNNORRT	NORTHERN	EHOPRTUY	EUTROPHY
EHLOPPRS	HOPPLERS		THRONNER	EHOPSSTY	PHYTOSES
EHLOPPRT	THROPPLE	EHNNORTU	UNTHRONE	EHORRSTW	THROWERS
EHLOPSSS	SPLOSHES	EHNNOSTU	UNHONEST	EHORRSTY	HERSTORY
EHLOPSSY	SPYHOLES	EHNNRSSU	SHUNNERS	EHORSSTT	SHORTEST
EHLORSST	HOLSTERS	EHNOOPTY	HONEYPOT	EHORSSTU	SHOUTERS
	HOSTLERS	EHNOORRS	HONORERS		SOUTHERS
EHLORSTT	THROSTLE	EHNOORRU	HONOURER	EHORSTUY	OUTHYRES
EHLORSTW	WHORTLES	EHNOORSS	SOREHONS	EHORTTUW	OUTTHREW
EHLORSTY	HOSTELRY	EHNOORSW	WHORESON	EHOSSSTU	STOUSHES
EHLORSUV	OVERLUSH	EHNOORTW	HONEWORT	EHPRSSSU	SPRUSHES
EHLORTTT	THROTTLE	EHNOOSSW	SNOWSHOE	EHPRSSUU	UPRUSHES
EHLOSSTT	SHOTTLES	EHNOOSTU	OUTSHONE	EHPRSTTU	TURPETHS
EHLOSSTW	THOWLESS	EHNOPRSW	PRESHOWN	EHPSSTUY	TYPHUSES
EHLOSSTY	THYLOSES	EHNOPRSY	HYPERONS	EHQRSSUU	QURUSHES
EHLOSTXY	ETHOXYLS	EHNOPSSS	POSHNESS	EHQSSSUU	SQUUSHES
EHLPSSTU	PLUSHEST	EHNOPSSY	HYPNOSES	EHRRSTTU	THRUSTER
EHLRSSTU	HURTLESS	EHNORRRS	SHNORRER	EHRSSSTY	SHYSTERS
	HUSTLERS	EHNORRST	NORTHERS	EHRSSTTU	SHUTTERS
	RUTHLESS	EHNORRTY	ERYTHRON	EIIILMSS	SIMILISE
EHLRSTTU	SHUTTLER	EHNORSST	SHORTENS	EIIILMSZ	SIMILIZE
EHLSSTTU	SHUTTLES	EHNORSSU	ONRUSHES	EIIILNRV	INVIRILE
EHMMOOOR	HOMEROOM		UNHORSES	EIIILPPR	LIRIPIPE
EHMMOOSS	HOMMOSES	EHNORSTT	THORNSET	EIIILRSV	VIRILISE
EHMMRRTU	THRUMMER	EHNORSTU	SOUTHERN	EIIILRVZ	VIRILIZE
EHMMSSUU	HUMMUSES	EHNORTUV	OVERHUNT	EIIIMMNS	MINIMISE
EHMNNOTY	ETHNONYM	EHNOSSUU	UNHOUSES	EIIIMMNZ	MINIMIZE
EHMNNSTU	HUNTSMEN	EHNOSTUU	NUTHOUSE	EIIIRRTV	TIRRIVIE
EHMNOOPR	NEOMORPH	EHNOSTUY	YOUTHENS	EIIIRSST	IRITISES
EHMNOORS	HORMONES	EHNPSSXY	SPHYNXES	EIIJKNRT	JIRKINET
	MOORHENS	EHNRSSTU	HUNTRESS	EIIJMPST	JIMPIEST
EHMNOOST	SMOOTHEN		SHUNTERS	EIIJNRSU	INJURIES
EHMNOOTW	HOMETOWN	EHNSSSTU	THUSNESS	EIIKKLLM	MILKLIKE
	TOWNHOME	EHOOPRRT	HOROPTER	EIIKKLLS	SILKLIKE
EHMNOOTY	THEONOMY	EHOOPRST	HOOPSTER	EIIKKLLT	KILTLIKE
EHMNOPSU	HOMESPUN	EHOOPRSW	WHOOPERS	EIIKKLNS	SKINLIKE
EHMNPRYY	HYPERNYM	EHOOPRSX	HORSEPOX	EIIKKNST	KINKIEST
EHMNPSTY	NYMPHETS	EHOOPRTY	ORTHOEPY	EIIKLLLY	LILYLIKE
EHMNSTTU	HUTMENTS	EHOOPSTT	PHOTOSET	EIIKLLMN	LIMEKILN
EHMOOOTZ	ZOOTHOME	EHOOPSTU	HOUSETOP	EIIKLLNO	LIONLIKE
EHMOOPRT	HOMEPORT		POTHOUSE	EIIKLLRS	SKILLIER
EHMOOPTY	HOMOTYPE	EHOOPSTY	OOPHYTES	EIIKLLSS	SKILLIES
EHMOORRS	SHROOMER	EHOOPTYZ	ZOOPHYTE	EIIKLLST	SLITLIKE
EHMOORST	RESMOOTH	EHOORSST	ORTHOSES	EIIKLMRS	MISLIKER
	SMOOTHER		RESHOOTS	EIIKLMSS	MISLIKES
EHMOORTU	OUTHOMER		SHEROOTS	EIIKLMST	MILKIEST
EHMOOSSS	SHMOOSES		SHOOTERS	EIIKLNOR	IRONLIKE
	SMOOSHES		SOOTHERS	EIIKLNRS	SLINKIER
EHMOOSST	SMOOTHES	EHOORSTV	OVERSHOT	EIIKLNRT	TINKLIER
EHMOOSSZ	SHMOOZES	EHOOSSSW	SWOOSHES	EIIKLPSS	PLISKIES
EHMOPRSW	MORPHEWS	EHOOSSTT	SOOTHEST	EIIKLPSW	WISPLIKE
EHMORSST	SMOTHERS	EHOOSTUU	OUTHOUSE	EIIKLRTT	KITTLIER

EIIKLSST	SILKIEST
EIIKLSTU	SUITLIKE
EIIKMPRS	SKIMPIER
EIIKMRRS	SMIRKIER
EIIKMRST	MIRKIEST
EIIKNNOS	NOISENIK
EIIKNNRS	SKINNIER
EIIKNNSS	INKINESS
EIIKNNST	KINETINS
EIIKNNSW	WINESKIN
EIIKNPST	PINKIEST
EIIKNRST	STINKIER
EIIKNSST	SINKIEST
EIIKNSTW	TWINKIES
EIIKNSTZ	ZINKIEST
EIIKPPRS	SKIPPIER
EIIKPSST	SPIKIEST
EIIKQRRU	QUIRKIER
EIIKRSST	RISKIEST
EIIKSSTV	SKIVIEST
EIIKSSVV	SKIVVIES
EIILLLVY	LIVELILY
EIILLMMR	MILLIREM
EIILLMMS	MILLIMES
EIILLMNR	MILLINER
EIILLMNS	MILLINES
	SLIMLINE
EIILLMNU	ILLUMINE
EIILLMRS	MILLIERS
EIILLNST	NIELLIST
EIILLNSU	SUILLINE
EIILLNSV	VILLEINS
EIILLNTV	VITELLIN
EIILLPSS	ELLIPSIS
EIILLRST	STILLIER
EIILLRVY	VIRILELY
EIILLSST	SILLIEST
EIILLSTT	LITTLIES
	TILLIEST
	TILLITES
EIILLSTW	TWILLIES
EIILLSUV	ILLUSIVE
EIILMMOS	MILESIMO
EIILMMOT	IMMOTILE
EIILMNNT	LINIMENT
EIILMNOT	LIMONITE
EIILMNSS	LIMINESS
EIILMOPT	IMPOLITE
EIILMPPR	PIMPLIER
EIILMPRS	IMPERILS
	LIMPSIER
EIILMPRT	PRELIMIT
EIILMPST	LIMEPITS
EIILMRSS	SLIMSIER
EIILMRST	LIMITERS
	MIRLIEST
EIILMRZZ	MIZZLIER
EIILMSSS	MISSILES
EIILMSST	ELITISMS
	SLIMIEST
EIILMSSV	MISLIVES
EIILMSTT	MILTIEST
	MISTITLE
EIILMSTY	MYELITIS

EIILNNOT	LENITION
EIILNORS	LIONISER
EIILNORT	TRIOLEIN
EIILNORZ	LIONIZER
EIILNOSS	ELISIONS
	ISOLINES
	LIONISES
	OILINESS
EIILNOST	ETIOLINS
EIILNOSV	OLIVINES
EIILNOSZ	LIONIZES
EIILNOTT	TOILINET
EIILNQTU	QUINTILE
EIILNRSS	RESILINS
EIILNRST	NIRLIEST
	NITRILES
EIILNSSW	WILINESS
EIILNSTT	INTITLES
	LINTIEST
EIILNSTY	SENILITY
EIILNSVY	SYLVIINE
EIILNTTU	INTITULE
EIILNTUV	VITULINE
EIILOPPT	POPLITEI
EIILOPRS	LIRIOPES
EIILOPST	PISOLITE
	POLITIES
EIILORST	ROILIEST
EIILORTT	TROILITE
EIILOSST	SOILIEST
EIILOTVV	VOLITIVE
EIILPPRR	RIPPLIER
EIILPPRS	SLIPPIER
EIILPPST	LIPPIEST
EIILPRST	TRIPLIES
EIILPRSU	PLURISIE
EIILPRTT	TRIPLITE
EIILPSST	PITILESS
	SPILITES
EIILPSTY	PYELITIS
EIILPSUZ	SPUILZIE
EIILQSSU	SILIQUES
EIILRRSW	SWIRLIER
EIILRRTW	TWIRLIER
EIILRSTT	SLITTIER
	STILTIER
EIILRSTU	UTILISER
EIILRTUZ	UTILIZER
EIILSSTT	ELITISTS
	SILTIEST
EIILSSTU	ULITISES
	UTILISES
EIILSTUY	TUILYIES
EIILSTUZ	TUILZIES
	UTILIZES
EIIMMNNO	MENOMINI
EIIMMNNT	IMMINENT
	MINIMENT
EIIMMNSU	IMMUNISE
EIIMMNTU	IMMINUTE
EIIMMNUZ	IMMUNIZE
EIIMMPRU	IMPERIUM
EIIMMRSW	SWIMMIER
EIIMMSSS	SEISMISM

EIIMMSST	MIMSIEST
	MISTIMES
EIIMNOPT	PIMIENTO
EIIMNOSS	EMISSION
	SIMONIES
	SIMONISE
EIIMNOSV	VISNOMIE
EIIMNOSZ	SIMONIZE
EIIMNOTV	MONITIVE
EIIMNPRS	PRIMINES
EIIMNRSS	MIRINESS
	RIMINESS
EIIMNRST	INTERIMS
	MINISTER
	MISINTER
EIIMNRSV	MINIVERS
EIIMNRTT	INTERMIT
EIIMNRTX	INTERMIX
EIIMNSTT	MINTIEST
EIIMNSTU	MUTINIES
EIIMNSTV	MINIVETS
EIIMOPRX	MIREPOIX
EIIMOPSS	MISPOISE
EIIMOPST	OPTIMISE
EIIMOPSZ	EPIZOISM
EIIMOPTZ	OPTIMIZE
EIIMOSSS	SEMIOSIS
EIIMOSSV	OMISSIVE
EIIMOSTY	MOYITIES
EIIMOSUX	EXIMIOUS
EIIMOTVV	VOMITIVE
EIIMPRRS	PRIMSIER
EIIMPRSS	MISPRISE
	PISMIRES
EIIMPRSZ	MISPRIZE
EIIMPSST	PIETISMS
EIIMPSTW	WIMPIEST
EIIMQSTU	QUIETISM
EIIMRRRS	SMIRRIER
EIIMRSTT	METRITIS
EIIMRSTW	MISWRITE
EIIMSSSS	MISSISES
EIIMSSST	MISSIEST
EIIMSSSV	MISSIVES
EIIMSSSZ	SIZEISMS
EIIMSSTT	MISTIEST
	SEMITIST
EIINNNPS	NINEPINS
EIINNOOR	ONIONIER
EIINNOSS	INOSINES
EIINNOSU	UNIONISE
EIINNOSV	ENVISION
EIINNOUZ	UNIONIZE
EIINNPSS	SPINNIES
EIINNQSU	QUININES
EIINNRTV	INVERTIN
EIINNSST	TININESS
EIINNSSW	INSINEWS
EIINNSTT	TINNIEST
EIINNSTW	INTWINES
EIINOPRS	RIPIENOS
EIINOPRT	POINTIER
	POITRINE
EIINOPST	SINOPITE

EIINOPTT	PETITION	**EIIPPSTT**	TIPPIEST	**EIKLLMOO**	KILOMOLE
EIINORRT	INTERIOR	**EIIPPSTZ**	ZIPPIEST	**EIKLLMPU**	PLUMLIKE
EIINORSS	IONISERS	**EIIPPRRSS**	PRISSIER	**EIKLLMSS**	MILKLESS
	IRONISES	**EIIPRRST**	STRIPIER	**EIKLLNOR**	KNOLLIER
	SIRONISE	**EIIPRRSU**	SIRUPIER	**EIKLLNSW**	INKWELLS
EIINORST	IRONIEST	**EIIPRRTW**	TRIPWIRE	**EIKLLNUY**	UNLIKELY
EIINORSV	REVISION		TWIRPIER	**EIKLLNXY**	LYNXLIKE
	VISIONER	**EIIPRSSS**	PRISSIES	**EIKLLOOW**	WOOLLIKE
EIINORSZ	IONIZERS	**EIIPRSST**	SPIRIEST	**EIKLLORV**	OVERKILL
	IRONIZES	**EIIPRSTT**	RISPETTI	**EIKLLOSS**	SKOLLIES
	SIRONIZE		TRIPIEST	**EIKLLOSU**	SOULLIKE
EIINOSST	INOSITES	**EIIPRSTU**	PURITIES	**EIKLLRSS**	RESKILLS
	NOISIEST	**EIIPRSTV**	PREVISIT	**EIKLLSSS**	SKILLESS
EIINOSTV	NOVITIES		PRIVIEST	**EIKLLSST**	SKILLETS
EIINPPRS	SNIPPIER	**EIIPRSTY**	PYRITISE	**EIKLMNNS**	LINKSMEN
EIINPPSS	PIPINESS	**EIIPRSVV**	SPIVVIER	**EIKLMNOO**	MOONLIKE
EIINPPST	NIPPIEST	**EIIPRTYZ**	PYRITIZE	**EIKLMNOS**	MOLESKIN
EIINPRRS	INSPIRER	**EIIPSSTT**	PIETISTS	**EIKLMNRS**	KREMLINS
EIINPRSS	INSPIRES		STIPITES	**EIKLMORV**	OVERMILK
EIINPRST	PRISTINE		TIPSIEST	**EIKLMORW**	WORMLIKE
EIINPSST	SNIPIEST	**EIIPSSTW**	SWIPIEST	**EIKLMOSS**	MOSSLIKE
	SPINIEST		WISPIEST	**EIKLMPPU**	PUMPLIKE
EIINPSSX	PIXINESS	**EIIPSTTT**	PITTITES	**EIKLNOOR**	OERLIKON
EIINPSTZ	PINTSIZE	**EIIPSTTU**	PITUITES	**EIKLNOPR**	PLONKIER
EIINPTUV	PUNITIVE	**EIIQSTTU**	QUIETIST	**EIKLNOSW**	SNOWLIKE
EIINQRRU	INQUIRER	**EIIRRSTW**	WRISTIER	**EIKLNPRS**	PLINKERS
EIINQRSU	INQUIRES	**EIIRRSTV**	REVISITS		SPRINKLE
EIINQSSU	QUINSIES		VISITERS	**EIKLNPRU**	PLUNKIER
	SQUINIES	**EIIRSTTU**	UTERITIS	**EIKLNRRU**	KNURLIER
EIINQSTU	INQUIETS	**EIIRSTTW**	TWISTIER	**EIKLNRSS**	SLINKERS
EIINQTUY	EQUINITY	**EIIRSTTZ**	RITZIEST	**EIKLNRST**	LINKSTER
	INEQUITY	**EIISSSST**	SISSIEST		STRINKLE
EIINRRTW	WINTRIER	**EIISSSTZ**	SIZEISTS		TINKLERS
EIINRSST	INSISTER	**EIISSTTV**	STIVIEST	**EIKLNRSW**	WINKLERS
	SINISTER	**EIISTTTW**	WITTIEST		WRINKLES
EIINRSSW	WIRINESS	**EIJJNTUY**	JEJUNITY	**EIKLNRTW**	TWINKLER
EIINRSTT	NITRITES	**EIJKKSSU**	JUKSKEIS	**EIKLNSSS**	SKINLESS
	STINTIER	**EIJKNOSS**	JOKINESS	**EIKLNSST**	LENTISKS
EIINRSTU	NEURITIS	**EIJKNSTU**	JUNKIEST	**EIKLNSSY**	SKYLINES
	UNITISER	**EIJKORRS**	SKIJORER	**EIKLNSTT**	KNITTLES
EIINRSTV	INVITERS	**EIJLLORS**	JOLLIERS	**EIKLNSTW**	TWINKLES
	VINTRIES	**EIJLLOST**	JOLLIEST	**EIKLOOPR**	PLOOKIER
	VITRINES	**EIJLMTTU**	MULTIJET	**EIKLOORT**	ROOTLIKE
EIINRTUZ	UNITIZER	**EIJLOSTT**	JOLTIEST	**EIKLOPRU**	PLOUKIER
EIINRTVY	INVERITY	**EIJLOSTW**	JOWLIEST	**EIKLOPRW**	PILEWORK
EIINSSSZ	SIZINESS	**EIJMNPSS**	JIMPNESS	**EIKLOPSU**	SOUPLIKE
EIINSSTU	UNITISES	**EIJMPSTU**	JUMPIEST	**EIKLORTY**	KRYOLITE
EIINSTTT	NITTIEST	**EIJNORST**	JOINTERS	**EIKLOSSU**	LEUKOSIS
	TINTIEST	**EIJNORTU**	JOINTURE	**EIKLOSTY**	YOLKIEST
EIINSTTW	TWINIEST	**EIJNOSTT**	JETTISON	**EIKLPSSU**	PUSSLIKE
EIINSTUZ	UNITIZES	**EIJNPRSU**	JUNIPERS	**EIKLRSSS**	RISKLESS
EIIOPRRS	PRIORIES	**EIJNRRSU**	INJURERS	**EIKLRSST**	KLISTERS
EIIOPSTV	POSITIVE	**EIJNRRUY**	REINJURY	**EIKLRTUZ**	KLUTZIER
EIIORRST	RIOTRIES	**EIJNSTTW**	TWINJETS	**EIKLSSTT**	SKITTLES
EIIORSST	RIOTISES	**EIJRSTUY**	JESUITRY	**EIKLSSTU**	SULKIEST
EIIORSTZ	RIOTIZES	**EIJSSSUV**	JUSSIVES	**EIKLSTTT**	KITTLEST
EIIOSSTT	OSTEITIS	**EIKKLNOO**	NOOKLIKE	**EIKMMRRS**	KRIMMERS
	OTITISES	**EIKKLNOT**	KNOTLIKE	**EIKMMRSS**	SKIMMERS
EIIOSSTZ	ZOISITES	**EIKKLNRS**	KLINKERS	**EIKMNNOO**	MONOKINE
EIIOTTTV	TOTITIVE	**EIKKLSTU**	TUSKLIKE	**EIKMNORS**	MONIKERS
EIIPPPST	PIPPIEST	**EIKKNRSS**	SKINKERS	**EIKMNOST**	TOKENISM
EIIPPQRU	QUIPPIER	**EIKKNRSU**	SKUNKIER	**EIKMNOSU**	MOUSEKIN
EIIPPRRS	RIPPIERS	**EIKKOOST**	KOOKIEST	**EIKMOPSS**	MISSPOKE
EIIPPRRT	TRIPPIER	**EIKKSTUY**	YUKKIEST	**EIKMORTW**	TIMEWORK

EIKMOSST	SMOKIEST	EILLMOST	MELILOTS	EILMNRST	MINSTREL
EIKMOSSU	KOUMISES	EILLMPSS	MISSPELL	EILMNSSS	SLIMNESS
EIKMOSSY	MISYOKES		PSELLISM	EILMNSSU	EMULSINS
EIKMPSSU	MUSPIKES	EILLMPTU	MULTIPLE	EILMNSTU	MUSLINET
EIKMRRSS	SMIRKERS	EILLMSST	MISTELLS	EILMNTUY	MINUTELY
EIKMRSTU	MURKIEST	EILLMSTU	MULLITES		UNTIMELY
EIKMSSSU	KUMISSES	EILLMUVX	VEXILLUM	EILMOOPS	LIPOSOME
EIKMSSTU	MUSKIEST	EILLNOPT	PLOTLINE	EILMOORS	SLOOMIER
EIKNNORS	EINKORNS	EILLNOPY	EPYLLION	EILMOOST	TOILSOME
	NONSKIER	EILLNOST	STELLION	EILMOOSV	MOOLVIES
EIKNNOST	INKSTONE	EILLNOTU	LUTEOLIN	EILMOPRR	IMPLORER
EIKNNPSS	PINKNESS	EILLNPSW	PINSWELL	EILMOPRS	IMPLORES
EIKNNRSS	SKINNERS	EILLNPUU	LUPULINE		PELORISM
EIKNOORS	ROOINEKS	EILLNSST	LINTLESS	EILMOPST	MILEPOST
EIKNOOST	NOOKIEST	EILLNSTY	SILENTLY		POLEMIST
EIKNOPSS	POKINESS		TINSELLY	EILMORRS	LORIMERS
EIKNORST	INSTROKE	EILLNSUV	LEVULINS	EILMORSY	RIMOSELY
EIKNORSV	INVOKERS	EILLNSVY	SNIVELLY	EILMOSTT	MOTLIEST
EIKNORTT	KNOTTIER	EILLNUVY	UNLIVELY	EILMOSTU	OUTSMILE
EIKNOSTW	WONKIEST	EILLOORW	WOOLLIER	EILMOSUV	VOLUMISE
EIKNPRRS	PRINKERS	EILLOOSW	WOOLLIES	EILMOUVZ	VOLUMIZE
EIKNPRSU	SPUNKIER	EILLOPSS	SLIPSOLE	EILMPPRU	IMPURPLE
EIKNPRTU	TURNPIKE	EILLOPTY	POLITELY		PLUMPIER
EIKNPSSU	SPUNKIES	EILLORST	TRILLOES	EILMPRRU	RUMPLIER
EIKNPSTU	PUNKIEST		TROLLIES	EILMPRSS	SIMPLERS
EIKNRRTU	RETURNIK	EILLORSU	ROUILLES	EILMPRSU	SLUMPIER
EIKNRSST	STINKERS	EILLORSZ	ZORILLES	EILMPRUY	IMPURELY
EIKNRSSW	SWINKERS	EILLORWW	WILLOWER	EILMPSST	MISSPELT
EIKNRSTT	KNITTERS	EILLOSSS	SOILLESS		SIMPLEST
	TRINKETS	EILLOSST	TOILLESS	EILMPSSU	IMPULSES
EIKNSSSU	UNKISSES	EILLOSTW	LOWLIEST	EILMPSTU	LUMPIEST
EIKNSSTT	SKINTEST	EILLOSVW	LOWLIVES		PLUMIEST
EIKNSTUZ	KUNZITES	EILLPRSS	SPILLERS	EILMRSSU	MISRULES
EIKOOPRS	SPOOKIER	EILLPSSS	SLIPLESS	EILMRSSY	REMISSLY
EIKOORST	ROOKIEST	EILLQSTU	QUILLETS	EILMRSTU	MURLIEST
EIKOOSST	STOOKIES	EILLRRST	TRILLERS	EILMRSTY	LYMITERS
EIKOPPRS	PORKPIES	EILLRSST	STILLERS	EILMSSTU	LITMUSES
EIKOPPRW	PIPEWORK	EILLRSSW	SWILLERS	EILMSSTY	MISSTYLE
EIKOPRST	PORKIEST	EILLRSTT	TESTRILL	EILMSTUU	MULTIUSE
EIKOPRSV	OVERSKIP	EILLRSVY	SILVERLY	EILMSUUV	ELUVIUMS
EIKORRWW	WIREWORK	EILLSSST	LISTLESS	EILMTTUU	LUTETIUM
EIKPPRSS	SKIPPERS		SLITLESS	EILMTTUY	MULTEITY
EIKPPSST	SKIPPETS	EILLSSTT	STILLEST	EILNNORS	ONLINERS
EIKPRRSU	SPRUIKER	EILLSTTT	LITTLEST	EILNNOST	INSOLENT
EIKRRSST	SKIRRETS	EILLSTUV	VITELLUS	EILNNOSV	NONLIVES
	SKIRTERS	EILMMNOS	MOLIMENS	EILNNOSW	SNOWLINE
	STRIKERS	EILMMPRU	PLUMMIER	EILNNOTT	NONTITLE
EIKRRSSU	SKURRIES	EILMMRSS	SLIMMERS	EILNNOTV	VINOLENT
EIKRSSTT	SKITTERS	EILMMRSU	SLUMMIER	EILNNPSU	PINNULES
EIKRSSTU	TURKISES	EILMMSST	SLIMMEST	EILNNSSU	LUNINESS
EIKRSTTY	SKITTERY	EILMMSTU	LUMMIEST	EILNNSTU	UNSILENT
EIKRSTWY	SKYWRITE	EILMNOOS	OINOMELS	EILNNTTY	INTENTLY
EIKSSTTU	TUSKIEST		SIMOLEON	EILNOOPP	EPIPLOON
EILLLNOY	LONELILY	EILMNOPT	PILOTMEN	EILNOOPS	POLONIES
EILLLOVY	LOVELILY	EILMNORS	MISENROL		POLONISE
EILLLPUV	PULVILLE	EILMNOST	MOLINETS	EILNOOPZ	POLONIZE
EILLMNNO	MONELLIN	EILMNOSU	EMULSION	EILNOOST	LOONIEST
EILLMNOS	SEMILLON	EILMNOSV	NOVELISM		OILSTONE
EILLMNOU	LINOLEUM	EILMNOTU	MOULINET	EILNOOSV	VIOLONES
EILLMNQU	QUILLMEN	EILMNOTY	MYLONITE	EILNOPPS	PLENIPOS
EILLMNST	STILLMEN	EILMNPSS	LIMPNESS	EILNOPPY	POLYPINE
EILLMNSU	MULLEINS		PLENISMS	EILNOPRS	PLERIONS
EILLMOPR	IMPELLOR	EILMNPSU	SPLENIUM		PROLINES
EILLMOPS	PLIMSOLE	EILMNPTU	TUMPLINE	EILNOPRT	TERPINOL

	TOPLINER	EILOPPPR	POPPLIER	EILPRSTT	SPLITTER
EILNOPRU	NEUROPIL	EILOPPRS	SLOPPIER		TRIPLETS
EILNOPSS	EPSILONS	EILOPPST	LOPPIEST	EILPRSTY	PRIESTLY
EILNOPST	POINTELS	EILOPPTY	POLYPITE		SPRITELY
	PONTILES	EILOPRRT	PORTLIER	EILPRSUU	PURLIEUS
	POTLINES	EILOPRSS	SPOILERS	EILPRSUY	PLEURISY
	TOPLINES	EILOPRST	POITRELS	EILPRTTY	PRETTILY
EILNOPTU	UNPOLITE	EILOPRSU	PERILOUS	EILPSSSU	PUSSLIES
EILNOPTY	LINOTYPE	EILOPRSV	OVERSLIP	EILPSSTT	SPITTLES
EILNORRS	LORINERS		SLIPOVER	EILPSSTU	STIPULES
EILNORRT	RITORNEL	EILOPRSY	PYROLISE	EILPSSUY	SPULYIES
EILNORSS	IRONLESS	EILOPRTT	PLOTTIER	EILPSSUZ	SPULZIES
EILNORST	RETINOLS	EILOPRTW	PILEWORT	EILQRRSU	SQUIRREL
EILNORTT	TROTLINE	EILOPRYZ	PYROLIZE	EILQRSTU	QUILTERS
EILNORTU	OUTLINER	EILOPSSS	PSILOSES	EILQRSUU	LIQUEURS
EILNORTW	TOWNLIER	EILOPSST	PISTOLES	EILQRSUY	SQUIRELY
EILNORVV	INVOLVER		PTILOSES	EILQSTUU	LUSTIQUE
EILNOSSU	ELUSIONS		SLOPIEST	EILRRSSU	SLURRIES
EILNOSSW	LEWISSON	EILOPSSV	PLOSIVES	EILRRSTU	SULTRIER
EILNOSTU	ELUTIONS	EILOPSTT	PISTOLET	EILRRSTW	TWIRLERS
	OUTLINES		PLOTTIES	EILRRTWY	WRITERLY
EILNOSTV	NOVELIST		POLITEST	EILRSSST	STIRLESS
	VIOLENTS	EILOPSTU	SOUTPIEL	EILRSSTT	SLITTERS
EILNOSTW	TOWLINES	EILOPSTX	EXPLOITS		STILTERS
EILNOSUV	EVULSION	EILOPSUV	PLUVIOSE		TESTRILS
EILNOSVV	INVOLVES	EILORRTU	ULTERIOR	EILRSSTU	SURLIEST
EILNOTUV	INVOLUTE	EILORSSS	RISSOLES	EILRSSTV	LISTSERV
EILNOTXY	XYLONITE	EILORSST	ESTRIOLS	EILRSSTY	SISTERLY
EILNOTYZ	ZYLONITE	EILORSSU	SOILURES		STYLISER
EILNPRSS	PILSNERS	EILORSTT	TRIOLETS	EILRSSUV	SURVEILS
EILNPRST	SPLINTER	EILORSTU	LOURIEST	EILRSSZZ	SIZZLERS
EILNPRSU	PURLINES		OUTLIERS	EILRSTTU	SLUTTIER
EILNPRUY	UNRIPELY	EILORSUV	RIVULOSE		SURTITLE
EILNPSSS	SPINLESS	EILORSZZ	SOZZLIER	EILRSTTW	WRISTLET
EILNPSST	PLENISTS	EILORTTY	TOILETRY	EILRSTTZ	STRELITZ
EILNPSSU	SPINULES	EILORTUV	OUTLIVER	EILRSTUV	RIVULETS
	SPLENIUS	EILORVWY	OVERWILY	EILRSTYZ	STYLIZER
EILNPSUV	SUPINELY	EILOSSST	LOSSIEST	EILRSUUX	LUXURIES
EILNQUUY	UNIQUELY	EILOSSTU	LOUSIEST	EILRSWZZ	SWIZZLER
EILNRRUU	UNRULIER	EILOSTTT	STILETTO	EILSSSTY	STYLISES
EILNRSST	SLINTERS	EILOSTUV	OUTLIVES	EILSSTTU	LUSTIEST
	SNIRTLES		SOLUTIVE	EILSSTTY	STYLIEST
EILNRSTU	INSULTER	EILOSTUW	OUTWILES		STYLITES
	LUSTRINE	EILOTVVY	VOTIVELY	EILSSTUU	LITUUSES
EILNRSTY	TINSELRY	EILPPPRY	PREPPILY	EILSSTVY	SYLVITES
EILNRTUV	VIRULENT	EILPPRRS	RIPPLERS	EILSSTYZ	STYLIZES
EILNRTWY	WINTERLY	EILPPRRT	TRIPPLER	EILSSWZZ	SWIZZLES
EILNSSTT	TINTLESS	EILPPRRU	PURPLIER	EILSTWZZ	TWIZZLES
EILNSSTU	UTENSILS	EILPPRSS	SLIPPERS	EIMMMNOT	IMMOMENT
EILNSSTW	WESTLINS	EILPPRST	PRESPLIT	EIMMMORZ	MOMZERIM
EILNSSVY	SYLVINES		RIPPLETS	EIMMNNOT	MONIMENT
EILNSTTU	LUTENIST		STIPPLER	EIMMNNTU	MUNIMENT
EILNSUWY	UNWISELY		TIPPLERS	EIMMNORS	MISNOMER
EILOOPRR	POORLIER		TRIPPLES	EIMMOPRU	EMPORIUM
EILOOPST	LOOPIEST	EILPPRSU	PERIPLUS	EIMMOPST	METOPISM
EILOOPTZ	ZOPILOTE		SUPPLIER	EIMMOSSV	MISMOVES
EILOORST	OESTRIOL	EILPPRSY	SLIPPERY	EIMMOSTT	TOTEMISM
	TROOLIES	EILPPRTU	PULPITER	EIMMPRRS	PRIMMERS
EILOORTV	OVERTOIL	EILPPSST	STIPPLES	EIMMPRST	PRIMMEST
EILOOSST	OSTIOLES	EILPPSSU	SUPPLIES	EIMMPRSU	PREMIUMS
	STOOLIES	EILPPSSW	SWIPPLES	EIMMPSSU	PESSIMUM
EILOOSTW	WOOLIEST	EILPPSTU	PULPIEST	EIMMRRST	TRIMMERS
EILOOSTY	OTIOSELY	EILPRSST	RESPLITS	EIMMRSST	MISTERMS
EILOOSTZ	ZOOLITES		SPIRTLES	EIMMRSSW	SWIMMERS

EIMMRSTT	TRIMMEST
EIMMRSTU	RUMMIEST
EIMMSSTU	MUMSIEST
EIMMSTUY	YUMMIEST
EIMNNOOT	NOONTIME
EIMNNOPT	IMPONENT
	PIMENTON
	POINTMEN
EIMNNOST	MENTIONS
EIMNNOTT	OINTMENT
EIMNNOUY	EUONYMIN
EIMNOOPS	EMPOISON
EIMNOORS	IONOMERS
	MOONRISE
EIMNOORT	MOTIONER
	REMOTION
EIMNOORV	OMNIVORE
EIMNOOSS	ISONOMES
	MONOSIES
EIMNOOST	EMOTIONS
	MOONIEST
EIMNOOSX	EXOMIONS
EIMNOPPU	PEPONIUM
EIMNOPRS	PROMINES
EIMNOPRT	ORPIMENT
EIMNOPSS	MOPINESS
	PEONISMS
EIMNOPST	EMPTIONS
	NEPOTISM
	PIMENTOS
EIMNOPTT	IMPOTENT
EIMNOPTV	PIVOTMEN
EIMNORSS	MERSIONS
EIMNORSU	INERMOUS
	MONSIEUR
EIMNORSW	WINSOMER
EIMNORTW	TIMEWORN
EIMNORTY	ENORMITY
EIMNOSST	MESTINOS
	MOISTENS
	SENTIMOS
EIMNPRSS	PRIMNESS
EIMNPSST	MISSPENT
EIMNPSTU	NUMPTIES
EIMNRSST	ENTRISMS
	MINSTERS
	TRIMNESS
EIMNRSSU	NEURISMS
EIMNRSTU	MUNTRIES
	TERMINUS
	UNMITERS
	UNMITRES
EIMNRSTY	ENTRYISM
	MISENTRY
EIMNSSSS	SENSISMS
EIMNSSTU	MISTUNES
EIMNSTTU	MINUTEST
EIMNSUZZ	MUEZZINS
EIMOORST	MOORIEST
	MOTORISE
	ROOMIEST
EIMOORTZ	MOTORIZE
EIMOOSST	OSTOMIES
EIMOPPRR	IMPROPER

EIMOPPST	MOPPIEST
EIMOPRRS	PRIMEROS
	PRIMROSE
	PROMISER
EIMOPRRT	IMPORTER
	REIMPORT
EIMOPRRV	IMPROVER
EIMOPRSS	IMPOSERS
	PROMISES
	SEMIPROS
EIMOPRST	IMPOSTER
EIMOPRSV	IMPROVES
EIMOPRSW	IMPOWERS
EIMOPRUU	EUROPIUM
EIMOPSST	STOMPIES
EIMOPSTY	PEYOTISM
EIMOQSTU	MISQUOTE
EIMORRSS	MORRISES
EIMORRST	MORTISER
	STORMIER
EIMORRTT	REMITTOR
EIMORRTV	OVERTRIM
EIMORRWW	WIREWORM
EIMORSST	EROTISMS
	MORTISES
	TRISOMES
EIMORSSV	VERISMOS
EIMORSTT	OMITTERS
EIMORSTU	MISROUTE
	MOISTURE
EIMORSTV	VOMITERS
EIMORSTW	MISWROTE
	WORMIEST
EIMORSTY	ISOMETRY
EIMORSVW	OVERSWIM
EIMORTXY	OXIMETRY
EIMOSSST	MOSSIEST
EIMOSSTT	MOISTEST
EIMOSSTU	MOUSIEST
EIMOSSTX	EXOTISMS
EIMOSSTZ	MESTIZOS
EIMOSSYZ	ISOZYMES
EIMOSTTT	MOTTIEST
	TOTEMIST
EIMOSTTU	TIMEOUTS
	TITMOUSE
EIMPRRST	PRETRIMS
EIMPRRSU	PRIMEURS
EIMPRSST	IMPRESTS
EIMPRSSU	PRIMUSES
EIMPRSTU	IMPUREST
	IMPUTERS
	STUMPIER
EIMPSSST	MISSTEPS
EIMPSSTU	SPUMIEST
	STUMPIES
EIMPSSTY	EMPTYSIS
	MISTYPES
EIMPSTTU	TUMPIEST
EIMQRRSU	SQUIRMER
EIMQSSTU	MESQUITS
EIMQSTUY	MYSTIQUE
EIMQSTUZ	MEZQUITS
EIMRRRSU	SMURRIER

EIMRRSSU	SURMISER
EIMRSSST	MISTRESS
EIMRSSSU	MISUSERS
	SURMISES
EIMRSSTT	METRISTS
EIMRSSTY	SMYTRIES
EIMRSSUU	MIURUSES
EIMRSTTU	SMUTTIER
EIMRSTUV	VITREUMS
EIMRSTUX	MIXTURES
EIMSSSSU	MISSUSES
EIMSSSTU	MUSSIEST
EIMSSTTU	MUSTIEST
EIMSTUZZ	MUZZIEST
EINNNORT	NONINERT
EINNOOTX	NEOTOXIN
EINNOPPT	PENPOINT
EINNOPRU	PREUNION
EINNOPRY	PYRONINE
EINNOPSS	PENSIONS
EINNOQSU	QUINONES
EINNORSS	IRONNESS
EINNORST	INTONERS
	NOINTERS
	TERNIONS
EINNORSU	REUNIONS
EINNORSV	ENVIRONS
EINNORTT	TONTINER
EINNORTU	NEUTRINO
EINNORTV	INVENTOR
	NOVERINT
EINNORWW	WINNOWER
EINNOSSS	NOSINESS
EINNOSST	TENSIONS
EINNOSSU	NONISSUE
	UNSONSIE
EINNOSSV	VENISONS
EINNOSTT	TINSTONE
	TONTINES
EINNOSTU	NOUNIEST
EINNPRSS	SPINNERS
EINNPRST	ENPRINTS
EINNPRSY	SPINNERY
EINNPSST	SPINNETS
EINNPSSU	PUNINESS
EINNPSSY	SPINNEYS
EINNPSTU	PUNNIEST
EINNPSXY	SIXPENNY
EINNRSTU	RUNNIEST
	STURNINE
EINNRSTV	VINTNERS
EINNRTTU	NUTRIENT
EINNSSTT	TENNISTS
EINNSSTU	SUNNIEST
EINNSSUW	UNSINEWS
EINNSSWY	SWINNEYS
EINNSTUW	UNTWINES
EINOOPRS	POISONER
	SNOOPIER
	SPOONIER
EINOOPSS	OPSONISE
	SPOONIES
EINOOPSZ	OPSONIZE
EINOORSS	EROSIONS

EINOORST	SNOOTIER	EINOSTUU	TENUIOUS	EIOOSTWZ	WOOZIEST
EINOORSW	SWOONIER	EINOSTVY	VENOSITY	EIOPPPST	POPPIEST
EINOORSZ	OZONISER	EINPPRRT	PREPRINT	EIOPPRTW	PIPEWORT
	SNOOZIER	EINPPRSS	SNIPPERS	EIOPPSST	SOPPIEST
EINOORZZ	OZONIZER	EINPPSST	SNIPPETS	EIOPPTTY	TIPPYTOE
EINOOSST	ISOTONES	EINPPSTY	SNIPPETY	EIOPQRSU	PIROQUES
EINOOSSZ	OOZINESS	EINPRRST	PRINTERS	EIOPQSTU	POSTIQUE
	OZONISES		REPRINTS	EIOPRRSS	PRIORESS
EINOOSTW	TWOONIES		SPRINTER	EIOPRRST	PIERROTS
EINOOSTZ	ZOONITES	EINPRRTU	PRURIENT		SPORTIER
EINOOSZZ	OZONIZES	EINPRRTY	PRINTERY	EIOPRRSU	SUPERIOR
EINOOTXX	EXOTOXIN	EINPRSST	SPINSTER	EIOPRRSV	PREVISOR
EINOPPRS	POPERINS	EINPRSTU	REPUNITS	EIOPRRTV	OVERTRIP
	PROPINES		UNPRIEST	EIOPRSSS	PROSSIES
EINOPRRS	PRISONER		UNRIPEST	EIOPRSST	PERIOSTS
EINOPRSS	PORINESS	EINPRTTU	INPUTTER		PROSIEST
	PRESSION	EINPSTTX	SPINTEXT		PROSTIES
	ROPINESS	EINPSTTY	TINTYPES		REPOSITS
EINOPRST	POINTERS	EINQRSTU	SQUINTER		RIPOSTES
	PORNIEST	EINQRTTU	QUITRENT		SPORTIES
	PROTEINS	EINQSSTU	INQUESTS		TRIPOSES
	REPOINTS	EINQSTTU	QUINTETS	EIOPRSTT	PORTIEST
	TROPINES	EINQSTUU	UNIQUEST		RISPETTO
EINOPRSU	PRUINOSE		UNQUIETS		SPOTTIER
EINOPRSV	OVERSPIN	EINQTTTU	QUINTETT	EIOPRSTU	ROUPIEST
	PROVINES	EINRRSSU	INSURERS		SPOUTIER
EINOPRTU	ERUPTION	EINRSSST	INSTRESS	EIOPRSTV	OVERTIPS
EINOPSSW	WINESOPS	EINRSSSU	SUNRISES		PIVOTERS
EINOPSTT	NEPOTIST	EINRSSTT	ENTRISTS		SORPTIVE
EINOPSTU	POUTINES		STINTERS		SPORTIVE
EINOPSWX	SWINEPOX	EINRSSXY	SYRINXES	EIOPRSUV	PERVIOUS
EINOQSTU	QUESTION	EINRSTTU	RUNTIEST		PREVIOUS
EINOQTTU	QUOTIENT	EINRSTTW	TWINTERS		VIPEROUS
EINORRSS	ROSINERS	EINRSTTY	ENTRYIST	EIOPRTTT	TRIPTOTE
EINORRST	INTRORSE	EINRSTUV	UNRIVETS	EIOPRTTY	PETITORY
	SNORTIER		VENTURIS	EIOPRTUZ	OUTPRIZE
EINORRTV	INVERTOR	EINRSTUW	UNWRITES	EIOPSSST	SEPIOSTS
EINORRTW	INTERROW	EINRTUUV	UNVIRTUE	EIOPSSSU	POUSSIES
EINORSSS	ROSINESS	EINSSSST	SENSISTS	EIOPSSTT	SPOTTIES
EINORSST	OESTRINS	EINSSTTU	NUTSIEST	EIOPSSTU	SOUPIEST
	TERSIONS	EINSSTTW	ENTWISTS	EIOPSSTX	EXPOSITS
EINORSSU	NEUROSIS		TWINSETS	EIOPSSTY	ISOTYPES
	RESINOUS	EINSSTUW	UNWISEST	EIOPSTTT	POTTIEST
EINORSSV	VERSIONS	EINSSTUX	UNSEXIST	EIOPSTTU	POUTIEST
EINORSTT	SNOTTIER	EINSSTXY	SYNTEXIS	EIOPSTTY	PEYOTIST
	TENORIST	EINSTTTU	NUTTIEST	EIOPSTUW	WIPEOUTS
	TRITONES	EINSTTTW	TWITTENS	EIOQRSTU	QUOITERS
EINORSTU	ROUTINES	EIOOPPRS	PORPOISE	EIOQSTUX	QUIXOTES
	SNOUTIER	EIOOPPST	OPPOSITE	EIORRRST	ERRORIST
EINORSTV	INVESTOR	EIOOPRST	PORTOISE		TERROIRS
EINORSTY	SEROTINY		ROOPIEST	EIORRRSW	WORRIERS
	TYROSINE	EIOOPRSW	SWOOPIER	EIORRRTU	ROTURIER
EINORSTZ	TRIZONES	EIOOPSST	ISOTOPES	EIORRSST	RESISTOR
EINORSUV	SOUVENIR	EIOOPSTV	POOVIEST		ROISTERS
EINORTTU	RITENUTO	EIOOPTYZ	EPIZOOTY		SORRIEST
EINOSSSS	SESSIONS	EIOORRSS	SORORISE	EIORRSSV	REVISORS
EINOSSST	SONSIEST	EIOORRST	ROOTSIER	EIORRSTT	RORTIEST
	STENOSIS	EIOORRSZ	SORORIZE	EIORRSTU	STOURIER
EINOSSTT	SNOTTIES	EIOORSTT	ROOTIEST	EIORRSTV	OVERSTIR
	STONIEST		TORTOISE		SERVITOR
EINOSSTW	SNOWIEST	EIOOSSST	OSTEOSIS	EIORRSUV	OUVRIERS
EINOSTTT	TOTIENTS	EIOOSSTT	SOOTIEST		REOVIRUS
EINOSTTW	NOWTIEST		TOOTSIES	EIORRSVV	REVIVORS
	TOWNIEST	EIOOSTTZ	ZOOTIEST	EIORRSVY	REVISORY

Code	Word(s)
EIORRTTU	TROUTIER
EIORSSTT	STOITERS
EIORSSTY	SEROSITY
EIORSTTU	TOUSTIER
	TUTORISE
EIORSTTV	VIRETOTS
EIORSTTW	SWOTTIER
EIORSTUV	VIRTUOSE
	VITREOUS
	VOITURES
EIORTTUW	OUTWRITE
EIORTTUZ	TUTORIZE
EIOSSSTT	TOSSIEST
EIOSSTTT	STOTTIES
EIOSSTTU	TOUSIEST
EIOSSTTW	TOWSIEST
EIOSSTUZ	OUTSIZES
EIOSTTTT	TOTTIEST
EIOSTTTU	TOUTIEST
EIOSTTUZ	TOUZIEST
EIOSTTWZ	TOWZIEST
EIPPQRSU	QUIPPERS
EIPPRRST	STRIPPER
	TRIPPERS
EIPPRRSY	PERSPIRY
EIPPRRTY	TRIPPERY
EIPPRSTT	TRIPPETS
EIPQRSTU	QUIPSTER
EIPRRRSU	SPURRIER
EIPRRSST	STRIPERS
EIPRRSSU	SPURRIES
	SURPRISE
	UPRISERS
EIPRRSTZ	SPRITZER
EIPRRSUV	UPRIVERS
EIPRRSUY	SYRUPIER
EIPRRSUZ	SURPRIZE
EIPRSSST	PERSISTS
EIPRSSSU	SUSPIRES
EIPRSSTT	SPITTERS
	TIPSTERS
EIPRSSTU	PURSIEST
EIPRSSTZ	SPRITZES
EIPRSTTU	PURTIEST
	PUTTIERS
EIPRSUVW	PURVIEWS
EIPRSVVY	SPIVVERY
EIPSSSTU	PUSSIEST
EIPSSTXY	PTYXISES
EIQRRSTU	SQUIRTER
EIQRSSSU	SQUIRESS
EIQRSSTU	QUERISTS
EIQRSTTU	QUITTERS
EIQRSTUU	SEQUITUR
EIQRSUZZ	QUIZZERS
EIQRUYZZ	QUIZZERY
EIQSSUZZ	SQUIZZES
EIRRRSST	STIRRERS
EIRRSSTV	STRIVERS
EIRRSTTU	TRUSTIER
EIRRSUVV	SURVIVER
EIRSSSTU	SUITRESS
	TSURISES
EIRSSTTU	RUSTIEST
	TRUSTIES
EIRSSTTW	RETWISTS
	TWISTERS
EIRSSTUV	REVUISTS
	STUIVERS
EIRSSUVV	SURVIVES
EIRSSUVW	SURVIEWS
EIRSTTTU	RUTTIEST
EIRSTTTW	TWITTERS
EIRSTTUX	TUTRIXES
EIRTTTWY	TWITTERY
EIRTTUWZ	WURTZITE
EISSSSTU	TUSSISES
EISSSTUW	WUSSIEST
EISSTTUW	WETSUITS
EISTTTUV	VUTTIEST
EJLLORSY	JOLLYERS
EJLOPSTU	PULSOJET
EJLORSST	JOSTLERS
EJLRSSUY	JURYLESS
EJMOPRUV	OVERJUMP
EJNORRSU	REJOURNS
EJNORSUY	JOURNEYS
EJNRSTUU	UNJUSTER
EJNSSSTU	JUSTNESS
EJOORSVY	OVERJOYS
EJOPPRST	PROPJETS
EJOPRSTT	JETPORTS
EJORSSTU	JOUSTERS
EJORSTUV	OVERJUST
EJOSSTTU	OUTJESTS
EKKLNPRU	KERPLUNK
EKKLOOSY	OLYKOEKS
EKKLOOSZ	KOLKOZES
EKKLRSSU	SKULKERS
EKKMORSY	KROMESKY
EKLLMSSU	SKELLUMS
EKLLNORS	KNOLLERS
EKLLOSSY	KYLLOSES
	YOLKLESS
EKLLRRSU	KRULLERS
EKLNOOOR	ONLOOKER
EKLNOPRS	PLONKERS
EKLNORSS	SNORKELS
EKLNOSST	KNOTLESS
EKLNPRSU	PLUNKERS
EKLNPSSU	SPELUNKS
EKLOOORV	LOOKOVER
	OVERLOOK
EKLOOPSW	SLOWPOKE
EKLORSSW	WORKLESS
EKLOSSTV	STOKVELS
EKLSSSTU	TUSKLESS
EKLSSTTU	SKUTTLES
EKMMORSU	MURKSOME
EKMMRSSU	SKUMMERS
EKMNOSSU	MUSKONES
EKMNOSUX	MUSKOXEN
EKMOOPRR	MOREPORK
EKMOOPST	SMOKEPOT
EKMOORSW	WORKSOME
EKMOOSSS	KOSMOSES
EKMOOSTU	OUTSMOKE
EKMOSSUY	KOUMYSES
EKMRSTUY	MUSKETRY
EKNNOORT	KENOTRON
EKNNOPSU	UNSPOKEN
EKNOOPRW	OPENWORK
EKNOORSS	SNOOKERS
EKNOORST	STROOKEN
EKNOPPSU	UPSPOKEN
EKNOPSSY	PYKNOSES
EKNORSST	STONKERS
EKNORSTT	KNOTTERS
EKNORSTW	NETWORKS
EKNORSUY	YOUNKERS
EKNRSTUY	TURNKEYS
EKOOOPRT	POKEROOT
EKOOORTV	OVERTOOK
EKOOPRRV	PROVOKER
EKOOPRRW	ROPEWORK
EKOOPRSV	PROVOKES
EKOOPRSY	SPOOKERY
EKOOPSTU	OUTSPOKE
EKOORRVW	OVERWORK
EKOORSST	STOOKERS
	STROOKES
EKOORSTW	KOTOWERS
EKOORSUU	EUROKOUS
EKOORTWW	KOWTOWER
EKOPRRSW	PREWORKS
EKOPRSTU	UPSTROKE
EKOPRSUY	KOUPREYS
EKORRSST	STROKERS
EKORRUVY	KURVEYOR
EKORSSTU	KURTOSES
EKORSTWY	SKYWROTE
EKPPSSUU	SEPPUKUS
ELLLMOWY	MELLOWLY
ELLLNSUY	SULLENLY
ELLLORRS	LORRELLS
ELLLOWYY	YELLOWLY
ELLMNOOS	MOELLONS
ELLMNOSY	SOLEMNLY
ELLMNOTY	MOLTENLY
ELLMNOUW	UNMELLOW
ELLMNPUY	LUMPENLY
ELLMOORS	MORELLOS
ELLMORRS	MORRELLS
ELLMOSTU	OUTSMELL
ELLMPSUU	PLUMULES
ELLNNOST	TONNELLS
ELLNNSSU	NULLNESS
ELLNOORV	LOVELORN
ELLNOOSW	WOOLLENS
ELLNOPRU	PRUNELLO
ELLNOSST	STOLLENS
ELLNOSSU	NOUSELLS
ELLNOSVY	SLOVENLY
ELLNOSXY	XYLENOLS
ELLNOUVY	UNLOVELY
ELLNPSSU	UNSPELLS
ELLOORRV	ROLLOVER
ELLOOSST	TOOLLESS
ELLOOSSW	WOOSELLS
ELLOOSTU	TOLUOLES
ELLOPRRS	PROLLERS
ELLOPRST	POLLSTER

Eight-letter anagrams

Code	Word(s)
ELLOPRTU	POLLUTER
ELLOPRUV	PULLOVER
ELLOPSST	PLOTLESS
ELLOPSTU	OUTSPELL
	POLLUTES
ELLORRST	STROLLER
	TROLLERS
ELLORSTY	TROLLEYS
ELLOSSSS	LOSSLESS
ELLOSSSU	SOULLESS
ELLOSSTU	OUTSELLS
	SELLOUTS
ELLOSSYY	LYOLYSES
ELLOSTTU	OUTTELLS
ELLOSTUW	OUTSWELL
	OUTWELLS
ELLOSTUY	OUTYELLS
ELLPPSSU	PULPLESS
ELLPPSUY	SUPPLELY
ELLPSSUW	UPSWELLS
ELLSSSTU	LUSTLESS
ELMMNOTU	LOMENTUM
ELMMNOTY	MOMENTLY
ELMMOPSU	PUMMELOS
ELMMORST	TROMMELS
ELMMOSUX	LUMMOXES
ELMMPSTU	PLUMMEST
	PLUMMETS
ELMMRSSU	SLUMMERS
ELMMRSTU	STRUMMEL
	TUMMLERS
ELMMRSUY	SUMMERLY
ELMMSSTU	STUMMELS
ELMNNOSU	UNSOLEMN
ELMNNOTU	UNMOLTEN
ELMNOOOP	MONOPOLE
ELMNOOSS	MOONLESS
ELMNOOST	MOONLETS
ELMNOPSU	PULMONES
ELMNORSS	NORMLESS
ELMNOSTW	SNOWMELT
ELMNPPSU	PLUMPENS
ELMNPSUU	UNPLUMES
ELMNUUZZ	UNMUZZLE
ELMOOPPS	POMPELOS
ELMOOPSY	POLYSOME
ELMOORST	TREMOLOS
ELMOORSY	MOROSELY
ELMOOSSY	LYSOSOME
ELMOPRSY	POLYMERS
ELMOPRTY	METOPRYL
ELMOPRVY	POLYMERY
ELMOPSYY	POLYSEMY
ELMORSSU	EMULSORS
ELMORSTT	MOTTLERS
ELMORSTU	MOULTERS
ELMORUUV	VERMOULU
ELMOSTTU	OUTSMELT
ELMOSTUU	TUMULOSE
ELMOSYYZ	LYSOZYME
ELMPPRSU	PLUMPERS
ELMPPSSU	PUMPLESS
ELMPPSTU	PLUMPEST
ELMPRSSU	RUMPLESS
ELMRRTUU	MULTURER
ELMRSTUU	MULTURES
ELMRSUZZ	MUZZLERS
ELNNNOOV	NONNOVEL
ELNNOOSU	UNLOOSEN
ELNNOPUS	NONUPLES
ELNNOPTU	NONUPLET
ELNNORSS	LORNNESS
ELNNOSSU	NOUNLESS
ELNNOSTY	NONSTYLE
ELNNRSTU	TRUNNELS
ELNOOPPR	PROPENOL
ELNOOPST	PELOTONS
ELNOOSST	SOLONETS
ELNOOSSU	UNLOOSES
ELNOOSSZ	SNOOZLES
ELNOOSTZ	SOLONETZ
ELNOPPRY	PROPENYL
ELNOPRVY	PROVENLY
ELNOPSTU	PLEUSTON
ELNOPTTY	POTENTLY
ELNOPTYY	POLYTENY
ELNORSSU	NOURSLES
ELNORSTU	TURNSOLE
ELNORSVY	SLOVENRY
ELNORTTY	ROTTENLY
ELNOSSST	LOSTNESS
ELNOSSSW	SLOWNESS
	SNOWLESS
ELNOSSTV	SOLVENTS
ELNOSSTW	TOWNLESS
	WONTLESS
ELNOSTTW	TOWNLETS
ELNOSTUZ	ZONULES
ELNOSUVV	VENULOUS
ELNOSUVY	VENOUSLY
ELNPPSUU	UNSUPPLE
ELNPRTUU	PURULENT
ELNPRUUY	UNPURELY
ELNPUUZZ	UNPUZZLE
ELNRSUUY	UNSURELY
ELNRSUZZ	NUZZLERS
ELNSSUZZ	SNUZZLES
ELOOPPRY	POLYPORE
ELOOPRSS	RESPOOLS
	SPOOLERS
ELOOPRSU	SUPERLOO
ELOOPRTV	OVERPLOT
ELOOPRUW	OWERLOUP
ELOOPSSS	SESSPOOL
ELOORSST	ROOTLESS
ELOORSTT	ROOTLETS
	TOOTLERS
ELOORSTU	TORULOSE
ELOORSUV	OVERSOUL
ELOORSWL	OVERSLOW
ELOOSSST	SOOTLESS
ELOOSSTT	TOOLSETS
ELOOSSTU	OUTSOLES
ELOOSSWY	WOOLSEYS
ELOOSTUV	OUTLOVES
ELOOSVVX	VOLVOXES
ELOPPRRY	PROPERLY
ELOPPSST	STOPPLES
ELOPPTYY	POLYTYPE
ELOPRRSU	PROULERS
ELOPRRSW	PROWLERS
ELOPRRSY	PYRROLES
ELOPRRTY	PORTERLY
ELOPRSSS	PLESSORS
ELOPRSST	PORTLESS
ELOPRSSU	SPORULES
ELOPRSTT	PLOTTERS
ELOPRSTU	PLOUTERS
	POULTERS
ELOPRSTW	PLOWTERS
ELOPRSTY	PROSTYLE
	PROTYLES
ELOPRSUV	OVERPLUS
ELOPRSYY	PYROLYSE
ELOPRXYY	PYROXYLE
ELOPRYYZ	PYROLYZE
ELOPSSST	SPOTLESS
	STOPLESS
ELOPSSSU	SOUPLESS
ELOPSSTY	STYLOPES
ELOPSSUU	OPULUSES
ELOPSTTU	OUTSLEPT
	OUTSPELT
ELOPSTUY	OUTYELPS
ELORSSTT	SETTLORS
	SLOTTERS
ELORSTUY	ELYTROUS
	SOUTERLY
	UROSTYLE
ELORTTTU	TROUTLET
ELOSSSTY	SYSTOLES
ELOSSTUU	SETULOUS
ELOSSWZZ	SWOZZLES
ELPPRSTU	PURPLEST
ELPPRSUY	RESUPPLY
ELPPSSTU	SUPPLEST
ELPRRSSU	SLURPERS
ELPRSSSU	SPURLESS
ELPRSSTU	SPURTLES
ELPRSTTU	SPLUTTER
ELPRSTUU	PULTURES
ELPRSUZZ	PUZZLERS
ELPSSSUY	PUSSLEYS
ELPSSTUU	PUSTULES
ELPSTUXY	SEXTUPLY
ELRRSSTU	RUSTLERS
ELRRSTTU	TURTLERS
ELRSSSTU	RUSTLESS
ELRSTTUY	SLUTTERY
ELRSTUUV	VULTURES
ELSSSTUY	STYLUSES
ELSSSTYY	SYSTYLES
EMMMNOTU	MOMENTUM
EMMNNOTU	MONUMENT
EMMNOOOS	MONOSOME
EMMNOORS	MONOMERS
EMMNOORT	MOTORMEN
EMMNOOST	MOMENTOS
EMMNOOSY	MONOSEMY
EMMNORSU	RESUMMON
	SUMMONER
EMMNORSY	MERONYMS

EMMNORYY	MERONYMY	EMOOSSTY	MYOSOTES	ENOOSSTT	TESTOONS
EMMNOSTU	OMENTUMS	EMOOSSXY	OXYSOMES	ENOOSTXY	OXYTONES
EMMNOSTY	METONYMS	EMOOSTUV	OUTMOVES	ENOPPRRU	UNPROPER
EMMNOTTU	TOMENTUM	EMOPPRRT	PROMPTER	ENOPRRSU	PRONEURS
EMMNOTYY	METONYMY	EMOPPRUV	OVERPUMP	ENOPRSST	POSTERNS
EMMOOORS	ROOMSOME	EMOPPSTU	UPTEMPOS	ENOPRSTT	PORTENTS
EMMOOSTY	MYOTOMES	EMOPRRSU	PROSUMER	ENOPRTUW	UPTOWNER
EMMOPRRS	PROMMERS	EMOPRSST	STOMPERS	ENOPSSST	STEPSONS
EMMOPRSU	SUPERMOM	EMOPRSSU	SPERMOUS	ENOPSSSY	SYNOPSES
EMMOPTTY	POMMETTY		SUPREMOS	ENOPSTTU	OUTSPENT
EMMRRRUU	MURMURER	EMORRRUU	RUMOURER	ENOQSTUU	UNQUOTES
	REMURMUR	EMORRSST	STORMERS	ENORRSST	SNORTERS
EMMRRSTU	STRUMMER	EMORRSSU	MORSURES	ENORRSTT	TORRENTS
EMMRSTYY	SYMMETRY	EMORSSSU	SMOUSERS	ENORRSUV	OVERRUNS
EMNNNOOU	NOUMENON	EMORSSTU	OESTRUMS		RUNOVERS
EMNNNOOY	NONMONEY		STRUMOSE	ENORRTUU	TOURNURE
EMNNOOOT	MONOTONE	EMORSUVW	OVERSWUM	ENORRTUV	OVERTURN
EMNNOORT	NONMETRO	EMOSSSTT	MOSTESTS		TURNOVER
EMNNOPTY	NONEMPTY	EMOSSTTW	WESTMOST	ENORSSSU	SOURNESS
EMNNOSTW	TOWNSMEN	EMOSSTVZ	ZEMSTVOS	ENORSSTT	SNOTTERS
EMNNOSYY	SYNONYME	EMOSTTTU	TETOTUMS		STENTORS
EMNNPSTU	PUNTSMEN	EMPRRTUY	TRUMPERY	ENORSSTU	TONSURES
EMNNSTTU	STUNTMEN	EMPRSSTU	RESTUMPS	ENORSTTU	STENTOUR
EMNOOPST	METOPONS		STUMPERS	ENORSTTY	SNOTTERY
EMNOOPTY	MONOTYPE		SUMPTERS	ENORSTUV	VENTROUS
EMNOORST	MESOTRON	EMPRSSUU	RUMPUSES	ENORSTUY	TOURNEYS
	MONTEROS	EMPRSTTU	STRUMPET	ENOSSSTT	STETSONS
EMNOORSU	ENORMOUS		TRUMPETS	ENOSSSUU	SENSUOUS
	NEMOROUS	EMRRSSTU	STURMERS	ENOSSTTU	STOUTENS
EMNOORSW	NEWSROOM	ENNNOORW	NONOWNER	ENPRRSSU	PRESSRUN
EMNOORTY	NOOMETRY	ENNNOOVW	NONWOVEN		SPURNERS
EMNOOSST	MOONSETS	ENNNORTY	NONENTRY	ENPRSSSY	SPRYNESS
	MOOTNESS	ENNOOORT	TENOROON	ENPRSSTU	PUNSTERS
EMNOOSUV	VENOMOUS	ENNOOOTZ	ENTOZOON	ENPRSSUU	PRUNUSES
EMNOOTTY	TENOTOMY	ENNOOPPT	OPPONENT		UNPURSES
EMNOOTUV	OUTVENOM	ENNOORST	NORTENOS	ENPRTTUY	UNPRETTY
EMNOOTWY	TOYWOMEN	ENNOORTV	NONVOTER	ENRRRTUU	NURTURER
EMNOPSSU	SPUMONES	ENNOOSTT	NONETTOS	ENRRSTUU	NURTURES
EMNORRSU	MOURNERS	ENNOPRSU	UNPERSON	ENRSSSTU	UNSTRESS
EMNORRTY	RETRONYM	ENNOPRUV	UNPROVEN	ENRSSTTU	ENTRUSTS
EMNORSST	MONSTERS	ENNOPTWY	TWOPENNY	ENRSSTUU	UNSUREST
EMNORSTT	SORTMENT	ENNORSST	STERNSON	ENRSTTUU	UNTRUEST
	TORMENTS	ENNORSSU	NONUSERS	EOOOPRSS	OOSPORES
EMNORSTU	MONTURES	ENNORSSW	WORNNESS		SOPOROSE
	MOUNTERS	ENNORSTU	NEUTRONS	EOOOPRSZ	ZOOSPORE
	REMOUNTS	ENNORTTU	UNROTTEN	EOOOPRTZ	ZOOTROPE
EMNORSUU	NUMEROUS	ENNOSSTU	NEUSTONS	EOOORRST	ROSEROOT
EMNOSSST	STEMSONS		SUNSTONE	EOOPPRRS	PROPOSER
EMNOSUUY	EUONYMUS	ENNPPTUY	TUPPENNY	EOOPPRSS	OPPOSERS
EMNOSUVY	EVONYMUS	ENNRSSTU	STUNNERS		PROPOSES
EMNRSSTU	MUNSTERS	ENOOORSV	OVERSOON	EOOPPRSV	POPOVERS
	STERNUMS	ENOOOSSZ	ZOONOSES	EOOPPSST	POSTPOSE
EMOOPRRT	PROMOTER	ENOOPPRS	PROPONES	EOOPPTTY	TOPOTYPE
EMOOPRSS	OOSPERMS	ENOOPPST	POSTPONE	EOOPRRSS	SPOORERS
EMOOPRST	PROMOTES	ENOOPRSS	POORNESS	EOOPRRST	PROTORES
EMOOPRSY	POMEROYS		SNOOPERS		TROOPERS
	PYROSOME	ENOOPSSY	SPOONEYS	EOOPRRTU	OUTROPER
EMOOPRSZ	ZOOSPERM	ENOOPSTT	POTSTONE		UPROOTER
EMOOPSSU	ESPUMOSO		TOPSTONE	EOOPRSST	STOOPERS
EMOORRST	RESTROOM	ENOORRVW	OVERWORN	EOOPRSSW	SWOOPERS
EMOORSST	MOROSEST	ENOORRSW	SWOONERS	EOOPRSTU	OUTROPES
EMOORSSU	UROSOMES	ENOORSSZ	SNOOZERS		PORTEOUS
EMOORTYZ	ZOOMETRY	ENOORSTU	OUTSNORE	EOOPRSTV	OVERPOST
EMOOSSTW	TWOSOMES	ENOORSVW	OVERSOWN		OVERTOPS

	STOPOVER		TROUTERS	FFGINPSU	PUFFINGS
EOOPRSTW	TOWROPES	EORRSUVY	SURVEYOR	FFGINSTU	STUFFING
EOOPRTUW	OUTPOWER	EORRTUUV	TROUVEUR	FFGIORTU	FOGFRUIT
EOOPSTTV	STOVETOP	EORSSSTU	TUSSORES	FFHIINSS	SNIFFISH
EOOPSTYZ	ZOOTYPES	EORSSTTT	STOTTERS	FFHIISST	STIFFISH
EOOQTTUU	OUTQUOTE		STRETTOS	FFHIISTY	FIFTYISH
EOORRRSW	SORROWER	EORSSTTU	OUTSERTS	FFHIKNSU	HUFFKINS
EOORRSST	ROOSTERS		TUTORESS	FFHILOOS	FOOLFISH
EOORRSVW	ROWOVERS	EORSSTTW	SWOTTERS	FFHILOSW	WOLFFISH
EOORSSTU	OESTROUS	EORSSTUX	SEXTUORS	FFHILOSY	OFFISHLY
EOORSSVW	OVERSOWS	EORSTTUW	OUTWREST	FFHIOPSS	SPOFFISH
EOORSTUW	OUTSWORE	EORSTTUY	TUTOYERS	FFHIRSSU	SURFFISH
EOORTTUV	OUTVOTER	EORSTUUV	VERTUOUS	FFHOOOST	OFFSHOOT
EOORTTUW	OUTTOWER	EOSSTTTU	STOUTEST	FFHOOSSW	SHOWOFFS
	OUTWROTE	EPPPRTUY	PUPPETRY	FFHOSSTU	SHUTOFFS
EOOSTTUV	OUTVOTES	EPPRRSUU	PURPURES	FFIILMOR	FILIFORM
EOPPRRSS	PROSPERS	EPPRSSSU	SUPPRESS	FFIILNSY	SNIFFILY
EOPPRRST	STROPPER	EPPRSSUY	SUPERSPY	FFIILNTY	FLINTIFY
EOPPRRSU	SUPERPRO	EPRRRSSU	SPURRERS	FFIILPSY	SPIFFILY
EOPPRRTY	PROPERTY	EPRRSSTU	SPURTERS	FFIINOOS	SOFFIONI
EOPPRSST	POPSTERS	EPRRSSUU	PURSUERS	FFIKLORT	FORKLIFT
	STOPPERS		USURPERS	FFIKLRSU	FRISKFUL
EOPPRSSU	PURPOSES	EPRRSSUY	SPURREYS	FFILLLSU	FULFILLS
	SUPPOSER	EPRRSTUU	RUPTURES	FFILLOPP	FLIPFLOP
EOPPRSSW	SWOPPERS	EPRSSTTU	SPUTTERS	FFILLTUY	FITFULLY
EOPPSSSU	SUPPOSES	EPRSTTUY	SPUTTERY	FFILNSUY	SNUFFILY
EOPRRSSS	PRESSORS	EQRRTUUU	TRUQUEUR	FFILRTUU	FRUITFUL
EOPRRSST	PORTRESS	ERRSSSTU	TRUSSERS	FFILSSTU	FISTFULS
	PRESORTS	ERRSSTTU	TRUSTERS	FFILSTUY	STUFFILY
	SPORTERS	ERRSSTTY	TRYSTERS	FFIMORSU	FUSIFORM
EOPRRSTU	POSTURER	ERRSTTTU	STRUTTER	FFINOOST	FINFOOTS
	RESPROUT	ERRSTTTU	STUTTERS	FFINOPRT	OFFPRINT
	TROUPERS	FFFGILNU	FLUFFING	FFINOPSS	SPINOFFS
EOPRRUVY	PURVEYOR	FFFILLUY	FLUFFILY	FFINOPST	PONTIFFS
EOPRSSTT	PROTESTS	FFFILOST	LIFTOFFS	FFJMOPSU	JUMPOFFS
	SPOTTERS	FFFMOOTU	FOOTMUFF	FFKLORSU	FORKFULS
EOPRSSTU	OUTPRESS	FFGGIILN	GLIFFING		FORKSFUL
	POSTURES	FFGGINRU	GRUFFING	FFLLOOSU	LOOFFULS
	SEPTUORS	FFGHIINW	WHIFFING	FFLMNOOU	MOUFFLON
	SPOUTERS	FFGHINOU	HOUFFING	FFLNOTUU	FOUNTFUL
EOPRSSUU	POURSUES	FFGHINOW	HOWFFING	FFLORRUU	FURFUROL
	UPROUSES	FFGHINSU	HUFFINGS	FFNORSTU	TURNOFFS
EOPRSSUV	OVERSUPS	FFGHIORS	FROGFISH	FFNSTUUY	UNSTUFFY
EOPRSSUW	POURSEWS	FFGHIRSU	GRUFFISH	FFOOPSST	STOPOFFS
EOPSSTTU	UPTOSSES	FFGIIKNS	SKIFFING	FFOORRUU	FROUFROU
EOPSSTTT	POSTTEST	FFGIILNP	PIFFLING	FGGGIINR	FRIGGING
EOPSSTTU	OUTSTEPS	FFGIILNR	RIFFLING	FGGGILNO	FLOGGING
EOPSSTTW	STEWPOTS	FFGIILNS	SIFFLING	FGGGINOR	FROGGING
EOPSTTUW	OUTSWEPT	FFGIINNS	SNIFFING	FGGGINRU	FRUGGING
EOQRRSTU	TORQUERS	FFGIINPS	SPIFFING	FGGHIINT	FIGHTING
EOQRSSTU	QUESTORS	FFGIINRS	GRIFFINS	FGGHIISS	FISHGIGS
EORRRTTU	TORTURER	FFGIINST	STIFFING	FGGHINTU	GUNFIGHT
EORRSSST	STRESSOR		TIFFINGS	FGGIILNN	FLINGING
	TROSSERS	FFGIKNOS	SKOFFING	FGGIINNR	FRINGING
EORRSSTT	STERTORS	FFGILMNU	MUFFLING	FGGIINRT	GRIFTING
EORRSSTU	ROUSTERS	FFGILNPU	PLUFFING	FGGIINRU	FIGURING
	TRESSOUR	FFGILNRU	RUFFLING	FGGIISZZ	FIZZGIGS
	TROUSERS	FFGILNSU	SLUFFING	FGGILNOR	FROGLING
EORRSSTW	STROWERS	FFGILRUY	GRUFFILY	FGGILNOS	GOLFINGS
	TROWSERS	FFGINNSU	SNUFFING	FGGINOOR	FORGOING
EORRSSTY	ROYSTERS	FFGINOPU	POUFFING	FGGINORS	FORGINGS
	STROYERS	FFGINORS	GRIFFONS	FGHIIKNS	KINGFISH
EORRSTTT	TROTTERS	FFGINOSW	SOWFFING	FGHIILNT	INFLIGHT
EORRSTTU	TORTURES		SWOFFING	FGHIINSS	FISHINGS

FGHIINST	INFIGHTS	**FGILNORU**	FLOURING	**FHIMNOOS**	MOONFISH
	SHIFTING	**FGILNOSS**	FLOSSING	**FHIMORSW**	FISHWORM
FGHILLTU	LIGHTFUL	**FGILNOST**	SOFTLING	**FHIMPRSU**	FRUMPISH
FGHILMTU	MIGHTFUL	**FGILNOSU**	FLOUSING	**FHINOSSU**	FUSHIONS
FGHILNSU	FLUSHING		FOULINGS	**FHINRTTU**	UNTHRIFT
	LUNGFISH	**FGILNOSW**	FOWLINGS	**FHINSSTU**	UNSHIFTS
FGHILRTU	RIGHTFUL		WOLFINGS	**FHIOOPTT**	PHOTOFIT
FGHINOOW	WHOOFING	**FGILNOTU**	FLOUTING	**FHIOPSSX**	FOXSHIPS
FGHINORT	FROTHING		OUTFLING	**FHIORSTY**	FORTYISH
FGHINOTU	INFOUGHT	**FGILNPRU**	PURFLING	**FHIPSSTU**	UPSHIFTS
FGHINRSU	FRUSHING	**FGILNPSU**	UPFLINGS	**FHKORSTU**	FUTHORKS
FGHIOPST	GIFTSHOP	**FGILNRRU**	FLURRING	**FHLLLOTU**	LOTHFULL
FGHIOTTU	OUTFIGHT	**FGILNSTU**	FLUTINGS	**FHLLOSTU**	SLOTHFUL
FGHLORUU	FURLOUGH	**FGILNSTY**	FLYTINGS	**FHLMORUU**	HUMORFUL
FGHNOORS	FOGHORNS	**FGILNUZZ**	FUZZLING	**FHLMOTUU**	MOUTHFUL
FGHNOTUU	UNFOUGHT	**FGIMNORS**	FORMINGS	**FHLNORSU**	HORNFULS
FGIIIKNN	FINIKING	**FGIMNPRU**	FRUMPING	**FHLOOSTU**	SOOTHFUL
FGIIINNX	INFIXING	**FGIMNRSU**	SMURFING	**FHLOOTTU**	TOOTHFUL
FGIIKLNS	FLISKING	**FGIMORRU**	GRUIFORM	**FHLOPSSU**	SHOPFULS
FGIIKNNS	KNIFINGS	**FGIMOSSY**	FOGYISMS	**FHLORTTU**	TROTHFUL
FGIIKNRS	FRISKING	**FGINNORT**	FRONTING	**FHLORTUW**	WORTHFUL
FGIILLNR	FRILLING	**FGINNORW**	FROWNING		WROTHFUL
FGIILLNS	FILLINGS	**FGINOOPR**	PROOFING	**FHLORTUY**	FOURTHLY
FGIILMNP	FLIMPING	**FGINOOPS**	SPOOFING	**FHLOSTUU**	OUTFLUSH
FGIILNNT	FLINTING	**FGINOORS**	ROOFINGS	**FHLOTUUY**	YOUTHFUL
FGIILNOO	FOLIOING	**FGINOOST**	FOOTINGS	**FHLRTTUU**	TRUTHFUL
FGIILNOS	FOILINGS	**FGINORST**	FROSTING	**FHNOSTUX**	FOXHUNTS
FGIILNPP	FLIPPING	**FGINORTU**	FOUTRING	**FHOOORST**	FORSOOTH
FGIILNRS	RIFLINGS	**FGINRRSU**	FURRINGS		HOOFROTS
FGIILNRT	FLIRTING	**FGINRSSU**	SURFINGS	**FHOOOSTT**	HOTFOOTS
	TRIFLING	**FGINRSTU**	TURFINGS	**FIIIMNST**	FINITISM
FGIILNSS	FISSLING	**FGINSTTU**	TUFTINGS	**FIIINNOX**	INFIXION
FGIILNST	STIFLING	**FGIORSTW**	FIGWORTS	**FIIINNTY**	INFINITY
FGIILNTT	FLITTING	**FGISSTUU**	FUGUISTS	**FIIKLRSY**	FRISKILY
FGIILNZZ	FIZZLING	**FGKLNOOS**	FOLKSONG	**FIILLMOP**	PLIOFILM
FGIINNST	SNIFTING	**FGLLMOOU**	GLOOMFUL	**FIILLMOS**	MILFOILS
FGIINNSU	INFUSING	**FGLLNSUU**	LUNGFULS	**FIILLMSY**	FLIMSILY
FGIINNUX	UNFIXING	**FGLNORSU**	FURLONGS	**FIILLMTU**	MULTIFIL
FGIINNUY	UNIFYING	**FGLNORUW**	WRONGFUL	**FIILLNTY**	FLINTILY
FGIINOQU	QUOIFING	**FGLOOOST**	FOOTSLOG	**FIILLSSU**	FUSILLIS
FGIINOST	FOISTING	**FGLORSUU**	FULGOURS	**FIILMNRY**	INFIRMLY
FGIINRRS	FIRRINGS	**FGLSSTUU**	GUTSFULS	**FIILMOPR**	PILIFORM
FGIINRST	FRISTING	**FGNOORSU**	FOURGONS	**FIILMPSY**	SIMPLIFY
FGIINRTT	FRITTING	**FGNOORTU**	UNFORGOT	**FIILNOST**	TINFOILS
FGIINRTU	FRUITING	**FHHIKOOS**	FISHHOOK	**FIILRTUY**	FRUITILY
FGIINRZZ	FRIZZING	**FHHOORST**	SHOFROTH	**FIILRYZZ**	FRIZZILY
FGIINSST	SIFTINGS	**FHIIKLLS**	FISHKILL	**FIILTTUY**	FUTILITY
FGIINSTT	FITTINGS	**FHIIKLMS**	MILKFISH	**FIIMMNSU**	INFIMUMS
FGIINSTW	SWIFTING	**FHIIKNSS**	FISHSKIN	**FIIMOPRR**	PIRIFORM
FGIINSZZ	FIZZINGS	**FHIILLTY**	FILTHILY	**FIIMOPRS**	PISIFORM
FGIIRSTU	FIGURIST	**FHIILNOS**	LIONFISH	**FIIMOSTY**	MOISTIFY
FGIKLNNU	FLUNKING	**FHIILRST**	FLIRTISH	**FIINNOSU**	INFUSION
FGILLNOW	WOLFLING	**FHIILSTY**	SHIFTILY	**FIINORTU**	FRUITION
FGILLNOY	FOLLYING	**FHIKLLLO**	HILLFOLK	**FIINOSSS**	FISSIONS
FGILMNPU	FLUMPING	**FHIKMNOS**	MONKFISH	**FIINTUXY**	UNFIXITY
FGILMNUY	FUMINGLY	**FHIKNORT**	FORTHINK	**FIIOPSST**	POSITIFS
FGILNNTU	GUNFLINT	**FHILLOOT**	FOOTHILL	**FIIQUYZZ**	QUIZZIFY
FGILNOOR	FLOORING	**FHILLORT**	HILLFORT	**FIKKLNOS**	KINFOLKS
FGILNOOS	FOOLINGS	**FHILMPSU**	LUMPFISH		KINSFOLK
FGILNOOT	FOOTLING	**FHILMRTU**	MIRTHFUL	**FIKLLLSU**	SKILLFUL
FGILNOOZ	FOOZLING	**FHILOPST**	SHOPLIFT	**FIKLLOSY**	FOLKSILY
FGILNOPP	FLOPPING	**FHILORSU**	FLOURISH	**FIKLNOSW**	WOLFKINS
FGILNOPS	FOPLINGS	**FHILORTY**	FROTHILY		WOLFSKIN
FGILNORS	ROLFINGS	**FHILPSSU**	SHIPFULS	**FIKLNSSU**	SKINFULS

Eight-letter anagrams

FIKLSSTU	KISTFULS	FLLNOSUY	SULFONYL	GGGIJNOS	JOGGINGS
	LUTFISKS	FLLOOPUW	FOLLOWUP	GGGIJNSU	JUGGINGS
FIKNORSW	FORSWINK		UPFOLLOW	GGGIKNSU	SKUGGING
FIKNOSSX	FOXSKINS	FLLRSUUY	SULFURYL	GGGILNOO	GOOGLING
FIKRSSTU	TURFSKIS	FLMNOOSU	MOUFLONS	GGGILNOS	LOGGINGS
FILLLUWY	WILFULLY	FLMNORUU	MOURNFUL		SLOGGING
FILLNSUY	SINFULLY	FLMOOORW	MOORFOWL	GGGILNOT	TOGGLING
	SULFINYL	FLMOOOST	TOMFOOLS	GGGILNPU	PLUGGING
FILLNUUW	UNWILFUL	FLMOORSU	ROOMFULS		PUGGLING
FILLOPPY	FLOPPILY	FLMORSTU	STORMFUL	GGGILNRU	GURGLING
FILLOPSU	SPOILFUL	FLNOOPSU	SPOONFUL	GGGILNSU	SLUGGING
FILLOSSY	FLOSSILY	FLNOORRS	FORLORNS	GGGILORY	GROGGILY
FILMNOOS	MONOFILS	FLNOOSTU	SNOOTFUL	GGGIMNSU	MUGGINGS
FILMOPRS	SLIPFORM	FLNOOTUW	OUTFLOWN		SMUGGING
FILMORRY	LYRIFORM	FLOOOPTT	POLTFOOT	GGGINNOS	NOGGINGS
FILMOSSU	MOFUSSIL	FLOOOSTU	OUTFOOLS		SNOGGING
FILMOSTU	MOISTFUL	FLOOPTTY	TOPLOFTY	GGGINNSU	SNUGGING
FILMPRUY	FRUMPILY	FLOORSSW	FORSLOWS	GGGINOPR	PROGGING
FILNNSUU	UNSINFUL	FLOOSTUW	OUTFLOWS	GGGINORT	TROGGING
FILNORSU	FLUORINS	FLOPRSTU	SPORTFUL	GGGINOSS	SOGGINGS
FILNOSUX	FLUXIONS	FLORTTUU	TROUTFUL	GGGINPSU	PUGGINGS
FILOOOPR	OILPROOF	FLRSTTUU	TRUSTFUL	GGGINRSU	RUGGINGS
FILOOSTW	WITLOOFS	FMNOOOOR	MOONROOF	GGGINSSU	SUGGINGS
FILORSST	FLORISTS	FMOOPRST	POSTFORM	GGGINSTU	TUGGINGS
FILORSTU	FLORUITS	FMRSSTUU	FRUSTUMS	GGHHIINT	HIGHTING
FILORSTY	FROSTILY	FNNOOORT	FRONTOON	GGHHINOU	HOUGHING
FILORWYZ	FROWZILY	FNNOORST	FRONTONS	GGHHISTU	THUGGISH
FILRSTTU	TRISTFUL	FNOOORTW	FOOTWORN	GGHIILNT	LIGHTING
FILSSTTU	FLUTISTS	FNOOPRSU	SUNPROOF	GGHIINNO	HONGIING
FILSTTUY	STULTIFY	FNOORRSW	FORSWORN	GGHIINNW	WHINGING
FIMMNOOR	OMNIFORM	FNOORSSU	SUNROOFS	GGHIINPT	PIGHTING
FIMMORRU	MURIFORM	FNOORTUW	OUTFROWN	GGHIINRT	GIRTHING
FIMMORSS	MISFORMS	FOOOPRST	ROOFTOPS		RIGHTING
FIMNORSU	UNIFORMS	FOOOPSTT	FOOTPOST	GGHIINST	SIGHTING
FIMOORRT	ROTIFORM	FOOORSTT	FOOTROTS	GGHIINTW	WIGHTING
FIMOORSS	ISOFORMS	FOOOSTTU	OUTFOOTS	GGHIIPRS	PRIGGISH
FIMOPRRY	PYRIFORM	FOORSTTX	FOXTROTS	GGHILSSU	SLUGGISH
FIMORRSU	URSIFORM	FOPSSSTU	FUSSPOTS	GGHIMSTU	THUGGISM
FIMORTUY	FUMITORY	GGGGIILN	GIGGLING	GGHINORU	ROUGHING
FIMOSTUY	FUMOSITY	GGGGIINR	GRIGGING	GGHINOST	GHOSTING
FIMRSTUU	FUTURISM	GGGGILNO	GOGGLING	GGHINOSU	SOUGHING
FINOOPSY	OPSONIFY	GGGGILNU	GLUGGING	GGHINOTU	OUGHTING
FINOPRST	FROSTNIP		GUGGLING		TOUGHING
FINOPSSU	SOUPFINS	GGGGINOR	GROGGING	GGHINOTY	HOGTYING
FINORSSS	FRISSONS	GGGHIILN	HIGGLING	GGHOOPRS	GROGSHOP
FINORSUY	INFUSORY	GGGHIINT	THIGGING	GGIIILLN	GINGILLI
FIOORSSU	FURIOSOS	GGGHIINW	WHIGGING	GGIIILNS	GINGILIS
FIORTTUY	FORTUITY	GGGHINOS	HOGGINGS	GGIIINNT	IGNITING
FIOSTTTU	TOFUTTIS		SHOGGING	GGIIJLNN	JINGLING
FIRSTTUU	FUTURIST	GGGIIJLN	JIGGLING	GGIIKLNN	KINGLING
FIRTTUUY	FUTURITY	GGGIIJNS	JIGGINGS	GGIILLNR	GRILLING
FJLLOUYY	JOYFULLY	GGGIILLN	NIGGLING	GGIILLNY	GILLYING
FJLNOUUY	UNJOYFUL	GGGIILNS	LIGGINGS	GGIILMNN	MINGLING
FKKLOORW	WORKFOLK	GGGIILNW	WIGGLING	GGIILMNY	GINGLYMI
FKKOORTW	KOFTWORK	GGGIINNS	SNIGGING	GGIILNNP	PINGLING
FKLMOOOT	FOLKMOOT	GGGIINPR	PRIGGING	GGIILNNS	SINGLING
FKLMOOST	FOLKMOTS	GGGIINPS	PIGGINGS		SLINGING
FKLNOOTW	TOWNFOLK	GGGIINRS	RIGGINGS	GGIILNNT	GLINTING
FKLNRTUU	TRUNKFUL	GGGIINRT	TRIGGING		TINGLING
FKLOORWW	WORKFLOW	GGGIINSW	SWIGGING	GGIILNPS	PIGLINGS
FKMOORRW	FORMWORK		WIGGINGS	GGIILNRS	RIGLINGS
FKNORSUW	FORSWUNK	GGGIINTW	TWIGGING	GGIILNTZ	GLITZING
FKOOORTW	FOOTWORK	GGGIJLNO	JOGGLING	GGIIMNOS	MISGOING
FKRSSSUY	SKYSURFS	GGGIJLNU	JUGGLING	GGIIMNPU	GUIMPING

GGIIMPRS	PRIGGISM	GGINNUVY	UNGYVING	GHIINNNY	HINNYING
GGIINNNR	GRINNING	GGINOORV	GROOVING	GHIINNRS	SHRINING
GGIINNNS	GINNINGS	GGINOOST	STOOGING	GHIINNST	HINTINGS
GGIINNOR	GROINING	GGINOOTU	OUTGOING		NITHINGS
	IGNORING	GGINOPRS	PROGGINS	GHIINNSW	WHININGS
GGIINNOS	INGOINGS	GGINOPRU	GROUPING	GHIINNUV	UNHIVING
GGIINNOT	INGOTING	GGINOPSU	UPGOING	GHIINOST	HOISTING
GGIINNOW	WONGIING	GGINORSS	GROSSING	GHIINPPS	HIPPINGS
GGIINNRS	RINGINGS	GGINORSU	GROUSING		SHIPPING
GGIINNRW	WRINGING	GGINORSW	GROWINGS		
GGIINNSS	SIGNINGS	GGINORTU	GROUTING	GHIINPPW	WHIPPING
	SINGINGS	GGINOSUV	VOGUINGS	GHIINRRS	SHIRRING
GGIINNST	STINGING	GGINPRSU	PURGINGS	GHIINRRW	WHIRRING
GGIINNSW	SWINGING	GGINPSYY	GYPSYING	GHIINRST	SHIRTING
GGIINNTW	TWINGING	GGINRSSU	SURGINGS	GHIINRSV	SHRIVING
GGIINNUV	UNGIVING	GGINSSUY	GUSSYING	GHIINRTT	TRITHING
GGIINPPR	GRIPPING	GGLLOOWY	GOLLYWOG	GHIINRTV	THRIVING
GGIINPSY	GIPSYING	GGLLPUUY	PLUGUGLY	GHIINRTW	WRITHING
GGIINRST	RINGGITS	GHHIILST	LIGHTISH	GHIINSSS	HISSINGS
GGIINRTT	GRITTING	GHHIINPS	PHISHING	GHIINSST	INSIGHTS
GGIINSSU	GUISINGS	GHHIINSW	WHISHING	GHIINSSW	SWISHING
GGIINSTU	GIUSTING	GHHIIRST	RIGHTISH		WHISSING
GGIIRRSS	GRISGRIS	GHHIISTT	TIGHTISH		WISHINGS
GGIITTUU	GUITGUIT	GHHILOSU	GHOULISH	GHIINSTT	SHITTING
GGIKKNOR	GROKKING	GHHIMNPU	HUMPHING		TITHINGS
GGILLNOY	GOLLYING	GHHIMOST	HIGHMOST	GHIINSTW	WHISTING
GGILLNUW	GULLWING	GHHINOOS	HOOSHING		WHITINGS
GGILLNUY	GULLYING	GHHINSSU	SHUSHING	GHIINSVV	SHIVVING
GGILLOOW	GOLLIWOG	GHHIOPST	HIGHSPOT	GHIINTTW	TWINIGHT
GGILMMNO	GLOMMING		HIGHTOPS	GHIINWZZ	WHIZZING
GGILMNOO	GLOOMING	GHHIORSU	ROUGHISH	GHIIORSV	VIGORISH
GGILNNOP	PLONGING	GHHIOSTU	TOUGHISH	GHIIPSSY	GIPSYISH
GGILNNOS	LONGINGS	GHHIRSST	SHRIGHTS	GHIIRSTT	RIGHTIST
GGILNNOU	LOUNGING	GHHOORTU	THOROUGH	GHIKLNTY	KNIGHTLY
GGILNNPU	PLUNGING	GHHOSTTU	THOUGHTS	GHIKLSTY	SKYLIGHT
	PUNGLING	GHIIIKNO	HIKOIING	GHIKNNTU	THUNKING
GGILNNUU	UNGLUING	GHIIILNS	SHILINGI		UNKNIGHT
GGILNOOP	GLOOPING	GHIIJNOS	JINGOISH	GHIKNSSU	HUSKINGS
GGILNOPP	GLOPPING	GHIIKNNT	THINKING	GHIKRSTU	TUGHRIKS
GGILNORW	GROWLING	GHIIKNPS	KINGSHIP	GHILLNOO	HOLLOING
GGILNORY	GLORYING	GHIIKNRS	SHIRKING	GHILLNOU	HULLOING
GGILNOSS	GLOSSING		SHRIKING	GHILLOTW	LOWLIGHT
	GOSLINGS	GHIIKNSW	WHISKING	GHILLSTY	SLIGHTLY
GGILNOSV	GLOVINGS	GHIILLNO	HILLOING	GHILMNSU	MULSHING
GGILNOSZ	GLOZINGS	GHIILLNS	SHILLING	GHILMPSU	GLUMPISH
GGILNOTU	GLOUTING	GHIILMST	MISLIGHT	GHILNOOS	SHOOLING
GGILNRUY	URGINGLY	GHIILMTY	MIGHTILY	GHILNOPP	HOPPLING
GGILNTTU	GLUTTING	GHIILNOT	LITHOING	GHILNOPS	LONGSHIP
	GUTTLING	GHIILNPR	HIRPLING	GHILNOPY	HOPINGLY
GGILNUZZ	GUZZLING	GHIILNRS	HIRLINGS	GHILNOSS	SLOSHING
GGILQSUY	SQUIGGLY		HIRSLING	GHILNOST	SLOTHING
GGIMMNSU	GUMMINGS	GHIILNRT	THIRLING	GHILNOSU	HOUSLING
GGIMNOOR	GROOMING	GHIILNRW	WHIRLING	GHILNOSW	HOWLINGS
GGIMNOOS	SMOOGING	GHIILNST	TINGLISH	GHILNPSU	INGULPHS
GGIMNPRU	GRUMPING	GHIILNTW	WHITLING	GHILNRSU	HURLINGS
GGINNNSU	GUNNINGS	GHIILOTT	OILTIGHT	GHILNRTU	HURTLING
GGINNOOS	ONGOINGS	GHIILTTW	TWILIGHT	GHILNRUY	HUNGRILY
GGINNOPP	PINGPONG	GHIIMMNS	SHIMMING	GHILNSSU	SLUSHING
GGINNOPR	PRONGING	GHIIMMNW	WHIMMING	GHILNSTU	HUSTLING
GGINNOPS	SPONGING	GHIIMNNU	INHUMING		SUNLIGHT
GGINNORW	WRONGING	GHIIMNST	SMITHING	GHILOPRS	SHOPGIRL
GGINNOSS	SINGSONG	GHIIMRST	RIGHTISM	GHILORSW	SHOWGIRL
GGINNOTU	TONGUING	GHIINNNS	SHINNING	GHILORSY	OGRISHLY
GGINNRTU	GRUNTING	GHIINNNT	THINNING	GHILPRTY	TRIGLYPH
				GHILPSTU	UPLIGHTS

Eight-letter anagrams

GHIMMNSU	HUMMINGS
GHIMNOPR	MORPHING
GHIMNOPU	GUMPHION
GHIMNOPW	WHOMPING
GHIMNORU	HUMORING
GHIMNOSS	MOSHINGS
GHIMNOTU	MOUTHING
GHIMNPTU	THUMPING
GHIMNPUW	WHUMPING
GHIMNSSU	SMUSHING
GHIMNSTU	GUNSMITH
GHIMPRSU	GRUMPISH
GHIMPSYY	PYGMYISH
GHIMRSSU	SIMURGHS
GHINNNSU	SHUNNING
GHINNOOR	HONORING
GHINNOPY	PHONYING
GHINNORS	HORNINGS
GHINNORT	NORTHING
	THORNING
	THRONING
GHINNOST	NOTHINGS
GHINNSSU	SNUSHING
GHINNSTU	HUNTINGS
	SHUNTING
GHINOOPT	PHOTOING
GHINOOPW	WHOOPING
GHINOOST	SHOOTING
	SOOTHING
GHINOOSW	WOOSHING
GHINOOTT	TOOTHING
GHINOOTW	WHOOTING
GHINOPPS	HOPPINGS
	SHOPPING
GHINOPPW	WHOPPING
GHINOPSS	GINSHOPS
GHINORSS	HORSINGS
	SHORINGS
GHINORST	SHORTING
GHINORSV	SHROVING
GHINORSW	SHOWRING
	SHROWING
GHINORTT	TROTHING
GHINORTW	INGROWTH
	THROWING
	WORTHING
GHINOSST	HOSTINGS
GHINOSSU	HOUSINGS
GHINOSSV	SHOVINGS
GHINOSSW	SHOWINGS
GHINOSTT	HOTTINGS
	SHOTTING
	TONIGHTS
GHINOSTU	HOUTINGS
	SHOUTING
	SOUTHING
GHINOSTW	SOWTHING
GHINOSUY	YOUNGISH
GHINOTTU	OUTNIGHT
GHINPPUW	WHUPPING
GHINPSSU	GUNSHIPS
GHINPTTU	PHUTTING
GHINRRUY	HURRYING
GHINRSSU	RUSHINGS

GHINRSTU	UNGIRTHS
	UNRIGHTS
GHINSSTU	HUSTINGS
	UNSIGHTS
GHINSTTU	HUTTINGS
	SHUTTING
GHIORTTU	OUTRIGHT
GHIOSTTU	OUTSIGHT
GHIPRSST	SPRIGHTS
GHIPRSTU	UPRIGHTS
GHIPRSUU	GURUSHIP
GHIPSSYY	GYPSYISH
GHLMOOOS	HOMOLOGS
GHLMOOOY	HOMOLOGY
GHLNNOOR	LONGHORN
GHLNOORU	HOURLONG
GHLNOOYY	HOLOGYNY
GHLNORSU	SLUGHORN
GHLOOORY	HOROLOGY
GHLORTUU	TURLOUGH
GHMNOOOY	HOMOGONY
GHMORSSU	SORGHUMS
GHMOSSTU	MUGSHOTS
GHMPSSUY	SPHYGMUS
GHNNOOOZ	GOHONZON
GHNOPRSY	GRYPHONS
GHNOPYYY	HYPOGYNY
GHNOSSTU	GUNSHOTS
	SHOTGUNS
GHNOSTUU	UNSOUGHT
GHNOSTUY	YOUNGTHS
GHOOOSSW	HOOSGOWS
GHOORTUY	YOGHOURT
GHOPRTUW	UPGROWTH
GHORSTUY	YOGHURTS
GIIILMNT	LIMITING
GIIILNNS	INISLING
GIIILNNU	LINGUINI
GIIILOTV	VITILIGO
GIIIMMNX	IMMIXING
GIIINNOS	IONISING
GIIINNOT	IGNITION
GIIINNOZ	IONIZING
GIIINNTV	INVITING
GIIINORS	SIGNIORI
GIIINRSS	GRISSINI
GIIINSTV	VISITING
GIIJMMNY	JIMMYING
GIIJMNOS	JINGOISM
GIIJNNOS	JOININGS
GIIJNNOT	JOINTING
GIIJNNRU	INJURING
GIIJNOST	JINGOIST
	JOISTING
GIIKKLNP	KINGKLIP
GIIKKNNS	SKINKING
GIIKKNRS	KIRKINGS
	SKRIKING
GIIKLLNS	KILLINGS
	SKILLING
GIIKLMNS	MILKINGS
GIIKLNNP	PLINKING
GIIKLNNS	INKLINGS
	SLINKING

GIIKLNNT	TINKLING
GIIKLNNW	WINKLING
GIIKLNRS	SKIRLING
GIIKLNST	KILTINGS
	KITLINGS
GIIKLNTT	KITTLING
GIIKMMNS	SKIMMING
GIIKMNPS	SKIMPING
GIIKMNRS	SMIRKING
GIIKNNNS	SKINNING
GIIKNNOV	INVOKING
GIIKNNPR	PRINKING
GIIKNNPS	KINGPINS
	PINKINGS
GIIKNNSS	SINKINGS
GIIKNNST	STINKING
GIIKNNSW	SWINKING
	WINKINGS
GIIKNNTT	KNITTING
GIIKNNTW	TWINKING
GIIKNORS	SKIORING
GIIKNPPS	SKIPPING
GIIKNPSS	PIGSKINS
GIIKNQRU	QUIRKING
GIIKNRRS	SKIRRING
GIIKNRSS	GRISKINS
GIIKNRST	SKIRTING
	STRIKING
GIIKNSSV	SKIVINGS
GIILLMNS	MILLINGS
GIILLMNU	ILLUMING
GIILLNOR	GRILLION
GIILLNOS	GILLIONS
GIILLNPR	PRILLING
GIILLNPS	PILLINGS
	SPILLING
GIILLNQU	QUILLING
GIILLNRT	TRILLING
GIILLNST	STILLING
	TILLINGS
GIILLNSW	SWILLING
GIILLNTT	LITTLING
GIILLNTW	TWILLING
GIILLNVY	LIVINGLY
GIILLNWY	WILLYING
GIILLOPW	POLLIWIG
GIILLPSW	PIGSWILL
GIILLTUV	GUILTILY
GIILLTVZ	GLITZILY
GIILMMNP	PLIMMING
GIILMMNS	SLIMMING
GIILMNNU	LUMINING
	UNLIMING
GIILMNOS	SMOILING
GIILMNPR	RIMPLING
GIILMNPS	LIMPINGS
	SIMPLING
GIILMNPW	WIMPLING
GIILMNPY	IMPLYING
GIILMNSS	SMILINGS
GIILMNST	MISTLING
GIILMNSY	MISLYING
GIILMNZZ	MIZZLING
GIILMPRS	PILGRIMS

GIILMPSU	PUGILISM	GIIMNOTV	MOTIVING	GIINPRSS	PRISSING
GIILNNNU	UNLINING		VOMITING		RISPINGS
GIILNNPP	NIPPLING	GIIMNPPR	PRIMPING	GIINPRST	SPIRTING
GIILNNPS	SPLINING	GIIMNPRS	PRIMINGS		STRIPING
GIILNNPU	UNPILING	GIIMNPRU	UMPIRING	GIINPRSU	SIRUPING
GIILNNTU	UNTILING	GIIMNPTU	IMPUTING		UPRISING
GIILNNTW	TWINLING	GIIMNRRS	SMIRRING	GIINPSTT	PITTINGS
	WINTLING	GIIMNRST	SMIRTING		SPITTING
GIILNNUV	UNLIVING	GIIMNSST	MISTINGS	GIINPSTW	WINGTIPS
GIILNOPS	PIGNOLIS	GIIMNSSU	MISUSING	GIINPSUZ	UPSIZING
	SPOILING	GIIMNSSW	SWINGISM	GIINPTTU	TITUPING
GIILNOPT	PILOTING	GIIMNSTT	SMITTING	GIINQRSU	SQUIRING
GIILNORS	LIGROINS	GIIMNSTU	MUISTING	GIINQRTU	QUIRTING
GIILNOSS	SOILINGS	GIIMNSTY	STIMYING	GIINQTTU	QUITTING
GIILNOST	TOILINGS	GIIMORRS	RIGORISM	GIINQUZZ	QUIZZING
GIILNPPR	RIPPLING	GIINNNOO	ONIONING	GIINRRST	STIRRING
GIILNPPS	LIPPINGS	GIINNNOT	INTONING	GIINRSTV	STRIVING
	SIPPLING		NOINTING	GIINRSTW	WRITINGS
	SLIPPING	GIINNNPS	PINNINGS	GIINSSSW	SWISSING
GIILNPPT	TIPPLING		SPINNING	GIINSSTT	SITTINGS
GIILNPPU	UPPILING	GIINNNRU	INURNING	GIINSSTU	SUITINGS
GIILNPPY	PIPINGLY	GIINNNST	TINNINGS		TISSUING
GIILNPRS	SPIRLING	GIINNNSW	WINNINGS	GIINSTTW	TWISTING
GIILNPRT	TRIPLING	GIINNNTW	TWINNING		WITTINGS
GIILNPSS	LISPINGS	GIINNOPR	PROINING	GIINSTUW	WINGSUIT
	SPILINGS	GIINNOPS	PIONINGS	GIINSWZZ	SWIZZING
GIILNQSU	QUISLING	GIINNOPT	POINTING	GIINTTTW	TWITTING
GIILNQTU	QUILTING	GIINNOQU	QUOINING	GIIORRST	RIGORIST
GIILNRSW	SWIRLING	GIINNORS	IRONINGS	GIIORSSV	ISOGRIVS
GIILNRTW	TWIRLING		NIGROSIN	GIIPRSTZ	SPRITZIG
GIILNRVY	VIRGINLY		ROSINING	GIJKLNOY	JOKINGLY
GIILNSST	LISTINGS	GIINNORT	IGNITRON	GIJLLNOY	JOLLYING
GIILNSTT	SLITTING	GIINNPPS	SNIPPING	GIJLNOST	JOSTLING
	STILTING	GIINNPRT	PRINTING	GIJLNSTU	JUNGLIST
	TILTINGS	GIINNPSS	SNIPINGS		JUSTLING
	TITLINGS	GIINNPSU	PINGUINS	GIJMNPSU	JUMPINGS
GIILNSTU	LINGUIST	GIINNRSS	RINSINGS	GIJNOSTT	JOTTINGS
GIILNSTW	WITLINGS	GIINNRSU	INSURING	GIJNOSTU	JOUSTING
GIILNSTY	STINGILY		RUININGS	GIJNTTUY	JUTTYING
GIILNSZZ	SIZZLING	GIINNRTU	UNTIRING	GIKKLNSU	SKULKING
GIILNTTT	TITTLING	GIINNRUW	UNWIRING	GIKKNNSU	SKUNKING
GIILNTTU	TITULING	GIINNSSW	INSWINGS	GIKLLNNO	KNOLLING
GIILNTTV	VITTLING	GIINNSTT	STINTING	GIKLLNOS	SKOLLING
GIILNTTW	TWILTING		TINTINGS	GIKLLNSU	SKULLING
GIILNZZZ	ZIZZLING	GIINNSTU	UNITINGS	GIKLNNOP	PLONKING
GIILOSST	OLIGISTS	GIINNSTW	TWININGS	GIKLNNPU	PLUNKING
GIILPSTU	PUGILIST	GIINNUVW	UNWIVING	GIKLNNRU	KNURLING
GIILRSST	STRIGILS	GIINOPST	POSITING		RUNKLING
GIILRTTY	GRITTILY		SOPITING	GIKLNNUY	UNKINGLY
GIIMMNPR	PRIMMING	GIINOPTV	PIVOTING	GIKLNOPR	PORKLING
GIIMMNRS	RIMMINGS	GIINOQTU	QUOITING	GIKLNRSU	LURKINGS
GIIMMNRT	TRIMMING	GIINORSS	SIGNIORS	GIKLORRW	WORKGIRL
GIIMMNRU	IMMURING	GIINORST	IGNITORS	GIKMNOSS	SMOKINGS
GIIMMNSW	SWIMMING		RIOTINGS	GIKMNPPU	PUMPKING
GIIMNNOP	IMPONING		ROISTING	GIKNNOOS	SNOOKING
GIIMNNOR	MINORING		ROSITING	GIKNNOPR	PRONKING
GIIMNNOY	IGNOMINY	GIINORSV	VISORING	GIKNNOQU	QUONKING
GIIMNNTU	MINUTING	GIINORSY	SIGNIORY	GIKNNOST	STONKING
	MUNITING	GIINORTZ	ROZITING	GIKNNOSW	KNOWINGS
	MUTINING	GIINORVZ	VIZORING		SNOWKING
GIIMNNUX	UNMIXING	GIINOSTT	STOITING	GIKNNOTT	KNOTTING
GIIMNOPS	IMPOSING	GIINPPQU	QUIPPING	GIKNNOTU	KNOUTING
GIIMNOST	MOISTING	GIINPPRT	TRIPPING	GIKNNOUY	UNYOKING
GIIMNOTT	OMITTING	GIINPPST	TIPPINGS	GIKNNPSU	SPUNKING

GIKNNRTU	TRUNKING
GIKNOOPS	SPOOKING
GIKNOOST	STOOKING
GIKNOOTW	KOTOWING
GIKNOPST	KINGPOST
GIKNORRW	RINGWORK
GIKNORST	STROKING
GIKNORSW	WORKINGS
GIKNSSTU	TUSKINGS
GILLMOOY	GLOOMILY
GILLMPUY	GLUMPILY
GILLNNSU	NULLINGS
GILLNOPR	PROLLING
GILLNOPS	POLLINGS
GILLNORS	ROLLINGS
GILLNORT	TROLLING
GILLNOST	TOLLINGS
GILLNOSY	LOSINGLY
GILLNOVY	LOVINGLY
GILLNPUY	PULINGLY
GILLNPYY	PLYINGLY
GILLNRUY	LURINGLY
GILLNSUY	SULLYING
GILLOOPW	POLLIWOG
GILLOPWY	POLLYWIG
GILLORVY	GILLYVOR
GILLOSSY	GLOSSILY
GILMMNSU	SLUMMING
GILMMTUY	MULTIGYM
GILMNOOS	SLOOMING
GILMNOPY	MOPINGLY
GILMNORS	MORLINGS
	SLORMING
GILMNORT	MORTLING
GILMNOSS	MOSLINGS
GILMNOSU	MOUSLING
GILMNOSY	SMOYLING
GILMNOTT	MOTTLING
GILMNOTU	MOULTING
GILMNOUV	VOLUMING
GILMNOVY	MOVINGLY
GILMNPPU	PLUMPING
GILMNPRU	RUMPLING
GILMNPSU	SLUMPING
GILMNSUY	MUSINGLY
GILMNUZZ	MUZZLING
GILMOOSY	MISOLOGY
GILMOOXY	MIXOLOGY
GILMPRUY	GRUMPILY
GILMPSSY	GYMSLIPS
GILNNOOS	GLONOINS
	LOONINGS
	SNOOLING
GILNNOSU	NOUSLING
GILNNOTU	NONGUILT
GILNNOTW	TOWNLING
GILNNOUV	UNLOVING
GILNNRSU	NURSLING
GILNNSSU	UNSLINGS
GILNNUZZ	NUZZLING
GILNOOOV	OINOLOGY
GILNOOPS	LOOPINGS
	SPOOLING
GILNOOPT	POOTLING

GILNOORT	ROOTLING
GILNOOSS	LOOSINGS
GILNOOST	LOOTINGS
	STOOLING
	TOOLINGS
GILNOOSY	SINOLOGY
GILNOOTT	TOOTLING
GILNOOVY	VINOLOGY
GILNOOWY	WOOINGLY
GILNOPPP	PLOPPING
	POPPLING
GILNOPPS	LOPPINGS
	SLOPPING
GILNOPPT	TOPPLING
GILNOPRU	PROULING
GILNOPRW	PROWLING
GILNOPSU	SOUPLING
GILNOPSY	POSINGLY
	SPONGILY
GILNOPTT	PLOTTING
GILNOPTZ	PLOTZING
GILNORSU	LOURINGS
GILNORTU	TROULING
GILNORVY	ROVINGLY
GILNOSSW	SLOWINGS
GILNOSTT	SLOTTING
GILNOSTU	TOUSLING
GILNOSVW	WOLVINGS
GILNOSWY	YOWLINGS
GILNOSZZ	SOZZLING
GILNOTUY	OUTLYING
GILNOTUZ	TOUZLING
GILNPPRU	PURPLING
GILNPPSU	SUPPLING
GILNPRSU	PURLINGS
	SLURPING
	SPURLING
GILNPRYY	PRYINGLY
GILNPSSU	PLUSSING
GILNPUZZ	PUZZLING
GILNRRSU	SLURRING
GILNRSTU	LUSTRING
	RUSTLING
GILNRTTU	TURTLING
GILNRTYY	TRYINGLY
GILNSSTU	SINGULTS
	TUSSLING
GILNSSTY	STYLINGS
GILNSTTU	SUTTLING
GILNTUUY	UNGUILTY
GILNUWZZ	WUZZLING
GILOOORS	ROSOGLIO
GILOOOST	OOLOGIST
GILOORSS	GIROSOLS
GILOORSU	GLORIOUS
GILOORVY	VIROLOGY
GILOOSSS	ISOGLOSS
GILOOSST	OLOGISTS
GILOOSTW	TWIGLOOS
GILOOSTY	SITOLOGY
GILORSTT	TRIGLOTS
GILOSSST	GLOSSIST
GILOSTUY	GULOSITY
GIMMMNSU	MUMMINGS

GIMMMNUY	MUMMYING
GIMMNOTY	TOMMYING
GIMMNSSU	SUMMINGS
GIMMNSTU	STUMMING
GIMMOSSU	GUMMOSIS
GIMMPSYY	PYGMYISM
GIMNNORS	MORNINGS
GIMNNORU	MOURNING
GIMNNOTU	MOUNTING
GIMNNOUV	UNMOVING
GIMNNSTU	MUNTINGS
GIMNOOOU	OOGONIUM
GIMNOOPR	PROMOING
GIMNOOPS	SPOOMING
GIMNOORS	MOORINGS
	SMOORING
GIMNOORT	MOTORING
GIMNOORV	VROOMING
GIMNOOSS	OSMOSING
GIMNOOST	MOOTINGS
	SMOOTING
GIMNOPRT	TROMPING
GIMNOPST	STOMPING
GIMNOPTU	GUMPTION
GIMNOPTU	RUMORING
GIMNORRW	RINGWORM
GIMNORST	STORMING
GIMNORSU	ROUMINGS
GIMNORSW	MISGROWN
GIMNOSST	GNOMISTS
GIMNOSSU	MOUSINGS
	MOUSSING
	SMOUSING
	SOUMINGS
GIMNOSTU	MOUSTING
	SMOUTING
GIMNOSYY	MISOGYNY
GIMNPRTU	TRUMPING
GIMNPSTU	STUMPING
GIMNRRSU	SMURRING
GIMNSTTU	SMUTTING
GIMNSTYY	STYMYING
GIMORSSW	MISGROWS
GIMPSSYY	GYPSYISM
GIMRSSUU	GURUISMS
GINNNOOS	NOONINGS
GINNNOST	STONNING
GINNNOSU	NONUSING
GINNNOSW	WONNINGS
GINNNPSU	PUNNINGS
GINNNRSU	RUNNINGS
GINNNSTU	STUNNING
	TUNNINGS
GINNNTUU	UNTUNING
GINNOOPS	SNOOPING
	SPOONING
GINNOOST	SNOOTING
GINNOOSW	SWOONING
GINNOOSZ	SNOOZING
GINNOPPU	UNPOPING
GINNOPRU	UNROPING
GINNOPRY	PROYNING
GINNOPSS	SPONGINS
	SPONSING

GINNOPSY	PYONINGS
GINNOPTU	GUNPOINT
GINNOPTY	POYNTING
GINNORSS	SNORINGS
	SORNINGS
GINNORST	SNORTING
GINNORSU	GRUNIONS
GINNOSST	STONINGS
GINNOSTT	SNOTTING
GINNOSTU	SNOUTING
	STOUNING
GINNOSTY	STONYING
GINNOSUW	SWOUNING
GINNPRSU	PRUNINGS
	SPURNING
GINNRSSU	NURSINGS
GINNRSTU	TURNINGS
	UNSTRING
GINNSTTU	NUTTINGS
	STUNTING
GINNSTUY	UNTYINGS
GINOOPPS	OPPOSING
	POGONIPS
GINOOPRS	SPOORING
GINOOPRT	TROOPING
GINOOPSS	SOOPINGS
GINOOPST	STOOPING
GINOOPSW	SWOOPING
	WOOPSING
GINOORST	ROOSTING
	ROOTINGS
GINOORTW	WROOTING
GINOOSTT	TOOTSING
GINOPPPR	PROPPING
GINOPPQU	QUOPPING
GINOPPSS	SOPPINGS
GINOPPST	STOPPING
	TOPPINGS
GINOPPSW	SWOPPING
GINOPRSS	PROSINGS
GINOPRST	SPORTING
GINOPRSU	INGROUPS
	POURINGS
GINOPRSV	PROVINGS
GINOPRTU	TROUPING
GINOPSST	POSTINGS
	SIGNPOST
	STOPINGS
GINOPSSU	SPOUSING
GINOPSTT	SPOTTING
GINOPSTU	POUTINGS
	SPOUTING
GINOPTTY	TYPTOING
GINOQRTU	TORQUING
GINORRWY	WORRYING
GINORSST	RINGTOSS
	SORTINGS
GINORSSU	SOURINGS
GINORSTU	OUTGRINS
	OUTRINGS
	ROUSTING
	ROUTINGS
	TOURINGS
GINORSTW	STROWING
	WORSTING
GINORSTY	ROYSTING
	STORYING
	STROYING
GINORTTT	TROTTING
GINORTTU	TROUTING
	TUTORING
GINOSSSS	SOSSINGS
GINOSSST	TOSSINGS
GINOSSSU	SOUSINGS
GINOSSSW	SOWSSING
GINOSSTT	SOTTINGS
GINOSSTU	OUTSINGS
	TOUSINGS
GINOSSTV	STOVINGS
GINOSSTW	STOWINGS
GINOSTTT	STOTTING
	TOTTINGS
GINOSTTW	SWOTTING
GINOSTUW	OUTSWING
	OUTWINGS
GINOTUVY	OUTVYING
GINPPPUY	PUPPYING
GINPPRSU	UPSPRING
GINPRRSU	PURRINGS
	SPURRING
GINPRSTU	SPURTING
GINPRSUU	PURSUING
	USURPING
GINPRSUY	SYRUPING
GINPSSUW	UPSWINGS
GINPSTTU	PUTTINGS
GINPTTUY	PUTTYING
GINRSSTU	RUSTINGS
	TRUSSING
GINRSTTU	RUTTINGS
	STURTING
	TRUSTING
GINRSTTY	TRYSTING
GINRSTUU	SUTURING
GINSTTTU	TUTTINGS
GIOOORSV	VIGOROSO
GIOOPRRS	PORRIGOS
GIOORRSU	RIGOROUS
GIOORSTU	GOITROUS
GIOORSUV	VIGOROUS
GIOPRRSU	PRURIGOS
GIOPRSSY	GOSSIPRY
GIOPRSTU	GROUPIST
GIORSTUY	RUGOSITY
GIOSTYYZ	ZYGOSITY
GJLMNOPU	LONGJUMP
GJOORSTT	JOGTROTS
GKKNOOSS	SONGKOKS
GKLOOOTY	TOKOLOGY
GLLLOORS	LOGROLLS
GLLOOPTY	POLYGLOT
GLLOOPWY	POLLYWOG
GLLOOXYY	XYLOLOGY
GLMMSSUU	SLUMGUMS
GLMNOOOS	MONOLOGS
GLMNOOOT	MONOGLOT
GLMNOOOY	MONOLOGY
	NOMOLOGY
GLMNORUW	LUNGWORM
GLMNRTUU	NGULTRUM
GLMNSUUU	UMLUNGUS
GLMOOOPY	POMOLOGY
GLMOOORS	MOORLOGS
GLMOORWW	GLOWWORM
GLMOOYYZ	ZYMOLOGY
GLMORSUW	LUGWORMS
GLNNOORS	LORGNONS
GLNOOOSY	NOSOLOGY
GLNOOOTY	ONTOLOGY
GLNOOPRS	PROLONGS
GLNOOPSY	POLYGONS
GLNOOPYY	POLYGONY
GLNOPRSU	LONGSPUR
GLNOPYYY	POLYGYNY
GLNORSTY	STRONGLY
	STRONGYL
GLNORTUW	LUNGWORT
GLNOSSUW	SUNGLOWS
GLNOSTTU	GLUTTONS
GLNOTTUY	GLUTTONY
GLOOOPSY	POSOLOGY
GLOOOPTY	OPTOLOGY
	TOPOLOGY
GLOOORUY	OUROLOGY
GLOOPRYY	PYROLOGY
GLOOPSSY	GOSSYPOL
GLOOPTYY	LOGOTYPY
	TYPOLOGY
GLOORSUU	ORGULOUS
GLOOSTUW	OUTGLOWS
GMMPSUUW	MUGWUMPS
GMNNOOOY	MONOGONY
GMNNOOYY	MONOGYNY
GMNOORSU	GUNROOMS
GMNOORSW	MORWONGS
GMORSTUW	MUGWORTS
GNNPRSUU	UNSPRUNG
GNNRSTUU	UNSTRUNG
GNOOORSS	GORSOONS
GNOOSSSS	GOSSOONS
GNOORSUW	WRONGOUS
GNOORTUW	OUTGROWN
GNOPRSTU	GUNPORTS
GNOPRSUW	GROWNUPS
GNOSTUUW	OUTSWUNG
GNPPRSUU	UPSPRUNG
GOOPRSST	GOSPORTS
GOOPRTUU	OUTGROUP
GOORSSTU	OUTGROSS
GOORSTUW	OUTGROWS
GOORTTUW	GOUTWORT
HHIIIOOP	PIHOIHOI
HHIILOPT	THIOPHIL
HHIINNST	THINNISH
HHIIPSST	PHTHISIS
HHILMOSS	SHLOSHIM
HHILPSSY	SYLPHISH
HHIMMOSS	MISHMOSH
HHIMNPSY	NYMPHISH
HHIMPSSU	SUMPHISH
HHINOOSW	NOHOWISH
HHINOPPS	PHOSPHIN

Eight-letter anagrams

HHIORSST	SHORTISH
HHKKSSUU	KHUSKHUS
HHMRSTUY	RHYTHMUS
HHOOPPRS	PHOSPHOR
HHOOSSTT	HOTSHOTS
HIIILMNS	NIHILISM
HIIILNST	NIHILIST
HIIILNTY	NIHILITY
HIIINRST	RHINITIS
HIIISSTV	SHIVITIS
HIIKMNST	MISTHINK
HIIKMRSS	SKIRMISH
HIIKNNSS	SHINKINS
HIIKNPSS	KINSHIPS
HIIKOPRS	PIROSHKI
HIIKOPRZ	PIROZHKI
HIIKQRSU	QUIRKISH
HIIKSSTT	SKITTISH
HIILLMMO	MILLIMHO
	MILLIOHM
HIILLSTT	LITTLISH
HIILMMSS	SLIMMISH
HIILMOST	HOMILIST
HIILMPSU	SILPHIUM
HIILMPSY	IMPISHLY
HIILMSTU	LITHIUMS
HIILMSWY	WHIMSILY
HIILMTUY	HUMILITY
HIILOPST	PISOLITH
HIILPSST	THLIPSIS
HIILPSSY	SYPHILIS
HIILRSTT	TRILITHS
HIILRSTY	SHIRTILY
HIILSSTT	SHITLIST
	STILTISH
HIILSTTY	SHITTILY
HIIMNSTT	TINSMITH
HIIMOPSS	PHIMOSIS
HIIMSSTT	SHITTIMS
HIINNNSY	NINNYISH
HIINNOST	THIONINS
HIINORST	HISTRION
HIINPSTW	TWINSHIP
HIIOPRSW	POWHIRIS
HIIORSST	HISTRIOS
HIIPPQSU	QUIPPISH
HIIPRTTU	PUIRTITH
HIIQRSSU	SQUIRISH
HIISSSSY	SISSYISH
HIISSTTT	TSITSITH
HIISSTXY	SIXTYISH
HIITTTZZ	TZITZITH
HIKKNSUU	INUKSHUK
HIKLNOST	HOTLINKS
HIKLORTY	KRYOLITH
HIKMNSUU	MINSHUKU
HIKMOSTZ	SHKOTZIM
HIKNNORS	INKHORNS
HIKNNSTU	UNTHINKS
HIKNOOSU	HOKONUIS
HIKNOTTU	OUTTHINK
HIKOOPRZ	PIROZHOK
HIKOOPSS	SPOOKISH
HIKOPSSY	KYPHOSIS

HILLMSUY	MULISHLY
HILLNOUY	UNHOLILY
HILLOOPT	LOPOLITH
HILLOOST	LITHOSOL
HILLOPST	HILLTOPS
HILLOSWY	OWLISHLY
HILLPSUY	PLUSHILY
HILLSSUY	SLUSHILY
HILMMOSU	HOLMIUMS
HILMNOOT	MONOLITH
HILMOOPT	PHILOMOT
HILMOPSY	MOPISHLY
HILMOPVY	MYOPHILY
HILMOSSW	WHOLISMS
HILMOTUY	MOUTHILY
HILMPPSU	PLUMPISH
HILMPRTU	PHILTRUM
HILMPSYY	SYMPHILY
HILMSTUU	THULIUMS
HILNOPSU	UNPOLISH
HILNORTY	THORNILY
HILNOSTY	THIONYLS
	TONISHLY
HILOOPYZ	ZOOPHILY
HILOOSTT	OTOLITHS
HILOOSTZ	ZOOLITHS
HILOOTTY	TOOTHILY
HILOPPSY	POPISHLY
HILOPSXY	OXYPHILS
HILORSTU	UROLITHS
HILORSUU	URUSHIOL
HILORTUW	OUTWHIRL
HILORTWY	WORTHILY
HILOSSTW	WHOLISTS
HILOSSTY	HYLOISTS
	THYLOSIS
HILOSTWW	WHITLOWS
HILOSTYY	TOYISHLY
HILPPRSU	PURPLISH
HILPPSUY	UPPISHLY
HILPRSUW	UPWHIRLS
HILSSTTU	SLUTTISH
HIMMOPRU	PHORMIUM
HIMMSSTY	MYTHISMS
HIMNOPRS	MORPHINS
HIMNOPRX	PHORMINX
HIMNOPSY	PHISNOMY
HIMNOSTY	THYMOSIN
HIMNSSTY	HYMNISTS
HIMOOPRS	ISOMORPH
HIMOPRRT	TRIMORPH
HIMOPRSS	ORPHISMS
HIMOPRSW	SHIPWORM
HIMOPRWW	WHIPWORM
HIMOPSSS	SOPHISMS
HIMOPSST	PHOTISMS
HIMORSST	RIMSHOTS
HIMORSTU	HUMORIST
	THORIUMS
HIMORSTW	MISTHROW
HIMOSTTV	MITSVOTH
HIMOTTVZ	MITZVOTH
HIMPRSTU	TRIUMPHS
HIMPSTUY	PYTHIUMS

HIMRSSTY	RHYMISTS
HIMRSTTU	MISTRUTH
HIMSSTTY	MYTHISTS
HINNORST	TINHORNS
HINNPSSU	NUNSHIPS
HINNSSUY	SUNSHINY
HINOORST	HORNITOS
HINOORSZ	HORIZONS
HINOPSSS	SHIPPONS
HINOPSSS	SONSHIPS
HINOPSSY	HYPNOSIS
HINOPSTW	TOWNSHIP
HINORSST	HORNISTS
HINORTXY	THYROXIN
HINOSSTU	SNOUTISH
HINPPSSU	PUSHPINS
HIOOOPRT	HOROPITO
HIOOOPRZ	ZOOPHORI
HIOOPRTT	POORTITH
HIOORSST	ORTHOSIS
HIOOSSTT	SHOOTIST
HIOPRSSW	WORSHIPS
HIOPRSUZ	RHIZOPUS
HIOPSSST	SOPHISTS
HIOPSSTU	UPHOISTS
HIOPSSTY	PHYTOSIS
HIORRSSY	SORRYISH
HIOSSTTU	STOUTISH
HIOSTTUW	WITHOUTS
HIPPPSUY	PUPPYISH
HIPSUYZZ	ZIZYPHUS
HJNNOOSS	JOHNSONS
HKKLOOSY	KOLKHOSY
HKKLOOYZ	KOLKHOZY
HKKOOPYY	HOKYPOKY
HKKOOSSY	SKYHOOKS
HKMNORRU	KRUMHORN
HKMOOORW	HOOKWORM
HKNNRSUU	UNSHRUNK
HKNOORRW	HORNWORK
HKNOOSWW	KNOWHOWS
HKOOOPST	POTHOOKS
HKOOPRSW	WORKSHOP
HKOORRUW	WORKHOUR
HKOOSVYZ	SOVKHOZY
HLLLOOWY	HOLLOWLY
HLLMNOOU	MONOHULL
HLLOPPRY	PROPHYLL
HLMOOSTY	SMOOTHLY
HLMORRSY	MYRRHOLS
HLNOOPPY	POLYPHON
HLOOSTUW	OUTHOWLS
HLOPRSTY	PROTHYLS
HLPRSSUU	SULPHURS
HLPRSUUY	SULPHURY
HMMNOOSY	HOMONYMS
HMMNOOYY	HOMONYMY
HMMOOORS	MUSHROOM
HMMRSTUU	HUMSTRUM
HMNOOOST	MOONSHOT
HMNOOOTY	HOMOTONY
HMNOORRW	HORNWORM
HMNOOSTU	UNSMOOTH
HMNOPSYY	HYPONYMS

	SYMPHONY
	HYPONYMY
	ZOOMORPH
HMOOPRSW	SHOWROOM
HMOOPTYY	HOMOTYPY
HMOORSUU	HUMOROUS
HMOORTUU	OUTHUMOR
HNNORTTU	NONTRUTH
HNNOSSTY	SYNTHONS
HNOOOOPR	OOPHORON
HNOOPPYY	HYPOPYON
HNOOPRSW	SHOPWORN
HNOOPRTU	HORNPOUT
HNOOPSTY	TYPHOONS
HNOORRTW	HORNWORT
HNOORSTU	SOUTHRON
HNOOSSTU	UNSHOOTS
HNOPPSTY	SYNTHPOP
HNOPRTUW	UPTHROWN
HNORSTUW	UNWORTHS
HNORTUWY	UNWORTHY
HNOSSTUU	UNSHOUTS
HNOSTTUU	OUTHUNTS
HNRSTTUU	UNTRUTHS
HOOOSTTU	OUTSHOOT
	SHOOTOUT
HOOPPSST	POTSHOPS
HOOPPSTY	PHOTOPSY
HOOPRRST	PORTHORS
HOOPSSTT	HOTSPOTS
	POTSHOTS
HOOPSSTU	UPSHOOTS
HOOPSSTW	POSTSHOW
HOOPSSTY	TOYSHOPS
HOOQSSUY	SQUOOSHY
HOORTTUW	OUTTHROW
	OUTWORTH
HOOSSTTU	OUTSHOTS
HOOSTTUU	OUTSHOUT
HOPPRRVY	PORPHYRY
HOPRRSUY	PYRRHOUS
HOPRSSTU	HOTSPURS
HOPRSTUW	UPTHROWS
HOPSSTTU	SHOTPUTS
HORRSTTU	THRUSTOR
HOSSTTUU	SHUTOUTS
HPRSTTUU	THRUPUTS
	UPTHRUST
IIIJJLNS	JINJILIS
IIIKLNPS	SPILIKIN
IIIKMNNS	MINIKINS
IIIKMNSS	MINISKIS
IIILLMMN	MINIMILL
IIILLMNP	MINIPILL
IIILLMNU	ILLINIUM
IIILLNOS	ILLISION
IIILMRSV	VIRILISM
IIILMUVX	LIXIVIUM
IIILRTVY	VIRILITY
IIIMMMNS	MINIMISM
IIIMMNST	INTIMISM
	MINIMIST
IIIMMPRS	IMPRIMIS
IIIMNSTT	INTIMIST
IIIMNTTY	INTIMITY
IIINORRS	IRRISION
IIINPRST	INSPIRIT
IIINQTUY	INIQUITY
IIINSSTU	SINUITIS
IIIOSTTU	OUISTITI
IIISSTTW	WISTITIS
IIJJSTUU	JIUJITSU
IIJLLNOS	JILLIONS
IIJMNOSS	MISJOINS
IIJNNOST	INJOINTS
IIJNNSTU	NINJUTSU
IIKKLNOS	KOLINSKI
IIKKMMUU	KUMIKUMI
IIKKNPSS	KIPSKINS
IIKLLNOS	SKILLION
IIKLLNSY	SLINKILY
IIKLMNPS	LIMPKINS
IIKLMPSY	SKIMPILY
IIKLMRSY	SMIRKILY
IIKLNOSS	OILSKINS
IIKLQRUY	QUIRKILY
IIKMNNOO	MONOKINI
IIKMNORS	KIRIMONS
IIKMNPSS	SIMPKINS
IIKNOSTT	STOTINKI
IILLLMUX	MILLILUX
IILLLPTU	LILLIPUT
IILLLPUV	PULVILLI
IILLMNOS	MILLIONS
IILLMRTU	TRILLIUM
IILLMUUV	ILLUVIUM
IILLNOOR	ORILLION
IILLNOPS	PILLIONS
IILLNORT	TRILLION
IILLNOST	STILLION
IILLNOSU	ILLUSION
IILLNOSZ	ZILLIONS
IILLNSST	INSTILLS
IILLNSTT	LITTLINS
IILLOPQU	PIQUILLO
IILLOPUV	PULVILIO
IILLPPSY	SLIPPILY
IILMMNSU	LUMINISM
IILMMPSS	SIMPLISM
IILMMSUU	SIMULIUM
IILMMSWY	SWIMMILY
IILMNORT	MIRLITON
IILMNOSS	LIONISMS
IILMNSTU	LUMINIST
IILMORSS	SIMILORS
IILMORST	TROILISM
IILMOTTY	MOTILITY
IILMPSST	SIMPLIST
IILMRSSY	MISSILRY
IILNNOOT	NOLITION
IILNNOQU	QUINOLIN
IILNNOST	NITINOLS
IILNNSSU	INSULINS
IILNOOST	INOSITOL
IILNOOTV	VOLITION
IILNOPST	PINITOLS
IILNORSS	SIRLOINS
IILNPPSY	SNIPPILY
IILNRTWY	WINTRILY
IILOOPPR	LIRIPOOP
IILOPRST	TRIPOLIS
IILOPSSS	PSILOSIS
IILOPSST	PTILOSIS
IILOPSTY	PILOSITY
IILORSTT	TROILIST
IILORSTV	VITRIOLS
IILOSSTV	VIOLISTS
IILPRSSY	PRISSILY
IILRSSTU	SILURIST
IILSSTTT	TITLISTS
IILSTUUV	UVULITIS
IILSTUVV	VULVITIS
IIMMMNSU	MINIMUMS
IIMMNOOT	MINIMOTO
IIMMNTUY	IMMUNITY
IIMMOORR	MIROMIRO
IIMMOPST	OPTIMISM
IIMMOPSU	OPIUMISM
IIMMSTTU	MITTIMUS
IIMNNOOT	MONITION
IIMNNOSU	MISUNION
	UNIONISM
IIMNNOTU	MUNITION
IIMNOOSS	OMISSION
IIMNOPRS	IMPRISON
IIMNOPST	MISPOINT
IIMNORTT	INTROMIT
IIMNORTY	MINORITY
IIMNOSSS	MISSIONS
IIMNOSST	SIMONIST
IIMNOSTX	MIXTIONS
IIMNPRST	IMPRINTS
	MISPRINT
IIMNPTUY	IMPUNITY
IIMNRSTY	MINISTRY
IIMOPSTT	OPTIMIST
IIMORSTY	RIMOSITY
IIMOSSTY	MYOSITIS
IIMOTTVY	MOTIVITY
IIMPRTUY	IMPURITY
IIMRRTUV	TRIUMVIR
IIMRSTTU	TRITIUMS
IIMRSTUV	TRIVIUMS
IIMSSSTU	MISSUITS
IIMSSTUW	SWIMSUIT
IINNOOPS	OPINIONS
IINNOPPT	PINPOINT
IINNOPTU	PUNITION
IINNOSTU	INUSTION
	UNIONIST
	UNITIONS
IINNPSST	TINSNIPS
IINNQSTU	QUINTINS
IINNSTTU	TINNITUS
IINOOPST	POSITION
IINOPSSS	ISOSPINS
IINORSST	IRONISTS
IINORSTT	INTROITS
IINOSTTU	TUITIONS
IINOSTVY	VINOSITY
IINRTTUY	TRIUNITY
IINSSTTW	INTWISTS

Eight-letter anagrams

IIOOPSTV	OVIPOSIT	IKNOPSTW	TOWNSKIP	ILNOOTUV	VOLUTION
IIOORRRR	RIRORIRO	IKNORSTW	TINWORKS	ILNOPRSU	PURLOINS
IIOOSTTY	OTIOSITY	IKNPSSTU	SPUTNIKS	ILNOPSSU	PULSIONS
IIOPRRTY	PRIORITY	IKORSSTU	KURTOSIS		UPSILONS
IIOPRSSS	PISSOIRS	IKORSTTU	OUTSKIRT	ILNOPSSW	SNOWSLIP
IIORRRSV	IRRISORY	ILLLMOPS	PLIMSOLL	ILNOPSSY	YPSILONS
IIORSSTV	IVORISTS	ILLLMPPU	PULPMILL	ILNOPSTU	UNSPOILT
	VISITORS	ILLLOOPP	LOLLIPOP	ILNORSST	NOSTRILS
IIORSTUV	VIRTUOSI	ILLLOOWY	WOOLLILY	ILNORSSU	SURLOINS
IIOSSTTU	OUSTITIS	ILLLOPPY	POLYPILL	ILNORSTU	TORULINS
IIPRSSTU	SPIRITUS	ILLMNOSU	MULLIONS	ILNORSTY	NITROSYL
IJJMSSUU	JUJUISMS	ILLMNRSU	MILLRUNS	ILNORTXY	NITROXYL
IJJSSTUU	JUJITSUS	ILLMOORS	MOORILLS	ILNOSSTW	STOWLINS
	JUJUISTS	ILLMOOST	TIMOLOLS	ILNOSSTY	TYLOSINS
IJJSTUUU	JIUJUTSU	ILLMOPRW	PILLWORM	ILNOSTTY	SNOTTILY
IJKLLOSY	KILLJOYS	ILLMOPSS	PLIMSOLS	ILNOSTUV	VOLUTINS
IJLNOQSU	JONQUILS	ILLMOSSY	LISSOMLY	ILNOSUVY	VINOUSLY
IJMPSTUU	JUMPSUIT	ILLMPSUY	PSYLLIUM	ILNPSUUV	PULVINUS
IJNNOSTU	UNJOINTS	ILLMPTUY	MULTIPLY	ILOOORSS	ROSOLIOS
IJNNSTUU	NINJUTSU	ILLNOORT	TORNILLO	ILOOPPRS	PROPOLIS
IKKLNORW	LINKWORK	ILLNOQSU	QUILLONS	ILOOPSST	POLOISTS
IKKLNOSY	KOLINSKY	ILLNORSU	RULLIONS		TOPSOILS
IKKMNOSU	KIKUMONS	ILLNPSUU	LUPULINS	ILOORSTU	RISOLUTO
IKKMOOOR	KOROMIKO	ILLOOPRW	POORWILL	ILOOSSST	SOLOISTS
IKKNORST	KIRKTONS	ILLOORSZ	ZORILLOS	ILOPPSTU	POPULIST
IKKORSSY	SIKORSKY	ILLOORTT	ROTOTILL	ILOPPTUU	OUTPUPIL
IKLLMORW	MILLWORK	ILLOPPSS	SLIPSLOP	ILOPRSTY	SPORTILY
IKLLOOTV	KILOVOLT	ILLOPPSY	SLOPPILY	ILOPSSTU	SLIPOUTS
IKLLOSSY	KYLLOSIS	ILLOPRTW	PILLWORT	ILOPSTTY	SPOTTILY
IKLLOSTU	OUTKILLS	ILLOPRXY	PROLIXLY	ILOPSUUV	PLUVIOUS
IKLLPSSU	UPSKILLS	ILLOPSST	POLLISTS	ILOQRTUU	LOQUITUR
IKLMNPSU	LUMPKINS	ILLORSTU	TROLLIUS	ILPPRTUY	PULPITRY
IKLMOOSS	LOOKISMS	ILLORSUY	ILLUSORY	ILRSTTUY	TRUSTILY
	LOOKSISM	ILLOSSYY	LYOLYSIS	ILRSTUUX	LUXURIST
IKLMOPSS	MILKSOPS	ILLOSTUW	OUTWILLS	ILSSSTTY	STYLISTS
IKLMORSW	SILKWORM	ILLOSTXY	XYLITOLS	IMMNOORS	MORONISM
IKLMORTW	MILKWORT	ILLOTTWY	WITTOLLY	IMMNOSSU	MUSIMONS
IKLMOSSY	SOYMILKS	ILLRSTUY	SULTRILY	IMMNOSUU	MUONIUMS
IKLNOOST	KILOTONS	ILMMSSSU	SLUMISMS	IMMOORTU	MOTORIUM
IKLNOOSW	WOOLSKIN	ILMNOOPS	POLONISM	IMMOPSTU	OPTIMUMS
IKLNOPST	SLIPKNOT	ILMNOOPU	POLONIUM	IMMOSSTU	STOMIUMS
IKLNOTTY	KNOTTILY	ILMNOSUU	LUMINOUS	IMMRSTUY	SUMMITRY
IKLNPSSU	SKULPINS	ILMNOTTU	MULTITON	IMMSSSTU	SUMMISTS
IKLNPSUY	SPUNKILY	ILMOPPSU	POPULISM	IMNNNOSU	MUNNIONS
IKLOOPSY	SPOOKILY	ILMORSTU	TURMOILS	IMNNOORS	NORIMONS
IKLOOSST	LOOKISTS	ILMORSTY	STORMILY	IMNNOOTT	MONOTINT
IKLOOSTT	TOOLKITS	ILMOSTUV	VOLUMIST	IMNNOSUU	NUMINOUS
IKLOSSSU	SOUSLIKS	ILMOSTUY	TIMOUSLY	IMNOOPPS	POMPIONS
IKMNNOSW	MISKNOWN	ILMPPTUU	PULPITUM	IMNOOPST	TOMPIONS
IKMNOOOS	OKIMONOS	ILMPSSTU	PLUMISTS	IMNOOPSU	OPSONIUM
IKMNOORS	OMIKRONS	ILMPSTUY	STUMPILY	IMNOORRS	MORRIONS
IKMNOOSS	MONOSKIS	ILMSSTUU	STIMULUS	IMNOORST	MONITORS
IKMNOSSW	MISKNOWS	ILMSTTUY	SMUTTILY		TROMINOS
IKMNPPSU	PUMPKINS	ILNNORSU	LINURONS	IMNOORTY	MONITORY
IKMNRSTU	TRINKUMS	ILNOOPRT	PLIOTRON		MORONITY
IKNNOPSY	PONYSKIN	ILNOOPSS	PLOSIONS	IMNOORVY	OMNIVORY
IKNNRSTU	TURNSKIN	ILNOOPSV	VOLPINOS	IMNOOSUX	OXONIUMS
IKNOOPRT	PINKROOT	ILNOOPSY	SNOOPILY	IMNOOPPSU	PUMPIONS
IKNOOORW	IRONWORK		SPOONILY	IMNOPRSW	PINWORMS
IKNOOSST	ISOKONTS	ILNOORSS	ROSINOLS	IMNOPSSU	SPUMONIS
IKNOPRSW	PINWORKS	ILNOORTW	TOILWORN	IMNORRSU	MURRIONS
IKNOPSST	INKSPOTS	ILNOOSST	SOLITONS	IMNORSTY	TRIONYMS
IKNOPSSY	PYKNOSIS	ILNOOSTU	SOLUTION	IMNOSTUU	MUTINOUS
IKNOPSTT	STINKPOT	ILNOOSTY	SNOOTILY	IMNRSTUU	UNTRUISM

	PROMISOR	**INOPSSSY**	SYNOPSIS	**KKOOSSUU**	KOUSKOUS
	IMPOSTOR	**INOPSSTU**	SPINOUTS	**KLLMNSUU**	NUMSKULL
	IMPOROUS	**INORSSUV**	UNVISORS	**KLLMOSSU**	MOLLUSKS
IMOOQSTU	MOSQUITO	**INOSSTUW**	SNOWSUIT	**KLNORSTY**	KLYSTRON
IMOORRTT	TRIMOTOR	**INPPRRUU**	PURPURIN	**KLOOORWW**	WOOLWORK
IMOORSTT	MOTORIST	**INPRRSTU**	SURPRINT	**KLOOOSTU**	LOOKOUTS
IMOORSTU	SUMOTORI	**INPRSSTU**	UNSTRIPS		OUTLOOKS
	TIMOROUS	**INPRSSTY**	TRYPSINS	**KLOOPRSW**	SLOPWORK
IMOORSTY	MOROSITY	**INPRSTTU**	TURNSPIT	**KLOSSTUU**	OUTSULKS
IMOORTVY	VOMITORY	**INRSSTTU**	INTRUSTS	**KMOOORRW**	WORKROOM
IMOOSSTY	MYOSOTIS	**INRSTTUU**	UNITRUST	**KMOORSTU**	MUSKROOT
IMOOSTUV	VOMITOUS	**INSSSTUU**	SUNSUITS	**KNNNOSUW**	UNKNOWNS
IMOPPRRU	PROPRIUM	**INSSTTUW**	UNTWISTS	**KNOOPSTT**	TOPKNOTS
IMOPRRSY	PRIMROSY	**IOOPRRSV**	PROVISOR	**KNOPPSTU**	POSTPUNK
IMOPRSST	TROPISMS	**IOOPRSSV**	PROVISOS	**KNOPRSTY**	KRYPTONS
IMOPRSTU	PROTIUMS	**IOOPRSSY**	ISOSPORY	**KNORRSTY**	KRYTRONS
IMOPSSST	MISSTOPS	**IOOPRSTT**	POSTRIOT	**KOOORSTV**	VOORSKOT
IMOPSSTU	UTOPISMS	**IOOPRSTY**	ISOTROPY	**KOOPRSTW**	TOPWORKS
IMORSSST	MISSORTS		POROSITY		WORKTOPS
IMORSSTU	TOURISMS			**KOORSTUW**	OUTWORKS
IMORSTTU	MISTUTOR	**IOORRSTY**	SORORITY		WORKOUTS
	TUTORISM	**IOORRTTT**	TROTTOIR	**KORRSTWY**	TRYWORKS
IMOSSSTU	MISSOUTS	**IOORSSTT**	RISOTTOS	**KORSTTUW**	TUTWORKS
	SUMOISTS	**IOORSSUV**	VOUSSOIR	**LLLMMSUU**	MULMULLS
IMOSSTUW	OUTSWIMS	**IOORSTTU**	TORTIOUS	**LLLOOPPY**	LOLLYPOP
IMPPPSUY	PUPPYISM	**IOORSTTY**	TOROSITY	**LLMOOPRS**	ROLLMOPS
IMRSSSTU	SISTRUMS	**IOORSTUV**	VIRTUOSO	**LLMOPRUU**	PULLORUM
IMRSSTTU	MISTRUST	**IOORSUUX**	UXORIOUS	**LLOOPRST**	TROLLOPS
IMRSSTTY	MISTRYST	**IOOSSTTU**	STOTIOUS	**LLOOPRTY**	TROLLOPY
IMRSTTUY	YTTRIUMS	**IOPPPRST**	PITPROPS	**LLOOPSTU**	OUTPOLLS
INNNNOOU	NONUNION	**IOPPRSST**	RIPSTOPS	**LLOORSTU**	OUTROLLS
INNNOOPT	NONPOINT	**IOPRRSUV**	PROVIRUS		ROLLOUTS
INNNOPRT	NONPRINT	**IOPRSSTT**	PROTISTS	**LLOPSTUU**	OUTPULLS
INNNORSU	RUNNIONS		TROPISTS		PULLOUTS
INNNORTU	TRUNNION		SPURIOUS		
INNNOSTY	SYNTONIN	**IOPRSTTU**	OUTSTRIP	**LLOSUUVV**	VOLVULUS
INNOOPRT	TROPONIN	**IOPRSTUU**	POURSUIT	**LMNOOOPY**	MONOPOLY
INNOOPRU	PROUNION	**IOPRSTUY**	PYRITOUS	**LMNOOPYY**	POLYONYM
INNOOPSS	OPSONINS	**IOPRSUVX**	POXVIRUS	**LMOOOOPR**	POOLROOM
	SPONSION	**IOPSSTTU**	UTOPISTS	**LMOOOORT**	TOOLROOM
INNOOPSU	UNPOISON	**IOQRSTTU**	QUITTORS	**LMOOPRTU**	PULMOTOR
INNOORST	NOTORNIS	**IOQRSTUU**	TURQUOIS	**LMOOPSYY**	POLYSOMY
INNOPRSU	UNPRISON	**IOQRTUXY**	QUIXOTRY	**LMOORSWW**	SLOWWORM
INNORTTU	NOTTURNI	**IORRSSST**	TSORRISS	**LMOOSSSU**	MOLOSSUS
INNOSSTU	NONSUITS	**IORRSUVV**	SURVIVOR	**LMOOTXYY**	XYLOTOMY
INOOOSSZ	ZOONOSIS	**IORSSTTU**	TOURISTS	**LMOPPRTY**	PROMPTLY
INOOOTXZ	ZOOTOXIN	**IORSSTTW**	TWISTORS	**LMOSTUUU**	TUMULOUS
INOOPRST	PORTIONS	**IORSSUUU**	USURIOUS	**LMRSSTUU**	LUSTRUMS
	POSITRON	**IORSTTUY**	TOURISTY	**LNOOOPRT**	POLTROON
	SORPTION		YTTRIOUS	**LNOOOPYZ**	POLYZOON
INOOPSSS	POISSONS	**IORSTUUV**	VIRTUOUS	**LNOOPPRY**	PROPYLON
INOOPSST	POSITONS	**IPPTTTUY**	TITTUPPY	**LNOOPSSU**	UNSPOOLS
INOOPSTT	SPITTOON	**IPRRSSTU**	STIRRUPS	**LNOOPSTU**	PULTOONS
INOOPTTU	OUTPOINT	**IPRRSTUU**	PRURITUS	**LNOOPSWW**	SNOWPLOW
INOORSST	ISOTRONS	**IPRSSTUU**	PURSUITS	**LNRSTUUV**	VULTURNS
	TORSIONS	**JJSSTUUU**	JUJUTSUS	**LOOOORSS**	OLOROSOS
INOORSSU	ROSINOUS	**JLNSTUUY**	UNJUSTLY	**LOOPPSUU**	POPULOUS
INOORSTT	TORTONIS	**JLOOSUYY**	JOYOUSLY	**LOOPPSUY**	POLYPOUS
INOORSTY	SONORITY	**JMOPSTUU**	OUTJUMPS	**LOOPRSTT**	STOLPORT
INOOSTTV	STOTINOV	**JNNOORRU**	NONJUROR	**LOOPRSUY**	POROUSLY
INOPPSST	TOPSPINS	**JNOORSSU**	SOJOURNS	**LOOPSTTU**	OUTPLOTS
INOPRTTU	PRINTOUT	**JNOOSUUY**	UNJOYOUS	**LORSSTUU**	LUSTROUS
INOPRTUY	PUNITORY	**KKMMOOOO**	MOKOMOKO	**MMNNOOSY**	MONONYMS
INOPSSSU	POUSSINS	**KKNOORTW**	KNOTWORK	**MMNOOOSY**	MONOSOMY
		KKOOOOTT	TOKOTOKO	**MMOORTTY**	TOMMYROT

MMOPSSTY	SYMPTOMS		WORMROOT		TURNOUTS
MNNOOOSS	MONSOONS	**MOOPSSSU**	OPOSSUMS	**NOSTTTUU**	OUTSTUNT
MNNOOOTY	MONOTONY	**MOORRSUU**	RUMOROUS	**NRSSTTUU**	UNTRUSTS
MNNOORSU	MONURONS	**MOORSTUU**	TUMOROUS	**NRSTTUUY**	UNTRUSTY
MNNOPRTU	NONTRUMP	**MOORSTUY**	UROSTOMY	**OOOOPRST**	POTOROOS
MNNOSSYY	SYNONYMS	**MOPRTTUU**	OUTTRUMP	**OOOOPRSSU**	SOPOROUS
MNNOSTUU	UNMOUNTS	**MORRSSTU**	ROSTRUMS	**OOOPRSTU**	OUTROOPS
MNNOSYYY	SYNONYMY	**MORSSTUU**	STRUMOUS	**OOORSTTU**	OUTROOTS
MNOOOPPS	POMPOONS	**MSSTTUUU**	TSUTSUMU	**OOPRSSSU**	SOURSOPS
MNOOOPRT	MOONPORT	**NNOOOPST**	PONTOONS	**OOPRSSTV**	PROVOSTS
MNOOORTW	MOONWORT		SPONTOON	**OOPRSTTU**	OUTPORTS
MNOOORXY	OXYMORON	**NNOOPRSU**	PRONOUNS		OUTSPORT
MNOOPRTU	PRONOTUM	**NNOOPSSS**	SPONSONS	**OOPRSTUU**	OUTPOURS
MNOOPSTY	TOPONYMS	**NNOOPSST**	NONSTOPS	**OOPSSSTT**	TOSSPOTS
MNOOPTYY	TOPONYMY	**NNOORSTY**	NONSTORY	**OOPSSTTU**	OUTPOSTS
MNOORSSU	SUNROOMS	**NNOORTTU**	NOTTURNO	**OORSTTTU**	OUTTROTS
MNOOSTTW	TOWMONTS	**NOOOPPRS**	PROSOPON	**OORSTTUU**	TORTUOUS
MNORSSTU	NOSTRUMS	**NOOORSSU**	SONOROUS	**OPPRRSTU**	PURPORTS
MNORSTUU	SURMOUNT	**NOOPRSSS**	SPONSORS	**OPPRSSTU**	SUPPORTS
MOOOPRRT	PROMOTOR	**NOORSSTU**	UNROOSTS	**OPRSSSUU**	SOURPUSS
MOOORRTW	MOORWORT	**NOORSTUW**	OUTSWORN	**ORRSSTTU**	TRUSTORS
	ROOTWORM	**NOPSSSTU**	SUNSPOTS	**ORSSTTUU**	SURTOUTS
	TOMORROW	**NORSTTUU**	OUTTURNS	**RRSSSUUU**	SUSURRUS